To the Little Company of Mary

40 Braemore Park

Churchtown Dublin 14

Feast of the Annunciation

25th March 2010

With deep appreciation for your work and charism.

Sincerely

Michael Ross SDB

Jesus Living In Mary

PRAYER TO JESUS LIVING IN MARY

O Jesus, alive in Mary,
Come dwell in us and reign,
Pour out your life in us,
No more to live but for you.

Shape there your noble virtues,
Your Spirit and his holiness,
Your maxims without flaw,
The passion of your charity.

Make us sharers in your mysteries,
That we might imitate you here below;
Send us the keenness of your light,
To guide our every step.

To the glory of your Father,
In the power of your Name,
Reign in us, through your Mother
Over nature and demon!
Amen.

St. Louis Marie de Montfort
Hymn 111, to the melody of the song "Reveillez-vous"
Translated by Rev. Charles Underhill Quinn

Thanks to Saint Louis of Montfort, I came to understand that true devotion to the Mother of God is actually Christocentric, indeed, it is very profoundly rooted in the Mystery of the Blessed Trinity, and the mysteries of the Incarnation and Redemption.

His Holiness John Paul II, from
Crossing the Threshold of Hope
Knopf, New York 1994

EDITORIAL BOARD

❖

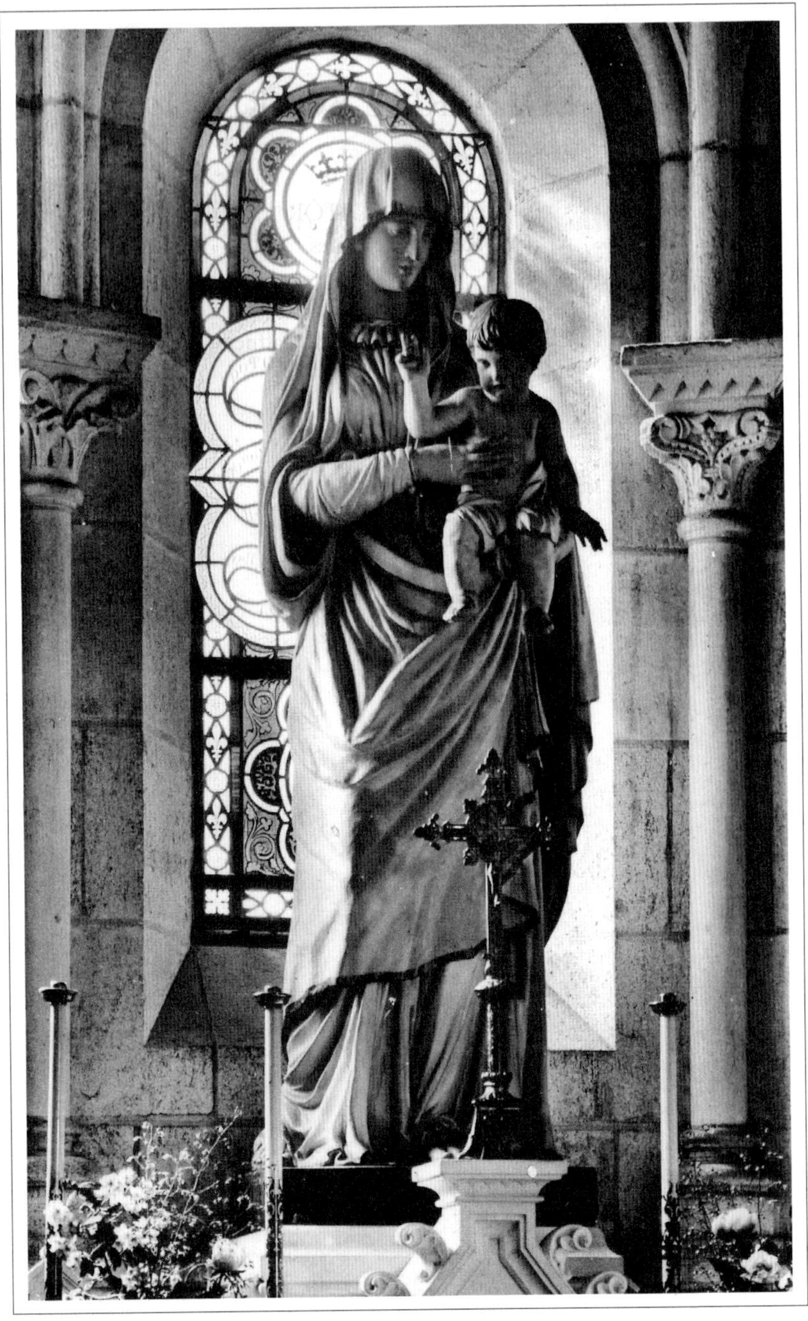

Our Lady of the Rosary from the parish church of St. Laurent-sur-Sevre, France.

It is believed that St. Louis de Montfort prayed often before this, one of his favorite statues. He preached his last mission and was buried before it.

Jesus Living In Mary

Handbook of the Spirituality
of
St. Louis Marie de Montfort

Montfort Publications
Bay Shore, NY

IMPRIMI POTEST
Gerald J. Fitzsimmons, S.M.M.
Provincial Superior

NIHIL OBSTAT
Rev. David Liptak,
Censor Librorum

IMPRIMATUR
Most Rev. Daniel A. Cronin,
Archbishop of Hartford

1994
Montfort Publications
26 S. Saxon Ave.
Bayshore, N.Y. 11706

Handbook Editorial Offices:
P.O. Box 667, Montfort Road,
Litchfield Ct. 06759

Designed and Typeset by
Sara Day Graphic Design, Beverly, Massachusetts

Front Cover Art by Vittoria Paravicini Bagliani: Cross icon depicts Virgin Mary and the Apostle John with Blessed Marie Louise and St. Louis de Montfort beneath. At bottom, St. Laurent-sur-Sevre.

Back Cover Art by Gisele A. Branchard: Weaving in which Mother Marie Louise holds scroll with the words "Yes, you will possess wisdom". Father de Montfort holds scroll saying "I am all yours and all that I have is yours". Photos by Robert Houser.

Back Flap Art (artist unknown): The Rennes Painting probably from the deathbed sketch of Montfort.

Front Flap Art: Wood statue of Our Lady of Wisdom which tradition holds to have been carved by Montfort. Photo by Robert Houser.

Printed in the United States of America by
Princeton Academic Press, Princeton, New Jersey

ISBN # 0-910-984-58-1

LIBRARY OF CONGRESS CATALOG CARD # 94-077726

Dedication

To God Alone

Dieu seul

St. Louis de Montfort's signed motto was: God Alone. He was dedicated to this goal, to this ideal alone. For the journey from God Alone to God Alone, he asked that it be the battle cry, one uttered with St. Michael the Archangel. He used the heart symbol as a reminder that the God who is worshiped is the God who is love.

Louis marie de montfort grignion

The deathbed signature of the saint on his last will and testament. April 27, 1716.

Contents

Foreword

It is a testimony to the beauty and power of St. Louis Marie de Montfort's teaching that, nearly three centuries after his death, Christians on five continents are still drawn to his example and his message. This Apostolic Missionary progressively opens for us a path of baptismal conversion and transformation that leads us toward selfless commitment in service of those in need and toward genuine and profound holiness. The presence of the Virgin of Nazareth in the life of the Christian becomes the crucible in which the fire of the Spirit forms Jesus Christ in us and us in Him.

Yet precisely this distance of three centuries requires that contemporary men and women seek guidance in interpreting Montfort's worldview and thought in light of the culture and theologies of the new millennium. If anything, St. Louis Marie de Montfort wonderfully understood the people of his time and place; three hundred years later he would surely seek companions who could reveal the treasures of Divine Wisdom to the men and women of our vastly different age.

The general councils of the Montfort Family—the Missionaries of the Company of Mary, the Daughters of Wisdom, and the Brothers of St. Gabriel—commissioned *JESUS LIVING IN MARY, Handbook of the Spirituality of St. Louis Marie de Montfort* with this end in mind. Most sincere gratitude is due to the editors: Fr. Stefano De Fiores, Fr. Alphonse Bossard, and Fr. Patrick Gaffney, as well as to all the authors and collaborators, without whose learning and dedication this volume would be impossible.

St. Louis Marie de Montfort wrote with fire and clarity, deeply rooted in the scriptures and in the theological tradition of the Church. Nevertheless, he always prized the Wisdom of God above all other human intellectual efforts. May this handbook be an instrument, a channel, for a deeper comprehension of Montfort's spirituality, but may Our Lady and the Holy Spirit prepare our hearts—like that of Blessed Marie Louise Trichet, Montfort's first disciple in this way of holiness—for the presence of the Wisdom of Love.

William Considine, S.M.M.
Superior General
of the Company of Mary

Preface

Apparently a collection of diversified topics, this *Handbook of the Spirituality of Saint Louis Marie de Montfort* hopes to offer the opportunity for a unique, profound and unified experience of the *Holy*. The volume enables an experience—however slight—of *mystery* in its deep meaning: a taste of what is beyond the senses, a knowledge of what cannot be grasped, a sight of what cannot be seen. The articles taken as a whole are an introduction to the wisdom of a giant among the saints, a vagabond Gospel troubadour known simply as the Father from the village of Montfort.

There is a double polarity which is clearly experienced as one plunges into the depths of the ecclesial grace God offered this missionary. There is, first of all, the feeling of profound satisfaction as one discovers the fulfillment for which one's very existence has almost unknowingly yearned. But as our spirit peacefully sighs, "I am at home here!," there is at the same time a subtle groan from deep within our being, "I do not want to be here!" It is as though a primordial battle is being fought within the profundity of our existence, a combat between good and evil, between life and death itself. And we know that we are not the only participants in this struggle. We are one with all peoples from the start of the human race to fulfillment; in fact, with all matter, even the farthest speck of existence in outer space. Our insatiable, sinful nature insanely demands to be constantly fed; far stronger still is the craving of the spirit for the Only who can fulfill our being itself.

The spirituality of Saint Louis Marie strongly lures us to free ourselves of those all too comfortable sinful shackles which prohibit unrestrained soaring into the brightness of eternal Light. By disclosing through present realities the ultimately triumphant and glorious end times, he urges us to listen not to the voice of the evil one which only leads to existential defeat.

Everything in Montfort cries out: "Choose Life, no matter the painful wrenching involved!" "Choose the Cross for it is only from its triumphant Wood that you pluck the fruit of eternal Life." "Choose Incarnate Wisdom and become a fool in the eyes of the world."

When through God's gift we actively let ourselves be drawn into God Alone, wonderful yet awesome transformations begin to occur. The inherent weakness of language makes it impossible fully to express the splendor of the path undertaken. It is the glory of the tenderness of God. It is the taste of the Trinity of Love. It is our fulfillment within the dynamic Lover who so powerfully divinizes us.

The montfort path is the same one which Wisdom took to enter the human family: the Immaculate Mary. Her spirit permeates every aspect of Father de Montfort's staunchly Christ-centered doctrine. To be bathed in her spirit is the turning point of our advance into a renewed baptismal consecration of union with the triune God.

The key, then, to an understanding of montfort spirituality is to grasp that this vagabond saint is unreservedly—madly, the world would say—in love with Love Itself, who becomes enfleshed through Mary's "Yes." Love-language is his vocabulary. Expressions which shock, like "slavery," "desire for the Cross," "the anger of God," "lose yourself in Mary," must be defined only through the help of the dictionary of love. His writings and most especially his canticles are a rendition of the Song of Songs.

This strong and uncompromising spirituality overflows into every aspect of existence. A life of evangelical freedom, totally trusting in God's loving providence; a servant's active love for the poor, the outcasts; an unflinching fidelity to the Church: they are some of the characteristics of those who integrate the saint's consecration spirituality in their life. Montfort's hope is to form a great squadron of men and women from every walk of life to live the gospel of Jesus Christ so valiantly that the Church will be constantly reformed and the earth renewed.

Too long has this treasure been hoarded. This *Handbook* is published so that all, most especially Montfort's beloved laypeople, can share in this saint's evangelical vision. Its appearance marks an important moment not only in the history of the communities Saint Louis de Montfort founded, but for the faithful throughout the world. This English edition has gone through drastic revisions since its anticipated audience is so broadly based. It is not intended just for English speaking Christians of the western world; on the contrary, its readers will include, among others, numerous Asians and Africans. The contents of this *Handbook* cannot respond to all the circumstances of such a wide group. Moreover, most of the authorities on Saint Louis de Montfort are—at least at this time—representative of the West and are understandably contextualized by its culture. Nonetheless, we are convinced that this volume will do immeasurable good in renewing the baptismal commitments of the faithful throughout the world. Theologians and spiritual authors will find in these pages insights into the teachings of Saint Louis de Montfort which have at times been misunderstood if not caricatured, since never explained—at least in English—as a whole. It is among the hopes of the editors that the real Montfort will come forth from these pages who will then challenge contemporary society—as he did his own—to a deeper and more powerful apostolic life in the Eternal and Incarnate Wisdom, the son of Mary.

To study the Handbook with profit, it is *strongly* recommended that the reader have at hand a copy of *God Alone: The Collected Works of Saint Louis Marie de Montfort*. The *Collected Works* and the *Handbook* are twin volumes which depend on each other.

The reader cannot fail to notice the hundred and more references to the *Hymns* of Father de Montfort which are interspersed throughout this volume. As yet these *Canticles* are not found in English although they form a major part of his works. This startling lack will be filled by winter 1995 when the English translation of the *Canticles* will at last be published. May the trilogy—*Collected Works, Handbook* and *Canticles*—form a powerful instrument of constant renewal within the People of God.

This volume could not have seen the light of day without the enthusiastic support and expertise of Richard Payne. To him and to all the contributors, assistants and benefactors, the Company of Mary offers heartfelt thanks.

Patrick Gaffney, S.M.M.
Montfort Pilgrimage and Retreat Center
Litchfield, Connecticut, July 8, 1994

Introduction

This book may be considered as a "barometer of the times." It records, bears witness, and gives meaning to our situation and anticipates history's path into the future. The editors of this handbook sought to capture what is essential in the spirituality of St. Louis Marie de Montfort, but they wished to remain concise. They sought what was perennial and deep, but they wished to remain current and clear. The past publishing success of works from or about the classical traditions of Christian spirituality that have appeared in many countries demonstrate that they respond to the pressing hunger in our contemporary society for what is "tried and true." Yet, carried away by the dizzying rhythms of present-day life, locked in a struggle with time and space, modern men and women want to know as much as possible and as quickly as possible.

This book represents a desire to respond concisely and profoundly to the need felt by many contemporary Christians to draw fully on the experience and the writings of the great missionary and spiritual father St. Louis Marie de Montfort (1673-1716).

Montfort's influence is widespread. It affects all levels of people and transcends cultural boundaries: from the ordinary Christian to Pope John Paul II, who has acknowledged that his own spiritual life is greatly indebted to his reading of *True Devotion to the Blessed Virgin.* St. Louis Marie de Montfort is the sole modern author he cites in his encyclical *Redemptoris Mater* (1987), as a "witness and teacher" of true Marian spirituality.

This is a timely and, indeed, necessary moment to present to the women and men of today, and especially to religious families who are inspired by Montfort, the whole of his spiritual legacy to the Church. We must render justice where it is due. During the three centuries that separate us from Montfort, his spirituality has been given serious study through the prism of this aspect or that: sometimes in the light of his devotion to Our Lady, at other times in the light of his love for Eternal Wisdom, of his apostolic inspiration, or of his prophetic vision of the latter times. Our duty now is to broaden those horizons and, without losing any of the contributions made in the past, encompass all of Montfort's major contributions to the field of Christian spirituality.

Since the publication in 1966 of the first French edition of the complete works of Saint Louis Marie Grignion de Montfort, an effort has been under way to make available worldwide the entire corpus of Montfort's writings. This book is part of that effort. It attempts to offer readers the joy of discovering in Montfort a spirituality that is not confined to those classical limits familiar to everyone (such as Christ Wisdom, the Cross, Mary, the apostolate, etc.). It embraces other themes as well, such as friendship, covenant, God, Holy Spirit, Providence, world, faith, hope, love . . .

Other characteristics make this handbook distinctive. Readers will not find an encyclopedic compendium of all of Montfort's themes; instead, the most important concerns of modern spiritual life are here. This book is not concerned with providing information but, rather, with giving readers the formation fundamental for true Christian living. Each article endeavors to serve as a short treatise. Although it gives special attention to Montfort's historical and spiritual milieu, the handbook is not a prisoner of the seventeenth century. While avoiding extrapolation, it attempts to speak the language of men and women of today and, as much as possible, incarnate Montfort spirituality in modern-day culture, taking advantage of certain advances in theology and the social sciences.

If the handbook is successful in performing this service, we undoubtedly owe its success to the contributors, who drafted the various articles with love and skill, the insightful expert advisers A. Bossard and P. Gaffney, and the diligent translators and secretaries. But above all we owe it to Father Gérard Lemire, recently superior general of the Montfort Missionaries, who, with the full agreement of Sister Ines of the Eucharist, superior general of the Daughters of Wisdom, and with Brother Jean Friant, superior general of the Brothers of Christian Instruction of Saint Gabriel, is responsible for the idea of this handbook on montfort spirituality.

May we express the wish that this handbook will embrace a wider circle of readers, leading to a personal, transforming, and definitive encounter with God, who through the saints lets a ray of His glory shine on the paths of history.

Stefano De Fiores, S.M.M.
General Editor
Rome, April 28, 1993

Abbreviations

A. God Alone, The Collected Writings of St. Louis Marie de Montfort

L	Letters
LEW	The Love of Eternal Wisdom
FC	Letter to the Friends of the Cross
SR	The Secret of the Holy Rosary
MR	Methods for Saying the Rosary
SM	The Secret of Mary
TD	True Devotion to the Blessed Virgin
PM	Prayer for Missionaries
RM	Rule of the Missionary Priests of the Company of Mary
LCM	Letter to the Members of the Company of Mary
WC	The Wisdom Cross of Poitiers
RW	Original Rule of the Daughters of Wisdom
MLW	Maxims and Lessons of Divine Wisdom
LPM	Letter to the People of Montbernage
RV	Rule of the Forty-four Virgins
RP	Rule of the White Penitents
PS	Pilgrimage of the Penitents to Our Lady of Saumur
CG	Covenant with God
W	The Last Will of Saint Louis Marie
MP	Morning Prayer
NP	Night Prayer
H	Hymns
RVP	Rules on Voluntary Poverty in the Early Church
MRL	Four Short Meditations on the Religious Life
LS	The Book of Sermons
HD	Dispositions for a Happy Death
N	Notebook

B. Documents of the Second Vatican Council

AA	Apostolicam actuositatem
AG	Ad gentes
CD	Christus Dominus
DH	Dignitatis humanæ
DV	Dei Verbum
GE	Gravissimum educationis

GS	Gaudium et spes
IM	Inter mirifica
LG	Lumen gentium
NA	Nostra ætate
OE	Orientalium ecclesiarum
OT	Optatam totius
PC	Perfectæ caritatis
PO	Presbyterorum ordinis
SC	Sacrosanctum concilium
UR	Unitatis redintegratio

C. Dictionaries, Reviews, and Other Sources

AAS	Acta Apostolicæ Sedis.
AGCM	Archives générales de la Compagnie de Marie. Viale dei Monfortani 65, Rome.
AGFS	Archives générales des Filles de la Sagesse. Via dei Casali di Torrevecchia 16, Rome.
ALLAIRE	[R. Allaire], *Abrégé / de la vie et des vertus / de la soeur / Marie-Louise / de Jésus, / Supérieure / des Filles de la Sagesse, / instituées / par M. Louis-Marie Grignon / de Montfort, Prêtre, Missionnaire / Apostolique.* / A Poitiers, / Chez Jean-Félix Faulcon, Imprimeur / de Monseigneur l'Evêque, & du Clergé. / Place et vis-à-vis Notre-Dame la Grande. / M.DCC.LXVIII. / Avec permission. 438 pp.
BESNARD I	C. Besnard, *Vie de M. Louis-Marie de Montfort.* Rome: Centre International Montfortain, 1981. Vol. 1, xiv-328 pp.
BESNARD II	C. Besnard, *Vie de M. Louis-Marie de Montfort* Rome: Centre International Montfortain, 1981. Vol. 2, 346 pp.
BLAIN	J.-B. Blain, *Abrégé de la vie de Louis-Marie Grignion de Montfort.* Rome: Centre International Montfortain, 1973. xviii-227 pp.
BSM	Bollettino di storia monfortana.
CM	Cahiers marials.
CLORIVIÈRE	*La Vie de M. Louis-Marie Grignion de Montfort / Missionnaire Apostolique / Instituteur des Missionnaires du Saint-Esprit et des Filles de la Sagesse* / par Mr. P. J. Picot de Clorivière, recteur de Paramé / M.DCC.LXXXV / Avec approbation et Privilège du roi. xii-587 pp.
DB	Dictionnaire de la Bible.
DMar	Documentation mariale.
DMon	Documentation montfortaine.
DS	Denzinger-Schönmetzer, Enchiridion symbolorum.
DSAM	Dictionnaire de spiritualité ascétique et mystique.
DTC	Dictionnaire de théologie catholique.
EM	Ephemerides mariologicæ.
EstMar	Estudios marianos.
EtMar	Etudes mariales.

FLORENCE	Sr. Florence and anonymous author, *Chroniques primitives de Saint-Laurent-sur-Sèvre.* Rome: Centre International Montfortain, 1967. xvii-202 pp.
GA	St. Louis Marie de Montfort, *God Alone: The Collected Writings of St. Louis Marie de Montfort.* Bay Shore, N.Y.: Montfort Publications, 1987.
GRANDET	J. Grandet, *La Vie / de Messire / Louis-Marie / Grignion / de Montfort, / Prêtre du Clergé.* / A Nantes, / Chez N. Verger, Imprimeur du / Roy & de Monseigneur l'Evêque. / Grand'rue, au nom de JESUS. / Avec Approbation & Privilège du Roy. / M.DCC.XXIV. xix-441 pp.
ITINERARIO	Stefano De Fiores, *Itinerario spirituale di S. Luigi Maria di Montfort (1673-1716) nel periodo fino al sacerdozio (5 giugno 1700). University of Dayton (Ohio), 1974 (vol. 6 of Marian Library Studies).*
MANSI	Mansi, *Sacrorum conciliorum nova et amplissima collectio.*
MARIA	H. du Manoir, ed., *Maria: Études sur la sainte vierge,* 8 vol.
Mar	Marianum.
MC	Apostolic exhortation of Paul VI "Marialis cultus."
NDM	Nuovo dizionario di mariologia.
NDS	Nuovo dizionario di spiritualità.
NRT	Nouvelle revue théologique.
Ob	San Luis-Maria G. De Montfort, *Obras.* Madrid: Biblioteca de Autores Cristianos, 1954, 1984.
OC	S. Louis-Marie Grignion de Montfort, *Oeuvres Complètes.* Paris: Editions du Seuil, 1966.
OM	S. Luigi-Maria Grignion de Montfort, *Opere.* Rome: Centro Mariano Monfortano, 1977.
PAPÀSOGLI	Papàsogli, *Montfort, A Prophet for His Times.* Rome: Edizione Monfortane, 1991.
PÉROUAS	Pérouas, *A Way to Wisdom,* Bayshore, N.Y. 1982
PG	Migne, *Patrologia,* series græca.
PL	Migne, *Patrologia,* series latina.
PMon	Perspectives montfortaines.
QM	Quaderni monfortani.
QOAH	Queen of All Hearts.
RDC	Regina dei Cuori.
Rmat	Encyclical *Redemptoris Mater.*
RMon	Rencontres montfortaines.
RPM	Revue des prêtres de Marie.
RSPT	Revue des sciences philosophiques et théologiques.
SC	Sources chrétiennes.
Smun	K. Rahner, ed. Encyclopedia of Theology: The Concise Sacramentum Mundi. Seabury, New York 1975.
CCC	*Catechism of the Catholic Church.* New York: Catholic Book Publishing Co., 1994.
VS	La vie spirituelle.

STATUE OF ST. LOUIS DE MONTFORT IN ST. PETER'S BASILICA, ROME.

The saint, the apostle of the Cross and rosary, crushes satan who clutches Montfort's ***True Devotion to the Blessed Virgin*** *(TD 114). Sculpted by Galileo Parisini.*

ADORATION

SUMMARY
I. ADORATION IN THE EXPERIENCE OF MONTFORT
II. ADORATION IN FRENCH SPIRITUALITY OF THE SEVENTEENTH CENTURY.
III. MONTFORT'S ILLUMINATION ON THE SUBJECT OF ADORATION:
1. The attitude of adoration;
2. Recipients of adoration:
a. An absolute "no" to idolatry,
b. Adoration of God,
c. "Adorable Jesus."
IV. ADORATION OF GOD IN OUR TIMES:
1. Idolatry or adoration?:
a. Liberation from modern idolatries,
b. Adoration in spirit and truth;
2. Return to the Trinitarian legacy.

"Let us adore forever / The Lord in his good things made. / Let us adore forever / The Lord in all that is." (H 50:1). Adoration of God is a constant refrain in Montfort; he invites the Christian community to adore the Lord always because He is God and reveals Himself in His gifts. Montfort reunites profound elements of adoration that aid in the discovery of an authentic spirituality.

I. ADORATION IN THE EXPERIENCE OF MONTFORT

A sense of God and God's presence was present in Montfort from his childhood. Blain, who remembers being shown his young friend's places for retreat and prayer, says, "He seemed to me to be so filled with God, so preoccupied with Him, that I was both confused and enlightened."[1] The search for silent and solitary places in which to make a retreat was constant in every stage of Montfort's life. But his rapport with God grew all along his journey, thanks to his own spiritual experiences and to his contacts with devout people of his time and with the poor.

During his time in seminary, under the influence of Boudon and Surin, Montfort succeeded in crystallizing his spiritual life in the love of God, which in turn implied remaining apart from all other creatures.[2] He took Boudon's exhortation literally: "Leave other creatures, contemplate God alone. . . . We must say to ourselves always, God alone, God alone."[3] *God alone* will be Montfort's motto, the hallmark of his excellence. For his part, Blain remarks that, after having abandoned the Sorbonne, Montfort "found more time to give to God and was free to follow his overriding attraction to retreat and prayer."[4] In addition, all his bodily mortifications, the subject of so much attention among the seminarians, were forms of this "perfect self-annihilation" of which Surin spoke and that served to enhance his adoration. There was an exception to this withdrawal from the presence of others: the "afflicted Christians"—to use Boudon's expression—whom we must honor because we see in them the "living images" of God.[5] Blain writes that, echoing Boudon's book, Montfort, while living in the community of La Barmondière, "felt a holy envy for the poor and afflicted; he honored and respected them as the living images of Jesus crucified. One day, seeing him escort to the door, hat in hand, a man who appeared rather insignificant, and surprised by such marks of respect, I asked him why he showed such respect to someone who did not appear to require it. He answered, 'It is because he is on the cross and we must respect and honor all those who have the good fortune to be thus attached.'"[6] There is a flash of this same attitude in the famous incident at Dinan in 1706, when he brought a poor leper to the missionary house, crying *"Open the door to Jesus Christ."*[7] This display of honor for the poor and sick goes hand in hand with true adoration for the person of Christ, Who is present in them. Around 1702, referring to a Benedictine of the Blessed Sacrament, Montfort said explicitly, *"I adore Jesus crucified in her"* (L 13).

Thus does Montfort's adoration become more Christological: he adores Jesus in the poor, and he enters into an adoring and atoning Eucharistic spirituality. In each case, he acts from a perspective of pure faith, without either visions or miracles: *"Faithful adorers give so much glory to God here on earth but they are so few, for even the very spiritual want to taste and see"* (L 19). For him, adoration of the Blessed Sacrament includes a sacrifice, an immolation, of which one's bodily attitude is only a symbol: *"What an honor it is for your body to be spiritually sacrificed in the hour of your adoration before the Blessed Sacrament!"* (L 19).

Throughout his ministry, Montfort notes the neglect of the Eucharist by priests and faithful. He makes complaint in his Hymns, especially in the "Act of Reparation to the Blessed Sacrament" (H 136), which he composed during the mission at Campbon in 1709, and which Besnard defines as almost an "elegy":[8] *"Let me cry, let me weep bitter tears to God above; / For Jesus is abandoned in his Sacrament of love; / Forgotten and insulted . . .* " (H 136:1). The link with adoration appears in the paradoxical situation of the *"King of glory,"* worthy of adoration and yet *"forsaken at our altars"* (H 136:1); *"The home for this adorable / Is often a sorry space; / The church is like a stable, / A plain, improper place"* (H 133:4). The missionary gives all his zeal to the task of restoring the houses of God, but his goal is to create a place that is appropriate for celebration of the mysteries of salvation, for adoration of the Blessed Sacrament, and for prayer. Besnard gives an example: "Fervent worshipper, angel at the altar, whether seen in celebration or contemplated in thanksgiving, but always in the church. It is impossible not to be deeply affected by the grandeur of the mysteries and the holiness of the ministry."[9]

Montfort's adoration is not restricted to the Eucharist, although it was undoubtedly the preferred setting. The universe was for him a truly divine milieu, offering the opportunity to adore God always and anywhere. Besnard, his biographer, gives us precious and profound testimony to this: "Everything served to elevate him closer to God, and one can say that he regarded this great universe as nothing but a vast and august temple that God fills with His majesty, desiring our adoration from everyplace therein. This thought pierced him so acutely that he was in a nearly constant state of adoration, bareheaded even when travelling, . . . so as to join exterior worship to that which he rendered unceasingly to the Supreme Being."[10]

Not only space but time as well became for Montfort a means of elevating himself to his Creator and of adoring His mysterious designs. The missionary encounters God in the events of his life, on his daily journey. If, for example, he remains in Paris around 1703 rather than return to Poitiers, it is because *"my Master led me there in spite of myself. He has his plan in all this and I adore his plan, though I do not understand it"* (L 15). And at the same time, he endeavors to know God's designs through prayer: *"Let us pray that God may make His holy will clear to us"* (L 33). In his last letter, written two weeks before his death, Montfort begins with a solemn declaration about the difficult life that the first Daughters of Wisdom were leading at La Rochelle: *"I worship the justice and love with which divine Wisdom is treating his little flock"* (L 34).

In all the biographical and autobiographical information we have of him, Montfort appears as a true adorer of God. In the universe and throughout history, among the poor and in the Eucharist, he encountered the divine presence and manifested his adoration before the mystery of God. Through his own experience and together with the spiritual men and women of his time, the saint knew how to speak of adoration with authority or sing of it in his hymns.

II. Adoration in French Spirituality of the Seventeenth Century

In order to place Montfort's statements about adoration in context, we must spend a moment looking at the spiritual figures of his century. They are usually grouped together as the "French school of spirituality."

A clear theocentrism characterizes the French, or Bérullian, school of spirituality. The honor of having renewed "the spirit of religion, the supreme worship of adoration and reverence to God"[11] is properly due to Cardinal de Bérulle. In the cardinal's words, God is so great, so "infinitely present and infinitely distant" that He must be adored "in His Essence and in His Persons, in His Being and in His operations."[12] The God of Bérulle, being a Trinitarian God, is above all else the Father. It is thus the Father whom we must "adore like the dawn, but an eternal dawn, and like a dawn at noon in the plenitude of its light."[13] Adoration is an interior attitude, consisting of "sublime thoughts of what we adore," but it leads to vital implications deriving from a "will marked by surrender, submission, and abasement"[14] and expressed externally by threefold adoration of the Trinity: "the first adoration in the morning when we adore it as the source and primary truth of our being; the second at noon, as the perfection of our being; and the third in the evening, as the object of our being."[15] Adoration is our first duty, but it must always yield to love, because "to love God is the greatest action that our spirit can take."[16] This means that our adoration must exist not in fear but by the law of grace and love.

For Bérulle, adoration is no less Christocentric than theocentric. In effect Bérulle "considers Christ a **result,** a **means,** an **example** of adoration."[17] Taking the mystery of the Incarnation seriously, the apostle of the Word Incarnate affirms, "We adore a God Who is eternal, but Who made Himself mortal; a God Who is invisible, but Who made Himself visible; a God Who is impassive, and yet Who made Himself prey to heat and cold, subject to the Cross and to death."[18] Bérulle presents Jesus as the perfect religious and adorer of the Father, to Whom, as a man, he renders infinite adoration: "You are now, O Jesus! This adorer, this man, this servant infinite in power, in quality, in dignity. . . ."[19] All Christians must become one with Jesus and strive to remain in a permanent state of adoration.

Bérulle's disciples follow in the footsteps of their leader by emphasizing important aspects or by drawing the central conclusions from his teachings. Thus Condren states that adoration is like a holocaust, an annihilation, a state of sacrifice, and that this sacrifice is "made first and foremost to adore God, to acknowledge His greatness, and to give homage to His divine perfections."[20] Olier, founder of the seminary of Saint-Sulpice, invites the faithful to live "the religion of Jesus Christ," to join in the adoration and praise that Jesus renders to his Father. And because Jesus renders this homage to his Father in the Eucharist, Olier "dreams of priests who prolong their adoration until they consume themselves before the Blessed Sacrament."[21]

Within this context, we can better understand the original contribution that St. Louis de Montfort made on the subject of the spirituality of adoration.

III. Montfort's Illumination on the Subject of Adoration

As we move from the thinking of Bérulle, Condren, and Olier to that of Montfort, we see Montfort's concern with abandoning a literary genre better adapted to the spiritual elites in favor of a language that is closer and more comprehensible to the people. At the same time, the missionary does not ignore the most profound ideas of his predecessors. In Montfort's thought, we can see particular attention to the nature of adoration and its objects.

1. The attitude of adoration

Montfort does not define adoration, but he readily ties it to abasement, sacrifice, and love. He writes that the body *"is sacrificed by fasting and watching before the Blessed Sacrament"* (L 18), and that it is an honor for the body *"to be spiritually sacrificed in the hour of your adoration before the Blessed Sacrament"* (L 19). Montfort understands that *"every mind should realize its inadequacy and adore"* (LEW 15) when confronted with the glory of Wisdom. The chosen means of adoring and rendering sovereign worship to the adorable Being of God is through prayer: *"That is where man does sacrifice / His body and his soul; / There he adores with Jesus Christ, / Trembling before all, / He humbly adores His majesty. . . ."* (H 15:4). This is not simply an optional posture. Men owe to God *"this perfect sacrifice / of a grateful heart,"* which consists of *"adoring God as we must"* (H 26:5). The adoration of God must be tied to love, and Montfort takes pleasure in repeating a refrain in the hymns: *"May we adore and love Him"* (H 116:7; 117:6; 132:1). For Montfort, then, adoration is a complex attitude, with both a negative aspect (self-sacrifice) and a positive aspect of acknowledgement, praise, and love.

2. Recipients of adoration

But to whom do we owe this attitude of adoration? Certainly not to idols, including the false wood and stone gods of idolatrous paganism (cf. TD 48, 50, 59, 64, 93; PM 17) as well as the objects of an exaggerated love among Christians: the flesh (*"the body naturally idolizes itself"* (LEW 201); the body, which *"becomes an idol / When too much gratified"* (H 33:14); women of society who are *"idols of beauty"* or *"idols of vanity"* (H 156,7; 33,112; 43,23). Montfort declares war on all forms of idolatry (H 33,112), but he invokes the aid of the Holy Spirit: *"Speak and crush the idols / That battle with your love"* (H 141:6).

a. An absolute "no" to idolatry. No earthly creature may receive the adoration of men (the Cross is unique, as Montfort will explain). Not even the Virgin Mary is an exception. On this subject, Montfort's teaching is categorical. Mary is certainly the *"living tabernacle of God, in whom Eternal Wisdom willed to receive the adoration of both men and angels"* (LEW 224), and Montfort invites us to view her this way: *"Let us adore Jesus / Living in the womb of Mary"* (H 87:1). She also promotes adoration; she is a means and model of adoration: *"It is through herself / That I adore and love"* (H 82:6). In the Magnificat, it is Mary personified who invites us to adore the Lord: *"May we adore and love Him . . . May we adore and bless / Our one true God!"* (H 85:2). She is the perfect adorer of Jesus, especially at the moment of Eucharistic communion, when with us she will receive her son; she will *"adore him profoundly, . . . embrace him intimately in spirit and in truth, and perform many offices for him"* (TD 270). However, Montfort is careful not to confer this adoring worship—even relative adoration—upon Mary herself: *"The cross is adorable / Mary herself is not"* (H 102:23). While Suarez adopts the language of "adoration" for Mary, with the qualifier "of dulia," Montfort unequivocally reserves adoration for God alone.

Indeed, *"It is not his wish* [i.e., the wish of Wisdom] *that the honor even of a relative adoration be given to any other creature however exalted, such as his most Blessed Mother"* (LEW 172). The saint consistently distinguishes between *"adorable Jesus"* (he uses the same adjective to describe the Heart, the Blood, the Cross of Jesus) and *"admirable Mary"* (H 28:17; 40:33; 63:1; 127:70). This theological rigor on the subject of worship is significant in a spiritual figure and missionary like Montfort.

For Montfort, God remains the only recipient of adoration, in the three Persons revealed in Jesus Christ and in the plan of salvation.

b. Adoration of God. Montfort's God is the God of biblical revelation, i.e., the Trinitarian God: Montfort adores God and desires that everyone acknowledge Him as the one true God. In SR 74 (which reflects Montfort's own thought) we read, *"All Christians have but one faith and adore one and the same God."* The ardent desire of the saint is that everyone adore the true God, and he prays vigorously for this: *"Jesus on the Cross, / Let your reign begin, / It is time, it is time. / All will adore and follow you then. . . ."* (H 164:17). The confession of faith in a unique God also forms a part of the rules that Montfort sets for the charitable schools: *"My God . . . I adore you and acknowledge you as my sovereign Lord and Master upon whom alone I depend"* (RW 292,1).

Montfort places us before the *"three adorable Persons"* (SR 41), beginning with the Father: *"Here I adore you, Father of my fathers, / All-powerful Lord, before Whom all is nothing"* (H 24:33). Faith in this God, unique in the Trinity of Persons, clearly becomes a doxology, which Montfort puts on Mary's lips in the Magnificat: *"He is our one and true God, / Let all adore and bless Him! / The cries of all ring out loud / As they sing and address Him: / Glory to the Eternal Father, to the Word Incarnate / And to the Holy Spirit as well / Who in His love unites Them with an ineffable bond* (H 85:6).

The saint does not ask for a simple adoration but a *"perfect adoration"* (H 15:37). Among the principal oracles of Incarnate Wisdom he cites the text of John 4:24: "God is a spirit and those who adore him must do so in spirit and in truth" (cf. LEW 145). In Hymn 136, lines 4–6, Montfort interprets this text to suggest the totality and sincerity of one's gift of oneself to God: *"In spirit, it is not shared, / . . . in truth it is not feigned . . ."* (H 139:5–6).

Montfort is not interested solely in the immanent Trinity, God *"in Himself,"* but also in the economic Trinity, God *"in his blessings"* (H 50,1). He adores the holy *"will"* (L 33), *"the justice and love with which divine Wisdom is treating his little flock"* (L 34), but also *"God's judgment"* (HD 20, H 8:39) and His *"blows"* (H 11:35; 101:50), i.e., the afflictions that we encounter in our journey through life.

c. "Adorable Jesus." The adoration that is directed to God in the Trinity is centered on the person of the *"adorable Jesus"* (LEW 8,223; SR 6; SM 78), acknowledged by the faith of the Church as *"true God and true* *man"* (LEW 223). At the same time, Jesus remains, in Bérulle's words, a "means" of adoration: *"Before his Father, he truly amazes, / He humbles himself every day, / He prays, he adores, he constantly praises, / He speaks for us in a powerful way"* (H 40:8).

Among the mysteries of Jesus, Montfort gives precedence to that of his childhood. He sings the mystery of Christmas in Bérullian terms, inviting us to adore the Christ child: *"The Eternal is become a day, the Word is now grown silent, / The All-Powerful is now an infant. / Let us acknowledge, / Let us adore . . . / Our God a tiny infant"* (H 57:1). The saint looks beyond the picture of a small infant lying in hay and, in the paradoxical encounter between divine grandeur and human weakness, adores the Lord: *"A God in all his majesty / Has become part of humanity / our likeness. / Let us go adore him . . ."* (H 57:5). He imagines the kings, prostrate before the infant Jesus, acknowledging his divinity among the signs of poverty: *"Your almighty power is for us to adore / Despite your appearance so lowly and poor"* (H 60:7). While expressing his admiration for Mary, Montfort reserves his adoration for her child: *"Dear child of Mary, / . . . She has an infant, our Lord Who is adorable, / Let us all greet / Let us humbly meet / This Mother who is admirable"* (H 63:1).

After this adoration of Jesus as an infant, Montfort adores him on the Cross. *"The Cross is adorable"* (H 102,23; cf. H 19:12; FC 1), he proclaims, while noting that it is a case not of absolute but of relative adoration (LEW 172). He explains this adoration in light of Wisdom: by the Passion and death on the Cross, the Cross *"became as it were deified and an object to be adored by angels and by men. Jesus now requires that all his subjects adore it as they adore him"* (LEW 172). The Cross, when it is received into the hands of God, is the mark of the faithful disciple of Jesus Christ (FC 3). Thus it becomes the true sign of the Christian (cf. H 109:23).

Regarding religious observances, Montfort does not fail to emphasize the value of adoration of the Eucharist. For the Daughters of Wisdom he ordains that *"each week they make at least an hour of adoration of the Blessed Sacrament"* (RW 134,2), but he believes that there should also be Eucharistic piety among the simple faithful whom he catechizes. In the hymn "The Rule of a Person converted during a Parish Mission," Montfort gives priority to an hour each month of Eucharistic adoration, asserting with Bérulle that Jesus is the sunlight of the soul: *"An entire hour each month is spent / In my primary devotion; / It is the Blessed Sacrament / I adore without reservation"* (H 139:60).

Finally, Montfort turns in satisfaction to adoration of the Heart of Jesus: *"O Heart of God, adorable Heart! / Heart, object of my total love"* (H 47:1); *"Mortal, adore with the angels / This Heart which must be adored"* (H 40:5). He does not look at the Heart of Jesus in isolation but in connection with the Trinity and with the Heart of the Virgin: *"Infinitely adorable Heart / In the Most Holy Trinity"* (H 40:9); *"He is adorable; I praise his Heart, / I praise with all proportion / His admirable Mother and her Heart. / So great is their union"* (H 40:33). One could hardly wish for greater theological precision in such simple, spiritual language.

IV. Adoration of God in Our Times

If Montfort finds places everywhere in which to adore God, today we speak of the "exile" of God and the Trinity from the daily lives of men and women.

On the one hand, we note the fact of God's absence from our world: "God's **habitat** no longer exists in this world, and if the heavens sing His glory, their song is a posthumous song. . . . The universe has become uninhabited."[22] Indeed, the word "adoration" has all but disappeared from vocabularies, even the theological vocabulary. Today one would say that the culture, at best, prefers to speak **of** God rather than speak **to** God in a context of prayer and adoration.

On the other hand, adoration among Christians seems to leave out the Christian concept of Triune God: "It scarcely seems to matter, in doctrines of faith as well as in ethics, that God is one and triune."[23] We often fall into a generic deism that excludes the Holy Trinity: "It is no exaggeration to say that we once again find the Trinity exiled from Christian theory and praxis. Yet it is perhaps this exile that gives rise to our nostalgia and motivates us to recover the beauty of the 'trinitarian legacy' in theology and in life."[24]

Even if his experience is not ours, Montfort helps us to recover the adoration of a unique God in the true biblical monotheistic sense and, at the same time, adoration of a specifically Christian God, the Trinitarian God. But it is up to us to make these essential dimensions live in the difficult context and the language of our times.

1. Idolatry or adoration?

Our age is not one of atheists but, rather, one of idolaters. In effect, the man who is living as if God did not exist but who cannot live without religion is resorting to supplementary gods, to whom he invariably offers incense in his own secret adoration. When a man no longer adores God, he replaces God with idols. Thus, before all else, it is necessary to free mankind from all idolatry with a profession of faith in the one God Who has revealed Himself throughout the history of salvation.

a. Liberation from modern idolatries. Notwithstanding the strict interdiction against directing one's adoration to possible rivals to God (cf. Deut 4:19, 5:7; Ex 34:14), the people of Israel fell back into the idol worship from which they had been wrenched away. The Bible recognizes two forms of idolatry: **perversion** and **substitution.** "The first arises with respect to Yahweh, when the image or even the name of God is manipulated or perverted; the second, when YHWH is replaced with other gods or false gods."[25] These same forms of idolatry exist in the world today. The idolatry of "perversion" exists when men and women, who are the image of God, are oppressed by new forms of slavery. And the idolatry of "substitution" occurs when mankind endows the works of his own hands with an absolute or divine character: the god of money, the god of power, the god of sex, the god of technology, etc.[26] As Montfort notes, citing the Bible, in order to adore God we must extricate ourselves from all idolatry. This is the most important liberation: freeing men and women from the diabolic circle of egoism so that they are open to adoration of God.

b. Adoration in spirit and truth. In response to the contemporary difficulty in finding places for encountering God, Montfort gives special value to the biblical verse of John 4:24: *"I serve God Whom I adore, / In spirit and in truth"* (H 139,4). The significance of this famous text in the Gospel of John does not lie in any affirmation of a worship that is purely internal, without rites, gestures, or forms. Certainly the text affirms the relative value of the material temple, because henceforth the Father wishes to encounter mankind only in the temple of the body, which Jesus restores to life (Jn 2:19–22). In the person of Christ, "we see a new **type** of adoration of God, in which the **place** of worship is unimportant."[27] True adorers no longer have any need for a national religion at Jerusalem or on Mount Garizim (Jn 4:20–23). They adore the Father *"in spirit and truth,"* which is to say in the Holy Spirit (in John "spirit" always refers to the divine Spirit), and in the revelation that is centered on the truth of Jesus (Jn 14:6). True adorers are the baptized, begotten by the Spirit (Jn 3:3–8). Wholly sanctified, they can adore by means of "a consecration of their entire being, spirit, soul, and body (1 Thess 5:23)."[28] True adoration is thus a gift from on high and takes the form of responding in love to the revelation, in Christ, of the true face of God.

2. Return to the Trinitarian legacy

The Trinity must be liberated from its exile and must no longer be considered a kind of spiritual theorem without any connection with the Christian life. We can encounter the three Divine Persons in the history of salvation, as in Karl Rahner's axiom "The economic Trinity is the immanent Trinity." Indeed, "if God in Himself were something other than the God Who is the subject of revealed history, we would have no other means of access in spirit and truth to the profundity of the Trinitarian life."[29]

The wonders that God has performed in the history of salvation are thus the road that leads the Christian, as it led the mother of Jesus (Lk 1:46–55), to praise and adoration of the Lord. And since this glory cannot be captured in history, there is always room for silence, amazement, adoration, especially with respect to the mysteries of the life of Christ and how they touch the Virgin Mary, and above all to those Montfort loved to emphasize: the Incarnation, the Cross, the Eucharist. *The Love of Eternal Wisdom* expresses from beginning to end admiration and adoration for the entire Trinitarian plan of salvation and for each mystery of Eternal Wisdom.

From Montfort's perspective, a life consecrated to Christ by the hands of Mary is an act of adoration, in its negative as well as its positive aspects. It implies a total sacrifice of oneself in the renunciation of Satan and of all forms of evil. It requires a total, perpetual gift that unites us with Christ *"because he is our last end. Since he is our Redeemer and our God we are indebted to him for all that we are"* (TD 125).

Spirituality for Montfort is incarnational. Montfort adores God in the poor and he takes care of them concretely. Certainly God remains God because He is transcendent, but we must discern His presence in the world of the oppressed. To adore this presence means to become involved in the disappearance from the world of the idolatries and ideologies that become the means of oppressing the children of God. The mystical character of adoration is nourished on history and reverts to history in prayer and engagement; its object is the coming of God's reign in the world.

G. Fenili - S. De Fiores

Notes: (1) Blain, 14. (2) Cf. S. De Fiores, *Itinerario,* 106–114, 176–183. (3) H. Boudon, *Les saintes voies de la Croix (The Holy Ways of the Cross),* Hérissant, Paris 1769, 109 and 123. (4) Blain, 46. (5) H. Boudon, *Les saintes voies,* 234. (6) Blain, 52. (7) Besnard I, 7–8. (8) Besnard II, 181. (9) Besnard II, 182. (10) Besnard II, 183. (11) F. Bourgoing, preface to P. de Bérulle, *Oeuvres complètes de Bérulle (Complete Works of Bérulle),* ed. Migne, Paris 1856, 101. (12) P. de Bérulle, *Oeuvres,* 1198. (13) Ibid., 334. (14) Ibid., 1210. (15) Ibid., 1199. (16) Ibid., 1245. (17) A. Molien, *Bérulle,* in DSAM 1 (1937), 1554. (18) P. de Bérulle, *Oeuvres,* 938.(19) Ibid., 183. (20) Ch. de Condren, *L'idée du sacerdoce et du sacrifice de Jésus-Christ (The Ministry and the Sacrifice of Jesus Christ),* Paris 1901, 41. (21) I. Noye and M. Dupuy, *Olier,* in DSAM 11 (1982), 745. (22) Ch. Duquoc, *La dislocazione della questione dell'identità di Dio e il problema della sua localizzazione (The Dislocation of the Question of the Identity of God and the Problem of Its Localization),* in Con 28 (1992) 4, 19. (23) J. Moltmann, *Trinità e regno di Dio (The Trinity and the Kingdom of God),* Brescia 1983, 11. (24) B. Forte, *Trinità comme storia: Saggio sul Dio cristiano (Trinity As History: An Essay on the Christian God),* Edizioni paoline, Cinisello Balsamo 1985, 14. (25) P. Richard, *Presenza e rivelazione di Dio nel mondo degli oppressi (The Presence and Revelation of God in the World of the Oppressed),* in Con 28 (1992) 4, 49–50. (26) Ibid., 50. (27) R. Schnackenburg, *Il vangelo di Giovanni,* Paideia, Brescia 1973, 1:646. *The Gospel According to St. John,* trans. Kevin Smith, Herder & Herder, New York 1968 (28) J. de Vaux and J. Guillet, *Adoration, in Vocabulaire de théologie biblique,* ed. X. Léon-Dufour, Cerf, Paris 1962, 17. *Themes of the Bible,* Fides, Notre Dame 1960 (29) B. Forte, *Trinità comme storia,* 19.

ANGELS/DEMONS

SUMMARY

I. ANGELS IN THE LIFE OF SAINT LOUIS MARIE:
   1. Montfort's devotion to the angels;
   2. Motives for this devotion.

II. DEMONS IN THE LIFE OF SAINT LOUIS DE MONTFORT:
   1. Fallen angels in the culture of seventeenth-century Europe;
   2. Saint Louis de Montfort and demons.

III. MONTFORT'S EXPLANATION OF PURE SPIRITS:
   1. The angels:
      a. Their identity,
      b. The angels and Our Lady,
      c. Angels at the service of human beings.
   2. The devil:
      a. Origin of devils,
      b. The devil and human beings,
      c. The devil and Mary.

IV. RELEVANCE OF MONTFORT'S TEACHING:
   1. Balanced stress on angels/demons;
   2. Rejection of Satan and baptismal renewal;
   3. Celebrating the angels.

The CCC declares: "The existence of the spiritual, non-corporeal beings that Sacred Scripture usually calls 'angels' is a truth of faith. The witness of Scripture is as clear as the unanimity of Tradition."[1]

Although obviously an element of Montfort's teaching, angels or devils are by no means central to his spirituality. Saint Louis Marie's teaching on this topic dovetails with the fundamental doctrine of Scripture and of the Church. Both his life and his works reveal a vivid awareness of the messengers of the Lord and of the fallen angels, the demons.

I. ANGELS IN THE LIFE OF SAINT LOUIS MARIE

1. Montfort's devotion to the angels

Even as a seminarian in Paris, Montfort was known for the veneration he had toward the angels: he "urged his confreres to show marks of respect and tenderness to their guardian angels."[2] He often ended his letters with a salutation to the guardian angel of the person to whom he was writing: "*I salute your guardian angel*" (L 7, 12, 20, 33). He saluted all the angels in the city of Nantes (L 33), a custom that, it appears, he repeated when he entered a new village or city.[3]

Of all the heavenly host, Michael the Archangel is the one to whom Montfort had the greatest devotion. Michael, whose name signifies "who is like unto God," is mentioned in Dan 10:13 as one of the "chief princes" who with Gabriel protect the Jews against the "prince" of Persia. In Dan 10:21 and 12:1, Michael appears as "the great prince who stands over your people." In Jude 9 Michael the archangel is caught up in a dispute with the devil over the body of Moses. The archangel is especially venerated as the leader of the angelic host in the battle between the dragon and the dragon's angels (Rev 12:7).

Saint Louis Marie's name is closely associated with Saint Michael, "*the prince of all the heavenly court*" (TD 8). The missionary considered Michael zealous for the glory of God (PM 28), conqueror "*in the tremendous battle which was fought out in heaven between truth, with St. Michael as its champion, and falsehood represented by Lucifer*" (RM 61). On his return from his long pilgrimage to Rome, Montfort made a retreat at Mont Saint Michel "to pray to this archangel to obtain from him the grace to win souls for God, to confirm those already in God's grace, and to fight Satan and sin."[4] In his retreats to soldiers, he usually organized them into a confraternity under the patronage of Saint Michael so that the results of the retreat would be lasting.[5] The soldiers were given "*small crosses of Saint Michael to wear*" (L 21). His reverence for Michael was such that some of his calvaries had a statue of the archangel. Describing the cross the saint erected at Salertaine, his early biographer Besnard writes: "Underneath, there was built a vaulted chapel with a beautiful altar on which was placed a large statue of Saint Michael."[6] The archangel is mentioned in two of the vagabond troubadour's hymns: H 21:2 and H 139:63. The first reference speaks of the archangel subduing Lucifer, the second again alludes to this conquest and adds that it is Michael who "*weighs all souls / for heaven or for the flames.*" This corresponds to the belief of the Church, for "in the Christian liturgy, Michael is the protector of the Church and the angel who escorts the souls of the departed into heaven."[7]

2. Motives for this devotion

One of the reasons why Saint Louis Marie de Montfort had such devotion to the angels is that veneration of the pure spirits was an integral part of his training and also of his culture. His college teachers, the Jesuits, were known for their zeal in propagating devotion to the angels. Montfort's seminary training under the Sulpicians brought him into contact with the thought of Cardinal de Bérulle and Olier, both of whom had deep veneration for the angels.[8] Furthermore, in the course of the seventeenth and eighteenth centuries, manuals of piety and treatises on the pure spirits were numerous. Preachers especially saw in this devotion an excellent means of leading their people to higher perfection. The faithful were invited to imitate the purity (i.e., total obedience) of the angels and to have recourse to their guardian angels, especially in times of difficulty.

Montfort did, however, not believe in angels simply because his age praised them. His forceful writings on angels would indicate that he intensely experienced on certain occasions the presence of his guardian angel. Tradition claims that several times he enjoyed a mystical vision of his angel, although Montfort himself never refers to such an incident.

II. Demons in the Life of Saint Louis de Montfort

The fallen angels, or demons, are far from forgotten by the missionary. Involved as he was in "*the reform of the Church and the renewal of the face of the earth*" (PM 17), he understandably experienced the power of evil. With the Church, he believed in not some abstract negative force but in personal spiritual beings who had at the dawn of creation refused to obey God. His vocation as retreat master and, most especially, as a preacher of parish missions, gave him occasion to speak on the devil. Sixty seven of his hymns (out of a total of 164) mention the devil, and some more than once. All the major works of Montfort contain references to the devil. It must be said, then, that this roving missionary believed himself to be at war with Satan, for he saw himself as the apostle of Jesus, who fought with the demons and who called the devil "a murderer from the beginning" (Jn 8:44). The CCC is clear on the existence of fallen angels.[9]

1. Fallen angels in the culture of seventeenth-century Europe

Christian civilization during the sixteenth century suffered a religious and moral crisis. Books on demonology multiplied, and the seventeenth century saw a great increase in books about demons, demonic possession, monsters, vampires, and genies. Witch hunting was common. But with the beginning of the Enlightenment during the eighteenth century, skepticism heightened, and the very existence of pure spirits—whether good or bad—was more and more rejected by so-called cultured society.

Saint Louis de Montfort lived at the junction of these two currents, the baroque coming to an end, the Enlightenment steadily growing. His doctrine on fallen angels was influenced by both these strands of thought.

2. Saint Louis de Montfort and demons

Since the evil influence of the rebellious angels was an obstacle in the ongoing conversion of his people to Jesus, Montfort referred to them in his mission sermons: "*Remember that Satan awaits you at the door in order to take from you that divine seed [the Word of God] for fear that you will use it for your salvation*" (LS 176). The missionary aimed at destroying not only the reign of sin in people's hearts but also the occasions of sin: "He also undertook to destroy the external works of Satan, such as books contrary to religion and good morals."[10]

Faced with cases of possession brought to him for help, Saint Louis de Montfort's primary aim was to bring about a deep conversion in the possessed person. "Montfort was more interested in chasing the demons from souls than using the means that the Church employs in chasing them from bodies. If the prescribed prayers of the Church were not efficacious in solving a case of diabolical possession, he saw it as a trap to make him lose time that could be better used to destroy the empire of sin."[11] Montfort himself, according to his early biographers, experienced the presence of Satan. Grandet gives several examples of these rather violent attacks,[12] which Montfort did not particularly fear, since he had full confidence in the power of Jesus and Mary. At the end of his life, the saint declared: "*It is in vain that you attack me. I am between Jesus and Mary. . . . I will sin no more*"[13]

III. Montfort's Explanation of Pure Spirits

Saint Louis Marie had to respond to a question that is quite contemporary: who are these spirits, angels and demons? His response is nothing more or less than what is taught by the Catholic Church.

1. The angels

a. Their identity. Montfort agrees with the classification of angels into nine choirs (TD 8) as established by Pseudo-Denys. Montfort also mentions the cherubim and seraphim (H 57:2), the angels (LEW 109), and the archangels (H 139:63). They surround the throne of God and constitute his court (H 127). They are God's servants and messengers (H 40:3-5; LEW 98, 110, 112), obedient to Him from the beginning. They sing God's praises (H 44:5; 65:2; 98:25). Their number is beyond our imagining; God is lavish in the creation of pure spirits.

When speaking about the angels, Montfort calls special attention to the guardian angels (H 110 is a prayer to one's guardian angel). "His explanation of the nature and of the role of our guardian angel is rich and remarkably concise. . . . He wishes to lead our soul to a devotion towards this prince of paradise who is always at our side."[14]

b. The angels and Our Lady. The one case where Saint Louis de Montfort can claim some originality in his preaching on the angels is when he speaks about the relationship of angels to Our Blessed Mother.

Montfort uses the angels as a point of comparison to bring out the grandeur of Mary. The angels ask each other questions about Mary: *"Quae est ista?"* (TD 3). God loves Our Lady far more than He loves the angels (TD 5). The angels themselves rejoice in the presence of Mary (TD 5). The angels praise her, even though she is incomprehensible to them (SM 19; TD 8). Mary has authority over the angels (TD 8), and she is more powerful than they (TD 27); the angels are pleased to obey her (TD 204). The "*Hail Mary well said . . . has the angels rejoice*" (TD 253). As, in Jewish tradition, the army of angels underlines the transcendence of God,[15] so, too, Montfort gives glory to Our Lady by placing at her feet the heavenly host.

c. Angels at the service of human beings. The total obedience of the angels, their complete adherence to God Alone, makes Montfort call them models for the human race. Their help as guardians of individuals and of communities is to be treasured. In emphasizing the horror of the first sin, Montfort writes: "*Adam came close to despair. He could not hope for help from angels or any of God's creatures*" (LEW 40).

The role of the angels is that of messengers of God and, in that sense, intermediaries between God and human creatures (LEW 109, 112). Angels warn human beings of the dangers they face if they do not agree to carry the Cross after Christ (LC 58). The guardian angels accompany each human person, "*guarding them in this life / against every dangerous incident*" (H 12, 18). As they did with Adam, the angels flee a person who has willingly rejected God; they quickly return, however, at the very first sign of repentance (H 98:25). Therefore, all people should respect guardian angels (H 139:64) and pray to them (H 110).

Montfort's veneration of the guardian angels, the subject of Hymns 110 and 121, is an expression of the faith of the Church: "From infancy to death," the CCC teaches, "human life is surrounded by their [guardian angels'] watchful care. . . . Already here on earth the Christian life shares by faith in the blessed company of angels and men united in God."[16]

2. The devil

Montfort often links together the devil and the world (e.g., LEW 199; LC 8, 41; RW 14), for he understands the world to be creation not yet turned to God. Anything, therefore, that is not motivated by an authentic religious purpose, whether it be theater, science, art, literature, etc., Montfort considers to be at best a waste of time and a possible means of distancing us from God. The "world," therefore, and "demons" are joined together in opposing the reign of Jesus Christ. The world in this sense is "*the synagogue of Satan*" (H 29:6) and "*the infamous Babylon*" (H 107:12). The missionary's interest in demons is not for the sake of increasing his knowledge; rather, he sees devils as a hindrance to his apostolate of reform and renewal.

a. Origin of devils. When discussing demons, Father de Montfort places himself in the tradition of the Scriptures as they are taught, prayed, proclaimed by the Catholic Church. Simply put, demons are fallen angels who are in an eternal rebellion against God: "*Satan fell because of pride*" (H 29, 68). He takes up the biblical symbol of the serpent to designate Satan (H 107:14-15), underlining the "*malice of this ancient serpent*" (TD 52). He also uses the biblical image of beasts of all sorts to represent the devil and his power of evil, as when he speaks of the future of his TD manuscript: "*I clearly foresee that raging beasts will come in fury to tear to pieces with their diabolical teeth this little book and the one the Holy Spirit made use of to write it*" (TD 114). But we are always to remember that Satan himself is a slave of God (TD 70). With Jesus Christ, therefore, we can conquer the ruses of the devil; this power he attributes especially to his Missionaries of the Company of Mary (PM 12, 13).

b. The devil and human beings. The devil, humiliated in seeing that human beings are called to take his place in heaven (H 127:74; LEW 43), tries to separate people from God. He attempts to drag as many as possible toward all sorts of sin in order to make them the reprobate, i.e., radically turned against the Lord. Montfort echoes the words of 1 Pet 5:8: "Your enemy the devil, like a roaring lion, prowls round looking for someone to devour."

c. The devil and Mary. Our Lady is the antithesis of Lucifer: "*What Lucifer lost by pride, Mary won by humility. What Eve ruined and lost by disobedience, Mary saved by obedience. By obeying the serpent, Eve ruined her children as well as herself and delivered them up to him. Mary by her perfect fidelity to God saved her children with herself and consecrated them to his divine majesty*" (TD 53). Satan has been conquered by Mary's "Yes," and therefore she is the enemy of the devil: "*The magnificence of the devil is even more humbled to see himself under the feet of the Blessed Virgin Mary, the most humble person who has ever been, than to feel crushed by the arms of the Almighty*" (N 70; cf TD 52). The devil also tries to fool people by leading them into false devotions to Our Lady (TD 90). But "*when the Hail Mary is well said, that is, with attention, devotion and humility, it is, according to the saints, the enemy of Satan, putting him to flight; it is the hammer that crushes him*" (TD 253). Devotion to Our Lady is, therefore, a powerful means of conquering any and all temptations of the devil. St. Louis Marie's doctrine reminds us that, like the angels, we are destined for service to God, not like the fallen angels, who fell from service to pride.

IV. Relevance of Montfort's Teaching

1. Balanced stress on angels/demons

Saint Louis de Montfort's treatment of the pure spirits, angels and demons, is nothing more than an authentic proclamation of the teachings of the Church. His insistence on the reality of the angels—guardian angels in particular—and the fallen angels, the demons, is an important instruction for all ages of the Church. Especially in an industrial age that considers anything "pure spirit" to be a product of man's fantasy, the teachings of this missionary can serve as a reminder of the truth of the Church's teaching. When angels become the sole property of the artist or poet, Montfort's writings and life sound a much needed alarm.

Although the style of Montfort's teaching is quite baroque at times, nonetheless his orthodox treatment of angels/demons is a refutation to extreme forms of "angel worship" that are found in some areas of the world. As twenty-first-century man searches for the transcendent in a highly secularized world, some have overstepped the boundary of the true and have landed in a morass of superstitions about angels and demons. To these mythical spirits they give names and duties foreign to the biblical teaching. Worse still, they meditate on these imagined angels with a veneration exceeding logic; devil worship is not, sadly, a thing of the past. Here also, Montfort's clear Christocentric Marian teaching—which is the context for his doctrine on angels/demons—can show the true path. Moreover, those who consider the devil a mere trifle or, at the other extreme, become involved in Gnostic dualism and think of the devil as equal to God will find in Montfort a needed antidote.

2. Rejection of Satan and baptismal renewal.

Montfort's linkage of the rejection of Satan and all his works with the renewal of the promises of Baptism is in total harmony with the Easter liturgy. The missionary, however, made this renewal an integral, if not an essential, part of his parish missions and retreats. Montfort urges us, then, to reject Satan and to renew our absolute allegiance to the Lord not only at Easter but every time we conclude a retreat or renewal program and even after a day of recollection. It is also, as it was for Saint Louis Marie, an occasion for a clarification of the role of angels, whose help we implore, and of devils, whose pomps and works we reject.

3. Celebrating the angels

Saint Louis de Montfort calls upon us to rejoice and praise God for the presence of the angels. Especially at the Divine Liturgy, where myriads of angels worship the Eucharistic Lord, we should advert to their presence; the Sanctus, which the Church calls upon us to sing with all the heavenly host, would appear to be a fitting moment to acknowledge the presence of the angels. The celebration of the angels puts us in communion with them, the adorers of God, a "place of theophany, a living manifestation of God" (P. Evdokimov). The conviction of the presence of pure spirits also "opens up our mind beyond the frontiers of the visible world. The cosmos in which we live is an extremely small reality in comparison with the spiritual universe, . . . and it is in the interior of this universe that the human world is located, with all its materiality, temporality. . . . The theology of the angels widens the limits of our vision of the world by opening up to us its highest dimension and grandeur, calling us to adore the one Creator of all."[17]

A. Delesalle - H. Stockert

Notes: (1) CCC, 328. (2) Blain, 53-54. (3) Cf. De Bérulle, *Opusc. 186: Pour se conduire chrétiennement dans les voyages et dans les affaires (In Order to Act in a Christian Manner on Trips and in Business),* in *Oeuvres (Works),* ed. Migne, 1856, 1263. (4) Grandet, 105. (5) Besnard, I, 252. (7) John L. McKenzie, *Dictionary of the Bible,* Bruce Publishing, Milwaukee 1965, 573. (8) H. J. Icard, *Doctrine de M. Olier (The Teaching of M. Olier),* Paris 1929, 185 and note 1. (9) CCC, 391-395. (10) Besnard I, 81. (11) Grandet, 23. (12) Grandet, 86-88. (13) Grandet, 260. (14) Fradet, *Les Oeuvres du Bx De Montfort Poète Mystique et Populaire Ses Cantiques avec Étude Critique et Notes,* Beauchesne, Paris 1929, 185. (15) Cf. Ph. Faure, *Les Anges (The Angels),* Cerf/Fides, La Flèche 1988, 24-25. (16) CCC, 336. (17) C. Rochetta, *Il problema degli angeli e dei demoni nella riflessione teologica odierna (The Problem of Angels and Devils in Contemporary Theological Reflection),* in B. Marconcini, A. Amato, C. Rocchetta, and M. Fiori, *Angeli e demoni. Il dramma della storia tra il bene e il male (Angels and Demons: The Drama between Good and Evil),* Edizioni dehoniane, Bologna 1991, 30.

APOSTLE

SUMMARY

I. MONTFORT'S APOSTOLIC JOURNEY:
1. The birth and blossoming of an apostolic vocation;
2. The apostolate, a dynamic reality in Montfort's life;
3. The development of an apostolic spirituality.

II. THE APOSTOLIC MISSION ACCORDING TO MONTFORT:
1. A link with the beginning: in the footsteps of the Apostles;
2. A way of acting apostolically;
3. A lifestyle: the vagabond apostolate;
   a. Breaking away,
   b. The journey,
   c. The end;
4. Unity: missionary/spiritual leader;
5. Paul of Tarsus and Louis Marie de Montfort.

I. MONTFORT'S APOSTOLIC JOURNEY

The distinguishing feature of Father de Montfort's life was its apostolic character. He was called to be a missionary. His vision was neither static nor worldly, despite innumerable influences to the contrary. His vocation to the apostolic life was not a fixed thing, a gift received in its entirety at birth. Rather, it was a dynamic reality, flourishing, ripening, knowing its moments of crisis, but constantly being reborn throughout his life journey.

1. The birth and blossoming of an apostolic vocation

Strangely, none of his biographers seemed interested in pinpointing the moment when Father de Montfort first heard his call to the apostolic life. Probably, it came quite early, certainly before he arrived in Paris. Blain states, "Once he had finished his philosophical studies, his only thought was to study theology in depth, so as to prepare himself for the apostolic life; that was his aim."[1]

A more important testimony is Louis Marie's own explicit confession to Fr. Leschassier in 1702, when he wrote about his personal inclinations, *"which have always been and still are for mission work"* (L 11).

It appears that the parish missions in Brittany had strongly influenced the birth of Montfort's missionary vocation, particularly those of Fr. Leuduger. Most likely he had heard about these from Fr. Bellier as early as 1687. In fact, when he began to look seriously at the idea of an apostolate, it was precisely this parish mission model that he recalls most naturally: *"I still harbor the desire I had in Paris to join Fr. Leuduger, a student of Fr. de St. Brieuc. He is a great missionary and a man of wide experience"* (L 5).

It is well known that Father de Montfort's vocation suffered many trials in the Sulpician milieu of Paris. Montfort's contact with Olier's writings as well as the example of Bayün, confirmed his choosing of an apostolic ministry that had a rich contemplative dimension, a ministry centered on the home missions, but open to the foreign missions.[2]

The teachings of his Sulpician masters, Brenier and Leschassier, followers of Tronson, recommended a life of fidelity to the Rule, which avoided all novelty, and demanded the practice of the "science of the saints." Forty years after its foundation (1643), Saint-Sulpice (with the exception of Bayün) seemed to have forgotten the mystical and missionary dimensions so beloved by Olier. In contrast to the Sulpician ideal, they presented a hidden and withdrawn life, so much so that, according to Leschassier, "when one is outside, cut off from the seminary community, one experiences being in a violent place, outside one's center."[3]

This heavily influenced Montfort's vocation, and he found himself in the belly of a paradox—faced with the opposites of contemplation and action. This he expressed in his famous letter of December 6, 1700 to Leschassier: *"I find myself, as time goes on, torn by two apparently contradictory feelings. On one hand, I feel a secret attraction for a hidden life in which I can efface myself and combat my natural tendency to show off. On the other hand, I feel a tremendous urge to make our Lord and his holy Mother loved, to go in a humble and simple way to teach catechism to the poor in country places and to arouse in sinners a devotion to our Blessed Lady"* (L 5).

These opposites within himself became complementary, mutual, and interdependent. There was a coincidence of them, a oneness in Love. He experienced a graced union of such opposites without their being dissolved, without their natural polarity being removed. He chose the itinerant life of an apostle, becoming a contemplative in action. Montfort gave expression to this in Hymn 22. It was inspired by Surin, yet remained missionary in nature: *"The die is cast, I will travel the world; / I have taken it into my head to wander / So as to save my poor neighbor. . . ."*[4]

We can see five factors that inclined Louis de Montfort to choose a missionary vocation:

a. He saw clearly that his strongest and deepest inclination was to preaching and to catechetics for the poor. Exercising the discernment of spirits, he concluded that since the desires were *"good and persistent,"* they were of God (L 5, 16) and were to be followed.

b. His pastoral contacts convinced him of the missionary need. He saw that the local Church should become more responsive to the need for preaching the Word to sinners and to the marginalized. As a result, he decided to dedicate himself to parish missions.

c. He first preached parish missions in the areas surrounding Nantes and Poitiers, and this experience confirmed Montfort in his apostolic vocation.

d. Montfort made a discovery of considerable importance in the first few years of his priestly life. It was that of Wisdom. He entered into a spiritual marriage with her (cf. L 20 of August 28, 1704). Wisdom was apostolic, he claimed in his famous conversation with Blain in 1714. It was a conversation that illumined his whole life up to that point. Wisdom inspired one *"to undertake great things for the glory of God and the salvation of souls"* (LEW 100).

e. Lastly, he considered the words of the Pope to be crucial. The Holy Father confirmed him in his call to preach parish missions in France. He approved of his methods and gave him the *ad honorem* title "Missionary Apostolic."[5] From then on, Father de Montfort did not doubt his apostolic mission, despite the inactive or difficult periods that were to beset him. In 1710, however, after the Calvary at Pontchâteau was demolished, he questioned whether he was called to the home or the foreign missions. He persuaded Des Bastières to come with him to Rome and to ask the Pope to send him to the East. Similarly, according to a 1714 letter, Montfort seemed ready to stay on at La Chèze (1712). There he even chose the spot where he wished to be buried, at Notre Dame de Pitié, provided his superiors did not decide otherwise.[6]

2. The apostolate, a dynamic reality in Montfort's life

To say that the missionary life consumed Montfort's life is to state the obvious. To the eyes of the world, he was first and last a missionary. It cannot be denied that he preached almost 200 missions between 1700 and 1716. Nor can there be any doubt that he saw himself as a missionary. This is evident not only from his missions and writings but also from incidents such as that at Sallertaine in 1712. Upon entering the house of a man hostile to the mission, he said to him, *"Well, Sir, you think I came here of my own volition. No, it is Jesus and Mary who have sent me; I am their ambassador."*[7]

We might say with Daniel-Rops, when speaking of the end of the seventeenth and the beginning of the eighteenth centuries, that Montfort was the vigorous "incarnation" of the "missionary spirit."[8]

Based on the biographical evidence, apostolic mission was at the heart of Montfort's life journey. Reflection on the structure and contents of his parish missions discloses the type of missionary that he was.

It is naive to think that all of the saint's time, from ordination to death, was devoted to giving parish missions. They were certainly the thread that ran through his life. But it was not an unbroken thread. Father Eijckeler notes three interruptions in Montfort's missionary activity: in Paris, between 1703 and 1704, after his expulsion from the Hospital in Poitiers; during his pilgrimage to Rome in 1706, which took six months; and in September 1710, after the interdict by the bishop of Nantes, which kept him idle until March 1711.[9]

Yet we must add also several other pauses: his stay at Saint-Lazare, from September 1707 to the summer of 1708; the time he spent in the hermitage of Saint-Éloi, in the summer/autumn of 1712; and at the cave in Mervent for more than a month in 1715. Also we should include some other journeys (to Paris in 1713 and to Rouen in 1714), pilgrimages (to Mont-Saint-Michel in 1706, and to Saumur in 1715), and retreats, as well as his times of sickness, especially his illness in 1711, which lasted nearly two months.[10]

These interruptions of his missionary calling only serve to underscore

Montfort's perseverance in it. In fact, his vocation suffered no real crises, save only what followed the destruction of the Calvary at Pontchâteau (1711). Indeed, these interruptions were very consistent with his mission, especially his journeys to Rome (1706), Paris (1713), and Rouen (1714) and his pilgrimage to Saumur (1716), all of which were directly concerned with either his own apostolate or that of the Company of Mary.

Over his life, the parish missions that Montfort preached varied both in number and in frequency. Approximately ten missions were spread over three months in the neighborhood of Nantes in 1701, roughly the same number in Poitiers and its suburbs in 1705, then not even ten between September 1706 and 1708 in Brittany around Rennes, where missions were rare. A renewed vigor followed in the Nantes area, between September 1708 and September 1710, with about twenty missions; finally, we come to the most intense period of his apostolate, in the dioceses of Luçon and La Rochelle (1711-1716), with a series of forty missions, which unfortunately were cut short by the death of the saint.

It is interesting to look beyond their general structure, to observe how the missions evolved.

L. Pérouas notes that in 1701 Montfort speaks of *"short missions"* (L 9), describing a brief ministry of catechetical teaching, preaching, and confessions that he carried on in the Nantes area. The following year, he described a seven-month stay in Poitiers as *"a continual mission,"* during which he heard confessions from morning till night almost every day, preached, visited the sick, and taught hymns (L 11). At that time, he speaks of his missions as being four or five weeks, with sermons, conferences, catechetical teaching, general confessions, communions, hymns, and processions. Finally, between 1711 and 1715, he speaks of more or less specialized gatherings, missions to women or to soldiers, which he described more as spiritual retreats.[11]

There were other variations during the different periods of Montfort's missionary life, as new insights shaped his ministry:

a. From being an independent missionary during the first period he became a member of a team led by Fathers Leuduger and Jobart in 1707-1708; then he was made director of missions that were given collaboratively with diocesan priests, religious, or lay brothers.

b. His missionary method acquired a new richness with the Covenant with God (GA, 501-503) after 1709. His missions were longer, had greater diocesan acceptance, and found new institutional approaches through schools, confraternities, etc., as well as follow-up parish missions, new ways of feeding the poor (first in Providence House, then in homes beginning in 1711), the construction of calvaries, etc.

In short, when Montfort defines the concept of mission in RM, it is a reflection of both his pastoral experience and his personal spirituality.

3. The development of an apostolic spirituality

The profound nature of Louis Marie's missionary vocation could not but help shape his spirituality. The apostolate became neither an ancillary nor an obstacle to the achievement of perfection. In fact, as early as his stay in Poitiers, Montfort noticed, with a certain sense of amazement, that his incessant activity was branching out into new forms of pastoral care that benefited the humblest classes of society. Far from weakening his life of ascetic virtue and union with God, he saw that the apostolate permitted immense spiritual progress. He received new insights, an increase of ease in speaking, and a greater opening of his heart to all (L 11). Later while meditating on apostolic zeal, he came to see it not only as salvific but as producing grace in abundance, leading to an incomparable glory. He prayed that his preaching would bring him not to a lesser but to a greater sanctity (H 21:11-15). In this way he was led to see the apostolic as the most divine of all works (H 21:12), as embodying the highest degree of perfection (LEW 30). In his writings intended for the Company of Mary, this idea is institutionalized, so to speak. Missionaries who followed in the footsteps of the Apostles were to have no fixed abode and were to be constantly occupied with giving missions (RM 2-6). PM ends with a call to priests who had fled to the desert or to places of solitude. He asks them to understand the apostolate, its pressing needs, and the priority it deserves (PM 29).

Pursuing this line of thought, Montfort not only shifted the emphasis from the contemplative life to the missionary life. He also discovered the apostolic purpose of crosses and purifications. They were not directly aimed at making one a friend of God. Rather, they sought to free an apostle from inordinate pride in a grace received or good accomplished. They prevented him from exalting himself in the presence of God (PM 46). The Cross was the lot of the missionary. It was intimately conjoined to apostolic wisdom (L 15; H 91:13, 31-32).

Montfort continued to live with the creative tension of contemplation and action. This can be seen in TD 196, where he gives priority to the contemplative life. He saw action (likened to a child's game) as the exception, with contemplation the rule.

Montfort spoke of the *"apostles of the end times."* He outlined an apostolic spirituality, with zeal as the virtue that raises one to sanctity before God (TD 47-59). Montfort might have overcome this ambivalence if his life had not been shortened by an early death. His mission apostolate had reached a high point when he died at the age of 43. A famous conversation with Blain in 1714 indicates two possible solutions. The first was experiential and mystical in nature. It was a spiritual integration through the graced presence of Jesus and Mary. This would have permitted Montfort to remain a contemplative, to live in intimate union with God in the midst of activity. The second was based on the principle of following Christ as Wisdom; by adopting his way of life, as reflected in his example and counsels. Montfort accepted the diverse vocations in the Church, including the Sulpician calling. But he chose the path of apostolic wisdom, for himself and his disciples. He saw in it a unique missionary charism, one capable of unifying the whole spiritual life.[12]

S. De Fiores

II. The Apostolic Mission according to Montfort

Montfort's first biographer tells us that during his pilgrimage to Rome in 1706, "Pope Clement XI gave him the title of Missionary Apostolic."[13] The term "apostolic" was a key word for Montfort. It properly described his "missionary path." Linked with the word "missionary," and having the etymological meaning of being "sent," it expressed something essential for St. Louis Marie. It pointed to a relationship with the Apostles of the early Church, and it gave a name to his dream for the Company of Mary and for himself.

1. A link with the beginning: in the footsteps of the Apostles

Montfort dreamed of missionaries *"called by God to preach missions in the steps of the Apostles, who were poor"* (RM 2), ready to suffer everything *"just as the Apostles were"* (PM 10), trained in *"the apostolic spirit"* (RM 12), never allowing themselves to be distracted from *"their apostolic work"* (RM 12), *"followers of the Apostles"* (PM 22), and following in all things the example *"which Jesus Christ, the apostles and apostolic men have handed down to us"* (RM 50). Montfort was himself such an *"apostolic missionary"* (RM 62), whose primary mandate came from the Pope himself. Finally, in the tradition of Saint-Sulpice and Olier, he sent his "White Penitents" on pilgrimage to Notre Dame des Ardilliers at Saumur *"to obtain from God through Mary's intercession good missionaries, who will follow the example of the apostles"* (PS 1). The emphasis in all this is too strong for us not to recognize something central for Montfort. What, then, was the significance of a *"missionary vocation"* (RM 2) for Montfort? What was this link to the Apostles? Why was it so important, if not indispensable, for him? Beginning with his earliest letters as a young priest to Leschassier, one can see his need to have his missionary orientation affirmed. And it was not by chance that he walked to Rome to seek this confirmation in 1706. Montfort needed to identify his apostolate, to feel himself in line with a movement within the Church, for fear "that I did not run my race in vain, or work in vain" (Phil 2:16). He felt led to drink directly from the spring of the Church's mission. So he turned to the Pope himself, and through him to the Apostles. In this way he discovered his true apostolic calling.

The origin of the Church's mission lies in this: Christ was sent by the Father "to announce good news to the poor" (Lk 4:18). In fact, just as the Father sent him, so Christ sent his Apostles. They walked in his footsteps and proclaimed the Good News to every nation. Founded by Christ through the Apostles and their successors, the Church in turn sent Montfort as Missionary Apostolic. He sent his Company.[14] In recalling these lines from the RM, we trace Montfort to the Apostles, from them to Jesus Christ, and from Jesus Christ to the Father and the Spirit. Through the Apostles, Montfort wanted to reach the *one who was sent*, the archetype, Jesus himself; to place himself in the main stream which takes its origin in the Trinity and is there at the birth of the Church. This is the first and most basic meaning behind his insistence on the Apostles. For Montfort, to be "apostolic" was to be an integral and vital part of the very movement that gave birth to the Church, a missionary movement that began with the Father, was realized in the Son, and was completed in the Spirit through the sending of the Apostles.

Montfort claimed this vital link both for himself and for his Company of Mary. It was his whole life. He clearly demonstrated it in the hundred or so missions that he preached. During the final ten years of his life he went from parish to parish. But beyond this he offers us a belief in the Second Coming of Christ, in the end times when the reign of God will be established, thanks to the *"Apostles of the end times"* (TD 58; PE 22). He wanted to be the first. The whole PM foresees the coming of such apostles: *"O Lord . . . It is indeed time to fulfill your promise"* (PM 5). Montfort, the Missionary Apostolic, thus sees himself as linked with both the beginning and the end of Church history. Thus reassured, he did not hesitate to pursue his proper mission: *"The die is cast. / I will travel the world . . ."* (H 22:1).

2. A way of acting apostolically

Montfort was not content with linking himself to the Apostles; he wanted to imitate them closely (PE 22) and to follow their example (RM 50). They were his models for exercising his mission, *"following their footsteps"* (RM 2). He insisted on going *"two by two"* (MR 52), *"on foot"* (RM 43), *"in complete dependence on Providence"* (RM 50), *"preferring . . . the poor to the rich"* (RM 7). He set out, always ready *"to be on the move and to suffer . . . just as the Apostles were"* (PE 10). Sent *"like lambs among wolves"* (RM 65), to do battle with the world, *"not like Religious who retreat from the world lest they be overcome, but like brave and valiant warriors on the battle-field, who refuse to retreat or even yield an inch"* (LC 2). These *"followers of the Apostles"* (PM 22), *"called by God to preach missions in the steps of the Apostles who were poor"* (RM 2), must avoid becoming settled, for *"the motto of the true missionary is one which enables him to say in all truth like St. Paul: instabiles sumus (we have no permanent home of our own)"* (RM 2). They should therefore be *"free from every other occupation and unimpeded by the administration of any temporal possessions which might hold them back . . . ready, like St. Paul . . . and other apostles, to run wherever God may call them"* (RM 6). In a word, they must be *"liberos,"* (Latin for child/free) a word on which Montfort gives a long commentary in PM 6-12.

Again, Montfort takes the Apostles as models for the specific ministry of the Word: *"These followers of the Apostles will preach with great power and effect. So powerful will their impact be that they will stir the minds and hearts of all who hear them"* (PM 22). Here it is good to recall two of Montfort's very rich insights into the true preacher, which remain relevant today. Commenting on the Lord's promise to his Apostles "I will give you a wisdom which your enemies will be unable to resist" (Lk 21:15), Montfort writes, *"How few preachers there are today who possess this most wonderful gift of eloquence and who can say with St Paul, 'We preach the wisdom of God' (1 Cor. 2:7). . . . They do not speak under the impulse of divine Wisdom or from a heart filled to overflowing with wisdom"* (LEW 97). In RM 62 he takes up again this description of an *"apostolic"* preacher: *"It is the easiest thing in the world to be a fashionable preacher. It is a difficult but sublime thing to be able to preach with the inspiration of an apostle."* And he concludes, *"The apostolic missionary should, therefore, preach . . . and he must first practice what he preaches"* (RM 62). We see here that Montfort has a certain interior spirit in mind. Here we come close to the meaning of what he termed "apostolic wisdom." He spoke at length about this with his friend Blain, who tells us about it in these words: "He added that there were different sorts of wisdom, as well as different degrees of wisdom; that the wisdom by which a community person should guide his life was one thing, and the wisdom of a missionary or an apostolic person another thing; that the community person did not have to undertake anything new but only to let himself or herself be guided by the Rule and the customs of the community. The missionary or apostolic person had to seek the glory of God instead of personal glory and to carry out new undertakings. . . . Those I suggested to him as models of wisdom were people of the first kind. . . . It was not the same thing for missionaries and apostolic persons. For these people always had to undertake something new. Some good work had to be done or defended. Inevitably people will always be talking about them. . . . And finally, if wisdom consisted in doing nothing for God, in not undertaking something for His glory, out of fear of what people would say, then the Apostles were wrong to leave Jerusalem. They should have shut themselves away in the upper room. Saint Paul should never have made so many journeys, nor should Saint Peter have attempted to plant the Cross on the Capitol."[15] Montfort drew his great evangelical inspiration from his models, the Apostles. He could sing joyfully of his life as a truly zealous missionary: *"When I go on my way, / my staff in my hand, / barefoot and without any carriage, / but also without any worries, / I march along in great state, / like a King with his court, / to the sound of the trumpet"* (H 144:1).

3. A lifestyle: the vagabond apostolate

The "vagabond apostolate" therefore became his life and the life he wanted for those who followed him. This imposed its own laws, to the point of becoming a lifestyle that Montfort passed on to his disciples. He said that the members of his apostolic band should be *"ready . . . to run"* (RM 6). He was, along with a few other founders of religious congregations, something of a pioneer, for he offered a style of religious life that was original.[16] Montfort himself was never a religious in the strict sense. But he never wanted to be alone (L 5; L 6). He yearned for a group, a band, etc.: *"Vis unita fit fortior" (In unity there is strength)* (PM 29). And here again, he makes reference to the disciples of Jesus, sent out two by two (RM 52). For his apostles of the road, he wrote RM, in which he sketched out an original lifestyle. Here, we see that he used special phrases to describe it, such as *"to set out on an adventure," "to be uprooted," "to leave Jerusalem,"* etc. An arrow could symbolize this lifestyle, one bearing the following inscriptions on its three main parts. On the feathered end "*break away*" (poverty), on the shaft *"undertake"* (obedience) and on the tip " *love*" (chastity).

a. Breaking away. This was the law of the vagabond apostolate, understood as: *"ready . . . to run"* (RM 6). For, as the ancient Romans used to say, "unnecessary baggage slows the walk." Our concern is with more than material baggage. Montfort strongly opposes those who prevent others from setting out, especially the *"habitatores quietis (lovers of the quiet life)"* (RM 2); and he also condemns *"what is being said daily, typically by all those worldly priests, those well-fed beneficed clerics, those pleasure-seeking ecclesiastics and those lovers of ease: 'I have bought a field . . . I have bought five yoke of oxen . . . have me excused . . . I cannot come'"* (RM 6). On the other hand, Montfort prays for *"men who are free, priests who are free with the freedom that comes from you, detached from everything, without father, mother, brothers, sisters or relatives and friends as the world and the flesh understand them, without worldly possessions to encumber or distract them, and devoid of all self-interest"* (PM 7). The idea of being a vagabond on the road gives a certain distinct color to the vow of poverty. What joy he found in living the freedom of the itinerant apostle. He sings of it enthusiastically: *"I travel about the world, / like a lost child, / wanting, despite others' objections, / neither goods nor money. / Having nothing, / I have everything"* (H 91:1; cf. H 22:22).

b. The journey. For Montfort this was *"leaving Jerusalem"*; it was boldness and enterprise. And here apostolic obedience found its place. It was not the facile obedience of either fleeing the world (FC 2) or hiding at home. He said that we had "only to follow in the footsteps and the practices of those who went before."[17] Such apostolic obedience is a difficult thing because it arises from a wisdom that upsets people. It "causes them to talk." It is a wisdom that does not conform to popular taste. Pioneers cannot set out without meeting this challenge. It is then that obedience becomes important, even essential, said Montfort. It is then that religious obedience becomes apostolic obedience. In his own life Montfort gave witness to this by giving to the bishops the same unconditional submission he gave to the Pope. For him there was no appeal from this obedience. It was total. It was an incontrovertible sign of what was good, an authentication of every mission.[18] Here, no less than in the case of poverty, Montfort is inflexible. The missionaries *"will obey their superiors in a wholehearted and undiscriminating manner. . . . In this Company, as in the Society of Jesus, it is obedience as we have described it which is the foundation and unshakable support of all its holiness and of all the blessings which God confers or will confer through its ministry"* (RM 19). He himself sings: *"I declare before God himself: / I would rather die, / even die condemned, / than be disobedient"* (H 91:28; cf. H 22:20).

c. The end. One always makes a journey for a reason. For Montfort, the reason for his journeys was of a personal one. He travelled in order to care for the souls of his brothers and sisters, especially the poor. His trips were made in the humble service of his neighbor (cf. H 22:1). He was moved by love of the Lord, who sent him. For Montfort love of neighbor was fused with the love of God Alone to become one Love, one source of energy and life. This was the unique religious character of our consecrated apostle. His consecrated chastity allowed him to separate from the world while his ascetical and contemplative life allowed him to reunite with those in it in loving service. This unselfish love is at the very root of Consecration. In Montfort's writings, it is expressed in a very forceful way: *"What, could I possibly see my dear brother's soul / perishing everywhere because of sin, / and not let my heart be touched by it? / No, Lord, no; it is too dear for that"* (H 22:1). He wanted to go off to India, then to North America; but the Pope sent him back to his own country.

But that is not enough: he continued to sing: *"I am a hunter of souls / for my Savior Jesus . . ."* (H 91:2). *"O my God, for your Gospel, / I want to suffer in town after town, / thousands of insults and evils. / If, by my life and the blood in my veins, / I can only destroy a single sin, / if I can touch only a single heart, / all my pains will be worth it."* (H 22:13). This completes the "apostolic" portrait of a consecrated person.

4. Unity: missionary/spiritual leader

Montfort being first of all a missionary, he drew primarily from this experience in giving the Church a unique spirituality, one centered on an apostolic Wisdom. He gave us the means to live this spirituality, centered on total Consecration through Mary to Jesus. Louis Marie did not live two separate lives. His spirituality was one. How can we discover such a vital unity? First we must recall that Montfort saw Jesus, the One sent by the Father, through the eyes of those he sent in the Spirit, his apostles. St. Louis Marie's spiritual writings reveal the unique way in which he contemplated Jesus in this missionary sense. We shall find there what some have called the descent of Wisdom's love towards men (LEW 65-71). For it is Wisdom, Jesus, who, *"in his pursuit of man . . . hastens along the highways, or scales the loftiest mountain peaks, or waits at the city gates, or goes into the public squares and among the gatherings of people, proclaiming at the top of his voice, 'You children of men, it is you I have been calling so persistently; it is you I am addressing; it is you I desire and seek; it is you I am claiming'"* (LEW 66). Montfort entered into communion with the wishes of Wisdom. He saw his path to perfection in the same way as he saw his mission. It came from the Father, and was realized in Jesus, God's Wisdom and Love for us. This is the root of his spirituality. He expresses this at the beginning of his Consecration: *"I thank you for having emptied yourself"* (LEW 223).

And at the center of this same movement, he discovered Mary. He then proclaimed this Credo: *"It was through the Blessed Virgin Mary that Jesus came into the world, and it is also through her that he must reign in the world"* (TD 1). Montfort consecrated himself to this apostolic life, and for it he took up his pen (cf. TD 110).

This corrects a too narrow view of his spirituality, one that ignores its missionary character by focusing on Montfort's relationship to God and to Mary while excluding his basic bond to his brothers and sisters. How could one possibly enter into communion with Wisdom Incarnate without at the same time entering into His Love for human beings? How could Louis Marie consecrate himself to Jesus through Mary, without the Consecration being a fulfillment of his mission; one that conjoined total abandonment of all goods with missionary poverty; one that conjoined unconditional surrender and the slavery of love with apostolic obedience; one that conjoined sacrificial love with consecrated chastity; one that saw all of this as the crowning glory of God's Kingdom? It is not surprising that all of Montfort's spiritual writings lyrically echo the missionary's song: *"God the Father wishes Mary to be the mother of his children until the end of time. . . . God the Son wishes to form himself, and, in a manner of speaking, become incarnate every day in his members through his dear Mother. . . . God the Holy Spirit wishes to fashion his chosen ones in and through Mary"* (TD 29, 31, 34). It is indeed to this realization of God's plan that the *"apostles of the end times"* are consecrated. For *"they will be like thunder-clouds flying through the air at the slightest breath of the Holy Spirit. Attached to nothing . . . they will shower down the rain of God's word and of eternal life. . . . They will be true apostles of the latter times to whom the Lord of Hosts will give eloquence and strength to work wonders and carry off glorious spoils from his enemies"* (TD 57-58). We discover "mission" to be at the very heart of Montfort's spirituality.

V. Paul of Tarsus and Louis Marie de Montfort

Finally, there is a personal affinity between Saint Paul and Montfort. They have many similarities.[19] Both were itinerant missionaries, both had strong characters, and both had deep prayer lives. It would be easy to quote Saint Paul each time we speak of Montfort. It is clear that, of all the Apostles, Montfort calls Paul *"the great Apostle"* (LEW 12; RM 49), or *"the great Saint Paul"* (H 21:16). He is the apostle who had the greatest influence on him. Montfort quoted Saint Paul no less than 220 times in his writings. They most closely resemble each other in the great theological themes that were significant and common to them: their Christology (cf. TD 61); Wisdom (LEW 15); the Cross (LEW 168/1 Cor 1:18-25); the renewal of baptismal vows (TD 126; RM 56/Eph 4:1; 23:4); the place of Mary at the very heart of the plan of salvation (TD 1/Gal 4:4-5); total Consecration to God (TD 120-121/Rom 12:1); the world and its false wisdom (RM 38; LEW 198/Rom 12:2). But perhaps we should underline those similarities which are particularly "missionary" or "apostolic." Here are some traits in St. Paul's "self-portrait" of a missionary; in them we can easily recognize Montfort: ardor (Phil 3:12-14/PM 1-5; H 22:1, 31); faith (2 Tim 1:12; Rom 1:16/LCM 1-3; TD 59); strength and boldness (2 Tim 1:7-8/PM 22, 28, 29; TD 56-7); zeal for souls (1 Cor 9:19/H 91; H 21; L 5; H 115; LEW ch. 6; TD 112); the ministry of the Word (Col 1:25; 1 Cor 2, 4; 2 Tim 4:2; 1 Cor 9:16/RM 60-62; PE 22; LEW 95-7; H 2:42); struggle (Col 2:1/H 22:4, 4, 18, 32; H 32:31; L 24; L 26); trials (1 Cor 4:9; 2 Cor 4:8-11; 11:23-33/L 16; L 26; H 91:2; H 22:13); sufferings (Col 1:24/LEW 175); discipline (1 Cor 9:27/L 10; TD 80-81); attachment to Jesus Christ (Phil 1:21; Gal 2:20/H 103; H 126; H 135; TD 67); disinterestedness (1 Thess 2:4; 2:9;

Phil 3:7-8/H 144; H 91; H 18); preference for the poor (1 Cor 1:26-27/L 6; H 91:22-23; H 144:20; RM 7); tenderness (Gal 4:19; 1 Cor 9:22; 1 Thess 2:7/H 22:1, 17; H 9:16, 18; H 14:1; LEW ch. 9); the humility of the servant (1 Cor 4:1; 1 Cor 15:9). These common traits suffice to illustrate how the term "Missionary Apostolic" was more than a title for Montfort. In the great tradition of Paul and the Apostles, this is what he really was. Montfort constantly leads us back to the wellsprings of the Church, to the great missionary themes that characterized the Church in world history. He takes us back so that we may recover some of the boldness and courage of the Church's early years. He does this in order to assist us in recovering the true missionary spirit of our age. In pointing out our roots, he transcends the limitations of his time and remains forever present and relevant for all time.

G. Dallaire

Notes: (1) Blain, 12. (2) For what touches on the preceding period, cf. S. De Fiores, *Itinerario.* Concerning the relationship of Montfort to Olier-Bayün, cf. 145-151, 186-187, 198-200. (3) Ibid., 232. (4) Surin's hymn (which finds an echo in H 91) begins thus: "I want to go and run about the world / where I shall live like a lost child. / I have a wanderer's spirit / having given away my all. / It is all the same to me whether I live or die; / It is enough for me that Love stays with me." (5) It seems that this is the correct interpretation of the *ad honorem* title, according to the study made by E. Sastre Santos, *Quaedam de «Missionarii Apostolici» titulo «ad honorem» noviter concessum,* (Certain remarks on the title *"Apostolic Missionary"* a title *"ad honrem"* recently granted) in *Commentarium pro religiosis et missionariis* 63 (1982), 372-386; 64 (1983), 170-185. (6) The letter of François Jagu, the rector of La Chèze, was published in H. Daniel, *Saint Louis-Marie Grignion de Montfort. Ce qu'il fut. Ce qu'il fit. (Saint Louis Marie Grignion de Montfort. Who he was. What he did.)* Téqui, n.p. 1967, 148 and 437. (7) Besnard I, 248. (8) H. Daniel-Rops, *Histoire de l'Église du Christ, (History of the Church of Christ)* A. Fayard, Paris 1958, 5/1:33O. (9) P. Eyckeler, *Comment Montfort faisait-il faire la Consécration? (How did Montfort have the consecration made?) A qui Montfort faisait-il faire la Consécration? (Who did Montfort have make the Consecration?) Aides d'animation montfortaine* 4, duplicated. (10) Concerning his illnesses, Grandet says that the saint, on his return from Rome, had a face "full of spots" (124); that with his heart of iron where penances were concerned, he fainted one day (43); and that he often suffered from colic, pain in the side, and headaches that were so bad that he could not open his eyes (372). Grandet describes the major illness he suffered in La Rochelle (372) and lastly his mortal sickness at Saint-Laurent, which lasted seven days (259-260). (11) L. Pérouas, *Grignion de Montfort, les pauvres, les missions,* Cerf, Paris 1966, 84-85. (12) Blain, 185-190. Cf. S. De Fiores, *Itinerario,* 172-183, 268-275. (13) Grandet, 101. (14) *The Montfortian Today,* Rome 1984, nos. 46-48. (15) Blain, 187-189. (16) This religious lifestyle of Institutes "consecrated to the apostolate" was recognized as such by the Church in a text of the Sacred Congregation for Religious and Secular Institutes, *Essential Elements of the Church's Teaching on the Religious Life, Applied to Institutes Consecrated to the Apostolate,* Vatican 1983. (17) Blain, 187-189. (18) Pope Clement XI said to Montfort, "Always work with a perfect submission to the bishops of the dioceses where you are called, and God will bless your labors in this way" (Grandet, 100). (19) A. Valentini, *Ma vie c'est une course. (My life is a race)* in DM 1 (1986), 1-20.

ASSOCIATIONS

SUMMARY

I. MONTFORT AND ASSOCIATIONS:
  1. Did Montfort himself belong to Associations?;
  2. Associations in Montfort's Apostolate:
    a. Beginnings of his apostolate,
    b. Confraternity of the Rosary,
    c. Other associations;
  3. Associations as the Manifestation of His Missionary Spirit:
    a. Submissiveness and freedom,
    b. Spiritual and apostolic dimension,
    c. Fidelity to the baptismal vocation,
    d. Marian Dimension.

II. IN THE MONTFORT SPIRIT: THE "MARY QUEEN OF ALL HEARTS" ASSOCIATION:
  1. Beginning of the dream:
    a. stages of practice,
    b. longing for "another kind" of confraternity;
  2. From hope to realization:
    a. A long silence,
    b. Birth and expansion of the confraternity;
  3. Decline and conciliar renewal:
    a. Crisis,
    b. Attempt at a fresh start,
    c. Conciliar renewal.

III. FROM THE PAST TO THE PRESENT: THE CHURCH TODAY:
  1. Associations of the baptized;
  2. Maternal role of Mary;
  3. Towards the Fulfillment of All Things in Christ Jesus.

I. MONTFORT AND ASSOCIATIONS

In Montfort's time there were numerous spiritual and charitable associations, some linked to orders or monasteries, others independent. Pious unions, confraternities, or Third Orders offered their services to all categories of the faithful in order to help them live a full Christian life. They were at this time "the form best adapted to the lay apostolate."[1] Montfort the missionary used existing associations and he created and formed new ones, leaving his distinctive imprint on all of them.

1. Did Montfort himself belong to Associations?

We know that Louis Marie de Montfort willingly became a member of several organizations.

While at the Jesuit College of Thomas à Becket in Rennes, he and a group of fellow students were attracted to an extremely zealous young priest, Julien Bellier, chaplain of the General Hospital. They were formed by this holy priest for a life of piety and practice of charity, particularly through the visits that they made during their free time to the sick in the hospital, where they served them meals and taught them catechism. No doubt this contributed to the young Louis Marie's love for the poor and sick.

Later, Louis Marie was admitted to the "Marian congregation" led by Father Provost, the philosophy teacher. This society received the elite of the pupils from the advanced classes. The program, under the aegis and protection of the Virgin Mary, aimed at an interior formation, which would be expressed in active testimony and various works of piety and apostleship. Admission was gained by an "oblation," by which one promised to honor Mary with a special form of reverence.

Although a seminary like Saint Sulpice in Paris is already a kind of association, Montfort the seminarian soon experienced the need for a smaller group where his piety to Mary could be more freely expressed. As such a group did not exist, he asked for and obtained permission to begin one. J. B. Blain, his fellow student, writes: "He would have liked to enroll everybody in a Confraternity of Slavery of the Holy Virgin. The book written by the late, holy Father Boudon inspired him with tremendous zeal, and he was given permission to follow these teachings and to exhort everyone else to do the same." All that was asked of him by Father Tronson, then the superior-general of the Company of Saint Sulpice, was that the words "slaves of Mary" in the formula of consecration be replaced with "slaves of Jesus in Mary"[3] (cf. TD 244).

More surprising perhaps was the desire that he expressed at the end of ten years of ministry and apostolic life, to be affiliated with the Third Order of Saint Dominic. His solicitude for personal sanctification certainly played a large role in this, as well as his need for fraternal support, specially after the ordeal at Pontchâteau. He made profession in the presence of the Prior and several religious belonging to the Third Order on November 10, 1710, at a Dominican priory in Nantes (cf. L 23).

2. Associations in Montfort's Apostolate

Soon after ordination in 1700, St. Louis Marie decided to unite the faithful in various associations that would provide mutual support as well as testimony for the Christian community. Sometimes he brought together what already existed, sometimes he set up groups that corresponded, more or less, to existing models, and sometimes he creatively instituted new ones.

a. Beginnings of his apostolate. While waiting to start his duties at the General Hospital in Poitiers in 1701, he used his free time to conduct various ministries with children, the homeless poor, and prisoners. He also established an association of students to form them for the an apostolate among their peers. This association nurtured several priestly vocations, one of whom was Alexis Trichet, brother of Marie-Louise. Once Montfort started at the hospital, he established a similar association for young girls, either residents or staff members. Marie-Louise Trichet and Catherine Brunet, the first two Daughters of Wisdom, belonged to it.

b. Confraternity of the Rosary. In all his missions and retreats, Montfort was an apostle of the Rosary. Echoes of his Rosary teachings and missionary practice have been left to us in SR. Everywhere he went he formed groups to pray the Rosary, and he encouraged them to join the "Confraternity of the Rosary." He asked for, and obtained in 1712, permission from the master-general of the Dominicans to incorporate these groups into the confraternity (L 23). As St. Louis Marie writes, *"This is a holy practice, which God, in his mercy, has set up in places where I have preached missions, in order to safeguard and increase the good brought about by the mission . . . There are even places where the Rosary is said in common every day, at three different times of the day. What a blessing from heaven that is!"* (SR 135).

c. Other associations. Similarly, in order to perpetuate the good results of his missions, Montfort introduced to numerous parishes associations that existed in other areas. In this way he established for men the Confraternity of White Penitents and for girls the Society of Virgins, two groups for which he himself wrote the Rules (RP, RV). For more courageous souls, he proposed the confraternity Friends of the Cross, which he saw as a great means to perseverance and sanctification; it was for this confraternity that in 1714 he wrote his famous FC. There was also the confraternity of Holy Slavery to the Mother of God (see below). We also know that on three occasions at least—in Dinan (1707), in Montfort (1707), and at La Rochelle (1711)—he established a Confraternity of Saint Michael for soldiers who had completed a spiritual renewal under his direction. He wrote and approved the Rules for this confraternity.

3. Associations as the Manifestation of His Missionary Spirit.

One of Montfort's preoccupations was to leave works in place at the end of the mission to keep it alive and thereby assure its benefits. Blain writes, "All ages and sexes, at whatever stage of accomplishment, found in his missions instructions that were both appropriate and particular. The young men had their own and the young women theirs. With the former, he gathered together those whom he saw had been deeply moved and brought them together in a type of congregation. With the young women, he took very particular care to remind them of ... the virtues applicable to their age and sex. . . . In order to help those young women who wished to consecrate themselves to God in the world . . . he established societies of virgins for which he prescribed rules of conduct, exercises of piety, and a way of life suited to their condition."[4]

While accomplishing all this, Montfort did not overturn everything that already existed. Instead, he took his inspiration from the fairly widespread pastoral structures of his time and built on them. From both his charism of apostolic wisdom and his personal experience, he was able to perceive quickly the contribution the associations could make to Christian fidelity and to realize how much the success and continuity of the mission depended on them. He made associations an integral element of his missionary method. Whether renewing what already existed elsewhere (Confraternity of Penitents and Society of Virgins) or creating something new in response to particular needs (Confraternity of Saint Michael), he always acted in the spirit and manner of a missionary. To appreciate his praxis in this domain, we can examine the writings he left us on this subject: the Rules (excluding the Rule for the Confraternity of Saint Michael, which did not survive) for the "penitents" and "virgins" (GA 493-499), SR, FC, and the hymn "The Good Soldier" (H 95).

Four other characteristic traits of this practice of Montfort should be emphasized.

a. Submissiveness and freedom "Work always in perfect submission to the bishops of the dioceses," Pope Clement XI said to Louis Marie. And Louis Marie remained faithful to this, even when his apostolic boldness led him to adapt or edit the Rules. When he found a strongly structured and recognized existent work, like the Confraternity of the Rosary, his concern was to animate and further its development not to supplant it.

Often enough, however, he did not find anything. Then he had to create and form something to respond to the needs of the parish. He began with associations that already existed, adapting them to the local parish and conforming them to diocesan regulations. It was in this way, for example, that he introduced the Confraternity of Virgins into the diocese at La Rochelle.[5] He must have acted in the same way with the Rule of the Confraternity of Saint Michael and with the others. His loyalty was unquestionable and in no way prevented his creativity according to what was locally needed. It is worth noting that these works were created within the framework of the parish community and were entrusted to the parish priest to be watched over and promoted (cf. RV 1).

b. Spiritual and apostolic dimension. These two inseparable qualities spring from one love: "Thou shalt love thy neighbor as thyself" (Mk 12:31; cf TD 171). Certainly, the primary aim of Montfort's confraternities was to ensure the perseverance of those converted at the mission and also to support them in their fidelity to the resolutions they had made. The congregation of White Penitents aimed at *"deterring men from drunkenness, immorality, swearing and slander"*; that of the Virgins had as its goal *"to protect girls from the corruption of the age."* Refraining from evil was the first condition to fortify the will to good; this was likewise the intention of other points in the Rules, such as regular meetings combining instruction and prayer, and faithfulness to prayer and the sacraments. Other groups (the Confraternity of the Rosary, the Friends of the Cross, and the Confraternity of Holy Slavery) were aimed at the more fervent, those seriously desirous of advancing their spiritual life.

The associations founded by Montfort aimed to make apostles of their members, in particular by witness and prayer. What Montfort asked of those who had made the parish mission at Montbernage indicates his continuous care to awaken the faithful to the apostolate: *"Remember, then, my dear children, . . . to have a great love for Jesus and to love him through Mary, to let your true devotion to your loving Mother Mary be manifest everywhere and to everyone, so that you may spread everywhere the fragrance of Jesus. . . . You must be living examples to all Poitiers and district. . . . I ask my dear women of St. Simplicien, who sell fish and meat, and other shopkeepers and retailers, to continue giving good example to the whole town by living what they learned during the mission"* (LPM).

What he asked of the entire parish community, he also asked, undoubtedly more forcibly, of those who had joined the associations.

Montfort's RP is precise: *"They will edify the faithful of both sexes by their example of Christian virtue"* (RP 5). The apostolic dimension of associations established by Montfort is underlined in the instruction which he gave to the White Penitents of St. Pompain at the time of their pilgrimage to Our Lady of Saumur: *"You will make this pilgrimage for the following intentions: 1 Firstly to obtain from God through Mary's intercession good missionaries, who will follow the example of the apostles by complete abandonment to divine Providence and the practice of virtue under the protection of Our Lady; 2 Secondly to obtain the gift of wisdom in order to know, love and practice the truths of our faith and to lead others to Christ."* (PS 1) After detailing the other points of the Rule for this pilgrimage, he concludes, *"If they make the pilgrimage in this way, I am sure they will be seen to be worthy of God, of angels and of men; and they will obtain from God through the intercession of his Blessed Mother, great graces not only for themselves but for the whole Church of God"* (PS 13).

In SR 78, 124, 127, etc., the apostle addresses his *"dear friend of the Rosary Confraternity."* Though he insists, above all, on the efficacy of this prayer—and comes back to it frequently—as a means of ridding oneself of sin and progressing in virtue (cf. SR 3, 71, 75, etc.), he sees it equally as a powerful means of apostolate, to obtain the conversion of sinners and their perseverance in grace. (cf. SR 1, 2, 101, 112, 113, etc.). His zeal urged people to enter the Confraternity of the Holy Rosary: *"There is nothing more divine, according to the mind of St. Denis, nothing more noble or agreeable to God than to cooperate in the work of saving souls and to frustrate the devil's plans for ruining them. . . . The Blessed Virgin, protectress of the Church, has given us a most powerful means for appeasing her Son's anger, uprooting heresy and reforming Christian morals, in the Confraternity of the Holy Rosary, as events have shown. It has brought back charity and the frequent reception of the sacraments as in the first golden centuries of the Church, and it has reformed Christian morals"* (SR 92; cf. 93-96).

c. Fidelity to the baptismal vocation. The way in which Montfort the missionary stressed associations for the faithful in order to extend and spread the fruits of parish missions, reveals the profound sense he had of the richness of Baptism. For him Baptism was the foundation. He wanted not only to renew the faithful's practice of the sacraments and prayer but, more profoundly, to make them aware of Baptism and its implications in accordance with the double commandment of love of God and neighbor. According to the directives he received from Clement XI, the preaching of parish missions had as its goal to *"renew the spirit of Christianity among the faithful"* and to see that *"baptismal vows were renewed"* (RM 56). Those who joined one or the other of the associations Montfort organized, did so in accordance with their baptismal commitment, in order to strengthen their faith and contribute by witness and prayer to the vigorous expansion of the Christian community .

Montfort's practice of joining the faithful to pastoral activity—the groups were led by the curate or a delegated priest—testifies to the advanced vision that he had of the role of the baptized in the apostolic mission of the Church. What we today call the "apostolate of the laity," which the Vatican Council reminds us was founded on Baptism (AA 3), Montfort lived and invigorated in his way and according to the pastoral needs of his time. Louis Marie, desiring an institute of missionaries to *"renew the spirit of Christianity among the faithful"* (RM 56) and to *"reform the Church"* (PM 10, 20), quite naturally included the baptized (today known as the laity) in this mission. For him, the work of salvation entrusted to the Church belonged not only to the priests and the religious, but to everyone who was baptized, complementing each other and supporting each other's functions. His practice confirmed the profundity of his theology of Baptism: all the faithful, by the fact of their Baptism, belonged wholly to the Church of Jesus Christ and were called to holiness. It was because of his certainty that the faithful were being called by God to holiness and service of the Church's mission that he set up the particular structures of support and witness that comprise the various associations.

d. Marian dimension. A fourth point must be emphasized as equally characteristic of the associations that were set up or renewed by the holy missionary: the Marian dimension, particularly in the form of devotion to the Rosary. Its recitation is demanded in every group. This is hardly surprising; Mary was present throughout Montfort's life and apostolate.

II. In the Montfort Spirit: The "Mary Queen of All Hearts" Association

The associations spoken about until now aimed principally at seeing that the parishes continued to benefit from missions and retreats.

Montfort dreamt of fostering yet another kind of association but was unable to bring his dream to reality. This was to be a new association, unique, widespread, and, along with the other associations, giving form to his deepest missionary vision: a "confraternity" that would gather together all the faithful everywhere who had decided to follow the spiritual and apostolic path as presented in TD. All who had made the *"consecration of oneself to Jesus Christ through the hands of Mary"* (cf. TD 121-130, 227), would be members of this confraternity.

This association finally came into being at the end of the nineteenth century, under the name of the Confraternity of Mary Queen of All Hearts. It spread rapidly until the last decades of this century, when it became sizably smaller. Having undergone its conciliar aggiornamento, it has now re-emerged as a valuable support for maintaining and promoting the montfort apostolic charism throughout the Church.

1. Beginning of the dream

Montfort's desire to have a confraternity of those who chose to follow him on the path he outlined in TD 227 began to be achieved in 1712. He was then at the peak of his missionary planning, which had expanded and matured over the years. He stated that he wanted *"to write down what I have been teaching with success both publicly and in private in my missions for many years"* (TD 110).

a. Stages of practice. We have seen how the young Louis Marie, while still a seminarian at St. Sulpice, established a society of Slaves of Jesus and Mary. Boudon's book, *Holy Slavery of the Admirable Mother of God,* was at the origin of this initiative. He was profoundly influenced by this book, which confirmed the doctrinal and spiritual vision that had emerged from his personal experience (cf. TD 118). It is worth noting that the teachings of Boudon and other authors on holy slavery was already well known in certain clerical circles, in monasteries, and among certain Christian leaders.[6]

Montfort could not keep his "secret of holiness" to himself. He believed everyone was called to a life of holiness by virtue of Baptism. (cf. SM 3-5; TD 118-120). If the teaching given during missions aimed at the renewal of the baptismal vows, it also intended to make available the doctrine of the Consecration to Jesus through Mary in the form of St. Louis Marie's version of holy slavery. Montfort himself attests to it when he undertook to extend his teaching on this point to a very large public (TD 110).

Did he establish in parishes where he preached—or among other groups—"confraternities of Holy Slavery of Jesus in Mary"? We know from Boudon's and Jobert's books that such confraternities existed here and there. It would have been astonishing if Montfort, whose sense and practice of the value of associations we know, had not set up associations to maintain the fidelity and fervor of people embarking on this spiritual path of perfection. Grandet's testimony could be interpreted in this way: "In all the parishes where he preached a mission, he established devotion to holy slavery of Jesus through Mary."[7] We know this was a fact in La Rochelle and, in all probability, in other dioceses. Some years after the death of Montfort, Father Mulot, his first successor, heard criticism on the subject of this practice. He asked the advice of E. de Champflour, bishop of the diocese, and received this response: "Some people have spoken against the Confraternity of Slavery, saying that we should not be enslaved to a creature. This is not the true sense of this confraternity. We must make them understand that it is a confraternity of enslavement to Our

Lord through the Holy Virgin, and not simply enslavement to the Holy Virgin. This explanation shows the goodness of the confraternity, which you can join the late Father de Montfort in blessing."[8]

b. Longing for "another kind" of confraternity. Montfort writes, *"Those who wish to take up this particular devotion, (which has not been made into a confraternity, although that might be wished for)"* (TD 227).

This expresses his unreserved desire that a new association be established, a different confraternity from others that had existed up until then, and one based on holy slavery of Jesus through Mary. It would be another kind of confraternity, uniting and supporting "*those who desire to take up the particular devotion*" proposed by Montfort. This spiritual practice consisted in submitting oneself entirely to the maternal influence of Mary, in order to better assure union with Jesus Christ, and in being faithful to the baptismal commitments to him (cf. TD 55, 82, 110-113, 120, 125). Although deeply indebted to his predecessors, especially Cardinal de Bérulle and Henri Boudon, Montfort gave to the doctrine of holy slavery his own imprint, quite different from that of Boudon and Bérulle. As Saint Louis Marie articulated the advanced spiritual conclusions of his understanding of consecration (confirmed by his own experience), he certainly realized that he was opening a new and unique road to gospel perfection for the simple faithful, one unknown to them yet easily accessible, sure, and fast. This profound conviction is present throughout TD: *"the interior and perfect practice of the devotion which I shall later unfold"* (TD 55); *"There are secrets enabling us to do certain natural things quickly, easily and at little cost, so in the spiritual life there are secrets which enable us to perform supernatural works, rapidly, smoothly and with facility. Such works are, for example, emptying ourselves of self-love, filling ourselves with God, and attaining perfection. The devotion that I propose to explain is one of these secrets of grace"* (TD 82); *"I am trying to fashion a true servant of Mary and a true disciple of Jesus"* (TD 111; cf. also 112, 113, 120, 130, 218, etc.).

We can see that Montfort the missionary envisioned and desired this new confraternity to aid the progress of those who had committed themselves to this "special" path. The association he was thinking of was, moreover, similar in spirit to his other projects with associations. Always in the forefront of his thoughts were a continuation and amplification of his basic apostolic mission: to *"renew the spirit of Christianity . . . [to] reform the Church"* Being a disciple of Jesus Christ implied, for this spiritual master, being an apostle of his reign. For Montfort the secret to holiness, to the spiritual path that he recommended, was a way of life that was apostolically rich and demanded two equal yet distinct conditions. Those who embarked on this journey are to be formed by Mary and to work ardently in her Son's service (cf. TD 50-59, 114, 118, 214, etc.). In wishing Christians to be involved in the Church's mission to this extent, it is most probable that Montfort desired that they have their own particular association.

We might wish that Montfort had left us a more detailed plan on this special confraternity, as he did for other associations. But he did not do so. Perhaps the rules and regulations given to the society at the parish of St. Donatien in Nantes (at the time of the inauguration of a statue of Queen of All Hearts in 1710) could have served as a rough draft. Unfortunately, however, these have not come down to us. Though we do not have precise regulations and directives, we do at least have—and this is of the utmost importance—a sense of the spiritual and apostolic zeal that should animate *"those who put into practise what it (i.e.,* TD*) contains."* The task for *"both men and women"* (TD 114) followers of Montfort is to live apostolically and ecclesially what Montfort saw to be a baptismal vocation.

2. From hope to realization

What ever became of Montfort's desire for the particular confraternity expressed in TD? It suffered the same fate as TD itself. It was forgotten after his death. Only later was it recognized.

a. A long silence. The premature death of Montfort doubtlessly meant that his first companions could not grasp the full height and breadth of the plans and projects that were dear to him. But once the first wave of emotion and indecision had passed, they started to work again, giving parish missions and retreats, keeping alive the spirit and methods they had inherited from this "missionary apostle." His successors continued in this way, at least until the French Revolution.

We read that towards the middle of the 1700's, "they [the Montfort Missionaries during their parish missions] aimed, above all, at leaving behind several responsible structures that saw to the care of souls. In this way, following the blessed example of their founder, they established confraternities of the Holy Rosary, the White Penitents, the Virgins, and Holy Slavery of the Mother of God, to which Father Mulot himself belonged."[9] We know so little about this period in the life of the community. The manuscript of TD remained unpublished, its doctrine unexplored. This was the case right up until the day it was found on a library shelf, having been preserved from destruction throughout the Revolution and its aftermath, *"hidden in the darkness and silence of a chest"* (TD 114). Since then it has been a dramatic best-seller, with more and more editions in more and more languages. Rapidly it left its mark on Marian doctrine and devotion, nurturing in particular a whole movement of "Consecration to Jesus through Mary."

b. Birth and expansion of the confraternity. In the spiritual movement that emerged from Montfort's precious writings, what became of the confraternity that he had so desired? Unfortunately it was a long time coming. It was only in 1899 that it was at last founded, with the title "Confraternity of Mary Queen of All Hearts." In establishing it in his diocese, the bishop of Ottawa, Canada, J. Th. Duhamel, was responding both to his personal desires and to the widely expressed wishes of Montfort's followers.[10]

The statutes of the new association stated: *"Aim:* this confraternity has as its aim the establishment and spread of the reign of Mary in our souls, in order to ensure the perfection of Jesus Christ's reign. *Practices:* Consecration to the Holy Virgin according as much as possible to the formula given by the Blessed L.M. de Montfort; daily renewal of this Consecration by a short prayer; and finally, the practice of dependance on Mary and continual action in union with her."

The title Mary Queen of All Hearts stems directly from Montfort's heart and mind. As a student at St. Sulpice, he occasionally went to Issy, where Father Tronson had erected a chapel dedicated to "Mary Queen of All Hearts." In 1706, at the end of the mission in Montbernage, an outlying district of Poitiers, Montfort transformed a barn into an oratory and erected there, for the inhabitants of the district, a statue bearing the inscription "Queen of All Hearts." And while preaching a mission at Saint Donatien in Nantes in 1710, he changed the name of a little chapel there to Queen of All Hearts.

We can see by this how dear this title was to Montfort. As he explains in TD, he saw it as imbued with a particular spiritual meaning. The title established the basis for a truly spiritual attitude towards the Blessed Mother, namely, that her motherhood of Christ continues with those who are joined to his Body as members. Montfort states, *"None of these things, I repeat, could she do unless she had received from the Almighty rights and authority over their souls. For God, having given her power over his only-begotten and natural Son, also gave her power over his adopted children, not only in what concerns their body—which would be of little account—but also in what concerns their soul. . . . But as the kingdom of Jesus Christ exists primarily in the heart or interior of man . . . we may call her, as the saints do, Queen of all hearts"* (TD 37-38). Thus the confraternity's choice of title could hardly be more fitting.

Scarcely had the confraternity been founded when numerous faithful, religious, and clergy, including bishops, flocked to join it. The following year a second confraternity was founded in France in the Luçon diocese, with its seat at St. Laurent-sur-Sèvre.[11] The dissemination of Montfort's spiritual and Marian doctrine was aided by numerous spiritual writers and theologians, and soon by the first Marian congresses.[12] The confraternities multiplied rapidly. By 1965 there were 140 centers worldwide, with memberships ranging from several dozen to thousands.

By Pius X's decree of April 28, 1913, the confraternity in Rome became the *arch*confraternity. All present and future confraternities would be attached to it. Likewise, in 1907 there came into being a priests' section of the archconfraternity, called the "Association of Priests of Mary Queen of All Hearts." The idea had been put forward the previous year at the Marian congress in Einsiedeln. This association had its own statutes, which defined a double goal: "First. The sanctification of their priestly life by the practice of complete devotion to Mary, as taught by Montfort; Second. To make this devotion the greatest means to an apostolate that would establish the reign of Jesus Christ through Mary in each individual, in the family and in society." Encouraged from its outset by Pope Pius X, who joined it himself, the association developed in France (particularly because of the *Review for Priests of Mary Queen of All Hearts*) and also in Italy, England, United States, Canada, Spain, Colombia, Mexico, and Vietnam.

3. Decline and conciliar renewal

The success of the association continued until the middle of the 20th century. At that time its members numbered around 500,000. It must be stressed, however, that this figure represented only a tiny proportion of the people who had consecrated themselves to Jesus through Mary according in the spirit of Montfort. Many of them were not aware of the confraternity. From 1940 onwards, the confraternity was affected by the many upheavals that beset society and the Church. And it benefited from the breath of fresh air brought by Vatican Council II.

a. Crisis. We are well aware of the upheavals caused by the Second World War (1939-1945), and the cultural changes that resulted. These changes were so numerous that they evoked crises in almost every area of life. Few could be easily dealt with in a short span of time. And Church teaching, both pastoral and spiritual, was not spared either. This is why we speak of the "Marian question" in the sixties and of the "Marian crisis" in the ten years that followed the Council.[13]

The confraternity also felt the repercussions of this with a gradual decline in membership. Perhaps this decline is to be explained, in part, by the lack of attention shown by the association to rethinking and adapting to new needs. Like many confraternities, it had refused to change and adapt, while still remaining faithful to its statute of "pious union," with its particular preference for personal spirituality.

b. Attempt at a fresh start. The authorities responsible, however, were not unaware of the problem. As a result of their work, the two Mary Queen of All Hearts associations received new statutes by decree of July 5, 1956.

Of the Mary Queen of all Hearts confraternity, we read: "1. *Composition and aim* - The Mary Queen of all Hearts confraternity is a pious union of the faithful which is not organized hierarchically. Its members wish to live and propagate Marian life as taught by Saint Louis Marie de Montfort, in order to facilitate and ensure sanctification. 2. *Relationship with the Company of Mary* - In the July 16, 1955, rescript the Holy See declared it to be a pious union having no distinct hierarchical organization, a true association of the Company of Mary, in the sense put forth by canon 686. 3. Faithful to the specific aim that determines constitutions approved by the Holy See, the Company of Mary will use this association to establish the reign of Christ through Mary, by zealously propagating Consecration to Mary Queen of all Hearts among the faithful."

On the Priests of Mary Queen of All Hearts association, the only difference is in the first paragraph: "The Priests of Mary Queen of All Hearts Association is a pious union of priests and clerics without a distinct hierarchical organization."

The two associations are considered, by a rescript from the preceding year, as "proper to the Company of Mary," in the manner of a Third Order. The association of priests, which had been considered up until now as a branch of the confraternity, became henceforth a separate association. The apostolic character of the confraternity is clearly expressed here, which was not the case in the statutes. The new canonical link uniting them to the Company of Mary, cooperatively joins the two associations in their specific Church mission: propagation of the work and reign of Christ in the world according to Saint Louis Marie de Montfort's method, the total Consecration to Jesus through Mary.

Some attempts at renewal and restructuring were undertaken here and there, with varied results. On the one hand, the negative effects of the Marian crisis were still present, and on the other, many of the missionaries' preoccupations inclined them to favor other apostolic activities. It is worth noting however, that in the same period other associations deriving from montfort inspiration were founded in several countries—proof that it was still alive, fertile, and active.

c. Conciliar renewal. Vatican Council II inspired renewal in all structures and associations in order for them to open to the Spirit of the new Pentecost. After accomplishing the aggiornamento of its own constitution, the Company of Mary still had to update the statutes of its two associations and to renew the spirit of both organizations. Vatican Council II's theological and spiritual reflections on Mary's place "in the mystery of Christ and the Church"—Montfort's imprint can clearly be seen[14]—could only gladden, encourage, and awaken those who were open to Montfort's missionary and Marian message.

An international commission for montfort associations was formed in the late 1980's.[15] New statutes were proposed and approved for the confraternity, which had become the Association of Mary Queen of All Hearts.

III. From the Past to the Present: The Church Today

The confraternity desired by Montfort still exists, endowed with a new title, Association of Mary Queen of All Hearts, and with new statutes reformulated to come into line with our entry into the postconciliar era. Renewing the statutes was not to be a simple cosmetic act. It had to be a true adaptation, one with integrity and in continuity with the montfort ideal. It had to convey the contemporary profundity of Montfort's charism and reiterate it, according to the Ecclesial Statutes of Associations.

Since the time of Montfort, many things have changed. There have been upheavals in every area of life. The Church, "in the world without being of the world," has not ceased contemplating and deepening the mystery of Jesus Christ. Vatican Council II was a major event of the second half of the century. In it the Church presented to us her understanding of herself and the mission received from her Founder. She also presented her understanding of man and his situation in the contemporary world. And she told us, as never before, what she understood to be the maternal role of the Blessed Virgin Mary today "in the Mystery of Christ and the Church," and consequently in the life of the faithful (particularly in LG, ch. 8). Bearing in mind the essence of this Church teaching, which is confirmed by the new Code of Canon Law, Father de Montfort must be "reread." When we do this, we quickly see the doctrinal elements at the root of his spiritual thought and apostolic work. Valued and confirmed by the highest authority of the Church magisterium, they are more than merely an encouragement. They are a call to fidelity.

1. Associations of the baptized

We have shown Montfort's sense of the value of associations and how he used them to encourage the faithful to live the spiritual and apostolic demands of their Baptism. This was not an innovation, but Montfort did show, very strongly and in his own way, the possibilities offered by an organized group. The confraternity was to continue in this way. The Second Vatican Council's constitution on the Church says, "The laity, however, are given this special vocation: to make the Church present and fruitful in those places and circumstances where it is only through them that she can become the salt of the earth." (LG 33).

And the new statutes say, "The Association of Mary Queen of All Hearts regroups the faithful who, with Louis Marie de Montfort as their guide, propose to fulfill their baptismal vows through total Consecration to Christ through Mary's hands" (*Statutes,* 1).

2. Maternal role of Mary

For Montfort, union with Christ by fidelity to baptismal vows becomes more assured by the Consecration that he recommends, which facilitates Mary's accomplishment of her maternal task. This is one of the fundamental convictions of his teaching and apostolate (cf. TD 35-59, 118-121, 15-183).

We can hear his echo in what the council says. The theme of Mary's spiritual maternity of the faithful is recalled in LG, ch. 8, in twelve of its seventeen paragraphs. In these texts the Church speaks of Mary's exemplarity and intercession (cf. LG 60-65) and concludes. "The Church, therefore, in her apostolic life too, rightly looks to her who gave birth to Christ, who was thus conceived of the Holy Spirit and born of a Virgin, in order that through the Church he should be born and increase in the hearts of the faithful. In her life the Virgin has been a model of that motherly love with which all who join in the Church's apostolic mission for the regeneration of mankind should be animated" (LG 65). For its part, the decree on the apostolate of the laity, says, "Perfect model of the apostolic spiritual life is the Blessed

Virgin Mary, Queen of Apostles . . . she remained intimately united to her Son and cooperated in an entirely unique way in the Savior's work . . . Everyone should have a genuine devotion to her and entrust his life to her motherly care" (AA 4).

The resolution that animates the Association of Mary Queen of All Hearts reads as follows: "Recognized as a true Association of the Company of Mary, . . . an extension of the Company of Mary, its members, taking sustenance from its spirit, work to maintain and extend its apostolic action in their environment and according to their vocations, in order to establish the reign of Jesus through Mary" (no. 2).

3. Towards the Fulfillment of All Things in Christ Jesus

To bring about the reign of Christ through Mary: this summarizes Montfort's apostolic spirituality (TD 13, 133, 217, 227). The more a soul is united to Mary and in communion with her virtues, dispositions and intentions, the more Christ can grow in it, as in Mary, and fulfill his work of grace. It is with this prophetic vision of growth into the fullness of Christ Jesus that the Association of Mary Queen of All Hearts and the Association of Priests of Mary Queen of All Hearts[16]—associated to the mission of the Company of Mary—today links itself.

J. Hémery

Notes: (1) J. Duhr, *Confrérie (Confraternity),* in DSAM II/1, 1477. (2) Blain, 50; S. De Fiores, *Itinerario,* 59-81. Cf. E. Villaret, *Congregations de la sainte Vierge (Congregations of the Blessed Virgin),* in DSAM II/1, 1575. (3) Blain, 50. (4) Blain, 160-161, passim. (5) Grandet, 385-386. (6) Cf. Th. Koehler, *Servitude (saint esclavage) (Slavery [Holy Slavery]),* in DSAM XIV, 730-745. (7) Grandet, 315-316. (8) Grandet, 439. (9) Cf. *Histoire de la compagnie de Marie (History of The Company of Mary),* St. Laurent 1924, 1:65-66. (10) Cf. the review *Le Règne de Jésus par Marie (The Reign of Jesus through Mary)* 1 (January 1900). The confraternity's seat was established in Our Lady of Lourdes parish, Ottawa. (11) *Le Règne de Jésus par Marie* 2 (April 1900). (12) Marian congresses: Fribourg (1902), Rome (1904), Einsiedeln (1906), Saragossa (1909), Trier (1912). (13) On the causes and effects of the Marian question and crisis, cf. R. Laurentin, *Mary's Place in the Church,* Compass Books, Burns & Oates, London 1965; S. De Fiores, *Maria nella teologia contemporanea (Mary in Contemporary Theology),* 3rd ed., Centro di cultura mariana "Madre della Chiesa," Rome 1991, 123-126. (14) Cf. H.-M. Manteau-Bonamy, *De Grignion de Montfort à Vatican II (Regarding Grignion de Montfort at Vatican II)* in CM 52 (1966), 120-126; A. Rum, *Il Trattato della vera devozione a Maria alla luce del Vaticano II,* (*The Treatise on the True Devotion To Mary in the Light of Vatican II*) in *La Madonna* 14 (1966), 3, 17-23. (15) The commission consequently also received a mandate to prepare a *Guide to Montfort Spirituality.* (16) The Association of Priests of Mary Queen of All Hearts, henceforth separate from the Association of the Faithful, certainly deserves equal attention. Since the Incarnation, Mary has been, and will be until the end of time, the most engaged, at the side of her Son, in the full accomplishment of his work of salvation in the world, in the place God has chosen for her. The more one is engaged in the salvation of human beings—by sacerdotal ministry, for example—the more one ought to belong to Mary in the mystery of Christ and the Church.

BAPTISM

SUMMARY

I. MONTFORT IN CONTINUITY WITH A CENTURY OF PASTORAL RENEWAL:
  1. The renewal of the seventeenth century;
  2. A privileged tool at the service of the renewal: parish missions;
  3. Parish missions and Baptism.

II. MONTFORT'S PRACTICE OF BAPTISMAL RENEWAL:
  1. From first awareness to definitive choice;
  2. A mandate of Clement XI;
  3. Parish missions shaped by baptismal renewal;
  4. Public solemn renewal of baptismal promises;
  5. Renewal through the hands of Mary.

III. MONTFORT'S TEACHING ON BAPTISM:
  1. Reference texts;
  2. Christocentrism;
  3. Baptism and Consecration;
  4. Baptism and Montfort's "slavery of love";
  5. Baptism and renewal;
  6. Baptism and perfect renewal through Mary.

IV. CURRENT VALUE OF MONTFORT'S THOUGHT ON BAPTISM:
  1. Baptism, point of departure for re-evangelization;
  2. Renewed and adapted teaching on Baptism;
  3. Baptismal renewal and Mary;
  4. Baptism and the Body of Christ.

To assist at one of Saint Louis Marie's parish missions was to witness a magnificent sight: a crowded church, splendid sermons, enthusiastic singing, elaborate processions, numerous confessions. It was an areawide event involving in one way or another all the people of the town. At the heart of everything was the specifically montfort characteristic of a parish mission: his version of the solemn renewal of the promises of Baptism. That event was the hub of everything else that made up a parish mission preached by Saint Louis de Montfort.

Baptism is, then, central to Saint Louis de Montfort's spirituality.[1] His teaching concurs with the CCC that "Holy Baptism is the basis of the whole Christian life, the gateway to life in the Spirit (vitae spiritualis ianua), and the door which gives access to the other sacraments. Through Baptism we are freed from sin and reborn as sons of God; we become members of Christ, are incorporated into the Church and made sharers in her mission."[2] In this dawn of the third millennium, when the Church calls for a "new evangelization," Montfort's insights into Baptism are a blessing for all Christians.

I. Montfort in Continuity with a Century of Pastoral Renewal

Saint Louis Marie's baptismal preaching is in direct continuity with a century marked by strong efforts to renew the faith among all classes of society.

1. The renewal of the seventeenth century

Although religious and political wars debilitated the France of the 1600's, it was also a period rich and fruitful in art, culture, and particularly religion. In spite of serious deviations (Jansenism, Gallicanism, Quietism), it was a great century for the Church in France. The backbone of the spiritual renewal was the strong influence of the members of the French school of spirituality, of which Montfort was one of the last.

The Council of Trent (1545-1563) sought to initiate a true Catholic reform (or Counter-Reformation). Its decrees were finally adopted in France by the Assembly of the Clergy in 1615 and enthusiastically received by those primarily responsible for the proclamation of the faith. The council's insistence on the renewal of the clergy was implemented especially through the establishment of new seminaries, thanks to Vincent de Paul, Cardinal de Bérulle, J.J. Olier, and Jean Eudes. With solidly educated clergy, work progressed on the ultimate goal of the council, the instruction of the Christian people in the faith.

2. A privileged tool at the service of the renewal: parish missions

The formation of the faithful should, according to the Council of Trent, be done chiefly through religious instruction. *The Catechism of the Council of Trent* (or *Roman Catechism*), published by Pius V, was a strong force in this regard.[3] The hoped-for renewal called forth by the Council of Trent, however, found a decisive tool in parish missions. A special period of intense teaching given to a community over several weeks (from three to five or even more) by itinerant missionaries, the parish mission called for popular methods to touch hearts and stimulate conversions. It was an extremely effective instrument of the renewal so desired by the Church of the seventeenth century. Religious orders, like the Jesuits, Dominicans, Capuchins, and Benedictines, all became involved in preaching parish missions, as did many of the leaders of the French school of spirituality and the Congregations founded by them: Vincentians, Oratorians, Sulpicians, Eudists. Teams of diocesan priests also took part in this "new evangelization."

3. Parish missions and Baptism

One of the chief characteristics of the Tridentine renewal, and one that became integrated with parish missions, was the insistence on the fundamental importance of Baptism. Time and again the *Roman Catechism* reminded pastors of their obligation to see that the faithful appreciated the Sacrament of Baptism and always remained faithful to this most radical of commitments to Jesus Christ (cf. TD 129).

Charles Borromeo, archbishop of Milan († 1584), was the most zealous in putting into practice the conciliar directives: he revived the custom of celebrating the anniversary of Baptism and introduced the fairly new practice of renewing the promises, or "vows," of Baptism. The renovation of baptismal promises as part of the Tridentine reform spread far and wide.

The public enactment of baptismal renewal became a part of parish missions by the middle of the seventeenth century. Julien Maunoir, a popular parish missionary of the time, integrated a baptismal-renewal ceremony into the end of the first week of the mission, usually on a Sunday afternoon. Another parish missionary, Jean Leuduger, with whom Montfort preached some missions, composed a formula of renewal that was to be signed by each person making the mission.

Father de Montfort was a successor to these many missionaries and reformers. But he brought special characteristics of his own to the practice of baptismal renewal during a parish mission.

II. Montfort's Practice of Baptismal Renewal

Heir of those who first implemented the Tridentine reform, Saint Louis Marie insisted that the renewal of baptismal promises should be celebrated regularly, most especially during a parish mission. His stress on Baptism developed early in life.

1. From first awareness to definitive choice

When the young Louis Marie began formal studies in Rennes, conciliar reforms had begun to bear fruit. The clergy, thanks to the vast improvement in seminary training, was better formed in theology and spirituality. The Christian people were better instructed in the truths of the faith. Central to this renewal was a greater insistence upon Baptism.

We can see the first sign of Montfort's deeper appreciation of this initial Sacrament when he renounced his civil identity and exchanged his family name for the place of his Baptism, the village of Montfort. He would be called only "*the Father from Montfort.*" It was a means of reminding himself and others that Baptism defines an individual far more deeply than family or national origin; it is the Christian's fundamental relationship, which in turn determines all others. A letter of October 1702 to his sister Guyonne-Jeanne is signed *De Montfort.* Several other letters, including one to his mother in 1704, are signed in the same way. Louis Marie spent only months at Montfort, the village of his birth; most of his youth was spent at the nearby town of Iffendic. It was, however, at Montfort that he was immersed into Christ Jesus. Montfort would then become his "family name."

There are other indications of his growing appreciation for the Sacrament of Baptism. While serving at Poitiers shortly after his ordination, he and a group of young people he organized restored the fourth-century baptistery of Saint John near the cathedral. We can also well presume that Baptism was a prominent topic in his preaching: writing to the inhabitants of Montbernage, a suburb of

Poitiers and a place where he preached, he declared, "*Do not fail to fulfill your baptismal promises and all that they entail*" (LPM 2).

2. A mandate of Clement XI

When the Father from Montfort wondered if he was on the right track preaching parish missions in northwestern France, he journeyed to Rome to seek the advice of the Holy Father, Clement XI. The Pope's words to the itinerant preacher were clear: "There is a large enough field in France for you to exercise your zeal; go nowhere else and work always in perfect submission to the bishops to whose dioceses you may be called."[4] Clement XI also bestowed upon him the title "Apostolic Missionary" and recommended that he teach Christian doctrine throughout the villages and towns of his area of France, renewing the spirit of faith through the renewal of baptismal promises.

Saint Louis de Montfort believed that the words of the successor of Peter were not only an encouragement but a mandate to continue his work as a parish missionary and to proclaim everywhere the renewal of baptismal promises. In 1707 and 1708 Montfort formed part of the team of Jean Leuduger, director of missions for the diocese of Saint-Brieuc in Brittany. In the course of some ten missions, Louis Marie was initiated in the methods of this great missionary, himself a disciple of the celebrated Fathers Maunoir and Huby. The climax of these missions was, as we have seen, a ceremony of renewal of baptismal promises, including the distribution of a printed formula for this purpose, which each one making the mission was asked to sign.

3. Parish missions shaped by baptismal renewal

In LS, sketches probably derived from his studies at Saint Sulpice, Saturday preaching was regularly consecrated to instruction on the Blessed Virgin and on the Sacrament of Baptism. When Father de Montfort became himself the leader of a mission band, first in the diocese of Nantes and then in Luçon and La Rochelle, he organized the missions according to the mandate given him by Clement XI. LS contains new outlines dating from this period, entitled "*Sermon-matter for a Mission, or Retreat, or the Renewal of Baptismal Promises.*" The collection comprises twenty-four subjects developing the formula "*I renounce the devil and all his pomps and all his works and I unite myself to you my Jesus*" (GA, 569-571).[5]

It seems clear that for Montfort Baptism and the renewal of its promises were no longer simply an integral element in a parish mission; they were, rather, the driving force, the means and the goal that gave the montfort parish renewal its special cachet and around which the entire mission was built. Preaching on the baptismal Consecration and leading the people in the renewal of its promises became the core of his renewal efforts. However much Saint Louis Marie owed to his illustrious predecessors in the field of parish missions, not one of them seems to have clarified to such a degree the apostolic meaning and demands of Baptism in order "to renew the spirit of Christianity."

4. Public solemn renewal of baptismal promises

The grandiose ceremony of the renewal of baptismal promises took place at the center of the montfort parish mission and was, in fact, its goal. As far as we can decipher from Montfort's sermon outlines on this subject, the ceremony probably occurred towards the end of the last week, before the planting of the mission cross. As his first biographer, Grandet, describes it, this parish renewal of baptismal promises had an elaborate, well-planned, festive character.[6] The ceremony began with a procession to a beautifully decorated outside altar. At the lead were the cross, colorful banners, standards of various organizations, musical instruments led or accompanied by the faithful, who walked in time with the hymns or the music or the prayers. Father de Montfort, bearing the monstrance, followed. At the altar of repose, after the chanting of the Gospel and the singing of hymns, Louis Marie preached a sermon. The long procession then began to weave its way back to the church, again with the joyful playing of music, the singing of hymns, and the chanting of prayers, including the Rosary. Each of the parishioners had a printed copy of the act of renewal - "*the covenant contract with God*" - which also listed practices for those who solemnly renewed their baptismal promises.

The ceremony appears to have included four phases:

- As the procession slowly made its way through the vestibule of the parish church, all passed in front of a deacon seated with the Gospel book open on his knees. Each one genuflected and venerated the holy book, saying, "I firmly believe all the truths of the Holy Gospel of Jesus Christ."
- Entering the church, they passed in front of the baptismal font, where a priest received them. Kissing the font, each renewed his or her vows with the formula, "With all my heart I renew the promises of my baptism and renounce forever the devil, the world, and myself [i.e., my evil inclinations]."
- From the baptismal font, the procession made its way to the Lady Chapel or a side altar of the Blessed Virgin, where the director of the parish mission, the Father from Montfort, held the small statue of Our Lady and the Christ Child (which he himself had carved); each one kissed it, saying, "I give myself entirely to Jesus Christ through the hands of Mary to carry my Cross after him all the days of my life."
- Then all gathered together at the baptistery to sing "the great Creed." And after an elaborate ceremony of veneration of the Gospel book, Saint Louis Marie reverently took it, walked up to the pulpit, and continued to preach on the new life to be led by all who were so privileged to renew through Mary their baptismal promises.

Undoubtedly there were variations from parish to parish on the renewal ceremony, as there were on the precise formula of the "covenant contract" that Montfort distributed (cf. CG). What must be emphasized above all is the great importance that Saint Louis Marie attached to this solemn, if not grandiose, ceremony of renewal.

5. Renewal through the hands of Mary

Montfort's imprint on the parish renewal of baptismal promises is nowhere more evident than in his linkage of Baptism with the role of Our Lady in salvation history. One of the sermons delivered at some of his parish missions a day or so before the solemn renewal is entitled: "*The manner of renewal through the Blessed Virgin Mary: Mother of the Head, Mother of the members, treasurer, advocate, terror of the devil, refuge, faithful virgin*" (GA, 571). Indicative of the importance Montfort attached to Mary's role was the gesture he introduced into the elaborate ceremony of renewal: passing by the altar of Our Lady, where he personally greeted the candidates for renewal with their printed formula and invited them to kiss the little statue of Mary and the Christ Child.

III. Montfort's Teaching on Baptism

It was Saint Louis Marie's sermons on Baptism that impelled the parishioners to take part in the elaborate ceremony of the renewal of the baptismal promises and to make it the highlight of their participation in the mission. Although the missionary has left us neither a separate work on Baptism nor a fleshed-out sermon on the subject, we can gather the main lines of his understanding of this Sacrament from his extant writings.

1. Reference texts

If our search for references is confined to the single word "Baptism," Father de Montfort uses the term over forty times, five of them in reference to the baptism of Jesus. Limiting ourselves to LEW, TD, and H, "Baptism" is found in LEW 19, 113, 223, 225; TD 68, 73, 120, 126-128, 130-131, 162, 232, 238; and Hymns 16, 17, 19, 27, 33, 98, 102, 109, 139. Although TD contains the most references to Baptism, a brief summary of the effects of the Sacrament is found in a couplet of his hymn "The Chief Mysteries of the Faith": "*Baptism of itself wipes out / original sin, / gives us grace, / opens Heaven to us, / makes us children of God himself and of the Church*" (H 109:8).

2. Christocentrism

What primarily emerges from these texts and their contexts is the Christocentrism of Montfort, a clear inheritance from the French school of spirituality. Saint Louis Marie's Christocentric doctrine permeates everything he writes: "*Jesus our Savior, true God and true man, must be the ultimate end of all our other devotions; otherwise they would be false and misleading. He is the Alpha and the Omega, the beginning and end of everything*" (TD 61). For Montfort, Christ is the raison d'être of all creation, following closely Saint Paul's thought, expressed especially in the

Captivity Epistles. In a few bold strokes, Saint Louis de Montfort summarizes his Christocentric teaching: "*If devotion to Our Lady distracted us from Our Lord, we would have to reject it as an illusion of the devil*" (TD 62). His famous proverb encapsulates everything: "*To know Jesus Christ . . . is to know all we need. To presume to know everything and not know him is to know nothing at all*" (LEW 11).

Baptism and Christocentrism go hand in hand. It is because of Montfort's insistence on the reality of baptismal immersion into Christ Jesus that his preaching is so Christocentric; it is because he is so centered on Christ the Lord that he is so taken up with Baptism. Infidelity to baptismal promises is nothing less, therefore, than infidelity to Jesus Christ: "*I must confess that I have not kept the vows and promises which I made to you (Eternal and Incarnate Wisdom) so solemnly at my baptism*" (LEW 223).

Since Baptism plunges us into the victorious dying of Jesus, the triumphant Cross is stressed in his teaching: "*Wisdom is the Cross and the Cross is Wisdom*" (LEW 180; cf. FC). Since Baptism is the beginning of such an intense participation in the divine nature (cf. 2 Pet 1:4), Montfort insists on a life of radical evangelical virtue. The initial Sacrament is, then, nothing short of the source and root of his teaching.

3. Baptism and Consecration

A constant concern of Montfort was to help the baptized to be aware of his or her absolute relationship with Christ Jesus and to grow in it. Baptism becomes, then, the foundation for his spirituality of total Consecration. In fact, it is the insistence on referring to Baptism as "*Consecration to Jesus Christ*" and thereby so clearly identifying it with his understanding of Consecration that is his most characteristic teaching on Baptism.

In the Christian economy of salvation, there is no Consecration to God that is not in union with Jesus Christ and a part of his own Consecration: "No one comes to the Father except by me" (Jn 14:6); "For their sake I consecrate myself so that they also may be consecrated in truth" (Jn 17:19).

This union with the Lord and his Consecration is achieved sacramentally by Baptism. In becoming a member of Christ's body, the newly baptized is established in filial relationship with God, becomes a sharer in the divine nature and, in and through Christ Jesus, consecrated to the Father and to His service. The baptized is, then, a sharer in Christ, priest, prophet, and king (1 Pet 2:9-10). This doctrinal foundation is at the root of Montfort's affirmation that Baptism "*consecrates us to Jesus Christ*" (TD 129) and that "*all our perfection consists in our being conformed, united and consecrated to Jesus*" (TD 120).

4. Baptism and Montfort's "slavery of love"

Saint Louis Marie constantly reminds us that Baptism brings about a radical, total belonging to Jesus. He found no other term to express this fundamental reality than the evangelical word "slavery," stripped of all servility and injustice. Montfort intended to underline the radical transformation of the baptized person and, still more, the newness of life consequent to Baptism: "*From what Jesus Christ is in regard to us, we must conclude as Saint Paul says, that we belong not to ourselves but entirely to him as his members and his slaves*" (TD 68).

There is a "before and after." "*Before baptism, we belonged to the devil as slaves, but baptism made us in very truth slaves of Jesus. We must therefore live, work and die for the sole purpose of bringing forth fruit for him*" (TD 68). This contrast of "before and after" is found time and gain in the missionary's writings (cf. TD 73, 126; SM 34, etc.). Justifying the wearing of little chains as a sign of this dependence, he writes: "*These little chains are a wonderful aid in recalling the bonds of sin and the slavery of the devil from which baptism has freed him. At the same time, they remind him of the dependence on Jesus promised at baptism*" (TD 238). He recalls holy persons who wore a little chain around their neck or arm "*to remind them, as they worked with their hands, they are slaves of Jesus*" (TD 242). It cannot be overstressed that slavery of love is for Montfort essentially different from slavery of nature or constraint, for baptismal slavery to Jesus Christ is neither debasing nor dehumanizing. On the contrary, it is the very peak of love and liberty: "*Voluntary slavery is the most perfect . . . for by it we give the greatest glory to God who looks into the heart and wants it to be given to him. . . . We must belong to Jesus as willing slaves who, moved by generous love, commit themselves to his service. . . . Baptism made us the slaves of Jesus. Christians can only be slaves of the devil or slaves of Christ*" (TD 70, 73). Faith is a belonging to: through Baptism we belong to the Lord not only as Creator and Sustainer but as Lover in Jesus Christ. The "belonging to" is so total that love seeks terms to express the depth of this relationship: "slavery" applied to our baptismal relationship with Jesus is clearly, for Montfort, the language of love.

5. Baptism and renewal

Montfort's teaching on Baptism is essentially directed towards the renewal of Christianity. It is not abstract theory, not theological speculation. It fulfills a special concern of his apostolic spirit: to renew the spirit of Christianity among the faithful by persuading them to renew their baptismal allegiance to Christ with all that such a step entails.

Saint Louis de Montfort sought to have his people open their hearts not only to the forgiveness of sins but to a dynamic new depth of fidelity to the Gospel in all its dimensions. Among the causes of infidelity to the Lord, the missionary singles out two: forgetfulness/ignorance and weakness in the face of the demands of baptismal life, a weakness heightened by the temptations of the world and the devil.

Louis Marie speaks of the first cause of infidelity when he writes: "*Does anyone keep this great vow? Does anyone fulfill the promises of baptism faithfully? Is it not true that nearly all Christians prove unfaithful to the promises made to Jesus in baptism?*

Where does this universal failure come from, if not from man's habitual forgetfulness of the promises and responsibilities of baptism?" (TD 127). The only real remedy for this ignorance and forgetfulness was to enlighten his people on the subject of the meaning, splendor, and demands of Baptism. Father de Montfort gives to the conscious and loving renewal of baptismal promises the title "Consecration." He thereby wished to underline that he was advocating a willing endorsement, a formal acceptance of the "*covenant contract*" previously made with God through godparents (TD 127).

6. Baptism and perfect renewal through Mary

The second cause explaining Christian infidelity to the vows of Baptism is, so Montfort believed, the weakness of mankind of itself, especially in face of the temptations of the world and the devil. His insistence on this point is so emphatic that he is not altogether free from Augustinian pessimism (TD 78-89); it must be said in the same breath, however, that his stress on the grandeur of man flowing from Baptism is far stronger than any comments he makes on the nothingness of man of himself. The question is, then, how to preserve the greatness of our baptismal life in the face of the alien value system of the world. Montfort suggests a way to be counterculture: a loving acceptance of Our Lady's maternal role and powerful intercession. The more we have recourse to the spiritual Mother of all the baptized, the more easily she can help us to journey in fidelity and to strive for perfection in Christ. This is the whole thrust of the first part of TD. "*The more one is consecrated to Mary, the more one is consecrated to Jesus. That is why perfect consecration to Jesus is but a perfect and complete consecration of oneself to the Blessed Virgin . . . or in other words, it is the perfect renewal of the vows and promises of holy baptism*" (TD 120).

IV. Current Value of Montfort's Thought on Baptism

As Montfort's time was an age of "new evangelization," so too is ours. As Montfort stressed Baptism and the renewal of its promises as an effective instrument of reform, we too can find in his practice a contemporary tool of evangelization. In fact, the renewal of our baptismal commitment is a necessity in order for the Church truly to be the *"Ecclesia semper reformanda."*

1. Baptism, point of departure for re-evangelization

Montfort's missionary program for renewal of the Christian spirit among the faithful was characterized by the primary and fundamental importance attached to Baptism. And rightly so, for Baptism, with its new life, manifested by a new conduct and spirit, is the Sacrament that establishes the fundamental identity of the Christian. To renew and strengthen the very root of the Christian life clearly contributes to a growing maturity among the people of God.

The Second Vatican Council, with some twenty references to Baptism, pointedly contributed to a reaffirmation of this Sacrament of initiation into new life in Christ. The powerful secularizing trends of the world today challenge the Christian and are so strong that some have been swept away in its flood. A renewal of the sense of Baptism and of its demands in contemporary society can only aid a Christian to appreciate and live the radical newness that this first Sacrament demands.

Pope John Paul II teaches: "It is of supreme importance that all Christians appreciate the extraordinary dignity conferred on them in Baptism."[7] Montfort appears as a master in the program of re-Christianization because of his constant teaching on Baptism and its demands.

The Gospel received with faith leads to Baptism (Mk 13:15-16). In this Sacrament the entire Christian existence is found in embryo. The Christian is not someone who was baptized by a rite sometime in the past; the baptized is and always remains a person who must become more and more one with Jesus in the power of the spirit (Acts 2:38). One cannot talk of Christian life and its demands, one cannot stress renewal and "new evangelization" without reference to Baptism itself.

2. Renewed and adapted teaching on Baptism

In the ecclesial context of his time and faithful to pastoral directives, Montfort gave proof of daring and imagination in bringing Christians to a realization of the grandeur of their Baptism. We are not to copy him to the last detail; he surely did not slavishly copy his predecessors. He was conditioned by the sacramental theology of his day; there are other points of emphasis in our time. But his apostolic spirit, his stress on a deeper knowledge and living of Baptism, and his insistence on the solemn renewal of baptismal promises are valid in every age of the Church.

In virtue of the principle that no one desires what is not known (*nil volitum quin cognitum*), teaching on Baptism must aim first of all at enlightening Christians to the radical and incredibly powerful transformation brought on by this Sacrament. Its essential role as the first gate to union with the Triune God and its foundational importance in every aspect of our life in Christ must be so underlined that hearers are stirred to a desire to live its reality more deeply.

Teaching and catechetical instruction (in a parish mission, a retreat, adult education classes, or a parish celebration) should take their inspiration from the Church's practice in the renewed baptismal liturgy. Going far beyond any presentation of the sacramental rite as a "thing," what needs to be highlighted above all is the newness and the quality of the relationship of life with Jesus and, through him, with the Father and the Holy Spirit, and indeed with all of God's family on heaven and earth. The rites themselves are the best means of preparing for a renewal of baptismal commitment. In this way, emphasis is given to the symbolic wealth of the celebration: words (the Word of God, the liturgical texts), gestures, material elements (water, oil, light), along with the different people involved. God comes to us through the senses. In a world more and more influenced by the audiovisual, the liturgy—heard and seen in all its power, rather than artificially conducted—offers unsuspected possibilities for teaching and catechetical instruction. This calls for an effort of reflection and imagination on our part.

3. Baptismal renewal and Mary

A characteristic note of Montfort's program for "renewing the spirit of Christianity among the faithful" and for making them *"true disciples of Jesus Christ"* (TD 111) was the place he gave to Mary in his teaching and in baptismal renewal. His goal is evident: to assure fidelity to Jesus Christ to the point of perfect, loving unity with him. His staunch advocacy of perfect Consecration to Jesus Christ includes as an essential element the reality of its Marian dimension. Although language, ceremonies, and emphases vary according to generation and culture, the renewal of baptismal commitment is not in line with Montfort's thought if it does not explicitly bring out the evangelical role of Mary in salvation history. There is no perfect renewal of the vows of Baptism that omits Our Lady. Her role is not an artificial one, imagined by this vagabond missionary. Rather, it is willed by God Himself. The Second Vatican Council and the supreme pastors of the Church have emphasized this maternal influence of Mary. Christians are entitled to know Mary as their spiritual Mother; this knowledge leads not only to imitation but to an openness to her efficacious maternal influence, which can only strengthen one's living in Christ Jesus, i.e., in one's baptismal reality.

Montfort is a witness to and a master of such a spirituality, which is rooted in the Incarnation and finds its image in John's taking Mary into his life as a "disciple" (Jn 19:27). Saint Louis de Montfort is not the only such witness, nor the first, but certainly the greatest and more relevant than ever. We cannot but see a need of our own times expressed in the prophetic words of Saint Louis Marie: *"God in these times wishes his Blessed Mother to be more known, loved and honored than she has ever been"* (TD 55; cf. 47-50, 113).

4. Baptism and the Body of Christ

At the root of Montfort's love for the poor and his demands that they share in the opportunities and wealth of the rich is his profound belief in the reality of Baptism. It is the Sacrament that makes individuals "family." It brings all together at the table of the Lord, erasing the differences imposed by society. It makes all understand that everyone shares in one fundamental vocation: Christ Jesus. God is hidden in my neighbor, as Saint Louis Mary sings (H 148), not only because we have all been created by the one God but also because we are called to be one in the Lord through Baptism. This has a radical effect not only on the relationship between poor and rich but also on international relationships. For Baptism clearly teaches that power is not for dominance but for service.

J. Hémery

Notes: (1) Cf. J.M. Bonin, *Consécration à Marie et promesses baptismales selon saint Louis-Marie de Montfort*, Centre Marial, Montreal 1960; M. Gendrot, *Vie baptismale et dévotion mariale chez Louis-Marie Grignion de Montfort*, in *De cultu mariano saeculis XVII-XVIII*, vol. 5 of *Acta congressus mariologici-mariani internationalis in Republica Melitensi anno 1983 celebrati*, Pontificia Academia mariana internationalis, Rome 1987, 81-111. (2) CCC, 1213. (3) *The Catechism of the Council of Trent for Parish Priests Issued by Order of Pius V* is not a manual for the faithful but for pastors, who would find in its clear, orthodox teaching a source for their sermons and conferences. (4) Grandet, 100-101. (5) LS also contains Montfort's resume of a conference given by Father Lechassier on the Sacrament of Baptism. It is not included in GA but can be found in OC, 1752-1754. (6) Grandet, 408-412. (7) *Christifideles laici* 64.

BEATITUDES

The Beatitudes (Mt 5:3-12; Lk 6:20-23) are central to the Gospel and central to Montfort's spiritual life and message as well. Montfort explicitly cites the Gospel Beatitudes only once in his writings. He quotes them as the direct words of Wisdom Incarnate, which must be believed and practiced by Christians if they are to be saved (LEW ch.10). The Beatitudes are found in LEW 151. Left out is the one in Mt 5:11-12: "Blessed are you when people revile you and persecute you for my sake." In PM 25 there is the spirit, though not the letter, of the Beatitudes. Montfort refers to the mountain from which Jesus continues to teach. The *"divine mountain"* is Mary. LCM reads like a detailed commentary on the first Beatitude, "Blessed are the poor in spirit." This article, however, will stress not so much the classical Beatitudes found in the Sermon on the Mount (Mt. 5: 3-12) as the "beatitudes" that Montfort himself composed.

I. THE BEATITUDES IN THE LIFE OF MONTFORT

"Beatitude," implying happiness, is not to be confused with "prosperity." But as Louis Marie lived in such a depth of union with the Lord, he enjoyed the sort of happiness that, according to the Gospel, is found in loving genuinely.

1. A disposition for happiness?

The name of Montfort is not always mentioned in connection with happiness. In fact, some are alienated from him because they misunderstand his insistence on the Cross. Others imagine that he had to overcome many obstacles before his personality blossomed. Some of his biographers declare that he did not appear very sociable as a child at home and as a student at Rennes and even at Saint-Sulpice; he delighted in prayer and action, rather than in forming relationships with his peers. From his ordination in 1700 right up to 1706 and even later, he seemed to be beset by failures and was suspended from priestly duties several times. He even appeared to draw down on himself enmities and desertion by others. His best friend, J.B. Blain, "who felt very desirous to follow him and act as a companion," eventually became uneasy about his frequent dealings with Montfort.[1]

It is undeniable that Montfort endured a great deal of suffering during his short life. What his biographers have called his "odd ways" aroused much opposition. This criticism would not have come his way if his makeup had been like that of his friend Blain, for example. Some of his sufferings were also due to the fact that he was a "prophet." The worldly-wise are ruthless with those who expose their foolishness. Not all who withdraw from the world do so because they have difficulty forming relationships. No one can say how much of Montfort's suffering was part of the "mystery of the Cross" that some people are called to share early in life and that "psychology" is powerless to explain. B. Papàsogli was probably right when she wrote, "If we could search the depths of Louis Marie's soul, we would find that deep down he was joyful."[2]

2. Signs of happiness

We can infer from the way he reacted on a number of occasions that he was truly joyful, for his reactions were not those of a sad or bitter man. First of all, he appreciated friendship, and all through his life he proved a loyal, faithful friend even to people, like Blain, whose views about the apostolic life almost totally clashed with his. In 1714 he made a long, exhausting journey just to meet him. All his biographers mention his special gift for touching hearts and even bringing priests to tears. And Blain adds somewhat mischievously that "priests are not easily moved to tears."[3] Montfort was manifestly at ease when dealing with poor and humble people, which may explain why his missions were so successful; this does not mean that he felt awkward with people in high positions, some of whom decided to mend their ways after one meeting with him. When he returned to La Rochelle from Rennes in 1714, he was given a hero's welcome.[4] The gift of close rapport with people, the way he attracted the crowds, his openness to all sorts of people of which he was aware (L 11) from the beginning of his priestly ministry, are signs that joy dwelt in the depths of his heart.

Several times he speaks of his happiness. He wrote to his sister Guyonne-Jeanne in 1702, two years after his ordination to the priesthood and when he was 29 years of age, *"Permit my heart to join yours in a flood of joy and my eyes to shed tears of gratitude and my hands to describe on paper the happiness which transports me."* This happiness was still abiding in him ten years later, when he wrote in TD, *"My heart has dictated with special joy all that I have written"* (TD 13). The reason for this was that he was sharing a happy experience: *"Happy are those who faithfully keep your [Mary's] ways"* (TD 200). In a hymn addressed to the *"priests and lay people who look with disdain on his way of life abandoned to Providence,"* he says, *"Oh, if only you were able to understand my happiness"* (H 28:40).

3. Happiness that the world cannot know

The sort of happiness that Montfort enjoyed is difficult to understand. It was not the degrading and more or less masochistic happiness of those who find pleasure in inflicting pain on themselves or on those they love. There are certain expressions of Montfort that, when taken out of context, appear to support this type of happiness, like the following words put on the lips of Jesus: *"Endure pain virtuously, this happiness is greater / Than the joy of being loved by me"* (H 11:16).

Saint Louis is talking, however, of "another sort" of happiness, the happiness mentioned in the Beatitudes, which brings joy in suffering but only to those who are "poor in spirit" or "meek" or "make peace" or are "persecuted for the cause of righteousness." When Montfort writes to his sister, *"I am content and happy in all my troubles. I think there is nothing in the whole world so welcome as the most bitter cross"* (L 26); when he invites other people to sing the Te Deum in thanksgiving for a severe humiliation that he has undergone;[5] when he proclaims his famous *"No cross, what a cross,"*[6] the joy he experiences is that experienced by Saint Paul when he wrote, "I am overjoyed in all our affliction" (2 Cor 7:4) or "I am now rejoicing in my sufferings for your sake" (Col 1:24). Why is *"nothing . . . so welcome as the most bitter cross"*? Because it is *"steeped in the blood of Christ crucified"* (L 26), permits a closer union with *"Jesus who suffered more than any of us"* (L 33), and makes missionary efforts fruitful (*"I have never had more conversions than after the most painful and unjust prohibitions"* [L 26]), or simply because it enables us to love, and to live our reality as God's children (H 148:9).

II. The Beatitudes in the Spiritual Message of Montfort

It has been said of the Beatitudes that they are not part of the Good News; rather, they encapsulate the whole Gospel. It could likewise be argued that they are not part of Montfort's message but encapsulate it.

1. The style of the Beatitudes

The Beatitudes are built in a three-part structure: the proclamation of a happiness—"Blessed . . ."; the subject (and the object) of this happiness—"the poor in spirit"; and finally the reason for this happiness— "for the kingdom of heaven is theirs." Montfort often follows the same style in expressing his message:

Not only does Montfort imitate the literary style of the Beatitudes but he also uses the same pattern and expresses their content, as shown in the following chart.

At times Montfort tries to go one better than the Beatitudes by adding a certain progression, as when he

"Blessed . . . are those who understand these eternal truths, . . . for they will shine in heaven like stars for all eternity" (LEW 153).
"Blessed, a thousandfold blessed, are those priests whom you have chosen with such care to dwell with you on this divine mountain . . . [for] they will become kings for eternity" (PM 25).
"Happy is that soul in which Mary . . . is planted . . . in which she has been able to grow and blossom . . . [and] in which she brings forth her fruit, . . . savors the sweetness of Mary's fruit and preserves it." (SM 78).
"What incomparable happiness!" "They even cast themselves into her virginal bosom, hide and lose themselves there, . . . [for] they are filled with pure love, they are purified . . . , and they find Jesus in all his fullness" (TD 199).
"How happy are those who faithfully keep your ways, your counsels and your commands," for "they are happy in this world, . . . at the hour of death, . . . [and] for all eternity" (TD 200).
"Blessed, indeed, are those Christians who bind themselves faithfully and completely to her as to a secure anchor, . . . those who enter into her as into another Noah's ark [for] the flood waters . . . will not harm them" or *"carry away their heavenly riches"* (TD 175).
"Blessed is the man who has given everything to Mary, . . . trusts in her, and loses himself in her, [for] he belongs to Mary and Mary belongs to him" (TD 179).
"What a joy and a privilege for us to enter and dwell in Mary, . . . [for in her] almighty God has set up the throne of his supreme glory" (TD 262).
"Be comforted, rejoice" "if you have trials and afflictions, if you suffer much persecution for justice's sake, . . . [for] all that is honorable, glorious, and virtuous in God and in his Holy Spirit is vested in you" (LEW 179).
"Your are indeed happy, Louise Grignion, if you are poor in spirit, abandoned, despised, and like refuse cast out from the house, . . . [for] then you will be truly the servant and spouse of Christ" (L 7).

says, *"Blessed are those . . . more blessed are those . . . but the most blessed are those . . ."* which he applies, for example, to those who understand the eternal truths, or to the soul in which Mary, the tree of life, is planted (LEW 153; SM 78). Finally, balancing the Beatitudes are the *"curses"* or *"woes of the world"* (LEW 6, 72; TD 199, 200), which are sometimes divided into three stages: in this world, at the hour of death, in eternity (cf. LEW 72).

2. The pattern Montfort employs in proclaiming the Beatitudes

The Beatitudes contrast true happiness, which only love secures, with false worldly joys. It can be argued that this was also Montfort's procedure in all his preaching and writings.

a. An invitation to happiness. During his missions, Montfort often dealt with *"the most terrifying subjects"* (SR 113), as was the rule in his days; his preaching, however, was basically an invitation to happiness, because he denounced the "woes of the world" when talking about these "terrifying subjects." We find evidence of this in the hymns, which are quite a faithful reflection of his preaching. It is noteworthy that these hymns generally present virtue in a most attractive manner, as in the following few examples:

> *"This is the way [of virtue] that secures happiness / And leads straight to heaven"* (H 3).
>
> *"One day I was contemplating the Lord / And I fell in love with what I saw: / It was a beautiful princess"* (H 4:1; Montfort is singing about virtue).
>
> *"In my songs I reveal / A thing of beauty . . . / Holy humility"* (H 8:1).
>
> *"They think I am a simple-minded girl / Who knows no joy and is despised,*
>
> *But the Gospel sings my praises / And I am as happy as can be"* (H 12:1; the topic of the hymn is virginity).

In the rest of his writings, which contain what Montfort had been *"teaching . . . in my missions for many years"* (TD 110), his call to happiness becomes an invitation to share an experience that involves frustration at being unable to do so fully, as suggested by such expressions as *"If people only knew," "If Christians only knew," "If only we could realize what Wisdom actually is"* (LEW 73), *"If only we knew the joy of a soul that perceives the beauty of divine Wisdom"* (LEW 10), *"If we knew the value of the Cross"* (LEW 177). The trouble is we do not truly know that beauty and joy (L13).

b. Montfort used the pattern of the Beatitudes. Montfort has written and preached in order to share his happiness. In each of his works we can trace one or several beatitudes. LEW seeks the *"infinite treasure [of divine Wisdom]"* (LEW 73): Happy are those who long for her and seek her, because *"nothing that you can desire can be compared with her"* (LEW 73). SM is about becoming holy: "Happy are those who find the secret of Mary, because she will make saints of them" (cf. SM 20). TD is a *"preparation for the reign of Jesus Christ"* and invites us to a similar sort of happiness: Happy are those who practice true devotion to Mary, for she is the way to Jesus. Even FC echoes the Beatitudes since the joy of the Cross is *"greater than . . . the greatest joys that can be experienced on earth"* (FC 34). Montfort wrote, *"Enclosed in the beloved cross is true wisdom and that is what I am looking for night and day"* (L 13). He was looking for the gift of Wisdom but also for Jesus himself, who became one with the Cross by an indissoluble bond: *"Wisdom is the Cross and the Cross is Wisdom"* (LEW 172, 180).

c. Montfort denounced false joys. The calamity is that the Cross (which is not any suffering whatsoever but suffering out of love) does not appear as "wisdom" but as a great stupidity. People run away from it with all their strength in their quest for a so-called happiness totally opposed to the Cross: wealth, pleasure, and power, which can only disappoint them. What Montfort sets out to do is denounce the false joys by showing that they are actually "woes," and to invite his audience to discern true happiness, which may come to them in the guise of what many think of as "misfortune." In a 92-verse hymn (H 29), Montfort describes the twelve major *"woes of the world"*; he goes into detail and ruthlessly denounces as many as ninety-six of them. They all, however, come from three main sources that could be termed: worldly pride, worldly heartlessness, and worldly lies. The joys which the world offers end in disappointment, do not satisfy humanity's deep aspirations (H 29:37,58,67), and are short-lived (H 29:41,42).

It is mainly the lies of the world that Father de Montfort attacks. He blames the world not so much for its sins as for its attempt to justify them by concealing them under the cloak of virtue, and for calling "truth" what are in fact blatant lies. In the hymn mentioned above he says:

The world is Satan disguised
Under attractive appearances . . .
He is so clever at misleading people
That only few can resist him.
He is extremely clever
At making sin look like virtue.
(H 29:8,36,16; LEW 79)

In its wickedness, the world goes even further: it attacks virtue, which it represents as "sin," and turns into "affliction" the true happiness promised by the Beatitudes (LEW 77, 78; H 39). Montfort invites us to call on the Holy Spirit to help us discern true from false virtue, true from false beatitudes. To aid us in this discernment process, Montfort denounces five *"snares of the world"* (H 30-34), and draws our attention to the most subtle of them all, *"human respect,"* to which he devotes a 152-verse hymn (H 34-39). Blain has described Montfort as "the man with the least human respect in the world,"[7] so it is not surprising that he should warn us strongly against the greatest obstacle to the spirit of the Beatitudes: *"Beware, though we such wiles enjoy, / Their hidden poison can destroy"* (H 39:132).

3. The message of the Beatitudes

What is the true happiness that Montfort invites us to enjoy? We are fully aware that it cannot be different from that held out by the Beatitudes, even if it is described in different terms and with a stress on the Wisdom of God.

a. The Beatitudes according to Montfort. It is possible that St. Louis' spiritual message may be summed up in the following beatitude: "Blessed are those who are wise in the Spirit, for theirs is the kingdom of heaven." Blessed are those wise people, for they know Jesus Christ. *"To know Jesus Christ incarnate Wisdom, is to know all we need. To presume to know everything and not know him is to know nothing at all"* (LEW 11). To know Jesus Christ means to "know" him in order to be able to love him and acquire the vital experiential knowledge of him, which is precisely the gift of Wisdom making us realize that we are loved by him (LEW 8, 64-65). To know Jesus Christ also means that we acknowledge him as *"an inexhaustible source"* of true riches, true joys, and true grandeur; he is the true love we are all seeking (LEW 63, 72, 181). He is *"infinitely eager"* to give himself to us: "Happy are those people wise with the very wisdom of Jesus, for they will also share his 'mind' and therefore the same Spirit and the same life" (Phil 2:5).

Those who have acquired Wisdom possess *"that infinite treasure which contains every good"* (LEW 206).

Wisdom is not only a "treasure" but also a "fruit" produced by Mary, who is the "tree." If we desire the fruit, we must possess the tree (TD 164). *"Happy is that soul in which Mary . . . is planted . . . happier again is the soul in which she brings forth her fruit"* (SM 78). Montfort adds: *"Happy, indeed sublimely happy, is the person to whom the Holy Spirit reveals the secret of Mary, thus imparting to him true knowledge of her. . . . That person will find only God and no creature in the most lovable Virgin Mary"* (SM 20). This brings us back to the beatitudes, mentioned earlier,[8] that celebrate the joy of those who have "taken her for their own" and live in her, with her, through her because it is Mary who gives us Jesus. She is the Mother who continues to give birth to all the members of the Body of Christ (LEW 204; TD 32).

A second Marian beatitude could be added to this and complete it. Happy are those whose "devotion to Mary is true and loving," for they have found an easy way to union with Jesus and they will be able to experience her *"sweet presence"* (SM 52). Any Christian who wants to follow Jesus has to carry his Cross, but with Mary he will be able to carry it joyfully and perseveringly (TD 152, 154).

Mary is not the only "dwelling place" where we can be certain that Wisdom resides. Wisdom is also to be found in the Cross, which is inseparable from Jesus (LEW 180). So we can say: Happy are those who live the mystery of the Cross, for they will encounter Jesus. This beatitude will only shock those who have not yet been shocked by the Gospel Beatitudes. Who but Christ could say, "Blessed are those who mourn. Blessed are those who are persecuted. Blessed are you when people revile you" (Mt 5:5,10,11)? Each of the Beatitudes promises joy as a reward for suffering endured in love and out of love. Montfort applies this to the Cross. At Baptism we have been buried with Christ into his death (in a sacramental manner), so that we too might share in his glory (Rom 6:3-5). Like the other Beatitudes the Beatitude of the Cross is only a small (or great) "Baptism" through which we continue our union with Wisdom.

b. Montfort and the Beatitudes. Although Montfort has his own beatitudes, we will attempt to show that in all his works he repeated in one way or another each of the Gospel Beatitudes.

"Blessed are the poor in spirit." LCM is an explicit commentary on this first invitation to happiness. Those who profess *"voluntary poverty"* are happy, because their hearts are rich and they lack for nothing; they are rich in faith and the other virtues; they are rich in divine consolations and even in heavenly glory (LCM 5-7). *"You are indeed happy if you are poor in spirit,"* Montfort wrote to his sister Louise Marie in a letter that has been described as "a hymn and a commentary on the first Beatitude."[9] The watermark of this Beatitude is embossed on every page of Montfort's life. The saint was truly "poor in spirit" to such a point that we could say that he was a "commentary"[10] on the first Beatitude. His life was nothing more than a translation of the "humility of God," the first of all the "poor."

"Blessed are the meek. Blessed are the merciful. Blessed are the peacemakers." Montfort lived out these three similar Beatitudes also, and he mentions them in his writings: "Happy are the meek" not only towards others whom they forgive *"from their heart"* (H 14:30-41), towards whom they are patient (H 11), and exercise their zeal in a fatherly way (H 21:18; 22:17), but also who are "meek" and "gentle" towards themselves (SM 51), and even in their relationship with God by a "tender" devotion to Mary (TD 107). Montfort has devoted a whole hymn to the "charms" of gentleness, which is, first of all, an attribute of Incarnate Wisdom (LEW ch.10) and of Incarnate Wisdom's mother, Mary (LEW 118; TD 199).

"Blessed are those who mourn. Blessed are those who are persecuted for righteousness' sake. Blessed are you when people revile you." The whole of FC as well as extensive passages from LEW (LEW 173-180; 194-202) are a commentary on these three Beatitudes and reflections on the "Mystery of the Cross."

"Blessed are those who hunger and thirst for righteousness." Montfort enters deeply into the spirit of this Beatitude when he speaks of the *"desire"* with which we should burn for social justice (H 18; H 29:49,80; H 150:8,14), and even more ardently for holiness, for Wisdom herself (LEW 54, 61), *"who is supremely desirable"* (LEW 181-183). Blessed are those who seek her ardently (LEW 54, 61); in so doing they only respond to the "infinite eagerness" of Wisdom to give herself to us (LEW 63), because she thirsted and hungered for us first (LEW 165).

"Blessed are the pure in heart." Montfort has pointed out that *"of the eight beatitudes it is only the pure in heart who are promised they will see God"* (MRL II). The hymn "Beauty of virginity" (H 12) is about purity of heart rather than purity of the body. The aim of devotion to the Blessed Virgin is to make us pure in heart (LEW 210, 211) by purifying not only the *"fruit"* of our good actions but most of all the *"tree"* that bears it, i.e., our heart (TD 146, 205; cf. Lk 6:43-45), so that it may be worthy to welcome Wisdom. In order to purify our heart, Mary rids it of any desire for a purely human reward (TD 110), and above all she rids it of any servile fear; she opens and enlarges it *"to obey the commandments of her Son with alacrity and with the holy freedom of the children of God"* (TD 215). She crowns this by giving *"herself completely in a wondrous manner"* and shares her purity with us (TD 144).

III. Relevance of Montfort's Beatitudes Today

The Beatitudes that Montfort lived out and taught by his way of life and his writings are relevant to our contemporaries and their aspirations, marked by a longing for happiness here and now, a search for unity, and a need for realism.

1. A longing for happiness here and now

A survey carried out in France in 1977 showed that people thought that the four main ingredients of happiness were health, love, freedom, and the family. Health was rated first by 90% of the people surveyed, love by 80%, freedom by 75%, and the family by 73%.[11] More recent surveys show that, apart from love, which thankfully remains one of the main driving forces, money, pleasure, and power are pursued by most of our contemporaries in their quest for happiness. It is noteworthy also that in the early 1990s people seem disillusioned with ideologies or "golden tomorrows" and long for happiness in immediate life experiences through personal relationships.

And it is happiness that Montfort offers. His entire teaching is punctuated with cries of "happy," "happy indeed," "a thousand times happy." His teaching holds out the promise of immense happiness, since it concerns the happiness of God Himself, of the Happiness Who is God! This happiness lies in relationship, since God is love and relationship by nature. Finally, it offers a happiness that is a life experience here and now, since Jesus—here and now—invites us to share his "mysteries" and, therefore, his life. Montfort seems to draw inspiration from Jn 1:45 and to say to our contemporaries, "I have found the One Who can give peace to your restless hearts, but you are vainly looking for Him in wealth, pleasure and power. He is the Eternal and Incarnate Wisdom, Jesus from Nazareth." He alone is true wealth, true joy and true power. Moreover, we need not discard our humanity in order to find Him, for He has made Himself a member of the human family. To our contemporaries who are so keen on the "promotion of the human being" in general and of women in particular, Father de Montfort reminds us of the marvel of the mystery of Mary, our sister within the human family, in whom we can find "only God" (SM 20). The great mystery of fraternal love, which Montfort expressed when he said, *"I must love as none other God hidden in my neighbor"* (H 148:1), finds its true fulfillment only in Mary, Mother of God.

2. A search for unity

It is because people live such scattered lives that they aspire for unity. They feel somewhat lost when confronted with a series of moral virtues in addition to the commandments that Jesus summed up so simply: "You shall love the Lord your God, you shall love your neighbor" (Mt 22:37-39). He spoke of the two commandments as one, since "the second is like the first." "Love suffices."[12] The Beatitudes prove attractive because they offer happiness without imposing any obligations, but, even so, there are perhaps too many of them. They should be reduced to one, which in a sense contains the whole of Montfort's message: "Happy are those who love" or, rather, "Happy are those who know they are loved," loved with a boundless love by Wisdom herself, for they will not be able to stop loving. *"In truth, to know what our Lord has endured for us [because he loves us] and yet . . . not to love him ardently is morally impossible"* (LEW 166; TD 138). But this is not the whole beatitude: "Happy are those who love . . ." Why? Because they love for the sake of loving and for nothing else. When he invites us to consecrate ourselves completely to Jesus through the hands of Mary, i.e., to experience the joy of loving, Montfort warns us that we should not seek any "reward." Love is its own *raison d'être.*

3. A need for realism

Although Montfort's entire message is the offer of happiness, which in this sense sounds attractive to our contemporaries, they are also afraid of it, since in his typically frank and blunt manner, the Apostle of the Cross never hesitates to remind us that "no one has greater love than this, to lay down one's life . . ." (Jn 15:13). The Cross stands at the very heart of all the Beatitudes in the shape of "poverty in spirit," "gentleness," "tears," "mercy," etc. This is a useful reminder for our contemporaries, who are so easily misled by the "beatitudes" of the world from which the Cross has been carefully eliminated. In contrast to widely publicized false joys, Montfort assures us that the true joy and happiness offered by the Gospel do not come cheap, because the promises of the Kingdom are not for the rich and powerful but only for the poor and the weak.

As Montfort translated the Beatitudes for his time, he would expect us to do the same for our times. A journalist with a sense of humor, Joseph Folliet, offered what he called his "Little Beatitudes" to the public, and they are still relevant today: "Blessed are those who can laugh at themselves, for they will always find something to laugh at. Blessed are those can tell a mountain from a molehill, for they will be spared a great deal of worry. Blessed are those who can keep quiet and listen, for they will learn more than they thought possible." Bishop Torija of Ciudad, Spain, wrote "Beatitudes for a time of high unemployment": "Blessed are those who are prepared to lose money in investing in order to create jobs, for they amass wealth for the eternal kingdom. Blessed are those who reject holding several jobs that are not necessary for them to live in dignity, for a place is reserved for them in the kingdom . . ."[13]

A few years ago, Daniel Ange offered "variations on the theme of the Beatitudes": "Blessed are you whom the Spirit makes poor, for the kingdom of God is yours. Blessed are you who do not resist love, for you will inherit the land of God . . ."[14]

The Montfort beatitudes must be adapted for our times. Their basic message is clear: "Blessed are those who believe. Blessed are those who hope. Blessed are those who love."

J. Morinay

Notes: (1) Blain, 224, 226. (2) B. Papàsogli, *Montfort, A Prophet for our Times* Edizioni Monfortane, Rome 1991, 192. (3) Blain, 309. (4) C. Besnard, V, 405. (5) Besnard, V, 529. (6) Besnard, V, 532. (7) Blain, 298. (8) Cf. p. 4. (9) B. Papàsogli, 142. (10) Ibid. (11) Théo, *Nouvelle encyclopédie catholique (New Catholic Encyclopedia),* Droguet-Ardant/Fayard, Paris 1989, 775a. (12) Name of a film on the life of St Bernadette Soubirous. (13) Théo, op. cit., 840. (14) In *Prier,* November 1982.

BEAUTY

I. INTRODUCTION

"You shall be quite beautiful and the world will love you if you love God" (Grandet, 3). This invitation, which the child Louis Marie Grignion made to his little sister, established a bond between the spiritual life and beauty. The anecdote may cause a smile, but the reality it expresses is basic: the experience of God is transfiguring. A transfigured face cannot help but be beautiful. It is the reflection of the beauty of God. As in the Song of Solomon, beauty does not exist without love.

When looked at in this light, beauty is to be found in the realm of "the experience of God." The inverted commas indicate that we wish to put aside any ambiguity as much as we can. The experience of God cannot be reduced either to a kind of positivism or to sentimentality. And what is more, we do not understand the experience of the beautiful as something merely aesthetic.

It is true that Montfort painted and sculpted. A certain aesthetic sense can be perceived in his missionary methods. He had a taste for beauty and good order in the processions and celebrations that he loved. They had to be spectacular and moving. He had a taste for the beauty and dignity of churches, chapels, oratories, and calvaries. Yet, as a look at the statues and canticles he left us will demonstrate, beauty as expressed through the perfection of forms was not his major concern. There is no real work of art in the Montfort canon. Art for art's sake does not exist, for the beauty of something handmade should not be the end point but should, rather, bring one to see more deeply inward (cf. H 2: 43).

Beauty is transitory (cf. H 137; 164). Beauty for beauty's sake is inadmissible, since we must connect *"the useful with the beautiful, the sturdy with the pleasing"* (H 33:37). Art is suspect, since it infers the artificial and, still worse, the fake (cf. H 33:25). As the mask of a deceitful world, art is a disguise (cf. H 2:5; 38, 119), a *"fine appearance"* (H 114:6), a *"beautiful invention"* (H 31:2), a kind of bait, a *"charm"* covering over the fishhook (H 29:36; 2,34; cf. 107:8; LEW 12).

Father de Montfort constantly railed against those arts which were mere distraction (cf. H 29; 31:32; 33) and hence *"perdition"* (H 1:34; 2,16,28,30,31; 32:4). In the context of luxurious display, they hide injustice (H 33: 55-57). Art is lying. By covering itself with the appearance of beauty, it dissociates the beautiful from the good or the true (cf. H 2, 18, 20). It changes vice into virtue and brings misfortune while promising happiness. It is a seducer, and Montfort would have nothing of this seduction. Wishing to lead people to the good and the true, he rejected art and its beauty (cf. H 2, 39,41).

In the search for the authentic good, only virtue is the bearer of beauty (cf. H 4:1,2; 6:2,40; 8:1,8; 9:3;12; 14:7; 15, 14; 20:4; 25:6,16; 36,65). This is why he cannot conceive of an aesthetic without an ethic. The *"fashionable society"* (LEW 78; FC 8; MLW 15; H 39:138; 103:25; 139:47), on the contrary, presents an aesthetic emptied of the ethical. We must withdraw, then, from this deceitful world, which offers merely an *"imaginary happiness"* whose beauty is nothing more than a *"sparkling display of pomp"* (H 4:23). Art produces only idols of beauty.

True beauty is not made by man's hands. It eludes human control. This beauty beyond all beauty, a beauty that is *"supreme"* (H 103:2; 157:36) and *"sovereign"* (LEW 19, 90; H 119:6; 127:7), is God Himself (LEW 17, H 127:20,57; 135:2).

Beauty can be shown but not demonstrated. Father de Montfort did not expressly treat of the beauty of God. But the theme is frequent enough, particularly in LEW, to attract our attention. In fact it appears at every stage where he is explaining *"in a simple way . . . Eternal Wisdom before, during and afterwhat his Incarnation"* (LEW 7). Wisdom is the face of beauty, its expression. Experiencing beauty is an interpersonal relationship with Wisdom. This relationship is acquired through the sense of sight: seeing and being seen. In beauty, Wisdom is seen as *"delectable knowledge (sapida sapientia), a taste for God and his truth"* (LEW 13).[1] Thus Montfort posits the bases for a theological aesthetic, of a knowledge of taste. He leads into the knowledge of Christ through taste. Tasting stirs up desire. Desiring enkindles love and keeps it alive.

Beauty reveals itself in order to be loved and allows itself to be seen in order to be known. Montfort develops this view of Wisdom on three levels: *"Starting with his very origin, we shall consider Wisdom in eternity, dwelling in his Father's bosom and object of his Father's love. Next we shall see him in time, shing forth in the creation of the universe. Then we shall consider him in the deep abasement of his Incarnation and his mortal life; and then we shall see him glorious and triumphant in heaven."* (LEW 14). Seeing and being seen, grasping and being grasped, man is taken up himself into the beauty that reveals itself to him. The beauty of God transfigures the one who contemplates it and transforms him into this very same beauty (cf. 2 Cor 3:18). A close bond unites being and seeing (cf. 1 Jn 3:2).

II. The Experience of Beauty

1. A science of taste

The first time we come upon beauty in LEW, we see it in the company of sweetness (LEW 1). Both words often go together in Montfort's work.[2] They have in common the fact that they both appeal to the experience of the senses, of sight and taste. Beauty and sweetness ask to be perceived and sensed: *"This good is conceived only in experience"* (H 56:36).[3] Of course, Montfort here means the "spiritual senses," since he invites us to see and taste the beauty and sweetness of Christ-Wisdom. He insists on the real possibility of an authentic experience of Christ. If Wisdom is beautiful and sweet, it is because there is something to see, taste, and grasp. This "grasp" is in the order of knowledge. Montfort sets up a theological aesthetic, i.e., the *"delectable knowledge"* of God (LEW 13).[4] It does not affect the understanding alone, since it is accompanied by true happiness. Here we learn *"the means for being happy"* (LEW 5; S 252).

2. A loving knowledge

This experimental knowledge of Wisdom has no other purpose than to lead to the love of this Wisdom (cf. LEW 8). In presenting it as beautiful and sweet, Montfort wants it to be loved by his readers. The experience of beauty is an element of a mode of teaching whose aim is to make Christ loved, and Christ himself uses it to make himself loved.

We love because we are attracted. We are attracted by what gives us pleasure. Pleasure is the enjoyment of beauty and sweetness.[5] The experience of beauty brings desire into play. Beauty is always provocative (cf. LEW 5, 66-69, 181). It flatters the senses and awakens affectivity and even sensuality. It wants to be charming and offers itself for enjoyment. It makes itself loved in order to be possessed (cf. LEW 2). It reveals itself and brings to itself those who contemplate it. The sight of beauty causes motion. It is always "ravishing." It captivates. The experience of beauty is not only the acceptance of a truth that is offered to us in the enjoyment of pleasure; it is also an "abduction" and a "capture."[6]

This rapture is both passive and active. It is passive because this ecstasy (attracted by beauty, man is beside himself) is produced by the Wisdom that attracts man and takes him in order to possess him. It is active because this being beside oneself is also the product of the will and the love of man who desires Wisdom, searches for it, and tends toward it.

The Calvary of Pontchateau

A primary symbol of obedience and trust, since upon completion Montfort was ordered to destroy it. Although deeply saddened by the request, he remarked that God wanted the Cross planted not on the hill but in the heart.

This double rapture is moved by love. This love is not gratuitous like *agapé-caritas.* It desires and pursues the mutual possession of the lover and the beloved: it is *eros-amor.* It goes beyond reason, and this is the scandal of Wisdom. It loves man with a desire that is vehement (cf. LEW 5, 47, 63-69) and excessive (cf. LEW 45, 64, 108, 155, 166; SR 67, 73; H 27:2; 40:12; 41:1,9; 42:14; 128:6; 132:2; 137:8; 158:5,13). In return, man must love it with the same desire (cf. LEW 54, 58, 72, 73, 131, 181-193; H 26:21; 44:2; 87:3; 128:6; 132:8; 135:4; 137:14; 158:13), to the point of intoxication (cf. LEW 10; H 40:22; 112:5; 129:4,7; 158:9).

The beautiful is the object of loving desire and is loving desire itself.[7] In the experience of beauty, a nuptial mysticism stands out that is not alien to Wisdom itself (cf. LEW 54 and 59 8,2). This notion of marriage geared toward the union of those who desire one another requires exclusiveness. Man can only desire Wisdom, the only desirable Good beyond all good (cf. LEW 8-12, 74, 181). It demands to be freed of all other desires and pleasures that are not ordered to the sole desire of Wisdom (cf. LEW 194-195). Our needs must be purified for true desire to emerge. Seeing the beauty of Wisdom requires purity of vision. A purification is necessary (cf. H 127:20). Montfort calls it *"mortification . . . that is total"* (LEW 196). It is a lengthy labor of divesting ourselves of all attachments in order to attach us solely to the possession of Wisdom (LEW 197-202). We rediscover *"God alone"* under the form of all or nothing: *"Leave all things and you will find all things by finding Jesus"* (LEW 202), and *"To know Jesus Christ incarnate Wisdom, is to know all we need. To presume to know everything and not know him is to know nothing at all."* (LEW 11).

3. The status of the book

Beauty sees itself as universal. By nature it is communicable. *"Eternal Wisdom, ever transcendent in beauty, by nature loves everything that is good, . . . and consequently nothing gives him more pleasure than to communicate himself."* (LEW 90). On the other hand, the experience of the beautiful can only be special: One cannot experience beauty in my stead. But it obliges one to speak and therefore to share: *"There is in you so much beauty and delight. . . . How can I remain silent?"* (LEW 1). Beauty amazes and cause a reaction. The book LEW had its origin in this amazement and disappointment: *"You are . . . so little known and so much slighted"* (LEW 1).

The experience of beauty is the point from which the book arose, but it is also its plan. In writing, Montfort allowed himself to experience desire: *"Look upon the strokes of my pen as so many steps to find you."* And he proposes to lead his reader to it *"so that those who read it may be filled with a fresh desire to love you and possess you"* (LEW 2).

The book is an invitatory. Montfort does not understand this experience of the beautiful as selfish enjoyment. For it is not enough to taste the truth for oneself; one must have others taste it by inviting them to have this experience themselves (cf. LEW 30, 153; RM 60; RP 1). By tasting and making others taste, the mystic is an apostle. As an invitation to see, the experience of beauty is apostolic.[8] These words of invitation, and the book they are found in, only find their authentication in Montfort's own experience.

To taste beauty to the point of being filled with it to overflowing opens up a breach. The person who has this experience will speak *"ex abundantia cordis"* (Mt 13:34), "according to the divine abundance that Wisdom communicates to him" and "according to what Divine Wisdom makes them feel" (Wis 7:15), according to *"what they have taken from books"* (LEW 97; RM 60). LEW is a book that springs *ex abundantia cordis.* Montfort does not so much seek to prove something as to touch hearts. His plan is "aesthetic." This can be construed from his desire to *"learn how to talk properly"* (LEW 1). To wish to "talk properly" is to seek *"unction"* and "mellowness" (cf. LEW 30, 97), which are signs not only of the grace to say things well but of the Spirit who impregnates what is written with His breath.

As an author, Montfort steps aside to allow the Spirit to speak. *"I did not want, my dear reader, to mingle my poor words with the inspired words of the Holy Spirit"* (LEW 5), he wrote after quoting the sixth chapter of the book of Wisdom (LEW 3-4). He shows Scripture more than he demonstrates it, and in this sense he is no exegete. He withdraws before the sacred text in order that it might appear in all its beauty: *"I shall not mingle my poor words with his for fear of diminishing their clarity and sublime meaning"* (LEW 20, before quoting Sir 24, 1-32). He is happy to present Scripture and allow it to do its work in revealing Christ, who is Wisdom. To read the Bible is to look at Wisdom, which reveals itself in it. The experience of beauty passes through the experience of the book. The Bible is the book in which Wisdom allows itself to be seen, the place where it seeks man and man seeks Wisdom. The Scripture is the mystery, the sacrament of the encounter of man with Christ.

This revelation and this search are of the nature of desire. Desire puts Wisdom in motion toward man and man toward Wisdom. The Bible is the book where this twofold tension is carried out. A man in search of Wisdom finds the expression of his own desire in Scripture, which is the exemplar and the pattern of desire. In LEW Montfort gives Solomon as an *"example"* to follow (LEW 2, 7, 54, 92, 183) to the point where the Old Testament ends and the New Testament begins. In the incarnation of Wisdom in Mary, the value of Solomon as an exemplar ends (LEW 220, 221).

The eternal possession of Wisdom is the purpose of the book. Its origin is the desire Wisdom has for man: *"This eternal beauty, ever supremely loving, is so intent on winning man's friendship that for this very purpose he has written a book in which he describes his own excellence and his desire for man's friendship. This book reads like a letter written by a lover to win the affections of his loved one"* (LEW 65; cf. LEW 63).

In Scripture, beauty allows itself to

be seen in order to be loved. "We write in order to be loved."[9] In the experience of the beautiful, Montfort returns to the book what cold and sterile science has taken from it: the ability to lead to genuine love. He brings us "to the point where we no longer read except in the Book of Truth where Eternal Wisdom is presented."[10]

III. The Beauty of Wisdom

1. Contemplating incomprehensible Wisdom

The experience of beauty can create the illusion that Wisdom can be understood through the spiritual senses. In fact, the beauty of eternal Wisdom is beyond any human grasp. It is incomprehensible in its divinity (LEW 15). Montfort shows presents a paradox: it is beauty but it cannot be seen. *"For here all human beings must close their eyes so as not to be blinded by the vivid brightness of his light"* (LEW 15). It is beyond all beauty, *"Something resplendent, / Sublime, immense, and infinite"* (LEW 19). Even if this *"dazzling and incomprehensible light"* can be vaguely discerned, it is no less true that "there are no words to explain it," and my idea *"fall[s] infinitely short of his excellence," Montfort adds, for "who can ever form an adequate idea of him?"* (LEW 19). This concept of the impossibility of looking face to face at eternal Wisdom and of saying something adequate about it because of its eminence comes from a negative or apophatic theology. The mystery of Divine Beauty remains inaccessible unless the Holy Spirit, *"adapting himself to our weakness,"* gives us an *"idea"* of it (LEW 16). Lifting the veil that hides Wisdom, the Spirit condescends to show some people this Divine Beauty (cf. LEW 17; S 25). It is in ecstasy that God reveals it *"to all you wish"* (LEW 19). We find once again the twofold movement of the experience of beauty: ecstasy and revelation. In revelation, God comes down to man. In ecstasy man is carried off to God. The beams of revelation cast man into ecstasy.

In the revelation of beauty there is a positive or cataphatic theology, since something true is said about this Wisdom (cf. LEW 17), but this "objective knowledge" does not allow us to grasp it, since it is man who in his rapture is seized by Wisdom.

Leaving aside a few momentary flashes, this contemplation of eternal Wisdom is beyond human experience. Only God the Father has knowledge of it. Only He can experience Divine Beauty. Indeed, *"God the Father was well pleased with the sovereign beauty of Eternal Wisdom, his Son, throughout time and eternity"* (LEW 19; Mt 17:5). The Father takes pleasure in looking on the beauty of His Son. The experience of beauty has its very source in the life of the Trinity. Montfort introduces beauty into the theology of the Trinity by showing (very rapidly it is true!) the relations between the Father and the Son in terms of aesthetics. Hence the contemplation of Wisdom is marked by the seal of infinity and incomprehensibility, signs of divinity.

2. Seeing Wisdom in creation

"For the greatness and beauty of created things give us a corresponding idea of their Creator" (Wis 13:5). This ascent of the experience of beauty, which goes up from the created world to the Creator, is practically absent in Montfort. This verse of the Wisdom of Solomon has inspired only one phrase in a hymn, *"What must the worker be, / If the work is so beautiful!"* (H 99:28). The rarity of this analogical rhythm is explained by the fact that his relationship to the experience of the beautiful remains problematical. Indeed, instead of causing our eyes to be raised up to God, the beauty of creatures can hold them captive. Instead of taking us to the adoration and knowledge of God, the experience of the beauty of creation can become idolatrous (cf. Wis 13:1-9). On the contrary, Father de Montfort used a descending movement. He begins with the beauty of Wisdom in order to reach the beauty of His creation (cf. LEW 31-34). The creative act is like "fireworks." *"Eternal Wisdom began to manifest himself outside the bosom of God the Father when, after a whole eternity, he made light, heaven and earth"* (LEW 31). Montfort describes Wisdom as an artist working on a work of art.[11] In creating beauty, Wisdom experiments with it as pleasure and play: *"I was with God and I disposed everything with such perfect precision and such pleasing variety that it was like playing a game to entertain my Father and myself"* (LEW 32). To sum up, creation is a holiday celebration given by Wisdom where we find the overflowing gratuitousness of excess (cf. LEW 33). But an understanding of this entertainment is not given immediately to the senses. The book of creation opens only through revelation, a "communication" of Wisdom itself (cf. LEW 23). Looking at creation in this way gives access to another experience of Divine Beauty in its twofold movement of revelation and enrapture. *"Eternal Wisdom has revealed these things [the mysteries of nature] to the saints. . . . At times they were so astonished at the beauty, the harmony and the order that God has put into the smallest things, such as a bee, an ant, an ear of corn, a flower, a worm, that they were carried away in rapture and ecstasy"* (LEW 34).

In hymn 157, Father de Montfort integrates the beauty of nature into a progressive, contemplative search for solitude. Nature is seen as a *"desert place"* and thus clashes with the world of men (cf. H 142:15-21). Flight from the inhabited world allows the rediscovery of pure nature unsullied by the sin of men, where the presence of the Creator shines through (H 157:18-19).[12] There the solitary inhabits a beauty not made by the hand of man, where he appreciates and sings about its slightest charms, and learns from it stimulating lessons (H 157:13,16).

"But if nature is so fair, / Grace has made it so, / Shaping a Paradise / . . . When the soul transfixed holds it so dear!" (H 157:20,21). Nature's beauty, then, offers it a *"pure and tranquil"* framework (H 157:14) where the soul can contemplate, but in order to contemplate Divine Beauty, it is not on the beauty of nature that the soul relies. No. The solitary soul retires to himself in that inner solitude where he finds Jesus Christ (H 157:23). Furthermore, in his retreat, hidden as he is in himself, nothing must distract him, not even outer beauty, if he truly wishes to contemplate Supreme Beauty (H 157:36).

3. Looking at Incarnate Wisdom

a. The paradox of beauty. The beauty of Eternal Wisdom has an indiscernible brilliance, a dazzling splendor. It is inaccessible because of too much light. But beauty calls for a representation. As a reflection of the beauty of the Father, Wisdom takes on its countenance by appearing in history. In the mystery of the Incarnation, *"God, the Incomprehensible, allowed himself to be perfectly comprehended. . . . God, the Inaccessible, drew near to us and united himself closely, perfectly and even personally to our humanity"* (TD 157; cf. 57,1). By becoming a countenance, the Eternal and Incarnate Wisdom opens the only possible access to the beauty of God. Only the Incarnation allows us to experience beauty within the paradox of the harmony of opposites: *"How gentle, attractive and approachable [comprehensible] is Eternal Wisdom who possesses such splendor, excellence and grandeur [incomprehensible]"* (LEW 5). This paradox is the paradox of Christology, the two natures of Christ in the oneness of his person.

b. Mary. In the Incarnation, God Himself experiences beauty. He experiences that ecstasy which causes Him to come out of Himself by becoming flesh in Mary. In her, God experiences beauty, first in creating *her—"[Wisdom] created the most holy Virgin, forming her . . . with even greater delight than He had derived from creating the universe"* (LEW 105)—and then in admiring her "virtues": *"The faithful care with which she corresponded to the graces of her Creator. . . . The angels and even God Himself were filled with rapturous admiration for her. Her humility, deep as an abyss, delighted Him. Her purity so other-worldly drew him down to her. He found her lively faith and her ceaseless entreaties of love so irresistible that he was lovingly conquered by her appeals of love"* (LEW 105, 107). *"You have enraptured God . . . / Attracted by your beauty, / He took human nature, / He could not help Himself,"* Montfort sings to Our Lady (H 63:5; cf. H 81:3).

The place and role of Mary in the Incarnation are not of the order of *"necessity,"* which would obligate God by reason of logical imperatives; they are the absolute gratuitousness of grace. Mary is never absolutely necessary (cf. TD 14, 21; SM 32) but always *"hypothetical[ly]"* necessary (cf. TD 39). In other words, it is a necessity without a reason, unless it be the necessity of "that's the way things are" (cf. TD 15).[13]

But grace obeys a logic that brings it together with beauty. What does the phrase *"Mary [has] found favor with God"* mean if it is not that *"God found her beautiful"* (cf. LEW 203; SM 7; TD 16)? Her beauty is the work of grace in her, her response to the divine initiative and her cooperation with it. Beauty and grace cannot be reasoned. Language is carried beyond the frontiers of concepts defined by the intelligence. Montfort takes them with him into this movement when he speaks of Mary. The exuberance of his images and words underline and hide the kindnesses, the liberties, and the excesses of God's love for Mary, in whom He has put *"unutterable marvels and beauties"* (TD 6, 7, 8, 10-12, 23; cf. LEW 208 and TD 262).

The treasures of grace and beauty prohibit saying anything that is not praise and jubilation. To say something about Mary presupposes a rapture that is like God's (cf. H 81:1; 82:1). To contemplate Mary's *"lovable beauty"* (cf. H 81:9) is to take *"delight"* and *"pleasure"* in it, following the Lord (LEW 208; H 87:3,8; TD 18). Beauty and grace do not exist without that limitless love which always takes us beyond what can be desired and imagined. This is how Montfort understands the Incarnation of a God who is "compelled," "attracted," and "vanquished" by beauty after the laws of *eros-amor,* love-eros.

c. The Infant Jesus. Jesus, child of Mary, is *"pure gentleness and beauty"* (LEW 118). A certain likeness unites him to his mother. Mary's beauty attracts God and the beauty of Wisdom attracts man (cf. LEW 117). In the experience of the beautiful, ecstasy has a twofold movement: from God to man and from man to God.

Jesus attracts man by the charm of his countenance, a most perceptible charm (cf. LEW 117). The manifestation of the beauty of God is the face of the Infant Jesus. The whole "experience of the beautiful" is in the crib: *"The shepherds who came to the stable to see him were so spellbound by the serenity and beauty of his face that they tarried for many days gazing in rapture upon him. The three Kings, proud though they were, had no sooner seen the tender features of this lovely child, than, forgetting their high dignity, they fell down on their knees beside His crib. Time and again they said to one another, 'Friend, how good it is to be here! There are no enjoyments in our palaces comparable to those we are experiencing in this stable looking at this dear Infant-God'"* (LEW 121). *"How good it is to be here"* (cf. H 58:9; 59:11; 66:8).

Contemplation of the beauty of Jesus is a transfiguration where sweetness is felt and where the pleasure of being with him is relished (cf. 58,9; 60,10). In this epiphany the beauty of Jesus is *"charming appeal"* (H 61:5; 9:5,6; 65:4), *"a countenance filled with allure"* (H 66:4), since he wishes to delight and touch deeply those who look at him (H 60:15; 61:5). Whether it is in the Christmas hymns or in the LEW, the beauty of Jesus elicits that love-eros where the eagerness of desire reaches the point of wanting to possess a set image of this beauty: *"Those who knew him could not prevent themselves from loving him, and distant kings, hearing of his beauty, desired to have a painting of Him"* (LEW 121).

Through his beauty Jesus attracts people to himself. Because of it, the first fellowship of Christians began with the sharing of their contemplative experience. This contemplation is the source and the outcome of an intense and gracious apostolate that takes the form of an invitation: *"Let us go and see young Jesus"* (LEW 121; H 57:5; 59:1,2; 60:2; 65:1-4; 66:1,4).

By stressing his beauty and his sweetness, these meditations on the Infant Jesus bring to light the positive aspects of sight and the "felt." But having this experience of God does not remove the scandal and obscurity of faith: *"The Most High, the Unfathomable, / The Eternal and Almighty One / Has come now to be born. / Is it possible? / The Eternal has become one day, the Word is silent, / The Almighty has become an infant"* (H 57:1; cf. 58:6,8; 59:4; 60:4; 66:6,7). The delightful contemplation of the mystery does not suppress it but, rather, reinforces its paradox. The scandal of the Incarnation is in the words *"That is not believable,"* (H 58:2) which calls for faith.

God's beauty is not limited to its appearance, since we must retain both the incomprehensible and the comprehensible together. It is a continual paradox: *"Almightiness in lowly estate"* (cf. H 60:7), *"Mightiness in helplessness, and bright light in this darkness"* (H 65:10), *"Greatness is in lowliness"* (H 60:13). This paradox resides in love-eros, that *"extreme love"* (cf. H 66:1,2; 66:7; 41:9,10) which takes the form of *kenosis, "loving eclipse of that divine sun"* (H 62:4; 66:5) that has "humbled itself to become one of us." This love-eros touches being itself and is the stripping of the self in *kenosis.* The Incarnation is God handing Himself over to men, and *"love alone makes this change"* (H 66:7).

d. The Eucharist. Father de Montfort speaks of the same "change" for the Eucharist. In this Sacrament, Jesus loves us to the extent of changing nature (cf. LEW 71; H 132:4). He *"loves us passionately"* (H 158:5). The excess of love reaches the point of *"loss,"* of *kenosis,* which is called *"obliterated glory"* (H 158:4), of *"utter humiliation"* (H 128:6). Here also we find the same words and the same expressions: *"The sun of truth / Hidden in darkness,"* his *"beauty,"* his *"divinity,"* his *"brightness,"* hidden *"under a lowly appearance"* (H 158:4; 132:2; 130:4). The same paradox appears again, since *"His brilliance is not tarnished / Though he lowers himself to our state"* (H 129:2). Faith is challenged: *"Oh, who could believe it?"* (H 128:1; 158:13). Faced with this same paradox, faith alone comes into play: *"The Most High, the Unfathomable, / Is here below confined. / Christians, ask not / Is it possible?"* (H 158:1).

The *kenosis* that affects Christ in the Eucharist is the darkness of the mystery. It is not an end in itself, since the love that bears it, the ecstasy of God toward man, orients it toward the *"all of us"* (H 129:7; cf. H 129:3; 131:7; 132:1; 158:5; 17:9) and the *"for us"* (H 57:2,4; 58:1,3; 64:1-4; 65:5; 67:1-73:12). If Jesus lowers Himself by *"emptying himself,"* it is *"in order to delight our hearts"* (H 129:1; 132:2). He takes us into his Eucharist because in it he himself is lost in *"his love that robs him of his life"* (H 41:23).

In him an active self-deprivation takes place, while in us a passive rapture. Such is the law of the experience of the beauty of Christ. Yet it arouses in the person who contemplates it the desire to come out of oneself—*"How can I not fly away? / Alas, I have no wings"* (H 116:9)—to look face-to-face at *"The One whose beauty enraptures / All the saints in glory"* (H 129:1; 133:3). Love-eros rediscovers its rights in continual invitations to savor its sweetness drawn from the Eucharist, to taste the pleasures it generously offers beyond all our desires (cf. H 44:8; 129:2; 131:4,6,9; 135:1). In this experience where all the senses are invited to enjoy his presence, Christ allows himself to be known to the point of ecstasy (cf. H 129:7). Beauty is experienced only in excess.

*e. **The Cross.*** Father de Montfort suggested the connection between the Eucharist and the Infant Jesus (cf. LEW 128). The same vocabulary of aesthetic experience unites the two themes. The same contemplative attitude nurtures them.

Montfort leads us still further by incorporating the Cross in the category of beauty. What he says of Mary he now says of the Cross: *"God's love could not resist / Such beauty or its plea, / Which bade Him keep a tryst / With our humanity."* (H 19:9 or 102:10; 123:2).[14] "Beauty awakens to love, and love takes us to ecstasy, that uncontrollable self-transcendence."[15] This beauty leads us to the love-eros of the wedding of the Cross: *"He took it, found it fair, / An object not of shame / But honor, made it share / His love's most tender flame."* (H 19:10 or 102:12; 164:13; LEW 168). This nuptial mysticism is always a surprise when connected with the Cross. It is the paradox of love and the Cross (cf. FC 50-53). The Cross testifies to love (cf. LEW 176) and incites us to love (cf. LEW 154, 155; H 19:27,28). Not to sense the love that is exhibited on the Cross is the real scandal: *"Is it possible, / . . . That your heart is so unfeeling?"* (H 71:13; cf. H 47:16; 137:13). What is *sublime, unfathomable and ineffable* (cf. LEW 168) in the mystery of the Cross is the conjunction of love and suffering, of seeing *"glory done away with"* in *"the excess of loving"* (H 137:3,8).

The beauty of the Cross is a mystery God reveals to the *"humble, [the] little"* (LEW 174; H 19:1). The light that springs from it is that of "beauty destroyed," the extreme of beauty in the extreme of ugliness. An experience of truly Christian beauty must pass through the contemplation of the Crucified. *In Him, God appears in the antithesis of Himself.*[16] Montfort shows us two transitions: to look at Christ, beauty disfigured; to look at Christ, beauty hidden.

The beauty of the Crucified is a disfigured beauty. It is the *"man of every sorrow"* (LEW 157; cf. Isa 53:3). It is the beauty of God covered over by the ugliness of men's sins, an ugliness hidden in the darkness of the conscience and at times disguised as counterfeit beauty. The Cross brings light to this shadow land and reveals its falseness. In showing us the crucified Christ and *"His countenance disfigured"* (H 70:6; cf. H 71:6; 73:6), Montfort invites us to see there our sin and be healed by it.[17]

Man was created "beautiful," in the image of God's beauty. In sinning, he has disfigured himself; he has become ugliness by losing his likeness to God (cf. LS 110). Beauty attracts, ugliness repels. Man's primordial beauty set him in a state of mutual attraction with divine communion. The ugliness of his sin leaves him lost and alone. Since he is no longer beautiful, he feels abandoned and unloved; he hides from God. The crucified Christ takes on himself the sum total of human ugliness, his solitude and abandonment. He descends to the depths of humanity's distress, which he then takes on himself. Indeed he is that *"behold the man"* (H 70:8; cf. Jn 19:5) who gives himself up *"for us"* in order to restore humanity and return it to its primitive beauty. The divine countenance disfigured in the crucified Christ transfigures man. The horror of the Cross already carries the glory of the Resurrection.

Beauty is pasted up on billboards everywhere and forces ugliness back into the shadows. There are the "beautiful people" and the "others," those whom we hardly mention, whom we hide away, the poor (cf. H 18:4). Misery is always associated with ugliness; the "poor beggars" are always "disgusting," repulsive, because they have lost health and fortune. In his "Hymn to the Daughters of Wisdom," Montfort reverses the world's laws of beauty: *"The cast-offs / Those whom the world abandons / Must move you the most"* (H 149:1). This reversal obeys the paradox of the mystery: beauty hidden in ugliness, *"God hidden in my neighbor"* (H 148-149), humanity disfigured. The poor man bears the stigma of sin, since he is its victim and he is *"The living image, / The lieutenant of Jesus Christ, / . . . Jesus Christ Himself"* (H 17:14). The poor are the *"dear members of the Savior"* (H 150:14). He has taken their *"ugliness"* upon himself (cf. 58,7.8).

The beauty of Christ is a veiled beauty. Montfort mentions a small thing that may seem trivial, although it is rich in significance: *"Some writers tell us that the Roman soldiers and the Jews covered his face in order to strike and buffet him more freely because there was in his eyes and face such a kindly and ravishing radiance as would disarm the most cruel of men"* (LEW 121; H 9:6). In linking beauty and cruelty, he joins together aesthetics and ethics. He connects the refusal to look at the face with the immorality of a violence that is uncalled for and blind. The face is the seat of beauty. In its nakedness it is exposed to violence and at the same time blocks all violence.[18] It is the face that says "Thou shalt not kill." He disarms "the most brutal." On Christ's face they see the endless temptation to murder. In order to do it violence, it must be veiled. The passion is the rejection of this face that, unprotected, gave itself over to men. Thus sin is unmasked as the absolute negation of this face that revealed the beauty of God, the negation of God Himself.

In this veiled face, led off to death, are reflected all the faces of those who since Abel are the victims of the violence of men. To veil this face is to refuse an encounter, a face-to-face dialogue, to refuse the responsibility that obliges us to answer for him by answering him. It is violence, which denies itself at the very moment it is the negation of the other. But the veiled beauty of the God-Man denounces this lie to God (Cain's "Am I my brother's keeper?" Gen 4:9) and the hatred that destroys humanity. To veil this face is to refuse the grace offered at the strongest temptation, to shy away from the "rapture" of love, to reject the outstretched hand. In some way it is the fundamental "no" said to God when a "yes" was still possible. When one becomes hardened to sin, the veil becomes mockery: *"They say to Him in mockery: / You see Him? How fair He is!"* (H 68:4; 69:7).

IV. Beauty and Divinization

1. Man and beauty

God alone is beautiful.[19] Beauty is a sign of divinity (cf. TD 49; H 25:9).

God creates only beauty. After the creative word comes the marvel of aesthetic delight: "And God saw that it was good/beautiful" (cf. Gen 1:4). His masterpiece is man.

This is where Montfort's anthropology is rooted. His vision of man is characterized by a tension: he is no longer what he was; he is not yet what he ought to be. He is stretched taut between his original beauty and his present ugliness. Ugliness masks and disfigures beauty. When our eyes are covered with darkness, we cannot see the light. This is why it is hard for man to perceive what his original beauty was (cf. LEW 37).

Created in the image and likeness of God (cf. Gen 1:26),[20] he is *"the living image of the Godhead"* (LEW 37; cf. SM 3), a microcosm, the whole of creation in miniature (cf. LEW 37). He was beauty and light, pleasing to God (once again a word for aesthetic delight). He knew Him perfectly and loved Him *"for God himself"* (LEW 38).

The beauty of man produces ecstasy. The soul delights the angels and God Himself because of its beauty. There is nothing on earth that is comparable to his beauty. This is why an ancient writer calls him *"immensum pulchri pelagus"* (LS 109). Man's original beauty is that of God. Moreover, did not the expression "immense ocean of the beautiful," here applied to man, designate God Himself?[21] *"Man was so godlike, so absorbed and rapt in God"* (LEW 38). Man is sustained by this twofold ecstasy, a creative ecstasy of God toward man and a divinizing ecstasy of man toward God. There once again beauty is spoken of as excess: *"Such was the generosity shown to man by Eternal Wisdom"* (cf. LEW 38).

"But, alas, . . . man sinned and by his sin lost his . . . beauty" (LEW 39; cf. S 110). Sin disfigures and deforms man's original beauty and tears up the portrait of Wisdom (cf. LEW 41). It has been said that Montfort laid too much stress on man's decline, that his anthropology was pessimistic (he would have said "realistic"). But this is not so. He does not let Adam fall into the despair of seeing himself as so "hideous" and "sullied"; he raises the challenge of one day seeing his original beauty restored. For Wisdom cannot stand seeing *"his masterpiece destroyed"* (LEW 41). Like a new creation, the Redemption will "repair" man's beauty in the Incarnation of the Word (cf. LEW 42). God *"Becomes what we are, / By making us become what He is"* (H 64:1).

In the Incarnation, the Word assumes the ugliness of men in order to give them the beauty of God. The return to beauty is divinization.[22] It is not only a recall of what man was in the beginning, but a call.[23]

2. Divinization

This call to beauty is our *"certain . . . vocation"* (SM 3). It is a radical change that affects and touches the totality of our being; *"Dust into light, . . . creature into Creator, man into God"* (ibid.). But this transformation is a work *"so difficult in itself, and even impossible for a mere creature to bring about"* (ibid.), for it is a question of being formed in Jesus Christ and of forming Jesus Christ in oneself. The "hand-made" is excluded. Only grace can achieve this "great masterpiece" (ibid.).

A comparison borrowed from the field of artistic creation permits Father de Montfort to elaborate on his thought about the restoration of the divine image in us. He compares the sculptor and the caster (cf. TD 219-221, 260; SM 16-18). These two different ways of making a work of art are two paths toward divinization. In the first path, the sculptor claims to achieve his goal by relying on his own strength and industry, where failure comes in one false blow of his chisel.[24] The second path, however, that of the caster, consists in handing oneself over to the work of grace. To reach God, it takes the same road that He took to come to us (cf. SM 35). It is therefore the most "economical." We easily recognize the ecstasies of beauty: an ecstasy of God toward man in the Creation and the Incarnation, and the divinizing ecstasy of man toward God. The link that allows us to pass from one to the other is the Incarnation. This central mystery is the pattern for our divinization and contains our origin and our end; our origin in that we are created in the image and likeness of God, and our end as the perfect and full achievement of our origin. Our divinization is modeled on the Incarnation.

It is here that Mary appears as the necessary vessel through whom transforming grace passes (cf. TD 125). Mary is God's "mold," *forma Dei,* made by the Holy Spirit. It is in her alone that God made man was formed according to nature by the hypostatic union, and it is also in her alone that man can be formed into God himself by grace. Thus, when "formed" properly in Mary, we shall have the beauty of Christ[25] in *"the perfection and the fulness of his age"* (LEW 214).[26]

The word "form" is interesting for more than one reason. For Montfort it designates the creation of man by Wisdom in the proclamation of his restoration in Christ (cf. LEW 42), the new creation in Mary, surpassing the first (cf. LEW 105), the Incarnation of Jesus in Mary's virginal womb (cf. LEW 108; SR 46; SM 12, 17; TD 16, 140, 220; H 63:6; 88:4; 155:5), and the birth of Jesus in the soul (cf. SM 12, 17, 67; TD 31, 33, 37, 219; H 155:16; 159:8,12). "To form" implies a twofold movement: from Creation to Redemption, from the Incarnation to divinization; a twofold birth of Christ in Mary and the soul (cf. LEW 214; TD 31, 33). The generation of Christ in the soul is also the generation of the soul in Christ.[27]

This twofold generation is accompanied by a reciprocal transformation: *"St. Augustine, speaking to our Blessed Lady, says, 'You are worthy to be called the mold of God (forma Dei).' Mary is a mold capable of forming people into the image of the God-man. Anyone who is cast into this divine mold is quickly shaped and molded into Jesus and Jesus into him. . . . He will become Christ-like since he is cast into the very same mold that fashioned a God-man"* (TD 219). *"Form them in Jesus and Jesus in them"* (TD 37; cf. LEW 214; TD 20, 212, 264). Montfort insists on this formula of mutual inclusion,[28] which also recalls the twofold rapture. This outflow of God toward man and of man toward God is not an assimilation of one by the other. The *"transformation into Jesus"* (TD 119) through Mary, who is *"so united to Christ and transformed to God"* (TD 164), is not a fusion but a *"union"* (ibid.; cf. SM 21; TD 27, 63, 120; H 90:59). This transforming union is the perfect consecration.

From the metaphor of the mold we come to emphasize the passive aspect. We must allow ourselves to be *"molded . . . by the working of the Holy Spirit"* (SM 18). Father de Montfort does not forget its active aspect: *"Remember that only molten and liquefied substances may be poured into a mold. That means that you must crush and melt down the old Adam in you if you wish to acquire the likeness of the new Adam in Mary"* (TD 221). It is not only renouncing the ugliness of sin. It is also renouncing oneself, *"[emptying] ourselves of self," "[dying] to self"* (TD 79, 81). Even more, it is a real kenosis, according to the example of Christ himself, who out of love for us took the form of a slave (cf. TD 72; LEW 223). We have to pass through the crucible of the Cross in order to rediscover original beauty. We must also agree to be an image, to receive for ourselves the image of the Father; in short, to agree to be a son.

The origin of our beauty is not in us. It is in God. Our beauty is shared. This active recognition Montfort calls dependence and submission, the slavery of love. Mary is the most beautiful of all creatures, because she is intimately aware of her total dependence, of her *"depths of nothingness"* (TD 25), because she knows that she is *"simply nothing"* (TD 14); *"[Mary] was relative only to God"* (TD 225). We must descend into this humility in order for the revelation of beauty to rise in us.

3. The beauty of the soul and the mission

To restore man in the beauty of the divine image is the saving mission of the Word, which Montfort describes with rare dramatic power (cf. LEW 35-46). It is absolutely intolerable that ugliness replace beauty, that unhappiness win out over happiness. Hence the blazing zeal of Wisdom, which "comes out of itself" to save man. From Wisdom the missionary learns to be *"deeply moved by the plight of poor Adam"* and to *"[listen] tenderly to man's sighs and entreaties"* (cf. LEW 41). *"The soul is so beautiful"* is the missionary's refrain, the reason for his apostolic love, which makes him go out into the world (cf. H 21:7; 22:2,3; 148:13). Restoring man's beauty received from God is the only sacred art.

V. Conclusion

Beauty runs through Montfort's work from beginning to end. The experience it proposes is stereotyped. It is a persistent theme from which a "theological aesthetic" unfolds.[29] It is composed of two aspects. The first is a "doctrine of perception, or fundamental theology," an aesthetic "understood as a doctrine of the discovery of the face of God revealing Himself." This perception is an experiential knowledge.[30] It is Wisdom as a "delectable knowledge," both revealed and revealing.

The second is a "doctrine of rapture, or dogmatic theology." The aesthetic here is the doctrine of the

Incarnation "of the divine glory, and of man called to share in it." It is here that the Redemption is rooted, and for man, "consecration." It is the twofold, two-sided rapture, of God toward man and man toward God. These two aspects become one when sight becomes a participation in the divine life.

The legitimacy of this rereading of Montfort's work is its own cohesion. But it holds only if the knowing subject accepts to be taken into the object of his knowledge. We can truly understand only to the extent that we are understood. God is never purely exterior. He is in what is most private about us. God touches us and we can experience it.

Feeling is at the heart of every aesthetic. Yet Montfort invites us to dismiss the realm of the senses in order to reach "pure faith." We have to go beyond spiritual consolations in order for our relationship with God to have the gratuitousness of *"pure love"* (cf. TD 214), to enjoy God alone and not His gifts. "Not to see, not to feel, not to taste" leads us to pure faith (LEW 187; cf. FC 4; SR 35; SM 51, 69; H 6:2,54).

By refusing every support, this renunciation thrusts the contemplative into utter darkness (cf. LEW 186; RW 136). He can rest on one word only: *"God has said it or promised it"* (LEW 187). It is no longer even necessary to see the beauty of Wisdom, to desire it, for the Word that elicits faith suffices (cf. LEW 186). The experience of the beautiful seems to have become useless. In fact, Father de Montfort introduces a second stage in purification: after purifying the "bodily senses" in order to allow the desire of God to appear, we must also purify the "spiritual senses." After "tasting" come disgust, boredom, and the dryness of the spirit. A new "way of feeling" appears in this agony. [31]

The presence of suffering and ugliness in the heart of beauty is mysterious and paradoxical, like the Cross in the case of love. But it leads to the very apex of experience, in the *"summit of the soul,"* where *"without any feeling of joy in the senses or pleasure in the mind, we love the cross we are carrying, by the light of pure faith, and take delight in it"* (FC 53).

O. Maire

Notes: (1) Cf. Plotinus, *Ennéades (Enneads),* VI, 7, 32; ed. E . Béhier, CUF, Paris 1938, 105. (2) Cf. St. Augustine, *De Trinitate,* VII, 1, 156, CCL 50, 249, or PL 42:936 (*sapientia* comes from *sapere*). This definition of Wisdom was very current in the twelfth century; cf. Saint Bernard, *Super Cant.,* 85, 8; PL 183:1191 (and 9, 3; PL 183:816); William of Saint Thierry, *Exposé sur le Cantique des cantiques (Explanation of the Song of Solomon),* 105, 115, ed. J.M. Déchanet, trans. M. Dumontier, SC 82, Cerf, Paris 1962, 236, 250, and *Lettre aux Frères du Mont-Dieu (Letter to the Brothers of Mont-Dieu),* 249, 287, ed. J. Déchanet, SC 223, Cerf, Paris 1985, 342, 374; Guerric d'Igny, *Sermons,* 3E, 195-196, SC 166, Cerf, Paris 1970, 284; Guigues II the Carthusian, *Lettre sur la vie contemplative (Letter on the Contemplative Life),* V, 121-125, 130-135; VI, 91-94, SC 163,

Cerf, Paris 1980, 92, 184; Hugh of Saint Victor, *Les cinq septenaires (The Five Septennaria),* 256, 257, in *Six opuscules spirituels (Six Spiritual Opuscula),* SC 155, Cerf, Paris 1969, 118; other references English Publication in H. U. von Balthasar, *La gloire et la croix. Aspects esthétiques de la Révélation (The Glory and the Cross. Aesthetic Aspects of Revelation),* vol. 1, *Apparition,* Paris 1965, 210, 242-245, 314, 315, 343. (3) Cf. LEW 10, 19, 34, 35, 59, 118, 121, 126, 131; TD 85; H 9:3; 50:2; 55:17,21; 66:4; 127:38. (4) With Montfort the word "to taste" often means "to have the experience of" (cf. L 13; LEW 1, 112; TD 82, 96, 163, 180, 197, 250), hence "to understand" (cf. TD 180, 199; H 40:6). (5) Cf. H 141:11. *"The wisdom of the cross [is] that knowledge of the truth which we experience within ourselves and which by the light of faith deepens our knowledge of the most hidden mysteries"* (FC 45). (6) Cf. St. Augustine, *Tractatus in Ioh.,* XXVI, 4-6, CCL 36, 261-263. (7) Cf. LEW 34, 107, 121; FC 4; SR 121; MR 19 (OC 410); H 4:1; 5:16; 9:5,6; 12:17,22; 21:15; 25:5,9; 34:12; 52:9; 61:6; 63:5; 81:1; 116:2; 126:1,7; 129:1; 134:4; etc.; cf. H 65:4 and S 24 and 64. (8) Cf. H.U. von Balthasar, *Apparition,* 99-101. (9) In H we cannot count these invitations to contemplate, to come see, and to look. Montfort likes to use imperatives and interrogations that call out, carry along, and gather together. (10) Roland Barthes, *Essais critiques (Critical Essays),* Points-Seuil, Paris 1981, 276. (11) Cf. William of Saint Thierry, *Exposé sur le Cantique des cantiques,* 2, 7, p. 203, 401 (12) LEW 32 mentions the characteristic terms of classical beauty: order, harmony, composition, balance . . . (13) This sin does not relate to ecology but to man's behavior in society, cf. H 157:11,14 (14) The same is true for the relationship between Mary and Christians, members of that Body of which Jesus Christ is the Head. Montfort's thought on the whole Christ (Body and Head) and on the twofold coming of Jesus into the world is derived from an "aesthetic," i.e. from a perception of harmony in the economy of salvation (cf. SM 58; TD 1, 13, 117) Hans Urs von Balthasar, *Apparition,* 9.22.49.50. - 75.85.158; cf. SM 12; TD 17, 20, 22, 32). (15) This twofold poetic sense runs throughout Montfort's writings, e.g., *"the tree of life,"* designating the Cross (SM 22; H 123:13), Mary (LEW 204; SM 67, 78; TD 44, 164, 218; H 81:7), and even the Rosary (cf. SR 6); the same verses of Scripture are applied to Mary and to Wisdom (cf. TD 175, 200, 201, 208, 264 and LEW 27, 28, 66, 67, 68). (16) In another sense, cf. H 19:17 or H 102:31,32. - Hans Urs von Balthasar, *La gloire et la croix,* vol. 3, *Théologie, Nouvelle Alliance (Theology: New alliance),* Paris 1976, 21. (18) The hymns of "the Octave of the Cross" (H 67, 73, 74) are constructed according to the same model. They are composed of three parts: 1. a meditation where an episode of the Passion is represented in a "sensory way" and the imagination is constantly appealed to by verbs that invite contemplation; *"let us contemplate," "let us go and . . . contemplate," "we see," "do you see?," "consider," "look,"* etc.; 2. Montfort's invitation to us to "enter the stage," take our position there, and to ask ourselves about conversion, about changing, and draw some conclusions from it; 3. a prayer ending the hymn (19) Cf. Emmanuel Lévinas, *Totalité et Infini. Essai sue l''extériorité (Totality and the Infinite. An Essay on Exteriority),* Nijhoff, The Hague 1971, 215-220 (Visage et éthique). (20) "All the world agrees in saying that the Godhead is the essential beauty," Gregory of Nyssa, *La vie de Moïse, (The Life of Moses),* trans. J. Daniélou, SC 1bis, Cerf, Paris 1987, 268; cf. Gregory of Nazianzus, *Discours (Discourses),* 31, 15, SC 250, Cerf, Paris 1978, 305 (and note 3). (21) *"His beauty, in making us in His image and likeness . . ."* (S 25). (22) Cf. *Plato, Banquet (Symposium),* 219d, ed. P. Vicaire, CUF, Paris 1989, 69. (23) To be beautiful and to see beauty are one and the same movement: "A soul would not see the beautiful without being beautiful itself! Let every being then first become divine and beautiful if he wishes to contemplate God and the beautiful" Plotinus, *Ennéades,* I, 6, 9, ed. E. Bréhier, CUF, Paris 1924, 106, or again, "People rightly say that the good and the beauty of the soul consist in becoming like God," ibid., I, 6, 6, p. 102 (24) For Pseudo-Dionysius, "beautiful" *(kalos)* came from the verb "to call" (*kaleo*) (25) This comes close to Plotinus's thought, which in some way puts God in the range of human endeavor: "Return to yourself and look: if you do not yet have beauty in you, act like the sculptor of a statue that is to become beautiful, . . . he polishes it until the divine burst of virtue is shown," *Ennéades,* I, 6, 9, p.105. With several Greek Fathers, "polish the statue" meant the purification brought about by asceticism *praxis.* (26) Let us not forget that *formosus* (beautiful) comes from *forma;* cf. H.U. von Balthasar, *Apparition,* 17, 98. (27) It is another way of looking at the whole Christ; cf. LEW 1, 227; SM 67; TD 33, 61, 119, 156, 164, 168. (28) The birth of Christ in the divinized soul is a major theme of Rheno-Flemish mysticism, particularly Tauler and Meister Eckhart. (29) Similar formulas in TD 32, 61, 63, 75, 144, 157, 179, 247; LEW 204. (30) H.U. von Balthasar, *Apparition,* 103-105. (31) Cf. St. Thomas Aquinas, *Summa Theologiae,* I, 43, 5, ad 2.

BIBLE

The Bible is, first of all, the text that Christians call the Old Testament and the New Testament. How did the text stand in Montfort's day? How much did it influence not only theologians and exegetes, pastors and preachers, but also the people of God? The answers to these questions necessarily involve a study of the history of the period in question. For the believer, however, the text of the Bible is more than just a text. It was given by Another and is received as the Word of God; it offers a dialogue and calls for a response. This is indeed its most important feature. Are the many Scripture quotations in Montfort's writings conducive to maintaining this dialogue? We will attempt to answer this question by analyzing his writings.

I. THE BIBLE IN MONTFORT'S TIME

In order to understand Montfort's attitude to the Bible as a preacher and spiritual writer, it is necessary to examine briefly the situation of contemporary French Catholicism with reference to the Bible.

1. The Council of Trent

The influence of the Council of Trent (1545-1563)—or, rather, the influence of the Counter-Reformation (from 1550 to the end of the Thirty Years War in 1648)—was still very much alive in France. A dominant concern of Church authorities was their opposition to the practices of the Reformed Church. The Protestant doctrines were often interpreted as a misreading of the Bible. Consequently, reading the Bible was seen as a mark of the "heretics." Nicolas Boileau (1636-1711), who was practically a contemporary of Montfort's, sums up the general sentiment in his "Satire XII sur l'Equivoque":

Then, rejecting all visible authority,
Each person was supposed to be an infallible judge of the faith,
And, though not approved by the Rome authorities,
Each Protestant set himself up as a Pope with a Bible in his hand.

The expression "with a Bible in his hand reflects the passionate debate that took place. We will now look at some of its characteristics and try to ascertain Montfort's position.

a. Authority of the Vulgate. It was mainly in the first period of the council (1545-1547) that the Fathers dealt with the theme of the Bible. They had focused their attention on four issues: the transmission of the Word of God through both Scripture and Tradition, the canonicity of Scripture, the status of the Vulgate, and the teaching and preaching of Scripture. All the discussions were colored by the diffuse but permanent background of the Protestant insistence on *Scriptura sola.* Many of the misuses, however, that had been made of Scripture seemed to be due to the fact that there was no official version of it. Several editions claiming to correct the mistakes made in the version of the Vulgate attributed to Saint Jerome were then in circulation, and this only added to the confusion. The Council Fathers decided to take action. While calling for a more accurate version of the "received" texts translated from the Latin, the Greek, and the Hebrew, they declared that the Vulgate, which had been used for centuries with the approbation of the Church, was to be regarded as "authentic in public lessons, discussions, sermons, and explanations." *Authentic* did not mean *inspired* or without faults but, rather, that no heresies had been found in it, as was the case for some recent versions. By itself the word *authentic* as used in the 1546 decree had a limited meaning. The meaning would be extended later on and become synonymous with "subject to absolute monopoly."[1] This was to be the *authoritative* version in the Roman Catholic Church. Obviously, it was the one frequently quoted by Montfort in his writings, sometimes in Latin, even though his readers had no knowledge of the language.

b. Vernacular languages. According to the Catholic authorities, not all versions of the Bible were suitable for reading, nor was everybody qualified to read it. If it was not read properly, it gave rise to all sorts of disorders. As a result, some bishops declared that it should not be made available to everyone. Others, who were in charge of areas coming under Protestant influence, opposed such bans on the basis that in his own time Christ spoke to the people in their own tongue and never used a scholarly language. The debate got bogged down, and the Council Fathers were unable to work out a common policy on the reading of the Bible in the vernacular.

They did, however, take a stand on another issue. At that time *Indexes,* or systematic lists of prohibited books, began to appear. The first of them was that published by the Sorbonne in 1544. The lists contained many translations of the Bible into the vernacular. The *Roman Index,* which was decided upon at the Council, was published by Paul IV in 1564. It was, however, prefaced by a series of rules, the fourth of which stated that the possession and reading of a book of the Bible was subject to prior approval by the bishop or inquisitor after consultation with the parish priest or confessor. Rule IV was made stricter under Sixtus V in 1590, then under Clement VIII in 1596, who made permission obtainable from the Holy See only. Rule IV was relaxed later, but it still prefaced every updated list of the books that Catholics were prohibited from reading, and it certainly acted as a deterrent.[2] But certain events promoted the reading of the Bible by laypeople in France. Port-Royal claimed not only that laypeople had the *right* to read the Bible but that it was a moral obligation, a *duty of state* for them to do so. Reading the New Testament and other sacred books was regarded as an obligation inherent in the very status of Christians. In the very fine preface to the *Nouveau Testament* "of Mons" published in 1667, Le Maistre de Sacy says that one should prepare for reception of the Eucharist by reading Scripture, in imitation of Jesus who prepared the disciples for the meal at Emmaus "by setting them aflame with love of his Word." It is in this perspective that the huge efforts made by Port-Royal to translate the sacred texts should be seen. From 1672 to 1693, Port-Royal worked on and published the Bible of the "Messieurs de Port-Royal," as Richard Simon called it. It became known mainly as the Bible "of Sacy." This was the version read by ordinary people and the one which Montfort used.

Finally, we would like to draw attention to a little-known event that had a strong impact on the French Church a few years before Montfort began his apostolic ministry. After the Edict of Nantes had been revoked in 1685, over a million books were distributed to "newly converted" laypeople on the initiative of the Church authorities (Harlay, P. de la Chaise, Pellisson). Half these books were copies of the *New Testament* by P. Amelote, the Psalms, and the *Imitation of Jesus Christ.*[3] No copies of the Old Testament were distributed. The Catholic Church had no official translation of the Bible in French, and the de Sacy version was not completed until 1693. This initiative, which was running more or less contrary to the Tridentine prescriptions and to the rules laid down by Rome in the *Index,* was more fraught with consequences than was suspected at the time. The distribution of books was designed to restore the balance between clerics, who alone had access to the sacred and inspired texts in Latin, and laypeople, who were only able to receive *oral instruction* in the truths of the faith through sermons, spiritual direction, and confession and were therefore dependent on clerics. In contrast to the traditional Church, which fostered more *emotional* "popular" devotions, as more suitable for laypeople, this *pastoral initiative promoting the written word* heralded a new Church, more intellectual, more individual, which, as a natural consequence, was to become more critical. Be that as it may, the distribution of books was a *fait accompli,* and from then on French laypeople had free access to the texts distributed to the "newly converted." It does appear that the Christians whom Montfort was dealing with in his missions had access to Scripture, directly if they could read, or indirectly through the medium of close relatives who read and explained it to them if they could not read. We know that Montfort always fostered popular devotions. In one of the hymns sung in his missions, however, he gives us a hint of his way of thinking concerning the reading of Scripture: *"Besides Scripture / I read devotional books / Propounding pure doctrine / Inspired by love"* (H 139:56).

Le Maistre de Sacy and the Messieurs of Port-Royal would have been at ease in his company. Though he mentions devotional books, *Scripture does come first.*

*c. **Preaching of Scripture.*** The Council of Trent also drew up a decree on the preaching and teaching of the Bible. The first draft of the decree was the object of long discussions, and the last chapter gave a description of the ideal preacher, who is to be guided by love of the truth and fidelity to Scripture. Was this text thought too spiritual for inclusion in a decree on discipline? As it was not included, was it widely known? Had Montfort heard about it? All that he says about *"preaching with the inspiration of an apostle"* in RM 60-65 might have been inspired by this text. Even the equivalent of what he says about gentleness (RM 65) can be found in it. And the passage about the servants of the Virgin Mary who *"bay like your watchdogs"* in PM 12 closely resembles the exhortation in the draft of the decree: "In order not to appear as if they were dumb dogs that cannot bark (Isa 56:10) and connive with the wolves, let them teach the truth and also refute the heresies."[4] In the preface to his *Introduction à l'Écriture Sainte* (Lyon 1699), Bernard Lamy points out the close link between preaching and the study of Scripture: "As a result [of the ignorance of Scripture], we have numberless ranters in our pulpits who do not deserve to be called preachers of the Word of God, as they seldom quote Scripture. They begin their sermons with a promise to explain Scripture, but the purpose of what they say afterwards is to delight the ears and minds of their audience with elegant turns of phrase and lofty-sounding ideas. They thus deprive the people of solid nourishment and leave them in ignorance of the science of salvation. Such so-called preachers are all the more to blame for neglecting Scripture as, unlike any other source, its wealth is inexhaustible."[5]

A quick look at *Father de Montfort's Book of Sermons*[6] is enough to reveal that in him Scripture and preaching are bound up together. This thick manuscript contains a large number of plans of sermons and lectures, but it does not give the texts of the actual sermons; it is, however, revealing of the ideas and of the probable content of his preaching. Montfort worked out his plans and summaries on the basis of a collection of sermons commercially available in the late seventeenth and early eighteenth centuries. These sermons gave many quotations from Scripture and the Church Fathers. Clearly, they were not homilies and had no bearings on the texts used in the liturgy.[7] They were talks on doctrine and of a very didactic nature; their purpose was to convince, and the quotations from Scripture or the Fathers, which were used out of context, were meant to prove the preacher's assertions. This is what Montfort did. He did not read Scripture for its own sake but geared it to his apostolic activity. As shown by the *"order of sermons"* for missions and retreats, which also gives the *sermon-matter* (LS 330-333), his activity was governed by his concern for teaching, and this did not foster a desire to read Scripture for its own sake. Having said that, Scripture remained the basis of his preaching, and it runs through his *Book of Sermons* together with comments by the Church Fathers.

2. Exegesis after the Council of Trent

a. The debates:

1. *Unanimous consent of the Fathers.* Naturally enough, the council took the view opposite to that of the Reformation on the subject of interpreting Scripture. The Protestant view is that each Christian can and may read and interpret *Holy Scripture* freely without reference to the Church or her teaching. The council took the view that the faith community that is the Church has a part to play when it comes to the reading of Scripture by believers. In order to keep "certain rebellious minds" within limits, the council decided that no one was to "rely on his own judgement and interpret Scripture contrary to the view that our Holy Mother the Church has held in the past and is holding now, and no one is to interpret Holy Scripture *against the unanimous consent of the Fathers.*[8]

The latter point was to become a rule for Catholic exegetes. The title that Le Maistre de Sacy gave to his Bible, *Sainte Bible traduite en français avec une explication tirée des SS. Pères et des Auteurs ecclésiastiques,* conformed entirely to the rule. In the preface to *Introduction à l'Ecriture Sainte,* Bernard Lamy of the Oratory, while a confrère of Richard Simon's and very keen to resort to the vernacular "to understand Scripture perfectly," cites the example of the Fathers, "who have handed on to us the books of Scripture as well as their true interpretation. They did not abandon the headspring to follow the course of the streams; they drew on Scripture for their devastating arguments that destroyed the heresies, and for the heavenly food that they gave to the Church for her nourishment."[9]

Did Montfort know about Lamy's handbook? In any case, he shares the views it expresses. He, too, turns to Scripture frequently in order to defeat heresy and draws on it as on a storehouse of arguments. But he does not confine himself to Scripture. For him, as for the council, the Spirit promised to the Church also speaks through Tradition, *"through the Fathers of the Church"* (TD 262). Whenever he wants to establish some point of doctrine on a solid basis to refute the *freethinkers,* he resorts to Scripture and the Church Fathers (cf. TD 25, 26, 32, 40, 41, 75, 93, 94, 130, 131, 141, 184, 185, 262, 264). This means that he had carefully read the books themselves or collections of quotations; he may have done this at Saint-Sulpice after he had been given the job of "looking after the library."[10] In any case, he knew them and was able to quote passages from them in Latin (TD 26)!

2. *The "new critics".* Bossuet had the first edition of Richard Simon's *Histoire critique du Vieux Testament* seized and withdrawn from circulation in April 1678. This triggered off a controversy between the "critics" and those in favor of traditional exegesis, who relied mainly on the Church Fathers. The controversy centered, however, around Richard Simon and Bossuet, and it turned out to be an uneven contest. Bossuet was then at the apex of his career and was very influential. Richard Simon had to fight him singlehandedly, although a letter from Bossuet mentions "a cabal of false critics headed by him [Simon] whose purpose is to destroy the authority of the Church Fathers and of the decisions of the Church."[11] What Simon says is "a strange historical exaggeration or the result of a singular mistake that we have to presume genuine."[12] Simon was fighting on his own, with no followers, no backing, and no allies. Bossuet continued the fight unremittingly, even after his death in 1704, for his posthumous works appeared in 1753, and one of them was *Défense de la Tradition et des Saints Pères.* Right from the preface, Bossuet attacks Simon violently: "We must no longer allow the new critics to attack the doctrine of the Fathers and the tradition of the churches." He places him among the priests who "share their views [the heretics'] and raise within the Church the standard of revolt against the Church Fathers." He makes Simon out to be a man who "glories in being a critic, that is to say, in weighing words in the scales of grammar" and "believes he can impose his views and settle questions of faith and theology by referring to Greek and Hebrew, which he is proud to quote. . . . What he is learning very well is how to esteem the heretics and to run down all the Church Fathers without exception, even those he pretends to praise."[13] This is a harsh judgement, which has been handed on down the ages until very recently; although Simon had faults, we must not forget that he worked out and pioneered textual criticism, and in his time he was the only one "who had envisaged the path along which the Church was to walk three centuries later."[14]

The controversy eventually spread to the general public. An ordinance dated September 29, 1702 condemned Richard Simon's translation of *Nouveau Testament de Notre-Seigneur Jésus-Christ,* published at

Trévoux in 1701, and prohibited on pain of excommunication all the faithful, "clerics and others, from reading or possessing a copy of the book." The ordinance was to be read and distributed by preachers, parish priests, and curates and posted up "wherever appropriate, so that no one could plead ignorance." In this ordinance, Bossuet stressed the fact that *Critique du Vieux Testament*[15] had been condemned previously. In Paris the ordinance of Cardinal de Noailles, which condemned Simon's version, on sale everywhere even in Paris,[16] was read out in the churches on Sunday, September 24, 1702. We can safely assume that the stir was still greater in theological circles. All who were interested in the Bible must have followed the controversy closely. Simon was censured by doctors in theology and professors from the Sorbonne. The controversy may have been kept out of the classes held there, but it must have had some effect on the teaching. As the theologians teaching at the Sorbonne did not deviate from scholastic theology, they must have given a cool reception to those whom Bossuet described as the "new critics."

When he was studying theology, or at any rate as a young priest, Montfort must have heard echoes of the controversy. In September 1702, when the ordinance of Cardinal de Noailles became public, he may have been in Paris looking after his sister Guyonne-Jeanne.[17] He had attended lectures at the Sorbonne from 1692 to 1695. Later on, at the "Little Seminary" of Saint-Sulpice, he may have attended the evening tutorials bearing on the lectures given during the day. His director, Fr. Leschassier, was reportedly "dean of the doctors at the Sorbonne."[18] Montfort defended a thesis on the question of grace, which was particularly delicate at that time, and he won the day by quoting "long passages from Saint Augustine and other Fathers of the Church in order to explain those which had been quoted at him."[19] This shows that he knew about the controversy. Should we repeat what Le Crom said, "From his lonely retreat Montfort was following the debates"?[20] What is undeniable, in any case, is that the term "critic," which was introduced into Catholic literary circles by Richard Simon,[21] was used by Montfort with the negative connotation that Bossuet had attached to it. Montfort applied it to the proud and self-important adversaries of *"the devotion"* he was promoting (TD 162, 167, 180, 226, 245). He puts critics into the category of *"evil men"* (TD 162) and "worldlings" (TD 226). When he uses it the word is synonymous with *"proud scholars"* (TD 26, 65, 93) and *"haughty"* (TD 245), *"people of independent and self-satisfied minds"* (TD 26, 93, 245). Montfort appears to side with Bossuet, who wrote in 1703, "Nothing is so contrary to the spirit of the early Christians as the spirit of modern critics."[22]

3. Literal meaning and prophetic meaning. Who was right? A small book, *Règles pour l'intelligence des Stes. Ecritures,* was published in 1716, the year of Montfort's death. The author remained nameless, but it was attributed to Jacques-Joseph Duguet, and it may throw some light on the question. The book, obviously, did not influence Montfort, but it gives principles that may help to explain his use of Scripture. Duguet maintains that we "always begin by establishing the literal meaning" (p. 13), which he calls *immediate* and which is "the meaning in history" (p. 14). But he strongly recommends looking for a second meaning, which he calls *prophetic,* that is to say, Christological, which gives unity and consistence to the whole of Scripture. Right from the first page, the principle, for its understanding is clearly set out: "Jesus Christ is the end of the law . . . and we cannot understand Scripture . . . unless we see him present in all of it." In contrast to those interpreting Scripture by means of allegories and to those, like Richard Simon, who interpret it literally, Duguet suggests a middle-of-the-road approach. He illustrates it with a comparison of a lute or zither, which he borrowed from Saint Augustine and which de Sacy[23] had used, and a comparison of the parable. "Although the whole of Scripture is centered around Jesus Christ, each of its parts does not tell us all about him; just like the whole of a parable is designed for a purpose, or main object, though not every detail is immediately relevant to the end. . . . Not every part of a lute produces harmonious sounds, but each of them is necessary for their production. According to Saint Augustine, it is the same for Scripture. The whole of it resounds with the name and mysteries of Jesus Christ, though not each individual part does. . . . We cannot expect each part to resound, but they all play a part in the overall effect"[24] (pp. 24-26). After all, this was an intelligent way to repeat the basic principle of the exegesis of the Church Fathers.

In the Middle Ages the traditional doctrine of the Church Fathers had been set out in the theory of the four meanings:

> *Littera gesta docet, quid credas allegoria,*
> *Moralis quid agas, quo tendas anagogia.*[25]

In the *literal* sense, the biblical account reports the "facts" of history. The other three senses are derived from it and help to understand the spiritual meaning. The *allegorical* sense reveals the hidden mystery of history, its saving dimension. The *moral* sense is the sense that Scripture has with reference to the *spiritual life* of Christians. In 1 Cor 10:6 Saint Paul speaks of the time that Israel spent in the desert and says, "These events happened as warnings to us not to set our desires on evil things as they did." Here Paul is referring to the historical events and not to the text of the Bible as such. But the biblical passage giving an account of the events takes on a paraenetic meaning[26] for us. The term used nowadays would be hermeneutics, or the meaning of the text as applied to us, in contrast to exegesis, which is concerned with the meaning of the text *at the time of writing.* It was on this typological sense that spiritual writers, including Montfort, preferred to concentrate. Finally, *anagogy* opens vistas on the future through hope. This typological interpretation flows directly from the Christ-centeredness of Revelation. Christ makes it possible to interpret the whole of Scripture in that way.

b. Spiritual writers and the Bible. In the late seventeenth century, exegesis was already largely concerned with the spiritual meaning of Scripture. In order, however, to understand Montfort's use of Scripture, we have to move from the tradition of the exegetes to that of the mystics and spiritual writers. For the mystics link their experience to the *Word of God,* by which they do not necessarily mean the biblical word. According to Saint John of the Cross, "The Father has uttered only one word, and this word was his Son; he still utters it in eternal silence, and it is in silence that the soul should listen to it."[27] In this silence, communication between God and the soul can be established, and the soul is given understanding of the mysteries of Christ. For this access to God is equivalent to an access to the Wisdom of God, Wisdom that ruled over the mysteries of salvation and their account in the Bible. For John of the Cross, the Cross of Jesus is where all the Wisdom of God is hidden, and Montfort would have agreed with him when he wrote: "The soul really desirous of Wisdom should first of all desire to enter more deeply into the mystery of the Cross, which is the way to life."[28] And the Cross, from which all mystical experiences originate, is also the key to the understanding of Scripture. "When Christ said on the Cross, 'All is accomplished,' and died, all the modes [of Revelation of the Old Covenant] ceased to exist, and along with them the ceremonies and rites of the Old Law."[29] It has been justly said, "Only the cry of Jesus on the Cross is univocal and admits of no allegory; the rest of the Bible and of authentic tradition is to be interpreted spiritually as the echo of that cry throughout the history of Revelation."[30] The mystics therefore do not confine themselves to the literal meaning of the Bible. They interpret it spiritually and find in it the Spirit whom they experience in their loving encounter with God. Their hermeneutics are spiritual and inspired by love. They realize that Scripture is meant for them personally, and they read it to increase their love of God. Montfort was one of them. He was not an exegete but a spiritual writer. Though his knowledge of Scripture was extensive, his reading of it was not scholarly but spiritual. This reading was part of his ardent quest for Wisdom. What mattered to him were not only the literal meaning of Scripture but the history of salvation that the text reveals and that is to be repeated today in terms of the discovery of Wisdom. . . . It is Wisdom, whom he identifies with Christ, that he discerns, senses, and recognizes in mere hints throughout Scripture. His reading is therefore not only prophetic and Christological but fully mystical. He did not question that Esau, Jacob, and Rebecca really lived in the days of old or that Jacob foreshadows Christ, and Rebecca, Mary, but he also believed that the story was handed down to us only to help our progress in the spiritual life. This is illustrated again by his reading of the Psalms in PM and by his reading of the Wisdom texts, which he construes as referring to Jesus and Mary throughout.

We will therefore leave critical reason behind—the exegete Richard Simon would probably not have gone along with Montfort and his "mystical fantasies"—and move into the higher sphere of prayer. It must be fairly obvious that the spiritual interpretation of Scripture is rooted in *lectio divina,* which belongs to the patristic and monastic tradition. *Lectio divina* is essentially reading in the Spirit, which is different from exegesis and from hermeneutics proper; nor does it consist in using Scripture for theological or homiletic purposes. It is "reading Scripture peacefully for its own sake, making the necessary efforts to reflect on it, *meditatio,* and being thus led as if naturally to prayer, *oratio.*"[31] In this sort of reading, the Holy Spirit is at work and presides over the inner confrontation between the Word and the heart that turns the reading into a real prayer.

Let us not dismiss mystical reading too hastily. It might tie in with the recent concern generated by the advances of the linguistic sciences, which have implications even for exegesis. Reading has now come under close investigation. What happens *in the act of reading?* How does the reader relate to the text and secretly connive with it? The text is not unconnected with the reader's subjective commitment. In its very essence, it contains propositions, injunctions, and requires to be read in a particular way. This is particularly true of the biblical text, which can be called Scripture, insofar as it is a life-giving text that therefore requires to be read in faith in order to lead to a personal commitment and an increase in life. "Those written [signs] have been *recorded in order that* you may believe . . . and that through this faith you may have life" (Jn 20:31).

In other words, the Bible is not just a text. Through it we hear the voice of Another. It is a living Word, an offer of dialogue. If I read it properly, I cannot but be challenged by the Word. If the dialogue part of it is left out, then the explanation of the Bible is incomplete. Should not the meta-language of the believing exegete aim at preserving the dialogic role of the biblical text so that what is said about a biblical text makes it possible to hear the Word of the Spouse, the living word of a loving God? In this sense, should not the literal meaning, the meaning as expressed at the time of writing, take on a spiritual, mystical meaning relevant to our present-day relationship with God? This is, at any rate, the way spiritual writers read Scripture, and it is also on this basis that Montfort's scriptural interpretations should be considered.

II. Montfort and the Bible

1. In his life

In order to determine how largely the Bible figured in Montfort's life, we could call to mind the picture, now traditional in montfort circles, of the wayfarer described by Grandet: "completely confident in divine Providence, carrying around with him a copy of the *Holy Bible,* his breviary, a crucifix, his rosary, a small statue of the Blessed Virgin, and with a staff in his hand" (p. 96, 478). We could also use Besnard's description of Montfort's furniture when he was staying on rue du Pot de Fer in Paris: "A shabby bed, an earthenware pot, a breviary, a *book of the Bible,* a crucifix, a picture of the Blessed Virgin, a rosary, his instruments of penitence, constituted all his furniture" (IV, p. 62). To his friend, who was reproaching him for his conduct and his ways, Montfort "showed his New Testament" (Blain, p. 185). Did he always carry it around with him, as Fr. Tronson, whom he had known at Saint-Sulpice, had recommended?[32] He made a point of copying in his "Notebook" (p.310) a passage from *Vie de Mr. de Renty* in which Saint-Jure says that towards the end of his life this holy man "only read the New Testament, which he always carried around with him." If Montfort did the same, it would give an extra outward indication of the importance that he attached to the Bible in his personal life.

In his apostolate, the Bible as a book was part of the apparatus he used during his missions. Besnard says that at Villiers-en-Plaine, in February 1716, "he took the book of the Holy Bible, which was very well bound, and had it carried under the canopy to the local church where the mission began that day" (V, 138). It was a bold way to emphasize the "real presence" of the Word of God, which would be the subject of his preaching during the mission. During the procession, which took place on the occasion of the "renewal of the Baptismal promises" during the mission, he gave pride of place to the book of the Gospel, which was carried in solemnity by a deacon, then venerated by the faithful; he "knelt down before taking it, then rising held it against his chest and preached so eloquently that all his audience burst into tears" (Grandet, 411). The whole performance was designed to highlight the Word of God at the expense of the one preaching it.

It is, however, his spiritual writings that best reveal to what extent Montfort turned to the Word of God for his nourishment.

2. In his writings

a. The Love of Eternal Wisdom. Of all his books, this is the most biblical and the most faithful to the biblical text. He did not use Scripture just to support a doctrine he had put forward previously. His starting point is the Book of Wisdom itself, which inspires the theological views he propounds and almost suggests the plan of his book. In this respect, Montfort is unique, as there are no other spiritual writers "who have based their teaching, as Montfort did, on this small Old Testament book written in Greek."[33]

1. *The Book of Wisdom.* Montfort keeps very close to the biblical text of the Book of Wisdom. He does not refrain from quoting whole chapters[34] from it; most importantly, he closely adheres to its internal development. The Book of Wisdom is generally divided into the main parts: chapters 1 to 6, chapters 7 to 9, and chapters 10 to 19, in accordance with the literary genre of the book. The Book of Wisdom belongs to the Greek genre

called eulogy or encomium, which is designed to "arouse admiration for a person and a desire to imitate him or to practice one of his particular virtues or qualities."[35] After the introduction, or exordium, Wis 6:24 [22][36] gives the plan of the rest of the book: "I will tell you what wisdom is and how she came to be, and I will hide no secrets from you, but I will trace her course from the beginning of creation." The eulogy is to be about the nature of Wisdom, her origin, and her works. Montfort follows this plan fairly closely and examines each of these points. He tells us about the origin and nature of Wisdom (ch. 2, 5-7), then he considers her works in creation (ch. 3) and throughout the Old Testament (ch. 4 and 8). Although Montfort goes beyond the scope of the Book of Wisdom by dealing at length with the Incarnation, he is still on the same track in considering the last chapter in the long history of salvation. He returns to the subject when dealing with the first two means to acquire Wisdom (desire and prayer), which are crowned with the Prayer of Solomon (ch. 15). But *"to be then in some way wiser than Solomon"* (LEW 221), he adds two further means: mortification, which is linked to the Cross of Christ, and devotion to Mary, who in the Incarnation had become *"mistress of divine Wisdom"* (LEW 205). It is clear that Montfort not only drew his inspiration from the Book of Wisdom but, by going beyond its scope and applying it to Christian living, also showed that he had fully grasped its implications.

Although the Book of Wisdom was Montfort's main source of inspiration and the general framework, as it were, of the rest of his writings, he drew on other sources as well. In this small book he seems to have tapped the current of Wisdom, and he quotes and comments on the main passages. He lays special emphasis on the well-known passages in which Wisdom is personified: he paraphrases chapter 8 of the Book of Wisdom (LEW 18, 32, 47, 66-68) and quotes the whole of chapter 24 of Sirach (LEW 20-28) . Besides, all the quotations and allusions referring to the Old Testament (more than 250 of them) bear on the theme of Wisdom. Even the passages from the New Testament are given a Wisdom tint and become Utterances of Wisdom Incarnate. The 72 utterances in chapter 12, which Montfort quotes without any comments or additions of any sort, sound as if they were spoken by Jesus, the teacher of Wisdom.[37] Montfort vanishes, as he does on several occasions, because he does not wish, as he puts it, *"to mingle my poor words with the inspired words of the Holy Spirit"* (LEW 5) or with the words of Wisdom (LEW 20). He thus allows the Gospel message to come through with its full force, as he did when summing it up in *The Wisdom Cross of Poitiers*.[38] He acted in the same way when he held up the book of the Gospel in front of the congregation during the ceremony of the renewal of the Baptismal promises and when the book lay wide open while those renewing their Baptismal vows and promises[39] were signing their *covenant with God.*

Although he drew largely on the Bible, Montfort's LEW remains his own work. He has woven scriptural quotations into it, but he is responsible for the arrangement of the warp and woof. He is a real writer, an author whose work is coherent and consistent throughout.

2. *His interpretation.* Montfort read the Book of Wisdom in the light of its becoming a reality in Jesus Christ. He read it with Christ in mind and in terms of the economy of the salvation history, which ends with the Cross, summit of the Love of Eternal Wisdom. In all Wisdom texts, Montfort saw Christ, Incarnate Wisdom, as a backdrop. He was fully aware that the word "wisdom" has several meanings. At the beginning of the book and somewhat in the manner of a teacher, he sets out the subject matter and defines the terms and the plan he is going to follow. He distinguishes true wisdom from false wisdom, natural wisdom from supernatural wisdom; then he divides supernatural wisdom into created wisdom, which is the gift of wisdom, *"the communication that uncreated Wisdom makes of himself to humankind,"* and substantial or uncreated Wisdom, i.e. *"the Son of God, the second person of the most Blessed Trinity. In other words, it is Eternal Wisdom in eternity or Jesus Christ in time."* To make his subject matter perfectly clear, he adds, *"It is precisely about this Eternal Wisdom that we are going to speak"* (LEW 13). Nothing could be clearer than this.

Montfort is able to reread the Wisdom texts of the Old Testament in this light because he has fully realized that salvation history cannot be split up. The New Testament helps him to understand the Old, and the Old enables him to better understand the spiritual realities of the New. He does not discuss the unity of the two Testaments, nor does he attempt to establish it. It is obvious to him. The identification of Wisdom with Jesus Christ, which is confirmed in the New Testament (cf. 1 Cor 8:6; Col 1:15-20; Heb 1:3; Jn 1:3),[40] sheds light after the event on the Wisdom texts of the Old Testament, especially on those in which Wisdom is personified. Montfort does not, however, level everything. He respects the stages in salvation history: the divine origin of Eternal Wisdom (ch. 2), the creation of the world and of man, followed by sin (ch. 3), Wisdom in the Old Covenant (ch. 4-6), the Incarnation and the life of Jesus (ch. 9-12), finally the Cross, which the "laws" of love make inevitable (LEW 168; ch. 13-14).

He acknowledges, however, that the same Spirit inspired both the New and the Old Testaments.[41] It can therefore be said that his exegesis of the Wisdom texts is a spiritual one. Some might say that his is an allegorical exegesis in the manner of the Church Fathers and in the strict etymological sense of the word "allegory, i.e., to say something more. It has indeed been pointed out that 'something more' is said of Wisdom when it is another name for Jesus Christ; and something more is said of Christ when looked at under the appearance of Wisdom."[42] But Montfort was not a professional exegete. His purpose was not to explain or comment on the original ancient texts. What he was seeking in them was the Word and what the Word was now saying to the believer. Montfort was a spiritual writer who lived and wanted others to live a spiritual, mystical experience, enabling them to "have experiential knowledge of the depths of God"[43] and making possible *"the communication that uncreated Wisdom makes to humankind"* (LEW 13). His listeners were those who "loved perfection and sought to realize their divine destiny" (LEW 14).The word "spiritual," as used in the present context, does not refer to the description of a technical scriptural meaning corresponding to a literal meaning, although this is the case where Wisdom is identified with Jesus Christ, but to an interpretation that may be useful in the spiritual life.

By reading Scripture in this way, Montfort respects the meaning that the Holy Spirit wanted it to convey. However, can it be maintained that he interprets it faithfully when he identifies Wisdom with the Cross and applies certain Wisdom passages to the Virgin Mary?

Everything that Montfort says about the Cross and universal mortification as a means to acquire Wisdom would be meaningless if no reference were made to Christ. It is because God, in his desire to save humankind, rejected the way of power and chose instead the way of love that the Cross, which is folly to men, has become the Wisdom of God. Montfort can therefore boldly assert: *"In all truth . . . Wisdom is the Cross and the Cross is Wisdom"* (LEW 180). When he applies to the Cross *"Hanc amavi a juventute mea"* ("I loved her from my youth") (Wis 8:2) (LEW 169), he admittedly[44] adapts, reading the passage from the Book of Wisdom out of context. Basically, however, he takes the biblical and spiritual logic to its conclusion for the overall Christological interpretation that is sanctioned by the New Testament. We notice something similar with the Blessed Virgin. It is by virtue of the mystery of the Incarnation and of her being the Mother of Christ that Mary, *"miracle of Eternal Wisdom"* (LEW 106), became *"mistress of divine Wisdom"* (LEW 205). This mystery enables Montfort to recognize Mary as the *dwelling place* Wisdom built for herself (Prov 9:1; cf. LEW 105), and he is justified in calling her the *"throne of Eternal Wisdom"* (LEW 208). Here again, the boldness of Montfort the spiritual writer is tempered by Montfort the theologian: *"Not that she is above him who is truly God, or even equal to him. To think or say such a thing would be blasphemous"* (LEW 205). He does say that Mary is wise (LEW 22), but it is Jesus and not his mother who is Wisdom.

Having thus established a solid foundation, we must admit that following in this the liturgical tradition,[45] Montfort does assimilate Mary with Wisdom, and Wisdom with Mary. In LEW 206, the pronoun "she" used in one sentence does not clearly refer to either Mary or to Wisdom. If it is indeed Wisdom who *"loves those who love her"* (Prov 8:17) and who, possibly, *"shares her blessings with them,"* in *"Jesus, the fruit of her womb,"* the adjective "her" can only refer to Mary. What is more, in TD 175, 201, Montfort applies to Mary the quotation from Prov 8:17, but in SR 52[46] he quotes the same passage and refers it to Jesus and Mary. In LEW 207 Mary is distinct from Wisdom, since *"she has given us incarnate Wisdom, Jesus her Son,"* but it is Mary that *"is ever on the look-out for those who are worthy of Wisdom,"* just as Wisdom is (Wis 6:16). Most importantly, it is to Mary that Montfort applies the well-known passage from Sirach 24:13: *"God has decreed that Mary should dwell in Jacob, make Israel her inheritance and place her roots in his elect and predestinate"* (LEW 213), but the same passage in LEW 23 retains its literal meaning.[47] Similarly, the ways to keep (Prov 8:32) refer to those of Wisdom in LEW 68 but to those of Mary in LEW 212. Mary is not to be identified with Wisdom for all that, for in adding that then *"we shall . . . easily and in a short time possess divine Wisdom,"* the distinction is being made perfectly clear. Nevertheless, when referring to Wisdom and Mary, Montfort shifts from one to the other easily, and he uses such subtle changes of meaning that they are sometimes imperceptible. Let us note, however, that whatever he says about Mary is only included because of its relevance to Jesus Wisdom. Montfort's interpretation becomes clear when considered within the overall context of the economy of salvation, in which Mary is the mother and mistress of Divine Wisdom because *"the Son God, Eternal Wisdom"* (LEW 205) chose to make himself subject to her.

This type of reading, called mystical, has been used by the saints down the ages. It follows from their spiritual experience. When Saint John of the Cross describes the Cross as the starting point of all spiritual experience and the key to the understanding of Scripture, what he says fits in perfectly with *The Love of Eternal Wisdom.* Without revealing any personal secrets, Montfort, who frequently uses the first person singular,[48] shares his personal experience. LEW reflects his own life, sufferings, prayer, and encounter with God. We only need to read his letters to realize this. In Letters 15 and 16, which were probably written in 1703, he shows that he is sighing *"night and day"* for Wisdom, whom he is hoping to obtain through the Cross and prayer. In Letter 20, addressed to his mother in 1704, he uses the mystical theme of spiritual marriage to describe his bond with Wisdom: *"In my new family—the one I belong to now—I have chosen to be wedded to Wisdom and the Cross for in these I find every good."* This makes the parallel clear.

In the same Letter 20, Montfort said, *"No one knows the secrets I am talking about, or at least very few people do."* He has written his book to reveal these secrets and inspire others with love for Wisdom. Unless we regard as a mere literary device the way in which he involves the reader in the book (cf. LEW 5: *"my dear reader"*; LEW 7: *"in your kindness"*; LEW 14: *"Let us now speak to chosen souls seeking perfection"*; the use of "we," which throughout the book creates a bond between writer and reader; the two Latin quotations *"Qui potest capere capiat."* and *"Quis sapiens et intelliget haec?"*, with which he ends the book and which are obviously meant for the reader), Montfort cannot be accused of writing for his own sake or of indulging in narcissism. He writes for the sake of other people.[49] His writing is an apostolic undertaking, as shown by the prayer with which he dedicates the book: *"Bestow your blessings and your enlightenment on what I mean to say about you, so that those who read it may be filled with a fresh desire to love you and possess you, on earth as well as in heaven"* (LEW 2). Commenting on Sir 24:30-31, "Whoever obeys me will not be put to shame, and those who work with me will not sin. Whoever makes me known will have eternal life," Montfort interprets the passage as suggesting three degrees of devotion, the highest one being perfection: *"Finally, seek to acquire the light and unction you need to inspire others with that love for Wisdom which will lead them to eternal life"* (LEW 30; see in LEW 95 how the Word and Wisdom are linked). Finally, he ends chapter 12, in which he has gathered together the great truths *"which Eternal Wisdom came on earth to teach us, having first put them into practice,"* by commenting on the three degrees mentioned in LEW 30: *"More blessed are those who believe them. Most blessed of all are those who believe them, put them into practice and teach them to others; for they will shine in heaven like stars for all eternity"* (LEW 153, which includes a quotation from Dan 12:3). This tells us the principles on which his vocation as a spiritual writer was based and his motives for writing books. Although Montfort wrote the book when he was a young man, probably about 1703-1704, *The Love of Eternal Wisdom* firmly lays down the main principles of what may be called the montfort spirituality[50] by basing them on Scripture itself. Montfort looks at everything from the angle of Wisdom, that is, God's loving design as set out in the Bible. This angle is that of the economy of salvation. In that vast perspective, each theme finds its place in relation to others. It is clear, for example, that the Cross and Mary are ordained to the acquisition and preservation of Wisdom, that is, to mystical union with Christ, who remains the goal of all efforts in the spiritual life.

The language of Wisdom seems to tail off in Montfort's later writings. Was this because of the demands of the missionary life and the needs to be supplied? The span between 1703-1704 and 1716, the year of his death, is a short one, and the spiritual man did not really change over that period. Actually he never grew old . . . He expressed his inmost thoughts in the letters he wrote at the end of his life, and we can find in them the accents of the LEW and the same desires. Letters 24 and 26, written in 1713, are all about the Cross. And in the last letter of those which came down to us, Letter 34, which he wrote about Easter 1716, he intermingled Wisdom and the Cross in every line. Together with *The Love of Eternal Wisdom,* his last letter encompasses the whole of Montfort's spiritual life and reveals its secret.

b. The Treatise on the True Devotion to the Blessed Virgin and The Secret of Mary. These two works appear to have been written at about the same time, probably towards 1713. The latter followed close on the former and gives a summary or abridgement of it: *"I will be brief"* (SM 2).[51] Actually, the important Scripture quotations in the *Secret of Mary* are condensed versions of those in TD; for example, Sir 24:13, on which he elaborates in TD 29-36, is commented on in just a few lines in SM 15. The same holds good for Ps 118:56 and Jn 19:27, which are given more development in TD 179 than in SM 66, and for Gal 4:19, which is quoted in Latin and translated in TD 33, but just given in Latin in SM 56. Consequently, what we will say about the Bible in TD holds true for SM as well.

1. *Overall view.* Montfort used a large number of Scripture texts in TD, but he uses them in different ways in TD and in LEW. TD contains about 140 explicit quotations, more than half of them from the Old Testament, and over 300 allusions, mostly to the New Testament. The explicit quotations are usually given in Latin and are very accurate. Only very occasionally does Montfort change or add to or adapt the text to make it fit his own idea (cf. TD 272, in which he adds *"Mariae"* to the words of Ps 16:2, and the adaptations of Jn 19:27 in TD 144, 179, 216, 266). Most of the allusions are incorporated into his thoughts and enter naturally into the stream of the sentences, shaping his language and turning his style into a real biblical style. Some passages, like TD 61, 68, 214, read virtually like fragments of Scripture.

The most striking feature of TD and SM is that most of the biblical passages they contain are interpreted in terms of the Virgin Mary in order to define her role in God's design in the mystery of the Incarnation, and also in the economy leading to this saving event and continuing it in the spiritual life of the faithful. Montfort's starting point in LEW was the Bible. And in TD everything hinges on the fact of the Incarnation as the fundamental biblical event par excellence, on which all the rest hangs, and this was how Montfort saw it. Now, whether we like it or not, Mary was involved in this event, and Montfort emphasizes this right from the start: *"It was through the blessed Virgin Mary that Jesus Christ came into the world"* (TD 1). This undeniable fact allows him to read the biblical texts with Mary in mind. Because the Incarnation took place in this way and because it was the means chosen by God to prove his love for us, it follows that Mary was necessary (TD 39). In the light of the will of God and of the Incarnation, the whole of the Old Testament, seen as heralding the New, takes on a different complexion for Montfort. All that seemed obscure or mysterious in it springs to life and is seen as prophetic, rather as if the secret code of the hieroglyphs had been cracked. Everything becomes a *type* announcing the mystery of Christ and the mystery of Mary, who cannot be separated from him: *"The types and texts of the Old and New Testaments prove the truth of this"* (TD 41).

It comes as no surprise to find in TD and SM the passages in which Saint Luke speaks of the Virgin Mary interpreted *literally.* Montfort quotes quite a few of them. He repeats that Mary is the only human being that "has found favor with God" (Lk 1:30; cf. TD 16, 44, 164); she was filled with the Holy Spirit and conceived God himself in her most pure womb (Lk 1:35; cf. TD 6, 16, 35, 44); she was proclaimed the servant and slave of the Lord (Lk 1:38; TD 72, 216, 267). He repeats Elizabeth's blessings (Lk 1:42-45; TD 33, 95, 225), the words of the Magnificat (Lk 1:48-55; TD 6, 148, 225, 255), and dwells particularly on the fact that Jesus chose to obey Mary (Lk 2:51; TD 18, 27, 37, 139, 156, 157, 196, 198). Montfort gives, however, a *spiritual meaning* to the biblical texts more freely and boldly in TD than he did in LEW. He hardly refers to the Book of Wisdom at all but quotes and gives a Marian interpretation to a few passages from the Book of Proverbs (8:17; TD 175, 201; cf. LEW 206; Prov 8:32; TD 200, cf. LEW 212). He applies to Mary the text of Prov 31:21 about the "capable" wife who clothes her servants in double garments, her Son's and her own: *"Omnes domestici ejus vestiti sunt duplicibus"* (TD 206, 208; SM 38). He dwells especially on Sir 24:13. In LEW he applied to Mary the words in which God ordered Wisdom to "make your dwelling in Jacob, in Israel receive your inheritance and place your roots in his elect and predestinate." In TD he comments on the quotation and allots parts of it to each of the Persons of the Trinity (cf. TD 29, 31, 34; SM 15). He also borrows from the Song of Songs to explain the mystery of Mary: a garden locked, a fountain sealed (Song 4:12; TD 5, 263; SM 20), tower of David (Song 4:4; SM 47), terrible as an army drawn up in lines of battle (Song 6:3; TD 50, 210). And in the invitation to God's banquet, he mixes the words of Wisdom with those of the Bride (Sir 24:26; Song 5:1; TD 208; cf. LEW 10).

Whereas LEW contains no reference to the Psalms, Montfort refers to this book about twenty times in TD. *"Sicut saggitae in manu potentis"* in Ps 126:4 is translated by *"in Mary's powerful hands, like sharp arrows"* (TD 56). He sometimes puts forward arguments in the manner of the Church Fathers. He uses *"Homo et homo natus est in ea"* from Ps 86:5 to show that Sion/Mary is mother not only of the first man, who is Jesus, but also of the second, who stands for all the elect. While cleverly claiming that Daniel is rather bold, he applies *"Haec facta est mihi"* from Ps 118:56 not to the Law but to Mary and dares to translate it as *"She was created for me"!* (TD 179).

2. *A few significant texts.* Gen 3:15 is the first of the significant passages that establish the role of Mary in the economy of salvation. After the Fall, God condemns the serpent, but he introduces in his verdict a word of hope for humanity. Montfort refers several times to the prophecy, which is the only one that he comments on in TD. He quotes it in full with its cross-reference in the text of the Vulgate: *"Inimicitias ponam inter te et mulierem, et semen tuum et semen*

illius; ipse conteret caput tuum, et tu insidiaberis calcano ejus" (Gen 3:15 (TD 51). The Hebrew text announced enmity between the serpent's offspring and the woman's and hinted that humanity would eventually triumph over the devil. This first glimmer of salvation has been called the *Protevangelium.* Later on, in the Greek text the second part of the sentence began with a masculine pronoun instead of a neuter as required by the generic "He will strike your head, and you will strike his heel"; consequently. victory over the devil was attributed to one of the woman's sons, and this gave rise to the messianic interpretation that the Church Fathers explained in detail. This interpretation which involves the Messiah necessarily brought Mary into play, and the Marian interpretation of the Latin translation *ipsa conteret* became fixed in the tradition, at least in the Roman Catholic Church. Obviously, Montfort had read the Vulgate, and in his view the woman is the first to be directly involved, and she will strike the serpent's head: *"ipsa conteret"* (TD 52-53), as will her offspring and her servants. The heel that the serpent strikes stands for the humble slaves and poor children of Mary. And it is with this humble *heel* that she will crush the serpent's head (TD 54). In PM the *"heel of this mysterious woman"* stands for the *"little company of her children who will come towards the end of time"* (PM 13), and RM states that in their preaching the missionaries are continuing the thousand-year-old battle (RM 61).

Among other texts dear to Montfort are Gal 4:19 and Eph 4:13, which illustrate and help to understand the maternal role of Mary in the economy in which we become children of God. Montfort applies to Mary what Saint Paul says of himself: *"We can attribute more truly to her what Saint Paul said of himself, Quos iterum parturio, donec in vobis formetur Christus: I am in labor again with all the children of God until Jesus Christ, my Son is formed in them to the fullness of his age"* (TD 33; cf. SM 56, LEW 214, and the allusions referring to "form" in TD 37, 219, 269). Montfort himself expresses clearly and distinguishes very well the literal meaning (what Paul says of himself) from the other meaning, which might be called allegorical, when applying the passage *"more truthfully"* to Mary (cf. LEW 214). On the basis of Eph 4:13, Montfort establishes a link particularly dear to him between the spiritual motherhood of Mary and the fullness of the age of Jesus Christ. He understands this to refer to the full spiritual growth, the mystical union with Christ. In his opinion, however, *"it is in the bosom of Mary that people . . . in a short time reach the fullness of the age of Christ"* (TD 156). He firmly believes that *"so few souls come to the fullness of the age of Jesus [because] . . . Mary is not formed well enough in their hearts"* (TD 164) and because they do not take the *quick. direct, perfect* way that leads to him (TD 168; cf. also SM 67, LEW 214). In this connection, it is worth noting that the Pauline expression, which epitomizes the whole spiritual journey, concludes both the first and the last numbers of LEW (LEW 1, 227).

On the subject of Mary's motherhood, we will now say a few words about a passage in Saint John's Gospel that Montfort seems to have deliberately left aside. In a book in which he frequently speaks of spiritual motherhood,[52] Montfort says nothing about the beginning of Jn 19:27, in which Christ on the Cross says to his mother and Saint John, "Here is your son. Here is your mother." Montfort knew Saint John's Gospel very well, as he quotes several times the second part of the verse referring to Saint John. Why did he choose to leave out[53] the first part, which Mariologists rightly regard as fundamental to establish Mary as Mother of the Church?[54] When addressing God the Father at the beginning of PM, he alludes to it, and this may help to justify the omission. He asks the Father to remember his Congregation, which *"you made . . . your own when you took it to your heart while your dear Son, dying on the Cross, bedewed it with his blood, consecrated it by his death and entrusted it to his holy Mother's keeping."* The words refer to the disciple whom Jesus loved. Similarly, the Company is entrusted to Jesus' Mother, and its members in their turn should regard Mary as all their good. Perhaps this is the right perspective in which to consider *"Da Matri tuae liberos"* in PM 6, which probably refers to Gen 30:1 and also calls to mind the words "Here is your son" spoken on Calvary.

Why is there no trace of the passage in Montfort's writings, apart from this allusion? Montfort gives no answer to the question. In TD 18 he evokes the scene on Calvary. In TD 5 he explains the word "woman," but his explanation has since been discarded. He quotes the second part of Jn 19:27 at least four times, adapting it in a number of ways, as some writers do when dealing with a favorite quotation to which they have given much thought: *"accepit eam discipulus in sua"* (TD 144), *"accepi eam in mea"* (accommodation to the first person, TD 179), *"accepi te in mea"* (accommodation to "I" and "you" TD 216), *"accepio te in mea omnia"* (adaptation to the present, to "I" and "you" with the addition of *"omnia"* TD 266); elsewhere he simply paraphrases the text: *"Like St. John the Evangelist at the foot of the Cross, I have taken her times without number as my total good"* (SM 66). But he never quotes "Here is your son" or "Here is your mother" [except for quoting these words from J. Nouet in HD 3b]. The reasons for this are probably to be found in the theological basis for the spiritual motherhood of Mary that Montfort no doubt borrowed from the Bérullian tradition. According to this tradition, it was at the Incarnation that Mary became Mother of Jesus and of *"all the members of his mystical body"* (TD 17, 20, 32, 140; SM 12; LEW 213, 214). Montfort, of course, could not know what recent Johannine exegesis has emphasized: the straining towards the "hour," which runs through Saint John's Gospel; the link between the mother of Jesus and this fateful "hour," which at Cana had not yet come (Jn 2:4) but had come on Calvary (cf. Jn 13:1; 17:1); consequently, the significance of Christ's going to the Father (Jn 13:1), of the mystery of his glorification (Jn 17:1), and of the fulfillment of Scripture (Jn 19:28,30). This fulfillment took place on Calvary, but Scripture was not fulfilled when the Word became flesh (Jn 1:14). Montfort could not be aware either of the ecclesiological significance of Mary's motherhood,[55] which was also proclaimed on Calvary but not earlier. In Montfort's way of thinking, it seems that the only, or almost only, purpose of the Cross is to testify to the love of Christ: *"the suffering he chose to endure to prove his love for us"* (LEW 154 and the whole of ch. 13). The impression we are left with is that, apart from Christ's final proof of his love for humanity, everything was accomplished, as it were, at the Incarnation, as far as Jesus, Mary, and her mystical motherhood were concerned. This was the view taken by Montfort and some theologians in former days. On the other hand, Montfort's reading of the second part of the verse, *"Accepit eam is sua,"* appears to tie in exactly with present-day exegesis. In TD 179 he writes, "I *have taken her for my own."* The beloved disciple has no other good but her, as if taking the mother of Jesus into his home was enough for him to be made a disciple. De la Potterie suggests that the Johannine expression (Jn 19:27) be taken literally, meaning "what belongs to the disciple 'as his own,'"[56] that is to say, what constitutes him a disciple, his relation to Christ. It is indeed by virtue of his relation to Christ that the disciple receives Mary in his life as a believer. Though Montfort might have argued the case differently, we must admit that his interpretation tallies well enough with the one suggested. What is being emphasized is not the fact that Mary lived *in Saint John's house* but that from then on Mary was his only good.

One last passage should help us to grasp not only Montfort's allegorical way of interpreting Scripture but also the use he made of Scripture texts in TD. We are referring to *"the story of Jacob who received the blessing of his father Isaac through the care and ingenuity of his mother Rebecca"* (TD 183).

Montfort deals at length (TD 183-200) with this type that *"the Holy Spirit gives us in Sacred Scripture."* He goes on to say, *"Here is the story as the Holy Spirit tells it. I shall expound it further later on."* He draws our attention to the fact that he, not the Holy Spirit, will expound it, though he does make the point that *"according to the early Fathers and the interpreters of Holy Scripture, Jacob is the type of Our Lord and of souls who are saved, and Esau is the type of souls who are condemned"* (TD 185).[57]

What we will concentrate on here is the use that Montfort makes of the biblical narrative. In TD 150 he tells his readers that he will relate *"the story of Jacob and Rebecca which exemplifies the truths I have been setting before you."* So he had already set out the "truths" before mentioning the "type." It has been pointed out that Montfort applies to the reprobate, symbolized by Esau, the marks of false devotions (TD 92-104), to the predestinate, symbolized by Jacob, the marks of true devotion (TD 105-110), and to Mary, prefigured by Rebecca, the motherly care shown to her slaves of love (TD 144-149). He had already expanded on all this. In other words, the "truths" are well established before he illustrates them by means of biblical texts. This was the method used at the Council of Trent; it consisted in turning to Scripture, the Church Fathers, and the Doctors of the Church to support theses that had been put forward and formulated previously. Montfort shows here that he was a man of his time, and he uses the same method in other places in TD.[58] The method, however, need not be chronological. It is not unlikely that Montfort was already convinced of the Scripture-based role of Mary in the economy of salvation before he reread Genesis and that he then found in this book some passages that could help him to explain or illustrate Mary's role in a way suited to ordinary people, and also possibly other details casting light on some particular aspects. He did not read Scripture as an exegete but as a spiritual writer.

This comes through clearly in TD and SM. In these works, he gives the spiritual meaning of Scripture and adapts it so as to go beyond the literal meaning without leaving the vast Christological framework in which Mary has her place. If we compare the whole of Scripture to a melody played on the harp, with the name and mystery of Jesus as its main theme, we can say that the short passages having Mary for their theme did not escape Montfort's practiced ear. And he has pointed them out to other people. But as he has said repeatedly, his aim is always to direct their attention to the main theme.

c. The trilogy: Prayer for Missionaries, Rule of the Missionary Priests of the Company of Mary, Letter to the Members of the Company. The three works form a trilogy, and they should be considered together.[59] We will, however, concentrate mainly on PM.

1. *The Prayer for Missionaries.* **Overall view.** The text takes up only eight pages in OC and is wholly Scripture-inspired. It contains 31 explicit quotations, 25 of which are taken from the Old Testament, and about 15 allusions to precise passages, mainly from the New Testament. On the whole, however, quotations from the Psalms predominate. They run through the texts, and Montfort uses them as naturally and as aptly as he does his mother tongue.

He addresses his prayer to each of the Persons of the Holy Trinity in turn, to the Father (1-5), to the Son (6-14), and to the Holy Spirit (15-25), and at the end comes back to *"great God"* (PM 26-28) and concludes with "God alone." Three biblical quotations give the prayer its rhythm and inspire it, so to speak; they correspond roughly to the three divisions[60] just mentioned. The first quotation is from Ps 73:2, and Montfort gives it in Latin: *"Memento"*—the Vulgate says *Memor esto*— *"Domine, Congregationis tuae. quam possedisti ab initio".* He elaborates on this in the first six numbers, but he emphasizes *"Memento"* again in PM 15, 18, and 26. This first quotation serves as a framework for the whole prayer and is therefore fundamental. It sums up the prayer and would make a fitting name for it. Two other texts describe the congregation that Montfort is praying for: Gen 30:1, which he adapted and applied to Mary and is the subject of PM 6-14, and the mysterious Psalm 67 (PM 10-17), which he quotes in Latin and does not translate and is the subject of PM 19-25. Among the other quotations, we must highlight Gen 3:15, which prophesies *"great enmity between the blessed posterity of Mary"*—the small company—*"and the accursed issue of Satan"* (PM 13). Montfort quotes the passage in Latin without translating it in PM 12 and comments on it in the following number. This text is fundamental, because it accounts for the warlike tone of the prayer, justified by the *"only enmity which you have instigated"* (PM 13). The reference to the prophecy about Mary also accounts for the military-sounding name by which Montfort calls his Congregation: Company of Mary.[61] *"Ab initio,"* which he uses in the context of Psalm 73, probably refers to the community in the wilderness and is linked with Gen 3:15, in which the humble Mary is commissioned *"from the beginning of time . . . to crush this proud spirit under her heel."* The other biblical texts may take up more space, but Gen 3:15 seems to have been the basic inspiration of Montfort's prayer. For it is to hasten the fulfillment of the prophecy that Montfort, using Ps 73:2, beseeches God to remember His promise, applies to Mary the petition in Gen 30:1, and outlines the characteristics of *"this noble company . . . under the cloak of obscure but divinely inspired words"* (PM 19) used in Psalm 67.

Exegesis and interpretation. Psalm 73 is a national lament. The first few verses tell us straightaway about the great misfortune that has brought Israel so low. The people of YHWH has been heavily defeated. The Covenant community has been ransacked. The foes have set the sanctuary on fire, there is no longer any prophet (v. 9). The situation is desperate. In its literal sense, the psalm describes the distress of the people under the reign of Nebuchadnezzar. Montfort applies the psalm to his time: *"The whole land is desolate, ungodliness reigns supreme, your sanctuary is desecrated and the abomination of desolation has even contaminated the holy place. . . . Will you never break your silence?"* (PM 5). As in former days, misfortune stirs memories of the past, of God's promises, and of the Covenant. Hope is restored. Now, as formerly, what happens belongs to salvation history. As in the psalm, *"Memento,"* which keeps hope alive throughout the Bible, runs through Montfort's prayer and strengthens it.

The reference to Gen 30:1 is more in the style of an adaptation. Montfort refers to the prayer of Rachel, who had borne no children to Jacob, but he changes the perspective completely. Rachel's prayer was on her own behalf: *"Da mihi liberos"*; Montfort prays to Jesus on Mary's behalf: *"Da Matri tuae liberos."* Bearing in mind what happened to Rachel later, however, Montfort's hope revives in spite of Mary having no children yet. And he may also have been thinking of the gift that the crucified Christ gave to his Mother on Calvary (Jn 19:26).

As for Psalm 67, on which Montfort draws to describe his missionaries, its state of preservation is the worst of all psalms and its meaning most obscure. Any translation can only be conjectural, as is any interpretation. Montfort, who speaks of *"the cloak of obscure words,"* is fully aware of this. The psalm is usually regarded as a hymn of thanksgiving referring to the great stages in the history of God's people, a sort of triumphal procession in honor of YHWH. The verses quoted by Montfort describe the wonders that God worked when he brought his people out of Egypt, and sings of the conquest of Canaan (vv. 12-15 appear to have been inspired by the story of Deborah in Judg 5), an epic relating how God was preparing a "habitation" for himself and his people. Epic inspiration, warlike songs, fighting, and enemy spoils—all this was suited to the huge battle that Montfort could feel was about to start. It is in the context of *mirabilia Dei* (cf. *innova signa, immuta mirabilia* from Sir 36:6 in PM 3) that Montfort envisages his Congregation. Here again, the words of the psalm are given a spiritual and allegorical meaning: the *"rain that you have stored up"* stands for his missionaries, children of Mary, who will have to restore the Church's heritage. The *"creatures and poor folk"* who will dwell in the *"heritage"* and the *"silver wings of the dove"* are also allegories. God's *"mountain,"* where the Lord delights to dwell, stands for Mary, in whom the missionaries should dwell.

But is the final battle really about to be waged? The atmosphere of PM is, without any doubt, eschatological. The missionaries envisaged by Montfort are identified with the *"apostles of the latter times"* whom he mentioned in TD 55-59. So the coming of the end raises the temperature of the "burning prayer." Like many others before him, Montfort reads the signs of the times: *"It is indeed time to fulfil your promise. . . . Torrents of iniquity flood the whole earth carrying away even your servants. . . . All creatures . . . lie groaning under the burden of Babylon's countless sins and plead with you to come and renew all things"* (PM 5). He urges God to act. He puts forward one reason after another, brings together the apocalyptic signs that he has collected from the Bible and from spiritual books. He himself, at least vicariously through his Company, wants to take part in the great final battle. But when will it be fought? He has no idea. Obviously he is eager for the fray, but his very eagerness betrays his ignorance.

Although he mentions three reigns, those of the Father, the Son, and the Spirit, he sees himself in the third, which is that of the Gospel. Even though he speaks of the *"Spirit of the Father and the Son"* (the Spirit sent by the Father in Jn 14:16 and by the Son in Jn 15:26), he shows that he is not deceived by the division into three reigns. He writes: *"Your reign, Spirit of the Father and the Son, is still unended and will come to a close with a deluge of fire, love and justice"* (PM 16). The reign of the Spirit, which is still unended, is therefore the reign of the Church, in accordance with the Johannine tradition, in which the coming of the Holy Spirit follows the glorious death of Jesus (cf. Jn 7:39). It is during that reign that his Company is to fight for love and justice (cf. *"Be mindful, Lord, of your Congregation, when you come to dispense your justice"* PM 5). This language is biblical; it belongs to the Last Judgement and is reminiscent of Mat 25:31-46, which also is about fire, love, and justice. But is the end near at hand? It is permissible to hope it is, to pray for its coming, and to try to read the signs of the times; we have no choice, however, but to say with Jesus, "About that day or hour no one knows, neither the angels in heaven, nor the Son, but only the Father" (Mk 13:32). Montfort echoes these words at the end of the passage about the apostles of the latter times: *"But when and how will this come about? Only God knows. For our part we must yearn and wait for it in silence and in prayer"* (TD 59).

Anyone reading Montfort's text carefully will notice that he always reads the Bible, particularly the Psalms, with Christ in mind. For him these texts are prophetic:[62] they are about Christ. Montfort's text traces the whole history of salvation, beginning with *"ab initio,"* continuing with the history of the chosen people at the time of Moses and throughout the history of Israel, and on to Montfort's time and beyond until the end of the *"era of grace"* (PM 6; cf. Lk 4:19).

All the events in that history happen because of God's loving wisdom and fulfil the promises. As the New Testament writers read and interpreted Scripture in the light of the mystery of Christ, so Montfort, like all spiritual writers, read Scripture in order to find in it his own history and to apply the deeds of God in the past to his own time. Bringing the hermeneutic cycle into play, he enters into the words of Scripture, and the words of Scripture enter into him. His reading of Scripture as a spiritual writer might be disputed by some, but it is the result of his faith. He is not naive and does not claim to say what the text meant at "the time of writing" or to have insights into the thought process of the ancient writers. Relying on God's faithfulness, he says what Scripture means now: "Today Scripture has been fulfilled in your hearing" (Lk 4:21).

2. *Rule of the Missionary Priests of the Company of Mary.* The Rule is the concrete expression in ordinary life of the ideal set out in PM. The biblical texts contained in it are comparatively few. However, some favorite texts recur there as well, for example, the reference to the mouth and wisdom that no opponent will be able to withstand in Lk 21:15 is mentioned in RM 60, though already quoted in PM 22 and LEW 97, and especially the reference to Gen 3:15. In RM 61 he quotes again *"evangelizantibus virtute multa"* from the famous Psalm 67, quoted also in PM 19. As Montfort is dealing with more practical details in the Rule, he draws more on texts by Saint Paul, particularly 1 Corinthians, and the gospel writers; he fleshes these out with quotations from the Old Testament but always with preaching in mind, as if drawing on a repertoire of biblical texts designed for preachers. He

is mindful, however, of the overall framework within which the preaching is to be done, and in a passage referring especially to preachers, he underscores again the enmity between the Blessed Virgin's offspring and the accursed offspring of the serpent (RM 61).

The contrast between RM and and RW is striking. Obviously, the two works do not develop along the same lines. In the 320 numbers making up RW, against 91 in RM, there are only three scriptural quotations and about ten allusions. The quotations (Sir 19:1 in RW 56, Rom 12:2 in RW 87, 1 Cor 9:22 in RW 129) are given in French, whereas the same quotations are given in Latin in RM 39, 38, 49. Of course, the two sets were designed for different people. Most important, however, a comparison between RM and RW reveals that the main biblical texts quoted in the former refer to the apostolic life, the ministry of the Word, whereas the few texts quoted in the latter refer to the interior life of the Sisters, their personal journey to holiness. Obviously, Montfort does not mean to make the mission the preserve of men; although the *"interior aim of the Congregation of the Daughters of Wisdom is the acquisition of Divine Wisdom"* (RW 1), the exterior aim is certainly apostolic, including as it does teaching children, caring for poor people in hospitals, running retreat houses, etc. It is noteworthy, however, that the distinction between interior and exterior aims is not made in RM, which throughout deals with the life of the Company only from the angle of the mission. The difference is certainly striking.

3. *Letter to the Members of the Company of Mary.* The last work of the trilogy is short and incomplete and is made up of only eleven numbers. It opens with a quotation of Lk 12:32: *"Nolite timere pusillus grex quia complacuit patri vestro dare vobis regnum."* The rest of the book is a paraphrase of the text and is concerned with complete confidence in Divine Providence and particularly with poverty. The first four numbers contain about fifteen quotations, but they give prominence to some important texts like Psalm 90 (LCM 3) and Mat 6:26-34 (LCM 4). But even in the following numbers, which are said to have been borrowed from Nouet,[63] the accent is strongly biblical, and Montfort once again repeats his favorite quotations from Psalm 67, for example in LCM 7 (cf. PM 19) and from Lk 9:62 in LCM 9 (cf. LEW 144). The work is a fine example of what might be called Montfort's biblical style.

d. Letter to the Friends of the Cross. The letter, which was probably addressed to a pious association called the Friends of the Cross, is said to be contemporary with TD, SM, and the trilogy.[64] It was mainly inspired by Scripture, even though Montfort drew on some spiritual writers[65] and on his own experience. Some parts of FC are nothing but a series of allusions to scriptural texts (cf. 6, 9, 10, 27, 29, 30, 33, 58). Montfort was a past master at arranging them. They inspire his thoughts, carry them along, and mould them to such a degree that it is sometimes difficult to tell Montfort and Scripture apart.

However, the key quotation on which the whole work hinges is Mt 16: 24: *"Si quis vult venire post me, abneget semetipsum, et tollat crucem suam, et sequatur me.* Montfort takes up again, comments on, and paraphrases virtually each individual word: *"Si quis"* (FC 14), *"Si quis vult"* (FC 15), *"Si quis vult post me venire"* (FC 16), *"tollat crucem suam": "suam"* (FC 18), *"tollat"* (FC 19), *"crucem"* (FC 20-40), *"sequatur me"* (FC 41-62). There are a few quotations, already commented on in LEW, that establish the link between Wisdom and the Cross. In FC 16 Montfort repeats the adaptation of Wis 8:2: *"hanc amavi a juventute mea"* (cf. LEW 169, 183); and FC 45, about praying for *"the wisdom of the cross, that knowledge of the truth which we experience within ourselves,"* evokes once again the infinite treasure of Wisdom referred to in Wis 7:14 (cf. LEW 62, 64). This short work gives convincing proof that Montfort's spiritual way of thinking is bound up with his constant pondering of Scripture.

e. The Secret of the Rosary. The composition of this work is not as original as that of his other books, and it contains fewer Scripture quotations. He uses them as a basis for assertions or in an allusive way. No one particular passage, however, is specially commented on or highlighted. Biblical references are notably more numerous when he considers the fifth decade, which is said to be "his own composition." His reflections on this decade contain 26 quotations out of a total of about 35 in the whole book, and he repeats the quotations referring to Wisdom that he has used frequently in other works: Jas 1:6 (SR 142; LEW 185; FC 45) and Wis 7:14 (SR 146; LEW 62, 64; FC 45).

f. The Book of Sermons. What we have just said about the composition of SR does not apply to LS. The book does not report what Montfort definitely preached, but it is an important document all the same. It gives us an idea of the environment in which Montfort developed his talents as a preacher. It tells us what sort of preaching was given in his days, what subjects were dealt with, what doctrine was taught, what points were emphasized, what theology was in current use (the small number of the elect, etc.), the content of the moral exhortations (reasons for which absolution could be delayed or refused, LS 656), how good the devotion or devotions that were then fostered. LS is like a cross section revealing Christian living and pastoral activity in those days.

Many people say that much of LS is not original. Yet he wrote most of the manuscript with his own hand, he arranged the plans of the sermons, he summarized them, added to them in various places, and supplemented them with his own ideas.[66] He had made a mental note of the important points in Fr. Leschassier's lectures. Reading through the book, one realizes what Montfort was exposed to in the way of theology and pastoral care during the hidden years at Saint-Sulpice, when he was preparing for the ministry that he was hoping to exercise,[67] and also during the years of his hectic missionary life, as several of the summaries and plans were written after 1705 or 1708, and others in the last years of his life.[68] In RM 60 Montfort writes: *"The preaching of God's word is the most far-reaching, the most effective and also the most difficult ministry of all."* In RM 35, 78, he invites the missionaries to prepare for preaching by study and prayer. What he suggests to others he had practiced in an exemplary way.

LS tells us how his mind was shaped, what thoughts flashed through it that he thought necessary to put down in writing so as to ponder on them while doing the demanding work of summarizing. For want of space, we cannot analyze the book in detail, but it would be fascinating to compare the summaries with the originals[69] and find out how Montfort's mind was working, what caught his attention, what he left aside and included or added. This would give us an inkling of how far his theological knowledge and his spiritual and pastoral experience extended.

One thing about the sermons that is blatantly obvious is the large number of references to Scripture and the Church Fathers. The passages are quoted mostly in Latin. Does this mean that preachers in those days addressed their audience in Latin? They probably gave their text in Latin, as was the practice before Vatican II, which introduced the vernacular into the liturgy. The Latin passages, however, especially those borrowed from the Church Fathers, with which the faithful were less familiar, were designed for the preachers, rather than for their audience. At the time of the Counter-Reformation, controversy[70] was prevalent, and preachers turned to Scripture and the Church Fathers to support their arguments. Montfort has drawn up long lists of *loca varia Scripturae* (N. 278, 318, 350, 407-408, 489, 612-618, 715-717) and of *testimonia ex Sanctis Patribus* (N. 34-40, 108-109, 149-152, 168, 192, etc.), all of them in Latin. The reason for this was that in order to give convincing proof, preachers needed to have the original text, or at least the Latin version, at hand. Besides, Montfort was aware that in controversies between him and the heretics, even *"the oldest French versions or the Vulgate"* were not authoritative enough, and he had *"to turn to the Greek text, which is the most reliable"* (N 366).

This, at any rate, shows that Montfort was aware of the theological debates taking place in his days. It also accounts for the natural ease with which he could use Scripture quotations in his works, as a man of his time during the Counter-Reformation, and as a preacher of parish missions, rather than as an exegete. Scripture had been familiar to him for a long time and he had assimilated it so thoroughly that by osmosis, as it were, it had become for him a natural means of expression.

III. Conclusion

Reading Montfort's works carefully, one finds that they are biblical all through. He refers to Scripture constantly and in many different ways. Sometimes he studies a whole book, for example, the Book of Wisdom. Sometimes he makes systematic syntheses, on the theme of Wisdom, for example, or on the role of Mary in the economy of salvation; these syntheses belonged to biblical theology even before it was known by that name. Sometimes he comments on, or paraphrases at length, specific passages, for example, Mt 16:24 in FC, Gen 27 in TD, or Psalm 67 in PM. At other times he puts forward arguments that he supports with a series of quotations, or he simply lets his prayer flow with the words of Scripture, as he frequently does with the Psalms.

His many quotations are not ineffective. A quotation refers to somebody else for confirmation or support, or simply to insert the text into a larger tradition. Authority, *auctoritates,* was the word used in the Middle Ages. The force given by *auctoritates* was due to the holy teachers quoted: their arguments were authoritative. Their names enjoyed more prestige than their words. The author of a quotation was more important than the quotation itself. Whenever Montfort quoted Scripture, something similar happened. The Holy Spirit was speaking[71] through the quotations. Montfort only needed to quote the first few words, and the Spirit took over, so much so that Montfort sometimes does not trouble to complete a quotation but leaves it unfinished and just adds "etc,"[72] as if the actual words hardly mattered. It may have been the case when he quoted Latin texts—Latin being a sacred language—to people who had no knowledge of Latin.[73]

The essence of a quotation is that it refers to somebody else, or in the case of Scripture, to Another. It enables him to express himself. This is noticeable in Montfort's work when, without adding any comment or anything else, he allows Scripture to speak for itself without mingling his poor word with those of the Spirit or of Wisdom (LEW 3-4; 20-28; 48-49; 191-192, the whole of ch. 12). The secret work that takes place is a particular characteristic of theological Christian speech, which, in the last analysis, is only reference to Somebody else. It is based on Somebody and on texts expressing His mystery. This was the view taken by patristic exegesis. Montfort's work, which is a long treatise on the Bible, belongs to the same tradition.

If he reads Scripture in a spiritual way, uses and adapts it, it is because he, too, firmly believes that "all Scripture is inspired by God and is useful for teaching, for reproof, for correction and for training in righteousness" (2 Tim 3:16). He rereads Scripture and rewrites it in order to live it out and bring others to do the same. This "editorial" work on the vast corpus of Scripture is theological in the full sense of the term. It belongs to the order of the understanding of the faith. The Jewish exegetes, for whom the text was a living reality, also reread and rewrote the texts. The practice has been a long-standing tradition among Christian exegetes, and the spiritual writers in particular gave it a new impetus. It is in this perspective that Montfort's biblical style becomes perfectly clear.

J.P. Michaud

Notes: (l) It was not until November 9, 1592, however, after all sorts of incidents in which Robert Bellarmine played a leading part, that Clement VIII finally promulgated the revised version, which was called the "Sixto-Clementine" Vulgate. (2) On this subject, see Guy Bedouelle and Bernard Roussel, *L'Écriture et ses traductions. Eloge et réticences (Scripture and Its Translations: Praise and Reticence),* in *Le temps des Réformes et la Bible (The Era of the Reforms and the Bible),* Bible de tous les temps 5, Beauchesne Paris 1989, 463-486, especially 468-476. For the history of the *Index* and of the versions in the vernacular, see Boudinhou, *La nouvelle législation de l'Index (The New Legislation on the Index),* Lethielleux, Paris 1925, 104-111. (3) On this subject, we strongly advise reading an important article by Bernard Chédozeau, *Les distributions de livres aux nouveaux convertis (1685-1687) et leurs incidences sur le status du laïc catholique (The Distribution of Books to New Converts [1685-1687] and Their Influence on the Status of the Lay Catholic),* in *XVIIème siècle,* 154 (1987), 39-51 (4) Cf. *Concilium Tridentinum,* Herder, Freiburg im Breisgau 1911, 5:75. See the commentary by Guy Redouelle in *La Réforme catholique (The Catholic Reform),* in *Le temps des Réformes,* 344-346. (5) Rev. Father Lamy, preface to *Introduction a l'Écriture Sainte (Introduction to Holy Scripture),* Jean Certe, Lyon 1699, 2-3. (6) Presentation by Mgr. Henri Frehen, Documents et recherches 5, Centre International Montfortain, 1983. (7) On some occasions, his biographers point out, he explained the Gospel of the day, cf. Besnard, IV, 213; V, 59. (8) *"Contra unanimem consensum Patrum."* Cf. DS 1507, or G. Dumeige, *La foi catholique (The Catholic Faith),* Publications de l'Orante 154, Paris 1969. (9) Lamy, preface to *Introduction a l'Écriture Sainte,* 2. (10) L. Le Crom, *Un apôtre marial: Saint Louis-Marie Grignion de Montfort (An Apostle of Mary),* Les traditions françaises, Tourcoing 1946, 73. (11) Letter dated 28 May 1702 to Mr. Edge Pirot, doctor at the Sorbonne, who had been censor of *Histoire critique.* Cf. Ch. Urbain and E. Levesque, *Correspondence de Bossuet (Correpondence of Bossuet),* Hachette, Paris, reprinted by Kraus Reprint Ltd., 1965, 13:334. (12) Paul Auvray, *Richard Simon (1638-1712). Étude bio-bibliographique (Richard Simon [1638-1712]: Bio-bibliographic Study),* Presses universitaires de France, Paris 1974, 176. (13) Cf. Bossuet, *Oeuvres completes,* published by F. Lachat, Louis Vives, Paris 1862, 4:viii-xii passim. (14) Jean Steinman, *Richard Simon et les origines de l'exégèse biblique (Richard Simon and the Origins of Biblical Exegesis),* Desclee de Brouwer, Paris 1960, 417. P. Auvray, *Richard Simon (1638-1712),* 174-177, gives a more qualified though similar opinion. (15) Cf. Bossuet, *Oeuvres completes,* 1863, 3:379-381. (16) *Les dernières années de Bossuet. Journal de Ledieu (The Last Years of Bossuet: Ledieu's Journal),* Desclee de Brouwer, Paris 1928, 1:310-311, 322. (17) Letter 12, dated autumn 1702, appears to have been sent from Poitiers: Montfort mentions his recent journey to Paris. (18) Le Crom, *Un apôtre marial,* 66. (19) J. Grandet, *La vie de Messire Louis-Marie Grignion de Montfort (The Life of M. Louis-Marie Grignion de Montfort),* N. Verger, Nantes 1724, 14. (20) Le Crom, *Un apôtre marial,* 74. (21) Simon makes the meaning clear in the preface to *Histoire critique du Texte du Nouveau Testament (Critical History of the Text of the New Testament),* Rotterdam 1689 (Minerva, Frankfurt 1968): "This work, which requires an accurate knowledge of the [Sacred] Books and a thorough research into the manuscript copies, is called Critique because one has to determine the best lessons to be kept in the text." Simon constantly refers in the preface to this "artistic term," making it clear against his adversaries that "the purpose of those practicing this art is not to destroy but to establish." (22) Bossuet, *Dissertation sur Grotius (Disseration on Grotius),* in *Oeuvres complètes,* 1863, 3:492. (23) In the preface to *Genèse (Genesis)* (1682), in order to determine the right measure of the spiritual or prophetic meaning, Le Maistre de Sacy writes, "We can compare it to a harp. . . . Similarly, not everything in Sacred Scripture is a type or a prophecy; however, the most insignificant things serve to join or link the most significant, which are prophetic and mysterious," quoted by Herve Savon, *Le figurisme et la "Tradition des Pères" (Figurism and the "Tradition of the Fathers"),* in *Le Grand Siècle et la Bible (The Great Century and the Bible),* Bible de tous les temps 6, 767. Cf. Saint Augustine, Contra Faustum, 22, 94. (24) J.-J. Duguet (attributed), *Règles pour l'intelligence des Stes Écritures (Rules for the Understanding of the Holy Scriptures),* Jacques Estienne, Paris 1716. This small book had a far-reaching influence. It was practically repeated in *Discours préliminaire, ou Introduction a l'intelligence des divines écritures (Preliminary Discourse, or Introduction to the Understanding of the Divine Scriptures),* which is found at the beginning of the new edition of *Sainte Bible contenant l'Ancien et le Nouveau Testament traduite en français sur la Vulgate par Monsieur Le Maistre de Saci, avec de courtes Notes pour l'intelligence du Sens littéral & prophétique (The Holy Bible, Containing the Old and the New Testament, Translated into French from the Vulgate by M. de Saci, with Brief Notes for the Understanding of the Literal and Prophetic Sense),* Guillaume Desprez, Paris 1759. (25) For the study of the four meanings, it is necessary to refer to the four-volume fundamental work by Henri de Lubac, *Exégèse médiévale (Medieval Exegesis),* Aubier, Paris 1959-1964. (26) Cf. G.

Martelet, *Sacraments, figures et exhortation en 1 Cor 10:1-11 (Sacraments, Figures, and Exhoration in 1 Cor 10:1-11),* in *Recherches de Science Religieuse* 49 (1956), 325-359; 515-559, which clearly brings out the paraenetic dimension, or the concern for "spiritual education," that belongs to the typological reading of Scripture. (27) *Counsels of Light and Love of Saint John of the Cross,* trans. E. Allison Peers, London, Burns and Oates, 1977; *The Ascent of Mount Carmel,* Trans. E. Allison Peers, Garden City, N.Y., Image Books, 1958, 2:22. (28) John of the Cross, *Cantique spirituel (Spiritual Canticle),* 36. (29) John of the Cross, *Montée du Carmel,* 2, 22. (30) Max Huot de Longchamp, *Les mystiques catholiques et la Bible (Catholic Mystics and the Bible),* in *Le temps des Réformes et la Bible,* 596. (31) Jacques Rousse, *Lectio divina,* in *Dictionnaire de Spiritualité (Dictionary of Spirituality)* vol. 9, Beauchesne, Paris 1976, col. 471. (32) Cf. L. Tronson, *Examens particuliers (Particular Examens),* LXVI, Paris 1887, 147. (33) M. Gilbert, *L'exegese spirituelle de Montfort (Montfort's Spiritual Exegesis),* in NRT 104 (1982), 684. After investigating the spiritual tradition of Wisdom for a long time, E. Catta, likewise, states, "No one before Montfort has set up this system, which is, as it were, exclusive . . . on the theme of Wisdom," cf. *Sedes sapientiae,* in *Maria. Études sur la Sainte Vierge (Maria: Studies on the Blessed Virgin),* ed. Hubert du Manoir, Beauchesne, Paris 1961, 4:794. It must be said that Wisdom literature enjoyed some vogue at the end of the seventeenth century (cf. *Dictionnaire de Spiritualité* under *Écriture Sainte et vie spirituelle,* col. 229: *Godeau,* and 237: *Bossuet;* and *France,* col. 918), but the emphasis was moralizing rather than spiritual. (34) Montfort quotes four whole chapters from the *Book of Wisdom*—ch. 6 in the introduction or preliminary observations LEW 3-4; ch. 10 in LEW 48-49; ch. 8 in LEW 53-61; and ch. 9 in LEW 191-192—and quotes the book about 150 times altogether. (35) Cf. M. Gilbert, *La Sagesse de Salomon, (The Wisdom of Solomon)* in *Les Psaumes et les autres écrits (The Psalms and Other Writings),* Ancien Testament 5, Desclee, Paris 1990, 331. (36) Montfort adopted the numbering used in the Vulgate. We give in brackets the number given in the Septuagint, in line with most modern editions of the Bible. (37) The term *"utterance,"* which belongs to the prophetic tradition, sounds strange in a sapiential context. We note the suggestion put forward by M. Gilbert, *L'exegese spirituelle de Montfort,* 686, who found that "utterance" could mean "burden" and was used in this sense in several prophetic texts (cf. Isa 13:1; 15:1; 17:1; 19:1, and especially Jer 23:33-40, which hinges on the double meaning of the Hebrew term *massa.* Now, "burden" can also refer to the instruction the sages give to their followers (Sir 6:25; 51:26). This would make it permissible to interpret in a sapiential perspective the words of Jesus in Mt 11:28-30: "My yoke is easy and my burden is light." Even though Montfort had not realized all the implications, it is permissible to interpret the word "utterance" in this sense. (38) OC carries a picture of it on p. 326. (39) Cf. GA, 501-503. (40) See Jean-Noel Aletti, *Sagesse, Nouveau Testament (Wisdom, NT),* in *Dictionnaire de Spiritualité* 14 (1990), col. 91-96. (41) It is the same Spirit that speaks in the Old Testament (LEW 5, 16, 48, 50, 52, 62, 63, 72, 88, 90, 190, 202) and in the New (LEW 13, 184, 194, 201). Similarly, it is Wisdom that expresses herself in one part of Scripture (LEW 6, 18, 20, 65, 66, 95, 179) as in the other (LEW 6, 70, 95, 153, 170, 173, 174, 184, 189, 195). (42) Olivier Maire, *Bible et mystique. Une lecture de l'Amour de la Sagesse éternelle de Saint Louis-Marie Grignion de Montfort (Bible and Mysticism: A Reading of the Love of Eternal Wisdom),* unpublished dissertation submitted for a diploma of licentiate in theology at Centre Sèvres, Paris, March 1989, 54. (43) This is the definition of the mystical experience by J. Maritain in *Les degrés du savoir,* Desclée de Brouwer, Paris 1946, 489. *The Degrees of Knowledge,* New York, Scribner 1938 (44) M. Gilbert, *L'exegese spirituelle de Montfort,* 683, n. 13: "Wis 8:2 is quoted explicitly in LEW 169, but it is adapted, and this is a rare occurrence in the book; the same passage is quoted again in LEW 183, and an explanation of the literal meaning is then given." (45) On this subject, see the brief and accurate article by Dom B. Capelle, *Les épîtres sapientiales des fêtes de la Vierge (The Sapiential Epistles of the Feasts of the Virgin),* in *Questions liturgiques et paroissiales* 27 (1946), 42-49. (46) *"'I love those who love me.' That is what Jesus and Mary say to us."* (47) The Marian interpretation of Sir 24:13 is repeated and expanded on in TD 29, 31, 34, 201, and in SM 15. Modern exegesis retains this interpretation, as shown by an article by M. Gilbert, *Lecture mariale et ecclesiale de Siracide 24:10 (15) (Marian and Ecclesial Reading of Siracide 24:10),* in *Marianum* 47 (1985), 536-542. (48) Cf. the use of "I" in LEW 1-2, 5, 7, 14, 19, 42-44, 88, 128, 167, 193, 202, 207, 215, 216. (49) This is expressed clearly in TD 112 and 114. (50) In the sense that it is a particular application of the Gospel spirituality. Each authentic spirituality emphasizes one particular aspect of the Gospel spirituality. This emphasized aspect is only a reference point on the basis of which the whole of the Gospel is to be lived out. Cf. *Spiritualité (Spirituality), Dictionnaire de Spiritualité* 14 (1990), col. 1152. In this connection, Montfort raises an interesting point when he identifies the Kingdom of God with Eternal Wisdom:

"For myself, I know of no better way of establishing the kingdom of God, Eternal Wisdom" (LEW 193). (51) Comparing the corresponding passages makes it evident that SM is a summary of TD. The large number of ellipses at the end of the numbers in SR (cf. 2, 3, 15, 19, 20, 36, 42, 46, 47, 48, 51, 53, 55, 57, 60, 62, 63, 64, 65) seems to confirm this. (52) In the book *Dieu seul est ma tendresse (God Alone Is My Tenderness),* O.E.I.L., Paris 1984, R. Laurentin speaks of "the small place that the spiritual motherhood holds in Montfort's writings" and of his "extreme reticence" on the subject (165-166). Montfort's reticence appears justified by the desire not to invite criticism from his adversaries. His many quotations in support of spiritual motherhood, which is essentially linked to giving birth to Christ, Head of the Mystical Body, seem to conflict with the idea of extreme reticence. (53) An explanation has been given recently by I. de la Potterie in *Marie dans le Mystère de l'Alliance (Mary in the Mystery of the Covenant),* Jésus et Jésus-Christ 34, Desclee, Paris 1985, 237-257. (54) In *GA.* it occurs only once and is not commented on in HD 36, 1781, p. 578. But the text was not written by Montfort. (55) Cf. I. de la Potterie, op. cit., p. 246-247. (56) I. de la Potterie, *Marie dans le Mystère de l'Alliance,* 250 *(Mary in the Mystery of the Covenant),* trans. Bertrand Buby, Staten Island, New York; Alba House, 1992. (57) Yet, further down, Esau's clothes are transferred to Jesus Christ (TD 206)! And Esau's good odor is that of Jesus Christ and his Blessed Mother (TD 207)! Are we entitled to assume that Montfort attributed unawares a double role to Esau? He was under no self-delusion, and his answer would probably be that a spiritual interpretation of the Bible allowed him to read into it more than a logical literal interpretation could provide. (58) Cf . TD 26, 40, 41: "The types and texts of the Old and New Testaments prove the truth of this . . . the many passages which I have collected from the Fathers and Doctors of the Church in support of this truth"; TD 130, 131, 141: *"Here are a few passages from the Fathers of the Church which I have chosen to prove what I have just said."* Thus the quotations from Scripture come afterwards and are used as proof. (59) Cf. P.L. Nava, *Il trittico monfortano: natura ed ermeneutica (The Montfort Triptych: Nature and Hermeneutic),* in QM 1 (1983) 110-111, 130. (60) PM 6, addressed to Jesus and acting as a link, is based on Ps 73:2 and serves to introduce Gen 30:1 (61) The *"bodyguard of handpicked men"* (PM 30), which with others is to make up the *"army drawn up in lines of battle"* mentioned in PM 29. What is more, all the vocabulary in PM 29 belongs to the military register: *"fight," "standard," "army drawn up in lines of battle," "attack," "sounded the call to arms."* (62) Cf. PM 14, in which he ascribes Ps 117:17 to *"another of your prophets";* for Ps 67 cf. also *"your prophet"* in PM 19. (63) J. Nouet, *L'homme d'oraison. Ses méditations pour tous les jours de l'année (The Man of Prayer: His Meditations for All the Days of the Year),* Paris 1866, 7:60-67. (64) L. Perouas thinks it was written four years after the order, issued in September 1709, to destroy the Calvary at Pontchâteau. The text is marked by moderation and prudence, indicating maturity, and this would make 1713 a likely date. Cf. L. Perouas, *Grignion de Montfort, Un aventurier de l'Évangile (Grignion de Montfort, An Adventurer of the Gospel),* Les editions ouvrieres, Paris 1990, 75. (65) Particularly M. Boudon, *Les saintes voies de la croix (The Holy Ways of the Cross),* 1671. (66) Cf. the passages mentioned by Frehen into which Montfort introduced his own ideas: p. 9, 12, 24, 28, 118; and the themes dealt with in his works: p. 9, 16, 28, 112. (67) Blain, 106, tells us that Montfort spent the period between his ordination on 6 June 1700 and his departure for the mission directed by Fr. Leveque at Nantes towards September of the same year "compiling and preparing material for sermons and collecting enough to enable him to preach on all sorts of subjects at any time, as he did later on." (68) Several outlines of sermons contained in the second part of the manuscript, which lists the subjects in alphabetical order, were probably written after 1705 or 1708. In this part, Montfort summarized a sermon by Massillon that was not published until 1705 or 1708 (cf. Frehen, viii) and one by Bourdaloue that was published towards 1707 (cf. Frehen, viii and 9, note b). All the signs are that Montfort wrote part 1 towards the end of his life (cf. Frehen, ii: "The various parts of the manuscript were not arranged chronologically: the second part was written first, whereas parts 2 and 3, which show identical features, were written in the last years of the missionary's life"). (69) The names of several authors whose works he summarized (J. Biroat, T. Cheminais de Montaigu, De la Volpilière, C. Joly, J. Lejeune, J. Loriot, C. Texier) are given in J.-P. Migne, *Collection intégrale et universelle des Orateurs Sacrés (Complete and Universal Collection of the Holy Orators),* Paris 1844-1866 . (70) Cf . LS 360-370, *méthodes pour convertir les heretiques.* Reference is made to the *"four Church Fathers whom they (the heretics) recognize and whose confession of faith they profess to follow"* (S 366), and also to *"the holy Church Fathers whose teaching they accept"* (S 367). (71) Cf. TD 18, 32, 34, 46, 68, 183; LEW 13, 16, 48, 50, 52, 62, 63, 88, 184, 190, 194, 201, . . . (72) Cf. LEW 173; TD 196, 248, 271, and, though this may look strange, in PM 5, 14. (73) Cf. LEW 6, 35, 99, 118, 173, 227; TD 70, 114, 173, 226; FC 4, SM 56.

BROTHERS OF SAINT GABRIEL

I. LOUIS MARIE DE MONTFORT, ACCOMPANIED BY A FEW BROTHERS

"Louis Marie de Montfort Grignion": such is the signature of the Apostolic Missionary affixed at the end of the Will he had just dictated to Fr. Mulot on April 27, 1716. *"I confide to His Lordship the Bishop of La Rochelle and to Fr. Mulot my small pieces of furniture and my mission books, to be preserved for the use of the four Brothers who joined me in a life of obedience and poverty"* (W).

1. A few companions

Throughout Montfort's missionary life, there are Brothers who accompanied him. Paradoxically, he searched for priests to continue his parish missions but, instead, found Brothers.

a. "The well-known Brother Mathurin."[1] In 1705 a young man named Mathurin arrived in Poitiers, hoping to become a Capuchin. He entered the Church of the Penitents to pray. Montfort happened to be present and gestured to him to approach. On learning Mathurin's plans for the future, Montfort invited him to remain and serve with him in the parish missions. The language Montfort used was that of the Savior calling the Apostles, 'Follow me,' and "at once this good man obeyed."[2] Mathurin joined Montfort in the parish missions and collaborated with him. Responding to a friend's request for aid, Montfort wrote: *"I will send Mathurin to you on Tuesday to say the Rosary publicly, to sing hymns, and to bring to our soldiers sixty small crosses of St. Michael"* (L 21). Mathurin became the missionary's faithful "traveling companion."

b. Brother Nicholas. The experiences of "this young man who accompanied Montfort on his travels" was similar to those of Mathurin. On January 29, 1711, Montfort wrote to Father de la Carrière, a priest of Pontchâteau: *"Please give my statues to the bearer of this letter and to Brother Nicholas. It is necessary to move them, both to relieve me of anxiety and to show obedience because it is God's will"* (L 22).

Nicholas was even obliged to give Father de Montfort the discipline. He struck him so hard that with each blow Montfort's shoulders bowed and he moaned as though it were in spite of himself that he was being struck. When questioned about it, Brother admitted that it was only on this condition that Montfort would accept him in his service."[3]

c. Brother John. Brother John was Montfort's confidant, "always ready to do anything he was asked." In 1715, Montfort wrote to Marie Louise and Catherine Brunet: *"The Bishop of La Rochelle to whom I have spoken about you and our plans thinks you should come here to begin the work we want so much. I will send you Brother John with a horse and some money to accompany you."* Shortly after, on April 4, he wrote, *"Send me news by Brother John if you cannot manage to come here yourselves"* (L 27, 29).

d. Brother James. This Brother appeared on the scene in the last two years of Montfort's life. The mission at Saint-Pompain began in December 1715, during a harsh winter. Nevertheless, each day before dawn Brother James ran through the icy streets of town summoning everyone to prayer: *"Arise, dear brother, come, my friend, / Let us arise before the sun, / God calls us to his festival, / The mission has begun. / So, be there ice, or be there snow, / To gain God's grace, to church we'll go"* (H 163).

"During the twenty-three months that I had the happiness of living with Father de Montfort, despite his travels and his occupations, I never once saw him pass a single day without saying Mass. He celebrated it with so much piety and such great devotion that he communicated this devotion to all in attendance."[4] Such was the testimony of Brother James, who, according to the parish chronicles, continued after Montfort's death to lead the Confraternity of the White Penitents and to teach in the grade school at Saint-Laurent.

2. Inheritors

In 1715 Father Mulot, the pastor of Saint-Pompain "a very zealous man of means," having planned for some time to hold a mission in his parish, chose Father de Montfort to preach it. The Brothers inherited a double function: helping in the parish mission itself and being of service to the parishioners. The apostolate of the Brothers is described in the following paragraphs.

The parish retreat was accompanied by catechism instruction (cf. RM), the singing of hymns, the recitation of the Rosary, and the organization of processions.

Charitable schools were founded only during Montfort's last years and within the framework of the pastoral options of the diocese of La Rochelle. Montfort's Will mentions this specifically: *"My few belongings and the mission books, that they preserve them for the use of these four Brothers . . . and for those whom Divine Providence will call to the same Community of the Holy*

Spirit." The Brothers also received a little house given by a kind woman on condition that "if there are no means of building here, one will provide for the Brothers of the Community of the Holy Spirit who teach in the charitable schools; all the furnishings that are at Nantes will be for the use of the Brothers who maintain the school as long as it exists."[5]

But if these charitable schools subscribed to a movement already begun by Jean Baptist de la Salle at Rheims, Paris, and Rouen, they cannot be divested of the missionary perspective that was proper to them and that did not appear in the work of Father de la Salle. "Father de Montfort's main preoccupation during the course of his missions was to establish schools for the boys and for the girls."[6] The teacher led them to Mass singing hymns; one student intoned the first verse and the others joined in. . . . Every day after class they recited five decades of the Rosary in honor of the Blessed Virgin."[7]

The Brothers are inheritors of the Montfort spirit. Hence, in no way were they merely temporary associates; they are rightly part of Montfort's family. Nor were they "Coadjutor Brothers," as found in the Society of Jesus or in Vincent de Paul's Priests of the Mission. Still less were they lay Brothers charged with only material concerns.

In this, Montfort seems to have forged ahead of his times. If he made the Brothers "heirs," was it not because in his missionary wisdom he felt them participants in his own experience? Besnard informs us that around the feast of Pentecost in 1715, after the mission of St. Armand, Montfort was exhausted and left for a few days rest at La Seguinière. As usual, "a few Brothers accompanied him." Ten months later he made the "holy pilgrimage to Our Lady of Saumur, to obtain from God good missionaries for his proposed Company of Mary." On the way he asked "two of the Brothers who accompanied him" to greet his sister at the convent of Fontevrault.[8]

With time his companions understood the desires of their "teacher" and "father." They began to realize how reciting the Rosary and singing hymns had made them instruments of conversion, even more, agents of conversion. Traveling with him, they gradually perceived the depth of his life for "God Alone."

Little can be said about his "companions" whom he made his "heirs," since the ecclesiastical mentality of the day paid little account to the category of "Brother." One need only recall the difficulties faced by Father de la Salle with the Brothers of the Christian schools.[9] Whether there existed a Rule or specific regulations for the Montfort Brothers remains another question, with the probability that a text did exist. In support of this hypothesis is Montfort's refusal of Communion to Brother Nicholas because he had not observed the rule regarding the nightly schedule.[10]

3. Brothers to care for temporal needs and to teach school

a. "Lay Brothers". Their presence is noted in RM, in a context that excludes the teaching of youth: *"Only priests who have been formed in seminaries are received into this Company . . . . Priests called by God to give missions in the footsteps of the poor apostles and not to be vicars, or to administer a* *parish, teach children or form priests in seminaries. . . . However, lay Brothers are admitted to take care of temporal affairs provided they are detached, robust, and obedient, ready to do all they are told to do. . . . Priests and Brothers alike must not accept even simple benefices and temporal possessions, even those they inherit"*[11] (RM 1-2, 4-5).

b. "To take care of temporal affairs". A typical case is that of Brother Peter at the mission of Vertou (1708), who was responsible for the missionaries' kitchen: "I command you to get up in an hour from now and come, serve us at table," which order of Louis Marie was carried out. "The Lord cured me." In the course of the mission of Montfort-la-Cane, mention is also made of the Brother-cook, who received the order to distribute food to nearly sixty poor people.[12] Grandet mentions several times the manager of the store: "rosaries, medals, booklets, instruments of penance . . . all this merchandise is in great demand"; he speaks also of small 'commodities'. Nor may the care of the mule and wagon be ignored. Was it not a Brother who fled with the receipts from the shop?[13]

c. Brothers teaching catechism and responsible for the activities of the mission. Some of these Brothers, having for their guide *"The Rules for Catechetical Instruction"* (cf. RM 79-91), also sang hymns, had the Rosary recited according to Montfort's method, and skillfully organized processions. These Brothers were entirely a part of his missionary enterprise. He consulted with them about the material organization, and he followed their advice "to the prejudice of his own." He shared with them, as with his priest-collaborators, "the collars and the clothing received."[14]

Then, in his boldness, Montfort daringly proposed to his Brothers that they "bind themselves by vows of obedience and poverty, regardless of the ministry they exercised, without discrimination." At Poitiers, Brother Nicholas learned the art of sculpting, Brother Gabriel assisted with the parish missions, and Brother Philip of Nantes and Brother Louis de La Rochelle ministered in the charitable schools. Although Montfort felt his health dwindling, it mattered little; he continued to "venture," even if he left behind but unfinished projects.

The Brothers were fully integrated in the Montfort community of Saint-Laurent and lived voluntary poverty there. Meals were very frugal; all except bread was lacking. Madame de Bouille wanted Father Mulot to train some Brothers at Holy Spirit (the name of the motherhouse at Saint-Laurent) and send them out to teach and catechize children in various parishes.[15]

II. The Brothers of Christian Instruction of Saint Gabriel, Formerly Called of the Holy Spirit.

On February 19, 1910, the Sacred Congregation of Religious signed the "Decree of Apostolic Approbation of the Brothers of Christian Instruction of St. Gabriel." In the summary of the Approbation, approved by Pope Pius X, we read: "The Brothers of Christian Instruction, formerly called of the Holy Spirit, whose motherhouse is in the diocese of Luçon, have for father, and invoke as such, Blessed Louis Marie Grignion de Montfort."

1. Brothers of the Community of the Holy Spirit

During the eighteenth century the life of the Community of the Holy

Spirit (the Company of Mary) was centered at Saint-Laurent. Research reveals the names of thirty-five Brothers and nearly fifty missionary priests who lived there. More helpful than names lifted from registers or enshrined in memories is knowledge about the services they rendered and the ministries they performed.

a. Brothers always ready to do whatever they were told to do. Complementary ministries demonstrated the originality of the Community of the Holy Spirit, and each had its prototype.

Brother Joseau had a ministry to the charitable schools. René Joseau, professed in 1722, whose ministry was "opening schools for the young and caring for the sick." Marie Louise of Jesus, whose confidant he was, said, "He has the spirit of God." He was the prototype of the first teaching Brothers. His reasons for becoming a Brother are revealing: "Because those at Saint-Laurent are poor. I wish to live like the poor, offering my small services to the poor who work for the glory of God and the salvation of souls."[16] His major ministry was in the charitable schools. Madame de Bouille encouraged R. Mulot, "faithful imitator of the well-known Montfort" to continue the schools of La Rochelle. To safeguard the unity of his young community, Mulot dared erase from a new edition of the Rule (1728) the adjective "vigorous" from the qualities necessary in a candidate for the Brothers. More importantly, he suppressed the prohibition "to teach youth" from the goals of the Company.[17] To preserve the memory of Montfort, whom he had not known, Joseau devised a souvenir notebook. "These are good things that could be used to write a new biography of the man of God," noted Sr. Florence, author of *The Chronicles of the Daughters of Wisdom.* When Brother Joseau died on May 2, 1755, his successor, Brother Joseph Metayer, had been prepared to take over his work. This ministry often included religious instruction as well as teaching in the schools.[18]

Brother Mathurin had a ministry of catechizing during the parish missions. The renowned Brother Mathurin participated in many missions during the span of fifty-five years, first as Montfort's companion from 1705 to 1716, then until 1755 with Montfort's successors. Thanks to the memoirs of Father Hacquet, the extent of this ministry is easily seen: of the 276 missions preached from 1749 to 1799, one or two Brothers participated in 250 of them with the missionaries. After Mathurin died, his successor was ready, for Brother Guerin had already practiced teaching in the schools for children, teaching catechism and singing hymns in church.[19]

b. The Brothers' "missionary memory" of Montfort. Whatever the service performed, the Brothers lived in the footsteps of their father, a life of faith that withstood all trials. "It was by faith that Montfort procured the conversion of so many sinners, that he loved the poor, and rejoiced in bearing the Cross." Some Brothers worked at preserving the texts of Louis Marie, such as Brother James, who copied the letter entitled *Secret of Mary and 15 Beautiful Meditations on the Blessed Virgin.* The wear and tear of time, however, has erased many specific details of their community life.

When in 1790 the dark clouds of the French Revolution arrived, there were eight Brothers in the motherhouse. Three Brothers, two of whom were thirty years old, were executed on the spot in February 1794, and three others were shot a few days later. "They can be considered martyrs, since they were massacred because of hatred for religion." They were joined in the holocaust by two missionary priests and at least twenty sisters.[20]

2. Gabriel Deshayes, the providential man[21]

In 1820, under the combined effects of the French Revolution and the politico-religious situation of the Napoleonic regime, the members of the Community of the Holy Spirit could be counted on the fingers of both hands—five or six priests and four Brothers, three for temporal needs and one for the charitable schools.

a. Gabriel Deshayes was "a man of the moment," extremely sensitive to the immense needs of his contemporaries, especially the poor. In his zeal he used every possible legitimate means to achieve his goals. "I do good; so much the worse for those who undo it!" At the age of twenty-five, he risked his life for God and souls by receiving abroad priestly ordination from the hands of a self-exiled bishop who had refused submission to the atheistic government of France. When Fr. Deshayes wanted something for God's glory, he sacrificed everything to achieve it. And he did everything possible to revive the almost defunct Community of the Holy Spirit. When he had completed his task, when the Spirit's fire consumed him, there were about twenty missionaries, compared to the four or five at the beginning of his administration; there were 150 Brothers, compared to four when he was elected; and 1700 Daughters of Wisdom, compared to 750.

b. Brothers of Christian Instruction of the Holy Spirit. Since 1824 there had been forty-two religious professions. These Brothers literally overflowed the Montfort motherhouse. And Father Gabriel Deshayes obtained official approbation for them under the name of Brothers of Christian Instruction of the Holy Spirit. This restored their authorization to teach. In addition, the formation of the Brothers was entrusted to some among themselves, all fresh from their own formation. Then he drew up for them Directories, Rules of Conduct, and sent them out into the parishes at the pastors' request. He even constructed new quarters for them. Further, on October 15, 1835, he had thirty-three of them leave the House of the Holy Spirit for the "Supiot House," which was promptly renamed "Saint Gabriel" to honor his patron saint. While he, Deshayes, remained the superior, Brothers Augustin and Simeon became directors of the young group. "In multiplying the Brothers I have simply realized the plans of Venerable de Montfort": this was the superior's response to the concern of a Daughter of Wisdom.

c. "My confreres, the Missionaries of the Holy Spirit, the Brothers of all the Congregations."[22] Brother Simeon, at the end of December 1843, remained secretary to Father Deshayes, even though Brother Simeon now lived at Saint Gabriel. He wrote the Will that was dictated to him by Fr. Deshayes: "I recommend myself in a special manner to the prayers of my confreres, the Missionaries of the Holy Spirit, the Brothers of all the Congregations, as well as to those of the Sisters and their students, especially the deaf-mutes. I recommend in a special way the matter of our holy Founder's beatification. As all the congregations are of equal interest to me, I beg them to be well united and to give each other mutual support."

3. Our founder

a. "A Brother, superior of Brothers". A reading of the official correspondence between Gabriel Deshayes and the civil administration makes it clear that he set himself up as a founder. "When I was curate at Auray, I was successful in forming a community of Brothers of the Christian Schools [of Ploermel]. This work prospered beyond my wildest dreams. Called to govern the Daughters of Wisdom, I relinquished the government of my Brothers to Father de Lammenais.... I brought six of the Brothers with me to form a core group at Saint-Laurent."[23] If the Rule of 1830 foresaw that the superior of the Missionaries would always be their superior, the Rule of 1838 stipulated that thenceforth, after the death of Fr. Deshayes, the superior would be a Brother. In 1853 the imperial decree of Napoleon III conferred on the Congregation the title so long desired, Brothers of Christian Instruction of Saint Gabriel.

4. Brothers of Christian Instruction of Saint Gabriel

The approbation of Rome for the Constitutions of the Brothers of Saint Gabriel states: "The general aim of the Brothers of Christian Instruction of Saint Gabriel is to glorify God by working, with the help of His grace, at their personal sanctification through the practice of the three simple vows of poverty, chastity, and obedience, through the True Devotion to the Blessed Virgin, Mother of Divine Grace, and by an exact observance of the Constitutions of their Institute. Their particular aim is to devote themselves to the education and Christian instruction of youth, especially the children of common folk in the primary schools. They are also engaged in the education of deaf and/or blind students. The manual works of the Institute are confided as much as possible to those whom the superiors judge apt to fulfill them. In certain very rare cases determined by the superiors, the Brothers may render to a parish some services related to worship. In their devotions to the patron saint of the Institute, the Brothers are distinguished by a filial love for the Blessed Virgin and by the imitation of their founder's virtues, especially his zeal for the education of young people."[24] A new text was approved by Rome in 1960: "The Brothers will have a special devotion for the mystery of the Incarnation and a particular devotion to the Holy Spirit, under whose name they have been founded. Consecrated to Jesus, Wisdom Incarnate, in and through Mary, they wish to commune with all her mysteries in their spiritual and apostolic life. . . In imitation of the Virgin, who had always been the humble servant of the Lord, and of Wisdom Incarnate, who had always accomplished perfectly the will of the Father, the Brothers delight to live in the spirit of dependence on Jesus and Mary even in the smallest details of daily life. As religious and disciples of

Saint Louis Marie de Montfort, the Brothers must be true friends of the Cross of Jesus."[25]

A dispute of many years between the Company of Mary and the Brothers of St. Gabriel on the precise roles of Father de Montfort and Father Gabriel Deshayes in the founding of the teaching Brothers was brought to an end in January 1968. A letter, signed by the general superiors of the Company of Mary (Cornelius Heiligers) and of the Brothers of Saint Gabriel (Roman Landry) declared: "Impelled by the spirit of unity, of charity, and of ecumenism, the General Councils of our two institutes have decided of common accord to reunite, to put an end in charity and, if possible, in unity to the unfortunate dispute that has separated us for almost eighty years. . . . In the measure in which we assume the ecclesiology of Vatican II, we must put in first place, beyond all historical consideration, the common montfort charism." Pope John Paul II emphasized to the Capitulants in their audience with him on January 5, 1989: "Like Saint Louis Marie during his missions, you must remind the baptized of the grandeur and obligations of their Baptism. You give great importance to the educational projects that you undertake with your lay collaborators . . . including the religious dimension of education and of catechizing. And like your first founder, you are anxious to give Mary her proper place in your apostolic ministry in order that through your action she may raise up disciples and evangelizers, whom the world needs as the twenty-first century dawns."[26]

III. The Spirituality of the Montfort Brothers of Saint Gabriel

"We are Montfort religious. As such, we are called to be disciples of Jesus Christ following in the footsteps of Montfort and to perceive in the Gospel the messages that he grasped, especially in what concerns Jesus Wisdom Incarnate and Mary's role in the economy of salvation." Such is the assertion of the General Chapter (1988-1989) as supreme authority in the Institute.[27] The montfort spirituality of the Brothers of St. Gabriel is expressed within a teaching community; it is manifested in their proper apostolate of forming boys and young men into the fullness of baptismal life.

1. Love of the Rule

The directive given to the earliest Brothers of Christian Instruction was precise: "Love our Holy Rule; esteem it, observe it faithfully everyday." During twenty years, the saintly Gabriel Deshayes led his communities with vigor: "I am sixty-two years old and I can say that I have never doubted Providence, and Providence has never failed me," and "had I but a week to live, I would press forward still."

Despite pressing situations, the spirituality of the Brothers was clarified. "You know, my dear Brothers, the way to obtain faith; it is prayer. Acquire the spirit of prayer; it is the key to heavenly treasures. Pray with the faith of the woman in the Gospel to whom Our Lord said, 'My daughter, your faith has saved you.' Pray with attention, purity of intention, fervor, and always in the name of Jesus, and you will pray well."

"Peace and charity" became the motto that gradually shaped the spirit of the young Congregation. "Let us love and serve Mary." In the Spirit, we come to embody its esprit de corps, family spirit. This spirit is indispensable if one is to be a true member of the community.[28]

2. Modest apostle of the Word Incarnate, servant of Mary

Everything takes time. There was another twenty-year cycle, confided to Brother Eugene-Marie when he was thirty-nine years old—twenty years to daringly open "horizons even more missionary and more evangelical." To sustain the educational mission of the Brothers, he gave spiritual and Christological instructions. "To be a complete Gabrielist, it is necessary that to the virtue of the religious we join the knowledge of the teacher and the enlightened zeal of the catechist. Nevertheless we must not forget that the Congregation must prepare its members to be teachers and catechists. It is not a question of great things today. You need not go far away to find occasions of self-denial. The sacrifice that God asks of you is to live your Rule, immerse yourself in its spirit."[29]

In a new edition of the Constitutions and Common Rules of 1874 it is written: "The spirit of the Brothers must be: towards God, a spirit of faith, of love, and of filial confidence in his divine Providence; toward themselves, a spirit of abnegation, of sacrifice, and of humility; towards their Brothers, a spirit of peace, of simplicity, and of charity that will make the Congregation one family in Our Lord Jesus Christ; towards their superiors, a spirit of filial docility and of respectful submission; towards the children and the Institute, a spirit of zeal and supernatural devotion."

Brother Eugene-Marie one day confided the source of his own spirituality: "Is not Mary proclaimed by the Church Mother of Divine Grace, the mother of all religious, the privileged children of God? This is what he understood, he of whom we are incontestably the grandsons, he whose tomb served as our cradle. I speak of the Venerable de Montfort, one of the apostles of devotion to Mary's maternity of grace and one of the prophets of her present glories in the Church. And was it not our venerated Father Deshayes's intention to have us honor the Infant Jesus and the double maternity of Mary? He gave us as sole mission the instruction of youth, as feast the Annunciation, as special protector Saint Gabriel."[30]

3. Sons of Montfort through the Cross.

"Expect to be pruned, hewed, chiseled under the hammer of the Cross; otherwise you will remain like rough stones which serve no purpose" (FC 28). During the twenty-four years of Brother Martial's generalate, the Congregation lived one of the bitterest seasons it had yet experienced. A simple glance back reveals why: the laws of laicization passed by the French government between 1880 and 1910, the hierarchy's uncertainty about secularized religious, and the deep uneasiness and discomfort of hunted lives, not knowing what risks to take. And then came World War I (1914-1918), menacing to wipe out the new foundations in the mission lands. To live through all this, which is definitely an impoverishment imposed by events and human beings, required a rare faith and the ability to readjust to life from day to day.

"We are in the process of examining our small part in the evangelization of the entire world,"[31] wrote Brother Martial. This meant to leave one's land, face other lifestyles, other climates, other cultures. This meant experiencing Montfort's *"abandonment to Providence"* by taking on a vagabond's role *"to save his poor neighbor."* After North America, where preparations were already made, after Africa, less known, came distant Asia, as far as the door of China. "God has his hour, and if you are still resolved to go to the missions, I announce that we have chosen you."[32] This letter of obedience came in response more than twenty years after the request. It meant leaving with one's meager baggage and, for bedside book, *The Common Observances.* It meant leaving with books that defined the life of a Brother of Saint Gabriel according to all the Roman canonical rigor, little inclined to spiritual consolations. But therein lies a mystery of grace and fidelity. For decades on end, in the ambiance of poverty, these books will be considered sacred. They will energize the life of religious pursued, displaced, but confident in God's time.

4. Heirs of the same past rooted in the first founder

"The providential mission of the Father is the continuous foundation confided to his children." The Spirit, *"deluge of fire, of love and of justice"* is always at work, as Montfort prayed (PM16). The Spirit purifies the inevitable dross of our lives, winnowing through the Gospel our humble daily fidelities and our lassitudes, refining by the Rosary, this "secret of sanctity for our conversion and salvation," so many lives immolated, so much common sanctity *"blessed for eternity!"* It is the Spirit who welcomes new vocations from foreign lands and other cultures. The fruitfullness of the founder can be seen in the concrete works of furure generations, works rooted in the world but which are not of it.[33]

The Spirit is still at work under the impetus of Vatican II, encouraging the Brothers to re-express their spiritual and apostolic motivation and to live it today and tomorrow through all races, peoples, nations, and languages.

J.-B. Rolandeau

Notes: (1) Florence, 130. (2) Grandet, 79. (3) Besnard II, 32-33. (4) Florence, 93. (5) Grandet, 224-225. (6) Grandet, 385. (7) Grandet, 384. (8) Florence, 131. (9) Cf. E. Tisserant, *Louis-Marie Grignion de Montfort, les écoles de Charité et les origines des Frères de Saint-Gabriel,* Pacteau, Luçon 1960, 254-255. (10) Besnard II, 146. (11) Grandet, 374-375. (12) J. Michel, *Claude-François Poullart des Places, fondateur de la Congrégation du Saint-Esprit (1679-1709),* Éditions Saint-Paul, Paris 1962, 218.(13) Grandet, 369. (14) Besnard, *Marie Louise,* 142ff.; cf. also E. Tisserant, *Louis-Marie,* 259. (15) J.-B. Rolandeau, *Pèlerinage aux commencements,* in *Magazine* 2 (1981), 15-38. (16) Florence, 95, 130. (17) Florence, 95. (18) Florence, 74, 77. (19) Florence, 95. (20) Dossier Deshayes, diocesan archives of Poitiers. (21) Dossier Lacombe, diocesan archives of Luçon. (22) J. Dalin, *Vie du vénérable serviteur de Dieu Louis Marie Grignon de Montfort,* Paris 1839, 545. (23) Circular of Brother Augustin, March 10, 1842. (24) Brother Sébastien, *Circulaire* 53, 1934. (25) *Réunion des conseils généraux de la Compagnie de Marie et des Frères de Saint-Gabriel, 23 décembre et 5 janvier 1968,* Tipografia poliglotta vaticana, Vatican City, 4-6. (26) Orientations of the 27th General Chapter, 1989. (27) Brother Eugène-Marie, 1872 *circular letter.* (28) Brother Eugène-Marie, *circular letter* 20, 1868. (29) Constitutions et observances régulières, 1874. (30) Brother Martial, *circular letter* 33, 1912. (31) Brother Martial, letter to Brother Fulgent, August 27, 1900. (32) Constitutions, 1923. (33) Brother Gabriel-Marie, *Esprit de l'Institut.*

CANONIZATION

SUMMARY I. INTRODUCTION.
II. BEATIFICATION AND CANONIZATION OF FATHER DE MONTFORT:
1. First steps;
2. The examination of the writings;
3. The examination of the virtues;
4. The examination of the miracles;
5. Towards beatification;
6. Towards canonization.

I. INTRODUCTION[1]

When speaking of beatification and canonization, it is not surprising or rare to hear from certain quarters remarks such as "Is it really useful to spend so much time and money on the canonization process, especially when the person is already in heaven and is thus without need of it, since it adds nothing to their essential happiness?" In spite of this critique, the Church continues to be responsive to the demands of the faithful by honoring in this way men and women of heroic virtue whom she believes to be models of encouragement for the people of God.

There are many explanations why so many great saints and authentic martyrs have yet to enjoy this great honor. Obviously, God's will offers the single significant reason. It is a fact that a canonization cause does require a great number of people to expend a great deal of money and effort over a long period of time. It also requires a special sensibility on the part of those who are furthering the cause. This partially explains why more religious than diocesan priests, and more priests than lay folk are canonized.

The main purpose of a canonization is not first to glorify a particular person. Rather it is to edify the faithful, who are always in need of new models of holiness. Also, communion with the saints increases and seals the union that exists between the triumphant and pilgrim Church. *Lumen gentium* affirms this: "It is not only through their example that we cherish the memory of those in heaven; rather we seek, by devotion to them, to exercise that bond of fraternal charity which unites and strengthens the whole Church in the Spirit (cf. Eph 4:1-6). Just as Christian charity brings us closer to Christ on our earthly journey, so does the communion of saints join the People of God to Christ, the fountainhead of all grace and life, on their eternal journey" (LG 50).

II. The Beatification and Canonization of Father de Montfort

Louis Marie de Montfort died at Saint Laurent-sur-Sèvre on April 28, 1716. He was beatified on January 22, 1888 and canonized on July 20, 1947, 231 years after his death.

There was a great lapse of time from the evening of April 28, 1716, when Christians spontaneously cried out, "Holy Father de Montfort is dead?" But a universal veneration of Montfort canonized him in anticipation of the event. His very first tombstone, which can be seen at Saint Laurent-sur-Sèvre, states unhesitatingly, "Died in the odor of sanctity." It must be noted also that Bishop de Champflour of La Rochelle on November 12, 1717, allowed the first exhumation of the body. It was found to be intact. In 1718 Bishop de la Poype of Poitiers had innumerable favors of a "miraculous" character attributed to Louis Marie committed to writing.

Why did the canonization of this celebrated missionary take so long? First, we must remember that his followers in the Company of Mary were few in number. Second, we should recall the tormented era in which they worked. The first biography of Montfort, by Grandet, dates from 1724, and the second, by Father de Clorivière, appeared in 1785. The end of the eighteenth century ushered in a period of immense social and religious upheaval.

1. First steps

In 1825, a dynamic, powerful man of many achievements, Father General Gabriel Deshayes, initiated the first preparatory steps of the beatification process. He undertook a long and exhausting pilgrimage to Rome. There he met the Dominican Fathers, who, mindful of the fact that Montfort had been a pious member of their Third Order, agreed to undertake his cause. Having accomplished this, Father Deshayes then met with Father Lamarche, prior of the order, who enjoyed the Holy Father's confidence. He gained from him a promise of full support. He also consulted a canon lawyer, who looked over Montfort's life and recommended that the cause be undertaken.[2]

Upon his return to Saint Laurent, Father Deshayes hastened to report on his consultations and the opinion of the canon lawyer in Rome. The community chose Father Deshayes as the postulator for France, and Father Lamarche as postulator in Rome. From that moment, the cause moved ahead with dispatch.

Bishop Soyer of Luçon established a tribunal composed of vicars-general and other dignitaries from his cathedral. This tribunal met for the first time at Luçon on August 4, 1829. It conducted its work either at Saint Laurent or at Luçon until July 1830 as it sought to establish the moral character and authenticate the miracles of Montfort. The tribunal received the testimony of many witnesses under oath. Among the numerous miracles attested to, four were chosen, and the results of their investigation sent to Rome. At the end of 1830, the Holy Father received the Acts of the process of canonization from two Fathers of the

Company of Mary, Fathers Hillereau and Jean-Baptiste Marchand. To these Acts were added a petition from the bishop of Luçon, twenty other cardinals, as well as archbishops and bishops of France. Their wishes were granted. The cause was entrusted to the Congregation of Rites in 1831.

On September 7, 1838, Pope Gregory XVI issued a decree that accorded to Montfort the title of Venerable, and thus gave his approval for the cause to be pursued.

On August 3, 1839, the "non-cult" process was started. Its goal was to establish that the proper judgement of the Church had in no way been compromised on this matter. The conclusion was favorable.

The success of the cause filled Father Deshayes with joy. And when others remarked to him that their work was going well, he inevitably would respond, "And the Father de Montfort affair is going well too!" Father Deshayes "would not live to see the beatification, but God allowed him to survive long enough to complete the task of postulator. The last official signature is his."[3]

2. The examination of the writings

The Congregation of Rites, charged with pursuing Montfort's beatification, ordered an ecclesiastical tribunal to convene on the matter at Saint Laurent from the end of 1841 to the beginning of 1842. When 291 of Louis Marie's writings were sent to Rome for examination and approval, one work was missing—his masterpiece, the *Treatise on True Devotion.* For it was only on April 22, 1842 that Fr. Pierre Rautureau rediscovered this precious work at the Montfort residence in Saint Laurent. The Treatise was sent immediately to the bishop of Luçon. A committee of experts examined it carefully and, under oath, declared it a signed work of Louis Marie de Montfort. This enabled the precious manuscript to be sent, in the very year of its discovery, to the Eternal City to join the 291 already there.

Then began a series of further investigations, in which the Congregation of Rites posed certain questions and sought the advice of a variety of theologians. The archives cite several dates when authorities dialogued and strongly discussed certain points: March 28, 1851, January 10, 1852, and during May of the same year. The cardinal "ponent" of the cause was Cardinal John Serafini.

Finally, on May 7, 1853, it was made public that the deliberations of the congregation had revealed nothing in the writings of Montfort that constituted an obstacle to the pursuit of his cause. The Holy Father approved and confirmed this rescript of the Sacred Congregation on May 12, 1853.

3. The examination of the virtues

Under the direction of Cardinal Clement Villecourt, pre-preparatory and preparatory assemblies were held on January 9, 1866 and July 16, 1867. By virtue of a special request from the postulator, another preparatory assembly was held on February 15, 1869. On July 27, 1869, under the direction of Cardinal Nicolas Clarelli Paracciani, the general assembly was held in the presence of the

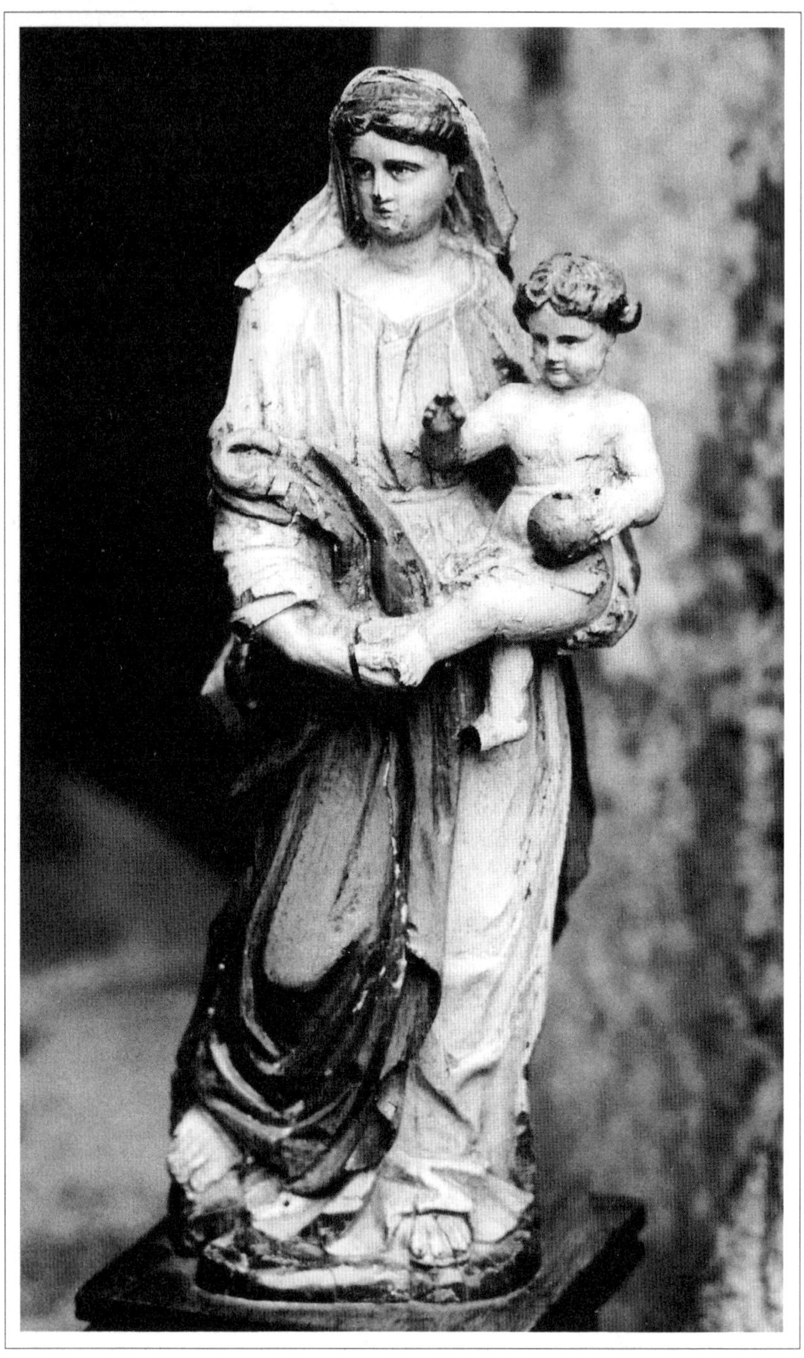

STATUE OF THE BLESSED MOTHER AND THE CHRIST CHILD

Tradition holds this to have been sculpted by Father de Montfort. It is found in the parish church of Saint Amand. Photo by Aartsen.

Pope. His Holiness, after welcoming the suffrages of the cardinals and consultant fathers, exhorted them to continue praying to obtain light and counsel so as to bring to a conclusion the work which had begun.

Finally, on September 29, 1869, the decree on the heroism of the virtues was issued. The Holy Father, Pius IX, in the presence of the prefect of the Congregation of Rites, the recorder of the cause and the defender of the faith, decreed "that the Venerable Servant of God, Louis Marie Grignion de Montfort, practiced the virtues of Faith, Hope, and Charity towards God and neighbor, the Cardinal virtues of Prudence, Justice, Fortitude, and Temperance, and the related moral virtues, to an heroic degree; to the effect in question, that one could proceed to the discussion of the four miracles."

4. The examination of the miracles

The miracles attributed to Father de Montfort are very numerous. Biographers state that various extraordinary favors were obtained through his intercession. Four of these were selected and proposed for examination by the Sacred Congregation.

The study of these miracles was very long. The affair seemed to be advancing slowly until, at the end of 1881, Bishop Catteau of Luçon, on his *ad limina* visit approached the Holy Father about the cause so dear to his diocese. Leo XIII was sympathetic to his plea.

These were the four miracles selected: in January 1845, the cure of Sr. Emmanuel, Daughter of Wisdom, of spinal paralysis; in July 1869, that of Sr. Saint-Lin, Daughter of Wisdom, of a chronic disease of the marrow; in March 1870, that of Reine Mallé, aged 10 years, pupil of the Daughters of Wisdom, of a tubercular arthritis of the hip and dislocation of the right leg; and finally, in April 1873, the cure of Sr. St-Gabriel, Daughter of Wisdom, of consumption of the lung that had been judged fatal, with abdominal cystic tumor and heart disease.

Pre-preparatory meetings were held under the presidency of Cardinal Aloysi Bilio, recorder of the cause, on June 12, 1883. A preparatory session took place at the Apostolic Palace of the Vatican on February 24, 1885. Then a general assembly was held in the presence of Pope Leo XIII at the Vatican on January 5, 1886. Finally, on February 21, 1886, Pope Leo XIII recognized the four cures as miraculous.

5. Towards beatification

Before the solemn beatification of Father de Montfort, it was necessary that a decree summing up the procedure should resolve the last doubt: "Now that there had been an affirmation of his virtues and four miracles, can we proceed with the solemn beatification of the Venerable Servant of God in full confidence?"

The doubt was proposed on May 25, 1887 at a general assembly in the presence of the Pope. All of the cardinals present, as well as the priest consultants, gave a favorable response. The Holy Father, however, deferred a final verdict, said the decree, "in order to pray to God beforehand to enlighten him in such a serious matter." Finally, on November 21, 1887, the feast of the Presentation of the Blessed Virgin, the Pope pronounced his solemn judgement and ordered publication of the decree, called a decree *de tuto,* which authorized proceeding confidently with the cause.

The process of beatification being complete, it would soon be possible for the faithful to venerate the precious remains of Father de Montfort. A decree from Rome dated November 9, 1886 had authorized the exhumation of his remains.

On August 18, 1887, the tomb was opened. Father de Montfort's tomb had been opened three times previously. The first was on November 12, 1717, with the authorization of the Bishop of La Rochelle. That ceremony, which took place at night, allowed the following facts to be noted: the missionary's face was well preserved; the body was "pitted" at certain points where it made contact with the earth; there was a pleasant fragrance of "little fennel-scented apples"; there was a mass of little flies with green wings, buzzing and singing like bees leaving their hive.

The tomb was opened a second time on November 30, 1812. It allowed the transfer of part of the relics to the montfort communities. A third opening took place on January 17, 1842 at the beginning of the process of beatification. On both these occasions, the coffin or the coffers containing Father de Montfort's remains were embossed with the episcopal seal.

On August 18, 1887, the bishop of Luçon, with an ecclesiastical tribunal, proceeded with the solemn opening of the tomb in the presence of several eminent persons, among them the superiors general of the montfort communities and a few witnesses. It consisted of an identification of the remains and a selection of relics for the beatification.

The solemn beatification of Louis Marie de Montfort took place on Sunday, January 22,1888.[4] The ceremony would have taken place in the choir of St. Peter's Basilica if the Pope had been entirely free, but because of the situation in which His Holiness found himself, it was held in the loggia, that is to say, in the large chapel to be found above the portico of St. Peter's. The ceremony was set for 10 o'clock. From 9 o'clock onwards, the crowds entered the loggia, and soon 3,000 persons were crushed into the enclosure, where lights and draperies focused attention on the four large tableaux representing the miracles selected for the beatification.

On May 8 of that year, Bishop Clovis-Nicolas-Joseph Catteau, of Luçon, announced in a pastoral letter, to be read on Pentecost Day in all the churches of the Diocese, the solemn triduum of Saint Laurent-sur-Sèvre. In this letter he wrote: "Never shall we forget the mysterious sensation that enveloped our whole being when, after the reading of the Brief of Beatification, the veil covering the Apotheosis of Father de Montfort suddenly fell and the Blessed one appeared to us, all bathed in light, ascending in glory surrounded by angels bearing the Cross, the Rosary, and the admirable

Book of Rules that he left to his children. While the Church on earth, for the first time, offered incense, the perfume of its homage, to the precious relics that we, a few months previously, had taken from the obscurity of the tomb, we witnessed the Heavenly Church salute with love this immortal victor."[5]

On June 4, 5, and 6, crowds gathered at the tomb of Blessed Father de Montfort in the parish church of St. Laurent-sur-Sèvre. On the final day of the triduum, 1,500 priests and 20,000 pilgrims formed a triumphant procession lasting three hours.

6. Towards canonization

After an interval of forty years, the cause of canonization was resumed. Captivated by the figure of Montfort and by montfort spirituality, the famous Cardinal Mercier made himself its herald. As early as 1925, he submitted for approval by the Catholic bishops a prayer requesting definition of the doctrine of the Universal Mediation of the Blessed Virgin, as well as the canonization of Montfort, her great apostle. Countless signatures of cardinals, archbishops, and bishops testify to the warm welcome that this step by the Primate of Belgium received. On October 7, 1927, Reverend Mother Pauline of the Sacred Heart, superior general of the Daughters of Wisdom, and on November 19, 1927, Very Reverend Father Henri Richard, superior general of the Company of Mary, sent their entreaty to the Sovereign Pontiff. Thus on January 27, 1928, the cause of canonization of Father de Montfort was resumed.

Two instant cures were presented: that of Sr. Gerard of Calvary, cured at Romsey, England, on April 8, 1927, and that of Sr. Marie Therese of the Visitation, cured at Saint Laurent-sur-Sèvre on June 24, 1934, both Daughters of Wisdom. The first was suffering from a very serious infection, a tubercular ulcerous lesion in the pelvic area, with two fistulas and bacterial consumption of both lungs; the second was suffering from tubercular meningitis. On February 1, 1939, Rome recognized the legal merit of the two examinations of these two cures carried out by the episcopal curias of Portsmouth and Luçon. On July 23, 1940 there was a pre-preparatory meeting of the Sacred Congregation of Rites for the examination of the two miracles, and on July 1, 1941 the preparatory meeting took place. These pre-preparatory and preparatory gatherings heralded the plenary meeting of December 16, 1941 in the presence of His Holiness Pope Pius XII. On January 11, 1942, the feast of the Holy Family, the Pope gave recognition to the two miracles, and the decree of approbation was read. On January 27, 1942, in a session that included the cardinals and was held in the presence of the Pope, opinion was voiced that it was safe to proceed to the canonization. The events of that period, however, resulted in the decree *de tuto* concerning the canonization being promulgated in Rome only on May 21, 1945.

Finally, on July 20, 1947, in the Basilica of St. Peter in Rome, the solemn canonization of St. Louis Marie de Montfort took place: "In honor of the Holy and Indivisible

Trinity. . . , after invoking divine help . . . , we decree and define that the Blessed Grignion de Montfort . . . be regarded as a Saint."[6]

After the invocation and special prayer of the new saint, the Sovereign Pontiff praised the missionary zeal of St. Louis Marie, his ardent devotion towards the Virgin Mary, and his obedience and loyalty to the Church. At his special audience for the many pilgrims from France and elsewhere, he repeated the same themes in a direct and homely style: "Hail to you, pilgrims gathered from various countries . . . , whose love for Mary binds you together, because all of you have come to honor the guide who leads you to Mary and from Mary to Jesus."[7]

Marie Claire Vienne-
Marcel Gendrot

Notes: (1) Fr. R. Rodrigo, O.A.R., published in 1991, under the aegis of the Holus Institutum Historicum Augustinianorum Recollectorum, a book valuable to postulators. It is entitled *Manuale per istruire i processi di canonizzazione (Manual for Preparing the Processes of Canonization).* (2) Abbé F. Laveau, *Vie de Gabriel Deshayes (Life of Gabriel Deshayes),* Vannes 1866, 201. (3) Ibid., 208. (4) Cf. *Béatification du serviteur de Dieu Louis-Marie Grignion de Montfort. Histoire du procès, décrets, cérémonies de la béatification (Beatification of the Servant of God Louis-Marie Grignion de Montfort: History of the Process, Decrees, Ceremonies of the Beatification),* Bideau et fils, Luçon n.d., 207. (5) Ibid., 44. On the ecclesial significance of Montfort's beatification, going beyond any provincialism, cf. S. De Fiores, *Per une "memoria" monfortana profetica ed ecclesiale (On a Prophetic Ecclesial "Memoria" of Montfort),* in QM 6 (1989), 3-5. (6) Cf. AAS 39 (1947), 329-330 - (21) Ibid., 410-411. Pius XII stated that "the Church leaves a fair margin of freedom to her children. She holds that true and perfect devotion to the Blessed Virgin is by no means so linked to interpretations that any particular one could claim a monopoly" (ibid., 413). (7) The parish church of Saint Laurent was built between 1888 and 1949 on the foundations of a church built at the beginning of the eleventh century and dedicated to St. Laurence, deacon and martyr. This church contains the tombs of Fr. de Montfort (†1716), of the Marquis of Magnanne, a great benefactor of the montfort family (†1750), and of Marie-Louise de Jésus, cofoundress of the Daughters of Wisdom (†1759). In 1963 the church received liturgical consecration and the title of "minor basilica."

CHARISMS

SUMMARY

I. CHARISMS IN THE CHURCH:
   1. A new appreciation of charisms:
      a. Before the council,
      b. The council,
      c. The charismatic renewal.
   2. Charisms: fact and diversity:
      a. From grace to charisms,
      b. Diversity and usefulness of charisms.

II. CHARISMS IN MONTFORT'S LIFE:
   1. The charisms of an apostolic missionary:
      a. A man led by the Spirit,
      b. The charism of apostolic wisdom.
   2. The charism of a founder:
      a. "Given the needs of the Church,"
      b. "To renew the spirit of Christianity . . . to reform the Church,"
      c. Apostles of fire . . . formed by Mary.
   3. Exceptional charisms:
      a. The charism of prophecy,
      b. The charism of discernment,
      c. The charism of healing, d. Other charisms,
      e. Other supernatural phenomena.

III. FROM MONTFORT TO THE CHURCH OF TODAY AND OF TOMORROW:
   1. The Church of Christ is also the Church of the Spirit;
   2. Witnesses to love in the way of Jesus Christ;
   3. Mary, spouse of the Holy Spirit, in the formation of apostles.

Over several decades we have observed in the Church a new interest in the manifestation of charisms, accompanied by renewed reflection on the doctrines concerning them. Charisms have always existed in the Church. Montfort is a unique witness to this in salvation history.

I. CHARISMS IN THE CHURCH

We are unable to understand or evaluate the charisms in Montfort's apostolic life without the deep inner experience of the Church: a Church the Spirit is unceasingly sanctifying and reforming with many and varied gifts.

1. A new appreciation of charisms

One characteristic of Christians today is a renewed sense of the presence and action of the Holy Spirit as manifest in spiritual gifts or charisms.

a. Before the Council. Prior to

1945-1950, little was said about charisms in the Western Church, except that they were exceptional graces accorded to privileged souls. Questions were raised by a number of apostolic movements about what was the effective and responsible role of the laity. As a result, the Church undertook a doctrinal study of the respective roles of clergy and laypeople. This was done both from the perspective of the institutional Church and its structures and from the perspective of the mystical Church and its spiritual gifts or charisms.

b. The Council. Influenced by this atmosphere of study, the Second Vatican Council addressed the question of charisms. It did so not in a direct and systematic way but indirectly within various documents, always strongly centered on the Scriptures (LG 4, 7, 12, 30; AA 3, 30; AG 4, 23, 28; DV 7; PO 4, 9).

We can summarize the conciliar thought on charisms in this way. Beyond the graces that come through the Sacraments, the Spirit gives to the Church *hierarchical gifts*, which are given to priests for the exercise of their ministry, and *charismatic gifts*, given to the faithful for the common good. Such charisms are given for the building up of the Church. They are freely given by the Giver of all gifts and received according to the disposition of the receiver.

The faithful have the right and the duty to exercise these charisms as long as they do so in a spirit of order and unity. Charisms are intended for, and subject to, the greater gift of charity, which alone unites and builds the Church (cf. 1 Cor 13:1-13; Eph 4:14-16).

c. The charismatic renewal. Since the council, the Church has undergone a prolonged period in which the Spirit has been strongly manifesting the power of renewal. It has made us more aware of charisms. From this larger phenomenon emerged a spiritual movement known as the charismatic renewal. It spread around the world. It is fundamentally a movement of prayer centered on Christ living in the Church, and it seeks to be attentive to the Spirit at work reforming and renewing the Church. The charismatic renewal from its inception was accompanied by a manifestation of numerous charisms. Some of the more obvious have been prophecy, interpretation, knowledge, healing, tears, speaking in tongues . . . The movement was greeted at first with surprise, reserve, and suspicion. But it was officially approved by the Church in 1975 after Paul VI detected certain signs of the Spirit within it. He declared it "an opportunity for the Church and for the world," as long as it remained faithful to certain basic spiritual principles.[1]

2. Charisms: fact and diversity

It is difficult to give in a few words an adequate definition of charisms. The Second Vatican Council wrestled with this difficult question in various documents. One such statement describes charisms as the Holy Spirit "allotting his gifts according as he wills (cf. 1 Cor 11:12) . . . also distributing special graces among the faithful of every rank. By these gifts he makes them fit and ready to undertake various tasks and offices for the renewal and building up of the Church, as it is written, 'the manifestation of the Spirit is given to everyone for profit' (1 Cor 12:7)" (LG 12). One sees that the same difficulty of speaking to the phenomenon of charisms exists among modern theologians.

What we are faced with is more than a problem of words. It is an immense challenge to wrap supernatural reality in natural language. Meanings of words vary considerably in their usage both in definition and perception. Isn't defining charisms like trying to catch the wind, a breath, or a breeze? For the mysterious source of life in the words of the Creed is "the Spirit, the giver of life."

a. From grace to charisms. But the difficulty of language must not stop us from speaking. Rather, it must challenge us to find ever more precise terminology for our times.

Etymologically, the word "charism" comes from the Greek *charis*, meaning grace, free gift. The word "grace" in current spiritual language gives expression to the primordial gift that allows Christians to participate in the divine life—in Christ. It is what makes a baptized person a child of God and a member of the Church.

Within this first or fundamental grace of the Christian life can be distinguished various graces or powers:

- the gifts of faith, hope, and charity, termed the theological virtues. Habitual aids to personal sanctification within our earthly state, faith and hope serve the higher virtue—charity (Mt 22:27-40; 1 Cor 13:13).
- the "spiritual gifts" termed charisms, which are gifts given for the benefit of the common good, for the building of the Church. The Spirit distributes them to many different people. They are given to each and every one according to the needs of the community. This does not mean that one should not remain open or ask for these gifts according to one's need or perception.

Though we speak here of charisms, it is important to remember that all graces come from the same Spirit and all charismatic gifts serve the higher gift of charity - the supreme charism: love of self and love of others are united in charity.

b. Diversity and usefulness of charisms. Charisms that serve the people of God are numerous. Isaiah (11:1-2), Saint Peter (1 Pet 4:10), and Saint Paul (Rom 12:6-8; 1 Cor 12:8-10) indicate a number of them. Neither is the list exhaustive or closed.

Given for the common good, charisms must be lived out in a spirit of service (1 Pet 4:10-11). They are always received by an individual according to his or her qualities, limits, tendencies, or faults. Therefore they can be used well or poorly can be expressions of charity or be an obstacle to it. Saint Paul intervened on this matter in order to restore order to the community at Corinth (cf. 1 Cor 14). Charisms can also be refused or stifled. But the Spirit cannot be stopped, for He is the master craftsman of God's plan for the world, from beginning to end (cf. Gen 1:1; Acts 22:17). He is the ultimate architect for the building of the Church, for the uniting of the members of the Body of Christ and their Head (cf. Eph 4:1-7; TD 20:34-36). The Holy Spirit bestows His gifts on unexpected people and places and in surprising ways. Thus does He unceasingly sanctify, purify, and renew the Church, moving her ever toward the accomplishment of the Body of Christ (cf. Eph 1:9-10; Col 1:18-20).

II. Charisms in Montfort's Life

One day Louis Marie de Montfort entered the Church of Jesus Christ through the waters of Baptism and took his place in history.

The Holy Spirit chose to give rich, powerful gifts to this rough, unpolished man with a fiery, generous temperament, gifts that would better enable him to serve the Church. He was an apostle, one nourished by the spiritual movements and reformers of his day. He awakened in the Church a spiritual movement possessing a new missionary zeal, one shaped by the end times. And he became its chief spokesperson. He was given an apostolic charism. It was a fundamental charism in the order of salvation, a charism that cast a light on Mary's maternity of Christ, the Incarnate Wisdom, and of the members of his Mystical Body—the Church.[2]

1. The charisms of an apostolic missionary

An old schoolmate of Louis Marie's at Rennes and later at Saint-Sulpice, Fr. Blain, tried to stay in touch with Montfort and his apostolic work. In 1703, aware of the criticisms that were then being levelled at Montfort, he wrote to Fr. Leschassier, asking for his opinion of Louis Marie and his ministry. He received this reply: "He is very humble, very poor, very mortified, very recollected. But I find it difficult to believe him to be led by the Holy Spirit."[3] Blain stopped following Montfort and his work (but later was obliged to revise his opinion of him).

One cannot become a saint and an apostle without permitting the Holy Spirit to inspire and lead.

a. A man led by the Spirit. Montfort did not speak directly to the subject of the charisms of the Holy Spirit. Formed, however, in Sulpician and Ignatian spirituality, his teachings throughout his writings reflect[4] a deep understanding of the doctrine of the workings of the Holy Spirit in the Church. But what stands out is the power that the Holy Spirit had in his life. It is impossible to understand the man, the way he behaved, or his apostolic work without seeing everything in light of the action of the Holy Spirit in him. One has only to listen to those who knew him. Blain reflected the attitude of his schoolmates and friends in the seminary when he wrote: "I have to say that he reflected the strength and impetuosity of the new wine of the

Holy Spirit from which apostles come. He is a madman, and a fool in the eyes of men, but a sage in the eyes of God. . . . His complete innocence is linked to his limitless penance, continuous prayer, and limitless mortification. He offers the Holy Spirit a pure heart ready for each and every undertaking."[5]

Recounting a meeting of Montfort and his brother, a sacristan for the Dominicans at Dinan, Fr. Blain says: "It was one of those meetings where men meet as they are—honestly and without shame. In him we see a man straight from heaven, one who allowed the impulses of the Holy Spirit to shape his actions; in short, a man who no longer lives except by Jesus Christ who works in him, a man fully mastered by the power of the Holy Spirit."[6]

Father Vincent, a Capuchin who occasionally helped in his missions, also gives witness to him: "In a word, listening to Fr. de Montfort, I thought I was listening to an angel. His face shone with the light of an ecstatic love. His words echoed what the Holy Spirit said to him in his heart. His voice, gestures, and presence reflected his union with God and the words that Jesus Christ placed on his lips."[7]

To understand the depths at which the Holy Spirit took possession of St. Louis Marie's heart, we must read again and try to grasp what he wrote about how the Holy Spirit formed, in union with Mary, the apostles the Church required to meet the needs of the times (cf. PM 15-25).

b. The charism of apostolic wisdom. To characterize the way the Holy Spirit acted in Montfort, one might describe it as "the gift of Wisdom." To be more precise, however, the caveat "apostolic" should be added to it. This gives one a sense of the originality and depth of his charism. Certainly the gift of Wisdom was primary. From it the other gifts flowed, and it served the higher gift of charity as well as the other theological virtues. It is referred to in Isaiah (11:2), in St. Paul (1 Cor 12:8), in the catechism's list of the Seven Gifts of the Holy Spirit. It is first attributed to Jesus (Lk 2:40, 52), and all other gifts come from it. St. Louis Marie defined it as *"the communication that uncreated Wisdom makes of himself to mankind"* (LEW 13). He wrote: *"When eternal Wisdom communicates himself to a soul, he gives that soul all the gifts of the Holy Spirit and all the great virtues to an eminent degree"* (LEW 99). Since true Wisdom is the firstfruits of love, one could call it "the Wisdom of love." It is that unique path of life whereby others are loved as Jesus loves them: *"Eternal Wisdom . . . invites men to come to him because he wants to teach them the way to happiness"* (LEW 5).

It is important to recognize that the gift of Wisdom gave rise within Montfort to a surprisingly dynamic apostolic quality. He prayed for it for himself and for his spiritual children (L 15, 16, 17; LEW 1; H 22:5; 103, 124, 125; PM 22; MR 60). Montfort called his women followers "Daughters of Wisdom." Though the word "Wisdom" was not used for the Missionaries of the Company of

Mary, we know that part of LEW is the text of a very special retreat that he gave at the seminary of Poullart des Places in Paris. It was in this retreat that Montfort made clear his intention to establish a Congregation of missionaries. He wanted this spirit of apostolic Wisdom, which he lived so completely, to infuse the community. Apostolic Wisdom is at the root of the montfort charism, because it is the gift of the Holy Spirit that most profoundly shaped Montfort himself (cf. L 20; MR 60-62).

How did the young priest Louis Marie come to receive this gift of the Spirit in such a unique and personal way? Why was he so imbued and inflamed by it that he initiated a new form of the apostolic life in the Church? To answer these questions, there is no more important source than Montfort's LEW. It doesn't permit us to recapture his life or pass on his spirit. But in it he shares his personal experience, offering it to us to help us discover our own.

In love with God from childhood, Louis Marie, helped by meditation and study, was fascinated by God's love for everyone and everything. Above all, this was most evident for Montfort by the way in which God entered history by becoming human with us, by saving us, by bringing happiness especially to the poorest of the poor, the lowest of the low, to the most forsaken, to the greatest sinners (LEW, chap. 2-3). This path of God's Wisdom and mercy Montfort saw to be most strikingly revealed in the words and deeds of Jesus Christ. He saw in him a living image of the Incarnate Wisdom of God alive in the world through Mary (LEW, chap. 4-6).

In contemplating this behavior of God's Wisdom in Jesus Christ, Montfort knew man best. He understood Who God was for man and who man was for God: a beloved creature whom God sought out in spite of, or perhaps because of, his poverty, misery, and sin. Thus were born his passion for Jesus Christ, Wisdom Incarnate, for the salvation of mankind, and his passion for loving and saving others, above all the poorest and most sinful.

Thereafter, it became ever clearer to Montfort that life's real Wisdom was opposed to all worldly wisdom. It was beyond all natural wisdom (LEW, chap. 7). It was sharing in the Wisdom of Jesus Christ. This meant that one was called to love others with him, to walk the paths of his Wisdom, to go to others and to prove to them how much God loves them, to make oneself lowly, simple, poor, to the point of accepting humiliation, abasement, suffering, and the Cross (cf. FC). Rarely has a disciple seen his Master, the Christ of Wisdom, with such depth.

Wisdom, thus understood by Montfort, was a participation in the Wisdom of love in Jesus, which necessarily manifested itself as apostolic Wisdom. It was humble and self-denying but also enterprising and courageous (LEW 100).

Nothing demonstrates this better than the saint's reply to Fr. Blain on the occasion of their last meeting in Rouen in 1714: "He showed me his

New Testament and wanted to know if I could restate what Jesus Christ practiced and taught and whether I could show a life more like his and that of the Apostles than a poor life, mortified, and rooted in abandonment to Providence; he said he had no other point of view but to follow that, and no other design but perseverance in it. . . . He added that there were different sorts of wisdom, as also different degrees: the wisdom of a missionary and apostolic man was distinctive. Missionaries and apostolic men had to promote the glory of God rather than their own and to carry out new schemes . . . always with some new undertaking, some holy enterprise or other to launch or defend."[8]

The gift of apostolic Wisdom is to receive Wisdom to the fullest degree. Montfort unceasingly asked for and obtained it, for it is the source of all gifts for every true apostle. Montfort gave witness to its light through his own personal experience (LEW, chap. 8).

Montfort's words and deeds were a living testimony to this gift. Through it he touched the hearts of countless numbers of people.[9]

2. The charism of a founder

As the gift of Wisdom is the primordial source of all spiritual gifts, it is not surprising to find it accompanied by other gifts or charisms. Charisms are gratuitously given by the Holy Spirit, or given in response to the prayers and desires of those who open their hearts to receive them. We have spoken of how this charism of Wisdom in Montfort attained its full apostolic dimension. It made him share intensely in Christ's love for men, especially the poorest and most alienated. The ardor of this love and the courageous power of this Wisdom soon awakened within him a new desire, one that could only result from the Holy Spirit alone. It was a Wisdom that attracted others to help him in his apostolic undertakings. It was a Wisdom that assured them a continuity of growth by reason of need.

a. "Given the needs of the Church". When Montfort arrived at the community of Saint-Clément to engage in the work of parish missions, he quickly assessed his task in the light of his own limitations. He felt the need for this reflection more acutely because he saw that a number of priests in the community did not share his apostolic concern. A great suffering welled up within him, a desire already become prayer, which he shared with Fr. Leschassier, his spiritual director: *"When I see the needs of the Church I cannot help pleading continually for a small and poor band of good priests to do this work [to teach catechism to the poor in country places] under the banner and protection of the Blessed Virgin"* (L 5).

Thereafter, this desire flowed like a river within Montfort. It rose and fell in rhythm to the waves of inspiration, but throughout his missionary life it remained within him, a deep current constantly drawing him forward. He was nourished and strengthened by prayer and by his experience *"of the needs of the Church,"* faced from within and without with the moral and spiritual infidelities of the world in which he lived (cf. H 38:116; 43:29; 47:9).

Montfort's wish for a foundation seemed confirmed and encouraged by Pope Clement XI when Louis Marie met with him in 1706 (cf. MR 56). Little by little the project became clear. His deep call to respond to "the needs of the Church" was extended. It would be further extended to other works that experience revealed to him. But they always had the same apostolic outlook. Included were the care of the sick and poor in hospitals, the Christian education and formation of children ("charitable schools") (cf. various letters to Sr. Marie Louise; RW 1, 275-292, and W). What in a certain sense confirms the supernatural origin of his establishing these apostolic foundations was the prophetically inspired manner in which he chose his first disciples: Marie Louise Trichet, Mathurin, Fr. Mulot, and Fr. Vatel.[10]

As years went by, our holy missionary, perhaps feeling his powers declining, became more and more preoccupied with seeing his works take root. Each had experienced their own difficulties, obstacles, and disappointments. He was moved by an immense desire, which he knew came from beyond himself, and by a recognition that each work was in some way a door to salvation for others. In PM he allowed this desire to burst forth from his heart, which could resist no longer. It was an ardent prayer, a cry of suffering and faith. In it he called upon each of the three Divine Persons in turn and with unprecedented boldness challenged their fidelity to remember what he was asking for: *"It is no personal favor that I ask, but something which concerns your glory alone, something you can and, I make bold to say, you must grant since not only are you true God. . . . Say but one word and it will be enough to send good workers to gather in your harvest, and missionaries worthy of the name to work in your Church"* (PM, passim).

Clearly the desires aroused by the Holy Spirit in the heart of the young missionary at Nantes grew and deepened with his apostolic experience. The "needs of the Church" observed at that time when he was teaching *"catechism to the poor in country places"* grew to include other great needs to be met in the Church.

Nowhere better than in PM do we sense Montfort as both mystic and apostle. In it he reveals his burning desire to do everything possible to fulfill God's will, expressed in the Heart of Jesus Christ - to save all men. Such was the Spirit of God's grip on Louis Marie's heart that it opened him to every aspect of the Church's mission in the world, and until the end of time.[11]

b. "To renew the spirit of Christianity . . . to reform the Church". In raising his heart to God in PM, undoubtedly a prayer that became Montfort's constant cry, he sought to meet the Church's need to replace several Congregations that had disappeared. But more than this, he wanted to realize something entirely new. He sought something more apostolic, something more adapted to the work of saving souls.

By temperament Montfort was wholly committed to the work at hand, totally enamored of perfection. Louis Marie never accepted, any more than his divine Model, the Christ-Wisdom, half measures or compromises with the false wisdom of the world. Nor did he ever cease to combat it with all his strength. He was all the more unwilling to compromise because he saw the Church's need for further reform despite the accomplishments of the Council of Trent. His sufferings became a prayer: *"Remember, Lord . . . Your divine commandments are broken, your Gospel is thrown aside . . . ungodliness reigns supreme, your sanctuary is desecrated and the abomination of desolation has even contaminated the holy place. . . . Will you let everything, then, go the same way? . . . Did you not give to some souls, dear to you, a vision of the future renewal of the Church?"* (PM, passim).

Louis Marie, a most loving, obedient priest and son of the Church, gave himself body and soul, through his missions and retreats, to the task of renewal. When he visited Rome in 1706, his spirit of zeal was confirmed with Clement XI's seal of approval. Montfort received from him the title of "Missionary Apostolic" and was given the assignment to return to his country to *"renew the spirit of Christianity among the faithful"* (MR 56). The Holy Father's directive was: "Work always with perfect submission to the bishops into whose dioceses you will be called." Montfort would have to suffer dearly to do this. He had to pay for his love of the Church and fidelity to his mission by accepting many misunderstandings and rebuffs from ecclesiastical circles. Yet his prayer for missionary apostles became all the more vehement, for he felt the Church could tolerate neither failure nor delays any longer. Thus, he prayed to the Holy Spirit, *"Spirit of the Father and the Son,"* whose reign *"is still unended and will come to a close with a deluge of fire, love and justice."* He pleads: *"Send this all-consuming Spirit upon the earth to create priests who burn with this same fire and whose ministry will renew the face of the earth and reform your Church"* (PM 17).

Reform the Church . . . renew the earth! Nothing less could be Montfort's apostolic goal. It might be considered pretentious and naive if one did not know that such ambitious desires came from the same Spirit who set ablaze the hearts of the Apostles in the Cenacle (Acts 2:3).

c. Apostles of fire . . . formed by Mary. Clearly, Father de Montfort's PM aims far and wide. Beyond the Congregations he wished to found, in order to save souls he wished to see come forth in the Church a totally new type of apostolic man. For every founder the sign of authenticity is the will to carry out and bring to fulfillment the work of salvation, which Christ realizes in the Church through the Holy Spirit, by adopting and imitating whenever possible the way the first Apostles lived and gave witness. This was certainly what Montfort wanted. He judged, however - and this was part and parcel of his special grace and charism—that there were certain characteristics of an apostolic missionary that could only be acquired through Mary. She was mother and teacher of Wisdom Incarnate to those who follow her (cf. Jn 19:25-27; TD 144, 179, 266). No one other than the *"Mistress of Incarnate Wisdom"* can show us how to die to self and become open to the gifts of the Spirit, her *"divine Spouse,"* particularly to the gift of Wisdom with its full apostolic character: *"Only through Mary then can we possess divine Wisdom"* (LEW 209), and *"once we possess Mary, we shall, through her intercession, easily and in a short time possess divine Wisdom"* (see LEW 203-214, 222-227).

Quite naturally we hear Montfort asking for such missionaries who would be offsprings of the Holy Spirit and of Mary: *"Holy Spirit, be ever mindful that it is you who, with Mary as your faithful spouse, are to bring forth and fashion the children of God. . . . All the saints who have ever existed or will exist until the end of time will be the outcome of your love working through Mary"* (PM 15).

Confident of the power of the Holy Spirit united with Mary, Montfort already saw a generation of new apostles arising. He realized how much the Church needed them as she moved to the end times, and that by means of *"the interior and perfect practice of the devotion [to Mary] which I shall later unfold . . . they . . . will consecrate themselves entirely to her service as subjects and slaves of love"* (TD 55).

Describing what *"these servants, slaves and children of Mary"* would be like, he wrote: *"They will be ministers of the Lord who, like a flaming fire, will enkindle everywhere the fires of divine love. . . . They will bring to the poor and lowly everywhere the sweet fragrance of Jesus. . . . Wherever they preach, they will leave behind them nothing but the gold of love, which is the fulfillment of the whole law. Lastly, we know they will be true disciples of Jesus Christ, imitating his poverty, his humility, his contempt of the world and his love. They will point out the narrow way to God in pure truth according to the holy Gospel, and not according to the maxims of the world"* (TD 55-59).

Was Louis Marie de Montfort a charismatic apostle of the Church? Yes, certainly, but in his own unique way. Through Mary he was wholly inspired by and steeped in the love and Wisdom of her son Jesus Christ, whose heart sought the salvation of each and everyone. Seized by the Spirit, formed by Mary always docile to the Spirit, Louis Marie found himself to be God's instrument for beginning a new spiritual movement in the Church. It was a new, multifaceted, but always profoundly apostolic movement designed to bring about the re-newal and reform of the Church.

3. Exceptional charisms

Montfort can only be understood as someone possessed and led by the

Spirit of Jesus Christ, the source of all holiness and apostolic spirit in the Church. To psychologize about certain eccentricities in his behavior would be to forget that the Holy Spirit took Montfort as He takes us - where we are and as we are. The God Who created us is the same God Who calls us to serve with our uniquely created temperaments and characters. The same generous God Who created us as humans is therefore the same God Who respects our own personal efforts and the rhythms of our human development. Saints, even though they seek to answer the radical demands of the Gospel, have their unique personality traits, like all of us. We have noted that in St. Louis Marie the power of the Holy Spirit was uniquely manifest in the form of a double charism. He was simultaneously an apostolic missionary and a founder of apostolic institutes. It is this which gives him his unique ecclesial personality. In truth, the two charisms were one within him. They arose from the same source, nourished each other, and were both equally sustained by the charism of his priesthood.

It must be added that his charism was so rich that we can single out within it several charisms rarely found in the same person (cf. Eph 4:11-13). Both priest and missionary, Montfort was also an evangelizer, pastor, and doctor. In addition, he had the unusual gift of "touching hearts" and leading them to conversion. While we have recalled and highlighted those charisms which enabled Louis Marie to stand out in history as the innovator of a new form of spirituality, we should not neglect or minimize the other charisms that were part of his missionary life. Such uniquely special charisms we see today in the charismatic renewal groups. In their own way, these gifts testify to the hold the Spirit had over Montfort and confirm his other fundamental gifts mentioned above. We know that they contributed to establishing his reputation as a man of God ("he is a saint . . . good Father de Montfort"), and gave credence to his apostolic activity and mission as founder.

Let us cite a few of these "secondary" charisms without going into detailed descriptions, which are to be found in most of the biographies of Montfort. Moreover, since such gifts are interrelated, an attempt to strictly classify them would appear arbitrary.

a. The charism of prophecy. The charism of prophecy is the most important gift after that of Wisdom. It seems to stem from it, especially in an apostle. In the Bible a prophet is God's spokesman. He is inspired by the Holy Spirit to proclaim God's Word to men (cf 1 Pet 21). The Spirit does not speak. That is the role of Jesus Christ, the Word of the Father made flesh (Jn 15:15; Lk 24:19).

The Spirit helps the prophet to understand and transmit Christ's Word to groups or individuals. The Spirit of God enables the prophet to instruct, exhort, admonish, or encourage them in any given situation (Jn 14:26; 15:13).

Without doubt, Montfort's gifts were very apparent in his preaching. Fr. Barrin, vicar general of Nantes, wrote, "His preaching was full of the grace of the Holy Spirit, and he converted countless heretics and sinners" (from the first epitaph on Montfort's tomb).

Probably a certain number of significant events should be attributed to this gift of prophecy in Montfort. Once Montfort appeared at the door of the Dinan missionaries carrying a homeless man on his back and crying: *"Open the door to Jesus Christ."* Another time Louis Marie simply presented a crucifix to those attending one of his parish missions with the words *"Are you not sorry for having offended him?"* During a disastrous flood in Nantes, he inspired courage among the boatmen with the exhortation *"Put your trust in God and you will not perish."* It is important to recall how he intervened prophetically in the vocation of the first members of his Congregations.

Sometimes a "prophet," is enlightened by the Holy Spirit concerning God's actions in history, and is led to foretell the future. Biographers have listed some twenty-five predictions in Father de Montfort's life. For instance, during his first voyage as a young priest on the boat taking him from Orleans to Nantes, he told three young men who were behaving scandalously that they would soon meet their death. It happened just as he said it would. At Poitiers he told Mme. d'Armagnac, who was close to death, that she would recover. She lived for twelve more years. At Montfort, his birthplace, where he had been prevented from building a calvary on a knoll, he proclaimed that the site would one day become a place of prayer. In 1850 the parish church was built on that spot. At Pontchâteau, after being ordered not to bless a calvary but to demolish it, he prophesied that one day it would be rebuilt and that people would see wonders worked there.

One must add to this the predictions he made to his friend Blain in 1714 and the famous prophecy concerning the fate of TD (TD 114).

b. The charism of discernment. Every Christian must use the gift of discernment to avoid the snares of the evil one (cf. Mt 7:16).

Certain people have this gift to a high degree, always to serve the good of the community, which seems to prove that it comes from the Holy Spirit (cf. Cor 12:10). "Never try to suppress the Spirit," says St. Paul. "Think before you do anything - hold on to what is good and avoid every kind of evil" (1 Thess 5:19-22). This charism was present throughout Montfort's life and accompanied his fundamental charism. One sees it in the way he analyzed and sorted out the different ecclesiastical wisdoms of the day. One sees it also in his apostolic conduct, how he conceptualized his missions and the way he carried them out. This can be clearly seen in his remarks to Blain at their last meeting in Rouen. We know also that he was spiritual director of a number of outstanding people: M. and Mme. de la Garaye at Dinan; M. de Magnanc and M. d'Orville at

Rennes; Mme. de Mailly and Mlle. Bénigne Pagé at La Rochelle. One of the most significant instances of his gift of discernment was his meeting at Saumur with Jeanne Delanoue, the foundress of the Sisters of Providence, who has since been canonized. This holy woman asked Montfort for advice on what penances God was asking of her. Father de Montfort prayed and, next day, having celebrated Mass, gave this reply, *"Yes, it is the Spirit of God which animates you and prompts you to this penitential life. Henceforth, then, be without fear and follow your inspirations."*

c. The charism of healing. Jesus healed the sick and the infirm and bestowed this power as a sign of his divine mission. Sending his disciples to proclaim the Good News, he gave them the same power (cf. Mt 10:19; Lk 10:9). The gift of healing, if not the most frequent, is at least the most striking and perhaps the most often mentioned gift in the lives of the saints. Saint Louis Marie de Montfort was abundantly blessed with such healing powers. Biographers attribute to him nearly thirty cures. It is not claimed that these were all miraculous cures, in the technical sense of the word. But they span his missionary life. Some examples: At Fontevrault in 1701, he cured a blind man with a simple touch of his hand. During the mission at Vertou in 1708, Brother Pierre fell dangerously ill and was unable to move. *"Do you have faith?"* asked Father de Montfort. "Alas, Father, I wish I had more than I have." *"Will you obey me?"* "With all my heart." The holy missionary laid his hand on his head and said: *"I order you to rise in an hour and come to wait on us at table."* One hour later Brother Pierre was on his feet, cured.

During his stay in Paris in 1713, Montfort was visited by a mother whose child was riddled with ringworm. *"Do you believe,"* he asked, *"that Jesus Christ's ministers have, in the name of their Master, the power to cure people suffering from different illnesses by laying hands on them?"* "Yes," said the mother, "I am convinced that if you ask God for my son's cure, God will grant it." Montfort placed his hand on the child and prayed, *"May the Lord heal you, and reward you for your mother's faith."* Immediately the ringworm disappeared, and the child was cured. Faith, prayer, and the laying on of hands—these are the marks of Montfort's healings. All are in the tradition of the gifts of the Holy Spirit as understood and experienced in the Church.

d. Other charisms. Without trying to list all of Montfort's gifts of the Spirit, it is nevertheless good to mention some further examples.

- *He could read hearts.* There are several instances of this. For example, at Landremont a woman hid three sins in confession. Montfort gave her a handkerchief stained in three places. She could not wash out the stains until she had confessed the sins.

- *He could multiply loaves of bread.* During the mission of La Chèze in 1707, "he multiplied loaves to feed the poor, who were his favorite companions." This is known from the testimony of the parish. At Pontchâteau during the construction of the calvary, slices of bread and bowls of soup were miraculously multiplied on the table of the widow Jeanne Guigan, a neighbor who out of the goodness of her heart fed Fr. de Montfort and many of his workers, who had come from great distances. The same miracle occurred in 1712 at Saint-Christophe-du-Ligneron.

e. Other supernatural phenomena. While they may not count as spiritual gifts, it is difficult not to cite in Montfort's life a number of exceptional happenings of supernatural origin. He himself made nothing of them: *"The wise man,"* he said, *"does not ask to see extraordinary things as seen by the saints"* (LEW 187; cf. SR 143). After noting that he had on several occasions suffered attacks by the devil (for example, at Poitiers in 1703, and on his deathbed at Saint-Laurent), we should recall above all that he was favored with several apparitions of the Blessed Virgin, nine according to witnesses. Once, at Pontchâteau, when he was coming to dine at the house of Jeanne Guigan, she saw him walking toward her in the company of a "beautiful lady dressed in white." The lady did not enter the house with him. Jeanne expressed her surprise to Louis Marie. *"You saw her?"* "Yes, I saw her clearly." *"You are very blessed. I hope you will always be worthy to see the Blessed Virgin."* At Landremont a woman on her way to church saw him walking down a garden path with a lady ablaze in light. At La Garnache in 1713, an altarboy surprised him in conversation with "a beautiful lady all in white who was standing in the air." At Roussay in 1714, two men testified to having seen next to M. de Montfort "a lady in white." Similar occurrences took place at Taugon-la-Ronde, at Fonteney-le-Comte in 1715, and at St.Laurent-sur-Sèvre during his last mission, in 1716, where he was surprised in the sacristy with "a lady in white." Fr. de Montfort explained, *"My friend, I was conversing with Mary, my good Mother."*[12]

III. From Montfort to the Church of Today and of Tomorrow

To conclude this survey of the many charisms Montfort received, we return to our starting point, that is, to the purpose of this study, which was to examine the work of the Holy Spirit in the life of Saint Louis Marie. It was to reflect on the way the Holy Spirit worked in the life of someone the Church has recognized as a saint, as one of her greatest sons, as one of her apostles, whose influence has never ceased to spread throughout space and time. We have mentioned—and the council has borne witness to the fact—that the term "charism" cannot be reduced to mean only extraordinary spiritual gifts. No matter how varied and visible such gifts were in the life of Louis Marie, no matter how important one might consider them to be, at the heart of Montfort's charism, and at the heart of the charism of the communities he founded, is something deeper. It is the gift of Wisdom, a participation in the Wisdom of Christ. It is this gift which makes Montfort the unique apostolic missionary and founder that he is. It is a charism derived from Christ's Wisdom in seeking others through love. Beneficiaries of this gift through grace, the Montfort family is called today to share its charism with others. The followers of Saint Louis Marie must always and everywhere strive to deepen the faith that motivates them to serve the "needs of the Church" in today's world. They must feel strongly impelled by the power of the Holy Spirit. For since the council, they have been called to change the face of the earth—to renew the Church and to bring the world family into a better age. Surely they must feel stirred by the powerful breath of the Spirit, Who since the council would seem to want to change the face of the earth, renew the Church, and carry humanity to a new age. Montfort's attentiveness to the presence of the Spirit in the salvific work of Jesus Christ, his willingness to surrender to the Spirit, and his generosity in letting himself be led in the way of Wisdom—the way of love—compels us to walk in his footsteps. Here three points merit some consideration.

1. The Church of Christ is also the Church of the Spirit

Since the Church images the Holy Trinity, to which she belongs (*Ecclesia de Trinitate*), she does not depend on us. For she is joined simultaneously and inseparably to the Father, Son, and Holy Spirit. In particular, she belongs to Christ by the grace of the divine life received from the Father and communicated to his members. She also belongs to the Spirit by means of the love poured out into the hearts of the baptized and by the gifts that accompany that love so as to bind the faithful together in love and build the Church. In her the reality of grace and the reality of love are mutually interdependent, as they are within Christ himself. It follows that the Church of Jesus Christ can only grow in itself and in humanity in rhythm with the workings of the Holy Spirit and in welcoming submission to His movement within us. The Sacraments themselves are the actions of Christ accomplished by the power of the Holy Spirit.

This role of the Spirit has been ignored too long in the Churches of the West. This has resulted in the work of salvation suffering a certain diminishment. In the long line of exceptional men of God who down the centuries have surrendered themselves wholly to the Spirit, Montfort stands out as a person of unusual stature. With St. Paul he says to us, *"My speech and my message were not in plausible words of wisdom but in demonstration of the Spirit and Power"* (1 Cor 2:4). In the light of the council, it is urgent for us to rediscover, along with a renewed conviction, the presence and role of the Spirit in the building up of the Church. We are called to stake all our power in His power. It is also urgent for us to be alive to the presence and role of the

Holy Spirit and His gifts, often quite simple, in the lives of those who have been baptized. It is no longer the time to worry about who is charismatic and who is not. The whole Church has been charismatic since its birth at Pentecost, and all Christians are charismatic by the fact of their own personal rebirth in the Spirit (cf. LG 9).

Everyone has received a share in the gifts (cf. 1 Cor 7:7) in order to contribute to the growth and renewal of the Church. This means that—without overlooking the gift of discernment—one should recognize in all ranks of the baptized—lay, religious, and ordained ministers—the gifts of the Spirit.

This means also that catechetical and pastoral teaching should help all the baptized to become more aware of this. It should prepare them by prayer to serve our ecclesial community with true fidelity.

The Holy Spirit comes to us during every age in the history of salvation freely, in his own unique way, and as the needs dictate. It seems in our time that He wishes to manifest Himself with new power, as He did in Vatican II and in the different spiritual renewals that have emerged since then. These collectively constitute what can be termed the charismatic renewal.

In his encyclical letter *Dominum et vivificantem* on the Holy Spirit (1986), John Paul II wrote in the same vein: "Guided by the Spirit of truth and testifying with Him, the Council has strongly reaffirmed the presence of the Holy Spirit, the Paraclete. In a certain sense, it has made Him 'present anew' in our difficult times. We understand better now in the light of that revelation how supremely important it is that all initiatives reinforce what Vatican II tried to accomplish." And he states: "The spirit of God, by a special and admirable Providence, is guiding hearts and renewing the face of the earth."

Living the Montfort charism today essentially means to go where the Spirit of history leads us, as Montfort did.

2. Witnesses to love in the way of Jesus Christ

To live the Montfort charism in our day is to show a deep love, modeled on the life of Christ, for our brothers and sisters, with a preference for the poor of all types, and in a certain sense joining them to save them. This way of loving others shown by Christ, the Wisdom of God, became in Montfort apostolic Wisdom, the fruit of a unique gift of the Spirit of Jesus.

Since Montfort's time, the world has changed, social structures have evolved, new problems have arisen in various spheres. The destitute have been left to their own devices in every country, rich or poor, and on every continent in the world. Whether they are materially, intellectually, or, above all, morally and spiritually poor, whether they are in city or suburb, whether in schools, hospitals, or businesses, they are loved by God and sought by Christ. They need to be loved, helped, taught, and, perhaps without realizing it, evangelized, because they have a right to hear the Good News. They look to apostles like Montfort, for they burn with a passionate love for Jesus Christ and are drawn to their brothers and sisters by the same apostolic charism. The Church has more and more need for such apostles in order to bring Christ's work in our evolving world to its fulfillment. Needed are men and women young and old, liberated from self and false wisdoms of the day, free to go where the Spirit leads in order to do God's loving will (PM 7:1).

Inspired no doubt by his charism, St Louis Marie foresaw, prayed for, and announced this new apostolic lineage that the Holy Spirit would raise up: *"They will be ministers of the Lord, who, like a flaming fire, will enkindle everywhere the fires of divine love"* (TD 56).

3. Mary, spouse of the Holy Spirit, in the formation of apostles

There seem to be two essential aspects of the montfort charism. The first is to live always in total submission to the Church of Jesus Christ and to let oneself be led by the Spirit, Who is its sole animator. The second is to become within the Church, by the power of the Holy Spirit, a true disciple and apostle of Incarnate Wisdom. But there is also a third aspect that characterizes this charism. It is to acknowledge Mary's mission as the Mother of Christ and of all Christians. She is also the faithful collaborator and spouse of the Holy Spirit in forming Christ and Christians, particularly apostolic Christians like Montfort—completely surrendered to the Holy Spirit. For it is in her maternal and teaching role that she helps us to overcome selfishness and to welcome the gift of God in Jesus Christ and his Spirit (cf. TD 118). *"The more he [the Holy Spirit] finds Mary, his dear and inseparable Spouse, in a soul, the more powerful and effective he becomes in producing Jesus Christ in that soul and that soul in Jesus Christ"* (TD 2; cf. also 25-26). Here again Montfort's words indicate why this does not come about in the soul: *"One reason why so few souls come to the fullness of the age of Jesus is that Mary, who is still as much as ever his Mother and the fruitful Spouse of the Holy Spirit, is not formed well enough in their hearts. . . . If we desire to have the Holy Spirit working in us, we must possess his faithful and inseparable Spouse Mary, the divinely favored one, whom, as I have said elsewhere, he can make fruitful"* (TD 164).

It is for us, then, to open our hearts to Mary and to the Holy Spirit by living and sharing Montfort's charism, now become our own in all its richness. By our fidelity we will hasten *"that happy day . . . when . . . the Holy Spirit, finding his dear Spouse present again in souls, will come down into them with great power; he will fill them with his gifts, especially wisdom by which they will produce wonders of grace"* (TD 217).

J. Hémery

Notes: (1) Paul VI, homily of May 19, 1975, in *L'Osservatore Romano,* May 21, 1975. See also A. Barruffo, *Charismatique,* in *Dictionnaire de la vie spirituelle,* Paris 1987, 118-119. (2) "If Christ is the original charismatic, Mary is the charismatic par excellence because she received the fullness of the Spirit, because she listened constantly to his voice, never saddened him, and actively participated in the birth of the Church at Pentecost." (3) Blain, 118. (4) See *Tables analytiques,* in OC, for many references to the Holy Spirit. (5) Blain, 33. (6) Ibid., 143. (7) Ibid., 164. (8) Ibid., 185-190. (9) See, for example, the evidence given by Father Martinet, SJ, ibid., 164-165: "Wanting to see for himself, he went one day with another priest to hear a sermon by Father de Montfort. Although on his guard, he was obliged, together with all the others present, including clerics, to pay tearful tribute to the preacher." (10) See in particular on this subject L. Le Crom, *Un apôtre marial: Saint L. M. Grignion de Montfort,* Pontchâteau 1946, chaps. 20-21. (11) Speaking of Montfort's "sense of his role within the Church," Benedetta Papàsogli wrote in *Montfort, a Prophet for Our Times,* Edizone Montfortane, Rome 1991, 401-402: "He knows himself to be called to renew the Church, to quicken its holiness. For this, an overwhelming epidemic of grace will be required: a wiping out of individualism and a new springtime of the Spirit. . . . The whole life story of Father de Montfort has been a prophetic sign of a reality destined to become ever more alive as it slowly and patiently comes to fruition in God's plan. From the humblest of beginnings, the charism will grow to giant proportions of creative power. From the tiny seed will come grace-filled fruitfulness for an apostolic brotherhood that will endure." On the meaning of the expression *"the latter times"* in Montfort (cf. *"the apostles of the latter times"*), see S. de Fiores, *Saint-Esprit et Marie dans les derniers temps selon Grignion de Montfort,* in *EtMar* 43 (1986), 131-171. (12) Such phenomena are merely visible manifestations of a closeness and an intimacy with her of whom he said that he bore her within, *"etched with strokes of glory"* (H 77:15). He himself testified that the Blessed Virgin "was so present to his mind and so engraved on his heart that he was unable to stir or to act, except in her, through her, and for her" (Grandet 312).

CHILDHOOD

I. MONTFORT AND CHILDHOOD

1. Montfort's childhood

Louis Grignion was born on January 31, 1673, in the small town of Montfort-la-Cane, which borders on the dense forest of Brocéliande. The newborn was baptized in the hands of the Montfort parish priest, Father Pierre Hindré, on February 1, and given the name of Louis. Grandet states that Montfort added the name Marie to his own name when he received the Sacrament of Confirmation, because of his great devotion to Mary, the Mother of God.[1]

Louis Grignion did not remain at home but was put in the care of a wet nurse, Mother André, who lived on a farm on the family property of La Bachelleraie, four kilometers from Montfort-la-Cane.

On July 16, 1675, Louis's father, Jean-Baptiste Grignion, purchased the lands of the Bois Marquer, the Plessis Bois Marquer, and La Chesnaie in the parish of Iffendic. From 1675 to 1685, between the ages of two and eleven, Louis lived in his family's newly acquired manor house. The family was not notably wealthy, but its members were conscious of their social position. Their income from the legal profession was negligible.

The first biographers of Louis-Marie (Grandet, Blain, Besnard) described his childhood as that of a saint whose character was angelic. They presented Louis as a human being who had been touched neither by original sin nor by the consequences of Adam's disobedience. He was not attracted to evil, had no difficulty practicing virtue, and was capable of tasting the joys of holiness.

However, it must be said that Louis had a normal childhood. He grew up with both feet planted on the ground. His psyche was influenced by the same growth factors that contribute to the development of any child.

Louis was the second of eighteen children in the household. The first, Jean-Baptiste, had lived only five months. Eight of the children lived to adulthood: Louis, Joseph, Gabriel, and Jean-Baptiste among the boys, and Guyonne-Jeanne (Louise), Renée, Sylvie, and Françoise Marguerite among the girls. As the eldest, Louis demonstrated a sense of responsibility and a great maturity that would only be strengthened with time.

Louis Marie benefited from his environment, from the warm affection that was showered upon him, and from his relationships with those around him. In short, he spent his childhood in a positive environment, which contributed toward making him the man and saint he was to be. This is confirmed by Father Gilbert, his first professor at Rennes, who said that even then the pious young man "was one of those whom God had favored with the marks of distinction."[2]

Thanks to the love and patience of their parents, the Grignion children grew strong in their sense of personal responsibility and confidence in themselves. But not surprisingly, Louis's father, responsible for raising a large family on a meager income, was easily provoked. He was, however, a solid Christian and a member of the confraternity of the Blessed Virgin. He raised his children in "the fear of God."

Louis's mother, Jeanne Robert, silently and humbly devoted herself to educating her numerous children. Pregnancies at short intervals and the birth of eighteen children had its effect on the health of Madame Grignion. Louis realized that his mother's situation was difficult and showed her compassion. From the age of four or five, according to his uncle Alain Robert, he "he supported his mother when he saw her afflicted, consoling her and encouraging her to suffer with patience."[3]

The church of Iffendic must have made a deep impression on the spirit of the young Grignion, laying a solid foundation for his unwavering faith with its stained glass windows magnificently depicting the mysteries of salvation history, its baptismal fonts where he assisted at the baptisms of his brothers and sisters and where he himself renewed his baptismal promises on many occasions. In this church he received the Sacrament of Confirmation and was instructed in the rudiments of the Christian faith.

Louis Grignion was shaped by these realities. His faith as a child echoed that of his parents and his entire community. But there was something else. The tender hand of God constantly guided him by means of a special grace, and this changed everything. Grandet and Blain point this out. A modern psychologist would call it religious conditioning. But in religious terms, it is obvious that God was forming Louis and that the first spark of his faith, like his first desire for God, was God's work.[4]

2. Montfort's concern for children and the establishment of schools

One of Montfort's concerns in his missionary life was to educate children in the faith. Charles Besnard says that the establishment of Christian schools and of the Daughters of Wisdom at La Rochelle preoccupied Louis Marie for the six or seven weeks he spent in that coastal town. The bishop assured him of the necessary building and money, but preparing for the opening of classes was a difficult task. Louis Marie, however, gave himself no respite and did not allow himself to become discouraged by the difficulty. To the great surprise of everyone, he overcame the obstacles and opened the boys' schools first, with three teachers whom he had chosen and with a priest to say Mass.[5] Montfort's concern with the educative aspect of the Church's mission, and for the Brothers who were fulfilling this mission, was so great that in his will he bequeathed his small pieces of furniture and his mission books *"for the use of the four Brothers who joined me in a life of obedience and poverty; namely, Brother Nicholas of Poitiers, Brother Philip of Nantes, Brother Louis of La Rochelle, and Brother Gabriel, who is at present with me."* He also put at the disposal of the *"Brothers of the community of the Holy Spirit to conduct charity schools" "two pieces of land given by the Lieutenant of Vouvant's wife, and a small house given by a good lady of rank"* (W).

To ensure that everyone, especially the poor, could benefit from the Christian schools he had established, Montfort insisted that the education be given at no charge. He established detailed regulations governing the teachers and students, the use of their time, the exercises to be adhered to, and the pious observances to be introduced.

He wished to educate children in the faith so that his missions would bear fruit for generations to come. Louis Marie himself trained the schoolmasters and instructed them how to teach in his way and draw the best from the students.

After the establishment of the charitable schools (schools for the poor) at La Rochelle, the young people remained neither rude nor ignorant, and the town's inhabitants were pleasantly surprised. As late as Besnard's time, the schools founded by Louis Marie were still in existence "for the use of the public, the honor of religion, and the glory of these two great men."[6] The two great men were apparently the Bishop of La Rochelle and Louis Marie de Montfort.

II. The "Spirit of Childhood" in the Seventeenth Century

Montfort's historical and spiritual environment was not indifferent to children. We need only remember the various institutions for children that resulted from the zeal of J.B. de la Salle, Démia, and Montfort himself, who was particularly interested in the development of children and the establishment of charity schools.

But it is also necessary to identify the shape of a spirituality of childhood, which reached "its historical zenith" in France during the seventeenth century.[7] In the reign of Louis XIV we find several spiritual writers whom Bremond called "the doctors of the spirituality of childhood."[8] They included well-known authors, such as Bérulle and Condren, but also others who were less well known, such as Amelote, de Renty, Saint-Jure, and the Sulpician Blanlo, who in 1665 wrote a book entitled *Christian Childhood*.[9] One reason for the seventeenth century's interest in Jesus' childhood and the spirituality of Christian childhood lies in the prevailing cultural conception of mankind. It was influenced by the occasionalist philosophy of Malebranche, by Protestantism, and by Jansenist rigorism. In general, they saw human nature from a negative point of view. Man was weak, a sinner who must be humbled, who must attain even the smallest of virtues in order to be saved. Spirituality required fidelity to the most obscure aspects of life.[10] This interest in small things might explain in part why seventeenth-century authors gave such attention to the mystery of Jesus' childhood.

It was true that for certain spiritual writers in the tradition, childhood possessed human qualities of happiness, beauty, and tenderness, which reflected higher supernatural ones. But this assumption would be incorrect for most spiritual writers of that time. As Bremond remarks, devotion to the childhood of Jesus "such as proposed by Bérulle offers little to comfort our understanding or soften our heart. Bare, austere, merciless, it speaks to us of humiliation and death."[11] In fact, for Bérulle and his disciples, childhood is the lowliest and most abject state of all, except for death.[12] Condren identifies four basic childlike qualities: smallness of body, dependence on others, subservience, and uselessness.[13]

As a result, the spirit of childhood, so fundamental to the Gospel, did not mean imitating the joy, trust, ingenuity, and candor of the young Jesus; rather, it meant imitating his absolute helplessness. Bremond interprets the phrase *"Nisi efficiamini sicut parvuli"* in Bérullian terms as "If you do not adhere to my state of childhood, you will not enter the Kingdom of Heaven."[14] This refers not to devotional practices but to a spirit, a condition, a coming together of interior dispositions. And this "spirit of childhood" requires "the annihilation of ourselves, docility before God, silence, and innocence" (Saint-Jure), "a state in which we are dead to everything" (de Renty), "no longer directing ourselves by our own spirit, but allowing ourselves to be moved and ruled by the Spirit of Our Lord Jesus Christ" (Blanlo).

This spirit of childhood, which does not proceed merely from a simple joyous contemplation, implies a relationship with the Cross, because Jesus in his cradle is destined for the Cross. It also implies a concrete relationship realized through charity: "The servants of the Holy Infant Jesus thought to aid one through action, not simply through an ideal devotion, as personified in the poor and abandoned little children" (Parisot).

After J.-J. Olier's encounter with Marguerite du Saint-Sacrement, the spirituality of the childhood of Jesus entered into his life and into the seminary of Saint-Sulpice. But Olier was also sensitive to the most positive and attractive aspects of Jesus's humanity: "The graces of this mystery are: innocence, purity, simplicity, obedience."[15] Montfort would draw on this spirituality of childhood and speak of it as an aspect of his personal approach.

We should also note that in the mystery of the childhood of Jesus, Mary, his mother, is always present. If the crib is humble and austere, Mary's womb is tender and venerable (Condren). Bérulle contemplates the "delights of Jesus in Mary," while his disciples pass quite naturally from Mary's biological maternity to her spiritual maternity of humankind. Olier calls Mary "the nursing mother of the Church,"[16] whereas Tronson, before Montfort, attributes to the Virgin Mary Ambroise Autpert's expression (and believed to be Saint Augustine's) *forma Dei* - to be shaped or formed in the mold of God.[17]

III. Childhood Spirituality in the Work of Montfort

1. Contemplation of the Infant Jesus

Montfort's perspective on childhood is not so austere as that of Bérulle. Certainly, Montfort does not forget that the Incarnation is a mystery of *kenosis* (cf. LEW 70). In fact, with Bérulle, the saint emphasizes Jesus' submission to Mary (he is not too familiar with the word "annihilation"), like *"a slave captured by love."* In effect, Wisdom *"did not come into the world independently of others in the flower of his manhood, but he came as a frail little child dependent on the care and attention of his Mother"* (TD 139). For Montfort, the idea of childhood is tied to that of dependence and, indeed, obedience. That is why he interprets the evangelical demand to become a child to mean giving the most complete obedience: *"You must become a child, / . . . A child obedient . . ."* (H 10:11). Later in the same hymn he writes, *"We will obey a child / . . . As a child I obey"* (H 10:24 and 40; cf. H 45:13; RW 297).

But Montfort's divergence from Bérulle's austerity is obvious when he contemplates Jesus in Mary's womb and in the cradle at Bethlehem. Mary's womb is the *"truly earthly paradise"* where the new Adam *"performed . . . so many hidden marvels"* (TD 248); *"There are in this earthly paradise untold riches, beauties, rarities and delights"* (TD 261). It is the glorious throne of Jesus, where can be found greater happiness than in the bosom of Abraham (TD 199).

When Montfort joyfully contemplates the Infant Jesus, *"like the Magi"* he is conscious of the *"tender features of this lovely child"* (LEW 121), and with the shepherds he exclaims, *"Oh, this child is beautiful!"* (H 58:9). He is delighted before *"this dear child"* who is the *"King of Heaven": "Oh this attractive child / has a divine face! / His tender eyes are secret charms / that speak in silence"* (H 61:5). Montfort's strongest impression of the cradle at Bethlehem is admiration for the amiability and beauty of the Infant Jesus: *"Oh little baby, / You are so lovable! / Oh little lamb, / You are so beautiful!"* (H 59:11). Montfort emphasizes Jesus' love for children by calling to mind the episode in the Gospel when the Apostles pushed the children away from him. *"On seeing this Jesus rebuked his apostles and said to them, 'Do not keep the children away from me.' When they gathered about him he embraced and blessed them with gentleness and kindness"* (LEW 124).

Montfort's positive conception of childhood enables us to understand the meaning he gives to Christ's invitation to become a child: *"If you want to get to heaven, you must become as a little child, that is, you must be simple, innocent and gentle as a little child"* (MLW 61).

In conclusion, Montfort avoids the unilateral perspective that views the Christ Child only in terms of humiliation and death. While he acknowledges limits to childhood, he sees love beyond the poverty, and beauty and power beyond the abjection: *"He is a child, but he is adorable, / He is abject, but he is lovable"* (H 60:11); *"And all do speak of him / In his divine childhood. / They see in his poverty, / His love is extreme"* (H 61:2). Although the Infant Jesus is forever linked to the Cross, there always remains this context of love (LEW 169).

2. Loving contemplation of children

Montfort's vision of childhood is not idyllic. His own experience leads him to perceive several habitual faults in children: *"a tendency to lack religious modesty in your bearing, which makes you act like a child"* (RW 176); *"children are naturally inclined to laugh a lot"* (RM 82); *"explained the Hail Mary word by word as he would to a group of children"* (SR 13); *"were you to cry like a baby or a woman"* (LEW 102); *"I can only lisp like a child"* (LEW 1).

At the same time, Montfort cites Mt 18:3: *"Beware of showing contempt for any of my little ones; their angels see the face of my Father"* (LEW 147), from which he derives his profound respect for children. Moreover, he applies to Jesus expressions of the most tender love for children: *"I love your age very much, / My dear little ones. / I have taken it for my own, / God who I am, / I am a child / And I love childhood . . ."* (H 93:3). Montfort addresses himself to children by entrusting to them the recitation of a part of the Rosary and by calling them *"dear little friends"* (SR 8). He recommends to catechists that they never strike children *"either with [their] hand or with the cane"* but, rather, that *"like a kind teacher, [they] encourage them by praising them, by promising and giving them rewards and by showing them affection"* (RM 80). In sum, *"the oil of love"* must outweigh *"the vinegar of fear"* (RM 80).

Montfort points to the qualities of children that make them good models for adults: obedience (H 10:11,24,40), tenderness (H 9:16; MLW 61), simplicity (MLW 61), filial trust in Mary (H 79:5; 80:10). These virtues of childhood are necessary for Christians—*"Become, through grace, / Like this child . . ."* (H 97:10)—but Montfort also wants to lead his people to spiritual maturity, to adulthood in Christ (TD 119, 156; LEW 227). This means abandoning and even scorning the games of superficial value that satisfy children: *"Before you can be a perfect man / You must be deaf, dumb, and blind / To all the little jokes and trifles, / Made for children and fools . . ."* (H 25:32).

3. Spiritual childhood and Marian spirituality

Abandoning oneself to Providence in complete trust like a child is an important aspect of montfort spirituality. To remain little is to recognize one's own nothingness and to expect everything from God, like little children who expect everything from their parents. Louis Marie wrote, *"Whatever happens I shall not be worried. I have a Father in heaven who will never fail me"* (L 2). Letters 7, 8, and 33 express the same confidence in the Providence of the Father, Who will always be present.

When Montfort preached devotion to Mary, he simply asked Christians to follow Jesus Christ, who was submissive and obedient to Mary and dependent on her (TD 18, 139, 156, 157). By offering himself to Jesus Christ through Mary, he took the shortest and most direct road to perfection: that of the child. In this way, he recognized his poverty, weakness, and smallness and gave himself totally to the almighty protection of God. By this simple means of acting like a child, Louis Marie shows us a shortened path to holiness. Those who have received the grace to follow this spiritual road therefore must be malleable like children; they must allow themselves to be shaped and molded according to the desires of the almighty Maker. They must abandon themselves wholly to Mary, body and soul, without reservation, so as to belong to Jesus. It is *"the safest, easiest, shortest and most perfect way of approaching Jesus"* (TD 55). To acknowledge one's own spiritual incapacity is to practice the spirit of evangelical poverty. To the same extent that we recognize our sins, our poverty, our weakness, and our smallness, we grasp the need to be saved, liberated, and loved by him who alone is capable of filling this need by his own strength. Mary is recommended to us as the way that leads to Jesus precisely so that it will be easier for us always to remain poor in spirit.

Montfort's exegetes have not failed to scrutinize "the close relationship between perfect devotion and spiritual childhood."[18] Montfort often links the words *"children and servants"* (LEW 222; TD 203, 208), *"children and slaves"* (LEW 227), *"servants, slaves, and children"* (TD 56, 113).

According to A. Lhoumeau, who devotes a chapter to *Spiritual Childhood*, "in order to easily recognize in our own devotion the spirit and practices of spiritual childhood, we have only to consider its object, its motives, and its practices."[19] For Montfort, Mary is venerated and "envisaged above all as Mother," i.e., in her spiritual maternity. It follows from this that we in Christ are the children of this same mother, and have infirmities, faults, and needs "analogous to those of natural childhood." Lhoumeau successfully characterizes childhood and slavery. In effect, "what is characteristic of childhood, its most salient trait, is to be in a state of dependence. . . . This state of childhood demonstrates to us clearly that our total dependence on the Blessed Virgin must be a slavery of love."[20]

For M. Th. Poupon, there is a special affinity between Montfort and Thérèse of Lisieux, even if at first glance the existence of a link between the Montfort path and the Theresian path appears surprising: "Humility and simplicity, charity and abandon, these are the rich virtues that characterize holy slavery; these are also the distinctive jewels of spiritual childhood."[21]

Whereas for Lhoumeau and Poupon the dependence of love is expressed in voluntary slavery and spiritual childhood, F.M. Lethel sees in Anselm's *"Fac totum tuum dilectione"* (Doing everything out of love) the basis for a different language from that of Montfort and Thérèse of Lisieux: "the deepest desire of love is always to give of oneself entirely, to the point of no longer belonging to oneself but of belonging entirely to the loved one, to the point of being possessed by him or her."[22]

If we can distinguish an itinerary of Marian spirituality that Montfort presents to Christians, it would begin with the state of childhood and end with the gift of oneself in the complete availability or slavery of love, leading to the liberty of the children of God that is the height or the fruit of perfect Marian devotion (TD 215).

IV. Actualization

Montfort's interest in children and his use of childhood to distinguish a level of spiritual life poses to us the challenge of interpreting his intuitions for contemporary life.

1. Mission of educating children

Montfort alerted us to the importance of school for educating children. Today this task is part of the Church's pastoral mission, which must take an active role in anything that touches the lives of mankind. In its declaration on Christian education, the Second Vatican Council proclaims "the primary rights of men with respect to education, especially those of children" (GE, preamble) and recognizes that "since it can contribute so substantially to fulfilling the mission of God's people, and can further the dialogue between the Church and the family of man, to their mutual benefit, the Catholic school retains its immense importance in the circumstances of our times too" (GE 8).

We must certainly recognize the fundamental educative role of parents, who, having given life to their children, "have a most solemn obligation to educate their offspring. Hence, parents must be acknowledged as the first and foremost educators of their children." It is their responsibility "to create a family atmosphere so animated with love and reverence for God and men that a well-rounded personal and social development will be fostered among the children" (GE 3). But parents must be assisted by society and the Church, which appoint authorized teachers to continue the task of education.

The children of Christian families pose a pedagogical problem: should education begin with their human development or with education in the supernatural, as the urgencies of biblical revelation would suggest? It is true that education may have several aspects: intellectual, affective, social, Christian, etc. But contemporary social sciences militate against any partial consideration of children's needs in favor of a complete and all-inclusive development.

From what we know of Montfort, it is clear that he achieved an educational synthesis that encompassed both ordinary school subjects (reading, writing, mathematics, etc.) and catechism simultaneously. He thus ensured a social education in a context of Christian instruction, following the pedagogy of his time.

It is interesting to note that the directions of Vatican II coincide with those of Montfort. The council, indeed, favors and promotes an education that "does not merely strive to foster in the human person the maturity already described. Rather, its principal aims are these: that as the baptized person is gradually introduced into a knowledge of the mystery of salvation, he may daily grow more conscious of the gift of faith which he has received" (GE 2). No dichotomy should be imposed between human development and Christian development. The purpose of the Catholic school is "to help the adolescent in such a way that the development of his own personality will be matched by the growth of that new creation which he became by baptism" (GE 8). That is why, for the council as well as for Montfort, the primary appropriate educative means is "catechetical training" (GE 4).

Beyond the content of an all-inclusive education, no educator can dispense with two attitudes that Montfort displayed to the highest degree: love for the children and living testimony to what one teaches.

2. Spiritual childhood, adult spirituality

We have noted that Montfort, while proposing the child as a model for the evangelical life, warned against our falling into spiritual infantilism. He labored to lead Christians to *"the fullness of the age of Christ"* (TD 156).

Today we are similarly trying to recover the authentic meaning of spiritual childhood in the light of the Gospel while at the same time avoiding "spiritual infantilism serving pseudo-adulthood."[23]

The NT teaching on this point is quite clear. On the one hand it is necessary to *"become like children"* to *"enter the kingdom of heaven"* (Mt

18:3), to receive the kingdom of God *"as a little child"* (Mk 10:13-16; Lk 18:15-17), to be *"infants"* to receive the revelation of the Father (Mt 11:26; Lk 10:21). This is, in its urgency, a permanent attitude, the essence of which is a radical availability to the Word of God and to His Kingdom. "What Jesus recommends is neither the innocence of children, nor their obedience, nor even their simplicity as such, but their humility and their receptivity, full of confidence."[24] We must regain the true evangelical message, beyond what is commonplace: "In the social parable of the child, its summit is his trusting behavior, not, as is so often mistakenly believed, his ingenuity. The child does not have the distrustful prudence of the adult but with spontaneity and trust remains open to whatever leads him, without calculation or prolonged reflection."[25]

On the other hand, "while the Gospels privilege children by endowing them with the symbolic value of authentic disciples, because of their availability to divine calls (Mk 10:15; Mt 18:3-4, 19:14), the Epistles of the New Testament often call on us to give up childhood '*so that . . . you may grow into salvation*' (1 Pet 2:2)."[26] This indicates that the Christian, while remaining childlike in his availability and openness to God, must not stop at the infantile stage characterized by instability (Eph 4:14) and by the inability to enter into the mystery of the Cross (1 Cor 3:1-3). He must become mature (Heb 5:11-14; 1 Cor 14:20), perfect (1 Cor 2:6), spiritual (1 Cor 3:1; 6:9).

Religious writers often quote Saint Thérèse de Lisieux when speaking of spiritual childhood and maturity: "I must remain little, and become more and more so."[27] This is because spiritual childhood is a mystical attitude of humble, filial trust, of total and conscious abandon.

So we must accept the words of Jesus on childhood in terms of life and hope. It is a question of becoming and of being reborn. In our current context, being reborn means to become spiritually young again, which implies that we live in joy like a child. To become a child means to refuse defeatism and pessimism. It is to be certain that life and the human adventure have meaning, that our history must be located in the present and also in the future, that the most fundamental hopes of humanity will have the last word. It is to become inventive and creative.

Insofar as Louis Marie rejected defeatism and despair at the worst moments of conflict, when confronted with difficulties and crosses, he was not only interpreting the words of Jesus but practicing them in his life.

3. Spiritual childhood in the hands of Mary

Montfort's tenderness toward the Mother of Jesus, who became our Mother by the plan of the Trinity (TD 30-32, 37, 85; SM 8-12, 22), finds unforgettable expression: *"Mary is my sole support, / In all my misery. / When cares press on me urgently / I say, just like a child, / Mother, mother, mother"* (H 79:5). In contrast to the Jansenist rationalistic devotion to

Mary, Montfort lives and offers a devotion that is *"trustful, that is to say, it fills us with confidence in the Blessed Virgin, the confidence that a child has for its loving Mother"* (TD 107).

Montfort does not stop, however, at true and tender expressions of love for Mary. Responding to the reality of Mary, Mother in the order of grace, he makes himself totally available to the spiritual maternity of the Blessed Virgin. He wishes to live as a child in Mary, depending on her for everything as a child in her womb would, until he is brought forth to eternal life (cf. TD 33).

But it is easy to see that this image of the child in the maternal womb, in slavery to his mother, is not the only expression of a filial life with Mary. The model or paradigm from which Montfort willingly draws his inspiration is that of an adult, a well-loved disciple who receives Mary as his mother and lives with her as her son: *"Like St. John the Evangelist at the foot of the Cross, I have taken her times without number as my total good and as often have I given myself to her"* (SM 66; cf. TD 179, 216, 266).

Contemporary exegesis underlines the importance of the presence of Mary at the foot of the Cross (Jn 19:25-27). This episode is constructed according to a "plan of revelation": Jesus shows us Mary's role in the story of salvation, and the reception that his disciples must give her. The disciples are represented by the "disciple whom he loved," who represents the perfect believer, characterized by intimacy with Jesus (Jn 21:21), fidelity (Jn 19:25-27), and the gaze of contemplation (Jn 21:7). To this adult disciple Jesus gives his mother like a precious treasure, which must be received "into his own home" (Jn 19:27). This is the inheritance of the disciple of Jesus: the Word (Jn 12:14, 17:8), the Eucharist (Jn 6:51-58), the Spirit (Jn 7:39, 14:17; 20:22), grace (Jn 1:16).

With these comparisons of the little child and the adult, Montfort seems to apply to a filial relationship with Mary the two orientations of the NT: to become a child is to become mature in Christ.

But the filial life with the Virgin Mary is not a closed circle. For Montfort, *"Mary is entirely relative to God"* (TD 225): she is not a stopping point for the faithful but projects them toward the Trinity and finally toward God the Father. Living with Mary in an attitude of trust and self-giving is, according to Montfort, only an introduction to living as children of the Father. This is the effect of Montfort's Consecration: *"Those who are led by the spirit of Mary are children of Mary, and consequently children of God . . ."* (TD 258).

J. Vettickal-
S. De Fiores

Notes: (1) Grandet, 2. But Sibold (*Le sang des Grignion, I* [The history of the Grignions]) believes, with good reason, that Montfort received the name Marie on his baptismal day; his godmother was named Marie Lemoyne. (2) Blain, 4. (3) Grandet, 2. (4) On Montfort's first religious expressions, cf. S. De Fiores, *Itinerario,* 19-33. (5) Besnard II, 109-111. (6) Besnard, II, 111. (7) François de Sainte Marie and Ch. Bernard, *Enfance spirituelle (Spiritual Childhood),* in DSAM 4 (1960), 709. (8) Henri Bremond, *Histoire litteraire du sentiment religieux en France depuis la fin des guerres de religion jusqu'à nos jours, 3:525* Paris; Bloud and Gay, 1921. Vol. 3, *A Litterary History of Religious Thought in France from the Wars of Religion Down to Our Own Times,* trans. K.L. Montgomery (New York; Macmillan Co. 1928) (9) Blanlo, *L'enfance chrétienne qui est une participation de l'esprit et de la grâce du divin Enfant Jésus Verbe incarné (Christian Childhood, a Participation of the Spirit and Grace of the Holy Infant Jesus, Word Incarnate),* Paris 1665. Several other authors should be added: É. Binet, *Les saintes faveurs du Petit Jésus au coeur qu'il aime et qui l'aime (The Holy Favors of the Baby Jesus for the Heart That He Loves and That Loves Him),* Paris 1626; R. Luyt, *La plus éminente sagesse du christianisme, Jésus-Christ enfant (The Most Eminent Wisdom of Christianity, Jesus Christ Child),* Paris 1648; C. Boussey, *Jésus en son bas âge pour servir de modèle à la jeunesse chrétienne (Jesus at a Young Age As a Model for Christian Youth),* 2 vols., Paris 1652; J. Auvray, *L'enfance de Jésus et sa famille, honorée en la vie de soeur Marguerite du Saint-Sacrement (The Childhood of Jesus and His Family, Honored in the Life of Sister Marguerite of the Blessed Sacrament),* Paris 1654; J. Parisot, *Explication de la dévotion à la Sainte Enfance de Jésus-Christ Notre Seigneur (Explanation of Devotion to the Blessed Childhood of Jesus Christ Our Lord),* Aix 1657; P. Floeur, *Le Prince de paix, l'Enfant Jésus (The Prince of Peace, the Infant Jesus),* Brussels-Mons 1662; B. Chaduc, *Dieu enfant (God Child),* Lyon 1682. (10) Cf. De Fiores, *Itinerario,* 202-203. (11) Bremond, p. 516. (12) *Oeuvres de Bérulle (Works of Bérulle),* 1007. (13) Condren, *Considérations (Considerations),* 58-62. (14) Bremond, 524. (15) Cf. E. Lévesque, *J.-J. Olier,* in DTC, 11/1:978. (16) *Oeuvres de Monsieur Olier (Works of Olier),* ed. Migne, 883. (17) *Oeuvres complètes de Monsieur Tronson (Complete Works of Tronson),* ed. Migne, 2:577. Cf. M. Quéméneur, *La maternité de grâce de Marie chez les spirituels français du XVIIe siècle, de Saint François de Sales à Grignion de Montfort (The Maternity of Mary's Grace among the French Spirituals of the Seventeenth Century from St. Francis de Sales to Grignion de Montfort),* in EtMar 17 (1960), 69-118. (18) A. Lhoumeau, *La vie spirituelle à l'école de Saint Louis-Marie Grignion de Montfort (The Spiritual Life in the School of Saint Louis Marie Grignion de Montfort),* Beyaert, Bruges 1954 (1st ed., 1901), 273. (19) Lhoumeau, *La vie spirituelle,* 273-274. (20) Ibid., 278-279. (21) M.-Th. Poupon, *Le poème de la parfaite consécration à Marie (The Poem of Perfect Consecration to Mary),* Library of the Sacred Heart, Lyon 1947, 418. (22) F.-M. Lethel, *Connaître l'amour du Christ qui surpasse toute connaissance. La théologie des saints (Knowing the Love of Christ That Surpasses All Knowledge: The Theology of the Saints),* Editions du Carmel, Venasque 1989, 216-217. (23) G. Rossetto, *Enfance spirituelle et NT (Spiritual Childhood and the NT),* in CM 85 (1972), 267. (24) M.-F. Berrouard, *Enfance spirituelle (Spiritual Childhood),* in DSAM 4/1 (1960), 691. (25) Rossetto, *Enfance spirituelle et NT,* 271. (26) S. De Fiores, *Itinéraire spirituel (Spiritual Itinerary),* in *Dictionnaire de la vie spirituelle (Dictionary of the Spiritual Life),* Cerf, Paris 1983, 553. (27) S. Thérèse de l'Enfant Jésus, *Manuscrits autobiographiques (Autobiographical Manuscripts),* Lisieux 1957, 245. Therese de Lisieux, *Autobiography; The Complete and Authorized Text L'histoire d'une ame,* trans. Ronald Knox (New York; Kenedy, 1958) (28) Cf. M. de Goedt, *Un schéma de révélation dans la quatrième évangile (A Plan of Revelation in the Fourth Gospel),* in *New Testament Studies* 8 (1962), 142-150, and *La Mère de Jésus en Jean 19,25-27 (The Mother of Jesus in John 19:25-27),* in *Keckaritomène. Mélanges René Laurentin (Keckaritomon: Miscellaneous Writings of René Laurentin),* Desclée, Paris 1990, 207-216; A. Serra, *Contributi all'antica letterature guidaica per l'esegesi di Giovanni 2:1-12 e 19:25-27 (Contributions to Ancient Jewish Litterature for the Exegesis of John 2:1-2 and 19:25-27),* Herder, Rome 1977, and *Maria a Cana e sotto la croce (Mary at Cana and beneath the Cross),* 2nd ed., Center of Marian Culture "Madre della Chiesa," Rome 1991; Ignace de la Potterie, *Mary in the Mystery of the Covenant,* trans. Bertrand Buby (Staten Island, New York, Alba House, 1992).

CHURCH

Ecclesiology is a formal area of theology which, more than others, has seen an enormous development in recent times. If, in truth, the concept of Church as a perfect society is several centuries old, it is only within the last hundred years, from Vatican Council I to Vatican Council II, that other dimensions have been studied in depth. The Council further developed the doctrine of the Church as mystery, as the people of God, as communion.[1] For this reason when one delves into the concept of Church in an author who lived long ago, especially a spiritual author whose writings were not rigorously scholastic, there is danger of revisionism, of projecting a contemporary theological understanding onto the past. Yet one should not be surprised to discover in an author such as Montfort someone far in advance of their times. But Montfort's ideas and insights should be considered in their basic simplicity, not as a systematic formulation. They should be seen as seeds which will grow and bear fruit later on. In this sense, Montfort remains a child of his times and should not be misread on this score. But once one sees these insights in their contextural meaning, it is reasonable to apply them to life today, within a different theological and spiritual setting.

I. MONTFORT AND THE CHURCH OF HIS TIME

Seventeenth century France was an extraordinary period for culture, politics, and the arts. Church life was no less rich or complex. Tridentine

Reform was in full swing. The doctrinal and moral changes it inspired ran the gamut from the teaching of bishops to priestly formation, from theological reflection to catechesis and preaching. Schools of spirituality and religious orders were born and reborn. Charitable institutions arose, and a new missionary impulse leapt beyond the bounds of Europe. Difficulties and uncertainties, however, were not absent. Movements sometimes became polarized, on the one hand by a too facile openness to novelties and on the other by an holding onto the past. In France Jansenism emerged and developed during this period,[2] and Gallicanism remained much alive. Each of these complex phenomena had a profound impact on the Church. Louis de Montfort received his formation at the very end of the seventeenth century and his ministerial experience was in the first years of the eighteenth century.[3] What choices did he make within the fabric of the church life of his time?

1. Within the context of the Catholic Reform

The Council of Trent (1545-1563) was a monumental historic event in the life of the Church. It was important both for what it said and what it did. It undertook a vast number of pastoral, canonical, liturgical, and disciplinary reforms. Urged on by a pagan Renaissance, the Church knew how to rebuild itself well and with vigor. Menaced by Protestantism, the Church discovered within herself the ability to transform an apparent decadence into a new vitality. This commitment to the reform of its institutions and to the renewal of its way of doing things that began in the sixteenth and seventeenth centuries has guided the Church into our present age.[4]

Post-Tridentine ecclesiology developed themes that are found over and over again in the authors of the era: the Church as a perfect society, its visibility and indefectibility, its infallible magisterium, the Church as the Body of Christ, and the necessity of belonging to her in order to be saved.[5] At the same time, one witnesses an evolution of what we might call "the mind of the Church," an awareness that comes from belonging to the community of believers. Within the ranks of the people of God there persisted a medieval heritage: various devotions, the veneration of relics and images, pilgrimages, seeking after indulgences. The religion of the people seemed encased in external practices and ceremonies.[6] Catholic humanists who, while affirming the inner and personal life and—not openly condemning the devotional practices—took refuge in an individualistic piety. The early Jansenists sought a more authentic prayer life, a more enlightened piety, and a more rigorous morality through the inspiration of the early Church.[7]

The Tridentine Reform sought a renewal of the everyday life of the local Church with initiatives for clergy and people alike. In France, with a population approaching 20 million at the time of Louis XIV, those involved in pastoral work constituted a massive presence. For the year 1702, it added up to the following numbers: 18 archbishops, 100 bishops, 140,000 pastors, 10,400 priors, 15,000 chaplains; among religious: 36,500 monks, 35,000 members of the major religious orders, 82,000 religious.[8] The reconstruction of the Church came from on high. It requried bishops devoted to their charges, and immediately France showed that it had capable and cultivated bishops. The priest was ordained and sent by his bishop. He was an official, hierarchical, and communitarian sign. A social charism among the presbyterate was evident: one was a priest for others, in a complex organism, where all the members were in solidarity with each other. A priestly spirituality developed, and seminaries were instituted to form the clergy.[9]

Montfort, in deciding to become a priest, agreed to take the path offered by the ecclesiastical institutions. He entered the seminary of Paris, finished all the required studies, and took on the priestly spirituality which eminent priests and directors of priests—such as Olier—were living and teaching to others.[10] In the parish of St. Sulpice, Montfort the seminarian, was initiated into catechetics and the works of charity. And even before his priestly ordination, he made up his mind not to stay permanently in a particular job but to become an itinerant missionary in service to the Church of the people. This was a fundamental perspective that would give unity to the personality and the work of Montfort. Many of his future choices can be understood in light of this decision such as his going about the countryside, missions to the people, catechism taught to the poor, the use of the language adapted to the popular culture, the use of hymns, recourse to devotional practices. At the beginning of the eighteenth century, Montfort was one of those rare representatives of the clergy of the Church in France to feel the need to update the teaching of the Church for the poor, and that meant the major part of the French population.[11] In all things, he wished to remain obedient to the Pope, the bishops, the local clergy and to accept the structures of the Tridentine Church.

2. The "science of the saints"

The vitality of the Church of the seventeenth century is to be seen not only in efforts at institutional reform but also in the richness, depth, and variety of its spiritual movements, which—while remaining in touch with earlier sources—took on original characteristics. Francis de Sales exercised an enormous influence; Bérulle was the head of a school of thought which saw theology and spirituality as inseparable. His disciples Eudes and Olier would leave a profound mark on the life of the Church. Port-Royal was a powerful magnet. Even if its doctrine was somewhat dubious and theology weak, its way of life, prayer, and mysticism gave it value. Its knowledge of Rheno-Flemish mysticism (Ruysbroeck, Harpius, Tauler) expanded and was influenced equally by the Italian spirituals such as Catherine of Genoa, Gagliardi, Scupoli, and Mary Magdalen de' Pazzi. The spiritualities of the major religious orders (Jesuits, Dominicans, Capuchins) were dominant. In the specific area of mysticism, they conjoined themselves to a more "abstract" movement, which taught that one must be in conformity with the will of God by annihilating oneself. In part this would lead to quietism. A more "positive" school had great influence and included Jesuit authors, like Lallemant, Coton, Saint-Jure and Surin, for whom conformity to the will of God and pure love, life in Christ, and docility to the Holy Spirit are the foundations for an apostolic zeal for one's neighbor. This school would give the Church some saintly people, among them secular priests like Boudon, religious like Mary of the Incarnation and Mathilde of the Blessed Sacrament, and lay people like Gaston de Renty and John Aument.[12]

On a more popular level we should mention another spiritual movement: psychological moralism (Nicole, Duguet). It tried to apply to the spiritual and mystical life the "knowledge of self," recalling Socratic thought: if man is made in the image of God, then the knowledge of man leads to the knowledge of God. But who is capable of this? Every day we discover something new in the world and in man; it is not possible to know everything. We see in profile a model of Christian life adapted to one's own status, in imitation of several saints and under the guidance of a spiritual director. Even without always being based on sound theological foundations, this movement presented a spirituality adapted to different situations in daily life, where a great deal of time was reserved for private prayer, for books of prayer, for practices of devotion, and for rules of a confraternity.[13] That which was written about the spiritual life was written within the context of the life of the faithful; within the family, professional and social life of each person. The writings were to be edifying to the ordinary person, spiritually and morally. They offered models of sanctity for married people, widows, country people, servants, soldiers, gentlemen, princes. Every group had its saints, prayers, images and feasts. Special attention was given to the sick and the dying; the art of dying "well" was one of the subjects most written about in Christian literature of the seventeenth century.[14]

In such a spiritual atmosphere—rich, varied and not without risk—Montfort made his first decisions. One such decision can be dated from when he was still a seminarian. He ceased to go to classes at the Sorbonne and instead took up study on his own. The fact is, having read Boudon and Surin, Montfort made a decision to study the "science of the saints."[15] He saw that no knowledge, even theological, no successful career, even ecclesiastical, constituted a true force for reformation in the Church. Rather, sanctity of life did. Among all those who sought renewal, Montfort looked first not to the bishops or clergy but, rather, to the lay people. He went to the people of God, and brought them the witness of his own sanctity. His holiness was that of an apostle who lived solely for God, inspired by Jesus Christ alone. To do this, Montfort borrowed from Bérulle and Olier, from Lallemant and other mystics. He wanted to offer a spirituality that, on the one hand, was well founded theologically while on the other hand one that avoided superficial moralizing. He wanted a spirituality that took into account the culture of the people, their need for "mystery" and, the concreteness and simplicity of their images, symbols, and external practices. Montfort's preaching, life witness, and writings were always along this line.[16]

Another proof of Montfort's popular genius as a missionary was his choice of Marian devotion as the "secret" of perseverance in the faith and as an efficacious synthesis of all those things involved in the following of Christ. Both its solid theological foundations and its interior and exterior practices could be well understood by the people. He placed everything at the service of renewal in the Church. The seventeenth century was also important for the development for Marian doctrine and devotion. At this time Mariology was born as a specific theological treatise, producing profound, fruitful studies and giving a solid foundation. Marian devotion continued to spread with positive although with risks of excess.[17] France, right up to the troubled times of the "Monita Salutaria" (1673), saw theologians, spiritual authors, and saints who were not afraid to live and recommend a fervent Marian devotion. Following upon this came the critical spirit of Protestantism, the Jansenist climate, and the first signs of enlightenment. They attacked the external practices of Marian devotions, judging them to be immoderate, if not superstitious. Montfort was faced with a double temptation when he studied theology at the beginning of the eighteenth century. The first was to restrain the rapid growth of Marian devotion. This would have given total credence to its critics, and infer that the theological foundations of Marian devotion were insufficient (more than one intellectual or "enlightened" theologian ceded to this temptation). The second temptation was to pursue these forms of devotion without worrying about enemies or heretics. On the level of the people, the latter involved a greater risk. Montfort reacted against both dangers. He unhesitatingly reasserted solid Marian devotion, making it the centerpiece of his pastoral work. At the same time, he kept in mind the lessons of history. He recommended that everyone avoid false devotions, while he carefully developed the theological basis for true devotion to Mary. He avoided renouncing authentic devotional practices, including external ones. Montfort knew how to create a proper balance through his choices. His sense of Church was rooted in tradition, it stopped him from vacillating in the face of what was going on at that time. It increased his sensitivity for the legitimate renewal of the Church, desired by the Council of Trent and it made him attentive to the dangers of those devotions which lack a strong theological foundation.

3. To Live the Church with the people

Montfort prepared himself to go out among the people. He taught catechism in the ghettoes of Paris, gathered together outlines of sermons, and wrote hymns. His desire was to *"go in a humble and simple way to teach catechism to the poor in country places"* (L 5). The life of a Christian community, especially in rural areas, was centered on the parish church.

Everyone was brought there for Baptism as soon as possible after birth. One received Communion about the age of 12 and, whenever the bishop showed up, Confirmation. Around the age of 25, a man and woman were married and at the end, at death, a person was interred in a cemetery ordinarily found next to the church, where it formed a sacred enclave.[18] Since Montfort, in his parish missions, wanted to renew the spirit of Christianity within a particular village, his pastoral work was based on these elements. He brought men, women and children to the church for catechism, preaching and general confession, Holy Communion and the celebration of the Eucharist, and the prayers for the dead. He concluded his mission with its crowning synthesis, the renewal of Baptismal promises. The days of the mission became a distillation of the whole Christian life. It was a way to recapitulate in a few weeks and in a Church setting, the spiritual events and concerns of a lifetime.[19]

Each week every person in the village came to the church, with the exception of the gravely ill or those at odds with the pastor. Everyone assisted at Mass, which was both a sign of faith and a community and social-get-together. On Sunday, a day of relaxation, everyone met at church and exchanged bits of news. When danger threatened the village, the church became a place of refuge and protection. The house of God was the house of all the people, a fulfillment of its primordial role. Conscious of the importance of the parish church, Montfort made it the point of reference of his work of missionary renewal. We must remember that particularly within the overall community of larger villages presided over by a pastor, there existed chapels, mission churches, and oratories connected to religious communities, and hospitals, or confraternities. Often these other churches received many of the faithful for prayer, for pious practices, and for special celebrations of feast days. They performed a positive function for several reasons. They offered people a place to pray, to hear sermons, to find spiritual directors. There was, however, a risk in them. They were often criticized for breaking the unity of the church community and of favoring the formation of elite groups of laypeople. [20] Montfort held to a Church for all the people and for the means of salvation of the universal Church (the sacraments and the liturgy) for all believers. Nevertheless, he also recommended prayers, devotions, and confraternities, not as a substitutes for the basic elements of the Christian life but rather as means for persevering on the path of conversion. The mission offered a road of conversion which began at the Baptismal font, continued at the confessional, and ended at the Eucharistic altar.

II. The Church in the Doctrine of Montfort

In the Christocentric Marian devotion of St. Louis de Montfort, there was an ecclesiological dimension.[21] Also it is important that he did not consider the church as a separate, formal, theological catagory. Montfort was a spiritual author and a missionary, not a professional theologian. His interest was in the conversion of souls. And yet, we find in his teaching, seen within the proper context of his time, a solid theological base.

1. Salvation history

To understand fully what Montfort wrote and taught, his teachings must be set within the context of his overall doctrinal and pastoral view. He was concerned with salvation history in its entirety. Montfort was profoundly conscious that the design of God to save humankind was a singular one, even if it came about in different ways.[22] The protagonists were always the same: on the one hand, the Three Persons of the Trinity and, on the other, mankind called to respond to the love of God. The complete parable of salvation history, as seen by Montfort, can be drawn from three of his most important works: LEW, TD, and PM. In LEW, he recounts the creation and the fall of man, the decision to save him, the Incarnation of the Word, the Wisdom of God made man not just through the cross, but through the totality of our human response. It is a call to search for, find, and live the Wisdom of God. TD puts devotion to Mary at the heart of this development, but only after illustrating the presence and role of Mary willed by the Trinity in salvation history. Authentic Marian devotion is then nothing other than man's response to God. PM, concise as it is, completes the story by showing how the saved individual, in his turn, is called to become an apostle in order to save his neighbor, renew the Church, and convert the world.

Time for the Church is that phase of salvation history which permits mankind to respond to God, to come to Him and and to let Him reign in our hearts. That is why Montfort speaks implicitly of the Church, as much in LEW 181-222 when he teaches one to search for Wisdom, as in TD 126-130 when he proposes that we live our Baptism through Consecration to Jesus Christ by the hands of Mary; and in PM 12 when he invites us to become apostles full of zeal for the evangelization of the world. The terminology is different but the meaning is equivalent to what today is meant by, "to be Church." For Montfort it was to conform oneself to Jesus Christ, the Incarnate Wisdom, in order that He may reign in our hearts and in the world (TD 61-62, 120). It is to be docile to the Holy Spirit and to Mary his faithful collaborator, in order that we may be formed into members of the Body of Christ (TD 34-36, 140). It is to be apostles of the end times in order to fight against evil and give final victory to the Lord Jesus Christ (TD 58). The design of salvation has come about in Christ who is the reason and foundation of all grace. But the description that Montfort had of the other periods of salvation history is uniquely that of the present age, the age of the Church, the time of conversion. Montfort, the missionary, is concerned with conversion. Thus he is conscious of being in the service of God for the time of the Church; and in the service of our neighbor in order that he may live the time of grace here and now, during this stage of salvation. It is true that in the seventeenth century they usually spoke of the individual salvation of every person in their meeting with God face-to-face. Consequently they saw the Church as the milieu within which each person might find his or her salvation. But it is equally true that they were conscious that all were called to conversion and that the means of grace were offered to all. They constantly used the image of the Mystical Body, of Christ as the Head and we the members (TD 32; FC 27). They sought to give witness to the belief that true believers form among themselves and with Christ a true oneness.

Furthermore, Montfort sees the Church as a time and a place for salvation (TD 50 64), where faith is professed (TD 2, 14, 25, 214) in the reception of the Word of God (TD 57; LEW 95-97; H 43:8; 141:5), in obedience to the Pope and the bishops (H 6, 50,57; 147:3; RM 22), and in meeting with God in the Sacraments (H 109:7-15), where our prayer of praise goes forth (TD 84, 95, 116), where spiritual fruit ripens (TD 68), but where there is expressed a need for renewal and reform (PE 5, 17), awaiting the final coming of Christ (SM 58; PE 5).

2. Other elements of strong ecclesial value

Not only salvation history but other aspects of Montfort's thought are ecclesial.

a. Incarnation. The mystery of the Word become man in Mary occupies a central place in the writings of Montfort. The influence of Bérulle is evident here. In the Incarnation all of the mysteries of the Redemption are already found. Therefore everything said of this mystery projects its light down through the centuries of Church history. In the Incarnation one discovers the action of the three Persons of the Trinity. The Father sends the Son through Mary. The Word becomes man in her. The Holy Spirit, forms Jesus Christ in the womb of Mary after having asked for her consent (TD 16).[23] God incarnates every day in the Church (TD 22). By Mary's mediation Jesus Christ came into the world. So by her mediation He will reign over the world (TD 1). Montfort wrote that at the moment of the Incarnation, Wisdom built the house of redemption. (LEW 105;24). He illustrated at length the role of Mary in the Incarnation and wished to teach an authentic devotion directed to Jesus Christ through Mary. Louis Marie drew from this mystery the rules of life for future believers. Jesus Christ is the one Savior of the world (TD 61). The Holy Spirit, forms the members of the Mystical Body in Mary in the same way that he formed Jesus in Mary (TD 20-21). Mankind's salutation and perfection consists in being conformed, united, and consecrated to Jesus Christ (TD 120). This will always be true right until the end of time. Mary was the path Jesus chose to come to us in the Incarnation. Therefore, she is the sure way to go to him (TD 50). Consequently, to speak of the Incarnation is to speak of the Church.

b. Paschal mystery. "Wisdom is the Cross and the Cross is Wisdom" (LEW 180); Montfort expressed his meditation on the paschal mystery in language appropriate to his time. The entire Letter to the Friends of the Cross (FC) is an exhortation to follow the path of the Cross of Christ. It is a road marked by suffering and death but, in the end, one crowned with glory for those who wish to follow him (FC 58). In the life and preaching of Montfort, the Cross was central. It was the search for the true Wisdom God, the turning away from the wisdom of the world, the object of asceticism (LEW 74 ff). the true Wisdom obtained by a universal mortification (LEW 194 ff). Persecution and the Cross were the life companions of a true disciple of Jesus Christ. In them he gave expression to the death and resurrection of Christ, to Easter. The paschal mystery is central to our faith and the foundation of ecclesial life. Baptized into Christ, we draw our salvation from the grace of the Sacraments. Montfort emphasized during the sermons and catechetical lessons of his parish missions that the proclamation of the Word prepared people for the Sacraments of Reconciliation and Eucharist. The conversion he obtained was a sealed "*covenant contract*"[24] and a renewal of one's Baptismal promises. It was a commitment to persevere. The montfort idea of Church is not to be found in theoretical formularies but, rather, in his pastoral missionary practice. The elements of his ecclesiology are clearly reflected in faith, Word and Sacrament, liturgy and life commitment.

c. Baptism and Consecration. These two words are a good summary of the specific characteristics of montfort spirituality. All of Montfort's missionary activity—his preaching, catechesis, celebrations, and written teachings—were dictated by a desire to renew Christianity among the faithful. His own personal understanding of the faith is to be found in the renewal of the Baptismal promises. It was a life commitment to become more faithful than ever before. Everything that Montfort wrote on Mary's role and presence in the mystery of God and salvation, and on the devotional life, taught Consecration to Jesus Christ through Mary. It led to one thing, to the renewal of Baptismal promises (TD 20, 126). We see Montfort the missionary and writer clearly in the way he identified Baptism with Consecration to Jesus through Mary. Montfort clarified the radical ecclesial character of the Sacrament of Baptism. In receiving and living this Sacrament, believers participate in the unique saving action of Christ who is Redeemer, Savior of the world and Lord of history. They become members of Christ's Body, the Church, the community of salvation. They join a pilgrim people on their way to God. Through each present moment, they live in Christ Jesus and in his Spirit, and know that they belong to God and to the community of the saved.[25]

d. Apostolate. Montfort very rapidly exhausted his human life in the service of God, in seeking the conversion of his neighbor and the renewal of the Church. His complete devotion to the apostolate came from his conviction that virtue's highest degree of perfection was *"to acquire the light and unction you need to inspire others with that love for Wisdom which will lead them to eternal life"* (LEW 30). In fact, *"Wisdom gives man not only light to know the truth but also a remarkable power to impart it to others"* (LEW 95).[26] In the history of montfort thought which begins in LEW, continues in TD, and concludes with PM, it is clear that the apostolate gives spirituality its true value. The apostolate is ecclesial by its very nature. Man's salvation consists in knowing Incarnate Wisdom, Jesus Christ, and in living in his Spirit. In order to find Jesus, one must find Mary (LEW 203; TD 85; SM 6). It is living the Consecration to Jesus through Mary, i.e. in order to carry Baptism to maturity, consecrated souls will dedicate themselves completely to the service of the Virgin Mary. In this way they will become ministers of the Lord who are tongues of fire, and clouds of thunder moved by the breath of the Spirit. They will propagate the Word of God, fight against sin, and bring home glorious victories (TD 56-59). By their ministry, the face of the earth will be renewed and the Church reformed (PM 17). Montfort called priests and laypeople, men and women to be apostles. His single standard was founded only on a capacity to live the Consecration to Jesus through Mary fully. Apostolic work should continue to progress in the Church. Why? Because *"in these latter times"* (TD 50) God wants to reveal Mary more then ever before. For she is the masterpiece of His hands. In the same way, the conflict between good and evil will daily become more acute. But a humble Mary will be victorious. She will raise up servants. She will endow them with divine charisms. These sons and daughters will do her work. They will be great in holiness and be superior to every other creature in their courage and zeal (TD 49-54).

e. Mary. The Marian dimension of montfort spirituality remains its best known aspect. It is what is highlighted the most. But one must not forget that without a Christocentric spirituality one cannot belong to this Gospel movement. From the start, Montfort insisted upon this. Mary is to be seen entirely in terms of her relation to God. She draws her total existence from the Lord. She is for the Lord completely (TD 61). Furthermore, Montfort's doctrine of Mary cannot be grasped correctly except in a Trinitarian and eschatological context. This was Montfort's central understanding. Consequently, the heart of his Mariology is ecclesial. Montfort stated that given the actual order of things, God chose Mary not only as necessary for the historical coming of Christ but for the realization of the reign of Christ down through the centuries (TD 15). In fact, Mary finds grace before God, for herself and for all human beings. She gave flesh and birth to Eternal Wisdom and today she incarnates him, in the believing faithful through the action of the Holy Spirit (LEW 203). Mary is Queen of All Hearts because she has received from God power over souls (TD 37). The Son of God, in fact, distributes his graces through her (TD 24). The actual role of Mary is, therefore, ecclesial. It is to give birth to Jesus Christ within the souls of the faithful. It is to give new sons and daughters to the Church, to the community of salvation. Such truths are seen by Montfort to be embodied in faithful people who have a devotion for Mary. She is, then, their model of faith. They are called to imitate her (TD 214). She gives them the example of how to be attentive to the Spirit, of how to be transformed into Christ (TD 218), for the greater glory of God (TD 222-225). This is how Montfort described the believer who travels in, through and with the Church toward a perfect realization of the reign of Christ.

III. Montfort Spirituality and Current Ecclesiology

Every reference to contemporary ecclesiology must take into account Vatican Council II. It was the culmination of the period of study and research that preceeded it. It was fully and consciously celebrated by the Church. It was a new departure which gave us a true modern ecclesiology. At the root of every conciliar document are new ecclesiological insights. Several treat this in a specific way. LG is concerned with nature, structure, and life of the Church. GS dealt with the Church and the world. SC treated the Church at prayer, the sacrament of salvation. AG considered the Church's missionary dimension. After centuries, ecclesiology once again began to develop. In the early post conciliar years other perspectives developed. They pointed to new "models" of the Church. Included are the Church as "Koinonia", which brought out the aspects of the church as communion-community, the Church as "Kerygma" which gave priority to the Church as Proclaimer of the Word, and Convoker of the assembly of the Lord, the Church as "Diakonia" which centered on the Church as Servant of God and of his people in love and glory, the Church as "Eschaton", which gradually defines the Church as the reign of God. Each of these models developed certain aspects of the Church. But none exhausted its mystery.[27]

Bearing in mind the ecclesiology of Vatican II, what is it relevancy to the spiritual doctrine of St. Louis de Montfort? Starting from our present understanding of the Church let's look back without forcing false similarities. Let's look for the "seeds" of our present understanding and how they have developed, grown and bore fruit, in our contemporary awareness of the church.

1. The reign of God

One of the most important results of the second Vatican Council was its rediscovery of the theology of salvation history. It bypassed an abstract method which more than once led the research of specialists down a dead-end street. The Council preferred to speak of history as a reflection of God's design of salvation willed by the Father, realized in the mission of his Son, and actualized each day among humans through the sanctifying work of the Spirit (LG 2-4). It is the reign of God, promised for centuries, manifest in Christ, that enters hearts through the presence of the Spirit. The Church is the seed of this kingdom. It is its beginning, the source of its growth, and its yearning for accomplishment. (LG 5). The life of the believer in the Church thus becomes a vital synthesis of this truth. The Church is called to build the reign of God, within its own heart and within the world. It draws its life from the Spirit, is victorious over and evil, and will continue until Christ comes in glory.

Montfort chose not to become a professor of the Sorbonne, but rather to dedicate himself to the people. He chose not to write for intellectuals but for simple people (TD 26). He had a predilection for a positive presentation of the history of salvation, by telling its story in dramatic form. The mystery of the Incarnation, prepared in the Old Testament and understood through the Cross, constituted the first reign of God, the first coming of Christ. Since then, the kingdom has begun to spread itself throughout the world (TD 1). Montfort always explicited the Trinitarian dimension of the action of God (TD 4, 16, 17-21, 22, 23, and in LG 2-4). People are called to have Christ reign in their hearts, since *"the kingdom of Jesus Christ exists primarily in the heart"* (TD 38). In this second coming, Jesus Christ must be known, loved, and served (TD 49). He *"must be the ultimate end of all our other devotions . . . [the] foundation for our salvation, perfection and glory"* (TD 61). By God's power, Jesus chases out demons and manifests the kingdom (LG 5). The battle against the reign of evil is seen to increase every day, in these end times (TD 50-51). But true believers will receive the power to obtain victory (TD 58). In this Trinitarian and salvation history context, the initiative comes from God and man collaborates. Men are joined together in history until the end of time. Montfort, like LG, prefers to use the theme of the kingdom.

2. Church, People

The most common criticism voiced about the ecclesiology of the past is that it was based upon on the more individualistic conception of salvation found among most of the theologians and spiritual authors of those times. Recently, the idea of the Church as the people of God, (an image so often found in the Bible) is taken up again as a fundamental one LG (9 ff). It was almost completely absent in Montfort's time. Thanks to Vatican II, the idea of the Church as the people of God in history has led to a renewed liturgical life, to a more evident missionary commitment, and to a more lively consciousness of our fraternal solidarity with believers and non believers alike. The benefits of this view of church can be seen in the Church's prayer life, her missionary and ecumenical spirit, her commitment to charity, her attitude of tolerance and patience with history, her sense of unity.

In his writings, Louis de Montfort appears to be a child of his times. In the Church, dispenser of the sacraments, salvation is sought and found. Through ascetical zeal and devotional practice, persons persevere in grace. Certain elements, however, merit particular attention. To be a saint means to free oneself from the spirit of the world and to fill oneself with Jesus Christ (TD 227), to renounce oneself and follow Christ (LEW 13), to acquire and conserve Wisdom (LEW 14, 223). It is not to isolate oneself in an individualistic asceticism but, rather, *"to inspire others with that love for Wisdom which will lead them to eternal life"* (LEW 30), to belong on Christ's side (LEW 7-12), to be apostles through whose ministry the world will be renewed and the Church reformed, where a welcome will be given to convert and non believers, to Moslems, Hebrews, and others (PM 17). If, consequently, we analyze the Montfort's choices on the pastoral level, we see there a clear sensitivity for the people of God whom he gathered together, the parish communities to which he preached missions. We see this in the liturgical assemblies which he convoked to listen to the Word of God, to celebrate of the Sacraments, to renew their Baptismal promises and to take part in processions. If the renewal of the Second Vatican Council has the same results (LG 13-17), it means that the same spirit animated both, but one expressed in different ways.

3. All are called to the same holiness

The Church is one people of God united by faith in Christ and participating in his Priesthood (LG 10-11), consecrated in his Baptism and called to his holiness (LG 40). Thus there exists a fundamental equality among all believers—between clerics and laypeople, religious and secular, men and women. However each has their own particular charism (LG 12) with different forms of expression for the same holiness (LG 41). The council brought about a great change in our way of thinking. It recognized that every state of life lived with an authentic faith, produces saints. Not only the monastic, priestly, and religious but also the lay and married states are open to heroic virtue, to the contemplative life, and to serving one's neighbor. The ways and means of sanctity first is charity and then it is listening to the Word of God, the Sacraments, prayer, and the exercise of virtue. (LG 42).

Montfort's point of view is in perfect accord with today's Church. For the spirituality taught by Montfort is founded on Baptism and on all the things that make up the following of Christ. It is a faith journey that begins with conversion from sin and leads to the highest points of mysticism. It is a simple way of arriving at full union with God accesible to all (TD 152). Holiness was certainly willed by God for every person (SM 3). The great saints and the apostles of the end times of the Church, *"both men and women"* (TD 114), will be true disciples of Jesus Christ, strengthened by his Word alone and by his Cross (TD 58-59). Before he put to paper his unique form of spirituality, Montfort taught it fruitfully in his missions for many years (TD 110). Occasionally his missions were for religious communities, but primarily they were for the faithful at large—for every type of person, age and state of life. His was a profoundly ecclesial spirituality. It was for all of the people of God.

4. Eschatological character

"And so the latter times have already arrived for us" (LG 48). The Church is already adorned with true holiness, albeit imperfect. We, the believers, "put on the armor of God in order to be able to stand firm against the ambushes of Satan" (ibid.). Strong in faith, we await the blessed hope, the glorious manifestation of Jesus Christ. The Church that marches through history is in communion with that portion of the people of God which possesses the full vision of the glory of God. For all those who belong to Christ have the same Spirit, they form one Church, because all are united to him.

Montfort showed a particular sensitivity for the future ages of the Church. He used a special terminology in describing the future stages of salvation history and the coming of the Kingdom of Christ (TD 49-59; SM 58-59; PM 2, 5-6, 13, 16-17), to the point of being wrongfully suspected of millenarianism.[28] In my judgement, there is no reason to judge his belief in the latter times to be any different from the one that prevailed during his era. It was an orthodox belief. Montfort awaited the glorious coming of Christ as *"the whole Church expect[s] him"* (SM 58), without offering a specific personal theological thesis. But it is clear that he saw the manifestation of the Kingdom of God as coming with increased acceleration. He pushed for a time of conversion, because the battle between good and evil is *"now more than ever"* decisive. Every time that he spoke of the future, there would occur expressions like *"more than ever," "more every day," "as soon as possible," "above all," "grows every day"* (TD 50, 51, 55, 113, 114). He had a dynamic way of convincing others that the time of salvation was now. He avoided putting things off, since the Lord was coming. As for the moment when he will come, *"only God knows"* (TD 59).

Setting his sights on the future of the Church and the world, Montfort looked at the faithfulness of the God of eternity, who never changes his way of acting (TD 15). This is the God whose love has continued throughout the centuries, was from the beginning and will be to the end. Between the past and the future there was a continuity, not a cyclical repetition. The future depends on the past. The past is the exemplar of the future. Such a view does not impede something new from happening. In the end, history progresses like a straight line and comes to an end. These are the end times. In them everything will be assumed, fulfilled, accomplished, for the glory of God and for eternity.

5. Mary

The relationships between past, present, and future, and their theological and their spiritual significance in salvation history, were seen and presented by Montfort through Mary. She was for Montfort the pass key to the different stages of salvation history in the life of the Church. Through Mary, God begins and ends his most important works (TD 15, 19). The Holy Spirit chose her as His collaborator (TD 20, 35). Through Mary the saints of the past have found grace before God. It will be the same in the future (TD 45). The apostle of the latter times saw the work of the Spirit in union with Mary. Through her all things are elevated, formed, and sustained (PM 6, 11; TD 35, 55-56). According to Montfort in every age of the Church, but more than ever, during the latter times, the central players emerge: the Holy Spirit, Mary, and the Saints. (TD 54). If everyone is called to holiness, to be great and exalted before God, then the time of grace given to everyone in the Church will be a time of perfect docility to the Spirit. Mary is the great *secret* for living fully in the Holy Spirit. Montfort taught the devotion to Mary, the Consecration to Jesus through her, the renewal of Baptismal promises, as the simple, but powerful, path to the fullness of the Christian life. It was a way to sanctity, to giving the Church more *great saints.* He believed that there would be more and more such holy people in the Church, as it approached the end times.

It is not by accident that the Second Vatican Council document on the Church ends with Mary (LG 52-69). Her presence in the mystery of Christ demands her continuing in the mystery of the Church. Mary thus becomes the image and model of the Church (LG 53, 63). She helps us to understand Christ and to enter into the mystery of his communion, which is the Church. Mary is the "model" of the Church (LG 63). What Mary has been and is, the Church is called to become—virgin and mother (LG 63-64). She is rich in virtues to imitate (LG 65), above all else her faith, her hope, and her love. At last, as sign of the people of God, Mary is glorified in God just as the Church anticipates the final destiny of every believer and of the entire community of the saved (LG 68).

In Montfort's journey of faith Mary has an analogous role. In effect, he presents the totality of God's universal plan of salvation through Mary —the work of the Trinity, and Christ's Incarnation and Redemption. Here, Montfort uncovers Mary's presence and role in the historical unfoldment of salvation. And from it emerges the fundamental principle of montfort spirituality. God came to us through Mary. We must return to Him through Mary. This is what the Council meant by the words of *Lumen Gentium's* Chapter 8 title - Mary in the Mystery of Christ and the Church (LG).

B. Cortinovis

Notes: (1) Cf. J. Frisque, *L'ecclesiologia nel XX saecolo,* (Ecclesiology in the XX century) in *Bilancio della teologia del XX secolo* (*Report on the theology of the XX century*), R. van der Gucht and H. Vorgrimler, vol 3, Roma 1972, 240-262; Avery Dulles, *Catholic Ecclesiology Since Vatican II* in Concilium 6 1986 (Synod 1985). (2) J. Leclerq, *Église, au temps de la Réforme et de la Contre-réforme,* (*The Church at the Time of the Reformation and the Counter-reformation*) in *DSAM* 4 (1960) 414-426; R. Taveneaux, *Le catholicisme post-tridentin,* (*Post-Tridentine Catholicism)* in *Histoire des Religions,* (*History of Religions*), H.C. Peuch, Gallimard, Paris 1972, II, 1049-1146 (3) Cf. G. Leclerc, *Zeger-Bernard van Espen (1646-1728) et l'autorité ecclésiastique. Contribution à l'histoire des théories gallicanes et du jansénisme,* (*Zeger-Bernard van Espen (1646-1728) and ecclesiastical authority. Contribution to the History of Gallican Theories and of Jansenism),* Zurich 1964, 11-16; R. Mandrou, *Louis XIV en son temps 1661*-1715, (Louis *XIV and His Times*), PUF, Paris 1973. (4) Cf. H. Jedin, *A History of the Council of Trent,* trans. Ernest Graf, B. Herder, St. Louis 1961.

(5) Cf. Y. Congar, *L'église de saint Augustin à l'époque moderne* (*The Church from Saint Augustine to Modern Times*) Paris 1970. (6) Cf. J. Delumeau, *Christianizzaione e dechristianizzazione fra Il XVI e il XVIII secolo,* (*Christianization and Dechristianization between the XVI and XVIII centuries*)in *Società e vita religiosa nell'Ancien Régime,* (*Society and Relgious Life in the Ancien Régime*), C. Russo, Guida, Napoli 1976, 533-579. (7) Cf. J. Carreyre, *Jansénisme* (Jansenism), in DTC 8/1 (1924) 318-529. (8) Cf. J. Saint-Germain, *La vie quotidienne en France à la fin du Grand Siècle,* (*Daily Life in France at the End of the 'Grand Siècle'*), Hachette, Paris 1965, 241; J. Queniart, *Les Hommes, l'Église et Dieu dans la France du XVIII siècle,* (*Man, Church and God in France of the XVIII century*). (9) Cf. J. Queniart, *Culture et société urbaines dans la France de l'Ouest au XVIII siècle,* (*Urban Culture and Society in Western France in the XVIII century*), Rincksieck, Paris 1978, 182-244. (10) Cf. De Fiores, *Itinerario.* (11) Cf. R. Mandrou, *Montfort et l'évangélisation du peuple,* (*Montfort and the Evangelization of People*), in RMon 11 (1974) 1-19. (12) Cf. L. Cognet, *La spiritualité française au XVIIe siècle,* (*French Spirituality in the XVII Century*), Paris 1949; J. LeBrun, *France, Le grand siècle de la spiritualité française et ses lendemains,* (*France, The 'grand siècle' of French Spirituality and the Days Following*), in DSAM 5 (1964) 917-953; B. Papàsogli, *Gli spirituali italiani e il 'grand siècle'. François de Sales - Bérulle - Pascal - La Rochefoucauld - Bossuet - Fénelon,* (*The Italian spiritual authors and the 'grand siècle'*), ed. Storia e Letteratura, Roma 1983; J. Dagens, *Bérulle et les origines de la restauration catholique (1575-1611),* (*Bérulle and the Beginnings of the Catholic Restoration, 1575-1611*), Paris 1952; R. Deville, *L'École française de spiritualité,* (*The French School of Spirituality*), Desclée, Paris 1987. (13) Cf. B. Chedozeau, *Religion et Morale chez Pierre Nicole, 1650-1680,* (*Religion and Morality in Pierre Nicole, 1650-1680*), thesis at the Sorbonne, Paris 1975. (14) Cf. J. Delumeau, *Rassurer et protéger. Le sentiment de sécurité dans l'Occident d'autrefois,* (*To Reassure and Protect. The Feeling of Security in the West of Former Days*), Fayard, Paris 1989; P. Aries, *The Hour of Our Death,* trans. Helen Weaver, Knopf, Random House, New York 1981; M. Vovelle, *La mort et l'Occident de 1300 è nos jours,* (*Death and the West from 1300 to our Day*), Gallimard, Paris 1983; A. Croix, *La Bretagne aux 16ème et 17ème siècles, La vie. La mort. La Foi,* (*Brittany in the 16th and 17th Centuries: Life, Death, Faith*), 2 vol., Maloine, Paris 1981. (16) Cf. P. Burke, *Popular Culture in Early Modern Europe,* Harper & Row, New York 1978; A. Bossard, *Il carisma del Montfort nel suo tempo: mediazione tra cultura colta e cultura populare,* (*The charism of Montfort in his time: mediation between educated and popular culture*), in QM 1 (1983) 86-96. (17) Cf. S. De Fiores, *Marie, De 1650 au début du 20ème siècle,* (Mary, From 1650 to the Beginning of the 20th century), in *DSAM* 10 (1980) 460-473; T. Koehler, *Marie, Du moyen age aux temps modernes,* (*Mary, From the Middle . Ages to Modern Times*), in *DSAM* 10 (1980) 440-459. (18) G. LeBras, *La practica religiosa nelle campagne francesi,* (*Religious Practice in the French Countryside*), in *Società ...* by C. Russo, 189-230. (19) Cf. S. De Fiores, *La 'missione' nell'itinerario spirituale ed apostolico di S. Luigi-Maria da Montfort,* (*'Mission' in the spiritual and apostolic itinerary of Saint Louis-Marie de Montfort*), in QM 2 (1985) 17-41. (20) Cf. I. Chatellier, *l'Europe des dévots, (Europe of the Devout),* Flammarion, Paris 1987. (21) Cf. L. Perouas, *Ce que croyait Grignion de Montfort ...,* (*The Way to Wisdom),* Mame 1973, 175-198; B. Cortinovis, *Dimensione ecclesiale della spiritualità di Grignion de Montfort,* (*Ecclesial Dimension of the Spirituality of Grignion de Montfort*), Pontifical Faculty of Theology "Marianum", Rome 1993 (ms). (22) Cf. P. Gaffney, *Le rôle de Marie dans l'histoire du salut* (*The Role of Mary in Salvation History*) in *Montfort, un maître spirituel pour notre temps,* (ms) Generalate of the Montfort Missionaries, Rome 1988, 189-213. (23) On the importance of Mary's consent, cf. P. Gaffney, o.c., 194-197. (24) Cf. H.M. Manteau-Bonamy, *St Louis-Marie Grignion de Montfort, théologien de la Sagesse éternelle au seuil du troisième millénaire,* (*Saint Louis Grignion de Montfort, Theologian of Eternal Wisdom at the Threshold of the Third Millenium),* in *Montfort, un maître spirituel,* o.c., 141-188: "For Montfort, there is no grace in Mary which is not ecclesial" (p. 174). (25) S. Epis, *Il "Contratto dell'alleanza con Dio": documento fondamentale della missione,* (*The "Covenant Contract with God": Fundamental Document of the Mission)* in QM 2 (1985) 166-177. (26) One of the sources for the "mysticism" of the apostolate seems to be Father Louis Lallemant; cf. *The Spiritual Doctrine of Father Louis Lallemant of the Society of Jesus,* Newman, Westminster, MD 1946. (27) Cf. A. Dulles, *Models of the Church,* Doubleday, Garden City, N.Y. 1974. (28) For different interpretations of Montfort's thought on the end-times, cf. S. De Fiores, *Le Saint Esprit et Marie dans les derniers temps selon Grignion de Montfort, (The Holy Spirit and Mary in the End-times According to Grignion de Montfort),* in EtMar 43 (1986) 131-171.

COMPANY OF MARY

SUMMARY

I. THE PLAN OF A FOUNDATION:
   1. From the time of priestly ordination to the first collaborators (1700-1705);
   2. Lay and priest associates (1705-1713);
   3. The Rule of the Missionary Priests of the Company of Mary (1713);
   4. The agreement with the Seminary of the Holy Spirit of Paris (1713);
   5. The pilgrimage of the Penitents to Saumur (1716);
   6. The Last Will and Testament (1716);
   7. The sojourn at Saint-Pompain (1716-1722);
   8. The petition presented to Clement XI (1719).

II. THE COMPANY OF MARY IN THE EIGHTEENTH CENTURY:
   1. The chapter of 1722: mission and vows;
   2. The petition addressed to Benedict XIII (1728);
   3. Benedict XIV and the oral approbation of the Rules (1748);
   4. Statutes and Regulations (1773).

III. THE COMPANY OF MARY BETWEEN THE REVOLUTION AND THE RESTORATION (1789-1841):
   1. The community of Saint-Laurent and the Civil Constitution of the Clergy;
   2. The "restoration" of Father Deshayes (1821-1841);
      a. The Brief of Praise of Leo XII (1825),
      b. The restoration of vows,
      c. The Constitutions of Father Deshayes (1832).

IV. TOWARD A NEW IMAGE OF THE COMPANY (1842-1880):
   1. Some key events:
      a. The discovery of the Treatise on True Devotion to the Blessed Virgin (1842),
      b. The approbation of the Institute by Pope Pius IX (1853);
   2. The Constitutions of 1872: the missions ad gentes;
   3. Missionary activity.

V. A COMPANY AT THE SERVICE OF THE UNIVERSAL CHURCH (1880-1994):
   1. Expansion of the Institute (1880-1940);
   2. The Constitutions of 1904 and 1949;
   3. The Company of Mary today.

I. The Plan of a Foundation

The path of Saint Louis Marie de Montfort as founder is closely linked to his personal apostolic experience. He dreamt of a company of missionaries who would evangelize the poor by means of parish missions. The idea of this "Company of Mary" obsessed Montfort during his entire missionary career from the first month of his sacerdotal ministry (1700) to his deathbed (1716).

1. From the time of priestly ordination to the first collaborators (1700-1705)

From the community of Saint Clement of Nantes, where he was sent *"to be formed for the preaching of parish missions,"* Louis Marie de Montfort wrote to Father Leschassier only seven months after his ordination (June 5 1700), *"When I see the needs of the Church, I cannot help but plead continually for a small band of good priests . . . under the banner and protection of the Blessed Virgin"* (L 5 [Dec. 6, 1700]). If we cannot see from these lines that the saint already at this date planned to personally found the community that he desired, his intentions for a foundation are, nevertheless, evident, and they will remain essentially unchanged up to the writing of RM in 1713. In L 5 the future of the Company *"of good priests"* is indirectly described: *"I feel a tremendous urge to make our Lord and his holy Mother loved, to go in a humble, simple way to teach catechism to the poor in country places and to arouse in sinners a devotion to our Blessed Lady and to go from parish to parish teaching catechism to the poor relying on Providence alone."*

The elements of the future foundation are already envisioned: a company of priests (RM 1); a Marian name (PM passim); the mission to preach the good news to the poor (RM 2) by means of catechetical instruction (RM 79-91); the role of devotion to Mary in the reconciliation of the faithful (SR; PM; TD; "Method of Penance"; etc.); abandonment to Providence (RM 10-18; LCM); and apostolic availability (PM 8-9; RM 6-7) in view of the *"necessities of the Church"* (L 5).

The original idea or intention of founding a company of priests enters into its first phase in a search for collaborators during the time of Montfort's stay at the hospital of Poitiers (1701-1705). In August 1702 at St. Sulpice, Montfort met his friend Jean Baptiste Blain. During their conversations, Montfort probably expressed the desire to have Blain with him as a collaborator in parish missions. Blain recalls, "I felt a strong attraction to follow him and be his companion." The hesitancy that Montfort's spiritual director, Father Leschassier, experienced concerning "the mystery" that Montfort was for him influenced Blain to such an extent that "this mystery . . . turned me against Montfort and prevented me from joining him."[1]

On August 15, 1702, another friend and fellow-student of the saint, Claude François Poullart des Places (1679-1709),[2] received the tonsure. According to Besnard, it seems that at this period or, at the latest, the following year, Montfort made this proposal to des Places: "He invited him to join him in the founding of this good work."[3] Poullart declined Montfort's invitation and added, "I feel no attraction at all for the missions." But he promised Montfort his support, "for I know the good that can be done too well not to help in this work with all my strength and to persevere in it with you. . . . If God graces me with success, you can count on missionaries. I will prepare them for you, and you will put them to work. In this way you and I will both be satisfied."[4]

In any event, the development of the relationship between the Seminary of the Holy Spirit in Paris and the successors of St. Louis Marie is linked to the promise of collaboration Poullart offered to Montfort.

2. Lay and priest associates (1705-1713)

In the seventeenth century France, short-term associations of parish missioners known as "missionary bands" worked in a diocese led by a "director of the mission" approved by the bishop of the diocese. Before the drafting of RM in 1713, in which the intentions of a foundation are transformed into a well-organized project that resembles the missionary institutions of the times, the strategy followed by Montfort seems to resemble that of a temporary association of parish missionaries. The association of Montfort with the team of Dom Jean Leuduger (1649-1722), disciple of Julien Maunoir (1606-1683), was of a temporary nature. Thus arose the distinction between temporary associate priests and long-term associate priests. Practically speaking, *"associates of parish missions"* were volunteers who formed a group of reserves, ready to assist in the preaching of parish missions when needed. They were more or less available, depending upon their parish duties and occupation.

In the former category of short-term associates were the unknown lay-brothers who worked intermittently with Montfort. There is no record of their names. Also in this category were Father Gabriel Olivier, a "diocesan missionary" who collaborated with Montfort during his apostolic activities in Nantes (1709-1710), and Gabriel François Grignion, brother of Louis Marie, who participated in the missions in La Rochelle in 1711.

At the beginning of Montfort's ministry in the diocese of La Rochelle, three priests joined him. The first was the Irishman Peter Keating, who on January 12, 1712, was named chaplain of Saint Louis Hospital, where Montfort resided. The following year he left this post to become pastor at La Seguinière. The second to join Montfort was Thomas Le Bourhis, a priest of the diocese of Nantes, who at the death of Saint Louis Marie remained at Saint-Laurent as a parish curate. The third was Father Clisson, whom Montfort mentioned in his will. These last-mentioned collaborators changed from temporary to long-term parish missionaries. Thus the distinction between temporary and long-term depended on evolving circumstances.[5]

On the other hand, among the long-term associates, certain young men should be named whom Montfort called "brothers." In 1705 Montfort asked Mathurin to follow him as a collaborator in the missions (even if Saint Louis Marie did not give him the name "brother").[6] Between 1707 and 1711, Brothers Jean, Pierre, Nicholas, and Phillip followed Montfort; between 1711 and 1716, Brothers Jacques, Louis, and Gabriel followed him. The chronology is uncertain, because the sources give only approximate dates.[7] Father Pierre Ernault des Bastières associated himself with Montfort intermittently from 1708, and more permanently from 1711 until January 1716, when he left Montfort. Special mention must be given to Adrien Vatel, the first permanently associated priest, from the beginning of 1715, and, from November of the same year, René Mulot, named by Louis Marie to lead the Company after his death. Montfort associated more closely to himself four brothers who pronounced vows of poverty and obedience (cf. W).

In LCM 1, written in 1713, Montfort alludes to *"a little flock, so few in numbers that a child can count you, puer scribet eos."* The little company (LCM 4) of 1713 was still at most an informal association of priests and laymen, personal collaborators with Montfort in the ministry of parish missions. The report of October 28, 1712, on the erection of the mission cross at Thaire, which occurred at the beginning of Montfort's ministry in the diocese of La Rochelle, is of capital importance in establishing the juridical standing of Montfort and the status of his associates. The saint is described as "Father Louis Marie de Montfort, missionary priest, approved by His Excellency the Bishop," and he signed the document as *"missionary priest,"* followed by "P.Keating, priest of the mission, and Thomas Le Bourhis, priest of the mission."[8]

In other words, Montfort is a diocesan missionary priest depending on the bishop, with two long-term associates. Only the priests of Saint Vincent de Paul officially added the name "priest of the mission." The qualification mentioned above places the two associates in close relationship with Montfort, who, however, is described in the document only as "approved by His Excellency the Bishop."

3. The Rule of the Missionary Priests of the Company of Mary (1713)

The intuitions expressed in the letter of December 6, 1700, to Leschassier became an organized project in the Triptych (the three documents dealing directly with the foundation of the Company of Mary), particularly in RM: a company of missionaries bound by private vows of poverty and obedience in the service of parish missions under the authority of the ordinary of the diocese and with a personal and community style marked by evangelical poverty in abandonment to Providence. Grandet synthesizes Montfort's project in these words: *"He thought of forming a body or community of twelve apostolic men who would have neither goods nor revenue, any more than the apostles did, and who would abandon themselves to Divine Providence for their subsistence, in order to go preach the Gospel in all dioceses according to the directives of the bishops. He even drew up rules for them containing points for a sublime perfection. The center of their Congregation was to be La Rochelle, and he had already associated with himself several priests, whom he had led to such great detachment that they followed him everywhere."*[9] Grandet's biographical sketch particularly emphasizes two aspects of Montfort's plan for a religious community: recourse to an apostolic typology in lifestyle and mission, and availability to the bishops. And there is a significant detail: the seat of the Company, like that of the diocese, should be in the city of La Rochelle. The writing of the Rule again moved Montfort to seek collaborators, and he turned again to the Seminary of the Holy Spirit and his friend Poullart des Places.

4. The agreement with the Seminary of the Holy Spirit of Paris (1713)

The successors of Poullart des Places were probably aware of the mutual promise exchanged by the two friends in 1702 or 1703. It is that promise which moved Montfort to go to Paris during the first two weeks of July 1713 to speak of his project and find support. Besnard is explicit about the motive for the journey: "he went there to renew his union with the priests of the Holy Spirit to recruit some missionaries."[10] The community of the Holy Spirit "was already numerous and consisted of excellent subjects from different countries who were remarkable for their piety and knowledge."[11] Montfort made official this associative agreement with the Seminary of the Holy Spirit in RM 1.

5. The pilgrimage of the Penitents to Saumur (1716)

According to Grandet, in March 1716 the local group of White Penitents of the parish of Saint-Pompain decided to organize a pilgrimage to Saumur. The purpose of the pilgrimage is described by Montfort: *"You will make this pilgrimage for the following intentions: Firstly, to obtain from God through Mary's intercession good missionaries, who will follow the example of the apostles by complete abandonment to divine Providence and the practice of virtue under the protection of Our Lady. Secondly, to obtain the gift of Wisdom in order to know, love and practice the truths of our faith and to lead others to Christ"* (PS). The pilgrimage of the penitents to Saumur is the last initiative taken by Montfort in favor of the Company of Mary.

6. The Last Will and Testament (1716)

On Wednesday, April 1, 1716, Father de Montfort was at Saint-Laurent-sur-Sèvre to prepare the mission that was to begin on April 5. He was joined very soon by two other missionaries, Fathers Thomas Le Bourhis and Clisson, and a little later by Jean Mulot, pastor of Saint-Pompain. During the mission, the pastoral visit to the parish by Etienne de Champflour, bishop of La Rochelle, was announced for April 22. That day Montfort enthusiastically organized a procession and went with it to meet the bishop at the outskirts of the parish. Upon his return, Montfort was exhausted because of a fever. From April 23 the illness progressed rapidly. On April 27, sensing that death was approaching, the founder dictated his last will to Father René Mulot, and the dying man signed it with a trembling hand. Considering the nature of the goods that Montfort bequeathed to his *"community of the Holy Spirit,"* as the community is called in the will, one easily concludes that they were for the work of parish missions: *"I confide to His Excellency, the Bishop of La Rochelle and to Father Mulot my small pieces of furniture and my mission books, to be preserved for the use of the four Brothers who joined me in a life of obedience and poverty. . . . If there is anything remaining in the purse, Father Mulot will use it like a good father for the Brothers and for himself. As the house at La Rochelle is reverting to its natural heirs, there will be left for the community of the Holy Spirit only the house at Vouvant given by an agreement."*

Mulot was named executor and at the same time was designated by Montfort as responsible for the "community of the Holy Spirit." This name in W supplanted the original title of the congregation desired by the founder and was used until the approbation of the Institute by Pius IX in 1853. The name "Community of the Holy Spirit" marks then, two distinct periods in the history of the Company.

7. The sojourn at Saint-Pompain (1716-1722)

Having withdrawn to the parish of Saint-Pompain, chosen as their place of residence after the death of Montfort, Mulot and Vatel began the work of parish missions again at Easter time of 1718. During this period, they enjoyed the hospitality offered them by René's brother, Jean Mulot, pastor of the parish, and in return they offered him their services in the parish. It is certain that Mathurin Rangeard was present in the parish from June 2, 1718. On the occasion of the visit of Bishop de Champflour to Saint-Pompain, the official report records an important fact on the juridical standing of "Fathers Rene Mulot, Vatel, and other priests living in the parish, who under our orders apply themselves to giving parish missions."[12]

On September 27, 1720, as a result of a request presented by Sr. Marie Louise of Jesus, Bishop de Champflour named Father Mulot superior of the community of the Daughters of Wisdom of Saint-Laurent-sur-Sèvre."[13] In the Statutes of 1773, drawn up by Besnard, the appointment was transformed into a true and natural *jus nativum,* expressed in very significant terms: "the superior of the missionaries being at the same time the superior by right of the Daughters of Wisdom" (ch. 2, par. 3).

8. The petition addressed to Clement XI (1719)

Grandet gives us a document of extraordinary importance for the history of the Company.[14] Its date is most probably July 1719. It is a petition addressed to Clement XI by Pierre Granier, pastor of Saint-Martin-de-Melle, and Jean Mulot, pastor of Saint-Pompain. The petition is supported by the attestations of the bishops of La Rochelle and Poitiers, dated August 1 and 8, 1719, respectively. The purpose of the petition was "to approve this newly formed mission and all those who will associate themselves with it, expected to be numerous in a short time, with the title of new apostolic missionaries of the Community of the Holy Spirit, to give missions in the dioceses to which they will be called." [15]

II. The Company of Mary in the Eighteenth Century

In 1722, thanks to the acquisition of a building near the tomb of the founder at Saint-Laurent-sur-Sèvre, the group was able to become a stable community, with the first taking of vows received by the newly elected superior, René Mulot. Progressively he and his companions, very quickly called "Mulotins," secured more qualified recruits through the intermediary of the Seminary of St. Sulpice of Paris, which sent them some priests. In 1722 there were three or four priests in the Company; there were thirteen in 1743, with some coadjutor brothers, among whom was Brother Mathurin, the first disciple of Montfort. During the entire eighteenth century, the Company never exceeded by much the number cited above, and during the lifetime of Father Mulot the missionaries of Saint-Laurent remained confined to a rather limited area, preoccupied with faithfully following the directives of their founder.

During the superiorships of Nicholas Audubon (1749-1755) and Charles Besnard (1755-1788), there was a slight evolution, as the Company accepted preaching retreats in colleges, hospitals, and religious communities.[16] The principal concern was to consolidate the institution by a formal approbation, obtained not without difficulties and obstacles in 1773 after a modification of the statutes of the community. This was the beginning of a new period, characterized by a better economic situation and by institutional stability. At first, limited to the parishes of the dioceses of La Rochelle and Poitiers, the missionaries widened the horizons of their apostolate and penetrated into the neighboring dioceses of Nantes, Angers, and Luçon. But during the eighteenth century, the range of the community remained strictly regional.

1. The chapter of 1722: mission and vows

As of April 6, 1721, the Company possessed a house at Saint-Laurent-sur-Sèvre, called the "Green Oak," even though it had been formally given to the board of the parish church by the buyers, the Marquis de Magnanne and Madame de Bouille.[17] It took a year to ready the house for use. After the 1721-1722 missionary season, "the priests and brothers gathered there for the summer vacation."[18] Besnard writes, "It was then that they thought of holding a formal election to choose a superior, who would be recognized as such by all the missionaries and whom they would all obey. For this intention, they all made an eight-day retreat, at the end of which, while all were assembled. Father Mulot rose and said that it was necessary that one must be chosen by the confreres to be recognized as superior, a position conferred on him by the bishop only with regard to the Daughters of Wisdom, not the missionaries, and that each one should think of the person whom he judged to be most capable."[19]

Besnard continues: "The choice was soon made, and all the votes were for Father Mulot himself,"[20] already chosen and designated by Montfort. Father René Mulot exercised the functions of superior general of the missionaries uninterruptedly until the year of his death (1749).

The act by which Mulot began his functions as superior general was the ceremony of vows attested to in the *Chronicles of Sr. Florence:* "All except two made vows in his presence according to the Rule."[21] It is an account of the first community celebration of vows after the death of the founder and the only evidence we have of an event of such great importance for the life of the Company.

2. The petition addressed to Benedict XIII (1728)

Like an echo of the one previously addressed to Clement XI, the petition to Benedict XIII in 1728 falls within the scope of the community's missionary pastoral plan: it reflects the image of a Company attentive to the demands of the mission and emphasizes its particular apostolic identity. The very year of the petition, the bishops of La Rochelle, Luçon, and Poitiers approved the "Rule of P. Mulot,"[22] confirming with their authority the fidelity of the Company to its mission. The words of the bishop of Luçon written at the end of the Rule do not sound like only routine praise: "We are no longer surprised that the priests who follow it faithfully do as much good as they do in our dioceses."[23]

3. Benedict XIV and the oral approbation of the Rules (1748)

In 1748 René Mulot sent three Fathers of the Company to Rome: P. F. Hacquet, C. Albert, and C. Besnard. It seems he wished to have the Rules of Father de Montfort approved. They left Saint-Laurent on July 28 and arrived in Rome on September 12. They remained there until September 30 and returned to the motherhouse on November 13. Thanks to the letters of presentation of the ambassadors of France, they were received in a private audience at the Quirinal by Pope Benedict XIV on September 27. This is an account of Father Hacquet: "The attendant introduced us in these terms: 'Tres Missionarii Sacerdotes Gallici.'" To Father Hacquet, who read to the Pope a French text that originally had been prepared in Latin, Pope Benedict XIV answered, "'Be assured, my dear Father, that I will do everything in my power for the well-being of your foundation. I am happy that priests give parish missions.' I presented him with the Rules of our society and of the Daughters of Wisdom. He took them, read some sections, and, since they were approved by the bishops of France, approved them and gave them his blessing, telling us to continue preaching parish missions."[24]

4. Statutes and Regulations (1773)

The manuscript presented to obtain legal recognition bears the title "Statutes and Regulations of the Missionaries of the Holy Spirit."[25] These statutes, contained in a manuscript of twenty-two pages (250 lines at most) are a pale reflection of the previous rule. The norms are strictly confined to the new requirements expressed by a legislation that tended to bring about uniformity in the religious life of the time by rigid institutional criteria. A decree of the King's Council of the State, resulting from the reform activity of the "Commission of Regulars," demanded for every Order a body of clear, precise, and permanent laws that "would be a sure protection against indiscipline and instability."[26] The demand for clarity and precision in the formulation of statutes is expressed again in the Edict of the King published in February 1773 (the very year official recognition was granted).

Faced with this requirement, Besnard purged the text of the founder's Rule of all elements foreign to the essential configuration of the ecclesial identity of the Company. He thus presented for royal approbation, a text that reflected by its literary style—even in its very title, "Statutes and Regulations"—a code adapted to a secular ecclesiastical association. The most evident novelty of the new statutes was the abolishment of the vows, which from 1722 had been regularly made according to the wishes of the founder. Why had such a serious decision been reached? One plausible reason is the intensely hostile attitude toward institutes of religious life, due to the policies of Louis XV through the Commission of Regulars, directed by Archbishop Lomenie de Brienne.[27] The formulation was very clear and left no doubt: every kind of bond was excluded for anyone who entered the Congregation. The Institute was reduced to a simple diocesan presbyterial association destined for "all works of the holy ministry." And thus the Institute was received into the civil organization: "We have approved and confirmed the two establishments that were formed in the village of Saint Laurent-sur-Sèvre, diocese of La Rochelle: one a community of secular priests with the title missionary priests of the Holy Spirit."

The reform of Besnard had been indicated or perhaps imposed by the political circumstances of the time and by the opportunity to preserve the existence of the Institute through legal recognition. The effects of the new modifications adopted by Besnard were not immediate.[28] After the Revolution of 1789, the identity and the cohesion of the group grew weak and provoked a period of laxity in the history of the Company. This was due in great part to the absence of canonical bonds.

III. The Company of Mary between the Revolution and the Restoration (1789-1841)

1. The community of Saint-Laurent and the Civil Constitution of the Clergy

From the first days of the Revolution, the Church of France was affected by the universal process of national regeneration. The clergy, which disappeared as an Estate, and renounced its privileges on the night of August 4 and gave over its property to the nation November 2, 1789. Equality and national solidarity had practical consequences for the Church. Even if these measures were not willingly accepted by all, they did not arouse excessive opposition, the more so because the clergy were guaranteed a suitable salary. On February 13, 1790, in the name of liberty the members of the Assembly banned solemn vows and suppressed institutions of contemplative life.

The final collapse of all canonical and legally recognized institutions came with the law of August 18, 1792. This law was the principal official decree to which the tribunals referred concerning men and women religious involved in teaching and hospital work, as well as concerning institutes that the legislative texts call "Ecclesiastical Secular Congregations." Being in the latter category under the name "Mulotins," the missionaries of Saint-Laurent were suppressed.[29]

One of the first worried reactions of the missionaries of Saint-Laurent to these decisions and, more generally, to the Revolution is contained in a January 6, 1790, circular letter addressed to the Daughters of Wisdom by Superior General Jean-Baptist Micquignon: "What I have reasons to dread are the effects that can result in the long run from dealings and indispensable relationships with a world whose faith is perverted. There are these talks that are poisoned by free-thinking, these erroneous maxims concerning religious matters that the appearance of some social virtues or the ostentation of some good works renders more insidious; it is, above all, defection. . . . What am I saying, my dear Daughters? Yes, I will say it—but with inexpressible heartbreak over the defection of those who should be your teachers in the faith. . . . Let your first care, in this time of infidelity, be to watch over the preservation and growth of your faith and to nourish an inviolable attachment to the Church and its head."[30]

The obligation for ecclesiastics to take the oath[31] provoked the missionaries of Saint-Laurent to take a clear position: they refused to take any oath whatsoever and favored an opposition movement against the oath and against constitutional priests. They opposed the oath by personal contacts or by letters, since preaching was then difficult or in certain cases impossible, and, above all, by distributing printed matter or simple manuscripts.

Very quickly, civil authority saw in the community of the Mulotins a kind of nest of counter revolutionaries. On June 1 and 2, 1791, the motherhouse of Saint-Laurent underwent a search by the National Guards, whose purpose was to find incriminating documents in order to refer the missionaries to the courts of the Republic. Having neither the competence nor the time necessary to evaluate the papers they found, the Guards seized everything they laid hands on. Among other things, they took sixteen letters not at all compromising for the writers nor for those to whom they were addressed. They were, however, considered inflammatory matter and as such were handed over to the director of the department of Angers and then sent to the "Committee of Investigation" in Paris. The Guards arrested Fathers Dauche and Duguet.

The Register of Arrests of the Directory of the department of Maine-et-Loire records on June 5, 1791, the accounts of the interrogations in the arrest of Fathers Dauche and Duguet. The superintendents of police seemed to have no doubt about the popular influence of the missionaries of Saint-Laurent: "For a long time the missionaries have played an important role in the provinces of Anjou, Poitou, Aunis, and Brittany. Known for their preaching, they have gained the confidence of the people. Their reputation has spread far through the Daughters of Wisdom, whom they instituted as a congregation and who serve in hospitals in several departments. It is by traveling all over the countryside, it is by taking advantage of the uneducated that they have achieved the reputation that they now enjoy."[32]

There were victims of the Revolution among the missionaries of Saint-Laurent. Toward the end of February 1793, the Republican Guards penetrated into the property of the Holy Spirit and massacred sixty-year-old Brother Bouchet, a native of Saint-Laurent, and Brother Jean, about thirty years of age. They impaled Brother Oliver. Brother Antoine was shot at Cholet with some Daughters of Wisdom. Brothers Joseph and Yvon were also victims on an unknown date. Fathers Dauche and Verger were denounced by a worker of the community of Saint-Laurent and arrested. Once it was known that they were not guilty of deeds attributed to them, a decree of the department of Vendée, dated October 27, 1792, condemned them to exile. They were, in fact, imprisoned on the island of Ré. Ordered several times to take an oath to uphold the Constitution, they were sent back to La Rochelle, where, having scarcely disembarked, they were literally torn to pieces by a furious crowd, which had been informed of their arrival.[33]

2. The "restoration" of Father Deshayes (1821-1841)

There is no doubt that what characterized the restoration of the Institute in the nineteenth century was the aim to be faithful to its origins. It was not easy to bring about an organization similar to the previous one, for the greatest number of founders and reformers—including Father Gabriel Deshayes (1767-1841)—possessed only a rather approximate knowledge of the religious life of former times. Nevertheless, the reformers presented their initiatives as a return to the original sources.

By the end of the Revolution, the Company of Mary had lost half its members. If in 1788 the missionary priests numbered between twelve and fifteen,[34] there were only seven signers of the account of the proceedings in a plenary meeting at Saint-Laurent on July 9, 1806.[35] The situation became more normal a little later in the nineteenth century; in 1820 the Company numbered at least ten

Fathers and five Brothers and did not appear preoccupied with increasing its numbers.

The Statutes and Regulations of Father Besnard remained in vigor until August 1817, when the missionaries forming the Congregation signed a new text consisting of only eleven articles that go back to the Statute of 1773. The document consists of less than two pages in the Register of Proceedings.[36]

Bishop Paillou of La Rochelle, who was also administrator of the diocese of Luçon, wrote on January 8, 1821, to the superior general of the Daughters of Wisdom on the situation of the Institute of missionaries: "I desire above all that you have a father superior who is zealous for the missions; that is the end that Father de Montfort proposed in instituting the Congregation. If this end is lost sight of, the Congregation of the Holy Spirit will destroy itself by that very fact, and you will have only chaplains. I greatly desire that this Congregation endure; but it can endure only inasmuch as it gives parish missions. I ask you to speak of all this to the pastor of Auray, who, I do not doubt, will think as I do and will neglect nothing in order to procure for you a good father superior and good priests willing to undertake parish missions."[37] On January 17, 1821, Father Gabriel Deshayes, vicar general of Vannes, pastor of Auray, and already assistant general, agreed to become the new superior of the Company of Mary and the Daughters of Wisdom.[38]

Thanks to Deshayes, the Company of Mary soon gave signs of renewal. Papal recognition, obtained through the personal efforts of Deshayes, inaugurated a long series of contacts with the Roman Curia to obtain the approbation of the Institute and its Constitutions and to have the honors of the altar accorded to the founder. Deshayes very much desired that the holiness of Father de Montfort be recognized.

a. The Brief of Praise of Leo XII (1825). The Brief of Leo XII opened the way for the Congregation to be recognized as an Institute of pontifical right, but it would only be with the Decree of the Sacred Congregation of Bishops and Regulars of November 14, 1853, that the community would be approved *"tamquam congregationem votorum simplicium."*[39]

b. The restoration of vows. Deshayes did not cease repeating, "There is no body because there is no bond."[40] But not all the missionaries were agreed to bind themselves by vows. Precipitous action could have jeopardized the very existence of the Congregation. Father Deshayes delayed until, in 1830-1831, it seemed to him that he could not wait any longer.

His decision to begin the dialogue within the community on the appropriateness of returning to vows coincided with the departure of two missionaries desirous of finding elsewhere the benefit of religious life. One of them, Father J. M. Hillereau (1796-1855), future titular archbishop of Petra and patriarchal vicar of Constantinople, returned at the earnest request of his superior. The new rules presented by Father

Deshayes categorically state (chapter 7, article 1): "To be members of the Company, the missionaries first, in the presence of the Superior, make simple vows of poverty and obedience for one year. They renew these vows annually, and at the end of five years of profession, if they themselves feel they are truly called by God and are judged to be so called in order to be irrevocably professed, they take the two vows of poverty and obedience in perpetuity."[41]

It is easy to see that the article on the vows was borrowed almost word for word from the Rule of Montfort (RM 8). Perhaps it is to respect the terminology of the founder that only the two vows of poverty and obedience are mentioned, while in reality, as is evident in the formula of profession written in the Constitutions, the missionaries made the three traditional vows, including the vow of chastity.[42]

c. The Constitutions of Father Deshayes (1832). The crisis of the Company, marked by the small number of its members and, even more, by its missionary awareness, is inevitably reflected in the tormented Constitutions of 1832, borrowed from either the Rule of Mulot (1728) or from the Statutes of Besnard (1773). The crisis of the parish missions, owing to the political situation, became a crisis of identity, and from this viewpoint the Constitutions of 1832 seem to reflect confusion in the missionary awareness of the Company.

If, on the one hand, the principle of availability is confirmed "to preach the Gospel everywhere with zealous activity," on the other hand, the apostolic horizon remained linked to the historical territory of the missionary presence of the Institute, western France: "They will limit themselves to French territory only, never thinking of the distant foreign missions, which would require new studies, thus diverting them from those that should completely occupy them."[43]

Fidelity to the founder remains unchanged in missionary methods: "To renew the spirit of Christianity, they will zealously use the exterior, edifying means whose salutary effects they have so often experienced, such as the renewal of baptismal vows, reparation to the Blessed Sacrament, devotion to the Blessed Virgin, etc."[44]

It suffices to skim the manuscript, starting with the significant title "Missions and Retreats,"[45] to verify even quantitatively that in the time of Father Deshayes, and subsequently even more so, retreats tended to be of equal importance in relation to the other activities of parish missions. Retreats followed some months after a parish mission, lasted ten to twelve days, and constituted a form of "follow up to the parish mission."[46]

IV. Toward a New Image of the Company (1842-1880)

The discussion aroused by the vows and the precarious church-state situation of the time marked the identity of the missionaries of Saint-Laurent in the Church in a way that was not always positive. The climate that had been created moved Father Deshayes' successor to continue the effort toward a return to the original identity of the Institute by going back to RM, written by the founder.

1. Some key events:

a. The discovery of the Treatise on True Devotion to the Blessed Virgin (1842). Having escaped the confusion of the Revolution, the manuscript remained forgotten *"in the darkness and silence of a chest"* (TD 114) until its discovery on April 22, 1842. The discovery of TD marks a turning point not only for the knowledge of the Marian doctrine of the founder but, even more significantly, for the very identity of the Institute. The Marian aspect connatural to its mission was clear evidenced, and it opened the way to a more serious reflection on the role of Mary. The Constitutions and the successive revisions record the signs of an evolution in the Marian awareness of the Company.[47]

b. The approbation of the Institute by Pope Pius IX (1853). Father General Joseph Dalin presented RM[48] to the Holy See for approbation. Father Dalin himself in an unsigned opuscule explained this decision as a return to the sources: "It was the same for the Company of Mary, where the need was felt more and more to return completely to the Rule of Father de Montfort and to the former customs of the Company."[49]

With the return to the original name desired by Montfort, Missionary Priests of the Company of Mary, the period of the title "Company of the Holy Spirit" ended. Restoration of their authentic name to the disciples of Montfort vigorously emphasized their identity as linked to an ecclesial mission.

2. The Constitutions of 1872: the missions ad gentes

The Constitutions edited by Father Denis in 1861,[50] which date back to a text approved *ad experimentum* on the occasion of the approval of the Institute (1853), express the following wish: "The priests of the Company of Mary should reproduce the public life of the Son of God, who went about doing good everywhere in Judea and even to the land of the infidels; whose every moment was employed in speaking of salvation with his heavenly Father or in making his Father known to all. In the footsteps of the Apostles, whose only occupation was prayer or the ministry of the Word, the Fathers of the Company will be always ready to carry the torch of the Gospel wherever obedience will call them, whether in France or in distant and infidel countries, if the Vicar of Jesus Christ so desires."[51]

In a letter dated February 3, 1872, the Congregation for the Propagation of the Faith informed the Congregation of Bishops and Regulars that there was no difficulty to inserting in the Constitutions of the Company of Mary a new article authorizing it to devote itself to missions in foreign countries.[52] This decision is of historical import. The Company thus broke with an isolation that kept it imprisoned within the limited horizon of Saint-Laurent since the foundation. It was with fortunate insight that the Constitutions of 1872[53] inserted the option of the mission *ad gentes* in a key text on the thought of the founder, taken almost word for word from RM 6.[54]

3. Missionary activity

A voluminous "Memorandum," containing the reports of the missions and retreats conserved in the AGCM, recounts the missionary activities of the Fathers from 1865 to 1878.[55] During the very year the first apostolic school (high school and 2 year college seminary) at Pontchâteau opened (1876), two things are striking: the enormous amount of work accomplished that year by the missionaries, and their fidelity to the apostolic directives of Montfort to preach missions and retreats.

V. A Company at the Service of the Universal Church (1880-1994)

1. Expansion of the Institute (1880-1940)

The Third Republic, first of all favorable to the Church, began a systematic policy of secularization in France as soon as power fell into the hands of the republicans. In 1880 the French government expelled the Jesuits, obliged each Congregation to file a request for authorization, and prohibited all unauthorized religious to teach. Other laws decreed the obligation of military service for clerics, the abolition of military and hospital chaplaincies, the laicization of cemeteries and courts, the possibility of divorce, and the abolition of Sunday rest.

At the same time, parish missions experienced much resistance. Municipalities prevented the holding of retreat exercises. The expulsions of 1880 and 1901 and the radical separation of church and state in 1904 contributed to the serious slowing down of missionary activity. Diocesan missionaries, helped by some secularized religious, continued their activities. They adapted their preaching, giving more importance to dialogue conferences and also to "living tableaux" that involved children, thereby giving the preacher the opportunity to evangelize the parents who attended these plays. The preachers did their best to answer the anticlerical objections to Christianity.

The decree of proscription struck all unauthorized French Congregations. The Company of Mary had the honor of being among the victims. The Fathers and Brothers were expelled *manu militari* from their different residences, but not without protests on their part and manifestations of solidarity on the part of the people. At Saint-Laurent-sur-Sèvre in particular, the clergy of the area and the people wanted to give proof of their esteem for, and solidarity with, the persecuted priests by objecting to those executing the unjust laws. The agents of the Republic permitted only five Fathers to remain as chaplains for the Daughters of Wisdom, together with Father Guyot, superior general (1877-1886).[56]

His successor, Father Armand Maurille (1887-1896), would have the joy of seeing Louis Marie de Montfort declared Blessed by Leo XIII on January 22, 1888. The dispersion of religious throughout the world increased the influence of missionary France. If the Third Republic opened a period of uncertainty for the Company within France, the expulsion revealed itself as providential, because it forced the Company to leave France. Thus the expulsion began an extraordinary movement of expansion that would see the little Company of Mary established in Europe and the other continents e.g., Holland (1881), Canada (1883), Nyasaland (Malawi) (1901), England (1891), United States (1903), Madagascar (1932), Zaire (1933), Indonesia (1938), and many others.[57]

2. The Constitutions of 1904 and 1949

The Constitutions approved on October 10, 1904, were structured on the model of the "Normae" edited in 1901 by the Congregation for Religious. They should be considered as an intermediate step in an institutional evolution that began with the approbation of the Institute in 1853 and ended with the Constitutions of 1949. The Company had experienced a profound upheaval brought about by multiple external and internal factors that helped give a new image to the Institute. The Constitutions of 1904 and, even more, those of 1949 reflect the image of a Company inclined to assume more decisively its role of evangelization in the universal Church.

The Constitutions of 1904 express the contemporary theology of religious life and the mind-set of the community. "The Company of Mary, founded in the beginning of the eighteenth century by Blessed Louis Marie de Montfort, has as its primary end the personal sanctification of its members by the observance of the vows of religion and the Constitutions of the Company and by devotion to the noble and holy Slavery of Mary, according to the method of the Blessed Founder."

Personal sanctification is achieved by the classical means (vows and observance of the Constitutions), but also "by devotion to the noble and holy Slavery of Mary, according to the method of the Blessed Founder."[58]

Father Lhoumeau (general from 1903 to 1919), author of valued publications on the spirituality of Montfort,[59] notes, not without a certain satisfaction, that "we must rejoice to see thus officially recognized, and by its own name, this devotion that characterizes the spirituality of our Institute" (letter of March 19, 1905).[60]

While holding a definite priority, the preaching of parish missions both in the Constitutions of 1904, as in those of 1949, were classed among the means that the Company uses to extend the reign of Christ through the reign of Mary.

3. The Company of Mary Today

The post-Vatican II general chapters of the Company of Mary have given a strong impetus to the renewal of the Institute. The changes have been structural, but primarily they have consisted of a profound interior renewal in the light of montfort spirituality. With close attention to the signs of the times and to the call of the Church, the chapters wished to discover anew and deepen their understanding of how to read, live, and announce the Gospel, and of the way of Montfort as evidenced in his life and writings, in particular in the Triptych (PM, RM, and LCM).

The renewal within the Company of Mary has strengthened the living of montfort spirituality and also the joyful obligation of explaining and propagating it. It has invigorated the apostolate intrinsic to its spirituality, of proclaiming to the poor the reign of Jesus through Mary. It has emphasized the importance of preaching, especially of parish missions and retreats. Responding to this new awareness of Saint Louis de Montfort's heritage, the Congregation for Religious and Secular Institutes approved not only the Constitutions of the Company of Mary but also the text of the founder's Triptych. At the present time, this approbation is unique among those of postconciliar Constitutions. In a remarkable passage, the decree declares: "The same Sacred Congregation equally approves as a legislative text the 'Original Rule,' preceding the Constitutions and composed of three writings of the founder, in such a way that for the norms the Constitutions have priority, but for the principles, the Rule has priority." This passage is of basic importance because of the consequences it has not only for the law of the Company but even more for its ecclesial identity and the very life of the Institute.

"This Sacred Congregation expresses the wish that, thanks to the faithful observance of these texts, the fondest desire of the founder may be realized: May the Lord use the Montfort Missionaries to form 'a company of guardsmen so that all give Him glory in His temple'" (PM 30).[61]

P. L. Nava

Notes: (1) Blain, 119. (2) On the personality of Poullart des Places, cf. J. Lecuyer, *En relisant Poullart des Places (On Re-reading Poullart des Places),* in *Cahiers spiritains* 3 (1977), 3-17; 5 (1978), 3-20; J. Michel, *Poullart des Places,* in DSAM 12 (1985), 2027-2035. (3) Besnard I, 278. (4) Besnard, I, 278-279. (5) Besnard I, 279. (6) Cf. P. Eyckeler, *Quelques Points d'histoire montfortaine,* vol. 1, *Des origines à M. Mulot, exécuteur testamentaire,* duplicated, Rome 1972, 43-53. (7) P. Eyckeler, *Compagnon de mission du Père de Montfort: Le frère Mathurin,* in *Spiritus* 13 (1962), 397-398. (8) Cf. P. Eijckeler, *Des origines,* 29-40. (9) Cf. the document in P. Eyckeler, *Des origines,* 51. (10) Grandet, 208-211. (11) Besnard I, 328. (12) Besnard II, 309. (13) Cf. P. Eyckeler, *Quelques points,* vol 2, *La société des missionnaires,* duplicated, Rome 1973, 11. (14) Besnard, *Marie-Louise,* 127-128. (14) The text of the petition and the relevant episcopal certificates are in Grandet, 269-274. (15) Grandet, 270. (16) Cf. Louis Pérouas, ed., *P.-F. Hacquet. Mémoires des missions des montfortains dans l'Ouest (1740-1779): Contribution à la sociologie religieuse historique,* Fontenay-le-Comte 1964, 1-10. It was probably Father Hacquet who played a part in the introduction of retreats. Pérouas puts forward the hypothesis that Mulot was against it. In fact, the running of retreats as ordinary ministry for the community of Saint-Laurent began the year after Mulot's death (1749), and until 1767 Hacquet was practically the only one engaged in that type of preaching. (17) Cf. J-F. Dervaux, *Folie ou Sagesse? Marie-Louise Trichet et les premiéres Filles de M. de Montfort,* Paris 1950, 323-324, especially note 34. (18) There is uncertainty on the number of priests and brothers at that time. It is certain that Mulot, Vatel, Le Valois, Guillemot, and Brothers Mathurin and Joseau were present, but it is not certain that Fathers Aumond and Toutant were there. (19) Besnard II, 277. (20) Besnard II, 277. (21) Florence, 105. (22) AGCM: "Règles des prêtres missionnaires de la Compagnie de Marie, établis par M. de Montfort, Approuvées par plusieurs Evêques." This manuscript has raised several problems of date and authorship. (23) The texts of the episcopal approbations are given ibid., 50-53. (24) Cf. J.-M. Texier, *Histoire de la Compagnie de Marie,* 1:90-105. The original of the account is preserved in the Archives of the Daughters of Wisdom at Saint Laurent-sur-Sèvre. (25) Texier, *Histoire,* 1:253. (26) The text of this decree is given in J. M. Prat, *Essai historique sur la destruction des Ordres religieux au dix-huitième siècle,* Paris 1845. (27) P. Chevalier, introduction to *Loménie de Brienne,* 1:34. (28) Cf. the remarks in L. Pérouas, *Réflexion historique sur l'apostolat des montfortains,* in DMon 40 (1967), 1-11. (29) Cf. J.F. Dervaux, *Le Droigt de Dieu: Les Filles de la Sagesse après la mort des fondateurs,* Cholet 1954, 1:112. The author deals at length with this stormy period in the history of the montfort family (51-31). (30) [J.M. Frissen], *L'atachement des congrégations montfortaines au Saint-Siège* (collection of texts attached to the *Circular of the Council,* August 30, 1962), Rome 1962, 11-12. (31) T. Tackett, *La Révolution, l'Eglise, la France,* Cerf, Paris 1986, 266-267. (32) Paris, Archives Nationales, D XXIX 39 L 392, 5-6. (33) Cf. the report on the death of the two martyrs in the death register kept in the city hall of La Rochelle, in Texier, *Histoire,* 2:51-53. The cause of death is modestly described in the official account as "popular emotion" (52). (34) Cf. Texier, *Histoire,* 2:71. (35) *Délibérations,* 1:3. (36) Ibid., 37-38. (37) AGFS: Sr. Agathange, "Chroniques de la Congrégation de la Sagesse," ms., vol. 5, 1916. (38) *Délibérations,* 1:50. (39) On the juridical nature of the Decree of Praise given by Leo XII, cf. P. L. Nava, *L'approvazione canonica,* 93-101. (40) F.Laveau, *Vie de Gabriel Deshayes,* Vannes 1854, 139-140. (41) AGCM, Arm. 2: "Règles et constitutions des missionnaires du St. Esprit," ms., St. Laurent-sur-Sèvre 1837. (42) Ibid., ch. 7, n. 1 (43) Ibid., ch. 1, art. 1. (44) Ibid., ch. 11, art. 10. (45) AGCM, Arm. 14: *Missions et retraites données par les Pères de la Compagnie de Marie de Saint Laurent-sur-Sèvre,* vol. 1 (1740-1864), vol. 2 (1862-1865). (46) In his *Mémoire,* Father Marchand recorded twenty-three six-to-seven week retreats between February 1823 and March 1830, two retreats lasting about two weeks, and an unspecified number of retreats lasting between ten and twelve days; cf. J.H. Frissen, *Mgr Julien-Marie Hillêreau,* 7. (47) Cf. [J.M. Frissen], *La place de la Vierge dans la vie personnelle de Montfort, la pensée du fondateur, l'histoire de la Compagnie (Textes et faits),* General Chapter, Rome 1964, 44 pages. (48) *Règle des prêtres missionnaires de la Compagnie de Marie,* Tipografia della Rev. Cam. Apostolica, Rome 1853. (49) J. Dalin, *Notice historique sur l'approbation des deux congrégations fondées par le Vén. Montfort,* Vincent Forest, Nantes 1854, 13. (50) *Règles et constitutions des missionnaires de la Compagnie de Marie,* Vincent Forest, Nantes 1861. (51) Ibid., part 1, ch. 1, nos. 1, 32, 33. (52) Archives of the Sacred Congregation for Religious and Secular Institutes: L 15, 2, 34. (53) The Constitutions of the Missionary Priests of the Company of Mary, approved for ten years by the apostolic decree of July 6, 1872, were the result of various initiatives already taken for the preceding approbation and had been used *ad experimentum* since November 14, 1853. (54) *Constitutions des prêtres-missionnaires de la Compagnie de Marie,* Oudin, Poitiers 1872, 9-10, VI,6. (55) AGCM, Arm. 15, "Missions et retraites données par les Pères de la Compagnie de Marie de Saint Laurent-sur-Sèvre . . . (1865-1878)," vol. 2, ms. (56) Cf. Dervaux, *Le doigt de Dieu,* 2:251-294. (57) On the origins of the foundations in and outside Europe, cf. the chronology in *La Compagnie de Marie: Origines des Provinces et des Missions, Statistiques à la date du 1er octobre 1951,* in *L'Echo des missions,* 220 (1951), 1-12. (58) *Constitutions des Prêtres Missionnaires de la Compagnie de Marie,* Vatican Press, Rome 1905, 5. (59) Cf. F. Fradet, *Le T.R.P. Lhoumeau, ancien supérieur général de la Compagnie de Marie et des Filles de la Sagesse,* Lille 1921. (60) On the Marian character of the Company of Mary, cf. [Frissen], *La place de la Vierge,* especially 23-44; D.M. Huot, *Engagement marial du montfortain: archaïsme ou exigence toujours actuelle?,* in DM n.39 (1967), 1-18. (61) Cf. Missionaries of the Company of Mary, *Montfortian Today,* Rome 1984.

CONSECRATION

SUMMARY

I. INTRODUCTION.

II. CONSECRATION IN SCRIPTURE:
   1. Consecration itself;
   2. Consecration of humanity through the covenant;
   3. Jesus, the Consecrated One;
   4. The Church a consecrated people through Baptism;
   5. Mary, the consecrated in Jesus:
      a. Mary, the model of Consecration,
      b. Mary, Mother of the consecrated.

III. CONSECRATION IN HISTORY:
   1. The beginnings;
   2. Immediate sources of the montfort Consecration:
      a. Cardinal de Bérulle,
      b. Henri Boudon.

IV. THE NATURE OF THE MONTFORT CONSECRATION:
   1. Trinitarian/Christocentric;
   2. Total;
   3. Baptismal renewal;
   4. Marian;
   5. Apostolic;
   6. Conclusion.

V. MOTIVES OF THE MONTFORT CONSECRATION:
   1. Perseverance;
   2. Interior liberty;
   3. Totally devoted to the service of God;
   4. Living for God Alone;
   5. Imitation of the Trinity;
   6. Union with Our Lord:
      a. An easy way,
      b. A short way,
      c. A perfect way,
      d. A secure way;
   7. A sharing of life with Mary;
   8. Charity towards our neighbor;
   9. Summary.

VI. THE EFFECTS OF THE MONTFORT CONSECRATION:
   1. The stripping of self;
   2. Participation in Mary's faith;
   3. Deliverance from scruples, cares, and fears;
   4. Great confidence in God and in Mary;
   5. Communication of the spirit of Mary;
   6. Transformation by Mary into the likeness of Christ;
   7. The greater glory of God.

I. INTRODUCTION

Although "Consecration" in montfort spirituality is used at times as an umbrella term denoting the totality of the saint's doctrine, it is employed by Louis de Montfort himself in two different ways that reflect degrees of the explicit giving of oneself to God. First, as one of many exterior expressions of true devotions to Our Lady signifying both a resolve to live as her own and an act of petition for her maternal care (cf. TD 116; LEW 215) in order to live the Gospel more fully. Second, as a dynamic state of life resulting from the perfect *"Consecration of oneself to Jesus Christ, Wisdom Incarnate, by the hands of Mary"* (LEW 223). This latter *"devotion"*[1] is also called *"perfect renewal of baptism"* (TD 120, 126), *"Consecration to the Blessed Virgin"* (SM 31), the *"perfect Consecration to Jesus Christ"* (TD 120), *"Holy Slavery of Jesus and Mary"* (SM 44), *"giving of oneself entirely and as a slave to Mary and to Jesus through Mary and after that to do all that we do through Mary, with Mary, in Mary and for Mary"* (SM 28; cf. LEW 219; TD 118), *"Consecration to Jesus by the hands of Mary"* (TD 35), *"Covenant Renewal"* (cf. CG), and the *"Tree of Life"* (SM 70–78).[2] It is this *"most perfect and most profitable of all devotions to the Blessed Virgin"* (LEW 219) that is considered in this article. From the variety of names Father de Montfort gives to this one Act of Consecration, it is already evident that it is the hub where a number of elements converge.

The study of the perfect Consecration is found in the fourth means of arriving at union with the Eternal and Incarnate Wisdom (LEW 203–222) and only after spending the greater part on devotion to Mary in general (LEW 203–218). Although SM touches on devotions to Mary, its clear aim from the very start is to give a concise teaching on St. Louis de Montfort's version of Holy Slavery. The specific explanation of the total Consecration begins with TD 120 and continues to the end of that work. It is at the beginning of this chapter (TD ch. 3) that we have the manuscript's first authentic title, which Montfort wrote in large letters: *THE PERFECT CONSECRATION TO JESUS CHRIST.* The entire first section of TD—dealing with devotion to Mary in general and its theological foundations—is an absolute prerequisite for an understanding of the perfect Consecration.[3]

II. Consecration in Scripture

Saint Louis de Montfort tells us that his teaching on perfect Consecration cannot be refuted without overturning the very foundations of Christianity (TD 163; cf. TD 180). To understand his claim, it is important to search its scriptural roots,[4] for Scripture as proclaimed, taught, prayed by the Church (i.e., Scripture-Tradition) is the *norma non normata,* the norm that has no other norm.[5]

1. Consecration itself

The term "Consecration" comes from the root "holy" (Hebrew *qds,* Greek *hag*) and fundamentally means that a person, place, or thing is sanctified, made holy (Greek *hagiazein*) to the Lord. To be consecrated or to be made holy conveys the idea, then, of being separated from the profane through a sharing in some manner in the life of God. For God Alone is the "Holy One," the "Holy One of Israel" (Isa 40:25; 60:14).

Holiness expresses, in its highest meaning, divinity itself. It has of itself a double polarity: the holy both attracts and wards off. It withdraws itself inaccessibly from our grasp; before its awesomeness we can only be silent. Yet nothing but this "other" can fulfill us in the very depths of our being. It is only in contact with the holy that we are interiorly liberated from the ambiguity of the self. The duality of abyss and presence does not signify a disharmony in the holy but the oneness of its holiness where we are both strangers and at home, experiencing distance in proximity. Gen 28 and 32, Ex 3 and 19, and Isa 6 display the typical combination of remoteness and proximity, awe and joy inherent in the holy.

Consecration, therefore, is the entrance into the holy, sharing in the life of the All-Holy One, God Alone. The more intense the proximity through Consecration, the more the awesome otherness of God becomes a vivid reality. Both polarities—the tender closeness of God and His awesomeness—are found throughout Montfort's writings, especially when describing Consecration to the Incarnate Wisdom.

2. Consecration of humanity through the covenant

Creation itself as the handiwork of the All-Holy One is "good" (cf. Gen 1:10, 12, 18, 21, 25, 31), holy, consecrated, although through original sin disfigured and deformed (cf. Gen 3; Rom 5:12–21). Holiness—Consecration—is especially attributed to the ground around the burning bush (Ex 3:5), the temple (Isa 64:11), special days (Neh 8:9), offerings (1 Sam 21:4), and priests (Ex 29), since these now pertain to the Holy. "Since holiness is a participation in the self-communication of God, in man it is a grace-given listening to God and a commitment to Him."[6] Holiness is shared with His people through the covenant, whereby Israel becomes a nation whom God has made peculiarly His own. The covenant with Noah, with Abraham, the covenant with Moses as the culmination of the Exodus event—all express God's desire to share His holiness, to consecrate His creatures. YHWH has consecrated them to Himself—made them holy—through His free, unmerited gift; they must accept this offer and thereby implement the Consecration freely initiated by their God. The chosen people do this by the acceptance of the ten words and the code of the covenant (Ex 24:3,7). Israel is now "the people of God," God's "chosen people," God's "holy people." "If only you will now listen to me and keep my covenant, then out of all peoples you shall become my special possession" (Ex 19:5). And the people accept and thereby implement the Consecration: "Whatever the Lord has said we will do" (Ex 19:8). According to Deuteronomy, intrinsic to God's Consecration of His people—which implies an active and responsible acceptance of God's offer, expressed in holiness of life—is the notion of mission. The consecrated nation Israel is not separated from others in the sense of isolation. Rather, it is to witness to the only God, deliverer and Lord of history (Isa 44:8).

Over and over again, Israel breaks its ratification of the covenant, in spite of numerous renewals at moments of national conversion.[7] When Israel deserts its God and had to be driven out of its holy frontiers during the exile because it had desecrated them, God nonetheless promises a new offer of covenant love (Jer 31:31–34) so that the Israelites may truly become the sheep consecrated to the Lord (Ezek 36:37–38). "I will make a covenant with them to bring them prosperity; this covenant shall be theirs forever, I will greatly increase their numbers and I will put my sanctuary forever in their midst" (Ezek 37:26; cf. 36:22–36).

3. Jesus, the Consecrated One

The fulfillment of God's promises of a new covenant is found in Jesus the Christ. He is in his Person "the Holy One of God" (Mk 1:24; Lk 4:34; Jn 6:69). The consecrated nation Israel becomes a Person, Jesus the Lord. In virtue of the Incarnation, he is the personal presence of the Holy in this creation. In him we see the two polarities of holiness: majestic awesomeness, remoteness ("Depart from me for I am a sinful man, O Lord" [Lk 5:8]) and proximity to the awesome ("It is well that we are here, let us make three booths" [Mk 9:5]).

Jesus Himself personally and lovingly accepts and ratifies his being as the Holy One. "As thou didst send me into the world, . . . for their sake I consecrate myself that they also may be consecrated in truth" (Jn 17:19). The incarnational Consecration of Jesus is not only ontological. It is also personal, subjective, willing, loving. He lovingly, willingly consecrates himself to the Father. And as the summit of all creation, he personalizes the ontological Consecration of this universe accomplished climactically through his redemptive Incarnation: "I consecrate them in truth." Heb 10:5–10 tells us that this personal Consecration of Jesus to the

Father begins at the Incarnation itself. It reaches its intensity in his Consecration from the Cross: "Father, into your hands I commend my spirit" (Lk 23:46).[8]

4. The Church a consecrated people through Baptism

In Jesus, then, the entire universe and, especially, all peoples are made holy, sanctified, consecrated. But as with the ancient Israelites, there is to be a response, an acceptance, for a gift becomes truly gift only when it is accepted. Jesus is the Consecration of the cosmos to the Father; he is also the acceptance of the Father's gracious love. The role of his "brothers and sisters" is to be one with him so that in the power of the Spirit all may be made holy, consecrated through Christ to God. The total, loving response of the intellectual creatures to Jesus' call, "Come, follow me," implements the transformation of all creation into God's holiness.

We enter into the victorious holiness of Christ through Baptism. The baptized person renounces everything that enslaves him to Satan in order to enjoy the freedom of belonging to Christ Jesus (Acts 2:38; 8:16–17; Rom 6:3; Gal 3:27). The Christian is God's chosen, dedicated in a special way to be at His service: "the slave of Jesus Christ" (Rom 1:1; Phil 1:1; Titus 1:1, etc.). The Christian accepts the Gospel as the rule of life and follows the Lord wheresoever he leads: he will carry his Cross after him all the days of his life (Lk 9:23). Baptism is, therefore, the fundamental Consecration of whoever in Christ believes in the Father, Son, and Holy Spirit (Mt 28:19). The Consecration of the world in Christ is personalized through its baptismal acceptance.[9] Anointed by the Holy Spirit (1 Jn 2:20–27), the Christian now is part of the New Covenant, a nation consecrated, a people whom God has chosen for His own to proclaim His marvels (1 Pet 2:9).

It is not surprising, therefore, that the baptized are called "the consecrated"; in Baptism they have put on Christ. They are part of the family of God, "consecrated in the Consecrated" (cf. Col 1:12–23). As in the OT, so in the NT the Consecration of the Church - the new people of God - is linked to God's free offer of salvation, which empowers our loving acceptance (2 Thess 2:13;2 Tim 1:8, 9). The majestic beginning of Eph declares the Church to be consecrated - holy - to God (Eph 1:4–2:22). Peter can therefore address his congregation: "To those of God's scattered people . . . who have been chosen by the provident purpose of God the Father, to be made holy by the Spirit, obedient to Jesus Christ and sprinkled with his blood" (1 Pet 1:2); "You are a chosen race, a royal priesthood, a consecrated nation, a people claimed by God for his very own to proclaim the triumphs of him who has called you out of darkness into his marvelous light. You are now the people of God who once were not his people" (1 Pet 2:9–10).

5. Mary, the consecrated in Jesus

Of all called by God to share in His holiness, to be consecrated to Him through Jesus Christ in the power of the Spirit, no one responds more fully than Mary, the Mother of the Consecrated One.

a. Mary, the model of Consecration. Mary, a member of the chosen people of God, is, then, herself a consecrated woman. Her life is lived in fidelity to the covenant, for she "hears the word of God and keeps it" (Lk 11:28; cf. Lk 2:19). Moreover, she is, in Luke's narrative, the *kecharitomene*: "the highly beloved one" (Lk 1:28), sharing in a unique way in the holiness of God. As a sign and model of this universe seeking a new Consecration to the All-Holy, she surrenders to the mysterious ways of the Holy One of Israel. The Infinite Word shares with her his total Consecration to the Father, so that she too may make—in him and through him—a total, loving Consecration of herself to the All-Holy: "Behold the handmaid of the Lord, let it be done unto me according to thy word" (Lk 1:38). The Magnificat song portrays her being: "He who is mighty has done great things for me and Holy is His Name" (Lk 1:49). She carries in her heart and womb the "Holy" (Lk 1:35) and becomes herself a uniquely "holy place," a new Ark of the Covenant bearing the Consecration of this universe, Jesus the Lord. She is the first of the consecrated in the Consecrated, sharing as none other in the redemptive Consecration wrought by her Son. Her courageous fidelity to her Son accompanies him even to the Cross, where she stands as the Church—the consecrated people of God—one with Jesus in his Consecration to the Father. Through the unmerited favor of God, she is the model of Consecration to the All-Holy, in and through the Incarnate Holy One who is Consecration itself.

Finally, in Montfort's thought Mary is the model of consecration, for she shares eminently in the holiness of Eternal Wisdom in virtue of her immaculate conception. The saint's strong belief in this prerogative of Mary—a century and a half before it was solemnly defined—is the context for his praise of Mary's holiness at the beginning of her existence: *"When the time appointed for the redemption of mankind had come, Eternal Wisdom built himself a house worthy to be his dwelling-place. He created the most holy Virgin, forming her in the womb of St. Anne with even greater delight than he had derived from creating the universe. . . the torrential outpouring of God's infinite goodness which had been rudely stemmed by the sins of men since the beginning of the world was now released precipitately and in full flood into the heart of Mary. Eternal Wisdom gave to her all the graces which Adam and all his descendants would have received so liberally from him had they remained in their original state of justice. The fullness of God. . . was poured into Mary insofar as a creature is capable of receiving it."* (LEW 105). Mary's heart, as Montfort teaches, is immaculate, all-holy, from the first moment of her conception (cf. SM 17; TD 50, 64, 145, etc.; H 75, 19-20). In anticipation of the redemptive Incarnation, Our Lady is consecrated from the first instant of her conception. She is of her very being, immaculate, all-holy, consecrated.

b. Mary, Mother of the consecrated. *In Mary's womb, the Consecration of this universe comes to be through God's grace and her representative consent.* Though no creature is necessary to the All-Holy, YHWH freely chooses her to be the representative of the people of God in accepting the New Covenant in Jesus Christ. In her the New Covenant takes place as Mary, summarizing Israel, speaks her **fiat,** echoing and voicing the assent of Israel to God's offer of His holiness: "We will obey and do all that the Lord has said" (Ex 24:7). "Mary, in particular, is heiress and the completion of the faith of Abraham."[10]

In her and through her, the definitive Consecration of the world becomes a reality. She is the spokesperson for the universe in accepting Consecration in "the Holy One" to be born of her, as is evident from Luke's Annunciation narrative (1:26–38). The pericope resembles more a covenant renewal (Mary, personification of the people of God, accepting God's offer of a new alliance; cf. Ex 19:8) than an OT birth-annunciation narrative like that of Samson (Judg 13:2–22). John also teaches this truth in his own fashion. Through the literary device of inclusion,[11] John depicts the faithful Mary as the antiphon of Jesus' entire ministry. The first antiphon is at Cana (2:1–11) where she is the woman who in the name of all called to the banquet requests the wine of new life (cf. Jl 4:18). The responding antiphon is the woman at the foot of the Cross (19:25–27), where she stands as the representative acceptance of the overflowing new wine of the Enfleshed Holy One, the universe's Consecration to the Father.

Moreover, at that culmination of the Consecration of the world to the Father, Mary is present not only as the Mother of the Lord but as the Mother of all who are contained in Him, of all the faithful. "Woman, behold your son . . . behold your mother. And from that hour, the disciple took her to his own" (Jn 19:26–27). Her spiritual maternity is promulgated from the throne of the Cross, and John takes her "to his own" (*eis ta idia*), into his very life. As Mary is to Jesus and Jesus to Mary, so she is now to the beloved disciple - the faithful - and the disciple to her.

II. Consecration in History

Saint Louis de Montfort's understanding of Consecration to Jesus through Mary must be placed in its proper historical context. He is the successor of centuries of development on this theme, which he then quite radically develops and molds into the core of a school of spirituality. Even in early Christian times, the followers of Jesus called themselves "slaves of Jesus Christ."[12] It is with difficulty, however, that we can trace the early stages of what could be equivalently called Consecration to Jesus through the hands of Mary.

1. The beginnings

The history of "Consecration to Our Lady" has been well documented.[13] What is of primary interest in this article are the immediate sources of Saint Louis de Montfort's total Consecration. Although he may have been introduced to the form of Consecration called Holy Slavery while studying with the Jesuits at Rennes, it is certain that he immersed himself in literature on the subject while a student and librarian at St. Sulpice in Paris.

As Father de Montfort himself notes, *"This devotion was practiced by several private individuals up to the seventeenth century when it became public"* (TD 159). But as practiced by these "private individuals,"[14] Holy Slavery appears to have lacked a strong Christocentric foundation and was highly involved in externals. Even when it became public, especially through the seventeenth-century school of spirituality, "it had not as yet reached the clarity and plenitude that it achieved under Saint Louis de Montfort. Moreover [the Consecration] is not addressed to Jesus, the Incarnate Wisdom, in dependence on Mary; it does not present to us the imitation of this filial dependence as its principal motive. Likewise, it leaves the spiritual maternity of Mary only in the shade."[15]

2. Immediate sources of the Montfort Consecration

Montfort's primary sources for his doctrine on Consecration appear to be Cardinal de Bérulle,[16] the founder of the French school of spirituality, and his disciples J.J. Olier[17] and H. Boudon,[18] although he finds the basic theological underpinnings especially in J.B. Crasset[19] and F.Poiré[20]. It appears that Bérulle and Boudon play the more significant roles in the developing of Montfort's own particular doctrine on Holy Slavery, or, as he more specifically terms it, the perfect Consecration to Christ through the hands of Mary.

a. Cardinal de Bérulle. Thanks to Cardinal de Bérulle, the devotion of Holy Slavery was made part of the French school of spirituality. Having become acquainted with the confraternities in Spain, he became its propagator in France.[21] This *"great and holy man"* (TD 162), however, did not merely import this devotion; he transformed it along the essential lines of his spirituality. Montfort speaks of the following developments introduced by the cardinal: *"He showed them that the devotion was founded on the example of Jesus Christ, on the obligations which we have toward Him and on the vows which we have made in holy Baptism . . . making them see that this consecration to the holy Virgin and to Jesus Christ by her hands, is nothing else than a perfect renewal of the vows and promises of Baptism"* (TD 162). The French school of spirituality "singled out as central and fundamental to all Christ's states his state of servitude. In the complete possession of Christ's humanity by the divinity, wherein the humanity of Christ lacks its own subsistence, its own personality, they saw the absolute condition of self-renouncement and clinging to God. From this state of 'infinite servitude' they drew the most fundamental characteristic of their spirituality - the deep, total renunciation of self that is at the same time total adherence to Christ and being possessed by Him. . . . Adoration, then, in the Bérullian sense, is a persisting state of renunciation, of self-surrender . . . grace in [the Christian] is a created copy of the state of servitude of Christ in the hypostatic union."[22]

Even as developed by this great spiritual author, the devotion of Holy Slavery, or total Consecration, differed from the spirituality that would be explained by Saint Louis de

Montfort. "On the part of Jesus, Bérulle assigns, as foundation of his Donation, the state of servitude of the Holy Humanity of the Incarnate Word; Montfort, the state of dependence of the Incarnate Word himself in relation to Mary in the entire redemptive work. On the part of Our Lady, Bérulle bases his Donation on the Divine Maternity and the Universal Sovereignty that flows from it; Montfort, on the spiritual maternity and the special dominion of Mary over the members of the Mystical Body."[23] Moreover, Bérulle's attitude towards Our Lady appears to be more reverential than loving.[24]

b. Henri Boudon. Boudon's work on Holy Slavery also had a profound effect on Montfort's understanding of perfect Consecration (TD 163). Here again, however, Saint Louis is not a copyist; he creatively analyzes Boudon's verbose explanations. This prolific writer does insist that any Consecration is ultimately to God Alone, for He alone merits the loving servitude of His creatures: this becomes an essential element of Montfort's understanding of the perfect Consecration. He also lists precisely what is given to Our Lady, such as our merits and satisfactions; Montfort will follow him closely on this point. But Boudon's Consecration is not made to Jesus-Wisdom, and its Marian dimension is founded on Our Lady's Queenship, not, as with Montfort, on her spiritual maternity. Moreover, "it is regrettable that according to the Bérullian tradition, he presents this generous transaction (Consecration) as a solemn pledge in virtue of which one surrenders his right over a thing; the Marian transaction of Boudon brings to mind the vow of Bérulle, the sacred covenant of St. John Eudes; evidently what is lacking is the clarity of synthesis and adaptation."[25] Strangely, Boudon's book on holy slavery ignores Bérulle's essential insight into the unity of Consecration and the renewal of the vows of Baptism.

Even as understood, therefore, by Montfort's proximate sources, Bérulle and Boudon, Holy Slavery of Love cannot be equated with Saint Louis de Montfort's perfect Consecration to Jesus the Incarnate Wisdom through the hands of Mary. The missionary's creativity, his pastoral ministry, and his own personal mystical experiences enable him to further develop, clarify, and synthesize the teachings of his predecessors to a point where his doctrine on Consecration takes on a new depth. Care must be had, therefore, in the use of the term "Holy Slavery" as understood in the Bérullian School to designate the montfort Consecration, since it substantially differs from the "Holy Slavery" generally attributed to the French school of spirituality.

IV. The Nature of the Montfort Consecration

The theological foundations for true devotions to Mary (TD 14–89) and the characteristics of authentic devotions (TD 90–117) form the general introduction to Saint Louis de Montfort's explanation of the *"perfect consecration to Jesus Christ"* (TD 120–273). There are no special theological roots for Montfort's perfect Consecration; it is but the full flowering of the principles he has laid down in the first section of TD.

The above scriptural examination of Consecration—although nowhere so expressed in the writings of Father de Montfort—is the solid substratum of the saint's total Consecration. Often in baroque language, this preacher to the "simple folk" does nothing more than proclaim the word of God and apply it in its fullest conclusions: the essence of his understanding of the perfect Consecration to Jesus Christ. The following appear to be the more important characteristics of Consecration as outlined by Saint Louis de Montfort in his writings and summarized in his Act of Consecration to the Eternal and Incarnate Wisdom by the Hands of Mary (LEW 223–227).[26] They remarkably mirror the scriptural understanding of Consecration.

Father de Montfort explains the nature of "perfect Consecration to Jesus Christ" in TD 120–134. In SM also, Montfort begins with an explanation of the nature of this way of life (28–34), and in a summary fashion he does the same in LEW 219. There are several essential elements intrinsic to the nature of Holy Slavery as fashioned by Saint Louis de Montfort.

1. Trinitarian/Christocentric

In LEW, SM, and TD—the three works dealing with perfect Consecration—the missionary makes it clear that Jesus is the goal of the covenant renewal. In fact, in his first fundamental truth of all devotions to Mary, he declares that if the final end is not Jesus Christ, it can only be called diabolical: *"If then we establish solid devotion to Our Blessed Lady, it is* ***only*** *to establish more perfectly devotion to Jesus Christ. If devotion to Our Lady removed us from Jesus Christ, we should have to reject it as an illusion of the devil"* (TD 62). And in the introduction to his explanation of the nature of perfect Consecration, he again is firm and explicit: *"All our perfection consists in being conformed, united and consecrated to Jesus Christ"* (TD 120). Montfort makes it clear from the outset that there is absolutely no such thing as Consecration—in the strict sense of the term—to Mary. In his eyes, that would be nothing short of blasphemous, for Mary is in herself a "nothing," a "pure (**i.e. nothing more than**) creature." Mary can only unite us with Christ: *"The greatest* ***means*** *of all and the most wonderful of all secrets for obtaining and preserving divine Wisdom is a loving and genuine devotion to the Blessed Virgin"* (LEW 203). The Christocentricity of the montfort Consecration is clearly and emphatically stressed: *"Jesus, our Savior, true God and true man must be the ultimate end of all our devotions; otherwise they would be false and misleading. 'We labor,' says St. Paul, 'only to make all men perfect in Jesus Christ.' For in him alone dwells the entire fullness of the divinity and the complete fullness of grace, virtue and perfection. In him alone we have been blessed with every spiritual blessing; he is the only teacher from whom we must learn; the only Lord on whom we should depend; the only Head to whom we should be united and the only model that we should imitate. He is the only Physician that can heal us; the only Shepherd that can feed us; the only Way that can lead us; the only*

Truth that we can believe; the only Life that can animate us. He alone is everything to us and he alone can satisfy all our desires" (TD 61).

The Trinitarian structure of the Consecration formula of LEW (23–227) is apparent. But in describing the perfect Consecration as Trinitarian/Christocentric, there are especially three qualifications to be underlined:

- The ultimate purpose of the Consecration is for the *"greater glory of God"* (LEW 227). As majestic as He is, it is the mighty God's tenderness and closeness that is accentuated by Montfort. The source of all, the Father, is the fountainhead of love.

- It is essential to Saint Louis de Montfort's understanding of the perfect Consecration that the goal be seen as Jesus, **the Eternal and Incarnate Wisdom** (cf. LEW). The attractive, tender, often feminine qualities of Wisdom as described especially in the sapiential books of the Bible are intrinsic to the goal that lures us to surrender all lovingly to Wisdom Incarnate. This is not a superficial element; rather, it profoundly affects his doctrine. The son of Mary, Jesus-Wisdom, caught up in the folly of the victorious Cross is the specific manner in which the saint wishes us to contemplate the Consecration of this world to God Alone; it is by becoming one with Jesus-Wisdom that we enter into this Consecration.

- Montfort lays particular stress on the truth that life in the Spirit is integral to the Consecration. The Consecration to Jesus-Wisdom necessarily entails a surrender to the overshadowing Spirit who both draws us into the Trinitarian life and sends us forth as "other Christs." *"The Holy Spirit, finding his dear Spouse [Mary] present again in souls, will come down into them with great power. He will fill them with his gifts, especially wisdom, by which they will produce wonders of grace"* (TD 217).

To be faithful to Montfort, any study of his Consecration should begin not with Mariology or Marian devotion but with the Trinity/Incarnation as outlined in LEW and TD.

2. Total

In the eyes of the modern reader, Saint Louis goes to extremes in demonstrating the totality of this Consecration to Jesus-Mary. Everything must be lovingly consecrated to the All-Holy. Following the authors of his time quite closely, he lists what we give to Our Lady and therefore more effectively to Christ: "*We must give her (1) our body with all its senses and its members; (2) our soul, with all its powers; (3) our exterior good of fortune whether present or to come; (4) our interior and spiritual goods, which are our merits and our virtues and our good works, past, present and future. In a word, we must give her all we have in the order of nature and in the order of grace and all that may become ours in the future, in the order of nature, grace and glory; and this we must do without the reserve of so much as one farthing, one hair, or one least good action; and we must do it also for all eternity and we must do it, further, without pretending to, or hoping for any other recompense for our offering and service except the honor of belonging to Jesus Christ through Mary and in Mary"* (TD 121).

This itemizing of what we freely consecrate is done by Montfort in order to try to get across the absolute totality of the Consecration. There is nothing whatsoever not included in this "perfect Consecration." We become "divested" of everything, for our career, plans, possessions, spiritual goods - even glory - is freely "made holy," i.e., subject to the overriding will of Jesus. There may be other ways of "itemizing" the totality of Consecration in contemporary circumstances, but the scope of the surrender envisioned by Montfort does not omit one iota (cf. LEW 225). What Montfort is speaking about is not ultimately the handing over of material things; rather, the Consecration entails a deeper personal relationship with Christ-Wisdom through Mary to a point that this relationship qualifies all others. Everything is seen, judged, planned, evaluated in the light of the Eternal and Incarnate Wisdom, the son of Mary. Montfort insists that we pour out *ourselves* totally, completely.

Montfort stresses the Consecration of our interior goods: *"Here everything is consecrated to Him, even the right of disposing of our interior goods and the satisfactions we gain by our good works day after day. This is more than we do even in a religious order . . . we strip ourselves as far as a Christian can, of that which is dearest and most precious, namely, our merits and our satisfactions"* (TD 123). The saint makes it clear that it is, of course, impossible to transfer our grace, virtues, and merits, for they constitute who "I" am in the eyes of God. We entrust them, however, to the care of Our Lady, i.e., we beg for her maternal care to persevere in the grace of God. The *"impetratory"* value of our life, however - the fruit of our good actions and prayers - we hand over to Our Lady so that she may apply them to whomsoever she wills. Even when we explicitly pray for someone or something, it is always with the proviso that it be her will - always one with Jesus - so that she can apply them in any way she wants. *"A person who is thus voluntarily consecrated and sacrificed to Jesus Christ through Mary can no longer dispose of the value of any of his good actions. All he suffers, all he thinks, all the good he says or does, belongs to Mary in order that she may dispose of it according to the will of her Son and His greatest glory without interfering in any way with the obligations of our state [of life]"* (TD 124). Montfort writes that even after Baptism, *"we remain entirely free either to apply them [the value of our good actions] to ourselves or to whom we please"* (TD 126). One of the reasons that Saint Louis Marie calls this Consecration *"perfect"* is precisely because it includes this "impetratory" value of all our good works.

The missionary calls for the most radical poverty possible, stripping ourselves of everything, of this "make-believe" ownership, for everything belongs to Jesus and Mary; all is for the glory of God Alone. Montfort's love for practical poverty is but an outgrowth of the loving acceptance of the reality of his existential poverty. All flows from our loving Father, Who redeems us - consecrates us - in Christ through the divinely willed consent of Mary. For Montfort, this is a clear, objective reality. To declare that we are anything of ourselves, that we of ourselves "own" anything is absurd. There is absolutely no self-redemption, no Pelagianism in Montfort's thought. All belongs to Jesus and Mary. Montfort is a realist: the truth that we are from every point of view **ab alio** (from the Other) must be sincerely acknowledged. The self-emptying, the **kenosis,** must be complete.

Two principles must be kept in mind in trying to interpret Saint Louis Marie on this subject of **total** Consecration. First, we are all intertwined, interrelated, interdependent. Everything we do or say affects everyone else in the Body of Christ. As process thought reminds us, every actual entity affects every other in the cosmos, even if it be at times in an infinitesimal way. This is especially true in the realm of our loving harmony - or disharmony - with God. Consecration or not, our good and evil actions affect all others. But more to the point, is it not the essence of all prayer, of all our good actions that "Thy Will be done on earth as it is in heaven"? Is that not the understood condition of everything we are and do? If it is not, then we can hardly say that we are Christian, that we are in harmony with God. In the perfect Consecration, however, we are explicitly and willingly making "Thy Will be done" the overriding rule of all that we are, of all that we do. In this sense, we *"give the value of all our good actions."* As Montfort points out, this is the foundation for a more profound life in the Spirit.

Second, in the language of popular piety, Montfort speaks of *"giving," "surrendering,"* yet he recognizes that we as redeemed creatures already do belong totally to Jesus the son of Mary. But offering all lovingly and freely through the power of the overshadowing Spirit results in a new depth of "belonging to" the Lord. The power of the Redemption, the intensity of our oneness in Christ through Mary is more firmly implemented in our lives by the perfect Consecration. The "I" freely empties itself into the "thou" so that it may be its true self. The Act of Consecration is not so much the pronouncement of a formula as the pronouncement of the self: a total and definitive loving "pouring out" into the All Holy. In the Act of Consecration, man finds his identity not in the pride of posing as being-in-itself but in the realistic humility of a loving, lived out relationship with the awesome yet so close "Other," Love itself.

3. Baptismal renewal

For Montfort, the two concepts, perfect renewal of the promises of Baptism and perfect Consecration, are synonymous (LEW 223, 225; TD 120, 126–130). Any authentic Consecration must be linked to Baptism; more so the perfect Consecration. Since Baptism is our immersion, our fundamental Consecration into Christ Jesus, then it is evident that a willing, loving Act of perfect Consecration to Christ Jesus can be nothing but a renewal of the vows of our Baptism. Montfort has left no special treatise on Baptism, but his TD, especially, implies a deep knowledge of its importance and its consequences.[27]

The Second Vatican Council recalls that "already by baptism, [the Christian] was dead to sin and is consecrated to God" (LG 44). It is through Baptism that man enters into the sphere of the Holy, for he is baptized into the death and Resurrection of the Consecrated One, Jesus the Christ. By Baptism, the Christian is consecrated, anointed by the power of the Holy Spirit: he participates in the essential Consecration of Christ. With Christ and by Christ, he is ordained to the glory of God and the salvation of the world. He no longer belongs to himself. He belongs to the Lord, Who shares with him His own life.

Montfort, following his sources, uses the term *"slave"* to illustrate the meaning of this fundamental and radical act of Baptism (TD 68–73, 126). "Slave," stripped of all connotations of oppression and servility and expressing solely the totality of "belonging to" another: it is apparent that in some contemporary cultures, the word is so inextricably bound with horrendous injustice that other expressions should be found as substitutes or as clarifications of what Montfort means by *"slavery."* Faith is a "belonging to" God Alone through Christ Jesus in the power of the Spirit. We enter into that special state of *"belonging to God"* through the Sacrament of Baptism: in this sense, through it we are the *"slaves of Jesus Christ."* As the missionary preaches to the people of his time, however, even before Baptism we belong to God through a *"slavery of nature."* We are His creation, we do not have existence of ourselves. Every breath we take, every heartbeat is the free gift of God; for creation is not something in the past, it is a present happening. Montfort describes our radical status as creatures as *"slaves of nature."* Now, according to the missionary, we have a choice: we can lovingly ratify this total dependence on God and become *"slaves of love"* or we can deny the truth of our belonging to God our Savior and become a *"slave of constraint,"* or *"slave of the devil"* (TD 126). Through Baptism, we become slaves of love, accepting that we are loved by God in Christ Jesus to such a point that we are being transformed into the holiness of God.

The perfect Consecration is precisely the renewal of this baptismal covenant: *"In baptism . . . he [the Christian] has taken Jesus Christ for his Master and Sovereign Lord, to depend on Him in the quality of a slave of love. That is what we do by this present devotion"* (TD 126).

The saint insists that there are three reasons the Consecration should be called *"perfect"* renewal of the vows of Baptism. First, "*in baptism we ordinarily speak by the mouth of another, our godfather or godmother, and so we give ourselves to Jesus Christ not by ourselves but through another. But in this devotion we do it by ourselves, voluntarily, knowing what we are doing*" (TD 126). It can be said that, whether Baptism took place when one was an infant or an adult, the perfect Consecration is the occasion for an ever deepening personal commitment to Jesus Christ, a renewal of the very foundation of our faith. Second, in Baptism we do not *"give Him [the Lord] the value of all our good actions,"* as was noted above. Third, in Baptism *"we do not give ourselves to Jesus by the hands of Mary, at least not in an explicit manner"* (TD 126), as we do in the perfect Consecration.

4. Marian

Montfort stresses that this perfect baptismal Consecration is necessarily Marian. The covenant renewal does not artificially unite Baptism and Mary; this is, as seen above, a **reality** of salvation history that the Consecration willingly and lovingly recognizes not only in theory but in a lived-out spirituality. The reason the saint can make what first appears such a strong statement is that his arch of Consecration is firmly embedded in the reality of the Incarnation.

In the present order of salvation - and there is in reality no other - the Consecration of this world takes place in Jesus Christ and through Jesus Christ because a woman says "yes." God will become man *"provided that"* Mary gives her consent (LEW 107). This is for Montfort the eternal pattern God follows in all the mysteries of salvation history, because they are *"contained"* in this headstream, this source, this beginning of the climactic Consecration, the divinization of the cosmos (cf. TD 248).

Saint Louis teaches, of course, that Jesus alone is the Consecration to the Father. But he must also insist, with the word of God as preached, taught, and prayed by the Church, that this incarnational Consecration takes place in Mary through God's grace and her divinely willed consent. It is, then, utterly impossible to separate the Consecration of this universe - the Eternal and Incarnate Wisdom - from the woman whose faith-consent is intrinsic to the Incarnation of Eternal Wisdom. Her salvific *fiat* brings about the Consecration of this world, inasmuch as her faith gives entry to the enfleshment of the Eternal Wisdom who is in his Person the Consecration of this universe to God.

Consecration to Jesus Christ must, therefore, be Marian. There are not, in Montfort's thinking, two consecrations. There is but one: we freely enter into the Holy One of God, the Incarnate Wisdom, in his full reality—the fruit of the faith-filled womb of Mary. *"We consecrate ourselves at one and the same time to the most holy Virgin and to Jesus Christ . . . to Our Lord as to our last End, to whom as our Redeemer and our God, we owe all we are"* (TD 125). To consecrate ourselves to Christ and exclude Mary is to consecrate ourselves to a chimera, a figment of the imagination, for there is no such person. In her, through her representative consent, our Consecration in Christ comes to be. We are called to freely and lovingly enter into that mystery: such is the Consecration proposed by Saint Louis Marie.[28]

It is through Mary's salvific consent at the Incarnation that she becomes Mother of the Consecration of this universe—Jesus—and, therefore, Mother of us all, for we are spiritually embraced in this Consecration (cf. TD 32; SM 12; LEW 213; H 104:21). It is through Mary's representative consent that Grace itself becomes enfleshed—Jesus—and she is rightfully, then, the spiritual Mother of all who share in that new life of grace which makes us holy to the Lord. The immediate foundation of the Marian dimension of the montfort Consecration is, then, her spiritual maternity.[29] And the spiritual maternity calls forth the Queenship, which is for Montfort primarily the effective maternal influence Mary exercises over the Body of Christ (TD 37, 38).

It follows that the perfect renewal of our Baptism is necessarily Marian. Baptism is our entrance into the Church, the consecrated people of the New Covenant: it is our entry into the Consecration, the Divinization of the world, who is Jesus.[30] Our baptismal covenant includes, therefore, this Marian Consecration. It is evident that when we speak of Consecration to Mary in montfort terms, we are using a short formula for Consecration to God Alone through the Incarnate Wisdom in the power of the Spirit, through Mary, our Mother. *"She is so completely transformed into you by grace that she no longer lives, she no longer exists, because you alone, dear Jesus, live and reign in her more perfectly than all the angels and saints"* (TD 63).

5. Apostolic

The ultimate purpose of the montfort Consecration is to bring about *"the reign of Jesus Christ"* (TD 227). He therefore preaches and writes in order *"to form a disciple of Jesus Christ"* (TD 111). In fact, Montfort firmly believes that he is called by God to raise up not only *"a great squadron of valiant soldiers of Jesus and Mary, a squadron of men and women to combat the world"* (TD 114) but also *"true apostles of the latter times"* (TD 58; cf. 23–27). Although this urgent call is directed primarily to priests, it must not be overlooked that his plea is universal: men and women of all ages, of all places are to become dynamic apostles of Jesus Christ. In the power of the Spirit, they will reform the Church and renew the face of the earth (TD 43; PM 17). The perfect Consecration, the lived-out baptismal covenant renewal, is the principal means he proposes for the formation of these apostles of Jesus Christ, and it is also the means they will use to bring about a renewal within the Church. His goal in promoting the perfect Consecration is to transform the members of the Body of Christ into an army of apostolic men and women who truly live the utter existential poverty of total Consecration and therefore, rich with the Spirit, *"perform great wonders in the world in order to destroy sin and establish the reign of Jesus Christ"* (SM 59).

The saint's theological foundation for this facet of the perfect Consecration is, again, the Incarnation. The sending of the Wisdom of the Father into the folly of this world is apostolic. As the God-man, he is both God's offer of the New Covenant carved in the hearts of men and its acceptance. The full flowering of his redemptive Incarnation, the Consecration from the victorious Cross, is already *"contained"* in the Incarnation itself (cf. TD 248). The redemption of the world is accomplished through and in Mary, the first beneficiary of the New Covenant and also its first missionary, bringing the Good News of the Incarnate Holiness to her relative Elizabeth and the yet unborn John the Baptist (Lk 1:39–45).

Montfort's more than 200 missions and retreats bear the imprint of this firm conviction. His early biographer, Grandet, tells us that the purpose of his parish missions was "to renew the spirit of Christianity by the renewal of the baptismal promises"[31] and adds, "In order that his people would better remember this truth, he had printed a formula of the renewal of the vows of Baptism and had the people sign them."[32] His mission processions were grandiose events solemnly dramatizing the perfect renewal of Baptism. The elaborate processions signified that we are a people on journey with Mary, choosing to follow the victorious crucified Jesus all the days of our life. Father de Montfort was convinced of the value of symbols, of dramatizing the truths of the faith. The processions, therefore, included lighted candles, symbol of Jesus the Light of the World, the renewal of the baptismal vows at the baptismal font, the entrusting of this new life to the Mother of God, the solemn pledge to accept the Gospel of Jesus Christ.[33] The end of the mission was a NT re-enactment of the "holy day" when Ezra and Nehemiah called upon all of Israel to accept the words of the Law that God had given them (cf. Neh 8).

The Consecration does not, then, close us up into ourselves. Rather, through a personal renewal of the faith, it is a renewed sharing in the life of the Missionary, Jesus. All who live the Consecration are to be living proclaimers of the New Covenant.[34]

6. Conclusion

Saint Louis de Montfort's creative weaving of these essential characteristics of Consecration cannot be found as such in his sources. His evangelical insight is a unique gift of the Spirit to the Church, as valid for its renewal today as it was in his time, even though his terminology and baroque expressions must be modified from culture to culture. Moreover, the saint does not give us an "Act of Consecration." Rather, since Mary is the person in whom and through whom Consecration - Jesus-Wisdom - comes to be, he calls for a way of life in Mary so that we may be more intensely consecrated in the Consecrated. It is especially this Marian spirituality - essential to a montfort consecrated life - which is considered in the following sections, keeping close to his explanations in TD and SM.

V. Motives of the Montfort Consecration

The longest section in TD on perfect Consecration is dedicated to the motives that recommend this devotion (135–212). About one third of this chapter is given to an allegorical explanation of the biblical narrative of Jacob (183–212), which serves as a summary of the entire section, whose evident emphasis is on the necessary Marian dimension of the Consecration to Christ. Already in TD 91 the saint has told us that the total Consecration to Jesus through Mary is *"the most perfect, the most agreeable to her, the most glorious to God, and the most sanctifying for ourselves."* And again, in TD 118, Montfort cannot resist anticipating his specific section on the motives of perfect Consecration, *"demanding from the soul, as it does, more sacrifices for God, ridding the soul more of itself and of its self-love, keeping it more faithfully in grace and grace more faithfully in it, uniting it more perfectly and more easily to Jesus Christ and finally being more glorious to God, more sanctifying to the soul and more useful to our neighbor than any other of the devotions to her."* In LEW 219, several motives are given: *"I have never found a practice of devotion to our Lady more solid than this one since it takes its inspiration from the example of Jesus Christ . . . [and none] more feared by the enemies of our salvation."* In SM 34 the missionary speaks of the *"excellence of this practice"* and then devotes several paragraphs (35–42) explaining reasons for this excellence, all of which are found under the title *"Motives"* in TD.

The primary reason for this lengthy treatment of the motives of perfect Consecration is that Montfort employs the term in a broad sense, encompassing not only foundational, universally accepted principles (e.g., Christian perfection consists in union with Jesus Christ) that motivate the will to embrace this devotion but also—and primarily—an explanation of the amazing fruits and results of this Consecration spirituality, which as **goal** move the will to the living of this perfect renewal of the vows of our Baptism. There is, then, an evident overlapping with the following sections on the effects of the perfect Consecration (TD 213–225) and its interior practices (TD 257–265).

1. Perseverance

There is no clear order in the arrangement of the motives of the perfect Consecration, as there is for the section on its effects. Yet the saint, both in SM and in TD, states, *"Were there but this one motive to incite in me a desire for this devotion, namely, that it is a sure means of keeping me in the grace of God and even of increasing that grace in me, my heart ought to burn with longing for it"* (SM 40; TD 173). The practical missionary realizes that the gift of perseverance, especially final perseverance, is a strong incentive to live the perfect Consecration (TD 87–89).

It is not that perseverance, which demands a special help of God,[35] can be strictly merited (cf. LEW 188). The difficulty is not that God does not will our perseverance, for such would go against the universal salvific will of God (1 Tim 2:4). Rather, in the unfathomable mystery of man's freedom and God's absolute primacy, the gift is not necessarily actualized. Without claiming that a person living the perfect Consecration is certain of final perseverance,[36] Montfort stresses that *"she [Mary] does obtain for those who attach themselves to her the graces of fidelity to God and perseverance . . . with an effectual and efficacious love [she] hinders them, through a great abundance of graces, from drawing back in the pursuit of virtue, from falling in the road and from losing the grace of her Son"* (TD 175).[37]

The key to Montfort's thought on how the Consecration brings about perseverance in grace is his expression *"losing oneself in Mary"* (TD 179), the *"faithful Virgin who by her fidelity to*

God repairs the losses which the faithless Eve has caused by her infidelity" (TD 175). Montfort speaks of Consecration to Our Lady as *"entrusting all that we possess to the Blessed Virgin . . . taking her as the universal depository of all our goods of nature and of grace"* (TD 173). In this mystical union with Mary, the saint himself has experienced Mary's maternal influence, an influence which is in keeping with her personality: the faithful Virgin who hears the word of God and lives it. It is this effective influence of the faithful Mary - which affects us so deeply because of our Consecration - that Montfort describes as *"entrusting our graces and virtues"* to her and thereby persevering in grace. Here again, Montfort emphasizes his firm belief in the Communion of Saints, in the interrelatedness and interdependence of all. By our lovingly accepting, through the Consecration, this powerful maternal relationship of Mary, thereby *"losing ourselves in Mary,"* her influence is intensified. We become more and more like her, the first Christian, the model disciple, the faithful Virgin, the Church consecrated to its Savior. In the language of the preacher-mystic, Montfort can, therefore, speak of those consecrated to her as receiving *"an augmentation of purity and consequently of merit and of satisfactory and impetratory value"* (TD 172), since we become one moral person with the Mother of Grace, Mary.

2. Interior liberty

"Losing ourselves in Mary" through this perfect renewal of Baptism not only is a means of perseverance but gives us a joyful interior liberty, the freedom of the children of God (Rom 8:21). Having so willingly and lovingly accepted to be embraced by the tenderness of God - in imitation and under the influence of Mary - the consecrated person is freed from all servile fear, from crippling scrupulosity, and trusts joyfully in the love of God (TD 215; cf. H 45:31; 104:9; TD 107, 170, 215, 264; SM 41).

3. Totally devoted to the service of God

Montfort can, therefore, declare that those *"consecrated to Jesus Christ by the hands of Mary,"* having explicitly and lovingly given all *"to Jesus and Mary without reserve,"* are *"devoted to his service entirely and without reserve, to the utmost extent possible"* (TD 135). Like Mary, those consecrated to the Lord through this perfect renewal of Baptism are free, loving *"slaves of love"* of Jesus Christ. It is the Spirit, the Spouse of Mary, Who therefore works through them in every facet of life for the good of the Body of Christ, especially of the poor.

4. Living for God Alone

While perseverance may be the motive that most moves Montfort's hearers to embrace the total Consecration, there is little doubt that ontologically the most important motive - and effect - of the total Consecration is that it is an excellent means of procuring the greater glory of God Alone (TD 151, 222–225). This overarching principle of Montfort's spirituality is the keystone of his teaching on total Consecration, the ultimate goal of all he preaches and writes. Everything is done for the glory of the good God Who so loves us. *"Is it not a simple matter of justice and of gratitude that we should give Him all that we can give Him? He has been the first to be liberal towards us; let us at least be the second"* (TD 138).

The greater glory of God is assured, because the Consecration is done through Mary, by *"entrusting ourselves to her"* (TD 179). For *"Mary is altogether relative to God; and indeed, I might well call her the relation to God. She only exists with reference to God. She is the echo of God that says nothing, repeats nothing but God. If you say 'Mary,' she says 'God.'. . . When we praise her, love her, honor her or give anything to her, it is God who is praised, God who is loved, God who is glorified and it is to God that we give, through Mary and in Mary"* (TD 255).

5. Imitation of the Trinity

In explaining the theology undergirding all true devotions to Mary, Montfort outlines the relationship of each of the Divine Persons to Mary (TD 14–39). He now draws the logical conclusion: if the Father, Son, and Holy Spirit give us the example of freely willed dependence on Mary, *"can we without extreme blindness dispense with Mary, can we fail to consecrate ourselves to her and depend on her for the purpose of going to God and sacrificing ourselves to God?"* (TD 140; SM 35). The Consecration Montfort advocates is in perfect conformity to the plan of salvation history as God has freely willed it. He has not come to us *"at the age of a perfect man, independent of others, but like a poor little child, dependent on the care and support of his Holy Mother"* (TD 139). *"Is it not most just, then, that we imitate this conduct of God?"* (TD 140). To do otherwise is to set up our own order of salvation, to lack humility. It is for Montfort incomprehensible to approach Eternal Wisdom in any other way than in the manner Wisdom comes to us: through Mary (SM 36). Severely wounded as we are through the sin of Adam, it is only fitting that we go to Jesus our God, our Friend and Brother (SM 36; TD 138) with and through this *"little girl"* (TD 18), who represents the human family in perfect conformity to Jesus.

6. Union with Our Lord

When discussing motives which should lead us to live the Consecration, Montfort accentuates the Christocentricity of his teaching by explaining that Mary is an *"easy, short, perfect and secure way of attaining union with our Lord"* (TD 152; LEW 212).

a. An easy way. This spirituality of the perfect renewal of our baptismal promises is first of all **easy**, for it is the way which Jesus Christ trod in coming to us - through Mary. Although it conforms to salvation history so beautifully, Montfort insists that it is not the only spirituality: *"It is true that we can attain divine union by other roads"* (TD 152). In fact, only a few saints have actually *"walked this sweet path to go to Jesus"* through a singular grace of the Holy Spirit. Moreover, even of those granted the grace of embracing this way, few live it fully and thereby experience the swiftness and facility with which it brings us to our goal, the Eternal and Incarnate Wisdom (TD 152). The Consecration is a *"secret,"* a "*singular grace*" of the Most High, a *"mystery."* It leads us—without any obstacle—to Jesus. Montfort's *"to Jesus through Mary"* does not mean that Our Lady is a hurdle that must be overcome in order to arrive at Jesus. Rather, she only enhances this direct union with Christ Jesus, she only intensifies our union with Christ in his Consecration of the universe to the Father. For how can she who is totally relative to God, so transformed by grace into the likeness of her Son, be anything but a positive catalyst in achieving the purpose for which we have been created, union with Christ Jesus?

Mindful of his insistence upon the Cross as an intrinsic element of his spirituality (LEW 167–180; FC), Montfort tells us that "easy" actually means being gifted with crosses, for those who are consecrated *"receive from her the greatest graces and favors of heaven, which are crosses"* (TD 154). Yet the missionary, speaking undoubtedly from his own experience, tells us that devotion to Mary, *" is the very sweetness of crosses"* (TD 154). We must not be confused by the baroque language of this saint of the early eighteenth century; the spirituality he advocates, the Consecration to Mary he recommends is not sentimental, spineless, weak. Rather, it is founded on the strength of "obedience unto death, even death upon a cross" (cf. Phil 2:8). Montfort's "easy" way is the courageous living out of the radical demands of the Gospel. He cannot tolerate halfway measures. He is a man of the absolute.

b. A short way. The perfect Consecration is also a **short** way to Jesus Christ. Again, the fundamental reason for this statement is the example of the Savior. Since he consecrates himself to the Father at the Incarnation in and through Mary, the shortest way for us to enter the Lord's Consecration is also in and through Mary.

c. A perfect way. Total Consecration is a perfect path uniting ourselves to Jesus Christ. Perfect for two reasons. Again, it is the path that Jesus took: through Mary; we can do no better. Second, Mary is the most perfect of pure creatures, a *"way without stain or spot, without original or actual sin, without shadow or darkness"* (TD 158), leading directly to Jesus Christ. In majestic terms, reminiscent of Pope Leo's famous Christmas sermon,[38] Montfort eloquently writes, *"The Incomprehensible has allowed Himself to be comprehended and perfectly contained by the little Mary without losing anything of His immensity. . . . The Inaccessible has drawn near to us and has united Himself closely, perfectly and even personally to our humanity by Mary without losing anything of His majesty. . . . He Who is has willed to come to that which is not and to make that which is not become He who is and He has done this perfectly in giving Himself and subjecting Himself entirely to the young Virgin Mary without ceasing to be in time He Who is from all eternity"* (TD 157). After each of these statements, Montfort draws the evident conclusion: it is by Mary that we too must draw near to God, that we *"who are nothing can become like unto God by grace and glory by giving ourselves to her so perfectly and entirely as to be nothing in ourselves but everything in her, without fear of delusion"* (TD 157). The example of the Eternal

Wisdom Who emptied Himself and is thereby exalted (Ph 2:6–11) teaches us that our divinization (**theosis**) can only take place through a total stripping of self (**kenosis**), which is realized in the living of the perfect Consecration. Montfort insists upon the nothingness of man in and of himself, of his corruption through original sin; far more does the saint stress the glory and exaltation of man divinized by grace, which is forever the fruit of Mary's womb.

d. A secure way. In. explaining that the Consecration is a **secure** way, Saint Louis de Montfort first underlines its conformity with the teachings of the Church, basing himself primarily on the findings of Henri Boudon. Montfort's conclusion is emphatic: *"Indeed, we cannot see how this devotion could be condemned without overturning the foundations of Christianity. It is clear then that this devotion is not new and that if it is not common, that is because it is too precious to be relished and practiced by everyone"* (TD 163; cf. SM 42; LEW 219; TD 118).

He appears to contradict himself, however, when he states that the perfect Consecration is a *"secret which the Most High has taught me, which I have not been able to find in any book old or new"* (SM 1). Montfort is speaking autobiographically here. Although he has read almost all the books that treat of devotion to Mary (TD 118; LEW 219), although he declares that Holy Slavery of Love is so ancient that we cannot even discern its beginnings (TD 159; SM 42), nonetheless his personal mystical experience of living the Consecration has disclosed a depth and clarity that he has not found in his studies.[39] From the Scriptures as explained, lived, prayed by the Church down through the ages, Montfort has formed a new school of spirituality based on living the perfect renewal of the baptismal vows. It is not a fad, it is not a dainty devotionette; it is a challenging way of life, demanding the practical acceptance of the very root of salvation history: the Incarnation, with all its integral components and consequences.

The second reason why the perfect Consecration is secure is that it is the very characteristic - the very personality of Mary - to lead us directly, quickly, intensely to union with Christ Jesus, in whom and through whom we are consecrated to the Father. To insinuate that she could lead us astray, that she would not enhance a direct union with the Lord, is to fashion a mockery, a caricature of Our Lady that has no resemblance whatsoever to the authentic Mary of the Scriptures as prayed by the Body of Christ, the Church.

7. A sharing of life with Mary

"Mary gives her whole self, and gives it in a wondrous manner, to him who gives all to her" (TD 144; cf. SM 55). The Consecration effects an intense mutual sharing of life with Our Lady. As we entrust to her maternal care our baptismal life in Christ, so she shares with us her incomprehensible union with Jesus. This truth - which is, again, an example of Montfort's mystical union with Christ in Mary - is founded on the incontrovertible principle that everything and everyone in the cosmos is interrelated, interdependent. Mary, the person

most intensely one with the climactic point of the universe, Christ Jesus, influences this world in an immeasurable degree.

Through the Consecration, we lovingly and formally accept this great gift, thereby making Mary's influence ever more effective: *"She causes him to be engulfed in the abyss of her graces, she adorns him with her merits, she supports him with her power, she illuminates him with her light, she inflames him with her love, she communicates to him her virtues"* (TD 144). The missionary again expresses this truth of Mary's maternal influence, so accentuated by living the Consecration, through analogies easily understood by his audience. *"That good mother purifies all our good works, embellishes them and makes them acceptable to her Son"* (TD 146). Her effective influence strengthens us to do everything for God Alone, thereby enabling us to surrender to the purifying Spirit who overturns the many idols of overconcern, overanxiety, attachments which hinder our union with Christ. She embellishes our good works: a graphic description of the truth that through the Consecration we form one moral person with Mary, model and representative of the human race in its total surrender to the Redeemer Jesus.

8. Charity towards our neighbor

Through the Consecration we formally and lovingly acknowledge that God may do with us and with our actions whatsoever he wants for His glory, for the advancement of the kingdom (SM 39; H 40:32; TD 171–172). The covenant renewal ratifies that in Christ Jesus, the Heart of the universe, we are linked to all creation, especially to our brothers and sisters in the Lord. The Consecration is, then, an expression of love for God and neighbor, the fulfillment of the Law. As Montfort explains in TD 214, this love for God and neighbor will express itself in action, enabling us to *"carry out great things for God and for the salvation of souls."*

9. Summary

The lengthy allegorization of the Genesis story of Rebecca who secures Isaac's blessing for Jacob instead of Esau (TD 183–212; cf. Gen 27) recapitulates all the motives drawing us to live the perfect Consecration. *"Of all the truths which I have been explaining with regard to our Blessed Lady and her children and servants, the Holy Spirit gives us an admirable figure in the Scriptures . . . the story of Jacob who received the blessing of his father Isaac through the skill and pains of his mother Rebecca"* (TD 183; SM 38). Here again, Montfort describes the **effect** of living the Consecration - from the point of view of its Marian dimension - as a convincing reason to embrace his teaching.

Montfort probably recounted this story many times in order to explain the meaning - and therefore the motives - of total Consecration. The narrative is clearly divided into two main sections: the summary of the biblical account (TD 184) and Montfort's allegorical interpretation, which comprises almost the entire section (TD 185–212), with the greatest emphasis on the role of Mary to those consecrated to her (201–212).

As a summary statement, the allegory reveals characteristics of total

Consecration that the saint believes central. In his comparison between Esau and Jacob, the source of the differences is that Esau—figure of the reprobate (those who freely refuse to accept God's empowering call)—is little prone to an **interior** life. Jacob on the other hand,—figure of the elect (those who lovingly accept God's invitation to share in divine life)—knows that *"while sometimes his brothers and sisters are working outwardly with much energy, success and skill, in the praise and with the approbation of the world, they on the contrary know by the light of the Holy Spirit that there is far more glory, more good and more joy in remaining hidden in retreat with Jesus Christ, their model, in an entire and perfect subjection to their Mother"* (TD 196). The missionary is not denying the importance of the active apostolate; his own life would belie such an opinion. But he firmly believes that the perfect Consecration involves primarily who we are, not what we do. The montfort version of the Holy Slavery of Love is essentially interior, a new way of life in Jesus, Wisdom, son of Mary, not primarily a new way of doing things. Montfort's intense missionary activity flows from his sincere, interior mystical union with Jesus in Mary. *"What is essential in this devotion consists in the interior"* (TD 226, 119).

Those who live the Consecration to Jesus in Mary live in that mystical *"interior."* There they will in a unique manner experience the maternal care of the new Rebecca, Mary (TD 201-212). They will taste her tender love, thus inspiring them to strip themselves of everything not the Lord's and to be clothed with the double garments of the life of Jesus and Mary. This empowers them to work great things for the glory of God and the salvation of their brothers and sisters. All is for God's greater glory, making us worthy to appear before our heavenly Father to receive His blessing even though we have no natural right to have it (TD 201-207). Moreover, as new Jacobs, those living the Consecration will know her overflowing bounty, for she will nourish them with Jesus, the fruit of life, whom she brings into the world (TD 208). She becomes in a special way their guardian and protector, directing them infallibly according to the will of her Divine Son (TD 209). She so protects them that they having nothing to fear (TD 210). Finally, she intercedes for them so that they may be united to Jesus in a most intimate union and so that she may keep them unshaken in that unity, preserving them in Jesus and Jesus in them (TD 211-212).

This allegorization of the biblical story of Jacob is for Montfort a summary motive for entering into the life of total Consecration. It not only powerfully expresses many effects of Consecration spirituality but also stresses the Trinitarian/Christocentric nature of Saint Louis' doctrine. Those who lose themselves in her will be formed in a short period of time into living copies of Jesus Christ in the power of the Spirit, for the glory of God Alone.

VI. The Effects of the Montfort Consecration

In the original manuscript of TD, one of the few titles Saint Louis de Montfort himself wrote is the marvelous effects which this devotion produces in a soul faithful to it (TD 213). Unlike his study of the motives to live the Consecration, the section on the effects (TD 213-225; SM 53-57) follows a progressive line of thought. It is, in a sense, a bare-bones outline of the spiritual life, a sketch of the montfort "path" of total Consecration. The seven steps the saint describes are—like the Teresian castles—not independent but dynamically interrelated and interlinked. Moreover, they cannot be isolated from the *motives* of perfect Con-secration and its *practices.* They are also highly autobiographical. They describe what Montfort himself experienced as he deepened his living of the perfect Consecration to Jesus through the hands of Mary. The saint stresses that these effects only follow upon the faithful living of the Consecration, which he will summarily describe in the next section.

1. The stripping of self

As the self-emptying of the Eternal Wisdom in the Incarnation is the first step to his exaltation (Phil 2:6-11), so too the first effect of the perfect Consecration is the total stripping of the self of all that is not the Lord's in order to participate in divine life (2 Pet 1:4). It is only in emptiness that we are filled. This *terminus a quo* of the journey into Infinite Light is stressed in vivid terms by the parish missionary: *"By the light of the Holy Spirit . . . you will understand your own evil, corruption and incapacity for anything good."* And again, Montfort makes use of expressions describing **man of himself** in terms quite repulsive to modern ears: *"You will think of yourself as a snail that spoils everything with its slime, or as a toad that poisons everything with its venom or as a spiteful serpent seeking only to deceive"* (cf. TD 79, 83, 173, 177, 178; FC 47; LEW 51). This knowledge (demanding a spirit of true humility, says Montfort) is not just for the sake of understanding our nothingness. The living of the Consecration *"demands from the soul more sacrifices for God, rids the soul more of itself and of its self-love"* (TD 118). The desire for Eternal Wisdom is the willingness to take all the means necessary to divest ourselves of everything not in conformity with our Baptism, even dying to ourselves. It is not just a velleity (LEW 181-183; FC 15, 61).

2. Participation in Mary's faith

The supernatural gift of faith gives us insight into the true meaning of life - Jesus - and, informed by love, strengthens us to follow the Light of Life wheresoever he may lead (H 6; FC 50, 53). Through this faculty, the person living the Consecration is enabled to belong to the Lord on every level of personality. On this easy path to Jesus, Mary's effective maternal intercession wins for us that gift of faith which she possessed to such an incredible degree (FC 57; TD 214). Montfort terms this a participation in Mary's active and courageous faith, which, with the permission of the Most High, she has retained even in the light of glory as gift for her servants.

It is this talent which impels us to leave the *terminus a quo* and *"gives us entrance into the mysteries of Jesus . . . into the Heart of God."* Saint Louis underlines not only the courage of this Marian faith but also its apostolic dimension: *"You will use [this faith] to enlighten those who are in darkness of the shadow of death, to inflame those who are lukewarm and who have need of the heated gold of charity, to give life to those who are dead in sin, to touch and overthrow . . . the hearts of marble and the cedars of Lebanon."*

3. Deliverance from scruples, cares, and fears

Nothing so freezes a soul in its journey to the inner castle, so Montfort constantly affirms, as servile fear of God, which manifests itself in the disorder of scrupulosity. There are times when, on this pilgrimage to contemplative union, the majesty and awesomeness of God become staggering, so overwhelming, in fact, that a person may fear to continue and may even turn back. The Divine becomes more "awe-ful" as we approach Him through faith. Reverence for God is definitely needed (Sir 1:14); rejected, however, must be all servile fear and scrupulosity. For God is not only majestic; God is also our "tenderness" (H 52,11: "*God Alone is my tenderness*").

True freedom is, then, an effect of living montfort Holy Slavery of Jesus in Mary: the freedom to run into the arms of Infinite Love, to let ourselves be embraced, to accept forgiveness, to accept acceptance. The effect of total Consecration is not hesitation, scrupulosity, timidity, or quietism but, rather, an active and responsible pure love that casts out fear so that our faith may be lived to the hilt. The barricades of fear, of an exaggerated sense of unworthiness, of refusing to accept that God yearns for us more than we can ever yearn for Him—all are destroyed through the living of the Consecration.

4. Great confidence in God and in Mary

Not only does living the Consecration remove the roadblocks; it also gives us the confidence to move on, to walk ever more deeply into the whiteness of Eternal light. Stifling fear is transformed into courageous assurance. We say to Our Lady, "*Totus Tuus*,"[40] so that we may confidently proclaim with her to the Lord, "I am your servant."

This confidence is not a "self-affirmation." Rather, it is the affirmation of our nothingness become our strength, for we are so identified with Mary, the Mother of Grace Itself, that we are filled with the Spirit. This joyful confidence becomes a hallmark of those who live the Consecration. An insurmountable conviction of God's infinite love for us becomes a dynamo of strength propelling us on our journey to the Lord. Trust in Providence becomes characteristic of those who live the Consecration.

5. Communication of the spirit of Mary

SM 55 declares that this effect is *"the most important of them all,"* for it means that *"it is no longer the soul that lives but Mary living in it, since Mary's life becomes its life."* For the missionary, this effect is the most important, because it is the turning point in our journey to Eternal Wisdom. To establish *"Mary's life in the soul"* is an absolutely essential element in his spirituality of total Consecration.

His reason for such a bold statement finds its source in his Marian theology. Introducing his explanation of total Consecration, St. Louis de Montfort writes, *"Of all God's creatures, Mary is the most conformed to Jesus . . . the more one is consecrated to Mary, the more one is consecrated to Jesus. That is why the perfect consecration to Jesus is but a perfect and complete consecration of oneself to the Blessed Virgin"* (TD 120).

We must, then, *"breathe Mary as the body breathes air."*[41] Every breath is one with her spirit: a total "yes" of radical discipleship to the Lord. As Eternal Wisdom in and through Mary consecrates Himself to the Father, so it is by becoming living copies of Mary that we become one with Christ's complete surrender to God. In his hymn *"The Devout Slave of Jesus in Mary,"* Montfort puts into verse this effect of living the Consecration: *"Here is what one cannot believe: / I bear her in my very heart / . . . Although in faith's obscurity"* (H 77:15). Montfort is certain that if this effect is achieved, the following two effects—the final goal of *"perfect consecration to Jesus Christ"*—will definitely be experienced.

6. Transformation by Mary into the likeness of Christ

The sixth (TD 218–221; SM 56) and seventh (TD 222–225) effects describe the term of our journey into the life of God. We are in the montfort inner castles. Father de Montfort has told us that the more we breathe Mary, the more we become one with the image of the Father, Christ Jesus. Grace is a sharing in the divine life in and through Jesus. The goal of Consecration's journey is to be one with Christ Jesus, a mystical and true union with Incarnate Love. This goal is realized *"without much toil,"* for we have lost ourselves into the "Holy of Holies," Mary, where we find the Incarnate Presence (**shekinah**), Jesus. But we more than find, more than gaze upon; we actually experience, taste, participate in the Consecrated One, Incarnate Infinite Love, Jesus (H 54, 55, 56).

Mary is the mold of God (SM 16; TD 219–221). Through this comparison, attributed to St. Augustine,[42] Montfort tries to summarize all the effects he has thus far described. To be poured into Mary we must be melted, i.e., we must surrender all. *"Losing ourselves in the fair interior of Mary,"* we take on her active, responsible and courageous discipleship and thereby become *"faithful portraits of Jesus Christ."* Montfort's analogy of Mary as the mold of God underlines one of his basic theological principles, which must constantly be kept in mind: the beginning is the never-to-be-repealed law governing all that flows from it. The Incarnation, the beginning and compendium of all mysteries, is the divinely willed pattern of all sanctification. God comes to us in the Infinite Beloved through and in the faith-filled womb of Mary. Therefore it is in and through this sacred mold of God that we become one with Jesus, or, as Montfort forcefully expresses our divinization by grace, *"at a light expense and in a short time he [the consecrated person] will become god because he has been cast into the same mold which has formed a God"* (TD 219).

7. The greater glory of God

The innermost castle of the montfort Consecration is entitled: all for the glory of God Alone. To lose ourselves in Mary, i.e., to be completely and lovingly open to her effective maternal influence, to become living copies of this woman who is *"relative only to God because she exists uniquely in reference to him . . . an echo of God, speaking and repeating only God."* (TD 225) is, then, to be one with the personal glory of God, Jesus, and through him, in the power of the Spirit, to become one with the Father, God Alone.

Through the living of the perfect Consecration, we are being dynamically drawn into the inaccessible Light of the Trinity Itself. Here we have for Montfort the ultimate goal, the greatest motive, the supreme effect of Consecration: a true mystical union with God Alone, Who is the keystone of the entire montfort structure.

VII. Particular Practices of the Montfort Consecration

Not only is this title from Saint Louis' own hand, so too are its divisions into *"exterior practices"* and *"special interior practices for those who wish to become perfect."* He has already spoken of practices of true devotions to Mary (TD 115–117). Here, however, he is describing the specific practices of the perfect Consecration itself. The practices presuppose a knowledge of the nature of the perfect renewal of the baptismal promises. These practices, specifically the interior ones, are the pulsing heart of total Consecration. Without them, it is nothing more than a cadaver.

1. Exterior practices

After a brief introduction (TD 226) explaining the necessity of *"certain external observances,"* Saint Louis Marie summarizes his thought: *"I will allude only briefly to some exterior practices which I call exterior not because we do not perform them interiorly but because they have something outward about them to distinguish them from those that are purely inward."* The TD manuscript itself (TD 226–256) numbers each of the seven external practices; SM 60–64 abbreviates them into four. Montfort stresses their importance: *"We must not omit [them] through negligence or contempt"* (TD 257); *"We must neither omit nor neglect [them]"* (SM 60).

a. Preparation for the Act of Consecration. The montfort Spiritual Exercises consist of three weeks, preceded, when the Consecration is first made, by twelve days of *"ridding themselves of the spirit of the world."* The missionary considers the topic of these twelve days to be of importance, for his seventh external practice is but a repetition of the identical subject (TD 256). The theme of each of the weeks dovetails with Montfort's consistent doctrine that in order to be united to Jesus Christ the Eternal and Incarnate Wisdom, we must first know ourselves,[43] our own failings, weaknesses, and need for God [first week] (TD 228). Then, having immersed ourselves in Mary, the mold of God [second week], we must pray for a deeper knowledge - a true experience - of Jesus, in whom and through whom in the power of the Spirit we are one with God Alone [third week] (TD 227–223). The Exercises echo the motives (TD 135–212) and effects (TD 213–225) of total Consecration.

It is evident that the life of total Consecration is not to be undertaken lightly. The Exercises are to be repeated yearly, the Consecration to be renewed if possible every day.

b. Prayers of those who live the Consecration. Of all the prayers listed among the exterior practices of true devotions to Our Lady in general (TD 116), Saint Louis Marie chooses three as of special importance for those who live the life of perfect Consecration. He numbers them the second, fifth, and sixth external practices: the Little Crown of the Blessed Virgin, the Hail Mary and the Rosary, and, finally, the Magnificat.[44] The fact that these three are singled out so emphatically - especially the Rosary - indicates the special role they must play in montfort spirituality.[45]

If the prayers Saint Louis Marie advises are Marian, it is because - as he consistently declares - the turning point of our journey into Christ God is our immersion into the spirit of Mary, which is the spirit of Jesus. In fact, it could be said that for Montfort, there is no such thing as a purely Marian prayer. Jesus and Mary are inseparable, she is the indissoluble spouse of the Holy Spirit, forever the daughter of the Father. Authentic Marian prayers are for this preacher Christocentric/Trinitarian.

c. The external sign of Consecration: little chains. While insisting that the wearing of little chains is not essential for those who have willingly recognized their loving slavery to Jesus in Mary, nonetheless the missionary strongly encourages that this practice not be omitted. Since Montfort is basically recommending some clear external symbol of our baptismal Consecration through Mary, the substitutes mentioned when describing external practices of devotion to Mary in general would also apply here: "*5. Carrying such signs of devotion to her as the rosary, the scapular, or a little chain*" (TD 116). The ordinary chain that many wear with a cross or religious medal, a ring clearly symbolizing discipleship, the religious habit, all are legitimate substitutes for the little chain. Each culture will have its own manner of externally manifesting one's Consecration, whether it be through a chain of some sort or through some other sign. Whatever it may be, the purpose of this recommendation should be fulfilled: *"First, to remind the Christian of the vows and promises of his baptism, of the perfect renewal he has made of them by this devotion and of the strict obligation under which he is to be faithful to them . . . second, to show that we are not ashamed of the slavery and servitude of Jesus Christ and that we renounce the slavery of the world, of sin and of the devil . . . third, to protect ourselves against the chains of sin and of the devil for we must of necessity choose to wear either the chains of sin and damnation or the chains of love and salvation"* (TD 238, 239). The chain or its substitute is, then, in Montfort's eyes a constant effective sign both to us and to others, and also to the devil, of our Consecration to Jesus in Mary.

d. A special devotion to the Incarnation. Since the theological foundation of Montfort's spirituality of total Consecration is built upon the mystery of the Incarnation, he recommends as an external practice a *"singular devotion to the great mystery of the Incarnation of the Word"* (TD 243). The fundamental reason for the veneration of this mystery is that it fulfills *"the two principal goals of slavery of Jesus Christ in Mary. . . first, to honor and imitate the ineffable dependence which God the Son was pleased to have on Mary for His Father's glory and our salvation . . . second, to thank God for the incomparable graces He has given Mary and particularly for having chosen her to be His most holy Mother"* (TD 243).

2. Interior practices

Again we have one of the relatively rare authentic titles in the TD manuscript: *"Special interior practices for those who wish to become perfect."* It is not that this interior life is to be considered optional for those who have made the Act of Consecration. As the formula itself demonstrates, anyone entering the life of total Consecration firmly desires *"to carry my cross after Him all the days of my life and to be more faithful to Him than I have ever been before. . . . [Immaculate Mary] grant the desire which I have to obtain Divine Wisdom. . . . O faithful Virgin, make me in all things so perfect a disciple, imitator and slave of the Incarnate Wisdom Jesus Christ, thy Son."* (LEW 224, 225, 226). Montfort himself is straightforward on this point: *"This devotion consists in surrendering oneself in the manner of a slave to Mary, and to Jesus through her and then performing all our actions with Mary, in Mary, through Mary and for Mary"* (SM 28). And again: *"I have already said that this devotion consists in performing all our actions with Mary, through Mary and for Mary"* (SM 43). Still more explicitly in TD 119: *"This devotion consists essentially in a state of soul."* The interior practices are, therefore, the very heart of the Consecration life flowing from the Act of Consecration.

These interior practices *"may be expressed in four words: to do all our actions by Mary, with Mary, in Mary and for Mary so that we may do them all the more perfectly by Jesus, with Jesus, in Jesus and for Jesus"* (TD 257). They are explicitly treated in both TD (257–265) and SM (43–52), although the order of the formulas and also their content are not precisely the same in SM and TD; it is the spirit of the Consecration life that Montfort is attempting to formulate.

a. By Mary. *"We must obey her in all things and in all things conduct ourselves by her spirit which is the Holy Spirit of God"* (TD 258). The missionary has already explained that to *"lose oneself in Mary"* is to become one with the spirit of Jesus and through Jesus to be one with the Holy Spirit for the glory of the Father (TD 179). And that spirit of Mary which must overrule our rebellious spirit is described by Montfort in emphatic terms: "*a spirit meek and strong, zealous and prudent, humble and courageous, pure and fruitful*" in the living of the Gospel (TD 258).

By Mary therefore demands that we first of all empty ourselves of our own spirit before doing anything - celebrating the Liturgy, teaching or attending a class, beginning household work or the daily chores - and then *"deliver ourselves to the spirit of Mary to be moved and influenced by it in the manner she chooses"* (TD 259). Although this is included in the daily renewal of the Consecration, the saint recommends that we formally *"renounce"* our spirit and release our selves into the spirit of Mary often during the day (TD 165, 259) *"in an instant, by one glance of the mind, by one little movement of the will, or even verbally"* (TD 259).[46] Montfort aims at creating a life of intense, peaceful union with Mary, through whom Divine Wisdom comes to us and through whom we enter into Divine Wisdom. *"We place ourselves as instruments in the hands of Mary that she may act in us and do with us and for us whatever she pleases for the greater glory of her Son and through her Son for the glory of the Father"* (SM 46).[47]

b. With Mary. This interior practice especially demands an authentic knowledge of the true Mary as depicted in the Scriptures in the light of their clarification by the Body of Christ. *"We must take our Lady as the perfect model of all that we do"* (SM 45). The practical missionary therefore calls upon us to *"examine and meditate on the great virtues which she practiced during her life: her lively faith . . . her profound humility . . . her divine purity . . . and so on with all her other virtues"* (TD 260). We copy Mary, for she is *"an accomplished model of every virtue and perfection which the Holy Spirit has formed in a pure creature for us to imitate according to our little measure"* (TD 260).

Stressing the contemporary ascending Christology, some declare that Jesus, and not Mary, is the human who is the paradigm of every virtue. Such an opinion, however, may easily bracket the truth that Jesus is our **God** in a fully human way. He is the Eternal Wisdom Incarnate. As Christ God, he is not - to use the scholastic term that Montfort often repeats - a *"pure creature."* All our perfection consists in being conformed to the Holy One of Israel, the Consecrated One, Jesus the Lord. No one is such an *"accomplished model"* of conformity to Jesus as Mary.

c. In Mary. This aspect of consecrated life is the culmination of the interior practices, the fruit of fidelity to living by and with Mary. It is life in the innermost montfort castle. It is **in** Mary that Incarnate Grace came to be through the gift of the Trinity and Mary's faith-filled consent. It is **in** Mary that we are intensely united with Wisdom and, through Wisdom, in the power of the Spirit, made one with God Alone. Although the theology undergirding this practice can scarcely be disputed, the precise meaning of *in Mary* is difficult to comprehend. And understandably so. It is the highest expression of the Consecration life. Its description by Montfort is in unfathomable, contemplative terms, vainly attempting to clarify in human language what he himself knows through experience. TD 261–263 are TD's most mystical sections. He himself writes that *"it is only the Holy Spirit who can make us know the hidden truth"* of the meaning "in Mary."

After describing Our Lady through the primary image of "the Paradise of God" where, therefore, the Trinity reposes, the contemplative missionary concludes, *"How difficult it is for sinners like ourselves to have the permission . . . to enter into a place so holy which is guarded by the Holy Spirit"* (TD 263). *"To enter into," "to lose ourselves in"* speak of an intense union of love between the soul and Mary, between her personality of total **fiat** to God and our weak surrender to Infinite

Love, between the woman fully consecrated in the Consecrated One, Jesus, and our fearful living of our baptismal Consecration. Montfort is attempting to describe a habitual state so penetrated with the spirit of Mary that we become one moral person with her. In her, at last, we have become one in the Consecration of this universe, the Eternal and Incarnate Wisdom. In this holy place, we will have nothing to fear and *"shall fall into no considerable fault"* (TD 264). It is in this *mold*, this *womb* - all images of the effective influence of Mary - that *"the soul shall be formed in Jesus Christ and Jesus Christ in it"* for the glory of God Alone.

Few there are, says the missionary, who will understand the depths of this mystery. Fewer still those who will enter upon this way. And rare, he says, are the souls who will persevere in the life of Holy Slavery and experience this mysterious but real oneness with Mary and thereby live to the full their baptismal Consecration in Christ Jesus (TD 119, 152; SM 70).[48]

d. For Mary. Living in Mary, it is understandable that we do everything for Mary so that our life can be lived more intensely for Jesus and, through him in the power of the Spirit, for God Alone. Mary is the *"proximate end, the mysterious milieu"* (TD 265) in whom everything we do is more perfectly turned only to the Lord. Montfort envisages this practice for Mary as including a truly apostolic life: *"We must undertake great things for this august Queen, we must stand up for her glory when it is attacked . . . we must speak and cry out against those who abuse her devotion to outrage her Son"* (TD 265).

VIII. Conclusions

1. The relevance of Montfort's doctrine

Montfort's teaching on the covenant renewal is of greater relevance today than it was in his time. He lived and preached in an age that, in spite of its excesses under the reign of Louis XIV, was still clearly Christian. Today the secularized West is in a post-Christian era. It is not only the lack of authentic church affiliation that characterizes our times but the demise of the significance of Gospel values in solving the personal and social problems of the day. Today man is Pelagian simply because the contemporary citizen of the Western world does not feel bound by the radical demands of the Gospel. No one denies the need of a renewal of the Church. And that is the ultimate purpose of Saint Louis de Montfort's perfect Consecration: *"to renew the face of the earth and reform the Church"* (PM 17; TD 56–59). He draws a blueprint for the formation of *"a great squadron of brave and valiant soldiers of Jesus and Mary, men and women, to combat the world, the devil and corrupted nature in those more than ever perilous times which are about to come"* (TD 114). The saint's teaching calls for and implements a solid renewal of our baptismal Consecration with all its practical consequences in order to bring about the needed reform and renewal. Small wonder that it has been so constantly extolled by the magisterium of the Church, especially in recent times.

2. The constant need of inculturation

Saint Louis de Montfort is, of course, a man of his times. His expressions, his stresses are all geared to the circumstances in which he lived and proclaimed the Word of God. In many contemporary cultures, verbal fidelity to the missionary's explanation of Holy Slavery could lead to a betrayal of his authentic thought. There is a constant need of "translating" the solid truth he teaches into the language and thought patterns of diverse cultures and, at the same time, of always being in harmony with the teachings of the Church. Montfort's writings on perfect Consecration are not only a gift to the Church but also a challenge: to adapt them faithfully to the mindset and the needs of constantly changing times.

There is also a need to explain the montfort covenant renewal within the context of the full teaching of Saint Louis de Montfort. At times, this demands a fleshing out of the core truth found in the saint's writings. For example, the interior practices of perfect Consecration should be brought to their completion by a more detailed explanation of "by, with, in, for" Jesus, which the saint declares to be - but never fully explicates - the fruit of "by, with, in, for" Mary. The same has to be done with Montfort's Spiritual Exercises, and with his description of our journey into the Heart of God, etc.

3. The necessity of the perfect devotion

Saint Louis Marie insisted upon the necessity of devotion to Mary in general (TD 39–42), especially for *"those called to any special perfection"* (TD 43–46) and, in a uniquely special way, for those *"apostles of the latter times"* (TD 47–59). In no way, however,does he speak about the necessity of adopting his spirituality of perfect Consecration. There are other ways of attaining a mystical union with Christ besides that outlined by Saint Louis de Montfort. In fact, he explicitly states that although it is an *"easy way,"* few saints have *"entered upon this way"* (TD 152). Nonetheless, *"we must draw all the world, if we can, to her service and to this true and solid devotion"* (TD 265). We should understand this to mean that people are to be attracted to it by its intrinsic appeal and never by any triumphalistic pressure. The fundamental simplicity of Montfort's teaching on perfect Consecration, its evangelical underpinnings, enable it to be adapted to, if not enhance, other schools of spirituality.

4. The Marian emphasis

The perfect Consecration Montfort proposes is **one.** It has, however, a variety of dimensions: Christocentric, baptismal, Marian, etc. Especially in TD and SM, Saint Louis Marie stresses and develops extensively the Marian aspect of the baptismal renewal, and this for especially three reasons. First, Our Lady's role is clearly an essential element in the present order of Redemption, Consecration. It is intrinsic to the very foundation of salvation history, the Incarnation. Mary must, therefore, play a predominant role in authentic Consecration theology and spirituality. Montfort has also personally experienced the efficacy of contemplative Marian spirituality in bringing about a new depth of union with the Lord. Second, the authentic Marian dimension is also, Montfort believes, the most unknown, the most misunderstood, and therefore the most neglected dimension of our life in Christ Jesus. It is a *"secret of the Most High"* (SM 1) that he is inspired to explain. Finally, as seen above, the montfort Consecration spirituality reaches its turning point in *"losing oneself in Mary,"* for it is in her and through her that our Consecration came to be. Mary is, then, the privileged entry into a constantly deeper baptismal life in Christ Jesus.

5. Entrustment or Consecration?

Pope John Paul II often uses the term "entrustment to Our Lady" rather than "Consecration to Our Lady," although he at times intermingles both expressions. Some prefer the term "entrustment" to Mary, "entrustment" to Jesus, because of its more mystical connotations of total trust and loving surrender.[49]

There is, however, another angle to consider concerning the use of one or both terms. Consecration taken in its strict sense is an act of adoration (*latria*), as its scriptural roots demonstrate; in this sense, it cannot be used with Mary as its object. In the broad sense, it is an act of veneration (*dulia*), denoting a petition for protection and intercession on our way to the All-Holy and can be used, e.g., in relation to any of the saints and most especially to the Queen of All Saints, Mary, where Consecration becomes an act of *hyperdulia*. It is in this sense that Montfort speaks of *"consecration to Mary"* among the practices of devotion to Mary in general (TD 116). The magisterium's more than occasional usage of "entrustment" over "Consecration" to Mary reminds the Church that Consecration strictly so called is nothing less than an act of worship of God. In other words, its "strict" meaning is coming to the fore.

P. Gaffney

Notes: (1) When speaking of the perfect Consecration as a "devotion," Saint Louis intends to convey the concept of an act of the will giving oneself completely to God; this interior spirit is made manifest in service to God and neighbor; cf. St. Thomas, *Summa Theologica* II-II, q. 82, aa. 1–2. (2) Montfort uses the analogy of *"the tree of life"* not only for the perfect Consecration but also for Mary (LEW 204; SM 67, 78; TD 44, 164, 218), the Cross (SM 22). (3) In introducing someone to the montfort Consecration, it may be better pastorally to begin with a study of LEW, which gives an overview of Montfort's spirituality. Emphasis must be given to the saint's understanding of the Incarnation and his strong Trinitarian/Christocentric stance. Only then should TD be studied, for it is a clarification of the fourth means of sanctity outlined in LEW. Finally, the summary of perfect Consecration in SM should be examined. And all, of course, must be read within the entire literary and historical context of the saint and within the present teachings of the Church, especially in Christology and Mariology. (4) Cf. P. Suarez, *La consécration totale à Jesus par Marie* (*The total consecration to Jesus through Mary*) in DMar (part 2, May 1986), 1–47; O. Procksch, *hagios*, in TDNT 1:88–112. (5) Cf. DV 7–10. (6) K. V. Truhlar, *Holiness*, in *SMun*, 637. (7) The Deuteronomic editing of the books of the OT interprets all the setbacks and evils inflicted on Israel as the result of unfaithfulness to its Consecration (cf. Judg 2; 2 Kings 17). (8) Jesus, the personal externalization within the human family of the All Holy God, is the summit of creation. In him creation is released from bondage (Rom 8:19–22) and is God's holy place. Yet there is a certain "becoming" in Incarnate Wisdom; cf. P. Gaffney, *Inexhaustible Presence: The Mystery of Jesus*, Dimension, Denville,

N.J. 1986, 150–151. Jesus becomes "fully" the Holy One when he conquers sin and death in his death and resurrection. Jesus can therefore say, "Father, glorify thou me in thy own presence with the glory which I had with thee before the world was made" (Jn 17:5); and even more to the point: "The Holy Spirit had not as yet been given because Jesus was not yet glorified" (Jn 7:39). Here "glory" can be considered the equivalent of "sanctified," "made holy," "consecrated." It is in his death/resurrection that Jesus, even in his transformed humanity, is transferred into the realm of YHWH. It is in the paschal mystery that he is fully the "Holy One of Israel." And from our point of view, this fullness (*pleroma*, cf. Eph 1:10) will only be accomplished when Christ is "all in all" (Eph 1:23) at the parousia, when all creation will, each in its own way, reach its destiny and be in the Holy Spirit one with the Holy One, Jesus, to the glory of God Alone. (9) The necessity of Baptism is to be understood according to the teachings of the Church. When baptism of water is impossible, baptism of desire suffices, even implicit desire. The *Letter of the Holy Office to Archbishop Cushing of Boston* (1952) is the clearest statement of the nature of the necessity of the Church and Baptism for salvation, stressing that belonging to the Church must be actual (*in re*) or, if that be not possible, through desire (*in voto*), even implicit desire (*etiam implicito*). The full text and commentary can be found in *American Ecclesiastical Review* 127 (1952), 307–311, 450–561; cf. *Sal Terrae* 41 (1953), 22–26; DS 3869–3472; LG 16; CCC 1260 clarifies: "Every man who is ignorant of the Gospel of Christ and of his Church, but seeks the truth and does the will of God in accordance with his understanding of it, can be saved. It may be supposed that such persons would have *desired Baptism explicitly* if they had known its necessity." (10) Pope John Paul II, *Angelus Message*, December 4, 1983, in *L'Osservatore Romano,* English Edition (12 December 1983), 2. (11) Inclusion: "At the end of a passage the Gospel will often mention a detail or make an allusion that recalls something recorded in the opening of the passage. This feature, well attested in other biblical books, for example, the Wisdom of Solomon, can serve as a means of packaging a unit or a subunit by tying together the beginning and the end." R.E. Brown, *The Gospel according to John, i–ixx,* Doubleday, Garden City 1966, cxxxv. (12) Besides the scriptural references, cf. article "Slavery." (13) Cf. J. Dayet, *Notre Consécration: Le mot de la tradition,* in *La Revue des Prêtres de Marie Reine des Coeurs,* (*Our Consecration: The Word of Tradition* in *The Review of the Priests of Mary Queen of All Hearts*) 26 (1939), 33–44, 65–72, 97–105, 162–169, 193–198, 226–230, 257–263, 290–296, 321–329; 27 (1940), 2–6, 33–38, 65–71; 28 (1941), 2–8, 33–37, 65–72, 97–104, 132–142; 29 (1942), 40–52; S. De Fiores, *Consacrazione,* in *Nuovo dizionario di mariologia,* (*Consecration,* in *The New Dictionary of Mariology*) ed. S. De Fiores and S. Meo, Edizioni Paoline, Rome, 398–40; P. Gaffney, *The Holy Slavery of Love,* in *Mariology,* ed. J.Carol, Bruce, Milwaukee 1961, 3:143–149. (14) The first confraternity of Holy Slavery appears to have originated in Spain on the August 2, 1595, under the leadership of Sister Agnes of St.Paul of the Franciscan Conceptionists at the convent of Saint Ursula in Alcala de Henares. With the exuberant dynamism so characteristic of Marian devotion at this time, Holy Slavery confraternities spread throughout Europe. Excesses crept into some of these and other pious associations that, at least from our vantage point, appear to have lacked a Christocentricity and at times to have been more involved in external manifestations - especially the wearing of chains - than in forming a true interior spirit. Rome condemned the abuses. For an example of a formula of Consecration at this time, see DM 3 (May-June 1956), 34–35. (15) Dayet, *Notre Consécration,* in *La Revue des Prêtres de Marie* 28 (1941), 37. (16) *Oeuvres Complètes,* 2 vols., 1644, reprint, Maison de l'Institution de l'Oratoire, Montsoult 1960. (17) *Oeuvres Complètes,* ed. Migne, 1856. Much of Olier's spirituality came to Montfort through one of his spiritual directors at St. Sulpice, M.Bayün. (18) *Oeuvres Complètes,* 3 vols., ed. Migne, 1856. For the Consecration, Montfort is especially influenced by Boudon's *Dieu Seul ou le saint esclavage de l'admirable mère de Dieu,* vol 2. (19) *La veritable dévotion envers la Sainte Vierge établie et défendue,* (*The true devotion towards The Blessed Virgin Established and Defrended*), De Launay, Paris 1708. (20) *La triple couronne de la Bienheureuse Vierge Mère de Dieu tissue de ses principales Grandeurs d'Excellence, de Pouvoir et de Bonté, et enrichie de diverses inventions pour l'aimer, l'honorer et la servir,* (*The Triple Crown of the Blessed Virgin Mary Mother of God woven from her Principal Grandeurs of Excellence, Power and Goodness, and Enriched with Multiple New Ways of Loving, Honoring and Serving Her*) Cramoisy, Paris 1639. (21) Cf. A. Molien, *Bérulle,* in DSAM 1547. (22) E.A. Walsh, *Spirituality, French School of,* in *The New Catholic Encyclopedia,* McGraw-Hill, New York 1967, 13:605. (23) Dayet, *Notre Consécration,* in *La Revue des Prêtres de Marie,* 29 (1942), 40; P.Poupon, *Le poème de la parfaite consécration à Marie,* (*The Poem of the Perfect Consecration to Mary*), Bellecour, Lyons 1947, 337–338, 361–364. (24) Cf. ibid.,

362. (25) Ibid., 369. (26) Montfort refers to a "Consecration" that is to be found at the end of TD. The present condition of the manuscript contains no such formula. The Act of Consecration is found only in the LEW manuscript. Although it surely expresses the saint's thought and is in full harmony with his teaching on total Consecration, it bears striking resemblance to other formulas of Consecration found in the first exercise of F. Nepveu, *Exercices intérieurs pour honorer les mystères de N.S. Jésus-Christ,* (*Interior Exercises to Honor the Mysteries of Our Lord Jesus Christ*) 2 vols., Paris 1791. (27) For a discussion of Baptism in the French School of spirituality especially as described by Jean Eudes, cf. Poupon, *Le poème*, 253–296. (28) "Every Christian Consecration begins with the Consecration of Mary on the day of the Incarnation and in a definitive way with the Consecration of the holy humanity of Jesus the Head in the womb of the most holy Mary; the Consecration flows from this as a stream from its source, as the fruit from the tree" Ibid., 251 (29) V. Devy, *La royauté universelle de Marie,* in *La Nouvelle Revue Mariale,* (*The Universal Royalty of Mary* in *The New Marian Review*) 8 (1956), 23: "Saint Louis Marie de Montfort has not based his slavery of love formally on the queenship but on the spiritual maternity of the Blessed Virgin." J. Ghidotti, in his resume of the conferences of the Montfort Missionaries at the 1950 Rome Mariological Congress in *Marianum,* 13 (1951), 96: "Without doubt—and this is the affirmation of all—the spiritual maternity in montfort Mariology holds the principal place."; cf. P. Gaffney, *The Spiritual Maternity according to Saint Louis Mary de Montfort,* Montfort Publications, Bay Shore 1976. (30) Baptism is the moment when Mary begins to exercise her office of Mother of the Church. That is why "we cannot speak of the Church if Mary is not present" (MC 28). (31) J. Grandet, 101. (32) Ibid., 395. (33) ìbid., 405–412, vividly describes the processions that Saint Louis de Montfort held during a parish mission; cf. P. Suarez, *La consécration totale*, 38–40. (34) This apostolic dimension of the Consecration is clearly evident in many societies that have taken Saint Louis as their spiritual guide and live the montfort Consecration. The Legion of Mary is one of the primary examples. (35) Cf. DS 832. Final perseverance is called a "great gift" by the Council of Trent, DS 826. (36) Cf. DS 805. (37) Montfort blames the inherent weakness flowing from original sin as the reason for the lack of perseverance (TD 177). He speaks of the cedars of Lebanon falling and eagles *"which had raised themselves to the sun, become birds of night"* (SM 40). It is the living of our total Consecration to Jesus through Mary that strengthens us to persevere in grace, even to the end. (38) Cf. *Sermo in Nativitate Domini,* PL 54:193–199. (39) Cf. Pius XII, *Discours aux pèlerins pour la canonisation, 21 juillet 1947,* (*Address to the Pilgrims for the Canonization, July 21 1947*) AAS 39 (1947), 412: "Incomparably more than his own human activity, he called upon divine help, which he attracted by his life of prayer." (40) This beginning of a short formula of Consecration (cf. TD 233, 216; MP 5) has become famous because adopted by Pope John Paul II as his episcopal motto. (41) For a magnificent insight into this montfort expression, read the poem of the famous English Jesuit author Gerard Manley Hopkins *Mary Compared to the Air We Breathe,* in J.Pick, *A Hopkins Reader,* Image Books, Garden City, N.Y. 1966, 70–73. For a comparison between Montfort and Hopkins' poem, cf. Sr. M. Teresa Wolking, *Mary Compared to the Air We Breathe,* in *QOAH* (Jan.-Feb. 1953), 13 (42) Cf. S. Augustinus (apocryphal), *Sermo 208,* in PL 39:2131; Tronson has the same expression, which he attributes to Saint Augustine, *Oeuvres Complètes de Monsieur Tronson,* ed. Migne, 2:577. (43) TD 228 terms this *"the foundation of all other graces."* (44) SM 64, presuming the Rosary, speaks of the Little Crown and the Magnificat. (45) At first sight it may appear astonishing that this contemplative missionary does not list any prayer to Jesus, and even more surprising that he does not include the celebration of the Sacraments among the prayers of those who have made the Consecration. A survey of the saint's writings makes it evident that he recommends the Sacraments and even frequent Communion to all Christians. Saint Louis sees no need of repeating what he considers so fundamental to a basic Christian life. (46) This interior practice - as all the others - presupposes the firm theological foundations of the perfect Consecration as described above and in the article "Mary." (47) Much of what Montfort includes under "by Mary" in TD is found under the rubric "with Mary" in SM. (48) For a profound yet concise explanation of the interior practice "in Mary," see the article written by a Ukranian rite monk, Joseph, *Finding Jesus in the Heart of Mary,* in *QOAH* (January-February 1991), 26 (49) Cf. De Fiores, *Consacrazione* in *Nuovo Dizionario di mariologia,* 412–413. De Fiores himself opts for what he calls the usage of Pope John Paul II "which pays attention to the substance (of the term) and attempts to express it in a variety of ways without being bound to one only expression." Ibid., 413; P. Gaffney, *Entrustment or Consecration?* in *QOAH* (May-June 1988), 8–9.

COVENANT

SUMMARY

I. USE OF THE WORD "COVENANT" IN THE WORKS OF MONTFORT:
   1. The Hymns;
   2. The Ark of the Covenant;
   3. Covenant and the Cross;
   4. Covenant and Wisdom;
   5. The covenant with God.

II. THEOLOGICAL CONTENT:
   1. Covenant contract and Baptism;
   2. The covenant as spousal relationship;
   3. The Ark of the Covenant;
   4. Characteristics of covenant.

III. RELEVANCE OF MONTFORT'S TEACHING ON COVENANT:
   1. Personal and communitarian aspects of the covenant;
   2. The renewal of baptismal vows;
   3. Covenant renewal as a new start;
   4. Montfort's clarity.

A study of covenant reveals that basic to all its types, historical, social or other, are three components: giving, receiving, and giving back. In this article we shall restrict ourselves to biblical covenants with their three components, as reflected in the writings of Saint Louis de Montfort.

I. USE OF THE WORD "COVENANT" AS EMPLOYED BY MONTFORT

The word itself occurs only twelve times in Montfort's works.

1. The Hymns

Almost half of the occurrences appear in H, and they would not seem at first sight to have much relevance to the biblical theme. Hymn 12:5 informs us that the covenant between the Virgin most pure and Jesus her Spouse is eternal. In his hymn "The Tenderness of Charity towards one's Neighbor," Montfort sings that one's neighbor *"is the son of the eternal Father, / and through a divine covenant, / is universal heir to the kingdom"* (H 14:17). In H 36:90 the victim of human respect is upbraided: *"Renegade Christian, have your way; / you are engaged in a horrible covenant; / you are but a monster in disguise."* In H 87:9, in honor of Jesus living in Mary, Montfort writes: *"They seem to be intertwined. / How beautiful this covenant!"* H 17:5, again referring to Mary, says, *"She is my Ark of the Covenant / wherein I find holiness."* The biblical theme of covenant is not the object of these citations—at least at first sight—except for the reference to the Ark of the Covenant.

2. The Ark of the Covenant

The Ark of the Covenant recurs twice more in Montfort's writings, in a rather surprising way. In FC, those who refuse to suffer patiently and are not resigned to carrying their Cross are told: *"You will be like the two oxen that drew the Ark of the Covenant, lowing as they went"* (cf. 1 Kings 12 according to the Vulgate, 1 Sam 6:12 in Hebrew and our modern translations). The same is applied to the worldly-wise in LEW 178: *"I seem to see in you the oxen that drew the Ark of the Covenant against their will, bellowing as they went, unaware that what they were drawing contained the most precious treasure upon earth."* The "precious treasure" refers to the fact that the Ark contained the Scrolls of the Covenant, the Decalogue (cf. Ex 25:16) and perhaps more (cf. Heb 9:4). These last two references from Montfort bring together the covenant and the Cross.

3. Covenant and the Cross

The relationship of covenant and the Cross appears again in LEW 172 - *"The bond between them is indissoluble, their covenant is eternal. Never the Cross without Jesus, or Jesus without the Cross"* - and indirectly in LEW 195, where we find the third means for acquiring Divine Wisdom, a universal mortification. Wisdom looks for people worthy of him: *"He has to search because there are so few and he can scarcely find any sufficiently unworldly or sufficiently interior and mortified to be worthy of him, of his treasures, and of his covenant."*

4. Covenant and Wisdom

The relationship of covenant and Wisdom is developed in LEW 20-28, where we find the whole of chapter 24 of Ecclesiasticus (Sirach), a text that is essential for an understanding of Wisdom, the basic element of Montfort's spirituality. Montfort introduces this passage: *"This is how divine Wisdom herself describes, in the twenty-fourth chapter of Ecclesiasticus, the effects of her activity in souls. I shall not mingle my poor words with hers for fear of diminishing their clarity and sublime meaning."* These words of Divine Wisdom end with verse 31 (according to the Latin Vulgate; verse 22 in our modern translations, which use the short Greek text), but Montfort adds verse 32 (=23), which is not part of the original but an explanation by Sirach, who says: "All this is the book of life, the covenant of the Most High, and the knowledge of the truth." "All this" means the description of Wisdom given in the preceding numbers. That Montfort should have retained this last verse and not the following ones, which are likewise Sirach's, is significant. For him, Wisdom is an expression of the Covenant of the Most High.

5. The covenant with God

The last of the twelve references to covenant pertain to the covenant contract. The first is in TD 126, where, having written that *"this devotion could rightly be called a perfect renewal of the vows and promises of holy baptism,"* he continues: *"Scarcely anyone makes a personal ratification of the covenant contract made with God through his sponsors"* (TD 127). The proof that he took this seriously is the fact that "he had a formula of this renewal of baptismal promises printed, which he got those who were literate to sign."[1] Several copies have been discovered entitled *"Covenant Contract with God"* (cf. CG), recalling the title of the book written by St. John Eudes, *Contrat de l'homme avec*

Dieu par le saint baptême (Contract of Man with God through Holy Baptism) (1654). We have, however, no proof that this book was available in the library at Saint-Sulpice or, if it was, that Montfort had read it.

II. Theological Content

1. Covenant contract and Baptism

The formula "covenant contract," unlike "Ark of the Covenant," does not so much evoke a concrete image of the covenant as its essential meaning. The legal aspect of pacts practiced by their neighbors, from whom the Israelites had copied them, helped the people of God to grasp the meaning of the bond that was offered to them by God: *"I will be your God, and you shall be my people, if . . ."* (cf. Dt 26,17-19, etc.).

The reference to Baptism reflects the New Covenant itself. What is significant here is that Montfort envisages not simply a renewal but a *ratification* (a legal term found also in TD 127 and in the formula of Consecration in LEW 225) of the covenant made by the godparents, all drawn up in legal terms: *"made before the Church, in such-and-such a place, on such-and-such a date"* (cf. CG 1-3).

It is interesting to note how well the covenant contract drawn up by Montfort is in keeping with his times. The formula of renewal and the practices that follow (the truths of the Gospel, the place of Mary, confession—reminding us that the missionary never ceases to call to conversion) all bear an authentic montfort stamp, expressed in the thought patterns and practices of his time and place. The saint's practices of popular devotion in connection with the covenant renewal (cf. H 139, *"Rule of a man converted during a parish mission,"* with its 71 verses) have been criticized. He is, however, simply reflecting the cultural context of the age. It is well to remember that the Gospel itself is a *living* word rooted in different cultures: the Gospel of Matthew employs a different approach to that of Luke or John. This is also a caution to those who would advocate using only the precise practices and formulas employed by Montfort in preaching the covenant renewal.

2. The Covenant as spousal relationship

Legal images of covenant are not the only ones to be found in Montfort's reading of the Bible. *The prophetic image of marriage*, itself essential to the covenant, is to be found throughout. For Montfort, it derives from the Wisdom aspect, which enlightens and facilitates the Law. The frequency of terms of love underlines their importance in Saint Louis de Montfort's spirituality in general and, in particular, his understanding of the covenant with God: *"spouse," "lover," "union," "womb," "breast," "desire," "seeking," "acquiring," "good," "happiness," "pleasing," "beauty," "grace," "sweetness,"* etc. It is impossible to recall all the terms used by Montfort in the rich vocabulary of love that he employs,[2] of realistic images. "Covenant" itself is, for Saint Louis Marie, a term of love. It is, therefore, in this context that we must understand the term "covenant" in H 12 on *"The beauty of virginity"* proclaims: *"He embraces me; I embrace him. / He is mine and I am his,"* and *"Since God lays himself down / upon my breast among the lilies,"* etc. Montfort clearly alludes to the Song of Songs, which speaks, in the words of popular love songs, precisely of the covenant between God and His people. The mystics, including Father de Montfort, use this vivid love language from the Song of Songs - hardly ever found in today's liturgy - when illustrating the covenantal relationship of God with man. To avoid confusing people, Montfort felt obliged to write verse 29, lest he be accused of denouncing marriage: *"It is not that I pretend / That marriage is evil."* He wrote this song to the tune of "I Have Nothing More to Claim": a clear indication that for him marriage can lay claim to no superiority over the divine union of the pure virgin.

Keeping in mind Montfort's insistence on the covenant with God—and therefore with our neighbor—as a love relationship, we can understand the expressions of tenderness in Hymn 14, expressions which are not easily assimilated when love of one's neighbor is seen as a duty, and often a painful one at that. The word "charity" itself no longer conveys its original meaning: love. The NT alone retains this interpretation, and Montfort follows suit. Even Hymn 36, *"The snare of human respect,"* can only be explained in the light of the alternative offered in Hymn 38, *"Please God, or please the world."* In his attempt to persuade us to prefer virtue, *"this infinite treasure,"* and *"this precious pearl which is never tarnished when one is in love with it"* (H 67), Montfort again uses the language of love. We should not be surprised, then, at the *"delights," "ravishments,"* and *"ardors"* of Hymns 77 and 87. All these terms take on an obvious meaning only when seen in light of the image of spousal relationship. All St. Louis Marie's references to the *"anger of God," "the snares of the world,"* to universal mortification, etc., can only be understood correctly if they are placed in the framework of the saint's insistence that God is love and earnestly calls us to an ever deeper union with Him; we are to respond joyfully and completely, no matter the cost.

3. The Ark of the Covenant

The three references to the Ark of the Covenant mentioned above now take on an added importance. If, as appears to be the case, the covenant is a major theme for Montfort (not just the term, but the reality behind it), we can understand the importance he attaches to the Ark, which *"contained the most precious treasure upon earth"* (LEW 178). Here we have not just an accidental symbol, in relation to Mary and the Cross, but something essential. May we not, like S. Lyonnet,[3] see Mary as "the holy Ark or the dwelling-place of God where his Son, the 'Holy One', the 'Son of God,' comes to live"? Charles Perrot thinks that "such an exegesis is not without interest, even if it presupposes, for Luke as well as for his readers, an astonishing facility for seeing allusions in the scriptural texts. For that reason, we ought not to rely too much upon it."[4] Montfort is not trying to settle exegetical debates. Rather, the missionary is insisting that the importance of Mary and the Cross in the economy of salvation derives from their function in the New and Eternal Covenant. For him, the mysteries of the Incarnation and the Redemption are the distinguishing marks of the NT.

4. Characteristics of covenant

In addition to the few explicit references to the covenant, Montfort's writings speak of *certain characteristics that are precisely those of the covenant.*

a. ***A new Law.*** The covenant carries with it *a new Law* (the covenant clauses with their different systems of law). This Law arises from an initiative that is always divine, and it derives from a promise (the theme of inheritance). Montfort's thought is heavily influenced by these ideas. This is exceptionally clear in PM: *"It is your work, great God. Make your divine purpose a reality."* But it is also the very basis of devotion to Mary: *"God has decided to begin and accomplish his greatest works through the Blessed Virgin"* (TD 15).

b. God's call and human cooperation. Another aspect of the biblical covenant is also present in LEW. While the covenant remains always the result of God's initiative, God commits Himself in it to a form of cooperation with the human being "that limits both the power of man and of God" (as André Neher says in his definition of the covenant). LEW is full of awareness of this weakness of God for the human being, *"whom he [Widsom] cannot help loving"* (LEW 45). At the same time, Montfort proposes maxims, rules, and practices (cf. the covenant's system of laws), which make the human being capable of remaining faithful to the covenant that God continues to offer. Finally, Montfort pays attention to the promises linked to the New Law. We have only to think of *"the marvelous effects of Wisdom in the souls of those who possess him"* (LEW 90ff.) or of *"the wonderful effects of this devotion in a soul which is faithful to it"* (TD 213ff.).

There are evident parallels between Montfort's understanding of covenant and current theology. In emphasizing covenant fundamentally as a Sapiential spousal relationship (demanding absolute fidelity) linked to Baptism—and its constant ratifications—with its Marian and apostolic dimensions, the roving missionary was quite innovative. His thought was mirrored in his contemporaries only in parts of stories about the saints, in moral commentaries on the Bible, and in a few spiritual authors.

III. Relevance of Montfort's Teaching on Covenant

In a world where the specific culture and context of Saint Louis Marie is no longer found anywhere, the thought of the missionary must be faithfully transposed and adapted to modern times and its own variety of cultures. This holds true for the particular practices surrounding man's relationship to the covenant. The principles on which Montfort bases his covenant spirituality are as valid as the Scriptures that proclaim them; Montfort's particular practices and stresses on the Gospel message, however, are time- and culture-bound.

1. Personal and communitarian aspects of the covenant

There is no question of erasing the individual and personal dimension of the covenant, especially now when several forms of individualism are extolling a subjectivism that goes further than Renaissance humanism. Ways must be found to integrate this personal responsibility with the ecclesial dimension, not to mention the planetary or even cosmic dimension, of which our world is becoming more and more conscious; such considerations are—understandably enough—

not stressed in Montfort's writings. Nonetheless, in LEW we find some striking passages on the drifting of society that would apply to the contemporary generation.

2. The renewal of baptismal vows

The Easter Eucharist includes a liturgical celebration of the renewal of baptismal promises: a covenant renewal ceremony. Saint Louis de Montfort's teaching on the "perfect" covenant renewal—Consecration—may be helpful in preparing the people for such an important rite. Moreover, as the missionary concluded parish missions and retreats with an impressive covenant renewal, it may be helpful to include such a ceremony in similar circumstances today.

The full significance of the ceremony can be accentuated by sharing with the community the stresses Saint Louis de Montfort connects with the renewal of baptismal promises: spousal, Marian, total, Trinitarian/ Christocentric, apostolic.

3. Covenant renewal as a new start

Saint Louis de Montfort insists strongly on a renewed life following upon the covenant renewal ceremony. The examples he gives of sins to be avoided and of piety to be lived, although time- and culture-bound, have value in principle. His stress on sincerity, on the totality of our belonging to the Lord, on not following contemporary idols, on a life lived in Mary, on the Eucharist and the other Sacraments, on the definite need for a spiritual guide and the regular celebration of the Sacrament of Reconciliation, on effective fraternal love, especially for the poor - all these can easily be transposed into the present-day context. Montfort's Path of Perfection is an overall view of the road to God Alone, which the saint kindly but forcefully encourages to all who renew the baptismal covenant with the Lord.

4. Montfort's clarity

Saint Louis Marie can also be imitated for the clarity with which he explained the consequences of a solemn covenant ratification. He never hedged; he never taught what would be contrary to the mind of the Church; he never watered down, not when it came to the reality of the spousal relationship inherent in the covenant renewal, not when it came to the sins that must be avoided and the virtues to be practiced after the covenant is ratified. The covenant sponsal contract embraces, as the saint explains following the Word of God, the totality of who we are and what we have. Sin, therefore, is absolutely to be rejected by all, especially by those who live the covenant ratification. Montfort upholds both the horrendous objective reality of covenant sins and also the incomprehensible love of God for sinful man.

Jean Audusseau

Notes: (1) Grandet, 395. (2) We might even speak of an "erotic" vocabulary, if the term had not taken on, in our modern language, a connotation of license and immorality in the use of sex, rather than of simple desire and pleasure (which can, of course be quite legitimate, as the Bible attests). Like the Bible, and any number of spiritual writers, drawing metaphors from very deep human experiences, Montfort has no difficulty in using this type of language to express the reality and the richness of the love relationship that God wishes to have with us. (3) *Le Récit de l'Annonciation*, in *l'Ami du Clergé*, 1956, 33. (4) *Cahiers Évangile*, (Gospel Notebooks) 18 Novembre, 1976, 47; cf. Jean-Paul. Michaud in *Cahiers Evangile*, 7 septembre, 1991, 31-32, 34, 40, 44-45.

CREATION

I. THE ECOLOGICAL CANVAS

If we define ecology as the relationship of human beings with the totality of creation, we see that Louis Marie de Montfort had a profound personal reverence for the fullness of God's created nature—in all of its mineral, vegetative, animal, and human forms.

1. The influence of the environment

In the letters he wrote at the age of twenty-seven and twenty-eight, Louis Marie often uses the adverb "here."[1] In this way he underlines his relationship to his surroundings and the influence they had on his evolution and his decisions. He seeks harmony in this relationship. He wants to avoid any milieu where he cannot live in a symbiotic relationship: *"I have not the slightest inclination to stay in the St. Clément community"* (L 9); *"I have no inclination at all to lead an enclosed life"* (L 9). On the contrary, he is looking for relationships where he will feel at ease: *"When I am teaching catechism to the poor in town and country, I am in my element"* (L 9).

2. Environment and health

Being in harmony with his environment seems to have been of benefit to the health of de Montfort. Disharmony distresses him. During one of the most painful missions he ever preached, at La Chevrolière, in 1708, "the missionary was afflicted with a violent colic and a continual high fever." His illness ceased at the end of his final sermon.[2] This fact is open to different interpretations, certainly, but it is a fact that in one of his writings, Louis Marie sees a connection between his health and his faith, his activities and his relationships: God *"has enlightened me [in Poitiers] to a degree I have never experienced before. He has given me the gift of making myself clear, a facility for speaking without preparation, a good health and a great capacity for sympathizing with everyone"* (L 11).

3. The ascetical life and health

At the very beginning of his priestly life, he takes note of his health in his life of self-denial: *"I am sleeping on straw; I do not have any lunch and I do not eat much in the evening. I am keeping very well"* (L 10). These statements have to be read in the context of the times. Louis Marie says that he has one good meal per day, "dinner"—which corresponds to our lunch—which was taken at eleven or eleven-thirty in the morning. Not to eat much in the evening, according to the understanding of someone of that time, did not preclude the eating of a goodly piece of bread, the essential food of those days.[3]

Louis Marie makes a connection between the use of the discipline, a violent mortification, and medicine. The discipline consisted in giving oneself lashes with a small whip reserved for this purpose, on the back and the upper part of the chest. This exercise, of religious inspiration, is quite harsh, but was included in the repertoire of medical practices of those days, along with clysters and bleedings.[4] The purpose of the discipline was for Montfort *"a specific remedy for lukewarmness,"* that is, for taking things easy (H 161). He insists that its use be limited in duration.[5] He attributes a medical quality to it: *"The discipline / is medicine. / Let everyone whip himself on the back . . . / Sickness / is cured by this. / The whip drives out moodiness / and pain."* (H 161:1,6).

4. A visual approach to nature

Louis de Montfort had a visual appreciation of nature. His sense of beauty expressed itself in painting, "for which he had a taste and a special talent." His ability amazed one painter who demanded a fee from him for instruction in art. He was then still a schoolboy at the Jesuit College in Rennes and did not have the money to pay. He copied a miniature and sold it for a gold piece so as to gain access to the painter's classes.[6]

In later years his attitude towards art changed. The superior of the ecclesiastical community in which he was living in 1693-1694 recognized his talents for painting, sculpture, and architecture and tried to persuade him to develop these talents by means of some basic training. The student, however, rejected the arguments of the superior and refused to develop his talents.[7] In practicing his art, the artist fashions himself and builds himself up, creating a more refined and more demanding self, whereas one of the conditions for following Jesus Christ is self-renunciation (Mt 16:24). While it is true that painting, even more than the other arts, is an expression of the relationship between the artist and his own body, this reluctance on de Montfort's part is an expression of a personal kind of evangelical asceticism. He would take up sculpture again later on, with a certain crudity due to his lack of technique. For example, he was to carve a statue of the Virgin to place on top of his pilgrim's staff.

5. In contact with nature

Louis Marie did a great deal of walking—along the roads, in the fields, among the trees, through villages and towns, and especially on the pilgrimages he made, such as those to Rome and Mont Saint-Michel in 1706. If he followed the normal pace of pedestrians of his time, he would have walked eight to ten leagues a day (twenty to twenty-five miles), which would have taken him about eight hours; and this would be repeated the following day to keep up with his schedule in terms of time and distance.

A pilgrim without any assets, he mocks in one of his hymns those who are chained to one place by their possessions, which at the same time cause them great bother (H 144). He himself has nothing to worry him: no horse, no carriage, no servants. Yet he has all he wishes, like a king at his court. God, in his Providence, supplies all his daily needs. He finds this worthy of public proclamation, even accompanied by trumpet blast: *"When I go on a journey [a pilgrimage], / my staff in my hand, / barefoot and without any baggage, / but also without any cares, / I make a stately progress, / like a king with his court, / to the sound of the trumpet . . ."* (H 144:1).

Compared with the hardships of the journey, the end point of the pilgrimage is a place of plenty. In his hymn to Notre Dame des Dons (Our Lady of the Gifts), Louis Marie sings of the abundance of good things, the beauty of the place, the rustic life (H 151). He sounds a triumphant note at Pontchâteau in 1709: *"Oh, we will see great marvels in this place!"* (H 164:9).

For the pilgrimage to Notre Dame des Ombres (Our Lady of the Shadows) at La Chevrolière in 1708, his tone is prayerful and intimate: *"It is through Mary / that Heaven wishes to entice us . . . / In the silence, / the shadows and the darkness, / Mary has hidden her beauty. / Heaven's wish is only / to show it forth clearly"* (H 155:1,14).

6. Chosen places

Louis Marie chooses certain places where he loves to linger. He was nineteen when Jean-Baptiste Blain visited a secluded spot with him in his parents' garden. He loved to be there and spent his most pleasant hours in this place.[8] He has his favorite places: the priory of Saint-Lazare in 1708, close by the wind-battered rock of Heurtebise; the wild heath of La Madeleine, near Pontchâteau, where he sets about the construction of a monumental calvary in 1709; and, towards the end of his life, the beautiful Forest of Mervent, where he serves his God with cheerfulness.

We see his love for these places in his hymn "The Good Shepherdess": *"These rocks, these shelters, / These sheep and lambs, / These woods and verdant pastures / are new singers . . . / Here, in the silence, / all things speak in truth, / all preach innocence / and simplicity"* (H 99:4,5,25).

7. The hermit's life

In a hymn entitled "A Sinner Converted during the Mission" (H 142), Father de Montfort speaks of the aspirations of a man of the world, a man of rank, who possesses goods and relations but chooses the life of a hermit: *"The die is cast, / I am going away to seek / a wood or a hole in a rock . . . / Oh! what secret happiness, / Oh! what holy and sweet peace / my heart experiences in these forests . . . / Alone with you, my sweet Jesus, / I want nothing but you"* (H 142:17,19,20).

This dream life becomes a reality for de Montfort as he hides himself away on several occasions during 1715 as a temporary hermit in the Forest of Mervent.[9] The *"hole in a rock"* that he dreamed of for the converted sinner is to be found in a place known as the Fawns' Rock: *"It is a deep cave / towards the North, in a rock, / which served as a hiding place / for the fawn and the tired hind"* (H 157:4).

The hermit makes his way to this spot through woods, following the rocky ridges or the little river known as La Mère (The Mother): *"Three ways lead to this retreat: / the main carriage-way, / a path through the woods, / and one beside the hidden waters"* (H 157:2).

In the early days of the Church, the hermits of Arabia or the solitaries of Egypt withdrew to those places where the dryness taught them how to strip themselves and how to search for God alone. In the rain-soaked and fertile lands of Europe, with their abundant vegetation, the forest becomes the hermit's desert.[10] In both cases, it is a question of seeking poverty, in which one may learn to depend on God alone. The surroundings change. The teaching is different: *"Here you hear the eloquent silence / of the rocks and forests / teaching nothing but peace, / breathing only innocence"* (H 157:13).

Down through the ages, the forest-dwelling hermits have nourished themselves on images: the tree's solid trunk is the image of tested and persevering virtue . . . Louis Marie speaks in the same vein, the same Western tradition: *"The rocks speak of constancy, / the woods of fruitfulness, / the waters of purity, / and everything of love and obedience"* (H 157:16).

Louis de Montfort, a hermit in the Forest of Mervent, does more than pray, more than simply renew his strength for future missionary endeavors. He hides himself away like Mary to serve God alone (TD 2): *"Let us hide ourselves away."* He goes there to adore God in total service: *"Far from the world in this hermitage / let us hide ourselves away to serve God"* (H 157:1).

He appreciates the cave in the Fawns' Rock as an exceptional natural place where nature favors grace: *"Could you ever find a place / where grace is more favored?"* (H 157:1).

He gets about a lot in this forest. He stops a while to take in the view from the highest point of the "plateau" above the cave: *"Up on the heights, you can see a plain, / churches and chateaux, / meadows and streams, / which charm one's vision and soothe one's pain"* (H 157:6).

He wanders along the valley of the Mère and is captivated by the view and by the life of the river, *"Abounding in fish / which delight in every way"* (H 157:7).

Water springs from the hillsides, the level ground, and the foot of the trees, while other secret springs are hidden away in the bed of the river: *"In the neighborhood are three clear springs / where the water, without tarrying, / gushes forth from high and low, / eventually to water the plain"* (H 157:9).

Louis Marie listens to the forest: *"You can hear the sweet harmony / of birds and of echoes"* (H 157:12).

Near the running water he finds himself between the migratory birds that have been passing through this region regularly for centuries—wild geese, lapwings, ducks, and wood pigeons—and the impressive fauna, ranging from toads to mosquitos, at the water's edge: *"You can see passing above your head / the birds according to their seasons, / and beneath your feet the fish, / while at your side are a hundred kinds of animals"* (H 157:17).

In the wildness of nature and the solitary life, he finds once again the primitive purity of the time before sin entered in: *"In these deeps everything is growing and is abundant / without the need of the laborer's hand. / By the hand of the Lord / this virgin soil is fruitful"* (H 157:10).

He lives in the presence of God the Creator: *"Here you see this powerful hand / which shaped the universe, / shining out clearly in these desert places, / in innocent nature"* (H 157:18).[11]

II. Montfort's Teaching on Creation and Nature

The word "nature" can signify the physical and biological environment of men and women, the world that is animal, vegetable and mineral; but it can also signify the characteristics proper to the human species.

We need to keep several things in mind when we read the term "human nature" in the works of St Louis de Montfort: the term is influenced by the times in which he lived; he does not treat of it as a teaching theologian but as a missionary; above all, his approach to human nature is that of a Christian mystic. And so it will be helpful when speaking of "human nature" to take as a starting point his personal experience.

1. Spiritual experience and knowledge

The first known seminal event in the life of Louis de Montfort took place on the road from Rennes to Paris, when the young man, just before his twentieth birthday, made the decision to trust himself entirely to the

Providence of God and to own nothing as his own.[12] Pious and fervent as he had been up to this point, he now made his definitive choice for God. During the following years, he made a total consecration of himself to Jesus Christ through the hands of Mary, following the impulse of his Baptism. The first known expression of a mystical life dates from his twenty-eighth year, when he was able to internalize the presence of God as Providence and of the Blessed Virgin: *"I find so much wealth in Providence and so much strength in the Blessed Virgin that my poverty is amply enriched and my weakness strengthened"* (L 8). The following year, he received from God what he would later call the *"gift of Wisdom."*[13] Rather than defining it at that point, he describes it: light for the mind and a facility for expressing himself and for speaking off-the-cuff without preparation (L 11). Two years later, during a stay in Paris (1703-1704), he had a mystical experience that he described in a number of his hymns. These contain enough indications for us to see there the passive purifications and the mystical contemplation proper to the "dark night of the soul" described by Saint John of the Cross.[14]

At that time he was cut off from the Sulpicians in the Parisian seminary where he had discovered the solid foundations of his spiritual life. He was in touch with his old confessor from the college at Rennes, who was then in Paris at the Jesuit novitiate. He studied also a book by another Jesuit, Fr. Saint-Jure,[15] and at this time wrote at least a part of *The Love of Eternal Wisdom.*[16]

2. A passing glance at creation

In the biblical texts he gathered together at this time, Father de Montfort underscores the creation of the universe: *"Eternal Wisdom began to manifest herself outside the bosom of God the Father when, after a whole eternity, he made light. . . . Eternal Wisdom is the mother and maker of all things . . ., not . . . simply the maker of the universe but also its mother because the maker does not love and care for the work of his hands like a mother does for her child"* (LEW 31). The human being *"is his supreme masterpiece, the living image of his beauty and his perfection, the great vessel of his graces, the wonderful treasury of his wealth and in a unique way his representative on earth"* (LEW 35, 37, 64). The sinner recalls to his mind a happier situation: *"But, alas, the vessel of the Godhead was shattered into a thousand pieces. This beautiful star fell from the skies. This brilliant sun lost its light"* (LEW 39). All of this has the stamp of a way of thinking characteristic of the Jesuits.[18] No doubt Louis Marie had rediscovered it through his old confessor at the Jesuit college. It has not been his habitual way of thinking since his time at Saint-Sulpice. And this momentary reference becomes blurred, to all intents and purposes, from 1704 on as quickly as it appeared.

3. A pessimistic vision of nature and the world

There is very little esteem for human nature of itself in the dominant trends of the seventeenth century. The followers of Bérulle emphasized the thinking of their master on the nothingness and corruption of a human being in serious sin: "By the end of the century, a pessimistic view of humanity had become more or less the norm in French spirituality."[19] Louis Marie illustrates very well the prevailing mentality, which is also his own, when he uses an image drawn from the baker's art. Pride is to the human being what yeast is to the dough. Both puff up and completely corrupt the element in which they reside: *"The sin of Adam has almost entirely spoiled and soured us, filling us with pride and corrupting every one of us, just as leaven sours, swells and corrupts the dough in which it is placed"* (TD 79). This pessimism about human nature was heightened during the seventeenth century by a very harsh doctrine of grace and predestination. Drawn from a reinterpretation of Saint Augustine, it was formulated by Jansen and spread through the Jansenist movement. It fostered mistrust of human nature and a suspicious way of viewing the body and all that is fleshly. It is a doctrine that is difficult to express in "propositions" and is so subtle as to affect even those who professedly fight against it. Jansenism was commonly known as "the novelty." Louis Marie, who is an optimist about nature in his Christocentrism, prays that he may be shielded from Jansenism: *"Preserve me from a great precipice: / scrupulosity in justice, / the spirit of novelty, / whether in my faith, my zeal or my conduct"* (H 22:30).

4. A brighter view of the world by way of the Redemption

The order of nature is reestablished by Jesus Christ: "With the coming of the God-man, there appeared in the world a new order whose source is Christ and whose characteristics are examined by Bérulle. The Incarnation, then, completely changes the problem of the relationship between God and the human being. It becomes unthinkable, from this moment on, to seek God apart from the Incarnation, that is, apart from the humanity of Christ."[20] Louis Marie is following Bérulle when he writes: *"Jesus came into the world . . . he must reign in the world"* (TD 1).

Jesus Christ *"came into the world"* through Mary. He was born of a woman who possessed our *"human nature at its purest"* (TD 85), purely and simply. Our nature does not, as does that of Jesus Christ, possess the hypostatic union, divine and human natures in one. Mary is a new earth for God.

Louis de Montfort expresses a poetic and mystical vision of creation from the standpoint of the Blessed Virgin. Mary is the *"masterpiece"* of God the Creator, the privileged *"dwelling-place"* of his presence in the *"universe"* (TD 5). She is *"the vast and divine world of God"* (TD 6). She is the sea of grace: *"God the Father gathered all the waters together and called them the seas (maria). He gathered all his graces together and called them Mary (Maria)"* (TD 23). The new world begins with her. It is a world created, like the first creation, by the Word of God, and by the Ave spoken to Mary: *"The Ave ravishes Mary's heart / and obtains her consent"* (H 89:7).

And just as in the first moments of the world, the Spirit hovers over her, covering her with just such a shadow, and the Word of God renews the world by a single word, the Ave: *"The earth was barren, / but, once the Angel had uttered the Ave, / it bears fruit, / it becomes fertile"* (H 89:9).

5. Images drawn from nature and his mystical knowledge

Saint Louis writes that the Christian can discover within himself, through mystical knowledge, the discord between grace and its opposite, sin. This type of self-knowledge is the first *"marvelous"* effect of the mystical life:[21] *"By the light which the Holy Spirit will give you through Mary . . . you will perceive the evil inclinations of your fallen nature and how incapable you are of any good"* (TD 213). Such knowledge as this is difficult to express. Louis Marie has recourse to mystical language, which is symbolic, to describe the relationship to God. Sometimes he draws metaphors from the social relationship with a royal personage (H 103:7), sometimes from human love and its intensity (H 103:7). He also uses comparisons from animal nature. He conjures up, from the earth or the water, from valleys, rivers and ponds, and sunken lanes, images of animals that are repellant, dangerous, or disturbing: *"You will consider yourself as a snail that soils everything with its slime, as a toad that poisons everything with its venom, as a malevolent serpent seeking only to deceive"* (TD 213). "These metaphors are used because we can know spiritual things only as images of things we can sense and because it is often difficult to find appropriate terms to express them."[22]

Louis Marie also says that we know by mystical knowledge, *"by the light of the Holy Spirit"* (TD 79), the natural human being, the human being without grace: our extreme pride, useless attachments, self-complacency, and desire for self-satisfaction, for domination of others, and for taking things easy. Once again he uses metaphors drawn from nature, relating to animals and trees: *"By nature we are prouder than peacocks, we cling to the earth more than toads, we are more base than goats, more envious than serpents, greedier than pigs, fiercer than tigers, lazier than tortoises, weaker than reeds, and more changeable than weather-cocks"* (TD 79).

The mystic in the Forest of Mervent had received self-knowledge (TD 213) and the power of self-denial (TD 79) as mystical graces. At that moment he was freed to rediscover primitive nature untouched by sin. "From then on, he has a freedom of spirit that extends in a general way to all things."[23]

III. The Human Being and Nature Today

1. Use and abuse

At the beginning of the eighteenth century, one-seventh of the French mainland was covered in woodland, not including the royal forests, like that of Mervent.[24] In 1699, Colbert had tried to control the forest exploitation, which until then had been of an anarchic nature, by means of a royal ordinance. His aim was to ensure the supply of wood for construction of buildings and, especially, merchant ships and warships. Felling in the royal forests, minutely regulated, was subject to decrees and letters patent: the woods, seen as national wealth, were placed under the special care of the king. The Office of Waters and Forests supervised the application of the rules. Colbert's ordinance was the source of the problem which arose later for Louis de Montfort over his cave at Mervent.

Beginning at the end of the seventeenth century, after the war of the Augsburg League (1697), there was a shortage of wood for the navy and the artillery. The wars had exhausted the supply, and the supervision of forestry operations had become draconian. Louis Marie seems not to have concerned himself with these national wartime matters of public service to king and nation. But Charles Moriceau, the seigneur of Cheusse, who was in charge of the regulation of waters and forests for Fontenay, was reminded by a royal attorney of his jurisdiction and made a visit, by virtue of his official functions, to the cave of the Fawns' Rock "on October 28, 1715, about eight o'clock in the morning."[25] He noticed that Father de Montfort had begun building a wall in front of the entrance to the cave, which was exposed to the southwest, with the aim of sheltering himself from the north wind, which would bring a chill to the air in the following months, and that he had removed five or six chestnut stumps to make way for the wall. The stumps, looked upon as matrices that must not be allowed to lose their precious nutritive properties, used to be cut very high to encourage new shoots (only later was this method of exploitation reconsidered). The stumps were useful for strengthening the wall. An offence had been committed, the reprehensible destruction of a productive part of the forest. Moriceau de Cheusse was satisfied with forbidding the building of the wall and requiring the priest to obtain written permission to stay in the forest.

The passing years have only increased the use of natural resources for warlike ends. And today, even more than at the beginning of the eighteenth century, the forest is threatened: the destruction of vast tracts of forest on a continent, without any renewal of these resources, can easily destabilize the equilibrium of the whole.

2. Technology, science, and nature

In Father de Montfort's days, the French people lived an integrated life in small village or urban communities. Poitiers, with 18,000 inhabitants, was generally considered *"a large town"* (L 6). France was a vast field of agriculture, meadows, and woods, where almost all the population worked. The land owners and many of the workers were irrevocably tied to production from the land. Integrated within nature, they occupied themselves with meeting the primary needs: food, shelter, clothing, and defence from predatory or wild animals. It was a question of survival in the famine years, such as the two that de Montfort himself endured during his life (1694 and 1709).

Since those days, technology has changed physical nature. Science has attempted to impose laws that have sometimes not been completely thought out: the optimism of days gone by has come up against some fundamental questions. The word "ecology," invented in 1866 by the biologist Haeckel, describes the conditions necessary for beings to exist. Different disciplines have studied these relationships. Since the beginning of the twentieth century, there has arisen a movement for the protection of nature.[26] At a most critical moment, after the dropping of the first atomic bombs (1945), it was realized that scientific rationalism had succeeded in giving birth to a monster. Over and above the term "ecology," there are questions of ethics, of morality, and of divine creation.

If we wish to learn something from Louis de Montfort, we can perhaps do no better than simply observe him living as a hermit in the Forest of Mervent, as someone for whom nature possesses not merely a certain charm but a mystery and a majesty in which one can decipher the traces of the Creator.

3. Goods for all

In former times, nature was looked upon as a nutritive soil. Louis de Montfort saw it as sufficiently abundant in all kinds of goods to ensure a frugal yet sufficient life for all living things: it is for him a patrimony, *"one which God himself gives . . . namely, the inexhaustible inheritance of his divine Providence"* (MR 5). Today, nature is looked upon above all as a capital to be exploited. Development, the creation of wealth, consumerism have all created a superfluity of goods and new sources of distress.

It was commonly accepted in the days of Louis Marie that the distribution of goods was incumbent on the rich, who were considered the managers of the goods of those who were poor (even if this was not always put into practice). In today's distribution of national or worldwide wealth, this teaching, which Father de Montfort put in verse, remains true: *"You should know that something that you hang on to / while it has no use for you, / belongs to the poor; it is theirs . . . / The poor have the right to ask for / all that is not necessary to you; / the rich must not hang on to it, / even though they may think differently"* (H 17:18).

4. Montfort spirituality and ecology

God's glory is the aim of Louis Marie de Montfort's spirituality (TD 151). The baptized Christian achieves this through belonging to Jesus Christ.

The Christian, if he is to belong to Jesus Christ, must have a total dependence on him, in his person, his material and spiritual possessions, and, for good measure, even all the merit that he may have been able to acquire (TD 121). Beginning with a consecration, the initial act of complete belonging, the Christian progresses to a permanent state of union (TD 119), of conformity and consecration to Jesus Christ (TD 120).

The way in which we live total consecration to Jesus Christ is purified by a similar consecration—made subordinately to Christ—to the Virgin Mary (TD 125) who gave him birth (TD 1). Mary, exempt from all sin, is neither selfish nor self-centered; she keeps nothing for herself (TD 149); she is wholly related to God (TD 225). Thus she is, in one's approach to Christ, a way in which there are no obstacles (TD 165), a way that will not fade, the immaculate way (TD 158), the perfect way (TD 157). Our consecration to Jesus Christ becomes perfect through the perfect way of Mary.

Louis de Montfort, employing the popular images of his day, speaks of the power of Mary over God in his anger,[27] but he recognized a deviation towards utilitarian prayer, a selfish recourse to Mary: *"The true subject of Mary does not serve his illustrious Queen for selfish gain. He does not serve her for temporal or eternal well-being . . . ; He loves her not so much because she is good to him or because he expects something from her, but simply because she is lovable. . . . How pleasing and precious in the sight of God and his holy Mother must these servants of Mary be, who serve her without any self-seeking. How rare they are nowadays!"* (TD 110).

Louis de Montfort saw clearly in his parish missions that total and perfect consecration—which he himself had practiced since his formation—was able to make a Christian disinterested: *"It is to increase their number that I have taken up my pen to write down what I have been teaching with success both publicly and in private in my missions for many years"* (TD 110). Thus there was born the *Treatise on True Devotion.*

Superstition, an expression of fear, gains ground in times of insecurity. It is a twisting of religion and a gathering together of all kinds of useless beliefs and practices. It offers worship to forces that it divinizes, in order to conciliate them, or it offers to God a worship that expresses a false understanding of the divinity.[28] In opposition to this selfish approach, Montfort offers one characterized by confidence and serenity: total consecration to Jesus Christ and, in order to render this perfect, consecration to the Blessed Virgin.

The *Treatise on True Devotion* describes a series of peaceful effects brought about by the relationship to Jesus Christ and to Mary: *"By the light which the Holy Spirit will give you through Mary . . . you will perceive the evil inclinations of your fallen nature"* (TD 213); the Virgin *"will rid your heart of all scruples and inor-*

dinate servile fear. . . . You will then cease to act as you did before, out of fear of the God who is love, but rather out of pure love" (TD 215); the Virgin Mary *"will fill you with unbounded confidence in God and in herself"* (TD 216).

Louis de Montfort experiences a special blessed detachment in the open fields and woods of the countryside. Fear is banished, spontaneity reigns. The new hymn "In Honor of Our Lady of thc Shadows" at La Chevrolière (1708) is a hymn to the woodland (H 155:12); the new hymn "On Solitude," (H 1/15), is a hymn to the forest of Mervent (H 157:2).

Nature is neither hostile nor menacing, but welcoming: *"In this woodland, / in these peaceful retreats, / in the shadow of these forests, / what benefit we find, / what silence and yet what language!"* (H 15).

The cave in the Forest of Mervent is a beneficial place for a hermit who desires to hide himself away there for the service of God, in the midst of a harmonious and eloquent nature (H 157:12-13). Louis de Montfort does not find in nature the incoherence or revolt of uncontrollable forces that the superstitious wish to conciliate. There is nothing here of the occult powers of springs, seen as either beneficent of malevolent, in which the superstitious drown themselves. Nature, for him, teaches only true and strong values in obedience to God (H 157:16).

Louis de Montfort, voluntarily poor and interested only in his relationship with God, does not make of nature an object to possess, to be exploited or destroyed at will. He respects nature: *"The sinner may never lay his criminal hands on it"* (H 157:19).

In the woodland cave to which he withdraws and in the undulating landscape through which he makes great strides, Montfort finds nothing disquieting. Serene nature is a help to the encounter with God (H 157:18). Nature is a paradise for the soul. Just as the cave favors grace, nature benefits the gift of grace: *"But if nature is so beautiful, / grace reaps the reward, / forming a paradise / when a soul is pure and faithful"* (H 157:20).

B. Guitteny

Notes: (1) The adverb "here" is used eight times in the letter of December 6, 1700 (L 5), twice in that of 16 September 1701 (L 9), once in that of November 3, 1701 (L 10), and three times in that of 4 July 1702 (L 11). (2) Clorivière, 187, 189. (3) P. Goubert, *La vie quotidienne des paysans français au XVIIe siècle; The Daily Life of French Peasants in the Severnteenth Century,* Paris, Hachette, 1982, 118: *The French Peasantry in the Seventeenth Century,* trans. Pierre Goubert, New York, Cambridge, 1986: "The purchase of flour or bread accounted easily for half the expenses of a modest or hard-pressed family. . . . An adult easily consumed three pounds per day. . . . There were large round loaves of grey bread made of wheat mixed with rye, or winter barley." Archives of the Département of Vienne, Rule of the Hôpital Général, *Estat de la Dépense qu'il faut pour l'entretien de l'Hôpital général des pauvres enfermés de cette ville de Poitiers (Account of Necessary Expenditures for the Maintenance of the General Hospital Hospital for the Sick Poor of the City of Poitiers)*: in 1691, a pound and a half of bread was given each day to every pauper. Later, the ration was reduced to one pound daily, owing to a lack of resources. (4) F. Bluche, *La vie quotidienne au temps de Louis XIV (Daily Life in the Time of Louis XIV),* Paris, Hachette, 1984, 144: *Louis XIV,* trans. Mark Greengrass, New York, F. Watts, 1990: Bleeding was the favored treatment under Louis XIV. Methodical doctors used bleeding without any hesitation as their principal remedy. They drew off corrupted or superfluous blood from their patients because they believed in the circulation of the blood. Louis de Montfort was granted this avant-garde treatment at the Hôtel-Dieu in Paris in 1695: "They did not close his vein until his body, drained of blood, could give no more" (Blain, 62). The clyster, today called the enema, was an injection of liquid into the intestine by means of a huge syringe used by the assistant apothecary. The liquid used was water, or milk, or boiled bran or grass. From 1680 on, brown sugar or catholicon ceased to be mixed with it, but honey continued to be used in the mixture (F. Bluche, *La vie quotidienne,* 146). (5) A slow reading of Psalm 51, which begins with the word "miserere" in Latin, would last two and a half minutes. (6) Blain, 6-8. (7) Blain, 45. (8) Blain, 19. (9) J. Fournée, *L'arbre et la forêt en Normandie (Tree and Forest in Normandy),* Flers 1985, 39-39: "In the strict sense, a hermit or anchorite is one who lives alone, completely separated from the world. . . . The term 'hermitage' is not used in so rigorous a sense in common parlance as in its literary definition." Common usage attributes the word "hermitage," then, to certain secluded spots, and the name "hermit" to those who hide themselves away there for a limited period. (10) G. Plaisance, *Les ermites forestiers (Forest Hermits),* in *Présence au désert (Presence in the Desert),* 1979. (11) The verses of this hymn, which are inspired by his physical presence in the forest, end with verse 19, AGCM: in manuscript number IV, a second copyist continues the hymn from verse 20. From this point on, it has more the sense of a catechism on the advantages of solitude and withdrawal than a description of the life of the forest. (12) Grandet, 350. (13) The gift of Wisdom is received from God to enable one to "know, taste, and enable others to taste, the truth" and to speak from the abundance of one's heart (MR 60). It is "an experimental knowledge of the truth, full of relish, which enables one to see, in the light of faith, the most hidden mysteries, in particular that of the Cross" (FC 45). (14) All the indications are that we should date from this period hymns 124, 125, 126 and 103; The Works of St. John of the Cross. *The Dark Night* and St. John of the Cross (1542-1591) were not a direct influence on St Louis de Montfort. They are useful here as a guide for the understanding of the Christian spiritual life, because they treat *ex professo* of what de Montfort confides to us as his own personal experience. R. Garrigou-Lagrange, *Les trois âges de la vie intérieure, prélude à celle du ciel (The Three Ages of the Spiritual Life, Prelude to That of Heaven),* Paris 1938, 2:16: *The Three Ages of the Interior Life: Prelude of Eternal Life,* trans. M. Timothea Doyle, St. Louis, B. Herder, 1948: "About the dark night of the soul, St John of the Cross speaks of graces dealt with by St Teresa in the six dwellings." (15) J.-B. Saint-Jure, *De la connaissance et de l'amour du Fils de Dieu, Notre Seigneur Jésus-Christ (The Knowledge of the Love of the Son of God, Our Lord Jesus Christ),* Paris 1688. The first edition was brought out in 1633. This was followed by numerous editions, often revised. The edition of 1688 is the twelfth. *L'homme spirituelle (The Spiritual Person),* Paris 1685, by the same author, which treats of the foundations of the spiritual life, probably was Montfort's inspiration for the four means to acquire Wisdom. (16) The original text of LEW is unknown. We possess only one copy, written out by two copyists of very different handwriting, neither of whom is St. Louis de Montfort (the first copyist: 1-134; the second: 135 to the end of the Consecration). GA is guilty of an obvious error in saying that we can recognize in it the handwriting of St Louis de Montfort (GA p.48). We do not know the state of preservation of the document (or documents) used by the copyists, nor whether the copy is true to the original text. Internal analysis suggests that certain texts towards the end of the book date from after 1703, for example, LEW 193 and 203-222. They are very like SR and TD (1712), whose ideas, terms, and expressions they reproduce; written as one block, they contain no references to other works in the text itself. (17) M. Gilbert, *L'exégèse spirituelle de Montfort (The Spiritual Exegesis of Montfort),* in NRT 104 (1982), 681: "The biblical text is not used as confirmation of an already enunciated doctrine; it forms the base, the foundation, and the source of this doctrine." (18) L. Cognet, *De la dévotion moderne à la spiritualité française (Modern Devotion in French Spirituality),* Paris, A. Fayard, 1958, 65-68. (19) L. Pérouas, *Ce que croyait Grignion de Montfort (Way to Wisdom),* Paris, Mame, 1972, 118. (20) L. Cognet, *De la Devotion,* 61. (21) In de Montfort's vocabulary, "marvelous" means "mystical." He says "marvelous effect" for "mystical effect," emphasizing the fact that it is an effect of the action of the Holy Spirit (TD 213, 79). (22) R. Garrigou-Lagrange, *Les trois âges,* 13. (23) John of the Cross, *The Dark Night,* Carmelite Publications, Washington D.C., 1974, p. 580. (24) E. Mireaux, *Une province française au temps du grand Roi, la Brie (A French Province in the Time of the Great King: La Brie),* Paris 1958, 153ff. (25) L. Brochet, *La forêt de Vouvant, son histoire et ses sites (The Forest of Vouvent: Its History and Its Places),* Fontenay-le-Compte 1893, 59-61. (26) P. Daubercies, *Nature,* in *Catholicisme,* Paris, 10:1095. (27) "To calm Jesus in his anger, is easy with Mary. I say to him: Behold your Mother, and at once he is appeased" (H 77:10); "At her prayer, God's anger is calmed" (H 155:3). (28) Magic is a form of superstition; witchcraft, a degraded and popular form of magic.

CROSS

SUMMARY

I. MONTFORT AND THE CROSS IN THE SPIRITUAL CONTEXT OF THE SEVENTEENTH CENTURY;

II. THE CROSS IN THE LIFE OF MONTFORT:
   1. His trials;
   2. The crucifix, the calvaries;
   3. How Montfort bore his Cross.

III. THE WISDOM CROSS OF POITIERS:
   1. The meaning of the Wisdom Cross;
   2. The symbols embedded in the Wisdom Cross;
   3. Inscription on the cross;
      a. Love of the Cross,
      b. Desire for Crosses,
      c. List of Crosses;
   4. How the Cross is to be carried;
      a. Humility,
      b. Submission,
      c. Patience,
      d. Obedience;

IV. THE LETTER TO THE FRIENDS OF THE CROSS:
   1. To whom it was addressed and its purpose;
   2. Contents.

V. THE TEACHING OF MONTFORT:
   1. The Cross in the life of Christ;
      a. The redeeming Incarnation,
      b. Christ longed for the Cross,
      c. Mystery of love and of Wisdom,
      d. Mystery of suffering and glory;
   2. The Cross in the life of Christians;
      a. Baptism and its obligations,
      b. The Cross and the perfect consecration to Mary,
      c. The Cross as a way to Wisdom,
      d. The Cross as a proof of love,
      e. Joy in carrying the Cross;
   3. Understanding Montfort's teaching;
      a. Christian logic,
      b. Wisdom or folly?

VI. THE CROSS TODAY:
   1. Paschal perspective;
   2. The language of the Cross;
   3. The Cross of the disciple;
   4. Relevance of the mysticism of the Cross today.

In the literal sense the word "cross" refers either to the ancient instrument of torture used to crucify those sentenced to death, a torture to which Jesus submitted himself, or to representations of the Cross such as crucifixes, calvaries, badges, decorations, etc. In the figurative sense, the word "Cross" refers to all that is entailed by the option for Christ in favor of the Gospel or in the service of the Gospel (Mt 5:11; Phil 1:29; 2 Thess 1:5; 2 Tim 1:8; 2:8 ff). The meaning has been widened to include the trials, obstacles, and difficulties met with in life and borne or accepted by Christian people in union with the sufferings of Christ to continue the mission of Jesus the Savior in the Church.

Very early on, the Cross of Christ was regarded as the greatest manifestation of God's love (Rom 5:6 ff; 8:32 ff) and the effective instrument of the wisdom and power of God reconciling humans with God (1 Cor 1:18 ff; Col 1:19 ff). According to the long spiritual tradition of the Church, the Cross is the crucible in which God fashions the saints. In its many forms it normally accompanies the decision to follow Christ (Mk 8:34) and to give one's life out of love, as he did.

I. Montfort and the Cross in the Spiritual Context of the Seventeenth Century

The spiritual features of a saint are the result, above all, of his faithfulness to the Gospel and of the work of the Holy Spirit. But any saint bears the marks of the centuries-old tradition of the Church and of the trends of the time and environment in which the saint lived. For example, Montfort was fond of comparing his deepest aspirations and life experience with those reported by well-established spiritual writers, while he remained himself as God was shaping him.

As far as the Cross is concerned, Montfort was greatly influenced by Henri Boudon's *Les saintes voies de la Croix,* Joseph Surin's *Lettres spirituelles,* Olier's writings, and the Sulpician environment in which he received his training for eight years.

Without doubt it was Boudon, the renowned archdeacon of Evreux, himself indebted to Louis Chardon's *La Croix de Jésus,* who exerted the most direct influence on the way Montfort approached the Cross. According to his fellow student Blain, his favorite book in his seminary days was *Les saintes voies de la Croix.* The book "inspired him with such a high esteem of, and a taste for, suffering and contempt that he kept talking of the happiness he derived from his crosses and of the merits of suffering."[1] According to Boudon, the Cross is such a precious gift for Christ and the Christian that it should be accepted with appreciation, love, and joy.

In order to unify the spiritual life, Surin stressed the total orientation of the soul towards God and its complete detachment from creatures, which involves voluntary exterior mortifications, besides the ordinary crosses met with in any Christian life. "In this respect, Montfort moves away from Boudon to follow Surin."[2]

Montfort was influenced by Olier's idea of the itinerant mission, which necessitates being radically poor and marked by persecution right from the start. In the formation given at St. Sulpice Seminary, the psychological trend introduced by Tronson was gaining ground at the expense of the mystical and apostolic orientation. The formation aimed indeed at bringing about an authentic spiritual life, though pervaded with an ideal of moderation, prudence, conformity in community living, and scrupulous observance of all the rules. Montfort never felt at ease within this rigid framework, which was like a mould into which he cast himself only out of obedience without inwardly adhering to it fully. The seminary was for him a place where he suffered in various ways from reproaches, mockery, humiliations, and contempt,[3] which may be partly accounted for by his lack of social adjustment resulting from his temperament. His missionary drive was held in check for some time, but this only led him to deepen within himself the mystery of Jesus crucified.

Montfort would gradually become himself only after he left St. Sulpice Seminary. He would continue his own spiritual and apostolic journey, always stamped with the Cross, as the logical consequence of his decision to live out the demands of the Gospel to the letter.

II. The Cross in the Life of Montfort

1. His trials

As a young priest, Montfort suffered from inactivity during his six-month stay in the community of St. Clement in Nantes. Then he had to feel his way around for five years before finding his way: he was rejected by Poitiers Hospital, then by the Salpêtrière Hospital in Paris; he was disowned by his former spiritual directors and abandoned by his long-time friends (L 15). In 1703 he lived alone in a dingy hovel under a staircase on Rue du Pot-de-Fer in Paris and felt *"more impoverished, crucified and humiliated than ever"* (L 16). Humanly speaking, it was a dreadful experience of rejection and humiliation for a 30-year-old man, but it was also a spiritual experience out of the ordinary for him, who kept praying longingly for the *"boundless treasure"* of Wisdom (L 15).

Montfort was confirmed in his ministry by Pope Clement XI in June 1706 with the title of "Missionary Apostolic," and the rest of his life was attended by the Cross. His preaching upset people and made enemies of some of them. His detractors disparaged him in the eyes of ordinary people (who looked upon him as "good Father de Montfort"), calling him a "vagrant," an "adventurer," a "hypocrite," a "demon-possessed man," and "Antichrist."[4] Several attempts were made on his life. Although he always strove to obey the directives of the bishops, several of them either placed him under an interdict or refused him entry into their territories as a result of slanderous reports or because of his excessive zeal. On these occasions his suffering was the greater as some of the faithful were thus deprived of the benefit of the mission. And those who accompanied him had no choice but to share his Cross.

In 1713 he wrote to his sister Guyonne Jeanne, *"If you only knew the half of the crosses and humiliations I have to bear, I don't think you would be so eager to see me; for I never seem to go anywhere without bringing something of the Cross to my dearest friends without any fault of mine or theirs. Those who befriend me or support me suffer for doing so. . . . I have for ever to be on the alert, treading warily as though on thorns or sharp stones. I am like a ball in a game of tennis; no sooner am I hurled to one side than I am sent back to the other, and the players strike hard. This is the fate of the poor sinner that I am, and I have been like this without rest or respite all the thirteen years since leaving St. Sulpice"* (L 26). This letter, like the following ones, was headed, *"May Jesus and his Cross reign for ever."* Until then he had headed his letters, *"May the perfect love of God reign in our hearts!"*

The aim of his preaching was to renew baptismal life in the faithful. He did not count the cost of *"fighting against the demons of hell or making war on the world and the worldly"* (L 24), and he invited his nun sister and her community to pray that he may *"obtain from Jesus the grace for me to carry the roughest and heaviest crosses as I would the light-as-straw ones and to resist with unyielding courage the powers of hell"* (L 24).

He died prematurely, before completing his work as a founder, which was the greatest sacrifice for a man who for sixteen years had never ceased to pray with confidence to obtain a company of missionary priests.

2. The crucifix, the calvaries

As a student, Montfort "always wore a crucifix and an embossed image of the Blessed Virgin."[5] "The crucifix and the image of the Most Blessed Virgin were throughout his life . . . his only resource in all his undertakings."[6] Pope Clement XI had attached to Montfort's ivory crucifix a plenary indulgence, to be gained by all who kissed it just before they died. During his last hours, he clutched it in his right hand and blessed those who visited him then.[7] In 1707 at Montfort-la-Cane, instead of giving a sermon, he pulled out the crucifix he had brought back from Rome, gazed at it for a long time, and burst into tears; then he left the pulpit without a word and offered the crucifix for all to kiss. The whole congregation was moved and repentant. He had achieved his aim.[8] He sometimes brandished his crucifix as a weapon of peace to part young people fighting a duel, or as a rallying symbol against licentiousness or obscenity. *"Let those who love Jesus Christ join me in adoring him."*[9] In August 1713, when the superior of the Holy Spirit community asked him for some token of friendship, he gave him "a small crucifix just a few inches long, saying, *'Of all my possessions this is the most valuable, and I give it to you'*; . . . the small crucifix was worn smooth with his many kisses."[10]

During his missions he gave out to those attending them small cloth crosses.[11] The climax of his missions, however, was the blessing of the calvary. Usually erected on a hill, the large cross reminded everyone of God's commitment to save humanity, and the faithful of their obligation to carry their Cross in the steps of their Master. It was also his way of engraving on the hearts of other people, as it was on his own, devotion to and love for Jesus crucified[12] while celebrating and perpetuating in an effective way the victory of Calvary.

In 1707, while in his native parish, he mobilized the local people for the erection not only of a cross but also of small oratories to be used as stations. The project failed.[13] He took it up again in 1708-1710 at Pontchâteau. It was a huge undertaking in which several hundred voluntary workers took part, working each day for sixteen months. A huge cross over 15 meters, flanked by those of the two thieves, and with statues of Mary, John, and Mary Magdalene, was erected on a 30-meter-high hill and was visible from a distance of 30 kilometers. Three chapels were added, and pine and cypress trees representing the mysteries of the Rosary were also planted. The calvary was completed by the scheduled date but destroyed shortly afterwards on orders from the misinformed bishop of the area.[14]

At Sallertaine in 1712, he started a less ambitious project, which included, all the same, a vaulted chapel dedicated to St. Michael, a round room called "the sepulchre," and statues of the characters in the Lord's Passion; it also included three crosses, a boundary wall, an access staircase, a huge rosary round the statue of Christ, etc. The blessing ceremony took place: "Hearts were changed, Jesus was glorified, and his Cross exalted."[15] But at the instigation of his enemies, the governor decided a few weeks later that the calvary was to be torn down. In these three instances, the same pretext was put forward: the calvaries, with their caves, moats, and boundary walls, might be used as fortresses or shelters by English troops in the event of an invasion. On each occasion the glorious Cross was robbed of triumph and popular veneration and turned into a painful Cross to be planted in the heart of all to bear lasting fruit. The calvary of his last mission, given at Saint-Laurent-sur-Sèvre, was erected the day after his death, a few hours before his funeral.

3. How Montfort bore his Cross

His immediate reactions during the weeks following the tragedy at Pontchâteau give a snapshot picture of how he faced up to it. He had first obtained the bishop's permission and all preparations had been made for the blessing ceremony to take place on September 13, 1710. At four o'clock in the afternoon he was informed of the King's notification to the bishop of Nantes that the ceremony was to be called off. He walked to Nantes during the night to find out more from the bishop. The cancellation was upheld. As scheduled, he began a mission at Saint Molf, in the same diocese, the following Sunday. In the first week the bishop forbade him to preach or hear confessions throughout the diocese. He shed tears while reading the bishop's letter. And yet the bearer of the message "saw that he was neither troubled nor bitter: on such occasions he merely suffered in silence." He called on the bishop again "in the hope that he would change his mind." Instead of this, the bishop told him that the Calvary of Pontchâteau was to be torn down. He then made a retreat in amazing serenity and breathed no word of the incident to anyone. To those who raised the subject, he said, *"I am neither sorry nor sad; I am content."*[16] Content in his apostolic suffering (L 26), Montfort invited those around him to thank God with him (L 24) and "recite the Te Deum."[17]

J. Bulteau

III. The Wisdom Cross of Poitiers

Several months after his ordination in 1700, Father Louis de Montfort agreed to be chaplain at the large poorhouse of the city of Poitiers, France. The disorder he encountered was far greater than he ever anticipated.

One of his principal means of reform was to organize a prayer group of about twenty pious women of the institution, all of them handicapped in one way or another. The young priest named the group Wisdom. These destitute women met in a small corner of the poorhouse, a blind woman their leader. In the Wisdom meeting room, Saint Louis de Montfort placed in a prominent position a large cross that he designed. On it he inscribed, in simple and forceful evangelical terms, the glory of suffering with Christ, the crucified Eternal and Incarnate Wisdom. The cross has become known as the Wisdom Cross, or the Cross of Poitiers.

At the invitation of Father de Montfort, a young girl from a well-known family of Poitiers joined the Wisdom group of handicapped paupers out of a desire to serve them. This teenager, Marie Louise Trichet, became the cofoundress of Montfort's Daughters of Wisdom. She was beatified on May 16, 1993, by Pope John Paul II in Rome. The original Wisdom Cross, venerated by Mother Marie Louise and forming a source of her strength, is preserved at the generalate of the Daughters of Wisdom in Rome.

1. The meaning of the Wisdom Cross

The mystery of the Cross, so central to the spirituality of Saint Louis de Montfort, is boldly expressed through the Wisdom Cross.

What is immediately striking is that Father de Montfort used a cross to symbolize Wisdom. What is Wisdom in the thought of the great saint? He tells us clearly in his masterful LEW: *"Supernatural wisdom is divided into substantial or uncreated Wisdom and accidental or created wisdom. Accidental or created wisdom is the communication that uncreated Wisdom makes of itself to humankind. In other words, it is the gift of wisdom. Substantial wisdom or uncreated Wisdom is the Son of God, the second person of the most Blessed Trinity. In other words, it is Eternal Wisdom in eternity or Jesus Christ in time. It is precisely about this Eternal Wisdom that we are going to speak"* (LEW 13).

Wisdom, then, in its fullest sense is Jesus Christ, the Eternal and Incarnate Wisdom of the Father. Yet Montfort depicts this Wisdom, Jesus the Lord, through the symbol of the Cross. He gives us his reason: *"Jesus has fixed his abode in the cross so firmly that you will not find him anywhere in this world save in the cross. He has so truly incorporated and united himself with the cross that in all truth we can say: "Wisdom is the Cross and the Cross is Wisdom"* (LEW 180).

The Wisdom Cross reminds us, therefore, that Jesus redeems us in and through the victorious Cross. He could have chosen another way. His will, however, is clear: he gives us eternal life by dying on the Cross. Jesus the Savior is inseparable from the Cross.

There is another reason why this work of Saint Louis de Montfort is called the Wisdom Cross. In the eyes of the world, the Cross and the message inscribed on it are sheer folly, yet they embody the deepest Wisdom accessible to humankind. Only the truly Gospel-wise can begin to grasp the truth manifested by the Wisdom Cross. It expresses the inspired teaching of Paul: "We preach Christ crucified, a stumbling block to Jews and folly to Gentiles, but to those who are called, both Jews and Greeks, Christ is the power of God and the Wisdom of God. For the foolishness of God is wiser than men and the weakness of God is stronger than men" (1 Cor 1:23-25).

2. The symbols embedded in the Wisdom Cross

The cross is embedded with five prominent symbols. At the very top, the IHS surmounted by a small cross: the familiar Greek abbreviation for the Holy Name of Jesus. At the head of the crossbeam, the entwined M and A, a symbol of Mary. Half way down the cross are the expressions *"May Jesus prevail, May his Cross prevail (Vive Jesus, Vive sa Croix)."* The words encircle a flaming Sacred Heart of Jesus, crowned with a cross as large as the Heart itself. At the bottom of the cross are two symbols: the crown of thorns, which encircle the three nails of the crucifixion, and a star, symbolizing Mary.

These images are essential interpretations of the text Father de Montfort inscribed on the cross. The central symbol and the most pronounced is the Sacred Heart of Jesus, the sign of Infinite Love Incarnate.

Saint Louis de Montfort's intense love for the Sacred Heart of Jesus probably stems from his association with the Visitation Nuns. It was at their Paray-le-Monial monastery that Our Lord revealed his Sacred Heart to Saint Margaret Mary Alacoque. Saint Louis' collection of hymns attests to his fervent devotion to the Heart of Christ, the great symbol of God's infinite love for us: "*The Heart of Christ loves us / without ceasing to love for even a moment / the Heart of Christ loves us as much as himself / with excess, infinitely*" (H 40:12; cf. H 40-44).

It is the Sacred Heart that interprets Montfort's writings on the mystery of the Cross. The Cross is the most powerful expression of the Heart of Christ for, it is on Calvary that the love of God for us is so manifest. The Cross is always to be seen, then, as the victorious love of the Heart of Christ for humankind.

Yet there is another side to Saint Louis' love for the Sacred Heart. It also is a call to repentance, to reparation, to suffering with Christ. Patience in bearing our crosses is the manifestation of our love for God, *"it is the proof which God requires to show our love for him"* (LEW 176). The fact that the Sacred Heart of Jesus is the most prominent aspect of the Wisdom Cross means that for Montfort the Cross is the great mystery of love: love of our God for us, and of our love for God.

The symbols of Our Lady are also essential in order to understand the meaning of the Wisdom Cross. Mary is the mother of the crucified Savior. She is the model of suffering with her Son. It is Mary who gifts us with the Cross of Jesus, it is Mary who shares with us her bravery in bearing the triumphant Cross, it is Mary, the guiding star who leads us safely to Jesus-Wisdom, our goal.

3. Inscription on the cross

The inscriptions on the cross are all written in capital letters. Some of the terms are so squeezed into the width of the cross that a few letters of the word are written in smaller print immediately alongside or above the word itself. The top portion of the cross and the crossbeam are inscribed with slightly adapted words from Sacred Scripture. *"Deny oneself, carry one's cross to follow Jesus Christ"* is found at the head of the vertical beam. The crossbeam carries in large letters *"If you are ashamed of the Cross of Jesus Christ, he will be ashamed of you before his Father."* The words of the Holy Spirit form the foundation for Saint Louis' personal thoughts inscribed on the Wisdom Cross.

Immediately under the crossbeam, Saint Louis de Montfort begins his brief commentary on the scriptural words he wrote at the top of the cross. His Wisdom Cross "sermon" is divided into two sections. First, a list of some of the crosses experienced by the followers of Christ and, more specifically, by the original Wisdom prayer group. Second, how the cross is to be carried.The sermon is prefaced by two phrases: *"Love the cross, desire crosses."*

a. Love of the Cross. The world would interpret this as masochistic; not so a Christian. Jesus Christ our Head dies for us upon the victorious Cross; those baptized into Christ are also immersed into the triumphant Cross. It is through the Cross that Jesus enters into his glory; it is only through the Cross that we share in his glory. Bearing the Cross is intrinsic to Christian life. Each Christian must become, in suffering, a sacrament of Jesus crucified. A love for the Cross, then, characterizes the follower of Christ. Not a sensual love, as the saint himself explains, but a love from the depths of the soul, springing from the desire to be totally conformed to our Head.

b. Desire for crosses. The expression desire for crosses repeats the divinely inspired thought of Paul: "But far be it from me to glory except in the Cross of our Lord Jesus Christ, by which the world has been crucified to me and I to the world" (Gal 6:14); "that I may know him [Christ Jesus] and the power of his resurrection, and may share his sufferings, becoming like him in his death, that if possible I may attain the resurrection from the dead" (Phil 3:10-11). Montfort, the man of the absolute, does not water down the radical demands of the Gospel. His desire for crosses is a forceful way of manifesting the yearning to be totally conformed to Christ Jesus in his dying so that the world may share in his rising.

c. List of crosses. The list of crosses that follows was easily recognizable by the destitute, sickly women who formed the first Wisdom community: *"contempt, pain, abuse, insults, disgrace, persecution, humiliations, calumnies, illness, injuries."* These crosses are also autobiographical. Saint Louis de Montfort's first years of priesthood were a series of difficulties that well fit the list he enumerated on the Wisdom Cross. Some would consider Montfort's list typical. However, he has not intended his naming of a variety of crosses to be universal. They fit him, they fit his Wisdom prayer group. The list is rather fluid, for the specific sharing in Christ's redemptive Cross may vary from month to month, even day to day. And recognition of crosses never prevents us from crying out with Jesus, "Abba, Father, all things are possible to thee; remove this cup from me," provided we continue with Jesus, "yet not what I will, but what thou wilt" (Mk 14:36).

4. How the Cross is to be carried

The symbol of the Sacred Heart of Jesus divides the two sections of Saint Louis' preaching. The first words of the second part are, then, *"Divine Love."* It is this unmerited and unconditional love of the Heart of Christ that prompts and strengthens Christians to carry their crosses. It is Divine Love that calls, further, from them the following four qualities that share in the victorious sufferings of Christ: *"humility, submission, patience, obedience."*

Why these particular four characteristics of bearing the Cross? They typify the manner by which Jesus himself carried his Cross to Calvary. They must, therefore, characterize every disciple on the way of the Cross.

a. Humility. The first quality needed to carry one's Cross is humility. In his canticle on humility (H 8), Saint Louis de Montfort sings of the necessity of recognizing who one truly is in order to be totally open to God's saving power. And the missionary speaks in strong terms of our sinfulness, of our nothingness. It is pride that would have a person think that he is "too good" to be asked to carry a Cross. It is pride that cries out, "Why me, Lord! I don't deserve this suffering."

For Montfort, the most serious effect of pride is that it blinds us to the privilege of taking up the Cross daily and following Jesus. It is only humility and her eldest sister, meekness (H 9), that enable us to be open to the Holy Spirit's teaching on the Cross. Humility permits us to understand that *"if you suffer much persecution for justice's sake, if you are treated as the refuse of the world, be comforted, rejoice, be glad, and dance for joy because the cross you carry is a gift so precious as to arouse the envy of the saints in heaven, were they capable of envy"* (LEW 179).

Humility is a chief characteristic of Jesus crucified, as Paul proclaims: "He humbled himself, becoming obedient unto death even death upon a cross" (Phil 2:8). Jesus, meek and humble of heart, is the model. With humility and meekness, we accept God's mysterious plan.

b. Submission. For Saint Louis de Montfort, submission is an expression of true humility. Jesus submits to the Father's will from the first moment of his conception in the womb of Mary (cf. Heb 10:5-9; TD 248). As the personification of true humility, Jesus says, "I can do nothing on my own authority . . . I seek not my own will but the will of him who sent me" (Jn 5:30). He willingly is subject to Joseph and Mary, he lives for thirty years in submission to Our Lady, because this is God the Father's plan for him. The Cross is the supreme example of his loving acceptance of the Father's will.

Submission is not something negative for this saint. Rather, it is the active and loving emptying of ourselves into the Other in order to become our true selves. It is to be in total harmony with the ground of all being, the source of all love, the goal of all creation: God alone.

Submission is the opposite of revolt. We do not carry the Cross complainingly (cf. LEW 178), we do not rebel against God's evident will. Rather, we pour ourselves into the mysterious will of God and become one with his plans for us, no matter how they may differ from our own. The true follower of Jesus is characterized by this loving oneness with Jesus and, in and through Jesus, a loving oneness with the Father. The submission of Jesus when called upon to carry his Cross, "Not my will but thine be done," must qualify the manner with which all Christians bear the Cross.

c. Patience. "Patience in bearing our cross" is the plea of Saint Louis de Montfort when praying the fourth sorrowful mystery of the Rosary. His hymn on patience is completely centered on bearing the Cross as Jesus did (H 11). The saint's understanding of patience is, then, intimately entwined with the Cross. It has as its primary meaning the strength *"to laugh in the midst of torments / to turn trials into charming pleasures / without any bitterness and without sadness / . . . invincible patience / the lesson of the dying Jesus"* (H 11:1). *"The patient man,"* sings the missionary, *"glorifies / the good Jesus with his cross / since he thus imitates his life / since he submits to his laws / since he fills by his suffering / what is lacking in his passion"* (H 11:4). In words that would bring ridicule from the worldly, Montfort teaches, *"Receive from the hands of God himself / your trials as great gifts / as marks that God loves you / as one of his dearest children"* (H 11:28). For Saint Louis, all this is the mark of true patience.

Just as Jesus did not complain, just as Jesus did not turn back on the way of the Cross, so too the follower of crucified Wisdom. The victorious Cross is, then, to be carried with joy, even in the midst of our tears (cf. H 11:32)—the meaning Saint Louis de Montfort gives to the expression "patience in bearing our cross."

d. Obedience. As the culmination and summary of the preceding three virtues, Montfort's Wisdom Cross devotes several lines to the necessity of the virtue of obedience in order to bear our crosses like faithful disciples.

Obedience is of the highest value in Montfort spirituality. Saint Louis de Montfort insists strongly upon it in his rules for his Congregations, the Company of Mary (Montfort Missionaries) and the Daughters of Wisdom. It is a primary characteristic of the *"apostles of the latter times,"* as described especially in PM. Loving obedience characterizes those who have made the perfect consecration to Jesus through Mary. So strongly does the saint stress obedience that he sings, *"To make the vow of poverty / and even of chastity / to practice austerities / with an extreme rigor / to suffer furious torments / and even martyrdom / to obey is worth far more / it is what God desires"* (H 10:3).

Again, this virtue holds such a prominent place in Montfort's spirituality of the Cross, because Jesus himself is the model of obedience in his suffering and death: *"He becomes an infant / in the womb of his mother / in order to obey . . . / he obeys right up to his death / . . . if he dies on the cross it is by the strength of his obedience"* (H 10:6, 8). The missionary echoes the thoughts of Paul's great hymn in Phil 2:6-11.

The result of Jesus' obedience is our very salvation: *"We have been rejected / by the disobedience [of Adam and Eve] / but Jesus has saved us all / by his obedience"* (H 10:5). It is, then, by obedience that one shares in the victory of the Cross (H 10:1, 16, 17).

In a summary statement, Saint Louis de Montfort declares that obedience is *"to obey the Lord / both in what we believe and in what we do / to submit both spirit and heart [to the Lord] / in order all the better to chant victory"* (H 10:1). His inscription on the Wisdom Cross details five qualities of obedience: *"complete, prompt, joyful, blind, persevering."* Complete, total obedience typifies the disciple who daily carries the Cross after Jesus. Montfort's insistence on total obedience surprises no one who is the least acquainted with his life and writings. He cannot tolerate halfway discipleship. Tepidity comes under his strong condemnation. If God has given Himself so completely to us, must we not give ourselves totally to God? This is especially true in bearing our Cross. Our union with the mysterious love of Christ must know no limits. As the Lord reveals his will unfolding each moment, our response—even when the moment is one of anguish—is marked by total obedience, a complete, loving surrender to Love Itself.

Obedience is to be prompt. In his hymn on obedience, where he goes into more detail on its qualities, Saint Louis numbers as the third quality *"Obey very promptly / without requesting that one wait / then you will be doubly obeying / the one who commands"* (H 10:29). Montfort begs God to send recruits to his Company of Mary who are always ready to obey promptly wheresoever the Spirit of the Lord calls them (PM 10). We do not put off a response to God's call to unite ourselves to his Cross. We do not delay in lovingly joining our heart to the pierced Heart of Christ. Wheresoever, whatsoever—our answer is the reply of Samuel: "I am ready!" (cf PM 10)

Immediately after listing *"prompt"* as a quality of obedience, Saint Louis de Montfort adds—in his hymn on obedience, in RM, and on the Wisdom Cross—"*joyful.*" The saint is not talking about "goosebump joy." It is the deep peace that no one, nothing can take away from us because we live in such union with Christ crucified. It is this peaceful joy that radiates from the Christian who is so completely one with the Lord, especially when experiencing incredible crosses. It was, so his biographers unanimously tell us, a characteristic of Montfort himself. In his bitterest moments, in his loss of everything he held dear, in the midst of his tears, there beamed a mysterious peace. He knew and shared with friends that he was at times treated unjustly; at times he sought a change of heart in those in authority who treated him so. Yet he obeyed, and obeyed joyfully. For such was his Master's attitude in bearing the Cross.

After detailing the importance of obedience in RM, he concludes, *"[The members of the Company of Mary] are permitted to state openly and straightforwardly the reasons they may have for omitting or for not undertaking what is commanded."* Montfort implies that in this dialogue the reasons given by the member of the community may convince the superior to retract what had been decided. But *"if their reasons have not prevailed, [they] must obey blindly and promptly"* (RM 27; cf. H 10:32). "Blindly means to obey even if we cannot agree with the decision" (RM 19; cf. H 10:31), provided, of course, that what is ordered is not contrary to the Gospel and does not *"run counter to their most important rules and vows"* (RM 22). The decision of the community, reached through prayer and openness to each other, is to be accepted as the will of God.

The final characteristic of obedience engraved on the Wisdom Cross is *"persevering."* The saint described *"inconstant"* devotees as *"those whose devotion . . . is practiced in fits and starts. Sometimes they are fervent and sometimes they are lukewarm. Sometimes they appear ready to do anything to please Our Lady, and then shortly afterwards they have completely changed"* (TD 101). Such persons are described as *"fickle," "changeable as the moon."* On the other hand, the *"constant"* or *"persevering"* person is one who is *"not changeable, fretful, scrupulous or timid"* (TD 09).

P. Gaffney

III. The Letter to the Friends of the Cross

1. To whom it was addressed and its purpose

Eight years after Montfort's death, Grandet wrote, "On the strength of the saying of Jesus Christ that requires his disciples to renounce themselves and carry their Cross and follow him . . . Montfort tried to inspire everyone with the love of the Cross. To inspire this devotion . . . he set up associations . . . including the word 'Cross' in their names; for their benefit, he wrote rules and prescribed practices that were all approved by the bishops. One of them is still in existence today in La Rochelle."[18] Besnard mentions one such association, founded in 1708 in the parish of St. Similien in Nantes.[19] The purpose of these associations was the same as that of all those set up by Montfort: to continue the work of conversion carried out during the mission and to secure its good results.

To the "Friends of the Cross" Montfort wrote a "circular letter" that "contains the gospel maxims necessary for salvation."[20] The original of this letter, which Montfort probably wrote while in Rennes (in 1714?) has not survived. The version published in 1839 by Father Dalin, superior general of the Company of Mary, appears in GA.

The framework of the letter is a commentary on Mt 16:24. Many biblical quotations are scattered throughout the text: no fewer than 75 quotations from, or references to, the OT, and over 150 to the NT. Montfort also quotes the Church Fathers and a number of saints. In several passages he keeps closely to Boudon's booklet *Les saintes voies de la Croix* (1671) (Cf. FC 18, 25, 26, 27, 35, 37).

2. Contents

The letter begins (FC 1-12) with an encouragement and a justification: the devils, the avaricious, the pleasure-seekers unite and make up the camp of the world; the Friends of the Cross also must unite to make up the camp of Jesus Christ. To be a Friend of the Cross is to choose the Wisdom of God; *"It is the genuine title of a Christian"* (FC 3). This is followed by the principles underlying the association (FC 13-40) and fourteen practical rules on how to carry one's Cross (FC 41-62).

"Christian holiness consists in this: (1) Resolving to become a saint: 'If anyone wants to be a follower of mine'; (2) Self-denial: 'Let him renounce himself'; (3) Suffering: 'Let him take up his cross'; (4) Acting: 'Let him follow me'" (FC 13). Montfort gives his own word-by-word explanation of this saying of Jesus.[21]

It is necessary for all to carry their Cross. No one can be or become a friend of Jesus without drinking from his cup. Crosses are the Father's sign that he looks on us as his dearly loved friends. As disciples of a crucified God, we have to learn to practice this all-important science (FC 26) in the footsteps of Jesus Christ. As members of his Body, Christians have to share his lot. It is fitting that as living temples of the Holy Spirit, they should be cut and chiselled before they are set into the edifice. Their only alternative is either to carry their Cross joyfully and patiently with the saints or to grumble and complain like the reprobate (FC 23-33).

When carried as it should be, the Cross becomes a *"yoke that is easy."* It is a source of progress and enlightenment; it is the fuel that feeds the love of God as wood fuels the fire; it gives strength and an unutterable joy that all the saints have experienced (FC 34). *"The greatest gift of God."* If we appreciated it, we would have Masses offered, make novenas, and undertake pilgrimages to obtain it. Is it not the source of glory even here on earth and then in heaven, since it turns humans into saints (FC 35-40)?

Suffering for suffering's sake is pointless. What does count is to walk in the footsteps of Christ and carry our Cross as he did his. Montfort sums this up in fourteen practical rules (FC 42-62): 1. Do not deliberately bring crosses upon yourself, since life brings its crop of them each day. - 2. Consult the good of your neighbor, avoiding all that the weak may take scandal at, and under the guidance of a wise person, ignore the criticism of the worldly-wise. - 3. Admire in humility the attitude and conduct of the saints whom the Holy Spirit prompted to seek crosses. - 4. Pray without ceasing for the Wisdom of the Cross coupled with the practice of it. Pray to understand from your own experience how it is possible to desire, seek, and find joy in the Cross. - 5. Without being upset, accept the humiliation brought about by your blunders and faults in your own eyes and in God's presence. - 6. God permits that you should be humiliated, tempted, and fall into sin to keep you from boasting and to purify you. - 7. Avoid the traps of pride, self-conceit, and self-love. - 8. Take advantage of little sufferings, even more than of great ones. The main thing is that you suffer for the love of God and turn everything to profit. - 9. Love the Cross, not with emotional love but with rational and, even more, with spiritual love—the love of the summit of the soul—which will lead you to love and appreciate suffering in faith. - 10. Suffer all sorts of crosses without exception or discrimination: be ready to lose everything and to be stripped of everything. - 11. With practice, four things will stimulate you to suffer in the right spirit: live under the eye of God, who looks with pleasure on those who carry the Cross cheerfully; consider the hand of God, who simultaneously permits affliction and upholds you with strength and gentleness; turn your thoughts and eyes to Jesus Christ, as he is the answer to all difficulties; look up to eternal glory in heaven and down to eternal punishment in hell. - 12. Never willingly complain against a person or thing that may afflict you. - 13. Always receive the Cross with gratitude. - 14. Under the guidance of a prudent director, take up some crosses of your own accord.

V. The Teaching of Montfort

In the light of the OT and the NT, Montfort interpreted in his own way God's eternal plan of love, life, and salvation for humanity. To realize this plan, God chose to become flesh to redeem the world. This choice is a mystery to humanity. Those who agree to walk along the road chosen by God find a meaning to life. Following Christ, they progress in Wisdom and love.

1. The Cross in the life of Christ

a. The redemptive Incarnation. The Incarnation is "*the first mystery of Jesus Christ; it is a summary of all his mysteries*" (TD 248); it makes all the other mysteries possible.[22] It was as Incarnate Word that Christ was able to be born, to teach, to suffer, to die, and to rise from the dead.

When he examines the mystery of the Cross Montfort looks at Christ suffering for our sake in his saving condition of Incarnate Word. Although Montfort describes it as "*the greatest mystery of Eternal Wisdom*" (LEW 167; cf. FC 26, H 19:1), his conviction and enthusiasm take nothing away from what he has stated about the Word becoming flesh. The mysteries of the Cross and the Incarnation can be regarded in turn as the great mystery, as successive stages in one global mystery, that of Christ saving humanity.

When choosing to become flesh, Christ chose a suffering condition, placing himself in a state of suffering, which is a direct consequence of joining the Word and "sinful flesh" in his very being.

b. Christ longed for the Cross. God chose the Cross to save humanity. Consequently, during his life on earth, Jesus' only desire and aspiration were to carry out the will of the Father: "*Incarnate Wisdom loved the cross from his infancy*" (LEW 169). "*Throughout his life he eagerly sought after the cross*" (LEW 170). Jesus' life was a longing for the Cross; "*his whole life . . . became one continuous cross*" (LEW 170).

This montfort teaching was influenced by seventeenth-century spiritual writers like Chardon, author of *La Croix de Jésus,* published in 1647. The theme of the longing for the Cross and of Jesus' continuous sufferings occurs in St. Robert Bellarmine († 1621) and St. Francis de Sales († 1622), both Doctors of the Church.[23] The Oratorians,[24] who influenced Montfort at St. Sulpice, as well as Olier[25] express a similar view. Boudon also lays emphasis on the condition of unceasing suffering in which the Word lived as a result of his Incarnation. "His whole life was spent in sorrow, because either he actually felt the pain caused by external thorns or his mind was afflicted by the vivid image he formed of them."[26]

When he describes the sufferings of Christ (LEW ch. 13), Montfort highlights their cause, their meaning: joyful love for humanity. It was for mankind's sake that Christ walked up to the Cross, embraced it (LEW 170), was joined to it (LEW 171), identified himself with it (LEW 172). After choosing it when he was "*in the bosom of his Father*" (LEW 170), he renewed his choice when he was "*in Mary's womb*" (LEW 170); "*all his pursuits, all his desires were directed towards the cross*" (LEW 170; cf. H 19).

c. Mystery of love and Wisdom. The mystery of the Cross is primarily a mystery of love, because it was generated by love. The Father loves Himself with a love of complaisance in His incarnate and crucified Word: "This is my Son, the Beloved" (Mt 3:17). The incarnate and crucified Son loves his Father with the same love with which the Father loves him eternally (cf. Jn 14:31). The Father cannot love his Son without loving him in his condition as a man of sorrows; the Son, in this same condition, welcomes the loving will of his Father. That is how the Holy Spirit, who is the reciprocal love of the Father and the Son, can be given to humanity.

For it is to humanity that God wants to show and give His love. "*In his infinite love he became our security and our Mediator with his Father*" (TD 85, 87). And he chose "*the cross and sufferings*" in order to "*give humanity proof of greater love*" (LEW 164).

Eternal Wisdom, Jesus Christ, could have won the hearts of men and women "*by his attractiveness, his delights, his magnificence and his riches*"; "*untouched by poverty, dishonor, humiliations and weaknesses,*" he could easily have triumphed over evil (LEW 168). He chose not to do so. "Instead of the joy that was set before him, he endured the cross" (Heb 12:2). As God chose the Cross, it has ceased to be foolishness, shame, or a stumbling-block; rather, it has become Supreme Wisdom, condemning short-sighted human wisdom, the earthly wisdom of which St. James speaks, love for the things of this world (LEW 80); the wisdom of the flesh, the love of pleasure (LEW 81); and diabolical wisdom, the love and esteem of honors (LEW 82). Here we have a summary of Montfort's argument. And God does not change. Eternal Wisdom united himself indissolubly with the Cross in an eternal covenant. No other way can therefore lead to him: "*Never the cross without Jesus, or Jesus without the cross*" (LEW 172). "*True wisdom . . . has fixed his abode in the cross so firmly that you will not find him anywhere in this world save in the Cross. He has so truly incorporated himself and united himself with the Cross that in all truth we can say: Wisdom is the Cross and the Cross is Wisdom*" (LEW 180).

d. Mystery of suffering and glory. The indissoluble union of Jesus Christ Wisdom and the Cross is consummated at Calvary, when they surrender to each other in a supreme embrace as "*upon a couch of honor and triumph*" (LEW 170-171). Christ gave and surrendered himself to the Cross. It had, so to speak, every right over him: it was necessary that he should suffer these things to enter into his glory (cf. Lk 24:26). His being stripped of everything, his physical and mental sufferings, the presence of his mother at the foot of the Cross, his being forsaken by his Father, all these are so many torments for the man of sorrows par excellence (cf. LEW 155-162). Montfort's mention of the Resurrection itself is almost limited to statements explaining the first glorious mystery of the Rosary (MR 4, 13, 27). This should cause no surprise, since the Resurrection itself, in Montfort's time, was not given a distinct or thorough study even in the manuals of theology. Yet the saint does treat of the Easter Ressurection mystery but only together with the Cross. For Saint Louis Marie, Easter does not come "after" Good Friday; glory does not come "after" the Crucifixion. Rather, Good Friday is Easter, the Cross is glory, the ignominious death on Calvary is victory. Like the writers of his day, Montfort celebrates "*the triumph of Eternal Wisdom in and by the Cross*" (LEW ch. 14).

Father de Montfort would definitely be disturbed by those who separate the Cross and glory. He would find incomprehensible those who distort the truth that we are an "Easter people" to mean that the Cross is now to be left aside. For Louis de Montfort, victory is only the Cross of our Lord Jesus Christ. This triumph of the Cross is epitomized in Hymn 19, which praises the victories of the Cross over the devil, the world, and the flesh and over its visible and invisible enemies on earth and in heaven; the third section deals at length with its glory and merit. Montfort looks on the Cross as a victory trophy worthy of adoration (LEW 172). Wisdom "*will go before him, borne upon the most brilliant cloud that has ever been seen. And with this Cross and by it, he will judge the world*" (LEW 172).

In the meantime, the Cross is a rallying sign for the soldiers of Christ to run from victory to victory (LEW 173), for "Christ crucified . . . is the power of God and the wisdom of God" (1 Cor 1:23-24). Its triumph is not merely eschatological; it manifests itself in this world through inner joy, peace and Christlike gentleness.

2. The Cross in the life of Christians

a. Baptism and its obligations. "All of us who have been baptized into Christ Jesus were baptized into his death. Therefore we have been buried with him by baptism into death, so that, just as Christ was raised from the dead by the glory of the Father, so we too might walk in newness of life" (Rom 6:3-4).

When plunged into the baptismal water, symbol of the Spirit, sinners are buried in the death of Christ; they come out of it as new creatures (Col 2:12; 2 Cor 5:17). Logically invited to live as "a new creation" (Eph 2:15), Christians have to fight sin all their lives. The conflict between the "old nature" and the "new nature," "the flesh and the spirit" entails renunciation and suffering. So, Baptism, which "extends the paschal mystery to all believers,"[27] brings the Cross in its wake. "Always carrying in the body the death of Jesus, so that the life of Jesus may also be made visible in our bodies" (2 Cor 4:10).

Montfort was familiar with St. Paul's teaching on Baptism. He lays particular emphasis, however, on the grace of adoption as God's children granted to the baptized. By becoming man the Word united himself with our nature and, as it were, goes on uniting himself with each Christian, who is really incorporated into his Mystical Body. The stress shifts towards the mystery of the Incarnation: "*God the Son wishes to form himself, and, in a manner of speaking, become incarnate every day in his members*" (TD 31). The consequence stated here ties in with the one drawn by St. Paul. We are not our own but belong to Christ (1 Cor 6:19), "*entirely his as his members*" (TD 68), and, for this reason, sharing in his Cross in a special way. The baptized who refuse the Cross are Jesus' treacherous persecutors (FC 27), unless they are dead members no longer sharing in the life of God's children in Christ. In the last analysis, "Christians are nailed to the Cross with Christ as a result of their Baptism."[28] The baptismal promises express the resolve to follow him in his sufferings: *"I give myself entirely to Jesus Christ to carry my cross after him."* The baptized share in the mystical espousal of Incarnate Wisdom and the Cross. As they are made Jesus' spouses in Baptism (H 27:11), the closer their union with Christ, the deeper the Cross sinks into their hearts.

b. The Cross and the perfect consecration to Mary. As the perfect consecration to Jesus through the hands of Mary is "*the perfect renewal of the vows and promises of holy baptism*" (TD 126), those who make it agree to carry their Cross "*every day of their lives.*" As the consecration consists in "*giving oneself, consecrating oneself and sacrificing oneself willingly out of love,*" "*sacrificing the right to* *dispose of oneself*" (SM 29), it entails of necessity some inner wrenches.

In addition, fasting and mortification of body and mind are among the practices recommended to honor Mary, whose universal mortification it is fitting to imitate (TD 108). The perfect disciples of Jesus in Mary long to carry out the Father's will, as did Christ, whom they have resolved to imitate "*without seeing, without tasting and without faltering,*" though they may be troubled by "*doubts, by darkness of the mind, by weariness and boredom of the heart, by sadness and anguish of soul*" (LEW 187). In various ways they "*taste the bitterness of the chalice from which we must drink to become proven friends of God*" (SM 22). Furthermore, those who have discovered Mary through a genuine devotion are more than anyone else assailed by crosses and sufferings "*because Mary, as Mother of the living, gives to all her children splinters of the tree of life, which is the Cross of Jesus*" (SM 22). She also grants to "*her greatest favorites*" the "*best graces and favors from heaven*" (TD 154). "*While meting out crosses to them she gives the grace to bear them with patience and even with joy. In this way, the crosses she sends to those who trust themselves to her are rather like sweetmeats, i.e., 'sweetened' crosses rather than 'bitter ones'*" (SM 22). These hard-sounding but realistic words were inspired by Montfort's own spiritual experience and can be trusted.

c. The Cross as a way to Wisdom. The Cross is "not so much a subject for contemplation and sentimental outpourings as a mystery to be deepened and put into practice."[29] It is not enough just to proclaim that Wisdom is the Cross and the Cross is Wisdom. One must be a real disciple of the Master: "*It is only Jesus, through his all-powerful grace, who can teach you this mystery and give you the ability to appreciate it*" (FC 26). "*The one among you who knows best how to carry his cross, even though in other things he does not know A from B, is the most learned of all*" (FC 26). But "*the number of fools and unhappy people is infinite, says Wisdom, because infinite is the number of those who do not know the value of the cross and carry it reluctantly*" (LEW 179).

So we should "*pray for the wisdom of the cross, that knowledge of the truth which we experience within ourselves . . . ask for it continually and fervently, without wavering or fear of not obtaining it.*, and *it will be yours. Then you will clearly understand from your own experience how it is possible to desire, seek and find joy in the cross*" (FC 45).

To know the mystery of the Cross, one must be humble, of little account, mortified, spiritually minded. This knowledge is a grace so "*special*" that it is granted only to "*those who make themselves worthy [of it] by their great fidelity and their great labors*" (LEW 174). As for appreciation of this "*great gift,*" which is "*greater than the gift of faith,*" God "*bestows this only on his best friends and only after they have prayed for it, longed for it, pleaded for it*" (LEW 175). "*It is the portion and reward of those who desire or already possess Eternal Wisdom*" (LEW 103); it is the sign, the emblem, and the weapon of all those chosen by Wisdom (LEW 173). It makes fruitful the preaching of missionaries: "*I have never had more conversions than after the most painful and unjust prohibitions*" (L 26).

d. The Cross as a proof of love. In a letter to Mother St. Joseph, a Sister of the Blessed Sacrament, Montfort encouraged her with these words: "*You are having to bear a large weighty cross. But what a great happiness for you! Have confidence if God continues to make you suffer. . . . The cross is a sure sign that he loves you. I can assure you of this, that the greatest proof that we are loved by God is when we are despised by the world and burdened with crosses*" (L 13).

For sinners the Cross is a "*loving punishment,*" a "*light and temporary punishment accompanied by consolation and merit and followed by rewards both here and in eternity*" (FC 21). If God ceases to send us crosses, we have reason to fear that he may look on us "*as an outsider*" or "*as an illegitimate child*" with no claim to "*a share in the inheritance*" (FC 25).

Montfort draws attention to the tact and thoughtfulness of God when he sends us crosses, as they are "*in proportion to our strength*" (LEW 103). Each of us receives "*his own cross and not that of another, which I, in my wisdom, have designed for him in every detail of number, measure and weight . . . which, out of love for him, I have carved from a piece of the one I bore to Calvary*" (FC 18).

In return for this, the Christians who welcome the Cross and take it up find in it an opportunity to show their love for God because the Cross detaches us from creatures and attaches us to Jesus Christ. It fuels our love for him and challenges us to welcome in a childlike way the loving will of the Father (LEW 176).

e. Joy in carrying the Cross. Bérulle has written, "The grace peculiar to the Incarnation is a grace of renunciation and suffering." He adds, "The characteristic feature of the spirit and love of Jesus is that he crucifies the souls dearest to him."[30] As Christ has accepted his condition as a man of sorrows, which was inescapable after his Incarnation, so through Baptism Christians agree to walk along the way of the Cross. They must be prepared to wage war on Satan and the world insofar as they take seriously, and resolve to live out, their baptismal commitment by consecrating themselves to Mary (TD 50, 54; PM 18). Their renunciation of the world will earn them contempt, humiliations, slander, and abandonment (FC 18). They must also "*detach their heart from material things, and possess them as though not possessing them . . . without complaining or worrying when they are lost. This is something very difficult to accomplish*" (LEW 197). In addition to this, Christ makes Christians share his own Cross in a variety of ways through sufferings, illnesses, spiritual trials, dryness, misunderstanding on the part of relatives and friends, hidden sufferings that no one else can ease (Cf. FC 18).

They have to *"deny themselves,"* that is, renounce their selfishness, strip themselves of the *"old nature,"* crush and melt it down (TD 221) by dying to themselves every day (TD 81) and courageously practicing "*total and continuous mortification*" (LEW 196). They must "*mortify the body, not only by enduring patiently their bodily ailments, the inconveniences of the weather and the difficulties arising from other people's actions, but also by deliberately undertaking some penances and mortifications such as fasts, vigils and other austerities"* (LEW 201).To deny oneself means first of all to renounce self-love, to avoid, with equal care, boasting about the crosses one has to bear (FC 48) and lamenting one's temptations or faults (FC 46).

When carried in the right way, the Cross brings joy to the soul. Words seem to fail Montfort when he describes the joy that he knew so well. "*Imagine the greatest joy that can be experienced on earth,"* he writes, *"the joy of a poor man who suddenly comes into a fortune, or of a peasant who is raised to the throne, or of a trader who becomes a millionaire, or of a military leader over the victories he has won, or of prisoners released from their chains"*—all these joys pale by comparison. "*The happiness of the one who bears his sufferings in the right way contains and even surpasses all of them"* (FC 34). The Cross means "Paradise on earth" for the simple reason that "through it we are united with God alone who is the center of our life and our end."[31]

And who can describe the heavenly glory that Christians win when, after death, their short-lived suffering is turned into "*a weight of everlasting glory"* (LEW 176)? "*Who can understand the glory gained in heaven by a year, and sometimes a whole lifetime, of crosses and suffering"* (FC 39)? "*You are indeed blessed when the world opposes you"* (MLW 9).

3. Understanding Montfort's teaching

a. Christian logic. At first sight, Montfort's way of acting and his teaching concerning the Cross appear to some to lack common sense. He regularly wore a hair shirt and whipped himself with the discipline, deprived himself of sleep and kept vigil beside the dead.[32] He feared that the mission at Vertou was going badly since everyone was praising it, and exclaimed, *"No cross what a cross!"* A few months before his death, he wished the Daughters of Wisdom *"a year full of struggles, victories, crosses, poverty and contempt"* (L 32). Without denying that Montfort thought little of unredeemed human nature, we have to look elsewhere to discover his underlying motivation for these actions and words.

His only references were *"God alone,"* Jesus Christ eternal and crucified Wisdom, and the Gospel. Through a spiritual insight and by grace, he came to realize that to save humanity, God Himself chose the way of suffering and death on the Cross. As a baptized person and a missionary, he owed it to himself to walk the same way. Walking in the steps of Christ involves choosing a way of life in opposition to that of the world. Fighting worldly wisdom brings sufferings, which are a source of life and guarantee fruitfulness. To follow Jesus Christ, one must also ruthlessly renounce oneself and sin. Montfort invites the "friends" of Jesus Christ to understand how necessary that renunciation is and to practice it uncompromisingly. And then, because he has experienced its sweetness when he was most abandoned, he can promise that they, too, will experience spiritual joy, the joy of the Beatitudes, which is a fruit of the Holy Spirit. It is only a short step from experiencing the joy generated by the Cross to wishing that others may share it, and Montfort took this step blithely. He was convinced that the victory of the Cross can only be assured at the end of the way of the Cross.

b. Wisdom or folly? Some of Montfort's statements or compressed turns of phrase, especially when he speaks of the Cross, may lead to false interpretations of his teaching. For example, in LEW ch. 14 he says, "*Wisdom takes his delight in it; he cherishes it more than all that is great and resplendent in heaven and on earth*" (LEW 168); "*Throughout his life he eagerly sought after the cross*" (LEW 170); the Cross is "*a delightful morsel of paradise*" (LEW 177); "*Wisdom is the Cross and the Cross is Wisdom*" (LEW 180). If these bald expressions are taken literally or removed from their context, they may lead us to believe that God is perverse and delights in human suffering. The language becomes clearer if we look on the Cross as the manifestation of the love of God for humankind and of his friendship with it. (cf. LEW ch. 6) "*The bond of friendship between Eternal Wisdom and humankind is so close as to be beyond our understanding.*" It is "*out of excess of love*" that "*he delivered himself up to death to save humankind*" (LEW 64), "*to draw closer to humankind,*" "*to give them a more convincing proof of his love*" (LEW 70; cf. LEW 71, 72). In another context, Montfort quotes Rom 5:8-9: "*Jesus Christ proved how well he loved us because though we were sinners—and consequently his enemies—he died for us*" (LEW 156). "*Such an excess of love is shown to us in this mystery*" of his suffering (LEW 155). God has compassion on humankind in their misery after the Fall. If there is any "excess" it is to be found on God's side first.

This does not, however, solve the mystery of the Cross or suffering. It becomes even deeper after God has chosen to suffer. For suffering is an evil that confronts humanity, and philosophers and religions have vainly tried to find an explanation for it, even though none exists; when faced with it, the only attitude worthy of a human being is to revolt against it in order to identify it, and to struggle to reduce or eradicate it; in this way, freedom will still give a meaning to life.

Evil and suffering are not willed by God, since he created humanity for happiness. But when confronted with evil, God chose to cast his lot with suffering humanity. This ultimate sharing made a separation that enabled humankind to "hope against hope" (Rom 4:18). On the Cross, God, in His apparent powerlessness, became credible by making Himself humankind's Good Samaritan and taking all suffering upon Himself (Is 53:4; cf. Is 53:3, 10). From then on nothing was able to separate humankind from the love of God manifested in Jesus crucified.

"*Never the cross without Jesus or Jesus without the cross*" (LEW 172) expresses this solidarity beautifully. Because in Jesus Christ God has thrown in His lot with all men and women who suffer and carry the Cross, He makes them able to face up to suffering, humanizes their lives even in the depths of distress, and therefore keeps the future open till the end of their existence on earth.

God did not spare His own Son but gave him up for us all (cf. Rom 8:32, 39; Jn 3:16) to reconcile the world to Himself (cf. 2 Cor 5:18-19): "It is [therefore] through Christ, and in Christ, that light is thrown on the riddle of suffering and death which, apart from his Gospel, overwhelms us" (GS 22). Jesus Christ proposes to his followers a new art of living, which is Wisdom in the eyes of God.

In his language and his way of acting, is not Montfort like those men who were "fools for God's sake"[33] and whose hearts were set on Jesus crucified, "fools for the sake of Christ" (1 Cor 4:10)? Like Ignatius Loyola and Francis of Assisi, John of the Cross and Teresa of Lisieux and many more, he made an unequivocal choice: to suffer and be despised for Christ's sake, to esteem nothing but the Cross, to ask for it earnestly (cf. LEW 177), to carry it from day to day. He was indeed an eccentric by worldly standards, but above all he was Christ-centered as a result of his continual self-denial: "It is no longer I who live, but Christ who lives in me" (Gal 2:20). "The saints understand the Cross. Following the example of God made man, they welcome their daily Cross as their most valuable possession. They love it throughout their life. . . . The Cross is the indispensable instrument with which the divine breaks into the human."[34]

VI. The Cross Today

1. Paschal perspective

The theology of the Cross of Christ and the place it holds in Christian living developed gradually through the apostolic period, during the first five centuries of the Christian era, in the Middle Ages, and in the post-Tridentine period. Devotion to the Passion of Christ, in religious orders and among lay people, has correspondingly taken various forms throughout the history of the Church. Its influence on the life of the Church was particularly noticeable during the late Middle Ages and after the Council of Trent; these periods were marked by such types of devotion as the stations of the Cross, the sorrowful mysteries of the Rosary, and popular preaching, which continued till the mid-twentieth century.[35] In the second part of the twentieth century, Christian spirituality, especially in the West, has tended to stress, instead, the Resurrection. But although the Easter alleluia is the triumphant cry hailing the victory of life over the death and suffering that took place on Good Friday, suffering and death are nonetheless present and necessary in the actual order of redemption. Death and resurrection are mutually inclusive, like the two aspects of the same mystery: the paschal mystery. To present one without the other, to emphasize one at the expense of the other, is very harmful to theology and spirituality alike.

Through Baptism Christians are reborn spiritually; they become children of God by being incorporated into Christ and his paschal mystery (LG 7; SC 6; AA 3; AG 14, 24, etc.).

It follows that they are to walk the path that the Son walked during his earthly life, the path of the Cross, which leads "to the glory of the Resurrection." No other course is open to them: without prejudice to the perspective of the new creation (Gal 6:15; LG 7), St. Paul's teaching (1 Cor 3:18-19; Gal 2:19; 6:11-14) is neither outdated nor obsolete.

Vatican II draws attention to the place held by the Cross in the paschal mystery; it speaks of the Church as flowing from the open side of Christ (LG 3; SL 5), as having the duty to proclaim the Cross of Christ as the sign of God's universal love and the source of all grace (NA 4), as the people of God following the narrow way of the Cross to follow Christ (LG 41; GS 38); it speaks of Mary united with her Son unto the Cross (LG 58), of missionaries not being ashamed of the scandal of the Cross (AG 24) but carrying out their apostolic work, which makes them resemble the suffering Christ (AA 16), of religious inspired by their love for the Cross (PC 25), etc.

The mystery of the Cross and Resurrection of Christ is a mystery of love (GS 52) and of liberation (GS 52; DH 11); it offers grace and life to the Church and humankind (SL 61); it brings every human activity to perfection (GS 38). It remains, however, an unfathomable mystery, because it is a mystery of excess: "the excess of divine love calls for an excess of foolish love in return."[36]

2. The language of the Cross

The image of the Cross of Christ in its traditional forms can still be seen everywhere. In some countries it can be seen at crossroads. The crucifix always occupies pride of place in churches and during sacramental celebrations. But those used to seeing it do not linger on the sight. Making the sign of the Cross has lost much of its evocative power. The Good Friday liturgy, though preceded by Lent, does not have a lasting impact on the life of the faithful. With the weakening of faith and the growth of religious indifference, the message of the Cross has lost some of its strength among the people of God.

On the other hand, concern for the poor, struggling against social inequalities, denouncing injustice, and solidarity with the oppressed and deprived in the Third and Fourth Worlds arouse growing interest. Is not devotion to the Cross being superseded by a commitment to helping suffering humankind, with whom Christ identified himself? "I was hungry, naked, in prison, a stranger, etc." (Mt 25:44-45). In preaching resignation, it is important that injustice not be simultaneously supported. The impact attached to the language of the Cross depends on who speaks it and who hears it. It is necessary to encourage the mysticism of the Cross as well as struggle against evil.[37] Insofar as the Church, through her teaching and the witness given by the faithful, deliberately sides with the poor—see the messages of Pope John Paul II during his apostolic journeys, the many men and women religious killed for defending the rights of the oppressed—she restores strength to the message of the Cross for herself and the world. The kind of devotion to the Cross that turns Christians in on themselves can only be deficient or false. On the other hand, the contemplation of Christ crucified, which opens us to human distress and leads us to commit ourselves politically or socially to witnessing to the presence of Christ, Savior and Liberator, amid the suffering, restores its essential meaning to the Cross of Christ.

For in itself the Cross is an unbearable burden. How many Christians confronted with trials or sufferings lay the blame at God's door: how can he be the "Father Almighty" and allow so many sorrows and atrocities to take place? When the Cross is too heavy, only the presence of a loving person—often silent but compassionate (in the literal sense of the word)—can help those who suffer to cope with their existence, purify their ideas of God, detach themselves from the inessential and cling to the essential, become hopeful again, and persevere in faith. The believers' cry uttered from the depth of their intolerable suffering echoes Christ's cry on the Cross and becomes a cry of love and an offering for the salvation of humankind.

3. The Cross of the disciple

Together with the Word of God, which explains its meaning, the paschal mystery is the light of the baptized on their journey through life. To accept ourselves as God's gift, with all one's strengths and weaknesses, and to live in dependence on our Creator in obedience and faith is no easy task. The struggle between the ever-present "old nature" and the "new nature" is never-ending; vigilance and asceticism are indispensable to foster the latter and curb the former. Unless one has a special vocation, to be discerned with the help of the Church, there is no need to seek extraordinary crosses. But humility, personal discipline in organizing one's time, and restriction in the possession and use of material goods are always necessary. Daily prayer, which is both effort and gift, and the reception of the Sacraments are permanent requirements. The trials we experience in our personal, family, and social life are unavoidable at every stage in life and challenge us to make choices and to steer the course of our life so that we may follow Christ more closely. A feeling of getting old, weak, dependent, and more or less neglected by those who are well and active is frequently the ultimate purification that a Christian is called upon to accept in love.

It is no small Cross to accept all others as they are, as mutual love between Christians means to be ready to lay down one's life for each other; Christians should, however, accept the Cross Christ offers to the members of a Church whose "law is a new commandment, that we love one another as Christ has loved us" (cf. Jn 13:34; LG 9).

All who wish to conform their life to the Gospel have to accept wholeheartedly even its harshest maxims (Mk 14:33; Jn 12:27; Lk 6:21). No real disciple is exempt from living the "now" of suffering and trial and experiencing the depths of abandonment. All of Christ's followers have to take Christ's words very seriously, "If any want to become my followers" (Lk 9:23) and "Follow me!" (Jn 21:19,22), and resist the temptation to take an easier way. Mary, the first disciple, had her soul pierced by a sword (Lk 2:35). Jesus allowed her to experience sorrow to the end, unto the foot of the Cross, where she watched her loved one die.

All who take the Gospel seriously go against the tide of the world and lay themselves open to mockery, abandonment even on the part of those near and dear to them (Lk 12:51-53), to misunderstanding, and persecution. Reflecting God's life in one's own existence usually involves the Cross.[38] But the baptized know that they do not have to fight single-handed. They advance "as followers of Christ," behind him and therefore with him, along the way already opened by the power of the Father: the way of the Cross and death leading to life. Christ's followers devote all their energy to eternal life, which is "already here"; they sustain and help it to grow with the Word of God and the Eucharist; they fortify it daily by their persistent efforts to accept their crosses and offer them in union with that of their Master. "When you suffer, hide your sorrow in that of Christ. Celebrate your Mass. If people watch you in bafflement, do not be troubled. Jesus, Mary, and the saints understand you. That is sufficient."[39]

4. Relevance of the mysticism of the Cross today

All the members of the Church are called to holiness (1 Thess 4:3; cf. Eph 1:4), whatever their walk of life and their functions. Under the guidance of the Spirit and in obedience to the Father, they follow Christ, poor, humble and Cross-bearing, that they may deserve to be partakers of his glory (cf. LG 39, 41). The larger the place held by Christ in their heart and in their life, the more clearly their holiness is visible. Examples of holiness abound in the history of the Church. Montfort is one of them. He experienced and desired the Cross. He appreciated its sweetness and praised its fruitfulness. The special charism of some founders has been to highlight one particular aspect of the Passion of Christ. Through their followers, they continue to remind other Christians of the reality of the suffering of Christ, which saved the world.

Some founders of well-known Church movements or Congregations speak in similar terms. "If I am the spouse of Jesus crucified, he has to embrace me. If I am one with Jesus, I too must suffer in order to share his suffering."[40] "I have one Spouse on earth, Jesus who was abandoned. I have no other God but him. In him is the whole of Paradise with the Trinity, and the whole of earth with humanity. Whatever is his is mine, and I do not want anything else. His is universal suffering. I will travel the world in search of him every moment of my life. Let me have all that is not joy, peace, beauty, serenity . . . whatever is not Paradise, because I find Paradise in the Heart of my Spouse. . . . Being united with my all-powerful Spouse, I will dry the tears of those who are suffering."[41]

J. Bulteau

Notes: (1) Blain, 34. (2) Stefano De Fiores, *La sapienza della croce nell'itinerario spirituale di san Luigi di Montfort,* in *Atti del congresso internazionale sulla Sapienza della Croce (Wisdom of the Cross in the Spiritual Itinerary of Saint Louis de Montfort in Acts of the International Congress of the Wisdom of the Cross) (Roma 1975),* LDC, Leumann 1976, 2:360-371. In the first section of this article we will keep close to what this writer says. (3) Blain, 58, 73. (4) Besnard I, 225. (5) Besnard I, 42. (6) Besnard I, 43. (7) cf. Besnard I, 102, Besnard II, 160. (8) Besnard I, 146-147. (9) Besnard II, 55-56. (10) Besnard I, 323. (11) Grandet, 402. (12) Besnard I, 147. (13) Besnard I, 147-148. (14) Besnard, I, 185-187. (15) Besnard I, 254. (16) Besnard I, 188-193. (17) Besnard II, 195. (18) Grandet, 401-402. (19) Besnard II, 22. (20) Grandet, 402. (21) cf. B. M. Ahern, *Croix,* in *Dictionnaire de la vie spirituelle (Cross in the Dictionary of the Sprirtual Life),* Cerf, Paris 1983, 236. It is probable that Jesus' saying on the necessity of carrying the Cross (Mk 8:34; Mt 10:38; 16:24; Lk 9:23; 14:27) does not refer to Jesus' Cross on Calvary but to the "yoke" mentioned by Jesus (Mt 11:29), or to all the sacrifices required of all who want to follow Christ, unless the saying refers merely to the Jewish custom of marking or anointing a person with a cross (+ or x, in the shape of the ancient letter tau). The saying might therefore have meant originally: "None of those who do not make the sign + (i.e., do not repent and dedicate themselves to God) can be my disciple." (22) Here Montfort uses the word "mystery" in the sense given to it in the seventeenth century: after St. Thomas, Bérulle refers here to the events in the life of Christ and Mary by which Jesus fulfils his mission as Savior and carries out God's plan or mystery in the Pauline sense (Eph 3:3) (23) Bellarmin, *In gemitu colombae (In the sign of the Dove)* III, 3, 153. (24) *Oeuvres complètes du Cardinal de Bérulle (CompleteWorks of Cardinal de Bérulle)* 1644, reprint Montsoult 1960, 754. (25) Letter 178, in *Lettres spirituelles de Mr. Olier, (Spiritual Letters of Fr. Olier),* Paris 1672, 436. (26) Boudon, *Les Saintes voies de la Croix (The Holy Ways of the Cross),* Paris 1769, 47. First approbation was dated April 12 and August 11, 1671. Comparison can be made between book IV, ch. 7 and FC 18, between book I, ch. 6 and FC 25, and between book IV, ch. 6 and FC 60. (27) F.X. Durrwell, *La résurrection de Jésus Mystère de salut,* Le Puy 1954, 369; F.X. Durrwell, The Resurrection, A Biblical Study, trans. Rosemary Sheed (New York; Sheed and Ward, 1960) (28) St. Thomas, *Contra Gentiles* IV, 71. Olier, *Lettres spirituelles,* writes, "The Cross of Jesus is the character and the seal of his covenant with the soul" (37), and "I would not be able to express the great desire I had that my whole life be spent on the Cross and, as St. Cyril of Jerusalem said, that I might be covered with crosses from head to foot, as required by baptism" (186). (29) J.A. Bizet, *Saint Louis Marie de Montfort et l'Ecole dominicaine du XIVème siècle,* in *Supplément de la vie spirituelle* 9 *(St. Louis de Montfort and the Dominican School of the XIV Century* in *Supplement of the Spiritual Life* 9*)* (1949), 60-67. (30) Bérulle, op. cit. 755 and 599. (31) Boudon, *Oeuvres complètes,* 66. (32) Blain, 24. (33) S. Breton, *Le Verbe et la Croix (The Word and the Cross)* Desclée, Paris 1981, 52-75. (34) C. Lubich, *Méditations,* Nouvelle Cité, Paris 1977, 101. The entry in her diary for September 20, 1964, reads, "Saint Louis Marie de Montfort has made me understand the central value of the Cross," *Diario 1964-1965,* Città Nuova, Rome 1967, 150. Chiara Lubich, Meditations (New York; New City Press, 1974) (35) B.M. Ahern, *Croix,* 232-235. (36) S. Breton, *Le Verbe et la Croix,* 62. (37) J. Moltmann, *Le Dieu crucifié,* Cerf-Mame, Paris 1974, 62-64. J. Moltmann, The Crucified God, The Cross of Christ as the Foundation and Criticism of Christian Theology, trans. R.A. Wilson and J. Bowden (New York; Harper and Row, 1974) (38) cf. M. Gourgues, *Le Crucifié (The Crucified One),* Bellarmin-Desclée, Montreal-Paris 1989, 164. According to M. Gourgues, this is the primary sense of the word "Cross" in the Gospel and the word refers to "the trials, separations, renunciations or wrenches involved when opting for faith or following Jesus Christ, receiving or spreading the Gospel." (39) C. Lubich, *Méditations,* 105. (40) Mother Teresa, *Par la parole et l'exemple (By Word and Example),* Nouvelle Cité, Paris 1990, 124. (41) C. Lubich, *Méditations,* 95.

DAUGHTERS OF WISDOM

SUMMARY

I. FOUNDATION:
   1. The project;
   2. The foundation;
   3. The long wait;
   4. La Rochelle;
   5. Marie Louise cofoundress.

II. TWO CENTURIES OF HISTORY:
   1. The reign of the Terror;
   2. The renewal;
   3. Antireligious laws;
   4. Changes;
   5. Internationalization;
   6. Contemporary evolution.

III. SPIRITUALITY.
   1. Evolution from birth of the Congregation to current times:
      a. From the birth of the congregation to the French Revolution,
      b. From the French Revolution to the beatification of Montfort (1789-1888): to Jesus through Mary,
      c. From the beatification to the canonization of Montfort (1888-1947): Consecration to Jesus Wisdom through Mary, an essential element of Wisdom spirituality,
      d. From the canonization of Montfort to post-Vatican II (1947-): apostolic religious life following Christ Wisdom.

I. FOUNDATION

The spirituality of Saint Louis de Montfort is expressed through the Congregations he founded. His teachings, especially on Jesus Wisdom and the Cross, is evident in the first order he established, the Daughters of Wisdom.

1. The project

"Daughters of Wisdom" is the name chosen by Saint Louis de Montfort for his religious Congregation of women. He had, we are told, been strongly drawn to "Daughters of Providence," reflecting his deep devotion to divine Providence. "Daughters of Wisdom," however, expressed his fundamental devotion to the Eternal and Incarnate Wisdom, and so we find in the original manuscript "Daughters of Providence" seven times erased and replaced by "Daughters of Wisdom" (RW 1).

The name "Daughters of Wisdom" (who in some English-speaking countries also called the Montfort Sisters or the Sisters of La Sagesse, and the congregation itself, La Sagesse) sums up Montfort's project as described by his first biographer, Grandet: "He planned to found a Congregation of women who, dedicated to Divine Wisdom the Incarnate Word and living according to his sayings, would be a counterwitness to the false wisdom of the world."[1] The project revealed also the spirituality that permeated his whole life and that he wished to communicate to his disciples. He did not, even as a seminarian, allow the charge of being singular deter him from living his radical interpretation of the Gospel. We find him years later, one year before his death, reproached by his friend Jean-Baptiste Blain for the singularity which had been for him a lifelong source of contradiction and humiliation. His response was unequivocal: *"One is easily and quickly classed as singular when one fails to follow the crowd or conform to its style of life, but if wisdom consists of refraining from undertaking work for God or his glory for fear of offending people, then the apostles should never have left Jerusalem, they should have remained shut up in the Cenacle, Saint Paul should never have undertaken his journeys, or Saint Peter attempted to raise the cross in the Capitol."*[2] Such was the wisdom Montfort proposed for those who preach the gospel. They must always live in opposition to the false wisdom and materialism of the age. It may be said he set his Daughters of Wisdom on the same path. It is essentially by fully living the *folly of the gospel* that the members of the community would be clear witnesses *in the world* to the Good News of Jesus Christ.

2. The foundation

In 1701 Montfort, twenty-eight years of age and ordained one year, arrived at Poitiers and entered the General Hospital which housed not only the sick but the homeless, the poor, derelicts and also some common criminals. Accustomed as he was to working with the poor, he was nevertheless profoundly shocked on finding an establishment where chaos reigned together with extreme poverty. Friend of the outcasts, he immediately set to work to better their lot by improved economic management and administrative organization. He introduced a plan of reform which, while improving the lot of the inmates, served only to expose the negligence and inefficiency of the administration, leading inevitably to the prompt dismissal of a chaplain who was far too zealous.

The reformer grasped the fact that the condition of the poor would never improve unless he could form personnel consecrated to their service. He composed a Rule of Life for the nurses; this, too, was refused. Montfort then turned to the inmates themselves: a small group of women, abandoned, physically handicapped, but spiritually endowed with a richness consisting of deep piety and true humility. He gathered them together in a room of the hospital and taught them meditation, self-renunciation, and Consecration to Jesus through Mary. A large cross hanging upon the wall at one end of the room bore the symbol of his teaching. On the door of the room was inscribed "Wisdom." The little group became the nucleus of the Congregation that would bear its name, and the rules they observed bore a strong resemblance to the Rule he presented to the first Daughters of Wisdom in 1715. RW is the realization of Montfort's own spiritual way, found in his early book and foundational work, LEW: contempt of riches, love of the poor, love of the Cross, Consecration to Jesus Incarnate Wisdom through Mary.

The small Wisdom group lasted only for a few months, from November 1702 to March 1703. Montfort had, however, found his future collaborator, who would become the cofoundress of the Congregation of which he dreamed: a young girl, Marie Louise Trichet. The initial encounter was truly providential. Marie Louise Trichet was seventeen years of age of a respected middle-class family of Poitiers. She was gentle, pious, and searching for her vocation. Drawn by the reputation for sanctity Montfort had acquired, she sought his advice in the confessional. *"Who sent you to me?"* Montfort asked. "My sister" was the reply. *"No, it was not your sister but the Blessed Virgin."* In a prophetic intuition, Montfort recognized in the young girl before him the one destined by Providence to be his helper in the realization of his great design.

Recognizing his holiness, Marie Louise chose him as her spiritual director. She participated in a retreat preached by Montfort at the hospital during Pentecost, 1702. Intent as she was in searching for her vocation, she pleaded for his help to enter a convent. His reply both upset and disturbed her: *"Come and live in the hospital."* His answer seemed ridiculous. The hospital was not a convent. Nonetheless, it was for the service of the poor, and living there would demand a thorough break with the values of the world. She took his proposal to the bishop. The reply was decisive: "There is no vacancy." The bishop was referring to an opening for a governess, the only post that would be considered fitting for a person of her social standing. Her reply was, "If they will not permit me to enter as a governess, perhaps they will accept me as an inmate." The incredible happened: the young lady, of simple but distinguished education, went to live at the hospital, not simply at the service of the poor but sharing their lot, eating the same coarse food, performing the same menial tasks, caring for the sick, cleaning the rooms, washing the linen, all in rather primitive conditions of hygiene. This was her novitiate. Several months passed until one day Montfort announced to her, *"I believe the time has come to give you a religious habit."* On February 2, 1703 - the foundation day of the Congregation - she was called to the chapel. The Father from Montfort blessed, and she received from his hand, the habit that would signify her separation from the world and her Consecration to God. Mademoiselle Trichet became Marie Louise of Jesus, and the habit she wore would from that day on be the garb, its form unchanged, of thousands of Daughters of Wisdom who would follow in her footsteps.

3. The long wait

The reforms introduced by Montfort won him the affection of the inmates but did nothing to endear him to the staff. It had become necessary to disband the little Wisdom group, which had aroused jealousy and recrimination. Reports of the situation reached the bishop and Montfort found himself obliged to leave Poitiers.

Marie Louise remained at the hospital, with no indication whether or when Montfort would return. He had already told her, *"Do not leave here before ten years. Even though it should take that length of time for the establishment of the Daughters of Wisdom, God will be pleased and his plans realized."* The young novice was not yet twenty-one years old. Alone in the licentious environment of the hospital, a governess without mandate, a religious without a rule, she would live a long and painful vigil.

The years passed. Montfort continued his missionary labors from town to town and village to village while his spiritual protegé heroically awaited the realization of her dream. In 1713 Montfort finally arrived at Poitiers, exhausted from his missionary labors. Not welcome at the hospital, he nevertheless succeeded in meeting Sister Marie Louise. After their long conversation, he decided to give her a companion, one she herself had discerned among the residents: Catherine Brunet, a governess already working with the poor in the hospital. A habit, identical to that of Marie Louise, was prepared and solemnly given to Catherine. She received the name Sister of the Conception and was to become for the young foundress an affectionate companion and firm support.[3]

4. La Rochelle

Bishop de Champflour of La Rochelle, finding his diocese woefully short of schools for the poor, approached Father de Montfort, whose missionary zeal had impressed him. A letter, characteristically brief and to the point, was soon written to his Daughters. Anticipating their reaction and hesitation, he wrote, *"I know you are doing a great deal of good where you are, but you will do infinitely more away from home and we know that since the time of Abraham right up to the time of our Lord and even to our own day, God sends his greatest servants out of their own country"* (L 27). The letter represents Montfort's constant challenge to the community to be totally detached, always ready to move on.

Poitiers was the birthplace of the Congregation. La Rochelle would see it take its first steps and acquire its future image. Montfort wanted his Daughters *in the world,* ready to answer the needs of the Church wherever they might arise. He directed them in the dual direction of charitable work and mission: *"Take the title 'Daughters of Wisdom' for the instruction of children and care of the poor"* (L 29).

La Rochelle saw the addition of two novices, Marie Valleau and Marie Régnier. The four pronounced their vows of religion in the chapel of the Sisters of Providence on August 22, 1715. They were soon joined by a fifth. The little community benefited for a short time of the presence of their founder, who had withdrawn to the Hermitage St. Eloi close by. Here he put the finishing touches to RW, to which he added the maxims or counsels of a saint:

> *Deprive yourself readily of something that others will not do without showing outwardly no regret at what you have done (*RW 41).
>
> *Do not deliberately think of the morrow...* (RW 28)
>
> *abandon themselves to the care of divine Providence* (RW 29).
>
> *when in doubt of the truth or goodness of a cause do not say, "What do people think?," or "What do they say of such and such a thing?" but "What does faith teach me? What does Jesus Christ say?"* (RW 95)
>
> *nourish your soul as much as possible on pure faith... do all your work in the presence of God and for Him alone...* (RW 136-138)

The same spiritual counsels were repeated throughout his correspondence with Marie Louise when, after his brief stay at La Rochelle, he returned once more to his missions. His last letter, in March 1716, speaks of the difficulties the congregation must face. His response: *"If you are a disciple at the school of divine Wisdom, you should rejoice to suffer the abandonment and contempt and alleged captivity, for these are the riches with which you will acquire divine Wisdom and the riches of the divinity of the Sacred Heart of Jesus. I expect far greater trials and obstacles which will put our faith and trust to the test. The congregation of the Daughters of Wisdom will not be founded on shifting sand or on silver or gold or by the work of human hands, but on the wisdom of Calvary"* (L 34). Words of a saint and his last testament. Twelve days later, while preaching a parish mission at the village of St. Laurent-sur-Sèvre, he was struck down by an illness that proved fatal. He died on April 28, 1716, and was buried in the parish church.

5. Marie Louise cofoundress

To Marie Louise, thirty-two years old, fell the responsibility of the foundation. Her first concern was to organize and consolidate the work begun. Another house and novitiate were essential. Providence would lead her, after much searching, to the village of St. Laurent-sur-Sèvre, near the tomb of the founder. She encountered complete misunderstanding from the parish priest. The latter, in welcoming the Sisters to his extremely poor parish, expected not only assistance with religious instruction of the children but financial assistance for his poor. In dire circumstances themselves, the Sisters were in no position to oblige. The situation was exacerbated when Marie Louise resolutely set about organizing her community along strictly conventional lines. All the parish priest had envisaged was a group of good ladies who would help out with the immediate needs of the parish; her long-term concern was to assure the future of the Congregation. Relations remained strained until mutual respect and the extreme charity of Marie Louise led to complete accord. Meanwhile, the motherhouse and novitiate developed; drawn by the extreme poverty and fervor of the beginnings, novices began to arrive, and the number of professed Sisters increased.

On leaving La Rochelle in 1719, Mother Marie Louise left behind two Sisters: Marie Valleau (Sister of the Incarnation) and Marie Régnier (Sister of the Cross), with the understanding that they should join the Sisters at Poitiers as soon as possible. Through a combination of circumstances, however, the separation came close to creating a schism. Ill-advised by successive directors and, doubtless, under pressure from their families (the two Sisters were from La Rochelle), they had exchanged their gray habit of the Daughters of Wisdom for a black dress complete with religious insignia and joined the Confraternity of the Cross, founded by Montfort himself during his stay at La Rochelle. Taking the name Daughters of the Cross, they were joined by other young ladies and continued to observe the rule of the Daughters of Wisdom. In 1724 they were six, known as the "Bourginettes," after Abbé Bourgine, their director and the administrator of Saint Louis Hospital. The question arose of naming governors for the hospital, and after consultation with Sister of the Incarnation, the deal was almost settled when news reached Marie Louise at Saint-Laurent. Deciding the time had come to put an end to an ambiguous situation, she left immediately for La Rochelle. The strong spiritual bond and mutual affection that still existed, coupled with the gentle persuasion of Marie Louise, effected a reconciliation and restored the unity of the congregation. Unity would remain a major concern of the foundress all her life. A recommendation in her last will and testament was to assure its continuance after her death.[4]

II. Two Centuries of History

1. The reign of the Terror

The Congregation continued to develop throughout the second half of the eighteenth century. The eve of the Revolution found it with 335 Sisters in seventy-five communities. The Civil Laws passed by the National Assembly in 1790, the Civil Constitution of the Clergy, and the obligation of the oath of allegiance, imposed first on teachers and later on medical personnel, led to the expulsion from their convents of religious who refused to conform and with the confiscation of their properties. The subsequent Law of 1792 abolished all religious Congregations in France. Cited in the decree were the Mulotins—as the Montfort Missionaries, headed by Father Mulot, the first successor of Saint Louis de Montfort, were then known—and the Daughters of Wisdom, who had resolutely refused to take the oath, which had been condemned by the Pope.[5] Several were arrested, thrown into prison, murdered, placed in the stocks, or massacred in their convents or on the roads. Others were deported or condemned to the guillotine. At the height of the Terror, the motherhouse at Saint-Laurent was ransacked, plundered, and finally set on fire by government troops. Thirty-three Sisters residing there were carried off to prison; four were guillotined; ten murdered; nineteen were left languishing in the prisons of the Revolution to die eventually of illness and exhaustion. "Lose everything rather than lose your faith" was the first directive of Father Micquignon, superior general, a directive reiterated by his successor, Father Supiot, whose own life was in constant danger as he traversed Vendée, exercising a clandestine ministry. The Sisters, faithful to the spirit of the founder, persevered throughout all the terrible events. Sister Ave, her hands immobilized in the stocks, continued to recite her Rosary. Sisters Solomon and Paul would mount the steps of the scaffold singing Montfort's hymn to Mary: *"I place my confidence, O Blessed Mother, in your help."*

2. The renewal

The Revolution over, the Sisters returned gradually to the establishments from which they had been banished. In 1800 they resumed the religious habit, and in 1802 they agreed to the Concordat.[6] The Congregation flourished, especially through the leadership of Father Gabriel Deshayes, general of the Montfort Missionaries and the Daughters of Wisdom. The success in the apostolates and the increase in the number of their establishments occasioned constant exhortations from the generalate recalling their commitment to poverty and humility. Teachers were warned of the dangers of triumphalism, ambition, and materialism. "Leave the honors and acclaim to others - for us obscurity and the last place, as recommended by our holy founder."

3. Antireligious laws

In the wake of the antireligious laws in France at the end of the nineteenth century and the beginning of the twentieth century, the Daughters of Wisdom found themselves expelled from 250 schools and institutions. One way of circumventing the law was laicization. This meant abandoning the religious habit and community life and severing links with the motherhouse. Many Congregations would opt for it. The Daughters of Wisdom did not. Several reasons were advanced, mainly spiritual. The exchange of the religious habit for secular garb, abandonment of community life, and breaking of links to the mother house would, in the opinion of the congregation, have disastrous consequences for the observance of the vows and the prayer life of the Sisters and for the very existence of the Daughters of Wisdom. Secularization was refused by the Chapter of 1903. The consequences of the decision were clearly perceived and accepted: the expulsion of thousands of Sisters, departure for foreign lands, change of work, financial difficulties. Yet it opened the Congregation to broader horizons. Forced departure would lead the Sisters to seek in other countries not only refuge but a larger field of apostolate, both pastoral and missionary. It was the expulsion of religious from France that was partly responsible for bringing the Congregation to England (1891) and the United States (1903).

4. Changes

The incredible upheaval in France was the harbinger of a period of instability that would continue into the twentieth century. Contrary to the preceding century, it was a time of constant change leading eventually to two world wars. The declaration of World War I coincided with the expiration of the delay on imposing the antireligious laws. The legislation called "L'Union Sacrée" had suspended the application of the law of 1904, saving at the last minute six schools of the Congregation.

5. Internationalization

In 1900 the Daughters of Wisdom were already established throughout Europe—in Belgium, Holland, Italy, and England—and beyond Europe, in Canada and Haiti. The antireligious laws proved to be an instrument of Providence for the expansion of the Congregation. The first motive had been the need to find a refuge for Sisters expelled from their convents. Inevitably the surrounding countries were the first choice. The Sisters from the north of France went to Belgium, those from the south to Italy, and those from the west to England. From 1902 to 1912, foundations followed in rapid succession beyond all expectation. This same period saw the first foundation in the United States, Colombia, and Shiré (present-day Malawi).

World War II brought isolation to the provinces, as well as its own particular problems and sufferings to each of them. One of the more serious was the painful evacuations of most of the communities of the north of France and Belgium, entailing the death of one Sister. Twenty-eight Sisters were buried under the ruins of their houses in Nantes, Angers, Valenciennes. For others, flight from bombed cities meant nights in air-raid shelters and forced evacuation.

Free from the horrors of war on its own territory, the Order in Canada and the United States continued to expand, and with the Atlantic closed to merchant shipping and all communication with Europe cut off, it provided generous aid and personnel to Haiti and Colombia.

6. Contemporary evolution

The year 1947 would bring the joy of the canonization of the founder, Father Louis de Montfort; and 1950, the transfer of the generalate to Rome, confirming the status as an international Congregation. In the 1960s the Congregation numbered 5,000 Sisters in 400 establishments and ten novitiates. Since Vatican II, the numbers have considerably decreased.

The most important event of this post-Vatican II period for religious Congregations was aggiornamento, the careful adaptation of the Constitutions, in fidelity to the sources, called for by the Council to meet the needs of the modern world. For the Daughters of Wisdom, Montfort's original Rule remains the fundamental inspiration. In 1965 the habit was modified. Customs and regulations not part of the Rule and often outdated and cumbersome were abandoned. Inspired by the Council and its "wind of change," a principle of subsidiarity, involving decentralization and participation with ensuing coresponsibility, led to a period of experimentation with a new mode of life. Lay clothes, professional work outside the Congregation by individual members, the breaking down of large communities into smaller units living outside institutions: all were signs of a desire for more diversified apostolic contacts, which in their turn demanded a change in way of life. Here and there, this led at times to excesses, resulting in painful departures. The *Rule of Life*, however, approved by the Sacred Congregation for Religious in 1985, placed the seal of approval on the better changes by giving guidelines for their application: A return to the sources aimed at a rediscovery of the charism of the founders: poverty and a love for the poor, spiritual values, and dependence on Mary. The Congregation is today represented on four continents, and its international character is being increaingly strengthened. Although the provinces of the Western world suffer from lack of vocations, new life is emerging in the Third World. The montfort charism continues to radiate.

M.Lepers

III. Spirituality

In the context of the history of the Daughters of Wisdom, the spirituality of the Congregation becomes quite clear. The different stages in the story of the community reflect different emphases in spirituality, giving a deeper insight into several essential aspects of the spirituality founded upon the writings and teachings of Saint Louis de Montfort.

1. Evolution from birth of the Congregation to current times

Although the fundamental elements of the spirituality of the Daughters of Wisdom are the fruit of permanent values found at all times,[7] we find that each epoch emphasizes one or another aspect, depending on the particular demands of the day. Three periods can be distinguished in the history of the spirituality of the Daughters of Wisdom, periods during which varying accents are noted in the way of living the montfort charism.

a. From the birth of the congregation to the French Revolution (1703-1789): evangelical radicalism. This period was dominated by Marie Louise of Jesus, who incarnated to the highest degree the spirituality of the Daughters of Wisdom. "She was not content," said Besnard, addressing himself to Jesus Wisdom, "to bear the beautiful name of Daughter of Wisdom; she wished to express in her conduct and in her actions all its ineffable significance and to become a living copy of your sublime virtues."[8] Strong spiritual life, long and profound prayer, ardent desire of Wisdom, proximity to and service for the poor under the austere program of the Cross, abandonment to Providence, confidence in Mary: such was the program of spirituality proposed by Montfort to the woman he helped become the first Daughter of Wisdom. To these were soon added separation from the family, adventures risked for God Alone, and finally a program of religious life that was both explicit and exacting.

Montfort's death bequeathed to Marie Louise's shoulders the responsibility for fidelity to this life's project, coupled with material insecurity and the painful search for God's Will. Marie Louise also watched over

Montfort's plan, protecting it, defending it, and giving it substance. She planted the spirituality of the Daughters of Wisdom in the hearts of the novices and maintained it in its radicalism through the years. Marie Louise accomplished her mission, leaving her Testament to her community, which had already spread throughout western France. Humility, poverty, detachment, union with one another - the entire program is found in her Testament. It embodies "the primitive spirit of our saintly founder," from which she exhorted the Sisters never to stray.[9]

What is admirable in Marie Louise is especially the balance and synthesis between contemplation and action according to the goals of RW 1. It has been justly written of Marie Louise: "She revealed herself during her entire life as a great mystic torn between solitude in contemplation and the devouring fire of the apostolate. The presence of God bursts forth through all her senses and behavior. Like Montfort, she only knows how to speak of God. And yet, like him, she is an activist. Her activity is the radiation of an overfull interior; it is contemplation in action. Like Montfort, she will be a remarkable organizer of hospitals, but the concern of her soul will not be the feminine taste for order, for cleanliness, nor even the maternal bent for the relief of the poor and the sick. Her concern will be souls; she will perform extravagant mortifications; she will have Montfort's audacity to lead back to God the rejects of humanity, vilified by misery and often by vice."[10]

The circular letters of the first superiors general of both montfort Congregations (Fathers Mulot, Audubon, Besnard, Micquignion, and Supiot) never failed to recommend fidelity to the spirit of true Daughters of Wisdom. In particular, Father Mulot, like Saint Louis Marie, identified Wisdom with the Cross: "Love the Cross, without which it is impossible to save oneself. . . . The Cross is not less lovable than Jesus Christ, since he chose it as his spouse. How sweet is the Cross to those who love Jesus. You cannot be a Daughter of Wisdom without loving the Cross; the habit and the name are worthless without that."[11] Father Besnard, especially, strove to revitalize the spirit of the Congregation by his initiatives, which resulted in some valuable documents: the sermon on Consecration to Wisdom, the explanation of the Rule of the Daughters of Wisdom, and the biographies of Montfort and Marie Louise.

Besnard wrote his sermon on Consecration to Wisdom in 1758, while Marie Louise, whom he mentions several times, was still alive. Beyond the structure of this sermon, which treats of the motives for loving Wisdom and refers to the Congregation founded by Montfort as the "house" of Wisdom, we find a vivid description of the rite of Consecration for which Besnard wished them to prepare. The Daughters of Wisdom are to gather around the statue of Wisdom, given by Montfort himself (and, unfortunately, not preserved for us): "This statue which you see before you will be an eternal monument to the desire that this great servant of God had to see daughters consecrated to Divine Wisdom." Besnard concluded his exhortation by inviting the Sisters: "Consecrate yourselves, then, my dear daughters, to Divine Wisdom, prostrate yourselves humbly at her feet. Honor her as Father de Montfort, your holy founder, honored her."[12]

The "Explanation of the Rule," dated 1758-1760, is not the exclusive work of Besnard but the culmination of the work of Marie Louise and of several Daughters of Wisdom "according to the counsels of our venerable Fathers Mulot and Audubon .... But it was Father Besnard who gave the final touch."[13] With Montfort, the text exhorts the Sisters to "ponder continually in your heart the truths of Divine Wisdom on which we are founded and established." After recalling these truths, which lead to "asking God with greater insistence for . . . Divine Wisdom," the text identifies the life of the Daughters of Wisdom with the state "that Jesus Christ Eternal Wisdom came to choose on earth." It is not a question of a life apart from the world but, on the contrary, "a life that is totally oriented to the service of one's brothers. . . . When we are sent into the hospitals to serve the poor . . . when . . . we go into their poor hovels to comfort them, visit them, cure their illnesses . . . do we not, there again, do what Jesus himself did?"[14]

In the biography of Marie Louise, Besnard enlightens us on the steps taken by Montfort to achieve the foundation of the Congregation of the Daughters of Wisdom. In Montfort's biography, he emphasizes the solid spirituality contained in the Rule of the Daughters of Wisdom. Above all, Besnard explains that "the special vocation and state proper to the Daughters of Wisdom is to crush underfoot all worldly wisdom, . . . to imitate Jesus Christ the Incarnate Wisdom both in his hidden life and in his public life."[15] He continues by interpreting the name of the Daughters of Wisdom in relation to Christ and by demanding that their lives reflect their name. "They are to become worthy of the beautiful name of Daughters of Wisdom, which was given to them to signify that under the auspices and the protection of the Blessed Virgin they are daughters of Jesus Christ, the Eternal Wisdom of God, of Jesus Christ, the Incarnate Wisdom."[16]

Father General Besnard magnificently commented on the two ends proposed by Montfort to the Daughters of Wisdom, that is to say, the acquisition of Wisdom and the works of charity. He highlighted their indissolubility and reciprocal dependence, opting for their reconciliation in practice: "When he distinguishes two ends in their state of life, one interior and the other exterior, it is only to develop more clearly his thoughts and plans. He wanted the two ends to be but one in their Institute and that each depend on the other. He was convinced that since nothing contributes more to our own perfection than to devote ourselves entirely to the edification and salvation of souls, nothing prepares us better to edify and save souls than to sanctify ourselves. So a Daughter of Wisdom who worked toward only one of these ends separated from the other would lose her way and would not respond to the plans of the holy founder. . . . He calls their attention to these two different forms of life; one, modeled on Martha, is fully preoccupied with serving others, and the second, modeled on Mary, has no other preoccupation than contemplation. He recognizes perfectly that the functions of these two states considered separately and to their full extent do not suit his plan, so he chose the best in each of them, joining both in such a way that, far from disturbing one another, they facilitate each other. For, however little Martha and Mary resemble each other, they are sisters and not enemies."[17]

Sustained by this Wisdom spirituality, the Daughters of Wisdom were ready to bear the great trial of the Revolution.

b. From the French Revolution to the beatification of Montfort (1789-1888): To Jesus through Mary. During these hundred years, the sad events of persecutions, anguish, and massacres follow each other for the montfort communities of Saint-Laurent-sur-Sèvre. The Wisdom community obeyed the orders of Father Micquignon, whose prophetic cry of alarm placed all on guard against the danger of losing the faith. He recommended "inviolable attachment to the Church and to its Head [the Holy Father], silence, prayer, unity within the Congregation, reception of the Sacraments, and fidelity to the Rule."[18] Likewise, in 1792 Father Supiot rejoiced with the Sisters of Poitiers "for having had the honor, the first in your city, of being persecuted, pursued for the faith and the name of Jesus Christ," and he exhorted them "to mutual charity and to obedience" in order to "experience the consolations of the life of a true Daughter of Wisdom."[19] In 1797 Father Supiot wrote to the community of Brest: "In the midst of afflictions that crush my heart, you are my crown and consolation. I am well pleased with you before the Lord. You have acted like true daughters of the Church."[20]

The period of the Revolution was honored with heroic deeds of fidelity to the Church and the Congregation; it was also drained of much strength. On January 17, 1821, the general superior, Mother Calixte, wrote: "We are going to have the consolation of seeing the spirit of the first Daughters of Wisdom be revitalized among us; . . . henceforth we shall all retrace the virtues of our holy foundress." And on March 4 of the same year: "We can no longer hide from ourselves that we have degenerated from the fervor of our predecessors. We all say that we wish to imitate our Mother [Marie Louise] de Jesus, and we believe that it suffices to say it, to think it, to desire it. But if we do not take the means, our desires will have no effect."[21]

We must emphasize here that the circular letters of the general superiors often speak of imitating Montfort or Marie Louise. Their experience must be taken into account. The thoughts of the superiors, however, are not focused on the founders but on Wisdom, Jesus Christ crucified.

Father General Denis wrote that "the acquisition of [Wisdom] is the first and interior end of your Institute." He reminded the Sisters: "Your special mission is to combat worldly wisdom with the folly of the Cross. . . . Study Jesus Christ . . . Wisdom."[22]

Following an initiative of Father Deshayes (1821-1841), Father Dalin in 1842 reestablished the custom that the Fathers of the Company of Mary (Montfort Missionaries) be the retreat masters for the Daughters of Wisdom, unifying more clearly their spiritualities. "United in the same spirit of filial dependence on Mary, led in the same way of abnegation and confident abandonment, the two families helped each other pursue the goal that had been proposed to them and that Montfort left them as marching order: 'To Jesus through Mary.'"[23]

The Marian accent proper to the montfort Congregations was reinforced by the rediscovery in 1842 of a manuscript of Father de Montfort hidden during the torment of the Revolution and lost from view, buried in the silence of a chest (TD 114). Entitled in 1843 by the editors *Treatise of the True Devotion to the Blessed Virgin,* this manuscript was received as a gift from heaven, a "treasure."

It had been the custom of the Daughters of Wisdom to take an oath every December 8th to uphold the doctrine of the Immaculate Conception. After the definition of the dogma in 1854 the decision was made to replace the promise with the Consecration according to the formula that Montfort himself gave. This decision was received enthusiastically throughout the Congregation.[24] A month of fervent preparation preceded the celebration, as was the intention of the founder.

In 1873 Father General Gabriel Denis edited a book that achieved great renown, *The Reign of Jesus through Mary,* written in the form of a manual for the Children of Mary, students in the boarding schools run by the Daughters of Wisdom.[25] The author hoped for religious and political restoration in the country: "In place of a persecuting and unbelieving France, will we not see a new, young France arise that will believe?" But, he added, "the work of restoration will not be truly undertaken until the day Christian piety fully recognizes the role of Mary in the plan of Redemption and the salvation of souls. This is why we must follow Father de Montfort's teachings, which reveal Mary's role." Father Denis' entire book, after an introduction on the "Slavery of Jesus in Mary," is a vade mecum to live this "devotion" in the prayers and actions of each day.[26]

The end of the nineteenth century was marked by the beatification of Montfort on January 22, 1888, followed by a great Marian movement. During the year 1892, General Superior Father Maurille wrote five circular letters to the Daughters of Wisdom proposing and explaining the doctrine of the "Holy Slavery of Jesus in Mary."[27] He also offered the Sisters a method of making their retreat in the spirit of the four weeks proposed by Montfort as preparation for the Consecration. When she announced the news of the death of

Father Maurille, Mother Marie-Patrice attested, "Thanks to his impetus, the Wisdom community has advanced further along the sure road that is Mary Immaculate."[28]

c. From the beatification to the canonization of Montfort (1888-1947). Consecration to Jesus Wisdom through Mary, an essential element of Wisdom spirituality. While keeping the ensemble of montfort spirituality, in the twentieth century the Wisdom community continued the Marian emphasis begun in the preceding epoch. It suffices to mention the publication of Father General Antonin Lhoumeau's masterful theological treatise *Spiritual Life at the School of Blessed Louis Marie Grignion de Montfort* (Ouden, Poitiers 1901). For Lhoumeau, perfect Consecration to Jesus through Mary is a "system of spirituality" with its proper ends, means, procedures, and effects." The end - the author states precisely in four chapters - is "Christ living in us," and Mary is the means. The gap in Father Lhoumeau's excellent book is the absence of references to LEW, which he only cites once. He makes up for this in his circular letters to the Daughters of Wisdom where he affirms, for example, that "without any doubt, no Christian can do without this Divine Wisdom; there are souls [i.e., the Daughters of Wisdom] who by state wish to profess it, and in perfection possess it."[29]

With Lhoumeau, a dual orientation begins that will endure a long time. On the one hand, it gives life to a process of interiorization that risks a dichotomy between religious life and works. Presenting the constitutions which had been approved by Rome, Lhoumeau noted, "Something has been added": The constitutions speak of a primary or principal end and of a secondary end. They offer a commentary that relativizes the works of charity and of the apostolate: religious life is first, and then the works. Works are not excluded by any means but are subordinate to the sanctification of the members.[30]

On the other hand, the constitutions insist on two notes of montfort spirituality that are mentioned in Pope Benedict XV's letter to Father Lhoumeau, "obedience to the Apostolic See and devotion to the Virgin Mary."[31] We must note that the Constitutions of the Daughters of Wisdom explain the Marian aspect of Wisdom spirituality by mentioning "the acquisition of Divine Wisdom through Mary"(no. 1).

Missionaries of the Company of Mary and Daughters of Wisdom worked together to spread Marian doctrine. The spirituality lived during this period was therefore strongly stamped with Saint Louis de Montfort's Marian devotion, forcefully recommended to the Sisters by Mother Marie Louise. Without in the least ever obscuring the end, Jesus Eternal and Incarnate Wisdom, the "means"—devotion to Our Lady—occupied an important place for the Daughters of Wisdom as well as for the Montfort Missionaries, as it did for the entire Church.

It was in 1929 that Father H. Huré published for the first time "the doctrinal treatise of Montfort exactly conformed to the manuscript, *The Love of Eternal Wisdom.*" And he added, "Without withdrawing anything whatsoever from the importance of the *Treatise on True Devotion,* it must nevertheless be admitted that Montfort produced two masterpieces, *The Love of Eternal Wisdom* and *True Devotion to the Blessed Virgin,* the second being a magnificent commentary on chapter 16 of the first book, and its indispensable complement. *The Love of Eternal Wisdom* is a major book. It alone gives us an overview of montfort spirituality and even a more exact and comprehensive idea of *True Devotion to Mary.*"[32]

Studies on Wisdom have been done by Poupon in his *Le poème de la parfaite consécration à Marie,* which proposes to explain "the Marian doctrine of Grignion de Montfort as found in his masterpiece *The Love of Eternal Wisdom* and to interpret it following the focus of his thought, Wisdom."[33] Montfort Father Olivier LeBorgne's writings on the Wisdom of love was the fruit of a double series of retreats given to the Daughters of Wisdom. The author thanks the sisters who welcomed eagerly the montfort message and states that he "had thought it beneficial to highlight all the Christological orientations of which the *Treatise of True Devotion* is full, and thus to establish Holy Slavery as the eminent means to obtain Wisdom. This point, he adds, "seems to have answered a strong need of souls, who sometimes find themselves torn between their interior end, which is Wisdom, and Marian devotion presented undoubtedly too unilaterally."[34]

Under the impetus of the Marian Year of 1954, Father General A. Josselin stressed Consecration spirituality and, in keeping with the Marian celebrations, underlined Our Lady's role: "What we desire is that you give the Blessed Virgin Mary a greater place in your life; that you be more attentive through the course of the year to let nothing be lost of the merits that you place in her hands; that your desires, your thoughts, your affections, your comportment be truly influenced by your Consecration. This Consecration has placed you in a state of Marian dependence, from which you cannot withdraw without renouncing at the same time your spirituality and your title of Daughters of Wisdom."[35] In his turn, Father General Cornelius Heilegers, basing himself on the life and writings of the founder as they have been lived down through the years, affirms: "The Congregation of the Daughters of Wisdom, like the Company of Mary, is a fundamentally Marian society. Both would be destroyed if the Marian emphasis were removed. It is more than an accidental element; it is of the very nature of the Institute."[36]

If, on the one hand, the canonization of Louis Marie de Montfort on July 20, 1947, mobilized the montfort family to live according to the spirit of the founder, it understandably did not authorize *all interpretations* of Montfort's Marian devotion.[37] Pope Pius XII declared this devotion "flagrans, solida ac recta,"[38] but this does not thereby canonize Montfort's specific devotional practices. He states precisely that the Church "is aware that true and perfect devotion to the Blessed Virgin is not so strongly linked to *these methods or techniques* that any one of them can claim the monopoly."[39]

d. From the canonization of Montfort to post-Vatican II (1947-): apostolic religious life following Christ Wisdom. The 1950s were touched by ecumenical and biblical currents. Books and studies on religion—even on theology—became easily accessible to all Christians. Gradually a number of Daughters of Wisdom were influenced by these currents, and perhaps "the home-made bread" (*le pain de chez nous*), i.e., the traditional spirituality of the community, seemed a bit stale, or perhaps had become insipid, because minds were scattered and feeding on multiple mannas.

Moreover, some theologians, basing themselves on the culture and language of the times, and often ignorant of Louis Marie's entire context were critical of Montfort's teachings.[40] Vatican Council II shed its light on the Marian question by affirming the legitimacy of devotion to the Mother of God, insisting on its Christocentric and liturgical character (LG 67-68). Even if the council did not mention Marian spirituality - as John Paul II has done explicitly in the encyclical *Redemptoris Mater* - it is not difficult to discern its convergence with Montfort's teaching.[41]

After Vatican II the Church appeared to go rather abruptly from intense popularity for Mary to a silence about her; the Christocentricity of devotion to Our Lady needed to be highlighted. Within the family of the daughters of Saint Louis de Montfort, the relationship to Mary needed to be more clearly articulated in light of Christ Wisdom.

The Congregation took steps in this direction. In 1973, on the occasion of the tricentennial of Montfort's birth, Sr. François du Christ hoped "to penetrate more deeply into the meaning of the vocation of the Daughters of Wisdom" by meditating on the mystery of the Incarnation. This mystery, "seeking to live for Christ, deepening our understanding of the meaning of our Baptism and the sense of our Consecration to God, this is 'acquiring Wisdom,' Montfort would say. But Saint Louis Marie reminds us that the Word lives in us only if, like Mary, we are docile to the Spirit." In her turn, Sr. Ludovic Marie launched a montfort Wisdom movement, inviting all Daughters of Wisdom to celebrate a montfort year (April 28, 1981-1982) in the company of Saint Louis Marie and Mother Marie Louise. "This will be a kind of jubilee year, during which each one, according to the expression of Leviticus 5:10, 'will regain possession of her inheritance'" (letter of April 28, 1981).

The revised Constitutions open a path by which all Daughters of Wisdom may become more and more "disciples of Wisdom," day after day more conformed to the Wisdom of God. Consecrated to announcing Jesus Christ in the world of today, each Sister's words, acts, mentality—in a word, her whole person—are called to conversion to true Wisdom in fidelity to the evangelical charism of Montfort and Marie Louise de Jesus. Sent to live this love in the midst of the world, the Daughters of Wisdom are urged by the Rule to be close to Jesus Wisdom and to those to whom they have been sent.[42]

In presenting the Rule of Life, Sr. Ines dell'Eucaristia, superior general of the Daughters of Wisdom, highlighted its basic characteristics. This Rule is at the same time "a destination, since it is essentially a reference to the richness of the past . . . and a point of departure, since it is the result of spiritual discernment in Chapter, which has permitted us to opt clearly to give priority to the apostolic commitment—this apostolic commitment which orients us toward those that the world rejects, that the Church reclaims with difficulty. The apostolic religious life of the Daughters of Wisdom is confronted with two great poles: the transcendent values, which manifest the supremacy of the Kingdom . . . , the values of the Incarnation, which show that the Kingdom is already here. . . . Rather than simply repeating the founders' charism, it must be re-expressed in the world and in the Church of today."[43]

The Daughters of Wisdom have as their mission in the Church and in the world to offer to God new opportunities so that the love with which He loves us may communicate itself to all people in order that, with the help of Mary, the reign of Jesus may come.

B-M. van den Hoof - S. De Fiores

Notes: (1) Grandet, 68. (2) Blain, 188. (3) AGFS: Sr. Agathange, "Chroniques," 89-90. (4) For more information on Blessed Marie Louise, see the article about her in this volume. (5) Only one Daughter of Wisdom took the oath to the Constitution. She retracted it later. (6) The small community at Angoulême lived heroically during the Revolution and refused to accept the Concordat but fell into the schism of the "Little Church." (7) Cf. the "main themes of montfort spirituality," i.e., God Alone; constant orientation towards Wisdom; poverty, humility, obedience; confident abandonment to Providence; love of the Cross, in the sense that Christ loved it for the salvation of humankind; love and service of the poor, who are the image of Christ; Marian life (Sacra Congregatio pro causis sanctorum, *Lucionen. Beatificationis et canonizationis servae Dei Mariae Ludovicae a Jesu (in saec.: Mariae Ludovicae Trichet) confundatricis Filiarum a Sapientia (+1759) Positio super virtutibus ex officio concinata,* Rome 1986, 139-142). (8) Besnard, *Marie-Louise,* 2. (9) On the Last Will of Marie Louise, cf Besnard, *Marie-Louise,* 402-405. (10) *Bulletin trimestriel [des Filles de la Sagesse]* 113 (July 1959) (11) AGFS, series DK: Letter of Fr. Mulot, Nov. 7, 1729. (12) AGCM: Besnard, "Discours pour la consécration à la Sagesse," in "Entretiens sur différents sujets de piété," ms., 11-17. The text of the *"consecration of oneself to eternal and incarnate Wisdom through the hands of Mary"* was known. Fr. Besnard had used it in the first chapter of the Constitutions. However, it would appear that the original formula was not in regular use. The formula used for the Consecration was the concluding prayer of the Little Crown or the prayer after the glorious mysteries. Here, however, the Consecration is addressed to Wisdom, so the question of the formula used in the rite of Consecration remains open. (13) Sr. Agathange, "Chroniques," 336. (14) AGFS: "Explanation of the Rule of the Daughters of Wisdom," published in *Positio,* 161-163, note 7. (15) Besnard II, 113. (16) Ibid., 114-115. (17) Ibid., 115-116. (18) Fr. Micquignon, letter of February 6, 1790. (19) René Supiot, letter "to Sr. Cyrille," 1792, Arch. Vienne, L460. (20) R. Supiot, letter to the Daughters of Wisdom in Brest, 1797, quoted in *Le doigt de Dieu. Les Filles de la Sagesse après la mort des fondateurs,* vol. 1, *1759-1800,* Cholet 1954, 292. The same author lists the Sisters who fell "victims to the Revolution": thirty-three Daughters of Wisdom, including fourteen who died by the guillotine or were massacred, and nineteen who died in prison (p. 312). (21) AGFS, series DK: Mother Calixte, letters of January 17 and March 4, 1821, in *Circulaires des Pères généraux.* (22) AGFS, series DK: Circulars of Fr. Denis, January 13 and April 8, 1859. (23) [Anonymous], *Congrégation des Filles de la Sagesse,* Letouzey and Ané, Paris 1925, 75. Cf. also Fonteneau, *Histoire de la congrégation de la Sagesse,* Oudin, Paris-Poitiers 1878, 308. (24) The interior and exterior practice of the slavery of Jesus in Mary existed in the Congregation at this time, since we know that the newly professed Sisters received the little chain. (25) *Le Règne de Jésus par Marie* by a missionary of the Company of Mary, Oudin, Poitiers 1873. (26) This program is given in the second edition: G. Denis, *Le règne de Jésus par Marie,* n.p., n.d., IX and XI. (27) Cf. AGFS, series DK: Circulars of Fr. Maurille (1887-1903). Note the shifts in the wording, which move slightly away from Montfort, who prefers the expression *"slavery of Jesus in Mary"* (TD 144-145) or *"the perfect consecration to Jesus Christ"* (TD 120); Fr. Maurille acknowledges that "the name that our Blessed Father prefers to give to this devotion is that of Slavery of Jesus in Mary." But in practice, Fr. Maurille prefers to speak of "perfect Consecration to the Most Blessed Virgin" (letter of April 18, 1892). (28) Mother Marie-Patrice, letter of 24 February 1903. (29) AGFS, series DK: A. Lhoumeau, letter of January 1914. (30) AGFS, series DK: A. Lhoumeau, letter of January 1906. (31) Cf. this letter of April 19, 1916, in AAS 8 (1916), 172-173. (32) H. Huré, preface to *l'Amour de la Sagesse éternelle,* "definitive edition," Pontchâteau 1929, ii. (33) M.-Th. Poupon, *Le poème de la parfaite consécration à Marie suivant saint Louis-Marie Grignion de Montfort et les spirituels de son temps: Sources et doctrine,* Librairie du Sacré-Coeur, Lyon 1947, 14. (34) O. LeBorgne, *Sagesse d'amour. Une retraite religieuse avec le Père de Montfort,* Rome 1963, 2. Among the works on Wisdom: J. Dayet, *La sagesse chez le B. Louis-Marie de Montfort,* n.p, n.d.; J. P. Richard, *La consécration plénitude de sagesse,* in *IIème Rencontre internationale montfortaine (Saint-Laurent-sur-Sèvre, 2-8 sept. 1958): Rapports et documents,* n.p, n.d., 68-87; A. F. Balmforth, *The Use of the Sapiential Themes of the Bible in the Writings of St. Louis-Marie de Montfort,* duplicated thesis, PUG, Rome 1964; R. Lack, *Sagesse biblique et le P. de Montfort,* duplicated, Saint-Laurent-sur-Sèvre 1968; J. Hémery, *Une attitude spirituelle de sagesse évangélique,* in CM 52 (1966), 153-170; S. De Fiores, *Ispirazione monfortana nella Congregazione delle Figlie della Sapienza,* lecture given at the Italian Provincial Chapter of the Daughters of Wisdom, Castiglione (duplicated); *Montfort un homme qui a rencontré Dieu en Jésus-Christ, Sagesse éternelle,* in *Dieu seul: A la rencontre de Dieu avec Montfort,* International Montfort Center, Rome 1981, 82-91; M. Gilbert, *L'exégèse spirituelle de Montfort,* in NRT 104 (1982), 678-691; B. Papàsogli, *Montfort moralista: "l'honnête homme" sotto processo,* in *La lettera e lo spirito: Temi et figure del Seicento francese,* Editrice libreria goliardica, Pisa 1986, 219-236; J.-P. Prévost, *Montfort et le courant de sagesse biblique,* in *Dossier Montfortain,* part 2 (May 1986), 1-19; H.-M. Manteau-Bonamy, *S. Louis-Marie Grignion de Montfort théologien de la Sagesse éternelle au seuil du troisième millénaire,* Éditions Saint-Paul, Paris-Fribourg 1986. (35) AGFS, series DK: A. Josselin, letter of October 25, 1953. (36) AGFS, series DK: Address given by Fr. Heiligers, quoted in the circular of Sr. Marie de Noël, superior general of the Daughters of Wisdom, April 22, 1958. It must be pointed out, however, that in the circular letter of August 2, 1959 (printed), the same Fr. Heiligers reverts to the four means to acquire and preserve Wisdom given in LEW. (37) Pius XII, *Litterae decretales: Beato Ludovico Mariae Grignion de Montfort. . . . sanctorum honores decernuntur,* July 20, 1947, in AAS 39 (1947), 274. (38) Pius XII, *"Soyez les bienvenus,"* address of July 21, 1947, in AAS 39 (1947), 413. (39) Cf. S. De Fiores, *La vicenda ecclesiale di Grignion de Montfort dalla beatificazione (1888) ad oggi* in QM 6 (1988-1989), 24-27, in which criticisms of Montfort by M. Cordovani (1946), C. Moeller (1964), K. Rahner (1965), G. Andreolli (1954), E. Schillebeeckx (1954), and H. Graef (1964) are to be found. (40) Cf. A. Rum, *Attualità post-conciliare della dottrina monfortana,* in *Madre e regina* 21 (1967), 4, 103-105; H.-M. Manteau-Bonamy, *De Grignion de Montfort à Vatican II,* in CM 52 (1966), 120-126; G. Giacometti and P. Sessa, *La novità della devozione monfortana alla Madonna* in *Rivista di ascetica e mistica* 12 (1967), 35-45, 148-157, 384-387. (41) *Règle de vie des Filles de la Sagesse,* n.p. 1985. (43) Circular letter of Mother Ines dell'Eucaristia, April 28, 1985, accompanying the text of the Rule of Life.

DISCERNMENT

SUMMARY

INTRODUCTION: NEED FOR DISCERNMENT IN MONTFORT'S TIME.

I. TWO SOURCES OF DISCERNMENT FOR MONTFORT:
  1. The Bible:
    a. Principles,
    b. Biblical foundation of Montfort's discernment,
    c. Trinitarian dimension of Montfort's discernment,
    d. Other biblical data for discernment;
  2. St. Ignatius and the spiritual currents of Montfort's time:
    a. Influence of St. Ignatius of Loyola,
    b. Other influences.

II. DISCERNMENT DURING MONTFORT'S LIFE AND SPIRITUAL ITINERARY:
  1. Priesthood;
  2. Active apostolate or contemplative life?
  3. Choice of pastoral work;
  4. Discernment in seeking perfection: the secret of Mary;
  5. Montfort's rules of discernment.

III. MONTFORT AS GUIDE TOWARDS DISCERNMENT:
  1. In Spiritual direction;
  2. In teaching about falsehood or truth:
    a. False or true Wisdom,
    b. False or true devotion to Mary,
    c. False or true friend of the Cross,
    d. False or true preacher.

IV. SIGNIFICANCE OF MONTFORT'S DISCERNMENT TODAY:
  1. Need for discernment in contemporary society;
  2. Christ Wisdom;
  3. Through Mary.

INTRODUCTION: NEED FOR DISCERNMENT IN MONTFORT'S TIME

A disciple of Christ must use spiritual discernment. This means that he should examine things attentively and continuously, in the light of the Gospel and on the basis of faith. He should look into the motivations that govern the personal choices of himself and others in order to discover God's salvific design for himself, the Church, the world and to live and act accordingly.[1]

In St. Louis Marie's time, the Church in France went through a turbulent period of Catholic reform after the Council of Trent. There was an increase in religious knowledge among ordinary people,[2] but too often it still remained superficial. Theologians and clergy hotly disputed Mary's role in the plan of salvation.[3] It was indeed a time that called for spiritual discernment. Montfort complained about the world's manipulation of the Gospel truths: *"Never has the world been so corrupt as it is now, for never has it been so cunning, so wise in its own way, and so crafty. It cleverly makes use of the truth to foster untruth, virtue to justify vice, and the very maxims of Jesus Christ to endorse its own, so that even those who are wisest in the sight of God are often deceived"* (LEW 79). And about devotion to Mary, he stated: *"It is all the more necessary to make the right choice of the true devotion to our Blessed Lady, for now more than ever, there are false devotions to her which can easily be mistaken for the true ones. The devil, like a counterfeiter and crafty, experienced deceiver, has already misled and ruined many Christians by means of fraudulent devotions to Our lady"* (TD 90).

Although the word "discernment" is rarely found in Saint Louis Marie's vocabulary (cf. LEW 92, 192; PM 19), his life and written works reveal him to be the epitome of discernment. Whether deciding on a particular form of his apostolate, advising people in spiritual direction, or simply choosing between truth and falsity, good and bad, he showed an exquisite ability to discern the mysterious workings of the Spirit in the circumstances of his life.[4] It is safe to say that the source of Montfort's spiritual discernment lay in his unremitting and prayerful search for Wisdom. Through it he sought to be *"mature in enlightenment, in holiness, in experience, and in wisdom"* (TD 156) through his total surrender to Mary.

I. Two Sources of Discernment for Montfort

1. The Bible

a. Principles. Holy Scripture makes it clear that a disciple of Christ must seek the will of the Father (cf. Jn 6:38-40; Mt 26:29; Rom 12:1-2; Eph 5:10-17), listen to the voice of the Good Shepherd (cf. Jn 10:3), and be guided by the Spirit of truth (cf. Jn 14:16-17; 20:22) in order to obtain eternal life (cf. Jn 15:26). Discernment is required, because there are many false prophets and not every spirit can be trusted (cf. 1 Jn 4:1). Imitating Christ demands entering the narrow gate and following the hard road that leads to life (cf. Mt 7:14). It means being open to growth in the Spirit,[5] as Christ himself had increased "in wisdom, in stature, and in favor with God and men" (Lk 2:52). The true disciple lived a holy life, because leading a sinful life meant belonging to the devil (cf. 1 Jn 3:8).

b. Biblical foundation of Montfort's discernment. Montfort's life and written works demonstrate convincingly that Holy Scripture was his central point of departure for discovering God's ways. In LS there are some short notes on its importance. The Bible is the authority of the Father, the voice of the Son, and the heart and soul of the Holy Spirit (cf. LS 313-314). The personal strength of this conviction of Montfort's was reflected in both his words and his deeds (cf. LEW 133-153). The best proof of this was probably his encounter with Jean-Baptiste Blain, which occurred towards the end of Louis Marie's life. When Blain reproached Montfort on the austerity of his life, the saint simply showed him the NT. Then Montfort went on to challenge Blain, asking if he could find fault with any practice or doctrine of Jesus Christ found in the Scriptures.[6]

Was there a central biblical principle guiding Montfort in discerning whether something was of God or of the Evil One? Yes, it was clearly his Trinitarian perspective.

c. ***Trinitarian dimension of Montfort's discernment*** *1. Unconditional confidence in God the Father.* A disciple of Christ is known by his complete confidence in the love and wisdom of the Father. This virtue marks him off from those of little faith, from nonbelievers who worry about food and clothing and who set their hearts on earthly things (cf. Mt 6:25-34). From his youth, Montfort showed an inimitable capacity for unconditional confidence in God the Father. Later he demanded this same attitude from his followers (cf. LCM; RW 5, 29). As a young student, his remaining in Paris was made uncertain when he unexpectedly lost his spiritual director and great benefactor. Nevertheless, he wrote to this uncle: *"I do not know yet how things will go, whether I shall stay or leave. . . . Whatever happens, I shall not be worried. I have a Father in heaven who will never fail me. . . . I never stop praying to Him and rely completely on His providence* (L 2). From his biography and his own writings, numerous other examples could be mentioned, making clear that his motto "God Alone" was a concrete reality in his daily life.

2. Jesus Christ the only Mediator. Nobody can be a true disciple of the Lord unless he adheres in faith and love to the divine person of Jesus Christ. In him salvation is mediated to the world (cf. Jn 1:17; 1 Jn 4:1; 1 Tim 2:5). It is important to emphasize this biblical and theological principle when dealing with Montfort's teachings, especially on the role of Mary. Sometimes, superficial readers of his works are tempted to conclude presumptuously that the saint, in citing Mary's unparalleled role in God's plan of salvation, might have eclipsed the role of the one Mediator, Jesus Christ. Montfort never tired, however, of explaining this incontestable truth: *"Jesus, our Savior, true God and true man, must be the ultimate end of all our devotions; otherwise, they would be false and misleading"* (TD 61; cf. TD 68, 84, 115, 117, 120, 125, 148, 245, 265; LEW 12).

3. Led by the Spirit of truth. The disciple of Christ must test the spirits in order to be guided by the Spirit of God Alone and remain faithful to the Beatitudes (cf. 1 Jn 4:1-2; Rom 8:5-17; Mt 5-7). Everyone moved by the Spirit is a son of God (cf. Rom 8:14). The true discipleship of Christ is recognized precisely through the presence of the Spirit. As an experienced spiritual master, Montfort made use of this biblical criterion of discernment. Without excluding other topics, what dominates is his teaching (a) on Christ Eternal Wisdom and (b) on perfect devotion to the Mother of God. He said of the former: *"Eternal*

Wisdom communicates her Spirit of enlightenment to the soul that possesses her. . . . This subtle and penetrating Spirit enables man, as it enabled Solomon, to judge all things with keen discernment and deep penetration" (LEW 92; cf. also LEW 182). And he said of the latter: *"Where Mary is present, the evil one is absent. One of the unmistakable signs that a person is led by the Spirit of God is the devotion he has to Mary"* (TD 166). For Montfort, to consecrate oneself to Jesus through Mary according to his method is to follow a path *"without fear of illusions"* (TD 168), because Mary is the mountain where the disciples encounter the true Christ, who *"will teach them in his own words the meaning of the eight beatitudes"* (PM 25).

d. Other biblical data for discernment. *1. Reciprocal love as a sign of belonging to Christ's company.* "By this love you have for one another, everyone will know that you are my disciples" (Jn 13:34-35; cf. Mt 25:31-40). Montfort was quite clear in his writings on this fundamental requirement for discipleship (cf. TD 171; SR 70; RM 44-49; RS 99-100, 112, 311, 316). No testimony, however, could be more convincing than his own life, marked as it was by an utter respect for the "new commandment," whose observance, according to Matthew 25, will be a decisive criterion for entering the Kingdom. An episode sums up his view. One evening he came home from preaching a mission at Dinan,[7] carrying on his shoulders a man who was miserably sick. When the door was not immediately opened to him, he cried out, *"Open to Jesus Christ!"* (cf. Lk 10:37).

2. Christ's criterion for what is authentic and what is false. Christ's criterion can be seen in the image of the tree that can be known by its fruits (cf. Mt 7:15-20; Gal 5:16f.). It was frequently applied as a method for discernment by Montfort. As a way of recognizing Mary's true devotees from the false ones, the true lovers of Wisdom from the false ones, the true friends of the Cross from the false ones, he invariably looked at their fruits, i.e., their way of life. A passage about presumptuous devotees of May can illustrate this: they are *"sinners who give full reign to their passions or their love of the world, and who, under the fair name of Christian and servant of our lady, conceal pride, avarice, lust. . . . If Mary made it a rule to save by her mercy this sort of person, she would be condoning wickedness and helping to outrage and crucify her Son. Who would even dare to think of such a thing?"* (TD 97-98).

3. Other Gospel images. Other Gospel images on discernment are likewise used by Montfort: the house built on rock or sand (cf. Mt 7:24-27; TD 61, 214; RM 64); children of light or darkness (cf. Jn 1:4-13; 3:19; 8:12; Eph 5:8f.; LEW 145, 199); the two ways (cf. Mt 7:13-14; TD 44, 152; FC 7-8; MLW 38).

2. St. Ignatius and the spiritual currents of Montfort's Time

Louis Marie never presented any explicit teaching on spiritual discernment, since it was beyond his scope as an active missionary. In order to gather information on the issue, his biographies and written works must be consulted. Of particular significance in this respect are his letters.

a. Influence of St. Ignatius of Loyola. *1. Contact with Jesuits.* There is no doubt that Montfort's regular contacts with the Jesuits furnished him with both the doctrine and the experience of Saint Ignatius' "discernment of spirits." Before joining the seminary of St. Sulpice in Paris, Montfort studied at the Jesuit College in Rennes,[8] where he was taught and guided by influential Jesuits.[9] Later on during his itinerant missionary life, "he usually went to the Jesuit Fathers in the places where he happened to be and followed their instructions."[10] Several times his biographers mention the fact that he made retreats with the Jesuits, especially at moments of painful persecution and great suffering.[11] He did so also in 1710 after the events at Pontchâteau, when "he withdrew to the Jesuits of Nantes, in order to make a week's retreat there and to find consolation in God."[12] In this way, the Jesuit Fathers deeply influenced Montfort's spiritual journey and were of decisive significance in his overall life orientation.[13]

2. Montfort and the Spiritual Exercises. His retreats with the Jesuits, which naturally brought Montfort into contact with Ignatius' method of the discernment of spirits, thus sharpened his personal understanding and practice of discernment. A revealing text is found in Besnard, who tells us that Montfort was called to give retreats at Saint-Brieuc to women who wanted to withdraw for a week to make the spiritual exercises. He adds: "By his own experience, Fr. de Montfort knew the inestimable advantages of the retreats so well that he was able to contribute to them with great zeal and love. . . . He was not unaware of the fact that the scope and sequence of his powerful systematic presentation of the great truths of religion was done according to the method of St. Ignatius, which contained an altogether unique grace to produce the most blissful effect on mind and heart. . . . At such retreats a person is best disposed to make a decisive life choice, one for both time and eternity."[14] In this connection, it is important to note that, like St. Ignatius, Montfort proposes a month's retreat (cf. TD 227-228). While he may have taken the idea from the founder of the Society of Jesus, the scope, method, and development of this montfort month is so different from Ignatius' Spiritual Exercises as to defy comparison.[15] Fundamental to Ignatian spiritual discernment in seeking the divine will is "an attitude of impartiality, unaffected by any irregular motive."[16] Montfort made this holy "indifference" his own, as his letters show (cf. L 6, L 9). Another indication of Montfort's familiarity with the Spiritual Exercises can be seen in certain images he uses in FC. Ignatius proposes a meditation on the two standards as a help to reach discernment.[17] Montfort speaks, in a similar way, of two parties or companies.[18] What is depicted by Ignatius and Montfort as containing the elements for discernment manifest some undeniable similarities. It is clear, however, that the latter introduces, in a markedly original and dynamic way, his own biblical perspectives on the twofold scene.[19]

3. Other references to Ignatius and his Society. (i) The ideal of seeking only God's glory in everything can be found in the life of all the saints. The motto of St. Ignatius was "For the greater glory of God,"[20] while Montfort's was "God Alone." It is, however, interesting to note that Ignatius' motto appears several times in Montfort's works.[21] Undoubtedly his use of "God Alone" as a motto was as much influenced by his contact with the Jesuits as by his reading of contemporary spiritual writers, such as H. Boudon, who explicitly uses "God Alone."[22]

(ii) In RM, Montfort proposes the Society of Jesus three times as an example to his own followers (cf. RM 15, 19, 66). Several times he refers to Jesuit Fathers in other works (cf. TD 26, 40, 117, 161, 242, 258; L 11, 31; SR 25, 54, 80: RM 6).

b. Other Influences. If the sons of Ignatius and their spirituality left their mark on Louis Marie, it is also true that he was equally influenced by the spiritual masters of the French school.[23] Bremond calls Montfort "the last of the great Bérullians."[24] R. Deville states, "All aspects of Bérulle or Olier—the primacy of God, contemplation of Jesus in his mysteries (notably those of the Incarnation and the Cross), union with Mary, and the apostolic spirit—are taken up again in a very personal way by Louis Marie."[25] On discernment, one element may be considered here in particular, the role of the Holy Spirit, who is at the base of Christian discernment. Montfort's teaching on God's economy of salvation often refers to the role of the Holy Spirit, especially in relation to Mary and her spiritual maternity for all Christians.[26] As will be seen later, devotion to Mary is for Montfort one of the unmistakable signs that a person is being led by the Spirit of God. Here we discover undeniable traces of influence from theologians of the French school, such as Bérulle,[27] Olier, and Eudes. But equally apparent is the influence of other spiritual writers[28] who wrote on devotion to the Blessed Virgin and whose books he consulted, according to his own testimony (cf. TD 118), when he was librarian at Saint-Sulpice. Particular reference should be made here to authors such as Poiré, Boudon, Lallemant, Crasset, and Tronson.

II. Discernment during Montfort's Life and Spiritual Itinerary

Four concrete examples of discernment are given below. Drawn from Montfort's life, they are followed by a summary of his principal means and rules for exercising discernment.

1. Priesthood

Louis Marie seemed able to discern his priestly vocation without undue problems. Blain says, "The priesthood was the only state of life that appealed to him, the only one that God meant for him."[29] Yet it is recorded that he had to be pressed by his spiritual director to receive the minor orders[30] and that just before his ordination, "he shuddered and was seized by a holy trepidation."[31] He felt himself unworthy of the Sacrament and therefore needed support and confirmation from his superiors to overcome his sacred awe. Once ordained a priest (1700), he had to decide how to serve the Church. His letters are an abundantly rich source of information on the minute discernment he made in order to arrive at the right choices. It is pertinent to analyze them here in a rather extensive manner in order to perceive Louis Marie's process for reaching discernment, a process that formed the pattern for the rest of his priestly life.

2. Active apostolate or contemplative life?

During his studies in Rennes and Paris, Montfort had shown a strong inclination to prayer, mortification, and contemplation.[32] His liking for solitude was also expressed in a letter from Paris to his uncle, Fr. Alain Robert (L 4). However, at the same time, he had already displayed, as a student, a great love for the poor and shown a keen interest in teaching catechism to youth,[33] which met "with prodigious success."[34] According to Blain, some of his former masters had badly wanted him to stay at Saint Sulpice after his ordination, but Montfort had declined this invitation, "because his attraction lay elsewhere."[35] He moved to Nantes to be initiated into pastoral work by preaching missions under Fr. René Levêsque.[36] After staying there for about three months, he wrote a letter to his spiritual director in Paris, Fr. Leschassier, to tell him *"briefly about his state of mind at the moment"* (L 5). Undoubtedly already acquainted with the method of the Ignatian Spiritual Exercises, he explained what was going on in his heart and how he was faced with a double choice: *"I find myself, as time goes on, torn by two apparently contradictory feelings. On one hand, I feel a secret attraction for a hidden life in which I can efface myself and combat my natural tendency to show off. On the other hand, I feel a tremendous urge to make our Lord and his holy Mother loved, to go in a humble and simple way to teach catechism to the poor in country places and to arouse in sinners a devotion to our Blessed Lady."* Montfort continues: *"When I see the needs of the Church, I cannot help pleading continually for a small and poor band of good priests to do this work. . . . Though I find it difficult, I try to suppress these desires, good and persistent though they may be. I strive to forget them and self-effacingly place myself in the hands of divine Providence and submit entirely to your advice which will always have the force of law for me."* This text is precious, since it reveals a number of telling elements in Montfort's discernment, viz., observation of the "movements of his soul" and of the signs of the times, continuous prayer, surrender to God's will with a spirit of blessed detachment, and obedience to his spiritual director. Montfort's dilemma was slowly solved in favor of an active missionary life when he came into contact with Madame de Montespan (*"I obeyed her blindly believing this was God's holy will, which was all I wanted"*) and met the bishop of Poitiers (cf. L 6, 9), and other events in the meantime were further signs to the young priest of what God wanted from him (L 8).

But once more Montfort thought of leaving the active ministry. After much opposition and suffering in the workhouse of Poitiers, he left in 1703 for Paris, where he became even *"infinitely more impoverished, crucified, and humiliated than ever"* (L 16). In these circumstances, he again considered withdrawing from this world to live a life of solitude and contemplation. Probably he rediscovered this inclination because of the grace-filled experience he had with the hermits of Mont-Valerian.[37] Besnard reports that he duly consulted a Jesuit Father on the issue, who told him that he should not abandon or even suspend his mission activities,[38] and Montfort obeyed as always.

3. Choice of Pastoral Work

After his ordination, the new priest considered going to Canada or India[39] as a missionary, but the refusal of his spiritual director to let him go was for him a clear sign of God's will.[40] The community of Nantes, to which he moved first, and afterwards the general hospital of Poitiers in no way fulfilled the call of his heart, because he had *"no inclination at all to lead an enclosed life"* but was *"in his element, when teaching catechism to the poor in town and country"* (L 9, cf. Lf). The young priest again used every means of spiritual discernment to discover God's will through complete surrender in prayer (cf. L 6, 11) and through submission to the various options of his director, whose advice was always decisive (cf. L 5, 6, 8, 9, 10, 11). He confessed, *"I wish to remain completely impartial to everything except what obedience requires of me"* (L 9). Striking at this stage as well was Montfort's attention to the events in his life that might be signs of God (cf. L 6, 11), his readiness to surrender to His divine will (cf. L 5, 6, 9, 11), and his desire to live an unsettled life, marked by the Cross, in order thus to follow in the footsteps of Christ (cf. L 11). All these elements helped Montfort in the long process of discerning the orientation his priestly life had to take. It came to an end when, *"following the enlightenment that the Spirit of God gave him,"*[41] he decided to leave the workhouse of Poitiers for good and started *"to rove the world with the mood of a vagabond"* (H 22:1), ready to serve God Alone in the way Christ would show him. The numerous conversions he made while preaching missions, his overwhelming spiritual successes, and the extraordinary trials he experienced were for him important additional elements of discernment (cf. L 11, 13, 15). When opposition and rejection, however, especially by Church authorities, made his missionary activity practically unbearable, Montfort decided to undertake a pilgrimage to Rome (1706). The confirmation of his vocation from God to be "Missionary Apostolic" in France by Pope Clement XI dispelled all further doubts about the correctness of his discernment.[42]

4. Discernment in seeking perfection: the secret of Mary

Through continuous discernment, Montfort was able to give a Spirit-led orientation to his apostolic life. More important, however, is Louis Marie's absolutely unique road to sanctity (cf. TD 118), which is both the fruit and culmination of his personal discernment. It is through the *"secret of Mary"* (SM 1), a means he was not afraid to propose to others as *"the safest, easiest, shortest and most perfect way"* (TD 55; cf. also TD 152-159) to union with Jesus Christ, Eternal Wisdom (cf. LEW 203). This *"mystery of grace unknown even to many of the most learned and spiritual of Christians"* (TD 21; cf. also TD 64) consists in the Consecration of oneself to Jesus Christ through Mary. For seeking perfection in this way, Montfort recommends all the means proposed by the spiritual masters (cf. SM 4; LEW 181-202). He also amply employs reading and study (cf. TD 118), but in the end he testifies that only the Holy Spirit can reveal this secret of sanctity, which is the *"immaculate way of Mary"* (TD 158; cf. SM 1, 20, 70; SR 150). The Saint's *"discovery"* consists in his discerning the truth that *"where Mary is present, the evil one is absent. One of the unmistakable signs that a person is led by the Spirit of God is the devotion he has to Mary"* (TD 166; cf. TD 258), because she draws the Spirit into the soul (cf. TD 36, 43, 55). Montfort's own experience made this truth an unequivocal criterion of his discernment for reaching sanctity: *"Through Mary I will seek and find Jesus; I will crush the serpent's head and overcome all my enemies as well as myself, for the greater glory of God"* (LPM 6; cf. TD 41, 110, 119, 130, 168; SM 53, 57; SR 77-78; RM 56).

5. Montfort's Rules of Discernment

Only by reading biographies of Father de Montfort and by analyzing his writings, in particular his letters, is one able to gather the rich combination of elements that ruled his profound discernment. Our review of his life permits us to list the following "common" forms of spiritual discernment and discernment of spirits: a) Docility to the Spirit and listening to God's Word (cf. L 15, 18, 27, 30, 32, 33; LEW 95, 97; RM 60; TD 59; SM 2; H 6,37, H 141). b) Surrender to the divine will and to Providence (cf. L 2, 3, 5-11, 15, 16, 33, 34; SM 4; PM 8; LCM; RW 5, 29) with an attitude of blessed detachment or *"indifference"* (cf. L 6, 9). c) Habitual checking of persistent inner movements of the soul in order to embrace only those coming from God's Spirit (cf. L 5, 6, 9, 16, 17; RW 21). d) An almost innate distrust of one's own activities, choices, and preferences (cf. L 5, 6, 9, 8, 10, 11, 15, 32, 33; LEW 202, 221; SM 69; RM 19; RW 72; MLW 79-85).[43] e) Complete openness of heart towards his spiritual director (cf. L 5, 6, 8, 9, 10, 32; RM 20; RW 6, 21, 59, 60, 94, 157; MLW 86). f) The constant seeking of confirmation from the authorities, and unconditional obedience to them (L 5, 6, 9-11, 33; LEW 202; LPM 1; RM 19-22; RW 46-65; H 10,10, 18, 19). g) Realistic analysis of the situation (cf. L 5, 6, 9, 11). h) Observation of the signs of the times and of any relevant events during the discernment process (cf. L 6, 8, 9, 15, 16, 22, 33, 34). i) Acceptance, even welcome, of adversities and crosses as confirmation of authentic discipleship of Christ (cf. L 11, 13, 14, 16, 24, 26, 27, 33, 34; FC 27-28; RM 60; WC; MLW 9-17, 28; H 19,3; H 102, 1). j) Filial trust in Mary (cf. L 7-11, 15, 24, 26; LPM 6; LEW 203-

227; SM; TD; RW 139-144; H 77, 79-84, 145, 155). k) Fasting, mortification, retreats, unceasing personal prayer, and requests to others for prayers in order to discern God's ways and Wisdom (cf. L 4, 6, 10, 11, 15-17, 33; LEW 184-202; SM 4; RW 172-179; MLW 29-37; LPM 6; H 157). It is pertinent to note here that the path to discovering God's ways invariably led Montfort to immerse himself in an ambience of prolonged solitude, silence, and prayer, enabling him to become ever more tuned to the Lord's voice.[44] l) Abundant blessings in the apostolate seen as signs of correct discernment (cf. L 8, 9, 11, 26). m) Peace and freedom of heart as confirmation of right discernment (cf. L 20, 26, 34; H 157,20-32).

III. Montfort As Guide towards Discernment

1. In spiritual direction

In LS are notes on the Christian's obligation to have a spiritual director because "the one who trusts himself, trusts a fool" and a soul without a director is "like a ship without a rudder or pilot" (cf. LS 142-143; LEW 202; RM 20; SR 128). Montfort was faithful to this practice in his own priestly life,[45] and this undoubtedly helped him to be formed into a "skillful master in the guidance of souls."[46] As a young, unexperienced priest, Louis Marie was at first apprehensive about guiding souls, because, as he wrote, *"this difficult and dangerous work requires a special calling"* (cf. L 6). But slowly he was drawn into pastoral activities, which made him spend long hours in the confessional. *"Wonderful conversions"* were brought about through his ministry of *"giving advice to a constant stream of people,"* because *"the Lord had enlightened him to a degree he had never experienced before, by granting him the gift of making himself clear, a facility for speaking without preparation, . . . and a great capacity for sympathizing with everyone"* (L 11). Montfort's name as a powerful preacher and a saintly director of souls became ever more famous,[47] and the impact of his apostolic ministry was overwhelming and enduring. His biographers describe numerous instances revealing his utter conversance with *"the ways of God"* in the direction of souls, since "he even seemed to discern their most intimate sentiments and to fathom, better than they themselves, the depth of their thoughts."[48] The startling conversion of Miss Pagé in La Rochelle and her subsequent entry into a monastery of the Poor Clares after an eight-day retreat with the saint is only one of the examples.[49] Perhaps his gift of profound discernment is nowhere more convincingly shown than in the way he called and accompanied his first collaborators, Marie Louise Trichet, Brother Mathurin, Adrien Vatel, and René Mulot,[50] and likewise in the way he confirmed Jeanne Delanoue, foundress of the Sisters of St. Anne, in her practices of mortification, about which some in her community were apprehensive.[51]

2. In teaching about falsehood or truth

Montfort the missionary intended to teach catechism in a humble way to the poor and the simple (cf. L5; TD 26). In doing so, he made abundant use of the Bible and interpreted it according to the spiritual exegesis of the times, always presenting the faith in utterly simple terms and images. One of his recurrent teaching methods was to make the faithful aware of a truth by inviting them to differentiate between true and false orientations in their daily lives.[52] By clearly depicting both sides of the coin, he led people almost imperceptibly to a clear discernment about which choice to make as disciples of Christ and how to grow from imperfection to sanctity. We will consider briefly the main themes of Montfort's teaching, in which he made use of this popular but, at the same time, sound method of discernment.

a. False or true wisdom. After explaining that there are several kinds of wisdom, Louis Marie unmasked for *"those who are spiritually mature"* the hypocrisy and malice of worldly wisdom *"lest they be deceived by its false glitter"* (LEW 74). *"The worldly wisdom consists in an exact conformity to the maxims and fashions of the world; a continual inclination towards greatness and esteem"* (LEW 75). The worldly wise man *"manages to make a secret but fatal reconciliation of truth and falsehood, of the Gospel and the world, of virtue and sin, of Christ and Belial"* (LEW 76). By contrast, uncreated Wisdom, whom chosen souls seeking perfection are to acquire (cf. LEW 14), is defined as *"the Son of God, the second person of the most Blessed Trinity. In other words, it is Eternal Wisdom in eternity or Jesus Christ in time"* (LEW 13). She communicates her subtle and penetrating Spirit of enlightenment to man, enabling him *"to judge all things with keen discernment and deep penetration"* (LEW 92). In fact, *"when divine Wisdom enters a soul, she brings all kinds of good things with her and bestows vast riches upon that soul,"* inspiring it *"to undertake great things for the glory of God and the salvation of souls"* (LEW 90, cf. LEW 100).

b. False or true devotion to Mary. Montfort states that it is important to recognize *"false devotions to our Lady"* (TD 90). He enumerates seven kinds that are false (TD 92-104). While some of these can easily be recognized by their bad fruits (cf. TD 97), others need deeper discernment. For instance, he unmasks as a *"very insidious inference"* the opinion of those who oppose honoring Mary, arguing that a true devotion to her would obscure the unique mediatorship of her Son. Montfort states bluntly: *"It is a subtle snare of the evil one under the pretext of promoting a greater good. For we never give more honor to Jesus than when we honor His Mother, and we honor her simply and solely to honor Him all the more perfectly. We go to her only as a way leading to the goal we seek—Jesus, her Son"* (TD 94). In this connection, in an original way the saint made use of the biblical story of Rebecca, symbol of Mary, and her two sons Jacob and Esau, symbols respectively of Mary's true and false devotees (cf. Gen 27; TD 183-211). Montfort's working method gave him a valid procedure to lead his contemporaries to discernment, based on biblical premises.

c. False or true friend of the Cross. According to Louis Marie, the great mystery of the Cross is to be learned in the school of Christ, the crucified God (cf. FC 11, 26). The enemies of the Cross are worldlings who belong to the company of the devil: they seek after wealth, enjoyment, honors, and the evil practices of the world (cf. FC 7-12, LEW 75; H 19:2). Instead, a sure sign of belonging to the company of Christ's disciples is the willingness to undergo persecution and to carry the Cross (cf. Mt 5:10-12; 19:3). It is in weakness that God's power to save comes out most clearly (cf. 2 Cor 12:10; 1 Cor 1:12; L 11, 26). It is in the folly of Christ's Cross that God's Wisdom shines out (cf. 1 Cor 1:17f.; L 15, 16). Probably in no other way than in this supreme test and proof of discernment, namely by suffering and being persecuted for Christ's name, Montfort has shown himself to be a faithful disciple of his Master. This is abundantly clear from his life,[53] and it is a recurrent theme in all his written works. *"The cross is a sure sign that He loves you. I can assure you of this, that the greatest proof which God requires to show our love for Him"* (LEW 176, 4).

d. False or true preacher. Montfort's description of false preachers is incredibly tart, almost cynical. These fashionable preachers have solely the tongue, mouth, and wisdom of men, and therefore they *"only beat the air and titillate the ears,"* yielding nothing more than *"popular admiration which occupies the mind of worldly people during the sermon and provides them with a subject of conversation when they meet socially after church"* (RM 60; cf. also H 4, 12; S 472). Montfort wanted his missionaries to preach the Good News in an entirely different way, namely, with great power, boldness, and wisdom (cf. RM 60-65; PM 22; TD 54). Throughout his priestly life, he practiced what he asked from his followers when he wrote: *"The missionaries will study and pray unceasingly that they may obtain from God the gift of wisdom so necessary to a true preacher for knowing and relishing the truth and getting others to relish it"* (RM 60). And the faithful of Montbernage had to pray in order *"to obtain from God the gift of speech or diving Wisdom"* (LPM 6), because *"the words that divine Wisdom communicates are not just ordinary, natural, human words but powerful, touching, piercing words, 'sharper than a two-edged sword,' words that go from the heart of the one through whom she speaks straight to the heart of the listener"* (LEW 96). The equation of "eloquence" with "Wisdom" by Montfort, in the context of missionary virtues, finds its explanation in his conviction that intimate union with Christ Wisdom infallibly produces in the preacher *"this great gift of the Holy Spirit"* (RM 60). Study and prayer are for Louis Marie not the only means to acquire Wisdom. The preacher must long for it day and night, must seek it through fasting, mortification, crosses and trials of every kind, and above all through a loving devotion to Mary (cf. L 13-16, 20, 34; LEW 181-222; TD 272; FC 45; PS 1).

IV. Significance of Montfort's Discernment Today

1. Need for discernment in contemporary society

In view of the sweeping changes that take place in today's world and affect all levels and areas of modern society, the Second Vatican Council (cf. GS 4) and many Church documents since stress the Church's responsibility to read the signs of the times and interprete them in the light of the Gospel.[54] "Discernment is at the heart of the Christian condition."[55] Montfort's life and works offer basic orientations on spiritual discernment, which show his familiarity with the Ignatian method. At the same time, however, he manifests his own unique and original approach to the issue. A number of elements and rules used by the saint have been listed above, but in final analysis, it is very hard to sum up, in distinctive categories, laws and codes by which he was governed when exercising discernment. In his apostolic life and ministry, Montfort was closely united with the mystery of Christ Wisdom, giving himself to the world through Mary. From this inscrutably singular and intimate relationship were born the rules that securely governed his own course of action and the guidance he gave to others. His works to discover their surprising topicality for spiritual discernment in modern times. While several apposite applications can be made, two are singled out as containing invaluable elements for contemporary spirituality.

2. Christ Wisdom

Although somehow becoming more open to religious issues today, our modern world is awash with numerous false norms and values that disorientate Christians in living out their faith (cf. GS 4, 7, 19-20). As a master pedagogue of Christian discernment, Montfort unfailingly unmasked the various forms of false wisdom that were current in his time and re-emerge under new appearances in our world.[56] His description of the *"commandments of the world"* is still entirely valid in our times (cf. LEW 74-89): *"You shall frequent fashionable society,"* etc. His sketch of the *"worldly-wise man"* is equally telling: *"He excels in the art of duplicity and well-concealed fraud without arousing suspicion. He thinks one thing and says or does another. He accommodates himself to everyone to suit his own end, completely ignoring the honor and interests of God. He manages to make a secret, but fatal, reconciliation of truth and falsehood, of the Gospel and the world, of virtue and sin, of Christ and Belial"* (LEW 76). Invariably, Montfort orientated souls to the source of all genuine Wisdom: *"To know Jesus Christ Incarnate Wisdom, is to know all we need"* (LEW 11). He had no fear to join battle against everything that came from the evil spirit, thus often drawing fierce criticism and painful persecution upon himself and becoming a sign of contradiction. In following the footsteps of Incarnate and crucified Wisdom, Montfort had, through personal experience,[57] discerned *"that the greatest proof that we are loved by God is when we are despised by the world and burdened with crosses"* (L 13). While our contemporary world still rejects the Cross as madness (cf. 1 Cor 1:23), the saint instead learned that *"the holy folly of the cross was the utterly infallible secret to attract blessings from heaven,"*[58] since, according to Saint Paul, God's power is at its best in weakness (cf. 2 Cor 12:7-10). "Le bon Père de Montfort," who was given the grace of touching men's hearts,[59] undoubtedly still provides today, through his life and works, and particularly through his teaching on the Incarnation and the Cross, rich sources of *"light and unction to inspire others with that love for Wisdom which will lead them to eternal life"* (LEW 30).

3. Through Mary

People searching for union with Christ find in Montfort a spiritual master who, with an unparalleled forcefulness of argument, confided to the Church the *"secret of Mary"* (SM, 1): *"The greatest means of all, and the most wonderful of all secrets for obtaining and preserving divine Wisdom is a loving and genuine devotion to the Blessed Virgin"* (LEW 203). Mary is *"the direct and immaculate way to Jesus and the perfect guide to Him; it is through her that souls who are to shine forth in sanctity must find Him. He who finds Mary finds life, that is, Jesus Christ who is the way, the truth, and the life"* (TD 50, cf. also 64, 158, 218). The saint came to this conviction through ample reading and study on the issue (cf. TD 118), but most of all through personal experience (cf. SM 53, 57; TD 41, 130; RM 56). Therefore, he is not afraid to make it an unassailable criterion of discernment: *"Where Mary is present, the evil one is absent. One of the unmistakable signs that a person is led by the Spirit of God is the devotion he has to Mary"* (TD 166). Montfort's message to the Church of today[60] is still as topical and timely as it was in his century, when he exhorted his audience: *"Whoever then wishes to advance along the road to holiness and to be sure of encountering the true Christ, without fear of the illusions which afflict many devout people, should take up with valiant heart and willing spirit this devotion to Mary which perhaps he had not previously heard about. Even if it is new to him, let him enter upon this excellent way which I am now revealing to him. . . . Let us then take this road and travel along it night and day until we arrive at the fullness of the age of Jesus Christ"* (TD 168; cf. Eph 4:13).

A. Van der Hulst

Notes: (1) *Discernment of Spirits* (translation of *Discernement des esprits,* in *Dictionnaire de Spiritualité* (*Dictionary of Spirituality*), Beauchesne, Paris 1957, 3:1222-1291), ed. E. Malatesta, Liturgical Press, Collegeville 1970, Introduction, 9; cf. also *Discernement,* in *Dictionnaire de la vie spirtuelle,* (*Dictionary of the Spiritual Life*) Cerf, Paris 1983, 271. (2) Cf. L. Pérouas, *Grignion de Montfort ou l'aventurier de l'évangile,* (*Grignion de Montfort or the Adventurer of the Gospel*) Ed. Ouvrières, 1990, 19-26. (3) Cf. J. Crasset, preface to *La véritable dévotion envers la sainte vierge établie et défendue,* (*The True Deovtion to the Holy Virgin Established and Defended*) Paris 1687; P. Eyckeler, *De Heilige Montfort, Louis Marie-Grignion,* (*Saint Montfort, Louis Marfe Grignion*) Maastricht 1947, 342-346; R. Deville, *L'école française de spiritualité,* (*The French School of*

Spirituality) Desclée, Paris 1987, 42-44; Papàsogli, 107. (4) This article makes use of an unpublished essay on *Discernement chez Montfort* (*Discernement in Montfort*) by G. Dallaire, Montreal 1991. (5) Cf. J.C. Haughey, *The Conspiracy of God,* Image Books, New York 1976, 12-19. (6) Blain, 178. (7) Besnard I, 114. (8) Cf. G. Durtelle de Saint-Sauveur, *Le Collège de Rennes depuis la fondation jusqu'au départ des Jésuites, 1536-1762,(The College of Rennes Since its Foundation Untill the Departure of the Jesuits)* in *Bull. Soc. Archéolog. d'Ille-&-Vilaine,* (*Bulletin of Archeology of Ille & Villaine),* 46 (1918), esp. 195. (9) Cf. S. De Fiores, Itinerario 35-71; Besnard I, 45. (10) Blain, 80. (11) Cf. Besnard I, 62, 94. (12) Cf. ibid., 191: Retreat under the direction of Fr. de Préfontaine. (13) Especially Fr. André Camus (Rennes, cf. Blain, 1) Fr. François Gilbert (Rennes, cf. Besnard I, 23); Fr. Philippe Déscartes (Rennes, cf. Blain, 61); Fr. Bertrand de la Tour (Poitiers, cf. Grandet, 454), and L. Martinet (Nantes, 1711). (14) Besnard I, 130. (15) The Ignatian Exercises aim primarily at helping a retreatant, through the experience of diverse spirits, to arrive at an unconditional availability and a new orientation of life towards God and one's personal sanctification. The montfort retreat is essentially meant as a preparation for consecrating oneself to Christ through Mary as a perfect renewal of the baptismal vows. Also, the means used by both differ greatly. The content of the month proposed by Montfort reflects little of Ignatius' Spiritual Exercises but has much more in common with the spirituality of the French school. (16) St. Ignatius of Loyola, *Spiritual Exercises,* trans. Corbishley and Clarke, Wheathampstead 1973, 197. (17) Cf. Spiritual Exercises, 4th day, 2nd week, nos. 136-147. Ignatius describes Christ and the forces of good as opposed to Lucifer and the powers of evil. The Savior teaches the Beatitudes and sends his disciples out to proclaim the Gospel, while the head of the enemy dispatches devils to seduce men into love for money, position, and pride. (18) Cf. FC 7-12: Montfort describes a small company of people, led along a narrow road by the suffering Christ. They strive to live according to the law of the Gospel and not headed by the proud Lucifer, is very numerous. These people follow a wide and pleasant road and are seduced by the attractions of the world. See also PM 26-30; TD 28, 50-54, 210. (19) These are: the wide and the narrow road (cf. Mt 7:13-14), the separation of the good and the evil on the right and the left (cf. Mt 25:33), and Christ's invitation to his followers to carry the Cross with him (cf. Mt 16:24), while those who follow the world urge each other to continue in their evil ways. (20) C. de Dalmaises, *Ignatius of Loyola, Founder of the Jesuits: His Life and Work,* St. Louis 1985, 69, 141. (21) Ignatius' motto *Ad maiorem Dei gloriam* is employed word for word in LEW 222, 225; SM 29; TD 122, 151 (twice). There are still many other expressions with the same content, though differently phrased: cf. L 13; LEW 164, 219; SM 46; TD 58, 70, 91, 118, 124, 139, 205, 222, 224; RM 62, etc. Cf. also L.L. Terstroet, *Maria en de glorie van God (Mary and the Glory of God),* Nijmegen 1946. (22) Cf. H. Boudon, *Oeuvres Complètes,* vol. 2, *Dieu Seul ou le Saint Esclavage de l'admirable Mère de Dieu (God Alone or The Holy Slavery of the Admirable Mother of God),* Migne, 1856, col. 377ff.; and R. Deville, *L'Ecole française,* 142-200. (24) H. Bremond, *Histoire litteraire du sentiment religieux en France depuis la fin des guerres de religion jusqu'a nos jours,* vol. 9, *La vie chretienne sous l'ancien regime,* Paris 1932, 272; *A Literary History of Religious Thought in France from the Wars of Religion Down to our Own Times,* K.L. Montgomery, Macmillan, New York 1928 (25) R. Deville, *L'Ecole française,* 143. (26) Cf. P. Gaffney, *Mary's Spiritual Maternity according to St. Louis de Montfort,* Montfort Publications, Bay Shore, N.Y. 1976. (27) An illustration of Montfort's "evolution" of Bérulle's doctrine of the Holy Spirit. The latter writes: "I wish that the Spirit of Jesus Christ be the Spirit of my spirit and the life of my life," P. de Bérulle, *Grandeurs de Jesus (The Grandeurs of Jesus),* in *Oeuvres Complètes,* Migne, 1856, col. 181. Montfort has in a unique way "developed" this idea by bringing in Mary's role and making it a prominent criterion for discernment about union with Christ: *"We should give ourselves up to the spirit of Mary to be moved and directed as she wishes. . . . The more we do so, the quicker we shall grow in holiness and the sooner we shall reach union with Christ, which necessarily follows upon union with Mary, since the spirit of Mary is the Spirit of Jesus"* (TD 259). Cf. also J. J. Olier, *Vie interieure de la Tres-Sainte Vierge (The Interior Life of the Blessed Virgin),* Paris 1866, 246-247. (28) Cf. B. Papàsogli, *Montfort a Prophet for Our Times,* Ed. Monfortane, Rome 1991, 103-100, 236. (29) Blain, 12. (30) Cf. Grandet, 18-19. (31) Besnard I, 51; cf. also S. De Fiores, *Itinerario* 71-79, 248. (32) Cf. Blain, 7-9, 25-32; Besnard I, 40. (33) P. Eyckeler, E. van Aelst, Maastricht 1953, 212. (34) Grandet, 20; also 15. (35) Blain, 107. (36) Cf. ibid., 108. (37) Cf. Besnard I, 64-66. (38) Cf. ibid., 62. (39) Cf. Besnard II, 211; cf. also S 502, note a. (40) Cf. Blain, 106; Besnard I, 52-53. (41) Besnard I, 76. (42) Cf. Eyckeler, o.c. 114-115. (43) Montfort is particularly apprehensive of the danger of illusions, visions, etc.; cf. LEW 186, 202;

SR 77-78; SM 17-18, 69; TD 62, 97, 157, 165, 167, 168, 209; H 10,19; 15,28, 30, 31, 39; 138,121. Cf. also St. Jean de la Croix, *La montée du Carmel,* Edit. Seuil, Paris 1947, 281-84; English edition: John of the Cross, *The Ascent of Mount Carmel,* trans. David Lewis, T. Baker, London 1906. (44) It has been recorded that Montfort spent a total of approximately four of his sixteen years of priesthood in solitude and retreat. (45) Cf. Blain, 60; also, on the same page, note 37; also FC 48. (46) C. Besnard, *La Vie de la Soeur Marie-Louise de Jésus, première Superieure des Filles de la Sagesse instituées par M. Louis-Marie Grignion de Montfort, Prêtre missionnaire apostolique (The Life of Sister Marie Louise of Jesus, First Superior of the Daughters of Wisdom Founded by Louis Marie Grignion de Montfort, Priest, Apostolic Missionary),* CIM, Rome 1985, 33. (47) Cf. Besnard I, 59, 77, 129-130, 146-147, 268-271, 287-289; 324-326; Besnard II, 39-40, 80, 100-102; J. Grandet, 124-125, 176-177, 201, 205-206. (48) Besnard I, 325. (49) Cf. ibid., 268-271; also 64-66: reform under the hermits of Mont-Valérien; 220-222: conversion of Mrs. de Mailly, etc. (50) Cf. Besnard, *Marie-Louis;* Besnard I and II, passim. (51) J. A. Mace, *Vie de Jeanne de la Noue, Fondatrice de l'Hospice de la Providence de Saumur et de la Congrégation des Soeurs de Sainte-Anne, Servantes des Pauvres (Life of Jeanne de la Noue, Foundress of the Providence Hospice of Saumur and of the Congregation of the Sisters of Saint Anne, Servants of the Poor),* P. Godet, Saumur 1845, 139-141. (52) Cf. TD 92, note 175. (53) Montfort's admirable resignation to God's will was manifest, e.g.: (a) during the painful treatment he received from spiritual directors, superiors, and Church authorities (cf. Besnard I, 46-47; 50-51; 61-62; 149-150; 310-311; Besnard II, 1-2; 34-36; 40; 205-210); (b) following the "trial of Pontchâteau" (cf. Besnard I, 180-193; Blain, 167-168). (54) Cf. *Life and Mission of Religious in the Church,* in *L'Osservatore Romano,* Jan. 26, 1981, Introduction. Cf. also John Paul II, *Pastores dabo vobis,* Libr. Ed. Vat., Rome 1992, no. 10; CCC 1676, 2846ff. (55) Paul-Andre Giguère, *Une foi adulte (An Adult Faith),* L'horizon du croyant, Novalis, Ottawa 1991, 91; quotation by G. Dallaire, *Discernement chez Montfort,* 1. (56) Cf. John Paul II, *Pastores dabo vobis,* nos. 7-8. (57) Besnard I, 225-227, 258-260; Besnard II, 39-40; 210-213 (58) Besnard I, 71. (59) Ibid., 151. (60) Cf. John Paul II, *RMat* 48; Paul VI, *Marialis cultus,* 27.

DISCIPLE

SUMMARY

I. THE FIGURE OF THE DISCIPLE IN MONTFORT'S THOUGHT:
   1. The identification of the Christian with the disciple;
   2. Discipleship and devotion to Mary.

II. DISCIPLESHIP IN THE NT PERSPECTIVE:
   1. Christian Discipleship;
   2. Radical requirements of Christian discipleship;
   3. The identity of the disciple.

III. SOME SIGNIFICANT ASPECTS OF DISCIPLESHIP:
   1. Sharing of the life of the Master;
   2. The radical nature of the discipleship of Christ;
   3. The presence of Mary in the life of the disciple;
   4. Serving the Kingdom.

There can be no doubt that, beginning with the apostles, the presence of disciples (in the widest sense of the word) is characteristic both of the ministry of Christ and of the Church throughout its history. Jesus Christ was sent by the Father to be the Shepherd of the Last Age, to gather together all the dispersed children of God (Jn 11:52), and He came to call all peoples to the obedience of faith (Rom 1:5), beginning with the lost sheep of the house of Israel (Mt 15:24).

He begins his ministry by calling certain disciples to follow him more closely than the rest in sharing his life and his mission. These belong to a wider circle of disciples, however, who all come into contact with the Master more or less directly. This wider circle surrounding Jesus is in turn surrounded by the crowds who accompany the Master, listening to his word and practicing a looser, less exacting discipleship.

When the risen Christ entrusts the Twelve with the mission of making disciples of all nations (Mt 28:19f) and gives them the mandate to be his witnesses to the ends of the earth (Acts 1:8), these tasks are in fact the continuation of Jesus' own mission, its extension in time and space. Making disciples is the fundamental task entrusted to Jesus and the Church; being a disciple is the life common to all believers without exception.

Given that disciples are so important in the NT, it is scarcely surprising that they are also important in the life and the thought of Montfort, whose single ambition was to live as the Apostles did, to relive exactly the experience of a disciple of the Lord.

I. THE FIGURE OF THE DISCIPLE IN MONTFORT'S THOUGHT

In Montfort's writing (as in the NT), the term "disciple" has many acceptations and refers to various categories of people. It can have a narrow, specific meaning; or it can have a wider, more general one when it refers quite simply to the Christian. It is therefore important to follow the developments of Montfort's thought in this respect and to emphasize the particular connotations of the term and concept "disciple" as it appears in various contexts.

1. The identification of the Christian with the disciple

Where LEW 64 speaks of the bonds of friendship between Eternal Wisdom and man, man is described as His brother, His friend, His disciple, His pupil, the price of His own blood and co-heir of His Kingdom. Montfort puts forward an overview resuming and synthesizing various aspects of the revelation. He begins by taking the various images and terms that biblical tradition interprets as referring to Divine Wisdom in general and applies them to Jesus, Wisdom Incarnate and crucified. The text introduces the term "disciple," with its connotation of "pupil" and other connotations belonging to the sapiential tradition, such as friend and brother, (Prov 8 passim, Bar 3:37f); but it also introduces traits belonging specifically to NT soteriology (the price of his blood, the co-heir of the Kingdom), which are derived from a different tradition.

In LEW 179 the Beatitudes, which according to the NT belong to all those who follow Christ, especially through suffering and persecution, are attributed to the disciples of Wisdom (who is still Christ crucified). Here the disciple of Wisdom is quite clearly the disciple of the Master's Cross.

FC 27 returns to this central figure, the disciple of the suffering and crucified Christ: *"If you are guided by the same spirit, if you live with the same life as Jesus, your thorn-crowned Head, you must expect only thorns, lashes and nails; that is, nothing but the cross; for the disciple must be treated like the master."* Hymn 35 can be read in the light of this, especially the close: *"But let us see only Jesus Christ, / Since He is our great model . . . / The Christian like his Savior, / The disciple like his Master, / the slave like his Lord"* (H 35:55, 58).

In SR 37, Montfort widens the concept of discipleship by emphasizing the importance of praying like Jesus. Whoever does not pray as the Divine Master prayed and taught others to pray is not his disciple. Prayer not only implies imitation of the Master - an important element in the concept of discipleship - but springs from an intimate communion with the Master himself, of whose Body we are members.

According to RM 52, one or two of the missionaries will announce the mission two weeks before it begins, as did the disciples whom Jesus sent two by two to the places where he was to go. Clearly then, the meaning of "disciple" is fleshed out and clarified in various contexts. As has already been remarked, however, the title of disciple in the widest sense remains applicable either to Christians as such or specifically to the future missionaries whom Montfort had in mind.

It should be noted that in LEW 197 Montfort groups together the Apostles, the disciples, the first Christians, and the religious who follow their example by renouncing all worldly possessions in order to possess Wisdom. Following Christ is closely linked to an attitude of complete detachment from material things. This passage can be aptly compared with the long, detailed Hymn 33, which is directed against luxury and worldly frivolities.

2. Discipleship and devotion to Mary

However bold it may seem, Montfort maintains in LEW 214 that one cannot be a son of God and disciple of Wisdom without being a son of Mary, nor belong to the elect without a sincere devotion to her. It should be noted that here the disciple is placed on the same level as the children of God and the elect; and there is also the typically montfort vision of the presence and decisive role of the Mother of the Savior in Christian experience.

The faithful Virgin—who also is a wise person—is invoked at the end of the prayer of Consecration. She is asked to make the believer *"so committed a disciple, imitator, and slave of Jesus, incarnate Wisdom"* (LEW 227).

Montfort strives towards the training of the perfect disciple, which is the aim of his entire spirituality. This goal is attained, it might be said, by the apostles of the end times. Indeed, in TD, Montfort rounds off his splendid description of such apostles by asserting that they will be *"true disciples of Jesus Christ"* (TD 59). They will imitate the Master's poverty, humility, contempt of the world, and love. They will have the two-edged sword of the Word of God in their mouths and the blood-stained standard of the Cross on their shoulders. Clearly, then, the follower of Mary is identified with the disciple of Jesus, whose sharing in the Master's sufferings is constantly emphasized. Montfort does not doubt for a moment that the two should be identified in this way. His aim is to fashion *"a true servant of Mary and a true disciple of Jesus"* (TD 111). The devotion he teaches leads us to perfect love of our neighbor and shows us that this is the way to be true disciples of Jesus, recognized by their love (TD 171): this is a view of discipleship different from the directly Christological one, so often emphasized, which entails sharing the Master's sufferings.

The ideal picture of the disciple remains for Montfort that of John the Evangelist: the disciple whom Jesus loved and confided to his mother. Montfort declares that this disciple - who represents all the others - is blessed (TD 179), will receive unbounded confidence (TD 216), and surrenders himself trustingly and in the manner of a son (HD 36). Montfort sees in him the model of the acceptance of Mary, a precious possession bequeathed to us by Christ on the Cross (cf. SM 66).[1]

In his writings Montfort pursues a highly practical goal; his intention is pastoral and spiritual. We should not expect a finished treatise nor an exposition of doctrine. Moreover, his vision is tied in with the specific concepts of his time and with his personal experience. So it will be useful to supplement Montfort's vision of the disciple in two ways: by examining fully the relevant biblical perspective and by discussing the outlook of our own time. This will help to reveal the full complexity and relevance of the montfort figure of the disciple.

II. Discipleship in the NT Perspective

1. Christian Discipleship

The term "disciple" (*mathetes*), which is of especial interest here, occurs up to 264 times in the NT, but exclusively in the Gospels and Acts (the reason for this will be discussed below). The basic connotation of this term is complete obedience to one person, realized in the form of the *sequela* (commitment to follow him). The pupil/master relationship is absent from the NT; it is replaced by the relation of disciple and Lord. This basic and characteristic attitude of the disciple is reflected in several significant points, which together define his position in the NT:

a. First of all, there is the unique and exclusive action of Jesus, who calls those he wants and lays down the conditions on which he will allow them into his following.

b. Whilst the pupil of the rabbis seeks doctrinal teaching so that he can become a rabbi himself, the relationship with Jesus is of a different kind; it involves a permanent discipleship, because there is only one Master, Christ.

c. Jesus is, therefore, the only Master, and his authority is normative. He can contradict the tradition of the Elders and he interprets God's Word and intentions with sovereign authority.

d. Jesus chooses his disciples from all stations in life, and in doing so fails to observe the separation of the clean from the unclean; his disciples even include publicans and sinners.

e. Jesus' call involves obedience to the Master and availability for mission, in the service of the Kingdom. He requires all his followers to make radical decisions and offer themselves unreservedly; he does so not on his own behalf but on behalf of the supreme authority of God, Who is the absolute form of his own person and of his mission.[2]

f. The disciple of Jesus will share the lot of the Master (cf. Mt 10:24f.; 16:24f.); disciple and Master share the same life, service, and destiny.

g. This sharing in the life of the Master extends to his Passion and the glory that follows on it. This raises the disciples up, so that they share in Jesus' authority and his life (cf. Mt 16:25; Jn 14:6). Their reward and their happiness are that their names are written in heaven.

2. Radical requirements of Christian discipleship

Whilst Jesus did not take social, religious, or dynastic privileges into account in choosing his disciples, the conditions he set his followers were radical and extremely exacting. He asks them to leave their home and family, to abandon their profession and way of life, and to follow resolutely in his steps. This means starting out on a risky and completely precarious existence, a life full of contradictions, in which no human help is available. The absolute nature of Jesus' conditions is typically illustrated in the case of the man who asks him for just enough time to bury his father before following him. Jesus replies sternly: "Let the dead bury their own dead; but as for you, go and proclaim the kingdom of God" (Lk 9:59f.). This was a scandalous thing to say, especially according to the Jewish mentality, for which burying the dead was an indispensable act of piety.

Another example of Jesus' radicalism is his request to the rich young man to give his possessions to the poor as the condition of becoming his follower (Mk 10:17-22). This attitude is also disconcerting to the Jewish mentality, which, while approving of the giving of alms, at the same time considers material possessions as a blessing from God rather than an obstacle. Jesus' request, which results from his choosing the side of the poor, has two effects: on the one hand, it provokes discussion on the prevailing mode of thought, and on the other, it presents poverty as one of the particular defining characteristics of following him.[3]

Even the request for celibacy, which is not addressed to everyone but only to a certain number "to whom it has been given," strongly emphasizes the requirements of the Master. Celibacy, in contrast with the beliefs of the Qmran community, indicates an absolute choice for the Kingdom of God.

Nevertheless, it must be remarked that whilst certain conditions are set for a few followers and so relate to discipleship in the strict sense of the word, requirements that are no less rigorous apply to all who wish to enter the Kingdom of God. The renunciation of riches, for instance, is a fundamental condition for entering the Kingdom; love of money is idolatrous and prevents entry. Similarly, the thirst for power is a serious obstacle on the road to salvation. In particular, it should be noted that in Matthew's version, the Sermon on the Mount, with its various conditions, is a call to happiness addressed to the crowds following Jesus (Mt 4:25; cf. 7:28).

3. The identity of the disciple

From this arises an important question: Who are the disciples? Or more precisely, what persons or what groups of people are covered by this term? It is only in later tradition that the disciples are identified with the Twelve. In fact, the Twelve, who represent the tribes of Israel and the whole of God's new people, belong to a wider circle of disciples whom Jesus chose from those who followed him; the seventy-two whom Jesus sends out on a mission (cf. Lk 10:1) are set apart from the rest of the crowd of followers. An exact account of names or numbers of disciples does not seem possible. What all the disciples have in common, beyond any possible distinctions between groups or individuals, is that they follow Christ, in the manner already described. As we have already seen, the passages of the Gospels relating to discipleship emphasize renunciation (Mt 23:7ff.), humility (Mt 18:1ff.), poverty (Mt 19:23ff.), and the prospect of suffering as the characteristics of the true disciple. But the basis of all is faith, the vital allegiance to the Master, who must be acknowledged before men (cf. Lk 12:8f.). Luke in particular considers this condition to be so important that after Gethsemani he stops using the word *mathetes* until Acts 6, where it reappears with a different connotation.

The term's change in meaning appears particularly clearly in the Gospel of John, in which it indicates Christians as a whole. Since no term such as *ekklesia* occurs in the Fourth Gospel, the believers are the *mathetai,* those who, according to Johannine terminology, have passed from darkness to light.

This meaning of disciple, i.e. "Christian," is still clearer in the Book of Acts, where the *mathetes* is the one who believes and bears witness to Jesus Christ.

In the Apostles' letters, there appear composite verb forms that serve to emphasize the relationship with Jesus in glory and with his Spirit. The *sequela* of Christ in this case obviously includes all believers. Such an expansion of the term "disciple" came about by a natural and almost inevitable process, as a result of the Resurrection of Jesus and the pouring out of the Spirit on the whole community. After the events of Easter, the early communities meditated deeply on the Passion and the death of the Master in the light of the Scriptures, and recognizing him as the Lord, they held him up as a model to all believers. In this way, to follow Christ came to mean to imitate him, as can be seen fully in 1 Pet 2:21-23. This is clear in Acts, especially in the martyrdom of Stephen (cf. Acts 8:60 and Lk 23:34); but it is also expressed in the epistles of Paul (passim) and in John. The theme of the imitation of Christ is subsequently stressed in the Apostolic Fathers, in particular by Ignatius of Antioch. "The *sequela* of Christ is to be always walking in his steps and participating in his death and his Resurrection, as Paul tirelessly emphasizes (cf. Gal 2:19f.; 2 Cor 4:16f.; Phil 3:10f.; Rom 8:17; etc.)."[4]

III. Some Significant Aspects of Discipleship

It will by now be clear that Montfort's life and thought are remarkably in tune with the NT concept of the disciple. His life is deeply marked by his commitment to following the crucified Christ and by the all-consuming passion to preach the Gospel to the poor. His "apostolic" way of life is the strongest proof of this, and this way of life is reflected in his writings.

Consequently, the relevant passages of the NT are reflected in Montfort's vision of the disciple, but with a number of special emphases linked to his spiritual and apostolic experience.

We shall refer to several of the relevant passages that seem to be the more obvious and decisive ones, and those that are more in tune with the outlook of our own time.

1. Sharing the life of the master

Above all, there is the sharing of the life of the Master. It has a particular emphasis on suffering, in line with the Synoptic tradition and in confority with the harsh experience of Montfort's life.[5] Nor should we forget that as man and as thinker Montfort constantly strove towards an intimate communion with Wisdom in order to become the true disciple of the crucified Christ. All other aspects of his life, including even the *"loving and genuine devotion to the blessed Virgin"* (LEW 203-222) are a means to achieve this fundamental experience. Certainly, from the point of view of the Johannine conception and the theological and ecclesial outlook of our time, the paschal and glorious aspect of the Cross of Christ could be brought out more strongly in Montfort's vision. This should not, however, cause us to forget that to be a disciple is to walk in the Master's footsteps towards Jerusalem, where the scandalous and paradoxical aspects of the Cross will be most clearly manifest, and where the confusion of the disciples - which is already clear along the way - will be completely revealed. Strong reference to the scandal of the Cross is especially salutary in our time, since now the glory of Resurrection is emphasized (though of course this is right in itself).

2. The radical nature of the discipleship of Christ

Another element of foremost importance that is linked with the first is **the radical nature** of the entry into Christ's following. Montfort and the NT both speak of it insistently. We are confronted with a disconcerting requirement of an absolute nature, as when Jesus says that one cannot turn back, even to bury his own father, and one must renounce all material possessions, family, and even his own life.

Montfort expresses himself with similar force; those who dedicate themselves to the service of the Kingdom must be completely free (cf. PM 7, 9) and follow the Master in poverty, humility, and contempt of the world (cf. LEW 133-135, 194; SM 46, 49; TD 59, 80f., 126f., 239, 259).

This decisiveness and absolutism are also particularly important in our time, in which a deep relativism is prevalent both in people's thoughts and in their actions, so that they are almost incapable of making rigorous and unconditional choices. It is worth repeating that to be a disciple is not simply to play a role; it is a way of being that irrevocably alters the life of every follower of Jesus, though not in such a way that he is set apart from others or—even less—isolated; rather, he enters on a road of ecclesial communion and solidarity with the world.

3. The Presence of Mary in the life of the disciple

The great importance accorded to the presence of Mary in the life of the disciple is characteristic of montfort spirituality. According to Montfort, it is impossible to belong to the elect without a true devotion to the Virgin (LEW 214). The true devotee of Mary is a true disciple of Christ (TD 111). Although her role is not limited to this, the Mother of the Lord makes of the believer a true disciple of Christ—always with the collaboration of the Spirit.

It is easy to detect the Johannine background of Montfort's vision of the disciple of Mary (cf. Jn 19:25-27). Of the various characteristics of the disciples, it was the filial relation to the Virgin that particularly struck Montfort, so much so that he makes a secret of it; it is, in fact, the secret of montfort spirituality. To acquire Wisdom, or—in other words—to be the disciple of the crucified Christ, God's Wisdom, he proposes four methods: ardent desire, continuous prayer, universal mortification, but above all a genuine devotion to Mary (LEW, ch. 15-17). We might be inclined to see in all this a personal and rather idiosyncratic vision on Montfort's part, but on reflection we realize that in fact it is a version of the Johannine vision discussed above: the "disciple whom Jesus loved"—the image of all true disciples—is confided by the crucified Lord to Mary, and he accepts her as his mother. This supreme NT revelation lends solid support to Montfort's position in this respect. It clearly rests on the general principle posited as the basis of his entire thought and constantly repeated: Jesus came into the world through Mary, and it is through her that he will reign over the world (cf. TD 1) and will be reborn in the hearts of the elect, his true disciples.

A study remains to be done, particularly widespread in our time, of Mary as disciple. Montfort never calls

Mary the "disciple of Christ." But this notion is never completely absent from his writing: for Montfort, Mary is of all God's creatures *"the most conformed to Jesus"* (TD 120).

4. Serving the Kingdom

One last characteristic of discipleship to which we must return is the service of the Kingdom, or the mission of witness that is entrusted to the disciple. Jesus chooses his followers in order to send them out into the world to announce salvation. This is the duty not only of the Twelve but of all the disciples. The evangelical mission struck Montfort so forcefully that he felt moved to live it out even in the most concrete ways. He feels he is called not only to evangelize the poor (cf. L 5) and to proclaim salvation to all corners of the earth (it should be recalled that he wished to be a missionary in Canada, and later in the Orient)[6] but also to live in the same poverty as the first missionaries of the Gospel, even in small details.

In RM 52 - as we commented above - he recommends that one or two missionaries should go ahead to announce the mission, like the disciples whom Jesus sent before him in pairs to the places where he intended to go. The fact that Montfort faithfully imitated even such a detail as this is a clear sign of his desire to recreate the content and style of the mission of Jesus and of the way of life of his disciples. He wants the missionaries to be able always to say with Jesus Christ, "The Lord has sent me to bring good news to the poor" (Lk 4:18) or with Paul, "Christ did not send me to baptize but to proclaim the gospel" (1 Cor 1:17) (cf. RM 2).

These ideals, which Montfort recommends to his missionaries, are above all a blueprint for life: *"The apostolic missionary must first practice what he preaches: 'coepit Jesus facere et docere'"* (RM 62).

According to Montfort, to become a disciple is, beyond doubt, to relive the experience of the Apostles in Jesus' footsteps, which he strove to achieve himself with exceptional commitment and faithfulness. He reveals as much in his famous conversation with his friend Blain in 1714. Montfort, only just over forty, was a man deeply marked, indeed almost destroyed, by the exhausting effect of the apostolic life and its hardships. Blain drew Montfort's attention to this and gently questioned the excessively radical life he led. By way of reply, Montfort showed him the NT and asked his friend if he could argue with what Jesus taught and lived. And he asked him to cite a style of life more conformed to that of Jesus and the disciples than his own. He added that, for his part, he fully intended to follow it faithfully.[7] In this direct testimony, we can perceive not only Montfort's experience but the very meaning of discipleship: an apostolic life in the steps of Jesus, Christ and Lord.

A. Valentini

Notes: (1) In H 77:4 Montfort enters into greater detail: *"Mary is my great treasure / And my all with Jesus."*. (2) Cf. R. Schnackenburg, *Il messaggio morale del Nuovo Testamento (The Moral Message of the New Testament),* Brescia 1989, 1:72f. (3) Ibid., 178ff. (4) Schnackenburg, *Il messaggio,* 80. (5) Cf. LEW 64, 179; FC 37; TD 59; H 35. See also the Letters, in particular L 13, 15, 16, 26. (6) Cf. Itinerario, 248ff., 273. (7) Cf. Blain, 331-333.

ECUMENISM

SUMMARY
I. VATICAN II AND ECUMENISM.
II. SAINT LOUIS DE MONTFORT AND ECUMENISM:
1. Montfort and the Calvinists;
2. Montfort, an unlikely patron of ecumenism?
III. RELEVANCE OF MONTFORT'S DOCTRINE:
1. The need for updating;
2. The need for charitable honesty;
3. The Marian dimension of ecumenism.
4. Ecumenism and the dialog with non-Christians.

The restoration of unity was one of the principal concerns of the Second Vatican Council (UR 1). In the words of a post-conciliar document, the Council "clearly asked Catholics to reach out in love to all other Christians with a charity that desires and works actively to overcome in truth whatever divides them from one another."[1] Since the council, this ecumenical commitment has been reaffirmed frequently and forcefully by the Popes.[2] Saint Louis de Montfort's doctrine contains useful insights into the work of restoring unity to the followers of Christ.

I. VATICAN II AND ECUMENISM

In UR, the Council Fathers declared that baptized believers in Christ enjoy a certain communion with the Catholic Church, albeit imperfect. They have the right to call themselves Christians and should be looked on as brothers by members of the Catholic Church. Many good things of the Church's life can exist outside her visible boundaries—the written Word of God, the life of grace, the theological virtues, the gifts of the Holy Spirit, as well as visible elements (UR 3). At the same time, the council strongly emphasized that the engagement of the Catholic Church in the ecumenical movement did not signify any change in her unique claims. It is in her, the visible society governed by Peter's successor and the bishops in communion with him, that the one Church of Christ subsists.[3] The separated brethren are not blessed with that unity which Christ wished to bestow on the members of his Body. It is through the Catholic Church alone that the *fullness* of the means of salvation can be obtained (LG 8). Thus Christian unity, the goal of ecumenism, does not mean the construction, through ecclesiastical mergers, of some utopian "new" Church, but rather the gathering of all Christians "into the unity of the one and only Church." This essential unity will increase until the end of time, but it nevertheless already "subsists in the Catholic Church as something she can never lose."[4]

The council distinguished carefully between the various non-Catholic Christian communities. In first place in UR come the separated Eastern Churches. These are Churches in the proper sense, possessing true Sacraments, "above all—through apostolic succession—the priesthood and the Eucharist," and so they are joined to the Catholic Church, despite all the tragic tensions of past and present, "in the closest intimacy" (UR 4). Then come the Churches and "ecclesial communities" that broke away from Catholic unity since the end of the Middle Ages: the Old Catholic Churches, the Anglican Communion, and the various Protestant denominations (UR 19).

When it outlines the practice of ecumenism, the council gives primacy to "spiritual ecumenism" (UR 7, 8). Without this "soul," the "body" of ecumenical activity and dialogue cannot live. The saint turns out to be the Church's best ecumenist, just as he is also the most effective practitioner for evangelization.[5]

J. Saward

II. Saint Louis de Montfort and Ecumenism

1. Montfort and the Calvinists.

It would be an anachronism to expect Saint Louis de Montfort to have been engaged in ecumenical dialogue as we know it today. He was, however, engaged in the apostolate to the Calvinists, not so much to share baptismal unity in Christ as to draw them to the Catholic Church. Since La Rochelle, with its concentration of Protestants, was an area evangelized by Montfort, he had to devise a plan on how to deal with them.

During the lifetime of Saint Louis de Montfort, the cold war—which at times heated up—between the Catholics and the Protestants was a sign of the age. Both sides had hardened their positions, at times refuting no more than a caricature of the other's faith.

Saint Louis Marie showed an interest in working with the Calvinists. The second part of LS—yet to be published in English except for a few entries found in GA, 558-571—contains a late insertion, "*Concerning Heretics,*" which Montfort copied from an anonymous author (S 360-370). The entry is divided into two parts: first, nine concise rules or "*Methods to Convert Heretics,*" and second, the much longer part of the entry, a "*Methodical Table to learn easily how to treat points of the faith against persons of the so-called reformed religion.*" This second part is itself divided into two: the first deals directly with "controversy," giving again summary rules to follow in any discussion with the Protestants, and the second with means "*to aid the more docile*" of the Protestants, who either a) believe *"that we [Catholics] can be saved in our religion"* or b) even "*desire to be instructed [in the Catholic faith].*"

The rules or methods for converting Protestants are apologetic arguments, e.g.: "*You only know which book of Scripture is the Word of God through the Church to which you formerly belonged; you are not able, therefore, to know the true meaning of disputed passages except through the same Church. . . . They [the Calvinists] must be told that when it is a question of salvation, the safest [path] must be taken, which they admit. Now, according to them and their council of Charenton, it is indifferent to believe in the Real Presence of Our Lord in the Eucharist, and according to us it is necessary to believe in it; therefore, the safest path is to believe in it. . . . They have to be shown that the . . . Church that recognizes the Pope as successor of Saint Peter is the true Church because it possesses the true mark, which is visible perpetuity without interruption since Jesus Christ up to the present."*

If Montfort followed these guidelines, which he transcribed into S, he would have also obeyed some practical notes that form part of his "Concerning Heretics": "*1. Never treat of two controversial points at the same time. . . . When one has thoroughly gotten to the bottom of one point, then another one can be treated. . . . 3. Never treat of open questions concerning religion, e.g., touching on the manner that Our Lord is present in the Blessed Sacrament, whether it be by adduction or reproduction, or how God predestines or how God gives grace"* (S 370).

Saint Louis Marie speaks of "*proving*" the Catholic position in order to convince the Protestants and to shake them in their beliefs. The best way "*to prove*" the Catholic faith is "*by Holy Scripture, which must always be treated with great respect. By the tradition of the Apostles, which is the foundation of everything we believe, because if tradition had not told us that Holy Scripture is such and such, we would not even know it, etc.; . . . by the contradictions . . . of sects and heresies; . . . by the authority of the councils, the Holy Fathers [of the Church], miracles, succession, etc.; by human reason, which aids faith"* (S 369).

These methods of trying to convince Protestants of the truth of the Catholic faith represent the standard approach at the beginning of the eighteenth century, especially evident in the statement *"outside the Church and outside salvation"* (S 367). The most important attitude of Saint Louis de Montfort in his apostolate to the Calvinists was not so common in his time: to do everything "*with charity*" (S 367).

More specific to Saint Louis Marie is the role of Mary in the hope of fulfilling the Lord's prayer, "May they all be one" (Jn 17:21). TD 49-59 and PM indicate Saint Louis de Montfort's conviction that Christ will only fully reign in the world through Mary; it is through her that all will be gathered into "*one flock and one shepherd*" (PM 30).

P. Gaffney

2. Montfort, An Unlikely Patron of Ecumenism?

a. Some difficulties. St. Louis de Montfort does not at first seem to be a suitable patron of ecumenism. To the modern ear, the words he uses to describe those outside the Catholic Church sound harsh and intemperate:

> *"Every heretic I detest / The pagan, the Turk, and the Jew, / The schismatic and the apostate, / Only the Catholic is my good"* (H 6, 32; cf. TD 30, 42, 64, 250).

Moreover, it is undeniable that St. Louis' writings about Our Lady have disturbed and confused some non-

Catholics. In the nineteenth century, Edward Bouverie Pusey, one of the original leaders of the Oxford Movement in the Church of England, cited St. Louis Marie as an example of the immoderate Marian piety that, to his mind, blocked the reunion of Rome and Canterbury. In the same period, Bishop Ullathorne, a Catholic of irreproachable orthodoxy, reported an example of how TD (Faber's translation) could disconcert an unprepared Protestant. A certain lady, the bishop tells us, was on the very threshold of the Catholic Church. She had only one unresolved difficulty: devotion to Our Lady. "De Montfort's book was put into her hands as the proper remedy, and it drove her away in terror."[6]

These examples do not disqualify St. Louis from the role of ecumenist. They prove only the need for his writings to be translated with linguistic accuracy, expounded with scholarly rigor, and presented with pastoral prudence. When they are thus unfolded, they will be seen to offer rich resources for the ecumenical endeavors of the Church.

In addition to the fact that Saint Louis Marie makes the distinction between formal and material heretics (TD 167) and would, then, be speaking about those involved in a knowing and willing alienation from the Church, the colorfulness of St. Louis Marie's language in his hymns is explained by their pastoral purpose. The missionary is reaching out to the common people. When souls are in danger, the refined vocabulary of the salons is useless. In the hymn cited above, he is urging Catholics to guard the pearl beyond price that God has lavished on them - the true faith in its fullness. The person speaking is not St. Louis Marie himself but the hypostatized virtue of faith. She detests the heretic as heretic, not as a human person made in the image of God. She simply preaches the teaching of St. Thomas Aquinas: heresy and apostasy are vices opposed, by definition, to the virtue of faith.[7] Faith cannot but "detest" them.

St. Louis' language would be inappropriate in our own time, but its vigor can still serve to challenge those tempted, through false irenicism, to minimize the claims of the Catholic Church. In the early years of the eighteenth century, the age of rationalist "Enlightenment," Louis de Montfort boldly preached fidelity to the Wisdom of God and His Church together with nonconformity to "the wisdom of the world." In a prophetic way, he foresaw the pressure that would be placed on Catholics, priests and laity, to attenuate their faith, to bring it into line with the "thoughts and maxims" of the world (RM 37), to make it look like just one of the many religions of mankind. Louis de Montfort is a "fool for Christ's sake," shocking us out of the tendency to indifferentism and any other compromise of our faith.[8] This is his first contribution to ecumenism.

As for his Mariology, it, too, can be an encouraging help, not an embarrassing hindrance, in the sacred cause of Christian unity. In RMat, Pope John Paul II said that he wished "to emphasize how profoundly the Catholic Church, the Orthodox Church, and the ancient Churches of the East feel united by love and praise of the Theotokos" (RMat 31). During the Marian Year, 1987-1988, the Holy Father gave practical expression to this shared love of the one Blessed Mother. Marian services in the various Eastern rites were celebrated in the course of the year, and when the Ecumenical Patriarch visited Rome in December 1987, the celebrations of the Divine Liturgy and Vespers that he attended included canticles, both Latin and Greek, in praise of the Ever-Virgin Theotokos.[9]

b. The Eastern Churches. The language of St. Louis' Marian devotion, which some western Christians find extravagant, is close in spirit of that of the Byzantine tradition. The Roman rite is restrained in its mentioning and invoking of the Mother of God, whereas in the East she appears on almost every page of the liturgical books.[10] In the Byzantine liturgy, while the Eucharistic Prayer is being completed by the priest, she is directly invoked in hymns sung by the choir. Newman mentioned this oriental exuberance in his response to Pusey's *Eirenicon*: "Is it not a very pregnant fact that the Eastern Churches, so independent of us, so long separated from the West, so jealous for Antiquity, should even surpass us in their exaltation of the Blessed Virgin?"[11] Many of the Marian titles in the TD can be found in the Byzantine liturgy and Fathers: *"Eastern Gate," "Sanctuary of the Godhead," "Repose of the Blessed Trinity," "Throne of God," "City of God," "Altar of God"* (TD 164).[12] Through Poiré, St. Louis Marie seems to have had access to some of the most important of the Greek Fathers, most notably St. Basil (FC 14), St. John Chrysostom (FC 37), St. Germanus of Constantinople (TD 165), and St. John Damascene (TD 41).

The objection could be made that St. Louis' advocacy of such typically Western devotions as the Rosary makes him unappealing to Eastern Christians. This need not be the case. The popular Byzantine Jesus Prayer, which often includes a Marian insertion ("through the prayers of thy Holy Mother"), is recited using a woolen prayer-rope similar to rosary beads. The praying of decades of the Hail Mary together with meditation on the mysteries of Jesus and Mary is also well established in the East, and not just among Eastern-rite Catholics. The Russian starets Father Alexander Guamanovsky used a prayer scheme in which "O Hail Mother of God and Virgin" was recited 150 times. He claimed that this "rule" had been given by the Mother of God to the Church in the eighth century and had been revived in the eighteenth by St. Seraphim of Sarov.[13] Bishop Seraphim Zvezdinsky had a plan for prayerfully "remembering" the fifteen mysteries of Our Lady's life from her Nativity to her Assumption and Coronation.[14] These Russian spiritual fathers are close in spirit to the author of SM and MR.

Perhaps the most striking affinity between St. Louis and the Russian Orthodox tradition is his theological meditation on Eternal Wisdom, that is to say, the Second Person of the Trinity seen as the Wisdom of the Father (cf. LEW; H 103, 124, 125,

126). Several Russian theologians of the late nineteenth century and early twentieth—V . Soloviev, P. Florensky, and especially S. Bulgakov—had a similar preoccupation and developed the doctrine of "sophiology."[15] This has always been controversial, however, and lacks the precisions and careful distinctions made by St. Louis Marie.[16]

*c. **Protestant Churches.*** To Protestants, St. Louis might appear to be an immovable stumbling block. Careful exegesis of his works, however, can contribute to ecumenical dialogue, especially on the subject of devotion to Our Lady. The fear of some Protestants that Catholics elevate Mary to the level of deity will be overcome by the forcefulness with which St. Louis confesses *"with the whole Church"* that *"Mary, being a mere creature coming from the hands of the Most High, is, in comparison with His infinite Majesty, less than an atom, or rather is nothing at all, since He alone is 'He Who is'"* (TD 14).

St. Louis Marie demonstrates throughout his works, in a way that should be enlightening for Protestants, that Catholic devotion to Our Blessed Lady is God-centered and Christ-centered. Our Lord Jesus Christ is the ultimate end of devotion to Mary (TD 61). Mary's whole mission on earth and in heaven is to bring Jesus to men and men to Jesus. Devotion to the Mother is the "easiest," shortest," and "surest" way to union with the Son (TD 152). It helps us renew our baptismal commitment to Christ (TD 126-130). It is to him that we consecrate ourselves through Mary. "*Since of all God's creatures Mary is the most conformed to Jesus, it follows that, of all devotions, the one that consecrates and conforms a soul most to Our Lord is devotion to the Blessed Virgin Mary, his mother, and that the more a soul is consecrated to Mary, the more it is consecrated to Jesus*" (TD 120).

The theology of St. Louis Marie issues a challenge to those Christians who have difficulties with Marian devotion. It invites them to ask themselves whether they truly believe in the Incarnation if they hold back their love from the Holy Virgin, in whose womb and by whose faith the Word was made flesh. Christological heresy, from Valentinus and Nestorius in the early centuries to the errors of our own time, has constantly sought to rob Our Lady of her unique role in the economy of salvation. Christological orthodoxy, by contrast, sees her as "*crushing all heresies*" (TD 166). In the words of Cardinal Newman, "She is called the Tower of David, because she has so signally fulfilled the office of defending her Divine Son from the assaults of His foes."[17]

St. Louis dramatically poses another question for the heirs of the Reformation. Can we be so confident that, with God as our heavenly Father, we have no need of an earthly mother in the order of grace? "*Just as in natural and bodily generation there is a father and mother, so in supernatural and spiritual generation there is a Father who is God and a Mother who is Mary*" (TD 30).

Father Louis Bouyer, convert and Oratorian priest, has argued that it is a kind of Monophysitism to accept human motherhood in the order of nature but not in the order of grace: "The most pernicious Docetism of Monophysitism is often the one we do not notice, in particular, Docetism toward ourselves, toward our new life as children of God. . . . The attitude of the Christian who imagines that, at the level of grace, it is sufficient for him to have a heavenly Father, and that he has no need of an earthly Mother, is a very dubious one. Does it not imply that Christian life and ordinary life have to remain on different levels, with nothing in common? There is no vainer illusion! There is no Christian life that is different from ordinary life. Christian life is that life placed under the immediate guidance of God without being cut off from its roots in history."[18]

A good case can be made for the thesis that the Christian bodies most vulnerable to the ravages of ideological feminism have been those traditionally reluctant to acknowledge the unique role of woman, of the Woman, in the drama of Redemption. In the Catholic Church, Cardinal Joseph Ratzinger has argued that Mary is the God-given "remedy" for all the Church's contemporary troubles, not least for extreme feminism. He confesses that he has learned to appreciate the wisdom of the principle, well liked by St. Louis Marie, *De Maria nunquam satis.* The young Ratzinger thought it was exaggerated. "Now—in this confused period where truly every type of heretical aberration seems to be pressing upon the doors of the authentic faith—now I understand that it was not a matter of pious exaggerations, but of truths that today are more valid than ever.[19]

In recent years, many Protestants have come to see the force of these considerations and are slowly rediscovering the person and mission of Our Blessed Lady. "Without her," writes the Reformed theologian Donald G. Dawe, "the redemptive mystery of her Son is lost. With her it is received with joy."[20] Over thirty years ago, Max Thurian, at the time a member of the Protestant monastic community at Taizé and now a Catholic priest, wrote a biblical Mariology, in which he argued that "instead of being a cause of division among us, Christian reflection on the role of the Virgin Mary should be a cause for rejoicing and a source of prayer."[21] The council took note of this new stirring: "It gives great joy and comfort to this most holy Synod that among the separated brethren, too, there are those who give due honor to the Mother of Our Lord and Savior."[22] The Council Fathers were thinking chiefly of the Orthodox, but there is no doubt that they were also celebrating the Marian re-awakening in the Protestant world.

Two years after the close of the council, the English Catholic layman Martin Gillet founded the Ecumenical Society of the Blessed Virgin Mary to promote ecumenical devotion to Mary and the study of her place in the Church under Christ. Having extended its activities and membership to the United States and other countries, the Society now holds regular international congresses.

Our Lady is widely recognized, both within the Catholic Church and outside, as the Mother of Christian Unity. It cannot be otherwise, for the reason that St. Louis himself adduces. If Mary is the "safest" and "surest" way to Jesus, then she is also the most secure and direct way to unity according to his will. This is Pope John Paul II's message in Rmat: "It is a hopeful sign that these Churches and ecclesial communities [in the West] are finding agreement with the Catholic Church on fundamental points of Christian belief, including matters relating to the Virgin Mary. For they recognize her as the Mother of the Lord and hold that this forms part of our faith in Christ, true God and true man. They look to her, who at the foot of the Cross accepts as her son the beloved disciple, the one who in his turn accepts her as his mother. Therefore, why should we not all together look to her as our common Mother, who prays for the unity of God's family and who "precedes" us all at the head of the long line of witnesses of faith in the one Lord, the Son of God, who was conceived in her virginal womb by the power of the Holy Spirit?"(RMat 30)

St. Louis de Montfort is a most worthy model for today's ecumenism. The resolute God-centeredness of his thought ("*God Alone*") points us to "the one thing necessary" in all our Christian strivings, whether for unity or for any other praiseworthy goal. This has been acknowledged recently by John Macquarrie, the Anglican theologian, in his collection of essays on ecumenical Mariology, *Mary for All Christians.* The text he quotes from TD will make a fitting conclusion to this article: "There have been few devotees of Mary so enthusiastic as Louis de Montfort, whose book on devotion to Mary is still widely used. But no one could be more forthright in making it clear that devotion to Mary is not an end in itself. . . '*When we praise her, love her, honor her or give anything to her, it is God who is praised, God who is loved, God who is glorified, and it is to God that we give, through Mary and in Mary.*'"[23]

J. Saward

III. Relevance of Montfort's Doctrine

1. The need for updating

A review of the guidelines Saint Louis de Montfort employed in his encounters with the Calvinists (cf. above) reveals the ecumenical situation in France at the turn of the eighteenth century. Thanks especially to the Second Vatican Council, attitudes have drastically changed since his day. Montfort definitely followed the mind of the Church as it was manifested during his life; he would expect this same obedience to be given to the Church today by those who claim to share his vision.

2. The need for Charitable Honesty

"Nothing is so foreign to the spirit of ecumenism as a false irenicism which harms the purity of Catholic doctrine and obscures its genuine and certain meaning" (UR 11). Montfort can never be accused of watering down the Catholic faith in an attempt to win over the Calvinists of his day. If there is one rule of ecumenical dialogue that he strenuously observed, it is this: avoid false irenicism, peace at any price. Although the contemporary ecumenical approach would find that he and his contemporaries were too unbending, seeking only "conversion" and not "convergence," his forceful stress on the truths of the Catholic faith is a helpful antidote to those who would dilute Catholic doctrine in order to achieve unity.

The need of presenting the truth "*with charity*" (LS 367) condemns any triumphalistic approach. Although the term "triumphalism" would be understood differently in Montfort's time, the words of Vatican II are to be observed in contemporary ecumenical dialogue: "Catholic theologians, standing fast by the teaching of the Church yet searching together with separated brethren into the divine mysteries, should do so with love for the truth, with charity and with humility" (UR 11).

3. The Marian Dimension of Ecumenism

An analysis of Montfort's writings indicates that he stresses the need for a clarification of Mary's role in salvation history as an integral part of ecumenical dialogue. Far from being a stumbling block to union, Montfort sees in Mary a unifying element bringing together all the baptized, provided that she is presented in her true Christocentric context. Moreover, Mary, a daughter of the Jewish people and the woman so revered by Islam, becomes an important point of contact for the monotheistic religions of the world.

4. Ecumenism and the Dialog with Non-Christians

The Incarnate Word declared "may they all be one: as thou, Father, art in me, and I in thee" (Jn 17: 21). The Vatican II Decree on Ecumenism (UR) should be seen in the light of The Declaration on the Church's Relations with non-Christian Religions (NA), which states: "In our times when every day we are drawn closer together, and the ties between various peoples are being multiplied, the Church is giving deeper study to her relationship with non-Christian religions. In her task of fostering love among men and even nations, the Church gives primary consideration to what human beings have in common and to what promotes fellowship among them." Montfort's belief in "the one true God . . . the God who is Love" is a constant call to live this unity and to share it with others as Incarnate Wisdom. The council was a prayer for unity in the spirit of Montfort's words: "*We must pray for Wisdom. And assuredly God who wants to be importuned, will sooner or later rise up, open the door of his mercy and give us three loaves of Wisdom, that is the bread of life, the bread of understanding and the bread of angels*" (LEW 190). In the spirit of "God Alone," the Church framed in NA, chap. 1, a universal call to unity with those who belong to the monotheistic religions of the world: "All men form but one community. This is so because they stem from the same stock that God created to people the entire earth (Acts 17:26)." The Church in NA, chap. 2, calls for Christians to discover those core values which are held in common across the boundaries of world religions: "The Catholic Church rejects nothing that is good and holy in these religions. . . . Let Christians, while witnessing to their own faith and way of life, acknowledge, preserve, and encourage the spiritual and moral truths found among non-Christians." Just as Mary is the Mother of Christ, and of the Church and of the Ecumenical Council dedicated to her, so she is the Mother of all peoples, and lands. She is the Mother of the re-creation: *"Nothing on earth can take from her what we place in her keeping"* (LEW 222).

P. Gaffney

Notes: (1) Pontifical Council for Promoting Christian Unity, *Directory for the Application of the Principles and Norms of Ecumenism*, n. 9, in *L'Osservatore Romano*, June 16, 1993, p. I. (2) On June 28, 1985, Pope John Paul II made this declaration to the Roman Curia: "The Catholic Church is committed to the ecumenical movement by an irrevocable decision, and she wants to contribute to it with all her powers." *Insegnamenti di Giovanni Paolo II* (*Teachings of John Paul II*), VIII/1 (1985), 1999; CCC, 820. (3) G. Philips, secretary of the Council's doctrinal commission and the principal redactor of LG, has offered this paraphrase: "This is where we find the Church of Christ in all her plenitude and all her power." *L'Eglise et son mystère au deuxième concile du Vatican: Histoire, texte et commentaire*, (The Church and its Mystery at the Second Vatican Council: History, text, and commentary), Paris 1967, 1:119. (4) Ibid, p. 249f. (5) According to Pope Paul VI, "The first means of evangelization is the witness of an authentically Christian life" (*Evangelii Nuntiandi*, n. 41; AAS 68 (1976), 31f.; cf. CCC, 821. (6) A letter to *The Tablet* (April 4, 1866) (*The Letters and Diaries of John Henry Newman*, vol. 22 (London, 19720, p. 344). (7) Cf.Summa Theologiae 2a qq. 11 & 12. (8) For a discussion of St. Louis as a "fool for Christ," see J. Saward, *Perfect Fools, Folly for Christ's Sake in Catholic and Orthodox Spirituality (*Oxford, 1980), pp. 185-196. (9) See *Liturgie dell'Oriente Cristiano a Roma nell'Anno Mariano 1987-1988*, (*Liturgies of the Christian East at Rome during the Marian Year 1987-1988*), Vatican City, 1990, pp. 153ff and passim. (10) See J. Ledit, *Marie dans la liturgie de byzance* , (*Mary in the Liturgy of Byzantium*), Paris, 1976. p. 11 and passim. (11) "*A Letter Addressed to the Rev.E.B. Pusey DD on Occasion of his Eirenicon*" in *Certain Difficulties Felt by Anglicans* in *Catholic Teaching Considered*, new edition, vol. 2 (London, 1900), p. 90. (12) For a list of Patristic figures applied to Our Lady, see the index in *Enchiridion Marianum Biblicum Patristicum* (Rome, 1974), pp. 2003-2013. (13) Jane Ellis (translator), *An Early Soviet Saint. The Life of Father Zachariah* (Springfield, 1976), p. 6f. (14) Ibid., p. 67f. (15) Cf.N. Zernov, *The Russian Religious Renaissance of the Twentieth Century* (London, 1963), pp. 138-150. (16) On Bulgakov's Christology, see L. Bouyer, *Le Fils éternel. Théologie de la Parole de Dieu et Christologie, (The Eternal Son. Theology of the Word of God and Christology)*, (Paris, 1973). (17) "Meditations on the Litany of Loretto for the Month of May" in *Meditations and Devotions*, new edition (London, 1965). p. 145. (18) *Le Trône de la Sagesse. Essai sur la signification du culte marial* (*The Throne of Wisdom. Essay on the Meaning of Marian devotion*), Paris, 1957, p. 239f. (19) *The Ratzinger Report. An Exclusive Interview on the State of the Church*, San Francisco, Ignatius Press 1985, p. 105f. (20) "From Dysfunction to Disbelief. The Virgin Mary in Reformed Theology," in A. Stacpoole OSB (ed.), *Mary's Place in Christian Dialogue. Occasional Papers of the Ecumenical Society of teh Blessed Virgin Mary*, 1970-1980 (Slough, 1982), p. 149. (21) *Mary, Mother of All Christians*, New York, Herder and Herder 1964, p. 7. (22) LG 69. (23) *Mary For All Christians*, Grand Rapids, William B. Eerdmans Publishing Co. 1991, p. 133.

EDUCATION

SUMMARY

I. PEDAGOGICAL CONTEXT OF THE SEVENTEENTH CENTURY:
   1. Primary schools;
   2. Secondary schools.

II. STAGES IN THE JOURNEY OF MONTFORT'S DEVELOPMENT:
   1. Primary education;
   2. Secondary education;
   3. Higher education.

III. MONTFORT'S PASTORAL GUIDANCE FOR THE EDUCATION OF THE BAPTIZED:
   1. Biblical orientation;
   2. Theocentric orientation;
   3. Marian orientation;
   4. Eschatological orientation;
   5. Baptismal orientation;
   6. Liturgical and pedagogical orientation.
   7. Concern for the poor.

IV. MONTFORT THE EDUCATOR:
   1. Establishment of charitable schools;
   2. General principles of education.

V. EDUCATION AND DEVELOPMENT TODAY:
   1. Christocentrism and pneumatology;
   2. Meaning of baptism and value of the laity;
   3. Presence of Mary;
   4. Value of spiritual guidance;
   5. Energetic devotion to schools.

I. PEDAGOGICAL CONTEXT OF THE SEVENTEENTH CENTURY

In order to understand better the milieu of Louis Marie's educational development and its implications for the establishment of the charitable schools (schools for the poor), it will be helpful to summarize the nature of schooling during his lifetime.

In the seventeenth century, schooling was considered a charitable activity and thus one of the works of the Church.

1. Primary schools

In the first half of the century, there were few primary schools, and there was no consistent principle of organization underlying methods and programs.[1] Where schools did exist, teachers, under ecclesiastical authority, used individual instruction, a primitive pedagogy based on fear of corporal punishment and a mechanical recitation of lessons.[2]

Between 1650 and 1700, three important and interrelated factors signaled the advent of pedagogy in primary schools and influenced the pedagogical thought of Louis Marie.

a. First, there appeared, probably in 1654, a treatise on pedagogical organization entitled *The Parochial School.* Edited by "a priest of a parish of Paris," Jacques de Batencour, the work marks the birth of modern pedagogy.

b. The Parochial School inspired the works and writings of Charles Démia, who founded charitable schools in Lyons beginning in 1667. He wanted to make Christians of the homeless children roaming the cities. Within thirty years, sixteen free institutions, administered by the Department of Schools, had been established.

At the end of his life, Démia published a book entitled *Rules for the Schools of the City and Diocese of Lyons* (n.d.). Inspired by *The Parochial School,* this volume is a compilation of pedagogical practices that Démia had instituted in the schools founded through his intervention.[3] In the preface to his volume, Démia emphasizes the profound ignorance that he discovered: "The children of the poor were in the furthest reaches of antisocial and libertine behavior for want of instruction."[4]

c. The third factor was the foundation of the Institute of the Brothers of the Christian Schools by Jean-Baptiste de la Salle and the establishment of several charitable schools, including one in Paris, from 1688 on. The shared method and teaching used by the Brothers, as well as the pedagogical characteristics of their instruction, were the subject of a publication by Jean-Baptiste de la Salle in 1720, under the title *The Administration of Christian Schools.* This manual was inspired largely by the ideas of Démia on pedagogical organization and by the Port-Royal method for teaching the native language.[5]

2. Secondary schools

Under the *ancien régime,* secondary education produced the most important doctrinal and pedagogical developments. There appear to be three reasons for this pedagogical ferment: the decadence of universities, the adaptation of secondary education, and the establishment of numerous colleges by religious communities. It is worthwhile to summarize the colleges run by the Jesuits, since it was within this framework that Louis Marie received his secondary education.

Toward the end of the seventeenth century, the Jesuits controlled more than 120 colleges, where they followed the *Ratio Studiorum* and pursued their own pedagogical direction.[6] The studies were organized with the goal of ensuring the moral, religious, and literary development of the student. The curriculum included four years of grammar, from its rudiments to versification, and one year of rhetoric, followed by several years of philosophy and theology. The courses were conducted in Latin, and Greek had priority over French. The exercises, for the most part, were in Latin. Study of rhetoric and classical literature served as training in the art of oratory. In addition to their formal education, the students were required to participate in theatrical presentations, literary exercises, and other extracurricular activities.

Elite groups of students were invited to participate in confraternities, which had originated in Italy, and been spiritually renewed through the Company of Jesus. In these confraternities, the Jesuits gathered together the best students with the aim of deepening their growth in the Christian life under the protection of the Virgin Mary. There were meditation, spiritual readings, the office of Our Lady, rosaries, fasting on the eve of the Blessed Virgin's feast days, and frequent confession and communion. In sum, they required from these youths an *oblatio,* or consecration, to Our Lady, whose virtues they strove to reawaken in themselves.[7]

II. Stages in the Journey of Montfort's Development[8]

1. Primary education

We know little about the earliest years of Louis Marie's development. He seems to have received his instruction in the small family school that was undoubtedly organized with the help of the priest of Iffendic.[9] His first biographers describe Louis Marie as a gifted child, very obedient, with a resolute look, attentive and passionate at his studies. He received the first lessons of his spiritual training from his parents. We also know that he loved very much to pray and kneel before an image of the Blessed Virgin and that his brothers and sisters followed in his steps. Louis Marie must have profited from the lessons he received, because at the age of twelve he became qualified to pursue secondary studies.

2. Secondary education

In the academic year 1684-1685, we find Louis Marie at Rennes pursuing his secondary education at the College of Saint Thomas à Becket, administered by the Society of Jesus. It was the foremost Jesuit college in Brittany, with more than 2000 students at the time of Louis Marie's matriculation. They received a quality education in accordance with the rules of the *Ratio Studiorum* and the pedagogical methods of the Jesuits. In this extremely rich spiritual and intellectual atmosphere, Louis Marie made progress that brought him to the attention of his masters, who saw in him a model not only of a life of prayer and piety but also of the intellectual life, and he won the major prizes at the end of the year.

Louis Marie was also noticed by Father Gilbert, professor of rhetoric, who completed his catechetical instructions with special visits to his student. His lessons and counsel must have been profitable, because Louis Marie was chosen by Fr. Julien Bellier to teach elementary level catechism and to visit the poor and sick in the hospitals. Other extracurricular activities interested Louis Marie: he enrolled in drawing and painting courses, in which he excelled. Louis Marie also belonged to the Congregation of the Blessed Virgin established at the college. We can thus conclude that, in addition to a remarkable intellectual development, the College of Rennes left as its mark on Louis Marie a deepening of the interior life and the beginning of an active, concrete, and popular apostolate. He was now ready for more advanced studies.

3. Higher education

Louis Marie had begun his theological studies at Rennes in 1692 under the direction of Fathers Magnon and Baron. Through the intervention of Mademoiselle de Montigny, a friend of the family, a woman offered to pay the costs for the student so that he might profit from the advantages of a more extensive education at the Seminary of the Sulpicians in Paris. Montfort read the will of God in this offer. Thus we find him in Paris, in a Saint-Sulpice community led by Claude Bottu de la Barmondière. In this establishment, intended specifically "for poor students, where they may give themselves to intensive Marian devotion,"[10] Louis Marie made remarkable progress. He enrolled in the regular courses of the faculty of theology at the Sorbonne. Studies in spirituality completed his course work. "Virtually every book dealing with the spiritual life passed through his hands," says Blain.[11] Forced to keep watch over the dead in the parish of Saint-Sulpice in order to avert financial crisis, Louis Marie occupied himself with prayer and meditation for four hours, spiritual reading for two hours, and study of his theological notebooks for the remainder of the time. After the death of Father de la Barmondière, Louis Marie was received into the Community of Father Boucher. We find him assiduous in his studies, concerned about the poor, and extremely faithful to the spiritual direction of Fr. Prévost. Following an extended stay at the Hospital, l'Hôtel-Dieu in Paris, Louis Marie came to the Little Seminary of Saint-Sulpice, which accepted poor ecclesiastics, thanks to the charity of Madame d'Alègre and Madame the Duchess of Mortemart. He was to remain there five years, from 1695 to 1700. His theological studies continued. After obtaining the baccalaureate, he chose not to pursue the three additional years of study that would enable him to complete his degree. In TD 118 Montfort affirms that he read nearly every book about devotion to the Virgin Mary.

It is also during these developmental years that he was given the task of teaching catechism to the poorest children of the district of Saint-Germain. He was directed in this effort by Fr. Baüyn himself, to whom he had confided his spiritual direction.[12] From these years of development in Paris, Louis Marie retained a solid theological training, an informed Marian spirituality, a knowledge of seventeenth-century mysticism, a life of extensive prayer, and an enhanced desire to help the poor, especially through catechism. After his ordination on June 5, 1700, the seeds of this study, in germination since Rennes in 1685, would bear fruit.

III. Montfort's Pastoral Guidance for the Education of the Baptized

Between 1700 and 1705, Montfort had several experiences in the apostolate. However, after his audience with Pope Clement XI in 1706, he became primarily, and in obedience to the Vicar of Christ, a Missionary

Apostolic. In his preaching, in his writings, in his preaching of parish missions, and in his education of children and adults in the faith—in what we may generally refer to as Montfort's pastoral activity—we can emphasize seven essential characteristics: it is biblical, theocentric, Marian, eschatological, liturgical, focused on renewing the baptismal promises, and marked by concern for the poor.

1. Biblical orientation

There are more than 1100 biblical citations in the writings of Saint Louis Marie de Montfort. He never tires of reciting or commenting on the Gospel. On the subject of acquiring the light of faith, Montfort does not hesitate to write, speaking of faith, "*Look for me in the Gospel, / I am there in every word*" (H 6:37). In the hymn on the rule for a convert, Montfort tells him to read the Gospel first (H 139:56). To the family he gives this advice: "*Fashion the family after the Gospel*" (H 33:117). A dozen other hymns testify to Montfort's concern to show that the Gospel is the rule of conduct for the Christian. The God that Montfort presents is rooted in the Bible. It is a God Who is faithful to all His promises (H 7:3) and slow to anger (H 51:10), a Father (H 7:7; 117:3) Who worries about all His creatures, even sinners, and Who overcomes all iniquity by His great goodness (H 14:31). Laurentin's remark about Montfort's theology could also be made of his pastoral approach: "With the history of salvation as its point of departure, it is rooted in the Bible and projected toward God's future."[13]

2. Theocentric orientation

The Trinity is the point of departure for Montfort's missionary catechism. "*God Alone*" is the most frequent formulation in his works; we find it in one form or another more than 130 times, especially in the hymns. He is conscious that all proceeds from the Father (LEW 19; SM 9). And the mystery of the Incarnation is central to Montfort's spirituality. His devotion to Mary rests completely on this fundamental intuition: we have only to remember TD 248. Hymns 57, 66 and 97 are centered on the mystery of the Infant-God. This Son Incarnate will die on the Cross from an excess of love for mankind: the theme of the Cross recurs over 200 times in Montfort's works. The mystery of the Incarnation also suggests the presence of the Spirit. Laurentin notes that the Spirit is foremost for Montfort. For him, Mary has received everything from the Spirit; she is related to the Spirit as she is to God and to Christ.[13]

3. Marian orientation

The mystery of the Incarnation implies the plan of the Father to send His Son by the power of the Spirit, on the condition that Mary consent. Montfort is struck dumb with admiration by Mary's "yes": "After Jesus Christ, the greatest object of Father Louis Marie's piety was the most worthy Mother of God."[14] He is convinced that the reign of Jesus will come through her (TD 1-13). Eighteen of Montfort's letters mention Mary. In LEW, about seventeen pages are devoted to the Virgin Mary; she is the direct subject of twenty-three hymns. Two books, TD and SM, pro-

STATUE OF MONTFORT AS THE PILGRIM TROUBADOUR, AND LOVER OF THE CROSS

Louis Marie sometimes afixed a Cross to the top of his walking stick as above. At other times he placed atop it a madonna that he had sculpted. His napsack holds the Bible. This statue is one of the most common portrayals of Montfort. Photo by Aartsen.

pose the way of Mary, which is both demanding and gratifying, as a means of reaching God. "In the two works, he openly moves from contemplating Mary in the mystery of the Incarnation, from which all else will forever flow, to proposing a secret of mystical and apostolic perfection."[15]

Among Montfort's methods of concretizing his pastoral discussion of Mary, we must emphasize his Consecration to Jesus through Mary and the recitation of the Rosary. Remember that the principal aims of Marian devotion, according to Montfort, are, above all, to *"honor and imitate the wondrous dependence which God the Son chose to have on Mary, for the glory of his Father"* and to *"thank God for the incomparable graces he has conferred upon Mary"* (TD 243). The fruit of this devotion to Mary is the transformation of the Christian in the image of Jesus Christ. *"Mary is a holy place . . . in which saints are formed and molded"*; *"but they are molded in Jesus Christ"* (TD 218, 54).

4. Eschatological orientation

Montfort's pastoral writings are marked by eschatology. Keeping in mind the past, particularly the covenant in Jesus Christ, we must reflect on what the future brings that is new and final. Montfort's pastoral approach, in conformity with the anthropology of his day, sets relative truths against the last things of mankind: death, judgment, heaven, and hell. The words "death, judgment, heaven, and hell" and their related concepts, "death, paradise, demon, and devil" occur more than 180 times in Montfort's works. The great eschatological truths are presented in the following hymns: 96, 116, 118-120, 127, 139, 142, 152-154, and 162. Montfort insists in his writings on the final days of the Church, when—by the intervention of the Holy Spirit, Mary, and the apostles of the latter times—the world will pass from sin to the reign of Jesus Christ (PM; SM 58-59; TD 47-59).

5. Baptismal orientation

The unique and fundamental Consecration of the Christian, established by Jesus Christ, is Baptism, by which we belong to Christ. Montfort understood well the importance of Baptism in the Spirit, the Sacrament of a new birth in the Spirit that is purifying and sanctifying. For that reason, he placed a high value on the renewal of the baptismal vows as a formal ratification of the initial choice. Missionary work almost always included renewal of the baptismal promises. Grandet emphasizes that the goal of Montfort's missions was "to renew the spirit of Christianity by renewing baptismal vows."[16] Even the Consecration to Jesus through Mary, as indicated in LEW 225, has as its object to "atone for infidelity to the unique Consecration of Baptism, disfigured by sin."[17] Thus Montfort made a rule for his missionaries: *"The missionaries will see to it that, as the Pope has commanded, the baptismal vows are renewed with the greatest solemnity. . . . Only those who have seen the results of this practice can appreciate its value"* (RM 56). This renewal is part of an appropriately prepared liturgy.

6. Liturgical and pedagogical orientation

The systematic project of bringing the New Covenant into being, a project carried out by the community of the Church through Christ and under the efficacious signs of the Holy Spirit, does not immediately suggest the liturgical nature of Montfort's pastoral work. It is, however, the pedagogical angle that interests us. Without the "necessary pedagogy, the liturgy cannot be renewed. The full and active participation of the faithful is required for the restoration and promotion of the sacred liturgy" (SC 18). Montfort's pastoral ministry calls for liturgical participation, especially in the Sacraments of Confession and Communion, after the renewal of baptismal vows (RM 56). He endeavors to enter into the mysteries of Christianity by means of processions, songs, mimes, pageants, and times of silence; he tries to touch the heart and the emotions as well as the mind. In the course of a parish mission, seven processions were normally held. Some of the hymns were even composed in the form of dialogue. Montfort used dramatization in his pastoral duties. The fifty couplets of Hymn 106 are a dialogue for five persons: Jesus, the company, the world, the angel, and the Christian. Such dramatization is even more notable in the seventy-nine couplets of Hymn 127, for which Montfort himself furnished the text, melodies, scenic directions, and even the design.[18] The dialogue required twenty persons and began with a prologue of prayer. It is also clear that his sermons on death and preparing for death, in particular, included mimes and moments of silence to make the experience more dramatic, so that the heart would be more deeply touched by the Spirit.

It should be also noted that Louis Marie's desire to educate in the faith was also expressed in spiritual direction. Having himself assiduously pursued spiritual direction in his developmental years, Montfort was to guide others wisely in the course of his apostolic activity. In his writings, Montfort remarks how necessary it is to consult at all times with a good spiritual director (H 10:38-43; 12:45; 13:67-69; 149:7; also FC 61 and TD 220); this practice can only bring positive benefits (L 29, 33; SR 128; H 139). In his parish missions, sinners and tormented souls would arrive in great numbers at his confessional in search of guidance and pardon. "Certainly he had an admirable talent for converting sinners," Grandet remarks.[19] There is no doubt that providing spiritual direction was one of his primary activities; J.B. Blain notes that during the more than 200 missions that he preached over the course of fourteen years, a considerable amount of time was spent in "his absorbing labors of spiritual direction."[20]

7. Concern for the poor

Like Démia and Jean-Baptiste de la Salle, Montfort was struck by the idleness of the young and by juvenile delinquency. However, his primary motive for establishing schools in La Rochelle seems to be the religious ignorance of the young and the strong influence of Protestantism. His instructions every Sunday at

Saint-Sulpice to the children and students attending boarding school, his experience as a catechist at Nantes, and his sense of organization led him quite naturally to this ministry.

Beginning in 1701, at the hospital of Poitiers, Montfort had the care of children and the poor. It is worth remembering that hospitals of the time generally included a benevolent school for young patients. The rule of Poitiers stipulated that the chaplain "will teach each of said poor people to read and to write and will free each of them from an hour's work a day so that they can devote themselves to their studies."[21] Thus Montfort saw nearly 200 children every day who were his to teach. He was happy to teach catechism to the poor; the task attracted him greatly (L 5). But as director general of the hospital, Montfort became overwhelmed with tasks to be accomplished and could no longer continue teaching. To ensure that the poor would still be taught, he asked the bishop of Poitiers, Monsignor Girard, to name a permanent teacher at the school.[22] He nonetheless continued at the hospital until the summer of 1702, when the new bishop, Monsignor de la Poype, named his replacement.

IV. Montfort the Educator

Two reasons entitle Montfort to be called a pioneer Christian educator: the establishment of charitable schools and his General Principles of education.

1. Establishment of charitable schools

Among the eleven goals and methods that made Montfort's mission fruitful, Grandet lists first "the establishment of Christian schools." He believed that one of Montfort's principal occupation during his missions was to establish Christian schools for boys and girls. Grandet states, in addition, that these missions produced lasting results wherever Montfort passed, because his holy methods enabled the grade schools to make his missions fruitful.[23] Similarly, Clorivière writes that one of Montfort's principal concerns "was to provide the parishes with good schoolteachers."[24] Were these schools short-lived? We cannot tell.

But Montfort's great desire was to establish schools that would be permanent. His most spectacular achievements in this field were in the town of La Rochelle. There he had been particularly struck by the danger of Protestantism. The young people of the town would have to be instructed in religion. He did not hesitate to buy a building in need of restoration; he himself became architect and entrepreneur. But the most important task was to find and train good teachers. That is why Montfort "himself went to the school every day to train the teachers in his methods of teaching and to provide a model for these disciples."[25]

For the schools for girls, he called on Marie-Louise Trichet, first Daughter of Wisdom, and several of her companions. These charitable schools were free and subject to the bishop.

For the schools for boys, Montfort chose several Brothers who followed him in his missions after 1705 and carried out the tasks of singing master, catechist, and schoolteacher. The methods and rules in these schools flowed from general educational principles.

2. General principles of education

Montfort's considerations on education can be grouped into four general principles:

a. An education whose primary goal is the glory of God and the salvation of souls—For Montfort, the primary aim of the school is the glory of God and apprenticeship in the Christian life. Like his contemporaries, Montfort felt that schools were the nurseries of the Church, where children, like young saplings carefully pruned and cultivated, eventually became fit to bear good fruit. The organization of his teaching reflects this preoccupation. Apart from two half-hours of catechism, the day included a morning offering before classes, memorization of prayers, recitation of the Rosary, and assistance at Mass. School for Montfort was a privileged means of evangelization.

b. An education in which the child is loved as a son and daughter of God—Montfort profoundly loved children and young people, in imitation of Jesus, who ordered the Apostles to let them come to him. His passion for catechizing the poor flowed from Jesus's burning love.

c. A free education for the poor of Jesus Christ—Montfort was partial to the poor and he wanted schools that were charitable and free, that could receive the poor and ensure their access to education. He instructed the teachers *"never, either directly or indirectly, under any circumstances, to request money or gifts of any kind from the children or their parents."*[26]

d. An education in which order and silence reign so as to improve the education—Montfort's educational thinking emphasizes the importance of order and silence; a minimum of organization and order is necessary to ensure a good education. To this end, he established rules for classes, admission requirements, a schedule of classes, and programs for study and piety (RW 275-292; RM 79-91).[27]

e. An active education geared toward the spiritual life—In his Rules for Catechetical Instruction (RM 79-91), Montfort gives his method, which is dominated by three concerns: "memorization, characterized by questions and brief, clear responses; attention to students, using 'little stories,' praise, and rewards, and questions directed toward many different students; and the placing of these lessons into the heart by prayer and 'tender exhortation.'"[28]

V. Education and Development Today

Certain characteristics of Montfort's pastoral approach still speak to the Church of today.

1. Christocentrism and pneumatology

Vatican II has again brought Christ to the fore as the center and end of all human history (DV 10), as Alpha and Omega, center of the human race (GS 4). Vatican II has also emphasized the role of the Spirit in the permanent sanctification of the Church (LG 4), so as to accomplish His work of salvation of souls (AG 4). Montfort's fundamental intuition, embodied in TD, derives its originality from the great mystery of the Incarnation. It would be to our advantage today to appeal to Montfort's pneumatology when educating in the faith. The mystery of the Spirit is too often missing from contemporary guidelines for education in the faith.

2. Meaning of Baptism and the value of the laity

Montfort also believes in the dignity of the baptized. In FC 5 he speaks of the royal priesthood of the baptized. Seen in this light, Baptism confers great merit on the laity. Montfort shares his missionary labors with his Brothers, and male and female parishioners alike join in his mission. This is the primary objective of *Christi Fideles Laici,* which invites the lay faithful to listen to Christ as it calls on them to work in his vineyard.

3. Presence of Mary

The role of Mary in the economy of salvation is another of Montfort's fundamental intuitions. We should also note the Trinitarian, Christological, and biblical aspects of this devotion, which agree with the standards established in *Marialis cultus* 25 and 29. And Consecration to Christ through Mary has lost none of its value, as John Paul II proposed it to all Christians in the encyclical *Redemptoris mater* (48).

4. Value of spiritual guidance

Montfort proposes to us that we grow in holiness by means of spiritual guidance, an idea that has expanded in recent years.

5. Energetic devotion to schools

Educational institutions are, first and foremost, societal institutions. They reflect the religious, political, scientific, and business state in which the culture finds itself.[29] Thus we cannot universalize completely from Montfort's society to ours. Nonetheless, there is much to be learned from Montfort's overall approach to education that has a broad perennial application. Today schools are dominantly public in character and no longer see a close tie between faith and learning. Separated from theology, they are secular in character and focused on pragmatic, materialistic, humanistic goals. Montfort would agree with Norbert Mette that "transformation, liberation, justice, and social solidarity presume the guidelines and goals of an education based on the Gospel."[30] Even among systems of education where the secular myth of teaching has explicitly absented itself from religion, their schools presume these same values, which were so basic to Montfort and his pastoral ministry of teaching. We must remember, however, schools are not the only place where learning occurs. They are not the only place where Montfort's approach to education can be followed. Other teaching ministries can serve to shape future pathways. The church has called Christians to serve refugees, the poor, and other marginalized and dispossessed people with programs of spiritual guidance and communication, especially those developed by the laity for the laity. The montfort charism is dynamic, open to development, to new forms of ministries. Wherever it is authentically practiced, education in the faith on all levels should be a natural consequence.

G. Croteau

Notes: (1) A. Léon, *Histoire de l'enseignment en France (History of Teaching in France),* University Presses of France, Paris 1967, 44-52. The History of Education Today (Paris; Unesco, 1985) (2) *Ancien régime,* in D. Demnard and D. Fourment, *Dictionnaire d'histoire de l'enseignment (Dictionary of the History of Teaching),* Delarge, Paris 1981, 34-39. (3) J. Charter, M.-M. Compère, and D. Julia, *L'éducation en France du XVIe au XVIIIe siècle (Education in France in the Sixteenth and Seventeenth Centuries),* Press of the Society of Higher Education, Paris 1976, 114-142. (4) J.-P. Gutton, *Dévots et petites écoles (Small Religious Schools),* in supplement of the *Revue Marseille,* no. 88, 9. (5) Cf. *Éducation et pédagogies au siècle des Lumière (Education and Pedagogies in the Age of Enlightenment),* in *1983 Acts of Colloquy of the Institute for Educational Sciences,* Catholic University of the West, 1985, 134 ff. (6) Cf. S. Sacchino, *Protrepticon ad magistros scholarum inferiorum Societatis Jesu (Protrepticon for Teachers of the Lower Schools of the Society of Jesus),* Mascardi, Rome 1625; J. Juventius, *De ratione discendi et docendi ex decreto Congregationis generalis XIV (The Method of Learning and Teaching from the Decree of the Fourteenth General Congregation),* N. Nestenius, Florence 1703; A. Schimberg, *L'éducation morale dans les collèges de la Compagnie de Jésus en France sous l'Ancien régime (Moral Education in the Colleges of the Company of Jesus in France under the Ancien Régime),* Champion, Paris 1913; G. Snyders, *La pédagogie en France aux XVIIe et XVIIIe siècles (Pedagogy in France during the Seventeenth and Eighteenth Centuries),* PUF, Paris 1965; G. Durtelle de Saint-Sauveur, *Le collège de Rennes depuis la fondation jusqu'au départ des jésuites (The College of Rennes from Its Establishment to the Departure of the Jesuits),* in *Archeological Society of the Department of Ille-et-Vilaine* 46 (1918), 1-241. (7) Cf. *Règles et observances de la Congrégation de la Sainte Vierge, érigée au collège de la Compagnie de Jésus, en la ville de Rennes, sous le titre de la Purification (Rules and Observances of the Congregation of the Blessed Virgin, Founded at the College of the Company of Jesus, in the Town of Rennes, under the Title of the Purification),* Vatar, Rennes 1676; E. Villaret, *Les Congrégations mariales (Marian Congregations),* vol. 2, Beauchesne, Paris 1947, and *Congrégation de la Sainte Vierge (Congregation of the Blessed Virgin),* in DSAM 2, 1479-1491. [Emile Villaret] *Abridged History of the Sodalities of Our Lady,* trans. William J. Young (St. Louis; Queens Work, 1957) (8) On this subject, cf. S. De Fiores, *Itinerario,* 19-264. (9) Papàsogli, 19. Cf. J. Hervé, *Notes sur la famille du Bienheureux Grignion de Montfort (Notes on the Family of the Blessed Grignion de Montfort,* extracts from the parish bulletin of Montfort-sur-Meu (1925-1927), Vatar, Rennes 1927; M. Sibold, *Le Sang des Grignion (The History of the Grignions),* International Montfort Center, Rome 1987. (10) R. Laurentin, *Dieu seul est ma tendresse . . . (God Alone Is My Tenderness . . .),* O.E.I.L., Paris 1984, 122, 144. (11) Blain, 34. (12) Cf. Faillon, *Histoire des catéchismes de Saint-Sulpice (History of Catechisms at Saint-Sulpice),* Gaume, Paris 1831. (13) Laurentin, 176. (14) Grandet, 312. (15) Laurentin, 203. (16) Grandet, 101. (17) Laurentin, 39. (18) OC, 1516, note 2. (19) Grandet, 101. (20) A. Blain, *Le Bienheureux de Montfort et les écoles charitables (Blessed de Montfort and the Charitable Schools),* Poitiers 1889, 13. (21) G. Bernoville, *Grignion de Monfort, apôtre de l'école et les Frères de Saint Gabriel (Grignion de Montfort, Apostle of the School and Brothers of Saint Gabriel),* A. Michel, Paris 1946, 77. (22) Besnard I, 67. (23) Grandet, 383-384. Pierre de Cloriviere, *Considerations sur l'exercice de la priere et de l'oraison* (Bruges; Desclee de Brower, 1961). *The Paths of Prayer: A Clear Portrayal of the Various Kinds of Active and Passive Prayer* (New York; Comet Press Books, 1958) (24) Clorivière, 343. (25) Besnard II, 110-111. (26) Besnard II, 110. - (27) Besnard II, 110-111. (28) L. Pérouas, *Grignion de Montfort, les pauvres et les missions (Grignion de Montfort, the Poor and the Missions),* Cerf, Paris 1966, 91. *Education and Sociology,* trans. Sherwood D. Fox (Glencoe, Ill.; Free Press, 1956). (29) E. Durkheim, *Éducation et sociologie (Education and Sociology),* Alcan, Paris 1934, 42. (30) N. Mette, *Éducation,* in *Dictionnaire de théologie (Dictionary of Theology),*Cerf, Paris 1988, 147.

END TIMES

SUMMARY

I. MONTFORT'S CONCEPTION OF EARTHLY TIME:
   1. Relationship between time and eternity;
   2. Appreciating the true value of time;
   3. Secrets for gaining time;
   4. Past, present, and future.

II. MONTFORT AND THE END TIMES:
   1. A progressive discovery;
   2. Sources:
      a. Bérulle and Saint-Sulpice,
      b. Eudist sources,
      c. Post-Joachimite sources;
   3. Scenario of the end times:
      a. First stage: tragic state of the Church,
      b. Second stage: divine intervention within salvation history,
      c. Third stage: the Second Coming and reign of Jesus Christ,
      d. Fourth stage: the deluge of the fire of justice and the Last Judgment;
   4. The protagonists:
      a. The Trinity,
      b. Mary,
      c. The apostles of the end times,
      d. Satan.

III. THE APOSTLES OF THE END TIMES:
   1. Who are they?
   2. Their activity;
   3. Their spirituality:
      a. Union with God,
      b. Apostolic zeal,
      c. The Marian experience,
      d. The experience of the Cross.

IV. AN ELABORATION OF MONTFORT'S THOUGHT:
   1. "Spiritual" interpretation;
   2. Eschatological interpretation;
   3. Millenarian interpretation;
   4. Attempt at resolution.

V. THEOLOGICAL EVALUATION:
   1. Prophetic character and verification in history;
   2. Scriptural and extrabiblical arguments;
   3. Theological arguments.

VI. CONSEQUENCES FOR MONTFORT SPIRITUALITY:
   1. The future: a key to the life of Montfort;
   2. Devotion to Mary.

I. Montfort's Conception of Earthly Time

On first encounter, Montfort does not appear to have a specific theory about the end times but shares the conception common to his period. On deeper examination, however, we find that while he assimilated several ideas of his day, in preaching for example,[1] he added interesting points of his own and, in particular, formulated an organic and original conception of the end times of the Church.

Montfort's era was a time of transition. The seventeenth century and the intellectual dominance of Bossuet were giving way to the eighteenth century and Voltaire.[2] The passage from the baroque culture to that of the Enlightenment also had an effect on the contradictory portrait we have received of the period. Those who lived in this time of wars, misery, famine, and infant mortality gave voice to a negative and pessimistic judgment on the period. In particular, the acute sense of sin and human frailty, on the one hand, and of eternal life, on the other, led to an emphasis on the perversity and decay of the time. They often found refuge in the past, in medieval legends, or in admiration of the fervor of bygone saints. This culture, which often made reference to the immutable workings of Providence, had difficulty coping with change, which was accused by Tronson of being the "daughter of time, mother of disorder."[3]

Within the milieu of Enlightenment culture, by contrast, the critical spirit of P. Bayle became more and more widespread, attempting to dissipate the shadows of the past with the light of reason and refusing to become resigned to the status quo. The historical criticism penetrated the ecclesiastical world and called into question the sacred legends and apocryphal texts of the Breviary; as a result, the bourgeoisie viewed the period as one of social progress and well-being. The past was regarded as an inheritance to be examined with suspicion and left behind.

What are Montfort's options with respect to his times? They appear clearly in his writings.

1. Relationship between time and eternity

For Montfort as for the Christians of his times, the primary term of reference for evaluating our time on earth is eternity. He often links time and eternity as two essential stages in the life of Christ Wisdom (LEW 13, 14, 19, 95, 223) and the life of humans (LEW 2, 51; TD 265; SM 69). Eternity is the axis of reference, a lasting phase, while our time on earth is brief, and valuable only insofar as it prepares us for blissful eternity: *"Your momentary suffering will be changed into an eternity of happiness"* (LEW 180).

The value of worldly time is relative: it must be directed toward eternity. Montfort coins the phrase *"in time and in eternity"* (LEW 2, 225; FC 21; TD 265; H 20:18; 77:20), which he applies to the glorification of God, to the possession of Wisdom, and to the gift of oneself to Christ through the hands of Mary. By contrast, those who give absolute value to their time on earth rather than eternity are *"blind," "impostors"* who *"to Heaven prefer the earth / . . . and time to eternity"* (H 29:72).

2. Appreciating the true value of time

For Montfort, earthly time is precious, *"of immense value"* (H 30:8), and not *"one single moment"* should be lost. He laments the time spent in the search for comfort and diversion (LEW 81) or the philosopher's stone (LEW 88), and in the useless company of others, even the devout (LEW 200). Montfort views time as a gift from God *"to acquire heaven / when our actions are just"* (H 30:7) and later as a totality that must be offered to God. Intermittent devotion to Mary, praying to her *"occasionally"* (SM 25) and serving her *"only for a time"* (SM 33), is not enough: we must consecrate ourselves *"to God through Mary"* as a slave of love, *"for life"* (SM 32-33, TD 71).

The time in which Montfort is interested has nothing to do with seasonal changes, even though he is admiring Wisdom when he expresses his *"wonderment at the changes we see in the seasons and the weather"*; they are the seasons of salvation. He is attentive to *"time marked for the redemption of men"* (LEW 33), which transforms time into a *"gift of the Holy Spirit"* and confers on it *"the price of Jesus' blood"* (H 30:8). When he dies, the sinner, like those who play with cards and dice, will have *"a thousand regrets / For having lost his time this way / In games and pastimes of today, / While never doing penance"* (H 30:8).

3. Secrets for gaining time

In his missionary work, Montfort fought to win earthly time for his listeners: it is a *"favorable time"* (H 105:10), even *"holy time,"* although it *"passes quickly."* We must profit by this time and forget our worldly preoccupations (H 115:1, and refrain). A refrain of the hymns is that earthly time is an opportunity, an auspicious moment that we must not allow to escape: *"it is time"* to love the Good Shepherd (H 94:5), *"it is time"* to plant the Cross on the Crescent (H 95:10), *"it is time"* for the Kingdom of Jesus to arrive (H 126:11), *"it is time"* for the sinner to repent his deeds (H 137:14), *"it is time"* to abandon the shrill, changing world (H 142:10).

Montfort is familiar with time that seems endless and time that is very brief. His search for Wisdom occupies him *"night and day"* (L 15; LEW 73, 188), like Solomon, who *"only received this gift after he had desired it . . . for a long time"* (LEW 183-184). Similarly, poverty is a hidden treasure for which he has *"searched for so long"* (H 20:1). But there are secrets for *"quickly"* obtaining marvelous effects (TD 82); one of these is Mary, who brings Wisdom to us *"easily and in a short time"* (LEW 212). Perfect devotion to Mary *"is a quick way and leads us to Jesus in a short time"* (TD 168), because it is the same road that *"Jesus took to come to us with giant strides and in a short time"* (TD 155). If we cultivate this devotion, then, the Tree of Life *"will grow so tall that the birds of the air will make their home in it"* (SM 78).

4. Past, present, and future

Montfort is acknowledging this tripartite division of time when he consecrates to Jesus, through the hands of Mary, *"good actions, past, present, and to come"* (LEW 225). He is sensitive to the past and the future at his side in his own time. Like Tronson and most others, he admires the fervor of the community *"at the beginning of the Church"* (H 20:12-13) and the happiness of mankind before original sin (LEW 35-39). In addition, he chooses an "apostolic" life—walking in the steps of the Apostles—and proposes to the Missionaries of the Company of Mary that they do the same (PM 22; RM 2, 6, 22, 43, 50).

As for the present, Montfort is quick to point to its negative aspects: the introduction of comfort and luxury, unlike the voluntary poverty and customs of the ancients (H 22), and of a critical spirit that laughs at the piety of simple folk and demolishes the *"miracles and stories"* of the past (TD 93). The present suffers in comparison with the past: *"My Good God, there is a difference / Between days gone by and now! / The ancients had intelligence / We all seem fools now!"* (H 33:40). Montfort is conscious of living in *"a time full of perversity,"* dominated by luxury, vanity, and malice (H 33:23, 35): *"hard times which are hard only because people do not have enough trust in God"* (LCM 4).

Nonetheless, Montfort welcomes certain aspects of this critical culture and is open to a revised post-Joachimite spirituality that opens onto the future: he desires a reformed Church and a transformed world. Therefore he looks willingly to the future, which he describes as a synthesis of the present and the past. Future times, *"the end times"* (TD 50, 54, 58), will be *"perilous times"* (TD 114) in which the devil *"intensifies his efforts and his onslaughts every day"* (TD 50). But it will also be a *"happy time"* when the Spirit and Mary will prepare the reign of Christ (TD 217). We must reflect on this future time to discover Montfort's prophetic design.

II. Montfort and the End Times

In order to penetrate Montfort's thoughts, we will look at his texts on the end times, attempt to recover the sources that inspired Montfort, and describe the protagonists and scenario of the end times.

1. A progressive discovery

Montfort devoted few pages in his writings to the end times (about 17 pages out of 1,700), but they form an elaborate and coherent whole that was the fruit of his reading, reflection, and prayer.

His perspective on the future of the Church and the world is not immediately apparent but becomes progressively clearer and more precise.[4] In LEW, Montfort makes no mention of the end times or, consequently, of the role that Mary and the Holy Spirit will play in them; he merely remarks that Wisdom will be preceded by the Cross, *"and with this Cross and by it, he will judge the world"* (LEW 172). In SM 58-59, Montfort speaks of the Second Coming of Christ to *"reign over all the earth and to judge the living and the dead"* and of the *"great men filled with the Holy Spirit and imbued with the spirit of Mary"* who will destroy sin and establish the kingdom of Jesus Christ. In PM, the saint does not explicitly mention the Second Coming of Jesus (although he does speak of the coming of God the Father in PM 5), but he emphasizes the Spirit-filled times to come (the special reign of the Spirit and the deluge of fire) and the apostolic spirituality of the Missionaries of the Company of Mary.

In TD 46-59, Montfort expressly refers to the *"end times"* (a phrase used in TD:35, and three times in 50, 54, 58). In these passages he writes at length on the works and the spirituality of the *"apostles of the end times"* (TD 58), and he speaks of the Second Coming of Christ and of his reign in the world, as well as of the roles of the Holy Spirit and Mary. In TD, the deluge of fire is not mentioned, but it exists interiorized or as seen in its effects (the apostles are like a blazing fire and driven by the Spirit). In other passages of the book, this perspective reappears in different forms: he speaks of the difference between the first and second comings of Jesus (TD 1, 13, 22, 158), and he foresees the participation of men and women of the laity in the battle against the devil and in preparation for the kingdom of Christ (TD 113-114). Montfort also writes of a *"happy time"* when Mary will reign over hearts, *"subjecting them to the dominion of her great and princely son"* (TD 217).

In other works, including H, the end times do not appear, but certain aspects of the subject are present, such as the necessity of the coming of Christ's kingdom and of its extension to the Crescent (H 126:11).

2. Sources

It is not easy to identify Montfort's sources for his thinking on the end times.[5] Current research indicates clearly that none of his predecessors had developed their thoughts on the subject to a comparable extent. Among his contemporaries, we find various elements scattered widely but never discussed with such coherence and organization as we find in Montfort. One or another of the musical themes may have been composed previously, but the symphony is the work of Montfort alone.

We can distinguish three sources on which Montfort apparently drew in his teaching on the end times.

a. Bérulle and Saint-Sulpice. We have no indication that Montfort possessed a doctrine of the end times during his seminary years in Paris. We find no such doctrine either in Bérulle, leader of what is called the French school of spirituality, or in Olier, founder of the seminary of Saint-Sulpice. In their spiritual works are found significant elements that may have influenced Montfort.

Bérulle, cited by Montfort in TD 162, speaks of the imminence of the kingdom of Jesus and of his Second Coming; he even asserts that priests are "on earth and in the Church to establish and hasten the glorious and desirable coming of Jesus."[6] Rather than reflecting on the role of priests in the end times, Bérulle discusses how the sacerdotal ministry is essentially oriented toward the "final coming of the Son of God."[7]

Olier also reflects on the formation of priests for his own time, and not for the end times as Montfort does. But Montfort does integrate into his thought two ideas that Olier proposed: reform of the Church by the sacerdotal ministry and the description of priests as "men of flames and fire."[8]

During his time at Saint-Sulpice, Louis Marie notes in LS two ideas that he will take up again in his writings: the *"deluge of fire"* that falls from Heaven and the *"difference between the first and second comings of Our Lord."*[9]

b. Eudist sources. Textual comparison seems to suggest a certain literary dependance in Montfort on Saint John Eudes; both writers discuss the general conversion predicted by several saints and the cry of "Fire! . . . Fire!"[10] On the other hand, Eudes says nothing on the subject of the apostles of the end times.

More certain and more direct was the influence exerted on Montfort by Marie des Vallées († 1656), the so-called saint of Coutances and the spiritual daughter of St. John Eudes. Louis Marie read her biography, which was written by M. de Renty, and cites her in his description of the great saints to come *"who will surpass in holiness most other saints as much as the cedars of Lebanon tower above little shrubs"* (TD 47). It is probably to Marie des Vallées that Montfort owes the scenario of the end times: the reign of sin, the trials ordained by the Antichrist, the reign of grace, the coming of Christ for the Last Judgment. Above all, he takes from her the idea of the "three deluges," in connection with the Father, the Son, and the Holy Spirit, and the affirmation that "all of this will be accomplished by the Blessed Virgin."[11] In Montfort's hands, the subject receives a more rigorously theological treatment than in de Renty's biography, which is wordy and given to inorganic and incoherent symbolism. Saint Louis Marie uses only that which enters into his theological perspective, and he then completes and develops it. Thus, he precedes the "three deluges" with the "three reigns" (PM 16), so that the vision of Marie des Vallées is made more positive, less somber.[12] Moreover, he invests the saints of the end times with a high evangelical and communal spirituality (PM 7-13, 18-25; TD 46-48, 55-59). And using several different arguments, he creates a theological foundation for the role of Mary in the end times, connecting her with the battle against evil, the work of the Holy Spirit, and the Second Coming of Christ (TD 49-56; PM 13, 15, 24).

c. Post-Joachimite sources. Montfort was probably not familiar with the work of Joachim de Flore (died 1202). Although there are numerous differences between them, Montfort and the Calabrian priest share a number of views: the tripartite division of history, including a third age to exist in time and on earth and ushered in by the Holy Spirit; the anticipation of an abundance of grace, as if for a new Pentecost (*"tempus maioris gratiae,"* according to Joachim); the announcement of the coming of "spiritual men" who will bring about the existence of the eternal Gospel. Like the religious orders that had appropriated it earlier, Montfort applies the Joachimite prophecy of the "spiritual men" to the prophetic roles of evangelical men from which saints such as Francis of Paola, Vincent Ferrer, and Catherine of Siena had profited. These names appear in St. John Eudes's work, but in inverse order. With respect to Vincent Ferrer, however, Montfort indicates that he had direct access to the source material, because he cites "one of his works."[13] Was he, then, familiar with the opinion of St. Vincent de Paul on the prophecy of Vincent Ferrer? There is nothing to suggest he was; in any case, he dissociates himself from that opinion by applying to the Missionaries of the Company of Mary the prophetic vision of Ferrer.[14] Similarly, Montfort's reliance on Mary of Agréda († 1665) seems to be slight; she is cited anonymously in TD 206, but not in connection with the end times.[15]

3. Scenario of the end times

Comparative study of the three works in which Montfort speaks of the end times (SM, PM, TD) leads us to distinguish four successive and intersecting stages. Together they make up the scenario of the final days of the Church.

a. First stage: tragic state of the Church. In the eyes of a missionary and mystic like Montfort, the state of the Church and the society of his time offered scarce consolation. Although historians argue that conditions at the close of the seventeenth century improved as a result of the intense pastoral commitment of the French clergy,[16] Montfort would disagree. In his converging texts, he refers to the *"universal failure"* of contemporary Christian practice (TD 127), to the *"corrupt kingdom of the world"* (SM 59) and the reign of the enemies of God (PM 4). The encroaching wave of sin takes on cosmic dimensions and does not spare even the Church herself: *"Your Gospel is thrown aside, torrents of inequity flood the whole earth carrying away even your servants. The whole land is desolate, ungodliness reigns supreme, your sanctuary is desecrated and the abomination of desolation has even contaminated the holy place"* (PM 5; see also PM 14: *"the ever-swelling flood of iniquity").* The Church herself has become a *"languishing heritage," "so weakened and besmirched by the crimes of her children"* (PM 20). Behind the domination of sin, Montfort sees the work of the devil, which is *"daily increasing until the advent of the reign of anti-Christ"* (TD 51). Montfort is so dismayed that he invokes his own death if divine intervention does not bring a change: *"Send me your help from heaven or let me die"* (PM 14). Thus does he feel compelled to send up a cry of alarm when confronted with such a grave and imminent danger: *"The House of God is on fire! . . . Help!"* (PM 28).

b. Second stage: divine intervention within salvation history. This intermediary stage is the most dynamic and active, because during this stage we pass from the reign of sin to the reign of Jesus Christ in the hearts of men and women. Montfort is convinced that the Kingdom of God in Jesus Christ should not be projected into the hereafter but must come into existence on earth, in this world: *"Is it not true that your kingdom must come?"* (PM 5). This is the leitmotif of TD from its first sentence: *"It was through the blessed Virgin Mary that Jesus Christ came into the world, and it is also through her that he must reign in the world"* (TD 1; cf. 13, 22, 49, 157, 217, 262). Who will be able to transform the world? For Montfort there is no doubt: God alone can accomplish such a task. He will intervene with *"a deluge of fire, love and justice"* through the mediation of the Spirit and the manifold acts of Mary (PM 13, 15, 24-25; TD 49-56). This divine intervention will be through and in mankind, especially through the *"apostles of the end times"* (TD 58). Their task will be twofold: *"destroying sin and setting up the kingdom of Jesus"* (SM 59).

c. Third stage: the Second Coming and reign of Jesus Christ. There is no doubt that *"the whole Church expect[s] him [God] to come and reign over all the earth and to judge the living and the dead"* (SM 58). This Second Coming of Jesus will lead successively to the reign of Jesus in the world and to the Last Judgment, although not in tandem. Here we see the characteristic vision of Montfort: the universal and stable reign of Jesus (PM 4) anticipated in time as an effect of his coming. Jesus *"comes in glory once again to reign upon earth"* (TD 158), *"the knowledge and the kingdom of Jesus Christ must come into the world"* (TD 13), *"you yourself will ask of Jesus, together with Mary, that he come with his kingdom on earth."* It is not a visible and personal advent of Jesus and a temporal kingdom, as millenarians would hope for; Montfort insists that the kingdom of Jesus is *"in the hearts"* (TD 113) or *"in our soul"* (TD 68). In other words, Jesus will reign when, by the intervention of Mary, he is known, loved, and served (TD 49). In TD 217, we have the logical and perhaps even chronological steps: reign of Mary, coming of the Spirit, reign of Jesus Christ. We also see here how montfort spirituality has as its goal the establishment of the kingdom of Christ: *"'When will that happy day come . . . when God's Mother is enthroned in men's hearts as Queen, subjecting them to the dominion of her great and princely Son?'"* (TD 217).

d. Fourth stage: the deluge of the fire of justice and the Last Judgment. Montfort describes the end of time and the world from a pneumatological and then a Christological perspective. In the first, the deluge of the fire of love will be followed by the deluge of the fire of justice, an expression of divine anger, which *"reduces the whole world to ashes"* (PM 16-17). In the Christological version, the reign of Christ in the world is followed, as if in continuation of his Second Coming or the Parousia, by the universal judgment: God will *"come and reign over all the earth and to judge the living and the dead"* (SM 58). Then thc end times themselves will end, and the true eschatology—that is, eternity—will begin.

4. The protagonists

In the four stages (tragedy, drama, happiness, and finally destruction and judgment) of the end times, various personages will play a role.

a. The Trinity. This is the principal and final Agent, Who is the origin of the plan for salvation and on Whom the glory of what has taken place in time reflects (TD 22; 50,6).

The three Divine Persons display Their efficacious works in the end times, beginning with God the Father, to Whom Montfort attributes *"merciful plans"* (PM 2); the selection, dispatch, and formation of the great saints at the end of time (TD 47-48, 57); the revelation of Mary (TD 50, 55); the enmity between Mary and her children and the devil and his children (TD 52, 54); and the knowledge of time and of how the end times will unfold (TD 59; SM 58).

The protagonist of salvation is Jesus Christ. His Second Coming on earth becomes real, and he once again reigns over men and judges them (SM 58-59; TD 48, 217); the purpose of the time of revelation is to lead us to know, love, and serve him (TD 49). The apostles of the end times will be *"the true disciples of Jesus Christ"* (TD 59). The Lord Jesus will again assume the power to give to Mary *"this new company so that you may renew all things through her"* (PM 6). The missionaries will be established on Mary, the mountain of God, and *"Jesus Christ, who dwells there forever, will teach them in his own words the meaning of the eight beatitudes"* (PM 25).

The work of the Spirit is preponderant and efficacious. The Spirit intervenes in the end times with a *"deluge of fire, love and justice"* (PM 16-17), like a new Pentecost. The Spirit will *"create priests who burn with this same fire and whose ministry will renew the face of the earth"* and renew the world (PM 17); the Spirit will sanctify them (PM 15), assemble them (PM 20-21), and send them on their mission (PM 9; TD 57).

b. Mary. She is one of the principal protagonists and supports, acting in many ways in the end times and in collaboration with the three Divine Persons. With the Most High and by His will, Mary forms the apostles and the great saints (TD 47, 59). With Christ, she does battle with the proud Satan (TD 52, 54; PM 12-13) and brings the years of grace to an end with the new company of missionaries that the Son, dying on the Cross, entrusted to her (PM 1, 6). With the Holy Spirit, Mary is entrusted with begetting the sons of God and forming the saints of the end of time (PM 11, 15). The end times bring the full revelation of Mary, not in the sense of a deeper abstract knowledge, but insofar as we will experience her presence. She will be revealed in her merciful love toward sinners, in her battle against the enemies of God, and in her support of the faithful disciples of Christ: *"In these end times Mary must shine forth more than ever in mercy, power and grace"* (TD 50,6). The Mother of God is a spiritual leader and teacher for the apostles of the end times, particularly the Missionaries of the Company of Mary. Montfort affirms this by applying to Mary the symbolism of the mountain: those who live in her grow in holiness and learn of contemplation and intercession. They are introduced to the logic of the evangelical beatitudes and participate in the mysteries of Christ that took place on the mountain: the Transfiguration, the Crucifixion, and the Ascension (PM 25).

*c. **The apostles of the end times.*** They are the necessary instruments for the realization of God's plan, as will be detailed below.

*d. **Satan.*** Satan establishes his own plan in opposition to God's plan. He will plot dire attacks on the heel of Mary (TD 54; PM 13), he will redouble his attacks (TD 50), and he will instigate wicked persecutions that will increase until the reign of the Antichrist (TD 51). The devil will lead the battle with the enemies of God, who will be his active intermediaries in the end times; trembling with rage, they are ready to break out in every direction, rebelling, uniting, and sounding the alarm (TD 48, 50; PM 5, 27, 28).

III. The Apostles of the End Times

Although this phrase, (TD 58) of Montfort, is used only once, it summarizes his thought on the end times. He describes at length the condition, activity, and spirituality of these apostles.

1. Who are they?

Their identity gradually becomes clear. Montfort speaks first of *"great saints"* (TD 47), *"great souls filled with grace and zeal"* (TD 48). He then refers to them as *"the valiant soldiers and loyal servants of Jesus Christ . . . . the true children and servants of the Blessed Virgin"* (TD 50,6; 52; 54), *"the elect"* (TD 55), *"these servants, these slaves, these children of Mary"* (TD 56). Finally he refers to their sacerdotal character: *"ministers of the Lord . . . . the children of Levi"* (TD 56), *"true apostles of the end times . . . . in the midst of other priests, ecclesiastics and clerics"* (TD 58). In his ardent prayer for vocations to the Company of Mary, he speaks of *"missionaries"* (PM 3, 20, 21, 25) and of *"priests"* (PM 2, 18, 25, 29). His proposed congregation of missionary priests forms the core of these apostles. But the activity and the mighty battles of the end times must not be reserved to them alone. In two other prophetic texts, Montfort speaks more generally of *"chosen souls"* in whom Mary will reign sovereign (TD 217), and he enlarges the horizon to embrace *"a mighty legion of brave and valiant soldiers of Jesus and Mary, both men and women"* (TD 114).

2. Their activity

The work of the apostles of the end times swings essentially around two poles, one negative, the other positive: *"destroying sin and establishing the reign of Jesus Christ"* (SM 59). The first pole involves a series of aggressive actions against the forces of evil: they *"will give battle, overthrowing and crushing"* (TD 48), they *"will thunder against sin, they will storm against the world, they will strike down the devil and his followers"* (TD 57), they *"will be the odor of death to the great, the rich and the proud of this world"* (TD 56). In the PM, along the same lines, Montfort foresees missionaries who will attack and overthrow the *"enemies of God"* (PM 8, 29), who will *"crush the head of the serpent"* (PM 12), *"address their ardent prayers to heaven, turning them into the weapons which will overcome or convert their enemies"* (PM 25). The positive pole, which is described in more detail, consists of actions directed at the reform of the Church and its extension into the world: their *"ministry will renew the face of the earth and reform your Church"* (PM 17). With this objective, the apostles of the end times will carry out sanctifying apostolic work: they *"will enkindle everywhere the fires of divine love"* (TD 56); *"wherever they preach, they will leave behind them nothing but the gold of love"* (TD 58); they will be the *"sweet fragrance of Jesus"* (TD 56). They will *"build the temple of the true Solomon and the mystical city of God"* (TD 48), and they will *"shower down the rain of God's word and of eternal life"* (TD 57). Moreover, they will work to extend the Lord's empire *"over the impious, the idolators and Muslims"* (TD 49), receiving the deluge of fire that will empower them to convert *"Muslims, idolators and even Jews"* (PM 17).

3. Their spirituality

Montfort's spiritual portrait of the apostles of the end times (TD 48) includes four aspects of their spirituality:

a. Union with God. They are *"great souls filled with grace"* (TD 48), *"rich in God's graces . . . . great and exalted before God in holiness"* (TD 54), *"closely joined to God"* (TD 56). The union with God (the Father) includes *"the gold of love"* (TD 56, 58), *"the frankincense of prayer"* (TD 56), *"the resolve to seek the glory of God"* (TD 58). In connection with the Son, Montfort calls the apostles of the end times *"true disciples of Jesus Christ"* and of the crucified Jesus because they are radical followers of the Gospel and they speak the Gospel *"in pure truth . . . . Their hearts will not be troubled, nor will they show favor to anyone"* (TD 59). With the Holy Spirit they live in total mystical availability: they *"will be like thunderclouds flying through the air at the slightest breath of the Holy Spirit"* (TD 57; cf. 58).

b. Apostolic zeal. They are the *"great souls filled with . . . zeal"* (TD 48), *"superior to all creatures by their great zeal"* (TD 54). The action of the *"true apostles of the end times"* (TD 58) consists of spreading *"the fire of divine love"* everywhere; they are themselves *"a flaming fire"* (TD 56). In the battle against evil and the enemies of God, these great saints *"will become, in Mary's powerful hands, like sharp arrows,"* and they will leave *"an odor of death"* among the worldly (TD 56). Their work will not be limited to reforming the Church, but will include extending it to *"the idolators and Muslims"* (TD 59).

c. The Marian experience. Montfort describes this with enthusiasm: *"these great souls . . . will be exceptionally* *devoted to the Blessed Virgin. Illumined by her light, nourished at her breast, guided by her spirit, supported by her arm, sheltered under her protection"* (TD 48; cf. also 55). They are *"those who belong to the Blessed Virgin,"* her *"true children and servants," "her humble slaves and children," "her heel,"* who will crush the head of the serpent (TD 54).

d. The experience of the Cross. There are various reasons for this experience: the need to be *"thoroughly purified by the fire of Great Tribulations"* and to carry *"the myrrh of mortification in their body"* (TD 56); the fact that they will be preaching devotion to Mary, which *"will make many enemies"* (TD 48); the description of the "heel" of Mary, which implies that they will be *"down-trodden and crushed"* (TD 54).

These four elements are found in the spirituality of the apostolic men whom Montfort describes in the PM. These apostles will be united with God, because they are *"enriched by the dew of heaven and the fat of the earth"* (PM 25); *"entirely dependent on Providence, who will feast to their heart's content on the spiritual delights you provide"* (PM 21); and endowed with *"their great love for Jesus Christ which enables them to carry his cross"* (PM 24); uniquely preoccupied with the *"glory"* of the Holy Spirit (PM 23), whose breath urges them forward to their mission (PM 9). In addition, they will burn with *"holy anger"* and *"ardent zeal"* (PM 21), because the Holy Spirit will create *"priests who burn with this same fire"* (PM 17) and who will have a *"perfect love . . . for their neighbor"* (PM 24). They will do battle against the enemies of God *"with the Cross for their staff and the Rosary for their sling"* (PM 8) and with an irresistible wisdom (PM 22, 25), and *"they will crush the head of the serpent wherever they go"* (PM 12). They will thus become the *"true children . . . . true servants of the Blessed Virgin"* (PM 11, 12), characterized by *"their true devotion to Mary"* (PM 12) and her maternal solicitude (PM 11, 25). Finally, they will experience persecutions and crosses, because *"the devil will lie in wait to attack the heel of this mysterious woman, that is, the little company of her children"* (PM 13).

Montfort expresses the spirituality of these missionaries using meteorological symbols (rain, snow: PM 20, 25), cosmic symbols (fire, sun: PM 12), and animals (dogs, lambs, doves, eagles, bees, deer, lions: PM 13), especially those of the four evangelists (man, lion, ox, eagle: PM 21). The key word that embodies this spirituality and that Montfort repeats six times, each time in a way that gives it new meaning, is *liberos,* in the twofold etymological sense of "free" and "son": the missionaries of the *"special reign"* of the Spirit are free of all human ties (PM 7). They will accomplish God's plans with a total availability; their means will be poverty (PM 8), always open to the breath of the Spirit (PM 9) and *"to the voice of authority"* (PM 10), *"true children . . . and servants of the Blessed Virgin"* (PM 11, 12).

IV. An Elaboration of Montfort's Thought

Exegetes of Montfort's thought do not agree on an interpretation of the "end times," particularly on the meaning of the "Second Coming" of Jesus and of his "kingdom" (SM 58; TD 1, 13, 22, 48-59, 158, 127). Three interpretations exist that we must grasp and attempt to conciliate.

1. "Spiritual" interpretation

According to the theologians Rosatini and Mercurelli, champions of Montfort's beatification, when the author of TD speaks of the Second Coming of Christ, he is referring not to the Parousia but to the "kingdom of Christ in this world. This kingdom is surely founded on Christ living in our hearts through faith, and he will come in all his fullness on that day when heresies have been vanquished and the shadows of our errors have been removed, and there will be one true flock and one true shepherd. It seems that God has chosen to accomplish this through Mary, she who has destroyed all of the heresies in the world."[17] For these two authors, the spiritual nature of the Second Coming derives from the fact that Montfort had already spoken of the spiritual kingdom of Christ and "of the role attributed to Mary in preparing for this event."[18]

This line of thought is also taken by H. M. Gebhard in 1918, in his commentary on TD.[19] With two arguments, he rejects the idea that the final coming of Jesus Christ will be that of the Last Judgment,[20] and he identifies this coming with "the arrival of Jesus . . . among men by means of grace."[21] In a similar but more eschatological vein, P. Oger states that "the final coming of Jesus Christ signifies the coming of Jesus Christ 'in the Spirit' (Saint Thomas) at the end of the world, not the supreme coming . . . 'against men' at the Last Judgment."[22] Another commentator on TD, A. Plessis, distinguishes among three comings of Jesus: the first took place with the Incarnation, the second "by means of his grace," and the third with the Last Judgment. Plessis declares that Montfort "does not speak explicitly of the immense distance between the first and second comings" and thus he is hesitant to link the "Second Coming" with the manifestation of Jesus by means of grace or to set it "in the time immediately preceding the Last Judgment," but he does maintain the three comings of Jesus.[23]

2. Eschatological interpretation

A. Lhoumeau gives a different interpretation to the Montfort texts. The second advent of Christ will take place "at the end of time in all the radiance of his glory. That is what we call the Parousia."[24] This coming is preceded by the end times, a "period of indeterminate length . . . that will be extreme and terminal, so to speak, in character." Montfort opens up "vast perspectives" on Mary's role in the Church in preparing for the Second Coming of Jesus.[25]

More recently, H. Frehen, after having examined Montfort's texts on the two comings of Jesus, comes down on the side of Lhoumeau against Gebhard. In fact, SM 58 and TD 158 scarcely allow for uncertainty, since both texts locate the first coming of Jesus *"in a state of self-abasement and privation"* (SM 58), *"secret and hidden,"* (TD 158), whereas the second is *"glorious and resplendent"* (TD 158). Thus the first coming, in grace, *"in an invisible manner"* (TD 22), cannot be confused with the second and final coming, which is manifest and visible. When he is confronted with determining the basis of this visibility or this radiance, Frehen rules out Parousia and falls back on the kingdom of Jesus, understood to be the perfect knowledge and service of Jesus himself.[26]

3. Millenarian interpretation

This interpretation has been put forward by L. Perouas, who considers "eschatological" interpretations of the end times inadequate. In effect, Montfort "envisions this marvelous era arising in the course of the earthly history of the Church. It would be more valuable to speak of millenarianism, the theory that predicts, at a given time, an earthly, collective, and total salvation." Saint Louis Marie would have borrowed certain elements from the predictions of Joachim de Flore and subsequent millenarian thinking, which is similarly weak and utopian.[27]

J. Séguy has devoted an article to Montfort and the apostles of the end times within the context of his research into the eschatological character of religious institutions. He expands the basis for a millenarian interpretation and emphasizes its centrality and importance in Montfort's thought.[28] Séguy distances himself from spiritual and eschatological interpretations, i.e., from identifying the Second Coming of Jesus with the existence of the Church (as in Gebhard) or with the Parousia (Frehen). Rather, he agrees with G. Barbera[29] that the Second Coming includes the earthly time of the Church and the true Second Coming, including the Parousia. He parts with Barbera, however, when he suggests, echoing the scenario uniformly put forth by Joachimite thinkers,[30] "an earthly triumph of the Church," "a period of indeterminate length, the 'kingdom of Jesus Christ,' between the Great Tribulation and the personal return of Christ for the judgment."[31] He underlines certain aspects of Montfort's thought: the kingdom of Jesus Christ is located "in history and is set on earth" (p. 30); the era of the Spirit has a fundamental Marian dimension, in that Mary will play a decisive role in the final days, a time that "will be pneumatological because of this Marian dimension"; the apostles of the end times are specifically the Missionaries of the Company of Mary . . . [32] Because several of these elements have been borrowed from Marie des Vallées (the division of history into three epochs, the reign of God as a spiritual triumph that will be realized in the world, the Great Tribulation, annihilation of the Antichrist, Parousia and universal judgment), Montfort must be placed in the "post-Joachimite tradition." Indeed, "it becomes legitimate to search in post-Joachimism for the coherence of Montfort's treatment of apocalyptic material."[33]

4. Attempt at resolution

The first two interpretations proposed here (Gebhard/Lhoumeau) are true in what they affirm, false in what they deny. The third (Séguy) forces the thought of Montfort in order to give him the ambiguous label "Joachimite." This evaluation becomes evident after making a few precisions concerning Saint Louis Marie's thought.

a. On the comings of Jesus, we must adhere strictly to Montfort's words, which describe only two: the first, and the second or last.[34] Thus, Montfort is adopting the language of the Church, which in its Credo confesses only two comings of Christ: at the time of the Incarnation and at the Last Judgment. Montfort considers each of these a discrete, complex event. In fact, his language is polyvalent: the word "coming" covers distinct events and partially different subject matter. The first coming includes the Incarnation and also the public life and the Cross (TD 18-19, 22; cf. PM 16); the second or last coming includes the spiritual reign, i.e., in the hearts of men and women of today, as well as his personal advent at the Parousia to judge the living and the dead (SM 58: *"to come and reign over all the earth and the judge the living and the dead"*; TD 158: *"When our loving Jesus comes in glory once again to reign upon earth").* Because Montfort includes in his understanding of Second Coming Jesus' dynamic reign in human hearts, he even calls this aspect *"glorious and resplendent"* (TD 158) in a way appropriate to the Parousia itself. As CCC 670 teaches: "Since the Ascension God's plan has entered into its fulfillment. We are already at 'the last hour.'" The Second Vatican Council declares: "Already the final age of the world is with us and the renewal of the world is irrevocably under way" (LG 48).

The missionary's use of the expression *"deluge of fire"* (PM 16-17) illustrates how Montfort intertwines concepts under one symbol when speaking of the end times. There is only one deluge (PM 16), but this deluge unfolds in two ways and in two stages with different effects: the *"deluge of fire . . . of pure love"* will produce reform of the Church and the conversion of peoples, whereas the *"deluge of fire . . . and justice"* or of divine anger *"reduces the whole world to ashes"* (PM 16-17).

It therefore appears that the spiritual (Gebhard, Plessis, Oger) and eschatological (Lhoumeau, Frehen) interpretations are one-sided. It cannot be underlined sufficiently that in the writings of Saint Louis Marie the Second Coming of Jesus includes the present earthly existence of the Church—Jesus now reigning in our hearts—as well as its eschatological fulfillment in the universal judgment. It is a *now* opening up to its *future* eternal completion. Therefore, to speak of *three* comings of Jesus is to contradict Montfort's text.

b. As for the millenarian interpretation of the end times, we must say that it not only creates confusion but does so by distorting Montfort's thought. In theological language, millenarianism constitutes "eschatological error, according to which Jesus Christ shall reign visibly for one thousand years on this earth at the end of the world."[35] This millenarian kingdom, in its modified form, includes the just rising from the dead.[36] This strict millenarianism is altogether alien to Montfort, who mentions neither the millennium (he never even cites Rev 20:3-5) nor the personal coming of Jesus to reign in the world together with the risen martyrs.[37] Séguy himself is forced to admit that these definitions do not suit Montfort at all or can be applied to him only with reservations.[38]

We must make the same distinction about Montfort's so-called Joachimism. There is no proof whatsoever of any direct dependence by the Breton missionary on Abbot Joachim; in fact, as stated above, Montfort may never even have known of him. The differences between them can only be termed enormous.[39] There are two surface similarities: the division of history into three periods (PM 16) and the conception of the earthly existence of the Church as a "reign of the Spirit" during which a new Pentecost ("deluge of fire") takes place (PM 16-17). These two points may be sufficient to classify Montfort within a post-Joachimite tradition, although Henri de Lubac states categorically: "We have found nothing clearly Joachimite, even as a passing breath, in the complete works of Saint Louis de Montfort."[40]

On a scenario for the end times, the texts of Montfort are limited in their scope. They refer to and describe stages and moments of the end times without placing them in sequence, and any attempt to establish exactly how these events unfurl is guesswork.

This is due to the fact, recognized by Séguy himself, that Montfort has not "systematically" addressed the subject of the final days of the Church.[41] In fact, the saint seems to exclude the existence of any clear demarcation setting off the various stages of the end times; rather, they appear to be more or less simultaneous and overlapping. Thus, for example, perfect devotion to Mary prepares one for the kingdom of Christ, on the one hand (this would then suggest a chronological succession: TD 217), whereas, on the other hand such perfect devotion is only possible during the kingdom of Christ, because it is Mary's task to fashion Christ in us (this would indicate simultaneity: TD 217-221). Similarly, the kingdom of Christ coexists with that of Satan or the Antichrist, because the children of Belial and the race of Mary will come face to face in the end times leading up to the final battle (TD 51-54). It follows that the coming of Christ is neither automatic nor instantaneous, but progressive and dynamic, just as the destruction of the kingdom of sin is not immediate but staggered over time. The retreat of the state of sin is tied to the advance of the reign of Christ, which is only possible with Mary's consolidation of the kingdom.

V. Theological Evaluation

If Montfort's teaching on the end times contained nothing that was original, there would be no reason to speak of it or justify it theologically. But the scenario of the end times, the interpretation of the Second Coming of Jesus, the presence of extraordinary saints, the deluge of fire, and the role of Mary are elements that are original and Montfort's alone. They have been neither rejected nor accepted but simply ignored by classical Catholic eschatology, which is generally content to single out, among the signs that precede the Parousia, the decrease in faith (Lk 18:8), the appearance of the Antichrist (2 Thess 2:3-11; 1 Jn 2:18-23), the preaching of the Gospels to every nation (Mt 24:14), and the conversion of Israel (Rom 11:25-26).[42]

In fact, several elements of Montfort's thoughts on the end times have provoked objections ever since the beatification proceedings. The first censor of the writings of this servant of God raised difficulties on two points: the necessity of the revelation of Mary in the Second Coming of Christ and the anticipation of great saints superior to those of the past. In the eyes of the Roman censor, these affirmations were not contrary to faith, but they were unclear and without a solid basis in Scripture.[43] Two other problematic elements of Montfort's teaching must be added: the view of the reign of Jesus in the interior of men and women as a time of an outpouring of grace (bearing some resemblance to the *"tempus amplioris gratiae"* of a Joachimite line of thought), and its preparation by the action of the Spirit and Mary (the deluge of the fire of love and the kingdom of Mary).

1. Prophetic character and verification in history

We can generally respond, as did the theologians who defended Montfort during the beatification proceedings, that because he was making a prophecy, we should not look for rational proofs: "If predictions of contingent future events had some kind of basis, they would no longer be prophetic."[44]

The censors themselves acknowledged both the extrinsic and intrinsic probability of Montfort's predictions. The extrinsic probability derives from the authority of the servant of God himself, who had stated 150 years earlier that the revelation of Mary by the Holy Spirit would increase in order to convert hearts to the kingdom of Christ. The realization of Montfort's prophecies, which can be seen in the spread of devotion to the Immaculate Conception and in the mass conversions in Europe (of years gone by) and in the "foreign missions" shows that he was right. The intrinsic probability of Montfort's predictions regarding the great saints derives from the very nature of the events concerning the reign of Christ in history or in the end times. In history, when Christ destroys false beliefs and reigns over the just, his reign will likely shine in the splendor of its holiness. In the end times, when the danger to the faithful from false prophets will grow, there can be no doubt that Divine Providence will come to the aid of its Church through the sublime saintliness of one of its servants.[45]

This kind of argumentation is not without interest, since it ties teaching to life, and prediction to verification in history. We cannot deny to Montfort the charism of prophecy, which his earliest biographers argue is demonstrated by the fulfillment of his predictions.[46] We will now examine the theological basis of these predictions.

2. Scriptural and extrabiblical arguments

Montfort is firmly convinced that the Kingdom of God must be realized on earth, as is demanded in the Lord's Prayer (Mt 6:10; *"Is it not true that your kingdom must come?"* [PM 5]). The request of the just and of creation itself that God may come into the world (Rev 22:20; Rom 8:22) cannot remain unanswered: *"the faithful on earth . . . cry out : Amen, veni, Domine, amen, come, Lord. All creatures, even the most insensitive, lie groaning under the burden of Babylon's countless sins and plead with you to come and renew all things: omnis creatura ingemiscit, etc."* (PM 5). Even the battle between Mary and Belial and their races is based on the Gospel, and remarked on at length by Montfort (TD 51-54; PM 12-13).

Since the Bible does not specify the modalities of the Second Coming of Christ— *"Holy Scripture . . . gives no clear guidance on this subject"* (SM 59)— Montfort relies on his interpretative understanding of Scripture as a whole and as clarified by the *"prophetic knowledge"* of great saints like Francis of Paola, Vincent Ferrer, and Catherine of Siena (PM 2), as well as the revelations of Marie des Vallées (TD 47). Certainly these arguments are not of equal value.

3. Theological arguments

On the connection between Mary and the Holy Spirit in the end times, Montfort elaborates a series of arguments that we do not find in his predecessors.

Curiously, however, he does not focus on the Biblical texts that mention the Spirit and Mary together. Thus he never cites Acts 1:14, which shows Mary in prayer in the cenacle in anticipation of the Spirit, nor the critical verse of Lk 1:35, which links Mary to the Spirit in the virginal conception of Jesus (this is implicitly cited in TD 44).

Montfort's argumentation is essentially theological: he assumes the biblical information and then deduces conclusions or laws relating to salvation history. His fundamental thesis is based on the mystery of the Incarnation and is clearly expressed in the opening of TD: *"It was through the blessed Virgin Mary that Jesus Christ came into the world, and it is also through her that he must reign in the world"* (TD 1). This theme recurs throughout the work and is expressed in increasingly eschatological terms, i.e., it is projected to the end of time: *"The salvation of the world began through Mary and through her it must be accomplished"* (TD 49; cf. TD 13, 22, 50, 158, 217, 262). As the root mystery of Redemption, the Incarnation "contains" everything that flows from it: as at the Incarnation, so too at the end of time.

Saint Louis de Montfort uncovers a typological rapport (of continuity and exemplarity) between the two comings of Christ, a rapport founded on the harmony of God's plan. Seeing the intimate and indissoluble action of Mary and the Spirit in the first coming of Jesus, the Incarnation, Montfort deduces that it will likewise exist for the Second Coming of Jesus, in the realization of his kingdom at the end times: *"Together with the Holy Spirit Mary produced the greatest thing that ever was or ever will be: a God-man. She will consequently produce the marvels which will be seen in the end times. . . . only this singular and wondrous virgin can produce in union with the Holy Spirit singular and wondrous things"* (TD 35). It is this unity of the Holy Spirit and Mary in preparing for the God-man's advent in the world, and its ultimate value for the history of salvation, that reveal the strength of Montfort's logic. Because the Incarnation is God's masterwork, it has a definitive quality. God does not change His direction: whenever the coming of Christ or marvelous works in the realm of holiness are at stake, Mary and the Spirit will always be at work.

Montfort develops at length the seven reasons that Mary's role in the Second Coming of Christ will increase (TD 50). We can restate in our own words these reasons for the revelation of Mary in the end times: 1. Mary personifies the law of humility/exaltation that is a constant throughout salvation history; having *"in her great humility considered herself lower than dust,"* she must be exalted. 2. Mary, a masterpiece of God, joins in the praise and glory of God; the more she is praised, the greater God is glorified. 3. Mary is the introduction to the reign of Jesus, as the Dawn relates to the Sun of Justice, as knowledge of her leads to knowledge of Jesus. 4. As the Eternal Wisdom entered this world through Mary, so he will come through her at the Parousia. 5. The way of Mary is characterized by its holiness, i.e., perfect union with Jesus Christ. This way must be followed by all those who would attain perfection. 6. Mary's role *("In these end times Mary must shine forth more than ever in mercy, power and grace")* is necessary to convert sinners, destroy the forces of evil, and support the faithful disciples of Jesus Christ. 7. In the final battle against the devil and his henchmen, Mary will ensure the triumph of Jesus Christ (TD 50; see also TD 51-54).

There is thus a continuity between the first and second comings of Jesus: both occur through the joint action of the Spirit and Mary. The second is not, however, simply a repetition of the first; their modality, their immediate goals, and their circumstances are different. Jesus came into the world the first time *"in self-abasement and privation,"* whereas he will come the second time to *"reign over all the earth and to judge the living and the dead"* (SM 58). Mary, who has participated in the self-emptying (*kenosis*) of Christ while remaining hidden in humility (TD 2-3, 49), will participate in the glorious manifestation of the Son; she will move from *kenosis* to glory, from secret to revelation (TD 49).

Montfort's perspective on the end times of the Church appears to be coherent and founded in different ways on Scripture, theology, and his own prophetic charism and that of other saints. Conciliar and contemporary theology confirms several elements of his perspective.

In particular it confirms Montfort's line of thought anticipating the eschatological reign in time (Jesus *"must reign in the world,"* TD 1). Theology today in effect tends to "insert the eschatological element more strongly into the Christ event" and to "consider what is still, one supposes, viewed too strictly as an event belonging to the future as an asset that is already present."[47]

Furthermore, theology is more attentive to the action of the Spirit in history. The perpetual renewal and extension of the Church are attributed to the Paraclete (LG 4), so that "a growth of the Mystical Body under the action of the Spirit"[48] can link with Montfort's thinking on the accelerated progress of sanctity and the missionary impulse in the final phase of history. Contemporary Mariology is increasingly sensitive to the link between Mary and the Holy Spirit in the different stages of the history of salvation.[49]

Nonetheless we do not yet find in recent theology all of the Spirit-related, Mariological, and ecclesial developments that are present in the writings of Montfort.

V. Consequences for Montfort Spirituality

The whole of Montfort's doctrine on time is precious for Montfort spirituality. montfort compels us to recall the past, to value the present in view of eternity, and above all to prepare for the future of the world. Montfort's coherent outline on the end times has consequences both for a correct understanding of Saint Louis Marie and for the Marian devotion that he taught.

1. The future: a key to the life of Montfort

Saint Louis Marie de Montfort's determination to become an itinerant missionary has often been explained as an expression of his desire to live the life of the early apostles. This explanation remains true, but it should be complemented with Montfort's projection toward the future. The prodigious activity that the missionary accomplished in his brief life was also due to the urgency he experienced in proclaiming the reign of Jesus Christ. This purpose is intrinsic to both his preaching and his writing. Although undoubtedly guided by the example of Christ Wisdom and the Apostles living in poverty, Montfort's existence is energized by the urgent need of transforming the reign of sin into the reign of Jesus Christ. The saint opens himself, therefore, to the breath of the Spirit and the maternal action of Mary, becoming a priest full of fire to reform the Church and renew the face of the earth.

2. Devotion to Mary

To read TD without the perspective of the end times—which for Montfort means the present time (*"these end times,"* TD 50)—gives the impression that Montfort is simply attempting to introduce his readers to *"the interior and perfect practice"* of Marian devotion. But there is one dimension of Montfort's Marian teaching that is often forgotten: his thought is eschatological and therefore Spirit-related and apostolic.

By indissolubly uniting Mary and the Holy Spirit as the begetters of Christ and Christians (TD 34-36), and by locating this action in the special reign of the Spirit, of the Father, and of the Son (PM 15-17), Montfort avoids the danger of Christomonism.

Moreover, this Marian spirituality cannot fall back on itself, because in Montfort's view it is projected toward the future and the kingdom of Jesus Christ. It is finalized and dynamically outstretched toward the fulfillment in history. Those who are consecrated to Christ through the hands of Mary will be bound to destroy the kingdom of evil, to establish the reign of God, and to spread His kingdom throughout the entire world. When they breathe Mary as the body breathes air, becoming living copies of her, then Jesus will be loved and glorified (TD 217). In other words, only when the Church becomes Mary will Jesus be "born" a second time and return to establish in the Spirit the fullness of the reign of the Father.

S. De Fiores

Notes: (1) In LS, Montfort copied five outlines on "time" from contemporary sermon writers (Lejeune, Laselve, Loriot). Cf. *Le livre des sermons du Père de Montfort (The book of Sermons of Father de Montfort),* International Montfort Center, Rome 1983, pp. 489-493. (2) See the description in the classic work of P. Hazard, *La crise de la conscience européenne, 1680-1715,* Fayard, Paris 1964. English translation: *European Thought in the Eighteenth Century, from Montesquieu to Lessing,* trans. J. Lewis May, Yale Univerisyt Press, New Haven 1954. (3) The maxim *Novitas filia temporis, mater perturbationis* (Novelty is the daughter of time and the mother of conflict) is reported by Gosselin, "Mémoires sur M. Tronson (Papers on M. Tronson)", ms., Archives of Saint-Sulpice, Paris, p. 183. (4) There are signs of this evolution in H. Frehen, *Le "second avènement" de Jésus-Christ et la méthode de saint Louis-Marie de Montfort (The "Second Coming" of Jesus Christ and the Method of Saint Louis Marie de Montfort),* DMon 7 (1962), n. 31, pp. 98-108. (5) The editors of *God Alone: The Collected Works of Saint Louis Marie de Montfort,* Montfort Publications, Bay Shore, N.Y., 1987). (6) P. de Bérulle, *Mémorial de quelques points servant à la direction des Supérieurs en la Congrégation de* *l'Oratoire de Jésus (Memorial of Several Points for the Direction of the Superiors of the Oratorian Congregation of Jesus),* in *Oeuvres complètes de Bérulle (Complete works of Bérulle),* ed. J.-P. Migne, Ateliers catholiques, Paris 1856 (original edition 1632), col. 833. (7) Ibid. Cf. M. Dupuy, *Bérulle et le sacerdoce: étude historique et doctrinale: Textes inédits) (Bérulle and the Ministry: A Historical and Doctrinal Study: Uncollected Works),* Lethielleux, Paris 1969, 174-176. (8) Cf. J.-J. Olier, *Mémoires autobiographiques (Autobiographical Memoirs),* 2:107 (cited by Etienne Michel Faillon, *Vie de M. Olier, fondateur du séminaire de Saint-Sulpice [Life of M. Olier, Founder of the Seminary of Saint-Sulpice],* Poussielgue-Wattelier, Paris 1873, 2:33); *Traité des saints ordres (Treatise on Holy Orders),* Langlois, Paris 1676, n.p. For a comparative study between the texts of Olier and those of Montfort, cf. Itinerario, 187-188; S. De Fiores, *Lo Spiritu santo e Maria negli ultimi tempi secondo s. Luigi Maria da Montfort,* in QM 4 (1986), 22-28. (9) Cf. *Le livre des sermons du Père de Montfort,* 242-243 (under the title *"Universal judgment,"* taken from P. Lejeune). (10) Cf. the synopsis of texts in S. De Fiores, *Lo Spirito santo e Maria,* 24-27. The cry of PM 28 can probably be traced to a letter of Saint John Eudes: "I went to Paris to cry out in the Sorbonne and the other colleges, 'Fire, fire, fire from the inferno that is burning the universe! Come, . . . you ecclesiastics, help to put it out'" (letter 39, July 23, 1659, in *Oeuvres complètes [Complete works],* 10: 432). (11) Cf. "Mémoire d'une admirable conduite de Dieu sur une âme particulière appelée Marie de Coutances. Copie d'un exemplaire écrit de la propre main de M. de Renty (Memoir of God's Admirable Guidance of a Special Soul Named Marie de Coutances. Copy of a Manuscript in M. de Renty's Own Hand)," ms., Bibliothèque Mazarine, Paris, n. 3177, pp. 58-59, 62, 69-70, 90, 92, 100. (12) The "three kingdoms" are mentioned by Madame Guyon († 1717) in the *Vita scritta da lei stessa* and in the *Discorsi Spirituali e cristiani,* vol. 1, disc. 63. Cf. H. de Lubac, *La posterità spirituale di Gioacchino da Fiore. I. dagli spirituali a Schelling,* Jaca Book, Milan 1981, 273-274. There is no indication that Montfort drew anything at all from the work of Madame Guyon. (13) Montfort was probably personally familiar with St. Vincent Ferrer's *Treatise on the Spiritual Life* in the 1617 edition published by Madame Julienne Morelle, who added the following commentary to the saint's text: "Here he foresees the condition of the apostolic men who must flourish before the end of the world. This conforms with the prophecy of Saint Catherine of Siena concerning the great renewal and reformation of the Church." A similar prophecy was familiar to T. Campanella, who in his *Articuli prophetales* (1607-1609) asserts that "it has been revealed to Joachim de Flore, to Catherine of Siena, and to Vincent Ferrer that the Holy Spirit must be widely distributed among several men, who will bring the renewal of the Church and the conversion of infidels." The same author, in book 20 of his *Theologia* (1613), foresees, after the victory of the Antichrist and before the end of the world, a temporal *pleroma* (Sabbath or golden age), of the Church, when the virtue inherent in Christianity will become manifest. (14) St. Vincent de Paul offers three interesting texts on the prophecy of St. Vincent Ferrer, but unlike Montfort, he does not believe that the Congregation is the object of this prophecy. The first text (1642) affirms humorously, "He is a fool who would imagine that Saint Vincent Ferrer prophesized about the Company, that in the end times one would see a company of priests who would greatly benefit the Church of God" (*Correspondance, entretiens, documents,* Gabalda, Paris 1923, 11:114-115; English translation, *Correspondence, Conferences, Documents,* ed. Pierre Coste, New City Press, Brooklyn 1985). Several years later Vincent returns to Ferrer's prophecy about the priests who "by the fervor of their zeal would embrace the entire earth," but this time he adds, more positively, "If we are not so meritorious that God should through His grace enable us to be those priests, may He at least give us their images and their precursors" (ibid., 75). The third text is along the same lines (before 1655); there he speaks with Ferrer of the "good priests and apostolic workers who give new life to the ecclesiastical state and dispose men toward the Last Judgment," and he concludes that we must become perfect "in order to cooperate with this revival that is wholly desirable" (ibid., 8). Cf. J. Séguy, *Monsieur Vincent, la Congrégation de la Mission et les derniers temps (Vincent de Paul, the Congregation of the Mission, and the End Times),* in *Vincent de Paul: Actes du colloque international d'études vincentiennes (Vincent de Paul: Records of the International Colloquy of Vincentian Studies),* Edizioni vincenziane, Rome 1983, 217-238. (15) It is easy to note a coincidence in thinking between Marie d'Agréda and Montfort on Mary's role in the end times, beyond some notable differences. Cf. Marie d'Agréda, *La cité mystique de Dieu,* Brussels 1715, vol. 3, 1.7, ch. 3, n.33, p. 31; English translation, *City of God,* trans. Fiscar Marison, Ave Maria Institute, Washington, N.J. 1971. (16) Cf. P. Broutin, *La réforme pastorale en France au XVIIe siècle (Pastoral Reform in France in the Seventeenth Century),* 2 vols., Desclée, Tournai 1956; L.

Cognet, *Crépuscules des mystiques (The Twilight of the Mystics),* (Desclée, Tournai 1958); Le Brun, *France. . . Le grand siècle de la spiritualité française et ses lendemains (France. . . The Great Century of French Spirituality and Afterwards),* in DSAM, cc. 917-153; L. Perouas, *Grignion de Montfort, les pauvres, les missions (Grignion de Montfort, the Poor, the Missions),* Cerf, Paris 1966, 47-48, 82-83. (17) S. Rituum Congreg., Lucion, *Beatificationis et canonizationis ven. Servi Dei Ludovici Mariae Grignion de Montfort. Positio super scriptis,* Rome 1851, 20. The two theologians imprudently refer to the *"septimo millennio"* of which Saint Gaudens speaks, following Rev 5:10; 20:4-6. This cannot be deduced at all from Montfort's texts, as the third censor will observe (cf. below). (18) Ibid., 23. (19) In *Regina dei Cuori* 5 (1918), 3-4. (20) "1. Simple logical order, followed by the Blessed, excludes such an interpretation. He has spoken at various times of God's role in the Incarnation, he speaks of this same role after the Incarnation. 2. He says this clearly, because he sets the first coming against the last, noting that the Second Coming began immediately after the first and will last until the end of time. When speaking of the role of the three Divine Persons 'in this end coming,' he says that they have and will have the same role forever . . . until the consummation of time" (Ibid,, 3-4?). (21) Ibid., 4. (22) P. Oger, note to *Trattato della vera devozione a Maria Vergine, Santuario di Maria regina dei cuori,* Redona di Bergamo, Rome 1945, 37. (23) A. Plessis, *Commentaire du Traité de la vraie dévotion à la sainte Vierge du Bx L.-M. Grignion de Montfort (Commentary to True Devotion to the Blessed Virgin by the Blessed L.-M. Grignion de Montfort),* Librairie mariale, Pontchâteau 1943, 83-84, 154. (24) A. Lhoumeau, *La vierge Marie et les apôtres des derniers temps d'après le B. Louis-Marie de Montfort (The Virgin Mary and the Apostles of the End Times according to the Blessed Louis Marie de Montfort),* Mame, Tours 1919, 10. (25) Ibid., 9-10, 13. (26) H. Frehen, *Le "second avènement,"* 98, 101-104. (27) L. Perouas, *Ce que croyait Grignion de Montfort et comment il a vécu sa foi (The Way of Wisdom),* Mame, 1973, 186. The author had admitted that there were in Montfort "certain indications of Marian millenarianism," which nonetheless were not essential to the work. *Grignion de Montfort: serait-il maximaliste? (Grignion de Montfort: A Maximalist?),* in CM 10 (1966), n. 52, p. 147. (28) "The apocalyptic theme is not marginal to the thought of Saint Louis Marie Grignion de Montfort. On the contrary, it appears to be central to his conception of the Christian life. Voluntarist and elitist, the Christian life is informed by a Marian devotion that is completely oriented toward the perspective of the Parousia." J. Séguy, *Millénarisme et "ordres adventistes." Grignion de Montfort et les "apôtres des derniers temps" [Millenarianism and "Adventist Orders": Grignion de Montfort and the "Apostles of the End Times"),* in *Archives de Sciences sociales des religions* 53 (1982), 23-24. (29) G. Barbera, *Tratatto della vera devozione a Maria ss.; di s. Luigi Maria di Montfort. Sviluppo logico et annotazioni. Maria nell'opera divina dell'escatologia,* nos. 49-59, in *Madre e regina* 22 (1968), 8-9, pp. 207-210; 11, pp. 271-274; 12, pp. 303-306; 23 (1969) 1, pp. 15-18. G. Barbera returns to this interpretation in the article *Montfort, homme de l'espérance (Montfort, Man of Hope),* in AA.VV. *Dieu seul. A la rencontre de Dieu avec Montfort (God Alone: The Encounter between God and Montfort),* International Montfort Center, Rome 1981, 145-163. Barbera draws a distinction between the first coming, accomplished in the Incarnation/Redempton/Cross, and the Second Coming, which will be realized in the life of the Church in the end times (TD 28-59) and will conclude with the "last coming" (TD 22, 49) (ibid., 48). This would indicate three comings of Jesus, as Plessis and Oger asserted. (30) This scenario unfolds as follows: the period of the Spirit, Great Tribulation, reign of the Antichrist, extraordinary saints, reign of Christ and the Spirit, Parousia and Last Judgment. (31) Ibid., 26. (32) Ibid., 30, 27-28. (33) Ibid., 30. (34) *"The first coming . . . . the last coming"* (TD 22); *"in the first coming . . . . in the second coming"* (TD 49); *"the difference betwen his first and his second coming"* (TD 158); *"the first time . . . . the second time"* (SM 58). (35) A. Piolanti, *Millenarismo,* in *Enciclopedia cattolica,* 8:1008-1009. This interpretation was spreading in the first centuries of the Church, on the reckoning of Rev, where there are six references to "a thousand years" ("He seized . . . Satan, and bound him for a thousand years," "they will reign with him a thousand years"). "Millenarianism must be counted among the systems that are erroneous, because it admits of not two but three comings of Christ" (A. Gelin, *Millénarisme [Millenarianism],* in *Dictionnaire de la Bible,* Suppl. 5 [1957], 1293), and he contrasts it with the conception of the Kingdom of God on earth, which includes suffering and persecution. (36) Cf. J. Pinkenzeller, *Chiliasmo,* in *Lessico di teologia Sistematica,* Queriniana, Brescia 1990, 95. (37) R. Laurentin agrees with this verdict; "On devra parler ici de millénarisme? Non, pour divers motifs." ("Is it a question of millenarianism? No, for several reasons.") In *Dieu Seul est ma Tandress,* O.E.I.L., Paris 1984.. (38) J. Séguy, *Millénarisme,* 36. (39) The states or kingdoms are not divided similarly; Montfort gives a different and greater, more decisive role to Mary in the reign of the Spirit than Joachim de Flore; the "spirituals" of Joachim de Flore are monks, whereas for Montfort they are missionaries, etc. Cf. S. De Fiores, *Lo Spiritu santo e Maria,* 19-20 (French edition, pp. 144-147). (40) *La postérité spirituelle de Joachim de Flore (The Spiritual Posterity of Joachim de Flore),* Lethielleux, Paris 1979, 232). H. de Lubac's statement seems too categorical for us. (41) It is surprising to see J. Séguy, *Millénarisme,* 29, speak of the "Montfort system [sic]" after having made this statement. (42) Cf. H. Rondet, *Fins de l'homme et fin du monde. Essai sur le sens de la formation de l'eschatologie chrétienne (The Ends of Man and the End of the World: An Essay on the Meaning of the Development of Christian Eschatology),* Fayard, Paris 1966, 136; M. Schmaus, *I Novissimi,* in *Dogmatica cattolica,* IV/2, Marietti, Turin 1964, 157-185; Ruiz de la Peña, *La Otra dimensión,* in *Escatología cristiana,* EAPSA, Madrid 1980, 163. (43) Cf. S. Rituum Congreg., Lucion. *Beatificationis et canonizationis,* 4-5. The third censor draws the same conclusion in ID., *II Positio super scriptis,* Rome 1853, 4. (44) S. Rituum Congreg., Lucion. *Beatificationis et canonizationis,* 24. (45) Ibid., 24-25. Cf. the development of the same arguments in *II Positio super scriptis,* 4, 9-17. (46) Particularly celebrated is the prophecy that TD would *"lie hidden in the darkness and silence of a chest"* (TD 114) until its discovery in 1842. (47) T. Rast, *L'escatologia,* in *Bilancio della teologia del XX secolo,* Città nuova, Rome 1972, 3:327. (48) J. Daniélou, *Essai sur le mystère de l'histoire (Essay on the Mystery of History),* Seuil, Paris 1959, 18. (49) R. Laurentin, *Marie dans la dernière économie selon les textes du Nouveau Testament (Mary in the Last Economy according to the Texts of the NT,* in EtMar 41 (1984), 89. Cf. E. Touron del Pie, *María en la escatología de Lucas,* in EstMar 31 (1981), 260-261; X. Pikaza, *El Espíritu santo y María en la obra de Lucas,* in EstMar 28 (1978), 151-168.

EUCHARIST

SUMMARY I. SEVENTEENTH-CENTURY THEOLOGY AND PRACTICE OF THE EUCHARIST:
1. The Eucharist according to the French school;
2. The Mass;
3. Communion and devotion to the Eucharist.

II. THE EUCHARIST IN THE LIFE OF MONTFORT:
1. Before his ordination;
2. After his ordination.

III. THE EUCHARIST IN THE WRITINGS OF MONTFORT:
1. The Sacrament of the altar;
2. Holy Communion;
3. The Mass;
4. The Eucharist and Mary.

IV. THE EUCHARIST AND MONTFORT SPIRITUALITY TODAY:
1. The summit of Christian initiation;
2. The Word of God and the Eucharist;
3. The Eucharist and mission;
4. Personal and ecclesial dimension;
5. The Eucharist with Mary.

I. SEVENTEENTH-CENTURY THEOLOGY AND PRACTICE OF THE EUCHARIST

Anyone wishing to grasp Montfort's way of thinking and teaching on the Eucharist must, first of all, discover the context in which the holy missionary lived. As the most authoritative members of the French school have produced an impressive corpus of doctrinal works in strict conformity to the Council of Trent, it is important to clarify their thought on the Eucharist, with special reference to the Mass, Holy Communion, and veneration of the Blessed Sacrament.

In the Middle Ages theoretical and practical emphasis was laid on the excellence of Christ's presence in the Blessed Sacrament. Although the two sometimes overlapped, a dividing line was drawn between the Sacrifice of the Mass and the Blessed Sacrament, received in Holy Communion or as an object of adoration. In line with this traditional distinction, the Council of Trent dealt with the subject in two separate sessions: the Eucharist was treated in the thirteenth and the Sacrifice of the Mass in the twenty-second.[1] When considering these questions, the Fathers of the Council of Trent were under pressure from outside the Church, because Protestant heterodoxy was seen as a threat, and from within, because of the widely felt need for appropriate renewal. In the dogmatic field, the council reasserted the Church's belief in the sacrificial value of the Mass and in Christ's Real Presence under the species of the bread and wine. In the pastoral and disciplinary field, the council strove to promote sacramental participation in the Eucharist, to restore dignity to worship, and to help the faithful to gain a better understanding of the rites and prayers of the Mass by providing appropriate explanations.

The distinction between sacrifice and sacrament, which was confirmed by the 1570 Missal and the 1614 Ritual,[2] was a signpost for post-Tridentine theological research as well as for pastoral practice, influencing the devotion of faithful and clergy alike. Consequently it was taken for granted that the priest offered the Sacrifice of the Mass, whereas the faithful attended the Mass and received Holy Communion or, as often as not, confined themselves to adoring the Blessed Sacrament at the Elevation or outside Mass. Thus the Mass was distinct from the sacramental presence of Christ, which was considered as the comfort of devout souls. All mention of the Mass was confined almost exclusively to highlighting the part played by the priest[3] or to explaining the sacrificial aspect of the Mass.

In the post-Tridentine period, the theologians devoted their efforts to examining and explaining how and why the Mass is a real sacrifice though not a repetition of the bloody sacrifice offered on Calvary.[4] For their part, and with a variety of emphases, those engaged in pastoral work did their best to stimulate interest in devotion to the Mass, keeping Communion as a separate subject, as was done by the Council of Trent.

The Mass was explained by reference to the categories of religious sacrifices considered generically, and occasionally with the help of medieval allegories; the Sacrament was examined in the light of philosophical concepts in an attempt to explain how the bread and wine were changed into the body and blood of Christ.

1. The Eucharist according to the French school

The essence of the sacrifice of the Cross and the nature of the Eucharistic sacrifice were among the topics considered most thoroughly by Bérulle, Condren, and Olier. All of them defended the "oblationist" view. Basing their arguments on Scripture, they maintained that the spiritual offering of Christ defined his priesthood, gave supreme glorification of the Eternal Father, and was the source of sanctification for sinful humanity.[5]

The interior or spiritual oblation,[6] which consists in total surrender to God's will, i.e., worship "in spirit and in truth," is best expressed exteriorly in the immolation on Calvary. What gives a sacrificial value to the death of Jesus is therefore his obedience and total dedication to the Father's will. This attitude towards the Father's will had begun at the Incarnation in Mary's womb; it reached its supreme height on the Cross, and continued in his life in glory. The Mass is the sacramental memorial of the spiritual oblation that permeates every mystery of the life of Christ.[7]

Although they did not break free from the dichotomy between sacrifice and sacrament, the members of the French school succeeded in basing their Eucharistic insights on Scripture. They situated their understanding within the history of salvation centered on the person of Jesus born of the Virgin Mary. The main points made by the various writers [8] clearly show a desire to encompass the total mystery of God and man.

In short, the view taken by the Bérullian School centers on the contemplation of the states of Jesus, inexhaustible sources of holiness, and on the importance of steeping oneself in these states in order to internalize them. Perfect conformity to the inner dispositions of the Word Incarnate comes about effortlessly through the mediation of the Blessed Virgin, who gave him her flesh and blood. The great devotion to Mary shown by the members of the French school was based on the mystery of the Incarnation, which is also the basis of the Eucharistic mystery, perpetuating "God with us for our sake."[9]

Pierre de Bérulle championed the Incarnation. His successor, Condren, had an extensive knowledge of Jesus' sacrificial and priestly mystery. Jean-Jacques Olier spared no effort to spread devotion to the Eucharist, as a memorial of Christ's mysteries. When he was parish priest of Saint-Sulpice, he was concerned to make the Mass the center of his parishioners' lives. In 1656 he published *L'Explication des cérémonies de la grande messe de paroisse selon l'usage romain (Explanation of the Ceremonies of the Parish High Mass according to Roman Usage);* he urged his parishioners to receive Holy Communion as the antidote to human weakness, and restored adoration of the Blessed Sacrament.[10] His views, which he shared with the rest of the French school, are summed up in a picture he himself painted; he had it reproduced and copies distributed to his parishioners. The picture shows "a monstrance with the Holy Spirit in the shape of a dove hovering above it; higher up is the Father with His arms outstretched and flanked by the Blessed Virgin and St. John bowing in adoration. In the center is the Host in the shape of a slain lamb in the midst of flames and, coming out of it, fourteen rays bearing the names of various acts of worship, such as adoration, love, praise, etc."[11]

In conclusion, it seems clear that the seventeenth-century leaders of the French school were driven by a desire to incorporate the advances of theology into the everyday life of the faithful. As both theologians and pastors, they left no avenue unexplored in their effort to offer a synthesis centered on the heart of Christian living, i.e., "living in Christ," or rather "letting Christ live in us." This is particularly clear in the case of the mystery of the Eucharist.

2. The Mass

One consequence of the advances of theology after Trent was that the parish clergy themselves discovered the value and significance of the Mass.[12] Without questioning the role of the priest, who alone is able to consecrate, "the eager desire to bring the congregation to share as closely as possible in the sacrifice of the Mass"[13] gradually spread, owing to the far-reaching influence of the French school and of the movements of that period (Augustinianism, Jansenism, etc.). The faithful themselves were expected to take part to some extent in the priest's offering of the sacrifice of Christ.[14]

By referring to liturgical texts, particularly those of the Roman Canon, it was easy to demonstrate the ecclesial dimension of the Eucharistic celebration. The idea of involving the congregation was promoted in their books on the liturgy by such experts as Bona, Mabillon, Martène, Muratori, Tommasi, and Lebrun. In this way they prepared the faithful to do better than just be present at Mass, which for various reasons, not least because it was in Latin, was beyond their comprehension. Options varied, controversies arose, and many lawful claims verged on heresy. Without going into a detailed examination, and leaving aside the problem raised by the seventeenth- and eighteenth-century French Missals, a few points should be highlighted.[15]

A large number of *Explicationes missae*[16] have come down to us. In literary or more informal language, according to the authors, they gave explanations of the texts used during Mass, and also of the actions and rites performed.[17] "Exercises," i.e. prayers and reflections,[18] were used as a sort of guidebook during Mass, and the celebrant translated or paraphrased some passages for the benefit of the faithful. These exercises had a large circulation in the late seventeenth century. Most people, whether they were literate or not, said the Rosary during Mass.[19] Although they stopped short of saying the Canon aloud—as the Jansenists did—the congregation in some cases took an active part by singing the Gloria, the Kyrie, and the Pater Noster together, by responding to the celebrant at some points during Mass, by giving the kiss of peace, and by receiving pieces of blessed bread.[20] After the Gospel reading, a homily was given that included prayers, pieces of advice, and announcements. It was still necessary to remind the faithful of their obligation to attend Sunday Mass, but the devout attended Mass daily in increasing numbers. Those attending the mission exercises, however, did not have to attend Mass daily; on the other hand, times were set aside during the mission for explanation of the "exercises."[21]

"Even though the people did not understand the significance of each of the Masses they attended, even though the meaning of the prayers and rites was far beyond their comprehension, they were aware that at the Consecration during Mass Jesus becomes present and continues to be present in the Host placed in the tabernacle or the monstrance for adoration during Benediction; they believed what is humanly unbelievable and derived from it all a stimulus for a particular life-experience."[22]

3. Communion and the devotion to the Eucharist

Towards the end of the Middle Ages, Holy Communion was rarely given during Mass, but instead either before or after, and very few people received it. The Council of Trent ruled in defense of the "private Mass" which was questioned by the Protestants, but it also expressed the desire that the faithful receive Holy Communion more frequently and that they do so with the dispositions required.[23] This teaching was repeated in the *Catechism,* which recommended that the faithful nourish their souls even every day, as they nourish their body.[24] In 1614 the Ritual of Paul V urged parish priests to do all they could to bring the faithful not only to honor the Blessed Sacrament but "to receive it frequently and with saintly dispositions, especially on the major feasts of the year." The Ritual also ruled, and gave reasons for it, that Holy Communion be given to the people immediately after the priest had communicated, unless a reasonable cause made it advisable for the faithful to receive Communion after Mass. In spite of this, "at the end of the seventeenth century—and all the evidence available confirms this—the celebrant alone communicated during Mass. . . . The practice was strongly attacked, however, by many liturgical experts and theologians."[25]

To this we must add that the Jansenists were extreme rigorists in the matter of Holy Communion, and various movements had their own ideas on the subject. Against this background, however, the French school persisted in promoting frequent Communion and evolved pastoral directives to help the faithful receive Holy Communion worthily and fruitfully.[26]

There was widespread interest in the adoration of the Blessed Sacrament as a means of expressing faith in the Real Presence and of venerating and serving the One who is King of heaven and earth. In the seventeenth century, the French celebrated devotion to the Eucharist with great splendor in Benedictions, long periods of adoration, expositions, and processions.[27] In some cases, Mass was celebrated in front of the Blessed Sacrament exposed, a custom that lasted up to the Second Vatican Council. Finally, much importance was attached to visits to the Blessed Sacrament, which renewed the feelings experienced at the time of Holy Communion: the sense of God's sovereign majesty, the memory of the Incarnation, Passion, and death of Jesus, the feeling of being but one heart with the Heart of Jesus, the thought of one's nothingness, and reparation for the outrages against the Sacrament of the altar.

II. The Eucharist in the Life of Montfort

It is not easy to describe the influence the Eucharist had on Montfort as an adolescent, as a seminarian at Saint-Sulpice, and as a missionary. The notebook that he kept during his priestly formation will be our principle source along with the comments of his friend Jean-Baptiste Blain.

1. Before his ordination

There are no records about the influence of the Eucharist on his childhood years. It can be reasonably assumed that at Saint Thomas à Becket school in Rennes, the Jesuits, who were great promoters of the devotion to the Blessed Sacrament, helped the young student in his study of the profound mystery of the Real Presence of Christ and inspired within him the desire to be closely united with Christ during holy Mass and during meditation before the Blessed Sacrament.

When telling us about the period the young Louis spent in Paris, Blain mentions Holy Communion on three occasions. He states that during the time he was in the community run by Fr. de la Barmondière, Montfort "received Holy Communion four times a week; he did so with so much devotion that just looking at him inspired one with devotion. Although his whole life was a preparation for this holy action, he used to prepare himself for this with particular devotion the day before. . . . His thanksgiving lasted an hour, and in order to make it in a quiet atmosphere and enjoy the presence of his Beloved, he would retire to the hidden recesses in the Church." [28] Blain also mentions the occasion when the young Grignion received Holy Communion at Chartres: "He received Holy Communion with a devotion and piety that the grace attached to the holy shrine seemed to bring to a climax; he continued in prayer for six to eight hours running . . . kneeling motionless as though in raptures."[29] Finally, Blain states that Louis Marie decided to take the vow of chastity when he was in "the church of Notre-Dame in Paris, where, out of devotion to the Blessed Virgin, he had made a practice of receiving Holy Communion every Saturday, together with a few other seminarians."[30] On the basis of Jean-Baptiste Blain's account, we can confidently say that Montfort received Holy Communion frequently, with devotion, and with Mary.

Louis Marie Grignion used to note down what he found striking in his teachers' classes and in his readings. These notes give us a glimpse of the teaching on the Eucharist that he received in Paris. Those which have been published are concerned with the Eucharist in general, the Mass, Holy Communion, and adoration of the Blessed Sacrament;[31] the unpublished notes are concerned with Mary and the Eucharist.[32] From Fr. Gaye, Montfort borrowed a few notes explaining the well-known *"O Sacrum Convivium"* (LS 328-330), and also a few brief reflections on *"the blessings we receive in Holy Communion"* according to the Gospel and the Fathers of the Church (LS 330). The notes he made in connection with Fr. Leschassier's teaching are concerned with the excellence of the Eucharist (receiving all the mysteries of Christ, which show the influence of the three Persons of the Holy Trinity; it is the feast of Jesus' friends; respect, purity, humility [LS 331]); he also drew on texts about the outrages against the Blessed Sacrament (unworthiness, lack of reverence in church), about the duty of reparation (priests ought to suffer with Christ), about the ways of making reparation (good example in church for the edification of the faithful, adequate preparation, [33] instructing the faithful about adoration of the Eucharist, acts of reparation to the Blessed Sacrament, visits and penance [LS 332-333]). We also find a list of the *"obstacles to fruitful Communion"* (persistence of venial sins, lack of mortification of the passions, inadequate faith). While he was still at Saint-Sulpice, he made notes highlighting that the Eucharist is a wonder of God's omnipotence, love, and liberality (LS 335). He dwells at some length on frequent Communion: he first establishes the biblical foundation ("Give us this day our daily bread" [Mat 6:11]), followed by an exhortation: *"Long for Holy Communion; ask your directors to give it to you. Never miss a single general Communion. Prepare for it and give thanks to God continually for this great grace"* (LS 336). Montfort gives three reasons to receive Holy Communion frequently: it is Christ's desire ("My flesh is truly food" [Jn 6:55]); it is the desire of the Church (the Council of Trent); it is very profitable to us (LS 337). LS 338 gives the central viewpoint of Saint-Sulpice on the Eucharist: *"the abundant love of Our Lord for us"* is contrasted with *"our extreme ingratitude."* Finally, the notes mention the priest-Eucharist relationship: *"As the life of a priest revolves around the Blessed Sacrament of the altar, including the Mass, thanksgiving, preparation, and distributing Holy Communion, he either saves or loses his soul according as he makes good or bad use of this Sacrament."*

Jean-Baptiste Blain says that as a seminarian, Louis Marie "composed hymns, which he used later during his missions";[34] it is not unlikely that at least some of the hymns about the Eucharist were written during that period.

Montfort's manuscript notebooks also include references to the Mass (LS 429-432; based on a sermon by C. Joly). He begins by quoting Mal 1:10-11; then, by way of introduction, he says: *"We should attend Mass as often as possible (i) because, of all the acts of religion, it is the one that gives most glory to God and (ii) because it is the one from which we can derive the greatest abundance of graces."* This is followed by the three parts of the sermon: (a) the Sacrifice of the Mass (incomparable greatness of *"the gift we offer to God," "humility of Christ offering himself to the Father,"* obligation of Sunday Mass, attention, interest;) (b) the teaching of the Council of Trent; (c) how we should attend Holy Mass (dignified posture, necessary interior attention). Quotations from Scripture and the Church Fathers are scattered throughout these notes.

In N, pp. 285-293, the young Louis Marie drew on Bernardin of Paris, d'Argentan, and Crasset for ideas on the link between Mary and the Eucharist; he expanded these ideas in his own way in his writings.

2. After his ordination

Louis Marie's Sulpician training for the priesthood enabled him to understand that the priest and Mass were bound up together. This relationship had been central in the thoughts and actions of those in the seminary.

In the Lady chapel of the church of St. Sulpice, Jean-Baptiste Blain attended the first Mass said by his friend. "I was there, and what I saw was a man looking like an angel at the altar."[35] It is noteworthy that the Mass he celebrated in Poitiers

Hospital opened an important chapter in his life: "As he was passing through Poitiers, he followed his inclination and went to the hospital to say Mass there."[36] The rest of the account, including the admiration he aroused and the desire of the poor people to keep him with them, is an invitation to us to reflect carefully on the celebration of Holy Mass as opening the mysterious path to genuine charity.

Blain also tells us about the puzzling encounter at Dinan between Montfort and his Dominican brother, whom he asked for permission to say Mass three days in succession.[37] This "fraternal encounter" provides a valuable piece of information, namely, that Montfort celebrated Mass every day, although it was not a general practice in those days.[38] We also learn at first hand that Montfort had a great desire to celebrate Mass in union with Mary: "The following day I suggested that in order to satisfy his devotion to Mary, he say Mass at the altar dedicated to the Blessed Virgin and called the altar of vows in the Rouen Cathedral."[39]

During the mission—which was to be his last—he was preaching at Saint-Laurent, Montfort wrote a letter, dated April 4, 1716, that shows how much importance he attached to celebrating Mass. The letter was a request to Bishop Nepveu of Nantes, who had forbidden him to preach and hear confessions, for permission to take a few days' rest in his diocese and be allowed to say Mass, which is the source of countless graces (L 33).

After he had been given a first-hand account, Blain describes a procession which was organized by Montfort during a mission and in which "the Blessed Sacrament was carried": "after a few moments' silent recollection in front of Jesus Christ enthroned on a altar . . . he addressed the crowd with so much force and persuasion that all those present burst into tears."[40]

The theme of the Eucharistic mystery is not often addressed by the biographers of Montfort, and yet we have to realize that it was central to the experience of the holy missionary. If we make allowances for the literary genre, the following passage from Besnard may help us to realize this: "Devout during his adoration, he was like an angel when saying Mass, such was the impression of those who watched him either saying Mass or during his thanksgiving, which he always made in the church. The greatness of the mysteries and the holiness of the celebrant struck the congregation forcibly. This reputation for holiness first spread in Poitiers Hospital; watching him recollected, motionless, lost in God in the chapel after Mass, the poor people said to one another, 'Come and see a holy man. He is the one we need to guide us along the way to salvation . . .' His face sometimes changed out of recognition when saying Mass: it became suffused with an unusual shade of red and looked as if luminous. People flocked to hear him say Mass and contended for the honor of serving it. Finally, he handled the Blessed Sacrament so devotedly and fervently and with such dignity that the faith of those who watched him was increased. His faith inspired him with respect for Jesus Christ, God and man, whose body was present on the altar, and wherever he was, his faith made him keenly aware of the presence of God, whose immensity fills the universe. Hence the recollected and devout countenance that he showed everywhere."[41]

III. The Eucharist in the Writings of Montfort

Montfort cared little for the "scholarly approach" to the mystery of the Eucharist; what he concentrated on was to make the revealed truths taught by the Church accessible to the faithful so as to help their faith and their faith-life.[42] This is made abundantly clear in his writings, which express his thought and testify to his missionary activity. He mentions the Eucharist in LEW, TD, SM, and RM; but he reveals his way of thinking and his ideas on the Eucharist especially in the hymns that were sung during Mass, adoration of the Blessed Sacrament, processions, etc.; they give us an inkling of the burning zeal that animated him when it came to helping people to understand and live the mystery of the Eucharist.[43]

Fr. Perouas has written: "If we look at all that Montfort has achieved in the liturgical field, we cannot but be amazed at the small place accorded to the Eucharistic celebration, despite the special emphasis laid on frequent Communion."[44] This is accounted for by the fact that parish missions were governed by long-standing principles that focused on personal conversion attested by confession and Communion. Missionaries hesitated, therefore, to make daily Mass an ordinary exercise during the mission. As a rule, they relied on the local clergy for the daily life of the parish and focused their efforts on providing religious instruction and hearing general confessions.[45] We must also keep in mind that St. Louis Marie's overriding interest was in the lay folk, and therefore he laid stress on Eucharistic devotions that were considered specifically their field: Holy Communion and adoration of the Blessed Sacrament. Although as we will see, he does preach on the Mass aside from the Communion, this was considered, above all, as the domain of priests. Montfort, who was people-oriented, was laying more emphasis on Holy Communion and veneration of the Blessed Sacrament than on the Sacrifice of the Mass, which, as people saw it then, was the business of priests.

Montfort's missionary career shows that he was increasingly interested in the celebrative aspect of worship: he wanted it to be dignified (reverence and good order inside the church, sanctification of Sundays and feast-days, interior and exterior dispositions for worthy reception of the Sacraments); he urged the people to take part (frequent Mass and Communion, hymn singing, processions).[46] These reflections suggested by the notes that Montfort made lead us to the thematic examination of the hymns.

1. The Sacrament of the altar

"Love's invention" is what Fr. Olier called it,[47] and it gave Montfort the key to his understanding of the "descent" of the Eucharist. The mystery instituted by Christ is the continuation in time of the love that prompted Eternal Wisdom to become man and die on the Cross (LEW 70; H 128:1). In order to remain with us, Jesus has left us the Eucharist: *"Eternal Wisdom, on the one hand, wished to prove his love for man by dying in his place in order to save him, but on the other hand, he could not bear the thought of leaving him. So he devised a marvelous way of dying and living at the same time, and of abiding with man until the end of time. So, in order fully to satisfy his love, he instituted the sacrament of the Holy Eucharist and went to the extent of changing and overturning nature itself"* (LEW 71). With characteristic sensitiveness, Montfort asserts that Jesus instituted the Eucharist before he died in order not to be separated from his mother and to be able to continue his heart-to-heart relationship with her after the Ascension (H 134:1-3). Indeed, the permanent presence of Wisdom among men is meant to be an interior rather than exterior fellowship: *"He does not conceal himself under a sparkling diamond or some other precious stone, because he does not want to abide with man in an ostentatious manner. But he hides himself under the appearance of a small piece of bread—man's ordinary nourishment—so that when received he might enter the heart of man and there take his delight"* (LEW 71). Montfort stresses not only the benefits of the Sacraments for us; he also views them, most especially the Eucharist and Penance, as a means invented by Jesus to fulfill the longings of his heart to love us.

To this descending dimension of the Eucharist, God's condescension, corresponds the "ascending dimension" of man's response, which all too often is marred by ingratitude. Hymns 128-134 give a detailed description of the encounter between God's Heart, beating in the Sacrament, and man's heart, with its mixture of greatness and meanness. The seven hymns, one for each day of the week, with the Saturday canticle dealing with the Eucharist and Mary,[48] were written in the form of a dialogue between Jesus and the faithful soul. Jesus in the Blessed Sacrament is addressed as *"spouse," "wisdom," "physician," "master," "friend," "brother," "way," "path," "gentle light"* (cf. H 129:5). The main themes of the Eucharistic spirituality promoted by the French school are there: faith in the Real Presence, the doctrine on the Eucharist and its grandeur, praise, adoration, thanksgiving, petition, reparation to the God-man present yet hidden and glorious yet humble, the humility of Christ and the perfect glory he gives to the Father, the gentle love of the Heart of Jesus, Jesus' search for sinners and the forgiveness granted to them, our personal unworthiness before the Most High. A few examples suffice: *"Since Jesus humbles himself / Because he loves us / His love urges us / To respond in kind: / Let us visit him often in the Eucharist"* (H 128:6). *"The Almighty, in his greatness / Equal to God the Father / In order to win our hearts / Lives in this mystery / I give you my flesh to eat. / Eat because I love you. / Drink my blood in great gulps / Even to intoxication"* (H 129:1, 7).

"Oh! How well the Blessed Sacrament / Can teach us in a short time / Without words and easily / The science of the virtues / Divine Wisdom! / This mystery is all about love / Or rather it is love itself" (H 130:1, 7). Since Christ abides in plenitude in the Blessed Sacrament (cf. H 5:33), Montfort urged the faithful to have devotion to the Eucharist. In the regulations designed for a man who became converted during the mission, we note the following pledge: *"My greatest devotion / Is to the Blessed Sacrament. / Every month without fail / I adore him for an hour"* (H 139:60). TD points out that *"Devotion to our Lady is the holiest and best after devotion to the Blessed Sacrament"* (TD 99).[49] The visit to the Blessed Sacrament is often mentioned in the hymns, together with the reasons for it and the blessings deriving from it (cf. H 128:6; 130:9; 131:1-9). A terse sentence tucked away in a letter to his nun sister speaks volumes about his own experience: *"Spend more time before the altar than in resting and eating"* (L 12).

One important ingredient of the visit to the Blessed Sacrament is reparation (cf. H 44:7; 133:8-9), involving an act of reparation for the outrages committed by Christians—priests and laypeople alike—against the Blessed Sacrament or the places of worship (cf. H 33:19; 43:5, 7; 67:3; 133:1; 136:1). It is interesting to note the connection established between devotion to the Eucharist and the Sacred Heart (cf. H 128:4, 8; H 131 mentions the Sacred Heart in every verse; see also H 44:7). During his missions, he stressed the importance of the act of reparation to the Blessed Sacrament (cf. H 158:11-12; LS 530) and also the importance of the procession for those who go to general communion in a body.[50] Benedic-tion of the Blessed Sacrament also rated high in his estimation (cf. H 158:13-14).

2. Holy Communion

Montfort was strongly convinced that Holy Communion conformed man and his life to Christ: *"When a just man receives Jesus Christ / He becomes another Christ / Is filled with his spirit / And his life"* (H 158:9).

The Blessed Sacrament is not there just to be visited and adored; Jesus gave us the gift of his body and blood with his soul and his divinity to transform us completely into himself: *"He gives us his flesh to eat / His blood to drink / His soul and his whole being / To change us into himself"* (H 132:3). In Holy Communion *"Jesus and the soul are one / They have everything in common"* (H 132:4), and the communicant can say with Saint Paul, "I live now not with my own life but with the life of Christ who lives in me" (Gal 2:20). These ever-valid reasons make Holy Communion supremely worthy of our longing; Hymn 112 fosters the desire of the faithful to be one with Christ, identifying them with stray sheep, with starving, thirsty, blind, or sick people, and with the centurion in the Gospel. When mentioning the feast given by Wisdom, Montfort suggests that we prepare for it as a community: *"Let us eat the living bread and drink the wine of angels / Frequently / As the saints did. / Let us eat and drink / And grow stronger / Let us eat and drink / And have our fill / And give praise to God."* (H 158:9)

At a time when Holy Communion was only received under one kind,[51] the repeated phrase *"Let us eat and drink"* is surprising; the use of the plural in a hymn meant to be sung by the congregation could only be conducive to a better understanding of the community dimension of Holy Communion.

In the plans of two sermons that have come down to us (LS 530-534), we note that during the mission, Montfort spoke of fervent, lukewarm, and unworthy Communion (LS 531, 533); this indicates that he was concerned about the preparation of the faithful for Communion, and he did his best to help them derive all possible benefit from it. In RM 56 he makes a point of telling the missionaries how they should go about preparing the faithful adequately to receive Holy Communion, which is meant to set the seal on their life in union with Christ: Holy Communion is to be preceded by the renewal of the baptismal promises and by confession. He stresses the importance of preparing children adequately for their first Communion during the mission by means of a good confession (RM 90). He draws attention to the dispositions required for Communion in one of the hymns: *"Happy the man who receives Communion / With a humble, faithful and pure heart / Who is not lukewarm or a hypocrite"* (H 5:34).

Montfort promoted fervent as well as frequent Communion. Although he laid stress on receiving Communion worthily, he encouraged people to receive it frequently.[52] The regulations mentioned above and meant for a man who became converted during the mission say: *"As a rule, every month / I receive the Sacraments / And more frequently if necessary / Depending on the times and places. / The more often I receive Communion / The better I live in Christ"* (H 139:22; see also LPM 2).

In those days devout souls were advised to receive Communion once a month;[53] it is not surprising, therefore, if Montfort urged all Christians to make serious commitments, as Communion calls for conversion. Writing to the first Daughters of Wisdom, he boldly says: *"Provided you do not fall into deliberate sin, receive holy communion every day for you both need holy communion very much"* (L 29). In RW the founder strongly recommends that the Daughters of Wisdom receive Holy Communion frequently, following the advice of their confessor and their superior (RW 147-151; 152-160); they are not to prefer *"devotions"* to receiving Holy Communion, or aim at enjoying *"spiritual consolations"* or look on themselves as privileged; rather, they are to receive Communion in order to *"sacrifice all things to Jesus crucified and annihilated"*; besides, they are to *"assist at Mass and receive holy communion with the community."* Montfort also prescribed that all the group of pilgrims to Our Lady of Saumur receive Communion together (PS 9-10).

3. Mass

It has been pointed out above that Montfort laid more emphasis on

Communion than on the Sacrifice of the Mass, as was done by those giving parish missions in those days.[54] The LS makes no mention of Mass (cf. LS 530-534); but the theme of Mass recurs several times in the Hymns. The Regulations designed for the man who has been converted contains this commitment: *"Whenever I can, I attend Mass / Every day devoutly / And in order to attend it I promptly drop / Whatever I am doing. / And I usually find afterwards / That things are going more smoothly"* (H 139:18). The holy founder laid down that his missionaries should say Mass daily, having first prepared themselves suitably, and they should make a half-hour's thanksgiving after Mass (RM 30).

Hymn 158 includes verses to be sung *"at Mass," "at the Sanctus," "at the Agnus Dei," "before Holy Communion."* The verse on Mass says: *"This is the perfect sacrifice / Containing all those of the Law. / It alone brings us / Salvation. / A God is sacrificed to God as priest and victim"* (H 158:6). The singing of these hymns during Mass—Blain tells us that he actually heard them sung after the Elevation and Communion at Saint-Laurent-sur-Sèvre [55]—shows that Montfort was doing his best to help the faithful take an active part in the Mass.[56] In this connection, we must note that he prescribed that his missionaries should say *"a rosary in the vernacular with the people in the morning during Mass before the sermon"* (RM 57).[57]

In Montfort's writings one does not find explicit mention of the priesthood common to the faithful, in the fullness of the Eucharistic sacrifice which comes to us through our union with the priesthood of Christ. On the other hand, Montfort does mention the offering of Christ to the Father in union with Mary: *"Father, I offer myself to you / Through the hands of Mary / That I may be sacrificed for all / As a host./ Here is my body, here is my blood, / Here is my dear Mother: / Immolate it all even now / If such is your will, Father"* (H 49:3). This quotation makes us realize the connection between *"Christ, the Eucharist, and Mary,"* and we thus move from the historical plane to the sacramental plane. Montfort never resorted to allegories to explain the Mass, and it may be added that the French school had already gone beyond that stage.

4. The Eucharist and Mary

The French school had a deep insight into the role of Mary at the Incarnation and, therefore, in all the mysteries of Christ. It is not surprising that Montfort experienced a further deepening of the mysteries through the Blessed Virgin. St. Louis Marie highlighted the Mary/Eucharist relationship.[58] The Sacraments, rooted in the economy of salvation, are essentially the actualization of the historical mysteries of Christ. Since Mary gave the Redeemer his flesh and blood, it follows that she cannot but be involved in the mysteries that are a unique memorial of the same flesh and blood, that is, the Eucharist.

In light of these theological principles, Montfort elaborated his teaching, which is full of grateful admiration for the Father, that the Father through the Holy Spirit has entrusted

His Son to Mary. This praise extends to Mary as well, as her *"fiat"* made it possible for us to share the Eucharistic body and blood of her Son: *"It was you, Virgin Mary, / Who gave us this body and blood / Which raises our status so high / that it is beyond the reach of the angels. May you be blessed throughout the world / For giving us such a great gift"* (H 134:11).

The Blessed Virgin's motherly care and concern for her faithful servants is epitomized in the fact that *"she gives them the Son she has borne, the Bread of Life"* (TD 208, which is full of scriptural quotations and allusions and is concerned with this particular theme). It is Wisdom who prepares the table and says, *"Come . . . eat the bread which is Jesus. Drink the wine of his love which I have mixed for you with the milk of my breasts"* (TD 208). With great sensitivity and in great depth, Montfort draws attention to the presence and action of Mary in the Eucharist without detriment to the excellence of the redeeming work of Christ. Mary is mediatrix of Communion: *"As Mary is the treasurer and dispenser of the gifts and graces of the Most High God, she reserves a choice portion, indeed the choicest portion, to nourish and sustain her children and servants. They grow strong on the Bread of Life; they are made joyful with the wine that brings forth virgins. They are carried at her breast"* (TD 208).

In the conviction that sacramental Communion necessarily involves the presence of Mary, Montfort concludes TD with an exhortation to receive Holy Communion in union with Mary. She receives in us and for us the Word of God made Bread. The reason for this is that she received the Word of God *"in her heart and in her body,"* as the Church Fathers put it. In the last few pages of TD (266-273), Montfort tells us why and how we should unite ourselves with Mary before, during, and after Holy Communion; his aim is to demonstrate clearly that in us and through us Holy Communion binds Christ and Mary together again. In other words, the union between Christ and Mary, which took place at a definite time and place, is repeated in a sacramental way when the faithful united with Mary receive Holy Communion.

In accordance with the thinking of the time, Montfort made no explicit mention of the ecclesial aspect of Holy Communion; if we make allowance for this, we can safely say that Montfort's teaching on the Christ/Mary/faithful relationship is extraordinarily clear from the theological standpoint. In practice, the relationship reflects the mystery of the oblation and communion that united in one heart Christ, Mary, and John at the time of the supreme sacrifice, which redeemed humanity (cf. Jn 19:25-27). It was precisely because he had in mind the conformity of the faithful to Jesus Christ, with Mary playing an all-important role, that Montfort envisaged and introduced the Consecration to Jesus through the hands of Mary, which he meant to be made in close connection with Holy Communion: *"They should go to confession and Holy Communion with the intention of consecrating themselves to Jesus through Mary as his slaves of love. When receiving Holy Communion they could follow the method given later on [cf. TD 266-273]. They then recite the act of consecration"* (TD 231; cf. also SM 61, 76).

In the method that Montfort suggests for receiving Holy Communion in union with Mary, the three Persons of the Holy Trinity are clearly involved; the prayers to the Father, the Son, and the Holy Spirit on the common basis of *"Lord I am not worthy"* (TD 267-269) highlight the relationship of each of the Divine Persons with the Eucharist and with Mary.

Finally, a theme dear to the heart of the missionary: the Eucharistic life of Mary, which he mentions in the hymn to the Blessed Sacrament on Saturdays (H 134). Jesus instituted the Eucharist in order to remain with Mary even after his death on the Cross and his Ascension; so he keeps coming back to her *"nourishing her with his own body which she nourished when he was an infant"; "in exchange for the milk of her most pure breast, he strengthens her with his divine Blood"*; the Blessed Virgin is the perfect model of all who receive Holy Communion.[59]

IV. The Eucharist and Montfort Spirituality Today

The gift of the Spirit, Who was given to the Church by the risen Christ on the evening of Easter Sunday (cf. Jn 20:22) and poured on his Spouse the Church as her Life-Giver on Pentecost Sunday, is constantly renewed in the Sacraments. Among the Sacraments, the Eucharist holds a special place, as it is the centripetal and centrifugal moment of the anointing by the Spirit: "Grant that we, who are nourished by his body and blood, may be filled with the Holy Spirit, and become one body, one spirit in Christ. May he make us an everlasting gift to you" (Eucharistic Prayer III). It is in this perspective and in the postconciliar spirit that we must accept Montfort's heritage, bearing in mind that the montfort Eucharistic spirituality can only bear fruit if it is nourished by the ongoing life, teachings, and worship of the universal Church.

1. The summit of Christian initiation

"Renew the spirit of Christianity among the faithful." This goal of Montfort was prompted by the Holy Spirit. He spent his missionary life trying to achieve it, and it is the gist of the message he left to his followers. The folly of Wisdom and the preferential option for the weakest are rooted in the likeness to the crucified Christ-Victor conferred on us in Baptism.

"To be a Christian means to live like one." Montfort was fully aware of this, and he focused his energy on making Christians aware of the grace and obligations of their Baptism and Confirmation, and on exhorting them to live out their commitments. His constant concern was to give a paschal dynamic to the life of the faithful, urging them to be totally open to grace so as to be freed from the slavery of sin and start a new life of loving service to God. This was one of his characteristics; but in order to grasp it properly, as well as the spirituality it generated, we must look at it as part of the Christian initiation. The purpose of this initiation is to bring Christians gradually to conform their lives to Christ's, and the most effective means to this end is the reception of the Eucharist, in which Christians are grafted on to Christ and have their lives renewed "Sunday after Sunday."[60] If we look at it from this angle, the reason that Montfort promoted the reception of Holy Communion will become evident to us. His perception of the relationship between Baptism and the Eucharist is confirmed by the fact that during the mission, Communion was to be given only to those Christians who had publicly and solemnly renewed their profession of faith and their baptismal promises (RM 56).

The Consecration to Jesus through Mary, seen as the perfect renewal of the vows and promises of holy Baptism (TD 120), should be regarded as part of Christian initiation and therefore be linked to the Eucharist. This ties in with Montfort's view, since he brings together the act of Consecration and the reception of the body and blood of Christ. The Eucharist is indeed the Sacrament of the new and eternal Covenant, which calls for the humble and total gift of self in return for Christ's gift of love, which no words can express. According to a widespread postconciliar practice, the Consecration is renewed after the liturgy of the Word as a response to it and in anticipation of the liturgy of the Offerings. It might be good however, if serious consideration were given to the value of making the Consecration after Holy Communion, as Montfort suggests. We would thus underscore the fact that the montfort Consecration finds its best expression in sacramental Communion, and make clear the commitment involved in receiving the Bread and Wine "consecrated and consecrators." In any case, it is clear that there is a connection between the montfort Consecration and the Eucharistic celebration, the supreme Consecration of baptized and confirmed Christians.

2. The Word of God and the Eucharist

The Second Vatican Council has helped us to take a comprehensive view of the Eucharist by restoring unity to the Holy Mass and presenting it as a celebration shared by the whole Church. SC requires that "richer fare be provided for the faithful at the table of God's Word" (SC 51) and reminds us that "the liturgy of the word and the Eucharistic liturgy are so closely connected with each other that they form but one single act of worship" (SC 56). The Eucharist and the Word of God can therefore no longer be kept apart when we consider Holy Mass or the adoration of the Eucharist outside Mass.[61]

The Eucharistic mystery is the accomplishment of the Word of God, "from the bread of the Word to the bread of the Eucharist." At Mass, the paschal sacrifice of the Lord, the liturgy of the Word announces the Communion of God and his people, which had been promised in the OT and was realized in Jesus Christ. The liturgy of the Eucharist actualizes what the Word has announced and brings about: Communion between God and the faithful in, with, and through Christ, in the Holy Spirit.

We are not saying that Montfort highlights the connection between the proclamation of the Word and the Eucharist as much as present-day theology does. We cannot deny, however, that his teaching on the Eucharist is based on Scripture, as examination of his hymns on the Blessed Sacrament has shown. It cannot be denied, either, that he understood and appreciated the celebrative side of the Eucharist. We celebrate because the Word is accomplished "here and now" in the Sacrament of the altar. We are called in a vital manner to offering worship "in spirit and in truth" that Jesus himself inaugurated. The gospel of the Annunciation, which is the bedrock of montfort spirituality, is most significant in this respect: the mystery of the Word taking flesh in the womb of the Virgin Mary by the working of the Holy Spirit evokes the mystery of the Word becoming Bread in the Church in order to be with her a single mystical living being.

3. The Eucharist and the mission

SC makes the following significant point: "The liturgy is the summit toward which the activity of the Church is directed; at the same time it is the foundation from which all her power flows. For the goal of apostolic work is that all who are made sons of God by faith and baptism should come together to praise God in the midst of his Church, to take part in her sacrifice, and to eat the Lord's supper" (SC 10). In another passage the Council Fathers say: "The most blessed Eucharist contains the Church's entire spiritual wealth. . . . Hence the Eucharist shows itself to be the source and the apex of the whole work of preaching the gospel" (PO 5). In the light of these principles, montfort spirituality, rich with the missionary experience of Montfort, which he handed on especially to the Company of Mary, is bound to acknowledge that the Eucharist is both the foundation of the mission and its ultimate goal; it is indeed in the Eucharist that the fruits of the mission mature when, sitting at the banquet of the Lamb, we enjoy indestructible Communion with him. This reminds one of Montfort quoting Wisdom, in which Wisdom is described as running about the streets and inviting people to the banquet of life.

4. Personal and ecclesial dimension

"Because there is one loaf, we, who are many, are one body, for we all partake of the one loaf" (1 Cor 10:17). The Second Vatican Council Fathers express this by saying: "The Eucharist makes the Church." These words are a strong reminder of the timeless purpose of the celebration of the memorial of the Lord's death and Resurrection. The "real presence" of Christ in history is the Church, living body in time and space, his beloved Spouse, "one flesh" with him; the Real Presence in the Sacrament of the altar is therefore geared to the upbuilding and increase of the Church.

The French school and the seventeenth-century movements have contributed to clarifying the Eucharist-Church relationship, but we cannot expect the theology and the pastoral directives of that century to go as deeply and as extensively as the relationship requires. Although Montfort urges the Daughters of Wisdom and the pilgrims to Our Lady of Saumur to receive Holy Communion together and frequently says in the plural, *"Come, eat and drink,"* his writings stress the personal character of Holy Communion. This should lead to the discovery of the community dimension, without losing sight of the real intimate relationship. Eucharistic spirituality should strike a balance between the personal and community dimensions.

If we apply to Mass what Montfort teaches about fervent Communion, which requires preparation and should influence the way we live, we come to the conclusion that the time before and after Mass should receive special attention.

5. The Eucharist with Mary

Though it is a unique and unrepeatable event, the Incarnation of the Word in Mary's womb is sacramentally perpetuated in the Eucharistic celebration, which makes God present with us for our sake.[62] What the eyes see changes but the reality is the same. As St. Justin wrote as far back as the second century, the sacrifice accomplished in the bread and wine is not "the sacrifice of the bread and wine," because we Christians "know that by virtue of the words of the prayer that comes to us from Christ, this bread and wine become the body and blood of the same Jesus who took flesh" (*Apologia* I, 66).

On this rich though simple theological vision, the French school grafted its teaching and stressed the link between the Incarnation and the Eucharist, rather than the link between Easter and the Eucharist. Montfort adopted this teaching and renewed it, adding the touch of his own charism. TD ends with instructions on how to practice this devotion at Holy Communion (see above), so that we can say that the reception of Holy Communion with Mary (or living the Mass through Mary) turns out to be a key aspect of montfort spirituality. The sacramental union that makes the faithful "one flesh" with the Son of God is the supreme expression of the Consecration received and lived out, of the covenant that affects and renews life. It is precisely this mystery, through which we become blood relations of Jesus, that brings the Virgin Mary into play, because "from her has sprung the mysteries of our salvation."[63] In reality, the determining presence of the Virgin, "faithful Spouse of the Holy Spirit," is not limited to the moment in time when she gave the flesh and blood of the Son of God to the world for our salvation. She is there again at the sacramental moment that repeats the unique event today. The words Saint Ambrose applied to Mary—*"throne-room of God's mysteries"*—and which Montfort repeats in TD 248,[64] are then found to be an apt description. The idea recurring in Montfort's writings, namely, that Mary forms the members since she has formed the Head, is realized in a concrete manner in the Eucharist: *"Her womb is, as the early Fathers call it, the house of the divine secrets where Jesus and the elect have been conceived"* (TD 264). Hence the link between Mary, the

Eucharist, and the Church.

The deep montfort insight opens up spiritual vistas based on the liturgy of the Church.[65] It is a question of rediscovering the mysterious links between Mary and the Eucharist. This can be done especially on the occasion of Marian feasts and solemnities, during Advent and the Christmas period, and when on pilgrimage to Marian shrines. As the Eucharistic celebration is the memorial of all the mysteries of Christ, we cannot ignore the admirable Mother of the Savior, as she is inevitably involved in all of them.[66]

Notes: (1) Cf. L. Godefroy, *Eucharistie d'après le Concile de Trente, (The Eucharist according to the Council of Trent),* in *Eucharistie (Eucharist),* DTC 5/2, 1326-1356; J. Rivière, *La Messe durant la période de la Réforme et du Concile de Trente, (The Mass during the Period of the Reformation and of the Council of Trent),* in *Messe (Mass),* DTC 10/1, 1085-1142. (2) The Ordo Missae in the Roman Missal of Pius V does not deal with the rite of the distribution of Holy Communion to the faithful; this rite, which is to be used even during Mass, is dealt with in the Ritual of Paul V under the heading "De Eucharistia." (3) The Missal of Pius V makes no provision for a congregation joining in the celebration: it does not mention the faithful or their taking part in the Mass; this is left to the priest's discretion. (4) Cf. A. Michel, *La Messe chez les théologiens postérieurs au Concile de Trente (The Mass in the Writings of Theologians after the Council of Trent),* in *Messe (Mass),* DTC 10/1, 1143-1316. On the subject of immolation and oblation in the explanation of Mass, see S. Marsili,

Teologia della celebrazione dell' eucaristia, in AA. VV., Anamnesis 3/2; *La Liturgia eucaristia: teologia e storia della celebrazione,* Marietti, Casale Monferrato 1983, 122-125. (5) Cf. J. Galy, *Le Sacrifice dans l'école française de spiritualité (Sacrifice in the French School of Spirituality),* Nouvelles éditions latines, Paris 1951 (includes a bibliography on the subject on pp. 388-389). (6) Olier established the feast of "the interior of Jesus" for celebration at the seminary and in the parish of Saint-Sulpice. (7) The distinction made by Bérulle between the actions and the states of Christ, with the emphasis placed on the latter, is well known. (8) See H. Brémond, *Histoire littéraire du sentiment religieux en France depuis la fin des guerres de religion jusqu'à nos jours* , vol. 3, *La conquête mystique (The Mystical Conquest),* Bloud et Gay, Paris 1921. English translation, *A Literary History of Religious Thought in France from the Wars of Religion down to Our Own Times,* trans. K.L. Montgomery, Macmillan, New York 1928. On the spirituality of the Oratory, see also A. Molien, *Oratoire de Jésus (Oratory of Jesus),* in DTC 10/1, 1104-1138, especially 1107-1130. (9) The index to J. Galy, *Le Sacrifice dans l'école française,* makes this clear. (10) On Olier's thought about the Eucharist, see the excellent synthesis ibid., 319-329. About the spirituality of the Mass and the pastoral thinking promoted by Olier, cf. Darrigau, *La messe et le prêtre dans l'ésprit de l'Ecole française de spiritualité (Mass and the Priest in the Spirit of the French School of Spirituality),* in AA. VV., *Histoire de la Messe: XVII-XVIII siècles (History of the Mass: Seventeenth-Eighteenth Centuries),* Librairie D.U.C., Paris 1980, 57-62. (11) Ibid., 57. (12) About Mass and the French school, cf. A. Michel, *La messe chez les théologiens,* 1192-1212; it may be helpful to refer to H. Brémond, *Le saint sacrifice,* in *Histoire littéraire,* vol. 9, *La vie chrétienne sous l'ancien régime (Christian Life under the Ancien Régime),* Bloud et Gay, Paris 1932, 129-206. (13) Ibid., 173. (14) The French Oratory gave a strong impulse to the efforts made to assert the values of Mass: "No effort was spared to draw together private prayer and the liturgy with a public character; the followers of Bérulle, especially Condren and Olier, promoted participation in the Sacrifice of Christ as the basis of any devotion. The liturgical aspect of a sacrifice offered by the Church was highlighted, and the faithful were encouraged to join in the action of the priest" (J. Jungmann, *Missarum Sollemnia,* Marietti, Casale 1953, 1:122; English translation, *The Mass of the Roman Rite, Its Origins and Development,* trans. Francis A.Brunner, rev. Charles K. Riepe, Benzinger Bros., New York 1959). (15) On the problematics, cf. J. de Viguerie, *La dévotion populaire à la messe dans la France des XVIIème et XVIIIème siècles (Popular Devotion to the Mass in France of the Seventeenth and Eighteenth Centuries),* in AA. VV., *Histoire de la Messe,* 7-25; J. Jungmann, *Missarum Sollemnia,* 1:121-136; *L'Eucaristia,* in A. G. Martimort, ed., *La Chiesa in preghiera,* rev. ed., Queriniana, Brescia 1985, 2:206-212; English translation, *The Eucharist,* trans. Matthew J. O'Connell, Liturgical Press, Collegeville, Minn. 1986. (16) Cf. Dom Oury, *Les explications de la messe en France du XVIème au XVIIIème siècle (The Explanations of the Mass in France of the Sixteenth and Seventeenth Centuries),* in AA. VV., *Histoire de la messe,* 81-93. (17) A significant example is given in François de Harlay, *La vraie manière de bien entendre la messe de paroisse tirée du Manuel de Rouen par le Commandement de Monseigneur l'Archevêque pour l'instruction des Familles (The True Manner of Hearing the Parish Mass Well, Taken from the Manual of Rouen by Command of the Archbishop, for the Instruction of Families),* 3rd ed., Rouen 1653 (the first edition was published in 1650). On pages 196-197, commenting on the expression *"Plebs tua sancta"* used in the Canon, the author says, "It does not say *Populus* but *Plebs,* which refers precisely to the humble people, the People of the Poor, as the Church is called in the Prophets, *Populum Pauperum.* The Church is the People of the Poor: she glories in her poor, who make up most of the People of God: the Church respects them . . . Plebs tua sancta; all these poor people to be seen in the streets and outside church doors are the People of God; all the poor village people are the holy souls to whom this expression refers." (18) Most of these texts are conducive to meditation on the Lord's Passion and arouse sentiments of adoration of God Incarnate, self-offering, sorrow for sins, desire for heaven, etc. (19) On reciting the Rosary during Mass, P. Stella, *L'Eucaristia,* cf. of MC (20) Cf. J. De Viguerie, *La dévotion populaire,* 16-19. (21) Cf. Ibid., 12. (22) P. Stella, *L'Eucaristia,* 147 (our translation). (23) Cf. section 13: 2 and 8 (DS 1638 and 1648-1649); section 22: 6 (DS 1747). See J. Dhur, *Communion fréquente,* in DSAM 2:1271-1273; on the French section, see H. Brémond, *La communion fréquente,* in *Histoire littéraire,* 9:45-128. (24) This was the line that even the Sacred Congregation for the Council always followed when answering questions about frequent Communion, which was only to be received on the advice of one's confessor. (25) J. De Viguerie, *La dévotion populaire,* 206-208; P. Stella, *L'Eucaristia,* 163-164. (26) Cf. Ibed, 58-59, P. Stella, *L'Eucharistia* o.c., 159, observed that for the devout of the 17th C. frequency of communion was weekly or almost never daily. (27) Cf. H. Bremond, *Histoire litteraire*, ix, o.c., 207-246 (L'Adoration reparatrice); R. Cabie, *L'Eucharistia*, o.c., 206-208; P. Stella, *L'Eucharistia*, o.c., 163-164. (28) Blain, 31. (29) Ibid., 100. (30) Ibid., 101. (31) We have been using the publication *Le livre des sermons du Père de Montfort: Documents et recherches (The Book of Sermons of Father de Montfort: Documents and Research)*, vol. 9, Centre international montfortain, Rome 1983. The passages quoted refer to the period before Montfort's ordination; see introduction, i-ix. (32) The unpublished notes are those contained in Montfort's N, which were transcribed with comments by Fr. Pierre Eijkeler, SMM (memeographed text). (33) See LS 339, probably by Fr. Leschassier again. (34) Cf. Blain, 70. (35) Ibid. 105-106. (36) Ibid., 112. (37) Ibid., 142-143. (38) Cf. J. De Viguerie, *La dévotion populaire*, 13. (39) Blain, 191. (40) Ibid., 163. (41) Besnard II, 182-183. (42) On the person and role of the seventeenth-century spiritual mediator between theologians and the people, see P. Stella, *L'Eucaristia*, 145-146. (43) Hymns 112, 128-134, and 158 are concerned with the Eucharist; some verses of Hymns 5, 44, and 139 also deal with the same theme. Though we do not know when they were written, we know that they were sung during the missions, and this is an important piece of information, as it allows us to regard them as reflecting, so to speak, what Montfort preached on the subject of the "Eucharist." (44) Cf. L. Perouas, *Grignion de Montfort: Les pauvres et les missions (Grignion de Montfort: The Poor and the Missions)*, Cerf, Paris 1966, 124. (45) Cf. Ibid., 124; J. De Viguerie, *La dévotion populaire*, 12. (46) Cf. L. Perouas, Grignion, o.c., 113-124. (47) J.J. Olier, *Explication des Cérémonies de la Grande Messe . . .*, in *Oeuvres complètes*, publ. Migne, 432-433: "Holy Communion is the invention devised by the love and religion of Our Lord Jesus Christ that his praise, adoration, and love of his Father, in paying homage to his Father, as he wants us to join him in offering it"; cf. J. Galy, *Le sacrifice*, 324-325. (48) The order in which they are given suggests that they were meant to be sung over a week during a mission. We must add Hymn 158, which in the first part deals with faith in the Real Presence, while the second part is a collection of prayers for the various stages of Mass. (49) This argues strongly in favor of Montfort's sound theological presentation. (50) On processions, cf. L. Perouas, *Grignion*, 122. (51) At that time many people were objecting to the prevailing practice, and arguments were put forward in favor of Communion under both kinds for the faithful; it appears, however, that Montfort, holding onto the teaching of the Council of Trent, stressed that the whole of Christ was really equally present under both species. It can be argued that his frequent realistic references to flesh and blood, eating and drinking, which were based on the Gospel, have something to do with the Eucharist-Incarnation relationship to which he attached so much importance. (52) Jansenism and Augustinianism placed less emphasis on this. The Ritual of Paul V urged parish priests to see that the faithful received Holy Communion frequently and with devotion, especially on the major feast days of the year. (53) Cf. L. Perouas, *Grignion*, 119. (54) Cf. Ibid. 120. (55) Blain, 204. (56) On the use of hymns and prayers, including the Rosary, during Mass as a remedy for absenteeism particularly during the parish missions, see J. A. Jungmann, *Missarum Sollemnia*, 1:125. (57) See Note 19. (58) On the same subject, see A. Lhoumeau, *La vie spirituelle à l'école du Bx L.M. Grignion de Montfort*, Mame, Tours 1920, 459-474 (Mary and Holy Communion), in which the author sets out to supplement Montfort's teaching on attending Mass in union with Mary. (59) Speaking of the Magnificat, Montfort mentions Gerson's view and suggests that we say the canticle after Holy Communion, in imitation of Mary, who used it in thanksgiving after Holy Communion; cf. SM 64 and TD 255. (60) Cf. Ordo Initiationis Christianae Adultorum and Ordo Baptismi Parvulorum, *praenotanda*, especially nos. 1-2. (61) Cf. *De sacra Communione et de cultu Mysterii Eucharistici extra Missam (On Holy Communion and the Cult of the Eucharistic Mystery outside Mass)*, editio typica, Typis Polyglottis Vaticanis, Vatican City 1973, nos. 26, 29, 44, 58, 71, 89, 95. (62) Sur les implications Incarnation Marie-Eucharistie, voir C. Maggioni, *Annunciazione Storia, eucloogia, telogia liturgica*, C.L.V. Roma, 1991, pp. 156-209. On the Implications of the Incarnation, Mary, Eucharist) (63) The expression is borrowed from a fifth-century Ambrosian preface: *"De cujus [Mariae] ventre fructus effloruit, qui panis angelici munere nos replevit. Quod Eva voravit in crimine, Mara restituit in salute. . . . Inde fusa sunt venena discriminis, hinc egressa mysteria Salvatoris"*; A. Paredi (publisher), *Sacramentarium Bergomense (Sacramentary of Bergamo)*, Monumenta Bergomensia 6, Bergamo 1962, no. 85. Cf. A. M. Triacca, *La Vierge Marie, Mère de Dieu, dans la liturgie eucharistique ambrosienne "Hinc egressa mysteria Salvatoris" (The Virgin Mary, Mother of God, in the Ambrosian Eucharistic Liturgy "Hinc egressa mysteria Salvatoris")*, in A. M.

Triacca A. Pistoia (publisher), *La Mère de Jésus Christ et la Communion des Saints dans la Liturgie (The Mother of Jesus Christ and the Communion of Saints in the Liturgy),* Conférences Saint-Serge, Paris, 1985, C.L.V., Rome 1986, 283-332. (64) Ambrose demonstrates the truth that the body of Christ is really present in the Eucharist by referring to the Incarnation: " The Blessed Virgin has given birth outside the order of nature. Well, we produce the body borne of her. Why seek the order of nature in the body of Christ when the Lord Jesus himself was born of a Virgin outside the order of nature? It is the same body of Christ that was crucified and buried. The Eucharist is therefore the Sacrament of his body." *De Mysteriis* 53, Sources chrétiennes 25 bis, 187.189. (65) On the mysteries of Christ celebrated by the Church "with" and "like" Mary, see Collectio Missarum de BVM, *praenotanda* nos. 4-18, especially 12-13, 17. See also: Congregatio pro Culto Divino, *Orientamenti e proposte per la celebrazione dell'anno mariano,* nos. 19-20, in *Notitiae* 23 (1987), 354-355. (66) Cf. SC 103; LG 53, 57.

FAITH

SUMMARY

I. THE VIRTUE OF FAITH IN THE LIFE OF SAINT LOUIS DE MONTFORT:
   1. Absolute confidence in God;
   2. Radical Gospel poverty;
   3. Intensity of prayer;
   4. Insight into the mystery of the Cross.

II. THE VIRTUE OF FAITH IN THE TEACHINGS OF SAINT LOUIS DE MONTFORT:
   1. General characteristics;
   2. Points emphasized:
      a. Faith must be simple,
      b. Faith must be pure,
      c. Faith must lead to practical commitment,
      d. Faith leads to trust in the Magisterium.

III. MONTFORT'S PERCEPTION OF MARY'S FAITH:
   1. Mary, the faithful Virgin;
   2. The faith of Mary and the Incarnation;
   3. Mary, model of faith;
   4. Mary shares her faith with us:
      a. Montfort's request,
      b. Sharing in the faith of Mary.

IV. RELEVANCE OF MONTFORT'S CONTRIBUTION TO THE SUBJECT OF FAITH:
   1. Faith in general:
      a. A faith based on the essentials,
      b. A faith lived in union with the Magisterium.
   2. The faith of Mary:
      a. In Lumen gentium,
      b. In the encyclical Redemptoris mater.

I. THE VIRTUE OF FAITH IN THE LIFE OF SAINT LOUIS DE MONTFORT

Saint Louis Marie's first biographer, Grandet, writes: "In short, all his actions, words, and sufferings were animated by a very lively faith, and he himself lived by faith. *Justus ex fide vivit* [The just man lives by faith]."[1]

It was in his home surroundings that he first found evidence of the faith he was to refine and affirm all through his life. Beyond any doubt, he saw evidence of it in his mother, Jeanne Robert, and also in his father; whose character should not be so blackened as to make him out to be almost "a profligate standing in the way of his children's religious and priestly vocation."[2] He was actually a good Christian. In a letter to his mother dated August 1704, Montfort attests his gratitude to both of them:

"I know that I owe you and my father a great debt of gratitude for bringing me into the world, for looking after me, bringing me up in the fear of God" (L 20). Montfort never renounced his cradle-faith: at no time did the awesome trials he had to endure lead him to lose his complete confidence in Divine Providence. On the contrary, he came out of his trials with his faith purified and intensified. He truly is "a believer who has opted for God Alone."[3]

1. Absolute confidence in God

"He believes in a God Who loves him, cares for him, and cannot fail him. No other sort of faith could account for his attitude of simple, filial, and unshakable confidence in Divine Providence."[4] At a time when he was in a state of complete uncertainty about his immediate future after the death of his benefactor, Father de la Barmondière, he wrote to his uncle Father Alain Robert in September 1694: *"I have a Father in heaven who will never fail me"* (L 2). These words reveal how intensely Saint Louis Marie was united to God as a caring, loving Father.

2. Radical Gospel poverty

On the strength of such confidence in God, Montfort is aware that he is not to be anxious. His poverty is essentially spiritual, the poverty of the Beatitudes, rooted in a profound conviction of faith. As a result, he will not really fear being stripped of everything if so be the will of God. This total, faith-inspired poverty pertains not only to material or emotional goods but even to spiritual ones as well, because through faith he is rooted in God Alone.

3. Intensity of prayer

Montfort is well aware that God can refuse nothing to the person who has surrendered all to Him. Thus, when ardently seeking for Divine Wisdom, especially in the years 1701-1704, he was certain he would be united with Wisdom. As a proof of this, we only need to read his letter to Marie Louise Trichet dated April-May 1703: "*I will never cease asking for this boundless treasure and I firmly believe that I shall obtain it even were angels, men and demons to deny it to me. . . . I believe . . . the promises of God too explicit*" (L 15). He is writing autobiographically when he says that "*lively faith,*" "*pure faith*" should animate the prayer of anyone wishing to possess Wisdom (cf. LEW 185-187).

He shows the same faith-inspired certainty in PM. Addressing Christ, he says: "*What am I asking you for? Something you can and, I make bold to say, you must grant*" (PM 6). With the boldness of a saint, he orders God, so to speak, to grant his prayer: "*Arise, Lord. Why is it you appear to be like one asleep? Arise in your might, your mercy and your justice*" (PM 30). We must consider, however, what he is asking for: "*It is no personal favor that I ask, but something which concerns your glory alone*" (PM 6). "*Thus, there will be but one sheepfold and one shepherd and all will make your temple resound with their praise of your glory*" (PM 30). Because the object of his request is dictated, as it were, by his faith, the promise made in the Gospel, "Ask and you shall receive" (Lk 11, 10), cannot fail to be fulfilled.

4. Insight into the mystery of the Cross

"*The Cross in mystery / Is veiled for us below; / Without great light to see, / Who shall its splendor know?*" (H 19:1). "*Let us believe / Let us believe with lively faith / Without the cross no one can be saved*" (H 11:9). Montfort was granted an extraordinarily deep insight into the mystery of the Cross because he had obtained "*the wisdom of the cross, that knowledge of the truth which we experience within ourselves and which by the light of faith deepens our knowledge of the most hidden mysteries, including that of the cross*" (FC 45).

II. The Virtue of Faith in the Teachings of Saint Louis de Montfort

Montfort's teaching on faith is scattered throughout all his writings.[5] Hymn 6, "*The Light of Faith,*" permeated with biblical references, is a miniature treatise on the subject. It can serve as a resume of the saint's thought on the virtue of faith.

1. General characteristics

Montfort begins with a descriptive definition of faith: "*I am a pure light / By which you believe everything firmly / Because it is God who assures it / Together with the Church*" (H 6:1). The missionary has in mind the Catholic faith, whose content, revealed by God and transmitted by the Church, is certain, sure. Faith is "*supernatural,*" and "*the senses are irrelevant when learning about faith*"; it is "*obscure but very beautiful*" (H 6:2); it is the foundation of hope, "*the wonderful argument in favor of what cannot be seen*" (H 6:3). Faith secures victory over the devil and the world (H 6:9-10); it makes prayer powerful (H 6:15), causes miracles to happen (H 6:16-18), gives strength and joy in trials, even to enduring martyrdom (H 6:19-21). It enables God to do His work in us (H 6:23-24) and discloses his secrets: "*I am the key opening the door / Into the mysteries of Jesus Christ / The wonders of the supernatural world / And the great secrets of the Holy Spirit*" (H 6:26).

2. Points emphasized

a. Faith must be simple. Faith is not, Montfort insists, the conclusion of a reasoning process: "*Simple faith is very beautiful and good, / Of great merit and great price. / I do not want anyone to try to 'prove' / The truths which I teach*" (H 6:40). Faith ought not to yield to the lure of novelty, which may lead astray: "*Keep clear of new doctrines / And new heretics as well: / They spread very subtle errors / Which create havoc everywhere*" (H 6:47). Montfort echoes Saint Paul (cf. Gal 1:7; 2 Tim 4:3-4). We must be careful, however, not to make a caricature of Montfort by thinking of him as a timid man totally unable to break with an immutable past. His illuminating teaching on Wisdom, Mary, and devotion to Mary is abundant proof that he regarded the deposit of faith as a store from which things new and old can be produced.

b. Faith must be pure. Faith will be pure if it rests only on the rock of the Word of God transmitted by the Church. It must therefore not be founded on "*fables,*" "*groundless sto-*

ries," or "*visions.*" According to Montfort, this does not mean that the genuine signs given by God should be ignored: "*As for authentic stories, / Believe them, but as good Christians*" (H 6:48). The theme of pure faith recurs often in his writings. In LEW 187, for example, he says: "*Simple faith is both the cause and the effect of Wisdom in our soul. The more faith we have, the more we shall possess Wisdom. The more we possess it, the stronger our faith. The just or wise man only lives by faith without seeing, without feeling, without tasting, and without faltering.*" In his *Prayer to Mary* he writes: "*I do not ask for visions or revelations, for sensible devotion or even spiritual pleasures*" (SM 69; cf. also LEW 186; FC 53; SM 51; TD 109, 214, 273). Montfort is calling for a total surrender on every level of personality to the God of truth, precisely because God is Truth.

We have to bear in mind these repeated warnings against attempting to ground faith upon visions or private revelations when Saint Louis Marie reports "stories" or "facts" to which he attaches some worth that is no longer acknowledged today. He was a man of his time, and people were less critical then than they are nowadays; moreover, he definitely was not a freethinker. He lived so intensely in the familiar presence of God that he had no difficulty in believing in divine actions so long as those reporting them seemed trustworthy and what was transmitted was in accord with the Scriptures as lived, taught, and prayed by the Church. It is clear that he would have had no difficulty in accepting the legitimate intervention of the Church in such matters, accepting whatever the decision of the Church might be. People voraciously hungry for the marvelous, for the extraordinary, make a great mistake if they turn to Saint Louis de Montfort for support. He puts the following in the mouth of faith: "*Be satisfied with the light I give. / Do not aspire to visions. / The Church is your mother. / Accept her decisions unreservedly*" (H 6:49).

c. Faith must lead to practical commitment. "*I am like a lifeless body / If am left unused. / I am as lively as a flame; / But without love I die.*" "*Beware of a sterile faith / Which believes everything but does nothing. / Rather, live out the Gospel, / Believing all it says and doing good*" (H 6:43—4; cf. among others LPM 1). True faith should make us "*the faithful*" and finds its expression in "*faithfulness*" in imitation of Mary. The two words recur frequently in Montfort's writings, especially when he refers to the faithful children, servants (or slaves) of Mary, i.e., those who have given themselves completely to her in order better to belong to Jesus (cf. among others LEW 212, 227; TD 50, 101, 135, 173, 209).

d. Finally, faith leads to trust in the Magisterium. In Hymn 6 Montfort comes back repeatedly to the statement made in the first verse. He puts these words into the mouth of faith: "*I am, in the visible Church, / The solid rock on which truth rests. / Most holy, infallible, invincible, / In spite of hell's fury*" (H 6:30); and "*Because the Church is so unshakable . . . / Believe her with obedient faith, / And every blessing will be yours*" (H 6:36). His obedience to the Pope is well known, and he reminds Catholics of their obligation: "*Believe Jesus speaking through his Vicar / When he pronounces on matters of faith. / Regard what he says as Teacher / As an oracle and sure law*" (H 6:50). This is in no way to be interpreted as infantile docility prompted by a fearful mind: the authentic foundation for the legitimate authority of the Sovereign Pontiff is well recognized by the saint.

III. Montfort's Perception of Mary's Faith

It is when he speaks of Mary that Montfort is most illuminating on the qualities of faith itself and on the way he lived it.

1. Mary, the faithful Virgin

The words "*faithful,*" "*faithfulness,*" and "*faithfully*" are certainly those which Montfort associates most frequently with Mary. She is the "*faithful Virgin*" (LEW 222, 227; TD 88, 89, 101, 102, 173, 175, 214), "*the faithful Spouse of the Holy Spirit*" (SM 15, 68; TD 4, 5, 25, 34, 36, 164, 269; PM 15); "*by her fidelity to God she makes good the losses caused by Eve's unfaithfulness*" (TD 175). The contrast between the "*faithful*" Mary and the "*unfaithful*" Eve accentuates the fruitfulness and effectiveness of Mary's faith.

2. The faith of Mary and the Incarnation

It was through her faith that Mary—according to God's mysterious plan—enabled the Word to become man for the salvation of the world. Where the "*holy people of the Old Law*" (LEW 104) had not succeeded, Mary did: "*He found her lively faith and her ceaseless entreaties of love so irresistible that he was lovingly conquered*" (LEW 107); "*The Blessed Virgin is only praised / For her faith in the Lord. / It was faith that consecrated her / The Mother of her Creator*" (H 6:22). "*O Wisdom, Come, then, by Mary's faith / You have not been able to resist her / She gave you life; / Through her you became incarnate*" (H 124:8). It was that perfect faith that, for its part, enabled Mary to become the "*worthy Mother of God.*"

3. Mary, model of faith

In order to perform our actions "*with Mary,*" says Montfort, "*we must look upon Mary, although a simple human being [a 'pure creature'], as the perfect model of every virtue and perfection, fashioned by the Holy Spirit for us to imitate, as far as our limited capacity allows. . . . For this reason, we must examine and meditate on the great virtues she practiced during her life, especially (i) her lively faith, by which she believed the angel's word without the least hesitation, and believed faithfully and constantly even to the foot of the Cross on Calvary*" (TD 260; cf. 108). Montfort is well aware, however, that we cannot do this by our own strength, so he suggests an effective means to achieve it: sharing in Mary's faith.

4. Mary shares her faith with us

This is a major aspect clarified by Montfort (cf., e.g., SM 51, 57, 68; TD 34, 144, 214).

a. Montfort's request. "*Worthy Mother of God, Virgin all-faithful, pure, / Share with me your faith / I will possess Wisdom through her / And all* *good shall come into me*" (H 124:7). Montfort's prayer shows how deeply convinced and conscious he was of the close connection between his faith life and the maternal influence of Mary. According to his perception of the mystery of the Incarnation, the Blessed Virgin's fruitful faith, which enabled her to become the Mother of Christ, is to be continued in us. In actual fact, the Holy Spirit commissioned her to "*reproduce her faith in us*": "*My well-beloved, my spouse, let all your virtues take root in my chosen ones . . . so that I may have the joy of seeing in them the roots of your invincible faith*" (TD 34). This goes for the other virtues as well, but it is significant that faith should be named first.

b. Sharing in the faith of Mary. TD 214 makes perfectly clear Montfort's view on the subject: "*Mary will share her faith with you. . . . Now that she is reigning in heaven she no longer has this faith, since she is seeing everything clearly in God by the light of glory. However, with the consent of almighty God, she did not lose it when entering heaven. She has preserved it for her faithful servants in the Church Militant.*"

Montfort is not unaware of the fact that in heaven faith gives way to vision. What are his grounds for saying that Mary has "*preserved*" it in order to share it with us? As he is speaking for "*the poor and simple*" (TD 36), he simply states the fact without going into details that might be above them. But we must keep in mind that Montfort lived in a spiritual atmosphere permeated by the teachings of the French school. One of the more important merits of that school was that, starting with Bérulle, it highlighted what could be called a theology (opening up to a spirituality) of the "states of Jesus." The first and fundamental of these is the Incarnation. What Jesus lived in his mysteries becomes, as it were, permanent, so that nothing of it was lost when he entered into glory. The salvific power (which in Montfort's time was called "virtue") of the mysteries has not been diminished, and it saves us today. (Recall the proclamation of the *Anamnesis* at the Eucharist). Saint Louis Marie's short prayers at the end of each decade of the Rosary are an example of this trait of the French School: "*May the grace of the mystery of [the Incarnation, Visitation, etc.] come down into our souls.*"

What is true of Christ the Head holds good also, making due allowances, for his members by virtue of their organic spiritual connection with him. This applies with much greater reason to Mary because of her exceptional union with Christ in the Incarnation. That is why Bérulle wrote: "In and through this mystery . . . she is empowered to give her Son to the world . . . and this power will last for ever and cannot be taken from her."[6] The "virtue" of Mary's faith, which enabled her to share in the Incarnation of the Word, is still at work in order that the Word may be received today, that he may be born and grow in us. As it is through faith that we become able to receive him, Mary can do no better than share with us her faith so that Jesus may be born and grow in us. It is in this wider context that Montfort's statement is to be explained and finds full justification.

Montfort continues with a beautiful description of Mary's faith, and the description would fit his own faith as well: "*Therefore the more you gain the friendship of this noble Queen and faithful Virgin, the more you will be inspired by faith in your daily life. It will cause you to depend less on sensible and extraordinary feelings. For it is a lively faith animated by love enabling you to do everything from no other motive than that of pure love. It is a firm faith, unshakable as a rock, prompting you to remain firm and steadfast in the midst of storms and tempests. It is an active and probing faith which like some mysterious pass-key admits you into the mysteries of Jesus Christ and of man's final destiny and into the very heart of God himself. It is a courageous faith which inspires you to undertake and carry out without hesitation great things for God and the salvation of souls. Lastly, this faith will be your flaming torch, your very life with God, your secret fund of divine Wisdom, and an all-powerful weapon for you to enlighten those who sit in darkness and in the shadow of death. It inflames those who are lukewarm and need the goal of fervent love. It restores to life those who are dead through sin. It moves and transforms hearts of marble and cedars of Lebanon by gentle and convincing argument. Finally, this faith will strengthen you to resist the devil and the other enemies of salvation*" (TD 214).

"*Pure*" faith animated by "*pure love*" is Montfort's ideal; throughout his life he showed a firm faith, unshakable as a rock, which enabled him to overcome all his trials. His faith admitted him into "the mysteries of Jesus": Jesus Wisdom, the triumphant Jesus crucified. "A courageous faith which inspires you to undertake . . . great things for God and the salvation of souls": this sums up Montfort's "missionary career."[7]

IV. Relevance of Montfort's Contribution to the Subject of Faith

Montfort's life and writings emphasize two aspects of faith.

1. Faith in general

a. A faith based on the essentials. While accepting authentic signs that God may give us—including Mary's "interventions" or "apparitions"—it may be helpful to point out that they are not of the essence of faith. They can help us only insofar as they refer us to "pure faith," by calling us to constant conversion. In this respect, the advice repeatedly given by Father de Montfort to exercise caution concerning reputed apparitions, locutions, etc., is very relevant today. It is clear indeed that Mary cannot possibly invite her children to rise against those whom her Son has commissioned to lead his Church.

b. A faith lived in union with the Magisterium. At a time when the authentic role of the Magisterium is questioned in various areas, it may be worthwhile to refer to Montfort's attitude towards the official teaching authority of the Church. The saint's experience was inevitably influenced by his time and his cultural background, as has been repeatedly underlined. Nonetheless, he set his mind and heart on the essentials. He was aware that faith is first and foremost a gift, in terms of its content and of our personal response to it; it cannot be the result of human endeavor. As a virtue it is a gift from the Holy Spirit; a gift of the essential truths, it must be received as the Word of God read according to the tradition of the Church. This tradition does not embrace the past only; rather, it is alive and continues in the life of the Church, the people of God. Therefore it is not the exclusive field of the Magisterium as such. The new insights and discoveries (which may enrich the faith) resulting from facing the many daunting contemporary issues and problems belong also to the field of research for theologians and to the experience of the faithful. Montfort's life and writings testify to this. The saint also firmly reminds us, however, that far from excluding confident and intelligent reference to the authentic teaching of the Magisterium, this attitude of openness posits it. It is a condition necessary for keeping in harmony with the faith of the Church, and Christ himself willed it to be so (cf. 1 Tim 3:15).

2. The faith of Mary

In this section we will concentrate on the teaching of the Second Vatican Council and on Pope John Paul II's encyclical *Redemptoris mater.*

a. In Lumen gentium. We have seen how much importance Saint Louis Marie attached to the faith of Mary. The faith of Mary appears as one of the keys to the proper understanding of LG, chap. 8: the whole of Mary's life on earth is described as a "pilgrimage of faith." Mary at the Incarnation is seen by the Council Fathers "not merely as passively engaged by God, but as freely cooperating in the work of man's salvation through faith and obedience" (LG 56); she "advanced in her pilgrimage of faith and faithfully persevered in her union with her Son unto the Cross" (LG 58; cf. LG 60); she is the model of the Church "in the order of faith," even in her maternal fecundity (LG 63; cf. LG 65); finally, "Mary, in a way, unites in her person and re-echoes the most important doctrines of the faith: and when she is the subject of preaching and worship she prompts the faithful to come to her Son, to his sacrifice and to the love of the Father" (LG 65). Montfort's wording is different. Nonetheless, it is easy to recognize his thought and, particularly with reference to the faith of Mary as model of the Church's faith, to supplement his teaching with the contributions made by Vatican II.

b. In the encyclical Redemptoris mater. Pope John Paul II himself tells us about the importance of the theme of Mary's faith: "In these reflections I wish to consider primarily that 'pilgrimage of faith' in which 'the Blessed Virgin advanced' [LG 58], faithfully preserving her union with Christ" (*Redemptoris mater,* 5). There are evident points of convergence with Montfort's teaching.

First of all, Mary's consent conditioned, as far as depended on her according to God's will, the accomplishment of the Incarnation: "The mystery of the Incarnation was accomplished when Mary uttered her fiat: 'Let it be done to me according to your word,' which made possible, as far as depended upon her in the divine plan, the granting of her Son's desire. Mary uttered this fiat in faith" (*Redemptoris mater,* 13).

Pope John Paul II agrees with Saint Louis de Montfort that through her faithfulness, Mary became the counterpoise to Eve's unfaithfulness: "From the Cross, that is to say, from the very heart of the mystery of the Redemption, there radiates and spreads out the prospect of that blessing of faith. It goes right back to 'the beginning,' and as a sharing in the sacrifice of Christ—the new Adam—it becomes in a certain sense the counterpoise to the disobedience and disbelief embodied in the sin of our first parents" (*Redemptoris mater,* 19).

Pope John Paul II describes Mary living her faith on earth as the one who lives to perfection "the obedience of faith" (*Redemptoris mater,* 12-19), i.e., a faith immediately incorporated into her life through her faithfulness to God's will. Montfort intends the same when he calls Mary the "faithful" Virgin par excellence.

These similarities between the teaching of John Paul II and Father de Montfort are hardly startling, since they concern common doctrine on Our Lady. But their teachings tie together in a special way when both declare that although Mary is now glorified, in a certain sense we share in her faith. Like Montfort, John Paul II points out that now that she is glorified, Mary no longer has faith: "The pilgrimage of faith no longer belongs to the Mother of the Son of God; glorified at the side of her Son in heaven, Mary has already crossed the threshold between faith and that vision which is 'face to face'" (*Redemptoris mater,* 6). Montfort did not explain how we can share in Mary's faith, but Pope John Paul put forward an explanation. To begin with, Mary is the one who initiates the faith of the New Covenant on the day of the Annunciation: "It is precisely Mary's faith which marks the beginning of the new and eternal Covenant of God with man in Jesus Christ; this heroic faith of hers precedes the apostolic witness of the Church, and ever remains in the Church's heart, hidden like a special heritage of God's revelation. All those who from generation to generation accept the apostolic witness of the Church share in that mysterious inheritance, and in a sense share in Mary's faith" (*Redemptoris mater,* 27).

"If, from the moment of the Annunciation, the Son—whom only the Father knows completely, as the one who begets him in the eternal 'today' (cf. Ps 2:7)—was revealed to Mary, she, his Mother, is in contact with the truth about her Son only in faith and through faith!" (*Redemptoris mater,* 17).

The mission that Mary carried out for the sake of the early Christian community she carries out for our sake today: "In the Upper Room Mary's journey meets the Church's journey of faith. . . . That first group of those who in faith looked 'upon Jesus as the author of salvation' (cf. LG 9) knew that Jesus was the Son of Mary, and that she was his Mother, and that as such she was from the moment of his conception and birth a unique witness to the mystery of Jesus, that mystery which before their eyes had been disclosed and confirmed in the Cross and Resurrection" (*Redemptoris mater*, 26). We are able to believe today because Mary believed first, and what we believe concerning the mystery of Jesus, God made man, is what she was the first to believe.

John Paul II's explanations supplement the attempts to explain Montfort's statements on Mary's shared faith in light of the views prevailing in the French school. In this regard, as in many others, John Paul II not only shows that Montfort's teaching is highly relevant but also demonstrates that it is possible to deepen the saint's intuition thanks to contemporary insights.[8]

A. Bossard

Notes: (1) Grandet, 285. (2) Itinerario, 21. (3) See *Dieu Seul (God Alone),* Centre international montfortain, Rome 1981, 76ff. (4) A. Bossard, *Saint Louis-Marie de Montfort*, in *Esprit et Vie*, July 12-19, 225. (5) Although LS gives evidence of the importance that Montfort attached to the theme in his preaching, it is not the book most likely to reveal his own way of thinking. It contains quotations and summaries of passages from writers he may have turned to either when he was at the seminary or when he was a young priest. The three plans of a mission or a retreat may also leave us unsatisfied, as the theme of faith is mentioned only twice. We should not jump, however, to hasty conclusions. In order to *"renew the spirit of Christianity among the faithful,"* the missionary did not hesitate to remind his hearers of the truths of the faith and urged them to make a deep commitment to keeping the faith by solemnly renewing their baptismal vows and promises. (6) Passage quoted by H. Brémond, *Histoire littéraire du sentiment religieux en France (Literary History of Religious Sentiment in France),* Bloud et Gay, Paris 1921, 3:96. It is necessary to read at least the whole of B in chap. 2 of *Le Verbe incarné (The Incarnate Word)*, 43-110, to form an idea of the importance of this theology. Montfort became acquainted with it through, among others, the Sulpicians, who follow the tradition of Olier. (7) It has inspired a beautiful prayer used by the Legion of Mary (8) Cf. A. Bossard, *Jean-Paul II actualise Grignion de Montfort (John Paul II Shows Grignion de Montfort's Relevance)*, in *Journal de la Grotte,* Lourdes, magazine no. 9, December 20, 1987.

FAMILY

SUMMARY

I. THE FAMILY AT MONTFORT-LA-CANE IN THE SEVENTEENTH CENTURY:
   1. Engagements and marriage;
   2. The establishment of a home:
      a. Birth and baptism,
      b. Nursing,
      c. Profane and religious education.

II. THE HISTORY OF THE GRIGNIONS:
   1. The Huguenot ancestors;
   2. The Grignions of Montfort.

III. MARRIAGE AND FAMILY IN THE WRITINGS OF MONTFORT:
   1. Writings and missionary catechism;
   2. The family, material possession of fortune;
   3. Mystical wedding.

IV. SPIRITUALITY OF THE FAMILY TODAY:
   1. The turning point of Vatican II.
   2. Pathways for experiencing Montfort's spirituality in the family:
      a. Family consecration,
      b. Participating in the dynamic love of Christ Wisdom for humanity,
      c. Life of fidelity to Mary within the covenant with God.

I. THE FAMILY AT MONTFORT-LA-CANE IN THE SEVENTEENTH CENTURY

1. Engagements and marriage

At the time of Louis Marie Grignion's birth at Montfort-la-Cane, Brittany, (1673), only about half of all children in that area of France reached adulthood. Few young men married before they reached the mature age of twenty-five. Young women, by contrast, generally found a partner before they turned twenty, and it was not uncommon for them to be married by the age of fourteen, especially in bourgeois society. Thus, Guillemette Dolliver, paternal great-grandmother of Saint Louis de Montfort, was only fourteen when she married François Saulnier in Saint-Pern, August 2, 1612.

Marriage was not a personal decision, regardless of the age of the participants. From the two sides, an extended family council discussed the advantages and disadvantages of the future union, and presided over the least details of the marriage contract in the presence of a notary. The registries of the County of Montfort still retain the conclusions of the family council authorizing, on February 7, 1672, the marriage of Jean-Baptiste Grignion to Jeanne Robert, with the marriage to take place three days later. Dispensing with this legal procedure was an offense punished severely by both the seigniorial and canonical authorities.

2. The establishment of a home

a. Birth and baptism. Well before the last month of pregnancy, family and friends of the future mother were ready to baptize the child in case of a premature birth. If the woman experienced difficulty in childbirth, Saint Joseph was invoked, and the infant would be dedicated to him. A considerable number of lay people administered baptism "in emergencies where there is danger of death"; records tell of one occasion in the rural parish of Coulon de Montfort, when a wine merchant "on his way to Saint-Malo," baptized the child of his host for the night.

All newborns were baptized within hours of their birth. Thus Louis Grignion was taken to the Church of Saint-Jean de Montfort less than twenty-four hours after his birth. In cases involving the firstborn of a noble or bourgeois family, the clergy sometimes granted an additional delay, but rarely of more than three days.

The attitude of clergy and parishioners toward illegitimate or abandoned infants clearly shows that, for them, birthright transcended blood affiliation. The faithful often argued with each other for the honor of becoming godparents to these children. When such infants died, the number of mourners at the funeral procession to the cemetery was often larger than at the death of "ordinary" newborns.

The baptismal name took precedence over the family name, which in the canonical view is simply the "surname." The predominant concern was that the baptismal name appear on the calendar of saints. In the sixteenth century, the bishops of Saint-Malo took advantage of pastoral visits to search the parish registries and officially give Catholic names to those children who were victims of unabashed laxism, even if this meant giving a girl, incorrectly named Phéline, the masculine first name of Félix.

Until 1610, the custom in Montfort was that a boy have a "big godfather," who "named" him, assisted by a "little godfather"; for girls, it was the reverse. This sponsorship was generally taken very seriously, especially on the issue of religious education: this spiritual parent was also considered the juridical equivalent of a legal guardian.

When a priest agreed to "name" an infant, the child's parents were overjoyed: they considered this a sign that the priest was willing to sponsor the secular and religious education, and indeed the vocation, of the child.

At Montfort, the godfather gave his "name" to his godson, and the godmother gave hers to her goddaughter; the second "name," if one was given, was that of the godfather for the goddaughter or of the godmother for the godson. This was true for the majority of Louis Grignion's brothers and sisters; Louis himself, though he appears in the baptismal registry under the sole name of Louis, after his godfather Louis Hubert, a doctor, also carries the name of Marie from the day of his baptism, after his godmother Marie Lemoyne.[1]

The bourgeois families of Montfort organized a large banquet at an eating-house to "welcome the coming of the infant." The clergy were invited, as well as the "co-fathers" and "co-mothers" of the neighborhood. The good priest sometimes made a note of the libations in the margin of the baptismal register.

b. Nursing. After several years of marriage, the number of young widowers with children, marrying for a second time was considerably greater than the number of young widows. There are several reasons for this phenomenon, not least of which is the elevated mortality rate resulting from the difficulties of premature pregnancy.

Bourgeois women were on average three times more prolific than rural women, who generally had only five or six pregnancies, spread out over time. For bourgeois women, wet-nursing of newborns was obligatory: this was an inflexible custom. A bourgeois woman was considered disreputable if she nursed her numerous children. Ten Grignion children were born at the manor house of Bois-Marquer in Iffendic; all ten were nursed by the successive tenant farmwomen at the neighboring manorial farms, mixed together with any number of foster brothers and sisters.

Few children of bourgeois families managed to overcome the heavy handicap that being wet-nursed placed on them. For a long time, however, this custom was tacitly accepted as a form of natural selection. Even the best of children were lucky to survive their mother. Thus, when Jeanne Robert, mother of Saint Louis de Montfort, died in 1718, she was survived by only one son and four daughters (of whom two were religious) of the eighteen children she brought into the world. Such numerous deaths explain how entire family lines, no matter how firmly rooted in the bourgeoisie of Montfort, could die out completely after three or four generations, in the space of one generation. Such was the case with the Grignions of Montfort.

c. Profane and religious education. The grammar school for boys in Montfort-la-Cane dated back to the twelfth century: the "scholastic" was normally an unbeneficed priest, although by the beginning of the eighteenth century he was often assisted by, or alternated with, a member of the laity. The school for girls, founded only in 1636, was run by Ursuline nuns. It was clear that the school for boys did not always boast instructors at the top of their profession.[2] In any case, parents themselves did not see the utility of grammar school attendance for their children: even bourgeois families willingly waited to have their sons enroll at the Jesuit "college" at Rennes.

Since the Grignions settled in the countryside of Iffendic in 1675, their children did not attend any grammar school. Only the boys were sent to the college at Rennes; the girls did not receive any instruction of their own.

The infants of Montfort were quite naturally caught up in the circumstances of the parish. They grew up within the daily lives of their parents, their godparents, their cousins; they accompanied them from an early age to church, to religious confraternities,[3] on "voyages."[4] They witnessed the extraordinary reception the town of Montfort gave to the poor pilgrims of Monsieur saint Méen.[5] Most homes were illiterate, and only rarely could the faith be passed on other than orally. The usual place for religious instruction was the parish church. At Sunday and feast day morning masses, a priest specially commissioned by the bishop gave the "homily," a catechism in the form of questions and answers, instead of the sermon. This had the additional advantage of simultaneously catechizing parents and adults.[6]

For reasons that are not altogether clear, the clergy did not admit children to confession and communion until they were fifteen. Rarely were those younger than this given the sacraments even if they were on the point of death: at best, the priest assisting them gave a simple blessing rather than Extreme Unction. Perhaps this was attributable to Jansenism, or to belief in the prolonged innocence of infants.

On the subject of confirmation, the parochial archives in Montfort as well as in Iffendic are silent. This does not mean that the seventeenth century bishops of Saint-Malo, who often visited the region, did not regularly confirm parishioners, but the lists and other written evidence are missing.

II. THE HISTORY OF THE GRIGNIONS

1. The Huguenot ancestors

The roots of the Grignions can be traced to Loudun (Poitou). From the end of the sixteenth century, the Grignions form what amounts to a family-held corporation of butchers, which divides into two enemy branches after the death of Calvin in 1534. One branch remained faithful to Catholicism, while the other (the richer and more important branch) only partially recanted after the successive persecutions following the Revocation of the Edict of Nantes; the more fortunate members of this branch found refuge in London.[7]

2. The Grignions of Montfort

The Grignions of Montfort had always displayed a remarkable ability to distinguish themselves from other Grignons, by the second "i" in their surname, by not palatalizing the "g," and by calling themselves "Grinion," exactly like their Huguenot relatives in London. This may have enabled the members of the Reformed branch of the family to distinguish themselves from the members of the Catholic branch.

Charles Grignion (1579-1630), baptised in the Protestant church of

Loudun in 1579, settled in Montfort-la-Cane (Brittany) in 1605, the very year in which Montfort and Loudun became the domain of the young Henri de la Trémoille (1598-1649), godson of Henry IV; he was raised in the Reformed religion. After the death of his father in 1604 he had become duke of Thouars and count of Loudun.

We cannot determine, for lack of precise documentation, whether Charles Grignion recanted his Protestant beliefs prior to or after his arrival in Montfort. We do know that he quickly assumed the position of royal notary for the county of Montfort. On September 8, 1606, he was admitted to the *Frairie Blanche (The White Brotherhood)*. However, no doubt because of his Huguenot youth, he was never fully accepted by the ultra-traditional bourgeoisie of Montfort. He never, therefore, became a godfather.

In 1611, he had married Louise Lechat (1593-1658), a completely illiterate woman but a member of the best branch of the local bourgeoisie, which had produced a great number of priests.

Eustache Grignion (1620-1669), their son, royal notary, baliff of several seignorial jurisdictions, mayor of Montfort and deputy to the States of Brittany, would have been ennobled by his position as collector general for the county of Montfort, had he not died prematurely at the age of forty-nine. He was the formidable Grignion. With his marriage in 1645 to Jacquemine Saulnier (1621-1683), he allied himself with what the county of Montfort considered the highest branch of the bourgeoisie and the lower nobility of regional squires. Through the Saulniers, the Grignions of Montfort gained the esteem of the bishops of Saint-Malo, residing near Paimpont in the principality, created by royal prerogative, of Saint-Malo-de-Baignon.

Jean-Baptiste Grignion (1647-1716), their son, in 1672 married Jeanne Robert (1649-1718), of a Rennes family whose members could be termed "saintly." He was a minor attorney at the court of Montfort but Jean-Baptiste's true vocation was that of a manager. Criticized by the clergy of Montfort for his authoritarian management style, he retired to Iffendic in the manor house of Bois Marquer. He had inherited from the Saulniers an impetuous and thin-skinned temperament, from which his family sometimes suffered. However, he managed not to shroud the household in too much gloom. As for Louis Grignion's relationship with his father, we should note the admiration that Louis held for him, to the point that while a young student at Rennes he imitated the paternal signature.

It has been established that Louis Grignion was very early taken into the charge of the Roberts of Rennes. After having been wet-nursed, he came to the family home at Bois Marquer in 1678; he left the village for Rennes in 1682. At that point the young boy was educated by his maternal uncle, Alain Robert. Even when his parents settled in Rennes in 1686, the young student was more influenced by the Roberts than by his often absent father. Nonetheless Louis himself admitted that he had inherited from the Grignions a temperament that tended to be excessively violent. His uncle Félix Grignion took this violence to an extreme:[8] his elder son, first cousin to Saint Louis, was condemned to death for premeditated murder.[9] In addition, two of his nephews became embroiled with the law, for desertion from the army and fraud.[10]

Louis wrote to his mother in 1704: *"I know that I owe you and my father a great debt of gratitude for bringing me into the world, for looking after me, bringing me up in the fear of God, and for all the other good things you have done for me"* (L 20).

III. Marriage and Family in the Writings of Montfort

1. Writings and missionary catechism

His writings are certainly not the sole or even the primary source for Montfort's thoughts on such fundamental aspects of life as Christian marriage and the family. Montfort himself admits that he has put into writing what he was in the habit of teaching during his popular missions. His vision of marriage and the family is essentially evangelical: he does not hesitate to remind his listeners that, whatever their condition in life, baptism necessarily carries with it a call to perfection. His sermons, like his writings, were not reserved for the souls of the elite. If his writings require from the reader (as they certainly do)—a depth of which not all Christians are capable—it is no less certain that Montfort has the evangelical boldness to remind the simplest members of his audience as well as the elite that all of the baptized are called to holiness.

Montfort's writings on marriage and family are to be interpreted in the light of his apostolate. During his parish missions, Montfort preached to children, young girls, young boys, men, women, and even soldiers in garrison towns. This missionary method resulted in writings that, when removed from their missionary context, sometimes appear to be independent of each other. These apparent paradoxes are particularly conspicuous in the popular genre that Montfort adopted, the hymn. Thus, in Hymn 12 entitled *"The Beauty of Virginity,"* he upheld the preeminence of the state of virginity over that of the sacrament of marriage; one of his purposes was to create or strengthen religious vocations by showing that dedicated virginity for the kingdom is a life of even greater fulfillment than the married state. In the margin of stanza 25 St. Louis Marie gives the *18th reason* for this preeminence: *"The folly and the evils of those who marry."* The stanzas under this heading consider negative aspects of marriage, well known to the married women of the time: *"What does one lose in marraige? / Will I say the truth?* [another copy of this hymn has: *One loses virginity*] */ In marriage one becomes a slave, / One* *loses tranquillity; / Ourselves we sully and we embrace / And often do we lose grace"* (H 12, 26); *"My companion will marry, / She fills me with pity! / I would rather lose life, / Even though someone swear friendship with me. / Women laugh at me for this and challenge me; / I am free, she's a slave"* (H 12, 27); *"I'm a woman and I am wise, / I avoid a great torment, / House and children are no prize, / Nor a husband who's discontent"* [another copy of this verse has: *"No children, no housework / nor a jealous husband"*] (H 12, 18).

And then the missionary adds in the margin of verse 29 a couplet to insure that his rustic language is not misunderstood: *"Marriage is not an evil"* and he sings: *"I do not maintain the view / That marriage is evil: / If God asks it of you, / Join with someone who's your equal . . ."* (H 29).

2. The family, material possession of fortune

On the sacrament of marriage and the Christian home, Montfort's missionary activity and related writings clearly conform to the traditional catechism of his time. It should however be noted that the saint emphasizes the importance of collective spiritual experience in the Christian home. When he speaks of the perfect practice of true devotion to Mary (SM 29), Montfort writes: *"We should choose a special feastday on which to give ourselves. Then, willingly and lovingly and under no constraint, we consecrate and sacrifice to her unreservedly our body and soul. We give to her our material possessions, such as house, family, income . . ."*

3. Mystical wedding

Montfort excels in giving a spiritual interpretation to marriage and the family. He summarizes perfect consecration to Jesus through the hands of Mary with this formula: *"in other words, it is the perfect renewal of the vows and promises of holy baptism"* (TD 120, 126). The baptized are a vital part of the divine family, and God is the Father of the family (SM 37). *"God the Father imparted to Mary his fruitfulness as far as a mere creature was capable of receiving it, to enable her to bring forth his Son and all the members of his mystical body"* (TD 17). *"It was with her, in her and of her that he produced his masterpiece, God-made-man, and that he produces every day until the end of the world the members of the body of this adorable Head . . ."* (VD 20). The mystical Body is thus presented as the brothers and sisters of the first-born Son of Mary, virgin and mother: a fundamentally Trinitarian montfort vision.

But Montfort's concept of spirituality is incomplete without the primary reference to Jesus Christ, *"Eternal Wisdom incarnate."* In Montfort's thinking, *"possessing and maintaining Wisdom"* and *"uniting with Jesus Christ through the hands of Mary"* are expressions that are more or less equivalent. This doctrine leads to the mystical wedding between the soul and divine Wisdom, a quest that Montfort's personal experience convinced him was accessible even to a very young child: *"Whoever wishes to find this precious treasure of Wisdom should, like Solomon, search for him, a) early and, if possible, while still young; b) purely and spiritually as a chaste young man seeks a bride; c) unceasingly, to the very end, until he has found him. It is certain that Eternal Wisdom loves souls so much that he even espouses them, contracting with them a true, spiritual marriage which the world cannot understand"* (LEW 54).

M. Sibold

IV. Spirituality of the Family Today

The attitude and thoughts of Montfort on the subject of family and marriage make evident that there are differences between his time and ours. And the fundamental difference is that in Montfort's time the family was sacrosanct, and today it is threatened by grave dangers, such as rampant divorce, abortion, drugs, radical feminism, same sex "marriages," etc. Although the spirituality of marriage has so beautifully flowered through the efforts of Vatican II—whose authentic teachings on this and all other points Montfort would surely uphold—there are some interesting insights of the saint on this subject which are still relevant today. His thoughts must, however, be placed within the context of contemporary theology in harmony with the Second Vatican Council.

1. The turning point of Vatican II

Certainly the ecclesiastical magisterium has always fought the tendency to discredit conjugal life.[11] Nonetheless, the exaltation of monastic life had in some areas made it appear, sad to say, that marriage was a second-rate vocation. CCC explains the Church's teaching: "Both the sacrament of Matrimony and virginity for the Kingdom of God come from the Lord himself. It is he who gives them meaning and grants them the grace which is indispensable for living them out in conformity with his will. Esteem of virginity for the sake of the kingdom and the Christian understanding of marriage are inseparable and they reinforce each other." The Catechism then quotes Saint John Chrysostom: "Whoever denigrates marriage also diminishes the glory of virginity. Whoever praises it makes virginity more admirable and resplendent. What appears good only in comparison with evil would not be truly good. The most excellent good is something even better than what is admitted to be good."[12]

The Constitution *Lumen Gentium* devotes chapter V to the "call of the whole Church to holiness," ruling out a monopoly by any category of the faithful, and explicitly mentioning "married couples and Christian parents" among those who are sanctified through their vocation.

In *Gaudium et Spes* it is affirmed that conjugal love "is caught up into divine love and is governed and enriched by Christ's redeeming power and the saving activity of the Church" (GS 48). That is why, in matrimonial life, the husband and wife "increasingly advance their own perfection, as well as their mutual sanctification, and hence contribute jointly to the glory of God" (GS 48—the entire number is important for a contemporary understanding of married love).

The term "domestic church" or "little church," used by the Fathers and revived by Vatican II to designate the family, is of great significance. Not only does it declare that marriage is the privileged "sign" and "place" of participation in and manifestation of the mystery of God's charity, but it also confers on the family an explicit ecclesial dimension. Thus, the family is not simply a "part" of the Church, but a "place" where the Church expresses Herself in a specific way and, in a sense, in Her totality.[13] The Christian family is, therefore, called to be a living Gospel for contemporary secularized society.

Vatican II ushered in a new period for conjugal and family spirituality, to which the magisterium of the pope and bishops is still contributing. Several movements in conjugal spirituality (like "Marriage Encounter") have flowered from the Council's clarification of marriage and the family.

2. Pathways for experiencing Montfort's spirituality of the family

Montfort's preferred manner of expressing spiritual realities is through the language of love, most especially marital love. He recognizes, then, that marriage is a disclosure of God, a privileged means of discovering the full meaning of the reality that "God is love" (1 Jn 4:16).

Saint Louis Marie believed that all Christian couples are called to experience married life in the light of the wedding at Cana, to which Jesus and his mother were invited (H 146,2). The presence of Christ and Mary in the Christian family indicates that family life with all of its joys and difficulties is to be lived in light of Gospel values. With their salvation in mind, Montfort insists on the unity of the married couple and on their loving sharing (H 109), implicitly suggesting that there is a spiritual path common to husband and wife. The Christian family that is consecrated to Christ through the hands of Mary must live this reality by clarifying, developing, and applying to itself several essential elements that are particularly dear to Montfort.

a. Family Consecration. First and foremost, the saint invites his readers to consecrate themselves to Jesus through Mary as slaves of love. Especially in light of the attention given to the family occasioned by the "Year of the Family" (1994) and the directives of the Holy See concerning family life, consecration should not only involve individuals as such but also the families and communities they form.

Even if Montfort were aware of collective consecrations (Louis XIII had consecrated all of France to Mary in 1638), he never mentions them in his works. On the contrary, he insists on the *"consecration of oneself to Jesus Christ, Wisdom incarnate, through the hands of Mary"* (LEW 223), that is, the eternal, total gift of an individual.

When, therefore, he insists that consecration is *"a perfect renewal of the vows and promises of holy baptism,"* his underlying assertion is that consecration represents a mature and responsible Christianity. Whereas in baptism the Christian engagement is made indirectly and unconsciously by means of the godparents, in other words *"by proxy,"* in consecration *"we give ourselves personally and freely and we are fully aware of what we are doing"* (TD 126). For Montfort, consecration is the offering of one's life to Christ, by the example of Mary and under her guidance, an offering that proceeds from the heart of the person who makes it. In his realistic and straightforward language—springing from love realities—he calls this consecration *"voluntary slavery,"* which is the greatest glory, because it represents a free choice of God, *"who looks into the heart and wants it to be given to him. Is he not indeed called the God of the heart. . . ?"* (TD 70).

Does this exclude consecration of the family? Far from it. Montfort includes the family in personal consecration, because he considers the family one of the *"possessions"* belonging to each person (SM 29; cf. TD 121). Offering the family to Jesus through Mary means that one submits one's family to the will of God and commits oneself to living within the family in accordance with the Gospel (cf. in TD 158-265, the interior practices of consecration). Leaving aside the question of the legitimacy of collective consecration, which implies engagement in the name of others or at least a prayer of intercession on their behalf,[14] Montfort falls decidedly on the side of personal consecration. As a result, following his line of thought, we must aim for a consecration of the family in which each family member personally undertakes to live an authentic Marian spirituality, adequately prepared to understand the nature and demands of such a life (TD 227-235). A family consecration made corporately presumes this individual consecration of each member.

If a family were to achieve this ideal it is clear that the consecration would assume a communitarian dimension: no longer a solitary, interior path, but one shared by the family, a "domestic church" engaged in giving witness to Christ in a secularized world. This is what Montfort calls *"joint salvation"* (H 146,9): the family *as family* working out its salvation, experiencing *as family* the total and irrevocable gift of self through Mary.

And even if the consecration is pronounced by only one spouse, and even if only by some but not by all the children of the family, the family is certain to experience the wonderful effects of the loving consecration for, de facto, the family is formally given over to Christ by the hands of Mary. This not only enhances the intercession of Mary for the entire family, but may also lead other family members to renew their baptismal promises through our Lady. The transformation this means for family life are evident.

b. Participating in the dynamic love of Christ Wisdom for humanity. There is in Wisdom, Montfort reveals, a dynamic, condescending love that leads Him to the most radical kenosis: *"Eternal Wisdom went so far as to become man, even to become a little child. . . . He hides himself under the appearance of a small piece of bread. . ."* (LEW 70-71). This logic of self-abasement and self-sacrifice is put into a context of ineffable love: *"The bond of friendship between Eternal Wisdom and man is so close as to be beyond our understanding. Wisdom is for man and man is for Wisdom"* (LEW 64).

Montfort cannot describe this interpersonal link between Wisdom and humanity without recourse to the symbolism of marriage: *"Eternal Wisdom loves souls so much that he even espouses them, contracting with them a true, spiritual marriage. . ."* (LEW 54). Humanity, in turn, cannot refrain from responding in love, which ends in an irrevocable gift of the heart (LEW 132), after a daily search *"as a chaste young man seeks a bride"* (LEW 54).

This interpersonal, loving encounter has a clear value for all of the Church and all of its members (cf. Ph 3:7-8; Rm 8:39; 2 P 3:18), but its sacramental sign is offered by marriage: *"This is a great mystery, and I am applying it to Christ and the church"* (Ep 5:32). To experience existentially the great mystery of the nuptial sacrament, the married couple should be urged to contemplate the history of Wisdom in His love for mankind. In this light, the couple—as sacrament of the love of Incarnate Wisdom for the Church—will live in mutual rapport and support. This is the logic of Wisdom that we find in Montfort and that he experienced in his relationship with the Church and with the poor of his time: to be *with* and *for* others. Conjugal spirituality must adopt similar language, especially if the married couple embraces the consecration to Christ Wisdom as proposed by Montfort.

The theological and spiritual importance of the example of Wisdom for married Christians is inescapable. On the basis of such a paradigm, their behavior, tempted to conform to prevalent worldly myths about power, fashion, possessions, egotism, will have to change radically, drawing its inspiration from the path of Wisdom, from the outpouring divine love.

c. Life of fidelity to Mary within the covenant with God. Montfort calls the act of consecration to Christ through the hands of Mary a *"covenant contract made with God"* (CG, TD 127). This expression quite naturally echoes the language of marriage and in fact the renewal of the marriage vows would be a welcome addition to Montfort's formula of consecration when prayed by couples. The relationship or covenant of God with his people, in accordance with the Biblical vision of Hosea and afterwards, is interpreted to be that of a spouse. It implies God's faithful love, a love that remains faithful even when the people desert Him and betray Him by idolatry.

The problem of remaining faithful to the covenant continues to be a difficult one for Christians, as Montfort noted in his day: *"We have had too many sad experiences of our fickleness and natural thoughtlessness. Let us be distrustful of our own wisdom and fervor"* (LEW 221). Even if husband and wife pronounce themselves faithful until death, a moment arrives when all is brought into question; the marriage risks failure, and often effectively ends. What does Montfort offer as a remedy for human inconstancy?

For the missionary saint there is a special means of attaining evangelical fidelity: daily life in harmony with the Mother of the Lord, and therefore in intense union with Christ her Son. *"This devotion, if well practiced, not only draws Jesus Christ, Eternal Wisdom, into our soul, but also makes it agreeable to him and he remains there to the rest of our life"* (LEW 220). Montfort's words bear a tone of certainty: continual union with Mary and adherence to her example and her maternal work represent *"a wonderful means of persevering in the practice of virtue and of remaining steadfast"* (TD 173).

This conviction stems from the very existence of Mary and her place in the history of salvation. *"She stands alone as the Virgin most faithful to God and to men. . . ; and she still keeps watch every day, with a special care, over all those who have placed themselves entirely under her protection and guidance"* (LEW 222). Montfort readily returns to this definition of Mary: *"Mary is the Virgin most faithful. . . . She obtains fidelity to God and final perseverance for those who commit themselves to her"* (TD 175). For Montfort, the roots of human infidelity are presumption, self-sufficiency, self-confidence (TD 173). As a result, men and women test their fragility and fall back on the worldly wisdom. Marian spirituality is an education in the mystical life, because it compels us to give primacy to the grace of God, and to place ourselves wholly in the hands of Mary, to be guided like her by the Spirit. With her prayers and her fidelity at every trial we face, Mary helps us every day to say "Yes" to Jesus.

Mary especially fulfills her maternal role in the sufferings and the crosses that accompany family life. In sickness, in lack of understanding between parents and children, the invocation of Mary and her presence give comfort and strength. She does not protect us from the crosses (SM 22) that are the normal consequences of human life and our journey in Christ's steps; rather she brings help and consolation with which to confront our crosses with courage: *"Oh Christians, do not grieve, / But call for Mary's aid. / Your pain she will relieve / Your faith in her repaid"* (H 80:3).

The consecration spirituality of Saint Louis de Montfort, no more than any spirituality, can not of itself be considered a panacea to cure all the family's ills. But it is, nonetheless, a sure road toward important objectives.

Pius XII recommended that families consecrate themselves to the Immaculate Heart of Mary, and noted its effects: "This act of piety will be for the married couple a precious spiritual aid in the practice of the duties of chastity and conjugal fidelity; it will ensure an atmosphere of purity in the home as children become older; what is more, the family that is invigorated by its devotion to Mary will become a living cell of apostolic force and renewal."[15]

P. Burrascano

Notes: (1) On the faith of his first biographer, Grandet, sucessive biographers of Louis Grignion have not hesitated to affirm that he "added the name of Marie on his confirmation day, as a mark of his attachment to the Blessed Virgin." There is nothing to this. We have several signatures of the young Louis, when he was a student with the Jesuits at Rennes; they invariably consist of his single baptismal name, "Louis." He will continue this practice until well after his ordination for the priesthood. It appears that the first time he signs his name "Louis-Marie" occurs in December 1703, at the professional registry of Mont-Valérien. This is a considerable time after his presumed confirmation date. (2) Mathurin-Allain Régnier, cousin of Saint Louis de Montfort, an odd priest who performed missionary work for a time with Father Mulot and his group, had been named "scholastic" of Montfort in 1699, and again in 1721, but dismissed before the expiration of his triennium as schoolmaster for having drawn his salary without ever having held class, "being absent most of the time." (3) In the three parishes of Montfort in the seventeenth century there were numerous confraternities, all of them charitable rather than pious in their aims. Among these, the oldest was the "Pure Confraternity," founded in 1431 in honor of the Nativity of Mary. (4) "Voyages" were pilgrimages to a holy place, whether near or far or indeed in the same parish. It is in this sense that a celebrated hymn of Montfort's composition must be understood; it begins, *"When I go on a voyage / With my stick in hand . . ."* (5) Located some leagues from Montfort, the fountain of saint Méen attracted pilgrims from all over the region, and indeed from abroad. Its water was reputed to cure "slave sickness," a skin malady that caused eruptions similar to those of leprosy. In order to have any hope of cure, the pilgrim of "monsieur saint Méen" was obliged to undertake this "voyage" in voluntary poverty, on foot, assuming the covering and lodging of a beggar, at least in the initial stages. Day after day these pilgrims became true indigents. They travelled as a group, and a considerable number died en route. The town of Montfort estimated that in 1633 more than 20,000 of them spent a night in the Hospital of Saint-Nicholas or in private homes. This sizable influx of the voluntarily destitute had brought about a large charitable movement on the part of the local population. (6) The bishops of Saint-Malo, in the course of their successive canonical visits, had insisted on this form of catechism that brought parents and children together. (7) Among these Huguenot Grignions, who were originally from Loudun and had settled in London after the Revocation of the Edict of Nantes, we shall mention: Daniel Grignion (1684-1763), watchmaker, who had three sons: 1. Thomas Grignion (1713-1784), reputable watchmaker and one of the first members of the London Society of Arts; 2. Reynolds Grignion (+ 1787), engraver; 3. Charles Grignion (like the ancestor of Saint Louis de Montfort) (1717-1810), engraver; Thomas Grignion, Jr., watchmaker; Charles Grignion, Jr. (1754-1801), painter of talent. (8) He will be imprisoned at Rennes for malpractice, in his position as community collector for the town of Montfort. (9) Jean-Mathurin Grignion (born in 1692), together with Antoine Elliot (another cousin of saint Louis), had assassinated squire Hubert de la Massue, gentleman of Redon, south of Rennes in 1722 in order to rob him. They were both condemned to torture on the wheel in absentia. (10) These were Félix Grignion (born in 1724) and Louis-Constant Grignion (1732-1793). The latter was a former student at the Seminary of the Holy Spirit in Paris, treated with veneration as the nephew of the great missionary on his admission; an "apostolic reader," an extravagant and megalomaniacal man, he was called the "abbot of Bois-Marquer" although he never attained holy orders. (11) "If anyone condemn human marriage and abominate the procreation of children, as the Manicheans and Priscillians, let them be anathema": Council of Braga in Portugal, of 561, DB, n. 461. Against the Armenians: "they say that concupiscence of the flesh is a sin and an evil, and that parents, even Christians, when they unite in the conjugal act, are committing a sin. . . , because in their view the matrimonial act is a sin, even within marriage. . ." (Decree of Benedict XII, in 1341). (12) CCC 1620; St. John Chrysostom, *De virg.* 10,1: PG 48, 540. The Catechism's entire sections on marriage and the family should be studied in order to grasp the contemporary teaching of the Church on these important points. (13) Cf. G. Volta, *La famiglia communità di Chiesa (The Family, Community of the Church)* in *Rivista diocesana di Mantova* 54 (1973) 230. (14) On collective consecration, cf. S. De Fiores, *Consacrazione (Consecrations),* in NDM 394-417; A. Rum, *Consécrations collectives à Marie (Collective Consecrations to Mary),* in CM, no. 137 (1983), 107-117; A. Bossard, *Consécration,* in *Voici ta Mère. Petit vocabulaire marial (Here is Your Mother. A short Marian Vocabulary),* in CM, no. 116 (1979), 17-19; A. Bossard, English translation: *Consecration* in *Dictionary of Mary,* Catholic Book Publishing Co., New York 1985, 53-57. J. de Sainte-Marie, *Réflexions sur un acte de consécration: Fátima, 13 mai 1982 (Reflections on an Act of Consecration: Fatima, May 13, 1982),* in Mar 44 (1982), 88-142. (15) Pius XII, Encyclical, *"The Pilgrimage to Lourdes,"* 2-7-1957.

FIDELITY

SUMMARY

I. WHAT IS FAITHFULNESS?:
   1. Human faithfulness;
   2. Divine faithfulness.

II. THE PATH FROM INFIDELITY TO FAITHFULNESS:
   1. Our essential infidelity;
   2. What Montfort requires:
      a. Baptismal promises,
      b. Mary, the path of faithfulness,
      c. The life of a consecrated person.

III. MARY, FAITHFUL VIRGIN:
   1. Faithfulness to God;
      a. Complete obedience,
      b. Motivated by love;
   2. Mary's faithfulness toward her servants:
      a. Safeguarding the deposit,
      b. Always ready to help,
      c. Unceasing presence.

IV. CURRENT RELEVANCE:
   1. Faithfulness in crisis;
   2. The path of faithfulness put forward by Montfort.

In the profile Montfort designs for the Christian consecrated to Christ through Mary, a long list would be needed to describe the qualities he includes. Among them, however, faithfulness is quite prominent. Its radical character gives it priority over all the others. Faithfulness is so basic, it must permeate everything. Nothing can be valid without it. This is why from the very start of his commitment, aware of his infidelity (*"ungrateful and unfaithful as I am"*), the Christian puts himself in Mary's hands in order to guarantee his faithfulness: "*Unfaithful sinner that I am, I renew . . . in your hands the vows of my baptism; . . . and I give myself totally to Jesus Christ, Incarnate Wisdom, so I may take up my cross and follow Him every day of my life so that I might be more faithful to Him than I have been up till now*" (LEW 225). Yet Montfort does not define here or elsewhere what faithfulness is, for his aim is not to give a theoretical explanation. He gives, rather, a description of the behavior of a faithful soul. Thus, *"taking up my cross and following Him all the days of my life"* is one element of faithfulness, even though the word itself is not used. Continued faithfulness is perseverance.

I. WHAT IS FAITHFULNESS?

Relating faithfulness and perseverance reveals both their uniqueness and what they have in common.

1. Human faithfulness

By itself, even if it does not exclude it, the word "faithfulness" does not contain the idea of duration or continuance.[1] Endurance itself is not faithfulness. One does not speak of the faithfulness of a halogen lamp, even though it might last for 2000 hours. Material things are alien to faithfulness, since it essentially contains a cognitive element. It can be found with animals who know their master and feel affection for him. Yet it is with human beings that faithfulness assumes its full meaning, because they are endowed with knowledge and freedom. It is with human beings that the duration-continuance element comes in, even if faithfulness cannot be limited to it. "Faithfulness is only understood as part of a starting option that can take on various appearances, depending upon the context. We are faithful to a promise, to a plan, to a commitment, to our word. Faithfulness, then, appears, in one sense, as steadfastness, as staying permanently with a choice that has been made."[2]

2. Divine faithfulness

Father de Montfort speaks several times of the "*faithful*" God: "*God infinitely faithful*" (L 7), "*Faithful to all His promises*" (H 7:3), "*faithful to His word*" (H 7; 77), and we should therefore *"hope in God so faithful"* (H 28:8). Although in Saint Louis Marie's writings the explicit term "faithfulness" is not used in connection with God, it is implied throughout his works and most especially in relation to Mary: *"Because God has decided to begin and accomplish His greatest works through the Blessed Virgin ever since He created her, we can safely believe that He will not change His plan in the time to come, for He is God and therefore does not change in His thoughts or His way of acting"* (TD 15).

"A God of faithfulness" (Deut 32:4). Over and over again the Bible calls God faithful; without number are the proofs of His faithfulness. He cannot be unfaithful without denying His very nature. All His attributes converge in this faithfulness by the very reason of His simplicity.

God cannot make a promise and then not keep it. God's faithfulness, then, is the foundation of our hope. "*I draw all my riches / From a God full of truth / Faithful to all His promises / In time and in eternity*" (H 7:3). Montfort repeats the thought of Hosea: "I will betroth you to me in faithfulness" (Hos 2:21).

II. The Path from Infidelity to Faithfulness

Montfort is vitally interested in the Christian's transition from infidelity to faithfulness. The knowledge he had of human beings and his vocation as an itinerant preacher permitted him to draw a realistic portrait of human infidelity, the *terminus a quo* of the journey into the faithfulness of God.

1. Our essential infidelity

The third of the basic truths of devotion to the Blessed Virgin is set forth in this way: "*The sin of Adam has almost entirely spoiled and soured us, filling us with pride and corrupting every one of us, just as leaven sours, swells and corrupts the dough in which it is placed. The actual sins we have committed, whether mortal or venial, even though forgiven, have intensified our base desires, our weakness, our inconsistency and our evil tendencies, and have left a sediment of evil in our soul*" (TD 79). In speaking thus of weakness and inconsistency, Montfort shows how our frail faithfulness actually is making it very difficult "*to keep the graces and treasures we have received from God. We carry this treasure, which is worth more than heaven and earth, in fragile vessels [2 Cor 4:7], that is, in a corruptible body and in a weak and wavering soul which requires very little to depress and disturb it*" (TD 87). For all these reasons, "*it is difficult to persevere in holiness*" (TD 89). This is why devotion to Mary is a safeguard against this weakness and inconstancy, provided we meet all the conditions of genuine devotion. For, being devout "*in fits and starts*" means joining the number of those fake devotees unworthy of being counted "*among the servants of the Virgin most faithful, because faithfulness and constancy are the hallmarks of Mary's servants*" (TD 101).

2. What Montfort requires

What is required is contained in a very tightly knit passage: "*As all perfection consists in our being conformed, united and consecrated to Jesus it naturally follows that the most perfect of all devotions is that which conforms, unites and consecrates us most completely to Jesus. Now of all God's creatures Mary is the most conformed to Jesus. It therefore follows that, of all devotions, devotion to her makes for the most effective consecration and conformity to Him. The more one is consecrated to Mary, the more one is consecrated to Jesus*" (TD 120). There are three main conclusions that can be deduced from this statement.

a. Baptismal promises. The whole Christian life is built on this initial, fundamental act, which St. Justin calls a "bath of conversion," in which sinful man encounters Christ his Savior, who meets him with the power of his Resurrection, possessing him irrevocably. The baptized person must be faithful to this first Consecration and its constant deepening and maturing. As a practical preacher, Montfort asks himself: "*Does anyone keep this great vow? Does anyone fulfill the promises of baptism faithfully? Is it not true that nearly all Christians prove unfaithful to the promises made to Jesus in baptism? Where does this universal failure come from, if not from man's habitual forgetfulness of the promises and responsibilities of baptism and from the fact that scarcely anyone makes a personal ratification of the contract made with God through his sponsors?*" (TD 127). The enlightened zeal of the missionary touches on an essential point of every Christian renewal. It will be a new start based on the very foundations of the faith and the most authentic tradition, "*since the Councils, the Fathers of the Church, and many authors both past and present, speak of consecration to Our Lord or renewal of baptismal vows as something going back to* *ancient times and recommended to all the faithful"* (TD 131). When faced with this infidelity, the formula of his *"consecration of oneself to Jesus Christ, the incarnate Wisdom, through the hands of Mary"* explicitly leads to: *"I, an unfaithful sinner, renew and ratify today through you my baptismal promises. I renounce forever Satan, his empty promises, and his evil designs, and I give myself completely to Jesus Christ, the incarnate Wisdom"* (LEW 225).

b. Mary, the path of faithfulness. Giving oneself to the Blessed Virgin has for its purpose a greater faithfulness to the Lord. *"The more one is consecrated to Mary, the more one is consecrated to Jesus."* (TD 120) Marian devotion taught by Montfort consists, then, *"in giving oneself entirely to Mary in order to belong entirely to Jesus through her"* (TD 121). Among the numerous reasons he mentions for consecrating oneself to Jesus Christ through Mary, the eighth and last is that it *"is a wonderful means of persevering in the practice of virtue and of remaining steadfast."* Referring to what was said about Mary's faithfulness to her servants by watching over what they entrusted to her, Montfort repeats: *"By this devotion we entrust all we possess to Mary, the faithful Virgin. We choose her as the guardian of all our possessions in the natural and supernatural sphere. We trust her because she is faithful, we rely on her strength, we count on her mercy and charity to preserve and increase our virtues and merits in spite of the efforts of the devil, the world, and the flesh to rob us of them"* (TD 173). In a long hymn describing the moral code "of a man converted in a mission" and the man's everyday new life and social relationships, the missionary has his convert sing: *"I am a devotee of Mary, / She is my help and my support, / She is the glory of my life, / After God she is all I possess. / So I may be faithful to God, / I make everything depend on her"* (H 139:60). He often repeats this same thought: devotion to Mary assures fidelity to God. *"If someone wishes to be faithful, / Let him come to the Mother of gifts"* (H 151:1); *"Mary is my good Mother, / To whom I always run for help, / To support my wretchedness, / To placate God my Father, / It is through her that I hope / Ever to persevere"* (H 94:9).

c. The life of a consecrated person. Our Lady is the one who makes us faithful to our perfect baptismal Consecration. We need not always look for the terms "faithfulness" and "perseverance" themselves. *"Let us, so to speak, bring Mary into our abode by consecrating ourselves unreservedly to her as servants and slaves. Let us surrender into her hands all we possess, even what we value most highly, keeping nothing for ourselves. This good Mistress . . . will give herself to us in a real but indefinable manner"* (LEW 211). Mary's devotee has nothing to fear. *"Mary is faithful: she will not permit anything we give her to be lost or wasted. She stands alone as the Virgin most faithful to God and to man. She faithfully guarded and kept all that God entrusted to her, never allowing the least bit to be lost; and she still keeps* *watch every day, with a special care, over all those who have placed themselves entirely under her protection and guidance. Let us, then, confide everything to the faithful Virgin Mary, binding ourselves to her as to a pillar that cannot be moved, as to an anchor that cannot slip, or better still, as to Mount Zion which cannot be shaken"* (LEW 222). To show this faithfulness of Mary, Montfort turns to biblical images in which God's faithfulness is symbolized, like Mount Zion, and "the rock" (Ps 92:15). The true devotee of Mary is identical with the devout faithful Christian. The terms are interchangeable.

The life of a consecrated person is fidelity. Consecration is the absolute gift that goes as far as the Cross. It must not be forgotten that in the very act of Consecration, the one who hands himself over to Jesus through Mary includes the Cross: "*to follow Him by carrying my cross and to be more faithful to Him than I have been up to this point.*"

III. Mary, Faithful Virgin

The basis of Mary's faithfulness is her sharing in the life of God. While He is faithful by nature, Mary, as a creature, can only be so by grace. God made her so perfectly in His image that she shares in His faithfulness. Montfort points this out in an expression that may never have been heard with this meaning but which states the idea very well, "*Mary is the wonderful echo of God*" (SM 21), or in a even more admirable way: "*Mary is entirely relative to God. Indeed I would say that she is relative only to God, because she exists uniquely in reference to Him. She is an echo of God, speaking and repeating only God*" (TD 225).

1. Faithfulness to God

In a sentence that in principle contains all the further developments that he will add about Mary's faithfulness to God, Montfort studies the initial period of her life up to the Incarnation: "*During the first fourteen years of her life the most holy Virgin Mary grew so marvelously in the grace and wisdom of God and responded so faithfully to His love that the angels and even God Himself were filled with rapturous admiration for her*" (LEW 107). As the Immaculate Conception, faithfulness is a constituent element of her personality. Not only do we say Mary is virginal but we call her *the* Virgin or the Blessed Virgin, a personification of this quality to a unique degree. We are also prompted to say that Mary is not only faithful, but *the* faithful one, just as we say of Christ, "Jesus Christ, the faithful witness" (Rev 1:5), using the word not only as a designation but also as a personification of the name: "Then I saw heaven opened, and there was a white horse! its rider is called Faithful and True" (Rev 19:11). Montfort develops this idea of faithfulness by introducing into it the notion of "deposit" in order to illustrate its application. This deposit is a contract entered into by two physical or moral persons. One, the deponent, entrusts to the second, a faithful guardian or agent, something that he must watch over and give back on demand. God does not entrust Mary with a deposit **because** she is faithful. He makes her faithful in order for her to keep His deposit. It is in this sense that we should understand Montfort's assertion "*It is impossible on the one hand to put into words the gifts with which the Blessed Trinity endowed this most fair creature, or on the other hand to describe the faithful care with which she corresponded to the graces of her Creator*" (LEW 105).

a. Complete obedience. This response is an obedience to the will of God. It is the meaning of the faithful servant found in many Scripture passages. In the parable of the talents (Mt 25:20-29), the servants are praised for their faithfulness and not for what their faithfulness produced. Without further specifying her faithfulness, Montfort calls Mary many times "*the faithful spouse*" in speaking of her relationship to the Holy Spirit (TD 4, 5, 34, 36, 164, 269). In TD 53 she is called "*perfectly faithful to God.*"

b. Motivated by love. Faithfulness is quite different from merely doing what has to be done along the lines of a scrupulous personal accounting. It is, rather, a flowering of charity that from the outset knows no limits. It is the Beatitudes' insatiable hunger and thirst for righteousness. It is called generosity and magnanimity, and according to St. Thomas it "tends to a certain excellence."[3] Just as, by definition, virtue always consists of something difficult, that excellence which is the property of magnanimity aims at things that are still more difficult. Persevering in these endeavors brings the virtue of fortitude particularly to the fore.[4] In the Annunciation's *fiat,* the fullness of the gift of self and the commitment to the divine will were already present. As Vatican II states: "By full-heartedly espousing the divine will of salvation without any sin holding her back, Mary handed herself over completely, as the handmaid of the Lord, to the person and the work of her Son" (LG 56).

2. Mary's faithfulness toward her servants

It is especially with her servants that Montfort develops the theme of the many-sided faithfulness of Mary. He sums it up in this prayer of praise: *"Advocate ever near us in life and in death, we praise you"* (MP 12). It is an echo of the Hail Mary: "Pray for us now and at the hour of our death." Vatican II expresses the same idea when it says that the motherhood of Mary "continues without interruption until the final consummation of all the elect. . . . Her motherly love makes her attentive to the brothers of her Son whose pilgrimage is not yet over . . . until they reach the homeland of the blest. This is why the Blessed Virgin is invoked in the Church under the titles of advocate, helper, mediatrix" (LG 62). We find the same ideas and words in Montfort: "*They will experience her motherly kindness and affection for her children. They will love her tenderly and will appreciate how full of compassion she is and how much they stand in need of her help. In all circumstances they will have recourse to her as their advocate and mediatrix*" (TD 55). The term "mediatrix," and not only the description of her mediation, occurs often, for example in MP 11, LEW 223, and TD 86.

a. Safeguarding the deposit. The total Consecration of oneself is likened to a deposit entrusted to Mary. "*In adopting this devotion, we put our graces, merits and virtues into safe keeping by making Mary the depository of them. It is as if we said to her, 'See, my dear Mother, here is the good that I have done through the grace of your dear Son. I am not capable of keeping it. . . . But, most powerful Queen, . . . keep a guard on all my possessions lest I be robbed of them. I entrust all I have to you, for I know who you are, and that is why I confide myself to you. You are faithful to God and man*" (SM 40). The same idea appears in a different form in TD 87, where Montfort shows that, given our weakness and frailty, it is very hard for us to keep the treasures received from God; and as for those who have trusted only in themselves: "*If they had only known of the wonderful devotion that I shall later explain, they would have entrusted their treasure to Mary, the powerful and faithful Virgin. She would have kept it for them as if it were her own possession and even have considered that trust an obligation of justice*" (TD 88).

b. Always ready to help. Mary is not merely an occasional help, in times of calamities and extremes. Her aid is constant, like that of a mother, and even more so, for her children and their needs could never escape either her attention or her capabilities. In a paraphrase of the second part of the Hail Mary, Montfort sings: "*You are our Mother, / O worthy Mother of God, / Help our wretchedness / At all times and everywhere, / Pray for us, sinners. / Hide us under your wing, / Be now our support, / Give us a good death, / And everlasting glory*" (H 109:40). And in his *"New Song of Our Lady of Gifts"*: "*Mary possesses in her domain, / The fullness of all goods. / Near to her we have no cares, / Fellow Christians, / She overflows with good / For her own*" (H 151:3).Everything comes through her hands: "*She is the Mother of grace, / She is its wondrous channel, / It is through her that all good comes, / here on earth, / That everything ascends and returns / To paradise*" (H 151:4). And then: "*In her we find all things, / Possessions, pleasures, honors and good health. / all these things for God alone she bestows / With kindness. / Upon her care the universe relies, / in truth*" (H 151:5). The couplets that follow enumerate the petitions of certain kinds of devotees: the vine grower, that his vine abound in grapes, the plowman for his fields, the afflicted, the needy. "*You will receive her assistance / Through your petitions, / Or else the gift of patience. / One or the other*" (H 151:8). The devotee of Mary can in all confidence speak to her: "*In your bounty / Comfort me in my wretchedness. / In your bounty, / Give me long-suffering or good health. / In you alone do I hope, / Show me that you are my Mother,*[5] */ In your bounty*" (H 145:4).

*c. **Unceasing presence.*** Mary's presence can be looked at from two points of view: either from that of Mary herself, or from that of her devotee. That Mary is present to her children means that no one escapes her constant motherly attention. Some find this truth hard to grasp because they liken the role of Mary to that of an earthly mother who cannot follow her children about or cater to all their needs. A moment of distraction is enough for a baby to be in danger on the edge of a swimming pool or in the street. But Mary's mode of knowledge is that of the elect in heaven. In the contemplation of the Divine Essence, they know everything that concerns them in accordance with the degree of perfection proper to each one.[6] Now Mary, mother of all the redeemed, knows the needs of all her children. Mary is present to us in this sense, and we are present to her even before we bring her our prayers and our wants. "For your Father knows what you need before you ask Him" (Mt 6,8). There is no passage in his work where Montfort shows this motherly presence better than in TD 201 to 213, when he explains *"the services which the Virgin Mary . . . lovingly renders to her loyal servants"* (TD 201). "*She loves them tenderly, more tenderly than all the mothers in the world together. . . . She loves them not only affectively but effectively, that is, her love is active and productive of good*" (TD 202). Paraphrasing the story of Rebecca and Jacob, he multiplies the ever watchful attentions of Mary. "*Like Rebecca she looks out for favorable opportunities to promote their interests, to ennoble and enrich them.*" And he gives the theological reason mentioned above: "*Since she sees clearly in God all that is good and all that is evil; fortunate and unfortunate events; the blessings and condemnations of God. She arranges things in advance so as to divert evils from her servants and put them in the way of abundant blessings. If there is any special benefit to be gained in God's sight by the faithful discharge of an important work, Mary will certainly obtain this opportunity for a beloved child and servant and at the same time, give him the grace to persevere in it to the end*" (TD 203).

But Mary's presence still has a subjective sense. It is the devotee's awareness and acceptance of Mary's action in him. Montfort writes of the hardships presented by the spiritual life: "*It is true that on our way we have hard battles to fight and serious obstacles to overcome, but Mary, our Mother and Queen, stays close to her faithful servants. She is always at hand to brighten their darkness, clear away their doubts, strengthen them in their fears, sustain them in their combats and trials. Truly, in comparison with other ways, this virginal road to Jesus is a path of roses and sweet delights*" (TD 152). Mary's faithful presence will be the strength of the apostles of the end times, who "*will be the most assiduous in praying to the most Blessed Virgin, looking up to her as their perfect model to imitate and as a powerful helper to assist them*" (TD 46). This presence of Mary can attain a mystical degree. "*Should you not savor immediately the sweet presence of the Blessed Virgin within you, take great care not to torment yourself. For this is a grace not given to everyone, and even when God in His great mercy favors a soul with this grace, it remains none the less very easy to lose it, except when the soul has become permanently aware of it through the habit of recollection*" (SM 52).

IV. Current Relevance

1. Faithfulness in crisis

All agree in admitting that today's world is going through a crisis of fidelity.[7] The most sacred commitments, like priesthood and especially marriage, have experienced massive infidelity. Common-law unions, even if they are sometimes lasting, are on the increase out of fear of a stable commitment. Because faithfulness is excluded from the outset, they are merely an open door to camouflaged infidelity. Today an aberrant definition of faithfulness is prevalent: "faithfulness to oneself," which is strangely thought to justify all sorts of deviations of thought and behavior. Such an attitude forgets that faithfulness also carries with it an altruistic relationship with a "Thou," a very noble value that imposes the moral obligation of keeping one's promises.

Still more serious is the fact that infidelity can be seen in basic values that up to now had always been considered to be beyond question. This is not only happening on the social level but even in the realm of the faith. The profound reason for infidelity is clearly a crisis of faith. When faith disintegrates and becomes ephemeral, it no longer has sufficient dynamism to motivate faithfulness. Conscience has reached a state of vagueness and indifference, and makes choices in opposition to the faith. The language of faith is eroded, piety disappears, devotions are relegated to the archival dustheap. Mary no longer has her place. She is dragged into the global process of the dechristianization of our age, where a twofold phenomenon is being manifested.[8] On the one hand, *acedia,* which is the lack of interest in the spiritual when faced with the appeal of the new values of science and technology; and on the other, *anomia* which is the rejection of established laws and systems, where each person looks for an absolute autonomy of thought and social behavior.

2. The path of faithfulness put forward by Montfort

It is as a realist, and without any pessimism, that Montfort treats of faithfulness. What he requires of a person who wishes truly to live his Marian devotion is motivated by his human and pastoral experience, which is never content with superficial enthusiasm. "*It is not enough to give ourselves just once as a slave to Jesus through Mary; nor is it enough to renew that consecration once a month or once a week. That alone would make it just a passing devotion,*" hence one that is unfaithful. It is not only repetitive acts that must be performed. A spirit has to be created. "*The chief difficulty is to enter into its spirit, which requires an interior dependence on Mary, and effectively becoming her slave and the slave of Jesus through her.*" As an experienced spiritual director, he is well acquainted with the spiritual life and its frailties. "*I have met many people who with admirable zeal have set about practicing exteriorly this holy slavery of Jesus and Mary, but I have met only a few who have caught its interior spirit, and fewer still who have persevered in it*" (SM 44).

H. M. Guindon

Notes: (1) E. Partridge, *Origins: A Short Etymological Dictionary of Modern English,* Greenwich House, New York 1983. (2) M. Gourgues, *Le défi de la fidélité (The Challenge of Fidelity),* Coll. Lire la Bible 40, Cerf, Paris 1985, 11-12. (3) St. Thomas, *Summa Theologiae* 2-2, q. 129, a. 4 ad 2. (4) Ibid., a. 5 c. (5) From the "*Hail O Star of Ocean*": "*Show Thyself a Mother.*" (6) St. Thomas, *Summa Theologiae* 1, q. 12, a. 6 c. (7) It is shocking to read that "we must not be in too much of a hurry . . . to complain today about a 'crisis of faithfulness.' For example, it is quite easy to juggle the most alarming statistics on the rate of divorce and separation. But should we not be careful about idealizing the past as the lost age of faithfulness? We know quite well that external fidelity can be deceiving. For example, was there always faithfulness in marriage in those days when the social climate hardly allowed acting in any other way? . . . May we not think that at this moment faithfulness —not without great pain and difficulty, it is true—is in the process of changing its appearance by doing itself over on the basis of personal options and convictions?" (M. Gourgues, *Le défi,* 12) (8) Cf. R. Faricy, *L'anomie et la Croix* (Anomy and the Cross), in *L'Indifférence religieuse (Religious Indifference),* Coll. Le point théologique 41, Beauchesne, Paris 1983, 250.

FREEDOM

SUMMARY I. THE MEANING OF FREEDOM:

1. Freedom "from";
2. Freedom "to."

II. THE PARADOX: HOLY SLAVERY AND FREEDOM:

1. Freedom in the life of Montfort:
   a. Freedom through obedience,
   b. Freedom through poverty,
   c. Freedom through chosen apostolate,
   d. Freedom through Consecration as slave of Jesus through Mary;
2. Freedom in the writings of Montfort:
   a. Scriptural basis of freedom through slavery,
   b. Freedom through baptismal promises,
   c. Freedom in TD,
   d. Freedom in PM and RM.

III. RELEVANCE OF MONTFORT FREEDOM TODAY.

I. THE MEANING OF FREEDOM

Freedom entails both a negative and a positive relationship. Negatively, freedom means "being free from"; positively, freedom means "being free to." Both are essential to a balanced understanding of freedom.[1]

1. Freedom "from"

To declare that someone is free from everything and everyone—from human relationships, from all relation to the world, food, air, etc.—and still is a being in the world is an evident contradiction. Although discussion may take place on the necessary breadth and depth of these relationships, nonetheless human freedom demands being in dependence. Only God is, in the absolute sense, free "from."

By the very fact that man is a creature, his very being is a dynamic relationship to the Creator, from whom he is receiving existence. To divorce oneself—to "free" oneself—from God would mean not to turn into dust but to be resolved into nothingness. Even if someone may wish to sever this relationship, there is no possibility of doing so. Creation is an ongoing event; every speck of existence, including human beings, is being created. One's existence itself, therefore, stipulates this relationship to God. There is no metaphysical possibility of being "free from" God the Creator; dependence upon Him is the required condition of freedom itself.

In and through the Eternal Wisdom, God has not only created all things but re-created them in the redemptive Incarnation. Redemption is an ontological fact that, independent of man's acceptance or rejection, penetrates this universe. In the present order of things—and there is no other—God in and through the Incarnate Wisdom creates and sanctifies all things. Freedom, therefore, means dependence on Jesus, the Way, the Truth, and the Life. And this to such a point that all other openings towards the infinite, all relationships enhancing the fundamental relationship to the Father, however powerful and beautiful they may be—whether persons or events—must indispensably (although not necessarily consciously) be through the opening to the infinite, the God-man, Jesus the Christ. In the present order of things, all gifts, all graces, existence itself—and therefore all freedom—entails dependence on Jesus who enjoys the primacy over all.

Down through the centuries, this truth has been expressed by saying that God Alone is "aseity," which is to say that He alone is "of Himself" (*a se*), only He is absolute freedom. Creatures by definition are *ab alio*, i.e., from the Other Who comes to us in Christ Jesus.

Presuming this ontological dependence and the interdependence on others, each person enjoys a certain independence from other creatures inasmuch as each individual is a distinct "I." This "I," with its freedom of choice, can only be enhanced by a free and loving acceptance of the root source of human freedom, God. Freedom is in direct proportion to dependence on God. The saint, then, is truly free. Our Lady is the liberated woman. Lovingly and totally dependent on God, she is the model of independence. She is Our Lady of Freedom precisely because from the depths of her being she declares: "Behold the slave girl of the Lord; let it be to me according to your word" (Lk 1:38).

2. Freedom "to"

Freedom is also "freedom to." If we understand the nature of freedom, it is apparent that freedom is a dynamic gift of God, the Father of all, not so that we may willingly turn from Him and from others. Rather, freedom is to serve God and neighbor. To be in loving harmony with God and with His creation is to be in harmony with ourselves. "To possess oneself" is not to turn *within* in a narcissistic distortion but to turn *without,* to be ever more in harmony with freedom itself, God, and with all others who flow from His free choice to be "for us." The gift of freedom is the call to the human race to serve God and one another.

Saint Louis Marie de Montfort is not an abstract theologian. His doctrine may well presume the above, but it is not, as such, the object of his writing or preaching. His interests are existential or, better still, incarnational. In order to assure the freedom of his hearers, he preaches Holy Slavery of love. All the abstract theory is contained in a practical, understandable fashion in his preaching of the total Consecration to Wisdom Incarnate through Mary. The Gospel paradox of slave-freedom, dependent-free, is at the core of his apostolate to reform the Church and renew the face of the earth.

P. Gaffney

II. The Paradox: Holy Slavery and Freedom

It is by no means an original insight of Saint Louis Marie de Montfort that makes him proclaim that to be a slave of Jesus in Mary is to be truly free. What is original is his development of this truth into a spirituality that governs the whole of life.

The clearest development of freedom is found in the writings, rather than the life, of Montfort. Not, of course, because he did not live what he preached and wrote but because it is not always easy to interpret his actions specifically in relation to the writings. In other words, we must trust what is written by Montfort more than what is written by his biographers, and certainly more than is written by his hagiographers.

1. Freedom in the Life of Montfort

a. Freedom Through Obedience. Not only was Saint Louis Marie intent on doing the will of God, he was equally determined to see this divine will mediated through human instruments of ecclesiastical authority and spiritual directors, even when these were palpably misguided, humanly speaking, and where they caused him deep humiliation and frustration and ran counter to what he saw and desired as his true apostolate. The greatest sign of Montfort's sanctity, sanity, and balance is that not once did he claim some charismatic enlightenment that superseded all ecclesiastical authority. Eccentric his behavior certainly was in human reckoning, and at times he seemed to lack a certain political prudence in his approach to authority; but never did he defy it. Yet we can say that the Montfort who always sought spiritual direction always needed it. And this, far from detracting from his character, enhanced it. It must also be pointed out that Montfort's dependence on spiritual advice and his seeking for authoritative recognition were not symptoms of pusillanimity; on the contrary, he was a man of strong will, energy, initiative, and decision. Those devoid of confidence and ideas do not perform the heroic work Montfort did, nor do they found religious orders. Nor do they become canonized saints. Yet, by being obedient, Montfort was becoming free by divesting himself of self-will and placing himself at the disposal of God through God's appointed earthly authorities. Psychologically and spiritually, Montfort, by obeying, was freeing himself of the need to agonize over what was indeed God's will. This is the opposite of indecisiveness, and it is not the "soft option." Three examples from the life of Montfort illustrate his freedom through obedience.

- In PM 7, Montfort asks for "*priests who are free . . . without worldly goods, without even a will of their own.*" The freedom through obedience is akin to that through poverty; obedience is a radical poverty. The first great test of obedience was also, in a not too pleasant way, freedom. When Montfort was ordained in 1700, he found himself a priest with no diocese (that of his birth was St-Malo) and no faculties for preaching or hearing confessions. This must have been a humiliating situation, and an angering one. Three months after ordination, when Father Lévêque came to the rescue by asking Montfort to join his team of missionaries at Nantes, Louis Marie went immediately to his spiritual director, Father Leschassier, to ask permission. This was given with ominous alacrity. Leschassier was not merely glad to be rid of Louis Marie but suspected that the Nantes appointment would test him to the limit, which it did. But Louis Marie, instead of leaving for Nantes in anger and without a permission he did not canonically need, asked leave from one of those who left him lingering without work around Paris for three months, at a time when a young priest is on the threshold of his priestly life, full of faith, energy, and enthusiasm. When Montfort discovered the impossible situation at Nantes, instead of departing not from cowardice but from the best of motives, he wrote to Leschassier and waited a long time for him to reply. While waiting for an answer, Montfort was without any priestly ministry. He had done scarcely any priestly work in his first year as a priest. Spiritually, it was perhaps his most fruitful year. In this sensitive part of any priest's life, Montfort left himself *free,* not to do but to be "done to"—by God, through the strange behavior of those who should have provided for him. This year of "idleness" was, to this dynamic man, a great act of detachment. At this point, Louis Marie was treated with virtual contempt; not only was he dispensable but, to the authorities, disposable.

• The second incident that shows Montfort's attitude to obedience was his trek to Rome in 1706 after being summarily dismissed by the bishop of Poitiers from his diocese. The action may seem to be the opposite of obedience, in that Louis Marie was going over the bishop's head. Yet it shows that he had the presence of mind to see no conflict between his desire to minister and his desire to obey. What surer font of authority than the Pope? When he saw St. Peter's Basilica, he fell to the earth, shedding tears of joy, not because of its grandeur (he has some harsh things to say about that sort of thing); unlike the Apostles, who marvelled at the beauty of the Temple because of its splendor (Lk 21:5), Montfort revered St. Peter's because it was the seat of the supreme spiritual authority on earth. The saint accepted the Pope's refusal to let him go to Canada and accepted his mission to evangelize France and to be obedient to the bishops there. Yet Montfort needed this papal directive and afterwards felt the freedom that comes from doing not his own will but God's. Yet his decisiveness in going to the fount shows that obedience is freedom;

that meekness is the opposite of weakness.

• The third incident is classical—the building and demolition of the Calvary at Pontchâteau. When the huge construction was due to be blessed and opened on the feast of the Exaltation of the Cross, Montfort suffered the very opposite of exaltation at the episcopal order to dismantle what was the joy not only of Montfort but of the peasants who toiled for him and trusted him. "*Let us plant the cross in our hearts,*" he said.

This obedience is not the freedom of refusing responsibility but the freedom that comes from detachment from one's own will. Not exactly the freedom of humility but the freedom of relaxing because of knowing that one is on the right course. But the freedom came at a high price, as all freedom does. Ironically, Montfort's treatment by authority gave him that other freedom he demanded from his missionary priests—freedom from fixed and secure appointments.

b. Freedom through poverty. It is a scriptural truism that possessions enslave; we cannot be the slave of God and mammon. If we choose God, then money serves us, not we money. PM 7 makes explicit the equation between voluntary poverty and freedom: "*Priests who are free from everything . . . without worldly possessions to encumber them.*" Montfort's freedom through poverty and through detachment from the "*world*" (in the Johannine sense of forces hostile to spiritual growth) was expressed in a dramatic and clean-cut way in his departure from Rennes for Paris and Saint-Sulpice. "The event [saying goodbye to family] takes on deep symbolism at the bridge of Cesson on the outskirts of Rennes. Having left all, he crossed the Cesson bridge to a new life of total dependence upon Divine Providence."[2] This evangelical detachment, also found in PM ("*without father, mother, brothers, sisters*"), did not blind Montfort to his fraternal duties to his sister Louise, whose rescuer and guardian he was on at least two occasions, at considerable suffering and inconvenience. Detachment, in this sense, is a sacrifice, not an excuse. This event was a crossing of the Rubicon, and it marked not merely a decisive moment to become a priest but to become a certain kind of priest—utterly detached. The incident was saturated in irony: Louis Marie was going to the sophisticated metropolis, to the famed Saint-Sulpice with its mixed aura of sanctity and learning, not unmixed with an aristocratic flavor and gentility. Yet this lad from the provinces, far from being nervous and from dressing for the encounter, became deliberately less presentable than he had been in Rennes; he gave his father's hard-earned money to a beggar, parted with his spare tunic, and went even further, exchanging his garb with that of the next beggar: "Carry no purse, no bag, no sandals" (Lk 10:4). For he had, in a different sense, "wiped off from his feet the dust" (Lk 10:11) of

Rennes, of security. He had also changed from a boy to a man. Theatrical perhaps—nothing wrong in that, provided it is not an empty gesture—but radical. Montfort was free—to serve. Such poverty distanced him not only from money but from friendship, respect, and acceptance. Another irony: his father gave him money, thinking it a wise investment if his son gained a lucrative benefice. If only he had known not merely the future but the past; if only he had known his son.

Montfort's poverty did not lead to the independence of not being sponsored. Not only did he accept the spasmodic charity of Madame de Montespan but, unlike the "unjust steward," he was not ashamed to beg. But he also slaved for a pittance, performing even the macabre task of "watching the dead." Poverty, in its physical deprivation, far from being liberating, makes for servility. It drives one to crime, to prostitution, to the slavery of addictions that act as a brief escape from a harsh world. Montfort's poverty was voluntary and evangelical. It did not impoverish; it enriched. It enriched not only Montfort but others.

The depths of poverty came quickly after ordination in his post as chaplain to the poor house in Poitiers. Here he refused to accept the situation fatalistically, as the poor usually do; he set about putting order into chaos, demanding, almost with spiritual menaces, money from the wealthy in Poitiers. He could do all this, antagonizing so-called administrators of the hostel, because he himself was thoroughly detached from wealth and reputation but not at all detached from the poverty of others. His simplicity, his literal acceptance of the Gospel, is an effect, as well as a cause, of this freedom. The one affects the other—a virtuous, not vicious, circle. W includes, most naturally and without any affectation, the casual statement "*I have no private money belonging to me.*" Yet he makes a plea for the prudent provision of some who cannot live up to his ideals and who may leave the religious life, for example, Brothers John, James, and Mathurin. And there is nothing at all judgemental in this bequest. The emotional heart that beat for Mary bequeaths the physical heart to be buried "*under the step of the altar of the Blessed Virgin Mary.*" It will be stepped on, as was its earthly owner, who owned little else.

c. Freedom through chosen apostolate. The word "chosen" seems at odds with Montfort's freedom through detachment. But Montfort "chose" his apostolate in the sense that he chose deliberately to accept any apostolate he was given. In fact, Providence ordained that his ministry would prevent him ever anchoring himself or casting roots in any one place.[3] His description as a "vagabond" is ironic and paradoxical. For although Montfort was pushed here and there, he knew exactly where he was going. And his destination had nothing to do with geography nor with planning a specialized destiny. His PM gives more detail on this matter; but the wandering of Montfort was within the confines of northwest France, not in the endless plains and forests of Canada, where he felt a strong urge to go. He was "rootless" but never "restless" and must never be regarded as a patron for the religious who drifts from dream to dream unimpeded by reality. Montfort, though incredibly energetic and active in his ministry and in temperament, was responsibly passive in the way he allowed God to bounce him, through ecclesiastical superiors, from pillar to post. Therein lay his freedom. Geographically and specifically varied as his ministry was, from a decaying mission house in Nantes to a poor house in Poitiers and a poorer poor house in Paris to, at last, a vigorous arduous tour on foot around the poorest parishes of Brittany, Montfort was *integrated.* His energy was dispersed; his motivation was always concentrated on bringing people to God and on doing God's will. His only possessions on his missionary journeys were a Bible, breviary, sermon book, and, of course, the Rosary. He was as free as a vagrant, but it was a freedom to work harder, to live poorer, to act more responsibly than the beneficed cleric. By being free of work that tied him to one place, by being thus able to make himself available for any pastoral work, Montfort was spiritually vagrant in this sense: he knew precisely that he was obeying God's will, he was inflexibly pointed in one direction, like Christ "setting his face towards Jerusalem" and death (Lk 9:51). He was "supple clay in the Potter's hands. An active and responsible living 'Yes'—like Mary—to the Holy Spirit."[4] Like Jesus, he had nowhere to lay his head, no social, geographical stability. This can be called insecurity or loneliness, or it can be called freedom. If it is imposed, the life of the vagrant is as confining as a prison; if freely chosen and properly motivated, it is a liberty that allows growth to maturity. All the parishes in which Montfort toiled, with virtually no clerical recognition, were the outcome of that choice to be free to do God's work.

d. Freedom through Consecration as a slave of Jesus through Mary. This most individual paradox of becoming truly free through becoming a slave of Jesus through Mary, though abundantly evident in Montfort's writing, has to be assumed in his life. We can say only that Montfort first dedicated himself to Jesus through Mary sometime during his seminary days and that it was influenced by many contemporary or near-contemporary writers, in particular by Boudon in *Holy Slavery of the Admirable Mother of God.*

2. Freedom in the writings of Montfort

a. Scriptural basis of freedom through slavery. Montfort uses Scripture, liberally but scriptural quotations are used as illustrations, after the manner of his age, rather than as the framework.[5] Nevertheless, Scripture not only abounds in examples of the paradox of freedom through slavery but is based on it.

Our fulfillment can come about only by being the "slave of one Master" (Mt 6:24). The keeping of this ethic is the only way to avoid radical conflict and becoming enslaved to addictive evil.

Since Montfort's Consecration is nothing but a perfect renewal of baptismal vows, which free us from the slavery of sin, it may be said to be based on the scriptural emphasis on Baptism. This theology is most clearly worked out in the middle chapters of Romans: "When you were the slaves of sin, you were free in regard to righteousness. . . . But now that you have been set free from sin, and have become slaves of God, the return you get is sanctification and its end, eternal life" (Rom 6:20, 22).

Later in the same letter, the Holy Spirit teaches that Baptism gives "freedom of spirit, the glorious liberty of the children of God," "set free from the bondage to decay" (Rom 8:21). The Galatians, who were once slaves of "the weak and beggarly elemental spirits" (Gal 4:8-9), are no longer slaves but sons (Gal 4:7). The paradox of freedom-slavery is more explicitly brought out in ethical duties of mutual love: "For you were called to freedom, brethren; only do not use your freedom as an opportunity of the flesh, but through love be servants of one another" (Gal 5:13).

The whole of Psalm 119 could be quoted, with many other psalms, to illustrate the paradox of obedience-freedom.[6] The paradox is not, therefore, original to Montfort, but its emphasis, admittedly nurtured by contemporary Sulpician spirituality, is peculiarly his.

b. Freedom through Baptismal promises. Montfort gives a comprehensive argument for Consecration to Incarnate Wisdom by showing how it is simply a perfect renewal of the radical Consecration that takes place at our Baptism. The emphasis is on the perfection of this Consecration: "*As all perfection consists in being conformed, united and consecrated to Jesus, it follows that the most perfect of all devotions is that which conforms, unites, and consecrates us most completely to Jesus. . . . It is the perfect and complete renewal of the vows and promises of holy baptism*" (TD 120). "Perfection" here means totality of fulfillment, and therefore freedom. Montfort explains this by showing that before Baptism "*every Christian was a slave of the devil*" (TD 126) and that we, conversely, gain freedom from this slavery by Baptism, through which we become a "*slave of love.*" Montfort is, of course, employing the theme pervasive in the Pauline letters, but he makes little, if any, direct reference to it, and he is clearly not immediately motivated by it. TD 127 quotes Thomas Aquinas and Augustine and, after them, Church councils—Sens and Trent. The point made by all sources cited is that Christians are exhorted to renew their baptismal promises. Montfort sees the Act of Consecration as being the same as those vows. In fact, it is "*more than we do at baptism, when ordinarily our godparents speak for us and we are given to Jesus only by proxy.*

*In this devotion, we give ourselves personally and **freely**, and we are fully aware of what we are doing*" (TD 126). Montfort is only being realistic when he says that few baptized have a habitual awareness of the significance of their baptismal promises, described by Aquinas and Augustine as the most important vows ever made (TD 127). The point made, however, is that by the Act of Consecration, an adult renews his baptismal vows and goes beyond them by freely accepting what they stand for; that is not possible psychologically as infants. Apart from stressing the freedom of the essentially adult Act of Consecration, Montfort shows how fundamental it is. It is not a devotion but central to our baptismal redemption.

In the Act of Consecration, the baptismal connection is central: "*But I must confess that I have not kept the vows and promises which I made to you so solemnly at my baptism*" (LEW 223). The baptismal vows are at the heart of Montfort's thinking when he defines his Holy Slavery: "*Before baptism, we belonged to the devil as slaves, but baptism made us, in very truth, slaves of Jesus*" (TD 68).

*c. **Freedom in TD.*** The entire theme of Montfort's spirituality is ultimately the Gospel paradox that we must lose our life in order to find it, that we "empty ourselves in taking the form of a slave," thereby "having that mind within us which was in Christ Jesus" (Phil 2:5-6). The paradox of freedom-slavery is scriptural and also typical of montfort spirituality. We have already mentioned the freedom through poverty in Montfort's life; it is equally evident in the only apparent impoverishment that comes from giving to Jesus through Mary the "*value of our good acts, past, present and to come*" (LEW 223). In an unacknowledged quotation from Paul, he speaks of giving everything, whether we eat or drink, or whatsoever else we do, to Jesus through Mary, and he talks of this as being "*richer*" than any monarch (TD 136). But the richness comes from not merely denuding ourselves of our will but from ensuring that Mary removes all residual self-centeredness. In quantitative language, we make a "good investment" when we place all in Mary's hands. But this is not naive or crude. On the contrary, it is ruthlessly realistic, since motives that are selfish so easily intrude and diminish, if not spoil, the value of the good we do. The psychological wealth, which is the most important, is found in Montfort's exclamation: "*How consoling!*" (TD 136). We are not creating a new fact but acknowledging what obtains anyway—total dependence on God. We are freed of the worry of wealth, which the moth, rust, and thief of selfish motives can damage or destroy.

The very heart of the slavery-freedom paradox is found in the profoundly psychological and spiritual treatment of TD 169. Here we are told that the "*holy slavery*" frees us "*from servile scruple and fear, which might restrict, imprison or confuse us,*" and enables us to see God as our loving Father, not an implacable Judge. Jesus "*inspires us with a generous and filial love.*" Love, not fear; filial (sons), not servile (slaves). It is a perfect echo of the Pauline clarion: "Because you are sons, God has sent the Spirit of his Son into our hearts, crying, 'Abba! Father!' So through God you are no longer a slave but a son, and if a son, then an heir" (Gal 4:6-7). Montfort's reference to being freed from scruples echoes what Paul then says almost immediately: "How can you turn back again to the weak and beggarly elemental spirits, whose slaves you want to be once more?" (Gal 4:9). Far from binding us by superstition and primitive fear, the montfort Consecration frees.

Freedom is not loneliness, nor is it disorientation and insecurity. Montfort unfolds another paradox by showing that we need stability in order to be free: "*Blessed, indeed, are those Christians who bind themselves faithfully and completely to her as to a secure anchor! The violent storms of the world will not make them founder*" (TD 175). This security-freedom is found in Psalm 1, as is the instability of the sinner: the just man is like a "tree planted beside running waters"; the wicked are "like chaff, scattered before the wind." Montfort refers to this psalm, without naming it, in TD 68: "*The Holy spirit compares us i) to trees that are planted along the waters of grace, and which bear their fruit when the time comes.*"

When Montfort defines "*slavery*" (TD 68-77), he refers, without giving precise location, to "*St. Paul [who] says that we belong not to ourselves but entirely to him as his members and his slaves, for he bought us at an infinite price—the shedding of his Precious Blood*" (1 Cor 6 and 12). Montfort distinguishes (TD 69) "*servant*" and "*slave*", although this distinction is made to stress the "binding" nature of slavery, it also serves to increase the love and freedom that causes such a bond. The paradox is heightened: the more total the slavery, which is of its essence total, the greater the love that inspires it. The paradox now becomes an oxymoron: "*Voluntary slavery,*" an apparent contradiction in terms, two words challenging each other. "*Voluntary slavery*" is "*the most perfect of all three states*" (TD 70).

d. Freedom in PM and RM. In TD, freedom is spiritual and psychological; in PM, it is apostolic. At the same time, we cannot too rigorously separate the two freedoms, since the motivation of the apostolate is clearly a total trust in Providence. So, detachment, besides being essential for Montfort's idea of apostolate, is likewise a chastening reminder of the detachment of the end times. It is this eschatological note that makes it an "ardent" prayer, as it is called in most languages.

"*Disponibilité*" is a key word of PM, often translated as "availability." "Rootlessness" does not convey the full meaning, and it is even doubtful as an English word in this context. "*Disponsibilité*" means "being totally open to any call made on us in the apostolate." Montfort himself usually describes it in negatives, which makes the meaning clearer.

In PM and RM, we see the basic

psychological and temperamental need Montfort had for freedom, as well as the spiritual and apostolic need. The relevant numbers of PM are 7-10. Montfort states that the first and most essential qualification of his missionaries is that they be "*free*"—"*liberos.*" "*What, then, am I asking for? "Liberos, men who are free, free with the freedom that comes from you, detached from everything, without father . . . and without worldly possessions to encumber or distract them, and devoid of all self-interest*" (PM 7). This is followed by the now familiar paradox: "*Men who are free, but still in bondage to your love*" (PM 8), "*free as the clouds,*" with a half-reference to the "Spirit blowing [them] where he will" (Jn 3:8). But now another paradox, freedom-obedience: "*Always ready to obey you [Christ] when authority speaks.*" Since "authority" means human instrumental authority, the freedom is not license to drift aimlessly and willfully. "For you were called to freedom, brethren, only do not use your freedom as opportunity for the flesh" (Gal 5:13). It is not an anarchic freedom but one that will "*carry out your will to the full*" (PM 8). We know from Montfort's life that he was always most scrupulous in doing this: Leschassier, the visit to Clement XI, the Calvary at Pontchâteau. It is an enriching and liberating obedience, perfectly in conformity with the Act of Consecration, in which all motives of self-interests are ruthlessly eradicated by handing them over to Mary. The freedom is radical; no compromise is allowed with the will of God. In RM, practical ordinances are laid down to exteriorize this freedom into the apostolate: "*The members of the Company avoid such work as being contrary to their missionary vocation so as to feel free at all times*" to evangelize the poor (RM 2). "*Such work*" includes "*curates, parish priests, teachers in colleges or seminaries, as so many other good priests are, God having called them to this work*" (RM 2). This quote shows a sensitivity not always apparent in such prophetic types as Montfort. In RM, we have the qualification needed for missionaries: the Latin term "*instabiles.*" Again, an irritating word to translate into English. "Total availability, ready to move on, whenever and wherever needed" seems to be the meaning. Montfort cites as exemplars St. Paul, Vincent Ferrer, and Francis Xavier (RM 6) as "*free from any other occupation*" than that of the missionary.

This impassioned plea for freedom must be seen in the context of eschatology. Otherwise it becomes more strident than vibrant.

III. Relevance of Montfort Freedom Today

Much has been said of paradox, of the striking confrontation of slavery-freedom. In today's world, in a world where slavery has been officially abolished, there are many forms of servitude even more oppressive than the slavery of the ancient world and of the medieval feudal system. There is the slavery of poverty, especially, but by no means only, in the Third

World and its concomitant debasement. There is the slavery of addiction: to drugs, alcohol, sexual deviation, phobias, anxiety states, and so on. There is, of course, an invincible desire for freedom from all this. There is also a growing desire for freedom—political, individual, religious, and economic. Yet we also see the desire to belong, to be part of a society. Life is a balancing act between preserving our sovereign individuality and not being isolated.

The total renunciation of self-centered motives, which Montfort's Act of Consecration entails, calls on Mary's maternal influence to correct wrong and selfish drives and to challenge us to grapple with self-indulgence, even at the level of the spiritual.

Saint Louis Marie de Montfort's Holy Slavery encourages us to consider at a more profound level wherein true freedom lies. Like Dante, Montfort's thought on freedom concludes: "Our peace, to do His will." That is the peace of the blessed in *Paradiso;* it is also the peace of the blessed, the happy on earth.

Gerard Mackrell

Notes: (1) For a concise study of freedom see J. De Finance, *Freedom,* in *New Catholic Encyclopedia,* McGraw-Hill, New York 1966, 95-100. (2) P. Gaffney, *Introduction,* in GA, ix. (3) Gaffney, five times in as many pages, refers to Saint Louis Marie as a "vagabond" or "itinerant" missionary. Cf. ibid, viii-xii. (4) Ibid., xii. (5) See the article *Bible* in this manual for a discussion of Saint Louis Marie's use of Sacred Scripture. (6) Psalm 119 (118), the longest in the psalter, appears to be principally a wisdom psalm that extols the beauty, joy, and freedom experienced in obeying God's law. Saint Louis Marie de Montfort quotes this psalm about ten times.

THE FRENCH SCHOOL OF SPIRITUALITY

SUMMARY

I. INTRODUCTION.

II. THE SOCIAL AND RELIGIOUS BACKGROUND:
1. Seventeenth-century French society;
2. Christianity in seventeenth-century France.

III. THE LEADERS OF THE MOVEMENT:
1. The founders: Bérulle and Condren;
2. A great missionary in the tradition of the Oratory: Jean Eudes;
3. Jean-Jacques Olier and Saint-Sulpice;
4. The Jesuit spiritual writers;
5. The role of women in the French school.

IV. SPIRITUAL DOCTRINE, SPIRIT, AND PEDAGOGY:
1. Christ-centeredness, the spirit of religion, adoration;
2. Mystical Christ-centeredness, Christian living, the spirit of Jesus;
3. The sense of the Church;
4. The French school and missionary activity;
5. A specific pedagogy;
6. The pessimism of the French school.

V. LOUIS MARIE DE MONTFORT, THE LAST OF THE GREAT BÉRULLIANS.

I. INTRODUCTION

Louis Marie de Montfort is undeniably linked to what is generally known as the French school of spirituality (at times called seventeenth century spirituality, the Bérullian school, the Bérullians). He received his formation at Saint-Sulpice Seminary (1692-1700) and later kept in close touch with his directors of formation; as a result, he is one of the best heirs and witnesses of the French school. H. Brémond has justly called him "the last of the great Bérullians." It must be noted at the outset, however, that although Montfort retained the main characteristics of the doctrine and teaching methods of Cardinal de Bérulle and Jean-Jacques Olier—among the many and varied spiritual writers used as his sources—he did it in a way distinctively his own.

In order to understand the thought, writings, and apostolic activity of St. Louis de Montfort, it is therefore important to be acquainted with the main features of the French school of spirituality.

In the nineteenth century, Bishop Gay made the main themes of the

French school accessible to a large audience. In the early part of the twentieth century, Dom Marmion's books, inspired by Bérulle, became very influential. But it was H. Brémond's works, published from 1915 on, that brought Bérulle and his followers out of obscurity: *L'Invasion mystique* and *La Conquête mystique* clarified how eminent, influential, and theologically profound the leaders of the French school were. The spiritual and apostolic current of the school now holds a significant place in nearly all the histories of spirituality. Some studies, such as the one by G. Salet (1938), have shown how deeply the Bérullian teaching was rooted in the thought of the Church Fathers. In the last thirty years or so, a large number of courses (and publications) have helped to make the wealth of that ever-relevant spirituality available to an increasingly large audience. Members of the communities founded by St. Louis de Montfort and by St. John-Baptist de la Salle are taking an active part in research and publication.[1]

This article—an attempt to give an overview of one of the principal foundations of St. Louis de Montfort's own spirituality—will first briefly present a general description of the French school and then develop some of the characteristics in more detail.

Since Brémond it has been customary to designate as the French school a powerful spiritual, missionary, and reform movement that animated the Church in France in the early seventeenth century. The movement was led by Bérulle, Condren, Olier, Jean Eudes, and St. Vincent de Paul. It had many followers: St. Louis de Montfort, St. John Baptist de la Salle, Louis Lallemant, etc.

The characteristics of the movement are:

- A deep mystical experience. Each of the leaders was a true mystic, nourished on Scripture, especially the writings of St. Paul and St. John.
- A stress on specific aspects of the Christian faith and Christian living: a sense of God's grandeur and of adoration; a relationship with Jesus lived out mainly through communion with his "states," his mysteries, his filial and apostolic sentiments; great devotion to the Holy Spirit, the Spirit of the risen Christ; the necessity for each Christian to surrender to the Spirit's action; a highly theological contemplation of Mary's mysteries.
- A mystical sense of the Church as the Body of Christ continuing and accomplishing the life of Jesus, his prayer and mission.
- A certain Augustinian view of man that underlines the pessimistic but also strongly stresses positive and optimistic elements: "man, pure capacity for God."
- An extremely strong apostolic and missionary commitment.
- A detailed and well-adapted method for instructing others: methods of prayer, vows of servitude, and various other commitments and Consecrations.
- A special concern for the dignity of priests, their holiness and formation.

The main Christian attitudes of the members of the movement are adoration and "religion" (respect and love) towards the Father, adherence or "communion" to the filial and apostolic sentiments of Jesus, surrender to his Holy Spirit, and "true" devotion to Mary, in whom Jesus lives and reigns and who introduces us into his mysteries.

II. The Social and Religious Background

We know a great deal about seventeenth-century France, for it has been well documented by competent historians. We will, however, highlight only some of the distinctive features of that period that may help to understand the apostolic commitments and the spiritual teaching of the leaders of the French school. What Lacordaire has said of others could be applied to them: "What sets noble hearts apart is their ability to realize the most urgent need of their contemporaries and to devote themselves to meeting it."[2]

1. Seventeenth-century French society

France was going through a period of revival after the wars of religion. In some border areas, however, like Lorraine and Picardy, the people were still living in poverty, and French peasants throughout the country and even around Paris were making a precarious living. It was in this period that the bourgeoisie grew. Its members lived rather close to the aristocracy, and the Christian renewal started with them. Most of those called "devout people" belonged to this "middle class."

2. Christianity in seventeenth-century France

French Christianity had a great vitality, initiated by the renewal of the previous century. Some, however, have described the Church in France in the early seventeenth century as being "in a pitiable state." Vincent de Paul said that "France's worst enemies are the priests."[3] The French clergy had not been adequately trained, and they received little support from the bishops, many of whom did not even live in their dioceses. The religious orders were beginning to experience a renewal in the wake of the Council of Trent, and the early seventeenth century saw an explosion of reforms and new foundations. The result was an extraordinary dynamism. But most ordinary Catholics were uneducated and not immune to the influence of superstition and witchcraft.

The Church in France was thus in a fairly sorry state, and though the Council of Trent had come to an end in 1563, the decrees it had issued were not "officially" received in France until 1615. Against this background, vigorous missionary efforts were carried out in France with lasting results. It is difficult to exaggerate the paramount importance of the parish missions, given in rural areas as well as in the cities and even at the court itself. All the leaders of the French school not only took part in them but also clarified the underlying theology of the parish mission. Bérulle, Vincent de Paul, and others saw the preaching of missions as the continuation of the mission of Jesus himself.

The missionary renewal went hand in hand with an educational renewal and with a multitude of apostolic initiatives. Madame Acarie's drawing room became a veritable center of Catholic revival, and the Company of the Blessed Sacrament, although giving rise to controversy, was very effective. The famous Tuesday Conferences brought priests together under the leadership of Vincent de Paul. There they exchanged ideas about their ministry and their spiritual life and planned the parish missions and their staffing. The Company of the Blessed Sacrament and Saint-Lazare Conferences spread to the provinces as well. Other apostolic undertakings were started to supply the needs of the foreign missions, e.g., the Company of the Associates of Our Lady of Montreal, which was established in the mid-seventeenth century, and the Seminary for the Foreign Missions, founded in 1663.

III. The Leaders of the Movement

1. The founders: Bérulle (1575-1629) and Condren (1588-1641)

The scope of this article does not make it possible to give more than a brief survey of their lives, which will help to situate them in the Church of the seventeenth century.

Bérulle was born in the department of Yonne in 1575 and spent most of his life in Paris. He was a precocious child. He received a very good education from the Jesuits and then studied at the Sorbonne. He became well acquainted with the best spiritual authors of his time, thanks to his visits to his cousin, Madame Acarie. Early in life he read the Rheno-Flemish writers, from whom he derived an acute sense of God's grandeur. Two retreats in 1602 and 1607 definitively oriented him towards highly Christocentric devotion: "Jesus, the fulfillment of our being . . ." In 1604 he made a journey to Spain and brought back a few Carmelite nuns of the Teresian reform. Their increase in number was spectacular, and between 1604 and 1660 no fewer than sixty-two convents were founded in France. Bérulle was their "visitator," and this brought upon him many difficulties. He proposed to the Carmelites that they take a vow of servitude to Jesus; this occasioned the marvelous (and difficult) *Discours sur l'état et les grandeurs de Jésus, (Discours on the State and the Grandeurs of Jesus),* published in 1623. In this work, Bérulle considers at length the "states and mysteries" of Jesus: "They took place in the past, but their power will never pass away." Of all the mysteries, the Incarnation was the one on which he centered his contemplation. He also paid special attention to the mystery of Jesus' infancy. His deep and loving devotion to Mary was rooted in these mysteries.

In 1611 he founded the Oratory of Jesus in order to "restore the state of the priesthood" and wrote an Office in honor of Jesus for the benefit of his confreres, whom he strongly urged to take the vow of servitude to Jesus.

Bérulle held various posts as a diplomat and reformer and was made a cardinal by Urban VIII in 1627, but he has gone down in the history of spirituality as an undisputed master and pioneer: "Without Bérulle something essential would be missing from the spiritual life in France and from Christian thought" (J. Dagens).

Charles de Condren succeeded Bérulle as superior of the Oratory. Though he did not leave many writings and did not carry out spectacular undertakings, his spiritual influence was profound: "Between 1630 and 1640 he was the spiritual director of all the saints in Paris." He was the driving force behind the foundation of seminaries by Olier, for, as his spiritual director (following Vincent de Paul), he exercised much influence upon him. He introduced Olier to the Bérullian way of thinking, especially on devotion to the Blessed Sacrament, and taught him his "little prayer": "Come, Lord Jesus, come and live in your servant."

Most of Condren's activities were connected with the Oratory. He established Oratorian communities at Nevers, Langres, Poitiers, and St-Magloire in Paris. He was elected superior general on Bérulle's death in 1629. He died in 1641.

Condren's spiritual doctrine was marked by a strong emphasis on sacrifice. He expressed the Bérullian theocentrism and adoration through sacrifice, immolation, and the state of victimhood. He frequently speaks of becoming nothing (*anéantissement*), of being consumed. The Eucharist is also central in his thought; at Mass "Jesus continues to offer the same sacrifice throughout the ages and multiplies the offering of himself on the altar every day." His doctrine was spread by two of his followers: Jean Eudes and Olier.

2. A great missionary in the tradition of the Oratory: Jean Eudes (1601-1680)

St. Jean Eudes, like St. Louis de Montfort, is regarded as the founder and inspirer of several religious communities: the Eudists, the Sisters of Our Lady of Charity, the Good Shepherd Sisters, the Sisters of the Sacred Hearts of Jesus and Mary, the Little Sisters of the Poor. The "Eudist family," as these Congregations are often called, is nourished by the example and doctrine of the great missionary and spiritual master, Jean Eudes. His theological thought is very much along Bérullian lines; it is very solid, though occasionally verbose.

Unlike Bérulle, Condren, Olier, and Vincent de Paul, Jean Eudes did not spend much time in Paris. He was born in Normandy in 1601 and died in 1680. He preached many missions, particularly in western France. Eudes founded several seminaries in Normandy and at Rennes. He was the leading spirit of the liturgical celebrations in honor of the Sacred Hearts of Mary (1648) and Jesus (1672). He published several books based on his missionary experience; some of them went through several editions even in his lifetime: *La Vie et le Royaume de Jésus (The Life and Kingdom of Jesus)* (first edition 1637), *Contrat de l'homme avec Dieu par le saint Baptême* (*Contract of Man with God through Holy Baptism)* (1654), *Le bon confesseur (The Good Confessor)* (first edition 1666), etc.

After twenty years as an Oratorian, he left the Oratory in 1643 to establish a seminary at Caen and also to found the Congregation of Jesus and

Mary. Jean Eudes never disowned the specifically Bérullian teaching he had received at the Oratory. His writings are the most accessible of all those by the Bérullians, and a few passages from them may be the best introduction to the spirituality of the French school. In his view, "Christian living continues and fulfills the life of Jesus Christ."[4] "When a Christian meditates, he continues and fulfills on earth the prayer of Jesus Christ; when he works he continues and fulfills on earth the labor of Jesus Christ. . . . We ought to continue and accomplish in us the states and mysteries of Jesus, and frequently pray to him that he will continue and accomplish them in us and in all the members of his Church. For the mysteries have not yet reached their full perfection and fulfillment. Though perfect and fulfilled in the person of Jesus, they are, nonetheless, not yet fulfilled and perfect in us, who are his members, or in the Church, which is his Mystical Body. . . . So, the Son of God's design is to accomplish and fulfill in us all his states and mysteries. His design is to complete in us the mysteries of his Incarnation, birth, and hidden life by forming himself in us and coming to birth in our souls by the holy Sacraments of Baptism and the divine Eucharist, by making us live a spiritual interior life hidden in God with him."[5]

During his long and very busy personal life, from the time he pronounced the "vow of martyrdom" at the beginning of his priestly life to his death, he practiced what he taught. In the many missions he gave—over a hundred—and in his countless activities, he "bore witness to Jesus Christ," as he put it. He expressed his mystical and apostolic Christ-centeredness in wonderful prayers to the "Heart of Jesus and Mary" ("Ave Cor") and in the "forenoon prayers," which were all focused on Jesus. He warned his followers: "The greatest of all practices . . . the greatest of all devotions . . . is to be detached from all practices . . . and to surrender to the Spirit of Jesus."[6] In his opinion, "the greatest work of all" is "that Jesus be formed in us" (cf. Gal 4:19). He devoted his whole life to repeating this teaching and to promoting the life and reign of Jesus in souls.

3. Jean-Jacques Olier (1608-1657) and Saint-Sulpice

As Montfort was born in 1673, he never met Olier, but he must have heard a great deal about him at Saint-Sulpice. Many characteristics of Montfort's message, as well as his own spiritual experience, are reminiscent of the founder of Saint-Sulpice. Perhaps too much has been made of the way J.-J. Olier's successors, especially L. Tronson, distorted and hardened the teaching given at Saint-Sulpice in its early stages.

Olier was born in Paris in 1608 into a family of lawyers. He was educated by the Jesuits in Lyon (1617-1624). After he had led a lukewarm Christian life for a few years, he experienced a true conversion of heart and considered becoming a priest from apostolic motives. Under the guidance of St. Vincent de Paul, he took part in the Spiritual Exercises at Saint-Lazare and was ordained priest in 1633. Prompted by St. Vincent de

Paul, he devoted himself to giving parish missions. He met Agnes de Langeac, Marie Rousseau, and Father Condren, and their influence was decisive in his founding a seminary at Vaugirard in December 1641, then at Saint-Sulpice, where he was appointed parish priest in 1642. He was convinced that parish missions could bear no lasting fruit unless they were based on a solid spiritual and apostolic formation focusing on union with Jesus Christ.

After going through the crucible of a psychological and spiritual trial between 1639 and 1641, he became an outstanding spiritual director. In imitation of Condren and the Oratorians, yet in a more personal way, he pronounced the vow of servitude to Mary in 1633, to Jesus in 1642. In 1644 he took the vow of victimhood, and in 1652 the vow of total oblation to the Trinity through Mary.

Olier dedicated himself to preaching parish missions in rural areas and to establishing seminaries (at Paris, Nantes, Viviers, Le Puy, Clermont), without neglecting his role as a zealous parish priest. In his last years he wrote a few spiritual books, which were to have a far-reaching influence: *La Journée chrétienne (The Christian Day)* (1655), *Le Catéchisme chrétien pour la vie intérieure (The Christian Catechism for the Interior Life)* (1656), *Introduction à la vie et aux vertus chrétiennes (Introduction to the Christian Life and Virtues)* (1657). He died on Easter Monday, April 2, 1657. It was not until 1676 that L. Tronson published the famous *Traité des saints ordres (Treatise on Holy Orders)*, drawing on Olier's writings but introducing into them some distorting shifts of emphasis, as a recent critical study has shown.[7] A number of manuscript works, especially "Mémoires," which he wrote at the request of his spiritual director, Father Bataille, are of great help in attempting to understand Olier's thought. It is his letters, however, that best reveal what sort of spiritual guide he was.

H. Brémond describes Olier as an excellent follower and witness of Bérulle's teaching. Four points in his spiritual message and teaching method constitute the essence of his legacy to the Church:

The first chapter of *Directoire spirituel de Saint-Sulpice (Spiritual Directory of Saint Sulpice)* can be considered the "principle and foundation" of his whole teaching: "The primary aim of the Institute is to live completely for God in Christ Jesus our Lord so that the interior dispositions of His Son may permeate the deepest recesses of our souls and enable each of us to repeat what St. Paul confidently said of himself, 'It is no longer I who live, but it is Christ who lives in me'" (Gal 2:20).[8]

The apostolic spirit—the Spirit of Jesus—is the source of all ministry in the Church: "Apostolic men and all the apostles of Christ are Christ-bearers, they bring him wherever they go; they are like sacraments, which bear him so that under their appearance and through them he may proclaim the glory of his Father."[9]

His method of prayer is entirely centered on Jesus and is a real school of prayer. An historian of spirituality has written: "We consider that the most practical contribution to

Catholic spirituality by the French school has been its resolutely Christ-centered approach to prayer, as aptly illustrated in what is called the 'Sulpician method.' This method comprises the successive stages: the stage of adoration: Jesus before the eyes; the stage of communion: Jesus in the heart; the stage of cooperation: Jesus in the hands."[10]

"O Jesus living in Mary" is the prayer that Olier learned from Condren and further adapted. It was and still is a prayer that "admirably sums up the teaching of Bérulle and his school."[11] H. Brémond writes that "it would be difficult to imagine a more perfect epitome of the French school."[12]

4. The Jesuit spiritual writers

The expression "Bérullian Jesuits" seems difficult to justify. Yet there was a mystical trend among the French Jesuits between 1610 and 1650, a current that had some kinship with the Bérullian movement. Father Pierre Coton (1564-1626) regularly attended the meetings of the Acarie Circle and deeply influenced the Christian public through his *Intérieure occupation de l'âme dévote (Interior Occupation of the Devoted Soul)* (1608), as well as a large number of Jesuits of the next generation whom he guided towards the mystical life. Father Louis Lallemant (1588-1635) was the moving spirit of a spiritual renewal that caused some concern to the Jesuit authorities in Rome. He was novice master at Rouen and trained a host of missionaries, spiritual directors, and writers. His followers were responsible for editing *Doctrine spirituelle,* which they systematized while keeping the core of his message and his "passionate emphasis on the interior life and union with God in purity of heart and obedience to the Holy Spirit."[13]

We know that Louis de Montfort used books by the Jesuit Jean-Baptiste Saint-Jure (1588-1657), the author of *De la connaissance et de l'amour du Fils de Dieu (Of the Knowledge and the Love of the Son of God)* (1633), *L'Union avec N.S. Jésus Christ dans ses principaux mystères (Union with Our Lord Jesus Christ in His Principal Mysteries)* (1653), and other books. The titles of the books alone tell us how much place the Incarnate Word held in the Christian life. The stress he laid on "application" and union with Jesus Christ ties in with the "adherence" promoted by Bérulle. Saint-Jure was the spiritual director of Renty and, for some time, of Marie des Vallées and Marguerite du Saint-Sacrement, and he also was in touch with the circles most influenced by Bérulle. The same cannot be said of Jean-Joseph Surin (1600-1665); after he had published his *Catéchisme spirituel (Spiritual Catechism)* (1659), however, his books became well known, and Montfort was acquainted with them.

During St. Louis' formation years and later, several books by Jesuit priests were published that showed how well they had assimilated Bérulle's teaching. The year 1686 saw the publication of *Vie du Père Rigoleau avec ses traités de dévotion et ses lettres spirituelles (Life of Father Rigoleau with His Treatises of Devotion and His Spiritual Letters).* Father Rigoleau was a disciple of Father

Lallemant, who also stressed interior purification and obedience to the promptings of the Holy Spirit. The same period saw the publication of the works of Father François Nepveu (1639-1706), who was mainly concerned with the link between Christ and the Christian soul: spiritual directors ought to "strive only to form Jesus Christ in souls."[14] The place he accords to the Incarnate Word in his works is clear evidence of the widespread influence of the French school at the end of the seventeenth century.

Montfort was also able to draw spiritual sustenance from other Jesuit spiritual writers, such as Paul de Barry, François Poiré, Julien Hayneufve, Jacques Nouet, Claude La Colombière, and Jean Crasset, but their writings were not concerned with the main themes of the French school.

5. The role of women in the French school

All agree that Blessed Marie Louise Trichet played an important role in Montfort's life. This is in keeping with the clear evidence that in the seventeenth century, women exercised a strong influence in religious circles, and particularly in the French school. P. Chaunu has described it as "the feminization of the Church in France during that period."[15]

Although French society kept women in a subordinate position, their influence was recognized and often fostered. It has been said that "the lot of women in France was a happy one: they were able to enjoy all forms of freedom and pleasure."[16] Catholic women especially played a leading role in Christian renewal.

Many contemplative Congregations for women, such as the Benedictines, were renewed; others, for example, the Visitation nuns and the Carmelites of the reform of St. Teresa, began to flourish in France. The number of convents increased considerably, and some, like Port-Royal, were popular spiritual centers.

Among devout people, a large number of groups of "secular daughters" came into existence, though some of them were short-lived. They were dedicated to God's service and engaged in many charitable works, such as nursing and teaching, without, however, forming a religious order as such. They heralded present-day secular institutes and societies of apostolic life. These women took no public vows, nor were they enclosed, and many of them wore no religious habit.

The world of pious women also included a number of laywomen who did not join any association but played an important part in the renewal process. Madame d'Herculais and Madame Hélyot were two of them.

Many women (nuns, "secular daughters," and independent laywomen) had connections with the French school in various degrees. Madame Acarie, who was a pioneer and close to Bérulle, exerted a far-reaching influence and, together with her cousin Madame de Sainte-Beuve, contributed to the foundation or the reform of the Benedictine convents at Montmartre and Soissons and of the Ursulines; she was particularly instrumental in bringing the Discalced Carmelites to France in 1604. She helped with the foundation of other

Carmelite convents before entering one herself. She certainly played a leading part in bringing the French school into existence.

Prominent members of the French school were influenced by women. Mother Agnès, Marie Rousseau, and Marie de Valence influenced and inspired Olier; Marie des Vallées influenced Jean Eudes; and Louise de Marillac had close ties with Vincent de Paul.

The most authentic Bérullian woman may have been Mother Madeleine de Saint Joseph, the first prioress of the first reformed Carmelite convent in France. She exerted considerable influence on the future prioresses of the forty original Carmelite convents in France. Her spiritual teaching was borrowed from both St. Teresa and Bérulle. She was responsible for spreading among the Carmelites the Bérullian doctrine of adoration, mystical Christ-centeredness through adherence to the states and mysteries of Jesus, and special devotion to the Mother of God. By infusing the Bérullian way of thinking into the Carmelites, she gave them a taste for doctrinal piety. A recent eloquent witness to this is Elizabeth of the Trinity.

The name Marie de l'Incarnation (Guyart) (1599-1672) should be added to those above. She was an Ursuline who lived at Tours and then Quebec, Canada. Although she was not typically Bérullian, her devotion to "the apostolic spirit that is the authentic spirit of Jesus" brings her surprisingly close to Olier's thought, as expressed in his writings.

Finally, Marguerite Bourgeois (1620-1700), who founded at Montreal the Congregation of Notre Dame, urged her Sisters to imitate Mary, the Mother of Jesus, especially in "going about and associating with people." Her writings show signs of influence by the teaching of Bérulle and Olier.

Though it may be more difficult to recognize the specific accents of the French school among the women of that period, their writings and religious commitments show that they drew inspiration from its members. It becomes clear, then, why so many religious Congregations founded in the seventeenth, eighteenth, and even nineteenth centuries acknowledge their indebtedness to the French school.

IV. Spiritual Doctrine, Spirit, and Pedagogy

1. Christ-centeredness, the spirit of religion, adoration

All the historians of spirituality have underlined the fact that Bérulle's experience and message are characterized by the sense of the grandeur, absolute perfection, and holiness of God. Although these qualities are typical of the monotheistic religions, for Bérulle and his followers, it is in Jesus alone, the perfect worshiper of the Father, that worship in spirit and in truth is fulfilled. Olier writes: "Our Lord Jesus Christ came into the world to bring reverence and love for his Father and to establish his kingdom and his religion. He bore witness to the respect and love for his Father that are the constituents of religion."[17]

Man responds to the grandeur of God by adoring Him to the extent that he gives himself completely to God: "We must consider God first rather than ourselves and act out of reverence for God rather than seek ourselves."[18] The reason for this is that "nothing is great except God and what gives him honor."[19]

These assertions of Bérulle were repeated by his followers and made an impression on his contemporaries. Condren, Olier, and Eudes, each in his own way, emphasized the grandeur of God and the importance of adoration and of the virtue of religion.

2. Mystical Christ-centeredness, Christian living, the Spirit of Jesus

This is the central core of the experience and teaching of the Bérullians. Their contemplation of the Incarnate Word and the relationship with Jesus that they advocate are at once traditional, deeply theological, and consistent. We are justified in claiming that there is a "Christology of the French school," in the sense of a dynamic spirituality of this "science of the saints" that they mentioned so frequently. The theological thought of Bérulle and his followers was concerned with the mystery of the Incarnate Word and with Christian living. They understood and presented Christian living as a specific, personal, and ecclesial relationship with the person of the risen Christ. This relationship, which is realized by the Spirit, essentially implies a relationship of adherence, communion, and eventually deep identification with Jesus Christ. All the members of the school (Olier, J. Eudes, J. B. de la Salle, Louis de Montfort) experienced the influence of the Holy Spirit, called the "Spirit of Jesus," and spoke a great deal about Him.

a. The Incarnate Word is at the center of the spiritual experience and message of the leaders of the French school. Pope Urban VIII reportedly described Bérulle as "the apostle of the Incarnate Word." We are evidently speaking of Jesus, living, risen from the dead, but contemplated in the mystery of his Incarnation.

This mystery is central to the faith of all Christians, and all schools of spirituality are "schools of Christ" (St. Bernard). Bérulle and his followers, however, made strenuous efforts to focus the attention, prayer, and activity of the faithful on the person of Jesus. According to them:

- Jesus is to be adored in the mystery of the Incarnation and in all his other mysteries (and "states"); this adoration is expressed in the Bérullian "elevations," in great devotion to the Eucharist, the Hearts of Jesus and Mary, the infancy of Christ, the Blessed Virgin . . .
- We must unite ourselves to Jesus ("adherence") through communion in his mysteries, his dispositions, and his Heart.
- Jesus comes and lives in us through faith, love, and our apostolic commitment. This "life of Jesus in us" begins at Baptism, and it is nourished and grows by our participation in the Eucharist and in meditation, which is nonsacramental communion.
- Jesus sends us, as he was sent by the Father and as he sent his

Apostles after they had been enriched with the gift of the Spirit.

- Jesus is linked to Mary in a unique, definitive way: she gave him his humanity, he lives in her, and she is still his mother and ours.

Many passages could be quoted to illustrate this. For instance, the *Discours sur l'état et les grandeurs de Jésus*: "A great mind of this century (Nicolas Copernicus) maintained that the sun and not the earth is the center of the universe. He maintained that the sun was motionless and that the earth, in conformity with its round shape, orbited the sun. This theory goes counter to all appearances that incline us to believe that the sun is constantly revolving round the earth. This new theory, which few astronomers accept, can be helpful and should be adhered to when applied to the science of salvation. Jesus is the great motionless sun around whom all things revolve. He is like his Father and sits at His right hand; like Him he is motionless and sets everything in motion. He is the real center of the world, and the world should continually move towards him. Jesus is the sun of our souls, and from him come all grace, enlightenment, and influence. The earth of our hearts should continually move towards him. . . Let us, then, turn to Jesus every movement and every affection of our heart; let us raise our hearts to him and praise God for his only Son and the mystery of his Incarnation with the following thoughts and words."[20] This is followed by an "elevation" to the Trinity.

b. Christian living is essentially Christ living in us. The words "Christian" and "Christian living" frequently recur in the speech and writings of Olier and of Jean Eudes especially. The terms possess a profound meaning for these Bérullians. Jesus is not only the Master to be listened to and followed, the King to be served, the Friend who wants to be close to us, but the Life of our life: "Christian living is the continuation and fulfillment of the life of Jesus. . . . When a Christian meditates, he continues and fulfills the prayer of Jesus" (Jean Eudes).[21] This is the application of Paul's words: "It is no longer I who live, but it is Christ who lives in me" (Gal 2:20). This identification takes place through the formation of Jesus in us (cf. Gal 4:19) by the Holy Spirit when we are in communion with the states, dispositions, and even the sentiments of Jesus. In more recent times, St. Theresa of the Child Jesus said to Christ on the day of her religious profession on September 8, 1890: "You, Jesus, be everything"; and shortly before her death she wrote, "I can feel that when I love my sisters, it is Jesus who loves them through me." Elizabeth of the Trinity prayed to Jesus to "come into me as Adorer, Restorer, Savior." She prayed to the Holy Spirit to "take possession of me so that the Word may, so to speak, become incarnate in my soul and that I may be to him an additional humanity in which he renews his mystery." This is perfectly in line with the teaching of St. Paul and Bérulle.

The reason that so much prominence is given to the Holy Spirit is, then, quite clear: He forms Jesus in us. For Jean Eudes, the secret of all secrets was to call on the Spirit. Olier said that we should "surrender to the Spirit," Who will then create in us the dispositions and sentiments of Jesus.

3. The sense of the Church

The leaders of the French school were steeped in the teachings of St. Paul and St. John and had an extensive knowledge of the early Church Fathers (which became, in turn, the primary source of St. Louis de Montfort's knowledge and love of the early Fathers). It is therefore not surprising to find that their insight into the mystery of the Mystical Body is highly theological. E. Mersch writes, "Some aspects of our incorporation into Christ can only be understood by reading some of their works."[22] Their teaching contained the germ of the recent theological advances concerning the Mystical Body as well as many of the ideas set out in the Second Vatican Council constitution LG. If Bossuet could say that the Church is "Jesus Christ expanded and communicated," he was, in fact, expressing in resume the thought of the entire Bérullian school.

There is no need to dwell on this aspect of their doctrine and of their contemplation. However, we will draw attention to the fact that their broad and deeply mystical vision of the Church contrasts starkly with the idea, then prevalent, of a Church with a highly centralized government preoccupied with legalistic matters. They did not look at the Church through rose-tinted glasses. They were well aware of her "stains and wrinkles"; but they still looked on her as the Spouse of Christ and ultimately as Christ himself. They were anxious to see the Church expand: "All we do in this world contributes to the 'construction' of the Body of Christ. All the saints have worked to this end."[23] They pointed out, however, that without Christ the Church is nothing and she can accomplish nothing except in Jesus.

"Beautiful as she is, the Church has many stains and wrinkles, whereas God is a stainless mirror; the moon can only give the light it reflects; likewise, the Church owes her light to the Sun. Just as the moon by itself is nothing and can give no light without the sun, so the Church is nothing by herself, and she is helpless without Jesus Christ our Lord."[24]

Jesus lives on in the Church. The Bérullians laid emphasis on two aspects of the mystery of the Church: liturgical prayer and missionary activity. In their view, the liturgical year offers opportunities to relive the states and mysteries of Jesus, and by their preaching and dedication, the missionaries, animated by the apostolic spirit of Jesus, continue and fulfill the mission of the Incarnate Word.

4. The French school and missionary activity

The criticisms leveled at the French school include those of concentrating exclusively on mysticism and of standing aloof from apostolic activities. According to some critics, the French school taught prayer and adoration but not a missionary spirit. Bérulle and his school would—according to this opinion—be far from the teachings of LG.

Such criticisms show that their authors are guilty of anachronism or are purely and simply ignorant of what actually took place in France in the seventeenth century. Admittedly, the current of spiritual and missionary renewal did not always progress smoothly, and some followers of the French school misinterpreted the thought of its founders. Having said that, we must be fair and acknowledge also that the seventeenth century in France was marked by great missionary activity, and the theological teaching of the spiritual masters of that period shows remarkable consistency, still of great value to the Church. The contribution of the Bérullians includes its vision of the Church from the "apostolic" angle as continuing the mission of Jesus, and not only their profound sense of Christian life and prayer.

One of the reasons that opinion is divided about the French school of spirituality is that such spiritual masters as Bérulle, Condren, Olier, Jean Eudes, and Vincent de Paul are too often depicted only as spiritual masters and mystical writers, whereas they were "apostolic" men, men of action, in touch with their times.

If we look closely at seventeenth-century France, we find that the mystical dynamism and the missionary development of that time went hand in hand; they stemmed from a keen sense of the Church and of the Gospel, coupled with total docility to the Holy Spirit, the Spirit of Jesus, the first One to be sent.

a. The seventeenth century saw great missionary activity in France. It is impossible to speak of the seventeenth-century spiritual and mystical masters without taking a close look at their apostolic commitments and examining the connection between their mysticism and their missionary activity. We must consider the seventeenth century's very strong missionary current *ad extra* within the wider framework of the pastoral and spiritual Christian renewal of that period.

• The controversies between Catholics and Protestants were of considerable interest at that time. First Francis de Sales, then Bérulle, Condren, and many others worked hard to bring Protestants back to the Catholic Church. This apostolate came high on the list of their priorities. To give only one typical example, Bérulle brought Mlle. de Raconis into the Catholic Church, then was instrumental in her joining a Carmelite Convent. Bossuet and Fénelon continued this apostolate later on.

• The "Home missions" developed considerably and were very successful in the seventeenth century. Vincent de Paul called his community the Congregation of the Mission. Many priests of the Oratory and others gave missions throughout France, working either independently or in connection with Vincent de Paul and his missionaries. Besides teaching at the Oratory, Jean Eudes gave 117 missions. Father Maunoir, a Jesuit priest working in Brittany, gave 375 missions. Vincent de Paul and his community gave as many as 700 missions. These figures may help to form an idea of the number of priests engaged in mission work.

In their letters, Vincent de Paul and Jean Eudes mention the sermons they gave, the size of their audience (as many as 20,000 on some occasions), the number of priests (sometimes several dozen) engaged in hearing confessions, etc.

• Great efforts were made to renew the liturgy and the teaching of catechism and to promote charitable activities in the parishes, e.g., by Bourdoise in the parish of St Nicolas and by Olier in the parish of Saint-Sulpice.

• Care of the poor and the reform of prostitutes were the constant concern of such great reformers as Vincent de Paul and Jean Eudes, and of many others as well.

• The training of priests was the constant preoccupation of the French school, whose members were aware that most priests—in spite of their great numbers, especially in the cities—sadly lacked almost any training whatsoever. Besides, the French school, especially Olier, wanted to make sure that the missions would bear lasting fruit, and this could only be done by a reform of the clergy.

• The education of youth in secondary schools (run by the Jesuits and Oratorians) as well as the education of poor children in "charity schools" developed tremendously in seventeenth-century France.

• An in-depth spiritual renewal took place in France in the early seventeenth century; this renewal brought in its wake the missionary and pastoral renewal. Referring to sixteenth-century Spain, Baruzi has written: "The people flocked to prayer"; the same could be said of some Catholic sections of the French population in the seventeenth century. Madame Acarie's drawing-room is a good illustration of this.[25] The spiritual and apostolic elite of Paris met there; they used their influence to bring a group of Carmelites from Spain to France (thanks to Bérulle's efforts, more than forty Carmelite convents were established within twenty-five years). It was there that spiritual and missionary experiences were shared for the benefit of all. In seventeenth-century France the people read the Bible and the writings of the spiritual masters a great deal, and religious art blossomed.

• The foreign missions fired many priests and lay people with enthusiasm. Canada attracted the Jesuits, as well as Recollects, Sulpicians, Ursulines, Augustinians, laypeople like Jeanne Mance and Jérome de la Dauversière, and many others who gave themselves wholeheartedly to the evangelization of Canada. Later Montfort himself seriously considered going there. The Capuchins and others left for the Middle East; the work of Jesuits like Alexandre de Rhodes in Vietnam was to bear lasting fruit. The seminary for the foreign missions opened in Paris in 1663.

b. Two meaningful words: "mission" and "apostolic". When they used the word "mission," the members of the French school, like Bérulle, Condren, and Vincent de Paul, were referring ultimately to the mission of the Incarnate Word. Similarly, the seventeenth-century French spiritual writers often used the word "apostolic": apostolic men, apostolic grace, apostolic spirit, apostolic dispositions, apostolic lifestyle, apostolic wisdom.

In the seventeenth century, "apostolic" did not just mean "relating to the Apostles," or living like the Apostles or the early Christians, or filled with zeal for the Gospel. To the members of the French school, it meant all this, but the core meaning was the spirit of Jesus, as illustrated by Marie de l'Incarnation when in her *Relation* of 1654 she spoke of one of the greatest graces she had received: "It was an emanation of the apostolic spirit, which is none other than the spirit of Jesus Christ."

The following examples illustrate the use of "apostolic" by members of the French school. Condren wrote to Olier about a missionary: "I seem to detect in him something of apostolic grace, for which I respect him and beg our Lord to grant some of it to you and me."[26] Before he left to give a mission at Montdidier, Olier wrote to religious living in Nantes: "I entreat you to pray earnestly and frequently that God may grant me the apostolic spirit. . . . With this spirit we will be able to do a great deal of good. . . . We must strive to obtain this gift."

When he spoke of his community, Olier often called it an "apostolic house," and he wrote: "If in a seminary there were three apostolic men with the Gospel virtues of knowledge and wisdom . . . they would suffice for the sanctification of the entire diocese."[27]

We notice something similar in Jean Baptist de la Salle's writings. In his *Meditations* for the time of a retreat, he draws the attention of his Brothers to the fact that they are "successors of the Apostles in your task of instructing the poor and teaching them catechism"; God has "given you the grace to share in the ministry of the holy Apostles."[28]

Long before Jean Baptist de la Salle, St. Francis de Sales, Peter Fourier, and Alix le Clerc had addressed nuns as "female apostles" (*apôtresses*), because through prayer or teaching these women were continuing the ministry of the apostles in their time.

The terminology used by the French school shows that its members were considering mission work from a theological point of view: it was the mission of the apostles themselves, and it had to be carried out in an apostolic spirit.

c. A theology and a spirituality of mission work: the contribution of the Bérullian school. All these men and women, so dedicated to promoting apostolic and missionary activity in their time, were driven by strong convictions:

- Jesus, who was the first to be sent by the Father, is the origin of every mission, of every proclamation of the Gospel. This theme recurs frequently in Bérulle's writings, especially in the *Discours sur la Mission des Pasteurs (Discourse on the Mission of Pastors)*.
- The zeal animating today's apostles, their apostolic spirit, is none other than the Spirit of Jesus, which

they share with him. Missionaries, apostolic persons, not only try to imitate Jesus but are bearers of Christ and borne by his Spirit.

In his "Mémoires," J. J. Olier writes: "During my meditation I have been granted the grace to understand that Our Lord has come to reside in the Blessed Sacrament of the altar in order to continue his mission until the end of the world and to reveal the glory of his Father. I also realized that all apostolic persons and the apostles are Christ-bearers: they take Our Lord with them wherever they go; they are, as it were, sacraments bearing Christ in order that under their appearance and through them he may proclaim the glory of his Father."[29]

Similar passages can be found in the writings of most members of the Bérullian school. They give ample evidence that their apostolic commitment was rooted in their faith and their spiritual experience. Their "communion" in the states and interior dispositions of Jesus led them to imitate the Heart of Christ in his universal charity and to "surrender to his apostolic Spirit."

The little-known prayer composed by J.J. Olier and hinting at the zeal of the Blessed Virgin for the Church runs along the same lines: "Jesus living in Mary, grant us a share in her holiness, through which she dedicated herself only to God; grant us a share in her zeal for your Church; and grant us to be so completely possessed by you that we may count for nothing so that like Mary we may only live through your Spirit to the glory of your Father. Amen."[30]

5. A specific pedagogy

Nearly all the spiritual masters, as well as the founders of world religions, have been remarkable teachers. We find evidence of this in the Old Testament with the oracles and deeds of the prophets, the sayings and writings of the sages, and the Psalms. Jesus himself was a great teacher, as were the Apostles and many holy Christians. The leaders of the French school sought to initiate their followers into a deep "Christian" life, rooted in the Word of God and finding its expression in prayer nourished by the great spiritual writers of the past; their Christian life included commitments, especially those inherent in Baptism, and in the form of vows of servitude.

The French school has left us formulated prayers like *"O Jesu, veni in me,"* which was composed by Condren and augmented by Olier to become "O Jesus living in Mary," so highly recommended by Montfort. Jean Eudes imitated Bérulle and composed the Office of the Heart of Mary in 1648 and the Office of the Heart of Jesus in 1672. He also promoted the recitation of several prayers, the best known of which is *"Ave Cor"*, a prayer to the Heart of Jesus and Mary.

The Bérullians punctuated their day with prayers and examinations of conscience. The texts of these were nearly always centered on Jesus, like the forenoon exercises composed by Jean Eudes, which were eminently Christological. The particular examinations by Tronson, in spite of their limitations, show a great pedagogical concern.

The best-known method of mental prayer worked out by the Bérullian school is that of Saint-Sulpice. It was originally a simple method, consisting in keeping Jesus before the eyes, in the heart, and in the hands. It was later cluttered, however, with a variety of acts designed to help beginners at the risk of becoming, like the particular examinations, too much of a "psychological" exercise.

During the parish missions organized by the apostles of the seventeenth century, a variety of methods were used to impart solid instruction to the faithful and prepare them for general confession and the renewal of the baptismal promises. Montfort used their methods in his own distinctive way. It would be interesting to compare his principles and methods with those of Jean Eudes and others.

6. The pessimism of the French school

One of the criticisms leveled at the leaders of the French school—and also at St. Louis de Montfort—is that they took an excessively pessimistic view of human nature. By insisting on the sinful condition of man and his nothingness as a created being, Condren's and Olier's views appear to go counter to what the Bible says about the "goodness" of creation and therefore to be at variance with the teaching of the Second Vatican Council.

In order to understand the way of thinking of the Bérullians, we must study them in context. They had their limitations, due to the time they lived in, and without wishing to defend them, we must say that their writings are worth reading today with great attention. Their idea of human nature and Christian self-denial challenges us today; it invites us to read the NT more carefully and to reread our own experience with closer attention.

We must, first of all, make a distinction between their view of human nature and the emphasis they placed on counting oneself as nothing (*anéantissement*) and dying to self in order to live; the two, of course, are connected. Bérulle, Olier, and Jean Eudes emphatically assert that we have to die to self but what is essential is life: "We must pray that God may grant us the state and spirit of death to self in order to live to Jesus, which we cannot do unless we die to self."[31] Olier points out first that, in imitation of Jesus, "we must die to self and immolate ourselves to God . . . count ourselves as nothing for the sake of the One we love . . . die to all created things . . . not just to one thing but to all." He goes on to say, however: "Love of the Cross and death to self are not the whole of the Christian religion. They are only the principles and foundations. They remove the obstacles to progress on our way to religion. . . . Religion is summed up in the words *'Sequere me,* Follow me.' St. Jerome himself points out that Christian and religious perfection does not consist in being stripped of all things, as some philosophers were. The perfection of the Christian religion consists in following the interior life and the holy and divine ways of Jesus Christ."[32] In addition, Olier is well-known for emphasizing the mystery of the Resurrection of Jesus, even though L. Tronson weakened this emphasis when he published Olier's writings in *Traité des saints ordres.*

We may, however, still think that the French school overemphasized the radical weakness of human nature and man's fundamentally sinful condition. Undeniably, some passages in their writings underline man's separateness from God rather than the "image and likeness" mentioned in the creation narrative. But unless we have a comprehensive knowledge of their writings, we cannot make the necessary qualifications. When "he listened to the birds singing" or watched the fire burning, Olier became almost Franciscan.

We have to bear in mind that the times were penetrated with Augustinianism and even rigorism. The extreme views adopted by Port-Royal are witness to this. We must also remember, however, that contempt for the world as advocated by Port-Royal and the Jansenists was promoted in reaction against the commitment "to the world" advocated by the Bérullians, priests and laypeople alike. The stand taken by Gaston de Renty is abundant proof of this.

Condren and Olier had read the works of St. Augustine and meditated many times on Rom 7 and on what St. John says about "the world" and the opposition between light and darkness. In addition, their pessimism was fostered by their human and spiritual experience. Olier's experience had been a particularly severe test for him. Few seem to have experienced as acutely as Olier the distress caused by the human condition and the anguish of opting to live the Christian life. This may be partly due to the fact that he was a highly sensitive man, and also to the interior and exterior trials that had made him "feel prostrate" during a crisis between 1639 and 1641. He came out of it, however, experiencing a new freedom, happy and filled with apostolic zeal. But he never forgot that dark period of his life.

We must also keep in mind that the leaders of the French school were real mystics. We have a long way to go before we can experience God and our nothingness as radically as they did. Their message to us, however, is an important one. Before them, St. John of the Cross had written about "the greatest and highest state we can attain in this world. It does not consist in amusements, indulging one's tastes, or spiritual sentiments, but in dying resolutely to all things interior and exterior."[33]

Finally—and this is perhaps the essential message of the French school—only in Jesus can humanity be both reconciled and re-created. Our aim should be total communion with Jesus, and the only way is total death to self. The way to Jesus is through the Cross, and "without him we can do nothing."

V. Louis Marie de Montfort, the Last of the Great Bérullians

What we have said so far should make fairly clear what H. Brémond meant by this expression. We will conclude by giving briefly the reasons Montfort belongs to the French school. Other articles in this manual point to additional reasons. What we are offering here are avenues for further exploration.

- As an apostle of Eternal Wisdom, i.e., the Incarnate Word, Montfort took up and developed in his own highly distinctive way Bérulle's idea of Christ-centeredness. When he considers at length the mysteries of Jesus lived in Mary and communicated by her, he develops Olier's thought and prayer. The fervent writings of Olier about the interior life of Mary are powerfully echoed by Montfort. In season and out of season, however, this "last of the great Bérullians" keeps pointing out that faith and Christian living demand that Christ be given absolute preeminence: *"Jesus, our Savior, true God and true man must be the ultimate end of all our other devotions; otherwise they would be false and misleading. He is the Alpha and the Omega, the beginning and the end of everything. We labor,' says St. Paul, 'only to make all men perfect in Jesus Christ.' For in him alone dwell the entire fullness of the divinity and the complete fullness of grace, virtue and perfection. . . . If then we are establishing sound devotion to Our Blessed Lady, it is only in order to establish devotion to Our Lord more perfectly by providing a smooth but certain way of reaching Jesus Christ. If devotion to Our Lady distracted us from Our Lord, we would have to reject it as an illusion of the devil. But this is far from being the case. As I have already shown and will show again later on, this devotion is necessary, simply and solely because it is a way of reaching Jesus perfectly, loving him tenderly, and serving him faithfully"* (TD 61-62).

• Like many of his contemporaries, Montfort was a missionary, but his activity was as firmly based on theology as Jean Eudes'. His concern for teaching the renewal of the baptismal promises and Consecration to Jesus through Mary fit in and further clarify the practices advocated by Jean Eudes. The secret that he reveals, i.e., the practice of holy slavery of love, is a continuation and, at the same time, a splendid union of the vows of servitude to Mary and to Jesus practiced and advocated by Bérulle and Olier. Montfort goes into great detail when dealing with the advantages of this practice and specifies its practical approach so that it may become an authentic and fruitful commitment. (St. Louis, although loud in his praise of Cardinal de Bérulle [cf. TD 162], does not hesitate to modify radically both the theological underpinnings and the practical specifics of the Consecration as it is generally taught by the Bérullians.) The short SM, which makes the specifically montfort Consecration to Jesus Wisdom through Mary easily accessible, cannot substitute for TD, which remains the classic on Marian devotion.

Of all the saints of that period and perhaps of all times, Father de Montfort probably delved deepest into the theological foundation of devotion to the Blessed Virgin to improve the Christian way of life of ordinary people. Pope John Paul II, who likewise considers TD a classic on Marian devotion, has said: "Montfort introduces us into the very interplay of Christ's mysteries, which nourish our faith, help it to grow, and make it bear fruit."[34]

• When considering the Cross, Montfort took a positive view and disapproved of suffering for the sake of suffering. His view is reminiscent of St. Paul and of Olier's *Pietas Seminarii Sancti Sulpitii (Piety of the Seminary of Saint-Sulpice).* Like Bérulle and Olier before him, Montfort maintains that the severe austerity of the Cross and of death to self is tempered by the love and maternal presence of Mary. He longs for an increase in the number of "*willing slaves who, moved by generous love, commit themselves to Christ's service after the manner of slaves for the honor of belonging to him*" (TD 73).[35]

R. Deville

Notes: (1) We are especially indebted to Pourrat, Gautier, G. Rotureau, L.Cognet, P. Cochois, M. Dupuy—whose works are mentioned in any general study of the French school itself—for their recent publications, which have supplied us with texts as well as a solid historical and theological basis for a better knowledge of the school of Cardinal de Bérulle. Cf. William M. Thompson, ed., *Bérulle and the French School: Selected Writings,* Paulist Press, New York 1989. The Montfort Missionaries publish a large number of studies and important documents; the recent foundation of the International Montfort Center in Louvain, Belgium, should spur on research into montfort spirituality. The De la Salle Christian Brothers publish a very interesting series of *Cahiers lasalliens.* (2) *Eloge funèbre de Mgr Forbin-Janson (Funeral Oration of Bishop Forbin-Janson),* Nancy, August 28, 1844, in *Oeuvres complètes, notices, et panégyriques (Complete Works, Notices, and Panegyrics).* (3) *Entretiens spirituels (Spiritual Conferences),* Dodin, Paris 1960, 502. (4) *Vie et royaume de Jésus (Life and Kingdom of Jesus),* part 2, Paris 1924, 166. (5) Ibid., part 3, 310-312. (6) Ibid., part 6, 452. (7) G. Chaillot, P. Cochois and I. Noye, *Traité des saints ordres (1676) comparé aux ecrits authentiques de Jean-Jacques Olier (1657) (The Treatise on Holy Orders [1676], Compared to the Authentic Writings of Jean-Jacques Olier [1657]),* critical edition, La Compagnie de Saint-Sulpice, Paris 1984. (8) *Pietas Seminarii,* transl. F. Tollu, Amiot, 1954, 163. Joseph Bruneau, *Our Priestly Life,* St. Mary's Seminary, Baltimore 1944. (9) "Mémoires," ii, 314. (10) John Saward, *Bérulle and the French school,* in *The Study of Spirituality,* SPCK, London 1986, 395. (11) Ibid., 386. (12) *Histoire littéraire du sentiment religieux—L'Invasion mystique: l'Ecole française (Literary History of Religious Sentiment—The Mystical Invasion: The French School),* Paris 1925, 98, note 1. (13) G. Bottereau in *Dictionnaire de spiritualité,* vol. 9, col. 133. (14) Preface to *De l'amour de Notre-Seigneur Jésus-Christ* (*On the Love of Our Lord Jesus Christ),* 1684. (15) P. Chaunu, *L'Eglise, culture et société (Church, Culture, and Society),* Paris 1984, 401. (16) *Femme,* in *Dictionnaire du Grand Siècle (Dictionary of the Grand Siècle),* Paris 1990, 579. (17) *Introduction à la vie et aux vertus chrétiennes,* chap. 1. (18) Bérulle, Op. de pit, XI, Migne, col. 1245. (19) Bérulle, letter 44, dated October 1608. (20) *Discours sur l'état et les grandeurs de Jésus,* 2, Migne, col. 161. (21) Op. cit., p. 165. (22) E. Mura, *Le Corps mystique du Christ, (The Mystical Body of Christ),* Desclée de Brouwer, Paris and Brussels 1936, 2:343. (23) Archives of Saint-Sulpice: Condren and Amelote, "Théologie chrétienne," ms. 347, p. 574. Cf. J. Eudes on the "formation of Jesus in us" in , part 2, 271-276. (24) Olier, "Mémoires," 2:321. (25) Cf. among others P. Cochois, *Bérulle et l'Ecole française,* Paris 1963, 8-11. (26) Letter 65 to M. Olier, in Auvray and Jouffrey, *Lettres du Père de Condren,* Cerf, Paris 1943, 201. (27) *Projet de l'établissement d'un séminaire (Project of Establishing a Seminary),* in I. Noye, *La tradition sacerdotale (The Sacerdotal Tradition),* Mappus, 1959, 10:228. (28) *Huitime méditation pour le temps de la retraite (Eighth Meditation for the Time of Retreat),* in *Méditations,* Paris 1982, 596 passim. (29) "Mémoires," 2:314. (30) Cf. I. Noye, *La prière à Jésus vivant en Marie (The Prayer of Jesus Living in Mary),* in *Cahiers marials* 123 (June 15,1980), 173-179. (31) Bérulle, Op. de pit, 144, Migne, col. 1183. (32) "Mémoires," 4:12-122. (33) *Monte du Carmel* II, 7, 8. (34) Cf. A. Frossard, *N'ayez pas peur: André Frossard, dialogue avec Jean-Paul II,* Robert Laffont, Paris 1982, 186. Engl. translation, *Be Not Afraid!* trans. J. R. Foster, St. Martin's Press, New York 1984. (35) TD 73.

Canonization of Saint Louis Marie de Montfort

The canonization of Saint Louis Marie de Montfort in St. Peter's on July 20, 1947. Photo by G. Felici.

FRIENDSHIP

SUMMARY

I. THE FRIENDSHIPS OF MONTFORT:
   1. His favorites;
   2. His friends in his family circle;
   3. In his student days;
   4. During his apostolic life;
   5. His friendships with women;
   6. In his spiritual life.

II. MONTFORT'S THOUGHT ON FRIENDSHIP:
   1. Human friendship;
   2. Friendship with God, the Supreme Good.

III. FRIENDSHIP TODAY:
   1. Value of friendship;
   2. Guidelines for a fruitful friendship.

I. THE FRIENDSHIPS OF MONTFORT

Montfort, who had so much difficulty winning followers for his Company of Mary, was not overly concerned about making friends for himself. His one concern was to bring to Jesus Christ the men and women he came into contact with that they might become friends of *"Eternal Wisdom"*; to this end, he used the most effective means, especially devotion to the Blessed Virgin.

To find out more about Montfort and his attitude to friendship, we will look at the friendships he formed in his dealings with men and women at various stages in his life.

1. His favorites

His favorites were ordinary people, especially those who were neglected or rejected, the poor (those we today describe as marginalized), and sinners. "Four hundred men and women, inmates of the general hospital [Poitiers] immediately recognize themselves in this priest, who resembles them."[1] Even though those poor people realized that Montfort was close to them, can we really say that they were his friends?

The case of the people of Montbernage explores this question. They were ordinary people who had benefitted from Father de Montfort's mission, and it appears that he regarded them as real friends. *"I beg my dear friends of Montbernage, who possess the statue of Our Lady, my good Mother and my heart, to continue praying even more fervently. . . . My dear friends, pray also for me"* (LPM 3, 6). "Montfort very soon felt comfortable" in the "lower parts of the town" of Poitiers, because there he was among poor people. They were really his friends.

If we are, however, to be fair to Montfort and look at people through his eyes, we must realize that he regarded all these people as being closer to him than friends. For Montfort, they were his brothers and sisters in Christ who needed his help to become saints and who in turn were a support for him on his journey to God.

2. His friends in his family circle

Louis Marie showed very special affection towards his sister Guyonne Jeanne because he found her *"more docile"* and realized that because of her attitudes, he could help her progress along spiritual paths. He gave her small gifts and flattered her feminine sensitivity and vanity, even promising her something that would not necessarily follow: *"If you love God, you will be very beautiful and the whole world will love you."*[2] His affection for Guyonne Jeanne was to continue his whole life long, as shown by the seven letters he wrote to her between 1701 and 1713. He hastened to Guyonne Jeanne's help when she was in a precarious situation (L 12) and opened his heart to her when he was in difficulties (L 26).

3. In his student days

Did Montfort, who in the hagiography of the day, "had hardly any dealings with his fellow-students,"[3] have any friends among those whose respect he commanded by his piety and his attitudes? It is enough to remember that he organized a collection to provide clothing for one of them.

Jean-Baptiste Blain tells us that one day he slipped away from his friends "and went to embrace . . . a poor beggar,"[4] but in this context the word "friends" is general. What we do know is that during the eight years he spent at the college in Rennes, he attracted the attention of several students, and two of them at least, Poullart des Places and J. B. Blain, kept in touch with him afterwards. These were lasting friendships. Montfort collaborated with Poullart des Places, who founded a seminary that supplied a few missionaries to the Company of Mary.

It can be said of Jean-Baptiste Blain that he was Montfort's greatest friend. He was one of those to whom he confided himself, as Blain himself says: "M. Grignion, who opened his heart to me easily about everything, told me in confidence . . ."[5] It was to him that he revealed how Mary was present to him. It was he who was in a position to criticize his "odd and extraordinary ways," and it was with him that in 1714 he exchanged views on the two ways of life: "in a stable community" and "in the field of the apostolate."

4. During his apostolic life

This period could be described as a period of setbacks. How many times was he refused and rejected before he could make a few friends among the clergy! At Poitiers Hospital he was assisted by Father Dubois, who presumably had some affection for the saint.

When the bishop of Poitiers divided the town into six areas and allotted one to each of the vicars general, one of them, Father de Rivarol, was very friendly towards Montfort. It may be assumed that if he remained there for nine months, it was not without reason: there must have been some friendship between them.

Father des Bastières, who worked with Montfort on the missions, was another of his friends, and he remained faithful to him to the end. L. Pérouas says that "his friendship with him was almost as great" as his friendship with Blain. It was to Father des Bastières that he confided that "he had almost run away as a teenager."[6]

We could name many other people with whom he was friendly, for example, Father Barrin, vicar general of Nantes, his friend and supporter in his dealings with the bishop of Nantes; and also some of his collaborators, like Father Vincent, Gabriel Olivier, and Bishop Champflour of La Rochelle, etc.

Can we say that he had ties of friendship with his followers? The Brothers, whose advice he sought and whom he asked to reprove him, certainly held a special place in his affections, but does that mean that he confided in them?

Did he experience friendship with laypeople, for example, with M. d'Orville, one of the "dignitaries" of Rennes? It really is impossible to know with any certainty.

5. His friendships with women

A certain number of women played a part in Montfort's life.

We will leave aside Marie Louise Trichet, whose advice he took when drawing up RW and to whom he wrote many letters, which, unfortunately, she burned by order of her confessor.

Some of these women, like Mlle. de Montigny and Madame de Montespan, protected him or helped him in various ways. Others called his teaching into question; one such was Madame d'Orion, who began by teasing playfully a saint whose "conversation was always very cheerful, edifying, and amusing."[7] Being beaten at her own game, she then took part in the exercises of the mission. Mlle. Pagé, who had come to make fun of the missionary from her chosen place in the church, was not only won over by the holy preacher, but entered the cloister of the Poor Clares (cf. H 143).

The Mlles. Dauvaise also had dealings with him; they belonged to the lower middle class and worked with him in the hospice for the incurably ill (L 33). It may be with them in mind that he wrote SM.[8]

6. In his spiritual life

It must be acknowledged that what Montfort loved and cherished during his life was the Cross. This was his great friend. He felt he could not live without it: *"No cross, what a cross!"* It was his friend in every circumstance, and he kept praising its qualities to those willing to listen to him, urging them to feel glad to suffer something for the sake of the divine Master and to carry their Cross *"cheerfully"* (FC 34).

It can be said, however, that his closest relationships were with Our Lord and Our Lady. He considered friendship with Mary indispensable and invaluable. He loved her because she is the way Jesus Wisdom took to come to us and therefore the way we go to Jesus Wisdom. But in no way was Our Lady the "ultimate friend" or the "ultimate end." *"Through Mary, in Mary, with Mary, for Mary"* is a way of life by which we may more deeply live *"through Jesus, in Jesus, with Jesus, for Jesus."* This is the "secret" for living as friends of Eternal Wisdom.

Wisdom was Montfort's supreme love. Won over by this *"gentle conqueror"* (LEW 5), he would preach Wisdom and do everything possible to bring men and women to consecrate themselves to Eternal Wisdom, who became incarnate in Mary.

II. Montfort's Thought on Friendship

Although Montfort has not written any treatise on friendship, he readily approached the subject.[9] His teaching was deeply rooted in his experience and can help Christians to live as friends of God and of all human beings. What Montfort has actually written on friendship can be brought together and looked at in a human as well as a divine perspective.

1. Human friendship

As we have seen, Montfort experienced friendship in his dealings with other people. In L he expresses his appreciation of friendship, especially when he seeks help for his spiritual journey or is in need.

He highly values the friendship of his spiritual director, Father Leschassier, who finds it difficult to guide him because of his "odd ways." Montfort promises never to abandon this *"friendship in Jesus and his holy Mother"* (L 6). When he feels he needs God's help particularly badly, he asks Marie Louise's prayers and urges her to *"enlist some good souls among your friends into a campaign of prayer"* (L 15). He repeats this request when he asks her *"to make a novena of communions . . . with some of our true friends, both men and women"* (L 16).

Montfort went through the painful experience of being deserted by his friends, and first of all by his spiritual director. In 1703 he wrote to Marie Louise from Paris to tell her about his loneliness and the indifference of all his former friends: *"My only friend here is God. Those friends I once had in Paris have all deserted me"* (L 15). He felt deserted physically, because people kept away from him, as well as psychologically and spiritually. He found it particularly hard when his actions were *"misinterpreted by . . . our best friends"* (L 13). In the same letter he ranks this trial among his bitterest crosses. He is convinced that being deserted and betrayed by one's friends is part of the divine strategy of Wisdom, who tests his friends *"in the crucible of tribulation like gold is tested in a furnace"* (LEW 100; cf. FC 18).

This is why Montfort distinguishes *three sorts of friendships:*

- *Bad* friendships, which are those among *"the friends of Venus"* (H 12:48), *"the friends of lies"* (H 29:3), and *"the friends of the world"* (TD 54). This sort of false, or at least calculated, friendship is that of "interested friends," and Montfort describes it as *"complimentary friendship."* He warns against this sort of friendship, which fits in with the commandment of the world, *"You shall make friends for yourself"* (LEW 78). It is an illusion. Montfort does not trust unaided human nature because he knows how fickle it is: *"Do not pin your hopes / On your friends or relations"* (H 28:35).

• *Natural* friendships, which do not rise above human considerations and are a danger to Gospel poverty. Montfort gives this piece of advice to the Daughters of Wisdom: "*Do not underestimate the danger of natural friendships, whether with your relatives or friends*" (MLW 5). Because charity makes it a duty to communicate with everyone, the Daughters are to *"avoid particular friendships, never seeking to converse more often with one than with another"* (RW 197). As he wants them to remain free in their apostolate, Montfort prays to Jesus that the Missionaries of the Company of Mary may be men *"without friends, as the world understands them"* (PM 7).

• Finally, *holy* friendships, which foster union with Jesus. Montfort desires that the Sisters foster *"a holy friendliness in the house"* (RW 311). He attaches much importance to the advice and guidance given by friends, especially by the spiritual director: *"In the interests of your spiritual progress / Follow the advice of a wise experienced friend"* (H 10:27). He prescribes that the superior of the community *"should choose a good friend among her Sisters to advise her on her defects"* (RW 319), and to all who want to prepare for Christian death, he suggests that they *"choose two good friends to help you"* (HD 7). Montfort considered that the best friendships were with the poor, who were his own *"real friends"* (H 18:8). With them he was on the most friendly terms: *"The poor beggars and the humble / Are my closest friends"* (H 108:3). In exchange for the friends he left behind for the sake of Gospel poverty in imitation of Jesus, he formed many new friendships with the poor: *"For one friend, a hundred friends / A hundredfold of everything"* (H 20:20).

2. Friendship with God, the Supreme Good

It was probably his positive experience of human friendship that led Montfort to interpret the history of salvation along the same lines. For him, God, who personally reveals Himself in Christ Jesus, is the *"real friend"* (H 55:24). God is *"the best friend of all"* (H 7:11). *"God alone"* is his *"friend"* (H 39:145). But God shows He is our friend in the person of his Son, Eternal Wisdom.

Divine Wisdom's characteristic is his unutterable friendship for humanity. Even before his Incarnation, he *"proved in a thousand ways his friendship for men"* (LEW 47). Montfort sees in the whole OT a manifestation of friendship on the part of Eternal Wisdom, appearing most of all as a loving and liberating power (LEW 48-50).

It is at the Incarnation that the friendship of Wisdom for humanity appears most strikingly. According to Montfort, the deepest and ultimate reason for the Incarnation is this love of friendship, which involves the *"rehabilitation"* of humanity (LEW 42). To form friends of God, that is, to divinize humanity, Wisdom wishes to *"convince man of his friendship; he wishes to come down upon earth to help men to go up to heaven"* (LEW 168).

The reason for the Incarnation is therefore God's love of friendship in all its Christological depth: *"Divine Wisdom became man only to stir the hearts of men to love and imitate him"* (LEW 117). In his love, Jesus, *"this dear friend of our souls, suffered in every way"* (LEW 157) and ended by dying *"in the arms of a dear friend,"* i.e., the Cross (LEW 171). The mystery of the Cross is revealed by Jesus to *"his best friends"* (LEW 175; cf. also 174).

The result of this divine initiative is that Jesus becomes *"our dearest friend"* (TD 138), *"our very dear friend"* (SR 68), our *"faithful friend"* (H 7:8). Montfort rates this friendship as the most valuable thing in life, as he himself says, quoting Henri Suso, *"I will always prize your friendship more than anything else on earth and you will always have the first place in my affections"* (LEW 101).

Friendship for Christ Wisdom is inseparable from friendship for the Cross. To be *"friends of Jesus Christ"* (LEW 180) is equivalent to being *"friends of the cross"* (FC 2, 4, 15; L 33; LEW 172). It is the rule for those who wish to follow Jesus along his way of love. It is Wisdom's way of showing his friendship for humanity, since he *"sends crosses to his friends in proportion to their strength"* (LEW 103).

Finally, Montfort regards Mary as *"our friend"* (SR 14, 53), and he invokes her as *"my friend"* (H 90:16). By giving her this title, he recognizes that Mary fulfills a mediating role between God and humanity *"in winning his friendship and favor"* (SM 37). Whoever finds Mary finds every good, *"every grace, continuous friendship with God"* (SM 21).

III. Friendship Today

1. Value of friendship

The ancient Greeks and Romans exalted friendship *(philia)* by distinguishing it from sexual love *(eros).* For Aristotle, friendship presupposes a certain equality and communion of feelings, even sharing the same way of life. Cicero, the author of *Lelius, seu de amicitia (Lelius, or on Friendship),* insists on the conformity of wills (*"idem velle, idem nolle,* to wish the same, to reject the same"). These writers of the classical age, however, fail to give an answer to two questions: the duration of friendship, fragile because based on natural virtue, which is weak, and its relevance to women, who were not recognized as men's equal.

The Bible exalts the friendship between Jonathan and David, whose similar feelings in life and in death formed a bond between them (cf. 1 Sam 18:1-4; 19:1-7; and 20 in its entirety; 2 Sam 1:4, 5, 17; 21:13-14; etc.). The Wisdom literature contains many texts on friendship, and the best-known highlight its beauty and rarity: "Whoever finds a friend has found a treasure. Faithful friends are beyond price. . . . Faithful friends are life-saving medicine" (Sir 6:5-16).

But it was Jesus who gave friendship its true dimension by his attitude towards men and women. He calls his disciples *friends* (Jn 15:15) because he has received them into his intimacy and revealed his secrets to them. Among his apostles, Jesus granted special favors to three, Peter,

James, and John, by allowing them to be present when he worked miracles, was transfigured, and underwent his agony in the Garden of Gethsemane (cf. Lk 9:28; Mk 5:37; 14:33). Jesus granted special favors most of all to the author of the Fourth Gospel, the "disciple whom he loved": he was his special friend, who was allowed to recline on the breast of the Master (Jn 13:23, 25); he was the friend who went all the way to the Cross, where he was given the Lord's Mother as a gift (Jn 19: 25-27); he was the friend who ran to the tomb (Jn 20:3, 4) and recognized the risen Christ by the Sea of Tiberias (Jn 21:7).

It is Jesus who answers the problems unsolved by pagan antiquity by showing that faithful friends go as far as laying down their life for their friends: "No one has greater love than this, to lay down one's life for one's friends. . . . He loved them to the end" (Jn 15:13; 13:1). Jesus showed his love of friendship towards women as well, especially the sisters of Lazarus, Martha and Mary, to whose house he retired from time to time (Lk 10:38; Jn 11:5). Another great friend of Jesus was Mary of Magdala, whom he called by her name and to whom he appeared first after his resurrection (Jn 20:16)?

It is in Christ that friendship reaches perfection. Only one who is deeply rooted in Christ can share in the Love that had no beginning; only one who is rooted in Christ can experience fully and in complete freedom the human reality of friendship with other human beings. This is how Christian tradition interprets friendship: "You and me, and Christ between the two of us." These words were written by a medieval abbot, Aelred of Rievaulx, who goes on to define friendship as "supernatural love that begins in Christ, develops according to his will, and ends in him."[10]

It is in this perspective that we can explain the many deep friendships between men and women saints: Francis of Assisi and Clare, Francis de Sales and Jane Chantal, Louis Marie de Montfort and Marie Louise of Jesus, etc.[11] Authentic Christian friendship, centered on Jesus, is a meeting place with God: "Of all human realities, nothing is more effective than friendship between friends of God to keep their gaze fixed ever more intently on God."[12]

Montfort is a genuine teacher in the matter of friendship. He gives us examples of faithful friendships with men and women; he invites us to discern between bad, natural, and holy friendships; and above all, he sets us, through Mary, on the road to friendship with Eternal Wisdom, which he considers to be the Supreme Good.

2. Guidelines for a fruitful friendship

Solid Christian friendship is perhaps still rare. Yet it is a fruit of the Redemption, an expression of the Gospel. For, after all, the Holy Spirit does not work in vain in the world, especially since the coming of the Messiah ("I will send you an advocate"). It cannot be in vain that his holiness has spread and keeps spreading. Cannot we say, however, that true friendship—as priceless as it is—is still rare because "sin is at work in the world"?[13]

Friendship needs an environment in which it can be born, blossom, and bear fruit. Is making friends, with or without worldly goods, synonymous with creating friendships? Or does it mean serving one's own interests and ensuring one's future? What binds together those who follow a leader and are prepared to die for him? Is it certain that they meet the requirements of friendship? These questions flow from the brief study of friendship in montfort spirituality. For Saint Louis Marie, the fundamental test of friendship is the simple "Do we love each other in Christ Jesus, for Christ Jesus, with Christ Jesus?" Such a criterion demands an authentic knowledge of the Lord as lived, prayed, and taught in his Body, the Church.

C. Le Bot

Notes: (1) Pérouas, 45. (2) Grandet, 1-2. (3) Blain, 2. (4) Blain, 13. (5) Blain, 105. (6) Grandet, 349. (7) Besnard II, 140. (8) *Les Chroniques de Soeur Florence (The Chronicals of Sister Florence),* International Montfort Centre, Rome 1967, 100-101. (9) Montfort used the words "friend" and "friendship" 224 times. (10) *De spirituale amicitia (On spiritual Friendship),* PL 195, 662. (11) Cf. E.M. Gentili, *Amicizia e amore (Friendship and Love),* in *Dizionario enciclopedico di teologia morale (Encyclopedic Dictionary of Moral Theology),* Edizioni paoline, Rome 1973, 28-43. (12) Simone Weil, *Attente de Dieu,* Paris 1950, 81. English translation, *Waiting on God,* Fontana, London 1951. (13) Brothers of Saint Gabriel, *Rule of Life, Constitutions, and General Statutes,* Rome 1986, 2, 9.

GOD

SUMMARY

I. THE EXPERIENCE OF MONTFORT:
1. The principal stages of his experience of God;
2. A God who communicates;
3. The structure of his experience of God;
4. God the Father;
5. The plans of God;
6. God Alone:
   a. God Alone in St. Francis de Sales,
   b. God Alone in Henri Boudon,
   c. God Alone in Montfort.

II. THE STUDY OF GOD:
1. The god of the philosophers;
2. The nature of God;
3. God, One and Triune;
4. Conclusion.

III. THE EXPERIENCE OF GOD IN OUR DAY.

The philosophy of language has clearly shown that the expression "to speak of God" is far from having a univocal meaning. Some wish to speak of God in the language of clear concepts. Others prefer the language of images, of metaphors, of parables. Still others prefer doxological and confessional language, because they do not want to lose sight of their involvement, commitment, and submission. Not far from this last choice is the rediscovery of the mystical tradition in which God reveals himself in the depths of the soul, in ecstatic experiences, in the consciousness of the *"docta ignorantia"* (learned ignorance), in the cloud of unknowing.

In the last few years, there has been a rediscovery of Montfort as a mystic. He is acknowledged to be someone who experienced the light of God's reality, and did so through his ministry of pastoral teaching. When he spoke of God, he ordinarily did so as someone who was moved, seized, touched. He was no dogmatician finding his greatest pleasure in scholastic argumentations and speculations. Rather, he was a practitioner, someone who knew how to develop a reciprocal relationship between his own experiences and the joys or sorrows of the people for whom and with whom he worked. God was for him a living reality.

I. THE EXPERIENCE OF MONTFORT

In large measure, Montfort thought and experienced God like a man of his time. He expressed the reality of God, and his own attitude towards God, through the images and concepts that he learned in his childhood, at the secondary school of Rennes, during his seminary years, and in his theological studies at Paris. He was influenced by Scripture and by the world of ideas of Ignatius of Loyola, of pseudo-Dionysius, and of Francis de Sales, among others. He lived in the context of the French school (Bérulle, Condren, Olier, Eudes), with its strongly Christocentric spirituality. Nonetheless, he was not a slavish follower but a man who succeeded in living with God in a manner that was completely personal. He had to find a balance between an orientation towards God and an orientation towards concrete circumstances, between verticalism and horizontalism. The result was a life in which can be found many typical aspects of the Christian struggle, of yearning to be in harmony with the God and Father of Jesus Christ.

1. The principal stages of his experience of God

It is difficult to discover what exactly was going on in Montfort when as a young child he spoke of God. What is clear is that since his childhood, he was emotionally linked to what cannot be reduced to the ordinary, to what is directly perceptible. He had the soul of a mystic; his common sense was moved by a presence of another order.

In an early stage, Montfort knew the temptation of searching for God outside all human relationship and outside the apostolate. In his final years, he recognized more traces of the will of God in the trials of his apostolate.

He discovered God in the unfolding of people's lives, of the poor primarily. That only reinforced his sensibility to the God of the Incarnation, of the Cross, of the total *kenosis*. Not that he had developed a very profound system of a theology in the manner of an Urs von Balthasar, for example. But he well knew what things meant or what they should mean.

What was dominant at first in Montfort was the orientation towards God Alone, God in Himself, detached from the world and from neighbor. This is by no means exceptional in the case of a mystic, especially if his character is somewhat special. He took his distance—distance of space—from his family (cf. Abraham, L 30) not for any lack of affection but because he thought he loved his mother more perfectly when "*flesh and blood have no part in it*" (L 20). He regularly withdrew into solitude, giving himself the discipline (a manner of chasing away the demons), listening so that God may speak in him, searching the will of God, trying to lose himself in God (H 28, 43) without reserve (H 153). He distrusted himself and was on the watch for any movements of the passions. He believed therefore that difficulties are a grace; in this sense, he welcomed "*crosses, humiliations and poverty*" (L 16). Montfort shared, along with people like Tronson, the certitude that man is a liar and traitor. This led him to think that it is best for man to keep to himself "*as a snail in its shell, which when it is hidden, seems to be something of value, but when it comes out is wretched and disgusting*" (L 4). In the light of the gospel, he realized more and more that the dynamic of God must be brought into everyday life. He also came to recognize that God is already present there. It cost him to be in harmony with all these tendencies but he always increasingly found the balance between these different poles or moments.

Montfort did not succeed in achieving this from the very start. Like someone who opens up only with difficulty because of character or nature, he searched for this equilibrium from his time in the seminary, principally through mortification and penance. To a certain degree, however, God was still the severe Father. Without diminishing these serious aspects of God, Montfort learned to know God as a force that moved him towards the exterior, the outside. He appreciated that God wills to share his existence with the poor and the suffering. The goodness of God is revealed on the Cross, where God takes to Himself the punishment and powerlessness of the world and supports its entire weight. And when Montfort was in the midst of his worst difficulties, at Paris in 1702-1703, he meditated and wrote LEW. He was not the troubadour of melancholy, but of joy.

2. A God who communicates

In his classical work on the mentality of the seventeenth century, Henri Brémond remarks: "God is our goal: this fundamental truth can be understood in two ways. It means either 'We are for God' or 'God is for us.' In other words, the proposition is both *theocentric* and *anthropocentric*, equally correct, moreover, under these two aspects."[1] God and man are considered from the point of view of their communicative nature. This same thought is found also in Montfort.

What is found in God and in his Holy Spirit, "*honor, glory and virtue*," wishes to pour itself out upon believers (LEW 179). Montfort is therefore perfectly in line with Holy Scripture, where the *kabod* or *doxa* (glory) of God is directed towards the earth and seeks to envelop it. God reveals Himself as an overflowing source of love.

This communicative nature of God is so much the more remarkable when the great difference between God and man is taken into account, a difference even greater after the sin of man. "*Nothing is more worthy of love than God and nothing is more deserving of hatred than self*" (TD 80). Nevertheless, God seeks out humanity and will not reject it. Spiritual theology of the times in which Montfort lived stressed surprise over this fact, no less than Luther or Jansen, but it kept a specifically Catholic tone in the conviction that man is truly sanctified by the grace of God and is capable of good. In spite of a sharp consciousness of the state of sin of man and of his weakness (Tronson), the ancient proverb "the glory of God is man" was not forgotten. When sin is considered by this mystical spirituality, it is never as a final determination of the status of the world but as a qualification seen from a determined and limited angle. The finality, the horizon that determines all is the "good," creation by God, the love and the mercy of God and His desire to communicate with humanity.

3. The structure of his experience of God

The life of faith corresponds in a certain sense to the breathing of God. This structure is seen clearly in LEW 30. Wisdom is *"the mother and the source of all good,*" but man must be open to her, let her descend upon him, "*because she only gives herself . . . to those who desire her and who seek her with all the zeal such a lofty aim deserves.*" Montfort describes the successive stages: "*listen*"; "*act*" (cf. LEW 61: "*ready to give up everything, to suffer everything, to undertake everything in order to possess her*"); "*acquire the light and the unction necessary,*" which will further allow us "*to inspire others with the love of Wisdom, in order to lead them to eternal life.*"

The experience of God lived by Montfort is strongly centered on Christology. The covenant with God is fulfilled by letting oneself be borne on the breath of God in the Incarnation. We must find there the goodness, gentleness, and depth of the Divine Life, even if there is still an eschatological growth possible (cf. LEW 127: the glory of the risen Lord "*perfects, in a certain sense, his kindness*").

The light of God appears after a somber night. A soul is often here on earth "*without any taste, knowledge, or light of glory, but with only the feeble light of faith*" (L 19). Nonetheless, abandonment has something gentle and attractive about, it for it leads to "*wisdom, to riches, to liberty, to the divinity of the Heart of Jesus crucified*" (L 34). When Montfort employs the terms "servant" and "slave," he expresses nothing other than the radical nature of Christian life, the loss of oneself in God in order to rediscover oneself. From all this it follows that Montfort lived God as space and movement far more than as a substance in itself.

For a mystic, the Being of God is less static, more dynamic, and more open. For man, that demands as a corollary openness, welcome, renouncing oneself, humbly allowing God to act. It is the opposite of the sinner often accentuated by Montfort. Sin is always a centering on self, the opposite of *kenosis* and of an anhypostatic life, i.e., not centered on self.

It is not a question of a human experience of Montfort and nothing more. The space of God has to be sought in prayer and liturgy. A place must be created for him. God is not to be taken for granted. Montfort prayed for many hours (L 6). He called prayer "*a flight of the spirit into its God*" (H 15:1). It is only on this road that the believer finds "*God Alone and . . . his holy Name, the only essentials* (H 15:35). Montfort may have lived a life of deep union with God, but he always remains convinced, according to the traditions of the French school, of the holiness of God and of the distinction between God and man. The love relationship maintains distance and is filled with gratitude, adoration, thanksgiving.

Distance and prayer do not suffice; whatever we experience through them must be completed or purified by obedience to spiritual directors. Montfort sought in Brenier (L 10) a guide known as the uprooter of all egoism. In encounters with others, he discovered the will of God and the demands of the Gospel. In dialogue, vocal or silent, he learned to see the presence of God and to understand divine movements. When, finally, he came out of all this as a missionary, he did it "*in view of the necessities of the*

Church" (L 5), convinced that "*God has willed to make use of me*" (L 11).

The place where God wants to be present is primarily the heart of man. That becomes evident in the heading of many of his letters: "*May the pure love of God reign in our hearts.*" In L 15, he adds "*with Divine Wisdom,*" which is developed into "*so that God alone may be there, God alone.*" Later, Divine Wisdom becomes more in focus and the heading is transformed into "*Long live Jesus, long live his cross.*" This is not a cheap slogan for Montfort but a heart-felt wish whose worth he has learned to recognize. He asks God to carve his countenance in us: "*Carve in me your divine face* (H 24:37).

In a letter dated 1715, we read: "*When God is asking his creatures for anything, he asks gently, leaving them entirely free but the longer we delay in responding to his gentle requests, the less we hear his voice, and the longer his voice goes unheeded the more his justice is asserted*" (L 30). God requests discreetly, which can give the dangerous impression that the call of God is somewhat delayed.

The manner Montfort understands God is typically Catholic. If man desires God, it is not in virtue of any quality of man but because God is looking for him and is attracting him. This divine action takes place without any expense to the freedom of man. Man must enter, by his own personal responsibility, into the possibility that God offers. "*The value and high standard of our actions correspond to the value and perfection of the grace given by God and responded to by the faithful soul*" (SM 5).[2]

4. God the Father

The world of God is a world of goodness, of tenderness, of gentleness, of mercy and pardon. This is the context in which Montfort speaks of the anger or the judgment of God. God never betrays his word (L 16). This was the backbone of Montfort's life. "Always united to God, always busy with his duties, always happy, he rests in the bosom of his heavenly Father in whom he has placed all his trust."[3] This is not some romantic feeling. Thanks to this attitude Montfort could swallow all his bitter pills! And his behavior was in agreement with St. Paul: "As dying and behold we live; as punished and yet not killed; as sorrowful yet always rejoicing; as poor, yet making many rich; as having nothing and yet possessing everything" (2 Cor 6:9-11).

Montfort lived trusting "*in the inexhaustible wealth of the motherly divine Providence, which has never failed us in all of our undertakings*" (L 33). True, Montfort speaks here, as we can tell by the context, of God as our mother, and this is in perfect agreement with other passages. Christ "*has a virgin Father in the heavens*" (MRL 2:2). According to LEW, the divine universe reveals itself as a fiancée who invites us to enter her home. Wisdom reveals herself to those who search for her (LEW 4). She is the queen of heaven and earth, of time and eternity. She came from eternity in order to enter into time and became flesh in Jesus Christ, but she is always present as Word and Spirit. She protects the earth from evil and fills man with blessings, but Montfort does not deny the presence of lies and folly.

Even if Montfort was inclined at times to stress the radicality of sin, he did not stop there because he was convinced that Wisdom "*takes the initiative herself*" (LEW 69) and, like a good shepherd, searches for the lost sheep (ASE 70). Christ says: "*I love them so much that I would be ready to die a second time for each one of them if there were reason to do so*" (LEW 130). It flows from this that God cannot resist our prayers and lets Himself be conquered by a living faith and a firm hope (L 16).

The will of God is a point of view that returns over and over again in Montfort. The divine unceasingly and freely wills to enter man to become man's place of repose (LEW 135). Following Jn 19:30 ("It is finished"), he writes, *"O Jesus you have entirely accomplished the will of your Father in everything"* (HD 39), and, after having cited Luke 23:46 ("Into thy hands I commend my spirit), *"O Jesus! You committed your spirit into your Father's hands before you died"* (HD 40).

The Father is *"from all eternity"* the source of creation (PM 1), the "thou" of the Son's prayer. He is "*mercy,*" who can raise up men all aflame (PM 12), the *"almighty"* (PM 3), *"goodness"* (PM 4), who accomplishes justice (PM 5). When Montfort speaks of the Father, he thinks in the most universal divine context, i.e., of God as the enduring source always present to whatever occurs (cf. the unity of creation and redemption in second Isaiah). God is "*great, just, good, true*" (S, in GA, 558).

In the *"Evening Hymn"* (H 53), everything is summarized very simply and directly: "*Let us forever bless / the Lord for all his blessings. / Oh! what a good Father he is! / He conserves us all / He supports us all / He teaches us all / He pardons us all / in spite of our misery.*" The majesty of God in no way contradicts the fact that God is Father, since Father is the majesty of mercy and of providence (cf. H 117). Father and Savior are practically identical.

Montfort tried to attract his disciples into that universe. "*I am your protector, I hold you in my hands, little company, says our eternal Father. I have graven you on my heart and on the palms of my hands in order to cherish and defend you because you have put your trust in me and not in men, in my providence and not in wealth*" (LCM 3). His words are not abstract language but, rather, a language founded on experience.

The word "Father" shows how sublime is this divine universe in Montfort's eyes; the word inspires confidence and is rich in love. It gives us the possibility of abandoning ourselves radically to the world of God, a world become visible in the Gospel of Jesus and in the lives of saints who have followed Jesus. What God signified for Montfort as a living reality was reflected in his own radical zeal as the encouraging, pardoning, challenging "good Father from Montfort."

All this appears at first to be contradicted by the place and the role that Montfort accords to Mary. The Father and Christ appear so exalted that humans are not able to reach them except by the intervention of mediators, like Mary (TD 147). TD 85 gives the spontaneous impression of the inaccessible grandeur of God or of "*infinite grandeur.*" Citing St. Bernard, Montfort speaks of the necessity of "*a mediator with the Mediator himself.*" We are in the realm of rhetoric, not dogma, if we understand this to mean that Mary is an accessory to intensify the distance of God. On the contrary, by her person and by her history, she precisely reveals a dimension of God as God reveals Himself through the events of Abraham, Isaac, and Jacob. Mary adds nothing to God Himself, but in her the nature and the Being of God are reflected in a specific manner. In his special devotion to Mary, Montfort finds God Himself, as—in an analogical manner—God is found in icons: God appears far more in persons than in the cosmos. Mary herself is *"the mold of God"* (TD 219-221; SM 16-18) or the school of the Spirit (TD 258) precisely by the manner in which, open to eschatology, she completely lets herself be led by God and by the Spirit of God (TD 258). When a passage like TD 85 leads one to the conclusion that in the eyes of Montfort, God would be above all a *"mysterium tremendum,"* or "like a Louis XIV at Versailles," [4] it seems evident that the reasoning process is not entirely correct.

Perouas presents an imposing number of quotations from Montfort where God does not appear at all like a God who is close but like "a demanding and all-powerful God."[5] I would like to remark again that it is evident that Montfort was a man of his times and that he did not find other language to translate his deepest experience of God. He was not an innovator in theology; he had to be content with ideas at hand, like ways of speaking and of expressing himself. Moreover, he was limited by his own nature. And in spite of all that, he reached an experience of God that was intimate and liberating.[6]

5. The plans of God

In PM, Montfort speaks of the "*designs of your mercy*" (PM 2). In salvation history, there is the "time" of the Father from the creation to the deluge, the "time" of Christ up to the Cross, and the "time" of the Holy Spirit up to the judgment (PM 16).

In this light, Montfort tried to understand, in his own age, the presence of God. He made use of models of the beginnings of Christianity but remained attentive to the specific situation of his epoch. How does God wish to manifest salvation in the history of his time, in the Church and society of the seventeenth and eighteenth centuries? What are the signs of the times? How must the fundamental Trinitarian and Marian structure of Christian life continue in his own day? At the same time, Montfort saw his own relation to God from a very personal point of view. He was not just any link in the chain but a person with his own beginnings and with a future of his own. Precisely because of that, his relationship to God and also his theology took on a living character. God is not an immutable state of things, but a living reality: hence, Montfort's research and prayer, with all the emotions that welled from within him. His trust in the merciful being of God, in his pardon and fidelity, was only a living

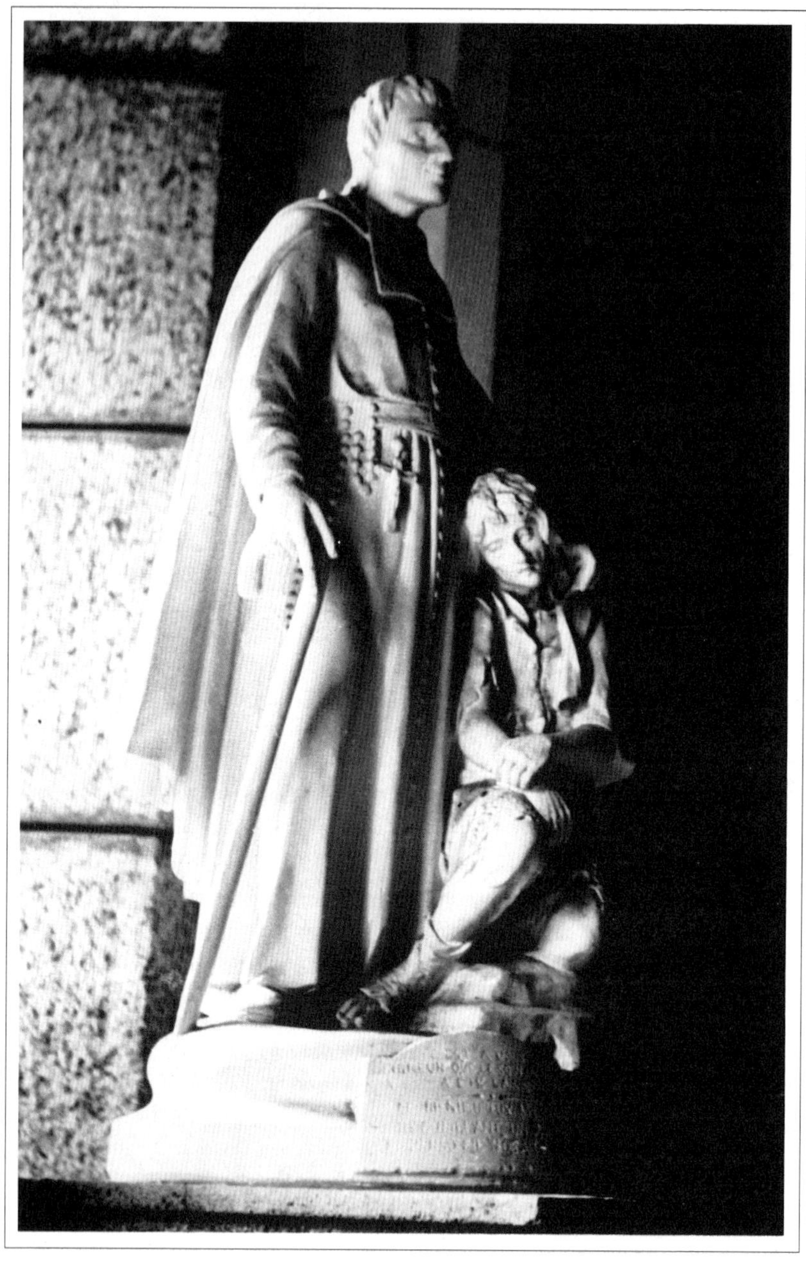

Montfort Caring for a Crippled Man

This statue of Montfort depicts his compassion for the suffering. "You are the members of Christ, a wonderful honor indeed, but one which entails suffering. If the Head is crowned with thorns, can the members expect to be crowned with roses? (FC. 27)". Photo by Aartsen.

reality because every aspect of his life was touched by the merciful God. "God has need of man"! (Suhard); "*Gloria Dei vivens homo* (The glory of God is man)" (Irenaeus).

The structure of salvation and of redemption is inscrutable both in origin and in its ways; but it is to come about through man. For Montfort, God is not a cheap stopgap. All the means of salvation are attempts by God to win over the heart of man (cf. LEW 104-132). The collaboration of man is enveloped from the beginning by the grace of God so that it may attain a personal quality. The grace of God respects man; in fact, seeks a partner in him (cf. Mary). Thus God lets Himself be entreated by man. PM is Montfort's most eloquent statement on this point.

For Montfort, the manner by which God seeks man is visible in Mary, because He has willed to fulfill her prayers made in silence, poverty, and humility (TD 3). This is the structure of grace and of redemption in someone already turned to the Lord. From this is born cooperation. Grace means that God wills to encounter man in his aspirations (TD 5). Montfort perceives this operation of grace in Mary's role in the Incarnation. Even though he fully recognizes that the initiative comes from God, he knows that God does not will to follow up the initiative by cornering her. Her own virginal, humble welcome corresponds to the fact that what happens to her depends completely on God. The "en-hypostatic" (the entry into God) requires an "a-hypostatic" (the emptying of self in total welcoming).

The Most High willed thereby to enrich her, to elevate her, to honor her, because during her earthly life, in her profound humility, she always emptied herself of self, humbled and hidden in the abyss of nothingness (TD 25). The "because" indicates cooperation and also its structure. It is not a question of any adaption of the normal order of causality but of an order that becomes visible only through Scripture.

For Montfort, this relation between God and man is to be renewed in each human life. Each one is called into this relation in his own concrete situation. Montfort tried to read his own vocation from the point of view of the needs of his time. That is what led him to the conviction that God wanted something of him and that God Himself willed that he win over others to be his collaborators in the apostolate. He was utterly convinced that God also willed to accomplish salvation history in him and through him, that God called him to found a Congregation. PM testifies to this concrete experience of God. Using the literary form of a prayer, PM is the result of a meditation, a conscious conviction of what God concretely wills. When Montfort prays in such an urgent manner, he gives space to God both in his own life and in that of others. Whoever reads PM or, better still, prays it, knows what the reality of God signifies for Montfort.

6. God Alone

"*God Alone*" signifies that for Montfort the universe is to be understood in terms of its ultimate reality—with God as its origin and purpose. What he means to say is seen when, for a plan of a mission sermon, he takes as his point of departure *"the greatness of God and the service given to him"* (S, in GA, 567).

a. God Alone in St. Francis de Sales. The expression "God Alone" is found already in the writings of Francis de Sales. In his well known *Introduction to the Devout Life* (1608), he compares the life of Christians in the world to the activity of moths. "These firebugs fly into the flames without burning their wings" (preface). "God Alone" indicates the mentality or the horizon of a Christian in the world: in and for the world but not of the world (cf. Jn). In order to be able to live for God Alone, "He has given you the understanding to know, the memory to remember Him, the will to love Him, the imagination to picture His blessings, eyes to see the marvels of His works, a tongue to praise Him, and also the other faculties." That appears to be a prophecy of the spirituality and the pastoral practice of Montfort. "God Alone," requests "a lively and attentive apprehension of the omnipresence of God, i.e., that God is in us and everywhere and that there is no place, no thing in this world where he is not present truly, so that, like birds always encountering the air no matter where they fly, wherever we may go, wherever we may be, we find God present. Everyone knows this truth, but not everyone is attentive enough to grasp it" (part 1, chap. 2). At the same time, it is important "to think that not only God is present where you are but that He is in a special way in your heart and in the depths of your spirit, which He vivifies and animates with His divine presence, being present there as the heart of your heart and the spirit of your spirit" (ibid).

b. God Alone in Henri Boudon. The plan for a retreat of ten days, entitled *God and I,* by Henri-Marie Boudon, one of the writers studied by Montfort, shows to what point Montfort was in the spiritual tradition of his time.[7] As Jesus went off into the desert in order to be with God Alone, so the soul should also go away from the world. The "God Alone" of Boudon is evidently a "God Alone in union with our good Savior" or "God Alone in three Persons and always God Alone in holy union with the Sacred Heart of our good Savior, the Savior of all men"; Boudon frequently employs these expressions in his letters. The first phases of the retreat are: "God Creator and I creature," "God offended and I acknowledging my crime," "God avenged and I punished," "God showing me the wicked state I am in and I desiring to move out from it," "God offering me the remedies for my evils and I accepting them," "God showing me my Savior as a divine original and I copying it," and "God reduced to nothingness and I reduced to nothingness." The conclusion is a series of meditations on obedience, suffering, and the Cross of Jesus and on "God sending His Holy Spirit and I made holy." The summit and the final point of this spiritual evolution occurs on the tenth day of the retreat: "God requesting my love and I giving it to him," "God wanting to be the only one envisaged and I envisaging only Him," "God willing that only His will be done and I conforming myself to His will," "to the greater glory of God." All this is nothing more than the development of the beginning of the Our Father. At the end of the retreat, Boudon formulates this prayer: "Yes, my God, I esteem only You, I have nothing to lose or gain except You, You are every good, outside of You there is but nothing and misery" (1516).

In "God Alone, or The Association for The Interest of God Alone," Boudon says, "we intend but one thing, which is the search of pure love, only for God Alone. Provided that God Alone be esteemed, honored, loved in himself, and in all things, according to His divine good pleasure, I am happy" (*Oeuvres complètes,* 1:429). And in a letter, he writes: "When God Alone is said, I have nothing else to say. The expression 'God first and then something else' is completely disgusting to me. When God is said, all has been said, and in first place, and in second place, and in third place, and forever" (ibid., 3:921).

c. God Alone in Montfort. In Montfort, we find this same world. The refrain of Hymn 24 sings: "*Let us therefore always keep in mind the presence of God.*" God is "*by essence and power present everywhere.*" This is not an abstract study, because *"God looks upon me here where I am."* The effect of this is "*joy and happiness, support and assistance.*" The presence of God is *"the soul's sun,"* which becomes full reality in the Beatific Vision. We can see God in every creature (sacramentality) and also in all those who guide us. But God must be sought first of all in our hearts; God is found "*in silence, in order to find God there more than in any other place.*" The omnipresence of God has, therefore, privileged places of intensity and fullness.

In another hymn, Montfort says: *"He is by his power / present everywhere / and the earth and the heavens / are full of his presence"* (H 50:5). The refrain says: "*Let us adore forever / the Lord in who he is.*" This truth calls out to man. This is what flows from H 139:12, where the prayer is spontaneously completed by a promise: "*I do another task / according to time and place / for God alone, in his presence / and not for my pleasure.*" Here the refrain says: *"I serve God with my whole heart, / that is my glory and my joy.*"

This is the way that Montfort sees the apostolic missionary. He must preach *"with holiness, having only God alone in view, without any interest except that of his glory and always practicing first what he teaches others"* (RM 62).

The "God Alone" of Montfort is not like the "alone's" (*"sola"*) of the reformers (faith alone, grace alone). Montfort, as a matter of fact, forcefully stresses that the Incarnation truly touches life. The more he stresses the sinful state of man, the more he emphasizes that it is not a determination without end but a qualification only seen from one determined angle. The infinity and the horizon that determines everything is the creative will of God, and his desire to communicate with humanity. Although Montfort frankly recognizes the sin of man and underlines it, he even more insists that God reaches out to man so forcefully and so truly that man becomes lovable. This is the nature of the divine dynamic. Montfort sees this realized in Mary, both as an invitation and as a requirement for those who seriously wish to be Christian.

II. The Study of God

Systematic theology of the seventeenth century moves essentially on the speculative plane. In universities and seminaries, the *Summa* of St. Thomas Aquinas served as the unifying thought, although it was read in "the decadent form of scholasticism of the end of the middle ages."[8] J. J. Olier (1608-1657), the founder of the seminary of Saint-Sulpice, wanted his professors to educate the seminarians "in scholastic theology, both positive and moral." The renewal of scholasticism was more in the realm of spirituality. And it was in the realm of spirituality that renewed interest in the thought of the Fathers of the Church took place in the sixteenth century. Between systematic reflection and spiritual experience, there is a rather considerable abyss. They are two quite separated lines.

This theological climate existed also in Montfort. What concerns systematic theology is taken from the views, opinions, and concepts of scholastic tradition. His study of God does not become alive until he lets himself be led by his own experience.

1. The god of the philosophers

Montfort does not approach the world of God as an order that man can understand by his own logical and classifying intelligence. He searches "*on all sides without method*" (LEW 2). Moreover, he has to use awkward words (LEW 20). And although it is evidently a matter of verbal exaggeration, it does indicate, nonetheless, that Montfort was conscious of apophatic spirituality (cf. Denis the Areopagite), of the wealth—far too great for us—of the divine reality and, finally, of the darkening of our intelligence by sin (LEW 36), by twisted passion and hostile feelings. The manner by which God communicates with Mary and the manner by which she responds cannot be expressed in words (LEW 105). In order to point out the incomprehensible ways of Wisdom, Montfort utilizes Rom 11:33 (LEW 168).

Consequently, it is not surprising that Saint Louis turns away from the wisdom of the philosophers, which he considers "*as useless and often dangerous for salvation*" (LEW 74). In this wisdom, the wisdom of the world is made apparent (LEW 79). "*I do not agree that the philosopher's stone is a possibility,*" writes Montfort, in the manner of Pascal (LEW 88). The authentic theology is, for Montfort, a knowledge deepened through the infinite Source of light that Wisdom grants (LEW 94). It is a short, simple road, even if it is a road that leads unfailingly to the Cross.

2. The nature of God

God is "*alone he who is*"; he is "*this great Lord, always independent and sufficient to himself*" (TD 14). "*What is God? A spiritual spirit, independent, immutable, infinite, immense, all-powerful, infinitely beautiful, unendingly holy*" (LS 5, 173).

These expressions recall abstract, metaphysical speculations. But for Montfort, they do not exist for themselves. They are only the threshold of the order of salvation and of grace. That is why speculative and emotional expressions are intermingled. "*God is charity.*" "*I am who am. . . . His providence [is] paternal, without indifference. . . . It is his essence: God is charity.*" (LS 24, 24) When Montfort writes in TD 14 that God "*has only to will to do anything,*" he wants to show the marvel of the choice of Mary. Speculation as a value in itself does not interest him. The same is found in TD 167: Montfort cannot know "*the Most-High, the Incomprehensible, the Inaccessible, He who is,*" other than that " *he has come down to us perfectly and divinely through the humble Mary,*" as someone who "*lets himself be understood,*" and "*has approached, united himself closely, perfectly and even personally to our humanity by Mary.*" When he adds afterwards, "*Without losing anything of his Majesty,*" he appears again, to a great extent, a child of his age, and he cannot develop his theology of the Cross as radically as Urs von Balthasar, Moltmann, and Pannenberg do today.

In his presentation of the thirteenth rose (SR 41), classical theology comes entirely to the foreground, but it is again remarkable to see Montfort unite it spontaneously to the structuring of the economy of salvation. As is well known, Montfort here follows quite literally other writers, but it is evident that he thought in the same fashion. After having outlined the eternal nature of the Trinity and the Trinitarian processions, he transfers spontaneously to a language far more direct. When God is called Father, it is in the sense of "*Father of men by creation, by conservation and by redemption, Merciful Father of sinners. Father of the just, Magnificent Father of the blessed*" (SR 41). The world of ideas of classical theology is completely present. "*We admire the infinite, the grandeur and the plenitude of God, who is named 'He who is,' that is to say who exists essentially, necessarily and eternally, who is the Being of beings, the cause of all beings, who is in everything by his essence, his presence and power, without being enclosed there. We honor his sublimity, that is to say, seated as on a throne, exercising justice on all humankind*" (SR 41). The final words of this citation are again quite meaningful: Montfort returns continually to the care of God for the world and for the salvation of men. It is not surprising, therefore, that one paragraph later, he speaks of the "*sovereignty of God and the justice of his laws,*" of "*his providence, his mercy, his power and his goodness*" (SR 41).

In his meditation on the fourteenth rose, the anthropological side appears more strongly. "*When we reflect that God is in heaven, that is to say, infinitely elevated above us by his grandeur and his majesty, we enter into the expressions of profound respect in his presence, seized by fear, we fly pride and we lower ourselves to nothingness*" (SR 43). Montfort concludes: "*The beginning of wisdom is the fear of God, it is by the fear of God that everyone avoids sin*" (SR 43).

"*God does not change in his thoughts, or in his conduct*" (TD 15).

This vision of the immutability of God does not result in an apathetic God. It flows precisely from the fact that man can be unfaithful to the God of the covenant. It is the base of the affirmation that what God has begun with Mary, he wants to complete with her.

In Hymn 51, the refrain goes: "*Let us exalt forever the Lord in his beautiful deeds.*" And the hymn declares: "*By him all things subsist / everything is submissive to him / even his enemies / and nothing resists him.*" The subsistence of God is placed in the perspective of his mercy. The hymn ends: "*He shows his glory in heaven, on earth his gentleness, / in hell his rigor / and everywhere, his victory.*" The Being of God and His good deeds are always, for Montfort, intertwined one with the other.

The definitions of the Being of God were a necessary limit to the reality Montfort experienced. God is great, elevated, all-powerful, all goodness, knowing all. The missionary was already structurally determined in his historical evolution by the existing discourse concerning God, both in the manuals of theology and in the tradition of piety; nonetheless he reached a point of expressing himself with always greater intensity, based on what he had lived and experienced.

And so a complex and, at the same time, personal concrete concept was formed. And in this concrete order can be seen the influence of Scripture and tradition, of the liturgy and of piety, of the numerous aspects of pastoral practice, of the faces of the poor, of his own troubles with the meaning of existing explanations; and thus he wrote his own hymn on God. And so there was born a symphony that survives him or in which he continues to live.

When Montfort spoke of the characteristics or the attributes of God, he was not speaking of a Being existing in Himself but of the characteristics that are disclosed and manifested to man. When he recognized in God certain proper qualities, they did not refer so much to any intellectual reflection but to what he had experienced, as a believer, in his frequent readings of Scripture and his "following" of God. The anthropomorphic character of the properties of God has its origin in the experiences that he lived as a believer, in the Incarnation of God. They must be anthropomorphic, otherwise there would arise the temptation to seek God in a world far from us, and the appearance of God on the faces of men would be hidden.

3. God, One and Triune

In LEW 14, Montfort utilizes the outline of the Thomistic tradition, leaving-returning (*exitus-reditus*). The background of what is said of the Almighty is the Eternal God who, in sovereign liberty and love, creates the world and humanity. Then there is the humility of the Incarnation and of mortal existence (going outside, leaving: *exitus*). Finally, there is the "return"—the "*glorious and triumphant presence in the heavens*" (*reditus*). The religious understanding of Montfort is determined by the Trinitarian model. He thinks of the Father as Creator, from Whom all flows and toward Whom all is oriented, of the Son as Word in time, of the

Spirit as the partner of graced man. For example, PM—like many other sections of Montfort's writings—is constructed in a Trinitarian format.

What this signifies concretely Montfort showed in the course of the years, when he understood God more and more from the point of view of what he himself personally grasped. He went more and more above intellectual theology and all relationship to God which would remain glued to a superficial moralism. Doubtlessly, for the most part he only knew how to express these experiences in the images, words, and concepts of his time and of his own tradition. But in order to discover there the interiority, the strength, the tenderness, we must always be attentive to what he did in the concrete and what he did not. God was for him a living grandeur, a reality that shone through what was done by his own hands, feet, eyes, ears, and mouth. If he could only with difficulty express himself in any other way than as a man of his time, he was, nonetheless, personal enough to give his own stamp (in the context of existing rules and customs), to the use of the word "God." The expression of his own experience of God was not done to astonish others or to make himself stand out, but simply because that is the way he experienced God.

According to the theology of the seventeenth century, Montfort speaks at times of God without another word, at other times he refers to the different Persons of the Trinity. When he wants to give different structures to the means of salvation, he speaks in a Trinitarian manner. And through the Trinitarian structure, he penetrates into the order of the economy of salvation, where he discovers the Christological centrifugal force and the eschatological dynamic that distinguish and grasp the people of God (and also Jesus inasmuch as the New Adam). The Trinitarian structure also gives him the possibility of bringing forward the secret of Mary and of clarifying it. But when he wishes to give full rein to this structure, he speaks of God and no more. The transition in PM 15, 18 is highly significant: first he addresses the Spirit directly (PM 15), then, by means of a consideration of the Trinitarian history of salvation (PM 16-17ab), it is a question of "*your Spirit* (PM 17c), and, finally, everything is expressed in *"Lord"* (PM 18), undifferentiated.

The absolute language about God and the Trinitarian language intersect, but in the change the semantic field of Montfort's understanding of God becomes apparent. The absolute and the transcendent have for him great value as reality, which unfolds in the distinct dimensions of Father, of Son, of Holy Spirit. Montfort establishes such a link between the treatise "On the One God" and the treatise "On the Triune God" that one and the other lose their abstraction. It follows, therefore, that his language about God is not cold but warm and interesting.

In order to describe the Eternal Trinity, Montfort begins with the economy of salvation, of Revelation. What thereby becomes expressed is the Being of God. Certainly, Montfort knows the distinction between "that which God is in

Himself and that which God is in relation to us," but this distinction plays only a small role in his writings.

The origin unfolds in time in such a manner that we have need of seeking new words to describe its nature and presence. To be truthful to the being of Jesus himself as God, we speak of the Son. To be able to indicate the different degrees of presence and describe the specific dynamic, we speak of the Spirit, the presence of God at the birth of concrete forms of the world. To speak thus responds to the structure of Revelation and goes into the linguistic field of Scripture. In order to avoid tritheism, Son and Spirit are described as proceeding from the Father. The Father is, therefore, always the dimension that contains all. But faced with all this, Montfort is finally without method; he simply follows the road of God's Revelation, going from one wonder to another.

It is not therefore surprising that LS begins with the exclamation *"Quis ut Deus* (Who is like unto God?)" (LS, in GA, p. 558). In a personal way, Montfort intermingles with his vision of God the role of power and of grace and the communicative structure both of God and of man. We can perceive this in the invocations of God in his spiritual testament at the end of LS: *"O my amiable Savior - to your divine Majesty - my God - my so gentle and so merciful Savior - O! my God, my sovereign, my final end - O! my God and my all, in time and in eternity, may I be all yours and all for you, as you are all for me - O! my beatitude, my light, my life - O! the God of my heart - O! Father Eternal, Father of mercies, Father of Lights from whom descends every perfect gift"* (LS 41-49).

Here theology is truly prayer. There is no longer a separation between the head and the heart. These words bear witness to a mystical ecstasy. It is, therefore, not strange that this testament ends up with the hope of dying *"in the love and by the love of my God and my most gentle Savior"* (LS 51).

The heart of Montfort was not in theological speculation or in scholastic reasoning. He knew them, but they did not lead him up into the very universe or Heart of God. The reality of God was for him, in the first place, something to be experienced, something that came upon him and accompanied him, and in such a fashion that Montfort, in the final analysis, could do nothing more than cry out, "*God Alone!*"

4. Conclusion

Montfort did not conceive of God in the context of a purely conceptual metaphysic or of a bourgeois morality, for he was too marked by the warm Christocentrism of the French school, by the spiritual tone of the Fathers of the Church, and by his own pastoral experiences.

The notions of objective knowledge taken from manuals of theology disappeared more and more and permitted a spiritual and mystical experience of God to enter into the foreground. That is what more and more characterized his words, his writings, and his hymns. Terms like "the Most-High" were stripped of their objective meaning. Even when he continued to use traditional terms or images, they were marked by his own experience and thereby took on a coloring, a warmth which was peculiarly his own. For Montfort, God became more and more a living reality, a reality which marked his own existence not in any ideological manner, flowing from a certain number of concepts, but flowing from his own spiritual life, a spirituality that was translated into his entire style of being, of perceiving, of living.

People called Montfort "the good Father," and that is surely the best qualification of the understanding of God and man as they converged in the person of Montfort. It cannot be denied that his psychology, his history, his theological and ecclesial milieus both energized him and frustrated him. Confronted with that, he became a saint, a man of salvation, an icon of the reign of God over humanity and of man, called to the image and likeness of God.

III. The Experience of God in Our Day

That the word "God" can arouse so many feelings and meanings is one of the most surprising and anguishing experiences of our time, particularly in the Western world. Cultural and religious pluralism is extending into all parts of the world. More and more people are confronted by close relatives for whom the word "God" calls up images, stories, and representations very different from their own world of ideas and feelings. It is surprising and upsetting.

Even more, we live in a cultural universe that is theoretically and practically atheistic. The canopy of heaven has disappeared for many; they live *etsi deus non daretur* (as if there were no God), without any meaning except a few scraps, of various sizes, of egocentric or altruistic human values. The world of consumerism rules. The existence of signs of a transcendent and universal reality is doubted; it is even neglected and ignored. The acceptance of a transcendent reality has strained relations with technical reason. Moreover, the value of God and of gods does not appear to have any solid usage. Their function consists, at best, in the control of contingent feelings, the sacralization of a "social religion," or the expression of subjective feelings.

For many people of our times, this is sufficient to keep God at a distance. And so much so that whoever begins to reflect seriously about God and to be preoccupied with the question easily loses face, becomes all entangled himself, and really does not know where he is going! Many people no longer risk this adventure, and so God becomes more and more a "so one says," a dimension that comes from another but not something that touches someone personally and is near. God is spoken of in the same way as a distant planet that a person has heard another explain. And today God is often spoken of by "experts" who simply repeat conclusions like amateurish laypeople or, totally uninterested, let the whole question drop.

For those who truly have the courage to confront the pluralist situation and the need of reform within the Church, the crisis of God may lead to a sudden awareness better and more profound than that which they themselves think, feel, and believe.

When God and the faith no longer are taken for granted, new possibilities are created to encounter God and to learn something of the lived adventure of saints both known and unknown.

We cannot simply repeat Montfort's adventure into God. Following the example of Jesus, Montfort searched for disciples and not for clones. We do not live in his age. Generally, we do not have his character. What we can certainly learn from him is that Christian life is not only an affair of the head but also of the heart—and of the hands and the feet. To begin to live with God entails much risk and suffering—Montfort attests to it. But his great experience is that a life in God gives incredible joy and fulfillment. Man has to move outside himself and place himself under the Word of God. There is no direct access to God. Man must move himself outside himself or, better, let God move him. There can be no question of "God Alone," of God who speaks heart to heart, until man is ready to undertake a voyage which must begin by a departure, a desert, a conversion.

W. Logister

Notes: (1) H. Brémond, *Histoire littéraire des sentiments religieux en France,* vol. 3, *La conquête mystique,* Paris 1925, 25. (2) This corresponds exactly with the theological anthropology of St. Thomas Aquinas: *"Donum gratiae iustificantis praecipue ordinat hominem ad bonum, quod est obiectum voluntatis et ideo ad ipsum movetur homo per motum voluntatis, qui est motus liberi arbitrii. . . . Non requiritur aliquis motus ex parte animae, sed sola continuatio influxus divini"* (*Summa Theologica,* I-II, 113, 3). (3) Besnard I, 30-31. (4). Perouas (5) Ibid. (6) According to L. Perouas, "Montfort was really influenced by the moralism of the late seventeenth century" (ibid., 125). In my opinion, Perouas's vision is influenced by the theological and spiritual climate of the 1970s with its optimistic image of man and its limited understanding of man's peccability. Yet Perouas also says: "As he progressed towards his human and Christian maturity, he recovered the best of this sponsal love in an encounter with God that was starker, more sacrificial, and more profound" (ibid., 159). (7) H. M. Boudon, (The Complete Works), Paris 1856, 2:1469-1516. (8) L. Cognet, *Das kirchliche Leben in Frankreich,* in H. Jedin, *Handbuch der Kirchengeschichte* (The Handbook on Church History), Freiburg, Basel, and Wien 1970, 5:106.

GRACE

"All good things come from above." Saint Louis Marie de Montfort's teaching on grace could be well summed up in that short phrase. "All good things come from above," that is to say, "All good things come from God." *God Alone!* is the foundational principle of Montfort's life and writings, perhaps most especially in his understanding of grace.

I. THE INCARNATION: ENTRY OF GRACE

1. Begging for grace

To say that all good things come from "above," i.e., God, implies that nothing good comes from "below," i.e., man. And it definitely is Saint Louis Marie's conviction that man on his own is incapable of good. Here "good" is not to be taken in the moral sense; rather, good is understood in its scriptural sense of leading to salvation. Through original sin, man of himself has become incapable of this good. The depth of meaning and the stress Montfort gives to the unbridgeable chasm separating sinful man from God is in no way any less than the thought of the Reformers themselves. Time and again the powerlessness of human works to bridge this gap demonstrates itself anew (Rom 3:30-24; Gal 2:16); man cannot span this chasm from his side, not even through good works or irreproachable conduct. Man can do only one thing: become a person of prayer who repeatedly cries out: "Lord, have mercy on me!"

It is this truth which influences Montfort—and so many others—to insist so strongly on the indispensable role of prayer and, above all, prayer of petition (cf. LEW 184-190). Prayer of petition at its core—no matter what precisely we may be praying for —is always a "begging for grace," for the grace of God, which He can grant or not (cf. SR 146). And it is precisely this fact which makes the concept of grace so difficult for contemporary men and women: they do not wish at any price to be dependent upon the grace of another, even of God. Yet it is specifically this acceptance of our total dependence upon the mercy of God that Saint Louis de Montfort—basing himself on the faith-understanding of Scripture—demands of his readers (cf. TD 143).

2. The bridge of grace

Montfort's life and writings clearly illustrate that there can be no discussion concerning the truth that God alone can overcome the chasm between God and man. The bridge God has built over the abyss of sin is grace. God's grace therefore belongs to "time", which begins with Creation and ends with the Second Coming of Christ; time understood as the opposite of eternity. The central event in this time and its absolute culmination is, according to Montfort, the Incarnation of Eternal Wisdom. For this reason, the mystery of the Incarnation is for Saint Louis de Montfort the entry of grace into human time. This holds true for the time before the Incarnation, during which God, in anticipation of the enfleshment of the Word, bestowed on man the grace necessary "*to obey His commandments and do salutary penance for any they might have transgressed*" (LEW 46-47). This holds true for the time of the Incarnation, which is stamped with the fact that in the Incarnation of Eternal Wisdom "*the complete fullness of grace*" (TD 61; LEW 88, 104; SM 12) is present among us. And it holds true for the time of the Ascension until the Parousia, during which the dynamism of God's grace is forever characterized by the inner structure of the mystery of the Incarnation. In the time of the Church, the very dynamism of grace, for Montfort, remains inseparably linked with the activity of the Holy Spirit and of Mary (TD 37). The mystery of the Incarnation leaves its imprint upon the entire history of salvation (TD 22).

II. Montfort's Concept of Grace

All grace comes from God, the originator of nature and grace (TD 213; SM 9). In the doctrine on grace, there are two poles that from the outset stand in tension to one another: nature and grace, God's sovereignty and human freedom. Montfort employs terminology that had become common in baroque scholasticism and speaks of the "*order of nature*" and the "*order of grace*" (L 30; LEW 58; SM 11; TD 32, 121; H 6:23). In this model, in which both orders are strictly differentiated from one another and exist relatively disconnected beside one another, grace is added more or less externally to human nature. Through faith opening up to grace, man is able to cross over from his "natural" world into the "supernatural" world of God.[1] This is what Montfort intends in his act of Consecration.

1. Existential

Montfort is not, however, interested in human nature in the abstract. The missionary has concrete man in mind, who, as he is here and now, clearly goes astray without God's grace. Saint Louis Marie's view of man is not philosophical but existential. This is also the characteristic of Augustine's doctrine on grace, as well as the Reformers'.[2] Certainly, man cannot find salvation without the grace of God, but he must, in his freedom, collaborate. Saint Louis de Montfort expresses this truth most strongly when he speaks of Mary's consent to the Incarnation, which, according to him, makes the Incarnation possible (LEW 107).

True, in this view grace appears as something external to the human being, but it is thereby a concretely tangible grace because it begins with human weakness. The missionary preacher does not speak theoretically, rather, he focuses on the concrete reality of man. In this way, his listeners have a clear starting point in any discussion on grace, whether it be the grace of virginity, or of conversion, or of a happy death. God's bending low over man and His help become concrete, and the effects of grace perceptible.

2. Trinitarian

As Montfort attributes the Incarnation event to the three Divine Persons, so also with grace. God the Father is the source of every grace (SM 9).[3] There is no grace that does not come from the Father and have its origin in Him. The characteristic of the Father is that He is the fountainhead, he "gives": *"The eternal Father yearns for nothing so much as to share the life-giving waters of His grace and mercy with us"* (SR 144) and "*to reign in our souls by his grace*" (SR 39). Above all, God desires to give us "*the greatest of all graces*" (LEW 104; H 103, 22:28), Eternal Wisdom, His Son, in whom reside "*the entire fullness of the divinity and the complete fullness of grace*" (TD 61; SM 12).

The quintessence of the grace of God is Jesus Christ, Eternal Wisdom (LEW 88, 104; TD 61). He is, as Montfort graphically expresses, *"the breast of the Father, full of grace and truth"* (SR 144; the phrase is omitted in GA). In him, God's grace encounters humanity in person. In the description of Eternal Wisdom's goodness and friendship toward humanity before, in, and after the Incarnation (LEW 41-51, 64-73, 117-132), Montfort depicts the divine-human countenance of grace and makes clear that all grace springs from the love of God for man. In Christ, God bends low over us in passionate love and affection, over every human need. That is the quintessence of grace, which again and again finds expression in individual, concrete graces. In the canticles on the Sacred Heart of Jesus (H 40-44), Montfort sings that Christ's heart is for humanity; it is *"the true treasure / of the grace of Jesus Christ; this Heart calms his anger, / obtains his grace and his favor"* (H 40, 15:21).

The third Divine Person, the Holy Spirit, is, in Montfort's words, "*the substantial love of the Father and the Son*" (TD 36; H 85:6). The characteristic grace of the Spirit may be designated, with Paul, as "God's love which has flooded our hearts" (Rom 5:5). The Holy Spirit, the bond of love between Father and Son, draws believers into the divine love through graces and gifts and enables them to respond through love of God and love of neighbor. Montfort's thoughts convey the impression that the Holy Spirit's special activity of grace in the history of salvation is first revealed in the Incarnation and can be read in the person of Mary. Montfort describes the Holy Spirit's activity of grace in Mary with the image of marriage ("*spouse of the Holy spirit*"), which suggests itself from the nature of the Spirit as Love. The Spirit's grace—the love poured out into the heart of Mary—enables her to speak her "*fiat,*" which God expressly receives. Only then can this grace become fruitful and Jesus Christ be formed in Mary (TD 16). In Mary, Montfort finds the model for the activity of the Spirit in Christians, in whom Christ is formed as in Mary. Every human "yes" to God and to Christ flows from the grace of the Holy Spirit and is intertwined with the consent of Mary. Montfort gathers from this that now—in the time after the Incarnation—the Holy Spirit's activity of grace can no longer be considered without Mary. In the generation of the members of the Body of Christ, together with their formation and sanctification, the Holy Spirit and Mary work together: Mary *is "the inseparable associate of the Holy Spirit in all these works of grace*" (TD 37).

III. Mary and Divine Wisdom

Mary is "full of grace" because the triune God has placed *all* grace in her in order that she can be the "*worthy Mother of God.*" For this reason, God creates "*His masterpiece,*" Mary, "*the masterpiece of grace*" (TD 50, 115). This favor, unique in the history of salvation, is the privilege that places Our Lady in a special and unique relationship to God. On the basis of this favor, Mary stands as the pinnacle of all the saints (H 75:25; 76:11).

Mary is receptive to God's grace to the highest degree. Montfort also emphasizes that Mary did not receive God's grace in vain; rather, she conformed to it in perfect faithfulness and has therefore constantly grown in grace (LEW 105; TD 222). Here the general structure of grace can be clearly seen. Man receives grace as unmerited gift; he must, however, accept it and conform to it so that it may become effective.

The fullness of grace that the triune God bestows on Mary, Montfort stresses again and again (LEW 105-107; TD 23), is completely and solely at the service of the Incarnation of Eternal Wisdom. But this is valid not only for the actual moment of the Incarnation of Eternal Wisdom; rather, it remains just as valid for the time after the Incarnation. God does not withdraw from Mary the fullness of grace that He has given her. Mary remains the "*mother of grace,*" because "*she gave existence and life to the author of all grace*" (SM 8-9; TD 211; H 151:4). Montfort can therefore say that *"it is his will that we should receive all gifts through her*" (LEW 207; SR 58; TD 23, 44, 208), that "*through her he [the Son] distributes his graces*" (LEW 207; TD 24; SM 10), and that Mary also distributes the graces and gifts of the Holy Spirit (cf TD 25). Saint Louis de Montfort derives from this truth certain of his Marian titles: "*Mediatrix of the graces and gifts of God,*" "*Treasurer,*" "*Treasury,*" "*Storehouse.*" These may sound quite strange to us today; nonetheless, they leave no doubt that the cause and the source of all grace is not Mary but rather God Alone. As Mother and Mistress of Wisdom Incarnate, she has "discretionary power" over God's graces. Since the Incarnation, every grace comes to us through her eternal "yes" (LEW 207; SM 10; TD 28, 44, 208; SR 58). Mary's special and unique role in God's activity of grace, according to Montfort, reflects the unique role assigned her by God in the Incarnation event: "*Mary is not only the Mother of Jesus, Head of all the elect, but is also the Mother of all his members,*" whom she bears through the grace of God (LEW 213).

In the same way, the divine activity of grace finds its highest fulfilment in the Blessed Mother. Montfort formulates what is included in the title "full of grace": "*She is completely transformed into God by grace*" (TD 27, 63). This transformation in God, the divinization of man (SM 3), is the actual goal of the Incarnation of Eternal Wisdom. It is also the goal of the montfort Consecration. Mary's particular role in Consecration consists in the fact that "*in her alone, by the grace of Jesus Christ, man is formed into God*" (SM 16). Here the actual goal of God's activity of grace is named—"*formed into God*" (divinized)—and the inner connection between grace and Incarnation becomes perceptible. In Mary, grace has already effected this transformation. For this reason, there is nothing to be found in Mary that might stand in the way of God's grace and could become an obstacle to it. The fullness of the grace granted her has brought Mary into perfect conformity with God. Mary's "discretionary power" over God's graces loses its ambiguity. True, Mary distributes God's graces "*to whom she wills, as and when she wills, and as much as she wills*" (LEW 207; SM 10; TD 25, 206). But this occurs by no mere whim, for the fullness of grace brings her will into total harmony with the will of God (TD 164). This perfect harmony with God is an expression of her sinlessness. The purity of heart completely realized in Mary makes her perfectly translucent of God's grace. "The more purely man receives God's grace, the more obviously he is prepared not to retain it for himself but to allow all others to participate in it".[4] Thus, Mary is the source "*where we can drink deep draughts of the living waters of grace*" (SM 20). Montfort therefore draws the conclusion that if we want to find the grace of God, we must really find Mary: "*The difficulty, then, is how to arrive at the true knowledge of the Most holy Virgin and so find grace in abundance through her*" (SM 23). This is an experience that many Christians bound to Mary will confirm. For to whoever turns to her, Mary does not show herself; rather, "she points through herself to the grace of God."[5]

IV. Means of Grace

Montfort's spirituality intends to lead Christians to union with Christ (LEW 7; TD 120). The means he recommends—desire, fervent prayer, mortification, and devotion to Mary (LEW 181-222)—may be understood as the means by which the Christian attains God's grace, because the greatest grace of God is Jesus Christ, Eternal Wisdom. At the same time, yearning after Wisdom is itself an effect of grace, a "*great gift of God*" (LEW 182). Yearning leads to prayer, which is absolutely necessary, for "*prayer is the usual channel by which God conveys his gifts, especially his Wisdom*" (LEW 184; cf. SR 144; H 15:7).

Among the many forms of prayer, the Rosary assumes a special status: "*God has attached to it grace in this life and glory in the next*" (SR 1). Montfort attributes the special efficacy of praying the Rosary to its power of enhancing communion with Christ and Mary. Those who finger the Rosary do not pray with their own words but, rather, with Christ's words and the angel's greeting. The Rosary is therefore "*this clear and ever-flowing water which comes from the fountain of grace*" (SR 38). Thus whoever truly prays the Rosary gains grace and is preserved from losing it. Montfort himself ascribes the success of his preaching to praying the Rosary.

Montfort clarifies mortification as especially the grace of fasting (H 16), silence (H 23), poverty (H 20); special attention, however, must be given to the grace of the Cross (FC; H 102), for Christ and the Cross are not separable (LEW 172). There is a special grace necessary if one wishes to discern the mystery of Christ's Cross (LEW 175), and imitation of the Cross exceeds purely human possibilities; it becomes possible only through the "all-conquering grace" of Christ and the Holy Spirit (FC 15, 26).

That the easiest, shortest, surest way to grace is, ultimately, solid devotion to Mary has already become clear. Mary is the Mediatrix of all graces. True devotion to Mary consists in a personal love relationship with the mother of the Lord; it finds its highest expression in total dependence upon her, which, among other effects, keeps us from losing the grace of God (LEW 222; TD 173, 174; H 80).

V. Relevance

1. Montfort and the "controversy of grace."

The fundamental problem of the doctrine of grace, at least as it has been taught in the West from Augustine up to the so-called grace controversy of the seventeenth century and beyond, is the dilemma: God or man? The question is how divine and human freedom, divine omnipotence and human autonomy, infinite and finite are reconcilable with one another. The history of Western theology shows that this problem is not completely resolvable in theory.[6] The relationship between God and man, between infinite and finite is not understandable through study. Wherever grace is the subject, we come into contact with the fundamental mystery of faith.

Montfort has a certain predilection for mysteries, for secrets. They are not puzzles capable of an eventual solution; rather, they are truths exceeding finite human reason, for which there is no sufficient theoretical explanation or "revelation"; it can only be practically experienced through a special "grace." In this sense, Montfort speaks of the *"secret of Mary,"* of the *"secret of the Cross"*; it is in this sense that the mystery of the Incarnation is the central secret of his teaching. In this very mystery, however, the intellectually insurmountable union of infinite and finite takes place in the Incarnation of Eternal Wisdom. In the God-man Jesus Christ the dilemma—God or human?—is finally overcome. Since the Incarnation, one can only say "God and man," even when man again and again obscures and distorts this "and." The place where this union of infinite and finite is consummated is Mary. Montfort's total devotion to Mary not only binds the believer to Our Lady but leads to the place where divine infinity and human finitude become one; "in" Mary humanity overcomes the false alternative "I or God" and finds the way to the true "God and I." It is saving and redeeming grace in fullness that the Christian finds in Mary. It is God Himself Who has taken flesh in her by the mystery of the Incarnation.

2. Trinitarian grace

It appears characteristic of Montfort's theological thinking that he consistently orients himself to God's revelation as Father, Son, and Holy Spirit. In his examination of the mystery of the Incarnation, he determines the specific role of each of the three Divine Persons. It is the triune God who, in a threefold-specific manner, comes to Mary in the Annunciation (TD 14-21). The examination of the self-communication of the triune God to Mary leads Montfort also to distinguish the specific role of the three Divine Persons in the work of grace. Through Montfort's clarification of grace in Mary, it is evident that grace in its ultimate analysis consists not in God sharing something but sharing Himself. It is God's personal coming to us, Father, Son, and Holy Spirit, and offering believers personal participation in the divine life.

Inasmuch as Montfort is guided in his "practical" understanding of grace by the Incarnation event, he holds fast to his Trinitarian stance, going beyond the doubts and hesitations of the theology of grace of his time. Saint Louis de Montfort inaugurates a new perspective, moving us toward a contemporary understanding of grace as *communio*.[7]

H. J. Jünemann

Notes: (1) Cf. G. Greshake, *Geschenkte Freiheit, Einführung in die Gnadenlehre (The Gift of Freedom: An Introduction to the Doctrine of Grace)* Herder, Freiburg 1992, 61-70. (2) Greshake, *Geschenkte Freiheit,* 79. (3) If Saint Louis de Montfort more often than not speaks of grace in a concrete fashion, S contains an outline explaining the essence of grace in eight points: *1. Grace is an ineffable gift of God.* Montfort broaches the fundamental problem of the doctrine of grace, which even today has not been satisfactorily solved: the relationship between the sovereignty of God and the freedom of humanity. *2. It is a great gift.* Here are to be found the distinctions between natural and supernatural, habitual and actual grace. *3. The necessity of grace. 4. The principles of grace*: the effective cause is God alone, the meritorious cause is Jesus Christ, the distributive cause is Mary. *5. The qualities of grace*: it is illuminating, mild, and pleasant, strong and victorious, humane and sociable; it brooks no delay, and upon rejection human beings are abandoned to their own devices. *6. Obstacles. 7. Means of attaining grace*: prayer. *8. Means of preserving and augmenting grace* (LS 36-40). (4) Hans Urs von Balthasar, *Maria in der kirchlichen Lehre und Frömmigkeit (Mary in the Doctrine of the Church and in Devotion),* in *Maria, die Mutter des Herrn (Mary, Mother of the Lord),* Secretariat of the German Bishops Conference, Bonn 1979, 42. (5) von Balthasar, *Maria in der kirchlichen Lehre,* 42. (6) Cf. G. Greshake, *Geschenkte Freiheit,* 87. (7) Cf. ibid., 132-133.

HOLY SPIRIT

The Holy Spirit is of the utmost importance for Montfort. The Spirit made of him a true prophet, moved by unusual, irresistible charisms. Montfort referred constantly to the Holy Spirit, and he even thinks of Mary only by reference to the Spirit. He said that she was *"entirely relative to God"* (TD 225; cf. 148), but he thinks of her as entirely relative to the Holy Spirit. He wanted to call his Company of Mary the *"Community of the Holy Spirit."* This formula recurs four times in his will. His spirituality serves as an antidote to Spirit-related emptiness. It provided the inspiration for the Legion of Mary, a movement that was poor and humble yet Spirit-related and fruitful (though these qualities, hidden beneath the Legion's external forms, went unnoticed by many). The charismatic renewal (that great twentieth-century movement of the Spirit) owes several of its most outstanding pioneers to this earlier movement. In particular, there was Cardinal Suenens, the first bishop to become involved in the movement (Paul VI entrusted him with guiding it), and Pierre Goursat, the humble founder of the largest and most international of the charismatic communities: the Emmanuel.

What exactly fashioned Montfort's life and theology, which bridged the seventeenth and eighteenth centuries? How are his life and work structured by the Holy Spirit, under what influences and towards what future? This is what the present study will attempt to establish.

I. THE HOLY SPIRIT IN THE LIFE AND TIMES OF MONTFORT

1. Montfort's influences and/or originality

History would have us explain everything by reference to antecedents and milieu. The presupposition of historical research is that the person studied (even if it were Jesus, according to David Flusser) has drawn everything from his or her milieu, arriving at a sort of composite of whatever is available within it. Such a working hypothesis can be fruitful and help to identify certain continuities, constants, and causal relationships. But it also inclines the researcher to miss the originality and uniqueness of the truly novel personality, especially in the case of that "singular" man, Montfort.

It has been assumed that Montfort was influenced by the Jesuits of Rennes, the masters of his college. They certainly guided him and trained him in prayer and in the service of the poor. They must also have talked to him about the Holy Spirit, about whom Montfort learned in the catechism and the liturgy of Pentecost. But it is simply not known how much they spoke of Him nor how influential they were in this respect. Did they collectively lay great emphasis on the Spirit? If they did, which individuals amongst Montfort's first teachers did so? There is no factual evidence to answer such questions.

Montfort arrived at the Seminary of Saint Sulpice in Paris (1692-1700) in the era of antimysticism. Fénelon's work *Maximes des Saints (Maxims of the Saints)* was not condemned until March 12, 1699; but from July 1694 to March 1695, Monsieur Tronson (1622-1700), the general superior of the Sulpicians, was already joining forces with Bossuet and Noailles to attack Madame Guyon and quietist mysticism. The Conference of Issy and the thirty-four resulting Articles proclaimed opposition to adventures in spiritual experience; Louis Cognet has called these events the *Twilight of Mysticism.*[1]

Monsieur Tronson had succeeded Monsieur Olier († 1657). The latter was a mystic prone to occasionally disconcerting impulses; but Monsieur Tronson established observance of the rules, method, and obedience. In his view and in that of his successor, François Leschassier (1641-1725), who was Montfort's spiritual director, there was no place for personal charisms. The slightest hint of novelty and originality was to be viewed as suspicious, particularly if it was a question of visions and revelations.[2]

In spite of the fact that they were often counterbalanced in an intelligent and useful fashion, Montfort's extraordinary transports and charisms were therefore misunderstood and curtailed. His masters counted not on his dynamism but on his unlimited obedience. In spite of this obedience and his faithfulness, Montfort's spiritual director finally washed his hands of the whole affair and left him to his own devices, as if in desperation.

2. A Synthesis of charisms and obedience

Although Montfort's disquieting qualities led him to be misunderstood and suppressed by his masters, the latter did train him in the doctrinal and spiritual theocentrism of the French school. The humble young man surrendered to the Holy Spirit. He thirsted for light, for complete dedication, for mission, for the unconditional service of God and man, especially the poor. He was able to obtain the mystic texts he craved in the seminary's library, where he worked.

3. A summary of influences

Montfort read the writings of Olier, who had influenced Monsieur Baüyn.[3] This influence inspired the basis of Montfort's thought.

Olier founded his seminary as an "apostolic house" made up of priests available for diocesan pastoral duties. Montfort founded the Company of Mary as a team of apostolic men, available for parish missions aimed at Christian revival.[4]

Olier affords a prophetic glimpse of the priests he wished to train: they are "rockets" that "fly through the air to wherever they are propelled by the impetuous force of love."[5] Montfort saw these future missionaries as *"thunder-clouds flying through the air at the slightest breath of the Holy Spirit"* (TD 57) or *"clouds that sail high above the earth . . . moving without let or hindrance, according to the inspiration of the Spirit"* (PM 9). In both texts Montfort replaces "love" by *"the Holy Spirit,"* which is indicative of his Spirit-filled nature.

Besides Olier, Montfort read the *Lettres spirituelles (Spiritual Letters)* of J.-J. Surin,[6] and also Marie des Vallées (cited in TD 47), Marie d'Agreda (TD 207), and Agnès de Langeac, whose experience impressed him deeply (he refers to it twice, in TD 170 and 242). In N, Montfort copied the following definition: *"It is the Spirit of Jesus Christ, his form and his life, that makes the Christian; just as the form and the life of man is the soul. . . . The Christian is a new creature . . . Erunt omnes docibiles Dei (Joann. 6:45). Quicumque Spiritu Dei aguntur, hi sunt filii Dei (Rom. 8:14)"* (N, pp. 306A/B, 308A).

Montfort was indebted to the influence of his friend Poullart des Places (1697-1709), founder of the Congregation of the Holy Spirit, with whom he instituted a prayer group at the Collège de Rennes (1685-1692), according to his biographer Besnard.[7] It is difficult to know, to what extent, for between these two men there was a preestablished harmony, based first and foremost on the place the Holy Spirit held in both their lives. Montfort wanted to call his own foundation the Community of the Holy Spirit; and the convergence between the two men's interests was so close, the exchanges between them so easy, that one might well wonder why they did not create a single Congregation. This was in fact due to the difference in their temperament and in their ideas on organization (Montfort strove for greater economy in this respect). The Holy Spirit Himself fostered the best in both these men, including their differences.

4. The Holy Spirit in Montfort's life

Montfort never created a monument or event that represented the Holy Spirit directly. This was not an oversight but resulted from the very nature of the Holy Spirit. The Third Person of the Trinity is invisible, unlike Jesus Christ and the Blessed Mother. He does not even have His own name (as do the Father and the Son), or any adequate iconographic form of representation. In 1707-

1708, however, Montfort restored a chapel, and in it he symbolized the objects of his leading devotions; not only did the name of Jesus, Our Lady of Wisdom, and the Rosary appear, but also, above the altar, the dove, the symbol of the Holy Spirit.

The difficulties Montfort encountered in defining the role of the Holy Spirit result from the fact that the Spirit does not show Himself. He characteristically disappears, both to light up Christ, as a spotlight is hidden so that it can light up the stage, and in order that each Christian, each community, each people might wake to self-realization. For Montfort, the Spirit was a presence. This presence was unobtrusive, in accordance with the nature of its working, becoming progressively more powerful in Montfort's life. As Louis Perouas observes: "Towards the end of Montfort's life, the Holy Spirit seems to occupy a much more important place than the Father."[8]

It is not clear that one ought to follow Perouas in minimizing Montfort's devotion to the Father; he certainly did practice this type of devotion, expressing it lyrically in his canticles to the Father (H 52:2, 8; 53). But Perouas is right to emphasize the increasing importance of the Spirit: "The disciples he desires will be led by the Holy Spirit (PM 9): he prays to the Spirit to send them to him (PM 15ff.). Their coming will announce the End Time, the era of the Holy Spirit (PM 15-16), of a purified, renewed Church, led entirely by the Spirit. . . . When he talks of the working of the Holy Spirit within Christians, Montfort adopts a warm and passionate tone, for instance in the following passages, which deal directly with Mary: TD 36, 217. These express the summit of Montfort's mystical experience."[9]

II. The Holy Spirit in Montfort's Theology

The Holy Spirit is mentioned seventy-four times in TD alone. Montfort synthesized his thinking poetically in Hymn 141, which is a brief *"treatise on the Holy Spirit."* He there presents the Spirit's "titles, His charisms, His work both within the soul and for the salvation of the world" (De Fiores) and insists that salvation cannot be obtained without the Spirit (H 141:10, 11). For Montfort, He is not the "unknown God," as O. Le Borgne observes.[10]

The coherence of all this doctrine can be perceived only in Montfort's personal experience, in his complete self-denial. This surrender placed him at the disposal of the Spirit, who worked in extraordinary ways in Montfort's paradoxical and stormy life.

1. The role of the Holy Spirit within the Trinity

The difficulties of expression that impeded Montfort are inherent in any theology of the Spirit. It is more difficult to objectify and formulate the Third Person of the Holy Trinity than the Father or the Son, who have names analogous to human-family relationships. The Spirit's role is more precisely expressed in Scripture. If the Holy Spirit is unobtrusive, if He is elusive, it is because of the mystery that is love. Unlike intelligence (and the generative faculty), which issues in fruit (the Son, or the Word), love is lost, for it is a gift.

The Holy Spirit is in fact the gift of the Father to the Son and of the Son to the Father. This gift is a Person, and this Person is relationship, as Thomas Aquinas explains. The Holy Spirit exists in primary relation to the Father, but also to the Son, however difficult it is to define this relation, which remains a bone of contention between East and West. The Father is nothing but a father, and the Son nothing but a son, as their mutual relationship defines them. The Holy Spirit is nothing but relationship: an anonymous relationship of love, for love has no content. It is in itself relationship, communication, which explains the impossibility of adequately expressing this mystery. Montfort, who is not a speculative but a spiritual thinker, writes that the Holy Spirit is *"the substantial love of the Father and the Son"* (TD 36).

He is not at all tempted to take refuge in modalism, unlike certain theologians of our own time, amongst whom modalism is enjoying a subtle revival. For him, the Holy Spirit is most certainly a living Person. He knows this from experience, and this experience informs and inspires everything he says and does, including everything he cites and uses in his writing.

Montfort mentions the Persons of the Trinity in the usual way, placing the Holy Spirit in third position, in accordance with Christian tradition and the French school. For Montfort, the Holy Spirit "is not a self-contained, static entity but plays a dynamic part in the realization of the plan for salvation. He is not effaced by the theory of appropriation, since He keeps his distinctive character. This way of speaking of the Spirit is inherited from the Bérulle school; and it echoes a theology influenced by the Greek model of the Trinity, according to which all three Divine Persons share in the action of salvation and the Spirit 'is the third element of the Trinity, which marks the transition to the created order, mediating salvation.'" [11]

Montfort mentions the role of the Holy Spirit within the Trinity only rarely and briefly: He is the *"substantial love of the Father and the Son"* (TD 36), the *"ineffable link"* that unites them by His love (H 85:6), the *"Spirit of the Father and the Son"* (PM 16).

Montfort borrows a striking and singular idea from Louis d'Argentan, the unfruitfulness of the Holy Spirit *"in God,"* to which we will return below, and the idea that the Holy Spirit becomes actively fruitful in Mary (TD 20-21).[12]

2. The role of the Holy Spirit in the work of salvation and the cooperation of Mary

Montfort does not forget the role the Spirit plays throughout the whole of the work of salvation, from the prophets to the mystery of Christ and our sanctification (TD 4, 50). He emphasizes the unity and permanence of the Spirit's action at all stages: *"The plan adopted by the three persons of the Blessed Trinity in the Incarnation, the first coming of Jesus Christ, is adhered to each day in an invisible manner throughout the Church and they will pursue it to the end of time until the last coming of Jesus Christ"* (TD 22).

Montfort stresses the role of the Spirit in the formation of Jesus Christ in Mary's womb (TD 20): *"Together with the Holy Spirit Mary produced the greatest thing that ever was or ever will be: a God man", "It was with her, in her and of her that he produced his masterpiece, 'God-made-man': a God-man"* (TD 35).

In a continuation of this most important work, it is the Holy Spirit's function to produce and form Jesus Christ within Christians. Montfort often speaks of the birth and growth of Christ in the soul, or the production of the *"children of God"* and *"members of Christ's body"* (TD 20, 35; SM 13, 67; MP 5; PM 15). He perceives a continuity between the conception of Christ in Mary and the birth of the elect today. Sanctification is a continuation of the Incarnation (Montfort's intuition is a development of the "wondrous exchange" of which the Church Fathers speak). The Spirit will do His utmost, with Mary, in the latter times (we will return to this point below).

The Holy Spirit is the craftsman of the spiritual progress of Christians *"that they may grow from strength to strength and from grace to grace"* (TD 34) towards their maturity in Christ, in Mary. Thus he asks the Holy Spirit *"that with her you may truly form Jesus, great and powerful, in me until I attain the fullness of his perfect age"* (SM 67).

In short, the Holy Spirit, Who kept Mary concealed in the Gospel (TD 4), wants to see her reproduced in His chosen ones (TD 24, 34). He hid her in the first coming of Jesus Christ but will reveal her in the second (TD 49). It is He Who reveals Mary's secret to us (SM 20, 70; cf. TD 229). Therefore we must pray to Him in order to know her (SM 2). To enter the place that is Mary is a special grace of the Holy Spirit (TD 263). This is to be *"most ready to be molded in her by the working of the Holy Spirit"* (SM 18).

The Holy Spirit even inspires loving slavery (TD 112, 114, 119, 152, 243; SM 20, 70) and its practices (TD 117), including the bearing of chains (TD 240, 241). He leads the faithful to such slavery (TD 119) and manifests its excellence (TD 112).

To give oneself to Jesus through the hands of Mary is to imitate the Holy Spirit, Who communicates His graces and His gifts exclusively through Mary (TD 25). Therefore it is necessary to pray to Him in order to prepare the Consecration (TD 228-230). He also reveals the value of the Rosary (SR 3).

In order to be sanctified, those who abandon themselves in Mary (cf. SM 18) to be formed by the Holy Spirit must practice a radical and persistent self-surrender involving the renunciation of selfishness, personal plans, and even spiritual gifts (TD 121, 135-137, 222, 259). Montfort requires true poverty, a complete emptying of the self that will liberate the believer from his own spirit and from the spirit of the world in order to render him open to Christian renewal.

This operation is compared to the action of molding (TD 220, 221; SM

16, 18), and on this basis he calls Mary the mold of God (TD 119, 219; SM 16): *"But remember that only molten and liquified substances may be poured into a mold. That means that you must crush and melt down the old Adam in you if you wish to acquire the likeness of the new Adam in Mary"* (TD 221).

This image is ambiguous, for it obscures the fact that it is a distinctive feature of the Holy Spirit to awaken each person, group, Church, and culture to its own resources and its own diversity: quite the opposite of a mold. But Montfort, who opposes a certain kind of activism, cultivates the passive ways that are essential to mysticism. He emphasizes above all the necessity for man to give up everything in order to receive the transcendent, transforming gift that comes from *"God alone."*

The Holy Spirit calls the soul to perfection (TD 257). He realizes this perfection by a fiery deluge of pure love (PM 16, 17); He sets us ablaze with His love (H 141:11-12; PM 17); He is also the divine sculptor Who shapes and polishes the stones of the heavenly Jerusalem (LEW 167). As the Spirit of truth, He enlightens us (H 7:4-6). As the Spirit of godliness, He purifies us (H 7:7-8) and sanctifies us (H 87:6; H 111:10-21). As the Spirit of strength, He fortifies us (H 7:9-10). The master of all knowledge (LEW 172), He teaches us to know ourselves (TD 79, 213, 228) and lives in the souls of the just (H 92:5). But He also inspires fidelity to even the least important of the community's rules in Montfort's missionaries (RM 24). Aware that the world is incapable of receiving Him (H 77:29-30), Montfort wants to open souls to Him.

For the Holy Spirit fashions the spiritual progress of Christians so, *"that they may grow from strength to strength and from grace to grace"* (TD 34), towards maturity in Christ. He is the source of Wisdom (LEW 118). Wisdom is the source of the gifts of the Holy Spirit (LEW 99), for the Heart of Christ is *"the wondrous fountain of all the gifts of the Holy Spirit"* (H 40:15); *"From this source of light, / The favorites of Jesus Christ / drew the greatest of mysteries, / The greatest gifts of the Holy Spirit"* (H 40:27).

So, in complete union with Christ and Mary, the Holy Spirit is the giver of virtues, graces, and gifts (LEW 99; SM 35; TD 25, 140, 217), especially the gift of Wisdom (TD 217; PM 22) and devotion to Mary (SM 1, 67, 70, 78; TD 119, 152, 229).

3. The Holy Spirit and Mary: identification or union?

Like Kolbe, Montfort was intensely aware of the close links, the privileged links, between Mary and the Holy Spirit. He has some difficulty expressing himself on this uncharted theological territory, and could not find a way adequately to define the mutual relationship of two clear spiritual truths. For to him it is quite obvious that the Holy Spirit is God, He is everything. He makes everything, even Mary, *"the true earthly paradise of the new Adam . . . this most holy place consists of only virgin and immaculate soil . . . with neither spot nor stain by the operation of the Holy Spirit who dwells there"* (TD 261).

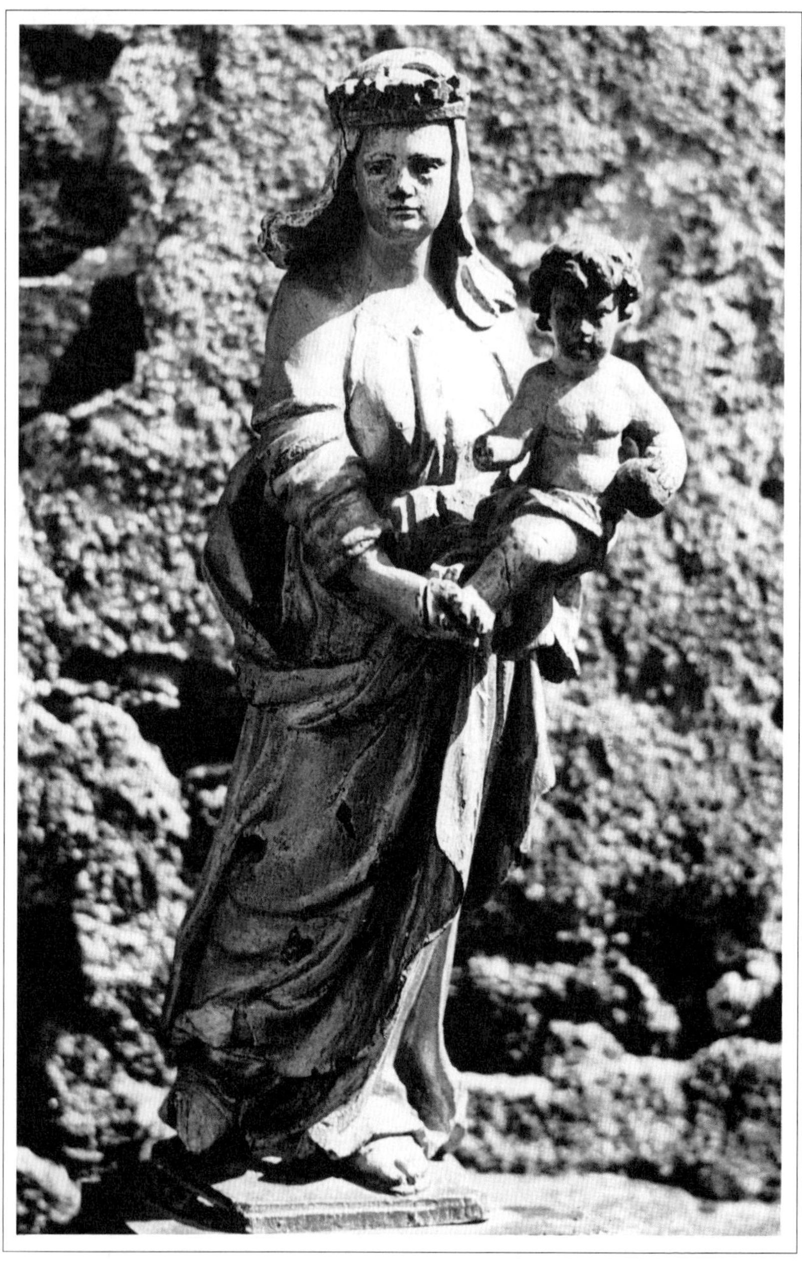

Our Lady of All Patience

In 1713, Montfort was invited to preach a mission to the parish of La Séguinière by its Irish pastor Peter Keating. Tradition says that while there Montfort restored an ancient chapel which he dedicated to Our Lady of All Patience. It is said that he sculpted this statue, and composed Hymn 145 for this oratory. Photo by Aartsen.

On the other hand, Mary seems to be everything herself, in a sense, for Montfort subordinates everything to her universal role, and the Spirit wills to work with her: *"God the Holy Spirit wishes to fashion his chosen in and through Mary. He tells her, "My well-beloved, my spouse, let all your virtues take root in my chosen ones that they may grow from strength to strength and from grace to grace. When you were living on earth, practicing the most sublime virtues, I was so pleased with you that I still desire to find you on earth without your ceasing to be in heaven. Reproduce yourself then in my chosen ones, so that I may have the joy of seeing in them the roots of your invincible faith, profound humility, total mortification, sublime prayer, ardent charity, your firm hope and all your virtues. You are always my spouse, as faithful, pure, and fruitful as ever. May your faith give me believers; your purity, virgins; your fruitfulness, elect and giving temples"* (TD 34).

Notwithstanding this tendency to unify and identify the two, Montfort does not confuse the roles of Mary and the Holy Spirit. For him, it is quite clear that the Holy Spirit is God and that Mary is a humble creature whom God required to make Himself a gift of human humility and weakness (TD 18, 157, H 57). It is indeed the Spirit Who brings everything about: *"Dear friend, what a difference there is between a soul brought up in the ordinary way to resemble Jesus Christ by people who, like sculptors, rely on their own skill and industry, and a soul thoroughly tractable, entirely detached, most ready to be molded in her by the working of the Holy Spirit"* (SM 18). Montfort perceives an identification, a spiritual coincidence between the Spirit and Mary: *"I have said that the spirit of Mary is the spirit of God because she was never led by her own spirit, but always by the spirit of God, who made himself master of her to such an extent that he became her very spirit"* (TD 258).

Here, as in everything that precedes, Mary appears as the epitome of the Church and the model to which any Christian soul must conform. Montfort adopts this view in conformity with the doctrine of the Church Fathers. We must be *"living copies of Mary"* (TD 217) and display the same docility towards the Holy Spirit who leads us to her. Between the Spirit and Mary there is a moral union, an affinity, and even an irrepressible attraction. Wherever Mary is, the Spirit comes: " *When the Holy Spirit . . . finds Mary in a soul, he hastens there"* (TD 36).

It seems that this attraction is reciprocal according to Montfort. The Holy Spirit comes to where Mary is, and Mary goes to where the Holy Spirit is. He leads to her, and she leads to Him Who brings everything about.

It is a mutual harmony. It is not that they can be substituted for each other, but their moral union means that the idioms expressing the maternal role of Mary and of the Spirit can be interchanged, whilst their roles are clearly distinguished ontologically.

Montfort seeks to express their complementary relationship, and he does so by contrasting the unfruitfulness of the Holy Spirit in God with His fruitfulness on earth with Mary, His complement, His representation, the expression of His power.[13]

Montfort finds it difficult to find a phrase to sum up this singular, privileged relationship, which is something whose existence he feels. The expression to which he returns most often in his writing is *"spouse of the Holy Spirit"* (TD 4, 5, 20, 21, 25 34, 36, 37, 49, 152, 164, 213, 217, 269; SM 13, 15, 76, 68; PM 15). He describes her as the dear spouse (TD 20, 35, 217), faithful spouse (TD 5, 34, 36, 89, 269; SM 15, 68: PM 20), inseparable spouse (TD 20, 269), fruitful spouse (TD 20, 21, 35, 36; PM 15).

The expression is inadequate, for the Holy Spirit is not the father of Jesus Christ, it is not He Who plants the seed as in the caricatured representation of the Holy Spirit given by the psychoanalyst Jones. It is necessary to retain an awareness of the limits of this formula, as Montfort did, at least implicitly.

What Montfort means is that this union, this loving covenant that identifies Mary with the Holy Spirit, makes of her not a transparent figure (for she is visible while the Spirit is invisible) but an expression, a representation, an image, an icon—but also a temple of the Spirit, for He dwells in her.

He dwells in us (LEW 176). And it is Mary who forms His chosen ones in herself and also gives Him *"temples"* (TD 34).

4. The Holy Spirit and the Church

Montfort is too centered on the contemplation of God, and especially on His life and His dynamic action in us, to have thought about defining the role of the Holy Spirit in relation to the Church: the Creed places Him before the Church, for He forms the Church.[14]

For St. Louis Marie, however, the Holy Spirit is definitely the architect or craftsman of the Church: *"You know that you are living temples of the Holy Spirit and that, like living stones, you are to be set by the God of love into the building of the heavenly Jerusalem. And so you must expect to be shaped, cut, and chiseled under the hammer of the cross. . . . It may be that this skillful and loving craftsman wants you to have an important place in his heavenly kingdom. So let him do what he pleases"* (FC 28).

But as De Fiores emphasizes, Montfort is not comprehensive in his treatment of the functions of the Spirit. He never speaks of the resurrection of bodies as the work of the Spirit, and "at the ecclesial level, he neglects the Pauline doctrine of the charisms. He does not even present the Spirit as a source of *unity* in the Church."[15] But all this is included in his metaphor of the architect. Moreover, he points out the marvels performed by the Spirit in the history of salvation and the marvelous age that He is preparing for the Church. The Spirit prepares for the age to come both in quantitative terms, when he speaks of the conversion of the pagans and the Jews (PM 5, 17, 35; TD 48, 50, 59), and in qualitative terms, when he speaks of the renewal and reform of the Church (PM 5, 17).

Montfort accepts the theory of the three reigns, aligning himself not so much with Joachim de Flore as with Marie des Vallées († 1659), *"whose life has been written by M. de Renty"* (TD 47). The third and last of these reigns is that of the Holy Spirit: *"The reign especially attributed to God the Father lasted until the Flood and ended in a deluge of water. The reign of Jesus Christ ended in a deluge of blood, but your reign, Spirit of the Father and the Son, is still unended and will come to a close with a deluge of fire, love and justice"* (PM 16).

This deluge of fire, which is a deluge of love and justice, has three functions, according to Montfort: a. the numerical increase of the Church by the conversion of all nations (PM 17); b. qualitative progress in Godliness by renewal and reform (PM 17); c. the creation of missionaries to help bring about this increase and reform (PM 17). The latter will be *"great saints,"* the apostles of the end times (TD 46-47, 58). They will be the ideal model of the apostolic Church. The Holy Spirit, *"God of truth"* (PM 25), will create these apostles; He is, according to Montfort, the source of all good inspirations (H 159:8), love of the Holy Scripture and joy (H 1, 14, 19, 30), even in the bearing of crosses (FC 44, 51). Montfort repeatedly refers to them as *"liberos,"* which means both children and free.

According to Montfort, the condition of such action of the Holy Spirit is absolute poverty (PM 7), giving oneself completely, renouncing everything in a radical and persistent fashion (TD 121, 135-137, 222, 229). On these conditions, one will be filled with the Holy Spirit (SM 57) and sent out by Him.

III. Present Relevance

In conclusion, the main lessons offered by Montfort are the following: 1. He was the prophet of a rediscovery of the Spirit, reacting against a growing Spiritual emptiness. He believed in the Spirit, its dynamism, its power, its future, which explains his eschatology (which is mysterious, not millenarian). 2. He inspired more or less directly many Spirit filled or charismatic renewals. He inspired Frank Duff, founder of the Legion of Mary, who brought out fully the practical side of Montfort's Spirit-related teaching. His teaching inspired such men as Cardinal Suenens, and Pierre Goursat, founder of the charismatic community of the Emmanuel, (which the Legion of Mary led to charismatic renewal). 3. Finally, like Kolbe, he was fascinated by the mysterious links between Mary and the Holy Spirit, which remain hidden and impenetrable. He experienced intensely their union and their mystical identification. But he did not believe them to be one and the same. He sensed the transcendence of the Holy Spirit and saw Mary as entirely relative to Him, entirely in reference to Him. In spite of these ontological differences, he did not set them apart from each other, but united them. And it is in order to express their personal relationship of love that he employed the approximate image of the spouse. Mary and the Spirit awake men to renunciation and willing slavery, to love and peace. They bring us back to the Father by the Son.

Everything Montfort writes is imbued with a deep experience and by a great mystical, charismatic, and eschatological vigor, inspired by the Spirit.

R. Laurentin

Notes: (1) L. Cognet, *Crépuscule des mystiques: Bossuet-Fénelon* (*The Twilight of Mysticism: Bossuet and Fénelon*), Desclée, Tournai 1958. (2) Cf. S. De Fiores, *Montfort, un homme disponible à l'Esprit* (*Montfort, a Man at the Disposal of the Spirit*), in the collective work *Dieu seul: A la rencontre de Dieu avec Montfort* (*God Alone: Encountering God with Montfort*), Centre international montfortain, Rome 1981, 93-94. (3) Cf. S. De Fiores, *Itinerario spirituale di S. Luigi Maria di Montfort (1673-1716) nel periodo fino al sacerdozio (5 giugno 1700) (The Spiritual Itinerary of St. Louis Marie de Montfort [1673-1716] in the Period up to His Priesthood [June 5, 1700])*, in *Marian Library Studies* 6 (1974), 191-203. (4) Ibid., 187-187. (5) J.-J. Olier, *Traité des saints Ordres* (*Treatise on the Holy Orders*), La Colombe, Paris 1953, 111. (6) Cf. S. De Fiores, *Itinerario*, 136, 171-176. (7) Besnard , 174-275. (8) L. Perouas, *Ce que croyait Grignion de Montfort et comment il a vécu sa foi* (*What Grignion de Montfort Believed and How He Lived Out His Faith*), Mame, Tours 1973, 158. (9) Ibid. (10) O. Le Borgne, *Introduction aux Oeuvres de Montfort (An Introduction to Montfort's Works)*, Centre international montfortain, Rome 1962, 1:B-9 (roneotype). (11) S. De Fiores, *Montfort, un homme*, 97, closes with a quotation from G. Philips, *Le Saint-Esprit et Marie dans l'Eglise* (*The Holy Spirit and Mary in the Church*), in EtMar 25 (1968), 14. (12) Cf. L. d'Argentan, *Conférences théologiques et spirituelles sur les grandeurs de la très-sainte Vierge Marie, Mère de Dieu* (*Theological and Spiritual Lectures on the Greatness of the Most Holy Virgin Mary, Mother of God*), Paris, 1687, 1, 4 and 3, 3, transcribed by Montfort in N, pp. 163 and 172. (13) Elsewhere I interpreted TD 20, where the Holy Spirit became fruitful through Mary, producing in her Jesus and his members, as the awakening and the actualization of the feminine and maternal powers of Mary (*Esprit saint et Marie en théologie mariale* (*The Holy Spirit and Mary in Marian Theology*), in NRT 99 (1976), 38. This interpretation is in accordance with the traditional doctrine according to which the Holy Spirit, infinitely discreet, awakens every person to himself and every community to itself at the same time as to Christ. The Holy Spirit disappeared before Him and before each personality, so that they can be formed in an internal rather than an external mold. This *pia interpretatio* possesses its own theological truth, but it is beyond TD 21, where Montfort does not speak directly of the fruitfulness of Mary but of the fruitfulness of the Holy Spirit, who is as nothing within the Trinity but is actualized in the Incarnation "by the mediation of the holy Virgin." The fact remains that this action in Mary does not amount to making her fruitful, it is not an exchange involving two parties (Montfort does not say so), but, according to Christian tradition, an internal awakening on the part of Mary to her feminine and maternal potentialities by a purely virginal generation in perfect affinity with the Holy Spirit. Cf. R. Laurentin, *Dieu seul est ma tendresse* (*God Alone is my Tenderness*), OEIL, Paris 1984, 181-193. (14) Y. Congar, *Je crois en l'Esprit saint* (*I believe in the Holy Spirit*), Cerf, Paris 1979, 2:13-25. (15) S. De Fiores, *Montfort, un homme*, 99.

HOPE

If faith points out the road, then hope gets us to take it, and love gives us the strength to mount its hurdles. Without hope we cannot explain the tireless persistence of Louis Marie de Montfort; nor, the dynamism of his short but intense life. No investigation of "what de Montfort believed" can be complete without an equally extensive search into what he hoped, so that we can get to know the source of his strength and courage, the projects closest to his heart, and the accomplishments he strove after. To do this, we shall attempt to follow his hope itinerary, the teaching he gives us on this theological virtue. But first, we shall examine the social and cultural context in which he lived.

I. THE HISTORICAL AND CULTURAL CONTEXT: HOPE BETWEEN DESPAIR AND PRESUMPTION

Montfort's notion of hope can be better understood when resituated into the social and cultural framework of seventeenth- and eighteenth-century France.[1] It was a rather gloomy time, when a minority of nobles and petty lords contrasted sharply with the vast majority of the people, who were poor. Food shortages were constant and were aggravated by frequent local wars, taxes, and abuse of power. Epidemics followed one after the other and with such frequency that they seemed part and parcel of daily life. Begging and prostitution came to be looked upon as professions. People became beggars or prostitutes with the same ease as those who chose to be soldiers, footmen, or craftsmen. Only a blurry line separated farm workers and beggars. The highways traveled by Montfort were a source of ever-present danger. They teemed with the starving, the plague-stricken, and troops on the march. From open ditches rose the cries of the dying. It was a scene of exasperation and despair that already foreshadowed a great revolution. At hope's other extremity, there was culture: it was the golden age of French literature and of a whole new way of thinking. Descartes and Pascal were barely gone when the first dawning of the Enlightenment appeared. There is no room for hope when reason becomes autonomous and creates its own happiness and salvation. In this period, culture sins by presumption.

Until this time, the teaching on hope had been noncontroversial. In its sixth session, the Council of Trent treated it along with faith, stating that above all we have to hope for salvation, which is to be earned. The Council also stressed its formal object: the promises, the mercy, and the faithfulness of God (DS, particularly 1526, 1535, 1541, 1548, 1581). In 1665, Pope Alexander VII had condemned laxist moral doctrine and specified that during his life a Christian should make acts of faith, hope, and charity (DS 2021). In 1687, Innocent XI, by the decree of August 28 and the constitution *Coelestis Pastor* of November 20, condemned Molinos, whose theses were at the root of the long-lasting problem of quietism (DS 2201-2269). Straight off the argument took fire on the question of hope. Molinos asserted that one could reach perfect union with God by means of passive contemplation alone, which each person could do habitually on his own with the help of ordinary grace. This dispensed a person from explicit acts of the virtues, the theological virtues included. Moreover, they claimed that perfect union with God required a fully disinterested love and a state of quiet and passivity, which made one indifferent to everything, even to one's own salvation (DS 2207, 2212, 2213, 2231, 2235). Louis Marie was already a seminarian at Saint-Sulpice in 1694-95 when Fénelon and Tronson gave a series of spiritual conferences in the seminary at Issy that were to give rise to Fénelon's *L'Explication des maximes des saints (The Maxims of the Saints Explained)* (Paris 1697) as a defense of the mystical theory of Madame Guyon. Fénelon's quietism was more reserved than Molinos's, and he avoided his excesses: on the level of holy indifference, one who is perfect no longer wants salvation for himself as an eternal liberation, as a reward of his own merits. Rather, with his whole will, as God's glory and good pleasure, salvation is destined as something that God wants and we want for him. Bossuet condensed the errors contained in Fénelon's work into four articles. The condemnation came from Rome on March 12, 1699 (a year before Louis Marie was ordained a priest) with Innocent XII's brief *Cum alias ad apostolatus* (DS 2351-2374): It is false to say that there is a spiritual state that excludes hope. On the contrary, hope is good even for the perfect. In the meanwhile, in a decree of December 1690, Alexander VIII had condemned certain Jansenist propositions, some of which concerned hope (DS 2310, 2313, 2314). On September 8, 1713, Clement IX, the same pope who seven years before had sent Montfort back to France, published the constitution *Unigenitus Dei Filius* against the 101 propositions of the Jansenist Quesnel (DS 2400-2502); numbers 53 to 67 dealing with hope. Ultimately, the quietists' and Jansenists' basic objection began with the presupposition that it is offensive to God for him to be the object of our hope. However, this is to misunderstand the very purpose of this virtue. Asserting that God is our end does not say that He becomes our means but that we are created for Him.

II. Montfort: A Life Marked by Hope

Louis Marie's life is under the sign of hope. Each page of Montfort's biography is shot through with hope. When studied in the light of the Roman document approving the beatification/canonization of Father de Montfort,[2] this fact takes on its full significance.

1. Heroic Hope

It is the beatification/canonization process itself—especially *Alia nova positio* of 1868—that contains the most significant insight into the heroic nature of Montfort's hope. On the feast of St. Michael the Archangel, September 29, 1869, Pius IX approved the decree on the heroic nature of Montfort's virtues. In the first document of 1868, hope occupies the entire second chapter (101-162). The 150 points that concern the canonical heroism of such a virtue are drawn from the biographies of Blain, Grandet, Besnard, and Dalin, and from writings and testimony produced during the apostolic process of beatification. These are divided into eight short chapters. In the first, it is shown that venerable Louis Marie desired and expected the bliss and mercy of God (1-12). In the second, that he cooperated with grace, he worked for his salvation, he strove to attain perfection (13-22). In the third, that he lived hope heroically with contempt for temporal goods and a soul unencumbered by the affective bonds of flesh and blood (23-52). In the fourth, that he was long-suffering and unshakable in adversity, in danger, and in need (53-79). In the fifth, that in temporal needs he had a marked trust in God, to which God responded by granting his requests (80-103). In the sixth, that he performed difficult tasks in adversity and need, even, at times, with inadequate means (104-118). Finally, in the last, that he urged others to trust in God, to undertake great projects, and to bear up under hardship (119-135). His heroic trust obtained miracles from God. The document *Novissima positio*, which followed in 1869, brought nothing new to light in regard to hope. It is evident that the matter was handled in accordance with the classical notion of hope: a theological virtue infused in the will, whereby, being grounded in God's goodness and omnipotence, we will desire Him as our supreme happiness. In order to possess Him, it is necessary to follow the means necessary to obtain Him.

2. Sapiential hope

For Montfort, rather than a series of theological actions, hope is such a markedly interior attitude that it structures his entire spiritual outlook. Whether in contemplation or in action, he lived the present as if it were an arrival point, but one that was already filled with the future. A "highway" or "path" seems the most adequate symbol for defining it, with its tireless forward course, free of every attachment or burden, as if it were the very breath of the future. This hope, which gave rhythm to his progress as a man, would still have been incomprehensible if no reference to Christ were made, to the "tasteful" experience of Wisdom: *"the taste of God and His truth"* (LEW). For Montfort, hope is a Wisdom experience. Taking into account the close bond that unites the theological virtues of faith, hope, and charity, we may recapitulate his hope in the framework of some of his most original expressions.

a. Trust in Providence. We must mention the connection between hope and Providence, elements so often united in Montfort's writing. If the missionary's hope was not indeed illusory, then it was precisely because it was anchored in the Cross and the day-to-day reality lived among, and with, the poor. God makes known His promise in the midst of the contradictions of the present, making Himself present and acting here and now. For Montfort, hoping in Providence means believing that the present already belongs to God and that He is orienting it to Himself, even if it does not yet exist in a perfect or definitive manner. The various multiplications of bread and flour brought about by Montfort are actually acts of hope in God as Providence.

During the building of the Calvary of Pontchâteau, another sign was added. At this gigantic building site,[3] thousands of volunteers learned to work "Montfort's way," namely, with Providence paying. They "came in groups of thousands to give their day's work, their sweat and their efforts to a man who had no other salary or recompense than what heaven had to offer. And since these men did not want to waste the time they freely gave out of love for God, each of them took on a heavier load than two salaried workers would have done."[4]

The mission itself became an experience of Providence for the poorest of the parish and the "proclamation of hope," of salvation, thus obtaining something far greater than any possession. To trust in God was added "trust in man". The mission proclaimed God's mercy to him and furnished him with a rich sign of the promise of eternity. The mission affirmed man's capacity to respond to divine grace under the action of that same grace.

b. Abandonment to God and to Mary. With Montfort, this is no quietist expression of pure passivity, but a filial act of faith in the veracity and fidelity of God, that counts on His love and omnipotence. This explains his act of voluntary deprivation and detachment at the Cesson bridge in 1692: "To leave his family to serve God in freedom."[5] "...In a total abandonment of himself to Divine Providence, without cares or anxiety for the future, even though he knew perfectly well that nothing was less assured than his own resources about which people so flattered him."[6] *"Whatever happens to me, I shall not be worried. I have a Father in heaven who will never fail me. He brought me here. He has kept me here until now and He will continue to treat me with His usual kindness. Although I deserve only punishment for my sins, I never stop praying to Him and rely completely on His Providence"* (L 2). As on the occasion of the death of M. de la Barmondière, hope was manifested especially when it was put to the test of the Cross. During the crisis of 1703, in that tiny room under the stairs on the rue du Pot-de-Fer, he wrote to Marie Louise Trichet: *"So you must put your trust in God. Be sure of this, that you will obtain from Him even more than you think. Heaven and earth would pass away before God would break His promises and allow anyone who hoped in Him to be frustrated in their hopes"* (L 16). And he is sure he can *"serve as a place of rest"* for Wisdom, for *"God Himself, great though He be, cannot resist your prayers. Fortunately for us He has shown He can be moved by a lively faith and a firm hope"* (L 16). Similarly, during the crisis of 1706 and at the time of the banning and destruction of the Calvary of Pontchâteau in 1713, "he merely went off to make a retreat with the Jesuits in Nantes. He immediately found there such great peace that the Fathers were only to learn from the outside, and three or four days later, about the events that had befallen him."[7]

Mary's presence and motherly assistance are important, especially in time of trial: *"There is nothing sweeter for me than the most bitter cross when it is soaked in the blood of Jesus crucified and in the milk of His divine Mother"* (L 27).

c. ***Risking for God.*** Certainty does not guarantee security. Faith does not do away with instability, precariousness, or the temporary nature of things. It means that we have to leave the safety of the boat and, like Peter, walk on the water, trusting only in the word of the Lord. Therefore, St. Louis Marie says that, when we must continually transcend the present in order to approach the absolute love of God, hope becomes daring and risks "always embarking on something new, founding some holy work."[8]

Among these "holy works" are the foundations of his religious communities, where he felt personally sure of God's word never once doubting it. This held true even when he had to advise Marie Louise about how long she would have to wait to become a religious. And when, dying, he had not as yet seen answered that great entreaty of hope, PM: *"I shall not die but I shall live and recount the deeds of the Lord"* (Ps 118, 17; PM 14). He relied completely on the God of his hope. "It was God's doing and not his."[9] *"If man is the first to put his hand to the work, nothing will come of it. It is your work, great God. Make your divine purpose a reality"* (PM 26).

We may say that even in the midst of trials and crises, in the anguish of waiting or at the moment of his adversaries' apparent triumph, Montfort's hope never suffered disillusionment precisely because he always entrusted everything to God and to God's domain. He based everything on the Cross and in expectation of the triumph of the Cross. His death was to be a perfect act of hope. *"Deo gratias et Mariae. I have come to the end of my career. I shall no longer sin."*[10] After death, hope is no more. Only love remains.

III. The Progress of Hope in Montfort's Thought

A breath of hope runs through Montfort's writing. As always, witness and teaching, life and doctrine go together.[11]

It is important to draw out a few characteristics of his understanding of hope from his writings.

1. The canticle of hope

Hymn 7 displays the *"solidity of hope."* It comes right after a hymn that treats of the *"excellence of charity"* (H 6). In all probability, it is something he wrote as a seminarian at Saint-Sulpice while he was composing rhyming songs about a tract on the virtues. He prized this work, and he was later to use it as a mnemonic device (one that seeks to utilize the memory) for catechizing the laity, the poor, and the people in the missions. The canticle offers us a quick and simple definition of hope: *"I am the virtue of hope, / I make us expect from the Lord / first grace and then its reward / through the merits of the Savior"* (first couplet). Only four verses, and yet in them we find both the source and the object of the theological virtues (the Lord), as well as the means (grace) and their meritorious cause (the merits of the Lord). There follow two symbols borrowed from patristic sources: The first is the *"firm and stable anchor / that makes instability stable,"* a symbol favored by St. Paul (Heb 6:18-19), and the second, *"the unshakable column / which holds up all holiness, / riches of an all truthful God, faithful to His promises / in time and in eternity"* (second and third couplets). Solidity and stability in God, faithful trust in God's word and help, are the rhyming theme throughout practically all of the thirty-eight strophes. They also touch on the following notions: 1. God's will is that we hope in Him; 2. the happiness of those who hope in God; 3. the misfortunes of those who trust in creatures; 4. the qualities of hope: supernatural, without human support, universal without exception, steadfast without despair; 5. the means for increasing hope. Theologians have suggested some twenty-odd motives of hope.[12] Montfort enumerates several, and he seems to treat them as one: God is our *Creator*, our *Friend*, our *Father*; Jesus is our *Savior*; Mary is our good *Mother*; God is *faithful* to His promises; and, finally, the *experience* of those who hope in God.

2. Christocentric hope

In LEW, Montfort echoes St. Paul: "Christ in you, the hope of glory" (Col 1:27). From the Wisdom perspective, Christ is the source of our hope. He is its foundation and guarantee, its object, and its mediator: the kingdom, the glory of the Father, and beatitude come to us through him.

a. The Incarnation. After sin, Adam *"came close to despair; he saw Heaven closed and no one to open it; he saw hell open and no one to close it"* (LEW 40). In the bosom of the Trinity, Wisdom reveals the decree of the Incarnation *"for the purpose of rehabilitating man in the state He formerly created Him"* (LEW 42), *"all the more so since He is an inexhaustible source of riches for man who was made for Him"* (LEW 63); *"[Wisdom] wishes to come down upon earth to help men go to heaven"* (LEW 168). Between these two extremes, beginning and end, Wisdom traces out an itinerary in a movement of death and Resurrection. From downward descent to the Cross and the Eucharist, *"He devised a marvelous way of dying and living at the same time, and of abiding with man until the end of time"*(LEW 71).

b. The Cross. The Cross constitutes a required stage in Wisdom's progress, and hope finds here a solid point of certainty because the Cross is, *"when it is well carried, the source, the food and the proof of love. . . . It is precious because it brings the one who carries it 'a weight of everlasting glory.'"* Indeed, it is through the Cross that *"the Holy Spirit cuts and polishes all the living stones of the heavenly Jerusalem"* (LEW 176). In the Cross, Christ's triumph is already anticipated for us, we now live the mystery of a God Who frees us and Who saves us by his death and Resurrection. *"While waiting for the great day of the last judgment, Eternal Wisdom has decreed the cross to be the sign, the emblem and the weapon of his faithful people"* (LEW 173). By the Cross, Wisdom traces in hope the road to true happiness, which is the possession of God. On the one hand, she inspires hope with a mistrust of the philosophical and empirical sciences, which claim to guarantee its full and definitive fulfillment in a secularized and nontranscendent future (*"natural wisdom,"* LEW 84-88). And on the other hand, she saves it from a subtle and wily compromise with the seductions of a happiness of this world, artificially constructed either by economic well-being (*"earthly wisdom,"* LEW 8) or by satisfying the appetites of the senses (*"carnal wisdom,"* LEW 81), or by the appeal of success and power (*"diabolical wisdom,"* LEW 82). It is only through a *"burning desire"* (LEW 181) that rises out of the deepest recesses of being that hope can open up for itself a road through the desert of the senses and the rejection of idols (LEW 194-202), toward the possession of true Wisdom. Hope is sustained by the three loaves obtained in prayer: *"the bread of life, the bread of understanding and the bread of angels"* (LEW 190).

c. Mary, the anchor of hope. Mary is the other solid base that supports the archway over which the road of hope travels in its journey toward God.

She brings about the hope of Israel (LEW 104-107; TD 16). She makes the Church share in her hope (TD 34, 35); she obtains hope for it; if there are some graces in us, some hope of salvation, they are a gift that comes from God through her (LEW 207). For, *"God gave her the power and the mission assigning to saints the thrones made vacant by the apostate angels who fell away through pride"* (TD 28). As a consequence, *"she is all the more necessary to men to reach their ultimate goal"* (TD 39-42). The Consecration made in her hands will open the heart *"with unbounded confidence in God and in herself"* (TD 216), since Mary is *"the wonderful means of persevering"* (TD 173ff.) until death, *"which is sweet and peaceful."* Mary is usually there herself to lead those consecrated to her into everlasting joy (TD 200). Like the Cross (LEW 172, 180) Mary is totally united to Christ (TD 63, 247) to the point of constituting a moral unity with him and of being absorbed in the same hope. *"For this reason, St. John Damascene compared her to a firm anchor which holds them fast* [i.e., those devoted to her] *and saves them from shipwreck in the raging seas of the world"* (TD 175); she is *"my life, my sweetness and my hope"* (MP 5, 13). And he even borrows St. Bernard's words: *"She is the one in whom I have put my greatest trust; she is the entire reason for my hope"* (LPM 6).

3. Hope in the future of the Church

The time between the first and last "coming" is the time of the Church, a time of watchful expectation, a time of mission, of the proclamation of the reign to come and of its being accomplished in *"a flood of fire, love and justice"* (PM 16), when *"the Lord will come a second time, as the whole Church awaits Him, to reign everywhere and to judge the living and the dead"* (SM 58). This transition from a personal hope to a collective one, that of the Church, is clarified by Montfort when he speaks of the comings of Jesus Christ. Christ is at once the One who has already come and the One who comes continually to *"become incarnate every day in His members through His dear Mother"* (TD 31) *"until the end of time, until the last coming"* (TD 22). During this period of waiting, the Church renews and reforms herself (PM 17). Montfort's times of expectation and eschatology are full of hope, either because they are not bound to precise times or specific dates (*"But when and how will this come about? . . . Only God knows. For our part we must yearn and wait for it in silence and in prayer."* TD 59) or because they are completely dependent on the active presence of Mary. God is entreated *"to renew all things through her and to finish the years of grace through her as You began them through her"* (PM 6). In Mary the Church already possesses God's triumph. This final dramatic time of history serves as an ideal reference point for all the difficulties the Church must overcome during her earthly pilgrimage. During these emergencies, the Church will always be able to count on *"the lowly and humble servant of God"* (TD 52) and on the end-time apostles, formed as they are by the Spirit, with Mary's collaboration.

IV. Relevance of Hope

"The joys and hopes, sorrows and distresses of the men of our time, of the poor especially and of those who suffer, are also the joys and hopes, sorrows and distresses of the disciples of Christ, and there is nothing genuinely human that does not find an echo in their heart. Indeed, their community composed of men, gathered together in Christ, led by the Holy Spirit in their progress toward the kingdom of the Father. They are bearers of a message of salvation to propose to all" (GS 1). In the thought of Vatican II's document, we can greet Montfort's message as a prophecy of hope.

1.The profound and very swift changes that have come about in human society over the last decades of the twentieth century are oriented toward hopes grounded in earthly realities, permanently excluding the supernatural. Moreover, they leave deadly contamination in their wake. Earthly paradises are derived from artificial paradises: superfluity is synonymous with economic well-being, drugs tranquilize human desires and aspirations, violence is an affirmation of one's personality. Marx, Freud, and Nietzsche have had faithful disciples who produced the extreme practical consequences of their theories. Within the churches, hope has happily once again found its central place in dogmatic and pastoral theology. One example is J. Moltmann's book *The Theology of Hope* (1964), which shows that "Christianity's conformity to the currents that surround it" is the sign of our present-day loss of an eschatological sense. This kind of conformism has to be overcome by hope in that future promised by God and announced by Christ's Resurrection. It is essential that the human community rediscover Christian hope so that it can discover the full dignity of man as created and redeemed by God for a future of eternal bliss.

2. Montfort hope is called Jesus Christ, the Eternal and Incarnate Wisdom, crucified so as to reveal to us the presence of an infinite Love in man's forward march and of a Providence that bends down to him. The Cross is a proclamation of joy and hope, a sign of permanent victory over evil and death, of an already acquired glory. It requires a commitment, because this life must come to its successful fulfillment.

3. A death culture has spread abroad and poisons our very existence—from abortion to euthanasia, from political or criminal massacres to the glorification of violence through the communications media. The *"total giving of the self to Jesus through the hands of Mary"* makes us aware that life is a precious gift at every moment. It is worth the *"trouble"* to live and *"risk"* for God so as to return the life that belongs to Him in its physical and spiritual integrity. This total giving is an entry into the dimension of the Resurrection. Death will be but the permanent manifestation of a life already begun. "The very act [of consecration] is rooted—may we say—in the history of that great paradox whose realm is the Gospel itself. It is not only a question of verbal paradoxes, but of ontological ones. The most profound among them is perhaps the paradox of death, expressed among other places in the parable of the seed that had to die in order to produce new life, the decisively confirmed paradox of the paschal mystery."[13]

4. On the world level, the lack of trust is the subtle evil that gnaws away at souls, the ever-threatening danger of uncontrollable nuclear or chemical warfare produced by a totalitarian

regime. The fear of the pernicious effects produced by an ecological disaster determined by human beings has a cosmic dimension. Irresponsible genetic experimentation also threatens the human race. These are but a few of the factors that produce a real and almost permanent feeling of anxiety, if not hopelessness. The Church and humanity are invited to lift their eyes to her who always precedes and who now shines on man's path "as a consolation" (LG 68). "May your Immaculate Heart be revealed as the light of hope for all."[14]

5. Also needed is hope and trust in man, who is the guardian of divine blessings on earth and who is destined to a future of eternal glory. And it is the whole of man, spirit and matter, that is destined to this divine glory, of which he is now certain since God's descent into humanity and His Easter victory. On this certainty rests the effectiveness of a "new evangelization" that will restore man's hope of being capable of building a civilization of love based on the Gospel.

G. Barbera

Notes: (1) On Montfort's sociocultural and religious environment, cf. P.Hazard, *La crise de la conscience européene, 1680-17 (Crisis of the European Conscience, 1680-17),* Fayard, Paris 1964; J. Le Brun, *Le grand siècle de la spritualité française et ses lendemains (The Great Age of French Spirituality for the Future),* under *France,* in DSAM 5 (1964), 917-953; P. Goubert, *Louis XIV et vingt millions de Français,* (Louis XIV and Twenty Million Frenchmen) Fayard, Paris 1966. (2) *S. Rituum Congregatio, Beatificationis et canonizationis ven. Servi Dei Ludovici Mariae Grignion de Montfort . . . Alia nova positio super virtutibus,* Typ. Brancadoro, Rome 1868. (3) Grandet, 154ff. (4) Blain, 166. (5) Blain, 17. (6) Besnard I, 11, 28. (7) L. Perouas, *Ce que croyait Grignion de Montfort,* Mame, 1973, 1199; English translation *Way to Wisdom.* (8) Blain, 188. (9) Blain, 186. (10) Grandet, 262. (11) Perouas, 114. (12) S. Harent, *Espérance,* in DTC 7 (1913), 632-645. (13) John Paul II, *Discourse to the Polish Bishops,* December 1987. (14) John Paul II, *Act of "affidamento" of the World to Mary,* April 25, 1984.

HYMNS

A perusal of the articles in this Handbook quickly reveals that Saint Louis de Montfort's hymns are essential for a full, authentic knowledge of both the man and his spirituality. This is true regardless of one's verdict on the poetic quality of his songs. This article will, therefore, examine the nature and general content of these songs, which comprise such a large share of Father de Montfort's writings.

The word "hymn" originally designated a chant of thanksgiving.[1] The Bible has preserved for us quite a number of these joyful songs of thanks, and they have become an integral part of Christian prayer. In the liturgy of the Hours, Christians sing the hymns of Moses and of David, of Anna, of Samuel, of Tobit and of Judith. The books of Wisdom and the writings of the prophets also contain hymns of praise. The best known canticles of the NT are the Benedictus of Zachary, the Nunc Dimittis of Simeon, and the Magnificat of Mary.

Hymn singing is an almost universal custom. People sing in their religious or secular meetings, whether the occasion be joy or sadness. In all countries and in every age, we find repertories of religious chants, coming from the ordinary people, written for ordinary people, speaking their language, and expressing their soul, their emotions, their beliefs. Some of these chants have survived the centuries.

I. MONTFORT AND THE TRADITION OF THE HYMN IN THE LIFE OF THE CHURCH

The hymns of Montfort elevate his spirituality. In the hymns, his life becomes a profoundly intimate and beautiful conversation with the Incarnate Word, who is the Sacrament of love. Hymns reflect the traditional symbolic language of ritual, especially the ritual of the Paschal Mystery—the Mass. In a world turned away from Jesus' humble presence in the flesh and from his Spirit of love, Who dwells within, Montfort's hymns awaken singer and reader alike to faith, to life's transcendent beginnings, endings, and processes. He sings: *"Your folly is wisdom / Abide with me. / Your dearth is abundance, / Abide with me. / With you, O what treasures / in our souls and bodies"* (H 103:13). Montfort's hymns are sometimes sublime in their mystic grasp of the majesty and wonder of God. Sometimes they are didactic and practical in their earthly grasp of the pastoral care for which the poor and dispossessed cried out. The hymns reveal the Father from Montfort to be a universal man, a suffering servant-disciple of the Incarnate Word, a saint for all times, especially for the end times. He is universal because his spirituality was a coincidence of opposites. He was a universal person because he embraced the paradox of the Cross. By choosing to live the unity of the Cross, he experienced in the Spirit the contemplative and active polarities of life as complementary, interdependent, and mutual. He humbled himself in order to become a slave to ultimate Freedom—to God Alone. The Louis Marie of the hymns was a mystic apostle—a hound of heaven, a pilgrim troubadour. His head was in heaven, and his feet on the ground. How did he arrive at such simplicity and purity? How is it that his life seemed a distilled essence of the Gospel? In the words of the ancient hymn: "Where there is charity, there is love. Where there is love, there is God." Montfort practiced charity because he followed Jesus. And following Jesus nearly, dearly, and clearly, he discovered Jesus' mother to be his own. She is the heart of a Christian open to the heart of her Son. She is the perfect human person. Just as Jesus came to life through his mother, so, too, did Montfort. His path to perfection was wisdom's path of becoming incarnate through Mary. *"O Jesus, alive in Mary, / Come dwell in us and reign, / Pour out your life in us, / No more to live but for you"* (H 111:1). Mary is mother of Jesus and thus the Mother of all. She rebirths those who turn to her with supernatural life and molds them in divine grace to conform to her son. She empties us of unfreedom and shapes us in the liberty of her son's will. *"Shape there your noble virtues, / Your Spirit and his holiness, / Your maxims without flaw, / The passion of your charity"* (H 111:2). Montfort shows that the foundation of the spiritual ascent to God is the practice of moral virtue. Virtues are lived, they become incarnate through the Blessed Virgin Mother, in the Spirit of love. She is perfect human selflessness, a Lady clothed in silent mystery, in faith, in the substance of what is unknown. But she gives us eyes for the invisible, for things unseen but hoped for—for faith. Her passion and understanding were pure because she humbly obeyed the perfect laws of her son. She said the "yes" heard round the universe and across the centuries. Montfort gives witness to her "yes." He leads us in singing to her son: *"Make us sharers in your mysteries, / That we might imitate you here below; / Send us the keenness of your light, / To guide our every step"* (H 111:3). With Louis Marie we are invited to enter the Temple of God, to stand before the Lamb of God on the heavenly altar, and to join in the chorus of heaven as the angels and saints sing the divine acclamation: "Holy, Holy, Holy, Lord God of power and might." Mary is the Temple of the Blessed Trinity. In Montfort's hymns, one is led to sing with her the great doxology: *"To the glory of the Father, / In the power of your Name, / Reign in us, through your Mother / Over nature and demon! Amen"* (H 111:4).

Montfort was a servant of the Lord whose mission was to renew the faith of the Church through parish missions. He sought to overcome unbelief by teaching people how to live contemplatively—how to be open to God Alone in every moment. St. Gregory the Great, the father of the Church's tradition of hymnody, saw hymns at the root of pastoral care—the ministry of helping people turn away from sin and back to God. "Now, that man is blind who is ignorant of the light of heavenly contemplation; who, oppressed by the darkness of the present life, does not behold the light to come as he does not love it, and, therefore, does not know whither to direct the steps of his conduct. Hence the Prophetess Anna said: 'He will keep the feet of His Saints, and the wicked shall be silent in darkness.'"[2] Montfort is depicted most often as a pilgrim troubadour carrying Cross, Bible, and Madonna to the people. He is seen "walking the walk" of the Christian soul's journey into God. He is seen singing with St. Paul: "Lift up the hands which hang down, and the feeble knees, and make straight steps with your feet, that no one halting may go out of the way, but rather be healed" (Gal 6:2). He is a troubadour because the God he sang to was the God who is Love. He dedicated his work, signing and sealing what he had accomplished to "God Alone." He replaced the i of the "Dieu Seul" (God Alone) with a tiny sketch of a heart. The "i" became love in God. Louis Marie reminds one of a troubadour or trouvère of the Middle Ages. Montfort was a vagabond singer, a composer of songs filled with heroism and love. He called people to a life of Christian chivalry. He called them to become Christian knights, to practice a chivalrous love in the court of Christ the King. The Lady of the court was Mary—the Queen Mother of All Hearts. He called them to take up arms, to become a knight of Christ like Michael the Archangel. He asked them to be ready to do battle with the forces of evil. A knight who took the sword took the Cross. Montfort's hymns called the people to spiritual chivalry, to become noble, courageous, and courteous and to set out on an adventurous journey in search of the Holy Grail—in search of Incarnate Wisdom. Montfort called his knights to do what knights have always done—to defend spiritual pilgrims. *"One road to heaven runs: / The highway of the Cross. / It was the royal Son's, / His road to life from loss. / And every stone of it / That guides the pilgrim's feet / Is chiselled fair to fit / In Zion's holy street"* (H 19:4). The hymns tell Christians that to set out on the mystic quest, they must first be consecrated to a moral life of fairness, valor, and protection of the poor—all of this through disciplined devotion to the Lady. *"A brave knight am I / I serve the King of Heaven, / whose throne is an invincible one / adorned with the Cross and the lily . . . thus I must live nothing contrary to truth, / nothing contrary to humility, / nothing contrary to charity / nothing contrary to purity"* (H 95:1, 6). Montfort continues a tradition of hymns to the one, true God, celebrated by another great singer and composer of hymns, St. Ambrose: "O Trinity of blessed light, / O unity of princely might, / The fiery sun now goes his way; / Shed Thou within our hearts Thy ray."[3]

Richard J. Payne

II. Hymns in the Life and Writings of Montfort

1. Hymns in the life of Montfort

In the West, since the birth of the modern languages, there appeared simple compositions, called ballads. In a religious period like the Middle Ages, these texts were called "songs of piety." Adapted slowly, both in structure and in language, to the ordinary folk, these "hymns" were sung to simple and popular airs.

Shortly before Louis Marie was born (1673), numerous authors of hymns were quite well known. Great writers like Pierre Corneille, Jean Racine, and Fénelon knew that even haphazard hymns from their pens would be well received. Fradet, in his excellent work on the hymns of Father de Montfort, lists many of the authors of popular hymns of seventeenth-century France. The majority of them were members of religious orders involved in evangelization, especially through parish missions and retreats.[4]

Louis Marie, who lived his childhood and youth in the shadow of churches, surely knew a number of these hymns and was certainly influenced by them. It is not astonishing, therefore, that Montfort saw quite early the part hymns could play in his apostolate. During his seminary days at Paris, he composed many hymns, as his friend and fellow student, J.B. Blain, attests.[5] All this, however, was preparation for his ministry as an itinerant preacher. The numerous hymns in circulation did not completely satisfy him, so he became a prolific writer of "religious songs."

2. Hymns in the writings of Montfort

OC, which unlike GA contains all the hymns of Saint Louis Marie, dedicates 812 pages to the hymns, compared to 846 for all his other works combined. The precise number of hymns is extremely difficult, if not impossible, to decipher. OC has published 164, and all of these are authentic. But there are several repetitions, and at times it is hard to determine whether or not a few of the hymns originally formed one piece. Keeping in mind these caveats, we can say that Montfort composed around 23,000 verses, which make up these 164 hymns.

One characteristic that is self-evident is the length of Montfort's hymns. Montfort seems rarely to be at a loss for ideas, and words to express them. More than half of these hymns contain 100 or more verses, and some even go beyond 400 verses. Hymn 127, a stage production, stretches out to 630 verses. Among the shortest, only 23 have less than 50 verses; these ordinarily are prayers and adaptations on prayers.

III. Hymns of Montfort

1. The manuscripts

The hymns, or canticles, are a beautiful inheritance that Father de Montfort left to his small community of missionaries. The montfort archives in Rome possess four manuscripts that contain the original texts written by Saint Louis Marie or copied by his close collaborators. Each manuscript was given a label during the beatification process. For practical reasons of identification, they were labeled Notebook #2, Notebook "Copy," Notebook #8, and Notebook #10. In this article, they are called Notebook #1, #2, #3, and #4. These manuscripts are in the form of long pads, 32 to 34 cm. long by 11 cm. wide ($12\frac{1}{2}$" to $13\frac{1}{3}$" long by $4\frac{1}{3}$" wide), except the third, which is more squat, 23 cm. by 9 cm. (9" by $3\frac{1}{2}$").

a. Notebook #1. This manuscript contains thirty-five hymns, all in Father de Montfort's handwriting, "writing that is delicate, tight, attractive in appearance, regular, and well formed," according to the description of Father Fradet.[6] In the margin, a resume gives the main idea of each couplet. At the beginning of each hymn, the author indicates one or several well-known tunes to which they could be sung.

Pages are missing from this first hymnal. But, this should cause no surprise, since Montfort wrote on pieces of paper that he tied by a thread to a makeshift cover.

This Notebook #1 is extremely valuable, first of all because it is written entirely in Montfort's handwriting, and second, serious studies have demonstrated that every piece is original.

b. Notebook #2. The lost sheets of the first Notebook have fortunately been preserved in the second. This one is marked "copy." It is, in fact, a faithful and complete copy of the preceding notebook plus the pages missing from Notebook #1. A faithful copy even to the least details: marginal notes, the embellishments that separate the verses, the capitalized words, etc.

This Notebook is written almost entirely in identical script, which is not that of Father de Montfort. Two other less skillful handwritings complete the transcription. It is evident that Montfort himself went over this Notebook and corrected when necessary. This copy contains an additional twenty authentic hymns.

c. Notebook #3. This manuscript is quite different from the others. It is in a more squat format still and contains a considerable number of pages (568), of which certain ones remained blank. These Notebooks were not considered precious relics but, rather, work instruments that were used daily. This third Notebook, besides being a hymnal carried from mission to mission, served as an all purpose memo pad for the mission band. The name of Brother Mathurin —the first Brother companion of Father de Montfort—appears inside the cover and twice at the end. We presume that this Notebook was used by the Brother, who accompanied the missionaries and collaborated in their apostolic work, especially in the singing of the hymns.[7]

We find four different handwritings in this third Notebook, including the very recognizable writing of Father de Montfort. None of the hymns contained in this manuscript is found in any other author; they are, therefore, the missionary's own work. These hymns, numbering ninety-four, are presented as "new."

d. Notebook #4. This hymnal, containing twenty of Montfort's songs, has come down to us with numerous blank pages. The handwriting of Saint Louis Marie is evident,. as well as the script of some of those who wrote in the other notebooks.

Fradet explains why editors are not in agreement on the exact number of hymns written by Montfort: "We have not taken into account the doubling done by editors who have split up the hymns they found to be too long at times."[8] At our current stage of research and study, we can assert that all the hymns contained in the four manuscript Notebooks are original and authentic. After serious study, Fradet concludes: "The manuscripts do not contain a single hymn that we can find in any previous collection."[9]

2. Dates of composition

H. Frehen, utilizing the remarkable work of M. Barré,[10] has attempted to date precisely the composition of certain montfort hymns.[11] From a detailed study of the manuscripts, involving close examination of the kind of paper used and of the handwritings, and comparison with the other works of the missionary, he concludes that hymns of the fourth notebook (H 137-163 in OC) date from the last years of the life of Father de Montfort. Unfortunately, he was unable to apply the same studies to the other manuscripts, and it is, then, impossible at this time to date each hymn. Suffice it to say that they were all composed sometime during his seminary days at Saint-Sulpice (Montfort was ordained in 1700) right up to his death in 1716.

3. Categories of hymns

Thanks also to Bishop Frehen, we can conclude that there are two major categories of montfort hymns: "inspired" and "didactic."

a. Inspired hymns. The inspired canticles flow as from a spring, spontaneously, on the occasion of a pilgrimage to a Marian shrine, or on the occasion of a joyful celebration, or simply to express the happiness of living in the solitude of the cave at Mervent.

Hymns that are found in this category are, for example, H 145 at Notre Dame de Toute Patience, H 151 at Notre Dame des Dons (composed on the occasion of the entrance of Marie-Anne Régnier into the Daughters of Wisdom), H 155 at Notre Dame des Ombres, H 159 at Notre Dame de Toute Consolation. H 143 recalls the conversion of Bénigne Pagé and her entrance into the Poor Clares. On occasions like these, the verses come to Montfort as easily as Hail Marys, flowing concurrently from his pen, his feelings of thanks, and his personal devotion.

b. Didactic Hymns. These hymns took a little more effort and time, which the saint had to find here and there in the midst of his studies and preaching assignments. That explains why hymns which were put in his collection as different hymns were, in reality, one and the same. Thus, Hymns 46, 100, and 101 have the same structure and are written in the same number of meters, the same persons are in dialogue, and the hymns may be sung to the same air as indicated on top of H 46. Hymns 19 and 102 on the triumph of the Cross are also one hymn. Montfort reworked these canticles, and the copiers inserted them into the Notebooks without necessarily checking out the preceding pages.

4. Audience

Montfort is, before anything else, a missionary. His hymns, sermons, and all his writings were addressed to the people whom he was evangelizing: for the most part, the country folk of northwestern France. Montfort went from one parish to another with his ever-growing collection of hymns to be sung during the parish mission. These hymns, especially the first ones presented in numerical order in OC, are truly a rhymed preaching intended to prolong and help retain the proclaimed Word. Montfort's determination to evangelize is the first motive for his hymn writing. But he also composed hymns to express feelings and devotions close to his heart, to honor someone, to underline a special event, and at times simply for the joy of writing a poem in honor of the Lord.

His numerous hymns in honor of Mary, the hymns expressing his joy at the entrance of Marie-Anne Régnier and of Bénigne Pagé into the cloister, the noels—all were written not only to edify but to express his own overflowing happiness.

His canticle to the Daughters of Wisdom (H 149) was inspired by the Rule of the Community that he was in the process of writing. H 157 on solitude betrays his happiness in the cave of Mervent and his own appreciation for the beauties of nature.

When he composed his hymn on the poor in spirit, inspired by the Beatitudes (H 144), he probably had in mind his small Company of Mary, which seemed to be taking shape among his several companions. In gratitude for permission to enter their Third Order, he sent the Dominicans at La Rochelle a hymn in honor of the canonization of the Dominican pope, Pius V (H 147). H 146 was a joyful wedding gift to friends.

Father de Montfort's hymns demonstrate a profound respect for the people for whom they were composed. The country folk were simple, often with little if any schooling. Yet the saint believed that beauty was the yearning of all, and he wrote elegant canticles for them. There is nothing banal in his collections of verse. His poetry is certainly not perfect, for he was far more preoccupied with content than with style. Nonetheless, there are some canticles that can only be classed as gems, and ultimately they were destined for his simple people.

5. Melodies

Some find it surprising that Saint Louis Marie used popular secular tunes for his sacred hymns and even for the most solemn of them. But even the melodies were for him a tool of evangelization. If he found a good one that caught the people's fancy, he would not hesitate to use it for one or more of his hymns. In examining all the melodies suggested, it appears that Montfort must have known the entire repertory of his time! The author did not always suggest a tune at the beginning of his hymns, but generally he did so. On the other hand, certain pieces that were quite lengthy, and made up of several choirs of people, had several tunes. H 127 is the best example of this: no less than eighteen different melodies are indicated. Fradet has discovered some of the original melodies to which the hymns were sung.[12]

Besides popular tunes, Montfort also made use of melodies of Christmas carols, and three times he suggests airs from drinking songs (cf. H 41, 151, 161).

6. Inspiration

Montfort found his inspiration everywhere, like the landscape painter for whom everything is the subject matter for his canvas.

The apparitions of the Sacred Heart to Saint Margaret Mary Alacoque (who died in 1690) are commemorated in Hymns 40-44, which may be considered one lengthy hymn of 165 quatrains. Other hymns are concerned with the principal preoccupations and writings of Father de Montfort. Thus, his hymns on the Eternal Wisdom are very close to his other texts on the same subject; they are among his most beautiful canticles (H 78, 103, 124-126); and bear a strange resemblance to Russian mystics who have written on the same subject.

There are thirty-seven hymns to Mary. They clarify many of the teachings expressed in TD and SM. The series of hymns for the octave of Christmas (H 57-66) not only are joyful but also preach a solid Christology.

Other subjects of the hymns include the themes proposed by Saint Louis de Montfort for the preparation for the Act of Consecration to Jesus through Mary: the *Spiritual Exercises* of montfort spirituality. Ridding oneself of the spirit of the world is the theme of Hymns 29-39, 106, and 107. He proposes as guides to know oneself the long hymns on the virtues and their practice in Hymns 4-28. The hymns to Mary and to Jesus complete this preparation for the Consecration.

Although many hymns contain references to the Holy Spirit, it is surprising that there is only one (H 141) that is specifically dedicated to the third Person of the Trinity.

7. Structure

The first series of hymns found in OC are truly sermons in verse, methodically composed. They contain an introduction and the division of the topic into sections or "points," followed by a conclusion and often by a final prayer. They are didactic verses, and they are not the most poetical. In a certain way, these hymns have an advantage over preaching. The hearer only has to listen and become a participant if the hymn interests him and the melody is good, by humming them. Montfort, the eloquent preacher, knew how to strike the imagination; the hymn, Montfort was convinced, is one of the most efficacious means to accomplish this.

Montfort also possesses a theatrical sense. His dialogue hymns are simple but forceful dramatizations (H 98 between the two sisters of the Third Order; H 99 between the two shepherdesses). At times, his songs demand the participation of several persons. In H 97, concerning the sinner converted during a parish mission, the *dramatis personae* include God the Father, the friend, the sinner, Jesus, the Holy Spirit, the angels, and finally a voice coming from the heavens designated "*The Echo.*" Three hymns, which really only make one (H 46, 100, 101), are a long conversation among the friend of God, an afflicted person, and Satan. H 119, on the despair of the sinner faced with death, and H 123, which presents the meeting of the faithful soul with Our Lord, are along the same lines. H 106 is even more detailed, for the actors include Jesus, an angel, the Christian, and two choirs: the followers of Jesus and the followers of the world. H 127 is nothing less than a short medieval mystery play, entitled *"The Abandoned Soul Delivered from Purgatory by the Prayers of the Poor and of Children."* Montfort includes a sketch of the stage settings, lists the *dramatis personae* (twenty) and the various choruses: souls in purgatory, the living, the poor, children. Saint Louis Marie not only composed all the parts to be sung but included in the margin all the stage directions. His artistic talent is clearly revealed not only in this production but in so many of his songs.

8. Theological and spiritual content

The Father from Montfort seems perfectly at ease in the composition of his hymns. Not all his verses are good poetry, but many are sublime, and all are about the glory of God: "*Here are my verses and my songs / If they be not beautiful, they are good / If they do not flatter the ears / They do rhyme with wondrous marvels*" (H 2:39).

The content of Montfort's poetry is more vast and more varied than his sermons and his other writings. The first section of the hymns in OC includes canticles comprising faith, hope, love, humility, meekness, obedience, fasting, almsgiving, poverty, zeal, silence, presence of God, modesty, gratitude, thanksgiving, abandonment to Providence, and contempt of the world (H 4-39).

There are several hymns on God (H 50-52, 114, 135, 153) and others on Jesus Christ and his great love for humanity (H 47-49, 54-56), the Cross and the Passion (H 61-73, 102, 123, 137, 138), the Eternal Wisdom (H 103, 124-126), and the Eucharist (H 112, 128-134, 136, 158); a beautiful series of noels (H 57-66); and hymns on the last things: heaven (H 116, 117, 152), hell (H 118, 120), and purgatory (H 119, 127). Hymn 109—nothing less than a catechism—is made up of 330 verses covering the fundamentals of the faith. There are hymns that defy classification. Two (H 22, 91) appear to be primarily autobiographical, singing the apostolate of a "zealous missionary." H 144 seems to have been composed for his Company of Mary, and H 149 is clearly for the Daughters of Wisdom. H 95 is to the good solider, H 96 to the good prisoner, and H 92 for members of Third Orders; H 46, 100, and 101 were written to console the afflicted.

Two hymns are invitations to the parish mission. Hymn 115 begins with the news that the parish mission is about to begin and suggests the program for the parish renewal. This is very much like Hymn 163, addressed to the inhabitants of Saint Pompain and inviting them to come to the mission. In reading these hymns, it is possible to picture the opening of a parish mission in Montfort's time. There is the impressive arrival of the preachers, sometimes twenty of them; they invade the parish accompanied by their helpers carrying objects, pictures, and banners to illustrate and dramatize the preaching. Brother Mathurin, Montfort's ever-faithful companion in his missionary work, used to go up and down the streets singing, "*Attention! Attention! the mission is open.*"(H 115:1) *"The Holy Journey,"* Hymn 162, stretches out the program of the retreat into a joyful program for life. There is, finally, H 152, entitled *"The Road to Paradise."* Montfort sang one of its verses on his deathbed: "*Let's go my dear friends / Let's go to Paradise.*"These were among his last words. They express the dominant thought of his entire life: to go to paradise leading a vast, jubilant—and singing —crowd with him.

O. Demers

IV. Literary Analysis of the Hymns of Montfort

Saint Louis de Montfort's hymns were—for the most part—meant to be sung in village churches, in the homes of the poor, and, therefore, by simple people. When we hear the term "mystical poet" we do not, therefore, think immediately of an early eighteenth-century preacher of parish missions in the countryside of northwestern France. Rather, our minds turn to figures like St. Francis of Assisi, Jacopone da Todi, and especially the great John of the Cross.

Yet this troubadour from Montfort is one of the mystical poets of the Church. From his youngest years, he surely got to know the songs of his village and of the ghettoes in the cities of Rennes and Paris. His artistic nature made him sensitive to the singing of workers in the fields, of gatherings in the village squares, to the wails at wakes, and to the singing in the celebrations at baptisms and weddings. For this reason, Louis Marie wrote his innumerable verses so that they might be sung by the ordinary people, not in a theater but in a country church or on the roadways. His poetry is the song of the masses.

Whereas the great writer of canticles, John of the Cross, succeeded in his mystical poetry to meld together biblical theology, classical humanism, and ancient popular chant, Montfort wrote simple songbooks for the people. Saint Louis Marie was well aware that his poetry would not be read in the Paris salons. He intended to produce songs that together would be a school of catechesis, of moral exhortation, and of prayer even in its highest states, and this for the country folk. These hymns are a monument also to the great saint who wrote them; they testify to his enthusiastic faith, his mystical, joyful prayer, his incredible love for the "ordinary" people, most especially for the poor.

His *ars poëtica* is found in his first two canticles: *"The Utility of Hymns"* and *"To the Poets of These Times."* In the first, the poet explains with biblical overtones the dignity and the high value of sacred song, which gives glory to God. The God of joy desires these joyful adorers; song is a sign of joy. Sacred song, according to this itinerant preacher-poet, lights the fires of love, by which we can respond to the new song God sings for us in Christ Jesus. The saints of the early Church sang, and St. Paul teaches, under divine inspiration: "Sing and celebrate the Lord with all your heart" (Eph 5:19). H 2 expresses the purpose of his chants: "*This is not to charm you, / You who think only of making rhymes. / Great poets, troublesome people, / I leave your ways to others.*" And then there follows a merciless attack against poets who do not sing of God and do not celebrate the name of Jesus. For the saint, these are all pagans; they search applause and glory; they mimic Virgil and Horace; they only are interested in the rhyme and rhythm of the day and are inflated by a base impudence; they sing of Bacchus and Venus, of impurity and idolatry. They think they are composing great verses, but since ordinary folk cannot understand them and—worse still—since they do not draw people to Jesus, they are quite useless. And the missionary does not spare unfaithful Christians who prefer these poisonous works to the Bible itself.

Louis Marie is careful not to give the names of these poets of his day, not for fear of defaming them but for fear of soiling his clean pages! How the country folk must have smiled at Montfort's biting words against the haughty. But when the missionary flogs the poets, he does not appear to be thinking only of cabaret singers. After all, they have no intention of imitating Virgil and Horace, and they surely are not renowned for "sublime verses."

Saint Louis Marie appears to be aiming at those people who produce poetry more for the sake of a poetic style than for the content. Yet he went even beyond this in his denunciation of the "poets of the day." It should be recalled that Louis Marie's short life saw some of the great lights of French literature: Molière died the year the missionary was born; the great Corneille died in 1684, Athalie de Racine in 1699. Yet Montfort believed that his battle-cry, *"God Alone!"* did not permit him to encourage his people to prefer classical works over sacred hymns. And even more: the missionary esteems as a waste of time or, rather, as utterly worthless and possibly dangerous whatever does not speak in some explicit manner of the infinite God of love. He is joyfully and enthusiastically caught up with the power of proclaiming the Gospel, the beauties of nature, binding the wounds of the ill, for they all speak so clearly of God. He himself—as his poetry so well demonstrates—was so captivated by the adorable Eternal and Incarnate Wisdom, Jesus crucified, that he could say with St. Paul: "I count everything sheer loss because all is far outweighed by the gain of knowing Christ Jesus my Lord, for whose sake I did in fact lose everything. I count it so much dung for the sake of gaining Christ" (Phil 3:8).

It would be erroneous to attempt to judge Montfort's "missionary" verses according to classical literary tradition and schools of poetry. Nonetheless, it must also be admitted that Montfort, the mystical poet, offers us pages of not only true poetry but verses of an exquisite, expressive power and tenderness reminiscent of Jacopone or of Villon.

Montfort lived and sang on a popular level. He knew, as his poetry attests, the great unity of God's creation; he believed that to exist, to pray, to evangelize, and to compose poetry are all—for the person living baptismal life—to praise God Alone. Garcia Lorca defined his own poetry as full of life and natural force in this way: *"Yo tengo el fuego en mis manos* (I hold fire in my hands)." Montfort could repeat the very same formula to describe his own poetry. It is filled with the fire of God.

G. Francini

V. Montfort's Hymnals after His Death

Montfort's successors, especially the Company of Mary, which continued his work of preaching parish renewals, made great use of the founder's hymns. The manuscripts were the work instruments that the missionaries always had at hand. They were instruments of evangelization.

At times the preachers added to their repertoire new hymns taken from here and there (without acknowledging the authors). Adapting to new circumstances, they followed Montfort's custom and revised some of the words or stanzas of the founder's hymns.

When Adrien Vatel, one of the first members of the Company of Mary, edited the hymns in 1725—less than ten years after Montfort's death—it is apparent that he did not consider the hymns a family treasure to be kept in the archives. There were six editions of the hymns of Father de Montfort in the eighteenth century and five more in the nineteenth, all of course in French. They borrowed from one another, and they all resembled each other by their lack of rigorous fidelity to the texts. It was only in 1929, with Father Fradet's monumental work, that there were a serious return to the sources and a meticulous study of Saint Louis de Montfort's poetry. The same fidelity to authenticity characterizes the hymns that appear in OC, published in 1966; the hymns are integrated with the other writings to form an imposing literary and spiritual monument.

This rapid overview shows that his hymns—at least the more popular ones—always held a place of honor among French-speaking Catholics. With the reform of liturgical music after Vatican II, many of the "old" hymns of all authors have been subjected to strong criticism. New popular songs fill the repertoire of parishes. Nonetheless, the hymns of Montfort are being "discovered" by Catholics of all languages, not primarily to add to existing hymnals but to be prayerfully read because of their solid content. Like his other works, they reveal a man who is unreservedly and publicly on the side of the Gospel and the Church. His hymns never hedge; they are not "piosity." They form an authentically Catholic program of life for which the present generation is desperately searching. For people who are not French speaking, the discovery of the writings of Saint Louis Marie in their own language has so renewed interest in the saint that it is hoped that the canticles of Montfort will soon be published in several modern languages.

O. Demers

Notes: (1) For a study of hymns in general, cf. J. Szövérffy, *Hymnology,* in *The New Catholic Encyclopedia,* New York: McGraw-Hill 1966, 7:287-295; M. Hueller, M. A. Bischel, and E.J.Selhorst, *Hymns and Hymnals,* ibid., 295-304. The best inroduction to the Hymns of Saint Louis de Montfort is F. Fradet, *Les oeuvres du Bx de Montfort, poète mystique et populaire. Ses Cantiques avec Etude Critique et Notes (The works of Blessed de Montfort, Mystical and Popular Poet: His Hymns with Critical Study and Notes),* Beauchesne-Grassin, Librairie Mariale, Paris, Angers, and Pontchâteau 1929 (with bibliography) (2) St. Gregory the Great, *Pastoral Care,* trans. Henry Davis SJ, Newman Press, Westminister, Md. 1950, 40-41. (3) Translated by John Henry Cardinal Newman, *The Church of the Fathers,* 4th ed., Burns, Oates, & Co., London 1868 (4) Fradet, *Les oeuvres,* pp. 1-2 of the chapter *Etude Critique* (5) Blain, 70 (6) Fradet, *Les oeuvres,* 9. (7) L. Le Crom, *Un apôtre marial: saint Louis-Marie Grignion de Montfort (A Marian Apostle: Saint Louis Marie Grignion de Montfort),* Librairie mariale, Pontchâteau 1942, 148-149. (8). Fradet, *Les Oeuvres,* 16. (9) Fradet, *Les Oeuvres,* 22. (10) M. Barré, *Chronologie des cantiques du Pere de Montfort (Chronology of the Hymns of Fr. de Montfort),* in DMon 33 (1963), 78-89; 34 (1963), 129-156. (11) Montfort Father H. Frehen, bishop of Iceland († 1986), produced several articles, amounting to 449 pages, printed under the title *Etudes sur les cantiques du Père de Montfort (Studys on the Hymns of Fr. de Montfort).* The first three titles were published in DMon 45 (1968), 1-16; 46 (1969), 17-40; 47 (1972), 41-58. The rest were published by the author in separate installments. (12) Fradet, *Les oeuvres,* 93-95.

ICONOGRAPHY

SUMMARY I. MONTFORT THE ARTIST:
- 1. Youth;
- 2. Art in service of the mission:
  - a. A restorer of churches and chapels,
  - b. The Calvary of Pontchâteau,
  - c. An inspired producer.

II. MONTFORT THE STATUE MAKER:
- 1. The Virgins of Roussay;
- 2. The Virgins of Choletais;
- 3. Our Lady of Wisdom;
- 4. The Crucifix of Saint-Lazare;
- 5. The Little Virgin and Child.

III. MONTFORT ICONOGRAPHY:
- 1. The Rennes Paining;
- 2. The Beauvoir painting;
- 3. Grotesque iconography and statuary;
- 4. The evolution of the montfort image in the twentieth century.

I. MONTFORT THE ARTIST

1. Youth

From an early age, Louis Marie had a taste for the arts, a feeling for the beautiful. Gifted with an uncommon intelligence and a studious pupil of the Jesuits at Rennes, he became interested as a youth in poetry and painting. These two activities earned the young artist a reputation as an eccentric.[1]

His fellow student, Jean-Baptiste Blain, called the free time he devoted to drawing and painting "innocent." He went on to say: "If he had any other more natural [talent], he limited himself to painting, for which he had a special taste and flair. If he had cultivated it, he most certainly would have excelled without a teacher. He taught himself how to draw very well and to paint miniatures. He had such a facility for art that he had only to see something in order to reproduce it. A painter he visited was so astounded that he used to stop working and hide everything related to his craft the moment the young Grignion came to his door. He wanted money if he was to become more receptive to the young man. But Louis Grignion had none (his uncle[2] told me this since I came back). Providence blessed him with a small but rather singular stroke of luck. A small, well-executed devotional painting fell into the hands of the young school boy, and he copied it so well that it was a perfect likeness of the original. A man who had a liking for this kind of work saw it and was so satisfied with it that he gave him a golden *louis* for it. It was this money that enabled the young Grignion to have better access to the painter."[3]

At the age of nineteen, Louis Marie left Rennes for Paris. There, under the aegis of the Saint-Sulpice Seminary, was a community of poor ecclesiastical students under the direction of M. de la Barmondière. Neither the historical monuments nor the many great palaces that gave the capital its reputation attracted Louis' interest. Fr. Blain notes: "The first thing Grignion sacrificed at the outskirts and entrance to Paris was his curiosity. He made a pact with his eyes not to let them see anything that could give them pleasure . . . nothing of that opulence, that splendor, of so many rare objects and art masterpieces that make Paris the most beautiful city in the world and attract so many strangers."[4] On the other hand, he often doffed his hat to salute a statue of the Blessed Virgin that otherwise caught no one's eye. "One day," Blain goes on, "surprised at seeing him doff his hat so often to someone unseen, I asked him who he was greeting. And he answered me that he was paying his respects to the images of the Blessed Virgin on the doors of the houses; they were indeed there but so indistinct that I had to strain to see them."[5] In Rennes and in Paris, he used to spend a long time admiring the statues of Mary adorning the Marian shrines and the altars of the Virgin. It is likely that he had begun to sculpt replicas of these "images."

Finding drawing to be a more "secular" art than sculpting statues and composing hymns, he resolved to sacrifice this artistic diversion. But his superior, Fr. de la Barmondière, found him to have a "great predisposition" for painting as well as for sculpture, architecture, and the other fields of knowledge requiring "a fine imagination." He ordered Louis Marie to cultivate and develop his talents. The future would justify the wisdom of that decision.

2. Art in service of the mission

Montfort was able to give free reign to his artistic soul during his days as an itinerant missionary. At the start of his career, he was an "apprentice" to such famous missionaries as Fr. Leuduger. Not wanting him to appear odd, they allowed him little expression for his many talents. During his later years in La Rochelle, he convincingly demonstrated that a fiery apostle and missionary could also be a genuine artist.

a. A restorer of churches and chapels. Appointed chaplain to the general hospital in Poitiers, Montfort busied himself there with projects that combined spiritual and material restoration. Wishing to obtain greater cleanliness and hygiene in the institution, he wanted to repair its chapel.[6] But a conspiracy forced him to leave the hospital before he was able to realize this plan. Desiring to become a missionary, he started his new apostolate in Montbernage, a working-class district near the church of St. Radegonde. There he transformed the barn of La Bergerie from a dance hall into the chapel of Our Lady Queen of All Hearts. In the middle of this improvised oratory he placed a crucifix.

He decorated the walls with fifteen standards, representing the fifteen mysteries of the Rosary. On one of the supports of the Joubert bridge existed the ruins of a little oratory dedicated to the Queen of the Angels. Built in the thirteenth century, it had been damaged by a flooding of the Clain river and later wrecked by the Huguenots. Under the guise of a memorial mission, Montfort undertook to restore the chapel. Upon its completion he placed in it a Madonna.

He did the same thing with the so-called Temple of St. John, where modern archaeologists had found Gallo-Roman remains. In principle, the clergy did not oppose its restoration, especially since Montfort intended to dedicate this future oratory to St. John the Apostle. This explains the capricious remark of the dean of the chapter of canons: "Fr. Grignion, weren't you transported to the island of Patmos, where God revealed to you that He wanted you to rebuild the Temple of St. John?" The missionary took up a collection for this work. He received many unexpected gifts. Volunteers helped him to transport stones and sand. As a result, in only a few months the Temple was restored "from top to bottom." This led the astonished people of Poitou to say, "Only a saint could have accomplished such a feat!"

In 1707, Montfort offered his services to a missionary team from Saint-Brieuc. People used to say that when St. Vincent Ferrer was preaching a mission there in 1417, he stood before the ruins of the chapel of Our Lady of Pity and exclaimed: "There will come a man who will be much badgered and ridiculed but despite it all will finish its restoration." During a mission three centuries later, Montfort took up the challenge. This restoration was to be his first great work. He drew up the plans, gathered the craftsmen, ordered the statues from a sculptor in Nantes, and directed their transport and installation. During some rare leisure moments in his itinerant missionary life, Montfort would often return to La Chèze to see the completion of the chapel, "one of the most beautiful in the diocese," according to Fr. Besnard.

Dismissed by Dom Leuduger, Fr. de Montfort went off to Montfort-la-Cane, his birthplace. There he found shelter in the priory of Saint-Lazare. For years this former house for lepers had fallen into disuse. It had become a two-family farm. For Louis Marie, Saint-Lazare was far from unknown. His grandfather had been the seneschal and sole judge there in 1666. And his own father, Jean-Baptiste Grignion, had been its farmer general. In Saint-Lazare as well, St. Louis Marie cleaned the chapel and restored order to it. More will be said later about Montfort's stay in Saint-Lazare.

In the diocese of Nantes there are several churches that Montfort restored. At the time, the general custom was to bury the dead in the church buildings. Arriving at the church of Campbon in February 1709, he found it in a sorry state. On its grimy walls hung the black mourning band with the coat of arms of the Coislin dukes. Tombstones were strewn everywhere.[7] First Montfort had the tombstones returned to the graveyard. Then he had the masons, stonecutters, and painters brighten the church itself. A few days later he got into trouble with seigniorial justice for whitewashing over the arms of the Duc de Coislin, the chief lord of the parish.

At Crossac, Montfort repeated his Campbon exploit. Fortified by several judgments of the Brittany parliament against those who wished to continue burying their dead in the church, the missionary profited from the good will of the parishioners and had them sign, before a notary, a surrender of their right to entombment inside the church building. After this, he had the tombstones removed and the sanctuary of the church paved, whitened, decorated, and repaired.

In the diocese of Luçon, he restored the chapel of Our Lady of Victory at La Garnache. In the diocese of La Rochelle, he restored the chapel of Our Lady of Patience at La Séguinière, and the church at Mervent.

Little by little, Montfort became aware of the advantage to be derived from having laypeople or religious assist him in the work of parish missions. Moreover, we know that Montfort, as founder of the Missionaries of the Company of Mary, had formally foreseen in his Rule that *"lay Brothers [be] admitted into the Company to take care of temporal affairs provided they are detached, robust, and obedient, ready to do all they are told to do"* (RM 4). And in W, he said: *"I have no private money belonging to me, but there are 135 pounds belonging to Nicholas of Poitiers."* Grandet points out that Montfort had sent "Brother" Nicholas to Poitiers to learn the "craft of sculptor" so that he might be able to decorate churches.[8] In RM, he stipulated that the Missionaries of the Company of Mary were to explain the prayers and the mysteries of the Rosary *"either by instructions or by pictures and statues which they have for this purpose"* (RM 57).

b. The Calvary of Pontchâteau. The Calvary of Pontchâteau in the diocese of Nantes remains Montfort's masterpiece, a monumental mission memorial that demonstrated his genius as an architect of religious art. Inspired by the achievements of Mont-Valérien, Montfort wanted an artificial mountain to become the "Holy Land" of the West of France—since *"The Turk still keeps Holy Calvary / Where Jesus Christ died"* (H 164:1). "The missionary engineer had drawn three concentric circles. The first marked the location of the Calvary. Between the second and the third, moats hollowed out by clearing away the shrubbery surrounded the holy mountain and protected it. A bit farther away, beyond the third circle, 150 fir trees were planted, intersected by fifteen cypresses that formed an immense rosary around the cross. A few chapels recalled the mysteries of Jesus and Mary."[9] "The Calvary Fr. de Montfort built a few leagues from Nantes, at so great an expense and labor, is a testimony without equal of the grace God gave him and the power he had over people's hearts. This work, which a governor of a province would scarcely have undertaken, and which would have cost a prince a vast amount of money, was not only attempted, but completed by the poorest of all priests. According to what people told me, he called upon farmers and laborers from ten or twelve leagues around and some from even farther away to work there. And these poor folk came to do his bidding with a zeal animated by his own, in throngs and thousands, to give their day, their sweat, and their painful efforts to a man who had no salary or recompense to give them other than what heaven could supply. I heard that over twenty thousand men came to work there, and since these men were not looking to waste the time they so freely gave for the love of God, each of them took a heavier load than two salaried people would have done, which is easy to believe. What happened was that this immense work of building a Calvary, which would have taken even a prince with fifty thousand men several months to build, was finished in relatively little time by the care and blessed ingenuity of a missionary zealot."[10] Its enormous size was the very reason for the loss of the Calvary of Pontchâteau. Fearing that the English might land on the coast and use its moats as trenches and its chapels as blockhouses, a royal edict ordered its demolition in 1710.

*c. **An inspired producer.*** A century after the death of their founder, the Missionaries of the Holy Spirit of Saint-Laurent-sur-Sèvre (as the Company of Mary was then called) were renowned for the splendor of their "mission pageants." They were a unique characteristic of Montfort's missions. Indeed, Montfort had an innate sense of how to create a religious production. He composed real medieval mystery plays and never hesitated to participate in a play himself, even to taking the part of a dead man on his way to judgment.

A handwritten page of Montfort's gives the details of the production, along with a supporting sketch, of a short mystery play of 650 verses entitled *"The Abandoned Soul Delivered from Purgatory by the Prayers of the Poor and Children"* (H 127). Here is the complete text: *"Dialog in the form of a canticle. Preface. In order to sing this dialog in a manner acceptable to God, edifying to our neighbor, and of benefit to the souls in Purgatory, it is necessary to:*

1. Begin with the Veni Creator Spiritus: Accende lumen sensibus; and then the Ave maris stella: Monstra te esse Matrem.

2. There must be twenty characters: God the Father, God the Son, God the Holy Spirit, the Blessed Virgin, the Guardian Angels, the Devil, the Abandoned Soul, Four Suffering Souls, Four Living Souls, Geneviève, Catherine, Agnes, Françoise, Armelle. And this is not counting the angels who surround God's throne nor the poor who will be praying in unison.

3. Each character learns his songs by heart, sings them unhurriedly, and will practice the ceremonies of which he is a part. Set up five chairs with the middle one higher than the others, and the actors will be positioned pretty much in this way: [there follows a small drawing by the author]."

The young Louis Marie certainly relished the great procession of the "consecration," which made Montfort-la-Cane famous throughout Brittany at the end of the seventeenth century. The whole city turned out. Behind the mayor and the aldermen were the harquebusiers, mounted or on foot, the count, represented by his squire, the dignitaries of the seigniorial court, with the herald of arms in his fancy *hoqueton,* the six paymasters carrying the chief banners of their parishes, the members of the various brotherhoods with their respective ensigns and standards, the troop of musicians that had come from Rennes, and the four chief worthies carrying the canopy. This was a format that one day would be reintroduced and brought to perfection by Montfort. The bishop of Saint-Malo personally carried the Blessed Sacrament. He was then greeted with great pomp at the town hall, a canon was fired, and upon their return a reception was held.[11]

Claude Masse, a military engineer at La Rochelle, had the good idea of sketching in comic-strip form the closing procession of the women's mission on August 16, 1711. Actually, this picturesque report proves Montfort to be a past master in the art of spectacular processions. In the mind of the saint, nothing was too beautiful for the eyes of God.

Here is the text of the explanatory captions that accompany Claude Masse's drawing: "A. Banner of the Jacobin Fathers (Dominicans), before which marched a large number of people of both sexes. B. A group of daughters of the common people, barefoot and dressed in white. C. A white standard for the same. D. A group of the daughters of merchants, most of whom were barefoot, carrying a cross, a candle, a rosary and a picture on which was written: contract of renewal of baptismal promises. E. A blue standard for the daughters of the townsfolk. F. Brother Mathurin,[12] missionary assistants, keeping the marchers in order and leading the singing of the different songs. G. The clergy also controlling and ordering the march and leading the singing of hymns. H. A red standard for married women, a few of whom were barefoot. I. Another standard for the young ladies of the town. K. Two ladies carrying torches. L. Two gunners' oboes that were played at the close of each of the verses sung by the women. M. The banner of Our Lady of the Seven Sorrows. N. A black and white standard for the Sisters of the Dominican Third Order. O. Navy men to maintain order and keep back the crowds present at various places. P. The cross of the Dominican Fathers with the rosary around it. Q. The chief dance masters and violinists of the town, whom the Father missionary railed against in his sermons and who were paid with a good supper, like the sargents and soldiers. R. Fr. Chauvet, the hospital chaplain and dispenser in reserved cases. S. Fr. M. Grignion,[13] the missionary's brother, who held a few procession rehearsals inside and outside the town in order to familiarize the women with its rubrics; he almost always carried the book of Gospels.[14] T. Fr. de Montfort, missionary and secular priest of the province of Brittany; he had given several missions, always using the rosary as a principle. V. Fr. Colusson, a Jesuit seminary professor, who followed a part of the procession. X. The Dominican Fr. Doiteau, who always accompanied the missionary in his processions. Y. Sergeants and soldiers from the regiments of Angles and La Lande, then garrisoned at La Rochelle, to control the crowds."[15] "This procession of women," Masse adds, "started at two o'clock from the Dominican church and passed in front of the town hall, where the Maréchal de Chamilly, then commander in this province, watched them march by along with the members of his court, which created quite an imposing spectacle. Women carried standards, and all sang the hymns and anthems in the missionary's style to all the latest tunes."

II. Montfort the Statue Maker

Quérard notes that in his travelling missionary team, Montfort had "a sculptor and a painter, whom he directed in the decorating of churches, chapels, and calvaries." But Grandet, whom he quotes, had added a moralizing intention that annoyed the purists: "On his missions he always had a painter and a sculptor with him in order to cover or redo those pictures and statues of the saints that were offensive or badly done."

In his leisure moments, Montfort himself became a sculptor. Tradition attributes to him a number of statues and other sculptures. Knowing Montfort's taste for the plastic arts and his love for Our Lady, it is almost certain that he made most of them, despite the lack of written documentation.

1. The Virgins of Roussay (May 1714)

"People have preserved as relics a few objects that belonged to the saint: a pearwood statue of Mary in the parish church, two other statuettes of the Blessed Virgin that were donated by him and adorn his restored chapel."[16]

2. The Virgins of Choletais

Maurice Laurentin made a special study of this series of madonnas in Saint-Laurent, La Séguinière, and Saint-Amand attributed to the saint. He concluded: "Examination and comparison both favor the tradition. They [the madonnas] are a bit clumsy and were obviously not done by a professional but by an amateur who had before him a fine statue that he copied. They reveal the gaps in training and the hesitancy of a gifted sculptor, but one who had little experience and who had never fully grasped the laws of anatomy and the rules of modeling. But they are not without skill. They have the charm of the feeling that inspired them. . . . They possess that essential quality of a sacred work which Paul Doncoeur calls chastity. They attract attention neither by their beauty nor by their worth. They do not move the art lover or dilettante in us. But they do move the believer. . . . Looking at these relics, a Christian understands the soul of a saint and the secret of his inspiration. For him the work of art was a means of action, a lasting sign of his spiritual teaching, and an instrument of an interior reform."[17]

The chief proof of the authenticity of all the works attributed to Fr. de Montfort is that they reveal a similar technique. The sculptures depict the Virgin draped like a patrician, holding the child with a globe in his hand. In their own way, they illustrate a trilogy of montfort characteristics:

1) Mary, 2) who is utterly submitted to Jesus Christ, 3) who is the Savior of the world.

These signs of montfort authenticity take on further importance when we compare these later works (1713-1715) with those earlier sculptures correctly attributed to the talents of Louis Marie. This brings us to the period in Montfort's life when he had been dismissed by Dom Leuduger and he had made his headquarters the priory of Saint-Lazare in Montfort, his birthplace. While there, he had some auspicious moments of "free time" at his disposal. This allowed him to use his artistic talents. We owe to this period a number of striking works.

3. Our Lady of Wisdom

Once the chapel of the old priory had been cleaned, Montfort immediately began to decorate it. He sought to make it a complete artistic unity, one that reflected his unique missionary vision. In addition, he decided to turn the priory into the oratory for the first montfort community (with Brothers Mathurin and Jean). Above the altar he placed a dove with silver wings, the symbol of the Holy Spirit, and below it the name of Jesus in large letters. Lastly, on the altar itself he placed the statue of Our Lady of Wisdom. In the sanctuary he installed a prie-dieu supporting a long rosary, whose chain was in forged iron with beads the size of walnuts. There was enough room to allow several people to recite it at the same time.[18]

4. The Crucifix of Saint-Lazare

The so-called Saint-Lazare crucifix is preserved in the bedroom where, according to tradition, Fr. de Montfort stayed. It is of the same rather clumsy technique mentioned by Laurentin about the Virgins of Choletais, as is the following piece.

5. The Little Virgin and Child

This is the little statue that Montfort carried on the top of his walking stick.

The authenticity of the first two such madonnas that Montfort made is beyond question. They served as models for the later sculptures that we have described above. Later other statuettes of the Virgin in the same montfort style were discovered. All came from the religious communities of Saint-Laurent-sur-Sèvre. One of them, which had been given to the Daughters of Wisdom of Mont-Saint-Michel, has been carefully preserved by the community of Pontorson.

III. Montfort Iconography

Besnard (1717-1788), the third successor of Louis de Montfort, gives the following portrait of him: "He was of above average height with a robust constitution. He had a noble manner with an air of kindness about him. He was considerate, affable, and good-natured. He had rather ruddy cheeks, a long face, a high and broad forehead, with large bright eyes that were often self-effacing, a gently aquiline nose, as people picture him, with a somewhat prominent chin, straight and quite short chestnut hair falling softly on the top of his head just above his forehead."

Besnard wrote these lines in 1767, some fifty years after Montfort's death. Although he may not have known the great missionary, he was on the mission band for five years with Fr. René Mulot, the saint's second recruit. Even then montfort iconography had already begun to be marketed throughout France in response to Fr. de Montfort's growing fame. When Fr. Adrien Vatel, the saint's first recruit (1715), announced Montfort's death to the superior of the Seminary of the Holy Spirit in Paris, he was able to include with his letter "two little engravings (or images)" of Fr. de Montfort.[19] This presupposes that working drawings for the engravings had already been made even before Montfort's death. Fr. Besnard was able to see these two engravings again in Paris in 1767. Is this engraving among those preserved in the Bibliothèque Nationale? We do not think so, since all of those engravings mention Fr. de Montfort's death. Furthermore, the engraving showing the Calvary of Pontchâteau gives such a tiny sketch of the missionary that nothing worthwhile can be obtained from it.

We possess two portraits of Montfort that might be called "prototypes," since it is apparent that they were used as models for all subsequent iconography of the eighteenth and nineteenth centuries.

1. The Rennes painting

Fr. Fernand Fradet writes: "When Marie Louise of Jesus, the first Daughter of Wisdom, came to Rennes in 1724, called there by the woman who was President of Montigny to set up the first school of her Congregation, she discovered, among the few pieces of furniture left to the institution by its first benefactress, a portrait of the founder, still jealously preserved today in the private clinic of Rennes. What was the origin of this canvas? May it be supposed that Montfort consented to pose for it? Did his universally benevolent charity allow him to give in to the entreaties of some noble friend? It is too bad that history gives us no details."[20] The author begins from the hypothesis that the Rennes painting was done during Montfort's lifetime. But there seems to be a simpler explanation. This painting was taken from Saint-Laurent-sur-Sèvre after Fr. de Montfort's death. The Marquis de Magnanne[21] was staying in Rennes in 1714 with M. Bédouët d'Orville—both of them were friends of the great missionary—when he acquired the house that was to become the first residence of the Daughters of Wisdom. In 1720, hence after Montfort's death, the Marquis entrusted the school founded by the saint to Mademoiselle Elisabeth Dauvaise, another great benefactress of the work of Fr. de Montfort. It is highly likely, then, that on May 12, 1722, when one of the representatives of Mademoiselle Dauvaise from Nantes took possession of the school in Rennes, she brought the famous painting along with her luggage.

The explanation Fr. Fradet gave of the original painting is even more valid for the Rennes canvas. "It is possible that a member of his family [Dupleix] was in Saint-Laurent-sur-Sèvre at the time of the Saint's death and that he was allowed to reproduce the features of the missionary as he lay on his deathbed."[22] It is probable that an artist made a quick death sketch, which then served as a model for the first painter. "The features of this odd painting are those one would find in the countless portraits that were to follow. Only the body was made to stand up. The hands remained joined and the eyes lowered. Later they were half opened in order to give the face a more lifelike expression. All that had to be done now was to surround the saint with the things that he loved best and were the symbols of his work."[23]

The fact that the original was "recumbent" explains the emaciated face and the extremely aquiline profile that successive reproductions were to exaggerate to the point of caricature. Besnard pointed this out in 1767. We may therefore rightly look upon the Rennes painting as the prototype and the Beauvoir painting as only a copy.

2. The Beauvoir painting

In 1888, the year of Fr. de Montfort's beatification, Fr. Deval, a Montfort missionary, was preaching in Beauvoir-sur-Mer, Vendée. He paid a visit to the octogenarian widow Dupleix in the company of the pastor of the parish. In her room, he noticed a painting that amazed him because the figure in the painting resembled the customary portraits of Fr. de Montfort.

"Convinced that he was in the presence of a genuine portrait and one painted by an eyewitness, he did not hesitate to ask Madame Dupleix for the old painting.' 'Never!' she replied, 'It is a painting that has been in my family for more than 150 years and must belong to the eldest of my children. I must leave it therefore to my eldest son, who is an officer. You may offer me many gold pieces for it, but I will never give it up, since our family cares about it so much.' 'But, Madame, you can't refuse. I think it is the portrait of Fr. de Montfort, who has just been beatified. Would you know the origin of this painting?' 'Undoubtedly it is by a family member, since we are so attached to it.' 'If you are willing to give it to me, I will pay for a beautiful statue of Blessed Louis Marie for the church in Beauvoir, and I would come and preach a triduum for its installation.' What the pastor had to say sounded like Montfort speaking, and soon Madame Dupleix gave in, saying that the replacement would please her son. The priest took away the treasure. It is what is called the 'Rome picture,' the most venerable and authentic of the portraits, since it is a barely retouched copy of the canvas. It shows the actual features of Fr. de Montfort as they were on the last day of his life."[24]

3. Grotesque iconography and statuary

Up to the beginning of the twentieth century, no one dreamed of being offended by the pictures of Montfort that today seem so grotesque to us. It is quite odd to note that there were fewer of the engravings and holy pictures inspired by the Rennes canvas in circulation than copies of the first pictures preserved in the Bibliothèque Nationale, which had been so badly recast. When there was a need to provide the areas that had been evangelized by Montfort with statues of his likeness, sculptors outdid themselves in the art of ugliness and caricature. In the Vendée we can still hear the expression "ugly as a Grignion." Proof of such distortions can be found in the ugliness of Montfort's statue in the Mervent grotto and the gruesome painting by Michel Poussin in the hermitage of Saint-Eloi in La Rochelle.

4. The evolution of the montfort image in the twentieth century

Today painters and sculptors have attempted to give Montfort a "better face." The results have been uneven. There have been different interpretations of the image of Montfort, based on the artistic taste, spirituality, and cultural period of the artists and those for whom they are creating. The richness and complexity of Montfort's personality lend themselves to varied and almost contradictory images.

Several artists, especially at the beginning of the century, portrayed Montfort as a contemplative who lived for Wisdom and who consecrated himself totally to Christ through Mary. Typical in this regard were the two Carrara marble statues from the chisel of the famous sculptor Paolo Bartolini. One is placed in front of the great Gothic chapel of the Daughters of Wisdom in Saint-Laurent-sur-Sèvre. The other is the Mary Queen of All Hearts statue, venerated in Rome at the shrine on the Via Romagna. The same attitude of ecstatic contemplation can be seen in the statue of Montfort, sculpted by H. Elström, in the church of Mary Mediatrix in Louvain and in the painting by G. Pranovi (1964) in the Montfort Marian Center in Rome. It depicts Montfort in solitude at the rue Pot-de-Fer in Paris. The colossal statue of Montfort in St. Peter's Basilica in Rome deserves special mention. The sculptor Galileo Parisini (1948) translated into marble TD 114, on the fate of the *"little book,"* in which with a motion of his hand the saint stops the devil from tearing it up.

From a popular perspective, another statue remains noteworthy. It is in the house where the saint was born in Montfort-sur-Meu. It depicts Montfort walking along, singing his famous hymn: *"So it is, throughout the world I run . . . / To save my poor neighbor"* (H 22:1). In the same house, the montfort artist Alessandro Leidi (1980s) depicts in his magnificent ceramic work a young Louis Marie with common but pleasant features. Jap Min created a cycle of paintings in 1953 for the chapel of the montfort scholasticate at Oirschot in Holland. We see Montfort taking his pen from Mary's Heart in order to write TD. Another shows the saint carrying the poor man of Dinan, who bears the features of the crucified Christ. Another depicts Montfort as the apostle of the latter days as he moves forward into the fire to destroy the reign of Belial and restore that of Jesus Christ.

During the 1990s something new was introduced into montfort art, the use of the icon. Following the rules of Russian and Greek icon painting, Vittoria Paravicini Bagliani produced an icon of Montfort in front of the grotto of Mervent; it leads into the interior world of the saint and into the mysteries he lived and proclaimed (1992).

Lastly, the so-called Montfort Canada statue, at the entrance to the Montfort Marian Center in Montreal. The Austrian artist Josef Zenzmaier, who conceived it in 1966, "deviated deliberately from the usual models. He made him rough and peasant-like. . . . But he especially wanted his work to be in motion and to have the walk of a resolute man charging into the wind. . . . But as if to counteract this animation, . . . his tilting head stops and centers on tormented shapes, expressions of his most secret contemplation."[25]

In the future, we expect to see interpretations of Montfort by artists from the young Churches of Africa or Asia. The new images of Montfort will certainly succeed in their purpose of remaining faithful to the prototype while inculturating him within their own context. No doubt they will still retain, however, a profound connection with Montfort's spirituality, which now belongs to the universal Church, to the Church of all times and places.

M. Sibold

Notes: (1) Let us note that the Huguenot Grignions of London (cf. article Family/marriage), who came from Loudun like the Montfort Grignions, during the eighteenth century excelled in the arts of watchmaking, engraving, and painting. We have a portrait of two of them. They show a striking similarity to Montfort's features in the Rennes painting (cf. below). (2) Alain Robert (1653-1735), who was sacristan of Saint-Sauveur de Rennes when he died. (3) Blain, 5-6. (4) Ibid., 19. (5) Ibid., 19-20. (6) Grandet, 67. (7) Also buried in the Campbon church were a great uncle of Fr. de Montfort, Pierre Grignion (1612-1640), his wife, Françoise Bécigneul (1613-1704), as well as one of their sons, Eustache Grignion (1638-1643). (8) Grandet, 311. (9) Le Crom, 229. (10) Blain, 166-167. (11) M. Sibold, *Le Sang des Grignion (The Blood of the Grignions),* Rome 1987, 82. (12) Mathurin Rangeard (1687-1760), who died at Saint-Laurent-sur-Sèvre as a tonsured cleric. (13) Gabriel Grignion (1682-1717). (14) Since La Rochelle had a large Protestant minority, Fr. de Montfort wanted to give prominence publicly to the Scriptures. (15) Archives of Charente-Maritime, Ms. B 501. (16) Le Crom, 279. (17) M. Laurentin, *Le bienheureux Père de Montfort statuaire. Le bienheureux Louis-Marie Grignion de Montfort est-il l'auteur de statues que la Vendée lui a attribué? (Blessed Louis Marie Grignion de Montfort, Statue Maker: Is He the Sculptor of the Statues Attributed to Him in the Vendée?),* L.-J. Biton, Saint-Laurent-sur-Sèvre 1936, 30-31. (18) This statue, mentioned since 1726 and hidden during the Revolution, is today in the oratory of the house of his birth in Montfort-sur-Meu. (19) Besnard II, 161. (20) *Histoire de la Compagnie de Marie (History of the Company of Mary),* Saint-Laurent-sur-Sèvre 1914, 1920. (21) Henri-François de Racappé, marquis de Magnanne (1664-1750), had a definitive influence in placing Montfort's religious communities in Saint-Laurent-sur-Sèvre. He died there in 1750. He was buried in the chapel of the Blessed Virgin opposite Fr. de Montfort. (22) A. David, *Le Père de Montfort par ses meilleurs historiens (Fr. de Montfort by His Best Historians),* Librairie Mariale, Paris 1947, 9 (23) A. David, *Le Père de Montfort,* 11. (24) Ibid. Under the signature of Th. Ronsin, a typed article is to be found in AGCM: "Quelques détails iconographiques relatifs au Bx Louis-Marie Grignion de Montfort de sa mort (1716) à l'année 1850 (Some Iconographic Details Relating to Bl. Louis Marie Grignion de Montfort from His Death (1716) to the Year 1850)," 6 pages. He mentions the following portraits of Montfort: 1. Montfort on his deathbed; 2. the Rennes picture; 3. the picture in Holy Spirit refectory in Saint-Laurent-sur-Sèvre; 4. an engraving by E. Desrochers; 5. an engraving by J. Massard; 6. an engraving done in Rome (1835-1836); 7. an engraving made after that of Rome; 8. a picture of Blessed de Montfort, of the Massard type; 9. an engraving by Bouasse-Lebel, no. 220; 10. a portrait of Montfort at Charpentier in Nantes; 11. a picture of Montfort, after the picture of Rennes and Saint-Laurent; 12. an engraving by Charles de Chergé; 13. a popular image, souvenir of the Mervent grotto; 14. a popular image, an announcement or remembrance of a mission. There follow four pages of Montfort correspondence. (25) B. Papàsogli, *L'homme venu du vent. Saint Louis-Marie Grignion de Montfort,* Editions Bellarmin, Montreal 1984, 7. English translation, *Montfort, a Prophet for Our Times,* Edizioni Monfortane, Rome 1991.

INCARNATION

SUMMARY

I. THE INCARNATION:
  1. A fundamental theme:
  2. The sources of Montfort:
    a. To Jesus through Mary,
    b. In the atmosphere of the French school,
    c. Deeply rooted in Scripture and the Church Fathers;
  3. How Montfort speaks of the Incarnation.

II. THE INCARNATION IN MONTFORT'S WRITINGS:
  1. In the light of LEW:
    a. Jesus Christ, Eternal and Incarnate Wisdom,
    b. "The prodigious excess of the love of God,"
    c. The Incarnation and the Cross;
  2. In the light of TD:
    a. The three Persons of the Holy Trinity played a part in the Incarnation,
    b. What the Incarnation involves for Christ and Mary,
    c. Incarnation and mission;
  3. The "mystery proper" to the perfect practice of the true devotion:
    a. "The mystery of Jesus living and reigning in Mary,"
    b. "The first mystery of Jesus Christ, the most hidden, the most exalted, the least known,"
    c. "It is in this mystery that Jesus . . . in cooperation with Mary, chose all the elect,"
    d. "It is in this mystery that he anticipated all subsequent mysteries of his life by his willing acceptance of them,"
    e. "The seat of the mercy, of the liberality and the glory of God";
  4. The fundamental mystery:
    a. The "state,"
    b. Montfort's spirituality is imbued with the mystery of the Incarnation.

III. THE RELEVANCE OF MONTFORT TODAY:
  1. The Second Vatican Council: "The supreme mystery of the Incarnation";
  2. The encyclical Redemptoris mater by Pope John Paul II;
  3. For an actualization and a development of Montfort's way of thinking:
    a. The Incarnation, Mary, and the Church,
    b. The "historic" dimension of the Incarnation,
    c. Mary, the guarantor of the identity of Jesus, true God and true man,
    d. The sense of the greatness of humanity.

IV. CONCLUSION.

I. THE INCARNATION

"Eternal and incarnate Wisdom, most lovable and adorable Jesus, true God and true man, only Son of God and of Mary always a Virgin" (LEW 223). These words, which sound like a profession of faith, not only introduce the *"Consecration of oneself to Jesus Christ Wisdom incarnate through the hands of Mary,"* but they also introduce us into the heart of the spiritual life of Montfort and the spirituality he has handed on to us. The Incarnation is not just one important theme among others; it is really *the* theme that gradually sheds light on the significant facets of spirituality. Montfort gradually wove round this theme his spiritual teachings into an organic whole.

1. A fundamental theme

The Incarnation, the divine manifest in the flesh, is Wisdom Incarnate. "Every spirit which acknowledges that Jesus Christ has come in the flesh is from God, and every spirit which does not thus acknowledge Jesus is not from God" (1 Jn 4:2-3). The wisdom of Wisdom Incarnate, the beauty of Beauty Incarnate, the love of Love Incarnate are manifest in creation. For creation was made through Jesus Christ and restored through Jesus Christ. *"Eternal Wisdom began to manifest himself outside the bosom of the Father, when after a whole eternity, he made light, heaven and earth"* (LEW 31). *"At times they [the saints] were so astonished at the beauty, the harmony and the order that God has put into the smallest things, such as a bee, an ant, an ear of corn, a flower, a worm, they were carried away in rapture and ecstasy"* (LEW 34). And so, too, was man created and restored in the Eternal Wisdom. *"We might say that Eternal Wisdom made copies, that is, shining likenesses of his own intelligence, memory, and will, and infused them into the soul of man so that he might become the living image of the Godhead"* (LEW 37). Thus the personal emanation of God is the person of incarnate Compassion.

The two classic forms of the spirituality of Christian compassion are reflected in two great saints of the twelfth century, St. Bernard of Clairvaux and St. Francis of Assisi. Both of their unique forms of spiritual compassion are found united in St. Louis de Montfort. First, there is St. Bernard's Song of Songs tradition of compassion as ecstatic Love Incarnate in Christ. *"It is certain that Eternal Wisdom loves souls so much that he even espouses them, contracting with them a true, spiritual marriage which the world cannot understand"* (LEW 54). Jesus is the personal embodiment of the Beloved, the personal emanation of the Father's ecstatic love of the human race and creation. St. Bernard states in his *Commentary on the Song of Songs:* "Show me, says the Bride, the place of such love and peace, and fullness, that as Jacob, yet abiding in the flesh saw God face to face, and his life was spared, so I too may look on Thee in Thy light and glory, by contemplation in trance of soul."[1] Christ, the Beloved of the Father, is the begotten of the Lover, the Father. *"Here we have the great wonder of heaven and earth, the prodigious excess of the love of God. 'The Word was made flesh.' Eternal Wisdom became incarnate. God became man without ceasing to be God"* (LEW 108). Jesus assumes the world into direct relationship with God Alone and restores that union when it has been broken. *"But what does the name of Jesus, the proper name of incarnate Wisdom, signify to us if not ardent charity, infinite love and engaging gentleness?"* (LEW 120). Thus, Jesus Christ becomes man so that man can participate in the divine life and, therefore, in a direct personal relationship with God. Thus, God has become man so that man can become God.

The second classical tradition of the incarnate Christ of compassion, and one also found in Montfort, is the tradition of St. Francis of Assisi. It is the incarnate Compassion who is the Suffering Servant. Montfort says that the greatest motive *"impelling us to love Jesus Christ the Wisdom Incarnate, the strongest, in my opinion, is the suffering he chose to endure to prove his love for us"* (LEW 154). The compassionate Savior takes upon himself the negativity of the human race. The radical self-sacrifice, which allows for the acceptance by Jesus of the sins and suffering of humanity as his own, is the expiation of the Passion become compassion. The Incarnation is the *kenosis* of Christ as suffering servant Incarnate. "Let your bearing towards one another arise out of your life in Christ Jesus. For the divine nature was his from the first, yet he did not think to snatch at equality with God, but made himself nothing, assuming the nature of a slave. Bearing the human likeness, revealed in human shape, he humbled himself and in obedience accepted even death—death on a cross" (Phil 2:5-9). This Suffering Servant theme, to which Francis gave witness, was illuminated powerfully by the other great Franciscan, St. Bonaventure: "God grant me this grace to obey as carefully the novice who enters the order today . . . if he were set over me as Guardian, as the most outstanding or ancient in the Order. For a subject ought to consider his superior not as a man but as God, for whose love he is subject to him."[2]

Thus in Montfort the tenderness of God manifest in and through the Incarnation is Redemptive. *"Incarnate Wisdom loved the cross from his infancy"* (LEW 169). Thus in Montfort's spirituality "Christocentrism" is "Trinitarian;" and the Incarnation is salvific. The Son, in Whom all things are created and restored, is the expression of the Father. The Son is the focus of the divine fecundity and unselfish self-expression. The Son is the Beloved of the Father, who is the Lover, the Parent or Source of compassion. The Son is also the Person Who fully returns that compassion, Who loves the Father. Their personal relationship, their intimacy, and their bond is the Holy Spirit. The spouse of the Holy Spirit is the Mother of God, the Temple of the Trinity chosen by God and prepared by her Immaculate Conception and confirmed in the virginal purity of her "yes" at the Annunciation. *"Only through Mary then, can we possess divine Wisdom"* (LEW 209). She is the mold of the incarnate Christ. She is the mold of the true Christian, the mother of each and every Christian.

"Accept, gracious Virgin, this little offering of my slavery to honor and imitate the obedience which Eternal Wisdom willingly chose to have towards you, his Mother" (LEW 226).

Richard J. Payne

2. The sources of Montfort

It was during the years he spent at the seminary in Paris (1692-1700) that Montfort consciously internalized the essential Christological dimension of his spiritual life.

a. To Jesus through Mary. Montfort's research on Mary, and the efforts he made to justify his devotion to Mary, gave him a deeper insight into the link between Mary and Jesus. This link is so essential that the *"divine Maternity"* is her raison d'être and her reason for acting. God chose her so that the Word might become flesh and thus become our Brother. Her mission is not only to give Jesus to the world, but also to reveal him, lead us to him, and unite us to him.[3] This is rooted in a deep understanding of the Incarnation.

b. In the atmosphere of the French school. In order to understand Montfort's teaching, it is indispensable to examine it within the spiritual and cultural context in which he lived and on which he drew heavily,[4] mainly the context of the French school.[5] It is significant that the writers familiar with that school, and particularly with its leader Bérulle, take it for granted that Montfort had close ties with it. H. Bremond, for example, who describes Montfort as "the teacher par excellence of Marian devotion," completes this description by saying that Montfort was "at once the last of the great Bérullians and an outstanding missionary."[6] Experts on Bérulle, Jean Dagens, the Oratorians A. Molien and P. Cochois, and a Dominican tertiary, Father Poupon, agree that Montfort was a follower of Bérulle.[7] Now, these authors seem to vie with each other in stressing that Bérulle's way of thinking revolved around the Incarnation.[8] Montfort could not be included among his contemporaries unless he had drawn on the same primary source of inspiration. Actually, he not only drew on it but enriched it as well.

c. Deeply rooted in Scripture and the Church Fathers. Montfort turned to the Bible and the Church Fathers for support throughout his writings. When he deals with the subject of Jesus, *"eternal and incarnate Wisdom,"* his references to Scripture, as an underpinning, assume even more importance. Such an importance, that they give his insight into the mystery of the Incarnation a very individual character, as we shall see later.[9]

3. How Montfort speaks of the Incarnation

Montfort approaches the Incarnation in his own way, as both a spiritual writer nourished on the Gospel and as a missionary. What he is concerned with is Jesus Christ as depicted in Scripture and influencing our lives. He shows unmistakable signs of belonging to the French school, although his style is definitely simpler and his terminology more concrete than Bérulle's or Condren's. Although Montfort was well aware of the meaning of words like "state" and "adherence," for example, he hardly uses them at all. When he does use these words, their meaning is different from what these authors gave them.

II. The Incarnation in Montfort's Writings

Montfort did not approach the Incarnation from the angle of speculative theology. What he wrote about the Incarnation has a wider scope and is more valuable. It is a meditation, full of wonderment and love, on the mystery of Jesus. We will now examine it and bring together the main themes dealt with in LEW and TD.

1. In the light of LEW

a. Jesus Christ, Eternal and Incarnate Wisdom. In Montfort's writings, the expression *"eternal and incarnate Wisdom"* recurs like a leitmotif. It is his way of identifying Jesus of Nazareth. The description indicates Jesus' divine nature as eternally begotten of the Father, as well as his human nature as conceived in Mary's womb. Gilbert has rightly pointed out that Montfort discovered the riches contained in the OT by linking it with Jesus: "Montfort rereads the Wisdom books as a framework, but the Old Testament gives way to the New when it comes to expressing the mystery: it is the coming of Christ, Incarnate Wisdom, that makes it possible to understand the Book of Wisdom and, consequently, all the Wisdom books."[10] For Montfort, the mystery of the Incarnation gives access to the mystery of Wisdom: when he speaks of Eternal Wisdom *"before the Incarnation,"* his thoughts are still with what he has found out about Wisdom in Jesus.[11]

His theology is perfectly right. He does not confuse the human and the divine natures of Christ. Though he clearly traces the stages in the carrying out of the divine plan, he always keeps in mind the unity of the Person. When he turns to Jesus and speaks about him, even when he mentions the *"humiliations"* of his humanity in most realistic terms, he never loses sight of the fact that he is talking about Eternal Wisdom: *"Substantial or uncreated Wisdom is the Son of God, the second Person of the most Blessed Trinity. In other words, it is eternal Wisdom in eternity or Jesus Christ in time"* (LEW 13).

His meditation is deeply biblical: it is based on the revelation of God Himself and of His love for humanity, which is shown in the economy of salvation (including the Incarnation).

b. "The prodigious excess of the love of God" (LEW 108). It is obvious to all believers that the Incarnation, which took place *"for our sake and for our salvation,"* is a mystery of love. Following Bérulle's example, the French school laid much emphasis on this.[12] Montfort followed in their steps and once again approached the mystery in his own way, especially through his interpretation of the Wisdom books.[13]

In his view, the love of God for us is revealed in the Incarnation as it took place in history.[14] In other words, in the *"economy of salvation."* Jointly with the Father and the Spirit, Eternal Wisdom decided to become flesh in order to *"restore"*[15] man after he had fallen victim to sin and was unable to save himself (LEW 40): *"I seem to see this lovable Sovereign convoking and assembling the most holy Trinity, a second time, so to speak, for the purpose of rehabilitating man in the state he formerly created him"* (LEW 40; cf. 104).

According to Montfort, what prompts Eternal Wisdom to take this initiative is his love of preference for humanity: *"Eternal Wisdom was deeply moved by the plight of Adam and all his descendants. He was profoundly distressed at seeing his vessel of honor shattered, his image torn to pieces, his masterpiece destroyed, his representative in this world overthrown. He listened tenderly to man's sighs and entreaties and he was moved with compassion when he saw the sweat of his brow, the tears in his eyes, the fatigue of his arms, his sadness of heart, his affliction of soul"* (LEW 41; cf. 104). Several things are worth noticing in this passage. It is undeniable that in LEW, in particular, Montfort dwells on the very special loving link between the Second Person of the Trinity and man (cf. LEW 35-38, 45, 47-50, 64-69). What Eternal Wisdom reveals of himself in the Incarnation enables Montfort to discover him better within the Trinity. And, conversely, the Wisdom books throw light on the mystery of Incarnate Wisdom.

This is a perfectly logical approach. The fact that it was the Word Who "became man" is an invitation for us to find the "reasons" that justify this decision; for, God never acts without some "reasons," even if his reasons are infinitely beyond our comprehension. As Montfort discovers in Christ's earthly journey a love for man carried to extremes (cf. LEW, chap. 9-11, 13), he attributes it quite naturally to Eternal Wisdom, for the person of Jesus is the 2nd Person of the Trinity. This accounts for the vocabulary borrowed from human love that he uses when speaking of the love that Eternal Wisdom bore man before the Incarnation.

Finally, the Incarnation is the result of the love of the Father and of the Spirit as well as of the Son. The contrast in LEW 42-45, between the attitude of the Father exacting justice and that of the Son pleading for mercy, should not be made too much of. Although Montfort's vivid description and his vocabulary are rather ambiguous, it would not be fair to quote only this passage as typical of his way of thinking. Many other passages could be quoted that can redress the balance. For example, this one about Incarnate Wisdom: *"She is a gift sent by the love of the eternal Father and a product of the love of the Holy Spirit. She was given out of love and fashioned by love. She is therefore all love, or rather the very love of the Father and the Holy Spirit"* (LEW 113).[16]

c. The Incarnation and the Cross. In order to find out Montfort's thought about the Cross, we have to look at this mystery in connection with the Incarnation because the Cross comes within the scope of the Incarnation.

The love of Eternal Wisdom for us leads Him to choose not only to become man but also to opt for a type of Incarnation making it possible for him to die on the Cross (LEW 167-168; cf. 163-164). In LEW 169, Montfort writes: *"Incarnate Wisdom loved the cross from his infancy. At his coming into the world, while in his*

Mother's womb, she received it from the eternal Father. He placed it deep in his heart, there to dominate his life, saying, Deus meus, volui, et legem tuam in medio cordis mei (Ps 39:9). My God and my Father, I chose this cross when I was in your bosom. I choose it now in the womb of my Mother. I love it with all my strength and I place it deep in my heart to be my spouse and my mistress."[17] Montfort goes on to show how Eternal Wisdom longed passionately for the Cross throughout his life on earth until it held him in its arms on Calvary (LEW 170-172). Finally, Montfort says that Wisdom and the Cross will be one *"in glory"* (Cf. LEW 172).

This is because the bond uniting Wisdom and the Cross is as indissoluble as the Incarnation, which binds them together: *"He espoused the cross at his Incarnation with indescribable love. At his coming into the world, while in his Mother's womb, he received it from his eternal Father"* (LEW 170). So Montfort is justified in writing: *"Do not think that, wanting to be more triumphant, he rejected the cross after his death. Far from it; he united himself so closely to it that neither angel nor man, not any creature in heaven or on earth, could separate him from it. The bond between them is indissoluble, their union is eternal. Never the Cross without Jesus, or Jesus without the Cross"* (LEW 172). Although the Cross implies suffering or trial in this world, this obviously does not apply after the glorification, except in the sense that glory is the fruit of the Cross. If we look at it in this perspective, it is clear that, for Montfort, love is central to the Cross, as required by the Incarnation, by the mystery of saving love.

This explains why Montfort concludes: *"Wisdom has so truly incorporated and united herself with the Cross that in all truth we can say: Wisdom is the Cross and the Cross is Wisdom"* (LEW 180).[18]

2. In the light of TD

Montfort cannot consider Mary without considering the Incarnation. In all she is and does, the Blessed Virgin refers us back to this mystery in all its dimensions.

a. The three Persons of the Holy Trinity played a part in the Incarnation. In TD, and more briefly in SM, Montfort makes it clear that the Father, the Son, and the Holy Spirit were involved in the Incarnation. He does so with reference to Mary in view of the aim he is pursuing.

Because the three Divine Persons freely chose to have need of Mary for the Incarnation, each of them in their own way took her into consideration (TD 16-21; SM 9-13). The love that the Father, the Son, and the Holy Spirit bore Mary and the riches with which they lavishly endowed her are justified by the role they entrusted to her. Now, her role did not consist merely in giving his individual humanity to the Word; she was meant to extend this role to the accomplishment of the whole Christ, Head and members. For according to the economy of salvation planned by the Trinity, from the first moment of its realization, the Incarnation is the beginning of the vast act of giving birth to the new humanity in Jesus Christ. This birthing will only come to an end *"at the end of time"* (TD 29). Montfort examines the two aspects in close connection and in a Trinitarian perspective. The *"power"* communicated by the Father to Mary for her to *"produce her Son"* extends to *"all the members of his mystical Body"* (TD 17); the Holy Spirit *"becomes actively fruitful in producing Jesus Christ and his members in her and by her"* (TD 21). Montfort's view is that when it comes to realizing the mystery of our salvation in Jesus Christ, the Persons of the Holy Trinity act in the same way as in the Incarnation: *"The plan adopted by the three Persons of the Blessed Trinity in the Incarnation, the first coming of Jesus Christ, is adhered to each day in an invisible manner throughout the Church and they will pursue it to the end of time until the last coming of Jesus Christ"* (TD 22). Then he draws conclusions from this about Mary herself and her maternal role towards us, as this role is part and parcel of her role as mother of the Incarnate Word (TD 23-36).[19] We are therefore directly concerned: our salvation *"began"* when Eternal Wisdom took flesh; the three Divine Persons had us in mind then, and Mary's consent concerned us objectively. Now, according to the principle laid down by Montfort, the *"beginning"* is an indication of how we are to continue to grow until we *"come to the measure of the full stature of Christ"* (TD 159; cf. 33, 119, 156, 164, 168). Consequently, if we consider our Christian life in the light of the mystery of the Incarnation, we realize that it is, as it were, a Trinitarian life in Christ under the motion of the Holy Spirit with the *"necessary"* presence of Mary.

b. What the Incarnation involves for Christ and Mary. We will confine ourselves to considering only a few aspects that Montfort emphasized which are important for an understanding of his spirituality.

Bérulle and his followers of the French school considered that in the Incarnation, Christ had "emptied himself."[20] Montfort does not reject the expression but he uses it very seldom.[21] On the other hand, he emphasizes *"dependence,"*[22] which is a more concrete term and refers to the attitude of *"obedience"*[23] to Mary that the Incarnate Word chose to adopt towards her. Montfort is aware that this attitude of dependence on Mary, and of obedience to her as her child, was adopted by Eternal Wisdom, that is, one of the three Persons of the Holy Trinity: *"God-made-man found freedom in imprisoning himself in her womb. . . . He glorified his independence and his majesty in depending upon this lovable Virgin in his conception, his birth, his presentation in the temple, and in the thirty years of his hidden life. Even at his death she had to be present so that he might be united with her in one sacrifice"* (TD 18). Montfort is talking not only about the "physical" dependence consequent on the Incarnation but also about the personal dependence of a son on his mother, which Christ fully accepted. This "state" of loving dependence is as permanent for Jesus as is his "state of Incarnation." So, Montfort does not hesitate to extend it to the condition of Christ in glory: *"Since grace enhances our human nature and glory adds a still greater perfection to grace, it is certain that our Lord remains in heaven just as much the Son of Mary as he was on earth. Consequently he has retained the submissiveness and obedience of the most perfect of all children towards the best of all mothers"* (TD 27; cf. LEW 205). Although he has retained this dependence, *"we must take care not to consider this dependence as an abasement or imperfection in Jesus Christ. For Mary, infinitely inferior to her Son, who is God, does not command him in the same way as an earthly mother would command her son who is beneath her"* (TD 27). Jesus' filial dependence on Mary must therefore be viewed in different ways according to the situation. It is different in glory from what it was on earth.[24]

The dependence of Jesus on Mary that results from the Incarnation becomes the foundation of Montfort's spirituality and of the obedience to Mary that it requires from us. It is a question of *"imitating"* Jesus (LEW 226; TD 139, 155-156, 157, 162, 198, 243; SM 63; H 76:2), and even of imitating the Trinity, Who chose to *"depend"* on Mary for the Incarnation (TD 140).

We must, however, realize that the imitation in question is not to be formal, or optional, depending after all on our personal initiative; it is made necessary, as we have seen, by the fact that the Incarnation of the Word in Mary entails for her a real spiritual motherhood in our regard; Mary is endowed with a corresponding *"power."* By becoming man, Eternal Wisdom actually involves us in a filial dependence on Mary, as far as our spiritual life is concerned. It is our responsibility to acknowledge and live it at our own level, as Jesus himself accepted and lived it at His own.

For Mary, it must be added that Jesus, Incarnate Wisdom is her whole raison d'être. It is therefore in the Incarnation, considered in its full extension and with its saving dimensions embracing all humankind, that we will find an explanation for Mary being so lavishly endowed by God, for her special relationships with the three Persons of the Trinity, and for her universal mission (cf., among others, TD 14-36). As Montfort says, Mary is the *"worthy Mother of God," "Mother of Jesus"* (TD 247; cf. TD 63), and it would be just as appropriate to call her "Mary of the Incarnation."

c. Incarnation and mission. Let us repeat that in Montfort's view, the way in which Jesus is to carry out his mission, even to the Cross, is already included, in a certain sense, in the plan for the Incarnation. The Incarnation is a mystery of love, proximity, and mystical identification, since Wisdom comes to sinful man in the total *"mission"* of Christ; that is, in the full accomplishment of the mystery of salvation. *"It was through the Blessed Virgin that Jesus Christ came into the world, and it is also through her that he must reign in the world"* (TD 1). By the same token, the association of Mary with the Holy Spirit in the Incarnation entails her permanent cooperation with Him until the mystery is accomplished. This holds good for the formation of the *"apostles of the end times"* (TD 55-59) and for the birth of the Company of Mary.[25]

3. The "mystery proper" to the perfect practice of the true devotion

Montfort shares with us his thoughts on the Incarnation in a very forceful way when he speaks of the *"mystery proper"* to the perfect practice of the devotion to Mary that he proposes (TD 243-248; cf. SM 63). Here is the main passage: *"Time does not permit me to linger here and elaborate on the perfections and wonders of the mystery of Jesus living and reigning in Mary, or the Incarnation of the Word. I shall confine myself to the following brief remarks. The Incarnation is the first mystery of Jesus Christ; it is the most hidden; and it is the most exalted and the least known. It was in this mystery that Jesus, in the womb of Mary and with her cooperation, chose all the elect. For this reason the saints call her womb the throne-room of God's mysteries, aula sacramentorum. It was in this mystery that Jesus anticipated all subsequent mysteries of his life by his willing acceptance of them. Consequently, this mystery is a summary of all his mysteries since it contains the intention and the grace of them all. Lastly, this mystery is the seat of the mercy, the liberality, and the glory of God"* (TD 248).

a. "The mystery of Jesus living and reigning in Mary". At first sight this definition of the Incarnation may appear rather restricting. In order to understand it properly, we must place it in its immediate context, that of the prefect practice of the true devotion, and *"Jesus living in Mary,"* both of which opens wider vistas.[26] Montfort uses the expression *"Jesus living and reigning in Mary"* to describe what the Incarnation brings about in Mary and, at the same time, what it should bring about in us: the life-giving reign of Christ in those who welcome it into their inmost being. To this, Montfort will add that Mary not only derives benefit from the extension of the mystery to us, but that she takes an active part in the process. In H 111 Montfort says, *"To the glory of your Father, By the power of your name, Reign in us through your Mother."*

b. "The first mystery of Jesus Christ, the most hidden, the most exalted, the least known". *"The first mystery"*—The context tells us that we are to interpret this as more than an indication of just a numerical order, as this would be obvious; Montfort did not mean to state the obvious. Because it is the first, this mystery is the source, the foundation, and all the others are to show how pregnant with meaning it is, for they express its potentiality.

"The most hidden"—Montfort deeply appreciates this aspect. It is true that of all the mysteries of Christ, the Incarnation is the one that proves most elusive to the grasp of our senses and of our imagination. And the vistas it opens up for our reason are breathtaking.

This is because it is *"the most exalted,"* the most elevated, the greatest mystery. It is, of course, not to be compared with the mystery of the Trinity, which is the mystery of mysteries.[27] But as Montfort considers it in the framework of the economy of salvation, it is the one that gives the deepest insight into the unfathomable depths of God, by giving a glimpse of His love. The other mysteries of Jesus are *"mysteries of salvation"* in relation to the Incarnation. They include the mystery of the Passion and Resurrection, which is the sign clearer than any other sign and draws its effectiveness from the mystery of Eternal and Incarnate Wisdom, Jesus Christ.

"The least known"—This is consequent on its being the most hidden. But Montfort does not seem resigned to this and does his best to make it more widely known.

c. "It is in this mystery that Jesus . . . in cooperation with Mary, chose all the elect". Montfort mentions again the aim of the Incarnation, which is our salvation. Mary is associated in a unique and universal way with the work of her son: *"In this mystery the elect / Have been given birth. / Mary and Jesus together / Have chosen them in advance / That they may share in their virtues / Their glory and their power"* (H 87:7). Does Montfort mean that from the moment of the Incarnation, Mary knew clearly and distinctly all who were to be her children? In the context of his time, it would not be surprising.[28]

d. "It is in this mystery that he anticipated all subsequent mysteries of his life by his willing acceptance of them". As a consequence, this mystery is *"a summary of all his mysteries since it contains the intention and the grace of them all."* In this passage Montfort expressed what is probably his deepest insight into the Incarnation as the source mystery that contains in advance, as it were, all that it makes possible.[29] It is true of the purpose of God, it is true in Jesus, who, from the moment he became man was the Savior, the *"grace,"* i.e., the gift, the communication par excellence of God to man. In and through the Incarnation, Christ in his very being is constituted the Head of saved humanity, the Source from which divine life will spring through all that he is and does. Far from being made superfluous, the other *"mysteries"* of Jesus appear like the realization in time of all the potentialities and *"intentions"* contained in that *"first"* mystery, so that the new humanity beginning with it may be born. The mystery of the Cross, for example, which leads on to the glory of the Resurrection, is the supreme realization of the redemptive Incarnation.

e. "The seat of the mercy, of the liberality and the glory of God". Montfort continues his consideration of the Incarnation as *"the mystery of Jesus living and reigning in Mary."* He sees it as the seat of divine mercy *"for us"* precisely because in it we find Jesus *"through Mary."* Mary is really the way of mercy by which Jesus came to us and by which we should go to him.

"The seat of liberality for Mary," because *"while the new Adam dwelt in this truly earthly paradise, God performed there so many marvels beyond the understanding of men and angels."* How could Jesus fail to repay his mother a hundred times over for what she gave him while she was carrying him in her womb?[30]

Finally, *"the seat of glory for his Father"*—Montfort knew better than to forget this purpose of the Incarnation: in Mary, Jesus *"gave more glory to God than he would have given had he offered all the sacrifices of the Old Law. In Mary he gave his*

Father infinite glory, such as his Father had never received from man" (TD 248). Jesus' dependence on Mary, consequent on the Incarnation, enabled him to *"give more glory to God his Father by submitting to his Mother for thirty years than he would have given him had he converted the whole world by working the greatest miracles"* (TD 18; cf. also 139). LEW presents the salvation of humanity as the means to obtain this glory and, therefore, as being the reason for the Incarnation (LEW 43).

4. The fundamental mystery

For Montfort, the Incarnation is not only an essential mystery: it is the fundamental mystery in the economy of salvation and the one at the heart of his spirituality.

a. The "state". Montfort does not use the term in the sense that Bérulle and the adherents of the French school did.[31] But he has perfectly grasped the deep reality they were trying to express, i.e., everything that Jesus achieved on earth has not purely and simply vanished into the past beyond recall. Though his *"actions"* as such were transitory, the interior dispositions from which they proceeded and that they expressed were not. We must, therefore, distinguish the *"actions,"* which are transient, from the *"states,"* which are permanent and retain all their saving power (their "virtue") for us.[32] The *"first"* state, which is absolutely fundamental, is the Incarnation. From this Montfort draws conclusions about, more especially, the filial relation between Jesus and Mary: through the Incarnation, and from then on, the Father's Son is established in *"the state"* of *"Son of Mary,"* and Mary herself in *"the state"* of *"Mother of Jesus."* Since her spiritual motherhood (of humanity) is ultimately based on the Incarnation, when it took place she also began to be in *"the state"* of *"Mother of humanity,"* which essentially *"qualifies"* her to play her role as mother.

b. Montfort's spirituality is imbued with the mystery of the Incarnation. The contemplation of Eternal Wisdom, Who took flesh in Mary for our salvation, pervades and characterizes Montfort's spiritual life. The mystery of the Incarnation, as he perceives it, is not only fundamental in itself according to an abstract theological view but is the *"mystery proper"* to his way of living in Christ with Mary and, therefore, to his life and spirituality. It acts in him like a welling spring that comes to the surface in his writings whenever the occasion calls for it.[33]

III. The Relevance of Montfort Today

The Second Vatican Council and Pope John Paul II give us grounds to say that Montfort's teaching is relevant today. Together with the recent advances in theology, they point the direction in which research is to be done to "actualize" Montfort's way of thinking and develop it.

1. The Second Vatican Council: "The supreme mystery of the Incarnation"

"Devoutly meditating on Mary and contemplating her in the light of the Word made man, the Church reverently penetrates more intimately into the supreme mystery of the Incar-nation and becomes ever increasingly like her Spouse" (LG 65). For the Council, and for Montfort as well, it is "in the light" of the Incarnation that we must try to discover Mary and also the Church.

Furthermore, the significant meaning of the expression "supreme mystery" must be emphasized. Although he phrases it differently, Montfort expresses the same thing (cf. among others TD 248) when he looks at the Incarnation from the viewpoint of the economy of salvation, as the Council did.[34]

2. The encyclical Redemptoris mater by John Paul II

The theme of the Incarnation runs through the encyclical, and in many cases it is dealt with along the lines adopted by Montfort.[35] For example, in the Encyclical, the mystery of the Incarnation is approached from the angle of the economy of salvation: pointing out how the Holy Trinity intervened in the Incarnation itself (RMat 1, 9); the consequences that result from this for Mary (RMat 8-9); and the fact that the reality of the Incarnation finds a sort of extension in the mystery of the Church, the Body of Christ. We cannot think of the reality of the Incarnation without referring to Mary, the mother of the Incarnate Word (RM 5. "Mary's mediation is intimately linked with her motherhood of Jesus" (RMat 38) and that, as a consequence, her spiritual motherhood is rooted in the Incarnation (RMat 20). All this is the more significant as John Paul II constantly refers to the Council in order to promote "a new and more careful reading of what it said about the Blessed Virgin Mary" (RMat 48).

3. For an actualization and a development of Montfort's way of thinking

The current teachings of the Magisterium, which take into account the modern advances of theological research, open up new vistas.

a. The Incarnation, Mary, and the Church. In Montfort's time, ecclesiology was inclined to center on the Church as an "institution." However, this does not mean that the "communion" aspect of it was ignored. Montfort can obviously not be blamed for not looking at it in the perspective of Vatican II. In his writings, especially in the way he looks at the mystery of the Incarnation, he offers enough raw material to integrate in an organic way, as it were, the relationship between Mary and the Church that is highlighted today.[36]

b. The "historic" dimension of the Incarnation. In RMat, John Paul II underlines the historic dimension of the Incarnation: it "marks" the moment when, with the entrance of the eternal into time, time itself is redeemed and, being filled with the mystery of Christ, becomes definitively "salvation time" (RMat 1). It is the "fundamental event in the economy of salvation"; it is recorded at the center of human history to direct it to its true goal. It establishes a "great transformation" that "belongs to the entire history of man, from that beginning which is revealed to us in the first chapters of Genesis until the final end" (RMat 52; cf. 11, 24).

Though Montfort is well aware of the "restoring" effect going back to the beginning of humanity, and that we are now in the "end times" moving towards the ultimate accomplishment, it is possible to widen his perspective by adding the proper historic dimension, insofar as it affects human history as such. Along the same lines, current theological research on earthly realities considered in the light of Creation and of the Incarnation can help us to nuance and enrich Montfort's vision.

c. Mary, the guarantor of the identity of Jesus, true God and true man. Finally, in connection with the present-day Christological currents, greatly concerned with highlighting the reality of the humanity of Jesus, presented as similar to ours in every respect (Christologies "from below"), Montfort draws attention to two things. First, it is essential to keep the realism of the Incarnation in order to avoid falling into a sort of Docetism, which destroys true faith. With his deep insight into Eternal Wisdom, which helps him to preserve the teaching of a Christology "from above," he warns us against an equally damaging drift that leads to leaving in the background, or even rejecting, the specifically divine character of the person of Jesus.

Besides, Montfort makes a point that always holds good, namely, that Christologists claiming to do without reference to *"the Mother of the Lord"* would be hard put to keep the balance required by faith in the mystery of the Incarnation. We have need of Mary to gain access to the mystery of Jesus in its entirety. From this point of view, again, she is *"necessary."* For, her motherhood makes her the privileged and indispensable guarantor of the realism of the Incarnation: she gave the Eternal Word the humanity that makes him our Brother. She is just as much the witness of his divinity, if we take seriously the title Mother of God, which refers us to the divinity and eternity of the One she brought forth in time. *"Eternal and incarnate Wisdom, most lovable and adorable Jesus, true God and true man, only Son of the eternal Father and of Mary always a Virgin, I adore you profoundly dwelling in the splendor of your Father from all eternity and in the virginal womb of Mary, your most worthy Mother, at the time of your Incarnation"* (LEW 223).

d. The sense of the greatness of humanity. Montfort is a realist: he sees humanity in its concrete situation, that is to say, bearing the scar of sin but redeemed by the wonderful love of God. His insistence on the misery of sinful humanity actually leads to the highlighting of its admirable dignity, created out of love, humanity is saved by love (cf., among others, SM 3; LEW 35-46, 64-71). Nowadays, when there is so much talk about human rights, and when the rights of the weakest are so frequently flouted in so many ways, it would be profitable to engage in a deep contemplation of the greatness of humanity as revealed to us in the Incarnation. It is none other than Christ, *"eternal and incarnate Wisdom,"*

Creator and Redeemer, who is the best guarantor of human values. It is Christ who protects the "inviolable rights of human beings" and of their dignity, from the very beginning till the last moment of their life on earth. Montfort can help us in this respect both by his teaching and his way of acting. He looked beyond the physical and mental misery of those he met and saw in them, especially the poor and those who were most despised, a reflection of the glory that the Incarnate Word sheds on them.

IV. Conclusion

What sets great spiritualities apart from others is that they delve deeply enough into the mystery of Christ to acquire in their essential elements a universal dimension that transcends the accidental characteristics reflecting the mind-set of a particular time or cultural milieu. That is why, without losing any of their rich teaching, they prove suitable for the integration of values highlighted in other times and places, This is true of montfort spirituality, which is rooted in the supreme mystery of the Incarnation.

Notes: (1) R. F. Littledale, *A Commentary on the Song of Songs Ancient and Medieval Sources,* 1869. (2) St. Bonaventure, *Mirror of Perfection,* chap. 46. (3) On this evolution and discovery, cf. S. de Fiores, *Itinerario.* (4) It is obviously possible to grasp the immediate meaning of Montfort's spiritual way and to act on it without studying the historical context (otherwise it would remain the preserve of scholars!). It is, however, important to be acquainted with the cultural environment in order to grasp the ins and outs of Montfort's theological and spiritual teaching. (5) It is beyond doubt that Montfort drew on all the material available to him that suited his personal concerns and his spiritual insights, consequently, we cannot restrict his sources to the members of the French school, like Bourgoing, Boudon, Olier, Saint Jure, and Nepveu, to say nothing of Bérulle himself. Besides, whenever these are mentioned, the precise references to them that we can establish thanks to N and the texts of the principal works (not least N) do not tell the whole story. Just as important is the fact that when he was at Saint-Sulpice, especially when under the influence of Olier, he lived in an atmosphere steeped in the teaching of the French school. Cf. H. Bremond, *Histoire littéraire du sentiment religieux en France* (History of Religious Feeling in France), vol. 3, *La Conquête mystique de l'Ecole française* (The Mystical Victory of the French School), Bloud et Gay, Paris 1921; S. De Fiores, *Itinerario spirituale di S. Luigi di Montfort,* passim. (6) Cf. Abbé A. David, *Le Père de Montfort par ses meilleurs historiens* (Father de Montfort by the Best Historians), Librairie mariale, Paris 1947, 113. (7) J. Dagens, preface to *Bérulle et les origines de la restauration catholique* (Bérulle and the Origins of the Catholic reform [1571-1611]), DDB, Paris 1952, 8 ("He [Bérulle] heralds the work of M. Vincent, Olier, Father Eudes, Father Grignion de Montfort"); A. Molien, *avant-propos* to *Les grandeurs de Marie d'après les écrivains de l'Ecole française* (The Greatness of Mary in the Writings of the French School), DDB, Paris 1934, 7, and especially preface, pp. 106-109; P. Cochois, *Bérulle et l'Ecole française* (Bérulle and the French School), Seuil, Series Maîtres spirituels, Paris 1963, 164-165; R.P. Poupon, *avant-propos* to *Le poème de la parfaite consécration Marie,* Lyon 1947, 7-17. We must also remember the work by Fr. Lhoumeau, S.M.M., who was the first to investigate Montfort's sources: *La vie spirituelle à l'école de saint Louis-Marie Grignion de Montfort (The Spiritual Life of the School of Saint Louis-Marie Grignion de Montfort),* Beyaert, Bruges 1954. H. Bremond thought highly of this work, which he studied carefully in one of its early editions. We must also mention the solid Préface by Father Huré, S.M.M., to the "typeset" edition of *L'Amour de la Sagesse Eternelle* (LEW), Librairie mariale, Calvaire de Pontchâteau (Calvary of Pontchâteau), 1929, 57-82, in which he widened the perspective, which had been mostly Marian until then, by showing the value of Montfort's book. (8) "The Incarnation holds a very central place in all of Bérulle's doctrine, "the apostle of the incarnate Word" (J. Dagens, *Bérulle et les origines (Bérulle and the Origins),* 291); cf. H. Bremond, *Histoire littéraire,* 43ff. Father Molien, *Les grandeurs de Marie (The Greatness of Mary),* 14, quotes, and expresses his approval of the following by Fr. Houssaye: "With inexorable logic he would always refer everything back to the the one source of the Incarnate Word." See also H.-M. Manteau-Bonamy, OP, *Maternité divine et Incarnation* (Divine Maternity and the Incarnation), Vrin, Paris 1949, 202-218. (9) We refer the reader to Fr. Gilbert, SJ, *L'exégèse spirituelle de Montfort* (The Spiritual Exegesis of Montfort), in NRT 5 (November-December 1982), 678-691. The author demonstrates both the quality of Montfort's biblical interpretation and originality (in his exegesis of the Book of Wisdom), p. 684. For his part, Father Grelot, SJ, *La Bible et la Parole de Dieu (The Bible and the Word of God),* Desclée, Paris 1965, wrote: "For a proper use of the texts relating to Wisdom, it is advisable to turn to the well-known Book of Eternal Wisdom by Blessed Suso and LEW by Saint Louis-Marie Grignion de Montfort. (10) Gilbert, *L'exégèse spirituelle* (Spiritual Exegesis), 688. (11) A study of Montfort's vocabulary in LEW is very illuminating. On many occasions the word *"wisdom"* used on its own refers to Jesus, e.g., LEW 11, 19, 73, 155, etc. Sometimes the expression *"eternal Wisdom"* refers directly to Christ, e.g., LEW 9, 11, 70, 71, 118, 131, 155, 167, 173, etc. The same is true for *"divine wisdom,"* e.g., LEW 6, 8, 95, etc. (12) As far as Bérulle is concerned, cf. P. Cochois, *Bérulle et l'Ecole française (Bérulle and the French School),* 87-89: "The Mystery of the Incarnation, is one of self-emptying for love," "The Incarnation, an ecstasy of eternal Love." (13) According to Gilbert, *L'exégèse spirituelle* (Spiritual Exegesis), 684: "This example of Montfort as a spiritual exegete of the Book of Wisdom is exceptional." (14) Montfort did not much care for theological speculation for its own sake. And he does not appear to have taken much notice of the celebrated theological controversy on the theme of the Incarnation. Supposing humanity had not sinned, would the Word have become man? To this question St. Thomas Aquinas answered in the negative, whereas Duns Scot answered in the affirmative. Similarly, in Montfort's time Bérulle linked the Incarnation to the Redemption, whereas Olier was inclined to think that the Incarnation would have taken place anyway. As for Montfort, he bluntly states that the Incarnation, as it actually took place, aimed at the salvation of humanity and, consequently, at the resulting glory of God. Should we go further and infer from the loving complicity that he discovered between Eternal Wisdom and humanity (by virtue of the Creation, and therefore before sin), that the logic of this love would have involved the Incarnation? Similarly again, since Montfort is so much concerned about the glory of God, and the Incarnation in itself can procure it in an unparalleled way, was he not inclined to share Olier's view? (15) Montfort uses the word "restore" several times to express the purpose of the coming of Incarnate Wisdom: to restore man by restoring him to the original dignity that he lost by sinning (LEW 40, 42, 95, 104; TD 156). (16) Throughout his writings, Montfort regards the Incarnation as a mystery of love. We shall see this when dealing with other themes. It is particularly noticeable in H 64:41, H 90:4. (17) The close connection between the Incarnation and the Cross is mentioned in, among others, FC 3, 16, and in H 28:2, H 97:9, 12. (18) All this presupposes that in order to understand Montfort's teaching, it is necessary to refer to what the French school says about the "states" of Jesus and their mystical permanence, the fundamental state in which all the others are rooted being the Incarnation. (19) In fact Montfort takes up this theme throughout TD and SM, as he does in LEW, chap. 17. (20) Cf. P. Cochois, *L'Incarnation, mystere d'aneantissement par amour* (The Incarnation, a mystery of self-emptying out of love), 87-88: in line with Phil 2:7; cf. also Poupon, *Le poème,* 45-49. (21) It occurs in the Consecration formula (LEW 223): *"I thank you for having emptied yourself in assuming the condition of a slave."* But it does not occur anywhere else in Montfort's major works. The word also occurs in H 158:4 on the Eucharist: *"See the vanished glory."* (22) Cf. TD 18, 27, 139, 243; SM 63. (23) LEW 205, 223, 226; TD 27, 139, 156, 157, 198. (24) Even in the latter instance, Montfort draws a clear distinction between the time of the hidden life and that of the public life: the fact that he mentions a form of dependence during the "thirty years" of his hidden life (TD 18 139, 198) prompts us to conclude not that all that time Jesus remained dependent on Mary like a young child does on its mother but, rather, that a radical change took place when he began his "public life." (25) PM is rich in explicit or implicit references to the Incarnation being fundamental, especially when Montfort speaks of the Son (PM 6) and of the Holy Spirit (PM 15). As for the maternal role of Mary in raising up and forming the missionaries for whom Montfort is praying (PM 11, 12, 13, 15, 20, 24, 25), we must remember how closely connected she is with the Incarnation. (26) N shows how deeply interested Montfort was in this theme, as he quotes passages borrowed from Argentan, Bourgoing, and Olier. Cf. Eyckeler, *Cahier de Notes,* xix, 176-178, 10, 185. It appears certain that he learned the prayer of Olier "Jesus, living in Mary" from the Sulpicians; he paraphrases it in Hymn 111 and adds the word *"reign": "Jesus, living in Mary. . . come dwell in us and reign";* he also wrote a hymn dealing at length with the presence of Jesus in Mary: *"In honor of Jesus living in Mary in the Incarnation"* (H 87). (27) Bérulle himself was careful not to rank the Incarnation above the Trinity: "After the mystery of the Trinity, there is no greater mystery." *De la Visitation,* in *Oeuvres de pieté,* Migne, 973). (28) Without any doubt, it is difficult for us to share Montfort's psychological perspective and to appreciate the expressions he used. But leaving aside the "psychological" side of it, we have to face the objective reality of the Incarnation, of which Mary was sufficiently aware to utter her fully conscious and responsible *"fiat."* According to Vatican II, on the day of the Annunciation she said yes to the saving love of God expressed in the mystery: "Embracing God's saving will with a full heart . . . she devoted herself totally as a handmaid of the Lord to the person and work of her Son . . . she served the mystery of redemption" (LG 56). There is no question in her having a clear and distinct Knowledge of those who were to be saved. The fact remains that, implicitly but really, we are concerned with the "yes" of Mary in union with her Son's divine will of salvation. It is in this sense that today we can try to sift the truth from Montfort's assertion. (29) In Montfort's time, the conscious acceptance by Jesus, from the first moment of his human existence, of all that he was called to accomplish, presented no problem. What Christ was humanly conscious of, however, especially at the time of the Incarnation, remains an unfathomable mystery that commands our respect. Montfort's assertion as a theological proposition can be defended. It was widely accepted and taught until relatively recent times. Be it as it may, here again it is wise to concentrate on the "objective" content of the mystery, which is enough to justify Montfort's assertion. (30) This is another theme that recurs in Montfort's sources, notably in Bérulle and Olier (cf., among others, Molien, *Les grandeurs de Marie,* chap. 17-19). (31) The reason may be quite simply that he does not want to use terms that are too complicated which would require an explanation for his audience of simple people.

(32) This is how Father Molien, *Les grandeurs de Marie,* 42, quotes Bérulle's thought on this point: "The Incarnate Word living on earth was in a new state that is permanent in heaven and in eternity. Undoubtedly the facts of his life occurred only once. They were carried out in the past, but their virtue remains and will never pass away, nor will the love with which they were carried out. . . . The Spirit of God, through whom this mystery was accomplished, the interior state of the exterior mystery. . . . The living disposition through which Jesus accomplished this mystery is stili alive, actual, and present to Jesus." The French school has highlighted in a special way a deep reality that sustains the Church, which keeps it alive for us in the liturgy and invites us to live it. (33) It does so, for example, when he speaks of the Eucharist (H 134), on the occasion of Christmas, as is only natural (H 57, H 61, H 63-66), when he speaks of the Sacred Heart (H 40, H 41). Although it is abundantly clear that Montfort does not speak only of the Incarnation and does not approach every subject only with immediate reference to this mystery, the fact that the subject comes up so frequently is significant. (34) Paul VI, *Signum magnum,* I, 3; RMat 27. (35) Pointing out these "convergences" does not mean that we have to go out of our way to see them as the result of a direct, still less exclusive, influence of Montfort. John Paul II, however, makes no mystery of the fact that he is imbued with Montfort's way of thinking, which explains why we find the same emphases in both of them. (36) See, among others, LG, chap. 8, no. 63-65; MC, introduction, 17, 19; RMat 1, 5, 24, 26, etc.

INCULTURATION

SUMMARY

I. INCULTURATION: "THE LAW OF ALL EVANGELIZATION" (GS 44).

II. THE HISTORY OF CATECHESIS AS THE HISTORY OF GLOBAL INCULTURATION:
  1. The cultural dialogue in the patristic era and the Middle Ages;
  2. The sixteenth-century evangelization of the American Indian;
  3. Inculturation in the Far East.

III. INCULTURATION AND THE MISSIONARY WORK OF MONTFORT:
  1. Christological criterion;
  2. Ecclesialogical criterion;
  3. Anthropological criterion.

IV. CONCLUSION.

I. INCULTURATION: "THE LAW OF ALL EVANGELIZATION" (GS 44)

For the Second Vatican Council, the history of evangelization has been and continues to be a process of cultural adaptation, of "communion with various cultural modes," "a living exchange . . . between the Church and the diverse cultures of people" (GS 58, 44). The council noted that the Church profits from the treasures buried within the diversity of human culture and that "from the beginning of her history, [the Church] has learned to express the message of Christ with the help of the ideas and terminology of various peoples, and has tried to clarify it with the wisdom of philosophers, too. Her purpose has been to adapt the gospel to the grasp of all as well as to the needs of the learned, insofar as such was appropriate. Indeed, this accommodated preaching of the revealed Word ought to remain the law of all evangelization [*'lex omnis evangelizationis'*]. For thus each nation develops the ability to express Christ's message in its own way. At the same time, a living exchange is fostered between the Church and the diverse cultures of people" (GS 44).[1] John Paul II's encyclical *Redemptoris missio* (December 7, 1990) emphasizes the necessity of inculturation of the faith as a serious and urgent ecclesial duty, especially today.[2]

II. THE HISTORY OF CATECHESIS AS THE HISTORY OF GLOBAL INCULTURATION

We intentionally speak of the history of catechesis rather than the history of theology as such because we take the word "catechesis" to include the multi-faceted evangelizing activity of the Church.

1. The cultural dialogue in the patristic era and the Middle Ages

Like the complex prepaschal catechesis *of Jesus* (which was not simply the spoken word but also included action, attitude, gesture, silence, witness, suffering: "the total experience"), the postpaschal catechesis *about Jesus* by the Apostles and the Christian community was highly articulated. It included preaching but also liturgical/sacramental and Eucharistic experience, expressed in everyday life. Communication of the faith was thus made complete through *kerygma* (the Word), *leitourgia* (the Sacraments, especially Baptism and the Eucharist), *diakonia* (service), *koinonia-ekklesia* (ecclesial communion), *martyria* (giving witness even through martyrdom).[3]

In the patristic era, for example, there was a very lively cultural dialogue with Stoicism and contemporary philosophical middle-Platonism. Non-Christian religions, which were rapidly multiplying in the Roman Empire at that time, also participated.[4]

Following the Greco-Roman example, even the grandiose conversions of the Germanic and Slavic peoples were modest attempts to inculturate the faith (with the adoption of practices, customs, language, legal behavior, religious expressions). Thus, the learned medieval summae can be considered not just innovative in methodology, but attempts to promote dialogue between Christianity, Islam, and Judaism (cf., for example, the *Summa contra Gentiles* of St. Thomas Aquinas). The great schisms themselves, in the East (1054) and in the West (in the sixteenth century) can be viewed as the affirmations of different "cultural" conceptions and traditions of Christian experience by particular communities, eastern or western.

2. The sixteenth-century evangelization of the American Indian

More than anything else, missionary activity has been a proven source of evangelical inculturation. The evangelization of the American Indian in the sixteenth century, for example, represents an exemplary parable of the process of inculturating the Gospel. The missionaries rejected the models of Germanic and Slavic evangelization and hoped to imitate the style of true Apostles: to refrain from using weapons, to respect the laws of the peoples, to defend the rights of the native inhabitants, to study and adapt to their psychology, to become familiar with their religious beliefs.[5]

However, the Spanish colonizers were violent and dishonest: a painful thorn of counterwitness. Nonetheless, the fact remains that evangelization triumphed over immense problems.

3. Inculturation in the Far East

Another significant example of inculturation of the faith in this period was the work of missionaries in the Far East, such as the Jesuits Robert de Nobili in India, Francis Xavier and Alessandro Valignano in Japan, and Michele Ruggieri and Matteo Ricci in China. Matteo Ricci made himself into "a Chinese man among the Chinese."[6] He became fluent in the language and gave himself the Chinese name Li Madou. He assumed the clothing of a Confucian man of letters; he wrote books in Chinese and lived in Peking from 1601 until his death in 1610. His interpretation of certain Confucian rites was impressive, albeit completely misunderstood (for example, in Benedict XIV's apostolic constitution *Ex quo singulari* in 1742). These rites were, in his view, not so much expressions of religion, as of filial respect and piety between those who govern and their subjects, between father and son or husband and wife, between elder and younger brother, among friends, between the living and the dead.

VI. Inculturation and the Missionary Work of Montfort

Basing ourselves on certain criteria of inculturation, we will endeavor to evaluate Montfort's personality and achievement in the context of the ecclesiastical culture of his time.[7]

1. Christological criterion

This is the first criterion of inculturation. Preaching the Gospel of Jesus Christ as a radical cure for human "nature" (fallen because of sin) and human culture by means of grace is an inculturation: "The law indeed was given through Moses; grace and truth came through Jesus Christ" (Jn 1:17). The inculturation process is actually a genuine incarnation of Christ and of his Gospel within a particular culture: "And the Word became flesh and lived among us" (Jn 1:14). Following the example of Christ, who judged and condemned the negative values of his time, the Gospel, too, continually evaluates the limitations and errors of the culture in which it exists. The reception given to the Gospel, the recognition of a culture's riches, and, at the same time, the purification or refusal of negative values enable a culture to rise and grow in a Christian way. The incarnation of the Gospel in a culture signifies the "conversion" of that culture to the Gospel and also the profound purification of that culture.

This was the existential experience of Montfort, who incarnated in his life and in his preaching the folly of the Cross (cf. 1 Cor 1:23). Confronted with the French culture of his time, licentious, irreligious, and profoundly ignorant of the poor in particular, Montfort became the herald of the Gospel by imitating Christ in his life and by preaching Christ's word in his parish missions. His vocation was to be a missionary of Jesus Christ, by example and preaching, by establishing religious communities of men and women.

His missionary work was especially addressed to the poor, the suffering, the humble, the marginalized, the sick. Montfort lived in poverty among the poor. He understood their language and their culture, so much so that they called him "he who so loves the poor."[8] According to R. Mandrou, a specialist in popular culture, "Grignion de Montfort is undoubtedly one of the rare clerics of the early eighteenth-century French Church who grasped the necessity of revitalizing Gospel instruction for the sake of the poor, who constituted the majority of the French people."[9]

In this way, he made a clear, motivated choice, preferring to devote himself not to the high theological culture of his time (academic, sterile, and often indifferent to the dramas of history), but to preaching and serving the people. Even in this choice, he preferred to model himself not after the models of the great orators of his day but on the popular preachers who evangelized the sordid peripheries of the large cities and the neglected countryside.

2. Ecclesiological criterion

Like Jesus, the Church lives in one time and place, in a particular society, in a specific culture. And, again like Jesus, the Church proclaims conversion to the Gospel to particular cultures (Mk 1:15). As the "body of Christ" (LG 7) and "sacrament of intimate union with God" (LG 1)—but also as a "community" and an "institution"—the universal and particular Church is thus, in history, the setting, agent, and guarantor for a true culmination of the inculturation process.

It is in the concrete reality of the life of the Church that inculturation is purified, carried out, and realized. For this reason, the historical Church is the setting for experiencing inculturation; it is the agency of inculturation; it governs the criteria for assessing the validity and legitimacy of inculturation. The postpaschal Christian community was the first to use inculturation as an ecclesial experience of both welcome to and purification of the "Hebraic religious culture." Both worship (where "the breaking of bread" replaced the ceremonies of temple and synagogue) and behavior saw the effects of this purification; circumcision was no longer imposed on converted pagans for this very reason (Acts 15:28-29): "For in Christ Jesus neither circumcision nor uncircumcision counts for anything; the only thing that counts is faith working through love" (Gal 5:6). The fundamental principle, however, remained the acceptance of authentic cultural values. Paul, for example, states: "Finally, beloved, whatever is true, whatever is honorable, whatever is just, whatever is pure, whatever is pleasing, whatever is commendable, if there is any excellence and if there is anything worthy of praise, think about these things" (Phil 4:8).

Distinguishing between faith and culture, between values and countervalues, is not always easy. Finding solutions is often arduous. But when they are adopted, they are to express the faith of the Church. That is why inculturation can be defined as an ecclesial method of incarnating and vitally reexpressing the Gospel, using a culture's own values, and purifying or denying those cultural realities that are opposed to the Gospel. Inculturation is a marvelous and mysterious exchange of gifts: "In one direction, the Gospel reveals to each culture the supreme truth of the values that the culture embodies and allows the culture to unleash that truth; in the other, each culture expresses the Gospel in an original way and reveals new aspects of it."[10]

Montfort's life and evangelical work fit perfectly into the framework of the Church of his time, and they are also in perfect obedience to the Pope, the bishops, and his other superiors. His constant and extraordinarily heroic obedience to his masters at Saint-Sulpice, even when they apparently did not agree with his choices, is significant. His pilgrimage to Rome and his official investiture by Pope Clement XI on June 6,

1706, when he was named "Missionary Apostolic," are the expression of a great ecclesial sensibility which enhanced the orthodox inculturation of his apostolate.

3. Anthropological criterion

According to this third criterion of inculturation, true evangelization becomes a grace-filled process of salvation of the human being, respecting the integrity of his nature and his culture. Conversion to Christ does not imply rejection of social or religious cultural values. On the contrary, conversion animates and fulfills these values in its gift of grace. Because each person is the object and the bearer of the Gospel, both as an individual and as a member of human and ecclesial society, inculturation reveals itself through the promotion and illumination of humanity and through the complete liberation of humanity from the negative realms of sin, death, injustice, meaninglessness, violence, poverty.

In this context, the work of Montfort was exemplary. He was a popular catechist. His language was simple, devoid of rhetorical flourishes, direct and clear.

One of his innovative means of evangelization was the use of hymns. His songs in the vernacular have no pretensions to being masterworks of pure poetry, but they are nonetheless lively, moving compositions, simple and yet full of evangelical wisdom. Montfort himself realized that not all his verses were beautiful. But he knew that they were good and that they preached the wonders of God (H 2, 39). His collection of religious hymns was a way of making faith live and flourish in the hearts, in the spirits, and on the lips of the simple and the humble; restoring smiles and joy to people who were often sad and desperate. More than the artifice of style, the hymns contain the salt and light of Divine Wisdom. Montfort, an implacable ascetic and penitent, reveals himself in his hymns to be a joyful promoter of happiness and evangelical peace.

Montfort's vivid language, punctuated with comparisons and proverbs, was borrowed from the people. He speaks of the devil as a *"counterfeiter"* (TD 90) and of the Christian without courage as a *"wet hen"* and a *"dead dog."* With the wisdom of the countryside, he reminds us that *"we must not believe that all that glitters is gold"* (TD 82). His pen sometimes produces charming parables, like that of the peasant who offers to the king, by way of the queen's hands, a sorry, wormy apple (cf. TD 47). The missionary saint is not afraid to adopt key words of popular culture, such as *"secret"* and *"contract,"* to express the vital and fundamental issues of Christianity, (for example, perfect devotion to the Virgin or the covenant with God).

We must acknowledge Montfort's Christian genius in "his capacity for synthesis, adapting popular values and promoting a highly demanding and indeed truly spiritual evangelical program. . . . Montfort demands personal awareness and renewal of baptismal promises, the passage from Christianity by proxy to a mature choice of Christ through Mary (TD 126), the total Consecration of oneself for time and for eternity."[11]

Inculturation guides the life of

God's people, by directing it toward concrete forms of social action and witness, characterized by justice, brotherhood, equality, participation, and communion. In this context, investigation into the practical and liberating aspect of the Christian message is of profound concern. The goal of Montfort's popular mission was not simply the practice of the Christian life but also the education of children and of the poor. As Grandet reports: "Grignion de Montfort's principal preoccupation in the course of his missionary work was to establish Christian schools for boys and girls."[12]

That was why the Daughters of Wisdom were given the task of assuming responsibility for the charity schools *"to instruct and promote their [the students'] spiritual welfare, a task performed out of pure charity"* (RW 281). In RW, Montfort gives a meticulous description of the rule to be adopted in these schools, to ensure adequate time (about three hours per day) and progressive training both for beginners and for more advanced students (RW 281-292).

IV. Conclusion

In his apostolic exhortation *Catechesi tradendae,* John Paul II describes the concept of inculturation this way: "The term 'acculturation' or 'inculturation' may be a neologism, but expresses very well one of the components of the great mystery of the Incarnation. We can say of catechism, as of evangelization in general, that it carries the strength of the Gospel to the heart of culture and cultures. For this reason, catechism will attempt to know these cultures and their essential components; it will learn their most significant expressions; it will respect their values and riches. In this way, catechism will be able to impart to these cultures the knowledge of the hidden mystery and to help them energize their own living tradition of giving original expression to Christian life, celebration, and thought" (no. 53).

Montfort aids us in this undertaking of evangelical inculturation by his own saintliness as well as by his application of Christological, ecclesiological, and anthropological criteria to his own missionary work. He teaches us how to listen to *"the cries of the poor"* (H 18) and to incarnate the entire Gospel, including the Cross, in the popular culture.

To be true followers of Montfort we must present an undiluted Christianity. Authentic montfort spirituality is Christianity in all its liberating and sanctifying fullness. It is a spirituality where the message and the medium are one. It is a spirituality communicated in understandable language and clear example.

A. Amato

Notes: (1) For the conciliar understanding of the term "culture," expressing the universality of mankind's ways of life, behavior, and expression in history and in society, cf. GS 53. For an adequate investigation into this theme, cf. H. Carrier, *Gospel Message and Human Cultures: From Leo XIII to John Paul II,* trans. John Drury, Duquesne University Press, Pittsburgh 1989; L. J. Luzbetak, *The Church and Cultures: New Perspectives in Missiological Anthropology,* Orbis, Maryknoll, N.Y. 1988; Pontificia Commissione Biblica, *Fede e culture alla luce della Bibbia, (Faith and Culture in the Light of* *the Bible)* Elle Di Ci, Leumann 1981; P. Poupard, *Il Vangelo nel cuore delle culture (The Gospel in the Heart of Cultures),* Città Nuova, Rome 1988; R. J. Schreiter, *Faith and Cultures: Challenges to a World Church,* in *Theological Studies* 50 (1989), 744-760. The *continuing* attention of the Church to dialogue with cultures led in 1982 to the establishment of the Pontifical Council on Culture, which since 1988 has published a monthly bulletin entitled *Church and Cultures.* (2) Inculturation is a *"grave and urgent necessity, especially today"* (*Redemptoris missio,* 52). (3) Cf. J. Daniélou and R. du Charlat, *La catechesi nei primi secoli (Catechesis in the First Centuries),* Elle Di Ci, Leumann 1982; E. Germain, *2000 ans d'éducation de la foi (2000 Years of Education in the Faith),* Desclée, Paris 1983); J. Longère, *La prédication médiévale (Medieval preaching),* Etudes augustiniennes, Paris 1983; C. Wackenheim, *La catéchèse (Catechisis),* PUF, Paris 1983. (4) For inculturation among the pre-Nicean and post-Nicean Fathers, cf. respectively the studies by F. Bergamelli and O. Pasquato, in A. Amato and A. Strus, *Inculturazione e formazione salesiana (Inculturation and Salesian Formation),* SDB, Rome 1984, 57-73, 75-115. (5) Cf. P. Borges Moran, *Metodos misionales en la cristianización de América. Siglo XVI (Missionary Methods in the Christianization of America, 16th Century),* Univ. Ed., Salamanca 1960. (6) "We made ourselves into Chinese in order to win the Chinese for Christ"—Matteo Ricci in a letter to his superior, writing in a mixture of Italian and Latin. Cf. *Opere storiche del P. Matteo Ricci sj (Historical Works of Matteo Ricci),* under the aegis of the Committee for National Monuments, with preface, notes, and tables by P. Tacchi Ventury, vol. 2, *Le lettere dalla Cina (Letters from China),* Tip. Giorgetti, Macerata 1913, 416. (7) Cf. A. Amato, *"Verbi revelati 'accomodata predicatio' lex omnis evangelizationis" (GS no. 44). Riflessioni storico-teologiche sull'inculturazione (Historical-Theological Reflections on Inculturation),* in *Ricerche teologiche (Theological Research)* 2 (1991), 102-124, especially 117-123. (8) A letter from 400 poor people of Poitiers to M. Leschassier, cited by Father Pauvert, *La vie du Vénérable Louis-Marie Grignion de Montfort (The life of the Venerable Louis Marie Grignion de Montfort),* Oudin, Paris and Poitiers 1875, 140. (9) H. Mandrou, *Montfort et l'évangélisation du peuple (Montfort and the Evangelization of the People),* in RMon 11 (1974), 18. (10) Commissione teologica internazionale, *Temi di ecclesiologia (Ecclesiological Themes),* 4, 2. (11) S. De Fiores, *Grignion de Montfort et la spiritualité populaire (Grignion de Montfort and Popular Spirituality),* in *Dossier montfortain* 4 (1984), 16-17. (12) Grandet, 382.

Le VENERABLE prêtre Louis Marie GRIGNON de MONTFORT missionnaire
apostolique. Instituteur des Missionnaires de la Compagnie de MARIE et de la Congrégation des Filles de la Sagesse, mort en odeur de Sainteté en 1716. âgé de 44 ans.

The Rennes Painting

Fradet suggests that this painting was probably painted by an anonymous artist from a sketch made of Montfort at his deathbed. The painting bears the inscription, "The Venerable priest Louis Marie Grignon de Montfort, apostolic missionary, Founder of the Missionaries of the Company of Mary and of the Congregation of the Daughters of Wisdom, died in the odor of sanctity in 1716 at the age of 44 years."

JESUS CHRIST

SUMMARY

I. Christology in the Seventeenth Century: Abstraction and Spirituality:
   1. Dogmatic theology;
   2. Spiritual theology.

II. Jesus Christ in Montfort's Spiritual Experience.

III. Montfort's Christology:
   1. The absolute nature of salvation in the biblical/ecclesiastical Christ;
   2. Jesus Christ, Wisdom Incarnate and crucified.

IV. Aspects of Montfort Christological Spirituality:
   1. The Christological spiritual journey;
   2. Notes on Christological spirituality.

Two of St. Louis de Montfort's more important works are of an outstanding Christological nature: LEW, which closes with the *"Consecration of Oneself to Jesus Christ, Wisdom Incarnate, through the Hands of Mary,"* and FC. In these works, Montfort presents Christian holiness as a life entirely won over by love of Jesus Christ, centered on him, so as to live *"through Him, with Him, in Him and for Him."*

It is a genuine and specific spirituality, which involves not only the knowledge of truth, ritual celebrations, and the external observance of rules and regulations; it is also a daily life lived consistently and exclusively in acceptance of Jesus Christ and his members. It is a deep, authentic experience of His commandment to love God and neighbor, with the help of the maternal intercession of Mary.

We will first outline the Christological context of Montfort's time, then concentrate on the person of Jesus Christ in the thought and spirituality of Montfort.

I. Christology in the Seventeenth Century: Abstraction and Spirituality

1. Dogmatic theology

From a theological point of view, the seventeenth century was a very complex period.The Jansenist conflicts, the crisis of quietism and, with Denis Péteau (1583-1652) and Louis Thomassin (1619-1695), and the appearance of historical theology, which marked the transition to the eighteenth century, the age of the triumph of reason.

The consolidation of "positive theology" caused a grave crisis for scholastic theology, which was already in decline, having become abstract, repetitive, and uncreative. The Christological themes that are most common in the *Summa Theologiae* of

St. Thomas Aquinas (the Incarnation, the elucidation of the person of Christ, the reconciliation of his freedom with his obedience to the Father) were discussed in a sterile fashion, in a climate of lively polemics between the various schools, often dealing with points of extreme and excessive abstraction.[1]

It is generally recognized that post-Tridentine theology is characterized by the study of the psychological unity of Christ (His knowledge and His awareness of himself). It has an emphasis on the meritorious and satisfactory aspects of the Redemption, expressed in juridical language, and in terms of justice.[2] As a result, the same values were emphasized in the works written by the faithful. There is also a serious gap in theological study concerning the Resurrection.

The Sorbonne of the eighteenth century and its theological speculation are symptomatic of the state of French scholasticism, which lacked new direction and was derived from the problems of the day. The masters of the famous University of Paris went so far as to condemn Descartes's doctrine on September 1, 1671, also condemning all those who denied the existence of "prime matter and substantial forms." This action aroused disappointment and laughter.[3]

The manuals of theology for colleges were first produced after 1680, when Montfort was attending the Sorbonne and the Seminary of Saint-Sulpice (1692-1700). One of the most famous teachers of the Sorbonne, Tournely, employed the method first used by Cano and the elegant form demanded by humanism.[4]

In the same period, however, theology and spirituality entered into a closer union in France, almost in reaction, or as a counterweight, to academic speculation, creaking and decrepit as it was. This was accomplished under the influence of the great masters of spirituality. A number of works are significant, such as *La Théologie affective ou saint Thomas en méditation (Affective Theology or St. Thomas in Meditation)* by Louis Bail (1610-1651), published in 1650; *La croix de Jésus où les plus belles vérités de la théologie mystique et de la grâce sanctifiante sont établies (The Cross of Jesus, in Which the Most Wonderful Truths of Mystical Theology and Sanctifying Grace are Established)* (1647) by the Dominican Louis Chardon (1595-1651), who aimed at a synthesis between theological science and mystical experience;[5] *La Théologie mentis et cordis (Theology of Mind and Heart)* (1668-1687) by Vincent Contenson (1641-1674), a Dominican who defended theology as the source of Christian holiness.[6]

2. Spiritual theology

The encounter of the individual with Jesus Christ is expressed more vividly in the French school of spirituality. The Christocentric tendency of this school is based on the contemplation of Jesus, the Word Incarnate, the perfect Servant and true Worshipper of God, in whom the acts of prayer and Redemption are considered a manifestation and an expression of his union with the Father. Over and above the contemplation of the mysteries of Jesus' humanity, Bérulle, the leader of this school, inculcated the desire for communion with him. Thus the Christian life came to be defined as a life of union with Jesus, according to St. Paul's expression "It is no longer I who live, but it is Christ who lives in me" (Gal 2:20). Other texts of similar content, either by John or especially by St. Paul (Jn 15:4; Eph 3:17; Phil 1:21, 2:5; Col 1:24, 3:1-4), were constantly taken as subjects of meditation by Bérulle and his disciples. According to Bérulle, "the apostle of the Word Incarnate," Jesus Christ, is the "source and the end of all life" for men from the moment of the Incarnation.[7] The mystery of the Incarnation is "the principle of our birth," and "we must no longer remain in ourselves or in our rooms. We must live in Jesus Christ."[8] Here, Bérulle develops his theory of the mysteries by distinguishing between external/transient events and an internal/perpetual state in Christ's life: "They are past in certain circumstances, and yet in a certain other respect they endure and are present and perpetual. They passed away, in that they were accomplished, but they are present, in that they continue to have a certain power. . . . This obliges us to treat matters pertaining to Jesus and His mysteries not as things past and done with but as living and present, and even eternal, and to see that we too have a present and eternal fruit to receive from them."[9]

According to Bérulle, the attitude of the Christian towards Jesus Christ consists in adherence to and dependence on Him. Christ's humanity is without human personality, and so subsists in the personal existence of the Word; therefore, we must renounce the possibility of being a whole, self-sufficient totality, and act only in complete reliance on Christ.[10] This explains the vow of servitude to Jesus (and to Mary) propagated by Bérulle. According to him, Jesus is the end and the fulfillment of our being: "Our first movement must be towards Jesus as towards our fulfillment; and in this search for Jesus, in this adherence to Jesus, in this deep and continual dependence on Jesus, are our life, our rest, our strength, and all our power to act; and we must never act except in unison with him, directed by him and drawing our spirit from him."[11] This spiritual Christocentrism later constituted the core of the spiritual education of priests inculcated by Olier, founder of the Seminary of Saint-Sulpice in Paris.[12]

Leschassier, Montfort's spiritual director, remained faithful to this Christocentric spirituality: "We so often repeat these words of St. Ambrose: 'Christ in us: a seal on the forehead, so that we will always confess his name; a seal on the heart so that we may always love him; a seal on the arm so that we may always work for him,' that we would cease to be faithful to the spirit of our fathers if we abandoned the holy practice implied by these three words: 'through Christ, with Christ, in Christ.'"[13]

The Seminary of Saint-Sulpice emphasized devotion to the Eucharist —"The Rule required that Communion be received every Sunday, feast day, and Thursday of the year"[14]— devotion to the Holy Infancy of Jesus, and especially devotion to Jesus living in Mary, to the point of consecrating oneself to Holy Slavery.

This period also saw the consolidation of devotion to the Sacred Heart of Jesus. Although it was of medieval origin, this form of devotion was definitively in place in the seventeenth century, as a balanced reaction against the severity of Jansenism and the arid abstraction of scholasticism. In the spirit of St. John Eudes (1610-1680), St. Claude de La Colombière (1641-1682), and St. Margaret Mary Alacoque (1647-1690), devotion to the Sacred Heart aimed to express the genuine worship of God's merciful love of humanity, which was revealed in Jesus Christ.[15]

The essential message of the French school of spirituality could be summed up in this statement: "It is in Jesus alone that humanity is at once reconciled and re-created. The aim is complete communion with Jesus, but the path can only be complete self-negation. The path of the Cross of Jesus is a necessary stage on the journey, for 'without him, we can do *nothing.*'"[16]

II. Jesus Christ in Montfort's Spiritual Experience

Both by vocation and from a sense of his mission, Montfort did not venture into the labyrinth of theoretical speculation. He lived in a state of intense involvement in the everyday practice of his discipleship, in the saving presence of the Cross of Jesus Christ, Wisdom crucified. When still young, he rejected the arid argumentation of the Sorbonne, preferring knowledge of the saints. In TD, he does not hesitate to accuse certain professional theologians of only knowing Jesus and Mary in an abstract, impersonal way: *"I am speaking of Catholics, and even of educated Catholics, who profess to teach the faith to others but do not know you or your Mother except speculatively, in a dry, cold and sterile way"* (TD 64).

In an atmosphere and a century characterized by extraordinary splendor and worldly glory, Montfort lived the strong and simple life of the foolishness of the Cross. In the letters that have survived, we are not surprised to see how the great apostle of devotion to Mary was sustained by a Christocentric and soteriological spirituality that was firm and fast. In other words, he founded his apostolic, saintly life on the hard, firm rock of the Cross. In a letter of January 1, 1713, to his sister Catherine of St. Bernard, he writes: *"You would be surprised if you knew all the details of the precious cross which has been sent to me from heaven at the intercession of our good Mother. Please thank my good Lord Jesus and ask your dear community, to whom I send my greetings, to obtain from Jesus the grace for me to carry the roughest and heaviest crosses as I would the light-as-straw ones and to resist with unyielding courage the powers of hell"* (L 24).

In another letter written two weeks before his death and addressed to Mother Marie Louise of Jesus, Montfort repeats that the community of the Daughters of Wisdom is founded *"not on quicksands of gold and silver . . . nor indeed on the strength and influence of any human being . . . , but . . . on the Wisdom of the Cross of Calvary"* (L 34).

Montfort's letters show that his spirituality is deeply rooted in the Wisdom of the Cross. The exclamation that recurs frequently in the letters of the last years of his life is characteristic: *"May Jesus and his Cross reign for ever! (Vive Jesus, vive sa croix)"* (L 26, 29, 30, 31, 33, 34). Letter 13, to a Benedictine nun of the Blessed Sacrament, probably Mother St. Joseph, a woman of very high spiritual perfection, offers a first synthesis of Montfort's spirituality of the Cross: *"You are having to bear a large, weighty cross. But what a great happiness for you! Have confidence. For if God, who is all goodness, continues to make you suffer he will not test you more than you can bear. The cross is a sure sign that he loves you. I can assure you of this, that the greatest proof that we are loved by God is when we are despised by the world and burdened with crosses, i.e. when we are made to endure the privation of things we could rightly claim; when our holiest wishes meet with opposition; when we are afflicted with distressing and hurtful insults; when we are subjected to persecution, to having our actions misinterpreted by good people and by those who are our best friends; and when we suffer illnesses which are particularly repugnant, etc. . . . Enclosed in the beloved cross is true wisdom and that is what I am looking for night and day more eagerly than ever. . . . After Jesus, our only love, I place my whole trust in the cross"* (L 13).

In the wake of Bérulle's Christocentric spirituality, Montfort harmoniously combined learning and piety in his life as priest and missionary. Like Francis of Assisi, he sought to imitate *without any qualifications* our Lord Jesus Christ, being poor amongst the outcasts and the disinherited who became his true friends (H 18:8).

In the seventeenth century, the poor were "an acute and disconcerning problem."[17] They received no consideration or respect in society; out of selfishness and under the influence of strict Calvinist ethics, the poor were turned away, mistreated, and despised. Montfort echoes this situation in H 18, *"The Cry of the Poor": "The rich man tells us: / I have neither penny nor halfpenny; And the great curse us / Calling us the rabble. / Bare-faced idlers! / Lowly breed! / This is what many say to us / Along with the mob."*

Under the influence of St. Vincent de Paul, Bossuet argued for "the eminent dignity of the poor" (1659), viewing them as representative of Christ in his poverty; consequently, *"to serve the poor is to serve Jesus Christ."*

Montfort drew on the same tradition. He internalized the pronouncement of Jesus (Mt 25, 40-45), which he implicitly cites: *"What is a poor man? It is written / That he is the living image, / the lieutenant of Jesus Christ / His most precious legacy / But, to speak even more clearly, / The poor are Jesus Christ Himself / In them men help or turn away / The supreme monarch"* (H 17:14).

This clarifies the Dinan episode, which was not a mere chance incident but is explained by Montfort's habitual vision of Christian faith: "One evening, in the street, he found a poor leper all covered in ulcers. He did not wait for this unfortunate man to ask him for help; he was the first to speak. He took hold of him, lifted him onto his shoulders, and carried him to the mission door, which was shut, for it was rather late. He knocked, shouting several times: 'Open the door to Jesus Christ!' The missionary who opened the door was astonished to see him carrying the poor man. He carried the precious burden inside, laid him in his own bed, and warmed him as well as he could (for he was numb with cold), while he himself spent the rest of the night in prayer."[18] What he asked of others he did himself as demonstrated in the Dinan episode. For Montfort, Jesus really lives in the poor.

III. Montfort's Christology

The writings of Montfort show that Christ is central to the profession of faith and the spiritual life. His writings contain certain passages on the person of Christ that render montfort Christocentrism especially significant.

1. The absolute nature of salvation in the biblical/ecclesial Christ

According to Montfort, Jesus Christ is the biblical/ecclesial Christ of the traditional understanding of the Catholic faith. He is Christ, the true God and true man of the NT and of the teaching of Chalcedon. He is Christ in his mysteries of obedience to the Father, in the *kenosis* of the Incarnation and of the Passion and death. He is Christ, to be contemplated and imitated as in the liturgical and spiritual tradition of the Church.

The first principle of devotion to the Virgin Mary is in fact the affirmation that Jesus Christ is the ultimate end of Marian devotion. In this connection, we shall transcribe a typical Christological passage that has lost nothing of its value and truth: *"First principle: Jesus, our Savior, true God and true man must be the ultimate end of all our other devotions; otherwise they would be false and misleading. He is the Alpha and the Omega, the beginning and end of everything. 'We labor,' says St. Paul, 'only to make all men perfect in Jesus Christ.'*

"For in him alone dwells the entire fullness of the divinity and the complete fullness of grace, virtue and perfection. In him alone we have been blessed with every spiritual blessing; he is the only teacher from whom we must learn; the only Lord on whom we should depend; the only Head to whom we should be united and the only model that we should imitate. He is the only Physician that can heal us; the only Shepherd that can feed us; the only Way that can lead us; the only Truth that we can believe; the only Life that can animate us. He alone is everything to us and he alone can satisfy all our desires.

"We are given no other name under heaven by which we can be saved. God has laid no other foundation for our salvation, perfection and glory than Jesus. Every edifice which is not built on that firm rock, is founded upon shifting sands and will certainly fall sooner or later. Every one of the faithful who is not united to him is like a branch broken from the stem of the vine. It falls and withers and is fit only to be burnt. If we live in Jesus and Jesus lives in us, we need not fear damnation. Neither angels in heaven nor men on earth, nor devils in hell, no creature whatever can harm us, for no

creature can separate us from the love of God which is in Christ Jesus" (TD 61).

There is here an admirable synthesis of Christology and of soteriology that goes to the essence of spirituality, and remains relevant today. Montfort founds his true devotion to Mary on the unquestionable affirmation that Christ is the sole and universal Mediator of salvation: *"If devotion to Our Lady distracted us from Our Lord, we would have to reject it as an illusion of the devil. But this is far from being the case. . . . This devotion is necessary simply and solely because it is a way of reaching Jesus perfectly, loving him tenderly, and serving him faithfully"* (TD 62).

Marian devotion is not a parallel form of Christianity, but a more certain and shorter route to arrive at Jesus Christ. The intercession of the Blessed Virgin is sought "*whether we want to enter his presence, speak to him, be near him, offer him something, seek union with him or consecrate ourselves to him*" (TD 143). All in all, this is a *"smooth, short, perfect and sure way of attaining union with our Lord, in which Christian perfection consists"* (TD 152).

Montfort deduces from the same Christological principle another consequence that is very important from several points of view, including an ecumenical perspective: the best way to qualify Marian spirituality is as His Christological.

In this connection, René Laurentin presents Montfort as initiating a reconversion to theocentrism: "What is important, historically speaking, is that Montfort, inheriting a tendency that began in Spain at the end of the sixteenth century (1595), brought about a revolution in the vocabulary of his predecessors by referring this Consecration to Christ and God Alone, positively and deliberately."[19] Laurentin also demonstrates that Montfort rectified the Mary-centered language that had been established by Los Rios, Rojas, Fenicki, van der Zandt, Boudon, etc., who often spoke of the slavery or the slaves of Mary. Montfort makes his position clear in several ways. Just before signing his letters, he employed up to 1705 essentially Christological formulae: *"priest and slave of Jesus in Mary"*; from 1704 he employed *"God alone,"* and the formula *"in Jesus and Mary"* remained until 1715, but without the word "slave."

In TD 244-247, while accepting the expressions *"slave of Mary, slavery of the Blessed Virgin,"* he clearly states his preference for Christological formulae: *"I think it preferable to say, 'slave of Jesus in Mary.' This is the opinion of Fr. Tronson. . . . It is better to speak of 'slavery of Jesus in Mary' and to call oneself 'slave of Jesus' rather than 'slave of Mary.' . . . In this way, we name this devotion after its ultimate end, which is Jesus, rather than after the way and the means to arrive there, which is Mary. . . . It is more appropriate for us to say, 'slavery of Jesus in Mary'"* (TD 244-246).

In TD 120-131, Montfort's Christocentric orientation reaches its peak. He entitles this part of his book *"Perfect Consecration to Jesus."* This is the first title of the manuscript to be written in large letters.

Montfort founds his spirituality on the baptismal vows, of which

Consecration is a perfect renewal. True to his own convictions, he names Consecration after its ultimate end (Jesus) rather than the way and the means to arrive there (Mary). In fact, we consecrate ourselves *"to Jesus because he is our last end. Since he is our Redeemer and our God we are indebted to him for all that we are"* (TD 125).

2. Jesus Christ, Wisdom Incarnate and crucified

Montfort, continuing the medieval tradition, and that of Bérulle,[20] takes pleasure in describing the mystery of the Infancy of Jesus in ten noels (H 57-66), and the mystery of the Passion of Christ: His suffering, death, and burial (H 67-74).

Devotion to the Sacred Heart of Jesus was important in the fight against Jansenist severity, in that it created a climate of trust and love in accordance with the message of the NT. Seven canticles dedicated to "loving devotion to the Heart of Jesus" form "a true poem" (F. Fradet) composed for the Visitandines (H 40-44, 47-48). The theme of these canticles is love, as in *"The One Who Loves Jesus"* (H 54-55), a love that Montfort contemplates in the Sacred Heart and wants to plant in the heart of the faithful: *"Let us love this heart since he loves us. / Love is rewarded by love, / But let us love with an extreme love / And purely night and day"* (H 44:2).

Finally, he does not hesitate to ask of Jesus the mystical grace of change (or transplantation) of heart: *"Finally, I make this bold request, / Remove from me my sinful heart / And may I have in this life / No other heart than yours"* (H 47:30).

In all his works, however, we notice a special vigor when he writes about Christ as Wisdom, and crucified Wisdom.[21] LEW, his Christological masterpiece, expresses in a coherent, developed synthesis the central intuition of montfort spirituality, which is entirely directed towards contemplation of the Cross. With inspired creativity, Montfort meditates on the paradoxical mystery of the crucified Christ, incarnate Wisdom of God. The work is a grand psalm of meditation on the Wisdom that is Jesus Christ, on the Wisdom that is the gift of Jesus to humanity, on the Wisdom that is a spousal union with Jesus on the Cross.

His exposition, full of biblical language and allusions to patristic and medieval tradition, begins by contemplating Eternal Wisdom as the object of the Father's love and as shining forth in the creation of the universe. Next, he meditates on Wisdom, first Incarnate and abased in the death of the Cross, then glorious and triumphant in heaven, and now the companion of humanity in the Eucharist.

Montfort then effects a far-reaching synthesis of Jesus' life on earth, contemplating its beauty and tenderness in a series of very apt expressions: *"But what does the name of Jesus, the proper name of incarnate Wisdom, signify to us if not ardent charity, infinite love and engaging gentleness?"* (LEW 120). The contemplation of Jesus turns into an inspired hymn to beauty: *"How beautiful, meek and charitable is Jesus, the incarnate Wisdom! Beautiful from all eternity, he is the splendor of his Father, the unspotted mirror and image of his goodness. He is more beautiful than the sun and brighter than light itself. He is beautiful in time, being formed by the Holy Spirit pure and faultless, fair and immaculate, and during his life he charmed the eyes and hearts of men and is now the glory of the angels. How loving and gentle he is with men, and especially with poor sinners whom he came upon earth to seek out in a visible manner, and whom he still seeks in an invisible manner every day"* (LEW 126).[22]

There follow sixty-two evangelical passages, without commentaries, that are juxtaposed to each other, and which sum up Montfort's teachings on salvation, concerning following Jesus, Wisdom Incarnate, and on being united to him.[23] They are the most detailed teachings of Jesus before Easter, those that define the original aspects of Christian life. The rules for the following of Christ set down by Montfort, and by the Jesuit A. Bonnefons before him (forty-nine oracles out of sixty-two listed by Montfort are taken from Bonnefons), begin and end with the themes of self-denial and the Cross: "If any want to become my followers, let them deny themselves and take up their cross" (Lk 9:23); "Blessed are those who are persecuted for righteousness' sake, for theirs is the kingdom of heaven" (Mt 5:3-10; cf. LEW 133, 151).

There is a close correspondence and friendship between God's Wisdom and every human: *"Wisdom is for man and man is for Wisdom. . . . Wisdom's friendship for man arises from man's place in creation, from his being an abridgment of Eternal Wisdom's marvels, his small yet ever so great world, his living image and representative on earth. Since Wisdom, out of an excess of love, gave himself the same nature by becoming man and delivered himself up to death to save man, he loves man as a brother, a friend, a disciple, a pupil, the price of his own blood and co-heir of his kingdom"* (LEW 64).

Refusing Wisdom, leads humanity into ignorance, blindness, folly, scandal, and sin (cf. LEW 72).

Accepting Jesus, Wisdom Incarnate, on the other hand, brings the gift of the light of truth and a surprising ability to communicate it to others (cf. LEW 95). Besides this, *"when Eternal Wisdom communicates himself to a soul, he gives that soul all the gifts of the Holy Spirit and all the great virtues to an eminent degree"* (LEW 99).

The meditation on Jesus, Wisdom Incarnate, continues with the contemplation of the sufferings of His Passion and death on the Cross. These are the events that bear witness to the salvific love of Eternal Wisdom, in all humanity: *"[Jesus] chose rather to endure the cross and sufferings in order to give to God his Father greater glory and to men a proof of greater love"* (LEW 164). According to Montfort, the Cross *"is the greatest secret of the King—the greatest mystery of Eternal Wisdom"* (LEW 167). The Cross becomes the spouse of Wisdom Incarnate in accordance with Jesus' prayer to the Father: *"My God and my Father, I chose this cross when I was in your bosom. I choose it now in the womb of my*

Mother. I love it with all my strength and I place it deep in my heart to be my spouse and my mistress" (LEW 169).

He states quite plainly that Wisdom *"was attached to the cross, indissolubly joined to it and died joyfully upon it as if in the arms of a dear friend and upon a couch of honor and triumph"* (LEW 171). Consequently, *"never the Cross without Jesus, or Jesus without the Cross"* (LEW 172). Wisdom has in fact established his dwelling place on the Cross: *"He has so truly incorporated and united himself with the Cross that in all truth we can say: Wisdom is the Cross and the Cross is Wisdom"* (LEW 180).

The Cross is the sign of Jesus and also that of the Christian: Wisdom *"has decreed the Cross to be the sign, the emblem and the weapon of his faithful people. He welcomes no child that does not bear its sign. He recognizes no disciple who is ashamed to display it, or who has not the courage to accept it, or who either drags it reluctantly or rejects it outright. . . . He enlists no soldier who does not take up the cross as the weapon to defend himself against all his enemies, to attack, to overthrow and to crush them"* (LEW 173).

Having celebrated Jesus, crucified Wisdom, Montfort presents the four methods of acquiring Divine Wisdom: the desire for Wisdom, continuous prayer, universal mortification, and a loving devotion to the Blessed Virgin. Devotion to Mary is treated at length because *"Mary must beget us in Jesus Christ and Jesus Christ in us, nurturing us towards the perfection and the fullness of his age"* (LEW 214). True devotion to Mary, *"if well practiced, not only draws Jesus Christ, Eternal Wisdom, into our soul, but also makes it agreeable to him and he remains there to the end of our life"* (LEW 220). Finally, LEW closes on the Consecration to Jesus Christ, Wisdom Incarnate, through the hands of Mary: *"I, an unfaithful sinner, renew and ratify today through you my baptismal promises, I renounce forever Satan, his empty promises, and his evil designs, and I give myself completely to Jesus Christ, the incarnate Wisdom, to carry my cross after him for the rest of my life, and to be more faithful to him than I have been till now"* (LEW 225).

Montfort's Christological spirituality has an explicit Marian dimension, for she nurtures a genuine life in the Spirit in union with Jesus Christ, Wisdom crucified and glorious.

IV. Aspects of Montfort Christological Spirituality

Montfort is a man who underwent a genuine encounter with Christ, i.e., with the biblical/ecclesial Christ, his person and his meaning in all their fullness, his existence before time and his life on earth, his mysteries and his living presence in the Church, in Mary, and in the poor. Montfort's doctrine is profoundly Christocentric.

1. The Christological spiritual journey

Whether in his Christological works, or those that are primarily Marian, St. Louis Marie offers a true teaching in Christian holiness as a filial life in Christ and in the Spirit according to Mary's example and with her help.

Montfort spirituality is based upon the beautiful words of Jesus: "I am the vine, you are the branches. Those who abide in me and I in them bear much fruit, because apart from me you can do nothing" (Jn 15:5). Montfort uses the formula *"us in Jesus and Jesus in us"* six times (LEW 214; SM 56; TD 20, 37, 61, 212). This is a phrase expressing mutual indwelling, because we belong to Christ's Body as its members and because Jesus Christ our Head grows in us. Montfort often returns to this doctrine of the Mystical Body (LEW 176, 213; FC 27; TD 17, 20, 21, 32, 36, 61, 68, 140, 168; SM 12).

Bérulle deduces rigorous spiritual requirements from the principle of our union with Christ: "adherence, dependence, conduct derived from Jesus,"[24] along with the constant need to empty oneself in order to become a "pure capacity" for Jesus. Montfort translates these spiritual requirements into more easily understandable terms: *"As all perfection consists in our being conformed, united and consecrated to Jesus"* (TD 120).

Montfort especially emphasizes our union with Christ (TD 43, 78, 117, 118, 120, 143, 152, 157, 159, 164, 212, 259) and our *dependence* on Him, expressed by loving slavery and complete self-surrender. He gives primacy to our total, loving oneness in Christ Jesus. He accords methodological priority to devotion to Mary, in the sense that she is the most perfect path leading to union with Christ. Vatican II, which placed the account of Mary in a Christological context, which substantiated this Christocentric Marian spirituality (LG, chap. 8).

In Montfort's thought, there are certain constants that together constitute a complete spiritual journey. We will simply list them here, since they are clearly found in his writings.

Montfort invites each of us to undergo a true conversion, including the desire to move progressively from a mediocre Christian life to a true and vibrant baptismal renewal and apostolic commitment (cf. TD 99, 126).

The consequence of this, and of a dynamic centering of our life on Christ, Wisdom Incarnate, is that our virtues are strenghthened, reducing almost to the point of extinction the power of evil and sin. According to Montfort, it is devotion to the Blessed Virgin that is to play the decisive role in this education in Christian virtue (cf. LEW, chap. 17, as well as TD and SM).

In this way, Montfort traces a spiritual route that contains two fundamental phases. The ascetic phase of the denial, through an increase in virtues, of the "old man" with his vices and his sins; and the mystical phase of union and communion with God the Trinity, accomplished through the mediation of Jesus Christ and the example and maternal intercession of Mary (cf. TD 120-225).

2. Notes on Christological spirituality

Several criteria of Christological spirituality can be deduced from Montfort's experience, which, with its clear Marian dimension is even more firmly anchored in Jesus Christ.

a. For Montfort, Christological spirituality is above all a life of devotion to the Trinity. The union with Jesus Christ, Wisdom Eternal and crucified, is a union with the Father in the Holy Spirit. We are children of the heavenly Father in His Son, Jesus Christ, thanks to the love of the Holy Spirit: christocentrism is not christomonism, for the latter calls for devotion to Christ while ignoring the Trinity. Christocentrism is essentially Trinitarian. In the chapter in LEW dedicated to the synthesis of the most important maxims of Jesus' teaching, Montfort first cites the pronouncement on following Christ (Lk 9:23), then that of St. John on the Trinity living within the faithful: "Those who love me will keep my word, and my Father will love them, and we will come to them and make our home with them" (Jn 14:23). In the famous page of TD on Christ as the ultimate end of devotion to Mary, Montfort shows once again that his Christocentrism is based on devotion to the Trinity: *"Through him, with him and in him, we can do all things and render all honor and glory to the Father in the unity of the Holy Spirit; we can make ourselves perfect and be for our neighbor a fragrance of eternal life"* (TD 61).

b. In everyday life, this life devoted to the Trinity is lived out in the ecclesial community; thanks to the Sacraments experienced as an interpersonal saving encounter with Jesus Christ. After the entry into Christ through Baptism, the Eucharist is rightly considered to be the supreme Sacrament of encounter and union with Christ and, through Him, with the Trinity. In this sense, Montfort recalls the saying of Jesus in the Fourth Gospel: "For my flesh is true food and my blood is true drink. Those who eat my flesh and drink my blood abide in me, and I in them" (Jn 6:55-56). For him, therefore, spiritual Christology is an ecclesial, sacramental life, above all a life based on the Eucharist. The union with God the Trinity in the Sacrament of the Eucharist effects and manifests daily communion with the Church. A life in Christ is, therefore, a life of union and communion in the Church, His Mystical Body. This sacramental life nurtures and develops a life of virtue consisting in ascetic striving and mystical accomplishment. Mary has a decisive role in this life of union with Jesus Christ: as can be seen in TD and SM.

c. The union with Jesus Christ in the Church becomes a witness, a discipleship, and a mission. That is to say that this union announces Christ in the world. This is why Christological spirituality is an apostolic and missionary life, according to Montfort. Like all saints and true mystics, Montfort offers a marvelous synthesis of contemplation and action, prayer and discipleship. Moreover, discipleship and mission among one's brothers and sisters are a sign, a consequence, and a necessary expansion of the life of union with the triune God. This recalls the maxim of Mt 5:16: "Let your light shine before others, so that they may see your good works and give glory to your Father in heaven" (cf. LEW 145). In Montfort, union with God is at the basis of service to others enabling the growth of life in the Spirit. This is what is called the grace of union, which makes of Montfort a great mystic and a great apostle. Discipleship is the fruit of prayer, of contemplation, of union and communion with God in Jesus Christ. The hymn of jubilation of Mt 11:25-26 completes Montfort's synthesis of the evangelical message of Jesus: "I thank you, Father, Lord of heaven and earth, for having hidden these things from the wise and prudent of this world and for revealing them to humble and little ones; yes, Father, for that is what it has pleased you to do" (cf. LEW 152).

d. Finally, for Montfort, discipleship strives towards the realization of a Christian culture. The Christian illumination of reality, through words and examples, results in a cultural life of fundamentally Christian inspiration. Culture is thus enriched with authentic human values, because they are inspired and supported by the truth of the Gospel. A life of union and communion with God the Trinity produces a culture which is a civilization of love.[25]

A. Amato

Notes: (1) Cf. L. Bouyer, *Le Fils éternel. Théologie de la parole de Dieu et christologie (The Eternal Son: The Theology of the Word of God and Christology),* Cerf, Paris 1974, chap. 21: *La christologie à l'époque moderne: entre la métaphysique et la psychologie (Christology in the Modern Age: Between Metaphysics and Psychology),* 443-468. Cf. also M. J. Congar, *Théologie (Theology),* in DTC 15 (1946), 441-502 (2) In the Christology of the seventeenth century there is an "exclusive preponderance of the meritorious-satisfactory prospective, entirely projected towards the problem of the equivalence between the 'atonement' accomplished by Christ and the divine offence, according to perfect justice." M. Bordoni, *Gesù di Nazaret Signore e Cristo. Saggio di cristologia sistematica,* Herder-PUL,

Rome 1986, 3:428. (3) Cf. E. Vilanova, *La escolástica en la Francia del siglo XVII,* in *Historia de la teologia cristiana,* Herder, Barcelona 1989, 2:810-814. (4) We should add that the Sulpicians were interested in another professor of the Sorbonne, Martin Grandin († 1691), whose lessons they had their students copy. In 1708 they worked on the three-volume edition of the works of Grandin, *Martini Grandini opera (The Works of Martin Grandin).* Cf. Y. Poutent, *Le XVIIe siècle et les origines lasalliennes. Recherches sur la genèse de l'oeuvre scolaire et religieuse de Jean-Baptiste de la Salle (1651-1719) (The Seventeenth Century and La Salle: Studies on the Genesis of the Scholarly and Religious Work of Jean-Baptiste de la Salle),* Imprimeurs réunis, Rennes 1970, 1:297, n. 10, and 1:302, n. 23. (5) For the influence of L. Chardon on Montfort, cf. Itinerario, 110-111. (6) The work of Contenson was completed by his fellow Dominican P. Massoulié. (7) P. de Bérulle, *Oeuvres de piété (Pious Writings),* chap. 32, in *Oeuvres complètes (Complete Works),* Migne, Paris 1856, 966. (8) Ibid., chap. 50, p. 1017. (9) Ibid., chap. 77, p. 1052. (10) Cf. E. Mersch, *Le corps mystique du Christ. Etudes de théologie historique (The Mystical Body of Christ: Studies in Historical Theology),* Paris and Brussels 1936, 2:314, where the author quotes *Les Oeuvres de piété,* chap. 9, 15, 109, 131, 133,. (11) P. de Bérulle, op. cit., CXLIX, 1181. (12) J.-J. Olier, *Mémoires (Memoirs*), 2:268. Cf. also *Maximes pour les séminaires (Maxims for Seminaries),* in *Oeuvres complètes de M. Olier (The Complete Works of M. Olier),* Migne, Paris 1856, col. 1145-1147. In his letters Olier requires of ecclesiastics "perfect establishment in Christ" through renunciation and adherence: *"Abrenuntio tibi Satana; conjungor tibi, Christe."* (13) Archives de la Compagnie de Saint-Sulpice, Paris, letter written by M. Leschassier, September 12, 1702, ms. 34. (14) Ibid., "Registre des Assemblées du Supérieur du Séminaire de Saint-Sulpice et de ses quatre consulteurs (The Register of the Assemblies of the Superior of Saint-Sulpice and His Four Consultants)," September 3, 1688, ms., p. 251. (15) Cf. G. Mucci, *Claude de la Colombière "perfetto amico" di Cristo,* in *La Civiltà cattolica* 143 (1992), I, 557-571. (16) R. Deville, *L'école française de spiritualité (The French School of Spirituality),* Desclée, Paris 1987, 175. (17) M. Marcocchi, *La spiritualità tra giansenismo e quietismo (Spirituality between Jansenism and Quietism),* Studium, Rome 1983, 57. (18) Besnard I, 144. (19) R. Laurentin, *Dieu seul est ma tendresse (God Alone Is My Tenderness),* OEIL, Paris 1984, 47. (20) Cf. I. Noye, *Enfance de Jésus, Dévotion à l' (Devotion to the Infancy of Christ),* in DSAM 4/1 (1960), 652-682. (21) Montfort himself, quoting Suso (LEW 101), reveals one of his distant sources of inspiration for this title. The Dominican Heinrich De Berg, known as Suso (1295-1366), was the author of several works on Divine Wisdom. (22) The merciful love of Jesus is celebrated with poetic fervor in the spiritual canticles, in which love of the Heart of Jesus is exalted above all: cf. H 40-44; 47-48; 54-55. (23) Cf. the whole of chap. 12 of LEW, 133-151. (24) P. de Bérulle, *Oeuvres de piété,* chap. 190, p. 722. (25) Cf. the call to the Beatitudes of Mt 5:3-10 in LEW 151. Cf. also FC, in which Montfort proposes a program of godliness and discipleship to the laity who remain in the world, to render their life there truly Christian.

LAST THINGS

SUMMARY
I. INTRODUCTION.
II. A PROPAEDEUTIC:
1. An object lesson;
2. The sermons:
a. Hell,
b. Judgment,
c. Death,
d. Purgatory,
e. Heaven;
3. Missions and retreats;
4. Preparation for death.
III. RHETORICAL ASPECTS OF THE DISCOURSE ON THE LAST THINGS.
IV. ETHICAL DIMENSION.
V. THEOCENTRIC AND CHRISTOLOGICAL DIMENSION.
VI. CONCLUSION.

I. INTRODUCTION

When we consider the role of the Last Things in montfort spirituality, we travel down abandoned and unused paths. Hell, purgatory, and the Last Judgment have been deconsecrated by modernity; they no longer evoke fear. Indeed, they evoke laughter in some people. A typical expression is: "Hell has become something akin to those stories about 'evil wolves' that parents tell to their children to make them wise, until the children become adults and realize that they were merely stories." Fear of hell bolsters authority. Others are shocked by such fear. They cannot accept the image of a vengeful God, an all-powerful God delivering vast numbers of the damned into eternal punishment (cf. LS I, 24-27, 93; II, 259). Even paradise is no longer "an attraction" (cf. LS II, 121). Once an object of desire, paradise has been perverted to the point of becoming the solution, in the next world, of the problems that we do not wish to solve here below. There is no longer any desire for that paradise after death[1] promised by those who, with outrageous injustice, build an earthly paradise for themselves.[2]

The image of a terrible God and a criminal humanity has given way to that of the merciful God Who cannot damn, and an innocent humanity that cannot be condemned. This radical reversal leads the practicing Catholic believer of our day to express a belief that in Montfort's day was associated with libertines: *"The Blessed God, he says, is so good, that when I die I will be pardoned"* (H 29:78 and H 23:29;

cf. H 106:22-25; H 150:16, 17; FC 10). This certainly represents a change in outlook!

The world has changed, and what was fact for a few has become the opinion of the majority: *"Without fear of hell or judgment / Nor of God, the devil, or vengeance, / The accursed sin fearlessly / Laughing with insolence; . . . They say their spirit is too strong / To groan and shed tears / To fear hell or death . . . / Though the souls of the good tremble at such thoughts"* (H 29:77-79; cf. H 29:27).

The Last Things lead us down unaccustomed paths because they lead us to examine some little-read texts of Saint Louis Marie de Montfort: LS and his hymns. In his hymns, Montfort gives us a definition of the Last Things in verse:

"OF THE FOUR LAST THINGS, DEATH, AND JUDGMENT: "Experience teaches me that I will die, / That hour draws near, / But when? I do not know. / The soul is freed from the body and is presented to God, / And receives His decree: / To be punished forever / Or to receive a great reward.

"OF PARADISE: Holy Paradise / is a place of delights, / that God, full of justice, / bestows on all His friends. / He invites all those to enter / Who died full of grace. / Forever they will live there, / They will praise God, and see Him / Face to face.

"OF HELL: Hell is rigorous and absolute / A place of torment / Where the unhappy sinner / Is punished for his malice. / It receives those who died / Without penitence. / Forever will they live there, / Burning and suffering, / Bereft of all hope" (H 109:18-20).

In the pages of his hymns and sermons, comes alive Montfort the preacher, whose missions were seen and heard by thousands of people. It is a very different Saint Louis Marie from the "confidential Montfort" of SM.

II. A Propaedeutic

1. An object lesson

Blain reminds us that Montfort was chosen by Father de la Barmondière to watch over the dead in the parish of Saint-Sulpice so that he could use the salary he received to pay for his room and board at the seminary.[3] This vigil was not simply an additional opportunity for the young Grignion to practice mortification;[4] it was also a true "object lesson." "It must not be forgotten that the saintly young man, who was so often the companion and guardian of the dead, did not neglect to look at them and to note how the vanity of the world and its pleasures appeared on their faces. He learned of the heavenly wisdom that scorns all that is crumbling and perishable and recoils in horror from the body, which rots and decays. He uncovered the faces of the dead, seeing their ugliness and appalling deformities, and contemplated the deceptive and fleeting charms of youth and beauty and the incredible folly of those who allow themselves to be seduced by them. Two of these corpses in particular . . . spoke to his heart and taught him a great lesson in the decay of mortal things."[5] In these lines we see the "classical" themes of *contemptus mundi,* of scorn for the world and its attendant vanities, scorn for the temporary things with which men surround themselves. These "corpses" present a spectacle that seems to come directly from the *danses macabres,* wherein Death mows down the Prince, the Abbot "of the first rank," the beautiful ladies of the court, etc. Death inverts those deceptive values of the world: "This beauty, which was idolized only a short time before, undergoes a horrible change and emits the foul stench of decay. . . . Montfort was forcibly struck by something else at such moments: he saw how the corpses of those who, only a few days before, had been worshipped were now mostly abandoned; often only a valet would remain in the house, while the rest of its inhabitants fled as from the plague."[6] This almost academic method of describing death foreshadows his preaching on the Last Things. The rich material is training for his parish mission.

This macabre scene collides with our sensibilities today, as it did with those of Charles Besnard, who, in his biography of Montfort, deleted from his description of this episode in Montfort's life everything that he found to be in "bad taste." He describes Montfort's vigil over the dead as an opportunity for methodical meditation on divine Judgment: "His spirit accompanied these souls to God's tribunal. There he saw them alone and incoherent, deprived of the imposing costume that adorned them on earth and that brought them the respect and homage and even adoration of other creatures. He saw them judged by the Just Judge, and by attempting to put himself in their place, he was pierced with the same feelings that they felt at that terrible moment."[7] Surely Montfort had no illusions about their prospects for eternal salvation; these souls had departed from bodies on which he could see "the horror of crime and the vanity of pleasures that were so clearly visible there."[8]

His vigils at the mortuary gave Father Montfort all the practical elements, all the examples he needed, to become a "good missionary." Those cadavers taught him, "at that moment, all that he would have to say, in his subsequent preaching, on the brevity of life and the vanity of mortal beauty."[9] Perhaps he drew on this experience when he spoke to the rowdy children of the Faubourg Saint-Germain and to those seminarians who were curious and listened in. "He spoke to those young people of death, judgment, and hell in moving and yet steady tones, so that they could not help crying, and they returned home imbued with those great truths that he had preached to them. . . . Monsieur Grignion had a rare talent for touching hearts, and these were merely his first attempts, preludes to the apostolic grace that our young missionary would subsequently display with such brilliance and success in the provinces."[10] His missionary efforts will be explored after examining LS, testimony to his final preparation for preaching and ministry.

2. The sermons

The second part of LS reverberates not so much with Father Montfort's preaching, as with his work in preparation for the ministry of the Word. Indeed, "the majority of the works in this part seem to have originated at

Saint-Sulpice: Montfort wrote them during his seminary days."[11] Outlines or summaries of sermons, taken from the "good books" of the day, lectures at Saint-Sulpice, and collections of scriptural and patristic texts that were indispensable for argument, form the basis of this collection. The bilingual citations, in French and Latin, contribute even more to the disorder of the collection. But Montfort arranged this jumbled material into a beautiful thematic order; the sermons proceed alphabetically from *"love of God" ("amour de Dieu")* to *"zeal."* This long list obviously includes the subjects that made up his preaching on the Last Things: hell (155-172), judgment of the sinner (240-251), universal Judgment (240-251), and heaven (314-330); we can also add purgatory (443-452) and death (288-306). This is a fair number of pages, but far from the 450 pages that make up the collection. We must not hastily accept the view that Montfort's preachings can be summarized by hell and divine anger. Let us look more closely at the contents of these "sermon ideas" that Montfort so loved to write, always remembering that they must be studied in the context of his personal works, like LEW and TD.

a. Hell. Several of these sermons are introduced with a verse from Scripture. At the outset, Montfort attaches to hell the Scriptural seal of truth, that none dare doubt. Using an array of biblical references, he describes six subjects for meditation: 1) after death, the pains of hell that await the impious; 2) thc "truth" of these pains; 3) the eternal fire of hell and other pains; 4) the just, rejoicing in the agonies of the damned; 5) the lamentations of the damned; 6) the great numbers of the damned. His patristic citations are "classical": he cites the testimony of St. Augustine and, especially, St. Gregory the Great. We may simply note the use of St. Gregory's *Book of Dialogues,* an actual treatise on the Last Things, which had a strong and lasting influence in the Middle Ages.[12] With Gregory, Montfort believed in the eternity of hellfire, a true corporeal fire, affecting the body and all the senses, but also affecting the spirit (LS 248). He also wrote that hell is at the center of the earth (LS 25), as if in a particular place; the symbol of the complete infernal confinement that encompasses the seven universal dimensions of humanity: within, above-below, before-behind, left-right.

More psychological is his description of the "worm of conscience" that gnaws away at the insides of the damned (cf. LS 258). The question of eternal damnation is more theological, because it involves the loss of God. This is a difficult question because we must first know what it means to possess God. All that we know is that the soul contains an infinite capacity, which can only be filled by God. To be deprived of God is extreme and unimaginable sadness. The intensity of eternal damnation is proportional to the intimate relationship of the soul with God (LS 392). For those who still doubt these *"great truths,"* Montfort writes that *"we must burn Holy Scripture and treat all of the Fathers as imposters, if the existence of hell is not an undeniable truth of faith, and we do not need the experience of our senses to believe a truth of faith"* (LS 252). We must acknowledge that today we are shocked at the expression that the saints in heaven *"rejoice over the agonies of the damned,"* even if this only means to express the loving justice of God. A justice which cannot force His creatures. The image of a vengeful and angry God does not truly convert anyone (Montfort notes this, as will be seen below); it only increases the ranks of those who could not believe in such a God.

b. Judgment. On this subject, too, several points begin with a verse from Scripture. While the citations from the Fathers of the Church are less numerous here than on the subject of hell, citations from Sacred Scripture are included under twenty-one titles (LS 408). The well-nigh scrupulously recorded minutiae of Montfort's cataloging brings to mind the exhaustive research into sins and their classification. *"Examination of thoughts, words, actions, and of the most hidden sins"* (LS 390). *"Our Lord will examine 1: concealed sins; 2: unrecognized sins"* (LS 401). God will carry out a rigorous examination; *"God will be terrible in His search for every sin. . . . God will perform a dissection"* (LS 409). And forgotten sins? God will not forget them. We can sense here the full weight of culpability and fear that has crushed so many souls. One aspect of patristic and biblical argumentation depends on "stories," *exempla*; they describe events in the lives of others that serve as an example and a lesson to us.[13] From the standpoint of "feelings," these stories establish the fear and shame of humanity: shame when sins will be revealed (LS 409) and fear of judgment, of the *"vindictive justice"* of God (LS 403). This fear is justified, because God is presented as a just judge whose *"decree is irreversible"* and to whom there is no appeal. *"Because God knows all (the omniscience of God with respect to sin), and because God is all-powerful and never acts out of passion, the soul will honor the justice of God even from hell, in spite of itself, because it neglected to honor His mercy with love here below"* (LS 392; cf. LS I, 26, 27). From the theological standpoint, we should note that divine justice and mercy, which since St. Anselm have uneasily coexisted, are here made separate: *"Mercy reigns during our time on earth, but justice reigns on the day of judgment"* (LS 418; cf. FC 22, 56; LS 284). This opposition between the justice and mercy of God brings us to a theological impasse, a blind alley down which Montfort was certainly not the first to travel. The division of divine attributes into "pure justice" and "pure mercy" has given deep existential torture to generations of Christian consciences. Montfort felt that his presentation of a God-Judge, watching out for the least sin and wreaking divine vengeance, would shake the spirit of his listeners and lead them to conversion (cf. H 8:18, 37; H 24:25-28; H 28:3). Today, we prefer to speak of the mercy of a God Who gives refuge to sinners. Father de Montfort believed in this as well. He wrote: *"We can see God as a powerful sanctuary / where a sinner will be safe from danger / or as a just judge / who is ready to judge us"* (H 24:18).

c. Death. Through death, we can judge life (H 120:19). Thus there are two deaths, that of the just person and that of the sinner. These two ways of dying are opposed to each other, just as the "predestinate" and the "reprobate" are opposed to each other (cf. TD 200). The just die a happy death, with sweet repose in the peace provided by a "good conscience" because, through God's mercy, this conscience is full of love and trust (LS 466, 471, 472, 477). The Blessed Virgin herself assists as the *"Throne of Wisdom"* in the death of the just (LS 477 and TD 33; cf. H 81:7 and SR 58), but the death of the sinner is horrible and unhappy. It is a death full of anguish and terror: terror, because *"all of our stories contain apparitions of demons at the moment of death and the agony of men, and of the saints and guardian angels abandoning the sinner"* (LS 468, 469; cf. H 120:15); anguish, because at that moment sinners see all of their sins (LS 465; H 120:3, 12, 16) and their future in Hell (LS 469). God abandons sinners to despair. The time for conversion is past, because they mocked him by living *"as though they had nothing to do with God"* (LS 470; H 120:6, 7; LEW 72). If sometimes sinners seem to die a tranquil death, as if they were not about to be damned, it is only because God is mocking them in turn (LS 470).

d. Purgatory. Montfort does not give citations either from Scripture or from the Fathers for purgatory. Instead, he invokes a "scriptural proof" from 2 Macc 12:38-45 and also cites several councils (LS 727, 738). But he is quite reserved about the nature of Purgatory: *"It is impossible to describe the extent of the agony that is suffered by the souls in purgatory"* (LS 730). He defines purgatory by showing how it is different from heaven and hell: *"Heaven is a place of love without unhappiness; hell is a place of unhappiness without love; purgatory is a place of love and unhappiness"* (LS 730). It is where sins that have not yet been *"satisfied"* are expiated (LS 729; FC 23; LS 356) and where the soul is purified so that it may be brought before the *"unsullied beauty and sovereign holiness"* of God (LS 728; H 127:20). The saints themselves are not immune from purgatory; they, too, commit "peccadilloes" (LS 729). No one can remain indifferent to the suffering of the souls in purgatory; thus, we must comfort them. The "prayers for the dead" summarize Montfort's preaching on purgatory. Prayers, alms, fasting, the Sacrifice of the Mass (LS 735; LS I, 17), etc., all help to ease the suffering of souls in purgatory (cf. H 29:81; H 119; H 127; H 139:65; MR 397, 424; Grandet, 319), and this is an unending concern (cf. SM 30, 31; TD 171, 172). We should remember that one of the reasons Montfort was dismissed from Father Leuduger's missionary team was his desire to "say Masses" for the souls in Purgatory.[14]

e. Heaven. Montfort wrote that the agonies of hell can only be understood in proportion to our knowledge of the joys of paradise, and his sermon notes on paradise; far from answering our questions, only restate them more insistently. In effect, he makes us acknowledge the weakness of our expressions and our temerity in attempting to speak of the joy of the saints. *"If the apostle, Saint Paul, were to have seen these secrets, he would not have been able nor dared to speak of them"* (LS 504)—an even greater reason for us to remain temperate. Only the exclamation "O!" is appropriate for referring to eternal Beatitude; it reflects both our summons and our amazement: *"O mankind, said Saint Gregory of Nazianzus, you are vast, because you can only be filled with God"* (LS 505). The question of paradise, which cannot be enclosed in a response, remains open. Into this opening there is a passageway: the desire that causes the heart to dilate when it perceives the dimensions of God. *"Here below the hearts of humanity are so small, but later they will contain God, and they will be swallowed up in God"* (LS 509). The vocabulary of desire is endlessly present in Montfort's sermon notes: ravishing and infinite beauty, ever greater joys and pleasures, delights, feasts, enjoyments. All awaken in us a dizzying desire for God (cf. H 116; H 117). Here we can trace the way of contemplation. Prayer, the sign of a mystical life, is an anticipation of heaven (LS 494). Intimate unity with God, the focus and the unique blessing of the soul, is the ultimate goal of the spiritual journey (LS 510, 513, 514, 177). This path of perpetual unity with God is marked by spiritual rapture (LS 505), the unique work of the Spirit. *"The Holy Spirit acts on the blessed and produces in them a love that is in some way infinite. The saints are in a constant state of ecstasy. That is to say, they have transcended their earthly existence"* (LS 511). The desire for heaven puts us in the illuminative way, *"because Beatitude consists of the most noble operation of the soul, which is that of understanding, in the possession of an eternal blessing which is produced by knowledge alone"* (LS 508). *"Knowledge of God does not always bring about His love here below, but in the other life it brings His love always and necessarily"* (LS 511).

In order to arrive at that knowledge of God Who is All Love, however, we must follow the *"way of love: we must empty ourselves of all other love"* (LS 512). We must take this purgative way because *"it is folly to pretend to taste the joys of the world as well as those of heaven. We must drink from the chalice of Our Lord before we can drink from the flood of His delights"* (LS 506). The way of glory passes through the Cross.

"Paradise" drawing us into the mystical life is the focal point of these sermons. Montfort offers some quite bold formulations to the attentive reader: *"Each saint possesses God, as God possesses Himself"*; *"The same charity that enabled God to become man enables each of the blessed to become God"* (LS 514); *"There is nothing that the heart of humanity desires more than God; there is nothing that God desires more than the heart of humanity"* (LS 511; cf. LEW 63, 64).[15]

2. Missions and retreats

These sermon notes become completely meaningful only when considered from the standpoint of their intended purpose: Montfort's missionary activity.

They occupy a singular place. The Last Things come at the beginning; at the beginning was the end: such is the paradox that gives meaning to the parish mission. Indeed, when we consider the order of preaching for a Lenten mission, (LS 530-531 or GA, 567-568) or for a four-week mission or retreat (LS 771 or GA, 568-569), we see that the sermons on the Last Things link the first two weeks.[16] We should note how they allude to the individual duty of each human being, and not to humanity as a whole. This is clear in the dissociation of the sermons on judgment; the personal judgment is treated as an integral part of the Last Things, whereas the universal Judgment is not discussed until the end of the mission or retreat. As a result, the Last Things are no longer grounded in eschatology. The preacher is attempting not so much to broaden the eschatological horizon of his listeners as to center their attention on the conscience. Thus, the notes speak of the personal examination or the examination of sins, which are closely related to personal judgment. The salvation of the soul is at stake.

Saving souls is the missionary's obsession (cf. H 21; H 22; H 91). In this he continues the mission of Christ (cf. LS 778; LEW 130; LS I, 90; II, 784). Otherwise, souls will be lost and fall into hell. They are damned because they live in sin, often without knowing it. Thus they must be told about it; they must be led down the path of salvation. The purpose of the Last Things is to dwell on this mysterious and sensitive point, which is decisive for repentance. In missionary work, repentance, confession, and the Last Things are mutually dependent. The Last Things are part of any path toward conversion. Here, the sermons are accompanied by the singing of hymns. This was a critical element of missionary practice, as we see in this preface to a book of mission hymns used by Montfort's successors: "The singing of hymns in missions is a very useful and simple method for teaching the true principles of religion, preparing hearts to receive the truths that the preacher lays before them from the pulpit, and leading them to feelings of true repentance; because anyone who wishes to observe this practice will see how the sinner progresses, by degrees, from the first moment that grace touches his heart, to that sure state of perfection. The preacher will begin by leading the sinner to a horror of sin in order to lead the sinner away from sin and induce him to make a retreat of several days during the mission, so as to meditate at length on the inconstancy and vanity of human things and on the thought of death, the fear of judgment, and the torments of fear, so that he may be raised up with the hope of happiness in heaven."[17] This itinerary of conversion reveals the true meaning of the Last Things. This method guides us along a coherent path. The hymns from such handbooks are grouped according to this itinerary, and the titles and subtitles clearly mark this path of conversion. "For opening the Mission. The mission is begun . . . The Lord Who calls you desires your conversion. Look for grace. This is the hour when you must change . . . Change your life. All sinners are invited to repentance. Come to confession. Horror of mortal sin. . . Dialogue between God and the converted sinner. Come back sinner, your God is calling you . . . God's loving search for sinners. God solicits the conversion of the sinner. The sinner is filled with fright but also trust, on seeing Jesus Christ on the Cross. Contrition. His sins make him greatly unhappy, and he weeps bitterly. Our Lord reveals the joy of heaven to the sinner who converts. He enters into retreat to detach himself ever more from the world and to think seriously on his Last Things. He meditates on the insubstantiality of things here below. He becomes disgusted with the world, the deceptive world. He meditates on the Last Things, the necessity of salvation. Death in general; the death of the sinner; the death of the just. He descends in spirit to the abyss of hell to interrogate the damned, to discover the cause, severity, and duration of their torments. He is sensitive to the cries of the souls in purgatory. He prays for them. He is present in spirit in heaven, to contemplate the beauty of God, by which the saints are made happy. Paradise. He interrogates the saints, to ask them about the joy they feel in this fortunate place. Enchanted with the pleasures of heaven, he longs for nothing else. Life itself becomes tiresome to him; he wishes to be reunited with his God. On his retreat, he renews the vows of his Baptism. It is time to undertake the covenant. He congratulates himself on his happiness" (from *Hymns,* unpublished manuscript).

If we associate the Last Things only with the flames of hell, with *"hyperbolas, exaggerations that frighten the world"* (LS 773; cf. LS 199, 564, 565), we condemn ourselves to never understanding them. Certainly the preacher elicits a psychological shock from his audience, but the outcome he desires most of all is spiritual: conversion. The title given to the first part of the hymns is explicit: *"Hymns on the motives that are most likely to affect the sinner who is thinking seriously of conversion during the Holy Mission."* In spirituality, the Last Things mark the usual path of the "beginners."

4. Preparation for death

On April 27, 1716, sensing that his end was near, Father Montfort dictated his testament to Father Mulot. It was written on one of the pages of a small booklet that was distributed at the conclusion of the missions, *Dispositions for a Happy Death.*[18] *Retreat for Preparing Oneself for Death, The Art of a Happy Life and a Happy Death, Spiritual Testaments, Preparation for Death,* etc.: such books were widely read during that time. Using these books, preachers and spiritual directors attempted to spread an asceticism, taken from the monastic orders, that would make life a practice for death because *"the art of dying happily is the most important and the most difficult of all the arts. That is why death serves as their [wise men's] everlasting apprenticeship during their lives and their unique and eloquent teacher"* (LS III,67).[19]

Father de Montfort devoted his "follow-up missions" to this particular task. Father Besnard writes as follows: "We have seen how it was his custom, after performing a mission in a particular place, to return there a short time later to ensure that his mission continued to bear fruit, and to perpetuate this outcome by means of a retreat. All the exercises on this retreat involved preparation for death. There was a series of meditations, wherein he developed, over several days and in great detail, everything that could be said on this interesting subject. Such a task must have required his complete absorption in the subject. He had seen death very near to hand, and one could say that he had only escaped it so that he could teach others to avoid being surprised by it. Therefore this retreat proved to be an excellent lesson for learning how to do something that is only done once; if one does not understand death, one loses eternal salvation."[20]

As the portal to the Last Things, preparation for death has two functions: it prevents us from committing sin, and it converts us and leads us to a life of repentance (cf. the notes of Father Vatel in LS III, 68). Preparing for a happy death means, above all, beginning to live a happy life (LS III, 86). Death embraces all of life and gives it true meaning. It is the mirror of life. It uncovers falsehood and reveals truth (LS III, 66). By placing this exercise at the conclusion of his mission, Father Montfort directs the renewed life of the convert toward obedience to its end. Death, always present, at once gives eternity to life, not by our escaping to the hereafter, but by revealing to us that only the present time is in our hands (cf. LS III, 804).

III. Rhetorical Aspects of the Discourse on the Last Things

The Last Things served the purpose of conversion. But how did they achieve this effect? Father Besnard, an experienced missionary, gives us some details on the "techniques" used by Montfort to "touch" hearts, to enlighten and instruct spirits. For example, during the retreat for preparation for death, he writes, Montfort "gave an emotional portrayal of the last act and denouement of life, wherein one could see the Christian seized by the fear of death, assailed by all the powers of hell, tormented by the remorse of his conscience, but given aid by the Church, assisted by the ministry of Jesus Christ, and no longer anticipating the irrevocable decree that would grant eternal recompense or punishment. This portrayal was lively and animated, as if the scene were a painting or a spectacle, and at its conclusion everyone was left with a resolution to live better so that they might die happily."[21] Father Montfort became a master at the art of mounting these "religious entertainments"[22] and at finding "pious tricks" that would lead to conversion. Canon Blain relates a significant story: "Young beggars, mendicants, the homeless—all played a distinctive part in his missionary exercises and his charity. He assembled them apart from the rest, catechized them, instructed them, and exhorted them in a way that was appropriate to their age and to their idle, errant, and vagabond lives. His ingenious zeal was constantly finding pious works for them and showing them the danger of their condition and the sins to which it exposed them, filling them with horror and preparing them for a true confession. To succeed in this, this old Capuchin told me, he set himself down in the middle of these poor young vagabonds and beggars, like a father among his children, and spoke to them with goodness and tenderness; and after catechizing them, he so identified with them that he could lead them to his objective, which was to relieve them of all embarrassment and confess their sins to him. With this in mind, he spoke of theft, leaving out nothing that might fill them with horror. When he sensed that they were moved, he urged them not to blush at their recognition of their own guilt: 'You have nothing to fear, my children, by admitting these thefts; and as evidence of repentance, raise your hand, all those whose conscience reproaches them with these thefts.' When the young criminals raised their hands, he led them, along with the rest of the group, outside the church, where he set fire to a bale of straw before their eyes, and, in the presence of those who were assembled there, he demanded to know the punishment that had been prepared for thieves. The fire of Hell, someone answered. Here is a small example of it, he then said forcefully; and continuing his discourse on the eternal torments that thieves suffer, he attempted to instill in them a great horror of theft and, at the same time, to oblige them to admit, in secret before a confessor and in all their simplicity, the errors by which they had publicly become known as criminals."[23] This is an excellent example of how the "rhetoric" prompted by the Last Things was merely a means to an end, which was confession and conversion.

Hymn 127, *"The abandoned soul delivered from purgatory by the prayers of children and the poor,"* gives us additional insight into these "plays." It is not simply a hymn but a "dialogue in hymn form" (cf. H 118; H 120; H 152), a true piece of theater: with twenty actors, a chorus, and a stage setting. Its subject is the agony and the duration of purgatory. Such atheme could be better illuminated by a theatrical work; even if the intelligentia find fault with his methods here, the end justified the means.[24] Agony and purgatory are acted out, with the future at stake. Agony involves the subject of death, whereas purgatory addresses hell and heaven. Montfort understood quite well that these latter two could not be included as part of the play. But they could, if necessary, be "described or depicted." These pious stage productions that Montfort directed were dramas. Only "the drama can lay bare those things that the plastic arts [or sermons] cannot reveal: What will the Judgment be like, or the prayers of intercession? What will Mary obtain for me, with Jesus at her side? How deep are the mysteries of the "communion of saints?" A dramatic presentation of those subjects, said by some to be too much, may in fact be not enough. In any case, it speaks to us with a power that is decisive for eternity."[25] When using such entertainment to describe the Last Things, Montfort emphasized their dramatic aspects, because he wished to evoke pathos. He hopes his audience will see and understand. But this scene was neither illustration nor recreation; He is not attempting to "amuse" his audience but to involve them in the action that is taking place. As they watch the participants portray the anguish of agony and the torments of purgatory, the spectators at Montfort's missions can only say to themselves, "It is true, I was a part of it." What seemed remote to them all at once becomes quite close at hand: "That man in agony, that is me," "That soul in Purgatory, could that be my father?" Moreover, they will say to themselves, "They are acting this out for my sake," "These missionaries are doing this for me." Caught in this theatrical rhetoric, they take part in the dialogue that is happening on stage; they become by taking turns the "response" in Hymn 118, the dying man in Hymn 120, etc. The drama in dialogue urges them on to identification. The spectators see it all happen before their eyes. This exteriorization gives them the necessary perspective, and enables them to become conscious of their fears and desires. Those who see Montfort's religious plays become actors in their own lives. These "pious productions," the itinerary of conversion described in the hymns and sermons, are narratives. If the events in these narratives were merely recounted, they would obscure the very paths they were meant to illuminate. In fact, the action, the activity on the stage, is produced by describing those very events, and the listeners and the spectators are made a part of the narrative. We should not be surprised at the tears that flowed freely at Father Montfort's missions.[26] He was aware of the force contained in "the orderly procession" of the "great truths of religion." He knew that those who meditated on those truths deeply and attentively could not remain indifferent to them.[27] The preaching of the Last Things succeeded insofar as men and women became conscious that its subject has their own duty. Montfort enabled them to become part of a "narrative theology." The narrative succeeds where concepts and beautiful words fail.

Another rhetorical element that Montfort used in his discourse on the Last Things was interrogation, the doubt that results from a question the answer to which is uncertain. *"It could happen that you will not"* be saved, he wrote to his mother (L 20; cf. H 14:39). The uncertainty of salvation: that is the question that haunts the Last Things (LS 178, 236-247, 355). This fundamental interrogation leads us to the question of "why" there is damnation. This is the only question to which we can respond (H 118) as if hell were the sole sure outcome. But the discourse on the Last Things is made possible by this affirmation: *"Hell is the only place we belong"* (cf. FC 21, 48, 58; TD 79; H 8:2, 16, 19-20; H 13:17; H 14:29; H 20:58; H 46:14; H 67:9-11; H 68:10-18; H 71:9; H 73:1; H 109:17; H 140:8). Divine justice condemns humanity to perdition. Ever since the Fall, men and women are lost or they lose themselves (H 1:27; H 2:30; H 14:29, 34; H 29:33; H 31:1; H 98:7; H 140:1; H 153:11; H 23:3). *"We become weak and fall to the depths by our own impotence. We fall into temptation, we fall into crime and then into damnation, and from one abyss to the next"* (H 15:9; cf. H 24:8; H 26:16). The metaphor of the Fall that Montfort uses so often, with the verbs "to fall" (H 7:19; H 13:17, 76; H 15:41; H 42:8; H 114:4; H 139:57; H 148:17;

cf. H 29:68) and "to plunge" (H 15:41, 42; H 28:26; H 31; H 29:62; H 36:85; H 100:4; H 142:15; cf. H 13:32; H 15:22, 28, 41, 42; H 16:9; H 20:25; H 29:46; H 30:15; etc.), emphasize the "naturalness" and *ineluctability* of this law of perdition—unless divine mercy intervenes (H 8:39; H 27:14, 15). We do not merit entrance to paradise. It is freely bestowed on us by mercy. We can only *desire* paradise (H 116; H 117). *"Seeing his place in hell"* can awaken the sinner from his slumber and set him on the road of conversion (cf. H 139:35). Repentance alone, sings Montfort, is the plank that can save sinners from their unmistakable loss of themselves (H 13:3).

Confronted with the uncertainty of their salvation and with the unforeseen moment of death that will decide their fate for eternity, human beings can act before the end arrives. Today wrestles with eternity. Death puts an end to this irretrievable time (H 114:7-9; H 139:15; cf. H 13:27; H 30:9). Tomorrow it will be too late (H 34:26, 32; H 36:64; LEW 72). Thus we must be converted *"without delay"* (H 13:24, 25) and catch death unawares, to fix the meaning of our entire lives. The Last Things underscore the urgency of conversion. For the everlasting question of our eternal duty as men and women, the Last Things do not simply inform and alert us about what lies ahead; rather, they reveal to us the true situation in which we find ourselves today. They are our ultimate summons to make a decision. The Last Things are brought before our eyes so that we do not postpone the moment of our conversion (H 13:6, 19; LS 169, 675-677, 696-698, 787). The mission is the privileged moment when we anticipate the Last Things. It is the place of judgment, where we are given the choice of justice or mercy. We must seize the grace that is available to us at that moment. God gives humanity a choice: to convert, or perish (cf. H 105; H 115; H 163). The pastoral treatment of the Last Things is completely directed toward closing the door to hell and opening the door to the confessional.

The rhetoric on the Last Things attempts to strike a perilous balance between justice and mercy, between fear and love. While Montfort, the popular parish missionary, frightened his audiences with his sermons on hell, he knew that the fear of punishment must not have the last word. In a long hymn on repentance, he sang: *"When repentance is produced / By the love of God alone, / Not by fear of punishment, / It has true merit"* (H 13:62). *"Fear leads to conversion, but love leads to a true conversion of the heart"* (LS II, 46; cf. LS II, 41). *"Those who do not act out of love are not truly converted, because the heart has not changed"* (LS II, 54, 55). For his part, Father Besnard makes the following comment, effective testimony to this double rhetoric: "While he spoke of God's justice in the way that was best suited to inspire fear, he did not forget to instill a sense of the infinite range of God's mercy, with the most moving words possible. After frightening the sinner, Montfort knew how to console him at the tribunal of reconciliation."[28] Missionaries had to be *"lions in the pulpit and doves in the confessional."*

IV. Ethical Dimension

Any theology on the Last Things must start with God: His justice and His mercy. The issue for humanity becomes apparent by implication: grace and freedom. These two pairs have a logical connection. Justice can only be performed on subjects that are free and responsible for their acts. Mercy is seen by men and women as grace, gift, and pardon.

The moral law that is imposed on man places him under judgment. The man under judgment must choose. This choice, given to him by his freedom, is called decision. The Last Things teach us that human activity, the fruit of this choice and this decision, has an irreversible element: it has eternal value, such that we could no longer act as if it did not.[29] Man's free will, as a fundamental choice, has in fact something "supratemporal" about it; it is an "unlimited responsibility." Eternity guarantees morality and protects it from absurdity. The *"freedom of man who is eternal"* (LS II, 261) establishes him face to face with eternal God.

A human act, inscribed in time, is indelible for all eternity (cf. LS 260, 261). Through faith, the eternal is rooted in time, and the believer discovers the paradox of his faith: it is within time itself that we find the eternal. For this reason, Montfort posits a singular equation between time and eternity: whatever is finitely posed in time is transposed with infinite power into eternity. Thus, a *"moment of vanity"* corresponds to eternal unhappiness (cf. H 29:19, 41; LS 814, 816); *"temporal pleasures"* correspond to *"eternal fires"* (H 114:4). This arithmetic allows us to *"change"* the temporal into the eternal (H 17:24; cf. H 35:49). Thus we can *"purchase heaven"* through almsgiving and charity (cf. H 17:30, 32, 34, 38, 39; H 18:9-11) and through the Rosary (SR 54, 146), or *"change eternal pain into temporal pain"* through penance, (H 13:65; cf. FC 21-23, 39; H 11:25, 26; H 16:26; H 96:2; H 100:49; H 123:9; H 153:21) and vice versa (H 34,19; TD 189). This assumption of time into eternity paradoxically may bring with it an attitude of depreciation toward the temporal, because it is made up of all that is opposed to the eternal: the body and the soul, the corruptible and the immortal, the earth and the heavens, the creature and the Creator (H 29:72; cf. H 12:10; H 28:14, 30; H 29:25, 28, 74; H 33:27; H 46:33; H 103:25; H 142:9; H 143:11; H 156:8; H 162:14). Therefore, the Last Things invite Christians to hold this deceptive world in contempt (cf. H 29ff.; H 106; H 107; H 108:9; H 114:5; H 142; LS 434-439, 454-458), to shun this world and look only upon heaven, their sole homeland (H 157:34).

V. Theocentric and Christological Dimension

Hymn 109 defines for us the four Last Things and then concludes with *"OF OUR LAST END": "God did not give me life, / Just for the fun of it, / But in order to know Him, / To love and serve Him. / That is my sole task, the rest is a trifle. / If I serve God now, / I will enjoy Him completely / In eternal glory"* (H 109:21; cf. H 26:11).

Losing God and losing oneself in God (H 28:43; LS 514): that is the stake posed by the Last Things. God is our only end because He is our origin: *"Your origin is to come from God, your end will be to return to God, your beatitude will be eternal enjoyment with God. With the first, you belong to God; with the second, you do all for God; with the third, God is everything to you"* (LS 791). The Last Things tell us of our relationship with God, but they are infinitely surpassed by the cry of the soul that desires to reach God, its unique center (cf. LS 280), with vehement prayer: *"O my God, my supreme good and my last end, . . . throughout time and eternity, . . . my God and my all! May I be entirely, completely yours, as you are entirely mine. . . . my blessedness, . . . , I long for you. . . . Until then, dear Lord, I will take no rest, I will languish out of love. My heart will beat continually within me, for you have made it for yourself, and it will never find rest until it finally rests in you"* (HD 47-48). God is the center because He is the beginning and the end. Between the soul and God there is a "concentration," because *"God is the center of my heart"* and *"our heart is the center of God"* (LS II, 2, 3; cf. LS II, 14). He is the God of the heart (LS I,67).

"Strictly speaking, our paradise will be God Himself" (LS 515). The soul cries to Jesus, *"Keep me in your heart, . . . / That he alone will be my paradise"* (H 131:10). By imitating and following Christ, we reconcile time and eternity, just as the Last Things had separated them (cf. H 20:17-21).

The Christocentrism of the Christian life is the primary fundamental truth of devotion to the Virgin Mary: *"Jesus, our Savior, true God and true man [Christological dimension] must be the ultimate end of all our other devotions. . . . He is the Alpha and the Omega, the beginning and end of everything. . . . If we live in Jesus and Jesus lives in us [another example of "concentration"], we need not fear damnation . . . nor devils in hell"* (TD 61). This famous text of montfort spirituality shows the extent to which Father de Montfort transcends his own discourse on the Last Things. The complex relationship that connects the beginning and the end gives structure to the Christology of TD. Such a Christology is not in the same conceptual category as the Last Things, and thus we are not restricted to the same categories of logic. When we contemplate Christ, our unique Redeemer and Savior, we are definitively beyond the realm of retributive justice.

LEW appears to beat a retreat from this soteriological standpoint. In effect, Montfort, like St. Anselm in his *Cur Deus Homo? (Why a God Man?),* makes the Incarnation dependent on the satisfaction exacted by divine justice after Adam's sin. Adam is desperate because he cannot make amends for his outrage against God. The offense against God is infinite, because God is infinite (cf. LS 261, 391). Thus the penalty, proportionate to the offense, is infinite, and humanity, whose nature is finite, can never erase such penalty. Adam *"saw heaven closed and no one to open it; he saw hell open and no one to close it"*

(LEW 40). He was damned forever; *"such was the well-deserved sentence God in his justice pronounced against him"* (LEW 39). Only a God made man can expiate mankind's infinite sin, can *"satisfy divine justice and appease God's anger."* The Word of God, identical to His mercy, thus debates the issue with divine justice. In order to rescue humanity, the Word will become incarnate. In this way the Incarnation, in this particular text, appears to be reduced to the sacrifice that the Son offers *"to his Father to comply with his justice, to calm the divine anger, to rescue us from the slavery of the devil and from the flames of hell, and to merit for us eternal happiness"* (LEW 45; cf. LEW 167). But we must note that Montfort is rather discreet on the subject of "satisfaction" and the "sacrifice offered to the Father."[30] He was wise enough not to pursue the metaphor of "redemption" too closely (cf. H 109:3). He was equally sensitive to the drama inherent in *"a kind of contest"* between Eternal Wisdom, mercy, and God's justice (LEW 41-46), serving as a prelude to the decree of the Incarnation.[31] But he did not view this simply as a "tactic"; he was undoubtedly convinced of the truth of this debate.

It would be clearly erroneous to reduce the whole of LEW to these few paragraphs taken out of context. In the end, hell does not have the last word, because the first word was addressed to paradise. From the very beginning of its existence, humanity has been called to eternal beatitude. Created in the image and resemblance of God, *"man was so godlike, so absorbed and rapt in God"* (LEW 38). Sin disfigured the divine image, but Wisdom sowed in humanity the hope of restoration. Wisdom could not endure the folly of perdition for his *"masterpiece"* (LEW 35, 41). Wisdom gave to mankind the desire to *"possess him," "on earth as well as in heaven"* (LEW 2). He is its center (LEW 12), the paradise that mankind searches for, and mankind is the paradise that Wisdom pursues in his *"loving search."*

VI. Conclusion

It is clear that we can no longer parrot Father de Montfort's sermons/notes on the Last Things. Nor can we revive his methods. But while we cannot repeat his words, we can certainly reread them. We owe it to ourselves to be attentive and receptive to the truths that his words contain.

Our world conceals death from us in a myriad of ways. Today we face the temptation to deny our finitude. But death has never been so much before us. We have never been so conscious of our responsibilities with respect to death. We obscure and exclude the meaning and gravity of life. In this context, to think about death is to consider the seriousness of life, to uncover the illusions and idols of this deceptive world: money, beauty, power, etc.

Montfort believed that hell was quite full. Today, many theologians are more guarded. But we must not go so far as to empty hell of its "truth" as a genuine possibility. Every passage in the NT on hell has the same goal: "to lead men and women to conduct their lives face to face with the genuine possibility of eternal perdition and to understand Revelation as an extremely serious call."[32] But this affirmation of the existence of hell must be accompanied by an invitation to conversion and a serious engagement with man's freedom, which renders him responsible for his acts. Man's greatness lies in his response to that freedom. More than simply information on the outcome of God's judgment, the discourse on the Last Things is a precaution against any lackadaisical attitude in the face of our ultimate destiny. The Last Things are a "wake-up call." Montfort was not one of those preachers who filled hell with others while tending to exclude themselves. He, too, could have said, "Hell awaits me personally, not hypothetically, but with just cause."[33] Confronted with this real possibility, Montfort describes two forms of despair: desperation and presumption (cf. H 7:28). Desperation is here the unwarranted anticipation of nonfullfilment; presumption is the unwarranted anticipation of fulfillment (cf. TD 97-98; LEW 217; LS II, 756). "Desperation is the descent into hell,"[34] the knowledge in advance that in the end there will only be despair (cf. H 120). Against hell, Montfort preached hope in divine love (cf. H 7:32-41); it is the devil who creates despair (H 101:39, 44). Montfort, who knew how to be practical, proposes several means for ensuring salvation, such as the Rosary (cf. SR 4, 29, 39, 50, 79, 104, 115, 132), because the Virgin Mary is all-powerful over hell (cf. H 7:31; H 15:33; H 76:6, 10; H 79:2, 7; H 82:6; H 88:12, 13; H 89:10, 12; H 90:36; H 104:12; H 159:7; H 190:40; TD 97). Other means may also be suggested. But it must not be forgotten that for Montfort this devotion presupposes a division of humanity into the *"predestinate"* (those who respond to God's call and therefore have heaven in the future, and the *"reprobate"* (those who refuse God's call and have hell as their goal). Reprobation is not a vocation but a "mystery of iniquity," a possibility of radical denial of God; God's subject who says "no" without looking back.[35]

In general, the language of the Last Things is impersonal, even though they affect us all personally. We speak of judgment, space, time, eternity, of what is felt. The theocentric dimension of Montfort's thought leads us to a true question: "What is our relation to God?" There is an interpersonal element to the Last Things. Beyond hell and paradise lies our *"contract of alliance with God."* We do not have to choose between the agonies of hell and the joys of heaven. By proposing that we renew our baptismal vows, Montfort invites us to make a more absolute choice: to renounce *"the devil, the world, sin and myself"* and to give ourselves *"entirely to Jesus through the hands of Mary, to carry my cross after him all the days of my life"* (CG 3). Far beyond death, judgment, purgatory, hell, and heaven, there is God Alone, for *"Our Lord is worth more than Paradise"* (LS II, 329). *"Yes, my dear love, I love you / not out of fear of punishment./ nor to gain recompense / but for yourself and yourself alone"* (H 5:46).

O. Maire

Notes: (1) According to Jean Delumeau, *La peur en occident, XIV-XVIII siècles (Fear in the West, 14th-18th Centuries),* Fayard, Paris 1978, Montfort is among those who exhorted his listeners to suffer their fate on earth so as to win recompense in the hereafter. Delumeau, *Le péché et la peur (Sin and Fear),* Paris 1985, 9, cites Hymn 108:15 as an example. We must qualify Delumeau's assertions when he writes that "the Church's insistence on [the horror of sin] and on [the obsession with damnation] led it to an astonishing devaluation, at every level of society, of material life and daily cares; Grignion de Montfort, at the beginning of the eighteenth century, sang to the faithful this significant hymn: 'Leave your wood for a while, carpenter, and ironsmith, take leave of your fire. Put away your work, laborer, and seek grace'" (H 163:7). This author has not truly understood St. Louis de Montfort nor the meaning and the stakes of a parish mission. (2) From the seventeenth to the eighteenth century, fear of hell and purgatory subsided; cf. J. Delumeau, *Rassurer et protéger (Reassurance and protection),* Paris 1989, 5. The great sermons on the eternal truths fell on deaf ears in France after the turning point of Vatican II. This may coincide with the cessation of traditional parish missions. (3) Blain, 22, 25-28; Besnard I, 31. (4) Ibid., 33. (5) Blain, 26. (6) Ibid., 27. (7) Besnard I, 33. (8) Blain, 27. (9) Ibid., 27. (10) Grandet, 15-16. (11) *Introduction* of Bishop Henri Frehen, SMM, III. (12) Cf. Adalbert de Vogué, SC 251, Paris 1978, 149-152; St. Gregory, *Dialogues,* vol. 4, SC 265, Paris 1980. (13) In LS 389, we find book 4, no. 40, 1 of the *Dialogues* of Pope Saint Gregory: "We must understand that, on occasion, souls that are still incarnate observe some part of the agonies of the hereafter. For some, it is for their edification; for others, for the edification of their listeners" (SC 265, p. 39). (14) Besnard I, 141-142. The care given to testaments is indicative of the "atmosphere of the time." Study of these testaments has enabled historians to "measure" the influence of the Last Things on the general population; cf. J. Delumeau, *Rassurer et protéger,* 520-521; N. Vovelle, *Piété baroque et déchristianisation (Baroque Piety and Dechristianization),* Plon, Paris 1973, 122-126, 318-337, 429-435; P. Chaunu et al., *Mourir à Paris (Dying in Paris),* Fayard, Paris 1978, especially 409-417. Montfort alludes in LS 734 to those who do not respect the clauses in testaments referring to prayers and Masses for the repose of the souls of the testators. (15) The importance of distinguishing between the Incarnation and the divinization of man cannot be overemphasized. It does not require much detective work to discover the patristic basis for these pages as recopied by Montfort, beyond the mere citation of the Fathers. (16) In St. Francis de Sales's *Introduction to the Devout Life,* the meditations on the Last Things are similarly placed; in Saint Ignatius's *Spiritual Exercises,* the meditation on hell comes at the end of the work. The order is completely changed in LS II, 532-534. (17) Edited by J. Felix Faulcon at Poitiers, 1756, 9, and 1776, 1779, 8. (18) This booklet was reissued in 1927, complete with notes, "contemporary engravings," and Montfort's W, by the publications office of the review *Règne de Jésus par Marie (Reign of Jesus through Mary).* (19) Cf. Gregory of Nazianzus, *Letters,* 31, 4 and 76, 1, and *Discourses* 27, 7; also Plato, *Phédon,* 80c. (20) Besnard, II, 6; LS III, 63-65, 66-86; cf. Besnard, Marie-Louise, 73-78. (21) Besnard II, 6-7. (22) Besnard I, 14, 85, 273. (23) Blain, 153-154. (24) Besnard II, 7; Blain, 153, 159. (25) Hans Urs von Balthasar, *La Dramatique divine (The divine drama),* Prolégomènes, Paris 1984, 1:94. (26) Besnard I, 115, 158, 219; II, 137. (27) Cf. Besnard I, 130. (28) Ibid., 35; cf. H 21:18 and H 22:17. On the failure of this rhetoric, see H 39:132. (29) Cf. Jacques Durandeaux, *De l'éternité, Temps réfuté ou Temps aimé? (On eternity: Disproven or Beloved?),* Desclée de Brouwer, Paris 1990. (30) By his sacrifice, Christ pacifies the anger of his Father; cf. H 128-134 and LS II, 327. (31) The little fable of the king, the queen, the peasant, and the apple (TD 147-150; SM 37), illustrating the mediating role played by Mary, our "advocate" (TD 83-85; SM 36), belongs to the same conceptual realm as the debate between Justice and divine Mercy. (32) J. Ratzinger, cited by H. Urs von Balthasar, *L'enfer, une question (Hell: A Question),* Paris 1988, 46; cf. CCC, 1033-1037. (33) Ibid., 37. (34) Isidore of Seville, cited by H. Urs von Balthasar, *Espérer pour tous (Hope for All),* Paris 1987, 21. (35) Karl Rahner, *Foundations of Christian Faith: An Introduction to the Idea of Christianity,* Seabury Press, New York, 1978, 435-444.

LEGION OF MARY

SUMMARY

I. MARIAN ORIGIN:
  1. First meeting;
  2. Second meeting.

II. ORGANIZATIONAL FRAMEWORK:
  1. Mary's army;
  2. Governing bodies.

III. METHODS AND TECHNIQUES:
  1. What is the objective of the Legion of Mary, and how does it achieve this objective?
  2. Through union with her;
  3. Marian Apostolate.

IV. LEGION SPIRITUALITY:
  1. Centered on the Holy Spirit;
  2. Centered on Christ.

V. MARIAN OUTLOOK:
  1. Sharing Mary's motherhood;
  2. Montfort's influence;
  3. The montfort way;
  4. Slave of Mary;
  5. Marian approach;
  6. "Fullness of devotion".

VI. PRODIGIOUS GROWTH.

The worldwide Legion of Mary has been called "a miracle of these modern times."[1] Cardinal Suenens wrote: "Today, two currents dominate the life of the Church: the Marian current and the apostolic current."[2] These two currents meet and blend harmoniously in the Legion of Mary, which has been a providential instrument in the hands of Mary and the Church for the spread of the Kingdom of God on earth.

To understand the relationship between Our Lady and the Legion of Mary, it may be well to begin by looking at a clear and authoritative definition of this lay organization. We take our definition from *The Legion of Mary Handbook*—VI. Edition, published by the *Concilium Legionis Mariae* in Dublin, Ireland: "The Legion of Mary is an Association of Catholics, who, with the sanction of the Church and under the powerful leadership of Mary Immaculate, Mediatrix of All Graces (who is fair as the moon, bright as the sun and—to Satan and his legionaries—terrible as an army set in battle array), have formed themselves into a Legion for service in the warfare which is perpetually waged by the Church against the world and its evil powers."[3]

What follows is a brief study of the Legion's Marian origin, organizational framework, methods and techniques, doctrinal and spiritual outlook, and, finally, growth and achievements. It seeks to clarify the relationship between the Marian doctrine of St. Louis de Montfort and the Legion of Mary and to justify the words of its founder, Mr. Frank Duff (1889-1980): "The Legion is Our Lady's spirit come to life in people."[4]

I. Marian Origin

Tracing the origins of the Legion, John Murray, former president of the *Concilium,* writes: "The nucleus of the Legion in its personnel was that little group attending the monthly Pioneer Council meeting in Myra House. It was in these informal 'talks' after the gathering that the spirit which characterized the Legion from its first meeting was formed. In a consecutive number of these talks, Mr. Frank Duff had outlined to his listeners the True Devotion to the Blessed Virgin, of Saint Louis Marie de Montfort. Those who established the Legion and guided the new movement from the first moment were those who had heard those spiritual talks each month at Myra House."[5]

1. First meeting

The historic first meeting of the Legion was held on the evening of September 7, 1921, the First Vespers of the feast of Our Lady's Nativity. It was in a modest "upper-room" of an apartment on Francis St., in an old and poor quarter of the city of Dublin, Ireland. In the center of the room, on a table covered with a white cloth, flanked by two lighted candles and two vases of flowers, was enthroned a statue of the Immaculate Conception, of the Miraculous Medal type.

This simple arrangement was the idea of one of the early arrivals and expressed the spirit of the organization that was about to be born. As the *Handbook* of the Legion puts it: "The Queen was there before those assembled. She stood waiting to receive the enrollments of those, who, she knew, were coming to her. They did not adopt her. She adopted them."[6]

At the hour agreed upon, this little group—fifteen girls, most of them in their late teens or early twenties; one layman, Mr. Frank Duff; and one priest, Michael Toher—knelt on the floor around the improvised altar. They recited the invocation and prayer to the Holy Spirit and then recited the Rosary. Their prayers ended, they took and considered together "how they could best please God and make Him loved in His world."[7]

They proposed together a program of work. They would visit an almshouse of the city to console the poor. Their concern would center chiefly on the women patients, and their visitations would be undertaken in a friendly, simple devotional manner with a willingness to listen patiently to the concerns of these people.

Those gathered that night were unanimous that this work should be organized to insure the regularity of these visits. In other words, it would be done seriously, methodically, or not at all. They decided to follow the format of the St. Vincent de Paul Society to a certain extent: a weekly meeting, prayer, spiritual talk, reports from each member on the previous week's work. They wanted an apostolate with and for Mary, in accordance with the teachings of St. Louis de Montfort.

2. Second meeting

There are accounts of the very first Legion visitations. A bedridden woman who had been away from the Sacraments for many years decided to "get right" again. Another woman, bedridden for five years, wrote on a scrap of paper a little note addressed to her daughter: "If I can see you once before death, then I shall die in peace." Another woman who had been living with a married man and who had nowhere else to go, upon being discharged from the hospital pleaded with the Legionary, "If I could only find a job, then I could make him return to his own wife." This woman asked if the kind visitor could perhaps help her in this difficult situation. These are just a few examples of their experiences.

Report after report authenticated the fruitfulness of this soul-to-soul Marian apostolate. The Legionaries understood their role as docile instruments in the hands of the Virgin Mary. Their intention was self-sanctification and the sanctification of others. Their message was to give Christ to the world through Mary.

A new organization was born . . . a spiritual army that was soon to encircle the globe: The Legion of Mary.

During the first four years of its existence, the organization was known as the Association of Our Lady of Mercy. Later, in November, 1925, it adopted the name Legion of Mary.[8]

II. Organizational Framework

The *Handbook* states: "The Legion is an army—the army of the Virgin Most Humble."[9] Like any army it must be built on discipline, tactics, and morale. It therefore calls for an "unrelaxed discipline," a discipline that is based on true humility and that must "bear on all the affairs of daily life and be ever on the alert for opportunities to promote the general object of the Legion, namely, to destroy the empire of sin, uproot its foundations and plant on its ruins the standard of Christ the King."[10]

Since the Legion "places before its members a mode of life, rather than the doing of a work," it provided "an intensely ordered system, in which much is given the force of rule that in other systems is merely exhorted or left to be understood, and in regard to every detail of which it enjoins a spirit of scrupulous observance."[11]

Despite some criticism of its inflexible rules, this point of faithful adherence to the Legion system in all its details is so important that the *Handbook* says that the Legion "deems a member to be a member to the degree to which he submits himself to the Legion system, and no more."[12]

1. Mary's army

Like any army, the Legion is composed of members who are in active service (active members) and those who support the troops by their work and their prayers (auxiliary members). Modeled on a military model, the Legion took its nomenclature from the old Roman legion. Using such Latin terms as *Praesidium, Curia, Senatus,* etc., gave the Legion a note of universality and unity.

The basic unit of the Legion is the Praesidium. This is the parish or institutional unit, and it ranges from approximately four to twenty active members, to which may be affiliated an indefinite number of auxiliary members, whose obligation it is to sustain the active members by their prayers and sacrifices. The prayers that the Legionaries, both active and auxiliary, must say every day are to be found on the official prayer card of the Legion, called the Tessera.

Each Praesidium is made up of four officers: president, vice-president, secretary, and treasurer. It holds its meetings once a week. Since the Legion "took root from the St. Vincent de Paul Society," it is to be expected that its method of procedure is much the same. It is invariable and consists of: 1. prayer to the Holy Spirit; 2. recitation of the Rosary; 3. spiritual reading; 4. reading of the minutes of the previous meeting; 5. verbal account of the preceding week's work, given by each member; 6. recitation of the Magnificat; 7. assignment of work for the coming week; 8. discussion based on the *Handbook*; 9. concluding prayers; 10. blessing by the spiritual director.

2. Governing bodies

It should be noted that "no praesidium shall be established in any parish without the consent of the parish priest or of the Ordinary."[13] In addition, no Praesidium can be organized in a locality without the express permission of the governing body immediately above it, called the Curia. This permission can only be given if the new group pledges itself to adhere faithfully to the rules and regulations as set down in the Legion *Handbook*.

When two or more Praesidia are established in a certain area, a higher body, called a Curia, is formed. This group is made up of all the officers of the Praesidia in the locality and chooses its own officers from among them. When one Curia is placed in charge of several Curiae, it becomes a Comitium. This body does not generally exceed the boundaries of a diocese. Above the Comitium is the Senatus, which is the governing body for a whole area. Finally, there is the Concilium, which is the central governing body of the Legion throughout the world. Its headquarters are located in De Montfort House, Dublin, Ireland.

To foster a higher spiritual level among its members, the Legion established the Praetorians.[14] This is not a distinct group but simply a higher degree of active service in the Legion. It comprises the following obligations: 1. the daily recitation of all the prayers contained in the Tessera of the Legion; 2. daily Mass and daily Holy Communion; 3. the daily recitation of some form of Office approved by the Church, such as the Little Office of the Blessed Virgin, etc.

III. Methods and Techniques

1. What is the objective of the Legion of Mary, and how does it achieve this objective?

The *Handbook* states: "The object of the Legion of Mary is the glory of God through the sanctification of its members by prayer and active cooperation, under ecclesiastical guidance, in Mary's and the Church's work of crushing the head of the serpent and advancing the reign of Christ."[15] It is interesting how the Legion *Handbook* identifies Mary's work with that of the Church, in what concerns "advancing the reign of Christ." This Legion objective gives it full right to be called Catholic Action.

Pope Pius XI once defined Catholic Action as "the participation of the laity in the true and proper apostolate of the Church." The Legion of Mary is Catholic Action founded on Mary. The Second Vatican Council's decree on the Apostolate of Lay People (AA) states that the "perfect model of this apostolic spiritual life is the Blessed Virgin Mary, Queen of Apostles. . . . Everyone should have a genuine devotion to her and entrust his life to her motherly care."

2. Through union with her

To recognize from the very outset the role and influence of Mary in the dual work of personal sanctification and the apostolate, and then to submit oneself fully to this maternal influence through intimate union with the Mediatrix of all Graces to become an instrument of conquest in her virginal hands is the secret of the Legionary apostolate—such is the method proper to the Legion of Mary. To be sure, there are many approved forms of Catholic Action. As Pope Pius XII pointed out: "'Catholic Action is not confined within a closed circle' . . . nor is it such that 'it pursues its object according to a special method and system,' so as to abolish or absorb the other active Catholic organizations."[16]

In other words, some organizations will stress the study and the application of the laws of psychology; others will concentrate their efforts on studying the social and intellectual milieu, etc. All of these are methods that, it will be readily conceded, merit our admiration and support. In the Legion of Mary, however, the method is entirely different. Placing itself, from the very outset, above all human strategy, it establishes a soul firmly in the realm of faith.

Since the Legionary's principal task is "to bring Mary to the world as the infallible means of winning the world to Jesus," it is obvious that "the Legionary without Mary in his heart can play no part in this."[17] Hence the necessity for each Legionary to seek union with Mary through imitation of her virtues and complete dependence upon her. "Its members thus grown into living copies of Mary, the Legion sees itself in truth a Legion of Mary, united to her mission and guaranteed her victory."[18]

3. Marian apostolate

This union with Mary, and imitation of her virtues, will inevitably lead to an apostolate that is essentially Marian, that is to say, an apostolate through which Christ will not only be seen in every person but will be tended to and cared for with the love of Mary herself. To quote the words of the *Handbook:* "In and through her Legionary, Mary participates in every Legionary duty and mothers souls, so that in each of those worked for . . . not only is the person of Our Lord seen and served, but seen and served by Mary, with the same exquisite love and nurturing care which she gave to the actual body of her Divine Son."[19]

For the Legionary, as for Mary herself, a crowd is never just a crowd. It is an assemblage of individual people, each meriting particular attention, infinite love. Hence the Legionary instruction: "The Legion must direct itself to the individual soul."[20] This is the way the Legion envisages the problem of people in the aggregate. It does not presume to belittle or ignore crowd psychology; rather, it seeks to transform that crowd by approaching and transforming the individuals in it.

In a word, the Legion method or technique is both spiritual and psychological. It is spiritual in that it is based on union with Mary; it is psychological in that it is based on sound elementary psychology.

IV. Legion Spirituality

This brings us to our fourth consideration: the Legion spirituality. Does the Legion have a spirituality of its own, a spirituality that can be universally adopted and that rests on good, solid theological grounds? If so, where is this spiritual doctrine to be found?

The spiritual doctrine of the Legion of Mary is to be found principally in the Legion *Handbook*. A storehouse of doctrine and action in which theory and practice intermingle freely—lest one should dominate to the detriment of the other—the Legion *Handbook* holds the key to a spirituality that has already reaped its fruits of holiness, and even martyrdom.

1. Centered on the Holy Spirit

The Legion's spirituality—symbolized in the Legion of Mary Standard—is centered on the Holy Spirit, the Sanctifier, the One Who not only overshadowed Mary in the work of the Incarnation, but also came down upon the Apostles on the day of Pentecost. The reason for this is obvious: The Legion is essentially Marian and apostolic. It must therefore be animated by the Holy Spirit both for the sanctification of its members and for their apostolic action.That is why every Legion meeting is opened with a prayer to the Holy Spirit. The Legion Promise, which marks the formal entry into Mary's Legion, is made directly to the Holy Spirit. The Legion Promise embodies the very spirit of the Legion. Readers may refer to the masterful commentary on the Promise by Cardinal Suenens in his book "The Theology of the Apostolate."[21]

2. Centered on Christ

Cardinal Suenens has pointed out that the Legion Promise, though directed to the Holy Spirit, is essentially Christocentric, since, in this Promise, "neither the Holy Spirit nor the Blessed Virgin has any meaning for us without reference to the mystery of the Incarnation."[22] He notes that Christianity has been defined as an exchange of two loves in Jesus Christ. First, the Love that descends from heaven to seal the sacred alliance is called the Holy Spirit. And second, the love that ascends to meet that Infinite Love is called Mary. The secret meeting place of these two loves is Christ Jesus.

The work of the Holy Spirit in the Church, therefore, is to bring to realization the work of Christ in the world, just as it is the work of Mary to lead us to Christ. In other words, the Legionary is asked to lend himself to the action of the Holy Spirit, in and through Mary, to serve Christ and to continue his mission on earth.

V. Marian Outlook

And this brings us to the Marian outlook of the Legion. "Under God," says the Legion *Handbook,* "the Legion is built upon devotion to Mary,"[23] not any kind of devotion, but an adequate devotion that can only be acquired "by union with her."[24]

As mentioned, the Legion seeks union with Mary through imitation of her virtues. The Legion seeks to identify itself with Mary, particularly in her motherhood of souls. Mary's whole life and destiny, says the *Handbook,* have been motherhood, first of Christ, then of men. "On the day of the annunciation she entered on her wondrous work and ever since she has been the busy mother attending to her household duties. For a while these were contained in Nazareth, but soon the little house became the whole wide world, and her Son expanded into mankind. And so it has continued: all the time her domestic work goes on and nothing in that Nazareth-grown-big can be performed without her. Any caring of the Lord's body is only supplemental to her care; the apostle only adds himself to her maternal occupations; and in that sense," concludes the *Handbook,* "Our Lady might declare: 'I am Apostleship,' almost as she said: 'I am the Immaculate Conception.'"[25]

1. Sharing Mary's motherhood

If Mary's motherhood of souls is her essential function in the Church today, then, the *Handbook* rightly concludes, "without participation in it [her motherhood of souls] there can be no real union with her."[26] In other words, "true devotion to Mary must comprise the service of souls. Mary without motherhood and the Christian without apostleship would be analogous ideas. Both the one and the other would be incomplete, unreal, unsubstantial, false to the divine intention."[27]

2. Montfort's influence

"To understand the spirituality of the Legion of Mary," said Cardinal Suenens, "one must know its history and especially, one must grasp the spiritual bond that links the Legion to the doctor of the Marian Mediation, St. Louis de Montfort."[28] And Bishop Patrice Flynn, of Nevers, once wrote: "The Legion spirituality is but the applying to the modern apostolate of the admirable doctrine of the French School, of St. John Eudes, Olier, and especially of Blessed Grignion de Montfort. The Handbook explains and comments upon, in its sometimes diffuse but always orthodox way, the classical treatise on True Devotion to the Blessed Virgin."[29]

That the Legion spirituality owes much to St. Louis de Montfort's writings is attested to by Mr. Frank Duff himself. The founder of the Legion said: "The Legion of Mary owes, you might say, everything to the montfort devotion."[30] And these words are but a faithful echo of the *Handbook,* which states: "It can be safely asserted that no Saint has played a greater part in the development of the Legion than he. The Handbook is full of his spirit. The prayers re-echo his very words. He is really the tutor of the Legion: thus invocation is due to him by the Legion almost as a matter of moral obligation."[31]

The Legion *Handbook* is full of Montfort's spirit and the Legion prayers re-echo his very words, for there is an intimate relationship between it and TD. "It cannot be denied," wrote Cardinal Suenens, "that the Handbook of the Legion of Mary is a striking follow-up of the Treatise on True Devotion. It takes up the same doctrine and carries it over into the field of effective and concrete action, within the reach of all men of good will."[32]

3. The montfort way

After pointing out that union with Mary entails sharing in her motherhood of souls, the *Handbook* invites each and every Legionary to read and study the writings of its "tutor," St. Louis Marie de Montfort. In chapter 27, *The Duty of Legionaries towards Mary,* we read that "Legionaries should undertake Montfort's *True Devotion to Mary,*" for the Legion of Mary strives to identify itself, so to speak, with the montfort way of spiritual life.

"It is desirable that the practice of the Legionary devotion to Mary should be rounded off and given the distinctive character which has been taught by St. Louis de Montfort under the titles of *'The True Devotion'* or the *'Slavery of Mary'* and which is enshrined in his two books, the *'True Devotion to the Blessed Virgin'* and the *'Secret of Mary.'*"[33]

Describing the nature of this holy slavery, the *Handbook* continues: "That devotion requires the formal entry into a compact with Mary, whereby one gives to her one's whole self, with all his thoughts, and deeds and possessions, both spiritual and temporal, past, present, and future, without the reservation of the smallest part or slightest little thing. In a word, the giver places himself in a condition equivalent to that of a slave possessing nothing of his own, and wholly dependent on, and utterly at the disposal of Mary."

4. Slave of Mary

Stressing the utter dependence of the slave of Mary, the *Handbook* goes on to say: "But the earthly slave is far freer than the slave of Mary. The former remains master of his thoughts and inner life, and thus may be free in everything that matters to him. But the surrender to Mary bears with it everything: each thought, the movements of the soul, the hidden riches, the inmost self. All—on to the final breath—is committed to her that she may expend it all for God."[34]

Lest this total Consecration to Jesus through Mary be mistaken for a mere passing act of devotion towards the Mother of God, the Legionary is immediately reminded that although the True Devotion is inaugurated by a formal act of Consecration, "it consists principally in the subsequent living of that Consecration. The True Devotion must represent not an act but a state."[35]

This state or attitude of the soul of the individual Legionary will blossom forth—as we have already shown—into a Marian apostolate. "The work of the Legion is essentially a hidden one. It commences in the heart of the individual Legionary, developing therein a spirit of zeal and charity."[36]

Through the Legion system, this zeal and charity will manifest themselves by direct personal contact in a soul-to-soul apostolate that will gradually raise the spiritual level of the entire community.

5. Marian approach

The nature of this Legion approach to souls is not only distinctly Marian but also clearly within the montfort tradition. As the *Handbook* says: "Souls are not approached except with Mary."[37] In other words, Legionaries are asked to bring Mary to the world by leading people to a "calm examination of the role of Mary" in God's plan of our redemption.[38] This will prompt them to give to others a full explanation of Mary's part in our lives and of the consequent "rich and full devotion" we owe her in return. Indeed, "how can Legionaries talk in any other terms of her?"[39]

Adopting Montfort's method of interior life with Mary, the *Handbook* takes up the formula "Through, With, In, and For Mary" and transposes it into the apostolic life of the individual Legionary. Here are a few of its slogans, so to speak: "Souls are not approached except *with* Mary."[40] To tell Legionaries to immerse themselves in their work is but the same thing as to urge them to bury themselves *in* Mary.[41] "The Legion apostolate operates *through* Mary."[42] And finally: "The Legionaries work *for* Mary, quite irrespective of the simplicity or the difficulty of the task."[43]

6. "Fullness of devotion"

Such is the Marian spirituality of the Legion of Mary—a spirituality that is totally Marian, totally montfort. It might be noted here that although the actual making of the act of Consecration, known as the Holy Slavery, is not enjoined as an obligation or condition of Legion membership but, rather, left to the discretion and free choice of each Legionary. Nevertheless, all Legionaries are reminded that the Legion "declares itself to be built on a fullness of devotion to Mary which approximates to, or is equivalent to, de Montfort's own special form."[44]

The Legion's founder, Frank Duff, stated: "It is desirable that every Legionary—not alone its Active Members, but likewise each one of its great host of Auxiliary Members—should possess a copy of Montfort's monumental exposition of the *True Devotion.* They should read it again and again, and fully comprehend it and bring it into wholehearted play in their spiritual life. Only then will they enter into the spirit of the Legion of Mary, to which, as the Legion itself declares . . . Montfort is veritably tutor."[45]

VI. Prodigious Growth

Is it any wonder that such an organization should have, within the lifetime of its founder, spanned the seven seas and reached the very "extremities of the earth"?

After experiencing a significant drop in numbers after Vatican II—as did so many communities and organizations within the Church—the Legion hopes to regain its ground and be a special instrument in the "new evangelization."

The Third World countries are a special sign of hope for increased participation in the Legion. By the mid 80's the Philippines had 15,500 Praesidia with nearly 200,000 active members. Hong Kong had 250

Praesidia, Indonesia almost 1,000, Japan 350, Taiwan 120. Korea had then over 7,000 Praesidia.[46] Recently at the close of the 2nd Marian year, at the request of the Korean Bishops, 150,000 active members of the Legion of Mary gathered at the Cheongju Stadium in Seoul, South Korea, representing 2 Senatus, 2 Regial, 70 Comitia, 700 Curial and 13,000 Praesidia.[47]

If a tree is judged by its fruits, and if the blood of martyrs is the seed of Christians, then the Legion of Mary has every reason to hope for a glorious future in the battlefront of Mary's, and the Church's, warfare against the forces of evil. And if Edel Quinn (whose cause for heroic virtue has already been introduced) is any indication as to what heights of sanctity the Legion's Marian spirituality can lead a soul, then we believe with the Legion and with St. Louis de Montfort that *"Mary has produced, together with the Holy Spirit, the greatest thing which has been or ever will be—a God-Man; and she will consequently produce the greatest of the saints that there will be in the end of time. The formation and the education of the great saints who shall come at the end of the world are reserved for her. For it is only that singular and miraculous Virgin who can produce, in union with the Holy Spirit, singular and extraordinary things."*[48]

R. M. Charest

Notes: (1) *Legion of Mary Handbook,* 6th American New and Revised Edition, 20 (H. E. Riberi) New York 1985. (2) Suenens, Leon, *The Legion of Mary—A work of God for our day,* in *Symposium on the Legion of Mary,* Dublin 1957, p. 3. (3) *Handbook,* pp. 1, 2. (4) Frank Duff, address to New York Senatus, December 1956, p. 2 (mimeo) (5) John Murray, *A Journey of a Thousand Leagues Begins . . . ,* in *Symposium on the Legion of Mary,* Dublin, 1957. p. 11. (6) *Handbook,* p. 2. (7) Ibid., p. 2; cf. F. Duff, *Miracles on Tap,* Montfort Publications, Bay Shore, N.Y. 1962. (8) Murray, Symposium, p. 10. (9) *Handbook,* p. 83. (10) Ibid., p. 128. (11) Ibid., p. 30. (12) Ibid., p. 31. (13) Ibid., p. 63. (14) Ibid., p. 157. (15) Ibid., p. 3. (16) *Bis saecularis,* September 27, 1948, in A.A.S., vol. 40, p. 393. (17) *Handbook,* p. 104. (18) Ibid., p. 106. (19) Ibid., p.106. (20) Ibid., p. 243. (21) *The Theology of the Apostolate,* by Msgr. Leon Joseph Suenens, Henry Regnery, Chicago 1955. (22) Maria, vol. III, 1954, Suenens, The Legion of Mary, p. 649. (23) *Handbook,* p. 9. (24) Ibid., p. 110. (25) Ibid. p. 110. (26) Ibid., p. 111. (27) Ibid. p. 111. (28) Maria, vol. III, p. 637. (29) *La Legion de Marie,* Nevers, France, p. 4. (30) Talk to Montfort Fathers, Bay Shore, N.Y., December 6, 1956; cf. QOAH, vol. VII., March-April 1957, p. 3. (31) *Handbook,* p. 46. (32) Marie, vol. VI, no. 3, p. 86. (33) *Handbook,* p. 114. (34) Ibid., p. 155 (35) Ibid. p. 155. (36) Ibid., p. 234. (37) Ibid., p. 254. (38) Ibid., p. 261. (39) Ibid., p. 261. (40) Ibid., p. 254. (41) Ibid., p. 143. (42) Ibid., p. 108. (43) Ibid., 140. (44) Frank Duff, *de Montfort Way,* Montfort Publications, Bay Shore, N.Y. 1947, p. 33. (45) Ibid., p. 35. (46) Aidan McGrath, SCC *Far East Report,* Queen, Nov./Dec. 1985. Bayshore, NY. (47) Maria Legionis, Dublin, Vol. 31, No. 4. (48) TD, No. 35.

All Handbook references (from 3 to 43): *The Official Handbook of the Legion of Mary,* new revised edition 1993, De Monfort House, Dublin 7, Ireland.

LITTLE CROWN

SUMMARY

I. ITS HISTORY:
   1. Inspired by the Scriptures;
   2. Previous versions of the Little Crown:
      a. The Triple Crown of the Mother of God,
      b. Salutation addressed to the Most Blessed Virgin.

II. ITS STRUCTURE:
   1. Introduction;
   2. Framework;
   3. The salutations:
      a. Crown of excellence,
      b. Crown of power,
      c. Crown of goodness;
   4. Concluding prayer.

III. ITS CONTENTS:
   1. Doctrinal value;
   2. Connection with Montfort's other writings.

IV. CONCLUSION.

The Little Crown of the Blessed Virgin is one of the prayers said traditionally in the montfort family. *"Montfort Prayers and Celebrations"* (published in Rome on December 8, 1986, by the generalate of the Montfort Missionaries), gives the text in Latin and in French with the following note: "The French text of the Little Crown, found in *Oeuvres Complètes,* 840-843, was settled upon by the 1859 general chapter of the Company of Mary which 'wanted to adhere as closely as possible in all things to the thought of the Venerable Father."[1]

I. ITS HISTORY

The text was published merely on the strength of that general chapter which also "prescribed that the morning and night prayers, recently published on April 14, be said throughout the Congregation. They are a faithful copy of the author's own manuscript."[2] This means that a copy did exist when this was published, but it has not yet been found. In the absence of the original, however, the evidence mentioned above is enough to establish the text as authentic. A similar question arises about the origin of SM, whose authenticity has been confirmed by internal criteria and rests on undeniable evidence.

1. Inspired by the Scriptures

The Little Crown was inspired by the well-known, difficult, and mysterious passage from Rev 12:1: *"A great portent appeared in heaven: a woman clothed with the sun, with the moon under her feet, and on her head a crown of twelve stars."* The only thing focussed on in the Little Crown is the twelve stars. Critical exegetes may find that the biblical inspiration is very slender, as only one part of the passage is considered, and in an accommodated sense at that. St. Bernard has made this passage famous by writing a sermon in which he elaborated on the last part: "She had on her head a crown of twelve stars. . . . Her head is indeed worthy of being crowned with stars whose brilliance it outshines and heightens. . . . Who could name the stars making up Mary's royal diadem? No human being would be able to describe this crown or say in detail how it was arranged. For very good reasons, however, we can recognize, it seems, in the twelve stars the twelve privileges of grace that constitute Mary's unique adornment." St. Bernard divided the privileges into three categories: "We can easily find in Mary privileges from heaven, privileges of the body, and privileges of the soul; if this set of three is repeated four times, the result is undoubtedly the complete series of the twelve stars sparkling in our Queen's diadem."[3]

The meaning of Rev 12, which some have regarded as "a crossroads of all the biblical avenues leading to Mary,"[4] is not clear unless it is considered as a whole, as it raises enormous problems for exegetes and mariologists alike. "Who is that woman crowned with twelve stars who, with great cries, is giving birth to the Messiah? Is she the Church, as suggested by the general symbolism of the Apocalypse? . . . Is she Mary?"[5] Following the recent in-depth study of Mariology and ecclesiology, it is now generally accepted that "Chapter 12 of the Apocalypse is about both Mary and the Church. John took pleasure in describing one under the features of the other. This is a device commonly used for drawing attention to a typological relationship between two realities."[6] However, there is no trace of this in the Little Crown, which, though doctrinally without blemish, is not didactic. Rather, it is a prayer that is expressed very freely, as can be gathered from the previous versions.

2. Previous versions of the Little Crown

We will not linger over the possible similarities with the earlier versions by Joseph Calasanz and Andrew Avellino or others that resemble it more or less; instead we will dwell on two noteworthy works.

a. The Triple Crown of the Mother of God. This work, which is a true Marian summa, was published in Paris in 1630.[7] Its author was the Jesuit François Poiré (1584-1637).[8] Montfort came across it in the library of Saint Sulpice and wrote a summary of it in N. He refers to it in TD 9. In TD 26, he speaks of *"solid proofs which can be read in full in Fr. Poiré's book The Triple Crown of the Blessed Virgin."* The title is derived from a centuries-old custom according to which "crowns were invented with the sole object of marking excellence and majesty."[9] A single crown, however, would not have been adequate to express the exalted queenship of the Mother of God. Just as the Church crowned the Vicar of Christ with "a triple crown to symbolize the fullness of the spiritual kingship vested in him," so the author meant to honor in this way the excellence, the power, and the goodness of Mary. In accordance with Rev 12:1, each of the three crowns will be adorned with twelve stars, or privileges, of Mary. Each crown constitutes a twelve-chapter treatise, plus an introductory and a concluding chapter at the end of each of the twelve. These acted as a reminder that Mary is to be honored, loved, and served. A fourth treatise is an invitation to accept all that has been said before in the *Triple Crown.* Among the practices of devotion mentioned in chapter 9, the writer suggests that "the Little Crown of twelve stars, which a large number of people recite daily, be said frequently."[10] The writer explains the structure of the prayer and how it should be said. After the mention of the "twelve privileges of the Mother of God," one Our Father and four Hail Marys are said. The first Our Father is said to give thanks to the Father, the second to the Son, and the third to the Holy Spirit for the privileges granted to Mary. He adds: "This does not mean, however, that the twelve salutations correspond exactly to the twelve prerogatives I have just listed; others may be substituted in their place, as the particular devotion of the person saying it is to be the guiding principle."[11]

b. Salutation addressed to the Most Blessed Virgin. This prayer was composed by St. John Eudes as a response, it is said, to a message from Mary.[12] It was inspired by the same passage (Rev 12:1) but structured, rather, on the model of an akathist hymn (Byzantine hymn to the Theotokos), with a series of acclamations. It consists of "twelve salutations" and twelve blessings in honor of the twelve stars in the crown of Mary in the Apocalypse. Each of the salutations begins with a Hail Mary:

> *"Ave Maria, filia Dei Patris, Ave Maria, Mater Dei Filii, Ave Maria, Sponsa Spiritus Sancti, Ave Maria, Templum totius Divinitatis."*[13]

After the twelfth salutation, St John Eudes continues the recitation of the salutation with the following paraphrase:

> *"Et benedictus fructus ventris tui Jesus, et benedictus sponsus tuus Joseph, et benedictus pater tuus Joachim."*

II. Its Structure

The two texts above offer a certain similarity. Like Montfort, John Eudes is indebted to Poiré, to whom he refers.[14] Despite the considerable differences between the two versions, it is difficult to believe that Montfort was not influenced by John Eudes.

1. Introduction

Like the Divine Office, the Little Crown begins with an invitatory: *"Dignare me laudare Te, Virgo sacrata. Da mihi virtutem contra hostes tuos"* (MP 2), which translated into English is *"Virgin most holy, accept my praise. And give me strength against your foes"* (MP 10). This formula is an antiphon from the Office of the Assumption, which was already in use in the ninth century, and occurs in the Antiphonal of Compiègne among other places.[15]

2. Framework

The set of three mentioned by St. Bernard recurs in the Little Crown, though in a different arrangement. Montfort divides the Little Crown into three sets of four salutations: one Our Father, four Hail Marys, each followed by a salutation to Mary, ending with a Glory be. Poiré leaves out the final Glory be[16] and does not mention it as part of the Rosary, about which he says, "A certain number of Hail Marys and Our Fathers."[17] It should come as no surprise that Montfort added the Glory be to each of the sets of salutations, as he did for the Rosary, which in his days did not include this doxology at the end of the decades.[18]

3. The salutations

In the first three parts of the Little Crown, the structure of the salutations is exactly the same: one Our Father; four Hail Marys, each followed by a salutation; and a Glory be. But the first part, which is purely laudatory, differs from the other two, in which a petition for the person saying the prayer is added to the salutation. This is an additional difference between Montfort's version and that of Poiré, who combines praise and petition in the three parts.

a. Crown of excellence. Following Poiré's example, some editions of the Little Crown have given this name to the first set of salutations. However, Montfort has not, nor has he used the same salutations. He highlights the divine and virginal maternity of Mary, from which all her privileges proceed, her peerless beauty, and the multitude of her virtues. *"You are indeed blessed, Virgin Mary, in having brought forth the Creator of the universe. You gave birth to the one who made you, while ever remaining a virgin"* (MP 10). Here Montfort combined two liturgical antiphons into one salutation: *"Beata es Virgo Maria, quae omnium portasti Creatorem"* and *"Genuisti qui te fecit et in aeternum permanes Virgo"* (MP 2).[19] The second salutation was taken from the Oratorio by Fulbert de Chartres which takes up the same idea, though it is expressed in the reverse order. In this text virginity is saluted first: *"Sancta et immaculata virginitas,"* which translated into English becomes *"Virgin holy and immaculate, no tongue can praise you worthily. For you bore in your womb the God whom the very heavens cannot enclose"* (MP 10).[20] The third salutation is the well-known antiphon *"Tota pulchra es,*

Virgo Maria, et macula non est in te." The word *"originalis"* used in the liturgical antiphon has been omitted, and the English version simply says *"And free from every stain of sin"* (MP 10). Finally, summing up in one salutation the bountiful graces granted to Mary, the fourth salutation says: *"Plures tibi sunt dotes, Virgo, quam sidera coeli"* (MP 2); That is, *"The gifts bestowed on you, Virgin Mary, outnumber the stars of heaven"* (MP 10).

*b. **Crown of power.*** This heading was used by Poiré, but Montfort did not include it in the Little Crown. It is noteworthy that from the fifth salutation onwards, the construction is different. Each salutation begins with the words *"Gloria tibi sit,"* which recur frequently in the liturgy with reference to God: "Glory to God in the highest," "Glory to you, God Most High,"[21] "Glory to the victorious Spirit,"[22] "Glory and praise to you."[23] As used in the Bible, glory (*kabod* in Hebrew) refers to what is weighty, important. In its vernacular sense, it is a reference to worth, as when we say of people that they are worth "their weight in gold."[24] Proportionately speaking, this expression exalts the excellence of Mary, just as the expression "Blessed be," whose meaning is similar, expresses praise and thanksgiving in both the Bible and the liturgy.[25]

The first salutation of the second part reads *"Gloria tibi sit, Imperatrix poli"* (MP 4), which, translated, is *"Queen of the whole world, we praise you"* (MP 11). The same title, used in the plural, *"Imperatrix polorum,"* dates back at least to the ninth century. Alcuin († 804) wrote many inscriptions or anagrams for churches or altars dedicated to Mary. One of them reads *"Virgo Dei Genitrix . . . Tu regina poli."*[26] The salutations following this repeat the traditional titles *"treasury of all God's graces"* and *"Mediatrix between God and man,"* with a petition that we may share in Mary's gifts and that she may intercede for us that the Almighty may be favorable to us. The last salutation refers to a time when the Church was fighting against pernicious heresies, particularly those of the Docetists, Gnostics, Arians, and Nestorians, all of which in their several ways were undermining the truth of the Incarnation. In those days the Church saluted Mary as the one who rooted out these heresies. In the third nocturn of the Roman Breviary, an antiphon on the feast of the Annunciation read "Rejoice, Virgin Mary, for you alone have rooted out all the heresies."[27]

*c. **Crown of goodness.*** In the last part, which Poiré calls "Crown of goodness," Mary is given titles that depict her as caring for all those suffering physically or mentally, in their bodies or their spirits: *"refuge of sinners", "mother of orphans", "joy of the just"*, and *"advocate ever near us in life and in death."* Here again Montfort drew on the traditional fund, which down the centuries people have enriched through their own experience of Mary's care and assistance of

Christian people. The Church has recognized her as the refuge of sinners who invoke her in the Hail Mary: "Pray for us, sinners." The expressions of this confidence are infinitely varied. Montfort may have borrowed the second salutation, *"Mother of orphans,"* from some unidentified ancient author. On the other hand, the expression *"Laetitia justorum," "Joy of the just,"* is similar to *"Laetitia sanctorum,"* which occurs in a Marian prayer "made up of titles" found in a manuscript reporting the customs of the monks of Monte Cassino. The prayer is said to date back to the early twelfth century.[28] The last salutation, *"Adjutrix,"* occurs in the prayer *"Oratio ad sanctam Mariam,"* found in the Book of Nonnaminster, which dates back to the middle of the eighth century: *"Adjutrix apud Patrem omnipotentem"*.[29] It also occurs in other places, for example, in an eighth- and ninth-century Anglo-Saxon collection of prayers known as the Book of Cerne: *"Esto mihi salvatrix et adjutrix apud deum et dominum nostrum iesum christum."*[30]

Each of the salutations in the three crowns ends with the acclamation *"Gaude, Maria Virgo: Rejoice, Virgin Mary. Gaude millies: Rejoice for ever and ever."* A large number of prayers inspired by liturgical antiphons repeat these acclamations in various ways: "Rejoice, Mary, Mother of God, ever a virgin. Rejoice, you who received joy from the angel. Rejoice, you who gave birth to the brightness of eternal light."[31]

4. Concluding prayer

Montfort has left us three prayers to Mary, which occur a. after the mysteries of the Rosary (MR 15); b. at the end of SM, as an appendix, along with a Prayer to Jesus: *"Prayer to Mary (for her faithful slaves)"* (SM 68); c. at the end of the Little Crown as a concluding prayer in Latin (MP 5) and in French (MP 13). Apart from a few minor modifications, they begin in the same way: *"Hail, Mary, daughter of God the Father"* (MP 13), *"Well-beloved daughter of the eternal Father"* (MR 15), *"Hail, Mary, most faithful spouse of the Holy Spirit"* (MP 13), *"Most faithful spouse of the Holy Spirit"* (MR 15), *"Hail, Mary, temple of the Blessed Trinity"* (MP 13). The last salutation does not occur in SM 68, and in MR 15 *"Hail, Mary"* is not repeated. Although the wording of the three prayers is different, the underlying thought is the same. Mary is addressed as Mother, Mistress, and Sovereign. The Little Crown is the only writing in which he calls her *"Queen of my heart."* He continues: *"My life, my consolation, my dearest hope, my very heart and soul. I belong to you entirely, and all that I possess is yours"* (MP 13). In SM 68 he writes: *"Hail, Mary, my joy, my glory, my heart and soul. You are all mine through God's mercy, but I am all yours in justice. Yet I do not belong sufficiently to you, and so once again, as a slave who always belongs to his master, I give myself wholly to you, reserving nothing for myself or for others."* The three prayers contain a formula of Consecration that in MR 15 reads: *"I consecrate myself to you with all that I have. I choose you today as my Mother and Mistress."* This is reminiscent of the *"Consecration of oneself to Jesus Christ, Wisdom incarnate, through the hands of Mary"* (LEW 225). In a sentence that epitomizes the life of complete dependence ensuing from the total gift of self, Montfort takes up a passage of the Consecration: *"Grant, gracious Mother, that I may be numbered among those whom you love and instruct, whom you guide, cherish and protect as your children"* (MP 13). Mary is to act as his Mother *"so that, through the Holy Spirit, your faithful spouse, and through you, his faithful spouse, Jesus Christ, your beloved Son may be formed in our hearts for the greater glory of God our Father, for ever and ever"* (MP 13). This conclusion is almost identical with the wording of the Consecration.

The influence of Saint John Eudes is most evident in this prayer. The beginning of the Little Crown's concluding prayer is a repetition of the salutations in "Salutation to the Blessed Virgin": "Ave Maria, Filia Dei Patris; Ave Maria, Mater Dei Filii; Ave Maria, Sponsa Spiritus Sancti; Ave Maria, Templum totius Divinitatis," which Montfort renders by *"totius sanctissimae Trinitatis."* In the same prayer, at the tenth Ave—corresponding to the tenth star in the crown mentioned in Revelation—John Eudes salutes Mary with the words "Ave Maria, Regina cordis mei" and continues with the words of the Salve Regina: "Mater, vita, dulcedo et spes mea carissima," which are identical with those in MP 5.[32]

III. Its Contents

The Little Crown is a compendium of all the mysteries of Mary and of the spiritual life lived in her dependence.

1. Doctrinal value

The series of salutations has nothing to do with "sterile or transitory affection, or with a certain vain credulity" reproved by Vatican II; rather it is inspired by "true faith, by which we are led to recognize the excellence of the Mother of God, and we are moved to a filial love towards our mother and to the imitation of her virtues."(LG 67) Although filled with the purest doctrine of the Church, the salutations are nonetheless pervaded with deep emotion. They are concerned with the divine maternity of Mary, her perpetual virginity, her universal mediation, her spiritual maternity, her ceaseless intercession, and her queenship, especially with regard to souls.

2. Connection with Montfort's other writings

A close examination of the Little Crown reveals that many passages—of which we give here only a few examples—correspond to Montfort's other writings in which he elaborates at length, and frequently the similar terms, the points mentioned in the Little Crown. A passage of TD says, *"God-made-man found freedom in imprisoning himself in her womb,"* and the first and second salutations of the Little Crown concern Mary carrying in her virginal womb the One who made her and *"whom the very heavens cannot enclose"* (MP 10). *"Treasury of all God's graces"* (MP 11) is reminiscent of TD 24, which says, *"God the Son imparted to his mother all that he gained by his life and death, namely, his infinite merits and his eminent virtues. He made her the treasurer of all his Father had given him as heritage. Through her he applies his merits to his members and through her he transmits his virtues and distributes his graces."* In MP 11, Mary is addressed as *"queen of the whole world,"* and TD 38 says that *"Mary is the queen of heaven and earth"* because *"it is principally in souls that she is glorified with her Son more than in any visible creature. So we may call her, as the saints do, Queen of all hearts"* (cf. MP 13). Finally, LEW 225 and 227 repeat MP 13, which gives a shortened version of the total consecration of oneself and, summarizing TD 201-212, repeats the principles guiding the life of dependence ensuing from the Consecration.

IV. Conclusion

The spiritual exercises prescribed for the Missionaries of the Company of Mary include *"the daily recitation of all fifteen decades of the Rosary, and the Little Crown of the Blessed Virgin at a convenient time"* (RM 29). However, the Little Crown is not mentioned among the prayers prescribed for the Daughters of Wisdom or as part of their devotion to the Blessed Virgin (RW 138-144). Interestingly, the Latin and vernacular texts of the Little Crown are included in GA as Morning Prayers to be said by both groups. The Latin text is given in MP 2-5 and, for the benefit of the Daughters of Wisdom, the vernacular text in MP 10-13. Montfort also recommends its recitation to all who have a genuine devotion to Mary. He merely mentions it as one of the optional exterior practices, such as *"the Rosary of six or seven decades in honor of the years Our Lady is believed to have spent on earth, or the Little Crown of the Blessed Virgin"* (TD 116). He describes the Little Crown as *"composed of three Our Fathers and twelve Hail Marys in honor of her crown of twelve stars or privileges."* In TD 234 he recommends its daily recitation *"if it is convenient."* TD 235 specifies that *"there are several ways of saying the Little Crown, but it would take too long to explain them here."* He suggests the following one, which he sets out elsewhere: *"Dignare me laudare te, Virgo sacrata; da mihi virtutem contra hostes tuos; then say the Creed, one Our Father, four Hail Marys and a Glory be; say again one Our Father, four Hail Marys, one Glory be; and so on. Conclude with Sub tuum praesidium."* [33] This is reducing the Little Crown to its simplest form, and it might be taken as enough to salve the conscience of those who have only a superficial devotion to Mary by giving them the impression of having done something to honor the Blessed Virgin. And so Montfort cautioned such people: *"I earnestly beg you, then, by the love I bear you in Jesus and Mary, not to be content with saying the Little Crown of the Blessed Virgin, but say the Rosary too, and if time permits, all its fifteen decades, every day"* (TD 254).

What conclusion are we to draw from all the above? Montfort recognizes that MP has a spiritual value as a means to keep up genuine devotion to Mary. As we have seen, its contents, its wealth of traditional doctrine, its inspiration drawn from the liturgy and the writings of ancient worthy authors, faithfully transmit the thought of the Church on Mary. The concluding prayer, in particular, summarizes the Mariology of Montfort in its speculative and emotional aspects. However, he does not single out this form of prayer as better than others that are equally good for most of those who have a genuine devotion to Mary. He mentions it as one of the *"exterior practices"* that, *"as far one's circumstances and state of life permit, should not be omitted through negligence or deliberate disregard"* (TD 257).

Since community prayers are the bearers of tradition, the Little Crown with its Marian invocations and consecration prayer, should be recited regularly. It is a treasure of authentic montfort spirituality and puts on our lips the praises sung by Montfort's followers from the earliest days. A certain creativity is also called for, so that the versicles correspond to the liturgical season.

H.-M. Guindon

Notes: (1) *Prières et célébrations montfortaines (Montfort Prayers and Celebrations),* duplicated ed., Rome 1986, 3. (2) Ibid. (3) P. Bernard, *Saint Bernard et Notre-Dame (Saint Bernard and Our Lady),* Desclée de Brouwer, Abbaye de Sept-Fons 1953, 183-184. (4) R. Laurentin, *Court traité de théologie mariale (A Short Treatise on Marian Doctrine),* P. Lethielleux, Paris 1959, 33. (5) M. J. Nicolas, *La doctrine mariale et la Théologie chrétienne de la femme (Marian Doctrine and the Christian Theology of the Feminine),* in *Maria,* 3:352. For more detail, cf. A Feuillet, *La Vierge Marie dans le Nouveau Testament (The Virgin Mary in the NT),* in *Maria,* 7:61. (6) R. Laurentin, *Court traité,* 33. (7) The Solesmes Benedictine monks published a new edition in two volumes of 788 and 856 pages respectively, Paris 1858; it is the edition referred to in this article: F. Poiré, .Paris 1858.. (8) F. Poiré, La Triple Couronne, 1:5. (9) Ibid., editors' preface, xi. (10) Ibid.,

2:689. (11) Ibid., 2:691. (12) "The servant of God to whom the Blessed Virgin addresses her message is clearly Fr. Eudes, as it is his usual way of referring to himself. But who was the messenger? An angel from heaven, or some soul privileged by God on earth, for example, Sister Marie? It is difficult to say. What is undeniable is that Fr. Eudes asserts that this method had been revealed to him by the Blessed Virgin." D. Boulay, *Vie du Vénérable Jean Eudes (The Life of the Venerable John Eudes),* vol. 1 (1601-1643), R. Haton, Paris 1905, 423. (13) Ibid., appendix, 97, note xix, *Salutation à la Sainte Vierge (Salutations to the Blessed Virgin).* (14) Ibid., 1:424, note 1: "It is written in golden lettering in the sacristy of Our Lady of Loretta, as reported by the author of the *Triple Crown of the Blessed Virgin,* treatise 4, chap. 60, 9." (15) PL 78:799A, 16, in H. Barré, *Prières anciennes de l'Occident à la Mère du Sauveur (Ancient Prayers of the West to the Mother of the Savior),* Lethielleux, Paris 1963, 36. (16) F. Poiré, La Triple Couronne, 2:690. (17) Ibid., 2:679. In SR 59 Montfort speaks first of the Lord's Prayer and the Angelic Salutation, then he says: *"In addition at the end of each decade, it is good to add the Gloria Patri, that is: Glory be to the Father, and to the Son, and to the Holy Spirit. As it was in the beginning, is now, and ever shall be world without end. Amen."* The way Montfort suggests this—"at the end of each decade it is good to add"—shows that it is a personal suggestion about something that nobody had done until then; it is therefore likely that this innovation, which later became a custom sanctioned by the Church, was first started by Montfort. In *Le Rosaire, Nouveau Manuel de la Confrérie (The Rosary, New Manual of the Confraternity),* St-Hyacinthe, 1942, 17, says about the Glory be: "The custom set in of saying it at the end of each decade, and it should be maintained." (19) Roman Vesperal, Maternity of the Blessed Virgin Mary, October 11, antiphons 1 and 2 of Second Vespers. (20) This text by Bishop Fulbert of Chartres reads: "Sancta et immaculata perpetua Virgo Maria, quibus te laudibus referam nescio, quia quem coeli capere non poterant, tuo gremio contulisti, et uberibus lactasti." PL 78:734C, in H. Barré, *Prières anciennes,* 160. (21) Feast of the Holy Trinity, Evening Prayer I. (22) Ibid., Morning hymn. (23) Ibid., Morning intercession. (24) It is the etymological meaning of "to esteem," from the Latin "aestimare," "aes" meaning bronze; therefore, to value as highly as bronze, which in the old days was most valuable. (25) S. De Fiores, *La place de Marie dans la prière de l'Eglise, Réflexion théologique (The Place of Mary in the Prayer of the Church, a Theological Reflection),* in EtMar 43 (1982), 106. (26) H. Barré, *Prières anciennes,* 50-51. (27) Montfort speaks of heresies on several occasions, especially in TD 167: *"Mary alone has crushed all heresies, as we are told by the Church under the guidance of the Holy Spirit: Sola cunctas haereses interemisti in universo mundo. . . . A devoted servant of hers will never fall into formal heresy or error."* (28) H. Barré, *Prières anciennes,* 254, 6. (29) Ibid., 55. (30) Ibid., 56. (31) Ibid., 282, note 12. (32) D. Boulay, *Vie du Vénérable Jean Eudes,* 97. (33) The influence of Fr. Poiré, who wrote, "It is customary to say the Creed at the end," is clearly visible here. In one of the methods for saying it, Montfort placed the Creed at the end. Fr. Poiré goes on: "However, some add the Salve Regina with the antiphon *Sub tuum Praesidium,* the verse *Ora pro nobis, sancta Dei Genitrix,* and the Prayer *Concede nos*" (F. Poiré, La Triple Couronne, 2:691), whereas Montfort ends with one of the three Prayers to Mary, following in this the example of ancient authors who wrote their *Oratio ad Sanctam Mariam.*

LITURGY

SUMMARY

"Every liturgical celebration . . . is a sacred action surpassing all others. No other action of the Church can equal its efficacy by the same title and to the same degree" (SC 7). Echoing the Second Vatican Council, the Catechism of the Catholic Church declares: "In the liturgy of the Church, God the Father is blessed and adored as the source of all the blessings of creation and salvation with which he has blessed us in his Son in order to give us the Spirit of filial adoption . . . The whole liturgical life of the Church revolves around the Eucharistic sacrifice and the sacraments."[1]

We cannot expect that Saint Louis de Montfort lived the magnificent liturgical spirit ushered in by the Second Vatican Council. Moreover, he was certainly not a liturgist in any technical sense of the term. As a preacher of parish missions, he was, nonetheless, quite involved in the liturgical life of his people. His liturgical apostolate—if the expression may be used—was, rather, to strengthen among the countryfolk of northwestern France the Tridentine liturgical reforms. This article will briefly examine some of the liturgical practices of his time and then try to discover the role of the liturgy in the life and teachings of the saint.

I. LITURGICAL PRACTICES OF XVII CENTURY FRANCE

A thorough study of the liturgy in France during the seventeenth century would include explanations of the work of Jean Mabillon (+1707)[2] and Edmund Martene (+1739),[3] Benedictines from Saint-Germain-des-Prés in Paris, along with the history of the liturgical reforms stipulated by the Council of Trent. However, not only is that field well documented,[4] but our interest here deals mainly with the liturgy as it was lived in the French countryside where Montfort exercised his preaching apostolate. We will, then, limit ourselves to some of the more important liturgical practices which were integral to Catholic life during Montfort's milieu.

1. The Sunday Liturgy

J.B. Thiers in his free-spirited, four-volume *Treatise on Superstitions* (1697-1704), makes reference to city churches where professional people, married women, and servants all assist at more than one daily Mass, each person praying his or her own devotions.[5] Few receive communion. In the country side, life on Sunday revolves around the Mass in the morning and Vespers in the afternoon. Sunday Eucharist was usually celebrated around ten o'clock, preceded by the blessing of holy water, and a procession inside or outside the Church accompanied by prayers and popular hymns. After the Gospel was sung in Latin, the pastor removed his chasuble and ascended the pulpit situated in the center of the nave. A series of announcements on a variety of topics, followed by the proclamation of the banns of marriage, and directives from the Bishop preceded the reading of the Gospel in the vernacular and the Sunday homily. The homily was a highlight of the Eucharistic liturgy; it was usually very long, often dealt more with morals rather than doctrine itself, and often did not relate directly to the readings of the day. J.J. Olier remarks that "when the sermon is over, very little of it is remembered by the common folk; yet, the long ceremonies are visual sermons. . .".[6] He also notes: "We know that Mass is a sacrifice that one offers to God, at which one must assist on the days specified by the Church, but that is about all. Few people know that our most important duty is to consecrate ourselves to God as victims."[7]

Communion, as a general rule, was received only on important feast days or to fulfill the Easter duty, even though the Council of Trent desired that the faithful be so disposed that they would receive communion at each Mass (22nd session, 1562). However, books like Antoine Arnaud's treatise, *On Frequent Communion* (1643) influenced the faithful to stay away from communion: for, as Saint Vincent de Paul noted, Arnaud had so exaggerated the dispositions necessary for the reception of communion that "even Saint Paul would not be worthy."[8] He also remarked that the reception of the Eucharist had become markedly less frequent. The influence of Jansenism on priests (often manifested in an extreme severity in the sacrament of confession) and people, strongly restricted the reception of Holy Communion. There were, however, two ceremonies which did involve all the people: the "kiss of peace" at the offertory procession when the paten (or a metal plaque on which a crucifix was engraved) was kissed by the people. And at the end of the Mass, there was the distribution of blessed bread. Devotion to the Blessed Sacrament itself was strong. Although confirmation was usually received at the age of seven, First Communion was only permitted at about the age of thirteen or fourteen.

The Council of Trent demanded that children from the ages of seven to fourteen be given an hour's catechism lesson every Sunday. This obligation of every pastor became widespread from about the year 1660.[9] Finally, Sunday would not be complete without parish Vespers, often introduced by an instruction for adults and followed by Benediction of the Blessed Sacrament.[10]

2. Popular Devotions

Popular devotions were strong at the time of Saint Louis de Montfort. The post-Tridentine reform tried to establish a separation between what is precisely "liturgy" and what is not, in order to eliminate anything which was "superstitious" in popular devotions. The life of the people of northwestern France was permeated with the faith which was firmly embedded in their culture. Integral to the life of every Catholic family was the frequent sign of the Cross (often made and even cut into the loaf of bread), the use of Holy Water, blessings of all kinds, and village processions on feasts and in times of danger and thanksgiving. Despite the opposition of the Jansenists, devotion to the Sacred Heart began to spread throughout France; in 1670, a Votive Mass in honor of the Sacred Heart was celebrated in the seminary of Rennes. The Angelus marked the rhythm of the day, the rosary was widespread. The Stations of the Cross—eighteen of them beginning with the Last Supper—became more and more popular.[11] Benediction of the Blessed Sacrament either in conjunction with Vespers, or as an independent ceremony, was becoming extremely common.

These popular devotions were the fertile ground for parish missions which hoped to bring about a revival of the faith among the people.

II. Saint Louis de Montfort and the Liturgy

Considering the strong faith of the times and Louis Marie's involvement with the Church, the liturgy definitely had a strong influence on him as a child, as a seminarian, and as a priest. The article will explore liturgical influences in both his life and writings.

1. Liturgy in Montfort's Life

The importance that Saint Louis de Montfort gave to prayer is an indication of his yearning to share in the life of the Lord. In his time, that clearly included sharing in the life of the parish church especially through devotion to the Eucharist. Saint Louis de Montfort lived the prayer life of the Church of his time. His respect for the Eucharist, for the reception of Communion, his love for the rosary and for devotion to the Sacred Heart and to Our Lady are well known. At the St. Sulpice seminary, renowned for the beauty of its liturgy, Montfort was for a time master of ceremonies;[12] this opportunity deepened his sense of the sacred and is probably one of the primary sources of his great awe and reverence for the sacred mysteries and for houses of worship. What he later prescribed for his Missionaries of the Company of Mary reveals his own practice: Mass is generally to be celebrated daily after adequate preparation and followed by a time of thanksgiving; the Divine Office is to be recited in community when possible and always with modesty, attention and devotion (cf. MR 28-36). His biographers speak of Montfort's Eucharistic life as accompanied by private devotions, silence, and sufficient time, so that nothing is hurried. The Eucharist was the center of his life.

Montfort was never a parish priest. His vagabond life was dedicated to preaching, most especially parish missions. During the weeks of a mission, the priests of the parish were still in charge of the daily liturgy and the regular activities of the parish. Montfort and his confreres were to bring the parishioners to a deeper level of life in Christ. This was accomplished not only by stirring catechetical sermons but by dramatizations, banners, decorations, elaborate and long processions—with plenty of loud hymn-singing—and often by general confession. The montfort seal is evident in the elaborate procession which intertwined the solemn renewal of the baptismal vows through Mary.

Saint Louis de Montfort's well-known clarity and tenderness as a confessor (surely not appreciated by those with Jansenist leanings) also characterized his missions. His evident devotion while celebrating Mass was itself a powerful sermon of sincere love for the Divine Liturgy. His Christocentric devotion to the Mother of God not only strengthened, but at the same time, purified the respect of his hearers for Our Lady.

Saint Louis de Montfort's mission sermons show his interest in the liturgy, for he insisted that respect be shown to the church as the house of God.[13] This is evident in his determination to refurbish a church—working alongside the parishioners—as part of his renewal of a parish. The house of God was repaired, cleaned, and if necessary, tombs of parishioners within the church were removed. Reverential silence out of respect for the Real Presence was strongly encouraged. He also urged full participation—as much as was permitted in his day—in every aspect of worship. He wanted the people to become involved—as a community—in the prayer life of the church. For Montfort, this included frequent and fervent communion, renewal of baptismal vows, consecration to Jesus through Mary, processions, pilgrimages, etc. Regular confession, spiritual direction and hymn-singing all were promoted. Visits to the Blessed Sacrament and Benediction were encouraged as an expression of belief in the Eucharistic Lord, as a source of peace and blessings. All ceremonies took place with a reverential, yet intimate, awe for the Lord, present among his people gathered in his name. Canon Blain's testimony about the devout manner that Sunday was observed at Saint Laurent-sur-Sèvre reveals Montfort's extraordinary efforts to enhance public worship.[14]

2. The Liturgy in Montfort's Writings

The explicit references to the themes of the liturgy and sacraments that we find in Montfort's works do not reflect the concerns of a liturgist, but of a preacher. His intention was to lead the simple people of the countryside into ways of prayer; the sacramental life of the Church was not neglected.

a. Preaching. Saint Louis de Montfort's missionary preaching was founded on baptism and anchored in the Eucharist. The goal of his parish missions was to help the faithful rediscover the path which leads from the baptismal font to the Eucharistic table. His sermons hoped to stir the people to correspond with the graces of baptism in order to arrive at a profession of renewed faith, ratified by confession and Holy Communion (cf. MR 56). This new life in Christ can only be sustained by frequent reception of the sacraments, as he wrote in LPM 2: *"Do not fail to fulfill your baptismal promises and all that they entail, say your rosary every day either alone or with others and receive the sacraments at least once a month"* (cf. H 139,22; CG 2, 4). The act of consecration to Jesus through Mary is presented by Montfort as a movement from baptism to Eucharist (cf. TD 120-125, 231, SM 61).

b. Instructions on the Sacraments. Integral to a parish mission at Montfort's time were instructions on the sacraments. The theme of Father de Montfort's preaching was the Holy Mysteries, explaining the doctrine of the sacraments, their effects and the dispositions necessary to receive them worthily. Hymn 109, 7-15, eloquently reveals the content of the sacramental catechesis that Montfort offered to his people. Each of the sacraments are reviewed in the light of the teachings of the Church: *"as the Church does, so do I believe in the seven sacraments."* The missionary employs familiar explanations: visible signs of invisible grace, the sacraments fill us with grace *"to make us holy, to nourish us and to help us follow in his footsteps"* (H 109: 15). The stanza on Confirmation (H 109: 9) may be used as an example of Montfort's sound theological vision. The sacrament is considered as a dynamic anointing of the Spirit which so fills man's heart that he can boldly live the faith. The preceding stanza on Baptism speaks about "being in Christ Jesus" while Confirmation is seen more as "acting in Christ Jesus." If Baptism is a rebirth in grace by receiving the Holy Spirit, Confirmation is a dynamic infusion of divine energy to those who have been baptized, blessing them with the strength to constantly profess all that the faith teaches, even at the risk of one's life.

c. Marian devotion. Saint Louis Marie's devotion to Mary, and most especially his consecration to Eternal Wisdom through Mary, is theologically based. Montfort stresses that the Marian dimension (union, invocation, praise of Our Lady) cannot be omitted from the liturgical ceremonies of Christ's mysteries, because the Blessed Virgin is irrevocably united to the historical mysteries of Christ our Redeemer.[15]

Montfort also exhorts everyone to celebrate fittingly the Marian feasts of the liturgical year and, in a special way, the feast of the Annunciation. He recommends exterior practices which flow from sincere interior dispositions (cf. TD 243-248; SM 63). Interspersed throughout his writings are numerous Marian antiphons and liturgical titles, which demonstrate how his Marian devotion was fed by the liturgy.

d. Sacred places, times and symbols. The significance of the church building did not escape Montfort; in fact, it was the object of his special concern. In MR 16, he recommends that the director of the mission should become involved in the repair of the church so that the example of the missionaries will help make the people more responsible for the holy place. Many hymns make explicit reference to this sacred place, e.g., "Christian silence" in the church (H 23: 31-32); interior attitude and external behavior in a church (H 33: 16-21; H 136, 9-15); care of the sacred vessels and furniture (H 136, 2-4); the decor and beauty of the church (H 133: 4-5); reparation for sacrileges committed in churches (H 139: 66-67; H 158: 11-12).

Concerning times of prayer, Montfort reminds the faithful to observe the liturgical calendar, especially the Sundays and feastdays, Easter duty, Lent, etc. (cf. H 109: 34). The missionary also insists on time for personal prayer: in the morning and evening, before and after meals, during the course of the day (H 139: 7-25, 53). He also recommends times of retreat (H 139, 69) and of silence (H 23: 14).

Montfort made extensive use of sacred symbols. Not only did he carve statues and crucifixes, but he also designed banners of holy scenes to be carried in procession. His mission crosses—which he himself often made—were erected at the close of a mission. Also the calvaries he had constructed were visible, and at times grandiose symbols of God's enduring love.[16] He distributed paper crosses to the faithful during the renewal of baptismal vows (cf. CG 2, n.5) as a constant reminder of their incorporation into Christ. Yet, he knew the risks involved in the use of sacred symbols and guarded against exaggerations (cf. RW 36).

e. Popular Piety. During Montfort's time, simple devotions compensated for liturgies that were frequently poorly attended—for a variety of reasons—and also poorly understood. Saint Louis Marie's "congregation" was made up of simple countryfolk. He shows a remarkable understanding of their language and culture, a talent he used to bring the people closer to the tenderness of God. This is the fundamental reason for his numerous hymns (so often based on popular melodies), his magnificent processions, pilgrimages, his methods and formulas of prayers. It should be noted, however, that Father de Montfort was intent to eradicate any "false devotions" (cf. TD 92-10, 105-113) and root out any signs of exaggeration or superstition. He also insists on a certain hierarchy in expressions of devotion, repeatedly stating that the Blessed Sacrament comes first (H 139,60; TD 99). H 139 contains what could be called an index of devotions which Montfort believed should be cultivated; they are listed in order of importance and separated by the refrain, *"I serve God . . ."* They include devotion to the Eucharistic Lord, to Our Lady, to Saint Michael the Archangel, to our guardian angels, and to the souls in purgatory.

III. The Liturgy and Montfort Spirituality

Montfort wanted to be a mediator between the liturgical teachings of his time—inspired by the Council of Trent—and the common people. So too, it would appear that montfort spirituality today calls for the faithful implementation of the liturgical directives of the Church. Moreover, it is evident from Saint Louis Marie's life and writings that "liturgical spirituality" and "montfort spirituality" are not to be placed side by side; rather liturgical spirituality is intrinsic to the correct understanding and living of montfort spirituality. There are several conclusions which flow from this principle.

1. The Celebration of the Word of God

The introduction of the Lectionary affirmed the sacramental importance of the proclamation/hearing of the Word of God in the liturgy. It is in the Liturgy that Scripture is the dynamic Word that the Lord himself proclaims to us here and now, re-creating us according to his Word.[17] Saint Louis de Montfort's insistence on the importance of the Bible and on the preaching of the Word must be implemented today by a contemporary understanding of the Scriptures and the proclamation of the Word of God. Often, in Montfort's time, the proclamation of the Word of God in liturgical ceremonies was not given the importance it merited. The sermon was at times only an opportunity to instruct the faithful about useful facts. Today the Liturgy of the Word must be understood as that moment when the Spirit of Christ speaks to the Church to form believers into the image of the Son.[18]

2. Participation

Saint Louis Marie's insistence on the participation of all in his spiritual exercises, is to be imitated today, but according to contemporary liturgical teaching. Moreover, his constant use of various means to bring people to a fuller living of the Gospel can also be followed; again using today's liturgical standards; this calls for not the discarding but the updating of pilgrimages, processions, consecrations, hymns which were so profitably employed by Montfort. Themes of montfort spirituality can be deepened by the celebration of appropriate Bible services.

3. R.C.I.A.

The Rite of Christian Initiation of Adults must be considered as the obligatory reference point for the renewal of Christian life, a fundamental theme of montfort spirituality. Saint Louis de Montfort perceived the renewal to be centered on Baptism; a fuller contemporary understanding would speak of a Baptism-Confirmation-Eucharist renewal. In keeping with the mind of the R.C.I.A., the Eucharistic celebration on Sunday should be considered an excellent weekly renewal of the faith professed in Baptism and Confirmation and also as a commitment to a life ever more in conformity with the radical demands of the Gospel. The R.C.I.A. should become a source for a revised preparation for the renewal of the baptismal promises which Montfort so strongly stressed.

4. Times and places of prayer

Since the Incarnation, time is no longer only *chronos* (the succession of moments: clock time), but *kairos,* the fullness of time charged with the presence of the Eternal One, a time of grace and time to correspond with grace. Participation in the mysteries of Christ through the liturgy have special effects during the diverse liturgical seasons (cf. SC 102). The Liturgical Year must therefore be the criterion for all instruction in the faith. Parish missions—the chosen means of Saint Louis' apostolate—and all preaching, catechesis, must seriously take into account the liturgical calendar and be guided by it.

Formation in daily prayer should be drawn from the content, rhythm and style of liturgical prayer, especially the Liturgy of the Hours.[19] Montfort's example should be followed in making people aware and respectful of sacred places (their cleanliness, orderliness, beauty) and of appropriate statues, icons, and religious articles.

5. Marian devotion

It is evident that Marian piety should be given a paramount role among those who live montfort spirituality. It should be cultivated both by liturgical sources and by popular devotions inspired by the liturgy. Marian solemnities, feast days, memorials and liturgical seasons are all fundamental celebrations of authentic Marian devotion. The texts—not only scriptural but the orations, antiphons, prefaces, etc.,—of the feasts and votive Masses of Our Lady, are the sure source of a deeper knowledge of Mary and of solid devotion to her. The rosary itself should spring from the liturgy and be in harmony with it.

6. The Act of Consecration to Jesus through Mary

The Act of Consecration advocated by Saint Louis de Montfort is clearly based, from every point of view, on the sacraments of initiation. It is then during these ceremonies that this deeper union with Christ is continually revitalized. The Eucharist, the culmination and unceasing renewal of life in Christ, is the most perfect offering of God to us and of us to God. It is not by chance that Montfort tells his readers that the Consecration should be made during sacramental communion.[20] His thought makes explicit, through the formula of Consecration, this commitment sealed through the Body and Blood of Christ; a commitment which entails Mary's active presence and presents her as the model of perfect conformity with Christ.

Although some advocate that the act of Consecration should be made within the celebration of Mass—either after the homily, or after the prayer of the faithful, or after communion—it appears more in conformity with contemporary liturgical life that the Mass should not be used as a framework or container for the act of Consecration. The formula of Consecration (LEW 223-226) because of its literary style, its stress on individual and not community Consecration, and also its length, make it inappropriate for use during the Eucharistic celebration. Although Saint Louis Marie suggests that it be recited after communion (cf. TD 231; SM 61, 76), it must be remembered not only that he was thinking of private recitation of the formula, but also that in his day communion was more often than not distributed before or after Mass. If it appears necessary that the Consecration be made at the time of the day scheduled for the Eucharist, it should be done at the end of the Mass, after the Postcommunion prayer and preferably after a procession to the altar or shrine of Our Lady.

C. Maggioni

Notes: (1) CCC 1130, 1113; cf SC 6. (2) J. Mabillon, *De liturgia gallicana libri tres,* Paris 1685; reproduced in PL 72:99-448., J. Mabillon and M.Germain, *Museum italicum seu collectio veterum scriptorum ex bibliothecis italicis eruti,* 2 vol., Paris 1687-1689, including in vol. 1 the *Missale gallicum* of Bobbio *(Liber sacramentorum Ecclesiae gallicanae)* and in vol 2, under the title *Liber ritualis sanctae romanae Ecclesiae,* a series of *Ordines* and other documents governing the ancient Roman liturgy; reproduced in PL 78:851-1406. (3) E. Martene, *De antiquis monachorum ritibus,* 2 vol., Lyon 1690, E. Martene, *De antiquis Ecclesiae ritibus,* 3 vol., Paris 1700-1702: vol 1, *De antiquis sacramentorum ritibus;* vol 2, *Benedictiones sacrae;* vol 3, *De variis ad ecclesiasticam disciplinam pertinentibus ritibus,* E. Martene, *De antiqua Ecclesiae disciplina in divinis officiis celebrandis,* Lyon 1706. (4) Cf. J.H. Miller, *Liturgy, Articles on,* in *New Catholic Encyclopedia,* vol III., McGraw Hill, New

York, 1986, 857-942. (5) "Some people say the Rosary or other prayers and offices unconnected with the prayers said at Mass. Others meditate silently on subjects of their own choice. Others, again, follow the prayers and actions of the priest, either in meditating on the various parts of the Sacrifice or in reading carefully the prayers said by the priest." N. Le Tourneux, *De la meilleure manière d'entendre la sainte messe (On the Best Manner of Hearing Holy Mass)*, new ed., Paris 1687, 13. (6) J.-J. Olier, *Explication des cérémonies de la grande messe de paroisse (Explanation of the Ceremonies of the Parish High Mass)*, Paris 1657, 6-7. Even aside from any Jansenistic influence, in country districts it was customary to communicate at most three or four times a year; the *Rituel de Paris* mentions Easter Sunday, Pentecost Sunday, and Christmas Day. (7) *Conférences ecclésiastiques de La Rochelle (Ecclesiastical Conferences of La Rochelle)*, 1676, 163. (8) Vincent de Paul, *Correspondance*, ed. Coste, Paris 1921, 3:318-331, 362-373. (9) Cf. *Rituel de Paris*, 64. (10) Collections of Latin songs for Benediction were assembled in that period, for example, C. Thuet, *Appendix à la pratique du catéchisme romain, contenant certaines prières eucharistiques et solennels saluts . . . lesquelles depuis quelques années cette dévotion ayant commencé, se continue et amplifie (Appendix to the practise of the oman Catechism containing certain Eucharistic prayers and Solmn Benediction . . . which since they began a few years ago, have continued and grown)*, Paris 1634, 348. (11) A. Parvilliers, SJ, *Les stations de Jérusalem pour servir d'entretien sur la Passion de Notre Seigneur Jésus-Christ (The Stations of Jerusalem to Serve as Conversation on the Passion of our Lord Jesus Christ)*, Paris 1680. There are at least fifty-three editions of this in French. (12) Cf. S. De Fiores, *Itinerario*, 243-244. (13) Cf. Grandet, 142-144, 149. (14) Cf. Blain, 202-205. (15) See also *Praenotanda*, 7-18, in *Collectio Missarum de Beata Maria Virgine*, Libreria Editrice Vaticana, Vatican City 1987; Congregazione per il Culto Divino, *Orientamenti e proposte per la celebrazione dell'Anno mariano*, Libreria Editrice Vaticana, Vatican City 1987, published also in *Notitiae* 28 (1987) 342-396. (16) In W, Montfort names the communities to which he leaves *"the statues of the Calvary, with the crosses and banners."* (17) Cf. SC 7, 24; *Institutio generalis missalis romani*, n. 9: "When the Scriptures are read in Church, God Himself speaks to His people, and it is Christ, present in his Word, who proclaims the Gospel." (18) "Therefore, whenever it is gathered by the Spirit in a liturgical assembly and announces and proclaims the Word of God, the Church recognizes itself perfectly as the new People in which the covenant, sealed of old, reaches its perfection and fullness. All the faithful, who through Baptism and Confirmation have become messengers of the Word of God, after receiving the grace of hearing it, are to announce this Word of God in the Church and the world, at least through their life witness." *Ordo lectionum missae*, no. 7. (19) Cf. SC 100; *Institutio generalis de liturgia horarum*, nos. 20-32. (20) "*They should go to confession and Holy Communion with the intention of consecrating themselves to Jesus through Mary as his slaves of love. When receiving Holy Communion they could follow the method given later on* (see TD 266-273). *Then they recite the act of consecration*" (TD 231; see also SM 61, 76). This shows that Montfort regarded the Sacrament of Holy Communion preceded by the Sacrament of Penance as the appropriate moment to set the seal on the intention of giving oneself entirely to Christ through the hands of Mary.

LOVE

I. INTRODUCTION

"Take and read; it is always love that speaks." These words of St. Augustine, referring to the Bible, could be equally addressed to the works of Montfort. While not writing a specific treatise on love, love alone was the well-spring of his life and the inspiration of his activities. His predilection for the poor, his zeal and missionary preaching, and his writings were inspired by love. Apostolate of word or pen, the aim remained unaltered: *"That all who heard be inflamed with a renewed desire to love and possess Divine Wisdom"* in time and eternity (LEW 2).

To speak of love is to speak of personal relationship. The word itself evokes qualities inherent in personal relationship: reciprocity, depth, faithfulness, total commitment, and joy. For Montfort it is this love relationship with God that permeates, explains, and nurtures all other relationships. God is the source of all things, and to Him all must return. The initiative rests always with Him. He it is who first loved us, and He will continue to do so for all eternity. At the heart of Montfort's spiritual experience is the discovery of Love that has come; the certitude that Love is present and a preoccupation to receive it; and the hope that Love will come again for the final accomplishment of all things.

Under this triple heading, the theme of love will be explored in Montfort's works to discover with him how Love has come, Love is present, and Love will come again; and to learn from him how to respond to it.

II. LOVE'S SEASONS

1. Love that has come

Love desires to "be with." In the Rue du Pot de Fer, Montfort had a religious experience of the presence of God. It was with the traits of Divine Wisdom, one from all eternity with God, and at the same time through his loving Incarnation one with man, that Montfort experienced the immanence of God's presence. Time and space both ceased to exist as Montfort communicated with the Presence that enveloped him. Do not seek for a treatise of speculative theology on the Incarnate Word from Montfort. He surpasses this and offers the reader instead a marvelous and loving contemplation of the mystery of Jesus.[1] In the context of a sort of long meditation, he strives to communicate to the reader his experience, a meditation where, with mutual enlightenment, Gospel and Wisdom literature meet and merge. The first book of Montfort, LEW, concerns the relationship between God and man, with love as the focal point—the initiative on God's part, the response on man's part. A simple reading of the book will reveal the theme of Love, not only as present but as the source, inspiration, and substance of the work.

In chapters 2 to 5 Montfort describes Divine Wisdom as coexisting with God before time began. She (Wisdom) is not only creator of the universe but, because of her love for it, *"Mother of the universe"* (LEW 31). In creating man, she *"enkindled the fire of the pure love of God"* in his heart (LEW 37). Man, however, because of sin, *"has a heart of stone for God"* (LEW 39). *"Wonder of wonders, with boundless and incomprehensible love, this loving and sovereign princess offers herself in sacrifice"* (LEW 45) to save man. In the time preceding the Incarnation, she will *"show her love for him in countless ways"* (LEW 47).

Montfort then takes a chapter to expound on what it is that impels Eternal Wisdom to act thus towards man. *"The bond between Eternal Wisdom and man is beyond comprehension. Wisdom is for man and man is for Wisdom. She loves him as a brother and a friend. For man to withhold his heart from Wisdom or to wrench it from her would constitute an outrage"* (LEW 64). Montfort concludes that the logical outcome of such a love could lead only to the Incarnation: *"Finally, in order to draw closer to men and give them a more convincing proof of her love, Eternal Wisdom went so far as to become man"* (LEW 70) and continues to plead, *"Come to me; do not be afraid; I am just like you. . . . I love you"* (LEW 70). Everything in the actions and words of Divine Wisdom prove her love and attachment to man, a love that culminates in the Eucharist, *"a marvellous and loving invention of Eternal Wisdom."* A way of living and dying at the same time, and of abiding with men until the end of time (LEW 71). Montfort continues to describe Incarnate Wisdom, his actions, his attitudes, his words, his death. He sums up what he has discovered: *"He was given out of love, fashioned by love; therefore he is all love, or rather the very love of the Father and the Spirit"* (LEW 118). His very name, Jesus, *"which is the proper name of Incarnate Wisdom,"* signifies his distinctive character, *"which is to love and save men"* (LEW 120).

Under the guise of gentleness, Montfort perceives love at work in Jesus Christ, gentle in his words, his actions (LEW 122), and his manner (LEW 124-30). This contemplation of Christ concludes with a chapter on his Passion, where once again love is the beginning and the end. *"Of all the motives compelling us to love Incarnate Wisdom, the strongest in my opinion is the suffering he chose to endure for our sakes"* (LEW 154). Because of that suffering endured for love, *"the cross when it is well carried is the source, the food and the proof of love"* (LEW 176).

Finally, Montfort gives the means for acquiring Divine Wisdom, which is to enter into a closer and ever more loving relationship with Christ, for *"He asks only for our heart"* (LEW 209).

This brief survey reveals that at the heart of Montfort's spiritual experience was an encounter with Love Eternal—the Son of God—who has taken on our human nature. The Incarnation event is willed and directed by the love God has for man. Following the Bérullian school of thought, Montfort also knows that this same love manifested in Jesus remains real and active today in each individual and in all creation.[2]

2. Love present

a. States and mysteries extended into the present day. In the thinking of the French school of spirituality, the whole life of Christ, his actions, words, joys and sufferings, are considered to be epiphanies or sacraments of the eternal love of God for man. His life reveals and communicates to the world that which has forever dwelt in the heart of God, and will forever dwell there. Montfort's spiritual experience was strongly influenced by this certitude. For him, the only response to this transforming love was complete acceptance. "Contemplate, commune with, cooperate with" this love: such is the foundation of the Christian life.

b. Identify with Love present. Montfort, then, would follow Christ, modelling his life on that of the Christ of the Gospels. He would live abandoned to Divine Providence, for like Jesus he could say, *"I have a Father in heaven who knows all my needs"* (L 2). Living thus, he would communicate with Christ in his complete trust in his Father in heaven.

He would emulate the gentleness of Christ, which implies both mercy and compassion. He, the preacher who could proclaim the Gospel without compromise, would also find it imperative to emphasize the mercy of God. His friend and collaborator Pierre des Bastières attests: "He had such a horror of fundamentalist morality that he believed those who preached it caused more harm to the Church than preachers and confessors who were too lax. 'I would rather,' he confided, 'suffer in purgatory for having been too lenient with my penitents than for having been too severe.'"[3]

The Rosary also became for him a means of responding to a love that is constantly present. For him, the Rosary is above all a contemplation of Christ in an effort to become part of "his mysteries." Contemplation in order to become: such is the whole meaning of this prayer through which we attempt to be joined with Christ (SR 66).

c. Mary, perfect vessel of Divine Love. Montfort realized early in his spiritual journey that of all creatures Mary alone had completely responded to God in faith. She who was "blessed because she had believed" (Lk 1:45) was filled with God through the Holy Spirit; to her, then, would Montfort turn to learn how he too could be "filled" with God, divine Wisdom. "By the expression 'Jesus living in Mary,' he depicted the mystery of the Incarnation accomplishing in Mary that which she in turn would accomplish in man."[4]

In Mary, who responded fully in faith, Jesus is fully present. In confiding himself totally to her, Montfort, too, would receive the fullness of Christ. His trust in her was such that he did not hesitate to make her the mistress of his whole being. His asceticism consisted in becoming supple in her hands, like liquid bronze: *"One places in a mould only that which is liquid and molten . . . the old Adam must be melted and destroyed"* (TD 219). Finally, fear must be cast out. Total abandonment, or Holy Slavery, as Montfort calls it, demands complete trust leading to a purification of the heart, preparing it to receive the God Who comes. In what does the Holy Slavery of which Montfort speaks consist, if not the will to remove all obstacles to God's love and to have sufficient confidence to say, "Lord, love me as you will." Such a commitment demands complete faith in love. Mary possessed it, and Montfort, having discovered this, resolved to emulate her through *"the perfect practice of true devotion"* to Mary. Because he wished to love God as she did, he chose her for his *"mother and mistress"* (LEW 225).

d. The Cross, where Love is to be found. In most of his writings and throughout his life, the Cross is present. For him, "the cross of Love" comes before "love of the cross," for the "cross of Love" is the great sign of God's love. Montfort, publicly humiliated, familiar with failure, could and did identify with the Christ of Golgotha. The Cross assured him of a place near Christ, a Christ close to those who suffer and Montfort close to him through his own suffering. While not seeking suffering for suffering's sake, he would teach us that we must, nevertheless, see it as an instrument of love: sent in love and received in love.

True love demands self-emptying, but as Varillon remarks, in the very act of loving we become aware of our loving, becoming thus once more prisoners of our egoism. In suffering, however, neither pride nor pleasure has a place; we can become pure love. Montfort witnessed around him, and experienced no doubt within himself, the subtle machinations of self-love. Experience had taught him that only the Cross, i.e. failure, deprivation, and humiliation, was capable of purifying the heart, emptying it to receive God.

e. The poor, sacrament of love. The outcasts, the marginalized, those without power or voice, all whom we designate "the poor," were for Montfort a "love" where he encountered and served his Lord. This was a constant in his life from his early years in college, when he visited the hospitals, until his death. The characteristic of love is to "be with, to be close." Montfort remained all his life close to the poor—physically, culturally, and spiritually.

First of all, physically: Montfort did not "talk" poverty; he lived it: in his food, clothing, shelter, bodily needs—his whole life style. He loved, and because he loved, he respected the poor, sharing their life, whether that of the sick, the outcasts who sought refuge in the hospices, or the peasants of Lower Brittany referred to by Blain with disdain as "sub-human."[5] Small wonder that the beneficiaries of his charity at the General Hospital of Poitiers repeatedly called for the return of "Father de Montfort, who so loves the poor." He shared their deprivations, their food, and the contempt in which they were held, for he chose to identify with the poor at a period in which they were particularly abused.[6]

Montfort was close to the poor in the language and practices he used when preaching a mission. Many of his eccentricities could be attributed to the fact of his being only too aware of the gap that existed between the culture of the clergy and that of the people, and to his desire to proclaim the message in a language and manner that would touch the ordinary people. He was sensitive to their need for visual aids, to see and touch. Could the motive for the erection of the Calvary of Pontchateau have been to give to the poor their own "Holy Land" (cf. H 164)? At a period of time when the Church, wary of a combination of magic and devotion, was distancing herself from popular religious ceremonies, Montfort corrected and used them as a means of evangelization.[7]

Finally, he was close to the people spiritually. He did not hesitate to call them to a deep and active faith. "He had confidence in the Christian potential of the simple faithful."[8] It was his desire to serve God in His little ones. Towards the end of his life, he ministered to another category of the poor, less apparent but nonetheless real: the spiritual poverty of the population of the Aunis. He turned his back on the spectacular conversions, and the enthusiastic crowds, for a work of evangelization far less rewarding. This is proof of the conviction in his heart that the poor, in whatever guise they presented themselves, were none other than Jesus Christ pleading for his love. To Mère Andrée, who nursed him, confused at having failed to recognize him, he replied, *"Forget Monsieur Grignion, he is of no account; think of Jesus Christ; he is all, and it is him that you find in the poor."*[9]

3. Love that is to come

Montfort was not the only one of the spiritual authors of his day to have reflected on and written about the last days. Unlike his contemporaries, however, he envisaged this final period of history as a final manifestation of the love of a changeless God. *"The plan adopted by the three persons of the Blessed Trinity . . . is adhered to each day in an invisible manner throughout the Church and they will pursue it to the end of time until the last coming of Jesus Christ"* (TD 22).

To emphasize his convictions concerning the end times, he would go so far as to correct certain of his sources, bringing what is too negative in them into line with his own more positive vision.[10] Where the visionary Marie des Vallées, whom he quotes as one of his sources (TD 47), speaks of "a coming in fire and judgement," Montfort writes instead of *"a coming of a fire of pure love"* (PM 16-17).[11]

What will they be like, these saints, apostles of the end times, if not *"Ministers of the Lord, who like a flaming fire will enkindle everywhere the flames of divine Love."* For they themselves *"will carry the pure love of God in their heart"* (TD 56) and *"leave behind them nothing but the gold of love which is the fulfillment of the whole Law"* (TD 58).[12] For Montfort, man's future is in love.

III. Conclusion

The great experience and intuition of Montfort was to have realized in the depths of his being that he was the unique object of the love of the Eternal Divine Wisdom. He encountered this Divine Wisdom in all its force and energy. Overwhelmed by a Love that enveloped and upheld him and even sacrificed itself for him, Montfort realized he had nothing to offer in return but his human misery. From Mary, through whom Love came into the world, he would learn how he, too, should receive him in his daily life. He would serve him in the least of his poor and, in so doing, would anticipate the last coming of Love at the end of time. For Montfort love is the guiding force of this great cosmic and human event, in some ways "the Law" of God himself (H 5:5). As *"perfect love casts out fear"* (1 Jn 4:18), Montfort could sing: *"Divine Jesus, I love you, / Not through fear, / Not for reward, / But for thyself alone"* (H 5:45-46).

G. Madore

Notes: (1) A. Bossard: *Incarnation,* notes of montfort summer session, Saint-Laurent-sur-Sèvre 1991, 2. (2) "The events of his (Jesus') life take place only once; they are over as regards their actual happening, but they are still present as regards their power, and their power will never pass away, any more than will the love with which they were accomplished." A. Molien: *Les grandeurs de Marie d'après les écrivains de l'école française (The Grandeurs of Mary according to the Writers of the French School),* DDB, Paris 1934, 42. (3) Th. Rey-Mermet: *Louis-Marie Grignion de Montfort,* Nouvelle Cité, Paris, 1984, 108. (4) A. Bossard, *Incarnation.* (5) J. Geraud: *Louis-Marie Grignion de Montfort, un point de vue du psychiatre (Louis Marie Grignion de Montfort: A Psychiatric Point of View),* in *Saint Louis-Marie Grignion de Montfort vu par l'historien, le psychiatre et le théologien (Saint Louis Marie Grignion de Montfort, Viewed by the Historian, the Psychiatrist, and the Theologian),* Montfort Generalate, Rome, 1973, 55. (6) R. Mandrou: *Grignion de Montfort et son temps: Perspectives historiques (Grignion de Montfort and His Times: Historical Perspectives),* in *Saint Louis-Marie Grignion de Montfort vu par l'historien, le psychiatre et le théologien,* 18-19. (7) Ibid. (8) Th. Rey-Mermet, *Louis-Marie,* 119. (9) Ibid., 76. (10) On this topic see S. De Fiores, *Le Saint-Esprit et Marie dans les derniers temps selon Grignion de Montfort (The Holy Spirit and Mary in the End Times according to Grigion de Montfort),* in *Bulletin de la Société Française d'Etudes Mariales* (1986), 133-171. (11) S. De Fiores, *Le Saint-Esprit,* 150. Montfort makes further reference to this final coming of love in TD 241 and perhaps in H 42:15. (12) The same idea is to be found in PM 8, 21, 24.

LOVE OF ETERNAL WISDOM

SUMMARY

I. REDISCOVERY OF A FUNDAMENTAL WORK.

II. BACKGROUND OF THE BOOK:
1. The manuscript;
2. The title;
3. The date of composition;
4. For whom was it written?

III. SOURCES:
1. Spiritual writers;
2. Biblical Wisdom:
   a. The Wisdom theme,
   b. The Book of Wisdom;
3. Montfort and Scripture.

IV. PROFILE OF THE BOOK:
1. Literary profile: structure and division;
2. Theological profile.

V. LEW AND ITS INTERPRETATIONS:
1. The silence of the biographers;
2. The definitive edition (1929) and the renewal of montfort studies;
3. Recent interpretations.

VI. RELEVANCE OF THE BOOK TODAY:
1. Christocentrism;
2. Theology of Creation;
3. Theology of the Redemption.

I. REDISCOVERY OF A FUNDAMENTAL WORK

Of all the works of Montfort, LEW can certainly lay claim to being the least known by people at large. We have lost count of the number of editions published of TD, SM, SR, and FC. But in the case of LEW, we had to wait until 1929 for a definitive edition, and translations into other languages had also to wait a long time and are still far less numerous than those of TD.

Nevertheless a number of those who know montfort spirituality well have not failed to note the great doctrinal value of LEW and its fundamental importance for an understanding of Montfort's work as a whole. Besides considering it "an academic treatise" and a "great work" equal to the TD, "the second being only a magnificent commentary on chapter 16 of the first and its indispensable complement. The Love of Eternal Wisdom is a fundamental book. It is this book alone which gives us the overall view of montfort spirituality."[1] J.-M. Dayet expresses a similar opinion: "Louis Marie Grignion de Montfort appears here, then, . . . as an undoubted contemplative and lover of Eternal Wisdom. This point of view is fundamental for a full understanding of his spirituality."[2] For his part. M. Quéméneur underlines the missionary dimension of the book: "While it is true that the last work of a writer expresses a more developed stage of his thinking, yet his first work, even if it is imperfect in its construction, is often the one that best reveals his interior strength and the direction he is taking. . . . This secret [the contemplation of Wisdom in search of humanity] was for Montfort the revelation of God's missionary dynamism and therefore of all missionary dynamism."[3]

If popular opinion has come down in favor of TD, is it because Montfort was less successful in popularizing his views on Wisdom? Or, rather, was this book less in touch with the tastes of the Christian public? Whatever the case, LEW deserves to be known widely today, especially in a period that is particularly restless and searching for a Wisdom that can give meaning to life and to the unfolding of history, and at a time when believers, to their great good fortune, have made renewed contact with a theology and a spirituality nourished primarily on the Bible.

II. Background of the Book

1. The manuscript

The manuscript, which is kept today at the General House of the Company of Mary in Rome, is in a remarkable state of preservation. It is easily legible and is, in the opinion of the editors of OC, in the handwriting of Montfort himself.[4] More recent and deeper studies of the handwriting of the manuscript, carried out by H. Frehen[5] and R. Paceri,[6] come to a different conclusion, however, and find in the manuscript the traces of four different copyists, among them Mulot, Vatel, and Besnard.

2. The title

The title can be read quite distinctly at the beginning of the manuscript. There is, however, a question about the use of the genitive *"of Eternal Wisdom."* Does this have a subjective or an objective meaning? In other words, did Montfort intend to give us his understanding of the love that Eternal Wisdom has for humanity, or was he more concerned with inspiring his readers to love Eternal Wisdom? The lengthy development of the theme of the first part of the work inclines us to opt for the objective interpretation, though the second can certainly not be excluded. Besides, the ambiguity in the title could well be deliberate and might be part of the richness of the work.

3. Date of composition

According to general opinion, LEW is a work of Montfort's youth, dating from the first years of his priestly ministry, perhaps during his stay in Paris (1703-1704) near the community founded by Poullart des Places. Montfort was one of the "poor scholars" whom this community welcomed and whose theological and spiritual formation it looked after. In the fifth book of his *Vie de Louis-Marie Grignion de Montfort (Life of St. Louis de Montfort)*, Besnard tells us: "I have it on the authority of the one who was superior of the house after M. Desplaces, and who had been his student, that one day M. Grignion preached to them on wisdom and gave a very beautiful paraphrase of the book of the Bible that bears this name."[7] The main theme of this preaching by Montfort and the explicit reference to Wis naturally make us think of LEW. Picot de Clorivière's reference to the same event is no less significant: "This conversation was like a paraphrase of those magnificent praises Solomon addresses to wisdom; but in examining this wisdom, he was at pains to point out that he was speaking not only of this wisdom given to Solomon, and still less of the wisdom of the wise men of the age, but also of the wisdom of the Gospel, of that wisdom Jesus Christ taught us by his example and by his words."[8]

Among those favoring a later date of composition are Dayet, who would place the preaching in Paris on Wisdom at the end of Montfort's life (for example, in 1713), and Frehen, who was led by a comparative study of the manuscripts of H 46 and H 100-102 and LEW and SR, to propose as the date of the writing or at least the copying of all of these works, "the last two years of Fr. de Montfort's life."[9]

The question of an earlier or a later date leads us to the following question: did LEW serve as the basis for these conferences on Wisdom, or was it the other way round? We have no proof either way, although it was Montfort's usual practice to present in writing what he had first of all taught and passed on in his preaching. But that does not imply a date for the written text much later than the events of 1703-1704.

To sum up, the reasons that favor dating the work around 1703-1704 are: 1. the appearance of both the vocabulary and the theme of Wisdom in the letters dating from this period (L 14-17, 20); 2. the evidence of Besnard on the conversations Montfort had with the seminarians gathered by Poullart des Places, whose content was close to the matter dealt with in LEW; 3. the more scholarly and theoretical character of the work, compared with the popular character of TD, where Montfort shows himself to be an accomplished popularizer with the benefit of lengthy missionary and pastoral experience. This does not exclude, however, the possibility that Montfort may have had his work transcribed during the last two years of his life.

4. For whom was it written?

Who is the *"dear reader"* whom Montfort addresses (LEW 5)? We have just seen that a first audience might well be those who benefitted from Montfort's preaching in Paris on Wisdom, namely, young seminarians in formation. This would explain the rather theoretical and scholarly nature of the work.

Another possibility is that he wrote LEW originally for the religious communities that he had founded and to which he was now offering a sort of "book of life." The correspondence he conducted with Marie Louise and the first moves he made to found the Daughters of Wisdom speak of the importance of the theme of the acquisition of Wisdom in Montfort's own spiritual journey and in that of the woman who joined him in his apostolic work. But there are absolutely no indications from Montfort himself or from the first Daughters of Wisdom to show that LEW was either written or received as a work primarily destined for the community of the Daughters of Wisdom.

The same must be said of A. Balmforth's position; he believes he can pick out "some interesting and positive signs to suggest that he was writing especially, if not exclusively, for the future Company of Mary."[10] He rightly recalls the missionary dimension of LEW and its many affinities with the ideal Montfort holds out to his future missionaries, and we cannot but agree with the general judgement expressed by Balmforth when he says: "Montfort wished this work to serve as an inspiration and guide for those whom he might gather around him to share his life and missionary activity."[11] We can scarcely go further than this, and there is nothing in Montfort's text (not even the Latin quotations) that allows us to restrict his intended audience to the disciples of Montfort alone. Above all, the distinction sometimes made between "missionary priests" and "ordinary lay folk" cannot be sustained; it is not only unthinkable today it was so even then in the idea of popular evangelization, which was so dear to Montfort.

Montfort is clearly writing for a much larger audience, whom he describes as *"chosen souls seeking perfection"* (LEW 14), which should not be interpreted here in an elitist or restrictive sense (as opposed, perhaps, to SM 1) but in the Pauline sense of those who have made an option for Jesus Christ and his Gospel (1 Cor 2:6), in other words, all Christians. Indeed, this is the most obvious sense in the light of the Beatitudes, which are quoted every so often in the text (LEW 10, 51, 153) and which remind us of those who hear the Word: "Rather blessed are those who hear the Word of God and keep it!" (Lk 11:28). Similarly, we could note how Montfort loves to emphasize the universal character of the audience that Wisdom looks for: "*What man would not love him and search for him with all his strength. All the more so since he is an inexhaustible source of riches for man who was made for him and infinitely eager to give himself to man*" (LEW 63; see also LEW 30).

III. Sources

In contrast to what he did in TD, where he claims to have "*read nearly all the books which treat of devotion to the Blessed Virgin*" (TD 118) and gives us a list of the writers who encouraged such a devotion (TD 159-163), Montfort shows himself in LEW to be in some ways more eclectic. Even though the allusions are sometimes brief, we can count about fifteen authors whom he quotes or saints whose testimony he cites: Gregory, Augustine, John Chrysostom, Rupert, Bernard, Thomas Aquinas, Henry Suso, Mary Magdalene de Pazzi, Teresa, John of the Cross, etc. There is nothing surprising in the breadth of his documentation. What is surprising is the fact that he makes no mention of his masters in the French school of spirituality, who nevertheless supplied him with a great deal of his material.

1. Spiritual writers

Among the spiritual writers who influenced Montfort's writing of LEW, three names stand out: Henry Suso, Jean-Baptiste Saint-Jure, and Amable Bonnefons. Of these three, only the first is explicitly quoted by Montfort (LEW 101-102, 132). Nevertheless his dependence on the other two is just as sure, as is shown by the countless similarities in wording and in the themes.[12] Still, there are also important differences in each instance.

Montfort may well have taken his basic inspiration and part of the title of LEW from the book by Henry Suso, a Dominican religious, since the French translation of the *Horologium Sapientiae* of Blessed Suso was called *Livre de la Sagesse Eternelle (The Book of Eternal Wisdom)*. It first appeared in a French version in 1392 and rapidly became very popular among spiritual people, second only to *The Imitation of Christ*. But the similarities between Montfort's text and that of Suso are, taken together, fairly slight, while the differences between the two are much more noteworthy.

The first important difference lies in the biblical character of Montfort's work. Suso, in a book which is about the same length as Montfort's, quotes exactly three verses of Scripture: Wis 8:2 (chap. 1) and Sir 24:19-20 (chap. 7), and it seems that for him Wis is in fact Sir (chap. 7). In this respect, Montfort is clearly different from his predecessor, as we will see later. A second significant difference lies in the place given to the mystery of the Cross. In Montfort, this theme is extremely important (parts of chap. 9-10 and the whole of chap. 13-14), but it is seen in a wider and more global view, which includes Creation, the history of salvation, and the Incarnation. In Suso, attention is focused entirely on the mystery of the Passion, and nothing is said of Creation or the other phases of the history of salvation.

Three other works are worthy of note. First of all, there is the monumental work of the Jesuit Jean-Baptiste Saint-Jure (1588-1657), *De la connaissance et de l'amour du Fils de Dieu Notre Seigneur Jésus-Christ (On the Knowledge and Love of the Son of God, Our Lord Jesus Christ)*, the first edition of which appeared in 1634. This volume would have had a particularly important influence, given that Montfort copies or makes a summary of whole passages of it (for example, in LEW 8-12, 66-67, 69, 154-166).

We should notice, once again, two significant differences. And again, the first concerns the biblical sources. The whole of Saint-Jure's book is deeply scriptural, and there are abundant quotations. But even here Montfort shows a clearly more systematic use of the Wisdom theme. While it is true that Saint-Jure gives a well-developed commentary, he limits himself to "two truly remarkable passages of Sacred Scripture that contain several motives to bring us to the love of our Lord Jesus Christ." These two passages are Prov 8 and Wis 6-8. This is certainly an important subject for him, but it is much less than the use Montfort will make of the Wisdom theme. The second difference is of a Christological nature. Both books are from the French school of spirituality, and their authors speak extensively of the same person, Jesus Christ. But among all the titles Saint-Jure gives to him, Wisdom is lacking. On this point Montfort is much closer to Suso.

We should add another book by Saint-Jure, which was certainly known to Montfort, since he borrows several passages from it in N 308. This is *The Spiritual Man, where the Spiritual Life is Treated in its Principles* (Marbre-Cramoisy, Paris 1685), from which Montfort takes the idea of Wisdom (pp. 392-393), the application of the Wisdom literature to the gift of Wisdom in imitation of Salazar (p. 392), and the first three means for acquiring Wisdom (pp. 403-407).[13]

We note also the more immediate influence of *The Little book of Life Which Teaches How to Live and Pray Well* (1st ed. 1650), by the Jesuit Amable Bonnefons (1618-1653), on chapter 12 of LEW. Indeed, the first forty-nine "*Oracles of Incarnate Wisdom*" are a copy of the complete list of "general rules for good living, found in the sacred words of our Lord Jesus Christ," that Bonnefons quotes. Montfort copied this list as a whole, but then added another thirteen, the last of which (Matt 11:25-26) has a very strong sapiential flavor and all of which are in line with the evangelical radicalism lived out by Montfort.

2. Biblical Wisdom

But the basic inspiration for Montfort comes first of all from the Bible. Certainly, his choice of Biblical sources and his interpretation of them owe a great deal to the exegesis of his day, notably to the translation and commentary of Le Maître de Sacy. But Montfort cannot be reduced to his sources, and we must recognize, with M. Gilbert, that none of his predecessors among the spiritual writers accorded quite so much importance to Wis (cf. below).

This biblical character of Montfort's little treatise did not escape the notice, as we shall see, of a first generation of interpreters of LEW (Huré, Dayet, Bombardier). But the most rigorous and complete study of this aspect remains that of M. Gilbert, SJ, a specialist on Wis and the other biblical Wisdom writings. In a well-argued study,[14] he shows Montfort's originality and the validity of his "spiritual exegesis." The publication of this article in a theological review of very high international standing must surely have made LEW better known in circles that have not always been reached by recent montfort studies. Several years later, the author of this present article took up again the question of the biblical sources of LEW.[15] Here we need not go into all the detail found in these two studies. But let us recall briefly the main lines.

a. The Wisdom theme. LEW displays an unusual characteristic, not only among the works of Montfort but within the whole corpus of Christian spiritual writing, in making systematic use of the Wisdom theme. Certainly, his other writings are also full of biblical quotations, but never before had he made a systematic effort to explore a complete theme in the Bible, including its fulfillment and its echoes in the NT as in LEW. That is what is so impressive. It presupposes clearly a remarkable mastery of the Bible as a whole, and a deliberate effort at synthesis. What is so striking here is not the detail of interpretation of some isolated verse or other but the fact that a vast network of texts is used: a large part of the Wis, some major chapters from Prov and Sir, the Prologue of Jn (filled with references to Wisdom), Jas (the only real Wisdom writing in the NT), and the passages that relate to the Wisdom of Jesus.

b. The Book of Wisdom. It is, nevertheless, as we might expect, Wis that claims the major share of attention in Montfort's reflection. No less than 140 verses (out of a total of 435 verses in Wis, or about one-third of the book) are cited by him, and are often quoted and commented upon. We should note, too, that Montfort used the central section of Wis, chapters 7-9: 65. Most of the verses quoted by Montfort in fact come from this section. Taken all in all, Montfort truly made Wis his own and used it as the basic framework of his own book, so much so that this can be seen as a veritable "paraphrase" (Besnard and Picot de Clorivière) of the biblical book. So we can validly ask, with M. Gilbert,[16] whether there is any other work in the Christian spiritual tradition that owes so much to Wis.

3. Montfort and Scripture

Over and above the interpretation of individual verses, the number of scriptural quotations and their importance in the whole structure of LEW lead us to take a wider look at the use Montfort makes here of Scripture.

a. Montfort shows a great respect for the text. Thus, for example, he presents us with long passages, while assuring us that he will add nothing to them (LEW 5, 20, 52). He sends his reader, as it were, back to the biblical text itself so that he may draw his own conclusions from it.

b. But at the same time, Montfort is unable to resist making his own commentaries. In the three numbers of LEW that we have just mentioned and in those that follow them, we can see how Montfort, far from treating Scripture in a static way, as something untouchable in itself, feels the need to move on to an application of the biblical text. So, in dealing with Sir 24, he adds, "*I make bold to offer a few comments . . .*" (LEW 5); or again, in the case of Wis 8, he introduces the sacred text with an indication that he wishes to *"quote them here, adding a few reflections"* (LEW 52). For him, it is clear that Scripture needs to be interpreted and applied to the present circumstances. Thus we find in his work a kind of Scripture reading quite opposed to fundamentalism or a magical use of the Bible.

c. Here Montfort appeals to a vast network of scriptural quotations and takes abundant material from a whole set of texts. His view of Scripture is global, and he sees a kind of dialogue between OT and NT. This has the advantage of putting things in perspective and ensuring a greater depth in one's spiritual progress.

d. For all that, Montfort is indebted to the exegesis of his own day. His allegorical reading of Sir 24 (LEW 20-30) is evidence of this, as is his acceptance of a time scale for the universe derived from the Bible—"*the 4,000 years since the creation of the world*" (LEW 104)—and of the calendar of the Incarnation (LEW 109-116), with the precise years, months, days, and even hours of the life of Jesus. We could not pretend, therefore, that Montfort's exegesis and modern exegesis agree on all points. But the basic agreement between them is so deep that, where Montfort's exegesis appears out-of-date or insufficient, we need have no fear about completing it or adapting it with the aid of the resources of modern exegesis.

IV. Profile of the Book

1. Literary profile: structure and division

The structure of LEW is apparently not difficult to establish, since Montfort twice tells us of the plan he intends to follow. First of all, he bases himself on Solomon's idea to give "*a faithful and exact description of Wisdom*"; he will follow this through by his own attempt "*in my simple way, to portray eternal Wisdom before, during and after his Incarnation and show by what means we can possess and keep him*" (LEW 7; see also LEW 12). Thus the two major divisions of his book are: a long discourse on "*what Wisdom is*" (chap. 1-14), and a more succinct reflection on "*the means to acquire Wisdom*" (chap. 15-17). We see immediately the disproportion between the two parts.[17] Montfort takes a long time to describe for us what Wisdom is, while the last part of the work is more in the style of an exhortation and comes from Montfort's pastoral concern. We are not dealing here with theory but, rather, with the spiritual path that will ultimately result in the acquisition and putting into practice of Wisdom.

Montfort does not simply take quotations from Wis but also, especially in the first part of his book, makes his own the literary structure announced in Wis 6:24[22]. In fact, like Solomon, he does all he can to show the excellence of Wisdom, by contemplating his "*origin*, his *nature*, and his *works in the course of history*" (cf. LEW, chap. 2-5).

Another point on the structure that cannot be accidental is that LEW begins and ends with a prayer. Such a bracketing serves the same purpose as Solomon's prayer, which comes at the apex of the central section of Wis (Wis 9). The first prayer, which reminds us somewhat of what Solomon says of the limitations of his mortal condition (Wis 7-8), is Montfort's own prayer as he writes his book, and it embodies the respect he has for the mystery he is about to explore. The second prayer, the Consecration prayer (LEW 223-225), is clearly intended for his readers and gives a good indication of where Montfort wants to lead them.

2. Theological profile

The unfolding of Montfort's reflections is, in fact, much more complex than the divisions he himself indicates.

Certainly, the major division into two parts is beyond doubt: in chapters 1-14, he describes for us what Wisdom is, and in chapters 15-17, he gives us the means to acquire Wisdom. In addition, this last part is itself very clearly divided by Montfort into four precisely identified means. That leaves us with the first part, which is by far the more complex. On the one hand, it is not clear what Montfort means by the expression "*after the Incarnation.*" Does this mean after Jesus' birth in Bethlehem, as the plan proposed by OC would seem to indicate? Or does it mean after the Ascension, as Montfort himself seems to indicate (LEW 14: "*And then we shall see him glorious and triumphant in heaven*")? On the other hand, the biblical quotations, because of their length, seem to impose their own logic, which in many cases seems even to take over from the plan announced by Montfort. It is therefore wise to be somewhat flexible in any attempt to make a synthesis of LEW.

LEW 1-7 form a whole and serve as a prelude or prologue. This prelude is made up of three elements: a prayer addressed to Wisdom, in which Montfort, in the style of the prophets of the OT and the NT, expresses his conviction that he is inspired to speak while remaining very conscious of his limitations (LEW 1-2); a quotation of Wis 6, which is an exhortation to seek wisdom with all one's strength (LEW 3-4); and finally a word to his readers (LEW 4-7), inviting them to join him in contemplating and seeking Wisdom.

The first chapter is also to be seen apart from the following ones. Here we have an introduction to the discourse, punctuated by questions, which tries to capture the attention and interest of the reader: "*Can we love someone we do not even know? . . . Why is Jesus, the adorable, eternal and incarnate Wisdom loved so little[?] . . . What good will it do us to know all the other branches of knowledge necessary for salvation if we do not learn the only essential one, the knowledge of our Lord Jesus Christ?*" (LEW 8:12). The whole chapter culminates in the expression of one of Montfort's major convictions: "*To know Jesus Christ incarnate Wisdom, is to know all we need. To presume to know everything and not know him is to know nothing at all*" (LEW 11). Notice in this first chapter the importance of the vocabulary of knowledge, with such words as "to know," "knowledge," "branch of knowledge," etc. Such a way of proceeding is very different from a devotion that might base itself on a fundamentalist, sentimental, or pietistic reading of Scripture. In order to love, Montfort says, it is important "*to know*" well, and before one can make the Word of God relevant to today, it is important to *understand* it well and take a global view of the history of salvation.

It is precisely this global view that the next thirteen chapters present, in two major sections: chapters 2-8 are centered essentially on the OT, while chapters 9-14 are dedicated to the mystery of the Incarnation.

Chapters 2-5 pick up, though in a different order, the three central themes of the eulogy of Wisdom pronounced by Solomon in Wis 6-9: the beauty and greatness of Wisdom in his origin, in his nature, and in his works. In chapter 2, Montfort first of all sets forth the Christological foundation of his reflection by immediately applying to Christ the texts of the OT that speak of the mystery of Wisdom. And, having examined his origin in God, he moves on to the opposite pole of Wisdom, "*the effects of his activity in souls*" (LEW 20), with his commentary applying Sir 24.

Chapters 3 and 4 complement each other admirably, in that they give us a synthesis of the two great theological themes of the OT, namely Creation and salvation. On the one hand, chapter 3 places us at the heart of the theology of the Wisdom writers, which is a theology of Creation, seeing the beauty of the world as a fruit of Divine Wisdom. The foremost revelation of Wisdom, its masterpiece, is to be found in Creation: "*If the power and gentleness of eternal Wisdom were so luminously evident in the creation, the beauty and order of the universe, they shone forth far more brilliantly in the creation of man*" (LEW 35).

This brilliant vision, however, is seriously marred by the appearance of sin (LEW 39-40). The contrast is striking and filled with pathos. But of course this is not the last word, and Montfort continues his reflection with a remarkable summary of the history of salvation, which he sees, just like the author of Wis (Wis 10), as stamped with the presence and the interventions of Wisdom. Clearly we are dealing here with a summary, both for the biblical author and for Montfort. As does his predecessor, Montfort accords very great importance to the events surrounding the Exodus. The second paragraph of LEW 41 ascribes to Wisdom a reaction analogous to that of YHWH confronted with the distress of the Israelites in Egypt (Ex 2:24-25; Deut 26:6-8), and in his conclusion (LEW 50), Montfort returns explicitly to the Exodus. Montfort's intention, then, is not to be exhaustive in his treatment but to go to the very heart of the OT and present Wisdom as at work especially in the salvation event.

Having spoken of the origins and the activity of Wisdom, Montfort returns to the eulogy, strictly so called, of Wisdom, whose "*beauty, . . . excellence and . . . treasures*" he is about to reveal to us in his commentary on Wis 7 and 8 (LEW 63). The eulogy unfolds in chapter 6, where Montfort describes the efforts of Wisdom to make himself known to humanity and to establish bonds of love with mankind. The signs of Wisdom's love are many, but Montfort recalls, most of all, the very fact that an inspired book is explicitly devoted to Wisdom, and he underlines the passionate tone of the discourse of Wisdom personified in Prov 8. The eulogy is then completed and the conclusion is obvious: "*Above all else let us seek and long for divine Wisdom*" (LEW 73).

But being a realistic man and knowing well his own times, Montfort knows very well that there is a choice to be made: "*But we must beware of choosing a wrong wisdom, because there is more than one kind*" (LEW 73). The conclusion should therefore be placed later, after one has been made aware of the illusion ("*hypocrisy and malice*") of false forms of wisdom as proposed by the world. In some ways, chapter 7 seems to differ from the rest of LEW and even from the Wisdom language. Yet Montfort continues to take up his stand within the Wisdom theme. On the one hand, he echoes here the very severe criticism levelled by Jas at "*earthly*" wisdom, while on the other hand it has to be remembered that biblical Wisdom is hardly gentle in regard to whatever is contrary to the Wisdom of God—this is seen quite simply as folly, vanity, and destruction. Biblical Wisdom is certainly not without its prophetic character.

Having denounced the illusion of false forms of wisdom, then, Montfort repeats his invitation—"*So let us remain with Jesus, the eternal and incarnate Wisdom. Apart from him, there is nothing but aimless wandering, untruth and death*" (LEW 89) —and completes his eulogy by describing the wonderful "*effects*" of Wisdom "*in souls*" (chap. 8).

Chapters 9-14 form the keystone of LEW, the mystery of the Incarnation. Montfort begins with the facts (chap. 9), giving us "*a summary*" of the life of Jesus Christ, the Word of God and Incarnate Wisdom, from the Annunciation to Mary to the Ascension "*on Mount Olivet*" (LEW 109-116). This gives him the opportunity to emphasize the unique role of Mary, in whom "*eternal Wisdom built himself a house worthy to be his dwelling-place*" (LEW 105). From this biographical summary, Montfort passes on to the theological interpretation with his reflections on the gentleness of Incarnate Wisdom (chap. 10-11). He bases himself primarily on the Christological title of Lamb of God and the meaning of the name "Jesus" (LEW 119-120). But he also goes through the Gospels, emphasizing the humility of Jesus and his love for the poor and for sinners, to whom he brings the good news of salvation through the medium of his looks, his words, and his actions.

Chapter 12 claims to be "*the summary of the great and important truths which eternal Wisdom came on earth to teach us*" (LEW 153), and it is made up entirely of quotations from the Gospel (together with a quotation from Acts 20:35). Here Jesus is presented as a teacher of Wisdom, and the Gospel as Wisdom for life.

At the end of this first part (chap. 13-14), Montfort leads us to reflect on "*the Cross . . . the greatest secret of the King—the greatest mystery of Eternal Wisdom*" (LEW 167). He sees in this the supreme manifestation not only of the Wisdom of God, considered folly in the eyes of men, but also of his love for humanity: "*Among all the motives impelling us to love Jesus Christ, the Wisdom incarnate, the strongest, in my opinion, is the sufferings he chose to endure to prove his love for us*" (LEW 154).

The second part, which is much shorter (chap. 15-17) is dedicated to the means to acquire divine Wisdom. First of all, "*like Solomon and Daniel we must be men of desire if we are to acquire this great treasure which is wisdom*" (LEW 183). Then Montfort lingers over the second means, giving us a veritable little treatise on prayer (LEW 184-193), which ends with the very beautiful prayer of Solomon asking for Wisdom (Wis 9). It is not surprising that Montfort devotes a whole chapter to the third means, "*mortification . . . that is total, continuous, courageous and prudent*" (LEW 196): this is precisely how Montfort understands the demands of the paschal mystery, and he will have occasion to return to this theme later and at more length in FC.

Then Montfort unveils for us "*the greatest means of all, and the most wonderful of all secrets for obtaining and preserving divine Wisdom . . . a loving and genuine devotion to the Blessed Virgin*" (LEW 203). In this final chapter of LEW, he recalls the unique closeness of Mary to Jesus Christ, Wisdom Incarnate, since she "*became the mother, mistress and throne of divine Wisdom*" (LEW 203). "*She became,*" that is to say, by grace and in virtue of her free response. Here also, Montfort is already mapping out the main themes of a later work, TD, for he tells us "*in a few words*" what "*genuine devotion to her involve[s]*" (LEW 215).

And finally, let us recall that LEW ends with a prayer. The exercise proposed by Montfort was not therefore something academic but, rather, existential. He does not even take care to issue any warnings to the reader, except at the very end (LEW 227): "*Qui potest capere capiat. Quis sapiens et intelliget haec?*" (Hos 14:10). LEW is, in some sense, like the prophetic books of Hosea and Jonah, an open book that calls for the response and the involvement of the reader.

V. LEW and its Interpretations

1. The silence of the biographers

If TD was indeed enclosed "*in the darkness and silence of a chest,*" in accord with the prediction made by its author (TD 114), one could say that LEW hardly enjoyed better fortune for the first two centuries following its composition. The manuscript was not published until 1856, and until the beginning of the twentieth century, the biographers and commentators on montfort spirituality maintained a general silence about LEW. We find no direct reference to the writing of LEW in the first biographers, and even after the renewal set in motion by the definitive edition of 1929, such writers as De Luca, Le Crom, Papàsogli, and Laurentin devote only a short paragraph to it. Even more surprising is the silence of A. Lhoumeau, who, in his remarkable treatise *The Spiritual Life at the School of Blessed Louis Marie de Montfort,* restricts himself to TD, even though his aim was "to set forth the dogmatic foundations of this devotion (i.e. the perfect devotion to the Blessed Virgin)" (preface of 1901) and even though the most important practice of this devotion is expressed in a formula of Consecration that belongs properly to LEW.

2. The definitive edition (1929) and the renewal of montfort studies

We had therefore to wait until 1929 for LEW to come back on the scene in montfort spirituality. Father H. Huré must be credited with recognizing its capital importance, and his long introduction to the definitive edition puts things in perspective.

Father Huré places Montfort primarily in the line of Pauline and Augustinian Wisdom. It was left to later interpreters to follow up the research and to emphasize how much Montfort owed, first of all, to the biblical theme of Wisdom.

The years following the appearance of the definitive edition of LEW and surrounding the canonization of Montfort saw Father Huré's intuition confirmed, and since that time it has not been possible to speak of montfort spirituality without relying on this capital work, LEW.

J. Bombardier, a Canadian Montfort, begins his introduction to montfort spirituality (four volumes) with a fascicle devoted entirely to a discussion of the Wisdom theme, which provides a sufficiently complete introduction to the questions about the writing of LEW as well as a synthesized presentation of almost all the chapters in Montfort's book. In his discussion of the sources from which Montfort drew in his composition of LEW, we find an interesting nomenclature and a heavily biased judgement. Since his work came before the start and the maturing of biblical renewal, we can well understand Bombardier's astonishment at the Christological use Montfort makes of OT Wisdom. Notice also that he links montfort Wisdom very closely with Augustinian Wisdom, to the point of seeing in them "not only a resemblance, but even identity" of view and content.

About a year later, Father Dayet published what can still lay claim to one of the best introductions to LEW.[18] His little book of eighty-four pages, first of all, gives a balanced judgement on the sources (both biblical and nonbiblical) of the work, and on the meaning of the word "Wisdom." The first part of his commentary is an excellent synthesis of LEW, while the second part is more concerned with showing what the totality of Montfort's spiritual experience gained from his contemplation of Eternal Wisdom. Fr. Dayet did not miss the opportunity to insert a long commentary on LEW in his presentation[19] of the sixth day of the third week of the exercises proposed by Montfort for preparing those who will make the Consecration. It was concerned precisely with gaining a better knowledge of Jesus Christ.

In his celebrated *The Poem of the Perfect Consecration to Mary*, Father Poupon, contrary to what the title might indicate, does not fail to emphasize the basically Christological slant of such a Consecration. And since his commentary traces the unfolding of the prayer of Consecration, he gives a prime place to the theme of Wisdom, notably in the first chapter of the first part, which is entitled *The mystery of light.*[20]

3. Recent interpretations

Since the end of the 1960s, L. Perouas has been making a systematic reexamination of the life and writings of Montfort. His efforts have profoundly influenced the renewal of montfort studies. His first work, *Grignion de Montfort, les pauvres et les missions* (1966), which was to give the impetus for a new way of approaching Montfort's texts, did not intend, as was supposed, to examine all Montfort's work. Thus, there is not a word about LEW.

But Perouas was to return to this on other occasions. In writing *A Way to Wisdom* (1973), he notes the originality of the theology presented in LEW, but does not accept that there is here a synthesis of montfort spirituality: "It would be a mistake to view this work today as a synthesis of montfort spirituality. This book brings together, undoubtedly, Montfort's favorite themes, but done at a moment of personal evolution."[21] He sees it therefore as a writing from a particular moment, written in the middle of a period of crisis and appearing, in Montfort, "at the same time as a transformation of his psyche, as progress in his faith and as an intellectual breakthrough."[22] We find the same position taken in the article *Louis-Marie Grignion de Montfort* that he wrote for DSAM[23] and in his book *Grignion de Montfort ou l'aventurier de l'Evangile.*[24]

The point of interest in the position taken by Perouas is that he stresses the great importance of the life context (the *Sitz im Leben* beloved of exegetes) that gave birth to LEW and that he emphasizes the contrast between this work and Montfort's other writings. He also has some very interesting things to say about "the language of lovers,"[25] although one must not give too psychological a slant to the reexamination of the text nor stress too much the finding of "the feminine side": these are considerations that throw light on a problematic area in our own day but need not necessarily be applied to a reading of Montfort's texts.

M. Gilbert, the exegete and respected specialist on Wis, for his part made a detailed study of "the spiritual exegesis employed by Montfort," which led him to acclaim the uniqueness of LEW among spiritual writings, principally due to the deep understanding Montfort had acquired of Wis: "It is truly surprising to see the impact of the Book of Wisdom on Montfort's treatise. I know of no other spiritual writing that has based its doctrine, as Montfort does, on this little Greek book of the Old Testament. . . . Montfort's standing as a spiritual exegete of the Book of Wisdom is quite exceptional."[26]

Finally, it seems that interest in LEW can only increase with the appearance in several languages of the complete works (Spanish, 1954; with a new edition in 1984; French, 1966, reprinted in 1982; Italian, 1977, with a new edition in 1990; English, 1988, reprinted in 1991), in which all the introductions emphasize the fundamental importance of LEW for the understanding of montfort spirituality and its application for today.

VI. Relevance of the Book Today

Far from being a marginal work, LEW opens up fundamental perspectives that, moreover, fit perfectly with the contemporary preoccupations and directions of Christian theology and spirituality.

1. Christocentrism

LEW has, first of all, the merit of being an eminently Christocentric work. This means that we are dealing with a spirituality and a theology that go to the very heart of the Christian mystery and bring us back to the essential question asked by the Gospels: *"And you: who do you say that I am?"* (Mk 8:29). Moreover, at a time when biblical studies are throwing fresh light on the diversity and richness of NT forms of Christology, LEW can help us to see an element of this diversity and what might be called an alternative Christology, one authentically of the NT because it is clearly evident in Jn's Prologue and in Col 1:15-20. The vision of a Christ Wisdom admirably puts the finishing touch to the reflection on the mystery of Christ attested to in the traditional titles of Messiah, Lord, and Son of God. In this way LEW helps towards a better understanding of the mystery of Christ.

2. Theology of Creation

LEW has also much to offer in that it is rooted in the biblical theme of Wisdom, the theology of which is first and foremost a theology of Creation. Even if it is important not to create an opposition between a theology of salvation and a theology of Creation, nevertheless the latter is very much more evident in the biblical Wisdom literature. The same could be said of LEW. Here more than anywhere else, Montfort gives us his theology of Creation and shows us, in line with the biblical theme of Wisdom, a vision of Creation that is basically optimistic. The widespread change in thinking brought about by Vatican II's GS shows the importance for today of a theology of Creation and of earthly realities, and the search for Wisdom proposed by LEW can easily be seen as a part of this new way of thinking.

3. Theology of the Redemption

Finally, the important renewal currently taking place in the theology of the Redemption[27] itself invites us to a deeper reexamination of what Montfort says on this theme in LEW. We know the importance he attaches to the Cross, and what he writes on this subject achieves great heights. LEW offers us a vision in which the theology of the Redemption is far from being an exaltation of suffering but is firmly anchored in the love God has for the world. Chapter 13, in fact, says clearly that it was not suffering that saved the world but the love Jesus Christ has shown for us in his sufferings. Montfort invites us to contemplate *"the sufferings he chose to endure to prove his love for us"* (LEW 154). LEW 154-166 often return to this theme of love. In addition, this thirteenth chapter would benefit by being reread and reinterpreted in the light of what modern theologians call "the suffering of God."[28] Such a rereading has already been attempted, in a very promising way, by J. Morinay in his book *Mary and the Weakness of God.*[29]

It is certainly true that LEW is not all that Montfort has to say. And this work could not, any more than could the Wisdom theme that finds its final achievement in the NT, exhaust all the dimensions of a Christian spirituality. We must seek elsewhere, in Montfort as in the Bible, for the prophetic dimension of challenge and commitment to the poor. This dimension, while not being absent in the Wisdom writings, is not as clear there as in the prophets of the Bible and in the Gospels. In this sense, we can only be glad that such writings as the PM and FC and certain of the hymns are there to complement LEW. But LEW remains a privileged witness to the theology of Montfort and to his own spiritual experience. It is also a guide of the highest value for Christians in search of *"true wisdom, eternal Wisdom, Wisdom uncreated and incarnate"* (LEW 14), Jesus Christ.

J.-P. Prévost

Notes: (1) H. Huré, preface to the definitive edition of *L'Amour de la Sagesse éternelle*, Librairie mariale, Pontchâteau 1929, 1-2. (2) J.-M. Dayet, *La Sagesse chez le Bienheureux Louis-Marie de Montfort (The Place of Wisdom in Blessed Louis-Marie de Montfort)*, Bureau des Prêtres de Marie, Saint-Laurent-sur-Sèvre 1944, 77. (3) M. Quéméneur, *Entreprendre de grandes choses (Undertaking Great Things)*, in *Cahiers Marials*, 52 (1966), 87. (4) OC, 88; see also H.-M. Guindon, *L'Amour de la Sagesse Eternelle (Love of Eternal Wisdom)*, in *Dossiers Montfortains*, 16 (1958), 65-68. (5) H. Frehen, *Etudes sur les Cantiques du Père de Montfort (Studies of the Hymns of Father de Montfort)* (a compendium of articles gathered together by the author). (6) Cf. D. M. Huot, *I manoscritti delle opere di S. Luigi-Maria da Montfort (Manuscript of the Works of St. Louis-Marie de Montfort)*, in QM 4 (1986), 16-127. (7) Besnard I, 280. (8) Picot de Clorivière, *La vie de M. Louis-Marie Grignion de Montfort (The Life of St. Louis-Marie de Montfort)*, Delalain, Paris 1785, 321-322. (9) H. Frehen, *Etudes*, 68-70. (10) A. Balmforth, *Pour qui le livre de "L'Amour de la Sagesse Eternelle" a-t-il été écrit? (Why did he write Love of Eternal Wisdom?)*, in *Dossiers Montfortains*, 41 (1967), 1. (11) Ibid. (12) See the parallels established by A. Guéry, *Etudes comparatives. I. Prière à la Sagesse Eternelle (P. de St-Jure/Montfort); II. Consécration de soi-même à Jésus-Christ, la Sagesse Incarnée, par les mains de Marie (Comparative Studies. I. Prayer to Eternal Wisdom (Fr. de St. Jure/Montfort) II. Consecration of oneself to Jesus Christ, Incarnate Wisdom at the Hands of Mary) (P. Nepveu/Montfort)*, in *Dossiers Montfortains (Montfortian Papers)* 32 (1963), 17-27; and by A. F. Balmforth, *"Oracles" de la Sagesse Incarnée: Montfort/Bonnefons*, in *Dossiers Montfortains, (Montfortian Papers)* 36 (1964), 129-135. (13) Itinerario, 221, n. 1. (14) M. Gilbert, *L'exégèse spirituelle de Montfort (Spiritual Exegesis of Montfort)*, in *NRT* 104 (1982), 678-691. (15) J.-P. Prévost, *Montfort et le courant de sagesse biblique*, Dossier Montfortain 2, Rome 1986, 1-19. (16) M. Gilbert, *L'exégèse*, 684. (17) The same observation is made, in a mystical perspective, in P. Humblet, *The Mystical Process of Transformation in Grignion de Montfort's "The Love of Eternal Wisdom,"* Titus Brandsma Institute, Daughters of Wisdom, Nijmegen, 1993, 6-9 (18) J.-M. Dayet, *La sagesse chez le Bienheureux Louis-Marie de Montfort*, Bureaux des Prètres de Marie, SaintLaurent-sur-Sèvre 1944. (19) J.-M. Dayet, *Les exercices préparatoires à la consécration de Saint Louis-Marie de Montfort (Exercises of Preparation for the Consecration of Saint Louis-Marie de Montfort)*, Les Traditions françaises, Tourcoing, 1957. (20) M.-Th Poupon, *Le poème de la parfaite consécration à Marie suivant saint Louis-Marie Grignion de Montfort et les spirituels de son temps. Sources et doctrine (The poem of Perfect Consecration to Mary of Louis-Marie Grignion de Montfort and the Spiritual Teachers of his Times)*, Librairie du Sacré-Coeur, Lyon 1947. (21) Perouas (22) Ibid. (23) *DSAM* 9 (1976), 1075. (24) Ed. Ouvrières, Paris 1990, 70-74, 87-88. (25) Perouas, 52. (26) M. Gilbert, *L'exégèse*, 684. (27) On this topic, see B. Rey, *Nous prêchons un Messie crucifié*, Cerf, Paris 1989; F. Varone, *Ce Dieu censé aimer la souffrance (This God who is Deemed to Love Suffering)*, Cerf, Paris 1984. (28) In the terminology popularised by F. Varillon, *L'humilité de Dieu (The Humility of God)*, Centurion, Paris 1974, and *La souffrance de Dieu (The Suffering of God)*, Centurion, Paris 1975, but owing much to the work of M. Zundel, from whom Varillon took much of his inspiration (cf. R. M. De Pison, *Le Dieu qui est "victime." Le problème du mal dans la pensée de M. Zundel (The God Who is Victim. The Problem of Evil in the thought of Zundel)*, in *Science et Esprit*, 52 (1991) 55-68. (29) J. Morinay, *Marie et la faiblesse de Dieu. Essai de présentation du message spirituel de saint Louis-Marie de Montfort (Mary and the Weakness of God. Essay presenting the Spiritual Message of St. Louis de Montfort)*, Nouvelle Cité, Paris 1988.

MAGNIFICAT

The Magnificat, song of the Virgin and of the people of God, has always held an eminent place in the community of believers, in liturgy as well as in personal piety. In the Byzantine tradition, since ancient times, it has been part of the morning celebration and sung virtually every day. The Magnificat is performed standing, with solemnity, during the "great censing" that precedes Lauds. In such a context, we might almost speak of the daily feast of the Magnificat.[1] The canticle has inspired hymnlike compositions called *Megalinària,* including *Timiotéran* and *Axion estin,* which are particularly cherished in Byzantine piety.

The Magnificat is also solemnized in the Armenian and Maronite liturgies in the daily morning psalmody, as practiced in the West in the old Gallican liturgy.

During the fifth or sixth centuries it was sung each day as part of Vespers. The Rule of Saint Benedict, written at Monte Cassino in about 530, gives the earliest evidence of this.[2]

The Magnificat has retained its central role in the liturgy while playing no less important a role in the spirituality and piety of the faithful over the centuries. There have been too many commentaries on the hymn to mention here,[3] and it would be nearly impossible to measure its impact on souls, which, as Montfort himself notes, has certainly been significant (cf. TD 255).

I. THE MAGNIFICAT IN MONTFORT'S LIFE AND THOUGHT

Montfort includes himself among those who have been fascinated with the Magnificat and have drawn strength from its spirituality. He does not often refer to the Magnificat, but we can perceive the place of honor he reserves for it in his own spiritual experience as well as in his theological and Marian doctrine.

He recommends that it be recited often, at important and solemn moments, after Holy Communion, for example (SM 64; TD 255), and before leaving this life (HD 24). *"The only hymn composed by our Lady"* (SM 64), the Magnificat allows us to participate in her spirit and to share her sentiments, in accordance with Montfort's conception of *"performing all our actions with Mary, in Mary, through Mary, and for Mary"* (SM 43; cf. TD 258-261). Montfort cites Saint Ambrose's exhortation: "May the soul of Mary be in each one of us to glorify the Lord; may the spirit of Mary be in each one of us to rejoice in God."[4] He invokes this citation explicitly on three occasions, at the culmination of both SM and TD, to indicate how the Christocentric and Marian spirituality that he teaches can live within us (TD 258) and to show us how the path of fidelity to Christ through Mary leads us to communication with the soul and spirit of Mary, giving joyful glory to God (SM 54; TD 217).

The Magnificat is a precious key to unlocking Montfort's mystical experience and spirituality. He counts it among the prayers and expressions that characterize true devotion to Mary (TD 116) and perfect Consecration (TD 255).

The significance and excellence of the canticle are due to certain of its characteristics that Montfort illuminates.

1. Hymn of Mary

The first is that it is a hymn of Mary, reflecting the exceptional richness of her interior world. In Montfort's words, it is *"the only prayer we have which was composed by our Lady, or rather, composed by Jesus in her, for it was he who spoke through her lips"* (TD 255). Not only is it a prayer suggested by the Holy Spirit; it is uttered by Jesus himself from the mouth of his mother. This is certainly a singular vision, but highly indicative of the communion between the Virgin and her Son and of the theological aspect of this sublime hymn.

2. Expression of praise and blessing

It is an **expression of praise and blessing** (SR 47), of thanksgiving and petition (SM 64). It is a prayer addressed to God in return for the blessings granted to the Virgin and continuously delivered to all those who place their trust in her: *"It is the greatest offering of praise that God ever received under the law of grace. On the one hand, it is the most humble hymn of thanksgiving and, on the other, it is the most sublime and exalted"* (TD 255).

3. Divine canticle

Montfort observes correctly that the Magnificat is a divine canticle that comes from Jesus in the Spirit and returns to the Father (cf. TD 255, 258). While remembering that we recite the Magnificat to *"thank God for favoring us"* (SM 64), Montfort does not completely explore the meaning of its "theological dimension": the celebration of God and

God's work in the history of salvation, especially the virginal conception of Jesus in the womb of Mary, the specific object of the Magnificat. For Montfort, its theological import lies in the fact that the Virgin, through her hymn, returns to the Lord the praise and benedictions that are addressed to her, like a faithful echo (cf. SR 47; TD 140, 225). On the other hand, the saint does evoke, albeit briefly and rather generally, the Trinitarian implications of this theological dimension; the hymn is *"most glorious to the Blessed Trinity, for any honor we pay to our Lady returns inevitably to God, the source of all her perfections and virtues. God the Father is glorified when we honor the most perfect of his creatures; God the Son is glorified when we praise his most pure Mother; the Holy Spirit is glorified when we are lost in admiration at the graces with which he has filled his spouse"* (SR 47).[5]

4. Prayer with the power of God

The Magnificat is a prayer with the power of God. It does not merely invoke the memory of the works of salvation but demonstrates their living efficaciousness: *"The learned Benzonius . . . cites several miracles worked through the power of this prayer. The devils, he declares, take to flight when they hear these words, 'He puts forth his arm in strength and scatters the proud-hearted'"* (TD 255).[6]

5. Prayer filled with mystery

Finally, the Magnificat is a prayer filled with mystery. It contains the secrets of God, which human thought cannot attain and which should only be approached in reverence and fear. *"Contained in it are mysteries so great and so hidden that even the angels do not understand them. . . . It was with apprehension that [Gerson] undertook towards the end of his life to write a commentary on the Magnificat which was the crowning point of all his works. In a large volume on the subject he says many wonderful things about this beautiful and divine canticle"* (TD 255).[7]

II. The Magnificat in Contemporary Thought

The difficulties presented by the Magnificat in the past were due to the great "mysteries" it contained and to its exceptional theological and spiritual wealth. Over the past century these difficulties have become of a different kind altogether.[8] We now find ourselves confronted with scholars, including a number of unbelievers, who have subjected the text of the Magnificat to technical analysis with quite varied and indeed disconcerting results. The (sometimes ingenuous) piety and devotion with which the canticle was approached for so many centuries have given way to the "scientific" method and criticism. Thus the Magnificat is now being studied with the use of ever more refined methods and techniques; if, on the one hand, these techniques have illuminated some important characteristics of the canticle, they have, on the other, frequently done harm to its theological richness and spiritual inspiration. The past few decades, however, have brought a favorable inversion of this tendency: exegesis has become more open to the theological and anthropological aspects of the text, with, in the case of the Magnificat, some notable results.

Leaving aside minor problematical questions, we would like to draw attention to some of the more valid acquisitions from recent exegesis.

The first is the scientific dimension of the research endorsed, in the Catholic realm, by the encyclical *Divino afflante Spiritu* (1943); the Pontifical Biblical Commission's letter *Sancta mater ecclesia,* and the Conciliar Constitution *Dei Verbum* have both insisted on this as well.[9] A rigorous exegesis, conscious of its responsibilities and its limits, has consistently brought forth valuable results. It has produced an impressive bibliography on the Magnificat[10]—clearly not limited to Catholic sources—that has enlarged our perspectives enormously. Particular study has been given to the literary genre and structure of the hymn, its place of origin, its transmission, its placement in the text of Luke 1-2 and in relation to the entire book of Luke, its potential relationship to the poetry of its period, and its Old Covenant background in the context of a biblical theology centered on the Christ event. The figure of the Blessed Virgin has been considered not simply in herself but as part of a relationship of living continuity between Israel and the Church. The song's impact on the actual history of the world, of a mankind still marked by violence and oppression and in need of true liberation, has also been studied.

We can now see the Magnificat as a dynamic, multidimensional song, compelling us to commit ourselves to God's plan. To proclaim the hymn means to assume the attitudes of concrete responsibility before God and the world. In what follows, we shall emphasize a few of these many dimensions.

1. Theological hymn

The theological dimension of the hymn is the most obvious and also the most important, on which every other aspect of the hymn depends. The Lord is not simply the direct object of the Virgin's song ("my whole being rejoices in God my Savior": v. 47)[11] but also the subject-protagonist, even from a literary standpoint, of the verbs from verse 48 through verse 54 that make up the powerful dynamic structure on which the entire song rests. J. Dupont has written a study of this passage entitled, with justification, *Le Magnificat comme discours sur Dieu (The Magnificat as a discourse on God):*[12] "The Magnificat does not define God; it speaks of God in terms of different aspects of His saving intervention, beginning with the Annunciation, of which Mary—according to Luke—is the first witness. The Magnificat locates the mystery of the Savior God and gives its coordinates."[13] In the words of *Redemptoris mater,* the canticle reveals "the truth about the God of the Covenant," a truth that has been obscured by sin and lack of faith. The Magnificat "sees uprooted that sin which is found at the outset of the earthly history of man and woman, the sin of disbelief and of 'little faith' in God. In contrast with the 'suspicion' that the 'father of lies' sowed in the heart of Eve, the first woman, Mary . . . boldly proclaims the *undimmed* truth about God: the holy and almighty God, who from the beginning is *the source of all gifts,* he who 'has done great things' in her" (*Redemptoris mater,* 37).

This theological "recentering" of the hymn seems to us to be one of the most notable rediscoveries that contemporary exegesis and theology have made.

2. Salvific hymn

The theological dimension is closely bound with its salvific dimension. This is no philosophical or abstract God but a living God Who acts in history and works among His people. Salvation, the central element of the biblical story and Revelation, occupies an exceptional place in the Magnificat. Within the song, all of past history is synthesized and future history is anticipated, and both are centered on the birth of the Savior.

The history of men and women in the ancient covenant, and the vicissitudes of Israel, the people of the covenant, are recapitulated in Mary, the servant of the Lord. Here we should note the link between verse 48 ("he has looked with favor on the lowliness of his servant") and verse 54 ("he has helped his servant Israel").

In a way, Israel's experience of grace is concentrated in Mary. Her song anticipates the voice of the Church, and in it resounds the eschatological praise of the redeemed. The Magnificat is "the song of the messianic times, in which there mingles the joy of the ancient and the new Israel. . . . It is in Mary's canticle that there was heard once more the rejoicing of Abraham . . . and there rang out in prophetic anticipation the voice of the Church. . . . And in fact Mary's hymn has spread far and wide and has become the prayer of the whole Church in all ages" (MC 18).[14]

3. Song of liberation

Few biblical passages have received so much attention and so successfully energized various contemporary groups and movements, not only religious and spiritual but also socially or politically inspired. The hymn of the Virgin has become an important point of reference for contemporary theology and spirituality and a basis for Christian involvement with society. Contact with the hymn has led theology to a rediscovery of its character as the word of salvation and liberation and has taught spirituality to unite praise and joy in God—in the experience of poverty—with the reality of involvement, in accordance with God's plan to overthrow the powerful and raise the lowly. The perspective of the Magnificat is in harmony with the liveliest contemporary expectations.

The song, which has been rediscovered both within and outside the Church, has been preeminently validated over the past several years in Latin America: "The Magnificat expresses well this spirituality of liberation. A song of thanksgiving for the gifts of the Lord, it expresses humbly the joy of being loved by Him. . . . But at the same time it is one of the New Testament texts which contains great implications both as regards liberation and the political sphere. This thanksgiving and joy are closely linked to the action of God who liberates the oppressed and humbles the powerful."[15]

The Magisterium of the Church has also turned its attention to the Magnificat as a hymn of liberation of the poor.[16] We refer in particular to the encyclical *Redemptoris mater.* The song of Mary not only reveals the truth about the God of the covenant but also—and precisely through this revelation—displays its preferential love for the poor, of which the song itself is the privileged expression. Through the Magnificat, the Church will become ever more aware that "the truth about the God who saves . . . cannot be separated from the manifestation of his love of preference for the poor and humble, that love which, celebrated in the *Magnificat,* is later expressed in the words and works of Jesus" (Rmat 37).

4. Ecumenical song

The ecumenical impulse not only inspired the body of work produced by the Second Vatican Council but is apparent in conciliar statements on the Virgin Mary (cf. LG 62, 67, 69). This aspect of the devotion to Our Lady is explicitly stressed by Paul VI, who believed ecumenism should be one of the fundamental characteristics of a renewed devotion to the Blessed Virgin (cf. MC 32-33).

Since ancient times, the Magnificat's vocation has been of reconciliation and communion: we need only remember how its daily recitation in the prayer of Lauds or Vespers has always united diverse Christian confessions in praise of God. In addition, this NT psalm contains an excellent synthesis of Hebraic spirituality.

III. The Magnificat in Montfort Spirituality

In order to give adequate due to the Magnificat, we must go beyond particular experiences and points of view and beyond a merely partial understanding of the hymn. In particular, the hymn requires a scientific reading, close attention to the salvation story contained within it, and a clear-sighted examination of its current reality.

1. Global and critical approach

The scientific character of research on the Magnificat has now brought us to a point of consensus such that it is becoming more difficult to distinguish among the diverse confessional origins of the hymn's exegetes. The value of exegesis in general has been strongly confirmed by the work on the Magnificat. Scholars of every religious persuasion have made the hymn the object of considerable research, and yet their various positions have converged. Without taking anything away from the secular tradition of the past, a "critical" reading has today become the basis for all subsequent progress.

2. Salvation History reading

Another fundamental aspect of any reading of the Magnificat is the story of salvation: the Magnificat is not an expression of individual piety or private sentiment but a liberation hymn celebrating God's great works of salvation on behalf of His servants, of those who fear Him, of Israel, of the redeemed. This is a powerful synthesis of the history of salvation that begins with the Exodus and reaches its fulfillment in the coming of the Savior, anticipating the eschatological aspect of the world's redemption.

3. Current-day reading

Finally, we must read the Magnificat in light of the contemporary vicissitudes of humanity, listening for the prophetic voices of the world's believers and of those who are building a society that is more worthy of God's plan and open to the salvific content of the Blessed Virgin's hymn. The Magnificat leads us to a "theological" reading of history, which, in all its contradictions, obliges us to rethink the canticle and extract from it the meaning of salvation for our time.

4. In communion with Mary

Montfort calls on his readers to recite it often and, especially, to give it a place in their prayer life. The Magnificat is a prayer that Scripture has placed on the lips of the Virgin Mary and that the Church places on the lips of believers. But Montfort is not content with simply reciting the hymn; he urges us on to an intimate identification with Mary, whose soul glorifies the Lord, whose spirit rejoices in God the Savior (cf. TD 258). The Magnificat sprang forth from the heart of Mary while she carried the Savior in her womb, and, as Montfort suggests, it should resound in the hearts of the faithful when they receive Jesus Christ, the Lord, in Holy Communion. Mary thus becomes the symbol of the Church who gives thanks to God for His saving interventions in the history of salvation, especially the coming of Christ in history and in hearts. We must recover the "piety" of the Magnificat and also its theological and ecclesial dimensions, with its great historical and salvific wealth, and with attention to the signs of our times. God's salvation is still at work in the world today; it must be celebrated and proclaimed.

A. Valentini

Notes: (1) G. Gharib, *Il canto del Magnificat nella liturgia bizantina,* in *Mater Ecclesiae* (The Magnificat Song in the Byzantine Liturgy) 13 (1977), 24. (2) Cf. Ph. Rouillard, *Il Magnificat nella liturgia attuale* (The Magnificat in the Present Day Liturgy), ibid., 65. See also A. Schweissinger, *Magnificat,* in *Lexikon für Theologie und Kirche,* 6:786. (3) For an investigation of studies on the Magnificat, cf. P. De Alva y Astorga, *Expositio nova litteralis cantici Magnificat* (The New Literal Explanation of the Magnificat), in J.-J. Bourassé, *Summa aurea de laudibus beatissimae Virginis Mariae,* Paris 1866, 13:677-682. (4) S. Ambrosius, *Expos. in Lucam,* 26, PL 15:1642. (5) Montfort takes this text from the work of the Dominican Antonin Thomas, *Rosier mystique de la très sainte Vierge (Mystical Rosebush of the Most Holy Virgin),* 2nd ed., Rennes 1685, second decade, chap. 8. (6) Rutilio Benzonio († 1613), bishop of Lorette and Recanati, author of *Dissertationes et commentaria in canticum Magnificat . . . libri quinque* (Dissertations and Commentaries on the Magnificat... five books), Venice 1606. The passage to which Montfort refers can be found in book 5, p. 134. (7) Cf. *Gersonii opera,* Paris 1606, 2:904-915. (8) We will simply mention one problem of textual criticism, raised at the end of the last century and continuing several decades into this one: the attribution of the Magnificat to Elizabeth, despite the near completeness of the codex and the virtual unanimity in assigning the hymn to Mary. This betrays some inconsistency, but the problem has been of interest to scholars for some time. It is indicative of the radical change in interest over time and of the ingenuous rationalism that has characterized certain areas of research (cf. A. Valentini, *La controversia circa l'attribuzione del Magnificat* (The Controversy concerning the Attribution of the Magnificat), in Mar 45 (1983), 55-93. (9) Cf. *Divino afflante Spiritu,* EB 557-562; *Sancta mater ecclesia,* 2; *Dei Verbum,* especially 12. (10) Cf. A. Valentini, *Il Magnificat: Genere litterario, struttura, esegesi* (The Magnificat Literary Genre, Structure, Exegesis), Bologna 1987, 269ff. (11) Our translation diverges from the usual translation in the hope of conveying the density and strength of the original. (12) In NRT 112 (1980), 321-343. (13) Ibid., 342. (14) On this central aspect of the Virgin's hymn, which takes up the triumphal hymn of Moses (Ex 15:1-18) or, to a greater extent, of Miriam (v. 21) and anticipates the hymn of the redeemed in the last Exodus (Rev 15:3-4), cf. A. Valentini, *Il Magnificat,* passim. (15) G. Gutierrez, *A Theology of Liberation,* Orbis Books, Maryknoll 1973, 207-208. (16) Apart from the positive references in MC 37, there is some critical reflection in the *Instruction of the Congregation for the Doctrine of the Faith on Liberation Theology,* August 6, 1984. This document expresses reservations about a "political reading" of the Magnificat: "The error does not inhere in bringing attention a political aspect to Biblical narratives (especially that of the Exodus), but in considering this their principal and exclusive aspect, which leads to a reductionist reading of Scripture."

MAN

SUMMARY I. MAN IN THE SPIRITUAL CONTEXT OF THE SEVENTEENTH CENTURY:
1. A Christology seen from above: God Alone;
2. Fallen man.
II. GREATNESS AND MISERY OF MAN:
1. The dignity of man;
2. The paradox of man;
3. Radical dependence;
4. Indigence;
5. Self-realization;
6. Consecration;
7. The tension between the ideal and the real.
III. MONTFORT'S PASSION FOR THE ABSOLUTE.

I. MAN IN THE SPIRITUAL CONTEXT OF THE SEVENTEENTH CENTURY

We cannot expect a systematic doctrinal teaching on the essence of man from someone who was primarily a missionary and only secondarily an author on spirituality. Correspondingly, in what follows, we can only try to bring out the basic features that Montfort lends to his idea of man. In order to throw light on the background of our subject, we can make two preliminary comments. The first is related to the Christology that helps to determine Montfort's thinking and his concept of man; the other is related to the general features that seventeenth-century spirituality attributes to man.

1. A Christology seen from above: God Alone

Montfort moves in the sphere of scholastic theology and the classical Christology characteristic of it. We must not forget this, even when considering his treatment of man. Classical Christology starts "above," with God, and moves down to man. Its starting point is not the Jesus of history but the Eternal Son made man. The Incarnation of the Son, the understanding of his person and his mission, derive from the God of the Trinity. Hence the well-known rudiments of scholastic theology: the Trinity, the Creation, the Fall (original sin), the Incarnation of the Word, who is true God and true man and who restores humanity to its original sinless state in order to bring it to eternal life. The initiative belongs to God Alone; man, including even the Second person in his human form, is considered to be receptive. God the Father sends his Son into the world so that he might take on human form and accomplish his task in perfect obedience. The center and the fundamental event with which all the rest begins is the redemptive Incarnation. The Death/Resurrection is left in the background. This divergence between Christology in the narrow sense and soteriology reduces both the understanding of the person of Jesus in his humanity and the extent to which we participate in his destiny, since salvation is only obtained by the death of Jesus and only the soul that finds itself in a state of grace at the moment of death is saved. This view of salvation impoverishes our humanity and devalues history. Consequently, the individual salvation of the soul constitutes almost the entire content of spiritual life.[1]

The communal aspect of salvation is scarcely considered. Similarly, the Church is not considered to be a community of brothers and sisters but, much more, an alternative society opposed to the world. Montfort's spirituality cannot be studied outside this Christological model—it is the opposite of the Christology that starts with man and with which we are more familiar. This initial remark helps to set the question in its proper context.

Finally, Montfort's life coincides with the middle of the scientific revolution of the seventeenth century, which increasingly attempted to explain the universe by reference to the chain of natural causes and laws that can be expressed in mathematical terms. God has no place in this view of the universe. Theology must increasingly defend itself against the claim that human reason is independent. Montfort, too, entered the polemic against this claim, which has certain consequences for the spiritual life (LEW 84-88; TD 83).

2. Fallen man

Seventeenth-century spirituality, including a certain concept of man, was more or less influenced in its different formulations by Augustinianism. St. Augustine had gained great importance among the champions of the Reformation, and the Council of Trent itself reflected the Augustinian tradition of the Middle Ages in essential respects. The dispute on the relation between nature and grace, particularly on the effects of original sin on human nature, is central. Post-Reformation teaching on the complete ruin of fallen man found new strength in seventeenth-century France in the system of Baius and, through Molinos and Quesnel, in Jansenism. Against such teaching, it was necessary to defend the concept of man's freedom under grace and the universal scope of God's will to save. The problem of the relation between human nature and the state of man after the Fall led to extreme responses: the Protestants depreciated human nature, the Pelagians overestimated it.

Both interpretations are important in the domain of spirituality. Both agree in saying that man has lost the divine endowment as a consequence of Adam's sin. But while the Pelagians maintain that man is restored to his pure nature, capable of natural goodness and possessing a healthy will that can resist evil inclinations and temptations, and even continues to be inclined to love God, the Protestant postition maintains that man no longer possesses any soundness in his nature and that he is still inclined towards evil. This second opinion was upheld by Augustinianism and Jansenism, while the first was held by Francis de Sales and the Jesuits.[2]

Montfort was in touch with both these tendencies. He came across the more optimistic view through his Jesuit masters of the Collège de Rennes.[3] There he was taught the necessity of separation from the world and a negative view of nature, since love of God and love of the world are irreconcilably opposed. Love of God renders renunciation, poverty, love of suffering, penitence, and mortification possible and indispensable.

Still more important was Montfort's acquaintance with the *Lettres spirituelles (Spiritual Letters)* of the Jesuit mystic J.-J. Surin, of the school of Lallemant.[4] Here Montfort came into contact with the idea of "pure love," which must be obtained by perfect self-negation, which consists in dying to everything and to oneself. This ideal and the experience of the infinite greatness of God, before Whom all creatures are reduced to nothing, led to a depreciation of the creature but, at the same time, allowed the development of a rich mysticism in the France of the first half of the seventeenth century.

As for Augustinianism, Montfort became acquainted with it through the spirituality of the French school and the Oratorians.[5] In fact, they did not profess the opinion that human nature is completely ruined by sin; they entertained, however, a certain disdain for fallen man, and this disdain appeared in different degrees in Baius, Jansen, Molinos, and Quesnel. Human love, the enjoyment of creation, the pursuit of happiness, the whole of human action is seen as bearing the stamp of sin.

This deeply theocentric doctrine emphasizes the indescribable greatness of God in contrast to the absolute nothingness of man, who cannot turn directly to God and must consequently incorporate himself in the Son made man and assimilate himself to Christ in all his "states." Bérulle's representation of man's nothingness had an increasing influence on his successors. For Ch. de Condren, man has the obligation of denying himself before the infinite greatness of God and rejecting everything that comes from nature. For J.-J. Olier, the "flesh," that is, everything human, deserves only disgust and rejection. Montfort insists (TD 79, 213, 228) that man can do nothing on his own. Man's sanctification can therefore never be the result of human activity. The first step in the spiritual life will therefore be universal renunciation and mortification. This is how evil inclinations must be reduced, permitting God to work in man.

II. Greatness and Misery of Man

With the Oratorians, Montfort maintains man's nothingness and always reaffirms that man is not capable of saving himself. The initiative can only come from God Alone. It is He Who is at work in the Incarnation. His Son becomes man to redeem man. In his representation of the history of salvation as the history of Eternal Wisdom's love for man, Montfort leaves no doubt that man, even after the Fall, is the object of God's love. Man of himself is incapable of good—and here Montfort is radical, perhaps in reaction to the independent tendency of human reason that was increasingly asserting itself, claiming to explain everything by its own strength and power. This attitude has consequences for the spiritual life (TD 83). Is this a loss of man's dignity (his original nobility)? No. Man remains what he is by his creation at the hands of Wisdom: *"An abridgment of Eternal Wisdom's marvels, his small yet ever so great world, his living image and representative on earth"* (LEW 64).

1. The dignity of man

This dignity is further increased and is perfected by an *"excess of love,"* thanks to which man is now *"a brother, a friend, a disciple, a pupil, the price of his own blood and co-heir of his kingdom"* (LEW 64). According to Montfort, human dignity does not originate in man himself. Man ultimately only possesses this dignity because, and as far as, Eternal Wisdom enters into relation with him. Everything else depends on this relationship; so it is immensely important that man should be open to this relationship and let himself be loved by Wisdom. In this, Montfort rises above all moralism and casuistry; in this, too, he justifies his ascetic effort to establish this relationship of love and to maintain it (LEW 7). His ways of expressing his *"universal mortification"* (LEW 194-202) may well be characteristic of his time, and the unusually severe penitential exercises that he imposed upon himself might well alarm us, even though Montfort is not unique in this respect. The important point remains, however, that the relationship to Wisdom is not given gratuitously; it costs man something, and so man proves his sincere will and his *"ardent desire."* Moreover, the words of St. Paul, to the effect that man, in a world of sin, must always be armed for the spiritual struggle (Eph 6:10-20), remain valuable. For Montfort, the decisive weapon of the Christian in this fight is the Cross received with love (LEW 173).

2. The paradox of man

According to Montfort, man after the Fall appears to be a living paradox. Man does not lose his original essence; sin does not destroy the fact that God said of his creation and also of man, "It was very good" (Gen 1:31). In another context, Montfort emphasizes the fact that God is unchanging (TD 15, 22). But sin, the harm it brings, and the concupiscence that Baptism does not eradicate stresses that Man, although sharing in God's life, is different from God. Man cannot resolve through his own strength this irreconcilable contradiction that he carries within himself. Ultimately, he can only wait passively and hope that God, instead, might solve it by making a gift of His creative love in spite of man's resistance.[6]

It is in the Gospel alone that Montfort sees the possibility of resolving man's inner contradiction. This possibility lies in the encounter with Christ, but this encounter must become a permanent alliance. Montfort says that the aim of all devotion is Jesus Christ (TD 61). Everything depends on knowing Jesus Christ, a knowledge that Montfort sees as a deepened experience of Jesus Christ, which can be called truly mystic (LEW 11).

Man turned in on himself, whom Luther calls *"homo incurvatus,"* i.e. man in a state of sin and without Jesus Christ, is the creature most worthy of pity; but man united to Wisdom Eternal and Incarnate becomes a *"man-God"* (SM 17; 3; TD 157), who by Christ, with him, and in him is capable of all things (TD 61; 56). In spite of sin, man united to Christ can re-attain what was originally given to him

(PM 18). In Montfort's writing, Mary seems to be the very model of humanity so conceived.

3. Radical dependence

In Montfort's thought, union with Christ takes the form of slavery. By this concept, Montfort characterizes man's dependence on his Creator and his relation to God, which man broke off through sin. The resulting separation is overcome if man accepts his dependence on God, and it is precisely by making himself the slave of Jesus Christ that he recovers his dignity and his freedom. This means that man imitates the conduct of Jesus Christ, who emptied himself and chose the humility of slavery so that all men might be freed from the slavery of sin. Man must in turn renounce his autonomy and recognize Christ as the only Lord.

Montfort goes one step further. Jesus makes himself a slave in order to assume in every last respect the life of man enslaved by sin (Phil 2:1-7). Sighs and entreaties, sweat and tears, fatigued arms, sadness of heart, and affliction of the soul: this is the destiny of man in the misery of sin (LEW 41). Clearly, Montfort is thinking of the living conditions of the poor of his time. He recognizes the true condition of man in general in the misery and the material and spiritual privation of men. If he decides to live in the same conditions himself, it is not only from love of poverty but to share, like Christ, as completely as possible the wretchedness of man the sinner. In doing so, he overcomes the contrast between rich and poor, which is what people generally see. For in reality, the rich and the poor live in the same state of wretchedness. Doubtless, material well-being can clothe and hide this wretchedness, but it cannot remove it. The experience of the rich Western nations clearly shows this today. They produce new forms of wretchedness, the wretchedness of anguish that is often unconscious and very complex and that is caused by the fact that man is no longer self-assured and no longer knows exactly who he is. It is necessary, however, to know who we are if life is not to become absurd. And man only reaches this knowledge, according to Montfort, through his encounter with Eternal Wisdom, Jesus Christ. It is only in his union with Christ that man discovers the truth of what he is. What must be done first of all, and constantly thereafter, is to listen to those words of God which form the fundamental traits of the picture of man according to the Bible (LEW 30).

4. Indigence

Man's powerlessness to obtain salvation through his own strength and his inability to reach the goal of Jesus Christ, Eternal Wisdom, justify for Montfort the necessity of a mediator with the Mediator himself (TD 83). It is an obligation, a necessity for man to use the help God offers him (TD 84). Of all these means of help, Mary has precedence, because she is Mother of Grace, *"royal throne of Eternal Wisdom"* (TD 27-44; LEW 208). But above all, it is she who produced the Head of the Mystical Body and who also produces its members (SM 12). The connection between Christ, Mary, and the Christian is based, according to Montfort, in the mystery of the Mystical Body of Christ. The consequence that he draws is that the Christian is the slave of Jesus Christ and, by analogy, he is also the slave of Mary (TD 70). This means that man essentially depends on Jesus Christ not only as his Creator but also as his Redeemer. This dependence is part of the definition of man according to Montfort.

5. Self-realization

In God's plan of salvation, the Redeemer comes to man through Mary, and Mary, by her *fiat,* shares in the Incarnation and at the same time in the Redemption. Thus man depends on Mary, on her *fiat.* This is a dependence of another type (TD 74) but no less wide in scope. In God's order of salvation, Jesus is de facto and always the Master of life, and Mary is de facto and always Mother and Mistress of life, whether man grasps it or not. But then, man only finds and realizes himself by accepting this dependence, which is always there from the start, and by living it out consciously. This is what happens in Montfort's Consecration to Jesus Christ through Mary. This is where the baptized draw the only possible and reasonable conclusion, in view of the wretchedness of their sin, their inability to save themselves, and the order of salvation as it is given by God. By recognizing their complete dependence on Jesus and Mary, by placing all that they possess in their hands, the baptized make themselves consciously dependent, radically so from every point of view; but it is precisely in this way that they attain true freedom, the freedom of the children of God (TD 169; 170; 215; SM 41). Consecra-tion in the form of slavery as intimated by Montfort signifies the most perfect realization of human freedom, for it implies an explicit choice and a free—and thus loving—acceptance of the relation to Christ that is accomplished in Baptism.

6. Consecration

According to Montfort, this relation to Christ, properly conceived, implies a relation to Mary, a relation brought about by the order of salvation as it is given to us. Montfort characterizes this relation by saying that everything must be done *"through Mary, with Mary, in Mary and for Mary"* (TD 257; SM 46-49). This is perfect Consecration. This unreserved giving to Mary implies letting oneself be formed and led by her in all things (TD 219-221, 258-259; SM 16-18). The aim of such giving is to attain the full stature of Christ (LEW 214; TD 33). In other words, it must lead the Christian to spiritual maturity. It is a long path, a lifelong one in most cases. It can be described as a slow and continual transformation of Baptismal grace. It draws its life from the existential experience of the love of God, calling man to an unconditional response, to the irrevocable giving of himself. This is a path of self-surpassing, which continually grows at all levels of human consciousness and finds its highest expression in a love that forgets itself. This Consecration encompasses *"our body with its senses and members,"* i.e. the self with its faculties; *"our soul with its faculties,"* i.e. the self as the deepest place of human motivation; *"our interior and spiritual possessions."* These are not necessarily to be sacrificed but are used according to the criterion of love (TD 121). In this love which gives unreservedly, human life attains a sovereign authenticity in its conformity with Christ's love.

Similarly, the unreserved and definitive gift of self corresponds to the way man's personality is structured. One can also judge a man's maturity according to how far he has learnt to give himself in this way.

Man can only become himself in the interpersonal relations that are realized through the giving and receiving of authentic love. An authentic relationship reaches its highest expression in mutual giving of one to another, in which both parties discover themselves as people in the reciprocal act of giving that unites them. The "I" becomes complete when it gives itself to a "you"; and the more successful this act of giving, the more self-aware man becomes. This giving of oneself through love is also the core of Christian love, both the love of God and love of one's neighbor. This love must lead to giving oneself because its ideal model is Christ.[7]

7. The tension between the ideal and the real

In Montfort's thinking, man is characterized by a deep internal tension between the ideal of the human being as God created him (LEW 35-38) and the reality of human life, which, in Montfort's eyes, is so marked by the consequences of sin. This is a deep and permanent human experience: it can be detected in the tension inherent in every human life, which is torn between the infinite aspirations, desires, and thinking of man and the finite nature and the limitations of the human condition—both experienced simultaneously. How will man manage this tension, which is not easy to bear? This is the crux of the matter. The answer lies in his life having a meaning and being a success.[8] Man's own inclination to avoid as far as possible all injury to his sense of self-worth does not make the task any easier. This is where we can detect those subtle forms of selfishness of which Montfort is speaking when he remarks that even the most disinterested and noble conduct is tainted with self-love (TD 78). Montfort turns forcefully against the temptation, ever present and so strong, to do away with the tension between the ideal and real life, between desire and moderation. How do people attempt to do this? Simply by making man alone responsible for his safety and well-being. This is the ultimate temptation, which urges man to make himself the center of the universe and claim to be omnipotent, at least to a certain point. To have all that one wants, to possess all that one desires, to receive instant satisfaction of every wish, to seek continually to assert one's own superiority: this is what Montfort calls the wisdom of the world (LEW 75-82), which he rejects categorically. For flight from the fundamental tension of human life into the illusion of human omnipotence results in man becoming a slave to himself.

For Montfort, the reality of the Incarnation also opens up a path that permits us to work with this tension. In fact, the Incarnation implies that it is not any human urge towards transcendence that is at the beginning of things but a movement of condescension on the part of God, which long precedes man's religious needs. This divine condescension signifies that in the person of His Son become flesh, God submits himself to human limitations down to their last detail (LEW 70; TD 17-19; 243). The Cross becomes the highest point of this tension in the life of God made man. It is also the powerful call to the believer to make the decisive choice; this choice does not do away with the tension we have already mentioned but, instead, means accepting and bearing it. For the Cross and the Resurrection finally reveal that it is not man, but God Alone Who fulfills the infinite aspirations of the human heart and makes it overcome its own limits.

Montfort builds his spirituality on this image of man, which he bases on the fundamental claims of the Bible, making of man a being who receives, who is laden with gifts—in stark contrast to man as he is seen by those who do not believe. This does not mean that he reduces man to a so-called mystic level, as if man could simply sit back and do nothing. But it remains true (and perhaps this is one of the sources of difficulty that people experience with the person and thinking of Montfort) that for him, man's existence is a reality defined by receiving: life is a pure gift of God. When man is no longer prepared to accept his role as recipient, when he no longer recognizes God as the eternal beginning and the goal of his life and prefers to live according to his own means, he falls into that frenzy of activity that began with original sin. Its destructive effects appear more and more worrying as the end of the twentieth century approaches, and in all aspects of life: in the way man organizes his own life, in the dissoluteness of social life, in the thoughtless pillaging of creation.

Whoever enters into Montfort's spirituality feels he is being invited to change his idea of man, to renew it by taking Revelation into account. This takes him onto the difficult path that leads from the old to the new Man. In the tension between infinity and the finite, he discovers and lives out the possibilities of life that God offers to him.

III. Montfort's Passion for the Absolute

The tension between the infinite and the finite, between the ideal and the reality of human existence, marked Montfort's life deeply. The key trait of his character was his thirst for the absolute. This included his unshakable passion for God Alone, which already appeared in his earliest years and in which he strove to combine all his energies as he increased in age and maturity. The same aspiration to the absolute, which leaves no space for mediocrity, imbued his personality as it developed. The question has been raised whether this inclination was strengthened by mental conflicts, caused according to some by Montfort's unsuccessful identification with his own father. Given the relatively small number of documents on which such an argument might be based, it is better to leave the question open.[9] What is more decisive here is that Montfort's inclination was strengthened, on the one hand, by his spiritual guides and his reading, which inculcated the ideal of Christian perfection and of pure love, and, on the other hand, by his discovery of the radical nature of the Gospel. Montfort was constrained to take the Gospel literally, with all the consequences this entails. This appeared quite clearly when he followed Jesus' command literally: "Let them deny themselves and take up their cross daily and follow me" (Lk

9:23). Montfort lived out this renunciation so completely that he caused people to accuse him of despising himself. In this he was influenced by the generally accepted way of thinking of the time: human nature is spoiled; we must suppress all its manifestations. But what appeared to be contempt of self was, rather, that forgetfulness of self whose model is the *kenosis* of God made man. And it was to become increasingly so.

It is important to live out the ideal of poverty just as radically; for Montfort, poverty is not only renunciation of material goods but renunciation of support of any kind in this world. For him, this is the sign and the starting point of an unshakable trust in Divine Providence. The same aspiration towards the absolute marks his spiritual life. Prayer was to occupy every free moment of his time; penance and bodily mortifications were to exceed the normal by far, both in quantity and form. This passion for the absolute urged Montfort to advance always further. But it also became the place where he experienced his limitations, both internal and external. He had to recognize that this passion, if it was not wisely controlled by him and no one else, would lead him to the limit of his strength and even jeopardize his life. He was constrained to recognize that it made of him an eccentric, fitting into no recognizable mold, because he exceeded the bounds of what was held to be good behavior in his milieu, and that by the same token it necessarily provoked incomprehension, rejection, and opposition. His impulsive, ardent temperament, led him to commit actions that were not only admirably brave but sometimes ill thought out and exaggerated and thus led him to be thought of as eccentric. The difficulties and failures of his life were caused by this. Montfort was forced to admit that he harmed himself by his singular qualities.

The conversation that Montfort had with his friend Blain less than two years before his death helps us to understand his personality. It shows us that Montfort was aware of the problem and that he made considerable efforts to eliminate his quirks.[10] Des Bastières, who worked with him for eight years, stated that Montfort managed to control his aggressive tendencies and use them constructively.[11] On this point, his ever-stronger closeness to Christ helped him greatly; indeed, this closeness increased in moments of crisis. His vital aim, to become like Christ and reach the full stature of Christ, led him to discover the gentleness and goodness of Jesus (LEW, chap. 10 and 11; LS 32-35). He made them increasingly his own, and this earned him the title "good Father Montfort."

His closeness to Christ also permitted him to confront the danger of quietist passivity and to transform the passive obedience that he had been taught at Saint-Sulpice into active obedience. Obedience remained a particular virtue for him, in the sense that God Alone takes the initiative. But for Montfort that does not mean that we need do nothing. On the contrary, we must *"listen to God with humble submission; act in him and through him with persevering fidelity . . . inspire others with that love for Wisdom which will lead them to eternal life"* (LEW 30). It is in this sense of obedience that man can realize the essence of Christian action and its ideal of a life according to the Gospel and according to the example of the Apostles. Then he takes on the ambition to make his life conform to the *"wisdom of the Apostles."*[12] Even if this means he will be accused of eccentricity. Here he expresses a high degree of self-confidence, as long as he is under the sovereign working of God; but this does not remove his suspicion of the malice of human nature and makes him hold firm to his rigorous penances and mortification of the body. But he can appeal to the example of numerous saints in this connection.

Humanity, as seen by Montfort, is characterized by a profound inner tension. Montfort neither sought to eliminate this tension, nor to accommodate himself to it (except when it threatened his life's ideals) nor did he take refuge in some extremism which saw nothing good outside of itself. Retaining his passion for the absolute, he realized, often painfully, that he could not divorce himself from reality. He knew that he had to remain in touch with the concreteness of his life, especially of himself as a person. This did not result in a lazy compromise for him. Rather it permitted him to identify his own ideals in given situations. Thus he avoided making his personal need for the absolute a framework of reality for others. Thus he was able to perceive the value of differing spiritual choices and directions. He succeeded in reconciling his passion for the infinite with the limitations of inner and outer reality. His life was ever more imbued with this resolve: to expect everything from God and His Holy Mother.

H. J. Jünemann

Notes: (1) B. Lauret, *Systematische Christologie, (Systematic Christology)* in P. Eicher (ed.), *Neue Summe Theologie, (Compendium of Theology)* Herder, Freiburg 1988, 1:141. (2) Cf. Ch.-A. Bernard, *Teologia spirituale, (Spiritual Theology)* Ed. Paoline, Rome 1982, 260-261. (3) Cf. S. De Fiores, *Itinerario,* 34-58. (4) Ibid., 176-183. (5) Ibid., 101-106. (6) O. H. Pesch, *Mensch/Menschwerdung,* (Man/Mankind) in *Praktisches Lexikon der Spiritualität, (Practical Dictionary of Spirituality)* Herder, Freiburg 1988, 871. (7) Cf. S. De Fiores, *Prospettive teologiche circa la consazcrazione a Maria, (Theological Perspectives Concerning the Consecration to Mary)* in S. De Fiores, S. Epis, and G. Amorth, *La consacrazione dell'Italia a Maria,* (The Consecration of Italy to Mary) Ed. Paoline, Rome 1983, 46-49. (8) Cf. B. Kiely, *Psycologie and Moral Theologie, (Psychology and Moral Theology)* Gregorian University Press, Rome 1980, 170-211. (9) R. Lagueux, *Approches psychologiques de la dévotion mariale chez Grignion de Montfort (Psychological Approaches to Marian Devotion in Grignion de Montfort),* in CM 52 (1966), 103-112; L. Perouas, *Grignion de Montfort, les pauvres et les missions (Grignion de Montfort, the Poor and Missions),* Cerf, Paris 1966, 33-46; *Ce que croyait Grignion de Montfort et comment il a vécu sa foi,* Mame, Tours 1973, 18, 30, 167; *(L. Perouas, A Way to Wisdom)* S. De Fiores, *Itinerario,* 31, 65, 74-77, 123, 226, 266-267; R. Laurentin, *Dieu seul est ma tendresse (God Alone is my Tenderness),* O. E. I. L., Paris 1984, 78, 117-118. (10) Blain, 184-189. (11) Grandet, 374. - (12) Blain, 188-189.

MARIE LOUISE OF JESUS

I. Biographical Profile

1. Childhood and adolescence

Marie Louise was born in Poitiers on May 7, 1684, and baptized the same day in the parish church of St. Etienne. Her parents, Julien Trichet and Françoise Lecocq, were deeply Christian. Marie Louise was the fourth child and third daughter of a family of eight.

The eldest, Jeanne, struck with paralysis at the age of thirteen, was cured three years later during a visit to Notre Dame des Ardilliers at Saumur. The second daughter, Elizabeth, a year older than Marie Louise and her inseparable companion, was known because of her extraordinary piety as "the angel of the family." The youngest, born after the death of two children in infancy, would later join the Congregation governed by her sister. Julien, the eldest son, who followed his father into the legal profession, was the only member of the family to marry. Alexis, a year younger than Marie Louise, was ordained priest in 1710. When the plague broke out in a prison camp, he volunteered to minister to the victims, contracted the disease, and died.

Her father held a distinguished post as magistrate at the Court of Justice of Poitiers. There was no lack of cases at the time, nor was there a lack of lawyers willing to defend them; not all of them, unfortunately, as honest as Monsieur Trichet, who refused to handle doubtful ones. Honesty does not always pay, and the family found itself living in reduced circumstances.

At the age of seven, Marie Louise was sent to the boarding school at Poitiers conducted by the Sisters of Ste. Jeanne de Lestonac; here she acquired the feminine and social accomplishments expected of a young person of quality in seventeenth-century France. In an atmosphere of simplicity and contemplation that was much to her taste, she gave free reign to her spiritual fervor, finding increasing inspiration in Mary. The product of an inner freedom, her faith, combined with love, was lived out daily.

We do not know just when the young girl's thoughts turned towards the religious life, but more and more frequently she was to be found on the road leading to the hospital, sometimes alone, sometimes in the company of her sister, with whom she attended Holy Mass daily in the cathedral. Together they would visit the poor in their homes as well as in the hospital.

2. The meeting with Montfort

In 1701, Father de Montfort went to Poitiers. He preached, heard confessions, and spent much time with the poor of the hospital, where he was to become chaplain. Returning from church, where she had listened to a sermon by Louis Marie, Elizabeth exclaimed to her sister, "That preacher is a saint."

Marie Louise had already decided to go to confession to this priest and perhaps confide to him her aspirations for the religious life. She entered the confessional. Scarcely had she begun to speak when the preacher interrupted her. *"My child, who sent you to me?"* "My sister," was the reply. *"No, my child, it was not your sister but the Blessed Virgin who sent you to me."* What prophetic words! From then on, the whole of Marie Louise's life, though she did not know it then, was set to bring about Montfort's idea: "A congregation of young women dedicated to Incarnate Wisdom, so as to confound the false wisdom of the world by the establishment of the folly of the Gospel among them."

She placed herself under the direction of this holy priest. After following a retreat preached by him, she became a frequent visitor to the small community of poor and infirm women founded by him, and of which he had become the chaplain. This, however, did not satisfy her aspiration for the contemplative life; she wished to enter a monastery. She sought his help, but this was not forthcoming, and during his absence she decided to enter the community of the Canonesses of St. Augustine at Chatellerault. She had no dowry, so she would have to be a lay Sister. This mattered little to her. But illness and a hint of Jansenism soon sent Madame Trichet to reclaim her daughter. On her return to Poitiers, she found Montfort. Her demands were renewed. "Shall I be a religious?" The response was unexpected but decisive: *"Go and live at the hospital!"*

3. The hospital in Poitiers

Poverty, corruption, and vandalism were rampant in Poitiers, as in most towns throughout the country. In Poitiers, capital of Poitou, a fine stone building had been erected: the General Hospital. Here were forcibly enclosed the town's beggars, cripples, drunks—the dregs of society—a world into which Montfort the young chaplain was determined to introduce some order, piety, and, if possible, a little joy. The rule of life he proposed for the governors was rejected. The rules that he introduced to ameliorate the lot of the inmates were regarded with suspicion or hostility. All the hospital offered the inmates was a common room; one bed for two, sometimes three; black bread; an unappetizing stew; and a uniform of grey calico.[1]

"Go and live at the hospital" was the direction given to a young girl who had already experienced the monastery and whose only dream was to return, to a young lady from a distinguished family and of a high education. "Go to the hospital." In what position? There was no vacancy for a governor. "Take me as an inmate," was Marie Louise's reply. "Go to the hospital." For how long? *"Do not leave this place even if it should take ten years for the congregation to be established; God will be pleased and his design accomplished."*

4. A long wait

Marie Louise obeyed. She left her family, and on February 2, 1703, she received from Montfort a religious habit and consecrated herself to God. For ten long years, the whole of her youth, she would live among the poor at their service, following alone the Rule rejected by the governors of the establishment. Gradually, the administration would confide to her financial and material responsibility; from 1708 she would substitute for the official bursar, until finally in 1711 she found herself in complete charge of the establishment. In the years of scarcity that were the sad characteristic of the end of the "Great Reign" and the beginning of the new century, and in the rigors of terrible winters that brought the poor and destitute in droves to the hospital, she carried out her functions with zeal and compassion. When the terrible epidemic of 1710 broke out, she found herself almost alone at the bedside of the sick, so great was the fear of contagion.

The years passed, with Montfort away on his missions in the west of France, letters at long intervals her only consolation.

In 1713, Montfort arrived at last at Poitiers. The conversations they had were long and fruitful; he gave her a companion, Catherine Brunet, chosen by her from among the governors. The long solitude was over.

5. The school at La Rochelle

In 1711, Montfort, with the approval of Monsignor de Champflour, bishop of La Rochelle, preached a mission there. During the course of the mission, the bishop confided to Montfort his great desire to build schools for the poor children of the diocese. Montfort, for his part, seeing the religious education of children as a fruitful outcome of the mission, was in full accord; the decision was taken to open two schools: one for boys and one for girls. For the latter, Montfort would enlist the help of the Daughters of Wisdom.

Marie Louise and Catherine Brunet, despite fierce opposition to their departure, left Poitiers for La Rochelle on March 23, 1715. A school was opened that in a short time would cater four hundred girls; a free school supported by the bishop and following the program and rules laid down by Montfort in his Rules for Charity Schools. It was so successful that it aroused the admiration of both the Jesuits and Bishop de Champflour himself. Not content with teaching academic subjects only, the school formed the pupils to good habits of discipline and piety. Marie Louise proved herself especially adept with adolescents, forming an association of thirty-three pupils in honor of the thirty-three years spent on earth by Jesus, Incarnate Wisdom. They followed a small rule of life drawn up by Marie Louise and approved by the bishop.

6. The Institution of the Daughters of Wisdom

Montfort withdrew from his missionary activities to spend time at the hermitage of St. Eloi at La Rochelle. While there, he put the finishing touches to the Rule of the Daughters of Wisdom. On August 22, 1715, Marie Louise and Catherine Brunet, together with the two ladies of La Rochelle who had joined them, Marie Valleau and Marie Régnier, made their religious profession at the hands of Montfort with the approbation of Bishop de Champflour. *"Call yourselves,"* he said, *"the Daugh-ters of Wisdom, for the teaching of children and the care of the poor."* And he added: *"God wants Marie Trichet to be the superior."* A community, a title, a Rule, a superior: the Institute was founded.

7. The death of Montfort

In the early days of May 1716, a messenger arrived with the sad news that Montfort had died while preaching a mission at St. Laurent-sur-Sèvre. Marie Louise, at thirty-two years of age, would, in the absence of a successor, assume the full responsibility for the foundation. Who was left after the death of the founder? A few priests, his missionary companions, who were not committed by vows; four Brothers with vows; three lay mission helpers, and, at La Rochelle, a female community that already had a structure, with a superior, three professed Sisters, and one novice. The numbers were negligible, but the numbers of Sisters especially would to grow rapidly. For the next three years, the school continued.

8. Foundation of the mother house

After the Sisters' departure from Poitiers, the situation in the hospital went from bad to worse. In 1719, the administration decided to ask the Sisters to return. But knowing that from now on it was a question of an established Congregation, they offered Sister Trichet the opportunity to install her mother house and novitiate at the hospital. Consumed by the desire to develop the Institute confided to her by Montfort, Marie Louise accepted, and with Catherine (Sister of the Conception) and Marie-Anne (Sister of St Joseph) she returned to her home town.

The administrators, however, interested only in the hospital, included in the contract two clauses unacceptable to the foundress: the board would name the superior, and half of the novices' dowry would accrue to the hospital. Not willing to compromise the autonomy of the Institute, Marie Louise refused. But then Providence intervened.

A chance meeting in the streets of Poitiers brought advice. Here, one day, the foundress met Jacques Goudeau, a pious layman, a disciple of Montfort. Before leaving for a mission, St. Louis Marie had confided to him the care of the sanctuary of Mary, Queen of All Hearts, at Montbernage. He suggested to Marie Louise that she contact Madame de Bouillé, a noble lady living in the neighborhood of Saint-Laurent: "She is in a position to help you," he said. For Marie Louise, this was a sudden and blinding revelation: Madame de Bouillé, a woman cured by Montfort; Saint-Laurent, the burial place of the founder. Was this not a sign from God?

The noble lady proved only too willing to help the daughters of the holy missionary. At first the dean of Saint-Laurent was well disposed to the proposed foundation. He called a meeting of the inhabitants; their act of agreement was registered at Mortagne on September 14, 1719.

One evening in June 1720, during the octave of Corpus Christi, Sister Marie Louise arrived at Saint-Laurent. Her first visit was to the tomb of her spiritual father, where she knelt in fervent prayer; then on to the "Maison Longue," the house purchased for her by Madame de Bouillé. She found it dilapidated, lacking the barest essentials. Here, in extreme poverty, the mother house of the congregation would function for several years. Bedding, clothing, and maintenance were nonexistent. Certain days would see the Sisters with only black bread for sustenance and, on one occasion, one egg for four Sisters.

Problems abounded, not least the opposition of the dean, M. Rougeau de la Jarrie, who had expected a kind of help for his parish that in their destitution the Sisters were unable to supply. One Sister gave classes to girls without asking fees; another visited the sick in their homes but had little to give them. And the community life, regulated by the bell that called the Sisters to prayers, seemed more conventual in style than was to the liking of the good priest. He had envisaged a parish team; the foundress, faithful to her mission, was set on establishing a novitiate.

The novices arrived, some of noble birth, others of humble origin; all were received with the same warmth. Marie Louise herself formed them with the greatest care in the religious life according to the Rule and spiritual doctrine of Louis Marie de Montfort. Silence, detachment from the world, poverty and mortification, prayer, a tender devotion to Mary, and an intense love of Jesus, Incarnate Wisdom, were taught more by her example than by word, gently in the joy of daily community living.

Madame de Bouillé, in her enthusiasm, wished to participate in this community life, but her two young children's natural exuberance was a constant obstacle to what little calm was possible. Her strongly expressed views, far from being the same as those of the superior, were often more in line with those of the dean. It became necessary that she should depart.

In separating itself from its benefactress, the community was depriving itself of valuable resources. Providence, however, came to their aid. With the dowries provided by certain novices, land was acquired that produced a certain amount of revenue. This, too, however, brought new problems in the form of hostile neighbors, who denounced the Sisters to the authorities as landowners evading taxes. The case was dismissed. Many years later, during the great drought of 1739, Marie Louise won the gratitude and affection of both people and parish priest when, having shared with them her reserves of wheat, she negotiated and obtained for them large provisions of rice from the authorities.

9. The montfort family at Saint-Laurent

Marie Louise also played a role in the establishment of the Company of Mary at Saint-Laurent.

There were two priests, Fathers Mulot and Vatel, and Brother Mathurin Rangeard, a lay Brother and faithful companion in their missions. When the superior of the Daughters of Wisdom founded her mother house, she recognized the need for a spiritual director, and who better than the priest designated by Montfort himself on his deathbed as his successor could fill this post? She requested and obtained permission from the bishop for R. Mulot to take up this duty and, at the same time, welcomed to Saint-Laurent M. Valois, who had joined the missionary group, all the while discerning and affirming the vocation of Brother Joseau, a faithful friend of the community. During a new mission at Saint-Laurent in 1721, the installation of the missionaries at the place of the tomb of their founder was decided. Thus, at the instigation of Marie Louise, Saint-Laurent became the place where the disciples of Montfort regrouped. In 1722, Montfort Fathers and Brothers gathered together in their new residence, elected their superior, and pronounced their vows in his presence.

They obtained from a nobleman, the Marquis de Magnanne, a relative of Madame de Bouillé, an ancient inn known as the "Green Oak," which served as residence during their breaks between missions. In 1723, the number of Sisters having increased to nine, their house, the "Maison Longue," proved inadequate, and a friendly exchange of residences took place between the two communities.

10. First foundations

Novices continued to arrive; the time had come to set up new foundations.

Montfort had predicted, *"There is a house at Rennes where you will go."* A true prophecy: the first Sisters to leave the mother house were destined for Rennes, capital of Brittany. In 1724, the Daughters of Wisdom took possession of a charitable school founded by the Marquis de Magnanne. The following year found them once more at La Rochelle, this time in the hospital, facing an extremely painful situation.

When Marie Louise left La Rochelle in 1719, she left behind two Sisters from that town, Sister of the Incarnation (Marie Valois) and Sister of the Cross (Marie Regnier). The separation, intended to be temporary, became protracted and came close to developing into a full-blown schism. The two Sisters, ill advised by successive directors and colleagues, abandoned both the grey habit and the name of Daughters of Wisdom. While continuing to observe the Rule given by Montfort, they functioned as an autonomous Institute, even receiving postulants. In 1725, they numbered eight and were staffing the schools of Saint-Nicholas, Esnandes, and Chaillé, when their director, M. Bourgine, acting in the name of the hospital board, offered them the administration of the general hospital.

At this point, Marie Louise intervened. She left for La Rochelle, and by dint of gentle persuasion, she brought about a reconciliation. She personally negotiated the contract between the hospital and the congregation. Later, at the request of the parish and the population, she proceeded to the Ile de Ré to establish a new community, that of La Flotte.

The Sisters at this date numbered twenty-four, including aspirants dispersed throughout five establishments: Saint-Laurent, Rennes, La Rochelle, Esnandes and La Flotte-en-Ré.

11. The development of the Institute

The Institute continued to develop. From 1729 to 1759, the foundress established thirty new communities, charitable establishments where the Sisters taught children, visited the poor, and nursed the sick without any payment; their expenses being met by the parishioners or benefactors.

There were also houses of "Providence," where the Sisters lived with orphans, the aged, and the handicapped confided to their care. Here they existed from day to day on voluntary donations.

There were the general hospitals, like the one at La Rochelle, or at Niort, where administrators hired their services: places of misery and often of filth and disorder, where they were expected to introduce a modicum of peace and happiness.

In all her foundations, Marie Louise proved herself both spiritual and realistic—realistic in her negotiation of contracts on the material environment and spiritual in her overriding concern for the spiritual welfare of her religious. She personally installed them in each new residence, remaining with them from three weeks to three months, or even longer, according to the circumstances; at Oléron , for example, this meant three years. A Sister would be designated to govern the mother house when this happened.

Later on, when she could no longer accompany the Sisters in new foundations, she would delegate a wise and experienced Sister. She never accepted an establishment if the conditions were incompatible with the observance of the basic Rules of the Institute. As at Saint-Laurent she had steadfastly refused to yield to the demands of the parish priest and her benefactress Madame de Bouillé, so at Poitiers she refused the enclosure of the Sisters requested by the bishop. However strong may have been her own attraction for the contemplative life, she remained faithful to the direction of St. Louis de Montfort, the founder. To the suggestion that she should introduce in the Congregation perpetual adoration of the Blessed Sacrament, one half of the community being at prayer while the other was at work, her reply was, "That was not the intention of Father de Montfort." Rather, following the example of the Blessed Virgin Mary, every Sister should be both Martha and Mary. This was indeed the specific role of Montfort's idea in the evolution of religious life of the eighteenth century.

12. The last years and death of the foundress

Combining the purest of mental prayer with continual activity, Marie Louise lived through her long adulthood, right up to the onset of old age.

At the age of 66, she made a last, long, and arduous journey on horseback to all of her foundations; a visit that gave to her the pleasure of finding all the Sisters living faithfully to the original Rule, and to the Sisters the joy of a final encounter and a chance to listen to her final exhortations. She returned to the mother house, never to leave it again.

A last painful trial, coming from her own community, awaited her. A Sister, who remains anonymous, started a campaign against her, with the intention of replacing her as head of the community. The new Father General, recently appointed and inexperienced, gave credence to the calumnies levelled against the foundress, who accepted the humiliations and reproaches in silence while continuing to govern with gentleness and self-effacement. When, at the end of a year, justice was finally done, she treated the instigator with the utmost charity and consideration.

Then she suffered an accident: a fall that occasioned months of suffering patiently borne. This was followed by a final illness, which heralded her meeting with her Lord. Her last hours were interspersed with frequent and joyful "Alleluias." Her last words were, "My Lord and my God."

This was in 1759, on the same day (28 April), at the same time, and even in the same place as Saint Louis Marie de Montfort, whose faithful disciple she had always been, had died. Her body lies next to his in the basilica at Saint-Laurent.

II. Her personality and Her Work

"What will become of this child?"—the exasperated exclamation of Madame Trichet. "You are mistaken, my dear!" was the reply of Monsieur Trichet. "God will do great things through her." Her personality was ambiguous from the start: reserved, timid, discreet, with a deep-rooted humility, she seemed to be introverted. Yet her faith, her balance, and her tenacity marked her for great things. Her serenity would exasperate some of her Sisters. Her obstinacy in following her own idea in opposition to the parish priest of Saint-Laurent would astound him. In her last years, her adamant opposition to the construction of ostentatious buildings at the mother house would be attributed by her detractors in the community to a deterioration of her mental powers. Until recent years, the tendency was to leave her in the shade, albeit in the shade of Saint Louis Marie. It must, nevertheless, be remarked that the parish priest did retract his unfavorable judgement. "I recognize the devil played his part," he remarked. The Father General, misled by the campaign waged against her, repented of his misjudgment and wrote her biography, the most important document about her. In a circular written the day following her death, he extolled her virtues. To the Daughters of Wisdom he wrote: "You have lost a real daughter of Montfort, a mother, a foundress, a model, a living copy of the virtues of Jesus Incarnate Wisdom."[2] Sr. Florence, her assistant for ten years, would affirm: "Her natural mind was capable of great things . . . . She had a foresightedness without equal, a mind that no detail escaped . . . . Her judgement and grasp of a situation were excellent."[3]

While not wishing to emulate the exaggerated eulogies of a certain style of hagiography, we must nevertheless recognize in Marie Louise not a speculative intelligence, but a sound judgement, a sense of reality, and a penetrating gift of discernment. She did not have extraordinary intuitions, but in them she showed balance and discretion. She did not dream of grand projects, but remained faithful to a demanding vocation, to the everyday calls on her energies, and was most effective in practical ways. Instead of a creative imagination, she showed, rather, a discretion and a wisdom that saved her always from excess and the lure of the spectacular, while her extraordinary energy helped her overcome trials and obstacles. Her strong fear of sin and her exalted understanding of obedience made her much more of a disciple than an innovator; yet, her care for human beings, allied with her gift of discernment, made her naturally a remarkable teacher. That is really what she was, as her tombstone, placed next to that of Montfort in the basilica in Saint-Laurent, says: *"Marie Louise of Jesus, foundress of the first Daughters of Wisdom."* The French word is *Institutrice*, one who founds, but also one who educates.

1. The foundress

On this point, we could ask two questions: What would Marie Louise have become without Montfort? And what would have become of Montfort's dream without Marie Louise?

Without Montfort, what would Marie Louise have become? No doubt a holy religious, probably a nun, and eventually an excellent superior of a community. Her desire to be a religious was obvious, but she would probably never have dreamt, left to herself, of founding a Religious Institute.

In fact, after her ill-fated spell in the novitiate of the Augustinian Canonesses, she tried three times to enter an established community. This was during the ten years of solitude in Poitiers. The first time, on the advice of her director in the absence of Montfort, Father Carcault, she asked to join the Daughters of Charity. But Bishop de Champflour forbade it: "You want to be a Grey Sister? Are you not one already?" A little later, she wanted to join the Benedictines of Calvary. Father Carcault gave his consent, provided Montfort should agree. But Montfort was forthright: *"Wait in patience and stay at the hospital."* Marie Louise, however, as the waiting grew longer, tried a third time, with the Carmelites of Montierneuf. This time, it was the Abbess who refused. And so, Providence returned her to Father de Montfort. Her vocation was to be his disciple and a cooperator in his life's work.

Marie Louise was first and foremost Montfort's disciple by the way she lived. She followed fervently the spiritual path traced out for her by the saint in LEW. Perhaps this is the book which he sent to the first Daughters of Wisdom, saying to them: *"Here is a book written for you."* The desire for Wisdom, continual prayer, universal mortification, dependence on Mary: Marie Louise made all these means pointed out by Montfort her own way to salvation. She kept faithfully, from the time of her harsh novitiate in Poitiers until her death, the rule of life mapped out by the founder. She taught its spirit and practice to the religious placed under her guidance. She defended it against all the abuses and softening with which even holy priests would try to dilute it, priests like Father Vatel or the dean of Saint-Laurent; against the suggestions of Madame de Bouillé, or the requests of the bishop of Poitiers: "That is not what Father de Montfort wanted," was always her irrefutable argument.

"She looked upon herself," says Pauvert, one of the biographers of Saint Louis Marie, "as a compliant worker putting into effect the plan of the master. If she had thought for a moment that the idea was her own, she would never have had the courage to fight all the obstacles that the nascent project was to encounter. She would have left it alone, believing that she had dreamed the impossible. But her burning faith in the holiness of the priest whose virtues she had seen gave her a trust in his promise and enabled her to hope beyond all hope." She was indeed, then, the disciple, to the point of heroism, of the one from whom, from her earliest youth, she had received teaching, example, and formation. That is why we could not imagine Marie Louise without Montfort.

On the other hand, what would have happened to Montfort's ideas for his foundations without Marie Louise? What would the beginnings of the Daughters of Wisdom have been like without her feminine influence, at once gentle and discreet? Certainly Montfort is a saint and a genius. His apostolic success was astonishing, the conversions he obtained extraordinary. And yet, according to his own words, he was like *"a ball in a game of tennis,"* always on the move, always the object of opposition. He initiated great plans without always seeing them bear fruit. RW, which he had dreamed of since 1702, would not be officially approved until 1715, by the bishop of La Rochelle. RM was only put together little by little, during his successive meetings with the seminary of the Holy Spirit in Paris in 1703 and 1713. It is true that the texts of these two are very precise, their spirituality is solidly based, and they bore much fruit; their harvest would be very great. Yet, it was not he who would gather in this harvest.

It was thanks to Marie Louise and the Marquis de Magnanne that the male disciples of Montfort found themselves gathered around the tomb of their founder. It was thanks to her that the Congregation of the Daughters of Wisdom got well started. This was not only because his death prevented the founder from completing his work but perhaps also because he himself, with his passionate temperament, was not really the right person to establish on a firm foundation a female Congregation. Pauvert was not mistaken when, while attributing to Montfort "the creative idea," recognizing in Marie Louise "the admirable instrument of its realization."[4]

Montfort reflected on, composed, and edited RW. But it was Marie Louise who founded the mother house, opened the novitiate, formed the first Sisters, established communities, and governed the Institute for more than forty years. Even during the lifetime of Montfort, we can see the discreet influence of Marie Louise on the definitive edition of the Rule. Several corrections in the manuscript give this impression, and we know that among other suggestions, she gave it as her opinion that a superior general appointed for life would present serious difficulties. "Mont-fort gave in to her advice." On the other hand, she gave very careful attention to the least little details, a tendency that would be accentuated in the Constitutions of 1760, which were drawn up under her guidance and control. Her femininity allowed her to escape a certain rigor and strangeness.[5] In codifying a certain number of customs, it seems that she gave a more monastic style to the Institute.

2. The teacher

More remarkable than her aptitude for governing was her extraordinary talent as a teacher. We find her at both La Rochelle and Rennes establishing, or reestablishing, discipline in large schools with a large enrollment. Her gift of discernment was employed in the formation of elite groups formed from among the older students.

The hospitals also profited by her talents. Not content with just ministering to the physical needs of patients, she and her Sisters always tried to introduce a modicum of peace, joy, and piety into the establishment. Documents from the hospital of Château d'Oléron, where Marie Louise stayed for nearly three years, testify that "never have the sick been better cared for, recovered more rapidly, or been more devout."[6]

Not unexpectedly, it was in the formation of the first Daughters of Wisdom that her gifts as educator were most evident. Relying always on the Holy Spirit, she nevertheless employed all her own personal gifts and intuitions, permeated with gentleness and goodness. The program was well balanced, with periods allocated to work, prayer, instruction, and relaxation. Temperaments also were taken into account. An admonition to her successor states: "Novices should be treated like fragile plants, but recently transplanted."

She knew how, following the advice of Montfort, to employ sterner measures, especially with the proud. When, however, necessity did require that she reprimand, "this was done only in private, in her own room or that of the recalcitrant novice whom she always sought out. Her speech on such occasions was so persuasive and gentle that it was impossible not to conform."[7]

She had a horror of duplicity. A novice pretending to fast while concealing bread beneath her mattress was promptly dismissed. At the same time, her reply to the singular penances of another novice that frightened her Sisters was, "Let her be; she has her reasons."

III. Her Writings

There are few remaining writings of Marie Louise: thirty letters in all, her "Spiritual Oratory,"[8] her "Spiritual Testament" (Besnard, *Marie-Louise,* 325), a ruling concerning the religious habit, and the Constitutions drawn up in collaboration with other Daughters of Wisdom. We find her signature also on receipts, account sheets, administrative documents, and a few contracts: signs of a woman engaged in apostolic action as well as spiritual combat. Fifty pages of "Memoirs," written under obedience to her Director, Father General Audubon, are unfortunately lost. We know she wrote of the early days of the Congregation, from 1701 to 1720, but above all she spoke of Montfort. It would have indeed been interesting to hear her own account of her relationship with her spiritual father, her first companions, her life at the hospital of Poitiers, and her apostolate at La Rochelle. For all this, we must refer to her biographer, who used the "Memoirs" for his book.

Little remains of her personal correspondence, especially of letters written in her own hand, only seven of which are among the twenty-nine quoted by Father Besnard, in whose possession they evidently remained. So few letters were preserved, yet we know from her own testimony that she kept a regular correspondence with the communities and with her own nieces and nephews. In the communities the messages were no doubt retained for a while, while some of the actual letters were confided to Father Besnard, who was diligently collecting all relevant material on the life of the foundress in preparation for a biography. The remainder disappeared during the troubled times of the Revolution, when the Sisters were expelled and the mother house pillaged and set on fire. Regarding the family letters, there is mention in the

Trichet family documents of a family legacy of letters that were evidently distributed among them; of these, however, only three remain in the possession of a descendant of her brother. Her business letters have completely disappeared, as have, with few exceptions, her letters of spiritual direction. We have the text of three letters written by her to Father Croissant near the end of her life, in which she outlines her personal plan of perfection. She must have given him permission to communicate these to her Father General, as they appear in her biography; we do not possess the originals.

Her family letters reveal a warm affection for her family, especially for her brother Julien, who remained close to his parents in Poitiers. At the time of her father's death, Marie Louise was in La Rochelle. She longed to be able to come to her mother and surround her with love and care, but duty prevented her, prompting her to ask her brother to take her place in doing "what little services she could render." Knowing her mother's means of livelihood to be reduced, she requested her brother to draw up a contract by which she renounced her right to any future inheritance, thus enabling him to provide her mother with a small supplement. In her letter of May 23, 1725, on the occasion of her mother's death, she expresses all her grief and affection. "Only God could have kept me from her, and it was not the least of my sacrifices. I cannot say more; my grief is too great."

Her tactful approach is seen in her correspondence with her Sisters. There is no authoritarianism here but, rather, a gentleness that anticipates all, and advice filled with tenderness and piety. She shares in their joys and difficulties, always in a spirit of faith. To a Sister provoked by an administrator she writes: "He is sent by God to try you." To a sick Sister: "Long live Jesus, long live his Cross! If we were really transformed by Divine Love, we should not complain of our illnesses." To another confiding her anxieties: "The Institutes founded by Father de Montfort are the work of God, and He is deeply concerned for their future and well-being. He will never abandon us if we are faithful to Him." These are the words of a woman of faith. But there are also the words of a mother: "Send me news of yourself. Were it only a few words, it would give me pleasure." To the community at the Château d'Oléron: "The affection I have for you is enhanced by the knowledge that I am also your mother in Christ."

To the superiors in the communities she constantly recommends obedience and humility; obedience to the hierarchy, humility in their relationships with the Sisters. To a superior complaining of her problems with a difficult Sister, she writes: "Have patience. Don't tell me you have been patient for a long time. Where would we be, you and I, if God tired of our infidelities?" Advising a Sister to break off from a too human friendship, she says: "I suggest you make a half hour's meditation at the feet of Christ and listen to what he has to say to you."

Marie Louise TRICHET, dite Marie Louise de JESUS,
1ère Supérieure des Filles de la Sagesse, morte le 28 Avril 1759,
Première élève de Mr de MONTFORT dans l'école de la Sagesse, elle
sut donner jusqu'à la Mort au Monde ses Mépris, aux pauvres sa Tendresse.

PORTRAIT OF MOTHER MARIE LOUISE

This painting preserved in the hospital of the Daughters of Wisdom, Rennes, was stylized to highlight the image of the cross. It recalls Montfort's words from his last letter, which was to her: "We want to found our Congregation on the Wisdom of the Cross of Calvary." (L 34). The painting is inscribed as follows: "Marie Louise Trichet, known as Marie Louise of Jesus. First Superior of the Daughters of Wisdom, died April 28, 1759. First student of Father de Montfort in the school of Wisdom. She knew how to despise the World, but offer its poor her tenderness."

IV. Her Spiritual Journey

1. Her search for divine Wisdom

"Jesus Christ Eternal Wisdom must be the end of all your desires. Desire Him, seek Him, for He is that precious pearl for the acquisition of which you must sell all you possess." Montfort adds: *"Whoever wishes to find this precious treasure of Wisdom should . . . search for him early and, if possible, while still young; purely and spiritually as a chaste young man seeks a bride; unceasingly, to the very end, until he has found him."* (LEW 54) A perfect account of the spiritual journey of Marie Louise. From her youth at the school of Montfort, she desired and sought Divine Wisdom, single mindedly, with complete renunciation of her own will, constantly and courageously with an ardor that increased with age.

On the occasion of her first meeting with Montfort at seventeen years of age, she was already committed to consecrating herself to God in the religious life. Montfort introduced her to the contemplation of Jesus Eternal Wisdom and the mysterious ways of the Incarnation and the Cross. He led her to leave her family and enter the hospital in the company of a group of poor women of whom he had formed a community named "Wisdom," placing her under the authority of a blind woman, saying: *"Mademoiselle Trichet must learn to obey."* He led her to heroic mortification in keeping with her aspirations, certain of which appear in our day to be exaggerated. Carrying malodorous linen at arm's length, she was ordered to carry it on her shoulders and to kiss the floor in the hospital yard. Following the guidance of her director, she gave herself to meditation and sought delight in a life "hidden, poor, and abandoned," the program inscribed on the large cross hung on the wall of the Daughters of Wisdom mother house. (see the article on the Cross).

The original Rule and especially the spiritual "counsels" added by Montfort are all imbued with the same principles, spelling out in detail the austere rules of the Cross of Poitiers. This Rule Marie Louise received, transmitted, and taught. She was formed by it; she embraced the spirit, not just the letter, and lived it as a means of acquiring the Divine Union to which Jesus called her. Thus, she was the first to live the charismatic vocation of a Daughter of Wisdom.

Humility, reserve, discretion, in short an apostolic simplicity, have made of Marie Louise a difficult subject for biographers seeking to penetrate below the exterior. Her life, actions, and certain of her writings reveal her as a woman of great faith and courage, a religious inflamed with the love of Christ, a faithful slave of Mary, and a missionary of her time. The Church, in proclaiming her Blessed in 1993, placed its seal on the heroism of her virtue.

2. Faith

A woman of faith and courage: such was Marie Louise of Jesus during the twelve years spent in the service of the poor in Poitiers, in the education of the young at La Rochelle, and especially in the formation of the first Daughters of Wisdom. Her faith sustained her through the trials of the first foundations, through solitude, poverty, and contradictions. Her meditation was, her biographer assures us, based on pure faith; she made it well, "humbling herself and becoming lost in the presence of God." Her constant admonition to her Sisters was: "Have faith. . . . We have not enough faith. . . . Let us renew our faith." Her repeated warning was against a sentimental piety that sought spiritual consolation: "Let us nourish our souls with the truths of faith without aspiring to visions or other extraordinary means that may lead us away from pure faith. Pure faith is the sure way to avoid falling prey to illusions."[9]

Her faith in the Eucharist was particularly strong. She received Communion daily and then spent half an hour in thanksgiving. While never allowing herself more time in chapel than the Rule allowed, she took every opportunity of prolonging her prayer. When passing the door of the chapel or sacristy, she would whisper a prayer. She was observed on occasion shedding tears of joy before the Blessed Sacrament. Her journeys were all marked by a visit to the chapel to adore the Blessed Sacrament, as was each departure.

Her union with God was continual, insofar as her occupations allowed. Besnard says that she managed "never to leave the center of her heart, where she had made herself a sort of interior cell." Unlike Montfort, she had no hermitage, but she prayed constantly in her "Spiritual Oratory."

Faith was the guiding light of her action as of her prayer. She sought nothing but God's will. In her youth she had sought it with a sort of anxiety, witness her several attempts to enter various convents; in later life she sought it in obedience, especially when it appeared obscure: obedience to the bishop, to her director, to the Father General. To a young novice who confessed, "Really I don't understand what 'living by the Spirit' means," she replied, "You have followed your own inclination and done your own will up till now; a spirit of faith teaches us to live only for God, to seek always his good pleasure. But we can only do this by submitting always to his Divine Will. It follows, then, that animated with a lively faith, our will is always in accord with what God allows should happen to us or asks of us through our superiors." Marie Louise practiced to the end of her life faithful obedience to the will of God manifested through her superiors and through events. A few days before her death, she asked a Sister to sing for her some verses of a hymn to Divine Providence by Father Surin: "Blessed Will of God / You are my sole delight / in heaven or on earth."

3. Humility

Love of God is synonymous with a hatred of sin. Marie Louise had a deep horror and fear of sin, together with an awareness of her own sinfulness. This was what gave rise to her humility, which was certainly not any lack of firmness of mind but, rather, a clear vision of her own nothingness before God, a conviction of the gratuity of all the graces received, and a repeated affirmation of her unworthiness: "I was placed here [in the post of superior general] for my sins, and because of my sins they leave me here." Towards the end of her life, victim of a campaign against her, unjustly accused by her Sisters, suspected and humiliated by her superior general, she remained calm and gentle, saying: "I am not upset; I deserve worse than that for my sins." We find in her life gestures of humility that may appear exaggerated, but are found also in the lives of the saints: kneeling at the door of the refectory, a cord about her neck, soliciting the prayers of her Sisters; prostrating herself before one or another of her Sisters, begging them to place their foot on her neck to humiliate her "as she deserved." Her real humility, however, was manifested in her everyday conduct, her gentle affability towards her Sisters, the respect she afforded them, her readiness to assume the most menial tasks, her preference for the company of the poor. Sr. Florence tells us of her readiness to give up her own opinion for that of others when neither principle nor the truth was at stake.

4. Obedience

Following the example of Montfort, Marie Louise practiced the virtues of poverty and obedience to an heroic degree. Yet where Montfort's predilection would seem to have been for poverty, hers was undoubtedly for obedience, as shown on numerous occasions. When Father Vatel, chaplain to the mother house and spiritual director of the community, requested that the rising time of 4 a.m. be changed to 5 a.m., causing consternation to herself and the Sisters, her reply revealed her spirit of obedience: "Real mortification is to found in perfect obedience."

She was a perfect example of the universal mortification prescribed by Montfort in LEW and into which she had been initiated in her early years. Frugal at meals, she never ate in between. She sought no comforts during her long and arduous journeys, nor relief from the hard work of moving to new foundations. Frozen in winter in an unheated chapel, she avoided the fire when entering the community. Corporal penance also had its place. The discipline, spiked bracelets, and prayers with arms extended were all means of renunciation and of opening her soul to divine grace. These were means that she also permitted to Sisters whom she considered capable of practicing them. They were considered the supporting pillars of her "Spiritual Oratory," where she communed with God. The principal support, however, was obedience resting on the sure foundation of humility.

Three letters written towards the end of her life to Father Croissant, her spiritual director, show us the lengths to which her passion for obedience drove her. They can be dated to approximately the end of 1756 or the beginning of 1757, for, commenting on them, Father Besnard tells us: "God, who brings light out of darkness, enabled Marie Louise of Jesus to draw from her persecutions an ever-increasing desire to resemble Jesus Christ crucified." During her great time of trial, she had asked her director to assign her a superior whom she would obey as God Himself, naming as the person she envisaged "the one whom she would find to be most repugnant to her own refined nature, someone who would be brusque, bizarre, anxious, and scrupulous . . . the most likely to make her suffer." Such a request is understandable only in light of the spirit that animated it. "I wish," she declared, "with God's grace to destroy all that which within me is displeasing to Him that I may have the joy of having God alone reign in my heart." "Destroy," for her, meant total transformation, not annihilation; total purification and Consecration of her will. Renunciation was not the only aspect of her resolution; there was also "joy": joy in "God alone." She found her joy in total and intimate union with God. Obedience did not come easily to her, as from a passive nature. She herself tells of the obstacles in the practice of it, speaking of "combat," "resistance," "the revolts of self love"; but "if nature rebels, I shall try not to listen."[10]

5. Joy through the Cross

To her director she once more declares her desire to be "a victim, of silence, obedience, of exterior and interior crosses." The word victim must be understood in its true sense as expounded by Father Besnard: "A state of perfect negation, fruit of her consuming desire to have Jesus reign supreme in her heart. There could be no divided loyalty; she was completely transformed in Christ." Far from being morbid, she affirmed her intense joy: "I cannot describe the consolation I receive from the Divine Jesus."

In April 21, 1759, a chill, followed by a high fever, gave her a presentiment that her death was close. From then on her thoughts were all on her approaching meeting with her Lord. After a fervent reception of the Viaticum, she blessed her Sisters with a small statue of the Blessed Virgin, the gift of St Louis Marie, dictated her "Spiritual Testament," and sank into semi-consciousness, murmuring from time to time a prayer to the Blessed Virgin or an Alleluia. Wishing to ascertain if she were still conscious, a Sister asked, "What does that mean? Alleluia?" The reply was prompt and clear: "That means 'Rejoice in the Lord!'"[11]

6. The way of Mary

"I do not believe," wrote Montfort, *"that anyone can acquire intimate union with our Lord and perfect fidelity to the Holy Spirit without a very close union with the most Blessed Virgin and an absolute dependence on her support"* (TD 43). That union and dependence Marie Louise practiced in the highest degree.

We do not know when or where she made her Consecration to Jesus through Mary as taught by by St. Louis de Montfort but that she did make it we are left in no doubt. In his letters to her, Montfort employs quite naturally and often the term *"Slavery."* In her exhortations to her Sisters, Marie Louise declares, "Your real Superior is Mary; I am but her servant." Father Besnard writes that he would not speak of her devotion to Mary "were it but the everyday devotion of ordinary Christians" but "she became transformed, lost in

Mary." She could only have arrived at that, he adds, "through the example and direction of Montfort." Through Mary, he says, "she acted and spoke, gave commands and gave thanks. Through her she received communion, considering herself unworthy to receive Christ. She offered him Mary's preparation and through Mary's thanksgiving she made her own." The life and mysteries of Mary were her daily meditation as she recited her Rosary. It was she who introduced the hourly Hail Mary into the community, and she loved to repeat: "Everything in the house belongs to Mary; for this reason we must spoil nothing and keep everything in order." Confronted with problems, she would turn to Mary: "Good Mother, you only need to make this your business. They are your daughters; take care of them for me."

V. Marie Louise Speaks to Us Today

1. Her missionary spirit

Marie Louise Trichet was given the task of governing a new type of Apostolic Institute, and this at a time when female religious had scarcely begun to venture outside their cloister. Her contemplative nature served to animate her mission. Consumed with a desire to love God more and more, "she was distressed," it was said, "by the fact the He was not loved by others." Like Montfort, she longed to go to "barbarous lands" or "to the poor women and girls of the rural areas of the country to speak of God and lead people to His love." Unable to do either, she would, together with her Sisters, pursue this aim where Providence had placed her, with the children, the poor, the sick in the hospitals and in their homes, the soldiers and sailors of Oléron, the Penitents of Poitiers, and the "converts" of Montbernage. In 1743, her dream of sending Sisters to Canada was about to be realized when it had to be abandoned for lack of finance. Unable to participate in the missionary labors of the Montfort Missionaries (Company of Mary), she addressed fervent prayers to God for vocations for the Company, and that He would bless their apostolate.

2. Her love of the poor

She was above all the missionary of the poor. Her predilection for the poor predated her entrance into the hospital, where she took them to her heart, dressed their wounds, washed their dirty linen; no service was too small. As bursar, her administration was wise and just. One severe winter, with the supplies exhausted, being approached by some beggars in rags, she was heard to murmur: "I wish I were cloth, so that I might clothe them." The famine of 1739 found her, having depleted the supplies of the mother house, begging the authorities to come to the relief of the hungry population of the district.

Practicing, as she had learnt from Montfort, abandonment to Divine Providence, she admitted all to the novitiate, poor and rich alike, daughters of nobles or daughters of peasants. She would quote Montfort: *"God will always bless the house which helps the poor."* She remembered them still on her death-bed, calling one of her benefactors and begging her to continue her care of the poor of the parish. Her option for the poor assured her of a place with the saints both of her own time and the present.

The cardinals responsible for examining her life for the cause of beatification recognized this. "The Servant of God," they wrote, "offers an example of how to work for the development of the whole human person in a spirit of sacrifice, looking for no reward, ever open to read the signs of the times with a serene and humble spirit."[12]

After lengthy investigations by teams of experts into her life and writings, Marie Louise Trichet, the first disciple of St. Louis Marie de Montfort, was beatified on May 16, 1993.

S. Lepers

Notes: (1) A heroic decision, which Montfort himself had not foreseen or suggested. (2) Charles Besnard, *Circulaire aux Filles de la Sagesse,* April 29, 1759, recorded in *La vie la soeur Marie Louise de Jesus, première superieure des filles de la sagesse, (The Life of Sister Marie Louise of Jesus, First Superior of the Daughters of Wisdom),* Center International Montfortain, Rome, 331. (3) Sr. Florence, 98. (4) Pauvert, *Vie du vénérable Louis-Marie Grignion de Montfort,* Oudin, Poitiers 1875, 150-151. (5) Constitutions, subtitled *"Explication de la Règle des Filles de la Sagesse, instituées par Louis-Marie Grignion de Montfort, missionaire apostolique, pour leur servir de Constitutions* (Explanation of the Rule of the Daughters of Wisdom, Founded by Louis Marie Grignion de Montfort, Apostolic Missionary, for Their Constitutions)." The editing of this document was finished in 1760 and the manuscript was signed in a chapter assembly on May 20, 1768. The original is in Rome. A copy kept in the archives of the mother house is 400 pages long. (6) Besnard, *Marie-Louise,* 230. (7) Ibid., 376. (8) For her "Spiritual Oratory," cf. ibid., 280. This concerns a retreat resolution. Marie Louise prays to Jesus to help her build, within herself, a place where he may live. She gives details, in a very imaginitive way, of the virtues that will be used in the construction: obedience, detachment, love of suffering, and prudence, which will be the pillars of the building; then piety, vigilance, gentleness, etc. (9) AGFS: "Constitutions des Filles de la Sagesse," chap. 3. (10) *Lettres de Marie-Louise de Jésus,* Scuola tipografica Pio XI, Rome 1981. (11) Besnard, *Marie-Louise,* 360. (12) Decree on the heroism of her virtues. (13) Sacra Congregatio pro causis sanctorum. *Beatificationis et canonizotionis servae Dei Mariae Ludovicae a Jesu (in saeculo: Mariae Ludovicae Trichet) confundatricis Filiarum a Sapientia († 1759). Positio super virtutibus ex officio concinnata,* Rome 1986.

MARY

SUMMARY

I. INTRODUCTION:
   1. Overall context of Montfort's Marian teaching:
      a. Montfort's overarching principle,
      b. Montfort's Trinitarian Christocentricity,
      c. Montfort's total spirituality,
      d. Montfort's vocation,
      e. Montfort's purpose in writing,
      f. Montfort, a preacher of his times.

II. MARY IN THE LIFE OF SAINT LOUIS DE MONTFORT:
   1. Marian climate;
   2. Family experiences;
   3. College years at Rennes;
   4. Study at Saint-Sulpice:
      a. Olier-Tronson dialectic,
      b. Theological studies,
      c. The "Monita" crisis,
      d. Holy Slavery of love;
   5. Apostolic ministry:
      a. Parish missions and retreats,
      b. Stress on renewal of baptismal vows,
      c. Personal spirituality,
      d. The approbation of the Pope.

III. MARY IN THE DOCTRINE OF SAINT LOUIS DE MONTFORT: THE INCARNATION:
   1. The Incarnation itself:
      a. Stress on the divinity of Jesus,
      b. The salvific Incarnation,
      c. The compendium of all mysteries;
   2. Our Lady's role in the Incarnation:
      a. Some presuppositions,
      b. The self-communication of the Trinity to Mary,
      c. The consent of Mary,
      d. First conclusion: Mary, associate of the Redeemer,
      e. Second conclusion: the unifying principle of Montfort's Mariology.

IV. MARY IN THE DOCTRINE OF SAINT LOUIS DE MONTFORT: THE SANCTIFICATION OF THE MEMBERS OF THE BODY OF CHRIST:
   1. Mediatrix of all grace:
      a. Mediatrix because full of grace,
      b. Mediatrix because of her consent;
   2. Mary, Mother of the redeemed:
      a. Spiritual Mother because graced by the Trinity,
      b. Mary, Mother of the redeemed through her consent;

I. Introduction

Saint Louis Marie de Montfort is known primarily for his devotion to Mary. There has not been one biographer who has not signaled out this trait; there has not been a mention of this saint in papal documents that has not underlined this characteristic. The vast majority of Catholics acquainted with the missionary immediately connect him to devotion to Our Lady and, in particular, to total Consecration or Holy Slavery. And there can be no doubt that to dissociate Marian devotion from Saint Louis de Montfort would be nothing short of the undoing of his very personality. His renown and enduring relevance in the field of devotion to the Mother of God is best summarized by Pope John Paul II's statement that Montfort is "master of Marian spirituality" (RMat 48). Montfort focuses our attention on the fundamental role of Mary in salvation history and, therefore, on the solid basis of Marian devotion. It is impossible to deny the extraordinary impact of his Marian doctrine upon the Church.

1. Overall context of Montfort's Marian teaching

The primary reason this vagabond preacher is known as the Apostle of Mary is his principal Marian work, *True Devotion to the Blessed Virgin Mary,* as it was erroneously called by its first publishers after its fortuitous rediscovery in 1842. It has become a religious best-seller. The popes have lavishly praised it, and it has become the springboard for numerous apostolic associations and entered into the fabric of many religious Orders.

Great harm can be done, however, to the true image of Saint Louis de Montfort if his Marian devotion and his principal Marian writing become the sum total of the saint's character. This has been done in the past, partly because of the impact of the discovery of TD, which relegated to the background his other writings and achievements as if they were not necessary for an understanding of his Marian devotion itself. Only by examining the total context can we appreciate his Marian teachings and thereby authentically promote his Christocentric devotion to the Mother of God. This point was brought out clearly by the second of the three theologians who examined Montfort's writings with a view to his beatification. The "fundamental principle of the entire Marian montfort doctrine," he wrote, "is the life of Jesus Christ in souls regenerated by holy Baptism."[1]

a. Montfort's overarching principle. Any study of Mary in the life and teachings of Saint Louis de Montfort must constantly keep in mind the motto he lived and the only one which he gave—somewhat like a battle cry—to his religious Congregations: *"God Alone!"* Evidently borrowed from his sources, especially H.Boudon,[2] it becomes the passkey to an understanding of his life and his writings (cf. SM 20, 21; L 10, 15, 19, 27, 32; TD 151, 225, 265, etc.). Everything flows from God Alone, everything returns to God Alone. This *exitus-reditus*—the coming from God and the return to God (the skeleton of Saint Thomas' *Summa Theologiae*)—is Montfort's bare-bones outline, as is evident from his principal work, LEW. If we are searching for the role of Mary in montfort doctrine, it must be situated within this overarching principle; it does not exist on its own. God is, for Montfort, *"God-Charity"* (TD 215; H 5; LS I, 60-72), the *"Good Father"* (cf. H 7:31; H 27-28; H 52-53; H 90:1; TD 215), the God of tenderness and loving care (H 52-53): *"I have a Father in heaven whose providence will never fail me"* (L 2). "These key formulas—God Alone, the Good Father—show the unity of the book. The loving folly according to which the Son of God, coming from the bosom of the Father, has taken the form of a slave in this world is fulfilled by the Cross and by the fiery gift of the Holy Spirit; it is completed in the filial return to God Alone, to the only Father, the source and the ultimate term of all love, in the Trinity as for humanity."[3]

An understanding of Montfort's evangelical Marian doctrine can only be grasped if we constantly gaze upwards at the keystone that ties all together: God Alone. And as Montfort insists, this God is Charity, Love itself (cf. 1 Jn 2:4, 8). When this preacher proclaims that it is through Jesus that God is "*calmed*,"[4] or that Mary "*calms*" Jesus our God, he is using an expression not only common to the Scriptures (cf. Rom 5:9) but suitable for the hearers of his time. In no way does he offend his overarching principle of God Alone, God Who is Love. Rather, it forcefully proclaims that Infinite Love is only effectively answered by Jesus' redemptive cry of love from the Cross (cf. LEW 154, 176). If Mary "calms" Jesus, Montfort is proclaiming that Infinite Love wills that the Mother of God be humanity's corporate personality in accepting acceptance, in total surrender to the Redemption won for us by Christ Jesus. She is the summary of the Church in total harmony with God through Christ Jesus. The analogy of "calming the wrath of God," in popular use in Western Christianity right up to the mid-twentieth century, may not appear appropriate in many contemporary cultures. But although the literary tool may not be always advisable today, the truth conveyed by Montfort is as solid as its scriptural foundation.

b. Montfort's Trinitarian-Christocentricity. Stated so emphatically in TD itself, Jesus Christ is the only Redeemer, the only Mediator, the only Way to the Father in the power of the Spirit (TD 61, 248). This essential Christian principle is a constant in everything that can be said about Montfort and, most especially, his Marian spirituality. So insistent is the missionary on Jesus Christ, the Eternal and Incarnate Wisdom of the Father, that he does not hesitate to declare that if devotion to Our Lady did not lead us to Jesus, it must be called a diabolical illusion (TD 62). A summary sentence of the saint is found in LEW: "*To know Jesus Christ the Eternal and Incarnate Wisdom is to know enough; to know everything else but not to know Jesus is to know nothing*" (LEW 11). Montfort's Marian devotion must be situated within and never outside the emphatic Trinitarian-Christocentricity of his life and writings (cf. MC 25).

c. Montfort's total spirituality . LEW gives a more complete picture of montfort spirituality than any other of his works. In it we encounter not only his theocentricity and his Christocentricity but also his stress on the Cross, which he exalts to the point of declaring: "*Wisdom is the Cross and the Cross is Wisdom*" (LEW 180). Montfort stresses that the Cross is to be adored, not Mary (H 102:23). The "emptying" of Incarnate Wisdom (cf. Phil 2:7) becomes the source for his phenomenal, practical love for the poor and for his utter simplicity of life: basic characteristics of montfort spirituality. The meekness and approachableness of the Incarnate Wisdom, so constantly stressed (cf. LEW 117-132), are also found detailed in his hymns (cf. H 9:3-14; H 97:3-9; H 130:4-6; etc.)—a veritable catechism of the Christian faith—along with his emphasis on the Eucharist (H 129-134; etc.) and love for the Sacred Heart (H 40-44; H 47-48; etc.). LS gives us outlines of some of his missions, during which, usually on Saturday, a sermon on Mary was inserted (cf. GA, 567-571). In other words, all Montfort's writings, their context, and his missionary, vagabond lifestyle form the essential framework for an authentic understanding of his Marian doctrine. Distortions will be attributed to his teaching on Mary if it is isolated from the total portrait of the saint and not inserted within the entire design of his spirituality.

d. Montfort's vocation. Saint Louis de Montfort is not a professional theologian. The pulpit is his rostrum, the crowded church his class. Saint Louis Marie is a missionary, a vagabond preacher to the masses, and his writings reflect his fundamental vocation. He is explicit on this point: "*I speak particularly to the poor and simple who being of good will and having more faith than the common run of scholars, believe more simply and more meritoriously* " (TD 26). It was never his intention to write a summa of Marian doctrine and devotion or to compose a Mariological treatise. And that is his genius: to proclaim the Gospel boldly, authentically, in words and style that truly enable his hearers —like Our Lady—to "hear the word of God and keep it" (Lk 11:28). Mary forms an integral part of the Good News, and the missionary here again displays a unique talent for proclaiming the core truth about her in a concise, stirring, down-to-earth manner, demonstrating how Mary is "*the* *greatest means of all*" (LEW 203) of arriving at union with Divine Wisdom. Although he heralds the truth "*quite simply*" (TD 26), this does not imply that his preaching is not founded on solid theological principles that he has integrated into his own life.

e. Montfort's purpose in writing. Montfort the author is identical with Montfort the missionary. But his principal Marian works—SM, TD, SR, and the hymns, especially 49, 74-90, 104, 111, 145, 151, 155, and 159—do not touch on all aspects of his Marian preaching. There is, for example, precious little about Mary's Assumption and Immaculate Conception or even Mary at the foot of the Cross, although we can presume that these did form part of his evangelizing.

His works on Our Lady have as their stated goal to form true disciples of Jesus Christ (TD 111, 114). He therefore decides to focus his more doctrinal Marian writings on a rather precise aim: to depict Mary at the very heart of the Christian mystery, the Incarnation, so that in her and with her we may live our baptismal commitment ever more fully in the Spirit, through Christ Jesus for the glory of God the Father.

f. Montfort, a preacher of his time. Finally, it is the glory of this roving troubadour of Our Lady that he speaks so eloquently and powerfully to the people of his age. He is not a man of the twenty-first century; if he were, he would have been a failure as a preacher in the early 1700s. He is, like all God's creatures, time- and culture-bound. We must not expect, therefore, to find in his writings on Our Lady topics like "Mary and the feminist movement," any more than we would expect a reference to Our Lady of Lourdes. It is remarkable how closely his doctrine does dovetail with Paul VI's MC and LG, chap. 8; nonetheless, it is, of necessity, couched in the culture, language, and thought patterns of the very beginning of the eighteenth century.

Although extraordinarily a man of the Bible,[5] Montfort does not interpret the sacred text as would a contemporary university Scripture professor. Like the Fathers of the Church, he searches for the depths of the spiritual sense of the Word of God, while accepting the historicity of the text itself.[6] His Marian applications are often to be taken in a spiritual sense distilled from the liturgy and not as strict scriptural proofs (cf. TD 29-34, 184-212).

His many Marian references to the Fathers of the Church—for which he must be commended—reflect an age when not only relatively few critical texts were available but also a time when sources obtainable were secondhand or thirdhand. Yet he does capture the thought of these early writers' teachings on Mary.

II. Mary in the Life of Saint Louis de Montfort

All experiences—indelible expressions of God's providence and of our response—are the means by which the mystery of one's personhood evolves. These encounters form dynamic, intertwined, concentric circles, beginning with the powerful influence of whatever is "family" and extending out through the networking of acquaintances, of embodiments of culture, to the farthest reaches of the cosmos, for everything and everyone in this universe are interrelated, interdependent.

Louis de Montfort's life is quite difficult to analyze, as the various attempts by biographers down through the years has proven. A fruitful method of examining his personality from the point of view of his Marian devotion is to use the symbol of the frontier, or boundary. Somewhat like the German-American theologian Paul Tillich, Montfort lived "on the boundary."[7] He experienced the tension of two or more opposing energies in almost every aspect of his life. This dialectic was never fully synthesized, resulting in a life of energetic paradox, similar to that of a person who truly embodies multiple cultures that can never be altogether blended. This is hardly to be classified offhandedly as a defect or handicap; it can be, as it is in Montfort, the source of an extraordinarily powerful, creative personality that has a unique and challenging ability to absorb diverse experiences and ideas while always striving for the ever-elusive perfect unity or harmony. The richness of such a personality produces an unsettled, dynamic, searching mind, a lifestyle that appears strange to others and impossible to categorize. It is also often marked—as it is in Montfort—by episodic withdrawal and discouragement, for it produces a sense of not being fully understood, not being fully at home in any one particular place.

Montfort would always be on the boundary between speculative knowledge and experience, between the contemplative and the active apostolic. He was never fully at home on one side of the boundary to the exclusion of the other. He had to live on both sides. This is evidenced in his mature Marian teaching, where, e.g., he insists on the burning apostolic zeal characteristic of a devotee of Mary (TD 56-59; cf. PM) and yet also stresses that the true child of Mary is one whose conquests are made at home, in a sedentary way, through prayer (TD 196). In spite of this insistence on solitude, he called all those in solitude to leave their retreat and join him in the open battle against the forces of Satan, the great enemy of Mary (cf. PE 29). He was a citizen of the baroque and of the beginnings of the age of the Enlightenment; he was the contemplative and yet the Missionary Apostolic; he was the hermit and the town-square preacher; he was the clear thinker, and yet his mystical experiences took him beyond the confines of the scholastic syllogism. He was a man of paradox. His life was lived on the boundary: an important context for an authentic understanding of his life and of his Marian teaching.

1. Marian climate

Life on the boundary is certainly true for the Marian spirit of Saint Louis Marie's age, for he was born and raised in what can be called the baroque age, the extravagant, maximalist period of seventeenth-century Europe, and yet he lived out his apostolic ministry in what has been termed the critical era of eighteenth-century Europe.[8] He was caught between both, and his life and writings manifest this tension. Most of the principal Marian authors he consulted are clearly baroque: F.Poiré,[9] J.B.Crasset,[10] L. F. d'Argentan,[11] P.Spinelli,[12] Cardinal de Bérulle,[13] H. Boudon,[14] and J. J. Olier.[15] It was an age that witnessed an explosion of Marian theses, of distinct tracts on Mary, of fervid expressions of devotion to the Mother of God, such as the "slavery of Mary" and the "oblatio" of the sodalities of Our Lady.[16] An example of this stress on the incomparable grandeurs of Mary was the great reluctance to call Mary our "sister," or even a "servant." During the baroque age, the danger was ever present of practically denying Mary's identity with us as creature and member of the Church.

Montfort, although steeped in the baroque through his studies, clearly became involved in the critical Marian epoch. In what was in some ways a reaction to the extravagance of the preceding years, the later Marian authors stressed a rational, nonemotional approach, a disregard for what was judged to be "superstitious," a proud, if not haughty, neglect of the past.[17]

Montfort's N contains primarily texts from the baroque author Poiré (N 1-127), to whom the missionary was heavily indebted for the most theological sections of TD (14-37). His option was for the baroque but not without accepting a number of the censures raised by "critical" authors. An example of this is seen in his repeated absolute insistence on the Christocentricity of all devotion to Our Lady (TD 61), in his condemnation of hypocritical and interested devotees (TD 102-103), in his explanation of Mary as not "absolutely" but "hypothetically" necessary in God's plan (TD 14, 39), in his "corrections" of any false impression that could be given concerning the authority of Mary over grace (TD 27, 76) and Mary's relation to the Spirit (TD 20, 21), etc. Being on the boundary helped Montfort to come to a balanced Mariology, even if his terminology remained baroque.

2. Family experiences

Here, too, Montfort was in a boundary situation, considering the opposing temperaments of his father and mother.[18] But to attribute his Marian devotion, if not every aspect of his life, to a supposed overattachment to a tender mother and a nonidentification with a choleric father is too facile a solution. God's grace expresses itself in many experiences that cannot be locked in as "Marian-oriented" or not. As important as his relations with his parents were—and they are impossible to know in detail—they formed one important aspect in a constellation of youthful experiences, including his attachment to his wet nurse and his admiration for his priest-uncle, Alain Robert. It cannot be forgotten that he was brought up in an area of France at that time renowned for its solid Catholic faith. Marian devotion was part and parcel of almost every aspect of his youth.[19]

3. College years at Rennes

Here, too, diverse currents flowed into the formation of Montfort's ever-developing understanding of the role of Mary. Father Descartes, his spiritual director, instilled in him a deep appreciation of God, Who is Love, and a Christ-centered spirituality. His conferences, together with the example of Louis Marie's professor of rhetoric, Father Gilbert, drew the young student from Montfort to a life centered on prayer and to an appreciation of solitude.[20] The boundary situation again appears when Louis Marie came under the influence of a young diocesan priest, Julien Bellier, whose ministry attracted him to an apostolic life among the poor. The Sodality of Our Lady, although aimed directly at forming an overall solid, apostolic Catholic, included a Consecration of self to Our Lady.[21]

Is devotion to Our Lady apostolic or contemplative? Where does she fit into the overall redemptive plan necessarily centered on Christ? If these were questions beginning to surface in the young student's mind, he still remained, according to his schoolmate Blain, characterized by a simple, special, tender devotion to Mary: "This devotion . . . was not a passing fancy, as in so many other children; it was a daily devotion. . . . If the young Grignion was in front of an image of Mary, it seemed as though he didn't know anyone and was in a sort of ecstacy. . . . He spent hour upon hour, immobile, without budging, at the foot of her altar praying to her . . . and consecrating himself to her service."[22] In fact, Blain, with characteristic flourish of his time writes: "The love for Mary was as if born with Monsieur Grignion, and it could be said that the Blessed Virgin chose him for one of her great favorites."[23]

4. Study at Saint-Sulpice

At the age of nineteen, Louis Marie made a decisive break with his family. His crossing of the hometown Cesson bridge, and the beginning of a long trek to the Seminary of St. Sulpice in Paris were decisive moments in his spiritual journey. There was a deep yearning in this young man to live, to experience, to taste what he had known through study and prayer: God is Love, His fatherly Providence never failing, and Mary is truly the tender, caring Mother. Four experiences in particular during his years at Paris played an important role in the formation of his Marian doctrine:

a. Olier-Tronson dialectic. Montfort was caught between the mystical spirit of Saint-Sulpice, as outlined by its founder, Jean-Jacques Olier, and the rigid, "proper" attitude of the then superior of the Sulpicians, Father Tronson, well represented by the director of the seminary, Father Leschassier. Through his spiritual director, Father Bayün, and through his incessant reading, he became acquainted with the teachings of the mystic Olier.[24] Montfort's own mystical bent was now caught in the dialectic of Olier-Tronson. Although he would, after a few years of priesthood, break with Tronson's clericalism and actually identify with the outcasts of society, he would never relinquish Tronson's insistence on strict obedience. He was also convinced of the need for a contemplative and a clear theological approach to spirituality. Montfort's Mariology deepened in its mystical dimension under the influence of Olier; its extremes were tempered by the reigning atmosphere of Tronson's demands for moderation. Saint Louis Marie accepted Tronson's stress (common to the French school of spirituality) on man's absolute nothingness of himself (cf. TD 79, 213, 228; H 8:14), but he also insisted with Olier upon man's grandeur with and in Christ Jesus (cf. H 64:1; SM 3; TD 82; etc). Montfort himself respectfully mentioned Tronson as the person who counseled him to use the more acceptable expression "slave of Jesus in Mary" instead of "slave of Mary" (TD 244).

b. Theological studies. Saint Louis Marie himself declared that he had read almost all the books that treated of Our Lady (TD 118). His friend Blain writes: "Almost all the writings that treat of the spiritual life passed through his hands."[25] During Montfort's lengthy stay at Saint-Sulpice, his work as librarian brought him into contact with some of the era's best writings on Mary. Especially through Crasset, he became acquainted with some Marian writings of the Fathers of the Church. His sincere interest in Marian doctrine and devotion is evidenced by N, which gives testimony of his great interest in this aspect of theological studies. His readings and studies gave him the opportunity to verify his own experiences and to broaden and deepen his knowledge and love of Our Lady. It also supplied him with theological foundations on which to build a Marian spirituality. Montfort's strong Trinitarian basis for his Marian writings, his emphasis on the centrality of the Incarnation, and his stress on Christocentric spirituality were not only in line with the spirit of Saint-Sulpice but were verified for Montfort through the books he critically examined. His theological studies helped foster a healthily discerning analysis of the Marian devotion of his time and gave him great confidence when he spoke about Our Lady.

c. The "Monita" Crisis. There can be no doubt that Saint Louis Marie knew well Widenfeld's work, *Monita salutaria,*[26] and books whose teachings contested the author, especially that of Grenier (N 296-302). This appears to have had a double effect on the seminarian. First, as we can tell from N, he studiously listed ideas taken from a variety of books on how to reply to any objections against devotion to Our Lady. Second, he seemed to understand that there was some truth in these criticisms leveled by Widenfeld (cf. TD 90), for, as already mentioned, he goes to great pains to insist that Jesus alone is the final end of all devotion, and definitely not Mary. Again, his Christocentricity was reinforced and the same time the authenticity of his solid devotion to Mary was strengthened.

d. Holy Slavery of love. If Saint Louis became acquainted with the devotion of Holy Slavery to the Mother of God at the Jesuit College in Rennes, it does not appear to have made any profound impression upon him. It was at Saint-Sulpice that he studied this devotion and in fact became enamored with it. His source was primarily the works of Cardinal de Bérulle and H. Boudon's *Dieu Seul ou le saint esclavage de l'admirable Mère de Dieu (God Alone or the Holy*

Slavery of the Admirable Mother of God). Saint Louis Marie clearly knew of the Roman decrees against the practice of holy slavery (N 302), yet he felt completely free to study Boudon's work thoroughly, for he was convinced that it did not fall under the abuses of the devotion, which alone were condemned. It appears that at first his discovery of this devotion to Our Lady so captured him that he wanted everyone at Saint-Sulpice to become a member of the Society of the Holy Slavery of the Blessed Virgin.[27] Saint Louis Marie's mature Marian devotion, however, would radically interpret the Holy Slavery of love of the French school of spirituality.

5. Apostolic ministry

Montfort's devotion to Our Lady had yet to be tried. It was through his sixteen years of ministry that he developed a Marian spirituality that was not only theologically sound but also adapted to the simple folk of the west of France.

a. Parish missions and retreats. An important factor in the development of Saint Louis Marie's Marian spirituality was the more than 200 retreats and missions he preached. Perhaps the principal influence on his Marian devotion was the "needs of the Church"—not just the Church in western France but the needs of the individual diocese, the village parish. There was, first of all, a need to simplify. Although not betraying the theological underpinnings, he insisted primarily upon an approach that could be understood by his people. TD, written probably only a few years before his death, demonstrates his ability to proclaim truths of the faith through examples, symbols, and analogies that appealed to his people, not necessarily to cultures of the twenty-first century. Monarchs, corsairs, dung heaps, rotten apples, molds, family life, pregnancy, birth, servants, and slaves become raw material for his explanations of the role of Mary. He was a theologian, in the sense that he was steeped in solid study. He was also an excellent Missionary Apostolic, using folksy hymns, stage productions, and elaborate processions to bring home to the people complex truths of the faith. Compared, for example, to Boudon's work on Holy Slavery, Montfort's TD and SM are concise, clear, and, at the same time, more theologically based than Boudon's verbose, extremely baroque writings.

b. Stress on renewal of baptismal vows. Another influence his ministry had upon his Marian devotion was the stress that Consecration to Jesus through Mary is the equivalent of the renewal of the vows of Baptism. He knew this in his seminary days, but it is only in experiencing the pastoral effects of such an approach that he fully realized its value and therefore insisted upon it to the point that it became a hallmark of his missions and retreats (cf. CG; RM 56). It was not only clearly enunciated but taught as the framework of a Marian way of life. Except for his well-known formula of Consecration, found solely in the LEW manuscript (LEW 223-227), only in TD, written after some years of missionary activity, does Saint Louis explain or even explicitly mention that the perfect Marian devotion is the perfect renewal of the vows of Baptism (TD 126-130).

*c. **Personal spirituality.*** His apostolic ministry significantly influenced his Marian devotion by deepening his own Marian spirituality. The profound changes brought about in his village missions convinced him of the need to be ever more immersed in living the faith, of being truly a *"child and slave"* of Mary, *"Mother and Mistress,"* in order to be filled with the Spirit for the glory of God Alone. Montfort was convinced that he could not effectively preach by words if his life was not a living Gospel (cf. H 91). It was through his proclamation of the faith in barracks, houses of prostitution, and town squares that the role of Mary in Christian life fully matured in the heart of this contemplative missionary. The results he achieved assured him that Mary had to be ever more deeply an integral element of his own life in Christ Jesus. He reached such a degree of mystical union with Mary, he was so totally open to her maternal influence, that he could sing: *"I have her image carved within me"* (H 75:11); *"I carry her in the center of my being"* (H 77:15). He could speak of the transforming effects of total Consecration, for he had deeply experienced them himself (TD 257-265). Although he was favored with mystical experiences of Our Lady,[28] he never desires *"visions or revelations . . . or spiritual pleasures"* (SM 69).

*d. **The approbation of the Pope.*** In an age of Gallicanism, Montfort displayed a radical obedience to the Holy Father (cf. H 6:50; H 57; H 147). When his confusion heightened on the direction his ministry should take—again, the boundary situation of a call to the foreign missions and a yearning to evangelize his own people—he, a simple, young, unknown priest, decided that he had to go to the Pope to discern the will of God. The effect of his pilgrimage to the Holy City, of his visit with Clement XI, was profound. He would follow the advice of the Vicar of Christ and return to his homeland, proclaiming the renewal of the baptismal vows. We can well presume that his discussion included his experience of Mary's influence in his life and preaching. Armed with the new role of Apostolic Missionary, Montfort returned to western France, convinced—as much as his personality permitted—that his life was to be the vagabond preacher of the reign of Christ through the reign of Mary. All was summed up in his conviction that the renewal of the promises of Baptism was the way to a reform of the Church. He needed no more convincing that Mary was intrinsic to this renewal. The essential lines of his Mariology were in place.

If there was one area where Montfort's personality and apostolic life did achieve a high degree of unity (always accepting the paradox intrinsic to Christian faith), it was in the frontier Jesus-Mary. His studies and contemplative insights had shown him that they are—although so distinct—one heart (H 40:36, 37; H 134:8). Devotion to Mary is devotion to Jesus, the center of all.

III. Mary in the Doctrine of Saint Louis de Montfort: The Incarnation

Mary's role in the Incarnation is the core of Saint Louis de Montfort's Mariology. In order to clarify this truth, we will first briefly consider some necessary, pertinent aspects of the Incarnation and then proceed to Our Lady's function in this. *"The Incarnation is the first mystery of Jesus Christ, it is the most hidden and it is the most exalted and least known"* (TD 248).[29]

1. The Incarnation itself

Faithful to the French school of spirituality, Montfort can declare that *"this mystery is a summary of all his mysteries since it contains the intention and the grace of them all"* (TD 248). Three points must be kept in mind about its relationship to Saint Louis Marie's Marian teaching.

a. Stress on the divinity of Jesus. Basing himself on the then current descending Christology, Montfort's stress is on the divinity of Jesus, although it by no means falls into the trap of docetism.[30] For Montfort, Jesus is clearly the enfleshed Second Person of the Trinity. In terms reminiscent especially of the Eastern Fathers of the Church, Montfort underlines that Jesus is God.[31] Any hesitations on this point, or Christological opinions that would effectively deny that Jesus is the Second Person of the Trinity in two natures, human and divine, are totally alien to his thought. This, of course, has important repercussions in his understanding of the mother of Jesus and also affects his vocabulary. Mary is a *"pure creature"* (TD 14), i.e., she is, in the totality of her being, creaturely, from the Other (*ab alio*). It would be blasphemous to predicate divinity of her except in an analogical way (the "divine Mary," TD 181; H 81:1; H 82:1; H 88:1; H 98:22; etc.),[32] for she is filled with divine grace in order to be the worthy Mother of God. Since Jesus is God, he, and he alone among all human beings, cannot be called a pure creature. This terminology is not Montfort's invention; it is the common language of scholastic thought. Jesus' humanity is part of creation (TD 248: Jesus gave God *"infinite glory which he had never as yet received from man"*); but it is a humanity, as the French school stresses with the early councils of the Church, that only exists as the humanity of God.[33] Mary is, then, in Montfort's writings, the greatest of pure creatures (SM 19). She is, therefore, the model of all virtues as found in pure creatures. Contemporary Christology, with its insistence on the humanity of Jesus, does not weaken Montfort's Mariology, for Our Lady is always subordinate to Jesus and is always surrendered to God the Father only through and in Jesus. She remains the model of all disciples of Jesus in her total active and responsible *fiat* to God the Father through the Son, in the power of the Spirit.

b. The salvific Incarnation. It is equally important, in probing Mary's role in Montfort's teaching, to be fully aware that for this vagabond preacher, the Incarnation is truly salvific (cf. MC 46). "*He who is has willed to come to that which is not and* *to make that which is not become He Who is and He has done this perfectly in giving Himself and subjecting Himself entirely to the young Virgin Mary without ceasing to be in time He Who is from all eternity*" (TD 157). In Mary's womb, Jesus has "*together with Mary, chosen all the elect. It is in this mystery that He has wrought all the other mysteries of His life by the acceptance which He made of them . . . that [He] has calmed His Father . . . and that He has made restitution of the glory which sin ravished from Him*" (TD 8). It is in this self-emptying of the Word (*kenosis*) that we are divinized (*theosis*): "*He becomes what we are in making us become who He is*" (H 64:1; cf. H 5:10; SM 3; TD 82; etc).

c. The compendium of all mysteries. Finally, it can never be overstressed that Montfort truly considers that all the mysteries of salvation are found in this compendium of salvation history, the Incarnation. The saint's reasoning is a simple and valid one: "*It is in this mystery that he has wrought all the other mysteries of his life by the acceptance which He made of them. 'When He comes into the world, He says . . . Behold, I come to do Thy will, O God' [Heb 10: 5-9]. Hence this mystery is an abridgment of all mysteries and contains the will and grace of all*" (TD 248; cf. H 10:6). Therefore, the miracles, the proclamation of the Kingdom of God, the death/Resurrection, the Church, the Sacraments, and all grace are rooted and "contained" in the Incarnation. The underlying philosophical reason is clear: the beginning is never merely the first point of a series of further moments in time. Rather, the beginning contains what follows and it is the never-repealed law that governs everything flowing from it. The beginning transcends and makes immanent the moments resulting from it; its structure is different from theirs qualitatively and not just quantitatively.[34]

Now if Our Lady intrinsically and in a unique manner cooperates in the Incarnation, the beginning of Redemption, "*the first mystery of Jesus Christ*" (TD 248), then she cooperates intrinsically and in a unique manner in *every aspect* of salvation history; the objective Redemption and the subjective Redemption form but one plan of God. This is the essential linkage between Mary's role in the Incarnation itself and her continued role in the consequence of the Incarnation, our sanctification. Since all salvation history is the immutable God's one plan, whose essential lines are found in the mystery of the Incarnation, Montfort can declare that "*considering things as they are, because God has decided to begin and accomplish his greatest works through the Blessed Virgin ever since he created her, we can safely believe that he will not change his plan in the time to come for he is God. Therefore he does not change in his thoughts or his way of acting*" (TD 15); "*The plan adopted by the three persons of the Blessed Trinity in the Incarnation, the first coming of Jesus Christ, is adhered to each day in an invisible manner throughout the Church, and they will pursue it to the end of time until the last coming of Jesus Christ*" (TD 22; cf. TD 1, 262, etc.).

2. Our Lady's role in the Incarnation

We are at the heart of Montfort's Marian doctrine. Her role in the Incarnation is also her role in everything that flows from this "*first mystery.*" Mary's function in the Incarnation implies a twofold dynamic, the Trinity freely pouring grace into her soul and Mary's faithful response: "*It is not possible to express, on the one hand, the ineffable communications of the Blessed Trinity to this most fair creature, and, on the other hand, the fidelity with which she corresponded with the graces of her Creator*" (LEW 105; cf. Lk 11:28). This is, for Saint Louis de Montfort, the basic plan of God in all the works of salvation, especially its summit, the Incarnation: call and response. As Pope John Paul II teaches: "Salvation comes from heaven but it also springs from the earth. The Messiah Savior is the Son of the Most High but is also the fruit of the womb of a woman, the Virgin Mary. The history of salvation . . . unfolds in a dialogue between him and his people. Everything is word and response. Mankind's response of faith must follow God's creative and salvific word. This logic is present to the greatest extent in the fundamental event of salvation, the Incarnation of the Son of God."[35] Basing ourselves on TD 1-21, this could be framed in the following statement: in the salvific mystery of the Incarnation, Mary is the worthy Mother and associate of God the Redeemer, thanks to the immeasurable graces granted to her by the Father, Son, and Holy Spirit, to which she totally surrenders herself by loving, representative consent. We will first examine some presuppositions of this thesis and then consider Montfort's explanation of the self-communication of the Trinity to Mary and her corresponding faithful consent in the Incarnation of Eternal Wisdom. The better to follow Saint Louis Marie's own methodology as given in TD, only in the next section will we treat of the Incarnation inasmuch as it reveals Mary's role in our sanctification.

a. Some presuppositions. It must first be stated that in Montfort's eyes, Mary, compared to God, is—like all humanity—a nothing: "*With the whole Church, I acknowledge that Mary, being a mere creature fashioned by the hands of God is compared to his infinite majesty, less than an atom, or rather is simply nothing, since he alone can say, 'I am he who is*" (TD 14). "*Mary is entirely relative to God. Indeed, I would say that she was relative only to God because she exists uniquely in reference to him*" (TD 225; cf. TD 25: "*hid herself even to the abyss of nothingness*").[36] There is absolutely nothing Mariocentric in the thought of Father de Montfort. Not only is she of herself "*nothing at all*" but Saint Louis underlines the fact that "*this great Lord, who is ever independent and self sufficient, never had and does not now have any absolute need of the Blessed Virgin for the accomplishment of his will and the manifestation of his glory. To do all things he has only to will them*" (TD 14). There is no self-redemption in Montfort's thought, and especially so for the masterpiece, Mary. All is grace, all is gift. She is totally turned to Christ; the only influence she can have on the faithful is in accord with this Christ-centered personality.

The Lord has no absolute need of Mary in the work of Redemption (cf. TD 14). She is necessary to God only because He freely wills it to be so (TD 39; cf. TD 63). Using the accepted theological terminology, Montfort calls this "*hypothetically necessary*," i.e., in the present—and only—plan of God. Since Mary is, then, necessary in the Incarnation because of God's free choice, she is necessary to all who enter into the mystery of the Incarnation. Mary is not optional in salvation history *as it actually is planned by God.* In the present order of things, to withdraw the "Mary-thread" from the fabric of salvation history is to unravel the entire tapestry itself. It would necessitate tearing pages out of the Gospels, like Jn 2, Jn 19, the infancy narratives of Lk and Mt, etc.[37]

b. The self-communication of the Trinity to Mary. Saint Louis de Montfort treats of this question *ex professo* in TD 14-21, 139-140 (cf. SM 8-13, 35). Montfort's doctrine on the Trinity's relationship with Mary at the Incarnation appears to be far more profound than declaring that sanctifying grace is a quality elevating us to a state of being pleasing to God and transforming us into temples of the Trinity.[38] The danger is ever present of modernizing Montfort, reading into his writings contemporary theological theories that are not his mind. Nonetheless, it is difficult to deny that Saint Louis Marie does speak of Mary being gifted at the Annunciation—in keeping with her creaturely status—with the life of Father, Son, and Holy Spirit, precisely in that which constitutes each of them as three distinct subsisting relationships of the one Godhead.[39] Saint Louis Marie himself struggles with human language, which of its nature conceals more than it reveals of the mystery of God and which can, therefore, only faintly approximate the ineffable union of Mary with the Trinity.

The Father

"*God the Father communicated to Mary His fruitfulness, in as much as a mere creature was capable of it, in order that He might give her the power to produce His Son*" (TD 17). In a short, concise phrase,[40] Montfort boldly declares that the Father shares with Mary—always in a manner consonant with her condition as a pure creature—that which constitutes Him precisely as the First Person of the Trinity: He is the dynamic source, the One Who generates. Mary and the Father have the identical Son, for the Father generates the Eternal Wisdom within the Trinitarian life and also empowers Mary to be the virginal mother of the Eternal Wisdom according to his humanity.

The Son

Not only do we find the actual enfleshment of the Second Person of the Trinity in the womb of Mary but the sharing with Mary of what precisely constitutes the Son as Son: his total dependence on the Father. For the Eternal Son, this dependence, this filiation, this "being-spoken" is, of course, without any hint of subordinationism, for he is "one in being with the Father," as the Council of Nicea (A.D. 325) infallibly declared. Three points are now to be underlined by Montfort:

First, the Eternal and Incarnate Wisdom expresses that filiation in and through Mary, for he lives in Mary, united to her by inexpressibly loving ties of sonship. "*He is that Infinite Wisdom who had a boundless desire to glorify God His Father and to save men; and yet He found no more perfect means, no shorter way to do it, than to submit Himself in all things to the Blessed Virgin*" (TD 139). Using the familiar Bérullian notion of "rest," Montfort considers the Son of God "resting" in the Father. At the Incarnation, Montfort declares, this eternal resting in the Father now takes place in Mary: "*The Word who in God His Father / Rests eternally, / Has willed to take you here in time / For his rest and for his mother*" (H 81:2; cf. TD 157).

Second, his characteristic of "dependence" on the Father is now expressed in an analogous manner in his dependence on Mary. Although Montfort can speak in general of the Trinity's dependence (always because of God's free choice) on Mary (TD 140), it is the specific characteristic of the grace given to Mary by the Son. "*He glorified his independence and His majesty in depending on that sweet Virgin, in His conception, in His birth, in His presentation in the temple, in His hidden life of thirty years and even in His death*" (TD 18). "*It is here that the human mind loses itself, when it seriously reflects on the conduct of Incarnate Wisdom who willed to give himself to men not directly though He might have done so, but through the blessed Virgin*" (TD 139).

This dependence of the Eternal Wisdom upon Mary so mystifies Montfort that he—following the florid language of the times—expresses it in the hyperbole of love: "*O Servant / All-Powerful, / To do everything, / You have only to wish it*" (H 75:15). "*The Son of God, the Eternal Wisdom, by making himself perfectly subject to Mary His Mother, gave her a maternal and natural power over Him, which surpasses our understanding. He gave her this power, not only for the length of His life on earth but also in heaven because heavenly glory far from destroying nature, perfects it. Hence, in heaven, Jesus is as much the Son of Mary as Mary is the Mother of Jesus. In this relationship, then, Mary has authority over Jesus, who, in a sense, remains subject to her because He wills it*" (LEW 205).

This filial submission to the Father (always insisting that there is no subordinationism) is shared in an analogous manner with Mary when Eternal Wisdom is conceived in her womb. He, the Head of the Body, the Church, freely and with infinite love "submits" himself to Mary. On this, Scripture is clear in describing the Annunciation itself. Montfort will conclude, as we will see below, that this same attitude found in the Incarnation of the Word must be found in all the members of the Head. Moreover, since Jesus is grace itself—she is "*the Mother of Grace*" (SM 8)—all grace is in a mysterious way "dependent" on her. But in no way does Montfort permit this dependence to be wrongly understood: "*We must take great pains not to conceive this dependence as any abasement or imperfection in Jesus Christ. For Mary is infinitely below her Son, Who is God, and therefore she does not command Him as a mother here below would command her child who is below her. Mary, being altogether transformed into God by grace and by the glory which transforms all saints into him, asks nothing, wishes nothing, does nothing contrary to the eternal and immutable will of God*" (TD 27).

Third, the Eternal Wisdom shares with Mary his total surrender of love to the Father. It is this aspect of the grace of God the Son that, when shared with Mary, becomes her loving *fiat.* The consent of Mary to the Father—the return of love—is so important in Montfort's Marian teaching that it will be seen separately in the next section. It should, however, be noted that this union of Eternal Wisdom and Mary in loving surrender to the Father is strongly stressed by Montfort in more ways than in her annunciation *fiat.* Jesus, incarnate only to save us by loving self-offering to the Father (TD 248, commenting on Heb 10:5-10), joins Mary to his total surrender to the Father: "*Their hearts, united very strongly / by intimate ties / are offered both together / to be two victims / in order to hold back the chastisement / which our crimes merit*" (H 87:6). Montfort can, in this sense, declare: "*Jesus Christ chose her for the inseparable companion of His life, of His death, of His glory and of His power in heaven and earth*" (TD 74). So intense is this union that the saint tries in vain to find words that can adequately express this alliance of Jesus and Mary: "*They are so intimately united that one is altogether in the other. Jesus is altogether in Mary and Mary is altogether in Jesus; or rather, she exists no more but Jesus alone in her and it were easier to separate the light from the sun than Mary from Jesus, so that we may call Our Lord, Jesus of Mary and Our Blessed Lady, Mary of Jesus*" (TD 247). With frustration, the missionary cries out: "*I turn here for one moment to Thee, O sweet Jesus, to complain lovingly to thy Divine Majesty that the greater part of Christians, even the most learned, do not know the necessary union there is between Thee and Thy Holy Mother. Thou, Lord, art always with Mary and Mary is always with Thee and she cannot be without Thee else she would cease to be what she is*" (TD 63). Because of Mary's mysterious sharing in the Son's life, Montfort can, therefore, conclude: "*What I say absolutely of Jesus Christ, I say relatively of Our Lady. Since Jesus Christ chose her for the inseparable companion of His life, death, glory, and power in heaven and upon earth, He gave her by grace, relatively to His Majesty, all the same rights and privileges which He possesses by nature*" (TD 74).

The Holy Spirit

Montfort's teaching on the free and loving communication of the Holy Spirit to Our Lady has been the subject of much discussion and controversy. It would appear that Pusey, Newman, and Faber were embroiled in it,[41] as were theologians in the mid-twentieth century.[42]

Before considering the important text of Montfort on the grace of the

Holy Spirit imparted to Mary at the Annunciation, it is well to recall Saint Louis Marie's insistence that Mary is totally relative to God, is a pure creature. Montfort need not repeat this on every page, since he makes it a key concept of his Marian doctrine. In no way, then, even when filled with outbursts of praise typical of the baroque age, does Montfort ever on any account substitute Mary for the Holy Spirit. On this point he is quite categorical: "*It is you alone [Holy Spirit] who form all the divine persons [i.e., the sanctified] outside of the Divinity*" (PM 15); "*Come, Holy Spirit, who form / the martyrs, the confessors / the apostles, the prophets / the great heroes, the great hearts*" (H 141:2). Mary, through the goodness of the Most High and only because of the mysterious Wisdom of God, is the "*inseparable companion of the Holy Spirit in all the works of grace*" (TD 90), "*the faithful and indissoluble Spouse*" of the Spirit (TD 85), and all this "*because of a singular grace of the Most High*" (TD 86). It appears that Montfort is declaring that Mary receives, in an evidently creaturely fashion, the distinctive grace of the Holy Spirit, Who is the Loving Who binds together the Father and the Son: "*Glory to the Eternal Father, / Glory to the Adorable Word! / The same glory to the Holy Spirit, Who by His Love, / unites them by an ineffable bond*" (H 85:6; cf. H 141:1). The same thought is expressed in TD 36, where the Holy Spirit is called the "*substantial Love of the Father and the Son,*" Who "*has espoused Mary in order to produce Jesus Christ.*"

If we hold, as mentioned above, that Montfort is teaching that each of the three Divine Persons takes possession of Mary according to each one's personal properties, then it must be said that the Holy Spirit communicates Himself to Mary precisely as the infinite Loving Who binds together the Father and the Son, Who takes possession of Mary for the Father and the Son. The Spirit is pure receiving, Who only exists insofar as He receives His Being from the mutual love between Father and Son. When the Spirit is sent by the Father through the Son, the "pentecost" results in the sanctification of those open to the Spirit, i.e., they are drawn into the Trinitarian life, made new creatures. Although this is true for all humankind, it is uniquely so for the Mother of God, who is overshadowed by the Spirit in the conception of the Wisdom of the Father. In a manner unsurpassed by any pure creature, Mary shares in the life of the Holy Spirit.

This entails, first, the sanctification of Mary to a degree that boggles the human mind. Montfort explodes in effusive exclamations (and yet rather calm, considering his contemporaries) when contemplating the grandeur of Mary: "*Oh, what grand and hidden things that mighty God has wrought in this admirable creature. . . . The height of her merits which she has raised up to the throne of the Divinity cannot be fully seen; the breadth of her charity which is broader than the earth is in truth immeasurable; the length of her power which she exercises even over God Himself*[43] *is incomprehensible, and finally, the depths of her humility and of all her virtues and graces is an abyss which can never be sounded. O height incomprehensible! O breadth unspeakable! O length immeasurable! O abyss impenetrable*" (TD 7). Montfort can then appeal to the proverb *"De Maria numquam satis*" (TD 10), "*Concerning Mary, there is never enough*," for so filled is she with the grace of God, so sanctified by the gift of the Spirit, that she eludes comprehension by anyone but God. Saint Louis Marie is by no means recommending a maximalist approach by quoting this ancient axiom. Rather, he is stressing that Mary's holiness makes her the "*paradise of God*"; she ever eludes our comprehension.[44]

Second, the empowerment of Mary to share uniquely—always in keeping with her creaturely state—in the Spirit's task of sanctification, of "*forming the saints.*" The Spirit is sent by the Father through the Son to possess all people for the Father and the Son. Mary shares in the work of the Spirit in the enfleshment of Grace Itself, the Eternal Wisdom of the Father: "*You [the Holy Spirit] have formed the Head of the predestinate with her and in her*" (PM 15), "*having produced in her and of her Jesus Christ, this Masterpiece, the Incarnate Word*" (SM 13). Again, it is only the foolishness of God's Wisdom that chooses Mary to be so united to the Spirit in the Incarnation of the Word of God. But "*things being as they are*," this is a fact of salvation history.

Mary, because she shares in the personal life of the Spirit in such a unique way, is called by Montfort—as she is by his contemporaries—the spouse of the Holy Spirit.[45] Montfort the mystic has a penchant for the term *"spouse."* He uses it for our relationship to Wisdom, for Wisdom's relationship to the Cross, for the soul's relationship to Jesus, etc.[46] Vatican Council II saw fit to approve LG, chap. 8, without including the term "spouse of the Spirit." Montfort's theology, dominated by the overarching theme of God's love, almost naturally employs such a title, and his context makes it clear that the term "spouse" is not used with any pagan connotations of marital intercourse between a god and a human being (cf. H 155:5). The expression is a valid one as employed by Montfort, but its use today should be controlled by the type of audience envisaged. After the Vatican Council, the term fell into disuse; but with its usage by Paul VI[47] and, especially, by Pope John Paul II,[48] the term is becoming more prevalent.[49]

It is also in the light of the above explanations that TD 20-21 is to be understood. Leaning on his predecessors, especially d'Argentan,[50] Montfort the preacher, the contemplative, declares that the Spirit, "*being barren in God, not producing another Divine Person, is become fruitful by Mary whom He has espoused.*" If Saint Louis Marie stopped here, as G. Philips implies that some members of the French school do, it must be said that this is a rather unfortunate way of expressing Trinitarian theology.[51] Speaking of the sterility of the Spirit within the Trinity *(ad intra)* and the Spirit's fecundity outside the Trinity *(ad extra)* can evidently lead to serious misunderstandings. But as Philips points out, Saint Louis Marie "felt the weakness and the danger, for he adds a restrictive commentary that brings him back to the reality of the current affirmations of theology."[52] Saint Louis Marie does this not only through the immediate context but by his overall thought gleaned from a study of all his writings and especially by the warning he gives us in TD 21: "*It is not that we mean that Our Lady gives the Holy Spirit His fruitfulness as if He had not it Himself. For as much as He is God, He has the same fruitfulness or capacity of producing as the Father and the Son, only he does not bring it into act. . . . But what we mean is that the Holy Spirit chose to make use of Our Blessed Lady, though He had no absolute need of her, to bring His fruitfulness into act by producing in her and by her Jesus Christ and His members.*"

c. The Consent of Mary. Mary's intrinsic role in the Incarnation—the never-to-be-repealed pattern of salvation history—is highlighted by Montfort not only when the missionary proclaims the graces shared with Mary by each Person of the Trinity but also when he reveals the meaning of Mary's loving consent to God's plan. Simply put, it is through her Yes, her *fiat,* that the redemptive Incarnation becomes a reality. There are five principal qualities of this consent of Mary that are found in the writings of Saint Louis Marie.

First, hypothetically necessary consent. True, her consent is not absolutely necessary; but it is evidently willed by God in the present order of salvation history and is, therefore, hypothetically necessary (TD 14, 39). This is clear from the way the Incarnation has unfolded, as narrated in the inspired Word of God (cf. Lk 1:26-38). "*The Eternal Wisdom,*" Montfort forcefully teaches, "*desired to become man in her, provided that she give her consent*" (LEW 107). Her Yes is, therefore, necessary in God's plan. "*May your faith be glorified, honored and praised! / This Savior has come to us / Only because you have believed / The word of an angel*" (H 63:4). "*It was for me, Divine Spirit, / That you formed Jesus Christ, / When Mary consented to it*" (H 27:9).

Second, freely given consent. Montfort insists that it was not a forced consent but flowed from her free will: "*This salutation was presented to terminate the most important affair of the world, the Incarnation of the Eternal Word*" (SR 45), and her freedom is implicit in stating that God would become one of us "*provided that*" she consent. Montfort insists, therefore, on her loving freedom at the Incarnation. "*God the Holy Spirit formed Jesus Christ in Mary but only after having asked her consent through one of the chief ministers of his court*" (TD 15).[53] Does she know what she is doing? For Montfort, this is a foregone conclusion, for he reads Luke's narrative not like a modern form critic but as a man of his times, understanding the Annunciation pericope as an historical account even in its details. And contemporary theology must say, in order to uphold Mary's freedom and God's characteristic of love, that Our Lady knew enough at the Annunciation to make an "active and responsible consent," as Paul VI declares in MC 37. She surely, say modern theologians, does not know all the details, but her Yes, like the consent given at a marriage, is a surrender to everything that will flow from her *fiat.*

Third, a representative consent. Montfort insists with St. Thomas Aquinas that her Yes at the Annunciation is given in the name of the entire human race: "[Mary] consents [to the Incarnation] in the place of the entire human nature, so that there would be a certain spiritual matrimony between the Son of God and human nature."[54] Again, St. Louis Marie tells us that "*the Son of God became man for our salvation . . . but after having asked her consent*" (TD 16). "*[Mary] found grace before God . . . for the entire human race*" (LEW 203). We could summarize Montfort's thought by saying that at the Annunciation, Mary, "*the little girl*" (TD 18; cf. TD 52, 157) of the human race, summarizes in herself the entire human family, desperately yearning for redemption. Through Mary, all humankind, the entire cosmos, says Yes to Wisdom's desire to enter our twisted human family. Montfort lyrically praises this consent of Mary when he sings: "*You have accomplished without battle / By your consent, / What all the earth / Desired so ardently*" (H 63:4). Pope John Paul II clearly expresses this characteristic of the consent of Mary: "Mary's response is personal, but it has also a community meaning. In her 'yes' flows the faith of ancient Israel and there is begun the faith of the Church. Her fidelity to the Lord, through a solidarity of grace, is a blessing for all who believe. The world's salvation is linked to her faith."[55]

Fourth, a salvific consent. Since the Incarnation is salvific, so too is the consent of Mary, which forms a necessary element of this mystery. "*It is in this mystery that Jesus, together with Mary . . . chose all the elect*" (TD 248). Wisdom would become man "*for our salvation . . . provided she would consent*" (LEW 107). The Second Vatican Council teaches: "The Father of Mercies willed that the consent of the predestined mother should precede the Incarnation, so that just as a woman contributed to death, so also a woman should contribute to life" (LG 56). And again, quoting Saint Irenaeus, it declares: "[Mary] being obedient, became the cause of salvation for herself and the whole human race" (LG 56). Pope Paul VI used expressions like "salvific motherhood," "salvific fiat"[56] and stated that "one perceives how through the assent of the humble handmaid of the Lord humankind begins its return to God."[57] These themes echo Montfort's insistence on the salvific nature of the consent of Mary: "*It was through Mary that the salvation of the world was begun*" (TD 49).

Fifth, an eternal consent. The consent of Mary enters into the fabric of salvation history itself. It is forever. As all gifts are given in virtue of the Redeemer, Jesus Christ, so too all gifts are also given in virtue of Mary's corporate consent to the Redeemer. Forever Jesus remains the fruit of her womb, the fruit of her faith (LEW 205). Forever Mary remains humanity redeemed by Christ, humanity actively and responsibly accepting the Redeemer. She is the *fiat* of all creation yearning for healing by the Savior; she is the symbol of the Church, open fully to the capital grace of Christ. Karl Rahner writes: "The absolutely unique Yes of consent of the Blessed Virgin, which cooperated in determining the whole history of the world, is not a mere happening that has disappeared in the void of the past. . . . She still utters her eternal Amen, her eternal Fiat, Let it be so, Let it be done, to all that God willed, to the whole great ordered plan of redemption, in which we all find place, built up on the foundation which is Christ."[58]

d. First conclusion: Mary, associate of the Redeemer. Mary's role as "associate of the Redeemer" is linked with the Incarnation. "*Their hearts united so strongly / By intimate bonds / Offer themselves conjointly / To be two victims / In order to hold back the punishment / That our crimes merit*" (H 87:6). Montfort can therefore sing: "*In this mystery [the Incarnation] the elect / Received their birth. / Mary united with Jesus / Chose them in advance / To have a part in their virtues / Their glory and their power*" (H 87:7). "*It is in this mystery that Jesus, together with Mary . . . chose all the elect*" (TD 248). Mary's cooperation in the Redemption is summarized in her consent to the salvific Incarnation. Montfort avoids the term "coredemptrix," although he was well acquainted with the expression and the teaching of his contemporaries through readings of Poiré and Grenier on this subject (N 91, 298). It is highly doubtful that he can be aligned with those who uphold immediate, formal coredemption.[59] Although insisting upon her great sufferings as foretold by Simeon (Lk 2:35), Montfort appears to limit her role as associate of the Redeemer to her perduring and ever intensifying consent. "*He glorified His independence and His majesty in depending on that sweet Virgin in His conception, in His birth, in His presentation in the temple, in His hidden life of thirty years and even in His death where she was to be present in order that He might make with her but one same sacrifice and be immolated to the Eternal Father by her consent just as Isaac of old was offered by Abraham's consent to the will of God. It is she who nourished Him, supported Him, brought Him up and then sacrificed Him for us*" (TD 18). If we put this statement in the entire context of his thought, Montfort is declaring that the Yes given at the Incarnation is the very personality of Mary; it is that Yes which accompanies Jesus throughout his life, death, and Resurrection.[60] It is that Yes which is Mary's role as associate of the redeemer (cf. H 90:18).

Another manner in which St. Louis Marie alludes to Mary's role in the Redemption is through the patristic Eve-Mary comparison: "*What Lucifer lost by pride, Mary won by humanity. What Eve ruined and lost by disobedience, Mary saved by obedience. By obeying the serpent, Eve ruined her children as well as herself and delivered them up to him. Mary by her perfect fidelity to God saved her children with herself and consecrated them to his divine majesty*" (TD 53;

cf. TD 175). Mary's fidelity is again signaled out as her cooperation in the Redemption.

e. Second conclusion: the unifying principle of Montfort's Mariology. Theologians search for that revealed truth from which all Mary's privileges may be "explained" and from which they flow by the hypothetical necessity of the will of God. The unifying—or prime—principle of Montfort's Mariology is nothing more or less than the finality in God's creation of Mary. Without hesitation, one turns to the mystery of the Incarnation. Like a golden thread, this mystery "*proper to the devotion*" (TD 243) he is teaching binds together his Marian doctrine. Montfort is by no means a speculative theologian, and his understanding of the Incarnation is not as an abstract truth but as it actually unfolds in salvation history. And the fundamental role of Mary in this mystery is the Divine Maternity: Mary the Mother of God, the *Theotokos.* Not Mother of God considered in the abstract but with all the intrinsic aspects mentioned above when we considered the union of the Trinity with Mary and her consent. This could be called the "concrete Divine Maternity," or the "Divine Maternity in its existential totality."[61]

Yet to declare that the Divine Maternity as understood by Montfort is his Marian unifying principle does not necessarily entail that it is the first step he takes in attempting to explain Our Lady. The ontological prime principle—the finality of God's creation of Mary—is not necessarily identical with the epistemological prime principle, i.e., the practical starting point used to arrive at the truth concerning Mary. The epistemological prime principle will vary from culture to culture, from age to age; the ontological prime principle (whatever one's opinion may be on this score) remains the same.[62] In trying to discern Montfort's epistemological prime principle, i.e., the first step he takes in coming to an authentic understanding of Mary, we would first have to admit that it must have varied, depending upon his audience. Montfort, good preacher that he was, surely adapted his explanations to his people. We can well presume, however, that his epistemological starting point involved the grandeurs of Mary. His was basically a descending Christology, and his Mariology also stressed majesty and awe, for such was the tenor of his times. He would hardly have been a good teacher within his culture if he had done otherwise. Today, in an age where ascending Christology is the favored methodology of Western theologians, the epistemological prime principle is often "Mary our sister," or "Mary the Disciple," or "Mary exemplar of the redeemed," etc. Montfort's Mariology remains "ardent, solid, and correct," as Pius XII affirmed;[63] many, however, are the varieties of starting points available to come to Montfort's centrality of the Incarnation.

Once arrived at the Incarnation, many modern Western theologians will retain throughout a different stress from Montfort's. Without denying the validity of his emphasis on Mary's grandeur, the primary accent today will be on the simplicity of Mary, on Mary as a member of the Church, as one of the redeemed: the ecclesio-typical model. Marian doctrine did not freeze with Montfort, and St. Louis Marie would be the first to recognize and accept the development of dogma within the Church. Nonetheless, the core content of Montfort's Marian thought, described above, remains not only valid today but also understandable and even appealing in its fundamental simplicity: at the Annunciation, Mary, this "*little girl*" of the human family, she who is so gifted by the Trinity, freely consents in the name of all to the salvific, liberating plan of God.

While we understand the epistemological prime principle as the broad context within which Montfort presented Mary, LS indicates that he never isolated the Mother of God while he was preaching a mission. In that sense, TD and SM abstract his doctrine on Mary from its *total* context. Montfort preached on Mary within the framework of the essential truths of the faith. And from what we can learn from a study of his life and writings, we can declare that a contemporary montfort study of Mary should begin with an expression of the saint's experience of God Alone: the God of charity, the God who is Love, the God Who is triune. This Infinite Love yearns to share and wills, therefore, to externalize Himself into this rebellious creation. The Wisdom of God comes into our family through its representative, Our Lady. This method also appears to be an excellent harmonization of both the ascending and descending methodologies: Mary, the little girl of the human family, nothing of herself (ascending, Antiochene) and—his principal stress—the Infinite Love Who comes to us in her and through her (descending, Alexandrian).

IV. Mary in the Doctrine of Saint Louis de Montfort: The Sanctification of the Members of the Body of Christ

"*The plan adopted by the three persons of the Blessed Trinity in the Incarnation, the first coming of Jesus Christ, is adhered to each day in an invisible manner throughout the Church, and they will pursue it to the end of time until the last coming of Jesus Christ*" (TD 22). The role of Mary in the Incarnation (the objective Redemption) dictates her role in the Church (the subjective Redemption). This essential link in Montfort's reasoning is enunciated at the very beginning of TD: "*It is by the Most Blessed Virgin Mary that Jesus Christ has come into the world and it is also by her that He must reign in the world.*"

As the three Persons of the one Godhead communicated themselves to Mary in order to bring forth Jesus Christ, so too, Montfort reasons, they preserve the identical plan in the prolongation of the Incarnation, the sanctification of the human race. Montfort, with tightly knit methodology, now clarifies the role of Our Lady in the sanctification of the members of the Body of Christ (TD 23-59).

Faithful to his method of showing how each of the three Divine Persons communicates Himself to Mary,

Montfort explains, first of all, that the Trinity's divinization of Mary makes her the Mediatrix of all grace (TD 23-28) and the Mother of the Redeemed (TD 29-36). He then explains two conclusions of these roles of Mary: she is the Queen of all hearts (TD 37-38), and she is necessary for salvation (TD 39-46) especially in the latter times (TD 47-59).

1. Mediatrix of all grace

Montfort first considers a basic truth of the Trinity's self-communication to Mary: she is full of grace, *for us.* "*God the Father . . . has a most rich treasury in which He has laid up all that He has of beauty and splendor. . . . Even His own Son and this immense treasury is none other than Mary* (TD 23); "*God the Son . . . has made her the treasurer of all that His Father gave Him for His inheritance. It is by her that He applies His merits to His members and that He communicates His virtues and distributes His graces*" (TD 24); "*God the Holy Spirit . . . has chosen her to be the dispenser of all He possesses. . . . [He] gives no heavenly gift which does not pass through her virginal hands*" (TD 25). She is "*the sole treasurer of his treasures, the sole dispenser of His graces*" (TD 44, SM 10, 21, etc.).[64]

This indubitably montfort doctrine—Mary, Mediatrix of *all* grace—is implicit in the very fact that to her has been given all grace, since she is the Mother of Grace, the Lord Jesus Christ, and also since her consent to the Incarnation of All Grace is done as the spokesperson of the entire human race. In her, through her representative consent, Incarnate Grace came to be. Montfort is faithful here to his understanding of the twofold formality of Mary's role at the Incarnation: the Trinity communicating itself to Mary and Mary lovingly and freely accepting that grace through her consent. Both form one reality: the dynamism of love.

a. Mediatrix because full of grace. Jesus is Incarnate Grace (cf. Titus 2:11). According to Montfort, every sharing in God's life is a grace of Christ, who is forever and everywhere the fruit of her womb. All grace then comes to us "*through Mary.*" Montfort does not consider Incarnate Grace as merely residing in Mary or being, so to speak, contained by Mary. Mary actually participates, as the Mother of God, to the extent permitted to a pure creature, in the life of her Son. Mary is not an unknowing instrument by which the Eternal Wisdom comes into this world. She is the loving Mother of the Lord and is united to him by love and knowledge uniquely proper to a mother. She therefore shares in his life in an absolutely unique manner. Jesus gives himself wholly to Mary, and Mary surrenders wholly to her Son, for is not he the best of sons and Mary the best of mothers?

And if grace truly is a sharing in the life of the triune God, who can deny that the immaculate Mary, Mother of Grace, shares in this life to a degree unsurpassed by any pure creature? To be graced by God is to share in some degree in this fullness of grace that is Mary's. She is the "Daughter of Sion," and in loving her, the Redeemer is loving all of us. Montfort is teaching us a profound and solid doctrine: Mary is the first and the uniquely beloved in the Beloved. And in her the redeemed—the Church—whose form and model she is, are loved also. The love of the Trinity for Mary is the love of the Trinity for the Church (cf. TD 22). In loving Mary, God in Jesus Christ loves us: such is his mysterious plan, his secret. She is truly, in this sense, the Mediatrix of all grace.

b. Mediatrix because of her consent. Divine Love is incarnate through the consent of Mary, which she gives in the name of the entire human race. She therefore accepts grace for us. She is the corporate personality representing humankind in its nothingness, in its yearning for healing; and in our name, as Rahner says, she agrees to be graced.[65] In this sense, all grace comes to us through Mary. This is not only Montfort's teaching but the common possession of the Church throughout the ages and stated by Vatican II. The truth is nothing more than a prolongation of her consent at the Incarnation. Montfort can say that Mary shares grace with us because "*her prayers and requests are so powerful with [God] that He accepts them as commands in the sense that He never resists His dear Mother's prayer because it is always humble and conformed to His will*" (TD 27). Glorified by her Son, she is the Mediatrix of intercession. This is not a task she is given; rather, it is her personality, for she is the eternal Yes of all creation to Jesus.

Montfort the missionary uses language ("*canal*," "*aqueduct*," "*treasury*," "*storehouse*," etc.) that in itself reifies grace, i.e., changes grace from a quality to a quantity, from the sharing of divine life to the reception of a thing. He is expressing the theology and language of his time. The saint would not want us glued to his terminology, as effective as it may have been for his hearers in Western France at the beginning of the eighteenth century. Each culture must find its own way of expressing the fundamental truth Saint Louis Marie is enunciating: she who, as representative of humanity, shares most intensely in Jesus' life, she who is the consent of the human race to the inbreaking of grace itself, is filled with grace, for us.

Mary is, then, the *"mediatrix of intercession"* (TD 86); Jesus is our *"Mediator of redemption"* (TD 84). He is the one Mediator between God and man. Never does Saint Louis Marie, in spite of a baroque language, withdraw Mary from her creaturely existence, redeemed by Jesus. It is only within the context of the Mediator of redemption, the Eternal and Incarnate Wisdom, that Mary is Mediatrix: precisely the teaching of Vatican II.[66]

2. Mary, Mother of the redeemed

The references that Louis de Montfort makes to the spiritual maternity abound in his writings. Our Lady is *"Our Mother,"* and the titles he gives to the Mother of all the predestined read like a special litany composed in honor of her spiritual maternity: "*My good mother,*" *"Mother of Sweetness," "My true Mother," "Mother of the Predestinate," "The best of Mothers," "Mother of Goodness,"*

"Mother of Gifts," "Mother of Grace," "My dear and well-beloved Mother," "His own dear Mother and Yours." In an echo of the Fathers, Mary is also the *"Mother of the Living," "Mother of Fair Love," "Mother of Christians," "Mother of His Members."* And so often this same truth is proclaimed without the term "Mother": "*Christians, lend me your ears, / Listen to me, you chosen / Because I recount the marvels / Of the woman from whom you were born*" (H 77:3).

It is evident that for Montfort, the spiritual maternity cannot be understood as an adoptive or legal function or in the sense that she merely acts towards us like a mother. Rather, with the three Persons of the Trinity and definitely subordinate to them, she is efficaciously and lovingly cooperating in our incorporation into our final goal, the risen Christ, the Eternal and Incarnate Wisdom. We are truly her children.

Moreover, this is for Montfort a dynamic role. The saint declares that "*all the predestinate, in order to be conformed to the image of the Son of God, are in this world hidden in the womb of the Blessed Virgin where they are guarded, nourished, brought up, and made to grow by that good Mother until she has brought them forth to glory after death, which is properly the day of their birth*" (TD 33; SM 14; LEW 213).[67] The entire cosmos is, we could say, "*in the womb*" of Mary, where she is—always in a subordinate manner—forming us into Jesus come to his full stature.

The foundations for such a vivid description of the spiritual maternity of Mary find their roots in Mary's role at the Incarnation. What immediately strikes the modern reader is that nowhere does Saint Louis Marie deduce Mary's motherhood of the human race from the words of Jesus on the Cross, "Woman, behold your Son. Behold your Mother" (Jn 19:26-27). Twice in TD, he does say that those who give themselves to Mary can declare with St. John, "*I have taken her for my own*" (TD 179, 216; cf. SM 66), implying that Mary's spiritual maternity is somehow found in the Johannine text. In PM, he declares that his Congregation was confided to Mary when Jesus died upon the Cross (PM 1). The text is never brought forward, however, as an explicit argument for the spiritual maternity. This is strange when we consider that in a small pamphlet of Father J. Nouet, SJ, *Dispositions for a Happy Death,* found among the saint's belongings when he died, there is a short commentary on Jn 19, referring this text to the spiritual maternity (HD 36). Again we are faced with the centrality, for Montfort, of the mystery of the Incarnation. His stress is on the root, the source, the compendium of all mysteries, the enfleshment of the Eternal Wisdom. We could say that Jn 19 is for Montfort a promulgation of the spiritual maternity but definitely not its origin.

a. Spiritual Mother because graced by the Trinity. Montfort employs three symbols to illustrate that Mary is the Mother of the redeemed because graced by the specific life of each of Persons of the Trinity. Concerning the Father: "*Just as in a natural and bodily generation of* *children there are a father and a mother, so in the supernatural and spiritual generation there are a Father, Who is God, and a Mother, who is Mary*" (TD 30); concerning the Son: "*One and the same mother does not bring forth into the world the head without the members or the members without the head. . . . So in like manner, in the order of grace, the head and the members are born of one and the same Mother*" (TD 32); concerning the Holy Spirit, the symbol is that of a spouse: Mary the Spouse is told by the Spirit, "*You are always my Spouse, as faithful, as pure and as fruitful as ever. Let your faith give me my faithful, your purity my virgins, and your fruitfulness, my temples and my elect*" (TD 34).

These are words not of a university professor but of a down-to-earth missionary who knows that his people are more convinced by examples and symbols than by abstract arguments. Nonetheless, his analogies are not without solid underpinning. And all three of them have basically one foundation: the three Divine Persons each lovingly communicate to Mary—inasmuch as a pure creature is capable—their specific personalities in order to bring about the Incarnation of Eternal Wisdom. But sharing in the life of the Eternal and Incarnate Wisdom is precisely what constitutes us as children of God. The mystery of the Incarnation of the Head includes, therefore, the birth of the children of God, since our graced life is "*contained*" in the divine life of the Savior. "We the many are one body in Christ," says St. Paul (Rom 12:5). Eternal Wisdom is enfleshed "for us and our salvation," offering his entire life even unto death for our Redemption. Christ is, of his very Person, Redemption, Salvation. Mary is Mother of the Redemption. Mary is empowered by the grace of the three Persons of the Trinity to conceive the Eternal Wisdom. She therefore carries all of us in her womb, since all of us are "in Christ Jesus," our Redeemer.

b. Mary, Mother of the redeemed through her consent. Montfort declares that there is a "*necessary consequence*" from the maternity of the Head to the spiritual maternity of the members (TD 32; SM 12; LEW 213). If Our Lady is an unknowing instrument of God, in whom Redemption is conceived without her consent, we could not say that Mary becomes our Mother because she is Mother of the Savior. To deny Mary an active and responsible consent, however, is blasphemous in the thinking of Montfort.

It is Mary's consent—with all the qualities mentioned above—that integrally undergirds the missionary's statement that we deduce the spiritual maternity from Mary's conception of the Head of the Mystical Body. In Montfort's eyes, Mary's consent to the Incarnation is not a blind act in which she is merely the unknowing instrument of the Lord. Such an opinion goes contrary to every page of his writings.[68] Mary's consent to the breaking forth into our human history of God's redemptive love is presumed by Montfort when he speaks about the necessary consequence from Mary's motherhood of Jesus to her motherhood of the members of his Body. If God is Love, he does not force. Love lures, Love requests, Love calls. Love never breaks down doors. And Infinite Love, possessed in three subsisting modes, requests the consent of Mary; Redemption comes into this world "*provided that*" she consent.[69]

3. The first consequence: Mary, Queen of all hearts

Because Mary is Mother of all, she is Queen of all hearts: "*Mary . . . cannot make her residence in [souls] as God the Father ordered her to do and, as their mother, form, nourish, and bring them forth to eternal life . . . unless she has a right and a domination over souls by a singular grace of the Most High . . . and so we can call her . . . the Queen of all hearts*" (TD 37-38). Inextricably united to the Savior's conquest by her cooperation in the redemptive Incarnation and, therefore, in all that flows from it, she shares in a unique way in his royal authority. Queenship is, for Montfort, a logical consequence of the fact that she is truly and effectively Mother of all. It is a Queenship only analogically similar to the queens of his age, for Mary's authority is a maternal one of love within the hearts of people, to influence them to surrender all to the overshadowing Spirit, so that Christ may be formed in them to the glory of the Father. Like the queen-mother of the kingdom of Judah, Mary sits upon a throne at the right of the monarch (1 Kings 2:19; TD 76). The biblical theme of the queen-mother (*gebirah*) is brought to its fulfillment in Mary, mother of the Messiah-King (cf. Is 7:14). Whoever accepts Jesus as King will enthrone the mother of the King beside him.

Her maternal Queenship connotes authority as vast as that of her Son but always—as is everything in Montfort's Marian doctrine—subordinate to and directed to Christ. Mary is, of her very person, as mother of the Redeemer and therefore Mother of the redeemed, a unique influence in this universe, lovingly luring all to surrender with her to Jesus Christ the King. Montfort's teaching is in accord with the famous text of "*Ad coeli reginam*": "Jesus Christ alone, God and man, is King in the strict, full, and absolute sense. Mary shares in his royal dignity in a secondary way, dependent on the sovereignty of her son. She is the mother of Christ God and is his associate in the work of Redemption, in the conflict with the enemy and in his complete victory. It is from this union with Christ the King that she reaches a height of splendor unequaled in all creation."[70]

4. The second consequence: Mary necessary for salvation

"*In the second place we must conclude that the most holy Virgin, being necessary to God by a necessity which we call hypothetical, in consequence of His will, is far more necessary to men in order that they may attain to their last end*" (TD 39).[71] Montfort is emphatic on this point: Mary is necessary for salvation because God freely wills it so. She is not optional. Even more so, Montfort insists she is necessary "*for those who are called to any special perfection*" (TD 43). And again, he repeats that core reasoning found throughout his doctrine: "*It was through Mary that the salvation of the world was begun and it is through her that it must be consummated*" (TD 49). If Mary is necessary to God in the Incarnation, she is necessary to all who will share in the Incarnation, since sanctification is nothing more than the extension of "*the compendium of all mysteries,*" the Incarnation of Eternal Wisdom. Then in the "*end times,*" when Satan will rise up—in vain—in a final diabolical surge to destroy souls, Mary will shine forth more powerfully than ever. For "*the most terrible of all the enemies which God has set up against the devil is His holy Mother*" (TD 52). Most terrible, because Mary is a "*nothing*" of herself, a "*little girl,*" and it is through her that the proud Satan is conquered.

The victory over Satan won in the abridgment of all mysteries, the Incarnation, must unfold out to the Second Coming of the victorious Lord. Those whom God chooses to engage in the front lines of this battle against the forces of evil will, then, necessarily be one with Mary in her total dedication to the Lord. In PM, the saint speaks of his missionary Congregation as in a special way involved in this battle and therefore in a special way one with Mary (PM 6, 12, 13).

5. Other Marian dogmas

Because of Mary's role at the Incarnation, Montfort stresses the ever Virgin Mother of God and associate of the Redeemer, the Mediatrix of all grace, Mary the spiritual Mother, Mary the Queen. The Immaculate Conception and the Assumption, however, are also found in his writings. Neither dogma was declared as such by the Church in Montfort's time. Nonetheless, they were Catholic teaching, and the missionary strongly upholds both prerogatives of Mary without developing them at any length, for they are not precisely within the scope of his Marian writings.

a. The Assumption. Although the references to the Assumption of Mary are relatively few and are found most of all in a listing of the mysteries of the Rosary (TD 3, 116; SR 64; MR 4, 13, 30; H 90:31; LS 221, 223 (part 2); N 10), the ultimate victory of Mary is presumed throughout his writings. That she shares, in the fullness of her personality, in the glory of her Son is, in fact, the primary perspective from which he views Mary. Outside the Annunciation, there are few events in Mary's life that attract his attention as an author of Marian works. That the Assumption itself is not given any special treatment is because it is not directly relevant to the purpose of his Marian writings.

b. The Immaculate Conception. Saint Louis de Montfort upheld the Immaculate Conception of Our Lady; of this there is no doubt. "*She is born immaculate / Never has sin / Tarnished her beauty*" (H 75:19). Without explanation, he puts in short rhyme the "*potuit, decuit, ergo fecit*" (God was able to do it, it was fitting that he do it, therefore He did it) reasoning on this privilege: "*I am struck that one reasons thus: / God was well able to do it / I uphold that He should have done it*" (H 75:20). In LEW, Montfort describes the Immaculate Conception: "*Eternal*

Wisdom built himself a house worthy to be his dwelling-place. He created the most holy Virgin, forming her in the womb of St. Anne, with ever greater delight than he had derived from creating the universe. . . . The torrential outpouring of God's infinite goodness, which had been readily stemmed by the sins of men since the beginning of the world, was now released precipitately and in full flood into the heart of Mary. Eternal Wisdom gave her all the graces which Adam and all his descendants would have received so liberally from him had they remained in their original state of justice. The fullness of God, says a saint, was poured into Mary, . . . masterpiece of the Most High, miracle of Eternal Wisdom, prodigy of the Almighty, Abyss of grace!" (LEW 105-106). And again, in the hymns, Montfort can say: *"Never did the least sin / soil her purity"* (H 88:6). For the most part, Montfort's writings clearly presume this initial privilege of Mary without making it a special study (SM 17; TD 50, 64, 145, 158; N 29).[72]

6. Summary: the titles of Our Lady

A summary of Montfort's Marian doctrine can be seen, to some degree, in the innumerable titles he lavishes upon her. Titles attributed to a person encapsulate the author's understanding of that individual and disclose his understanding of the "selfhood" of the person. What Vincent Taylor states about Christology can also be applied to Mariology: "The question, who Jesus is, is approached best by considering how men named Him, for it is by His names that He is revealed and known."[73]

Approximately 200 titles are used by Montfort to designate Our Lady. Many refer to the spiritual maternity, as shown above. The majority are reflections of the baroque: "*O Marvelous Virgin*," "*O Stunning Prodigy*," "*Clear Image of the Trinity*," "*The Immense Ocean of All His Grandeurs*," "*Paradise of the Trinity*," "*Abyss of grace*," "*Holy of Holies*," etc. At the same time, Montfort, again on the boundary, insists that she is "*servant*," "*a nothing*," "*less than an atom*," "*the most obedient of the servants of the Lord*," "*the little girl*." With the French school, Saint Louis de Montfort stresses the greatness with which God has freely endowed this nothingness who is Mary. If all are, in Bérulle's words, "*un néant capable de Dieu* (a nothing capable of God)," Mary is for Montfort a nothing who is the "*masterpiece of all his grandeurs*." She is "*all-powerful*," yes; but always as a servant of Jesus, a servant of God.

The titles often emphasize that Mary is the "*rest*" of the Trinity and also of the redeemed: a concept dear to the French school of spirituality and implying being at home, finding one's peaceful joy, the place of one's activities. This is expressed in relationship to God, e.g., "*Resting-place of the Trinity*," "*Sacred place of repose*," "*Paradise of God*," "*the tabernacle of God*," "*Royal throne*," "*His sure dwelling*." Yet it is not a sleep to which Montfort refers. Far from it. God works wonders as He reposes in Mary. She is God's "*masterpiece*," the "*immense ocean of all his grandeurs*," the very "*mirror of the divinity*," the "*divine Mary*." This is in accord with

Montfort's teaching that the Most High accomplishes such wonders in her. In other words, the titles Montfort attributes to Mary designate a dynamic, free pouring forth of God's life into Mary to a degree unparalleled in a pure creature. She is God's "*Holy-Place*," where God accomplishes his greatest miracles of grace. God is present in her to share divine life with her, not only for her but for others.

Mary is for us, as she is for the Trinity and in a unique way for the Incarnate Wisdom, a resting place: "*My rest of love*," "*My place of rest*," "*My oratory*," "*Milieu of mysteries.*" Yet to live in Mary through total surrender is to experience the divine life of which she is filled for us ("*even for us,*" H 90:52). She is, therefore, "*the woman who nurses me*," "*my Flame*," "*Mother of Grace*," "*Mother of Gifts*," "*Remedy for the Incurable*," "*Sure Refuge of sinners,*" "*Our all-powerful Queen*," "*Mother of Fair Love,*" "*Joy of God's servants*," "*Tree of Life*," "*treasurer of the Lord*," "*New Eve*," "*the canal*," "*the aqueduct of all God's graces*"; she is the mother "*who feeds us with a milk all divine*" (TD 264). We "*repose*" in Mary to be fed with divine Life. It is especially the sharing of Mary's faith,[74] which Montfort calls an "*unshakable rock*," "*courageous,*" a "*flaming torch*," *the restorer of life*," inflaming "*those who sit in darkness and the shadow of death,*" that we see the apostolic, missionary dimension of living in Mary (TD 214).

Mary is the contemplative apostle. So too are those who dwell in her, for in her reposes the triune God, pouring forth as in a torrent His grandiose gifts of grace to be shared by the other members of the Body of Christ: the basic theme of the titles given by Montfort to Mary.

VI. Relevance and Prospects of Montfort's Marian Doctrine

Montfort's Marian teaching is not complete. But as has already been noted, he never intended to write a manual of Mariology. His purpose is to form a squadron of apostles of Jesus Christ, and so he stresses the fundamental root of the faith, the Incarnation of the Lord and Mary's role in this compendium of all mysteries. The saint's Marian teaching is best studied within the context of contemporary Mariology as a whole; then his stresses can be more clearly understood.

1. Challenge to the contemporary world

Saint Louis de Montfort's bold teaching that we are called to live the total, loving *fiat* of Mary is a great challenge to the self-sufficient citizen of the contemporary world.[75] His Marian doctrine is nothing less than the call to a profound renewal of the faith, to a life in harmony with the radical demands of the Gospel in imitation of Mary and with the effective aid of her maternal influence. If original sin and personal sin are not popular topics today, it appears to be primarily because the demands of the Gospel are so watered down that a neo-Pelagianism vainly attempts to answer the crises of the day. Saint Louis de Montfort's clear insistence on living Mary's total fidelity to the Word makes us understand the radical need for God.

In a world that theoretically accepts the reality of globalization yet appears impotent to face its challenges, Montfort's teaching offers insight and practical means of implementing this new world order, this "global village." In Mary, the spokesperson for this universe in its yearning for wholeness, we come together as the redeemed brothers and sisters of Jesus Christ; we are all her children. It is clear through Montfort's doctrine on Mary—one with the scriptural portraits of the Mother of God—that it is only by an active and responsible total surrender to the Lord that the victory of the Cross can be implemented. We cannot just roll up our sleeves and bring about the Kingdom of God. Understanding that without the Lord we can do nothing, like Mary we release ourselves totally into the tenderness of God in order to be divinized and thereby be in harmony with the world, with ourselves, with each other, for we are in obedient harmony with the source of all, God Alone. Montfort's Marian teaching brings us to the very core of our faith.

Especially, then, in this post-Christian age, Montfort's teaching on Mary is highly relevant, for Montfort's Mariology—most especially his "*perfect*" devotion to Mary—is nothing less than a call to live the Gospel to the hilt, a clear cry for renewal, to turn away from everything that is not God Alone. It is rejected especially by the highly secularized West, which cannot tolerate joining in with Mary's active and responsible *fiat*. In a haughty, do-your-own-thing age, an era marked by little if any doctrinal or moral restraints—characteristics of the West—Montfort's doctrine is as acceptable as Jeremiah's was to the people of Jerusalem. The saint's boldness in his proclamation of Mary as the model and of the necessity of joining in with her representative surrender to the Lord is highly unpalatable to the self-sufficient, rugged-individualist citizen of the first world.

Montfort leaves us with no doubt about the permanent validity and relevance of devotion to the Mother of God. The saint makes it evident that only an erroneous understanding of God's self-disclosure permits one to neglect Mary. At the same time, his teachings, if faithfully followed, prohibit deviations in the Christian's veneration of Our Lady.

Yet it also holds a strange fascination for modern man. For underneath the thick facade of "I'm OK; you're OK," there hides a deep-down emptiness, yearning to be filled. Montfort's teaching on this courageous "*nothing*," a "*little girl*" who is truly filled with Infinite Love only by surrendering to the Spirit, becomes the sign of hope. The more so because, in Montfort's eyes, she represents us in our yearning to be healed and in our divinization. We could go so far as to say that Montfort's Marian teaching appears to be needed by the jaded, fundamentally fearful modern man and woman. With Mary as Mother and Queen, we "*lose ourselves*" in God, Who *is Love* (H 28:43), and joyfully and fearlessly put ourselves at the service of the Body of Christ.

2. Development of Montfort's Marian doctrine

Nonetheless, contemporary insights must permeate Montfort's Marian teaching not only so that it speaks more effectively to modern men and women but also so that its powerful roots may flower. The inculturation of Montfort's Marian teaching in the variety of cultures that make up the world appears to be lagging behind the development of Marian devotion itself; there is a danger that strict fidelity to the "language" of Montfort may in today's times be a betrayal of his authentic thought. The interdependence and interrelatedness of all things and all peoples—a foundation of much of Montfort's Marian teaching—must be more fully taken into account so that we can better understand Mary's role in salvation history, especially as Mediatrix, Mother. Moreover, Mary must be seen within the context of everyone, especially today's poor, the marginalized, and those suffering injustice under the extremes of capitalism or socialism. We can, then, better understand that when we speak about Mary, we are ultimately speaking about the omnipotent love of our Redeemer and about ourselves as liberated by Christ. Montfort's Marian teaching has the raw material for a magnificent Mary-Church analogy, but it has yet to unfold. The ramifications of his stress on the role of the Spirit in the divinization of Mary have not yet been sufficiently plumbed. Montfort's doctrine on Mary offers healthy insights to the feminist movement of Western society, but this investigation has not yet been truly deep. And there are the seeds within Montfort's Marian teaching for an excellent ecumenical dialogue about Mary: her nothingness of herself, her total relativity to God, the strong Christocentricity of his Marian doctrine, his stress on Consecration as the equivalent of the renewal of baptismal promises, his overarching principle: God Alone. Montfort's Marian doctrine is a gold mine that has been discovered but as yet scarcely dug.

P. Gaffney

Notes: (1) Because of his poor eyesight, the first of the three theologians called to review the writings of Montfort could only read the TD and thereby could not know the global context of montfort spirituality. The promoter of the faith, in presenting the reports to the cardinals, expressed deep concern about this and underlined the importance of "the fundamental principle" as outlined by the second reviewer. *Positio super scriptis beatificationis et canonizationis Ven. Servi Ludovici Mariae Grignion de Montfort,* Rome 1851, 23. (2) H. Boudon, *Oeuvres Complètes (Complete Works),* vol.2, *Dieu Seul ou Le Saint Esclavage de l'Admirable Mère de Dieu (God Alone or the Holy Slavery of the Admirable Mother of God),* Migne, Paris 1856, 475: "O God alone, God alone, God alone and always God alone!" (3) R. Laurentin, *Dieu Seul est ma tendresse (God Alone Is My Tenderness),* O. E. I. L., Paris 1984, 198. (4) The roving missionary's references to the biblical expression "*the wrath of God,*" found mostly in his popular hymns—"*anger,*" "*wrath,*" "*to calm God*" (cf. SM 66; H 119:16; H 128:3; H 131:3; H 104:2; H 88:12; H 82:7; H 75:1; TD 52, 172)—must, as its multiple citations in Scripture (cf. Mt 3:7; Jn 3:36; Rom 1:18, 3:5, 9:22; Eph 5:6; etc.), be understood as expressing a profound truth: Infinite Love betrayed by those who freely walk away from Love into estrangement, out of Light into darkness. Sin is its own punishment. Montfort uses the biblical image of the anger of God to illustrate to his hearers Infinite Love's yearning to have the sinner return to his senses: "*Listen to me. Like a Good Father, I complain / That for a long time I have been searching for a child / Up till now, I've held back my anger. / O! must punishments be used?"* (H 98:1). (5) Montfort's Bible was among the few items he carried in the knapsack flung over his shoulder. His implicit and explicit quotes from Sacred Scripture are well more than several hundred. (6) Cf. H. de Lubac, *The Splendor of the Church,* Paulist, Mahwah, New Jersey 1963, 218-235, tracing the Marian interpretation of the Song of Songs. (7) Tillich saw himself as a person living his existence "on the boundary." Cf. P. Tillich, *On the Boundary: An Autobiographical Sketch,* Charles Scribner's Sons, New York 1966. Although the comparison between Tillich and Montfort is not without its weaknesses, it is interesting to read a description of the "boundary situation," which appears to apply to Montfort's intellectual and personal development, in L. Gordon Tait, *The Promise of Tillich,* Lippincott, Philadelphia 1971, 11: "It is the condition . . . [that] is the basis of creativity; it presupposes always being receptive to new possibilities. Life in the boundary situation is difficult, dangerous, tense, exciting—but fruitful and rewarding." (8) For an excellent discussion of this entire period, especially in its Marian ramifications, cf. S. De Fiores, *Il culto mariano nel contesto culturale dell'Europa nei secoli XVII-XVIII* in *De Culto Mariano Saeculis XVII-XVIII* (Marian Devotion in the European Cultural Context in the 17th and 18th Centuries), Pontificia Academia Mariana Internationalis, Rome 1987, 2:2-57. (9) F. Poiré, *La Triple Couronne de la Bienheureuse Mère de Dieu tissue à ses principales grandeurs d'Excellence, de Pouvoir et de Bonté et enrichie de diverses inventions pour l'aimer, l'honorer et la servir* (The Triple Crown of the Blessed Mother of God, Women from Her Principal Grandeurs of Excellence, Power and Goodness and Enriched with Diverse ways of loving, honoring and serving Her), Cramoisy, Paris 1639. (10) J.B. Crasset, *La véritable dévotion envers la Sainte Vierge,* De Launay, Paris 1708. (11) L. F. d'Argentan, *Conférences théologiques et spirituelles sur les grandeurs de la très sainte Vierge Marie, Mère de Dieu* (Theological and Spiritual Conferences on the Grandeurs of the Blessed Virgin Mary, Mother of God), Paris, 1687. (12) P. Spinelli, *Maria Deipara Thronus Dei* (Mary Mother of God, Throne of God), Tarquini Longhi, Naples 1613. (13) Cardinal P. de Bérulle, *Oeuvres Complètes,* reproduction of the original ed. (1644), Maison de l'Institution de l'Oratoire, Montsoult 1960. (14) H. Boudon, *Oeuvres Complètes,* Migne, Paris 1857. (15) J. J. Olier, *Oeuvres Complètes,* Migne, Paris 1856. (16) Cf. S. De Fiores, *Il culto mariano nel contesto culturale dell'Europa,* 17-18. (17) The most important Marian work of this period is a sixteen-page pamphlet composed in 1673 by a lay Catholic of Cologne, Adam Widenfeld: *Monita Salutaria B. V. Mariae ad cultores suos indiscretos* (Salutary Warnings of the Blessed Virgin Mary to Her Indiscreet Devotees). For a study of Widenfeld's work, cf. P. Hoffer, *La dévotion à Marie au déclin du XVIIe siècle. Autour du Jansenisme et des "Avis salutaires de la B. V. Mariae à ses dévots indiscrets"* (Devotion to Mary at the End of the 17th Century Concerning Jansenism and the "Salutary Warnings"), Cerf, Paris 1938. (18) Cf. L. Perouas, *Grignion de Montfort, les pauvres et les missions,* Cerf, Paris 1966, 36-37. (19) Cf. Blain 2:12. (20) Blain 21, speaks of this tendency in describing some summer days spent with Louis Mary at the Grignion home at Iffendic: "He showed me some secluded spots in his garden for prayer, places where he liked to be and where he spent the greater part of his time." (21) This "initiation" into the sodality proclaimed Mary as the *"Domina, Patrona, et Advocata"* and included the words *"Accept me, Therefore, as your servant forever."* Cf. Crasset, *La véritable dévotion,* 465. For a study of the influence of the Sodality on Montfort, cf. Itinerario (22) Blain, 17. Blain speaks with an exuberance about Montfort, especially his Marian devotion and also his apostolic lifestyle. Is some of this hyperbole? Considering the state of hagiography at the time, most probably. (23) Blain, 16. (24) H. de Lubac, *The Splendour of the Church,* Paulist, Glen Rock 1963, 338, n. 130, points out that Olier's *Vie intérieure de la Sainte Vierge* "only just escaped being placed on the Index on account of certain exaggerations; cf. C. Flachaire, *Dévotion à la Vierge,* p. 104: Henri Bremond, *Histoire littéraire du sentiment religieux,* 3:494-495. . . . According to Fr. Congar these exaggerations were perhaps the result of 'a certain monophysicist tendency.'" Montfort avoided the extremes of Olier. The saint cannot be accused of the heresy of monophysitism, which for all practical purposes denies the humanity of Jesus, teaching that Jesus is of one nature, and that divine; cf. n. 31 below. (25) Blain, 52. (26) Cf. S. De Fiores, *La devozione mariana del Montfort nel contexto della polemica degli 'Avvisi salutari' di Widenfeld,* in Mar 36 (1974), 40-69. (27) Blain, 28. (28) Cf. R. Laurentin, *Dieu Seul est ma tendresse,*

136, n. 18, for a list of the apparitions of Our Lady to Montfort that biographers of the saint recount. (29) Cf. N 175-178, 185 for references to the works of d'Argentan, Bourgoing, and Olier that Montfort used to explain the mystery of the Incarnation. (30) The full humanity of Jesus is stressed, e.g., in LEW 104-132, 154-166, and the noels, H 57-66. Montfort's understanding of "full humanity," however, is similar to that of Saint Thomas (cf. *Summa Theologica* III, q. 4, a. 2, q. 5) and not to the contemporary Antiochene Christological thought as represented, e.g., by N. Pittinger, *Christology Reconsidered*, SCM Press, London 1970. (31) H 55:17 sings of Jesus: "*The Supreme Beauty,/ The Supreme Light,/ The Supreme Goodness,/ True God of God the Father.*" And Mary is clearly the Mother of God: "*Mother of Fair Love, May all praise you everywhere / For having given to us this Infant-God / For having given day to the Light, / Being to the true God, life to our Father*" (H 60:12); cf. Cyril of Alexandria's statement: "If anyone confesses not Emmanuel to be God in truth and the holy Virgin on this ground to be Theotokos since she brings forth according to the flesh the Word of God who became flesh, let him be anathema" (PG 77:120). (32) In this ecumenical age, the appellation "*divine*" Mary would unnecessarily offend. It is, however, still used in expressions like "St. John the Divine," "The Divine Liturgy," "The Divine Office." English theologians were customarily called divines. In the secular world, the term is currently used for opera stars ("Diva") and even for one's appearance. (33) "In the complete possession of Christ's humanity by the divinity, wherein the humanity of Christ lacks its own subsistence, its own personality, they [writers of the French school] saw the absolute condition of self-renouncement and clinging to God. From this state of 'infinite servitude' they drew the most fundamental characteristics of their spirituality." E. A. Walsh, *Spirituality, French School of*, in *The New Catholic Encyclopedia*, McGraw-Hill, New York 1966, 13:605. (34) W. Kasper, *Jesus the Christ*, Paulist Press, New York 1976, 140, applies this principle to the Easter experience of the first Apostles; cf. A. Darlapp, *Anfang*, in *Lexikon für Theologie und Kirche*, 1:525-529. (35) John Paul II, *Angelus Message of Sunday, 4 December*, in *L'Osservatore Romano* (English edition), December 12, 1983, 2. (36) Montfort is echoing his sources, especially Cardinal de Bérulle, who wrote: "What is man? A nothing capable of God." Quoted by H. Daniel-Rops, *The Church in the Seventeenth Century*, E.P. Dutton, New York 1963, 58. (37) Paul VI uses the expression "intrinsic element of Christian worship" when speaking of devotion to Mary (MC 56; cf. MC 58). Since, as the Holy Father declares, "devotion must match its doctrinal content" (MC 38), he is declaring that Mary is also intrinsic to salvation history. (38) Montfort's explanations appear, in the final analysis, as more consonant with a modern understanding of grace as not primarily in the realm of efficient causality (i.e., God does something to us, grace as a created quality) but in the realm of quasi-formal causality (i.e., God actually sharing life, grace as uncreated), the self-communication of God. And Saint Louis Marie appears to declare that God communicates Himself to Mary precisely as triune, each Person taking possession of her according to His personal properties. In doing so, he is not denying that the activity *ad extra* of the three Divine Persons is one and the same and is ascribed to one of the Persons only by appropriation (DS 3326). His forceful language, however, would have us believe that this is a valid principle only when we speak about efficient, and not quasi-formal, causality. Cf. K. Rahner, *Trinity, Divine*, in *Encyclopedia of Theology: The Concise Sacramentum Mundi*, Seabury Press, New York 1975, 1758; P. Gaffney, *The Spiritual Maternity according to Saint Louis Mary de Montfort*, Montfort Publications, Bay Shore 1976, 19-20. This contemporary understanding of grace is applicable therefore to all, but in a special way to the woman destined to be the Mother of God. (39) Montfort's writings make it clear that the Divine Persons interpenetrate (*circuminsessio* of the West, *perichoresis* of the East), since they are relational realities. In other words, each one implies the others. The missionary's constant grouping together of the Father-Son-Holy Spirit makes this evident. (40) N 171 sums up the thought of d'Argentan on this point. (41) Cf. J. Pintard, *La maternité spirituelle de Marie selon les théologiens du XIX siècle* (The Spiritual Maternity of Mary According to Theologians of the 19th Century), in EtMar 17 (1960), 140. Pintard does not appear to realize that the text under discussion by Pusey and Newman is taken from these numbers of the TD; cf. J. Stern, *Le Saint-Esprit et Marie chez Newman et Faber* (The Holy Spirit and Mary in Newman and Faber), in EtMar 26 (1969), 37-56, and his bibliography; cf. J. H. Newman, *A Letter Addressed to the Rev. E. B. Pusey in Certain Difficulties Felt by Anglicans*, vol. 2, London 1885. (42) Cf. De Rosa, *La fecondità dello Spirito Santo* (The Fecundity of the Holy Spirit), in Mar 10 (1948), 65-72; P. Oger, *Intorno ad un passo . . .* (Concerning a passage . . .), in Mar 10 (1948), 369; J.M. Alonso, *Hacia una Mariología Trinitaria* (Towards a Trinitarian Mariology), in EstMar 10 (1950), 183. (43) This is always understood in the full context of

Montfort's writings as mentioned above; cf. TD 27. (44) Her holiness is so astounding that Montfort can declare that the patriarchs could not merit the Incarnation (LEW 104) and "*there was found only Mary who by the sublimity of her virtue attained to the very throne of the Divinity and has merited this infinite treasure*" (TD 16). The missionary would be speaking about merit in a strongly analogous sense, i.e., Mary's unmerited gift of holiness is so intense that it was fitting that God answer her prayers for the coming of Divine Wisdom. (45) Cf. S. De Fiores, *Le Saint-Esprit et Marie chez Grignion de Montfort* (The Holy Spirit and Mary in St. Louis de Montfort), in CM 99, 195-215. (46) The term *"spouse"* is found throughout the writings of Montfort and used in a variety of ways. A sampling: the Cross is the spouse of Eternal Wisdom (LEW 168); the soul is the spouse of Eternal Wisdom (LEW 54); Mary is the spouse of the Spirit (SM 13, 15; TD 21, 25; H 114:16); the Holy Spirit is the Spouse of Mary (SM 10; TD 152); Jesus is the Spouse of the soul (H 112:1); God is Spouse (H 4:22); God is the Spouse of Mary (LS 214). Mystical union under the symbol of spouse was the common interpretation of the Song of Songs in Montfort's time. (47) MC 26. (48) Pope John Paul has not hesitated to use the expression in RMat 26: "The Holy Spirit had already come down upon her, and she became his faithful spouse at the Annunciation." (49) Many contemporary theologians still have strong hesitations about the expression "spouse of the Holy Spirit"; cf. R. Laurentin, *Dieu Seul est ma tendresse,* 181-194. (50) Cf. N 163, where Montfort copies the following from d'Argentan: "[The Holy Spirit] produces in her a divine person, ie., Our Lord, although he produces no divine person in eternity." (51) Cf. G. Philips, *Le Saint Esprit et Marie dans l'Eglise, Vatican II et Prospective du Probleme* (The Holy Spirit and Mary in the Church, Vatican II and an Overview of the Problem), in EtMar 25 (1968), 31-32; M. Dupuy, *Le Saint Esprit et Marie dans l'Ecole Française* (The Holy Spirit and Mary in the French School), in EtMar 26 (1969), 27-32. (52) Cf. G. Philips, *Le Saint Esprit et Marie,* 32. (53) Paul VI strikingly reflects this teaching of Saint Louis: "The Blessed Virgin's free consent and cooperation in the plan of redemption. . . . Mary, taken into dialogue with God, gives her active and responsible consent not to the solution of a contingent problem but to that event of world importance, as the Incarnation of the Word has rightly been called" (MC 37). (54) *Summa Theologica* III, q. 8, a. 1. (55) Pope John Paul, *Angelus Message,* 2. The Holy Father in the same address calls Mary "the heiress and the completion of the faith of Abraham. Just as the patriarch is considered 'our father' in faith, so Mary, for all the more reason, must be claimed as 'our mother' in faith. Abraham is at the beginning, Mary is at the summit of the generations of Israel. . . . Mary's words recall the words of the children of Israel at the foot of Sinai on the day of the covenant: 'We will do everything that the Lord has told us!'" (56) MC 5, 6. (57) MC 28. (58) K. Rahner, *Mary, Mother of the Lord: Theological Meditations,* Herder and Herder, New York 1964, 100-101. (59) The expert on Mary Coredemptrix, J. B. Carol, in his monumental work on the coredemption, *De Coredemptione B. V. M., Disquisitio Positiva,* Vatican City 1950, 348-349, is rightfully doubtful that he can include Saint Louis de Montfort among those who support his thesis of Mary's immediate cooperation in the objective Redemption. Cooperation through consent is itself not considered sufficient by Carol to declare Mary "immediate" Coredemptrix. (60) Notice that Jn "encloses" the entire public ministry of Jesus with the faith of Mary: the beginnings at Cana (Jn 2) and the culmination at the Cross (Jn 19). (61) Saint Louis de Montfort's sources agree that the Divine Maternity is the unifying principle of all that can be said about her. E.g., H. Boudon writes in *Dieu Seul,* 171: "Her greatest happiness and the source of all the other favors that heaven has given her is the Divine Maternity." And the missionary himself sings: "*She is the Mother of Jesus, / Nothing greater can be said of her. / There is the glory of glories, / The crown of crowns, / May all mortals intone, / In heaven, on earth and everywhere: / Mary is the Mother of God, / She is the mother of Jesus, / Nothing greater can be said of her*" (H 88:20, 21). (62) For an excellent study of the meaning of "paradigm" and its application to contemporary Mariology, see Patrick J. Bearsley, SM, *Mary the Perfect Disciple: A Paradigm for Mariology,* in *Theological Studies* 41 (September 1980), 461ff. Bearsley clarifies the distinction between the ontological and the epistemological prime principle. (63) AAS 39 (1947), 331. (64) The possible exception mentioned by Montfort in SM 23 is only apparent: Montfort is again alluding to the fact that God has absolutely no need of Mary in sharing His saving love, and so intent is he on stressing this point that he will say that it would be rash to say that he does not bypass Mary at times. The missionary is not saying —and, in the context of his entire doctrine, it is not the thought of Montfort—that God de facto ever does so. Whether this is specifically the thought of his source for this statement, Crasset (N 46), can be debated without demanding that Montfort's teaching on this point has to be identical to what he read in another author. Saint Louis does have a creative mind, and while we note the literary dependences, he should be allowed to speak for himself. For a different explanation of this text, cf. GA, 285, n. 35. (65) K. Rahner, *Mary, Mother of the Lord*, 105: "For our salvation you said Yes, for us you spoke your Fiat." (66) Whether the term "Mediatrix" should be employed depends upon the audience. In an ecumenical age, it may unnecessarily confuse, even with the clarifications of the Vatican Council. If so, other terms and other symbols, flowing from the particular culture, must be used to express this fundamental truth, that because of Mary's necessary role in the Incarnation—the compendium, the beginning of all mysteries—she must be considered the mediatrix by which God shares life with us. (67) Montfort attributes this text to Saint Augustine; cf. Gaffney, *The Spiritual Maternity*, pp. 59-61. (68) Saint Louis Marie would have no part with those authors who appear to be making a clear dichotomy between what could be called the Mary of history and the Virgin of faith, declaring, against the constant teaching of the Church, that, without any foundation in historical reality, Mary is the symbol of the believing Christian. Montfort insists on the basic reality and fundamental authenticity of Mary's role in the Incarnation as depicted by the Scriptures. That the Lucan Annunciation scene is couched in literary forms found in the OT (cf. Judg 13:2-5) and language borrowed directly from earlier inspired writings (cf. Zeph 3:14-17), no one can deny (cf. *Behold Your Mother of Faith: A Pastoral Letter on the Blessed Virgin Mary*, USCC, Washington 1973, 21-33). But to conclude from this that Lk 1:26-38 is a total, although justifiable, fabrication is to confuse the literary instrument with the truth conveyed. The Church has constantly insisted on the reality of the active and responsible consent (cf. MC 37) of Mary to the redemptive Incarnation. (69) K. Rahner, *Mary, Mother of the Lord*, 100-101, puts this truth—so central to montfort spirituality—most beautifully: "The absolutely unique Yes of consent of the Blessed Virgin which cooperated in determining the whole history of the world, is not a mere happening that has disappeared in the void of the past. . . . She still utters her eternal Amen, her eternal Fiat, Let it be so, Let it be done, to all that God willed to the whole great ordered plan of redemption." (70) AAS 46 (1954), 625-640. (71) The necessity of Mary for salvation is analogous to the necessity of the Church in order to be saved. The *Letter of the Holy Office to Archbishop Cushing of Boston* (1952) is the clearest statement of the nature of the necessity of the Church for salvation, stressing that belonging to the Church must be actual (*in re*) or, if that is not possible, through desire (*in voto*), even implicit desire (*etiam implicito*). Cf. DS 3869-3872; LG 16. The full text and commentary can be found in *American Ecclesiastical Review* 127 (1952), 307-311, 450-561; cf. *Sal Terrae* 41 (1953), 22-26. (72) Cf. J. M. Hupperts, *L'Immaculée Conception dans la doctrine mariale de Saint Louis-Marie de Montfort,* in *Virgo Immaculata,* Congres mariologique de Rome, 1954, Academia Mariana, Rome 1956, 151-172. (73) V. Taylor, *The Names of Jesus*, St. Martin's Press, New York 1962, 1. (74) Montfort is referring to the effective influence of Mary upon us, so that in the power of the Spirit we resemble her in her total surrender to the Lord. We all affect each other in varying degrees. After Jesus, no human being so influences the human family—because of the will of God—than Mary. (75) Cf. C. Bilo, *L'homme d'aujourd'hui face au salut* in, *Dieu Seul. A la recontre de Dieu avec Montfort*, Centre International Montfortain, Rome 1981, 11-19.

MILIEU

SUMMARY

I. FRANCE IN MONTFORT'S TIMES:
   1. An overview of eighteenth-century France;
   2. Structures and divisions of the French territory:
      a. The religious structures,
      b. Administrative and juridical structures,
      c. The division into areas according to landscape features;
   3. Montfort in western France.

II. THE SOCIOPOLITICAL, ECONOMIC, AND CULTURAL CIRCUMSTANCES:
   1. The sociopolitical and economic situation:
      a. The political scene,
      b. The economic situation;
   2. The social strata:
      a. The clergy,
      b. The nobility,
      c. The common people or third estate;
   3. The cultural circumstances:
      a. The two cultures,
      b. Sociocultural perceptions.

III. RELIGIOUS MENTALITY AND PRACTICE:
   1. The socioreligious mentalities:
      a. The mentalities in the regions,
      b. The mentalities of the social classes;
   2. Religious mores:
      a. Worship,
      b. Morality,
      c. The life of faith,
      d. The clerical life,
      e. Religious life.

IV. THE INFLUENCE OF HIS TIME ON MONTFORT'S LIFE AND WRITINGS: A MAN WHO THROUGH HIS HOLINESS TRANSCENDED HIS TIME:
   1. Montfort's ties with the three social orders:
      a. His ties with the bourgeoisie,
      b. His ties with the clergy,
      c. His ties with the common people and the poor;
   2. From a mission in time and space to a timeless mission in the Church.

If the various writings of Saint Louis Marie de Montfort are difficult to read, and if we are surprised by the main events of his life and the characteristics of his attitude and work, it is because they must be seen within their cultural and historical context.[1] This article—which draws heavily on a course given by Fr. L. Perouas—does not set out to give explanations. Rather, it seeks to highlight the atmosphere of the times, i.e., the historical, sociological, and cultural context which was the background of Montfort's life and mission. The aim of this article is to spur us to further reading, research work, and reflection. It is our hope that it will be a signpost on the road to a better understanding of Montfort's contemporaries, of their mind-sets and of their lifestyles: of what influenced him as a man and as a missionary priest. This article does not claim to be exhaustive. In order to give a comprehensive picture of Montfort, we would need to bring together his many facets. Even if this were possible, God, who made every saint, would insure that some things would elude us.

I. France in Montfort's Time

When Montfort began his missionary work in the early eighteenth century, the national boundaries and political structures of Europe were very different from today. National boundaries still as ill-defined as they were in the Middle Ages, gave rise to constant quarrels: the Austrian Empire and the great kingdoms of France and England were continually waging war, either internally, in order to achieve unification, or externally in order to establish their political, economic, maritime, and colonial supremacy.

1. An overview of eighteenth-century France

The boundaries of the kingdom were roughly the same as those of present-day France. Some provinces, however, like Lorraine or Savoy, were not fully part of the kingdom. The total area was nearly 500,000 square kilometers. The total population of France was nearly 19 million. It was the most densely populated country in Europe. The average birthrate per family was five. The death rate was high, with life expectancy no more than forty years.

2. Structures and divisions of the French territory [2]

The most striking feature of France in this period was that it was made up of many closely interwoven political, juridical, administrative, and religious structures. They were like many different size frames placed one on top of another.

a. The religious structures. Since the beginning of its history, France had been divided into dioceses. In 1700 their number was much larger than it is today. Their sizes varied widely, and their boundaries did not fit juridical or political divisions. In Montfort's time there were twenty or so dioceses in western France. The diocese of Poitiers was made up of over 600 parishes, whereas the diocese of Avranches numbered only 67. The dioceses were divided into areas headed by archpriests or deans having jurisdiction over a group of parishes. The geographical location and size of the parishes varied greatly, with a larger number of them in urban areas. In Poitiers, for example, there were no fewer than 20 parishes. They were basic administrative units, responsible for keeping the records now held by registry offices. The parish priests informed their parishioners of the latest legislation and news in their Sunday sermons.

b. Administrative and juridical structures. The province was the oldest and most important political and administrative division. In Montfort's day, people felt they belonged to a province, e.g., Normandy or Brittany, rather than to the French kingdom. A province was, in a way, a nation within a nation. It had its own rights, customs, traditions, trade and commerce, which determined the local way of life, culture, and language.[3] In 1700 there were twenty-seven French provinces, of very unequal size, each relatively independent. The provincial government was divided into a great many sections for administrative purposes: one of them dealt with military matters, another with finances, another with taxes, and another with juridical matters. In some provinces the parliament was the highest authority and dealt with fiscal and juridical matters. The provincial law courts had jurisdiction over a number of bailiffs and other court officials. At the top of the juridical administration was an intendant, who was the king's representative in the province, and who had a number of subdelegates. Vested with extensive powers, he controlled and governed everything within his jurisdiction, and thus upheld the centralized power of the state. This outdated form of administration was not really efficient. It required a large body of highly paid functionaries with varying degrees of efficiency, who were difficult to manage properly. Most of them were officials who had bribed their way into posts, which they would later hand on to their children.

c. The division into areas according to geographic and economic factors. There was a further division, based on a region's economy and terrain. This was particularly noticeable in western France. The wooded-countryside areas were strikingly different from the flat-countryside areas. In the wooded areas, the bottom soil was impervious to water and contained many springs. People lived in scattered hamlets or in remote farms. Their fields were fenced in with thick hedgerows and trees. The soil was poor, and farmers could only raise low-yield crops every three years. In some areas half the land was barren and given over to heath and trees. By contrast, the flat-countryside areas lay on chalky soil with few springs. Thus, people tended to live in clusters of houses near the center of the parish, or in a couple of villages in the open country, with fenceless fields, where their cattle pastured after the harvest. The land in the flat areas was fertile, and 80 percent of it was sown with wheat. It yielded a good harvest every second year. The differences of terrain perhaps accounted greatly for the two ways of life, the two mind-sets. In the wooded areas, the population was scattered, inward-looking, and individualistic. Their primary concern was to become economically self-sufficient.

In the flat areas, the clustered houses were conducive to trading and to a more communal way of life. There were many wooded areas in Brittany, Normandy, Anjou, and Poitou. These had wide flat areas on the fringes. There were other very unique regions, but they were less extensive and not so strikingly different as the two types we have just considered. There were the coastal areas, with their farming and fishing population: with many craftsmen and shopkeepers, especially near the ports of La Rochelle, Nantes, and Saint-Malo. There were the marshy areas, where cattle-breeding was prevalent and the suburbs of some large towns, for example Montbernage. The Loire valley was a heavily traveled area with many rural trading centers, where fairs were held regularly, etc. Whatever the area, whether large or small, rich or poor, those who gave parish missions there, had to take its geographic and economic peculiarities into consideration.

3. Montfort in western France [4]

Louis Marie Grignion was born at Montfort-sur-Meu in the Rennes valley. His native village was part of the diocese of Saint-Malo and lay in the heart of the province of Brittany. He gave most of his missions in the provinces of Brittany, Poitou, and Aunis, and only a few in the neighboring provinces of Normandy, Anjou, and Saintonge. He carried out most of his missionary work in the dioceses of St.-Malo, Rennes, Saint-Brieuc, Poitiers, Nantes, La Rochelle, and Luçon. He also passed through the dioceses of Coutance, Bayeux, and Saintes. He received his priestly formation in Paris and exercised his ministry there in various forms, and on several occasions. His missionary work was clearly influenced by the geographical, administrative, and socio-economic circumstances prevailing in France at the time.

II. The Sociopolitical, Economic, and Cultural Circumstances

Around 1700 the political and economic prospects in France were rather gloomy in the wake of a series of unfortunate events.

1. The sociopolitical and economic situation

a. The political scene. It can be summed up in one word: absolutism. Since 1661, when he became king, Louis XIV was the embodiment of the state, having taken all power to himself. His role was puffed up by politicized theologians who made him out to be "God's assistant."[5] At the court at Versailles, his seat of royal grandeur, the king lived a life of self indulgent pleasure and luxury. From this place he wielded power over his subjugated people; its upkeep was costly, and it kept the king remote from the real problems and difficulties of ordinary people. From 1680, and especially after 1700, the political situation kept deteriorating. The king turned within himself, hardening his stand on some of his mistaken and arbitrarily made decisions. These included his conflict with the Pope over his appointment of bishops, the revocation of the Edict of Nantes in 1685, and, above all, his endless ruinous wars, such as that of the Spanish

Succession from 1701 to 1714. The war affected the northern and western parts of France most severely. At Pontchâteau and Ile d'Yeu, it hindered Montfort's missionary activities in the Atlantic coastal region.[6] As a result of the war, new taxes were levied and the number of militiamen increased. Ordinary people, already hard hit by the economic crisis, bore the brunt of these new measures. The troubles grew tragically worse at the end of Louis XIV's reign, and more and more people denounced the general malaise. In *Remonstrances*,[7] Fénelon wrote, "It is not only a question of bringing the war to an end abroad, but also of providing food for the population within the country."

b. The economic situation. In the sixteenth century, the growth of navigation and foreign trade, the colonization of the Americas, and the abundance of precious metals gave rise to a dramatic economic expansion. This fostered the coming into existence of a new social class—the middle class. In the seventeenth century, on the other hand, Europe was plunged into economic stagnation. And the depression grew periodically worse because of political problems, wars, bad weather and ensuing poor crops. The end of Louis XIV's reign was marked by a series of linked crises in 1693, 1698, and 1713. Their effects were felt for years. The soaring prices of foodstuffs made it virtually impossible for the population to get adequate supplies. The slump in business was aggravated by countless taxes, inequitably levied. These problems turned ordinary poverty into extreme misery, giving rise to revolts, that were then ruthlessly quelled.[8] Montfort's early biographers mention a few incidents in his life which suggest the crisis nature of the times, especially around the years 1693[9] and 1706.[10] The population fluctuations, however, offer the best clues to those difficult days. From 1696 to 1716, the death rate and the birth rate were almost level. The number of people dying of famine was alarmingly high. The misery endured by ordinary people prompted some to become vagrants, beggars, or thieves in both urban and rural areas. All of this culminated in a subhuman way of life. This accounts for Montfort's commitment to serve the poor.

2. The social strata

Since the Middle Ages, French society consisted in three strictly hierarchic and rather self-contained orders: the clergy, the nobility, and the third estate, i.e., the common people.[11] Praying, fighting, and working had been the respective roles of the three orders in medieval society. This social structure remained unquestioned for the most part, until the seventeenth century. In the seventeenth century, one notes a gradual irreversible shift "from a social order-based society to a social class-based one. That is, from a society established by social privilege to one determined by wealth." Money became the "source of power and esteem" (L. Perouas). The bourgeoisie, the new moneyed order, began then to assert itself. At the same time, within each order, social homogeneity was eroded, and the gap between the haves and the have-nots widened.

a. The clergy. This was the highest social order in the kingdom and generally the richest. Canonically, the clergy included both religious, and secular priests, i.e., bishops and priests in charge of dioceses and parishes. The most noticeable social inequality was to be found among the secular clergy. Under the terms of the 1516 concordat, the king appointed the archbishops, bishops, and abbots. He selected them from among the nobility and, only occasionally, from among the bourgeoisie. Parish priests and other secular priests, who came from the common people, had little if any social contact with the "high clergy" and almost never became bishops. Bishops lived on huge incomes generated by the land donated to the Church, and on tithes levied on crops. Such income was shared in a grossly uneven way. Most was kept by the high clergy, who would pass on only a meager portion to the parish priests and curates.

b. The nobility. The nobility occupied the second most dominant place in society, because of the political privileges which they enjoyed. Some privileges were merely honorary, but other privileges such as tax exemptions came with royal appointments and were more substantial. These royal appointments included high ecclesiastical posts, well-paid court positions, the diplomatic service, the armed forces, or the government administration. In addition to tax advantages from court appointments, the nobility owned a great deal of land for which they received taxes directly. People became royalty by birth and by wealth. There were the "royalty for life" who were the actual descendants of medieval knights. There were those who were made nobles because of some great social service, but many were raised to the nobility only because of their wealth. Certain privileged nobility lived at court on pensions provided by the king, and owned mansions or manor houses; less privileged nobility lived in the country where they eked out a meager existence, through their land taxes and farming. Such nobles were impoverished, possessed little political influences and felt particularly threatened by the rising bourgeoisie.

c. The common people or third estate. The lowest order, the third estate was by far the largest and the most varied. Traditionally it did the hard work required by landowners and clergy, and paid nearly all the taxes. In 1700 not a single town, outside Paris, numbered more than 100,000 people. About 20 percent of the active population lived in towns and the rest, mostly farmers, lived in the country.

Rural society included many divisions in status, from the farmer to the day laborer (who had no status). Between the well off to the destitute, there was a whole range of people living in varying degrees of poverty. Their lives were generally harsh. They depended on the landowners and their homes were wretched. Their incomes were contingent on the weather and the crops and on the whim of the rich.

The urban society could be divided roughly into the bourgeoisie, the "middle class or common people," and the poor or "little people." The bourgeoisie which had grown considerably in the sixteenth century, controlled the wealth of the country, and aspired to seize power. Included in this middle class were professional people, such as lawyers and doctors, business people, such as industrialists, wholesale merchants, ship owners, bankers, heads of corporations, and merchant navy captains. There were bourgeoisie by function and those by trade—high, middle, and low levels. Most were well educated and enterprising, interested in intellectual and artistic activities, and concerned about educating their children, and about their future careers.

In Montfort's days, 85 percent of La Rochelle's population was made up of common people who were engaged in about 60 trades or professions and possessed quite varied incomes. Badly housed, poorly educated, frequently exploited and generally despised, the common people had to bear the brunt of hardships in times of crisis, famine, and epidemic.

The poor were the underclass in the full sense of the term. They were the homeless and unemployed, and also those lacking steady work. Also included among the poor were the journeymen, farmers evicted from their tenanted farms, the elderly and infirm who could not earn a living. Also, there were the tramps and beggars who inhabited the roads and the streets, sometimes in gangs, posing a constant threat to the safety of the population. Some poor were locked away in poorhouses, where they were fed and had a roof over their heads. Locking away the poor began in 1660 when between 300 and 400 of them were locked up in Poitiers, 200 at Fontenay-le-Comte, and 400 at La Rochelle. These people lived in such tragic conditions that Saint-Simon wrote: "The poorhouses are a disgrace to the poor, for whom life is already a torment."

French society in 1700 was based on inequalities but was seemingly stable.

3. The cultural circumstances

To gain a thorough understanding of a particular era, it must be seen from a cultural perspective. Some have defined culture as "social heredity." A more accurate definition might be that it is the total configuration of inherited and learnt forms of behavior shared by a given group of people.

a. The two cultures. Reading Montfort today and understanding him is not easy. His life, attitude, and language belong to the "social legacy of a different time and place." Part of a "total configuration," it must be understood through "transculturation" as Fr. Perouas suggests. That is to say, one must try to analyze the cultural elements pervading Montfort's work and spirituality. This is all the more difficult since the culture of his times is extremely hard to decipher. We know about the so called "intellectual" culture of the period—the *grand siècle* in France. It was a high point of civilization in virtually every field—academic, artistic, and religious. But this high culture was accessible only to the educated social classes. There was another type of culture which has long gone unacknowledged. It was the culture of the mostly uneducated people. The French historian Robert Mandrou[12] authentically describes the popular culture of the era in his book, *Blue Library of Troyes.* It reproduced a large collection of short booklets, which were distributed by hawkers and meant for a popular readership of the time. The booklets reflect the traditional oral culture of the period. Included are a variety of literary genres and styles. The key word is "secret." The booklets were best sellers because they fulfilled the need of the poor for escape. Montfort found himself at the meeting point of these two cultures. He stood between two sets of attitudes, each determining people's behavior.

b. Sociocultural perceptions. The sociocultural attitudes were many, and depended on the individual person and the social class that they belonged to. The times were very gloomy marked by a seemingly irreversible fatalism. Bereft of hope for the future, ordinary people turned to an idealized past. This gave rise to a passive attitude of resignation, one marked by a longing for escape through fantasy and dreams. Festivals and feasts were the result. People longed for heaven, where they would experience an entirely different society. This attitude fostered a somewhat naive return to the early Church, and to a romanticized era of simple purity (the clergy's teaching strengthened this attitude). Fostered was a belief in a purely transcendent order of things which made the present immutable. Any change which departed from such a determined order was sinful. It was clear, then, why the clergy of the times denounced and condemned the attitude of the bourgeoisie who sought to advance their social status. They also condemned the attitude of the educated social classes who sought a future marked by greater freedom and happiness.

Obviously, the attitudes to society varied with the social classes. Ordinary people saw society as a relationship between the rulers and the ruled and were generally resigned to their plight. They desired justice but saw it primarily as something to be obtained in the afterlife. The aristocracy and the bourgeoisie perceived society inversely one from another. Conscious of being superior to ordinary people by birth or wealth, the nobility and the bourgeoisie both despised the poor. They looked on them as backward, unrefined, and superstitious. But the clergy, who cherished medieval values, saw the upper and lower classses as complementary, designed as such by Providence. They believed that the nobility and the wealthy were meant to be the charitable patrons of the poor.

As was said, this was a period which emphasized belief in a great variey of forms of the "supernatural" life. The term "supernatural" in this context refers to those images of God, religion, and the extraordinary phenomena which cannot be explained by natural laws.

The theological and spiritual outlooks of the period derived from two main currents of thought. There were the "humanists," and for them God was near. Humanity had access to

God through its own efforts. Without denying grace, they relied on human nature, reason, and freedom for discerning what was right and doing it. This inspired a religion which stressed will power, organization, and devotional practice. The Jesuits were closely associated with this current. On the other hand, there were the "Augustinians," for whom God was far away, "wholly other." God transcended humanity in such a way that few would have access to Him, understand Him, or please Him. Consequently, religion was filled with adoration and awe and reverential fear but emphasized human weakness and infirmity and inner dispositions at the expense of strength, goodness and outer actions. This became the nature-grace controversy for these two perceptions gave rise to widely different attitudes towards God's mystery and presence in the world and in human relationships.

Popular perception was akin to a sort of simplistic Manichaeism. Ordinary people explained what eluded their immediate comprehension, by resorting to the supernatural, attributing most things to God or Satan. They looked to the supernatural hoping for some just reward, and sought out myths, legends, and marvelous tales to help them escape from their humdrum lives.

The bourgeoisie's religious perception shows that they approached life more concretely—generally from an economic perspective. Their social relationships were filled with planning and little risk taking. The bourgeoisie looked on poverty as a fault, but more as a sign of social failure than as an evil thing. Thus their perception of God's action appeared to be rather at odds with the Christian idea of Providence. But they remained animated, over all by a deep and vital faith, as witnessed by the large number of priestly and religious vocations that came from the bourgeois class.

III. Religious Mentality and Practice

The general mentality and religious practice of the people was a natural consequence of the perceptions mentioned above. These were the social and outer manifestations of such religious perceptions. It is important to take a closer look at them if we are to form an accurate idea of Montfort's ministry.

1. The socioreligious mentalities

The mentalities varied widely and there were almost as many of them as there were regions and social classes. Montfort's mission reflects his profound grasp of the unequal forms of consciousness which prevailed at that time.

a. The mentalities in the regions. The parish missions that Monfort offered in western France were to people from areas of the country which possessed a great many different social outlooks with many fundamental differences. Regions thus varied in socioreligious mentality, based on their geographic composition. Some people came from wooded-country areas and others from flat-country areas. The former tended to be more individualistic and suspicious, but courageous, generous, obedient, and with a faith inclined to mysticism. The latter were more welcoming and sociable but rather listless, stingy, and more independent. They were more materialistic but also more down-to-earth. Therefore, people came to the parish missions with their differences of attitude and behavior. In wooded-country districts, people tended to place more value in religion, whereas those in the flat-country districts tended to be more lukewarm or indifferent. Such stark differences must be qualified but there is a general truth here. People living in the marshy regions were perhaps more listless when it came to religious practice and those living on the sea coast were generally more enthusiastic but lacking depth. But the Catholic urban population had perhaps the widest variety of different religious attitudes and behaviors.

b. The mentalities of the social classes. Each order or class for the most part had its own ways of thinking. The nobility's image reflected that of a king who ruled by divine right. Most of its members valued religion, seeing it as something that brought stability. But the impoverished lords jealously clung to their rights and did not take kindly to the clergy or bourgeoise using their religious influence or their wealth to rise to equality with them.

Because they were hard working and active people, the middle-class were the mainstay of the urban parishes. They funded them and ran their programs such as the confraternities, and contributed greatly to the poor, and their children were educated in the local schools run by such orders as the Jesuits or Oratorians. At La Rochelle the influence exerted by these two religious Orders reflected the division mentioned above between the "humanists" and the "Augustinians."

Because "the times were hard," ordinary people seemed irreversibly alienated from a proper religious balance. As was said, they tried to compensate for the tough lives by indulging in various forms of escapism—such as licentiousness or occultism. The churches therefore were filled with feasts and festivals with special celebrations of patron saints and pilgrimages, which combined religious and secular rituals. These festivals were filled with dancing, theater, etc. A parish mission, including its sermons, hymn-singing, processions, and Sunday mass was also an opportunity for people to escape into a well kept, brightly lit church. Parish fairs, weddings, and other get-togethers broke the monotony of their lives. Even church functions reflected a touch of the occult escapism mixing magic and superstition, especially related to the veneration of relics and to the keeping of esoteric secrets. In 1700 ordinary people did not live an individualized form of religion but tended to be carried along by the group, depending on rules imposed from above, and upon set prayer formulas and traditional practices.

The poor, especially the beggars and tramps, were keenly conscious of being marginalized. And, as a result, they questioned the society that rejected and oppressed them, and the Church which seemed to look on them as sinners, as failed Christians. But even those who only occasionally practiced their religion were generally not without religious faith.

As for the clergy, their mentality in 1700 was a middle class one. They for the most part had a standard of living and way of life which far exceeded that of the ordinary people both socially and economically. Their mentality was based on this superior position, which set them apart from the common people and made them aloof. They tied this sense of superiority to a lofty theological image of Christ as the triumphant highpriest. From this image, they derived a pre-eminent dignity for the priesthood, almost angelic. Consequently, the clergy looked down on popular entertainments, shunned women, and had little regard for everything unspiritual and this meant especially anything pertaining to the body. Their vision was dualistic, somewhat akin to Catharism. They tended to repress their feelings. Finally, their mentality became overly inward-looking, inflexible, and servile. Training in the seminaries had laid great emphasis on the teachings of the Council of Trent. The Council had stressed the priest's dependence on the bishop and on the ordinances and regulations governing the priestly function "to the point that they did not dare do anything without permission."[13] This is a far cry from the prophetic "*Liberos*" in PM.

Then from 1640 on some scholars and specialized historians like the Bollandist Jesuits and the Benedictines of Saint-Maur began systematically to interpret "religious" texts from a historical point of view. This gave rise to a critical movement, the aim of which was to sift out authentic historical reality from myth or legend. As a result, some types of popular religion were shaken to their foundations. More importantly, thanks to scientific and medical advances, some disturbing phenomena, attributed until then to the devil, were accounted for scientifically. After 1670 there were almost no more witchcraft trials. Science and its particular form of concrete inquiry tended to deminish the prevailing transcendentalism. Empirical positivist thinking began to replace an experience of the majesty of God. Montfort strongly denounced such "*skeptics*," "*critical devotees*," and "*proud scholars*" (FC 17; TD 26).

2. Religious mores

In the late seventeenth century, it was almost inconceivable for anyone to be without religious faith. Everyone was baptized. Most people accepted the doctrine and discipline of the Church. The general atmosphere was Christian, with Catholicism the only religion recognized by the state. There remained some traces of Protestant influence in certain areas, like the diocese of La Rochelle. But even there persecuted Protestants had been forced to return to the Church after the revocation of the Edict of Nantes in 1686.

a. Worship. Although entirely made up of nominal Catholics, the general population was not equally devout. With few exceptions, people made their Easter duty. Sunday Mass was not attended by everyone, since some parishioners were prevented from going to church if they lived too far away or had to harvest their crops, or if bad weather prevented the journey. It was general practice in those days for people to receive Holy Communion at only two or three major religious feasts during the year. Most houses of worship were renovated in the seventeenth century and although many parishes were poor, the parishioners showed their devotion by keeping their churches in good repair. The vitality of the parishes was attested to by the many large donations of money as stipends for Masses for the dead and for other celebrations or for pilgrimages. The seventeenth century also saw the emergence of many confraternities, like those of the Blessed Sacrament, the Rosary, the Virgins or the Penitents. In addition, a variety of confraternities were founded to help the poor. FC, which is both an exhortation and a set of rules,[14] was written by Montfort for the Confraternity of the Friends of the Cross.

b. Morality. Morals were generally very good relative to what exists today. The records left by the parish priests are proof of this. At the same time they throw some light on certain aspects of the Church's attitude to sin in those days. The records denounce in the first place public transgressions of sexual morality, which were few. In a diocese lacking fervor like La Rochelle, between 1 and 2 percent of the marriages were invalid, and 1 percent of the births were illegitimate. Parish priests tended to denounce the occasions of sin as well, especially the drinking and dancing in public houses on Sundays, feast days, and market days. They also challenged mixed dancing at local festivities, weddings, and parties. Such occasional forms of relaxation undoubtedly led to abuses but not all of them deserved such condemnations. The records show that a greater leniency was shown to private faults, like missing Sunday Mass, fraud, usury, and dishonest dealings. The following were regarded as minor faults: quarrels, fights, even longstanding disputes among families, villages, parishes, social groups, and private individuals (including the parish priests). These occurred over issues such as legacies, neighborhood interests, precedence, or authority. Such constant bickering, however, was proof of a sad lack of harmony, forgiveness, and love. Montfort endeavored to restore these virtues in his missions.

c. The life of faith. In the wake of the Council of Trent, Catholics had broadened and deepened their knowledge of the faith. Seminary training, publication of catechisms, regular Sunday sermons, the teaching of catechism to children in parishes, coupled with religious teaching in schools and in the recently established "charitable schools," effectively combated religious ignorance making it a rather rare occurrence. Diocesan catechisms, like the one published at La Rochelle in 1676, are evidence that the teaching methods were generally well suited to the people. This was no mean achievement at the time.

However, it remains a mystery as to how much of the teaching was actually absorbed by parishioners, most of whom were illiterate and only able to learn by rote.

d. The clerical life. Although the number of vocations had decreased, there were still more than enough priests to serve the parishes. The decline in numbers brought about a deep change in the financial, intellectual, and social status of the priests. In 1700 the priests received a fixed income that varied between 400 and 1,500 *livres.* This was enough for a decent, though not comfortable, lifestyle. Nearly all the priests had been educated in seminaries. Some of them had attended university. Most had at least thirty books in their bookcases, a sign of a fairly decent cultural level for the period. Finally, around 1700, a group of priests emerged who were conscious of their social position. They were not inclined to practice a great deal of detachment or evangelical poverty. Their ministry tended to be more fixed than transient, and functional rather than missionary.

e. Religious life.[15] In the seventeenth century, many abbeys and convents founded in the Middle Ages possessed vast riches but showed little religious vitality, whereas the Orders founded in the sixteenth century in the wake of the Counter-Reformation displayed a great spiritual and apostolic drive. The Jesuits, Ursulines, and Capuchins were engaged in apostolic work which included teaching and caring for the needy. The clerical communities were also engaged in preaching parish missions. New and dynamic types of religious Congregations came into existence in the seventeenth century. Among them were the Oratorians, Vincentians, Daughters of Charity, and De La Salle Brothers. Their members came from all types of social background. They led a more modern sort of life. They dedicated themselves to difficult apostolic work and remained close to the people. Although these Congregations did valuable work in the dioceses, they often did not follow the diocesan pastoral directives strictly. They broadened their sphere of action and became increasingly engaged in social work. In the late seventeenth century, when the country was torn by wars and bedeviled with economic crises, these religious Congregations played a leading role. They did so because of their awareness of the rights of the people, especially of the poor. They sought to obtain justice, education, and a better life for the socially dispossessed. It might even be said that these Congregations came into existence in response to the overall needs of the poor, to the tragic call of a society powerless to help its destitute, sick and illiterate. St. Vincent de Paul, for example, brought to the fashionable society of his time, a "social" understanding of the Gospel. Such Congregations devoted themselves to "caring for the poor" in hospitals and at home. They looked after orphans and abandoned children. They set up charitable institutions and established "charitable schools" for the education of poor children. A great spirit of solidarity inspired these foundations and kept them going. Bishops, the Christian people with their confraternities, and even the civil leaders of cities and provinces came to realize how important these educational and charitable institutions were. They supported their growth with donations, grants, and endowments. The whole nation was gradually brought to an awareness of its duty in providing mutual support and in sharing their resources with those in need. As a result, the populace began to realize the value of evangelical poverty and the obligation it entailed. This conformed to Montfort's ideas and, in part, prompted his uncompromising attitude of service towards the poor.

IV. The Influence of His Time on Montfort's Life and Writings: A Man Who through His Holiness Transcended His Time

Louis Marie de Montfort could not escape being influenced by his social era, though at times he appeared to be either behind or ahead of his times. Though he distanced himself from the middle class, he belonged to it. It was his family's background, and from it came his vocation and clerical formation. Montfort chose through his missions to become one with the ordinary people, especially the poor.

1. Montfort's ties with the three social orders

a. His ties with the bourgeoisie. We know that his father, Jean-Baptiste Grignion, was an ambitious man who worked with grim determination but with little success to improve his social status. What is even more evident is the way St. Louis Marie distanced himself from his family for the sake of the Gospel: "*In my family—the one I belong to now—I have chosen to be wedded to Wisdom and the Cross, for in these I find every good, both earthly and heavenly*" (L 20). Although he severed his ties with his family, he owed to their bourgeoisie status the fact that he was educated at the Jesuit school in Rennes. As well it was through his parents' connections among the nobility, that he gained admittance to Saint Sulpice Seminary. From his bourgeoisie background he inherited a number of attitudes and qualities, such as a spirit of enterprise, independence, and respect for authority. These qualities stood him in good stead when he gave missions and acted as a spiritual guide. In his writings he even used banking terms. He spoke of managing spiritual wealth, and called Mary the dispenser and treasurer of God's gifts (TD 178). But having said this, Montfort's way of life was in direct opposition to his bourgeoisie origins. He wedded himself to poverty and lived in complete surrender to Providence.

b. His ties with the clergy. At the Seminary of Saint Sulpice in Paris, Montfort received the best theological and spiritual formation available at the time and was nourished on Scripture, the Church Fathers, and the mystics of the period. His mind, thought, and heart were steeped in all of this espccially as it came to him through the French School; his writings mirrored the great tradition but in a personal, albeit original way. He alternated between periods of intense and highly internalized religious formation (which included long periods of meditation, prayer, and mortification) and periods of practical formation in the apostolic work of actively caring for the poor and teaching catechism. The fact remains, however, that the training he received at Saint Sulpice did shape him. The seminary's numerous rules had as a primary purpose turning a would-be priest into a holy man, set apart from the world. The seminary tended to produce priests who remained closer to the bourgeois population than to the poor. They made good servants of the Church, solid religious functionaries but they tended to remain more often establishment types rather than men given to risky apostolic activities. We know how vigorously Montfort reacted against this concept of priesthood, from the time he left the seminary until the end of his life. Although this was the accepted image of the priest in clerical circles, he showed a complete disregard for it when, early in his priestly life, he threw in his lot with the poor. His formation, however, had left its mark on him, as shown by the style of his letters to Fr. Leschassier, superior of Saint Sulpice Seminary (L 5, 6, 10). In them he gave signs of still being influenced by his seminary teachers. But shortly after, Montfort chose to break with them. Rejecting the social appearances of such a clerical lifestyle, he clung only to the essentials of the priesthood which he had been taught in the seminary.[16] As a priest of Christ, he wanted to imitate Jesus closely, the way the Apostles had done. He wanted to be poor, detached, free, and available (PM 7-10), and concerned with the urgent needs of the Christian people, especially those who were the poorest and most uneducated or "*those whom the world neglects.*" His attitude unsettled and challenged people. Breaking from the clerical image of the period, he distanced himself from his fellow priests, and accepted to be treated as a "madman." He allowed himself to be denounced and driven from various dioceses without ever fighting back or rebelling. He remained obedient to the bishops and to a Pope who confirmed him and his work by granting him the title of "Apostolic Missionary." Montfort belonged to the clergy through filial obedience to the hierarchy and dedication to his priestly mission, but he strongly opposed the tendency on the part of the clergy to become socially or culturally established or fixed.

c. His ties with the common people and the poor. Montfort deliberately chose to become one with the common people, to throw in his lot with the poor. At the Cesson bridge on the outskirts of Rennes, while on his way to Paris, he took off the clothes of a bourgeois cleric and put on the clothing of a poor servant priest. He never took it off. His clerical garb would thereafter remain rough and simple. In his mind, this was the best way to identify himself with the suffering Christ. But for him there was no taint of morbid enjoyment of such suffering in this, rather, there was a pride in the restoring of value to a despised condition, of dignity to those without possessions. It was also a way of showing his gratitude (L 6). But there was much more to it. Montfort sought to make despised human beings aware of their dignity and he worked to change their hostile attitude at being social outcasts into one of responsibility and solidarity. He tried to make poor disabled women members of the first Community of Wisdom. He was a shining example of faith in human ability and in the future of humanity, one based on the dynamic presence of Jesus Christ's saving action. Montfort remained close to the ordinary people, identifing himself with them whether they lived in the suburbs of Montbernage, or in some country district. He wanted to teach them catechism, to evangelize them and he worked among them living from hand to mouth at the bottom of the social ladder. He opened them to the opportunities which the faith life offered them. Although he came from a bourgeois and clerical background, he entered wholeheartedly into the culture, mentality, and customs of the poor. He purified and transcended such social realities instead of destroying them. In so doing, he was a true missionary, one attuned to his audience, one who adapted his preaching to those he served, and one who used whatever resources he found among them to evangelize them. He borrowed words like *"marvel," "treasure,"* and *"secret"* from the language of the popular culture of his time. He set hymns to popular tunes. He used pictures, banners, liturgical ceremonies, processions, and calvaries which reflected their public entertainments. Although his way of teaching was not original to him, the way he adapted it to those he served was, and the results were certainly unique. He renewed and revived them, infusing those around him with his prophetic vigor and energy. As a true missionary, he enlisted the help of ordinary people in the work of undertaking "great things for God," like the Calvary at Pontchâteau. He insured the lasting fruits of his missions by leading those who attended to make individual and collective commitments, such as the renewal of their baptismal promises. He left them rules governing their prayer life, set up confraternities, and established devotional practices, such as CG and the Marian Consecration. Like a true missionary, he adopted the way of life of the Apostles, and of those threatened with misery and famine. He lived in poverty and with confidence in the Providence of God, all the while adapting himself to the popular mentality of his age.

2. From a mission in time and space to a timeless mission in the Church

Montfort met with opposition in his life. He lived at a time when humanity, society, culture, perceived salvation in Jesus Christ differently from the way we perceive it today. Some have reproached Montfort for both idealizing the past and prophetically, or even apocalyptically, envisioning the future. But here again he wanted to touch the mentality of his time and the unique way in which people longed for Jesus Christ. He put spiritual reality into two camps, the camp of God and the camp of the Evil One. This may appear too radical and simplistic, and some might say that it smacks of Manichaeism. But it was the spiritual language of an era marked by religious and political wars. Was it not a language which made it easy for the people to understand the choice involved in baptism? It is rather futile to fit Montfort into a social category. Monfort was no exclusivist either in his writings or in his missions. He designed his missions so that they would reach everybody, all social orders and classes, from the nobility to the poor, including the rich bourgeois. He called all to conversion and salvation. The best proof of this was the mission he gave at la Rochelle in the winter of 1711 which had a huge scope. It engaged the whole population of the town, and all of its social, economic, and political groups, including the bishop, the military governor, and those in its military garrison.

Influenced by history, family, society, and the Church, and with a particular culture and formation, Montfort was in every respect a man of his time. Yet, in spite of these realities, he remains an elusive, bewildering even baffling figure. His message took the Gospel literally, and he identified so completely with the poor, in whom he saw the image of the suffering Christ. He understood the baptismal commitment, and Mary's role in the economy of salvation history. All of this was rooted in but transcended his times. His missionary teaching is timeless. He is a man for our times, if we translate him into our present culture. In Jesus Christ, Montfort's message is a universal one.

P. Pénisson

Notes: (1) L. Perouas, *Ce que croyait Grignion de Montfort*, Mame, Tours 1973, 206-207; English translation, *A Way to Wisdom: Louis Marie Grignion de Montfort and His Beliefs*, Montfortians Yesterday and Today. (2) L. Perouas, Séminaire intermontfortain d'Avrillé, July-August 1971, typed notes. (3) P. Goubert, *Mazarin*, Edition Fayard, Paris 1990. (4) L. Perouas, *op. cit. 1* map, p. 8. (5) Henri Daniel-Rops, *L'Eglise des temps classiques—Le grand siècle des âmes*, Fayard, Paris 1958, 214-219; English translation, Daniel-Rops, *The Church in the Classical Times: The Great Century of Souls*, trans. John Warrington, Dutton, New York, 1964. (6) Besnard I, 189, 239. (7) Daniel-Rops, *L'Eglise*, 265-268. (8) L. Perouas, *Grignion de Montfort, un aventurier de l'Evangile (Grignion de Montfort, an Adventurer of the Gospel)*, Editions ouvrières, Paris 1990, 11-12. (9) Blain, 28. (10) Grandet, 151. (11) J. Michaud, *1492-1789: La Renaissance et les Temps Modernes (1492-1789: The Renaissance and Modern Times)*, Classique Hachette, Paris 1974, 220-244. (12) R. Mandrou, *De la culture populaire en France aux 17ème et 18ème siècles. La Bibliothèque Bleue de Troyes (Popular Culture in France in the 17th and 18th Centuries: The Blue Library of Troyes)*, Edition Stock, Paris 1964. (13) Blain, 83. (14) Grandet, 401-402. (15) Daniel-Rops, *L'Eglise*, 107-115. (16) Blain, 187-190.

Our Lady of Wisdom

Probably sculpted by Fr. de Montfort, this wooden statue was found at Saint Lazare in the village of Montfort. There the saint restored an ancient priory (1713-1715), turning it into the community's first oratory. Tradition suggests that Montfort refurbished the chapel with the help of Brothers Mathurin and Jean. Above the altar Montfort placed a dove with silver wings. It is said that below it on the altar, he placed this madonna.

MODEL

SUMMARY I. MODELS IN MONTFORT'S LIFE:
1. Persons;
2. The works of spiritual masters.
II. MODELS IN MONTFORT'S WORKS:
1. The Trinity;
2. Jesus Christ Wisdom;
3. Mary;
4. The saints;
5. The Apostles:
a. A life of poverty abandoned to Divine Providence,
b. Burning with zeal for the Lord,
c. Wisdom crucified,
d. The apostolic community,
e. Mary, Mother of the montfort apostles.
III. MONTFORT AS MODEL.

A "model" should be understood in the context of human and spiritual growth. A model's function is to share with another person the ideals which he himself has lived; the model's values, then, become principles of behavior for other persons and, "a means of historical continuity for society." [1] For the model to fulfill his role and effectively contribute to the education of another, he must be chosen consciously.

A model not only clarifies "real life" for another but often represents what the subject would like to become; the model is, then, the "ideal image of the self." It is according to the behavior and values of the model that the subject evaluates himself, corrects himself, and matures. From one point of view, the model is chosen only to be outmatched and thus reinterpreted in an original way by the subject when the model is God.

I. MODELS IN MONTFORT'S LIFE

1. Persons

We do not know exactly what Louis Marie's family or other personal relationship models were, nor what influence they may have had during his childhood. Following Grandet, we might mention a deep affection between the child Louis and his mother Jeanne Robert.[2] She became, one can presume, a model which influenced his understanding of Our Lady.

When Louis Marie moved to Rennes, it marked the beginning of his human and Christian adventure. The adolescent Montfort had his first contact with the Jesuits at the College of St. Thomas Becket, and they served as a springboard for his later Sulpician experience in Paris. During this whole period (from 1684 to 1700, the year of his ordination), Montfort had contact with people and institutions that would profoundly influence his personality. They were the models from whom Louis learned in a most special way, the art of the interior life and of the apostolate.

Fathers Descartes, Gilbert, and Bellier were among the first of his instructors to have an influence on him. They initiated him into a more intense spiritual life. From Fr. Descartes he learned loving intimacy with God and a knowledge of the mysteries of Christ. He also learned to appreciate a life of poverty where God was the sole possession.[3] These are also themes he learned from Fr. Gilbert, whose "pious behavior" made him the butt of jokes and mockery on the part of the students of the Jesuit school. Louis imitated and developed this behavior, while at the same time learning from his teacher how to bear crosses, insults, and pain in silence. During this Rennes period, he also experienced the influence of another teacher, Fr. Bellier. He introduced Louis to the love of the poor (expressed by the charity Bellier showed toward them) and to the missionary ideal (Bellier participated from time to time in the activities of Father Leuduger's parish mission team). At Rennes Louis joined the Marian Sodality, which was directed by Fr. Prévost. The montfort ideal of Christian perfection and of a concrete love for the poor found a favorable environment in the intense spiritual climate of the Marian Sodality. This especially influenced Louis in his devotion to Mary. During these years it was to take on the quality of an affectionate and stable relationship toward the Mother of God.

When he was a student in Paris, his love of poverty received a decisive impetus within the environment of Father de la Barmondière's residence for poor seminarians. He lived the rules of the house quite strictly. He refused stipends in order to be utterly poor and "*have no personal possessions.*" In doing this, he accepted as a normal condition of life the insecurity of the poor, deprived of any economic support and laid open to the uncertainty of tomorrow. In this way, he could become rooted in an absolute trust in God's Providence (cf. L 2).[4] Perfectly linked to love, voluntary poverty had a twofold direction: toward God and toward his brothers and sisters in need. In Paris, Montfort continued to help the poor in all the ways he could. He found a model in the person of Fr. de la Barmondière, who, despite the fact that he had a considerable personal fortune, lived like a poor man and spent his time in works of charity. Montfort cherished his regularity in prayer, his disregard for Paris society, his practice of penance, his Marian devotion and his apostolic zeal. Montfort also imitated Father Bayün's practices of penance, poverty, patience in illness, and Marian devotion to the point of slavery. But before everything, he imitated the mystical orientation of his spiritual life (the splendor of God expressed in a horror of sin and the fear of desecrating the Sacraments, as well as in the experience of God's infinite bounty). He also imitated the strongly apostolic dimension of his spirituality.

2. The works of the spiritual masters

During his formation period, Montfort came in contact with the central persons and spiritual movements of his time and with the classical works of the spiritual masters. He was profoundly moved by certain ones who became genuine models for him.

Montfort's behavior and his doctrine on the Cross were influenced by the works of H. Boudon (1624-1702), including *The Holy Ways of the Cross.*[5] On a Marian level, Montfort changed some of his attitudes in response to another of Boudon's writings, *God Alone, or the Holy Slavery of the Admirable Mother of God.* Louis Marie's devotion to shrines and images of Our Lady, as well as his entry into a confraternity of "Holy Slavery," flow in great part from his readings of Boudon.

In the formation years at Saint-Sulpice, Louis Marie came to know the writings of Surin. He discovered in those works a spiritual man, completely centered on the love of God who lived on a supernatural plane. Montfort learned how to pray for hours, through a spiritual and sapiential rather than a speculative theological approach. He discovered in Surin an apostolic passion to defend the love of God, and extraordinary penances as indispensable means of acquiring the virtues. Surin's spirituality, which at this particular time permitted Montfort to unify his spiritual life, he subsequently surpassed. Louis Marie found the unifying center of his life in the experience of Jesus as Wisdom and in the living example of Christ and his poor Apostles.

At the Saint Sulpice Seminary, Montfort came to know another model of the spiritual life, J.J. Olier (1608-1657). In addition to imitating his external behavior (e.g., speaking of God during recreation, kissing the wounds of the sick, making pilgrimages, renouncing academic degrees and ecclesiastical stipends), Montfort drew from Olier an important aspect of his Marian spirituality, the doctrine of Jesus living in Mary. A number of passages from TD were in fact developed from notes taken from the *Letters of M. Olier.* They are the pages where Montfort speaks of the profound union of Mary and Jesus, based on the mystery of the Incarnation of the Word in her womb, which the saints called *aula sacramentorum, "the throne-room of God's mysteries"* (cf. TD 246-248).

Montfort again borrowed from Olier certain ways of looking at things that marked his apostolate. In the first place, there was the idea of the Company of Mary itself, which he had been thinking of since 1700 (cf. L 5), as an "apostolic group." Louis was to broaden his understanding of this idea, in that those who were to follow this path would burn with zeal to renew the spirit of Christianity among Christians themselves (cf. RM 2). The very notion of a priest as a man burning with zeal and marked with the royal dignity of

Christ, which for Montfort was manifested especially in voluntary poverty (cf. LCM 6, 8), was influenced by Olier.

The years that followed immediately upon his ordination to the priesthood (1700) were governed by the discovery of Wisdom, thanks to the reading of the works of Saint-Jure. From him Montfort took the very idea of Wisdom and the first three means for obtaining it: a burning desire for Wisdom, continuous prayer, and universal mortification (cf. LEW 181-202). The writings of Saint-Jure intensified Louis Marie's solid Christocentricity.

II. Models in Montfort's Works

1. The Trinity

Among the reasons Montfort gives as proofs of the goodness of God and of the "*perfect practice*" of true devotion, there is God's very own way of acting. Montfort asserts that to consecrate oneself to Christ through Mary is to imitate the Trinity itself in the "*dependence*" the triune God chose to have on Mary (TD 140). In TD, as in SM 35, he gives the motives for it: the Father gives us Christ, makes us His children, and gives us His graces through Mary; the Son came to us through Mary and invites us to go to him via the same path; the Holy Spirit forms Christ and the members of his mystical Body in union with Mary, just as it is through her that He communicates His graces. For all these reasons, Montfort can say: *"It is only right then that we should imitate His [God's] conduct"* (TD 142).[6]

2. Jesus Christ Wisdom

In H 44:14, Montfort describes the twelfth practice of devotion to the Heart of Jesus: imitation. This consists in identifying one's thinking with that of Christ and in deciding to walk along behind him. Furthermore, Jesus Christ is *"the only model that we should imitate"* (TD 61), because in him is the fullness of divinity and grace. Montfort here is referring to Eph 4:13, where St. Paul invites us "to mature manhood, measured by nothing less than the full stature of Christ."[7]

Above all, Jesus is to be imitated in his submission to Mary. In TD 18, Montfort reviews the whole human adventure of Jesus from the point of view of the *"dependence"* he had on his mother. That would include the humility and obedience of Jesus, so clear in the mystery of Jesus living in Mary. Montfort sees in Christ's conception, his birth, His presentation in the temple, and in the sacrifice of the Cross irrefutable evidence of Christ's dependence on Mary. He reminds us that it was Mary who "*nursed Him, fed Him, cared for Him, reared Him and sacrificed Him for us.*" And this manifests "*the independence and majesty of Christ,*" i.e. the freedom of love (another attitude to be imitated). Those who consecrate themselves to Mary, Montfort says, *"behave in the same way as Christ by utterly and completely submitting themselves to her"* (TD 196).

Accepting the Cross like Christ is a second requisite of Montfort's in the imitation of Jesus. Its principle is asserted in FC 42. In this passage, Montfort invites his followers not to seek crosses voluntarily for themselves but, rather, *"to imitate our Lord, of whom it was said, 'He did all things well.'"* Why and how are we to imitate Wisdom crucified? Montfort answers this "why" in LEW 173-80, where he reflects on the theme of the Cross in relation to man. Since the Cross is the victory standard of Jesus, it is the same for his friends. It makes us more like Christ and worthy of being sons of the Father, members of Christ, and temples of the Spirit. When it is borne well, the Cross is the sign of the love we have for God and a proof of the love God has for us. Finally, it brings joy, peace, and an "*immense weight of glory in heaven.*" What the imitation of Christ crucified means for man in the concrete is explained in FC 18. Here, in referring to the spatial dimensions of "*breadth, length and depth*" of the Cross, Montfort seems to indicate three modalities of imitation. The first (the "breadth" dimension) recalls the solidity of the Cross, which is even heavier than foreseen; the second (the "length" dimension) stresses the patience needed to bear crosses by remaining faithfully united to the One crucified; the third dimension (that of "depth") returns us to the inner moral sufferings that allow us to sacrifice ourselves with Christ.

To imitate Christ crucified, to live in his Cross, is also to abide in Wisdom, which has set up its dwelling place there and has so intimately united itself to the Cross: *"Wisdom is the Cross and the Cross is Wisdom"* (LEW 180). To search for Christ crucified is to search for Wisdom, and to find Wisdom is to find Christ crucified.

3. Mary

The essential practice of true devotion to Mary, Montfort says in SM 45, is to do everything with her: *"This means that we must take her as the accomplished model for all we have to do."* And this "*all we have to do*" is made explicit in TD 260: take her as *"the perfect model of every virtue and perfection."* After reading the two texts side by side, we may conclude that one of the ways that the Virgin Mary is a model is through the superlative nature of her virtues. Montfort mentions three in TD 260: *"Mary's faith, her profound humility and her godlike purity."* In TD 108, he asks his readers to model themselves on the ten chief virtues of the Virgin Mary: *"her profound humility, her living faith, her blind obedience, her continuous prayer, her universal mortification, her godlike purity, her fervent charity, her heroic patience, her evangelical gentleness and her godlike wisdom."*

In other montfort texts, Mary is seen not only as a model to be imitated but as the one who models us into the image of Jesus Christ (cf. TD 33). Mary is in fact the mold in which Christ was formed (cf. TD 220). And this is why a person who gives himself to her *"is quickly shaped and molded into Jesus and Jesus into him"* (TD 219). As a means to a deeper life in Christ, Our Lady goes beyond the understanding of "instrument" to become a vital, personal, maternal presence with the devout soul, who then finds himself glorifying God with the very soul of Mary and rejoicing in God with her spirit: *"Her spirit will take the place of yours"* (TD 217).

4. The Saints

In the eyes of those who look upon them, the saints (those of the past and those of today, canonized or not) are models to be imitated in their devotion to the Blessed Virgin, chosen as an easy path for reaching Christ (cf. TD 152). In the stormy sea of this world, these souls are bound to Mary and in such a way that they are saved. This is why Saint Louis de Montfort can say: *"Blessed, indeed, are those Christians who bind themselves faithfully and completely to her as to a secure anchor!"* (TD 175). But the imitation of the saints does not only have to do with their attachment to Mary. In fact they are also to be imitated insofar as they have let themselves be formed by her. *"The formation and the education of the great saints who will come at the end of the world are reserved to her"* (TD 35). And they will be enlightened, nourished, generated, sustained, and preserved by her with the mission to destroy evil and to rebuild the city of God, which is Mary herself as the sheltering womb of God (cf. TD 98).

Finally, from the texts of Montfort, we are able to draw up a series of virtues typical of saints: humility, prayer, abandonment to Providence, obedience to God, mortification (cf. SM 4; RM 19; H 8:24; H 16:12), praying the Rosary (cf. SR), devotion to Mary (cf. SM 1, 6; TD 156), hope (cf. H 7:2), charity (cf. H 14:6) steadfastness (cf. H 38:120), and finally the love of the Cross (cf. LEW 175).

5. The Apostles

Montfort looks upon the Apostles as models of his missionaries of the end times.[8] He speaks of them in TD 55-59 and in the Triptych (PM, RM, and LCM), where Montfort traces a profile of them characterized by five basic qualities. They are the same characteristics that Montfort requires for the members of his Company of Mary:

a. A life of poverty abandoned to Divine Providence. To live in voluntary poverty and in the abandonment to Divine Providence constitutes one of the primary characteristics of an apostolic person, in Montfort's thought. This distinguishes the manner of living the apostolate (the refusal of funded missions and a living that depends on salaries from the people) (cf. RM 50);[9] the style of life of the missionaries during a parish mission (detachment from the self in order to cling to God; detachment from things and persons; detachment from the outcome of the mission) (cf. PM 7-10, 23); and the idea itself of the missionary's status understood as "itinerant," with docility to the motion of the Spirit, Who sends the missionary where He will. Trust in God (cf. LCM), love for real poverty, which accepts the fact that one earns one's living by missionary work, and experience of the privations that accompany poverty in the matter of clothing, housing and travel are all intrinsic to a life of voluntary poverty (cf. LCM 9-11).

b. Burning with zeal for the Lord. Poor and abandoned to Divine Providence, Montfort's apostolic missionary has a passion for the Kingdom of God and the salvation of man (cf. H 21). It is only obedience that keeps zeal from taking an undisciplined and inhibiting course, because it gives direction to the total availability required of missionaries (cf. PM 21; RM 19-27).[10] Montfort's zeal finds its specific focus in fervent and sound preaching. Filled with the Spirit of God and with a thorough familiarity with the Word of God, the missionary can light the way for his hearers so that they may be converted to the love of God (cf. RM 60-64). Preaching can become a centrifugal force, in the sense that it is always capable of affecting the missionary himself, urging him on to a deeper union with Christ. To do this, Montfort asks his followers to be constantly concerned about their own sanctification (cf. H 22) by fulfilling the duties it requires: asceticism, prayer, retreats, study. Zeal also possesses its own special characteristics. It is gentle like the zeal of Christ because it brings man closer to the very tenderness of the Master; it is creative and enterprising; it urges one to become all things to all (cf. H 21:17-24; H 22:19-21, 25-28).

*c. **Wisdom crucified.*** There is, in Montfort's eyes, an identity between Wisdom and the Cross (LEW 180). There is, therefore, an identity between the authentic preacher of Wisdom and the Cross (cf. PM 24-25). In the school of Wisdom crucified, the missionary learns how to be wise according to the Cross, thus becoming a sign of contradiction to the world. In fact, to follow the *scientia sapida* of the Cross is to place oneself naturally in conflict with the wisdom of the world (cf. RM 37), because its principles and pseudo-values are rejected. Moreover, the apostle lives the Pauline motto of nonconformity to the mentality of the world (cf. Rom 12:2). Humiliations, mockeries, calumnies, and conflicts are the Cross that the missionary carries with Christ. An apostolic person must therefore be well trained in order to make a total commitment to such an evangelical life.

*d. **The apostolic community.*** The montfort community is presented as a group of people gathered together, ready to set out as "itinerants" on the mission where the Spirit of God and obedience is calling them (cf. PM 9-10; RM 6). The mission to which the missionaries are called actually gives form to the community because it sets up its rhythms of life and prayer (cf. RM 66-67). Yet community is also a prerequisite of mission because it is "together," as a united and compact group, that apostolic men live the mission of evangelization in the midst of the people of God, especially among the poor. Montfort insists upon community apostolate. In its life, the community has a special rhythm, with moments of prayer and common life that cannot be neglected except when certain mission commitments may dictate otherwise. The apostolic community lives poverty and obedience in a total abandonment to Divine Providence, which provides for all the missionary's needs (cf. RM 45).

*e. **Mary, Mother of the montfort apostles.*** It is in a threefold way that Montfort describes the relationship between Mary and the Company of Montfort's apostolic men. Above all, Mary is the Mother who generates, feeds, and sustains her missionaries.

She makes them strong to enable them to accomplish the mission to which they have been called. She acts through her children in their very apostolate. Her motherhood is a missionary motherhood (cf. PM 11; TD 54-56; SM 59).

Since Mary is Christ's mother, it follows that her motherhood in regard to the missionaries consists also in conforming them to the image of her Son. To the precise extent that apostolic men become part of Mary's household and abide in her, they will be progressively and unceasingly configured to Christ, and they will learn from Christ himself, who abides in Mary permanently, to live in accordance with the spirit of the Gospel Beatitudes (cf. PM 25).

This relationship with Mary leads to the experience of Christ the Savior. Living in Mary brings about intimacy with the Son. Christ the Savior came to humanity by means of the Virgin Mary, and it is through her that he is to reign in the world, thus extending over all the lordship of love. Mary's place in the saving plan of God is intrinsic; to pull the Mary-thread out of the weaving of salvation history is to destroy the tapestry as God has designed it. For this reason, preaching Mary and a tender devotion to her plays a central and precise part in the evangelizing activity of Montfort's missionaries of the Company of Mary (cf. PM 12; RM 57).

III. Montfort as Model

We may speak of Montfort as a model from two points of view: those of imitation in particular (exemplification) or in general (exemplary nature).

Montfort may be considered, first of all, as a model to be imitated in the here and now. This imitation of Saint Louis Marie's ways enables us to live a life in keeping with Gospel values. In this perspective, we can think of his devotion to the poor, the tenderness and patience of his behavior, his great mastery of self, his creativity in preaching, and his style of living as a poor man, humble and abandoned to Divine Providence. Choosing Montfort as a model requires solid knowledge of his life and teachings, which influence us to choose the Montfort model instead of so many others set forth by modern culture. The choice carries with it all the implications that flow from such a decision.

To consider Saint Louis Marie as a model in general, it is not so important to consider what Montfort "is" as to see him as a person who strongly directs us towards the Absolute. His life, whether in its entirety or in individual actions, here becomes the sign of the Other to whom we are sent: God Alone. In this sense, the Montfort model is a means whereby we arrive at a personal encounter in the Spirit with God and with His Son, but with a special evangelical stress on Mary. We are now in the domain of "charism" understood as an "experience of the Spirit" (*Mutuae relationes,* 11), as a means of entering into the life of the divine archetype, God.

R. Gabbiadini

Notes: (1) S. De Giacinto, *Modello,* in G. Flores d'Arcais, ed., *Nuovo Dizionario di Pedagogia,* Paoline, Brescia 1882, 834. (2) Grandet, 2. (3) An echo of this placing of oneself on the side of Divine Love with its practical consequences can be found in FC 7-12. (4) "Poverty thus returns to its mystical and theological aspect: it is a detachment from the realm of the ephemeral in order to be anchored in the absolute, in God Alone." S. De Fiores, *Itinerario,* 95. (5) Boudon's recommendations concerning behavior, although strange to contemporary ears, are rather typical of the spirituality of the French school. Cf. ibid., 104-105. (6) On the connection between the Trinity and Mary, TD 14-39 are enlightening. These texts describe a threefold bond between the Virgin Mary and each of the Persons of the Trinity. The first bond results from the mystery of the Incarnation, where, after giving Mary her fruitfulness, the Father generates the Son through her (cf. TD 16, 17); the Son, by permitting himself to be "imprisoned in her womb" (TD 18), became man for us in Mary and through Mary (cf. TD 16, 18, 19); the Spirit, though sterile in God, became fruitful by forming Christ in Mary (cf. TD 16, 20, 21). The second bond results from Mary's mission (the relationship between the Trinity, Mary, and humanity). The Father makes Mary the immense treasury of His graces and gathers them together in her, just as all the waters come together in the sea (cf. TD 23); the Son makes Mary the merciful channel through which he showers his mercies on human beings (cf. TD 24); the Spirit communicates His gifts to Mary and makes her the administrator of what He possesses (cf. TD 25). The third bond is that intervening between the Trinity and the Church, where the Father generates children for Himself through Mary (cf. TD 29-30); still through her, the Son wishes every day to become incarnate in his members (cf. TD 31-33); finally, the Holy Spirit wishes to form the elect in and through her (cf. TD 34-36). (7) In TD 62, Montfort asserts that Jesus Christ is the ultimate goal of the veneration given to the Virgin; or better, "*this devotion is necessary, simply and solely because it is a way of reaching Jesus perfectly, loving Him tenderly, and serving Him faithfully.*" We imitate Christ, of whom Mary is the mold (cf. TD 129). Mary's life is a life that follows Christ, the perfect model. (8) As regards the basic characteristics of missionaries of recent years, see R. Gabbiadini, *"La formazione dell'uomo apostolico nella congregazione montfortana. La 'Ratio Montfortana' del 1987; analisi del testo e rilievi critici"* (*The Formation of an Apostolic Man in the Montfort Congregation. The Montfort 'Ratio' of 1987: Analysis of the Text and Critical Notes*), dissertation for the licentiate in the science of education, given at the Pontifical Salesian University, Rome 1991, 33-61. (9) On the custom of funded missions, see P. L. Nava, *"La missione al popolo di s. Luigi di Montfort: natura e metodo"* (*Montfort's Mission to the People: Nature and Method*), Sussidi di animazione montfortana 5, Rome 1984, 25-26; S. De Fiores, *La "missione" nell'itinerario spirituale e apostolico di s. Luigi Maria da Montfort* (*The "Mission" in the Spiritual and Apostolic Itinerary of Saint Louis de Montfort*), in QM 2 (1985), 27 (10) On obedience in Montfort's works, see H. Frehen, *Le "caractère particulier" de la Compagnie de Marie suivant le P. de Montfort (The 'Particular Character' of the Company of Mary, following the Thought of Father de Montfort),* in DM 41 (1968) 6-12.

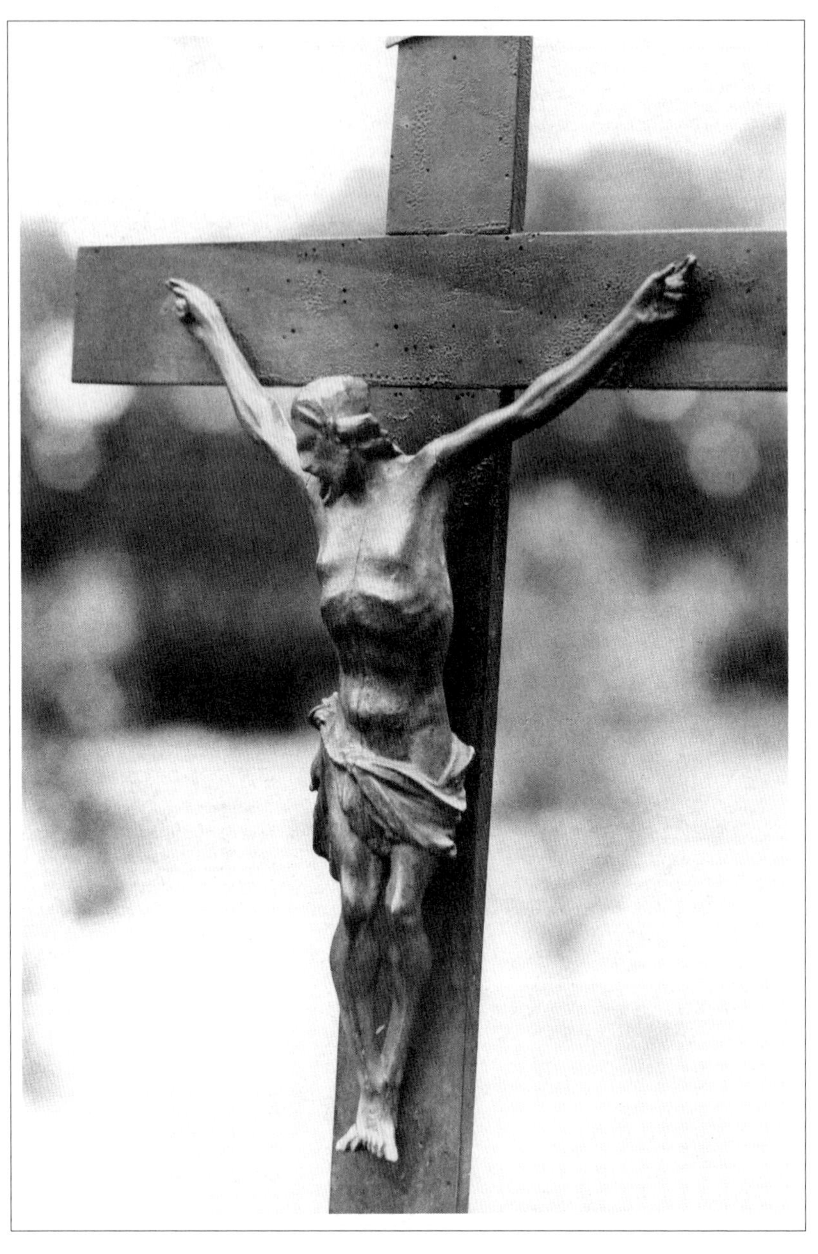

THE CROSS OF ST. LAZARE

Tradition holds that this crucifix was carved by St. Louis de Montfort in 1707, during the time he spent restoring the chapel of St. Lazare. Photo by Aartsen.

MONTFORT, LOUIS MARIE DE

SUMMARY I. VARIOUS INTERPRETATIONS OF MONTFORT'S PERSONALITY:
1. Devotional biographies: Montfort the extraordinary saint;
2. Historical-psychological biography: Montfort the spiritual man;
3. Realistic biography: Montfort the man of the streets.

II. BIOGRAPHICAL JOURNEY OF MONTFORT:
1. Family Milieu;
2. Secondary studies at Rennes;
3. The trip to Paris;
4. Among the Sulpicians;
5. At Nantes with Fr. Lévêque;
6. With the poor in Poitiers;
7. The search for Wisdom (1703-1704);
8. Missionary life from 1706 to 1710;
9. In the dioceses of Luçon and La Rochelle (1711-1716).

III. THE INCULTRATION OF MONTFORT'S MESSAGE TODAY:
1. God the Absolute: Goal of all Peoples
2. Abandoning oneself to divine logic, to Christ Wisdom;
3. Regard for the feminine point of view in Christianity;
4. A life orientated toward the coming of the reign of Christ into the world.

A presentation on Saint Louis Marie de Montfort (1673-1716) is essential to a handbook centered on his spirituality. Rather than duplicate what the other articles have said about Montfort, this article will seek to discover the thread that connects his spirituality to his unique personality.

Part I, will focus on the various interpretations of Montfort's life by his different biographers. Part II, will then present our own biographical profile of Montfort. Part III, will attempt to discern Montfort's major challenge to us today.

I. VARIOUS INTERPRETATIONS OF MONTFORT'S PERSONALITY

With characteristic emphasis, one of his biographers, Pauvert, noted in 1875: "Historians have written more about this humble country missionary, who rarely preached in cathedrals, than about the great orators or kings of the past."[1] This observation is even more true today. We now have more than a hundred biographies of Montfort.[2]

Rather than deal with each one, they will be grouped into biographical models, which interpret Montfort's persona in different ways.

Certain of Montfort's characteristics are present in all of the biographies, but they assume a greater or lesser importance in each. Underscored here will be the unique outlook of each biography. 1) how their authors responded to the question: "Who in the final analysis was this man Montfort?"; 2) how particular biographical types or models were born; 3) how they result not so much from a biographer's individual point of view as from the ecclesial and cultural milieu within which each was written.

1. Devotional biographies: Montfort the extraordinary saint

The first four biographies of Montfort, by Grandet, Blain, Besnard, and Picot de Clorivières, were all written in the eighteenth century. They reflect the hagiographical method current then—the devotional biography. Such an approach reflected little of the critical sensibility that had dominated most of the seventeenth century through the works of the Bollandists, the memorialists of Port-Royal, and Jean de Launoy († 1674), the famous "saint hunter."

The first four biographies thus can be characterized as devotional biographies. They sought to edify, praise, eulogize, idealize.[3] Grandet, in particular, focused on the events in Montfort's life that would tend to edify a reader. But they did so by portraying Montfort's specialness. They revealed him as "an unusual example of someone living a poor, humble, mortified, and crucified life." Beginning with the saint's childhood, this is how Montfort's life is depicted.[4] Blain is more of a eulogist of Montfort than a biographer. Although he did not hide "what the world would see as surface defects in Montfort,"[5] he exalted the virtues of his hero, as if everything came easily and naturally to him.[6] Lacking a deep critical sense, such early biographies are filled with anachronism, incoherence, and overgeneralization.[7]

Despite such limitations, Montfort's early biographers provide us with very valuable material. They have preserved for us numerous eyewitness accounts and original documents, and they offer a solid historical foundation for reconstructing many of the truths of Montfort's life.[8] They also remind us of certain extraordinary or unusual traits in Montfort's personality and behavior.

Beginning with his preface, Grandet highlights the prevalent conflicting opinions about the nature of Montfort as a person; and like the other devotional hagiographers of his time, Grandet centered on those aspects of Montfort's saintly nature that were of an unusual, extraordinary, supranormal or superhuman character. He said of Montfort that "worldly men deemed him strange, good men unique." He emphasized those things which made Saint Louis Marie appear eccentric and remote rather than ordinary and accessible. Thus Grandet presented him as someone more to be venerated than imitated. He dwelt on such things as Montfort leaving his head uncovered both winter and summer, kneeling to pray when he entered a house, throwing himself at the feet of fellow travelers, allowing himself be disciplined by them, traveling on foot everywhere, and sleeping in stables rather than with his family when he was in the area where they lived. He depicted Montfort as someone constantly seeking opportunities for humiliation and for poverty, and as someone who did things that caused him to be thrown out of several dioceses.[9]

To justify such unusual behavior, Grandet invoked God, Who guided Montfort's earthly journey. But thankfully a theological intuition made him avoid taking this attitude to the extreme and thus completely isolating Montfort. Happily, Grandet set Montfort within the living tradition of holiness, beginning in the OT, continuing in the NT, and fulfilled in the communion of saints. In the end, Grandet saw Montfort as reflecting God's Wisdom in choosing certain saints "to fight the counterfeit wisdom of the world by being fools for Him and His Gospel." Thus Grandet portrayed Montfort like the saints of old, as someone so filled with the Spirit that he became elevated almost to "a new species of being." The following passage from Grandet highlights such a sapiential or Spirit-inspired interpretation of Montfort: "One must concede that God's ways relative to His saints are very different from God's ways relative to ordinary humans. . . . To the latter He measures His Spirit in weight and number, to the former He gives Spirit spontaneously, abundantly, immediately without concern for them being able to support such fullness so far above their natural ability. Therefore saints have been obliged to do extraordinary things to lessen the burden and offer solace to those who would find such things incomprehensible. The Holy Spirit, in the words of the prophets, would descend upon them so violently and powerfully that He would transport them far beyond themselves, making them appear to a normal human person like a new species of being."[10]

Blain took this approach to explain things when, after presenting the "singular and extraordinary ways" of Montfort several times,[11] he apologized for the saint's behavior by recourse to the Holy Spirit and Wisdom. He then seems to take an anthropological perspective. He no longer considers Wisdom within God but rather within Montfort, who is following in the footsteps of the Apostles: "I believe it can be said that he experienced the power and spontaneity of the new wine of the Holy Spirit like the Apostles, and like them he was thus made wise in the eyes of God but an insane fool in the eyes of the world. . . . This was the holy intoxication that is the summit of true Wisdom.[12] In 1714, during his famous discussion with Blain, Montfort gave us a symbolic gesture that remains the hermeneutic key to understanding his life. Taking his New Testament from its case, he dramatically quoted those verses which revealed what it meant to be an apostle of Christ. His path was not to follow "the wisdom of the community" but, rather, "the wisdom of a Missionary Apostolic." It consisted in "creating new designs of things" for God's glory.[13]

We find the same outlook in Besnard, who duplicated in his own way Grandet's apologia for Montfort.[14] As Montfort's successor in leading parish missions, Besnard accentuated Montfort's commitment "to teach the simple people and to evangelize the poor."[15]

2. Historical-psychological biography: Montfort the spiritual man

The nineteenth century's "romanticized" conception of history influenced hagiography in two main ways. 1) Although a biography should relive the outer events of a saint's past, it was more important to describe the interior drama of his soul.[16] 2) The nineteenth-century biographies of Montfort in no way betray this historiographic orientation. In fact, none of them is very concerned with reviving or reenacting for the reader Montfort's historical setting or with sketching the actual dramatic events of his life story. The biography of Dalin (1839), for example, is content to "verify and correct, as needed, the different details of the history, . . . to put them in order and to clarify them."[17] Two biographies were prepared for the Montfort's beatification, one by Fonteneau and the other by Persiani. The latter is almost a translation of the former (1887). They limited themselves to recounting the events that took place and did not go into Montfort's psychology.[18] On the other hand, the work of Pauvert (1875) made some noticeable progress. The author not only published a collection of Montfort's unpublished letters and established a chronology of the first years of his priesthood; he also proposed an interpretation of Montfort's life, seen as nature's immolation. Pauvert presented Montfort as the "hero of the Cross," a protest and witness that went to the heart of the atmosphere of sensuality pervading his century.[19]

The four volumes Quérard (1887) completed on the life of Montfort form the largest work devoted to the Breton missionary. The author found fault with his predecessors because they "did not dare present their hero in the true light of day, neither the height nor the breadth, neither the beauty nor the greatness of his missionary work." For Quérard, the "providential missionary work" of Montfort made him "an extraordinary ambassador of the Almighty," the "leader of a new school, . . . a prophet, precursor, and apostle of the great reign of Jesus and Mary on earth."[20]

It was not until the early twentieth century (1927) that A. Crosnier's biography was published. Crosnier's subtitle underscored how his style of hagiography was influenced by nineteenth-century romanticism: *Blessed Louis-Marie Grignion de Montfort, a Great Sower of the Good News: The History of a Life, the History of a Soul.* Though he clearly affirmed that Montfort "grew in virtue and in grace and entered more and more deeply into intimacy with Jesus and Mary," the author neither detailed Montfort's outer life story nor recounted the saintly missionary's interior life. He preferred to stop "at the threshold of the mystery of divine friendships."[21]

In a similar nineteenth-century vein, just before Montfort's canonization, there appeared the *"saggio biografico"* authored by De Luca (1943). The author took into account the literary and spiritual milieu of seventeenth-century France and attempted "an interpretation of his [Montfort's] soul based on known events of his biography."[22] In a discreet,[23] synthetic way De Luca introduced his readers to Montfort's spiritual life. He pointed out the "phases" and "laws" of his growth and development. He described Montfort's "seasons of holiness" as he climbed the ladder of mystical ascent. "In fact, at Paris he must have had the first in a series of mysterious, dizzying high points that characterized his mystical life. . . . His voice and speech would betray him. They expressed that luminous resoluteness and firmness which are the privilege of someone continually living in close proximity to God. His everyday life betrayed this as well, but of its details we know practically nothing."[24]

A thesis of S. De Fiores (1974) explicitly studied the spiritual journey of Montfort, although it limited itself to the period up to his priesthood. The author highlights "the mystical and theological aspects of Montfort's life as they evolved."[25] He was careful first to set them in the context of "the French school of spirituality," within the precise milieu, often neglected, in which Montfort was formed and from which his spiritual experience emerged. Assiduous research into the archives, especially those of the Sulpicians and the Jesuits, allowed him to reconstruct the vital aspects of Louis Marie's story: the mystique of liberating poverty, the saint's ascetical follies, choice of the science of the saints, Slavery of Love of Jesus in Mary, etc. The end result was exemplified in the contrasting outlooks of Montfort the seminarian and his spiritual director, F. Leschassier, who came from "different spiritual streams and had contrasting temperaments."[26] Louis Marie drew on the mystical and missionary currents of the authors he preferred, i.e., Olier, Surin, and Boudon, thus placing himself outside those principles of formation inspired by Tronson. Freeing himself from his Sulpician conditioning, Montfort passed through a contemplative and acosmic type of spirituality into a spirituality where the apostolate became the most divine work (H 21:12). At Paris Montfort had already attained a high degree of union with Jesus Christ, a "unity of the spirituality of pure love, with a taste for God Alone and a detachment from worldly distractions."[27] This was a provisional path, since through his conversations with Blain, he uncovered two fundamental aspects of his spirituality: "the first, its experiential and mystical nature—the unity of the spiritual life through the grace of the presence of Jesus and Mary. This allowed Montfort to realize an intimate contemplative union with God through action. The second is the principle of following

Christ, Incarnate Wisdom, by imitating his way of life through his example and counsel."[28]

3. Realistic biography: Montfort the man of the streets

Of the different genres of biography that purport to describe the events of someone's life, today "the realistic biography is much in favor. . . . The truths of the human side of the life, including the actual work of the saint, are thus given a primacy of value."[29] Without forgetting the era or milieu in which the saint lived or his accomplishments, today's biographer gives his subject realistic flesh and bone. He makes the saint truly human.

Such a method is clearly apparent in the four works dedicated by L. Perouas to Grignion de Montfort (1966, 1973, 1989, 1990). The author separated himself from his predecessors by describing Montfort, his life, and his pastoral work using a historical-critical and psycho-sociological approach. It was truly a "reinterpretation" that modified the traditional image of the saint but was justified in its attempt to bring out Montfort's human reality. "Every analysis of the pastoral work of a man must begin with the man himself and also with the milieu in which that man worked."[30] In contrast to earlier biographies, which explained everything with reference to the supernatural, Perouas believed that "it was legitimate to abstract from the reality of grace without at the same time minimizing in any way the primacy of the action of the Spirit."[31] Focusing on Montfort's psychological reality, Perouas held that the Breton saint's path was a "tormented journey" because he had difficulty dealing with a strained relationship with his father and because he had a violent temper. His long and arduous journey toward a balanced life came to a "certain maturation for Father de Montfort when he was in his forties."[32] An analysis of factual events in Montfort's history allows us to conclude that "through his increasing responsiveness to the Holy Spirit, he learned to accept himself despite the events that tormented his existence. . . . We can, today, by turning back the clock of history, admire how, in the depths of his soul, God wrote straight with crooked lines."[33]

A similar psychological interpretation can be seen in the other works of Perouas. Montfort is "like a tree growing out of rock," a man in whom there was "something abrupt, rough-skinned, savage, rocklike." His journey was marked with crises: a vocational crisis, culminating in his "great forsakeness" at rue Pot-de-Fer in Paris in 1702; a crisis in his apostolic ministry, especially in 1710, when the Calvary of Pontchâteau was destroyed; a personal crisis around 1713, when Montfort experienced "biologically and psychologically a turning point in his own existence"; and, finally, when he was "supremely laid bare" by the precarious state of his two foundations.[34] Montfort, however, never became a victim of his difficulties. "At every crisis he instinctively found himself and returned to his work among the people."[35]

Generally more acceptable than

Perouas' Freudian psychological interpretation[36] is his understanding of Montfort's ministry in the context of the sociological and pastoral realities of his times. Therefore the "relative uniqueness" of Montfort's missionary activity is more easily seen when contrasted with his content and method. Montfort's preaching gave the "Virgin Mary her proper place next to Christ in the economy of salvation and in man's personal response"; his preaching insisted on the Christian virtues, on the Rosary, and on the exigencies of Baptism. Montfort "manifested to a high degree a universal missionary vision, a preferential love for the poorest of the poor, along with his own 'radical poverty' and 'hope in God.'"[37] Perouas remarks that none of Montfort's works offer a complete or definitive synthesis of his spirituality. Rather, his concepts of God, of Jesus, Incarnate Wisdom, of Mary, and of the Church are modified and developed throughout his total faith journey.[38]

To write the life of a saint, a modern hagiographer must be a multifaceted person. A writer must critically examine every document deemed authentic and relevant. He must study and bring to life the saint's cultural and spiritual milieu and truthfully portray both the various chronological events and the inner drama of the saint's life. We should also add that today the intimate meaning of a saint's life for those living today is of greater importance than a complete recounting of all known biographical details. Consequently, a biography must offer both the cultural and the spiritual aspects of a saint's life.

S. De Fiores

II. Biographical Journey of Montfort

January 31, 1673, to April 28, 1716: only forty-three years and three months of life on earth. When we look at all that the Father from Montfort did in so short a time and all that he has left us, there is reason to be stupefied. If we add that his priestly ministry covered not quite sixteen years from his ordination on June 5, 1700, such astonishment can only grow. His missionary activity took him into almost two hundred parishes. He found time to be concerned with the poor, with his foundations, with going on retreat. He travelled on foot for thousands and thousands of miles. How did he find time to write? For beyond the legacy of his personal example, we have his surprisingly large and important corpus of writings, which remain remarkably relevant to us today. Who was this man? What has he to say to us today? To discover answers, in this section we will follow Montfort through a brief retelling of his life journey. Along the way, we will point out several significant events that reveal how and what he lived. We will not attempt here to present in a synthetic and organic manner the key aspects of his spiritual patrimony. But it is important to add that without his writings, we would be missing certain salient aspects of his life.

1. Family milieu

Our saint's family background is well known.[39] His father, a not very successful lawyer, was not without ambition but was continually faced with financial worries. These problems the family came to know quite well. There were eighteen children, of whom seven or eight died very young. These difficulties happened to a man who was a difficult sort of character. Thus our saint's family atmosphere was not as serene as one might have wished it to be.

The role of first-born fell to Louis Marie when the actual first-born child of the family died at the age of five months. During his childhood, he suffered from his father's outbursts of anger, and probably more because of the tears of his meek, pious mother than because of himself.

His father's ambitious attachment to worldly position had an effect on Louis Marie, for he took an exactly opposite stance as soon as possible.

We must not, however, make the situation look too dark. Jean-Baptiste Grignion was a staunch Christian and made sure that he transmitted his faith to his children, providing them with a solid human and religious education. Undoubtedly he was helped in this by his wife, Jeanne Robert, who had three brothers who were priests. Three of the Grignion sons became priests, and two of the daughters became nuns.

2. Secondary studies at Rennes

In 1685, Louis Marie entered the College of St. Thomas Becket run by the Jesuits at Rennes.[40] He stood out as a serious student, but more so for his piety and devotion to the Blessed Virgin and his love for the poor. The young people of the school, though not living fast and loose, were still full of that turbulence of life so normal to those their age. Louis Marie appeared to them somewhat distant, to some even unsociable.

He had a close relationship, however, with certain of his instructors, such as Fathers Descartes and Gilbert, and he knew how to form solid friendships, which would remain for many years. Examples of this were Claude Poullart des Places, who in the future was to become the founder of the Seminary of the Holy Spirit in Paris, and Jean-Baptiste Blain, whose recollections would later become so precious to the montfort community.

3. The trip to Paris

Louis Marie heard the call to the priesthood. In the autumn of 1692, he left for Paris in order to do his "seminary" training there. His departure was marked by an event that reveals an essential aspect of Montfort's spiritual personality. He refused to accept a horse offered to him "to make half the trip," which was over 300 kilometers (180 miles). His uncle Father Alain Robert and his brother Joseph accompanied him up to the outskirts of the city of Rennes, bidding him farewell at the Cesson bridge.

Once alone, there was nothing more urgent for the young man than to give to the first poor person he encountered all the things that he had been forced to accept for his stay in Paris. He gave to a beggar at the bridge his extra clothes and all his money, ten *écus*. He exchanged the new suit he was wearing for the poor man's rags.

How can this act of radical detachment be explained? Was it an adolescent reaction against an overbearing father with an excessive desire for material goods? This problem had at times poisoned the atmosphere of the Grignion household. Was it now conjoined to juvenile enthusiasm? Such a psychological explanation is insufficient, because this attitude of Louis Marie towards material goods was not of a fleeting nature. It was to be the permanent rule of his life.

His friend Blain testified: "This trip, being the first, was also a model for so many others to come, which his zeal for souls saw him multiply in the future. What I mean to say is that he had to be apostolic, poor, humbled, accepting of pain and fatigue, and abandoned to Divine Providence. It was this last virtue which I admired the most in him when he departed."[41]

Perhaps it was premature for Fr. Blain to call this his entrance into "the apostolate." The same might be said for abandonment to Providence, which was truly at the heart of Montfort's actions. He possessed an absolute confidence in his heavenly Father. He was convinced that he would never be deceived by Him. As a consequence, he became effectively detached from seeking security in earthly or material goods, in human power or influence. His sense of "poverty" had a directly theological dimension. It was a simple expression of his faith.

This is not to say that Louis Marie rejected recourse to all natural or human means and supports. He knew how to solicit such things at certain times. For example, he came to the aid of the Daughters of Wisdom when they needed material assistance. But his faith was not in such things; it was in God Alone.

An almost immediate consequence of his radical detachment was his capacity to give without measure to those deprived of the necessary means of life. One can speak of both his material poverty and his spiritual poverty. Montfort's attitude toward the poor had its root in the poverty of his own faith.

4. Among the Sulpicians

At Paris, Montfort placed himself under the guidance of the Sulpicians.[42] In the beginning he was welcomed and guided with affection by Fr. de la Barmondière, and later by Fr. Bayün. But beginning in 1696, others, especially his spiritual director, Fr. Leschassier, found him hard to understand. Though he showed an obedient willingness to seek and follow their advice, they found his behavior strangely "out of tune."

At Saint Sulpice, little by little, the well-codified ascetical trend of Fr. Tronson had supplanted the more mystical orientation of Fr. Olier. For Fr. Leschassier, the ideal for a "good ecclesiastic" was to be found in surrendering himself to the balanced mold of the "common rule." It had no room for fantasy and even less for extravagance. This "rule" was not so much the written rule, which Louis Marie obeyed assiduously; rather, it was an image of the model seminarian.

Montfort was a generous, passionate seeker of God whose fervor and good will were obvious. But it was also obviously impossible for him to conform himself to an established framework. Should not certain excessive or extravagant acts also be considered a sign of uniqueness of character? Could such behavior be inspired by the Holy Spirit? But could not such a quasi-impossibility of freeing himself manifest an unconscious attachment to his "own judgment," which might not be very balanced?

The truth is more easily discovered in light of Montfort's entire journey than here in its beginnings. The Holy Spirit was truly at work in him. Over time Louis Marie would rid himself of the roughness and imperfections in his character. He did not understand half measures that compromised with the spirit of the world. The inner Master continued working to mold him into a saint and apostle, even through the trials and difficulties that resulted from his being misunderstood by others.

Montfort throughout his life would remain more of an enigma "for the sages and wise men," than for the "poor and little ones," who spontaneously recognized him as a man of God, as someone they could trust. For a long time, even his friend Jean-Baptiste Blain would have reservations about him. Only after their Rouen meeting in 1714 did he drop his prejudices.

Montfort was never a troublemaker. He didn't do sensational things for shock value. His apparent anticonformism resulted from something much deeper, something immensely more praiseworthy. It was rooted in the absoluteness of God and in the radicalness of the Gospel. He drew concrete conclusions without being preoccupied with how they might impact on himself. He would have willingly renounced any of his uncommon character traits, but not his uncommon commitment to do Christ's will unfailingly.

Fr. Blain asked his friend "whether he ever hoped to find people willing to follow the type of life he led. In response, he showed me his New Testament and asked me if I could improve on what Jesus Christ had said and done. Could I show him a better life than that of his Apostles, one of poverty and mortification based on abandonment to Providence?"

Blain reproached him: "But where do you find in the Gospel valid examples of your odd or unusual ways of doing things. Why haven't you given them up? . . . He replied that truthfully he had not intended his actions to be odd or unusual, that he had paid no attention to his actions in natural terms; yet if his actions caused humiliation, then they were not without purpose. As for the rest, he said if acts of charity, mortification, and other such uncommon practices of heroic virtue were considered odd or unusual, then in that sense he would be happy to be considered odd or unusual. If being uncommon was a defect, then it was one shared with every saint."[43]

For Montfort, Saint Sulpice was more than a time of trial, testing, and conflicting spiritual lifestyles. It prepared him for the misunderstandings and rejections that he would later experience. Even though he opted for the *"science of the saints"* rather than that of the worldly wise, he did receive a solid theological formation; he was thus able to bring together, notably on the Marian plane, important documentation that would later make it possible for him to translate and to communicate his spiritual experience into several major works.

Discovering the devotion *"of holy slavery,"* he enthusiastically made it his own, giving it new dimensions. He realized, deepened, and was shaped in his Christ-centeredness by a profound grasp of the mystery of the Incarnation. This allowed him to integrate organically his exceptional Marian piety, to bring it to the very heart of his Christian life, and to discover its ultimate implications. It set in place the essential foundations of his spiritual life.

Already composing hymns and sermons, he had begun to anticipate his future apostolate.

5. At Nantes with Fr. Lévêque

After his priestly ordination, June 5, 1700, his desire to depart for the missions of Canada was not fulfilled. He went to Fr. Lévêque in Nantes, hoping to be trained for a ministry in parish missions. But his hope was unrealized, and the young priest, so on fire with apostolic zeal, had to cool his heels. He found himself inactive, in a community where he was ill at ease. Though he handled the situation with maturity and sensitivity, he managed to communicate the strain this left him under, as well as his desire for the active apostolate, something that would never leave him.

Writing with total candor of heart to Fr. Leschassier, who remained his spiritual director, he said: " *With conditions as they are, I find myself, as time goes on, torn by two apparently contradictory feelings. On the one hand I feel a secret attraction for a hidden life in which I can efface myself in combat, my natural tendency to show off. On the other hand, I feel a tremendous urge to make our Lord and his holy Mother loved, to go in a humble and simple way to teach catechism to the poor in country places and to arouse in sinners a devotion to Our Blessed Lady. This was the work done by a good priest who died a holy death here recently. He used to go about from parish to parish teaching the people catechism and relying only on what Providence provided for him. I know very well, my dear Father, that I am not worthy to do such honorable work, but when I see the needs of the Church I cannot help pleading continually for a small and poor band of good priests to do this work under the banner and protection of the Blessed Virgin"* (L 5).

This is a remarkable text. Already it contains Montfort's basic life orientation. It shows how he was being led to understand and live out his mission during this early period. It reveals as well his vision of a foundation and of how he planned to make it a reality. It was natural that he would experience a tension between the desire for the hidden life of solitude, on the one hand, and for the active apostolate, on the other. What Montfort said was not unusual, and in fact he found ways to live both a contemplative and an active life.

6. With the poor in Poitiers

For the first time in his life, he spent five months in forced inactivity. But though Providence closed one door, it opened another. Madame de Montespan, who was a benefactor of his sister Sylvia and had helped her to enter the Abbey of Fontevrault, invited Louis Marie to come and assist at the ceremony where his sister received her religious habit. During his stay at the monastery, the young priest met with Madame de Montespan a number of times. She was interested in his future and recommended that he visit the bishop of Poitiers and speak to him about his projects. Montfort agreed, but upon his arrival in Poitiers, he found that the bishop was away. How would he find what to do? He wrote to Fr. Leschassier: *"I thought of going to the hospital at Poitiers, and being of material help to the poor, even if I couldn't serve them spiritually. I went into their little church to pray and the four hours I spent there waiting for the evening mealtime seemed all too short. However it seemed so long to some of the poor, who saw me kneeling there dressed in clothes very much like their own, that they went off to tell the others and they all agreed to take up a collection for me. Some gave more, some less; the poorer ones a denier, the richer ones a sou. All this went on without my knowing anything about it. Eventually I left the church to ask the time of supper and at the same time to ask permission to serve the poor at table. But I misconceived the situation for I discovered they did not eat together and I was surprised to find out that they wanted to make me an offering and had told the doorkeeper not to let me go away. I blessed God that I had been taken for a poor man wearing the glorious livery of the poor and thanked my brothers and sisters for their kindness.*

Since then, they have become so attached to me that they are going about saying openly that I am to be their priest, that is their director, for there has not been a regular director in the poorhouse for a considerable time, so abandoned has it become" (L 6).

This event is quite revealing. How can one explain the feelings of sympathy, the attraction, that the poorhouse residents felt for this unknown priest? Quite simply! Montfort himself gives the reason: *"Some of the poor . . . saw me kneeling."* But what was so unusual about seeing a priest praying in church? In this case, it was this unknown person's attitude, the length of time he spent in prayer, so absorbed in contemplation that no one dared disturb him. And then there was the fact that they saw him *"dressed in clothes very much like their own."*

These two reasons seem to explain the behavior of the poor. They took up a collection among themselves to help him out. Instinctively they sensed that this priest, so close to God and to them, understood them deeply. In spite of their social differences, he was *"one of them,"* to the degree that after the initial contact, they wanted him for themselves. *"They are going about saying openly that I am to be their priest."* And one of them wrote to Bishop Girard, asking that he be assigned to them.

This was not the only time that he helped people materially. He had been doing this his whole life. Montfort attracted *"the poor"* to himself because he loved them. This love for the poor is one of the keys to his spiritual physiognomy.

The poor of Poitiers would almost immediately get their wish. When Montfort returned to Nantes, Fr. Lévêque gave him first one and then several other missions to preach in the countryside. He did this with surprising success for someone who was just beginning his ministry.

But on August 25, 1701, a letter came from Bishop Girard asking him to fulfill the wishes of the residents of the poorhouse in Poitiers. Montfort accepted, but on September 16 he wrote to Fr. Leschassier: *"The only thing that would make me want to go to the poorhouse at all would be the hope of being able to extend my work later into the town and the countryside and so be able to help more people"* (L 9). Mission work was his only goal.

At the poorhouse, his devotion and sense of organization worked marvels and in time also aroused the hostility of certain malcontents. He was forced to leave Poitiers in the spring of 1703. But during his first stay, he had met Marie Louise Trichet and Catherine Brunet. They both would forever remain faithful to him and would become, a dozen years later, the first two Daughters of Wisdom.

He was not, however, finished with the poorhouse at Poitiers, for "his" poor wanted him. Here is the beginning of the letter dated March 9, 1704, that they sent to Fr. Leschassier: "We, four hundred poor, petition you very humbly, for the great love and glory of God, to return to us our venerable pastor, him who loves the poor so much, Fr. Grignion." Could one think of a more beautiful compliment?

Once again, however, after a very encouraging beginning, new difficulties arose, and he became disconcerted. His final farewell to the poorhouse at Poitiers occurred in 1705.

7. The search for Wisdom (1703-1704)

From the spring of 1703 to March 1704, Montfort lived in Paris. He first headed toward the immense poorhouse of la Salpêtrière, where 5,000 impoverished people lived. For five months he devoted himself to their care. He was very effective, but this incited the ire of those who opposed such fruitful change, and they attacked him. At the end of just five months, they asked him to leave. But where was he to go? He found lodgings on rue Pot-de-Fer, near the Jesuit novitiate. Fr. Blain testifies that it was a "tiny nook, under a staircase, where the sun practically never shone. All I saw there was a clay pot and a miserable bed, good only for beggars and wretches."[44] Such extreme poverty did not disturb Montfort, because we know that he remained full of joy while he stayed there.

But another terrible trial awaited: Fr. Leschassier's public rejection of him. Montfort had always considered him his spiritual director. But Fr. Leschassier no longer wanted to assume the cumbersome responsibility of someone who was such an open source of embarrassment to him. From his point of view, Montfort would never settle down and would always find some way to be asked to leave. Montfort had become fair game for the public rumor mills. They ridiculed him about his manners and the way he dressed. Fr. Leschassier didn't want to compromise his reputation and that of the Seminary of St. Sulpice. His role as Montfort's spiritual director had become too burdensome. Since Montfort refused to understand Fr. Leschassier's letters of resignation, his director chose to confront him publicly on the issue, in front of all of the seminarians gathered at the vacation house in Issy. Fr. Blain, who was present, described it: "He was mortified when, the day he arrived at Issy, this wise superior, who was there with the community during vacation, received him with an icy stare and shamefully sent him away, with a dry and scornful air, without wishing to talk to him or to listen to him."[45] This time the break with Saint Sulpice was complete. Montfort suddenly found himself alone. Humanly speaking, his life journey seemed to have come to a dead end. But Saint Louis Marie even more intensely lived his motto "God Alone" in the several months of forced solitude and inactivity that followed.

Montfort's spiritual path was centered on a passionate search for Wisdom. Wisdom, for him, was Jesus Christ, the Eternal Word made incarnate for our salvation. It was also to live for him, and with him to enter into the depths of God's design of love for the world. This design was expressed in the folly of the Cross, because the Wisdom of God was contrary to the wisdom of the world.

Beginning at Poitiers, Montfort proclaimed this in a spectacular way. He lived it in the way he cared for the organization of services to the poor. He sought to give to the administrators a spiritual foundation for their work. He began grouping the women administrators of the poorhouse into a religious Congregation. To this end, he composed a rule and proposed it to them. But he met with their refusal. Then, "like the servant who allowed the beggars and the cripples into the bridal chamber, he selected from among the residents of the poorhouse a dozen young girls. He took them from among the most disenfranchised: the lame, the tubercular, the blind. In a way, they will become the first Daughters of Wisdom, . . . they will try out the Rule whose spirit its founder infused into them through the [spiritual] exercises that they would practice. At the head of this unusual community, Montfort placed a blind woman!"[46] This was a veritable challenge to the wisdom of the world. It was not by chance that Montfort gave the name Wisdom to the place where this little group met. And it was not by accident that he placed on the wall a cross covered with emblems and words. It was a kind of summary "of the spirituality that he wished to give to his Daughters."[47] For him as for St. Paul, *"Wisdom is the Cross and the Cross is Wisdom"* (LEW 180). One must, therefore, enter by way of the Cross in order to acquire Wisdom. Montfort began by living himself what he asked others to live. He wrote this more than likely at the end of April or the beginning of May 1703 to Marie Louise Trichet: *"Keep on praying, even increase your prayers for me; ask for extreme poverty, the weightiest cross, abjection and humiliations. I accept them all if only you will beg God to remain with me and not leave me for a moment because I am so weak. What wealth, what glory, what happiness would be mine if from all this I obtained divine Wisdom, which I long for day and night!*

"I will never cease asking for this boundless treasure and I firmly believe that I shall obtain it even were angels, men and demons to deny it to me. I believe strongly in the efficacy of your prayers, in the loving kindness of our God, in the protection of the Blessed Virgin, our good Mother; I believe too that the needs of the poor are too urgent and the promises of God too explicit for me to be making a mistake in seeking Wisdom. For even if the possession of divine Wisdom were impossible, according to the ordinary workings of divine grace, which is not the case, it would become possible because of the insistence with which we ask for it. Is it not an unchangeable truth that everything is possible to him who believes?

"Another thing that makes me say that I shall possess Wisdom is the fact that I have encountered and still encounter so much persecution night and day" (L 15).

What we wish to underline from this dramatic text is Montfort's passionate desire to acquire and to possess Wisdom, which is Jesus Christ, and also the fact that in order to obtain it, Montfort was joyously ready to forget the price by travelling the way of the Cross. Finally, he possessed the unshakable assurance that he would obtain what he coveted so deeply. What is the source of such assurance? This question demands careful reflection. It was the efficacy of the prayers of both Marie Louise and himself, the goodness of God, the protection of the Virgin, the need of the poor. At the time he wrote this letter, Montfort was at the poorhouse of la Salpêtrière; it is very significant that he depended on the "needs" of those to whom he was sent as the foundation for his confidence in obtaining Wisdom. He had a right to what was needed for him to accomplish the mission given to him by the Lord. Montfort naturally integrated his pastoral ministry and his spiritual life, because both finally depended not upon himself but on the Lord, from Whom he received all and to Whom he owed all. The ultimate foundation of his confidence was "the word and the promise" of God, to which he responded with the total force of his faith.

Montfort decided to raise the price, so to speak, in his letter of October 24, 1703, also addressed to

Marie Louise Trichet. He had been thrown out of la Salpêtrière and found himself alone in a small room on rue Pot-de-Fer in Paris. He wrote: *"I feel that you are still asking God that by crosses, humiliations and poverty I may acquire divine Wisdom. Be brave, my dear daughter, be brave. I am grateful to you; I feel the effects of your prayers for I am infinitely more impoverished, crucified and humiliated than ever. Both men and demons in this great city of Paris are waging against me a war that I find sweet and welcome. Let them slander me, scoff at me, destroy my good name, put me into prison, these are precious gifts, tasty morsels, great and wonderful things. They form the accoutrements and retinue of divine Wisdom which he brings into the lives of those in whom he dwells. When shall I possess this loveable and mysterious Wisdom? When will Wisdom come to live in me? When shall I be sufficiently equipped to serve as a place of rest for Wisdom in a world where he is rejected and without a home. . . . So pray, entreat God, plead for me to obtain divine Wisdom. You will attain it completely for me; for this I am quite convinced"* (L 16).

The tie between the prayers of Marie Louise Trichet and the trials that beset Montfort was clearly established. He was living with many crosses, a sign that he would finally receive what he wanted. Let us note some important truths. Suffering tested Montfort by letting him see his dear Wisdom, Jesus Christ, "thrown down and despised" there in the city of Paris. This was necessary if he was to offer Wisdom a heart able to receive her and respond to her will for men. That is what Montfort was thinking of. Such was the depth and character of his love for Christ.

His spiritual work during this period, 1701-1704, was accompanied by a profound doctrinal breakthrough on this theme of Wisdom. Invited in 1703 to give several conferences at the Seminary of the Holy Spirit, founded by his friend Poullart des Places, he presented a commentary on the Book of Wisdom. It appears that it was also during these years, 1703-1704, that he wrote LEW, the book that presents the most complete synthesis of montfort spirituality. This period, marked by poverty and many other trials, thus came to be seen as a very rich and very fruitful period.

Before he left Paris, Montfort was asked once again to bring order and peace to the hermits of Mont-Valérien. To everyone's satisfaction, he was able to accomplish this work in several months. This showed that there were at least some people who recognized his worth, who had confidence in him.

8. Missionary life from 1706 to 1710

Even though he had been asked to leave the poorhouse there, Montfort returned to Poitiers and began the missionary apostolate to which he was called. In the densely populated suburb of Montbernage, he experienced the full flowering of his dream. There he preached an immensely successful parish mission. His mission left behind an oratory dedicated to

Mary Queen of All Hearts, which the people restored. He was then welcomed by a number of other parishes of the city. His success as a missionary could no longer be denied. Had his path clearly opened? Was he now to realize his full apostolate? But something happened that set his ministry back. He preached a mission in a parish directed by the Congregation of Notre Dame du Calvaire. He touched the people's hearts so deeply that those who made his mission brought their licentious books and pictures to the church for them to be burned. And this was done. But without Montfort's knowledge, while he was preaching in the church, some people, gathered outside at the pile of indecent literature, crowned a grotesque mannequin figure, reputedly representing the devil. Several backbiters immediately informed the vicar general of the diocese, Fr. de Villeroi, about what was happening. He was someone who didn't have many good things to say about Saint Louis Marie. He came running, entered the church, and interrupted the preacher. Montfort could do nothing about the situation. Fr. de Villeroi proceeded to insult him publicly. As was his manner, Montfort humbly accepted what he said. But this did not bring an end to the matter. Bishop de la Poype, who was absent when this happened, was told upon his return about this incident in a way that incriminated Montfort. In deference to his influential vicar general, the bishop threw Louis Marie out of his diocese.

Montfort thus considered it his duty to leave. But he did not go alone. For from that moment on, he had a constant companion, one who remained faithful to the end. They met in the church of the Penitents. After a brief conversation, Montfort saw that the young man, whom he had never met before, wanted to consecrate himself to the Lord. Montfort simply said to him, *"Follow me."* Mathurin Rangeard, soon to be called Brother Mathurin, obeyed.

Montfort didn't know where to go or what to do. Once again his ministry seemed blocked. Since he was apparently unable to work in France, it occurred to him that he might be called to leave for the foreign missions. He had considered this possibility from the beginning of his priesthood, and it returned again. But who was going to tell him if this was what the Lord wanted him to do?

A sort of foolish project then presented itself. "In order to discern the will of God on such an important question, he was drawn to consult the oracle and first superior of all Christians, the head of the Church and all within it. Montfort became persuaded that if he was to make God's orders his own, he should throw himself at the feet of Pope Clement XI to offer himself to him and to go wherever he pleased to send him."[48] He went to Rome, and his mission was revealed to him by the Holy Father himself in the following words: "Father, you have a big enough field of endeavor to exercise your zeal in France. Don't go elsewhere. Always work in perfect submission to the bishops into whose dioceses you will be called. In this way God will give His blessing to your work."[49] And Clement XI conferred on his visitor the title Missionary Apostolic.

His future laid out in such a manner, Montfort returned to France as he had come to Rome, on foot. He passed by Ligugé to pick up Brother Mathurin, who was patiently waiting for him there. Then, with him he headed for Brittany, the country of his birth. After several side trips, he arrived at Dinan and joined a group of priests who were giving missions in that city. A renowned episode, heavy with significance, occurred there, one that has remained strong in the memory of each of his chroniclers since then.

One evening Montfort, while on a trip, came across a "poor man, leprous and covered with ulcers. He did not wait for the man to implore him; he spoke to him first, took him on his shoulders, and carried him up to the door of the missionaries' house, which was closed because of the late hour. He knocked, crying out several times: *"Open the door to Jesus Christ, open the door to Jesus Christ."*[50] We mention this because it was such a simple and deep expression of Saint Louis Marie's vision of faith. He did not love the poor simply "out of love for Jesus Christ" but also because they revealed Christ himself and his love. His love reached out to the poor in themselves and for themselves, as they were. They were for him, mystically but really, Jesus himself. Indeed, Jesus did not say, "That which you do to the least of those who are mine, do it for the love of me." He said, "You do it to me." Here we discover one aspect of the secret of "him who loves the poor so much."

After the mission at Dinan, Montfort, always in the company of Mathurin, headed for St. Brieuc in order to join up with the group of missionaries led by Dom Leuduger. Inheritor of the work of Fr. Maunoir, disciple and follower of Father Huby, Dom Leuduger continued the great tradition of the "Breton mission." His reputation and influence were both strong. About twenty priests worked with him on a permanent basis, and occasionally, as needed, others joined him. The collaboration between the experienced missionary and Montfort was fruitful from more than one point of view. But it did not last too long. In August of the same year, 1707, during the mission at Moncontour, the mission team broke up.

The pretext used to send Montfort away seems quite weak. It was over a collection of Mass stipends taken up for the souls in purgatory. The group had made it a point of honor never to ask for money. It is hard to believe, knowing how disinterested Montfort was in material things, that he would transgress the spirit of poverty. Whatever actually happened, he was asked to leave. It is quite possible that some members of the group found it difficult to accommodate themselves to Montfort, to his ways and to his success with the people.

Undoubtedly, however, there was a deeper reason: a difference in the way they conceived of mission. It was a difference more of spirit than practice. When he was on his own, free to organize the missionary activities as he wished, Montfort did so "in an apostolic way." This meant, according to Fr. Blain, "in a great spirit of simplicity, poverty, penance, and abandonment to Divine Providence."[51]

In this spirit, which was opposed to that of Fr. Leuduger, he objected to the "funded missions"—those whose costs were covered by the generosity of benefactors in high places: bishops, lords of the manor, the King himself. He carried over into his missionary practice a sense of his own personal poverty. It entailed a complete abandonment to Divine Providence.

Once again, Louis Marie found himself without an apostolic ministry. He profited from the situation by making a retreat. With Brothers Mathurin and John, he occupied the hermitage of Saint-Lazare in the town of Montfort, his birthplace, fixing up and decorating a chapel there. It became a center of attraction for people from the surrounding countryside. Now that Montfort no longer traveled about, people came to him. This included certain priests from the area, who invited him to preach in their parishes.

Everything appeared to be working out for the better until the spring of 1708. The bishop of Saint-Malo passed through the village of Montfort. He had very little regard for the hermit of Saint-Lazare, whatever his motives might have been. His Jansenist tendencies might have played a part in this outlook. He ordered Saint Louis Marie not to preach any more, except in parish churches, of which the chapel of Saint-Lazare was not one. Understanding that his presence in the diocese was no longer wanted, the Missionary Apostolic decided to leave.

The diocese of Nantes welcomed him. Up to the end of 1710, Montfort went about the diocese giving missions. Besides *"the Brothers who accompanied him,"* he was joined, at least for a time, by priest collaborators—Fr. des Bastières and Fr. Olivier. Fr. Barrin, Bishop de Beauveau's vicar general, was on his side.

Under these circumstances, Montfort could begin to give his full attention to structuring his personal method of mission. Borrowing the normal ways of doing things at the time, he added to them his personal touch. His spiritual orientation included: living *"on Providence," "dependent on the people"*; attending in a particular way to the poor; Mary's place in prayer, notably the practice of the Rosary; the Wisdom of the Cross; and, above all, renewing the vows and promises of Baptism.

Among the means employed to renew the Christian education of the people were the hymns; Montfort composed his own. There were also the great processions; he became a master in the art of organizing and staging them. In order for a mission to have a continuing effect, he made sure that he organized groups of laypeople, often as confraternities, beginning with those centered on the Rosary.

He knew how to insert his conviction into his sermons. With him, teaching took on the power of witness. To

Fr. Hindré, rector of Bréal, near Montfort, who was astonished at the success of his preaching, he said in confidence: *"Dear friend, I have traveled more than 2,000 leagues on pilgrimage asking of God the grace to touch souls; He has answered me."*[52]

The grandiose project of the Calvary of Pontchâteau in 1710 demonstrated the exceptional hold that Montfort had on the crowds. It expressed in action the major themes of his life and of his preaching. But it also caused his expulsion from the diocese of Nantes.

9. In the dioceses of Luçon and La Rochelle (1711-1716)

This marked the last stage of his life. Unreservedly supported by Bishop de Lescure of Luçon and especially by Bishop de Champflour of La Rochelle, Montfort had at last found the terrain where his zeal could be employed in complete freedom. Saint Louis Marie, from personal conviction, wanted so much to work "with perfect submission to the Bishops" because he had a profound sense of the Church and also because it was the wish of Pope Clement XI. He was now able to do it with peace of mind.

It is also true that he had matured. He did not give up any of his evangelical radicalism, nor did he submit to the spirit of the world, which was always a horror for him. His efforts to master the natural violence of his character were not in vain. He became more mellow and, in a sense, wiser. He adapted himself more easily to the human and religious milieu of his apostolate. No longer do we see the spectacular reactions that, though coming from his desire to be faithful to the Gospel, appeared extravagant in the eyes of many.

Since we cannot follow Montfort on all of his fruitful journeys, some of the salient events of this period should be noted here. There are more than a few. Undoubtedly, it was around 1713 that he wrote the little book that is best known today, TD, which after its rediscovery and publication in 1842 made its author known throughout the entire world.

Under Bishop de Champflour, he became occupied with the education of children. Toward that end, he worked to renew an already existing institution that no longer responded to the needs of those for whom it was destined; this was the "charitable" or free school. A school for boys was organized. For the girls' schools, he called on Marie Louise Trichet and Catherine Brunet from Poitiers, who, for the last ten years, had been awaiting the realization of his promise to found with them the Daughters of Wisdom. The time had come.

One project remained that Montfort held close to his heart: the *"little and poor company of good priests"* to preach missions *"under the banner and the protection of Mary,"* which he had already spoken about to Fr. Leschassier in 1700. This project had also ripened. Montfort thought of it again but now with all the richness of his experience, on a spiritual level as well as on a practical level. Thus he blessed us with his writing of RM and the extraordinary text of PM. The manuscript of RM seems to date from the spring of 1713. At that time, Montfort had with him on a permanent basis only a few lay companions, the senior of whom were Mathurin and John, who did not wish to take vows. He had not succeeded in recruiting permanent priest collaborators until then. But the faith and hope that had animated his search for Wisdom ten years before had lost no impetus. With the same vehemence and the same confidence, he cries out to God even today in PM for apostles who share his heart.

He combined action with prayer. Claude Poullart des Places had promised to send him missionaries formed in the Seminary of the Holy Spirit. His friend was dead, but his work endured. In August 1713, Montfort arrived in Paris to share with Poullart des Places' successors his compact with their founder. He was warmly received, and his effort was not in vain. Several of the first Fathers of the Company of Mary were recruited from the Seminary of the Holy Spirit, although this would occur only after Montfort's death.

In June 1714 Montfort left for Rouen to pay a visit to his friend Fr. Blain. Did he have a secret hope of convincing the canon of Rouen to join him in preaching missions? Certain excerpts from their meeting make this hypothesis quite plausible. Besides, it was quite in accord with Montfort's concerns at the time.

When he died on April 28, 1716, at the close of the mission at St. Laurent-sur-Sèvre, there were two priests with him: Fr. Vatel, whom he recruited at La Rochelle in February 1715, when he stopped him from embarking for Canada, and Fr. René Mulot, whom Montfort had recruited in October of the same year, when Father René had asked him to preach a mission for his brother, the pastor of Saint-Pompain. Humanly speaking, neither of the two seemed to possess the qualities required to continue Montfort's work. At the moment of his death, they were without any binding ties to the missionary's small team. And yet they would take up the torch. Montfort's prayer had been heard.

The spirituality that animated this great saint is treated throughout this Handbook, but especially in the articles *God, Wisdom, Holy Spirit, Cross, Mary,* and *Montfort Spirituality.*

A. Bossard

III. The Inculturation of Montfort's Message Today

According to the criteria of modern hagiography, we must frankly ask this question: what can the life of a saint from centuries ago mean for men and women who live in a culture and place so different from his own?

This question is more than apropos of Montfort since he has at last broken out of the restraining limits of western France. The beatification (1888) and the canonization (1947) have made the holy missionary a worldwide figure and placed him outside provincial borders. The extraordinary distribution of especially TD and SM in numerous languages has contributed much to making him known almost everywhere. Furthermore, the presence of the montfort family throughout the world has made Saint Louis Marie a citizen of all continents; he is surely at home in the non-Western world.

Lastly, to speak about Montfort and forget the necessity of an appropriate inculturation would be equivalent to a literal repetition, of a fundamentalist nature. It would contradict the healthy creativity that the Spirit brings to the different ages of the Church.[53]

Pouring Montfort into the mold of our times is a very delicate operation. Father de Montfort could be manipulated and reduced to particular cultural descriptions. One could focus on certain aspects of the saint, as he relates to certain values or aspirations in vogue today in various cultures. Montfort would then become a kind of litmus paper, changing his colors to fit the cultural conviction of each and everyone. With this sort of manipulation, Montfort would lose his uniqueness. He would in a sense be created by the whims and options of others. But it should be remembered that Montfort cannot be enclosed within a limited framework. He can often serve as an antidote to evils inherent in diverse cultures.

Members of each culture should interpret Montfort according to their own symbolic and ecclesial world and make him part of their own milieu. But first, at the base of every systematic reflection, one should stay in touch with the living experience of Montfort and assimilate his inner evangelical dynamism. This kind of work is made easier by the fact that Montfort, even though he belongs to his own time, presents a uniqueness that, in a certain sense, places him above and beyond his own century and distinguishes him from various contemporaries.

This inquiry, although made primarily from a Western perspective, is conscious of the fact that the montfort family, as with the Church at large, presently finds itself in a vast range of cultures, which are continually evolving. Fundamental values emerge, however, that constitute the common patrimony of the industrialized world: a keen sense of personal and social liberty, grown more so since the crumbling of totalitarian systems; a desire for a high standard of living, of quality of life; justice on a worldwide scale to eliminate the vast ranks of poverty and marginalization; harmony between the sexes; etc. But with these common aspirations, there cohabits fears about the future of the world: the apocalyptic man has been born, divided between certitude and fear.

This contemporary man who encounters Montfort clearly perceives that he is not able to get around certain of his a priori challenges.

1. God, the Absolute: Goal of all Peoples

The most profound and essential message of Montfort seems to be that expressed by G. de Luca: "The first impression that I had in reading one of his biographies for the first time was the following (which was his design and his motto): God Alone

. . . . He did not inhabit the world, he did not reside in himself; his home was God. Every time he went out among men, he seemed to burn like a raging fire from some secret and profound source. He carried the anger and the splendor of such an eruption in the night. He entered into solitude to be with God. He went out among men in order to give God."[54]

In truth, this sense of a transcendent and condescending God dominates the experience of Montfort. His life is a hymn to the presence of God (H 24). He speaks of God as the totally Other, (*totaliter aliter*): *"The Most High, the Incomprehensible, the Inaccessible, He who Is"* (TD 117), before Whom we are nothing. And yet the God of Montfort is incarnate in Jesus, close to each creature, *"infinitely condescending and proportioned to his weakness"* (SM 20).

The instruction given to the Daughters of Wisdom *"Do all your works in the presence of God and for God alone"* (RW 138) Montfort had realized in his own life. He disappeared in order that all the glory would return to God: "*What is it I ask of you? Nothing for myself, all for your glory*" (PM 6).This theocentric view he borrowed from one of his preferred authors, the archdeacon Boudon, who had written two works entitled *God Alone.* This motto must not be interpreted in a philosophical or metaphysical sense. God Alone exists, whereas creatures are nothing. "When Montfort speaks of 'renouncing oneself,' . . . the 'oneself' that he wishes us to detach ourselves from is not exactly our personality but, rather, the base of egotism within us. That comes also from the fact that we do not always put ourselves in the same perspective as his, a truly mystical perspective."[55] Such a view indicates the primacy of the merciful action of God, Who does not destroy either the human person or his or her collaboration. It only excludes a redemption brought about by his or her own initiative independent of the plan of God: "*It is you alone who will make this assembly; if man puts his hand to it first, nothing will come about*" (PM 26).

The mystical perspective is the fundamental interpretative key to the historical experience of Montfort, which can be defined as a life in rhythm with God. This explains why prayer occupies the day of this holy missionary, why it animates his retreats and inflames the contemplative dimension of his life. His holiness consists in "letting God do it," not in a quietist sense but in the sense of being totally disposed to His action, putting all his energy into serving the God of salvation. Montfort's intense missionary activity as well as the constancy of his charitable service to the poor are evidence of the fact that he recognized the primacy of God. He saw that this does not bring about man's demise but, on the contrary, leads to a radical commitment to the divine project—to bringing life in its abundance.

For a man or woman of today, taken up with secular activism or imprisoned in the convoluted materialistic and individualistic values of our age, Montfort is both a challenge and an alternative. He is a witness to an encounter with God in the concreteness of one's life and of history. He is a mediator, in Christ, between historicity and divinity. From this viewpoint, the unique quality of Montfort is his call for us to turn away from an existence that is morally trite because it is not rooted in God. Rather, he calls us to live from supernatural grace which infuses nature with a vitality and life, to realize its full "human" character.[56] In this way, we overcome the conflict between a saint as an "exceptional individual" and the call of everyone to sanctity. We thus discover in Montfort's spirituality a vocational path suitable for every Christian. Truly, we are all called to have God at the center of our heart, to have Him as the master of our lives, to have Him as our single source of meaning, to recognize his sovereignty. Montfort took God seriously. And he drew from this recognition its consequences. Thus he lived in God's presence from moment to moment, dialoguing and collaborating from moment to moment along his life path.

2. Abandoning oneself to divine logic, to Christ Wisdom

To make a place for God in one's own life is to receive His logic, which is entirely transcendent, disconcerting, and paradoxical. Inspired by Isa 55:8, Montfort cries out: *"Oh! that the thoughts and the ways of Eternal Wisdom are far from and different from those of humans, even the wisest!"* (LEW 167). Further, the holy missionary accepted the ways of God without debating them. He had arrived. He had come to Wisdom by totally giving himself to Wisdom (LEW 59, 132). He understood that true Wisdom is *"a savory science, sapida scientia, or the taste of God and of his truth"* (LEW 13). Therefore we can legitimately say that for Louis Marie, Wisdom "is the 'eye of the heart' open to the logic of God. It is, in reality, the knowledge of Christ, the participation in the light of the One who is substantial and uncreated Wisdom."[57]

As very few others have, Montfort perceived in a living way the difference, the opposition between the Wisdom of God and that of men. This appears concretized in the model of wisdom of his time and ours, which is anthropocentric rather than theocentric. Distancing himself from it, he describes it well in LEW 76-79.[58] Montfort sees *"respectable man"* as the personification of *"humanistic man"*—one closed to divine revelation and thus *"anti-Gospel man": "A worldly sage is a man who, being led only by the light of his senses and human reason, only seeks to cover himself with the appearance of being Christian and respectable, without caring too much about pleasing God"* (LEW 76).

Louis Marie's horizon of reality is altogether different. It is the divine logic revealed in Christ Wisdom. In him he learned the value of the two realities that the world refuses to appreciate: the Cross and the poor. According to a sublime and incomprehensible plan, Wisdom chose the Cross to save the world (LEW 168).

Wisdom became flesh, incorporated himself in the world in such a way, united himself with the Cross in such a way that we can truly say with Montfort that *"Wisdom is the Cross and the Cross is Wisdom"* (LEW 180). It follows from this that the Cross *"is also the witness that God asks of us to show him that we love him"* (LEW 176), in such a way that we cannot call ourselves Christians without being *"friends of the Cross"* (FC 3). Montfort went so far as to pronounce, at Vertou in 1709, this paradoxical phrase: *"No Cross, what a Cross!"* meaning that the Cross is inevitable for one who wishes to follow Jesus (Mt 16:24). From our impoverished human experience of reason, the Cross remains incomprehensible (LEW 178, 179), but for the person who accepts it, it is the source of superhuman Wisdom: *"It enlightens the mind and gives to it more intelligence than all the books in the world"* (LEW 176). Truly, the Cross introduces us to a new knowledge of God unknown to the world of antiquity: Revelation under the guise of weakness, defeat, absurdity and folly. The Cross reveals a *kenosis* of God, which does not simply bring us down but, rather, raises us to the divine logic of solidarity and subsidiarity. The Cross breaks apart our myopic view of justice, which values money—as a substitute for Wisdom, as a substitute for the logic of love, which demands self-sacrifice and forgiveness. It is the value of this logic that will stop the spiral of violence and buy back a sense of the other by a merciful love.

By introducing us to Divine Wisdom, Montfort's role here is one of initiator; it is, however, important to understand and follow this Wisdom as it flows from his teaching.

Wisdom is not identified uniquely with the Cross but also with the poor. Basing himself on the word of Jesus, who identifies himself with man in need (Mt 25:40, 45; cf. H 18:8), Montfort defines the poor man as *"the lieutenant of Jesus Christ"* and, even more, as *"Jesus Christ himself"* (H 17:14). Montfort offers us an eloquent sign of this vision of faith in the episode at Dinan (1706), when he hoisted upon his shoulders the ulcerous poor man whom he met on his trip and knocked at the door of the missionary house, crying out: *"Open to Jesus Christ!"*[59] He had not elaborated a theology on the nature of the presence of Christ in the poor, but through gestures like this one, he demanded it. In any case, our neighbor remains the sacrament of our union with Christ. Our poor neighbor is our forgotten neighbor, the Christ who has been rejected down through the centuries.

Faced with the failure of modern post-Enlightenment ideologists and ideologies and their discoveries, we cannot fail to notice the overwhelming need for us to rediscover Divine Wisdom. It is incarnate Wisdom who will teach us an art of living that will help us avoid our past failures. Vatican Council II affirms this: "Our times, more so than past centuries, have need of that Wisdom, in order that all these new discoveries may become more humane. In fact, the future of the world is in peril unless wiser men rise up" (GS 15).

3. Regard for the feminine point of view in Christianity

Montfort was—and no one contests this point—one of the saints who received the charism to give a very high value to the person and to the role of Mary in the spiritual life. It is evident that his vision is not limited to the figure of Mary but is broadened to embrace the whole panorama of salvation history.

The mother of Jesus, in fact, is a maternal presence and an ideal model in the life of Montfort,[60] who, in a significant gesture, set forth as one of his last wishes that his heart be buried *"under the step of the altar of the Blessed Virgin"* (W).

Mary, as every one of his works shows, is the structure of his thought. She is fundamental to Wisdom's plan: in Wisdom's journey to mankind and in mankind's journey to Wisdom (LEW 105-108, 203-222). In the design of God, Mary is the maternal Mediatrix of grace, in such a way that without her one cannot attain holiness (SM 6-22). Her role is essential in the mystery of the Incarnation. Her action in the world is necessary to the mystery of the Church. Devotion to her becomes an indispensable condition for the preparation of the reign of Jesus Christ (TD 1-13). The passing of the reign of sin into the reign of Jesus Christ cannot come about without a full out-pouring of the Spirit. Therefore, Mary must have a role in the end times, since she cooperates with the Paraclete in bringing about the great salvific work of history (SM 58-59; TD 49-59; PM 15). In the *"Covenant Contract"* with God that Montfort called for in his missions, Mary was the foundation of faith in Christ and in his Cross (CG 1). To separate Montfort from Mary, would be to deprive his teaching of its essential component.

This attention given to Mary is part of his general tendency to value the presence of woman within the Church and to draw attention to the feminine aspects of Christianity. He, in fact, underlines two feminine attributes of God: Providence and Wisdom. He calls Providence *"the Mother of Love"* (H 28:19) and Wisdom *"the spouse"* with whom we can contract a true spiritual marriage (LEW 54; L 20).

Devotion to the Blessed Virgin becomes for him a means to uncover the tenderness of God (H 52:11), his maternal visage. As Fr. Zundel already observed before John Paul I: "God is more Mother than all mothers. God is infinitely Mother: as much as He is infinitely Father. And perhaps precisely there is the most profound significance of devotion to the Virgin in the Church of her Son: . . . to manifest in her, as in a living sacrament, the maternal tenderness of God."[61]

The Marian devotion Montfort proposes to us undoubtedly carries with it many different aspects: theological, Christological, Trinitarian, ecclesiological, anthropological, eschatological, etc. It is the task of his disciples to explicate these essential dimensions, following the directives of Vatican Council II and of MC. Marian spirituality especially must not be separated from the promotion of woman in civil and Church law. That Mary is a woman is not a petty fact. It is a dimension that characterizes her whole being. It explains the maternal mission which she has been given. A person who has recourse to Montfort and discovers the saint's profound devotion to the Mother of Jesus can not possibly ignore the invitation to welcome her within his or her own spiritual life, by a total gift of self. We must go to God through a thorough examination of certain aspects of our way of loving that can only be expressed in feminine and maternal terms. Then, in the name of the "blessed among women" (Lk 1:42), we will learn to treat women as persons called to assume their own unique roles and responsibilities in society and in the Church.

4. A life oriented toward the coming of the reign of Christ into the world

Whatever different interpretations one might have of Montfort's life, he will always remain a missionary. That is a too evident fact, given his actions, for anyone to ignore. In fact, we might even define Montfort as the personification of the Church's missionary calling.

There are two hermeneutical keys to understanding Montfort's missionary vocation: a. his sense of the past, his recovery of the apostolic life of Jesus and of the Apostles; and b. his sense of the future, his vision of preparing for the reign of God. Montfort must be seen against the horizon of the end times.

Montfort suffers from that agony of true missionaries, the urgency of proclaiming the Gospel of salvation. Montfort's urgency is best expressed in his elaborate strategy for the Company of Mary and for every person who accepts his Company's call to consecrate himself or herself to Christ through Mary.

The last years of Montfort's life coincided with a renewed interest in those foundations which he had already envisioned in the early years of his priesthood. Around 1713 he drew up RM. In 1715, he composed RW. As he sensed his energies failing, Montfort never retreated into himself but, rather, looked ahead to the future. He foresaw the coming of the reign of Jesus on earth. He saw this reign in both the divine promise and the expectation of the faithful. He saw that to realize this reign would be the fulfillment of a new Pentecost. He saw it as a deluge of the fire of love, as an interior coming, as a continuation in time of salvation history, as the ultimate renewal of the sanctity of the Church, one that would transform the world through the preaching of the Gospel to all the nations. This transformation he saw to be the work of the entire Trinity, especially through the Holy Spirit, with the collaboration with Mary, in preparing the apostles of the end times and sending them forth into the world to establish there the reign of Jesus Christ.

Montfort considered himself to be a missionary of the end times, which he believed to have already begun (TD 50). Montfort's missions were addressed to all people. They were not confined to people of any specific social dimension. In fact, if we closely examine the text of CG, we see that it does not go beyond a personal commitment to live faithfully the promises of Baptism. TD was intended to extend Montfort's mission of preaching into writing (TD 110) and designed to prepare people for the reign of Christ in the world. By implication, it demonstrates his call to conversion and reform, which he points to clearly in PM 17.

The means or privileged instrument to attain this end is the gift of oneself to Mary. It is the school of filial life toward the Father. It is fidelity to Christ and openness to the Holy Spirit. From Montfort's point of view, devotion to Mary is in no way confined to practices of devotion or to an individualized interior life. It is essentially apostolic and oriented toward the future. Mary brings us into an intimate relationship with the Holy Spirit in the final phase of the Church. She brings us into the reign of Christ. The Marian devotion proposed by Montfort is missionary in character. It is a Mariology that is Spirit-filled and Christological—a rarity today.

The living witness of Montfort gives us a uniquely personal vision of the Church as God's people. Montfort's message is one of personal relationship, of love. His message was not the mission that people came to hear. Rather, his mission was the people themselves who attended the missions. They were the mission. Persons were the reason for and measure of mission: human persons in relation to the Persons of God through Mary, persons serving God's reign in the world. For this seventeenth-century Breton missionary, mission was the heart of the Church. It was her essential form, her raison d'etre in the world.

S. De Fiores

Notes: (1) Pauvert, *Vie du vénérable Louis-Marie Grignion de Montfort (Life of the Venerable Louis Marie Grignion de Montfort)*, Oudin, Paris 1875, xx. The author mentions the biographies already published of Grandet, Picot de Clorivière, and Dalin, and also the manuscripts of Blain and Besnard (p. xx-xxiv). (2) Cf. *Bibliography of Saint Louis-Marie de Montfort*, in *Echo des Missions* 223 (1954), 3-12; *Special Monographs on Saint Louis-Marie de Montfort*, ibid., 227 (1954), n.p. The number of biographies of Montfort, some short, others more developed, up to 1954 is seventy-nine. Since that date, at least thirty-four others have been published. (3) Cf. P. Pourrat, *Biographies spirituelles (Spiritual Biographies)*, in DSAM 1 (1932), 1715. (4) Grandet, iii, 2-4. (5) Pauvert, *Vie du vénérable Louis-Marie*, xxiii. (6) Blain, *passim*. We find in Blain "oratorical procedures that are those of a preacher more than of a historian." E. Lett, *Les premiers biographes de Saint J.-B. de la Salle (The First Biographies of Saint J.B. de la Salle)*, Ligel, Paris 1954, 339. (7) Reproaches aimed at Grandet by later biographers: e.g. Pauvert, *Vie du vénérable Louis-Marie*, xx; P. Eijckeler, *Le testament de Saint Louis-Marie Grignion de Montfort (The Testament of Saint Louis-Marie Grignion de Montfort)*, Van Aelst, Maestricht 1953, 202-204; L. Perouas, Grignion de Montfort, les pauvres et les missions, Cerf, Paris 1966, 137, 141 (on the confraternities and the schools). (8) Bremond considers Grandet

The small wooden statue carved by St. Louis Marie and placed on top of his walking stick. Photo by Robert Houser.

The front of the restored house in Montfort-la-Cane (today Montfort-sur-Meu) where Louis Marie was born in 1673.

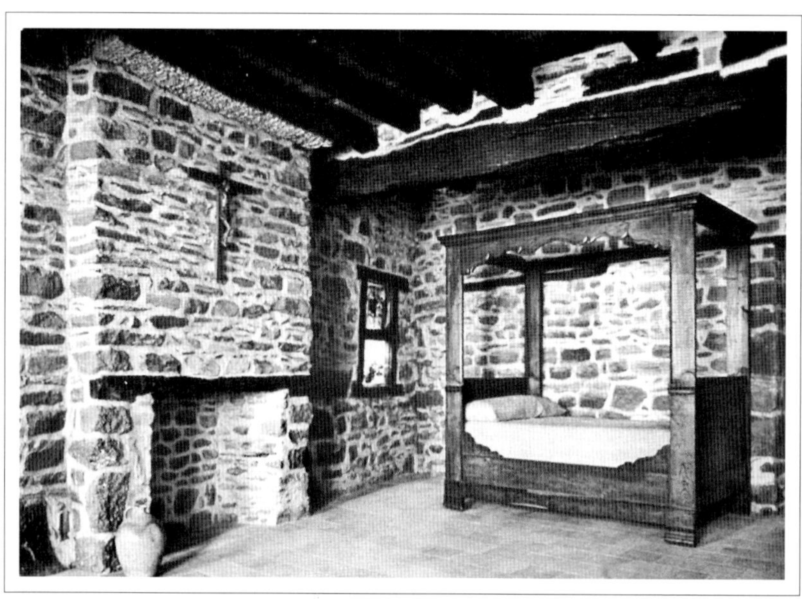

Room where Montfort was born in 1673.

Ancient gate to the village of Montfort which dated to the Middle Ages and which was demolished in 1897. (Cl.Arch. Photo).

Nineteenth century painting of Montfort and the Meu River. Photo by Aartsen.

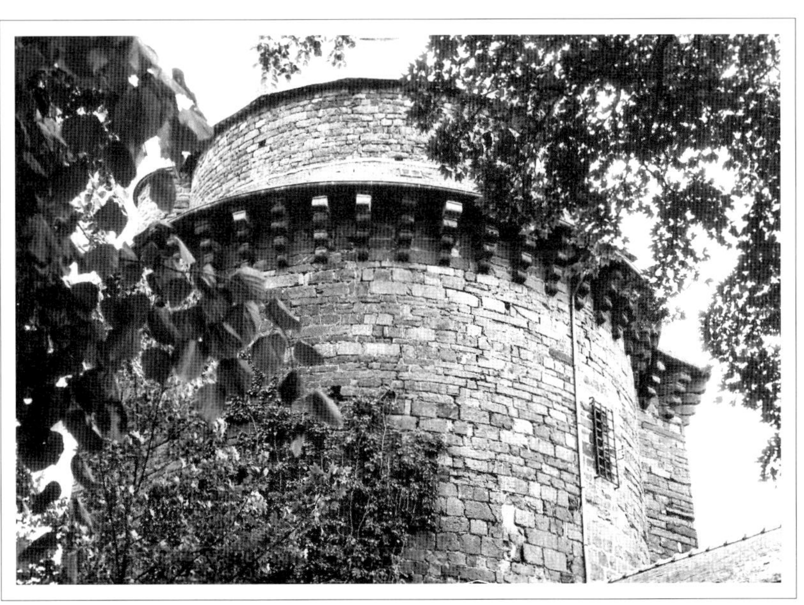

Medieval ramparts of the village of Montfort. Photo by Aartsen.

The church of St. John the Baptist where Montfort was baptized.

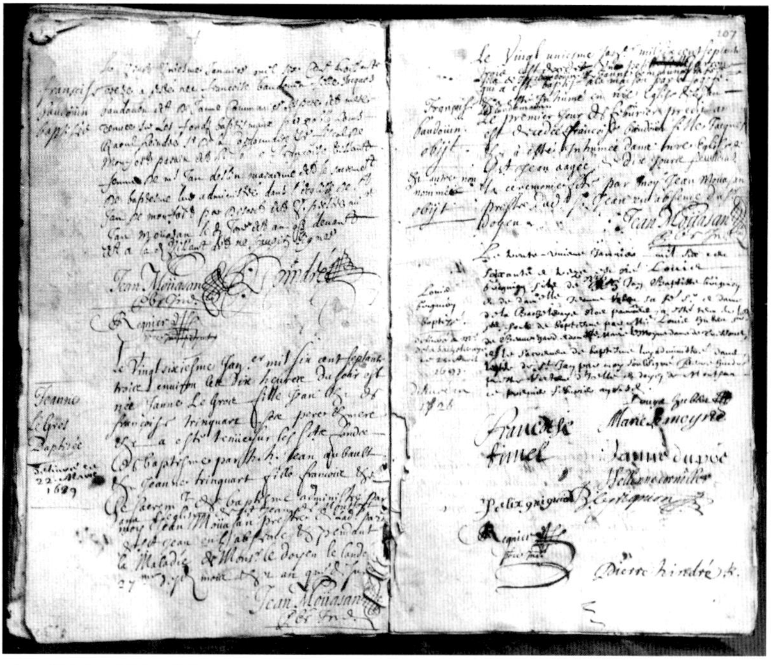

Louis Marie's baptismal record. Photo by Aartsen.

The Bois-Marquer farmhouse in Iffendic where St. Louis Marie lived as a child from 1675-1685. Photo by Aartsen.

Fireplace in kitchen of Bois-Marquer. Photo by Aartsen.

Map of the period showing Montfort, Iffendic and environs.

Montfort's parish church in Iffendic.
Photo by Aartsen.

Font in the parish church of Iffendic where St. Louis Marie renewed his baptismal promises.

Interior of the parish church at Iffendic. Photo by Aartsen.

The city of Rennes as it looked in the 17th century.

The Jesuit College of St. Thomas Becket. Picture preserved in the Rennes Archeological Museum.

The bridge at Cesson over the Vilaine River. Montfort met a beggar here while on his way from Rennes to Paris to begin studying for the priesthood in 1692. Louis Marie gave the man his money and exchanged clothes with him. From that time forward, the Saint lived by divine providence.

Painting that depicts Montfort offering his cloak to the beggar at the Cesson bridge.

Notre Dame Cathedral in Paris from an early 18th century drawing. Here, prior to ordination in 1699, Louis Marie knelt and pronounced a vow of chastity through Mary to Jesus.

The Church of St. Sulpice. Here in the chapel of the Virgin, Montfort said his first mass.

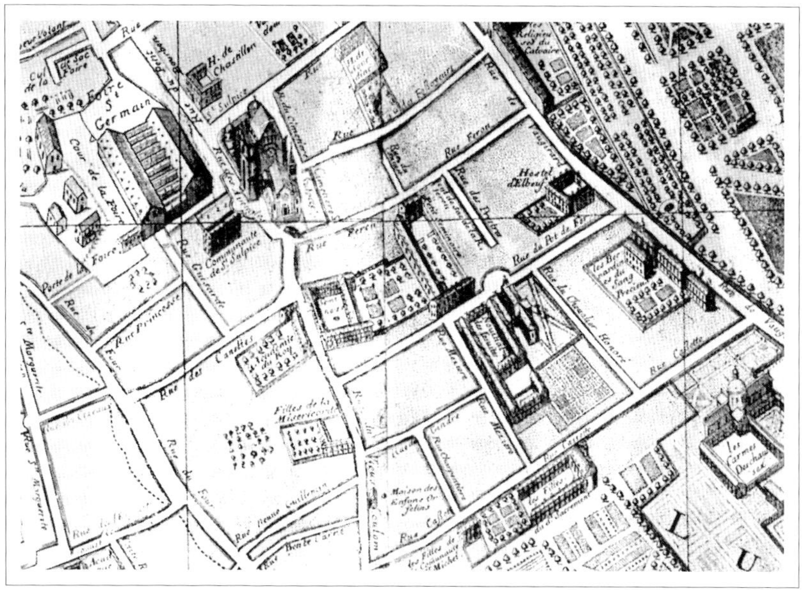

The St. Sulpice quarter of Paris where Montfort studied for the priesthood, from a 1710 drawing.

Jean Jacques Olier (1608-1657). Parish priest of St. Sulpice and founder of the seminary which Montfort attended.

François Leschassier (1641-1725). Fourth Superior General of St. Sulpice.

Claude Bottu de la Barmondière (1631-1694). Parish priest of St. Sulpice from 1678 until 1689 when he founded the community of Poor Clerics which admitted St. Louis Marie de Montfort.

Bazan de Flamanville, Bishop of Elne near Perpignan. On May 5, 1700, Louis Marie was ordained to the priesthood by this schoolmate from the seminary of St. Sulpice.

Chartres Cathedral. Located on the Beauce plain west of Paris, this great gothic shrine to Our Lady, is a medieval masterpiece in stone, glass and wood containing a great relic of the Blessed Mother—the veil that tradition says she wore at the birth of Jesus. St. Louis Marie went on pilgrimage here prior to his ordination to the priesthood in 1699. Photo by Aartsen.

Mont St. Michel. A city, mountain, monastery, cathedral located on the channel coast. Like Chartres, it became a central place of pilgrimage in the Middle Ages. An island at high tide, part of the mainland at low tide, it is dedicated to St. Michael the Archangel. Montfort went on pilgrimage here upon his return from Rome in 1706 after being made "apostolic missionary" by the Holy Father. Photo by Aartsen.

Michael the Archangel miniature from a 13th Century Psalter. Montfort was especially devoted to Michael whose name means "who is like unto God". The archangel is revered in the tradition as prince, protector and warrior. He is venerated as leader of God's people in their battle against the forces of evil and untruth. (TD 8, PM 28, RM 61). Photo by Aartsen.

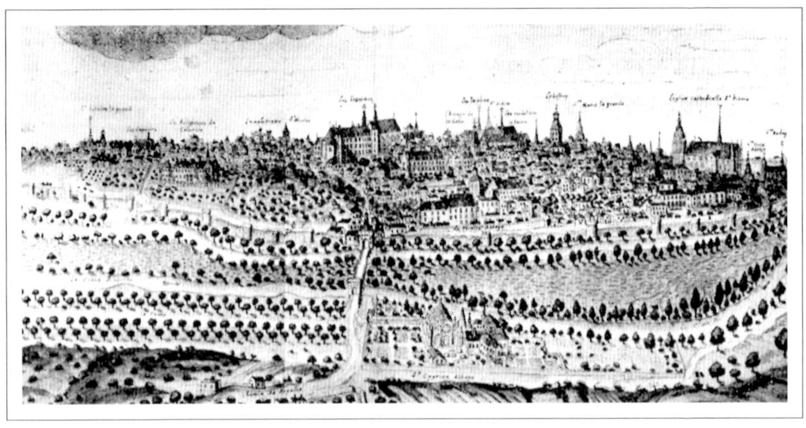

Poitiers at the time of Montfort. During the years 1701 to 1705, Louis Marie was chaplain at the Poorhouse, began his mission work, and met Marie Louise Trichet here. Photo by Bloudet Gay

Notre Dame La Grande in Poitiers. Montfort, during his time in the city, loved to pray in this church. Photo by Leuy-Neurdin

The Poorhouse in Poitiers where Montfort was chaplain, and where the Congregation of the Daughters of Wisdom was founded. Photo by V. Belebeau.

Entrance to the Chapel in Montbernage. A barn used as a dance hall by the young people called la Grange de la Bergerie was renovated by Montfort and transformed into this Chapel of Mary, Queen of All Hearts.

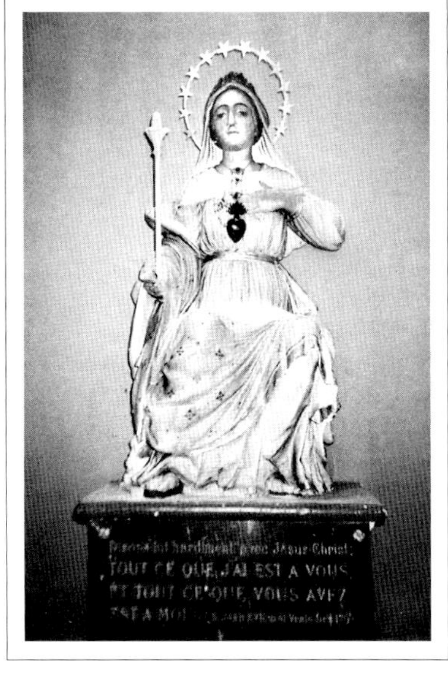

Statue of Mary, Queen of All Hearts, placed in the Montbernage Chapel by Montfort during his mission of 1705.

Portrait and signature of Marie Louise of Jesus, the first Daughter of Wisdom. Born in 1684, she met Montfort in 1702 at a retreat the Saint gave at the Poitiers poorhouse in preparation for Pentecost.

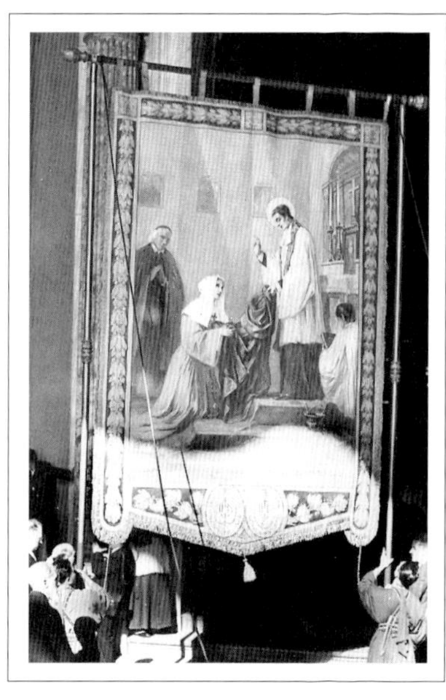

Banner from Montfort's canonization ceremony in 1947. It depicts Marie Louise receiving her habit from Montfort in Poitiers, February 2, 1703.
Photo by G. Felici.

Julien Trichet, father of Marie Louise. A devout man who was a respected magistrate in the city of Poitiers. Photo by Aartsen.

Françoise Trichet, mother of Marie Louise, a woman of great faith who gave birth and successfully raised six children.
Photo by Aartsen.

The old Jesuit college in Poitiers that later became the town hall. Students from this school helped Montfort in his apostolic work.

John Claude de la Poype de Vertieu, Bishop of Poitiers from 1702 to 1732. He favored Montfort and called him back from Mont Valérien to work with the poor of Poitiers in 1703.

The Calvary of Mont Valérien where Montfort went to serve a troubled community of hermits. It is said that it was this Calvary that inspired him to build Pontchateau.

Classical engraving of Montfort, the Catechist, spontaneously teaching young people in front of Notre Dame la Grande in Poitiers.

The city and shrine of Loretto. Montfort, travelling to Rome on foot in order to obtain the Holy Father's blessing visited here in 1706. Believed to be the house of the Virgin Mary's Annunciation, tradition says that it was transported from Nazareth in the thirteenth century.

Clement XI, whose papacy spanned the years 1700 to 1721, on June 6, 1706, granted Montfort an audience, blessed him, and bestowed on him the title, "Apostolic Missionary".

A view of the Vatican and St. Peter's Basilica from the Tiber River with Hadrian's tomb in the foreground. In Montfort's papal audience, Montfort was told by the Holy Father not to go to the foreign missions, but to remain in France under obedience to the bishops, "By this means, God will bless all you do."

Cardinal Tommasi. The Holy Father's confessor. There is the possibility that while in Rome, Montfort was the guest of the Theatines of St. Andrew, and thus of Father Tommasi, a theologian and future Cardinal who was later beatified. It has been said that he introduced Montfort to Clement XI.

Brother Mathurin Rangeard (1687-1750). The first Montfort brother. Louis Marie met him in Poitiers in 1705. He assisted Montfort on his missions by leading the singing of hymns, reciting the Rosary, and teaching catechism.

Claude Poullart des Places, Founder of the Congregation of the Holy Spirit. Montfort visited with him while in Paris in 1703.

The Temple of St. John. An ancient fourth century baptistry in Poitiers with a pool for baptism by immersion. It is said that St. Hilary was baptised here. Montfort did some restoration work on the structure.

The poorhouse of Salpêtrière on the Left Bank in Paris. By an edict of Louis XIV in 1656, all beggars and vagrants were to be shut up in this building. It housed five thousand dispossessed people when Montfort ministered there in 1703.

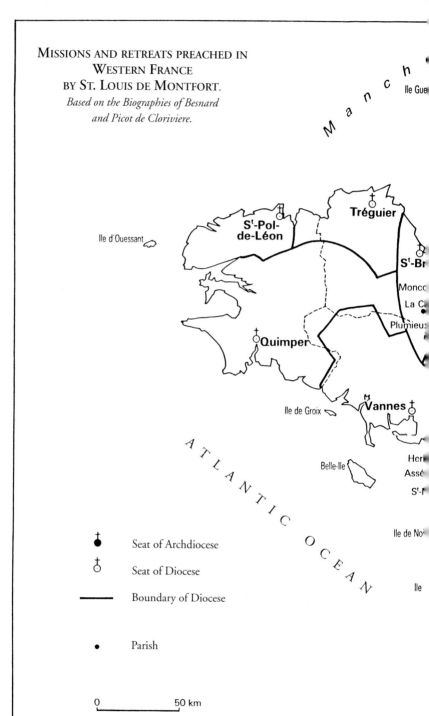

Missions and retreats preached in Western France by St. Louis de Montfort.

Based on the Biographies of Besnard and Picot de Cloriviere.

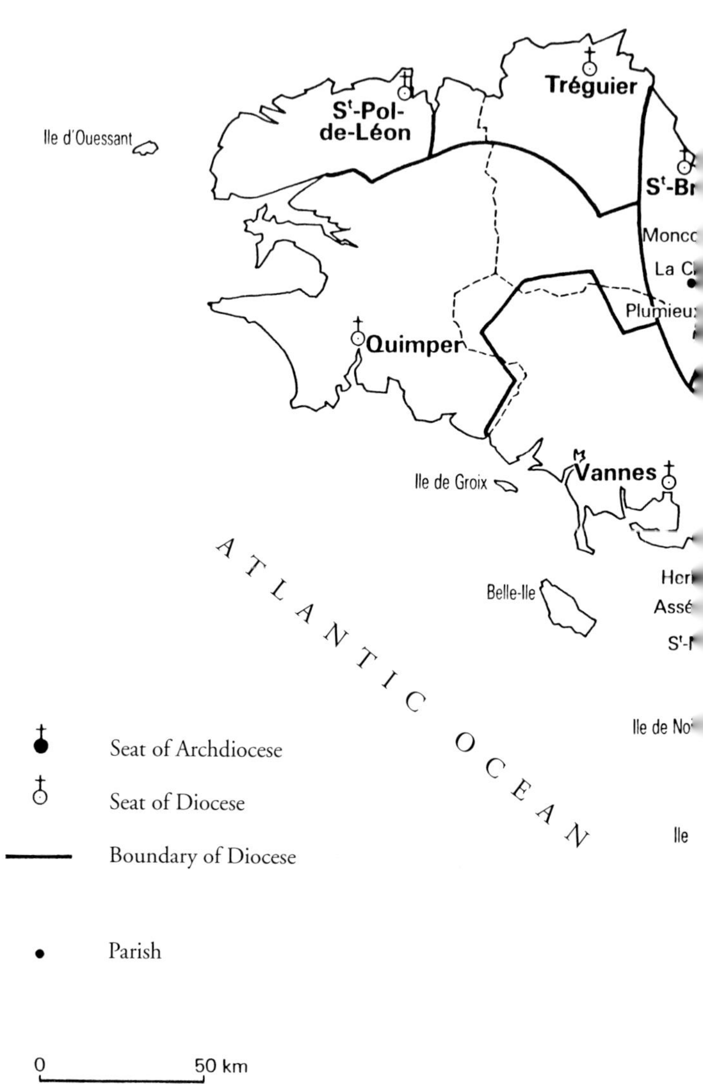

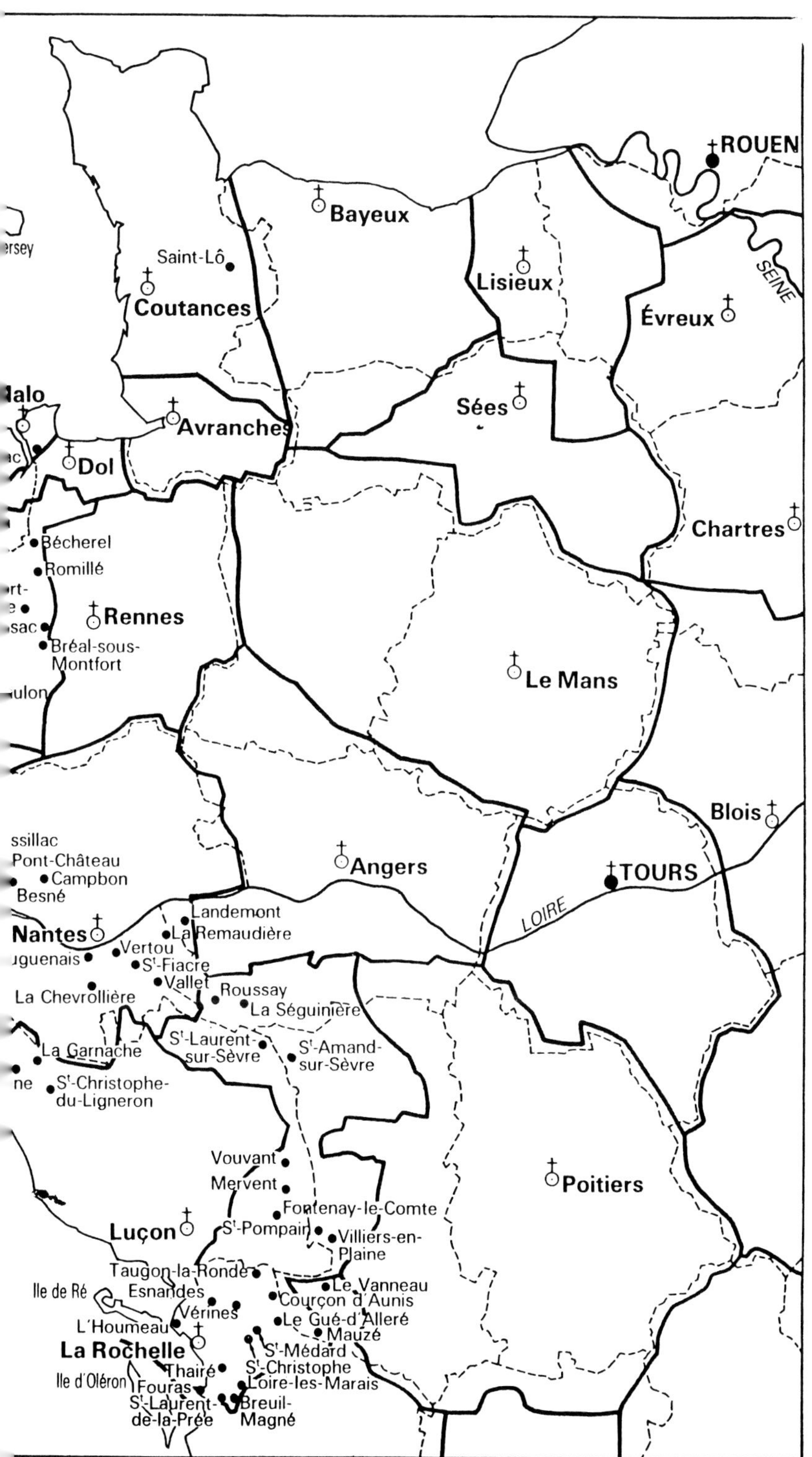
ROUEN
Bayeux
Lisieux
SEINE
Évreux
Saint-Lô
Coutances
Sées
Avranches
Dol
Chartres
Bécherel
Romillé
Rennes
Bréal-sous-Montfort
Le Mans
Blois
ssillac
Pont-Château
Campbon
Besné
Angers
TOURS
LOIRE
Landemont
Nantes
La Remaudière
Vertou
St-Fiacre
Vallet
Roussay
La Chevrollière
La Séguinière
St-Laurent-sur-Sèvre
St-Amand-sur-Sèvre
La Garnache
St-Christophe-du-Ligneron
Vouvant
Mervent
Poitiers
Fontenay-le-Comte
Luçon
St-Pompain
Villiers-en-Plaine
Taugon-la-Ronde
Ile de Ré
Esnandes
Le Vanneau
Courçon d'Aunis
Vérines
L'Houmeau
Le Gué-d'Alleré
Mauzé
La Rochelle
St-Médard
Thairé
St-Christophe
Ile d'Oléron
Fouras
Loire-les-Marais
St-Laurent-de-la-Prée
Breuil-Magné

An eighteenth century engraving of Montfort as Missionary of the Cross. Artist unknown.

Bronze sculpture of Montfort venerating the cross. Signed by L. J. Briton and P. Belquin, 1886.

Mosaic of Montfort by Fr. Sandro Leidi, a Montfort Missionary.

Roadside statue of Montfort in Venée. Photo by Aartsen.

Baptism of St. Louis de Montfort: a ceramic by Fr. Leidi.

Displayed by the local parish priest is a Cross erected by Montfort during his mission to St. Pompain. It is preserved in a tiny chapel there.

A modern painting by Giulio Carminati portrays Montfort in 1706, carrying a leper back to the community house, and calling out at the entrance, "Open the door for Jesus Christ."

The door to the community house in Dinan, where tradition says the event of Montfort and the leper took place. Photo by Aartsen.

La Rochelle as it appeared in the late seventeenth century.

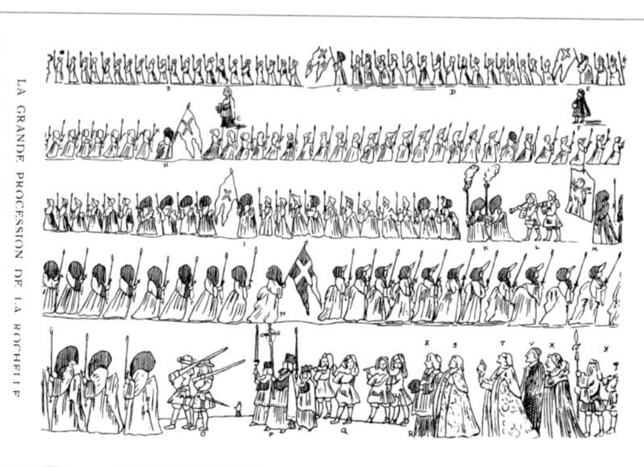

The Great Procession of La Rochelle organized by Montfort in 1711.

Etienne de Champflour, a Sulpician priest who became Bishop of La Rochelle from 1703 to 1724.

This little hermitage was given to Montfort. It is located in the parish of St. Eloi in La Rochelle. Louis Marie came here often between missions and retreats. Here he wrote True Devotion to the Blessed Virgin and The Rule of the Daughters of Wisdom.

The Calvary of Pontchateau as it appears today. Photo by Aartsen.

CONTRACT D'ALLIANCE
avec Dieu.

Vœux ou promesses du St. Baptême.

1. JE croy fermement toutes les veritez du St. Evangile de Jesus-Christ.

2. Je renonce pour jamais au Demon, au monde, au peché & à moi-même.

3. Je promets moyennant la grace de Dieu qui ne me manquera point, de garder fidélement tous les Commandemens de Dieu & de l'Eglise, évitant le peché mortel & ses occasions, entr'autres les mauvaises compagnies.

4. Je me donne tout entier à JESUS-CHRIST par les mains de MARIE, pour porter ma Croix à sa suite tous les jours de ma vie.

5. Je croy que si je garde fidélement ces promesses jusqu'à la mort, je seray eternellement sauvé, mais que si je ne les garde pas, je seray éternellement damné. En foi dequoi j'ai soussigné.

Fait en face d'Eglise dans la Paroisse de
ce l'an 1709.

Contrat d' Alliance signé par le P. de Montfort.

Donné par lui à la Mission de Pont-Château en [illegible],
il a été conservé dans la famille Paboeuf de Travers
et donné à la résidence le 8 février [illegible].

Covenant Contract with God. Montfort had these printed and passed out in 1709. This copy signed by him is displayed in the chapel at Pontchateau. Photo by Aartsen.

The crucifix from Father de Montfort's first calvary, preserved in the chapel of Pontchateau. Photo by Aartsen.

An eighteenth century engraving of Montfort preaching a parish mission.

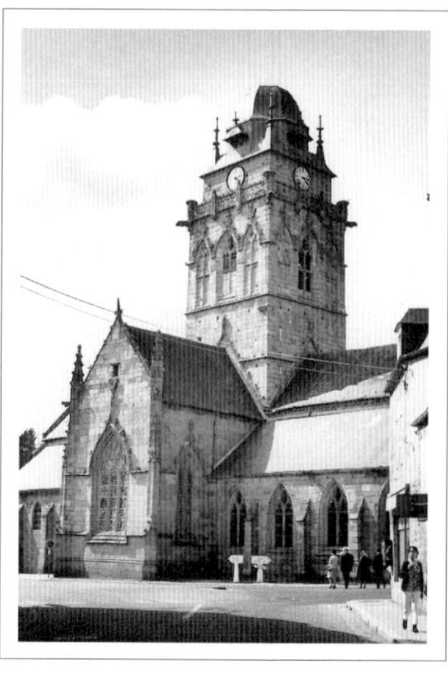

The Church of Villedieu-les-Poèles, a shrine of the diocese of Avranches, where Montfort said Mass on August 15, 1714. Photo by Aartsen.

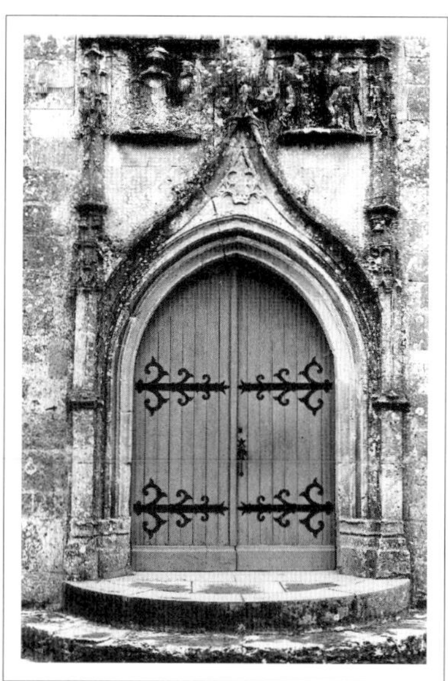

Entrance to the Church of St. Pompain where Montfort preached a mission. Photo by Aartsen.

Door of the church at Vouvant in which Montfort preached a mission. Photo by Aartsen.

The cross of Father de Montfort in the forest of Mervent.

A contemporary icon by Vittoria Paravincini Bagliani depicts Montfort at the cave in Mervent. Photo by Robert Houser.

Top row: The Annunciation; Montfort, Apostle of Mary. Center row: Montfort, Father of the Poor; Montfort, Apostle of the Cross. Bottom row: Montfort, Prayer for Missionaries; Montfort, Apostle of the End Times (All Frescos by Jaap Min, 1953)

Chêne Vert. The first residence of the Montfort Missionaries in St. Laurent-sur-Sèvre (1722-1723). The house was later occupied by Mother Marie Louise of Jesus and the first Daughters of Wisdom.

Maison Longue. The first residence of the Daughters of Wisdom in St. Laurent-sur-Sèvre (1720-1723). The house was later occupied by the Montfort Missionaries.

Saumur, Montfort led a pilgrimage from the parish of St. Pompain to Our Lady of Ardilliers. Photo by Aartsen.

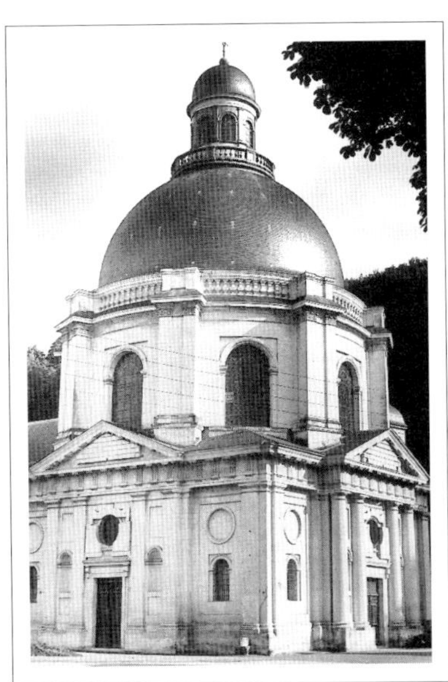

Chapel of Our Lady of Ardilliers in Saumur. Photo by Aartsen.

Altar of the Virgin Mary in the chapel of Our Lady of Ardilliers. Photo by Aartsen.

Panoramic view of St. Laurent-sur-Sèvre. Photo by Aartsen.

Interior of the parish church of St. Laurent-sur-Sèvre.

The old parish church of St. Laurent-sur-Sèvre's chapel of the Blessed Virgin. On the left is the original tomb of Montfort.

René Mulot. Fr. de Montfort's first successor as Superior of the Montfort family (1715 to 1749).

Gabriel Deshayes (1767 to 1841) restored Montfort's work after the agony of the revolution.

Jean Baptiste Blain. College friend of St. Louis Marie, author of a Memoir on Montfort.

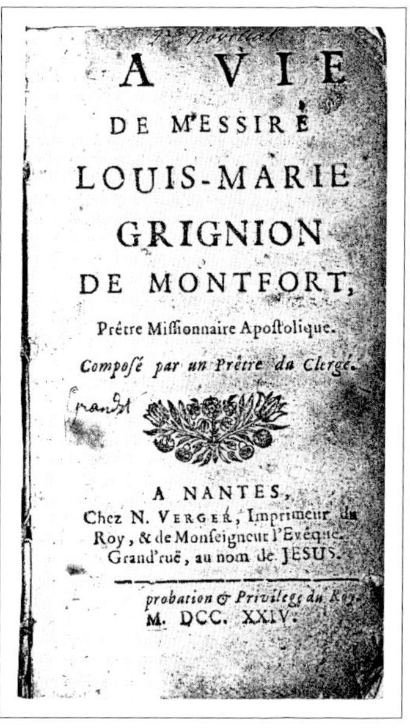

A VIE
DE MESSIRE
LOUIS-MARIE
GRIGNION
DE MONTFORT,
Prêtre Miſſionnaire Apoſtolique.
Compoſé par un Prêtre du Clergé.

A NANTES,
Chez N. VERGER, Imprimeur du
Roy, & de Monſeigneur l'Evêque.
Grand'ruë, au nom de JESUS.

probation & Privilege du Roy.
M. DCC. XXIV.

Title page of Grandet's biography of St. Louis de Montfort published in 1724.

The death of Montfort.

Votive light at the Tomb. Photo by Aartsen.

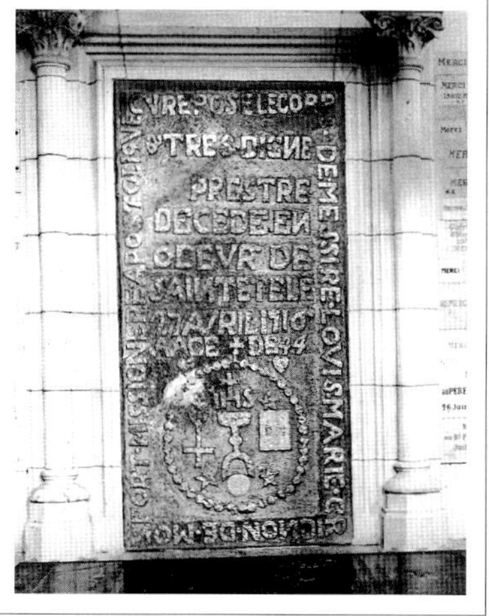

Tomb in the Basilica of Saint Laurent-sur-Sèvre. Under the magnificent marble canopy lie the remains of St. Louis de Montfort and Blessed Marie Louise.

Opening of Canonization ceremony of St. Louis de Montfort, St. Peter's Basilica, Rome, July 20, 1947. Photo G. Felici.

Pius XII sitting on the papal throne as ceremony begins. Photo G. Felici.

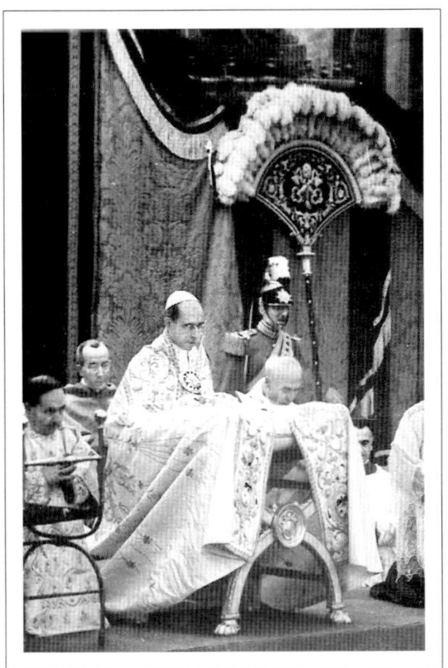

The Holy Father presides at the Canonization ritual. Photo G. Felici.

Closing recessional of the ceremony. Photo G. Felici.

"the very honest and interesting memorializer of Angers." H. Bremond, *Histoire du sentiment religieux en France depuis la fin des guerres de religion jusqu'a nos jours (History of Religious Devotion in France at the End of the Wars of Religion Until Today)*, Bloud et Gay, Paris 1920, 4:225. Besnard, on his part, protests that he wants to write a historical work: "I looked up all the material necessary so that nothing in his life would be omitted that appeared to me to be interesting; and I used the remembrances that were the most sure, so that I would only say the truth." Besnard I, 5. (9) Grandet, vii-x. (10) Grandet, xiv, xv. (11) Blain, 72, 90, 185-187.(12) Blain, 32-33; cf. also 90-91. (13) Blain, 185-190. (14) Besnard I, 5-13. (15) Besnard I, 13. (16) P. Pourrat, Biographies spirituelles, 1716. (17) Dalin, *Vie du vénérable serviteur de Dieu Louis-Marie Grignon de Montfort missionnaire apostolique (Life of the Venerable Servant of God, Louis-Marie Grignion de Montfort Missionary Apostolic)*, Le Clerc, Paris 1839, 6. (18) Fonteneau, *Vie du Bienheureux L.-M. Grignon de Montfort (Life of Blessed L.M. Grignion de Montfort)*, Oudin, Paris 1887; G. Persiani, *Vita del beato L. Maria Grignion di Montfort*, Befani, Rome 1887. Fonteneau points out the heroic virtues of Saint Louis Marie without knowing which he should give first place to: "In Montfort every virtue shows itself with the same brightness, with the same perfection, so that it is difficult to say which one should hold first place" (p. 490). (19) "The most outstanding characteristic is to have completely immolated nature. Living according to a supernatural principle, or, as the promotor of his cause said, only seeing through the eyes of faith, he possessed neither the ideas nor the impressions of other men. This was the cause of his strong and saintly originality. The immolation of nature, the exclusive worship of a supernatural principle such was the double spectacle that rendered his life so edifying to pious souls, so easily understood by those who have the least notion of the Christian ideal." Pauvert, Vie du vénérable Louis-Marie, xi. (20) J.-M. Quérard, *Vie du bienheureux Louis-Marie Grignion de Montfort (Life of Blessed Louis-Marie Grignion de Montfort)*, H. Caillière-Librairie de St-Paul-Lanoë et Métayer, Rennes-Paris-Nantes 1887, 1:iv, vi, xxxiv. This author's same perspective already appeared in his *La mission providentielle du vénérable Louis-Marie Grignion de Montfort dans l'enseignement et la propagation de la parfaite dévotion à la sainte Vierge comme préparation au grand Règne de Jésus et de Marie dans le monde (The providential mission of venerable Louis-Marie Grignion de Montfort on the teaching and propagation of perfect devotion to the Blessed Virgin as preparation for the great Reign of Jesus and Mary in the world)*, Haton-Fougeray-Lanoë et Métayer, Paris-Rennes-Nantes 1884. For a short appreciation of Quérard, cf. A. Laveille, Blessed L.-M. Grignion de Montfort, J. Poussielgue, Paris 1907, 550. (21) Manuscript in the General Archives of the Company of Mary, Rome, II, 80. -(22) G. De Luca, *Luigi Maria Grignion da Montfort. Saggio biografico,* Postulazione generale monfortana, Rome 1943, xii; 2d ed. (including the other works of De Luca on Montfort), Edizioni di storia e letteratura, Rome 1985. (23) "To study the [divine] element is not as easy as studying the natural element: only someone, in fact, who is close to God sees God, and we poor sinners are also at a distance from God, being immersed in pure nature. Furthermore, the divine life in man is a secret of God, and for someone who has given himself to God, a jealously kept secret in the fullness of humility." Ibid., 288. (24) Ibid., 107. Cf. 129, 287. (25) S. De Fiores, *Itinerario spirituale di s. Luigi Maria di Montfort* (1673-1716) *nel periodo fino al sacerdozio (The spiritual journey of Saint Louis-Marie de Montfort up to the time of his priesthood)*, [5 giugno 1700], in *Marian Library Studies* 6, University of Dayton, Dayton, Ohio 1974, 5. (26) Ibid., 234. (27) Ibid., 183. (28) Ibid., 275. (29) P. Pourrat, *Biographies spirituelles (Spiritual Biographies)*, 1717. (30) L. Perouas, *Grignion de Montfort, les pauvres et les missions (The poor and the missions)*, Cerf, Paris 1966, 7. (31) Ibid., 35. (32) Ibid., 29. (33) Ibid., 171-172. (34) Perouas (35) Ibid., 105. In his later works, L. Perouas, *Grignion de Montfort et la Vendée,* Cerf, Paris 1989, 30, 31, 33, went one better yet, describing the young Montfort as "an extreme case," "a problem child." Because of a supposed deficiency in his initial formation, Montfort would even be "a youth carrying a heavy handicap," of which he was not conscious but which conditioned him throughout his spiritual and missionary journey (*Grignion de Montfort ou l'aventurier de 1'évangile [Grignion de Montfort or the Gospel adventurer]*, Les Editions ouvrières, Paris 1990, 28). (36) The psychoanalytic method of interpretation seems today to be a "reductionist measure" because it "reduces" the sources of psychic life to infantile conflicts. "All such 'explanations' deny the obscure labyrinth of solid facts. It tends to be a substitute for reality - a mixture of intentions, necessities, and accidents - a few selected life scenarios, which become a simplistic mold for the logic of someone's behavior and words. . . . Reports, relationships, and new facts can easily contradict this theory." D. Madelénat, *Biographie,* in *Encyclopaedia universalis,* suppl. 1, Le savoir, Paris 1984, 194. (37) L. Perouas, *Grignion de Montfort, les pauvres et les missions,* 170. (38) Cf. *La doctrine et l'expérience de Grignion de Montfort,* in *Ce que croyait,* 113-198; *De l'idôle [sic] & l'icône, in Grignion de Montfort ou l'aventurier,* 59-80. (39) Cf. J. Hervé, *Notes sur la famille du bienheureux Grignion de Montfort* (*Notes on the Family of Blessed Grignion de Montfort),* G. Vatar, Rennes 1927; M. Sibold, *Le sang des Grignion,* vol. 1, International Montfortian Center, Rome 1987; S. De Fiores, *Itinerario,* 19-33. (40) Cf. G. Durtelle de Saint-Sauveur, *Le collège de Rennes depuis la fondation jusqu'au départ des jésuites* 1536-1762, in *Société archéologique du département de l'ile-et-Vilaine* 46 (1918), 1-241; S. De Fiores, *Itinerario,* 19-81. (41) Blain, 23-24. (42) For the entire period, cf. the analysis of S. De Fiores, Itinerario, 82-264. (43) Blain, 332-334. (44) Blain, 220-221. (45) Blain, 115. (46) J.-F. Dervaux, *Folie ou Sagesse? Marie-Louise Trichet et les premières Filles de Saint L.M. de Montfort (Folly or Wisdom? Marie-Louise Trichet and the First Daughters of Wisdom of Saint Louis-Marie de Montfort),* Ed. Alsatia, Paris 1950, 70. (47) Ibid., 72. (48) Blain, 328. (49) Grandet, 100. (50) Besnard I, 114. (51) Blain, 281. (52) Besnard I, 151. (53) "Models are not only paths; they often become obstacles. If one determins types of holiness, one is inclined to attach oneself in an exaggerated manner to a form from the past and impede one from new applications of the Gospel." C. Duquoc, editorial, *Modelli di santità,* in Con 15 (1979), 9, 21. (54) G. De Luca, *Luigi Maria,* 300-302. (55) Perouas (56) Cf. L. Zanzi, *Storicità e santità, questioni metodologiche,* in *La scuola cattolica,* 119 (1991), 135-182, esp. 143-156. (57) Papàsogli (58) Cf. B. Papàsogli, *Montfort moralista: 1. "l'honnête homme" sotto processo,* in *La lettera e lo spirito. Temi e figure del Seicento francese,* Editrice libreria goliardica, Pisa 1986, 219-236. (59) Cf. Besnard I, 114. (60) Cf. [J. Frissen], *La place de la Vierge dans la vie personnelle de Montfort, la pensée du Fondateur, l'histoire de la Compagnie (The place of the Virgin in the personal life of Montfort, the thought of the founder, the history of the Company),* duplicated, Chapitre général, Rome 1964, 44. (61) M. Zundel, *Poème de la sainte liturgie, Desclée de Brouwer (The Poetry of the Holy Liturgy),* 223.

MONTFORT SPIRITUALITY

I. INTRODUCTION

Different articles in this Handbook analyze the spirituality that Montfort lived and transmitted through his life and writings. It is not intended that these few pages reproduce or substitute for the other articles. Rather this is an attempt to formulate a synthesis of the spirituality of Saint Louis de Montfort. The Handbook article *Path of Perfection* contains a general introduction to the meaning of "spirituality in the Catholic tradition generally." We will therefore limit ourselves here to the specific school called montfort spirituality.

A number of authors have summarized this path to union with Wisdom. This article will critically examine a few of them (II). We will then present a systematic synthesis of our own (III) and briefly describe the journey into this spirituality in today's ecclesial context (IV). Finally, we will try to underline certain aspects of contemporary interest in montfort spirituality (V).

Montfort certainly accepts the Christian life completely, with its hierarchy of truth and values; he does, however, stress certain elements of Christianity which constitute the pillars of his spirituality: God Alone, Christ-Wisdom, the Cross, the Holy Spirit and the Virgin Mary, the apostolic and eschatological dimensions.

During his short life of forty-three years, Montfort did not develop a complete and systematic exposition of his path of perfection. Commentators have attempted to develop from Montfort such a systematic presentation. One after another, they have offed a range of interpretations which, understandably, reflect each one's historical milieu.

II. Principal Interpretation

A panoramic view of the principal interpretations of montfort spirituality permits us to catch a glimpse of the different spiritual movements that developed from the end of the nineteenth century until today. Instead of bringing them together under some common denominator, each will be briefly treated.

1. The Reign of Jesus through Mary (J. M. Quérard, 1884)

Father Quérard was convinced that Montfort's earlier biographers did not understand the saint's mission because they did not sufficiently consider the importance of his Marian devotion. He intended to fill this gap by his work, *La Mission Providentielle du Vénérable Louis-Marie de Montfort (The Providential Mission of Venerable Louis Marie de Montfort).* Written in 1859, about seventeen years after the rediscovery of the TD manuscript, it was only published on the eve of Montfort's beatification.

In essence, the thesis of Quérard consisted in this: to reveal Montfort not only as "a first-class theologian" and the "leader of a new superior theological school" but also as the "precursor of the Second Coming" of Jesus Christ and of the "great epoch of the renewal of Christianity in the world."[1] In order to support his thesis, he stressed that Montfort preached a "perfect" devotion to Our Lady and that he also explained Mary's role in the Second Coming of Jesus Christ.

Montfort is distinguished from his predecessors (Bérulle, Olier, Boudon) —Quérard affirms—in that he teaches devotion to Mary, the Holy Slavery, as "a perfect and new method." It is a "superior devotion" that, far from being introspective, "extends itself to every facet of Christian life." A devotion that "implies all the other devotions. . . . It contains all of them." Furthermore, this devotion is not a occasional act but rather a constant attitude, which "puts us in continual relationship with the Blessed Virgin, because we do not breathe, so to speak, except through her . . . and, as a result, simultaneously in Jesus Christ."[2] In order for us to live this devotion, the Rosary takes on such an importance that Montfort consecrated a whole book to it, SR.

Perfect devotion to Mary has as its aim the reign of Jesus Christ, or his Second Coming into this world. This coming—as Quérard affirms—"will be grandiose, this second and last coming . . . will be glorious." It "represents a length of time, the end times, a period of centuries perhaps." The author offers us an interpretation that we do not find in the writings of Montfort: Quérard believes that the reign of Mary and of Jesus "will perhaps lead . . . up to this mysterious era of a thousand years of the book of Revelation, when Christ will reign on earth with some of the just."[3] As proof of his hypothesis, Quérard brings up a text (erroneously) attributed to Montfort, "Life of the Blessed Virgin Mary for young children in the form of a Catechism with questions and answers," which affirmed that the Blessed Virgin "will return [to earth] at the end of the world with her Son."[4] And Quérard concludes, in line with a spiritual millenarianism: "It is thus that the apostle of the end times ties into all his writings this mysterious coming of Jesus and Mary in this world."[5]

The interpretation of Quérard, if we exclude the millenarianist perspective, underlines the eschatological tension of devotion to Mary, strongly focused towards the reign of Jesus in this world. The author only cites LEW once, thus ignoring the sapiential dimension. Further, he does not give us an organic synthesis of all the aspects of montfort spirituality.

2. "The Spiritual Life at the School of Blessed L. M. Grignion de Montfort" (A. Lhoumeau, 1901)

In a work published in 1901 and reprinted in 1953—*La vie spirituelle à l'école du Bienheureux L.M. Grignion de Montfort* (*The Spiritual Life at the School of Blessed de Montfort*)— Father Lhoumeau, a future superior general of the Company of Mary (1903-1919), proceeds on a more solid theological plane. Like Quérard, he is convinced that he must fill in an empty area. This time, however, it is not a question of the relative silence on the Marian aspect in Montfort but, rather, of the fact that there has not yet been a sufficient emphasis on "the perfect devotion to the Blessed Virgin, called the Holy Slavery to Mary . . . which, according to the thought of St. Louis Mary de Montfort, is a system of spirituality, a special form of interior life, and not only an ensemble of pious practices."[6] According to Father Lhoumeau, we should give to Montfort the title "head of a school of spirituality." Without thinking of TD, and even less of SM, as a "methodical and complete treatise of spirituality," without pretending that he is teaching a "new" doctrine, we must nevertheless admit that Montfort has truly united "in a homogeneous whole certain points of view in which he more vividly clarified several issues and developed to the limit their practical consequences." Montfort's system is original, and we might say that "the spirituality of Father de Montfort is distinguished by a particular form, of which he is the veritable author."[7]

The thesis of Lhoumeau is that the doctrine of Montfort possesses "a purpose, a means, certain procedures and effects, which have special characteristics and constitute a distinct spirituality." He demonstrates this thesis in the five parts of his work, the first two treat the doctrinal and the last three are devoted to the spirituality.

The purpose of montfort spirituality is union with God considered under the aspect of "Jesus Christ living in us." Evidently, such a purpose is common to all schools of spirituality. Montfort, however, brings forth a particular aspect: "To make Jesus live in us through that total and absolute dependence that is called Holy Slavery."[8]

To attain this purpose Mary is the great means. She "is an essential part of montfort spirituality . . . because she is the one who gives it its specific form and its distinctive properties. In fact, the formal object of this devotion is the mediation and queenship of Mary; and its proper act is the Consecration. It is called the Holy Slavery of Mary; and that is its true name, which explains its very nature."[9] In giving us a "theology of the Virgin Mary" according to Montfort, Lhoumeau insists on the "spiritual maternity" of Mary, "the culminating point, the principal function of her mediation, based on her Divine Maternity." And he is able to conclude that "in this devotion Mary is seen as Mother."[10]

The "special methods" of montfort spirituality are "the two practices, one inner, and the other outer," which make up "an act of Consecration that is accomplished by the recitation of a formal prayer." This outer act demands an inner disposition that "will animate all our acts with the spirit of this Consecration and will create in us in a habitual dependence on Mary."[11]

The effects of living holy slavery are treated in terms of the different phases of the spiritual life: the purgative way (purification), the illuminative way (progress in virtue) and the unitive way (union with God, transformation of the soul in Mary, filial confidence and freedom, etc.).[12]

This synthesis of Lhoumeau may be considered as the classical interpretation of montfort spirituality, the most organic and the most widely accepted in the Church. The author enlightens in a masterly fashion the different aspects of montfort spirituality (particularly the Christocentric purpose), and distinguishes this spirituality clearly from any sort of devotionalism. One drawback is that Father Lhoumeau scarcely makes mention of LEW (cited only once) and does not probe deeply enough into Montfort's theology of the Cross; moreover, he could have placed more emphasis on the apostolic dimension of Montfort's spirituality.

3. "The Love of Eternal Wisdom," Powerful Synthesis of Montfort Spirituality (H. Huré, 1929).

With the *editio typica* of 1929 (the first edition is dated 1856), H. Huré, father general of the Company of Mary, marked a turning point in the interpretation of montfort spirituality.

Although exuberant about the qualities of TD, the author emphasizes the importance of LEW as the other masterpiece of Montfort. LEW is a "book of capital importance. It is this book and this book alone that gives us montfort spirituality as a whole and can even give us a more exact and more comprehensive idea of *True Devotion to Mary.* Only *The Love of Eternal Wisdom* puts us in permanent contact with the end to acquire and with the evangelical asceticism we must possess in order to live as true slaves of Jesus through Mary."[13]

Unlike Father Lhoumeau, Father Huré does not, systematically and in a specific work, present his sapiential interpretation of montfort spirituality. His synthesis is found in the introduction and in the footnotes for LEW. He gives precise reasons why LEW "constitutes . . . a most powerful synthesis of spirituality, an entire body of illuminating doctrine capable of bringing about in people not only the reign of Jesus but his perfect reign." He points out the double structure of this work when he distinguishes "the great loving efforts of Divine Wisdom and the entirely loving response of the soul that has listened to, understood, and followed his incredible call."[14] It is then that we understand "that everything begins from Christ Wisdom and everything ends there."[15]

Father Huré outlines the idea of Wisdom in Christian spirituality and he concludes from this that "neither before nor after Blessed de Montfort, have we seen a work like his, . . . and constituting such a powerful synthesis."[16] LEW is a veritable treatise that is "not piecemeal." Everything is found there and in an organized way: "The proposed purpose, the nature and manifestations of Wisdom, its effects, its examples, its words or oracles, and the four means to obtain it."[17] Father Huré clarifies well how Wisdom is both person and gift: "The proper object that Blessed de Montfort expounds is, first of all, the Eternal and Incarnate Wisdom, Our Savior Jesus Christ. But since this Wisdom is communicated to us through created gifts . . , he will also speak of an accidental and created Wisdom, which is the communication that the uncreated Wisdom Himself gives to men."[18]

Father Huré is careful to add that he does not wish in any way whatsoever to supplant TD. He also underlines "the essential role of . . . [true devotion to Mary] in montfort spirituality," making clear that it "loses something of its value and significance if it is not set within the spiritual method of Blessed de Montfort, about which only this treatise openly gives us the design." Father Huré is convinced that "if we consider Marian devotion on its own, as completely autonomous, and totally independent of the treatise on Wisdom, we will certainly not have the same idea as Blessed de Montfort himself had of it. How come? Because *True Devotion* is only a means, directed toward something else: the acquisition of Eternal Wisdom."[19] In summary, "all things begin with Wisdom and end with Wisdom, but pass through Mary, who is the means."[20]

The merit of this interpretation is undeniable: LEW itself affirms a clear Christocentric-sapiential orientation. And further, the accent placed on the originality of LEW in the context of Christian tradition shows that the spirituality of Montfort may not be reduced to its Marian dimension, even if this is clearly Christocentric, since one of its essential characteristics remains its sapiential perspective. The weakness of the work of Father Huré is found only in not having developed *ex professo* and in a systematic manner the montfort synthesis: he does not bring out the organic coordination of the principal elements that emerge from the whole montfort corpus.

4. The Glory of God Alone by Means of Union with Christ and Mary (H. Frehen, 1966-1967)

In a course, never published, on montfort spirituality, H. Frehen, a montfort theologian who became bishop of Reykjavik († 1986) dealt with the specific elements of montfort spirituality, which he considered to be: the greatest glory of God (final end), union with Christ (proximate end), union with Mary (means), and sinful man who renounces himself and gives of himself.[21] He searched through all the works of Montfort without exception in order to find texts that would embody these essential elements. He cited as prime examples of basic formulas of montfort spirituality CG 4; LPM 6; RW 203; H 49: 1-2; H 141:15. His course, therefore, developed the three themes, God, Jesus Christ, Mary.

Resolutely theocentric, Montfort immerses us in the presence of God, in an atmosphere which remains close "both to the majesty of Sinai and to gospel tenderness." More precisely, he "realized a magnificent synthesis between theodicy and the theological treatise on the Trinity." In fact, "the initiative of the Trinity, in Montfort's vision, extends to each and every salvific work understood in its broadest sense, including the Incarnation, the earthly life of Christ, and also the sanctification of man." Montfort brings out in a special way that "the predominant and first role in the sanctification of man belongs to the Holy Spirit." It even seems that Montfort is not content with simply "attributing" to the Holy Spirit the sanctification of man in the classical sense: "All works outside the Trinity are common to the three Persons of the Trinity." Such a doctrine is true for efficient causality, but in the realm of quasi-formal cause, each of the Divine Persons gives Himself in accordance with His personal properties. Mary herself is also considered by Montfort in strict relationship with the Trinity.

After establishing the Christocentrism of Montfort, Frehen reasons: "The principal mystery of the life and the personality of Christ is the Cross. Now Christ in his relationship to the Cross is called by Montfort Christ Wisdom. Therefore this aspect, Christ Wisdom, constitutes the principal and specific aspect of the Christological vision of Father de Montfort." The mystery of the Cross occupies the center of the mystery of

Christ, since even the Incarnation and the other mysteries "are ordered toward the Cross."[22]

On Christ Wisdom the attitude of the Christian is expressed in certain formulas dear to Montfort: to be united or give oneself to Christ-Cross (CG 1, LEW 225), to obtain and preserve Wisdom (LEW 220, MR 15), to reproduce in oneself the life of Christ (MP 5; TD 44, 50; LEW 214; SM 67), the realization of the reign of God (TD 1, 13, 22, 49, 113, 133, 258; H 3:1, 4), the slavery of love (TD 118, 120). But the attitude of Christians is above all "to be in conformity, united, and consecrated to Jesus Christ" (TD 120). This formula, which includes a relationship to the baptismal promises and to the Cross, is concretely summarized in the montfort version of the slavery of love.[23]

Montfort speaks of Mary in relationship to the plan of the Trinity for salvation (TD 16-48); in her work for the reign of Christ in the world (TD 1). He insists on Mary's transcendence as Mother of Christ and, consequently, sees her in intimate relationship with the Father and the Holy Spirit (MP 2-5; TD 5-6, 16-17, 22-23). For mankind, Mary is the treasurer of grace, all-powerful queen and spiritual Mother (TD 23-38). "A special devotion to Mary is, therefore, necessary; and later Montfort will say that following Christ's example this devotion must be lived through the slavery of love." We experience the maternity and sovereignty of Mary by being entirely submissive to her through love and not by fear or force.[24]

The synthesis of Frehen is founded upon *all* the works of Montfort. The accent put on the mystery of the Cross seems, however, to diminish the fundamental importance of the Incarnation. Furthermore, different elements of montfort spirituality appear to be seen in opposition to each other rather than seen in their organic unity.

5. Way to Wisdom (L. Perouas, 1973)

The methodology adopted by Perouas in his presentation of montfort doctrine resides in his refusal to separate theology and experience.[25] It is from the very heart of this experience that insights are discovered "which go beyond and balance out his doctrine on man and God, on Mary and the Church."[26]

Montfort underscores the corruption of sinful man and asks that he "renounce his very self," i.e., that he empty himself not of his own personality but of that foundation of egoism which resides in man. Perouas reminds us that Montfort's perspective is mystical, which does not stop at the metaphysical essence of man but at his position before the gratuitous gift of God. From such a perspective, Montfort "gives the impression of minimizing and, at times, of forgetting the active collaboration" of the Christian in his own sanctification. Yet, in reality, he insists on a total gift of self to God "and speaks less of letting himself be taken over by God than of making his Consecration according to a precise method." Such an attitude is explained by the moralizing influence at the end of the seventeenth century, which understated at times the importance of the mystical dimension. Montfort's experience contained the two tendencies: the vision of the man who despises self and wishes to live apart from the world and that of man who wants to realize his own desires (cf. L 5). As entirely submissive as he was to his superiors and, above all, to Jesus through Mary, Montfort "sensed, from his own experience, that man was made for affection, for freedom, for action, for creativity. It is in the tension of existing between these two realities that we best discover the feeling which Montfort had for man."[27]

Faithful to Augustinian thought, Montfort experienced *God Alone,* his preferred motto, which expresses the great, incomprehensible, inaccessible (TD 157), and far-off God. This God, considered, so Perouas believes, "almost as the Sun King, must be served totally, without division, without alloy," and it is very important to calm him in his anger (LEW 45; SM 66; TD 85) and not to approach him directly (TD 18). Montfort, however, stresses God as a "good father. . . . From his youth, Louis Marie perceived the All-Powerful as Providence, sovereign Monarch, angry Father, and yet a God close to him."[28]

The closeness of God is perceived in the Incarnation, which "is truly at the center of Montfort's doctrine." It is a mystery of self-emptying and of dependence on Mary, which mystifies us (TD 18, 139). Montfort lingers on the birth of Jesus, to which he dedicates eleven hymns; a little on Jesus' apostolic life (LEW 114); and quite a bit on the Passion, which is the object of eleven hymns and two chapters in LEW. "This choice shows us," says Perouas, "that Montfort comprehended with difficulty the depth of humanity that the Incarnation signified. And yet Jesus Christ was, for him, very much a living being."[29] In fact, he speaks of Jesus Christ living in us (TD 61) and of the active permanence of the events of his life (MR).

It is certain that Montfort encountered God in the Sacraments and in the Bible, but also in the poor (H 18:8). This is revealed in the episode at Dinan, where he cried out, "*Open up to Jesus Christ.*" When he was approaching thirty, he discovered Jesus Christ as Wisdom, personified as a feminine figure. Thus his love for God becomes spousal: a decisive moment in his journey toward maturity.

At the end of his life, Montfort brings to the fore the role of the Holy Spirit. Through Mary, he finds the Spirit in abundance (TD 36, 217). It is above all to her that he directs his prayer to obtain the apostles of the end times (PM 15-16), which is the period of a "purified, renewed Church, led entirely by the Spirit."[30]

The interpretation formulated by Perouas of the figure of Mary in Montfort is extremely critical and seems, at times, to lack objectivity and coherence. Led by the mentality of his times, Montfort would have unconsciously diminished the figure of Mary, for he never mentions her intelligence, her will, her body. "Nor does he ever show us Mary in action; her holiness appears that much more beautiful inasmuch as she let herself be molded by God without contributing anything; her Divine Maternity is that much more admirable in that she only consented to it."[31] And yet, at the same time, Montfort would be guilty of one of those excesses of maximalism in associating Mary to Christ, presenting her as "analogous to him" (cf. TD 74) and giving to her by grace the same rights and privileges that belong to God by nature.

Dipping into the spiritual currents of his time, especially into Augustinianism, Montfort liked to consider the Church as the Mystical Body, of which Christ is the Head and the faithful are the members (TD 32; FC 27). The concept of Church, as he saw it, tends to limit itself to the "predestinate," those who live in the state of grace.

If Father de Montfort saw in the Church a reality that was at first invisible, mystical, that does not mean that he rejected its external, social aspect. The best indication of this was his "total fidelity to the hierarchy.[32] In fact, Montfort always generously manifested during his lifetime a perfect obedience to the Pope and to the bishops in whose dioceses he worked.

Montfort criticized and castigated the different categories present in the Church of his time: Religious, theologians, pious people, priests, etc. He spoke of the Church *"so weakened and so soiled by the crimes of her children"* (PM 20). He denounced its terrible burden, because he wished a pure Church, one with a different appearance: poor, abandoned to Providence, apostolic, and full of initiative as it was in the first ages of Christianity and as it will be in the end times. In apocalyptic language which is even a little millenarian, says Perouas, "Father de Montfort depicts the far off-future of the Church. It will truly be the reign of the Holy Spirit. The Church will have found a marvelous power to convert the Turks and the Jews; within its own walls there will appear Christians greater than those who have appeared up to that time, because they will be formed by Mary."[33]

It is quite evident that Perouas did not wish to offer an organic synthesis, particularly of the spirituality of Montfort. What he develops lacks an explicit systematic formulation.

6. God Alone: Meeting God with Montfort (1981)

In this research document produced by authors from around the globe, all aspects of montfort spirituality converge within a presentation of Montfort as "a man of God," as the one who "had an experience of God that was quite personal and who witnessed to this in an original manner."[34] The mystical dimension is a particular need perceived by contemporary society. It is present in Montfort, in a totally absorbing way. It explains every other dimension.

In the first part, dealing with man's salvation today, Father Bilo describes the situation of man in the twentieth century, as slowly coming to the conclusion that "the building of a just and human world cannot happen without God." Montfort responds to this "need for God who is near and who calls man to collaborate with him." He teaches man how to live in communion with Christ Wisdom "in a living and personal relationship." For the people of today who are conscious of their responsibilities and social commitments, Montfort presents to us a God of love, who invites us to live in true solidarity with the poor.[35]

Montfort was a man who truly encountered God. He combined an intense apostolic activity with an exceptional experience of God (Bossard, Fabry). Louis Marie's entire life is guided by the fundamental option for *God Alone,* the triune God.

Montfort lived his relationship with God, Father and Providence (L 2, L 33; LCM 4-5; TD 169, 215; H 28). He encountered Him in prayer, in his missions, in the trials of life, in Mary, in the poor (Parrado, Jo van Osch).

Even more, Montfort encountered God in Jesus Christ, Eternal and Incarnate Wisdom. That was true for his entire missionary life, even if the beginning and the end of his apostolate seem more profoundly marked by a sapiential note. In attributing to Christ the title Wisdom, Montfort brings out four aspects of this mystery in harmony with biblical Revelation: 1) Christ as "fullness," infinite treasure for mankind (LEW 62); 2) as "Word" that reveals and transforms and whose pronouncements one must believe in order to be saved (LEW 133-153); 3) as "Love" in his dynamic bending low to man; 4) as "Cross," since *"Wisdom is the Cross and the Cross is Wisdom"* (LEW 180).

The relationship of Montfort with the Holy Spirit is both profound and original. The mystical perspective applies well to Montfort's anthropology, whose pessimistic affirmations wish to simply prove "the impossibility of self-salvation." This pervades equally the entire Marian experience of Louis Marie, for whom the Virgin is the "*mysterious milieu*" (TD 265) where we can live in the liberty of the children of God, encounter Christ, and be docile to the Spirit (Bossard).

The third part of the volume, which was written by Father Jan van Osch, describes the correspondence between the journey that permitted Montfort to encounter God and the theological views of today. Van Osch points out that by his motto *"God Alone,"* Montfort proclaims that "the unreasonable (for us) Wisdom of His love is found at the origin of every Christian act."[36] He comes to the aid of contemporary man to discover the true relationship between morality and mysticism, introducing ethics into the loving response to the gratuitous love of God, Who necessarily has priority. It is thus that the holy missionary lived, being at ease in the mystical field, recognizing in his submission to authority "the concrete expression of his openness to the Holy Spirit." A total receptivity to the love and the Wisdom of God is the fundamental attitude of the Virgin Mary. "For Montfort . . . the

Secret of Mary consists in the fact that the continual attention given to the feminine figure of Mary as it appears in the divine plan of salvation renders the Christian more open to God as He is in reality, to God Who became man, Who suffered and was humiliated right up to death on the Cross. He is convinced that the relationship to this 'woman,' the New Eve by the side of the New Adam, is able to accelerate and make more perfect the union of men with God."[37]

Montfort is an example to be followed "in the sense that the purpose of all his efforts at renewal is always God Alone and His Kingdom." He teaches that "every effort at Church renewal and all human attempts at betterment can only bear fruit if they are carried on and conducted by the Spirit of God."[38]

This work, *God Alone: Meeting God with Montfort,* offers important insights as well as an original interpretation of the givens of montfort spirituality. But there is such a variety of authors within its three parts that the work cannot be called an organized whole.

7. God Alone Is My Tenderness (R. Laurentin, 1984)

As his contribution to the movement to proclaim Montfort a Doctor of the Church, Laurentin examines Saint Louis Marie from a theological perspective.[39] He states that Montfort's theology is "a theology of the history of salvation. . . . It is a Trinitarian theology." He distinguishes in it three points that include the presence of Mary: the Incarnation, the Cross, and the Holy Spirit.

"This [the Incarnation] is the very center of his [Montfort's] living theology: the descent of God to the lowliness of our humility and a taking of us into the divine plenitude."[40] In the "foolishness of a transcendent God," we find the basic intuition of Montfort, which gives a profound unity to his thought: *"It is through the Blessed Virgin Mary that God came into the world, and it is also through her that he must reign in the world"* (TD 1). Along with the Greek Fathers, Laurentin interprets this principle in the sense that "it is through Mary that God became man so that man could be divinized." The mission of Mary consists, in fact, in being the *forma Dei,* the mold of God. By this image Montfort "expresses . . . the admirable exchange by which the Son of God is formed as a man in Mary in order that we may be formed in the image of God . . . , i.e., divinized." Mary is the embodiment and the sign of our paradoxical God: *"God is at the same time infinitely holy and raised up, infinitely condescendent and proportioned to man's weakness"* (SM 20). Seeing this total gift of love on the part of God, we also should give our all (H 57:2). It is in this context that the Holy Slavery of Montfort is situated.[41]

The juncture of the Incarnation and the Cross, which is central in the life and preaching of Montfort, is the Trinity: "In the bosom of the Father, Jesus is desirous of the Cross and becomes incarnate in order to lovingly embrace it." Montfort does not insist on the link between the Cross and Mary but, rather, on their difference: *"The Cross is adorable. / Mary is not"* (H 102:23; cf. LEW 172). We are surprised that he does not allude to Mary near the Cross nor to the Co-redemption. "It is above all because he puts the filial link of the Incarnation within the maternal womb of Mary. . . . For him, everything is found at the point of departure."[42]

"The theology of the Holy Spirit according to Grignion de Montfort is, like that of the Incarnation and the Cross, the expression of a hope . . . . It is a theology of the history of salvation. And the departure point is, here again, Trinitarian."[43] The Holy Spirit occupies a place of principal importance in the writings of Montfort. In Mary and with her He is the one Who accomplishes the work of the Incarnation of the Word; in her and with her it is again He Himself Who forms Christ in Christians, especially during the end times (PM 15-16). The title *"Spouse of the Holy Spirit,"* attributed to Mary by Montfort, even though it expresses authentic values, remains, however, "inadequate and ambiguous"; according to Laurentin, it would be preferable to substitute other expressions.

The synthesis of Laurentin is especially valuable because of his insistence on the theocentrism and the work of the Holy Spirit in montfort spirituality. But he, too, does not insist enough on the sapiential and apostolic dimensions of Montfort's spirituality.

III. Systematic Synthesis

The principal elements of montfort spirituality have already been well described in the different articles of this Handbook. We will attempt to weave these together into a general, organic presentation.

To remain faithful to its roots, the interpretation of montfort spirituality must take into account the bipartite division present in the works of Montfort: the descending movement of God towards man and the ascending movement of man towards God. This rhythmic call-response, so evident in the works of Montfort (especially in LEW and TD), must therefore be preserved if we wish to remain faithful to Montfort's biblically based structure.

The statement that sums up montfort spirituality is the following: "Responding to the love of the Father, expressed in salvation history by the mission of the Word and the Holy Spirit, and living for God Alone, Father and Providence, by means of the total Consecration of oneself to Christ Wisdom, in the docility of the Spirit, in communion with Mary, within the ecclesial community that announces the reign of God." Or even this other formula, which covers the essential: "To God Alone, by Christ Wisdom, in the Spirit, in communion with Mary, for the reign."

The meeting point of these two movements is the totality of the gift, which belongs above all to God, Who gives Himself to the world by an infinite and paradoxical love, especially in the Incarnation and in the paschal mystery of Jesus. The total donation of oneself also characterizes man, who pledges himself to return to God by preparing the reign of Christ in the world in the absolute docility of the Spirit and by identification with Mary, type of the faithful Church.

1. Descending Movement:

"All things come from the Father through Christ Wisdom, in the power of the Spirit, in collaboration with Mary, in the ecclesial community." This fundamental assertion contains several basic elements of Montfort that must be underscored.

a. Everything begins with the Father. The action of God in history, revealed in Holy Scripture, is an essential part of montfort spirituality. Montfort sums up his concept of God in the motto *"God Alone,"* repeated 150 times. The expression indicates, first of all, that God is the absolute value. Creatures, including Our Lady herself, are not excluded unless they cause us to be separated from God. Their value is that much more insofar as they refer and lead us to God. And Montfort is able to affirm: "*I desire God Alone and the soul*" (H 91:12). Or further, on the subject of Mary: "*That person will find only God and no creature in the most lovable Virgin Mary. . . . It is God Alone who lives in her*" (SM 20, 21). Thus "God Alone" equals "God is all," which must suffice: *"God Alone, and that suffices"* (H 28:23); "*God Alone is my tenderness, / God Alone is my support, / God Alone is all my well being, / my life and my riches*" (H 52:11).

The motto, God Alone, also expresses that God is Father/ Providence, on Whom depends all of salvation history and one's personal life. "*God the Father, from whom every perfect gift comes as from an essential source*" (SM 9). In LEW, Montfort contemplates Wisdom in eternity: "*From his beginnings, we contemplate him in eternity, living in the bosom of the Father, as the object of his kindnesses*" (LEW 14). And it is in the inner life of the Trinity that Montfort places the decision of Eternal Wisdom to come into the world: "*The decision is made and completed: Eternal Wisdom, or the Son of God, will become man*" (LEW 46). It is from the Trinity and—from its very interior—from the Father, named by Montfort before the Son and the Holy Spirit (TD 4-5, 16, 17, 23, 29), that is born the plan of salvation, in which Mary also is involved (TD 22).

In perfect harmony with biblical tradition, Montfort proclaims his profession of Christological faith: "*Jesus, true God and true man, only Son of the Father and of Mary always virgin!*" (LEW 223). He prefers, however, to consider Christ as Savior and Life: *"Jesus Christ Our Savior is the alpha and the omega, the beginning and the end of all things, . . . our only way who must lead us, our only truth whom we must believe, our only life who must give us life and our sole all in all things, who must be sufficient for us*" (TD 61).

The title Montfort likes to attribute to Christ is Wisdom. According to LEW, this title brings out four aspects of the mystery of Christ: the "fullness" (LEW 9), the "Word" (LEW 95), the "Love" that comes down to man in a humbling kenosis (LEW 70-71), and the "Cross" (LEW 180).

Interpreting these four aspects in terms adapted to our contemporary situation, we can recognize four attributes of Christ Wisdom. First, Christ is the unique Mediator of Salvation: we proclaim Christ as the "unique Mediator between God and mankind" (1 Tim 2:5; cf. 1 Cor 8:6). This given of our faith excludes every possibility of self-salvation and implies a vital relationship with the living person of Christ, the very center of the Good News and of the Christian life. Second, Jesus, the Word of God, is the Master of life. He transmits to every person the Wisdom coming from God, and indicates to us how we should act in order to enter into life. The radical demands of the Gospel are imperatives. Third, Montfort contemplates Christ Wisdom in his kenosis of love, the Incarnation, so foreign to human standards (LEW 167). In such a dynamic of condescending love, we find certain Christological mysteries especially dear to Montfort: the Incarnation, the key mystery, which contains all the other mysteries (TD 248); the infancy of Jesus (H 57-66); the Eucharist (LEW 71); the Sacred Heart (H 40-44; H 47-48). The presence of Christ in the poor and those who suffer according to Mt 25:31-46 is also evident in the life of Montfort (recall the episode at Dinan: *"Open up to Jesus Christ"*). Finally, at least as much as the Incarnation, Montfort underlines the importance of the Cross, which he identifies with Wisdom: "*Wisdom is the Cross and the Cross is Wisdom*" (LEW 180). Like St. Paul (1 Cor 2:2), he announces Jesus crucified. Like him, he does not exclude the Resurrection but understands the part for the whole. It is necessary that today we explain the paschal mystery in its totality, seeing the Cross as inseparable from the Resurrection: it is the Cross of the Risen One. Salvation comes to us through the paschal mystery celebrated in the Sacraments of the Church.

Montfort spirituality also underlines that to the Person of the Holy Spirit belongs the realization of salvation history as a regenerative, unifying, and missionary force. With Montfort it is correct to underscore the work of the Holy Spirit in the Incarnation of the Word—when, with Mary and in Mary, "*he produced his masterpiece, which is God made man*" (TD 20)—as well as His role in the birth and the growth of Christ within all mankind (TD 20-35; SM 13-67). The times of the Church coincide with the "*special reign*" of the Spirit, which seemingly implies an acceleration of His Pentecostal presence in the final phase of the "*end times*" (PM 15).

The economy of salvation is revealed in Jesus Christ, the Word become Incarnate in Mary by the operation of the Holy Spirit. The plan of the Trinity (TD 14-37) and the journey of Wisdom toward man (LEW 105-106) go through a woman: Mary. With Montfort, we must underline certain aspects of the figure of this woman.

"*Excellent masterpiece of the Most High*" (TD 5), Mary is, of her being, "*entirely relative to God*" (TD 225). The fundamental collaboration of Mary with the Father consists in her maternal action towards Jesus and Christians, an action that we should consider, with Montfort, as a participation in the fruitfulness of the Father (TD 17).

Wisdom finds in Mary the person worthy of welcoming Him (LEW 105). And the proposal of God encounters in her the most adequate response (LEW 106). Mary is not only the Seat of Wisdom; she is the person who welcomes Him in faith and puts herself totally at His service (LEW 107). The one who imitates Mary becomes the Church welcoming the Word of God in his life.

The relationship of Mary with the Spirit is found on the level of a communion of love and of collaboration. Montfort expresses that reality by calling Mary fruitful and faithful "*spouse*" of the Holy Spirit (TD 20-21, 35-36, 269). The formation of the saints becomes, therefore, the united effort of the Spirit and of Mary, each one of course on a different level. The Spirit makes of Mary His new creation (cf. TD 261) and the type of the Church in the fields of holiness, of virginity, and of maternity (cf. TD 261). She is for Christians the model of availability and of docility to the Spirit.

The saving work of the Trinity is realized in the Church, which is "the sign and the instrument of the intimate union with God and of the unity of all of humankind" (LG 1). With Montfort, we must point out the visible aspect of the Church—endowed with the Sacraments and its ministers, guided by the Pope and bishops—and the invisible aspect, the Mystical Body. Within the Church, Montfort assesses the priceless value of Baptism, which has made of its members a consecrated people with the mission of extending the reign of God up to its definitive realization.

2. Ascending movement

There is no other path for man than that revealed by God in salvation history. Consequently, we can say that "man responds to the love of the Trinity by living for the glory of God Alone the Consecration to Christ Wisdom, in the docility of the Spirit, in the welcome of Mary, and in ecclesial communion, with a view to the announcing of the reign of God."

If God is the supreme value, the principle from which existence and salvation come, man must adore Him in spirit and in truth, live in his presence, conduct himself as His child, and work for His glory. Everything must be oriented toward the glory of God, which means toward the praise of God for His action in salvation history, especially for the redemptive work of Christ. Montfort also inspires us to purify our intentions: we must not look for our own proper interests but, rather, the accomplishment of the will of the Father through pure love: "*Having only God Alone in view, without any other interest than that of his glory*" (RM 62); "*They do all their actions for the greater glory of God*" (RW 203); "*Reign in me with your power, / in order that I may glorify him / God alone eternally*" (H 141:15).

Christ is mankind's infinite treasure (LEW 64-67); man arrives at saving encounter with him by the gift of his heart (LEW 132). This is accomplished by the perfect Consecration to Christ, which brings with it the renunciation of Satan and the total gift of oneself to Christ by the renewal of the baptismal promises (TD 120-130).

The Spirit recalls to our minds the Gospel (Jn 14:26), makes us cry out "Abba" (Gal 4:6; Rom 8:15), and dispenses life to us (Jn 6:63) and the charisms necessary for the edification of the Church (1 Cor 12:4-11; 14:12). Like Montfort, we follow the Spirit especially in our daily actions, trying to identify ourselves with Mary, whose spirit is "*the Spirit of God*" (TD 258); we also follow the Spirit in the apostolate, allowing ourselves to be guided by the Holy Spirit without putting affective or economic obstacles in the way (PM 7-9).

Montfort speaks of a unique Consecration to Christ through Mary. There are those who prefer, today, to reserve the Consecration to Christ and to find other words to recognize the maternal and exemplary function of Mary in Christian life. Montfort has recourse to a multitude of expressions to proclaim such a recognition, and he often uses the answer of the beloved disciple, who welcomes Our Lady into his own (Jn 19:27; cf. TD 144, 179, 216, 266; SM 66). Thus, in giving himself up in a filial relationship to Mary, the Christian, like the Apostle John, "accepts among his personal goods" the mother of Christ and introduces her into the entire area of his interior life, which means, into his human and Christian "I" (RMat 45). In the journey of man toward Wisdom, Mary represents the "perfect way," which assures an intimate and faithful union with Christ (LEW 220-221; TD 157-158).

The baptized person is part of the ecclesial community, in which he shares in the priestly, prophetic, and royal function of Christ. As such, he must follow the liturgical route: celebrate with his brothers and sisters the divine mysteries, frequent the Sacraments, meditate on Sacred Scripture, and give witness to the Lord by his life and his speech. Every Christian must live this ecclesial spirituality, which is intrinsic, therefore, to montfort spirituality. All are invited to take "Mary as a model of the spiritual attitude with which the Church celebrates and lives the divine mysteries" (MC 16). The disciple of Christ will avoid every individualistic attitude, focusing his entire attention on being with others and for others, in conformity with the principles of solidarity and subsidiarity. He will strive to enter into the pastoral life of the community according to the directives of the Pope and the bishops.

"What the soul is to the body," affirms the *Letter to Diogenes,* "Christians are to humanity." The Christian must not separate himself from the world but remain in the world to be the salt of the earth and the light of the world (Mt 5:13-14).

He is sent into the world to announce and realize salvation (Mk 16:15; Mt 28:19-20). The reign of God fills a central role in the NT and also in the life of Montfort. This must be the purpose of every prayer of the Christian, but it also entails a commitment of life and witness. Jesus will reign, when, through Mary, he becomes better known, loved, and served and when his commandments are better observed (TD 13, 49, 62).

IV. The Path of Montfort Spirituality

More important than systematic synthesis of the essential points of montfort spirituality, is to outline how one can live this spirituality in one's daily life. Montfort is not ignorant of the fact that the spirituality which he has proposed cannot be improvised. He saw that it cannot be realized automatically: *"This secret becomes great only in the measure in which the soul uses it. Be very careful not to keep your arms crossed, doing no work"* (SM 1). A preparation is necessary, an initiation and a constant exercise are indispensable in order to penetrate this secret more and more deeply and to move through the different stages that make it up. In short, a true initiation into the mysteries of the spiritual life is demanded.

1. Preparation

In order that the act of *"consecration of oneself to Jesus Christ, the Incarnate Wisdom, by the hands of Mary"* (LEW 223-227) may not be reduced to a simple formula without influencing one's life, it must be prepared for by serious reflection and prolonged prayer. This is the reason that Montfort prescribes a month of preparation for a formal commitment to the Consecration: at least twelve days to empty oneself of *the "spirit of the world which is contrary to that of Jesus Christ"* (TD 227), a first week *"to ask for knowledge of themselves and contrition for their sins"* (TD 228), the second week *to "know the Blessed Virgin Mary"* (TD 229), and the third to "*know Jesus Christ* "(TD 230). Even though the act of Consecration is a personal act, Montfort does not separate it from the liturgy: he prescribes that it be done after sacramental confession and Holy Communion (TD 231).

The directives given by Montfort are quite valuable because they urge us to free ourselves, by a spiritual exodus, from the vain wisdom of this world and to know man, Mary, and Christ more profoundly. What must be avoided, however, is a nonchalant repetition of this montfort Consecration formula.

The contents of the preparatory month should be updated according to CCC, which, following Vatican Council II, offers the fundamental truths relating to the world (67-68: the Creator), to man (82-92: Man, the Fall; 365-423: Man's Vocation), to Mary in the mystery of Christ and the Church (107-111; 207-209), and to Jesus in his mysteries (96-150).

The preparatory month must also be harmonized with the liturgy. The more appropriate period seems to be

Lent, when the catechumen repeats the cry of the man born blind, which Montfort places on the lips of those preparing for the Consecration: "*Lord, that I may see!*" (cf. TD 228). During Lent the Church invites the faithful to recall their Baptism (SC 109) and prepares them for the solemn Easter Vigil service, the heart of the liturgical year, during which we renew our baptismal promises; it is then that we welcome Mary as a gift of the crucified Lord (cf. Jn 19:15-27).

2. Initiation

Montfort takes into consideration both the purpose to be attained and the route to take: "*As this devotion essentially consists in a state of soul, it will not be understood in the same way by everyone. Some—the great majority—will stop short at the threshold and go no further. Others—not many—will take but one step into its interior*" (TD 119).

The aim is the assimilation of Christocentric-Marian spirituality. Moved by the Holy Spirit (TD 258), identified with Mary, the model of perfection (TD 260), "*proximate end . . . , mysterious milieu . . . easy means*" (TD 265), forms us in Jesus Christ (TD 264), enabling us to live more intimately by him, with him, in him, and for him (TD 257). Montfort does not intend here something transitory nor simply exterior. He speaks of someone with an interior and stable attitude: "*Finally, who will remain in it [in the interior] permanently?*" (TD 119). In practice, it is a matter of acquiring availability and docility to the action of the Spirit and to the maternal collaboration of Mary, in order to be formed in Jesus Christ, which is to say, in order to arrive at spiritual maturity.

The way that leads to this end is the application of the fourfold formula "*do all one's actions by Mary, with Mary, in Mary and for Mary, in order to do them more perfectly by Jesus Christ, with Jesus Christ, in Jesus Christ and for Jesus Christ*" (TD 257). Such an exercise may seem at first glance to complicate the spiritual life; rather it facilitates it. We have here a method that is required in order that the option for Christ through Mary may bring about a deeper and more apostolic life. Obviously it is in no way necessary to simultaneously practice the four formulas: it suffices to experience them one at a time.

The repetition suggested by Montfort of a formula that actualizes the paschal rhythm of death and Resurrection, of leaving behind our egoism and bringing forth new life in the Spirit is quite efficacious: "*I renounce myself and give myself to you, my dear Mother*" (TD 259). Better still, because it is more explicitly Christocentric, the following formula that Montfort counsels us to recite often is perhaps more important: "*Tuus totus ego sum, et omnia mea tua sunt: I am all yours and all that I have is yours, O my Jesus, through Mary, your most holy Mother*" (TD 233).

S. De Fiores

3. The Montfort Spirituality Path of Perfection

Saint Louis de Montfort's path of perfection is characterized by the same qualities of his consecration to the Eternal Wisdom through Mary: christocentric/Trinitarian, total (therefore involving the Cross), baptismal, marian and apostolic, as explained in the article *Consecration.*

There are however, varying degrees in the living of this consecration. Saint Louis de Montfort does not exclude beginners from this perfect renewal of the baptismal promises; it evidently can only enhance the path of those in the illuminative (advanced) and unitive (perfect) ways. In fact, this consecration spirituality will of its very nature unfold into an extraordinary depth of union with God Alone through Wisdom Incarnate in the power of the Spirit. It is claimed that the majority of those Christians who seriously set out on the way of perfection remain in the illuminative way. Although Montfort appears to imply this opinion (cf. TD 118), he urges his "*poor, simple folk*" (cf. TD 26) on to the highest stages of union with God.

Nowhere does this saint of the common people formally detail stages of growth into Trinitarian life. He does speak about varying intensities of living his consecration spirituality: "*As this devotion essentially consists in a state of soul, it will not be understood in the same way by everyone. Some—the great majority—will stop short at the threshold and go no further. Others—not many—will take but one step into its interior. Who will take a second step? Who will take a third? Finally who will remain in it permanently? Only the one to whom the spirit of Jesus reveals this secret. The Holy Spirit himself will lead this faithful soul from strength to strength, from grace to grace, from light to light, until at length he attains transformation into Jesus in the fullness of his age on earth and of his glory in heaven*" (TD 118).

What are these steps? The closest we can come to the mind of Montfort appears to be found in the effects of total consecration as outlined especially in TD 213-225, supplemented by his thoughts taken from his other works. The editors of Saint Louis Marie's *Complete Works* recognize that "These effects [the 'wonders of grace' foretold in TD 35] are presented according to a certain progressive order of the spiritual life" (GA p. 391, note 361). It is evident that Montfort is describing the stages of growth of someone who is already living the consecration and, it can be presupposed, is already in the illuminative way. However, using the seven "*wonderful effects of this devotion*" as the bare-bones outline, his path can well be applied to even the beginners who undertake the road of Montfort's consecration spirituality. The various degrees do show an ascending progression to union with the Lord. They are to be understood as essentially intertwined; none exists independently of the others. Although already noted in the article *Consecration* as the effects of perfect devotion to Our Lady, they are considered here as the steps on the path of perfection.

a. Knowledge of Self. "*By the light which the Holy Spirit will give you through Mary, his faithful spouse, you will perceive the evil inclinations of your fallen nature and how incapable you are of any good apart from that which God produces in you ...*"

In a certain sense, this step is the most important since it marks the beginning, the start of the journey itself. The heart of this first of the stages is that we deepen our knowledge of self in the light of a new depth of knowledge of God. In the brilliant light of God's holiness, we perceive our nothingness. To be penetrated with our own nothingness outside of the framework of God's redemptive sharing of his holiness can only lead to discouragement if not despair. Montfort, finely tuned to the workings of the soul, never calls for an inward gaze into our sinful nothingness without stressing the infinite, forgiving Love Who is God.

His demand that a person serious about the spiritual life regularly seek the counsel of a wise spiritual director who knows the path well (cf. LEW 202; H 139:68) also forms part of the context of this first stage.

The saint also calls for—even at this initial step—a recognition of all the other pilgrims on the way to the Lord. In baroque language, he declares: "*The humble Virgin Mary will share her humility with you so that, although you regard yourself with distaste ... you will not look down slightingly upon anyone*" (TD 213). The foundational concept implied so often in Montfort that all persons are intertwined, interrelated, is to be seen also here at the first step.

This initial stage presupposes that "*desire*" for holiness so insisted on by Montfort as his first means of acquiring Divine Wisdom (cf. LEW 181-183). It is a desire—the determination to take all the means to arrive at the goal, no matter the cost—and not just a wish (velleity) that characterizes the person willing to examine the depth of one's own sinfulness. And as he tells us in LEW, this desire will express itself in mortification—the willingness to be stripped of all false idols—and in continuous prayer (LEW 184-193) marked by sincere petition springing from simple faith for the great gift of Divine Wisdom. Montfort's magnificent canticles on the desire for Wisdom powerfully express the basic content of this first step (cf. H 103, 124, 126).

b. Joyful Enthusiasm. The second stage on our way to "God Alone" is marked primarily by joyful enthusiasm. With the zeal of a Montfort who as a youth tried to enlist all his fellow students into the Confraternity of the Holy Slavery, the traveler is convinced that nothing stands in the way of union with God, nothing too difficult, no demands too great. The reason for this burst of energy is the experience that Our Lady shares her gift of faith with us. The Annunciation 'Yes' which personifies her, is in varying degrees, the life of the voyager into God. "*It is a lively faith ... it is a firm faith ... it is a courageous faith ... it inflames those who are lukewarm and need the gold of fervent love*" (TD 214). The faith is sincere, the experience of Mary's support is real. Yet understood in the light of the entire voyage, it appears to be a youthful enthusiasm which has yet to be sorely tested.

c. Overcoming Roadblocks. This step presumes a letdown after the initial burst of enthusiasm. Roadblocks spring up along the way, especially scruples, fears, overconcern (TD 215; cf. TD 168-169, 263). Saint Louis de Montfort insists throughout his writings that there can be no true advance into God Alone unless the traveler is imbued with pure love understood not in any quietistic sense but as an active and responsible surrender to the Lord like Mary's *fiat.* This presupposes for Montfort, a conviction that God is love so that "*you will look upon him as a loving Father ... you will speak to him as a child does to its Father. If you should have the misfortune to offend him, you will humble yourself before him and beg his pardon. You will offer your hand to him with simplicity and lovingly rise from your sin. Then peaceful and relaxed and buoyed up with hope you will continue on your way to him*" (TD 215).

Overanxiety, overconcern about the future, about sinfulness, about our responsibilities all have to be stripped away or else the path appears to be so rugged and the terrain so threatening that there is a serious danger of turning back. The answer to this almost insurmountable problem is, so Montfort simply states, to release ourselves into the tenderness of God. And this too is a gift of Mary, the Mother of Fair Love. Montfort gives strength to the sinner surprised by a sudden fall, or to the soul who for the first time experiences the malice of one's sinfulness. The cure lies in destroying the travesty we make of God when, filled with servile fear or painful overanxiety, we forget the fundamental truth of our faith: God is Love.

d. Unbounded confidence. Peaceful, active and responsible trust is the characteristic of this fourth stage of our journey. With the roadblocks removed, we continue on the way with a new depth of calm, total trust in God's Providence and the maternal care of Our Lady. There is a steadiness now in the travel since the person lives the truth that there is a "*Father in heaven who cannot fail me*" (L 2), and Mary is the "*Mother of saving grace,*" upon whose breast "*all good things come to me*" (TD 216).

It is as if the traveler no longer looks down on all the ruts and sharp rocks in the road but now looks up to the loving God who carries him on eagle's wings. Crosses are experienced, to be sure; yet more than ever, they are borne with extraordinary calm and trust for they are known to be "*dipped in honey*" by Our Lady (cf. TD 154).

e. Lost in Mary's Spirit. The turning point of the entire journey is found here in the fifth step: the travelers "*hide themselves completely in the depths of Mary's soul, becoming living copies of her*" (TD 217). "*You must offer yourself to Mary, happily lose yourself in her, only to find God in her*"

(SM 70; cf. TD 222, 264). This is really the specific crux of Montfort's spiritual path of perfection, an essential element which is one of the chief distinguishing marks of his spirituality. This is achieved only through the great gift of the Holy Spirit who alone gives entry into this "*paradise of God*." It is both the result and cause of being faithful to the interior practices Saint Louis Marie explains: to do all our actions, with Mary, in Mary, by Mary, for Mary, so that they may be done more perfectly through, with, in and for Jesus-Wisdom (cf. SM 45-49, TD 257-265).

Lived in its intensity, this stage of the path brings with it the mystical experience of Our Lady's presence: "*I carry her in the very center of myself,/ engraved with lines of glory, / Although in the obscurity of faith*" (H 77:15). "*Should you not savor immediately the sweet presence of the Blessed Virgin within you, take great care not to torment yourself. For this is a grace not given to everyone, and even when God in his great mercy favors a soul with this grace, it remains none the less very easy to lose it, except when the soul has become permanently aware of it through the habit of recollection*" (SM 52).

The mystical marriage of the soul with God takes place in Mary. In a true, mystical sense, we are Mary in whom Jesus lives and reigns. Since it is in Mary that Eternal Wisdom became incarnate and offered himself as victim and priest for the human race, so too it is in the soul transformed into Mary that Wisdom becomes again, in a mystical way, enfleshed.

f. To Live Jesus. Lost in Mary, the soul is formed into Jesus Christ. Mary is the mold of God who formed Christ-Wisdom; she is the mold in whom we must be poured in order to become living copies of Christ-Wisdom.

This step on the montfort path of perfection is a further clarification of step five. Saint Louis de Montfort is so insistent that all authentic devotion to Mary must be Christocentric (cf. TD 61-67), that he is careful to clarify that "*losing oneself in Mary*" is to say that we become more and more Jesus. Again, keeping the entire spectrum of Saint Louis de Montfort's teaching in mind, it cannot be stressed enough that this transformation into Christ is nothing more or less than transformation into the Eternal and Incarnate Wisdom. Jesus as Wisdom is another of the essential and characteristic traits of Saint Louis Marie's path of perfection. It is specifically under the aspect of Wisdom that Jesus is both present reality and future goal. As the soul unfolds more deeply into Wisdom, so too the entire universe, living the age of Mary, is unfolding more and more through an intrinsic ordination, into the fruit of her womb, the Alpha and Omega Who is Jesus. "*The Holy Spirit himself will lead this faithful soul from strength to strength, from grace to grace, from light to light, until at length he attains transformation into Jesus in the fullness of his age on earth and of his glory in heaven*" (TD 119).

To "*lose oneself in Mary*" is not to speak of quietistic passivity. On the contrary, it is marked by an active zeal for God and for neighbor as is evident from all the writings of the saint and from the clear example of his life.

g. For God Alone. The goal of the journey, the '*terminus ad quem*' of the montfort path of perfection: to live in God Alone. Montfort's stress in TD is to show how losing ourselves in Mary is another way of expressing that we live in God for she is the "*echo of God.*" "*Mary is entirely relative to God. Indeed I would say that she was relative only to God because she exists uniquely in reference to Him*" (TD 255). This marian path of perfection transforms us also so that we too live a life only in reference to God.

Everything according to Montfort, flows from this God of tenderness and everything finds its fulfillment in God. Having been transformed into Jesus, through the power of the Spirit we walk into the blazing light of the Father. This Trinitarian experience is intrinsic to Montfort's way. God is "*tasted,*" "*experienced,*" "*known*" as Father, source and goal of all. The experience of the tenderness of the Father is a critical criterion of our advance in holiness.

It is not, Montfort says, that we will never fall again once we live in the experience of the Holy of Holies; he says that he has seen the stars of heaven [the saints] fall (cf. TD 88). That is why he constantly speaks of the importance of meditation, and of the rosary—which is for Montfort a Gospel meditation with the background music of the Hail Mary—of formulated prayers, both vocal and private. His insistence on the daily rosary, the reading of the Scriptures, is indicative of his concern that those who are so favored with God's grace never think of themselves in elitist fashion as people who do not need the ordinary means of sanctification.

God Alone, goal of all montfort spirituality, is never separated from love of neighbor. The way of Mary is essentially intertwined with the apostolate. Montfort's goal is to form a "*mighty legion of brave and valiant soldiers of Jesus and Mary, both men and women*" (TD 114), whose contemplative life constantly overflows to service of one's neighbor especially in "*the end times*" (TD 55-59).

Conclusion. The path Saint Louis de Montfort outlines is the one he himself lived and which he preached to the simple, country people of northwestern France. It is in many ways a distinct and singular path of christian spirituality. The power it encloses is coupled with, or better still, flows from its marked stress on the tenderness of God and the maternal care of Mary. It is a path which—adapted to each one's own gifts—leads each person and through humanity, the entire cosmos, "*quickly, perfectly, directly, surely*" (TD 168) to the goal, Jesus the Eternal Wisdom, and through Christ in the power of the Spirit to the glory of God the Father.

P. Gaffney

V. Contemporary Interest

For centuries montfort spirituality has exercised its influence on a worldwide scale and with a never-weakening force. Near the end of the second Christian millennium (1987), it received the height of official recognition with the explicit mention made by John Paul II in RMat 48.

The spreading of the writings of Montfort are the source of the present interest in his spirituality. Based on the experiences of the saint, they transmit with conviction what he lived and preached. It is difficult to deny the fascination that the holy missionary exercises through his writings. Using the cultural means of his times, he has succeeded in transmitting a message that goes beyond frontiers and centuries.

Some of the treasures of montfort spirituality that are particularly relevant to our times are the following:

1. Christocentric perspective

The Christological question, always so highly relevant, is often answered today in a manner that diminishes the figure of Christ. There are those who consider him to be a great moralist and to have a tendency to see only the human in him. On the contrary, Montfort offers a profound and orthodox vision of Jesus. Above all, he gives witness, in pages rich with feeling (TD 61-67), of his personal experience of Christ. Continually Christ is considered in Montfort's works as the *"final end"* (TD 61, 68, 115, 117, 120, etc.) of the spiritual life. For Montfort, the Son of Mary is not among so many others but "*Our Savior, true God and true man*" (TD 61): he is the spiritual life's ultimate and absolute reason, and its fullest realization.

Most especially in LEW, Jesus is at the very center of Montfort's reflections. In the midst of the conflicts of his day among various forms of humanism, some hostile, and others indifferent to the faith, Saint Louis vigorously proclaimed the truly superior Wisdom through the events of the Incarnation and the Cross and in the direct words of Jesus. Everything must be seen in Him and through Him.

Every element in montfort spirituality leads back to this divine-human center, to Christ Wisdom: Baptism, the Cross, the apostolate, love for the poor, Mary. In a very special manner, Montfort sees the spiritual relationship with the Mother of the Lord intrinsically oriented toward filial life in Christ and in the Spirit. He castigates with words of fire (cf. TD 98-99) the "*presumptuous devotees*" who continually outrage Christ by their sins *"under the pretext that they are devotees of Our Lady"* (TD 97).

An especially marvelous insight of Montfort is that he founds his spirituality on Baptism (TD 120-131). This Sacrament of Christian initiation, in fact, contains in seed the entire development of the spiritual itinerary. It is from here that the demands of Christian life flow. Mary is the way to the faithful observance of the baptismal promises. Montfort thus unifies the spiritual life in the gift of the heart to Jesus Christ.

2. Mary: An understanding of woman according to the divine plan

Women are looking for new areas of responsibility in society and in the

Church. Even though Montfort does not propose direct solutions to modern-day questions such as those raised by the feminist movement, he powerfully exalts the figure of woman in the person of Mary. Recognizing the active and responsible participation of the Virgin Mother in salvation history does not leave woman in a subordinate state. In her function as collaborator in salvation history, Mary represents a principle of self-comprehension as much for man as for woman. And she also leads us toward the discovery of the paternal and merciful face of the Father (TD 169, 215) as well as of his maternal traits (cf. Is 49:14-15). The divinely willed value of Mary constitutes the Marian dimension of montfort spirituality. She can contribute to the humanization of the world by injecting her values of receptivity, of the gift of self, of protection for all life: values especially dear to the feminine world.

3. Projection toward the future

Faced with the evil use of scientific discoveries and the accumulation of nuclear arms, contemporary man wonders about the future of the world. Apocalyptic visions slip into his soul. Montfort is not unmindful of such preoccupations; he responds to them not to satisfy vain curiosity but, rather, to lift the veil that covers the final phase of human history. He foresees a tomorrow of battles between diabolical and salvific forces. The latter are those of the Holy Spirit, Christ, Mary, and their kin, whose number includes the apostles of the end times. These forces prepare for the Second Coming of Christ. They consist in his reign within hearts and the world, and are accomplished without marvels or spectacular events. Marian spirituality itself is entirely oriented toward the reign of Christ, for which it is the best and most perfect preparation.

Montfort spirituality is thus seen as rooted in the past, immersed in the present, and projected toward the future. It proves to be, therefore, a spirituality entirely prepared to confront and to accompany history. Like Christianity, of which it is only a particular facet, it is not fearful of encountering the challenge of different cultures; it penetrates them in order to purify, promote, and elevate them.

S. De Fiores

Notes: (1) J.M. Quérard, *La mission providentielle du vénérable Louis-Marie Grignion de Montfort dans l'enseignement et la propagation de la parfaite dévotion à la sainte Vierge comme préparation au grand regne de Jésus et de Marie dans le monde (The Providential Mission of Venerable Louis Marie Grignion de Montfort in the Teaching and the Propagation of the Perfect Devotion to the Blessed Virgin as Preparation for the Great Reign of Jesus and Mary in the World),* Haton-Fougeray-Lanoè/Metayer, Paris/Rennes/Nantes 1884, 192, 159; cf. M. Audran, *Les différentes formes de la spiritualité du* *bienheureux Louis-Marie Grignion de Montfort (The Different Forms of the Spirituality of Blessed Louis Marie Grignion de Montfort),* in *Cahiers thomistes* 3 (1928), 521-541. (2) Quérard, *La mission providentielle,* 51, 55-69. (3) Ibid., 239-242. (4) Ibid., 244. The book attributed to Montfort is also cited on page 219. (5) Ibid. (6) A. Lhoumeau, *La vie spirituelle à l'école de saint Louis-Marie Grignion de Montfort (The Spiritual Life at the School of Saint Louis de Montfort),* Reyaert, Bruges 1953 (1st ed. 1901), 7. (7) Ibid., 7-9. (8) Ibid., 8. (9) Ibid., 8-9. (10) Ibid., 132, 274. (11) Ibid., 9, 220, 254. (12) Ibid., 224-362. (13) H. Huré, *Préface à L'amour de la Sagesse éternelle (par la "Vraie dévotion à Marie") puissante synthèse de spiritualité par le Bienheureux L. M. de Montfort (Preface to The Love of the Eternal Wisdom [by Means of the "True Devotion to Mary"]: A Powerful Synthesis of Spirituality by Blessed L. M. de Montfort),* editio typica, Librairie Mariale, Pontchâteau 1929, II-III. (14) Ibid., historical Introduction, [4]. (15) Ibid., [80]. (16) Ibid., [6]. (17) Ibid., [80]. (18) Ibid., 55. (19) Ibid., 275-276. (20) Ibid., 277. (21) H. Frehen, "Corso di spiritualità monfortana," Montfort Scholasticate, Rome 1966-1967, 21-24. (22) Ibid., 59, 62. (23) Ibid., 52-56, 79-85. (24) Ibid., 88-103. (25) L. Perouas, *Ce que croyait Grignion de Montfort et comment il a vécu sa foi,* Tours, Mame 1973, 139. English edition, *A Way to Wisdom,* Montfortians Yesterday and Today, Bay Shore, 1982. (26) Ibid., 114. (27) Ibid., 115-138. (28) Ibid., 144, 154-555. (29) Ibid., 148. (30) Ibid., 139-159. (31) Ibid., 161-162. (32) Ibid., 180. (33) Ibid., 175-189. (34) G. Barbera et al., *Dieu Seul: A la recontre de Dieu avec Montfort (God Alone: Meeting God with Montfort),* Centre international montfortain, Rome 1981, 4. (35) Ibid., 11-19. (36) Ibid., 24-28, 29-49. (37) Ibid., 67-74, 75-81. (38) Ibid., 87-88. (39) Ibid., 198. (40) R. Laurentin, *Dieu seul est ma tendresse (God Alone Is My Tenderness),* O.E.I.L., Paris 1984, 144. (41) Ibid., 146-159. (42) Ibid., 159-176. (43) Ibid., 176-195.

MORTIFICATION

I. INTRODUCTION

"If any man would come after me, let him deny himself and take up his cross and follow me" (Mt 16:24). These Gospel imperatives are spoken to Jesus' followers of all times and they are highlighted by Saint Louis de Montfort,[1] as they are by CCC.[2] The contemporary teaching of the Church states: "The way of perfection passes by way of the Cross. There is no holiness without renunciation and spiritual battle. Spiritual progress entails the ascesis and mortification that gradually lead to living in the peace and joy of the Beatitudes: 'He who climbs never stops going from beginning to beginning, through beginnings that have no end. He never stops desiring what he already knows.'"[3]

Mortification is, therefore, an understandably important theme in the life and writings of Saint Louis Marie de Montfort. He uses the word mostly in its traditional sense: "the deliberate restraint that one places on natural impulses in order to make them increasingly subject to sanctification through obedience to reason illumined by faith."[4] Father de Montfort speaks of self-denial, carrying the Cross, disciplining by austerities inherent in one's state of life or even self-imposed renunciation of the world, worldly goods, and worldly company.

This article will discuss the influences on Monfort's understanding of and doctrine on mortification. It will also attempt to demonstrate how mortification was present in his life and teaching, and the relevance of Montfort's doctrine of mortification.

II. THE IMPACT OF BERULLIAN SPIRITUALITY

Saint Louis Marie de Montfort is known as the last of the great Bérullians. His views and teaching on mortification should be seen in the context of the

Bérullian or French school of spirituality, which exercised considerable influence on him together with other currents of thought.

1. God Alone

Asceticism is a hallmark of Bérullian spirituality. Essentially, the Bérullian asceticism embodies the double movement of total renunciation of self and total clinging to God. In fact, the total renunciation of the self is only authentic and valid to the extent that it frees us to cling to God Alone. The focus should be on *"God Alone"* —and Montfort will stress that in God Alone we find our neighbor, especially the poor and the brokenhearted—and not on oneself. Nothing should be motivated by self-will or self-seeking; rather, the contemplation of God Alone should move one to action. "It is these two aspects of the Bérullian heritage that mark most deeply the personal experience of Louis de Montfort."[5] Theocentrism—a life focused on God—is the constant aim of Bérullian mortification. Yet it must be constantly stressed that this centering on God—most especially for Montfort—includes a practical love for one's neighbor.

2. Motives of mortification

Not only did Bérullian mortification seek to be united with *"God Alone"*—the first motive for mortification—but it is also the means to overcome the radical weakness of human nature and man's fundamentally sinful condition: a second motive for mortification. This strong stress by some members of eighteenth-century spirituality on the weakness of man in the light of original and actual sin is termed Christian pessimism. According to this view, the body, or the flesh, is to be mortified continually to subjugate its evil tendencies, so intense because of original and actual sins. Bérulle's thought is summed up in his famous text: "Of ourselves we have no right to anything but nothingness, sin, and hell—in other words, nothingness from start to finish. . . . Sin is a second nothingness and worse than the first—a nothingness opposed to God, resistant to God—and hell is the consummation of, and permanent establishment in, this wretched nothingness."[6] Montfort echoes this attitude when he writes: *"Never give your body all it demands. With permission, refuse it even some lawful satisfaction"* (RW 74).

Bérullian spirituality, however, was staunchly Christ-centered. Only in Jesus can humanity be both reconciled with God and re-created. The aim of the spiritual life is total communion with Jesus. The way to Jesus is through the Cross, and here we have a strong third motive for mortification: carrying the Cross like Jesus. The Cross held a preeminent place in the French school. In imitation of Jesus, who carried the Cross and died on it, and in order to live in him, we must die to self and to all created things and immolate ourselves to God. This aspect of Bérullian spirituality seems to have particularly influenced Montfort. During his formative years in Paris, a book that he devoured and that became a foundation for his meditation was *The Holy Ways of the Cross* by Henri Marie Boudon, an exponent of French spirituality. A strict interpretation of poverty and an impassioned fidelity to the Cross characterize the teachings of this book.[7]

Bérulle's doctrine on the total surrender of the humanity of Christ to the Divine Person can also be considered a fourth motive for total self-abnegation. Bérulle's concept of Consecration—Holy Slavery—is modeled on the truth that the humanity of Christ so totally clings to the Divine Logos that the human nature has no ontological personality of its own. This total self-emptying, the *kenosis*, is, then, a call to the followers of Christ to practice mortification to belong as much as possible to the Divine Word.

Saint Louis de Montfort followed the French school quite closely in finding motives for a life of penance and mortification. As we will see, however, he modifies these reasons in accord with his own experience of an evangelical, apostolic life.[8]

III. Mortification in Montfort's Life

Moved by the gifts of the Spirit expressing themselves through his own temperment—described as energetic, passionate, aggressive, fiery, and yet gentle and affectionate—and encouraged by the religious climate of his time, Montfort led a life of rigorous mortification. He willingly gave up the comforts of life because he firmly believed that *"wisdom is not found in the hearts of those who live in comfort"* (LEW 194).

1. Youth

Louis Marie surely practiced mortification even as a young man preparing for the priesthood. It appears that he fasted frequently, something that must have been particularly difficult for him because his appetite was hearty and his constitution sturdy. While studying in Paris under severe economic strain, he used to go three times a week to keep all-night vigils at wakes held in the parish of Saint Sulpice. Here his intense, habitual asceticism came to the fore, as it appears that he refused the light refreshment offered to sustain him during the long hours of the night. He habitually wore a hair shirt. His use of the discipline was often severe. Papàsogli calls him "one of the most mortified saints of the century."[9]

Though one spiritual director discouraged his intense practice of mortifications, others encouraged Montfort in its pursuit. While he was studying in Paris, Father Prévost, who was his confessor for some time, did not hesitate to ask him to give up the only material object in the world to which he had an attachment: his little statue of the Blessed Virgin.[10]

2. Missionary apostolate

Montfort's sixteen years of priestly, apostolic ministry witnessed his most intense period of mortification. As a priest in the early eighteenth century France, he was entitled and expected to live the dignified life of the first estate. He chose, however, the lifestyle of a poor vagabond preacher with few possessions. It was this thought-out choice which became the source of many of his mortifications: his identity with the outcasts qualified his food, clothing, shelter, friends, and, to a great extent, his reputation among priests and bishops. When Saint Louis de Montfort tells his Congregation of missionary priests that their principal mortification is to be found in their hardships as itinerant preachers, he is speaking from experience. (cf. LCM 10)

Saint Louis Marie's primary penances and mortifications flowed from his life as a vagabond, homeless preacher of parish missions. Montfort lived the rule he gave to his Missionaries of the Company of Mary: "*Their motto will be: do not follow the ways of the world. Consequently, they will avoid, as far as is consistent with charity and obedience, whatever savors of worldliness*" (RM 38).

But this is not to say that penitential acts did not abound in his rather short life. Montfort was a firm believer in being spiritually fit. He never wanted to be taken by surprise by some providential call to a Cross that might overwhelm him. His chosen penances prepared him, so he was convinced, for any eventuality and helped him to be totally centered on the Lord in his life and preaching. Mortification gave him the opportunity to imitate Christ and atone for his own sins and the sins of others.

Many of his biographers believe that Saint Louis de Montfort's penances erred on the side of extravagance. Perhaps so. But the custom of the times, his motives, and also the fact that he would never undertake a serious penance without the permission of his spiritual director soften such a judgement.[11] Most of the accounts of Montfort's penances are repetitions of chapter 11 of Grandet's biography, where he almost gleefully describes in vivid terms "his daily austerities, which exceeded by far the natural forces of man."[12] In spite of Grandet's attempt to place Saint Louis Marie outside the realm of the human, he does imply that many of these mortifications were at times omitted by the saint when preaching missions.[13]

Montfort considered the practice of mortification an indispensable means of holiness and salvation taught by the Gospels, explained by the masters of the spiritual life, and practiced by saints (SM 4).

Clearly, mortification held a prominent place in Montfort's life. A lack of mortification, he firmly believed, was incompatible with serious Christian life. In FC, he writes: *"Be careful not to admit into your society those delicate and sensitive people who are afraid of the slightest pin-prick, who cry out and complain at the least pain, who know nothing of the hair-shirt, the discipline or other instruments of penance, and who mingle, with their fashionable devotions, a most refined tediousness and a most studied lack of mortification"* (FC 17).

IV. Montfort's Teaching on Mortification

In his writings, Montfort presents solid teaching on mortification. For him, it should be understood and practiced in the context of our relationship with Christ; it is universal, and it is far more than external acts.

1. Christocentric mortification

What is most striking about Montfort's teaching on mortification is its Christ-centeredness. Christian life is about acquiring and possessing Jesus Wisdom and remaining with him. In his principal work, LEW, he says: *"So let us remain with Jesus, the eternal and incarnate Wisdom. Apart from him, there is nothing but aimless wandering, untruth, and death. 'I am the way, I am the truth, I am the life'"* (LEW 89).

For Montfort, Christ is, above all, the one who suffered and died for us on the Cross. The mystery of Christ is the mystery of the Cross. *"Never the Cross without Jesus, or Jesus without the cross"* (LEW 172). Eternal Wisdom has fixed his abode in the Cross so firmly that we will not find him anywhere else in the world, least of all in the souls of those who live in comfort. *"He has so truly incorporated and united himself with the cross that in all truth we can say: Wisdom is the Cross and the Cross is Wisdom"* (LEW 180).

As his writings demonstrate, Montfort was a contemplative of the mystery of the Cross and a singer of its praises. The Cross is glorious and worthy of adoration. *"Through his [Christ's] dying upon it the cross of ignominy became so glorious, its poverty and starkness so enriching, its sorrows so agreeable, its austerity so attractive, that it became as it were deified and an object to be adored by angels and by men"* (LEW 172). Because of its eternal union with Christ, the Cross has a permanent significance. At the last judgement, Christ will judge the world with his Cross and by it. It is a greater gift than even the gift of faith (LEW 175).

The mystery of the Cross is the mystery of God's love. The Cross is the soundest proof of divine love. *"Among all the motives impelling us to love Jesus Christ, Wisdom Incarnate, the strongest, in my opinion, is the suffering he chose to endure to prove his love for us"* (LEW 154). For our part, we respond to God's love by carrying our own crosses. *"The cross was the proof God gave of his love for us; and it is also the proof which God requires to show our love for him"* (LEW 176).

The Cross is precious to us for many reasons. It makes us resemble Jesus Christ. It is the means of union with Christ. Jesus Christ accepts as his own only those who carry their crosses. It enlightens the mind and is the source of an understanding that no book in the world can give. It is an *"abundant source of every delight and consolation; it brings joy, peace, and grace to our souls"* (LEW 176). It gives the one who carries it the weight of everlasting glory. It changes momentary suffering into an eternity of happiness (LEW 180).

Christians are called to participate actively in the Cross of Christ. *"Make no mistake about it; since incarnate Wisdom had to enter heaven by the cross, you also must enter by the same way"* (LEW 180). For Montfort, this is what mortification is about, i.e., carrying the Cross through, with, and in Christ and participating in his paschal mystery. *"All those who belong to Christ, incarnate Wisdom, have crucified their flesh with its passions and desires. They always bear about in their bodies the dying of Jesus. They continually do violence to themselves, carry their cross daily. They are dead and indeed buried with Christ"* (LEW 194).

Mortification is necessary because self-denial and renunciation of the world and self are ways to possess Incarnate Wisdom. In LEW, Montfort lists mortification among the four means necessary to acquire Wisdom. A relationship with Christ is impossible without mortification. *"Do not imagine that incarnate Wisdom, who is purer than the rays of the sun, will enter a soul and a body soiled by the pleasures of the senses. Do not believe that he will grant his rest and ineffable peace to those who love worldly company and vanities"* (LEW 195). Though the Incarnate Wisdom is eager to give himself to us, it is a sad truth that there are so few who are "*sufficiently unworldly or sufficiently interior and mortified to be worthy of him, of his treasures, and of union with him*" (ibid).

The call to mortification, Montfort points out, is found among the principal utterances of Wisdom Incarnate himself, which we must believe and practice if we are to be saved. He gives a list of sixty such utterances, and the very first is the call to self-abnegation and to carry the Cross: "*If anyone wishes to follow me, let him deny himself, take up his cross and follow me. Lk. 9:23*" (LEW 133).

Many wise and honest people living in this world simply do not know the value of the Cross, because they are too fond of sensual pleasures and seek only their own comforts. That is the reason the Cross is not welcomed, why it is even rejected. In a letter to a religious, Montfort wrote: "*If Christians only knew the value of the cross, they would walk a hundred miles to obtain it, because enclosed in the beloved cross is true wisdom*" (L 13).

There is also another problem. Many Christians know the value of the Cross in theory because so much is written and spoken about it. But in practice, "*people lose courage, complain, excuse themselves, and run away as soon as the possibility of suffering arises*" (LEW 174).

2. Universal mortification

Mortification is required of all at all times. It has a perennial significance. Montfort speaks of it as universal. He explains universal mortification as total, continuous, courageous, and prudent. "*Wisdom is not satisfied with half-hearted mortification or mortification of a few days*" (LEW 196). Genuine mortification is courageously applied to the senses and faculties, mortifying the eyes, sense of smell and taste, the faculties of mind and will, and their inordinate and useless affections (RW 170).

Universal mortification penetrates the diverse areas of human life. Its highest point is the giving up of our worldly possessions—expressive of interior poverty—which is the quickest, the best, and the surest means to possess Wisdom. Montfort recognizes that this may not be easy for all or even within the vocation of all. Hence, he recommends detachment of the heart from material things, possessing them as though not possessing them (LEW 197). Not following the showy fashions and the false maxims of the world and fleeing from the company of worldly people are important areas of mortification.

Mortification of the body, according to Montfort, is indispensable in our efforts to possess Wisdom. Speaking of bodily mortifications, he says that accepting our life as it is and living it patiently everyday by enduring our bodily ailments, the inconveniences of the weather, and the difficulties arising from other people's actions is mortification enough. To this we may add some voluntary penances and mortifications, such as fasts, vigils, and other austerities practiced by holy penitents (LEW 201). This balanced advice on the subject of mortification seems surprising coming from a person so "mortified" as Father de Montfort; yet it is basically the very route that he himself followed. His advice to his Missionaries on the subject of mortification is simple: "*The Rule does not prescribe any corporal penances. This is left to their own fervor controlled by obedience. They will, however, abstain from meat on Wednesdays and fast on Fridays or Saturdays and, on the evenings of these two days only a light meal is to be served*" (RM 36).

It is true that bodily mortifications are difficult. The body idolizes itself, and the world considers all bodily penances pointless. But Montfort warns: *"Beware of thinking that bodily mortification is not necessary to acquire Wisdom, for Wisdom is never found in those who live a life of ease and who gratify their senses"* (RW 172). He advises caution, however, in the practice of bodily mortification. Both excess and defect are to be avoided here. And again, Montfort's common sense is evident: *"Although certain great and holy people have sought and asked for crosses and even by their peculiar behavior have brought sufferings, scorn and humiliations upon themselves, let us be content with admiring and praising the marvelous work of the Holy Spirit in their souls. Let us humble ourselves at the sight of such sublime virtue without attempting to reach such heights ourselves"* (FC 44).

It is also important to note that for Montfort, mortification is not synonymous with a gloomy spirit. Rather, it is a source of joy, for it brings with it the knowledge of obeying the command of the Lord and of imitating him. *"You will find in it [mortification, the carrying of the Cross] a delight beyond anything you have known. . . . The joy that comes from the cross is greater than that of a poor man who suddenly comes into a fortune or of a peasant who is raised to the throne, greater than the joy of a trader who becomes a millionaire"* (FC 34).

3. Interior and small mortifications

Montfort points out that interior mortifications are more important than exterior ones, even though the latter are not to be disregarded. The conquest of selfishness, or self-will, is the greatest challenge. Even the good results of difficult practices of mortification may be spoiled by self-seeking. Hence he recommends that all exterior acts of mortification be done under obedience. *"For exterior and voluntary mortification to be profitable, it must be accompanied by the mortifying of the judgement and the will through holy obedience, because without this obedience all mortification is spoiled by self will and often becomes more pleasing to the devil than to God"* (LEW 201).

Montfort also teaches that little mortifications are often more meritorious than great ones because they are less apt to give rise to vanity. Small interior acts of mortification made for God, for example, repressing useless words and glances or checking a movement of anger or impatience, etc., could turn out to be great victories. In this connection, he specifically asks—in his down-to-earth language—to mortify *"1) a certain natural activity that inclines you to hurry and to accomplish much; 2) changing moods that rule you and displease your neighbor; 3) your tongue, which always wishes to talk, laugh, mock etc.; 4) a tendency to lack religious modesty in your bearing, which makes you act like a child, laugh like a fool, jump around like a juggler, and eat and drink like an animal"* (RW 176).

Special devotee of the Blessed Virgin Mary that he was, Montfort sees Mary as the best example of universal mortification. He lists mortification as one of her ten principal virtues, which should be imitated by those who are devoted to her. Acts of interior or exterior mortification may be performed as one of the five principal practices of true devotion to her (TD 108, 116).

V. The Relevance of Montfort's Teaching on Mortification Today

While some people may be put off by what appear to contemporary man as excesses in Montfort's own practice of mortification, his teaching on this point is important and relevant for every one. What is particularly appealing is the Christocentrism of his teaching on mortification. Montfort does not think that "mortification" performed for its own sake has value. The pains and agonies of the athlete in order to get in shape cannot be considered for that reason alone as mortifications. Acts of penance and mortification become meaningful, useful, and necessary as our participation in the mystery of the Cross of Christ and as means for our union with him. It is their relation to Jesus that turns daily hardships into mortifications.

Montfort's concept of universal mortification also has a lasting impact. Mortification is for all. All Christians are called to it. It should affect our entire life all the time, not merely one or other aspect of our life at a given time. In other words, mortification is a permanent part of the Christian life. This teaching of Montfort is relevant especially today, when more and more people seem to think less and less of mortification and asceticism as an integral part of the Christian or spiritual life.

His teaching that interior and small mortifications are as important as, if not more important than, exterior and greater mortifications should also not be forgotten. As in many other things, quality is more important than quantity: "*God considers not so much what we suffer as how we suffer*" (FC 49). Mortifications are much more than rituals. True mortification should change our lives, behavior patterns, and relationships for the better. Acts of mortification should have a healthy impact on the daily lives of those who perform them. Montfort's teaching on mortification points to that.

T. Myladil

Notes: (1) FC is fundamentally a commentary on the call of Jesus to carry the Cross after him. It is not only a treatise on the Cross; its highly practical content makes of it a booklet on mortification. Montfort considers mortification—the carrying of the Cross—to be a response to this command of the Lord to take up one's Cross daily. (2) CCC 2029 is nothing more than Mt 16:24, summarizing the necessity of mortification to achieve holiness. (3) CCC 2015. The quote is from St. Gregory of Nyssa, *Hom. in Cant. 8.* (4) P. F. Mulhern, *Mortification,* in *The New Catholic Encyclopedia,* McGraw-Hill, New York 1966, 9:1153. (5) B. Papàsogli, *Montfort: A Prophet for Our Times,* Edizioni Monfortane, Rome 1991, 105. (6) Cardinal de Bérulle, *Opuscules de piété,* Aubier-Montaigne, Paris 1944, 439-440. (7) Papàsogli, *Montfort,* 75-76. (8) It is important to note that Saint Louis de Montfort stresses in his version of Holy Slavery not the dependence of the humanity of Christ on the Divine Person but the loving mutual surrender of Jesus to Mary and Mary to Jesus. This point, often overlooked, has repercussions throughout Montfort's doctrine. (9) Papàsogli, *Montfort,* 80. (10) Ibid., 39. (11) There is no doubt that Saint Louis de Montfort's mortifications were intense: "Given the excesses of his nature, his great desire for perfection and that zeal of his which is a mixture of nature and grace, it is not surprising that his practice of mortification errs on the side of extravagance rather than restraint." Ibid., 46. Montfort surely would not think that he was "extravagant" in his penances, especially since they were constantly held in check by his obedience to his directors. (12) Grandet, 341-345. (13) Ibid., 342: "He observed this same style of life [i.e., one of great mortifications] often enough during the time of missions," which implies that often he at least lessened his mortifications while undergoing the rigors of a parish mission.

MYSTIC

INTRODUCTION: MYSTICISM AND MYSTERY

Psychological and sociological research within the last few years point out that more and more people are seeking a stable foundation in the Absolute. A new religiosity has developed that is characterized by a search for experience, unity, and cosmic totality. Thus there has emerged a special interest in what is called a "mystical" experience. But in the course of the discussion on what "mystical" means (often almost entirely outside Christian tradition), it is finally noted that the concept has been completely emptied of any content. "Mystical experience" has been leveled off to a point where often it has no other meaning than "daily experience."

Against this minimizing tendency, it must be remembered that according to the classical Christian understanding, mystical experience is one of the highest and most intense human experiences. The adjective "mystical" (hidden) describes from the very start something that is connected to the mystery of God's love for us manifested in Christ.[1] "Mystical" cannot be separated from "mystery." It is not an experience that originates in the center of a person but an objective reality: the revelation of God in Jesus Christ. It is first of all Jesus Christ himself who is mystical, for in him the salvific action of God becomes visible, the mystery that forms the core of the Christian proclamation. The Christian is involved in this mystery through the

Sacraments of Baptism (mystical rebirth) and Eucharist (mystical food).

The term "mysticism" becomes another manner of expressing the contemplation of divine mysteries. In the power of the Holy Spirit, contemplation admires the divine truths and is called "mystical" because, on the one hand, these truths are totally penetrated with mystery and, on the other, they are not able to be grasped by human intelligence or be manipulated by it. The milieu of mystical contemplation is sacramental union, mystical union of the creature with God in Jesus Christ. Thus, mystical contemplation has as its goal unity with God in the encounter with Jesus Christ.

I. Montfort in the Mystical Context of the Seventeenth Century

1. The "golden age" of French mysticism

With the rediscovery of the dignity of man in his own individuality—which occurred during the transition to modern times—the interior aspect of experience (the subjectivity) was certainly strongly stressed; nonetheless, the objective aspect was maintained. It was not until the seventeenth century, the "golden age" of French mysticism, that in reaction against the rationalist and empirical spirit of the age, there was a more determined turn toward mysticism and the adjective "mystical" began to change meaning.

From the adjective "mystical" comes the noun "mystic." The negative semantic content of the adjective, in the sense that man cannot program it of himself, gives a mysterious character to the noun. The "contemplative," who "looks at" the mystery of God, becomes "the mystic," surrounded by something of the mysterious and of the extraordinary, a person of "contemplation," a manner of plunging oneself into the mysterious reality of God. Its study becomes "mysticism," an esoteric science, reserved to a few rare people. And so a new scientific branch is born that has for its object mystical events and experiences, the extraordinary: the "science of the saints," mystical theology. As an experiential science, it is often opposed to scholastic theology and, as such, is detached from it. It therefore follows that theological truth acquires a cold and rational aspect. This revolution leads to a polarization between a radical rejection and an unlimited exaggeration of the "mystical" phenomenon that leans ever more towards the extraordinary. The quarrels about quietism at the end of the seventeenth century reflect this polarization.[2]

2. Montfort and the "science of the saints"

Montfort was one of the last representatives of the apex of French mysticism and was also at the threshold of another epoch, called the age of Enlightenment because it tended to consider suspect all mystical phenomenon and to limit the life of piety as much as possible to the ordinary.

From his childhood, Montfort had a pronounced passion for the absolute. He could not adopt as a rule of life the "ordinary," which in reality only means an undeveloped Christianity, immobilized in its very beginnings. For him, the only goal to be considered is Christian perfection, to which all the baptized are called (SM 3).

In his "systematic" yearning for this perfection, he found the support of his directors in spirituality. But it is likewise the proper theme of the "science of the saints," towards which Montfort turned from 1695 on. He reflected the influence of the mystic J. J. Surin, whose *Spiritual Letters* strongly impressed Montfort.[3] Louis Grignion found in Surin the ideal of a total renouncement of all earthly reality so as to benefit from the pure love of God and of intimacy with Him. This idea of a withdrawn and hidden life for God Alone had, at this time, the favor of the directors of the Seminary of Saint Sulpice. They gave it priority over the active life of a missionary. Montfort recognized this in the writings of J. J. Olier and in the person of J. J. Bayün, his spiritual director from 1692 to 1695.[4] The conflict between these two ideals was only resolved by Montfort after long interior struggles, which lasted through the first years of his priesthood and which finally clarified and confirmed his missionary vocation.

In turning towards the science of the saints, Montfort entered into contact with a great number of spiritual authors of his time (TD 90, 159-163) and, through them, with the movements influencing the period of the apex of French mysticism in the seventeenth century. Among these currents, a few must be cited: German mysticism of the fourteenth century, the mystical traditions of the Cistercians and of the Spanish Carmelites, and Italian mysticism.[5] Montfort lists the names of their representatives.

This also fashioned his language. It is not the cold language of theological science but the emotional, colorful language of the science of the saints,[6] with a particular preference for the concepts of "*secret*" and "*mystery*" and for the word "*love.*" And his criticism of a purely rational and empirical science (LEW 84-85) and of a "*speculative, dry, sterile and indifferent*" theology (TD 64) must be understood as the echo of the science of the saints. Beyond any oratorical emphasis, the words of Montfort give insight into how much he was personally taken up by mystery. He did keep, nonetheless, a healthy levelheadedness in the face of extraordinary mystical experiences so much appreciated at that time, like visions, revelations, miracles, etc., and likewise in the face of the false mysticism of quietism, characterized by passivity, which asks no collaboration from the soul. Against this, Montfort insisted on the absolute necessity of personal effort, of collaboration with grace (SM 1, 4; TD 99, 108), and of universal mortification (LEW 184-203) and on the priority of pure faith, which goes beyond experiences perceptible by the senses (LEW 186; SM 51; TD 109, 214).

Montfort found his vocation in missionary service. He was an apostolic missionary, and his entire life took its meaning from his determination to "*renew the spirit of Christianity among Christians*" (RM 56). It is this motivation which gave birth to his writings. Thus, he did not leave us any autobiographical notes on his personal experiences of faith but only rare allusions in his letters and in the dialogue reported by J. B. Blain.[7] In his writings, his experience of personal faith is revealed tightly interwoven with his vision of theological truth and his pastoral experiences.

II. The "Experimental Knowledge of God" in Montfort in the Light of the Pauline Mystery

Mysticism, according to the classical definition, is "the experiential knowledge of God," *cognitio Dei experimentalis* (Bonaventure). Montfort's writings are characterized by a successful unity between experience of the faith and knowledge of the faith, a unity in which knowledge of the faith has become alive. Knowledge and love are the two poles (LEW 8) around which everything moves: loving knowledge and knowing love, both oriented totally towards the mystery of God.[8]

Montfort's "experiential knowledge" of God is most forcefully seen in LEW. This work was the fruit of a lengthy *lectio divina*, whose meditation centered on Divine Wisdom. The key to his understanding is found in 1 Cor 1-2; faced with the conflicts at Corinth, Paul brings out the great worth of the only true mystery of God.[9] It was in the Pauline mystery of the Wisdom of God, which in the eyes of men is folly, that Montfort continued his research. This mystery was revealed to him ever more profoundly when he looked back at the Wisdom of OT.[10]

1. Wisdom is folly

If in the sapiential literature of OT, Wisdom was already personalized, she became personified according to the intuition of the French school. Divine Wisdom, which appears in OT as a woman, is Jesus Christ, "whom God made our wisdom" (1 Cor 1:30). In him is revealed the mystery of God, but in the form of folly and of weakness and therefore in opposition to all human wisdom and power. What Montfort—along with Paul—discovered ever more profoundly is the "mysterious passion that God expresses under the form of 'folly,' which impels Him even into the weakness of humbling Himself."[11] For Montfort, that was an entirely other thing than dry, arid articles of faith. That this knowledge became for him the key to his own life, or that his experience of his life led him to this knowledge, is, in the final analysis, without importance. But this knowledge was inscribed ever more deeply in the experience of his life and helps us to understand it. In his own life, this divine folly took, in a certain sense, a new form. The more that this knowledge penetrated him thoroughly, the more he easily succeeded in accepting the experiences of folly that continually crossed his life, without losing any interior peace. And he succeeded in living these divine truths more simply and peacefully.

But Montfort learnt also, more and more, that from this folly of God arises the dynamic of an unlimited liberty. Faith-filled weakness and folly share in the weakness of God crucified, liberating a force that is stronger than man's and a wisdom that is wiser than all human wisdom. The life of Montfort testifies to this. He gave witness to a radical life style expressed in trust in Divine Providence, in voluntary poverty, and in the limitless acceptance of suffering. He appeared so foolish that toward the end of his life even his friend Blain thought of him this way.[12] Nevertheless, it was this same style of life that was transformed into a strength going beyond all understanding.

Montfort points this out when he writes: *"I find such riches in this divine Providence and so much strength in the Blessed Mother, that they suffice to enrich my poverty and support my weakness"* (L 8). *"I never made so many conversions than after the most anguishing and unjust interdicts"* (L 26). The experience of this liberty and of this strength is reflected in the collection of characteristics he foresaw for future members of his missionary community: *"Liberos—men who are free with your liberty"* (PM 7-12).

2. Passion of Divine Love

The mysterious passion that impelled God into the folly of the Incarnation Montfort recognized as love. This knowledge changed the representation he had of God: from the Almighty Lord to the loving Father. This became the central point of his experiential knowledge of God; with Paul and John, he discovered the "central factor" of the mystery of God, which is revealed in Christ Jesus: the love of God. He can, therefore, say that Christ-Wisdom is *"the love of the Father and of the Holy Spirit"* (LEW 118; cf Jn 3:16). From this point of view, Montfort can reread salvation history as the history of Divine Wisdom, in which is incarnated God's eternal plan of salvation and which wins the final victory in the folly of the Cross. In his presentation, Montfort follows the outline of classical theology: Trinity—Creation—Original Fall—Incarnation; but by presenting it under the form of dramatized history, he is able to make a far more immediate impression than under the form of abstract teaching. Salvation history is the history of the love of the Eternal Wisdom for man, the history of *"an incomprehensible friendship"*; *"Wisdom is for man and man is for Wisdom"* (LEW 64). This friendship finds its culminating point in the spiritual marriage of Wisdom with the soul (LEW 54).

In order to describe the love union between Christ and the soul, Montfort takes up one of the most ancient symbols of Christian spirituality, spousal union. With the same symbol, he characterizes his own experience: *"In the new family to which I belong, I have espoused Wisdom and the cross"* (L 20).

3. Wisdom and Cross

In Wisdom and the Cross are found the Pauline vision of mystery. The Cross of Christ is the definitive revelation of the Wisdom of God, Who wills that salvation be accomplished in Christ crucified (1 Cor 1:24). Montfort concentrates Pauline thought into this one point: *"Wisdom is the cross and the cross is Wisdom"* (LEW 180). And after maturely reflecting on the love of Wisdom for the Cross (LEW 167-171), which culminates in the *"marriage in blood"* on the Cross (LEW 171), he says:

"*Never the cross without Jesus or Jesus without the cross*" (LEW 172). But this Wisdom is Wisdom in mystery, accessible only to those to whom God has revealed *"the greatest secret of the Eternal Wisdom"* (LEW 167, 174; FC 26). This discovery is accomplished in faith. To those who welcome the Word of the Cross in the obedience of faith, this secret of Wisdom is revealed before their eyes as the culminating point of the love of God (LEW 154), while human and earthly wisdom is revealed as dangerous wisdom, precisely because it strips the Cross of its essential content (LEW 174; FC 36).

Thus Montfort describes in all its cruelty the agony of the Cross—he describes even to the least details what Christ has suffered on the Cross (LEW 154-166)—but at the same time, he recognizes that precisely in that is revealed the excess of love of God. The Cross is no longer the expression of the anger of God but the proof of his love (LEW 176). That is why Montfort is able to take up again the symbolism of espousals, when he has Wisdom declare: "*I love the cross with all my strength and I place it in the midst of my heart so that it may be my spouse and my mistress*"; and the suffering of Wisdom culminates in the marriage of blood on the Cross: "*He dies with joy in the embrace of his beloved friend, as on a bed of honor and triumph*" (LEW 171).

The presentation of the *"triumph of eternal wisdom in the cross and by the cross*" (LEW, chap. 14; H 19; H 102) permits the Johannine vision of the Cross to shine through, in which the Cross is the authentic revelation of the glory of God (LEW 170), which is not the glory of the Almighty but of the surrender by Love to its very extremes.

4. Surrender even to extremes

Surrender, abandonment, even to extremes, became for Montfort the principle of life. For the Cross is not only the objective reality of salvation; it is not only and simply object of the kerygma. It is precisely the "*Word of the Cross,*" which took flesh in Jesus Christ. Montfort already recognizes the mystery of the Cross in the mystery of the Incarnation (LEW 169). It is not "no matter which" Christ who becomes man but Christ crucified. It is the Incarnation in view of the agony of the Cross, and because of that the entire life of Christ is situated under the sign of the Cross. The only model of Christian life (LEW 173; FC 19) is therefore Christ in his voluntary humbling and nothingness, the Model of life that Paul presents in Phil 2 (LEW 16-17); Montfort makes this the theme of FC. In explaining the words of Jesus, "Whoever wishes to be my disciple, let him renounce himself, take up his cross, and follow me" (Mt 16:24; Lk 9:23), he shows how Christian life is completely situated under the mystery of the Cross. To be Christian, to become like unto Christ, to be united to Christ, is not possible without the Cross. Jesus must be followed on the way of voluntary nothingness, of humility, of service, of abandonment even to the extreme. In other words, Montfort—following Paul—says: to become a slave, we must knowingly and willingly follow the example of

Jesus Christ, the suffering Servant of God (TD 18, 72-73, 139). This means nothing else than to welcome the Cross in our own lives, permitting it to become the determining force of our lives, letting ourselves be crucified with Christ (1 Cor 1:18-31; Gal 6:14; LEW 173; FC 19). This includes the Yes to our own weakness and lowliness; and like Paul, Montfort considers weakness, trial, suffering, and failure because of the Cross as *"the sufferings of Christ,"* to a point of regarding such *"crosses"* as the greatest gifts of God for the Christian (FC 35-39; LEW 174-175; TD 154; H 102), because through the Cross conformity to Christ becomes a reality.

That is why the Cross also determines the relation of the Christian to the world, which "cannot be an unrestrained acceptance of the world nor a total satisfaction of being in the world."[13] Looking upon the Cross, the Christian will tend far more to serve the world than to be served by it; in so doing, the unconditional service to the world is in harmony with the distance from the world (which always remains a world disrupted by sin) and also with a radical asceticism. But it is precisely this forgetfulness of self in *kenosis* and this abandonment without reserve following the example of Christ that leads the Christian to this paradoxical experience of joy in suffering (FC 51), and even through suffering. This is what Montfort says in colorful language, in phrases like "*cross . . . in sugar*" (TD 154) or "*candied crosses*" (SM 22). Formally, Montfort describes this experience as the love of the Cross, which is not a love for suffering but always love for Christ; it is "*the love of the summit of the soul. . . . Without any feeling of joy in the senses or pleasure in the mind, we love the cross we are carrying by the light of pure faith and take delight in it*" (FC 53). The fruits of this love of the Cross are conformity to Christ, dignity of divine filiation, a sense of life, love, joy, interior peace, and, finally, eternal glory (LEW 176; H 123).

The personal experiences of Montfort in his following of Christ carrying his Cross dovetail perfectly with his sources, thus assuring an indissoluble unity in his life. In this regard, reference should be made above all to the *Holy Ways of the Cross*[14] of Boudon but also to the *Mysticism of the Passion* of Henry Suso, which Montfort cites explicitly (LEW 66, 101-102) and for which "a suffering sent by God and accepted by man is a sign of divine predilection, as the suffering of Christ is a sign of the gracious attention of God."[15] For Montfort also, the Cross is the sign of the chosen, the sign of election and of the special favor of God (LEW 174-175; SM 22).

5. Christ in us: the goal and the center of montfort spirituality

"The perfect friend of the Cross is a true Christ-bearer, or rather, another Christ" (FC 4). This is the experience to which Paul gives witness in Gal: "If I live, it is no longer I but Christ who lives in me" (Gal 2:20; FC 4). For the mystery of God that has been revealed in Christ crucified is at the same time the mystery of "Christ in you, the hope of glory" (Col 1:27). This mystery of "Christ in us" is

precisely at the heart of the thought of Montfort. Whether he speaks of *"union with Christ"* (TD 120), "*the acquisition and the conservation of Wisdom*" (LEW 14), "*the consecration to Jesus Christ"* (TD 120), or *"the perfect renewal of the vows of baptism"* (TD 120), it is always a matter of Christ in us, of this Christ who has come to pitch his tent among us, which is the fruit of the grace of Baptism. The missionary effort of Montfort had as its object to open the entry to "*Christ in us*" in such a way that this living presence of Christ in us becomes a tangible experience.

6. Christ in Mary and in us: the mystery of the Incarnation

"Christ in us." In no other person has this mystery been realized as marvelously and tangibly as in the person of Mary: "*You are, Lord, always with Mary and Mary is always with you and cannot be without you: otherwise she would cease being who she is: she is so transformed in you by grace that she no longer lives, that she is no longer; it is only you, my Jesus, who live and reign in her, more perfectly than in all the angels and the blessed*" (TD 63; SM 21). For in the Incarnation, Jesus has fixed his abode in Mary, has entered the body of Mary, and has taken possession of her maternal powers. That is why Mary is the archetype of all those who through faith are open to Christ. Her openness, her sense of welcome, and her availability permit the Holy Spirit to produce in her the Son of God (TD 20). The contemplation of the mystery of the Incarnation, which Montfort considers as the representative mystery of his spirituality (TD 243)—completely in line with Bérulle and Olier—is the contemplation of Christ in Mary (TD 246-248); it is in this mystery that the permanent and indissoluble unity of Christ and Mary finds its foundation (TD 165; H 87).

But Montfort discovered in the mystery of the incarnation yet another dimension, which he designated as "*an unknown secret of grace"* (TD 21). For the mystery of the Incarnation is also the mystery of the Holy Spirit, Who in and through Mary produces Jesus Christ and his members (TD 21). Not only does the Holy Spirit act with Mary in the Incarnation of the Son; the extension of the mystery of Christ in us by Baptism and the production of the growth of Christ in us are the common work of the Holy Spirit and of Mary. Montfort calls Mary the "*dispenser of all the graces of the Holy Spirit* (SM 10, 13, 67; TD 240); with her the Holy Spirit produces all the children of God (TD 33; SM 56; LEW 214). The formation and the education of these children of God are the task of Mary (TD 35; PM 15), so that they "*may become perfect and that they may present Christ in the fullness of his age"* (Eph 4:13; LEW 214; TD 33, 61, 119, 156, 164, 168).

In Montfort's eyes, the experiential knowledge of the common action of the Holy spirit and of Mary in order to produce Christ in us recalls the theology of the birth of God, according to which Mary contributes to the birth of the Divine Word in the heart of man. "With this formula of the birth of God in the heart, an allusion is made to the mystical touch by God, and by that fact man, the created, is implicated very intimately in this event."[16] In popular Catholic tradition, Mary is spontaneously perceived as the one in whom this mystical life is accomplished, as the type of the intimate encounter of God.

As there has always been a mysterious unity among the Holy Spirit, Jesus Christ, Mary, and the Christian, the contemplation of the mystery of the Incarnation can and must have this result: that the presence of Christ develops in the believer the same effects as in Mary—the spirit of her holiness, the fullness of her power, the perfection of her ways, the truth of her virtues, the communion with her mysteries, as Olier has described in his prayer "O Jesus Living in Mary," which Montfort thought of so highly (TD 246; H 111). And that is why it can also be deduced that whoever takes Mary as his model assimilates her manner of living and accomplishes everything "by, with, in, and for" her (TD 257-265; SM 43-49), thus becoming like her and thereby, at the same time, like unto Christ (TD 120). When the soul is entirely penetrated by the spirit of Mary, *"which is the spirit of God"* (TD 120), and the soul is transformed into Mary, then is realized—as an unmerited gift of God—this experience that Montfort has designated as "*the grace of the permanent presence of Jesus and Mary in the soul.*"[17]

III. The Mystique of the Permanent Presence of Jesus and Mary

The summit of his own experiential knowledge of God Montfort declared to be *"the permanent presence of Jesus and Mary in his soul."* It is one of the rare personal testimonies on his spiritual evolution that he left us. For he was, in his entire being, an apostolic missionary, and he had no intention to give us a detailed exposé of his faith experience.

A rapid glance at his life and writings makes it evident that his experiential knowledge of God was not the result of spectacular spiritual experiences nor of any revelation suddenly fallen from the sky. His experience of union with Christ was not a strange event; it was not a unique, rare, and passing experience. Rather, it was the experience of the permanent presence of Christ in the soul, rooted in human existence; this experience is the fruit of a maturing process of man in his totality. We see here the reflection of the experience of the Johannine "permanence" (Jn 15:4), which is a free gift but calls for an openness and receptivity on the part of the believer, with an attitude that is a committal of his entire human existence (TD 78-82). It is finally the total abandonment that Montfort calls *"slavery"* (TD 121) and that so marked his life.

His spirituality of Consecration to Jesus Christ by Mary in the form of slavery should be understood as a means of leading to a life of the continual presence of God, which Montfort describes in detail in his hymn "*The holy practice of the presence of God*" (H 24). In this hymn, Montfort expresses his personal experience in poetic language: "*God residing in us more than in any other thing / It is in our hearts that His majesty is to be sought, / it is there that it is seen / in all its clarity. / God chose our hearts to be his throne and domain, / He attracts us there to taste night and day / his sovereign beauty / and his divine love*" (H 24:23-24).

To live constantly in the presence of God does not signify simply to be always conscious of the omnipresence of God. Rather, it means living in faith and trust in the dynamic goodness and love of God. It entails an abandonment, without any deviation, to the loving Providence of God, Who cares for man even to the least details, a Providence that Montfort himself lived to a point where no one, no suffering could shake him.

The radical poverty of Montfort can, finally, only be understood on the basis of the "foolish" trust that he placed in the Providence of God and that is rooted in the experience that is the core of all authentic mystical experience: in the experience of God as the absolute *Thou*. From his childhood, Montfort had the boldness, through grace, to address the *Thou* of God in all simplicity.

In all this, he was led by Mary herself, who forms and guides us (TD 219-221, 258-259; SM 16-18). Under the guidance of Mary, Montfort plunged his roots into an ever more profound attachment to Christ. With Mary, his desire ever intensified for union with Christ Wisdom (L 12, 14, 15, 16), to whom he knew he was joined by a mystical marriage (L 20). The union with Christ, received as a gift, became a permanent union and a continual presence in Jesus and in Mary. The mystery of "Christ in him" was the motor and the strength of his life and of his apostolic service, which consisted in assisting Christ to burst forth in the ordinary lives of the baptized.

IV. Perspectives for an Authentic Experience of God

In the pluralism of ideologies in the present world, Christianity can no longer pretend to be the only one presenting an absolute meaning and valid responses to the fundamental questions of life. This does not contradict the claim of having absolute truth, but it does oblige each Christian in particular—and the Church—to make its religious conviction plausible. This can only succeed when faith finally becomes a personal decision. At this threshold of the twenty-first century, "the Christian can not simply act like everyone else and assume that the faith is simply gift, but must understand that he is to lay hold of it through a personal decision." His faith must "be lived in a more profound and conscious manner and therefore in a manner more constructive of personality."[18]

Now this is exactly the preoccupation of Montfort. With his spirituality of Consecration to Jesus Christ through Mary, his goal is precisely to lead the Christian in his life and his faith to a conscious decision, responsible and personal. The Consecration is, according to him, a "*perfect renewal of the vows and promises of holy baptism*" (TD 120), which finally does not mean anything other than to grab hold of the faith in a "personal decision." The effects of this Consecration, as Montfort has described them on the basis of his own personal experience, can be summed up in the two key phrases "transcendence of self" and "authenticity." They are the fruits of a faith that becomes ever more profound, more conscious, and more constructive of personality.

This process can only succeed if the quality of the sense of the faith itself becomes for the believer a conviction. It must become an authentic experience of faith that leads to belief. Montfort wants to lead man to this kind of experience, which gives the faithful a sure and indestructible foundation. It is an experience of the *Thou* of God, a *Thou* Whom we meet in Jesus Christ. Across all the changes in time, culture, and theology, Montfort is strongly touched by what K. Rahner has formulated: "Religious man of tomorrow will be a mystic, someone who has experienced God, or else he will no longer be."[19]

Montfort had sensed the importance of the mystical experience, of incomparable importance when the faith is at stake. If today the most important mission of the Church must be that of preparing the road toward this experience, then the "little mystical way" of Montfort appears now and always as such a path for the Christian.

H.J. Jünemann

Notes: (1) L. Bouyer, *Mysterion. Du mystère à la mystique (Mysterion: From Mystery to Mysticism),* O.E.I.L., Paris 1986, 12, 98. (2) J. Sudbrack, *Mystik. Selbsterfahrung - kosmische Erfahrung - Gotteserfahrung (Mysticism: Experience of Self, of Cosmos, of God),* Grunewald, Mainz 1988, 30-39. (3) Itinerario, 170-183. (4) Ibid., 184-200. (5) Cf. B. Papàsogli, *Gli spirituali italiani e il "grand siècle." François de Sales - Bérulle - Pascal - La Rochefoucauld - Bossuet - Fénelon (Italian Spirituality in the "Great Century"),* Ed. Storia e leteratura, Rome 1983. (6) This colorful language of Montfort is often baroque and poses a problem for some Western readers. (7) Blain, 184-189. (8) For an analysis, in a mystical perspective, of the words "to know" and "to love" as found in LEW, see P. Humblet, *Le processus de transformation dans "L'amour de la Sagesse éternelle" de Grignion de Montfort (The Process of Transformation in "The Love of Eternal Wisdom" by Grignion de Montfort),* Institut Titus Brandsma/Filles de la Sagesse, Nimegen/Berg en Dal 1991, 10-12. (9) Bouyer, *Mysterion,* 13-30, 127-141. (10) H. Frehen, *De Liefde tot de Eeuwige Wijsheid en Synthese van Montforts Spiritualiteit (The Love of Eternal Wisdom a Synthesis of Montfort's Spirituality),* in *Montfort. Zijn geestlijke Vorming en Levenswerk,* Maastricht 1947, 197-217; H. M. Manteau-Bonamy, *S. Louis-Marie Grignion de Montfort, théologien de la Sagesse éternelle au seuil du troisième millénaire (St. Louis de Montfort, Theologian of the Eternal Wisdom at the Threshold of the Third Millenium),* Editions Saint-Paul, Paris/Fribourg 1986, 26-28. (11) S. Breton, *Saint-Paul,* PUF, Paris 1988, 113; cf. LEW 41-46. (12) Blain, 185-190. (13) F. J. Ortkemper, *Das Kreuz in der Verkündigung des Apostels Paulus (The Cross in the Preaching of the Apostle Paul),* KBW, Stuttgart 1967, 99. (14) S. De Fiores, o.c., 106-112. (15) G. Hinricher, *Kreuzesmystik (Mysticism of the Cross),* in: *Praktisches Lexikon der Spiritualität (Practical Lexicon of Spirituality),* Herder, Freiburg 1988, 737. (16) J. Sudbrack, *Mystische Spuren (Mystical Traces),* Echter, Würzburg 1990, 311. (17) cf. Blain, 191. (18) J. Sudbrack, *Mystiche Spuren,* 89. (19) *Schriften zur Theologie (Theological Writings),* 5:22.

Mary Queen of All Hearts

This statue sculpted by Paolo Bartolini, is to be found in the Italian Provincial House chapel on the Via Romagna in Rome.

NOELS/CHRISTMAS

SUMMARY

I. INTRODUCTION.

II. CHRISTMAS IN MONTFORT'S TIME:
   1. Montfort's childhood;
   2. Reaching maturity at the seminary:
      a. The essence of Bérulle's thought,
      b. Absolutism,
      c. Disdain of infancy,
      d. A new emphasis.

III. MONTFORT'S VISION OF CHRISTMAS:
   1. Christmas in Montfort's preaching;
   2. The hymns.

IV. A LITERARY ANALYSIS AND DISCUSSION OF THE CONTENT OF MONTFORT'S CHRISTMAS HYMNS:
   1. Omnipotence reduced to infancy;
   2. The Virgin Mother;
   3. Infancy;
   4. A personal experience of God.

V. CHRISTMAS IN MONTFORT'S SPIRITUALITY:
   1. The spirituality of the Incarnation;
   2. The spirituality of loving dependence;
   3. The spirituality of hope and joy.

I. INTRODUCTION

The angels at Bethlehem sang of joy. Yet the ambiguous historical origins of Christmas, especially since it was celebrated during the pagan festivals of the winter solstice, repressed some of its spontaneity.[1] The Latin hymns of the fifth to the thirteenth centuries reflect this. These hymns, composed by monks, were theological rather than realistic or closely concerned with life. They dealt above all with the Incarnation and the Nativity as part of the Redemption, probably in reaction to the 5th century errors of Nestorianism. Little effort was made to imagine the scene of the stable in Bethlehem. Little interest was shown in the Infant as an infant, and little sensitivity was displayed towards the human side of the Nativity. St. Bernard, in his first sermon on the Nativity, limited himself to stating that "the God of Majesty, in emptying Himself, conformed Himself not only to the earthly body of mortals but also to the weak and infirm age of infancy."[2] Six centuries later, Cardinal de Bérulle was to express exactly these ideas. This monastic spirit is reflected in the hymns of the Church composed by monks. Not until Jacopone da Todi (1230-1306) do feelings of a more human kind appear. It was difficult for faith to blossom in a popular religion steeped in superstition, in a Christianity mixed often indiscriminately with paganism. Fear of punishment was often stronger than joy. The world was haunted by evil spirits and goblins, whose evil influence could only be warded off by charms and offerings. Luckily, the thirteenth century brought the sweetness and joy of an Italian sun to this dark picture.[3] A happier, more human religion appeared, which saw in the Infant of Bethlehem not only a theological mystery but an Infant full of charm—God, of course, but a God Who felt with us the cold of winter and the rough straw of the crib. At the same time, in 1223, three years before his death, Francis of Assisi was authorized by the Pope to popularize this vision. This was also the time (though some locate it as early as the middle of the tenth century, when the people ceased to understand Latin) when lighter Christmas songs began to appear in the vernacular, called mixed noels, in which Latin and the ordinary languages alternated: "Let us celebrate the birth / Nostri Salvatoris / Who is the delight / Dei nostri Salvatoris." This genre persisted until the time of Louis XIV. As the songs circulated between different regions, the form as well as the melody changed. One author, who seems not to have known Montfort, writes that "apart from a few rustic Christmas songs, the eighteenth century produced little French poetry of any charm."[4] It is perhaps significant that the first collection of truly French noels came from Poitou, which is very close to Montfort's region. These songs were published in Paris in 1520 under the name Lucas Le Moine, curate of St. Georges at Puy-la-Garde, in the diocese of Poitiers. The author was apparently an uncle of Rabelais who hid himself under this name.[5]

II. Christmas in Montfort's Time

In order to grasp the significance of Christmas in Montfort's spirituality, we must return to the Brittany of his time, and as far as we can reconstruct its religious climate. We must enter the world of beliefs and practices in which the people lived and breathed. Its environment was a convergence of religious, social and agrarian realities. Across the centuries, Christian festivals developed which reflected the rhythm of the seasons, and the cycles in cultivating the land. Popular religion was shaped in a world dominated by such a deeply-rooted lifestyle. It left its mark on even the most alienated souls. "They remained faithfully devoted to their ancestors, they loved the times past, they respected the old ways, they cared for the primordial soil."[6]

1. Montfort's childhood

Montfort's biographers do not describe what Christmas was like within his family circle. But it was probably similar to that of most of his contemporaries. The Christmas of 1672 preceded his birth on January 31 by scarcely a month. His mother Jeanne Robert was already eight months pregnant when the Christmas bells rang. Her son's birth so close to Christmas, could not have left her indifferent to Mary's giving birth to Jesus. Moreover,she had undergone a very painful experience when she lost her firstborn boy four days after his birth. It is unclear how soon after his birth little Louis Marie was turned over to the wet nurse named Mère André, a peasant from la Bachelleraie. Louis Marie remained with her about two years. Like all Breton children, Louis Marie was to have memorable evenings round the hearthfire—"long winter evenings peopled by ghosts."[7] Brittany was the classic land of myth and legend. It blended its Celtic and Christian spiritual experience into an enchanted story telling tradition. Christmas Eve was a special time for telling tales. It was no time to be a skeptic about fantastic people, places and events. It was commonplace for the drowned to return from the sea, for the damned to raise their tombstones.[8] When he returned to his family, Louis Marie lived at Bois Marquer, attending the church at Iffendic. Louis Marie, already a child imbued with an immense sensitivity to the spiritual world, experienced a great deepening of his faith during this period. This fact was particularly evident from the way he treated his younger sister Guyonne. In Montfort's rural home, Advent was a period of waiting, of expectation, both in in terms of the agrarian and the religious life cycles. The low sun, the long evenings, the first gorse flowers and the holly already announced the approach of Christmas, which was always celebrated in grandiose fashion in the French provinces.[9] When Christmas came, the children cleaned their clogs carefully, then placed them at the foot of the chimneypiece and the following day discovered what "little Jesus" had put in them—very small gifts, for toys were still unknown. At church, Louis Marie listened to traditional hymns. He was impressed by this huge house "of the good God," by its decoration, by the Latin that he did not understand and that added to the mystery. His eyes and ears were open to the ceremonies and to the engravings in the stone, "visible and eloquent signs that are the missal of the poor."[10] If Chateaubriand was able to describe the stunning effect of Christmas, of the New Year, of Twelfth Night, on his child's soul—"I experienced an extraordinary religious feeling"—we can easily imagine what Louis Marie might have felt, but with still more intensity since the action of the Holy Spirit was already so manifest within him.[11]

2. Reaching maturity at the seminary

The traditional faith Montfort acquired during his childhood and adolescence was further strengthened and developed in Paris. There he had many new teachers, some in person others in books. The Holy Spirit integrated everything for Montfort, and transformed him into a spiritual master able to teach by word and deed, by preaching and writing. The men to whom he entrusted his soul for spiritual direction were holy priests,most of whom greeted his ascetic tastes with surprising approval.

a. The essence of Bérulle's thought. Everything can be summed up in this saying of Bérulle: "What is man? A nothing capable of God." According to pope Urban XIII, Bérulle was the apostle of the greatness of God. He was inspired by the power of theocentric religion, a spirituality perfectly embodied in the Word Incarnate. This spirituality aimed to imitate and to take in more fully Christ's attitudes or "states" (a word coined by the French school in order better to express the permanence of Christ's mysteries) .

b. Absolutism. The sublimity of such a doctrine is open to the danger of absolutism, from which certain of Bérulle's disciples were not exempt. When the greatness of God was considered next to the nothingness of the creature, the latter can logically appear quite abject. The Incarnation was an absolute self-abasement, of which Christmas was the realization. "From the throne of those glories where the Son of God lives by his first, eternal birth, he humbles himself and descends to earth and the womb of the Virgin to be born a second time. . . . And our senses perceive him, not as on high but as very humble."[12] In this Olympian contemplation, there is nothing to soften the heart. "The harsh reality hidden beneath 'the grace and kindness that appeared to us with this Infant' is the self-abasement of the Word Incarnate."[13]

c. Disdain of infancy. At their most extreme, the disciples of Bérulle went beyond these high considerations. Not only did they fail to speak of the humanity of the Christ Child, exalting instead his divinity, but they fell into an exaggerated way of speaking which expressed nothing but contempt for the state of infancy. For Condren, the crib merely portrayed a wretched creature who "appears to be no more than an infant," who is "a composite of four types of wretchedness: smallness, poverty and dependence on others, subjection, uselessness." Therefore he seems to want Jesus "finally to discard the shameful exterior of the state of infancy" as quickly as possible.[14] Bérulle similarly asserted that infancy was "the most vile and abject state of human nature after the state of death."[15] This attitude was taken to what Bremond described as an extreme state of "inane fanaticism" by a certain Jean Garat, abbot of Chancelade, who could never bring himself to touch small children, for the veil of the flesh "always exhaled qualities so malignant that there was a danger of infection."[16]

d. A new emphasis. Others avoided such excesses, while maintaining the same principles. Gaston de Renty, "one of the first disciples of the early followers of Bérulle,"[17] wrote: "The infancy of our Lord . . . teaches us self-emptying and docility before God. . . . The soul does not rise to anything by itself but, on the contrary, empties itself absolutely and allows itself humbly to be led with . . . the simplicity of a pure, abandoned attitude."[18] We need only introduce the happy images and thoughts that the vision of a child evokes into the formulation of Bérulle, and the austere doctrine becomes gentle. Self-abasement is replaced by self-surrender; and self-negation is replaced by simplicity.[19] After Bérulle, were John Eudes and especially Margaret Mary Alacoque. The new emphasis we have just noted was largely influenced by the devotion to the Sacred Heart that began in Montfort's time: he was born in 1673, the year of the great revelations of the Sacred Heart to St. Margaret Mary.

III. Montfort's Vision of Christmas

Montfort was imbued first with the traditional religion of his family and milieu and second with the spiritual education which he received at the hands of his spiritual directors, who followed Bérulle's teachings. How did he express this double legacy in his life as preacher and author? He was too much of an individual to be merely the reflection of the influences to which he had been exposed. He absorbed all aspects of these influences in his own very rich nature. "He was human with the best of human values, displaying love of men and the temperament of an artist, sculptor, and poet. He was singularly human without being a humanist."[20] It was through this rich nature that he saw Christmas. If the mystery of the Incarnation was fundamental for him, it was in the mystery of the Nativity that the Incarnation was rendered visible and became "what we have seen with our eyes, what we have looked at and touched with our hands" (1 Jn 1:1). While Bérulle lowered his gaze to this holy humanity only to see its weakness, poverty, and abjection, Montfort contemplated its beauty, gentleness, and charms. It would be appropriate here to emphasize his talents as sculptor. Several representations of Virgin and Child are traditionally attributed to him, especially the one that never left him until death, an Our Lady of Wisdom. The child whom Mary carries in her arms is always an extension of Christmas. The Magi do not necessarily find the Infant in his crib. Fra Angelico represents him on the knees of Mary. Whatever the pose, the background of a Virgin and Child is always that of Christmas: "They saw the child with Mary his mother" (Mt 2:11). In this, Montfort showed his balance, compared with the Bérulle school, which was too absolute in its disdain of the world. "There is a spirituality of human values, of the accomplishment of creation, of the action of grace [which Montfort knows well: LEW 36, 39]. And there is a spirituality of the Cross, of detachment, of the radical surpassing of this world of sin: this spirituality is reached via asceticism."[21] Like Francis of Assisi, Montfort knew both types of spirituality well and blended them perfectly together. Christmas tempered the rigors of Calvary.

1. Christmas in Montfort's preaching

All the great preachers have a series of sermons on Christmas. Bossuet preached two before the Court.[22] He dealt with Christmas eight times in his *Elévations sur les mystères (Elevations on the Mysteries)*.[23] There is nothing similar in Montfort. None of his sermons is entitled "Christmas." Should we conclude that he never spoke on this theme?[24] In fact he touches on the mystery of Christmas in many ways. In his last mission sermon at Saint-Laurent-sur-Sèvre, several days before his death, he deals with *"The Love and Gentleness of Jesus Christ"* (LS 1710). Even if we only possess the title, it is reasonable to suppose that he may have returned to ideas explored in Hymn 9 on "*The Charms of Gentleness*," where he mentions the mystery of Christmas: *"From his Infancy He delighted / The Shepherds and the Kings / With such power / That they were ruled by Him. / His smiles, His air of gentleness / Spoke so eloquently / That He won them all over / In total silence*" (H 5). There is a striking similarity between SM 9, Hymn 9, and LEW 121, where Montfort speaks of Wisdom: "*The face of our loving Savior is so serene and gentle that it charmed the eyes and hearts of those who beheld it. The shepherds who came to the stable to see him were so spellbound by the serenity and beauty of his face that they tarried for many days gazing in rapture upon him.*" In SR 8, he relates the story of two little sisters who were saying their Rosary when a beautiful lady appeared to them and took away the younger sister. When she was found three days later, she said that the lady had taken her away to a beautiful place and that she "*had also given her a baby boy to hold . . . and that she had kissed him again and again.*" In MR 19, in the sixth Hail Mary of the Birth of Jesus, he mentions "*the ravishing beauty of her divine child.*" Finally, in TD 18 the idea of the dependence of Jesus is foregrounded instead, in the tradition of Bérulle: "*He glorified his independence and his majesty in depending upon this lovable virgin in his conception, his birth . . . even at his death.*" The historical fact of Christ's birth therefore gives precedence to this spiritual dimension, which embraces his whole life.

2. The hymns

Montfort dealt with the theme of Christmas especially in the hymns. It is regrettable that we do not know under what circumstances he composed the ten noels or hymns on Christmas. They add up to 785 lines. The first nine, Hymn 57 to Hymn 65, are numbered (the first, the second, and so on), each with a title: the Noel of the Angels, of the Shepherds, of the Children, of the Kings, of Pious Souls, of Zealous Souls, of the Children of Mary, of Spiritual Souls. The ninth merely bears the title *"Christmas."* A tenth, Hymn 66, *"The Noel of Schoolchildren,"* is added. Hymn 63, *"Noel of the Children,"* especially exalts Mary, who "*has just borne this adorable Lord*" (H 63:3). "*This Savior only came to us / Because you believed / The word of an angel*" (H 63:4). The only true allusion to Christmas is to be found in strophe 8: "*Jesus loves the stable / But especially loves our heart.*" Hymn 64, with its authentic flavor of Bérulle's thought, is dedicated to *"spiritual souls."* Here attention is concentrated on the Incarnation. God "*becomes what we are, making us become what He is*" (H 64:1). The rest of the hymn proceeds by a series of contrasts. "*This very high Lord lowers himself / To raise us to Heaven, / He comes down into our lowliness, / To give us his glorious being*" (H 64:2). There is nothing pessimistic here. On the contrary, everything opens out onto hope, as does the liturgy, in this Irenaean expression: "*In the admirable exchange of the Eucharistic sacrifice you make us share in your own divine nature.*"[25]

Hymn 65 is quite different from the hymns just mentioned: it is sensitively constructed and recalls the mystery of Christmas in simple terms. A great deal of joy is expressed in the cadence of this hymn: "*A great*

Master / Has just been born to us, / A new King / Rules over us from the crib" (H 65:1); "*He is called / A God made Man / The Son of God / Incarnate in this place*" (H 65:3).

Finally, Hymn 66 is the *"Noel of the Schoolchildren."* Here again there are a different rhythm and a varied description of the mystery. "*Friends, I hear the song of the Angels, / How sweet and melodious it is! / They announce in their praises / A new-born child, King of Heaven. / They say he is in swaddling cloths / Let us adore Him with them*" (H 66:1). *"Do you see Him in a stable? / His mother holds Him in her arms. / Ah, how beautiful He is, how lovable! / How full of charms His face is! / Ah, how sweet, how affable He is! / Let us go to Him, let us make haste*" (H 66:4).

Here and there in other hymns, scattered allusions to Christmas are found. Devotion to the Sacred Heart, revealed to St. Margaret Mary, tended to humanize the aridity of Bérulle's outlook. H 57:6 is subtly inspired by such devotion in the following couplet, in which, addressing Mary, Montfort says: "*You have charmed the Savior, / Beloved Heart, / He gave Himself, / He became God made Man!*" Another brief allusion is found in Hymn 90, in the eighth Hail Mary of the first Decade, "*I salute you, Mary, / In the birth of the Savior,*" which has the following conclusion: "*Oh Virgin and Mother, / I revere you, / Produce Jesus in my heart*" (H 90:14).

Hymn 97 is entitled *"The Great Lesson of the Children Whom One Must Resemble to Enter Heaven."* The hymn does not strictly speak of Christmas, but the birth of Jesus is evoked in an attempt to recapture the spirit of evangelical infancy. The hymn resembles a thesis in the way it sets out its opening proposition: "*Whoever wishes to be / An all-powerful King / According to our Master, / Must become like a child. / Let us therefore go to listen to / A little baby; / Let us therefore learn his gentle lesson*" (H 97:1). The description of the mystery follows: "*Jesus rests / In this crib . . . he wishes to appear / As a one-month-old infant / He speaks as Master there / Let us listen to His voice*" (H 97:2). Montfort is sensitive to the Infant Christ's charms: "*See His face / Filled with sweetness. / Do you see the image of our Savior? / His infancy speaks through silence, / His air of innocence / Preaches to powerful effect*" (H 97:3). The following quatrain closes as follows: "*Through grace, become / Like this child, / And you will take your place / In the firmament*" (H 97:10).

Christmas also inspires H 55:18, which condenses the whole mystery of the Incarnation into four lines: "*He is born of Mary. / In His temporal existence He is named, / Jesus, the Word Incarnate, / Or else the Son of Man.*" There is also an unexpected comparison with Christmas in H 48:6, 7, dedicated to the Sisters of the Visitation: "*It is a great glory for you / That this Heart of the Lamb / Was born in a fashion amongst you: / Your house is His cradle. / If He wanted to be born amongst you, / It is to grow and increase, / You must make Him known, / You must make Him shine forth.*" Finally, it is Jesus Christ, offered by Mary, who becomes the model of our own act of offering. In H 49:2, we read: "*Behold your dear Son, / Oh Father of light, / Listen to His infant cries, / Grant his prayers. / We offer Him to you now / Through the hands of*

Mary: / Be calmed; this dear Child gives you / Infinite glory."

H.-M. Guindon

IV. A Literary Analysis and Discussion of the Content of Montfort's Christmas Hymns

1. Omnipotence reduced to infancy

The fact that Montfort consecrated ten special hymns to Christmas, combined with other references scattered through other works, clearly shows how much he was aware of the mystery of the Incarnation. It is the "*mystery of Jesus living and reigning in Mary . . . the first mystery . . . the most hidden; and it is the most exalted and the least known. . . . It was in this mystery that Jesus anticipated all subsequent mysteries of his life*" (TD 248).

By her intimate union with the Son—the sole center of the Incarnation—Mary, too, becomes central; according to Montfort, she becomes the sign that reveals God, the "*infinitely holy and exalted God*" Who is "*at the same time infinitely solicitous for him and understands his weakness*" (cf. SM 20). This is the Christological formulation—Laurentin noted this—anticipating the Marian formulation that Péguy employs when he writes: "*To the one who is infinitely celestial / Because she is also infinitely terrestrial . . . / To the one who is the highest princess / Because she is the closest to men . . . / To the one who is infinitely distant / Because she is infinitely near . . . / The one who is infinitely our Queen / Because she is the most humble of creatures.*"[26]

The infinite nature of God's transcendence and the weakness that God takes on in Christ without ceasing to be God is marvelously expressed by the poet with a dogmatic precision and a real beauty in the first noel: "*The Most High, the Incomprehensible / The Eternal and the All-powerful / Has just now been born. / Is it possible? / The Eternal is one day old, the Word remains silent / The All-powerful has made Himself an Infant, / Let us acknowledge Him / Let us worship, let us praise, / Let us praise, let us love / And let us recognize / Our God, reduced to Infancy*" (H 57:1).

Montfort's artistic temperament is revealed here from the start; it is lofty and solemn and employs expressions that form antitheses as a sculptor works stone. The opening, which is clear and immediate, stresses the infinity of God's greatness, and the strophe closes in an expression of the infinity of human limits that employs imagery and chiaroscuro. And then we find the following, delicately expressed in a series of contrasts: *eternity reduced to a day*; the Word, the living Word of the Father *reduced to silence*; and omnipotence humbled in the person of a *powerless infant*. Theological rigor is here lightened by poetry. Thanks to this, the paradox of transcendence in immanence emerges in the full unfurling of love, in its expression and its consequences. To God Who gave everything, let us also give everything. Divine love, which has rendered possible the equation of absolute greatness with the smallness of the infant, in a "wonderful exchange" requires love in return: "*If our dear Lord is born for men / And to render them blessed / We owe Him, just as they do / What we are*" (H 57:2).

And at the same time, in a dazzling

flight, the angels sing glory to God in heaven, peace on earth, and goodwill among people, and they bring the good news to the shepherds, who are told to leave their flocks to go and worship the newborn, the true Lamb (a subtle allusion to the Passion in the middle of the joy of Christmas, for Christmas and the Cross are the dual manifestation of a single mystery). The rugged shepherds guess that their miserable life is to change: "*How worthy this day is! A God of all majesty / Made Himself, in humanity / Our likeness*" (H 57:5).

He Who created humankind in His own image and likeness now creates Himself in the image of humankind to search out His poor creatures, even the most lowly, to restore them to their original dignity. And Mary, always present in all Montfort's noels — the Mother and the Child — is congratulated "*for having given life to her Savior,*" having "*charmed the Lord*" (H 57:6). These congratulations are also a form of thanks and veneration.

2. The Virgin Mother

It is Our Lady who inspired Montfort to write TD, and he never ceased to sing of her in loving devotion. "*The Most High God came down to us in a perfect way through the humble Virgin Mary, without losing anything of his divinity or holiness. . . . God, the Incomprehensible, allowed himself to be perfectly comprehended and contained by the humble Virgin Mary without losing anything of his immensity. . . . God, the Inaccessible, drew near to us and united himself closely, perfectly and even personally to our humanity through Mary without losing anything of his majesty. So it is also through Mary that we must draw near to God*" (TD 157). This explains the constant presence of Mary in Montfort's Christmas hymns: the Virgin and Child are Christmas and are the perpetual continuation of Christmas. And the shepherds, sent by the choir of angels, sing and invite the King in the stable to sing. Moved, grateful, and adopting a conscious attitude of humble sincerity, they address the Infant Christ: "*Hail, dear Child long awaited, / Be welcome amongst us. / We come to pay homage to you, / We are only simple country folk, / We are without refinement*" (H 58:4). And Jesus replies: "*It is an excellent honor to me / To love me most dearly*" (H 58:11).

And after these happy expressions, with their rich human and divine content, the shepherds address their feelings of gratitude to the Holy Mother: "*We bless you a thousand times / Oh Most Blessed Virgin Mary, / You give life to us all / By giving us the fruit of life*" (H 58:10).

This concept and attitude are repeated in the "*Noel of the Kings*" with new, sensitive expressions: "*Mother of the most wonderful love, may you be praised in every place / For having given us this Infant-God / For having given birth to light, / And life to the true God, life to our Father*" (H 60:12).

The contemplation of the Mother of God arouses in the poet such deeply tender feelings that the rough exterior of the ascetic yields as he describes an admirable Virgin and Child in the "*Noel of the Pious Souls*" (H 61). "*How good it is to see the Savior / On His Mother's breast! / He presses against her heart / gently. / He kisses her tenderly, / He clings to her side, He embraces her. / His smiles, His tender and charming air / Fills her with grace*" (H 61:4).

This marvelous portrait, which Montfort painted with delicate feeling, certainly does not recall the Virgins of the Renaissance. It recalls, instead, an icon such as that of Vladimir, of great intensity of feeling and extraordinary artistic sensitivity, but above all a work of deep spirituality, one not flawed by sentimentality. And Montfort's language, at once noble and accessible, recalls the *Praise* of Giovanni Domici (1356-1419), that masterpiece of spiritual poetry, which takes up the theme of Mary's maternal delight, dear to Jacopone de Todi, and elaborates on it: "Tell us, gentle Mary, with what desire / You looked upon your Son, Christ my Lord! / When sometimes He slept a little during the day, / You woke Him, desiring Paradise, / So softly you went, without a sound, / And you placed your face on His holy face, / And then you said to Him, with a maternal smile: / Awake . . ."

No less beautiful was the Marian flower in Montfort's garden of popular poetry. In Hymn 63, inspired with human tenderness, St. Louis Marie contemplated, celebrated in song, and prayed to the Child Jesus and to his Virgin Mother. It is an enthusiastic celebration of Mary and her Son in nine verses of eight lines each. *"Noel of the Children of Mary"* weaves together a seamless eulogy to the marvelous Blessed Virgin Mother,and to her amazing prodigy: to she who broke the chains of evil and fulfilled the prophecies of the OT through her maternity. Thanks to her who overcame the serpent, "*Heaven receives . . . a new glory*" (H 63:3). Montfort's words speak of the faith of she who gave us the Savior, and the charm of her purity, her power through humility, her beauty that vanquished God and made Him come down to earth to become our Brother. Montfort dwelt on the greatness of God, Who showed His power by making His finest masterpiece in Mary; on the loving tenderness of the Child towards the Mother whom He had chosen for Himself, a pure, strong, and fascinating Mother. In Montfort's words the theology of the Fathers becomes a lyrical contemplation: "*Jesus loves the stable / But especially your heart, / It is His agreeable bed, / It is his palace of honor. / He makes your breast his most glorious throne . . . / Oh gentle tenderness, / Oh tender smiles, / Oh holy caresses / Which this dear Son bestows on you!*"

And the Virgin is blessed to be the privileged place which has embraced the whole of immensity: "*Happy is your womb . . . / to have contained immensity, / To have nourished, to have carried / Eternal Wisdom!*"(H 63:8-9).

3. Infancy

Péguy is one poet who most eloquently celebrated both the artistic beauty and the theology of the Infancy, and did so with a deeply engaging tenderness. The first flower, the first day, the baby, everything was memorable, full of wonder: shaped by amazement, freshness and newness, everything great or small is beautiful. And Baptism is the Sacrament of infants, the first Sacrament. It contains in seed everything which will be. It is a beginning which contains the power of the future. The first day is the finest day, and Baptism is the Sacrament of the first day.

Péguy offers a song to the innocence of the child: *The Porch of the Mystery of the Second Virtue* is taken up again in his *Mystery of the Holy Innocents.* In it he relives and rejoices in infancy, longing for that age of undiminished freshness, for that stage of human life which offers the finest and purest mirror of new creation.[27]

In brief, the theme of infancy, with its beauty and freshness, was dear to Montfort, too. He and Péguy considered the Incarnation to be the fundamental mystery. Both celebrate Christmas ceaselessly with their vital faith and passionate feeling. Cardinal de Bérulle—the apostle of the Word Incarnate—brought out the absolute infinity of God in contrast to the nothingness of humankind; he exalted the divinity but neglected the humanity of the Christ Child. And some of Bérulle's followers who were also Montfort's teachers were excessive in their disdain for infancy as an abject, useless, and powerless state, the most contemptible except for death itself. In spite of his severe view of a world immersed in sin, Montfort appreciated the beauty of creation. He saw Christmas not from the viewpoint of a rigorous and moralizing theologian but from the perspective of a person who loved humanity. For among other things Montfort was endowed with the temperament of an artist and poet. He was clearly "human without being a humanist." For this reason, he contemplated and celebrated the beauty of Christmas, being attracted to the tenderness of the marvelous Child. All his noels are tender songs to the gentleness which emanated from the most beautiful Child: "*Most sweet infant*" (H 57:2); "*How beautiful this infant is, how sweet it is to be close to his cradle*" (H 58:9). Even the Magi prostrated themselves to worship, with authentic feeling, "*at the feet of his Infancy, in respect, love and silence,*" enjoying "*the ineffable gentleness which is to be experienced here, near this gentle Savior,*" and they wished to prolong their stay "*to contemplate your most sweet charms*" (H 60:10, 15). With the same delicacy of feeling, he celebrates the divine Infancy in the *"Noel of the Pious Souls"*: "*How small He now is, / But how lovely! / How many charms adorn this Child's / divine face. / His gentle eyes are secret charms / Which speak without words*" (H 61:5).

Two animals are present. In their silent way, they invite people to lovingly and humbly praise the Infant. These unusual cantors sing: "*Love this good little king*" (H 61: 3).

Then the saintly poet turned his attention to the Blessed Virgin and exclaimed: "*How charming you are in your purity.*" And he adds: "*Let me kiss Him all I want! I am charmed to see this beloved child.*" And the schoolchildren, too, are in ecstasy before a new family group: *"His mother holds Him in her arms / Ah! How beautiful, how lovely He is / How charming his face is*" (H 66:4).

A whole swarm of happy children race to pay homage to the Child Jesus, in the *"Noel of the Children"* (H 59)—a festival of innocence for the innocent Lamb. The children, deeply moved on seeing the newborn Infant's wretched surroundings, want to save him from the poverty of the stable. They are touched, and invite him and his Mother to come and live in their homes where they can serve him completely, so that he might lack nothing. Montfort in this hymn synthesizes and integrates his devotion and theology, in and through Jesus' relationship with children in the Gospel. It is filled with very joyful expressions, and delicate feelings. There is a rhythm in the canticle which seems to spring directly from the saint's grateful faith. It is overflowing with deep divine and human meanings. It needs no commentary. Its meaning leaps out from every line, beautifully.

Jesus greets the children: "*You see here / In me, your own Infancy* [Péguy's "Christ-children"] */ May I also see / In you Innocence, / Simplicity, / Charity. / Adorn your heart, / It is my home, / It is where my greatness / Is always pleased to be, / It is my gift, / It is my incense*" (H 59:8-9). And marvelously, the children reply: "*Take, King of Heaven, / Our children's hearts . . . / How sweet it is / To be in this stable! / Oh little Child, / How lovely you are! / Oh little lamb, / How beautiful you are!*" (H 59:10-11).

4. A personal experience of God

The ten Christmas hymns do not all attain the same poetic level. Some of them, or some of their verses, are purely catechism lessons, expressed in rhyme, for instance, the *"Noel of Zealous Souls"* (H 62).

However, even in these less poetic lines, where some preacher is reproaching a miserly, worldly soul or where some proud potentate is refusing the treasure of true Wisdom offered to them by the infant King, there are sparks of brilliance. This is seen, for example, when Montfort defines the emptying of the All-Powerful into the state of infancy: "*the loving eclipse of this divine Sun*" (H 62:4). And one cannot help admiring in his various compositions his faculty for feeling and imagination in the way he develops various aspects of the Gospel story, in words and music. It is certain that Montfort's poetry is always in the service of evangelization. His free flowing popular lyric poetry deservedly and reasonably should be called a "spiritual discipline" in the most positive sense of this phrase.

Montfort's poetry is religious poetry, even if it is also didactic. It interprets and explains the doctrine and discipline of the faith. It communicates above all an experience of God and of the Virgin. The poet's lyricism, often naive, aspires only to celebrate the eternal advent of Christmas, which is at once in time and beyond time.

G. Francini

V. Christmas in Montfort's Spirituality

On first sight, certain passages of Montfort can fail to show that he is imbued with the spirituality of Christmas. Other passages, even while speaking of Christmas, appear to have little connection with his spirituality. We must therefore look beyond the literal meaning of both types of passage, as in the following quotes, which are inspired by Bérulle: "*The infinitely holy and exalted God is at the same time infinitely solicitous for us and understands our weaknesses*" (SM 20); and "*The Most High, the Incomprehensible One, the Inaccessible*

One, He who is, deigned to come down to us poor earthly creatures who are nothing at all" (TD 157). The Nativity is indicated by the words "*our weaknesses*" and "*come down to us.*" Expressed here are not only the union of great and small but also the absence of disdain for the small, which is instead called upon to grow: "*The Most High God came down to us in a perfect way through the humble Virgin Mary, without losing anything of his divinity or holiness*" (TD 157).

On the other hand, we cannot reach the same conclusion simply on the grounds that Montfort writes, "*Let us give Him instead our souls / Let us deliver our hearts to His flames / Let us go in mind to the stable / To kiss His little feet*" (H 64:8), or says to Christ, "*Lovely Infant / Reign over us as Sovereign, reign over us*" (H 9). Christmas remains the mystery of the Infant-God: "*The All-Powerful made Himself an Infant*" (H 57:1). Along with the Incarnation, this is the fundamental mystery to which the whole of Christian spirituality returns. Everything related to birth and infancy and their many aspects has a certain affinity with Christmas. Bérulle and his disciples concentrated on this affinity, but where they only saw humiliation and abjection, Montfort sees this mystery in a completely different way, though considering the same elements and often using the same language. Smallness and powerlessness become in Montfort loving dependence on a maternal Providence.

1. The spirituality of the Incarnation

Christmas begins in Mary's womb before being made concrete in the crib. Montfort has this truth in mind: "*I adore you profoundly . . . in the virginal womb of Mary, your most worthy Mother, at the time of your Incarnation*" (LEW 223). From this moment on, the Consecration recognizes our belonging to Christ (TD 32), who already unites all his mystical members. "We must say that we originate in the Virgin's womb, from which we emerged one day like a body attached to its head."[28]

2. The spirituality of loving dependence

Montfort links these three terms: "*servants, slaves, children of Mary*" (TD 56). This progression in dependence finally leads to a relationship of filial love, which is emphasized many times: "*You will give them birth, feed them and rear them*" (TD 31). "*They will experience her motherly kindness and affection for her children*" (TD 55). Wisdom Incarnate did not wish to come into the world independently of others, in the flower of his manhood, but he came as a frail little child, dependent on the care and attention of his mother (TD 139). Montfort's whole spirituality is centered on this maternal function of Mary towards the newborn Christ wholly dependent on his mother; for us, this state lasts all our earthly life, our true birth coming about in glory after death (TD 33).

3. The spirituality of hope and joy

Christmas is a festival of hope and joy because it fulfills the hope of salvation. Montfort celebrated this joy, which was for a long time suppressed by a religion of fear and pessimism, of deviant spirituality: "*Be blessed, O*

Mary, / You are our happiness, / And you give us life / by giving us this amiable Savior" (H 64:11). In SM 68, we read: "*Hail, Mary, my joy,*" and in MP 12: "*Mary, joy of those who serve the Lord.*" This joy which Mary communicates to us is her own joy. In H 57:6 we read: "*O pure and divine Mary, / We admire your happiness: / To your Savior / You gave life.*" Mary, who at Christmas created our happiness by giving us the Savior, is always "in the act" of giving him. Her maternity is in the order of grace the continuation of what began with Christmas. Montfort here meets with the most current Church teaching: "Christmas is an extended commemoration of the Divine Maternity . . . of her who gave birth to the Savior of the world" (MC 5). "This maternity of Mary in the economy of grace is continued uninterrupted to the consummation of all the elect" (LG 62). John Paul II has recalled "the most special maternal cooperation" of Mary, not only in the past but also to prepare the future at the end of this second millennium (RM at49).

H.-M. Guindon

Notes: (1) H . A. Miles, *Christmas in Ritual and Tradition, Christian and Pagan*, T. Fisher Unwin, London 1912, 34. (2) St. Bernard, *Oeuvres complètes* (*Complete Works*), trans. Dion-Charpentier, Paris 1867, 7:369. (3) W. R. W. Stephens, *The English Church from the Norman Conquest to the Accession of Edward I*, London 1901, 309, in H . A. Miles, *Christmas*, 35. (4) H . A. Miles, *Christmas*, 63. The author refers to H. Lemoignon, *Vieux Noëls composés en l'honneur de Notre-Seigneur Jésus-Christ (Old Christmas Hymns Composed in Honor of Our Lord Jesus Christ)*, Nantes 1876. (5) R. Louis, *La Nativité de Notre-Seigneur Jésus-Christ (The Nativity of Our Lord Jesus Christ)*, Paris 1911. (6) *Histoire des Diocèses de France (History of the Dioceses of France)*, vol. 18, *Le Diocèse de Nantes (The Diocese of Nantes)*, Beauchesne, Paris 1983, 252-253. (7) B. Papàsogli, *Montfort, A Prophet for Our Times*, Edizione Monfortane, Roma, 1991, 18. (8) *Histoire et liturgie, coutumes et legendes, littérature et poésie (History and Liturgy, Customs and Legends, Literature and Poetry)*, Desclée De Brouwer, 1894, 23. (9) Lambert, *Dieu change en Bretagne (God is Changing in Brittany)*, Cerf, Paris 1985, 23. (10) Papàsogli, 18. (11) G. Davailly, ed., *Histoire religieuse de la Bretagne (A Religious History of Brittany)*, H.L.D., Chambray 1980, 160-161. (12) Bérulle, 352. (13) Bérulle, 985. (14) Condren, *Considérations* 54-62, in Bremond, 3:520. (15) Bérulle, 1007. (16) *Le Portrait fidèle des abbés et autres supérieurs réguliers et de leurs religieux dans la vie du père Jean Garat, abbé de Chancelade (The True Portrait of the Abbots and Other Regular Superiors and Their Religious in the Life of Father Jean Garat, Abbot of Chancelade)*, by a regular canon of the Abbey of Notre Dame de Chancelade, L. Roche, Paris 1691, 148. (17) Bremond, 264. (18) *La Vie de M. de Renty par le Père Jean-Baptiste Saint-Jure (The Life of M. de Renty by Father Jean-Baptiste Saint-Jure)*, Paris 1652 in Bremond, 527. (19) Ibid., 528. (20) Laurentin, *Dieu seul est ma tendresse (God Alone Is My Tenderness)*, O.E.I.L., Paris 1984, 110. (21) Ibid., 67. (22) J.-B. Bossuet, *Oeuvres complètes (Complete Works)*, Flachat, Paris 1862, 8:241-242. (23) Ibid., 267-278. (24) No conclusion can be drawn from this silence. Montfort is called "the perpetual orator of his privileges and his greatness," yet he has scarcely one sermon of three pages and only a few mentions in the 477 pages of sermons that Montfort left. (25) Prayer over the Offerings, fourth Wednesday of Easter time. (26) Ch. Péguy, *Le porche du Mystère de la deuxième vertu (The Porch of the Mystery of the Second Virtue)*, I, 572-574. (27) Cf. Ch. Péguy, *Il clima della speranza*, introduction, translation, and notes by G. Francini, Padua 1982, 86, 119ff. (28) Saint Pius X, *Ad diem illum*, February 2, 1904.

OXFORD MOVEMENT

I. INTRODUCTION

1. The Movement

The Oxford Movement is the name given to the actions and endeavors of a group of clergymen at Oxford University in the 1830s who sought to restore Catholic faith and practice within the Anglican Church. Its leaders were the professor of poetry, John Keble (1792-1866); the Regius Professor of Hebrew, Edward Bouverie Pusey (1800-1892); and the vicar of St. Mary's and fellow of Oriel, John Henry Newman (1801-1890). Keble's sermon on "National Apostasy" on July 14, 1833, is generally regarded as the movement's beginning, and Newman's reception into the Roman Catholic Church on October 9, 1845, as the end of its first phase.

2. Newman, Pusey and Montfort

Newman's conversion was a "parting of friends," the leaving, for the sake of the truth, of almost every person and thing humanly dear to him. On February 22, 1846, he said goodbye to Littlemore, the retreat of his final Anglican years; to Oxford, in which he had hoped for a "perpetual residence"; and to Dr. Pusey, his once close comrade and friend. The two men were not to meet again for another twenty years. When they did, it would be in a tense atmosphere of controversy, and the name of Louis de Montfort would figure in the debate.

II. THE MARIAN CONTROVERSY

1. In General

Newman called to see Keble in his vicarage at Hurscly on September 12, 1865. They did not recognize each other. "How mysterious that first sight of friends is! For when I came to contemplate him, it was the old face and manner, but the first effect and impression was different."[1] Newman was taken aback to discover that Pusey was also paying a visit. "As we three sat together at one table, I had as painful thoughts as ever I recollect, though it was pain, not acute, but heavy. There were three old men, who had worked vigorously in their prime."[2]

At dinner Pusey was "full" of a new book, which would soon provoke a masterly rejoinder from Newman. It was a work of high polemic with the surprising title *An Eirenicon.*[3] Pusey argued that the reunion of Canterbury and Rome was impeded by the excesses of Catholic piety, not least in relation to the Blessed Virgin Mary. Newman was astonished by the title of Pusey's book. In a letter to Keble, he says that if Pusey "is writing to hinder his own people from joining us, well and good, he had a right to write as he has done—but how can he fancy that to exaggerate, instead of smoothing contrarieties, is the way to make us listen to him?"[4] Pusey offers the bread of peace but delivers the stone of polemic.

2. The Montfort Issue

One of the authors accused by Pusey of holding extravagant Mariological opinions is St. Louis de Montfort. Pusey is shocked, among other things, by his adaptation of John 1:13: "Souls born not of blood, nor of flesh, nor of the will of man, but of God *and Mary*,"[5] and by the bold assertion that "*the Holy Ghost chose to make use of Our Blessed Lady to bring His fruitfulness into action by producing in her and by her Jesus Christ in His members.*"[6]

In letters to Pusey and Keble in October 1865, Newman says that he has never even heard of "de Montfort."[7] The implication is that Pusey throws together minor devotional writers with major dogmatic theologians such as Suarez. Any "extravagances" de Montfort and others like him may have "put out" are unknown to the majority of Catholics in England. "They do not color our body. They are the opinions of a *set* of people—and not even of them permanently."[8] Why does Pusey not refer to English Catholic books of piety, such and *The Garden of the Soul*, which is very widely used and "free from such extremes"?[9]

Newman does not condemn St. Louis Marie. He is just disconcerted by what he has heard of TD and wants to be reassured. On December 4, 1865, he asks Charles Russell, "What do you think of Pusey's quotations from de Salazar, de Montfort, Oswald, etc. about the Blessed Virgin? Are they not startling and unusual?"[10] (These authors are not, of course, of the same order. Oswald was a wild extremist, and his *Dogmatische Mariologie* was eventually placed on the Index.) In his eagerness for second opinions, Newman consulted Edmund O'Reilly, SJ, who had been professor of dogmatic theology at the Catholic University in Dublin. His judgement was that though he too was "startled" by some of the passages quoted by Pusey, he "doubted whether [he] ought to be so. . . . It is quite possible that some may be true and none heterodox."[11] Newman came to the conclusion that St. Louis Marie had not been well served by his translator, Newman's fellow Oratorian and Oxford convert

Frederick William Faber. Writing to Pusey, he asks: "Have you heard . . . that Faber's translation of de Montfort is *very* incorrect? He did it when he was too near death to be able to be accurate. De Montfort does not say some of the things which are most startling in the English."[12]

III. Newman's Marian Apologia

1. The Letter to Pusey

On November 28, 1865, Newman went out to Rednal to write his *Letter to Pusey.* It is a classic of Mariology and a model of apologetics. Although the book does not try to defend St. Louis Marie's writings, its explanation of the Church's "true devotion to Blessed Virgin" reveals the agreement in all things needful, despite differences of temperament and style, between the sainted Breton and the venerable Briton. Incidentally to his main object, Newman provides a kind of hermeneutic for reading and evaluating those passages which he and others have found difficult in the works of St. Louis Marie.

2. Church Tradition

Newman argues from the Fathers of the Church: to them he owed his conversion, and from them, too, he learnt to understand and embrace Marian doctrine and devotion. "The Fathers made me a Catholic, and I am not going to kick down the ladder by which I ascended into the Church."[13] In similar fashion, St. Louis Marie regularly quotes from the Fathers and claims that his theses on devotion to Our Lady can be supported from their writings. If he does not do so, that is because of the audience for which he is writing: not Puseyites but peasants. "*If I were speaking to the great minds of our day, I should prove at greater length from Sacred Scripture and the holy Fathers, from whom I should quote passages in Latin, all that I am saying simply. . . . But I am speaking mainly to the poor and simple, who, being of good will and having more faith than the average scholar, believe with more simplicity and more merit. And so I content myself with telling them the truth simply without stopping to quote all the Latin passages*" (TD 26).

3. Christology

In his *Letter to Pusey,* and in several other places, Newman confirms the truth of St. Louis Marie's central doctrine by referring to religious history: "True devotion to the Mother is the 'easiest,' 'shortest,' and 'surest' way to union with the Son, and when devotion to Mary grows cold or dies, faith in Jesus as Lord, God, and Saviour is certain to wither away" (cf. TD 152ff.).

"If we look through Europe, we shall find, on the whole, that just those nations and countries have lost their faith in the divinity of Christ who have given up devotion to His Mother and that those, on the other hand, who had been foremost in her honor have retained their orthodoxy. Contrast, for instance, the Calvinists with the Greeks, or France with the North of Germany, or the Protestant and Catholic communions in Ireland. . . . In the Catholic Church Mary has shown herself, not the rival, but the minister of her Son; she has protected Him, as in His infancy, so in the whole history of the Religion. There is then a plain historical truth in Dr. Faber's words [in the preface to his translation of TD], which you quote to condemn, *'Jesus is obscured, because Mary is kept in the background.'*"[14]

Newman suggests that the hesitations of some Protestants about Our Lady's role, under Christ, as intercessor and advocate betray a woefully inadequate Christology. If we take from the Blessed Virgin her intercessory mission and transfer it to Christ, we shall be diminishing, not enhancing, his glory.

"If we placed Our Lord in that center, we should only be dragging Him from His throne and making Him an Arian kind of a God; that is, no God at all. He who charges us with making Mary a divinity is thereby denying the divinity of Jesus. Such a man does not know what divinity is. Our Lord cannot pray for us, as a creature prays, as Mary prays; He cannot inspire those feelings which a creature inspires. To her belongs, as being a creature, a natural claim on our sympathy and familiarity in that she is nothing else than our fellow. She is our pride—in the poet's words, 'Our tainted nature's solitary boast.' We look to her without any fear, any remorse, any consciousness that she is able to read us, judge us, punish us. Our heart yearns towards that pure Virgin, that gentle Mother, and our congratulations follow her, as she rises from Nazareth and Ephesus, through the choirs of angels, to her throne on high, so weak, yet so strong, so delicate, yet so glorious, so modest and yet so mighty."[15]

Newman's sober teaching, rooted in orthodox Christology, corresponds exactly to Montfort, *"Our Lord is our Advocate and our Mediator of redemption with God the Father. It is through Him that we must pray with the whole Church, triumphant and militant. It is through Him that we have access to the Majesty of the Father, before whom we should never appear unless supported and clothed with the merits of His Son, just as young Jacob came before his father, clad in goatskin, in order to receive his blessing. But have we no need of a mediator with the Mediator Himself? Is our purity great enough to unite us directly to Him, and by ourselves? Is He not God, in all things equal to His Father, and consequently the Holy of Holies, as worthy of respect as His Father?"* (TD 84-85).

4. Against Heresy

Mary keeps reverence for the God-man intact. Both Newman and Montfort are warning us against the crypto-Arianism that may be lurking behind disdain for devotion to Mary. Newman speaks with special authority as the translator and permanent disciple of St. Athanasius, the implacable adversary of the "Ariomaniacs." He offers a challenge to souls that are cold-hearted towards Our Lady: Do you truly confess the Son to be true God, and do you accept that without ceasing to be true God, He has become true man by taking flesh from the Virgin? If this is your faith in Jesus, how can you hold back your affection for Mary? "I say, then, when once we have mastered the idea that Mary bore, suckled, and handled the Eternal in the form of a child, what limit is conceivable to the rush of thoughts which such a doctrine involves? What awe and surprise must attend upon the knowledge that a creature has been brought so close to the Divine Essence?"[16]

IV. Newman and Montfort

1. Mary and Salvation

The effort to harmonize Newman and St. Louis Marie has a major obstacle to surmount. Montfort appears to argue that devotion to Mary is necessary to attain salvation, whereas Newman seemingly rejects the thesis, both in his private correspondence and in his public *Letter to Pusey.* Writing to Keble, he says: "There is all the difference in the world between saying that 'without her intercession no one is saved' and 'without her invocation no one is saved.' . . . I never can deny my belief that the Blessed Virgin prays efficaciously for the Church, and for individual souls in and out of it. Nor can I deny that to be devout to her is a duty *following* on this doctrine—but I never will say, even though St. Bernardine said it, that no one is saved who is not devout to her, and (though I don't know St. B's writings) I do not think *he* would have said it had he not been in his own Christendom."[17]

Newman returns to this last thought in the *Letter to Pusey.* The claim that no human being can be saved who has not had some explicit devotion to the Blessed Virgin, if taken as a universally applicable proposition, is unsustainable. In particular circumstances, however, in the Brittany of St. Louis Marie or the Sienna of St. Bernardine, it can be defended. The man raised in a Protestant culture may have no devotion to the Blessed Virgin other than what is implied by confessing the Son of God as incarnate from her by the Holy Spirit; it would be quite wrong, on those grounds alone, to deny the possibility of his salvation. On the other hand, the man who was raised in a Catholic culture and has absorbed devotion to the Mother of God from an early age cannot cast it off without placing himself in grave spiritual danger. The first is the orphan who one day may discover his mother; the second is the son who was raised in her presence but now turns unthankfully away. On the one hand, regrettable omission; on the other, culpable neglect. "To say . . . dogmatically that no one can be saved without personal devotion to the Blessed Virgin would be an untenable proposition; yet it might be true of this man or that, of this or that country at this or that date. . . . If an Italian preacher made [this statement], I should feel no disposition to doubt him, at least if he spoke of Italian youths and Italian maidens."[18]

There is one other consideration. It appears quite clear that for Montfort, explicit devotion to Our Lady is necessary for salvation in the sense that the goal is not utterly unattainable without it, but it is more expeditiously reached by this means.[19] The cultus of Our Blessed Lady is the *"safest, easiest, shortest and most perfect"* way to union with Christ the Savior (LEW 212; TD 152). Moreover, it strengthens within us that humble childlikeness of soul without which we cannot enter the Kingdom of Heaven (cf. Mt 18:3). "*The Most High came down to us perfectly and divinely through the humble Mary, without losing any of His divinity or holiness; and it is through Mary that the very little must ascend perfectly and divinely to the Most High without having anything to fear*" (TD 157; LEW 135). Placing ourselves in Mary's arms helps protect us from the pride and presumption that blocks off the saving grace of Christ. Here Montfort's spiritual theology touches its deepest level.

2. Church History

In trying to reconcile Newman and Montfort, we can usefully turn for instruction to Church history. At the Council of Florence in 1439, the Greeks were persuaded of the orthodoxy of the *Filioque* by supporting texts not only from the Latin Fathers but also from the Greek (especially St. Cyril of Alexandria). Their view was that "saint cannot contradict saint": if some of the Fathers without doubt taught the *Filioque,* then the patristic texts that they thought denied it had to be reinterpreted.[20] The modern mind may find this a rather naive view of the tradition. Surely, comes the objection, it is indisputable that saintly theologian has contradicted saintly theologian. Did not St. Thomas Aquinas oppose the Immaculate Conception, while Bl. Duns Scotus defended and expounded it? If we examine the matter more closely, we shall find that the naiveté is but a holy simplicity. There is a harmony among the saints, if only we are prepared to train our ears to hear the daring polyphony that the Holy Spirit orchestrates out of their voices. Thus, with regard to the Immaculate Conception, we can say that despite his failure to perceive the possibility of preservative redemption, all that St. Thomas was trying positively to affirm (for example, that Jesus Christ is the Redeemer of every human person without exception) is not only compatible with the doctrine of the Immaculate Conception but is one of its essential premises. Similarly, we can harmonize St. Louis de Montfort and Ven. John Henry Newman by saying that in their very different ways, they were both attempting to show the Christ-centeredness of true devotion to the Blessed Virgin. The title of one of Newman's discourses on Our Lady could easily have come from the pen of Montfort: *The Glories of Mary for the Sake of Her Son.* "We praise and bless her," says Newman, "as the first of creatures, that we may duly confess Him as our sole Creator."[21] This is also the fundamental principle of St. Louis Marie. According to him, Our Lord Jesus Christ is the "final end" of Marian devotion. *"If . . . we establish solid devotion to the Most Blessed Virgin, it is only in order to establish solid devotion to Jesus Christ more perfectly, to provide an easy and certain way to find Jesus Christ"* (TD 61).

For both these great Catholic doctors, Our Lady is the supremely Christ-centered person. Her whole mission is to bring Christ to us and us to Christ; for this she was predestined and created, for this she was engraced from her conception; this is the office she fulfilled on earth and now continues forever in heaven. To go to Jesus through Mary is, therefore, to take the straightest and swiftest path.

3. The Communion of Saints

The truly Catholic heart is open to the whole Communion of Saints. The attachment of a religious to the founder of his Order does not blind him to the achievements of other saints and Congregations. As Dante shows us in the *Paradiso*, the loyal son of St. Dominic can and should be unrestrained in his praise of St. Francis. In something of the same spirit, this article has tried to find correspondences between St. Louis de Montfort and the converts of the Oxford Movement. Other resemblances could be added to the list. For example, the Oxford men, like St. Louis Marie, challenged the complacent assumptions of "the world," "this present age." If need be, they were ready to be dismissed as fools for their fidelity to Eternal Wisdom.[22] And then there is St. Louis Marie's love of the hymn, the *cantique*. His conviction that song has the power to sustain doctrine and lift up the soul to God was shared by the men of the Oxford Movement, both those who remained Anglican (Keble and Isaac Williams) and those who became Catholics (Newman, Faber, Caswall). In conclusion, therefore, as a sign of a surprising spiritual kinship, here are two verses from St. Louis de Montfort and two from Edward Caswall, convert clergyman and Oratorian. They have a single center: the Eucharistic Christ. "*O Jesus, our dearest Spouse, / Our God, our brother, / Come, come be born in us / Through thy Blessed Mother, / So that we through thee may go / To thy heavenly Father. / Come by thy humility / To make us all infants / Come by thy sanctity / To give us back innocence. / Come by thy charity / To reign without resistance*" (H 87). "O Jesus Christ, remember, / When thou shalt come again, / Upon the clouds of Heaven, / With all thy shining train; / When every eye shall see thee / In deity revealed, / Who now upon this altar / In silence art concealed. / Remember then, O savior, / I supplicate of thee, / That here I bowed before thee / Upon my bended knee; / That here I owned thy presence, / And did not thee deny, / And glorified thy greatness / Though hid from human eye. / Accept, divine Redeemer, / The homage of my praise; / Be thou the light and honor / And glory of my days. / Be thou my consolation / When death is drawing nigh; / Be thou my only treasure / Through all eternity."[23]

J. Saward

Notes: (1) Letter to Ambrose St. John, in *The Letters and Diaries of John Henry Newman* (= LD), London 1972, 22:52. (2) Ibid. (3) *The Church of England a Portion of Christ's One Holy Catholic Church, and a Means of Restoring Visible Unity: An Eirenicon, in a Letter to the Author of "The Christian Year,"* Oxford 1865. (4) LD 22:67. (5) cf. Pusey, *Eirenicon, The First Letter to the Very Rev. J.H. Newman, D.D. in explanation, chiefly in regard to the reverential love due to the ever-blessed*

Theotokos, London, Rivingtons, London 1869, 164. Louis Bouyer—convert, Oratorian, and Newman scholar—has shown the importance of remembering that through our incorporation into Christ, we are children at once of God and Mary. The attitude of mind that contents itself with adoptive sonship of the divine and heavenly Father without seeing the need of a human and earthly Mother is a species of "Docetism with regard to ourselves." Natural life and supernatural life do not operate on two unconnected planes. In nature I am the child of a father and mother, and in grace I am the child of both God and Mary. Cf. *Le Trône;* English translation: *Woman and Man with God: An Essay on the Place of the Virgin Mary in Christian Theology and Its Significance for Humanity*, Darton, Longman & Todd, London 1960. (6) TD 20-21; Pusey, *Eirenicon*, 164. St. Louis Marie's daring speculation is not unorthodox and is carefully explained by him in a passage that Pusey, in his typically selective way, does not quote: "*This does not mean that the Blessed Virgin gives the Holy Spirit fruitfulness as if He did not have it. Because He is God, He has fruitfulness, or the capacity to produce, just as Father and Son do, even though He does not put it into act and does not produce another divine person. But it does mean that the Holy Spirit, through the Blessed Virgin, whom He deigns to use without absolutely needing her, puts His fruitfulness into act, producing in her and through her Jesus Christ and His members*" (TD 21). Since the death of St. Louis Marie, both the papal Magisterium and individual theologians have given increasing attention to the link between the Holy Spirit and Our Lady. Pope Paul VI, in MC, called for further research on this "hidden relationship" (no. 27). (7) LD 22:68, 83. (8) Ibid., 89. (9) Ibid., 91, to Keble. (10) Ibid., 117. (11) Ibid. (12) Ibid., 294. (13) John Henry Newman, *A Letter Addressed to the Rev. E.B. Pusey, D.D. on the Occasion of His Eirenicon,* in *Certain Difficulties Felt by Anglicans in Catholic Teaching Considered,* new ed., London, New York, and Bombay 1900, 2:24. (14) Ibid., 92f. The same point is made, and at even greater length, in *The Glories of Mary for the Sake of Her Son,* in Newman's *Discourses Addressed to Mixed Congregations,* new ed., London 1892, 348. (15) Newman, *Letter to Pusey,* 85. (16) Ibid., 82f. (17) LD 22:68. (18) Newman, *Letter to Pusey,* 104f. (19) Cf. St. Thomas Aquinas, *Summa Theologiae,* 3a, 1, 2, on the sense in which it was necessary for God to become man for our salvation. (20) See J. Gill, *The Council of Florence,* Cambridge 1959, 227ff. (21) Newman, *Discourses,* 344. (22) See John Saward, *Perfect Fools: Folly for Christ's Sake in Catholic and Orthodox Spirituality,* Oxford 1980, chap. 10, 11. (23) *The Westminster Hymnal,* no. 82.

PARISH MISSIONS

SUMMARY

I. PARISH MISSIONS IN THE SEVENTEENTH AND EIGHTEENTH CENTURIES:
   1. "Home missions" in relation to "foreign missions";
   2. The evolution of "home missions":
      a. First generation;
      b. Second generation;
      c. Third generation.

II. THEOLOGICAL AND ECCLESIOLOGICAL PRESUPPOSITIONS OF MISSION:
   1. The Trinitarian source;
   2. The influence of Scholasticism and the Bérulle school;
   3. Synthesis.

III. TARGETS OF MISSION: THE POOR:
   1. Who are the poor?;
   2. Mission and social instances of the poor.

IV. THE PROCLAMATION OF GOD'S WORD IN MISSION:
   1. Preaching in the seventeenth century;
   2. The proclamation of the Word in Montfort:
      a. The word of God is for everyone;
      b. The Word used for conversion: "touch the heart."
   3. Methods of proclaiming salvation:
      a. The Sermons and the order of preaching;
      b. The Catechism of the parish mission.

V. THE AIM OF MISSION:
   1. The pastoral of conversion;
   2. Faithfulness to the promises of Baptism;
   3. Consecration and Baptism;
   4. The Covenant with God.

VI. RELEVANCE TODAY.

I. PARISH MISSIONS IN THE SEVENTEENTH AND EIGHTEENTH CENTURIES

"Towards the end of the Seventeenth century and the beginning of the Eighteenth . . . the spirit of mission . . . is embodied vigorously by one man: Saint Louis Marie de Montfort,"[1] Montfort is both the heir and the custodian of a great missionary tradition begun in the early seventeenth century by a number of eminent figures: St. Vincent de Paul (1581–1660), Michel Le Nobletz (1577–1652), St. John Eudes (1601–1680) and Blessed Julien Maunoir (1606–1683). Montfort brought such creative dynamism and such apostolic ardor to the preaching of missions that he can be considered the last of the great

French missionaries. However, in order better to understand Montfort's concern for mission, we must briefly recall the genesis and evolution of "home missions" throughout the seventeenth century.

1. "Home missions" in relation to "foreign missions."

As home missions sprung up in France in the first half of the seventeenth century, they displayed certain points of similarity with foreign missions. Reconstructing the beginnings of the home missionary movement in France is a complex task, for subsequent historiography often gives the name "mission" to any kind of preaching. The term "mission" is an umbrella term covering a great number of fairly diverse pastoral forms of missionary activity, which came into existence and developed over a long period of time. The topic can be clarified by reconstructing the history of the first mentions of the term "mission" as it was applied to apostolic activities within France.

In 1609–1610 the Jesuits set up a post which they described as a "mission" at Béarn, a Protestant region. In 1613 the Oratory, created two years earlier, accepted a four-year preaching foundation which in the relevant contract is designated by the word "missions." In 1617 the Capuchins went ahead with a plan of three years' standing, initially aimed at Protestant regions, officially known as the "mission of Poitou." This mission is closely linked to the activity of Father Joseph of Paris (1577–1638) who, as early as 1616, was able to give a strong impetus to the Order's missions.

The Capuchins saw France's religious situation as scarcely different from that of India, perhaps because they found in missionary work that fundamental unity which springs from any religious vocation. It is therefore completely understandable that all the missions would be entrusted to the same authority and organized in the same fashion. Documents of the time present the home missionary as one who is restoring or even initiating a Christian environment, as though he were a religious arriving in a region with no clergy or place of worship at all. The sending of *relationes* to Rome and the granting of faculties by the Holy Office helped to reinforce the assimilation of the home to the foreign missions.[2]

The missionary activity organized in France by the Sacred Congregation *Propaganda Fide* was successful. The study of the archives of the Sacred Congregation would, according to B. Jacqueline, yield useful documentation on the number of Protestants embracing Catholicism in the course of the seventeenth century. No one can doubt the weakening of Protestantism in France during that period. Cardinal Ludovisi, in his letter to the Nuncios which announced the erection of the Sacred Congregation *Propaganda Fide* (*Inscrutabili Divinae,* June 22, 1622) already presented the dangers of the "dechristianization of the West," and recommended that the missionary activity of the Sacred Congregation *Propaganda Fide* should be developed among the faithful.[3]

All the evidence shows that the

enthusiasm for missions *ad gentes* that the young Montfort felt during his seminary training never waned and found clear expression in the *Prayer for Missionaries:* a constant concern for the salvation of believers and infidels whom the Church's mission has not yet reached. It is this conviction which inspired the great missionary enterprises of the era and impressed strongly on Montfort the universality of the call to salvation, the fundamental value of the missionary spirit.

2. The evolution of "home missions."

The first half of the seventeenth century saw the birth of what can be called the generation of "pioneers." The concept of "home missions"—which is linked to the ideal of the "foreign missions"—is most dynamic at this time because it is rooted in a realization of the misery and needs of the population. The missions aimed above all to catechize the rural parishes whose priests did not truly carry out the ministry of the Word.

If, after the Council of Trent, so many missionaries were active in Catholic Europe, it is also because the parish clergy failed to break away from the past and to rise to the task of the care of souls.[4] The missions thus inaugurated a great period of "Christianization," particularly in France. There, the missionaries tried to penetrate into the rural world and modify it radically, while the preachers of the fourteenth and fifteenth centuries had preferred to speak to the population of the towns. And while all France's social classes in the seventeenth century were affected by the missionaries' apostolate, the preachers concentrated on the common people, for the lower levels of the population, whether in town or country, were considered the least Christianized. Methods varied, for in the absence of precedents the main concern was to respond to the situation the missionaries found. St. Vincent de Paul probably had the clearest vision at the time. He created the first "missionary" congregation to be consecrated specifically to the "poor people of the country."[5]

a. First generation. During the first half of the century, the missionary who went out into the countryside did not differ radically from his counterparts leaving for the New World. The image of the "interior Indies," which referred not only to France but also to the religious situation of southern Italy, met with great success among the clergy who were interested in pastoral renewal. It illustrates the state of mind in which the Catholic campaign of reconquest was undertaken.[6] To embark on a mission to regions of mixed faith was to grapple with the excesses of both religions. "It is therefore quite arbitrary," asserts Dompnier, "to try to distinguish between missions aiming at the conversion of the Protestants from other missions whose aim was the education and strengthening of the Catholics."[7]

In the light of all this, the mission appears as an enterprise that aims to reappropriate a given region by the Church. The vocabulary employed by the missionaries supports this conclusion, including military terms and metaphors borrowed from the Gospel parables, e.g. seeds and sowing. These images imply that the faithful are passive. The missionary is the man who takes the initiative: he sows and he harvests, or he fights. People are the hearers of the word that is sown, or they are the territory that is fought over. It is the priest who comes, in God's name, to tear souls away from the devil. Moreover, these images imply that the missionaries place particular emphasis on religious practice, the external sign of internal adherence to the true religion. "In coming to bring people back to the fold or to win people over, perhaps they were often more concerned to be able to display tangible results—the number of confessions, of communions, of conversions, etc. than to ensure a deep transformation in behavior. This latter concern probably only set in during the last decades of the century."[8]

b. Second generation. A second generation of missionaries can be located in the years 1650–1690. This is the era when the reform begun with the Council of Trent reached the clergy, and when the parish priests progressively attached more importance to the litugy and to the administration of the sacraments, along with the teaching of the catechism. One might therefore believe that the missions would become rarer or even disappear, given that their need to act as substitutes for the local clergy had been reduced. On the contrary, the missions multiplied, for two reasons. First: between 1660 and 1680 there was the introduction of new approaches: retreats, the renewal of the promises of Baptism, and a variety of prayer groups. Second: the missionaries' role as substitute had decreased, and they devoted themselves to a periodic revival, an extraordinary pastoral, in which the "great truths" and imposing ceremonies intended to move souls were emphasized more than before. The spectacular side of the missions is to be explained by the intention to impress the public, whose mentality was still unpolished and in need of a simple and forceful religious teaching. This was manifest in the bonfires of books and useless things, the imposing constructions of crosses, the allegorical writings, and the "living tableaux" organized to recall the principal scenes of the Bible or the works of the most popular saints.

c. Third generation. Between 1690 and 1700, with the disappearance of the great religious figures of the century, the generation of development came to an end. Henceforth the principal concern was to remain broadly faithful to approaches inherited from the past, while attempting to improve them in certain respects. An "institutional" vision of the missions had been adopted; the new generation aimed at the conservation of tradition. During the course of the century, then, the term "mission" underwent a profound transformation in terms of aims much more than methods.[9]

Nevertheless, the evangelical effort was not to weaken during Montfort's time, even if someone had already noticed "that the Missions are beginning to become less useful than formerly."[10] The Church had again felt the need to relaunch this type of apostolic effort. Thus, after a period of relative calm and satisfaction between 1685 and 1690, came a second wave of Catholic reform. The first quarter of the eighteenth century saw the missions of the Doctrinarians in the southwest of the reign,[11] and those of the Oratorians in the region of Avignon.[12] The priests of the Community of St. Clément of Nantes worked in their own region, often in collaboration with Montfort's missionaries,[13] whom F. Lebrun defines as "the great specialists of the home missions of eighteenth-century France."[14] The Vincentians worked in Upper Brittany,[15] the Capuchins in the whole kingdom.[16]

Montfort's apostolic life (1700–1716) must be placed in the context of the third generation of missionaries of Christendom in order that his personal choices and pastoral preferences might be understood.

II. Theological and Ecclesiological Presuppositions of Mission

1. The Trinitarian Source

PM teaches a Trinitarian theology of mission organized according to a three-part plan: mission—renewal—reign. On the basis of this teaching, Montfort adopted in RM 56 the formula *"to renew the spirit of Christianity among the faithful"* by the means of the mission to the people. The theological and ecclesial perspective and the subsequent missionary methodology go hand in hand. Montfort adopts the criterion of the *Ecclesia semper reformanda,* which had become rooted in the Church's consciousness after the Council of Trent (even if around 1700 the Church's situation was better than in previous centuries). He resorts to missions to the people as the preferred though not exclusive means of guaranteeing this renewal at the level of the local church.[17]

Even if Montfort adopted the only form of mission present in the France of his time—which was the only possible form in a Christian country—nevertheless, his work was inspired by a personal vision of the Church's mission. There is no other way to explain the dynamics of the mission seen as the *"renewal of the spirit of Christianity in Christians."* This formula, probably derived from Olier,[18] is taken up by St. John Eudes in his Constitutions[19] and is proposed afresh by Montfort in RM 56. In order to arrive at the correct interpretation of this formula, we must place it in the theological context of mission expressed in PM.

The theological and ecclesial perspective of PM opens up a broader horizon than that implied by the method Montfort chose to follow in the missions to the people. In concrete terms, Montfort expresses the pastoral implication of the ecclesial mission of the institute: that the mission to the people is a prolongation and an historical realization of the mission of the Company which is called upon to *"renew the spirit of Christianity in Christians"* (RM 56).

2. The Influence of Scholasticism and the Bérulle School

The theological outline of mission in PM is rooted in the thinkers of

Scholasticism, and more immediately in the spiritual doctrine of Cardinal de Bérulle and his school. The spiritual thinkers of the period, enamored with the mystery of the Triune God (cf. ST I, q. 43), attempted to express by the term *missio/missiones*—sending or mission—first, the dynamism within the Divinity (*missio interior; missio ad intra; processiones aeternae*)[20] and second, the creative power of God manifested especially in the redemptive Incarnation of the Word of God (the new creation), and in the sending of the Spirit of God at Pentecost (*missio exterior, missio ad extra: processiones temporales).*[21]

This theological outline of PM is also to be found in TD and provides us with one of the key elements we need to interpret the Marian masterpiece: *"The plan adopted by the three persons of the Blessed Trinity in the Incarnation, the first coming of Jesus Christ, is adhered to each day in an invisible manner throughout the Church and they will pursue it to the end of time until the last coming of Jesus Christ."*[22] This outline can also be applied analogically to the mission of Montfort's Company of Mary. It would be more correct to say that this plan of God "animates" the mission of the Company. Montfort does not adopt it extrinsically, as if the mission of the Company were to be superimposed on a Trinitarian mission, but rather he resorts to the concept of participation, by which the mission of the Company is born of the dynamism within the Trinity and emanates from this dynamism according to the model of *missiones ad extra.*

Quite clearly it is within the context of salvation that the terms "renew" and "renewal" take on their fullest meaning. In PM in particular is to be found the full doctrinal expression of "mission": it is presented as an event of Salvation in the life of a Christian community. The *"Directives to be Followed during their Missions"* drawn up by Montfort in RM require that one or two missionaries should go ahead to announce the mission two weeks before it begins (RM 52). This is so that the missionaries, as Montfort asserts, "*prepare the way for Jesus Christ.*" The announcement of the mission is not merely a means of pastoral pedagogy, but aims rather to make the parish community understand this event of grace. The community, once it has been prepared for the mission, is to pray, *"in order to be worthy of the grace of the mission."*

The mission is therefore announced to the Christian community as an event of Salvation: *"The mission of the apostolic men is a continuation and an imitation of that of the Son of God who said to His disciples: 'I send you as my Father sent me'. Now, just as our Lord came to save us, we are sent to you for this same reason. This will be the aim of our sermons and catechism lessons,"* (LS 778). Montfort confirms that the consciousness of being sent is at the root of the missionary mandate: *"Finally, let them remember that it is Jesus Christ who is sending them just as He sent the apostles"* (RM 65).

3. Synthesis

A few conclusions can now be drawn:

a. *"To renew the spirit of*

Christianity," means to reawaken the consciousness of the *Ecclesia semper reformanda.* It is the consciousness of the "already" and the "not yet" that must safeguard the Church, the sign and preparation of the coming of the reign of Christ, by means of a "reform" in the heart of the Christian community.

b. Montfort places the mission of his Company (RM 56) within the historical/salvific dynamism of Trinitarian mission and in the context of the preparation and coming of Christ's reign. Consequently, the *"consecration to Jesus Christ through the hands of Mary"* as the spiritual path to a renewal of Christian identity is the methodological missionary option Montfort prefers for the preparation of the Church for the Second Coming of Christ. Mary collaborates with the Trinity in the "work of all times," i.e. the Incarnation of the Word in the life and the history of men.

c. Consequently the eschatological perspective of the Company's own mission (RM 56), prefigured by the apostles of the end times, can be correctly interpreted according to its original *sitz-im-leben:* the coming of the reign of Christ by the coming of the reign of Mary.

III. Targets of Mission: The Poor

1. Who Are the Poor?

While mission must embrace all humanity, it must favor the poorest, according to the words of Isaiah, which were repeated by Jesus and adopted by Montfort in his life and in RM 2: *"The Lord has sent me to preach good news to the poor."* The missionaries always made this phrase their motto.

The theme of the poor is complex: within it the problem of Montfort's personal attitude towards the poor is intertwined with the values of evangelical poverty. Saint Vincent de Paul realized that at the heart of christendom in France and in all of Europe various groups were "religiously marginalized." In the society of the *ancien régime* there were many homeless individuals, vagrants wandering from town to town. For all practical purposes, they had no parish life and lived outside the religious system. Hence Montfort's emphasis on the poor, his desire to bring back to the practice of the faith a group living so radically on the periphery of society.

"In our minds, the image of St. Louis-Marie Grignion Montfort is inseparable from those to whom he felt called"[23] writes V. L. Tapié. The discovery of the poor marked Montfort's adolescence, and it is to the poor that he dedicated the first years of his ministry. This precise social and religious orientation of Montfort rests in part on a personal theological vision: the poor are the close friends of Jesus Christ and, much more, they are Jesus Christ himself.[24]

Indeed, in the *ancien régime* the poor continued to benefit from the Franciscan idealization which they had undergone in the Middle Ages. Begging remained more or less sacred. To stop a poor man from begging meant attacking all these values. The idea that the poor keep their aura of Godliness is suggested by too many documents for it not to have been true. The custom of choosing a godfather and godmother from the poor, or even among vagrants, is very significant. The concept of the poor man as representative of Christ finds expression in these and many other customs. Such behavior is not fundamentally different from that of Montfort who, one evening, carrying a poor man on his shoulders, shouted before the door of the house at Dinan where he was staying: *"Open up to Jesus Christ."* Interpreting this spiritual orientation of Montfort, Besnard was to write: "He saw only Him [Christ] in the poor; he venerated Him in them, he saw them as a sacrament which contained Jesus Christ hidden beneath their exterior. 'A poor man,' he used to say, 'is a great mystery; one must know how to penetrate this mystery.'"[25]

But there is also a world of the poor of which society disapproved and which it clearly marginalized. J. P. Gutton asserts: "To write the social history of the poor also means writing the history of a 'separation,' of an 'expulsion' from society."[26] Often it is precisely with a connotation of the *asocial* that the poor appear in Montfort's texts, in particular in his Hymns where he acknowledges that the *"demon"* calls them *"poor dog"* (H 46:11); *"wretch, utter rabble"* (H 46: 21; cf. H 107); *"barefaced idlers, evil breed,"* (H 18:5) and so on. Montfort reiterates a well-known fact; however, the manner he presents it is quite original. It suffices to quote, for instance, the famous hymn, "The Cries of the Poor" (H 18), in which social marginalization is a *curse,* and alms for the poor is the remedy for the deep *wound* of pauperism.[27] As a result the poor man is, simultaneously and alternately, a blessing and a disgrace, holy or a moral deviant.

However, a new concept of the poor had begun to take root as early as the beginning of the seventeenth century, which during Montfort's time began to gain acceptance: poverty is still represented by marginal and asocial people, but at the same time it affected most of the population, and especially the farming world, the vital strength of the country. In other words, the poor become a people. The result is an image of a fragile society with no security, with more than half of the population living at subsistence level.[28]

Montfort's preference for the poor is therefore a preference for those levels of society at the very edge of subsistence and more generally for the "poor people" of the countryside. Montfort requires of his missionaries that *"the poor are to be the special objects of their care. They must never refuse to help them, materially when possible, and spiritually, even if they say only one Hail Mary"* (RM 47). Moreover Montfort's personal habit of always inviting a poor person to his table becomes an instruction for his missionaries: *"After each catechetical instruction, they will provide a meal for all the poor of the parish who have attended the instruction and every morning and evening they will bring one of them to eat at their table"* (RM 48).[29]

The "poor of the parish" apparently are to be assisted by the local

Christian community. A passage of Besnard alludes to the participation of lay persons in the pastoral of charity organized at the time of the mission: "This is the plan which he had proposed and which he followed precisely. He would invite the women and young ladies of the Parish, giving a little speech on the merit of good works and especially of giving alms. He told them that his custom was that the poor should be fed during the mission, in order to be able to gather them all together and instruct them in the ways of Christianity, of which most of the poor were ignorant. He exhorted them to lend a hand in this good work. Then he would find a house in the vicinity, where every day a pot of food would be boiled up for the poor. Everyone was invited to contribute to this, each according to his means. The meal was prepared by those pious persons who had taken on this responsibility."[30]

2. Mission and Social Instances of the Poor

In the seventeenth century debates on pauperism were often suspected of being an attempt to justify social inequalities and to show the mass of the poor as an obstacle to the affluent society. In this context, poverty was seen, quite categorically, either as punishment for a moral shortcoming or as the negative byproduct of a fundamentally just and beneficial social process (as though it were nothing more than a fact of nature which could not be eliminated), which public and Christian charity had a duty to alleviate.[31]

The spiritual and apostolic perspective adopted by Montfort in his missions had to reckon with the social reality of the poverty created by the system of fiscal injustice imposed on France by Louis XIV's economically disastrous reign. The minutes of a parish meeting of November, 1715—drawn up during the mission Montfort gave at Vouvant—inform us of a legal dispute between the people and a certain tax collector. The locals named the Mayor, Louis Guéry, as their representative who called a meeting during which he announced that, if necessary, the taxpayers were ready to go to court. Montfort agreed to side with the poor of the parish of Vouvant to help them claim their rights by law.[32] Montfort's name does not figure in the document drawn up by the lawyer Bernier. The missionary had not attended the meeting, but that does not mean that he was not involved in the affair. We know that in the missions he often went to great lengths to resolve disagreements between individuals and families. In the Vouvant affair there is formal proof of his intervention. That he did not hesitate to take part openly in favor of the people emerges from several lines of a hymn he composed during this mission. Here we read: "*Pray, poor people, eaten up, / By excessive cuts [into your earnings] / You will be relieved of them / without court proceedings. / Come, poor laborers, / you will have in abundance*" (H 159: 6). It is possible that these words were less a promise to the poor than an invitation to abandon a lawsuit, but there is no doubt that the first words contain a condemnation of arbitrary and unjust taxes. The tax collectors were certainly aware of Montfort's sympathies, and in all probability it was they who gave the chief tax collector Philippeau the idea of accusing Father de Montfort of breaching the peace and of having his mission notes seized.[33] This episode is extremely revealing, showing a Montfort who is not at all a stranger to the social justice concerns of his time, such as those which had already begun to develop in the second half of the seventeenth century around representative figures such as Fénelon, La Bruyère, and the Abbot Fleury.[34]

IV. The Proclamation of God's word in mission

1. Preaching in the seventeenth century

The preachers of the beginning of the seventeenth century tended—as Montfort complained several times—to preach sermons which were *"popular . . .* [and] *which very often produce admiration but not instruction"* (SR 114). In Montfort's estimation, these preachers think above all about impressing the public with constant quotations in Latin and references to extraordinary events of profane or sacred history. Each preacher plays the role of the erudite: interminable, confused sermons, perhaps barely suitable for an educated urban audience but meaningless for most of the Christian people. If one really wants to convert people one must deliberately end this practice and begin to make oneself understood. Therefore missionaries must not let themselves be carried away by their "eloquence," for the task is not to speak well, but to instruct.[35]

St. Vincent de Paul recommends to his members "the little method" he himself had perfected. This consisted, first and foremost, in organizing the content of the sermon according to a rational outline which could be changed according to the requirements of the argument in question. It was a whole style and a language. It was the return to evangelical preaching, the use of familiar examples, and a direct and natural tone. This meant avoiding pedantic quotations and profane authors. It meant a certain caution in using allusions; it meant respecting heretics, who were not to be attacked but before whom the truths of Catholicism were to be simply set out; it meant concern for the effective conversion of souls and an absolute absence of vanity. The "little method" could be summarized, according to Vincent, in a single phrase: simplicity in preaching.[36]

Montfort shares in this same tradition and he reflects its requirements. In RM he portrays in caricature the figure of the *"fashionable preacher"* (RM 60) and contrasts it with that of the *"apostolic missionary"* who *"preaches the simple truth, avoiding all pretentiousness and discarding all fables, false statements and dissembling. He must be bold and speak with authority, showing neither fear nor human respect. He must preach with all charity and give offense to none. His intention must be holy and centered on God alone. God's glory must be his sole preoccupation and he must first practice what he preaches: coepit Jesus facere et docere"* (RM 62).[37] Paragraphs 60–65 of RM all deal with the qualities of the apostolic preacher. The qualities listed and the type of preaching recommended reflect themes common at the time.[38]

Another typical aspect of the preaching of the period is the cultivation of drama, which reached its peak in the eighteenth century with Father Bridaine, and which probably was also expressed in the seventeenth century. Emotional reactions, such as shedding tears at the most pathetic moments of the sermon, were so widespread at the time that they even touched the most hardened and reserved among the faithful: the missionary thus allocated a role to the audience in the cause of converting individuals.

The main aim of the "pathetic" sermons (generally given in the evening) was apparently to create an atmosphere that might favor the reception of the (often terrifying) content of the sermon. The church was lighted by candles, and the shadows that their weak, trembling light threw into the half-light was a sight that increased the terror aroused by the missionary's tone and his words. J. Delumeau spoke of the "pastoral of fear." It was believed that the fear inculcated in this way was salutary and that it led the faithful to make a general confession, which was the fundamental justification of the mission.[39]

Drama is therefore not merely a scenic expedient, but an integral and essential element of missionary preaching. "Drama is not only the expression of the taste for demonstration," asserts B. Dompnier, "but was thought to be fundamental in provoking an emotional reaction, which was important."[40] Moreover, the preachers, "with the help of an appropriate pedagogy, solicited a reaction from those assembled whom they led . . . into making a show of themselves for themselves."[41] This is an aspect which is of foremost importance as we seek to understand the range of technique of preaching of the "home missions" of the *ancien régime.*

The very announcement of mission must take the form *"of an appeal to the people's feelings"* (RM 52), in order to find souls inclined to receive the word. Like many preachers of his time, Montfort aimed to move people's hearts through his sermons. The biographical sources emphasize the "pathetic" aspect of Montfort's sermons. Besnard writes: "He never preached without moving his listeners to tears."[42] During the mission of Moncontour (in the diocese of St.-Brieuc), he passed his ivory crucifix along the rows of pews to be kissed: "Having listened to the words full of unction which the missionary spoke while he had his crucifix pass from row to row to be kissed, they could not hold back their tears and they shed them abundantly with the rest of the congregation."[43] A similar scene occured in the mission of St. John's Parish in Montfort's home village.[44] The kissing of the crucifix prepares the grace for the reception of absolution in the mission of Valette (diocese of Nantes). A sudden storm and the "noise of thunder and the lightening threw everyone into consternation. The feeling of fear helped to bring the people to contrition.[45]

2. The Proclamation of the Word in Montfort

In this way one can briefly schematize Montfort's position on the pastoral currents of his time. Far from being favorable to an anti-Jansenist system, as has often been asserted, he was able to draw on the Augustinians, who were supporters of Jansenism, and also their opponents, who were motivated by a commitment to orthodoxy. He was as sensitive to the pedagogical concerns of the opponents to Jansenism as to the influence of the Augustinians, who had helped complete his vision of Christianity. Nothing expresses this balance of Montfort better than his concern for the Rosary, in which he combines a taste for external practices and popular images with the spirit of communion in the mysteries of Christ, distinctly reminiscent of Bérulle. In the domain of pastoral action he collaborated with the Augustinians, who were later to die in schism, as much as with the self-declared anti-Augustinians, such as Monsignor E. de Champflour, bishop of La Rochelle. Far from being a man of the traditional party, as people have wished to see him, Montfort seems today to be a man of mediation who was able to reconcile the best of conflicting tendencies.

a. The word of God is for everyone. In parish missions, the word of God undeniably occupies a central place in Montfort's missionary practice: *"The preaching of God's word"* is *"the most far-reaching, the most effective and also the most difficult ministry of all"* (RM 60). The effectiveness of the mission would be compromised if the missionaries, through their sermons, *"only beat the air and titillate the ears"* (RM 60). Montfort is convinced that people go to the mission *"to hear only God Himself / In each preacher"* (H 141:5) and to *"fill themselves with God / And His words of life"* (H 157:33). Montfort places the announcement of the word and the conversion of the faithful in close relation: *"I received your light, / Your grace and my pardon, / In the last mission / When listening to the sermon"* (H 139:3).

Around 1700 the announcement of the word by preaching the catechism and, especially in Montfort's case, by the missionary hymns, remains of the highest priority for all missionaries. Montfort believes too deeply in the need for knowledge in conversion not to place this ministry at the forefront of this pastoral, without neglecting the validity of its content.[46] For Montfort, *"the church and the word of God are for everybody"* (RM 53).

b. The Word used for conversion: "touch the heart." The preacher of the seventeenth century must *"pierce, move, and convert the most hardened hearts"* (SR 51) with *"powerful, touching, piercing words [. . .] which go from the heart of the one through whom he speaks straight to the heart of the listener"* (LEW 96).

The metaphor of the heart is current in the seventeenth century and implies a heavy emphasis on a connection with the will and with feelings; indeed, the image of the heart recalls the *apex mentis* of the spiritual writers.[47] A recent study by A. Sauvy refocused attention on the fact that the form of the heart admirably suits baroque art, so much so that it became a universal symbol. It is found everywhere, in religious and profane works and even in alchemy, and very often it is at the center of the symbolism of the "mission tableaux," a tradition dear to the Breton missions.[48] The return to an "abandoned" God really meant "a new heart and a new spirit" (Ezk 18, 30–32). The announcement of the word of God in mission was also destined to uproot *"the lies which originate in hell"* from a heart which is *"the citadel where the tyrant has locked himself in"* (RM 60). If the Word does not enter the heart to transform it, *"[the tyrant] is not unduly alarmed by all the hubbub going on outside"* (RM 60).

3. Methods of proclaiming salvation

In addition to the composition and singing of hymns (cf. the article "Hymns" in this work), there are two other means of proclamation Montfort adopted and modified.

a. The Sermons and the order of preaching. LS [49] does not contain the actual preaching of Montfort, nor does it provide us with summaries, for Montfort composed the manuscript to have at his disposal a collection of notes to serve as a stock of basic material for the missions to the people. The great number of sermon outlines and the quantity of themes dealt with attest not only to the interests connected with Montfort's long-term planning, but, more immediately, to the general content of the announcement. The content perfectly reflects the traditional needs of the mission of Christendom.

The manuscript is divided into three parts, and the order of the parts is not chronological. The second part is the oldest and includes an alphabetical collection of sermon themes, of which the greatest number must be attributed to Montfort's time in Paris at Saint-Sulpice (1695–1700). The first and the third part date from the last years of Montfort's missionary experience.

It is the first part which is of interest here. This part develops one of the mission's programs, *"Order of Sermons for a Lenten Mission"* (LS 530–31). The mission began with the first Sunday of Lent and ended on the Tuesday after Easter, for a total of thirty-eight days. The opening of the four-week mission invited the faithful to reflect on the greatness of God and on His service; the two following weeks centered on the theme of penance/confession, while the conclusion, the fourth Sunday of Lent, was related to the theme of reconciliation and the forgiveness of sins. In parallel, the themes of the "Last Things" were approached: death, particular judgment, Hell, and Heaven.

The Monday of the third week

opened a cycle of sermons on the theme of the love of Jesus Christ which ended on the Thursday of the fourth week on the love of God. The missionary proposed different thoughts, spread across a period of eleven days, on habitual sins—like lying, slander, anger, impurity—and on the corresponding positive attitudes inspired by Christian virtues—like humility, gentleness, obedience, purity, and patience—to conclude with the theme of prayer and of the qualities of devotion to Mary.

The *"reparation to the Blessed Sacrament"* was set for the Friday of the fourth week. The following Sunday, Passion Sunday, the preacher spoke to his congregation on the occasions of sin, in particular lawsuits and dancing. The following day was for the themes of faith and almsgiving; the devil and his temptations, the guardian angel and devotion to him; contempt of the world and its maxims; the above-mentioned sermon on the love of God; and finally, the name of Jesus and the crucifix. On the Saturday preceding Palm Sunday there was the sermon on the renewal of the promises of Baptism, which precedes the sermon on Fervent Communion and Unworthy Communion. A sermon on the Holy Rosary concluded the celebration of the Palms.

The fifth week, Holy Week, was to include a series of sermons on good works and the familial duties of parents and children. On Good Friday it was indispensable to speak on the theme of the Passion, while on Saturday the subject was the Passion of the Blessed Virgin Mary. Easter Sunday was obviously dedicated to the same theme: the Resurrection of Jesus Christ and, to finish, the resurrection of the body and general judgment. On Easter Monday the missionaries spoke of priests and the closing of the mission, and could not fail to recall the theme of perseverance. The address known as the "Farewell Discourse" sealed the end of the Lenten mission.

The first part of the Book of Sermons also includes a "Sermon-matter for a Mission, or a Retreat, or the Renewal of Baptismal Promises." This is probably the program of mission which is most typical of Montfort. It comprises twenty-four sermons divided into four different thematic groups having as their common factor the central formula of the Covenant with God: *"I renounce the devil, his pomps and his works and I unite myself with you, my Jesus."* The subject-matter is divided as follows: five days consecrated to the opening section; two to "*I renounce his pomps*"; nine to "*I renounce his works*"; and eight to "*I unite with Jesus my Savior.*"

In the first five days (on "I renounce the devil") the mission starts off on the theme *"On God's side. On the devil's side."* The congregation is made to feel it is standing before two options, a situation that can only be resolved by freely choosing salvation. Into this process of liberation from the negative forces which prevent men from belonging to God, Montfort introduces the theme of the innocence of Baptism in relation to the *"excellence of the soul"* (fifth sermon). The key to reading this first series is in its conclusion: the importance of salvation, one of the fundamental aims of the missions of the time. From this perspective the mission was even seen as a kind of urgent intervention for the salvation of the faithful who were threatened by damnation.[50] However, Montfort already opens in this first section an itinerary of Baptismal spirituality, which leads to the fourth section concerning the renewal of the promises of Baptism.

The second series of sermons, on renunciation of the devil's pomps, proposes afresh an indispensable theme: contempt of the world and its vanities, for the world is "*the enemy of truth.*"

There follows the third section (on the renunciation of the *"works of the devil"*) which presents mortal sin—preceded by a sermon on devotion to Mary *"for a true and prudent repentance"*—and in which the traditional theme of interior and exterior penance is taken up again as a way of approaching fervent communion, which is the basis of a witness to the believer's faith through good works. This third cycle of preaching concludes with the theme of Heaven, already broached in the *"Last Things"*: death, particular and general judgment, and eternal suffering. The section concerning the last realities is normally linked to the theme of penance and confession.

The fourth section ("*I unite with Jesus my Savior*") opens with the theme of loving union with Jesus Christ, made explicit in what follows by the theme of charity towards our neighbor. The last four sermons of this cycle are dedicated to Baptism and the renewal of the promises of Baptism, with Montfort's typical emphasis on the *"necessity of renewing them [. . .] through the Blessed Virgin Mary."* The liturgy of the renewal of baptismal promises precedes the last sermon of the mission on perseverance.

b. The Catechism of mission. It is only in 1670 that the institution of the parish catechism began to spread through France but by the end of the century it had been established almost universally. The turning point is between the seventeenth and eighteenth centuries, when each bishop, in the context of the reform of his diocese, intended to publish his own manual of catechism, "the only to be taught in his diocese." This is how the diocesan manuals came to multiply. Not a year went by without a new text appearing: the newly-appointed bishop would have his predecessor's manual reprinted, or he reworked it, resumed or expanded it, and he borrowed from the catechisms of other dioceses more or less explicitly, unless he wished to compose a new one or entrusted its preparation to the director of his seminary. The aim was always the formation of the "good Christian" who would live a life in the service of God. Of course, the catechisms do not escape the influence of the doctrinal currents of the period. The revocation of the Edict of Nantes (1682) brought about a renewal in Catholic manuals of apologetic passages directed towards the "newly converted." The Jansenist and anti-Jansenist polemic easily led to the replacement of any bishop's manual by his successor's, where the two showed different tendencies.[51]

Montfort drew up "*Rules for Catechetical Instruction*"—appended to RM—around 1713, during his time at La Rochelle. The catechetical tradition of the mission to the people was henceforth a given, and Montfort himself does not fail to recognize its importance: "*The catechist has the most important function of the whole mission, and the one who is appointed catechist by obedience must do all he can to fulfill his function worthily. It is more difficult to find an accomplished catechist than it is to find a perfect preacher*" (RM 79). The catechist is reminded of an "*abridged catechism for the use of missionaries from which the children can learn in seven short lessons all that is necessary for salvation. I say 'in general' because, in the case where the parish priest of the locality has given the children a sound instruction based on another catechism with a different wording, the missionary must use this catechism. He thus avoids confusing the minds of the children who learn more by rote than by reasoning*" (RM 91).

It seems that Montfort's experience convinced him of the usefulness of a catechism adapted to his mission to the people. The text of RM would seem to afford proof of this: there existed an "Abridged Catechism for the Use of Missionaries,"[52] a small manual whose length took into account the average duration of a mission (three to four weeks). Hymn 109, which is presented as a summary of the mysteries of the faith, seems to have been composed during Montfort's stay at Saint-Sulpice, when he was designated the catechist of the young and of the "lackeys" of the Saint-Germain district of Paris (where the Parish of Saint-Sulpice was located).[53]

The essential elements of the Sulpician catechetical school were subsequently to be reflected in RM. These included learning by rote, repetition, rewards, amusing little stories, and a designated seat during the lessons (RM 80–91). However, the aim of the instruction is subordinate to the goal of the moral transformation of the children: prayer, the hymns, and especially moving exhortation on the great truths are to transform knowledge into an attraction to a true conversion to God (RM 83). The Sulpician catechisms led Montfort to explore the relationship between the renewal of the promises of Baptism and the consecration to Christ through Mary, which are the mainsprings of his missionary preaching.

V. The Aim of Mission

1. The Pastoral of Conversion

In the language of the seventeenth century, by "conversion" is meant *moral* conversion, experienced and understood within the Christian faith. The pastoral of conversion was not only linked to the sacrament of penance (confession was an exercise of the greatest importance in the missions) but also took its place in a pastoral of Christian instruction.

Conversion, moreover, was not considered merely "personal" but was linked to the needs of the parish community. It certainly involved the inner life of personal conscience, but it also involved day-by-day behavior, including the fact of living together in a social context. In other words, confession serves as an intermediary stage on the way to the true aim of mission pursued by all the missionaries of the time: conversion.[54]

In his missions, Montfort like other missionaries of his time not only required a "moral" conversion, but one reaching beyond mere morality into the domain of faith. Conversion, like preaching, must transform the heart. Drawing inspiration from a sermon of Lejeune, Montfort was to say that *"penance is a change: Be converted! It changes our heart,. . . our whole heart . . . Be assured that conversion has been as nothing if this change has not taken place in the heart."*[55] The confessors and preachers of the time all say as much. Confession during a parish mission is understood to be a general confession. It was quite common to use a written memory-aid that could be read in the confessional before the confessor. Besnard recalls that "the paper which they held to help them remember what to say was often quite wet with their tears."[56]

2. Faithfulness to the Promises of Baptism

Montfort includes two plans for sermons on Baptism. The first (drawn up immediately after a lecture by Leschassier)[80] mainly sets out the truths of the promises of Baptism; the layout is the same as in the programs of mission. The body of the sermon explains first the excellence of the grace of Baptism, then the renunciation of Satan, and third, faithfulness to the promises of Baptism to emphasize adherence to Christ. The text suggested is borrowed from St. Paul: "As many of you as were baptized into Christ have clothed yourselves with Christ" (Ga 3:27). And in perfect parallel to this he develops the theme of the "Receive this garment" of the liturgy of Baptism. Finally the practical part follows: *"1. Contrition for the past; 2. Proposal for the future; 3. Renewal of the promises of Baptism."* In this sermon, as in the programs of mission, the plan is always the same: the ascetic aspects of the renunciation of Satan, and the positive aspect: adherence to Christ. Renunciation is a preliminary condition (penance): the aim is total adherence to Jesus Christ (reconciliation).

The subject of the second sermon (which might perhaps also be attributed to Leschassier[58]) is the promises of Baptism. The first item of para. 161 parallels TD 128. The outline focuses on the theme of the renunciation of Satan and his works: *"Men make a point of honor of keeping their promises and not breaking their contracts: people say 'he is a man of his word'. What, then, of God?"* The second point of the outline relates to the *"necessity of fulfilling them to avoid damnation."* The practices suggested are resumed as follows: *"1. Contrition for all past failures. 2. Renewal. 3 Meditation on these obligations."*

3. Consecration and Baptism

Every consecration is an awakening to the "new life" which follows on

Baptism.[59] The first allusion to the relation between Baptism and consecration is to be found, apparently, in the *Narré* of Cardinal de Bérulle. The true contribution of Bérulle's thought is the discovery of the potentialities contained in the sacrament of Baptism. The Sulpicians M. de Lantages and M. de la Chétardie, disciples of Bérulle, clearly expressed this relation in their catechisms. It is Father Julien Maunoir (1606–1683) who introduced into parish missions the solemn renewal of the promises of Baptism. His disciple, Dom Leuduger (1649–1722), with whom Montfort collaborated for less than a year, continued the tradition. In his book *Bouquet de la Mission*, in which he presents a "formula of renewal," Leuduger associates the commitment of renewal of the promises of Baptism with the religious vows: "Christianity is the religion of Jesus Christ: all Christians are religious, they have all taken the vow to keep this religion; they must therefore, following the example of those who bear the name of religious, renew, as the Fathers say, their Baptismal vows." The influence of Bérulle, in the form of the "spirit of religion" dear to the Oratorian missions, seems clear. His formula presents "an act which contains the Covenant which we have made with God."[60] He therefore asks people to prepare themselves for renewal through confession, then through communion.

It is interesting to note that Our Lady is not mentioned in Eudes' or Leuduger's formula of Baptismal renewal. "Mary is practically absent from Bérulle's doctrine of Baptism; Providence was to entrust the task of enriching and completing it to Montfort," says Poupon.[61] Montfort's most important contribution is probably the role he attributes to the Virgin Mary in his mission apostolate. In this he owes much to the spiritual thinkers of the seventeenth century, in particular the Sulpicians. Nevertheless his representation of Mary is decidedly more catechetical. And in relation to the doctrine of the other missionaries, Montfort presents the function of Mary as more closely linked to the Trinity's plan of salvation.[62]

4. The Covenant with God

Grandet, the first biographer of Montfort, writes: "He had a formula for renewal of the Baptismal vows printed which he had signed by those who could write."[63] This is the "Covenant with God." This document is of utmost importance. The missionary handed it out to all who had attended the mission, i.e., all those who had attended the different services and were inclined to accomplish the essential act of the mission, the renewal of the Baptismal vows. Each signed the document and carefully guarded it. Leuduger explained this recourse to signing a document by stating that, "if this practice of signing the contract appears new or extraordinary to anyone, let him read Chapters 9 and 10 of the second book of Esdras, where it is stated that the Jews, after their return from captivity in Babylon, signed in their own hand the covenant which they had made with God."[64]

The formula of May 4, 1709,

made at Pontchâteau reads: *"1)* [Profession of faith:] *I firmly believe all the truths of the Holy Gospel of Jesus Christ. 2)* [Renunciation of Evil:] *I renounce forever Satan, the world, sin and myself.* 3) [Promise of faithfulness:] *With the help of God's grace, which will never be wanting to me, I promise to keep faithfully all the commandments of God and of the Church, and avoid mortal sin and its occasions, especially bad company. 4)* [Consecration:] *I give myself entirely to Jesus Christ by the hands of Mary, to carry my Cross after him all the days of my life. 5)* [Clause concerning Salvation:] *I believe that if I keep these promises faithfully until death, I shall be eternally saved, but that if I do not keep them, I will be eternally damned.* [Signature:] *In testimony of this I affix my signature.* [Closing formula:] *Signed in the presence of the Church in the parish of Pontchâteau, on this 4th day of May in the year 1709. L. M. de Montfort"* (CG 1).

This text expresses in five brief paragraphs an exceptional summary of the Christian spirituality that Montfort offers to the faithful in his missions. It serves to explain to those who sign it the content of the mission seen as the announcement of salvation: the truths of the faith of the Gospel professed by the Christian; the commandments of God and the Church; the priority of grace in the believer's response to the commitment of the Christian life; our conformity to Christ by a path of faith guided by Mary's presence; the urgent problem of one's own salvation represented as the alternative to breaking the promises of Baptism. The Parish community witnesses the Covenant with God, entered into by the faithful.

It is worth emphasizing that the name of the Virgin Mary is invoked in the very act of renewal of the promises of Baptism, or the gift of self to Christ.[65] She is mentioned in the Covenant not only to pay honor to her, or to express a particular esteem towards the Mother of God, but because she must be present, given that we cannot consecrate ourselves perfectly to Jesus except through her. Montfort means to explain to Christians that perfect devotion to the Virgin, far from being a gesture with no actual impact, is a true realization of the commitments deriving from Baptism. Other missionaries also recommended devotion to the Virgin, but they did not do so with the same force, and, especially, they did not expressly establish any particular link with the renewal of promises of Baptism.[66]

The renewal of the promises of Baptism—the highest aim of Montfort's missions—expressed a solemn commitment, sealed in the Covenant, to live as true Christians. There is no need to emphasize the similarity, of structure and content, between CG and the ceremony of renewal described by Grandet,[67] with its extraordinary thematic and liturgical relevance. One could describe this ceremony as the liturgical version of the scriptural texts of the covenant renewal ceremonies.

VI. Relevance Today

Evangelization is an essential aspect of the Church's mission. Montfort had a clear awareness of this: *"Christ did not send me to baptize but to preach the gospel"* (1 Co 1:17; cf. RM 2). Missionary evangelization aims to convert individuals and peoples and unite them around Christ to form in Him a community which is the sign and sacrament of salvation.[68] This evangelization represents an earnest aspiration on Montfort's part and forms the basis of his concept of the universal vocation to holiness.

The evangelizing Church must constantly be evangelized itself. Montfort is well aware of this. When he did criticize the Church of his time, it was for fear that evangelical zeal was weakening. This is why he writes: *"Your divine commandments are broken, your Gospel is thrown aside"* (PM 5). The Church, situated within the world and often tempted to yield to so many idols, needs continually to hear the great works of God proclaimed in order to uphold and deepen the faith of its members.

There exist several ways and means of evangelization, among which the explicit announcement of the Word occupies a special place. Montfort does not hesitate to write that *"The preaching of God's word is the most far-reaching, the most effective and also the most difficult ministry of all"* (RM 60).

Everyone needs to be catechized and evangelized. We know that in the missions under the *ancien régime,* the catechesis of different social groups was the substructure of the mission. Montfort sets down "Rules for Catechetical Instruction" in the conviction that *"the catechist has the most important function of the whole mission"* (RM 79).

This evangelization is directed to individuals, groups, communities and associations, and also to the masses—to all those who profess themselves Christians and who belong to the Church in one way or another. Montfort's formula, designed *"to renew the spirit of Christianity among the faithful"* (RM 56), reflects this wide pastoral horizon.

This is a comprehensive evangelization, aiming for the renewal and deep transformation of persons, communities, and cultures, but it is also a "new evangelization" because "in the countries which possess a long Christian tradition, as sometimes in the youngest churches . . . whole groups among the baptized have lost their acute sense of faith, they no longer even recognize that they are members of the Church, and they lead an existence far removed from Christ and his Gospel."[69]

In the perspective of this new evangelization, the parish mission in its variety of contemporary forms helps Christians discover the requirements of constant conversion to Christ begun in Baptism. This is the program Montfort adopted when he centered the whole mission on the perfect renewal of the Baptismal vows. The directive of Pope John Paul II, echoing the thought of Father de Montfort, must be heeded: "Traditional missions, which have often been too quickly abandoned and which are irreplaceable in renewing Christian life periodically and vigorously, must be resumed and renewed."[70]

P. L. Nava

Notes: (1) H. Daniel-Rops, *Histoire de l'Église du Christ* (History of the Christian Church), vol. V/1: *L'Église des temps classiques. Le grand siècle des âmes* (The Church in the Age of Classicism. The Great Century of Souls), A. Fayard, Paris 1958, 330. (2) Cf. B. Dompnier, *Mission lointaine et mission de l'intérieur chiz les capucins francais de la premiére moitié du XVIIe siécle* (The French Capuchin Foreign and Home Missions in the First Half of the XVI Century) in *Les réveils missionnaires en France du Moyen Age á nos jours (XIIe-XXe siécles)* (The Missionary Awakenings in France from the Middle Ages to Our Day [XII-XX Centuries], Acts of the Colloquium at Lyons, May29-31 1980, organized by the Society of Ecclesiastical History of France together with the Society of the History of French Protestantism, Paris 1984, 95. (3) Cf. B. Jacqueline, *La sacrée Congrégation de Propaganda Fide et le réveil de la conscience missionnaire de France au XVIIe siècle* (The Sacred Congregation of Propaganda Fide and the Awakening of Missionary Conscience in Seventeenth-Century France), in *Les réveils*, 116–17. (4) Cf. J. Delumeau, *Cristianità et cristianizzazione. Un itinerario storico,* (Christianity and Christianizing: An Historical Itinerary), Marietti, Torino 1984, 182–223. (5) Cf. L. Mezzadri, *San Vincenzo de Paul,* Edizioni paoline, Cinisello B. 1986, 113–124. (6) Cf. B. Dompnier, *Le vin de l'hérésie. Image du protestantisme et combat catholique au XVIIe* (The Wine of Heresy. The Image of Protestantism and the Catholic Struggle in the seventeenth century), Le Centurion, Paris 1985, 203. (7) Ibid., 204. (8) Ibid., 205. (9) On the development of popular missions, cf. L. Pérouas, *"Missions intérieures et missions extérieures françaises durant les premières décennies du XVIIe siècle"* (Home and Foreign Missions during the First Decades of the seventeenth century), in *Parole et Missions* (Word and Missions) 27 (1964) 644–58. The rigorous historical synthesis of B. Peyrous is indispensable: *"Missions paroissiales"* (Parish Missions), *Catholicisme* 9 (1980) 401–31. (10) The influence of this crisis in popular missions towards the end of the seventeenth century is explored in *Le parfait missionaire ou instructions très-utiles à tous les prêtres, pour travailler avec fruit à la vigne du Seigneur,* (The Perfect Missionary or Very Useful Instructions for All Priests to Work Fruitfully in the Vineyard of the Lord),G. Buitingh, Quimper 1696, 35. (11) Cf. J. Viguerie, *"Les missions intérieures des Doctrinaires toulousains au début du XVIIIe: un missionnaire, le père Jean-Baptiste Badou"* (The Home Missions of the Doctrinaires of Toulouse at the Beginning of the eighteenth century: A Missionary, Father Jean-Baptiste Badou), in *Revue historique* (Historical Review), 93 (1986) 41–64. (12) Cf. M. Vénard, *"Les missions des oratoriens d'Avignon aux XVIIe–XVIIIe siècles"* (The Missions of the Oratorians of Avignon in the Seventeenth and Eighteenth Centuries), *Revue d'histoire de l'Église de France* (Review of the History of the Church in France) 47 (1961) 16–39. (13) Cf. M. Faugeras, *"La communauté missionnaire de Saint-Clément de Nantes. Mission et cathéchèse au temps de Grignion Montfort"* (The Missionary Community of St. Clément of Nantes: Mission and Catechesis in the Time of Grignion Montfort), *Annales de Bretagne et des Pays de l'Ouest* (Annals of Brittany and the Western Regions of France) 81 (1974) 553–76. (14) F. Lebrun, *La predicazione nel XVIII secolo,* (Preaching in the XVIII Century) in J. Delumeau, ed., *Storia vissuta del popolo cristiano,* SEI, Turin 1985, 570. (15) Cf. F. Lebrun, *"Les missions des Lazaristes en Haute-Bretagne au XVIIe"* (The Missions of the Vincentians in Upper Brittany in the seventeenth century), *Annales de Bretagne et des Pays de l'Ouest,* 89 (1982) 15–37; Id., *"La pastorale de la conversion et les missions intérieures: l'exemple des Lazaristes en Haute-Bretagne au XVIIe"* (The Pastoral of Conversion and Home Missions: The Example of the Vincentians in Upper Brittany in the seventeenth century), in *La conversion au XVIIe. Actes du XIIe colloque de Marseille* (Conversion in the seventeenth century. Acts of the Twelfth Colloquium of Marseilles) (January 1982), Marseille 1983, 247–55. (16) Cf. B. Dompnier, *"Les missions des capucins et leur empreinte sur la Réforme catholique en France"* (The Missions of the Capuchins and their Influence on the Catholic Reform in France), *Revue d'histoire de l'Église de France* (Review of the History of the Church in France), 70 (1984) 127–47; Id., *"La pastorale de la peur et la pastorale de la séduction. La méthode des missionnaires capucins"* (The Pastoral of Fear and the Pastoral of Attraction: The Method of the Capuchin Missionaries), in *La conversion au XVIIe,* 157–73. (17) For the ecclesiology of the French school, cf. E. Mersch, *Le corps mystique du Christ. Études de théologie historique* (The Mystic Body of Christ: Studies in Historical Theology), Paris-Brussels 1951, vol. 2, 301–44. (18) In connection with the historical and ecclesiastical context of the time, one of M. Olier's constant concerns was that of working towards the "renewal of Christianity in order to show that it is conformed to its institution" (*Mémoires* XXX 2, 247). During the summer of 1642, M. Olier became parish priest of Saint-Sulpice with responsibility for running the Seminary, and he was to become increasingly aware of his own vocation. Certainly he felt called to work "to renew Christianity [. . .] first by the way of the peoples, by showing them what they must do as Christians." This perspective goes beyond the previous pastoral practice of the missions in which M. Olier had participated. Cf. G. Chaillot, *"La pédagogie spirituelle de M. Olier d'après ses 'Mémoires'"* (The Spiritual Pedagogy of M. Olier according to his "Memoirs"), in BSS 2 (1976) 27–64; the text of the memoirs is on p. 49. Cf. also the synthesis of Olier's thought by G. Gaillot, *"Critères pour la formation spirituelle des pasteurs. La tradition pédagogique héritée de M. Olier"* (Criteria for the Spiritual Education of Pastors: The Pedagogical Tradition Inherited from M. Olier), BSS 4 (1978) 15–23. (19) J. Eudes, *Les Statuts et Constitutions de la Congrégation de Jésus et Marie* (The Statutes and Constitutions of the Congregation of Jesus and Mary), in *Oeuvres Complètes* (Complete Works), Beauchesne, Paris 1909, t. 9, 145: "The second particular aim of the Congregation is that its sons by their example, by their prayers, by their instructions, by the practice of the priestly functions, and especially by the exercises of the Missions, dedicate their efforts to renew the spirit of Christianity in Christians, and to make Jesus Christ our Lord live and reign in them." A study on the missions of Eudes that is already a classic is that of Ch. Berthelot du Chesnay, *Les missions de Saint-Jean Eudes. Contribution à l'histoire des missions en France au XVIIe* (The Missions of St. John Eudes: Contribution to the History of the Missions in Seventeenth-Century France), Paris 1967. Cf. also the recent monograph of P. Milcent, *Un artisan du renouveau chrétien au XVIIe siècle. Saint-Jean Eudes* (A Craftsman of Christian Renewal in the seventeenth century), Cerf, Paris 1985. (20) "The same God, contemplating the origins of the divine persons existing in the unity of his essence, did not want there to be any other source and origin of His divinity in the state of the Church than that of the mission . . . and He wants the mission to occupy the same rank among men as procession to divine persons, which according to St. Augustine, these two terms 'mission' and 'procession' say one and the same thing": P. Bérulle, *la mission des pasteurs en l'Église, sur l'article 31 de la Confession de foi* (On the Mission of the Pastors of the Church, on Article 31 of the Confession of Faith), in *Oeuvres Complètes du cardinal de Bérulle* (Complete Works of Cardinal de Bérulle), Reproduction of the Princeps edition (1644), Maison d'institution de l'Oratoire, Montsoult 1960, t. I, 65. (21) "The Holy Spirit, Spirit, I say, Sovereign, existing eternally and not created, only comes and only works in God's Church through mission": Ibid., 72. (22) On the theological principle of the Incarnation as an essentially Trinitarian event in relation to TD, cf. the rich essay of M. Quéméneur, *"La maternité de grâce de Marie chez les spirituels français du XVIIe de François de Sales à Grignion Montfort"* (Mary's Maternity of Grace among the French Spiritual Thinkers of the seventeenth century, from François de Sales to Grignion Montfort), ÉtMar 17 (1960) 69–118, especially 112–14. (23) V.-L. Tapié, *"Spiritualité et action de St. Louis-Marie Montfort"* (Spirituality and Action of St. Louis-Marie Montfort), in *Quelques-unes des conférences prononcées à l'occasion du 250e anniversaire de la mort de saint Louis-Marie Montfort* (Some of the Lectures Given on the Occasion of the 250th Anniversary of the Death of St. Louis-Marie Montfort), Édition montfortaine, Rome 1967, 64. (24) Montfort composed numerous canticles whose theme is the poor and poverty. The wonderful Canticle 108, "The Treasures of Poverty," is of great beauty; in it, Montfort addresses the poor through Jesus' mouth in the following terms: *"Those who appear the last / Are all the first in my sight. / The poor beggars and the humble / Are the closest friends. / For they have my appearance"*: H 108:3. (25) Besnard II, 216. (26) J. P. Gutton, *La società e i poveri* (Society and the Poor), Milan 1977, 10. (27) The date of composition of Canticle 18, "The Cries of the Poor," seems to correspond to Montfort's stay in the Hôpital at Poitiers: cf. *H. Frehen, Études sur les cantiques du Père Montfort* (Studies on Montfort's Canticles), Reykijavik ms., 212. (28) Cf. Ph. Sassier, *Du bon usage des pauvres. Histoire d'un thème politique (XVIe–XXe)* (Right Conduct towards the Poor: History of a Policitical Theme), Fayard, Paris 1990. (29) In RW a comparable arrangement is prescribed for the Daughters of Wisdom. Montfort had the opportunity of enjoying the famous "portion of the Blessed Virgin" among the Benedictine nuns of the Most Holy Sacrament on the occasion of his stay at Rouen in the course of the summer of 1714 (Blain, 191–92). This custom was begun by the founder of the Benedictine nuns, Catherine de Bar, the famous Mother Mectilde of the Blessed Sacrament (1614–1698) who introduced it in her institution: cf. (Anonymous), *Catherine de Bar Fondatrice des Bénédictines du Saint Sacrement 1614–1698* (Catherine de Bar, Founder of the Benedictine Nuns of the Blessed Sacrament), Fondation de Rouen, Rouen 1977, 152, n. 8. (30) Ibid., 242–43. On the bread for the poor in the mission, cf. Besnard II, 184. (31) Cf. B. Geremek, *La potence ou la pitié. L'Europe et les pauvres du Moyen Age à nos jours* (Gallows or Pity: Europe and the Poor from the Middle Ages to the Present Day),

Gallimard, Paris 1987, 187–262. (32) Cf. P. Eijckeler, *Quelques points d'histoire montfortaine* (Several Points of Montfort History), vol. 1: *Des origines à M. Mulot exécuteur testamentaire* (From the Origins to M. Mulot, Executor of the Will), Rome 1972, 108–27. (33) Besnard II, 134. (34) Cf. F.-Z. Cuche, *Une pensée sociale catholique. Fleury, La Bruyère, Fénelon* (Catholic Social Thought in Fleury, La Bruyère and Fénelon), Cerf, Paris 1991. (35) Cf. the collective work, *"La prédication au XVIIe"* (Preaching in the seventeenth century), in *Journées Bossuet: Actes du colloque de Dijon* (On Bossuet: Acts of the Colloquium of Dijon) (1977), Paris 1980. (36) Cf. J. M. Roman, *S. Vincenzo de'Paoli,* 305–307. (37) The paragraph quoted from RM clearly has its source in recollections of a sermon by Massillon, *Sur la parole de Dieu* (On God's Word), resumed by Montfort in S I, 33–36, where he sets out the qualities of the good preacher. (38) As an example, cf. J. Eudes, *Le prédicateur apostolique contenant les qualités et les dispositions extérieures et intérieures du Prédicateur évangélique* (The Apostolic Preacher Containing the Qualities and the External and Internal Dispositions of the Evangelical Preacher) in *Oeuvres complètes* (Complete Works), Paris 1907, vol. 4. (39) The famous historian's trilogy is well known: J. Delumeau, *La peur en Occident (XIVe–XVIIIe)* (Fear in the West), Fayard, Paris 1979; Id., *Le péché et la peur. La culpabilisation en Occident (XIIIe–XVIIIe)* (Sin and Fear: The Apportion of Blame [The Thirteenth to the Eighteenth Centuries]), Fayard, Paris 1983; Id., *Rassurer et protéger. Le sentiment de sécurité dans l'Occident d'autrefois* (Reassure and Protect: The Feeling of Security in the West of the Past), Fayard, Paris 1989. (40) B. Dompnier, *Le missionnaire et son public. Contribution à l'étude de la prédication populaire* (The Missionary and His Public: Contribution to the Study of Popular Preaching), in *La prédiction au XVIIe* (Preaching in the seventeenth century), 125 (section discussion, 123–128). (41) Ibid., 117. (42) Besnard I, 135. (43) Besnard I, 141. (44) Besnard I, 145–47. (45) Besnard I, 161. (46) Cf. L. Pérouas, *Grignion Montfort,* 89. (47) Cf. L. Cognet, *"Cor et Cordis affectus,* 4: *Le coeur chez les spirituels du XVIIème"* (The Heart in the Spiritual Thinkers of the seventeenth century), DSAM 2 (1953), 2300–2307. (48) A. Sauvy, *Le miroir du coeur. Quatre siècles d'images savantes et populaires* (The Mirror of the Heart. Four Centuries of Scholarly and Popular Imagery), Cerf, Paris 1989, 50–52. (49) On the state of the L.S. manuscript and its problems, cf. H. Frehen, *"Étude curieuse sur le manuscrit du Livre des sermons du P. Montfort"* (Curious Study on the Manuscript of the Book of Sermons of Father Montfort), DMon 38 (1967) 1–8, continued in DMon 39 (1967) 1–8; P. Eijckeler, *"Lettre sur la date du manuscrit du Livre des sermons"* (Letter on the Date of the Manuscript of the Book of Sermons), DMon 41 (1967) 1–6; answer of H. Frehen, *"Encore sur la date du Livre des sermons Montfort"* (More on the Date of Montfort's Book of Sermons) DMon 42 (1968) 1–12. (50) Cf. B. Dompnier, *Le venin de l'hérésie* (The Poison of Heresy) 198–200. (51) Cf. the collective work, *Aux origines du catéchisme paraoissial et des manuels diocésains de catéchisme en France (1500–1660)* (The Origins of the Parish Catechism and the Diocesan Manuals of Catechism in France, 1500–1660), Desclée, Tournai 1989, 304; E. Germain, *Deux mille ans d'éducation de la foi* (Two Thousand Years of Teaching of the Faith), Desclée, Tournai 1983, 94–109. (52) It has been supposed that Montfort was citing one of his texts. The original manuscript of RM does not support such a supposition. However, RM 91 alludes to a text that was used or at least known. P. Eijckeler, *"Le cathéchisme des missions. Un problème difficile à resoudre"* (The Catechism of the Missions: A Difficult Problem to Resolve), DMon n. 48 (1972) 1–8, puts forward the hypothesis that we might find this "abridged catechism" in Canticle 109, which is entitled "The Principal Mysteries of the Faith in Canticle Form" and which comprises forty couplets. Montfort had added the subtitle, "The Catechism of Mission." Moreover, from 1759 onwards in editions of Montfort's Canticles there appears a text entitled *Abrégé de ce que doit croire et savoir un chrétien* (Summary of what a Christian must Believe and Know). This is a catechism which, according to Eijckeler, parallels Canticle 109. Perhaps the *Abrégé* to be a reproduction of the "Abridged Catechism of the Missionaries" indicated by Montfort in RM 91. The Montfort scholar A. Guéry seems to be of this opinion; in an unpublished study *(Recherches sur le "Catéchisme abrégé des missionaires"* (Study on the "Abridged Catechism of the Missionaries), Gouts-Rossignol 1974, typed text of 35 pages), he effects a careful analysis of H 109 and of the *Abrégé* published in 1759, identifying its probable source as a catechism of the Sulpician Joachim Trotti de la Chétardie (1636–1714), who in 1696 had taken possession of the parish of Saint-Sulpice. (53) For Montfort's catechetical training at Saint-Sulpice, cf. De Fiores, Itinerario 198–200. (54) Cf. P. Dumonceaux, *"Conversion, convertir, étude comparative d'après les lexicographes du XVIIe"* (Conversion, Converting: A Comparative Study Based on the Lexicographers of the seventeenth century), in *La conversion au XVIIe,* 5–15. (55) On the signs of true penitence: S II, 667. (56) Besnard I, 289. (57) Cf. LS II, 158–159. (58) Cf. LS II, 160–162. (59) Cf. J. Finance, *Consécration,* in DSAM 2 (1953), 1578–1579; R. Daeschler, *"Baptême [Commémoration du]"* (Baptism [Commemoration of]), DSAM 1 (1949), 1239. (60) J. Leuduger, *Bouquet de la mission composé en faveur des peuples de la campagne* (Mission Bouquet composed for the People of the Country), [14th ed.], L. Prud'homme, Saint-Brieuc 1853, 9–12. (61) M.-Th. Poupon, *Le poème de la parfaite consécration à Marie suivant Saint Louis-Marie Montfort et les spirituels de son temps. Sources et doctrine* (The Poem of Perfect Consecration to Mary according to St. Louis-Marie Montfort and the Spiritual Thinkers of His Time: Sources and Doctrines), Lyon 1947, 283. (62) Cf. J. Tranvouez, *"La Vierge Marie dans la pastorale de Grignion Montfort"* (The Virgin Mary in the Pastoral of Grignion Montfort), CM 10 (1966) 90–98. (63) Grandet, 395. (64) J. Leuduger, *Bouquet de la mission,* 12. (65) Cf. A. Bossard, *"Le don total au Christ par Marie selon Montfort"* (The Total Gift to Christ through Mary according to Montfort), CM 17 (1973), 31–32; Id., (Consecrating onself to Mary), CM 28 (1983), 95–106. (66) Cf. J. Tranvouez, *"La Vierge Marie,"* 94–95. (67) Grandet, 409–10. (68) Paul VI, Apostologic Exhortation *Evangelii nuntiandi* (1975), 15:51–53; John Paul II, Encyclical *Redemptoris missio* (1990), 9–10:31. On this encyclical, cf. E. Dal Covolo—A. M. Triacca (ed.), *La missione del Redentore. Studi sull'enciclica missionaria di Giovanni Paolo II,* (The Mission of the Redeemer. Studies on The Missionary Encyclical of John Paul II), LDC, Turin-Leumann 1992. (69) *Redemptoris missio,* 33. (70) John-Paul II, Apostolic Exhortation *Cathechesi tradendae* (1979), 47.

PATH OF PERFECTION

I. INTRODUCTION

In order to understand fully the montfort path to perfection outlined in this Handbook, especially in the article *Montfort Spirituality*, it is necessary to have a good grasp of the theology of Christian perfection and the various roads that lead to the perfection of charity. Thanks in great part to the Second Vatican Council, and especially its document LG, devout Christians from every walk of life are aware of their obligation to strive for the perfection of charity.[1] The people of God are supposed to be the holy people of God. In fact, throughout the twentieth century, the Church has been blessed with theologians and saints who have reminded the faithful of their lofty vocation as Christians. It suffices to recall the teaching and influence of St. Thérèse de Lisieux, Blessed Elizabeth of the Trinity, St. Maximilian Kolbe, Dom Columba Marmion, Reginald Garrigou-Lagrange, John Arintero, Gabriel of St. Mary Magdalene, Thomas Merton, and Joseph de Guibert. These persons and numerous others prepared the way for the profound renewal of the Church that was eagerly awaited when Pope John XXIII summoned the bishops from all over the world to the Second Vatican Council in 1961. A fundamental doctrine that has been repeated again and again since the close of the council is the teaching of Christ himself: "You, therefore, must be perfect, as your heavenly Father is perfect" (Mt 5:48). St. Paul could therefore write to the Thessalonians: "This is the will of God, your sanctification" (I Thess 4:3).

The Church, whose mystery is set forth by this sacred council, is held, as a matter of faith, to be unfailingly holy. This holiness of the Church is constantly shown forth in the fruits of grace that the Spirit produces in the faithful, and so it must be; it is expressed in many ways by the individuals who, each in his or her own state of life, tend to the perfection of love, thus sanctifying others. It is therefore quite clear that all Christians in any state or walk of life are called to the fullness of Christian life and to the perfection of love. The forms and tasks of life are many but holiness is one. Each one, however, according to his own gifts and duties, must steadfastly advance along the way of a living faith, which arouses hope and works through love.[2]

Running parallel to the efforts at renewal and *aggiornamento* of the Church is the rediscovery of the saints. The saints and mystics are key figures in the life of the Church. They can show the rest of the faithful what it means to be an authentic disciple of Christ. Chosen by God from every walk of life, they are living proof that holiness is not restricted to an elite class in the Church. This is the same doctrine that was taught by the Venerable Louis of Granada, OP, in the sixteenth century and by St. Francis de Sales in the seventeenth century. These two authors addressed their writings specifically to the laity.

Bishop Christoph Schonborn, OP, the general editor of CCC, has stated: "What is unusual for this kind of document [the Catechism] are the many references to the testimony of saintly men and women. The saints alone are sufficiently universal, Catholic, to speak to everyone in words that are born of the light and truth of faith. How could one doubt that the words of a St. Catherine of Siena, a St. Teresa of Avila or the "Little Flower" will have the power to cross all cultural and human boundaries to tell everyone, in a language impassioned by the love of Christ, the ancient and ever new truths of the Good News of Christ?"[3]

It is precisely in this context that we are to understand the teaching of Saint Louis Marie de Montfort on the stages in the path of perfection. As is well known, the path to perfection is for Montfort a Marian path; Mary is present throughout the entire journey to guide the soul and lead it to a full sharing in the mystery of Christ, and through him to the Trinity.

If, as Bishop Schonborn has stated, the saints are sufficiently universal to cross all cultural boundaries in order to bring to the faithful the Good News of Christ, how much more can his mother Mary do so. Saint Louis Marie stated this truth in the very first sentence of TD: *"It was through the blessed Virgin Mary that Jesus Christ came into the world, and it is also through her that he must reign in the world"* (TD 1). This is a pivotal principle in Montfort's description of the path that leads to perfection, and it constitutes one of the distinctive elements of his spirituality.

II. Meaning of Perfection

Before we can discuss the stages of growth on the path to perfection and the means that must be used in order to reach the goal, we must first define what we mean by the term "perfection." We look first at the meaning of the words used in this context, that is, the etymological definition. Our English words "perfection" and "perfect" come from the Latin verb *perficere* which means "to make completely or to bring to completion." Hence, that is perfect which is complete or finished; it lacks nothing that is proper to its nature. At the risk of being too technical for those who are not trained in philosophy or of seeming to go into great detail unnecessarily, we must nevertheless not only define our terms but make necessary distinctions. Only in that way can we obtain a clear understanding of the theology of Christian perfection and the means for attaining it.

1. Philosophical notion

As we have stated, a thing is perfect when it has all the being, all the reality, that is due to it in accordance with its nature. For example, a newborn baby is said to be physically perfect if it is in good health and has all the vital powers due to an infant; a blind man is physically imperfect because he lacks the use of a faculty that is due to a human being; but it is not an imperfection if a human person lacks wings, because flying is not an activity proper to humans.

We say that the very word "perfection" is an analogous term, which means that it can be applied to a variety of things but not with precisely the same meaning in each case. For example, there are differences in the meanings of the word "perfection" when applied to God, to a human being, to a thoroughbred horse, and to a Parisian croissant. Each one may be perfect in its class or genus, but there is a vast difference when they are all listed in the hierarchy of being. The result is that when we use these analogous terms, we are saying that various objects are partly the same and partly different. To speak precisely and correctly in theology, it is absolutely essential to know how to use analogous terms.

Further distinctions must be made when we try to classify the three types of perfection: a) when a being is integrally whole and entire in accordance with its specific nature (perfection *in esse*); b) when it has all the faculties, parts, or powers necessary for proper functioning, e.g., a living organism or a machine (perfection *in operatione*); and c) when it attains its proper goal or achieves its purpose (perfection *in assecutione finis*).[4]

The first type of perfection is also called substantial perfection, and in this sense, everything that exists is perfect to the extent that it exists. The other two types of perfection are something over and above substantial perfection: either as a perfection in operation or functioning (e.g., the perfection of a violinist playing at a concert) or the perfection that results from attaining one's goal (e.g., the perfection represented by graduation from a university or being awarded the gold medal at the Olympics).

All that we have said about perfection thus far pertains to the purely natural order, and it is within the scope of unaided human reason and observation. Nevertheless, the wisdom of the pagan philosophers has been a great boon in the development of theology and has helped Christians to give a reason and sometimes a defense for their faith.

2. Biblical teaching

When we turn to Sacred Scripture, we find numerous references to perfection. First of all, we praise and adore the perfection of God, for He transcends every human and angelic perfection to an infinite degree. It was this awareness of God's transcendence that fostered the apophatic theology of pseudo-Dionysius and likewise produced the abstract spirituality of the early French school.

God's essence is existence; his name is Yahweh, "I am who am" (Ex 3:14). The philosophers interpret this by saying that God is Pure Act and contains in Himself all possible perfections. More than that, He is the source of all perfections; it is only because of God's perfection that we can attribute perfection to any creature. This is part of what is meant when the theologian says that God is the First Cause uncaused.[5]

The OT speaks of God's sanctity or holiness rather than his perfection. The reason is that God is of a completely different order than the things of this world, and His attributes far transcend anything we can comprehend. Can we say that they spoke this way because they did not understand the use of analogy? Whatever the reason, the OT writers speak of the perfection of God's creation and the perfection of His Law, but they do not apply the word to God.

When God chose a people as His own, however, He commanded them to be holy. "Be holy, for I am holy" (Lev 11:45); "Walk in my presence and be perfect" (Gen 17:1)." Yahweh must be served "with a perfect heart" (1 Kings 8:61). The holiness of God's chosen people was found in their observance of the Law: "Happy, perfect in their way, are those who walk in the Law of Yahweh" (Ps 119).

In the NT, Jesus reveals that the most holy God is our Father and a God of love. He challenges his followers to "be perfect, even as your heavenly Father is perfect" (Mt 5:48). But their perfection is to be measured not only by obedience to the Law but by obedience to the "new commandment" of Christ. The children of God are commanded to strive for the perfection of love, love of God and love of neighbor. In this regard, they are to walk in the footsteps of Jesus, meek and humble of heart (cf. Lk 9:23; Mt 11:29).

3. Theological conclusions

If now we subject the three types of philosophical perfection to theological analysis, we can identify them as follows: substantial perfection (*in esse*) is sanctifying grace, which is the very soul of the supernatural life and the basis of our status as children of God. Without sanctifying grace, a person is spiritually dead and can do nothing of supernatural merit. Functional or operational perfection (*in operatione*) is the virtue of charity, because love is the springboard of all our actions, even on the purely natural level. On the spiritual level, we have the statement attributed to St. Augustine: "Love God, and do what you will, you won't sin." Finally, perfection in reaching the goal (*in assecutione finis*) is likewise charity, but there is a twofold application here. The goal in this life, in view of our call to holiness, is the perfection of charity; the goal in eternity, in the glory of the beatific vision, is to love the Lord our God with the totality of our being. Let us now discuss briefly the important conclusions that follow from these theological statements.[6]

a. *Christian perfection consists primarily in charity.* Christ taught that the most important precept is the precept of charity (Mt 22:35-40; Mk 12:28-31), and St. Paul's teaching on charity is explicit and abundant. For example: "But above all these things have charity, which is the bond of perfection" (Col 3:14); "Love is the fulfillment of the Law" (Rom 13:10); "So there abide faith, hope and charity, these three; but the greatest of these is charity" (1 Cor 13:13). In the papal bull *Ad conditorem,* Pope John XXII stated explicitly that "the perfection of the Christian life consists principally and essentially in charity."

This does not mean that the other virtues, such as faith and hope and the moral virtues, are not essential to Christian perfection and sanctity. It simply means, as St. Paul teaches, that without charity we are nothing, but with charity we reach the fullness of Christian perfection, and this requires the practice of the other virtues proper to our state in life.

b. *Christian perfection increases in the measure that one's love is more intense and inspires the acts of the other virtues.* There are two parts to this conclusion. First of all, we say that the individual is more perfect and holy if one's acts of love are more intense. Jesus commanded his followers to love the Lord their God with their whole heart and soul, mind and strength; that constitutes perfection. Secondly, an ardent love will prompt one to practice the other virtues as well as charity, and especially those pertaining to one's state of life. Nevertheless, as St. John of the Cross has stated, in the evening of life we shall be judged by love. Hence, it is not what we do that makes us holy but the love with which we do it.

c. *All Christians are obliged to strive for the perfection of charity.* The fundamental obligation stems from the very nature of sanctifying grace, which is meant to increase in us, and from the commitment made at our Baptism in Christ. St. Paul says that we must struggle until we attain "to the mature measure of the fullness of Christ" (Eph 4:13). He also tells us: "This is the will of God, your sanctification" (1 Thess 4:3). Finally, Pope Pius XI stated in his encyclical on St. Francis de Sales: "Let no one think that this obligation pertains only to a select few and that all others are permitted to remain in an inferior grade of virtue. They are all obliged to this law, absolutely and without exception."[7]

III. Nature of Christian Perfection

Having seen the meaning of perfection in general and the obligation of all baptized Christians to strive for the perfection of charity, we now ask what constitutes Christian perfection. We have already referred in passing to sanctifying grace and the virtue of charity because they are key elements in the life of the spirit. Without them, there can be no supernatural life in the soul and consequently no growth in the spiritual life.

1. Sanctifying grace

There is nothing in our fallen human nature that can lay a claim to the supernatural life; it is a gift that God gives us through the sanctifying grace received at our Baptism in Christ. Indeed, sanctifying grace is the very soul of our spiritual life and the basis of any merit we have before God. It is also our passport to heaven and the Beatific Vision, but even here on earth, says St. Peter, sanctifying grace makes us "partakers of the divine nature" (2 Pet 1:4). Consequently, St. Thomas Aquinas has stated that the minimum degree of sanctifying grace in a soul is greater than the good of the entire universe.[8]

The truth of this statement becomes evident when we consider the effects of sanctifying grace, which are beautifully summarized by St. Paul: "You have received a spirit of adoption as sons, by virtue of which we cry: Abba! Father! The Spirit himself gives testimony to our spirit that we are the sons of God. But if we are sons, we are heirs also: heirs indeed of God and joint heirs with Christ" (Rom 8:15-17).

The first effect of grace is to elevate us to the supernatural order, as we have seen. The three effects listed by St. Paul hold a place of eminence: through sanctifying grace we become adopted children of God, heirs of the kingdom of heaven and co-heirs with Christ our Brother. St. Augustine states that whoever says "our Father" to the Father of Christ calls Christ Brother.[9] As a result of the soul's intimate union with God through grace, it is justified and made pleasing to God; in addition, St. Paul tells us: "You are the temple of the living God" (2 Cor 6:16). What does this mean except that the entire Trinity dwells in the soul that is justified by the reception of sanctifying grace? And thus the promise of Christ is fulfilled: "If anyone love me, he will keep my word, and my Father will love him, and we will come to him and make our abode with him" (Jn 13:23).

2. The supernatural organism

There is a remarkable similarity between the natural human structure and what we call the supernatural organism. In the natural order, the human soul, which is spiritual, is the principle and source of human life and activity. Nevertheless, it is not immediately operative; it functions through the spiritual powers of intellect and will. Similarly, sanctifying grace is the principle and source of our supernatural life and activity, but it functions through the infused virtues and the gifts of the Holy Spirit. All these powers are given to the Christian with the first infusion of sanctifying grace, received at Baptism. Thus we read in CCC: "The grace of Christ is the gratuitous gift that God makes to us of his own life, infused by the Holy Spirit into our soul to heal it of sin and to sanctify it. It is the *sanctifying* or *deifying* grace received in Baptism. It is in us the source of the work of sanctification" (no. 1999).

"Human virtues acquired by education, by deliberate acts and by a perseverance ever-renewed in repeated efforts are purified and elevated by divine grace. With God's help, they forge character and give facility in the practice of the good" (no. 1810).

"The moral life of Christians is sustained by the gifts of the Holy Spirit. These are permanent dispositions which make man docile in following the promptings of the Holy Spirit. . . . They complete and perfect the virtues of those who receive them. They make the faithful docile in readily obeying divine inspirations" (nos. 1830, 1831).[10]

St. Thomas Aquinas says: "It is not fitting that God should provide less for those he loves that they may acquire supernatural good, than for creatures whom he loves that they may acquire natural good."[11] Indeed, by their very nature, grace and the infused virtues are meant to increase, even to perfection. Hence, from the moment of Baptism, every Christian is called to be holy and to strive for the perfection of charity.

Not only that, but even a newly baptized infant already has all the spiritual faculties and powers it needs to attain to the perfection of the Christian life, just as any healthy infant already has the potentiality to become an integrated adult person. That is why theologians and spiritual directors insist on the necessity of cooperating with the graces received. There is an excellent reminder attributed to St. Augustine, to the effect that the God who created us without our help will not save us without our help.

We cooperate with grace by performing the works of virtue: the theological virtues of faith, hope, and charity, and the moral virtues of justice, temperance, prudence, and fortitude that pertain to our state of life. With the repetition of the acts of virtue, the individual gains facility in their use and the habit of virtue becomes, as it were, a second nature. On the other hand, if a person ceases to perform virtuous actions or does so but rarely, it becomes very difficult for that person to live the Christian life.

If, however, the acts of virtue are sufficiently perfected, the individual is then disposed to be acted upon by the Holy Spirit. This involves the operation of the gifts of the Holy Spirit, which constitutes *mystical* activity because it is no longer under the control of the individual; it is the work of the Holy Spirit. The soul is docile, passive, and receptive; it is led by the Spirit.

From what has been said, it should be evident that the perfection to which all are called is a "mystical" perfection. Therefore, we cannot label mystical experience and activity as something "extraordinary" or put mysticism in the class of charismatic graces (*gratiae gratis datae*). The supernatural life of grace is meant to increase in us even to the "plenitude of Christ." The seven gifts of the Holy Spirit are given to us together with the sanctifying grace received at Baptism; they are not meant to lie dormant but to be activated by the power of the Holy Spirit. The fact that the majority of Christians do not seem to reach this state of perfection in this life does not negate the fact that all are called to the perfection of charity.

3. The love that is charity

Having seen the elements of the supernatural organism—sanctifying grace, the supernatural virtues, and the gifts of the Holy Spirit—which are given to every soul in the state of grace, we are now in a position to consider the virtue of charity and its role in the spiritual life. We already drew some conclusions concerning charity when we discussed the meaning of perfection; now we must ask precisely what kind of love is charity.

The reason for asking the question should be apparent: love operates on various levels of the human psyche. Saint Louis Marie de Montfort makes the following distinctions when treating of love: "*There are three kinds of love: emotional love, rational love, and the supernatural love of faith. In other words, the love that resides in the lower part of man, in his body; the love in the higher part, his reason; and the love in the highest part of man, in the summit of the soul, that is, the intelligence enlightened by faith*" (FC 50).[12]

It is crucial for the devout Christian striving for the perfection of charity to be correctly informed on the precise nature of the love that is charity. The simplest way to answer the question is to state, with

St. Thomas Aquinas, that the theological virtue of charity is "friendship."[13] What he means is that this infused supernatural virtue operates through a type of love that constitutes friendship, a love that wishes well to another person. It is a mutual benevolent love. Now, it is in this context that Jesus said to his Apostles: "I have not called you servants, but friends" (Jn 15:15). Therefore, the love that is the bond of this relationship and communication of friendship is the love that is charity.

The friendship love that is charity is not only a virtue; it is the most excellent of all the virtues, as St. Paul says: "So faith, hope, love remain, these three; but the greatest of these is love" (1 Cor 13:13). In fact, there can be no perfect Christian virtue without charity, as St. Paul also teaches: "If I should distribute all my goods to the poor, and if I should deliver my body to be burned, and have not charity, it profits me nothing" (1 Cor 13:3).

Since charity is love, and love is the source of all our actions, whatever the Christian does should be motivated by charity. The greatest challenge and the most common source of failure is in the area of self-centered love. Our fallen human nature is so prone to seek self that St. Alphonsus Liguori is reputed to have said that the struggle against selfish love does not end until a few hours after death. That is why spiritual writers constantly urge the practice of self-denial, even to the point of self-annihilation. The justification of such severe asceticism is found in the command of God Himself: "You shall love the Lord, your God, with all your heart, and with all your soul, and with all your strength" (Deut 6:5). And there is no terminus or limit to our love of God because, as St. Augustine taught, God gives us the grace to love Him, and when we love Him, He gives us the grace to love Him more.

J. Aumann

Notes: (1) Cf. *Dogmatic Constitution on the Church,* in *Vatican Council II: The Conciliar and Post-Conciliar Documents,* ed. A. Flannery, Costello, Northport, N.Y. 1975, 396. (2) See ibid., 396-398, *passim.* (3) Christoph Schonborn, OP, *The Divine Economy Interwoven through New Catechetical Work,* in *Reflections on the Catechism of the Catholic Church,* ed. J. P. Socias, Midwest Theological Forum, Chicago 1993, 83. (4) Cf. *Summa Theologiae* I, q. 6, a. 3. (5) Cf. ibid., q. 20, aa. 1-3. (6) For a more detailed explanation, cf. A. Royo and J. Aumann, *The Theology of Christian Perfection,* Priory Press, Dubuque 1962, 121-155. (7) Pope Pius XI, *Rerum omnium,* January 16, 1923, AAS, vol. 15, p. 50. (8) Cf. *Summa Theologiae* I-II, q. 113, a. 9, ad 2. (9) St. Augustine, *In Joannem,* PL 35:1565. (10) See CCC 484, 445, 450. (11) *Summa Theologiae* I-II, q. 110, a. 2. (12) Cf. FC 50. Some contemporary theologians and psychologists offer a slightly different classification: natural or instinctual love; emotional or psychic love; rational love (which can be concupiscible or benevolent); and the generous, friendship love that is charity, a supernatural infused virtue. (13) See *Summa Theologiae* II-II, q. 23, a. 1.

PEACE

SUMMARY

I. MONTFORT'S EXPERIENCE:
1. Home;
2. Education;
3. Family;
4. Adult working life;
5. Time to pray and reflect;

II. MONTFORT'S DOCTRINE:
1. Contemplative response to Christ Wisdom;
2. Experience and the Cross;
3. Identity and character;

III. THE PRESENT DAY:
1. Revitalize Baptism, self, and evangelism;
2. Meeting failure and change.

"Peace," as used in the Gospel, does not mean the absence of trouble, but what follows when God's will is done (cf. GS 78). "Thy kingdom come, thy will be done on earth as it is in heaven" (Mt 6:10), is the key to peace. At one with God's will there is peace in the individual, environment, and world. The crucial question is, therefore, "What shall I do Lord?" (Ac 22:10).

I. MONTFORT'S EXPERIENCE

1. Home

Montfort's first experience of the tension between peace as a gift from God and the imperfections of everyday life came at home. His father's social aspirations were not met by life nor shared by his son. This frustration only reinforced his father's temper. It has been suggested that Montfort's approach to life, and especially his literal identification with the poor, developed through "unconscious revenge" on his father's values.[1] Might it not have been, rather, a graced insight into the nature of the Gospel, discovered within the family and society in which he lived? Clearly, his father's strivings brought little peace. Around him he saw the poor as permanent and hopeless failures in that school of life. Destitution and indigence "were two of the great festering sores" in seventeenth-century France, and some attempts to deal with them made the poor feel "harried and unwanted."[2] Domestic and social life as Montfort experienced it offered little hope of peace. Did the Gospel offer a better way?

2. Education

At school in Rennes, he and others were encouraged by Father Bellier to do as he did and to care for the poor and sick in the general hospital. Montfort never deviated from that course. Always the poor received from him practical, sympathetic help, a man "ready to share not only the Gospel of God, but also our own selves because you had become very dear to us." (1Th 2:8) A sensitive man would find a strand of peace there.

As a student for the priesthood, Montfort was "systematically humiliated" by some of his teachers.[3] He could rationalize the ridicule of fellow students, perhaps, but what was he to make of it from respected teachers? It left its mark on him. "What shall I do Lord?" In that context, equilibrium could only be found in translating what was happening to him into what he knew to be the Gospel. He developed and lived radical dependence on Providence, making his own the Pauline tradition of "folly": "the foolishness of God is wiser than men." (1Co 1:25) Thus he found peace in answer to friends like M. Blain, who "took the opportunity to point out to him the many things which people objected in his behavior and in his eccentricities; but then he would refute my arguments with such apt and sound answers that I wondered where he got them from."[4] Perhaps a life of unflagging Gospel integrity found its own logic and peace.

3. Family

That same thread governed his relations with his family. *"I have done all God asked me to do for them in a spirit of love . . . poorer than all of them . . . Let them think of me as dead . . . I place them . . . into the hands of him who created them"* (L20). He adds, *"no one knows the secrets I am talking about, or . . . very few"* (L20). This did not come from some responsibility-free young bachelor alone in the big city.

4. Adult Working Life

At times, Montfort was at odds with some bishops, priests, authorities, and lay people. When he asked, "What shall I do Lord?" mission work abroad suggested itself. After advice and a meeting with Pope Clement XI, his commitment to work in France was confirmed. Always he followed what he took to be God's will in the directives of the pope and bishops. His correspondence gives a paradigm illustration of his general approach and how he found peace.

Newly ordained, he went to Nantes with *"a tremendous urge to make our Lord and his holy Mother loved"* (L5), especially among the poor. Very disappointed, he analyses the situation with a young man's judgment. He sees no future there. He indicates alternatives, but in writing to his director says, *"but I put aside all these ideas . . . I await your advice on whether I should stay here, in spite of having no inclination to do so, or go elsewhere. In the peace of Christ and his holy Mother, I am completely at your command.*" (L5).

Invited to work in the poor house in Poitiers, he accepts after taking advice. Although it *"is a house of discord where there is no peace whatever,"* he trusts that Christ and *"good Mother Mary will turn it into a holy place, one that will become rich and peaceful."* (L 10) Several times he asks, *"am I doing the right thing?"* For example, when he is unwilling to dine with the staff, he writes: *"I explained to the bishop that even in the poor house I do not wish to be separated from my mother divine Providence and . . . happy to share the meals of the poor and . . . no fixed salary . . . Have I done the right thing?"* (L10).

5. Time to Pray and Reflect

Welcomed initially, *"as a man sent from God,"* (L 11) inevitably, after considerable achievement, the combination of "new broom" and a radical evangelical lifestyle aroused antagonism. *"During this painful period I kept silent and lived in retirement putting my cause in the hands of God . . . in spite of opposite advice given me. To this end, I went for a week's retreat to the Jesuits"* (L 11). This is a recurring and important pattern in his grasp of peace. Active as one of Christ's *"bodyguard of handpicked men who will protect your house, defend your glory and save the souls that are yours,"* (PM 30) he yet knew when to withdraw and make time for rest and contemplation, as well as writing. His hymns on "The Wisdom of Silence" (H 23) and "On Solitude" (H 157) give a glimpse of the peace he then found at one with God's will and the natural world.

II. Montfort's Doctrine

1. Contemplative Response to Christ Wisdom

He begs God *"to look upon the strokes of my pen as so many steps to find you,"* (LEW 2) which again is the Gospel way to peace. God gave Himself in Christ, Eternal and Incarnate Wisdom, through the foolishness of Incarnation, Cross, and Resurrection (cf. 1Co 1:21–25), and *"how gentle, attractive and approachable is Eternal Wisdom who . . . invites [us] to come to him because he wants to teach [us] with a smile"* (LEW 5:117–132). Yet this gift is transcendentally beyond us (*"all should be silent . . . every mind should realize its inadequacy and adore"* [LEW 15]) so that, *"if we receive this great gift where are we to lodge him?"* (LEW 209). To prepare for and foster such a presence, *"the great way, the wonderful secret . . . (is to) bring Mary into our abode by consecrating ourselves unreservedly to her as servants and slaves"* (LEW 211). In turn, she *"who never allows herself to be surpassed in generosity will give herself to us in a real but indefinable manner; . . . In her, eternal wisdom will come and settle as on a throne of splendor"* (LEW 211). Mystics such as Montfort know that God does not ask our help: He asks for us. Our Lady's guiding presence will encourage a response *"that is total, continuous, courageous and prudent"* (LEW 196). So guided, *"Incarnate Wisdom . . . will grant his rest and ineffable peace"* (LEW 196).

2. Experience and the Cross

From the heart of that insight, Montfort found peace. He developed this in SM and TD: *"experience will teach you . . . and fill you with delight"* (SM 53). Writing (and living) from within the Pauline tradition of folly, he is explicit that *"you must expect to be shaped, cut and chiseled under the hammer of the Cross . . . So let him do what he pleases; he loves you, he knows what he is doing"* (FC 28). The *Wisdom Cross of Poitiers* and the *Pilgrimage Rules to Our Lady of Saumur* make that point. Montfort, no more than the Gospel, bypassed the Cross on the way to peace.

3. Identity and Character

Montfort is emphatic that in first pursuing Wisdom, it is "*a mistake to make charity towards your neighbor your chief end, for if in time you were not engaged in serving your neighbor, you would become troubled, sad, and discouraged. If . . . your primary purpose is your own sanctification . . . by the accomplishment of the will of God . . . then you will remain at peace*" (RW 4). Equally, fear of the future, *"is to make you lose your peace of soul . . . or time"* (RW 5). The contemplative insight, therefore, is primary. If all else is an expression of that, there is peace. In Christ, what one does is an expression of who one is. Writing for a congregation of missionary priests and brothers that did not then exist, Montfort says, *"it is not enough simply to be unafraid, God wants you to hope for great things from Him and to be filled with joy by reason of this hope"* (LCM 5). Such insight would produce *"men who are free, but still in bondage to your love and your will; men after your own heart . . . free as the clouds . . . moving . . . according to . . . the Spirit . . . Mary's children . . . (who) will look kindly on their fellowmen, fearlessly on your enemies, impartially on themselves, and when they look on you, . . . will be carried away in contemplation"* (PM 8-11, 21). Such people are at one with themselves, their environment, and their God. They know and communicate peace, as Montfort does in much of his writing.

III. The Present Day

1. Revitalize Baptism, Self, and Evangelism

"The kingdom of God is . . . righteousness, peace, and joy in the Holy Spirit" (Rm 14:17) is an acceptable description of life in God as a present reality. To achieve this means work, *"to renew the spirit of Christianity among the faithful. Therefore . . . see to it, as the Pope has commanded, (that) baptismal vows are renewed with the greatest solemnity"* (RM 56; LPM 2–5). To revitalize

Baptism and its implications is mainstream renewal, an essential pre-condition for evangelical peace (PM 5–6). Montfort further advocates genuine personal renewal in the evangelist or teacher, with the possibility of radical Gospel living (RM2). The apostle "Paul, slave of Christ Jesus . . ." (Rm 1:1) takes his identity from his Lord, as does Montfort, "*slave of Jesus in Mary*" (L passim). This is root and branch renewal. To enjoy peace at that level of being is to glimpse what they saw in faith.

All his life he tried to dismantle the institutional and economic violence of an unjust society by personally identifying with the poor and organizing practical care. The catalyst for change and so peace has to be the authentic Gospel; therefore to follow or preach other than the Christ of the Gospel may lead to illusion and oppression, the antithesis of peace. Thus Montfort advocates authentic preaching. He had high regard for its value, cost, and difficulty (RM 60–65).

Communicating the Gospel is inevitably culturally conditioned. In a contemporary culture where words are cheap, communication often easy and superficial, and secular media dominant, "*study and pray unceasingly . . . (to) obtain . . . the gift of wisdom . . . for knowing and relishing the truth and getting others to relish it*" (RM 60) is positive advice for possessing and sharing peace.

2. Meeting Failure and Change

Montfort knew failure and personal hurt "*like a ball in a game of tennis . . . and the players strike me hard.*" (L26) Individual temperament is part of this, of course, but inescapably, much of it is because, "we impart a secret and hidden wisdom of God . . . None of the rulers of this age understood this; for if they had, they would not have crucified the Lord of Glory" (1 Co 2:5–16). If that is one assessment of contemporary society, peace clearly has to be paid for (PM 27–30), and the price is not cheap. Authentic Gospel living may mean that, "*we love the cross we are carrying by the light of pure faith*" (FC 53). Unease and loss of identity and meaning can be the fearful results of change in society and church. No longer are we sure of who we are or what we are doing. If we are disoriented whenever circumstances change, we shall never know peace, because our peace is then dependent on a variable outside ourselves. For Montfort, changing and crucifying circumstances were often a chance to retrench and ask advice. Living in an unjust society and an unhealthy Church, he was helped to keep his balance by making his own and developing the Bérullian and Jesuit contemplative traditions he found in Paris and Brittany. He worked hard (L 21) and exhausted himself trying to make a better society and Church, but fulfillment, identity, and, ultimately, peace were not in what he did. The contemplative insight was the reality on which he stood, in the overriding conviction that *"Jesus is always and everywhere the fruit and Son of Mary, and Mary is everywhere the genuine tree that bears that Fruit of life, the true mother who bears that Son."* (TD 44) He never left the shade of that tree, with which he was one in Baptism. Many, clerical and lay, share that insight today.

D. Macdonald

Notes: (1) S. De Fiores, *Montfort's spiritual development until 1700,* in *Montfortian Encounter* No. 11. (2) L. Cognet, *"Ecclesiastical Life in France,"* in H. Jedin and J. Dolan, *History of the Church,* vol. VI, New York 1981. English translation of *Handbuch Der Kirchensgeschichte* vol. V., Verlag Herder, Freiburg im Bresgau 1970; R. Mandrou, *Montfort and the Evangelisation of the Poor,* Rome 1973 (English translation), in *Montfortian Encounter* No. 11. (3) R. Mandrou op. cit. (4) Blain, 228.

PENANCE

SUMMARY
I. THE PENITENCE CANTICLE.
II. THE SACRAMENT OF PENANCE IN THE PARISH MISSIONS OF THE SEVENTEENTH CENTURY.
III. MONTFORT'S EXPERIENCE.
IV. MONTFORT AS CONFESSOR AND MISSIONARY:
1. The use and value of the Sacrament of Penance;
2. "The Procedure of the Sacrament of Penance."

After briefly reviewing Saint Louis de Montfort's hymn on penitence, this article, while touching on some of his penances will focus on penance—the Sacrament of Reconciliation in his life and preaching. First we will consider Montfort's understanding of the virtue of penitence: the penitent sinner's turning away from sin and back to God. Included here are the acts of atonement required of a true penitent (for the rejection of God's personal love)—contrition, confession, and satisfaction for sin.

I. THE PENITENCE CANTICLE

Saint Louis Marie has written an entire treatise on penitence in Hymn 13, *"The Necessity of Penitence."* The study comprises ninety verses and is clearly divided according to the brief outline at the margin of each stanza. Following a brief definition, Montfort discusses five points: the necessity of penitence, the need for not postponing penitence, the usefulness of penitence, its qualities, and, finally, the means of accomplishing penitence.

From the very start, Montfort insists that penitence, which *"destroys all sin"* and is "*the plank which saves a sinner from his evident loss*" (H 13:2, 3), is "*more pleasing than one thinks*" (H 13:1). The saint understands penitence as conversion of sinners to God (v. 4), but since this is accomplished by painful wrenching from all that is not God—by mortification—Montfort speaks of Jesus Christ himself as the example of penitence (v. 6), inasmuch as Jesus practiced mortification, resisting all temptation (cf. Heb 4:15). Fourteen reasons are brought forward for the practice of penitence, and the example of the saints is a strong one: *"Look at the saints, if you please: Although often very innocent, They have all been penitent / During their entire life*" (v. 11). This practice of turning to God constantly in spite of the allurements of a sinful world—no matter the cost involved —is necessary especially "*when one has lost innocence, for one can no longer recover it / one can no longer repair it / except by penitence*" (v. 14).

Montfort the missionary devotes the greatest attention to the necessity of not postponing departing from sin and turning to God. Seventeen reasons are brought forward for seizing "*this day*" to turn to the Lord. An especially beautiful verse is addressed to young people who think that conversion can wait until some future time: "*Give to God your youth / Consecrate to Him your first desires*" (v. 21). "*God gives you today his grace / Designed to convert you: / Tomorrow you will not be able to use it / For it flies and passes*" (v. 25). There is a burning urgency in Montfort's preaching: "*From this moment then, without waiting / No longer war against the Most High! / Do penance for it is necessary*" (v. 37). Montfort's third point, the usefulness of penitence, stresses in its sixteen reasons the joy that conversion of heart brings to "*God the Father, this very Good Father [who] / Always receives a penitent / Embraces him like his own Child*" (v. 40), and "*what joy to the Faithful Shepherd [Jesus Christ]*" (v. 41), to the Holy Spirit (v. 42), to our guardian angel (v. 43) and to all of heaven (v. 44). Montfort strongly insists, however, that conversion should not be faked or "*simulated,*" for then the so-called penance only damns (vv. 53-56). The qualities of penance are primarily that it be interior and from the heart, entire, humble, and loving: "*When penitence is produced / By Love of God alone / Not by fear of punishment / Then its merit is so great*" (v. 62). The practical director of souls concludes his treatise with a few directives on the means to do penance; the first one is: "*Choose a good confessor, / A firm and wise director, / for he is necessary for you*" (v. 67). Montfort lists the attitudes that one must have with the spiritual director: candor, openness of heart, obedience. Other means to an ongoing conversion are frequent recourse to the Sacrament of Penance; corporal penances done with discretion, for "*they have very marvelous effects*" (v. 71); prayer; the intercession of Our Lady; and almsgiving. The hymn concludes with a fifteen-verse prayer and an act of contrition, including a petition to Mary: "*Pray for me, Virgin Mary, Certain Refuge of Sinners / Say but a word in my favor / And my soul is healed*" (v. 88).

II. The Sacrament of Penance in the Parish Missions of the Seventeenth Century

The Sacrament of Penance had been carefully formulated by the Council of Trent. In its first version, that of Bologna in 1547, as in its definitive redaction in the fourteenth session of the Council in 1551, the decree on penitence had coherently clarified the Catholic conception of the faith in contrast to Protestant doctrine. Against the Lutheran denial of the sacramental nature of Penance, the Council of Trent had reiterated the divine institution of this Sacrament, its necessity for salvation, and the forms of sacramental confession (cf. DS 1701-1715). In doing so, the Council had only reconfirmed the centuries-old liturgical and spiritual tradition of the Catholic Church.[1] The Tridentine doctrine, drawn from the *Catechismus ex decreto Concilii Tridentini ad parochos (Catechism of the Council of Trent)* of 1566, became one of the pillars of the Christian religious and sacerdotal education of the post-

Tridentine Catholic reform.[2]

In seventeenth-century France, a renewed parish catechesis was already found in some places around 1600. With the help of a wonderful range of catechisms, it was firmly established at the end of the century.[3] The Sacrament of Penance assumed a quite special role in the preparation for first Communion, as in the reception of the other Sacraments, and also in preparation for the seasonal confessions of Christmas, Lent, Easter, Assumption, and All Saints day.[4] French catechisms abounded in this period. Among the best known are those of Cambrai, Lyons, and Reims and those prepared by Bossuet and Tressan.[5]

The catechesis and the practice of the Sacrament of Penance also had an important place in the parish missions that flourished in Europe in the seventeenth and eighteenth centuries and were intended to revitalize the religious practice of the people in town and country. During these missions, great emphasis was laid on conversion; there were, for example, "sermons referring to the most dramatic moments of the Christian life, i.e., the Passion and death of Jesus Christ, the Last Things, sin and repentance; processions; the Way of the Cross; auto-da-fés of books or objects inciting sin; general confession; general Communion; the solemn promise of radical reform and perseverance; the institution of confraternities; the founding of schools and pious works; and the introduction of retreats and of the life of devotion and meditation."[6]

In reality, the missions had two fundamental aims: first, the preaching of Catholic doctrine and the reconversion of Catholics who had been won over by heresy or who were threatened by it, and second, the practice of the Sacrament of Penance.

Among the great missionaries and French catechists of the seventeenth century are Michel Le Nobletz (1577-1652), the Jesuits Julien Maunoir (1606-1683) and St. Jean-François Régis (1597-1640), and all the teachers of spirituality and founders of the "golden century" in France, like J.J. Olier and the Sulpicians, Vincent de Paul and the priests of the Mission, François Bourgoing and the Oratorians, John Eudes and the priests of the Congregation of Jesus and Mary, and Montfort and his followers. "In the missions there appear without fail the children's catechism (which generally takes place in the early afternoon) and the 'full catechism' for adults (towards sunset, or else morning and evening). Often there is also a catechesis specifically for boys undergoing preparation for their first Communion, which is solemnly celebrated as the conclusion of the mission."[7]

III. Montfort's Experience

The great masters of Christian priestly spirituality had already used the Sacrament of Penance as an effective Sacrament of conversion and holiness prior to the Council of Trent, and afterwards they did so even more. Montfort's spiritual and priestly experience is also to be understood against this background, i.e., an intense sacramental life aimed at the maturing and strengthening of virtuous habits through the Sacrament of Penance.

In the course of his classical education at the College of the Jesuits at Rennes (1685-1693), the young Montfort was able to experience his first period of spiritual maturing in an attitude of simplicity and enthusiasm. This was to flower into a vocation to the priesthood and the missionary life. The confessor of the College at the time was Father Philippe Descartes, a Jesuit and nephew of the famous philosopher. He therefore heard the confessions of the young Montfort. We know how important spiritual direction and the Sacrament of Penance were at the time in the pedagogical and spiritual tradition of the Jesuits, along with appropriate reading, common prayers, retreats, and good companions. In 1688, the young Louis was admitted to the Marian sodality. Among the most important obligations of this group was commitment to an intense spiritual life, sustained by purity and frequent practice of the Sacraments. In addition to the influence of living in this atmosphere, Montfort's spiritual formation was also enriched by his own extraordinary virtues, which found their truest expression in the unimpaired generosity of this young man.

Beyond his Marian fervor, characterized by a deep spirit of prayer and an irresistible charitable urge to help the poor and the unfortunate, Montfort was endowed with a firm desire to undertake rituals of penitence: "Scourges, iron chains, and other similar instruments of mortification were used by him."[8]

In 1692, when Montfort arrived in Paris on foot and with no material means, he could not enter either of the residences of the Seminary of Saint Sulpice. When he was admitted to "the little seminary" in 1695, he provided tangible proof of a great spirit of penance. Continual mortification, deliberate and accepted, was a characteristic of his spiritual temperament, which inclined him to a great deal of work, little sleep and food, and sharing the little he had with the poor. The lesson of death—in Paris he had to watch over the dead in order to make a living. In Paris, people were dying all around him. Montfort liarned even more about the ephemeral nature of the body and its pleasures, and also the physical disorder brought about by sin. One of Montfort's biographers asserts unequivocally: "He lived in a state of penitence because, precisely on account of his innocence, he understood the unbearable seriousness of sin. He mortified himself so much that his spiritual masters told him to show more restraint."[9]

In Paris, his first spiritual director was Father de la Barmondière, former parish priest of Saint-Sulpice, a man who lived austerely and possessed great virtue. It was to him that Montfort made his general confession covering his whole life, which, remarked M. Blain, "only served to expose the innocence of his soul and the great gifts with which God had enriched him."[10] In Paris, he received

Communion four times each week.[11] Subsequently, his spiritual director at the smaller Saint Sulpice was Father Brenier; there followed six months of misunderstandings, humiliations, and inexpressible mortifications for Montfort, who bore everything with humility and patience. Another of his spiritual directors, who was scarcely more understanding than Brenier, was the Sulpician Father Leschassier.

The heroic exercise of the virtue of penitence, accompanied by the frequent practice of the Sacrament of Penance, was a constant characteristic of Montfort's life.

IV. Montfort as Confessor and Missionary

The Sacrament of Penance and the virtue of penitence were not only a living experience of personal sanctification but also the principal aim of Montfort's apostolate to the people, especially those who were poor, ill, indigent, rejected, and marginalized.

1. The use and value of the Sacrament of Penance

In a letter of July 4, 1702, to Fr. Leschassier, Montfort stated that the two principal occupations of his apostolate at Poitiers were teaching catechism to the people and the administration of the Sacrament of Penance: "*In the meantime, for about two months, I gave instructions to the beggars that I encountered in the town and lived entirely at his Lordship's expense. First, I taught them in the church of St. Nicholas and then, as their numbers increased, I gathered them every day in the market hall and heard the confessions of many of them in the church of Saint Porchaire. . . . Since I arrived here it has been like preaching a mission every day. From morning till night I am hearing confessions and giving advice to a constant stream of people*" (L 11).

In fact, Montfort is aware that conversion and penitence are a central Christian reality (FC 9; LEW 138) and that confession, Communion, prayer, and the renunciation of sin are important means of salvation for everyone (TD 126; LEW 80-81). Indeed, it was in the course of spiritual direction and within the context of the Sacrament of Penance that Marie Louise Trichet met Montfort at Poitiers in 1701; she was seventeen at the time and would later become cofoundress of the Daughters of Wisdom.

Montfort also essentially codified his spiritual and apostolic experience in the Constitutions of his Congregations. In RM, for example, priests returning from mission are invited either to apply themselves to prayer and penance (RM 33) or to "*study in order to perfect themselves more and more in the art of preaching and hearing confessions*" (RM 35). Then he emphasizes the aim of their missionary work: the renewal of the spirit of Christianity among Christians, by the ministry of the Word of God (RM 60), the administration of the Sacrament of Penance (RM 58), and the renewal of the baptismal vows (RM 56).

According to the timetable of missions, missionaries might spend most of their time in the ministry of confessions (around four hours in the morning and almost as much in the afternoon): "*They will take their places in the confessional as soon as they can before or after the sermon and remain there until 11 a.m. precisely*" (RM 69); "*Recreation ends at one o'clock sharp and then they say Vespers and Compline together. After Vespers, they return to the confessional, unless the Director gives them other work to do, and they remain there until about five o'clock, depending on the season of the year*" (RM 74).

The missionaries were to take special care in teaching catechism to the children, especially when they were being prepared for their first Communion, by an adequate confession (RM 90). Montfort is aware of the fact that catechesis and the ministry of confession are tiring commitments. Because of this, he exhorts his missionaries willingly to experience the effects of poverty, for instance, "*the labor it entails in the pulpit or the confessional by which you earn your bread by the sweat of your brow*" (LCM 10).

The Sacrament of Penance is also an essential aspect of the religious life of women. In RW, on the subject of the frequency of the Sacraments, it is established that nuns must "*go to confession regularly every week to the confessor chosen by the community*" (RW 145). The Sisters are exhorted to guard against scruples (RW 159) and to be concerned with attaining perfect contrition: "*strive more to rouse yourself to contrition than to recall all your sins*" (RW 160). To the man who was converted during a parish mission, Montfort counsels daily Mass (H 139:18) and the practice of the Sacraments (i.e., confession and Holy Communion) ordinarily once a month (H 139:22). Monthly or frequent Communion in Montfort's time was a practice strongly condemned by the rigorism of the Jansenists. In his rhymed treatise on penitence, Montfort teaches: "*Approach the sacrament of confession often / But with determination to amend one's life / For to do otherwise / Is to damn oneself without ceasing*" (H 13:70).

Montfort exhorts his missionaries to be very restrained both in their preaching and in hearing confessions. For instance, as preachers, they must avoid criticizing other preachers, losing their temper, referring directly or indirectly to an individual in the audience, indulging in a barrage of affected or exaggerated condemnations of rich or important people, and "*censuring and criticizing priests and giving detailed accounts of their sins*" (RM 63).

While he was very severe towards himself, Montfort was very merciful to sinners. Grandet describes him in the confessional in the following terms: "Father de Montfort was gentle even in the tribunal of penitence: he always avoided these two grievous excesses which used to cause and today still cause such great evil in the Church: excessive rigor and excess moral laxity. From the pulpit he thundered out against all vices, but he was at once firm and gentle in confession; he had a singular gift for touching hearts, in the confessional as well as the pulpit. But he was so horrified by oversevere morality that he believed that strict confessors did a hundred times more damage in the Church than those who were lax. . . . Meanwhile, although M. de Montfort had the reputation of being extremely severe, great sinners more often went to him for confession than to any other missionary."[12]

Following the example of Jesus the Good Shepherd, Montfort preferred to approach the most hardened sinners, the worst, the most obdurate, to incite them to conversion. And for these sinners he sacrificed the whole of his life.

A. Amato

2. "The Procedure of the Sacrament of Penance"

Montfort alludes to a *"Méthode Uniforme que les Missionnaires Doivent Garder dans l'Administration du Sacrement de Pénitence pour Renouveler l'Esprit du Christianisme (Uniform Procedure to be Followed by Missionaries in Administering the Sacrament of Penance in order to Bring about a Renewal of the Christian Spirit"* (RMW 59). Perhaps an outline of this work can be found in Montfort's book of Sermons under the title *"Méthode du Sacrement de Pénitence (Procedure for the Sacrament of Penance)"* (LS 156); this could refer to the *Méthode uniforme,* given that no work of this title by Montfort has survived.

We can deduce the content of the *Procedure* from two works by St. John Eudes: *Avertissements aux confesseurs missionnaires (Advice to Missionary Confessors)* (1644) and *Le Bon Confesseur (The Good Confessor)* (1667),[13] in which the earlier work was taken up and expanded. These works were themselves inspired by *Avertissements aux Confesseurs (Advice to Confessors)* by St. Francis de Sales and *Instruzioni dei confessori (Instructions for Confessors)* by St. Charles Borromeo.[14] These manuals were written as the result of the new requirements of penitential practice and theology sanctioned by the Council of Trent (session 14, 1551), which brought about a deepening but also a certain hardening in the sacramental celebration of confession. The very title of the confessor's manual referred to above establishes a connection between the "procedure" in question and the pastoral aim of mission as Montfort defines it in RM 56.

The second part of the sentence that sets out the meaning of *"renewing the spirit of Christianity"* is interesting: *". . . they are not to give absolution or communion to any penitent who has not first renewed his baptismal promises"* (RM 56). In fact, the *Procedure* prescribes the renewal of the promises of Baptism after contrition and before absolution.[15]

Montfort institutes a close relationship of subordination between the aim of mission ("*renewing the spirit of Christianity*") and the reconciliation obtained by the renewal of the promises of Baptism. This mediation has a preparatory function: the Sacrament of Reconciliation would be purely palliative if the Christian had not first radically renewed his awareness of the dignity that Baptism conferred on him, by agreeing to fulfill the commitments or the "promises/vows" of his Baptism. These themes will be developed accordingly in TD 120-131.

In choosing this method, Montfort adheres to a fundamental point introduced into pastoral life and catechesis by the Council of Trent (DS 1671-72), which calls Penance "a more laborious kind of Baptism" and, in doing so, refers to Tradition, which had also defined Penance as a "second Baptism."

In line with the practice after the Council of Trent and the missionary tradition of his time, sacramental absolution of the penitent was not infrequently delayed in well defined cases.[16] Montfort copied into LS a quotation from St. John Eudes that justifies this practice: "*Experience shows the usefulness of refusing absolution. Almost none of those who immediately received absolution was converted, and the vain ghost of absolution casts or drags a great number of souls into Hell. A penitent who has received absolution no longer thinks about conversion or penitence. He is quick to sin because he will be quickly absolved.*"[17]

The delay of absolution was "at the center of great debates in the seventeenth century."[18] It was a threat used by the confessor to break the sinner's resistance and oblige him to change his life, given the danger of going to hell if he were not absolved. Until the middle of the seventeenth century, the dominant doctrine of manuals for confessors tended towards indulgence to the faithful. Montfort was to keep a sense of proportion, and he wrote that his missionaries "*must not be either too strict or too lax imposing penances or granting absolution but must hold to the golden mean of wisdom and truth*" (RM 59).

On the occasion of the mission to Vanneau, in the diocese of Saintes, which probably dates back to the spring of 1714, after the ordinary of the district refused the faculties of the diocese to all the members of the mission team, Montfort — as one of his collaborators testifies — said "that he had never been subjected to a clearer penance in his life." For after the general confession of sins, the plan was "the following day to begin to absolve the penitents to prepare them for general communion," and Montfort was deeply hurt because "he was obliged to leave in a state of sin" all the faithful who had already confessed their sins.[19]

Bénigne Pagé, somewhat by chance, attended Father de Montfort's sermons. She was inspired to leave a worldly life to enter the cloister of the Poor Clares. Father Besnard tells us that at her conversion, Saint Louis de Montfort urged her to make a general confession. Besnard writes that "she used eight days [to prepare] for it."[20]

Montfort's insistence that the promises of Baptism be renewed before sacramental absolution takes place was based on his conviction that this renewal is already a conversion ("*metanoia*"), considered not only as a preliminary phase but, rather, as a precondition of sacramental reconciliation.

Indeed, Montfort reiterates the

links between Baptism and penitence in his pastoral practice, already defined as a method in the popular mission of his time. Penitence is a condition of baptism (Acts 2:38), i.e., incorporation into Christ and the Church through faith. Baptism is a radical, total conversion: the baptized die to sin and live in faithfulness to Christ; it is a regeneration in the Spirit of Christ.

P.L. Nava

Notes: (1) Cf. A. Amato, *I pronunciamenti tridentini sulla necessità della confessione sacramentale (The Tridentine Pronouncements on the Necessity of Sacramental Confession),* LAS, Rome 1974. (2) Cf. the critical edition of the catechism: Father Rodriguez, I. Adea, F. Domingo, R. Lazentti et M. Merino, eds., *Cathechismus Romanus,* Ed. Universidad de Navarra 1989. For the Sacrament of Penitence, cf. 286-337. (3) E. Germain, *Parler du salut? Aux origines d'une mentalité religieuse (Speaking of Salvation? At the Origins of a Religious Mentality),* in *La catéchèse du salut dans la France de la Restauration (The Catechesis of Salvation in the France of the Restoration),* Beauchesne, Paris 1967, 291. (4) Cf. J. Delumeau, *Le péché et la peur. La culpabilisation en Occident XIIIème-XVIIème siècle (Sin and Fear: Guilt in the Western World, from the Thirteenth to the Seventeenth Centuries),* Fayard, Paris 1983, 300-301. (5) Cf. P. Braido, *Lineamenti di storia della catechesi e dei catechismi. Dal "tempo delle riforme" all'età degli imperialismi (1450-1870), (Outline of the History of Catechesis and Catechisms: From "the time of the Reform" to the age of Imperialism (1450-1870)*, Elle DI CI, Leumann 1991, 162-164. (6) Ibid., 178. (7) Ibid., 188. (9) G. De Luca, *Luigi Maria Grignion de Montfort,* Edizioni di Storia e Letteratura, Rome 1985, 2, 121. (10) Blain, 24. (11) Ibid., 31. (12) Grandet, 375-376. (13) LS 652-660. (14) On the genesis and content of the works just mentioned, cf. P. Milcent, *Un artisan du renouveau chrétien au XVIIe, St. Jean Eudes (An Architect of the Christian Renewal of the Seventeenth Century: St. John Eudes),* Cerf, Paris 1985, 423-433. (15) J.-J. Olier, who knew the life and works of St. Charles Borromeo well, wished to present the famous archbishop of Milan as the most authoritative adviser of confessors, which led to the many editions of his *Instructions aux confesseurs.* On February 1, 1657, the General Assembly of the Clergy of France recommended that it be distributed. The success of the work, in spite of certain interpretations, demonstrates the esteem that St. Charles Borromeo enjoyed. Cf. R. Darricau, *La posterità spirituale di San Carlo Borromeo in Francia nei secoli XVII-XIX (The Spiritual Posterity of Saint Charles Borromeo in France in the Seventeenth to Nineteenth Centuries),* in *La Scuola Cattolica,* 112 (1984), 751-752. (16) Cf. LS 655. (17) Cf. Ibid., 657. (18) J. Delumeau, *L'aveu et le pardon. Les difficultés de la confession aux XIIIe-XVIIIe siècles (Confession and Forgiveness: The Problems of Confession in the Eighteenth and Nineteenth Centuries),* Fayard, Paris 1990, 87; cf. chap. 7, p. 79-90. (19) Cf. the account in Besnard II, 8. (20) Besnard I, 270.

Our Lady of Wisdom

A classic sculpture, which entered montfort iconography from the Sulpician tradition of the French school of spirituality.

PILGRIMAGE

SUMMARY

I. SAINT LOUIS MARIE DE MONTFORT AND THE PILGRIMAGE TRADITION.

II. MONTFORT'S MAJOR PILGRIMAGES:
1. Chartres: Notre-Dame de Sous-Terre;
2. Saumur: Notre-Dame des Ardilliers:
   a. 1700,
   b. 1701,
   c. 1706,
   d. 1716;
3. Loreto and Rome;
4. Mont-Saint-Michel;
5. Holy sites created or restored by Montfort.

III. MONTFORT'S MOTIVATIONS AS A PILGRIM:
1. The grace of touching hearts;
2. The search for God;
3. Profound communion with Mary.

IV. PILGRIMAGES WITH SAINT LOUIS MARIE:
1. Montfort's tomb;
2. Following Montfort's steps;
3. Lourdes;
4. The pilgrimage from Saint-Pompain to Notre Dame des Ardilliers, Saumur.

V. A MODEL PILGRIM FOR TODAY AND THE FUTURE.

I. SAINT LOUIS MARIE DE MONTFORT AND THE PILGRIMAGE TRADITION

Several statues show Saint Louis Marie de Montfort as a pilgrim on the road, his gaze seemingly fixed on the hereafter rather than the passing geography. He carries the knapsack and staff that are the hallmark of the pilgrim and, at the end of his staff, the crucifix blessed by Pope Clement XI; he holds the statuette of "his good Mother" in his left hand, and his rosary is at his side. Throughout his life, he retained the bearing of a pilgrim: he requested charity "*for the love of God*," and as soon as the object of his pilgrimage came into view, he removed his shoes and approached barefooted.

The word "pilgrimage" comes from the Latin *peregrinus.* The root word is *per-agrare,* meaning "to travel a distance." To be a pilgrim was to travel far, to go to a foreign country and sojourn there. Later, "pilgrimage" came to mean a journey to a holy place, with a religious purpose.[1]

The origins of pilgrimages can be traced back even beyond Christian antiquity. Cultural anthropology has revealed three stages of pilgrimage: a. the victory over space, wherein pilgrims must break the routine of their daily life and journey elsewhere to change themselves from within; b. the contact with a sacred place by means of the *abrazo,* or embrace of a stone or statue, or by leaving a souvenir of one's passing (a votive offering, inscriptions on the walls, etc.); c. the encounter with the divinity and the hereafter, which the holy place brings to mind.[2]

We frequently see the words "way, road, path" in the Bible. The Semites habitually expressed spiritual realities with concrete terms. They used these words to describe mankind's way of life, moral conduct, and religious bearing. Abraham, who left Ur in Chaldea, exemplifies the spiritual pilgrim on the way of perfection. Since Abraham, all men of faith have been pilgrims marching in the desert toward the promised land. We are the people of God on pilgrimage.

Jesus said, "I am the way" (Jn 14:6), and thus forced us to reevaluate all worship tied to a particular place. The first Christians referred to early Christianity as "the Way" (Acts 9:2; 18:25; 19:9, 23; etc.). Although the Mosaic law requiring three pilgrimages had been abolished, pilgrimage in the early Church developed into an act of spontaneous and private devotion. In the West, pilgrims were attracted to the tombs of the Apostles Peter and Paul in Rome; in the East, they travelled to biblical sites, to the tombs of martyrs and saints, and to the dwelling places of well-known monks.[3]

In the Middle Ages, an entire spirituality of pilgrimage developed. There were two categories of pilgrims: those who hoped to obtain a bodily cure through a miracle and those who hoped to gain salvation for their soul; it often happened that both purposes fused into one.

At the close of the sixteenth century, from 1692 to 1700, Saint Louis Marie resided at the seminary of Saint Sulpice in Paris. In the short book *Practices of Slavery to Jesus in Mary,* a publication of the seminary, it is stated: "Once each month, out of devotion, two gentlemen travel in the name of the seminary, on a pilgrimage to a church or chapel dedicated to the Most Blessed Virgin; if they desire, they may receive Holy Communion there, as may be observed in every pilgrimage one makes."[4] Jean-Baptiste Blain reports that in the company of several seminarians who were chosen from among the most fervent, Louis Marie went every Saturday to receive Communion at Notre-Dame de Paris. There he loved to kneel before "his Good Mother."[5]

In the eyes of the directors of Saint Sulpice, three pilgrimages were especially important: Chartres, Notre-Dame des Ardilliers at Saumur, and Loreto in Italy. Saint Louis Marie made all three, and many more besides, placing him in the tradition of the great pilgrims. He could have composed the motto that Newman chose for himself and indeed illustrated much later: "I am a pilgrim." "A pilgrim of the infinite," wrote Father Morineau in his portrait of St. Louis Marie, "a sublime vagabond," whose pace was so quick that the world proved too confining for him. His steps led him to teach mankind the meaning of life.[6]

II. Montfort's Major Pilgrimages

1. Chartres: Notre-Dame de Sous-Terre

Blain, a confidant of Louis Marie, described this pilgrimage to Chartres.[7] The seminary at Saint Sulpice traditionally chose two seminarians each year "to travel on pilgrimage to Notre-Dame de Chartres. Montfort, on being chosen, received this happy commission with all the joy of his soul." So, in the summer of 1699, he made the pilgrimage to Notre-Dame de Sous-Terre with his fellow seminarian Bardou. The journey took three days, which they spent alternately in silent meditation and in praying the Rosary. For meals, they requested bread in villages; they spent their nights in a barn. With Bardou, Montfort felt free to follow the impulse of his zeal. On the road, he "spoke of God to laborers and the poor whom he saw near and far, then rushed to catch up with his brother seminarian." His time in Chartres was spent in intense prayer. At the altar of Notre-Dame de Sous-Terre, "he received Communion in an excess of fervor and piety brought on by the grace of his surroundings. He persevered in prayer for six successive hours, on his knees, unmoving, as if in ecstacy." He spent the day in contemplative prayer, to the astonishment of his companion: "How is it that Grignion can converse with God for so long?"

2. Saumur: Notre-Dame des Ardilliers

Because de Foix, du Ferrier, and Olier—founders of Saint Sulpice seminary—had made a pilgrimage to Notre-Dame des Ardilliers in 1641, this shrine of Our Lady was a favorite pilgrimage center for the seminarians of Saint Sulpice. Louis Marie de Montfort made this pilgrimage several times.

a. 1700. Just after being tapped to be a part of the community of missionaries directed by René Lévêque at Saint-Clément of Nantes, in September 1700, he traveled to Nantes. His journey took him to Saumur, to the holy sanctuary of Notre-Dame des Ardilliers.[8] There, at the beginning of his priestly ministry, he prayed to Mary for the works that he planned to undertake.

b. 1701. At the beginning of October, Father de Montfort left Saint-Clément de Nantes for the General Hospital at Poitiers, responding to an urgent appeal by the bishop, Monsignor Girard. This was a new mission, and so he went to Notre-Dame des Ardilliers to request God's mercy. He made a novena of prayers and distributed the money that Lévêque had given him to the poor who frequented the holy church, a concrete gesture of renouncement conforming to his missionary ideal.[9]

c. 1706. Father de Montfort returned from Rome, where Clement XI had invested him with the title Apostolic Missionary. His mission had been clearly defined: the Pope "enjoined him to apply himself to teaching Christian doctrine to the children and the people and to make the spirit of Christianity flourish once again through the renewal of baptismal promises."[10] After a short stop in Poitiers to join Brother Mathurin, his faithful companion, he travelled to Notre-Dame des Ardilliers. He wished to entrust this new departure in his missionary life to the care of Mary and her sanctuary. He remained several days at Saumur. It was during this pilgrimage that he met St. Jeanne de la Noue, foundress of the sisters of Providence; he reassured her and encouraged her to persevere in her "extraordinarily austere" way of life.[11]

d. 1716. At the beginning of Lent 1716, thirty-three White Penitents of Saint Pompain proposed to Montfort that they make a pilgrimage on foot to Notre-Dame des Ardilliers de Saumur. Father Montfort agreed to their request and composed a highly detailed rule for them, indicating the objective of the pilgrimage and the means of accomplishing it: *The Pilgrimage to Our Lady of Saumur made by the Penitents to obtain from God good Missionaries* (PS).[12] The two priests whom they had appointed to accompany them, Fathers Mulot and Vatel, were given the task of directing the pilgrimage. The purpose of the pilgrimage was clearly stated: *"You will make this pilgrimage for the following intentions: Firstly, to obtain from God through Mary's intercession good missionaries, who will follow the example of the apostles by complete abandonment to divine Providence and the practice of virtue, under the protection of Our Lady. Secondly, to obtain the gift of wisdom in order to know, love, and practice the truths of our faith and to lead others to Christ."*

Montfort insisted that the thirty-three Penitents pray in common and that they always walk together as a group, except through villages, where they were to travel in twos. In particular, the rule recommended mutual charity, frequent silence, mortification, and complete obedience to their designated superior. The chapter on mortification bluntly states: *"Unless they are prevented by sickness they try to fast during the whole pilgrimage."*

We should note *"the day's timetable."* Montfort planned every detail. Upon their arrival in Saumur, the Penitents were to march two by two, feet bare; at the hour of Mass and Offices, they would refrain from singing so as not to disturb the ceremonies; at other times, their superior was to request permission from the sacristan to recite the Rosary. They were all to take Communion on the first day and the following day, *"provided they have not committed any serious sin."*

In this famous rule, the favorite devotions of Montfort are revealed, together with some of his prayers and hymns. The effort he demanded for an entire week from thirty-three lay people is quite astonishing.

On their return, Father de Montfort himself made one last sojourn to pray at Notre-Dame des Ardilliers with several brothers: Mathurin, Jacques, and Gabriel. After this pilgrimage, he journeyed to Saint-Laurent-sur-Sèvre for his last mission. His "holy pilgrimage" on earth ended on April 28, 1716.

3. Loreto and Rome

At Poitiers, Father de Montfort had encountered a climate of opposition that threatened to obstruct his missionary activity and render all his work useless. Dismissed by his bishop, he decided to travel to Rome and request the advice of the Pope to see where God called him next. It was a long journey. He traveled in poverty; he gave away the coins in his pocket and required the same of his companion en route. He ate and lodged "as Providence led him."

On his way, he took the opportunity to stop and pray at a place frequented by pilgrims: the Holy House of Loreto. Happy to follow the example of his masters at Saint Sulpice, he prayed and meditated at length on the mystery of the Incarnation, the foundation of his spirituality. He remained there fifteen days.

Rome marked the last stage of his long pilgrimage. As soon as he saw the dome of St. Peter's basilica, "he prostrated himself, his face pressed to the ground. When he arose, he removed his shoes and traveled the final distance barefoot."[13] Montfort was granted an audience with Clement XI on June 6. He admitted to having been seized with an extraordinary respect in the presence of the Pope, believing he saw Jesus Christ himself in the form of his Vicar. This interview gave Montfort the answer to his questions and a definitive direction to his career. As a memento of this pilgrimage, he carried back with him his indulgenced crucifix, attached to his pilgrim's staff.[14]

4. Mont-Saint-Michel

Saint Louis Marie was named an Apostolic Missionary by Clement XI. From Rome he returned to France, sought out Brother Mathurin at the abbey of Ligugé, and made a retreat of eight days at the parish house of clerical friends near Poitiers. When he finished his retreat, his plans were decided: he would commit his new missions to the protection of the Most Holy Virgin Mary and the Archangel Saint Michael. With Brother Mathurin, he went to Notre-Dame des Ardilliers and, passing by Angers, proceeded on to Mont-Saint-Michel.

The two pilgrims arrived there on September 28, 1706, the eve of the feast of the archangel. To this unique setting, an incomparable encounter of nature and art, Montfort came to live, as it were, a soldier's vigil at the foot of Saint Michael. The next day, the feast day, he spent in prayer. Since his days at Saint Sulpice, the missionary had nourished a special devotion to the holy angels. Now he required the aid of Saint Michael, the conqueror of Satan and patron of France, the apostolic field conferred on him by the Pope. At Mont-Saint-Michel he drew the apostolic strength to make him invincible in spiritual combat.

5. Holy sites created or restored by Montfort

The saint made all of his journeys on foot, travelling from parish to parish, from Rennes to Paris, Paris to Nantes, Nantes to Poitiers, and so on, living like a pilgrim. He himself created, or restored, various sites of pilgrimage: in 1705 at Montbernage in

Poitiers, the sanctuary of Mary, Queen of All Hearts; in 1707 at Montfort-sur-Meu, the chapel of Our Lady of Wisdom, and at la Chèze in Brittany, the chapel of Our Lady of the Cross; in 1710, the chapel of Mary, Our Lady Queen of All Hearts, at Nantes and the Calvary of Pontchâteau; in 1711, at La Garnache, the chapel of Our Lady of Victories; in 1712, Our Lady of Good Help in the church of Sallertaine; in 1713, the chapel of Our Lady of All Patience at La Séguinière, near Cholet.

III. Montfort's Motivations as a Pilgrim

Saint Louis Marie de Montfort is justifiably considered a great pilgrim. He appears to have travelled many thousands of miles on foot. Why did he make so many pilgrimages? We can discern from his writings some of the motivations that led him to undertake his numerous journeys.

1. The grace of touching hearts

In 1708, toward All Saints' Day, Montfort preached at Bréal, in Brittany. The parish priest, Father Hindré, was astonished at his success and expressed his surprise. Montfort confided, *"Sir, my dear friend, . . . I have made more than two thousand leagues on pilgrimage to ask from God the grace of touching hearts, and He has answered my prayer."*[15]

When leaving for Rome, he revealed the missionary motive behind his journey in a letter to the townspeople of Montbernage: *"I ask you all, in general and individually, to follow me with your prayers on the pilgrimage which I am going to make for you and many others. I say, 'for you,' because I am undertaking this long and difficult journey in dependence on the Providence of God to obtain from him through the prayers of Mary, your perseverance. I say, 'for many others,' because I bear in my heart all the poor sinners of Poitou and elsewhere, who are sadly placing their salvation at risk. They are so dear to my God that he gave all his blood for them and would I give nothing? He undertook such long and arduous journeys for them, and would I undertake none? He went so far as to risk his own life and wouldn't I risk mine too?"* (LPM 6).

His pilgrimages were missionary in character, as his travels always were: *"I am a hunter of souls / For my Savior Jesus"* (H 91:2). Even during his pilgrimage to Notre-Dame de Chartres, he was prone to wander off the road to evangelize. Later he wrote: *"I've taken on a vagabond spirit / To save my poor neighbor"* (H 22:1).

Montfort's pilgrimages were characterized not only by their missionary goals but also by their apostolic style: he traveled without any money, abandoning himself totally to Providence. On his return from Rome, a priest asked him, "Why didn't you travel by horse?" And the pilgrim is supposed to have simply replied, *"The apostles never traveled by horse."*[16]

Like the pilgrims of the Middle Ages, Montfort considered pilgrimage a path of penitence, but he added his own apostolic intentions. The trials of the road, with the sweat and physical exhaustion; the sun, the rain, and the cold; the difficulties of finding lodging and shelter; the various attitudes of the people he encountered: these basic elements of a pilgrimage held enormous penitential value for Montfort. And at the conclusion of his journey, he presented his fatigue as an offering, a prayer: *"St. Augustine . . . tells us, 'The one who does not mourn in this world like a stranger and a pilgrim will not rejoice in the world to come as a citizen of heaven'"* (FC 25).

In PS, he again describes this spiritual attitude of the penitent, calling on the Penitents to fast and to walk barefoot at times. Always a missionary, he offers up his repentance in order to carry out the work of the Gospel: *"Oh my God, for your Gospel, / I wish to suffer from town to town . . ."* (H 22:13).

Ever faithful to himself, Father de Montfort counsels obedience during a pilgrimage as the best penance: *"I roam throughout the world / Like a lost child . . . / All of my worth / Comes from my obedience"* (H 91:1). This hymn, which depicts the life of the "good missionary," also depicts Father de Montfort, pilgrim of the Absolute, a pilgrim who takes part in this form of popular religion while maintaining great fidelity to the institutional Church. We have seen how, a few weeks before he died, he traveled on a pilgrimage to ask for missionaries and the gift of Wisdom (PS).

2. The search for God

The pilgrimage is also a search for God in Jesus Christ, a search he expresses with his entire being. He sings this ardent hymn: *"Seek, my feet, seek / The sovereign beauty; / Run quickly, draw near, / Make my pain end / The pain of love. / Jesus is my love / My night and my day"* (H 54:12).

The existence of a true pilgrim is characterized by a new vitality which deepens his sense of God, and thus of prayer. He knows he is on the pathway to God, because here below there is no lasting city (H 13:14). Montfort writes: *"A Friend of the Cross is one who is holy and set apart from the things that are visible, for his heart is raised above all that is transient and perishable, and his homeland is in heaven; he travels through this world like a visitor and a pilgrim"* (FC 4).

Montfort's spirit, being solicitous of God, demanded this alertness. Pilgrimage expressed his march toward Christ. He was a pilgrim throughout his life, with prayer in his heart and on his lips. In PS, he is describing his own spiritual approach to prayer when he says that the pilgrims must engage in "continual prayer" on their journey. On the other hand, he himself would stop at length to pray at sites of pilgrimage along his way.

His heart and his voice sang on the pilgrim's road: *"When I travel, / My staff in my hand, / Feet bare, without belongings, / But also without sadness, / I walk in great ceremony / Like a king in his court"* (H 144:1). When he travels this way, his whole bearing is completely captured by those two words that he so often used to close his hymns: *"God Alone."*

A pilgrimage, with the cadence of walking, enabled Montfort to find the words and the rhythm for his hymns. His pilgrim's soul was a singing soul. "Sing and walk," wrote St. Augustine, in a sermon on the Easter season. Whenever the two men stopped on their route, Brother Mathurin would write what Montfort had composed as he walked. Several hymns were thus the products of his travels, and a number of them expressed the spiritual poverty of the pilgrim, such as the *"New hymn for the poor in spirit"* (H 144) and *"The holy voyage"* (H 162).

3. Profound communion with Mary

For Montfort, the pilgrimage was also an opportunity to experience a profound union with Mary. His friend Jean-Baptiste Blain thus described his departure for Paris at the bridge of Cesson, near Rennes: "His eyes always returning to heaven, his heart at Saint Sulpice, the constant invocation of Mary on his lips: thus did he take leave of Rennes."[17]

He often considered pilgrimages a gift that he offered unstintingly to the Virgin Mary. In SM, he suggests that a pilgrimage would be one way of offering to Our Lady each year the homage that is due her (SM 62).

Montfort was sensitive to the efficacy of signs and symbols. He preached Jesus Christ and the Virgin Mary with all his being, with his words and his writings, in his way of life and his travels, even in his dress. He moved through towns and countryside with "his rosary, his staff complete with the Cross, his striking and unforgettable features—his great aquiline nose, his large mouth, the look of fire in his long, oval-shaped face—his ravaged, tireless body, and his powerful voice."[18] Saint Louis Marie was a true pilgrim of God.

The intense desire and search for God, constant prayer, penitence, and obedience to Mary: these qualities form the spiritual profile of the eternal pilgrim such as Montfort. Indeed, we see in him the four means of obtaining Wisdom that he describes in LEW 181-222.

IV. Pilgrimages with Saint Louis Marie

1. Montfort's tomb

Upon Montfort's death, his own tomb became a place of pilgrimage. "Each day, more and more of the faithful would arrive in Saint-Laurent-sur-Sèvre; some had traveled a great distance, and most of the pilgrims proclaimed that their prayers had been answered. Several cures were attributed to the Servant of God."[19] The tomb of Saint Louis Marie de Montfort and the tomb of Blessed Marie Louise of Jesus still attract both individual pilgrims and groups. Each year, at the beginning of October, a large regional pilgrimage to the Basilica of Saint-Laurent-sur-Sèvre is organized. Since 1989, the mother house of the Montfort Missionaries has received pilgrims during the summer. The pilgrims arrive not merely from different regions of France but from other countries as well.

2. Following Montfort's steps

It is becoming more and more customary for members of the Montfort Congregations, and others who live Saint Louis Marie's spirituality and are thus part of the extended Montfort Family, to make a pilgrimage not only to his tomb but to the places where Father de Montfort spent his life: his birthplace at Montfort-sur-Meu and its surroundings, Rennes, Dinan, La Chèze, Pontchâteau, Nantes, Vallet, Mervent,

Saumur, Poitiers, La Rochelle. They come not out of curiosity to see the old stones and walls and houses that attract so many others but because these places evoke Montfort's life and make his message speak even more eloquently to contemporary men and women. These ten-day-or-more pilgrimages, especially when lived in the context of prayer and study of the texts of Montfort, often conclude with the perfect renewal of the baptismal vows.

3. Lourdes

Since 1949 an immense montfort pilgrimage to Lourdes, France, takes place every year at the end of April, around April 28, the feast day of Saint Louis Marie de Montfort. Approximately 10,000 people, including more than 800 sick people, take part; 1,800 volunteers, 1,200 stretcher bearers, many nurses, and 40 doctors serve the sick. Montfort Missionaries from all over the globe—renewing Louis Marie's love for pilgrimages—regularly conduct pilgrimages to Lourdes, where a large statue of Saint Louis Marie adorns the walk leading to the upper basilica.

4. The pilgrimage from Saint Pompain to Notre-Dame of Ardilliers, Saumur

As mentioned above, Montfort several times went on pilgrimage to Saumur. In 1712 he wrote a "rule" for the thirty-three who made the pilgrimage to Our Lady of Pity of Ardilliers at Saumur, asking them to pray for vocations to his Company of Mary. Since 1982 a group of Brothers of St. Gabriel, with other members of the Montfort family, retrace Montfort's route in order to recapture the same spirit, the same faith, and the same supplication. As much as possible, the directions Saint Louis Marie gave for the pilgrimage of 1716 are observed. Like Montfort, they make the pilgrimage on foot from Saint Pompain to Notre-Dame des Ardilliers, with the goal of "*obtaining true missionaries and Wisdom through Mary.*" The words of Father Montfort give them encouragement: *"I am sure . . . they will obtain from God through the intercession of his Blessed Mother great graces not only for themselves but for the whole Church of God"* (PS 13). They travel two by two, without choosing their walking companions, alternating between prayer, silence, and conversation.

On their arrival in Saumur, a large group of friends welcomes them and joins the celebration that concludes the pilgrimage.

V. A Model Pilgrim for Today and the Future

Today the meaning and power of going on pilgrimage appear to have been rediscovered. Some thought it would disappear after the upheavals of the 1960s, but in fact the opposite has happened. The number of pilgrims traveling to Lourdes, Rome, Jerusalem, and other cities has increased. More than twenty million pilgrims travel through Europe each year. Guadalupe alone receives a similar number. John Paul II has said that pilgrimage is "a key to our religious future." And Raïssa Maritain, quoted by her husband Jacques, wrote, "Our great spiritual need today is to contemplate our paths."[20] She meant that our everyday lives are a path to God. All men and women are pilgrims who search for some meaning in their lives; who question themselves, look within themselves and beyond themselves; who search for truth, and look for places, simple or grandiose, which seem to them to carry a message. Life's pilgrimage is the journey to the Promised Land, Jesus. A pilgrim's journey to a holy site, with all its hardships, joys, penances, is a summary of life's journey to God. The pilgrimage not only summarizes this life but, made with sincere prayer, calls down God's blessings so that the pilgrim will arrive safely and for all eternity in Jesus, the Holy One of God.

Saint Louis de Montfort's way of perfection is nothing less than a Marian pilgrimage into the blazing light of God Alone. His four means of attaining union with Wisdom characterize the pilgrimage: the Christian sets out with an intense desire to know God, to march on with a prayer in his heart and on his lips, and to practice mortifications by accepting joyously the difficulties of the journey.

"'Leave all things and you will find all things by finding Jesus Christ, incarnate Wisdom,'" wrote Saint Louis Marie (LEW 202). His missionary life is marked by renunciation of all else to follow the way of Christ. His pilgrimages are so filled with grace, for they are always Marian. As John Paul teaches, "The Blessed Virgin Mary continues to 'go before' the people of God. Her exceptional pilgrimage of faith represents a constant point of reference for the Church, for individuals and for communities, for peoples and nations, and, in a sense, for all humanity" (RMat 6).

So that we may be pilgrims throughout our lives, Saint Louis Marie exhorts us to fix our gaze on Jesus Christ: *"He is our model of living, / Let us imitate his feelings, / Try to follow him, heart to heart / In his steps and in his movements"* (H 144).

F. Garat, E. Guil

Notes: (1) A. Solignac, *Pélerinages, Introduction (Pilgrimages, Introduction),* in DSAM 12/1 (1984), 890. (2) Cf. A. Dupront, *Pélerinages et lieux sacrés (Pilgrimages and Sacred Places),* in *Encyclopédie universelle* (1972), 12:729-734. (3) Cf., for example, J. Henninger, H. Cazelles, M. Join-Lambert, *Pélerinages dans l'ancien Orient (Pilgrimages in the Ancient Near East),* in *Dictionnaire de la Bible,* suppl. 7 (1966), 567-589; S. De Fiores, *Itinéraire spirituelle (Spiritual Itinerary),* in *Dictionnaire de la vie spirituelle (Dictionary of the Spiritual Life),* Cerf, Paris 1983, 549-564; Fr. John, *Le chemin de Dieu. Etude biblique sur la foi comme pélerinage (The Way of God: A Biblical Study on the Pilgrimage of Faith),* Taizé 1983. (4) The manuscript of this work, which is in the archives of Saint-Sulpice in Paris, is attributed to the Sulpician A. Brenier (1651-1714), founder of the Sulpician residence where Louis Marie Grignion was a student from 1695 to 1700. (5) Blain, 101. (6) B.-M. Morineau, *Saint Louis-Marie Grignion de Montfort* Flammarion, Paris 1947, 9, 12. (7) Blain, 98-101. (8) Le Crom, *Un apôtre marial, Saint Louis Marie Grignion de Montfort (1673-1716) (A Marian Apostle: St. Louis Marie de Montfort),* Librarie, Mariale, Pontchateau 1942, 85. (9) Ibid., 97. (10) Besnard I, 102. (11) Ibid., 104. (12) The Rule has come to us through Grandet, with some minor differences, and through Besnard (cf. OC 814). (13) Le Crom, *Un apôtre marial,* 160. (14) Grandet, 95-100. (15) Besnard I, 151. (16) Cf. Grandet, 101. (17) Blain, 18. (18) G. Rigault, *Saint Louis-Marie Grignion de Montfort,* in *Les Traditions Françaises (The French Traditions),* Tourcoing 1947, 48. (19) Le Crom, 376. (20) J. Maritain, *Le paysan de la Garonne (The Peasant of the Garonne),* Desclée de Brouwer, Paris 1966, 340.

POPES/BISHOPS

"When Louis Marie Grignion de Montfort . . . came to this august city of Rome, to venerate devoutly the tomb of Blessed Peter, he learned from our predecessor pope Clement XI . . . that he was destined to preach the truth of the Gospel, not to the foreign nations as he had wished, but rather to regenerate Christian practice in the heart of his own country. This is why, submitting quite willingly to this invitation, Louis-Marie Grignion de Montfort returned to France, and during his life left no stone unturned in responding by energetic apostolic activity to the invitation and plan of the Sovereign Pontiff."[1] It is with these words that Pope Pius XII began his homily on the occasion of Montfort's canonization on July 20, 1947. This article may be considered a commentary on the words of the Holy Father.

I. FRANCE AND GALLICANISM DURING MONTFORT'S LIFETIME

1. Montfort's *sensus fidei.*

To understand Montfort's ecclesial attitude—which entails his attitude toward the popes and the bishops—it is necessary to recall the incredible struggle between the opposing forces of "Ultramontanism" and "Gallicanism,"[2] which existed in the Church from the Council of Trent down to Vatican I. The former looked toward Rome and the Holy See, the latter looked to the church of France. St. Louis de Montfort was well acquainted with these movements. He was richly endowed with a sense of the faith and gifts of the Spirit that guided the disciples of Christ. This guided him to recognize the primary role of the pope and the bishops.

2. Montfort's "Roman spirit."

In Montfort's time France was troubled by the controversy surrounding Jansenism and Gallicanism. Church doctrine "was the root and foundation of Jansenism's moral notions and, at least indirectly, of its attitude toward discipline;"[3] however, Jansenism did not consider infallible, nor consequently binding, the judgment of the Church on the theses held by Jansenius in the Augustinus. In the best of cases it hid behind an "obsequious silence" which precluded inner assent to the Roman decrees. In 1705, the year before Montfort's Roman pilgrimage, the Bull *Vineam Domini* of Clement XI rejected the theory of the Jansenists. Thus it is true that in the west of France, evangelized by Montfort, people still lived in the beneficent atmosphere of the *Pax Clementina* (1669) until the beginning of the eighteenth century, when the conflict rekindled. But it is also true that, "we would fall into the opposite mistake were we to refuse to consider the undoubted repercussions of the Jansenist struggle on Louis's career, sent back as he was to the heart of the Gallican Church, furrowed with rebellion."[4] Montfort never let himself be won over by Jansenist ideas: *"Jansenism, away with you!"* (H 139:55). As for the Gallican controversies, which accompanied the Jansenist ones in the eighteenth century, "a complex frame of mind, defiant of Roman authority, jealous of its own independence, very attached to its own ways, faced with State interference, was then quite widespread in France."[5] "It cannot be said," observes G. De Luca with a touch of irony, "that in the France of that day there was an excessive devotion to the papacy."[6]

II. Montfort's Relationship with the Pope and Bishops

The study of Montfort's relationship with the hierarchy will first examine, in chronological order, the Popes and Bishops Montfort encountered, followed by an attempt to evaluate the often strained relations between the missionary and those in ecclesiastical authority.

1. Bishops Montfort Encountered.

a. Henri Bazan de Flamenville, Bishop of Perpignan (d. 1721). Around 1693–1694 Montfort was his collaborator in the evangelization of the footmen of Paris. It was he who ordained him priest on June 5, 1700.

b. Antoine Girard de la Bournat, Bishop of Poitiers (d. 1702). In April 1701, Montfort told him about *"the attraction he had for working for the salvation of the poor"* (L 6). The bishop *"rather curtly"* thanked him for the information (L 6). Later, Bishop Girard, impressed by the petition addressed to him by the management of the local poorhouse, called Montfort back, spoke to him "more calmly," and ordered him to write to his spiritual director, Fr. Leschassier, to ask him to decide what should be done (cf. L 6). Toward the end of August 1701, the bishop wrote to Montfort in these words: "Father, those at the poorhouse continue to want you with them . . . I even think that Mme. de Montespan was kind enough to write you about this. But now I think I owe it to you to write to you myself that their desires, together with what Fr. Leschassier took the trouble to tell me, lead me to believe that God wishes you at their side, if your bishop [the bishop of Nantes] is willing."[7] Louis Marie felt that he had no inclination *"to withdraw into his shell"* (cf. L 9), and the letter from the bishop, spokesman for the poor, was possibly the long-awaited sign. Thus, without much delay, he went to Poitiers on October 20, 1701. Bishop A. Girard greeted him "with open arms" (L11), and offered him room and board at the seminary "while waiting for hospital authorities" (L 10; cf. L 11). In the meanwhile, he taught *"catechism to the poor beggars of the town with the approval and the help of the Bishop"* (L 10). He made himself poor with the poor, as he himself wrote to Fr. Leschassier on November 3, 1701: *"I explained to the Bishop that even in the poorhouse I do not wish to be separated from my mother, Divine Providence, and with this in mind I am happy to share the meals of the poor and to have no fixed salary. The Bishop agreed heartily to this and offered to act as a father to me"* (L 10). *"The Bishop, unable to resist the insistent appeals of the poor any longer, allowed [him] to go to the poorhouse shortly after All Saints Day"* (L 11). Once there, with the bishop's consent and that of the whole administration (cf. L 11), Montfort served the poor in the refectory and went round the town begging for something extra for them (L 11). With the approval of the bishop he gave a conference each week to thirteen or fourteen schoolboys who were the elite of the local Jesuit school (cf. L 11). But in the poorhouse there was *"a quick-witted girl who is the craftiest and proudest girl I have ever met"* (L 11). For this reason, Montfort wrote to Fr. Leschassier on July 4, 1702, *"I am afraid that Bishop de la Poype, like his predecessor, has been greatly deceived by her, because he was too credulous. If you judged it proper you could warn him about this"* (L 11).

c. Jean-Baptiste de Saint-Vallier, Bishop of Québec (d. 1727). Montfort's relationship with this missionary bishop, alumnus of Saint-Sulpice, is described by De Fiores: "The affinities of temperament and spirituality of Bishop de Saint-Vallier and Montfort explain the deep friendship that existed between them and attested to by first-hand sources. The bishop of Quebec intervened on behalf of Montfort: recommending his sister to the future Bishop of Poitiers, Antoine Girard, praising his behavior, acting as a mediator in order to avoid the destruction of the Calvary of Pontchâteau. When he asked to leave for Canada, probably in September 1700, Montfort did not fail to think of Bishop de Saint-Vallier in whom he would have found understanding and help for the accomplishment of his vast missionary plans."[8]

d. Jean Claude de la Poype de Vertrieu, Bishop of Poitiers (d. 1732). "A generous and very spiritual shepherd,"[9] he received Montfort like a father who at the end of the summer of 1702 returned from Paris to Poitiers. Giving him discreet assistance, he allowed him to attempt a complete reform of the poorhouse and to admit, among the poor, Marie Louise Trichet.

But in the spring of 1703, the position of the young chaplain became unbearable. "Louis reacted severely to the indecent behavior of a boy, which released a storm of complaints, and the bishop who had been misinformed acted on impulse. Tired with this priest who put him in such an awkward position, he forbade him to say Mass," although "once the situation was clarified, not in a few days but a few hours, the prohibition was rescinded." After this "harsh action of the good bishop,"[10] around Easter 1703, Montfort set out for Paris where he passed through a veritable calvary of rejections. Yet it was to this man of God that Fr. Madot, delegated by the cardinal of Paris, entrusted the reform of the hermits of Mont Valérien.

In the meanwhile things in Poitiers were changing. In two letters, now lost, Bishop de la Poype asked Louis Marie to return while at the same time the residents of the poorhouse were clamoring for Montfort, their "angel" and "venerable shepherd." Louis Marie then returned to Poitiers where the bishop supported him and the poor loved him. Yet in a very short time new jealousies cropped up in his regard. "He sought counsel from Bishop de la Poype who had not withdrawn his confidence and who evaluated objectively the chaplain's untenable position."[11] Finally, Montfort shook the dust from his feet, and left the poorhouse for good. The Bishop then gave him lodging in the House of Penitents and Montfort had his first encounter with missionary work.

When the missionary was preaching in the church of Our Lady of Calvary, Father de Villeroi, one of the vicars general of the diocese, reprimanded him publicly, expressing disapproval of one of Montfort's personal initiatives. "Louis Marie got down on his knees. His face was ashen and expressionless. When the other man withdrew, he said merely, *'My brothers, we were ready to plant a cross at the door of this church. It was not God's will. Our superiors were against it. Let us plant it then in the midst of our hearts.'*"[12] The following day the church was full. Father Révol, another vicar general, friend of Louis Marie's, and the Bishop-elect of Oloron, went into the pulpit and thanked Montfort with great feeling, with the explicit purpose of repairing the damage done. But the news of what had happened at Our Lady of Calvary had already reached Bishop de la Poype. Although he appreciated and understood Montfort, and had granted him generous protection in other difficult moments, he now felt obligated to sacrifice him to keep the peace. Father de Montfort "had barely begun to preach a retreat to the Dominican nuns of Sainte-Catherine when a letter reached him containing the order of the Bishop to leave Poitiers immediately. The blow was a hard one for Louis Marie, not only because of the break with the now familiar atmosphere but because this new ordeal cast a thick shadow over the most precious ideal of Father de Montfort's life: the preaching ministry."[13]

He then decided to go to Rome to "see Peter" (Gal 1:18). Before leaving he wrote a letter to all who had profited from the missions he preached: *"If God preserves my life, I will pass by here again, and stay for a while subject to your illustrious Bishop, who is so zealous for the salvation of souls and compassionate with our failings"* (LPM). Back from Rome, Montfort showed up in

Poitiers, but his presence sounded so loud an alarm that an order came from Bishop de la Poype asking him to leave the town without delay. Montfort took refuge in a religious house for six days of prayer. He then left Poitiers for good and made his way to Brittany.

A few years later he was again in Paris looking for vocations for his Company of Mary. Before going back to La Rochelle, he met in Poitiers with the first two Daughters of Wisdom, Marie Louise Trichet and Catherine Brunet. The next day Louis Marie received an "invitation" from Bishop de la Poype to get out of Poitiers within twenty-four hours.

e. Pope Clement XI (d. 1721). In the beginning of 1706, five years of difficulties came to a head. Not knowing what God was doing with him, Montfort expressed to Clement XI his availability for whatever ministry the Pope wished. "Louis Marie asked to be sent into the Church by the Church."[14] The conversation he had with Clement XI was decisive in Montfort's life. "Father, you have in France a large enough field for your zeal. Go nowhere else, and always work in perfect submission to the Bishops of the dioceses to which you will be called. Because of this God will bless your labors." The Pope conferred on him the title "apostolic missionary" and graciously blessed a small ivory cross that Louis Marie presented to him and that he would later attach to his pilgrim's staff.

f. Vincent-Francis Desmaretz, Bishop of Saint-Malo (d. 1739). In 1707, after a short missionary experience with Dom Leuduger, Louis Marie withdrew to the Saint-Lazare hermitage near the town of his birth. Bishop Desmaretz of Saint-Malo, known for his Jansenist sympathies, listened to the rumors circulating about the apostolate of the reclusive priest. It was said that Montfort opposed an exaggerated sense of autonomy on the part of the local clergy, and had spoken against the canons of the Cathedral, etc. Louis Marie was therefore forbidden any form of ministry in the diocese of Saint-Malo.

When he was ready to withdraw, there was a dramatic turn of events. Msgr. Hindré, pastor of Bréal, had come to see Bishop Desmaretz for the precise purpose of having Father de Montfort preach a mission in his parish. Surprisingly, the Bishop responded affirmatively.[15] In the spring of 1708, Bishop Desmaretz came back to the town of Montfort. "This time his speech was unambiguous and terse. He forbade Louis Marie to preach outside of parish churches, including in the prohibition the hermitage chapel [of Saint-Lazare]."[16]

g. Gilles de Beauveau de Rivau, Bishop of Nantes (d. 1717). After leaving Saint-Malo, Montfort went back to the diocese of Nantes, where he preached with remarkable success during 1708–1709.

During the mission at Pontchâteau he launched the idea of a monumental Calvary. After more than a year of work everything was ready for the dedication. However, on September 13, 1710, Montfort received a message from the bishop forbidding him to proceed to the blessing of the

Calvary scheduled for the next day. Montfort left immediately for Nantes on foot to plead with Bishop de Beauveau. He was unsuccessful in getting the prohibition rescinded, which had come to him like a bolt from the blue. Late in the morning of the following day, Louis Marie was back at Pontchateau. The missionary informed them that on orders of the local Ordinary, no blessing would take place. Bishop de Beauveau had concealed that the real reason for his prohibition was that he had received an order from the King to destroy the Calvary. Although he tried to defend the missionary, the Bishop felt Montfort's behavior was imprudent. While he was preaching a mission at Saint-Molf, Father Olivier, one of his co-workers, came to him with a letter from the bishop forbidding Montfort any ministry whatsoever in the diocese of Nantes and ordered him to get far away from the Calvary of Pontchâteau, never to return. Louis Marie returned to Nantes to speak with the bishop, who finally decided to let him know that the order for the demolition of the Calvary had come from higher up. He marveled at Montfort's calm and told his vicar general: "Father de Montfort has to be either a great saint, or an arrogant hypocrite!" Montfort spent the next eight days making a retreat at the house of the Jesuits in the city. He said nothing about what had happened, and there was nothing in his behavior that gave any indication of his distress, even though he had burst out in tears when first informed of the Bishop's demand to destroy the entire site of the immense calvary.[17]

h. Étienne de Champflour, Bishop of La Rochelle (d. 1724) and Jean-François Salgues de Lescure, Bishop of Luçon (d. 1723). After the drama of Pontchâteau, these two pastors opened "the doors of their dioceses to the missionary, who from this point on would be carrying with him a collection of prohibitions and limitations in the ministry. For the first time he met two genuine shepherds, especially Bishop de Champflour, who were to show him constant and unfailing consideration. Holy prelates like the bishop of Poitiers and prudent ones like the bishop of Nantes, while keeping their esteem for Louis Marie, allowed themselves to be influenced by opinions adverse to the missionary. Both the bishops of Luçon and La Rochelle remained loyal to him."[18] The favor the bishop of La Rochelle showed Montfort did not falter when faced with enemies who accused Louis Marie: "Three canons well versed in theology were commissioned by Bishop de Champflour to check Louis's preaching and they upheld his orthodoxy. From this moment, the bishop gave him his complete confidence."[19]

On the subject of free schools for boys, a project very dear to St. Louis Marie's heart, he met with Bishop de Champflour and had lengthy discussions with him in the spring of 1714. In the beginning of 1715, on the verge of completing the foundation of the girls' schools, Montfort wrote to Sister Marie Louise of Jesus and Sister Conception: *"I have spoken several times to His Lordship, the bishop of La Rochelle, about you and about our plans and he thinks you ought to come here and begin the work we want so much. He has rented a house for the purpose until another house can be bought and suitably furnished. . . I am writing you on behalf of the bishop, so keep this confidential"* (L 27). On April 22 1716, Bishop de Champflour paid a pastoral visit to Saint-Laurent-sur-Sèvre, where Montfort was preaching his last mission. "Louis was moved. It was a bit like receiving his bishop in his own house. A rare opportunity was given him to show his loyalty and gratitude to the shepherd who had given him asylum and who had been a father and a friend to him the last five years. What turn would Father de Montfort's life have taken if he had never met Bishop de Champflour? We understand the missionary's excitement and his generous desire to have a celebration for his guest."[20] The saint died six days after the bishop's visit. In his will of April 27, 1716, Montfort left the bishop of La Rochelle and Father Mulot his personal property and mission books (W).

i. Monseigneur Le Pileur, Bishop of Saintes (d. 1726). On his return trip to Paris via La Rochelle, Montfort stopped in 1713 to preach in the parish of Vanneau in the diocese of Saintes. He was in the middle of the mission when the bishop, unfavorably informed about the missionary, withdrew from Montfort the right to exercise his ministry. Only the intervention of the pastor succeeded in keeping the mission from being interrupted.

j. Monseigneur Turpin de Grissé de Sanzai, Bishop of Rennes. In the spring of 1714, Montfort took a trip to Rouen where he wanted to meet his friend Blain. He made a long stop at Rennes and asked the bishop for permission to preach, but to no avail. He ended up by making an eight day retreat with the Jesuits.

k. François Rolland de Coëtanfao, Bishop of Avranches (d. 1720). After leaving Rennes, Montfort continued on to Avranches, arriving there on August 14, Assumption Eve. "The next day he presented himself to the bishop with the testimonial letters of Bishop de Champflour, but he met with a bitter surprise. The bishop forbade him to say Mass, and this on Mary's solemnity. A desperate ride on a horse rented for the moment brought Louis Marie outside the inhospitable diocese. He arrived before noon at Villedieu-les-Poêles in time to beg the bewildered pastor to allow him to celebrate Mass."[21]

l. Monseigneur François de Nesmond, Bishop of Bayeux (d. 1715). "The next stopping place (after Avranches) was Caen in the diocese of Bayeux, which was hosting its bishop, François de Nesmond. After the recent refusals he had met with, Louis found in this prelate a fatherly welcome and an invitation to stay in the town to exercise his ministry."[22]

2. An evaluation.

a. Montfort's obedience. Montfort always worked in complete compliance with the bishops in the dioceses to which he was called; it is not known of any time that he did anything contrary to their orders.[23] His obedience was never a mere "obsequious silence." Obedience, seen in the light of God's will, caused Montfort's initiatives to mature "through the unpredictable changes between the great deeds and the weaknesses of the Church in its historical expression";[24] it also made his own missionary activity all the more zealous without ever allowing that holy inner freedom to fade out. Like any disciple of Christ, "he learned obedience in the school of suffering" (Heb 5:8). "This man, who at Saint-Sulpice learned to obey . . . had continually to risk anew the confrontation of his charism with the institution in a painful tension of unity."[25] In this sense, it also appears that there was a development in Montfort's attitudes. The day after one of the most frustrating experiences Montfort ever had, the demolition of the Calvary of Pontchâteau, Pierre des Bastières said: "I thought I would find him overcome with sorrow . . . But I was quite surprised when I saw him happier and more content than I who needed consolation more than he did."[26]

b. Montfort's persecution. How then can it be explained that a great number of the bishops Montfort encountered made him leave their dioceses like a priest in disgrace? If it is true that "the fate of some saints in their lifetime is one of the darkest mysteries of the Church,"[27] it must also be acknowledged that these difficulties with the hierarchy are almost impossible for the biographer to explain. "Looking at all the solutions attempted," said Henri Daniel, "without any one of them being fully satisfying, we might wonder whether it is simply beyond solution. Yet however disturbing it may be, it is of such significance that we have to face up to it and not minimize it . . . several of the ecclesiastical authorities [who expelled Montfort] are rightly remembered with veneration."[28] The same author then proposes his own solution according to which none of the measures taken by the bishops against Montfort could be attributed to doctrinal differences or to Jansenist intrigue. He adds that logically, judging him from the outside, Montfort must have seemed to be a great saint, or perhaps a hypocrite.

G. De Luca seems to join Henri Daniel in his "judgment of Solomon" when he writes, "Today we do not think we have to defend any eccentricity of Louis Marie's. We do not accuse his accusers, but we do not think we have to excuse the saint. . . . He received public condemnations and prohibitions from the civil and church authorities. He was hunted down like a dog, he was held up to ridicule as a pretender, pitied and shunned like a fool. He was never cowed by such adversity and stayed calm, obedient, courageous and smiling. The strength of his own temperament changed into this new strength, the strength of gentleness."[29]

The judgment of Cardinal Tedeschini on those who did not understand Montfort and persecuted him seems more severe. "His enemies, these sterile Christians who tolerated neither adherence to the head of the Church nor a breath of love in the holy ministry, opposed him every step of the way and along with them, all those people who were influenced by calumny or led on by the corrupt. And among their number, unfortunately, as with Christ, there were not lacking certain Church authorities who were ill-disposed toward him, whose names I would rather not recall, and who took no account of the immense services Montfort rendered to people's souls. On many occasions they did not hesitate to inflict on him the most painful suspensions for a priest, those that concerned the sacred ministry. They were misinformed, set against him, and God permitted them to do what they did; they undoubtedly intended to achieve a greater good. Despite all this Montfort bowed to their authority with humility and docility."[30]

The words of Daniel-Rops in regard to Montfort are à propos: "It was not inappropriate that the Christianity of the *grand siècle* be reminded that the theology of the Beatitudes is not one of human prudence, and that there is no more violent scandal than that of the cross. . . Louis Marie Grignion de Montfort was a loner in his time, a kind of unpredictable bastion of the religious life, totally outside the austere and rather conformist norms in which the ideal of priesthood was firmly set at the time. An eccentric if you will, but there have been a number of eccentrics in the Church who nevertheless played an important rôle in its life. . . . Even better, he was a fool for God."[31] This is an explanation that pleased Grandet and Blain, the first biographers of Montfort. Grandet appeals to God's law of the history of salvation (cf. 1 Co 1:27) according to which He chooses certain saints and makes them, through the outpouring of the Spirit, "men of a new species," to "combat the false wisdom of worldly men by the apparent folly of His gospel."[32] "As a man of the absolute," De Luca adds, "Montfort lived as he believed."[33] Montfort's absolute obedience to the Gospel, then, basically explains why he was misunderstood and persecuted during his life.

While accepting this Gospel explanation, Montfort himself is obliged to add another more human one. He candidly acknowledged to Blain the "eccentric" ways that he came by "naturally" and which brought him the privilege of humiliation.[34] Yet he is well aware that beyond the bounds of nature, every Christian life, when taken seriously, and every genuine proclamation of the Gospel are inseparable from the Cross. Suffering becomes a source of a fruitful apostolate. He admits this himself to his "very dear sister," Sister Catherine de Saint-Bernard, in a letter that has nothing pathologically self-centered about it:

> *"I have forever to be on the alert, treading warily as though on thorns or sharp stones. I am like a ball in a game of tennis; no sooner am I hurled to one side than I am sent back to the other, and the players strike me hard. This is the fate of the poor sinner that I am and I have been like this without rest or respite all the thirteen years since leaving St. Sulpice. However, my dear sister, thank God for me for I am content and happy in all my troubles. I think there is nothing in the whole*

world so welcome as the most bitter cross, when it is steeped in the blood of Christ crucified and in the milk of his holy Mother. Besides this inward happiness, there is the great merit of carrying the crosses. I wish you could see mine. I have never had more conversions than after the most painful and unjust prohibitions" (L 26).

III. The Pope and the bishops in Montfort's Writings

Montfort recognized in the *"Bishop of Rome"* (H 142:2) the *"Vicar of Jesus Christ, / An organ of the Holy Spirit"* (H 147:3). From this he draws conclusions: *"Believe Jesus in His Vicar, / In all that touches on faith, / And take what he says as Pope / As an oracle and certain law"* (H 6:50); *"I believe what the Holy Father says, / Despite the shrewd hounds of hell, /He is my leader and my light, / I see nothing, he sees most clearly"* (H 6:57). In his methods for reciting the rosary Montfort recalls the *"faith and obedience to the pope as Vicar of Jesus Christ"* (MR 16). And to justify the form of devotion to Mary he fosters, the saint appeals to the bulls and indulgences accorded to it by the popes (cf. SM 42) and to the *"great indulgences of Gregory XV"* (TD 160). He mentions *"the different popes who have approved this devotion"* (TD 163), adding that *"no pope has condemned it"* and that *"it could not be condemned without overthrowing the foundations of Christianity"* (TD 163). Montfort also names the pontiffs who were devoted to the Holy Rosary: Pius V, Leo X, Gregory XIII, Julius III, Innocent III, Urban VIII (cf. SR 80, 93, 132). It was to Blessed Pius V, canonized on May 12, 1712, that Montfort dedicated his Hymn 147. Montfort's missionary work and his religious foundations constitute an act of obedience to the mission received from Clement XI in 1706. Saint Louis Marie stipulates that his missionaries should have people renew their baptismal promises in accordance with the order received from the pope (RM 56). They were to recite the Roman breviary (RM 31).

In evening prayer Montfort includes an act of faith: *"My God, I firmly believe all that the Catholic, Roman and Apostolic Church believes and teaches, because you, the sovereign Truth, have revealed it"* (NP 14). Montfort also urges obedience to the bishop, shepherd of the local Church, not only by his example but in his writing as well: *"With regard to the government of the community they [the Daughters of Wisdom] obey the bishop"* (RW 54). In a parallel way the missionaries of the Company of Mary *"will obey the bishop of the diocese to which they belong, the Vicars-General and other ecclesiastical superiors who represent the bishop"* (RM 22).

IV. Relevance of Montfort's Obedience to Popes and Bishops

Obedience to the Holy See is intrinsic to montfort spirituality. The same can be said of all Catholic schools of spirituality; yet, because of Montfort's staunch fidelity to Rome while in the midst of Gallican tendencies among the French hierarchy, respect for the papal Magisterium is even more pronounced in his heritage. Moreover, Saint Louis Marie's recourse to Pope Clement XI to resolve a fundamental crisis in his life is also a significant sign, not only for the communities he founded, but for all who follow his steps. He alludes to the famous dictum, *"Roma locuta est, causa finita est,"* not only concerning pronouncements ex cathedra but in regard to the ordinary Magisterium of the pastor of all the faithful (cf. H 6:50, 57). His teaching appears to be an early rendition of the famous text of Vatican II: "Loyal submission of the will and intellect must be given, in a special way, to the authentic teaching authority of the Roman Pontiff, even when he does not speak ex cathedra in such wise, indeed, that his supreme teaching authority be acknowledged with respect, and that one sincerely adhere to decisions made by him, conformably to his manifest mind and intention" (LG 25; cf. CCC 892).

Benedict XV, on the occasion of the bicentenary of Blessed Louis Marie de Montfort's death (1916), summarized this aspect of montfort spirituality in a handwritten letter to the Father General of the montfort family: "Among the reasons that make your two communities (Company of Mary and Daughters of Wisdom) so respected, we mention two that are of special importance, that were left to you as an inheritance by your founder: reverence for the apostolic see and devotion to the Virgin Mary. A very enlightening proof of such a devotion . . . is the fact that your members have been in the first rank of those to be relentlessly ill-treated by both the Gallican and Jansenist heretics because they seemed so attached to the Roman pontiff and for the same reason they had to suffer all sorts of acts of cruelty during the French revolution. . . . Furthermore, these two elements [reverence for the apostolic see and devotion to the Virgin Mary] are closely interconnected: the person who truly loves Mary, being incapable of not loving Jesus—for through the intermediary of the Mother we go directly to Jesus—must for this reason have attachment and devotion to the Vicar of Christ."[35]

The bishops who expelled Saint Louis de Montfort from their dioceses, whatever their motives, have become witnesses to the saint's joyful obedience. Although he believed that at times he was treated unjustly and did not hesitate to lay his case before them hoping for a change of decision, he obeyed when he lost his appeal—not begrudgingly, not bitterly, but bolstered by a week's retreat to strengthen him, lovingly praising God for the occasion of such a cross. At times his reputation was clearly damaged by well-intentioned but irresponsible superiors, and the claims of his detractors that he was a fool were thereby strengthened. Instead of curling within himself in discouragement and self-pity, these so called failures became occasions of incredible growth. There is little doubt that it was his deep faith that endowed him with this ability. Saint Louis de Montfort is clearly an example to contemporary Christians and, in a special way, to many preachers and theologians who, at least in this regard, feel a close affinity with him.

A. Rum

Notes: (1) Pius XII, "Homily on the occasion of the canonization of Louis-Marie de Montfort (7-21-1947)," in AAS 39 (1947) 330. (2) G. Martina, *La Chiesa nell'età dell'assolutismo, del liberalismo, del totalitarismo. Da Lutero ai nostri giorni* (The Church in the Age of Absolutism, Liberalism, Totalitarianism: From Luther to Our Times), Morcelliana, Brescia 1974, 364. (3) Ibid., 332. (4) B. Papàsogli, *L'homme venu du vent. Saint Louis-Marie Grignion de Montfort,* Bellarmin, Montréal 1984, 247. English translation: *Montfort, A Prophet for Our Times,* Edizioni, Monfortane, Rome, 1991. (5) G. Martina, *La Chiesa,* 187. (6) G. De Luca, *Luigi Maria Grignion de Montfort. Saggio biografico,* Edizioni di storia e letteratura, Rome 1985, 203. (7) Quoted in OC, 25, n. 1. (8) De Fiores, 251. On Bishop de Saint-Vallier, cf. Anon., *Monseigneur de Saint-Vallier et l'hôpital général de Québec* (Bishop de Saint-Vallier and the Gereral Hospital of Quebec), Darveau, Québec 1882; T. Ronsin, *Le Bx de Montfort et Mgr de Saint-Vallier* (Blessed De Montfort and Bishop de Saint-Vallier), in *Messager de Marie reine des coeurs* 30 (1933) 271–76. (9) Papàsogli, 167. On this bishop cf. G.-J.-C. Paulze-d'Ivoy de la Poype, *Un évêque de Poitiers au XVIIe siècle, Mgr J.-Cl. de la Poype de Vertrieu* (A Bishop of Poitiers in the 17th Century: J.C. de la Poype de Vertrieu), Poitiers 1889. (10) Papàsogli, 173–74. When Montfort's biographers speak of the "prohibitions" to which he was subjected, they do not mean to say that he received some particular ecclesiastical censure that is defined by the word "interdict": cf. the note of Cardinal Villecourt in A. Pauvert, *Vie du vénérable Louis-Marie Grignion e Montfort,* Oudin, Paris-Poitiers 1875, 643. (11) Papàsogli, 228–29. (12) Ibid, 228-229. (13) Ibid, 230. (14) Ibid, 231. (15) Ibid, 272. (16) Ibid. (17) On the drama of Pontchâteau, we have given a summary here of pages 297–300 of Papàsogli. (18) Papàsogli, 307. (19) Papàsogli, 310. On this bishop cf. A. de Lantenay, *Étienne de Champflour, évêque de La Rochelle, avant son épiscopat. Mélange de biographie et d'histoire* (Stephen de Campflour, Bishop of La Rochelle Before His Episcopate: Both Biography and History), Bordeaux 1885; L. Pérouas, *Le diocèse de La Rochelle de 1648 à 1724* (The Diocese of La Rochelle from 1648 to 1724), Sociologie et pastorale, Paris 1964, 256–397. (20) Papàsogli, 411. (21) Papàsogli, 368–69. (22) Papàsogli, 369. (23) Grandet, 339. (24) Papàsogli, 178. (25) Papàsogli, 231. (26) Grandet, 304. (27) I. Silone, *L'avventura di un povero cristiano* (The Adventure of a Poor Christian), Mondadori, Milano 1968, 181. (28) H. Daniel, *Saint Louis-Marie Grignion e Montfort. Ce qu'il fut, ce qu'il fit* (St. Louis de Montfort: Who He was and What He Did), Téqui, Toulouse 1967, 12. (29) De Luca, 237, 233. (30) Card. F. Tedeschini, *Discorso inaugurale in lode di San Luigi Maria di Montfort* (Inaugural Discourse in Praise of St. Louis Marie de Montfort), (December 8, 1948), Typ. Pio X, Roma, 28–29. (31) H. Daniel-Rops, *L'Église des temps classiques. Le grand siècle des âmes,* Fayard (The Church of Classical Times. The *grande siécle* of souls), Paris 1958, 330. (32) Grandet, preface. (33) De Luca, 234. (34) Blain, 184–90. (35) Benedict XV, "Letter to Fr. Antonin Lhoumeau," April 19, 1916, in AAS 8 (1916) 172–73.

POVERTY

SUMMARY

INTRODUCTION

Father de Montfort interpreted, understood, and incarnated the ideal of evangelical poverty. He did so, though, in a social, economic, cultural, and religious context radically different from today. To imitate Montfort's poverty in every aspect would be anachronistic and practically impossible. However, to imitate does not mean to copy exactly. To imitate implies first of all to contemplate and to admire. This leads one to discover and to assimilate the truest and purest motivations of one's model. In this way one can discern what is common to and different from one's own spiritual journey. We must accomplish everything within the context of our own unique lives. We must recognize the reality of the new forms and new situations of poverty that are characteristic of our modern world. For example, we cannot be oblivious to our contemporary capacity for mass producing goods, which has become integral to our way of life. It has increased immensely the wealth of those who control these means of production, and has intensified the problem of the lack of an equitable sharing of the world's resources. The Word of God, the Gospel, is always there to clarify the ultimate meaning of wealth and poverty. Montfort taught and gave witness in his life to the value of authentic poverty. Other spiritual authors also enlighten our understanding, encouraging us to live the Gospel's attitude to the poor and suffering. The Gospel message is a universal one, which calls us to make the best possible use of the goods that we possess or control today.

I. Two Preliminary Observations

1. Our Social Awareness

It is difficult to speak of poverty or suffering without personal experience, or without at least having been close to the poor and their suffering in the style of the good Samaritan of the Gospel (Lk 10:29–37).

Montfort did not produce any treatises on poverty. Apart from two hymns (H 20, 108), which treat of the *"treasures of poverty"* and are illuminating but brief instructions on the subject, no sustained discourse on poverty can be found. However there are enough solid indications, precise allusions, ardent exhortations (for example in LCM), and even realistic descriptions to warrant the conclusion that the theme of poverty is uppermost in his thought and is definitely an essential aspect of his spirituality. It is, in a sense, the door opening up to the fuller meaning of total Consecration, Mission, Providence, Incarnation, the Cross, Charity, Alms, Humility, etc. In reading his biographies,[1] it is apparent that for Montfort poverty was a real spiritual experience, strong, original, and deep, which left its mark on his entire existence and governed his life. From his youth he always deliberately wanted to draw near to and be close to the poor with respect, tenderness, piety, and veneration. This speaks volumes on the love he felt for the poor in the purest evangelical spirit. As with many saints (e.g. Francis of Assisi, Benedict Joseph Labré), it could be said that he rediscovered and reappraised evangelical poverty by identification with the poor.

2. The Problem of Impartial Objectivity

There is a serious difficulty, almost an impossibility, of treating themes on poverty with absolute and unruffled objectivity. Complex, confrontational, and even contradictory feelings and thoughts arise within and around us, ranging from rejection and contempt to welcome and commiseration, from ignorance and indifference to involvement and effective solidarity with the poor, from passive and fatalistic acceptance to revolt and rejection of imposed conditions. Our reactions reveal the measure of human and spiritual as well as personal and social maturity or immaturity. No doubt Father de Montfort, opting for the evangelical preference for the poor and poverty, got himself into an uncomfortable and even conflicting situation with his family, his friends, and certain social and ecclesiastical groups. Finally he received frank approval only from the poor themselves[2] and from his most fervent and loyal disciples such as Marie Louise Trichet and the first Daughters of Wisdom.

II. Aspects of Real Practical Living

1. Who Are the Poor?

Given that community living is a struggle, it could be said that the poor are those who do not manage 'honorably' to survive the struggle for life. They could be individuals, families, groups, or even entire populations. They are poor simply because they are deprived, prejudiced against, stripped of elementary needs of life. Other adverse factors also confront them. Despite themselves they are disadvantaged in the struggle for life.

At the source of poverty there could be "natural" causes such as climatic, geographic, historical, and cultural factors. These, normally, would not explain the poverty of masses of people in one sphere nor poverty on an international scale. Poverty reveals itself swiftly and smoothly, not only as a social phenomenon, but more so as a social evil, a physical and moral evil. It is spawned by a malignant and malicious society quite incapable of producing the fruits of justice and humanity one might expect. Thus the poverty of those who are poor seems to be the exact opposite of wealth, and the result of the selfish indifference and injustice of the well-to-do.

The consequences for the poor are a life of privation and abasement, extreme limitation of their freedom and power of action, an outlook of dependence and frustration, effective marginalising which puts them at the bottom of the social ladder and makes them rebels, outcasts of society, excluded from and denied everything valuable, and led by way of poverty to premature and undeserved death. Thus the great resource of the poor person, and to some degree his salvation, resides within his own being and in what remains of his humanity, his driving force and ingenuity, his qualities of heart and soul and his sense of solidarity—provided that these have not been ravished, enslaved to those dark and lying powers that feed on his poverty.

From all this, it seems that there is little margin between poverty and Gospel. *"The poor are evangelized"* can mean two things. The first is that to be truly evangelized one must be poor in one way or another. The second is that the Gospel truly is good news, first of all for the poor, since the promise of freedom, salvation, and life is for them.

2. The Poor in Montfort's Time

To have full insight into the social situation in France in the seventeenth and eighteenth centuries, one must refer to specialized treatises on the subject.[3] Clearly Montfort—like any contemporary saint, and like his biographers—had no intention of analyzing or issuing conclusive descriptions of the society of his epoch in his writings. However those holy people were not lacking in delicate insight and observation. Anyone immersing himself in their writings easily discovers the atmosphere, the stamp of life, the social levels within which facts unfolded and points were made. Examples such as those of the peasant and his apple (TD 147), the miller, the sculptor (TD 220–22), and allusions to clothing and fashion, worldly gatherings, and such, allow us to recast in imagination the complex and variegated society of the mainly rural France of the *ancien régime*, in which the middle-class were set to carve a decisive role for themselves between the nobility and the proletariat.

With broad strokes Montfort divides this society into rich and poor,[4] and the social and geographic landscape into town and country (RM 7). In the towns live the people of status, the robed and the sword-bearing, and there also are found the merchants and the jacks-of-all-trades. But if we follow Montfort into the slums of Poitiers, the suburbs of St. Donatien and St. Similien at Nantes, or the Loges de Fontenay and Villeneuve at La Rochelle, we find ourselves in the midst of poor, humble folk and squalid bands of deprived, untutored children. We also know that Montfort visited and frequented general hospitals, which in most towns welcomed and housed hundreds or even thousands of poor and sick people (the *"cloistered poor")*.

But if Montfort required his future missionaries to prefer country over town (RM 17), that was because the vast majority of the population lived in the country, poor and neglected. Large landowners were few compared with the tenant farmers, servants, and day laborers who seasonally and down the years became beggars and tramps. All these little folk were held in preference by Montfort. M. Blain, friend and colleague of Louis Marie, noted very early on his extreme love of poverty and the poor and his apostolic abandonment to Providence.[5]

3. The Poor in Montfort's View

a. The religious concept. Montfort saw everything, especially the reality of the poor, from the standpoint of faith. Precisely in them he saw and served Jesus Christ himself. His formation, which above all was theological and spiritual, and the special grace which inspired him, spontaneously raised his vision to that level. He considered and saw all things in their relationship to God, the Creator and Savior. To the question, "What is a poor person?" he himself replied: *"It is written / he is the living image, / the lieutenant of Jesus Christ, / his finest heritage. / But to put it better, / he is Jesus Christ himself"* (H 17:14); or: *"They are true likenesses / of Jesus Christ, poor for us. / They are his brothers just like him, / worthy of being honored by all"* (H 20:17). "The poor person is a great mystery which must be grasped. Beatus qui intelligit super egenum et pauperem."[6]

Thus, in the eyes of Montfort, the poor are the intimate friends of Jesus Christ—his chosen portion, his lieutenants, his elders, that is to say those from whom the heritage is derived; even more, they are Jesus Christ himself. Of this last definition he gave a striking example when he hailed the doorkeeper of the house at Dinan where he was lodging when he returned one evening carrying a leper on his back: *"Open up to Jesus Christ!"* "He entered bearing his precious burden, settled the poor man on his own bed, warmed him as best he could, then passed the rest of the night in prayer."[7] Here one must see and read in outline the chapter on judgment of Matthew 25 (cf. H 17).

b. A realistic view. An evangelical view of the poor and poverty does not preclude realism in a view of things or in action. When a man like Montfort suffers deprivation, abandonment, or rebuff in an unjust and humiliating manner, it is very difficult for him not to ask, "Why?" as Job did. On many occasions Montfort preferred to suffer in silence, peace, and joy, plumbing the depths of the mystery. Such complaints as sprang from his sensitive heart were very few, but they gushed out with rare vigour as cries of grief and cries to arouse dormant consciences. It is in that sense that one must understand Hymn 18, "The Cries of the Poor," and hearken to the reply of God, Who in His Goodness and Justice shows Himself as the God of the poor: *"O dear poor at heart, / I hear your just complaints; / I feel your grief; / I receive the same blows. . . / All the evil done to you, / is done to me. / Anyone who alleviates your suffering / shows his love for me"* (H 18:7–8).

c. Good and bad poor people. Montfort is not so naïve as to be unable to distinguish between good and bad poor people. About the latter he presents a list describing their failings and vices, such as impatience, avarice, idleness, and impiety (H 20:43–46). But when it comes to alms, moral judgments take second place: *"Simply see God alone / in all the wretched. / Give to them, only for him, / your charitable help. / Be they good or wicked, / You give to Jesus. / Enough that he is to be found in them / in his own person"* (H 17:42; cf. RW 128).

d. Dignity of the poor. What matters is to give back to the poor an awareness of dignity and stature, of true wealth and happiness. *"For the kingdom of my glory / belongs to their poverty. / Believe me, the poor man is master / of all my joy"* (H 20:8). These words of Jesus to the poor are a repetition in popular language of the first Beatitude, as are: *"I will make you, poor little ones, / great lords in paradise / and true kings,"* (H 108:12) and: *"A truly virtuous man, / were he the poorest of beggars, / is far more respectable / than all kings and doctors, / if they have no virtue in their hearts"* (H 4:13). Similarly: *"He has made you his kings and priests by the Christian faith and the priestly ordination he has conferred on you, and your voluntary poverty gives you an additional right to be called kings"* (LCM 5).

e. Justice and charity. One had to wait for the industrial revolution of the nineteenth century for the theme of social justice to penetrate consciences and public debate. Montfort is not a precursor in this sphere of ideas. He did not feel the "social question" to be a matter of urgency.

However, taught by Scripture and the holy Fathers, Montfort did not fail to promote the rights of the poor and the duties of the rich. *"Do not deprive the poor man of his due, / says Holy Scripture. . . / Know that any possession you hold onto, / even when useless to you, / belongs to the poor; it is his, / as the Gospel says"* (H 17:16–17).

In the sphere of charity Montfort was not content with transient deeds. He knew that no enterprise would bear lasting fruit unless established subject to precise rules carefully drawn up. He attempted in the General Hospital at Poitiers a reform of customs and rules for the benefit of the *"cloistered poor."* But it was at La Rochelle that he successfully devoted his energy, in concert with Bishop de Champflour, to the founding of charitable schools for the instruction of poor children of the town. The Daughters of Wisdom were founded in response to this double need: to teach children and to care for the poor.[8]

It is interesting to note that his short admonitions on the duties of justice are found in the hymn *"The value of alms."* We know that for a Christian it is difficult to separate the virtues of justice and charity even when putting conscious emphasis on one or the other. Certainly, Montfort during his life and in his preaching put the emphasis on charity, that quite divine virtue exercised by alms in many forms.

f. ***Alms.*** Montfort practiced almsgiving as a matter of course. "I could rightly call him the begging brother for the poor, for he made that his life's task. Nothing of his own, nothing which did not belong to the needy. Money, clothes, as a matter of course, stayed in his hands no longer than necessary before passing to the needy."[9] "Counting, if possible, all the poor whom this worthy priest, so poor himself, nourished during the entire course of his missions, it will be seen that he has perhaps sustained, single-handedly, more than all those clergy who had a better idea of how to put the goods and wealth of the Church to use."[10]

g. Sharing one's table. Where Montfort excelled was in his sense of sharing with the poor. Just as he wanted to share their way of life to the limit, so also he contrived to gather the poor to his table as being his best and greatest friends. For him the table was always for sharing with the poor, welcomed with joy and honored. The lesson was repeated at every turn of his life, each time he was somewhat in command of the situation: at Poitiers, Rennes, Montfort, Pontchâteau—to the point where it became the norm in the mission he gave in Lower Poitou. He made it a rule for his missionaries in the course of a mission (RM 5, 16, 48, 89), and for the Daughters of Wisdom, *"who, in honor of the Blessed Virgin, will give food to a poor person every day"* (RS 139). *"All my entourage and my glory / are these poor beggars. / If I have to eat and drink, / I share with them"* (H 144:20).[11]

4. Evangelizing the Poor

Like many other missionaries, Montfort took as his motto (RM 7) the evangelical text (Lk 4:18) adopted by Jesus from the prophet Isaiah (61:1). Indeed, amidst all the services, all the honors he could bestow on the poor, above all his works of charity, he could not overlook the most important: announcing the Gospel of Jesus Christ. Like St. Paul he made it a duty. In the first years of his priesthood (1700–1706) Montfort sought his missionary path amid numerous difficulties. Finding it was what troubled him most, and he mentions it in all his letters to his spiritual director, Father Leschassier (L 5, 6, 9, 10, 11). Torn between the service of the poor in difficult conditions, and the needs of the mission, he came to define his missionary project in these terms: *"I feel a tremendous urge to make our Lord and his holy Mother loved, to go in a humble and simple way to teach catechism to the poor in country places and to arouse in sinners a devotion to our Blessed Lady"* (L 5). *"When I am teaching catechism to the poor in town and country, I am in my element"* (L 9). At that time, therefore, his vision of his missionary work was restricted to catechizing. He aimed at a somewhat reduced audience, viz. the poor, meaning by that the poorest, such as beggars, tramps, and those poor closeted in hospitals.

Later, especially after his visit to Pope Clement XI (1706), the objective of his mission broadened; it became *"to renew the spirit of Christianity"* (MR 56) by means of parish missions. The audience extended to the bulk of the people and thereby to folk of every condition. However, even then Montfort did not abandon his preference for the poor, having *"a greater obligation to the poor than to the rich"* (MR 89). Every day of the mission, after catechetical instruction, soup was prepared, uniting the participants around the same table unless they were received at the table of the more generous families (RM 47, 48). There is no doubt that this emphasis on the poor gave the mission an unprecedented evangelical quality. It could be a sign of authentic conversion and of effectiveness in the mission. Montfort sharply rebukes the recalcitrant worldling: *"You have nothing for your neighbor / but a pitiless heart. / You have nothing but contempt / for the wretched poor"* (H 107:6; cf. H 29:80). On the other hand, the converted worldling never ceases praising poverty and charity: *"Poverty and deepest humility, / poverty at its worst, / most fruitful charity: / These are all your assets in this world, / Poverty"* (H 143:24).

What are the most pressing motives, the deepest reasons, for these preferences and missionary tactics in favor of the poor? Quite simply, to *"share in the most tender inclinations of the heart of Jesus, (our) model"* (RM 7). These are the choices and practices of Jesus, the poor one.

5. Montfort's Poverty

There is no preferential love of the poor without some personal involvement in poverty. Not content with loving the poor, serving them, sharing his board, handing out to them all he had, and catechizing them, Montfort also wished to *be* poor like them, in close touch with them.

Never was he happier than when treated as a poor person, as we see each time he arrived at a town or place where he was unknown. In a letter to Father Leschassier he describes the first reception accorded him by the poor of Poitiers, who, he said, *"all agreed to take up a collection for me."* In conclusion: *"I blessed God that I had been taken for a poor man wearing the glorious livery of the poor and I thanked my brothers and sisters for their kindness"* (L 6).

Certainly he was not just playing the poor man, but truly being one. He was really poor because he lived his poverty in the presence of God, finding in Him all the unfailing richness of Providence. He was really poor because he consented to suffer all the upsets and all the trials which are the normal lot of the poor. Montfort fully appreciated the intimate bond created by the poverty of Jesus Christ and his own personal poverty, no less voluntary than that of Jesus. He also valued the bond created by the poverty of the poor—his friends and brothers, with whom he associated in the name of Jesus Christ—and his own poverty, which was as real and effective as theirs. Only saints, by the simplicity of their outlook on faith and the interior coherence that moved them, are capable of this kind of powerful and flawless theological synthesis. This is illustrated by the testimony of J. Grandet, his first biographer: "Father de Montfort, supported by these great truths of Faith (the poverty of Jesus Christ and the apostles), made himself poor, renounced his patrimony and all kinds of benefices, took a vow of poverty and persuaded all the workers who followed him in his mission to do likewise."[12]

It cannot be overlooked that at times poverty and deprivation reached extreme limits in his life, especially when the Church through some bishops stole from him such rightful goods as good reputation, open friendship, the faculties needed to exercise his ministry, acceptance, and understanding. It is reported that only once did a complaint pass his lips: *"Is it possible that a priest could be so treated in the seminary?"*[13] In 1703 he wrote to Marie Louise Trichet: *"I am infinitely more impoverished, crucified and humiliated than ever."* Montfort knew from experience that poverty never came alone; it came with *"sufferings, humiliations and other crosses which his servants must carry all the days of their life"* (FC 7): *"They form the accouterments and retinue of divine Wisdom which he brings into the lives of those in whom he dwells"* (L 16).

III. Doctrinal Aspects

1. Poverty and wealth

a. Wealth/poverty. In Montfort's words and spirit these two words are intentionally and closely connected, as if to invite us to grasp an entrenched, enigmatic truth. One cannot speak of poverty, implying lack, privation, denial, without at the same time speaking of the opposite, wealth which connotes ideas of plenitude, abundance, life and happiness. All aspire to such plenitude of life and happiness, and exert all their efforts to obtain it. After all, this aspiration is rooted in a fundamental, inalienable right. By contrast, poverty, especially extreme poverty—"wretchedness"—is an evil to flee from or to fight. Who fails to see that the poverty that results in stunting our being and diminishing life in every aspect is to be rejected and condemned? Our deep human calling is to life, with the inalienable right to a sufficient share of the goods necessary for its maintenance and conservation and for developing and procreating. Among these necessary goods are a degree of status and a degree of familial or social ownership of possessions. The social doctrine of the Church caps this by corroborating, explaining, applying to circumstances of time and place this universal maxim, which is also that of Scripture and Christian Tradition.[14] Montfort is not unaware of this truth (e.g. TD 207), but spiritual man that he is, this is not what he directly expounds and develops.

The truth he prefers is different. It relates to the difficulty or danger posed by a certain kind of wealth to the Christian. Speaking of the *"rich at heart,"* Montfort says, *"It [wealth] is full of idolatry / against his [the Christian's] sovereign God. / It is full of barbarity / towards the poor and one's neighbor"* (H 20:36).

b. Idolatrous wealth. The difficulty experienced by the budding Christian as to possession and use of this world's goods arises from considering two orders of things. In the first, thanks to the Gospel, we learn to see God as the Supreme, Absolute Good, Infinite, alone able to fulfill us now and for eternity. Consequently, every other good has worth that can only be relative, symbolic, supplementary, or instrumental (Montfort speaks of *"material, temporal and perishable things"* [TD 137]). On this score no good in this world can bear comparison with God, the Supreme and Infinite Good. According to the Gospel, the Kingdom of Heaven is the greatest treasure to be found, and one should be prepared to leave and sacrifice everything in order to gain it (Mt 13:44–46; Mk 10:21; Lk 12:33–34; 14:33). Even though this world's goods are necessary, we refuse to give them absolute primacy, or to bow to them as to another god. However, we know the danger is there and plagues us always. The human heart has an infinite yearning, yet is inherently limited: it attaches itself to the goods of this world and pursues them as alone true and final, and thus becomes insatiable.

On this point the teaching of the Gospel is perfectly clear and explicit. Father de Montfort takes this Gospel teaching into account and incorporates it into his thought and life, so that what might at first sight appear to be a problem for him can be seen as a sign of his maturity and complete freedom of spirit. One who is stripped of everything, after the spirit of the Gospel, becomes entirely free to love and serve God and *"to save his poor neighbor"* (cf. H 22:1). The person dedicated to God can experience the goods of the Kingdom—such as pardon, grace, insight, wisdom, virtues, spiritual gifts (cf. 1 Cor 1:5), and even apostolic mission—as true goods, since they affect us and enrich us not in what we have but in what we are, not by their quantity but their quality. We are thereby reminded that "having" is an illusion of being, and that no wealth of having can compensate for or replace the wealth of being and living in God. The former without the latter represents failure and true human and spiritual poverty. Poverty by contrast is the condition *sine qua non* that allows us to be *"rich in God": "Provided I stay / very poor and rich in God"* (H 91:16; 137:16). *"I hail you Mary / in your rich poverty"* (H 90:55).

c. An outrage to our neighbor. The second difficulty with regard to worldly possessions experienced by even a fervent Christian arises from the rooted and sordid selfishness to which he, as all mankind, is born, molded, educated, sustained, and almost enveloped (by reason of a gamut of cultural, judicial, philosophical, and ideological concepts that aim rather to protect the individual than to encourage growth of personality). This selfishness, often mixed with fear, is called cupidity or avarice, and is clearly the greatest obstacle to the spirit of communion and to the formation of truly human and Christian communities.

On the one hand, we know from all our catechetical instruction that the human being is called by God to giving, to sharing, to communication and solidarity with his brothers and sisters, in the image of his Creator Who is Love. On the other hand, the hard reality of daily life in a complex world pushes the Christian, only human, to look upon the next human being, not as a brother or sister, but as a rival, if not an enemy. Thus the civilizing action of love and universal brotherhood is constantly blocked by the cult of gain, which is at once a cult of inequality, injustice, conflict and violence.

Father de Montfort could have no idea, even by presentiment, of the wars and revolutions that would batter the world and tear Christianity apart in the following centuries. However, in unmasking and denouncing the false wisdom propounded by the world in opposition to the divine Plan, in guiding the faithful to surrender themselves by absolute consecration to Jesus through Mary, by shifting the core of the struggle towards each one's heart, by practice of evangelical poverty in a spirit of sharing and service, and by appealing to and rallying good Christian folk, he strove in the best way possible for the Kingdom of God, always a kingdom of truth, life, justice, grace, holiness, peace and love. *"This attachment to earth, / this cupidity, / sparks war everywhere, / causes all evil. / How fatal is its revenge! / It hardens the heart. / It emaciates the soul, / and plunges it into total gloom"* (H 28:26).

2. A Question of Wisdom

"Goodness, how wisdom is needed / to unmask that treacherous value / which compels even the wise / to pursue it to destruction!" (H 20:28).

Problems concerning poverty and wealth and their connection are themselves problems concerning wisdom. Wisdom may derive from a purely human and worldly viewpoint, or from a viewpoint of faith helping us to see things according to God's vision in the light of revelation. At a personal or community level conclusions will vary. Divine Wisdom alone can instruct us, guide us, enrich us. *"How unfortunate are the rich and powerful if they do not love. . . Wisdom!"* (LEW 6). On the other hand, *"Wisdom is so rich and generous; how can anyone who possesses him be poor?"* (LEW 59). *"When divine Wisdom enters a soul, he brings all kinds of good things with him and bestows vast riches upon that soul. 'All good things came to me along with him'"* (LEW 90).

Thanks to this Wisdom we know how to place supreme and utter worth on the blessings of salvation in Jesus Christ. We know also that these endowments are eminently communicable, bonds of brotherly and sisterly communion, since they are given entirely and freely and destined for all men and women. In this line of thought we are invited and called upon to recover the true significance of earthly goods, be they material, cultural, or technical. It would, first, consist of a sense of submission to the supreme Good, God and his Kingdom. Then in a sense of communication and service to all, beginning with the poorest, in such a way that material goods become again instruments of communion and salvation, no longer roots of division, oppression, hate and death.

The standard for this struggle is the Cross of Christ which, material, vile, and abject as it is, received the signal honor of being the instrument of our redemption. *"It is our natural and supernatural philosophy, our divine and mystic theology, our philosopher's stone, which by patience transforms the basest metals into precious ones, the bitterest pains into delight, poverty into riches, the most profound humiliations into glory"* (FC 26).

3. The Poverty of Jesus Christ

In the life and thought of saints everything springs from contemplation and imitation of Jesus Christ. So it is with Montfort, struck by the poverty of Jesus: *"A God defenseless / before the beauty of poverty, / loving it to the point of / assuming the poverty of our humanity"* (H 20:4). Montfort has Jesus declare: *"In poverty I find / such splendor and majesty / that I espouse it"* (H 108:4).

Montfort closely observes the pattern of Eternal Wisdom: *"in order to draw closer to men and give them a more convincing proof of his love, eternal Wisdom went so far as to become man, even to become a little child, to embrace poverty and to die upon a cross for them"* (LEW 70, cf. Ph 2:8 ff). He was struck by the infinite disparity between the wealth, splendor, and glory of the Word, Wisdom of God, and the poor, lonely, suffering life of the Savior. Such is the mystery of Divine Wisdom: *"To smother us in wealth, / his Majesty became impoverished; / to cradle us, / this great Lord became poor and lowly"* (H 64:4; cf. 2 Cor 8:9). In "The Treasures of the Cross," Jesus says: *"In my wisdom I find / treasures in poverty, / splendor in humility, / greatness in lowliness"* (H 123:3)

The conclusion is that Jesus became poor by free choice: *"I chose poverty / to make it respectable. / I chose poverty / to enrich it with holiness"* (H 58:7). By dint of resemblance, Jesus is also the friend of the poor: *"I cherish and make much of / those who here below / are considered wretched. / Those who seem to be last / for me are first. / Those poor little beggars / are my best friends / for they are my counterparts"* (H 108:3). In return the poor look upon Jesus as their friend: *"The poor, on seeing him poorly dressed and simple in his ways. . . felt at ease with him"* (LEW 124). To them was addressed *"the first beatitude, / the greatest utterance ever made, / needing long study: / Blessed are the poor in spirit"* (H 20:7).

Finally, if Jesus is poor in this world, that is merely to demonstrate his richness in God: *"In the midst of poverty, / Jesus is rich in truth, / in all abundance, / since he is replete, clothed / in all the great treasures of virtue"* (H 4:4).

4. Slavery of Love and Poverty

"Mary is my great wealth, / my all next to Jesus, / my honor, my tenderness, / the treasure of my virtue" (H 77:4).

Perfect consecration to Jesus through Mary is the complete offering we make to them of all that we are and all that we have. After the gift of ourselves, we give *all that we have* and yield even the right to dispose of ourselves and everything belonging to us, without exception. In the TD Montfort explains the scale and depth of this offering (TD 121ff). He insists more on interior than exterior goods or fortune, undoubtedly with the intention of attacking the precise point at the core of our being where our aspirations and desires are born and become embroiled. Left to ourselves, we will be betrayed by our desires (cf. RW, MRL). True devotion to Mary, therefore, is in a way the education of desire.[15]

In particular our *desire to possess* is so strong and tenacious that it is found within the coils of our souls and is hidden in every aspect of our spiritual life. Within us there are totally reserved and protected areas, such as our desires, our rights, our liberty, etc. Strictly speaking these areas cannot be called the *"evil that is rooted in us,"* but they are our most sensitive areas—most fragile, most exposed, most touchy; easily and quickly they risk being clouded and led astray in the absence of light and divine grace. The practice of our Marian consecration therefore becomes therapeutic: it reeducates and redirects us towards God and our neighbor in a way that is sacrificial and God-centered, and frees us from bondage and selfishness. In a school of radical poverty we learn to live without regard *"for selfish gain"* (TD 110) and *"to rid ourselves so easily of the possessiveness which slips unnoticed even into our best actions"* (TD 137). We can develop within ourselves a sense of free service, generosity, magnanimity and welcome, person to person, "one poor person to another."

At this point of our spiritual experience and encounter with God, *poverty becomes synonymous with humility*. Normally, at any rate, poverty should lead to humility. Montfort imbues the words *"lowly"* and *"poor"* with the significance of the humility of those who mutually recognize themselves, by some experience or other, as limited, deprived, conditioned, and needy. He associates the words *"poor"* and *"sinful"* to imply that we are poor in the sight of God and in need of His gracious mercy by reason of our sinfulness. The well-known formula "poor sinner," consecrated by use and much employed by Montfort, far from losing impact, as in such expressions as "poor folk," "poor peasant," etc., here retains its fuller sense. We are poor, even wretched, before God when we are alienated or cut off from Him by sin. Thereupon we understand better that God alone can endow us anew by the grace of Jesus Christ. *"How loving and gentle he [Jesus, Incarnate Wisdom] is with men, and especially with poor sinners whom he came upon earth to seek out in a visible manner, and whom he still seeks in an invisible manner every day"* (LEW 126). With Montfort we can also sing of the Virgin Mary: *"She is my Ark of the Covenant / where I find holiness. / She is my robe of innocence / with which I clothe my poverty"* (H 77:5).

5. Voluntary Poverty

"True happiness on earth consists in voluntary poverty and imitation of me" (MLW 1).

In the catalogue of all forms of human poverty, real or imagined, often tainted with as much vice as virtue, there is one kind calling for special attention: voluntary poverty, or poverty of heart and spirit. For *"only the voluntary poor / are the predestined poor"* (H 20:43). This poverty is not come to under protest and with detestation, but is chosen with love, accepted with a full, patient heart, and assumed with *"great zeal." "It is a virtue for the courageous, / not for the faint-hearted"* (H 20:22).

This poverty is *voluntary,* a free choice of the will (LFC 7, 14–16, 54, 57). It is a considered response to the Master's call: *"If anyone, therefore, wants to follow me thus abased and crucified, he must glory, as I did, only in the poverty, humiliations and sufferings of my Cross"* (LFC 17). This poverty is entirely inspired by the Gospel (see the main oracles of the Eternal Wisdom in LEW 133 ff), and in particular by the eight Beatitudes. If it is spiritual, it is no less real and effective: *"Try to put into practice / this holy spirit of poverty; / otherwise it is fanciful / and full of pride"* (H 20:49). This spirit of poverty is also the open door to *"faith . . . your secret fund of divine Wisdom"* (TD 214), and a sign of authentic conversion. *"The poor in spirit are rich in faith and the other virtues"* (LCM 7; H 108:2). Voluntary poverty is a source of joy and happiness: *"Holy poverty of heart / is the true happiness / of the children of Light"* (H 108:7). The one who is poor in spirit is *"rich in divine consolations"* (LCM 7). *"He even counts heavenly glory as part of his wealth,"* for *"The man who is truly poor in spirit possesses God himself in his heart"* (LCM 7–8).

One chooses to live poverty by contemplation of Jesus Christ who willed to be poor and identified himself with the poor. *"Poor Jesus, I want to follow you, / poor as the poor, until death"* (H 20:59). Jesus chose poverty in solidarity with the poor who, lacking possessions and human support, put all their trust in the Lord. These are the poor of YHWH in the Old Testament and *"the poor filled with faith"* in the New Testament, those of the Church and the whole world (for whom Mary, *"lowly, humble handmaid of God"* [TD 52], is the unique example and the compassionate Mother [H 159:4–6; H 151:5–7]).

At every opportunity Montfort sought to involve as many as possible, friends, relatives, spiritual directors, fellow missionaries, to follow him in the path of voluntary poverty (L 7 and L 12 to his sister, Jeanne Guyonne; L 20 to his mother; L 30 to Anne Régnier). To a community of lay-people he proposed the *Rules of Voluntary Poverty of the Early Church* (GA 549-551), the first part of which (nos. 1–9) is a plan of the *"fundamental truths of this poverty of spirit."* Montfort does not hesitate to give to his Company the name of *"company of the voluntary poor"* (RM 18).

In RW, out of a total of thirty-nine allusions to the poor and poverty, there are nine references to the work of the sisters regarding the poor (organization, service, care, etc.), nine references to their customs and community life (habit, meals, room, personal relationships, etc.), and finally ten references to their spirit or virtue of poverty and to the poverty of Jesus Christ. Of these, the most important would be those referring to the spirit of poverty, *"preferring to lose their gown and cloak rather than hold on to one or the other and lose peace of heart and poverty of spirit"* (RP 10). In the hymn *"To the Daughters of Wisdom"* we find the same insistence on the spirit of poverty: *"O Daughters of Wisdom, / help the poor who are shunned, / those bowed down by grief, / the ostracized, the rejected. / Those whom the world spurns / should appeal to you most"* (H 149).

6. "In the steps of the poor Apostles" (RM 2)

If evangelical poverty must be enjoined on all Christ's disciples to some degree, it specifically concerns those dedicated to apostolic mission. Evangelical poverty then becomes apostolic poverty, for it has to do with the apostles in the exercise of their mission (Mt 10:9–16). It is rooted in the example of the apostles themselves: the example of St. Peter, "who entered the great city of Rome without entourage, penniless, friendless, with only a stick in his hand and as dowry the poverty of a crucified God";[16] that of the great St. Paul, who "made so many journeys,"[17] with destitution, persecution and adversity of every kind (2 Cor 4:7–18, 6:1–10); and that of all those apostolic men who followed and emulated them. More profoundly, it is rooted in the example and teaching of Jesus, the Incarnate Wisdom and the envoy *par excellence* of the Father to such poor sinners as we are.

If an apostle has to be poor, stripped of everything and attached to nothing, *"free from every other occupation and unimpeded by the administration of any temporal possessions which might hold them back"* (RM 6), that is so that he may respond to the needs of the mission without ambiguity, in the greatest freedom and with perfect docility to the Holy Spirit. His abandonment to Providence also shows clearly that the work to which he is dedicated is strictly God's work and not his own, and that it is supported chiefly by the charity and solidarity of Christian communities.

Montfort observes with sadness and nostalgia that for lack of this detachment not enough good is achieved in the Church. *"How many useless priests, / with great talents, sterile / for want of detachment"* (H 22:24). *"We do not see in our midst / such true apostles as those / who shone in days gone by. / There are no longer any voluntarily poor ones; / a secure position is required; / even though obliquely, / money is wanted for their own concerns"* (H 22:25). *"Priests, let us follow in the steps / of a God poor and crucified; / since He begs us, / let us hearken to his voice, / think only of his concerns, / march under his flag, / be voluntarily poor; / that is the better part"* (H 28:42–43).

Montfort required apostolic poverty of his collaborators and missionaries (RM 10–19), and he strove to inculcate it by means of precise rules concerning house, way of life, alms from the faithful, Mass offerings, etc. Every material preoccupation was to be eliminated through the effect of abandonment to Providence. It must however be noted that Montfort was not ignorant of the real needs that a community of missionaries could face both for living and the work of the mission. Proof of that lies in his RM (RM 12, 15–18), and in particular in his will,[18] which is a real deed of management and administration, drawn up and signed in due form, in which Montfort indicates that goods from different sources are destined for different institutions, works, and persons.

IV. Conclusion

One could sum up Montfort's spiritual doctrine on poverty—seeing it as a triangular form which depicts the relationships between Jesus Christ, the poor, and Christ's apostles. Side one shows the connection between Jesus Christ and the poor: Jesus Christ loves the poor and prefers to identify himself with them and proclaims a Gospel of liberation; the poor accept Jesus as their Savior and go to him and the Heavenly Father, moved by the Holy Spirit, by faith, hope, and charity. Side two shows the connection between Jesus and an apostle. Jesus Christ is the Incarnate Wisdom, Master of Wisdom, instructing and commissioning; the apostle, at once disciple and friend of Wisdom, knows that he can achieve nothing unless united with and dependent on his Master; with Jesus he learns to do the will of the Father, abandoning himself to Providence. Side three shows the relationship between the poor and the apostle, a mutual friendship established and strengthened by fraternal sharing and evangelical interchange, dignifying the poor and building the Kingdom conforming to the Beatitude: *"Happy the poor in spirit; theirs is the Kingdom of Heaven"* (Mt 5:3).

There can be no doubt that poverty is an essential element of Montfort spirituality. Montfort poverty of spirit yearns to share the wealth of Jesus and Mary; however, to enjoy authenticity, it must express itself in simplicity of life and in sharing with the poor. Identification with the poor entails being the voice of justice and mercy for the disenfranchised, the new immigrants who experience prejudice, the single parent, the handicapped, the homeless vagrant, the hungry. The montfort spirit of poverty cannot remain speechless when a wealthy country manipulates a poorer one for its own profit. But above all, montfort poverty must be firmly rooted in the total lived out surrender of the self to the Eternal and Incarnate Wisdom through Mary.

M. Lemarié

Notes: (1) The first and oldest biographers (Grandet, Besnard, and Blain) seem to have best seen the importance of various aspects of poverty in St. Louis Marie de Montfort. (2) See the letter from the poor of Poitiers: "We, four hundred poor people. . ." in Le Crom, *Un Apotre Marial: Saint Louis-Marie Grignion de Montfort* (A Marian Apostle: Saint Louis Marie Grignion de Montfort), Librairie Mariale, Pontchateau 1942, 128. (3) See L. Pérouas, *Grignion de Montfort, les pauvres et les missions (Grignion de Montfort, the poor and the missions),* Cerf 1966, 74–87; 161–70; *Grignion de Montfort, un aventurier de l'Évangile* (Grignion de Montfort, An Adventurer of the Gospel), Paris 1960, esp. ch. 1. (4) *"They will bring to the poor and lowly everywhere the sweet fragrance of Jesus, but they will bring the odour of death to the great, the rich and the proud of this world"* (TD 56). (5) Blain, 18. (6) "Not only had he [Fr. de Montfort] an exceptional predilection for poverty, but I make bold to say that his tenderness towards the poor went to excess! He looked upon them as sacramental, holding Jesus Christ in their repellant exterior. 'A poor man,' he said, 'is a great mystery to be unravelled'; '*Beatus qui intelligit super egenum et pauperem*'. By such principles M. Grignion not only cherished and embraced the poor as children and brethren; he honoured and respected them as lords and masters. When he came across some in the street he hailed them, spoke to them cap in hand, kissed them, washed their feet, set them at his right hand at table, served them first of all with the choicest morsels, drank from their glasses and ate their left-overs. He embraced the ugliest, full of ulcers. He left the table only when no poor person remained, saying: 'I'm off to find the good Jesus.' Every day during missions he had soup served to any poor people who turned up; he even supplied clothing made up by pious persons in the course of the mission, and finally established 'ladies of charity' in the parishes and from them sallied forth to visit the poor and the sick and help with their needs. That was one of his chief objectives in the institution of the Daughters of Wisdom. He had the poor walking two abreast in all processions. With Cross raised at their head and Rosary in hand, he instructed and taught them to love God with all their heart, and to serve him faithfully, thus setting poverty to holy use" (Grandet, 354–57). (7) Besnard II, 114. (8) L 29:4; RS 1. (9) Blain, 23. (10) Besnard II, 217. (11) See L. Pérouas, *Grignion de Montfort,* 140, 163n. 20. (12) Grandet, 347-348. (13) Blain, 179. (14) On this topic cf. *Gaudium et Spes,* 11–33; Paul VI, *Populorum Progressio,* (1967), 6, 14–22; Jean Paul II, *Centesimus Annus* (1991), 33–34; and the documents of the Latin American Bishops from Medellin and Puebla. (15) Montfort's thought is shot through with references, implicit and explicit, to the threefold concupiscence. The desire to have or to possess is the first of these, and poverty of heart is the remedy for this. There is an up-to-date presentation of this traditional doctrine of the Church in J. Morinay, *Marie et la faiblesse de Dieu (Mary and the Weakness of God),* Nouvelle Cité, Paris 1988, ch. 1. (16) Grandet, 98. (17) Blain, 185–90, provides the whole of the conversation between Louis Marie de Montfort and Jean Baptiste Blain. (18) Cf. P. Eijckeler, *Le testament d'un Saint, étude historique (The Testament of a Saint, Historical Study),* Maastricht 1953.

PRAYER

SUMMARY

I. PRAYER IN THE SEVENTEENTH CENTURY:
   1. "The great century of souls";
   2. The seminary of Saint-Sulpice;
   3. A God Incarnate.

II. MONTFORT, MAN OF PRAYER:
   1. Montfort as he prayed;
   2. The beggar of prayers;
   3. The teacher:
      a. Prayer of faith,
      b. Prayer of pure faith.

III. THE MISSIONARY'S PRAYER:
   1. The Rosary;
   2. Other forms of prayer;
   3. Consecration to Jesus through Mary.

IV. THE MIND AND THE HEART:
   1. Doctrinal prayer;
   2. Affective prayer.

V. PRAYER TODAY:
   1. Prayer beyond formula;
   2. Montfort, witness of prayer.

Prayer is both simple and complex: simple, for it is conversation with the Beloved; complex, for it stems from the very nature of our religious experience, and hinges on the psychological evolution of that experience, from childhood to adult life.[1] Prayer is also complex in respect to its practice: unbelievers see no reason to address a being they believe does not exist; believers of all levels, from the nonpracticing to the fervent, with whom prayer is either sporadic or habitual, are driven by utilitarianism or by grateful filial love. No matter how simple or complex, we cannot sidestep the subject, because it bears on everything in the universe: all creatures must give worship to their Creator, from those that were granted intelligence ("Therefore mortals fear him; he does not regard any who are wise in their own conceit" [Jb 37:24]) to the inanimate creatures of the cosmos ("We know that the whole creation has been groaning in labor pains until now" [Rm 8:22]). We must examine how St. Louis Marie de Montfort, at one moment in the Church's history, enhanced the sense of God and of the worship due Him for Christians then and now, through his life of prayer and his teaching.

I. Prayer in the Seventeenth Century

1. "The great century of souls"

This phrase of Daniel-Rops well expresses how Christian life, on the spiritual level, was thoroughly renewed in the seventeenth century, just as profane life, on the cultural level, had been similarly renewed in the preceding century with the Renaissance. A galaxy of saints and other great spiritual figures like Francis de Sales, Vincent de Paul, John Eudes, Bérulle, Charles de Condren, Olier, and, among the laity, Gaston de Renty, had a deep impact on both society and the Church. Implementation of the Tridentine decrees created a better educated and more saintly clergy. Bishops such as Cospeau,[2] bishop of Nantes and later of Lisieux, friend of Bérulle and John Eudes, with whom he carried on a correspondence, were highly effective instruments of Catholic reform.

2. The Seminary of Saint-Sulpice

Jean Jacques Olier established the Society of Saint Sulpice in order to train priests in piety, learning, and the apostolate. He adopted bérullian doctrine and made it the basis of his plans. "The paramount aim of this Institute," he wrote, "is to live supremely for God, in Christ Jesus Our Lord, so that the interior dispositions of the Son reach into the depths of our heart, and each will be able to say what Saint Paul said of himself: 'I live, but it is no longer myself, it is Christ who lives in me.'" Bérullian doctrine professes the virtue of religion to the utmost extent. Before the grandeur of God, the soul is struck dumb with wonder. Such grandeur gives rise to a deep feeling of adoration that simultaneously releases an overflowing joy, expressed in the "O" of admiration in the presence of the mystery: "O Jesus living in Mary." We see this often in Bérulle and his disciples. It has been called an "elevation," the purest form of prayer, whereby one honors and glorifies God while neither requiring nor desiring anything in return: gratuitous prayer of pure contemplation. For Olier, "living supremely for God" is an echo of this.

3. A God Incarnate

The God of Bérulle is not simply the Supreme and Transcendent being. He is God Incarnate in Jesus Christ, from whom arises the permanent states or attitudes that we must reproduce. These attitudes are interior, which is why they are called "states," and they are "mysteries" because of their depth (to distinguish them from "acts" which are exterior and transient). Again we discern the meaning of Olier's words when he spoke of "the interior dispositions of the Son" that must "reach into the depths of our heart." Insofar as it begins with God and leads to Jesus Christ, bérullian doctrine has as its focal point the Incarnation and the related mystery of the "only Son of Mary, Jesus Christ our sovereign Lord." Mary is therefore not merely a simple accessory of devotion, but an integral and essential part of the mystery of the Word Incarnate: without her God's plan—because of His free choice—would be impossible, in the present order of salvation (and there is no other).

II. Montfort, Man of Prayer

Montfort's prayer and extraordinary contemplative life coexisted with intense apostolic activity. Through his incredible interior gifts he appears as a practitioner of prayer, a beggar of prayers, and a teacher of prayer.

1. Montfort as he prayed

In the spiritual environment described above, Montfort's life of prayer, which had been pronounced in his childhood and adolescence, matured. From his youth he had showed an inclination toward prayer. His younger sister Guyonne-Jeanne (Louise), with whom he was very close, learned her piety from him. "He would secretly draw her away . . . with her young friends, to lead her in prayer to God."[3] During his journeys to and from school, he never failed to stop in a chapel or church in Holy Savior, his parish; according to his uncle, Father Alain Robert, he sometimes stayed there an hour. Similarly, one of his biographers notes that "whenever he was on his way to class, he never failed to enter the church of the Carmelites to pray, and he often spent a considerable time before the image of the Virgin."[4] He loved to kneel down before the Madonnas he saw on the corners of houses. As a member of the Sodality of Our Lady, he was faithful in reciting the office of the Blessed Virgin; he already prayed the Rosary daily and dedicated time to mental prayer. His friend Blain relates that upon his arrival in Chartres for a pilgrimage, "Montfort went in haste to bow down before the image of the holy Virgin . . . . The next day . . . he remained in prayer for six or eight hours at a time, from morning until noon, on his knees, unmoving and as if in ecstacy. After the noon meal . . . he began prayer again, in the same posture and with equal devotion, that was as lengthy as his morning prayer, lasting until the evening hour or until he was told that he must leave."[5] Blain also recounts that, as a seminarian, Montfort watched over the dead every other night in order to earn some money, and that during this time he spent "four hours in prayer, two hours in spiritual reading, and two hours in sleep."[6] At his first Mass, celebrated eight days after his ordination, he appeared "like an angel at the altar," according to Jean-Baptiste Blain. A prolonged thanksgiving followed each of his Masses. Traveling long distances as a pilgrim, he was always conscious of the presence of God, and he therefore went without a hat. In one of his letters he speaks of his *"secret attraction for a hidden life"* (L 5), and seems to refer to this desire in another letter: *"During this time I made a short retreat in a little room where I enclosed myself, in the middle of a large town where I knew nobody"* (L 6). However, he did leave his room to provide help to the poor of the general hospital. *"I went into their little church to pray and the four hours I spent there waiting for the evening mealtime seemed all too short,"* but he acknowledged that the poor who saw him kneeling there thought it quite a long time (L 6). On many occasions he withdrew into solitude, at the cave of Mervent and at the retreat of Saint-Lazare. On his return from Rome, he spent fifteen days at Mont Saint-Michel.

2. The Beggar of Prayers

The communion of saints is the basis for their intercession and the intercession of God's friends here below: "The fervent prayer of the just is very powerful."[7] Montfort often reminded his correspondents of this. To his sister Guyonne-Jeanne (who was about to become Sister Catherine of Saint Bernard) he wrote, *"Continue asking pardon of God and of Jesus, the eternal High Priest, for the offenses I have committed against his divine majesty in the Blessed Sacrament"* (L 12). A subsequent letter to his sister indicates that these offenses were *"half-hearted communions"* (L 19). *"Thank God in my name for the crosses he has given me and which he keeps within limits to suit my weakness"* (L 14). *"Keep on praying, even increase your prayers for me; ask for . . . the weightiest cross, abjection and humiliations"* (L 15). He asked that others join in praying for him: *"So, my dear daughter, I ask you to enlist some good souls among your friends into a campaign of prayer especially from now until Pentecost, and to pray together for an hour on Mondays from one to two o'clock. I will be praying at the same time. Write and send me their names"* (L 15). The object of this prayer is often Wisdom: *"Pray that I may receive divine Wisdom and get others to pray"* (L 17).

3. The Teacher

Montfort taught what he practiced. He noted that prayer is second only to desire among the means of obtaining Wisdom. *"The greater the gift of God, the more effort is required to obtain it. Much prayer and great effort, therefore, will be required to obtain the gift of Wisdom, which is the greatest of all God's gifts. . . . Prayer is the usual channel by which God conveys his gifts, especially his Wisdom"* (LEW 184). His Hymn 103 is a contemplative sigh, directed at Wisdom, in twenty-nine stanzas; all but one of the stanzas has the same structure, twice repeating the same line, in an insistent litany: *"Come to me"*: *"Son of God, supreme beauty / Come to me. / Without you I am anathema / Come to me. / With you I will be a king, / But a king that bows before your law"* (H 103:2). *"O Word, equal to Father, / Come to me. / Light of all lights, / Come to me. / With you I will see clearly, / And I will crush hell itself"* (H 103:3). *"Jesus, Wisdom uncreated, / Come to me. / Jesus, Wisdom incarnate, / Come to me. / With you, what could be happier? / But what hell exists without you!"* (H 103:4). *"A thousand times I desire you / Come to me. / Without you I suffer martyrdom, / Come to me. / With you I will have all that is good / Without fear of want"* (H 103:12).

a. Prayer of faith. For Montfort, all rests on faith, *"a strong and lively faith, not wavering, because he who wavers in his faith must not expect to receive any gift from the Lord"* (LEW 185). In this case he is referring to the gift of Wisdom, but it clearly applies to everything else as well. Thus he himself prayed, *"Come, O Wisdom, come! Hear this, a beggar's* *plea / By Mary's womb, by every gush / of Blood her Jesus shed for me, / Confound us not, nor bid us hush"* (H 124:1). Notice the "us" of the conclusion, wherein Jesus, Mary, and the suppliant are united. Montfort's faith is founded on the weight of the prayer of Jesus and Mary, united with his own. This faith is emphatic and persevering, unafraid to importune and confident of eventually being fulfilled. Witness the insistence with which he pleaded for his Company of Mary. *"When I see the needs of the Church I cannot help pleading continually for a small and poor band of good priests"* (L 5). His ardent PM has this same impassioned tone. *"We ought not to act, as so many do, when praying to God for some grace. After they have prayed for a long time, perhaps for years, and God has not granted their request, they become discouraged and give up praying, thinking that God does not want to listen to them. They deprive themselves of the benefit of their prayers and offend God, who loves to give and who always answers, in some way or another, prayers that are well said"* (LEW 188). As an illustration of this he cites the example of the man who arrives at his friend's house late at night and aggressively requests some bread (cf. Lk 11:5–8). *"This man knocked and repeated his knockings and entreaties four or five times with increased force and insistence . . . . At length the friend became so annoyed by the persistence of the man that he got out of bed, opened the door and gave him all he asked for"* (LEW 189). Montfort prays with similar insistence in his hymn on "the desire for Wisdom": *"Why do you prolong my painful martyrdom? / For you I languish night and day"* (H 124:2). *"My Beloved, Open!. I knock at your door. / . . . . If you do not want me to belong to you. / At least allow me in that case / The privilege of seeking you / Though finding not your hiding-place"* (H 124:3–4). But faith carries all before it—especially Mary's faith: *"Worthy Mother of God, Virgin all-faithful, pure, / Lend me your faith; lift me on wings / Of faith, that I may mount secure / To Wisdom's height, and have all things. / By Mary's faith then come, O Wisdom heaven-sent! / You leapt to her as light to flame; / She gave you your embodiment, / In her Incarnate you became"* (H 124:7-8).

b. Prayer of pure faith. Montfort's demands are those of a true spiritual Master, equal to St. John of the Cross. Such pure faith does not mean *"counting on consolations, visions or special revelations. Although such things may be good and true, as they have been in some saints, it is always dangerous to rely on them. For the more our faith is dependent on these extraordinary graces and feelings, the less pure and meritorious it is"* (LEW 186). Therefore, *"the wise man does not ask to see extraordinary things such as saints have seen, nor to experience sensible sweetness in his prayers"* (LEW 187). This describes Montfort's own prayer to Mary: *"May the light of your faith dispel the darkness of my mind"* (SM 68). *"As for my portion here on earth, I wish only to have a share in yours, that is, to have simple faith without seeing or tasting"* (SM 69). He speaks on several occasions of prayer and faith. They are so closely interwoven that it is impossible to put one before the other; they are bound like body and soul. A prayer without faith would be like a corpse without a soul. The faith that animates prayer can itself be the object of prayer. In his hymn on faith, Montfort writes, *"You should often make this prayer: / Increase my faith, dear Lord, / Enable it to spread / From my head to my heart"* (H 6:53). *"Give me a faith that is simple and pure / Which accepts all without seeing or feeling / . . . . Pray for me, faithful Virgin. / I ask only that you increase my faith"* (H 6:54–55).

III. The Missionary's Prayer

Jesus expressed a fundamental law of the economy of grace when he said, "Apart from me you can do nothing" (Jn 15:5). This law is based on our complete and essential dependence on God; however, this dependence does not mean that we must become robots. There are always two actors: God and His creature. Mankind can do nothing without God, but God does not carry out His plan of salvation unless we freely open ourselves to His mercies. Montfort himself was imbued with this feeling. He was convinced that he was *"unable to do anything conducive to [his] salvation"* (TD 79). Thus he resorted to prayer. This conviction also permeated his apostolic work. His preaching could not be effective unless God touched the hearts of his listeners and disposed them to turn toward Him. The missionary requires the grace that will render his ministry fruitful. "I will give you words and a wisdom that none of your opponents will be able to withstand or contradict" (Lk 21:15). This is why Montfort so often prayed and asked others to pray that he would be granted this Wisdom. *"How few preachers there are today who possess this most wonderful gift of eloquence and who can say with St. Paul [1 Co 2:7], 'We preach the wisdom of God'"* (LEW 97). There are several forms of prayer that Montfort values especially highly and that he often recommends.

1. The Rosary

For Montfort, the Rosary has a dual function. It is both worship and catechesis, summarizing the mysteries of Christianity. He loved to describe it as the Gospel in tableau form. The very title of his work *The Secret of the Holy Rosary for Renewal and Salvation* (written before his Rule for the Missionary Priests for the Company of Mary and only published two hundred years after his death in 1911) indicates his opinion of its effect: *"renewal and salvation."* Its origin is further proof: *"It was given to the Church by St. Dominic, who had received it from the Blessed Virgin as a means of converting the Albigensians and other sinners"* (SR 11). That is why it is the preferred weapon of her missionaries, *"true servants of the Blessed Virgin who, like a Dominic of old, will range far and wide, with the holy Gospel issuing from their mouths like a bright and burning flame, and the Rosary in their hands"* (PM 12).

At the beginning of his work on the admirable secret of the Holy Rosary, Montfort addresses his readers as *"dear ministers of the most high God, you my fellow priests who preach the truth of God,"* so that they will keep in their hearts and in their mouths the truths that are revealed in the Rosary. *"Please keep them in your heart so that you yourselves may make a practice of the Rosary and taste its fruits. Please have them always on your lips too, so that you will always preach the Rosary and thus convert others by teaching them the excellence of this holy devotion"* (SR 1).

The priest or director who is given its secret *"will say the Rosary each day and will encourage others to say it. God and his blessed Mother will pour abundant grace into his soul, so that he may become God's instrument for his glory; and his word, though simple, will do more good in one month than that of other preachers in several years."* Montfort concludes: *"It will not be enough for us to preach this devotion to others; we must practice it ourselves"* (SR 1-2). Montfort repeats his counsel to priests and directors of souls, but in stronger terms, in the RM, as a guide for their apostolate, the purpose of which is *"to renew the spirit of Christianity among the faithful"* (RM 56). We can see Montfort's practical, methodical temperament in this passage from RM: *"During the whole of the mission, they must do all they can by the morning readings and by the conferences and sermons, to establish the great devotion of the daily Rosary."* To ensure that this can be done, *"they will enroll . . . as many as possible in the Rosary confraternity."* The Rosary is also included in the catechism classes given during the parish mission: *"They will explain the prayers and mysteries of the Rosary either by instructions or by pictures and statues which they have for this purpose."* Montfort would not have hesitated to utilize modern video technology. He ends by saying, *"They will give the people the example by having the Rosary recited aloud every day of the mission, saying all fifteen decades in French* [i.e., not in Latin] *with the offering of the mysteries"* (RM 57).

2. Other Forms of Prayer

Although the Rosary looms large in Montfort's perspective, he does not neglect other forms of prayer. Among external practices of true devotion to the holy Virgin, he also mentions the chaplet of five decades, which comprises one-third of the Rosary. With certain groups he refers only to the chaplet; the Rosary appears to be optional.

He acknowledges other practices that were common in his day: *"The Rosary of six or seven decades in honor of the years our Lady is believed to have spent on earth,"* or the fourteen Our Fathers and Hail Marys in honor of her fourteen joys; a certain amount of genuflecting or bowing each morning while saying *"Hail Mary, Virgin most faithful"* sixty or one hundred times in order to obtain her faithfulness, or, in the evenings, *"Hail Mary, Mother of Mercy,"* to be pardoned for the day's sins (TD 116).

He also mentions the *Little Crown*

of the Blessed Virgin, three Our Fathers and twelve Hail Marys in honor of her twelve stars or privileges. He suggests still other liturgical prayers, depending on the liturgical season, such as the *Alma,* the *Ave Regina coelorum,* the *Salve Regina,* and the *Regina coeli,* as well as the *Ave Maris Stella* and the *Magnificat* (TD 116).

3. Consecration to Jesus through Mary

Montfort composed several prayers, including those to Wisdom (LEW 1), a prayer for Wisdom [*O God of our fathers . . .*] (MR 11), and to Jesus and to Mary (SM 66-69), in addition to composing his methods for saying the Rosary and his inspired writing "vocation prayer," PM. However, in Montfort's missionary perspective, consecration ranks above all else.

This consecration is made to Jesus Christ: *"I give myself entirely to Jesus Christ"* (CG), through the hands of Mary: *"I, an unfaithful sinner, renew and ratify today through you my baptismal promises"* (LEW 225). Mary thus takes into her charge the consecrated soul and ensures its continuing growth, which can only be accomplished in her. Montfort prays to the Virgin that he become *"in everything so committed a disciple, imitator, and slave of Jesus, your Son, incarnate Wisdom"* and thereby be given *"the fullness which Jesus possessed on earth, and . . . the fullness of his glory in heaven"* (LEW 227).

IV. The Mind and the Heart

Created in the image of God, man has both intelligence and a will, and they are mutually dependent. We cannot love what we do not know, but once we are brought to this knowledge, intelligence, by action of the will, will attempt to gain even greater knowledge of the object that it loves. Montfort is thinking of this law of nature when he says of devotion to Mary that *"it comes from within the mind and the heart, . . . the high regard we have for her greatness, and the love we bear her"* (TD 106). This explains why his prayer is so rich in its doctrinal content, which aids intelligence, and so full of tender confidence, *"the confidence that a child has for its loving Mother"* (TD 107).

1. Doctrinal Prayer

Montfort prayer is highly doctrinal, profoundly theological, and Bérullian in approach, and yet it is comprehensible to all. He articulates the truths of Christian dogma in formulas that are intricate but clear.

For example, in his methods for reciting the Rosary, Montfort speaks of the *"unity of one, living and true God"* and of the Trinity: of the *"eternal Word, equal to his Father and who with him produces the Holy Spirit by their mutual love,"* of the *"Holy Spirit who proceeds from the Father and the Son by the way of love"* (MR 16). He then mentions *"the creation of the soul and the formation of the body of Jesus in the womb of Mary by the Holy Spirit"* (MR 17) and *"the coming forth of the eternal Word from the womb of Mary without breaking the seal of her Virginity"* (MR 19). Montfort recalls the life of Mary: *"the eternal predestination of Mary to be the masterpiece of*

God's hands," her *"Immaculate Conception"* and her *"fullness of grace and reason in the very womb of St. Anne"; "her fullness of pre-eminent virtue"; "her divine Motherhood and her relationship with the three persons of the most Holy Trinity"; "her resurrection and triumphant Assumption"* (MR 30). For Montfort, Mary is *"queen of heaven and earth . . . . treasurer and dispenser of the graces of God, the merits of Jesus Christ and the gifts of the Holy Spirit . . . mediatrix and advocate of men . . . nurturing Mother of sinners"* (MR 31).

In a Bérullian approach, Montfort honors God with each Our Father in the Rosary for His Immensity, His most adorable Majesty, His Wisdom, His Holiness, His unspeakable Beauty, His unlimited Omnipotence, His Providence, His unattainable Glory (MR 17-31).

Bérulle's great work, the *Discourse on the State and Grandeurs of Jesus,* is full of the words "greatness" and "ineffable." We find them similarly in Montfort. He writes, *"There is not and there never will be, either in God's creation or in his mind, a creature in whom he is so honored as in the most Blessed Virgin Mary"* (SM 19). Mary derives her greatness from the greatness of God within her. And everything that Bérulle most admires in what is "ineffable" can be seen in this passage: *"Mary is God's garden of Paradise, his own unspeakable world, into which his Son entered to do wonderful things"* (SM 19).

Although these passages are not integral parts of a prayer, the admiration that permeates them, transporting the writer and the reader, turns them into a kind of contemplative prayer. It is in this sense that, in order to show how Mary is not an obstacle but rather a means to prayer, Montfort could write, *"Rest assured that the more you turn to Mary in your prayers, meditations, . . . seeing her, if not perhaps clearly and distinctly, at least in a general and indistinct way, the more surely will you discover Jesus"* (TD 165). The admiration that emerges from a passage like this is expressed in increasingly elevated language. Confronted with the greatness of Mary, he cries, *"What incomprehensible height! What indescribable breadth! What immeasurable greatness! What an impenetrable abyss!"* (TD 7). His "Consecration of oneself to Jesus Christ, Wisdom incarnate" opens with a passage of splendid sublimity, even closer to the style of the French School: *"Eternal and incarnate Wisdom, most lovable and adorable Jesus, true God and true man, only Son of the eternal Father and of Mary always Virgin, I adore you profoundly, dwelling in the splendor of your Father from all eternity and in the virginal womb of Mary, your most worthy Mother, at the time of your Incarnation"* (LEW 223). It would be difficult to give a more compact doctrinal presentation of the mystery of the Word incarnate. In the text of this consecration he again addresses Mary in the same Bérullian style: *"Gracious Virgin . . . O admirable Mother . . . Mother of mercy . . . Virgin most faithful"* (LEW 226-227).

2. Affective prayer

As doctrine leads to admiration, admiration expresses itself in outbursts of the soul. Montfort composed several prayers to Mary that illustrate these feelings. At the end of the Rosary St. Louis Marie prays: *"Hail Mary, well-beloved daughter of the eternal Father, admirable Mother of the Son, most faithful spouse of the Holy Spirit, glorious temple of the Blessed Trinity. . . . Hear, O my Queen, the prayers of a heart that desires to love and serve you faithfully. . . . O my hope, my life, my faithful and immaculate Virgin Mary"* (MR 15). The opening of his *Prayer to Mary* (SM 68) and the prayer that comes after the *Little Crown* follow the same lines: *"Virgin most faithful . . . Gracious Mother . . .O Queen of heaven . . . O daughter of the King of kings"* (MP 13). In his *Night Prayer* we find the well-known prayer, *"O Jesus living in Mary"* (NP 20).

But, more than any of his other writings, his hymns, appropriately for a lyric genre, display Montfort's most ardent feelings. They could be quoted endlessly. *"A thousand times my heart desires you, / Divine love, come to me: / To be without you is to martyrdom, / Come to me and give me the law"* (H 5:40). *"Here is my body, here is my soul: / All are yours, O queen of heaven, / Light your flame so it shines over all, / Sacrifice everything to your fires"* (H 5:41).

We should particularly note his hymns to the Sacred Heart. *"Hear my divine lament. / Friends of the Heart of my Savior, / If I open my breast / It is to allay the grief of my heart"* (H 43:1). *"Speak, my heart, speak, my tears. / Sigh, cry, a thousand times. / Wherever I feel such strong alarms / Then I have neither words nor voice"* (H 43:2). *"You wish to ask me now / Why my heart is afflicted, / Why I sigh and I cry. / Ah, my Jesus has been so attacked"* (H 43:3). The following stanza would be an excellent prayer to repeat often: *"O my Jesus, my love, I love you / From the depths of my heart, / Above all, I love you"* (H 45:30).

V. Prayer Today

1. Prayer Beyond Formula

For many people, even the pious, prayer is a rote oral statement ("to know one's prayers"); they cannot believe that any prayer that does not come wrapped in that verbal packaging is truly prayer, although in fact their lives are often permeated with thoughts of God. This is to confuse essence and appearance. The Gospel speaks of Anne, the prophetess, a widow, eighty-four years old, who never left the temple: *"she worshipped there with fasting and prayer night and day"* (Lk 2:37). Her service to God lay not simply in words but in her constant prayer and thoughts of God there in the temple. However, as it is traditionally defined, "prayer" always refers to God. Saint John Damascene saw in prayer "an elevation of the soul" toward God,[8] and Saint Augustine also noted its "affective" character, but every definition includes lovingly recognizing an attribute of God, and letting it form us more perfectly in His Image. Therefore, we can elevate ourselves before God by recognizing His Greatness, and adoring it; by remembering His blessings, and expressing our thanks to Him; by becoming conscious of His rights, and asking His forgiveness for having ignored or scorned them; and finally by requesting His help in our need.

By our very nature we always tend to disguise our feelings in that verbal packaging. This is true of prayer as well. It is first and foremost "an affair of the heart," or, in St. Augustine's thinking, "a loving attempt to approach God." Only as a last resort does it become visible, like a volcano that carves out an opening so that its flames can escape. We can pray very well without a formula, just as we can pray mechanically by repeating words without truly praying.

The Second Vatican Council spoke of "the spiritual bond linking the people of the New Covenant with Abraham's stock" (NA 4). The Jewish liturgy was "the symbolic and direct setting of the encounter with God."[10] This was not an intellectual concept, a theology, but an experience of life, so that prayer in Judaism was not part of some other realm. It was a part of the life of Israel under the Torah. Worship meant becoming familiar with what it contained. So, over time, prayer moved away from being a precise formulation. "Its value is in its spontaneity, in the outpouring of the heart."[11] It was this liturgy on which Jesus, Mary, the Apostles, and the first Christians were all nourished.

2. Montfort, Witness of Prayer

"There are spiritual and religious values present in today's culture, and man, notwithstanding appearances to the contrary, cannot help but hunger and thirst for God."[12] Montfort is a great witness for our time to this hunger and thirst for God. He made it his motto: "God alone." He is a witness as much for priests as for the Christian people who, by the force of his missionary zeal, were led to God. John Paul II remarks as well that "an intimate bond exists between the priest's spiritual life and the exercise of his ministry."[13] As members of the laity are invited to intensify their activity on behalf of the Church, by virtue of their baptism, this principle, which is true for all of us, is new impetus for them to live a more intense life of prayer and in closer union with Christ and, through him, in the Holy Spirit, with the Father. Mary is a *"smooth, short, perfect and sure way"* (TD 152) of entering into intense union with Christ. Those who have consecrated their lives to Mary become so closely one with her that, even without words, they can live a life of continuous prayer. *"We must gradually acquire the habit of recollecting ourselves interiorly and so form within us an idea or a spiritual image of Mary. She must become, as it were, an Oratory for the soul where we offer up our prayers to God"* (SM 47). In this silent intimacy, *"we naturally turn to Mary for help, with never a fear of importuning her or displeasing our Lord"* (TD 106).

H.M. Guindon

Notes: (1) Cf. M. Parent, *Expériences de Dieu* (Experiences of God), Ed. Paulines-Médiaspaul, Montreal-Paris 1983); 22-23. (2) Y. Durand, "Nantes," in *Histoire des diocèses de France 18* (History of the dioceses of France), Beauchesne, Paris 1985); 93–94. (3) Grandet, 2–3. (4) Clorivière, 17. (5) Blain, 100-101. (6) R. Laurentin, *Dieu seul est ma tendresse* (God alone is my tenderness), O. E. I. L., Paris 1984, 77. (7) Fifteenth ordinary Sunday, response after first reading. (8) "Ascensus mentis in Deum," *De Fide orthodoxa,* vol. III, 24, PG 94, 1090. (9) "Oratio namque est mentis ad Deum affectuosa intentio," *Sermo* IX, n. 3. (10) C. di Sante, *La prière d'Israel* (The prayer of Israel), Descleé-Bellarmin, Paris-Montreal 1986); 12. (11) R. Le Déaut, A. Jaubert, K. Hruby, "Le Judaisme" (Judaism), DSAM 2 (1975), 109. (12) John Paul II, *I Will Give You Shepherds* (apostolic exhortation), 46. (13) Ibid., 24.

PRIEST

SUMMARY

I. TYPOLOGY OF THE PRIEST IN THE TIME OF MONTFORT:
  1. The characteristics of the priest in the post-Tridentine Church:
    a. "New priests for new faithful";
    b. Situation of the clergy before the tridentine renewal.
  2. The reformers of the French clergy;
    a. The Oratorian School;
    b. Saint Sulpice;
    c. Other artisans.
  3. Identity and mission of the priest;
  4. The Dimensions of priestly spirituality;
    a. Theocentrism;
    b. Christ the mediator;
    c. Mary;
    d. Mystical orientation;
    e. Separation from the world.

II. MONTFORT, A PRIEST BOTH MYSTIC AND MISSIONARY:
  1. As seminarian and young priest:
    a. At Rennes;
    b. At Saint Sulpice in Paris.
  2. Priestly life:
    a. Priest, both mystic and missionary;
    b. Christ Wisdom and devotion to Mary;
    c. Poverty;
    d. Pastoral sense.
  3. Relations with the clergy of his day.

III. THE PRIEST IN THE THOUGHT OF MONTFORT:
  1. Jesus, priest and victim;
  2. The type of priest desired by Montfort;
  3. The offering of the Eucharist in union with Mary;
  4. The universal priesthood.

IV. THE PRIESTLY DIMENSION IN MONTFORT SPIRITUALITY:
  1. Vows of Baptism and priestly promises;
  2. Baptismal life and sacerdotal commitment;
  3. Mary, bearer of the priestly spirit of the risen Christ;
  4. The heavenly priesthood.

I. Typology of the Priest in the Time of Montfort

Without any doubt, Montfort is "a man of his century" said [H. Daniel-Rops]. He is also one of the best witnesses of his century's sulpician and berullian spirituality, which he modified and enriched by his life and writings.[1] Montfort was a priest both mystic and missionary, a combination not well known and in need of additional study.

1. The Characteristics of the Priest in the Post-Tridentine Church

a. "New priests for new faithful". Fifty years after the closing of the Council of Trent (1545–1563), France appeared to be "a mission country without missionaries."[2] With the assembly of the clergy of 1615, a pastoral ideal was put in place which demanded "new priests for new faithful."[3] By 1640 the Tridentine reform was underway in France and seminaries were opened.

If the first half of the seventeenth century was the generation of pioneer priests, the second was the time of holy priests who possessed the grace to touch hearts both in preaching and in the celebration of the liturgy.[4] As a consequence, pastoral work improved: catechizing insisted upon the sacraments and preaching on the pedagogy of prayer and the renewal of the vows of baptism.

b. Situation of the clergy before the Tridentine renewal. Around 1600, the clergy was extremely numerous in France, but its lifestyle was decadent, its moral sense deficient, and its cultural preparation limited. Pastorally, the priest was underemployed. He was attentive to benefices but lacking in zeal and piety. In addition to being a notable person and a leader within his own jurisdiction, a priest was "a man apart," more feared than loved, more endured than accepted. In 1659, Vincent de Paul told the priests of his community: "The church has no worse enemies than its priests."[5] And, taking into account the over-abundance of priests and the lack of priestly service to the faithful, he concluded: "There are too many bad priests."[6] The situation clearly got better under Louis XV (d. 1774) and his successor, Louis XVI (d. 1793). Little by little the corrupt and over-privileged clergy, typical of the epoch of the Council of Trent, was reduced to such a few that at the beginning of the French revolution in 1789, the priest was a man fully trusted by his parishioners.[7]

2. The Reformers of the French Clergy

"The formation of good priests is really a masterpiece of this world," affirmed Vincent de Paul.[8] The principal artisans of this masterpiece were Bérulle and the Oratory, and Saint Sulpice Seminary, which lived within the halo of the berullian school.[9]

a. The Oratorian School. The goal of the Oratory was "to raise up the state of the priesthood" with a program not so much of reform as of sanctification. Its founder, Cardinal de Bérulle (1575–1629), desired to rehabilitate the priesthood in the eyes of the faithful, who feared or faulted priests. Charles de Condren (1588–1641), who succeed Bérulle as superior of the Oratory, was very attentive to the spiritual discipline needed for a minister of God. Saint

John Eudes (1601–1680), an authentic Bérullian, was a man of action and of recognized holiness, a true missionary and the founder of several religious institutes. He dedicated himself to the formation of the clergy. In his mind, the seminary was "a school of piety and an academy of holiness" more than a school of theology.[10] He promoted the annual clergy retreats of eight to ten days.

b. Saint Sulpice. The "Land of Saints," Saint Sulpice is the matrix and the nursery of the French clergy. The seminary was founded by J. J. Olier (1608–1657), a priest and mystic, a missionary and reformer. With its four communities of seminarians, Saint Sulpice's purpose was the spiritual and theological formation of candidates for the priesthood. The second director of this work was A. de Bretonvilliers (1621–1671), a guardian and faithful interpreter of the apostolic ideal of the founder. However, the pedagogical orientation changed with L. Tronson (1622–1700), who bent sulpician spirituality towards a spiritual and moral psychologism. He attributed the primacy of all priestly virtues to obedience and insisted on the observance of the slightest details of the rules. With the collaboration of Brenier and Baüyn, he founded, around 1684, the "Minor Seminary" for the less fortunate aspirants to the priesthood.[11] He was the superior general when Montfort entered the seminary at Paris. With A. Brenier (1641–1714)—the same priest who tested the vocation of Louis Marie—the psychologism of Tronson attained its greatest development. A true champion of mortification, Brenier enjoyed a reputation of sanctity among the seminarians. J. J. Baüyn (1641–1696), a convert from Calvinsism, displayed another orientation: that of a man "so full of God and so empty of everything else."[12] He had a great esteem for the priesthood which he considered as an angelic dignity and a source of responsibility towards the Church. He renewed in the seminary of Saint Sulpice the examples and the ideals of Olier. Montfort received from Baüyn, his spiritual director from 1692 to 1696, a clear mystical and missionary orientation. Father Leschassier (1641–1725), the successor of Tronson in the direction of Saint Sulpice, was a person of extraordinary virtue enjoying a reputation of prudence and wisdom. Chosen by the seminarian Montfort as spiritual director, he took great interest in Montfort for some time, guiding him along a spiritual and apostolic path.

c. Other artisans. Among those who gave themselves to the formation of the clergy, the figure of Vincent de Paul (1581–1660) stands out. He believed it necessary to give Christian instruction to the poor and therefore, first of all, to reform clerics in order to be able to reach the people through them.[13] Montfort wanted his missionary priests to model themselves on those of Vincent de Paul (RM 7, 66). Claude Poullart des Places (1679–1709), founder of Holy Spirit seminary, dedicated his resources to the support of poor candidates looking for the possibility of studying for the priesthood. Louis Marie de Montfort asked his missionaries of the Company of Mary to prepare themselves both in knowledge and virtue in des Places's seminary in Paris (RM 1). Along with the founders of seminaries are the Jesuits (instituted in 1543) who also collaborated in priestly formation as spiritual directors and in various other ways. They were always the friends of Montfort (TD 161; RM 15, 19).

3. Identity and Mission of the Priest

In the context of the French school, there developed a profound understanding of the nature of the priesthood and its functions. "To govern a soul is to govern the world,"[14] and the sacerdotal mission is to form Christ in souls. The priest is the sacrament of Jesus, the one High Priest. It is in the name of Christ that the priest acts and works, having been clothed with salvific divine authority. In the celebration of the Eucharist, the priest cooperates with God the Father in the Father's glorious generation of the Son in time. The source of the incomprehensible dignity of the priesthood is in its function: priests are called "with reason, not only angels but also gods since they represent, near to us, the immortal power and sublimity of God."[15]

Therefore, a holiness greater than that of a religious is demanded of a priest; his life must be a total immolation. The young aspirant to the priesthood must prepare himself in the house of formation at least like a novice in the cloister pursuing religious life.

At Saint Sulpice the priestly spiritual formation was carried out with vigor. Brenier partially lost the intuition of Olier since he gave so much attention to the smallest practices, to blind obedience, to total disdain of the world; but Baüyn accentuated the responsibility the priest takes on in relation to the mystical Body. *The Treatise on the Duties of a Good Parish Priest* (F. V. Hersé, 1660) exhorts priests in charge of souls to cultivate "the heart of a mother," while Olier himself yearns that the heart of a priest be as large as the Church in the world.

4. The Dimensions of Priestly Spirituality

a. Theocentrism. For Bérulle and his school, priestly spirituality is theocentric: "In the first place, it is absolutely necessary to consider God and not oneself . . . and to act only for the pure honor of God."[16] To be a priest signifies, before all else, to put first in one's own life the love of God and service to one's neighbor. Olier accepted to be a parish priest at the end of a spiritual retreat, during which he consecrated himself to God by a special vow of service towards every member of the Church.

b. Christ the mediator. Bérulle made a vow of perpetual service to Christ-mediator—Son, servant and adorer of the Father—since Jesus himself is "in the service of the Father." Following their founder, the priests of the Oratory pronounced a vow of perpetual service to the Lord. In like manner, Charles de Condren and Olier consecrated themselves to Christ by the formula: "I offer myself in the person of Jesus, perfect victim and faithful servant, to live and to die in following his example, in the continual dispositions of victim and of service."[17] The consecration of oneself in union with Jesus flows from the "*consummatum est*" of the passion and from two sacraments of the covenant: Baptism and Eucharist.

c. Mary. Devotion to the Blessed Mother is one of the great theological themes of the seventeenth century (TD 161). Bérulle's vow of servitude to Mary follows on the vow of service to Jesus Christ, which is theologically founded on the vows of Baptism. Montfort better unites the perspective of Bérulle and identifies consecration to Mary as the perfect renewal of the baptismal promises (TD 120, 162).

Olier, who calls himself a slave of Mary (TD 170), affirms that Our Lady carried in her womb all creatures; in her God forms the Son in all of his extension—Christ the Head and his entire ecclesial body.[18] He decided that the patronal feast of the Sulpician seminary be the Presentation of Mary in the temple, November 21. This is a feast day of the clergy (as is February 2, the Presentation of Jesus in the temple) on which the clergy present at the seminary renewed their priestly promises through the hands of Mary, a practice which Eudes successfully adopted.

Tronson suggested to Montfort that he modify the formula *"slave of Mary* to *slave of Jesus in Mary"* (TD 244).[19] Brenier taught dependence on Our Lady and Baüyn adhered personally to the practice of holy slavery; Leschassier, although not fully adhering to the slavery of love, did profess devotion to Our Blessed Mother. This clear Marian dimension explains the innovation of Charles de Condren and of Olier concerning the celebration of the Eucharist for the intentions of Mary.

d. Mystical orientation. While Olier insisted simultaneously on the mystical and apostolic aspect, the seminary of Saint Sulpice stressed the profound piety required of the minister of God, even if this meant placing limits on preaching and pastoral work. Tronson accentuated the dignity of the priest and his sanctification by means of eucharistic devotion and separation from the world. For him, the observance of the rule is preferable to any personal charisms.[20] Even Bérulle and de Condren, although with different nuances, chose obedience and total oblation to the will of God as the principle of holiness, fed by eucharistic devotion and the Mass, the center of all devotion. Boudon and J. B. Saint-Jure recommended the love of the cross which is the masterpiece of the Wisdom of God.[21] The priest, therefore, must suffer with Christ in order to make reparation with him for sin. Brenier preferred little practices, blind obedience, disdain for the world, and finally, Baüyn enclosed spiritual direction around the Mass, confession, fidelity to the little rules. In conclusion, the new type of priest had to be modest, obedient, charitable, zealous, and pious.

e. Separation from the world. Olier wanted priests to live separated from the world in order to busy themselves only with heavenly realities. Not without reason he requested *"the profession of death to the world, and the profession of the folly of the gospel."*[22] Leschassier echoes his sentiments in recommending to the priest trained at St. Sulpice seminary the love of a life withdrawn from the world, consumed in eucharistic adoration, and in the service of the liturgy: outside of his own community, the priest is in a frightful state and far from his own center. He taught that "suffering is worth more than acting."[23] The perfection of the priesthood consisted above all in abnegation: he will be attentive to the rule and, if necessary, keep in check pastoral work.

II. Montfort, a Priest Both Mystic And Missionary

1. As seminarian and young priest

a. At Rennes (1684–1692). In 1684, Louis Marie entered the college of the Jesuits at Rennes and for eight consecutive years followed the complete course of the humanities. The college counted about two thousand students, all non-boarders, and from a variety of social backgrounds. The courses were free. The spiritual director, Father Descartes, opened up to the young Louis Marie the ideal of divine love which is to be found in abandonment of any human supports. The example and the conferences of J. Bellier oriented him towards the service of the poor,[24] an apostolate made even more attractive by the example of his uncle priests, Gilles and Alain Robert. Contact with Father Provost and his friendship with his fellow student, Claude Poullart des Places, developed within him devotion to the Virgin Mary.

During this period, an ideal of piety and of apostolic commitment in the context of evangelical poverty and mortification begin to mature in Montfort. The priestly vocation appeared to him not like climbing the ladder to a higher social class that enjoys special privileges, but as a ministry lived in poverty and in abandonment to Providence. He had already left his family in order to seek virtue and to serve God freely.[25]

b. At Saint Sulpice in Paris. In 1692, at the age of 19, Louis Grignion went to Paris in order to prepare for the priesthood. He was welcomed among *"the poor students"* of Claude Bottu de la Barmondière and then among those of Father Boucher, where the extreme poverty touched on misery. As if in compensation, their love for studies was intense. Finally, he was admitted to the Little Seminary of Saint Sulpice, which was reserved for students with little or no money. He began his theological studies at the Sorbonne, but chose to continue his education at the seminary itself: he intended to study exclusively because of his yearning for God.[26] He never did doctoral work for he chose to remain among "the simple folk": he would be a preacher to the masses, while also being "a humanist and poet, . . . a master of classical language."[27] At the seminary, he was given the task of librarian, a charge which gave him the opportunity of reading and transcribing into his notebook many citations concerning Christ and the Virgin Mary. It also was the occasion to begin composing hymns, which he would utilize in his future apostolate.

In the course of these eight years, during which he matured in his desire for missionary life, he intensified his prayer and mortification and deepened his devotion to Mary, who would guide his spiritual life and ministry. While assimilating the works of certain masters of spirituality, he was distancing himself—without even realizing it—from the orientation of Tronson, so measured, so filled with prudence and moderation.

2. Priestly Life

In June, 1700, Louis Marie was ordained a priest. His priestly life would unfold for a period of sixteen years. After a rather slow beginning, which lasted six years, and a pilgrimage to Rome (1706), where the Holy Father named him "missionary apostolic," he at last became the preacher of parish missions in the west of France.

a. Priest, both mystic and missionary. After leaving Saint Sulpice, where he felt as though he were living "in a shell" (L 4), Montfort passed from contemplative spirituality—to be more precise, the spirituality of the hidden life of the seminary—to an apostolic spirituality. He refused all offers to be part of the formation team in charge of seminarians, so that he could fully dedicate himself to catechizing and preaching. In the eyes of Montfort, the apostolic life is not a danger, but a means of holiness and of growth in perfection (H 22:23). He began his apostolate in the midst of the rejects of Poitiers society at the city hospice. With the permission of the bishop he went to Paris, where he experienced absolute solitude and total abandonment to Providence. During the summer of 1703, in a closet under the stairway of Pot-du-fer Street in Paris, while he deepened his thought on Wisdom, he discovered again his vocation as an itinerant missionary and he balanced his yearning for a hidden life with his missionary calling. He liberated himself from scrupulous subjection to a multitude of little obligations in order to give priority to the interior movements of the spirit. He thereby restored the mystical and missionary value of the priesthood: he immersed himself in the midst of society even if it were at the price of an extremely poor life and subject to misunderstandings and persecutions.[28]

b. Christ Wisdom and devotion to Mary. "*I have espoused Wisdom and the cross where are all my treasures*" (L 20), Father Louis Marie wrote to his mother on August 28, 1704. The mystical marriage with Christ, Wisdom crucified, constituted henceforth the foundation of his prayer; even his innate "singularity" was now defined as a "wisdom." In reality, the way or path of Jesus Wisdom was illuminated by a secret: the maternal presence of Mary permitted him to live the "*slavery of love*" as the offering of his own life to God. He thus conformed himself to the obedience of the Son of God continuing in his flesh the offering of Jesus, who wished to depend on his Mother. The art of living was based on an abandonment or forgetfulness of self. The soul, stripped of everything but regenerated in the womb of Mary, received the characteristics of the Lord, the crucified servant. Living with Jesus in Mary, Montfort the priest accepted the rigorous discipline of renouncing his own will in order to live as the humble sacrament of ecclesial service.

c. Poverty. The discovery of Christ Wisdom led Montfort the priest to abandon himself to Providence in voluntary poverty, which he believed necessary both for the spiritual life and for the apostolate (H 22:1). The poor priest is a king who is filled with the possession of God (PM 25; ACM 5:7; TD 135) and enriched with spiritual goods. Poverty is a free choice in a social and ecclesiastical system which could strongly affect his priestly life.[29] Following the example of J. B. de la Salle, he refused a canonry which Madame de Montespan offered him (L 6:9) and he affirmed that he would never exchange Providence for any benefice (L 6) because, so he wrote, *"If God has risked his life, should not I risk mine?"* (LPM 6; cf. H 91:6).

Love for poverty called him to the service of the outcasts. In March 1704, the poor of Poitiers welcomed him with a great festival. He was as poor as the poor; he dressed and ate like them and became a beggar for them. On their part, they never hesitated to proclaim him "their true priest." They defined him, so to speak, as "the one who so loves the poor."[30] Gifted with the grace to touch hearts, "he possesses a heart so tender that it is found in none other." He took care of the poor and the rejects of society with the hands of a mother: he is "the good Father from Montfort."

d. Pastoral sense. He not only esteemed catechizing, preaching, and the renewal of the vows of baptism by the means of slavery of love, but Montfort also revealed gifts of being a missionary organizer and an innovator in pastoral work. He restored churches, erected crosses and calvaries, painted banners, organized processions and pilgrimages, instituted or restored confraternities (L 11 and n. 1), founded religous communities, composed methods of popular prayer, and wrote hymns to be sung during the celebrations of the mission. In sum: he constructed a method of preaching and a style of pastoral work unique in their form and content.[31]

3. Relations with the Clergy of His Day

In general, Louis Marie was not accepted by the bourgeois and lay world. That should not surprise anyone; but what does cause surprise are the disputes and frequent refusals on the part of different bishops, of priests and even of his friends and collaborators who became hostile or even defiant. Some examples stand out: Leschassier, his director, who pushed him aside without listening to him; or Blain, who, when accusing him of wanting to canonize his own ideas, begged him to be more condescending to the common rules of social life.

Montfort was rebuffed by the well-settled clergy because of his "singularity,"[32] misunderstood because of his evangelical radicalism. In reality, he was a priest who was upsetting and disturbing,[33] for the very reason of his "originality" which followed him everywhere. Up to the end, he carried with him the hair shirt of his singularity. But to be singular is his wisdom, which makes him apt to preach *"like the apostles"* (RM 60–61).

He sought especially in his last years to converse and collaborate with everyone, even if for a poor priest like him there was no institutional mediation that could protect him. It is not without reason that he describes himself like a ball in a game of tennis: *no sooner am I hurled to one side than I am whacked back to the other"* (L 26).

By conscious choice, he tended to dissociate himself from priests who loved tranquility and a sedentary life (RM 2, 12; L 5), from fashionable preachers who actually did no more than beat the breeze (RM 2, 60), from priests quite secure and worldly (RM 6). We can then understand more easily his reply to Blain: *"Let me walk in my own way; more so because it is the road which Jesus Christ taught by his example and his counsels."*[34] He himself chose his own collaborators, priests, and lay people,[35] and he invited good priests everywhere to unite with him in his missions (L 5; PM 29).

III. The Priest in the Thought of Montfort

1. Jesus, Priest and Victim

According to the French School, Jesus is the true and principal priest since he is the mediator and the victim, the offerer and the victim of God most high. For Louis de Montfort, Christ is the high priest who enters and leaves this world by the eastern gate who is Mary (TD 262). In the Wisdom of the Cross (LEW 159; FC 45; H 19:1), Jesus is the priest and victim who offers himself to the Father by the hands of Mary. In truth, God the Son wanted his Mother present at Calvary in order to be able *"to make with him but one and the same sacrifice and in order to be immolated by her consent to the eternal Father as formerly Isaac was offered by the consent of Abraham to the will of God. It is Mary who fed him, nourished him, took care of him, raised him and sacrificed him for us"* (TD 18; cf. LG 61).

2. The Type of Priest Desired by Montfort

Having assimilated sulpician spirituality in the line of Olier, Montfort considered as central in the life of a priest the sacrament of the altar: the celebration of Mass (L 33), thanksgiving, preparation for the Eucharist, administration of Communion (S 338). He is conscious of the sacerdotal commitment required by the sacrament of Confession (RM 56, 58–59). Naturally, the sacramental life is accompanied and preceded by the preaching of the word of God (RM 2, 50, 60–65; H 22), to which Montfort gives priority in his pastoral method. He therefore asks God to raise up poor missionaries, courageous and disinterested (PM 21). The type of priest that Montfort yearned for had to be a missionary (L 5), a preacher according to divine Wisdom (LEW 97; H 4:12), one who gives to souls the Word Incarnate.

Six months after his ordination—December, 1700—he begged God to create *"a little and poor company"* of itinerant apostles who, free from the system of benefices, live abandoned to Providence (L5, 6; RM 7, 19; LS 320).[36] They are to be priests filled with fire who, like the apostles (RM 2), dedicate themselves to preaching the word in order to renew the spirit of christianity. He requests from them a style of life that corresponds to their commitments: they are to love the Eucharist (RM 30), to obey the bishops (RM 22), not to accept parishes (RM 2), to fly from a sedentary and quiet life in community (RM 7, 66). Above all, the members of the community must cultivate study and prayer in order to taste and to make others taste the divine word (RM 60). In conclusion, the missionary priest as seen by Montfort *"leads a life so poor, so hard, so abandoned to Providence,"* that such a life is not possible except for *"extraordinary men."*[37]

Montfort also treats of "wicked" priests of his time: *"ministers who are poor in the midst of the great divine treasures"* (LS 296), who consider the priesthood a means of obtaining honors and fortune; fashionable preachers—false prophets—who trust in their own capabilities. The good priests—good preachers (RM 61–65) formed and inspired by Wisdom (LEW 47, 90, 119, 122), worthy ministers who uphold the Church by the holiness of their life (S 290)—should not mix in with them (H 32, 31, 34).

3. The Offering of the Eucharist in Union with Mary

The Marian dimension of priestly spirituality of the French School has already been touched upon. Against this background, Montfort does not speak of the priesthood of Mary; he does declare that she has immolated and sacrificed her Son by her loving surrender, by *"her consent to the eternal Father"* (TD 18). This thought is based upon F. Poiré and also Bernardine of Paris (N 285–92), authors who deepened the theme of communion with Mary at the moment when the priest at the Eucharist receives the body of her Son in sacramental communion.[38] The innovation of founding masses to be applied to the intentions of Mary comes directly from Charles de Condren: only this godlike Mother is prepared to offer Christ in a continual, new, and perfect manner.[39] Olier spread this practice, exhorting priests to offer Mass—especially on Saturdays—for the intentions of Mary. He disclosed that it was the Mother of the Lord herself who requested this service.[40]

Montfort says nothing explicitly concerning this, but he does write that because of Our Lady's hypothetically necessary *fiat,* Christ immolates himself by means of Mary (H 49:3) from the beginning of redemption, since his sacrifice to the Father begins at the incarnation in the womb of his Mother. He teaches that by consecration to Jesus through Mary, one entrusts to Mary the liberty, the rights and the merits of one's soul, since she is the depository of spiritual goods (SM 40; TD 176, 216) and the treasury of all divine grace (LEW 207; SM 19; TD 24, 28, 44, 206, 20).

He declares that the consecration to Jesus through Mary respects the obligations of a priest who has to celebrate Mass for a particular intention (TD 124; cf. H 139:18). Granted that the Eucharist of the priest continues the one and the same sacrifice of Christ, the Son of Mary, it could be held that it is according to the spirit of Montfort to celebrate the Eucharist, in the measure that is possible, for the intentions of Our Lady.

4. The Universal Priesthood

Montfort treats only in an indirect manner of baptismal priesthood. Moreover, this theme does not appear, at least in any explicit fashion, in the writings of the masters of the French School (although Bérulle, in his *Rule of the Oratory* makes allusion to the priesthood of the faithful[41]). In the thought of Olier, the priest is quite different from a lay person. And Montfort, following his masters on this point, copied a note in his *Book of Sermons* which declared that the minister of God is above the people (LS 295, 298).

However. there is another affirmation of Bérulle, upheld in part by Olier and even by Quesnel, which says, "Each christian can and must offer his very self at the Mass."[42] This assertion is, perhaps, a reaction to the Protestant critique which, basing itself on 1 Pt 2:5.9; 1 Cor 12:12–27, undervalues the hierarchical priesthood defining it as a "specialized caste."[43] Catholics did not completely reject the Protestant affirmations, but they affirmed that the priest does not bear the title of "priest" *(sacerdos)* except in Christ and through Christ, the one priest of the NT; one theologian stressed the scriptural appellation "royal priesthood," applying it to all the faithful.[44] Montfort does the same when he directly refers to the royal priesthood: *"You are a chosen race, the royal priesthood"* (FC 4) and *"You are kings and priests of God . . . by your christianity and your priesthood"* (LCM 5). The Friends of the Cross, therefore, are within royal priesthood of the Lord.

The baptismal priesthood in Montfort is articulated in the context of the universal vocation to holiness (FC 28; SM 2–5; LS 169–80): the word of God, by the Incarnation, has come to divinize the human race, the masterpiece of His hands, and to take to himself a holy people (TD 68; LS 170).

The pastoral method of Montfort the priest must not be neglected. In his missions he had the simple people participate materially and economically and also in liturgical or devotional collaboration which he requests of the people (Mass and Communion, processions, hymns, Rosary, and especially the renewal of the vows of Baptism in the Covenant Contract). Nonetheless, the substantial difference remains between the hierarchical priesthood and the universal priesthood. But Montfort considers the dignity of the priest from a pastoral point of view, that is to say, in service to the people. He does not speculate on the priesthood in itself and never considers the priesthood as founding the specialized and privileged caste of ecclesiastics. The dignity Montfort attributes to the baptized heightens the worth of both the universal priesthood and of the ministerial priesthood.

It should be remembered that as a priest, Montfort belonged to the first estate; he had contacts with the nobility, the second estate; his family was of the bourgeoisie; yet he freely opted to identify with the common people, and especially with the poorest of the poor.

IV. The Priestly Dimension in Montfort Spirituality

Montfort did not develop the sacerdotal dimension of Christian spirituality, although he did indicate its substance in delineating the practical realites of living the consecration to Christ through Mary. Today, this dimension must be explicitated not only for ordained priests (for the baptismal promises cannot be separated from priestly promises), but also for each Christian called through Baptism to participate in Christ's prophetic and royal sacerdotal dignity. The exercise of this priestly function unites both ordained ministers and other faithful with the heavenly priesthood of Christ and with the glorious heavenly community, in the midst of which emerges the figure of the Mother of Jesus.

1. Vows of Baptism and Priestly Promises

Saint John Eudes taught that baptismal life prolongs in the faithful the Incarnation, or sacerdotal life of Christ. The sulpician school affirmed that through Baptism all are inserted into Christ the priest. In order to make Christ the priest live in Christians—priests of God by Baptism (LCM 5)—Montfort prescribes the renewal of baptismal promises as the conclusion of the parish mission (CG; RM 56). The Sacrament of Orders (episcopacy, priesthood, diaconate) consecrates certain Christians as ministers of Christ-Priest so that the baptized, by the intermediary of the ordained ministry, may live their royal priesthood.

But what relation is there between the baptismal vows and the presbyteral promises? The renewal of the baptismal promises has for its goal to make Christians live as daughters and sons of God (H 109:8), to make them living members of the Body of Christ (TD 68; LS 158–68), to help them to become servants and collaborators of the Spirit (TD 73, 126). The priestly promises—Montfort does not speak precisely of them—require celibacy (in the Latin rite), obedience to and collaboration with the bishops, the ministry of the word, the celebration of the mysteries of Christ, particularly the Eucharist and sacramental reconciliation, the ministry of prayer and a more intense union with Christ, the supreme pastor and sovereign priest.[45]

The two types of promises are complementary precisely because they are functionally diverse. The ordained ministers are exhorted to live their priestly promises generously in order to announce and celebrate the Lord, so that the duties of sacramental life and the gift of prayer may be awakened in the faithful. In this manner, because they are baptized, the faithful are assured of their rights as daughters and sons of God, i.e., the right to the food of the word, of the Eucharist, of the sacrifice of praise, and of the gift of evangelical fraternity. These rights of the faithful are at times neglected by priests who lack a mystical and missionary spirit, and are perhaps little known by Christians, because the consecrated ministers do not always wholly realize their sacerdotal promises.

In other words, the renewal of the promises of Baptism recall to the baptised that they are daughters and sons of God and that because of this title they have taken on certain precise duties. The promises of the priesthood recall to the priest that he is minister for people: his rights as son of God have now become for him inescapable duties towards all the people of God.

2. Baptismal Life and Sacerdotal Commitment

Preaching, since the Council of Trent, stresses the vows of Baptism. The grace of Baptism and the sacraments connected with it must, as a consequence, be "re-newed." During the parish missions, Montfort made certain that the faithful renew their baptismal promises after having confessed their sins and received communion (RM 56, 90). To live baptism—particularly after the renewal of Vatican II—signifies renewing the strength of the three sacraments of Christian initiation: Baptism, Confirmation, Eucharist. These sacraments are distinct but inseparable and also inclusive of sacramental reconciliation.

The text of the consecratory prayer of priestly ordination says: *"Innova in visceribus eorum spiritum sanctitatis"*[46] (Renew, Lord, in their hearts your spirit of holiness), an evident allusion to the sacerdotal spirit already received in the three sacraments of initiation. This happy theological rediscovery of the sacerdotal meaning of Christian initiation has again placed before the eyes of the Church its "ministerial" vocation, a ministry exercised in the sacrament of service: fruit, in its turn, of an precise option, the Church wants to be poor in order to serve people.

3. Mary, Bearer of the Priestly Spirit of the Risen Christ

Mary, Mother of Christ, chief and sovereign priest, also becomes, by the new Passover, Mother of the members of the Body of the Church (cf. Jn 19:26–27). Now into this line of thought, Olier, who called for the reform of priestly orders to renew the entire church, projected a Marian solution: in the Cenacle, Mary did not receive the sacrament of priesthood but the Spirit and apostolic grace.[47] In the Cenacle, therefore, the Virgin Mary, as the queen of the apostoles (PO 18), is the bearer of the priestly spirit of the risen Christ (AA 1:14).

In his historical Incarnation, the Lord received from his Mother the capacity to be a priest of the Father (TD 18, 63, 246–48, 261–64; H 49:3, 90:15);[48] a priest who announces the gospel of grace, who offers his own body at the sacrifice of the cross and as supreme Shepherd, leads all back to divine life.

In the sacramental economy, the Lord exercises His eternal priesthood in the person of ordained ministers. Yet before there is ministerial priesthood, the Virgin Mary conceives the Christ, the first priest of the new covenant. Mary is the perfect type of God's priestly people.[49] Proclaimed by Paul VI "Mother of the faithful and of pastors,"[50] she is the aid of priests (PO 18; OT 8) and the pure mirror who illumines the triple sacerdotal ministry.

a. Mary accepts the salvific word and responds by the self-offering and sacrificial *fiat*. During the public ministry of her Son, she follows him as a pilgrim of faith (LG 58; MC 17; RMat 2), up to her courageous presence near the cross and the sepulchre. In the Magnificat, she proclaims "the marvelous works," historical and salvific, realized in her (Lk 1:46–55). And after the Resurrection and Ascension of her Son, she listens to the teaching of the apostles[51] and praises God in tongues for the mysteries accomplished in the world (AA 2:4).

b. Associated with her Son in the redemptive work (LG 55-62; MC 20), she offers herself together with Christ priest and victim, in the presentation in the temple, at the paschal supper and next to the cross. Prophetically, at the marriage feast of Cana, she anticipated the paschal mandate of her Son ("Do this in memory of me" [Lk 22:19]) when she says to the servants: "What ever he will say to you, do it" (Jn 2:5).

c. After Easter she does not return to Nazareth near the family clan, but remains in the Cenacle as a vigilant and attentive mother of the new family of the Savior here on earth (MC 18). And above all else, she, Spirit-bearer, directs all to the Spirit, source of filial life and of unity in the Church. Among the promises of Baptism, there should be included today the fidelity to the Spirit who is affirmed in the pentecostal sacrament of confirmation.

4. The Heavenly Priesthood

Jesus, supreme and eternal priest (Heb 4:15–26, 9:11, 10:21), is the heavenly God-Man who offers himself as a perpetual oblation to the Father and prepares for his disciples a royal dwelling place (Jn 14:2-4).

Glorious woman, clothed with the sun that never sets (Rev 12:1–6) and royal gate of heaven, the Holy Mother is the throne of Incarnate Wisdom. While from her virginal bosom she presents her Savior Son to all, she always addresses to them this pressing appeal: "Come and contemplate the Christ!," glorious icon of the Father; "come and listen to the Master!" word of life; "come, eat the body and drink the blood of Christ!" in the banquet of the eschatological wedding feast (Rev 19:7–9, 21:9, 22:17–20).

Like an "angel at the altar,"[52] Montfort, priest both mystic and missionary, emerges from the depths of three centuries as a prophetic voice that proclaims *"the infinite treasure of the eucharist"* (L 33), the salvific value of the preaching of the word, the love of the Eternal and Incarnate Wisdom who is in his person, Kingdom of Heaven (cf. LEW 193).

Disciple of the Master of divine Wisdom (1 Cor 1:24) and at the school of Mary (MC 21), the priest is identified to the Lord who is superior to the angels (Heb 1:4). "Christian with christians and priest for them,"[53] he is the minister of the Eucharistic table in the assembly of the Lord, the pastor who increases the joy of the brethren (2 Cor 1:24), the guide of the elect towards the heavenly home.

The celebration of the supper of the Lord extends to infinity the sacrifice of earthly and heavenly salvation until the Savior has raised all men to himself in the bosom of the Father (Jn 12:32). The sacramental life, the liturgy of praise, the Marian dimension of Christian life (RM 45–46) prolong the incarnation of the Word, give the irresistible breath of the Spirit, and make the Father of mercies known. So the faithful—baptized, confirmed, and Eucharist-fed—with Jesus, supreme priest of their faith (Heb 3:1) and illuminated by Mary, the Woman clothed with the sun, call everyone to the house of the Lord so that all may eternally glorify the universal Father in the temple of His glory (PM 30).

S. Gaspari

Notes: (1) R. Deville, "L'École française de spiritualité" (The French School of Spirituality), *Bibliothèque d'histoire du christianisme* 11, Desclée, Paris 1987, 9, 139—citing H. Bremond—affirms that Louis de Montfort is the last of the greast Bérullians. (2) Cf. P. Lafue, *Le prêtre ancien et les commencements du nouveau prêtre. De la contre-réforme à l'aggiornamento* (The Priest of Former Days and the Beginnings of the Priest of Today. From the Counter-Reformation to the Aggiornamento), Plon, Toulouse 1967, 65–74. (3) R. Deville, *L'École française,* 15–27. (4) In relation to "the great century of french spirituality" or "the great century of souls", cf. J. Le Brun, *France,* VI: *Le grand siècle et ses lendemains.* (France, VI: The 'grand siècle' and its Tomorrows) DSAM 5 (1964) 917–53; R. Deville, *L'École française,* 7–13 (5) Cf. *Vincent de Paul* in R. Deville, *L'École française,* 18. (6) Citation in P. Pierrard, *Le prêtre français* (The French Priest), 26. On the "bad priests" and "clericalism, here is the enemy," cf. ibid., 5. (7) Concerning the improvement of the clergy during the reign of Louis XV and at the eve of the French revolution, cf. P. Pierrard, *Le prêtre français,* 49–54. For the situation of clerics before the Council of Trent, cf. P. Lafue, *Le prêtre ancien,* 15–32 et passim. On the subject of the deplorable state of priests in France around 1600, cf. M. Dupuy, "Bérulle et le sacerdoce. Étude historique et doctrinale. Textes inédits" (Bérulle and the priesthood. Historical and Doctrinal Study. Unpublished Texts), *Bibliothèque d'histoire et d'archéologie chrétienne* 7, Lethielleux, Paris 1969, 31–42;. (8) Cf. de Paul, dans P. Pierrard, *Le prêtre français,* 26–29. (9) For the reformers of the French clergy, see, *Le prêtre français,* 21–42; R. Deville, *L'École française,* 23–27;. (10) Text of J. Eudes in P. Pierrard, *Le prêtre français,* 37. (11) The price of room and board was the only difference between the two institutions. (12) Blain 48; cf. De Fiores, 191–203. (13) The precise text of Vincent de Paul as related by P. Perrard, *Le prêtre français,* 29: "If it is such a great undertaking to instruct the poor . . . it is still more important to instruct clerics since, if they are ignorant, the people they lead will also necessarily be ignorant." (14) R. Deville, *L'École française,* 120; cf. 101–23. (15) *Catechismus ex decretis concilii tridentini ad parochos* (Catechism from the Decrees of the Council of Trent for Pastors) Regensburg 1896, II, 7.2. Concerning the dignity of the priest, cf. M. Dupuy, *Bérulle et le sacerdoce,* 131–38, 165–67, 176–77 et passim; concerning the identity and the mission of the priest according to the French School, cf. J. Galy, *Le sacrifice,* analytical index, 397–99; R. Deville, *L'École française,* 25–27, 113–17. (16) H. Bremond, *Histoire littéraire du sentiment religieux,* (Literary History of Religious Sentiment) 3. *La conquête mystique: l'École française* (The Mystical Conquest: The French School), Bloud et Gay, Paris 1923, 29. (17) E.-M. Faillon, *Vie de Monsieur Olier, fondateur du Séminaire de Saint-Sulpice,* (The Life of Monsieur Olier, Founder of the Seminary of Saint Sulpice) 3, Poussielgue-Wattelier, Paris 1873, 193; cf. I. Noye-M. Dupuy, *Olier,* DSAM 11 (1982) 744; cf. 740–45. (18) Cf. E. Théorêt, *La médiation mariale dans l'École française* (The Mediation of Mary According to the French School), Vrin, Paris 1940, 32. According to Olier, the Virgin Mary is both the one who inspired the seminary and its queen. Cf. E.-M. Faillon, *Vie de Monsieur Olier,* 3, 62–67. The Mariology of the French School takes its definitive form from the founder of Saint Sulpice. Cf. P. Pourrat, *La dévotion à Marie dans la compagnie de Saint-Sulpice,* in *Maria* (du Manoir) 3, 153–62; R. Laurentin, *Maria. Ecclesia. Sacerdotium. Essai sur le développement d'une idée religieuse* (Mary. Church. Priesthood. Essay on the development of a Religious Idea), Nouvelles Éditions Latines, Paris 1952, 341–84. On Marian devotion in seventeenth century France, cf. J. Le Brun, *France,* DSAM 5 (1964) 944–45. (19) Cf. Blain, 50. The term "slaves of Jesus in Mary" is clearly an authentic Bérullian and Sulpician expression. (20) Cf. J. Gauthier, *Ces messieurs de Saint-Sulpice* (These Priests of Saint Sulpice), Fayard, Paris 1957, 48. For a rather complete idea of the lifestyle at the Seminary of Saint Sulpice during the time of Father L. Tronson, cf. De Fiores, 155–58, with particular attention to the notes, taken from the archives of Saint Sulpice. (21) Cf. H.-M. Boudon, *Les saintes voies de la croix,* (The Holy Roads of the Cross) in *Oeuvres complètes,* 2, Migne, Paris 1856, 109–12; J.-B. Saint-Jure, *De la connaissance et de l'amour du Fils de Dieu Notre Seigneur Jésus Chris,* (On the Knowledge and Love of the Son of God, Our Lord Jesus Christ), Mabre-Cramoisy, Paris 1688, 21, 33–35; G. Rossetto, *La Sapienza è la Croce* (Wisdom and the Cross), in Collectif, *La missione monfortana ieri e oggi. Atti del 2° Convegno intermonfortano* (The Montfort Mission Yesterday and Today. Acts of the Second Intermontfortian Reunion) (Rome, September 5-8, 1984), QM 2 (1985) 42–56. (22) Cf. De Fiores, 154, 189. Leschassier sought a life style that was death to the world and to its spirit: ibid., 232. (23) Ibid., 228, 232, 164–65. Terms like "self-emptying," "immolation," "mortification," and "death to human nature" reveal a pessimistic understanding of man. On this point, cf. R. Deville, *L'École française,* 173–75; De Fiores, 101–106, 271, 282. Montfort himself is well aware of human weakness and fragility (cf. L 12, 32; PE 26). But human nature is restored by God through the gift of creative Wisdom (cf. ASE 90–100). On the original beauty of nature, cf. H 157: "New Hymnn on Solitude." (24) Concerning Bellier, cf. R. Deville, *L'École française,* 140–141; De Fiores, Itinerario 78–80, 267, 277. On the poverty of Montfort, who even as a youth was totally abandoned to Divine Providence, cf. Grandet, 349–50. (25) Cf. Blain, 16 17. (26) Blain, 46; Grandet, 13–14. (27) B. Papàsogli, *L'homme venu du vent. Saint Louis-Marie Grignion de Montfort*, Bellarmin, Montréal 1984, 282. English Translation, Montfort, A Prophet for our Times, Edizioni Monfortane, Rome 1991. On Montfort the writer, cf. J. Fréneau, *Saint Louis-Marie de Montfort écrivain* (Saint Louis Marie de Montfort, Writer), DMon 47 (1972) 1–16. (28) Concerning Montfort's understanding of the priesthood, cf. De Fiores, Itinerario 188–89; on his break with Saint Sulpice cf. 258–64. (29) Responding to a pastor who wanted to know who he was, Montfort replied: "I am a poor priest who goes up and down the highways of this world searching for souls" (Clorivière, 418). (30) J.-M. Quérard, *Vie du bienheureux Louis-Marie Grignion de Montfort* (Life of Blessed Louis Marie de Montfort) 2, Rennes-Paris-Nantes 1887, 278; cf. *Letter of the Poor of the Poitiers Hospital to Father Leschassier*, in De Fiores, Itinerario 281. (31) Cf. Grandet, 465; S. De Fiores, *La «missione» nell'itinerario spirituale apostolico di s. Luigi-Maria da Montfort* ("Mission" In the Apostolic Spiritual Itinerary of Saint Louis de Montfort), QM 2 (1985) 17–41; R. Mandrou, *Montfort et l'évangélisation du peuple* (Montfort and the Evangelization of People), RMon 11 (1974) 1–19. (32) When B. Papàsogli asks if the singularity of Montfort is a charism, she replies that in any case, grace did make up for certain deficiencies of nature. (*L'homme venu du vent,* 99; cf. also 93–107, 281; De Fiores, Itinerario 38, 189, 225–27, 275–77). On this subject, cf. the conversation of Montfort with Blain in September, 1714: Blain, 185–90. (33) Cf. P. L. Nava, *Un prete scomodo* (A Troubled Priest), *Madre e Regina* 42 (1989) 11, ii–iv; S. Gaspari, *La scelta missionaria del Montfort* (The Missionary Choice of Montfort), *Madre e Regina* 40 (1986) 2, 5–6. (34) Blain, 186. In N 306, Louis Marie wrote: "What makes a Christian is the Spirit of Christ, the Spirit's strength and life." (35) For example, he chose A. Vatel (d. 1748) the first priest of the Company of Mary: originally assigned to the foreign missions, he was called by Montfort to follow him; he also called Brother Nicholas who accompanied him on his missions until the saint's death. (cf. L 11; T). (36) Clorivière, 310–11 declares that the Company of Mary is distinguished from other communities by "a truly apostolic perfection." (37) Blain, 185–86. (38) For F. Poiré, cf. R. Laurentin, *Maria, Ecclesia, Sacerdotium,* 259–61, 265, 355, 389, 633, 635. For Bernardine of Paris, 284–88, 221–22. (39) Charles de Condren's explanatory text is: "I place her Son, Jesus Christ, into the hands (of Mary) by this foundation, inasmuch as I can, and I beg her with my whole heart to offer it herself to God in this daily sacrifice as she does offer it and has offered it, in time and in eternity, on earth as in heaven." Cf. J. Galy, *Le sacrifice,* 256n. 40. (40) Ibid., 256, 326. (41) The annotation on the priesthood of the faithful is the work of Bourgoing, cf. J. Galy, *Le sacrifice,* 90. (42) Ibid., 354. (43) Cf. P. Pierrard, *Le prêtre français,* 10–13; J. M. R. Tillard, *Sacerdoce,* DSAM 14 (1988) 27–31. (44) D. Soto, *De iustitia et iure* (On Justice and Right) VII, 5, 1, Lyon 1559, upholds that the laity are priests but in a lower way. (45) Cf. Pontificale Romanum, *De ordinatione episcopi, presbyterorum et diaconorum,* Editio typica altera, Typis Polyglottis Vaticanis 1990: promises of the bishop, 40–42; of priests, 60–62; of the deacon, 108–110. (46) Ibid., 75. (47) On Olier, cf. S. De Fiores, *Itinerario,* 187. Concerning the theme of 'Virgo Sacerdos' in the spirituality of the French School, cf. R. Laurentin, *Maria, Ecclesia, Sacerdotium,* 375–82. (48) Cf. E. Campana, *Maria nel culto cattolico,* 2. *Il culto di Maria nelle devozioni particolari, nei sodalizi e nei congressi mariani* (Mary in Catholic Devotion, 2. Marian Devotion in Particular Devotions, in the Marian Sodalities and Congresses) Marietti, Torino-Roma 1933, 726; R. Laurentin, *Maria, Ecclesia, Sacerdotium,* 294–304. (49) On Mary *Typus Ecclesiae*, cf. LG 63 (which cites Saint Ambrose); MC 16; RM 44; I. Biffi, *Maria tipo della Chiesa popolo sacerdotale,* (Mary, type of the Church, A Priestly People) in *La Madonna* 30 (1982) 70. (50) Paul VI, *Discours au terme de la troisième session du concile Vatican II* (Discourse at the Closing of the Third Session of Vatican Council II), (Novenber 21, 1964), AAS 56 (1964) 1015. (51) Saint Ambrose relates that Mary learned from the pastors of the Church and constantly paid attention to the apostolic directions: *In Ev. Lucae Hom.* 2, 54, in PL 15, 1572B; cf. S. Gaspari, *Lettura mistagogica di testi biblici per la mariologia* (Mystagogical Reading of Biblical Texts For Mariology), Regina mundi Institute , Rome 1986, 227–67 (manuscript) (52) Blain, 105–106. (53) The expression recalls the celebrated text of Saint Augustine: «Vobis enim sum episcopus, vobiscum sum christianus» ("For you I am a bishop, with you I am a Christian"), *Disc. 340,* 1: *In die ordinationis suae,* PL 38, 1483.

PROVIDENCE

SUMMARY

I. PROVIDENCE IN ITSELF.

II. MONTFORT'S LITTLE TREATISE ON PROVIDENCE:
1. The definition of providence;
2. The existence of providence;
3. The extent of providence;
4. Confidence in providence;
5. Qualities of trust in providence;
6. Final Prayer and Resolution;
7. Conclusion.

III. THE ROLE OF PROVIDENCE IN THE LIFE OF SAINT LOUIS DE MONTFORT:
1. Years preceding his ordination:
   a. His departure from Rennes;
   b. Trust in the midst of difficulties;
   c. Life of surrender to providence.
2. Priestly life:
   a. The Founder;
   b. Pilgrimage to Rome;
   c. Contradictions on all sides;
   d. Living by providence;
   e. Necessity of work.

IV. PROVIDENCE IN THE WRITINGS OF SAINT LOUIS DE MONTFORT:
1. Letters,
2. True Devotion and Secret of Mary:
   a. Mary's role in God's care of the universe;
   b. The consecration.
3. The Rules;

V. RELEVANCE OF MONTFORT'S TEACHING ON PROVIDENCE:
1. Insistence on the grandeur of God;
2. Abandonment to God's will;
3. The need for human response.

All agree that Providence plays a principal if not dominant role in the spirituality of Saint Louis de Montfort. His well known phrase, *"Whatever happens I shall not be worried. I have a Father in heaven who cannot fail me"* (L 2), typifies his entire life. It can be said that trust in Providence is so profound in Montfort's being that it forms a constitutive element of his personality. After a brief review of Church doctrine on the subject, the saint's teaching on Providence will be summarized by first examining his canticle treatise on the subject, then by studying his life of abandonment to divine

Providence, and finally, by investigating the emphasis on Providence in some of his writings.

I. Providence in Itself

"The universe was created in a 'state of journeying' *(in statu viae)* toward an ultimate perfection yet to be attained, to which God has destined it. We call 'divine Providence' the dispositions by which God guides his creation toward this perfection: 'By his Providence God protects and governs all things which he has made, 'reaching mightily from one end of the earth to the other and ordering all things well.' For 'all are open and laid bare to his eyes,' even those things which are yet to come into existence through the free action of creatures.'"[1]

Providence is, then, the concrete and immediate solicitude of God the creator, present and dynamically active at the most profound roots of everything which exists. The Catechism of the Catholic Church strongly declares that "the sacred books powerfully affirm God's absolute sovereignty over the course of events: 'Our God is in the heavens; he does whatever he pleases' (Ps 115:3). And so it is with Christ, 'who opens and no one shall shut, who shuts and no one opens' (Rev 3:7). As the book of Proverbs states: 'Many are the plans in the mind of a man but it is the purpose of the Lord that will be established' (Pr 19:21)."[2]

There is nothing that escapes this sustaining, creative care of God, for there is nothing real except through Him. It is evident that belief in this immediate concern of God which directs every thing and everyone to the final purpose of the universe—the manifestation of His Glory—demands a firm faith. Evil in the world, which at times seems to be overwhelming, both on an individual and collective basis, can well test one's faith in the good God's continual, loving creation.

It is not that man's input is to be disregarded. In fact, Providence is the cause of man's freedom and calls for its activity.[3] The term "Providence" expresses the relationship between God and His world; it is a denial of deism (implying that God abandons the world to itself after creation) and also of pure passivity (pushing dependence on God to the extreme of denying man's cooperation). Theology insists upon the action of God working through man *(concursus divinus)*, stressing always that God alone is first cause and the sovereign master of His plan; He freely wills man's cooperation. The precise nature of this interplay is impossible to gauge, most especially when it is a question of evil. Faith demands belief in the All-Holy God's sovereignty and at the same time a clear affirmation of the freedom of man in this ongoing creation, unfolding towards the fulfillment of God's reign. In the final analysis, we can only repeat with the word of God: "We know that in everything God works for good for those who love him" (Rm 8:28).

Because of this concrete and immediate loving care of divine Providence for the least and the greatest events in history, "Jesus asks for childlike abandonment to the Providence of our heavenly Father who takes care of his children's smallest needs."[4] The Sermon on the Mount speaks of our response to Providence: "Do not be anxious about your life, what you shall eat or what you shall drink nor about your body, what you shall put on . . . Consider the lilies of the field, how they grow; they neither toil nor spin; yet I tell you, even Solomon in all his glory was not arrayed like one of these . . . Therefore do not be anxious . . ." (Mt 6:25–33).

In order to cover the topic as Saint Louis de Montfort explains it, Providence will be taken in the broad sense, comprising not only God's orderly governance of the universe to its final goal, but also the trustful response of human beings to God's strong yet gentle care.

II. Montfort's Little Treatise on Providence

The hymns of Saint Louis de Montfort are often profound, practical catechetical sermons put to verse. For example, the first section of the canticles covers subjects like Charity, Faith, Hope, Humility, Meekness, Obedience, Patience, Virginity, etc. Hymn 28 follows this pattern; it is a forty-four verse "little treatise on Providence," covering the meaning of Providence (28:1), the existence of Providence (28:2–3), the extent of Providence (28:4–5), the confidence we must have in Providence (28:6–20), the qualities of Providence (28:21–24), and concluding with *"Prayer and Resolution"* (28:25–44). The outline itself and the number of verses allotted to each section make it evident that the missionary is not writing a theoretical, speculative paper on the subject. Rather, his goal is eminently practical. Only the first five verses are dedicated to Providence as the governance of the universe by God. The other thirty-nine stanzas deal with man's response, and of these nineteen are devoted to the final exhortation, *"Prayer and Resolution."*

1. The Definition of Providence.

As in many of his other teaching canticles, Father de Montfort begins with a definition, putting into one verse the core of his understanding of Providence: *"Let us admire providence / Which leads everything to its end, / This supreme prudence / And this sovereign order / Which knows, rules and arranges / Strongly yet gently, / Everything even to the least thing / Without any disorder."* Montfort follows rather closely the thought of Aquinas, who considers Providence the principal part of the virtue of prudence, whose object is the proper ordering of things toward their final end.[5]

There is a triple stress in the missionary's general understanding of Providence, found not only in this hymn but throughout his writings. First, God is supreme. *"God alone"* is in charge, as the first cause of the entire universe. Following a thought so basic to the French School of spirituality, the missionary underlines the grandeur of God. His approach is clearly theocentric (stressing God) not anthropocentric (stressing man). Second, Montfort insists that there is nothing whatsoever that acts "on its own," outside of God's knowledge, orderly rule, and arrangement of the universe. Even the farthest speck of existence in outer space, Montfort would declare, is not only known by God but is part of his orderly plan dynamically tending to the fulfillment of God's eternal purpose. Third, God's Providence is carried out *"fortiter et suaviter,"* strongly and gently. In the first stanza, Montfort implicitly points to the fundamental truth of his entire structure of spirituality: *"God Alone,"* and this God is Love. It is God who gently rules all and who leads all to their end, and nothing can conquer God's will. Yet, God, who is Love, does not force: all is done from love and therefore with infinite love. Montfort, the missionary to *"the poor and the simple"* (TD 26), avoids all academic speculation on the question of the supremacy of God's governance of the universe and man's free will.

In the margin next to the first stanza, this gospel troubadour writes: *"Essence and definition of providence."* This core definition will be expanded and explained in the following verses of the hymn. If we were to limit our study to this stanza alone, it would appear that man plays no role in the unfolding of God's plan to its ultimate fulfillment. This is far from his teaching, as can be seen not only in this hymn but especially in his own way of life of "total abandonment to divine Providence." His stress in the definition is on God. H 51 again praises this care of God: *"His tender Providence / Rules everything strongly, / Conducts everything wisely, / Without anyone else even thinking about it"* (v. 3). And this fatherly concern is directed especially towards man: *"Not a leaf may fall / Without his express command, / Over everything his Providence watches, / But in a special way over us"* (H 11:29).

2. The Existence of Providence

The missionary's first point, as clearly expressed in the margin of the manuscript, is *"the truth of Providence,"* which englobes six proofs that divine Providence is a reality. His marginal notes indicate clearly what they are: the order in the universe, the change of seasons, the movements of the stars and planets in the skies, the testimony of conscience, the punishment of even hidden sins, and the witness of every creature that God is always present within it, mysteriously leading it. His expressions—again reminiscent of Thomas Aquinas[6]—are easily understandable by his audience. They encompass objective phenomena that can be compressed into one—the orderliness of creation itself—and subjective reasons that again can be resumed into one—mysteriously, God's ruling, orderly presence is experienced primarily by one's conscience. Saint Louis de Montfort is not arguing with atheists or deists. On the other hand, he requests that one peacefully and sincerely gaze into the magnificence of creation and into the depths of one's being. The missionary seems assured that such a person will come to accept the mysterious Providence of God.[7]

3. The Extent of Providence

Nothing whatsoever escapes the sovereignty of God, declares Montfort; nothing whatsoever is withdrawn from his supreme, orderly rule, this continuous creation. *"From the first of the archangels down to the least worm,"* this wisdom of God knows and rules all in a hidden way, often beyond our comprehension; He guides all things freely to the fulfillment of the divine plan. *"Over each thing, He watches / And the fools do not think of it. / Without him, even the least leaf / Cannot fall to the ground / He rules the thunder / The wind and the clouds in the air/ And the dust of the earth / And the storm on the sea"* (cf. H 11:29).

As mentioned above, intrinsic to the saint's understanding of Providence is the response of man to God's loving care. The rest of the canticle centers on this response.

4. Confidence in Providence

The longest explanatory segment in the hymn is devoted to the third point, the confidence one should have in Providence. Fifteen motives are brought forth by the missionary to inspire his people to a total abandonment to God's Providence. After recalling that God is a loving Father who knows all our cares and wants us to hope in His love for us—the first four motives—Father de Montfort presents nine reasons that are nothing more than a hymnal paraphrase of Matthew 6:24–34, excerpted from the Sermon on the Mount. In simple rhyme, impossible to capture in English, Montfort repeats the words of Jesus: *"Do not be anxious / Avoid the troubles of pagans / Who make their primary concern / To love and seek earthly goods. / Not having faith to believe, / They think of the future; / Tomorrow, what will we have to drink, / To eat, to be clothed? And please do not become / Anxious about your body / For your soul far surpasses / Your body and your treasures. / It is your soul which I have filled / With my infinite treasures/ How could you think that I would forget / Your food and clothing? Consider, I beg you, / The birds in the millions / Who do not have for their poor life / Any reserves or barns. / Your loving Father / Makes sure that they lack nothing; / And you, worth far more, / Would ever lack what you need? . . . Look at the magnificence / Of the lilies of the fields and all the flowers. / Solomon in all his power / Never had such splendor. / If they have this beautiful glory / Without working, without spinning, / You who are worth so much more, / Must I not clothe you? . . . First and before all else / Seek the eternal goods / The Lord and his justice, / His kingdom and his love. / Win by this sacrifice / Your daily bread . . ."* (vv. 9-14). Montfort's marginal note introducing the section on these words of Jesus is revealing: *"Especially we must try to understand this great secret of the Savior which he came to teach us thereby doing us so great a favor: Hope in God so faithful, Repose in the bosom of his fatherly goodness, Without worrying about tomorrow."* Providence is, in Montfort's eyes, a secret—a mystery—which motivated divine Wisdom to become incarnate in order to share his beauty with us. The Sermon on the Mount of the Eternal and Incarnate Wisdom appears to be for Saint Louis the strongest motive for trusting totally in Providence.

Yet Jesus teaches us not only by words. The fourteenth motive instructs us to follow the example of the Lord who so trusted in the Providence of the Father, as did Our Lady and all the saints: *"They had, almost without any trouble / Food and clothing, / And that sovereign meekness / Of perfect detachment* (v. 19)."

The final motive is a reminder that to turn away from God's Providence and to put our trust in human support is not only harmful but *"cursed are those who so trust, /the Holy Spirit tells us, / But happy are those who depend / on God alone through Jesus Christ* (v. 20)."The loving care of the

Father is mediated to us through Our Lord Jesus Christ. For Montfort, this is the only route to follow.

5. Qualities of trust in Providence

In the first quality of trust in God, Montfort declares that God can accomplish His will even if man does not collaborate and in the same breath puts emphasis on the divinely willed human cooperation in the work of Providence. Similar to his discussion in SM 23 of Mary's universal mediation, the saint appears to be making a distinction between what can be done in theory and the actual manner in which God carries out His will.[8] The first quality of any authentic abandonment to God is, therefore: *"Trust in Divine providence is prudent and laborious."* This is elucidated in stanza 21: *"It is absolutely necessary that the trust / Which you have placed in God / Be joined with prudence / According to time and place. / Even though God may accomplish an event/ And that we do nothing, / Nonetheless, it is absolutely necessary that we do it / And even that we work at it well."* Montfort is attempting to balance—without explaining—the Grandeur and Sovereignty of God as primary cause of all things with the human response. It is clear from Montfort's life (as will be seen) that, in his eyes, this human response is part and parcel of the entire picture of Providence; but he also makes this belief explicit in LEW, where he twice boldly declares with strong words that the human person is the *"vicar on earth"* of Wisdom; it is in and through this vicar that the orderly governance of the world is carried out (LEW 35, 41).[9]

The second quality of trust in God is repeated often in his works: nothing whatsoever is to be withdrawn from this loving trust in God. It must be universal, for *"God is our Father and infinitely liberal."* The third quality is perhaps the most difficult: *"Be calm . . . when your plans are turned upside down* (v. 23)." Becoming irritated when we don't get our way is harmful, he sings. His advice for those times when everything seems to crash about us is, *"to love God alone who loves you so / And who never leaves you. / Throw yourself entirely into God."* Montfort is calling for a life lived in God alone so that when Providence's cross seems too heavy to bear, we will be sustained by our faith conviction that infinite Love is intensely sharing life with us. Finally, trust in God must be humble and thankful, recognizing His tenderness.

6. Final Prayer and Resolution

The lengthy conclusion to this Hymn on Providence is a fiery call—especially to the clergy—to make the interests of God one's goal, and not the interests of "the world": money, power, and prestige. In strong language he rebukes those who ridicule him for his total abandonment to God's loving care: *"Men of the church and lay folk / If you despise my way of life / Know that I detest yours / Which leads to death. / Oh, if you could only understand / My joy and your unhappiness, / Without hesitation, from all your goods / You would detach your hearts"* (v. 40). His call to *"voluntary poverty,"* to *"lose ourselves in God,"* will, he firmly believes, enable all to become apostles leading others to heaven. For this vagabond saint, Providence implies not only a universal trust in God but also a resolve to make God alone and His Righteousness our only goal. It is always to be recalled that for Montfort "God Alone" includes essentially loving service to all our brothers and sisters in God. The motto of Saint Louis Marie is not only vertical (outstretched to God) but also horizontal (outstretched to neighbor).

7. Conclusion

Some of the principal points stressed by Saint Louis de Montfort in this little treatise on providence are: God, the creator of all things, is Love and tenderness; He governs all out of love, leading everything, infallibly yet freely, to the final goal; man is called upon to work arduously (there is no quietism in Montfort) for the kingdom of God and His justice. Providence implies God's presence in all things as continuing Creator, and also calls forth in us full trust, a total abandonment to his divine plan, even and especially when nothing seems to make sense.

III. The Role of Providence in the Life of Saint Louis de Montfort

The saint's Providence Canticle does not detail his full thought on the topic. It is clarified and made more complete by examining the manner that he himself lived his teaching. His years preceding his ordination and his life as a vagabond priest reveal his growing abandonment to the Providence of God.

1. Years Preceding his Ordination

Three aspects of Montfort's youth can be singled out as examples of his total dependence on God alone.

a. His departure from Rennes. At the age of nineteen, having completed eight years at the Jesuit college in Rennes, Louis Grignion decided to pursue his theological studies at Saint Sulpice in Paris. The young man bade goodbye to family and friends at the bridge of Cesson at the outskirts of Rennes. The event takes on deep symbolism. Having left all, he crossed the Cesson bridge to a new life of total dependence upon divine Providence. So convinced is he that God is truly his loving Father, that he gave to the first beggars he met his money and baggage, and even exchanged clothes with one of them. With total abandon he gave joyful, free expression to his deep desire to experience the loving care of God. Begging for food and shelter along the way, he walked to Paris arriving in the rags of a beggar. He was finding his freedom in an active and responsible total surrender to God's loving, tender, intimacy.[10] His friend John Blain writes: "From that time forward he gave himself over to divine Providence, leaving all his troubles behind, confidently and peacefully. The thought that God might not care for him never even entered his head. If he had a purse full of gold or a letter of credit for six thousand pounds to be drawn on a bank in Paris, he could not have had more security."[11]

b. Trust in the midst of difficulties. Difficulties abounded as Louis Marie began his seminary studies. He had been told that a friend of a friend would pay the boarding fee at the seminary. When he arrived in Paris he discovered that the person had no intention or ability to do so. Louis Marie was overjoyed to learn that he would have to reside in a community "of the poor students who lived in common quarters adjoining the seminary of St. Sulpice. It was a sharing in the life of the poor and in the hidden life that Jesus led for about thirty years in order to prepare Himself for his priestly ministry."[12] This becomes a pattern in his life: his plans are torn up by God and God calls forth from Louis Marie total trust without revealing the divine strategy. Examples of Louis Marie's response of total trust even in the midst of serious difficulties are numerous: e.g., during his illness as a seminarian, which brought him to death's door; in his difficulties adjusting to seminary community life; in his struggle to pay for room and board, which forced him to beg for assistance and to work during the nights keeping vigil at wakes. His trust in the Providence of God was often severely put to the test. His solution was not to run back home to Rennes, but to trust even more in God's loving care, come what may.

c. Life of surrender to Providence. However, there is another side to the young man's trust in Providence, which is underplayed by his more exuberant biographers. Montfort the seminarian trusts in divine Providence; however, it is not a quietistic abandonment. He knows that God's infallible overall plan is realized through creatures and therefore does not hesitate to ask for help or to accept assistance when it is offered. He understands that divine Providence calls upon him to work for his daily bread. The young Louis Marie does not expect that his tuition will float down from heaven or that he can do without professional help in his illness. Providence, as he writes in his little treatise, demands prudence and hard work. This is a trait that characterizes his life of surrender to Providence. Trusting in God and doing nothing is not St Louis' formula for total abandonment to God. He searches for people to help pay the expenses at the seminary, he seeks work to earn his tuition, he pours out his heart to his superiors and directors in order to accomplish God's will.

2. Priestly Life

Almost every aspect of Saint Louis de Montfort's priestly ministry is stamped with his amazing trust in divine Providence. Several facets of his apostolate will be highlighted to substantiate this statement.

a. The Founder. The founding of both the Daughters of Wisdom and the Company of Mary illustrate the missionary's radical abandonment to the will of God. After inviting Marie-Louise Trichet to help at the Poitiers General Hospital, he began to realize his dreams of a congregation of women who would be representatives of the Eternal and Incarnate Wisdom in quest of the poor and the outcasts of society. However, he never approached this project as if it were his own, or as a businessman attempting to launch some new enterprise. He is convinced that he is no more than God's loving apostle. After giving Marie Louise a religious habit and instructing her in the ways of Divine Wisdom, he left her for ten years, keeping in touch only by letter. He had done what he could; moreover, his ministry obliged him to move on. If the congregation is the will of God, then it will definitely survive. It is not carelessness or a lack of concern for Marie Louise; rather, the congregation of the Daughters of Wisdom is too precious a gift of God for him to "take charge." God in his Providence must oversee and bring to birth this new community.

His yearning to found a congregation of missionaries, proclaimers to the poor of the reign of Christ through Mary, dates from the earliest years of his priesthood. Yet aside from the faithful Brother Mathurin, he found no one who would join him in fulfilling this hope. So convinced is he that God's Providence wills the congregation that he wrote an ardent prayer for missionaries, a rule, and a letter to all the future members of the Company of Mary before the community even existed (LCM). His prayer for this Company indicates his stress on the Providence of God: *"[Almighty God], be mindful of your Congregation, for it is you alone who must, by your grace, make it a living reality. If man is the first to put his hand to the work nothing will come of it. If he contributes anything of his own to what you are doing, the entire undertaking will be warped and come down in ruins"* (PM 26).[13] Thwarted in every way, he still was convinced that God desires such a congregation of priests and brothers. At his death only two priests and a few brothers were counted as his followers. None had taken vows. But Saint Louis Marie dies assured that the Providence of God will raise up the congregation.

b. Pilgrimage to Rome. For Saint Louis de Montfort, Providence entails first discerning God's will and then carrying it out through the power of the Holy Spirit. Providence, therefore, connotes obedience to God. Since God works through creation, through events, and through others, Providence includes obedience to God as manifested through His representatives. First and foremost, this means obedience to Jesus as revealed in the Scriptures and to Our Lady whose will is always one with her Son. It means obedience to the Church, the Body of Christ, and in a special way to its chief pastor, the vicar of Christ, the bishop of Rome. Caught up in dilemmas on all sides, the young Father Louis from Montfort made a decision to seek the advice of the Holy Father in order to discern God's will. His pilgrimage to the Holy City was made on foot even though war was being waged between France and Italy—so confident was he that God wanted him to consult the vicar of Christ. The words of Pope Clement XI assured him that his itinerant preaching in western France was of God and gave Montfort the confidence he needed. He spent the rest of his life fulfilling the wish of the Holy Father, assured that it was God's providential will for him.

c. Contradictions on all sides. Father de Montfort was faced with opposition that tested his total abandonment to God's Providence. Several times bishops forbade him to preach in their dioceses. Unjust treatment at times brought him to tears; God's Providence was often a heavy cross to bear. He spoke with confidants about the injustice that some local ecclesiastical authorities inflicted upon him. Yet he obeyed, certain that God's Providence would bring good out of evil; he would even praise God for the gift of such a cross.

Montfort's interpretation of divine

Providence is evidenced in his attitude when told by the local bishop to destroy the Calvary at Pontchateau on the very day it was to be blessed. He did not sit by and watch the destruction of a project he firmly believed would strengthen the faith of the people. The bishop was wrong and the missionary knew it. He went immediately to the bishop to change the prelate's mind. Only after having done all he could to keep the Calvary intact —and having failed to convince the bishop—did he accept the fact that in some mysterious way, God's inscrutable Providence is permitting the evil for some greater good of the church. *"We had hoped to build a Calvary here,"* he reportedly told the waiting crowd, *"but God wills that we build it in our hearts."* And he set about obeying the bishop's orders to destroy the site.

d. Living by Providence. Perhaps the clearest evidence of Montfort's total abandonment to divine Providence is his strange lifestyle: a vagabond missionary, with his few belongings packed into a knapsack slung over his shoulder, a walking stick with a cross or statue of Our Lady on its top, moving from town to town freely proclaiming God's reign. He is absolutely certain that God's fatherly care will always envelop him, giving him food to eat, water to drink, and a place to sleep. He describes this life à la Providence in one of his canticles: *"With stick in my hand / My bare feet on the road, / I speed through the land / For I carry no load. Like a bird in the tree / With no worry or care / My heart is quite free / For no burden I bear. / With no cash for tomorrow / I live day by day / And I know that I follow / The far better way"* (a paraphrase of a few verses of H 144).

e. Necessity of work. Although Saint Louis de Montfort's trust in Providence knew no bounds, he never interpreted God's loving care as a dispensation from personal work. Quite the contrary: it was only by laborious seeking that God's will unfolded; it was only by steady, painful toil that God's will is fulfilled. When his sisters were in need, he did not only pray for them. He sought help, requesting aid from some wealthy women, including Madame de Montespan, the former mistress of Louis XIV. He insisted that the founding of the Company of Mary was God's work, but he recognized that this meant that he himself must be God's hands in forming the community by writing the *Rule*, by seeking recruits, and by begging his friend, Claude Poullart des Places, to direct seminarians to his proposed congregation. Preaching God's word, as Providence willed him to do, in no way freed him from laborious preparation, as his *Book of Sermons* testifies. Total abandonment to God's Providence implies action on our part.

IV. Providence in the Writings of Saint Louis de Montfort

The direct and implied references to Providence abound in the writings of Saint Louis de Montfort. In addition to his cantique on Providence studied above, there are passages relating to Providence especially in his Letters, in his *Triptych* (PM, RM, LCM), and in his Marian classics, TD and SM.

1. Letters

Ten of the thirty-four letters of Father de Montfort which have been preserved explicitly mention "Providence." Letter 7, addressed to his favorite sister, Guyonne-Jeanne (whom he affectionately called Louise), contains the most references. Its theme is to prompt the young girl not to be so concerned about the future: *"What God wants of you, my dear sister, is that you should live each day as it comes, like a bird in the trees, without worrying about tomorrow. Be at peace and trust in divine providence and the Blessed Virgin and do not seek anything else but to please God and love him . . . if you serve God and his Holy Mother faithfully you will want for nothing in this world or the next."* Even his early letters, written as a seminarian, refer to the loving care God constantly shows him. When Father de la Barmondière, his superior and director at the seminary, died, the young Louis Grignion's future as a seminarian was placed in serious jeopardy. In this difficult situation, he wrote to his uncle priest: *"I do not know how things will go, whether I shall stay or leave, as Father de la Barmondière's last will and testament has not yet been made known. Whatever happens I shall not be worried. I have a Father in heaven who can never fail me. He brought me here, he has kept me here until now and he will continue to treat me with his usual kindness. Although I deserve only punishment for my sins, I never stop praying to God and rely completely on his providence"* (L 2). Several months later, the young seminarian wrote again to his uncle, informing him that *"God, in his loving providence, without my ever having thought of it,"* had indeed taken care of him through the intermediary of some benefactors and that he was able to continue his studies at St. Sulpice. Yet God's loving Providence never forces: *"When God asks his creatures for anything, he asks gently leaving them entirely free."* But to delay in fulfilling God's will places us in danger, for *"the longer we delay in responding to his gentle request, the less we hear his voice"* (L 30). *"I only want to do God's will"* (L 6) is a primary theme of all his correspondence, coupled with a complete, loving trust in God (L 8, 9, 10, 25, 33).

2. True Devotion and Secret of Mary

The originality of Montfort on the theme of Providence rests especially in his understanding of the place of Mary in God's governing of the universe in and through the Eternal and Incarnate Wisdom. His Marian classics, TD and SM, are the principal sources for his Marian theology and also for the foundations of the consecration to Jesus-Wisdom through Mary, which encompasses a total abandonment to God's Providence.

a. Mary's role in God's care of the universe. That Providence is to be attributed to God alone as primary cause, the missionary leaves no doubt. However, the Lord of all makes use of others in the governing of the universe. Jesus, the Eternal and Incarnate Wisdom, true God and true man, is in his very reality the essential and only mediator (cf TD 61). He alone is King *"by nature"* (TD 38), he alone is *"the beginning and the end of all things,"* (TD 61) he alone is God's plan itself and its fulfillment, for through Wisdom and for Wisdom all things are created and governed (LEW 31–38). *"After creating all things, Eternal Wisdom abides in them to contain, maintain, and renew them. It was this supremely perfect beauty who, after creating the universe, established the magnificent order we find there. It was Wisdom who separated, arranged, evaluated, augmented and calculated everything"* (LEW 32).

We can summarize the saint's thought on Mary and Providence by piecing together various elements of his teachings on God, Jesus, and Our Lady. Because the Trinity freely chose Mary to be the "Yes" of the universe in accepting and, in this sense, bringing about the Incarnation, Our Lady plays a unique role in every aspect of salvation history (TD 14–36). It is through her consent that our redemption, the Eternal and Incarnate Wisdom, came to be (TD 16). The Incarnation, as the first of all mysteries, is the pattern of all the works of grace (TD 248). God comes to us in Jesus Christ who is always and everywhere the son of Mary, the fruit of her representative faith (TD 44).

Montfort insists then that Jesus, the Eternal and Incarnate Wisdom, *"shares his power with his holy mother"* (TD 76). *"Such is the will of the Almighty who exalts the humble, that the heavens, the earth and hell itself, willingly or unwillingly, must obey the commands of the humble Virgin Mary. For God has made her queen of heaven and earth, leader of his armies, keeper of his treasures, dispenser of his graces, worker of his wonders, restorer of the human race, mediatrix on behalf of men, destroyer of his enemies and faithful associate in his great works and triumphs"* (TD 28; H 77:8, 81:6). The saint underlines, therefore, that *"Whatever belongs to Jesus by nature, belongs to Mary by grace"* (TD 74). The governing of the universe takes place through Jesus and belongs to him by nature as the incarnate Son of God. Mary, the inseparable companion of Jesus, even *"of his glory and of his power in heaven and on earth"* (TD 74), shares by grace in this role of the Incarnate Wisdom. Providence, then, governs us through Jesus Christ in union with his mother, Mary.

The same conclusion is reached when considering Montfort's teaching on the spiritual maternity. Mary is truly the mother of the Christ who is in himself the goal, the fulfillment of God's Providence (TD 61). As the Daughter of the Father, Mother of the Son, Spouse of the Holy Spirit (SM 68), she, the living Yes of all creation to God's desire to espouse us in Christ, is the spiritual mother and queen of the universe (TD 37–40). Mary is, then, the Mother of the whole Christ, head and members (TD 32–33), Mother of the fulfillment of God's plan when all shall be one in Christ Jesus in the power of the Spirit, for the glory of God alone. As the true Mother of all, and as the Yes of the human family, she is the mediatrix of the gifts of God. The gift of God's loving care, which governs all things to their goal, comes to us in Christ Jesus through Mary, as the eternal surrender of the cosmos to God's plan, Jesus the Lord. In this sense, Our Lady is, in Saint Louis de Montfort's eyes, intrinsic to the mystery of Providence.

b. The consecration. Saint Louis de Montfort's *"Act of consecration to the Eternal and Incarnate Wisdom through the hands of Mary"* (LEW 223-227) is a recognition of God's Providence and of a total loving surrender to his purpose. His design for the universe is to incorporate all things into the Beloved, the Eternal and Incarnate Wisdom, through Mary. The consecration, an act of *latria,* is addressed ultimately to the God-Man, Jesus Christ, the goal of all creation. However, in light of the Incarnation, it is evident for Montfort that Jesus the goal comes to us and we to him through Mary (TD 1); she is the unique means of union with Christ. The consecration is, then, the loving acceptance of this providential plan of God—Jesus our goal, Mary the unique means—and the consequent emptying of all the idols set up in its place. This was done in Baptism (at least implicitly); the consecration is the renewal of our baptismal promises, accepting lovingly and freely the governance of the universe, and in particular of our own life, the way that God so wills.

For Montfort, the more that we live this baptismal consecration whereby we freely accept divine Providence, the more intense our freedom. Liberty is in direct proportion to our surrender as slaves of love to God's plan in Christ Jesus. It is the consecration, the total abandonment to God's Providence, that sets us free; fabricating our own plans outside the Lord's is enslavement.

As Montfort outlines in the effects of the consecration (TD 213–25), Mary prompts all of us to surrender actively and responsibly to God's will for us; she strengthens us by her maternal intercession so that our response may resemble hers, a *fiat* to God's mysterious ways (TD 201–12; 214–16).

3. The Rules

Abandonment to divine Providence is an important element in the Rules the saint drew up for his congregations. In the first number of his Rule for the community of women, he calls the congregation the Daughters of Providence, finally erasing that title and substituting Daughters of Wisdom. His insistence on total trust in Providence is apparent. Moreover, he writes that the Sisters *"abandon themselves, in everything, to the cares of divine providence which will help them in the manner and time that providence so wills."* In his Hymn to the Daughters of Wisdom, he sings: *"Establish everything on providence / Without thinking of tomorrow. / Disregard that so-called prudence/ Which wants a sure support"* (H 149:2).

It is especially in the *Triptych* of the Company of Mary that the saint stresses trust in the Providence of God. The PM is a clear indicator of Montfort's understanding of total abandonment to divine Providence. With an incredible boldness, he begs God to create this congregation that he so ardently desires and that he so strenuously tries to establish; yet he recognizes that it must be God's will, it must be the result of God's love. If man takes charge instead of God, the entire project is lost (PM 26). He prays for a group of men whose preaching will *"reform the church and renew the face of the earth,"* who will be apostles ushering in the kingdom of Christ through Mary. In order to do this, they must *be "men according to your own heart, O Lord, who without any will of their own . . . carry out your desires . . . men always at your hand, always ready to obey you"* (PM 8, 10),

". . . men abandoned to your providence" (PM 20), *". . . the Lord's bodyguard of handpicked men"* (PM 30), known for their *"abandonment to providence and their devotion to Mary"* (PM 24).

In order to enter the Company of Mary, a candidate must surrender all material goods and rely totally on divine Providence: *"Priests and Brothers alike must not accept even simple benefices and temporal possessions, even those they may inherit. If they did have any before entering the Company, they must return the benefices to those who presented them. What they inherited must be given to their relatives or to the poor, having first taken the advice of a good counselor. They thus exchange their paternal inheritance for one which God himself gives them, namely, the inexhaustible inheritance of his divine providence"* (RM 5). *"Their sole resource must be God's providence . . . the community will supply all that is necessary in the way of food and clothing, depending on what providence supplies to the community"* (RM 10-11). *"The missionaries will not become settled in any one place, as communities, even the most regular, normally do. Instead of this undesirable stability they will be more solidly grounded in God alone, provided that they always yield themselves without reserve to the care of providence"* (RM 12). *"They must rely on divine providence for all things. God would sooner work a miracle than fail to supply the needs of those who trust in him. They are not, however, forbidden to mention in public or private their state of dependence on providence and the rules they follow in this matter"* (RM 14).

The short but powerful LCM is an appeal to all the professed of the congregation to live a life of poverty, totally trusting in divine Providence. The founder places these words on the lips of the eternal Father: *"I have graven you on my heart and on the palms of my hands in order to cherish and defend you because you have put your trust in me and not in people, in my providence and not in wealth"* (LCM 3). St. Louis de Montfort then himself addresses each member of the community: *"These are the marvelous promises which God has made to you through his prophets. They will be yours provided you put all your trust in him through Mary. Entirely dependent as you are on God's providence, it is up to him to support you and to increase your numbers . . . fear nothing whatsoever and sleep in peace in your Father's arms"* (LCM 4). Saint Louis de Montfort again combines two elements in his explanation of living in total abandonment to divine Providence: complete trust in God joined with prudence and hard work: *"earn your bread by the sweat of your brow"* (LCM 10).

V. Relevance of Montfort's Teaching on Providence

Saint Louis de Montfort's theological, ecclesial, and general cultural context differ greatly from that of contemporary society. Not surprisingly, his teaching runs counter to several present currents. The autonomy of humankind in formulating its destiny is a characteristic of many modern men and women of the First World (the industrialized countries). The marvelous technological advances with repercussions most especially in First World society have influenced some to disregard, for all practical purposes, God's governing presence in every particle of creation. With the emphasis on rugged individualism, the notion that God has an infallible plan for the human race appears outlandish. As always, the personal and collective calamities and perennial injustices raise serious doubts in many minds that God's loving care is a reality. Montfort's insistence that God governs all things in Christ Jesus through Mary and that we should have total abandonment to the designs of so loving a Father appears to many rather quaint, at best.

Without denying the need to update the expressions of Saint Louis Marie, it must be said that Montfort offers a healthy confrontation with contemporary thought. Three points especially should be noted which make his teaching relevant for today's society.

1. Insistence on the Grandeur of God

Montfort's stress on the absolute supremacy of God is needed in a neopelagian world. The missionary's teaching recalls not only the Sermon on the Mount but also the words of Paul: "For he has made known to us in all wisdom and insight the mystery of his will, according to his purpose which he set forth in Christ as a plan for the fullness of time, to unite all things in him, things in heaven and things on earth. In him, according to the purpose of him who accomplishes all things according to the counsel of his will, we who first hoped in Christ have been destined and appointed to live for the praise of his glory" (Ep 1:9–12).

Connected to this stress on the grandeur of God is the saint's emphatic teaching that God's greatness does not distance Him from creation. Rather, it is precisely His Majesty which enables Him to be so intimately present within us. For the Omnipotence of God is love. This loving presence in every particle of creation—most especially in human persons, directing all freely to the final goal—is an important lesson for a society so filled with fear of tomorrow while attempting to handle burdensome responsibilities without God. Montfort appears to be crying out to the present generation: "You are loved by God who dwells within you, there is purpose in life, your goal is glory with Christ, the son of Mary; do not be frozen by fear."

2. Abandonment to God's Will

Montfort calls upon us to be who we really are. To ignore God's will and to do whatsoever one pleases, to withdraw Christ from the goal of all creation and set up aims with no relation to the Lord, is to live a counterfeit existence. *"Seek the Lord and His righteousness, His Kingdom and His Love,"* (H 28:14) is the only prescription for a fully human life. Such is the meaning of abandonment to God's will. The missionary is a realist and at times will call this surrender—nothing more than an acceptance of our reality—a heavy cross. He himself experienced grave and painful illnesses, extreme poverty with all its consequences, injustices from authorities, betrayal by friends, the death of loved ones, apparent failure after failure; and yet there was in the midst of his tears a deep peace if not a joyful lightheartedness. He knew that in some mysterious way God's will was being accomplished; he was convinced of the loving care of the Trinity who continually shared life with him and rejoiced in the experience of the presence of Mary. "Thy will be done," was his formula for peace. He calls this total abandonment to God. It is a lesson that every generation must constantly learn.

Saint Louis's teaching on the consecration to the eternal and incarnate Wisdom through Mary encompasses total abandonment to divine Providence. Seen in this light, the consecration with its liberating "slavery of love" takes on a clearer and more urgent meaning.

3. The Need for Human Response

Taken out of context, excerpts from the saint's teaching may appear to neglect human cooperation and to overstress trust in God, as if we were to do nothing, but such is definitely not his thought. Providence, as God's continual creation, is the ground and source of our freedom, which must be used to promote the glory of God. True, the missionary's stress is on God's sovereign, loving care; yet that means that we are to be open to that care by hard work. Following his example, that implies boldly living the gospel, protesting injustices, standing up for the truth even at the cost of one's life, seeking help and advice, creatively proclaiming the good news of Jesus Christ to the poor and the marginalized. To be open to the guiding Spirit is to be filled with zeal for God's glory. This is, for Montfort, intrinsic to a balanced understanding of "abandonment to God." His teaching offers a corrective to any quietistic understanding of the response to God's loving care.

P. Gaffney

Notes: (1) CCC 302. The Catechism is quoting Vatican Council I, Dei Filius 1 (DS 3003) and also Ws 8:1 and Heb 4:13. (2) CCC 303. (3) Cf. Ernst Niermann, *Providence,* in Smun, 1314–15: "There is no rivalry or competition in the relation between divine and creaturely freedom. Divine freedom is the transcendent cause which enables the creatures to be free. The exact relationship is a controversial question in theology." (4) CCC 305. Cf. also CCC 322: "Christ invites us to filial trust in the providence of our heavenly Father (cf. Mt 6:26–34), and St. Peter the apostle repeats: 'Cast all your anxieties on him, for he cares about you' (1 Pet 5:7) cf. Ps 55:23)." (5) Summa Theologiae, II-II, 49, 6 and ad 1. (6) Ibid., I, 22, 2. (7) Saint Louis de Montfort seems to refer to the text of Paul: "For what can be known about God is plain to them, because God has shown it to them. Ever since the creation of the world his invisible nature, namely his eternal power and deity has been clearly perceived in the things that have been made. So they are without excuse" (Rom 1:19–20). (8) *"God, as the absolute Master, can give directly what he ordinarily dispenses only through Mary, and it would be rash to deny that he sometimes does so. However, St. Thomas assures us that, following the order established by his divine Wisdom, God ordinarily imparts his graces to men through Mary."* Saint Louis de Montfort is discussing the question of Mary, mediatrix of all graces. All his writings insist on this privilege, and SM 23 must be read within that context and not considered as some momentary hesitation about the universality of Mary's mediatrix role. The text of Montfort is to be understood in the light of LG 60, 62. (9) Cf. CCC 307: "To human beings God even gives the power of freely sharing in his providence by entrusting them with the responsibility of 'subduing' the earth and having dominion over it (cf. Gn 1:26–28)." (10) Cf. Grandet 8–9. (11) Blain, 24. (12) B. Papàsogli, *Montfort: a Prophet for Our Times,* Edizioni Monfortane, Roma 1991, 61. (13) Cf. ibid., 414.

THE PSALMS

I. INTRODUCTION

The Psalter is the hymn book of Israel, or to be more precise, the songbook of the Temple.[1] The numbering of the psalms has caused some confusion since Psalms 10 to 48 in the Hebrew Bible are one figure ahead of the Greek and Vulgate, which join 9 and 10 and also 114 and 115, but which divide 116 and 147 into two. The Hebrew numbering is followed in this article.

The book is a collection of one hundred fifty psalms, which may be divided structurally into hymns of praise (e.g., 33, 46–48, 96–100, 145–150) that celebrate the glory of God; psalms of suffering or laments that are national (e.g., 44, 60, 83, 85) or individual entreaties (e.g., 5–7, 69–71, 140–43); and psalms of thanksgiving (e.g., 18, 21, 30, 65–68). This tripartite division is by no means watertight, for often one psalm has characteristics of all three types.

However, the above division is based upon the principal theme of the psalms, which calls for a certain structure. Based primarily on content, the psalms may be divided into several categories, e.g., historical narratives (e.g., 105–106, 135–36); those entirely devoted to liturgical worship (e.g., 15); royal psalms wherein the king appears to be the speaker or the subject of the piece (e.g., 2, 18); and wisdom psalms, which seem to show an affinity with the content of OT wisdom literature (e.g., 1, 34, 37).

This divinely inspired prayer book of the Old Testament was recited by Jesus, Our Lady, and the apostles. It is also the official prayer of Christianity, which sings the psalms in the light of the Incarnation, death, and Resurrection of the holy one of Israel, Jesus the Christ.

The psalms run the whole gamut of human emotions and experience, from despair, mourning, even wish for revenge, to compassion and bold hope. For the most part, they are the inspired voice of humanity crying out to God, an authentic and at times startling voice, which seems to echo the depths of the soul.

II. Saint Louis de Montfort and the Psalms

1. Montfort's Knowledge of the Psalms.

Montfort has without doubt drunk often from this fountain of Christian spirituality. Grandet tells us that the Holy Bible and the Breviary were his constant companions, and from these he came into daily prayerful contact with the psalter. Evidence that his spirituality is steeped in the psalms is the fact that there are numerous references to the psalms in his writings.

By temperament Montfort was an artist and a poet endowed with an esthetic sense. His poetic soul would have vibrated with the psalms of praise as he felt the joy in God, in Eternal Incarnate and Crucified Wisdom, in Mary, in the poor, and in nature. The psalms of lamentation would have found echoes in his soul as he faced persecution from his enemies and the rejection of bishops, always putting his trust in *"God Alone"* (Ps 62). He not only loved the psalms but composed himself many songs and canticles inspired by these canticles: e.g., H 117 is a paraphrase of Psalm 113, and H 160 a paraphrase of Psalm 117.

2. Montfort's Interpretation of the Psalms

Montfort's exegesis is similar to that of spiritual writers of his age, such as Bossuet and the followers of Bérulle. He "develops" scripture texts to support what he writes. Occasionally he comments on a scripture text, as in FC. In other places, he paraphrases the Bible text. Sometimes he interprets the same text in different ways in different contexts (e.g. Psalm 84: 1-3 in TD 196 and in HD 48). He is against a too scientific exegesis, and this causes him to sometimes interpret the Bible in an unusual way, as in his commentaries on Psalm 68 in PM 19–25. Most often, however, his faith leads him to an interpretation that helps him go beyond the literal text to discover the spiritual or mystical sense inspired by the divine author and to find the application that is apposite to the present situation. M. Gilbert, a modern exegete, calls Montfort's interpretation a "spiritual exegesis."[2] The originality of his exegesis comes from his ability to uncover the hermeneutic keys of Eternal Wisdom and of Mary and to find "an abundance of meaning" in the texts that he uses.[3] Saint Louis Marie's interpretation of the psalms is spiritual if not mystical at times and is very different from contemporary scholarship in its concerns and content.

His contemplative reading of the

psalms became a treasury for his preaching and also for his writings. The rather free interpretation the saint gives to some of the psalms will become evident in the course of the article. Psalms speak to Father de Montfort exactly where he is, in the circumstances before him, and he finds in them the voice of God guiding him, according to the mind of the Church. At times his understanding of a verse or two of a psalm has little if anything to do with what appears to be the original meaning; Montfort freely accomodates it to light up the path God has picked out for him.

Even a cursory study of Montfort's writings demonstrates that he was intent on basing his doctrine on scriptural foundations. Psalms is the book of the Old Testament most often cited, and after the Gospels of Luke and Matthew it is the book most often referenced. There are at least seventy-eight explicit citations and forty-nine allusions to the Book of Psalms interspersed in the works of the saint. A few of the explicit quotes will be studied in order to give the reader a grasp of the manner Saint Louis prayed the psalms.

III. Examples of Montfort's Interpretation of the Psalms

Montfort's use of the psalms can be divided into texts dealing with God, with Jesus, with Mary, and with man.

1. Psalms Dealing with God

• In SR 39 Montfort is commenting on the Our Father and more precisely on the first petition, "Hallowed be thy name." He explains the meaning of these terms: *"The name of the Lord is holy and to be feared, said the prophet-king David, and heaven, according to Isaiah echoes with the praises of the seraphim who unceasingly praise the holiness of the Lord, God of hosts."*

The psalm cited is 99:3: "Let them praise thy great and terrible name! Holy is He!" This is the last of the enthronement hymns celebrating YHWH as the Victorious King of all creation. It is a chant of praise to the holiness of His Name, the cry of the people extolling the reign of YHWH. Like some modern commentaries, Saint Louis de Montfort refers his readers to a similar thought found in Is 6:3: "Holy, Holy, Holy is the Lord of hosts; the whole earth is full of His glory." It is remarkable that Louis Marie beautifully concludes his commentary on this verse of the Our Father by stating: *"We pray that all may be holy because God himself is holy"* (SR 39). The absolute Holiness of God is not, for the missionary, only to be adored and praised; thanks to the mercy of the All-Holy, this Holiness of God is to become our life.

• TD 70 explains that there are three types of slavery: *"natural slavery, enforced slavery, and voluntary slavery."* And Montfort is quick to add: *"All creatures are slaves of God in the first sense, for 'the earth and its fullness belong to the Lord.'"* Saint Louis Marie is quoting Psalm 24:1: "The earth is the Lord's and the fullness thereof." The psalm itself is victorious praise of YHWH the Creator and Lord of the universe; its words recall the Genesis account of creation. Everything then belongs to the Lord, the farthest speck of existence belongs to the Lord. All are *"slaves of God"* by nature.

• PM 30—the conclusion of Saint Louis' fiery prayer for missionaries—quotes two psalms, 68:2 and 44:23 in the Latin: *"Exsurgat Deus et dissipentur inimici ejus!" Exsurge, Domine, quare obdormis? Exsurge." ("May the Lord rise up and his enemies be scattered! Lord, Arise! Why are you sleeping?")*

Psalm 68 is recognized as probably the most obscure and therefore the most difficult of the psalter. The RSV translation reads: "Let God arise, let his enemies be scattered." Whether the psalm is a triumphal hymn or, more likely, a series of short ancient hymns is of little interest here. Montfort interprets the psalm quite literally, begging the Lord to destroy all His enemies so that His kingdom may come.

Psalm 44, on the other hand is a lamentation of a people oppressed by the enemy. Verse 23 is an urgent appeal to YHWH to rise up from His sleep and come to the aid of His people. With these two verses the ardent prayer of Montfort for missionaries reaches its climax.

• Psalm 90:11: "Who considers the power of thy anger?" is quoted in FC to underline the gravity of sin: *"Dear Friends of the Cross, we are all sinners . . . if punishment for our sins is put off till the next world, then it will be God's avenging justice . . . which will inflict the punishment, a dreadful, indescribable punishment: 'Who understands the power of your anger?'"* (FC 21, 22). This wisdom psalm, a cry of national lament, underscores the eternal nature of God and the passing sinful nature of man. In this psalm, man appears as the object of God's anger (vv. 7, 9, 11) and judgment. Montfort wanted to convince the Friends of the Cross that if we sinners do not accept the cross and sufferings here below, we will be punished in the next world by the terrible anger of God. However, the knowledge of God's anger should make wisdom enter our hearts.

a. Jesus. It is somewhat surprising that the principal Christological work of Montfort, LEW, makes only one reference to Psalm 40:8, a Christological psalm. FC mentions only this verse and psalm 22:6 when referring to Christ.

• Psalm 40:8 is referrred to in FC 16: *"I . . . Who came into the world only to embrace the Cross, to set it in my heart,"* and in LEW 16: *"At his coming into the world, while in his Mother's womb, he received it [the cross] from his eternal Father. He placed it deep in his heart, there to dominate his life, saying: 'My God, and my Father, I chose this cross when I was in your bosom. I choose it now in the womb of my Mother. I love it with all my strength and I place it deep in my heart to be my spouse and my mistress.'"* The psalm itself reads: "I delight to do thy will, O my God, thy Law is within my heart." In this psalm of thanksgiving, a poor man of YHWH, saved from great danger, thanks God in peace and offers himself to God. The verses 7–9 are a prophetic meditation on true worship, which does not mean sacrifices but the observance of the Torah of God, which is in the heart (cf. Jr. 31:33). The Letter to the Hebrews, radically changing the Septuagint version of this psalm, turns it into a messianic text and places it on the lips of Christ (Heb. 10:5–10). Montfort, deepening the Christian interpretation of the Old Testament, identifies the *"will and the law of God"* with *"the cross."* LEW 169 combines Psalm 40:9 with Wisdom 8:2 and says that Incarnate Wisdom has put the cross deep in his heart. FC 18 presents Jesus as following the words of Psalm 40:8–9 as an invitation to anyone who wishes to follow him in his humiliations.

• Psalm 22:6 is found in FC 16: *"If anyone wants to follow me who so humbled and emptied myself that I have become rather a worm than a man."* The verse of the psalm itself reads: "But I am a worm and no man, scorned by men and despised by the people." Montfort applies v. 6 to Jesus and considers Psalm 22 as messianic, since the opening of this psalm, an individual lament, occurs on the lips of Jesus crucified. Even though v. 7 is not used in the New Testament, it describes the abject humiliation of the psalmist who, as the Servant of YHWH, *"is despised and rejected"* by men (Is. 53:3). In these words, according to Montfort, Jesus describes his *kenosis* as he invites the Friends of the Cross to follow him.

• Psalm 84:9 is cited in PM 4: *"Look upon the face of your anointed one."* Psalm 84 is the great chant of the pilgrim journeying towards Sion, the house of YHWH. The official prayer of the temple (v. 9) gives the prayer for the anointing of the Lord, the Hebrew king (cf. Ps 1:2). However, after the fall of the davidic dynasty, these supplications were transformed into pleas for the coming of a definite and perfect Messiah. In PM 4, after giving other reasons, Montfort asks God to look on the face of his 'anointed,' his only son Jesus so that the missionary's plea for a new congregation, the Missionaries of the Company of Mary, may come about.

• Psalm 30:9 is cited in PM 4: *"What value do you see in my death?"*. The RSV has: "What profit is there in my death, if I go down to the Pit?" Montfort reminds God of the agony and shame Jesus endured and makes of the text a loving complaint of Jesus in the Garden of Olives. It forms part of Saint Louis Marie's plea to God to raise up his community of the Company of Mary. This psalm itself is a song of personal thanksgiving for deliverance from mortal danger. Verse 9 accepts the traditional idea of Sheol of the Old Testament, as a place of silence where God is not praised.

*b. **Wisdom.***In LEW, so steeped in the wisdom books of the Bible, Montfort cites three psalms.

• Psalm 34:8 ("O taste and see that the Lord is good!") is found in LEW 10: "*Taste and see.*" In this psalm, the poor person, who prays to the Lord in his distress for delivery, asks his hearers to taste and see how the Lord is good. Montfort makes this an invitation of Divine Wisdom to taste the joy and sweetness of this wisdom.

• Psalm 107:43 ("Whoever is wise let him give heed to these things") is found in LEW 33 and 227: *"Let he who is wise consider these things."* This psalm, a hymn of thanksgiving of the community, ends with an invitation to anyone who is wise to understand the "steadfast love of the Lord." In LEW, the "wise person" is the one who has received the gift of Wisdom from the Eternal Wisdom, and "these things" are the mysteries of nature revealed by the marvelous power of

Divine Wisdom. In LEW 227, the verse is the last phrase of the book.

• Psalm 4:2 (How long will you love vain words, and seek after lies?") becomes in LEW 181: *"How long will you go on loving vain things and seeking what is false?"* All want good things but often seek them in vanity and lies. Montfort suggests a burning desire as the first means of acquiring Divine Wisdom and exhorts his reader to desire Wisdom in place of vanity and deceit.

c. ***Missionaries.*** In PM Montfort uses the psalms thirteen times. He calls the band of missionaries for whom he is praying *"the congregation"* (PM 1–6), borrowing from Psalm 74:2: "Remember thy congregation which thou hast gotten of old." Quoting Psalm 106:47, Montfort prays in PM 18: *"Lord, gather us from the nations."* The readiness of the missionaries of the Company of Mary to respond to the call of obedience is described by citing Psalms 57:7 and 108:1: "My heart is steadfast, O God, my heart is steadfast!" and also psalm 40:7: "Behold I come." In PM 14, showing his confidence in God he makes allusion to Psalm 34:6: *"this poor man cried and the Lord heard him"* and cites Psalm 118:17: *"I shall live and recount the deeds of the Lord."* In PM 17, he cites Psalm 19:6: *"there is nothing hid from its heat,"* an allusion to the deluge of fire of the pure love of God, which the Almighty will send for the conversion of all nations.

In PM 19 we find the longest passage from the psalms, 68:9–16. In PM 19:25 Montfort gives a liberal and somewhat personal exegesis of this psalm which, as mentioned above, is most probably the most difficult psalm of the entire psalter.[4] *"The abundant rain with which the Lord nourishes his faltering heritage," "the creatures"* who live in the heritage of the Lord, *"the animals"* prefigured by the mysterious animals of Ezekiel (1:5–14), all become symbols of the missionary saints he is requesting in his prayer. It is to them that *"the Lord gives his commands."* In all the missions that they undertake, their only goal will be to give glory to the Lord for *"the spoils"* he has won from his enemies. *"The silver wings of the dove"* are given them because of their complete dependence on Providence and their devotion to Mary. They will be *"covered in gold like the wings of the dove"* by their perfect love for their neighbor and for Jesus Christ. *"The mountain of God, . . . mysterious mountain"* is no other than Mary, the well-beloved elect of God. Happy those missionaries of the Company of Mary that God has chosen as his own to live with him on the divine mountain of all delights. Montfort uses Psalm 68:10 in LCM 7, and 68:13 in TD 58, always with reference to the missionaries and apostles of the end times for whom this ardent prayer is made.

In TD 59, he says that God knows when these apostles of the end times will come and that, for our part, we must long for these times and wait for them in silence and prayer. He finishes with Psalm 40:1: "I have waited patiently for the Lord," or as Montfort transcribes it: *"I have waited and waited."* He concludes the rousing Prayer for Missionaries with Psalm 29:9: *"And in his temple all cry 'Glory.'"*

2. Marian Texts

Montfort's Marian use of the psalms can be divided into images and allusions.

a. Images. Following patristic exegesis, and sometimes going beyond it to personal spiritual exegesis, Montfort uses several images of the psalms in referring to Mary.

• *Mother.* In his remarks on the need for devotion to Mary and her role in the sanctification of souls, in TD 32 he borrows from Psalm 87:5: "In her all are born." In the canticle of Sion, symbol of Jerusalem, Sion appears as a mother, which enables it to be applied to the Mother of the Lord.[5] The word "born" in v. 4, 5, and 6 introduces the idea of the maternal womb. Sion becomes the womb of a fruitful mother from which all nations are born. Using Sion as the symbol of Mary, Montfort says in TD 32: *"According to the explanation of some of the Fathers, the first man born of Mary is the God-Man, Jesus Christ. The second is simply man, child of God and Mary by adoption."* In TD 33, when he says that Jesus is always the fruit of the womb of Mary, he declares with Saint Augustine that all the just are also formed in her womb. Again in TD 264, he repeats this text in the context of the interior practice of doing everything *"in Mary,"* and how *"her womb, as the Fathers say, is the room of the divine sacraments, where Jesus Christ and all the elect are formed."*

• The fourth wonderful effect of TD, *"a great confidence in God and Mary"* paraphrases Psalm 131:1–2: "O Lord, my heart is not lifted up, my eyes are not raised too high, I do not occupy myself with things too great and too marvelous for me. But I have calmed and quieted my soul like a child quited at its mother's breast" (cf. TD 216). Montfort applies to Mary the image of abandonment to God shown in the relationship of a child resting on the lap of his mother, and ends: *"It is on her breast that all good things come to me."*

• *The daughter of the King, the fiancée.* In his introduction to TD, Montfort recalls Psalm 45:13: *"All the glory of the daughter of the King is within"* (TD 11). Traditionally, the Church has used this royal wedding song in liturgical celebrations of the Blessed Virgin Mary. The poet keeps his attention on the daughter of the king, become fiancée and queen of another king. She appears all glorious, adorned with a glory like the divine glory. Montfort applies the *"interior"* of the palace to the *"interior"* of the daughter of the king, Mary, and understands that her external glory is as nothing compared to that which she received internally from her creator. He uses Psalm 45 in TD 196; and in TD 46, he makes the Marian application of Psalm 45:12.

• *The ark and the dwelling.* Explaining the connection between Holy Communion and the living of perfect consecration, Saint Louis Marie recommends: *"Implore him (Jesus) to rise and come to the place of his repose and the ark of his sanctification,"* recalling Psalm 132:8, "Arise, O Lord and go to thy resting place, thou and the ark of thy might." Using the only psalm that mentions the ark, Montfort makes of Mary the dwelling place of Jesus and the ark that of his sanctifying power, and makes this text a prayer to Jesus before Communion.

• In TD 196 he mentions Psalm 84:3–4 and addresses it to *"Lord Jesus"* instead of to the "Lord of hosts." He adds: *"Lord Jesus, how lovely is your dwelling place! The sparrow has found a house to dwell in and the turtle-dove a nest for her little-ones! How happy is the man who dwells in the house of Mary, where you were the first to dwell! . . . 'How lovely is your dwelling place, Lord, God of hosts!'"*

• *The City of God.* In TD 48, Montfort adapts Psalm 59:13–15: *"They will be converted towards evening, and will be as hungry as dogs. Suffering this hunger, they will go around the city in search of something to eat."* Providing a spiritual exegesis of "city," "hunger," and "evening," he goes on: *"This city, around which men will roam at the end of the world, seeking conversion and the appeasement of the hunger they have for justice, is the most Blessed Virgin who is called by the Holy Spirit, the City of God."* The text also seems to refer to Psalm 87:3: "Glorious things are spoken of you, O City of God." In the first paragraph of TD 48, Montfort speaks of *"the mystical city of God, that is to say the most blessed Virgin, who has been called by the Fathers of the Church the temple of Solomon and the City of God."* TD 266 applies to Mary, the City of God, Psalm 46:5: *"God is in the midst of her: she can not be moved."*

• *The mountain of God.* Reference has been made above to PM 25, where, using Psalm 68:14, Montfort speaks of the mysterious mountain of God, which is no other than Mary, *"whose beginnings you established on the heights,"* making reference also to Psalm 87:1: "on the holy mount stands the city he founded."

• *The way.* Explaining the pertfect practise of true devotion as the best way to attain the Lord, Montfort says that, if someone were to give him another way, no matter how perfect, *"I would choose the immaculate way of Mary,"* referring to the "way" of Psalm 18:32: "God . . . has made my way safe."

b. Allusions. Montfort makes at the very least seven allusions to Mary based on the psalms. Psalm 119 is a psalm of the Torah in which each of eight verses in each stanza contains a reference to the law of God in three different ways. In TD 200 he applies the commandments of v. 21 to Mary's orders. In TD 216 he adds the invocation: *"Holy Virgin"* from v. 94. In TD 179, he translates v. 56 by: *"Mary is made for me,"* and in SM 66 by *"Mary is in me."* In SR 46, he notes that the *"new song"* of Psalm 144:9 *"is the salutation of the archangel"* to Mary. In TD 272, he recalls Psalm 17:2: *"let your eyes see nothing in me but the virtues and merits of Mary."* And in TD 56 the "arrows" of Psalm 127:4 are the *"children of Mary."*

3. Texts Concerning Man

A rapid glance at some of Montfort's psalm references to man can be grouped according to theme.

a. Invitation to praise. In TD 271, speaking about the practise of total consecration after communion, Father de Montfort suggests an invitation to all creation to thank, adore, and love Jesus through Mary, and mentions Psalm 95:6: *"Come, let us adore."* In SR 141, speaking of the good fortune of those who join the confraternity of the daily rosary, he uses psalm 84:4: *"Blessed are those who dwell in thy house, ever singing thy praise!"*

b. The sinful nature of man. When he speaks of our spoiled nature, Montfort paraphrases and expands Psalm 51:5: *"Our bodies are so corrupt, that they are referred to by the Holy Spirit as bodies of sin, as conceived and nourished in sin and capable of any kind of sin"* (TD 79). Praising Wisdom for confiding to Mary all the graces we receive through total consecration, he alludes to Psalm 119:141 and notes: *"But bitter experience has taught me that I carry these riches in a very fragile vessel and that I am too weak and sinful to guard them by myself"* (TD 173). In LEW 129, in order to show that Incarnate and Glorified Wisdom continues to be lovable in heaven, he tells us how a dissipated man was converted by the words of psalm 51:1: *"O God, have mercy on me."*

c. Human suffering and the Cross. In FC 45 Montfort strongly recommends a prayer to obtain the wisdom of the cross and using Psalm 51:10–12, he advises: *"If you stand in need of such (the spirit to carry crosses courageously), pray for wisdom, ask for it continually and fervently without wavering or fear of not obtaining it and it will be yours."* In FC 51, he writes that the joy of suffering does not come from the body but from the soul and goes on to cite Psalm 84:2: *"In that way, someone who is suffering greatly can say with the psalmist 'My heart and my flesh ring our their joy to God the living God.'"* In FC 54, to exhort the acceptance of all sorts of crosses, he uses the words of Psalm 57:7 and 108:1: *"My heart is ready, O God, my heart is ready."* He changes the exhortation "to praise" to the exhortation to *"suffer all sorts of crosses."* In FC 58, to suggest the reward of a crown in heaven as a reason for accepting suffering, Psalm 69:7 is cited as saying: *"We suffer persecutions for the reward,"* instead of the literal: "for thy sake."

d. Death. The seven short pages of HD have six quotations from and two allusions to the Psalms. HD 24 notes: *"Recite, if you can . . . the psalm: "I rejoiced because they said to me"* (122:1). HD 33 evokes Psalm 51:10: *"Create in me a pure heart, O my God. Wash me completely from my fault; purify me from my offense."* In HD 46, he appeals to Psalm 31:1 and 71:1: *"I have my refuge in you, Lord; keep me humble always"* ("let me never be put to shame"). In HD 48 there is reference to Psalm 116:9 *"the land of the living"* and further on, a reference which combines two quotations and a reference: *"My soul is thirsting for God, the God of my life"* (Ps 42:2); *"How lovely is your dwelling place, Lord of hosts"* (Ps 84:1); *"I will be satisfied when your glory appears"* (Ps 17:15). In HD 49, Montfort recalls Psalm 150:6: *"Let everything that breathes praise the Lord."*

IV. The Psalms in Contemporary Montfort Spirituality.

Even though the reading of the psalms is necessary for all Christian spirituality, they hold a special place within the hearts of those inspired by Saint Louis de Montfort. Although his manner of interpretation may not be ours, nonetheless, it is evident that he is totally imbued with both the spirit and words of the psalms. His contemplative praying of the psalter opened up for him magnificent vistas not accessible through a cold, academic study of "the psalms as literature."

Nonetheless, praying the psalms is not always easy. First, the psalms may appear as strange expressions of centuries ago, hardly relevant in the third millenium. Life experiences are perhaps necessary to be in tune with many of the psalms.[6] Anguish, joy, praise, victory coupled with sickness, and lamentable defeat and fear of death all resonate throughout the psalter. The psalms give words to our innermost feelings. Like Saint Louis de Montfort, our own life experiences and our own community events are to interpret the psalms, as the psalms themselves interpret us.

Secondly, the psalms of revenge shock us and scandalize us. We avoid them, taking out a few verses from a few psalms, or give them a spiritual meaning. We ought to recognize that vengeance is not only found in the psalms but in ourselves, and that we all have a tendency to hatred. This revenge should be humbly acknowledged and completely confessed; only then can it give way to the mercy of God, as in the psalms of complaint. There is always, however, the "wrath" of God. It should be seen as another face of divine compassion, a way of speaking of the moral order in which God is acting in favor of his "people." In the psalms, as elsewhere in the Bible, God acts for his "faithful"—that is, the just—and in the name of "the poor and oppressed" against their oppressors. The "compassion" of God for Israel becomes "revenge" against Israel's enemies. God's victory is assured.

Third, the psalms of creation and nature, such as Psalm 104, recall to us our duties of working for the protection and conservation of the environment and the ecosystem, which we have received from the hands of the creator, God.

Saint Louis de Montfort's intense love for the hymns of Israel inspired him to see God's loving, triumphant hand in all events of his life and in the history of the universe. The hymns empowered him to proclaim the victory of God in Christ Jesus and our duty and privilege of implementing that victory in spite of individual and collective difficulties.

T. A. Joseph

Notes: (1) For bibliography on the psalms and a concise introduction and commentary, cf. John S. Kselman and Michael L. Barré, "Psalms," in *The New Jerome Biblical Commentary*, R. Brown, J. Fitzmyer, R. Murphy, eds., Prentice Hall, Englewood Cliffs, N. J. 1990, 523–552. (2) Cf. M. Gilbert, *L'exégèse Spirituelle de Montfort* in NRT, Nov. -Dec. 1982, pp. 678-691. (3) Cf. J. S. Croatto, *Biblical Hermeneutics*, Orbis Books, New York 1987, 20–35. (4) Cf. the work of M. Zappella, *Psalm 68 and the Prayer for Missionaries. Exegetical notes,* QM 4 (1986) 110–17, where he states that Montfort "shares with the psalmist a reading of history of salvation, understood as a dwelling of God with his people" (p. 116). Cf also C. Carniti, *Psalm 68. Literary Study*, LAS, Rome 1985. (5) The Septuagint translates the first part of verse 5: "the mother of Sion says to man," creating a problem among the sages from Augustine up to certain modern experts, who, to keep the term "mother," have altered the text of the Hebrew. Cf. Ravasi, *The Book of the Psalms*, vol 2, 795. Cf also the notes 56 and 57 of GA 379–80. (6) Cf. W. Brueggemann, *Praying the Psalms*, St. Mary Press, Minnesota 1986.

REIGN

SUMMARY

I. INTRODUCTION:
1. The centrality of the reign of God in the Gospels;
2. The centrality of the reign of God in montfort spirituality.

II. THE NATURE OF THE KINGDOM.

III. THE SOURCES OF MONTFORT'S CONCEPT OF THE REIGN:
1. Scriptural;
2. The French school of spirituality.

IV. TRINITARIAN REIGN:
1. The reign of the Father;
2. The reign of Jesus;
3. The reign of the Holy Spirit.

V. MARY AND THE REIGN OF GOD:
1. Mary shares in the reign of God;
2. Mary, Mother of the personal embodiment of the Kingdom.

VI. THE REIGN OF CHRIST THROUGH THE REIGN OF MARY.

VII. THE PERFECT CONSECRATION, THE MEANS OF BRINGING ABOUT THE REIGN OF CHRIST.

VIII. THE INHERITORS OF THE KINGDOM.

IX. THE PROCLAIMERS OF THE KINGDOM:
1. Apostles of the end times;
2. The members of the Company of Mary;
3. Priests throughout the world;
4. All men and women.

X. THE TIME OF THE REIGN.

XI. THE REIGN OF PURE LOVE.

XII. CONCLUSION:
1. Basic insight into montfort spirituality;
2. The eschatological character of montfort spirituality;
3. The missionary character of montfort spirituality;
4. A clarification of devotion to Mary.

I. INTRODUCTION

God is love (1 Jn 4:8). God's reign is the salvific rule of omnipotent Love embodied in Christ Jesus and extended through the Holy Spirit. This reign becomes fully operative when accepted in the interior of humankind's heart, thereby "making all things new" (2 Cor 5:17).

The kernel of Saint Louis de Montfort's spirituality can be summarized in his prayerful exclamation to Jesus: *"Ut adveniat regnum tuum, adveniat regnum Mariae. 'Lord, that thy reign may come, may the reign of Mary come!'"* (TD 217). The vagabond missionary's life goal was to implement the reign of Jesus Christ in the power of the Spirit for the glory of God Alone. He was convinced that this kingdom arrives only through the reign of Mary. "Montfort in the Church of God . . . is, before all else, the prophet and the apostle of the reign of Mary and, through that, of the reign of Jesus Christ."[1]

1. The centrality of the reign of God in the Gospels

"And Jesus went about all the cities and villages, teaching in their synagogues and preaching the gospel of the kingdom" (Mt 9:35). The reign of God is the central issue for Jesus. He is consumed with the call to proclaim the Kingdom: "I must preach the Good News of the kingdom of God in other cities also, for I was sent for this purpose" (Lk 4:43). The importance and centrality of the reign of God in NT theology is difficult to exaggerate, for it is clearly *the* message of the Lord, a message which cannot be separated from his person. In the Gospels themselves, "the herald is already being presented as the one heralded."[2]

The Kingdom is identified with a poor, itinerant preacher. He himself is the proclamation of the reign. "In the coming of Jesus, the kingdom of God is arriving in a hidden way. Origen described the situation by saying Jesus was the *autobasileia*—the kingdom of God in person. To be more precise, we would have to say that Jesus is the kingdom of God in the form of concealment, lowliness and poverty. In him the meaning of his message is made visible and tangible; in him is made manifest what God's kingdom is. . . . Person and 'cause' cannot be separated in Jesus. He is cause in person. He is the physical embodiment and personal form of the coming of the kingdom of God."[3] In Christ Jesus the Kingdom of God has come upon us (cf. Lk 11:20). To mobilize all one's forces in the service of the Gospel is to be an apostle of the reign of God.

2. The centrality of the reign of God in montfort spirituality

Although Saint Louis de Montfort has no special work, or even a section of his writings, specifically devoted to the reign of God, nonetheless this theme encapsulates the saint's life and teachings. Saint Louis Marie was consumed with the burning desire "*to destroy sin and establish the reign of Jesus Christ over that of the corrupt world*" (SM 59). He was, like Jesus, the Missionary of the Father, above all the herald of the Kingdom of God.

Montfort's life and writings bear out this truth. Seventeen of his thirty-four letters or fragments of letters have the greeting *"May the pure love of God reign in our hearts"* (cf. L 2, 3, 5, 6, 7, 8, etc.). The salutation in his later letters, "*May Jesus Christ and his Cross reign forever! (Vive Jésus, Vive sa Croix)*" (cf. L 26, 27, 29, 30, etc.), not only calls for the reign of Jesus but makes it known that Jesus reigns from the Cross (cf. FC).

Father de Montfort describes TD as *"the preparation for the reign of Jesus Christ"* (TD 227); the conclusion of his introduction to TD also summarizes his writing: "*If then, as is certain, the knowledge and the reign of Jesus Christ must come into the world, it can only be as a necessary consequence of the knowledge and reign of Mary*" (TD 13). The opening sentence of the TD manuscript, as we now possess it, sets the stage for the entire work: *"It was through the most holy Virgin Mary that Jesus came into the world and it is also through her that he has to reign in the world*" (TD 1). The reign of Christ through the reign of Mary, "is the central point of montfort doctrine and practice. . . . All his Marian activity is entirely oriented to the rule of Jesus Christ as he never ceases saying (TD 62 and 227)."[4] His burning desire, the impelling force of his life, is that "*Jesus Christ, my dear Master will reign more than ever in the hearts of men*" (TD 113).

Father de Montfort describes those who have made the Consecration to the Eternal and Incarnate Wisdom through the hands of Mary as people *"who breathe only the glory and the reign of Jesus Christ by his holy Mother and who sacrifice themselves completely to bring it"* (TD 133). He portrays Mary as the disciple in whom Jesus lives and reigns in a degree unimaginable (TD 248) and therefore sings the beautiful Sulpician prayer "O Jesus living in Mary" (cf. TD 246; H 111:1, 4). His plea to Jesus is that *"to the glory of your Father, / In the power of your name / Reign in us through your Mother / Over nature and demon. Amen*" (H 111:4). The purpose of the Incarnation itself is that God may reign: *"By the Ave Maria, the Great Jesus will reign"* (H 89). His purpose in founding his missionary Congregation, the Company of Mary, was that it may "*reform the church, renew the face of the earth,*" so that the reign of God may come (cf. PM 5). His future members of the Company are told by Montfort that by being poor in spirit, the Kingdom of God is theirs (LCM 5, 7, 9). They form the core of *"a great squadron of brave and valiant soldiers of Jesus and Mary, of both sexes, to combat the world, the devil and corrupted nature"* (TD 114) in order to *"extend His empire"* over all (TD 59).

Although somewhat neglected in early studies of Montfort's spirituality—as the biblical theme of the Kingdom was in theology manuals—the reign of Jesus Christ is a passkey unlocking the ultimate driving force of Montfort's life and writings.

II. The Nature of the Kingdom

It is not without purpose that Father de Montfort prefers the term "reign" over "Kingdom." "Kingdom" has connotations of a territory, a land, a realm, which is not its primary meaning in the thought of Saint Louis Marie. "Reign" stresses the dynamic, penetrating, current rule of the God of love among those who accept that rule. These inheritors of the Kingdom experience its corresponding "interior" transforming effects, which overflow on the world itself. This thought coincides with contemporary theology, which prefers to translate the scriptural *basileia tou theou* (the Kingdom of God) by "the lordship or reign of God since *basileia* means primarily the exercise of royal power, sovereignty and dignity, and only secondarily the realm or territory."[5] Montfort expressly says: "*The kingdom of Jesus Christ consists principally in the heart or the interior of man —according to the words 'The kingdom of God is within you'—in like manner the kingdom of Our Blessed Lady is principally in the interior of man; that is to say, his soul*" (TD 38; cf. TD 113). Not that Saint Louis Marie does not envision the final, ultimate transformation of the universe itself. Montfort speaks of a reign that includes "*the reform of the church and the renewal of the face of the earth*" (PM 17), of great things being accomplished "*in the world*" (SM 59) and "*on the earth*" (TD 272). This can only be achieved, however, by transforming human hearts. It is this "interior" transformation of humankind—the result of the reign of Jesus Christ through the reign of Mary—to which he principally dedicates his life and writings, so that there will be truly an evident reform of the church and a visible renewal of the face of the earth.

The missionary's interpretation of the scriptural reign of God is dynamic. As Kingdom parables often denote growth (cf. Mk 4:30-32), so Saint Louis Marie emphasizes the unfolding of the Kingdom. He dedicates himself wholeheartedly to the development of the total rule—the lordship of Christ—within the hearts of all so that humankind may be lead in the Spirit to the interior castle of the Father, God Alone, God Who is Love (TD 215; H 5). The Kingdom is a present reality, inasmuch as God's reign imparts new life to the world now; but Montfort's view of the biblical Kingdom of God is primarily eschatological. He looked forward with extreme urgency to the fullness of that reign and yearned to be a faith instrument in bringing it about. He was intent, therefore, to form others—through the perfect renewal of Baptism—to be an army filled with the Holy Spirit to transform the reign of Satan into the reign of Jesus Christ. This goal ahead mesmerized the saint. His life and writings were a response to the challenge consuming him: the reign of God must be constantly intensified and thereby become a full reality in the hearts of humankind and in the world itself.

Montfort understood this scriptural reign of God as the fruit of the Holy Spirit working through Mary. His contemplative praying of the *protoevangelium* (Gen 3:15) and the Lucan Annunciation narrative (Lk 1:26-38) convinced him that the Gospels are proclaiming that the reign of Christ Jesus will only come about through the reign of Mary. For, as she is the indissoluble Spouse of the Holy Spirit (TD 85), the Spirit is operative through her in a unique and all-encompassing way, forming not only the Head of the Mystical Body but also "*all the divine persons outside of the Trinity*" (PM 15).

III. The Sources of Montfort's Concept of the Reign

The sources from which Montfort drew the essential lines of his teachings on the Kingdom of God were primarily the Gospels and the French school of spirituality.

1. Scriptural

Saint Louis de Montfort was a man imbued with a love for the inspired Word of God. The Bible was the principal source of his preaching and writings. Texts from the Word of God literally abound in his works.

Without doubt, Montfort's contemplative study of the Scriptures was the primary root giving rise to his teachings on the Kingdom of God. When the saint writes to his sister, "*Seek ye first the kingdom,*" (L 7) he is reflecting his own living of this text (Mt 6:33). As the reign of God is the principal theme of the preaching of Jesus, so it is not surprising that it became the principal theme of the proclaimer of Jesus. Montfort was determined to fulfill the central petition of the Lord's Prayer, "Thy kingdom come" (Mt 6:10).

Montfort's spirituality is founded upon the Annunciation narrative (Lk 1:26-38); so too his doctrine on the reign of God. God, Who is King from all eternity (cf. FC 55; PM 25, etc.), reigns in person among us in Jesus the Lord: *"the reign of God, the Eternal Wisdom"* (LEW 193). It is in Mary's womb and through her hypothetically necessary consent that Jesus, the reign of God, came to be. Mary herself, then, is filled with the glory of the Kingdom; she is Queen (TD 38) alongside and subordinate to Christ the King (TD 38; SR 36, 89).

2. The French school of spirituality

Although the topic of the Kingdom of God is part of the Ignatian Exercises that Saint Louis de Montfort experienced during his studies at Rennes and during his several retreats at Jesuit residences, it would appear that the French school of spirituality was the primary contemporaneous source where Montfort culled his material for his teachings on the Kingdom of God. Olier and John Eudes—and Eudes' enigmatic *dirigée,* Marie des Vallées[6]—play a principal role in Montfort's understanding of the reign of Jesus Christ and of the end times, so intertwined with the saint's formulation of the Kingdom.

John Eudes represents the influence of many of the French school on Montfort's understanding of "reign." In his *Kingdom of Jesus* he repeats a Sulpician theme dear to Montfort: "This must be our desire, our concern, and our principal occupation: to form Jesus in us, i.e., to have him live and reign in us and to have his spirit reign in us, his devotion, his virtues, his sentiments, his inclinations and dispositions . . . that he may be established and reigning in everything."[7] "O Jesus, only Son of God, only Son of Mary, I contemplate and adore you living and reigning in your most holy Mother." [8] Charles de Condren also used expressions that would find a place in the preaching and writing of Montfort: "The reign of sin," "the empire of the devil," "establishing the reign of God."[9] Saint Louis de Montfort was not a copyist; he digested, contemplated, and integrated the treasures of a variety of authors and of diverse schools of spirituality. His creative spirit then intertwined these various strands into a new synthesis of the biblical theme of the Kingdom of God.

IV. Trinitarian Reign

Montfort's stress on the Trinity is integral to his concept of the reign of God. His doctrine on the triune God is not something merely theoretical; it is lived, experienced, flowing from his mystical union with the three

Persons of God. Like Elizabeth of the Trinity centuries after him,[10] Montfort expresses what he has himself tasted in the depths of his being. God reigns as triune.

Consistent with his implication that grace is in the realm of quasi-formal causality, each Person of the Trinity reigns in the Christian according to His individual properties. This becomes evident in the saint's description of Mary as the daughter of God the Father, the Mother of God the Son, and the Spouse of the Holy Spirit (cf. TD 16-36). God reigns in Mary in three distinct ways, as three distinct Persons of the one Godhead.[11]

Montfort the mystic-apostle is not speaking of three different reigns or three different kingdoms. All three Persons must reign in the soul simultaneously, for, as relational realities, one Person cannot reign without the other (*perichoresis*). [12] The soul is possessed by the one God in three distinct and noninterchangeable ways.

This helps us to understand the missionary's famous statement, borrowed substantially from the enigmatic Marie des Vallées: *"The reign especially attributed to God the Father lasted until the flood and ended in a deluge of water. The reign of Jesus Christ ended in a deluge of blood, but your reign, Spirit of the Father and the Son, is still unended and will come to a close with a deluge of fire, love and justice"* (PM 16). The expression cannot be violently wrenched from the entire context of Montfort's Trinitarian thought and used to uphold some variation on a heterodox Joachimite division of the reigns of God.[13] Such an interpretation goes counter to the most fundamental thought of the saint on the reign of the Trinity.[14]

1. The reign of the Father

The Father reigns in the soul precisely as the origin, the source, the fountainhead of all holiness, as the Infinite Lover (H 52 passim; H 53), the eternal infinite Speaking, the *"good Father"* (H 109:33, 38; H 52:2), the "*God of tenderness*" (H 109:26; H 52:11; etc.), "*Father loving us even to excess*" (H 109:2). God Alone is the source from which the Son and Holy Spirit proceed without any subordination. The Father is the Lover pouring Himself out. All things flow from the Father; all return to the glory of God Alone.[15] The Father, termed "the Ancient of Days" (Dan 7:13) to signify His eternity, is the eternal dayspring, eternal dawn, creative outpouring of life. This mighty God of tenderness reigns not only in the brightness of eternal light but also "*here on earth*" (TD 217), "*in this world*" (H 109:35, 37). It is to the glory of God the Father that we are led through Jesus in the power of the Spirit.

Adapting in a positive manner the ominous words of the mystic Marie des Vallées, Montfort describes the special reign of God the Father as culminating at the Flood in a deluge of water. The Flood may well signify the blocking by man through sin of any depth experience of God's reign as Father, Abba. Not that the Father ceases to reign; tragically, his reign is not accepted by creatures. It will be through the Incarnate Son, through a deluge of blood, and in the Spirit through a deluge of love, that we can again cry out from the depths of our spirits, "Abba, Father" (H 7:31).

One could summarize by saying that according to Montfort, the First Person of the Trinity reigns in us precisely as the good Father of Infinite Love, the God of tenderness, the source and goal of all (cf. H 52; H 53).[16] This reign is truly experienced through the redemptive Cross of Jesus and the outpouring of the Holy Spirit.

2. The reign of Jesus

The Son reigns precisely as the Beloved, as the Wisdom of the Father, as the infinite and eternal being-spoken, the Word. He is the divine Second Person of the Trinity, Who is now personally externalized in and through this creation. The infinite Lord has sent His beloved son (Mk 12:6) into the vineyard; the Word of the Father is made flesh (Jn 1:14). The Incarnate Wisdom is the reign of God (LEW 193), "the physical embodiment and personal form of the coming of the kingdom of God."[17] He has come so that we may have life and have it more abundantly through the "*deluge of blood,*" as he reigns on Calvary. His lordship in us is always marked by the Cross (cf. FC passim).

Any sharing in the divine life, any entry into the reign of God must, then, be in and through Jesus. "*He is our only Way who can lead us; our only Truth whom we must believe; our only life who can animate us; and our only All in all things who can satisfy us*" (TD 61). All of our perfection, our life in God Alone, comes only, Montfort insists, through the Son, in the power of the Spirit. This could be paraphrased as saying that the reign of God is a gift, unmerited, to which we have access only through the culmination of all creation, Jesus, the personal epiphany of the Wisdom of the Father.

Although the reign of God in person, Jesus is only fully manifest as the reign through the paschal mystery. Even in the womb of Mary at the moment of his conception, he has come to do the will of the Father (cf. TD 248), to redeem humankind through his life, death, and Resurrection. There is, then, in Jesus a dynamic "becoming" in his presence as the Kingdom of God. Having taken on the opaqueness of our humanity, which was in rebellion against the Creator, he becomes more and more transparent of who he is from the first moment of his conception: the reign of God. His Resurrection is the climactic epiphany of the reign. It is only when glorified that he, as the victorious Eternal and Incarnate Wisdom, is the sender with the Father of the Holy Spirit.

Yet from our point of view, Jesus does not fully reign. Although the supreme gift of the Father, he is not fully known and loved by all. Here we are at the core of Montfort's theology of the reign of God. Each person must inherit the reign of God by repentance and faith: "The kingdom of God is at hand. Repent and believe in the gospel" (Mk 1:15). The *metanoia,* the *kenosis* of each human being must be complete: the emptying of self of all other reigns, of everything that impedes the permeating of the divine rule in us. We must forcefully turn away from sin, acknowledge the nothingness of ourselves, our sinfulness, our rebellion. This repentance however, cannot be separated from faith: the total, active, and responsible surrender of the self to God. Through grace's empowering call, we must release ourselves into the reign of God Who is Jesus. That means, for Montfort, the total, absolute, surrender on every level of being to Jesus (cf. TD 121-125). Through Jesus, in the Spirit, we experience the Father. It is only in total surrender that we are conquerors, only in losing that we find ourselves, only in dying to self that we live. Only by lovingly accepting who we are[18]—slaves of Jesus—do we share in the reign of God. This is Montfort's goal: to proclaim this truth by every means possible, to attract all to a life of sharing in the divine omnipotence of love, of partaking in the reign through the obedience of faith for the glory of God Alone. Only through this growth of the reign of God among people will the Church be reformed and the earth renewed. This is the craving of his life, the all-consuming drive propelling him to proclaim everywhere and to all: Let Jesus Christ be known and loved. Let Jesus Christ reign in our hearts!

3. The reign of the Holy Spirit

The Holy Spirit reigns in the soul as the infinite breath of the Father, the Loving uniting the Lover and the Beloved (TD 36; H 141:1), as the ecstasy of pure receiving from Father through the Son. These Persons are three intrinsic personal relationships in which the one Love Who is God subsists.

In Montfort's concept of the reign of God, the Holy Spirit plays a unique role. It is the Spirit—pure receiving—Who at the Incarnation shares this property so that the humanity is the pure receiving of the divinity, binding the humanity to the divinity hypostatically: the Incarnate Wisdom of God, the lordship enfleshed. After the Resurrection, the Spirit is sent by the Father through the Incarnate Son to draw all people into the life of God. Pentecost—the outpouring of the Spirit—binds Christians together in the love of God, forming the one Body of Christ for the glory of the Father. In the Spirit, through the glorious embodied reign—the Son—we are led back into the Father.

The Spirit overshadows Mary, reigning in her as the deluge of pure love, forming within her the personal form of the reign of God. It is, then, this deluge of pure love that must be poured out on all people (cf. Joel 2:28-29), transforming them into inheritors of the reign of God. Montfort prays for this deluge (PM 16, 17), this continual Pentecost, so that the reign of God may come into the hearts of all totally surrendered to divine love. "*Mary has produced, together with the Holy Spirit, the greatest thing which has been or ever will be—a God-Man; and she will consequently produce the greatest saints that there will be in the end of time*" (TD 35).

V. Mary and the Reign of God

The role of Mary in the theology of the reign of God is essential, according to the thought of Saint Louis de Montfort.

1. Mary shares in the reign of God

No pure creature[19] so shares in the reign of God as Mary. In her we see the supreme exemplification of the conditions to enter the Kingdom: turned away from sin and turned—

actively, responsibly—to the Lord. She is the Immaculate Conception, the sinless one, and therefore totally poor, empty of self. She is also total response to the Trinity's empowering call to share in divine life through Jesus, her Son. She is the first participant in the reign; she shares in its fullness as no other. Her life is also a pilgrimage of faith, of a deepening share in the reign through her ever-intensifying consent to God's inscrutable will.

Mary is the holy one in the Holy, Jesus the Lord. So intensely does she share in the Incarnate Holiness, her Son, that she forms with him but one heart (H 40:36, 37; H 134:8). In her, God reigns supreme. No one participates in the life of the Incarnate Son, the reign of God, as his mother. Through her divine motherhood and her fullness of grace, she shares in the reign of God beyond what the mind can fathom (cf. TD 5-7). Mary is the model of participation in the Kingdom, for she is "poor in spirit," "pure in heart," "like a little child"—the requirements laid down by Jesus for entry into the reign—in total surrender to Infinite love. To gaze upon her is to see in a living person what is meant by entering the Kingdom of God.

Mary, as the "first" in the reign of God, is expressed by Montfort in analogies of presence, sharing: she is "*the paradise of God*," "*the tabernacle of God*," "*the resting place of the trinity*," etc. (cf. TD 262).

2. Mary, Mother of the personal embodiment of the Kingdom

It is through the Incarnation—the root of all mysteries—that the reign of God becomes an enfleshed reality in our creation. Mary's *fiat* gives entrance to the inbreaking of the victorious life of the Beloved, Who conquers the reign of Satan. God has made Mary's consent hypothetically necessary so that the Kingdom of God may rise upon the ashes of the kingdom of Satan. It is in the name of all creation, held bondage to sin, that Mary surrenders to the overshadowing Spirit so that the Father may speak his Eternal Word—establish His reign—in Mary's bosom, for us. Through her salvific and eternal Yes, she is the "*cause of our joy*," for through her divinely willed assent God reigns in this world (cf. LEW 107; H 27:9; SR 45; TD 15, 49).

VI. The Reign of Christ through the Reign of Mary

If it is through Mary that the reign of Christ in this world has begun, it is only through Mary that the reign of Christ can be implemented and reach fulfillment. "*If then, as is certain, the knowledge and the kingdom of Jesus Christ are to come into the world, they will be but a necessary consequence of the knowledge and the kingdom of the most holy Virgin Mary, who brought Him into the world for the first time and will make His second advent full of splendor*" (TD 13; cf. TD 1, 22, 262). Montfort's thought centers on the Incarnation, the summary of all the mysteries of the faith (TD 246-248). The Incarnation is the beginning, the never-to-be-repealed law governing God's plan of salvation. For the beginning is not only the first; it encapsulates everything that flows from it. The reign of Christ is, therefore, the prolongation and fulfillment of the

Incarnation. And as the Incarnation calls for the salvific, effective, eternal, representative role of Mary,[20] then it is only through Mary's divinely willed cooperation that Jesus reigns in the world. The full flowering of the reign of Christ finds its root in the Incarnation, where Mary's Yes plays an intrinsic, hypothetically necessary role. Mary must, then, play an intrinsic role, willed by God, in the growth of the reign of God within human hearts. "*The conduct which the three persons of the Most Holy Trinity have deigned to pursue in the incarnation and the first coming of Jesus Christ, they still pursue daily, in an invisible manner, throughout the whole church; and they will still pursue it even to the consummation of ages in the last coming of Jesus Christ*" (TD 22).

As the inseparable Spouse of the Holy Spirit (TD 34, 36), she is indissolubly united to the Spirit (TD 85) in His role of drawing all into the reign of God through the deluge of pure love. The Spirit works through Mary in forming the Head; the Spirit works through Mary in forming the members (PM 15; SM 13; TD 32). The deluge of pure love—the Holy Spirit—brings about the bonding of the humanity to the divinity hypostatically at the Incarnation through the consent of Mary. The deluge of pure love—the Holy Spirit—gives entry for all peoples to the reign of God through the eternal consent of Mary.

It is not that God has any absolute need of Mary in order to reign in this world. But as Montfort consistently repeats, since God has chosen Mary as the means by which He will reign in this world, it is only through Mary's reign in us that we enjoy the participation in the life of the King. According to God's plan, which does not change (TD 15), the age of Mary is the time when the Spirit ever more intensely overshadows the cosmos and brings forth Christ in our hearts for the glory of God the Father (TD 217). This reign of Mary will bring with it the return of those separated from the Catholic Church and the entry of non-Christians into the Church (TD 50). The reign of Satan was begun by a man, a woman, and a tree; the reign of Christ will overcome the kingdom of Satan in the same way in which the devil conquered: a tree, the Cross; a New Adam, Jesus the Lord; a New Eve, Mary (cf. TD 52-54).

The reign of Mary implies total openness to her effective rule as Mother and Queen, enabling us to be like her in total surrender to the deluge of pure love, the Holy Spirit. Christ, embodiment of the reign of God, will then be formed more intensely in our hearts. Mary, the first disciple, the first Christian, enthrones the King in her heart and in her womb by her loving, total *fiat*. When we enter into Mary and lose ourselves in her dispositions, Christ will capture our hearts in the power of the Spirit, to reign as King. Such is the inscrutable plan of God. When Mary is Queen, Christ will truly be King. "*Ut adveniat regnum tuum, adveniat regnum Mariae*" (TD 217). It is the age of Mary that will usher in the reign of Christ: "*When will that happy time come when the divine Mary will be established as Mistress and Sovereign in hearts in order to submit them fully to the empire of her great and princely*

Son? When will souls breathe Mary as the body breathes air? When that time comes wonderful things will happen on earth. The Holy Spirit, finding his dear Spouse present again in souls, will come down into them with great power. . . . When will that happy time come, that age of Mary, when many souls . . . will hide themselves completely in the depths of her soul, becoming living copies of her, loving and glorifying Jesus?" (TD 217). *"Sooner or later the Blessed Virgin shall have more children, servants and slaves of love than ever; and that by this means, Jesus Christ, my dear Master, shall reign in hearts more than ever"* (TD 113). "*Mary has to be made known and revealed by the Holy Spirit in order that through her, Jesus Christ may be known, loved and served*" (TD 49; cf. TD 50).

VII. The Perfect Consecration, the Means of Bringing About the Reign of Christ

Devotion to Our Lady intensifies oneness with Christ, the reign of God. In LEW 193 Montfort therefore can say: "*For myself, I know of no better way of establishing the reign of God, Eternal Wisdom, than to unite vocal and mental prayer by saying the holy Rosary and meditating on its fifteen mysteries.*" Perfect devotion to Mary is synonymous with the perfect Consecration, whose goal is the implementation of the reign of Christ in the hearts of all (LEW 227). This perfect renewal of Baptism entails losing oneself in Mary (TD 259), taking on her spirit, so that with her, in her, by her, and for her we can live more perfectly in Christ Jesus. It is not only a formula to be pronounced but, above all, a life to be lived, a life in total and loving conformity to reality: Jesus is Lord who comes to us through Mary.

Montfort, therefore, sees the need of proclaiming the Consecration so that the reign of Christ may be more intensely lived in the hearts of all people. If only the poor, the pure in heart, those who are like children, enter the Kingdom of God, then the Consecration fulfills these evangelical conditions, for it is a total stripping of pride, a *kenosis* of everything that we claim as our own, so that our lives may be lived with Mary and under her maternal influence for God Alone. Since the Consecration is the perfect renewal of the baptismal vows, the Gospel lived to the hilt, it is a sure means of entering into the Kingdom who is Jesus. "*That time [the age of Mary] will not come,*" writes Saint Louis de Montfort, "*until people shall know and practice this devotion [the life of total Consecration] which I am teaching*" (TD 217; SM 259).

VIII. The Inheritors of the Kingdom

The personal commitment (faith) demanded by Jesus for participation in the Kingdom is equivalent to saying that the Kingdom is for the poor. For faith is the living-out of the reality of our utter existential poverty. Its opposing concept is pride, haughtiness, self-righteousness. Jesus tells us: "Unless you turn and become like children, you will never enter the kingdom of heaven" (Mt 18:3). The Gospels stress this point by depicting

Jesus as "proclaiming the gospel to the poor" (cf. Mt 9:35; 11:5). The reign is for those who "labor and are heavy laden" (Mt 11:28), for "tax-collectors and sinners" (Mt 11:19), for the sick, the lame, the deaf, the blind. So insistent is Jesus that the Kingdom is only for the poor that he proclaims in the first Beatitude, which summarizes them all: "Blessed are you poor, for yours is the kingdom of God" (Lk 6:20). He boldly proclaims: "I came not to call the righteous but sinners" (Mk 2:17); and addressing some of the haughty religious leaders of the day, he states: "Truly I say to you, the tax collectors and harlots go into the kingdom of God before you" (Mt 21:31).

It is on this scriptural foundation that Montfort founds his proclamation of the Kingdom to the poor. It is one of the most predominant elements of his life; it is an essential element of his spirituality, an integral part of the rules given to his religious Congregations. His writings are not for the proud and haughty but for "*the poor and simple*" (TD 26, 65). It is only those who carry the Cross with Jesus who share in the glory of his reign (LEW 180; FC 9, passim). Montfort's identification with the poor, to a point that baffled the ecclesiastical authorities, is founded upon his obedience to the Gospel, Good News for the poor of the Kingdom of God (cf. Mt 11:4-6).

IX. The Proclaimers of the Kingdom

Montfort yearns to form a squadron of men and women who are not only sharers in the reign but who become Spirit-filled instruments in bringing about the reign of Christ. These apostles of the end times live the baptismal perfect Consecration to Jesus Christ through the hands of Mary. Baptism is of its every nature apostolic; Marian devotion is of its very nature apostolic.[21] The Consecration, as the renewal of our baptismal vows with its explicit Marian dimension, propels those who live it to proclaim the reign of Christ, no matter the cost. Whoever lives the Consecration authentically is of necessity an apostle of the reign of Christ. As Montfort insists, devotion to Our Lady—and particularly the perfect Consecration—is a requisite for these apostles. It not only preserves them in the reign of God but is their weapon in conquering the empire of Satan.

1. Apostles of the end times

These proclaimers of the Kingdom Montfort creatively terms "*apostles of the end times*." "Apostles," for they are truly sent by the Spirit to kindle the fire of divine love throughout the world, to renew the face of the earth and reform the Church. They are apostles of "the end times," i.e., they bring about the flowering of the reign of Christ, which takes place as the universe approaches ever more closely to its goal, Omega, the triumphant reign of Christ the King, when all creation will be a shout of Alleluia to the Lord. In a certain sense, these apostles bring about the end times by their bold, charismatic preaching. Their apostolate instills a greater knowledge and love of Mary and, therefore, of Jesus. The Spirit, the deluge of pure love, works through them, binding all people to the Father and the Son and thereby giving entry into the very life of the Godhead. "*We are given to believe that, towards the end of time and perhaps sooner than we expect, God will raise up great men filled with the Holy Spirit and imbued with the spirit of Mary. Through them, Mary, most powerful Sovereign, will work wonders in the world, destroying sin and setting up the kingdom of Jesus her Son upon the ruins of the corrupt kingdom of the world*" (SM 59).

2. The members of the Company of Mary

Specifically, these apostles of the end times comprise for Montfort, first of all, his Company of Mary. To this chosen bodyguard of God's house and glory (PM 30) the Lord has, in a special way, given the charge of renewing the earth and reforming the Church, thereby bringing about the reign of Christ through Mary. PM describes this company as the core group of the apostles of the end times. Living the Consecration themselves, shining examples of the reign of Christ through the reign of Mary, wherever they go they destroy the empire of Satan and establish the reign of Christ. In the thought of Montfort, entry into the Company of Mary is admission into the "*garde-corps (bodyguard)*" whose purpose is to establish the reign of Christ through Mary.

3. Priests throughout the world

But Montfort is no elitist; in no way does he limit these apostles of the reign to the Company of Mary. His is an urgent call, a heartfelt plea to all priests to join with him in battle against the forces of evil (PM 29; TD 56-59). His call is for a renewal of authentic priestly life, a plea to priests to shake off any lethargy and be who they are by their ordination: the sacramental expressions of Jesus Priest-Victim. Like so many of the French school of spirituality who became involved in the renewal of the clergy—Vincent de Paul, Jean-Jacques Olier, John Eudes—so too Montfort sees that the reign of Christ will come about when the priests are exemplary proclaimers of the Kingdom of God. But Montfort is not involved in the teaching or academic formation of clerics, and he prohibits his Company of Mary from engaging in it. His role is, rather, to call all priests to a profound interior renewal of their priestly vocation as effective announcers of the reign of God.

4. All men and women

The missionary's squadron of apostles of the reign is not a snobbish clerical organization. It also involves laymen and laywomen who, by their living examples and apostolic life, will join in this incursion into the realm of Satan and plant the victorious standard of the Cross of Christ the King. These laity must be filled with the spirit of Mary, the Spouse of the Holy Spirit; they must know and cherish their life of Consecration to the Eternal and Incarnate Wisdom in order to share more fully in the reign of Christ her Son. They are to be the children of Mary and, therefore, apostles of her Son who fearlessly bring about the reign of Christ especially to the poor, the disenfranchised, the rejects of society (TD 47, 48, 114).

Montfort is calling, therefore, for a revolution of love in order to implement the reign of Christ. Faithful to the Good News, he overturns accepted values of the world for the radical demands of Jesus Christ. In the eyes of the world, his plan to establish the Kingdom of God—identical to the Gospel plan—is foolishness. Its strength can only be experienced by people of faith who under the effective influence of Mary, Mother and Queen, freely release themselves wholeheartedly into the life of a renewed and vibrant baptismal vocation.

X. The Time of the Reign

When will the reign come about? As stated in a more detailed manner in the article *End Times* in this Handbook, the time of the reign of God has been interpreted by Gebhard and Plessis as simultaneous with a "spiritual reign," "the coming of Jesus among us . . . through grace."[22] There are, therefore, three advents of Jesus: the Incarnation, grace, and the Parousia. According to these authors, Montfort situates his teachings on the reign of Christ within the "second" coming, i.e., through grace. The primary text used for this opinion is TD 22: "*The plan adopted by the three persons of the Blessed Trinity in the incarnation, the first coming of Jesus Christ, is adhered to each day in an invisible manner throughout the church and they will pursue it to the end of time until the last coming of Jesus Christ.*"

Frehen, however, following the lead of Lhoumeau, interprets Montfort's vision of the reign of Christ as connected to the Parousia itself: "The reign of Jesus, connected to the Second Coming of Jesus Christ, consists in an 'entire reign,' that is to say, that Jesus Christ is perfectly loved and perfectly served; this demands, as a necessary presupposition, that he be 'perfectly known.'"[23] Frehen stresses Montfort's words: "*When our loving Jesus comes in glory once again to reign upon earth—as he certainly will—he will choose no other way than the Blessed Virgin by whom he came so surely and so perfectly the first time. The difference between his first and second coming is that the first was secret and hidden but the second will be glorious and resplendent. Both are perfect because both are through Mary*" (TD 158; cf. TD 22). Frehen believes that when Montfort speaks about the reign of Jesus Christ, he is speaking about the necessary presupposition for the Second Coming of the Lord, the Parousia, i.e., that Jesus be perfectly known and loved, and thereby glorious and resplendent.

J. Séguy considers the reign of Christ as explained by Montfort as an earthly triumph of an undetermined length of time between the time of the Church and the Parousia.[24] According to this classification, Montfort is implicitly following a Marian adaptation of the millenarian thought of Joachim of Flore,[25] an opinion strenuously and rightfully denied by R. Laurentin[26] and Cardinal de Lubac.[27]

A critical study of the time of the reign of Christ as envisioned by Saint Louis de Montfort has been done by S. De Fiores.[28] According to this opinion, Montfort conceives four stages for the final times of the Church. First, the reign of the Antichrist (cf. SM 59; TD 51; PM 4, 5, 13, 20). Second, an intermediate stage: the reign, or the age, of Mary.

This era entails the work of the Holy Spirit, the deluge of love (PM 16, 17), and the apostles of the end times (TD 58), which inaugurate a horrible combat between the devil and the children of Mary (TD 48, 54). Third, the reign of Jesus Christ (SM 58; TD 48; PM 4); Montfort is anything but precise on the length of this reign because he is speaking not of a literal Parousia but a dynamic and intensifying knowledge, love, and service of Jesus leading to the fullness of the reign.[29] Finally, everything is fulfilled by the deluge of fire and of justice (PM 16), which reduces all the earth to ashes (PM 17) and, probably after this deluge, the final Judgment by Christ: "*God will come a second time . . . to judge the living and the dead*" (SM 58).[30]

The division of the first three phases should not be considered as clearly distinct successive moments. Although the writings of Father de Montfort lean to such a sharp division, this is more for the sake of clarity, characteristic of the preacher to the masses. In reality, there would seem to be an overlapping of the first three periods: the time of evil; the flourishing of the reign of Mary and therefore of the working of the Holy Spirit and of the apostles of the end times; the flowering of the reign of Jesus upon earth, reaching its fulfillment in the visible Parousia.

The reign of Jesus Christ is, then, a dynamic eschatological concept. It is a "happening," going on now secretly, for the most part, but it will flourish as Mary's reign intensifies, so that the Holy Spirit's deluge of love will overcome the evil of the world. The full flowering of the reign will be the Parousia, when Jesus will come again in glory with Mary and all the saints to transform the universe into the realm of God in the power of the Holy Spirit.

XI. The Reign of Pure Love

Montfort makes several references to the reign of pure love. As noted above, many of his early letters contain the greeting, "*May the pure love of God reign in your heart.*" The reign of the Holy Spirit is termed a "*deluge of fire of pure love*" (PM 17). Those who implement the reign of Christ are "*ministers of the Lord who like flaming fire will enkindle everywhere the fires of divine love*" (TD 56). This pure love "*God only shares with those who have died to themselves and whose life is hidden with Jesus Christ in God*" (TD 81, 154). The grace of pure love is a gift, an effect of total Consecration, "*so that you will then cease to act as you did before, out of fear of the God who is love, but rather out of pure love. You will look upon him as a loving Father and endeavor to please him at all times. You will speak trustfully to him as a child does to its Father*" (TD 215).

At first sight, the expression "*the reign of pure love*" smacks of quietism. "Dispute over quietism or dispute over pure love have become synonyms."[31] There is, however, no heretical quietism in Montfort's spirituality. The "pure love" as explained by extreme quietists—a love so "disinterested" that it permits one to give into temptation[32]—has no place in the life and writings of Montfort. The apparent misuse of the expression "pure love" by some Spanish and French quietists does not destroy the orthodoxy of the phrase.

The reign of pure love is, for Montfort, found especially in Mary, in her total, active, and responsible abandonment to the overshadowing Spirit. She is addressed, "*O All-aflame / with divine Love*" (H 90:30; cf. H 84:5). The opposite of pure love for Saint Louis de Montfort is "*self-love,*" and the saint insists upon the constant battle needed to destroy this idol so as to center our entire lives on Jesus Christ (H 5:20, 30; TD 81, 146, 149, 197; LEW 202). The reign of pure love, then, that Montfort wishes for his readers is the Holy Spirit, the infinite Loving of the Father and the Son, which enables us to live for God Alone. It destroys scruples and servile fear, immersing us in the God of love (TD 107, 169, 215, 264). The reign of pure love as illustrated by Montfort shows how his teaching steers in between the Scylla and Charybdis of his day, Jansenism and quietism. Montfort insists upon the love and approachableness of God (against Jansenism) but he also insists upon the need for the constant struggle to empty ourselves of all idols (against the quietistic pure love).[33]

XII. Conclusion

A brief study of the theme of the reign of God in montfort spirituality leads to some important conclusions.

1. Basic insight into montfort spirituality

The reign of God can serve as an epistemological prime principle not only for the doctrine of Saint Louis de Montfort but also for his life. The concept undergirds montfort spirituality, and all aspects of it may be seen as spin-offs of this fundamental truth: "The time is fulfilled. The kingdom of God is at hand, repent and believe in the gospel" (Mk 1:15). Montfort, man of the absolute in his life and writings, was dedicated to the fulfillment of this inaugural sermon of Jesus. His preaching, his religious Congregations, his indefatigable drive, his penances, his unequivocal dedication and total commitment—all resulted from the urgency he experienced to extend the reign of Christ.

2. The eschatological character of montfort spirituality

It is a travesty to depict the spirituality of this vagabond missionary as introverted, turned into itself. Rather, Saint Louis de Montfort is open to the future, yearning for the coming of the fulfillment of God's rule. His spirituality is dynamic, tending to the goal ahead, when the Kingdom of God will be established on the ruins of the empire of evil. There is a vigorous thrust towards the future, towards the victorious fulfillment of salvation history, which lies at the very foundation of his spirituality.

In order to be proclaimers of the fulfillment of the reign, those devoted to Our Lady must involve themselves in "the joy and hope, the grief and anguish of people of our time, especially of those who are poor or afflicted in any way . . . nothing that is genuinely human fails to find an echo in their hearts. For . . . united in Christ and guided by the Holy Spirit, [they] press onwards towards the kingdom of the Father" (GS 1).

3. The missionary character of montfort spirituality

It is the reign of God that forced Montfort to go into every sector of the population and animated him to volunteer for the remotest missions of the Church. His spirituality does not remain in the Upper Room. Filled with the boldness of the Spirit, those who follow him are ipso facto missionaries. They experience an unquenchable zeal to go to every town and place to proclaim that the Kingdom of God has come in Jesus and that through Mary, the Spouse of the Spirit, we must implement that rule of Infinite Love.

4. A clarification of devotion to Mary

The essential Marian dimension of montfort spirituality is the direct opposite of a narcissistic attitude. Rather, it spurs us on to bring forth Christ in the souls of men, to strip ourselves of everything in order that Jesus be known. The Christocentrism of montfort Mariology is seen even more clearly in light of his doctrine on the Kingdom of God. The age of Mary is not an end in itself. It is pregnant with Jesus, the embodied reign of God. It must experience the birth pangs of struggle with evil in order to bring forth the King. The more we *"lose ourselves in Mary,"* the more we will live the reign of Christ and become bold apostles ushering in the victorious rule of God.

The communicating of a deeper knowledge and love of Our Lady has as its goal a deeper knowledge and love of Our Lord so that he may reign in our hearts (TD 49, 50). Devotion to Our Lady is for those willing to risk all in living the radical demands of the Kingdom. It is for those willing to be dynamic signs of the Church of the eschaton. When Christians breathe Mary as they do air, especially through total Consecration to the Eternal and Incarnate Wisdom, we have present one of the signs that the goal is at hand, that the fullness of the reign is fast approaching.[34] "When the Church is 'Mary,' Christ will be able to be born and finally to reign in the world."[35] "The Mother of Jesus . . . is the image and beginning of the church as it is to be perfected in the world to come. Likewise she shines forth on earth until the day of the Lord shall come (cf. 2 Pet 3:10), a sign of certain hope and comfort to the pilgrim People of God" (LG 68).

P. Gaffney

Notes: (1) J. M. Hupperts, *Pour elle (For Her),* Série Immaculata 5, Secretariat Marie-Médiatrice, Louvain 1957, 24. (2) J. Fitzmyer, *The Gospel according to Luke (I-IX),* Doubleday, Garden City, NY 1981, 153. (3) W. Kasper, *Jesus the Christ,* Paulist Press, New York 1976, 100-101; cf. Mk 10:29, where it appears there is an identification of Jesus with the Good News. Cf. J. Fitzmyer, *The Gospel according to Luke,* 153. (4) J. Hupperts, *Pour Elle,* 56. (5) P. Hunerrmann, *Reign of God,* in *The Concise Sacramentum Mundi,* Seabury, NY 1975, 1349; cf. R. Schnackenburg, *Note on Theological Terminology,* in *God's Rule and Kingdom,* Herder & Herder, New York 1963, 354-357. (6) Cf. S. De Fiores, *Le Saint Esprit et Marie dans les derniers temps selon Grignion de Montfort (The Holy Spirit and Mary in the End Times according to Grignion de Montfort),* in EtMar 43 (1986), 133-171. (7) St. Jean Eudes, *Royaume de Jésus (Kingdom of Jesus),* in *Opera Completa,* 1:271ff., cited in *Lectionnaire propre à* *la congrégation de Jésus et Marie (Lectionary Proper to the Congregation of Jesus and Mary),* Paris 1977, 56-57. (8) S. Jean Eudes, *Royaume,* 432; *Lectionnaire,* 129. (9) Charles de Condren, *Pièces diverses,* ed. Auvray des Lettres, 541, cited in *Lectionnaire,* 167. (10) Cf. Jean Lafrance, *Elizabeth of the Trinity: The Charism of Her Prayer,* Darlington Carmel, 1983. (11) Montfort shows a remarkable knack of getting across profound Trinitarian theology in many of his hymns, e.g., "*In God there are Three Persons / Father, Son, Holy Spirit / Three infinitely Good, / I believe it for God has said it. / Three make only one God for the Three have only one Essence: / The Father is God, the Son is God, / The Holy Spirit is God. / All equal in substance*" (H 109:2). (12) Cf. W. Kasper, *The God of Jesus Christ,* Crossroad, New York 1982, 283-285; cf. DS 1331. (13) Cf. J. Séguy, *Millenarisme et "Ordres adventistes": Grignion de Montfort et les "Apôtres des Derniers Temps" (Millenarianism and "Adventist Orders": Grignion de Montfort and "The Apostles of the End Times"),* in *Archives de Sciences sociales des religions,* 53/1 (January-March 1982), 29-30. (14) The literary genre of PM must also be a hermeneutical tool in deciphering Montfort's understanding of the reign of the Father, the reign of the Son, and the reign of the Holy Spirit. He is caught up in contemplative prayer, in a lovingly violent pleading with God that springs from the center of his soul, begging God to send missionaries all aflame to proclaim the Kingdom of God. The text is not from an academic treatise on *De Deo Trino.* Using analogies borrowed from mystics, Montfort speaks of the triple reign of the triune God: a deluge of water, a deluge of blood, a deluge of love. The text cannot be wrenched from the total context of his Trinitarian teachings without distorting the thought of the saint. (15) Cf. R.Laurentin, *Dieu Seul est ma tendresse, (God Alone is my Tenderness),* O. E. I. L., Paris 1984, 198. (16) Cf. ibid., 195-198. (17) W. Kasper, *Jesus the Christ,* 101. (18) Montfort is speaking about an explicit, faith acceptance of the reign. But if that is not possible, a desire—whether actual (*in re*) or, if that also is not possible, through desire (*in voto*), even implicit desire (*etiam implicito*)—gives entry into the Kingdom. Cf. DS 3869-3872; LG 16. (19) Mary is a "pure creature" (TD 14), i.e., she is, in the totality of her being, creaturely, *ab alio.* Modern Christology stresses the full humanity of Christ, insisting correctly that it is "creaturely." Because of the hypostatic union, however, the humanity of Jesus is the humanity of the Second Person of the Trinity. Jesus, therefore, cannot be called a "pure creature," a term that can be applied to all other human beings, who are, of course, ontologically human persons. (20) Montfort is interested in the present order of salvation, for in reality there is no other. And as is evident from the development of salvation history, Mary's consent is hypothetically necessary (i.e., not necessary in itself but only because of God's free will) in salvation history; cf. TD 14, 15, 39. (21) Spontaneously addressing the members of the 1987 general chapter of the Montfort Missionaries, Pope John Paul II, speaking directly to the superior general, said: "You have pointed out that the two elements go together: Missionary and Marian. . . . This has been stressed in the encyclical *Redemptoris Mater* and likewise in the teaching of Vatican II in *Lumen Gentium,* chapter 8." The full text of the address of the superior general and of the Holy Father's response can be found in QOAH (May-June 1991), 11. (22) Cf. H. M. Gebhard, SMM, *Commento al Trattato della vera devozione a Maria Vergine (Commentary on the Treatise of the True Devotion to the Virgin Mary),* in RDC 5 (1918), 3-4; A. Plessis, SMM, *Commentaire du Traité de la vraie dévotion (Commentary on the Treatise of the True Devotion),* Librarie Mariale, Pontchâteau 1943, 83-84, 152-171. (23) H. Frehen, *Le second avènement de Jésus Christ et la "méthode" de Saint Louis-Marie de Montfort (The Second Coming of Jesus Christ and the "Method" of Saint Louis Marie de Montfort),* in Dmon 7 (1962), 101; cf. A. Lhoumeau, *La Vierge Marie et les apôtres des derniers temps d'après le B. Louis-Marie de Montfort (The Virgin Mary and the Apostles of the End Times according to Bl. Louis-Marie de Montfort),* Mame, Tours 1919, 7-14. (24) J. Séguy, *Millenarisme et "Ordres Adventistes;"* cf. L. Perouas, *Ce que croyait Grignion de Montfort et comment il a vécu sa foi,* Mame, Paris 1973, 186-187; English translation, *Way to Wisdom.* (25) Cf. M. F. Laughlin, *Joachim of Flore,* in *New Catholic Encyclopedia,* 7:990-991. (26) Cf. R. Laurentin, *Dieu Seul est ma tendresse,* 268. (27) H. De Lubac, *La posterité spirituelle de Joachim de Flore (The Spiritual Posterity of Joachim of Flore),* Paris, Lethielleux, Paris 1979, 232. (28) S. De Fiores, *Le Saint Esprit et Marie dans les derniers temps selon Grignion de Montfort (The Holy Spirit and Mary in the End Times According to Grignion de Montfort),* in EtM 43 (1986), 133-171. (29) Ibid., 143. (30) Ibid., 144. (31) Jacques Le Brun, *La question du l'amour pur (The Question of Pure Love),* in DSAM, 12B:2824. (32) Cf. T. K. Connolly, *Quietism,* in *New Catholic Encyclopedia,* 12:26-28. (33) This authentic total abandonment—demanding so much from the soul as Montfort insists—has become well known through the popularity of Father de Caussade, *The Joy of Full Surrender,* Paraclete Press, Orleans, Mass. 1986. (34) Cf. De Fiores, *Le Saint Esprit et Marie,* 145-146. (35) Ibid., 171.

REPARATION

SUMMARY

I. INTRODUCTION.
II. TYPES OF REPARATION IN THE WRITINGS OF MONTFORT:
  1. Reparation as healing or restoration;
  2. Reparation for public offenses.
III. SAINT LOUIS DE MONTFORT AND REPARATION OF OUTRAGEOUS INSULTS TO GOD:
  1. Catherine de Bars and the Benedictines of the Blessed Sacrament;
  2. The Visitation and Saint Margaret Mary;
  3. Atonement for outrages:
    a. Letters;
    b. Hymns.
IV. CONCLUSION.
V. EVALUATION:
  1. The problem;
  2. The solution.
VI. RELEVANCE.

I. INTRODUCTION

Reparation is an ambiguous term. Even in profane use it may be employed in the sense of repair of a damaged object or an act of justice whereby payment of some sort is made for damage done. In religious use it has a variety of meanings. It means principally the work of redemption accomplished by Our Lord Jesus Christ, in the sense of "repairing the damage done" by Adam's revolt and the sin of his progeny; Christ restores us to God's friendship. The term is also used in a generic way for restitution for injuries, usually when moral theology cannot measure precisely what such payment would entail. In popular devotional literature and also in ascetical theology, reparation is the making of amends for insults given to God through sin, either one's own or another's. Through Saint Margaret Mary's devotion to the Sacred Heart of Jesus—a devotion stemming through Saint John Eudes back through Saints Gertrude and Mechtilde and Saint Francis' devotion to the Five Wounds and Passion of Christ—"reparation" took on a more distinctive meaning. Saint Margaret Mary saw Christ's heart and his love ignored and ridiculed; the response of man is to be reparation through adoration, prayer, and sacrifice.

After a brief review of Saint Louis de Montfort's use of the term "reparation," the article will touch on his teaching of reparation as making amends for the insults given to our Lord through sin and negligence of his love.

II. TYPES OF REPARATION IN THE WRITINGS OF MONTFORT

The root "*repar*" is found in Louis Marie's writings about forty times in such terms as reparation, reparatrice, repairer, to repair. The object of this "reparation" may be creation, humanity, Heaven, the Honor of God, and of course scandals and injustices. In most cases Montfort does not use the word as contemporary spirituality defines it, as compensation for an outrage against love.[1] Occasionally he refers to reparation in ways that are unrelated or tangential to spirituality, e.g., repair of church buildings (RM 16), reparation for damage caused by an enemy (SR 99), for damage done to the property of others (H 29), or for honoring the devil (H 100; cf. also the word *"irreparable"* and the loss of *"what one knows not how to repair"*: H 12:30; H 115:1; H 139:15).

1. Reparation as healing or restoration

It was in the writings of Poiré[2] and Grasset that Montfort first encountered the idea that Mary, in unity with her Son, atones for the fallen world. He also knew Eadmer of Canterbury's assertion that, through her piety, Mary had "succeeded most worthily in atoning for the fallen universe—*ut reparatrix perditi orbis dignissime fieret.*"[3] In LEW and TD, "reparation" means restoring the universe and, in particular, healing the wounds of mankind caused by sin. When Adam became a slave of the demon and the object of God's anger, *"nothing could restore his privileges"* (LEW 40). Wisdom, by whose word *"everything was made and everything was restored"* (LEW 95), chose *"to become man in order to restore fallen humanity"* (LEW 104; see also TD 156; H 13, 14). In Mary, Jesus *"has perfectly restored the glory"* that sin had taken from the Father (TD 248). Mary, the *"restorer of the human race"* (TD 28), is completely united with the Son; as she gains the fidelity and perseverance of those who commit themselves to her, she *"makes good the losses caused by Eve's unfaithfulness"* (TD 175). According to Alain de la Roche, *"who restored the devotion of the Rosary"* (SR 27), *"by this prayer* [the Angelic Salutation] *the whole world was restored"* (TD 250; see also SR 49). Through the Angelic Salutation, the ruins of heaven have been repaired and *"the empty thrones in heaven have been filled"* (SR 45).

2. Reparation for public offences

Montfort cites the example of the preacher who at one time had preached against the Rosary and then *"publicly acknowledged his former error"* (SR 32), and that of the woman who had given herself to the devil and felt *"an intense desire to make amends for this terrible deed"* (SR 109). He called on the Daughters of Wisdom to make public reparation for their faults (RW 53, 306) and invited them to atone for *"the scandals of all of your brothers"* (H 37, 112; it is unclear whether he is referring to those who have committed these acts or to those who have been their victims). We know that Montfort founded confraternities for the reparation of such public wrongs.

III. Saint Louis de Montfort and Reparation of Outrageous Insults to God

After examining some of the historical roots of Montfort's desire "to make amends" for insults to the Lord, a study of his letters and hymns will reveal his own thoughts on reparation for outrages committed by Christians against divine Love.

1. Catherine de Bars and the Benedictines of the Blessed Sacrament

Montfort was familiar with the spirituality of Catherine de Bar (Mechtilde of the Blessed Sacrament, 1614–1698), the foundress of the Benedictines of the Blessed Sacrament, if only because his sister Guyonne-Jeanne had joined the order in 1702. Since the beginning of the seventeenth-century, Christianity had known some great profanations of the Blessed Sacrament, which renewed attention to the atonement dimension of adoration and gave rise to various societies for the Blessed Sacrament. The first monastery was officially established on March 12, 1654, and the queen herself was present to read an official proclamation of atonement. In the view of Catherine de Bars, the adoration offered by the religious was rooted in their status as victims, as a result of their unity with Christ in the Eucharist. They were obligated to make reparation for those who did not pray. Catherine de Bars, however, did not consider herself among the "innocent victims" offering their lives in reparation, but rather as among the sinners atoning for sins against the Lord, especially in the Eucharist. We can see her influence at the beginning of the eighteenth century in formulas for atonement and exercises of reparation that were included in various manuals for adoration and for confraternities of the Blessed Sacrament.

2. The Visitation and Saint Margaret Mary

While at the Monastery of the Visitation at Poitiers, Montfort, although he never mentions her name or convent, in all probability became familiar with Saint Margaret Mary (1647–1690), a nun of the Order of the Visitation at Paray-le-Monial, she had mystical experiences which led to devotion to the Sacred Heart. An apparition in 1673 was the starting point for her mystical life. In it Jesus invited the future saint to exchange her heart for his. She was no longer simply his slave, but the object of his passionate love. This in a way goes beyond the kind of "slavery" advocated by Cardinal Pierre de Bérulle (died 1629), founder of the Oratory of France and also of what Brémond has called the French School of spirituality. Saint Louis de Montfort considers "*slavery of love*" a recognition on our part of the tender and passionate love of God for us in Jesus Christ.

Margaret Mary had another apparition, in 1675, in which Jesus lovingly complained that, even among those consecrated through religious vows, his love for mankind was returned only with ingratitude. Our Blessed Lord requested that the first Friday after the octave of the Feast of the Blessed Sacrament be established as a feast day to honor his Sacred Heart and to atone for the insults inflicted upon it. Devotion to the Sacred Heart is characterized by *redamatio*, the atoning love of the faithful who have in some way experienced the love that Christ has first given them and who wish to give their love to Christ in return.

3. Atonement for outrages

Atonement for outrages is discussed both in Montfort's letters and in his hymns.

a. Letters. In his letters, Saint Louis de Montfort uses the term "victim" to indicate a person whose life is spent in atonement for the insults offered Our Lord through sin but especially to the Eucharistic Lord. To his sister, admitted to the monastery of the Benedictine

Nuns of the Blessed Sacrament, he wrote: "*You are now immolated, truly, deeply and for ever. Let no day pass without offering yourself in sacrifice as a victim. Spend more time before the altar praying than in resting and eating*" (L 12). Montfort encouraged her to live the life of a sacrificial victim, in the spirit of the Benedictines of the Blessed Sacrament, and to atone for him: *"It is a source of great of happiness and a great honor for me to have someone so near to me offering loving sacrifices to make up for the faults* ["outrages"] *I have, alas, so often committed against Jesus in the Blessed Sacrament"* (L 19; cf. also Letters 17, 18). He even addresses her, in light of her vocation, as "*Dear victim in Jesus Christ*" (L 19).

b. Hymns. The Cantiques of Montfort call for reparation to Jesus for insults commited against him in general and most especially in the Eucharist and to his Sacred Heart.

- Amends for injuries to Jesus in General. Montfort's hymns invite us to make amends for songs that are offensive to God's honor (H 1:23), and to restore, through penance, the *"glory and honor of the Lord"* (H 13:12) while also making amends for *"the outrages / against Jesus at his Passion"* (H 13:13). He notes that *"To righteousness, repentance / Makes an atonement of honor"* (H 13:38).
- Amends for Injuries to the Eucharistic Lord. He particularly invites us to atone for the outrages inflicted on the Blessed Sacrament: *"Make honorable amends / To Jesus dishonored / Even in a sacred place . . . / Cry, angels, cry, / Cry and atone / For this excess, this supreme insult"* (H 158:12). H 136, *"Reparation (Making Amends) to the Most Holy Sacrament of the altar,"* is a nineteen verse bitter satire on the customs of his times which so often ignored if not insulted the Eucharistic presence: "*Let us moan, let us bitterly weep / . . . For Jesus in the Most Blessed Sacrament / Is Forgotten, Insulted even in His Extreme Love* (H 136:1). After detailing the disgraceful state of the church building, the missionary does not hesitate to point out the blasphemous attitude of some of the people towards the Blessed Sacrament, but reserves his sharpest barbs for the cleric in charge of the church. His hymn ends with the prayer: "*Pardon, my sweet Jesus, both for them and for us / Have pity on us, have pity on you yourself! / Ah!, that we would be able to atone these outrages / By your own Blood and our weak homage*" (H 136:18).
- Reparation and devotion to the Sacred Heart. Montfort demands reparation for the outrages inflicted on the Blessed Sacrament, especially in the seven hymns that are expressly written to foster devotion to the Sacred Heart (H 40–44, 47, 48). There we see devotional characteristics that can be traced to Paray-le-Monial: Jesus' reproach that his love is insulted, *redamatio,* and acts of reparation.
- *Jesus' love insulted.* The Sacred Heart is the symbol of the love that the Son bears for us and that he demonstrated by surrendering himself completely to the Father for our sake (H 40, 41; also H 132:7: *"My heart has exhausted itself for you").* But this love is too often insulted: *"All of my labors are tossed to the ground / My blood, my Heart, my charity"* (H 42:16). He is overwhelmed by non-Christians, heretics, and, especially, malicious Catholics, who *"surpass the cruelty"*

of the others and who show *"only indifference"* toward his Heart (H 43:13, 17).

• *"Redamatio" (returning love with love) and the offer of comfort.* The Heart of Jesus *"looks for solace"* to give to the penitent soul (H 42:2). *"Your tears give me pleasure,"* it says to that soul. *"I have suffered many affronts / So that I can be here now for you. / Make amends with your homage"* (H 42:5.33). *"My Heart loves and desires you, / For you my heart was pierced, / My heart longs for your heart"* (H 43:38). *"Let us love this Heart, because it loves us, / Love is paid with love"* (H 44:2; cf. also H 47:18; H 132:8; H 133:9; H 135:4).

• *Acts of reparation.* The act that is *"The most glorious to the Lord . . . / Is to restore His honor"* (H 44:17). We must *"atone for the injury / That we have done to this divine Heart"* (H 44:18) and make *"honorable amends"* (H 133:9). Hymn 47, entitled "Reparation to the Heart of Jesus," asks for pardon on behalf of many different sinners, from the unfaithful laity to wicked priests. For a missionary such as Montfort, pious desires alone do not make reparation: *"It is the end that I crown / And not the beginning,"* says Jesus in the hymn. The invitation to the *"Princes of France"* to love the *"victorious heart,"* accompanied by a promise of victory for their troops (H 42:30), may be our oldest written trace of Saint Margaret Mary's message to Louis XIV.

IV. Conclusion

The theme of reparation (in the spiritual sense) is not explicitly discussed in the prose works as it is in the hymns. But we can assume that Montfort was aware of what was happening at Paray-le-Monial while he wrote these works. His spiritual experience led him down many different paths. He affirmed the goodness of the Lord, who is touched by the misery of fallen humanity. Divine Wisdom brought together the members of the Trinity, so to speak, *"for the purpose of rehabilitating man in the state he formerly created him"* (LEW 42). Montfort also writes of the love that is ridiculed by all, even by Christians (FC 11), and he discusses the satisfactory value of atonement for sins committed (TD 122, 171). Like Margaret Mary, he affirms the *redamatio*—the response of love to the gift of love—but Montfort sees this as a total, all-inclusive response. It refers not to specific practices of atonement, such as on the first Friday, but to making a complete gift of oneself, a consecration. To make such a gift is in Montfort's view the ideal in any Christian life; and although Montfort never explicitly mentions it, reparation would certainly be encompassed by this gift. He does not discuss reparation when he speaks of the works undertaken by the friends of Wisdom *"for the glory of God and the salvation of souls"* (LEW 100), nor when he explains why the Cross is *"precious"* (LEW 176) and why we should consecrate ourselves to Jesus through Mary (TD 135–37), nor even when he explains how consecration gives greater glory to Jesus Christ (TD 222–25). But this act of consecration does indeed contain an element of reparation. In this act we in effect acknowledge how much Wisdom has done for us through love, and, simultaneously, we acknowledge our own unfaithfulness (LEW 223, 225). By offering ourselves through the mediation of Mary, we are truly honoring Jesus Christ, because *"we are showing that, because of our sins, we are unworthy to approach his infinite holiness directly on our own"* (SM 36; cf. TD 223).

V. Evaluation

1. The problem

Treading unconsciously in the footsteps of the late medieval nominalists, and forgetting that mankind is joined by a constitutive, essential link with its Creator, modern Western thinkers have too often set mankind and God in opposition to each other, as if in the present order of things man could go his way and God His own. Some contemporary thinkers then reject God; the others reject mankind. Even for some members of the French School, who were anxious to assert God's greatness, creation itself and mankind in particular were considered as somehow "separate" from the Creator and Redeemer —to such an extent that it was said that "the entire universe should be destroyed for His glory."[4] From this perspective, reparation provides additional grounds for man's destruction: his sin.

2. The solution

Although Montfort is generally grouped with the French School, there is no problem of this kind in his writing. Saint Irenaeus's statement that "the glory of God is a living person"[5] reflects Montfort's conception of mankind's relationship with God. But there is no sanctimony in Montfort's optimism: he thinks of mankind as disfigured, precisely because its connection with God has been substantially damaged by sin. Reparation necessarily implies restoration of the glory of God, *redamatio*, and the Cross. It also implies service to man and to society, as many encyclicals, dating back to Leo XIII's *Rerum novarum* (1891), as well as the Second Vatican Council (GS 3), have affirmed.

VI. Relevance

Montfort can contribute to a spirituality of atonement precisely because he enables the Christian to overcome artificial distinctions between various kinds of reparation, and thereby to experience reparation in its profound unity, in accordance with the highly comforting yet incredibly urgent teachings and examples of Wisdom incarnate (LEW 173). Montfort's unifying theme of Wisdom not only clarifies the meaning of "reparation," but also brings contemporary man face to face with the horror of insulting our brother, Jesus the Eternal and Incarnate Wisdom.

From another standpoint, Saint Louis Marie's teaching on reparation shows an essential interrelatedness of all within the Body of Christ. The insults to the Lord committed by an individual affect the entire creation, the blasphemies of nations even more so. Montfort therefore hopes to offset this lack of harmony by acts of reparation, especially by acts directed to the Eucharistic Lord; for love of Jesus expressed by even one individual helps to restore the relationship of this universe with God in Christ Jesus.

J. Stern - P. Gaffney

Notes: (1) É. Glottin, "Réparation," in DSAM 13 (1988), 394. (2) Cf. in particular *Triple couronne* (Triple crown), second Treaty, ch. VI; cf. Montfort's *Notebook,* 57–60. Montfort used the 1639 edition. (3) *De excellentia Virginis Mariae,* c. 9 (PL 159, 573D); cf. A. Cabassut, "Éadmer," in DSAM 4/1 (1960), 4. Montfort attributes this text to Saint Anselm and also to Saint Bernard. (4) Attributed to Condren (1588–1641) by his biographer, Amelote; cf. A. Molien, "Condren," in DSAM 2 (1953), 1376. (5) *Contra haereses,* IV, 20, 7.

RETREATS

SUMMARY I. RETREATS IN THE SEVENTEENTH CENTURY:
1. Religious reform in France in the seventeenth century;
2. Retreats as an element of reform;
3. The end of the age of Louis XIV and the beginning of the eighteenth century.

II. THE RETREATS INSTITUTED BY MONTFORT:
1. Autobiographical evidence:
a. Letters,
b. Rules,
c. Hymns,
d. True Devotion;
2. Biographical testimonies:
a. The decisive and painful events of his life,
b. Places of retreat;
3. The apostolic life and retreats:
a. Mission-retreats,
b. Retreats for nuns.

III. THE SPIRITUAL RETREAT TODAY:
1. What is understood by the spiritual retreat today?;
2. The content of the spiritual retreat;
3. Several forms of the spiritual retreat.

I. RETREATS IN THE SEVENTEENTH CENTURY

1. Religious reform in France in the seventeenth century

The seventeenth century in France saw a spiritual upsurge that marked the life of the Church for a long time; it has been named the "golden age of spirituality." It was a time of reform, for the Church bore the heavy weight of an ignorant, lazy, and sometimes even corrupt clergy: there were too many of them in the towns, they had received little training, they were motivated often by financial gain, and they had a status that dispensed them from pastoral work but ensured a good income. As for the people, they were marked by ignorance and superstition of all kinds. This is the context in which a whole reform movement developed and widened in the course of the first part of the seventeenth century. This movement was both pastoral and deeply spiritual.[1]

2. Retreats as an element of reform

The parish mission movement developed as a result of this reform. In the first decades the missions of the likes of Michel Le Nobletz or of Vincent de Paul had a double aim: to catechize the people in the rudiments of the faith and to have the people begin a new life in Christ by means of a general confession. The organization of the missions thus brought them closer in nature to what today would be termed retreats. Among a whole range of methods employed in order to develop the spiritual life, the retreat was clearly impressive. It was introduced both by the Jesuits and by the Franciscan Recollects of the Strict Observance and became so widespread that new houses for the "recollections" needed to be built. All the large towns and many country regions soon had such houses. In Paris the Saint-Lazare house of retreat was very well attended. For eight or ten days, people kept silence, were recollected, meditated, prayed, and listened to a director speaking on religious matters; then general confession was made and Communion received; the good Catholic left the house in excellent spirits.

Other methods were added to this movement directed towards the people. There were the growing influence of the colleges of the Jesuits, the Oratorians, and others, and the creation of the "exercises for ordinands," which contributed to the training of the clergy. In the fall of 1628, Vincent de Paul, in response to a request from his bishop, preached the first retreat of those to be ordained. This met with considerable success. The archbishop of Paris wanted to have the exercises in his own diocese; once he had seen how they went, he required that these exercises take place there in the future. Gradually this movement spread to several other dioceses of France.

3. The end of the age of Louis XIV and the beginning of the eighteenth century

In 1660 the extraordinary era of the "great century of souls"[2] was already waning, and a new chapter of the Church in France was soon to begin. In fact, in 1660 Vincent de Paul died, preceded by eminent reformers such as Jean-Jacques Olier, Le Nobletz, and others. These deaths were omens, although, of those great figures who led the Church in its admirable effort of renewal; there were a few who, like John Eudes, survived and tried to continue the effort. Three tendencies developed out of this situation: the decline of the dynamism of the seventeenth century, the appearance of the new spirit of the eighteenth, and the opposition of various pastoral currents. At the beginning of the seventeenth century, the missions were therefore a means of doctrinal education for the people, leading to individual conversions. For the clergy, the "exercises" were a means to ensure their own theological training. Through these efforts many advances were made: the retreat movements, practice of the renewal of the baptismal vows and the propagation of prayer. In approximately the 1690s, at the latest in 1700, the major preoccupation was to continue being the faithful heir to the past, improving on it only in a small number of ways.

II. The Retreats Instituted by Montfort

1. Autobiographical evidence

Montfort lived through the turn of the century (1673-1716), a time when the weakening of efforts for renewal in the Church was becoming more pronounced. His personal reaction to the "retreat movement"—one of the great means of reform for the clergy as well as the Christian people—is important to discover.

a. Letters. In order to understand his attitude to this situation, we must consider that although Montfort harbored a secret love of the secluded life, he also felt a great desire to attract people to a greater love of Our Lord and his Blessed Mother.

In the letter of December 6, 1700, to his director, Father Leschassier, Montfort expressed his spiritual state in the following terms: "*On the one hand, I feel a secret attraction for a hidden life in which I can efface myself and combat my natural tendency to show off. On the other hand, I feel a tremendous urge to make our Lord and his holy Mother loved, to go in a humble and simple way to teach catechism to the poor in country places and to arouse in sinners a devotion to our Blessed Lady*" (L 5).

Montfort certainly drew on energies from the great spiritual reforms of the past, which included retreats. As we learn from the letter written to his uncle Alain Robert on September 20, 1694, he participated in organized retreats: "*I was not able to reply to your letter as soon as I wished because I was making a retreat at St. Sulpice in preparation for the reception of minor orders which, thanks be to God, I have now received*" (L 2).

Retreat into solitude also had a quite special attraction for Montfort, having a central place in his personal life at those decisive moments and times of testing that marked his missionary life.

Montfort spoke of his habit of making retreats in letters to his director Leschassier. After he was obliged to wait for the bishop of Poitiers for four days, he wrote: "*During this time I made a short retreat in a little room where I enclosed myself, in the middle of a large town where I knew nobody*" (L 6).

Again, on July 4, 1702, when his ministry at the Hospital was threatened, he wrote: "*During this painful period, I kept silent and lived in retreat putting my cause into the hands of God and relying on his help, in spite of opposite advice given to me. To this end I went for a week's retreat to the Jesuits*" (L 11).

b. Rules. The program of the missions preached by Montfort was similar to that of the retreats: a time of preaching and prayer that led to a total conversion to Christ. In 1713, with his future congregation in mind, Montfort wrote: "*The purpose of these missions is to renew the spirit of Christianity among the faithful,*" In the chapter of RM entitled *"Prayers and Spiritual Exercises,"* he recommends that they make *"at least one day of recollection every month"* after they have returned from their missions, and that "*outside the times when they are giving missions . . . the time allotted during the mission for preaching and hearing confessions is devoted to study, prayer and retreat*" (RM 78).

In RW, he wrote: *"Each month they make a retreat of one day; and every year a retreat of ten days"* (RW 134). Montfort entrusts the work of retreats to the Daughters of Wisdom as part of the *"exterior aim"* (RW 1).

It is clear that in his life, Montfort favored retreats as a means of sanctifying himself and wished to pass it on to those men and women who would follow him.

c. Hymns. Montfort also spoke of retreat in another sense, a mystical sense, to signify the soul's encounter with God, in a strengthening and reassuring exchange.

Thus, in his canticles to the Sacred Heart of Jesus, he sings: "*This is the holiest retreat / Where all sin is avoided, / Where the most imperfect soul / Becomes most holy with little effort*" (H 40:18). "*Let us all make our retreat / In his sacred side*" (H 72:19). "*Dear lamb, keep your retreat / To avoid the wolves / To listen to me and to speak in secret*" (H 106:37).

d. True Devotion. In a comparable sense, he took up the term "retreat" in TD, where he uses an allegory that might appear simplistic to modern interpreters: the biblical figures of Esau and Jacob as symbols of the punished reprobate and the chosen. The love for solitude appears to mark the chosen: "*They stay at home . . . , they . . . love the interior life . . . in the company of the Blessed Virgin . . . whose glory is wholly interior*" (TD 196).

2. Biographical testimonies

a. The decisive and painful events of his life. Montfort told his director that he was both a man drawn to solitude and a missionary to the people. The biographers point out that it was quite "costly" for him to acquire biblical radicalism. But a retreat was always the new starting point that helped him to see more clearly the loving hand of God.

Biographers point out several retreats that he made in the course of his active missionary apostolate.

On his return from Rome in 1706, strengthened in his vocation of Apostolic Missionary, he decided to pause at the famous abbey of Saint-Martin of Ligugé, which belonged to the Jesuits at the time. Obliged by Monsignor de la Poype to leave the diocese of Poitiers, he withdrew to the home of a priest who was a friend of his for a retreat of eight days in order to ask the Holy Spirit to direct his steps at this decisive moment of his life.

In September 1710, the failure of the Calvary of Pontchâteau brought him back to his usual method of spiritual renewal. He went on a week's retreat at the house of the Jesuits in Nantes. "This is the calming remedy to which he turns when his heart is heavy."[3] This was a painful but decisive moment in his life; he emerged from this retreat like a new man who had come to a deeper understanding of the fact that God's ways include the Cross.

In 1714, once the bishop of Rennes had refused to accord him faculties in his diocese, he went on a retreat "with the Jesuits" near the College of Saint Thomas. For a week he lived in contemplation of Jesus Christ; and it is in the fervor of this retreat that he composed the circular letter to the Friends of the Cross, deeply engrossed in the mystery of God Incarnate crucified.[4]

In 1714, before leaving for Normandy and while reflecting on the importance of this journey, he withdrew from company in order to prepare himself by means of a fervent retreat.

b. Places of retreat. Not only did Montfort frequent houses of retreat, as, for example, those of the Jesuits, but he chose isolated places in order to immerse himself deeply into retreat.

His stay beneath the staircase of a wretched hovel on rue Pot-de-Fer in Paris was one of his prolonged retreats, where, filled with contemplative prayer, it appears that he wrote LEW (1703-1704), or at least a part of it.

The hermitage of Saint-Eloi at La Rochelle was also one of the places where he loved to withdraw between apostolic works. It is most probably there that he wrote TD in the fall of 1712. As well as Saint-Eloi, he chose other isolated areas, such as the grotto of Mervent and the hermitage of Saint-Lazare.

In these places far removed from the world, he sought tranquillity, peace, and contact with God in an atmosphere his ardent and mystic soul required.

3. The apostolic life and retreats

a. Mission-retreats. Whoever surveys Montfort's life can see that his love for a secluded, contemplative life was present even during his active parish missions. Clement XI named him an Apostolic Missionary, and Montfort gave meaning to this title through his activity both in popular missions and in retreats organized for different groups of people.

Grandet relates that he was preaching a retreat in 1706 to more than two hundred persons of the Third Orders of St. Francis and St. Dominic. "There he was," remarked Le Crom, "at last a recognized missionary and, we might add, an up-to-date one. First the popular soup kitchens, then the closed retreats: the holy Breton priest, with his air of sanctity, was a man of progress."[5]

From 1707 to 1708, he joined Leuduger for the preaching of parish missions that could just as well have been called closed retreats. For "during the holy exercises, the church was really the center of existence for the people of the parish: catechism lessons, songs, prayers, examinations of conscience, and sermons followed each other all day long. At such times, the public squares of our towns resembled monastic cloisters."[6] This type of mission utilized as far as possible the excellent method of closed retreats.

But either on account of his collaborators' jealousy or Montfort's eccentricity, the Father from Montfort was rejected by Leuduger, the director of the mission band. According to Vincent F. Desmaretz, bishop of Saint-Malo, it was because Montfort ceaselessly preached God's mercy and the tenderness of the Blessed Virgin and because beggars and vagrants followed him everywhere.

L. Perouas tells us that in 1706 Montfort spoke of *"mission"* in reference to his recently completed preaching in the poor areas of Poitiers. Everything seems to indicate that it was a kind of retreat. It took people out of their regular parish routine. Montfort increasingly adopted the term "mission" to describe this time of prayer and reflection which was common at the time. In 1711 and 1715, he termed what his colleagues merely called "retreats" by the names: *"women's mission"* and *"soldiers' mission."*

b. Retreats for nuns. While Montfort preached retreats to penitents, he also gave several retreats to nuns. In 1712, at La Rochelle, he agreed to provide a retreat for the Sisters of Charity of St. Augustine. On various occations, he preached retreats to the nuns of the Order of Visitation of La Rochelle. The Sisters of St. Joseph of Providence, the Poor Clare nuns of the convent of Ave Maria, the nuns of the Sacred Heart of Ernemont, and countless others benefitted from his preached retreats.

As for the themes that Montfort dealt with during retreats, there only remains an outline in LS 769-770 and an *"Order of retreat"* for four weeks in LS 771. From the mission to La Garnache in 1712, Montfort returned in "follow-up missions" to the parishes he had evangelized. He emphasized "dying happily" and handed out the short work HD.[7]

III. The Spiritual Retreat Today

1. What is understood by the spiritual retreat today?

In the seventeenth century, the retreat centered on conversion and individual salvation. At the outset, its function was the reform of the clergy and the instruction of the Christian people. Gradually it shed a certain doctrinal rigor, moved on to Christian morality, and rose to a spiritual, even mystical, level under the influence of the great saints who marked this period.

The idea of organized spiritual retreats preached in a retreat house for a week or a month has been passed down to us through the religious families that have preserved and lived this tradition.

The retreat, however, has evolved enormously both in form and content and has spread from religious houses to take its place in the midst of God's people for persons of all ages and situations in life.

2. The content of the spiritual retreat

The spiritual retreat today is centered on the Word of God. Increasingly it begins with people's experience in order to lead them to read their spiritual story in the light of the ever-living Word. It also tries by its content to lead Christians to a life lived in relation to God, a relation initiated by God (1 Jn 4:19).

The modern Christian who has progressed from an intellectual faith to a faith that is a vital response to God increasingly desires to have a personal experience of the Gospel and divine life. The retreat, in various forms, permits him or her to attain this encounter, this experience.

The retreat is a milieu where, far from feverish and noisy activity or only in privileged moments, the Christian can enter into a dialogue with God and with himself. Modern culture has changed the content of the dialogue radically, but the aim remains the same: the Christian must consciously place Christ at the center of his or her life, for "in reality the mystery of man can only be explained by the mystery of the Word incarnate . . . and reveals to him the sublimity of his vocation" (GS 22).

3. Several forms of the spiritual retreat

The phenomenon of our having passed from awareness of individual salvation to the recognition of a collective and even cosmic salvation gives rise to a profound change in our encounter with God and the way we express it.

The traditional closed retreat, of variable length and spent in total or partial silence under the direction of a guide, still has a place today, especially among religious.

There is also an accompanied or organized retreat of six to eight days, centered on personal prayer rather than on content presented by a speaker. It is an encounter with God in solitude, an internalization of the texts of the Holy Spirit. This process aims to make individuals open to the working of God and to accustom them to discern His call so that they can respond with ever increasing faithfulness.

There are likewise the "thirty-day retreats" integrated into the normal routine of life. Without abandoning daily occupations, the individual sets special time aside to be in silence and meditate on the Word of God. This form of retreat is carried out under the direction of a competent director.

The young of today need special forms of the retreat, like simple days of recollection and weekends dedicated to conversation and to prayer in which people search together for answers to life's problems. Taizé has proven to be admirably successful in drawing today's youth into days of retreat and reflection.

Montfort spirituality not only draws its followers into times of solitude but also calls on them to provide times and places of retreat to others, especially to the poor. Saint Louis de Montfort's life and writings, combined with a contemporary imitation of his creativity, are the important ingredients for Spirit-filled contemporary retreats.

H. Robitaille

Notes: (1) R. Deville, *L'Ecole française de spiritualité (The French School of Spirituality),* Desclée, Paris 1980, 17ff. (2) H. Daniel-Rops, *Histoire de l'Église du Christ (The History of the Christian Church),* Grasset, Paris 1962-65, 7:31-32, 243ff. (3) B. Papàsogli, *Montfort, A Prophet for Our Times,* Edizioni Monfortane, Rome 1991, 37-38. (4) Besnard I, 154. (5) L. Le Crom, *Un Apôtre marial, St. Louis-Marie Grignion de Montfort (1673-1716),* Librairie Mariale, Pontchateau 1942, 182. (6) Ibid., 183 (7) L. Perouas, *Grignion de Montfort, les pauvres et les missions (Montfort, the Poor, and Missions),* Cerf, Paris 1966, 84.

The Wisdom Cross of Poitiers

Preserved in the Mother House of the Daughters of Wisdom in Rome, Montfort made this cross in 1701-1703. The article in the Handbook "Cross" explains the significance of the Wisdom Cross for Montfort.

ROSARY

SUMMARY

I. Introduction:

II. The Rosary in the Life and Missions of Montfort:
   1. "With his Rosary in his hand;"
   2. In his missions;
   3. Montfort and the Dominican Order;
   4. Efficacy of the Rosary during missions.
   5. Directives to missionaries.

III. The Rosary in Montfort's Writings:
   1. An "exterior practice" of Marian devotion;
   2. A teaching on the Rosary;
   3. The legacy of a tradition;
   4. A secret . . . destined for everyone;
   5. In spite of contradictory advice;
   6. Praying with faith;
   7. "My Hail Mary, my touchstone;"
   8. Meditation on the mysteries;
   9. "The easiest of all prayers;"
   10. "From my own experience;"
   11. A blessed way of praying the Rosary:
   12. Final advice;
   13. A set of instructions: the 150 motives.

IV. Montfort's Methods of Reciting the Rosary:
   1. The method of offering of the decades:
   2. The method of adding phrases;
   3. The Rosary said with a reflection before each Our Father and Hail Mary;
   4. A Rosary in hymns:

V. The Rosary in Montfort spirituality:
   1. A devotion centered on Jesus Christ;
   2. Learning about Jesus through the mysteries of the Rosary;
   3. Special devotion to the mystery of the Incarnation;
   4. "Long live Jesus, long live his Cross";
   5. The place of the Rosary in Montfort's Spiritual Way.

VI. Conclusion: Montfort and the Rosary Today.

I. Introduction

Over the last two centuries, Montfort's doctrine has played an important part in bringing about a renewed interest in praying the Rosary. How can montfort spirituality contribute to the practice of praying the Rosary in our contemporary world, which seems to be searching for methods of prayer?

At the time of the French Revolution, the practice of saying the Rosary was common among Catholics. Rosary confraternities were established in most parishes. Pauline Jaricot of Lyons added great impetus to this devotion with her "Living Rosary" (1826). The Rosary carried by Our Lady at Lourdes also contributed to the popularity of this prayer. Pope Leo XIII, who was personally very influenced by the discovery of the *Treatise on the True Devotion,* published an encyclical on Marian devotion, and on the Rosary in particular, every year from 1883 to 1901.

The history of devotion to the Rosary, which for a long time had been encumbered by the legend of Alain de la Roche, was gradually clarified by historians: from the time of Esser and Thurston, to significant articles on the Rosary by W.A. Hinnebusch in the *New Catholic Encyclopedia* (1967) and by P.A. Duva in the *Dictionnaire de Spiritualité* (1988).[1] Devotion to the Rosary also has benefited from the study, in the years prior to Vatican II, of the biblical sources of Marian piety, and from the teachings of Paul VI in *Marialis Cultus* (1974), Nos. 42–55.

Today there seems to be a new hunger for "spirituality" and a desire for the support of those "methods of prayer" that have been tested and proved worthy by tradition. Montfort helps us rediscover, pray, and live the Rosary.

II. The Rosary in the Life and Missions of Montfort

1. "With his Rosary in his hand"

It is evident from any biography of Montfort, such as Father Le Crom's work,[2] that throughout his life the Rosary was one of the most common expressions of Louis Marie's Marian piety. With Rosary in hand, "He was affectionate and devoted to his brothers and sisters. Louise-Guyonne was his favorite and in his desire for her to practice virtue, he would take her aside while the others played, and they would say the Rosary together."[3]

In 1699, he made a pilgrimage to Chartres with some students of the Seminary of Saint-Sulpice. "When they spoke, they spoke only about Our Lady; when they prayed together, they recited the rosary, said their breviary and sang hymns from the Psalm Book of Saint Bonaventure."[4] Later he was seen arriving at Ligugé, "his hat under his arm and his Rosary in his hand."[5]

In 1706, at the Dominican convent of Dinan, where his brother Joseph-Pierre was chaplain, he asked to celebrate Mass at the altar of Blessed Alain de la Roche, the famous preacher of the *Office of Our Lady.*[6]

2. In his missions

When Montfort left the poorhouse at

Poitiers and undertook his first missions, the Rosary was the principal practice that he recommended. In 1705, at Montbernage, he erected a crucifix in the center of a barn: he had transformed the structure into an oratory, and had decorated the walls with fifteen banners, representing the fifteen mysteries of the Rosary. There, in order to obtain grace from God, the Rosary was recited before a statue of the Blessed Virgin every evening.[7]

Before Montfort left Poitiers, he wrote to the people of Montbernage: *"Remember . . . to have a great love for Jesus and to love him through Mary. . . . Do not fail to fulfill your baptismal promises and all that they entail. Say your Rosary every day either in private or in public and receive the sacraments at least once a month."*[8]

At La Chèze, in the diocese of Saint-Brieuc, Montfort established the Society of Virgins, the Society of the Friends of the Cross, and the Confraternity of the Rosary, in order to maintain the results of his parish mission. The entire Rosary was recited three times daily: morning, noon, and evening.[9]

To aid in praying the Rosary, Montfort used a variety of props. At Montbernage there were the fifteen banners representing the fifteen mysteries of the Rosary. At the end of the mission of Sallertaine, Montfort erected a cross, "whose beams bore a large Rosary wrapped around the Body of Christ."[10] At the Hermitage of Saint-Lazare, very close to his native town, Montfort devised something novel: "In the sanctuary on a kneeler there was a large Rosary with iron links and beads as large as nuts which several people could finger at the same time."[11]

At the majestic Calvary of Pontchâteau, the Rosary had the place of honor: a field of 150 fir trees, interspaced with 15 cypress trees, formed an immense Rosary and several small chapels recalled the mysteries of Jesus and Mary."[12] At Saint-Donatien in Nantes he had fifteen banners on the Rosary carried in procession, and during his homilies he used fifteen paintings on the mysteries.[13] In his *Testament*, dictated on the eve of his death, he said, *"I give to each parish of Aunis where the Rosary will be continued to be recited, one of the banners of the Holy Rosary."*[14]

3. Montfort and the Dominican Order

Saint Dominic is considered by all to be the "originator" of the Rosary. Consequently, his order held a monopoly on founding and directing Rosary confraternities, especially from the time of Pope Pius V.[15]

Since Montfort was also a great preacher of the Rosary, he decided to become affiliated with the Dominican family by entering their Third Order. He made profession at the hands of the Prior of the Convent of Nantes on November 10, 1710.[16]

In May, 1712, he wrote to the Master General of the Dominicans to ask him for *"permission to preach the Holy Rosary wherever the Lord calls me, and to enroll into the Rosary Confraternity with the usual indulgences as many people as I can. I have already been doing this with the permission of the local Priors and Provincials."* Montfort made his request through the Provincial of France, and it was granted.[17]

4. Efficacy of the Rosary during missions

At La Rochelle, a Protestant town, it seems that Montfort showed particular zeal for the Rosary; he preached his first three missions there, in the church of the Dominicans, during the summer of 1711.

According to Besnard, "The apostle of the Rosary . . . used this heavenly devotion very advantageously to convert the Protestants, who had based some of their false doctrines on the Albigensian heresy. He left the controversies to those whom the Bishop had designated for this ministry, and dedicated himself to stimulating devotion to the Holy Rosary, and to explaining the mysteries that are called to mind at the beginning of each decade."[18] The conversion of an important Protestant woman, Madame de Mailly, "caused a great sensation and convinced several people who were hesitant." It was specifically stated that "until her death in 1749, she was faithful to the daily recitation of the Rosary."[19]

According to the testimony of a priest, who had known Montfort in Paris during the summer of 1713, "No one was a more faithful disciple of Saint Dominic when it came to the devotion to the Rosary. He recommended its practice to everyone, and he confided that he himself had obtained from God, through the intercession of the Blessed Virgin, the conversion of the most obstinate sinners. He had a book on the marvels of the Holy Rosary, which he explained with such unction that everyone was amazed. I believe that he influenced more than a hundred thousand people."[20]

He summarized his beliefs in such expressions as: *"Believe in the power of the Rosary; no sinner has ever resisted me once I have collared him with my Rosary."*[21]

In September 1714, Montfort visited his good friend J. B. Blain, then a canon at Rouen. Blain relates two incidents in which Montfort challenged two very different groups of people with his Rosary.

The first episode took place among the Sisters of Ernemont, to whom he had preached a retreat, terminating it with a homily on the Blessed Virgin. After he had preached on the Rosary with great ardor and love, they asked him to "give them a demonstration" and to recite it himself, using his own method. He did so "with such tender devotion to Mary" that he inspired everyone to deep piety. He was remembered for his Rosary, which had fifteen decades and was worn openly on his belt. Thus, he was called the "priest with the big rosary."[22]

Another episode took place several days later, on a ferry crossing the Seine. As Blain described it, "It was a real Noah's Ark. . . . Ordinarily about two hundred people were on board, returning home on market days. It was not exactly the most propitious place to talk about God. . . . However, as soon as our missionary embarked, he knelt down in front of everyone, and with his large Rosary in his hand, invited them to pray with him. The sight of the holy priest inviting them to say the Rosary became a joke for the group. They were happy to have such a butt for their laughter. When they finished laughing, he invited them again to say the Rosary. The laughter began again, and continued for quite a while. After that, the devoted priest, whose zeal seemed to grow with each humiliation, invited them for the third time, to say the Rosary. He asked them so dynamically and devoutly, that he convinced the group to say the Rosary in its entirety, and to listen to his homily which lasted until the boat landed. This story was told to me by an eyewitness."[23]

5. Directives to missionaries

Each time that Montfort gave direction on Christian life, he mentioned the Rosary, whether it was in the *"Covenant with God"* that he wanted signed at the end of the missions (CG), in the *"Rule of the Forty-four Virgins"* (RV), or in the *"Rule of the Penitents of Saint Pompain on Pilgrimage to Our Lady of Saumur"* (PS). *"Without attracting extraordinary attention, you may carry a Rosary and wear a crucifix over your heart . . . in their procession they will sing hymns, they will recite the Holy Rosary, and they will pray silently. . . . During the day they will recite the entire Rosary in two groups"* (PS 2-5).

In his directive concerning the Rosary, Montfort was particularly insistent on its use for the personal prayer life and missions of the Missionaries of the Company of Mary. *"Every day they will say all fifteen decades of the Rosary as well as the Little Crown of the Blessed Virgin."* In their missions, *"to renew the spirit of Christianity among the faithful . . . during the whole of the mission they do all they can to establish the great devotion of the daily Rosary and they will enroll as many as possible in the Rosary Confraternity (they have the faculties for this); they will explain the prayers and mysteries of the Rosary, either by instructions, or by pictures or statues which they have for this purpose; and they will give the people good example by having the whole Rosary recited aloud in French every day of the mission at three different times with the offering of the mysteries . . . this is one of the greatest secrets to have come from heaven"* (RM 29, 52, 56–57).

Let us conclude our consideration of the place of the Rosary in the life and missions of Montfort with two beautiful expressions from the *"Prayer for Missionaries."* Montfort asks for missionaries who will be *"men after your own heart . . . like David of old, with the Cross for their staff and the Rosary for their sling,"* and for *"true servants of the Blessed Virgin, who, like Dominic of old will range far and wide, with the Holy Gospel issuing from their mouths like a bright and burning flame and the Rosary in their hands"* (PM 8, 12).

III. The Rosary in Montfort's Writings[24]

1. An "exterior practice" of Marian devotion

In the TD, the Rosary is cited among the principal exterior practices of devotion to the Blessed Virgin:

"Enrolling in her confraternities. . . . Singing her praises. . . . Giving alms and fasting in her honor. . . Carrying such signs of devotion to her as the Rosary, the scapular, or a little chain. . . . Reciting with attention, devotion and reverence the fifteen decades of the Rosary in honor of the fifteen principal mysteries of Jesus Christ, or at least five decades which is a third of the Rosary." The traditional list of the joyful, sorrowful, and glorious mysteries follows (TD 116).[25]

Even if some proud people *"consider the Rosary to be a devotion suitable only for ignorant and illiterate people,"* Montfort affirms, *"I know no surer way to discover if a person belongs to God than by finding out if he loves saying the Hail Mary and the Rosary"* (TD 250–51).

At the beginning of his ministry, Montfort wrote: *"For myself, I know of no better way of establishing the kingdom of God, Eternal Wisdom, than to unite vocal and mental prayer by saying the holy Rosary and meditating on its fifteen mysteries"* (LEW 193).

We should not be any more concerned than Montfort himself was regarding the term "exterior practice" (cf. TD 226). We already perceive the essence of what he thinks about the Rosary and his insistence on praying it: insistance on the daily rosary, vocal and mental prayer, the Our Father and Hail Mary, and meditations on the mysteries of Jesus Christ. For Montfort, these would always be deeply important.

2. A teaching on the Rosary

Among Montfort's manuscripts one finds an explicit teaching on the Rosary, in which there are two different forms: a) a text written primarily for parish priests and preachers: *"The admirable secret of the Holy Rosary for conversion and salvation"* (SR), which has two *"blessed methods for the recitation of the holy rosary;"* and b) An outline of instructions for the people in the form of the Rosary, *"150 motives which oblige us to say the Rosary"* which Montfort inserted in his *Book of Sermons.*[26]

3. The legacy of a tradition

In the first pages of SR, Montfort refers to the sources of his book on the Rosary: *"All I have done has been to copy from very good contemporary authors and, in part, from a book written a short time ago, The Mystical Rose Tree, by Fr. Antonin Thomas, O.P."* (SR 33)[27] In comparing the texts one perceives that Montfort had in hand the second edition (Rennes 1698).[28] This was very probably the *"marvelous book on the rosary"* that he had with him in Paris in 1713.[29]

Montfort began writing his SR in the Notebook (N), which he began keeping during his seminary years at St. Sulpice. He copied into it many Latin and French texts on the Rosary, in particular those of the Franciscan John of Carthagena.[30] Also cited are texts by the Jesuits Boissieu and Spinelli and the Dominican Cavanoc. He cited one or more texts on abandonment by Alain de la Roche, in particular *Apology* and *Psalter of the Virgin Mary,* which Montfort knew in their Latin versions.[31] It is evident that SR is for the most part a faithful rendering of the Dominican tradition of the Rosary, as explained by Alain de la Roche.[32]

Montfort accepted this tradition unconditionally, as did the Church of his time, (save for a few critics), for it had been approved by the popes since Pius V. Montfort was a missionary, not an historian. We might add that in the context of the Counter-Reformation, the Rosary appeared like a sign and a providential weapon against "heretics," very similar to how it had been used by Saint Dominic against the Cathars.

In order to highlight the montfort spirituality of the Rosary, we shall concentrate on what Montfort considered essential to this prayer tradition and what he added to it.

4. A secret . . . destined for everyone

Antonin Thomas addressed his *The Mystical Rose Tree* to the Directors of the Confraternity of the Holy Rosary—that is, to priests. His intention was to supply them with material for preaching and for directing confraternities. He assured them that "it is the secret of winning the hardest hearts and of converting the most despairing people, of conserving penitent souls in the state of grace . . . and of helping those people who aspire to perfection, to make great strides in virtue." Montfort, after having written his *"little book,"*[33] also addressed it with touching fervor to priests and above all to that company of missionaries about whom he never ceased to dream: *"Ministers of the Most High, preachers of the truth, trumpeters of the Gospel . . . Let us not be satisfied, my dear brothers, to counsel it* [the Rosary] *to others; we must practice it ourselves . . . Let us imitate Jesus Christ, who began by practicing what he preached"*(SR 1–2).

Then Montfort spoke directly to sinners, to pious people, and to little children: *"Poor sinful men and women, I, a greater sinner than you, wish to give you this rose, which is crimson because the precious blood of Jesus Christ has fallen on it. . . . Even if you are on the brink of damnation, even if you have one foot in hell, even if you have already sold your soul to the devil, . . . sooner or later you will be converted and will amend your life and save your soul, if you say the Holy Rosary devoutly every day until death"* (SR 3–4).

Truly the Rosary is for everyone: *"Let the learned and the ignorant, the just and the sinners, the great and the small praise and honor Jesus and Mary night and day by saying the Holy Rosary"* (SR 8).

5. In spite of contradictory advice

There have always been critics of the Rosary. Montfort was aware that his life and preaching were opposed to those of many clergymen and well-known people. He was often careful to justify himself in speaking to the humble and the sinners: *"if I thought that the grace God has given me to know by experience the efficacy of preaching the Holy Rosary to convert souls would move you to preach this beautiful devotion in spite of the fact that priests are not in the habit of doing so these days, I would tell you how I have witnessed the most wonderful conversions it has wrought, but instead of all this I think it will be quite enough for this little summary if I tell you a few ancient yet authentic stories about the Holy Rosary."* (SR 2; cf. 17, 33).

It is not surprising that Montfort seemed to accept without difficulty anecdotal stories of the sort that critical contemporary historians would never accept. He was a man of his times. It is evident from what he says that he discerned clearly the difference between divine faith, human faith, and *"pious faith."* We know that he saw the difficulty in being neither *"too credulous nor too critical"* (SR 33). This keeps us from caricaturing him as a person with an insatiable desire for the unusual.

6. Praying with faith

Speaking of the Creed that was recited on the crucifix of the Rosary, Montfort highlighted the need for faith as the *"root, foundation and beginning of all Christian virtues"* (SR 34). *"Since faith is the only key which opens all the mysteries of Jesus and Mary for us, we must begin the Rosary by saying the Creed very devoutly, and the stronger our faith the more merit our Rosary will have. . . . One must not be looking for sentimental devotion and spiritual consolation in the recitation of the Rosary, nor should one give it up because the mind is flooded with countless involuntary distractions nor because one experiences a strange distaste in the soul. . . . Neither feelings, nor consolations, nor sighs, nor transports, nor the continual attention of the imagination are needed to say the Rosary well. Faith and good intentions are quite enough"* (SR 35).

7. "My Hail Mary . . . my touchstone"

When speaking of the prayers of the Rosary—the Our Father and the Hail Mary—Montfort followed the second decade of *The Mystical Rose* Tree step by step. He repeated word for word what seemed truly useful, skipped several paragraphs or even whole chapters that seemed very complicated, and added his own personal comments here and there. We will examine closely what he says about the Hail Mary, highlighting his original contributions.

Montfort repeated everything that referred to the Incarnation, the Mother of God, and the glory of the Holy Trinity, and he added this conviction: *"The Angelic Salutation is a most concise summary of all that Catholic theology teaches about the Blessed Virgin"* (SR 44).

At the beginning of the subsequent chapter of *The Mystical Rose Tree* Montfort found these words, attributed to Mary by Alain de la Roche: "It is a probable and imminent sign of eternal damnation to have an aversion for the Rosary, to be lukewarm and negligent in the recitation of the Angelic Salutation which has saved the world; and on the contrary, it is a great sign of predestination to be devoted to it" (*The Mystical Rose Tree* II, 10). Montfort felt challenged; he affirmed and completed the thought using Alain's Latin quote, and added his personal comments: *"Heretics, all of whom are children of the devil . . . have a horror of the Hail Mary. . . . Among Catholics, those who bear the mark of God's reprobation, think but little of the Rosary. . . . Even if I did not believe what was revealed to Blessed Alain, even so my own experience would be enough to convince me of this terrible but consoling truth . . . that a devotion which appears to be so insignificant can be the infallible sign of eternal salvation, and its absence can be a sign of God's eternal displeasure.*

The Hail Mary, the Rosary, is the prayer and the infallible touchstone by which I can tell those who are led by the Spirit of God from those who are deceived by the devil. The Hail Mary is a blessed dew that falls from heaven upon the souls of the predestined, giving them a marvelous spiritual fecundity. . . . The Hail Mary is a sharp and flaming blade which, joined to the Word of God, gives the preacher the strength to pierce, move, and convert the most hardened hearts." (SR 50–51)[34] After these very personal asides, Montfort takes up the text of *The Mystical Rose Tree* from where he left off: *"This divine salutation."* He pauses once again to include two other statements of Alain de la Roche cited by John of Carthegena, which he had copied a long time previously in his notebook: *"The court of heaven rejoices and earth is lost in wonderment whenever I say Hail, Mary"* (SR 55).

Finally he excerpted exactly the beautiful paraphrase of the Angelic Salutation that followed in *The Mystical Rose Tree:* "Are you in the miserable state of sin?" Evidently, Montfort loved to cite this text which concurred admirably with his own personal devotion, and with his pastoral zeal.[35]

To transmit his love for the Hail Mary to Christians, Montfort composed a hymn with twenty-six stanzas: "The Triumph of the Hail Mary," with its well-known chorus: *"Through the Hail Mary / Sin will be no more. Through the Hail Mary / Jesus we adore"* (H 89).

8. Meditation on the mysteries

"Those who pray the Rosary say it better if they say the Hail Marys while meditating on the life, passion, and glory of Jesus Christ. Meditation is the soul of this prayer. The Rosary without meditating on the sacred mysteries of our salvation would almost be a body without a soul, excellent matter, but without the form which is the meditation, and which distinguishes it from other devotions" (SR 61).

Montfort has taken these two statements from *The Mystical Rose Tree* (IV, I), the first from Blessed Alain's tradition. Pope Paul VI, (in MC 47) repeats the same idea: *"Without contemplation, the Rosary is a body without a soul."* We are now at the heart of the Rosary.

The numbering of the fifteen mysteries (SR 62–64) is identical to that in *The Mystical Rose Tree* with two slight differences: the Presentation of Jesus in the Temple comes before the Purification of the Blessed Virgin; and the crucifixion of Jesus is completed by his death on Calvary. While summarizing, Montfort made his own the teaching of Father Antonin Thomas on the meditated Rosary, in the fourth, fifth, and sixth decades of *The Rose Tree.* The titles that Montfort added at the beginning of the twenty-second, twenty-third, and twenty-fourth roses highlight what seemed most important to him: *"The meditation of the mysteries conforms us to Jesus; the Rosary is a memorial of the life and death of Jesus; the meditation of the mysteries is a great means of perfection."*

Montfort adds a personal remark: *"A Christian who does not meditate on the mysteries of the Rosary is very ungrateful to Our Lord and shows how little he cares for all that our divine Savior has suffered to save the world"* (SR 70).

9. "The easiest of all prayers" (SR 76)

There was lively debate in the spiritual centers of Montfort's time concerning the importance of meditating on the mysteries of the Rosary. Montfort alludes to this debate when he mentions the *"false Illuminists and Quietists of our times."* He is certainly referring to the notion of Quietism, revived in France in 1685 by the publication of *A Short and Easy Way to Pray* by Madame Guyon. Saint Sulpice considered as suspect anything related to "Illuminism," and Father Tronson was at Bossuet's side in 1694–1695, at the Seminary of Issy, to question Madame Guyon about her doctrine. In 1698, Bossuet published his rigorous treatise *On Quietism.*[36]

These were precisely the years when Montfort was a student for the priesthood. Torn between his spiritual fervor and his Sulpician formation, he was certainly knowledgeable about the essence of the debate: should one consider as opposites "prayer of the mind" and "prayer of the heart," meditation and union with God, the practice of virtue and infused prayer?

The Mystical Rose Tree (V, 9) answers the questions that Montfort pondered: "There are three types of prayer: meditation, which is a form of reasoning within oneself . . . ; contemplation, which is the union of a soul with God . . . ; and the prayer of the heart. . . . It is this last type of prayer that one engages in ordinarily while meditating on the mysteries of the Rosary, and considering lovingly and gratefully Jesus Christ in the stages of his hidden life—his suffering life and his glorious life to encourage oneself in the practice of virtue and the avoidance of sin. Prayer of the heart is the balance between meditation and contemplation, it shares the advantages of both, and is the end toward which they tend, which is the love of and transformation into Jesus Christ."

But Montfort knows very well that this debate will do nothing for his *"dear member of the Rosary Confraternity"* (SR 78). So he gives free rein to his heart and to his pen: *"Never will anyone be able to understand the marvelous riches of sanctification which are contained in the mysteries of the Holy Rosary. . . . Nor is there anything in the world more moving than the wonderful story of the life, death and glory of Our Savior, unfolding before our eyes in the fifteen mysteries. How could there be any prayer more wonderful and sublime than the Lord's*

Prayer and the angel's Ave? . . . For learned men and women, these mysteries are the source of the most profound doctrine, while simple men and women find in them a means of instruction well within their reach. We need to learn this easy form of meditation before progressing to the more sublime heights of contemplation. . . . It is dangerous, not to say fatal, to give up saying the Rosary under pretext of seeking a more perfect union with God. . . . Believe me, dear member of the Rosary Confraternity, if you genuinely wish to arrive at a high degree of prayer in all honesty and without falling into the illusions of the devil so common with those who practice mental prayer, say the whole Rosary every day, or at least five decades of it . . . on the other hand, if while saying the Rosary, God in his infinite mercy draws you to himself as forcibly as he did some of the saints, let yourself be drawn to him, let God work and pray in you and let him say your Rosary in his own way" (SR 75–77).

For Montfort, the Rosary was more than an easy way of prayer available to everyone: it was a spiritually sure way to the highest forms of union with God. *"The Rosary, recited while meditating the mysteries, brings about marvelous results: it gradually brings us a perfect knowledge of Jesus Christ; it purifies our souls from sin; it gives us victory over all our enemies; it makes the practice of virtue easy; it enflames us with the love of Jesus Christ; it enriches us with graces and merits"*(SR 81). Knowledge and love, practice of the virtues and grace; the Rosary is a complete prayer. And Montfort concluded, *"It must not be imagined that the Rosary is only for women, and for simple and unlearned people; it is also for men, and for the greatest men"* (SR 95).

10. "From my own experience" (SR 113)

The fourth decade of SR is somewhat deceiving: there Montfort copies entire pages from *The Mystical Rose Tree* on "the marvels that God has performed through the Rosary," and these marvels are of almost no interest to us today. But at the end Montfort abruptly adds: *"I, who write this, have learned from my own experience that the Rosary has the power to convert even the most hardened hearts. . . . When I have returned to Parishes where I have preached missions, I have seen tremendous differences between them. In the parishes where the people had given up the Rosary, they had generally returned to their sinful ways, wheras in places where the Rosary is said faithfully, I found the people were persevering in the grace of God and advancing in virtue day by day. . . . Dear reader, if you practice and preach this devotion, you will learn more by your own experience than from any spiritual book"* (SR 113–114). Montfort was not a theoretician but a spiritual master, and a missionary who knew how to judge the tree of the Rosary by its fruits.

11. A blessed way of praying the Rosary

With Montfort, we shall now look at the eighth decade of *The Mystical Rose Tree* or "the guidelines for reciting the Rosary devoutly and fruitfully." These include the states of grace, attention, humility, and universal charity. Here we have a practical method of reciting the Rosary while meditating on the mysteries of our Redemption in order to imitate the virtues of Jesus and Mary and to plead for our neighbors' needs. Montfort also tells us how to pray the Rosary in two choirs. Finally a series of fifteen meditations is suggested.

The fifth decade is by far the most personal, starting with this beautiful prelude: *"It is not so much the length of a prayer as the fervor with which it is said which pleases God and touches his heart. A single Hail Mary said properly is worth more than a hundred and fifty said poorly . . . . Let us consider how we should pray if we want to please God and become more holy"*(SR 116–117).

a. State of grace. (cf. *The Rose Tree* VIII, 1). This is a delicate issue, and a pastoral one. One could cite the words of Cardinal Hugues: *"One must be as pure as an angel to approach the Blessed Virgin and say the Angelic Salutation"* (SR 118).

Between the rigidity of the Jansenists and the moral laxity of the Quietists, Montfort suggested in *The Mystical Rose Tree* an excellent alternative: *"To say the Holy Rosary well, one must be in the state of grace or at least be fully determined to give up sin"* (SR 117). This allowed him to add this comment: *"We earnestly advise everyone to say the Rosary: the virtuous, that they may persevere and grow in the grace of God; sinners, that they may rise from their sins"* (SR 118).

b. Sufficient attention. (*The Rose Tree* VIII, 2). This is another problem inevitably encountered by anyone who truly tries to pray. *"For God listens to the pleas of the heart rather than to the voice. It would be gravely irreverent to pray with voluntary distractions and this would make saying the Rosary useless and even sinful"* (SR 119). Here again, Montfort, like a good teacher, highlights that he is speaking about voluntary distractions. *"Of course, you cannot say the Rosary without having a few involuntary distractions . . . but you can say it without voluntary distractions, and you must try to lessen involuntary distractions and control your imagination . . . above all, do not fail to offer each decade in honor of one of the mysteries, and try to form a picture in your mind of Jesus and Mary in connection with that mystery"* (SR 120).

c. Invoking the Holy Spirit. *"After you have prayed the Holy Spirit for the grace to say your Rosary well, recall for a moment that you are in the presence of God"* (SR 126). *The Mystical Rose Tree* does not mention the Holy Spirit, but Montfort insists that we do so, and at the beginning of his first method he writes: *"Veni, Sancte Spiritus."*

d. Practical advice. From his own experience Montfort knew what would improve prayer the most: *"Whenever you say the Rosary, be sure to ask for some special grace or virtue, or strength to overcome some sin. . . . Control your tendency to hurry and pause at times while saying the Our Father and the Hail Mary. . . . Whenever possible, the Rosary should be said kneeling, with hands joined, clasping the Rosary. . . . But it can be said while walking or even working . . . If you cannot find the time to say five* *decades continuously, say a decade here and a decade there; you will in this way be able, in spite of your work and other demands on your time, to complete the whole Rosary before going to bed"*(SR 126–30).

e. The Rosary said in common. *"Of all the ways of saying the Holy Rosary, the most glorious to God, the most salutary for our souls, and the most terrible to the devil is that of saying or chanting the Rosary publicly in two choirs. God is very pleased when people pray together. . . . If you live near your parish church or a chapel, go there at least every evening, with the approval of the pastor, together with all who want to participate and say the Rosary in two choirs; do the same at home or in a neighbor's house if a church or chapel is not available"* (SR 131–34).[37] Today many people who pray the "family Rosary" find these words very encouraging.

12. Final advice

Like all good preachers, Montfort concludes with a powerful expression: *"Say the Rosary often with faith, humility, confidence and perseverance"* (SR 136). Then he developes each of these aspects with the help of the Gospel on which he had often meditated.

Montfort insisted, *"Never omit the least part of your Rosary, even if you experience boredom, distaste for prayer and discouragement . . . like a brave follower of Jesus and Mary, say the Our Fathers and Hail Marys without seeing, feeling or tasting, concentrating as well as you can on the mysteries"* (SR 143).

Having arrived at the end of his treatise on the Rosary, Montfort says freely, *"To arm yourselves against attacks . . . from those who are considered 'respectable' and even from devout people who have no use for the Rosary, I am going to tell you simply some of what they say every day. . . . What is this babbler of the Rosary saying? He is lazy! All he does is finger his beads, it would be much better for him to work, rather than amuse himself with such foolishness! He thinks that all you have to do is say your Rosary and good luck will drop from heaven . . . how many saints have never said it? . . . The Rosary is fine for little old ladies who can't read . . . Forget about exterior devotions; true devotion is in the heart, etc. . . . Finally, dear brothers and sisters, the daily Rosary has so many enemies that I consider the grace of persevering in it until death as one of the greatest favors God can give us"* (SR 148–50).

13. A set of instructions: the 150 motives

Montfort's LS does not contain a single sermon on the Rosary. The third mission sermon on Palm Sunday, probably in the evening, speaks of the Rosary.[38] But, under the title *"150 Motives for saying the Holy Rosary"* (cf. MR 32-37), we find an outline in Rosary format with a reflection for each Our Father and Hail Mary, but without any allusion to the customary mysteries. It seems to be a type of memory aid that Montfort devised spontaneously for speaking to people in parishes. Several passages are especially worth noting.

> V. *"The Hail Mary is a divine compliment which wins the Virgin Mary's heart. . . . It is the prayer of Catholics and of souls who are destined for heaven"*

VI. *"The Rosary is the divine summary of the mysteries of Jesus and Mary . . . . After Holy Mass, saying the Rosary is the best thanksgiving one can make, because it is both a memento and a re-enactment of what Jesus did and suffered for us."* [39]

XV. *"Of the different ways to say the Rosary . . . say only the Our Father and Hail Mary with the intention of the mystery . . . add a few words pertinent to each mystery . . . make a small offering at each decade . . . genuflect at each Hail Mary," etc.*

The outline in *"150 Motives"* . . . gives us a precise idea of what Montfort preached about the Rosary to the people.[40]

IV. Montfort's Methods of Reciting the Rosary

The strength of the Rosary lies in its uniting the body, the mind, and the heart. It consists of a sequence of specific prayers known by everyone; it suggests fifteen specific themes to meditate on, which encompass the core of the mystery of Christ; finally, it puts one in contact with Mary, our Spiritual Mother.

Like all his great predecessors—Dominic the Carthusian, Alain de la Roche, Sprenger, Castellano, and even Father Antonin Thomas—Montfort suggested different "methods" to say the Rosary well, that is, to meditate on the joyful, sorrowful, and glorious mysteries of Jesus and Mary (cf. SR 154).[41]

1. The method of offering of the decades

This method consists in saying or listening to simple formulas before each prayer to be recited. (cf. MR 1-5, 7-13)

a. Introductory prayers. Besides the *"general intention of the Rosary,"* one may develop an instruction on the Trinitarian structure of Christian prayer in union with Mary and all the saints (cf. MR 1).

b. The mysteries of the Rosary. The fifteen formulas have an identical format: *"We offer you O Lord Jesus, this first decade in honor of the mystery of your Incarnation," "this second decade in honor of the Visitation of your Holy Mother to her cousin Saint Elizabeth."* Let us take note of some variations. The decade of the Nativity is offered to the Child Jesus, and the decade of Pentecost to the Holy Spirit. The fourteenth decade is offered to Jesus, but in honor of the mysteries of the Immaculate Conception and of Mary's Assumption. Montfort's method is simple: *"Above all, do not fail to offer each decade in honor of one of the mysteries, and try to form a picture in your mind of Jesus and Mary in connection with that mystery"* (SR 120).

c. The grace of the mysteries. During the great discussions of the seventeenth century on the "ways of prayer," the Illuminists and the Quietists were accused of being insufficiently concerned with the practice of the virtues, with striving to lead a moral life. That is why *The Mystical Rose Tree* insists on the imitation of the virtues of Jesus and Mary, as Montfort also did: *"The chief concern of the Christian should be to try to be perfect . . . the Christian must always have before his eyes the life and virtues* *of Jesus Christ"* (SR 65). That is why he said, *"Always be sure to ask, by this mystery and through the intercession of the Blessed Virgin, for one of the virtues that is most evident in that particular mystery or one of which you are in special need"* (SR 126). This request is expressed in the offering of each mystery: *"We ask you by this mystery and through the intercession of your Holy Mother, profound humility."* It is also recalled after the decade has been recited: *"May the grace of the mystery of the Incarnation descend into our hearts and make them truly humble"* (MR 2).

Here we find once again an explicit application of what the French School, following Bérulle, said of the states of Jesus (the profound sentiments which motivated Christ in his mysteries, and which have permanent value). If his acts are completed, his states last forever; and they should penetrate us in such a way as to transform us gradually into his image. This communion with the states of Jesus should allow us to say with Saint Paul, "it is no longer I who live, it is Christ who lives in me" (Ga 2:20). It is Mary's mission to form us into Jesus Christ, and to form Jesus Christ in us. She is there to help us interiorize this grace of the mysteries, upon which we meditate in the Rosary.

2. The method of adding phrases

After the method of "Offering Each Decade", Montfort suggests a *"shorter method of celebrating the life, death and glory of Jesus and Mary, and of decreasing distractions. To do this, a word or two is added to each Hail Mary of the decade reminding us of the mystery we are celebrating. The words should follow the name of Jesus in the middle of the Hail Mary"* (MR 6). Then Montfort suggests a list of fifteen "phrases" corresponding to each mystery. The first decade then becomes "Hail Mary . . . and blessed is the fruit of your womb, Jesus becoming man. Holy Mary . . ." The following decades of Hail Marys includes *"Jesus sanctifying"* . . . Then, *"Jesus born in poverty . . . Jesus sacrificed . . . Jesus holy of holies . . . Jesus in his agony,"* to *"Jesus raising you up,. . . Jesus crowning you."* This venerable method of phrases, older than the Rosary itself[42] is very useful to unite the heart to the voice, the mind to the word. It integrates vocal prayer with the meditation of the mysteries, and simultaneously highlights the fact that these are Jesus' mysteries that we meditate with Mary. It also encourages creativity because there are no limits on the choice of the phrases.[43]

3. The Rosary said with a reflection before each Our Father and Hail Mary

In Montfort's LS, under the title *"Summary of the life, death, passion and glory of Jesus and Mary in the Holy Rosary"* (MR 16–31) there is a plan for saying a short reflection before each prayer of the Rosary; *"Credo: 1. Faith in the presence of God, 2. Faith in the Gospel, 3. Faith in and obedience to the Pope as vicar of Jesus Christ. Pater: unity of one, living and true God, 1. Ave: to honor the eternal Father. . ."* For each of the one hundred fifty Hail Marys of the decades a different focus is suggested, which allows us to expand on the theme of each mystery. For example, the mystery of the Finding of Jesus in the temple spans the whole life of Jesus up to Holy Thursday: *1. Ave: To honor his hidden, laborious and obedient life at Nazareth. 2. Ave: His preaching and his being found in the temple among the doctors. 3. Ave: His fasting and his temptations in the desert. 4. Ave: His baptism by St. John the Baptist. 5. Ave: His wonderful preaching. 6. Ave: His astounding miracles. . ."* (MR 21).

The mystery of Pentecost may give rise to a vast catechesis on the Holy Spirit. As for the mystery of the Assumption, it celebrates the whole life of Mary, including her eternal predestination, her immaculate conception, her fullness of grace, her nativity, etc.(MR 30).

The meditated Rosary is solid catechesis, organized around the fifteen mysteries of the Rosary.[44]

4. A Rosary in hymns:

a. *"The new Rosary or crown of the Blessed Virgin"* (H 90). The stanzas of this hymn correspond to a Rosary with five decades. The first decade is dedicated to the joyful mysteries of Mary—from her *"pure conception"* and birth, to the finding of Jesus in the temple. The second decade is dedicated to the sorrowful and glorious mysteries, up to the *"descent of your Spouse"* (Pentecost). The third decade honors Mary's life, death, Assumption, and Crowning in heaven. What follows is a Marian litany: Virgin and Mother, Full of grace and beauty, Sovereign of the universe, Treasurer of divine gifts, Mirror of the Divinity. . .etc. The end of each stanza is often a request, very similar to the *"grace of the mystery."*

The *"New Rosary"* is a beautiful spiritual poem, in which Montfort freely expresses his Marian piety, without the confining structure of the mysteries of the Rosary.

b. *"A Hymn on the Rosary."* This hymn is found only in Fradet's collection of Montfort's cantiques.[45] The first five stanzas are a brief instruction on the Rosary, a summary of the *"150 motives."* Then follows a stanza on the Creed and one each for the fifteen customary mysteries. The stanzas are very simple: *"An Angel from Heaven came down/And greeted Mary;/ She conceived by the Holy Spirit/ Jesus, our Life"*. . .There is a petition after each mystery. Undoubtedly the Creed, the Our Father, the Hail Mary and the Gloria were recited after each stanza.

Summary: We have seen at least four of Montfort's methods of worthily reciting the Holy Rosary: making offerings, adding phrases, providing reflections for each Our Father and Hail Mary, and hymns. It seems that he did not use the method of including biblical verses for each Hail Mary, which is a practice that comes from the modern biblical renewal.

V. The Rosary in Montfort Spirituality

After having examined what Montfort explicitly said about the Rosary, we shall now look at his writings to discover what might contribute to a Spirituality of the Rosary, and also to discover what influence the Rosary might have on one's spiritual life.

1. A devotion centered on Jesus Christ

The Rosary has been faulted with being a "Marian devotion" which risks obscuring somewhat the central and unique focus on Jesus Christ. This was certainly not true of Montfort.

Montfort's faith and piety were resolutely centered on Jesus Christ, Incarnate Wisdom. For him, *"If devotion to Mary distracted us from Jesus Christ, we would have to reject it as an illusion of the devil"* (TD 62). On the contrary, according to Montfort, true devotion to Mary is *"an easy, short, perfect and sure means of attaining union with Jesus Christ"* (TD 152). *"Mary is the surest, the easiest, the shortest and the holiest of all the means of possessing Jesus Christ"* (LEW 212).

Montfort loved the Rosary because he found in it an efficacious means of meeting Jesus Christ, particularly by means of the *"short phrases"* attached to the name of Jesus.

2. Learning about Jesus through the mysteries of the Rosary

"Why is Jesus, the adorable, eternal and incarnate Wisdom loved so little if not because he is either too little known or not known at all" (LEW 8). Full knowledge of God is not *"esoteric knowledge,"* a human speculation on the unknowable mysteries and greatness of God. It is a discovery of the love of God through the mysteries of the life, death and glorification of Jesus, Incarnate Wisdom. The *"summary of the divine life"* of Jesus, from his Conception to his Ascension is very close to the mysteries of the Rosary (cf. LEW 109–116). This is why Montfort insists that the Rosary be *"recited while meditating on its mysteries,"* for in this way it *"raises us unconsciously to the perfect knowledge of Jesus Christ"* (SR 81).

In particular, the structure of the joyful, sorrowful and glorious mysteries helps us to efficaciously focus our meditation on what is essential in the mystery of Jesus Christ: Incarnation, Cross and Glory.

3. Special devotion to the mystery of the Incarnation

Those who are truly devoted to Mary should esteem highly devotion to the great mystery of the Incarnation (TD 243) because *"this mystery is a summary of all his mysteries"* (TD 248).

We have already said that for Montfort, the first mystery of the Rosary is almost always designated "the Incarnation," not the Annunciation. One could even say that one of the principal bases of the TD (and thus with even stronger logic one of the principal bases of the perfect practice of the true devotion), is precisely *"the Incarnation, where we find Jesus only in Mary . . . Jesus living and reigning in Mary"* (TD 246).

In the Rosary, this special devotion to the Incarnation is expressed not only in the first mystery or in the joyful mysteries (e.g., the Visitation or the Nativity), but throughout the whole Rosary by the recitation of the Hail Mary: Jesus, the fruit of your womb . . . Mother of God. In this way, all the mysteries are associated with the Incarnation.[46]

4. "Long live Jesus, long live his Cross"

Surely, one of the reasons for Montfort's devotion to the Rosary is his strong experience of the mystery of the Cross, meditated in the sorrowful mysteries. To pray the Rosary in the spirit of Montfort, one must allow oneself to be filled with Montfort's love for the Cross, and to follow Jesus: *"If anyone wishes to come after Me, he must renounce himself, take up his cross and follow me"* (FC 13).

In the Rosary with Mary we already experience the Cross in the poverty of the Crib (Nativity) in the prophecy of the *"piercing sword"*(FC 31) and in the three days of anguish spent searching for Jesus. With Mary we accompany Jesus as he carries his Cross to Calvary and in his last prayer on the Cross. But it is also with Mary that we enter into the joy of Easter and of the Ascension, which draws us to Heaven. The Rosary can make us gradually become *"Friends of the Cross."*

5. The place of the Rosary in Montfort's Spiritual Way

Every "true devotion" leads one to live ever more intensely with Mary. Life in Mary attains exceptional intensity through what Montfort calls *"the perfect practice of the true devotion."* This demands that intention *"to perform all one's actions through Mary, with Mary, in Mary and for Mary in order to perform them more perfectly through Jesus Christ, with Jesus Christ, in Jesus and for Jesus"* (TD 157). It is evident that the Rosary assists us in meditating on the conduct and sentiments of Mary as found in the Gospel, *"especially: her lively faith, by which she believed the angel's word without the least hesitation, and believed faithfully and constantly even to the foot of the Cross; her deep humility . . . , her truly divine purity"* (TD 260). The mystery of the Visitation implores *"that Mary's spirit be in each of us to glorify the Lord"* (TD 258).

The Rosary leads us to *"look upon Mary as a perfect model of every virtue and perfection fashioned by the Holy Spirit for us to imitate, as far as our limited capacity allows"*(TD 260). The Rosary prayed regularly helps us to remain in the beautiful interior of Mary with delight (TD 264). The recitation of the fifth glorious mystery, the "Coronation of Mary" encourages us not to remain idle, and to undertake and carry out great things for our illustrious queen (TD 265).

The Rosary in having us repeat untiringly, *"Holy Mary, pray for us,"* teaches us to have recourse to Mary with great confidence, as *"our Mediatrix of intercession"* (TD 86).

Thus, one sees that there is a close link between the spiritual way of Montfort and devotion to the Holy Rosary: both are rooted in contemplation of the mystery of the Incarnation. Meditation on the mysteries of the Rosary is a privileged way of living day by day with Mary in order to live more perfectly with Jesus.

VI. Conclusion: Montfort and The Rosary Today

For a century, the work of historians, biblical scholars, and theologians, as well as the doctrinal teachings of Vatican II (cf. LG. chapter 8) have elicited a profound renewal of Marian devotion, and thus a renewal of interest in the Rosary.[47] But Montfort's spiritual experience and his undying devotion to the Rosary have never aged. Montfort encourages us to deepen our meditation on the Rosary, in light of the Incarnation, the Cross, and our desire for Heaven. On the practical level, he helps us to rediscover the method of *"phrases"* attached to the name of Jesus.[48] Our times demand Spiritual Masters; Montfort is one who shows us the way to union with Jesus Christ, the only Savior.[49]

J. -C. Laurenceau

Notes: (1) A. Duval, *Rosaire* (Rosary), in DSAM, Vol. 13, Beauchesne, Paris, 1988, 938–80. This is a synthesis of the history of the rosary from the beginnings to the present day, with a complete bibliography. (2) L. Le Crom, *Un apôtre marial: saint Louis-Marie Grignion de Montfort* (A Marian Apostle: Saint Louis Marie Grignion de Montfort), Librairie mariale, Pontchâteau, 1942. (3) Ibid., 10. (4) Ibid., 77. (5) Ibid., 165. (6) Ibid., 177–78. (7) Ibid., 137–38. (8) Ibid. 154; cf. LPM 2. (9)Ibid. 189–190. (10) Ibid., 268. (11) Ibid., 200. (12) Ibid., 229–32. (13) Ibid., 439; cf. 351. (14) Ibid., 371; OC 832. (15) Cf. A. Duval, *Rosaire*, 952–55. (16) Le Crom, *Un apôtre marial* (A Marian Apostle), 245. (17) Ibid., 284–85; cf. L 23. (18) Le Crom, *Un apôtre marial*, 258, 283; cf. 255. (19) Ibid, 286. (20) Ibid., 311. (21) Cf. Ibid., 306. (22) According to Le Crom, Father de Montfort's seal showed "a religious on his knees with a rosary hanging from his cincture", ibid., 333.

(23) L. Pérouas, *Grignion de Montfort ou l'aventurier de l'Évangile* (Grignion de Montfort a Gospel Adventurer), Ed. Ouvrières, Paris, 1990, 100–101. Cf another intervention in Rennes, Le Crom, 339. (24) The Rosary is also mentioned in H 12:43; 15:33; 89:25; 90; 92:4,16,22; 93:5; 95:8; 115:13; 139:20; 147:4; 159:14. Additionally, in H 109 Montfort paraphrases the Our Father and the Hail Mary. (25) Other mentions of the rosary in TD are at 42, 229, 254. (26) Despite the indication of Our Father and Hail Mary, we regard this text as didactic. This sort of presentation of a teaching on the rosary, taking the form of fifteen decades, was common at the time. (27) Fr. Antonin-Thomas (Drugeon) was born in Rennes and took the habit of the Domnicans at Dinan Priory in Brittany on August 15, 1653. He died in 1701 at the age of seventy and was buried in the Chapter Room of the Priory at Dinan. Besides *Rosier mystique,* his known works are *Les marques les plus sensibles de la tendresse de la T. S. Vierge envers l'Ordre des Frères Prêcheurs* (The Most Touching Marks of Tenderness shown by the Blessed Virgin to the Order of Friars Preachers) (1688) and a translation of *Traité de la Vie Spirituelle* by St. Vincent Ferrer. It is worth noting that Alain de la Roche also took the habit at Dinan Priory about 1445. Cf. J. Quétif et J. Echard, *Scriptores Ordinis Praedicatorum,* published by R. Coulon, Rome, 1909. (28) *Le Rosier mystique de la T. S. Vierge Marie ou le T. Sacré Rosaire (inventé) par S. Dominique* (The Mystical Rose Tree of the Blessed Virgin Mary or The Sacred Rosary of St. Dominic). . . went through two editions in Fr. Antonin-Thomas's lifetime: one at Vennes (i.e. Vannes, where St. Vincent Ferrer died: cf. Preface) in 1686, and the other at Rennes in 1698. The two editions are in the Bibliothèque du Saulchoir, Paris. (29) Cf. Le Crom, *Un apôtre marial,* 311. (30) Jean de Carthagène (d. 1618), cf. DSAM, Vol. 8, 323. (31) Probably in *B. Alanus de Rupe redivivus, de Psalterio seu Rosario Christi ac Mariae. . .* by J. A. Coppenstein, o.p., Fribourg/Br 1619 or Cologne 1624. The latter warns us, *"Materia Alani, forma mea."* (32) Concerning Alain de la Roche (d. 1475), see A. Duval, *Rosaire,* Vol. 13, 946–49; or *La dévotion mariale dans l'Ordre des Frères Prêcheurs* (Marian Devotion in the Order of Friars Preachers), in *Maria,* Vol. 2. Beauchesne, Paris, 1952, 739–82. (33) Cf. SR 1. (34) This passage of SR is almost identical to TD 249–53. Other mentions of the Hail Mary in TD 8, 9, 95. (35) See also the paraphrase of the Hail Mary in two verses of H 109:39–40. (36) See the dictionary *Catholicisme* (Catholicism) under *"Guyon et Quiétisme"* (Guyon and Quietism) and DSAM under *"Guyon et Oraison"* (Guyon and Prayer). (37) The stress on the fifteen decades of the Rosary prayed every day, "as all the confrères used to do," ties in with the preaching of Alain de la Roche, who asked his confrères to pray every day the Psalter of the Blessed Virgin, i.e., 150 Hail Marys. (38) Cf. OC 1745. (39) On the connection between the Rosary and the Eucharist, see also SR 88. (40) Also informative on the Rosary are the first five verses of *Rosaire en cantique* , ed. Fradet (S. 31). (41) The various methods proposed by Montfort are grouped together in GA, 233–62, quoted in MR; except the *Rosaire en cantique.* (42) The "short clauses" of the Rosary had been forgotten until about 1950, except in German-speaking countries. The historical studies of Dom Gourdel, Klinkhammer, and Heinz take us further back than Dominic the Carthusian to the Cistercian nuns of the diocese of Trier, who, by about A.D. 1300 already said the Hail Mary with short clauses like, "Jesus adored by the Magi," "Jesus tempted by the devil," and "Jesus who washed his disciples' feet." Cf. Duval, DSAM. Vol. 13, 943–46. (43) The practice of short clauses, which was reintroduced in France in the years 1967–1968 (Esnard, Eyquem-Laurenceau) is mentioned favourably by Paul VI in *Marialis Cultus,* No. 46. It is a pity that the word *"clausule"* used in the original (Latin or Italian) has been left out of the French and English translations. (44) The first method indicates the "Glory be . . ." Cf. SR 59. (45) *Le Rosaire en cantique* is not included in the *Oeuvres Complètes* (1966) nor in *God Alone* (1987) because the work was not included in Montfort's manuscript notebooks, but Fradet regards it as "undeniably authentic" (cf. Fradet, 777). (46) Paul VI is in perfect agreement with Montfort when, in *Marialis Cultus* No. 46, he writes, "As a Gospel prayer, centred on the mystery of the redemptive Incarnation, the Rosary is therefore a prayer with a clearly Christological orientation." (47) Among the recent works that have benefited from this renewal is R. Barile, *Il Rosario, Salterio della Vergine,* EDB, Bologna, 1990. After some courageous historical clarification, the author proposes a judicious revision of the fifteen mysteries, with short clauses. (48) In the *Livre d'Or,* new edition, Librairie Mariale Nouvelle Cité, Paris, 1989, the Montfort Rosary of the Daughters of Wisdom, which combines offerings and short clauses, is followed by the refreshing proposal of a Rosary "in the spirit of Father de Montfort" with 150 short clauses to be added to the name of Jesus. (49) For more on the Rosary, cf. Brother Gabriel-Marie, *Notre rosaire ou le Secret d'aller à Jésus par Marie* (Our Rosary or the Secret Path to Jesus through Mary), *St. Gabriel, St. Laurent-sur Sévre, 1958.* Brothers of Saint Gabriel, Saint-Laurent-sur-Sèvre, 1958.

SACRED HEART

SUMMARY
I. INTRODUCTION.
II. SEVENTEENTH-CENTURY FRANCE:
  1. A mystical era;
  2. Gradual development;
  3. Christ, the Heart of God.
III. THE DISCOVERY OF THE HEART OF JESUS:
  1. Contribution of the French school;
  2. The promoters:
    a. Francis de Sales,
    b. John Eudes,
    c. Margaret Mary Alacoque.
IV. MONTFORT, A FOLLOWER OF BERULLE OR OF ST. FRANCIS DE SALES?:
  1. Montfort and the Order of the Visitation;
  2. Montfort and devotion to the Sacred Heart:
    a. In his writings in general,
    b. In the hymns,
    c. Similarities with St. Margaret Mary.
V. RELEVANCE TODAY.

I. INTRODUCTION

Saint Louis de Montfort promoted and spread devotion to the Sacred Heart of Jesus to a far greater extent than is generally realized. The silence of his biographers on this subject[1] is surprising, not to say baffling. It is especially surprising when one considers the fact that his hymns on the Sacred Heart number no fewer than 905 lines; this is to say nothing of the mention he makes of the Heart of Christ in his other writings.

II. SEVENTEENTH-CENTURY FRANCE

Speaking of seventeenth-century France from the viewpoint of our present subject means speaking mostly about Paris.

1. A mystical era

"Paris in the seventeenth century witnessed a high point in its religious history. . . . The main themes of the history of Paris and those of French Catholicism merge into one."[2] Religious institutions, such as monasteries, convents, and seminaries, as well as works of mercy carried out by individuals or organizations were concentrated there. Besides, great religious and mystical figures such as Bérulle, Olier, Vincent de Paul, Madame Acarie, and Louise de Marillac lived there: "As the city was the capital of the country, some founders, e.g., St. Francis de Sales, moved there and, through their influence or their presence, played an essential part."[3] Between 1600 and 1660, more than eighty monastic institutions sprang up in the city. The influence exerted by St. Francis de Sales was considerable. Three convents of the Visitation were established there. "The first convent, which marked the beginning of the Order, was established in Faubourg Saint-Antoine by St. Francis de Sales himself and St. Jane Chantal."[4] It produced a wealth of religious literature. Our modern "pocket editions" came long after "those publications in a small format . . . dealing with daily Christian living and spiritual subjects. Even after many reprints, they were in great demand in Paris."[5]

As early as 1609, de Sales' *Introduction to the Devout Life* had a considerable influence in Parisian circles. The *Treatise on the Love of God,* whose publication was delayed by the foundation of the Order of the Visitation in June 1610, appeared in 1616, after it had been touched up to take account of the comments received from the early members of the Order.

2. Gradual development

Devotion to the Sacred Heart was still being refined somewhat in its expression and proper purpose. This article will not attempt to trace its history but will highlight the most significant stages of its development. The word "heart" occurs more than 600 times in the Bible, where it is often connected with the loins (Greek *nephroi*: kidneys, reins), with a similar meaning. Among the ancients, the kidneys or reins (loins) were the seat of physical and emotional life: *"Prove me, O Lord, and try me; test my heart and loins"* (Ps 26:2). The heart, the innermost part of man, refers to all that concerns the mysterious interior of a human being. Its meaning, however, remains general and vague. "It is not essentially the seat of feelings, which is in the loins, but, rather, the seat of knowledge: God is the one *'who tests the loins and hearts,'"* that is, the one who knows the feelings and thoughts of man (Ps 7:9).[6] The heart also means the faculty of memory: "He remembered his covenant, and showed compassion according to the abundance of his steadfast love" (Ps 106 [105]: 45); "Mary treasured all these words and pondered them in her heart" (Lk 2:19). We learn things by heart, that is, we commit them to memory. The Italian *ricordare* (root *cor*: heart) means "remember." The biblical word "heart" therefore takes us back thousands of years to the origins of that cultural anthropology that has left its mark on our modern languages, and refers to all that has to do with affectivity. A person who is unfeeling is described as "heartless," and one extremely kind as "having a heart of gold." Memory is influenced by the heart. We remember something we have enjoyed and carry bitter memories of something we disliked. Conditioned by this anthropological element, the language of faith could not remain unaffected by our use of the word "heart." Even though faith does not belong to the order of the senses ("True devotion consists neither in sterile or transitory affection . . . but proceeds from faith" [LG 67]), it is not divorced from the heart.

3. Christ, the Heart of God

"God is love" (1 Jn 4:8). Paradoxical as it may sound, however, God does not have a heart. Being a pure spirit, his love is entirely spiritual. It was to come down to our level, as it were, that he became man. "God so loved the world that he gave his only Son" (Jn 3:16). "And the word became flesh" (Jn 1:14). "Sacrifices and offerings you have not desired, but a body you have prepared for me" (Heb 10:5); a body, therefore a heart. In giving us His Son, God gave us the One who, like Him, is all-loving. Having become man, Infinite Love Incarnate will love us in the way human beings love. All that affects us emotionally has repercussions on the organ called our heart, through the extremely complex network of the sympathetic nervous system. The heart dilates when we are joyful; when we are sorrowful, our heart "contracts." Strong emotions can even lead to death. "I am deeply grieved, even to death" (Mt 26:38). The various feelings of Jesus are evident all through the Gospel: "Love one another as I have loved you" (Jn 15:12). "Jesus loved Martha and her sister and Lazarus" (Jn 11:5). When the disciples returned from their mission, "he rejoiced in the Holy Spirit" (Lk 10:21). He shared our sorrows. At the tomb of Lazarus, "Jesus began to weep" (Jn 11:35). When he met the widow whose only son was being carried out of the town, "he had compassion for her" (Lk 7:13). "He who is the image of the invisible God is himself the perfect man. . . . By his incarnation, he, the Son of God, has in a certain way united himself with each human being. He worked with human hands, he thought with a human mind. He acted with a human will, and with a human heart he loved" (GS 22).

III. The Discovery of the Heart of Jesus

To discover the love of Jesus is one thing, but to discover what is meant by the "Heart of Jesus" is quite another. None of the disciples who shared his life doubted his love; and yet none of them, not even John, "the disciple whom he loved" (Jn 19:26), made any explicit mention of his Heart. The expression is fairly recent, its meaning in this modern sense must be clear. St. Augustine says that St. John "rested his head on his Master's breast, meaning by this that in his inmost heart he drank from the most exalted secrets."[7] St. Anselm speaks of "the love of his heart for us."[8] St. Bernard wrote that "the secret of his heart is revealed through the wounds in his body."[9] These are generalities applicable on the whole, and not to every person who "opens his heart." To infer from this that the quotations above refer to the Sacred Heart, as modern piety understands the term, would clearly be to force their meaning.

1. Contribution of the French school

The gradual development mentioned above reaches its high point with the French school. When Pope Urban VIII described Bérulle as "the apostle of the Incarnate Word," he summed up the contribution of the French school to the spirituality of his days. The Incarnate Word is the historical Jesus, the Christ whose mystery had been investigated in the theological speculation of the Middle Ages. The French school inquired deeper into his human and divine reality, into his personal condition as God made man and into the interior riches of each event in his life. These are so pregnant with meaning that the members of the French school called them "mysteries," and the dispositions of Christ who experienced them, "states." "The mysteries of Jesus Christ took place in definite circumstances, and they last and are present and enduring in another manner. . . . Therefore, the spirit, the state, the virtue, the merit of the mystery is ever present."[10] To contemplate these states of Jesus is to focus one's attention on his interior life as Incarnate Word. From this it is only a short step to move on to the seat of all the feelings of Christ, his "Heart," which, through his Hypostatic Union with the person of the Word, is worthy of adoration, like his entire holy humanity. Devotion to the Sacred Heart had now found what it had been searching for. By assimilating the feelings, the states of the Incarnate Word, Christians entered the theocentric current of religion and adoration through the inmost part of the Incarnate Word, the Heart of Jesus, so that it has been said that "Bérulle had brought about a revolution in the spiritual world of his days: theocentrism, a term that may sound strange but is almost necessary."[11]

2. The promoters

Thanks to the French school, devotion to the Sacred Heart became accredited, as it were. Even though allusions to the Heart of Jesus occurred here and there in previous writings, they lacked the precision and the wide implications of those of St. Francis de Sales and, even more, those of St. John Eudes and St. Margaret Mary.

a. Francis de Sales. Francis de Sales was born in 1567 and died in 1622. He was born a few years before Bérulle (1575-1629), and though they were contemporaries, their lives followed different courses. Their ideas about the person of Christ tallied, but they expressed them differently. Francis de Sales' *Treatise on the Love of God*, which was nine years in the making and is the "perfect manifestation" of his spirit and of his heart at "the highest point of genius and holiness,"[12] presents the doctrine on the Sacred Heart that he instilled into his Daughters of the Visitation. A few passages from his book reveal both his teaching and his style. Right from the start of his *Treatise on the Love of God*, in the *Dedicatory Prayer*, he addresses himself to Mary and Joseph, a "peerless pair," in whom "the Sun of justice . . . experienced the delights of the affable love of his Heart for us . . . O beloved Mother of the Beloved . . . I beseech you by the Heart of your loving Jesus who is the King of all hearts . . . animate my soul and those of all who will read this with your all-powerful favor with the Holy Spirit."[13] He keeps coming back to the subject of the Sacred

Heart in a variety of ways. "We say that someone who is impervious to the divine touch has a heart of iron or a heart of stone. . . . On the contrary, a loving heart, malleable and tractable, is a melted, liquefied heart: My heart, says David (Ps 22:15) referring to Our Lord on the Cross, my heart is like wax; it is melted within my breast."[14] The following is in a more mystical vein: "'I run,' says the Spouse, 'but shall I ever capture the prize I am running for, which is to be united heart-to-heart . . . with my God, my Spouse and my life? When shall I be able to pour my heart into His Heart, and He pour His heart into my heart, and thus happily united we will live inseparably as one?'"[15] Finally, speaking of the union of the soul with God, he writes, "O sweet Jesus, draw me ever deeper into your Heart that your love may engulf me and that I may be overwhelmed with its delight."[16]

b. John Eudes. Born in 1601 and Bérulle's junior by twenty-six years, St. John Eudes was one of his most authentic followers. First a member of the Oratory, he left it to found his own religious Congregations and promote devotion to the Sacred Heart. St. Pius X called him "its [devotion to the Heart of Christ] Father, its Doctor, and its Apostle." Influenced by the teaching of the French school and St. Francis de Sales, especially as set out in the *Treatise on the Love of God,* and also by the revelations of St. Gertrude and St. Mechtilde, he was the theoretician, so to speak, of devotion to the Sacred Heart and explained the expressions of his predecessors. He did not separate Mary from Jesus but united them in one and the same devotion, beginning with Mary, who gave Christ his Heart. For him the union of the Son and the Mother is so close that he refers to "the Heart of Jesus and Mary" and devotes to the Heart of Jesus the whole of book 12 of his most important work, *The Admirable Heart of the Most Holy Mother of God.* Won over to devotion to the Heart of Jesus by Bérulle's devotion to the Incarnate Word, he combined with it the gentleness and devotional warmth of St. Francis de Sales. He changed the somewhat individual and private character of the devotion into a devotion for the whole Church by writing for the benefit of his communities an Office and a Mass, which were later approved by several bishops before spreading throughout the Church. Leo XIII described him as "the author of the liturgical devotion of the Sacred Hearts of Jesus and Mary." In 1765 Clement XIII approved the Office and Mass for use in Poland, and the nuns of the Visitation were allowed to celebrate the feast throughout their Order. In 1856 Pius IX made the feast obligatory throughout the Church.

c. Margaret Mary Alacoque. Born in 1647, twenty-five years after the death of St. Francis de Sales, Margaret Mary joined the Order of the Visitation at Jesus' request. A cousin of hers who was an Ursuline urged her to join the Ursulines, but Christ is reported to have said to her, "I do not want you to live there but at Sainte-Marie (Paray-le-Monial)."[17]

"As soon as I heard the word 'Paray,' my heart swelled with joy."[18] After she had visited the convent on May 25, 1671, an inner voice said to her, "This is where I want you to live." She entered the convent on June 21 that year and took her solemn vows there on November 6, 1672. Within a short time, in silence and humility, she was granted the most eminent mystical graces. On December 27, 1673, feast of St. John the Apostle, she rested her head on the breast of the Master for a long time, as St. John had done. "My divine Heart loves humanity, and you in particular, so passionately that I am no longer able to contain within myself the flames of my burning love and I have to spread them through you."[19] Her mission was made clearer in the course of subsequent apparitions. On the first Friday of each month, "the Sacred Heart appeared to me in the form of a sun shining brilliantly. . . . And on one occasion . . . flames were shooting out from all over his sacred body, especially from his adorable breast . . . and when he uncovered it I saw his all-loving and all-lovable Heart, which was the source of the flames. It was then that he revealed to me the unutterable marvels of his pure love, which he carried to excess towards humanity, from whom he received only ingratitude and lack of appreciation. . . . You will be pleasing to me if you supply for their ingratitude to the best of your ability."[20] Jesus asked her to receive Holy Communion on the first Friday of each month and to spend a Holy Hour in prayer on Thursday and Friday nights. In the meantime, her physical sufferings multiplied and she was frequently misunderstood, but she bore all this heroically, with the help of Mary who had said to her, "Take heart, my daughter, . . . you still have a long and difficult way to go, . . . but do not let this frighten you, as I will not abandon you and promise to protect you."[21] The revelations of St. Margaret Mary have contributed to spreading devotion to the Sacred Heart even more than the more doctrinal writings of Bérulle and St. John Eudes. They were more within the capacity of ordinary people, who adopted the practices they recommended: Communion on the first Friday and the Holy Hour. St. Margaret Mary urged Father Croiset in particular to make the desires of the Heart of Jesus known. "If you knew how earnestly I desire that he should be known, loved, and glorified, you would not refuse to work for this as hard as you can. Unless I am mistaken, this is what he expects from you."[22] St. Margaret Mary died the following year on October 17, 1690, but on January 17 she had written with increased urgency: "I cannot refrain from telling you that the Holy Spirit does not suffer delays gladly, and if you keep putting it off, I fear he will withhold the graces meant for you and give them to somebody else."[23] In June 1691 Father Croiset published his book *La dévotion au Sacré-Coeur de Notre-Seigneur Jésus-Christ, (The Devotion to the Sacred Heart of Our Lord)*, which was followed by *Abrégé de la vie de Soeur Marguerite-Marie Alacoque (Summary of the Life of Sister Margaret Mary Alacoque)*.

IV. Montfort, A Follower of Berulle or of St. Francis de Sales?

It is accepted that Montfort received a great deal from the French school during his formation years at Saint-Sulpice Seminary. His writings are pervaded by the teaching he was given there. His devotion to the mystery of the Incarnation and to Jesus Christ, Eternal and Incarnate Wisdom (LEW 223), justifies his well-known title "the last of the great Bérullians." But his personality kept him from becoming slavishly dependent. He assimilated the teaching of his masters, Bérulle, Olier, John Eudes, but remained open to the other trends of thought of his day. St. Francis de Sales influenced these trends to a great extent. Montfort knew his writings and both refers to them explicitly and alludes to them. In TD 152, he speaks of *"some saints, not very many, such as . . . St. Francis de Sales, who have taken the smooth path [Mary] to Jesus Christ."* In SR 80, he quotes as an example *"St. Francis de Sales, the great spiritual director of his time,"* who bound himself by vow *"to say the whole Rosary every day for as long as he lived,"* which is confirmed in SR 130.

1. Montfort and the Order of the Visitation

Montfort was also acquainted with the Order of the Visitation. He may have been brought into contact with it by Father Barrin, vicar general of Nantes and spiritual father of the convent in that town, who held the missionary in high regard and had urged his return in 1708. Between 1710 and 1714 he had further opportunities to meet the nuns of the Visitation. Sister Marie-Madeleine de Santo-Domingo de la Bouveray had opened her heart to "a holy ecclesiastic called Father Grignion de Monfort" who, she reports, came back "in visions, three years after his death, and visited her for several months."[24] Hymn 48, dedicated *"to the Nuns of the Visitation,"* is proof that he knew them well. He thinks they are *"fortunate / In having this great Heart to love"* (H 48:1). In this hymn he highlights devotion to the Sacred Heart but in connection with St. Francis de Sales. The Sacred Heart *"has taken you [the Visitation Order] as his possession / He has established his dwelling among you / He is also your inheritance / And this is an uncommon lot"* (H 48:2). The word "inheritance" connotes a filial kinship with a father who bequeaths his possessions to his children, which is what St. Francis de Sales did to the Order of the Visitation even before the Sacred Heart had made his requests to St. Margaret Mary.[25]

The verses following this make the meaning clear: *"From the Cross on Calvary / Through Mary he came down / Into the heart of your holy Father / And there was absorbed completely"* (H 48:3). Clearly, Montfort is referring here to St. Francis de Sales, as confirmed by what follows: *"This holy and charitable Father / Who was an eminent loving teacher / Has given you this lovable Heart / that you may burn with his fire"* (H 48:4). When the Order of the Visitation was founded in 1610, John Eudes was only nine years of age. It was only thirty years later that he began propagating devotion to the Sacred Heart. Montfort was therefore justified in writing: *"It is for you a great honor / That the Heart of the Lamb / Was born, as it were, among you / Your house was his cradle"* (H 48:6).[26] Even before St. John Eudes had given devotion to the Sacred Heart its public character, the teaching they had received from their founder had brought it to the attention of the community of the Visitation nuns. Even though he refers explicitly only to St. Francis de Sales, at the time of writing Montfort was well aware of the requests made by the Sacred Heart to St. Margaret Mary, as they seem to have inspired the following verses, which gently hint at the initial difficulties encountered even within the community: *"If in your house he willed to be born / It is to grow and increase. / You ought to make him known / And reveal his splendor"* (H 48:7). *"He dwells among you; / Be ablaze with his fire"* (H 48:8). *"God has entrusted to you / The most valuable treasure. / It rests with you, dear Sisters, / To make it productive."* Even if they are doing so already, they need to do more. *"Try to be still more perfect / And more faithful in this regard"* (H 48:9-10). Montfort refers to this "holy Father," who had been canonized in 1665. The nuns of the Visitation are to cultivate three loves: *"Between three Hearts take your places; / Jesus, Augustine, and Francis; / But let the first, who is full of grace / Gather you all in one rather than three"* (H 48:11). Montfort mentions St. Augustine because St. Francis de Sales adopted the Bishop of Hippo's Rule for his daughters. Montfort himself drew inspiration from St. Francis de Sales when he wrote the Original Rule of the Daughters of Wisdom and borrowed from it (cf. RW 68 and RW 311-318).

2. Montfort and devotion to the Sacred Heart

At the time when Montfort was preaching and writing, devotion to the Sacred Heart had been spreading for nearly a hundred years. It is difficult to pinpoint the influences he came under. The use of similar expressions, unless they are really typical and identifiable, is not enough to determine their origin. But one thing is certain: Montfort had a strong devotion to the Sacred Heart.

a. In his writings in general. All that he has written about the love of Eternal and Incarnate Wisdom, who *"became man only to stir the hearts of men to love and imitate him"* (LEW 117), is suggestive of what could be said of the Sacred Heart. *"He is a gift sent by the love of the eternal Father and a product of the love of the Holy Spirit. He was given out of love and fashioned by love. He is therefore all love, or rather the very love of the Father and the Holy Spirit"* (LEW 118).

A comparative study of LEW and the hymns would be illuminating. It is interesting to compare, for example, *"But how describe the gentleness of Jesus in his dealings with poor sinners: his gentleness with Mary Magdalene, his courteous solicitude in turning the Samaritan woman from her evil ways, his compassion in pardoning the adulterous woman taken in adultery?"* (LEW 125) with *"This heart runs driven by love . . . / He sits down by a well / Not to rest there / But for the sake of the Samaritan woman / Whom he wants to save and win over"; "It is because his heart is gentle / So tender and loving / That he brought Mary Magdalene to repentance"; "Let us admire the gentleness / Without a trace of sternness / With which he deals with the adulterous woman / Whom he delivers from the clutches of her accusers"* (H 41:16, 17, 19, 20).

LEW 155 sets out *"the circumstances surrounding the sufferings of Eternal Wisdom"*; Montfort sums them up: *"This dear friend of our souls suffered in every way exteriorly and inwardly, in body and soul"* (LEW 157). This is echoed in H 41:24ff. In LEW 181, he gives the means to obtain Wisdom: desire, prayer, mortification, and, finally, Mary. In H 42:25, he adds something else: *"Do you desire divine Wisdom / Who makes people wise in God's eyes? / Do you wish to taste God's bliss? / My heart is his fiery throne."*

He wrote in a letter to Marie Louise of Jesus about Easter 1716, shortly before his death—thus revealing the thoughts that occupied his mind: *"I worship the justice and love with which divine Wisdom is treating his little flock, allowing you to live in cramped quarters here on earth so that later you may find spacious dwellings in his divine heart"* (L 34). The idea of "dwelling in his divine heart" recurs in H 40:29: *"This Heart is the cleft in the rock . . . Sheltering those who are perfect"*; then, bringing together the Hearts of Jesus and Mary, after the example of St. John Eudes, he writes: *"Christian soul, give yourself without reserve / To these miraculous Hearts"* (H 40:37). Before this he had written: *"This is the sacred door / Leading into the Spouse's sacred alcove"* (H 40:22).

In a letter he wrote to his sister Guyonne-Jeanne, who was then a nun of the Blessed Sacrament under the name of Sister Catherine de Saint-Bernard, he gives thanks to God that she has become *"a perfect victim of Jesus Christ, an adorer of the Blessed Sacrament and one who is called to atone for so many bad Christians and unfaithful priests"* (L 19). The idea of victim is connected with the reparation requested by the Heart of Jesus. Even though he does not use the expression "devotion to the Heart of Jesus," it is implied. In other contexts Montfort associates the idea of reparation and victim with the Blessed Sacrament: *"Let us make amends / To his Heart so despised / Since this most lovable Heart / Has given all for our sake"* (H 133:9). *"O Sacred Heart, set us ablaze . . . / Here are our hearts, consume them / Turn them on your altar / Into a pleasing sacrifice"* (H 132:9). *"To make amends for these crimes / We offer you our hearts / Take them and sacrifice them / At the foot of your altar."*[27]

The Sacred Heart is also mentioned in other places. The prayer that Montfort suggests accompany the third of *The Seven Last Words of Jesus* (*"Woman, behold your Son . . . Behold your mother"*) reads as follows: *"O Jesus, when you were dying, you manifested the tenderness of your heart for your Blessed Mother, and you confided to her all your disciples in the person of Saint John. Place me, I beg you, under her protection and give me the heart of a son to honor her"* (HD 36). Finally, HD 49 reads, *"Eternal Father . . . by the loving heart of Jesus Christ our Lord, I offer you countless acts of thanksgiving for all the blessings you were pleased to bestow upon me purely out of your goodness."*

b. In the hymns. Through his magnificent hymns on the Sacred heart of Jesus, Montfort contributed much to spreading adoration of the Heart of Christ.

From the theological standpoint, the Sacred Heart hymns are clearly along the lines of Bérulle's teaching. Whose Heart is it? *"It is the Heart of the Son of Mary / And of God's only Son"* (H 40:4). Because of the Hypostatic Union, he is worthy of adoration: *"Mortals, worship with the angels / That Heart that must be worshipped / In the most Holy Trinity"* (40:9). He is the only Mediator (1 Tim 2:5): *"Before his Father at all times / He praises, adores, entreats / He speaks on our behalf powerfully"* (H 40:8). *"It is that great wounded Heart that calms / And disarms an angry God"* (H 40:20). *"That Heart calms his anger / Obtains his grace and favor"* (H 40:21). It is full of all the gifts and virtues and is the source of life: *"O great Heart, wonder of the world / That contains all things . . . / All the Holy Trinity"* (H 40:32). *"From this source of light / The favorites of Jesus Christ / Have drawn the greatest mysteries / The greatest gifts of the Holy Spirit"* (H 40:27). *"O great Heart, O profound abyss / Of profound humility / O great Heart, O sublime throne / Of perfect charity"* (H 40:31).

In the following verses, the influence of St. John Eudes is apparent even in the wording. The inseparable presence of the Heart of Mary is emphasized, and a "proportionate" devotion is given to her with all the required nuances: *"In praising this adorable Heart / I praise in due proportion / The Heart of his admirable Mother / So close is their union"* (H 40:33). *"It is only you that I adore / Heart of my God, glorious Heart / But in adoring you I honor / The Heart of the Queen of Heaven"* (H 40:34). The Heart of Mary is the origin of this human and divine Heart: *"From the blood of her heart all aflame / The Heart of Jesus was formed; / They have but one heart and soul / Both of them invite you / To look on them as one"* (H 40:36). For Montfort, too, the Heart of Christ and the Heart of Mary form but one Heart: *"Our hearts were only one victim / During our life on earth / The two of them were firmly bound / And in heavenly love, now only one"* (H 42:28). From the spiritual point of view, H 41:1 sets out a program: *"Let us enter this marvelous Heart / To love as he did."* The following three verses draw attention to the obligation to love God, do his will, and take up one's Cross (H 41:3, 4, 5).

c. Similarities with St. Margaret Mary. Montfort knew about the revelations of the Sacred Heart either because he had read Father Croiset's book or because of his contacts with the nuns of the Visitation.[28] Hymn 42 on devotion to the Sacred Heart, Hymn 43 on the outrages against the

Heart of Jesus, and Hymn 44 on the practices of devotion to the Heart of Jesus tie in with the requests that the Sacred Heart made to St. Margaret Mary. In Hymn 43, which is thirty-eight verses long and concerns the outrages against the Heart of Jesus, Montfort mentions the profanations committed in his time: *"How many infamous heretics / Have profaned your sacrament!"* (H 43:5). In another place he mentions witchcraft, which was common in those days—*"Alas! how many have used witchcraft / To hand over the host to demons"* (H 43:12)[29]—and other profanations, which he sums up when he alludes to the revelations that had taken place at Paray-le-Monial twenty-five years earlier but were not to reach the general public until the end of the century. *"Never before has the world been / So full of enemies of God / Crime and war are rife everywhere / And Jesus lamented this not long ago"* (H 43:20); *"It was in his Heart that our Master / Harbored all his secrets of love / Before he revealed them / And brought them to light"* (H 40:25). Among the practices of devotion, he mentions love (H 44:2), adoration (44:3), Consecration (H 44:4), speaking about it (H 44:6), joining confraternities (H 44:26), and making reparation—an idea unknown before St. Margaret Mary: *"The most useful practice / Which gives our Lord most glory . . . / Is to make reparation"* (H 44:17). Jesus asked St. Margaret Mary to offer her suffering "particularly for consecrated souls,"[30] which Montfort expresses thus: *"Alas! how many bad priests /Wolves in sheep's clothing / How many traitors like Judas / More cruel than the tormentors!"* (H 43:29); *"I have suffered countless outrages / to be with you now. / Atone for them by honoring me / I beg you with all my heart"* (H 42:33).

V. Relevance Today

Although some of our contemporaries show a certain lack of enthusiasm for devotion to the Sacred Heart (and some of its iconography is admittedly in poor taste), this devotion is bound up with the very foundation of our faith,[31] which acknowledges that Christ is one person—the Eternal and most adorable Wisdom—in two natures, human and divine. We are therefore justified in worshipping his Heart as an appropriate object of the adoration given to him and as the most profound expression of what humanity of all ages has recognized as the symbol of their noblest sentiments. Adoration of the Heart of Christ is strong testimony that this man Jesus is personally our God. The Heart of Jesus is the Heart of our Incarnate God.

Devotion to the Heart of Jesus gives a new, "intelligent" (= *intus legere,* "to read deep within"), and penetrating insight into the Word of God, who has kept on saying to humanity from the beginning of its history, "I will take you for my wife . . . in steadfast love and in mercy" (Hos 2:21-22). Jesus carried this love to extremes during his earthly life by lavishing blessings on those suffering physically and mentally: "They were astounded beyond measure, saying, 'He has done everything well: he even makes the deaf to hear and the dumb to speak'" (Mk 7:37).

How have humans repaid him? Their fickle hearts have repeatedly broken "the everlasting covenant" (Is 24:5) that God made with them and have repaid Him only with ingratitude. Montfort said in his time, *"It was that blood-stained mouth / That spoke seventeen hundred years ago / In a dying and living voice / Words that I can hardly understand"* (H 41:37).

These words are no less relevant at the threshold of the third millennium: *"As the world nears its end I open / My heart burning with love for sinners. / But to my advances they respond / Only with cold indifference"* (H 42:15). In 1990, on the occasion of the three-hundredth anniversary of the death of St. Margaret Mary, Pope John Paul II wrote to Bishop Raymond Séguy of Autun that St. Margaret Mary "was conveying to us an ever-relevant message," and he urged that it be made "more widely known." At a time when humankind worldwide fills the air with groans of misery and loneliness and rushes headlong after false and elusive happiness, the Sacred Heart repeats with more aptness than ever: "Come to me, all you that are . . . carrying heavy burdens, and I will give you rest" (Mt 11:28).

All the writings of Montfort are pervaded with these sentiments of the Heart of Jesus. Like his writings, his social and missionary activity was steeped in the compassionate understanding of human beings that characterizes the Hearts of Jesus and Mary. In this connection, reading his writings again with a different approach may be necessary for some who have only a superficial knowledge of him. The new evangelization is a much talked about topic nowadays, but the implication is that the world has lost the sense of the Good News that Christ brought two thousand years ago, and, in its bewilderment, looks to a host of self-styled saviors, as shown by the vast number of new religions. We live in a time of great confusion; the sheep are scattered, and the number of "lost sheep" keeps growing. *"Oh, I have lost a precious soul / My sheep has gone astray / My sacred Heart is deeply grieved / Because my sheep has surrendered to my worst enemies"* (H 98:7). It takes missionaries of Montfort's stamp to care for the lost sheep. *"Shall I stand by and see, indeed, / My brother die in sin / With heart unmoved? / Great Lord, not I!"* (H 22:1). In the spiritual economy, in the eyes of the Heart of Jesus, there is neither inflation nor recession. In the year 2000, as in year 1 of the Christian era, the value of a human soul is the same. *"God alone knows its invaluable price / . . . The price of the blood of Jesus Christ"* (H 21:6).

Montfort's writings make it clear that once devotion to the Sacred Heart has been renewed in the light of Scripture and with the help of reliable human sciences, it can be a radical remedy for the evils of our day, especially in the struggle against the tendency to regard each human being as a mere interchangeable number. "In this context, the heart of Jesus reminds men and women that their immortal destiny transcends their economic power and their social role within societies of mortals; they are the object of a personal love as individuals on the part of the One who, for the sake of all human beings, agreed to take a human body of flesh and bone and assume the human sufferings of all human hearts of all times (cf. Mt 8:17; Is 53:4) through his Incarnation, which was not only ontological and physical but also psychological and universal in its effects. Vatican II had good reason to declare in two successive sentences: 'By his Incarnation, he, the Son of God has in a certain way united himself with each man . . . and with a human heart he loved'"(GS 22).[32]

H.-M. Guindon

Notes: (1) Not a word of it, not even "Sacred Heart" in R. Laurentin, *Dieu Seul est ma tendresse (God Alone is My Tenderness),* O.E.I.L., Paris 1984; in T. Rey-Mermet, *Louis-Marie Grignion de Montfort,* Pneumathèque/ Nouvelle Cité, Montreal/Paris 1984; or in the biography by Papàsogli. In his book *Ce Coeur si passionné (This Heart So Passionate),* Saint Paul Publications, Paris/Fribourg 1974, Jean Ladame writes, "The devotion to the Sacred Heart also had zealous apostles after St. John Eudes, for example, St. Louis Marie de Montfort," 56. (2) B. Porcheron, *Le Diocèse de Paris (Diocese of Paris),* Series Histoire des diocèses de France (History of the Dioceses of France) 20, 1:226-227. (3) Ibid. (4) Ibid., 233. The official register of the foundations of the Visitation mentions the first foundation in Paris on May 1, 1619, and that of Paris II by Paris I on October 21, 1627. (5) Ibid., 287. (6) J. Dheilly, *Dictionnaire biblique (Dictionary of the Bible),* Desclée, Tournai

1964, 202. "The heart is not only an organ that conditions the biological vitality of man but it is also a symbol. It expresses the whole interiority of man, with his inner spirituality" (John Paul II, general audience of June 20, 1979, *Documentation Catholique* [Catholic Information Services] no. 178, July 15, 1979, 676). (7) *Traités sur l'Evangile de saint Jean (Treatises on the Gospel of St. John)*, 18, 1. (8) PL 158:762. (9) In *Cant.*, Sermon 61, 4. (10) Bérulle, Oeuvres Complètes, 1052-1053. (11) Bremond, *L'Ecole française (The French School)*, 23; *Bérulle*, in *Dictionnaire des Connaissances religieuses (Dictionary of Religious Understanding)*, vol. 1, col. 787. (12) A. Molien, Ibid., vol. 3, under *François de Sales.* (13) *Oeuvres*, Gallimard, 1969, 334. (14) *Traité de l'Amour de Dieu (Treatise on the Love of God)*, book 4, chap. 12, loc. cit., 644-645. (15) Ibid., book 1, chap. 9, 378. (16) Ibid, book 8, chap. 1, 665. (17) *Vie et oeuvres de Sainte Marguerite-Marie (The Life and Works of St. Margaret Mary)*, introduction by Professor Darricau, vol 1, *Autobiographie (Autobiography)*, Saint Paul Publications, Paris/Fribourg 1990, no. 26, 58. (18) Ibid., no. 33, 64. (19) Ibid., no. 53, 82-83. (20) Ibid., no. 55, 85-86. (21) Ibid., no. 60, 89. (22) Letter 130 to Father Croiset, April 14, 1689, ibid., vol. 2, chap. 1, p. 424. (23) Letter 135 to Father Croiset, January 17, 1690, ibid., vol. 2, chap. 1, p. 508-509. (24) Etienne Catta, *La Visitation Sainte-Marie de Nantes (The Visitation Convent of Saint Mary of Nantes)* (1630-1792), Series Etudes de théologie et d'histoire de la spiritualité 13, Librairie philosophique J. Vrin, Paris 1954, 463. See also *Abrégé de la vie et des vertus de notre très honorée soeur Marie-Madeleine de Santo Domingo de la Bouleveray (Summary of the Life and Virtues of Our Very Honored Sister Marie-Madeleine de Santo Domingo de la Bouleveray)*, in *Année Sainte des religieuses de la Visitation Sainte-Marie (The Holy Year of the Religious of the Visitation of Blessed Mary)*, vol. 9, November, Annecy-Lyon 1870, 488-490; Sr. Marie-Madeleine died in the convent in Nantes on 18 November 1725, aged sixty-two years with forty-four years of religious life. (25) The extraordinary increase in the number of convents of the Visitation during the first hundred years of its existence certainly played an important part in spreading this devotion even before St. Margaret Mary. "The Order established 149 houses in the eighteenth century, including 132 before 1660 and 87 during the lifetime of St. Jane Chantal, who died in 1641" (R. Devos, *Les Visitandines d'Annecy aux 17ème et 18ème siècles, Mémoires et Documents [The d'Annecy Visitations of the Seventeenth and Eighteenth Centuries: Memoires and Documents]*, Académie Salésienne, Annecy 1973, 84:80). One of the early superiors, Mother Hélène-Angélique Lhuillier (1592-1655), who was under the guidance of St. Francis de Sales and joined the Visitation in 1621, said the year before her death, "We shall have the honor of being called daughters of the Sacred Heart." These words are attributed to St. Francis de Sales himself. He said, "The nuns of the Visitation, who are happy to keep their Rule, will be allowed to bear the name of evangelical daughters; they were established during this time with the particular purpose of being imitators of the two virtues closest to the Sacred Heart of the Incarnate Word, namely, gentleness and humility, which are the basis and foundation of their Order and entitle them to the privilege and incomparable grace of bearing the name of Daughters of the Heart of Jesus" (*Vie et oeuvres de Sainte Marguerite-Marie*, 1:319). Etienne Catta, *La Visitation*, chap. 1, p. 454, n. 4, attributes this passage to Mgr. de Maupas, *Vie de saint François de Sales (The Life of St. Francis de Sales)*, Paris 1657, 2d ed. 1669, 310. (26) Along the same lines, A. Molien has written: "In founding the Visitation, St. Francis de Sales prepared for it a cradle in which it was able to grow and then spread worldwide." *Coeur de Jésus (Heart of Jesus)*, in *Dictionnaire des Connaissances religieuses (Dictionary of Religious Knowledge)*, vol. 2, col. 250. (27) Montfort also wrote to his sister: *"The true Sister of the Blessed Sacrament is a real victim, body and soul"* (L 18). (28) St. Margaret Mary wanted the requests of the Sacred Heart to be made known, though not by herself. On January 17, 1790, the year of her death, she wrote to Father Croiset, "As for your wish that I should tell you more about the graces granted by the Sacred Heart, as you intend to mention them in your book, I will from now on keep silent on this subject. I have already told you that I do not wish to be known in any way." Letter 135, in *Vie et oeuvres de Sainte Marguerite-Marie*, 2:508. (29) Backed up by documents, Funck-Brentano, *Sorcellerie (Sorcery)*, in *Dictionnaire des Connaissances religieuses*, vol. 6, col. 422, speaks about the Black Masses requested by Madame de Montespan. (30) *Vie et oeuvres de sainte Marguerite-Marie*, vol I, no. 46, 76. (31) C. Pozo, *La teologia del Corazón de Jesús en la actual crisis del pensamiento teologico (The Theology of the Heart of Jesus in the Current Crisis of Theological Thought)*, in *El Corazón en el Mundo de Hoy (The Heart in the World of Today)*, Semana de teologia y pastoral, Valladolid 1975, 37-55. (32) B. de Margerie, *Sacré-Coeur, dévotion au (Sacred Heart, Devotion to)*, in DSAM 13 (1991), 301.

SAINT

SUMMARY

I. MONTFORT'S PATH TOWARD SAINTHOOD:
   1. The evolution of Montfort's sainthood;
   2. The marks of Montfort's holiness;
   3. His reputation for holiness.

II. MONTFORT'S WRITINGS ON HOLINESS:
   1. The sources of holiness;
   2. The origin of holiness;
   3. The Holy Spirit through Mary;
   4. A secret of holiness;
   5. Models of holiness:
      a. Jesus Christ;
      b. Mary;
      c. The saints.
   6. Cooperation needed;
   7. The development of sanctity;
   8. The goal of sanctity.

III. MONTFORT, FOUNDER OF A SCHOOL OF SPIRITUALITY?:
   1. The Montfort spiritual tradition;
   2. Following the Montfort way of holiness.

I. MONTFORT'S PATH TOWARD SAINTHOOD

Montfort is among the saints who attained Christian perfection through a special gift of the Spirit. He did so by the "*smooth, short, perfect and sure*" Marian path of total consecration to the Eternal and Incarnate Wisdom, through Mary (TD 152). He knew well the grace-filled effort required for any true encounter with holiness, but his *"Good Mother"* was at his side to light up the darkness. She supported him as he faced battles and obstacles (cf. TD 152). She helped him use properly the gifts God had given him (cf. TD 54).

Upon his baptism into Christ Jesus on February 1, 1673, the young Louis become a son of God, a sharer in the Divine Nature and thus truly holy. Pauvert writes that later Louis Grignion would drop his family name and take that of Montfort,[1] in tribute to the place of his baptism: "a significant choice, indicative of the character of this hero of the Cross, in whom divine grace would take root and flourish."[2] Given that Montfort was a Christian who was faithful to the reality of baptism and to a life shaped by Christ's death and resurrection, his path toward sainthood can be seen as a progressive, ascending journey toward perfection to *"the measure of the full stature of Christ"* (Ep 4:13).

1. The evolution of Montfort's sainthood

Biographers have described and analyzed the various stages of Montfort's holiness, including infancy (the stage of beginners, *incipientes*), adolescence (those who advance, *proficientes*), and maturity (the perfect, *perfecti*). De Fiores correctly states: "Montfort's perfection was not fully realized at birth; he did not hold the same attitudes and profess the same doctrines from the beginning of his life to its end; rather, he appears as a person who was to pursue, over time, an uneven, divergent itinerary, but progressively acquiring the fundamental tenets of his own spirituality through dynamic grace, in harmony or in contrast with his environment."[3]

Thus any discussion of the evolution of Louis Marie's sainthood must be predicated on our great respect both for the free and unforeseeable action of the Holy Spirit (cf. Jn 3:8) and for Montfort's freely given response. In effect, "among the saints we always find the principles of newness and renewal . . . a surprise, a reaction" and we must also respect "that freedom that God has chosen to grant only to His saints."[4]

His biographers are unanimous in observing that Montfort's outstanding holiness had its beginnings in his childhood: in his love for prayer and the poor, in his filial tenderness toward his mother and toward Mary, and in his attention to others. His adolescence, which was spent at the Jesuit college in Rennes, saw him grow in wisdom and grace, so much so that "the friendships he made at school, in the Church, and in the ecclesiastical world in which he moved indicate that Louis Marie had, over the years, gained the admiration of his fellow students, his teachers, and even his most virtuous friends. They all openly said even then that he was a saint."[5] H. Daniel observes, "If Louis Marie had died at the age of twenty-two, he would have left us with an image of a young saint rather like Aloysius Gonzaga, bearing the same tender devotion to Mary, the same horror of sin and scandal, the same absorption in God. We would admire him unreservedly. From his father he inherited a temperament that he himself admitted would, without God's grace, have made him the most terrible man of the century."[6] But Montfort outlived Aloysius Gonzaga and, although he never reached old age, he continued on his unique path toward sainthood.

Montfort's sanctity—even in his youth—does appear to be truly profound, so much so that he was a mystery to many. Father Leschassier himself, Montfort's spiritual director, found it difficult to believe that the saint had been led by the Holy Spirit. When after Montfort's death he was reproached by Blain for being so hard on the great missionary, he candidly admitted: "You can see that I do not recognize saints." [7]

We can recognize moments of intense spiritual experience in Montfort's journey toward Christian perfection, moments of transfiguration that reveal the inner light of his holiness, resulting from an intimate and friendly communion with God.

The letters that survive from the years 1694 to 1716 nearly always begin with a strong desire of Montfort's soul: *"May the perfect love of God reign in our hearts"* (cf., e.g., L 2, 3, 5, 6). This desire explodes in three great hymns to charity (H 5, 14, 148) that are like tongues of fire irrupting from a heart full of passionate love for God and neighbor. The hymn is sung by the voice of charity: *"I enable the faithful soul / To ascend to God in a chariot of fire, / I join that soul to God in marriage, / And transform all in God's sight"* (H 5:10). *"Charity embodies in itself / The most perfect holiness"* (H 14:6).

After his ordination, the young Montfort felt a strong attraction to solitude and the hidden life (cf. L 5), the silence that is the true home of saints, where they pray to God in peace and where they secretly *"taste my fires and receive my characteristics"* (H 5:36). For Louis Marie this close communion with God led him to desire to do God's will only and forever (cf. L 6), in the profound conviction that in faithful obedience to God—with Mary and in Mary—he would become rich in grace (cf. TD 54).

In 1704, after having desired so greatly and invoked so often the infinite treasure of divine Wisdom, after having yearned endlessly for this Wisdom, Montfort said good-bye to his mother, telling her of his happiness in mystical union with Wisdom: *"In my new family—the one I belong to now—I have chosen to be wedded to Wisdom and the Cross for in these I find every good, both earthly and heavenly. So precious are these possessions that, if they were but known, Montfort would be the envy of the richest and most powerful kings on earth"* (L 20). De Fiores remarks that Montfort, after traveling a tormenting road of purification and grace, attained the mystical state of "constant delight in the presence of Jesus and Mary even in the midst of his missionary activity."[8] Montfort himself confides: *"Here is something one will not be able to believe: / I carry her in the midst of me / Engraved with the marks of glory / Although in the obscurity of faith"* (H 77:15).

2. The marks of Montfort's holiness

"Our eye, which is sometimes dazzled by the splendor of the light that emanates from Saint Louis de Montfort, must, so to speak, examine its source." Thus spoke Pius XII on July 21, 1947, to the pilgrims who had come to Rome for the canonization of Louis Marie.[9] As he added Montfort to the calendar of saints, the Pope spoke of his incessant devotion to prayer, his humility, his love for evangelical poverty, his penitence, his abnegation, his constant mortification, and his ardent devotion to the Virgin Mary.

As we examine the records of his beatification and canonization proceedings, the numerous biographies of his life, and his spiritual writings, we can see that Louis Marie's holiness bears three essential characteristics: it is Trinitarian, Christocentric, and Marian. The point where these concerns meet is the focal, unifying, and dynamic point of his life, his apostolate and teaching. Montfort arrived at that stage through contemplation of the salvific and irrevocable plan that the Father, Son, and Holy Spirit realize in the fullness of time and will continue to realize as the history of salvation continues throughout the centuries: Christ came into the world through Mary, and through Mary he must reign in the world (cf. TD 1). Montfort brought these concerns together in perfect, harmonious agreement in the threefold acclamation that closes TD: *"Glory to Jesus in Mary! Glory to Mary in Jesus! Glory to God alone!"* (TD 265).

"The Father gave and still gives His Son only through her. . . . God the Son was prepared for mankind in general by her alone. Mary, in union with the Holy Spirit, still conceives him and brings him forth daily. It is through her alone that the Son distributes his merits and virtues. The Holy Spirit formed Jesus only through her, and he forms the members of the Mystical Body and dispenses his gifts and his favors only through her" (TD 140).

In this light of faith, the Trinitarian and primordial source of grace and holiness *("Glory to God alone!")* becomes Christocentric *("Glory to Jesus in Mary!")* and Marian *("Glory to Mary in Jesus!").*

Montfort's spiritual journey centers on, and can be summarized by, consecration to Jesus Christ: *"God has laid no other foundation for our salvation, perfection, and glory than Jesus"* (TD 61). *"The most perfect of all devotions is that which conforms, unites, and consecrates us most completely to Jesus"* (TD 120).[10] This is why Montfort so often mentions Paul's exhortation to the Christians at Ephesus: *"until all of us . . . come to the measure of the full stature of Christ"* (Ep 4:13; cf. TD 33, 61, 119, 156, 164, 168; LEW 1, 214, 226).

From this emphasis on Christocentrism comes the ardent prayer (cf. TD 67) that rises in Montfort's soul and that he invites us to recite each day in order to receive the gift of Christ's love. It is tempting to connect this prayer to Pascal's Memorial, the famous "night of fire" in the Year of Grace 1654. That same inflamed love for Christ gives rise in Montfort's heart to his prayer to the Holy Spirit, requesting missionaries to live on the mountain that is Mary, *"on which Jesus Christ, who dwells there forever, will teach them in his own words the meaning of the eight beatitudes. It is on this mountain that they will be transfigured as he was on Mount Thabor; that they will die with him as he died on Calvary, and from it, they will ascend to heaven as he did from the Mount of Olives"* (PM 25). Love of Christ carries Montfort forward on his spiritual journey and in his intense missionary work: love of Christ, Eternal and Incarnate Wisdom; love of the Cross, the Eucharist, and the Heart of Christ, translated into preferential love for the poor.[11]

The Christocentrism of Montfort's spirituality necessarily entails devotion to Mary: *"The greatest means of all, and the most wonderful of all secrets for obtaining and preserving Divine Wisdom is a loving and genuine devotion to the Blessed Virgin"* (LEW 203). Montfort's approach has the allure of a syllogism in this well-known text: *"As all perfection consists in our being conformed, united and consecrated to Jesus it naturally follows that the most perfect of all devotions is that which conforms, unites, and consecrates us most completely to Jesus. Now of all God's creatures Mary is the most conformed to Jesus. It therefore follows that, of all devotions, devotion to her makes for the most effective consecration and conformity to him. The more one is consecrated to Mary, the more one is consecrated to Jesus"* (TD 120). Montfort experiences this consecration to Mary in a progressive spiritual itinerary: "At the outset, Montfort views her in terms of affective human expressions. . . . Later, he is conscious of living in unity with the Virgin, who is wholly spirit, brought to life in the Trinitarian God: *'Mary is all . . . relative to God . . . she who does not exist except in relation to God . . . or the echo of God, saying and repeating only God.'* One must be a slave of Mary *('consecrating oneself and sacrificing oneself entirely, without limit')* before one can receive the Holy Spirit . . . which is to allow oneself to be molded by the Spirit in Christ's image: *'They cast themselves in Mary and lose themselves in her in order to become the true portrait of Jesus Christ.'"*[12]

It should be emphatically noted that Montfort not only wrote about holiness; it was something he lived, a reality he strongly experienced. What he writes is for the most part autobiographical; he is sharing with his readers not an abstract way, but a path of holiness he himself has trod. *"Experience alone will teach us the wonders wrought by Mary in the soul"* (SM 57). Montfort similarly cites experience as the best introduction to the way of Mary: *"Experience will teach you much more about this devotion than I can tell you, but, if you remain faithful to the little I have taught you, you will acquire a great richness of grace that will surprise you and fill you with delight"* (SM 53).

3. His reputation for holiness

After Montfort's death, the bishop of La Rochelle, Étienne de Champflour, wrote to Father Mulot: "I will always believe that he was a great saint before God. Wherever he preached, he was met with gratitude, esteem, and devotion."[13] For his part, the bishop of Poitiers, Jean-Claude de la Poype, affirmed on November 29, 1718, that Montfort "gave us an admirable example of penance, prayer, zeal, and charity, over the several years that he lived in our diocese."[14] Jean-Baptiste Blain tells the story of traveling as a pilgrim to the tomb of Louis Marie and encountering at Saint Laurent-sur-Sèvre, "crowds of pilgrims, from both near and far, who came to visit and honor the place where the body of the holy priest lay in repose."[15] The reputation for holiness that accompanied Montfort from his youth and throughout his life, despite malicious rumors, grew and spread "through all of France" as we read in the decree on the heroic practice of his virtues.

II. Montfort's Writings on Holiness

Montfort reveals to us the *source* of holiness (the Trinity), describes its *origin* (the Christian vocation), indicates its *authors* (the Holy Spirit working through the Mother of the Lord), reveals its marvelous *secret* (true devotion to Mary), proposes *models* of holiness (Christ, Mary, and the saints), reminds us of the necessity of mankind's *cooperation* in order to acquire it (the virtues), traces the development of its *intensity* (the three stages of the spiritual life), and speaks to us of its final *goal* (eternal life).

1. The sources of holiness

The source and origin of all holiness is the one and indivisible Trinity, in and through Christ. One page in TD is filled with Biblical passages that Montfort uses to emphasize Jesus' central role in Christian life, e.g.: *"For in him alone dwells the entire fullness of the divinity* [Col 2:9] *and the complete fullness of grace, virtue and perfection. In him alone we have been blessed with every spiritual blessing* [Ep 1:3] "(TD 61).

In a hymn dedicated to the Sacred Heart of Jesus, Montfort invites Christians to draw on the sources of holiness in the Savior: *"This is the source of life / On whom all the saints have drawn, / This is the beautiful fire / In which their hearts were embraced. / . . . Here is the most holy retreat / Where we avoid all transgression, / Here the most imperfect soul / Can easily become the most holy"* (H: 40, 16, 18).

2. The origin of holiness

Above all, Montfort reminds mankind, which is created in the image of a living God and saved by the precious blood of Christ, that God wishes us to become saints on earth, like Christ, and to become a part of His glory for all eternity. *"It is certain that growth in the holiness of God is your vocation. All your thoughts, words, actions, everything you suffer or undertake must lead you towards that end. Otherwise you are resisting God in not doing the work for which he created you and for which he is even now keeping you in being"* (SM 3).

He goes on to define sainthood with an exaltation that is reminiscent of the opening of St. Teresa of Avila's *Interior Castle,* where she compares the beauty and dignity of the soul in God's grace to a crystal that is completely transparent: *"What a marvelous transformation is possible! Dust into light, uncleanness into purity, sinfulness into holiness, creature into Creator, man into God! A marvelous work, I repeat, so difficult in itself, and even impossible for a mere creature to bring about, for only God can accomplish it by giving his grace abundantly and extraordinarily. The very creation of the universe is not as great an achievement as this"* (SM 3). Finally, in his role as a spiritual teacher, Montfort suggests the necessary means of attaining saintliness: *"sincere humility, unceasing prayer, complete self-denial, abandonment to divine Providence, and obedience to the will of God. The grace and help of God are absolutely necessary for us to practice all these"* (SM 4–5).

3. The Holy Spirit through Mary

Pope Paul VI referred to the "hidden relationship between the Spirit of God and the Virgin of Nazareth, and . . . the influence they exert on the Church" (MC 27). Montfort is noteworthy among spiritual theologians for his efforts to make this vital relationship between the Holy Spirit and Mary visible.[16] In a classic passage from TD he reveals the links between

Mary and the Holy Spirit in the Trinitarian economy of salvation as well as the reciprocal relationship between life in the Spirit and devotion to Mary: *"God the Holy Spirit wishes to fashion his chosen ones in and through Mary. . . . The formation and the education of the great saints who will come at the end of the world are reserved to her, for only this singular and wondrous virgin can produce in union with the Holy Spirit singular and wondrous things. When the Holy Spirit . . . finds Mary in a soul, he hastens there and enters fully into it. He gives himself generously to that soul according to the place it has given to his spouse. One of the main reasons why the Holy Spirit does not now work striking wonders in souls is that he fails to find in them a sufficiently close union with his faithful and inseparable spouse"* (TD 34–36).

4. A secret of holiness

While it is true that Montfort believed that life in the Spirit and devotion to Mary are inseparable in any journey to Christian holiness (cf. TD 14–42)—specifically for those who are called to a particular perfection (cf. TD 43–46), the children of Mary (cf. TD 56), and the apostles of the end times (cf. TD 47–54)—it is also true that in his Marian writings Montfort proposes and recommends a special form of holiness that he calls *"perfect devotion to Mary,"* the keynote of his own spirituality.[17] Here is how he describes this secret of holiness, the filial sacrifice in Mary's hands: *"I have seen many devout souls searching for Jesus in one way or another, and so often when they have worked hard throughout the night, all they can say is, 'Despite our having worked all night, we have caught nothing.' . . . But if we follow the immaculate path of Mary, living the devotion that I teach, we will always work in daylight, we will work in a holy place, and we will work but little. There is no darkness in Mary, not even the slightest shadow since there was never any sin in her. She is a holy place, a holy of holies, in which saints are formed and molded"* (TD 218).

In his hymns, Montfort speaks of receiving grace and gaining happiness for having discovered such a marvelous secret of saintliness: *"All through her / Nothing without her, / This is my secret / For becoming perfect"* (H 75:9); *"I do all things through her. / This is the surest way / To do God's will, the spur / And key to sanctity"* (H 77:19).

5. Models of holiness

Montfort is a teacher, an expert in the spiritual life: he educates us in holiness not only by teaching a sound ascetic and mystical theology but also by providing us with models of such holiness.

a. Jesus Christ. Jesus is the teacher and the exemplar of all Christian sainthood. Montfort asserts this vigorously in both LEW and TD: *"Eternal Wisdom alone enlightens every man that comes into this world. He alone came from heaven to teach the secrets of God. We have no real teacher except the incarnate Wisdom, whose name is Jesus Christ. He alone brings all the works of God to perfection, especially the saints, for he shows them what they must do and teaches them to* *appreciate and put into practice all he has taught them"* (LEW 56). Montfort again emphasizes the unique mediation of Christ in the order of salvation and holiness: Jesus Christ *"is the only teacher from whom we must learn; the only Lord on whom we should depend; the only Head to whom we should be united and the only model that we should imitate"* (TD 61).

In his hymns, Montfort describes Jesus as a model of humility (H 8:9–10), tenderness (H 9:3–11), obedience (H 10:5–8), patience (H 11:13–14; 41:1–37), charity toward others (H 14:11, 40), prayer (H 5:10), poverty (H 20:2–8), silence (H 23:18), thankfulness (H 26:6), modesty (H 25:6), and love of the Cross (H 19:6.9–12).

b. Mary. For Montfort, Mary is *"the perfect model of every virtue and perfection, fashioned by the Holy Spirit for us to imitate, as far as our limited capacity allows"* (TD 260). Since Mary is the *"great queen of virtue"* (H 4:22), the Christian must imitate all of her virtues, and particularly her ten primary virtues: *"deep humility, lively faith, blind obedience, unceasing prayer, constant self-denial, surpassing purity, ardent love, heroic patience, angelic kindness, and heavenly wisdom"* (TD 108). Montfort mentions several of Mary's other virtues that the Christian should imitate: poverty (H 25:8–9), silence and ability to listen (H 23:19), modesty (H 25:8–9), thankfulness (H 26:11–12, 24), and her abandonment to Providence (H 28:17).

c. The saints. The saints are also exemplary models of Christian perfection: *"The saints seek perfection, full of ardor, / for their grandeur and beatitude; / Unhappy are they who do not have this (desire) / Or who do not make the saints / Their principal study here below!"* (H 4:8).

Among the virtues of the saints, we must imitate:[18] the splendor of their humility (H 8:15), the charm of their tenderness (H 9:14), the excellence of their obedience (H 10:10), their strength of patience (H 11:19), the beauty of their virginity (H 12:16), the necessity of their penance (H 13: 8, 11), the tenderness of their brotherly charity (H 14:13–15), their joy of pardon (H 14:37), their blessed solitude (H 5:36), the frequency of their prayer (H 15:10), their power of fasting (H 16:6), the generosity of their alms (H 17:11), their love for the Cross (H 19:15–17; H 37:91), the treasures of their poverty (H 20:15–16), the flame of their zeal (H 24:16), the wisdom of their silence (H 23:2), their experience of the presence of God (H 24:12), the pleasant appeal of their modesty (H 25:10), their thankfulness (H 26:8), their abandonment to Providence (H 28:17–18), and even their innocent games (H 30:3).

In all, fifty saints are mentioned in Montfort's writings.

a. Of these, just over half are listed in SR: Agnes (128), Augustine (37, 40, 53, 88), Albert the Great (88), Alphonsus Rodriguez (25), Antoninus (51), Bonaventure (30, 53), Bridget (72), Charles Borromeo (80), Catherine the martyr (128), Cyprian of Carthage (36), Dominic (11, 16, 19, 20, 22, 26, 31, 51, 61, 66, 79, 90), Francis of Assisi (25, 32, 130), Francis Borgia (80), Francis de Sales

(80, 130), Francis Xavier (8), Gertrude the Great (54), Jerome (40, 73), Gregory of Nyssa (65), Louis IX, king of France (98), Mechtilde of Helft (48), Michael the archangel (79, 81), Peter of Verona (34), Pius V (80, 93), Teresa of Avila (8), Thomas Aquinas (69, 76, 88), Thomas of Villanova (80).

b. Those named in *True Devotion* are: Augustine (8, 33, 40, 67, 127, 145, 219, 230), Alphonsus Rodriguez (258), Ambrose (217, 258), Anselm of Canterbury (40, 76), Bernardine of Siena (27, 40, 76, 141, 152), Bernard (27, 40, 76, 141, 152), Bonaventure (8, 27, 40, 75, 85, 86, 116, 152, 174), Cecilia (170), Cyril of Jerusalem (40), Dominic (42, 249, 250), Ephrem (40, 153), Francis of Assisi (42), Francis de Sales (152), Germanus of Constantinople (40), John Capistran (249), John Damascene (40, 41, 152, 182), Gregory the Great (199, 226), Laurence the martyr (222), Michael the archangel (8), Odilo (159), Thomas Aquinas (40, 127), Vincent Ferrer (48).

c. In *The Love of Eternal Wisdom:* Augustine (30, 213), the Apostle Andrew (175), Arsenius the Great (200), Carpas (130), Francis of Assisi (166), Francis of Paula (166), John Chrysostom (9, 21, 175), John of the Cross (177), Gregory the Great (60), the Apostle Peter (175), Peter of Alcantara (177), Teresa of Avila (177), Thomas Aquinas (94, 163).

d. In *The Secret of Mary:* Augustine (14), Ambrose (54), Bernardine of Siena (10), Bernard (10), Thomas Aquinas (23).

e. In the *Prayer for Missionaries:* Francis of Paula (2), Catherine of Siena (27), Dominic (12), Michael the archangel (28), Vincent Ferrer (2).

f. Finally, in the *Letter to the Friends of the Cross:* Augustine (58), Catherine of Siena (27), Elizabeth of Hungary (54), John Chrysostom (37), Ignatius the martyr (32, 34).

Montfort spoke prophetically of the Marian secret of sainthood and had a natural sympathy for saints who, like himself, had followed the virginal and immaculate way of Mary to grow in wisdom, maturity, and holiness: *"There have been some saints, not very many, such as St. Ephrem, St. John Damascene, St. Bernard, St. Bernardine, St. Bonaventure, and St. Francis de Sales, who have taken this smooth path to Jesus Christ, because the Holy Spirit, the faithful Spouse of Mary, makes it known to them by a special grace. The other saints, who are the greater number, while having a devotion to Mary, either did not enter or did not go very far along this path. That is why they had to undergo harder and more dangerous trials"* (TD 152). Drawing on this observation, Montfort formulates a new argument for Christians to embrace perfect devotion to Mary: it is an easy way *"of attaining union with our Lord, in which Christian perfection consists"* (TD 152).

6. Cooperation needed

Everyone in the Church is called to saintliness. But sainthood is expressed through the external manifestation of virtuous acts. For this reason, *"the saints seek perfection, full of ardor, / for their grandeur and beatitude"* (H 4:8). *"Through virtue the saints have /*

Consummated all their plans" (H 36:68). *"Without virtue, all is lost"* (H 4:14). We must thus abandon the worldly spirit that prevents us from becoming holy (H 29:27) and subdue our concern about the opinions of others (H 38:120). Montfort speaks of *"poor saints"* (H 23:33), hypocrites who waste their time chattering before God, blind persons whose false holiness will lead them to perdition (cf. H 23:33).

Devotion to Mary must be holy; only then will it lead those who practice it to avoid sin and to imitate the virtues of the Virgin (cf. TD 108). Those who wish to be virtuous must remember that Mary is the queen of virtue (cf. H 4:22): we must request virtue of her, and from her we shall receive it (cf. H 104:8). We must follow the example and the virtue of the saints: *"We must confound our lack of courage / By contemplating the holiness / Of all the saints, our brothers. / Beside these powerful giants, / We are idle dwarves, / Filled with human misery. / They are made of iron and fire, / And we are fragile as glass before God"* (H 4:19).

Among the numerous virtues that Montfort considers part of a spiritual path, two in particular should be emphasized: obedience, which Montfort describes to the Company of Mary as *"the foundation and unshakable support of all its holiness"* (RM 19), and charity, which *"in itself contains / The most perfect holiness. / It is the fulfillment of the law; / Without it, there is no law"* (H 14:6; cf. H 17:29).

7. The development of sanctity

Montfort's spirituality is dynamic: those who adopt it are introduced to the itinerary of spirituality and accompanied throughout their journey; it guides Christians through the stages of (a) purification, (b) illumination, and (c) union. The month-long exercises in preparation for consecration to Jesus by the hands of Mary (outlined by Montfort in TD 227–33) reveal this path of (a) purification: liberating oneself from the worldly spirit that is counter to the spirit of Jesus Christ; (b) illumination: charismatic knowledge of Mary and of her way of living, dynamic presence in the mystery of Christ and the Church, and thus in the spiritual life of the Christian; and (c) union: filling oneself with Jesus Christ by means of Mary.

The Marian element of Montfort spirituality, far from diminishing the dynamism of this march toward saintliness, in fact enhances it. In order to describe this dynamism, Montfort invokes the Biblical narrative of Rebecca and Jacob, in which he sees depicted a life of consecration to Jesus Christ by the hands of Mary: *"What does this good Mother do when we have presented and consecrated to her our soul and body and all that pertains to them without excepting anything? Just what Rebecca of old did to the little goats Jacob brought her. (a) She kills them, that is, makes them die to the life of the old Adam. (b) She strips them of their skin, that is, of their natural inclinations, their self-love and self-will and their every attachment to creatures. (c) She cleanses them from all stain, impurity and sin. (d) She prepares them to God's taste and to his greater glory"* (TD 205).

This purification is followed by illumination: *"Once this good Mother . . . has stripped us of our own garments, she cleanses us and makes us worthy to appear without shame before our heavenly Father. . . . She clothes us in the clean, new, precious and fragrant garments of Esau, the first born, namely, her Son Jesus Christ. . . . Finally, Mary obtains for them the heavenly Father's blessing"* (TD 206–207). We are thus led to union with Christ (cf. TD 152–168): *"Furthermore, once Mary has heaped her favors upon her children and her faithful servants and has secured for them the blessing of the heavenly Father and union with Jesus Christ, she keeps them in Jesus and keeps Jesus in them. She guards them, watching over them unceasingly, lest they lose the grace of God and fall into the snares of their enemies. 'She keeps the saints in their fullness' (St. Bonaventure), and inspires them to persevere to the end"* (TD 212).

8. The goal of sanctity

If "Mary raises up, develops, and crowns the saints,"[19] and if the death of the saints is their *dies natalis*, then their entire life must be considered their formation in the womb of Mary, mother in the order of grace. On this subject, Montfort writes, *"St. Augustine, surpassing himself as well as all that I have said so far, affirms that in order to be conformed to the image of the Son of God all the predestinate, while in the world, are hidden in the womb of the Blessed Virgin where they are protected, nourished, cared for and developed by this good Mother, until the day she brings them forth to a life of glory after death, which the Church calls the birthday of the just"* (TD 33).

But the fact that the saints dwell in Mary's womb does not mean that they are passive and inert. We must imitate Mary's virtues until the end. For Montfort, the greatest inducement to embrace perfect devotion to Mary is that it is *"a wonderful means of persevering in the practice of virtue and of remaining steadfast"* (TD 173). He places these consoling words on the lips of the Virgin: *"Happy are those who practice my virtues and who, with the help of God's grace, follow the path of my life. They are happy in this world because of the abundance of grace and sweetness I impart to them out of my fullness, and which they receive more abundantly than others who do not imitate me so closely. They are happy at the hour of death which is sweet and peaceful for I am usually there myself to lead them home to everlasting joy. Finally, they will be happy for all eternity, because no servant of mine who imitated my virtues during life has ever been lost"* (TD 200).

III. Montfort, Founder of a School of Spirituality?

The conviction is ever-growing that Saint Louis de Montfort founded a school of spirituality, an outgrowth of the Bérullian school and of many other strands of holiness in the Church.

1. The Montfort spiritual tradition

In his encyclical *Redemptoris Mater*, John Paul II includes Saint Louis Marie de Montfort among the many witnesses and teachers of Marian spirituality, and describes the specific nature of this spirituality: "Saint Louis Marie Grignion de Montfort . . . proposes consecration to Christ through the hands of Mary, as an effective means for Christians to live faithfully their baptismal commitments" (RMat 48). Fundamentally, of course, there is only one uniform school of Christian spirituality in the Church. However, the Spirit, "according to His own richness and the needs of the ministries, distributes His different gifts for the welfare of the Church" (LG 7). In this sense, we can speak of diverse forms or schools of Christian spirituality.

In his book *The Spiritual Life at the School of the Blessed Louis Marie de Montfort,* A. Lhoumeau discerns in Montfort's teaching a true "system of spirituality."[20] "A century later, Lhoumeau's assessment remains completely valid, and the numerous and ever-multiplying studies of Montfort's works since that time have demonstrated that this assessment rests on an increasingly sure foundation. A. Martinelli, for example, has asserted that Montfort's TD forms the "basis for modern Marian spirituality."[21] For his part, John Paul II has invited us to be faithful "to the inexhaustible source of spirituality that Montfort left for us, by teaching us the meaning of true devotion to Mary."[22]

R. Deville recently described Montfort as one of the great heirs of the Bérullian school. He summarizes Montfort's mission and his particular grace as follows: "In many aspects of his thought and teaching, Montfort remains one of the best witnesses of the French School; Brémond unhesitatingly referred to him as the 'last of the great Bérullians.' He is certainly a part of the Bérullian tradition, but with his own particular emphases, notably on the subject of eternal Wisdom. He colors and enriches that tradition . . . with his long, loving contemplation of the Wisdom of God, which is the person of the Word incarnate." Deville also observed that, among the teachers of what is called the French School, and perhaps "among all of the saints, Grignion de Montfort has probably done the most to put this theological study of devotion to Mary at the service of the lives of the most ordinary Christians. John Paul II, a great reader of *True Devotion to the Blessed Virgin,* could say: 'Grignion de Montfort introduces us to the ordering of the mysteries in which our faith lives, enabling it to grow and become fruitful.'"[23]

Among the elements that make up montfort spirituality, the dominant motifs are the *Trinitarian, Christocentric,* and *Spirit-filled* elements that characterize Montfort's pedagogy of baptism. His missionary work and his writings were all concerned with preparing for the reign of Jesus Christ and with renewing personal consecration to Eternal and Incarnate Wisdom. And the Marian element is intertwined throughout his thinking. On the subject of Mary's presence in God's salvific plan, Montfort suggests that we live with, in, and for Mary, the mother and model of Christian life, to experience the fundamental, constitutive consecration of baptism into Christ Jesus. This synthesis can be expressed as follows: "Montfort received in the

Church the charism to express, with great vigor, the marvels and demands of baptism, which consecrates us to the Father, the Son, and the Holy Spirit, and at the same time to illuminate clearly the theological and pastoral value of true devotion to the Mother of the Lord. With this secret of grace, we can become alive to the duties that our covenant with God entails and that make us Christians, and thus to the fundamental consecration of baptism."[24]

In this way, the path of holiness that Montfort describes becomes the path that baptism laid down before us. Thus, with God's help, we must maintain and perfect the holiness that becomes ours when we receive this sacrament of spiritual rebirth. By renewing his or her baptismal promises in the hands of Mary, the disciple of Montfort will journey toward holiness, conscious "of his elevation, or rather, of his rebirth to the most happy reality of being the adopted Son of God, to the dignity of being a brother or sister of Christ, to the grace and joy of the indwelling of the Holy Spirit, to the vocation to a new life."[25] The itinerary that Montfort proposes can thus be called an easy, short, perfect, and certain path, open to everyone, a path to sainthood for "daily . . . or ordinary time." If trust in Mary *"makes us give Jesus and Mary all our thoughts, words, actions, and sufferings and every moment of our lives without exception"* (TD 136), then the consecrated Christian finds comfort in the thought that *"everything is done for Jesus and Mary. Our offering always holds good . . . unless we explicitly retract it"* (TD 136).

2. Following the Montfort way of holiness

From the time of the rediscovery of TD in 1842 until today, many have followed the path that Montfort proposed.

We can agree that "Montfort spirituality has been accepted by and given a place of honor in the contemporary Church. No book or dictionary on spirituality can ignore him."[26] It surely could be said that the deep, renewed devotion to Our Lady so resembles Montfort's thought that he could well be named its precursor.

In his encyclical *Redemptoris Mater,* John Paul II notes that "in our own time too new manifestations of this spirituality and devotion are not lacking" (RMat 48). John Paul II's example and word, signified by his motto "*Totus tuus,*" invite the twentieth-century Church to scrutinize and carry out Montfort's spiritual message as a path toward Christian holiness.[27] The Pope himself has expressed this message in new and personal terms based on his own experience: "Grignion de Montfort even shows us the working of the mysteries which quicken our faith and make it grow and render it fruitful. The more my inner life has been centered on the mystery of the Redemption, the more surrender to Mary, in the spirit of Saint Louis de Montfort, has seemed to me the best means of participating fruitfully and effectively in this reality, in order to draw from it and share with others its inexpressible riches."[28] In these words of John Paul II we can hear a distant echo of Paul VI's exhortation to the montfort family on January

31, 1973, the three-hundredth anniversary of Montfort's birth: "There are still greater secrets of your Father to be discovered; you must live and proclaim Jesus Christ, eternal Wisdom; you must bring others to know and love Mary as the surest path to Jesus."

If it is true that "Saint Louis-Marie de Montfort's spiritual legacy has been received by countless souls, even beyond the religious congregations he founded"; if it is also true that "the montfort movement is strengthening, extending throughout the world" and that "new forms of social communication are accelerating and multiplying the spread of Montfort's message in the world,"[29] then we must rejoice with all our hearts. This heralds a new springtime of holiness.

A. Rum

Notes: (1) According to Grandet (p. 45), Louis-Marie first used the name "de Montfort" in a letter to his sister Guyonne-Jeanne (L 12, October 1702). On August 28, 1704, in a letter to his mother, he called himself simply "Montfort": "*. . . Montfort would be the envy of the richest and most powerful kings on earth*" (L 20). (2) A. Pauvert, *Vie du vénérable Louis-Marie Grignion de Montfort . . . (Life of the venerable Louis-Marie Grignion de Montfort*), Oudin, Poitiers-Paris 1875, 12. (3) De Fiores, *Itinerario,* 4. (4) G. De Luca, *Luigi Maria Grignion de Montfort. Saggio biografico* (*Biographical Essay*), 2nd ed., Edizioni di storia e letterature, Rome 1985, 152. (5) Ibid,. 85. (6) H. Daniel. *Saint Louis-Marie Grignion de Montfort. Ce qu'il fut, ce qu'd fite,* (St. Louis de Montfort, Who He was and What He Did), Téqui, Toulouse 1967. 27. (7) Blain, 227. (8) De Fiores, 264. (9) Pius XII, Discourse of the pilgrims gathered for the Canonization of St. Louis-Marie de Montfort, July 21, 1947, in AAS 39 (1947), 411. (10) The first authentic title for the manuscript of TD was *"The perfect consecration to Jesus Christ"* (TD 120). Montfort wrote it in large letters to indicate its importance. (11) Apart from LEW and FC, one can find various hymns that Montfort composed in honor of Christ's passion and Cross, the Eucharist, and the Sacred Heart of Jesus. In RM 7, Montfort exhorts his missionaries to share in *"the most tender inclinations of the heart of Jesus, their model."* (12) T. Goffi, P. Zovatto, *La spiritualità del Settecento (The Spirituality of the Eighteenth Century),* Edizioni dehoniane, Bologna 1990 175–176. (13) Grandet, 440. (14) Grandet, 440. (15) Blain, 201. (16) Cf. S. De Fiores, "Le Saint-Esprit et Marie chez Grignion de Montfort" (*The Holy Spirit and Mary in Grignion de Montfort*) in CM 20 (1975), n. 99, 195–216. (17) A. Rum, "La spiritualità mariana di s. Luigi Maria Grignion de Montfort," (*The Marian Spirituality of Saint Louis Marie Grignion de Montfort*) in E. Ancilli, ed., *Le grandi scuole della spiritualità cristiana* (*The Great Schools of Christian Spirituality*), Edizioni O.C.D., Rome 1984, 577–596. (18) Often, in the margin of his hymns, Montfort wrote, *"The examples of the saints."* (19) Pius XI, for the canonization of Jeanne Antide Thouret. (20) A. Lhoumeau, *La vie spirituelle a l'école du Bx. Louis-Marie Grignion de Montfort* (The Spiritual Life at the School of Blessed Louis Marie de Montfort), Oudin, Paris 1901). (21) In *Palestra del Clero,* February 1965, 207. (22) John Paul II, *To the General Chapter of the Brothers of Saint Gabriel,* 1985. (23) R. Deville, *L'école française de spiritualité* (The French school of spirituality), Desclée, Paris 1987, 162. (24) A. Rum, *La spiritualità,* 584. (25) Paul VI, Encyclical *Ecclesiam suam,* August 6, 1964, 23. (26) Ibid., 591. (27) Cf. M. Comin, "Movimento mariano monfortano," (*Montfort Marian Movement*) in A. Favale, ed., *Presenza di Maria nelle aggregazioni ecclesiali contemporanee* (*Presence of Mary in the contemporary ecclesial societies*), LDC, Leumann 1985, 15–28. This article gives an insight into the influence of montfort Marian spirituality on the progress of the Church. (28) A. Frossard, *"Be Not Afraid!": Pope John Paul II Speaks Out on his Life, his Beliefs, and his Inspiring Vision for Humanity,* St. Martin's Press, New York 1984, 126. (29) B. Cortinovis, "Presentazione" (Presentation), in S. Luigi Maria da Montfort, *Opere (Works)* vol. I: *Scritti spirituali* (*Spiritual Writings*), Edizioni monfortane, Rome 1990.

SALVATION

SUMMARY

I. INTRODUCTION:
  1. The etymology of the word;
  2. From the profane to the religious sense;
  3. Salvation as God's loving kindness.

II. SALVATION IN THE SEVENTEENTH CENTURY:
  1. Parish missions;
  2. Jansenism.

III. MONTFORT AND THE SALVATION OF HIS NEIGHBOR:
  1. Aspirations of the young priest;
  2. Montfort the missionary;
  3. His plan for his mission:
    a. Prayer for Missionaries,
    b. Rule of the Missionary Priests of the Company of Mary.

IV. MONTFORT'S VISION OF SALVATION:
  1. An all-encompassing vision;
  2. A unified concept:
    a. The Rosary,
    b. The Cross,
    c. Perfect Consecration to Jesus Christ through Mary.

V. CONCLUSION.

I. INTRODUCTION

This article will present a general overview of the meaning of salvation and consider the method Saint Louis de Montfort employed to proclaim God's healing love in and through Christ Jesus. The word "salvation," a familiar one in the Christian language, has a long history. We can better understand its significance for us today if we briefly review this history and clear away the historical accumulations that have obscured the word's meaning.

1. The etymology of the word

Words become as familiar to our lips as the feel of coins in our fingers. Just as coins become worn and illegible, words lose their original meaning through repeated use. Such is the case with the word "salvation." The concept can trace its lineage to the Sanskrit word *sarvah,*[1] from which its rich etymological history derives. The root, *sar,* became *sal* in the Latin languages. Thus, for example, we have the French word *salut* and the English "salute," to wish someone good health, as well as the words "salutary" and "salubrious," promoting health. Later, the word "salvation" became associated with a danger from which one escapes, something that threatens the integrity of a material or physical good.

2. From the profane to the religious sense

From the beginning of our existence, mankind has been surrounded by dangers. Pagans turned to their gods to ask for help and protection. The OT understanding of salvation springs from concrete experiences: deliverance from mortal danger, healing from serious illness, freedom from captivity, victory in battle (cf. Ps 7:11; 22:22; 86:2; etc.). It is not only individuals who cry out for liberation but the nation as a whole. To these chosen people, God revealed His name (Ex 3:14) and, at the same time, revealed Himself as the Savior of His people (cf. Ex 3:16). Every subsequent revelation has contained this duality: God in His transcendence and God the Savior. "Your Redeemer is the Holy One of Israel" (Is 41:14). Judith, in her prayer, "cried out to the Lord with a loud voice and said, . . . thou art God of the lowly . . . savior of those without hope" (Jdt 11:1, 9). This notion of total healing of the people of God developed concurrently with the concept of the God of the covenant in the history of Israel, and of the breaking of this covenant through sin. Understanding of one allowed for understanding of the other, as we see in Zechariah's hymn: "Blessed be the Lord God of Israel, for he has looked favorably on his people and redeemed them. . . . He spoke through the mouth of his holy prophets from of old, that we would be saved from our enemies. . . . Thus he . . has remembered his holy covenant . . . to grant us that we, being rescued from the hands of our enemies, might serve him without fear, in holiness and righteousness" (Lk 1:68ff). Mankind's greatest misfortune is to be separated from its Creator, especially if this separation should become final. Salvation—and here we return to the word's distant etymological origins—signifies man's complete flowering, in the fullness of his being, into eternal life. "And this is eternal life, that they may know you, the only true God, and Jesus Christ whom you have sent" (Jn 17:3). This is the good news, the Gospel brought to the world by Christ and by those who followed him, proclaiming his message of salvation: "To you is born this day in the city of David a Savior, who is the Messiah, the Lord" (Lk 2:11).

Although the NT employs for salvation the term *sotería,* which can mean both bodily health and the well-being of spiritual life, in NT it is a religious term and is almost never applied to purely earthly conditions. In its fullest sense, salvation *is* Jesus: "Today," Jesus says to his host, Zacchaeus, "salvation has come to this house" (Lk 19:9; cf. Lk 18:42). Those who turn to him in loving surrender encounter and accept God's forgiveness personally enfleshed. They are "healed," "saved" in and through a dynamic, mutual relationship with Christ Jesus.

3. Salvation as God's loving kindness

"In this is love, not that we loved God but that he loved us and sent his Son" (1 Jn 4:10). Cut off from God because of sin, mankind finds salvation only through God's merciful initiative. "It was because the LORD loved you and kept the oath that he swore to your ancestors, that the LORD has brought you out with a mighty hand, and redeemed you from the house of slavery, from the hand of Pharaoh king of Egypt. Know therefore that the LORD your God is God, the faithful God who maintains covenant loyalty with those who love him and keep his commandments, to a thousand generations" (Deut 7:8-9). This love takes the first step. "When Israel was a child, I loved him, and out of Egypt I called my son. The more I called them, the more they went from me .... Yet it was I who taught Ephraim to walk, I took them up in my arms; but they did not know that I healed them. I led them with cords of human kindness, with bands of love" (Hos 11:1-2, 3-4). In spite of mankind's forgetfulness and rebellions, throughout the history of His people, God has never ceased to follow them with His love and to renew His pardon. He was not content to speak to them through His messengers, the prophets; He came Himself, in His Son. "For God so loved the world that he gave his only Son, so that everyone who believes in him may have eternal life" (Jn 3:16). This Son is Jesus, whose name means "YHWH saves."

II. Salvation in the Seventeenth Century

The seventeenth century was a time of solid spirituality and extraordinary religious vitality that led to the development of saintly priests, including several who were canonized: Francis de Sales, Vincent de Paul, John Eudes. There was a sincere interest in the salvation of sinners and the task of leading them back to their Christian obligations. Some theologians, however, propounded doctrines on the role of divine grace and salvation that proved excessive, and their deviations led to a subtle and tenacious heresy called Jansenism,[2] which was so rigorous that it closed the doors of hope and divine mercy to sinners, doors that had been so bounteously opened by the entire prophetic tradition.

1. Parish missions

As Montfort was preparing himself for his ministry of parish missions, France could already boast of generations of pioneers in this apostolic ministry dedicated to the conversion and salvation of all. In 1625, Vincent de Paul founded the Congregation of the Mission,[3] approved by Urban VIII in 1633. The priests of the Oratory, the Jesuits, the Capuchins, and the Eudists all were involved in forming mission teams. Toward the close of the seventeenth century and the beginning of the eighteenth, Brittany and the west of France were the scene of an impressive outbreak of evangelizing activity, due to the establishment of numerous monasteries and a revival of Christian life at every level in society. Missionaries traveled in groups of six to twelve or sometimes, as among the Capuchins, twelve to twenty. Several would preach, while others would hear confessions for eight, fifteen, or thirty hours.[4] "They wished to convert and instruct sinners and at the same time lead them to holiness" (Bremond).

These missions were supported by "endowments," sometimes worth thousands of *livres*. The missions themselves had to be renewed every five or ten years.[5] History has left us some celebrated names, such as Le Nobletz, Maunoir, Leuduger, and also the Father from Montfort.

2. Jansenism

Before Christian people felt the effects of its moral teachings in the form of an excessively rigorous administration of Penance and the Eucharist,[6] Jansenism was the product of an elite of theologians and spiritual figures.[7] With the intention of presenting St. Augustine's doctrine on grace in all its purity, the Dutch theologian Cornelius Jansen (Jansenius)—encouraged by Jean du Vergier de Hauranne, Abbot of Saint-Cyran and a friend and fellow graduate of the University of Louvain—taught that human nature was so thoroughly corrupted by original sin that it was incapable of doing good; as a result, the unfaithful were unable to love God. The sole remedy was grace, but God granted grace only to those who were predestined—those who were redeemed by Christ, whereas God is "the Savior of all people" (1 Tim 4:10). At Jansenism's most extreme, this interior grace was said to be so irresistible that humans were deprived of their freedom and could not collaborate in their own salvation. In July 1705, eight months before he was to meet with Montfort, Pope Clement XI reiterated the condemnation of his predecessors Urban VIII (1643) and Innocent X (1653). Certainly Clement must have had the religious situation in France in mind when, after listening to Montfort, then a young priest of only six years, he made him a part of his apostolic plans, saying, "You have a great field in France in which to exercise your zeal. Stay in France, and always work with a perfect submission to the bishops of the dioceses to which you are called. By this means, God will give His blessing to your works."[8] Montfort returned to France with the title of "Apostolic Missionary."

III. Montfort and the Salvation of His Neighbor

Cicero would have said, "One is born a poet, but one becomes an orator." One is a gift of nature; the other, the result of art. In the words of his friend Blain, Montfort was "born for the apostolic life." His earliest childhood years presaged his future, as he strove to initiate his young sister, Guyonne-Jeanne, into prayer: a missionary wholly dedicated to the salvation of his fellow human beings.

1. Aspirations of the young priest

In a letter dated December 6, 1700, scarcely six months after his ordination, Montfort confided to his spiritual director, Leschassier, the superior at Saint-Sulpice, his desire for the apostolic ministry of preaching. Although the members of Saint-Sulpice had been watching over Montfort and had expected that he would remain there, they regretfully allowed him to leave and advised him to visit a holy priest at Nantes, named René Lévêque, who had established a community of priests intended for parish missions. This experience, as Montfort reveals in that same letter, was disappointing, and he describes it in detail (L 5). Several months later, he wrote again to Father Leschassier: *"As you know, I have not the slightest inclination to stay in the Saint Clément community"* (L 9).[9] He was torn between his attraction to a life in seclusion and his *"tremendous urge to make our Lord and his holy Mother loved, to go in a humble and simple way to teach catechism to the poor in country places and to arouse in sinners a devotion to our Blessed Lady"* (L 6). He cites the encouraging example of a good priest, unnamed: *"He used to go about from parish to parish teaching the people catechism and relying only on what Providence provided for him."* Then he reveals the plans that he had probably harbored since his ordination and that tortured him inside: *"When I see the needs of the Church I cannot help pleading continually for a small and poor band of good priests"* to carry out this apostolic work (L 6).

2. Montfort the missionary

On the strength of his mission from the Pope, Montfort resumed the hard apostolic labor he had dreamed of. *"It is done, I roam through the world, / I have the spirit of a vagabond / To save my poor neighbor. / What! I see the soul of my dear brother / Perish everywhere from sin / And my heart is not touched? / No, no, Lord, that soul is too dear to me"* (H 22:1). *"I see this soul, so beautiful, / Fall into eternal death. / Shall no one feel any sorrow? / What! I see the blood of God who loves / Spread among all in vain / And His prize forever lost? / I would rather be anathema"* (H 22:2). We hear there an echo of St. Paul, who cried out: "I have great sorrow and unceasing anguish in my heart. For I could wish that I myself were accursed and cut off from Christ for the sake of my own people" (Rom 9:2-3). Montfort castigated evil everywhere that he found it. He describes at length, in LEW 75-82, the false wisdom, worldly, carnal, and diabolical, against which he does battle. He returns to this theme in ten hymns, numbers 29 through 39. In the first, made up of ninety-two stanzas of 6 lines each, or 552 lines in all, he speaks of every sin from all levels of society: pride among the great; indolence, self-complacency, ignorance among the peasants; drunkenness, slander; even in the religious Orders, envy and discord. *"Injustice in the palace, / Scandals before the public; / In secret beds and places, / Filthy impurities"* (H 29:19). *"See the world and its misfortunes. / Can we love anything so miserable? / Can we follow its adherents / In their deplorable fate? / Let us all cry out together: Woe, woe / Woe to this deceitful world"* (H 29:91). We must imagine these words on the lips of a preacher who is burning with passion, in order to grasp the effect they must have had on his audience. This preacher was animated with the Spirit of the ancient prophets: "They proclaim their sin like Sodom, they do not hide it. Woe to them! For they have brought evil on themselves. . . . Woe to the guilty! How unfortunate they are, for what their hands have done shall be done to them" (Isa 3:9, 11). How many times did Jesus himself condemn the world? "Woe to you who are full now, for you will be angry. Woe to you who are laughing now, for you will mourn and weep. Woe to you when all speak well of you, for that is what their ancestors did to the false prophets" (Lk 6:25-26). "Woe to me if I do not proclaim the gospel!" said St. Paul (1 Cor 9:16). This was Montfort's view, in spite of the dangers he encountered from those on both ends of the religious/theological spectrum who tried on several occasions to kill him.[10] He preached without any endowment to ensure his subsistence, relying totally on Divine Providence.[11] His only companion at that time was a young man to whom Montfort said one day, like Christ, "Come, follow me." This man became Brother Mathurin. Less than three years before he died, in August 1713, Father de Montfort traveled to Paris to find heirs to his spirit and to throw his coat, like Elijah, over some new Elisha (2 Kings 2:13). He had prayed for thirteen years to have missionaries for his little Company who would continue his proclamation of salvation.

3. His plan for his mission

It was during this long gestation that Montfort carried in his heart and in his prayer the missionaries whom he wished to associate with him. PM gives a general description of his ideal missionary for his Company. RM describes his intentions for his Company in more detail. Its author's clear and methodical mind is apparent throughout and expresses perfectly his expectations for the mission.

a. Prayer for Missionaries. This work, more than any of his other writings, displays the purity and transparency of his apostolic ardor and indicates how deeply he took the salvation of souls to heart. It should certainly not be classified as simply one prayer among others. Its spiritual quality is exceptional, akin to what one finds in the highest reaches of the mystical life, the sixth mansion, wherein St. Teresa of Avila places the zeal of souls. Something similar animated Montfort. He wanted to convert sinners and ensure their salvation so that he might restore to God the glory that sin had taken from Him. *"But above all, bear in mind your dear Son . . . his cruel death and the blood he shed, all these cry out to you for mercy, so that, by this Congregation, his kingdom may bring down the empire of his enemies and rise upon its ruins"* (PM 4). With all the strength and familiarity of Elijah speaking to YHWH (cf. 1 Kings 18:27), he cries out: *"Be mindful, Lord, of your Congregation, when you come to dispense your justice. . . . Your divine commandments are broken, your Gospel is thrown aside, torrents of iniquity flood the whole earth carrying away even your servants. . . . Will everything come to the same end as Sodom and Gomorrah?"* (PM 5). One cannot help thinking of St. John of the Cross's remark about how few souls arrive at that intense degree of charity that bears fruit in an apostolate, a doctrine that conforms to the teaching of St. Thomas Aquinas: "The preaching of the divine word must proceed from the fullness of contemplation."[12] As a young priest, Montfort must surely have received, at the moment of his ordination, a special grace of the Holy Spirit, in light of the mission he was to accomplish. When Samuel anointed David, "the spirit of the LORD came mightily upon David from that day forward" (1 Sam 16:13). The imprint of the Holy Spirit is apparent in the words that fall from his pen: *"Would it not be better for me to be dead, Lord, than to see you offended daily so deliberately and with such impunity and, daily, to stand, myself, in ever-increasing danger of being swept away by the ever-swelling flood of iniquity?"*—as if it were a question of his own salvation. *"I would rather die a thousand deaths than endure such a fate. Send me your help from heaven or let me die"* (PM 14). His zeal had no limits except those of the absolute reign of God. *"When will it happen, this fiery deluge of pure love with which you are to set the whole world ablaze and which is to come, so gently yet so forcefully, that all nations, Moslems, idolators and even Jews, will be caught up in its flames and be converted?"* (PM 17).

b. Rule of the Missionary Priests of the Company of Mary. The deepest desire of Montfort's soul, even before his sole companion had joined him at his side, was codified in the Rule that stipulates what he wanted from his missionaries. Their apostolic objective took priority, and they were to dedicate themselves wholly to the task of saving souls, and that task alone. Others could train priests or form seminarians. *"Only priests who have already completed their seminary training are to be admitted to the Company"* (RM 1). All other occupations, no matter how beneficial, were to be abandoned *"as being contrary to their missionary vocation so as to feel free at all times to repeat after Jesus Christ: pauperibus evangelizare misit me Dominus, the Lord has sent me to preach good news to the poor, or, as the Apostle said: non misit me Dominus baptizare sed evangelizare, Christ did not send me to baptize but to preach the gospel"* (RM 2). *"The purpose of these missions is to renew the spirit of Christianity among the faithful. Therefore, the missionaries will see to it that, as the Pope has commanded, the baptismal vows are renewed with the greatest solemnity. They are not to give absolution or communion to any penitent who has not first renewed his baptismal promises with the rest of the parishioners"* (RM 56). Montfort was not, of course, acceding to the rigorism of Jansenism, but he clearly wished to convey the seriousness of this step. Montfort was not the sort of confessor that worldly people seek for themselves. *"They go looking for some broad-minded confessor (that is how they describe lax confessors who shirk their duty) to obtain from him on easy terms the peaceful sanction for their soft and effeminate way of living and a generous pardon for their sins"* (LEW 81). Montfort maintained in himself and required of his missionaries a healthy balance in the work of the confessional: *"They must not be either too strict or too lax in imposing penances or granting absolution but must hold to the golden mean of wisdom and truth"* (RM 59). The true preacher in Montfort's eyes is the man who has the gift *"for knowing and relishing the truth and getting others to relish it"* (RM 60). This is a difficult thing; it requires that we receive from God, *"as a reward for one's labors and prayers, a tongue, a mouth and a wisdom which the enemies of truth cannot withstand"* (RM 61). Such preachers *"have received the gift of proclaiming God's eternal word,"* and *"all the members of the Company of Mary must one day be preachers of this caliber"* (RM 62).

IV. Montfort's Vision of Salvation

However eloquent he must have been, to judge from the crowds that pressed round to hear him speak, Montfort was not only a prestigious preacher but a holy preacher with only one ambition, one reason for being, which was to have his people experience the need for salvation and to find that need fulfilled in Christ Jesus. Like the prophet Elijah, he was consumed with zeal for God: "I have been very zealous for the LORD, the God of hosts; for the Israelites have forsaken your covenant" (1Kings 19:10).

1. An all-encompassing vision

Montfort's viewed salvation not simply as bringing the sinner out of moral misery but also as bringing him or her to a stable and progressive Christian life. Montfort was not a preacher who, on completing a parish mission, simply left to begin new work elsewhere, as if he had merely carried out a contract to do missionary work in that area for a couple of weeks. Montfort articulated a universal vision of his mission. Preaching led to conversion, but conversion was only a way station, not the final destination. Perseverance and progress in virtue were needed. "Better is the end of a thing than its beginning" (Eccles. 7:8).

2. A unified concept

Saint Louis Marie speaks of *"the means of saving . . . souls, such as confession, holy communion, prayer, etc"* (LEW 80). There are, however, three means of salvation proposed by Montfort that should be given special attention: the Rosary, the Cross, and most especially the baptismal Consecration renewal through Mary.

a. The Rosary. In one of his methods for saying the Rosary, Montfort dedicated the tenth decade to *"the conversion of sinners, perseverance for the just"* (MR 9). Montfort knew that perseverance could be obtained through prayer, which is why he established the Rosary everywhere. The Ave Maria *"obtains indulgence / And grace for the sinner, / To the just go fervor / And perseverance"* (H 89:16). *"I, who write this, have learnt from my own experience that the Rosary has the power to convert even the most hardened hearts. . . . When I have gone back to parishes where I had given missions, I have seen tremendous differences between them; in those parishes where the people had given up the Rosary, they had generally fallen back into their sinful ways, whereas in places where the Rosary was said faithfully I found the people were persevering in the grace of God and advancing in virtue day by day"* (SR 113).

b. The Cross. The mystery of the Cross is a cornerstone of Montfort's doctrine; he is traditionally referred to as an apostle of the Cross and the Rosary. The Cross plays a critical role in every one of his written works, because "God has destined us not for wrath but for obtaining salvation through our Lord Jesus Christ, who died for us" (1 Thess 5:9-10). It would be impossible for us to speak of salvation without speaking of the Cross. Montfort's all-encompassing vision of salvation required that he address this essential point. As mentioned above, his mission was not short-term—it did not end with conversion. Its ultimate outcome was a life given wholly to God, a life in which we fulfill the potential promised by our Baptism and live the mystery of the Cross. This does not simply mean leading a virtuous life; rather, it means authentic holiness, as Montfort himself expressed it so clearly. It was with this goal in mind that he often founded the Association of the Friends of the Cross on the completion of a parish mission, which normally lasted several weeks. Those who had followed thirty-three sermons of the mission were eligible to join. After solemnly planting a large cross, Montfort would distribute to each member a small embroidered cross, to be pinned to his or her sleeve as a reminder of discovered truths. For many years after his death, one of these groups continued to exist at La Rochelle, with about sixty members. For Montfort, this was a way of encouraging perseverance in Christian perfection. *"Christian holiness consists in this: 1. Resolving to become a saint: 'If anyone wants to be a follower of mine'; 2. Self-denial: 'Let him renounce himself'; 3. Suffering: 'Let him take up his cross'; 4. Acting: 'Let him follow me'"* (FC 13). It is rare indeed today to hear words as urgent as those Montfort spoke to his Friends of the Cross!

c. Perfect Consecration to Jesus Christ through Mary. Montfort's logical mind would never have allowed him to leave out of his vision of salvation *"the greatest means of all, and the most wonderful of all secrets for obtaining and preserving divine Wisdom"* (LEW 203), which is perfect devotion to Mary, the act of "*losing ourselves*" in Our Lady so that she can mold us into Jesus Christ. This is, in Montfort's view, a *"perfect renewal of the vows and promises of holy baptism"* (TD 120). Here again we see the same urgent demands for holiness: *"Chosen soul, living image of God . . . , God wants you to become holy like him in this life and glorious like him in the next"* (SM 3). This is salvation. He tells the soul in whom he is confiding his secret of Mary: *"Inspired by the Holy Spirit, I am confiding it to you, with these conditions: . . . That you use this secret to become holy and worthy of heaven"* (SM 1). Saint Louis Marie gave his people, through his preaching of total Consecration, a solid means of living their faith, a program of life that, precisely because it so intensifies union with Our Lady, is such an excellent means of living in Jesus Christ, our salvation.

V. Conclusion

Our faith proclaims: "For us men and for our salvation he came down from heaven; by the power of the Holy Spirit he was born of the Virgin Mary and became man." Basing himself on this truth, Montfort writes: *"The salvation of the world began through Mary and through her it must be accomplished"* (TD 49). Montfort's voice no longer resounds in the churches of Brittany, but his works still speak to us. Their message is a vibrant, undiluted call to salvation. Two hundred and fifty years after Montfort, the Second Vatican Council endorsed a similar vision (LG 52), and John Paul II, for his part, has referred to the "precise place in the plan of salvation" of the Mother of the Redeemer (RMat 1). The Vicar of Christ has not hesitated to point out explicitly Saint Louis de Montfort's Consecration as "an effective means for Christians to live faithfully their baptismal commitments" (RMat 48).

H. M. Guindon

Notes: (1) R. Grandsaignes d'Hauterive, *Dictionnaire des racines des langues européennes (Dictionary of the Roots of European Languages),* vol. Sal-V, Larousse, Paris 1987, 129. (2) *Dictionnaire practique des connaissances religieuses* (Practical Dictionnary of Religious Knowledge), Letouzey-Ané, Paris 1925, 3:1145. (3) "He was alone in Paris in having established an institution that was dedicated exclusively to missionary work." B. Porcheron, *Paris I,* in *Histoire des diocèses de France* (History of Dioceses in France), Beauchesne, Paris 1987, 20:244. (4) "These missions, which were one of the great novelties of Tridentine pastoral activity, multiplied in number. They were conducted along standard lines that various accounts and narratives describe: preaching, conversion of sinners, confessions, communions, solemn ceremonies and processions, with shocking and dramatic sideshows that were a part of the pedagogy of such missions. . . . There is no indication that these missions bore any lasting fruit." Ibid., 246. (5) In 1678 a lawyer, Pierre Lebardier, founded a mission at Montoir to provide for the Capuchins at Croisic every seven years. Y. Durand, *Nantes,* in *Histoire des diocèses de France,* 1985, 18:136. (6) Even though severity seemed to be the rule in the second half of the seventeenth century (B. Häring, *La Loi du Christ* [The Law of Christ], Desclée, Tournai 1960, 1:45), an excessive number of confessors were accused of leniency and of leading sinners to damnation because it was necessary to postpone or deny absolution until the penitent could give proof of his or her improved conduct. Le Camus, bishop of Grenoble, wrote: "In a town like Grenoble or Chambéry . . . there are scarcely forty persons to be absolved out of four thousand, if we have to find converts to absolve them: if confessors are doing this, it is scandalous." H. Baud, *Genève-Annecy,* in *Histoire des diocèses de France,* 1985, 19:141. (7) This includes disciples of Bérulle. At Lyon, "the Oratorians had welcomed the new doctrine." J. Gadille, *Lyon,* in *Histoire des diocèses de France,* 1983, 16:141. "Jansenism came to Nantes from the Oratory. . . . The congregation was won over by the theories of Jansen." The same was true of the Benedictines with Dom Louvard, who convinced the faculty of theology at Nantes (Durand, *Nantes,* 139f). (8) Grandet, 100. (9) The goal of this community was to conduct parish missions. Its founder provided "more than sixty" such missions, but it was languishing at the time of Montfort's stay there, and later it became contaminated with Quesnelism after the bull *Unigenitus* condemning Jansenism, and its members were "appealers" of the bull at the next council (Durand, *Nantes,* 139). (10) Some young libertines who were told to leave one mission waited for Montfort for four hours at a street corner. He never came. "We would have cracked his skull if he had come by." On the other hand, his speech was immensely successful. "After the men, three thousand women followed the mission in an atmosphere of intense piety." Father Gabriel-Marie, *Louis-Marie Grignion de Montfort, routier de l'évangile* (Louis-Marie Grignion de Montfort, Traveler of the Gospel), Saint-Laurent-sur-Sèvre/Montreal 1966, 127, 129. (11) Montfort formally excluded these foundations: *"They will give all their missions in complete dependence on Providence and must not accept any endowment for future missions as do some communities of missionaries founded by the King or by private persons"* (RM 50). (12) *Summa Theologiae* I-II, q. 188, a. 6.

SECRET OF MARY

SUMMARY

I. TEXT AND ITS HISTORY:
  1. The sources;
  2. State of the text;
  3. Editions;
  4. Literary genre and addressee(s);
  5. Title;
  6. Date.

II. ANALYSIS.

III. CONTRIBUTIONS OF SM:
  1. The first part:
    a. Introduction,
    b. Goal of our life and means of attaining it,
    c. "Necessity" of Mary;
  2. The second part: the exposition on "what perfect devotion to Mary consists in":
    a. What this "devotion" consists in,
    b. The manner in which the interior practice is presented;
  3. The two final prayers and the Tree of Life:
    a. Prayer to Jesus,
    b. Prayer to Mary for use by her faithful slaves of love,
    c. "The cultivation and growth of the tree of life, in other words the way to make Mary live and reign in our souls."

IV. THE SECRET OF MARY FOR TODAY.

I. TEXT AND ITS HISTORY

1. The sources

The spiritual "way" articulated by St. Louis Marie de Montfort in SM is identical in substance with the "way" found in TD. The sources are the same. This also holds for the personal experience that constantly emerges in both writings. This article, therefore, should be read in conjunction with the one on TD.

2. State of the text

We do not have Montfort's original manuscript. Its text has come to us by way of two copies. One is preserved in the archives of the Company of Mary, and the other in the archives of the Daughters of Wisdom. The few variants in the text in no way affect its essential content.

The copy used by the editors of OC bears the following heading: "Copy of a manuscript that the late Father de Montfort had written by hand and sent to a person of piety." Sister Florence, a Daughter of Wisdom, in her valuable chronicle (which ends in 1761) observes: "By the same channel we received this admirable letter on the devotion of the Holy Slavery of Jesus in Mary, which Father de Montfort wrote to a religious Sister of Nantes." There were three prayers that were later placed at the end of the letter: one was addressed to Jesus, another was for those preaching Holy Slavery, and the third was entitled 'Multiplication of the Philosophers' Stone, or Cultivation of the Tree of Life.'"[1] According to the editors of OC, the "same channel" of which Sister Florence speaks "is doubtless Joseau and Brother Jacques. A companion of Montfort since 1714. Brother Jacques settled at Saint-Laurent-sur-Sèvre in 1716 and became friendly with a young man named Joseau, to whom he gave Father de Montfort's writings to be copied" (GA 263).

In any case, the copy dates from the first half of the eighteenth century. Despite the loss of the original manuscript, the text is without doubt attributable to St. Louis Marie de Montfort. Indeed, its content and style alone are signature enough.

3. Editions

While fragments of the text are found in various biographies of Father de Montfort, only in 1868 did a first edition make its appearance. Even then the text was not complete. In 1898 Father Lhoumeau published the text almost in its entirety; the only omissions are of certain passages bearing on the wearing of little chains as a sign of the Consecration of the slaves of Jesus in Mary.[2] The Lhoumeau edition itself contains a certain number of explanatory notes. It is to Father Huré that we owe the first *"typica"* edition, one in complete conformity with the manuscript, "furnished with an interpretive reflection at each important break in the text, briefly that summarized and contextualized the preceeding text" (preface, p. iv). As well, marginal numerals were used, "which provided the uniformity of references, despite the diversity of editions" (ibid., p. v).

The editors of OC, while retaining the marginal numbering introduced by Father Huré, have undertaken a painstakingly minute revision of the text. This has resulted in "the correction of certain textual mistakes found in the previous editions" (GA 264).

It was not until the manuscript of TD was rediscovered, published, and met with prompt success that the interest and value of SM came to light. It is a small booklet size work that has known a growing success in the footsteps of TD. It is difficult to give the exact number of editions of SM. A very reasonable estimate would be 350 editions.

4. Literary genre and addressee(s)

The text is presented in the form of a "*letter*," which the author addresses to a "*soul*"—someone that Saint Louis Marie wishes to convince of the excellence of the spiritual way. The letter was addressed to a specific person. The manuscript confirms this. It states that it is a "copy of a manuscript that the late Father de Montfort had written by hand and sent to a pious person." This is supported by Sister Florence's statement about "this admirable letter, which Father de Montfort wrote to a religious Sister of Nantes, on the devotion of Holy Slavery of Jesus in Mary."

None of the hypotheses to identify this individual are particularly compelling. However, this does not seem to be a matter of the primary importance. The fact that St. Louis Marie sent his "letter" to one "person of piety" rather than another changes little concerning the understanding of the text. Indeed, while the tone Montfort employed is personal (as is also the tone in a number of passages of his other writings), the text itself teaches us next to nothing about the precise person to whom it is addressed. It says nothing about the person's state, milieu, character, current difficulties, etc. Unless we find a personal indication in the reference in SM 2 to what little time the reader has at his or her disposal, this tells us little about the individual. The only conclusion we can draw about the addressee is that she is a person of good will and can understand the message being communicated. Otherwise, apart from the doctrinal knowledge and profound spiritual experience to which the text testifies, Montfort tells us nothing about the precise individual. If this is a letter, it is very different from the saint's extant personal letters. Were it not for the statements that we cited, we might imagine a sort of "circular letter," intended for a number of persons and yet sent to particular individuals, of whom Montfort would have thought of more especially as he wrote it.

A personal style, where an author addresses himself directly to a reader, can be a literary device and altogether appropriate for such a work of general interest. In the case of SM, it is not artificial. Apart from certain cultural expressions or constructions that obviously do not have the same meaning for us today, there is no reason why contemporary readers should not see themselves as other than directly and personally addressed by Montfort. The style endows the text with a freshness and simplicity, not the least among its values.

5. Title

Like TD, we owe the title of the work not to St. Louis Marie but to its first publishers, and it is an appropriate one. First, Father de Montfort is fond of the popular word "secret." Second, in SM 20, he speaks of a *"secret of Mary": "Happy, indeed sublimely happy, is the person to whom the Holy Spirit reveals the secret of Mary, thus imparting to him true knowledge of her. Happy the person to whom the Holy Spirit opens this enclosed garden for him to enter, and to whom the Holy Spirit gives access to this sealed fountain where he can draw water and drink deep draughts of the living waters of grace"* (SM 20). The expression "secret" has a strong, complex meaning for him. In herself, Mary is a secret. That is, she is hidden (cf. TD 2-13), too beautiful, too precious, too great, too filled with God, for us to be able to understand her. Only the Holy Spirit can give us access to her wealth, since the Holy Spirit is the author of that wealth.

Another meaning of the word "secret" for Montfort is that Mary can enable us to enter into the very mystery of God. She is the "*wonderful means*" given to us by God to permit us to arrive at holiness, which is union with Jesus Christ. Saint Louis Marie calls for a life experience of "*drawing*" on Mary and of "*drinking deep draughts of the living waters of grace.*"

Finally, for Montfort, what he calls the "*perfect practice of the true devotion,*" by which we strive to make all possible room for Mary in our life in order to reach Jesus and to be united with him, is the "*secret of holiness*" (H 77:19), it is "*his*" secret. For it is the means, according to him the best means, of arriving at the goal the Lord suggests to us. This is the secret he seeks to reveal to his reader: *"Here is a secret, chosen soul, which the most High God taught me*" (SM 1). It is a secret rooted in Mary. Since Montfort is convinced that it is his mission to make known her place in the divine plan, the title, *Secret of Mary,* is well chosen.

6. Date

When it comes to determining the date of the booklet composition, the scarcity of precise data counsels us to be cautious. There is, of course, Sister Florence's notation indicating that the writing was sent to a religious Sister of Nantes, but this only tells us that it was in this city that Father de Montfort found her. Various differences between this writing and TD could suggest a certain time lapse between the two writings. But since Father de Montfort seems to be writing—and rather hurriedly—a long-thought-out teaching here and since the literary genre is somewhat different in the two cases, it is difficult to force this argument. Montfort's control of his subject and style invite us to see in SM a work of his maturity.

II. Analysis

The manuscript used by the editors of OC is a continuous text, with only an occasional "1" or "2" to indicate items in a list. It is thanks to internal criticism, then, that it has been possible to propose divisions. While the marginal numerals added by the *"typica"* edition of 1926 have been retained by the editors, the latter have rather thoroughly recast the divisions and the wording of their headings. They have been concerned to show a kind of parallelism between the structure of SM and that of TD. The outline proposed is as follows:

Author's Introduction (1-2)

I. Necessity of Having a True Devotion to Mary (3-23)
  - A. The grace of God is absolutely necessary (3-5)
  - B. To find the grace of God, we must discover Mary (6-22)
  - C. A true devotion to the Blessed Virgin is indispensable (23)

II. What Perfect Devotion to Mary Consists In (24-65)
  - A. Some true devotions to the Blessed Virgin Mary (24-27)
  - B. The perfect practice of devotion to Mary (28-65)
    1. What it consists in (28-34)
    2. The excellence of this practice of devotion (35-42)
    3. The interior constituents of this Consecration and its spirit (43-52)
    4. The effects that this devotion produces in a faithful soul (53-59)
    5. Exterior practices (60-65)

Supplement
  - Prayers to Jesus and to Mary (66-69)
  - Prayer to Jesus (66-67)
  - Prayer to Mary (68-69)

Care and Growth of the Tree of Life (70-78)
  1. The Holy Slavery of Love: The Tree of Life (70)
  2. How to cultivate it 71-77)
  3. Its lasting fruit: Jesus Christ (78)

One need only glance at the outline of TD in GA to observe that with a certain flexibility—TD being notably more developed—the basic structure is the same. It is the same spiritual way or path, founded on the same profound considerations. Thus, it is unnecessary to repeat here what is said on this subject in the article on TD. On the other hand, it is useful to take note of certain more explicitly supported points, as well as several variants that can be observed in SM. And at least in certain cases, it is important to emphasize their significance.

III. Contributions of SM

1. The first part

a. Introduction. *"Here is a secret, chosen soul, which the most High God taught me and which I have not found in any book, ancient or modern"* (SM 1). St. Louis Marie is making three assertions here. First, he states that he is about to reveal a secret. Here he means a hidden reality which is at the same time an exceptional means to attaining the goal, which in this case is holiness, the perfection of the Christian life. Next, he states that he has himself received this secret directly from the Most High. Montfort is aware of the grace that he has obtained to know Mary and her mission and to take her into his life, "to himself," like John the Apostle. We must take this statement seriously, for it means that we can attain this knowledge of Mary only through grace. Finally, Montfort tells us straight out that he has not found this secret *"in any book, ancient or modern"* (SM 1). Now, inasmuch as he asserts elsewhere that his secret "devotion" is old, that it has been approved by the Holy See, and has been practiced by *"many saints and illustrious people"* (SM 42; cf. TD 18, 159). How are we to reconcile these apparently different assertions?

Montfort indeed would have found the Holy Slavery of the Mother of God in various authors (especially in Boudon), along with various formulas of Consecration. But the fact remains that he was able to bestow upon this form of Marian devotion a new and original expression. In a certain sense, he had transformed it, and what he expounded and proposed, he had not found it in books.[3] For that matter, since it is a "secret" it takes on its whole meaning only when one *who lives it by putting it in practice.* It cannot simply be discovered by readings. *"This secret becomes great only insofar as a soul makes use of it. . . . As you go on using this secret in the ordinary actions of your life, you will come to understand its value and its excellent quality"* (SM 1).

b. Goal of our life and means of attaining it. The method employed by Montfort to demonstrate Mary for us is basically the same in SM and TD. More briefly in SM, it articulates in precise theological terms, the goal of life: *"Chosen soul, living image of God and redeemed by the precious blood of Jesus Christ, God wants you to become holy like him in this life and glorious like him in the next"* (SM 3). We are made in the image of God by creation and saved, by Christ. He explains that we do not belong to ourselves: and that we receive the goal of our life from the One from whom we receive life and salvation. God wants simply for us to share in divine holiness here in this world, in order to share in the divine glory in the next. Thus, right from the outset, and in few words, the whole love of God is set before our eyes. It follows that we must respond to it.

"*It is certain that growth in the holiness of God is your vocation.*" There is no point in looking elsewhere. Our calling does not depend on us but on God's love for us. That sets out a path for us. We ought to set out on it without any reservations: *"All your thoughts, words, actions, everything you suffer or undertake must lead you towards that end. Otherwise you are resisting God in not doing the work for which he created you and for which he is even now keeping you in being"* (SM 3). How are we to find this grace? In finding Mary: *"It all comes to this, then. We must discover a simple means to obtain from God the grace needed to become holy. It is precisely this I wish to teach you. My contention is that you must first discover Mary if you would obtain this grace from God"* (SM 6). Montfort then sets forth, much more briefly than in TD, the arguments upon which his conviction is based (SM 7-23).

*c. **"Necessity" of Mary.*** SM 24, which concludes this part, poses a minor problem of interpretation. *"The difficulty, then, is how to arrive at the true knowledge of the most holy Virgin and so find grace in abundance through her. God as the absolute Master, can give directly what he ordinarily dispenses only through Mary, and it would be rash to deny that he sometimes does so. However, St. Thomas assures us that, following the order established by his divine Wisdom, God ordinarily imparts his graces to men through Mary. Therefore, if we wish to go to him, seeking union with him, we must use the same means which he used in coming down from heaven to assume our human nature and to impart his graces to us. That means was a complete dependence on Mary his Mother, which is true devotion to her"* (SM 24).

At one moment in the relatively recent past, when Mariologists were deeply concerned with debating the question of the "universal mediation of Mary," the interpretation of this text of Montfort acquired a particular importance. Some Mariologists had difficulty in accepting from Montfort what seemed to them to be a distortion of the principle of the universal mediation.

Very simply, St. Louis Marie's concern is different from that of a university professor. He is a preacher of parish missions. He knows, however, that he must take certain precautions in order to base his conclusions on solid ground, and not leave himself open to being criticized for "exaggerations" in his conceptualization of Mary's mission, and in the practice of the devotion to her whom he heralds.

Montfort, the good theologian that he is, makes a distinction. He knows perfectly well that God is *"absolute Master"* (SM 23) and that "*this great Lord, who is ever independent and self-sufficient, never had and does not now have any absolute need of the Blessed Virgin for the accomplishment of his will and the manifestation of his glory. To do all things he has only to will them*" (TD 14). God alone can determine, in all Wisdom and Love, what is to be accomplished in the divine plan and the ways to accomplish it. If Mary is "necessary," it is because God wills her to be necessary, and she is necessary to the extent that God wills it.

It is possible, and very useful, therefore, to seek out the pathways that the Lord has actually chosen in order to come to us, and the ways that same Lord asks us to take in order to come to him. But God's ordinary actions teach us that He wishes to use Mary in communicating and obtaining grace. Montfort showed this in the preceding numbers. It is what is important to him. Obviously God, in his absolute divine power, could have done otherwise. Has God at times actually done so? Will God do so? For Montfort, such questions remain purely hypothetical. He has no need to be burdened with them. He took all of the necessary precautions lest he be accused of unduly encroaching upon the mystery of God. He was careful to avoid proposing a false notion of the person of Mary and her mission. Montfort simply presented his teachings in a positive way. Then we meet Montfort's profound vision of the Incarnation. In it he perceives the manner of God's action. He saw everything as flowing from this mysterious source, for Mary and for us. "*If we wish to go to him, seeking union with him, we must use the same means which he used in coming down*" to us.[4]

2. The second part: the teaching on *"what perfect devotion to Mary consists in"*

Having briefly indicated that there are *"several true devotions to our Lady,"* Montfort arrives at the one dearest to his heart: the perfect practice of true devotion. Once more, we must refer to the article on TD. It presents montfort teaching on this theme in a much more developed fashion. Two observations suffice:

a. What this "devotion" consists in. St. Louis Marie's definition of his perfect practice of the true devotion is, in a way, more synthetic and more precise than the one we find in TD: *"Chosen soul, this devotion consists in surrendering oneself in the manner of a slave to Mary, and to Jesus through her, and then performing all our actions with Mary, in Mary, through Mary, and for Mary"* (SM 28). There are two elements which make up the spiritual path for Montfort. He clearly defines and relates them: 1) the total Consecration (or total gift) of oneself to Jesus through Mary; and 2) what he calls in TD the *"interior practices"* (TD 257) and in SM 60 simply the "*interior practice.*" He restates the principle that this interior practice is of the essence of the spiritual way in question: *"I have already said that this devotion consists in performing all our actions with Mary, in Mary, through Mary, and for Mary"* (SM 43). While it is not difficult to draw this conclusion on the basis of the presentation in TD, it must be acknowledged that on this important point, SM furnishes a clearer and more explicit formulation.

b. The manner in which the interior practice is presented. The interior practice is presented with several variants in SM and TD: *"Performing all our actions with Mary, in Mary, through Mary, and for Mary"* (SM 43); *"Doing everything through Mary, with Mary, in Mary and for Mary, in order to do it more perfectly through Jesus, with Jesus, in Jesus and for Jesus"* (TD 257).

The first difference strikes the reader immediately. The order of the prepositions is not the same. Ultimately, this is not very important in and of itself.

A closer examination reveals that not quite the same things are said by way of explanation of the prepositions "through" and "with." In SM 45, to act "*with Mary*" means that Mary is taken *"as the accomplished model for all we have to do."* In TD 260, the same idea is expressed in more developed fashion: *"We must look upon Mary, although a simple human being, as the perfect model of every virtue and perfection, fashioned by the Holy Spirit for us to imitate, as far as our limited capacity allows."* But next Montfort will state in SM under "*with Mary*" what he has developed in TD under "*for Mary*": that we must renounce ourselves in order to commit ourselves to Mary.

Further, the explanation of "*for Mary*" in SM is very brief: *"We must never go to our Lord except through Mary, using her intercession and good standing with him. We must never be without her when praying to Jesus"* (SM 48). This idea is a familiar one in Montfort (cf., e.g., TD 142-43), and he develops it in very rich fashion in TD 258 in order to explain "*through Mary*": it is a matter of obeying Mary "*always and being led in all things by her spirit, which is the Holy Spirit of God.*" We find something of the kind in SM 55: "*This devotion faithfully practiced produces countless happy effects in the soul. The most important of them is that it establishes, even here on earth, Mary's life in the soul, so that it is no longer the soul that lives, but Mary who lives in it. In a manner of speaking, Mary's soul becomes identified with the soul of her servant.*"

Thus, "*in Mary*" is presented somewhat differently. In SM: *"We must gradually acquire the habit of recollecting ourselves interiorly and so form within us an idea or a spiritual image of Mary. She must become, as it were, an Oratory for the soul where we offer up our prayers to God without fear of being ignored. She will be as a Tower of David for us where we can seek safety from all our enemies. She will be a burning lamp lighting up our inmost soul and inflaming us with love for God. She will be a sacred place of repose where we can contemplate God in her company. Finally, Mary will be the only means we will use in going to God, and she will become our intercessor for everything we need. When we pray we will pray in Mary. When we receive Jesus in Holy Communion we will place him in Mary for him to take his delight in her. If we do anything at all, it will be in Mary, and in this way Mary will help us to forget self everywhere and in all things"* (SM 47).

In TD 261-64, not altogether the same things are said about "*in Mary.*" In SM, it is a question, first, of a certain activity on the part of anyone who seeks to live "*in Mary.*" It is up to that individual to form, within himself or herself, a little "*idea or a spiritual image*" of Mary, with all of the consequences and advantages that might accrue. In TD, Montfort begins by describing the splendor of Mary, that *"true earthly paradise of the new Adam"* (TD 261), a splendor that the Holy Spirit was at pains to describe (TD 262); and it is this Spirit alone Who, by a "*special grace,*" can grant *"the unfortunate children of Adam and Eve, driven from the earthly paradise,"* access to this new paradise (TD 263). True, Montfort adds that this grace is to be *"obtained by our fidelity"* (TD 263). The effects described in TD 264 in no way contradict what is said in SM. It is only that they tend to be different, including the last, which reiterates an idea that is of the utmost importance for Montfort: we ought to be *"delighted to remain in Mary,"* in order that *"we may be formed in our Lord and our Lord formed in us"* (TD 264).

A second difference can be noted. In TD the Christocentrism of the interior practice is explicitly and strongly maintained. It does not appear in the same way in SM. A closer examination, however, reveals that this essential reference to Christ is actually present, first, in the act of total bestowal of self *"to Mary, and to Jesus through her"* (SM 28), and, next, when there is question of the "spirit" of this devotion, *"which requires an interior dependence on Mary, and effectively becoming her slave and the slave of Jesus through her"* (SM 44).

What can we conclude from these two variants? Perhaps simply that we should not adopt hidebound formulas, interesting and expressive as they may be, but ought to undertake to discover the overall spirit. And from this viewpoint, the differences we find in SM and TD only underscore the wide-ranging wealth of such formulas. Instead of seeking to discover contradictions in them, it would be better to see their complementarity.

3. The two final prayers and the Tree of Life

a. Prayer to Jesus. This is a prayer of thanksgiving to Jesus: *"Most loving Jesus, permit me to express my heartfelt gratitude to you for your kindness in giving me to your holy Mother through the devotion of holy slavery"* (SM 66). After a mention of the benefits of belonging to Mary comes a little development that is very interesting because it forcefully asserts that it is the desire of Jesus himself that we give ourselves utterly to his Mother. It refers to the example of John at the foot of the Cross: *"Like St. John the Evangelist at the foot of the Cross, I have taken her times without number as my total good and as often have I given myself to her. But if I have not done so as perfectly as you, dear Jesus, would wish, I now do so according to your desire. If you still see in my soul or body anything that does not belong to this noble Queen, please pluck it out and cast it far from me, because anything of mine which does not belong to Mary is unworthy of you."* (SM 66).

This text is important for grasping the spirit that is at the heart of the montfort Consecration and of the life that ought to follow from it: Mary is a gift that Jesus himself has given to us (hence the reference to John), and the only way to thank him for it is to make place for Mary in our life, as Jesus desires. Furthermore, if we are able to give ourselves utterly to Mary, is it not because Jesus gives us the grace to do so?

The prayer ends with an appeal to the Holy Spirit, whose association with Mary is appropriately recalled: *"Holy Spirit, grant me all these graces. Implant in my soul the tree of true life, which is Mary. Foster it and cultivate it so that it grows and blossoms and brings forth the fruit of life in abundance"* (SM 67). To this purpose, Montfort asks the Spirit to give him *"a great love and a longing for Mary, your exalted spouse. Give me a great trust in her maternal heart and a continuous access to her compassion, so that with her you may truly form Jesus, great and powerful, in me until I attain the fullness of his perfect age"* (SM 67). These last words plainly refer to the essential goal of the montfort way as an authentic and complete spirituality that will lead to the perfect age of Christ. They also refer to the primary mission of Mary, in her association with the Spirit, that of forming Jesus Christ in us.

b. Prayer to Mary for use by her faithful slaves of love. The prayer that follows begins with a salutation to Mary very much like the one that we find in the prayer at the end of the *"Little Crown"* (cf. MP 13), with an added statement: *"You are all mine through God's mercy, but I am all yours by justice"* (SM 68). This assertion sheds new light on the relationship of reciprocal belonging between Mary and each person. Mary belongs to us "by mercy," while we belong to her "by justice"—by reason of all that she has done for us.

Quite naturally, this leads the person uttering the prayer to a renewal of Consecration: *"I am all yours by justice. Yet I do not belong sufficiently to you, and so once again, as a slave who always belongs to his master, I give myself wholly to you, reserving nothing for myself or for others"* (SM 68). The mention of Jesus, to whom this Consecration is ultimately directed, comes later: *"Finally, most dearly beloved Mother, grant, if it be possible, that I may have no other spirit but yours to know Jesus and his divine will. May I have no soul but yours to praise and glorify the Lord"* (SM 68).

The following expression included in the prayer is especially relevant: *"I do not ask for visions or revelations, for sensible devotion or even spiritual pleasures"* (SM 69), recalling the *"pure faith"* that *"will cause you to depend less upon sensible and extraordinary feelings"* and of which we read in TD 214.

Finally, the triple Amen that concludes the prayer has no equivalent elsewhere in Montfort's work: *"The only grace I beg you in your kindness to obtain for me is that every day and moment of my life I may say this threefold Amen: Amen, so be it, to all you did upon earth; Amen, so be it, to all you are doing now in heaven; Amen, so be it, to all you are doing in my soul. In that way, you and you alone will fully glorify Jesus in me during all my life and my eternity"* (SM 69).

c. "The cultivation and growth of the tree of life, in other words the way to make Mary live and reign in our souls." The expression *"Tree of Life,"* which Montfort uses on a number of occasions, does not always have the same application. In SM 22, it refers to the Cross of Jesus, and in H 123:13, the Cross is Mary's Tree of Life. In LEW 204; SM 67, 78; TD 44, 164, 218, 261; and H 81:7, Mary herself is the Tree of Life, and the fruit she bears is Jesus, as is explicitly stated in the majority of occurrences (cf. LEW 204; SM 78; TD 44, 164, 218, 261).

Saint Louis Marie begins by proclaiming the happiness of those who, thanks to the Holy Spirit, can have access to *"a secret of which very few people are aware. If you have discovered this treasure in the field of Mary, this pearl of great price, you should sell all you have to purchase it"* (SM 70).

But what the Holy Spirit alone has planted must be cared for and cultivated: *"If the Holy Spirit has planted in your soul the true Tree of Life, which is the devotion that I have just explained, you should see carefully to its cultivation, so that it will yield its fruit in due season"* (SM 70).

"This tree, once planted in a docile heart, requires fresh air and no human support. Being of heavenly origin, it must be uninfluenced by any creature, since a creature might hinder it from rising up towards God who created it. Hence you must not rely on your own endeavors or your natural talents or your personal standing or the guidance of men. You must resort to Mary, relying solely on her help" (SM 71).

Not that we are to wait passively for this tree to bear its fruit! Therefore:

1. By raising and tending the tree: *"The person in whose soul this tree has taken root must, like a good gardener, watch over it and protect it. For this tree, having life and capable of producing the fruit of life, should be raised and tended with enduring care and attention of soul. A soul that desires to be holy will make this its chief aim and occupation"* (SM 72).

The work of the gardener is to prune away anything that might hinder the growth of the tree. Accordingly, *"by self-denial and self-discipline you must sedulously cut short and even give up all empty pleasures and useless dealings with other creatures. In other words, you must crucify the flesh, keep a guard over the tongue, and mortify the bodily senses"* (SM 73).

2. *"You must guard against grubs doing harm to the tree. These parasites are love of self and love of comfort; . . . for love of self is incompatible with love of Mary"* (SM 74).

3. *"You must not allow this Tree to be damaged by destructive animals, that is, by sins."* And not only sins that deal death but even *"venial sins, which are most dangerous when we do not trouble ourselves about them"* (SM 75).

Over and above this struggle with what might assault the health of the tree, there is the whole positive aspect of a true spiritual life:

4. *"It is also necessary to water this Tree regularly with your Communions, Masses, and other public and private prayers. Otherwise it will not continue bearing fruit"* (SM 76).

5. Finally, we must not fear difficulties and contradictions, which are the lot of all who seek to follow Christ faithfully: *"This devotion to our Blessed Lady will surely be called into question and attacked. But as long as we continue steadfastly in tending [this tree], we have nothing to fear"* (SM 77).

Well protected and well cultivated, the Tree of Life will grow and "*will yield in due season the sweet and adorable Fruit of honor and grace, which is Jesus, who has always been and will always be the only fruit of Mary.*" This enables Montfort to conclude with the proclamation of a beatitude: *"Happy is the soul in which Mary, the tree of life, is planted. Happier still is the soul in which she has been able to grow and blossom. Happier again is the soul in which she brings forth her fruit. But happiest of all is the soul which savors the sweetness of Mary's fruit and preserves it up till death and then beyond to all eternity. Amen."* (SM 78).

IV. The Secret of Mary Today

Montfort's vocabulary and rhetorical style reflect the language of his times. Thus, sometimes he answers our contemporary questions and sometimes he doesn't. To cite but two examples: the Christian's duty to be committed to temporal tasks and the work of building the city of God on earth is practically left unaddressed. A concern with the quest for Christian perfection is situated on a very spiritual and very personal level, with scarcely any insistence on the apostolic commitment properly so-called, at least as it is conceived today.

Without contesting the fact of these limitations, two observations are in order. The first is that no one can blame Montfort for being a person of his time. The second is that SM is only one of the works that Montfort has written: his other writings enable us to complete and better understand the richness of his spiritual way.

Furthermore, SM and TD are clearly complementary. A reading of SM can be a good introduction to that of TD. At the same time, readers of TD can discover certain of its aspects better by referring to SM, which must not be taken as a pale compendium of the longer work. It has its own wealth and particular power of persuasion.

For that matter, the simple and concise form of this booklet renders it easily approachable even today, as is demonstrated by the success that it always enjoys. In a certain sense, while less documented and less developed than TD, SM is more accessible to certain persons. Indeed, certain difficulties occasionally raised in connection with TD are far less applicable to SM. For example, what some might call Montfort's "pessimism" is scarcely in evidence in the latter work.

As to content, that remains altogether current. Suffice it is to recall what is said of the content of TD and of the testimonials it inspires. A Christian spirituality that, in a balanced way, has accorded to Mary only the place that the Lord Himself has conferred upon her has the whole future ahead of it. In SM, as in TD, Montfort does not hesitate to assert: *"We are given reason to believe that, towards the end of time and perhaps sooner than we expect, God will raise up great men filled with the Holy Spirit and imbued with the spirit of Mary. Through them Mary, Queen most powerful, will work great wonders in the world, destroying sin and setting up the kingdom of Jesus her Son upon the ruins of the corrupt kingdom of the world. These holy men will accomplish this by means of the devotion of which I only trace the main outlines"* (SM 59; cf. TD 46-59).

A. Bossard

Notes: (1) *Chroniques de Soeur Florence (Chronicals of Sister Florence),* Archival Source, 95. (2) This "omission" is explained by criticisms that the wearing of this symbol could have occasioned. Certain abuses provoked by the wearing of these little chains had led the Holy See, at the end of the eighteenth century, to proscribe their usage and to condemn certain books of particular confraternities. While aimed only at the abuses, these condemnations nevertheless cast a pall over this practice. The prudence of the editors of SM is understandable. On all this, see GA, 394, n. 419. (3) On this question, see the article *True Devotion* in this Handbook. (4) On the central character of the mystery of the Incarnation in Montfort's spirituality, see especially the articles *Incarnation, True Devotion,* and *Mary* in this Handbook.

SICK

SUMMARY I. MONTFORT IN HIS TIME:
1. Health situation in the seventeenth century;
2. Montfort's experience of illness;
3. Montfort and the sick.
II. MONTFORT'S TEACHING.
III. THE SUFFERING PATIENT TODAY:
1. A presence to the sick;
2. Illness, suffering, and the spiritual life;
3. Pastoral service to the sick and dying.

I. MONTFORT IN HIS TIME

1. Health situation in the seventeenth century

Life was precarious for most of the population in seventeenth-century France. Precisely those "cataclysms that, for long centuries, people had prayed to avert—pestilence, famine, war"—now burst over their heads.[1] The plague itself had receded and disappeared after 1650, but it raged on in the minds of the people. They thought they saw it everywhere. *La peste,* "pestilence," "plague," was the term used at the time for diphtheria, typhoid, smallpox, typhus, and "purple fever"—in other words, any severe epidemic. Epidemics were brief but most deadly. Even today,in Brittany—at Plourin, for example —one finds votive chapels erected precisely to ward off the plague. Hippocratic medicine was helpless in the face of diseases of this kind, except for the ones called *chaleurs* and *fièvres* ("heats" and "fevers"). The presence and availability of the medieval hospital with its medical equipment had grown by leaps and bounds in the fifteenth and sixteenth centuries.[2] The years 1693-94, 1698, and 1709-10 figure among the seven years of the century in which the death rate peaked. Brittany was very much affected in 1673-75.[3] Montfort was born in 1673. Wars regularly added their own quota of misery to that of famine, epidemics, destruction, massacres, and fires.

2. Montfort's experience of illness

Endowed with a robust constitution, Montfort never had any great interest in his health. He ate little, slept on a thin pallet or even the bare floor, often took the discipline, and walked throughout the countryside of northwestern France, in addition to his pilgrimage on foot to Rome. His preaching activity can only be called exhausting. Yet throughout all this, his health appears to have been strong enough to continue a highly demanding ministry.

On at least two occasions, there was fear for his life. The first was when he was twenty-one years of age and living in Father Boucher's community in Paris. In this instance he was transported to the Hôtel-Dieu and subjected to repeated bloodletting, which ultimately exhausted his already enfeebled body. Here he acquired a personal, deep-seated knowledge of solitude and abandonment amidst an energetic struggle with illness and death. Once he began to recuperate, his recovery was rapid. His early biographers admired his patience, gentleness, and acceptance of the will of God.[4]

In the fall of the year 1713, at the age of forty, during a mission that Montfort preaching at Mauzé, he was suddenly hit by most violent pains. He went on with his mission, concluded it, then went to the La Rochelle hospital, to remain there for two months. A severe fever, caused by a rather large abscess, raged unabated, and he was subjected to frequent probings and to delicate operations with the means available at the time, all of which he bore with strength and courage. He would ask the physicians not to go easy with him, and it is said that he would murmur during the procedures, "*Long live Jesus! Long live his cross! Is it not altogether just that he be loved?*" In the face of ninety-nine-to-one odds, Montfort lived.

Biographers also indicate a dangerous scare in 1708, at Chevrolière: "violent colics and a constant high fever," due to his constant preaching of parish missions. Again he pulled out of the illness in spite of the blood-letting cures of the physicians. In 1711, in the course of the La Rochelle mission, Calvinists poisoned his soup. Although he survived, he would ever after feel "weakened and feeble."[5]

Worn out with his labors, Montfort died at the age of forty-three. Stricken with an apparent pleurisy in the midst of a mission that he had been unwilling to interrupt, he asked to celebrate the Sacrament of confession and to receive Holy Viaticum and Extreme Unction,[6] and his life was over.

3. Montfort and the sick

The "General Hospitals" of Montfort's time were the poorhouses; more places of refuge for the poor and outcast than for the sick. Extreme poverty is the fertile soil of illness; it was Louis Marie's apostolate to the poor that brought him into the apostolate to the sick. At Poitiers, sharing the life of the poor of the Hospital, Montfort became deeply interested in the welfare of the sick poor. He not only ministered to them spiritually but he also cared for the sick physically, making their beds, washing their clothing, and cleaning the wards and bathrooms and assisting in their medical care. When someone with a contagious disease was thrown out into the street, Montfort would have the poor person carried back in and would care for him himself, secluding him from the others lest they might be infected, then would assist the victim in a happy death.[7]

Montfort, by vocation a member of the first estate, the clergy, by blood a member of the bourgeoisie, through friendship tied in with some members of the nobility, was by evangelical choice one with the absolute destitute, sharing their life and serving them first with the Word and, to the extent possible, with food and care. His attitude is clearly revealed in the oft-repeated incident at Dinan in 1706, when he came upon a leper, all covered with ulcers, lying in the street. "He lifted him upon his shoulders" and carried him to the missioners' house, where, in response to his knocking, the cry came, "Who's there?" In reply, Montfort called out, *"Open up to Jesus Christ!"* then entered, laid the leper in his own bed, and cared for him as best he could.[8]

For Saint Louis Marie, the poor—and in a special way the sick poor—are unique sacraments of Christ. He was able to minister to the most difficult cases because he truly saw in them the suffering Jesus. His respect for the handicapped was based on his belief that they were chosen by God to be special manifestations of the Cross. His words and actions, he hoped, would help them understand their dignity and accept their Cross even joyfully.

At Nantes, Montfort encouraged the foundation of a hospice for "incurables"—that is, paupers who were physically unable to beg their bread. He supported those in charge and gave them advice in their undertaking.[9] At the same time, he lent his support to a "convalescent" establishment. His foundation of the Daughters of Wisdom is in itself an indication of his deep concern for the poor, especially the sick poor, since the care of the handicapped and the sick is among their "exterior aims" (cf. H 149; RW 1).

Superstition attributed many a sickness to sorcery and the devil. Montfort struggled with this mentality, instructing the people as best he could.[10]

II. Montfort's Teaching

For Montfort, illness is one of life's crosses which the Christian must carry (L 13; H 46). We find the word "illness" on the famous Wisdom Cross at Poitiers. By his life, Montfort shows us that we must struggle with disease and seek to heal it. At the same time, he describes the human being's gravest maladies as a preparation for death.

A readiness to accept one's terminal illness figures among the "proximate dispositions" for meeting the Lord: "*Suffer sickness patiently, for God sends it to us. It can withdraw us from exile. It enables us to expiate our sins, and bravely to accept our death at its hands*" (HD 5).

Hymn 46 summarizes the essentials of Montfort's teaching about sickness. On stage come three characters: the Sick Person, the Devil, and the Friend of God. The Sick Person focuses on his affliction (colic, gout, fever, toothache, asthma, or sciatica). He suffers, he burns with fever. He is like a poor beast, overwhelmed with pain to the point of death and not knowing what to do. A very saint would waver. And the Sick Person reflects: *"What misfortune! What a mournful lot! I would rather die than be permanently ill! What have I done to the Lord?"* (H 146:10). This miserable patient feels neglected by all those around him, even by his physician, and he plots vengeance. The Devil drives the Sick Person to discouragement, rebellion, and blasphemy: *"Look! Everyone's leaving you alone /*

Like a sick dog. / No one gives you / any help or support" . . . How I pity your misery! / Cold soup, stale bread / a piece of bad meat, / They're making a fool of you, that's for sure! . . . Keep far from your door / the Father confessor / His presence only brings / Fear and pain" (H 46:11, 22, 32). The Friend of God naturally takes the opposite tack from that of the Devil in order to assist the sick person to suffer well. His words meant to be comforting and seem a little strong to contemporary ears: God scourges us as a Father; He chastises us to test us; He gives us grace at every moment; suffering is better than hell. Gaze upon Jesus crucified: does he not suffer more than we? Suffering wins us an eternal reward; one day of sickness is of more value than excellent work throughout a whole year; at the end comes victory. After each strophe, the refrain nails the Sick Person's Cross to the Cross of Christ: *"Cross of Calvary, / So quickly passing and so dear!"*

The last two strophes are a prayer placed on the lips of the Sick Person. He adores, he accepts, he asks God's help: *"My God, I adore You / In your decisions; / If you strike again / Powerfully help me. . . . In your Blood I drown / My sins and my troubles, And I embrace with joy / Any new suffering you may send*" (H 46:37, 38).

The hymn so well describes the situation of the sick person overwhelmed with unbearable suffering. The teaching of the Friend of God, however, is doubtless more appropriate for the healthy than for the sick; this short "skit" was meant to be acted out not in the presence of the ill but of those who are well so that they may prepare for the inevitable day when sickness envelops them.

Hymns 145, to Our Lady of All Patience, and 159, to Our Lady of All Consolation, emphasize Mary's motherly role with the poor sufferer. Montfort names her the "*remedy of the incurably ill*" in both hymns and "*health of poor sinners.*" He invites the sufferer to pray to her.

Not only because of the culture of his day but more so because of his theology of the Cross, Montfort sees suffering and sickness as a "healthy punishment" for sin and a privilege of sharing in the sufferings of Christ. He does not hesitate to accept the medication that the medical profession was able to supply in his day; his trust in God, however, is apparently far deeper than his trust in doctors, or, better still, whatever medicine is able to accomplish is but the loving hand of God reaching out to heal.

III. The Suffering Patient Today

Montfort spirituality has always included a special concern for the sick. The teachings and examples of Father de Montfort and Mother Marie Louise call forth a loving union with all those who share in the Cross of Christ. What is asked for is not only a union of prayer but a practical, supportive presence, to the extent possible. The sick are, in so many ways, "the poor" who need to experience God's loving care through the love shown by the members of the Body of Christ.

Montfort spirituality also gives strength in one's own suffering. Saint Louis Marie's profound teaching on the Cross, his constant reminders of the love of Jesus and Mary for all, and his beautiful doctrine on Providence and the ultimate victorious outcome of all things in Christ Jesus are thoughts to be thoroughly learned well before serious illness strikes. As an aid to this apostolate to the sick, we close with a few remarks on this ministry.

1. A presence to the sick

Many feel awkward in the presence of the seriously ill. Perhaps this is especially felt by those who have not as yet experienced a brush with death. Yet the seriously ill person has to experience loving presence, especially of loved ones.

Being present to persons stricken with disability means taking them as they are—sick or hurt—and trying to help them live in their new situation. It means trying to understand them without judging them or even attempting to "put ourselves in their place," since each person is unique and singular. It means accepting their reactions, their questions, their silence. It means not running away despite the sense of confusion and sometimes helplessness that they so often awaken in us. It means "being there," and being glad to be there, taking them seriously—with discernment—being true, credible, being a vessel of hope, even when an attitude of defiance, persecution, or revenge is manifested. It means not simply shrugging off a request for euthanasia but perceiving the immense distress it implies and the cry for help it conveys.

One who is present to the sick has need of balance, courage, love, openness, humility, sincerity, and quite often a sense of humor. His or her role is to be reassuring and to offer a sense of security, telling the sick person the truth that he or she can bear, distinguishing moral from psychological guilt (actual guilt from mere guilt feelings), responding to spiritual need, facilitating the elucidation of anguished questions and the positive element of life, helping the suffer to reject any useless or wicked suffering—rebelliousness, resentment, false notions of God.

Love and compassion will respect the solitude and sense of dispossession of self that opens the way to God, Who is the Utterly Other —especially when medicine can no longer do anything, so that now the sick person is no longer the object of care but only the subject of love.

2. Illness, suffering, and the spiritual life

A time of illness can be a time of rebellion and blasphemy, or one of hope, love, and grace. Suffering without love is unlivable. The sick person is sometimes reduced to a cry, a supplication often without a response. The Passion narratives and many of the psalms begin to take on new meaning. Faith does not suppress the senseless aspect of certain sufferings. God seems absent when they supervene. The presence and compassion of those around may restore courage. After all, God is present in the very experience of absence. In Jesus, God bestows on each one of us the opportunity to face our own suffering and to cooperate with the divine enterprise that is the salvation of the world. Christ identifies with the sick person: "I was sick and you visited me" (Mt 25:36).

Illness has the character of a test. It also has an educational value for those able to consider it from the standpoint of the reign of God. In discovering, thanks to faith, the redemptive suffering of Christ, human beings also discover their own sufferings there. Thanks to faith, they find those sufferings enriched with a new content and a new meaning.

3. Pastoral service to the sick and dying

Christians seek to promote a pastoral ministry of health, one calculated to keep account of the dignity and the rights of the patient. The Church reminds physicians of their duties, which include "respect for life in all its forms, respect for the freedom of patients to choose their conditions of existence in function of their own hierarchy of values."[11]

If the saints of the miraculous cures are no longer as much in vogue as in years gone by, pilgrimages (to Lourdes, for example) continue to offer the gravely ill the opportunity to express their cry to Mary, Health of the Sick, to feel accepted and respected in their dignity, to take their place as members of a people sensitized to the "Gospel of suffering" —a community of persons who pray with them and for them. They discover their usefulness at work in the Church and weave new bonds. They find serenity and go their way with more love, faith, and hope; for they have accepted and offered their life of suffering for a filling up in their flesh of what is lacking to the Passion of Christ for his Body that is the Church (Col 1:24).

The Church further asks for the "protection, at the moment of death, of the dignity of the human person and the Christian conception of life against an abusive technicity" or therapeutic relentlessness. Indeed, some have begun to speak of a "right to death"—not the right to put oneself to death, or to have oneself put to death as one wishes (euthanasia), but the right to die in human and Christian dignity, in all serenity and in the presence of other, genuinely caring, respectful persons.[12]

J. Bulteau

Notes: (1) R. Mandrou, *La France au XVIIe et XVIIIe siècle (France in the 17 and 18th Centuries)*, Presses universitaires de France, Paris 1970, 91. (2) Ibid., 93. "When the General Hospital of Paris was founded in 1656, with the intention of endowing it with capital as a 'necessary establishment'—even after the creations of St. Vincent de Paul—the move was so well received that in the following years, the monarchy recommended its imitation in all of the cities of the kingdom" (ibid.). (3) Cf. H. Méthivier, *L'ancien Régime (The Ancien Régime)*, Presses universitaires de France, Paris 1971, 66, 69. (4) Besnard II, 37-38. (5) Besnard I, 166, 232. (6) Besnard II, 156-58. (7) Besnard I, 71-72 (8) Ibid., 15 (9) Besnard I, 194-95; Besnard II, 22; L 33. (10) Besnard II, 97-101. (11) F. J. Paul-Cavallier, *Mourir vivant (Dying Alive)*, Mediaspaul, Paris 1990, 23. (12) Congregation for the Doctrine of the Faith, *Déclaration sur l'euthanasie (Declaration on Euthanasia)*, in *Documentation Catholique*, no. 1790, July 20, 1980, 699.

SILENCE

SUMMARY

I. RHYTHMS OF SILENCE IN MONTFORT'S LIFE.

II. CANTICLE OF SILENCE:
1. Silence as victory over evils of the tongue;
2. Value of silence;
3. Rules for speaking well;
4. A Message to sanctimonious people;
5. Prayer.

III. SPIRITUAL DIMENSIONS OF SILENCE ACCORDING TO MONTFORT:
1. Sanctification of silence;
2. Silence and spiritual maturity:
   a. Silence and Wisdom,
   b. Silence and cultivation of the Tree of Life.

IV. SILENCE AND MONTFORT SPIRITUALITY TODAY:
1. Need for silence today;
2. The Montfort spirit.

I. RHYTHMS OF SILENCE IN MONTFORT'S LIFE

A liking for silence was a constant in Montfort's life, and many of the rhythms of silence were evident over the course of his life. Silence had a variety of meanings and motivations for him in the course of life's trials. Sometimes his silence seemed an avoidance of the world—a tendency to isolation and inactivity. Actually, though, the silence of Montfort's lived experience was a silence filled with reverence for God. It was a silence that not only led him to prayer, but flowered into an active zeal to communicate with others in order to glorify God. Even in childhood—according to Grandet, his first biographer—he was "distancing himself from the company of young people his age, from worldly persons, and [he was] avoiding taking part in their amusements," and Louis Marie "would withdraw to some corner of the house to pray."[1]

It is particularly interesting that his childhood experience of silence and prayer did not turn Montfort into himself. Instead, it caused him to become more unselfish, especially in to comforting his mother. He urged his younger sister and his companions to prayer.[2]

At Rennes, according to his hagiographer, Blain, Louis Marie was socially reserved.[3] The example, influence, and training of the Jesuits—his teachers at the College—fostered in him a taste for God. He was struck by the heroic silence of Father Gilbert, when the boys ridiculed him.[4] In his youth, Louis Marie was regarded by his fellow student Blain as "born with a most profound memory, and with a constancy of prayer."[5]

At Paris, this tendency to silence grew, since the director of his residence, Father de la Barmondière, "placing no limits on his own fervor, gave free rein to that of his disciple." Then Louis' fervor became "practically continuous, nothing could stop it, so strongly did he seem drawn to God. He prayed several hours a day, and gave a great deal of time to spiritual reading."[6]

It is certain that under the influence of mystical authors like Surin, and following his own inclination, Louis Marie opted for the "science of the saints." Silence, recollection, mortification, and austerities were its important ingredients.[7] Even in his leisure time he chose recollection. He wanted only to converse with Jesus and Mary.

His superiors judged his intense life of contemplation to be dangerous. They prevailed upon him to relax during his periods of recreation. On a pilgrimage to Chartres as a seminarian, he experienced a remarkable time of union with God and the Blessed Virgin, interrupted only by the zealous deeds it moved him to perform. Kneeling before the Blessed Virgin in the underground chapel, "he persevered for six or seven continuous hours, from early morning till noon, motionless, and as if in ecstasy."[8] His companion was amazed at how a young person could be recollected for nearly an entire day without interruption. He was in awe at how Montfort remained in a kind of profound prayer of ectsacy.[9]

At the Saint-Clément residence for priests in Nantes, Montfort lived a special period of silence, devoting himself earnestly to the task of spiritual discernment. He had moved into the community of Father Lévêque, intending to be trained for the missions, but he had become disappointed: the community prevented him from realizing his hope. This difficulty thrust him into a period of deep discernment. In it he discovered the nature of his *"secret attraction for a hidden life in which I can efface myself and combat my natural tendency to show off"* (L 5).

Later, after the failures in the Poitiers and Paris poorhouses, he would wonder "whether, in order to abandon himself to this powerful attraction [to prayer], he should not refrain from, or at least suspend for a time, the functions of the ministry."[10] But Montfort came to see this ostensible calling to the eremitical life as a temptation against the apostolic vocation which won out in him. He wrote, *"my own inclinations . . . have always been and still are for mission work"* (L 11).

Montfort himself testified to the meaning of silence when, in 1702, at Poitiers, he was the object of criticism and persecution because of the reforms he had introduced in the poorhouse: *"During this painful period, I kept silent and lived in retirement putting my cause into the hands of God and relying on his help. . . . To this end I went for a week's retreat to the Jesuits"* (L 11). Montfort's silence was not a simple absence of words or activity. It belonged to the mystical dimension of "Yahweh's poor," who, in trusting silence, looked to God for salvation (Lam 3:26; Ps 37:7; Isa 10:15). It was a silence filled with trust in God Alone—a silence bound to the Cross, the consequence of evangelical choices. Whenever he met the Cross, then, Montfort did not complain but turned to silence, accepting with reverence God's will. This was how the missionary behaved when the vicar general of Poitiers publicly reprimanded him for indiscreet zeal.[11] Not that Montfort was insensitive to humiliations and crosses; the famous case of the Pontchateau calvary was proof enough of this. On September 13, 1710, he received an emissary of the bishop of Nantes who ordered him not to proceed with the blessing of the site. The missionary traveled all night to Nantes to speak to the bishop, who confirmed what he had ordered Montfort to do. Father Olivier attested that a few days later, while reading a letter in which the bishop demanded that he destroy the Calvary, Montfort burst into tears.[12]

Periods of silence punctuated Montfort's life. Sometimes it was by necessity, at other times it was by choice. The bishops prevented his missionary activities, but he profited from these periods of rest by living a life of more intense prayer and by writing the works that extended his preaching on the subjects dearest to his heart: Wisdom, the Cross, the Rosary, and so on. He also tasted the *"eloquent silence"* (H 157:13) of a nature as yet unspoiled by the heavy footstep of man. The Mervent woods, the hermitages of St. Eloi and St. Lazare, are three places dear to Montfort and to the montfort tradition. They remind us of the missionary's determination to alternate between proclaiming the Word in action, and listening in silence. Montfort's silence was always the silence of the contemplation of God Alone, *"the silence of adoration and wonderment in the presence of the Ineffable, a silence of ongoing availability to God, a silence in the spirit of the beatitudes, which Wisdom has taught us in order to set us free from the blindness in which sin has cast us"* (LEW 153).

Montfort's writings later explained his idea of silence and furnish us with a key for the interpretation of the silent rhythms that punctuated his existence.

II. Canticle of Silence

Montfort devotes an entire metrical composition, forty-nine couplets long, to silence: *"The Wisdom of Silence"* (H 23). We shall use this canticle as a starting place in order to enter into Montfort's idea of silence. This hymn, like those on other virtues, actually constitutes a little treatise. A very precise order has been observed in its mode of presentation. The marginal notes offer us (although, unfortunately, they break off at couplet 31) the essential structure of the canticle, which has five parts. After giving a basic definition of silence, *"the closing of the mouth and heart to creatures in order to be perfect and to glorify the Lord"* (H 23:1), Montfort dedicates several couplets to illustrating the five points of his idea of silence.

1. Silence as victory over evils of the tongue (2-11)

Inspired by the well known passage Jas 3:5-10, against intemperance in language, Montfort groups together the motivations which guard a person against the inordinate use of the tongue. He disciplines this *"little piece of flesh"* (H 23:3) and uses a flood of metaphors to do so: *"poisoned dart," "sword soft but deadly," "terrible monster"* (H 23:3, 4, 7). Montfort lists the sins commited by the tongue: swearing, cursing, outbursts, blasphemy, and so on. He concludes by calling the tongue the *"compendium of all iniquities"* (H 23:5) and proposes silence as the *"infallible remedy"* for this great evil (H 23:7). Putting the title of the canticle to use, Montfort contrasts the chatterbox with the wise person: the former is a *"big ball full of air, . . . an empty pot"* (H 23:8-10).

2. Value of silence (12-20)

While the first point urges an avoidance of the sinful use of the tongue, the second dwells in a positive way on the "*excellence of silence.*" The basic idea was that silence was not some empty, sterile thing but a reality filled with hidden treasure, fostering a high spirituality. Silence is the "*divine training school*" of divine thoughts and intense joys (H 23:12), "*a divine school for learning to speak well*" (H 23:13), "*the father of prayer, . . . the companion of wisdom, . . . the book of the wise and the ignorant*" (H 23:14-16). Silence interiorized a faith which without it would become *"sterile and wavering"* (H 23:17). Saint Louis Marie gives concrete examples of silence: God, Who spoke very little *ad extra,* "outside," but so much *ad intra,* "within"; Christ, who "*for thirty years kept silence*"; Mary, who "*stored up in her heart the most divine words*"; the saints, for whom silence was a "*beatitude*" (H 23:18-20). Montfort adds that the lesson of silence also comes from the "*sages of Greece,*" who preserved their quiet precisely in order "*to obtain the gift of a great wisdom*" (H 23:20).

3. Rules for speaking well (21-32)

Having convinced the reader of the importance of silence, Montfort moves on to outlining the practical norms: *"how"* and *"when"* to speak. Surely one must speak *"prudently,"* in order to avoid irreparable evils; *"rarely,"* in order to accord listening the primacy; *"truly,"* without lying; *"charitably,"* in order to edify; *"wisely,"* without being persistent; *"modestly,"* or in a low voice; *"humbly,"* without adopting a magisterial tone; and *"holily,"* without hypocrisy or human respect (H 23:23-29). As to times and places, Montfort specified that one should avoid speaking in church, since it would be *"an irreverence"* to God (H 23:31-32).

4. A Message to sanctimonious people (33-43)

Taking as his point of departure the question of speaking in church, Montfort delivers a humorous diatribe against sanctimonious people. Playing on words, he bemoanes the *"blindly devout,"* who ceaselessly chatter and risk *"holily to be damned by devout language"* (H 23:33). His description of a devout chatterbox is well done: *"Talking of every idle thing, / prattling 'round the clock, / gazing first this way, then that, / racing from street to street, / nosing into any novelty— / O pious one and lost!"* (H 23:24). Tirelessly, Montfort proceeds in this tone, with women especially in mind: "*Oh, yes, the nasty thing loves to talk! / she cannot shut her mouth! / bad talk, grumbling, babbling— / Her one sole business!*" (H 23:37).

He poetically attacks the "*faddish devout*" person. He could not abide her pretentious patristic references ("*She cites Augustine, Jerome, Hilary*") publicly displaying her knowledge. Noticing, however, that she has gone too far, she decides to break off: "*I'm saying too much, I'll stop*" (H 23:43).

5. Prayer (45-49)

Montfort feels a need to conclude the hymn by imploring God to help him to control his tongue and begin then to practice silence. He asks for the strength to curb his tongue, and for a "*burning coal*" to purify his lips. Taking up once more his initial idea of silence, Montfort proposes to close off his senses to creatures and to open his heart to God Alone: "*Lord, speak to my heart!*" (H 23:46). A speech addressed to God Alone is the wise person's ideal (H 23:47).

On this note, of contrasting God and creatures, Montfort brings his Canticle of Silence to a close. Precisely because of this note, it should to be situated in the Saint-Sulpice period, when the influence of Surin and Boudon especially encouraged Louis Marie the seminarian to concentrate on prayer and silence.

III. Spiritual dimensions of Silence According to Montfort

The topic of silence also appears in Montfort's other writings—sometimes from different points of view not considered in Hymn 23. We shall try to point them out, grouping them under two aspects dear to Montfort's heart.

1. Sanctification of silence

Montfort insisted on the exterior observance of silence. To the Daughters of Wisdom he recommended they be very firm in "*keeping silence and seeing that it is kept in the community and in the school*" (L 29). He regarded silence as necessary in the schools (RW 282), given children's tendency to laugh and shout. He asked the missionaries of the Company of Mary to keep silence, especially during meals, and when they retired for the night (RM 34, 72, 77). He recommended that the Daughters of Wisdom "*faithfully observe silence at all times save during the two hours of recreation after meals and whenever charity, obedience or the duties of their office require them to do otherwise*" (RW 75). As we see, it was not a question of setting rigid rules and observing them mechanically. Silence was not an absolute value but something to be ruled by charity and obedience. When a Sister interrupted her silence because her task demanded it, she should not see herself at fault (RW 262). With his practical sense, Montfort put the

Daughters of Wisdom on their guard not only against the "*longing women ordinarily have to talk*" (RW 82) but also against "*being so taciturn by their misplaced silence that they become ordinarily burdensome in any conversation*" (RW 229).

Silence and speech ought to be regulated, Montfort went further and demanded that silence be sanctified. "*Sanctify your silence*" (RW 85). How was one to sanctify silence? While linking silence both with Wisdom and with the Cross (TD 273; LEW 200; H 100:45), Montfort prefered to join silence to prayer—to "*your holy silence and your continual prayer*" (PS 3:2): "*They will . . . engage in silent prayer*" (PS 3:4). "*I love to pray in secret, in silence*" (H 12:24). "*Sanctify your silence by vocal or mental prayer, according to your inclination*" (RW 85). The silence that St. Louis Marie wanted was an open space for an encounter with God in prayer.

For Montfort, the special places of silence were in the outer world and within the inner "I." In the presence of natural creation—in the shadows of the forest, beside clear waters, at the mouths of deep caverns, and amidst all the beauties of nature, he experienced an "*eloquent silence*" (H 157:13) and cried out, "*What silence! What talk!*" (H 155:12). Nature actually conveyed spiritual messages, which sometimes protested the pollution generated by human beings: *"These immobile rocks / look innocent enough— / but condemn the cities / with their air so vile!"* (H 99:24). While God was everywhere, there was a special inner, hidden place where the divine presence reigned: the human heart. Montfort made Augustine's invitation his own—"*In teipsum redi*: return within thyself!"—when he said: *"Let us all return within ourselves, / in secret, in silence, / to see God present there / more than in any other place"* (H 24:39).

2. Silence and spiritual maturity

Montfort's discourse on silence was connected with the Marian Christocentric spirituality that he lived and taught to others. From this standpoint, silence wais necessary for acquiring Wisdom and for the cultivating of the "Tree of Life."

a. Silence and Wisdom. First, it was Wisdom Incarnate that furnished us with the example of an ineffable, paradoxical silence. The mystery of the Incarnation brings us into the silence of that wonder-filled nine months' sojourn for Jesus in Mary's virginal womb; *"From the outset He would fain / repose in silence there, / to offer Himself to the Father Eternal / upon the altar of her heart"* (H 134:2).

Montfort's hymns spoke of the manger of Bethlehem as the paradox of the Eternal Word of the Father, reduced to the silence of a tiny, speechless infant! Montfort manifested his astonishment in Bérullian terms: *"The Eternal is one day old. / The Word falls silent"* (H 57:1). All wrapped in silence, little Jesus was nonetheless eloquent with his smile and his tenderness, which ravished the hearts of the shepherds and the magi (H 9:5). Montfort insisted: *"This dear child, today / speaks to us in*

His silence" (H 61:2) and revealed to us, in poverty, his immense love. As a grown-up, Jesus continued to give us examples of a life of silence, when he kept silence for thirty years at Nazareth (H 23:18) and sojourned for forty days in the desert: *"All without drinking or eating, / in silence, in prayer"* (H 16:7).

If silence marked the coming of Wisdom among us, then it ought to typify, as well, those who go in quest of Wisdom. For Montfort, it will not do merely to declare that "*the sage is a silent one*" (H 23:11). One must endow silence with a Christological dimension: "*Be silent with others, so as to converse with the divine Wisdom*" (LEW 200). It was not surprising that Montfort insisted on "*mental prayer,*" which, as words fall still, "*disposes the soul to listen to the voice of Wisdom, to savor his delights and possess his treasures*" (LEW 193).

b. Silence and the cultivation of the Tree of Life. Montfort revealed his secret of holiness in *The Secret of Mary*. It is an abbreviation of his Marian doctrine and spirituality anyone can understand and appreciate. In its conclusion, he included a little code for the spiritual life, entitled "*Care and Growth of the Tree of Life*" (SM 70-78). He identified six counsels for cultivating this Tree. He developed the primary forms of behavior in a Christian who welcomed Mary into his or her life and wished to be receptive, open, and available to God. He nuanced that complex attitude which gives birth to authentic silence, and which manifests its profound wealth. The Tree is planted in the soul by the Holy Spirit. It is one's gift of oneself to Jesus through Mary's hands. It must be cultivated. To this end, Montfort exhorts us to rein ourselves in, to enter and to remain in an atmosphere steeped in silence: the silence of a gaze directed on God, of attention to God, of contemplation (SM 72). It is plain, then, that one cannot rely on one's simple human talents, or on the support of other people. One must impose silence on the instinctive need for human props. One must have recourse, instead, to the help of Mary (SM 71). If one's gaze is fixed on God, the divine light shows the obstacles that harm the cultivation of the Tree of Life—useless pleasures, vain occupations—and it shows the soul the need for mortification and self-control. Here Montfort's reference to silence is explicit. One must "*keep a guard over the tongue, and mortify the bodily senses*" (SM 73). In order to cultivate the Tree of Life, continual prayer is very important—a prayer overflowing with faith, and made strong by public prayer and the Sacraments (SM 96). At this point, Montfort foresees that "*the storm-winds of temptation will threaten to bring it down, and snow and frost tend to smother it*" (SM 77). This was the fate foreseen for TD as well. It will be buried "*in the darkness and silence of a chest*" (TD 114). This should not be surprising for it falls into the divine logic of the first being last and the last first. The fruit of the Tree of Life is Jesus, who is, was, and will always be the fruit of Mary. Happy the soul "*which savors the* *sweetness of Mary's fruit and preserves it up till death and then beyond to all eternity*" (SM 78)!

IV. Silence and Monfort Spirituality Today

In view of man's need for silence today, Montfort's thoughts on it seem especially relevant.

1. Need for silence today

It is clearly evident that in today's world, there is an urgent need to rediscover an atmosphere of silence. We live in a noisy society with a pop culture overwhelmed by the deafening sound of its music. Noise camouflages the ceaseless, unconfessed fear of discovering an inner void. Carl Jung, the celebrated psychologist observed: "Most people fear silence when the continual noise assaulting their worldly antennae falls still. For one must constantly be acting, speaking, whistling, singing, coughing, or mumbling something. The need for noise is all but insatiable, even if at times the noise is unbearable." Personal growth is arrested by such a banal form of existence. People may never achieve authentic existence because they remain mired in world of chatter. "Prattle is the shame of language," Blanchot said.[13] One must agree: chatter is "speaking for speaking's sake—emitting noises, not sounds; and unfortunately, in our day babbling has become our speech, from the politician to the theologian."[14] Yet everywhere we see a quest for silence and for great relaxation. People are fond of taking vacations in a rural atmosphere, far out in the country, where the air is pure. This may be in order to "defend ourselves," says Romano Guardini, "against the everlasting flow of chatter that floods the world, like a person afflicted with bronchial congestion who earnestly wants to breathe freely." The attraction to yoga, Zen, a technique enabling a so-called immersion in the river of being, the quest for spiritual masters of the East, for experts on the inner rather than on the outer world, all seems to be on the upsurge. Schools of prayer, hermitages, and charismatic groups of all forms and types are multiplying. Nor do we lack books on silence, or theological symposia on silence. What we do lack is more people who will seek their mysterious silence in the authentic "eternal silence" of the Father, Who is the "hidden depth of utterance, the goal and native land of the obedience of faith in the *Verbum*, the Word."[15] The need for silence is evident. On one level it is a need with its origin in the stress of physical and psychological fatigue; in discouragement, in the bitter, unaccepted realization of one's own limits, helplessness, failures. On a deeper level it is a call to rest in God.

Fruitful silence is taught by Holy Scripture: "It is good to wait in silence for the salvation of the Lord" (Lam 3:26). "Silence before him, all the earth!" (Hab 2:20). Silence implies casting our gaze upon God, upon His transcendence, upon His love. This is the faith of silence. It listens in order to respond in prayer and obedience. It is a humble silence, which defeats selfishness and discovers God, the Absolute, the Ineffable.

2. The Montfort spirit

Montfort lived this gospel silence before God Alone. He listened to God's Word. The lesson emerging from Montfort's life is that one must learn to alternate between silence and word, between contemplation and proclamation, between direct dialogue with God and missionary activity among one's brothers and sisters. Montfort portrayed silence in its various dimensions, presenting it as a positive reality, as a path to Wisdom and as a basic factor in spiritual growth. Human beings must discover that it is essential that their lives lead to God, and to live in God's presence. Otherwise they will remain outside life, like a fish out of water, Montfort says (H 24:19). Silence has meaning and fecundity if it is conscious of the presence of God. Montfort sings this for thirty-nine couplets, in which he sets forth the motivations and counsels concerning the "*holy practice of God's presence*" (H 24). And above all, Montfort proposes silence before the mystery of God and assimilation of the Wisdom of the Gospel. "The mystery of Christ as Eternal Wisdom, incarnate in Mary for man's salvation, is the radiant center of montfort spirituality, the 'unifying' viewpoint that imparts a particular coloration to a way of living the whole Christian life."[16] In the elements and nuances of the particular montfort shading of the Christian life, we find, doubtless, that intimate silence of the soul that, in Montfort's school, reveals a secret of sanctity in an incarnational spirituality. Here is the mystery of contemplative silence, of wonder in the presence of a God "*truly lavish with himself in his desire to be with man!*" (LEW 71). Through the mighty realism of his couplets, a style of his era, Montfort displayed a vision of the specific, concrete sufferings of the Passion, suffered and endured by Jesus without a murmer. Piously, in seven hymns (H 128-34), he sang of the silence of the incarnate word in the Eucharist. We note the nuances in feelings Montfort expressed about various aspects of Jesus' silence in the Eucharist. They are praise, wonder, gratitude, and lament at humans' incomprehension, and desire for reparation by a great love. And Father de Montfort's silence is a contemplation of the pleasure and satisfaction of Jesus in his Eucharistic relationship with Mary. Sister Marie Louise of Jesus, Montfort's disciple, contemplated this mystery of silence in a mystical state, feeling called as she did to become an image of the silence of God throughout eternity and the silence of Jesus in the Eucharist.[17] And this is the silence of Wisdom, says Montfort. Silence is the guide and guardian of the soul, the fuel of its flame. Silence and Wisdom are inseparable (H 23:15). Only through an experience of authentic silence, an interior attitude of freedom, humility, and contemplation, can we fully grasp Montfort's call to center our lives on the quest and contemplation of Wisdom, who has become flesh for us. Here we discover the mystery of Mary, her place willed by God in the divine salvific plan: "An associate of unique nobility, and the Lord's humble handmaid" (LG 61). In his spirituality, Montfort proposes attitudes to be fostered by "*special interior practices for those who wish to be perfect*" (TD 258-65). Montfort's proposal cannot be lived apart from a profound silence: a silence of the soul that allows itself to be guided by the Spirit of God, Who has power to lead it to the gift of mystical silence. This is the gift to which Montfort himself testifies when he says: "*Behold the unbelievable: / I carry Our Lady in the midst of me, / graven in strokes of glory, / Although in the darkness of faith*" (H 77:15).

I. Chiari

Notes: (1) Grandet, 3-4. (2) Ibid., 2-3. (3) Blain, 2. (4) Ibid., 2-4. (5) Ibid., 8. (6) Ibid., 25. (7) Itinerario, 178-79. (8) Blain, 100. (9) Ibid., 101. (10) Ibid., 117. (11) Grandet, 92. (12) Grandet, 161-62. (13) M. Blanchot, *L'amitié (Friendship)*, Gallimard, Paris 1971, 145. (14) M. Baldini, *Le dimensioni del silenzio nella poesia, nella filosofia . . . (The dimensions of silence in Poetry, in Philosophy, Etc.)*, Città Nuova, Rome 1988, 9. (15) B. Forte, *Teologia della storia: Saggio sulla rivelazione, l'inizio e il compimento (Theology of History: Essay on Revelation, the Beginning and the Fulfillment)*, Edizioni Paoline, Cinisello Balsamo, Italy 1991, 63-64. (16) A. Bossard, *Le mystère de la Sagesse éternelle incarnée en Marie pour le salut du monde (The Mystery of the Eternal and Incarnate Wisdom in Mary for the Salvation of the World)*, in DMon (September 1986), 2. (17) *Lettres de Marie Louise de Jésus*, private printing, Generalate of the Daughters of Wisdom, Rome 1981, 11.

SIN

I. INTRODUCTION

"Cry out full throated, spare not, lift up your voice like a trumpet; declare to my people their transgression, to the house of Jacob their sins" (Is 58:1). This *Introit,* which was sung for the feast of Blessed Louis Marie de Montfort (*Clama, ne cesses*), underlines the missionary's powerful call to repentance. Saint Louis Marie's vocation was to be a preacher of renewal and reform, especially through parish missions; the proclamation of the horror of sin and the infinite mercy of God is a prominent and central element of his ministry.

After reviewing some prerequisites for an authentic understanding of Montfort's doctrine on sin, the article examines St. Louis's explanation of the nature of sin, the kinds of sin, its consequences, and the forgiveness of sins, which strengthens the resolve to take the means necessary to avoid sin. The article closes with some brief reflections on the relevance of Saint Louis Marie's teaching on sin for contemporary men and women.

II. The Context of Saint Louis Marie's Doctrine on Sin

In order to grasp Saint Louis de Montfort's understanding of the "mystery of iniquity" three points especially should be underlined.

1. Montfort, the parish missionary

It is to be expected that a priest engaged in bringing about the reform of the Church (PM 17) would preach resolutely against sin. And that is precisely what Montfort did.[1] Boldness and urgency form the persistent, repetitive background beat of all Montfort's preaching on sin. Sinful transgressions are the destructive force engulfing individuals and the entire human family. They offend Jesus, holding back the reign of love: sinners must either change the direction of their lives without delay or risk the fires of hell. With Jesus, the missionary cries out: "The time is fulfilled, the kingdom of God is at hand, repent and believe in the Gospel" (Mk 1:15). The time is "now" and repentance is not to be put off for one moment (H 94:5; 126:11; 137:14) for the kingdom of God is already present in Jesus (LEW 193) and we must strive for its fulfillment by turning away from sin and turning towards the Gospel, the Eternal and Incarnate Wisdom.

Montfort's conviction that it is his vocation to destroy sin and establish the reign of Christ through Mary is found throughout his writings.[2] He joyfully puts the meaning of his vocation to song: *"I run around this world, / I have taken on a vagabond spirit / in order to save my poor neighbor / What! Should I see the soul of my dear brother / perish all around by sin, / without it touching my heart?"* (H 22:1); *"I cannot rest an hour / nor stay in the same place, / seeing Jesus so offended! / Alas! everywhere they wage war against him. / Sin reigns all over. / Souls fall into the fire / I want to cry out like a clap of thunder"* (H 22:12); *"If by my life and the blood of my veins / I destroy one only sin, / If I bring about only one heart touched by you / You are paying too much for all my troubles"* (H 22:13). His parish missions are a call to the village to seek *"pardon for sins committed"* (H 163:12).

Writing autobiographically, he indicates one of the chief roles of the apostles of the end times: *"They will give battle, overthrowing and crushing heretics and their heresies, schismatics and their schisms, idolators and their idolatries, sinners and their wickedness"* (TD 48). *"They will be like thunder clouds flying through the air at the slightest breath of the Holy Spirit . . . They will thunder against sin, they will storm against the world, they will strike down the devil"* (TD 57).

2. Montfort's overarching theology

In order to understand Montfort's sense of sin, one must first grasp his overarching theology embodied in his *Collected Writings* and explained in the many entries of this *Handbook* (particularly the articles on "Trinity," "Sacred Heart," and "Love"). Montfort spirituality is, in the final analysis, a path to the Triune God. Thus, montfort spirituality entails a personal, intimate, and loving relationship with God. The montfort disciple lives a mystical marriage, a spiritual espousal, a Song of Songs relationship with God, belonging to God as the beloved of the Divine Lover. The immense mystery of God's triune nature as a community of persons yet one love is the starting point and the goal of Montfort's spirituality. In the words of the Song of Songs, the bridegroom says to all of us, "How beautiful you are, O my love," and the bride responds, "How beautiful you are my love" (Sg 1:15—16).

It cannot be emphasized enough that the entire corpus of Montfort's writings must be placed in its authentic framework: the tenderness of God who is Love itself. The saint revealed in a rather unique way the degree to which his love model of salvation is central to his teaching, by choosing it as the theme of the final sermon he would preach. Knowing that he was in the grip of death, he struggled to the pulpit to preach once more before he would go to the Lord. It was to be his farewell gift to the parish of St. Laurent, and also to his friend, Bishop de Champflour, who was present that evening. In a sense it was to be the summary of his teachings, his final word. The topic was apparently not difficult for him to choose: the tenderness of God in Jesus Christ, a theme that he was convinced moved people to repentance.[3] (A probable outline of the sermon is found in LS 80–90; the content is spelled out in LEW 117–32.)

It is Montfort's conviction that God is merciful that made him known as the simple "good Father from Montfort." Louis Marie's insistence that God shows tender mercies cannot be twisted into alignment with some contemporary thought denying eternal punishment. Far from it: Montfort knew the ugliness of sin and did not hesitate to preach the horrors that await the damned. But his call to forgiveness, his appeal to heed the tender mercy of God, qualifies all his preaching. Montfort cannot seem to find the terms to explain the abomination of sin; he is far more lost for words when trying to express the forgiving love of God.

3. Montfort's sanctity

Montfort's thought on sin must also be contextualized by the historical truth that he was a great saint—in fact, an extraordinary saint. There is clearly present in Father de Montfort a deep, sincere conviction not only of his own sinfulness but of the sinfulness of all people. His words seem to echo Paul's: "All have sinned and fall short of the glory of God" (Rom 3:23). It would, in fact, be quite shocking not to find that experience of sinfulness in his life, for the closer one is to God, the more that person experiences distance; the more immersed in Holiness, the more sensitive to sin.[4] It is only the great saint who can tastes the horrible bitterness of sin even the slightest. And as vehement as Montfort is in declaring himself "by nature" nothing, he becomes even more passionate about his dignity and power "in Christ Jesus." Sensitivity to sin is a hallmark of Saint Louis de Montfort, as it is for all those who live so deeply within the All-Holy, Love Itself.

Montfort is, therefore, extremely conscious of his own sinfulness. His vocation to preach to sinners does not spring from any elitism or triumphalism: he sincerely counts himself as one of the greatest sinners: *"Although I deserve only punishment for my sins"* (L2); *"I only spoil things whenever I get involved in them"* (L 4); *"Our human nature is so spoilt"* (TD 83); *"Providence has established spiritual ties between me and several other persons who are sinners like myself"* (L 9). He thinks of himself as a *"wretched sinner"* (L 15, 16), a *"poor sinner"* whose *"criminal hands"* (L 15) hold the Holy of Holies every day. *"I beg the prayers of all the 'Friends of the Cross' so that God will not punish my sins"* (L 33); *"Poor men and women who are sinners, I, a greater sinner than you"* (SR 3); *"Dear Friends of the Cross, we are all sinners; there is not one of us who has not deserved hell, and I more than anyone."* (FC 21) He too calls upon the mercy of Christ Jesus and in the power of that love does not fear to undertake great things—joyfully—for God and the salvation of souls (cf. TD 214).

He speaks also in his own name when he has his congregation sing: *"In your blood I drown my sins and my evils"* (H 46:38); *"My sins have only merited an eternal death"* (H 79:2). Montfort himself surely prayed the formula of consecration he placed at the end of LEW, which includes: *"I . . ., a faithless sinner . . .it is by this means (i.e., through Mary) that I hope to obtain from you contrition and pardon for all my sins"* (LEW 223). The preacher, Saint Louis Marie, applies to himself first of all the harsh language, characterized by dramatic emphasis, describing the weakness of sinful humankind: *"by nature we are prouder than peacocks, we cling to the earth more than toads . . . more envious than serpents, greedier than pigs . . . we have nothing in us but sin"* (TD 79). Montfort does not exclude himself when speaking to sinners: *"because of* our *sins"* (SM 36).

II. The Nature of Sin

1. Sin in general

"But thou, our God, art kind and true and patient. . . . To know thee is the whole of righteousness, and to acknowledge thy power is the root of immortality. We have not been led astray by the perverted inventions of human skill or the barren labors of painters, by some gaudy painted shape, the sight of which arouses in fools a passionate desire for a mere image without life or breath. They are in love with evil" (Wis. 15:1–6). Sin is choosing resentment over compassion, ugliness over beauty, deceit over wisdom.

Sin is a moral evil. And as Montfort tells us, sin is rarely presented as evil but rather as good. *"In general, they do not teach sin openly, but they speak of it as if it were virtuous, or blameless, or a matter of indifference and of little consequence. This guile which the devil has taught the world in order to conceal the heinousness of sin and falsehood is the wickedness spoken of by St. John when he wrote, 'The whole world lies in the power of evil', and now more than ever before"* (LEW 199). Montfort throughout his ministry presents a clear and direct warning to sinners, to be aware of God's righteous justice and of the eternal punishment in Hell that awaits those with unforgiven grave sins: *"Every sin, says St. Augustine and Tertullian, is a debt which we contract with God, and in his justice requires payment"* (SR 40). But Montfort first and foremost gave witness, as compassionate confessor and teacher, to the gentleness and unfathomable mercy of God.

2. Sin as rupture of covenant love

Montfort conceives of sin not so much as an abomination, or a revolt, or a betrayal, but more as the breaking of a relationship with Love who is God. His own thundering against sin flows directly from his conviction that sin is nothing less than a *disdain* for Infinite Love Incarnate (cf. L 7; LEW 1, 72; H 13:81). Although he can speak of rules that cannot be broken without sinning, his underlying concept of sin is not based on a legalistic model but on the model of the spousal relationship. Montfort appears to grasp that calling sin an infraction of the Law places us immediately within the context of God's love, since the Law is intrinsic to God's free, loving covenant with man.[5] *"You should consider your sins in the light of God's holiness"* (FC 48).

3. Sin as lack of harmony

It is for this reason that he speaks of the horror of sin; for sin is *"against God Himself"* (cf. H 13:81; 98:17). As his many hymns on the passion of the Lord and the Sacred Heart show, sin is *"against Jesus"* (H 98:7) and also against the Holy Spirit (98:13). To sin is to be out of order, to be in disharmony with the Source of all; thus sin can also be against creation itself (H 157:19). At the same time, Montfort insists that sin is also a transgression against one's brothers and sisters (cf. H 2; 148). In a special way sin is also an offense against Our Lady. Since Mary plays a part in the redemption of sins, to refuse redemption, to refuse forgiveness, to break out of harmony with her Son is to disrupt harmony with the woman who is perfect harmony with Christ. *"Sinners, we by our crimes make Mary and Jesus two very innocent victims"* (H 74:7).

In the light of the above, it can be said that Montfort has the raw material for building a contemporary understanding of sin as against both God and neighbor. "Just as love of God and love of neighbor form a unity, so too sin is against both."[6] "It might be said that sins solely against God are impossible. Every sin is at least against the self (and hence is its own punishment), and God encounters us with his gifts and invitations in our fellow men, especially in Christ."[7] Contemporary teaching of the Church states in the same vein: "The sinner wounds God's honor and love, his own human dignity as a man called to be a son of God, and the spiritual well-being of the Church, of which each Christian ought to be a living stone."[8]

III. Kinds of Sin

1. The sin of the angels

"Behind the disobedient choice of our first parents lurks a seductive voice, opposed to God, which makes them fall into death out of envy" (cf. Gen 3:1–5; Wis 2:24).[9] God created the angelic world out of the self-effusiveness of his love. Angels are immaterial supernatural beings of intelligence set apart for the service of God (Ps 88:6; Jb 5:1). The angels share in the Divine Life, and were given the gift of freedom in order that they might know and love God. Lucifer, joined by other angels, chose self over God (cf. 2 Pet 2:4). Lucifer (meaning "the light bearer") is hereafter known as Satan (meaning "the opposer") or the Devil (meaning "the accuser"). Saint Louis de Montfort, closely following his predecessors, tells us that *"Saint Michael, armed with his zeal / Struck the rebel Lucifer / And plunged him from heaven into fire"* (H 21:2). *"Satan fell because of pride."* (H 29:68). An allusion to this primordial battle may be found in Rev 12:7–9: "Then the war broke out in heaven. Michael and his angels waged war on the dragon. The dragon and his angels fought, but they had not the strength to win, and no foothold was left to them in heaven." The devil, humiliated in seeing that human beings are called to take his place in heaven (H 127:74; LEW 43) tries to separate people from God through sin. Montfort echoes the words of 1 Pet 5:8: "Your enemy the devil, like a roaring lion, prowls around looking for someone to devour." Montfort refers to *"the self-sufficiency of proud Lucifer"* (FC 18) and *"that self-complacency of Lucifer"* (FC 48) and *"what Lucifer lost by Pride"* (TD 53). Montfort presupposes that all sin, even original sin, is to be placed within the context of the fall of the angels.

2. Original sin

Saint Louis's treatment of original sin[10] is found principally in LEW, where he gives a synopsis of salvation history.[11] After characterizing the first human creatures as *"His supreme masterpiece, the living image of his beauty and his perfection, the great vessel of his graces, the wonderful treasury of his wealth and in a unique way his representative on earth,"* Montfort dramatically describes the horror of the first sin: *"The vessel of the Godhead was shattered into a thousand pieces. This beautiful star fell from the skies. This brilliant sun lost its light. Man sinned and by his sin lost his wisdom, his innocence, his beauty, his immortality. In a word he lost all the good things he was given and found himself burdened with a host of evils. His mind was darkened and impaired. His heart turned cold towards the God he no longer loved . . .*

Adam could see God's justice pursuing him and all his descendants" (LEW 39–40); *"The sentence of death and eternal damnation has been pronounced against man and his descendants"* (LEW 44). *"Even from birth, / This sin* (original sin) *reigns in us; / Adam, by his offense, has infected all of us"* (H 109:16). Man, created to be divinized by God in glory, chose to divinize himself. Satan convinced Adam and Eve to eat of the Tree of Knowledge of Good and Evil. Using envy of God as the basis for temptation to the sin of Pride, he said, "Of course you will not die . . . your eyes will be opened and you will be like gods knowing both good and evil" (Gen. 2:5). The Fall—man's envy, pride, hatred, and attempted overthrow of God—was followed by man's envy, pride, hatred, and murder of his neighbor.

Saint Louis de Montfort's thought on original sin dovetails with the theology of his time on this subject. The question of the historicity of the Genesis account and the subsequent issues concerning original sin were, of course, unknown to him. His teaching on sin of our first parents is in harmony with the contemporary doctrine of the Church on this point: "The 'tree of knowledge of good and evil' symbolically evokes the insurmountable limits that man, being a creature, must freely recognize and respect with trust . . . In (original) sin man preferred himself to God and by that very act scorned him . . . Created in a state holiness, man was destined to be fully 'divinized' by God in glory. Seduced by the devil, he wanted to 'be like God,' but 'without God, before God, and not in accordance with God'. . . All men are implicated in Adam's sin."[11]

3. Actual sin

The actual sins of man are the personal and individual offenses committed against an all-loving, all-just, and personal God. Evil is that which turns man away from the incarnate and redemptive God of Love. Sin is what disrupts a person's intimacy with and commitment to God. It is what erodes the human beloved's spiritual marriage to the Divine Lover. Montfort states: *"All natural evils which befall us, from the smallest to the greatest, come from the hand of God. The same hand that killed an army of a hundred thousand men on the spot also causes a leaf to fall from the tree and a hair from your head; the hand which pressed so heavily on Job gently touches you with a light tribulation. It is the same hand which makes both the day and the night, sunshine and darkness, good and evil. He has permitted the sinful actions which hurt you; he is not the cause of your malice, but he permits the actions"* (FC 56).

To sin is to choose voluntarily a moral privation. The degree of evil that exists depends on how serious the privation is objectively and on the character of the subjective knowledge and intention of the person who is choosing a particular privation. Sin is an evil human act. It is a word, deed, desire, or omission in opposition to the eternal law of God. Serious sin requires a deliberate act. It requires the adequate exercise of the intellect and will. To understand the degree of sin one must consider "what" was done, "why" it was done, and the circumstances surrounding both. Sin is so often a subtle reality, disguised as a good. In the words of Montfort, *"You must not allow this Tree* [Holy Slavery of Love] *to be damaged, by destructive animals, by sins, for they may cause death simply by their contact. They must not be allowed even to breathe upon the Tree, because the mere breath, that is venial sins, which are most dangerous when we do not trouble ourselves about them"* (SM 75). According to the theology of his time, Saint Louis speaks of *"the sin named actual, whether mortal or venial, . . . committed freely, knowingly"* (H 109:16).

His distinction between the two types of sin is traditional: *"Grace is always lost by a mortal sin . . . venial sin cools the charity of the Holy Spirit, its punishment is temporal"* (H 109:17). In LS, the missionary has this note: *"Mortal sin is an incurable evil in its very nature since no natural remedy is able to cure it, nor can man, nor the angels, etc."* (LS 625). Saint Louis's description fits in with the teaching of the Catechism issued by Pope John Paul II: "Mortal sin destroys charity in the heart of man . . . venial sin allows charity to subsist, even though it offends and wounds it."[12]

IV. Consequences of Sin

1. Weakness of sinful man

Father de Montfort is very much the parish preacher when he says that *"the sin of Adam has almost entirely spoiled us and soured us . . . we have in us nothing but sin and deserve only the wrath of God and the eternity of hell"* (TD 79). That a deep, crippling scar remains in the baptized is forcefully taught by Montfort: *"Our soul, being united to our body, has become so carnal that it has been called flesh . . . Pride and blindness of spirit, hardness of heart, weakness and inconstancy of soul, evil inclinations, rebellious passions, ailments of the body—these are all we can call our own"* (TD 79). *"You must realize that through the sin of Adam and through the sins we ourselves have committed, everything in us has become debased, not only our bodily sense, but also the powers of our soul"* (FC 47). *"By the light of the Holy Spirit given you through Mary ..you will perceive the evil inclination of your fallen nature and how incapable you are of any good apart from that which God produces in you as Author of nature and of grace. As a consequence of this knowledge, you will despise yourself and think of yourself as a snail that soils everything with its slime, as a toad that poisons everything with its venom, as a malevolent serpent seeking only to deceive"* (TD 213). What saves Louis Marie from despair is his complete trust in God who is Love, in Jesus who is all Love manifested especially through the victorious Cross, in the Holy Spirit who is the loving of the Father and the Son, and in Mary, the Mother of Fair Love. In Jesus, the threefold concupiscence is overcome: *"A Friend of the Cross is an all-powerful king, a champion who triumphs over the devil, the world and the flesh in their three-fold concupiscence"* (FC 4; cf. FC 6, 9, 12). Montfort's insistence on the "nothingness" of man—which is not removed by the grace of baptism—is overwhelmed by his conviction that man is "omnipotent" in Christ Jesus.

Moreover, this experience of his weakness "by nature" never impeded his joyful creativity and his determination to reform the Church and renew the face of the earth. He is not (as some of his writings read out of context would lead one to believe) a heavy, morose man, pessimistically harping on sin: far from it. When he writes the introduction to his hymn book, he tears into prophets of gloom: *"Since God is in eternal bliss, He wants his servants happy!"* (H 1:10). It was precisely this mystical taste of his own nothingness which was at the same time a taste of God's omnipotence. And all, claims the saint, are called to share in the infinite love who is God. Priests, religious—in fact all men and women are to rise up and overturn the power of sin (PM 29). Montfort assures us that the slimy toads, the proud peacocks, and the greedy pigs perform incredible wonders in building the City of God. They are personal instruments of the Spirit to the extent that they recognize their absolute nothingness and are open to the omnipotence of God.

a. Christological Statement. Saint Louis Marie's sincere conviction of his sinfulness and of the impossibility of doing anything "on our own," is primarily a Christological statement. He is affirming with the divine word of Scripture that "all things were created through him and for him. He is before all else that is and in him all things hold together" (Col 1:16-17); and he adheres literally to the words of Jesus: "apart from me you can do nothing" (Jn 15:5). Only in and through Christ Jesus, the saint would insist, do we have any worth, for all creation derives its meaning from Christ as its highest point. His doctrine on the utter destruction left in man in the wake of sin is an affirmation of the primacy of Christ, who, through this sinful world, brings about the kingdom. Everything is grace, the grace of Christ Jesus. Montfort experiences, then, a Gospel paradox: "without me you can do nothing," and "nothing is impossible with God." Even as divinized by the Lord, Montfort would say, we must be conscious of the truth that it is only by grace that we are made whole. Montfort's "joy in the Cross," his seeming delight in proclaiming his nothingness and the nothingness even of Mary and of all creation, is never to be considered in isolation from its essential context: Christ's divinization of creation precisely in its emptiness. Since no one is so much a "slave of the Lord," since no one has so emptied oneself of self as Our Lady, she is, then, the summit of those divinized in and through Christ Jesus.

b. Nature and grace. "The intrinsic orientation of man in Christ radically excludes any dualism between nature and grace. The merely natural relationship of man to God, possible in the abstract . . . does not and cannot exist in fact."[13] Man is of his very nature in the present economy of salvation open to the infinite, and only the infinite will satisfy him. The cosmos itself has been affected in its very being—ontologically—by the redemptive Incarnation.

Montfort, like writers before and after him, continuing even up to Vatican II, speaks as if grace were superimposed on sinful nature, and did not totally penetrate and in principle heal it. Nature and grace are for this saint always in mortal conflict. His language about *"this wicked world,"* which is *"the universal assembly of sinners"* (H 29:5), and the utter misery of man in himself should be understood today as placing significant emphasis on the power of concupiscence intensified by the sin of the world, and on the absolute necessity of the grace of Jesus Christ.

Whatever may have been Montfort's underlying theology, his thought must be interpreted to mean that whatever does not foster a deeper relationship with Christ should be avoided. To deepen this relationship, experience proves that we must stand as beggars of God's grace. The problem involves more than outright sin; it embraces whatever may be even remotely called an occasion of sin. The "world" that lures us, in our inherent weakness, away from total surrender to the Lord and into sin would include, for Montfort, village dances, cabarets (H 31), games of chance (H 30), luxury (H 33), poetry for itself (H 2), etc. The list appears broad and long to modern men and women. However, the total historical and moral context of Montfort's time is difficult for us today to grasp; our primary concern should be to recognize honestly in our own "world" those things that are sinful and also those that so easily and so powerfully remove us, in our inherent weakness, from the Lord. Contemporary Christians surely can list modern activities that would fall into such a category, e.g., many TV sitcoms, some modern types of dancing, etc. However, in all this it must be remembered that Montfort stresses far more the power of God's forgiveness than of man's sin.

V. Forgiveness of Sins

1. Jesus, friend of sinners

If Montfort so strongly believes that his vocation is to proclaim Good News to sinners, it is primarily because that was the vocation of Christ Jesus. He has the Eternal and Incarnate Wisdom plead: *"Do not be afraid, it is I. Why are you afraid? I am just like you; I love you. Are you afraid because you are sinners? But they are the very ones I am looking for; I am the friend of sinners . . . come to me and I will unburden you, purify you and console you"* (LEW 70). Jesus *"tender and mild towards all, especially towards poor sinners"* (LEW 126), is *"the friend of sinners"* (LEW 125), who requests *"to be struck in the place of sinners"* (LEW 130) for *"I love sinners so much,"* . . . *"that I would be ready to die a second time for each one of them if that were necessary"* (LEW 130). Montfort's theology of love is the absolutely essential framework for any attempt to understand his doctrine on sin. Sin's malice derives from the rupture of the love relationship God has established with us; its redemption flows from the Infinite

Love Who is God. *"Where are you fleeing, O sinner so filled with crimes? why are you putting yourself so far from me? / You'll fall into the abyss / My Heart calls out to you . . . Come close!"* (H 42:8). A hymn that was quite popular in French-speaking lands for about two centuries expresses beautifully this yearning of Jesus for the sinner: *"Come back, O sinner, it is your God who calls out to you / Come quickly and submit to his law. / You have been already too rebellious;/ Come back to Him, since He comes back to you"* (H 98:3). When Montfort urges oil rather than vinegar for the treatment of sins, he is proclaiming his conviction that stressing God's love is more powerful than insisting on the wrath of God: *"Get far from me you austere zealous people / so filled with rigors and anger / pretexts for charity! / A little vinegar with plenty of oil /. . . converts the greatest sinners / as we see in the Gospel"* (H 22:17).

2. Jesus, redeemer of sinners

Jesus is not only friend of sinners (cf. Mt 11:19) but far more so the redeemer, the only medicine who can heal the wounds of sin: *"How sweet his conduct towards all sinners! . . . / On the Cross, he uses all his strength / To obtain grace for the poor sinner, And even for his own executors so filled with rage and envy, / who by a thousand evils take away his life"* (H 9:10). He includes a rather detailed description of the sufferings of Jesus in order to reveal the infinite love that God has for sinners and to demonstrate that in that love, all sin is forgiven (cf. H 67–73). His refrains, especially in H 68, sing the dirge: *". . . It is for us, O sinner, that he endures such sufferings! . . . Oh! We are the ones, we sinners, who merit such sorrows!" "Jesus, your immense Love/ Having Carried our Sins . . ."* (H 71:9).

His boldness in language can only be explained by his own mystical experience of God's merciful forgiveness for himself and for others: *"In piercing Him through, they actually comfort Him,/ for the lance is making a passage / for the fire devouring his Heart / to enter the heart of the sinner"* (H 41:36). *"Finally,"* Montfort bursts out in a cry of love: *"my request is bold: / Remove from me this sinful heart / so that I will have in this life / no other heart but Yours"* (H 47:30). *"Oh abominable sinners! It's over, Jesus is dead. / We are all culpable, What will become of us?/ It is for us, O sinners, that He dies in sorrows"* (H 73:1). *"Ah! Sinner, God for you dies out of Love!/ It is time to weep over your deed, / it is time that you love him in return"* (H 137:14). The Cross is victorious for it becomes for us the true Tree of Life bearing the bread of angels as food for sinners. *"He (Jesus) has closed hell, / pulled out of prison our ancestors, / opened eternal glory, / made universal peace./ Finally, Jesus is Conqueror / for the salvation of the sinner. / Let us all sing: Alleluia! / And then, Ave Maria!"* (H 84:3).

Montfort attributes to the Eucharist the saving power that he attaches to the Cross: *"Come, O sinners, Find in the Eucharist / the True Life / with all its goods; / Come hide yourself here, place yourself safely / in the midst of my Sacred Heart, / to encounter there sorrow / and the pardon of your offenses"* (H 131:5); in the Eucharist, *"A God immolates himself / to God as priest and victim /. . . to press Him to pardon us"* (H 158:6).

3. Mary and sinners

To speak of Our Lady in the context of sin we must state, first of all, that she is the Immaculate Conception, the Mother of the Divine Forgiveness who is Jesus. She is the Mother who in a mysterious way brings the new life of Jesus to man.

There is no doubt that Saint Louis Marie fervently upheld the dogma of Mary's fullness of grace from the first moment of her conception. It is as the holy one sharing so fully in divine life that she is the *"refuge of sinners,"* a title especially dear to Saint Louis de Montfort (cf. LEW 224; SR 58; H 7:9). As the Immaculate One, she shares so intensely in the life of God that she too shares in God's mysterious yet infinite love for sinners: *"(Mary), thou who art always filled with compassion for those in need, who never despise sinners or turn them away . . . gentle Mother of pity . . ."* (SR 58). *"These two hearts (Jesus and Mary) love sinners"* (H 87:10).

Mary participates by her total "Yes" in the redemption wrought by her Son, and Montfort can therefore write: *"Sinners, we make of Jesus and Mary two innocent victims by our crimes. Ah! . . . may we never sin again!"* (H 74:7; cf. H 87:6).

It is fundamentally because of Mary's role in the redemptive incarnation that Montfort speaks of her actual tasks as mediatrix of God's forgiving graces. The role she plays in the pattern of all mysteries, the Incarnation, is the role that she plays throughout salvation history. And it is in her and through her faith-filled womb that Incarnate Forgiveness comes into a rebellious world. It is through her "Yes"—which indicates her very personality—that divine forgiveness is forever granted. Saint Louis Marie's Hymn on the Ave Maria is filled with references to the power of the *Hail Mary* uttered by Gabriel (cf. H 89); Mary's role in the destruction of sin through her consent is again stressed by Montfort (H 89:7).

VI. Means of Avoiding sin

Saint Louis Marie insists that anyone sincerely desiring to live a life free from serious sin must avoid all occasions of sin. He also recommends the means found in all manuals of spirituality, e.g., a life of prayer, frequenting the sacraments, a spiritual director, etc. There are, however, some means to avoid sin on which Saint Louis especially insists.

1. Mindfulness of God's love

The primary means to avoid sin, taking all Montfort's works into account, would be to understand and accept the Infinite Love that God is for us. To be ever-conscious of being loved by Love Itself, a love that pursues and never rests, makes one understand that sin is a rupture of a spousal relationship. Montfort can therefore sing: *"Come, O Holy Spirit, God all aflame / Be again my Spouse. / Pardon, Pardon,*

God of my soul, / May I return to grace with you! (H 98:21). *"Father, you love us / as your true children / . . . O God of charity, Pardon, mercy! / O God full of goodness, Be merciful! (H 127:39). "Pardon, my tender Jesus . . ." (H 136:18).* With this motive, Montfort hopes all can say *"I would prefer to die at this very instant than to commit a mortal sin"* (RW 292).

Conscious of this great love, even after having fallen into sin, we quickly reach out for the loving hand of God, which yearns to lift us up: *"If you make a blunder which brings a cross upon you whether it be inadvertently or even though your own fault, bow down under the mighty hand of God without delay and as far as possible do not worry over it. You might say within yourself, 'Lord, here is a sample of my handiwork.' If there is anything wrong in what you have done, accept the humiliation as a punishment for it* . . . (FC 46). *"Do not despair, do not get upset when you fall into some sin, but humble yourself and ask me pardon"* (MLW 78). And Montfort gives insight into the sins of saints: *"Frequently, even very frequently, God allows his greatest servants, those far advanced in holiness, to fall into the most humiliating faults so as to humble them in their own eyes and in the eyes of others."* (FC 46).

2. Devotion to Our Lady

Devotion to Our Lady is Montfort's strong remedy for those in sin and for those hoping to avoid sin. Not only does the consecration bring about a share in Mary's faithfulness, but her intercession is especially strong for her children who have fallen: *"Are you in the miserable state of sin? Then call on Mary and say to her, 'Ave,' which means 'I greet you with the most profound respect, you who are without sin,' and she will deliver you from the evil of your sins"* (SR 57). In particular, Montfort insists on the power of the Rosary to keep us from sinning and to bring us to the Lord for pardon: *"If by chance your conscience is burdened with sin, take your Rosary and say at least a part of it in honor of some of the mysteries of the life, passion and glory of Jesus Christ, and you can be sure that, while you are meditating on these mysteries and honoring them, he will show his sacred wounds to his Father in heaven. He will plead for you and obtain for you contrition and the forgiveness of your sins"* (SR 83). *"We earnestly advise everyone to say the Rosary: the virtuous that they may persevere and grow in the grace of God; sinners, that they may rise from their sins"* (SR 118).

The perfect baptismal consecration, so ardently advocated by Montfort, entails a life "in Mary"; and, St. Louis Marie assures us, *"Those who live in her will never sin"* (TD 264).

VII. Relevance of Montfort's Teaching on Sin

Saint Louis Marie's doctrine on sin is highly relevant for contemporary society, which has to a large extent lost a sense of sin.

1. Sin exists

The missionary insists first of all that sin definitely exists. To say that because of the redemptive Incarnation, *all* is now good, without qualification, is to deny the obvious. The effects of original and personal sin are real; the polluted atmosphere of the world—the sin of the world—is difficult to resist, and Montfort reminds us over and over again of these pitfalls. Saint Louis Marie asks for "confession," i.e., an admission that we have done wrong and that all is not to be excused through recourse to human weakness. Only in that honesty can there be forgiveness. That there are situations that reduce the voluntarium he surely admits; but in a society that stresses free choice and a purely subjective norm of morality, Montfort rises like a powerful prophet to denounce a world alienated from God and turned within itself.

2. Social sins

Montfort sounds quite contemporary in constantly insisting on love of neighbor and the horror of sins against one's brothers and sisters. His thought has to be broadened to take in the magnitude of contemporary international relations where "neighbor" also means another country, another race, another nationality. It would be totally out of harmony with his doctrine not to denounce the sins of injustice and prejudice which can become part of the very fabric of "civilized society."

3. The mercy of God

Montfort's heightened sensitivity to sin is only outweighed by his conviction of God's mercy; again, we encounter the capstone of Montfort spirituality, God Alone who is overflowing Love. The saint's insistence that sin must never cause a person to turn further within him or herself or to grovel in guilt, is pure Gospel. It also indicates the attitude of the Church in all its members towards those who are "in sin." God is forgiveness to all who sincerely confess their guilt; the Body of Christ must be likewise.

4. Asceticism

The reality of man's weakness is strongly expressed in Montfort's thought. All strength is given to us in and through Jesus Christ, the Son of Mary, for the order of salvation is the order of the redemptive Incarnation. Montfort therefore prescribes asceticism as a powerful means to remain in grace, to live in Jesus Christ in spite of the triple allurements of concupiscence. Mortification and penances, avoiding occasions of sin, and showing fidelity to one's state in life, are not principles to be tossed aside without dire consequences. Spiritual flabbiness is the cause of spiritual death. Montfort's doctrine on the Cross is an essential part of his doctrine on both the meaning of sin and the means to avoid sin. The joyful asceticism demanded in living the baptismal consecration must be proclaimed to modern men and women in order that they may reach the true fulfillment God has planned for them.

5. Frequent use of sacraments

The Eucharist and the Sacrament of Reconciliation are among the prime means that Montfort requires of those who are serious about persevering in their life in Christ. The necessity of frequenting the sacraments is of no less importance today than it was in the eighteenth century. The

Sunday Eucharist especially, combined with Montfort's recommended monthly confession and spiritual direction are means that cannot be discarded by anyone who is serious about avoiding sin so as to live forever in Christ Jesus.

6. Avoidance of moral relativism

There has been a not-too-subtle return of an ancient Gnostic danger of separating the experience of God, or the mystical life, from the practice of virtue, the moral life. The result is a confused abstract esotericism and a practical moral relativism. This contradicts the lives of the saints and certainly the example and doctrine of Saint Louis de Montfort. Living according to the Christian moral law is a process of becoming that goes beyond self selection, good intentions, trying hard, or an exercise in probability. Life always presents people with new mountains for them to climb to God. For everyone on the path to perfection, yesterday's practice of virtue may seem today to have been presumptuous, egotistical, or self-deceptive. It may appear to have been a defense mechanism, rationalization, or escape. The evil one uses such deceitful defenses against moral rectitude in his attempt to subvert our relationship with God. This has been true not only for individuals but for whole civilizations.

7. Sin and psychological development

Another important consideration is the effect of modern depth psychology on our contemporary understanding of sin. So much of this modern science has been devoted to the study of the abnormal self from a post-enlightenment analytical, empirical, and positivistic perspective, one for the most part divorced from a Catholic spiritual perspective. The benefits of modern depth psychology will be discerned by history. But clearly it has tended to reduce immorality to psychic pathology. If a sickness results from a falling away from the Absolute, from God's laws, then a therapy not including a return to such laws will fail. If they are to be seen in a legitimate way, human mistakes, weaknesses, and failures must be seen in their relationship to God, sin, and evil. To reduce sin to an anthropocentric reality is to avoid its true reality, which is found in man's relationship or lack of relationship with God. Not all sin is the sin of human weakness. Sin is not about something, it is about someone. Sin cannot be considered merely as the absence of a psychological or physical healing: sin has to do with the character of a person's relationship with God and with falling short of the Ideal. To deal with sin merely from a humanistic point of view is to deal with the symptoms, rather than causes of human problems. And in the end it rejects true healing. Therapy that attempts to remove guilt while avoiding its cause increases guilt. Psychological abnormalities cause illusion, allusion, or delusion and their concomitant obsessions or compulsions. But to reduce sin to the level of the individual psyche is to create an epidemic of such behavior.

P. Gaffney - R. Payne

Notes: (1) Saint Louis Marie's first biographer, Grandet, includes an entire chapter to explain the missionary's "implacable hatred for sin." He begins the chapter by stating: "Monsieur Grignion, having learned by faith that mortal sin, which inflicts death to the soul, is the greatest evil in the world, the sovereign evil, as God is the sovereign good, the one evil and the source of all other evils, fought without any limits against sin . . . it is his zeal against all sins which brought on him persecutions, calumnies, injuries, contradictions on the part of the devil, the world and the flesh whose empire he absolutely wished to destroy" (Grandet, 320–21). (2) In addition, the saint's LS contains sermon notes on venial sin (567–74) and mortal sin (577–631). Most of the notes are taken from Lejeune, some from Joly. (3) "Burning with fever, he went up to the pulpit . . . his voice weak. The congregation believed that he was going to pass out . . . he chose for the subject of his last sermon the meekness of Jesus. More than ever before, he spoke from the abundance of his heart." Such is the description of Montfort's final sermon as given by Louis Le Crom, *Un Apôtre Marial: Saint Louis-Marie Grignion de Montfort (A Marian Apostle: Saint Louis Marie de Montfort)*, Librairie Mariale, Pontchateau 1942, 36. (4) Cf. Klaus Hemmerle, *Holy*, in *Encyclopedia of Theology: The Concise Sacramentum Mundi*, Karl Rahner, ed., Crossroad-Seabury, New York 1975, 640–41. (5) Cf. Piet Schoonenberg, *Sin*, in Rahner, ed., *Sacramentum Mundi*, 1580: "Men do evil against him (Yahweh) by transgressing his law, but this law functions in the covenant. Sin is hated by Yahweh as Lord of the covenant and so its most definite expression is in idolatry, forbidden in the first command of the Decalogue and denounced by the prophets." (6) Ibid., 1581. (7) Ibid. Schoonenberg goes on to state: "God encounters us with his gifts and invitations in our fellowmen, especially in Christ. But it iis necessary to stress today that it is God, with his initiative transcending our reality, who meets us in this way." (8) CCC 1487. (9) CCC 391. The Catechism goes on to quote the Latern Council IV (DS 800): "The devil and the other demons were indeed created naturally good by God, but they became evil by their own doing." (10) For a contemporary understanding of the traditional meaning of original sin, cf. Karl Rahner, *Foundations of Christian Faith: An Introduction to the Idea of Christianity*, Crossroad-Seabury, New York 1978, 106–15. (11) CCC 396, 398, 402. The quote "be like God but without God, before God, and not in accordance with God" is taken from St. Maximus the Confessor. *Ambigua:* PG 91, 1156C. (12) CCC 1855. (13) Juan Alfaro, *Nature*, in Rahner, ed., *Sacramentum Mundi*, 1034.

SLAVERY OF LOVE

SUMMARY

I. HISTORY:
1. History of the word "slave";
2. Confraternities;
3. Decisions of the Church;
4. French spiritual writers:
   a. Pierre de Bérulle,
   b. Henri-Marie Boudon.

II. SAINT LOUIS MARIE AND THE HOLY SLAVERY OF LOVE:
1. In his writings;
2. In his missionary and personal life;
3. Doctrine:
   a. Meaning of a language,
   b. Scriptural foundations,
   c. Liturgical foundation: Baptism,
   d. Spiritual deepening,
   e. Liberation,
   f. The small chains.

III. HOLY SLAVERY TODAY:
1. The fullness of freedom;
2. The essential.

Saint Louis Marie de Montfort asked his followers to acknowledge that they were slaves of the love of Jesus Christ through Mary, and even suggested that they wear small chains (TD 236-242) as an external sign of this condition. This might cause surprise and even offense today. In order to clear up any misunderstandings, we will first consider the Consecration of Holy Slavery in its historical context.

I. HISTORY

The Consecration of Holy Slavery was one of the main features of the spirituality of the French school, on which St. Louis Marie drew heavily. It was a cultural and spiritual legacy of Catholic Spain, where it was born in the sixteenth century. It referred to a biblical tradition and spread to a number of countries.

1. The history of the word "slave"

The word "slave" (in Latin *sclavus, slavus*) was first used in the tenth century. The German lords and Spanish caliphs used to recruit their "slaves" from the Slav countries; in the thirteenth century, the Italian merchants renewed this practice. As a result, the word came to refer to any human being owned by another.[1]

In the Latin documents referring to the confraternities of the Holy Slavery, the words *mancipium, manci-*

patus are used. The terms are also found in the Middle Ages with reference to the serfs who could not be removed from their lords' land. It is this kind of slavery that is referred to in the examples given in the tradition of the Holy Slavery of Love. It must be kept in mind that the Church had her slaves, who could not be removed from the land belonging to a diocese or a monastery. There were also voluntary slaves, and this accounts for the Consecration made by Blessed Marinus († 1016 cf. TD 159) and Gautier de Bierbach († 1222?), as well as the offering of himself to Mary by Odilon of Cluny († 1049), who wore a rope round his neck.

As the Consecration is an act of Christian devotion, it is not so much its relation to actual slavery that matters but, rather, its foundation in Scripture and Tradition. In Scripture the Greek word *doulos*, translated by *servus* in the Vulgate version, referred to slavery as it was known in ancient times and to spiritual realities: our complete dependence on God and, in accordance with St. Paul's teaching, our acknowledgment of Christ's sovereignty. Thus, when St. Luke says that Mary was the *doulê*, the slave or servant of the Lord (cf. Lk 1:38), the meaning is to be understood in the spiritual sense. St. Paul urges us to imitate Christ, who "took the form of a slave, being born in human likeness" (Phil 2:7).

The Marian terms *servus, servitus Mariae* spread in the Orient as well as in the West.[2] Around the year 500, Melodius addresses the Blessed Virgin as "the hope of your servants."[3] Before the year 600, Pseudo-Augustine[4] begs to be excused for daring to call Mary the Spouse "of my Lord," while acknowledging that he is "not only a worthless servant but also a sinful one" who speaks to her "in trembling." In Spain St. Ildefonsus of Toledo († 667) wrote prayers which have become part of the Mozarabic liturgy, and also a prayer to Mary begging "that we may ever live as your slaves."[5]

In the sixteenth century the word "slave" was part of the vocabulary of the spiritual masters of the "golden age" of religious history in Spain. St. Ignatius Loyola († 1556), in his *Exercises,* no. 114, contemplates the birth of Christ and looks on himself as "an unworthy slave" (*esclavito*) of Mary, Joseph, and the God-man. According to Blessed John of Avila (1499-1569), Mary prayed to God that she might be "the slave of the young woman who is to conceive and bear you while ever remaining a virgin." St. Joseph was the first person to declare himself a slave of Mary: "When he considered that Mary was the Mother of God . . . he gave praise to God Who had chosen him as spouse of the Blessed Virgin and offered himself to her as her slave."[6]

2. Confraternities

It is therefore not surprising that the explicit devotion of Holy Slavery to Mary first appeared in Spain. The first confraternity of the Slaves of the Mother of God was established in honor of the Assumption of Mary by a Franciscan nun of the Immaculate Conception. She was Sister Ines Bautista de San Pablo, in an Ursuline convent at Alcala de Henares, between

1575 and 1595. It was canonically established on August 2, 1595. A Franciscan monk, Juan de los Angeles († 1609), rewrote the rules of the confraternity, and Melchor de Cetina (1618) wrote the final version, which he gives in chapter 12 of an *Exhortación*.[7] He did so at the request of the nuns because the practice of the Holy Slavery to Mary was spreading throughout Spain. In 1612 a Benedictine monk, Anthony d'Alvarado, founded the confraternity of the Blessed Virgin in exile and wrote a *Guide* for use by Slaves of the Blessed Sacrament and the members of his own confraternity. In 1615 a member of the Order of Mercy, Peter de la Serna, published a set of rules for the Slaves of Our Lady of Mercy. The order had been founded for the purpose of ransoming the captives held in slavery by the Turks, and the members of the confraternity shared in the prayers, merits, and work of the members of the order.[8]

The Trinitarian Simon de Rojas († 1624), who had approved Peter de la Serna's rules, founded the renowned confraternity of the Slaves of the Name of Mary, approved in 1616, which the royal family joined. This encouraged Simon, and he sent to the Netherlands, then under Spanish rule, an Augustinian, Bartholomew de los Rios († 1652), who founded a confraternity there (approved in 1631). De los Rios wrote a six-volume treatise on Holy Slavery, "*De Hierarchia Mariana*," which is his most widely known work.

The devotion spread to Germany, Poland, Luxembourg, and France. The Theatine Francesco Olimpio promoted it in Italy by publishing a *Brief Exercise* for use by the "chained Slaves of the Mother of God."[9]

The nuns of Alcala de Henares declared themselves slaves "out of love for our Lord and the Immaculate Conception of Mary in order to serve them"; "they offered themselves to our Redeemer and his glorious Mother and surrendered to them, body and soul, as living victims."[10] They were therefore not only spouses of Christ but also slaves of his most holy Mother. The Blessed Virgin "took for herself [the title of slave] when the Word of God took possession of her heart, was made flesh in her womb, and became her Son . . . *Ecce ancilla Domini*." The Son of God himself "emptied himself, taking the form of a slave" (Phil 2:7).[11]

3. Decisions of the Church

De los Rios was the first to mention the wearing of small chains, and Francesco Olimpio also mentions it in his book. The practice led to abuses and tendentious interpretations. During the papacy of Clement X, the practice was placed on the Index, as were some confraternities (July 5 and October 2, 1673), and the apostolic brief "*Pastoralis Officii*" (December 15, 1675) proscribed the wearing of small chains. The condemnation and the proscription were confirmed by Pope Benedict XIV in an Index decree issued in 1758. These decisions were directed, however, against the abuses and by no means against the devotion of Holy Slavery or the use of the term in spiritual books.

4. French spiritual writers

Montfort in N gives the names of a number of spiritual writers who influenced him in his seminary days. With reference to the devotion of Holy Slavery, Bérulle and Boudon played a prominent part (TD 159-163).

a. Pierre de Bérulle. For Bérulle († 1629) the Holy Slavery was not just any form of devotion. The spirituality he lived earned him the title of "apostle of the Incarnate Word": he strove to adhere as perfectly as possible to all the mysteries of the life, death, and Resurrection of the Word made flesh, who had become the Servant of God, a "slave," in order to save us. Bérulle summed up his teaching on the subject in the heading of a text approved in 1620: "Desires or elevations to God were prompted by the mystery of the Incarnation. There were opportunities to offer oneself to Jesus in the state of slavery. This we owe him as a consequence of the ineffable union of the Divinity with humanity. This is done in order to offer oneself to the most Blessed Virgin in the state of dependence and slavery, which we ought to assume in her regard as the Mother of God, and because she has a special power over us as a result of this admirable condition." In 1623 he published the texts in *Discourse on the State and Grandeurs of Jesus.* He begins with an elevation to the Trinity, to Christ, and to Mary. This is followed by the vow of offering oneself "to Jesus Christ in the state of perpetual servitude . . . by the bond of perpetual servitude." He completes this with the offering to Mary: "I consecrate and dedicate myself to Jesus Christ in the state of perpetual servitude to his most holy Mother, the Blessed Virgin Mary; in perpetual honor of the Mother and the Son, and in honor of her quality as Mother of God; I offer myself to her in this state and quality as a slave; and I give myself to her grandeur in honor of the offering that the Eternal Word made of himself as Son, through the mystery of the Incarnation, which he chose to accomplish in her and through her." Bérulle identifies his vow with "the solemn profession of the Christians at Baptism,"[12] basing his assertion on the Catechism of the Council of Trent (art. 1, c. 31). For him, "it is a vow of the worship Jesus rendered, of which he himself in person is the author and initiator; it is the first and oldest worship, with the Apostles as its first . . . directors"[13] The vow of servitude (Bérulle used "slavery" less frequently), is strictly conformed to the fundamental truth of our relation with God as creatures. "This state of servitude ought not to appear suspect or strange to anyone; it is the correct, fundamental state of a creature in relation to God. For a creature is essentially a servant or, better still, a slave of the Creator; and it is the primary, general, absolute, and universal condition of a creaturely being. . . . It is a primitive state, in respect of nature as well as grace."[14]

b. Henri-Marie Boudon. The title of Boudon's († 1702) book, *God Alone or the Holy Slavery of the Admirable Mother of God,* tells us that his devotion is based on "God Alone," which later became Montfort's well-known motto. Boudon was a follower of St. Francis de Sales and Bérulle. He called to mind "the total and irrevocable offering [to Mary] made long ago, of all that I am in the order of nature and the order of grace. . . . My interior as well as my exterior life, and generally all that is mine, belongs more to you than to myself." Like Bérulle, he belonged to Mary in "the state and condition of a slave." He wrote his book in order to "win hearts . . . secure slaves" for Mary, and "in honor of the state and form of servitude that the Eternal Word took on himself, making himself nothing in your pure womb and becoming your subject."[15] According to St. Francis de Sales, devotion is "a love that prompts us to serve with a ready and loving will." The devotion of Holy Slavery is this kind of devotion to Mary "without any reservation."[16] In his "meditation preparatory to offering himself to the most Blessed Virgin as a slave" (583-584), he first called on the Blessed Trinity, then on Christ; and because God chose to give himself to us through Mary and wants us to give ourselves to him through her, "I take and choose her as my very good and most dear Mother, my most holy Patron, my faithful Advocate, my dear Mistress, my Sovereign and Queen, and vow to be her servant and slave for the rest of my life."[17]

II. Saint Louis Marie and the Holy Slavery of Love

1. In his writings

In his writings, St. Louis Marie recommends that we consecrate ourselves "*as slaves,*" that is to say, that we consecrate "*completely and for all eternity our body and soul, our possessions both spiritual and material, the atoning value and the merits of our good actions, and our right to dispose of them. In short, it involves the offering of all we have acquired in the past, all we actually possess at the moment, and all we will acquire in the future*" (LEW 219). This entails a complete surrender through the hands of Mary. "*We should choose a special feastday on which to give ourselves*" (SM 29); "*This is an occasion for receiving Holy Communion and spending the day in prayer*" (SM 61). "*At least once a year on the same day, we should renew the act of consecration.*" "*We should give our Lady some little tribute as a token of our servitude and dependence . . . homage paid by slaves to their master.*" "*This tribute could consist of an act of self-denial or an alms, or a pilgrimage or a few prayers*" (SM 62). In accordance with the tradition of the confraternities, Louis Marie recommends that "*in token of their slavery of love, the slaves of Jesus in Mary wear a little chain*" (TD 236) "*either around the neck, on the arm, on the foot, or about the body*" (SM 65). He makes clear, however, that this practice can be omitted without detriment to the essential feature of the Consecration, but "*just the same, it would be wrong to despise or condemn it, and foolhardy to neglect it*" (SM 65) without a good reason.[18]

Holy Slavery is, however, primarily a way of living, a spirit, a spirituality, as surrendering to Mary means "*performing all our actions with Mary, in Mary, through Mary, and for Mary*" (SM 28).

2. In his missionary and personal life

In his biography of St. Louis Marie, Grandet writes, "In every parish where he gave a mission, he established the devotion of the Holy Slavery of Jesus living in Mary."[19] He also draws attention to the fact that Bishop de Champflour authorized Father Mulot to "bless the small chains as the late Father de Montfort used to do."[20]

St. Louis Marie practiced what he preached, as attested by the fact that he died like a chained slave, "wearing small iron chains on his arm, round his neck and on his feet; in his right hand he held the crucifix to which Clement XI had attached indulgences, and in his left hand he clutched a small statue of the Blessed Virgin that he always carried with him."[21] It is not known when he made his offering as a slave,[22] but he has handed on to us the formula of Consecration as a conclusion to LEW: "*With the whole court of heaven as witness, I choose you, Mary, as my Mother and Queen. I surrender and consecrate myself to you, body and soul, as your slave.*" This is followed by the surrender mentioned above (LEW 225 and 219).

He signed himself "*slave*" only between 1700 and 1702, then once again in 1704, stating that he was "*priest and unworthy slave of Jesus in Mary,*" or "*slave of Jesus living in Mary.*"[23]

3. Doctrine

a. The significance of the term. In considering the Slavery of Love within the context of Montfort's writings, we should note that in them the saint explained that his relationship with Christ and Mary took various forms.

In LEW, he did not consider Holy Slavery in itself, as Boudon did, but, rather, as a description or a quality of the Consecration: "*Consecrating ourselves entirely to her [Mary] and to Jesus through her as their slaves. It involves consecrating to her completely and for all eternity our body and soul*" (LEW 219). Montfort views the Consecration in a Wisdom perspective: it is "*the greatest means of all . . . for obtaining and preserving divine Wisdom*" (LEW 203). Here Montfort acknowledges his debt to his predecessors, to whom he refers the reader explicitly: "*There are several books treating of this devotion*" (LEW 219).

The words "*in the manner of a slave*" also occur in SM 28, 32, but always within the context of surrender or Consecration: "*Happy the person who . . . consecrates himself entirely to Jesus through Mary as their slave*" (SM 34). The larger perspective in which the total gift of self is placed is that of holiness (SM 3-22). Montfort regards the Consecration as a "*secret*" that he has not found in "*any book, ancient or modern*" (SM 1).

In the central part of TD (120-134), Montfort becomes more clearly aware than ever of the novelty of the devotion that he recommends: "*I have never known or heard of any devotion to Our Lady which is comparable to the one I am going to speak of*" (TD 118). He calls this devotion "*the perfect consecration to Jesus Christ,*" which was the authentic title of the manuscript and which he had written in large letters as a heading before what is now TD 120.

The explanation that he gives does not mention the Slavery of Love. He does not reject it, since he mentions it again in the same central section when he speaks of the Council of Trent "*exhorting the faithful to remember and to hold fast to the belief that they are bound and consecrated as slaves to Jesus*" (TD 129). When he explains the essential part of the Consecration, however, Montfort does not mention the Holy Slavery explicitly.

This is even more noticeable in CG, a printed statement which Montfort had his people sign at the close of the parish mission. The central part of the formula used in the Covenant gives only the bare bones: "*I give myself entirely to Jesus Christ by the hands of Mary to carry my cross after him all the days of my life.*" It is clear that in his desire for inculturation with ordinary people, Montfort used the sort of language they could easily understand: he has replaced the Holy Slavery and even the total Consecration with complete surrender, and Wisdom with Jesus Christ and the Cross. He also left out the titles of Mother and Mistress given to Mary, and the list of possessions surrendered to her. In his hymns Montfort does not refer to the Holy Slavery, except in Hymn 77, which he entitled "*The devout slave of Jesus in Mary.*" Similarly, in his letters, he frequently signs himself "*unworthy slave of Jesus in Mary*" from 1700 to 1702, but then he omits the word "slave," except in L 20 (August 28, 1704). This less frequent use seems to indicate the relative significance of the word and its declining importance, which is consonant with his life in its last twelve years.[24] After these preliminary reflections, we can now consider the thought of Montfort on slavery.

St. Louis Marie distinguishes between three types of slavery: (i) natural slavery, and all creatures are slaves of God in this sense, as He is their Creator and Master; (ii) enforced slavery, which includes the devils and the damned; (iii) voluntary slavery, "*the slavery of love and free choice, the kind chosen by one who consecrates himself to God through Mary, and this is the most perfect way for us human beings to give ourselves to God, our Creator*" (SM 32). God is the God of the heart.

Along with Boudon (cf. TD 71), Montfort makes a clear-cut distinction between a servant, who remains his own master, and a slave, who is the property of his master. Only through the slavery of free will can anyone belong entirely to Jesus Christ and his Mother (TD 71, 72).

In TD, Montfort explains several ways of expressing our belonging. His own usual and favorite way is Christ-centered:[25] "*slave of Jesus in Mary*" (TD 244-245). The advantages he sees in it are: (i) "*We avoid giving pretext for criticism*"; we describe the devotion by stressing its ultimate end, Jesus Christ, rather than Mary, who is the means to this end; however, "*we can very well use either term without any scruple, as I myself do.*" (ii) It fits in better with the mystery of the Incarnation: we say we are "*slaves of Jesus . . . dwelling and reigning in Mary,*" according to the beautiful prayer "O Jesus, living in Mary." It is the mystery that this devotion honors: "*It is the first mystery of Jesus Christ; it is the most hidden, and it is the most exalted. . . . In this mystery Jesus in the womb of Mary and with her cooperation, chose all the elect . . . anticipated all subsequent mysteries of his life by his willing acceptance of them*" (TD 244-247).

b. Scriptural foundation. The devotion practiced by the Ursuline nuns at Alcala de Henares was inspired by Scripture, and St. Louis Marie's also was based on Scripture. The Slavery of Love consists in following the example of Christ and Mary. Jesus took the form of a slave (Phil 2:7) "*out of love.*" Mary "*called herself the handmaid or slave of the Lord*" (TD 72). St. Louis Marie reminds us that St. Paul considered it an honor to be called "*slave of Christ,*" and several times in Scripture the Christians are referred to as "*slaves of Christ*" (TD 72). Jesus is our model, and he points to us the ways of God, the Father's secret, Mary. "*Our good Master stooped to enclose himself in the womb of the Blessed Virgin, a captive but loving slave, and to make himself subject to her for thirty years*"(TD 139). This conduct of Divine Wisdom is beyond human comprehension. "*Consumed with the desire to give glory to God, his Father, and save the human race, he saw no better or shorter way to do so than by submitting completely to Mary. What better and shorter way of giving God glory than by submitting ourselves to Mary as Jesus did*" (TD 139)? Such is the example given by the three Divine Persons: through Mary the Father gives his Son and every grace; through Mary the Son was formed and is formed in us all; through Mary the Holy Spirit formed Christ and forms him in us. "*With such a compelling example . . . we would be extremely perverse to ignore her and not consecrate ourselves to her. We would be blind if we did not see the need for Mary in approaching God and making our total offering to him*" (TD 140).

c. Liturgical foundation: Baptism. The missionary wanted the faithful to make a "*perfect renewal of the vows and promises of holy baptism*" (TD 120, 126). "*Before baptism every Christian was a slave of the devil because he belonged to him*" (TD 126). Through Baptism he is set free and "*chooses Jesus as his Master and sovereign Lord and undertakes to depend upon him as a slave of love*" (TD 126). These are the words of the Catechism of the Council of Trent; we have to "devote and consecrate ourselves for ever to our Redeemer and Lord as slaves (*non secus ac mancipia*)" (cf. TD 129). This dependence is professed perfectly when "*we give ourselves to Jesus Christ through the hands of Mary*" (TD 126).

d. Spiritual deepening. For St. Louis Marie "*the slavery of love and free choice . . . is the most perfect way for us human beings to give ourselves to God our Creator*" (SM 32). This involves "*the most radical and complete*" dependence,[26] which is born of love, leads to love (TD 75-76, 113, 126), and ends with the freedom of the children of God (SM 41; TD 169-170, 215). As A. Lhoumeau explains, "It is not a question of a double belonging, to God and Jesus on the one hand, and to the Blessed Virgin on the other; belonging to Mary is the continuation and the consequence of belonging to Jesus and the means of achieving it: '*Depending on her care / The better to depend / On Jesus*'" (H 77:8).[27] Stating that we are slaves of Jesus through Mary is not enough, however, and we have to live through Mary, with Mary, in Mary, and for Mary, in order to live more perfectly through Jesus, with Jesus, in Jesus, and for Jesus (cf. TD 257ff.). On what grounds does Mary accept us as her slaves? First of all, because we are slaves of Jesus. Montfort gives the following theological explanation: "*What I say in an absolute sense of Jesus Christ, I say in a relative sense of the Blessed Virgin.*" Christ chose her as his "*inseparable associate in his life, death, glory and power in heaven and on earth*"; "*he has given her by grace in his kingdom all the same rights and privileges that he possesses by nature*"; so, "*they have the same subjects, servants and slaves*" (TD 74). Besides, Mary is acknowledged as "*Queen and Sovereign of heaven and earth.*" But Mary is only the means, not the ultimate end. Every Christian spirituality warns its followers of the difficulty of renouncing sin and of making the uphill journey to holiness (cf. TD 78ff.). Through the Slavery of Love we surrender our whole being and life to Mary, thus enabling her to give us a share of her dispositions, to unite us perfectly with Jesus and to form him more fully in us. The Marian way is an easy, short, perfect, secure way.

e. Liberation. The Slavery of Love is a new Beatitude, as it were. "*Happy, very happy indeed, will the generous person be who, prompted by love, consecrates himself entirely to Jesus through Mary as their slave, after having shaken off by baptism the tyrannical slavery of the devil*" (SM 34). The Slavery of Love makes us free: "*Since we lower ourselves willingly to a state of slavery out of love for Mary, our dear Mother, she out of gratitude opens wide our hearts enabling us to walk with giant strides in the way of God's commandments*" (SM 41).

f. The small chains. Iron chains are "*ignoble*" in the eyes of the world, but they are "*glorious*" when worn as "*the chains of Jesus Christ, because by them Christians are liberated and kept free from the shackles of sin and the devil*" (cf. Rom 6:22). "*Thus set free we are bound to Jesus and Mary . . . by charity and love as children are to their parents*" (TD 237). Father de Montfort is fond of quoting Hosea 11:4: "I led them with bands [Montfort uses 'chains'] of love" (cf. TD 237). "Love is strong as death" (Song 8:6). Death will destroy our bodies, "*but the chains of our slavery, being of metal, will not easily corrupt . . . and will be transformed into chains of light and splendor*" (TD 237). The small chains are a constant reminder of our baptismal promises and of their renewal. We ought to realize how much St. Louis Marie was aware of the importance of external signs and symbols; he demonstrated this when he died wearing his small chains and holding his crucifix and a small statue of Our Lady. In his opinion, too many Christians are forgetful of their baptismal vows and neglect wearing external signs reminding them of their vows (TD 238).

III. Holy Slavery Today

In Spain between 1877 and 1956, several religious foundations included the word "slaves" in their name (e.g.,

Slaves of the Sacred Heart, of the Heart of Jesùs [or of the Eucharist] of the Immaculate Heart of Mary, of Christ the King).[28] A major development took place in Poland. It occured on May 3, 1966, at the Shrine of Our Lady at Czestochowa, on the occasion of the thousandth anniversary of the evangelization of Poland. Cardinal Wyszynski addressed a prayer to God the Father, and then consecrated the whole nation to Mary, Queen of Poland, according to the devotion of Holy Slavery, for the service of the Church: "*We, the baptized children of God born in Poland and all those whom our country defends, place ourselves under your eternal and maternal yoke that the freedom of the Church may prevail throughout the world and in our native land and that the Kingdom of God may be established on earth.*"[2]

1. The fullness of freedom

John Paul II renewed the Consecration on June 4, 1979, and explained its paradoxical significance. In essence, those who love God want to belong to Him. Now, "the fact of 'not being free' in love is not perceived as slavery but as an affirmation of freedom and its realization. The act of Consecration as slaves therefore indicates a singular dependence and a boundless confidence. In this sense, slavery (lack of freedom) expresses the fullness of freedom."[30]

2. The essential

St. Maximilian Kolbe has tackled the language problem that arises when trying to describe a perfect spiritual relationship with Mary. "All try to emphasize the most perfect form of Consecration possible, even though their words and their immediate meaning show some difference. Thus, the expressions 'servant of Mary,' 'servant of the Immaculate,' may suggest an idea of renunciation in acknowledgement of the servants' work. The expression 'son of Mary' may suggest the legal obligations of a mother towards her son. Even the expression 'slave of love' is not universally accepted; although the stress is on love, the idea lingers in the mind that a slave only remains such against his will. Some prefer 'thing and possession.' Obviously, all these expressions and any other possible ones eventually point to the same reality: all those using them want to consecrate themselves completely to the Blessed Virgin."[31] This shows that Kolbe was aware of the language problem.

In times past, several writers have placed great emphasis on the word "slavery" as used by Montfort because it expresses his thought accurately and undeniably suggests the idea of our dependence on God. "The term 'slavery' is accurate and in accordance with the language of the tradition."[32]

As the word "slavery" was rejected in certain circles, other writers suggested that it be no longer used. They argued that instead of evoking "an attitude of willing dependence that prompted a renunciation of all things out of love for Jesus and Mary," it suggests the unjust and unnatural condition of a master with the unrestricted right to use his slave. "As a result," they asked, "Is it advisable to tell modern readers that whenever they come across the word in Montfort's writings, they should engage in the complicated process of substituting an inappropriate meaning for the literal one?'"[33]

In between are the middle-of-the-road writers like A. Josselin, a past superior general of the Company of Mary, who wrote in 1959: "I am not talking about the use but rather the abuse of such terms as 'slavery' and 'slave.'" He added: "Although quite accurate, the terms do stir up unpleasant memories in some countries, and there is nothing we can do about this. We have to allow for historical events and not use the terms unthinkingly. Other words could be used that imply the same thing, 'complete surrender,' 'Consecration,' 'belonging,' 'total dependence,' etc. Perhaps we could use them in circumstances where we are aware that 'slave' and 'slavery' may sound offensive."[34]

In our opinion, using various expressions to refer to the Consecration to Jesus through Mary is best because it shows an awareness of the limits of any language to express fully the realities of life. Besides, Montfort himself used a variety of words and expressions, such as "*the most perfect devotion*" (LEW 219), "*consecration*" (LEW 219; TD 120, 231), "*slavery*" (LEW 226; SM 32; TD 244-245), "*placing everything in Mary's hands*" (LEW 221-222; SM 31), "*offering*" (LEW 222; TD 121, 124), "*giving*" (LEW 222, 225; SM 28-31; CG; TD 120, 126), "*entrusting*" (SM 40; TD 179), "*belonging entirely*" or "*totus tuus*" (TD 179, 216, 266; SM 66). John Paul II accepts the various terms, but he seems to prefer *affidamento* ("commitment, entrustment") and "Consecration." He also emphasizes that we should welcome Mary into our human and Christian *"I"* (RMat 45). He points out that a person fulfills himself through self-giving in love; the montfort Consecration is meant to be a giving of self out of the most personal and complete love.

T. Koehler

Notes: (1) Le Crom, *Esclavage (dans la spiritualité chrétienne) (Slavery [in Christian Spirituality]),* in *Catholicisme,* 4:421-424; Ch. Verlinden, *Slavery (History of),* in *New Catholic Encyclopedia,* 283-285; ibid. *L'origine de sclavus, esclave, (The Origin of "Sclavus," Slave),* in *Archivium Latinitatis Medii Aevi,* 17, 97-128. (2) Th. Koehler, *Servitude (Saint Esclavage) (Servitude [Holy Slavery]),* in DSAM, 14:731; cf. P. Gaffney, *The Holy Slavery of Love* in J.B. Carol (ed.), *Mariology* vol. 3, Bruce. Milwaukee, 1961, 143-149. (3) *Hymn. 13 de Nativ.* 4.13, SC 110, p. 146. (4) Sermon 195.2., PL 39:2108. Cf. H. Barré, *Prières anciennes de l'Occident à la Mère du Sauveur (Ancient Western Prayers to the Mother of the Savior),* Paris 1963, 22. (5) *Oracional Visigotico* (*Visigoth Prayer Book*), Barcelona

1946, 75. (6) *Serm. 75* (on Saint Joseph), in *Obras (Works)*, BAC, II, Madrid 1953. (7) Melchor de Cetina, *Exhortación*, BAC 46, in *Misticos Francescanos Espanoles (Spanish Franciscan Mystics)*, ed. J.B. Gomis, Madrid 1949, 805-809. Cf. J. Ordonez Marquez, *La Cofradia de la esclavitud en las Concepcionistas de Alcala* (*The Slavery Confraternity among the Conceptionists of Alcala)*, in EstMar 51 (1986), 234. (8) Pedro de la Serna, *Estatutos y Constituciones que han de guardar los Esclavos de Nuestra Senora de la Merced, (Statutes and Constituions to be Observed by the Slaves of Our Lady of Mercy)*, Seville 1615; cf. L. Aquatias, *Piedad mariana en la Orden . . . de la Merced (Marian Piety in the Order . . . of Mercy*), in *Alma Socia Christi*, vol. 7, Rome 1952, 491-582. (9) Cf. DSAM 14:735-737. (10) *Regla y Constiotuciones Generales de las monjas franciscanas de la Orden de la Immaculada Concepcion de la Bienaventurada Virgen Maria (Rule and General Constitutions of the Franciscan Nuns of the Order of the Immaculate Conception of the Blessed Virgin Mary)*, ed. Burgos, 1975, chap. 2, n. 5, p. 17 and chap. 2, n. 2, p. 16. (11) Juan de los Angeles, *Cofradia y devocion de las esclavas y esclavos de Nuestra Senora la Virgen Santisima* (*Confraternity and Devotion of the Slaves of the Most Blessed Virgin*), BAC III, 46, *Misticos Francescanos Espanoles*, 691-698. (12) *Oeuvres . . . de Bérulle*, Migne, 625-630. (13) Ibid., 377-378. (14) Ibid., 618. (15) *Oeuvres*, Migne, 2:370-371. (16) Ibid., 377-378. (17) Ibid., 583-586. (18) The advice he gives is that "*if the chains are not made of iron, they should be made of some other metal for the sake of convenience*" (ibid.) (19) Grandet, 315. (20) Ibid., 439. (21) Le Crom, *Esclavage*, 374. (22) According to E. Villaret, *Marie et la Compagnie de Jésus,(Mary and the Company of Jesus)*, in *Maria. Etudes sur la Sainte Vierge (Mary:Studies on the Blessed Virgin)*, ed. du Manoir, Beauchesne, Paris 1952, 2:961, Montfort became acquainted with the Slavery of Love while attending the Jesuit college at Rennes. De Fiores agrees that the Slavery of Love was promoted by the Jesuits Jégou and Nepveu at the college in Rennes, but he does not think that Louis Grignion embraced it then. Blain's silence on the subject suggests that Montfort discovered the Slavery of Love at Saint-Sulpice when he read Boudon (*Itinerario*, 70-71). (23) R. Laurentin, *Dieu seul est ma tendresse (God Alone Is My Tenderness)*, Paris 1984, 196, analyzes the signatures and finds that *"God alone"* becomes more frequent. (24) Ibid., 48. (25) R. Laurentin shows "how Montfort corrected the expression 'Consecration to Mary' by relating the Consecration to Christ." Whereas his predecessors, Sister Ines-Bautista, Los Rios, Fenicki, Boudon, etc., commonly said "*the slavery of the Mother of God*," Montfort prefers the expression "*slave*" or "*slavery of Jesus in Mary*" (L 5, 6, 8-12, 20; LPM 6; TD 236-237, 244-245, 252), or "*consecration to Jesus through Mary as slaves of love*" (SM 34, 44, 61; LEW 219; TD 231). It must be admitted that Montfort frequently speaks of Holy Slavery with reference to Jesus as well as to Mary: TD 56, 68, 72-77, 113, 135, etc. (26) A. Lhoumeau, *La vie spirituelle à l'école de saint Louis-Marie Grignion de Montfort (The Spiritual Life at the School of Saint Louis Marie Grignion de Montfort)*, Beyaert, Bruges 1954, 99. (27) Ibid., 96. For his part, A. Bossard perceives the dynamic of the Consecration as follows: "The Consecration recommended by Montfort involves only one movement towards Christ. . . . But the movement implies two distinct relationships: one with Mary, the 'perfect means,' and the other with Christ, 'our ultimate end.'" *Se consacrer à Marie* (*To Consecrate Oneself to Mary*), in CM 28, no. 137 (1983), 101-102. (28) Cf. *Dicc. de Hist. ecl. de Esp.*, 2:806-808. (29) M. Zalecki, *Notre-Dame de Czestochowa*, DDB, Paris 1981, 98-99. (30) *Documentation Catholique* 76 (1979), 615. (31) St. Maximilian Kolbe, *Gli scritti (The Writings)*, Italian translation, Firenze 1978, vol. 3, no. 1329, p. 776. See further references in the index on p. 1051, under *consacrazione illimitata.* (32) Ibid., 127. M. Th. Poupon, *Le poème de la parfaite consécration à Marie (The Poem of the Perfect Consecration to Mary)*, Librairie du Sacré-Coeur, Lyon 1947, 337, states that "those trying to do away with the term . . . water down the spirituality of the holy poet and even change its nature." (33) R. Graber, *La donation totale à Jésus par Marie (The Total donation to Jesus through Mary)*, taken from the preface to the German edition of *Le Livre d'Or (The Golden Book)* (1960), in DMon 8 no. 32 (1963), 12. (34) A. Josselin, *Vraie Dévotion, âme de notre ministère* (*True Deovtion, Soul of Our Ministry*), at International Montfort Marian Meeting, Rotselaar, July 26-August 4, 1956, in *Acts of the Rotselaar Meeting*, Generalate of the Company of Mary, Rome 1956, 14.

TENDERNESS

SUMMARY

I. TENDERNESS IN THE LIFE OF MONTFORT:
  1. A violent person with tender gestures;
  2. Tenderness as an apostolic strategy.

II. THE WRITINGS OF MONTFORT ON TENDERNESS;
  1. In keeping with his time;
  2. The place of tenderness in the works of Montfort:
    a. The tenderness of Wisdom;
    b. The tenderness of Mary.

III. FOR A SPIRITUALITY OF TENDERNESS.

I. TENDERNESS IN THE LIFE OF MONTFORT

To speak of the tenderness and gentleness of Saint Louis de Montfort may astound some people, since he thought of himself as the most terrible man of his century. The life of this missionary was a harsh conquest of himself, a continual struggle to transform himself into the image of Christ, *"in order to be humble and gentle / and to walk in his footsteps"* (H 9:27). It is surprising to note the important place given to tenderness in the first as well as the last writings of Louis de Montfort. This man, called at times excessive, violent, and quick tempered, has left us "a secret" through his writings on the tenderness of Jesus and of Mary. His tenderness and gentleness give us pause in the midst of a world of violence, war, and aggression.

1. A violent person with tender gestures

Born of a quick-tempered father and a patient mother for whom he had a particular affection, Montfort was endowed with a strong and vigorous constitution. The first of his gestures that his biographers record are, nevertheless, stamped with tenderness. As a child, he consoled and encouraged his mother to endure her sufferings patiently.[1] Grandet recounts this same affectionate concern toward his favorite sister, Guyonne-Jeanne. Although Montfort had a tendency toward anger, Blain insists on "his great tenderness and docility." As an adolescent, he distinguished himself by novel and radical manifestations of compassion towards the poor. Whether at Rennes, at Cesson, at Paris, or at Poitiers, this young man with a fearsome temperament loved the neglected with tenderness and an excessive and passionate affection. His friend Blain once even came upon him as he embraced and washed the feet of a poor person.

The temperament of Montfort underwent severe trials. His directors at Saint-Sulpice, particularly Leschassier and Brenier, made him undergo deeply felt humiliations:

"He approached his persecutor in a joyful manner as though to thank him, and he spoke candidly to him as though he had been flattered."[2] The tenderness of this young man, who was naturally violent, could be called heroic. It seems that by the end of his seminary training, "he learned that striving for evangelical meekness must become one of the pillars of his personal commitment to sanctity."[3] He joyfully sang: *"A saint is entirely affable, / tender, courteous, charming, / kindly, agreeable, / without any sign of anger"* (H 9:17).

Even in his worst trials, as in the destruction of the Calvary of Pontchateau, he tried to maintain a semblance of tenderness. It had become for him a road to sanctity: "This peace," assured Father de Préfontaine, "this tranquility, this evenness of disposition from which he did not swerve during eight days astounded me. . . . This patience . . . , the serenity, the joy itself which appeared on his face despite a shock so crushing for him, made me regard him as a saint."[4]

During his whole life, Montfort made unheard of efforts to conquer his impulses. Des Bastières did not hesitate to compare him to St. Francis de Sales: "That is the character of Father de Montfort . . . he made unbelievable efforts to overcome his natural impetuosity; he came to terms with himself and acquired a charming virtue of tenderness."[5]

This long journey, this laborious work on himself, transformed his personal relationships: "Bearing in mind what he himself was and what the mentality of his time was, his evolution seems to be a human success, a great success."[6]

This did not keep him from making, till the time of his death, what appear to us to be hasty and odd remarks, and from performing extreme (from today's point of view) penances. But his experience among the poor, the sinners, and the little ones made him ever more human and more capable of understanding others and of sharing in their sufferings and their weaknesses. In this harsh combat waged against himself, a new man appeared: his explosive reactions became rarer, and he became more and more open and receptive. His trials made him gentler and more compassionate. His gentle features were transformed into features of goodness which today could be called humane. A letter of Madame d'Oriou, whom he knew toward the end of his life, bears witness to this long maturation: "He took everything happily, and conveyed to me, joyfully, very gentle moral principles . . . I never found in him any scrupulosity, either for himself or for others. He had only what every true Christian ought to have, and always: great tenderness. Although he was born with a very quick temperament, he was always master of himself in everything."[7]

At the time that he met with Marie Louise Trichet to confirm her as Superior of the Daughters of Wisdom, it was to tenderness that he exhorted her: *"You must be very firm, but tenderness should prevail over the rest."* Besnard attests that Marie Louise gave much attention to and showed great affection toward all her daughters, as Montfort had recommended: "It was through her tenderness that she was able to support for more than forty years, the various moods of so many of her daughters. She sought them out, spoke to them with a goodness and tenderness that disarmed them . . . . It had to be without a doubt, that Sister Marie of Jesus acquired a great control over herself and a heroic tenderness so as to maintain, in the midst of so many contradictions, her peace of soul and her equanimity of behavior which were manifested in her whole being."[8]

2. Tenderness as an apostolic strategy

At the hospital at Poitiers, where he lived as one of the poor, we can see that Montfort "had a special gift for accommodating the poor without approving of their conduct: *"I tell them frankly, though gently, their faults which are, drunkenness, quarreling, and scandalous behavior.*" (L 11). "To reproach with zeal and tenderness" those who offended God were the main concerns of Montfort, who preached ceaslessly the mercy of God (which did not always please the bishops or certain Jansenist priests). According to Father de Préfontaine, he had a gift and an extraordinary grace to win hearts.

His tenderness toward sinners did not hinder his apostolic daring, which sometimes incited him to rather violent actions at the time of his missions. At Roussay, he broke open the doors of a tavern, overturned the tables, and led the people to the Church; at La Rochelle, he dared to break into houses of prostitution, and from the pulpit he would thunder against blasphemers, swearers, and those who sang wicked songs. Father des Bastières maintains, nevertheless, that in these missions, he was both tender and firm. This is also the picture that Montfort portrays of himself: *"I support mightily / the weak person close to falling, / I take him back gently, / without fear that he will persecute me, / but to stop sin, / I will be very firm"* (H 38:124)

It is in the confessional that he seems to practice best a tenderness marked with firmness: *"I would prefer to suffer in purgatory for having had too much tenderness toward my penitents, than to have treated them with hopeless severity."*[9] His gestures of tenderness toward the poor and sinners, his sermons, which touched the hearts of his audience, led the crowds to call him "The good Father from Montfort." This man, capable of a violent temper, was sincerely moved by a repentant lay brother who had harmed him: "he received him with angelic tenderness, and addressed him in such a touching way that the poor young man, having admitted his fault, cried bitterly."[10]

For Montfort, the difficulties, the attacks on his missions were occasions to delight in the love of God for him: *"Both men and demons in this great city of Paris are waging war against me, a war that I find sweet and welcome. Let them slander me, destroy my good name, put me in prison, these are precious gifts, tasty morsels, great and wonderful things."* (L 16) He revealed the secret of Wisdom and sanctity in his missions and in the confessional by his gestures, his words, and his writings. If he preached tenderness it is because he was convinced that his action had an influence on hearts: conversion is at the center of the mission of Montfort, who spares nothing so that the penitent can turn to God. The hymns he composed on the tenderness of Jesus often included reference to the tenderness and mercy of God toward sinners; it was evident that he wanted to put into practice what he wrote: *"But how describe the tenderness of Jesus in his dealings with poor sinners: his tenderness with Mary Magdalene, his courteous solicitude in turning the Samaritan woman from her evil ways, his compassion in pardoning the adulterous woman taken in adultery, his charity in sitting down to eat with public sinners in order to win them over?"* (LEW 125).

This apostolic strategy he passed onto Marie Louise. Besnard has described her practices of tenderness: "It was by her tenderness that she gained the confidence of the poor and the sick in all the hospitals where she resided and they looked upon her as their mother."[11]

II. The Writings of Montfort on Tenderness

It is surprising to note how often the theme of tenderness appears in the works of Montfort. What interests Montfort is not so much the virtue of tenderness as the tenderness of God, of Wisdom, and of Mary. There are no systematic exhortations on tenderness, but instead long contemplations of God, which resulted in TD, LEW Hymn 9, and his sermon on "The Love and Tenderness of Jesus." (LS, 1st part, 80-40).

1. In keeping with his time

During his years of study at Rennes and more so at Paris, he read all the spiritual writers of his time, including Olier, Bérulle, Nouet, Saint-Jure, and Surin. With these authors tenderness was very important. In a century when the image of a distant, all-powerful, and majestic God was stressed, it is surprising to find tenderness come forward as an outstanding virtue, one that encompasses all the others: "The virtue of tenderness is the summation of Christianity, for it presupposes, in itself, the destruction of all self interest as was done by Jesus Christ."[12]

Father Saint-Jure and Father Nouet, whose works[13] had a profound and noticeable influence on Montfort, strongly insisted on the acquisition of goodness and graciousness: "Tenderness is a characteristic of saints and sign of predestination."[14] Bérulle, who had a strong influence on the spirituality of his time through his preaching on devotion to the mysteries of the infancy of Jesus, had also written a chapter on goodness. For him, one had to be aware of Jesus Christ and pay heed to his humility, his charity, and his goodness: one had to "open one's heart to them, so as to be marked by them . . . His tenderness tends to make us tender."[15]

Among the authors Montfort consulted, tenderness was defined as docility, meekness, or a filial abandonment to the will of God and a conquering of aggressive tendencies. The spirituality of the seventeenth century considered tenderness as a private virtue that invites one to imitate a God who became incarnate, made

Himself a little one, and worked to win hearts by His tenderness. This virtue was interpreted by spiritual writers as a demanding love for one's neighbor, and supposed a total renouncement of self: "This tenderness is but a participation in that of God. It is an essential tenderness and when it renders the soul a participant, it is so fundamental to the soul that there is no longer anything of the body or the soul . . . to the extent that all that transpires is accomplished in tenderness."[16]

2. The place of tenderness in the work of Montfort

Like his spiritual masters, Montfort dared to suppose the nearness of the All-Holy God and insisted on the tenderness of Wisdom and of Mary. It is from the aspect of tenderness that he presents all the mystery of a God who became incarnate through love. If Chapters X and XI of "The Love of the Eternal Wisdom" go into long detail about *"the charming beauty and ineffable tenderness of Incarnate Wisdom,"* the first chapters of this treatise speak of the tenderness of Eternal Wisdom who is of himself tender, approachable, and winning (LEW 5). For Montfort there is nothing so tender as Wisdom (LEW 53), whom he calls *"tender conqueror"* (LEW 5).

a. The tenderness of Wisdom. There are almost fifty occurrences of the terms "tenderness," "meekness" in LEW. The chapters on tenderness in LEW were largely inspired by the writings of Father Nouet, which Montfort had summarized during his years of study. In "The Man of Prayer," Nouet develops the charms and tenderness of Jesus.[17] It is to Wisdom that Montfort attributes this virtue; not only to Incarnate Wisdom, but also to Eternal Wisdom. Contrary to Nouet, Montfort connected beauty to the tenderness of Incarnate Wisdom (cf. GA pp. 562-566). Although inspired by Nouet and Saint-Jure, Montfort had his own logical outline and describes the tenderness of Wisdom in eternity, before his incarnation, at the time of his incarnation, during his life on earth, and in his glorious life: *"Wisdom was born of the tenderest, the gentlest, and the most beautiful of all mothers . . . because he is Eternal Wisdom, tenderness and beauty itself"* (LEW 118); *"There came from his eyes and his countenance a ray of beauty so tender"* (LEW 121). The combinations of tenderness and beauty, tenderness and gentleness, and tenderness and love are often inseparable when Montfort speaks of Mary or of Wisdom. The tenderness of Wisdom is subordinate to his love, so humanity may love God and allow itself to be drawn to him: *"With this knowledge of Eternal Wisdom, shall we not love him who has loved us and still loves us more than his own life; and whose beauty and tenderness surpass all that is loveliest and most attractive in heaven and on earth?"* (LEW 131).

In his "Sermon" (LS pp. 32–35; cf. GA pp. 562-566) it is with love that tenderness is closely associated: *"Of the love and of the tenderness of Jesus."* On the other hand, the outline is practically the same as in the tenth and eleventh chapters of LEW. Hymn 9 takes up this contemplation of the tenderness of Jesus in his exterior, his childhood, and his conduct and adds that the Christian should practice this tenderness according to the example of the saints. For Montfort, tenderness is the most excellent quality of the heart. It is through tenderness that one wins the heart of God, the heart of one's neighbor, and the hearts of sinners. In this same Hymn, one can find the themes that inspire Montfort to practice tenderness, including the desire to imitate Jesus in his tenderness: *"I am, in my behavior / rough as a bull; / make me in following him / as gentle as a lamb"* (H 9:28); *"I am full of anger / pardon me, Lord"* (H 9:27); *"When someone angers you / suffer all gently. . . . Tenderness has, in itself / a secret power / Which makes for all a rule / a perfect peace"* (H 9:24).

In Hymn 41, when Father de Montfort sings of the loving excess of the heart of Jesus, he teaches that tenderness is the fruit of love, which prescribes a most gentle behavior. Here charity and tenderness merge: *"How tender and approachable is his heart. / He speaks with little children; / how courteous and charitable he is / How exalted is his appearance!"* (H 41:14); *"With what poise and wisdom / This heart full of goodness / wins over the sinner / It is a miracle of charity"* (H 41:18). In imitation of Divine Wisdom, the *"wise man should be graciously firm and firmly gracious"* (LEW 53).

The whole life of Christ is viewed in the light of tenderness in LEW in the "Sermon," and in Hymn 9.

The frequent references by Montfort to the tenderness of the heart of God and of the heart of Jesus lead us to believe they are not the simple reflections of youth, much less the manifestations of an unbalanced person who transfers his feminine fantasies to God. The notion of tenderness occurs constantly in the work of Montfort. It developed, however, as he contemplated Christ in his mysteries and in his hidden and public life. And he considers the Cross of Christ as the ultimate tenderness: *"I am content and happy in all my troubles, and I do not believe there is anything in the world sweeter for me than the bitterest cross when it is steeped in the blood of Jesus crucified"* (L 26).

b. The Tenderness of Mary. If, as J. B. Blain points out, the love of Mary was inborn in Louis Grignon, it was equally manifested by a most tender piety toward his *"beloved Mother,"* his *"good and dear Mother,"* as he liked to call her. His affectionate relationship with Mary is evidenced in a language both mystical and realistic: *"The Blessed Virgin, mother of tenderness and mercy, never allows herself to be surpassed in love and generosity. When she sees someone giving himself entirely to her in order to honor and serve her . . . she gives herself completely in a wondrous manner to him"* (TD 144).

Montfort also portrays in affectionate language the conduct that should mark a true devotee of Mary: *"they rely on her mercy and kindness to obtain forgiveness for their sins through her intercession and to experience her motherly comfort in their troubles and anxieties"* (TD 199).

Montfort understood that God comes to us through Mary, He communicates Himself to us gently through her, and she leads us to Jesus with the tenderness of a mother: *"She is his mystic channel, his aqueduct, through which he causes his mercies to flow gently and abundantly"* (TD 24). The tenderness of Mary is made most explicit when Montfort speaks of Mary as one who makes the cross bearable. He attributes to Mary the precious gift of crosses: *"Mary, as Mother of the living, gives to all her children splinters of the tree of life, which is the cross of Jesus"* (SM 22). But she also sweetens the bitterness: *"This good Mother . . . dips all the crosses she prepares for them in the honey of her maternal sweetness and the unction of pure love"* (TD 154). This language conveys how intensely true devotion to Mary is stamped with tenderness and gentleness (cf. TD 107). She is like an evangelical echo of the words of Jesus: "Take my yoke upon your shoulders and learn from me, for I am gentle and humble of heart. Your souls will find rest" (Mt 11:29).

Tenderness is very often expressed in feminine and maternal images. Saint Louis de Montfort also sings without reserve of the tenderness of the Father, His goodness, His gentleness: *"He is my dearest Father, / He takes great care of me, / He holds me close to him, / He helps me in my distress. . . . /His tenderness caresses me / His grace cures me . . . God alone is my tenderness, / God alone is my support"* (H 52:8, 10, 11). *"You will look upon him as a loving Father and endeavor to please him at all times. You will speak trustfully to him as a child does to its Father."* (TD 215) The filial love full of tenderness and gentleness, which he expressed in his first work LEW, is again present in the work of his maturity, TD.

III. For a Spirituality of Tenderness

It would appear that the message of Montfort on gentleness and tenderness is quite relevant for today's world. Without locking ourselves into the flowery language of another century, we can, through an attentive reading of Montfort, rediscover the prodigious beauty of a God who makes Himself one with our humanity. In contemplating the tenderness of Wisdom and of Mary, Montfort stresses for us that the Power of God is not domination but a power of gentleness, tenderness, of humanization. The Omnipotence of God is love. If *"Wisdom is for man and man is for Wisdom"* (LEW 64), the gentleness of Wisdom should remind us of our human and divine dimension. Montfort presents the tenderness of Jesus as a secret of eternal life, a mystery of rejoicing and creativity (cf. LEW 5, 118, 119). It is from the tender Father that the Son is born in time, through the gentlest of mothers, Mary. It is through tenderness that Wisdom Incarnate draws hearts to his friendship (cf. LEW 117). In studying these montfort texts on tenderness, we are called to deepen our own faith experience in regard to God and to Mary: *"He is a gift sent by the love of the eternal Father and a product of the love of the Holy Spirit. He was given out of love and fashioned by love. . . . Jesus is eternal Wisdom and therefore pure tenderness and beauty"* (LEW 118).

In the numerous passages on the gentleness of Wisdom and of Mary, we find the Incarnation at the heart of the history of salvation, and at the heart of human experience itself: *"Behold that Eternal Wisdom who, to captivate our hearts and to take away our sins, has gathered unto his person all that is meek in God and in men, in heaven and on earth"* (LEW 119).

In the midst of conflict and division Montfort's beautiful stress on tenderness—in his life and writings—should encourage us to think of peace, and even more so to "make peace." Furthermore, the reflection of Montfort on tenderness and his efforts to reproduce it in his gestures and actions remind us that love is tenderness, beauty, wisdom, goodness, and gentleness.

Tenderness, as an evangelical quality and as a beatitude, has something to say to our afflicted world. For believers, it is an assurance of the kingdom already present: "Blessed are the gentle, they shall possess the land" (Mt 5:4). The pages of Montfort on the tenderness of Wisdom recall this text of St. James: "Who is wise and understanding among you? By his good life let him show his works in the meekness of wisdom. . . . The wisdom from above is first pure, then peaceable, gentle, open to reason, full of mercy and good fruits, without uncertainty or insincerity" (Jm 3:13, 17).

P. T. Daviau

Notes: (1) Grandet, 2. (2) Blain, 77. (3) B.Papàsogli, *Montfort, A Prophet for Our Times,* Edizioni Monfortane, Rome 1991, 132. (4) Grandet, 451. (5) Grandet, 373. (6) Perouas, 105 (7) Besnard II, 140–141. (8) Besnard, Marie Louise, 375. (9) Grandet, 376. (10) Grandet, 374. (11) Besnard, Marie Louise, 374. (12) J. J. Olier, *Introduction à la vie et aux vertus chrétiennes* (Introduction to Christian Life and Virtues), nouvelle edition (new edition), Téqui, Paris 1889, 261.-(13) J. B. Saint-Jure, *De la connaissance et de l'amour du Fils de Dieu, notre Seigneur Jésus Christ* (On the Knowledge and the Love of the Son of God, Our Lord Jesus Christ), nouvelle edition (new edition), Palmé, Paris 1873; J. Nouet, *L'homme d'oraison, ses lecture spirituelles pour toute l'année* (The Man of Prayer, His Spiritual Readings for the Entire Year), vol. 6, part 3, Périsse, Paris-Lyon 1837. (14) Nouet, *L'homme d'oraison,* 443. (15) Bérulle, *Correspondances* (Correspondence), vol 3, Dagens, Paris-Louvain 1939, 550. (16) Ibid. (17) Nouet develops the theme of tenderness over more than a hundred pages: *L'homme d'oraison,* 350–453.

TRINITY

SUMMARY

I. INTRODUCTION: SOME PROBLEMS IN APPROACHING THE TRINITY.
II. HISTORICAL BACKGROUND ON SPIRITUAL MEANING.
III. THE TRINITY IN SAINT LOUIS DE MONTFORT: GENERAL OVERVIEW.
IV. THE TRINITY IN MONTFORT AS A MYSTERY OF LOVE:
   1. The Father;
   2. The Son;
   3. The Holy Spirit;
V. RELEVANCE OF SAINT LOUIS DE MONTFORT'S TRINITARIAN DOCTRINE:
   1. Insistence on the Trinity;
   2. Experience of the Trinity;
   3. The missionary dimension;
   4. The Marian dimension;
   5. Understanding of community.

The Trinity is the most basic and at the same time the loftiest of Christian mysteries. It is most basic because it underlies and encompasses all other Christian mysteries: Creation, Incarnation, Redemption, sanctification, and the Beatific Vision. It is loftiest because it is the ultimate revelation of the inner life of God. It reveals God's inner life as divinely interpersonal: a life of mutual giving and receiving of love, a love that simultaneously overflows itself and is yet contained in its deepest intimacy. It is a life of boundless creativity, producing within itself sublime expressions of artistic beauty, a life so abundant that it overflows even the realms of divinity and shares its fecundity with creatures, imparting to each and every creature its Trinitarian reflection of love and creativity.

Saint Louis de Montfort experienced and preached the loftiness and intimacy of the mystery of the Trinity. As in the case of many great theologians and preachers before him, his own spiritual life and mystical experience were focused on the Trinity, and the Trinity provided the energy and the content of his preaching. For him the Trinity was not primarily a formula showing God as distant from us and beyond our comprehension. Rather, the doctrine of the Trinity reveals the deepest dimension of the God of love and at the same time the deepest dimension of human beings as Trinitarian images, and of all the panorama of creatures as vestiges of the Trinity.

This article will (I) address some problems in approaching the Trinity; (II) sketch some highlights in the history of Christian theology and spirituality that form a background to Montfort's own theology and spirituality of the Trinity; (III) provide an over-view of his teaching on the Trinity; (IV) study the Trinity in his writings as a mystery of love; and (V) explore the relevance his Trinitarian teaching for ministry and the spiritual life.

I. Introduction: Some Problems in Approaching the Trinity

Throughout history Christians have approached the Trinity from two major perspectives: the formulation of the doctrine and its spiritual meaning. Both are of paramount importance, for they mutually support and presuppose each other. In teaching and preaching, however, often the formulation of the doctrine has overshadowed its meaning for the spiritual life of the faithful. In fact, teaching and preaching often stop at the level of formulation without even opening the door to spiritual meaning.

Awareness of the mystery of the Trinity emerged in the early Christian communities through their contact with the person of Jesus of Nazareth as the Christ. His very person as well as his teaching and preaching revealed his relation to the Father and to the Holy Spirit. In the early Church the names of the Father, Son, and Holy Spirit appeared in prayers and in the liturgy, for example, in the baptismal formula. The Gospel of John, with its prologue and Jesus' discourse at the Last Supper, became a basic text for both a doctrine and a spirituality of the Trinity. In this emerging awareness, Christians began to perceive in the OT the symbolic foreshadowing of the Trinity, which led to later Trinitarian theologies of history.

In a struggle against the Arian heresy, the foundational Trinitarian creed was formulated at the Council of Nicea in 325. Christ as eternal Logos was declared to be of the same substance as the Father. In 381 the First Council of Constantinople added to the Nicene Creed a similar affirmation about the Holy Spirit, thus solemnly establishing the classical credal formula for belief in the mystery of the Trinity. Its importance is attested to by the fact that to this day this Creed is said at Mass.

The impact of the Nicene-Constantinople creed, as well as many other creeds, has led to an almost exclusive focus on the Trinity from the perspective of doctrinal formulas. Derivatives of this are visible in the emphasis placed on Trinitarian formulas in catechisms and in teaching and preaching the Trinity. This trend has also had an enormous influence on both historical and speculative theology, especially in the recent past. For an entire century before Vatican II, neoscholasticism focused on establishing Trinitarian formulas, either against various heresies or in refining concepts within Christian belief. Whole generations of priests were trained almost exclusively in this perspective. Although the affirmation of belief, formulated with verbal and conceptual precision, will always remain an essential element of Christianity, it needs to be supplemented, especially at the present time, by the perspective of the spiritual meaning of the doctrine of the Trinity.

II. Historical Background on Spiritual Meaning

In addition to formulating the doctrine of the Trinity, the Christian community since ancient times has explored its spiritual significance. In fact, the Trinitarian formulation in the Nicene Creed was explicitly conceived as a technical expression of a spiritual experience. Athanasius, the leading theologian at the council, began with the fact that the Christian community had an experience of being divinized. Since this experience of divinization was brought about through Christ, he argued, Christ as Logos must possess the same substance as the Father.[1]

Having arisen, then, out of a spiritual experience, the credal formula can be seen as an expression of this experience, and the creed can serve as a point of departure to evoke this experience. The problem of the Trinitarian formulas and the abstract theologies derived from them has not been due to the formulas themselves but to the split between these formulas and the spiritual experience they have expressed in the past and can continue to express today.

In the West, Augustine responded to an Arian objection that Christians, by affirming the Father, Son, and Holy Spirit, really believed in three divine substances and therefore three Gods. He answered by using the distinction between substance and relation. There was only one divine substance and the Persons were constituted by mutual relation, each sharing in the single divine substance.[2] This approach, which focused on the problem of three and one, led to the formulation of a major Trinitarian creed[3] and laid the foundation for the very abstract Trinitarian theology that flourished in the thirteenth and again in the twentieth century.

At the same time that Augustine was developing this abstract formula, he was meditating on the human soul as image of the Trinity.[4] He himself had mystically experienced the Trinity in the depths of his soul. As a consequence, for him the Trinitarian God was more intimate to him than he was to himself. It was this Trinitarian image that constituted the dignity of each human person and provided the basis for the spiritual journey that reaches its culmination in union with the Trinity.

In the twelfth century, theologians focused on the Trinity as the perfection of love. Chief among these was Richard of St. Victor, who in his treatise *On the Trinity* stated that there must be a plurality of Persons in God in order for God to share in the highest form of love. For we do not say that one possesses the perfection of love if one has love only for oneself. The perfection of love requires that love flow out of itself and into another who responds with mutual love. Finally, love reaches another level of perfection in mutual love for a third. In this perspective, human interpersonal love is a mirror of the Trinity.[5]

Bernard of Clairvaux applied to the Trinity the passionate language of the Song of Songs. Like many other interpreters, he saw in this marriage hymn from the OT a symbol of God's passionate love for the human soul and the soul's passionate love for God. In eighty-six sermons, Bernard plumbed this mystery of divine and human love, seeing the bridegroom as the Logos, the Beloved of the soul, and perceiving the bride as the symbol of the soul that has fallen deeply in love with the divine Beloved.

Bernard begins with the image of the kiss found in the first verse of the Song: "Let him kiss me with the kiss of the mouth." As Bernard proceeds, he describes a spiritual journey that begins with love, proceeds through love, and culminates in the loving union of the soul with the Beloved. It is not surprising, then, that Bernard sees the inner life of the Trinity as a life of love. "The Father," Bernard says, "loves the Son and embraces him with a special love." This love between the Father and the Son is the Holy Spirit. Therefore the bride "asks boldly to be given the kiss, that is, the Spirit in Whom the Father and the Son will reveal themselves to her."[6]

This love tradition flowed into the thirteenth century through the early Franciscan school, especially through Bonaventure, its chief theologian and spiritual writer. Inspired by Francis of Assisi, he developed the metaphysics of love into a comprehensive system based on the Trinity. In fact, in treating the Logos as the offspring of the Father, he claimed: "This is our entire metaphysics, that is, emanation, exemplarity, consummation: to be illumined by spiritual rays and led back to the Highest Reality."[7] It is important to underscore the fact that Bonaventure and others in this tradition did not abandon intellect for affectivity nor treat love merely as the practical expression of a purely speculative system. Quite the contrary: with their intellects they penetrated into the depths and dynamism of divine and human love and there found the principles for understanding all of reality.

Bonaventure focused on the fecundity of love, its inner dynamic to share with the beloved its own richness and at the same time its desire to be united with the beloved. This fecundity of love is found primarily in the Father, who is the fountain-fullness of divinity (*fontalis plenitudo*). In focusing on the Father in this way, Bonaventure situates himself in the mainstream of the Greek Fathers' approach to the Trinity. This fountain-fullness wells up in the Person of the Father and expresses itself in the generation of the Son, His perfect Image and Word, the Art of the Father, as Bonaventure calls him, following Augustine. The Son turns back to the Father in the love of union that is the Holy Spirit. This inner circle of love, as Bonaventure calls it, overflows in the outer circle of love, which is Creation. Since Creation flows from the inner life of the Trinity, it manifests the Trinity and leads back to the Trinity.[8]

In the growing awareness of divine and human love, there emerged in the twelfth and thirteenth centuries a heightened awareness of the meaning of person, both human and divine. Since the late patristic period, the person had been seen through Boethius' definition as "an individual substance of a rational nature."[9] This formulation can lead to a radical individualism. In the twelfth and thirteenth centuries, theologians balanced this perspective with that of mutual relation with another person. Developed eloquently in Richard of St. Victor, this approach reached a high point in Thomas Aquinas' definition of a divine Person as "a subsisting relation."[10]

In the twelfth century and reaching a high point in the thirteenth, there developed another aspect of love—the love of compassion—which flourished in devotion to the humanity of Christ. The self-communicating love of the Trinitarian life responded in compassion for the plight of the human race. This divine compassion expressed itself concretely in a Trinitarian way: in the Incarnation of the Son, with his suffering, death, and resurrection, along with the sending of the Holy Spirit.[11]

III. The Trinity in Saint Louis de Montfort: General Overview

It is in the light of the tradition outlined above that one must understand Montfort's Trinitarian teaching. This does not imply that he explicitly quoted these authors or made reference to them. Rather, they are the classical writers who have given expression to the Trinitarian tradition of which Montfort himself is a part. This tradition, which sees the Trinity as the mystery of the fullness of divine love, flows as a great river throughout Christian history, integrating into an organic whole doctrinal formulations, speculative theology, and mystical experience. It is in the context of this tradition, then, that we can best appreciate Montfort and the contribution that he can make to our own times.

The mystery of the Trinity is pervasive in Montfort's writings. Although love is at the center, he also presents the mystery in formulas of faith that reflect the great Trinitarian creeds. Like many classical authors before him, he often divides his work according to the Father, Son, and Holy Spirit and, further, into many patterns of three, in a way reminiscent of Bonaventure and Dante.

A summary of Trinitarian faith is found in his canticle on *"The Principal Mysteries of the Faith"* (H 109:1-2). It represents his basic teaching on the Trinity, which reflects the Trinitarian creeds and which he put into hymn format so that it could be easily sung and remembered by his people: *"Listen, Christian soul / What the faith teaches you; / In order that you retain it, / Sing devoutly: / I believe in one only God, Father exceedingly good, / The infinite Being, everywhere present, / And the all powerful Creator / Of heaven and earth.*

"In God there are three persons / Father, Son, Holy Spirit/ Three infinitely Good, / I believe it, God has said it. / Three make only one God for three have only one essence: / The Father is God, the Son is God and the Holy Spirit is God, / All equal in substance."

In SR the same thought is repeated: *"Father . . . who dost beget a Son like Thee, eternal, consubstantial with Thee, who is of the very same essence as*

Thee; . . . the Holy Spirit who is God like Thee, three persons adorable but one only God." MR Montfort suggests that when we pray the Rosary, the first Our Father should honor *"the Eternal Word, equal to his Father and who with him produces the Holy Spirit by their mutual love,"* and the third Hail Mary, *"the Holy Spirit who proceeds from the Father and the Son by way of love."*

The major works of Montfort are divided according to a Trinitarian pattern. In addition to the approximately forty times that the term "Trinity" occurs in his writings (e.g., LEW 13, 42, 208; SR 4, 11, 22; TD 5, 22, 50, 262; H 40; H 90; H 109), the centrality of the Trinitarian mystery in the life and teachings of Montfort is evident in his custom of often dividing his material into the role of the Father, and of the Son, and of the Holy Spirit. In the most theological section of TD (1-37), there are seven sets of "threes" explaining the role of each Person of the Trinity in relation to Mary: 4, 5, 6, 16, 17-21, 23-25, 29-36. In this part of TD, the saint over and over again describes Mary's union to each Person of the Trinity to illustrate her greatness: *"God the Father gave his only Son to the world only through Mary. . . . The Son of God became man for our salvation but only in Mary and through Mary. God the Holy Spirit formed Jesus Christ in Mary but only after having asked her consent; . . . God the Father gathered all the waters together and called them seas. He gathered all his graces together and called them Mary. . . . God the Son imparted to his mother all that he gained by his life and death, namely his infinite merits and his eminent virtues. . . . God the Holy Spirit entrusted his wondrous gifts to Mary, his faithful Spouse."*

IV. The Trinity in Montfort As a Mystery of Love

That the Trinity is a mystery of love can be seen in Montfort's teaching on each of the divine Persons:

1. The Father

Echoing the Greek Fathers in the East and Anselm and Bonaventure in the West, Montfort focuses on the Father as the fecund source of self-communicating love. The very term "Father" *"honors his fecundity . . . for he engenders a Son from all eternity"* (SR 41). It is *"in his womb"* that the *"only Son"* rests from all eternity (LEW 14, 19), and it is from the infinite Love who is Father that the Spirit flows (MR 16). It is clear that the Father, the First Person of the Trinity, is, then, for Montfort the *"fons totius Trinitatis."* The Father is infinitely good (H 27:1), *"loving to excess,"* as Montfort so often repeats not only of the Father but of Eternal Wisdom as well (LEW 45, 64, 108; SR 67; HD 8; H 128:6, H 158:5). It is this originating Love, this love source who is Father, that clearly distinguishes the First Person of the triune God (LEW 14, 31, 104, 107, 169, 223).

The Father is the loving source not only in the inner life of the Trinity but in the economy of salvation as well. The Father is *"the essential source"* from whom *"all perfect gifts and all graces flow"* (SM 9). He is the

Father of lights from which every good gift originates" (HD 49). The most striking insistence of Montfort about the First Person of the Most Blessed Trinity in the economy of salvation is the term "Father," found extensively throughout his writings. In his commentary on the Our Father, Saint Louis Marie writes: *"We captivate the heart of God by invoking him by the sweet name of Father"* (SR 39). He is, first of all, the Father of Our Lord Jesus Christ, who has come to us from the Father's bosom (LEW 14, 104, 107, 223; SR 72; H 81:2). In Jesus Christ, the mighty God is also our Father, for *"when we pronounce the name Father, we remember that we receive our existence from God . . . who has sent his only Son to be our Savior"* (SR 43, 46).

The primary characteristic of God the Father, Who engenders the Son from all Eternity and Who is our *"ABBA, Father"* (H 7:31), is his goodness (H 27:1), tenderness (H 13:20; H 28:24; H 52:11). As seen above, He is Love itself, and even His chastisements are proof of His infinite love for us (H 98:1). His loving care for us *"never fails"* (L 2). Since we all have the same loving Father, we are all brothers and sisters (H 148:5), and we are therefore to be apostles to each other, to love the God hidden in our neighbor, especially the poor (H 148:16; H 149:1). The expressions "loving Father," "good Father" are found on almost every page of his writings.

Montfort boldly declares that the Father, Love itself, the source and goal of all, shares with Mary His fruitfulness, inasmuch as a pure creature is capable of it, so that she may generate the eternal Son in time (TD 17). In an analogous way, Montfort sees the Father sharing life with all His children who like Mary totally open themselves to His yearning to love us.

God the Father, source and goal of all people, lovingly draws everything to Himself in Christ Jesus. Montfort's path of perfection, found in the effects of Consecration (TD 213-225), is fulfilled in the blazing light of the Father, God Alone (TD 151).

In this teaching, Montfort is giving expression to his own mystical experience of the Father, an experience that radiated through his life and writings. Although called a "fiery preacher"—for he would not hesitate to call sin by its name and to describe its horrendous repercussions—he nonetheless attracted hundreds to the confessional where he was the loving Father welcoming home the strayed. The very name given to him by the people, "the good Father from Montfort," demonstrates how intimately he "tasted" the goodness of the Father and shared it with others.

2. The Son

Out of the Father's fecundity, the Son is born. He is begotten of the Father, united in being with the Father: *"Father, thou who throughout eternity dost beget a Son like Thee, eternal, consubstantial with thee, who is of the very same essence as thee; and is of like power and goodness and wisdom as thou art"* (SR 41). *"He was given out of love and fashioned by love. He is therefore all love, or rather the very love of the Father and the Holy Spirit"*

(LEW 118; cf. LEW 9, 117-132). He is within the womb of Love itself, the Father (LEW 14, 31, 104, 107, 169, 223; SR 72; TD 6); he is the Beloved (LEW 19; FC 6; PM 23; H 65:16).

In a striking image reminiscent of the Greek Fathers, Saint Louis de Montfort describes the Son as the *"mamilla Patris," "the breast of the Father"* (LEW 10; SR 144; LCM 3): *"If only we knew the pleasure a soul tastes who knows the beauty of Wisdom, who sucks the milk of this breast of the Father, we would cry out with the Spouse: 'meliora sunt ubera tua vino: the milk of your breasts is sweeter than delicious wine and all the sweetness of creatures'"* (LEW 10).

It is not surprising that Montfort should develop the theme of Divine Wisdom as the beautiful expression of the Father, for love does not remain silent but expresses itself in beautiful words and images. This expressive aspect of love is developed in the classical Trinitarian love traditions of Augustine, Anselm, and Bonaventure. In this tradition, theologians speak of the Son as the Art of the Father, the unsurpassably beautiful expression of the Father. Montfort echoes this tradition when he writes that the Son as Eternal Wisdom is *"the substantial and eternal idea of divine beauty"* (LEW 17). *"God the Father was well pleased with the sovereign beauty of Eternal Wisdom, his Son, throughout time and eternity"* (LEW 19). Montfort's own life can be seen as a reflection of this aspect of the Trinitarian mystery. He was indeed inspired and inflamed by the creativity of the Father's artistic expressiveness, and he produced his own expression of this in preaching, composing poetry and songs, and staging productions to dramatize the message of love that was at the heart of both his preaching and his mystical experience.

The Son is the Eternal Wisdom of the Most Blessed Trinity: *"Substantial or uncreated Wisdom is the Son of God, the second person of the most Blessed Trinity. In other words, it is Eternal Wisdom in eternity or Jesus Christ in time"* (LEW 13). Again, as LEW forcefully teaches, it is love, gentleness, that characterizes Eternal Wisdom: *"[Incarnate Wisdom] is a gift sent by the love of the Eternal Father and a product of the love of the Holy Spirit* (LEW 118). Montfort considers the Eternal Wisdom the personification of Wisdom as found in the Sapiential books of the OT— "a pure emanation of the glory of the Almighty . . . the reflection of eternal light, the spotless mirror of God's majesty, the image of His goodness" (Wis 7:25-26; LEW 16)—and repeats the beginning of the Gospel of John, adding a short commentary: *"In the beginning was the Word—the Son of God, or Eternal Wisdom—and the Word was in God and the Word was God"* (Jn 1:1-2; LEW 17).

It is out of love that the Son as Wisdom becomes incarnate for us. Since the Incarnation is the central and "compendium" mystery (TD 243-248), the references to the Son of God are understandably found throughout the writings of the missionary. It is at the Annunciation that God the Son forever enters the human family, that redemption becomes a reality—by becoming truly Mary's child through virginal conception—thanks to her active and responsible consent. Jesus and Mary become "one heart" (H 40:37; TD 263, 47; H 87:9). It is in her that he continues his "dependence" on the Father—without any hint of subordinationism—inasmuch as he is constantly "being generated" by the Father (cf. H 81:2; TD 157). Moreover, this "dependence" is expressed in an analogous way in his *"dependence"* on Mary (TD 27). Finally, the Son shares his divine life with Our Lady, thereby "divinizing" her, making her *"his inseparable companion"* (TD 74; cf. H 87:6; TD 247, 63). He communicates to her his total surrender to the Father so that she, too, may be *"the slave of the Lord"* (Lk 1:38, TD 72). Jesus is "for Mary" so that she may fully be "for Jesus" (TD 225) and thereby, in the power of the Spirit, totally for the Father.

The Incarnate Son is the Son of God who reposes in the bosom of the Father from all eternity (LEW 14, 31) and in the bosom of Mary from the time of the Incarnation (LEW 233). Sent by the God of love, the Incarnate Wisdom is *"all love"* (LEW 118), so approachable and yet our awesome God. He is the highest point in the cosmos, for he is the God-man (SR 82; TD 68), the Savior of all (H 10:5), the Beloved of the Father (FC 6), the only Way, Truth, and Life (LEW 89; FC 6). The evident conclusion is that our entire life must be centered on Jesus, for it is only through the Incarnate Second Person of the Trinity that we enter the glory of the Father (TD 63, where the Christocentrism of Montfort is so strongly expressed). To turn away from the Incarnate Wisdom is to fall into the foolishness of sin, which brings about eternal damnation. Centering our life on Christ through total surrender is, then, to be "divinized," to become inheritors of eternal life. In this sense, Jesus becomes "incarnate" within us, since our entire being is molded into him (TD 219).

The life of the Eternal and Incarnate Wisdom is "for us," thereby revealing that God-Trinity is for us. He is born for us (H 58:1), dies for us (LEW 54), rises for us (H 84:3) so that we may conquer in him and through him. He awaits our petitions so that he may answer. His gift is to reconcile us with the Father. *"Wisdom is for man and man is for Wisdom"* (LEW 64).

The Son of God, the New Adam, is, then, the source of eternal life (LEW 11). For through the victorious Cross he wins for us a share in his own divine life. Montfort appears to be stunned that this mighty God, the radiance of the Father (LEW 126), is also *our* brother and *our* spouse (H 87:12). It is by taking up our cross daily and following Jesus, as Mary did, which calls for a total surrender, a constant living of our baptismal vows, a Consecration to Jesus the Incarnate and Eternal Wisdom, that we arrive at the fullness of the glory of God Alone. We must be one with Eternal and Incarnate Wisdom, thereby becoming fools for Christ's sake, so that we conquer the foolish sinfulness of the world.

This Trinitarian/Christocentricity of montfort spirituality is highly pronounced. Mary, in herself a "nothing" (TD 14), is integral to salvation history because of the Trinity's inscrutable will that she be hypothetically necessary (TD 39) in God's plan of leading all through Christ Jesus to the Father.

3. The Holy Spirit

Montfort's preaching on the Holy Spirit is so important and so pervasive in his writings that it is detailed elsewhere in this *Handbook* (cf. *God, Holy Spirit,* and *Mary*). A brief overview of the Spirit in the life of the Trinity will suffice.

Saint Louis Marie's doctrine on the inner life of the Trinity includes two central statements on the Holy Spirit. First, God the Holy Spirit, one in being with the Father and Son (H 109:2), is the infinite relationship of divine love binding Father and Son: *"The substantial love of the Father and the Son"* (TD 36); *"Father and Son, who from your mutual love produce the Holy Spirit who is God like unto you"* (SR 42); *"Glory to the Eternal Father, Glory to the Adorable Word! / The same glory to the Holy Spirit / Who by his love joins them with an ineffable bond"* (H 85:6). The Holy Spirit is also depicted as the infinite *"fire," "flame"* of love within the Trinity: *"Come Holy Spirit, God of flame"* (H 98:21); *"Come, Father of Lights / Come, God of Charity, / . . . Let there descend into my soul / a coal of your fire / which penetrates it with flame / and fills it with God"* (H 141:1).

Second, Montfort in a celebrated passage of TD 20-21 attempts to clarify the role of the Spirit within the Godhead: *"God the Holy Spirit who does not produce any divine person, became fruitful through Mary whom he espoused. . . . This does not mean that the Blessed Virgin confers on the Holy Spirit a fruitfulness which he does not already possess. Being God, he has the ability to produce just like the Father and the Son, although he does not use this power and so does not produce another divine person. But it does mean that the Holy Spirit chose to make use of Our Lady, although he had no absolute need of her, in order to become actively fruitful in producing Jesus Christ."* Saint Louis Marie repeats this teaching in PM 15: *"Holy Spirit . . . within the Trinity, none of the divine Persons is begotten by you. Outside the Trinity, you are the begetter of all the children of God. All the saints who have ever existed or will exist until the end of time, will be the outcome of your love working through Mary."*

This thought, borrowed and critically adapted from d'Argentan, makes two assertions about the Holy Spirit within the Godhead: the Spirit does have the same ability to produce like the Father and the Son, for the Spirit is of one substance with them. Here Montfort is repeating Saint Thomas Aquinas (*Summa Theologiae* I, 41, 5). The missionary also declares that the Spirit does not produce another divine Person within the Trinity, for the relationship which constitutes the

Spirit is pure reception, pure gift. The Father through the Son and with the Son is the giver, the Holy Spirit is pure recipient. Montfort is echoing and simplifying the rather awkward words of Cardinal de Bérulle: "The sterility of the Holy Spirit is a sterility that, because it flows from the fertility of God, ends in the fertility of God, i.e., in the fecundity of a Divine Person, operating outside itself. . . . It is unique to the Holy Spirit to be sterile and fertile at the same time. It is sterile in itself and fertile outside itself." [12]

Montfort has captured the mystery of the Trinity as community. This is called *perichoresis,* or, as the Latins term it, the *circuminsessio,* of the three Persons of the Trinity. Echoing Richard of St. Victor, Montfort perceived that one Person is inconceivable without the others, since they are love relationships. The Father, as pure loving self-giving, cannot exist without the Beloved and the Loving; the Spirit, the Loving uniting the Father and the Son—or the Love poured out from the Father through the Son—cannot exist without the other two Persons. We deduce, then, from Montfort's teaching on the Incarnation that the one God is the Lover (Father) and the Beloved (Son) and the Loving (Spirit). For Montfort, God is not a *solitary* God; God *is* community.

Montfort's mysticism appears to reach its most profound depth in his contemplation of the Holy Spirit's union with Mary at the Incarnation. The Spirit communicates Himself to Mary precisely as the infinite Loving Who binds together the Father and the Son, Who then takes possession of Mary for the Father and the Son. The overshadowing Spirit draws Mary—who actively and responsibly lets herself be drawn—into the intimate life of the Trinity itself. Mary herself becomes then a *"mirror of the Divinity"* (H 90:40). Living the Trinitarian life in the Holy Spirit, she is the *"paradise of the Trinity"* (H 90:58; LEW 208), sharing as a creature in the holiness of God in a manner incomprehensible, which reaches its fulfillment in her final *"fiat"* as she is assumed into heaven. The term that would summarize Montfort's profound understanding of the Spirit's relationship with Mary is *"faithful and indissoluble spouse"* (TD 85).

Moreover, Mary, whom the Spirit has espoused in order to produce Jesus Christ (TD 36), shares in a unique manner in the formation of the saints, since she is called upon to share in the formation of the Saint in whom all the saints form one Body. Since the sanctification of the greatest saints, especially those of the end times, is the work of the Holy Spirit (TD 55-58), Mary, *"the inseparable companion of the Holy Spirit in all the works of grace"* (TD 90), is integral to the Spirit's task of leading all to the fulfillment of the kingdom of God (TD 59). Therefore, the Spirit—*"the deluge of fire"* (PM 16)—renews the face of the earth together with His spouse, who is joined to him in all the works of grace by an inexplicable, eternal union.

In an analogous way, as the Spirit espouses Mary, so too with all the redeemed. In the light of Montfort's theology of the Incarnation, the espousal takes place in Mary and through Mary. The wonders of the Holy Spirit, the vigor of the continual Pentecost, then, are intensified to the extent that the Holy Spirit sees his inseparable spouse, Mary, in a soul: *"Rest assured that the more you turn to Mary in your prayers, meditations, actions and sufferings, seeing her, if not perhaps clearly and distinctly, at least in a general and indistinct way, the more surely will you discover Jesus. . . . Mary is far from being an obstacle to good people who are striving for union with him"* (TD 165).

It is the Holy Spirit Who, then, draws the soul into the intimacy of the Trinity itself; it is the Spirit Who divinizes a soul by making it his "temple" and forming that person into the very image of Christ. It is the Holy Spirit Who pours forth dynamic Love into our hearts.

Because of the never-to-be-repealed law of the Incarnation, the great saints of the end times, called to bring about the ultimate fulfillment of God's victory, are formed by the Spirit with Mary. It is the Spirit Who lures us out of the Cenacle into the proclamation of the glories of God, Who forms us into *"true apostles"* (TD 58). The apostolate, especially the final burst of God's liberating, healing power culminating in the reign of Christ through the reign of Mary, is carried out by people—especially by the members of the Company of Mary—"filled with the Holy Spirit." These apostles will be imbued with the spirit of Mary, for *"when the Holy Spirit, her spouse, finds Mary in a soul, he hastens there and enters fully into it. He gives himself generously to that soul according to the place it has given to his spouse. One of the main reasons why the Holy Spirit does not now work striking wonders in souls is that he fails to find in them a sufficiently close union with his faithful and inseparable spouse"* (TD 36).

It is evident, then, that in the order of redemption, the three Persons of the Trinity, having willed her consent to the Incarnation, also will her active presence in the full flowering of the Incarnation, culminating in the glorious Second Coming of the Savior. Mary is also the model of how the Trinity works with us—who, like Mary, actively and responsibly release ourselves into the infinite light of the Trinitarian God—for the greater glory of God Alone.

IV. Relevance of Saint Louis de Montfort's Trinitarian Doctrine

In his preaching and his life, Saint Louis de Montfort opened to others the mystery of Trinity as fullness and perfection of divine love. As a creative channel of this classical love tradition, he has much to offer to our times.

1. Insistence on the Trinity

Perhaps the most vital effect of Montfort on today's work of evangelization is the saint's clear insistence on the Trinity. In an age where it appears that the majority of Christians either ignore the Trinity or misunderstand it, Saint Louis de Montfort challenges us by permeating his doctrine with solid Trinitarian teaching.

2. Experience of the Trinity

Montfort proclaims solid Trinitarian thought, however, not for the sake of abstract intellectual learning. His purpose is to lead the people into a deeper understanding: into a profound, experiential, mystical experience of the Trinitarian life within them. It is impossible to enter Saint Louis de Montfort's spirituality without being drawn to a life within the Trinity itself. Montfort recalls to us that this profound experience of the Trinity is the calling of every Christian.

3. The missionary dimension

His Trinitarian doctrine, however, is not turned in to itself. Just as the Incarnation—the masterpiece of the Trinity—is essentially "missionary," so too the Trinitarian mystic, in the eyes of Montfort, is essentially missionary. Integral to the formation of the great apostles of the end times is their deepening knowledge and experience of the Trinity, the ultimate source and the ultimate goal of their proclamation of the kingdom. Christian missionary endeavor is essentially Trinitarian.

4. The Marian dimension

In many ways distinctive of Saint Louis de Montfort is his insistent teaching on the divinely willed role of Mary in the Trinity's divinization of creation. He boldly tells us today that if faith is weak, if the indwelling of the Trinity is not truly alive and central in our experience, it is because Mary—the Trinity's companion in all works of grace—is not sufficiently united to souls. With Gospel logic he proclaims to our age that forgetfulness of Mary can only lead to a weakening of the living of the Trinitarian mystery with all the consequences involved. Is it possible that this "secret of sanctity"—a life lived in Mary—is the fundamental reason for the weakness of Trinitarian awareness and experience in so many Christians? Montfort would never doubt it.

5. Understanding of community

Saint Louis de Montfort's Trinitarian doctrine paves the way for a deeper understanding of community, for not only does he insist that the Trinity refers to love relationships but he also affirms that human beings are created to the image of the Trinity (LEW 35, 64; SM 3).

If God is community, if God is dialogue and we have been made to God's image, then it follows that we are meant for community. In fact, since the Persons of the Trinity are pure relationality, then it could be said that relationship is, in the concrete order, essential to the full understanding of the human person: persons are made for community. Since, as Montfort asserts, the Trinity is the community of love relationships, human communities must mirror within and outside the core group not hatred but love. Dialogue, depth sharing—applied differently in diverse cultures—must characterize human community, for they are intrinsic to the community called God-Trinity. Moreover, since the triune God wills to be "for us," as Father de Montfort repeats, so too should the human community not be turned within itself but reach out "for others." Community "at a distance" through fax, phones, and computers is hardly the full imaging of the interrelationality and interpersonality of the Trinity and can never, therefore, be considered the ideal of family or community life.

The important practical dimensions of a spirituality flowing from the knowledge and experience of the triune God are many. Montfort's Trinitarian teaching in the classical love tradition can be as vital for us today as it was when he preached so dynamically and profoundly in his own time.

E. Cousins - P. Gaffney

Notes: (1) St. Athanasius, *Against the Arians.* (2) St. Augustine, *On the Trinity,* 5. (3) See the Athanasian Creed, which in fact is not derived from Athanasius but Augustine. (4) St. Augustine, *On the Trinity,* 5-15. (5) Richard of St. Victor, *On the Trinity,* 3. (6) St. Bernard of Clairvaux, *On the Song of Songs,* 8, 1 and 2. (7) St. Bonaventure, *Collations on the Six Days,* 1, 17. (8) St. Bonaventure, *Disputed Questions on the Mystery of the Trinity,* q. 8. (9) Boethius, *On the Person and Two Natures,* 3; for a critical treatment of Boethius' definition, see Richard of St. Victor, *On the Trinity,* 4. (10) Thomas Aquinas, *Summa Theologica,* I, q. 29, a. 4, corp. (11) See St. Bonaventure, *The Tree of Life.* (12) William M. Thompson (ed), *Bérulle and the French School: Selected Writings,* Paulist Press, Mahwah, N.J., 1989, 132 (Discourse on the State and Grandeurs of Jesus, Fourth Discourse on the Unity of God in this Mystery).

TRIPTYCH

SUMMARY

I. THE MANUSCRIPT:
   1. Time and place of composition;
   2. Genesis: experience and tradition.

II. NATURE AND STRUCTURE:
   1. Prayer for missionaries;
   2. Rule of the missionary priests;
   3. Letter to the members of the Company of Mary.

III. THE COMPANY OF MARY IN THE TRIPTYCH:
   1. Name of the institute;
   2. Apostolic community:
      a. "In the footsteps of the poor apostles";
      b. Apostolic vocation;
      c. Aggregation and incorporation;
      d. Deviation from vocation;
      e. Community and mission.

IV. SPIRITUALITY OF THE COMPANY OF MARY:
   1. Trinitarian perspective;
   2. Marian dimension;
   3. Priority and primacy of evangelization of the poor;
   4. Anthropological component;
   5. Vows and missions:
      a. Evangelical poverty;
      b. Apostolic obedience.

V. CONCLUSION.

The Montfort triptych[1] groups together the three writings defined as the fundamental Rule of Saint Louis Marie de Montfort for the Missionaries of the Company of Mary: the "Prayer for Missionaries," the "Rule," and the "Letter to the Members of the Company of Mary." It is a unique document, not only because of its particular structure, but more importantly because of its basic inspiration. There is nothing quite like it among the other religious constitutions of the seventeenth and the beginning of the eighteenth century.

I. THE MANUSCRIPT

A 17 x 11 cm. chestnut brown leather binding covers Father de Montfort's triptych manuscript. The text is comprised of three parts, which follow each other consecutively. The pagination is written in Montfort's hand, showing that there was no doubt in his mind that it was a single document.[2] The montfort triptych does not include a title for PM, nor indeed for the entire manuscript. Those who saw it in its original state give no indication that it ever had a title. If it did have one, its wording would greatly help in interpreting the manuscript.[3]

1. Time and place of composition

Joseph Grandet, Montfort's first biographer, was one of the people who actually read the triptych manuscript. In chapter seventeen of his biography he presents the beginning of PM, and at the end of the book he intimates that he would also have liked to include RM, but since it was too long he would publish it separately.[4] Unfortunately, however, he never fulfilled that promise. Nevertheless, we owe the beginning of PM to Grandet,[5] since in its present state the manuscript is missing the first two pages. He does not provide any other information on either the place or time of the writing of the triptych.

Grandet's scanty information was added to by Father Charles Besnard, Superior General of the Company of Mary from 1755 to 1788. Besnard devoted nearly the whole of book five of his biography on Montfort to describe the genesis and development of the plan for the Company of Mary.[6] Besnard's writing provides us with a good framework from which to reconstruct the events that led Montfort to establish his company.

Saint Louis Marie fully developed his ideas for a company of missionaries between the second half of 1712 and the beginning of 1713. Besnard affirms that Montfort's decision to found his institute came to fruition during a period of retreat: "Not content with offering his prayers and adorable Sacrifice [of the Mass] for the accomplishment of this great and holy work, he also fasted, made pilgrimages, joined his tears to his prayers, and even drew blood in the severe mortification of his flesh. It was during a retreat that he finally decided to actively pursue the formation of the new society, and to devise for it a Rule which would join intense reflection and study of sacerdotal perfection to a zealous undertaking of apostolic work."[7]

Besnard indicates that it was during this retreat that Montfort quite suddenly made the decision to go ahead with his long-standing plans to institute the Company of Mary. However he had not as yet written the Rule. Saint Louis Marie decided to consult his Ordinary, Étienne de Champflour, the Bishop of La Rochelle,[8] before proceeding to put his thoughts into writing. Besnard writes: "Though he had endeavored in many ways to know God's will, if no mistakes were to be made there remained a still surer path. This was the path of obedience. And this was the path he chose to follow, beginning with the submission of his proposal to the judgment and decision of the bishop in the diocese where he resided. The bishop was Étienne de Champflour of La Rochelle, a very enlightened prelate who supported and was in favor of anything that seemed to him to contain the spirit of God. The Bishop was completely sympathetic to Father de Montfort's views and he approved his project and promised to do all he could to facilitate the enterprise and assure its success."[9]

We can date this meeting between Montfort and his bishop somewhere during the summer of 1712, before the resumption of missionary activity in the autumn period.[10] However, even de Champflour's explicit support did not hasten Montfort's drafting of the Rule. It was as if he needed still more time to distill, through missionary experience, the idea that had matured in silence and prayer. For a variety of reasons, he delayed the composition of the Company's Rule until the end of the mission season.[11]

In the autumn of 1712, Montfort began giving missions again. The first took place at Thairé, where the cross was erected on October 28. On January 1, 1713, the founder wrote a letter to his sister at Rambervilliers, in which he talked mostly about the theme of the cross and did not mention the Company project.[12] At the beginning of 1713, he preached a mission at Courson, and this was followed by other missions not mentioned by his biographers. The season finished with a mission at La Séguinière where his friend and collaborator, the Irishman Peter Keating, had been installed as parish priest.[13]

Thus Montfort, during the interval between the autumn-winter missions of 1712 and the spring of 1713, was able to breathe life into the project he had been thinking about for such a long time. Whenever the parishes where he preached were close enough to his Saint Eloi hermitage at La Rochelle, he would always take the opportunity of going there for a few days. It appears that the plan for the new missionary congregation was drawn up during these intermittent periods of solitude during missions. The plan was definitively completed by the end of June, 1713, when he left for Paris.[14]

However, later passage of Besnard's seems to allude to a definitive version of the text which Montfort prepared before he met with the superiors of Holy Spirit seminary in Paris, in July of 1713. He writes: "He described his plan and also read them the Rule that he had devised for those of their students, and any others, who might care to join him in order to follow the same vocation. His project was warmly applauded and all the priests and directors agreed to help him in the formation of students capable of sustaining and perpetuating his good work. As a result of this declaration, which can be regarded in some ways as a kind of contract, Louis Marie wrote these words at the beginning of RM: '*There is a seminary in Paris where young clerical students who are called to the mission in the Company receive academic and spiritual training to prepare them to become members.*' To make sure the readers would remember these words he included them a second time in the body of the work."[15]

The structure of the manuscript points to successive drafts attempting to integrate the three parts. Unfortunately, we do not have any record of this activity, but it probably happened during the period between the summer of 1712 and the summer of 1713.

2. Genesis: experience and tradition

The basis of the triptych is rooted in the many experiences of Father de Montfort; his personality, the spiritual and pastoral directions of the Church and of society in his time, and, especially, the living tradition of popular missions.[16] In fact, the triptych was written in the course of parish missions then actually being preached by the saint.

The incomparable thematic richness of PM reflects the complex motives that inspired it and form its base: they matured throughout Montfort's life. The mission theology formulated in PM was probably influenced by the thought of Thomas Aquinas as well as of Bérulle. The fundamental elements of the institution, already expressed by Montfort from December 1700 *("a small and poor company of itinerant missionaries, giving themselves up to Providence, and under the standard and protection of Mary"* [L5]), become focused in PM. The project becomes more and more precise as the elements of his original intuition are further distilled: the missionaries of the Company of Mary will not be tied down to any one place, but they will be always available and free to fly at the breath of the Spirit wherever their action against the reign of Satan, and in support of the reform of the Church, may be needed. Always vitally important are the *"priests all aflame"* with the love of God (PM 17), following in the steps of the apostles (RM 2).

Certain of these elements are also found in J. J. Olier's (1608–1657) original conception of the seminary of Saint Sulpice.[17] In his view, the seminary was an "Apostolic House," in which everything is directed towards reproducing the spirit of the Twelve Apostles; the members of the house were to be filled with zeal to spread the Church of Jesus Christ throughout the world. The seminary is therefore called the "smallest portion" of the Church; it does not belong to any particular diocese and it does not receive any benefits, so that its members may realize the ideal of the priest animated by the interior fire of the Holy Spirit. Fundamentally, Olier's and Montfort's texts converge in the idea of an apostolic company characterized by its lack of fixed roots in any one place, the total availability of its priests, and its devotion to the Blessed Virgin Mary. Various passages from Olier's writings correspond so well with Montfort's thinking, particularly in PM, that one has to conclude that Montfort relied considerably on Father Olier. Montfort's originality consisted most of all in the transfer of the "Apostolic House" into a vibrant company of apostolic missionaries destined to renew Christianity among Christians. De Fiores further clarifies: "while Olier plans formation of priests for his day, Montfort 'projects' his missionaries towards the future and the reform of the Church in the context of the end times."[18]

PM employs a series of images taken from military language: *"a troop of nimble deer," "a battalion of bold lions"* (PE 18). The final section (27–30) is particularly rich in examples: *How is it that scarcely one soldier lines up under your standard? . . . Let all the worthy priests . . . those still in the fight . . . come and join us.* Vis unita fit fortior, *with the cross as our standard let us form a strongly disciplined army drawn up in lines of battle. Let us make a concerted attack on the enemies of God who have already sounded the call to arms"* (PE 28–29); *"a chosen company of soldiers"* (PE 30).

These phrases of themselves hardly indicate an influence stemming from Saint Ignatius of Loyola, who founded the Company of Jesus. In fact, Saint Ignatius' use of the word "company" was very vague and undefined, until a year before his death. In its most primitive sense, what was meant by "Company of Jesus" was simply companions of Jesus.[19] In fact, being "armed" in the Company of Jesus has a direct relationship to "going to war for God under the standard of the Cross." Ignatius does not have any military intentions, but he wants to indicate the depth of the involvement in the Reign of God and total abandonment to it. The Cross becomes its own standard, and the service of its members is obedience to Christ and to his Vicar on earth, the Pope.[20]

Military terminology in Montfort's writing, therefore, corresponds to the then prevalent demand for boldness on the evangelical front; this was a characteristic of other religious and apostolic institutions and was typical of the age of Counter-Reformation. However, this recourse to military metaphor should not be seen as a kind of apostolic aggression. The saint's use of military terms is based on the model of the archangel Saint Michael (PM). As Michael shouted: "Who is like unto God," so too the missionaries must proclaim that God is king. Michael also serves as an example of the boldness and courage of missionaries in the face of the opposition with which historically the announcement of salvation is greeted (RM 60–61). However, there is a strong ignatian influence on the concept of the vow of obedience in relation to the very mission of the Company of Mary (RM 19), and to the community life of its members.[21]

It is impossible to ascertain with any certainty from RM whether there was a material dependence on the constitutions of other congregations of the time. However, there are certain analogies between the text of RM and that of other missionary communities. Montfort himself referred explicitly to the Congregation of the Mission of Saint Vincent de Paul (cf. RM 7, 66) and to Saint Ignatius of Loyola's Company of Jesus (cf. RM 15, 19, 66).[22]

Sections of the *allocutio,* "To the Members of the Company of Mary," echo *Man of Prayer* by Jacques Nouet, especially 5–11, which are linked to the theme of the voluntary or evangelical poor.[23] The theme of voluntary poverty was at the heart of a burning debate on the poverty of priests, which greatly upset the ecclesiastical and monastic communities of the time. The result of this debate was that "the seventeenth century, except for notable exceptions, appeared to scorn the value of voluntary poverty; with the decrease in mystics it had fallen out of favor, and it was not approved by the clergy itself."[24] Montfort was therefore proposing that his associates take on a way of life—voluntary, evangelical poverty—that was counterculture, clearly going against the grain of society.

II. Nature and Structure

The triptych as such was first published in 1932, for the collection, *Vade-mecum du montfortain* (Handbook for the Montforts), published by H. Huré, then father general of the Company of Mary.[25] In the presentation of the booklet, extracted from his circular of May 31, 1931, he sums up the aim of the edition: "to present the Rule of our holy Father in a pocket volume, with the 'prayer for missionaries' as preface, and the *allocutio* as conclusion."[26] It was clearly grasped that the three parts formed a coherent whole since their pages were "numbered consecutively."[27] Similarly, the *Complete Works* (1966), present the triptych as a trilogy.[28]

The publication of the three parts as a single work is due not only to the unity of the manuscript itself, but, more profoundly, to its single basic theme: The Company of Mary. It follows that the reading of the text should be done considering the Trilogy as a whole, not as three distinct works.

Constitutions appeared in the sixteenth to seventeenth centuries as new orders and congregations were founded; they were generally presented as large and complex collections of norms and ordinances in which everything was defined and prescribed with minute and prolific prescriptions. Montfort's *Rule of the Daughters of Wisdom* (1715), easily fits into this category. Moreover, to facilitate the smooth running of the institution, constitutions also specified the aim of the institute concerning its government, the rights and duties of each member according to his standing and his function, etc. The triptych is, strangely enough, much closer to various Rules of Medieval origin, whose principal role was to propose an ascetic code of life within the context of the spiritual life; they contained only general precepts of a disciplinary nature inherent to the observance of the "regular life."

The montfort triptych can be classified as one of the great contributions to the tradition of popular missions, for it stands above all else as a universal model for apostolic life. The legal or normative aspect is not dominant; the text of RM is subordinate to and framed within the spiritual and mystical dimension of PM and LCM. The net result is a kind of "template rule" for those who choose an apostolic form of life.[29]

1. Prayer for missionaries

Grandet tells us that the first part of the triptych is a "fervent and eloquent prayer."[30] Besnard prefers to call it "a kind soliloquy that he placed at the head of the document."[31] Picot de Clorivière says that "each word is a burst of flame."[32] Closer to our time, the oratorian W. Faber,[33] in the preface to the first English edition of TD, written in 1862, says: "Since the Apostolic Epistles it would be hard to find words that burn so marvelously as the twelve pages of his prayer for Missionaries" (TD edition 1946, ix).

What is most striking about PM is its fire-like spirit, which burns from beginning to end. It is not a literary artifice; neither is it what some today would term a result of a "spiritual high." Rather, it is one of those rare cases in which writer and text are completely fused. It could be said that in this composition Montfort reaches the height of his spirituality. It is as if a fiery volcano burst forth burning magma that solidified into words.

A somewhat classical style[34] is softened by a conversational format filled with words and images from the Bible, and in particular from the Psalms. The Prayer is a montage of symbols and figurative representations. PM is an authentic mystical creation. Even a cursory glance at the triptych shows the incredible level of spiritual perfection that Montfort's inspiration attained.

The Trinitarian structure itself raises this urgent plea to the very heights of the Trinity. With the emotional repetition of questions and of key terms such as *"Liberos,"* there is a more and more intense build-up in the prayer imploring the Trinity to grant Montfort's plea for a company of missionaries, the Company of Mary.

The prayer is both revelation and recall: revelation in the sense of a subjective mystical enlightenment, i.e., an intuition of the truth through a depth of contemplation; recall in the sense of a remembrance of biblical themes like the repetitive, mysterious beat of Psalm 73:2: "*Memento Domine Congregationis tuae quam possedisti ab initio,"* which is written into the structure of the prayer. This theological recall is to show that the Company of Mary is on the same level as the other marvels of the Lord, the God of all history: *"Renew your wonders and perform other miracles"* (Si 36, 5; PM 3). In the same way the *"Memento"* of PM has a salvific content. The request for redemptive intervention on the part of God is answered by the sending of the Company, a sign of salvation in action. Again "*from the beginning*" (PM 1), ties the Company to God's "*mercy of times past*" (PM 4). The Company is His "*divine purpose*" (PM 26).[35]

PM, a true literary and vocational masterpiece, was created in an ecstatic moment of contemplation in which all of Montfort's thinking about the Company was clarified. The result is a kind of synopsis of everything he wanted to say about the Company of Mary.[36]

2. Rule of the Missionary Priests

Grandet is flatteringly appreciative of RM: "It is very fine and quite perfect, but as it is so long we will do an abbreviated analysis of it."[37] However, as we know, Grandet only published the text of PM. Besnard is just as flattering when he calls RM "a very beautiful work that admirably conveyed the apostolic spirit."[38]

Perhaps more than his predecessors, it was the Jesuit, Picot de la Clorivière, who discerned that RM, far from being limited because so short, was open to all necessary modifications depending on time and place. "Some regret that Saint Louis Marie did not go into detail; however, he intends to write no more than an outline concentrating on the essential structure which is always to be animated by PM and LCM. If anything else would be needed, it could be added later, either by him or his successors. He believed that the inner covenant, engraved on the hearts of the members by the Holy Spirit, would have more power than all the rules that he could have given, and that would be enough for those apostle-like men who would form the future company."[39]

As Clorivière consulted the works of Grandet and Besnard, who only give a simple resume of Montfort's original Rule,[40] it is only natural that he also saw RM as a simple essay. A rather strange exception to the prevalent understanding of RM is the opinion of the Promoter of the faith, Andrea M. Frattini, who in *Posito super scriptis* (1815), writes: "In the second part [of the Triptych] there is a fully developed Rule for missionaries, as much in what regards their particular conduct, as in what regards the work of holy missions."[41] As he did not have the same stereotypes to refer to, Frattini's opinion differs from other preconceived judgments. The Jesuit Giovanni Ferrone (1794–1876), in a view expressed to the Sacred Congregation of Bishops and Regular Clergy, defines the character of the Company of Mary as being "sui generis" and qualifies Father de Montfort's Rule as "very simple."[42]

In the twentieth century, the hagiographer Mgr. Laveille, inspired in his turn by Pauvert, introduced a more positive tone: "Nothing more supple than this Rule exists."[43] More recently, Cardinal Tisserant called the text "an outline of a Rule."[44] Father Le Crom, a Montfort, deplores the lack of detail in what concerns the problems of government; on the other hand he does say that Montfort believed more in experience than norms, recalling a similar statement made by Louis Marie to his friend Blain.[45]

Montfort did not write RM for an institution or congregation in the accepted sense. Rather, he had in mind a team of itinerant missionaries engaged for nine months of the year in preaching parish missions and retreats. The Rule should therefore not be viewed as if it applied to an established community with an organic structure of government containing highly specific roles and a series of rigorous and punctual practices. When the Rule is seen in this way, the project does appear to be no more than an outline or draft. What the Rule actually does is to present the criteria for the apostolic life of an itinerant community whose lifestyle is both modeled on the preaching of parish missions and actually spent in preaching parish missions.

3. Letter to the members of the Company of Mary

The last section of the triptych, the *Allocutio,* is entitled "Letter to the Members of the Company of Mary." It is an exhortation on voluntary poverty expressed as abandonment to Providence and as apostolic detachment.

Father de Montfort closely ties together abandonment to Providence and the mission of the Company of Mary. The character of the Company is based on the salvific mission that God the Father entrusted to His Son, a mission in which the apostles participated, and through them the missionaries of the Company of Mary.[46]

In LCM Saint Louis de Montfort's vision of the poverty of the Company of Mary is highly radical. Not only does LCM bring to the fore the lifestyle and mission of the Company, but it also makes clear the specific though not exclusive character of the institute in the Church. For Saint Louis Marie, the very concept of an apostolic way of life transcends any exclusively individual needs. The very title stresses the strong community dimension, as do the terms "company" and "associates"; so much so that communitarianism becomes a characteristic of the entire montfort foundation. The authenticity of the apostolic nature of the itinerant group is realized through poverty: solidarity with the people to be evangelized and trusting openness to loving Providence.

In LCM the law of poverty becomes liberty; self-affirmation no longer exists; the gift of self to others is a way of life; total adherence to the salvific plan of God is a requirement. Apostolic poverty is total availability, which translates the demands of metanoia even to the structural level of government, to the control of property, and, most especially, to the demands of mission. From this perspective, LCM always remains an upsetting, challenging, and prophetic document for the Company of Mary.

III. The Company of Mary in the Triptych

1. Name of the institute

Montfort adopted the word "company" (from the medieval Latin: *cum pane* = "those who share the same bread"; in this case, those who share the same mission) with full recognition of its institutional and spiritual spin-offs. The use of the word "company" for missionary institutes was widespread in the sixteenth and seventeenth centuries. Generally, however, the term usually referred to groups of diocesan missionaries—mission teams—like those under the Dom Jean Leuduger, which operated on a strictly regional level.

Montfort, in adopting "Company of Mary," no doubt based it on the names currently in use during that time. However, his Marian option reflects an evident spiritual and missionary choice, which finds in PM a profound theological justification. The members belong to Mary and she to them.

2. Apostolic community

a. "In the footsteps of the poor apostles" (RM2). Throughout the history of the Church the "Apostolic College" has often been depicted as a kind of premier religious institution or community. Those who did not find it sufficient to live the evangelical counsels on a personal level often endeavored to establish a religious community, citing the "apostolic community" as their example. This was a characteristic of the promoters of a poorer, purer, more holy and missionary church: if the Church becomes like the apostles, it will respond more faithfully to Christ's message.

Montfort did not concern himself with theoretical claims. For him, the model of the poor apostles was an authentic example of behavior, a recall of the radical demands of following Christ and of the community that it engendered. He formally prescribed in RM a missionary life *"in the apostolic style."* In the ecclesiastical language of the seventeenth century, both missionaries and preachers were usually called "apostolic," but this qualification had two distinct meanings.

When applied to a missionary, it signified that his powers emanated from the highest Church authority; the "apostolic missionary" was therefore theoretically someone who had received approval and ultimately "special powers" from the Roman Congregation for the Propagation of the Faith. However, several French bishops believed that the missionaries they sent into their diocese were invested, by their authority, with powers and duties that were rightfully theirs by fact of apostolic succession.

The second meaning of "apostolic" referred to a way of preaching commonly employed by a popular missionary, which had therefore become particular to him.

The two meanings clearly reveal the importance of the relationship to the Twelve Apostles. Whenever someone in Montfort's time wanted to talk about missionary activity, the "apostolic" attribution indicated that the missionary, like the apostles, had been sent to announce the Gospel.

b. Apostolic vocation. Montfort believed that an apostolic life was primarily a calling which took its initiative from God Himself: "*The priests who enter must be called by God to preach missions in the steps of the Apostles who were poor*" (RM 2). Therefore the vocation of the Company of Mary clearly does not equate with a generic call to the priesthood, for it was based by Montfort on the perception of a real apostolic fitness. The founder thus demanded a definite, clear, and conscious choice from those who were *"called by God to preach missions"* in the company and to *"receive academic and spiritual training to prepare them to become members"* (RM 1). He excluded anything that might compromise the apostolic dynamism of the institution and anything that would even remotely transform the candidates into "*habitatores quietis*" (RM 2). It followed that the suitability of the candidate for the missionary vocation demanded a clearly apostolic choice of life. Montfort warns of this in an imperative: *"He must."*

c. Aggregation and incorporation. The missionary groups of the time were formed through the membership of its occasional and regular collaborators. Montfort even uses "associates" in the title of LCM. They formed the core on which Montfort counted for the evangelical efficacy of his missionary community.

Two different levels of membership are evident in RM: aggregation and incorporation.

With regards to the conditions of aggregation: before being admitted to the Company, the candidates had to return any benefices and they had to cede their inheritance to their relatives or to the poor (cf. RM 5). Personal money had to be deposited *"into the purse of Providence"* (RM 17). These conditions of Montfort are in line with the criteria for the suitability of candidates to the apostolic vocation (RM 2).

Montfort uses the expressions *"before entering the Company"* (RM 5) and *"enters the Company"* (RM 17). He foresaw here a stage of aggregation, a period of "candidacy" before the more final and definite incorporation into the company: *"If before or after making his vows, one of the missionaries"* (RM 18); Montfort thereby implies the possibility of being temporarily associated—aggregated—while awaiting permanent membership, which involved taking simple vows: *"To be accepted as permanent members of the Company, they must, first, in the presence of the Superior, make simple vows of poverty and obedience for one year. These vows are renewable annually. Then, if, at the end of an unbroken five-year period spent in the Company, they themselves feel they are truly called by God to belong to the Company and are judged to be so called, they take the two vows of poverty and obedience in perpetuity"* (RM 8). It is clear from this that Montfort demanded at the pronouncement of first vows the intention of a final commitment.

In order to leave the Company after having taken final vows, it was sufficient to obtain a dispensation from the bishop. Montfort also covered dismissal from the institute in the case where *"one of its members, even after final vows, should his behavior become an occasion of scandal, rather than edification, in spite of the steps taken to correct him"* (RM 8), as well as in the case of express disobedience (cf. RM 25).

d. Deviation from vocation. Once he had established the apostolic mission of the Company, Montfort outlined the ecclesiastical functions that were to be considered as *"subtle temptations":* the missionaries were not allowed to be curates or parish priests, or teachers in colleges or seminaries (cf. RM 2). These interdictions are more strictly formulated in RM 9.

The subtle temptations are given more space. Montfort was faced with the situation of *"several good communities which were established in recent times by the holy inspiration of their founders for the purpose of preaching missions"* and which, *"under the pretext that they could do more good,"* truly deviated from their original goal. *"Some turned to educational work, others to the training of priests and clerics. If they still give a few missions, these are only incidental and unplanned."* Paragraph 2 of RM reflects how completely conscious Saint Louis Marie is of the fact—based on the historical experience of his time—that following *"in the steps of Apostles,"* far from being an empty anachronism, is a guarantee of institutional identity. This must not be distorted by simple solutions that distance the Company from its original inspiration; this would inevitably cause the institute to lose its significance, meaning that it would no longer be the "sign" that it is meant to be in the life of the Church; it would lose its raison d'être.

The last part of the text elucidates the basic idea that Montfort holds most dear. The distortions that so many communities experienced resulted from losing some of "*the holy inspiration of their founders,"* they were transformed into *"habitatores quietis,"* and spent *"years that are entirely sedentary."* It is this mentality of being rooted and settled that the founder wanted to avoid at any price.

e. Community and mission. Mission was the goal of the community, but it was also an integral part of the communal and institutional life. In fact, mission is seen by Montfort as not only a pastoral task, but the very form of the community. The mission life is not by accident and in passing. Rather, the montfort community cannot exist without mission, or exist independently of it: the mission is not extrinsic to the community, but is rather part of its very being. The mission—as modeled by Montfort in his preaching of parish missions and retreats—is not only the result of a pastoral choice but is the space, or better still, the form of the community's realization and expression.

Community life expressed in community apostolate (the mission) and in community prayer is clearly the rule of the founder, both in the course of missions and during the summer "rest" (RM 28-35; 67-78). However, communal life, in the strict sense of the term as applied typically to a settled or monastic community, is periodic according to RM: it comprises the summer months from July to September, when they continue to perfect themselves for the next round of itinerant preaching. Montfort clearly takes a stand against all forms of settled life that would undermine the necessary apostolic force of the community. Any kind of stability is perceived as institutional fossilization and implies the failure of the community. Montfort's desire for a rootless, mobile community *("instabiles")* ever ready to pull up stakes and move on to where Providence calls, reflects his missionary ideal.

This concept of the Company is clearly stated in RM 12. Dealing with the restrictions on fixed property it is one of the longest and is perhaps the most casuistic of all the passages. Once the basic criteria had been formulated, *"Within the realm of France, the Company will own two houses and never more than two,"* Montfort waived this rule only in the case of some benefit accruing from other houses that the Company eventually might receive from divine Providence; he specified, however, that these houses must belong to the local bishop.

This idea of a company whose structure is subordinate to its mission is decidedly prophetic, in the sense that the organization of the Company depends on its mission: the *ordo societatis* is legitimized by the *ordo missionis.*

The company Montfort planned is therefore opposed to monastic stability and to a priesthood in the service of a settled community. It is a dynamic mission band which has as its house not the monastery but the world to be evangelized. The company must, then, be free from attachments such as the benefit system in order to devote itself exclusively to the prophetic service of the Word. These characteristics disclose the true identity of the Company within the Church.[47]

IV. Spirituality of the Company of Mary

The spirituality of the Company of Mary can be said to flow from the triptych. Without tackling the subject *ex professo,* Montfort presented certain constituent elements of this spirituality in this triple work. The full picture of what can be called the spirituality of the Company must also take in more clearly the vital aspects of Wisdom, Mary, Consecration, the Cross, Providence, End Times, and Reign, which should be studied in the articles under those titles.

1. Trinitarian perspective

The mission of the Company is born from the Trinity as a prolongation of the Triune God's own salvific mission. Montfort's theological option, deeply entrenched in the theology of the Word Incarnate of the Bérullian School, is reflected in the structure of PM which reveals the salvific functions of the Persons of the Trinity. Thus, the founder developed a Trinitarian theology of salvation applied to the mission of the Company and its members. What he is talking about here is a particular flow of movement, coming from the Trinity and going toward the Trinity, through the historical mediation of the Company of Mary.

2. Marian dimension

In Montfort's historical and salvific "remembering," Zalmon mountain (cf. Ps 68:14) appears as a symbolic representation of the Virgin (PM 25). In connection with this symbol, Saint Louis Marie interprets Psalm 68 as God's search for a dwelling place and also man's search for a home. The mountain rises high as the symbol of the function of Mary in the history of salvation, predestined as she is to be the dwelling place of her Company. "The link established by Montfort between Mary and the Company appears in all its glory: in this way a dwelling place for *'the poor missionaries, entirely dependent on Providence'* (PM 21), is assured. Such a space becomes a memorial, a guarantee of the divinity's presence as well as a magnetizing center. . . . Like the temple of Jerusalem, a center of attraction for all people; the *devotion* to Mary—a new sanctuary for the Lord of all armies; it universalized the mission of *these followers of the apostles* and placed it in the sphere of the present Kingdom, already here and yet to come (PE 22)." [48] The missionaries live on the top of the mountain that rises high above the others, the holy mountain of Mary.

Protagonist after the Trinity, Mary brings about the renewal of the Church through its apostles. Jesus Christ himself will give to his Mother a company to renew the world through Mary, and the time of grace will come to a close (PM 6).

It then becomes clear that the specific name, Company of Mary, is not a mere attribution but a much more deliberate act of belonging to Mary. The Company is a gift from God the Son to Mary: *Da Matri tuae liberos.* This secures the Marian component of the Institute: through Mary the Company takes its place in the history of salvation to renew the Church. This living *"in Mary"* expresses itself in all aspects of the Company; the saint who stipulates so few regulations in RM does insist that, *"Every day they will say all fifteen decades of the Rosary and also the Little Crown of the Blessed Virgin at a convenient time. The purpose of these heaven-sent devotions is to call down the blessing of God on themselves and their ministry. They experience daily the efficacy of these prayers"* (RM 29).

3. Priority and primacy of evangelization of the poor

As so many of the missionaries of his time, he too states: *pauperibus evangelizare misit me Dominus* (Lc 4, 18; cf. RM 2). Evangelization (RM 2) and catechism (RM 79-91), oriented towards the renewal of Christian spirit in Christians themselves (RM 56), enjoy an absolute primacy in relation to what is called today sacramentalization: *non misit me Dominus baptizare sed evangelizare* (1 Co 1, 17).

The role of converting magical and sociological Christianity to Christianity lived consciously and in a responsible way is a task assigned by Montfort to his Company. For this to happen, he insisted on the solemn renewal of baptismal promises; this was a personal involvement with the intention of a lifelong, on-going conversion.

The poor and the marginalized, that is, the groups of humanity desperately in need of support, are the ones to whom the announcement of salvation is to be made. In announcing the Gospel to the poor and giving them preference, the Company of Mary would model itself on the example of Christ, and in this way fulfill the Church's mandate. The Company is, therefore, to detect the signs of the times, and to fill in the pastoral gaps that have resulted in the marginalization of certain of God's people.

4. Anthropological constituent

PM 6–12 opens with the citation from Gn 30:1: *"Da Matri tuae liberos, alioquin moriar: give me children or let me die"* (PM 6).

The Saint uses the Latin word *liber* (plural: *liberi*) meaning "free" and also "sons". This term is explained by Montfort who gives it a particular weight in the expression: children and servants. In fact the word *liberos,* as intended by the Saint, explains the double situation of missionaries: free (PM 7–10) and at the same time slaves of Jesus in Mary (PM 11–12).

The terminology also clearly indicates a significant double aspect of the word "consecration": the missionaries are consecrated to Mary as children and servants in order to live more intensely consecrated to Christ, thereby becoming men totally free to announce the Gospel.

In this central part of PM, the originality of Montfort concerning devotion to Mary in the mission context is evident. He understands consecration as a path of interior liberty. The profile of the person consecrated in view of living within a Marian mission band discloses two types of freedom: *freedom from* everything and everyone that would impede living in the footsteps of the apostles; and *freedom for* total service to others in the apostolic life envisaged by Montfort.

5. Vows and missions

In RM Montfort adopted simple vows of poverty and obedience. The qualification "simple," in the context of the seventeenth century, is synonymous with private.[49] However, the phenomenology (so to speak) of the vow and the responsibilities that derive from it are very fluid.[50] Montfort opted for what was then the current custom, in order to insure the possibility of an episcopal dispensation for someone who would leave the institute or for someone the community expels. However, he explains the demands of the vows for those living an apostolic life in terms of the purest evangelical radicalism.

The very strong link between vows and mission makes it understood that vows are not a religious option tacked on to the apostolic commitment. Rather, the apostolic life demands the vows with the view of a total commitment to the cause of mission in the Company.

a. Evangelical poverty. Poverty for St. Louis de Montfort is an expression of apostolic detachment and its roots are found in following the example of Jesus who from his riches made himself poor.[51] The apostle loves the company of the voluntarily poor Christ, so that the follower of Jesus can also minister to the poor. This is also the reason for Montfort calling his Institute the *"Company of* *the voluntarily poor"* (RM 18).

Montfort delved more deeply into this view of apostolic detachment in the second part of LCM by quickly examining the message of the Beatitudes, a theme evident in LEW.[52] We come into contact here with a strong point in Montfort's teaching: he demands total self-emptying, surrendering the "centrality of the self." With this in mind, he lists practices to maintain this *"rich treasure of your poverty and this great realm that you have conquered."* If missionary life provides material security denied to so many of the poor, the effort towards generous service must be even greater. The practices are the concrete expression of voluntary poverty, willingly accepted, and freely offered, so that freedom may grow, and with it total renunciation for the Kingdom of God.

b. Apostolic obedience. Obedience for Montfort means that both the demands of the community and of the mission interpenetrate. The style of apostolic life remains unaltered whether the missionaries are giving a mission or whether they *"have completed their mission schedule and return to enjoy the rest which divine Providence provides for them and counsels them to take"* (RM 35;cf RM 78).

The style of life of the montfort community entails the complementarity of community *in* mission and community *of* mission. It follows that the relationship between authority and mission is interdependent. As has been emphasized, the mission of the Company cannot be confined to a pastoral method. Mission rather is the fundamental *form* of the community. Thus a superior's authority must be perceived in the context of a community in mission, which is the definition of the montfort community. The mission itself and those it serves thus becomes the center of authority, and not something merely internal to the community.

"Each member must faithfully discharge the duties entrusted to him and will not, unless directed to do so by obedience, pry into the work of another in order to find out what he is doing or how he is doing it" (RM 23). Montfort sets forth here the missionary's personal responsibility to carry out his duties faithfully. The missionaries form a group: *"vis unita fit fortior"* (PM 29). However, Montfort does not exclude but, on the contrary, urges dialogue, which implies some individual responsibility: *"They are, however, permitted to state openly and straightforwardly the reasons they may have for omitting or for not undertaking what is commanded"* (RM 27). In this the founder is within the thinking of the traditional teams and communities involved in parish missions. An understanding between the mission band and the superior of the mission is the guarantee of the *good order of the Company.* This dimension of the dialogue is made clearer in the *Rule of the Daughters of Wisdom* (1715), which in relation to the text of the *Rule of the Missionary Priests of the Company of Mary* (1713), shows the evolution in the founder's thought with regard to the authority-obedience relationship: *"They may, and often should, present their reasons for doing or not doing a certain action"* (RW 50). The incidental *"and often should"* emphasizes a precise duty and

not a mere permission. Far from demanding a purely passive obedience, Montfort on the contrary pushes for personal responsibility.

V. Conclusion

The originality of the montfort triptych consists in the combination of three texts in a single document, which by virtue of their contents and literary genre, fulfill the following functions:

1. The spiritual and theological foundations of the true mission of the Company of Mary are clearly enunciated in the PM as explained above.

2. The structural dimension of the community's apostolic ministry—popular missions—and its spirituality of following Christ in evangelical radicalism (*apostolica vivendi forma* and vows in view of the mission), as well as submission to the Spirit and to Mary (as outlined in TD and SM) are all placed in the *Rule of the Missionary Priests of the Company of Mary.*

3. LCM proposes once again a fundamental dimension of the apostolic spirituality so dear to Montfort: the voluntary poverty of the missionary. Service for the reign of God demands this as a sign of an apostolic vocation for evangelization of the poor.

The triptych constitutes a rule of apostolic life which remains to this day a valuable support and guide to authentic evangelization. In the grace shared by the founder with his Company, resounds the voice of the Spirit, who calls for a *sequela Christi* in which *"the truth will be a Company."*[53]

P. L. Nava

Notes: (1) The name "montfort triptych" has officially been used in the Company of Mary since 1975 cf. The Montfortorian Today, Rome 1975, 3). (2) The manuscript is in its third printing. The original was verified at the beginning of 1957. (Cf. with regard to this D. M. Huot, *Traite prêtres de la vraie dévotion. La voix du manuscrit* [Treatise on True Devotion. The manuscript's voice], DMar 2 [1957] 25n.–26). For a wider and more detailed presentation of the manuscript, cf. H. M. Guindon, *La Régle des prêtres missionnaires de la compagnie de Marie. Présentation materielle* (Rule of the Missionary Priests of the Company of Mary. Material presentation), DMar 3 (1958) 57–58. (3) In its original form the manuscript started on page 3 and ended on page 82. At the end of the text a note in pencil (in a unknown hand) said: "Memo. The last section was 6 leaves (24 pages). Now it begins on page 65. This section is therefore missing 3 recto-verso or 6 pages." The unfortunate loss of the first and the last leaves of the manuscript—which cuts out the beginning of PM and the end of LCM—has also deprived us, probably, of a title which would definitely have contributed to a more correct interpretation of the triptych. (4) "We are not presenting here, as promised, the Rule of the Company of Mary, because it is too long; we will publish it separately as we deem this more appropriate" (Grandet, 251). (5) Grandet, 244–45. (6) Besnard I, 273–328. (7) Besnard I, 186. (8) For the character and episcopate of Mgr. Étienne de Champflour (1702–1724), cf. the classic work of L. Pérouas, *Le diocèse de La Rochelle de 1648 à 1724. Sociologie et Pastorale* (The Diocese of La Rochelle from 1648–1724. Sociology and Pastoral), Paris 1964, 256–360. (9) Besnard I, 286. (10) Cf. P. Eijckeler, *Quelques points d'histoire montfortaine, Ier vol.: Des origines à Monsieur Mulot exécuteur testamentaire* (Several Points of

Montfort History, vol. 1: From its Origins to Mr. Mulot, Executor), Rome 1972, 58–59. (11) Besnard I, 286–87. (12) The addressee was Sr. Catherine of Saint Bernard (Guyonne-Jeanne) who entered the Benedictine order of Rambervilliers in October 1702. (Cf. L 24). (13) P. Eijckeler, op. cit., 58. (14) Besnard I, 299. (15) Besnard I, 315. (16) V. Devy's view of the influence exerted over Montfort by his contemporaries remains valid: *Saint Louis-Marie Grignion de Montfort, "le dernier des grands berulliens,"* (Saint Louis Marie Grignion of Montfort, "the last of the great berullians"), *Revue de l'Université d'Ottowa* (University of Ottowa Review) 18 (1948) 249–315. More recently, B. Papàsogli, in her general introduction to Montfort's works, gives an excellent synthesis of the sources and spiritual currents underlying the montfort production: *Opere*, vol. 1: *Scritti Spirituale* (Works, vol. 1: Spiritual Writings), Edizioni, Monfortane, Rome 1991, 21–71. (17) On Olier's idea of seminary cf. BSS generally, especially from 1976, and in particular G. Chaillot, *"La pedagogique heritée de M. Olier d'après ses Memoires"* (The Legacy of Olier's Teachings Based on His Memoirs), BSS 2 (1976) 27–64; Id., *"Critères pour la formation spirituelle des pasteurs: la tradition pédagogique heritée de M. Olier"* (Criteria for the Spiritual Formation of Pastors: The Legacy of Olier's Teachings Based on His Memoirs), BSS 4 (1978) 15–23; id., *"Monsieur Olier educateur spirituel des pasteurs d'après les sources principales du Traité des saints ordres"* (Father Olier, Spiritual Teacher of Pastors According to the Principal Sources of the Treatise of Holy Orders), BSS 4 (1978) 205–38; Id., *"J. J. Olier et la formation pastoral des clercs"* (J. J. Olier and the Pastoral Formation of Clerics), BSS 15 (1989) 12–17; Id., *"Aux sources de l'esprit missionaire de Jean-Jacques Olier"* (At the Source of Jean Jacques Olier's Missionary Spirit), BSS 17 (1991) 18–29; A. Giraldo, *"La formation sacerdotale dans la compagnie de Saint-Sulpice hier et aujourd'hui"* (From the Past to the Present: Sacerdotal Formation in the Company of Saint Sulpice), BSS 5 (1979) 27–42. (18) S. De Fiores, *"Le Saint-Esprit et Marie dans les derniers temps selon Grignion de Montfort"* (The Holy Spirit and Mary in the End Times According to Grignion de Montfort), EtMar 43 (1986) 148–49. (19) Ibid., 60. Cf. M. Olphe-Gaillard, *"La vie commune et l'apostolat dans la compagnie de Jésus"* (Communal Life and Apostleship in the Company of Jesus), in Collectif, *La vie commune* (Communal Life), Le Cerf, Paris 1956, 61–74; *"Sant'Ignazio di Loyola, fondatore della Compagnia di Gesu"* (Saint Ignatius of Loyola, Founder of the Company of Jesus), *La Civiltà cattolica* Catholic Life 142, 3 (1991) 111–24. (20) *"La Compagnia di Gesu nel 450 anniversario della sua fondazione"* (The Company of Jesus on the 450th Anniversary of its Foundation), *La Civilta cattolica* Catholic Life 141, 3 (1990), 455. (21) Cf. P. Blet, *"Note sur l'origine de l'obéissance ignatienne"* (Footnote on the Origins of Ignatian Obedience), *Gregorianum* 25 (1954) 99–111; Id., *"Les fondements de l'obéissance ignatienne"* (The Foundation of Ignatian Obedience), *Archivum historicum societatis Iesu* (Historical Archive of the Company of Jesus) 25 (1956) 514–38. (22) Regarding the profound influence of the Jesuits during the visit to the Saint Thomas Beckett College of Rennes (1648–1692), cf. S. De Fiores, *Itinerario*, 34–51. (23) Cf. J. Nouet, *L'homme d'oraison. Ses méditations pour les jours de l'année* (Man of Prayer: Daily Meditations for the Year), Paris 1866, vol. 7, 60–67. (24) Cf. P. Christophe, *Les Pauvres et la pauvreté du XVIe siecle à nos jours, IIe partie* (Poverty and the Poor from the sixteenth century to the present, second part), Desclée, Paris 1987, 67–84. (25) *Vade mecum du montfortain* (Montfortian Vademecum), Mame Editions, Tours 1932, pro manuscripto, 64. This edition was presented in the Institute's official bulletin *L'Écho des missions* (Mission Echo) 104 (1932) 3–6, where it was affirmed that the edition "is as faithful to the original text as is possible. Note that we say, as is possible" (at 4). In fact many inaccuracies were found in it: cf. J. Frissen, *"Transcriptions fautives dans notre Vademecum"* (Transcription Errors in the Vademecum), DMon 33 (1976) 76–77. (26) Vademecum 5. (27) Cf. *L'Écho des missions* (Mission Echo), 104 (1932) 4. (28) OC 673. (29) Cf. Ph. Maroto, *Regulae et particulares constitutiones singulorum regligionum ex jure Decretalium usque ad Codicem*, in *Acta congressus iuridici internationalis VII saeculo a Decretalibus Gregori IX et a XIV a Codice Iustiniano promulgatus* (Rome, 12–17 November 1934), Rome 1937, vol. 4, 215–47; in particular the definition of Rule and Constitution, 214; J. Gribomont, *Regola. Visione generale filologicastorica delle regole e coistituzioni religiose*, in *Dizionario degli istituti di perfezione* (Dictionary of the Institute of Perfection) 7 (1983) 1411–14; G. Rocca, *I codici legilslativi dei chierici regolarie e degli istituti del '600–700* (The Legislative Codes of Regular Clerics and of Institutes of 1600-1700), ibid. 1435–49. (30) Grandet, 224. (31) Besnard I, 284. (32) "The prayer that Montfort placed at the top of his project is comprised of nothing more than a collection of fervent aspirations which he used frequently. One cannot read it without feeling in oneself some of the holy saint's enthusiasm. Everything in it gives evidence of the most ardent zeal, each word is like a burst of flame; and in his depiction of Mary's children one has to see oneself" (Clorivière, 303–4). (33) About W. Faber (1814–1863), cf. R. Plus, *L'oratorien Faber.*

L'écrivain, le maître spirituel (Faber the Oratorian: Writer and Spiritual Master), in NRT 72 (1950) 296–301, with bibliographical appendix. (34) Cf. J. Freneau, *Saint Louis-Marie Grignion de Montfort, ecrivain* (The Writer, Saint Louis Marie Grignion de Montfort), DMon 47 (1972) 10. (35) Regarding the structure of PM, cf. H. Frehen, *"Le caractère particulier de la compagnie de Marie suivant le P. de Montfort"* (The Particular Nature of the Company of Mary According to Fr. de Montfort), DMon 40 (1967) 12. For the contents cf. J. Bombardier, *"Prière pour l'Eglise. Prècis de la Priere de St L-M de Montfort"* (Prayer for the Church: Summary of St. L. M. de Montfort's Prayer) DMon 46 (1969) 1–5. Regarding certain literary precedents reflecting the theme of PM, with particular reference to St. Franci Xavier and to St. John Eudes, cf. J. Bombardier, *"Deux precedents de la Prière embrasée"* (Two precedents of the Prayer for Missionaries), in DMon 37 (1966) 1–6. (36) Cf. P. L. Nava, *"Il Trittico monfortano: natura e ermeunetica. Riflessioni sulla 'Regola.'"* (The Montfort Triptych: Nature and Harmeneutic. Reflections on the 'Rule'). QM 1 (1982) 112–15. (37) Grandet, 244. (38) Besnard I, 304. (39) Clorivière, 312. (40) Cf. the text of the *Rule* in Besnard I, 300–4, and in Clorivière 304–10. (41) S. Rituum Congregatio, *Positio super scriptis*, Rome 1851, 31. (42) Cf. *S. Congr. de' Vescovi e Regolari, Super approbatione Instituti et Constitutionum . . .*, Rome 1853, 25. (43) A. Laveille, *Le Bx L.-M de Montfort (1673–1716) d'après des documents inédits* (The Blessed L. M. de Montfort: the Unedited Documents), Poussielgue, Paris 1907, 392. (44) E. Tisserant, *Luigi-Maria Grignion de Montfort, le scuole di carita e le origini dei fratelli di San Gabriele* (Louis Marie de Montfort, the School of and the Origin of the Brothers of Saint Gabriel), Tip. del Senato, Rome 1943, 248. (45) Cf. L. Le Crom, *Un apôtre marial. Saint Louis-Marie Grignion de Montfort (1673–1716)* (A Marian Apostle: Saint Louis Marie Grignion de Montfort), Les Traditions Françaises, Tourcoing 1946, 406. (46) Cf. H. Frehen, *"Le caracterè particulier de la compagnie de Marie suivant le P. de Montfort"* (The Particular Nature of the Company of Mary According to Fr. de Montfort), DMon 41 (1967) 1–15. (47) Picot de Clorivière (1785) had already discerned this particular character of the Company: "The idea he gives of the Company of Mary is noble and sublime; it demands of its members an unusual degree of perfection, this not only from the simple faithful but also from fervent Clergymen and good Religious; in short, a truly Apostolic perfection. This idea also sets this new Company apart from all the others like it which consecrate themselves to Mission work. Among these, there are none which do not also embrace other zealous and charitable works, sometimes in great number, but this variety of works, as good as they might be, prevents the company from devoting all its resources and attention to this principal work; the Company of Mary, on the contrary, confines itself only to this work, in order to be a body of light infantry, always ready to speed on its way, whenever requested by the good Bishops, and wherever the people most urgently are in need of them." (48) M. Zappella, *Il salmo 68 e la Preghiera infuocata*, QM 4 (1986) 116–17. (49) Cf. D. M. Huot, *"La Règle des prêtres missionnaires de la compagnie de Marie. II. Présentation juridique"* (Rule of the Missionary Priests of the Company of Mary. II. Judicial Presentation), Dmar 3 (1958) 76–77. (50) Cf. R. Lemoine, *L'époque moderne 1563–1789. Le monde des religieux* (The Modern Age 1563–1789: the Religious World) (*History of Law and Institutions of the Western Church*, vol. 15/2, under the direction of G. Le Bras and J. Gaudement), Paris 1976, 3–7. (51) Cf. I. Noye, *La formation du clergé à la pauvreté dans la seconde moitie du XVIIe* (The Clergy's Embrace of Poverty in the Second Half of the Seventeenth Century); J. Meuvret, *La situation materielle des membres du clergé séculier dans la France du XVIIe. Possibilites et limites des recherches* (The Material Situation of Members of the Secular Clergy in Seventeenth-Century France: Possibilities and Limitations of Research), RHEF 54 (1968) 47–58; J. P. Devaise, *Clergé rural et documents fiscaux. Les revenus et charges des prêtres de campagne au nord-est de Paris, d'après les enquetes fiscales des XVIIe et XVIIIe siècles* (Rural Clergy and Fiscal Documents: Revenues and Charges of Country Priests in the North-East of Paris According to Fiscal Inquiries During the Seventeenth and Eighteenth Centuries), RHMC 17 (1970) 921–52. (52) Chapter 12 of LEW presents *"the principal utterances of Wisdom Incarnate which we must believe and practice if we are to be saved."* This is not merely about the clever juxtaposition of evangelical passages. In this central part of his work, Montfort takes the Lord's actual words as the guide line for the inspiration of those who seriously wish to live in accordance with Jesus Christ and Eternal Wisdom Incarnate. The chapter ends with a paragraph reserved for the eight Beatitudes according to Matthew (Mt 5.3–10); cf. LEW 151, 153). On the mountain of Zalmon, symbolic image of Mary, the missionaries will receive a great lesson: *"Jesus Christ, who dwells there forever, will teach them in his own words the meaning of the eight beatitudes"* (PM 25). (53) A. Manaranche, *Prêtres à la manière des Apôtres pour les hommes de demain* (Future Priests in the Mold of the Apostles), Centurion Editions, Paris 1967, 82.

TRUE DEVOTION

Summary

I. The Origins of True Devotion to the Blessed Virgin:
   1. The Notebook;
   2. The use of the Notebook;
   3. The use of the Fathers and Scripture;
   4. How Montfort used his sources in True Devotion.

II. Observations on True Devotion to the Blessed Virgin:
   1. The manuscript:
      a. Discovery of the manuscript;
      b. Condition of the manuscript;
      c. Date and place of composition;
      d. Intended readers;
   2. The title and divisions in the various editions:
      a. From the first editions until today;
      b. Observations on the editions.

III. Analysis and Principal Content:
   1. First part: True Devotion to Mary (1–117):
      a. Introduction;
      b. "God has decided to begin and accomplish His greatest works through the Blessed Virgin" (14–36);
      c. The necessity of devotion to Mary (37–59);
      d. Basic truths of devotion to Mary (60–89);
      e. Choosing and practicing true devotion to Mary (90–117);
   2. Second part: The perfect practice of true devotion (118–273):
      a. The perfect consecration to Jesus Christ (120–134);
      b. "The motives which recommend this" (135–182);
      c. The Biblical representation of this devotion: Rebecca and Jacob (183–212);
      d. "Wonderful effects of this devotion" (213–225);
      e. "Particular practices of this devotion" (226–265);
   3. Some general remarks:
      a. True devotion and perfect practice;
      b. The missionary dimension of Marian devotion;
      c. Marian devotion and Christian life;
      d. Receiving Mary's spiritual maternity.

IV. "True Devotion To The Blessed Virgin" and Contemporary Christianity:
   1. Chapter 8 of Lumen Gentium and true devotion to Mary;
   2. True devotion to the Blessed Virgin and John Paul II:
      a. The Marian piety of Karol Wojtyla and true devotion;
      b. The official teaching of John Paul II.

V. Conclusion.

True Devotion to the Blessed Virgin, considered by most to be the masterpiece of Saint Louis Marie de Montfort, is undeniably the work that has most effectively spread his name and the specific devotion to Mary that marked his spiritual journey. This article will deal briefly with the sources of the book, its contents, and its relevance for contemporary men and women.

I. The Origins of True Devotion to the Blessed Virgin

The development of Saint Louis Marie's personal devotion to Our Lady is well documented in the *Handbook* (cf. articles on Saint Louis de Montfort, Mary, and Consecration). We will limit ourselves, therefore, to a study of the written sources of the TD.

"Having read nearly every book on devotion to the Blessed Virgin" (TD 118); *"I shall quote one only of the many passages which I have collected from the Fathers and Doctors of the Church"* (TD 41). Montfort accumulated a significant amount of literature. As Librarian at Saint-Sulpice he could take advantage of his privileged circumstances and consult the works that interested him.[1]

1. The Notebook

Montfort's notebook (N) has proven exceptionally useful in identifying his sources. Through patient research, Father P.H. Eyckeler has succeeded in tracing the majority of passages that Montfort copied or summarized in his notebook to their original authors, so that we can see the authors from whom Montfort borrowed and who contributed indirectly to *True Devotion.*[2] Study of the notebook reveals Montfort's preoccupations while he kept it. Several broad fields of interest emerge: general information on Marian doctrine, such as is found in Poiré (whose influence is scattered throughout TD); the necessity of true devotion and the signs of true and false devotion (from Crasset); responses to those who object to devotion to the Holy Virgin in general and holy slavery in particular, as well as arguments in support of such devotion (from Crasset, from whom Montfort gathered considerable Patristic documentation, and from others such as Grenier and the Capuchin d'Argentan); and passages referring to some particular issue discussed in TD, e.g., devotion to the Virgin as a sign of predestination (from d'Argentan, Carthagena, Bourgoing, Boissieu, Nicquet, and others), the particularly important theme of *"Jesus living in Mary"* and the Incarnation (from d'Argentan, Bourgoing, Olier, and others), the communion of Mary or, as it becomes in TD, with Mary (from Bernardine of Paris and Boissieu), consecration and the baptismal vows (from Bérulle). Toward the end of the notebook there are texts that testify to his interest in Jesus as the center and consummation of the spiritual life (notably from Saint-Jure and Nepveu).[3]

2. The use of the Notebook

There are several important observations to be made on Montfort's use of his notebook as he composed the book that is now called *True Devotion to the Blessed Virgin.*

To begin with, it is interesting to discover which texts Montfort chose to use and which he ignored in the authors he consulted. On one hand, he chose texts based on his own interests (and we know that he was more interested in what bore directly on the spiritual life rather than in the purely speculative); on the other hand, his spiritual intuition, applied to balanced theology, led him to put aside some exaggerated material (as can be found notably in Poiré). Certainly not everything that he copied into his notebook found its way into TD.[4] His deepening personal and pastoral experience enabled him to sort his texts and choose what he needed. As a result, we cannot draw a pure and simple connection between his text and his sources.

In addition, the extent to which St. Louis Marie was genuinely influenced by the authors we find in his notebook is not proportional to the amount of space they occupy there,[5] nor to the number of direct references to their work in the text of TD.[6] There are some works that Montfort read that were especially influential for him but that are mentioned very little in his writing or not at all, such as Boudon's book, *God Alone, or the Holy Slavery of the Admirable Mother of God.*[7]

Finally, we must still return to the authors' original texts to determine what Montfort chose to adopt and what he passed over, and to understand the meaning of the "summaries" that he occasionally composed instead.[8] This task can sometimes illuminate the meaning these authors gave to words such as "predestined" or "predestination." Boissieu or D'Argentan argued that, without prejudicing the sovereign and mysterious action of God, predestination to salvation, which God desires for all mankind because "God desires that all men should be saved," requires the freely given response of mankind. Those who accept grace are thus "predestined," whereas those who refuse it fall into "reprobation." Rather than attempt to discover predestination in God (where it is and will remain for us an unfathomable mystery), they prefer to examine it at the existential level, stating that predestination and reprobation appear to depend on the will of mankind.[9] With this we can see much more clearly how St. Louis de Montfort (who had no need to become involved in theoretical considerations on this subject) uses these words, particularly when he speaks of devotion to Mary as a preeminent mark of predestination.

3. The use of the Fathers and Scripture

The importance that Montfort attached to Scripture and the Tradition is evident. Most of the patristic references in TD can be found in the works cited in N, notably in Crasset;[10] a number of Scripture passages are also taken from those works.

4. How Montfort used his sources in TD

When we see the abundance and the precision of the documentation on which Montfort drew,[11] it is tempting to wonder whether TD is not simply a compilation of many different authors whose works Montfort more or less plundered. However, this is not the case.

First of all, we have seen how Montfort selectively chose his texts while compiling his documentation. This was one way of putting his own imprint on the material he collected. His information also reveals one of his abiding traits in all its richness: he would listen and learn, and he wanted to obey, but his obedience was never blindly conformist. He perceived the world around him in a way that was part of his nature but that also derived from a spiritual intuition connected to the inspiration of the Spirit: Montfort emerges as a true mystic. His readings nourished him spiritually, but to some extent they were filtered through his own experience. And as he progressed in his journey, his ability to discern what could be integrated into his personal synthesis and what would allow him to convey that synthesis continued to grow. In TD he presents us with the product of his rumination and assimilation, renewed and developed,[12] so that it became "his own"; his work is personal and, on a number of points, original.

II. Observations on True Devotion to the Blessed Virgin

The manuscript has its own history and is itself capable of speaking to us; likewise, the way in which it has been edited reveals how the book has been understood at different points of its history.

1. The manuscript

a. Discovery of the manuscript. On April 22, 1842, a montfort father, Father Rautureau, the librarian at the Mother House in Saint-Laurent-sur-Sèvre, discovered a manuscript that attracted his attention; on looking at it more closely he immediately recognized the stamp of Father de Montfort. The superior general at the time, Father Dalin, identified the handwriting as that of Father de Montfort and, when he had become aware of the manuscript's contents, declared to the congregation, "We have found a treasure!" He was right.[13] How could such a treasure have lain in oblivion for more than a century? For reasons we do not know, Father Montfort never published it, although his intention as he wrote the book was certainly to bring it before the public (TD 112). Why did Montfort's earliest successors neglect to carry out this project? We have no answer to that question, but history tells us that it was through neither oversight nor disaffection with the Marian aspect of the founder's spirituality: they faithfully respected Mary's role in their missions;[14] among the Daughters of Wisdom, Marie Louise of Jesus would in no way renounce this inheritance.[15] In any case, during the French Revolution the manuscript was entrusted to some local farmers, along with some other items that were thought to be in danger of being destroyed, and was buried in trunks underground, lending prophetic significance to the following passage in the book: *"I clearly foresee that raging beasts will come in fury to tear to pieces with their diabolical teeth this little book and the one the Holy Spirit made use of to write it, or they will cause it at least to lie hidden in the darkness and silence of a chest and so prevent it from seeing the light of day"* (TD 114).

b. Condition of the manuscript. Evidence suggests that the manuscript is materially incomplete.[16] The editors of the *Complete Works* calculated that somewhere between eighty-four and ninety-six pages must be missing from the beginning of the work.[17] Must we conclude that we have only a portion of the book that this holy missionary wrote? An internal examination suggests as much. On three occasions the text refers to the first part of the book: in TD 227 *("as I have recommended in the first part of this preparation for the reign of Jesus Christ")*, again in TD 228 *("Every day they should say the Litany of the Holy Spirit, with the prayer that follows, as indicated in the first part of this work")*, and in a further reference to the *"first part"* in TD 256. In addition, in TD 230, Montfort speaks of *"the prayer of Saint Augustine which they will find at the beginning of the second part of this book,"* although in fact this prayer is at TD 67. Add to this that the manuscript we possess has no title (which is not typical of Montfort), and we can scarcely avoid concluding that a "first part" has been lost and that, based on what we read in TD 227, the entire work was to be a *"preparation for the reign of Jesus Christ."* This confirms the essentially Christological objective of Marian devotion in general, and its perfect practice, as Montfort describes them.

The manuscript may be truncated at its end as well as at its beginning. TD 231 and 236 give rise to this suspicion, because they refer, respectively, to an *"act of consecration"* and to a blessing for little chains, said to be found *"at the end of this book,"* like the method for communion which can in fact be found at the end of TD.

Also, the manuscript includes only five subtitles, and the first does not appear until TD 120.[18]

c. Date and place of composition. The few elements that give us a clue as to the book's date and place of composition are derived from internal examination and can only be considered approximations. The first reference is the following statement from Montfort: *"I have taken up my pen to write down what I have been teaching with success both publicly and in private in my missions for many years"* (TD 110). One senses that Montfort has such command of his subject that, as soon as he has taken up his pen, the words and sentences flow effortlessly. In addition, the work is so well organized that it suggests long meditation. This leads us to the conclusion that it was a work of St. Louis Marie's maturity.

We cannot conclude much from the allusion in TD 159 to the death of Father Boudon *("who died a short time ago")* in 1702. The phrase is simply too vague.

How long did it take Montfort to write the work? The hypothesis that it was largely written in one continuous burst of inspiration is not unlikely.[19] The book would have to have been written during an adequately long period of tranquillity in the missionary's life. The autumn of 1712, when he sojourned at the hermitage of St. Éloi in La Rochelle, was one such period. That is "the date that has traditionally been favored."[20]

d. Intended readers. Montfort spoke of his intention of addressing his book to *"the poor and simple"* rather than to *"the so-called intellectuals"* (TD 26). He did not aim his work at an educated or cultural elite. He used a relatively simple style and vocabulary, and a method of argumentation that is largely accessible. Our saint undoubtedly merits the title of a born mediator between scholarly religion and popular religion.[21] Even today, experience demonstrates that he accomplished his objective: many persons of simple faith find themselves completely at ease with the text of TD. He also fulfilled another objective, probably unintentionally: his book has unfailingly given rise to interest from and reflection by theologians, who continue to find it profoundly rich and contemporary.

2. The Title and Divisions of the Various Editions

a. From the first editions until today. Since 1842, the year it was discovered, publication of the manuscript has been an ongoing preoccupation. "Permission" was granted by René-François Soyer, bishop of Luçon, on December 18, 1842, and the work appeared in 1843. The person responsible for this first edition was "a Director of the Seminary of Luçon," now identified as Augustin Grillard, who entered the Company of Mary on October 6, 1851.[22] The first editors chose the title by which the book is universally known today, *Treatise on True Devotion to the Blessed Virgin.* They also divided the book into sections in order to make it more accessible: after an "Introduction" (1–13), they proposed a "First part. On devotion to the Blessed Virgin in general" (14–114), followed by a "Second part. On the most excellent devotion to the Blessed Virgin, or the perfect consecration to Jesus through Mary" (corresponding to 115–273).

This division points to the distinction between *"true devotion"* (the object of the first part) and *"perfect practice of true devotion,"* i.e., *"total consecration of oneself to Jesus by the hands of Mary,"* or *"holy slavery,"* according to Montfort (the object of the second part). In light of this, the title *Treatise on True Devotion to the Blessed Virgin* seems completely appropriate, because it does not solely encompass either *"true devotion to the Blessed Virgin"* or the *"perfect practice"* of this devotion.

In 1921, a new French edition appeared,[23] divided differently, with "a system of progressive numbering."[24] In place of the two parts of the previous editions there were eight successive chapters, with an Introduction (1–13) and a supplement (266–273). Although there were reasons for making these modifications, they do not seem to have put a stop to an evolution in expression that was already in progress and that would not be without consequence: *"true devotion"* had come to be discussed entirely in terms of its *"perfect practice."* This is not an unusual phenomenon in language: a generic term that is used to apply to a whole, eventually comes to refer to an essential element of that whole. The initiated can grasp the correct meaning (one hopes), but others may become lost. It is not at all difficult to find multiple examples of this kind of drift in meaning.[25]

With the 1966 edition of the French *Complete Works,* we come to a third stage. The traditional title was retained; "however, we thought it useful to add as a subtitle for the work, the description that Father de Montfort himself used, in TD 127: *'Preparation for the Reign of Jesus Christ.'*"[26] This has the advantage of emphasizing the Christological objective of the work. The editors once again divided the book into two parts: "Necessity of devotion to Our Lady" (1–59), and "In what devotion to Mary consists" (60–265), with a "Supplement: Method of practicing this devotion at Holy Communion" (266–273).

There were evident and worthwhile reasons for choosing this approach. One can still argue that the divisions adopted by the book's first editors ought for the most part to be retained, in order to highlight the book's structure. The work would then be ordered as follows: I. True devotion to the Blessed Virgin (1–117): 1. Necessity of devotion to Our Lady (1–59), 2. In what devotion to Mary consists (60–117); II. The perfect practice of devotion to Mary (or: The way of Montfort) (118–273), with the same divisions that are found in GA.

In this way, two important points would immediately be made clear. The first is the fundamental distinction between *"true devotion"* and its *"perfect practice."* The second is that the original cast of Montfort's mind, as it is displayed throughout the book, including the first part (if we assume that what is missing is equally specific), is evidence of a personal method for understanding and presenting consecration in holy slavery, so that it becomes his own, in a sense, and he can present *"the perfect practice of true devotion"* as an authentic spiritual path.[27]

b. Observations on the editions. In 1902 there were sixty-seven editions of TD in eight languages; in 1956, there were 253 editions in eighteen languages. We can form an idea of the amazing international distribution of TD through a brief sampling of some publication figures for 1902 and 1956, not counting editions published by the montfort missionaries: In Germany/Switzerland/Austria, there were five editions in 1902 and in 1956, twenty. In England, there were nineteen editions in 1902 and in 1956, thirty. In America, there were three editions before 1902 and about a dozen editions in 1956. The same trend is true for the Netherlands and Italy, not to mention the Spanish-speaking countries. In addition, there have been editions of Montfort's writings in fifteen countries where the montfort community has never had a presence.[28] This is notable, because it demonstrates that others, outside of the montfort family, have undertaken to spread the word about the Marian way of Montfort, which is all to the good. Although the montfort family recognizes that its founder's message belongs to the entire Church, it must also be aware that the family of Saint Louis Marie is the living custodian of the treasure. It does, therefore, fall to the montfort community to ensure, as far as possible, that the purity of this message be respected and, in particular, that it not be used for partisan or sectarian ends, as it sometimes, unhappily and deplorably, has been.

At the time of writing, there are about four hundred editions in more than thirty languages. The momentum of the book worldwide shows no sign of slowing down.

To what is this success due? We can attribute it partly to the intrinsic value and universality of Montfort's work. It can also be attributed to the concordance—especially evident today—between the crux of de Montfort's doctrine and the teaching of the Magisterium.

III. Analysis and Principal Content

In order to analyze the major teachings of TD, we will follow the divisions proposed in GA, except with respect to the two principal parts.

1. First part: true devotion to Mary (TD 1–117)

a. Introduction (TD 1–13). TD 1–13 can be better understood if the reader keeps in mind that they were to introduce a second part, the *"Preparation for the Reign of Jesus Christ,"* and that as a result they are joined to what was to have preceded them. The main reason that Montfort speaks of Mary, which he does *"with special joy"* (TD 13), is that it is through Mary that Christ must become known (TD 13) and through Mary that he must come to reign more and more, because it is through her that he *"came into the world"* (TD 1, 13). We can already see here the principal lines of approach that Montfort will develop: Mary's reason for being, and thus Father de Montfort's reason for speaking of her, is Jesus Christ; Mary's essential link with her Son, and the reason for her role in the coming of Christ's kingdom, can be found in the mystery of the Incarnation. Thus, as Mary becomes better known in all her wealth and splendor, as God made her and reveals her to us (because only He knows her [TD 2–6, 10–13]) so too will Jesus become better known. It is from this perspective that Montfort can adopt for his own purposes the *De Maria nunquam satis,* but his context insures him against an excessive application of the axiom, because he is already speaking of fundamental first truths (TD 61–89). This Christological absolutism, which he early on asserts quite strongly, gives St. Louis Marie's text a tone that illuminates all true Marian devotion.[29]

b. "God has decided to begin and accomplish his greatest works through the Blessed Virgin" (TD 14-36). TD

14 and 15 have the value of fundamental truths, not to be forgotten. Montfort tells us that *"God has decided to begin and accomplish his greatest works through the Blessed Virgin."* But he immediately affirms that, whatever Mary's greatness and however important a role we must acknowledge for her in carrying out the plan of salvation, she owes all to God, Who gives in absolute gratuitousness, and Who has no need except that which originates in His will. Because God is God, the place that Mary holds in the realization of the Incarnation indicates for us the place she must always hold in carrying out the plan of salvation.

What then is Mary's role in the Incarnation? The three Persons have freely decided that They need her to play a role in an association wherein her dignity and responsibility are perfectly respected (TD 16). But Montfort goes considerably further, tying Mary's maternity toward the Word made flesh to her maternity of grace toward us, always conforming to the design of the three divine Persons and dependent on their action (TD 17-22). Here again we see—and his notebook confirms—how Montfort drew on the ideas of the authors he had studied but gave those ideas an expression and strength that were entirely his own.

TD 22 is itself a small masterwork of profundity, concision, and preciseness. In it, Montfort seeks the light within the mystery of the Incarnation that will allow him to affirm that Mary's maternal mission toward us will continue *"to the end of time until the last coming of Jesus Christ"*; for him, in effect, the entire plan of salvation is carried out according to what might be called "the law of the Incarnation," and this law requires Mary's presence and maternal action. Therefore, Mary receives from the three divine Persons all that is necessary for her to fill the maternal mission toward us with which she has been entrusted (TD 23–36).

We should note several things here. The first is the importance of the Trinitarian aspect, which becomes all the more forceful as the three divine Persons are perceived concretely through their action in Mary, and this action is completely directed toward our salvation. If we read closely, we will realize that God's love and attention toward Mary are the sign and token of His love for us. Here as elsewhere when he grapples with other mysteries of faith, the Father from Montfort draws his inspiration above all from the "economy," i.e., the history of salvation, as his frequent study of the Fathers and Scripture in particular has revealed it to him. We find in Montfort an excellent example of living Trinitarian theology.

Second, St. Louis Marie does a remarkable job of explaining and locating the association of Mary and the Holy Spirit, which allows him to describe its most profound consequences for spiritual life in general (TD 34–36, 43), for what Montfort calls *"the apostles of the end times"* (TD 49, 57), and for all those who wish to undertake perfect practice of true devotion (cf., e.g., TD 258–59). We can trace this inspiration to the

Bérullian tradition, with which he was in contact through Saint Sulpice, but which he raised to a quite extraordinary level (prompting Cardinal Suenens to say, "Montfort has written pages on the subject of the relationship between the Holy Spirit and Mary that have never been equaled"[30]). In this way, he gives the title *"Spouse of the Holy Spirit,"* which was common among other authors and of which he is especially fond, a new meaning for the tradition of spiritual maternity. For Montfort, the completely spiritual association of the Spirit and Mary, by which they carry out the Incarnation, can only continue and lead in time to their giving birth to the whole Christ, i.e., Christ as the Head of the Body and us, its members.[31]

c. The necessity of devotion to Mary (TD 37–59). Mary is necessary to us because God has freely willed that she should be. This conclusion follows naturally from what has been said before (TD 39), but, because Montfort knows well that what should be obvious will nonetheless be disputed, he gives several arguments (TD 43–45). Then he discusses two consequences of this. First, the more one is called *"to a special perfection,"* the greater is one's need for Mary (TD 43–45). Second, as the battle against the forces of evil grows fiercer, Mary's presence and aid will become even more necessary (TD 46–59).

d. Basic truths of devotion to Mary (TD 60–89). The *"truths"* that Montfort presents, *"basic"* to all true devotion to Mary, are all the more valuable for *"the remarkable and sound devotion"* that he wishes to teach us (TD 60), and which he calls *"the perfect practice of true devotion."*

The *"first principle"* expresses Father de Montfort's Christological absolutism with a force, even a vehemence, that would be difficult to equal (TD 61–62). In effect, it is respect for this first truth that justifies "all devotion," but it also allows Montfort to propose, later on, its most extreme possible consequences. We should note the degree to which Montfort unburdens his heart in 65–67, which are written in a confidential tone.

Similarly, the *"second principle"*—*"We belong to Jesus and Mary as their slaves"* (TD 68–77)—also has general implications for all Marian devotion, but it finds its ultimate application in holy slavery, as presented by Montfort. Here again, Jesus is primary, in an absolute sense. Mary's *"relative"* place with respect to Jesus is once again underscored with remarkable theological accuracy (TD 74). It is worth mentioning that Montfort, as if carried away by his own impetus, already begins to justify his conception of holy slavery (TD 75–77).[32]

The three other *"principles"* (TD 78–89) may require commentary because of their manner of expression, since they are influenced by the cultural climate in which the saint evolved, as should be expected. But we must be careful not to allow the basic truths they contain to slip away from us, even if they prove shocking to a contemporary mentality.

e. Choosing and practicing true devotion to Mary (TD 90–117). We can only emphasize the accuracy of Montfort's observations on false devotion (TD 92–104). They may have been inspired by Crasset and Tronson, but they bear the stamp of Montfort, including his style. This is also true of the *"marks of authentic devotion"* (TD 105–14) and the *"principal practices"* (TD 115–17).

Observe that, for Montfort, by virtue of these principles, all *"true"* devotion to Mary must be closely joined to Christian life and its demands.

2. Second part: the Perfect practice of true devotion (TD 118-273)

Here we have arrived where Montfort has been leading us: to *"the perfect practice of true devotion,"* his own path, which he owes to the legacy he inherited from his precursors and his own additions to that legacy.[33] We should note how, in TD 119, he acknowledges that there are degrees of this devotion, and also that we can only attain the fullness of such devotion through the Spirit of Jesus.

a. "The perfect consecration to Jesus Christ" (TD 120–34).[34] This is the first subtitle from Montfort's own hand: it refers to the perfect practice of devotion to the Blessed Virgin who will lead us perfectly to Jesus, in accordance with the first principle of all true devotion. Our explicit and absolute completion in Christ is, as we have previously noted, one of Montfort's principal contributions, allowing him to push the gift of oneself to Mary and dependence on Mary to their ultimate consequences.[35]

The objective is to advance toward union with Jesus, in which Christian perfection consists. *"Now, of all God's creatures Mary is the most conformed to Jesus. It therefore follows that, of all devotions, devotion to her makes for the most effective consecration and conformity to him . . . 'That is why perfect consecration to Jesus is but a perfect and complete consecration of oneself to the Blessed Virgin, which is the devotion I teach; or in other words, it is the perfect renewal of the vows and promises of holy baptism'"* (TD 120).[36] We now find ourselves at the very heart of the Christian life, centered on Christ and established by baptism and the promises it entails (cf. TD 126–131).

In order to *"belong entirely to Jesus Christ"* through Mary, one's gift of oneself must be total and absolute. With a precision and meticulousness that invite us to take him very seriously, Montfort explains exactly what this gift consists of (TD 121). It is so radical as to include surrendering our *"merits,"* insofar as this is possible (TD 122–23). However, the "totality" of this gift does not conflict in any way with the obligations of our *"state of life"* (TD 124).

But how can we address such a gift to Mary? It seems to involve an act of *latria* that ought only to be addressed to God.[37] In a few authoritative words, Montfort responds to this objection: if the gift of oneself to Mary and to Jesus is identical in extent, it is not identical in its nature. This gift does not stop with Mary, but passes through her, because she is *"the perfect means to unite himself to us and unite us to him,"* so that we may reach Jesus, *"our last end. Since he is our Redeemer and our God we are indebted to him for all that we are."* It follows that *"we consecrate ourselves at one and the same time* [i.e., by the same act] *to Mary and to Jesus"* (TD 125). This is extremely important. If we do not understand that this complete gift of oneself must finally be addressed to Jesus Christ, we are not truly understanding St. Louis de Montfort. Neither is our understanding complete if we think that we can make this radical consecration to Mary alone, for in that event we would open ourselves to charges of "mariolatry." Nor is our understanding complete if we see in Montfort's formulas only a manner of speaking that should not be taken literally, for in that case we would rob the act of consecration of its content. In each case, we are distancing ourselves from Montfort, who, more than his predecessors, was adept at finding the right expressions and making accurate explanations.

b. "The motives which recommend this devotion" (TD 135–82). This section, in which Montfort discusses reasons for undertaking this "perfect practice," does not require particular comment. We need only emphasize the importance of the second motive: this devotion *"helps us to imitate Christ"* (TD 139–40). Regardless of whether a given "spiritual path" integrates every other essential element of Christian life, none is worthy of the name if it does not acknowledge the value to be gained in imitating Christ. Submission to Mary is a true but not the only element of montfort spirituality; to some extent it gives this spirituality its "evangelical" basis.[38] The fifth motive runs along the same lines: *"This devotion is a smooth, short, perfect, and sure way of attaining union with our Lord, in which Christian perfection consists"* (TD 152–68). Here we are invited to imitate Jesus by following the same path that he took to come to us. Note the care that Montfort takes to show, like Boudon (or Jobert) before him, that this devotion is rooted in the Christian tradition.

c. The Biblical representation of this perfect devotion: Rebecca and Jacob (TD 183–212). Montfort consciously distinguishes between the story of Rebecca and Jacob *"as the Holy Spirit tells it"* and his own account of the story (TD 183). This account allows him to return to two themes that are dear to him: devotion to Mary as a sign of predestination, and Mary's maternal devotion to her children and the *"good services"* that she renders to them (TD 185-212).

d. "Wonderful effects of this devotion" (TD 213–25). The section on the *"wonderful effects"* that *"this devotion"* must produce if it is faithfully undertaken, can be read as Montfort's personal testimony of his own experience. He felt these effects, from the humility that true knowledge of oneself brings (TD 213), to *"a share in Mary's faith"* (TD 214), *"the gift of pure love"* (TD 215), *"great confidence in God and in Mary"* (TD 216), the *"communication of the spirit of Mary"* (TD 217), our *"transformation into the likeness of Jesus"* through Mary, with the remarkable image of the *"mold of Mary"* (TD 218–21), and finally, *"the greater glory of Christ"* (TD 222–25). It is here especially that we can speak of a spiritual "self-portrait."

e. "Particular practices of this devotion" (TD 226–265). Montfort himself does not insist on the distinction between *"exterior practices"* (TD 226–56) and *"interior practices"* (TD 257–66).

The first exterior practice he speaks of is the solemn act of consecration. We must be suitably prepared for this, and the preparation is to be serious and lengthy (one month). Although another method of preparation may be used, the consecration requires sufficient time for reflection and prayer; otherwise, such an act of devotion might be rendered commonplace. In addition, this must be truly *personal* in character: St. Louis Marie speaks of the *"signature"* of the act of consecration.

All the practices that he lists are valuable (and Montfort tells us that the list is far from exhaustive [TD 226]). Of particular interest, however, are the special devotion to the mystery of the Incarnation (TD 243–48) and the devotion to the chaplet (or the Rosary), because of their close and almost organic connection to the spirit of perfect practice as described by Montfort.

With the interior practices (TD 257–265), we come to an essential aspect of both the Marian way of Montfort and of the act of consecration. On this point, SM is perfectly clear: perfect practice *"consists in surrendering oneself in the manner of a slave to Mary, and to Jesus through her, and then performing all our actions with Mary, in Mary, through Mary, and for Mary"* (SM 28; cf. 43). SM and TD are speaking of the same *"interior practice,"* although the order of the formulas is different and the Christological end is made more explicit in TD 257.

If interpreted literally, the terms used in TD 257—*"for those souls who feel called by the Holy Spirit to a high degree of perfection"*—may present some difficulty: are we to conclude that, in Montfort's view, only a privileged elite can observe this practice? This depends on how we take the word "privileged." If we take Montfort's statements as a whole, we realize that he is in no way referring to those who are privileged according to the criteria of the world. If, on the other hand, we understand him as referring to those who are privileged with grace, we might find agreement if we also understand that all are called to evangelical perfection and that God's grace is offered to all so that we may achieve it. But, as with predestination, the appeal may be heard or refused. Thus we cannot invoke this passage in deciding to whom we will deliver Montfort's message, any more than we can decide to whom we will proclaim the Gospel. *"Qui potest capere, capiat,"* and no one can identify in advance those who will be able, because of special grace or generosity, to "grasp" what is offered them.

In any case, in order to carry out the project of life included in the act of consecration, it is evident that one must strive to live with Mary so that one can better live with Jesus. Otherwise one's act of consecration may have no future. The gift and total abandonment of self that are *part* of the act of consecration are not *prerequisite* to that consecration. In that case, only those who were already established in the fullness of perfection would be capable of it, which is certainly not Montfort's intention. We must thus conclude that there is a "plan," and that what allows us to contemplate this plan seriously is a consciousness that Christ invites us to participate in it (*"Be perfect as your Father in heaven is perfect";* cf. SM 3) and an efficacious desire to offer ourselves in an act of trust and hope. Efficacious desire is a desire that will lead to a genuine effort toward realizing the gift of oneself with the intention of becoming consecrated. Interior practices are the best method for accomplishing this, provided we carry them out tirelessly. This is why Montfort could say that his way was *"sure"* and, as it were, unfailing.

By way of conclusion, Montfort gives us an example of his devotion: *"This Devotion at Holy Communion"* (TD 266–73).

3. Some General Remarks

a. True devotion and perfect practice. It is very important to recognize the distinction between a true devotion to Mary and perfect practice of true devotion according to St. Louis de Montfort. The first has by right been imposed absolutely on all of us, because God desires it; it can and must be made an *obligation* for all those who are aware of the mission that God Himself entrusted to Mary. We also have a pastoral duty to bring other faithful Christians to true devotion.

On the other hand, while we can propose perfect practice, it cannot by any means be made an obligation for all of us; nor can we simply assert that perfect devotion to Mary is impossible unless we adopt the way advocated by Montfort. Therefore, we must also make a distinction between an attitude toward Mary that may reach perfection in some other way than that explicitly advocated by Montfort (although it will include essential aspects of Montfort's approach, in spirit if not in fact), and *"perfect practice"* of true devotion. The term "practice" here refers to precise methods, codified to some extent, that one consciously attempts to put into use.

Montfort is justified in describing his practice as perfect, because it demands the radical step of giving oneself to Christ and because Mary exists as its *"perfect means"* (TD 120–26). He is also justified in emphasizing the relative ease of this practice and the advantages that it offers for advancing toward perfection, thanks to the gift of oneself to Mary and the constant collaboration with her (cf., e.g., TD 152–68). He never suggests that this is the only way of attaining perfection in Christian life. The strength of Montfort lies in his having presented, as no one had before him, 1) true devotion to Mary and why it is necessary, and 2) the consecration to Mary and holy slavery to her, which led him to total consecration to Christ at

Mary's hands. In this way, the word "consecration" takes on its full theological value, embodying all that it should.

b. The missionary dimension of Marian devotion. It would be surprising if Montfort had not grasped and articulated the apostolic dimension of all true Marian devotion. Although he does not include this dimension among the visible marks of true devotion, we would not be betraying him to consider it one. It is naturally connected to Mary and her mission: if she was made to lead us to Christ and help us to know him, how could she not urge her children forward on this same path? Whatever can be said of true devotion (e.g. TD 48, 57–59, 62, 113) can *a fortiori* be said of its perfect practice (e.g. TD 171–72, 214, 265).

c. Marian devotion and Christian life. Because, in Montfort's view, all true devotion to Mary has Christ and union with Christ as its ultimate objective, it cannot be pushed to one side of the Christian life; in fact, it must be placed at the very heart of Christian life. And the greater the devotion to Mary, the more apparent it must be that union with Christ is its goal. Therefore, perfect practice is equivalent in effect to the perfect renewal of baptismal promises. This explains why it is truly *"simple,"* because it includes no obligations that are new to those who wish to embrace it. After we are consecrated, we must attempt to accomplish all that our state of life requires, in the spirit of interior practice. Again, we need to find methods of doing this, and so it is useful to have recourse to these particular practices, which are flexible and bountiful and can be observed *"as far as one's circumstances and state of life permit"* (TD 257).

d. Receiving Mary's spiritual maternity. At the beginning of *True Devotion,* Montfort immerses us in the atmosphere of Mary's spiritual maternity toward us, which he sees as the direct (and, in God's plan, necessary) extension of her maternity toward Jesus. For Montfort, Mary becomes our Mother by virtue of the Incarnation. He thus sees in Mary's behavior toward Jesus the model of her behavior toward us; he also sees in Jesus' dependence on Mary, for his life and his worldly education (because in terms of his mission he is clearly the Teacher), the model of what must be our dependence on her, as children of God. Mary has dominion over us, exerts power over us, which is why we are dependent on her (TD 37, 74–77), but we must realize that it is in the end a dominion or power that is based on her divine maternity extending into spiritual maternity. Therefore, our dependence, our *"slavery,"* must be characterized by filial love.

III. True Devotion to the Blessed Virgin and Contemporary Christianity

The present-day appeal of TD is reflected in the new editions that are published regularly in many languages, and this appeal seems to be increasing rather than decreasing. This is a clear sign that the book continues to respond to needs and expectations. But two major reasons for this enduring appeal today deserve to be noted.

1. Chapter 8 of Lumen Gentium and True Devotion to Mary

We must begin by emphasizing that the Second Vatican Council wished to place its Marian teaching in a context that is broadly similar to that in which Montfort developed. The title of Chapter 8—"The role of the Blessed Virgin Mary, Mother of God, in the mystery of Christ and the Church"—expresses a fundamental preoccupation of the Council: to contemplate the Virgin, from the standpoint of Scripture and Tradition, in her most profound reality, viz., in her relationship with Christ. Here we discover the fundamental reason for Mary's existence and her relationship with the Church (i.e., with us), which is derived from her relationship with Christ in the mystery of salvation, as God's plan decrees. We can immediately see that this is also Montfort's perspective.

Therefore, we will find the same conclusions, beginning with Mary's mission in the Church in general and with respect to each of us in particular, and the need for the Church and for each of us to respond to her mission. In other words, devotion to Mary is necessary. Although the Council does not use the word "devotion," it is led to draw the same conclusion: "Taught by the Holy Spirit, the Catholic Church honors her with filial affection and piety as a most beloved mother" (LG 53); "This sacred Synod intends to describe with diligence the role of the Blessed Virgin in the mystery of the Incarnate Word and the Mystical Body. It also wishes to describe the duties of redeemed mankind toward the Mother of God, who is mother of Christ and mother of men" (LG 54). Montfort would be entirely comfortable with these affirmations.[39]

Thus, the Council's approach, based on Scripture and Tradition, was within bounds that Montfort would recognize. Of course, the Council could draw on contemporary exegesis and patristics, whereas Montfort could draw only on those available in his day. But the path that each took to discover Mary and her mission is largely the same. So it is not difficult to enrich Montfort's text with the contributions of Vatican II.

There is another issue to be raised. We have seen that Montfort was not content with a solid intellectual foundation for his arguments. He also referred to his own personal and pastoral experience, in his conviction that the Spirit was with him always. Likewise, the Synod was ready to cite the experience of the Church: "The Church does not hesitate to profess this subordinate role of Mary [i.e., her maternal role in total dependence on Christ]. She experiences it continuously and commends it to the hearts of the faithful, so that encouraged by this maternal help they may more closely adhere to the Mediator and Redeemer" (LG 62).

The Council insists several times on the absolute primacy of Christ and on Mary's relative status next to him (with which Montfort would be fully in agreement), so that it can illuminate true Marian piety in all its aspects.[40] The "marks" of genuine devotion that Montfort described can be found in Lumen Gentium, if in rather different language.[41] Here are two texts, the first from Vatican II, the second from Montfort, that demonstrate how far they agree on the nature of true devotion: "Let the faithful remember moreover that true devotion consists neither in fruitless and passing emotion, nor in a certain vain credulity. Rather, it proceeds from true faith" (LG 67); *"a good and faithful servant of Mary is guided in all his life by faith in Jesus and Mary, and not by feelings"* (TD 109).

We should also note how Mary is empowered by her elevation to glory to exercise fully her spiritual maternity. And for both Vatican II and Montfort this maternity becomes the site and the setting for our vital and contemporary encounter with her.[42]

It should be clear that underscoring these points of agreement is not to suggest that Vatican II addressed every issue that Montfort raised (beginning with the perfect practice of true devotion) or that Montfort is the sole author or devotee of Mary with whom such a strong connection could be established. But it is comforting and important to see that this basic agreement exists. Father H.-M. Manteau-Bonamy, an expert at the Synod, gives us this explanation: "Knowing that Monsignor Philips had drafted the outline for 52–59, and seeing that he liked to invoke Mary's role as a new Eve, I asked him, 'Did you consult Father de Montfort's *True Devotion to the Blessed Virgin?'* and he answered, 'I did not have it physically in front of me, but it was in my memory and in my heart while I was drafting this outline.'"[43]

2. True Devotion to the Blessed Virgin and John Paul II

John Paul II has made no secret of his ties to Montfort. We will discuss what bearing the saint has had on his personal piety and his teaching as the vicar of Christ.

a. The Marian piety of Karol Wojtyla and True Devotion. Pope John Paul II has himself spoken of his encounter with Montfort in TD and its consequences for his life:

"My life reached a decisive turning point when I read this book. I say 'turning point' although in fact it was part of an interior journey that coincided with my secret preparation for the priesthood. It was then that this singular book fell into my hands, one of those books of which one can say that simply 'having read' it is not enough. I remember carrying it with me for a long time, even to the soda works, to the point that there were lime stains all over its beautiful cover. I realized right away that there was something fundamental contained within that baroque style. From that point on, the devotion of my childhood and even of my adolescence to the Mother of God gave way to a new attitude, a devotion rising from the depths of my faith, as if from the very heart of the trinitarian and Christological reality."

"Whereas previously I had held back for fear that devotion to Mary would obscure Christ rather than give him precedence, I understood with the light of Grignion's book that in truth it was entirely different.

Our interior relationship to the Mother of God is the organic outgrowth of our connection to the mystery of Christ. So it is impossible that one should prevent us from seeing the other."[44]

In fact, quite the contrary: "'true devotion' to the Blessed Virgin reveals itself more and more clearly in those who advance in the mystery of Christ, the Word incarnate, and in the trinitarian mystery of salvation, which has this mystery at its center. We might even say that Christ himself appoints his mother to those who strive to know and to love him, as he did at Calvary for his disciple John."[45]

This account in itself, independent of the personality of the man who is giving it, is extraordinarily revelatory of how Montfort's teaching always remains contemporary. John Paul II did not hesitate to follow it to its very conclusion, to the perfect practice of true devotion. The papal motto he has chosen, "Totus tuus," calls this to mind.

b. The official teaching of John Paul II. It would be a labor of love to look for possible traces of Montfort's influence in the many pronouncements of the Pope, and to understand the light by which John Paul understood and used Montfort's writing.[46] We will confine ourselves to the exceptional contribution made by his encyclical on the Mother of the Redeemer to the subject of perfect practice.

For John Paul II, the Marian Year "is meant to promote a new and more careful reading of what the Council said about the Blessed Virgin Mary" (RM 48). He is referring not only to the *doctrine of faith,* but also to "*the life of faith*, and thus of authentic 'Marian spirituality,'" which, "like its corresponding *devotion,* finds a very rich source in the historical experience of individuals and of the various Christian communities present among the different peoples and nations of the world." And here he introduces a passage that speaks directly of Montfort: "In this regard, I would like to recall, among the many witnesses and teachers of this spirituality, the figure of Saint Louis Marie Grignion Montfort, who proposes consecration to Christ through the hands of Mary, as an effective means for Christians to live faithfully their baptismal commitments." This passage gives an excellent summary definition of perfect practice. And without resorting to triumphalism, we might note that this is the sole reference in the encyclical to a "spiritual teacher" and the specific path that he proposes. We cannot ask for clearer testimony to the contemporary quality of Montfort's message as presented in TD.

V. Conclusion

Montfort is one of those persons who leave an indelible mark on the history of the Church because of the intensity of their experience of God, thus they attain a kind of universality and permanence, transcending the marks of their own culture and era. This was the case for Saint Louis de Montfort.

A. Bossard

Notes: (1) As evidence we have the catalog of the Library of Saint-Sulpice, in five volumes, in Montfort's handwriting, now kept at the Bibliothèque Mazarine in Paris. Cf. M. Quéméneur, "Le catalogue de la Bibliothèque de St.-Sulpice" (The Catalog of the Library of Saint-Sulpice), DMon 9 (1964), 35. (2) P.-H. Eyckeler, S.M.M., *Le Cahier de Notes—Manuscrit de saint Louis-Marie de Montfort—notes et commentaire* (The Notebook—Manuscript of Saint Louis-Marie de Montfort—Notes and Commentary), roneographed edition. The following authors are quoted most often by Montfort, according to Father Eyckeler's list: F. Poiré, S.J., *La triple couronne de la Bienheureuse Vierge Mère* (The Triple Crown of the Blessed Virgin Mother), a book to which Montfort refers explicitly (TD 26); J.-B. Crasset, S.J., *La véritable dévotion à la Sainte Vierge* (True Devotion to the Holy Virgin); L.-F. D'Argentan, Capuchin, *Conférences sur les grandeurs de la Sainte Vierge* (Discussions Concerning the Greatness of the Holy Virgin); J. de Carthagena, *Homiliae Catholicae de Sacris Arcanis Deiparae Mariae;* P. Grenier, *Apologie des dévots de la Sainte Vierge* (Apologia for Devotion to the Blessed Virgin). Montfort drew on other authors as well, not the least of whom were Bérulle, Olier, Boudon, Boissieu, and Bernardine of Paris. (3) Saint-Jure's *L'homme spirituel* (The Spiritual Man), *Conduites pour les principales actions de la vie chrétienne* (Principal modes of conduct for the Christian life), *La vie de M. de Renty* (The Life of de Renty); Nepveu's *De l'amour de N. S. Jésus-Christ* (On the Love of Our Lord Jesus Christ). Father Eyckeler chose to attribute certain passages without references in the latter part of the notebook to Olier: Eyckeler, *Le Cahier de Notes*, 304, 309b. (4) One example: in his notebook (p. 57) he summarized the fourth star of the second crown of Poiré: "The most Blessed Virgin is the spouse of Our Lord", a title which is found nowhere in TD or in Montfort's other writings. (5) Father Eyckeler has noticed that, with respect to his analysis of Poiré, Montfort's method led him to study the texts of d'Argentan and Cartagena, subsequently complemented by texts from Crasset and Grenier. Father Eyckeler concludes that Montfort did not find Poiré's arguments adequate. (6) See for example Father Eyckeler's remark on Boissieu's work, *Le chrétien prédestiné par la dévotion à Marie* (The Christian Predestined through Devotion to Mary): "the influence of this book on Montfort's Marian doctrine is much greater than the rather few number of citations would suggest": Eyckeler, *Le Cahier de Notes*, XXI; cf. XVI on d'Argentan and XIX, n. 3, on Olier. (7) And yet Blain, 50, suggests that Montfort was directly inspired by this work during his time at Saint-Sulpice. All that we find in Montfort's notebook are a few passages from the *Avis catholiques touchant la véritable dévotion de la Bienheureuse Vierge* (Catholic Views on True Devotion to the Blessed Virgin), a work that is not in the Saint-Sulpice catalog (cf. Eyckeler, *Le Cahier de Notes*, 159–60). (8) Father Eyckeler suggests that this is particularly necessary for the texts of Grenier (Eyckeler, *Le Cahier de Notes,* XVII), but it is certainly true in other cases as well. (9) Cf. Boissieu, *Le chrétien prédestiné par la dévotion à Marie* (The Christian Predestined through Devotion to Mary) Lyon 1686, part one, chs. 1–4; d'Argentan, *Conférences sur les grandeurs de la Sainte Vierge* (Discussions concerning the greatness of the Holy Virgin), disc. 1, art. 1. (10) Cf. Eyckeler, XV. (11) The notes for the edition in OC give some idea of this documentation, as well as the work of Father Eyckeler, XI-XXIV. But more research, in particular a detailed critical examination of Montfort's method for using his sources, remains to be done. (12) See below, II.2.a–b. (13) Cf. TD, preface to the second edition, Paris 1843, x–xiii; also introduction to the photographic edition, Rome 1942, xviii–xx. (14) Ibid., xvii. (15) Cf. Besnard, *La vie de Soeur Marie-Louise de Jésus* (The Life of Sister Marie-Louise of Jesus) International Montfort Center, Rome 1985, 360–65. (16) Preface to the second edition, xii–xiii. (17) OC, 483. (18) Here are the subtitles supplied by Montfort (with current numbering): "The perfect consecration to Jesus Christ" (120); "The wonderful effects which this devotion produces on a soul that is faithful to it" (213); "Particular practices of this devotion—Exterior practices" (226); "Special interior practices for those who wish to be perfect" (257); "Method of practicing this devotion at Holy Communion" (266). (19) Father Eyckeler believes nonetheless that Montfort "had largely composed his Marian doctrine as early as 1703," and that when he began work on the final draft, "he inserted passages that were written earlier": Second Montfort International Conference, Saint-Laurent-sur-Sèvre, September 2-8, 1958, 17. (20) See OC, 481–82. (21) On Montfort and popular religion, see R. Mandrou, "Montfort et l'Évangélisation du peuple" (Montfort and the Evangelization of the People), in *Rencontres Montfortaines,* n. 11 (1974), 1-19; S. De Fiores, "Grignion de Montfort e la spiritualità popolare" (Grignion de Montfort and Popular Spirituality) in *AA.VV., Missioni al popolo per gli anni '80* (Rome 1981, 519ff; A. Bossard, "Il carisma del Montfort nel suo tempo: mediazione tra cultura colta e culturale popolare" (The Charism of Montfort in His Time: Mediation between Educated and Popular Culture) in QM 1 (1982), 86-96. (22) See the Introduction to the photographic edition, xxii. (23) Mame edition, Tours 1921. We can only discuss here the evolution of the various French editions. (24) Ibid., x. The Italian edition of 1919 was the first to divide the work into numbered paragraphs (cf. OC, 485). (25) At the 1906 Marian congress in Einsiedeln, this kind of shift in meaning appeared clearly in several connections: in the work of Joseph Péré, S.M.M., the theme of "true devotion" is discussed from the outset in terms of "holy slavery": *La vraie dévotion et la morale* (True Devotion and Morals), Acts of Congress, Revue Mariale, Lyon 1907, 234–46); or in the work by H. Clemens, S.M.M.: *De la diffusion parmi les fidèles de la parfaite consécration à Jésus par Marie* (On the Spread of Perfect Consecration to Jesus through Mary among the Faithful), Ibid., 269–88. In 1956, at the International Montfort Conference at Rotselaer, Father Josselin, Superior General of the Company of Mary, said, "Finally, the third unintelligent method (of presenting Montfort's message) is to consider True Devotion and Holy Slavery as identical, which is counter to Father Montfort's way of thinking. This is undoubtedly because we have to some extent forgotten the Pope's reminder to us in his address to the pilgrims following the Canonization. We must admit that one can love and serve the Most Blessed Virgin outside of Holy Slavery. Otherwise we would be accused of building a 'monopoly.' And it is never pleasant to hear that said." (Reports and Resolutions of the Conference, 14.) And yet, at this same conference, Father Ghidotti admitted as self-evident on the level of vocabulary that "by a kind of tacit agreement, in the expression 'true devotion,' the word 'true' recalled the 'Consecration of oneself to Jesus Christ, Wisdom Incarnate, through the hands of Mary'" (although he claimed that on the intellectual level the two can be distinguished): Ibid., 33. In a remarkable account, *Comment étudier et présenter la Vraie dévotion* (How to Study and Present True Devotion), Father Frehen, S.M.M., reacted vigorously, and quite fairly, against this habit, and noted in passing how dangerous it could prove, such as in certain translations of *True Devotion:* Ibid., 44–47). (26) OC, 484. (27) On this subject, cf. A. Bossard, "Marie, 'milieu mystérieux' pour rejoindre le Christ" (Mary, "mysterious setting" for Becoming United with Christ), in *Dieu seul* (God Alone), 119 and ff. (28) Reports and Resolutions of the Conference at Rotselaer, 71. (29) Therefore we can presume that Montfort went beyond the sources on which he drew. For those sources, particularly those that can be found in his notebook, we can refer to the notes in OC. (30) L.-J. Suenens, *Une nouvelle Pentecôte* (A New Pentecost) DDB, Paris 1974, 241. (31) One of the censors of Montfort's writings at the beatification proceedings had raised the following objection: the renewal of baptismal promises is an act of latria that can only be addressed directly and immediately to God; he also suggested that the total gift of oneself, as described by Montfort, referred to latria and thus could only be made to God. Cf. *Lucionen. Beatificationis et canonizationis Ven. Servi Dei Ludovici Mariae Grignion de Montfort—Position super scriptis,* Rome 1851, 11–13; also the responses that had already been mounted to these objections, *Responsio ad adnotationes R.P.D. Promotororis fidei,* 34. In themselves, the assertions were just, but their application to Montfort's teaching was not. This indicates how important it is to make necessary distinctions in order to convey the doctrine of Saint Louis Marie correctly. (32) We must take this point into account if we wish to grasp exactly how Montfort understands the title "Spouse of the Holy Spirit": as soon as he offers an explanation, he speaks in terms of spiritual maternity, even when his point of departure is Mary's association with the Spirit for the Incarnation: TD 20–21, 36. Most often he simply speaks of the united action of Mary and the Spirit in us, e.g., of spiritual maternity: TD 25, 34, 36, 164, 213, 217, 269. This is also the case when the term "Spouse" is attributed to the Holy Spirit and its relationship to Mary: TD 36, 152. (33) We must understand that Montfort is very particular about his use of the words "slave," and "slavery"; he justifies it by appealing to the Word of God, which lends irrefutable strength to his argument. If we decide for whatever reason that we can no longer use these terms, we must search for words that capture everything that this concept entails—not an easy task. (34) When we read the opening sentence of TD 118 *("Having read nearly every book on devotion to the Blessed Virgin . . . , I can now state with conviction that I have never known or heard of any devotion to our Lady which is comparable to the one I am going to speak of"),* we must remember (a) Montfort's subsequent efforts to show that the devotion he is teaching is not "new" (TD 159), (b) his remarks in LEW 219, and (c) his unequivocal assertion in SM 1: *"Here is a secret, chosen soul, which the most High God taught me and which I have not found in any book, ancient or modern."* One way of resolving these statements would be as follows: as he presents it to us, the perfect practice of true devotion has no equivalent among his sources; in this respect it is genuinely new, and so he is entitled to call himself its inventor. It is difficult to identify the extent to which he was conscious of the originality of his path; he unhesitatingly credits his inspiration to God Himself (SM 1, TD 119). (35) Cf. the title of his profession of consecration in LEW 223: *"Consecration of oneself to Jesus Christ, Wisdom incarnate, through the hands of Mary."* (36) Compared with Jobert and Boudon, in whose writings the theologal or Christological aspect is always present but usually only implicitly or indirectly so, Montfort crosses a threshold that tranforms our way of understanding holy slavery: Jobert, *La dévotion du saint esclavage de la Mère de Dieu* (The Devotion of Holy Slavery to the Mother of God) Orleans 1785 [1668], 3–4; Boudon, *Dieu seul ou le saint esclavage de l'admirable Mère de Dieu* (God Alone Or the Holy Slavery of the Admirable Mother of God), 1667, First Treatise, chs. 1–2 (the imprimatur for the first edition is dated December 5, 1667). Similarly, the "prayer for consecration of oneself to the Blessed Virgin as a slave" at the end of Jobert's book, replicated in almost perfect detail at the conclusion of Boudon's book, proves interesting when compared with Montfort's in LEW 223–27. On a number of issues, there are points of contact, yet one can see the path traveled by Montfort. (37) It was undoubtedly through Bérulle (cf. the *Notebook*, 302–303) that Montfort was led to join, and almost to consider as identical, "consecration of oneself to Jesus Christ by the hands of Mary" and the renewal of baptismal vows and promises. But he was capable of exploring the relationship between the two in depth and perceiving an organic connection, whereas for Bérulle, according to Father Eyckeler, "this question was only secondary, a piece of luck in a way, allowing him to escape from the difficulty he encountered when he called his 'donation' a vow": *Notebook,* xix. (38) This issue of imitating Jesus's dependence on Mary in the Incarnation and on his chosen path is certainly present in Jobert and Boudon, including their acts of consecration or offering. But Montfort introduces and develops this issue in a way that renders it much weightier and more significant. (39) Cf. the affirmation of the special character of Marian ("this devotion is altogether special," LG 66, which can be connected to TD 39, for example). (40) Cf., e.g., LG 60: the Unique Mediator and Savior (compare with TD 61); LG 66: "While honoring Christ's Mother, these devotions cause her Son to be rightly known, loved, and glorified, and all His commands observed. Through Him all things have their being (cf. Col. 1:15-16) and in Him 'it has pleased [the eternal Father] that . . . all his fullness should dwell' (Col. 1:19)" (cf. TD 13, 49, 62, e.g.). (41) For *"true devotion to our Lady is interior"* (TD 106), cf. LG 67; *"trustful"* (TD 107), cf. the passages wherein the Council adopts a vocabulary with clear affective resonance to speak of the relationship that we must establish with Mary, such as LG 53, 62, or 67; *"holy"* (TD 108); *"constant"* (TD 109), cf. LG 67. (42) The quite strong language used in Lumen Gentium to describe Mary after the Assumption, i.e., as she is today ("By her maternal charity, Mary cares for the brethren of her Son who still journey on earth"), could be used as a title for whole chapters of TD. However, there is one important aspect of Mary's maternity toward us, notable in Chapter 8 of LG (at 58, 61), to which Montfort seems to attach less importance than we do today: the proclamation by Christ on the Cross of Mary's maternity toward his disciple (Jn 19:25–27). It is true that today, especially with the teaching of the Magisterium, it is impossible to discuss Mary's spiritual maternity without referring to this passage. But it can be easily and naturally integrated into Montfort's teaching, especially as he often referred to John taking Mary "for his all" (TD 144, 179, 216, 266). (43) H.-M. Manteau-Bonamy, *S. Louis-Marie Grignion de Montfort, théologien de la Sagesse au seuil du troisième millénaire* (St. Louis-Marie Grignion de Montfort, Theologian of Wisdom on the Eve of the Third Millenium), Éd. Saint-Paul, Paris 1986, 54. (44) André Frossard, *"Be Not Afraid!" Pope John Paul II Speaks Out on his Life, his Beliefs and his Inspiring Vision for Humanity,* St. Martin's Press, New York 1982, 124–27. (45) Ibid. (46) We should observe in particular how John Paul II uses the terms *"affidamento"* and "consecration" with respect to the relationship with Mary as such, and the significance of this use depending on the context. He definitely uses the term "consecration" when, following Montfort, he speaks of the total gift of oneself to Christ by the hands of Mary: RMat 48.

IL BEATO LUDOVICO-MARIA GRIGNON DI MONTFORT
FONDATORE DEI MISSIONARII DELLA COMPAGNIA DI MARIA,
E DELLA CONGREGAZIONE DELLE FIGLIE DELLA SAPIENZA

Mother Mary Louise Receives the Habit

This traditional painting portrays Montfort presenting Blessed Marie Louis of Jesus with the habit of the Daughters of Wisdom at the General Hospital in Poiters on February 2, 1703. Anachronistically, Brother Mathurin and Fr. Mulot are pictured in attendance. Nearly 10 years later the Congregation of the Daughters of Wisdom was officially founded in La Rochelle on October 17, 1712.

VIRTUES

SUMMARY

I. VIRTUES PRACTICED BY MONTFORT:
  1. Two comprehensive testimonials;
  2. Practice of some virtues in particular;
  3. Special difficulty with certain virtues;
  4. Meaning of these virtues and their unity;
    a. Virtues and holiness;
    b. Virtues and devotion to Mary;
    c. Meaning and unity of Montfort's virtues.

II. MONTFORT AND THE VIRTUES:
  1. The "Treatise on the Virtues" in Father de Montfort's hymns;
  2. Virtues of the Christian and the apostle;
    a. Virtues of the Christian;
    b. Virtues of the apostle;
  3. Reflection on the meaning of these virtues and their unity;
    a. Virtues and virtue;
    b. Virtues of the Christian and those of the world;
    c. Virtues and love;
    d. Virtues and the consecration.

III. VIRTUES OF MARY:
  1. Virtues of Mary
  2. Mary and the virtues;
    a. Mary, model of the Christian virtues;
    b. Mary, mother who shares her virtues.

IV. VIRTUES OF JESUS:
  1. Virtues of God;
  2. Virtues of Jesus.

V. MONTFORT VIRTUES TODAY:
  1. Some difficulties;
  2. Effective directions for today;
  3. Useful reminders for today.

I. VIRTUES PRACTICED BY MONTFORT

One cannot separate the virtues practiced by Father de Montfort from those he called others to practice, such as in his set of hymns known as the "Treatise on the Virtues." One of Montfort's dominant virtues was precisely that his preaching and his own life were one. A priest who worked with him and knew him well, Father Dubois, writes: "What was unique in the life of Father de Montfort was his integrity. At no moment did he appear different from his ordinary self . . . on retreat or in public functions, with the poor, with the rich, in drinking and eating, alone or in company, and so on."[1]

1. Two Comprehensive Testimonials

There are two key testimonials to the virtues of Father de Montfort. One was written at the beginning of his active life, the other at the end. The two can be regarded as containing a basic list of his virtues. The first is a letter from Father Leschassier (Louis Marie's spiritual director) dated May 13, 1701: "I have known Father Grignion for some years. God has outfitted him with many graces, and he has responded faithfully. He has appeared to me, as to so many others who have examined him closely, to have been constant in the love of God and the practice of prayer, mortification, poverty, and obedience. He has a great deal of zeal in helping the poor and instructing them. He has industry and perseverance in many matters. He appears rather single minded, and his manners not quite to the taste of a goodly number of folk. He has such a high idea of perfection, plenty of zeal, and little experience."[2]

The second list of virtues comes to us from his biographer Blain, who speaks to us of his friend's death: "He died as he had lived, as a saint, with the liveliest sentiments of faith, the most tender piety, the most perfect abandonment to God, the purest charity, and a trust in and tenderness toward the holy Virgin that is practically without precedent."[3]

2. Practice of Some Virtues in Particular

The whole life of Father de Montfort would have to be analyzed in order to show how he practiced each of the virtues that made a saint of him. Suffice it to cite some of these virtues, without distinguishing between what might be called the basic Christian virtues and the properly apostolic virtues.

With Montfort, personal poverty, self-abandonment to divine Providence, and love for the poor, were perhaps one and the same virtue. He chose poverty, traveling always on foot, "in the manner of the apostles," begging for his bread along the route, renouncing the benefices that would have brought him security (L 6, 20). He wrote to his mother (L 20) excusing himself for not being able to help his brothers and sisters *("For the moment, I have no worldly goods to give them for I am poorer than all of them"):* he does not wish to *"exchange divine Providence for a canonry or a benefice"* (L 6), for this would be *"to be separated from my mother, divine Providence"* (L 10). This choice also enabled him to enter into solitude with the world of the poor, to be one with those in whom he recognized the very face of Jesus. "His tenderness for the poor, if I may make bold to say so," writes Blain, "went quite to excess. He regarded them as a sacrament, containing Jesus Christ hidden beneath their repulsive exterior. A poor person, he used to say, is a great mystery. One must be able to penetrate it."[4]

In the radiant warmth of this love for the very poorest shine two other virtues that Louis Marie practiced to a heroic degree, both of which find their crown in mercy and love of enemies: a love of others as his brothers and sisters, and graciousness. When Montfort sings, in his canticle of charity: *"Who should be surprised / that I love my neighbor so?"* (H 148:4), we have a strong feeling that he is expressing his own experience. He who possessed a heart "more tender than anyone else's" had a more than motherly tenderness for his neighbor, especially for the very poorest. *"The Christian and fatherly love I bear you,"* he writes to the people of Montbernage, *"is so great that you will always have a place in my heart as long as I live and even into eternity"* (LPM 1). Altogether naturally he is called "the good Father from Montfort." But his goodness appears in its full light—in its full holiness—in the forgiveness he accords those who have done him harm. For Father Brenier, who humiliated him "fully, at length, and publicly" the whole time he was his spiritual director, his penitent has only words of gratitude: *"I take the liberty of greeting Fr. Brenier and humbly thanking him. God only knows all the good he has done for me"* (L 10).

However, Louis Marie obtained this forgiving graciousness only at the price of painful battles and fervent prayers. He himself testified to Father des Bastières that, "if God had destined him for the world, he would have been the most terrible man of his century"; but, his friend adds, "he bent unbelievable efforts to conquer his natural impetuousness, succeeded in the end, and acquired this charming virtue of graciousness. . . . It was painted on his face, it burst forth in all his dealing."[5] His last sermon, just before his death, was to be on *"the tenderness of Jesus"* (LS 1718–26).

This graciousness doubtless has its roots in two other deeply integrated virtues, which were, it appears, the basis of Montfort's holiness, and which he lived as essential apostolic virtues. They allowed him to practice self-effacement, in order to let Christ himself speak and act in him. Humility led him to obey, and obedience needed humility. "These two virtues appeared in very tangible ways in all of Father de Montfort's actions," Besnard writes. "He was always seen blindly submitting to the most rigorous and most unexpected orders. Perhaps he would never have acquired them [these virtues] had the desire to be humiliated, and despised, not tempered his great zeal and the freedom of the gospel."[6] It is beautiful to see Louis Marie writing to the people of the outlying districts of Montbernage, to whom he has just preached a mission: *"dear women of St. Simplicien who sell fish and meat, and other shopkeepers and retailers"* (LM 5). Although only thirty-two years of age, he noted: *"Surrounded by all this I am very weak, even weakness personified; I am ignorant, even ignorance personified and even worse besides which I do not dare to speak of"* (LM 6). But again, barely a month before his death, he concluded a letter: *"Humility! Humiliations! Humiliations! Thanks be to God for them,"* after having asked to be prayed for, *"so that,"* he wrote, *"God will not punish my sins and refuse true conversion of heart to all the poor who listen to my preaching"* (L 33).

Although he directed his missioners *"to state openly and straightforwardly the reasons they may have for omitting or for not undertaking what is commanded"* (RM 27), he sings: *"I tell it before my very God: / I had rather die, / and die anathema, / than disobey"* (H 91:28).

One sees that this person had taken

obedience, like humility , to an "all-consuming extreme."[7] As early as the days of Saint-Sulpice, he could not resist, Blain tells us, "making use of innocent subterfuges and little tricks" to obtain explicit permission to perform acts of even the smallest details of community life.[8] At Poitiers, again, he felt the need to consult constantly his spiritual director, Father Leschassier, on the tiniest decisions that he had to make: *"Am I doing the right thing? . . . Have I done the right thing? . . . Am I doing the right thing?"* (L 10). Montfort obeyed the bishops with scrupulous exactitude, throughout his whole apostolic life. It is no doubt significant that among all of the things he was reproached for, the only one he did not accept was that of disobedience: "He was convinced," Blain tells us, "that obedience was the mark of the will of God. One must never depart from it. But his conscience made him irreproachable on this subject. At all times and in all circumstances, he was ready to obey, and to do nothing without the approval of his superiors."[9]

A study like this one does not permit a detailed examination of every virtue that made Louis Marie a saint. We should, though, speak of his courage, his apostolic zeal, his heroic mortification, his love of crosses, his virtue of religion. He always practiced fervent adoration in prayer, the four cardinal virtues—justice, fortitude, prudence, and temperance—and the three great theological virtues that have God as their object: faith, hope, and love.

However, wisdom was for him the crown of virtues: Certainly nothing is higher than faith, hope, and love, but as with these theological virtues, wisdom was for Montfort not so much a virtue as a gift. St. Louis Marie himself speaks of the gift that is greater than faith (also a virtue). It is "the cross," or more precisely, the enjoyment and actual possession of the mystery of the cross (LEW 175). The great foolishness of the cross was for Montfort the wisdom of love. In this sense we can say that Montfort's greatest virtue was wisdom. Wisdom was central when he began the "Wisdom" prayer group in the poorhouse at Poitiers,[10] in order *"to confound the false wisdom of the people of the world";* when he dreamt of erecting a gigantic Calvary at Pontchâteau; when he shared his meals with paupers, (letting them treat him as poorly as they pleased);[11] when he obeyed the least justifiable order of a superior. Montfort was, very simply, *wise,* because he possessed the true wisdom of love which is folly, the very folly of God (1 Cor 1:21–24).

3. Special Difficulty with Certain Virtues

It is always difficult to "put one's finger on" the mystery of holiness. Ordinarily, progress in virtue and the practice of the beatitudes will render a Christian more "human." The demands of gospel love know no measure, and demand everything, without reserve. Such demands are difficult to reconcile with a purely human outlook in which the supreme criterion would be some kind of balance.

Some have said that throughout most of his life, Montfort appeared to have had difficulty in forming deep personal relationships. "Socially maladjusted" and "inable to particpate in common social structures" have been said of him. It has been observed that he never succeeded in "enlisting genuine collaborators while he was alive."[12] However, such a judgment, even if correct, should also take into consideration the amazing apostolic successes of Louis Marie: the truly amazing conversions he brought about, the deep, lasting attachments of certain collaborators such as Father des Bastières, the altogether spontaneous affection felt for him by the poor of Poitiers: *"They have become so attached to me that they are going about saying openly that I am to be their priest"* (L 6). If Montfort had difficulty in relating to others, then how can we explain that, as early as 1702 (when he was only twenty-nine), he could testify how God had given him *"a great capacity for sympathizing with everyone,"* and that he was *"highly praised by nearly everyone in the town"* (L 11)? He who some say "disqualifies himself because of his moralistic statements to and about women" is the same one who would "forge very delicate friendships with female personages throughout his life":[13] Marie-Louise de Jésus, Catherine Brunet, and others. One should properly speak of Montfort as a "rare human, with a tender capacity for love."[14]

It has also been asserted by some that Montfort suffered from a low self-esteem, a difficulty in loving himself,[15] for he sees himself like a *"snail in its shell, which, when it is hidden, seems to be something of value, but when it comes out is wretched and disgusting"* (L 4). However, it must be noted that in the next letter, a few months after his ordination, he does not hesitate to express his feelings, his *"tremendous urge"* to sow a love of Our Lord and Our Lady in human hearts, an urge he finds to be *"good and persistent."* As humble as he was, he did not bat an eyelash about founding a new congregation of priests before he had even begun his own ministry (L 5).

Saint Louis Marie's insistence on *"God Alone"* is also considered to be another of his faults. It is said that he risked forgetting that he was a human person who needed to love other persons. But such words and phrases should not be taken out of context. To say that Montfort had little regard for himself as a person, or for his neighbor, is clearly contradicted by even a superficial glance at his life and writings. Montfort insisted: *"Though God perform a work, / And we do nothing there, / still must we perform it / indeed, and do it well"* (H 26:21).

Again, he asked that the Daughters of Wisdom *"abandon themselves to the care of God's divine Providence, . . . as though they expected to receive food and care directly from an angel sent from heaven."* Yet, that they *"undertake manual work to help earn their living, as though they expected nothing from God"* (RW 29).

Such open-minded care is scarcely compatible with the fault with which Father de Montfort is most reproached: his "individualism." His Sulpician masters, for whom the term "individual" was synonymous with "stubborn," showed no pity in seeking to rid their disciples of such singular tendencies. Toward the end of his life, in 1714, his friend Blain reproached him: "'But where, in the Gospel,' I told him, 'will you find instances and examples of these unusual individualistic ways of yours?'"[16] Montfort in response made a distinction between three kinds of individualism: the first was from personality, temperment or nature, the second was evangelical, and the third might be called missionary. If it was the first, he would be helped to notice it for he would be humiliated by it—which would prove useful. If it was the second, it was a fault possessed by every saint in helping them to avoid conforming to worldly wisdom. Third, if it was the third it would tend to support his becoming a better missionary by avoiding settling down in one community."[17]

4. Meaning of These Virtues and Their Unity

Having thus considered the criticisms made of Montfort for his lack of "humanness," perhaps now it might be helpful to reflect briefly on all of his virtues.

a. Virtues and holiness. First, all of the virtues practiced by Montfort should not be confused with his holiness. His friend Blain, who admired him so much, spoke of the "mystery" of Louis Grignion. Blain wrote: "He was an avowed saint, and his praises were sung now for his great modesty, now for his recollection, now for his humility, often for his great mortification and his austerities, at other times for his love of poverty and the poor, for his charity and his zeal, and especially for his great tenderness and devotion toward the Blessed Virgin. And you ask whether he trod the path of the saints?"[18]

"He is most humble," declared Father Leschassier, "very poor, very mortified, very recollected. And yet I find it difficult to believe that he is led by the good Spirit."[19] Almost all of his life, to be sure, according to his friend Blain, Montfort posed "a problem for spiritual persons."[20] This problem has been solved, in a sense, by Louis Marie's canonization. But at least we are reminded that holiness is not a collection of virtues. Holiness consists in the practice of the theological virtues, whose pathway is more one of beatitude than virtue. It is a path of "poverty of heart," and it is compatible with many a fault. The secret of this path is hidden from the prideful and revealed to the humble. For Montfort the path was his consecration to Jesus through Mary.

b. Virtues and devotion to Mary. Devotion to the Virgin Mary is without doubt a virtue, and in the classic sense of the term. Within all of Louis Marie's virtues (including the theological ones), and within his holiness, there is the great secret of his consecration. Had Montfort merely been content in acquiring and practicing virtue at the price of a demanding asceticism, he would have *"sculpted his statue"* and never succeeded in *"forming Jesus"* in a way that was *"natural"* (cf. TD 220). He did better than that: he let himself be led by the Holy Spirit (TD 258). Montfort was a very "mortified" person, and his mortifications doubtless were beyond what saints normally imposed on themselves. But the profoundest mortification that he chose was his spiritual asceticism, which consisted in his becoming a soul *"thoroughly tractable, entirely detached, most ready to be molded in [Mary] by the Holy Spirit,"* without any reliance on its *"own skill and industry"* (SM 20), casting itself into Mary, *"the 'living mold of God'"* (SM 18, citing St. Augustine).

With the devotion to the Mother of God, one might say that, in Louis

Marie, the virtue of mortification shifted: it was spiritualized, deepened. In renouncing self-reliance, and a life lived of himself, he installed death (and hence life) at the very wellspring of his being. He did this in order that it might no longer be he who lived, but Mary (and hence Jesus) who lived in him. With the consecration to Jesus through Mary, it could be said that Montfort's mysticism becomes asceticism.

c. Meaning and unity of Montfort's virtues. We should see Montfort's life of virtue and holiness in the light of the consecration. In this way we will better understand what the practice of virtue meant to him. For him virtues were not just a series of habits to be acquired or commandments to be observed. They were the practice of that *"necessary and fruitful death,"* without which it is impossible to bear fruit (TD 81); to put it positively, they establish within the person, the life and mind of Jesus, incarnate Wisdom (Ph 2:5).

These virtues find another source of unity, as it were, in a focus on mission. Montfort practiced humility, obedience, and poverty, to the point of appearing to be a fool in the eyes of the world. He did so, of course, because these were the virtues of Jesus and he wanted to live them in his own life. But he also chose to live them because he was a missionary. Missionaries did not come from themselves, nor did they proclaim themselves. In order to be someone truly sent, and not to proclaim oneself but He who sends, one must be humble, poor and obedient. One must live what he preaches.

II. Montfort and the Virtues

This section considers the virtues Montfort taught and preached.

1. The "Treatise on the Virtues" in Father de Montfort's Hymns

We find a first listing of the virtues in LEW: *"When Eternal Wisdom communicates himself to a soul, he gives that soul . . . all the great virtues to an eminent degree. They are: the theological virtues—lively faith, firm hope, ardent charity; the cardinal virtues—well-ordered temperance, complete prudence, perfect justice, invincible fortitude; the moral virtues—perfect religion, profound humility, pleasing gentleness, blind obedience, complete detachment, continuous mortification, sublime prayer, etc."* (LEW 99).

In the *Hymns* one finds a far more complete collection of virtues. If we count as virtues mental and vocal prayer, contempt for the world, the cross (as a way of life), praise, thanksgiving, and so on, then we may say that Father de Montfort sings the virtues in nearly 80 of the 164 hymns; i.e., almost half.

A possible catalogue of the hymns on the virtues would be the following:

a. Hymn on virtue in general: "Esteem and Desire of Virtue" (H 1).

b. Eleven hymns on the theological virtues—faith: "Lights of Faith" (H 6); hope: firmness of hope (H 7), "Joys of Paradise" (H 116); charity: generally, "Excellence of Charity" (H 5); love of God: "New Canticle on the Love of God" (H 135, 138), "Serving God in the Spirit" (H 153); love of neighbor: "Tenderness of Charity" (H 14), "Hymn of Charity" (H 148); love for the poor: value of alms (H 17), "Cries of the Poor" (H 18).

c. Forty hymns on the moral

virtues—one on the virtue of religion: "Service of God in Spirit and Truth" (H 153); four on the virtue of humility: "Splendor of Humility" (H 8), "Good Odor of Modesty" (H 25), "Children's Great Lesson" (H 97), "New Canticle of the Poor in Spirit" (H 144); two on the virtue of trust: "Abandonment to Providence" (H 28), "Miseries of this Life, and Trust in God" (H 114); one on the virtue of graciousness: "Charms of Graciousness" (H 9); one on the virtue of obedience: "Merit of Obedience" (H 10); one on the virtue of patience: "Strength of Patience" (H 11); one on the virtue of chastity: "Beauty of Virginity" (H 12); four on the virtue of penitence: "Need for Penitence" (H 13), "Power of Fasting" (H 16), "The Penitent Who Loved Much" (H 94); "Specific Nature of Tepidity" (H 161); four on the virtue of mental and vocal prayer: "Splendors of Prayer" (H 15), "Wisdom of Silence" (H 23), "Holy Practice of the Presence of God" (H 24), "New Canticle on Solitude" (H 157); one on devotion to Mary: "Zealous Devotee of Mary" (H 80); two on the virtue of poverty: "Treasures of Poverty" (H 20), "Treasures of Poverty," once more (H 108); one on the virtue of gratitude: "Duties of Gratitude" (H 26); fourteen on contempt for the world: "Misfortunes of the World" (H 29), "Snares of the World: Games of Chance" (H 30), "Dancing and Balls" (H 31), "Comedy and Shows" (H 32), "Luxury" (H 33), "Human Respect" (H 34–39), "Condemnation of the World" (H 106), "Farewell, Mad World!" (H 107), "Vanities of the World" (H 156); three on the mystery of the cross: "Triumph of the Cross" (H 19, 102); "Treasures of the Cross" (H 123).

d. Nine hymns on the virtues to be practiced in certain conditions of life—For religious: "To the Religious of the Visitation" (H 48), "The Good Sisters of the Third Orders" (H 92), "To the Daughters of Wisdom" (H 149); for virgins: "Beauty of Virginity" (H 12); for children: "The Good Child" (H 93); for soldiers: "The Good Soldier" (H 95); for prisoners: "The Good Prisoner" (H 96); for shepherdesses (and country folk): "The Good Shepherdess" (H 99); for married persons: "New Canticle for the Christian Wedding" (H 146).

e. Sixteen hymns on virtues to be practiced in certain situations—for persons afflicted with scruples: "The Scrupulous Person Converted" (H 45); for persons who live in affliction: "Consolation of the Afflicted" (H 46, 100, 101); for persons undergoing trials: "Strength of Patience" (H 11), "Miseries of this Life and Trust in God" (H 114); for persons to whom a mission is being preached: "Christ's Call to the Sinner to Take Advantage of the Mission" (H 105), "The Mission Opens" (H 115), "Wake-Up Call of the Mission" (H 163); for converted sinners: "The Sinner Converted by Mary's Intercession" (H 79), "Rule for a Converted Person" (H 139), "The Converted Sinner" (H 140), "Resolutions of a Converted Sinner" (H 142), "Canticle on the Conversion of a Worldly Woman" (H 143), "The True Christian" (H 154); for persons on pilgrimage: "Holy Journey" (H 162).

f. Three hymns on the apostolic virtues: "Flames of Zeal" (H 21), "Resolutions and Prayers of a Missionary Perfected and Zealous" (H

22), "The Good Missionary" (H 91).

This catalogue is incomplete. Furthermore, some hymns are listed twice, since they illustrate two categories of virtues. Finally, some hymns that are prayers rather than expositions have been omitted.

Although the theological virtues are certainly represented, there is no specific hymn devoted to a cardinal virtue. It must be remembered that the *Hymns* are not the only works of Montfort which present the virtues. The *Sermons* speak of them, as well, and, in a sense, the missioner's entire work is organized in function of them.

2. Virtues of the Christian and the apostle

It would impossible here to illustrate every virtue whose praises Montfort sang. The texts themselves should be thoroughly studied. Here we indicate certain key Christian virtues of the Christian, especially those that are uniquely apostolic.

a. Virtues of the Christian. *Faith, hope,* and *love.* Faith, hope, and love bring one to God so strongly that, in a sense, they "overcome" God. Faith, especially Mary's, and her love, actually attract and "force" God: *"'So great was the love of Mary,' explains St. Augustine, 'that it conquered the omnipotent God'—O quantus amor illius qui vincit omnipotentem"* (LEW 107).

Humility. Humility may be the most important moral virtue for Montfort. In the *"earthly paradise of the new Adam,"* the cardinal virtues are but the four branches of the great *"river of humility that gushes forth from the soil"* (TD 261). Humility, too, like the theological virtues, has the power to attract God, to overcome or *"surmount"* God: *"He is insurmountable, / but the humble one is His conqueror; / with an ineffable strength, / that one wins His heart"* (H 8:4).

Bound up with obedience, humility enables its practitioner to *"make more progress in virtue than others"* (RW 64). At one with the Beatitude of "poverty of heart," such a soul becomes like a theological virtue. The soul reaches God all the more easily for God's incarnation in Jesus reveals God to her, and fills her with humility. "Humility" becomes a synonym for "perfection." The true devotion that Montfort undertakes to explain *"is more perfect,"* Montfort makes bold to say, *"because it supposes a greater humility to approach God through a mediator rather than directly by ourselves"* (TD 83).

Trust and abandonment. From humility a whole constellation of virtues emanate: poverty, trust, abandonment to divine Providence. All have their goal in the withdrawal of the Christian from self in order to become open to the other. It is an experience of total letting go into the hands of the Father. There is no contempt for action here. One must toil at the work of God, and *"toil well"* (H 28:21), as if one expected nothing of God (RW 29). But one should preserve sufficient openness of spirit not to forget that activity, important as it is, is never anything but a *"virginity"* in need of fecundation by the Spirit in order to bear fruit.

When, in TD, Montfort describes the behavior of the predestined, he cites the virtues that seem to him to be important for the Christian. Christians are interior persons. They have a taste for retreat and prayer. *"It is true, at times they do venture out into the world, but only . . . in obedience";* doubtless because we are ourselves more obviously in action than in prayer (TD 196; cf. 187, 191). They rely not on themselves, but on God and Mary (TD 186, 194, 199). They are submissive and obedient (TD 193, 198). They imitate the Blessed Virgin (TD 195, 200), and love her (TD 193, 197).

b. Virtues of the apostle. Every Christian must be an apostle. The virtues of the one are the virtues of the other. But it is possible to single out some more typically apostolic virtues.

Zeal. Zeal is the shape of a love become a missionary love. Montfort sings of a raging *"fire"* with which he would have all apostles burn. *"No single hour can I rest, / nor sit one minute still: / I see Jesus offended!"* (H 22:12). *"Might I see this soul [my neighbor's], so lovely, / fall into death everlasting? / I had rather be anathema. Ah, Lord, they all outrage you / in the human being, your beautiful image! / Shall I keep silent? Shall I bear it? / Rather death itself!"* (H 22:2–3)

When we prefer to die, or even to be separated from Jesus, rather than see a neighbor going to perdition; when I am able to declare: *"I am ready to sacrifice my time, my health and my life for the souls of the poor in this neglected house"* (L 6); or when I can tell someone who threatens me with death, *"I had rather a thousand times the salvation of your soul than ten thousand lives like mine"*[21] —then I shall be a *"perfected, zealous missionary"* in the spirit of Montfort (H 22).

Freedom. "Freedom" could be the name of a whole cluster of apostolic virtues: detachment, poverty, abandonment to divine providence, obedience. The apostle must be detached from all things, not only in order to be *"free as the clouds that sail high above the earth, . . . according to the inspiration of the Spirit"* (PM 9), but also the better to let Christ shine through us and act of himself. *"What, then, am I asking for?"* cries Montfort in the burning Prayer for Missionaries. *"Priests who are free with the freedom that comes from you, detached from everything, without father, mother, brothers, sisters or relatives and friends as the world and the flesh understand them, without worldly possessions to encumber or distract them, and devoid of all self interest"* (PM 7). The virtue of poverty is significant in this respect. It permits us to remove ourselves from all that prevents us from depending on God and on others. Shall we therefore fall back into slavery? By no means. If we depend completely on God, we shall be able to, and shall actually, work *"prodigies of grace."*[22]

Prayer. Prayer may not be directly a virtue. Saint Thomas sees it as an act of the virtue of religion.[23] But Father de Montfort asks his missioners to apply themselves to it *"unceasingly,"* as well as to study, *"that they may obtain from God the gift of wisdom so necessary to a true preacher for knowing and relishing the truth and getting others to relish it"* (RM 60). *"It is the easiest thing in the world,"* he adds, *"to be a fashionable preacher. It is a difficult but sublime thing to be able to preach with the inspiration of an apostle"* (RM 60), *"under the impulse of divine Wisdom"* (LEW 97), with words *"that go from the heart of the one through whom he speaks straight to the heart of the listener"* (LEW 96). But such a gift, for the apostle, is the fruit of toil and prayer (RM 60).

Finally, prayer, in the form of *"devotion to the Virgin Mary,"* enables the apostle to join the grand combat between light and darkness, plunging into the very heart of the conflict with the weapons of God (TD 54).

3. Reflection on the Meaning of These Virtues and Their Unity

a. Virtues and virtue. In the seventeenth century, the word "virtue" in the singular had a very different meaning from the plural. In the singular it denoted a strength. It is masculine (the Latin *virtus*): it wells up from the depths of being and expresses that being. We have it in Hymn 4, *"Esteem and Desire of Virtue in General":* the *"virtue of God,"* the divine *"vapor of His everlasting glory"* (H 4:2), which we are called to take as our teacher, is the very love, or holiness, or wisdom, of God.[24] In the plural, the "virtues" are closer to what we call "virtues" today.

With Father de Montfort, it is also necessary to set the virtues in relationship with a whole series of realities which he calls the *"graces of God"* (LEW 207), which are all contained in *"Wisdom"* (LEW 206). Montfort likes to associate virtues with graces, frequently in phrases consisting of three members (sometimes in correspondence with the persons of the Trinity): virtues and graces (TD 173, 174); virtues, graces, and lights (TD 119); virtues, graces, and perfections: In Jesus alone *"dwells the entire fullness of the divinity and the complete fullness of grace, virtue and perfection"* (TD 61); virtues, merits, and good works (TD 121, 122); virtues, graces, and treasures (TD 178). In Hymn 4, virtue comes from the Father: it has been expressed by Jesus, and it is the Spirit who brings us to it (H 4:2–3, 6).

b. Virtues of the Christian and those of the world. When Montfort invites us to enter into the Wisdom of God, he is quite aware that this Wisdom of Love is altogether opposed to that of the world, which itself has created a universe completely contrary to that of the Gospel (LEW 199). The world, too, has such *"virtues as courage, finesse, tactfulness, shrewdness, gallantry, politeness and good humor. It stigmatizes as serious offenses, insensitiveness, stupidity, poverty, boorishness and bigotry"* (LEW 77). But the world is not content to oppose the Gospel. Its wickedness runs deeper. It actually cloaks sin under the appearance of virtue, and virtue under the appearance of sin. *"In general,"* the worldly *"do not teach sin openly, but they speak of it as if it were virtuous, or blameless, or a matter of indifference"* (LEW 199). A hymn like the one on the "Axioms of the World" (H 39) shows vividly how *"worldly"* persons can attack new converts by showing them that their virtues are nothing but sin: *"Drop that meditation! / 'Tis a dangerous thing. / It can be a temptation: / woe to the lazy soul!"* (H 39:135).

One senses a particular resentment in Montfort for that prototype of worldly virtues, the seventeenth-century *"honest man"* or *"wise man"* of the world (LEW 76). Papàsogli has marvelously described this virtuous person: "[Here is] the person of calculation, not risk—who will never know the irrevocable generosity of 'going for broke'; the person of the useful, not of piety. . . . It is not the great darkness of the world [that guides this person], but the 'bourgeois' side, and the common measure; not atheism, but a diminished God, shrunken to the skimpy measure of human selfishness."[25]

At bottom, it is not so much the "libertine," such as Molière's Don Juan, that Montfort resents, but precisely this *"honest man."* Don Juan at least had the merit of being frank, while the *"wise man"* of the world (LEW 76) has replaced holiness with the appearance of virtue, and the folly of the cross with a human equilibrium made up by and large of social conventions. In the eyes of this *"fool of God"* who is Montfort, the great sin is the tepidity and compromise of anyone who dares try to make the *world* agree with the Gospel.

c. Virtues and love. It might seem surprising that, in his list of virtues, Montfort has so little room for the four "cardinal" ones: prudence, justice, fortitude, and temperance. True, no hymn is specially reserved for them. But prudence is not neglected: Montfort recommends it in almsgiving (H 17:41), in mortification (LEW 202), and even in zeal (H 22:20). Are not certain virtues, like modesty (H 25) and obedience (H 10), forms of prudence? And is not also *"wisdom"* the authenticity, and immense prudence of love? Likewise, while Montfort speaks little of social justice, emphasizing instead charity toward the poor. Their cry, which he makes his own, is a cry for that justice: *"Know that what you hold so fast, / when no longer of use to you, / belongs to the poor. Those things are theirs! / You owe them that gilded furniture, / those precious pearls!"* (H 17:18). And let us not forget that our consecration to Jesus through Mary is itself a matter of justice, even before being an affair of love (TD 68:142; SM 68). Nor is fortitude ignored: it is only another name for *"graciousness"* (H 9) and *"patience"* (H 11), the courage to face *"the world, the demon, and the flesh"* (PS 20). Fortitude is the virtue diametrically opposed to the notorious *"human respect,"* which is composed of nothing but *"fear,"* which Montfort vigorously combats (H 34–39).

Thus, if St. Louis Marie speaks so little of the cardinal virtues, it is surely because these virtues are essentially qualities of balance and measure. While for him the attractive, magnetic thing is the great imbalance: the grand folly of love, manifested in Jesus' Cross. Not for nothing did Montfort laud this *"Queen of virtues"* (H 5:5) in eight Hymns. Without it, life is useless (H 5:18), sanctification impossible (H 5:6), and virtue itself sin (H 5:12). But with love, not only do all virtues take on meaning and life, they also become easy and sweet to practice (H 5:7), since they are loved: *"Love makes me love obedience, / seek poverty, / flee pleasures, / embrace suffering"* (H 45:20).

d. Virtues and the consecration. This theological love is at once the motive, the fruit, and the goal of our consecration to Mary in the spirit of Montfort. It is the motive because consecration ought to be *"moved by generous love"* (TD 73), the love at work in *"one who loves God with a* *pure and unselfish love"* (TD 151). After all, faith has revealed to this person that he or she is loved by God, that *"Jesus, our great friend has given himself (first) without reserve, body and soul."* Our consecration is ever but love's response to a first Love that has, so to speak, beaten us to it. Among the fruits of this consecration, its *"wondrous effects,"* we find the *"pure love of which Mary is the treasury."* Mary, that *"Mother of fair love, will rid your heart of all scruples and inordinate servile fear"* (TD 215). Finally, the goal of the consecration is not primarily our own interest, not even our spiritual interest (TD 110), but, as always, love, since its two main ends are to *"honor and imitate the wondrous dependence which God the Son chose to have on Mary,"* and to *"thank God for the incomparable graces he has conferred upon Mary"* (TD 243).

In focusing our minds and hearts on this gratuitous love, the consecration is the font of its costly demands. It delivers us from a too moralistic asceticism. To be sure, we must do violence to ourselves, as the saying goes, in order to acquire the virtues and practice them. Montfort was very severe with those *"presumptuous devotees"* who renounce *"any great effort to correct"* their faults (literally, *"without doing great violence to themselves in order that they be corrected"*), *"believing that their devotion to our Lady gives them this sort of liberty"* (TD 97). *"Nothing in our Christian religion is so deserving of condemnation"* (TD 98). But the virtues are primarily to be received directly, like love, from she who has practiced them to perfection in order to share them, for she is our Mother. Mary who *"shares her virtues"* with the one who has succeeded in delivering and despoiling himself from that to which he is most attached, receives *"her humility, faith, purity, etc."* (TD 144), and a great trust in God (TD 216).

In the end, Father de Montfort invites us not so much to practice our own virtues as to make a gift of them. For three great reasons, he calls us to offer them up together with all of our other interior and spiritual goods and with our merits and our good works (TD 121). The first reason is that, if our good works are impure and sullied by self-love (SM 49), and secret pride (RW 159), then the tree that has produced this fruit must itself be pruned and purified. "There is no such thing as a good tree producing worthless fruit" (Lk 6:43). The tree of our virtues must be tended, that our works may be purified. The second reason is that it takes a great deal of love to give everything and keep nothing back. We must establish and enthrone love from the outset and give up everything there and then. Finally, if I want my life to be Christian—that is, to be the actual life of Christ in me—then it must be his own virtues that lead me, his own spirit, his own wisdom that guide me. "If the Spirit is the source of our life, let the Spirit also direct our course" (Ga 5:25).

What does Mary do when we have given her our virtues? She purifies them, she strips us of them, like old garments, to clothe us "in the clean, new, precious and fragrant garments of . . . her Son Jesus Christ." That is, she dispenses to us his *"merits and virtues"* (TD 206). And since she adds her own as well, we are, as Montfort says, *"clothed with double garments, her own and those of her Son"* (TD 206).

III. Virtues of Mary

Mary is not only the prefiguring of the Church (LG 63), she is the perfect model of all of the virtues of a Christian (LG 65). She is also the mother who shares them with us in the life that the Holy Spirit gives us through her. Therefore it is of the greatest importance for us to study her virtues as Montfort presented them.

1. Virtues of Mary

In TD 108 we find a list of the *"ten principal virtues"* of Mary: her *"deep humility, lively faith, blind obedience, unceasing prayer, constant self-denial, surpassing purity, ardent love, heroic patience, angelic kindness, and heavenly wisdom."* In TD 144, Father de Montfort refers to this list, taking up three virtues that are reemphasized further on: *"her lively faith, . . . her deep humility, . . . her truly divine purity"* (TD 260). In LEW, he shows us a Mary wise, charitable, generous, faithful, and so on (LEW 222). There are other lists as well (TD 34, 261; LEW 107; SM 15). On the basis of these various listings, we may make three observations:

a. While charity occasionally occurs in a list, in Mary *"love"* is above everything. This is evident whenever Montfort crisply distinguishes between the love with which Mary inflames us and *"her virtues"* which she shares with us and in which we find faith (TD 144).

b. Aside from love, we may say that Mary's three main virtues are faith, humility, and purity: By her lively faith, she believed the angel's word without the least hesitation, and believed faithfully and constantly even to the foot of the Cross on Calvary. Her deep humility made her prefer seclusion, maintain silence, and submit to every eventuality and put herself in the last place. Her truly divine purity has not and will not be equaled this side of heaven (TD 260).

c. These three key virtues seem to have, in Montfort's eyes, a kind of theological scope: faith, of course, but humility and purity as well. All three, joined in Mary to *"her ceaseless entreaties of love,"* had the effect not only of touching God, as it were, but of actually attracting or seducing God, as it were, *"conquering"* God! *"She had won his heart"* (LEW 107). *"Her humility, deep as an abyss, delighted him (se charma[26]). Her purity so other-worldly drew him to her. He found her lively faith and her ceaseless entreaties of love so irresistible that he was lovingly conquered by her appeals of love"* (LEW 107).

The better to grasp their range and purview, it will be useful to see all of these virtues of Mary in a single panorama. There are not only "the depths of her profound humility," there is also *"the height of her merits, . . . the breadth of her love, . . . the greatness of the power which she wields over one who is God"* (TD 7). Furthermore, Montfort associates Mary's virtues with her privileges, her actions, and her grandeur (TD 115). On a deeper level, he links them, especially her faith and her love, to her motherhood, which is not primarily a reality of flesh, but a deed and work of the Spirit who finds faith and love: *"Christian, through Mary's heart / you love the heart of Jesus, / for Jesus has taken life in her heart and her virtues.* (H 40:35).

Happily, Mary's virtues are inseparable from her life, her being, her calling—her whole person, invested by the Spirit who is faith, hope, love.

2. Mary and the Virtues

It is not only a matter of discovering Mary's virtues. We must also wonder what they mean in relation to us. For us, Mary is a model of virtues, to be imitated, and a *"treasurer"* (LEW 207), a mother who shares them with us.

a. Mary, model of the Christian virtues. The imitation of the Blessed Virgin's virtues is for Montfort one of the characteristics of the *"predestined"* and one of the interior practices of the consecration. Like little Jacob in the Bible with respect to his mother, Rebecca, the predestined *"keep to the ways of the Blessed Virgin, their loving Mother—that is, they imitate her and so are sincerely happy"* (TD 200). Without this imitation, devotion to Mary would be but "exterior," and thereby false (TD 96).

"We must look upon Mary . . . as the perfect model of every virtue and perfection, fashioned by the Holy Spirit for us to imitate, as far as our limited capacity allows" (TD 260). This is also one of the interior practices of the consecration. In order to *"do everything with Mary, . . . in every action . . . we should consider how Mary performed it or how she would perform it if she were in our place,"* and therefore *"examine and meditate on the great virtues she practiced"* (TD 260). In the same passage in which he speaks of living *"with Mary"* and taking her as our model, Montfort adds that *"Mary is the great, unique mold of God, designed to make living images of God"* (TD 219). This plainly shows that, in his eyes, to imitate the virtues of the Mother of Jesus is much more than to strive, by oneself, to resemble an external model while keeping control of the experience. On the contrary, this imitation means allowing ourselves to be transformed by the model that then becomes a *"mold"* to shape us (TD 219–20; SM 16–18). When all is said and done, it is less a matter of "gazing upon" than of being gazed upon. It is more a matter of allowing oneself to be molded by the image contemplated than to mold oneself to its likeness.

b. Mary, mother who shares her virtues. This image of the *"mold"* that is Mary, who fashions us to the image of her Son, paves the way to better understanding that she is not only a model, but also a mother, who communicates her own virtues. Actually, this sharing of virtues is part of an entire series of phenomena that might be called the gift that Mary makes of herself in response to the one we make of our persons (by consecrating ourselves to Jesus through her). *"She gives herself completely in a wondrous manner"* to *"someone giving himself entirely to her"* (TD 144; cf. 216). But in giving herself to her *"consecrated one,"* she is not content to share her virtues with her devotee: *"She engulfs him in the ocean of her graces, adorns him with her merits, supports him with her power, enlightens him with her light, and fills him with her love"* (TD 144). And Mary bestows not only her own virtues, but also, as we have seen, those of Jesus (SM 38; TD 206).

All of this helps us to understand that it is not so much that the Mother of God communicates to us a whole arsenal of virtues, but rather that she shares a life, shapes a face, to which no *"feature of Jesus Christ"* (SM 17) is lacking. She gives birth to a person, that of Jesus. All of the blessings that she shares with us so *"generously"* are naught in comparison with *"that infinite treasure which contains every good, Jesus"* (LEW 206), and *"of her fullness we have all received"* (LEW 207). The virtues she shares with us are already the traits of the face of Wisdom, that fruit of her faith and the Holy Spirit.

IV. Virtues of Jesus

May we speak of the virtues of Jesus, who is God? Are not virtues rather a possession of the Church, something attaching to the response of love of the children of God to the antecedent love of the Father, manifested in Jesus? Are the virtues not part of the spiritual equipment that the Christian receives with the grace of baptism? And yet, beyond the shadow of a doubt, one may speak—however briefly—of the virtues of God and Jesus.

1. Virtues of God

Although in the seventeenth century the word "virtue" does not always have the same meaning that we give it today, Montfort does not hesitate to speak of the *"virtue of God"* (H 4:4), which is nothing else but God's love, wisdom, or holiness. *"All that is . . . virtuous in God,"* he says elsewhere, is *"invested in"* the one who attains to the carrying of his or her cross (LEW 179). *"God of goodness, give me / the virtues of your heart!"* (H 4:21).

It is interesting, for example, to observe that Hymns 4 ("Virtue in General"), 5 ("Charity"), and the hymn on the Holy Spirit (H 141), are almost perfectly parallel. God's virtue, indeed, is love—God's very nature (1 Jn 4:8–16): generated in the divine heart from all eternity, this virtue has complete authority over God, since it is this that has led God to become a human being on earth (H 5:3–4). But if God is love and nothing else, it would doubtless be better to speak not of the divine "virtues," but of the "attributes" of God: justice, graciousness, mercy, and so on—or, therefore, to say that all of God's virtues are contained in the divine love.

The greatest virtue that this love contains is surely, in Montfort's eyes, humility. True, Montfort never speaks explicitly of the humility of God.[27] But the *"poverty"* of the divine heart is everywhere present. If the Triune God, in the wisdom of love (Father, Son, and Spirit), has willed to depend upon Mary not only in order to effect the wonder of the Incarnation, but also to continue its mystery today in the Church, it is because God is humble. Humility is not only a human virtue, which inclines us to approach God only through mediators (TD 143). It is also, and principally, a divine virtue—the virtue that has inclined the Almighty, in Jesus, to work the marvel of a God who "made himself nothing," in Mary's womb, and thereupon "in obedience accepted even death—death on a cross" (Ph 2:7–8).

2. Virtues of Jesus

It is this humility, as well, that we must emphasize if we wish to speak of the virtues of Jesus. Of course, Wisdom itself is only love—*"the very love of the Father and the Holy Spirit"* (LEW 118). Then it is in this love that the fullness of the virtues dwells, like that of the graces and the perfections (TD 61), and the Heart of Jesus is the sole source of all of the virtues (H 130:8). But his humanity, molded and reared by Mary, the *"Queen of the virtues"* (H 4:22), and Joseph, comes forward as our *"only model"* (TD 61). Among all of Jesus' virtues, Montfort especially loves to underscore his humility, which is only part and parcel of his obedience and graciousness, which in turn are identical with his charity and his wisdom.

His humility. Montfort contemplates Christ's humility especially in the three great mysteries of the Incarnation, the Cross, and the Eucharist. It is humility that *"reduces"* the Word to silence and God to infancy (H 57:1). It is humility that, still today, *"Draws him from glory, / to hide his majesty / in a poor ciborium,"* (H 130:4) and makes of God, in the mystery of the poor, *"the neediest / of all the wretched"* (H 17:15).

His obedience. "Of all the Savior's virtues / the very exemplar, the miracle / midmost in his heart" (H 10:5). After all, it is in being obedient not only to his Father, but to Mary and Joseph as well, that Jesus has rendered glory to God and has saved human beings (TD 139).

His tenderness. In LEW, Montfort has devoted no less than two chapters to Jesus' *"graciousness"*: We find the actual word, *"meekness," (tenderness, graciousness)* at least forty-five times. We see how sensitive the one they called the "good Father from Montfort" was to this characteristic of Jesus' love for children, the poor, and especially, sinners (LEW 10, 11:124, 125).

His charity. We should have to cite all of the hymns to the Heart of Jesus (H 40–44, 47) in order to illustrate that *"infinite charity"* by which Jesus *"became our security and our Mediator with his Father"* (TD 85), that charity which has led him to give himself to us wholly and entirely, *"body and soul"* (TD 138), and impels us today to *"Undertake / a grand return of love"* (H 128:6).

His wisdom. Provided we regard wisdom as a virtue (after all, it is also a gift, and Father de Montfort identifies it with the very person of Jesus), wisdom is that prudence of love that has inspired and animated all of the Savior's choices, in contrast with the wisdom of the world. In being willing to become *"nothing"* and to depend upon Mary, in freely living the great scandal of the cross, Jesus has experienced the greatest of the wisdoms, that of love. In identifying Jesus with the virtue of wisdom and the experience of his cross (*"Wisdom is the Cross and the Cross is Wisdom,"* LEW 180), Montfort plainly shows that Jesus' virtues are not distinct from his person and his life. In Jesus, virtues and life are one.

V. Montfort Virtues Today

Can Montfort's teaching on the virtues, and the manner in which he lived them, be of interest to us today? Surely, various aspects of what Montfort—the man of the Absolute—practiced and taught seem difficult to accept for our world. However, the montfort doctrine and practice of the virtues are filled with solid directions for our contemporary world and offer support to the ongoing reform of the Church. Finally, prescinding from a baroque style and expressions inevitably marked by his age, Montfort's life and message present some useful reminders for today.

1. Some Difficulties

Contemporary Christians find Montfort's practice of the virtues excessive. The Christian life is for everyone, Blain said, but Montfort's life, "so poor, so harsh, so abandoned to Providence, was . . . for extraordinary persons, and not for the common person, who could not reach so high."[28] Examples of Montfort's unique actions appear excessive, like drinking from the same glass as a person with a contagious disease. It is mortification beyond a doubt, but, in order to overcome ourselves, must we actually drink the pus that had just drained from a sick person, as an early biographer claims Montfort had done?[29] It is true, as well, that Jesus asked persons to leave their families to follow him, but must this detachment be pushed to the point of not visiting our parents when we are actually in town?[30] True, these actions can only be judged in their full context, which is impossible to reconstruct today. Nonetheless, they are for modern men and women definitely excessive.

Do not all of these virtues Montfort explains (thirty or more, in the *Hymns*) bring us to the practice of the Law—a legalism—from which the Spirit ought to deliver us? Today we would prefer to replace this morality by love alone—or perhaps by the simplicity of the Beatitudes.

Whatever the worth of these arguments may be, it cannot be denied that an entire generation today has trouble accepting virtues like humility and obedience. They seem to encourage a certain passivity, or to foster a destruction of the person, since they involve a self-abasement and a dependency, which might appear to prevent one from "being oneself." Are human beings so wicked that they need such a great number of virtues in order to set their nature right? What is needed, it is claimed, is a bit more confidence in human beings and in life: as the saying goes, "just let it all happen!" And what is this "slavery" that Montfort teaches? How can it be meaningful to moderns who thirst for freedom?

Much of the misunderstanding of Saint Louis de Montfort is due to the fact that his words are strong, if not shocking. They imitate the Gospel. Regretably Montfort's thoughts are often considered piecemeal instead of taken as a whole. But it cannot be forgotten that "the good Father from Montfort" truly stands out in the history of hagiography as an outstanding saint. To follow him is to imitate Jesus without any "ifs" or "buts." Montfort does not go "beyond" the Gospel; he lives it to the hilt as we must do in our generation, in our times, in our context.

2. Effective Directions for Today

The virtues that Montfort practiced and taught do have a role to play in contemporary society. First, they find an echo in a whole series of current values. Modern theology (especially spiritual theology) comes very close to Montfort in its insistence on the three theological virtues, especially love and hope, which are the very basis of the "consecration." We likewise observe in many of our contemporaries a great thirst to serve freely, out of love for our brothers and sisters, doubtless in reaction to a world of output and profit that crushes us.

In response to this thirst, Montfort proposes the wholly disinterested character of true love, whether in devotion to Mary (TD 110), in apostolic zeal (H 21:22), or in service to the poor (H 17:42–43). In reaction, as well, to a hard, aggressive, pitiless world, we hear so much today about "gentleness." Montfort, for his part, speaks of *douceur,* gentleness or tenderness, and most of all of the irresistible gentleness or graciousness of Jesus Wisdom: *"Nothing is so gracious as Eternal Wisdom"* (LEW 53). But he also lauds the gentleness, the graciousness of Mary, and that of devotion to her: true devotion to Our Lady is tender and trustful (TD 107). Finally, the "preferential option for the poor," which is one of the official choices of the Church today, and of so many religious congregations, corresponds completely to Montfort's symbolic gesture in crossing the bridge of Cesson that day when, according to a biographer, he "crossed over to the poor."[31]

Above and beyond all of the virtues that Montfort explicitly names, there is one that particularly enchants the young of today (as it has those of all times), as well as those new communities so eager for the absolute, striving for a somewhat "foolish" or "insane" way of living the Gospel of the Crucified One. It could well be called the virtue of radicalism. The Gospel is a book of life. We have no right to be satisfied with reading it without putting it into practice, "as is" (without seeking to accommodate it to our comforts), here and now. It is this montfort radicalism, this absolutely total living of the Gospel which so attracts young people today. Does Jesus ask us to invite to our table "the poor, the crippled, the lame, and the blind" (Lk 14:14)? Montfort attends a big family dinner with his friends: every vagrant he can find.[32] Has Jesus not said, "When I was ill you came to my help. . . . Anything you did for one of my brothers here, however humble, you did for me" (Mt 25:36–40)? At Poitiers, Louis Marie undertakes to care personally for a pauper "covered with infection, . . . rejected by all public medical personnel, on the point of being abandoned and ejected from the general hospital—the poor house." He offers him "all of the services required by a disease so dangerous and so disgusting, . . . right up to the moment of death,"[33] for this pauper is *"Jesus Christ himself"* (H 17:14). Many of the objections mentioned above have another side to the coin: they tug at the heart of a young person who wants to give all. It is not a question of the specific examples of Montfort's total giving of self; it is rather the determination to avoid, like Montfort, any half-way measures.

Two other aspects of the "Treatise on the Virtues" can help us a great deal today. First, their insistence on the virtue (or gift) of wisdom, that compendium of the whole of montfort moral thought. Perhaps we should recognize that we live a fool's life when we claim to be in quest of evangelical wisdom. And so it is with great joy that our contemporaries (even unbelievers!) discover that the virtues Montfort invites them to practice, such as humility and even faith, are also and first of all divine virtues. Does not the just one, according to TD, live by the faith of Jesus (TD 109)?

3. Useful reminders for today

It has been observed that, when Montfort speaks to us of faith and love, quite often he adds the adjective, *"pure"*: *"pure love"* (TD 214, 215); *"pure faith"* (SM 51). This insistence is surely not useless today, when we are so ready to say, "All you need is love," forgetting that we so easily seek ourselves, and that self-love (so easy to detect and denounce in others) is first of all in us (e.g. SM 49, 146). Montfort invites us today to discern the true meaning of "love."

He reminds us that there is no true love without humility and obedience. If these virtues are rather out of fashion today, perhaps the reason is that we have forgotten certain evangelical truths of which Montfort reminds us. On the path of humility and obedience, God has gone before us. It is in gazing upon a God who "made himself nothing, . . . in obedience," that I learn: *"We must descend if we would rise"* (H 8:23), and the obedient one *"sings ever of victory"* (H 10:16–17). God has not been content to be the first to love (1 Jn 4:10, 19). God has willed to do so precisely along the pathway of obedience and humility (TD 18, 139; H 8:8–9, 10:5–8).

In the same spirit, Montfort insists on another virtue so difficult to practice today: perseverance, or fidelity. To those who might be tempted to live so called "successive fidelities," or "limited engagements," out of fear of a permanent commitment, Montfort brings understanding and hope. Yes, Montfort says, perseverance is difficult, even impossible: *"It is difficult to persevere in holiness because of the excessive corrupting influence of the world"* (TD 89). But the miracle of fidelity is possible, provided only we do not rely on ourselves, and place all our trust in God. Perseverance, too, is one of the *"wondrous effects"* of the consecration to Jesus through Mary's hands. Montfort's path of perfection calls us to the incredible fulfillment of a permanent commitment to God first of all and within that commitment, a pledge to serve—forever—our brothers and sisters.

J. Morinay

Notes: (1) *Un Apotre Marial: Saint Louis-Marie Grignion de Montfort (1673-1716)* (A Marian Apostle: St. Louis Marie de Montfort), Librairie Mariale, Pontchateau 1942. Le Crom, 381–82. (2) Le Crom, 90. (3) Blain, 350. (4) Besnard 5:216. (5) Grandet, 373–74. (6) Besnard 1:314. (7) B. Papàsogli, *L'homme venu du vent: Louis Marie Grignion de Montfort,* Bellarmin, Montreal 1984, 189. English edition: *Montfort, A Prophet for Our Times,* Edizioni Monfortane, Rome 1991. (8) Blain, 140. (9) Blain, 339. (10) Le Crom, 102. (11) Le Crom, 358. (12) Papàsogli, 61, 95, 339. (13) Papàsogli, 134. (14) Papàsogli, 40. (15) Pérouas, 124. (16) Blain, 333. (17) Blain, 334–37. (18) Blain, 223–24. (19) Blain, 225. (20) Blain, 222. (21) Besnard 1:223. (22) J. Picot de Clorivière, *La vie de M. Louis Marie Grignion de Montfort, missionnaire apostolique . . . ,* (The Life of Louis Marie de Montfort, Apostolic Missionary), Delalain, Paris 1785, 323. (23) *Initiation théologique,* Cerf, Paris 1952, 3:867. (24) In seventeenth-century translations of the Old Testament, God's "virtue" is primarily God's power: cf. Ps 65:7, 11:6. (25) Papàsogli, 208, 210. (26) "To charm," in the seventeenth century, has a very strong sense: it means to attract someone or something in such a fashion that the latter is all but helpless (as in "serpent's charm"). (27) Cf. Father Varillon's beautiful book, *L'humilité de Dieu* (The humility of God). (28) Blain, 331. (29) Grand, 472–74, 66; Le Crom, 131. (30) Le Crom, 174. (31) Papàsogli, 48. (32) Le Crom, 180. (33) Le Crom, 131.

WISDOM

The contemplation of Christ as Wisdom and a perception of the spiritual life as the quest for genuine Wisdom, figure among the most singular traits of the spiritual journey and the work of Louis Marie de Montfort. Over and above the various influences we can discover under the pen of the author of LEW, one fact remains incontestable: Montfort establishes himself as one of the rare Christian authors to make Christ as Wisdom the cornerstone of his spirituality and his key to biblical sapiential thought, with the O.T. Book of Wisdom the fundamental source of this inspiration. While we may not isolate Montfort from his century and his predecessors, neither may we deny the extreme originality of his vision of Wisdom.[1]

I. MONTFORT'S QUEST FOR WISDOM ALONG HIS SPIRITUAL AND MISSIONARY PATH

1. Context of his formation

Young Grignion de Montfort's spiritual route can be established by a study both of the sources and of the testimony of the biographers who have addressed the question. For the period of his philosophical and theological training before his ordination to the priesthood, we may refer to De Fiores' detailed study, which includes an examination of Louis Marie's spiritual formation.[2] But even with such a fine study in hand, it remains extremely difficult—in fact, impossible—to determine the triggering element that would have induced Montfort, while he was still in his formation, to define his spirituality in terms of a quest for Wisdom[3] or incited him to draw his inspiration directly from the biblical Wisdom literature. True, it is possible to see in the references he makes to the work of Saint-Jure in N, 392ff., "a prime factor sensitizing Montfort to the Wisdom theme and impelling him as well to read and utilize the sapiential books."[4] But that would be all that we could say, and the treatment Montfort accorded the sapiential books of the Bible would far surpass, in extent as well as depth, the work of the authors of the French school of spirituality. Among the immediate influences on Montfort, however, we ought not neglect the contribution of Father Descartes, his spiritual director at the College of St. Thomas in Rennes. LEW contains accents akin to those found in Father Decartes' two works, *Le Palais de l'amour divin (Palace of Divine Love)* and *Les divers emplois de l'amour divin (The Manifold Uses of Divine Love);* Montfort's vocabulary, however, is not only more innovative but decidedly more sapiential.

2. Testimony of the letters

The situation is different, however, for the period dating from his ordination to the priesthood in 1700 to his death in 1716. And in the front rank we must point to the letters, which probably furnish the first references to the use of the term "wisdom" in Montfort's works. They also testify to a very marked evolution in Montfort's spiritual and missionary journey.

Of the thirty-four letters that have been preserved, nearly one-third (L 14-17, 20, 28-30, 33-34) address the Wisdom theme in one way or another. A mere examination of the chronology of the letters in question immediately shows a powerful concentration on the topic at the two poles of Montfort's ministry—that is, around the years 1703-04 and 1715-16. Thus it is said that the Wisdom theme becomes "strikingly dormant" in the missionary's career, as his correspondence remains silent on the subject for a good ten years.[5]

The first mention that we can date with certitude is from the spring of 1703 (L 15). It appears as a variant in the formula of salutation used by Montfort in the preceding letters. To his usual greeting, *"May the perfect love of God reign in our hearts,"* Montfort adds, "*with divine Wisdom.*" It should not be forgotten that this letter is the first to be addressed to Marie Louise Trichet, who not only would become a religious, as Montfort predicts to her in the conclusion of his letter, but would be his most faithful disciple and, finally, his partner in the foundation of the community of the Daughters of Wisdom.

We should also emphasize another happy coincidence. Montfort's last letter, written shortly before the missionary's death in 1716, is addressed to this same Marie Louise Trichet, now Mother Marie Louise of Jesus.

Here the Wisdom theme plays a role at center stage, since Montfort invites Marie Louise to interpret and to experience the trials that she is undergoing with her young community in the context of the mystery of Divine Wisdom: "*I worship the justice and love with which divine Wisdom is treating his little flock, allowing you to live in cramped quarters here on earth so that later you may find spacious dwellings in his divine heart which was pierced for you to enter. How pleasant and safe is this sacred refuge for a soul truly possessing Wisdom!*. . .*If you truly seek to be a disciple of divine Wisdom and one chosen among so many, then this unkind treatment you are suffering, the contempt, the poverty, the restrictions, all these should be pleasing to you since they are the price you have to pay to obtain Wisdom and true freedom and become partakers of the divinity of the heart of Jesus crucified*" (L 34).

Consequently, Montfort asks her to "*found our community of the Daughters of Wisdom, not on quicksands of gold and silver,*" but "*on the Wisdom of the Cross of Calvary*" (L 34).

Montfort's letter to his mother, written in August 1704, so characteristic of the young priest's evangelical radicalism, furnishes an important key for an understanding of the manner in which he experienced what might be called the mysticism of his priestly celibacy. We read: "*In my new family—the one I belong to now—I have chosen to be wedded to Wisdom and the Cross for in these I find every good, both earthly and heavenly. So precious are these possessions that, if they were but known, Montfort would be the envy of the richest and most powerful kings on earth*" (L 20).

We cannot escape the parallel between these lines and the highly original commentary that Montfort makes on Wis 8:16: "*Whenever I go into my house, says Solomon, even though I am alone, I will take my rest with Wisdom because Wisdom's company is always pleasing, Wisdom's companionship is never tedious but always satisfying and joyful*" (LEW 98). The words "*even though I am alone*" are not part of the biblical text but are an expression of Montfort's personal interpretation.

3. The Love of Eternal Wisdom

Inasmuch as LEW is the subject of another article in the present Handbook, we shall here investigate only the significance of this work in Montfort's experience of the quest for Wisdom.

While the letters of 1703 and 1704 were written during a period called by Perouas "the time of crises,"[6] the treatise LEW stands out somewhat as the resolution of a crisis. Not that Montfort claims to have reached the end of the evangelical adventure or believes himself sheltered from the storm. Here we need only consider his protestations of humility and avowals of "*incompetence and ignorance*" (LEW 7; cf. LEW 1). But the exposition of the topic is at once magisterial and serene. The composition is a powerful synthesis of biblical Wisdom and a treatise on the Christian life, situated in a comprehensive view of salvation history. It is the Incarnation that sets the tone for the entire book. Creation, however, is not neglected, and while we may regret the fact that, in keeping with the theology of his time, Montfort does not stress the mystery of the Resurrection, we find sublime pages in LEW on the Love that saves by the victorious Cross.

LEW is a work of the saint's youth; it is also a masterpiece. It situates his Christological perspective, from which, as starting point, Montfort views his spiritual experience and apostolate. It already enunciates, in very condensed terms, the great themes of his preaching and writings: the mystery of the Incarnation, the demands of a Wisdom inspired by the Gospel, the foolishness of the Cross, and the unique place of Mary in the mystery of salvation.

4. The hymns and the sermons

Montfort's hymns are of undeniable catechetical interest and, by virtue of their popular character, afford us a better perception of the teaching addressed by Montfort to the public at large. Of the 164 hymns that have come down to us, only 5 bear explicitly on Wisdom (H 78; H 103; H 124-26), while Hymns 19 and 102, which are manifestly parallel and devoted to the "*Triumph of the Cross,*" contain numerous sapiential echoes. Indeed, they present the Cross in terms unmistakably reminiscent of LEW, chap. 14. Just as Wisdom is a mystery that surpasses understanding, so also is the Cross: "*The Cross is a mystery / profound, here below. / Without brightest light, / unknowable it remains. / Who can comprehend it? / A lofty mind alone. / Yet grasp it we must / if we would be saved*" (H 19:1).

Stanzas 10-11 of the same hymn apply to Jesus the spousal language of pseudo-Solomon (Wis 8) in order to speak of Jesus' quest for Wisdom: "*So fair He found it, / He made it His crown, / and companion everlasting: / bride of His heart! / From tenderest childhood, / His heart would sigh— / sigh for the presence / of this Cross He loved. / Yea, from His youth, / He sought [it], / and with mighty stride!*" (H 19:10-11).

The hymn's finale focuses on the acquisition of Wisdom today. After all, Wisdom seeks disciples still: "*Wisdom everlasting / seeks, yet today, / a heart that will be faithful / and worthy of this gift*" (H 19:25).

The last strophes (28-31) then present, in terms very much akin to the biblical discourse on Wisdom, the Cross as that treasure par excellence that is to be sought at the cost of all else besides and fills the human heart to overflowing: "*I take thee for my life, / my pleasure, my honor, / for my single beloved, / my unique beatitude*" (H 19:29).

As for the hymns explicitly consecrated to Wisdom, these fall first and foremost under the sign of prayer. Except for the first stanzas of Hymn 125, which take the form of an exhortation, all is ardent supplication and dialogue with God. Hymn 78, for example, brief as it is, is a fine paraphrase of the prayer in Wis 9 "*that asks for Wisdom,*" and Montfort adds a Marian note in the second and last strophe.

Hymn 103 is surely the most important of those that Montfort devotes to Wisdom. First, we observe the wealth of Christological titles (*"divine Wisdom," "Son of God," "beauty supreme," "Word equal to His Father," "Light of Light," "God become a human being," "immortal Spouse,"* and so on), along with the intensity bestowed on the note of supplication with the recurrence of the refrain, *"Come dwell in me!"* The hymn reaches its climax in a declaration of the greatest assurance of being heard: *"I would walk in Thy footsteps: / come dwell in me! / Behold the grace of graces: / come dwell in me! / With Thee I walk in gladness, / to the Cross and to the skies! / Jesus, Child of Mary, / come dwell in me! / She it is who prays within me: / come dwell in me! / Thou, in my exile, / be my every bounty. Amen"* (H 103:28-29).

Hymns 124-26 form a unified canticle on the Wisdom theme. While shorter than Hymn 103, they are no less compact. There is the very beautiful and classical Hymn 124, which opens with the words *"O Wisdom, come, behold, a poor one begs"* and continues in ardent accents: *"I seek thee night and day! / Come, my soul desires thee, / come, for I am faint with love"* (H 124:2).

Here we find the actual words of the Beloved of the Song of Songs. The same thrusts recur in Hymn 126: *"O divine Wisdom, / I love thee with a burning fire! / Thou art my mistress, / I thy lover! / Thee alone below / I seek and love. / Beholding thy charms / I am beside myself!"* (H 126:1)

As for the sermons, we find none on Wisdom. There is only S 9 (GA 562-566), entitled, "*On the Love and Gentleness of Jesus,*" which recalls the sapiential themes. We find the same divisions as in LEW, chap. 10 ("*The Captivating Beauty and the Inexpressible Gentleness of Incarnate Wisdom*"). The theology is the same in both cases, and it scarcely comes as a surprise that we see Montfort concluding his second point with a reference to Jesus as Wisdom: "*Behold that Eternal Wisdom who, to captivate our hearts and to take away our sins, has gathered into his person all that is meek*" (LS 120). Do we have here a sermon from the beginning of the missionary's career, before the appearance of the Wisdom theme in his work? Or on the contrary, would this be a sermon from the period when the theme was so strikingly dormant in the saint's work? At all events, judging solely from LS, it appears that Montfort did not preach on the subject of Wisdom as such.

5. Ten years' silence?

In addition to this notable absence of the Wisdom theme in Montfort's popular preaching, a great deal of attention has been called in recent years to its near disappearance during the zenith of the Breton priest's missionary career, 1704-14.[7] Only the last two years of Montfort's life see the reappearance of the theme with some force: in his last letters, which are usually addressed to the Daughters of Wisdom.

The period from 1704 to 1714 is surely the most productive from the literary viewpoint, since it is in this period that SM, PM, SR, FC, RM, RW, and TD were composed. Indeed, other thematic topics and other perspectives emerge here, and the Wisdom theme appears only now and then. When it does appear, it assumes a certain importance. A brief survey of the works concerned will enable us to form a better idea of the place of Wisdom in them.

SM contains only one reference to Wisdom. This work, which, in the light of God's free choice, defends the crucial importance of devotion to Mary, *"following the order established by [God's] divine wisdom"* (SM 23). Otherwise no appeal is made here to the acquisition of Wisdom as one of the fruits to be sought by this devotion, nor do we find in the closing prayer to Jesus (SM 66) the Christological title Wisdom.

Neither does PM contain more than a single reference to Wisdom (PM 22), and it not a direct one, as it is a quotation in Latin of Lk 21:15 about the assistance that Jesus will give to the word of his Apostles in the midst of persecutions. The same verse of Scripture will be taken up once more and commented on at length in RM 59-60.

In SR, we discover two references, one of them ambiguous (SR 142) and the other expressing a clear meaning (SR 146). The first is a citation of Jas 1:6 on the importance of asking for Wisdom in prayer; but here it seems that Montfort refers to Wisdom only secondarily, the better to illustrate the importance of praying with faith and with the certitude of being heard. The accent is not on the acquisition of Wisdom. The second occurrence, on the other hand, leaves no doubt: "*So, dear members of the Confraternity, persevere in asking God for all your needs, both spiritual and material, through the holy Rosary; especially should you pray for divine Wisdom, which is 'an infinite treasure' [Wis 7:14], and there can be no possible doubt that you will receive it sooner or later, provided you do not give up and do not lose courage in the middle of your journey. 'You still have a great way to go, Grandis enim tibi restat via,' [1 Kings 19:7]"* (SR 146).

Given the highly popular character of SR and the practices that Montfort expounds there, we may have here one of the missing links that help us appreciate the importance of Wisdom in the missionary's preaching and activity.

FC, which is actually a further development of LEW, chap. 13, 14, and 16, contains three allusions to wisdom. The first (FC 17) consists of a very brief reference to the "*worldly-wise,*" of whom Montfort has already drawn an anything but flattering portrait in LEW 75-83. The second (FC 18) sees in the Cross assigned to each person a particular choice on the part of Divine Wisdom. The third is much more important. Here Montfort develops the fourth of the fourteen rules that he addresses to those of his disciples who choose to "*suffer and carry our cross in the footsteps of Christ*" (FC 41). We note that in this passage Montfort once again transfers to the Cross a vocabulary he has used apropos of Wisdom (the words underlined in our quotation): "*You may, and should, pray for the wisdom of the cross, that knowledge of the truth which we experience within ourselves and which by the light of faith deepens our knowledge of the most hidden mysteries, including that of the cross. But this is obtained only by much labor, great humiliations and fervent prayer. If you stand in need of this strengthening spirit [Ps 50:14] which enables us to carry the heaviest crosses courageously; of this gracious and consoling spirit [Lk 11:13], which enables us, in the higher part of the soul, to take delight in things that are bitter and repulsive; of this sound and upright spirit [Ps 50:12] which seeks God alone; of this science of the cross which embraces all things; in short, of this inexhaustible treasure by which those who make good use of it win God's friendship [cf. Wis 7:14]—if you stand in need of such, pray for wisdom, ask for it continually and fervently, without wavering [cf. Jas 1:5, 6] or fear of not obtaining it, and it will be yours. Then you will clearly understand from your own experience how it is possible to desire, seek and find joy in the cross"* (FC 45).

TD, which most commentators date to 1712, is, of course, Montfort's best known work, and it remains one of the great classics of Marian theology and spirituality. The strongly Christocentric nature of Montfort's argumentation in this work has always been acknowledged. It is no less certain that the foundations of his argumentation had already been laid in the final chapter of LEW, in which he sets forth *"the greatest means of all, and the most wonderful of all secrets for obtaining and preserving divine Wisdom": "a loving and genuine devotion to the Blessed Virgin"* (LEW 203). Now, what of the theme of Wisdom in TD, this other masterpiece of Montfort's? While it is not dominant, it may be more present, and more important, than we might have suspected.

The book contains at least fifteen references to Wisdom—itself an impressive fact. Of that number, no less than six (TD 18, 80, 139 twice, 168, 240) make of it a Christological title and refer us to the person of Christ and his incarnation, while another two refer more generally to Wisdom in God (TD 175, 272). Thus, more than half of these references confirm the character of the theological vision of Montfort, for whom the mystery of God and Christ translates in terms of Wisdom.

Furthermore, we should cite TD 240-41, where Montfort argues on the basis of a sapiential text, Sir 6, whose echoes resound in the NT itself (Mt 11:28-30): "*Dear friend, break the chains of sin and of sinners, of the world and the worldly, of the devil and his satellites. 'Cast their yoke of death far from us' ['Dirumpamus vincula eorum et projiciamus a nobis jugum ipsorum' (Ps. 2:3)]. To use the words of the Holy Spirit let us put our feet into his glorious shackles and our neck into his chains ['Injice pedem tuum in compedes illius, et in torques illius collum tuum' (Sir 6:25)]. Let us bow down our shoulders in submission to the yoke of Wisdom incarnate, Jesus Christ, and let us not be upset by the burden of his chains ['Subjice humerum tuum et porta illam, et ne accedieris vinculis ejus' (Sir 6:25)]. Notice how before saying these words the Holy Spirit prepares us to accept his serious advice, 'Hearken, my son,' he says, 'receive a counsel of understanding and do not spurn this counsel of mine' ['Audi, fili, et accipe consilium intellectus, et ne abjicias consilium meum' (Sir 6:24)]. Allow me here, my dear friend, to join the Holy Spirit in giving you the same counsel. 'These chains are the chains of salvation' ['Vincula illius alligatura salutis' (Sir 6:31)]"* (TD 240-41).

On four occasions, Montfort alludes to the Wisdom of Mary (TD 4, 108, 156, 217). This gift is hers because of her proximity to Jesus, source of all Wisdom; it has been granted to her in order to be shared with us as we await the plenitude of the mystery of Christ: "*It is in the bosom of Mary that people who are young grow mature in enlightenment, in holiness, in experience and in wisdom, and in a short time reach the fullness of the age of Christ [cf. Eph 4:13]*" (TD 156; see also TD 214, 217).

True, the allusions are scattered, but the fact remains that they can be comprehended only in the light of the magisterial exposition that Montfort had made on Wisdom less than ten years before, when he wrote LEW, and they suffice to show that nothing of this basic theme has been retracted.

When he wrote RM, which seems to have been essentially complete by June 1713,[8] Montfort was obviously interested only in the missionary dimension of Wisdom, whether on the attitude to be taken in the practice of the Sacrament of Penance—"*They must not be either too strict or too lax in imposing penances or granting absolution but must hold to the golden mean of wisdom and truth*" (RM 59)—or, especially, on his missionaries' primary activity, preaching: "*The preaching of God's word is the most far-reaching, the most effective and also the most difficult ministry of all. The missionaries will, therefore, study and pray unceasingly that they may obtain from God the gift of wisdom so necessary to a true preacher for knowing and relishing the truth and getting others to relish it. It is the easiest thing in the world to be a fashionable preacher. It is a difficult but sublime thing to be able to preach with the inspiration of an apostle, to speak like the wise man, ex sententia (with true understanding [Wis. 7:14]) or, as Jesus Christ says, ex abundantia cordis (from the fullness of one's heart [Mt 12:34]), to have received from God as a reward for one's labors and prayers, a tongue, a mouth and a wisdom which the enemies of truth cannot withstand: mercedem linguam . . . os et sapientiam cui non poterunt resistere omnes adversarii vestri [Lk 21:15]*" (RM 60).

Once more, Montfort comments upon what he had sketched in LEW in describing the "*marvelous effects*" of Wisdom. Thus, RM 60-61 must be read as a direct expansion of LEW 97.

There remains, finally, RW, whose text was in broad circulation from 1715 onward; it probably was written by Montfort that same year. This text contains some ten references to Wisdom, of which three invoke only the commonplace sense of the terms "wise" or "wisdom." Among the remaining more meaningful uses, three especially stand out. The first is the finest possible definition of the community's raison d'être: "*The interior aim of the Congregation of the Daughters of Wisdom is the acquisition of Divine Wisdom*" (RW 1). But the second is no less important, as it presents, in the chapter on obedience, the example to be followed or model to be imitated, Wisdom Incarnate: "*Holy obedience, practiced with all possible perfection, is the special virtue that should characterize the Daughters of Wisdom. Just as divine Wisdom, who reigned in the heavens, came down to earth to obey from the first moment of his incarnation to his death, so, following his example, his daughters have left the world to subject their mind and will to the yoke of obedience*" (RW 46).

Finally, the third of the more important occurrences of the term "wisdom" demonstrates the objectively theological character of the Wisdom recommended by Montfort to his daughters. He insists on the bonds between Wisdom and faith: "*As faith is the foundation of all religion, so is it the basis of all wisdom and perfection; hence faith, the daily bread of the Daughters of Wisdom, is the motivating force of all their thoughts, words and actions*" (RW 202).

Montfort does not omit recommending the concrete deeds of a Wisdom to be lived in day-to-day affairs: Wisdom in conversations (RW 250), the Wisdom of silence (RW 175), as well as Wisdom in the exercise of authority (RW 294).

6. Foundation of a community of Wisdom

Montfort's quest for Wisdom constituted one of the major stages of his own spiritual journey. This fact alone renders it worthy of consideration. But it is not a matter of an experience confined to the saint's personal pilgrimage. Quite the contrary, it overflows into his missionary career, and it has the great merit of having produced disciples. The biographer Picot de Clorivière, reporting the crosses Montfort had to bear at the Poitiers Hospital, makes no effort to conceal his admiration for the "great things" that Montfort's project of establishing a congregation of Wisdom would entail: "But the Lord placed wickedness in the service of the great things His servant was to do for His glory. This is how I must describe the establishment of a Congregation that, one day, would produce great fruits and render to the faithful of countless places the most important services, under the beautiful name of Daughters of Wisdom." [9]

Montfort, the initiator of the project, managed in short order to find an exceptional disciple, capable of uniting in the same passionate search and of carrying its project to term. Very early, indeed from the moment of his first allusion to Wisdom (L 15), Montfort had not the least hesitation in sharing his desire for Wisdom with a young woman of Poitiers, Marie Louise Trichet, and in leading her upon an evangelical adventure in which Wisdom would play such a decisive role. The young priest relied on the fervent prayers of this new disciple and associate in order to obtain the treasure of Wisdom: "*I will never cease asking for this boundless treasure and I firmly believe that I shall obtain it even were angels, men and demons to deny it to me. I believe strongly in the efficacy of your prayers, in the loving kindness of our God, in the protection of the Blessed Virgin, our good Mother; I believe too that the needs of the poor are too urgent and the promises of God too explicit for me to be making a mistake in seeking Wisdom. For even if the possession of divine Wisdom were impossible, according to the ordinary workings of divine grace, which is not the case, it would become possible because of the insistence with which we ask for it. Is it not an unchangeable truth that everything is possible to him who believes? Another thing that makes me say that I shall possess Wisdom is the fact that I have encountered and still encounter so much persecution night and day. So, my dear daughter, I ask you to enlist some good souls among your friends into a campaign of prayer especially from now until Pentecost, and to pray together for an hour on Mondays from one to two o'clock. I will be praying at the same time. Write and send me their names*" (L 15).

And so Montfort is not alone. Louise Trichet and "*some good souls among her friends*" are invited to "*enlist*" in the "*campaign.*" Nor will they delay to do so. A few months later, Montfort could write to his "*Dear Daughter*": "*I feel that you are still asking God that by crosses, humiliations and poverty I may acquire divine Wisdom. Be brave, my dear daughter, be brave. I am grateful to you; I feel the effects of your prayers*" (L 16).

Not that he did not beg, in concluding this letter, as well as in his next to Louise Trichet, a continuation of the prayers. With Montfort, then, the personal quest for Wisdom penetrated the marrow of his bones.

To the discourse on Wisdom, which was particularly intense in the first years of his ministry, now, after the fashion of the biblical prophets, Montfort joined the language of symbolic acts. Besides the solemn and significant symbol of the name of the new group, Daughters of Wisdom, Montfort would posit three acts that, over a period of a dozen years, marked the first steps of the new association, which later became a religious Congregation. The first two stand in intimate connection: the formation of the very first association of Wisdom, and the ideal of life that Montfort inculcated in that association by bestowing on it what is ordinarily referred to as the Wisdom Cross of Poitiers. Besnard describes these two actions of Montfort: "Following the example of Jesus Christ, Eternal Wisdom, he chooses the most base and abject objects in the eyes of the world. He gathers together on the grounds of the Hospital the poorest of the poor: eighteen to twenty sick ladies, all covered with ulcers—anything but favored by nature, but virtuous and pleasing in the eyes of the Lord. Faithful servant that he is of the Head of his household, he gathers in the blind, the lame, to be seated at the festive board. He seeks out a suitable place for the implementation of his plan. It will become the cradle of his community. He gathers them all together in a room apart, separated from the wards of the Hospital. He calls this place "Wisdom." He places a superior in charge. But what a superior! A poor, sick girl like any of the rest of them, but the simplest, most prudent, most pious, and most obedient. He places in the middle of the room a great cross, which is a piece of foolishness according to the world but which is the Wisdom of Jesus Christ. He wants them to be called by the lovely name Daughters of Wisdom.[10]

The third and last of the symbolic acts occurred only at the close of Montfort's missionary career, when he gave to Marie Louise of Jesus and her companions a gift of a statue of Our Lady of Wisdom. The deed is all the more significant for the fact that Montfort seemed to be quite attached to this statue, taking it with him on his missionary journeys. Unfortunately, it is impossible to know how Wisdom was represented through this "mysterious statue," but its very existence and the testimony we have from Marie Louise of Jesus about it are a further indication of the importance of the spirituality of Wisdom throughout Montfort's missionary career. We know the fact through Besnard's writings: "She always made her treasure and consolation this mysterious statue of Wisdom that the servant of God had given her. She has told us, time upon time, its history. 'Father de Montfort sent it to us,' she said, 'from Nantes to La Rochelle around the year 1715, when we were setting up charity schools there. "*I send you, my dear daughters,*" he stated, "*Wisdom along with the messenger*" (meaning that he was always united with Wisdom). We have simply set it on a table, and we pray before it often, always begging for Wisdom. Father de Montfort had a particular devotion to this figure, which represents Wisdom as Solomon depicts it in the Book that bears his name.'"[11]

The saint's last letters, composed in 1715 and 1716, likewise furnish insights on the Wisdom community that Montfort wished to found: *"The day for the establishment of the Daughters of Wisdom has at last arrived"* (L 28). Among the recommendations he addresses to the new community, the fourth leaves no doubt whatever about the name and the kind of mission he wishes to entrust to it: "*Call yourselves the 'Community of the Daughters of Wisdom for the education of children and the care of the poor'*" (L 29). Identity and mission are in strict association here: the spirituality of Wisdom has a properly evangelical, missionary dimension.

That the spirituality of Wisdom should emblazon the standard of a religious congregation is a unique fact in the history of the institutes of consecrated or apostolic life. This unique character is all the more astonishing in view of the countless institutes, male and female, bearing the names of titles of Christ or aspects of his mission: Sacred Heart, Precious Blood, Blessed Sacrament,

Holy Cross, Good Shepherd, Christ the King, and so on.[12]

II. Wisdom according to Montfort

1. Toward a definition

Just as with the biblical notion of Wisdom, Montfort's understanding of the term is far from being univocal and spans a multitude of meanings. Dayet himself recognized this fact: "The word 'Wisdom' in Montfort, as in Saint Paul and traditional terminology, presents more than one meaning."[13] There is no doubt, however, about the "primary meaning" of the term "wisdom" in Montfort: "Under the appellation 'Wisdom,' Montfort intends to designate especially the Son of God, generated by the Father from all eternity, who became a human being in the womb of the Virgin Mary Jesus Christ, Wisdom at once Eternal and Incarnate."[14] Then, secondarily, Montfort intended by Wisdom "the created qualities so magnificently accompanying [Jesus'] presence in the soul either actually, or striving to be, holy."[15]

The complexity of the notion of Wisdom in Montfort has also been brought out by Le Texier[16] in some fragmentary, incomplete notes. He introduces distinctions that come very close to Montfort's language, it is true, but he also appeals to the authority of Thomas Aquinas, whom he frequently cites. Aware of the subtleties of certain distinctions in Montfort, Le Texier actually speaks of a "certain confusion" generated by a "continual shift from essential Wisdom to a Wisdom that is personal by appropriation."[17] While the foundations of the distinctions established by Le Texier may be open to question and while the word "confusion" may well translate the malaise of the interpreter rather than the data of the text, we must acknowledge with him the equivocal character of the term in Montfort, as well as a number of sudden transitions from one meaning to the other in Montfort's work.

The distinction proposed by De Fiores appears more apt. He speaks of Wisdom "as a *person,* that is, Jesus Christ," and of Wisdom "as a *gift,* that is, Jesus Christ's communication to human beings."[18] Such a distinction has the twofold merit of emphasizing the basically Christological distinction of the notion of Wisdom in Montfort along with its functional or "economic" dimension, according to which Wisdom appears in a context of covenant in salvation history.

Montfort's view of Wisdom, then, is both fragmented—he himself gives a number of distinctions or quasi-definitions—and centered, for he refers everything to the mystery of Christ Wisdom, essentially a mystery of covenant and salvation for humanity.

In LEW, chap. 1, Montfort first proposes a definition based on etymology. "*In the general sense of the term wisdom means a delectable knowledge [sapida sapientia]—a taste for God and his truth*" (LEW 13). We note, furthermore, the importance accorded in this first chapter to the vocabulary of cognition (see the article *Love of Eternal Wisdom* in this Handbook). Wisdom, in Montfort, is bound up with knowledge. But at the same time, Montfort defines very clearly the context of his quest by the addition of the adjective "*delectable*" ("*savoreuse*"). The knowledge in question here is not a theoretical, abstract, cold knowledge but a knowledge that one can taste and that enables one, as it were, to come alive. Here, too, the vocabulary is revealing: in LEW especially, but also in the Hymns, Montfort speaks a great deal of "*tasting,*" "*loving,*" "*cherishing,*" "*treasure,*" "*sweetness,*" "*pleasure,*" "*delight,*" etc. The etymological definition, then, permits him to introduce and, in a sense, justify the type of discourse he proposes on the topic of Wisdom.

But more than etymology is at play here. Montfort also proposes distinctions of a more philosophical character, which he draws, this time, from his scholastic training: "*There are several kinds of wisdom. First: true and false wisdom. True wisdom is a taste for truth without falsehood or deception. False wisdom is a taste for falsehood disguised as truth. This false wisdom is the wisdom or the prudence of the world, which the Holy Spirit divides into three classes: earthly, sensual, and diabolical [Jas 3:15]. True wisdom may be divided into natural and supernatural wisdom. Natural wisdom is the knowledge, in an outstanding degree, of natural things in their principles. Supernatural wisdom is knowledge of supernatural and divine things in their origin. This supernatural wisdom is divided into substantial or uncreated Wisdom and accidental or created wisdom. Accidental or created wisdom is the communication that uncreated Wisdom makes of himself to mankind. In other words, it is the gift of wisdom. Substantial or uncreated Wisdom is the Son of God, the second person of the most Blessed Trinity. In other words, it is Eternal Wisdom in eternity or Jesus Christ in time*" (LEW 13).

Several distinctions are drawn here. First, between *true and false wisdom,* which calls for judgment and interpretation on the part of the reader. We also find two more essentialistic distinctions: first, between *natural wisdom* and *supernatural Wisdom*—a distinction that would not easily hold in light of recent studies on biblical Wisdom and in light of the theological and biblical renewal of Vatican II. Finally, we have a distinction between *accidental, created,* wisdom and *substantial, uncreated* Wisdom—which has lost none of its validity today and would only call for a bit of rethinking of its formulation, primarily for accidental wisdom.

In addition to these essentialistic definitions, Montfort likewise has a tendency to define Wisdom in an inductive fashion—that is, by way of a detailed description of the effects produced by Wisdom in those who seek it: a spirit of discernment (LEW 92), knowledge that instills life (LEW 93-94), capacity for communication and prophetic witness (LEW 95-97), a "*relish for everything that comes from God*" (LEW 98), gifts of the Spirit (LEW 99), apostolic daring and strength in trial (LEW 100). Here Montfort appeals to his own experience and sense of observation. In doing so, he harks back to biblical tradition, for which Wisdom always gives in superabundance, in incalculable richness: *"'He [Wisdom] entered the soul of the servant of God and withstood fearsome kings with signs and wonders' (Wisdom 10:16)"* (LEW 90).

Indeed, it is from the Bible, even more than from etymology and philosophy, that Montfort borrows the essentials of his "definition" of Wisdom. On the one hand, he quotes and comments on the main texts of the OT on personified Wisdom—Prov 8, Sir 24, Jas 6-8 (cf. LEW 16-17, 20-30, 65-68)—just as he does with their application by the NT writers to the person of Jesus (LEW 16-19). He devotes an entire chapter to Wis 7-8 (LEW 52-62), which describes in a beautiful way "*the excellence of Eternal Wisdom*" (LEW 52). At the same time, when he attempts to define the gift of Wisdom, it is again from Jas 7-8, complemented by Wis 10-11, in order to show *"the countless effects Eternal Wisdom produces in souls"* (LEW 91; see also all of LEW, chap. 8). The NT figures importantly in this chapter as well, as Montfort has drawn from it the distinction between "*earthly, sensual, and diabolical*" Wisdom (LEW 13, quoting Jas 3:15), which will serve as the basis of chapter 7, "*Choice of true Wisdom*" (LEW 74-89).

Montfort's understanding of Wisdom is extremely rich in connotations, (etymological, philosophical, experiential, biblical, and, of course, theological). Moreover, there are three fundamental lines of Montfort's theology of Wisdom.

2. Christ Wisdom

The great originality of Montfort's views on Wisdom resides first and foremost in his Christological reading of the biblical texts on Wisdom. It is here that he reveals what J. Hémery calls "St. Louis Marie's charism"—his "particular view of faith in *Christ known as the Wisdom of God,* come among human beings in order to reveal to them the fullness of the Father's design of love and teach them, true master of Wisdom that he is, by example and word, the way to beatitude."[19]

While the OT abundantly illustrates the varied meanings of the word "wisdom," reflection on this theme leads us to shift questions in another direction. From "What is wisdom," we have come to the question "Who is wisdom" (cf. Job 28, Prov 8, Sir 24, Wis 6-8). For Montfort, it is evident that this is the great question. And for him, the answer is the same as for Paul (1 Cor 15-20) and John (Jn 1:1-18): Wisdom is Jesus Christ, creative Word and Word of God become flesh. In LEW, we find more than forty instances where Montfort designates Christ as Wisdom, mostly in terms of "*Eternal Wisdom*" and "*incarnate Wisdom,*" thus referring to the mystery of his origin in God and to his presence among us in the Incarnation. From the very beginning of LEW, Wisdom's identification with Jesus Christ is strongly emphasized: *"So often were these last words* [Mt 19:24; cf. Mk 10:25, Lk 18:25] *repeated by divine Wisdom while on earth*" (LEW 6). And again, "*Why is Jesus, the adorable, eternal and incarnate Wisdom loved so little . . . ?*" (LEW 8). The identification becomes even more explicit as Montfort sets John's Prologue in relationship with the major OT texts on Wisdom in God (Wis 7:25-26, Prov 8:23-24): "*He is the substantial and eternal idea of divine beauty which was shown to St. John the Evangelist . . . when he exclaimed, 'In the beginning was the Word—the Son of God, or Eternal Wisdom—and the Word was in God and the Word was God.' . . . This is the Eternal Wisdom of which Solomon often speaks in his books when he says that Wisdom was created*" (LEW 17-18; cf. Jn 1:1).

The book's title, it is true, carries no explicit reference to the Incarnation, but the structure Montfort proposes and the development of his reflection invite us to read that title in a Christological sense: "*Following the example of this great man [Solomon], I am going, in my simple way, to portray Eternal Wisdom before, during and after his Incarnation*" (LEW 7). The identification is explicit once more in the enunciation of his project: "*Substantial or uncreated Wisdom is the Son of God, the second person of the most Blessed Trinity. In other words, it is Eternal Wisdom in eternity or Jesus Christ in time. It is precisely about this Eternal Wisdom that we are going to speak*" (LEW 13).

Biblical Wisdom is not the whole of Scripture, any more than the title "Wisdom" is the whole of NT Christology. But both OT and Christological Wisdom afford us a better grasp of the great unity between salvation history and the loving presence of God in the works of creation. Through his Christian rereading of OT Wisdom, then, Montfort helps us to a better understanding of the unity between both Testaments as the unity between the first and the new covenants.

3. Evangelical and missionary Wisdom

The Wisdom Montfort proposes is none other than the Wisdom of the Gospel. To paraphrase a turn of thought most dear to him, we might even say that for him "Wisdom is the Gospel and the Gospel is Wisdom." This identification emerges in his very project for LEW: he devotes an entire chapter to the "*principal utterances of Wisdom Incarnate which we must believe and practice if we are to be saved*" (LEW, chap. 12 [LEW 133-53]). This sampling does not represent Montfort's entire structure where Wisdom is concerned. As he himself intimates, it is only an abridgment. But it is also a way of referring directly to the Gospel, which Saint Louis Marie perceives both as prophetical (in oracles) and as sapiential (in oracles precisely of Wisdom). Beyond any doubt, it is from the Gospel that Montfort invites Christians to draw all of their Wisdom.

That the Gospel is the principal source of Wisdom for him is illustrated also by his well-known response to his friend Blain in their celebrated exchange in 1714. To the objections raised by his friend to his seemingly strange conduct, Saint

Louis Marie responded that his behavior was dictated by the Wisdom of the Gospel.[20]

Since, however, the Wisdom theme in Montfort is less known than his Marian teaching and since Wisdom does not figure in his sermon outlines, it might be objected that Wisdom had no deep impact on his missionary career, even though it was embedded in his personal experience. But the truth is quite the contrary, and it is again the conversation with Blain that best illustrates the repercussions of evangelical Wisdom on the life of the missionary: "He added that there were different kinds of wisdom, just as there are different degrees—that the wisdom guiding a community person in his or her conduct was not the same as the *wisdom of a missionary and apostolic person*—that the former was not a matter of new undertakings; . . . that it was not the same with *missionaries and apostolic persons,* for whom there is *always something new to be undertaken,* some holy work to be established or defended; that it was impossible not to get them talked about and get everyone in agreement; that, finally, if Wisdom was not to be put to work doing new things for God and undertaking something for His glory, for fear of what people might say, then the Apostles had been wrong to leave Jerusalem."[21]

It is the Missionary Apostolic who speaks here, and quite obviously his conception of Wisdom has nothing to do with calculated prudence. The Wisdom that instills Montfort's life is a Wisdom that thrusts him to *"undertake"* things, to *"leave Jerusalem,"* like the Apostles of times gone by, in order to do *"new things for God."* It is not surprising, then, to see him recommend to his religious community of men that they esteem the gift of Wisdom as being of the highest utility for ensuring success in their preaching (RM 60).

4. Paradoxical Wisdom of the Cross

Montfort's celebrated maxim "*Wisdom is the Cross and the Cross is Wisdom*" (LEW 180) admirably expresses how closely connected these two realities are in his thought. LEW, chap. 14, "*The Triumph of Eternal Wisdom in and by the Cross,*" is profoundly influenced by Pauline thought (1 Cor 1-2). Like the Apostle, Montfort bows in wonder before the paradoxical paths of Divine Wisdom: "*How remote and how different are the thoughts and the ways of eternal Wisdom from those of even the wisest of men*" (LEW 167), he cries, and again with Paul: "*O the depths of the wisdom and knowledge of God! How amazing is his choice and how sublime and incomprehensible are his ways! But how inexpressible his love for that cross!*" (LEW 168; cf. Rom 11:33).

The roots of Montfort's sapiential theology are broader than its Pauline origins. That theology is inscribed in the larger framework of a biblical theology in which the mystery of God is perceived under the sign of what a great contemporary theologian, François Varillon, has called the "humility of God" and the "suffering of God," or what Mornay, for his part, calls "the weakness of God."

"*Do you think that Jesus, now that he is triumphant and glorious, is any the less loving and condescending? On the contrary, his glory, as it were, perfects his kindness. He wishes to appear forgiving rather than majestic, to show the riches of his mercy rather than the gold of his glory*" (LEW 127).

In Montfort, the identification of the Cross with Wisdom is evidenced in Hymns 19 and 102, which manifestly borrow from the vocabulary of Wisdom in order to speak of the mystery of the Cross: *"In this princess / we truly find / grace, wisdom, / and divinity . . . / God found irresistible / her beauty so rare: / the cross has descended him / into our humanity!"* (H 102:9-10).

The importance attributed by Montfort to the Cross is altogether justified. Here, for the NT writers, is the supreme, decisive deed by which Incarnate Wisdom accomplished the world's salvation: "Jesus knew that his hour had come and he must leave this world and go to the Father. He had always loved his own who were in the world, and now he was to show the full extent of his love" (Jn 13:1). Montfort lacks an explicit theology of the Resurrection. He does not, however, entertain the least doubt that Golgotha alone is not the Cross. The Cross is the "*power of God*" (1 Cor 1:18). To use his own words, he speaks of the triumph of the cross: *"By it has Jesus Christ / thrown hell into chains, / laid low the rebel, / and conquered the universe"* (H 19:6).

Here is the Cross in all its glory, and Montfort's gaze is ever upon Christ's victory and the judgment of salvation that flows from it: that victory "*will have the cross carried in triumph by the Angels, and will sing to it canticles of gladness. It will follow this cross, which will stand high on the brightest-shining cloud that has ever been, and it will judge the world with it and by it*" (LEW 184). "*From His youth did he it follow, / with giant stride. / Of tenderness and love he died / in its arms. / I desire a baptism, / once he cried— / the cross I so love, / the object of my love!*" (H 19:11).

Here, then, is a theology of the Cross that could very well be included in current theological perspectives, provided certain expressions were updated and certain of his Christological premises reexamined, notably those bearing on the "consciousness of Christ" (LEW 169-70 and H 19:10 not being without their difficulties for today's understanding of the implications of Jesus' humanity). Apart from these reservations, Montfort's discourse on the Cross remains altogether pertinent and rich in theological and spiritual insights.

5. Mary and Wisdom

Our concern here is only how Montfort's Marian thought is integrated into his teachings on Wisdom.

First of all, a concrete fact: Montfort carried with him on his missions a wooden statuette, apparently carved by himself, and christened by him "Our Lady of Wisdom." Preserved and treasured at the Generalate of the Daughters of Wisdom, it is a Madonna and Child;

the Child is holding the world in his hand and has a playful expression on his face, reminding one of the Wisdom taking "delight in mankind" (cf. Prov 8:22-31). Mary is not presented alone but, rather, in her relationship with Wisdom Incarnate.

Montfort's teaching on Wisdom preceded and, in a way, framed his Marian teaching. While his devotion to Mary can be traced back very far in his spiritual pilgrimage, it is no less certain that as a spiritual author, Montfort has first given us a developed Christology. His Marian doctrine flows from that Christology and is understandable only in its light. It is not to be wondered at, then, that he should have devoted the first sixteen chapters of LEW to establishing his vision of Wisdom before furnishing us, in the seventeenth and last chapter, with his Marian doctrine.[22]

For Montfort, Mary's connections with Wisdom are manifold. But here again our saint begins with the mystery of Christ. If Mary is capable of guiding us in the quest for Wisdom, it is by reason of her proximity to Him who is not only the source of Wisdom but who is very Wisdom in person, Jesus Christ. In a rather bold phrase, Montfort says of Mary: "*She became the mother, mistress and throne of divine Wisdom*" (LEW 203). "*She became*"—suggesting the underlying reality of the economy of salvation. It is by virtue not of some necessity but of God's good pleasure and Mary's free response that she has become what she is in salvation history.

For Montfort, it cannot be a question of Mary's being able to have some precedence or superiority vis-à-vis the Divine Wisdom: "*Mary is also mistress of divine Wisdom. Not that she is above him who is truly God, or even equal to him. To think or say such a thing would be blasphemous. But because the Son of God, Eternal Wisdom, by making himself entirely subject to her as his Mother, gave her a maternal and natural authority over himself which surpasses our understanding. He not only gave her this power while he lived on earth but still gives it now in heaven, because glory does not destroy nature but makes it more perfect* (LEW 205). And again: "*If it is true to say that Mary is, in a sense, mistress of Wisdom incarnate, what control must she have over all the graces and gifts of God, and what freedom must she enjoy in giving them to whom she chooses*" (LEW 207).

As for the expression "*Throne of Wisdom*" (Sedes Sapientiae) and its Marian application, this figure had already seen a long history of liturgical usage, even before being popularized by the Litany of Loretto: Prov 8 and Sir 24 have been used in the Roman liturgy for the feasts of the Blessed Virgin ever since the seventh century.[23] In other words, Montfort has not given us any innovations on this point. Nor indeed should we be surprised to see him invoking, on this subject, the witness of the Fathers of the Church. In the following text we observe the abundance of synonyms for the word "*dwelling*"—these, as well, inspired by the famous text of Sir 24: "*Moreover, Mary is the royal throne of*

Eternal Wisdom. . . . That is why the Fathers of the Church call her the tabernacle of the divinity, the place of rest and contentment of the Blessed Trinity, the throne of God, the city of God, the altar of God, the temple of God, the world of God and the paradise of God. All these titles are most correct with regard to the different wonders which the most high God has worked in Mary" (LEW 208).

Quite evidently, the liturgical and montfort exegeses are "accommodation" and make no claim to convey the first meaning of the texts of Prov 8 and Sir 24, whose reference is to Wisdom in God. In fact, even from the viewpoint of a Christian rereading, it is Christ, and not Mary, who accomplishes what is said of Wisdom. But the liturgical and the montfort intuition remain correct, precisely inasmuch as it is in Mary that Jesus Christ Wisdom became incarnate. Mary, in our humanity, is the *dwelling place, the tabernacle, the place of rest* of Jesus Christ, God's Wisdom.

III. Montfort among the Pedagogues of Wisdom

The question of Montfort's sources has been the subject of numerous studies by the commentators, and it has long been established that by virtue both of his extensive reading and of his docility to his teachers during his theological and spiritual training, Montfort was mightily influenced by the theology of his time, especially by the French school of spirituality. Here we may refer to the commentators Lhoumeau, Plessis, Poupon, Catta, and Perouas, among others. As for the more specific case of the sources for LEW, Father Huré remains an excellent reference,[24] and that study can be complemented by more recent ones.[25] For the biblical sources, Gilbert's study is the best and most complete.[26]

We must, however, attempt to bridge a little gap here. What of LEW and two sources that antedate the productions of the French school: Augustine, and the Franciscan Wisdom tradition?

1. Montfort Wisdom and Augustinian Wisdom

A certain number of commentators on the montfort corpus appeal to the great Augustine for a grounding of the Montfort notion of Wisdom. Father Huré, indeed, in his *Introduction historique,* reserves Augustine the lion's share, according him some twenty pages out of about eighty. The monumental accomplishments of the Doctor of Hippo have much to offer, it is true, on the subject of Wisdom: "Key word in the language of the philosophers, ["wisdom"] is a key word, as well, in the theological language of Saint Augustine."[27] Besides, Augustine was one of the first great commentators—and one of the rare ones coming before the Middle Ages—to deal with Wis: he cites that book at least 760 times, commenting on some 150 verses, or roughly the number (140) cited by Montfort in LEW alone. It would be interesting to compare the commentaries of the two authors in order to see both their convergences and divergences.

On the other hand, we must not forget that in large part, Augustine understands wisdom in the philosophical sense,[28] while Montfort appears rather reticent when it comes to philosophical wisdom (LEW 84-88). Besides, while Montfort cites Augustine in LEW 30, 107, 213, Augustine's influence remains diffuse. Montfort generally shares an Augustinian view of the human being and salvation. But this is all that we can say, and it is unclear to what extent Montfort may depend on specific texts of Augustine that deal with Wis.

2. Montfort Wisdom and Franciscan Wisdom

A less thoroughly explored avenue is that of the parallels between Montfort's Wisdom and the Franciscan Wisdom tradition. Audusseau has studied them in some notes—whose nonexhaustive, provisional character he acknowledges—bearing mainly on texts of Angelo of Foligno, Bonaventure, and, finally, Francis of Assisi.[29] It is regrettable that this author did not return to the subject later so as to solidify his argumentation and the parallels. But the fact remains that his conclusions show profound affinities between Montfort's texts and the Franciscan texts and demonstrate that, indeed, there is a tradition of Christian Wisdom. The search remains to be pursued and refined, especially about Montfort's ties with Francis of Assisi, Angelo of Foligno, Raymond Lull, and Bonaventure, all of whom are cited in LEW or other works of Montfort.[30]

IV. Relevance of Montfort Wisdom

It would scarcely be an easy task to popularize Montfort's discourse on Wisdom—Montfort himself not having completely taken up the challenge of a like enterprise!—but there can be no doubt that his vision of Wisdom might respond to more than one felt need crying out in the hearts of Christians today.

First of all, in his teaching on Wisdom, Montfort is far from expressing a mere marginal, or peripheral, devotion. His devotion goes to the essential: it is centered on Christ. And the Christ Montfort proposes for our contemplation and imitation is not just any Christ, of vague or indeterminate delineation. The Christ Montfort proposes is none other than Christ as Eternal and Incarnate Wisdom, whose stamp creation has borne since its origins—precisely the element of coherence and cohesion in the whole created universe. This Christ is God's dwelling place among human beings, and Love crucified—the supreme manifestation of God's love for human kind.

In the second place, the montfort Wisdom has the great merit of sending us back to the Bible itself. In these times of a biblical renewal, no more appropriate undertaking could be imagined. So much remains to be rediscovered—especially in the Wisdom writings themselves, so long misunderstood by Christians, which offer a unique outlook on the mutual relationship between God and the world and on the deep meaning of human realities.

Finally, at a moment when so many cults and new religious groups (some even calling themselves "wisdom" or "sophia") propose esoteric spiritualities that so often go in tandem with gnostic tendencies (proposing a salvation that would be obtained by virtue of the mere possession of certain knowledge), Montfort's teaching also has the great merit of clearly revealing the radical evangelical demands of a Wisdom that must necessarily be lived, a Wisdom that is acquired only by way of a personal appropriation of Jesus' paschal mystery.

J.-P. Prévost

Notes: (1) Three major indices illustrate this singularity of Montfort's in the history of spirituality. First, Wis was little commented upon before the Middle Ages, and lack of interest in the history of its spiritual rereading extends, for all practical purposes, to our very day. Cf. M. Gilbert, *Sagesse de Salomon* (Wisdom of Solomon), in DSAM 14 (1990), 66. As a spiritual commentator on Wis, then, Montfort is an exception and, thereby, an especially important witness. Second, apart from the acceptance of Wis as a book of the Bible, it must be said that the Wisdom theme is scarcely dominant in the history of Christian spirituality. In order to convince ourselves of this, we need only consult the principal contemporary dictionaries of spirituality. For example, the *Dictionnaire de la Vie Spirituelle*, Cerf, Paris 1983, contains no article devoted expressly to Wisdom, while DSAM 14 (1990), 72-132, which presents an excellent synthesis of biblical Wisdom, gives most of its attention in the historical part of its study to the philosophical dimension of the theme in Christian antiquity and up to the sixteenth century. Montfort is not even considered in this historical part! Third, Montfort seems to have created a "precedent without a sequel" when he founded a religious community *of Wisdom,* which bears the name Daughters of Wisdom and the core of whose spirituality is the acquisition of divine Wisdom. (2) Itinerario, 296. (3) We know of a goodly number of theological works that have had a general influence on Montfort. But it is difficult to specify which of these works would have given him the taste and the means to pursue a systematic study of biblical Wisdom. Furthermore, we shall seek in vain to determine who, among Montfort's professors or spiritual directors, might have guided him into the ways of Wisdom. Itinerario, 255-58, seems to confirm this impossibility, since the treatment it accords the "discovery of Wisdom" goes beyond the study's own precise chronological framework, which is the spiritual itinerary of Montfort up until June 5, 1700. (4) De Fiores, *Montfort, un homme qui a rencontré Dieu en Jésus-Christ, Sagesse éternelle et incarnée* (Montfort, a Man Who Met God in Jesus Christ, Eternal and Incarnate Wisdom), in *Dieu Seul: A la rencontre de Dieu avec Montfort (God Alone: Encountering God with Montfort),* Documents et Recherches 1, Centre International Montfortain, Rome 1981, 84. (5) Ibid., 85. (6) *Louis-Marie Grignion de Montfort,* in DSAM 9 (1976), 1074. (7) L. Perouas, *Grignion de Montfort ou l'aventurier de l'évangile,* Editions Ouvrières, Paris 1990, 71: "Thereafter [after 1704], any mention of Wisdom is scattered, or even absent, until 1713-14." We have similar words from the pen of T. Rey-Mermet, *Louis-Marie Grignion de Montfort: 1673-1716,* Nouvelle Cité, Paris 1984, 64-65: "This identification of Wisdom and the Cross will disappear in the following years [after 1704]. . . . After 1711, in the writings of his maturity, designating the Son of God with the title Wisdom becomes extremely rare." The observation is correct on the frequency of occurrence of the vocabulary of Wisdom, but in no way is the theology of LEW cast aside. It still appears "in filigree" in some of Montfort's works and continues to be very powerfully expressed, his writings aside, in symbolic actions that we shall examine a little further on. (8) Cf. Besnard I, 315. (9) Clorivière, 2:103-104. (10) Besnard, *Marie-Louise,* 27-28. (11) Ibid., 353. (12) The comparison is easy to make between, on the one hand, the variety and multiplicity of the other Christological titles borne by the religious institutes and, on the other, the exclusive character of the title of Wisdom given to the Congregation of women that Montfort wished to establish. We need only refer to the list of institutes that still exist today in, for instance, *Annuario Pontificio per l'anno 1992,* Libreria Editrice Vaticana, Vatican City 1992, 111*, 2328. On the basis of this list, we see that in Italy there is a female institute dedicated to Our Lady, Throne of Wisdom, which actually seems to be of relatively recent origin and numbers 105 members. The reference to Christ as Wisdom, unlike what Montfort meant by the name he gave his Congregation of Wisdom, is thus present only indirectly. The Oblates of Wisdom, an institute of men, of rather recent American origin, bases its spirituality on Saint Louis de Montfort (13) J. Dayet, *La Sagesse chez le bienheureux Louis-Marie de Montfort* (Wisdom According to Blessed Louis Marie de Montfort), Bureau des Prêtres de Marie, Saint Laurent-sur-Sèvre 1944(?), 9. (14) Ibid. (15) Ibid., 10. (16) F. Le Texier, *La Sagesse selon St. L. M. de Montfort* (Wisdom According to Saint Louis de Montfort), in DMon 8 (1963), 1-5. (17) Ibid., 3. (18) De Fiores, *Montfort, un homme qui a rencontré Dieu,* 86-87. (19) J. Hémery, *Une attitude de sagesse évangélique* (An Attitude of Evangelical Wisdom), in CM 152 (1966), 157-58. (20) Blain, 185-86. (21) Ibid., 187-88. (22) L.-M. de Montfort, *L'Amour de la Sagesse éternelle (par la "vraie dévotion à Marie"): Puissante synthèse de spiritualité* (The Love of the Eternal Wisdom [by "True Devotion" to Mary]: A Powerful Synthesis of Spirituality), ed. H. Huré, Librairie Mariale, Pont-Château 1929, 276. For the profoundly Christocentric nature of Montfort's Marian theology, see also the great classic commentaries on TD, such as Lhoumeau (pp. 30ff.), Plessis (pp. 175-88), and Poupon (39-67). (23) Louis Bouyer, *Le Trône de la Sagesse: Essai sur la signification du culte marial* (The Throne of Wisdom: Essay on the Meaning of Marian Devotion), 2nd ed., Cerf, Paris 1961, esp. 74-77; B. Capelle, *Les épitres sapientiales des fêtes de la Vierge* (The Sapiential Epistles and the Feasts of the Blessed Virgin, in *Questions liturgiques et paroissiales* 27 (1946), 42-49; E. Catta, *Sedes Sapientiae,* in *Maria: Etudes sur la Sainte Vierge,* ed. Julien du Manoir, Beauchesne, Paris 1961, 6:689-866; Gilbert, *L'exégèse spirituelle de Montfort,* in NRT 104 (1982), 688-90. (24) H. Huré, *Introduction historique: L'idée de "sagesse" dans la spiritualité chrétienne et l'oblation qui s'y rattache* (Historical Introduction: The Idea of "Wisdom" in Christian Spirituality and the Oblation Connected to It), in Montfort, *L'Amour de la Sagesse éternelle.* (25) We shall not enter into this question, about which so much has been written; the reader may simply refer to the article *Love of Eternal Wisdom* in this Handbook. (26) Gilbert, *Exégèse spirituelle de Montfort,* 678-91. (27) *Le livre de la Sagesse (The Book of Wisdom),* in *Biblia Augustiniana: A.T. (Biblia Augustiana: OT),* Etudes Augustiniennes, Paris 1970, 368. (28) R. Holte, *Béatitude et sagesse: Saint Augustin et le problème de la fin de l'homme dans la philosophie ancienne* (Beatitude and Wisdom: Saint Augustine and the Problem of the End of Man in Ancient Philosophy), Etudes Augustiniennes, Paris 1962, 435. (29) J. Audusseau, *Sagesse franciscaine et sagesse montfortaine (Franciscan and Montfort Wisdom),* in DMon 7 (1962), 60-80. (30) Citations of Francis of Assisi: LEW 166; SR 25, 32, 130; TD 42; H 20:16; H 25:13; Angelo of Foligno: SR 68; Raymond Lull: LEW 87; Bonaventure: SR 30, 52; TD 8, 27, 40, 75, 76, 85, 86, 116, 152, 174.

ZEAL

SUMMARY I. MANIFESTATIONS OF ZEAL IN MONTFORT'S LIFE:
1. Zeal for the glory of God;
2. Montfort's zeal for Mary;
3. Montfort's zeal for the poor and outcast.
II. ZEAL IN MONTFORT'S WRITINGS:
1. Autobiographical testimonials in the letters;
2. In the hymns:
a. Hymn 21: "Flames of Zeal";
b. Hymn 22: "Resolutions and Prayers of a Perfect, Zealous Missioner";
c. Remarks on zeal in other hymns of Montfort.
III. APOSTOLIC ZEAL IN RESPECT FOR HUMAN FREEDOM.

The term "zeal" etymologically means to be hot or to begin to boil. It refers, therefore, to a rather vehement emotion or movement of the will in relation to a cause. In its fullest sense it refers to energetic and forceful activity in favor of some project. "Zealot" usually implies a fanatical or at least excessive dedication to someone or to some ideal. St. Thomas Aquinas presents zeal as an intense impulse of love and friendship: "Zeal, considered from any of its aspects, flows from an intensity of love. . . . The love of friendship seeks the good of the friend. When it is intense, then, it impels the one who loves to act against anything that might impede the friend's good. Thus, those are said to be zealous for their friends if they strive to repress words or deeds contrary to these friends' good."[1]

Montfort rides in the wake of the Angelic Doctor. For him, too, zeal flows from an intensity of love, just as flames come out of a fire. Indeed, he entitles one of his hymns, "Flames of Zeal." And that hymn begins: *"Sing we all, and burn with flames / of zeal for souls' salvation! / Zeal comes of love of God, / nor ever can abide / offense to God, our Sovereign, / or brook it that our neighbor / be assaulted. Come, make we / examination of its excellence, / examination of its excellence!"* (H 21:1).

In PM Montfort speaks of the jealous zeal of Moses, who seeks to satisfy God's holiness by appealing for a conversion of heart and the destruction of idols (PM 25) and of the burning zeal of the prophet Elijah, who summons the chosen people to restore fidelity to the covenant with God.

I. MANIFESTATIONS OF ZEAL IN MONTFORT'S LIFE

The saint's biographers offer abundant witness to the zeal that welled up within Saint Louis de Montfort from the love he had for God, for the Mother of the Lord, and for his neighbor.

1. Zeal for the Glory of God

From his youth, Montfort "breathed only zeal for the salvation of souls."[2] Episodes of this zeal for the glory of God and the salvation of his sisters and brothers occur all through his life. Wherever he saw offense to God, he was unable to abide it, and felt the greatest exasperation. His blood boiled in his veins, and he sometimes intervened rather violently. At Poitiers, he once caught sight of a young man harassing some ladies, and vigorously put an end to it. At Saint-Donatien one evening, he entered a cabaret, overturned tables, and smashed musical instruments. His character was no stranger to such reactions. He himself acknowledged his violent temper. Predominant in his life, however, was a constructive zeal, which committed him to seek in all things the glory of God. Indeed, Montfort's burning desire, the raison d'être of his life as a person of action and a missioner, was the extension of the Reign of Jesus through Mary, through the operation of the Holy Spirit, for the glory of the Father.

From the intensity of his love for God's glory, a project to found a community of missionary priests and brothers arose in Montfort's heart: *"It is no personal favor that I ask, but something which concerns your glory alone"* (PM 6). The missioner was also consumed with zeal for the Lord's house: "He always joined his preaching to a campaign for the restoration of churches."[3] At Poitiers he restored the Church of Saint John the Evangelist, at La Chèze the Chapel of Our Lady of Mercy, and at Campbon the parish church that lay in ruins.

2. Montfort's Zeal for Mary

Montfort manifests his zeal for devotion to the Blessed Virgin in LEW, SM, and, especially, TD. "He was captivated by the person of Mary in Scripture. He contemplates her at Cana, where Jesus manifests his glory for the first time, and he contemplates her again at the foot of the cross (Jn 2:1, 19:25–27). He contemplates her in her relationship with God, in herself, and with regard to us. . . . He encourages the Marian devotions and recommends meditation on the life of Jesus and Mary during the recitation of the rosary (LEW 193; TD 249–54). From his childhood, he already was in miniature, if I may say so, what he was so magnificently at a more advanced age: zealous panegyrist of the Blessed Virgin, perpetual orator of her privileges and her grandeurs, indefatigable preacher of devotion to her. Even as a youngster, his biographers tell us that he enjoyed speaking about Our Lady. As a preacher of parish missions, he was joyfully determined to spread devotion to her and to increase the number of men and women who would lovingly serve her."[4]

3. Montfort's Zeal for the Poor and Outcast

Montfort's predilection for the lowly and afflicted, the *anawim* of his time, is an echo of Zephaniah's appeal in behalf of justice for the weak and the small (Zp 2:3). With Zephaniah as with Montfort, poverty took on a moral, eschatological dimension. Today, a concern for the poor is expressed in the activity of movements fighting world poverty or waging campaigns for human rights. Montfort could only exercise this zeal in behalf of persons in his immediate vicinity. How appropriate, then, the inscription on his tomb today: *"Quid cernis, viator? / Virum charitatis igne consumptum"* ("What dost thou behold, O traveler? A man consumed with the fire of charity!")

II. Zeal in Montfort's Writings

1. Autobiographical Testimonials in the Letters

Surely no other type of document better reveals an author's true personality than his or her letters. This is certainly true in the case of Montfort. We need only page through the few letters that have been preserved in order to discover the signs of the inner flame of his zeal.

A note addressed to Father Leschassier, Superior of Saint-Sulpice, manifests Montfort's *"tremendous urge to make our Lord and his holy Mother loved"* (L 5). In Letters 6 and 9 he reiterates his ardent desire to teach catechism to the poor, and Letters 9 and 11 indicate the intensity of his concern for the temporal and spiritual welfare of the poor of the hospital in which he worked.

In Letter 11, which he wrote in 1702, Montfort repeats that his greatest attraction is for the missions. This desire gradually became more concrete, and at the end of his life his letters demonstrate his zeal for the cause of God. In Letter 27, to Marie-Louise, he urges her and Catherine Brunet to leave Poitiers for La Rochelle. Citing the example of Abraham, he exhorts the pair to be willing to risk something for God: *"I know you will have many difficulties to overcome but an enterprise which is going to do so much for the glory of God and the salvation of men will have its way strewn with thorns and crosses. If you don't take risks for God, you won't give anything worthwhile"* (L 27).

Letters 28, 29, 30, and 33 evince, besides Montfort's zeal, the urgency of the task to be undertaken by the Daughters of Wisdom. The pressing tone of Letter 30, addressed to Marie Régnier and inviting her to return to the La Rochelle community, is especially significant. The letter opens: *"The grace of the Holy Spirit does not permit of delay"* (L 30).

Letter 34 was the last addressed to Marie-Louise. The expressions of zeal that Montfort employs in this communication have been constants throughout his life. They have tempered and matured, but they have never ceased developing: zeal for the Cross, and zeal for divine Wisdom. No power on earth can separate him from these. In LPM, Montfort manifests the same *"divine jealousy"* that Paul experienced in his soul with regard to Christians he had evangelized: "Remember, then, my dear children, my joy, my glory and my crown (Phil. 4:1), to have a great love for Jesus and to love him through Mary. Let your true devotion to your loving Mother Mary be manifest everywhere and to everyone, so that you may spread everywhere the fragrance of Jesus and, carrying your cross steadfastly after our good Master, gain the crown and kingdom which is waiting for you" (LPM 2).

2. In the Hymns

A number of Montfort's hymns praise the zeal of any servant of God.

a. Hymn 21: "Flames of Zeal." Hymn 21 begins by identifying the source of Christian zeal: *"Zeal comes of love of God"* (v. 1) and neighbor. The flames of zeal flash forth from the very fire of love in the bosom of the Trinity, and they return there. *"What pleasure to God our Father, / when, for love, we aid / poor sinners' salvation!"* (v. 3). Montfort cites the joy of, *"the sweet Savior . . . / in finding some lost child— / whose price? The blood He shed!"* (v. 4). *"A single word of heartfelt zeal / has more than once flung wide the door / to touche some hardened heart. . . . / Just then, the Holy Spirit comes, / And peace is struck for everlasting"* (v. 5).

But the flame of love that bursts forth for the glory of the Father, the Son, and the Holy Spirit (vv. 3–5) kindles zeal for the good of our brothers and sisters as well (v. 16). They deserve that we should be concerned with their salvation. After all, *"our neighbors' dignity is great"* (v. 6), and *"their immortal soul . . . so noble, so great, and so lovely!"* (v. 7). Of ourselves they beg help and light, that they may wrench free of the clutch of evil (vv. 8–9), and rediscover the path of good (v. 10). Fed by love, the flames of zeal radiate with fervor, and fill with graces the soul that is their hearth (v. 11). Zeal is a most meritorious, divine virtue (v. 12), and its effects are precious; for it covers a multitude of sins (v. 13), prepares its practitioner for a sweet and holy death (v. 14), and leads to an incomparable glory, in heaven (v. 15). A "zeal" that would be practiced from selfish motives, rather than those of love, is a false zeal. Christian zeal is recognizable by certain characteristics: it is supernatural (v. 17) and sweet (v. 18),[5] after the example of Christ, the Good Shepherd (vv. 19–20). It is industrious and universal (v. 21), modest and disinterested (v. 22). It is accompanied by abandonment to Providence (v. 23). It is invincible (vv. 24–25), humble, and obedient.

b. Hymn 22: "Resolutions and Prayers of a Perfect, Zealous Missioner." Hymn 22 transfers, as it were, the flames of zeal, of which we hear in Hymn 21, to a missioner of flesh and bone. The three opening lines of the hymn perfectly fit St. Louis Marie de Montfort, the zealous missioner of the Reign of Christ through Mary: *"The die is cast: / I scurry 'cross the world, / rootless to the very quick of me— / to save my poor neighbor!"*

The first verses of the hymn cry the missioner's love for his brothers and sisters in need of spiritual help. But since love for one's neighbor proceeds from love for God, the good missioner asks God for the holiness, the truth, and the fervor needed to overcome evil and convert souls (v. 4). He asks for the gift of wisdom and charity that transform him into a *"a man divine"* (v. 5) by truly sharing in the divine nature.

In his zeal, the missioner is animated and guided by the Father's *"interests,"* and encouraged and strengthened by the joy of pleasing the Father (v. 6). In vv. 7 and 10 there are echoes of PM: *"For a grain of sand, they scour sea and land alike, / their labor past conceiving. / For Thee, then, O my God, shall I lack zeal? / To win the blood of my God, / shall I not stir from my place? / O what contempt, / O what contempt! / Were this some unbeliever here?"* (v. 7). *"A soldier, drumming 'cross the land, / enlistments wins from every side. / 'To arms!' he cries, and sudden there's a regiment. / But to defend an injured God / what cavalry is here? / Who ever takes up holy arms? / Alas, alas! / Alas, alas! / No thought for that!"* (v. 10).

The missioner casts his regard over fields now white for the harvest, and from deep in his heart wells a prayer to the Lord of the harvest, to send forth laborers of the Gospel (v. 9). Rising up as well is a reproach to the *"false devout,"* all closed off in the shell of their selfishness, for their *"cruel rest"* (v. 11). And especially, a renewed commitment surges: an engagement to work for the good of human beings—one's brothers and sisters (v. 12)—and for the cause of the Gospel (v. 13). The missioner toils with a humble, trusting heart (vv. 14–15), joining action to contemplation (v. 16). Montfort is moved to express this ideal in a number of mottos or slogans: *"How I would make Thee loved, O Lord!"* (v. 18); *"May I become / all things to all!"* (v. 19); *"Thou alone, my God, and souls' salvation!"* (v. 28); *"Make of me Thy missionary!"* (v. 31).

The qualities of zeal are proposed, not in abstract fashion, as in Hymn 21, but as invocations in the missionary's own prayer, which asks for a zeal that will not be austere. After all, a little vinegar and much oil win minds and hearts (v. 17). And so this zeal will be modest, kind, and heavenly (v. 19), obedient, humble, and prudent (v. 20), disinterested (v. 21), trusting (v. 22), and vibrant with initiative (v. 29). A missionary zeal lives in poverty: *"All monies are a brackish pool. / They soil a soul. How generous / it otherwise had been!"* (v. 26). *"It relies on the providence of God"* (vv. 22–23, 24–27).

Hymn 22 closes with a prayer to Jesus and Mary. The missionary asks Jesus to kindle his soul with the fire of his own love (vv. 28–29), to guide him by wisdom (v. 30), and to support him with his strength (v. 31). He asks Mary for her help: *"Mary, my good Mother, / send thou a whole army / to my aid!"* (v. 32). He also asks her for wisdom and strength, that his word *"may grow and bear fruit."* He confides to her his desire, *"that I may grow in holiness, / and glorify my God."* (v. 32).

Montfort must have composed Hymn 22 during his missionary life; unlike Hymn 21, which was probably written at his desk in the years of his youth at Saint-Sulpice. It is in Hymn 22 that he speaks of a humble, prudent zeal: *"Now, through my own experience, I have learned: / a burning zeal is a terrible thing, / unless it be all humble, meek, and wise— / submissive to the laws of human nature"* (v. 20).

Mary's spirit is presented as *"zealous yet prudent, humble yet courageous,"* just as we find it in TD 258. Just as in PM Montfort begs his Lord to send him missionaries of *"burning and prudent zeal"* (PM 21). Hymn 22 attributes more importance to poverty, which ought to be both actual and affective in a zealous missioner. It may well allude, between the lines, to that abandonment to Providence that Montfort has chosen for himself and now proposes to his followers (cf. RM 10–18; LCM).

Finally, Hymn 22 presents a missionary zeal so enlivened and filled with the spirit of Mary that we easily discover, here again, Montfort's own experience and a part of the spiritual legacy that he has bequeathed to his religious families.

c. Remarks on zeal in other hymns of Montfort.[6] Hymn 32:31–34 is an appeal to priests to be courageous shepherds of their flock. Hymn 46:6 exhorts all Christians to speak of the Heart of Christ, and to preach with courage Christ's greatness and the attractions of his goodness. In H 47:20–26 Montfort's impassioned cry summons all the earth to the love of Christ. Hymn 139:67 is fired with a zeal for the glory of God, which is being profaned.

Hymn 130:3 celebrates the Heart of Christ, which in the Eucharist burns with such intense zeal. Saint Michael the Archangel (H 21:2, 138:6), along with Moses and St. Paul (H 21:16), are consummate models for Christian zeal to imitate. The true devotee of Mary, as well, given over completely to her service, appears as an example of Christian zeal (H 80).

III. Apostolic Zeal in Respect for Human Freedom

Since Montfort's times, the apostolate has acquired certain qualities that are based on a contemporary reading of the Bible and a consciousness of human freedom. Certain expressions of zeal that are comprehensible in Montfort's milieu and culture of the seventeenth century may not be viable in our times. The reason Montfort still speaks to us today is his sincere, fervent love for God and human beings, and his having lived a life utterly consecrated to the proclamation of the Gospel. Deeds that may appear inopportune, or even violent, in Montfort—as in Christ himself (Jn 2:15)—are the exception rather than the rule. Montfort's habitual behavior, marked by a welcome of the sinner, commitment to preaching, and charity, won him the appellation, "the good Father from Montfort."

In the light of the New Testament, Christians must not allow themselves to be contaminated by a thickheaded, unenlightened zeal, even when it is rooted in a religious spirit. Christians look to Jesus, who condemned the extreme reactions (Lk 9:54–55) of James and John, those "sons of thunder" (Mk 3:17), and will mount the very Cross rather than resort to violence (Mt 26:51–55).

Thus, zeal is not rejected in itself. On the contrary, Paul insistently calls us to be zealous. Zeal is a good thing when lived for love of Christ, who himself was zealous for God (Jn 2:17). And so the Apostle expressly praises the missionary zeal that seeks to attract others (cf. Ga 4:18; also 2 Co 11:2, where Paul justly speaks of a "divine jealousy"). Finally, there is as well such a thing as a positive zeal for others' good (2 Co 7:7, 9:2), which translates into a manner of being and acting stamped with goodness, and with a love that takes precedence over every other solicitude (1 P 3:3–4; T 2:14).[7]

Enriched by a deep respect for the human being—that icon and child of God—Montfort's missionary zeal retains its value today. It thrusts us to continuous, tireless, and courageous commitment to the Reign of God in our world. Montfort refers especially to Christ as Wisdom, who is the principle of apostolic dynamism, and at the same time, of tenderness. He appeals as well to the Blessed Virgin Mary, whose spirit is *"gentle yet strong, zealous yet prudent, humble yet courageous, pure yet fruitful"* (TD 258). Montfort's proposal, a gift and consecration of self to Christ through the hands of Mary, is altogether valid and a precious secret of holiness.

A. Rum - Mary Firth

Notes: (1) ST II–II, q. 28, a. 4, c. (2) Blain, 13. (3) Pauvert, *Vie du vénérable Louis-Marie Grignion de Montfort* (Life of the Venerable Louis Marie Grignion de Montfort), Oudin, Poitiers 1875, 175. (4) Blain, 10. (5) For zeal in its quality as "tender," cf. a piece of advice for missionaries that Montfort himself borrows from Saint Francis Xavier: "At every moment, seek to be in an agreeable humor, and wear a cheerful, serene countenance. Never allow the least shadow of anger or sorrow to cross your face. Otherwise those who see you will not open their hearts, and will not have in you all of the confidence that will be necessary if they are to profit from meeting with you" (LS 502). (6) A number of Montfort's hymns manifest the fire that consumed him for the house of the Lord: H 23:31, 28:29, 33:18–21, 43:14–16,23-28, 47:7, 133:6, 136:9–15, 158:11–12. (7) H.-C. Hann, "Zelo" (Zeal), in *Dizionario dei Concetti Biblici del NT* (Dictionary of Biblical Concepts), Dehoniane, Bologna 1976, 2036.

Acknowledgments

Now that the privileged task of editing this volume has been completed, it is a joy to thank the many people who so willingly assisted in its publication.

In addition to the contributors and to the professional translators, the editors of the English edition of the *Handbook* express their gratitude to the members of the Company of Mary of the American Province, especially to Father Gerald Fitzsimmons (Provincial), Fathers Frank Allen, Edwin Blydenburgh, Roger Charest, Theodore Murphy; to Fathers Marcel Gendrot, Superior of the Mother House at St.Laurent-sur-Sèvre, Guy Jacob of Montreal and Jean-Louis Courchesne of the Generalate in Rome for assistance in securing illustrations for the *Handbook*; to Father Dorio Huot, for many years of Rome, presently of Montreal, for his scholarly, clear advice which was always deeply appreciated; to the members of the Company of Mary of the Great Britain and Ireland province, especially to Father Robert Douglas (Provincial), Fathers Paul Allerton, Fred Scragg (Assistant General), Lawrence Handley, Wilfrid Jukka and to Sister Jean Hickey of the English province; to the members of the Daughters of Wisdom of the American province, especially to Sisters Eileen Burton, Rachel Bouchard, Edna Butler, Veronica Byrne, Alice Crowell, Rosemary Gaffney, Ann Nielsen, Gertrude O'Brien, Margaret Oehrlein, Josephine Thomas, Anne Werner; to the Brothers of Saint Gabriel, especially to Brother Julien Rabiller of London, England, and Brother Adélard Faubert of Montreal, Canada.

The secretaries deserve special mention: Father Michel Bertrand, General Secretary of the Company of Mary, Rome, and Sister Marie-Paule, formerly secretary of Father General, Rome; Cindy Cassotto, secretary of the montfort editorial office at Litchfield, Connecticut; project volunteers Diana Casey, Debby DiAngelo, Millie Higgins, Tom Higgins, Andy Lach, Tom McDermott, Aline Nelson, and Pat Zuccarelli. Thanks are due to Robert Houser of Litchfield for his expert photography work, to Sara Day for her beautiful layout designs, to Joseph Carey for accomplishing so well the difficult task of Copy Editor, to Steven Riecker and the Princeton Academic Press, to *Wordworks* for compiling the topical index, to Lynn McNamee for her assistance with the endnotes, to Robert White and Michael Guerin for giving up part of their summer vacation to assist in the publication of this volume. The montfort community of Litchfield, Brother Alfonso, Ken Footit, Fathers Ronald Lloyd, Flavius Gamache and George Werner, has shown exemplary patience and support in the many months they have had to put up with the varied activities of the editorial team!

The editors of the English edition wish to thank Stephen Payne for his magnanimous service at the computer day in and day out for the last several months; his constant and faithful updating of the computer files for the entire editing process was an essential element in publishing the *Handbook* of montfort spirituality.

Finally, in a special way the editors wish to thank Sisters Yvette and Marie Franck of the Daughters of Wisdom. Their joyful and skilled dedication to the publication of the Handbook was invaluable. An index to such a massive volume, even though found at the book's back door, more often than not becomes the front door to interested readers. Sisters Marie and Yvette who prepared the Proper Name and Biblical indexes for Jesus Living in Mary, with such care and precision, not only gained the last word but became the welcoming doorkeepers offering hospitality and direction to those who would enter this treasurehouse of montfort spirituality.

In conclusion the editors wish to express their deep gratitude to Mary Robert, a devotee of Mary.

List of Contributors

AMATO, Angelo, SDB: Dean of Theology, Salesian Pontifical University, Rome (Italy). Articles: *Inculturation, Jesus Christ, Penance* (co-author).

AUDUSSEAU, Jean, SMM: Licentiate in Theology and Holy Scripture, Marseille (France). Article: *Covenant.*

AUMANN, Jordan, OP: Formerly Professor of Theology, Pontifical University of St. Thomas Aquinas (The Angelicum) Rome; retreat master and author, St. Thomas Aquinas Priory, River Forest, Illinois (USA). Article: *Path of Perfection*

BARBERA, Gaetano, SMM: specialist in Mariology, Bergamo (Italy). Article: *Hope.*

BOSSARD, Alphonse, SMM: Doctor of Theology, Rector of Notre-Dame du Marillais Sanctuary (France). Articles: *Faith, Incarnation, St. Louis Marie de Montfort* (co-author), *Secret of Mary, True Devotion.*

BULTEAU, Jean, SG: Bachelor of Philosophy, Bachelor of Religious Sciences, La Mothe-Achard (France). Articles: *Cross* (co-author), *Sick.*

BURRASCANO, Pietro, SMM: Licentiate in Moral Theology; founder of the *Centro Famiglie incontro* of Pozzuolo Martesana (Italy). Article: *Family* (co-author).

CHAREST, Roger M., SMM: Director of the Marian Center; managing editor, *Queen of All Hearts*, Montfort Publications, Bayshore, New York (USA). Article: *Legion of Mary* .

CHIARI, Ismene (Sister Bernardetta dell'Immacolata), DW: Specialist in Mariology, Rome (Italy). Article: *Silence.*

CORTINOVIS, Battista, SMM: Doctor of Theology, specialist in Mariology; Provincial Superior, Rome (Italy). Article: *Church.*

COUSINS, Ewert: Professor of Theology, Fordham University, New York,

General Editor, *World Spirituality Encyclopedic History* (USA). Article: *Trinity* (co-author).

CROTEAU, Georges, SG: Doctor of Educational Science, Toronto (Canada). Article: *Education.*

DALLAIRE, Gilles, SMM: Instructor in Montfort Spirituality, Montreal (Canada). Article: *Apostle* (co-author).

DAVIAU, Pierrette, DW: Bachelor of Pedagogy, Doctor of Letters; Director of the Institute of Social Communication at Saint Paul University of Ottawa (Canada). Article: *Tenderness.*

DE FIORES, Stefano, SMM: Doctor of Theology; Professor of Mariology, Gregorian and Salesian Pontifical Universities; the Pontifical Faculty of the "Marianum", Rome (Italy). Articles: *Adoration* (co-author), *Apostle* (co-author), *Childhood* (co-author), *Daughters of Wisdom* (co-author), *End Times, St. Louis Marie de Montfort* (co-author), *Montfort Spirituality.*

DEMERS, Odilon, SMM: Bachelor of Pastoral Theology, Montreal (Canada). Article: *Hymns* (co-author).

DELESALLE, Agnès, DW: Specialist in pastoral liturgy, assistant for the development of priests and the laity, diocese of Tours (France). Article: *Angels/Demons.*

DEVILLE, Raymond: Specialist in the spirituality of the seventeenth century, Superior General of the Company of Priests of Saint Sulpice, Paris (France). Article: *French School.*

ÉVENOU, Jean: Expert in liturgy, Congregation of Divine Worship, Rome (Italy). Article: *Liturgy* (co-author).

FENILI, Giuseppe, SMM: Doctor of Theology, Santeramo (Italy). Article: *Adoration* (co-author).

FRANCINI, Giorgio, OSM: Professor of Italian literature, Rome (Italy). Articles: *Noels* (co-author), *Hymns* (co-author).

FRITH, Mary (Sister Philip-Mary), DW: Specialist in theology and Holy Scripture, Chorley (Great Britain). Article: *Zeal* (co-author).

GABBIADINI, Rosino: Specialist in educational science, Ravenna (Italy). Article: *Model.*

GAFFNEY, Patrick, SMM: Doctor of Theology; Professor Emeritus of theology, Saint Louis University, St. Louis, Missouri; Montfort Missionaries, Litchfield, Connecticut, (USA). Articles: *Consecration, Cross* (co-author), *Ecumenism* (co-author), *Freedom* (co-author), *Mary, Reign, Sin* (co-author), *Trinity* (co-author), *Providence, Reparation* (co-author).

GARAT, François, SG: Licentiate in Religious Studies, Mortagne-sur-Sèvre (France). Article: *Pilgrimage* (co-author).

GASPARI, Sergio, SMM: Doctor of Biblical Theology; Professor of liturgy, Rome (Italy). Article: *Priest.*

GENDROT, Marcel, SMM: Doctor of Philosophy, Licentiate of Canon Law, Saint-Laurent-sur-Sèvre (France). Articles: *Associations* (co-author), *Canonization* (co-author).

GUIL, Emmanuel, SMM: Spiritual director and retreat master, Le Marillais (France). Article: *Pilgrimage* (co-author).

GUINDON, Henri-Marie, SMM: Doctor of Theology, Ottawa (Canada). Articles: *Noels* (co-author), *Fidelity, Little Crown, Prayer, Sacred Heart, Salvation.*

GUITTENY, Bernard, SMM: spiritual director and retreat master, Meaux (France). Article: *Creation.*

HÉMERY, Jean, SMM: Staff of the Basilica of St. Louis Marie de Montfort, spiritual director and retreat master, Saint-Laurent-sur-Sèvre (France). Articles: *Associations* (co-author), *Baptism, Charisms.*

JOSEPH, T. A., SG: Doctor of Letters, Licentiate of Sacred Scripture, visiting Professor of Sacred Scripture, Hyderabad (India). Article: *Psalms.*

JÜNEMANN, Hermann Josef, SMM: Master in Spirituality; Director of the Marian Montfort Center, Salzburg (Austria) and assistant Director of the INternational Montfort Center, Louva in (Belgium). Articles: *Man, Mystic, Grace.*

KOELHER, Théodore, SM: Doctor of Theology; former director of the Marian Library, Dayton, Ohio (USA). Article: *Slavery of Love.*

LAURENCEAU, Jean, OP: Theologian, spiritual director and retreat master, Lille (France). Article: *Rosary.*

LAURENTIN, René: Doctor of Letters, Sorbonne; Mariologist, Évry (France). Article: *Holy Spirit.*

LE BOT, Corentin, SG: Licentiate of Letters, Rome (Italy). Article: *Friendship.*

LEMARIÉ, Michel, SMM: Specialist in social sciences, Buenos Aires (Argentina). Article: *Poverty.*

LEPERS, Simone, DW: Licentiate in Pilosophy and Pedagogy; Archivist of the mother house of the Daughters of Wisdom, Saint-Laurent-sur-Sèvre (France). Articles: *Daughters of Wisdom* (co-author), *Marie-Louise.*

LOGISTER, Wiel, SMM: Doctor of Theology, Professor of Theology at the Catholic University of Tilburg (Netherlands). Article: *God.*

MACDONALD, Donald, SMM: Spiritual director and retreat master, Montfort Missionaries, Manila, (Philippines). Article: *Peace.*

MACKRELL, Gerard, SMM: Spiritual director and retreat master, Andover (Great Britain). Article: *Freedom* (co-author).

MADORE, Georges, SMM: Provincial Superior, Montreal (Canada). Article: *Love.*

MAGGIONI, Corrado, SMM: Doctor of Liturgy, Congregation of Divine Worship, Rome (Italy). Articles: *Eucharist, Liturgy* (co-author).

MAIRE, Olivier, SMM: Licentiate in Natural Sciences, Rome (Italy). Articles: *Beauty, Last Things.*

MICHAUD, Jean-Paul, SMM: Doctor of Theology, Licentiate in Sacred Scripture, Professor of Theology at Saint Paul University, Ottawa (Canada). Articles: *Bible.*

MORINAY, Jean, SMM: spiritual director and retreat master, Chezelles (France). Articles: *Beatitudes, Virtues.*

MYLADIL, Thomas, OCD: Doctor of Theology, Fordham University; retreat master and teacher, New York (USA). Article: *Mortification*

NAVA, Pier Luigi, SMM: Licentiate in Canon Law; Director of "Quaderni Monfortani," Rome (Italy). Articles: *Company of Mary, Parish Missions, Penance* (co-author), *Triptych.*

PAPÀSOGLI, Benedetta: Doctor of Letters; Professor of literature, University of

Messina; hagiographer, Rome (Italy). Article: *Hymns* (co-author).

PAYNE, Richard J.: Executive Director, Arcadia House; publisher and editor, founding editor *The Classics of Western Spirituality, World Spirituality - Encyclopedic History,* and the forthcoming *The Classics of Eastern Spirituality,* Goshen, Connecticut (USA). Article: *Sin* (co-author), editor's notes - *Ecumenism, Incarnation, Hymns.*

PÉNISSON, Jean, SG: Instructor in modern letters, Professor of history and educational sciences, Center for Pedagogical Development, Marseille (France). Article: *Milieu.*

PRÉVOST, Jean-Pierre, SMM: Doctor of Biblical Theology, Licentiate in Sacred Scripture; Professor of Theology, Saint Paul University, Ottawa (Canada). Articles: *Love of Eternal Wisdom, Wisdom.*

ROBITAILLE, Hélène, DW: Professor of religious studies, Rome (Italy). Article: *Retreat.*

ROLANDEAU, Jean-Baptiste, SG: Specialist in Montfort history and spirituality, Saint-Laurent-sur-Sèvre (France). Article: *Brothers of Saint Gabriel.*

RUM, Alberto, SMM: Writer, Montfort Marian Center, Rome (Italy). Articles: *Pope/Bishops, Saint, Zeal* (co-author).

SAWARD, J.: Professor, St. Charles Borromeo Seminary, Philadelphia (USA). Articles: *Ecumenism* (co-author), Oxford Movement.

SIBOLD, Marcel, SMM: Specialist in Montfort research (France). Articles: *Family* (co-author), *Iconography*

STERN, Jean, MS: Theologian, archivist of the mother house of the Missionaries of Our Lady of La Salette, Rome (Italy). Article: *Reparation* (co-author).

STOCKERT, H. R.: Priest of the Byzantine Rite of the Diocese of Passaic; Communications Director of the diocese, Granville, New York (USA) Article: *Angels/Demons* (co-author)

VALENTINI, A., SMM: Doctor of Theology; Professor of Theology, Rome (Italy). Articles: *Disciple, Magnificat.*

VAN DEN HOOF, Bernadette, DW: Licentiate in Philosophy and Letters, Brussels (Belgium). Article: *Daughters of Wisdom* (co-author).

VAN DER HULST, Adrianus, SMM: Masters in spirituality; Director of scholastics, Manila (Philippines). Article: *Discernment.*

VETTICKAL, J. (Antony Francisco), SG: Specialist in educational sciences, Tiruchirapalli (India). Article: *Childhood* (co-author).

VIENNE, Claire (Sister Marie-Claire), DW: Graduate in religious studies, Saint-Laurent-sur-Sèvre (France). Article: Canonization (co-author).

Translators

Frank Allen, SMM; Paul Allerton, SMM; Eileen Burton, DW; Rachel Bouchard, DW; Edna Butler, DW; Veronica Byrne, DW; Ann Crowell, DW; Adélard Faubert, SG; James Fowler and the Alliance Francaise; Mary Firth, DW; Rosemary Gaffney, DW; Lawrence Handley, SMM; Jean Hickey, DW; Wilfred Jukka, SMM; Ann Nelson, DW; Julien Rabiller, SG; Gertrude O'Brien, DW; Margaret Oehrlein, DW; Stephen Perry; Fred Scragg, SMM; Carol Marshall Stopforth; Rev. Charles Underhill Quinn; Ann Werner, DW.

Bibliography

The following bibliography is limited to a sampling of some of the works on montfort spirituality. Additional references may be found in the end notes of the various articles in this Handbook.

I. The Works of Saint Louis Marie de Montfort

God Alone: The Collected Writings of Saint Louis Marie de Montfort, Bay Shore, Montfort Publications, 1987.

This volume includes most of the works of Saint Louis de Montfort. It contains only a few pages of the Book of Sermons and omits the saint's Notebook; both of these works have yet to be translated into English. Only eleven of the saint's 164 hymns are found in *God Alone.* The entire corpus of Father de Montfort's "*Cantiques*" will be published in English at the end of 1995 by Montfort Publications, Bay Shore.

Gendrot, M.(ed.) — *Make Way for Jesus Christ,* Montfort Publications, Bay Shore, 1984. This small volume contains excerpts from various writings of Saint Louis de Montfort.

II. Biographies of Saint Louis de Montfort

Included in this list are only some of the better known biographies of more than 100 pages. They are listed chronologically:

1. 18th Century: -

Anonymous [Grandet] — *La vie de Messire Louis-Marie Grignion de Montfort, prêtre missionnaire apostolique, composée par un prêtre du clergé,* Centre international montfortain, Rome, 1993 (original text), 1994 (modern French text) (Nantes 1724), 487.

Besnard, Ch. — *Vie de M. Louis-Marie Grignion de Montfort,* Centre international montfortain, Rome 1981, 2 t., XVI-334, 346 (ms. from around 1770, at AGFS).

Blain, J.-B. — *Abrégé de la vie de Louis-Marie Grignion de Montfort,* Centre international montfortain, Rome 1973, 255 (two ms. of the work, edited 1722-1724, at AGCM).

Picot de Clorivière, J.	*La vie de M. Louis-Marie Grignion de Montfort, missionnaire apostolique, instituteur des missionnaires du Saint-Esprit et des Filles de la Sagesse,* Delain Jeune/L. Hovius-/E. G. Blouet, Paris/Saint-Malo/Rennes 1785, 587.

2. 19th Century:

Anonymous	*Vie du vénérable Louis-Marie Grignion de Montfort,* chez Lefort, Lille 1861, (2ème éd.), 106.
Anonymous	*Der Selige Ludwig-Maria Grignion von Montfort, der grosze Apostel und Diener Mariens in 17 Jahrhundert, Selig gesprochen den 22 Januar 1888,* Werkes von heiligen Paulus, Freiburg (Schweiz) 1890, 209.
Anonymous	*Vie populaire du bienheureux L.-M. Grignion de Montfort,* Plihon et Hervé, Rennes 1891 (2ème éd.), 227.
Anonymous [Cruikshank]	*Blessed Louis-Marie Grignion de Montfort (Missionary Apostolic, Founder of the Company of Mary and the Daughters of Wisdom) and his devotion,* London, New York 1892, 2 t., 359 and 417.
Anonymous [Dalin]	*Vie du vénérable serviteur de Dieu Louis-Marie Grignion de Montfort, missionnaire apostolique et instituteur de la congrégation des missionnaires du Saint-Esprit de Saint-Laurent-sur-Sèvre, et de celle des Filles de la Sagesse,* Le Clerc et Cie, Paris 1839, 582.
Babonneau	*Le bienheureux Grignion de Montfort, tertiaire dominicain, apôtre du Sacré-Coeur, de la croix et du rosaire. L'homme, la parole, l'oeuvre,* L'Année dominicaine, Paris 1888, 120.
Boutin, H.	*Histoire populaire du bienheureux Louis-Marie Grignion de Montfort,* L.-J. Biton, Saint-Laurent-sur-Sèvre 1893, 264.
Chauvin, P. M.	*Le bienheureux L.-M. Grignion de Montfort,* H. Gallières, Rennes 1888, 215.
Fontenau, P.	*Vie du bienheureux Louis-Marie Grignion de Montfort, missionnaire apostolique, fondateur des Pères de la compagnie de Marie, des Soeurs de la Sagesse et des Frères du Saint-Esprit,* Oudin, Paris 1887, 563.
Fonteneau, P.	*Vie populaire du vénérable serviteur de Dieu Louis-Marie Grignion de Montfort, fondateur des Pères de la compagnie de Marie, des Soeurs de la Sagesse et des Frères du Saint-Esprit,* Imprimerie Bourgeois, Nantes 1885, 138.
Gaignet, J.	*Vie populaire du vénérable Louis-Marie Grignion de Montfort,* F. Bideaux, Luçon 1879, 105.

Kerkhoffs, A. *Levensschets van den Gelukzaligen Louis-Marie Grignion de Montfort, apostolisch missionaris en stichter des missionarissen-congregatie van't Gezelschap van Maria (Compagnie de Marie) en der congregatie van de Dochteren der Wijsheid (Filles de la Sagesse),* Druk van M. Alberts, Gulpen 1886, 171.

Pauvert, A. *Vie du vénérable Louis-Marie Grignion de Montfort, missionnaire apostolique, fondateur des prêtres missionnaires de la compagnie de Marie et de la Congrégation des Filles de la Sagesse,* Oudin, Paris/Poitiers 1875, 684.

Persiani,. G. *Vita del Beato Ludovico Maria Grignon [sic] di Montfort, sacerdote del terzo ordine di San Domenico, Fondatore de' Missionari della Compagnia di Maria e delle Figlie della Sapienza,* Befani, Roma 1887, 263.

Quérard, J.-M. *Vie du bienheureux Louis-Marie Grignion de Montfort, missionnaire apostolique, du tiers ordre de Saint-Dominique, fondateur des missionnaires de la compagnie de Marie, de la congrégation des Filles de la Sagesse et des Frères de la communauté du Saint-Esprit,* Caillère, Rennes 1887, 4 vol., 580, 610, 621, 654.

3. 20th Century:

Anonymous [Texier, J. M.] *Un apôtre de la croix et du rosaire, le bienheureux Louis-Marie Grignion de Montfort, fondateur de la compagnie de Marie et de la Sagesse,* E. Petithenry, Paris [1902], 164.

Bernoville, G. *Grignion de Montfort, apôtre de l'école, et les Frères de Saint Gabriel,* A. Michel, Paris 1946, 372

Bolger, E. C. *Life of St. Louis-Marie de Montfort,* Montfort Fathers, Liverpool 1952, 157.

Bombardier, J. *Saint Louis-Marie Grignion de Montfort, missionnaire en pays chrétien,* Les éditions montfortaines, Nicolet-Dorval 1947, 142.

Buondonno, P. *San Luigi-Maria Grignion de Montfort (1673-1716), fondatore dei Missionari della Compagnia di Maria e delle Figlie della Sapienza,* Centro mariano monfortano, Redona di Bergamo 1947, 514.

Chaigne, L. *Le bienheureux Louis-Marie Grignion de Montfort,* J. de Gigord, Paris 1937, 167.

Christoflour, R. *Grignion de Montfort, apôtre des derniers temps,* Éditions du vieux colombier, Paris 1947, 223.

Clénet, L.-M. *Grignion de Montfort, le saint de la Vendée,* Perrin, Paris 1988, 309.

Crosnier, A. — *Un grand semeur évangélique Louis-Marie Grignion de Montfort, histoire d'une vie, histoire d'une âme,* ms. of 401 pages, at AGCM

Daniel, H. — *Saint Louis-Marie Grignion de Montfort. Ce qu'il fut, ce qu'il fit,* Téqui, Toulouse 1967, 518.

David, A. — *Saint Louis-Marie Grignion de Montfort,* Bonne Presse, Collection «Les Saints de France», Paris 1947, 126.

Id. — *Le Père de Montfort par ses meilleurs historiens: René Bazin, Henri Brémond, Daniel Rops, Garrigou-Lagrange, Pierre de la Gorce, Cardinal Mercier, Jean Yole, etc...,* Librairie mariale, Paris 1947, 157.

De Luca, G. — *S. Luigi M. Grignion de Montfort. Saggio biografico,* Postulazione generale monfortana, Rome 1943, 317 (second edition, including other works of de De Luca on Montfort: Edizioni di storia e letteratura, Rome 1985, XX-380.

Demarchelier, E. — *The Queen's Herald,* The Birchlay Hall Press, Lancashire 1964, 181.

Diéres Monplaisir, L. — *Vida del Beato Luis María Grignión de Montfort, Fundador de la Compañía de María y de las Hijas de la Sabiduría. Autor del Tratado de la verdadera devoción a la santísima Virgen,* Librería nueva, Bogotá 1942, 157.

Eijckeler, P. — *De Heilige Montfort, Louis-Marie Grignion, 1673-1716, Apostolisch Missionaris, Stichter van de Paters Montfortanen (Gezelschap van Maria) en van de Dochters der Wijsheid,* E. van Aelst, Maastricht 1947, 255 (2nd ed. 1958).

Windeatt, Mary Fabyan — *Our Lady's Slave: The Story of Saint Louis Mary Grignion de Montfort,* St. Meinrad's Abbey, St.Meinrad's 1950.

Gabriel-Marie, Fr. — *Grignion de Montfort, routier de l'évangile,* Maison St-Gabriel, St-Laurent-sur-Sèvre 1966, 184.

Guinefoleau, H. — *Saint Louis-Marie Grignion de Montfort. Sa vie, sa doctrine, sa mission, son influence jusqu'à nos jours,* ms. of 125 pages (1948), at AGCM.

Jac, E. — *Le bienheureux Grignion de Montfort (1673-1716),* chez Lecoffre, Collection «Les Saints», Paris 1903, 233.

Jongen, H. — *De Zalige de Montfort. Heraut van Maria's Rijk,* Drukkerij-uitgeverij Lannoo, Thielt 1944, 123.

Lammot, J. — *Un nouveau Saint français: Louis-Marie Grignion de Montfort,* S.I.L.I.C., Lille 1949, 110.

Laveille, A. *Le bienheureux L.-M. Grignion de Montfort (1673-1716), d'après des documents inédits,* Ch. Poussielgue, Paris 1907, 560.

Laveille, A. *Le bienheureux Louis-Marie Grignion de Montfort et ses familles religieuses*, Mame, Tours 1916, 440.

Le Crom, L. *Un apôtre marial, Saint Louis-Marie Grignion de Montfort (1673-1716),* Librairie mariale, Pontchâteau 1942 (another edition: Les traditions françaises, Tourcoing 1947), 479.

M'Geoy, T. *Blessed Grignion de Montfort, his life, labours, pilgrimages, and apostleship to Mary,* Browne and Nolan, Dublin-Belfast 1913, 150.

Miglioranza, C. *San Luis María Grignión de Montfort*, Padres monfortianos, Buenos-Aires 1987, 286.

Morineau, B. M. *Saint Louis-Marie Grignion de Montfort,* Flammarion, Collection «Les grands coeurs», Paris 1947, 192.

Ny lalam-piainan'i *Md. Louis-Marie de Montfort,* Fianarantsoa 1982, 192.

Papàsogli, B. *Montfort, un uomo per l'ultima Chiesa,* Gribaudi, Torino 1979, 416 (2nd ed.: Edizioni monfortane, Roma 1991, 474). English Translation: *Montfort, A Prophet for Our Times,* Edizoni Monfortane, Roma, 1991.

Pérouas, L. *Grignion de Montfort, les pauvres et les missions,* Cerf, Paris 1966, 184.

Pérouas, L. *Ce que croyait Grignion de Montfort et comment il a vécu sa foi,* Mame, Tours 1973, 214. English Translation: *A Way to Wisdom: Louis Marie Grignion de Montfort And His Beliefs,* Montfortians Yesterday and Today, Bay Shore, 1982.

Pérouas, L. *Grignion de Montfort et la Vendée,* Cerf, Paris 1989, 130.

Pérouas, L. *Grignion de Montfort ou l'aventurier de l'évangile,* Les éditions ouvrières, Paris 1990, 112.

Rey-Mermet, Th. *Louis-Marie Grignion de Montfort,* Nouvelle Cité, Paris 1984, 158.

Rigault, G. *Le bienheureux Louis-Marie Grignion de Montfort,* Editions Publiroc, Marseille 1930, 224. English Translation: *Saint Louis de Montfort: His Life and Work,* Port Jefferson, Montfort Fathers, 1948.

Rivière, E. *San Luis María de Montfort,* Padres monfortianos, Bogotá 1947, 356.

Soto, J.F. — *San Luis María de Montfort*, Centro mariano monfortiano, Lima 1980 (2ème éd.), 320.

Valderrama, J. — *Tha'nh L.M. Mon-pho*, Fons vitae, Saïgon 1959, 117.

Waach, H. — *Ludwig Maria Grignion von Montfort*, Franz-Sales Verlag, Eichstätt-Wien 1966, 306.

Some Dictionary Articles Articles On Montfort:

De Fiores, S. — *Luigi Maria Grignion de Montfort*, in *Dizionario degli istituti di perfezione* 5 (1978) 755-764.

Frissen, G. M. — *Luigi-Maria Grignion de Montfort*, in *Bibliotheca sanctorum* 8 (1967) 357-366.

Gaffney, P. — *Grignion de Montfort, Louis Marie, St.*, in *New Catholic Encyclopedia* 6 (1967), 805.

Guérin, P. — *Le v. Louis-Marie Grignon [sic] de Montfort [...]*, in *Les petits Bollandistes. Vie des Saints [...]*, Bloud et Barral, Paris 1876, t. 15, 320-337.

Moreri, L. — *Montfort (Louis-Marie Grignion de)*, in *Le grand dictionnaire historique*, Chez les libraires associés, Paris 1759, t. 7, 725.

Pérouas, L. — *Louis-Marie Grignion de Montfort*, in DSAM 9 (1976) 1073-1081.

Tranvouez, J. — *Louis-Marie Grignion de Montfort*, in *Catholicisme* 7 (1975) 1128-1133.

III. Commentaries on Montfort Spirituality:

A. The Series DOCUMENTS ET RECHERCHES

Published under the direction of Marcel Gendrot, s.m.m., formerly Father General of the Company of Mary. The volumes are published at the International Montfort Center, Montfort Generalate, Rome. The new International Montfort Center at Louvain, Belgium, will be offering courses and publications concerning montfort spirituality.

Documents:

I. — *Les chroniques de la Soeur Florence.* 1967.

II. — Chanoine BLAIN, *Abrégé de la vie de Louis-Marie Grignion de Montfort.* 1973.

III. — Ch. J.-B. BLAIN, *Summary of the life of L.M. Grignion de Montfort.* 1977.

IV. — Charles BESNARD, *La vie de Messire Louis-Marie Grignion de Montfort, missionnare apostolique.* (vol. Premier) 1981.

V. Charles BESNARD, *La vie de Messire Louis-Marie Grignion de Montfort, missionarie apostolique.* (Vol. Second) 1981.

VI. *Le Livre des Sermons du Père de Montfort.* 1983.

VII. Charles BESNARD, *La vie de la Soeur Marie-Louise de Jésus, première supérieure des filles de la Sagesse.* 1985.

VIII. Charles BESNARD, *La vita di Sr Maria Luisa di Gesù, Prima superiora delle Figlie della Sapienza.* 1988.

IX. Joseph GRANDET, *La vie de Messire Louis Marie Grignion de Montfort, prêtre, missionnaire apostolique.* (texte original) 1993.

X. Joseph GRANDET, *La vie de Messire Louis-Marie Grignion de Montfort, prêtre, missionnaire apostolique,* (texte en francais moderne, notes et tables) 1994.

XI. *En direct avec Marie-Louise de Jésus,* Ecrits - Paroles, 1994.

XII. *Gabriel Deshayes,* 1995

Recherches:

I A.A. VV, Dieu seul, *A la rencontre de Dieu avec Montfort,* 1981.

B. Books and Articles Relating to Montfort Spirituality

AA.VV. *Circulaires des supérieurs généraux des Filles de la Sagesse,* 16 vol., Rome, Generalate of the Daughters of Wisdom (private printing)

AA.VV. De singulari missione B.V. Mariae cultruque ei debito juxta doctrinam S. Ludovici-M. de Montfort, in *Alma SociaChristi, Acta congressus mariologici-mariani Romae anno sancto 1950 elebrati,* vol. 8, Academia mariana internationalis, Rome 1952.

Agudelo, F. *Naturaleza de la esclavitud mariana según el Padre de los Rios y San Luis Maria de Montfort,* Bogotá, Centro Mariano Montfortiano, 1958.

Allaire, R. *Abrégé de la vie et des vertus de la soeur Marie-Louise de Jésus, Superieure des Filles de la Sagesse, instituées par M. Louis-Marie Grignon de Montfort, Prêtre, Missionnaire Apostolique.* A Poitiers, Chez Jean-Félix Faulcon, Imprimeur de Monseigneur l'Évêque, & du Clergé. Place et vis-à-vis Notre-Dame la Grande. M.DCC.LXVIII.

Audran, M. *Les difféentes formes de la spiritualité du bienheureux Louis-Marie Grignion de Montfort*, in *Cahiers thomistes* 3 (1928) 521-541.

Barbera, G.M. *Montfort, homme de l'espérance*, in *Dieu seul. A la rencontre de Dieu avec Montfort*, Centre international montfortain, Rome 1981, 145-163.

Barré, M. *Chronologie des cantiques du Père de Montfort*, in DMon n. 33 (1963) 78-79; n. 34 (1963) 17-40; 129-156.

Bombardier, J. *Introduction à la Spiritualité Montfortaine*, Missionaires Montfortains, Dorval, ms. 1962.

Bonin, J.M. *Consécration à Marie et promesses baptismales selon saint Louis-Marie de Montfort*, Montréal, Centre Mariale, 1960.

Bonin, J. M. *Consécration à Marie et promesses baptismales, selon saint Louis-Marie de Montfort*, Centre Marial, Montréal 1960.

Bossard, A. *Le don total au Christ par Marie selon Montfort*, in CM 17 (1973) 23-48.

Marie "milieux mystérieux" pour rejoindre le Christ, in *Dieu seul. A la rencontre de Dieu avec Montfort*, Centre international montfortain, Rome 1981, 113-144.

Se consacrer à Marie, in CM 28 (1982) 146-162.

Jean-Paul II actualise Grignion de Montfort, in *Lourdes, Journal de la Grotte, Magazine*, N° 9 (20 décembre 1987), 35-40.

Les grands spirituels et notre temps: Saint Louis-Marie de Montfort, in revue *Esprit et Vie*, 1990 nn. 24-25, 26-27, 28-29, 30-31.

Catta, E. *Louis-Marie Grignion de Montfort*, in *RMon* 13 (2975) 1-21.

Cortinovis, B. *Dimensione ecclesiale della spiritualità di Grignion de Montfort*, Rome, Pontifical Faculty of theology, "Marianum" 1993. Doctoral Thesis, private printing.

David, A. *Le Père de Montfort par ses meilleurs historiens*, Paris, Librairie Mariale 1947.

Dayet, J.M. *Pour mieux aimer Marie avec le Père de Montfort*, Luçon, Pacteau, 1947.

Total Consecration to Mary, Translated by A. Bouchard, Bay Shore, Montfort Publications 1958

Dayet, J.-M. La Sagesse chez le Bx Louis-Marie de Montfort, St. Laurent-sur-Sèvre, Bureaux des Prêtres de Marie 1944.

DeFiores, S. *La devozione mariana del Montfort nel contesto della polemica degli "Avvisi salutari" di Widenfeld*, in Mar 36 (1974) 40-69.

La Figura di Maria nel Trattato della vera devozione, in *Miles Immaculatae* 19 (1983) 1-3, 50-68.

Il culto mariano nel contesto culturale dell'Europa nei secoli XVII-XVIII, vol 2, Pontificia Academia Mariana internationalis, Rome 1987, 1-57.

Le Saint-Esprit et Marie in les derniers temps selon Grignion de Montfort, in EtMar 43(1986) 131-171.

Grignion de Montfort et la spiritualité populaire, in *Dossier montfortain* 1984, n° 4, 1-27.

Itinerario spirituale di s. Luigi Maria de Montfort (1673-1716) nel periodo fino al sacerdozio (5 giugno 1700), "Marian Library Studies" University of Dayton (Ohio) 1974.

Le Saint-Esprit et Marie chez Grignion de Montfort, in CM 20 (1975) 195-216.

Montfort et l'impossibilité de l'auto-salut, in *Dieu seul*, 106-112. *Le Saint-Esprit et Marie chez Grignion de Montfort*, in *CM* 21 (1975) 195-215.

Montfort, un homme disponible à l'Esprit Saint, in *Dieu Seul. A la rencontre de Dieu avec Montfort*, Centre international montfortain, Rome 1981, 92-105.

La figura di Maria nel Trattato della vera devozione, in *Miles Immaculatae* 19 (1983) 1-3, 50-68.

Denis, G. *The Reign of Jesus Through Mary*. Translated by A.Somers, s.m.m., Bay Shore, Montfort Fathers 1960.

Dervaux, J. F. *Folie ou sagesse....? Marie-Louis Trichet et les premières filles de M. de Montfort*, Alstia, Paris 1950..

Le doigt de Dieu. Les Filles de la Sagesse après la mort des fondateurs, I. 1759 à 1800. II. 1800 à 1900, Farré et Frelon, Cholet 1954-1955.

Dethier, P. *L'Esclavage de Jésus en Marie chez Grignion de Montfort à la lumière de l'Amour de la Sagesse Éternelle et du Traité de la Vraie Dévotion*, Louvain, Université de Louvain, ms. 1981.

Devy, V. *Saint Louis-Marie Grignion de Montfort. Le dernier des grand bérulliens*, in *Revue de l'Université d'Ottawa* 18 (1948) 294-315.

Eijckeler, P. *Le Testament d'un Saint. Étude Historique*, Maastricht, E. van Aelst 1953.

Epis, S. *Un grande piccolo libro. Trattato della Vera Devozione a Maria*, Roma, Edizione Monfortane 1992.

Fabry, F. *Le grand témoin et Montfort vu par lui-même*, in *Dieu seul. A la renvontre de Dieu avec Montfort*, Centre international montfortain, Rome 1981, 19-66.

Fradet, F. *Les oeuvres du Bx de Montfort, poète mystique et populaire. Ses cantiques avec études critiques et notes*, Beauchesne, Paris 1929.

Frehen, H. *Le second avènement de Jésus-Christ et la "methode" de saint Louis-Marie de Montfort*, in DMon 7 (1962) n. 31, 98-108.

Études sur les cantiques du Père de Montfort, in DMon n. 45 (1968) 1-16; n. 46 (1969) 17-40; n. 47 (1972) 41-58.

Le caractère particulier de la compagnie de Marie suivant le P. de Montfort, in DMon n. 40 (1967) 1-16; n. 41 (1967) 1-16; n. 42 (1968) 1-12.

Corso di spiritualità monfortana, Roma, Studentato monfortano, 1966-1967 (private printing).

Frissen, J. *L'attachement des congrégations montfortaines au Saint-Siège (Collection of texts)*, Roma, Montfort Generalate (private prinitng).

Gabbiadini, R. *La formazione dell'uomo apostolico nella congregazione monfortana. La "Ratio Montfortaine" del 1987: analisi del testo e rilievi critici*, Rome 1991 (thesis for the masters in education, presented to the Pontifical Salesian University, Rome).

Gaffney, P. *The Spiritual Maternity of the Blessed Virgin Mary According to Saint Louis de Montfort*, Bay Shore, Montfort Publications 1976.

Light, Wind and Water: Life and Spirituality of St. Louis de Montfort, Bay Shore, Montfort Publications 1989.

The Holy Slavery of Love, in *Mariology* (ed. J.B. Carol), vol. III, Milwaukee, Bruce 1961, 143-161.

St. Louis Mary Grignion de Montfort and the Marian Consecration, in *Marian Studies* 35 (1984) 111-156.

Gebhard, H. M. *Commento al Trattato della vera devozione a Maria Vergine*, in *Regina dei Cuori* I (1914)-XII (1925), XIX (1932)-XXI (1934).

Gendrot, M. (éd) *Saint Louis-Marie de Montfort, un docteur pour l'église de notre temps?*, Rome, Montfort Generalate (private printing) 1985.

Montfort, un maître spirituel pour notre temps, Rome Montfort Generalate (private printing) 1988.

Vie baptismale et dévotion mariale chez saint Louis-Marie Grignion de Montfort, in *De cultu mariano saeculis XVII-XVIII.* Acta congressus mariologici-mariani internationalis in Republica Melitensi anno 1983 celebrati, vol. 5, Pontificia Academia mariana internationalis, Romae 1987, 81-111.

Ghidotti, G. *La consacrazione monfortana, Teologia e pastorale della consacrazione a Maria*, Messaggero, Padova 1969, 149-161.

Gilbert, M. *L'exégèse spirituelle de Montfort in Nouvelle Revue Théologique*, nov.-dec. 1982, pp. 678-691.

Gonzalez, J. *La Esclavitud Mariana o Perfecta Devoción a la Santissima Virgen según la Doctrina de S. L.M. de Montfort*, Medellin, Granamerica, 1963.

Humblet, P. *Le Processus de Transformation dans "l'Amour de la Sagesse Éternelle" de Grignion de Montfort*, Institut Titus Brandsma-Filles de la Sagesse, Nijmegen-Berg en Daal, 1991 (private printing).

Huot, D. M. *Traité de la vraie dévotion. La voix du manuscrit*, in DMar 2 (1957) 25-26.

Hupperts, J.M. *Saint L.M. Grignion de Montfort, Vie et Doctrine, Doctrine & Textes*, Bruges, Beyaert 1961.

Série *"Immaculata."* I-V, Louvain, Sécretariat Marie-Mediatrice 1957.

Huré, H. *Préface à L'amour de la Sagesse éternelle (par la "Vraie dévotion à Marie") puissante synthèse de spiritualité par le Bienheureux L. M. de Montfort*, édition "type", Pontchateau, Librairie mariale 1929.

Ibañez, J.& Mendoza, F *Consagración mariana y culto de esclavitud a Maria*, in EstMar 51 (1986) 63-171.

Laurentin, M. *Le bienheureux Père de Montfort statuaire. Le bienheureux Louis-Marie Grignion de Montfort est-il l'auteur de statues que la Vendée lui attribue?* Saint-Laurent-sur-Sèvre, L.-J. Biton, 1936.

Laurentin, R. *Dieu seul est ma tendresse. René Laurentin présente L.-M. Grignion de Montfort*, O.E.I.L., Paris 1984.

Le Crom, L. *La spiritualité de saint L.M. de Montfort*, in DMon 6 (1961) n. 29, 63-78.

Lepers, M. *Dieu écrit droit*, Casa generalizia Figlie della Sapienza, Roma 1976, 1978, 1980, 3 vol.

Le Texier, F. *La Sagesse selon St. L. M. de Montfort*, in *DMon* 8 (1963), no 32, 1-5.

Lhoumeau, A. *La vie spirituelle à l'école de saint Louis-Marie Grignion de Montfort*, Beyaert, Bruges 1953 (first edition, 1901).

La vierge Marie et les apôtres des derniers temps d'après le B. Louis-Marie de Montfort, Mame, Tours 1919.

Macdonald, D. *Alive to God: A Preparation for the Renewal of Consecration in the Spirit of Saint Louis Marie de Montfort*, Liverpool, Montfort Press 1993.

Manteau-Bonamy, H.M. *S. Louis-Marie Grignion de Montfort théologien de la Sagesse éternelle au seuil du troisième millénaire*, editions Saint-Paul, Paris-Fribourg 1986.

Mora, E. *Musica e Cantici nell'Evangelizzazione di San L.M. di Montfort*, Roma, Istituto di Musica Sacra, ms. 1976.

Morinay, J. *Marie et la Faiblesse de Dieu*, Paris, Nouvelle Cité 1988.

Nava, P.L. *Il trittico monfortano: natura ed ermeneutica. Riflessioni sulla "Regola"*, in QM 1 (1983), 96-121.

Oger, P. *La coroncina illustrata. Preghiera antica, preghiera dei santi. Metodo di s. Luigi Maria di Montfort per recitarla con frutto*, Bergamo, Tipographia monfortana, 1978.

Papàsogli, B. *Wisdom of the Heart, Blessed Marie Louise of Jesus*, Bay Shore, Montfort Publications 1993.

Pérouas, L. *L'image du montfortain au XVIII siècle*, in DMon n.40 (1967) I-II.

Réflexion Historique sur l'apostolat des montfortains, in Dmon n.43 (1970), 1-8.

Plessis, A, *Manuel de Mariologie Dogmatique*, Rennes, Les Nouvelles de Bretagne, 1947.

Mariologie Montfortaine. Commentaire du Traité de la vraie dévotion, Pontchateau, Librairie Mariale, 1943.

Poupon, M. Th. *Le poème de la parfaite consécration à Marie suivant saint Louis-Marie Grignion de Montfort et les spirituels de son temps. Sources et doctrine*, Librairie du Sacré-Coeur, Lyon 1947.

A Jésus par Marie. La Parfaite Consécration à Marie selon St. L.M. de Montfort, Librairie du Sacré-Coeur, Lyon 1948.

Quéméneur, M. *La consécration de soi à la Vierge à travers l'histoire*, in CM 3 (1959) 119-128.

Essai sur la spiritualité de saint L.-M. de Montfort, in DMon n. 29 (1961), 63-68.

Rolandeau, J. B. *Dans la foulée de saint Louis-Marie: la vie des premiers frères*, in DMon n. 39 (1968) 1-15.

Sankalé, L. *Avec Marie au pas de l'Esprit: Le Secret de Marie lu aujourd'hui en paroisse*, Paris, Fayard 1990.

Sibold, M. *Le Sang des Grignion*, Centre International Montfortain, Rome 1987.

Séguy, J. *Millénarisme et "ordres adventistes": Grignion de Montfort et les "apôtres des derniers Temps"*, in *Archives des sciences sociales des religions* 53/1 (1982) 22-38.

Charisme, Sacerdoce, Fondation: Autour de L.M. Grignion de Montfort, in *Social Compass*, XXIX/1, 1982, 5-24.

Sessa, P. & Giacometti, G. *La novità della consacrazione monfortana*, in *Rivista di ascetica e mistica* 12 (1967) 35-45, 148-157, 384-387.

Sigouin, C. & M. Belotti *The Totus Tuus Journey*, Manila, Bahay Maria & Montfort Missionaries, 1988.

Suarez, P. *Manual del Consagrado*, Lima, Centro Mariano Montfortiano 1985.

Suarez, P. *La consécration total à Jésus par Marie*, in DMon 2 (mai 1986) 1-47.

Texier, J.-M. *Histoire de la Compagnie de Marie*, Saint Laurent-sur-Sèvre, vol.1, 1914; vol. 2, 1924.

Les Martyrs de la Compagnie de Marie pendant la Grande Révolution, Saint Laurent-sur-Sèvre 1927.

Texier, P. *Orientation de la catéchèse missionnaire de saint Louis-Marie Grignion de Montfort.* Dissertation ad licentiam in scientïs religiosis, Romae 1964.

Tisserand, E. *Louis-Marie Grignion de Montfort. Les écoles de charité et les origines des Frères de Saint-Gabriel*, Pacteau, Luçon 1960

van Osch, J. *Comment Montfort voit Dieu et le rencontre in la prière*, in *Dieu seul. A la rencontre de Dieu avec Montfort*, Centre international montfortain, Rome 1981, 75-81..

Waach, H. *Ein Heiliger der Gegensätze. Bemerkungen zu Leben und Lehre des hl. L.M. Grignion de Montfort* in Jarhbuch für Mystische Theologie, 1963, 9-43.

C. Reviews

The Company of Mary (Montfort Missionaries) publishes reviews in several countries, dealing with montfort spirituality on a popular level. For the United States: *Queen of All Hearts*, published at Montfort Missionaries, Bay Shore, N.Y. 11716.

Afterword

The resurgence of interest in the teachings of Father de Montfort has prompted many to seek ways of networking those who live his consecration spirituality. We do, therefore, urge those who integrate his doctrine in their lives, to enroll in the Association of Mary Queen of All Hearts; we would ask priests to join the Association of the Priests of Mary. Addresses of some of the centers in certain English speaking countries are given below. We also suggest that those interested in the spirituality of Saint Louis de Montfort subscribe to the montfort review, *Queen of All Hearts*, which is a means of clarifying and updating the saint's teachings and also of dialogue among the members of the associations. We again strongly request that all interested in Saint Louis de Montfort's spirituality have the necessary companion volume to the *Handbook*, God Alone: The Collected Works of Saint Louis Marie de Montfort.

We also pray that some young men and women studying this volume may be drawn by the Holy Spirit to dedicate themselves to the living and proclaiming of Montfort's spirituality by entering the core montfort family: the Daughters of Wisdom, the Missionaries of the Company of Mary and the Brothers of Saint Gabriel, the three religious communities who trace their ancestry back to Saint Louis de Montfort himself. Although montfort spirituality belongs to the entire Church, the custodians of this treasure, as Pope John Paul II has reminded the Company of Mary, are his "children," these "*servants of the Blessed Virgin Mary who will range far and wide with the holy Gospel issuing from their mouths like a bright and burning flame and the Rosary in their hands and bay like your watch-dogs, burn like fire and dispel the darkness of the world like a sun*" (PM 12). We ask all to join in Montfort's Prayer for Missionaries, so that "*the face of the earth may be renewed and the Church reformed.*"

For subscriptions to the review, *Queen of All Hearts*, write to:

Montfort Publications
Montfort Missionaries
Bay Shore, NY 11706

For all information concerning the Associations and vocations to the montfort family, contact:

In the USA:
Montfort Missionaries, Litchfield, CT 06759.
In the United Kingdom:

Montfort Missionaries
54A Parson Street
Hendon, London NW4 1QX

In the Republic of Ireland:
Montfort Missionaries
Monaghan

In the Philippines:
Montfort Missionaries
121 9th Street
New Manila, Q.C. 1112

In India:
Guru Mandir
22 Lalitha Mahal Road
Siddarthanagar P.O.
Mysore 570 011

In Canada:
Montfort Missionaries
463 Riverdale Avenue
Ottawa, Ontario K1S 1S1

In Africa:
Montfort Missionaries
P.O. Box 76252
Nairobi, Kenya

Any questions or comments concerning this volume may be directed to:

The Montfort Handbook
Montfort Missionaries
Litchfield, Connecticut 06759
USA

For information on Montfort Spirituality seminars and retreats:

Montfort Missionaries
The Retreat House
Litchfield, Connecticut 06759

Shortly before the *Handbook* went to press, we received the news of the sudden death (on September 20, 1994) of Father Charles Underhill Quinn, of the Archdiocese of New York. He translated a number of the articles for this work and had begun translating the *Hymns* of Saint Louis de Montfort which were scheduled for publication in several months. A fine poet himself, he had a magnificent grasp of Father de Montfort's canticles. Father Quinn dubbed himself a "convert to Saint Louis de Montfort," since it was only in the light of the articles in this *Handbook* that he said he understood the "real Montfort," so different from what he had learned by hearsay. The last lines of Saint Louis de Montfort's *Hymns* translated by Father Charles Underhill Quinn, perhaps the night before his massive heart attack, are H 13:90:

To live and die with joy
And so full of hope.

Patrick Gaffney, S.M.M.
Handbook of the Spirituality of Saint Louis de Montfort
Litchfield, Connecticut
September 29, 1994

Feast of the Archangels Michael, Gabriel and Raphael

Index

Subject Index:

Proper Name Index:

Biblical Index:

OLD TESTAMENT

NEW TESTAMENT